Preface

This is the seventh edition of the *Report on Business Canada Company Handbook*. This year, we have enhanced white pages of the Handbook by adding almost 100 new companies to this section. These companies trade on the Toronto Stock Exchange. They are included in the Handbook based on the size of their assets.

Bryan Boulton, David Curry, John F. Grennan, Vivian Hood, G. Trevor Leong, Sean T. McLoughlin, Douglas Tripp, and Tsang Kwong-Ping were the financial analysts who worked on the Handbook this year. Mary-Jane Wilson was our corporate information coordinator. Helena Huiqun Jin, Brenda Tabe, Sham Arora, Gerard ter Hofstede, and Mike Kimber provided software development and support. We would also like to thank Julie Bassett and Sandy Salem.

Globe Information Services markets a number of targeted directories and financial databases including the **Canadian Federal Government Handbook**, **The Guide to the Canadian Financial Services Industry**, **Corporate Canada Online**, and the **Report on Business Corporate Database**. Globe Information Services continuously gathers and analyzes financial information and news on thousands of Canadian companies. For up-to-date information on companies in the **Handbook** and other Canadian companies contact our Financial Services Group at (416) 585-5561 in Toronto, (800) 268-9128 toll-free, or by fax, (416) 585-5249.

Table of Contents

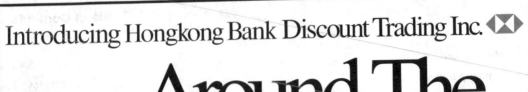

ARRANGEMENT OF COMPANIES

The white pages of the **Report on Business Canada Company Handbook** provide current news, ratios and price performance charts, and annual and quarterly financial information for 503 major Canadian public companies. These companies include the current TSE 300, and the next largest companies by assets that trade on the TSE.

One full page is devoted to each company. Companies are grouped by industry and arranged alphabetically, within each industry. The **Handbook** uses the same industry groupings as the **Report on Business Corporate Database**. A company index follows this section of the **Handbook**.

The earnings table preceeding each section lists each company in that industry group. The table lists earnings per share for the current year and the mean earnings estimates for the subsequent two fiscal years. Earnings estimates are provided by First Call Corporation. Industry summaries compiled by both Globe Information Services and INVESTEXT follow each earnings table.

The colour pages are an alphabetical directory of all the companies that appeared in the July 1995 **Report on Business 1000**, including public and private companies, crown corporations, and cooperatives. Each entry lists the address, stock symbol, description of business, senior executive, assets, revenue, and net income from the most recent annual report, and rankings from the ROB 1000.

SOURCES OF INFORMATION

The bulk of information in the **Handbook** is provided from a range of Info Globe Online databases including: the **Report on Business Corporate Database**, **The Globe and Mail Online**, and **Marketscan Plus**.

Globe Information Services is constantly gathering and organizing financial information and news on thousands of Canadian companies. For up-to-date information on companies included in the **Canada Company Handbook** and other Canadian companies contact our Client Services department:

- (416) 585-5345 Toronto
- (800) 268-9128 Toll-free
- (416) 585-5249 Fax

First Call Corporation is a unique partnership between major Wall Street brokerage firms and Thomson Financial Services, a leading supplier of financial research, analyses, and software products to the worldwide investment and corporate communities. Established in 1984, First Call is the only real-time source of commingled equity research and earnings estimates.

The **INVESTEXT** database was employed in the compilation of the **Handbook**. INVESTEXT is a database which offers the complete text of company and industry reports written by analysts at more than 150 of the world's leading investment banks and consulting and research firms. INVESTEXT currently includes over 210,000 reports which cover 12,000 companies and 53 industries. Copies of all reports are available online or from Thomson Financial Networks.

INVESTEXT
Thomson Financial Networks
11 Farnsworth Street
Boston, MA   02210
(800) 544-5651   Canada
(800) 662-7878   U.S.
011 44 071 815-3860   U.K.
(617) 330-1986   Fax

The following section includes a sample company page with sections labelled for your convenience. Major sections are:

- Summary stock market information
- Fundamental information
- Stock graphs
- Business description
- Current news synopsis
- General information.

SAMPLE COMPANY PAGE

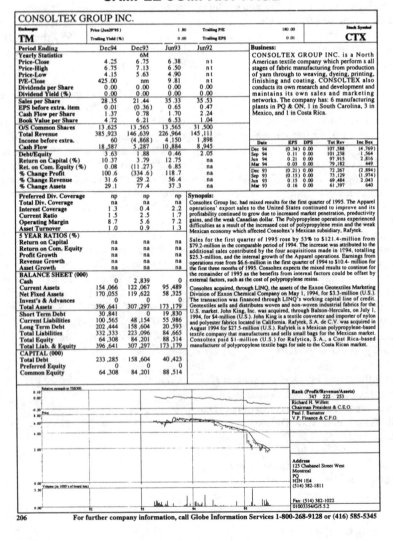

CONSOLTEX GROUP INC.

Exchange	Price (Jun29'95)	1.80	Trailing P/E	180.00	Stock Symbol
TM	Trailing Yield (%)	0.00	Trailing EPS	0.01	**CTX**

Period Ending	Dec94	Dec93	Jun93	Jun92
Yearly Statistics		6M		
Price-Close	4.25	6.75	6.38	n t
Price-High	6.75	7.13	6.50	n t
Price-Low	4.15	5.63	4.90	n t
P/E-Close	425.00	nm	9.81	n t
Dividends per Share	0.00	0.00	0.00	0.00
Dividend Yield (%)	0.00	0.00	0.00	0.00
Sales per Share	28.35	21.44	35.33	35.53
EPS before extra. item	0.01	(0.36)	0.65	0.47
Cash Flow per Share	1.37	0.78	1.70	2.24
Book Value per Share	4.72	6.21	6.53	1.04
O/S Common Shares	13,625	13,565	13,565	31,500
Total Revenue	385,923	146,639	226,964	145,111
Income before extra.	60	(4,868)	4,150	1,898
Cash Flow	18,587	5,287	10,884	8,945
Debt/Equity	3.63	1.88	0.46	2.05
Return on Capital (%)	10.37	3.79	12.75	na
Ret. on Com. Equity (%)	0.08	(11.27)	6.85	na
% Change Profit	100.6	(334.6)	118.7	na
% Change Revenue	31.6	29.2	56.4	na
% Change Assets	29.1	77.4	37.3	na
Preferred Div. Coverage	np	np	np	
Total Div. Coverage	na	na	na	
Interest Coverage	1.3	0.4	2.2	
Current Ratio	1.5	2.5	1.7	
Operating Margin	8.7	5.6	7.2	
Asset Turnover	1.0	0.9	1.3	
5 YEAR RATIOS (%)				
Return on Capital	na	na	na	
Return on Com. Equity	na	na	na	
Profit Growth	na	na	na	
Revenue Growth	na	na	na	
Asset Growth	na	na	na	
BALANCE SHEET (000)				
Cash	0	2,839	0	
Current Assets	154,066	122,067	95,489	
Net Fixed Assets	170,055	119,622	58,325	
Invest's & Advances	0	0	0	
Total Assets	396,641	307,297	173,179	
Short Term Debt	30,841	0	19,830	
Current Liabilities	100,565	48,154	55,986	
Long Term Debt	202,444	158,604	20,593	
Total Liabilities	332,333	223,096	84,665	
Total Equity	64,308	84,201	88,514	
Total Liab. & Equity	396,641	307,297	173,179	
CAPITAL (000)				
Total Debt	233,285	158,604	40,423	
Preferred Equity	0	0	0	
Common Equity	64,308	84,201	88,514	

Business:

CONSOLTEX GROUP INC. is a North American textile company which perform s all stages of fabric manufacturing from production of yarn through to weaving, dyeing, printing, finishing and coating. CONSOLTEX also conducts its own research and development and maintains its own sales and marketing networks. The company has: 6 manufacturing plants in PQ & ON, 1 in South Carolina, 3 in Mexico, and 1 in Costa Rica.

Date	EPS	DPS	Tot Rev	Inc Bex
Dec 94	(0.34)	0.00	107,588	(4,769)
Sep 94	0.11	0.00	101,238	1,564
Jun 94	0.21	0.00	97,915	2,816
Mar 94	0.03	0.00	79,182	449
Dec 93	(0.21)	0.00	72,267	(2,894)
Sep 93	(0.15)	0.00	73,129	(1,974)
Jun 93	0.15	0.00	69,484	2,043
Mar 93	0.16	0.00	61,397	640

Synopsis:

Consoltex Group Inc. had mixed results for the first quarter of 1995. The Apparel operations' export sales to the United States continued to improve and its profitability continued to grow due to increased market penetration, productivity gains, and the weak Canadian dollar. The Polypropylene operations experienced difficulties as a result of the increased cost of polypropylene resin and the weak Mexican economy which affected Consoltex's Mexican subsidiary, Rafytek.

Sales for the first quarter of 1995 rose by 53% to $121.4-million from $79.2-million in the comparable period of 1994. The increase was attributed to the additional sales contributed by the four acquisitions made in 1994, totalling $25.3-million, and the internal growth of the Apparel operations. Earnings from operations rose from $6.6-million in the first quarter of 1994 to $10.4- million for the first three months of 1995. Consoltex expects the mixed results to continue for the remainder of 1995 as the benefits from internal factors could be offset by external factors, such as the cost of polypropylene resins.

Consoltex acquired, through LINQ, the assets of the Exxon Geotextiles Marketing Division of Exxon Chemical Company on May 1, 1994, for $3.3-million (U.S.). The transaction was financed through LINQ's working capital line of credit. Geotextiles sells and distributes woven and non-woven industrial fabrics for the U.S. market. John King, Inc. was acquired, through Balson-Hercules, on July 1, 1994, for $4-million (U.S.). John King is a textile converter and importer of nylon and polyester fabrics located in California. Rafytek, S.A. de C.V. was acquired in August 1994 for $27.5-million (U.S.). Rafytek is a Mexican polypropylene-based textile company that manufactures and sells small bags for the Mexican market. Consoltex paid $1-million (U.S.) for Rafytica, S.A., a Cost Rica-based manufacturer of polypropylene textile bags for sale to the Costa Rican market.

Relative strength to TSE300

Price

Volume (in 1000's of board lots)

Rank (Profit/Revenue/Assets)
747   222   253

Richard H. Willett
Chairman President & C.E.O.

Paul J. Bamaiter
V.P. Finance & C.F.O.

Address
125 Chabanel Street West
Montreal
PQ
H2N 1E4
(514) 382-1811

Fax: (514) 382-1022
01003354/G/5.5.2

STOCK MARKET INFORMATION

This section gives the ticker symbol and the Canadian and American stock exchanges where the company stock is listed. The primary exchange is listed first. The latest closing market price date for the majority of companies in the **Handbook** is June 29, 1995.

Stock exchange codes are: **T**-Toronto; **M**- Montreal; **V**-Vancouver; **W**-Winnipeg; **Z**-Alberta; **A**-American; **N**-New York; and **Q**-Nasdaq.

FUNDAMENTAL INFORMATION

The fundamental information is derived from a company's annual and quarterly financial statements. Financial items are indicated as dollar amounts, percentages, or ratios. Dollar amounts are reported in Canadian currency and in thousands of dollars, unless otherwise indicated. For ratio calculations, figures are converted to Canadian dollars and annualized. Annual and quarterly information is restated or reclassified where applicable. Share information is split adjusted. Financial items having negative values are enclosed in parentheses.

Certain financial information is not available for all companies. The following codes may be used when a number does not appear: **na** - not available; **nc** - no common shares trading; **nd** - no debt; **nm** - not meaningful; **np** - no preferred shares; and **nt** - no shares trading.

The **Handbook** uses four different presentations to reflect the differences in financial reporting requirements for different types of companies. They are: Banks; Finance (eg. trust, insurance and investment companies); Real Estate Management and Development; and General (eg. industrial, resource and communications companies).

For a detailed explanation of each financial item, please refer to the **Definitions of Financial Terms** beginning on page DEF-1.

The **Yearly Statistics** section contains five years of financial information. All financial items in this section apply to all companies in the **Handbook**.

The section beginning with **Preferred Dividend Coverage** contains three years of financial ratios. Preferred Dividend Coverage and Total Dividend Coverage apply to all companies. All other financial items in this section are presentation specific.

The **5 Year Ratios** section contains three years of key ratios. All financial items in this section apply to all companies.

The **Balance Sheet** and **Capital** sections contain three years of financial information. Two items — Total Equity and Total Liabilities — apply to all companies. All other financial items in this section are presentation specific.

The **Quarterly** section contains information from the eight most recent quarterly financial statements. All financial items apply to all companies. Quarterly data represent the incremental period between the dates given.

STOCK GRAPHS

The graphs in the **Handbook** are designed so that price and volume movements for each stock can be seen at a glance for each week during the past five years, or since the stock has been publicly traded. Market information is taken from the primary exchange on which the stock trades. The information is current as of the week ended June 30, 1995.

Three graphs are displayed for each of the companies in the **Handbook**. The graphs display three types of information:

- strength compared to the TSE 300
- stock price
- stock volume, in thousands of board lots.

Relative strength is calculated by dividing the stock price by the TSE 300 index. The result of this division is the ratio between the stock price and the TSE 300 index. The relative strength indicator is then adjusted to normalize the value by subtracting the beginning ratio from each day's value. The result of this adjustment is to set the day-one value at zero for easier analysis. When the relative strength indicator is moving up, the stock is performing better than the TSE 300 index. When the indicator is level, the stock is performing the same as the TSE 300 index. When the indicator is moving down, the stock is performing worse than the TSE 300 index.

The stock price graph displays the high, low, and close prices, as well as the five-week (solid line) and 40-week (dotted line) moving averages. All prices have been stock split adjusted. A logarithmic scale is used to better facilitate the analysis of price movements. Wherever a company name change, merger, or amalgamation has occurred, every effort has been made to display the complete price history of the company stock.

The volume graph displays the volume of shares traded, in thousands of board lots, during each week. The highest recorded volume for the stock during the five-year period, rounded up to the nearest hundred, is displayed on the vertical axis.

BUSINESS DESCRIPTION

This section provides an overview of a company's line of business. It lists primary and secondary activities, and gives the location of company operations, mines, properties, and markets. The business description may also list company products and include subsidiary and major shareholder information.

CURRENT NEWS SYNOPSIS

The synopsis, or summary, provides context for all other company information and covers any or all of the following:

- industry trends
- company events (eg. sales contracts, takeovers, share offerings, layoffs)
- key executive appointments
- fundamental information on a company's geographic and product divisions.

This section provides a 12-month capsule of company events. The majority of summaries cover events from July 1994 to June 1995. Where possible, changes were made to summaries up to the date of printing.

GENERAL INFORMATION

This section provides an investor with the means to obtain additional information on a given company. Included are company rankings of profit, revenue, and assets from the latest **Report on Business 1000**, the names and titles of up to five top company officers, and the head office address, phone, and fax number.

FIRST CALL

First Call Corporation is a unique partnership between major Wall Street brokerage firms and Thomson Financial Services, a leading supplier of financial information, research, analyses, and software products to the worldwide investment and corporate communities. Established in 1984, First Call is the only real-time source of commingled equity research and earnings estimates.

First Call provides instantaneous electronic access to: analyst morning meeting notes and intraday research broadcasts from 50 North American brokerage firms; real-time earnings estimates contributed directly by analysts at more than 260 leading firms; 100 fundamental data items on 5,500 companies; and full-text corporate news from more than 1,000 corporations in the U.S. and Canada. The system serves as a comprehensive source of financial research for money managment professionals. A variety of search methods and screens make First Call a versatile tool for managing the daily volumes of investment research.

FIRST CALL RTEE
(Real Time Earnings Estimates)

The First Call RTEE database delivers earnings estimates on 6,000+ publicly-traded companies, including more than 610 Canadian companies. Estimates on interlisted companies are provided in both Canadian and U.S. dollars. Estimate revisions are received as they happen, and the proprietary First Call consensus is updated immediately, providing users with the most up-to-the-minute information available.

RTEE features over 150 data items including: current and previous consensus estimates by quarter and year; actual earnings; standard deviation; recommendations; and revision dates. Additional contributing brokers are added to the system regularly and more than 50 quality control checks are performed on each data item to ensure accuracy.

First Call RTEE is available in a variety of formats to best suit the investment style of individual users. First Call earnings estimates can be received online, via fax or printed reports, on computer tape or diskette, and via third-party market data systems. For further information:

First Call Corporation
22 Pittsburgh Street
Boston, MA   02210
(800) 366-9992
(617) 261-5679   Fax

Page	Company				Fiscal year end	EARNINGS Last Year	Estimate this year	next ye..
3	Alcan Aluminium	AL	$US		Dec-94	0.34	2.92	4.20
4	Arimetco International	AR X	$US		Jun-94	0.10	0.22	0.32
5	Brunswick Mining and Smelting				Dec-94	0.71	1.03	1.00
6	Cameco				Dec-94	1.56	1.81	2.11
7	Canada Tungsten Mining				Dec-94	0.04	0.03	0.07
8	Cominco	C LT.			Dec-94	0.47	1.66	2.15
9	Denison Mines				Dec-93	(0.18)	na	na
10	Dia Met Minerals				Jan-95	(0.02)	na	na
11	Falconbridge				Dec-94	0.94	1.97	2.43
12	Gibraltar Mines				Dec-94	(0.44)	0.10	0.13
13	Global Stone				Sep-94	0.25	0.34	0.44
14	Inco		$US		Dec-94	0.26	2.22	3.46
15	Inmet Mining				Dec-94	0.38	0.90	0.93
16	Kerr Addison Mines				Dec-94	1.09	1.52	1.67
17	Lytton Minerals				Dec-94	(0.00)	na	na
18	Minera Rayrock		$US		Dec-94	(0.02)	na	na
19	Novicourt				Dec-94	0.00	0.29	0.58
20	Princeton Mining				Dec-94	(0.09)	0.21	0.16
21	Rio Algom				Dec-94	1.48	2.75	2.79
22	Westmin Resources				Dec-94	(0.60)	0.37	0.58

@ 5/24/2

Estimates from First Call Corporation, 22 Pittsburgh Street, Boston, MA 02210   (800) 366-9992   Fax (617) 261-5679

Globe Information Services © **1995**

...ring 1994, a sharp increase in metal consumption in Western countries combined with increased activity by commodity funds, resulted in price increases for most metals. Both industrial and developing countries exhibited strong economic growth. In 1994 and 1995, the economies of Europe and Asia joined the United States economy in a period of sustained growth, and demand for base metals increased significantly. Since the beginning of 1994, base metal inventories have declined, and price increases have followed.

This economic expansion may be more prolonged and more broadly based than previous cycles. This is because industrial countries are curbing inflation by raising interest rates early in the cycle, and the number of developing countries is growing. Many mining companies expect that 1995 will be a strong year as the Japanese economy expands, and world economic growth becomes more balanced.

Copper

Improvements in the price of copper and the lower Canadian dollar resulted in a turnaround in the fortunes of copper mining companies in 1994 and 1995. Reductions in operating costs also played a major role. The London Metal Exchange (LME) copper price opened 1994 at 78 cents (U.S.) per pound and moved steadily upward to close the year at $1.38 (U.S.). Western world refined copper consumption surged in 1994 by 6.7% to reach 9.90 million tonnes.

Copper consumption in the Western world should continue to increase in 1995. Demand will outstrip supply despite significant increases in mine and metal production and a slowing down of the U.S. housing and automotive industries. Also, an anticipated decline of the U.S. dollar versus the Japanese yen could hurt the Japanese economy which could curb demand for copper from Japan. The continuing strong demand and projected lower inventory levels are expected to sustain copper prices in 1995 at an average of $1.30 (U.S.) a pound in 1995.

Zinc

Zinc-coated steel, or galvanizing, accounts for about 50% of zinc demand in the Western world. Galvanized steel sheet mainly is used in the manufacture of automobiles and in construction. In North America, close to 90% of all automotive steel is galvanized.

After several years of small consumption increases, zinc consumption in the Western world began to rise sharply in 1994 at a 3.5% growth rate to reach 5.72 million tonnes. Strong growth occurred in the U.S., Western Europe, and the East Asian economies. Some growth occurred in Japan. The LME zinc price opened 1994 at $0.45 (U.S.) per pound, fell to a yearly low in April of $0.41 (U.S.) per pound, and closed the year at $0.515 (U.S.) per pound.

With the economies of the major nations growing in tandem, zinc consumption should continue growing at a strong rate in 1995. Small increases in mine and metal production and some decrease in the outflow of East Bloc metal should cause metal inventories to drop in 1995 for the first time since 1990. Although zinc prices have improved, there remains a large world stockpile of the metal that is more than twice the traditional level. Analysts expect only a modest improvement in zinc prices in 1995.

Lead

In 1994, refined lead consumption in the Western world increased sharply by 5.3% to reach 4.73 million tonnes as all major consuming regions, except Japan, showed healthy increases. Metal consumption should continue to increase in 1995. Analysts expect that small increases in mine production in the West plus secondary production as well as a decline in East Bloc outflows will cause a significant metal deficit and declining metal inventories in 1995. Batteries are the major use for lead, accounting for more than 65% of demand in the Western world. The LME lead price opened 1994 at 21.2 cents (U.S.) a pound, fell to a yearly low in April of 19.3 cents (U.S.) a pound, and closed the year at 29.5 cents (U.S.) a pound.

Nickel

Nickel demand was strong in 1994. Nickel consumption in Western countries increased by 9% to approximately 752,000 tonnes. A 10.5% increase in stainless steel production and a shortage of stainless steel scrap drove the demand. This is in addition to the 9.4% increase in 1993. Nickel consumption in the Western world should increase by 5% to 796,000 tonnes. The LME nickel price opened 1994 at $2.36 (U.S.) a pound and continued its rise to close the year at $4.02 (U.S.) a pound.

Increased nickel consumption in the Western world continued in 1995. All the market areas in the West should grow in 1995. Markets in China and Eastern Europe should remain at 1994 levels. Stainless steel production continues to be the largest single-use end market for nickel, accounting for more than 60% of the worldwide nickel consumption. Stainless steel production has nearly doubled since the early 1980s.

Aluminum

Following three years of depressed prices due to a severe glut of aluminum, inventories began to decline, and prices rose steadily during 1994. The price of aluminum was as low as $0.50 (U.S.) a pound in early 1994. It should reach close to $1 (U.S.) a pound by the end of 1995. By the end of 1995, demand should eat up the world surplus of the metal which was about one million tonnes in April 1995.

The dominant factor behind the change in market climate was the strong, 8% growth in demand for primary aluminum. This demand was the result of accelerating economic growth in the Americas and recoveries in Europe and Asia.

ALCAN ALUMINIUM LIMITED

Exchanges	Price (Jun29'95)	40 .87	Trailing P/E	24 .77	Stock Symbol
TMVN	Trailing Yield (%)	1 .06	Trailing EPS	1 .22	**AL**

Period Ending	Dec94	Dec93	Dec92	Dec91	Dec90	Business:
Yearly Statistics	US	US	US	US	US	
Price-Close	35 .63	27 .75	22 .63	23 .25	22 .50	
Price-High	38 .13	29 .63	26 .38	27 .75	28 .50	
Price-Low	27 .38	21 .63	19 .13	20 .63	19 .63	
P/E-Close	55 .93	nm	nm	nm	7 .09	
Dividends per Share	0 .30	0 .30	0 .45	0 .86	1 .12	
Dividend Yield (%)	1 .15	1 .40	2 .42	4 .24	5 .81	
Sales per Share	36 .63	32 .30	33 .97	34 .74	39 .09	
EPS before extra. item	0 .34	(0 .54)	(0 .60)	(0 .25)	2 .33	
Cash Flow per Share	2 .74	1 .41	1 .10	1 .70	3 .54	
Book Value per Share	19 .17	18 .28	19 .06	21 .17	22 .20	
O/S Common Shares	224 ,685	224 ,060	223 ,807	223 ,420	222 ,667	
Total Revenue	8 ,325 ,000	7 ,307 ,000	7 ,665 ,000	7 ,830 ,000	8 ,919 ,000	
Income before extra.	96 ,000	(104 ,000)	(112 ,000)	(36 ,000)	543 ,000	
Cash Flow	614 ,000	316 ,000	246 ,000	380 ,000	792 ,000	
Debt/Equity	0 .53	0 .60	0 .60	0 .61	0 .51	
Return on Capital (%)	6 .00	1 .31	1 .63	1 .35	12 .10	
Ret. on Com. Equity (%)	1 .79	(2 .92)	(3 .00)	(1 .16)	10 .91	
% Change Profit	192 .3	7 .1	(211 .1)	(106 .6)	(35 .0)	
% Change Revenue	13 .9	(4 .7)	(2 .1)	(12 .2)	(1 .4)	
% Change Assets	1 .8	(3 .3)	(6 .2)	1 .6	12 .0	

ALCAN ALUMINIUM LTD. is the parent company of a multinational industrial group engaged in all aspects of the aluminum business. The activities of the Alcan Group include bauxite mining, alumina refining, aluminum smelting, manufacturing, sales and recycling.

Date		EPS	DPS	Tot Rev	Inc Bex
Mar 95	US	0 .75	0 .08	2 ,455 ,000	174 ,000
Dec 94	US	0 .19	0 .08	2 ,252 ,000	48 ,000
Sep 94	US	0 .27	0 .08	2 ,196 ,000	66 ,000
Jun 94	US	0 .01	0 .08	2 ,068 ,000	7 ,000
Mar 94	US	(0 .13)	0 .08	1 ,809 ,000	(25 ,000)
Dec 93	US	(0 .17)	0 .08	1 ,860 ,000	(36 ,000)
Sep 93	US	(0 .08)	0 .08	1 ,824 ,000	(13 ,000)
Jun 93	US	(0 .18)	0 .08	1 ,873 ,000	(35 ,000)

				Synopsis:
Preferred Div. Coverage	4 .6	0 .0	0 .0	
Total Div. Coverage	1 .1	0 .0	0 .0	
Interest Coverage	2 .0	0 .4	0 .5	
Current Ratio	2 .0	1 .8	1 .7	
Operating Margin	5 .4	1 .9	1 .7	
Asset Turnover	0 .8	0 .7	0 .7	

Synopsis:

Alcan's turnaround in 1994 and 1995 was due to better conditions in the world aluminum industry and to its cost reduction efforts over the last four years. The company expects further improvements in 1995 and 1996 as it benefits from higher prices for fabricated products and the eventual return of the 15% of smelting capacity that it closed in 1994 in response to oversupply.

5 YEAR RATIOS (%)			
Return on Capital	4 .5	7 .5	12 .8
Return on Com. Equity	1 .1	4 .5	9 .8
Profit Growth	(35 .2)	na	na
Revenue Growth	(1 .7)	(3 .3)	2 .1
Asset Growth	0 .9	2 .6	5 .7

Following three years of depressed prices brought on by a glut of aluminum, inventories began to fall and prices rose steadily during 1994. The dominant factor behind the change in market climate was the strong, 8% growth in demand for primary aluminum. Demand grew in response to accelerating economic growth in North and South America and recoveries in Europe and Asia. The strongest growth came from the transportation, construction, and beverage can markets. By the end of 1995, demand should eliminate the world surplus of the metal, which was about one million tonnes in April 1995.

BALANCE SHEET (mil)			
Cash	27	81	149
Current Assets	2 ,821	2 ,402	2 ,655
Net Fixed Assets	5 ,534	6 ,005	6 ,256
Invest's & Advances	1 ,193	1 ,053	923
Total Assets	9 ,989	9 ,810	10 ,146
Short Term Debt	265	328	499
Current Liabilities	1 ,384	1 ,335	1 ,545
Long Term Debt	2 ,206	2 ,322	2 ,287
Total Liabilities	5 ,328	5 ,361	5 ,527
Total Equity	4 ,661	4 ,449	4 ,619
Total Liab. & Equity	9 ,989	9 ,810	10 ,146

Alcan has brought its raw material costs to below the world average. In the smelters, cost reductions continue, and despite operating in 1994 at only 85% of capacity, average unit costs were held to 1993 levels. Alcan continued on its goal of optimizing its world-wide network of rolling operations. Capacity expansions and the acquisition of a plant in Germany have made Alcan the world's largest producer of rolled aluminum products. Meanwhile, during 1994, Alcan sold about 20 downstream fabricating businesses, following its strategy to focus its resources on core activities.

CAPITAL (mil)			
Total Debt	2 ,471	2 ,650	2 ,786
Preferred Equity	353	353	353
Common Equity	4 ,308	4 ,096	4 ,266

Alcan's sales by product in 1994 were: rolled products, 44%; extruded and drawn products, 16%; other fabricated products, 6%; ingot products, 18%; and non-aluminum products, 16%. The company's fabricated and non-aluminum sales by market in 1994 were: containers and packaging, 34%; transportation, 8%; electrical, 9%; building and construction, 22%; and other, 27%. Its sales by country were: Canada, 12%; United States, 40%; South America, 7%; Europe, 34%; and Asia and Pacific, 7%.

Rank (Profit/Revenue/Assets)
50   6   23

John Evans
Chairman
Jacques Bougie
President & C.E.O.
Suresh Thadhani
V.P. & C.F.O.

Address
1188 Sherbrooke Street West
Montreal
PQ
H3C 3A7
(514) 848-8000

Fax: (514) 848-8115
A0001748/G/1.1

ARIMETCO INTERNATIONAL INC.

Exchanges	Price (Jun29'95)	1.85	Trailing P/E	9.74	Stock Symbol
T	Trailing Yield (%)	0.00	Trailing EPS	0.14	**ARX**

Period Ending	Dec94	Dec93	Dec92	Dec91	Dec90
Yearly Statistics	US	US	US	US	US
Price-Close	1.28	1.85	3.35	3.70	1.30
Price-High	2.20	3.80	5.75	4.50	1.80
Price-Low	0.98	1.44	2.85	1.25	1.00
P/E-Close	6.87	nm	32.43	nm	nm
Dividends per Share	0.00	0.00	0.00	0.00	0.00
Dividend Yield (%)	0.00	0.00	0.00	0.00	0.00
Sales per Share	0.80	0.69	0.92	0.56	0.34
EPS before extra. item	0.10	(0.20)	0.07	(0.02)	(0.08)
Cash Flow per Share	0.19	(0.06)	0.17	0.03	(0.05)
Book Value per Share	1.45	1.35	1.51	0.85	0.76
O/S Common Shares	28,739	28,689	26,366	20,399	17,295
Total Revenue	23,424	19,366	22,597	10,498	4,904
Income before extra.	2,749	(5,395)	1,661	(432)	(1,181)
Cash Flow	5,516	(1,785)	3,911	616	(646)
Debt/Equity	0.39	0.34	0.32	0.80	0.31
Return on Capital (%)	5.83	(9.23)	4.94	0.01	(3.08)
Ret. on Com. Equity (%)	6.85	(13.73)	5.82	(2.85)	(15.18)
% Change Profit	151.0	(424.9)	484.1	63.4	0.3
% Change Revenue	21.0	(14.3)	115.2	114.1	506.3
% Change Assets	10.4	(1.1)	64.2	78.5	33.7

Business:

ARIMETCO INTERNATIONAL INC. is a natural resource company engaged in the production of cathode copper through acid leaching of predominantly copper oxide ores, followed by solvent extraction and electrowinning. The company has interests in ten mineral properties, five of which contain former producing copper mines.

Date		EPS	DPS	Tot Rev	Inc Bex
Mar 95	US	0.06	0.00	6,451	1,477
Dec 94	US	0.05	0.00	7,227	1,728
Sep 94	US	0.02	0.00	6,721	494
Jun 94	US	0.01	0.00	5,080	238
Mar 94	US	0.01	0.00	4,679	288
Dec 93	US	(0.10)	0.00	3,728	(2,703)
Sep 93	US	(0.05)	0.00	5,055	(1,539)
Jun 93	US	(0.03)	0.00	5,236	(961)

	Dec94	Dec93	Dec92
Preferred Div. Coverage	np	np	np
Total Div. Coverage	na	na	na
Interest Coverage	7.1	0.0	5.1
Current Ratio	1.7	2.7	3.0
Operating Margin	12.0	(23.0)	6.9
Asset Turnover	0.4	0.3	0.4
5 YEAR RATIOS (%)			
Return on Capital	(0.3)	na	na
Return on Com. Equity	(3.8)	na	na
Profit Growth	na	na	na
Revenue Growth	96.0	na	na
Asset Growth	33.7	na	na
BALANCE SHEET (000)			
Cash	810	1,186	7,944
Current Assets	16,915	17,421	20,267
Net Fixed Assets	43,965	37,701	34,286
Invest's & Advances	129	163	1,499
Total Assets	62,098	56,250	56,872
Short Term Debt	5,849	2,069	2,420
Current Liabilities	9,915	6,372	6,689
Long Term Debt	10,473	10,916	10,368
Total Liabilities	20,566	17,466	17,058
Total Equity	41,532	38,784	39,814
Total Liab. & Equity	62,098	56,250	56,872
CAPITAL (000)			
Total Debt	16,321	12,985	12,788
Preferred Equity	0	0	0
Common Equity	41,532	38,784	39,814

Synopsis:

After having gone through a difficult period as a result of low copper prices, permitting difficulties, and production problems, Arimetco International Inc. will concentrate on its North American copper operations. The company has developed a huge reserve position, as large as most major producers, and must now focus on development. At December 1994, the Arimetco had about 19.8 billion tons of ore reserves, with an average copper grade ranging from 0.25% to 0.80%.

Permitting of the company's 100% owned Zonia mine in Arizona is expected during the second quarter of 1995, with completion scheduled by year-end. The project should produce 22 million pounds of copper annually at a cash cost of $0.54 (U.S.) per pound. This property has approximately 47 million tons of ore reserves with a 0.33% average copper grade. Capital costs will be $17.5-million (U.S.), most of which will be financed with debt.

The Mesaba project in Minnesota is one of the company's important development properties. In October 1993, Arimetco bought a 100% leasehold interest. This project contains one of the largest undeveloped copper reserves in North America (1,906 million tons of ore reserve, with a 0.80% average copper grade). The company expects to develop this project with a joint venture partner.

Sales in 1994 rose to $18.9-million (U.S.) from $16.1-million (U.S.) in 1993, due to higher copper prices and a higher volume of copper sold. Copper production for the year was 19,935,047 pounds at a net cash cost of $0.58 per pound on a weighted average basis. In 1994, Arimetco sold its copper at an average price of $0.95 (U.S.) per pound, compared with an average price of $0.87 (U.S.) in 1993. A hedging program kept Arimetco's price realizations below the COMEX average price of $1.07 (U.S.) per pound.

Each operation was re-engineered during the year to correct operating deficiencies. Also, Arimetco developed new ore, which enhanced recoveries and lowered operating costs at both the Johnson and MacArthur mines.

Rank (Profit/Revenue/Assets)
474   639   511

H. Roy Shipes
Pres., Chairman & C.E.O.

Harold E. Davis
V.P., C.F.O. & Treasurer

Address
335 N. Wilmot Road
Suite 400
Tucson
AZ
85711
(602) 748-2600

Fax: (602) 748-2626
01000829/G/1.2

For further company information, call Globe Information Services 1-800-268-9128 or (416) 585-5345

BRUNSWICK MINING AND SMELTING CORPORATION LIMITED

Exchanges	Price (Jun29'95)	9.87	Trailing P/E	12.34	Stock Symbol
TM	Trailing Yield (%)	2.53	Trailing EPS	0.80	**BMS**

Period Ending	Dec94	Dec93	Dec92	Dec91	Dec90
Yearly Statistics					
Price-Close	10.75	9.63	8.75	7.00	8.00
Price-High	11.13	9.63	10.50	9.38	11.00
Price-Low	9.63	7.38	7.00	6.50	6.75
P/E-Close	15.14	nm	21.34	nm	12.50
Dividends per Share	0.25	0.15	0.50	0.25	0.70
Dividend Yield (%)	2.33	1.56	5.71	3.57	8.75
Sales per Share	8.39	6.47	7.96	4.54	7.20
EPS before extra. item	0.71	(0.57)	0.41	(0.53)	0.64
Cash Flow per Share	1.80	(0.35)	1.16	(0.41)	1.22
Book Value per Share	5.70	5.21	5.91	5.96	6.74
O/S Common Shares	40,584	40,127	39,924	39,096	38,979
Total Revenue	359,969	261,957	338,656	188,711	285,773
Income before extra.	28,889	(22,704)	16,176	(20,836)	25,021
Cash Flow	72,340	(13,859)	45,611	(15,845)	47,371
Debt/Equity	0.26	0.36	0.26	0.39	0.04
Return on Capital (%)	16.43	(13.03)	9.46	(13.15)	11.91
Ret. on Com. Equity (%)	13.12	(10.21)	6.90	(8.40)	9.70
% Change Profit	227.2	(240.4)	177.6	(183.3)	(15.7)
% Change Revenue	37.4	(22.6)	79.5	(34.0)	(17.2)
% Change Assets	7.1	(4.5)	(0.6)	14.0	(9.8)

Preferred Div. Coverage	np	np	np
Total Div. Coverage	2.9	0.0	0.8
Interest Coverage	21.7	0.0	7.2
Current Ratio	1.8	1.3	1.8
Operating Margin	7.5	(16.1)	7.6
Asset Turnover	0.8	0.6	0.7
5 YEAR RATIOS (%)			
Return on Capital	2.3	1.9	8.0
Return on Com. Equity	2.2	2.1	7.0
Profit Growth	(0.5)	na	(3.8)
Revenue Growth	0.9	(5.0)	3.8
Asset Growth	0.9	0.1	1.3
BALANCE SHEET (000)			
Cash	0	70,815	70,815
Current Assets	207,805	168,277	185,104
Net Fixed Assets	229,155	241,998	244,487
Invest's & Advances	0	0	0
Total Assets	439,390	410,275	429,591
Short Term Debt	60,570	75,175	53,541
Current Liabilities	114,904	128,388	101,060
Long Term Debt	0	0	8,050
Total Liabilities	207,969	201,367	193,595
Total Equity	231,421	208,908	235,996
Total Liab. & Equity	439,390	410,275	429,591
CAPITAL (000)			
Total Debt	60,570	75,175	61,591
Preferred Equity	0	0	0
Common Equity	231,421	208,908	235,996

Business:

BRUNSWICK MINING AND SMELTING CORP. LTD. is engaged in mining and metallurgical operations at its facilities in New Brunswick. The company mines lead, zinc, silver, and copper and smelts lead. The company also makes diammonium phosphate, a fertilizer. Brunswick is 63% owned by Noranda Inc.

Date	EPS	DPS	Tot Rev	Inc Bex
Mar 95	0.26	0.00	98,061	10,588
Dec 94	0.43	0.10	116,222	17,545
Sep 94	0.02	0.00	72,663	620
Jun 94	0.09	0.15	82,844	3,681
Mar 94	0.17	0.00	88,240	7,043
Dec 93	(0.01)	0.00	68,964	(156)
Sep 93	(0.29)	0.00	37,942	(11,610)
Jun 93	(0.10)	0.15	64,566	(4,168)

Synopsis:

Brunswick Mining and Smelting's improved financial performance since early 1994 is the result of increased metal production at the Brunswick Mine and higher metal prices when priced in Canadian dollars. The economic recovery in North America has had a positive impact on metal prices and particularly on lead consumption. Productivity improvements and cost control measures implemented during the past three years also contributed.

Although zinc prices have improved, zinc stockpiles remain at twice the traditional level. Further improvement in zinc prices, a key parameter affecting Brunswick's profitability, is expected to be relatively modest in 1995. The zinc concentrate supply should move from the shortage of 1994 to a balanced position in 1995 and eventually, in 1996, to a slight surplus.

The Brunswick Mine will operate at full production throughout 1995. Exploration is continuing on projects in New Brunswick and Newfoundland, with a strong focus at Halfmile Lake. Brunswick invested $7.9-million during 1994 in mineral exploration with the aim of replacing depleted ore reserves at its mining operations or discovering new ore bodies. The program will continue with similar funding in 1995.

New feed treated at the smelter increased 28% to 211,297 tonnes in 1994, but is still limited by blast furnace capacity. Modifications to the hearth may be attempted in 1995 in order to increase throughput and reliability. Additional supplies of concentrate from the re-opened Heath Steele mine and the purchase of custom concentrate should enable the smelter to operated on a more continuous and productive basis.

In 1994 net revenue by product was: zinc, 46%; lead products, 16%; copper 10%; DAP, 9%; silver, 9%; bulk, 8%; and other, 2%.

Rank (Profit/Revenue/Assets)
167   230   241

Michael J. Knuckey
Chairman & C.E.O.
Derek G. Pannell
President

Address
P.O. Box 3000
Bathurst
NB
E2A 3Z8
(506) 546-6671

Fax: (506) 548-8379
B0004526/G/1.1

CAMECO CORPORATION

Exchanges	Price (Jun29'95)	41.25	Trailing P/E	26.79	Stock Symbol
TM	Trailing Yield (%)	1.21	Trailing EPS	1.54	**CCO**

Period Ending	Dec94	Dec93	Dec92	Dec91	Dec90
Yearly Statistics					
Price-Close	31.13	28.50	17.50	13.50	n t
Price-High	31.13	28.50	18.25	15.50	n t
Price-Low	21.75	17.00	16.63	13.13	n t
P/E-Close	19.95	20.21	116.67	13.11	n t
Dividends per Share	0.50	0.50	0.50	0.25	0.00
Dividend Yield (%)	1.61	1.75	2.86	1.85	0.00
Sales per Share	6.68	5.89	5.87	6.12	7.60
EPS before extra. item	1.56	1.41	0.15	1.03	2.21
Cash Flow per Share	2.68	2.55	2.45	2.68	2.37
Book Value per Share	23.35	22.35	21.48	21.83	23.55
O/S Common Shares	52,262	52,047	51,981	51,934	41,534
Total Revenue	350,047	313,144	248,025	301,173	373,090
Income before extra.	81,144	73,036	7,970	47,893	91,621
Cash Flow	139,434	132,631	127,242	124,406	98,553
Debt/Equity	0.05	0.07	0.15	0.14	0.36
Return on Capital (%)	6.78	6.52	1.50	5.05	9.07
Ret. on Com. Equity (%)	6.81	6.41	0.71	4.54	9.83
% Change Profit	11.1	816.4	(83.4)	(47.7)	289.6
% Change Revenue	11.8	26.3	(17.6)	(19.3)	16.8
% Change Assets	5.6	(1.9)	0.2	(3.2)	(6.4)

Date	EPS	DPS	Tot Rev	Inc Bex
Mar 95	0.23	0.13	59,260	12,018
Dec 94	0.34	0.13	96,469	17,359
Sep 94	0.35	0.13	76,517	18,056
Jun 94	0.62	0.13	118,022	31,940
Mar 94	0.26	0.13	58,122	13,789
Dec 93	0.50	0.13	108,535	25,907
Sep 93	0.31	0.13	66,356	16,164
Jun 93	0.24	0.13	79,309	12,620

Preferred Div. Coverage	np	np	np
Total Div. Coverage	3.1	2.8	0.3
Interest Coverage	19.4	7.5	1.6
Current Ratio	3.6	5.1	6.8
Operating Margin	24.3	25.3	25.8
Asset Turnover	0.2	0.2	0.2
5 YEAR RATIOS (%)			
Return on Capital	5.8	5.5	6.0
Return on Com. Equity	5.7	4.8	5.8
Profit Growth	28.2	5.4	(33.2)
Revenue Growth	1.8	4.3	4.3
Asset Growth	(1.3)	(3.0)	12.8
BALANCE SHEET (000)			
Cash	20,460	0	45,008
Current Assets	229,866	247,206	264,731
Net Fixed Assets	997,581	972,821	991,613
Invest's & Advances	20,000	20,000	0
Total Assets	1,426,762	1,350,872	1,376,483
Short Term Debt	0	6,831	0
Current Liabilities	63,818	48,882	38,779
Long Term Debt	61,568	74,927	170,008
Total Liabilities	206,390	187,825	259,977
Total Equity	1,220,372	1,163,047	1,116,506
Total Liab. & Equity	1,426,762	1,350,872	1,376,483
CAPITAL (000)			
Total Debt	61,568	81,758	170,008
Preferred Equity	0	0	0
Common Equity	1,220,372	1,163,047	1,116,506

Business:

CAMECO CORP. is one of the world's largest uranium producers, supplying about 10% of the western world's uranium consumption requirements. The company's products are used to generate electricity in nuclear energy plants around the world. Cameco also mines gold and explores primarily for uranium and gold.

Synopsis:

In 1994, Cameco achieved increases in revenue (14%), net earnings (11%), sales volumes of uranium concentrates (13%) and of uranium conversion services (25%) despite relatively abundant supply and continuing low spot market prices. Cameco supplied more than 10% of the western world's uranium consumption of about 134 million pounds. Cameco feels there will be a shortfall between consumption and existing supply of uranium as early as 1997. The shortfall may be well in excess of 50 million pounds a year by the end of the decade.

Electricity demand is increasing at a modest rate in the industrial world and at an annual growth rate approaching 7% in the developing countries. There are 431 nuclear power plants around the world that generate about 17% of the world's electricity. North America, with 131 reactors, is the largest customer region for Cameco, followed by Asia and Europe. During the next several years, the Asian market will be the growth area for nuclear power.

Cameco's strength as a producer is anchored by its two-thirds ownership of two of the world's largest, lower cost, high-grade uranium mining operations at Key Lake and Rabbit Lake. Its two Saskatchewan uranium development projects at McArthur River and Cigar Lake, in which Cameco holds about 50% ownership, promise to surpass the existing operations in size and in grade. These four Saskatchewan properties account for 85% of the 500 million pounds of uranium reserves which Cameco controls.

The company wants to increase its uranium concentrate sales by 25% by the end of the decade, increasing its share of the growing western world market. Cameco will make efforts to acquire uranium resources outside Canada. Cameco also wants to become a significant gold producer, with 250,000 ounces of production annually by the year 2000, doubling to 500,000 by 2005. The company's share from Contact Lake in northern Saskatchewan and Kumtor (Kyrgyzstan Republic) should account for most of the first phase of these production objectives.

Relative strength to TSE300

Price

Volume (in 1000's of board lots)

Rank (Profit/Revenue/Assets)
87   234   132

Bernard M. Michel
Chair., President & C.E.O.

Thomas J. Gorman
V.P. Fin., C.F.O. & Treas.

William Allan
Sr. V.P. & C.O.O.

Address
2121 - 11th Street West
Saskatoon
SK
S7M 1J3
(306) 956-6318

Fax: (306) 956-6318
C0002655/G/1.1

CANADA TUNGSTEN INC.

Exchanges	Price (Jun29'95)	1.63	Trailing P/E	nm	Stock Symbol
TM	Trailing Yield (%)	0.00	Trailing EPS	(0.12)	CTG

Period Ending	Dec94	Dec93	Jan93	Dec91	Dec90
Yearly Statistics					
Price-Close	1.80	1.40	1.50	3.00	2.00
Price-High	2.31	1.85	3.10	3.50	5.25
Price-Low	1.40	0.85	1.35	2.00	1.50
P/E-Close	nm	46.67	nm	nm	nm
Dividends per Share	0.00	0.00	0.19	0.20	0.20
Dividend Yield (%)	0.00	0.00	12.67	6.67	10.00
Sales per Share	0.41	0.49	0.88	0.86	0.41
EPS before extra. item	(0.09)	0.03	(1.88)	(0.12)	(0.33)
Cash Flow per Share	(0.09)	(0.05)	(0.21)	0.04	(0.26)
Book Value per Share	1.43	1.52	1.49	3.58	4.04
O/S Common Shares	29,929	29,874	29,806	20,756	18,942
Total Revenue	14,205	18,836	19,715	18,044	8,085
Income before extra.	(2,717)	967	(41,211)	(2,451)	(6,316)
Cash Flow	(2,724)	(1,403)	(4,630)	825	(4,691)
Debt/Equity	nd	0.06	0.02	0.01	0.02
Return on Capital (%)	(5.91)	2.21	(68.33)	(3.09)	(7.55)
Ret. on Com. Equity (%)	(6.16)	2.15	(69.45)	(3.25)	(7.93)
% Change Profit	(381.0)	102.3	(1,581.4)	61.2	(24.1)
% Change Revenue	(24.6)	(4.5)	9.3	123.2	(32.5)
% Change Assets	(1.4)	7.1	(39.1)	4.0	0.0
Preferred Div. Coverage	np	np	np		
Total Div. Coverage	na	na	0.0		
Interest Coverage	nd	na	0.0		
Current Ratio	4.4	12.7	5.2		
Operating Margin	(30.9)	(21.6)	(18.7)		
Asset Turnover	0.2	0.3	0.4		
5 YEAR RATIOS (%)					
Return on Capital	(16.5)	(16.5)	(17.3)		
Return on Com. Equity	(16.9)	(16.9)	(17.7)		
Profit Growth	na	na	na		
Revenue Growth	3.4	9.6	11.6		
Asset Growth	(9.7)	(10.3)	(11.5)		
BALANCE SHEET (000)					
Cash	17,184	14,444	9,113		
Current Assets	19,171	19,537	14,260		
Net Fixed Assets	34,706	34,840	36,222		
Invest's & Advances	0	280	575		
Total Assets	53,878	54,657	51,057		
Short Term Debt	0	0	0		
Current Liabilities	4,376	1,533	2,747		
Long Term Debt	0	2,520	946		
Total Liabilities	11,094	9,206	6,620		
Total Equity	42,784	45,451	44,437		
Total Liab. & Equity	53,878	54,657	51,057		
CAPITAL (000)					
Total Debt	0	2,520	946		
Preferred Equity	0	0	0		
Common Equity	42,784	45,451	44,437		

Business:

CANADA TUNGSTEN is a mining company in the business of exploration, development and operation of base and precious metal mines. The Company's assets include a 70 per cent interest in the Andacollo heap leach copper project in Chile, various Tungsten properties and a protfolio of exploration properties. Aur Resources Inc. holds 45.3% of the shares of Canada Tungsten Inc.

Date	EPS	DPS	Tot Rev	Inc Bex
Mar 95	(0.01)	0.00	251	(428)
Dec 94	(0.11)	0.00	(61)	(3,223)
Sep 94	(0.02)	0.00	4,280	(534)
Jun 94	0.02	0.00	5,464	581
Mar 94	0.02	0.00	4,522	459
Dec 93	0.05	0.00	7,744	1,433
Sep 93	0.04	0.00	4,808	1,126
Jun 93	(0.02)	0.00	3,452	(565)

Synopsis:

In August 1994, Aur Resources Inc. bought 48% of the issued common shares of Canada Tungsten from Cyprus Amax Minerals Company. Aur had intended to merge its operations with Canada Tungsten. However, in January 1995, the two companies could not agree on the terms of the merger. Following the share acquisition, Aur management assumed responsibility for the day to day operations of Canada Tungsten.

Canada Tungsten's major undertaking is the development of the Andacollo copper project in Chile. Andacollo should begin initial production in late 1996. Financing for the project should be arranged by September 1995.

In January 1995, the company and its 30% Chilean partner exercised an option to buy Andacollo from the Chilean government. The initial payment was $500,000 (U.S.). As well, the partnership agreed to the following: a further payment of $770,000 (U.S.) upon start-up of mining operations; 10 annual payments of $350,000 (U.S.); and 10% of net profits after pay-back.

A production feasibility study for Andacollo was completed in late 1994. It indicated that the 35 million tonne heap leachable copper deposit could be developed into an open pit mining operation. The mine is capable of producing 44 million pounds of cathode copper annually over a mine life of 11 years with a capital investment of $69-million (U.S.). Production costs were estimated at $0.54 (U.S.) per pound of copper produced. Pay-back of the pre-production development costs would be achieved in approximately four years given a copper price of $1.00 (U.S.) per pound. Currently, the partnership is evaluating the potential for new copper and gold deposits in the Andacollo area.

Canada Tungsten's net earnings and losses for 1995 and 1996 will be affected primarily by costs for administration, exploration, and facilities under care and maintenance. It sold its only producing mining asset, the Aurora Partnership gold mine in Nevada, in December 1994.

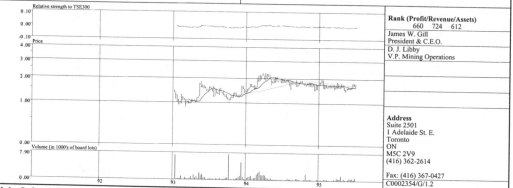

Rank (Profit/Revenue/Assets)
660 724 612

James W. Gill
President & C.E.O.

D. J. Libby
V.P. Mining Operations

Address
Suite 2501
1 Adelaide St. E.
Toronto
ON
M5C 2V9
(416) 362-2614

Fax: (416) 367-0427
C0002354/G/1.2

COMINCO LTD.

Exchanges	Price (Jun29'95)	25.12	Trailing P/E	13.09	Stock Symbol
TMVA	Trailing Yield (%)	0.00	Trailing EPS	1.92	**CLT**

Period Ending	Dec94	Dec93	Dec92	Dec91	Dec90
Yearly Statistics					
Price-Close	24.88	20.25	17.75	21.38	21.25
Price-High	26.50	21.50	23.50	25.75	28.00
Price-Low	18.63	13.63	17.13	19.50	19.13
P/E-Close	15.36	nm	nm	nm	32.69
Dividends per Share	0.00	0.00	0.40	0.50	0.50
Dividend Yield (%)	0.00	0.00	2.25	2.34	2.35
Sales per Share	13.81	12.37	18.47	17.76	17.69
EPS before extra. item	1.62	(1.46)	(0.42)	(0.56)	0.65
Cash Flow per Share	1.74	(0.65)	1.18	0.62	2.52
Book Value per Share	12.73	10.97	12.37	12.85	13.97
O/S Common Shares	79,495	79,456	79,456	79,440	79,333
Total Revenue	1,254,641	1,082,779	1,558,646	1,335,017	1,417,545
Income before extra.	132,076	(113,210)	(30,167)	(41,309)	54,756
Cash Flow	138,462	(51,468)	93,526	45,773	199,949
Debt/Equity	0.48	0.64	0.61	0.60	0.44
Return on Capital (%)	15.93	(4.65)	2.67	(0.29)	6.83
Ret. on Com. Equity (%)	13.71	(12.54)	(3.33)	(4.20)	4.65
% Change Profit	216.7	(275.3)	27.0	(175.4)	(74.5)
% Change Revenue	15.9	(30.5)	16.8	(5.8)	(11.9)
% Change Assets	7.7	(6.6)	(2.5)	0.2	0.4
Preferred Div. Coverage	44.2	0.0	0.0		
Total Div. Coverage	44.2	0.0	0.0		
Interest Coverage	5.7	0.0	1.0		
Current Ratio	2.1	2.2	2.3		
Operating Margin	10.5	(18.5)	0.5		
Asset Turnover	0.4	0.4	0.6		
5 YEAR RATIOS (%)					
Return on Capital	4.1	5.5	11.6		
Return on Com. Equity	(0.3)	1.0	8.3		
Profit Growth	(9.3)	na	na		
Revenue Growth	(4.9)	(8.3)	3.5		
Asset Growth	(0.4)	1.4	4.7		
BALANCE SHEET (000)					
Cash	46,112	12,327	18,969		
Current Assets	632,336	506,216	682,375		
Net Fixed Assets	1,720,497	1,634,949	1,658,794		
Invest's & Advances	42,678	83,620	48,743		
Total Assets	2,445,970	2,271,220	2,432,567		
Short Term Debt	56,517	43,493	76,648		
Current Liabilities	303,711	225,058	302,679		
Long Term Debt	505,496	622,022	622,502		
Total Liabilities	1,269,130	1,234,280	1,281,752		
Total Equity	1,176,840	1,036,940	1,150,815		
Total Liab. & Equity	2,445,970	2,271,220	2,432,567		
CAPITAL (000)					
Total Debt	562,013	665,515	699,150		
Preferred Equity	164,996	165,743	167,692		
Common Equity	1,011,844	871,197	983,123		

Business:

COMINCO LTD. is an integrated natural resource company with activities in mining, smelting and refining and mineral exploraiton. The company produces zinc, lead, copper, ferronickel and other metal products. It also mines zinc, lead, copper and other minerals at mines in Canada, the United States, Mexico and Chile.

Date	EPS	DPS	Tot Rev	Inc Bex
Mar 95	0.32	0.00	326,500	26,100
Dec 94	0.84	0.00	379,741	67,776
Sep 94	0.20	0.00	294,500	16,700
Jun 94	0.56	0.00	318,900	45,300
Mar 94	0.02	0.00	261,500	2,300
Dec 93	0.12	0.00	307,179	10,090
Sep 93	(0.89)	0.00	214,000	(70,200)
Jun 93	(0.22)	0.00	270,900	(16,300)

Synopsis:

In 1994, Cominco Ltd. dealt successfully with operating problems at its Red Dog mine and brought into production the new Quebrada Blanca copper mine in Chile. After three years of losses, the company achieved net earnings of $132-million. This turnaround in results was due to improved copper prices and the lower Canadian dollar. Production improvements at the key Red Dog and Trail operations, and Highland Valley Copper's significantly improved operating profit, were the main reasons for the sharp increase in profitability.

During 1994 and 1995, the economies of Europe and Asia have joined with the U.S. in a period of sustained growth. Demand for base metals is up, and base metal inventories have fallen while prices rise.

The Quebrada Blanca mine opened in September 1994. It is expected that production will steadily increase in the first half of 1995 and will reach capacity at 75,000 tonnes of copper per year. The mine cost $342-million (U.S.) to open, excluding capitalized interest. In early 1995 Cominco and Marubeni Corp. bought the Cajamarquilla zinc refinery in Peru. Cominco's share of the $108-million purchase price was $90-million (U.S.).

In late 1994, Cominco Ltd. sold its remaining interest in Cominco Fertilizers for $125-million, bringing the gross proceeds from the sale to $371-million. This sale largely completed the company's divestiture of non-core businesses, allowing it to focus on the exploration, mining, smelting and refining of base metals -- primarily zinc, copper, gold, and nickel. Exploration projects are now underway in the United States, Canada, Mexico, Peru, Bolivia, Chile, Turkey and Greenland.

By May 31, 1995, Cominco Ltd. bought the 44.3% of Cominco Resources International Ltd. that it did not already own. It by offered Cominco Resources shareholders one Cominco Ltd. share for every 6.15 Cominco Resources shares.

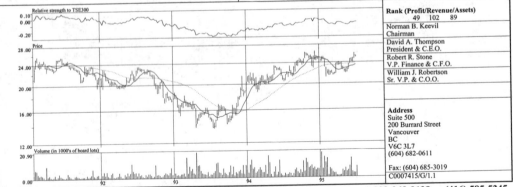

Rank (Profit/Revenue/Assets)		
49	102	89

Norman B. Keevil
Chairman

David A. Thompson
President & C.E.O.

Robert R. Stone
V.P. Finance & C.F.O.

William J. Robertson
Sr. V.P. & C.O.O.

Address
Suite 500
200 Burrard Street
Vancouver
BC
V6C 3L7
(604) 682-0611

Fax: (604) 685-3019
C0007415/G/1.1

DENISON MINES LIMITED

Exchanges	Price (Jun29'95)	0.30	Trailing P/E	30.00	Stock Symbol
TM	Trailing Yield (%)	0.00	Trailing EPS	0.01	**DEN.B**

Period Ending	Dec93	Dec92	Dec91	Dec90	Dec89
Yearly Statistics					
Price-Close	0.25	0.16	0.22	0.70	4.00
Price-High	0.40	0.35	1.00	3.45	6.88
Price-Low	0.16	0.07	0.20	0.45	3.70
P/E-Close	nm	0.36	nm	nm	nm
Dividends per Share	0.00	0.00	0.00	0.00	0.24
Dividend Yield (%)	0.00	0.00	0.00	0.00	6.00
Sales per Share	1.49	2.83	5.03	4.93	4.91
EPS before extra. item	(0.18)	0.44	(1.71)	(4.83)	(0.47)
Cash Flow per Share	0.40	0.50	0.69	0.31	0.74
Book Value per Share	(4.44)	(4.55)	(3.80)	(2.38)	2.38
O/S Common Shares	64,143	64,143	64,143	64,143	64,143
Total Revenue	121,729	386,706	317,038	318,282	336,904
Income before extra.	7,122	47,153	(91,144)	(291,268)	(4,278)
Cash Flow	25,869	31,861	44,513	19,730	47,409
Debt/Equity	na	na	na	6.35	0.52
Return on Capital (%)	na	308.94	(14.05)	(64.41)	5.89
Ret. on Com. Equity (%)	na	na	na	nm	(19.23)
% Change Profit	(84.9)	151.7	68.7	(6,708.5)	96.4
% Change Revenue	(68.5)	22.0	(0.4)	(5.5)	(23.6)
% Change Assets	1.1	(75.6)	(19.4)	(36.4)	(21.8)
Preferred Div. Coverage	na	na	na		
Total Div. Coverage	na	na	na		
Interest Coverage	2.7	9.2	0.0		
Current Ratio	3.5	2.2	1.1		
Operating Margin	(12.4)	(75.3)	(5.3)		
Asset Turnover	0.8	1.6	0.7		
5 YEAR RATIOS (%)					
Return on Capital	na	45.6	(14.0)		
Return on Com. Equity	na	na	na		
Profit Growth	na	11.6	na		
Revenue Growth	(22.8)	(3.4)	(5.4)		
Asset Growth	(37.3)	(39.5)	(21.5)		
BALANCE SHEET (000)					
Cash	16,861	19,718	23,341		
Current Assets	90,070	82,250	84,393		
Net Fixed Assets	24,859	31,261	142,906		
Invest's & Advances	1,639	1,787	4,121		
Total Assets	116,568	115,298	473,027		
Short Term Debt	0	0	5,468		
Current Liabilities	25,640	36,844	76,089		
Long Term Debt	91,924	80,449	122,950		
Total Liabilities	218,735	224,587	529,660		
Total Equity	(102,167)	(109,289)	(56,633)		
Total Liab. & Equity	116,568	115,298	473,027		
CAPITAL (000)					
Total Debt	91,924	80,449	128,418		
Preferred Equity	182,511	182,511	186,861		
Common Equity	(284,678)	(291,800)	(243,494)		

Business:

DENISON MINES LTD. is a Canadian company with energy resource related interests, including interests in uranium deposits in Saskatchewan and Australia, uranium recovery operations in Louisiana and oil and gas operations in Greece. Roman Corp. Ltd. of Toronto is the company's largest shareholder.

Date	EPS	DPS	Tot Rev	Inc Bex
Mar 95	0.01	0.00	17,492	5,526
Dec 94	0.03	0.00	16,568	6,603
Sep 94	(0.06)	0.00	21,264	321
Jun 94	0.03	0.00	26,647	6,603
Mar 94	(0.05)	0.00	21,209	1,692
Dec 93	0.03	0.00	45,800	6,856
Sep 93	(0.06)	0.00	23,745	588
Jun 93	(0.06)	0.00	29,305	1,176

Synopsis:

In May 1995, Denison Mines announced an agreement with its two bankers regarding the company's restructuring plan. In exchange for forgiving the $40-million it owes the Toronto-Dominion Bank and the Bank of America, Denison will give the two banks a total of 10% of the newly restructured company. Also, Denison will issue the two banks a $30-million note. The note will be paid off only after Denison pays for the clean up at the now closed uranium mine in Elliot Lake, Ontario. Besides the amounts owed to the banks, Denison owes money to Canada Mortgage and Housing Corp. and preferred and common shareholders.

In April 1995, Denison received regulatory approval to withdraw the surplus amount of $19.1-million from the company's pension plan. The withdraw applies to pensions owned by salaried employees. Of the total amount, Denison applied $14.7-million equally to the company's bank debt and the Elliot Lake reclamation trust fund.

As of April 1995, Denison had contributed about $14.4-million to the Elliot Lake reclamation trust. Denison's efforts continue towards the demolition and clean up of mine site buildings. As well, it will cover the tailings basin with water to prevent any future acid generation.

In November 1994, Denison common shares resumed trading on the Toronto and Montreal Stock Exchanges. The trading resumed after the Ontario Securities Commission lifted its restriction on Denison's shares.

Rank (Profit/Revenue/Assets)
241   433   470

Helen E. Roman-Barber
Chairman

William James
President & C.E.O.

Address
Suite 320
40 Dundas Street West
Toronto
ON
M5G 2C2
(416) 979-1991

Fax: (416) 979-5893
D0000940/G/1.4

DIA MET MINERALS LTD.

Exchanges	Price (Jun29'95)			11.75	Trailing P/E		nm	Stock Symbol
T	Trailing Yield (%)			0.00	Trailing EPS		(0.02)	**DMM.B**

Period Ending	Jan95	Jan94	Jan93	Jan92	Jan91
Yearly Statistics					
Price-Close	12.88	29.50	19.25	4.50	0.13
Price-High	33.00	33.50	30.00	4.56	0.36
Price-Low	10.00	18.50	2.30	0.16	0.10
P/E-Close	nm	2,950.00	nm	1,800.00	260.00
Dividends per Share	0.00	0.00	0.00	0.00	0.00
Dividend Yield (%)	0.00	0.00	0.00	0.00	0.00
Sales per Share	na	na	na	na	na
EPS before extra. item	(0.02)	0.01	(0.01)	0.00	0.00
Cash Flow per Share	(0.02)	0.02	(0.01)	0.00	0.00
Book Value per Share	0.66	0.84	0.22	0.18	0.18
O/S Common Shares	26,915	21,462	20,367	18,719	17,145
Total Revenue	1,951	946	46	60	7
Income before extra.	(650)	235	(230)	47	5
Cash Flow	(452)	299	(228)	(13)	7
Debt/Equity	nd	nd	nd	nd	0.03
Return on Capital (%)	(3.10)	2.09	(5.85)	1.46	na
Ret. on Com. Equity (%)	(3.63)	2.09	(5.85)	1.48	na
% Change Profit	(376.8)	202.0	(588.7)	892.5	na
% Change Revenue	106.2	1,961.3	(23.0)	755.8	na
% Change Assets	0.3	288.3	33.9	10.7	na

Business:

DIA MET MINERALS LTD. is in the mineral exploration business with a primary interest in diamonds. Its principal properties are located in the Northwest Territories and Alberta.

Date	EPS	DPS	Tot Rev	Inc Bex
Apr 95	0.00	0.00	393	(77)
Jan 95	(0.01)	0.00	400	(457)
Oct 94	0.00	0.00	671	38
Jul 94	(0.01)	0.00	547	(183)
Apr 94	0.00	0.00	393	(48)
Jan 94	0.01	0.00	875	170
Oct 93	0.01	0.00	336	231
Jul 93	0.00	0.00	120	14

Preferred Div. Coverage	np	np	np
Total Div. Coverage	na	na	na
Interest Coverage	nd	nd	nd
Current Ratio	15.4	27.0	14.8
Operating Margin	(97.2)	(311.2)	(1,043.5)
Asset Turnover	na	na	na
5 YEAR RATIOS (%)			
Return on Capital	na	na	na
Return on Com. Equity	na	na	na
Profit Growth	na	na	na
Revenue Growth	na	na	na
Asset Growth	na	na	na
BALANCE SHEET (000)			
Cash	11,316	12,669	1,336
Current Assets	12,033	13,261	1,425
Net Fixed Assets	6,568	5,284	3,351
Invest's & Advances	0	0	0
Total Assets	18,601	18,545	4,776
Short Term Debt	0	0	0
Current Liabilities	783	491	96
Long Term Debt	0	0	0
Total Liabilities	783	595	270
Total Equity	17,818	17,950	4,506
Total Liab. & Equity	18,601	18,545	4,776
CAPITAL (000)			
Total Debt	0	0	0
Preferred Equity	0	0	0
Common Equity	17,818	17,950	4,506

Synopsis:

In Dia Met's annual report, the company said it will continue to focus on its diamond projects in the Northwest Territories. The 1995 winter sampling program was completed on 10 kimberlite deposits relating to the Dia Met/BHP joint venture. The joint venture partners say diamonds found on the property in the Northwest Territories are among the highest quality. The deposits are comparable to any top 10 pipes in the world.

Subsequent to its January 31, 1995, year end, Dia Met granted an option to a third party entitling the party to acquire a 49% interest in the Alberta River claims. In exchange for the option, Dia Met will receive, on or before July 10, 1995, $1-million. The money will then be used to finance exploration to be conducted on the claims by Dia Met. If after the $1-million has been spent and further development is warranted, costs will be divided on a joint basis between the two parties.

Dia Met stated in their annual report that subsequent to the company's year end of January 31, 1995, the company granted options to directors and employees to buy 641,000 Class A shares at a price of $9.25 per share. The options are exercisable on or before February 21, 2005.

As of the end of January 31, 1995, Dia Met had no long term debt. However, if the Lac de Gras property goes into production, Dia Met will have to fund its joint share of the $500-million (U.S.) mine. The BHP Diamond joint venture states that BHP must advance up to $500-million (U.S.) to place the first mine into production. Dia Met must then repay its proportionate share advances by BHP, plus interest.

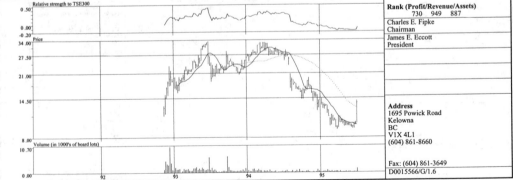

Rank (Profit/Revenue/Assets)
730 949 887

Charles E. Fipke
Chairman

James E. Eccott
President

Address
1695 Powick Road
Kelowna
BC
V1X 4L1
(604) 861-8660

Fax: (604) 861-3649
D0015566/G/1.6

FALCONBRIDGE LIMITED

Exchanges
TM

	Price (Jun29'95)	24.50	Trailing P/E	14.50	Stock Symbol
	Trailing Yield (%)	0.41	Trailing EPS	1.69	**FL**

Period Ending	Dec94	Dec93	Dec92	Dec91	Dec90
Yearly Statistics					
Price-Close	24.50	n t	n t	n t	n t
Price-High	24.63	n t	n t	n t	n t
Price-Low	17.00	n t	n t	n t	n t
P/E-Close	26.06	n t	n t	n t	n t
Dividends per Share	0.00	0.00	0.00	0.00	0.00
Dividend Yield (%)	0.00	0.00	0.00	0.00	0.00
Sales per Share	14.00	14.33	16.51	nm	nm
EPS before extra. item	0.94	(0.44)	0.75	nm	nm
Cash Flow per Share	3.33	1.04	2.90	nm	nm
Book Value per Share	9.82	2.41	2.10	nm	nm
O/S Common Shares	176,487	100,000	100,000	10	10
Total Revenue	1,994,642	1,434,775	1,664,400	1,757,242	2,070,194
Income before extra.	131,252	(44,462)	74,807	20,548	91,022
Cash Flow	466,634	104,223	289,619	224,550	364,481
Debt/Equity	0.34	7.52	9.27	1.82	1.88
Return on Capital (%)	13.31	1.53	9.05	5.28	12.05
Ret. on Com. Equity (%)	13.30	(19.74)	11.42	1.88	14.14
% Change Profit	395.2	(159.4)	264.1	(77.4)	(76.9)
% Change Revenue	39.0	(13.8)	(5.3)	(15.1)	(15.7)
% Change Assets	14.4	(8.2)	(24.6)	(0.8)	1.5
Preferred Div. Coverage	np	np	np		
Total Div. Coverage	na	na	na		
Interest Coverage	4.5	0.4	2.0		
Current Ratio	2.8	1.4	1.6		
Operating Margin	17.2	4.5	15.3		
Asset Turnover	0.7	0.6	0.6		
5 YEAR RATIOS (%)					
Return on Capital	8.2	11.4	17.1		
Return on Com. Equity	4.2	12.9	21.9		
Profit Growth	0.0	na	20.1		
Revenue Growth	(4.1)	(7.7)	3.9		
Asset Growth	(4.5)	(0.6)	0.8		
BALANCE SHEET (000)					
Cash	307,548	31,829	108,231		
Current Assets	1,005,634	544,513	678,299		
Net Fixed Assets	1,850,222	1,911,040	1,986,733		
Invest's & Advances	0	0	3,589		
Total Assets	2,901,903	2,536,939	2,762,314		
Short Term Debt	108,000	182,437	178,527		
Current Liabilities	364,731	391,356	424,570		
Long Term Debt	473,389	1,627,466	1,765,360		
Total Liabilities	1,169,301	2,296,147	2,552,686		
Total Equity	1,732,602	240,792	209,628		
Total Liab. & Equity	2,901,903	2,536,939	2,762,314		
CAPITAL (000)					
Total Debt	581,389	1,809,903	1,943,887		
Preferred Equity	0	0	0		
Common Equity	1,732,602	240,792	209,628		

Business:

FALCONBRIDGE LIMITED is an international resource company engaged in the exploration, mining, processing and marketing of metal and mineral products including nickel, ferronickel, copper, zinc, cobalt and precious metals. The company has operations in Canada, Norway, and the Dominican Republic.

Date	EPS	DPS	Tot Rev	Inc Bex
Mar 95	0.55	0.10	618,500	96,250
Dec 94	0.55	0.00	596,535	81,352
Sep 94	0.32	0.00	528,300	55,500
Jun 94	0.27	0.00	453,500	46,000
Mar 94	(0.08)	0.00	420,800	(7,600)
Dec 93	(0.07)	0.00	346,353	(7,362)
Sep 93	(0.11)	0.00	371,100	(11,400)
Jun 93	(0.02)	0.00	360,700	(2,400)

Synopsis:

Falconbridge issued common shares in June 1994, after being taken private in 1989. The $1.341-billion received for the issue went primarily to repay debt. This will allow Falconbridge to raise money to develop its Collahuasi and Raglan projects.

The strengthening economic recovery had a major impact on metal markets in 1994 and this has continued into 1995. Prices for most of Falconbridge's products have improved and nickel sales volumes continued to climb throughout 1994 and the first half of 1995, driven largely by demand from the stainless steel sector. Nickel markets have improved, compared to the oversupply that curtailed production between 1990 and 1994.

While 44% of revenues generated in 1994 were from the sale of nickel and ferronickel, 28% was from copper sales, 11% from zinc and 17% from cobalt and other products. The average prices in U.S. dollars per pound realized by Falconbridge during 1994 (1993) for nickel were: $2.91 ($2.48); ferronickel, $2.78 ($2.43); and copper, $1.06 ($0.86).

The Collahuasi project in northern Chile is one of the world's largest known undeveloped copper properties. Falconbridge is moving towards a production decision in 1995. Collahuasi has almost two billion tonnes of ore grading 0.90% copper. The company's one-half share of Collahuasi's planned output would double Falconbridge's mined annual copper production by 137% at 1994 levels, with a planned production rate of 60,000 tonnes per day. Copper reserves at Collahuasi should last 50 years.

The Raglan nickel project in northern Quebec should be a highly competitive producer in the future, with cash operating costs estimated to be significantly less than $2.00 (U.S.) per pound of nickel. Raglan would increase the company's annual refined nickel production from Falconbridge mines, at 1994 levels, by 56%.

Rank (Profit/Revenue/Assets)
51   69   72

Alex G. Balogh
Chairman
Franklin G.T. Pickard
President & C.E.O.
Lars-Eric Johansson
Sr. V.P. & C.F.O.

Address
Suite 1200
95 Wellington Street West
Toronto
ON
M5J 2V4
(416) 956-5700

Fax: (416) 956-5757
F0000142/G/1.1

GIBRALTAR MINES LIMITED

Exchanges	Price (Jun29'95)		6 .50	Trailing P/E		nm	Stock Symbol
TV	Trailing Yield (%)		0 .00	Trailing EPS		(0 .33)	**GBM**

Period Ending	Dec94	Dec93	Dec92	Dec91	Dec90
Yearly Statistics					
Price-Close	7 .00	6 .50	5 .00	6 .25	6 .88
Price-High	9 .38	6 .50	8 .20	8 .75	11 .38
Price-Low	5 .00	4 .60	4 .75	5 .50	6 .25
P/E-Close	nm	nm	19 .23	23 .15	8 .38
Dividends per Share	0 .00	0 .00	0 .05	0 .20	0 .50
Dividend Yield (%)	0 .00	0 .00	1 .00	3 .20	7 .27
Sales per Share	0 .82	3 .29	5 .47	5 .60	6 .72
EPS before extra. item	(0 .44)	(0 .82)	0 .26	0 .27	0 .82
Cash Flow per Share	(0 .28)	(0 .06)	1 .37	1 .08	1 .31
Book Value per Share	4 .15	4 .59	5 .60	5 .39	5 .32
O/S Common Shares	22 ,890	22 ,881	12 ,041	12 ,041	12 ,041
Total Revenue	21 ,603	47 ,800	67 ,338	69 ,136	84 ,558
Income before extra.	(10 ,080)	(11 ,298)	3 ,107	3 ,244	9 ,888
Cash Flow	(6 ,445)	(775)	16 ,501	12 ,947	15 ,825
Debt/Equity	0 .02	0 .01	nd	nd	nd
Return on Capital (%)	(15 .65)	(24 .31)	10 .31	8 .16	31 .88
Ret. on Com. Equity (%)	(10 .08)	(13 .11)	4 .70	5 .03	15 .92
% Change Profit	10 .8	(463 .6)	(4 .2)	(67 .2)	(59 .3)
% Change Revenue	(54 .8)	(29 .0)	(2 .6)	(18 .2)	(19 .2)
% Change Assets	(7 .7)	39 .4	7 .9	(2 .8)	(5 .9)
Preferred Div. Coverage	np	np	np		
Total Div. Coverage	na	na	5 .2		
Interest Coverage	na	na	nd		
Current Ratio	4 .1	13 .1	4 .7		
Operating Margin	(98 .9)	(51 .0)	8 .1		
Asset Turnover	0 .2	0 .3	0 .7		
5 YEAR RATIOS (%)					
Return on Capital	2 .1	17 .5	25 .6		
Return on Com. Equity	0 .5	9 .9	15 .0		
Profit Growth	na	na	(6 .1)		
Revenue Growth	(27 .2)	(0 .9)	(1 .9)		
Asset Growth	4 .9	7 .4	(0 .1)		
BALANCE SHEET (000)					
Cash	5 ,534	44 ,519	9 ,958		
Current Assets	28 ,949	63 ,651	28 ,476		
Net Fixed Assets	83 ,037	59 ,521	58 ,343		
Invest's & Advances	0	0	8 ,000		
Total Assets	121 ,986	132 ,183	94 ,853		
Short Term Debt	0	0	0		
Current Liabilities	7 ,136	4 ,870	6 ,032		
Long Term Debt	1 ,984	1 ,006	0		
Total Liabilities	27 ,030	27 ,191	27 ,480		
Total Equity	94 ,956	104 ,992	67 ,373		
Total Liab. & Equity	121 ,986	132 ,183	94 ,853		
CAPITAL (000)					
Total Debt	1 ,984	1 ,006	0		
Preferred Equity	0	0	0		
Common Equity	94 ,956	104 ,992	67 ,373		

Business:

GIBRALTAR MINES LTD. is a copper and molybdenum mining company. It has operations and exploration activities in British Columbia and Chile. Placer Dome Canada Limited owns 44.4% of the company's shares.

Date	EPS	DPS	Tot Rev	Inc Bex
Mar 95	0 .03	0 .00	23 ,269	714
Dec 94	0 .02	0 .00	13 ,071	416
Sep 94	(0 .26)	0 .00	3 ,702	(5 ,952)
Jun 94	(0 .12)	0 .00	1 ,686	(2 ,661)
Mar 94	(0 .08)	0 .00	3 ,144	(1 ,883)
Dec 93	(0 .31)	0 .00	9 ,882	(5 ,096)
Sep 93	(0 .26)	0 .00	12 ,220	(3 ,174)
Jun 93	(0 .29)	0 .00	14 ,452	(3 ,452)

Synopsis:

The strategy of Gibraltar Mines Limited focuses on growth through the exploration and acquisition of copper properties exploitable through SX-EW technology. SX-EW amenable deposits generally have lower capital and operating costs than sulphide deposits of similar grade. Gibraltar will concentrate on properties amenable to open pit mining. It will target deposits such as Lomas Bayas in Chile, which holds between 50 and 150 tonnes of ore.

As Gibraltar's only working asset, the continued operation of the McLeese Lake mine in British Columbia remains a key part of Gibraltar's strategic plan. The mine resumed full production in September 1994. Production resumed mainly because of improved copper prices, lower exchange rates, and cost reductions. Copper prices rebounded from around $0.80 (U.S.) per pound in January 1994 to reach a high of $1.39 (U.S.) in December 1994. The B.C. government also agreed to defer certain government levies. The mine had been closed since December 1, 1993. Gibraltar implemented new smelting and refining contracts, and negotiated and implemented a hedging program to support the restarted operations.

Gibraltar bought Lomas Bayas in October 1994 for $19.3-million (U.S.) or $0.015 (U.S.) per pound of estimated recoverable copper. The acquisition study assumed a 20,000 tonne per day crush and leach SX-EW operation producing 45,350 tonnes (100 million pounds) per year of cathode copper. Gibraltar estimated capital spending would be $156.5-million (U.S.), and operating costs would be $0.52 (U.S.) per pound. Project development should finish in the fall of 1996.

During 1994, Gibraltar spent $7.1-million on exploration. For 1995, exploration activities will center on northern Chile, around Lomas Bayas and the nearby Fortuna de Cobre copper oxide property.

Rank (Profit/Revenue/Assets)
943 707 443

Ian G. Austin
Chairman

William H. Myckatyn
President And C.E.O.

Paul B. Sweeney
Sr. V.P. & C.F.O.

Address
266 Oliver Street
Williams Lake
BC
V2G 1M1
(604) 398-6211

Fax: (604) 398-8671
G0001435/G/1.2

GLOBAL STONE CORPORATION

Exchanges	Price (Jun29'95)		4.60	Trailing P/E		17.04	Stock Symbol
T	Trailing Yield (%)		0.00	Trailing EPS		0.27	GLS

Period Ending	Sep94	Sep93	Sep92
Yearly Statistics			8M
Price-Close	5.50	4.80	n t
Price-High	7.25	5.25	n t
Price-Low	4.50	2.63	n t
P/E-Close	22.00	48.00	n t
Dividends per Share	0.00	0.00	0.00
Dividend Yield (%)	0.00	0.00	0.00
Sales per Share	2.90	2.30	0.00
EPS before extra. item	0.25	0.10	na
Cash Flow per Share	0.60	0.31	0.00
Book Value per Share	3.06	2.05	0.15
O/S Common Shares	19,388	12,800	3,000
Total Revenue	47,406	16,748	0
Income before extra.	4,256	724	0
Cash Flow	9,649	2,272	0
Debt/Equity	0.50	0.14	1.68
Return on Capital (%)	13.53	25.87	na
Ret. on Com. Equity (%)	9.96	5.44	na
% Change Profit	487.8	na	na
% Change Revenue	183.1	na	na
% Change Assets	204.7	2,024.9	na

Preferred Div. Coverage	np	np	np
Total Div. Coverage	na	na	na
Interest Coverage	4.5	1.5	na
Current Ratio	2.7	4.3	0.1
Operating Margin	15.5	23.6	na
Asset Turnover	0.5	0.5	0.0

5 YEAR RATIOS (%)			
Return on Capital	na	na	na
Return on Com. Equity	na	na	na
Profit Growth	na	na	na
Revenue Growth	na	na	na
Asset Growth	na	na	na

BALANCE SHEET (000)			
Cash	6,727	4,930	72
Current Assets	22,900	8,440	91
Net Fixed Assets	77,403	24,475	23
Invest's & Advances	0	0	0
Total Assets	100,303	32,915	1,549
Short Term Debt	840	68	750
Current Liabilities	8,525	1,974	1,102
Long Term Debt	28,496	3,553	0
Total Liabilities	41,019	6,740	1,102
Total Equity	59,284	26,175	447
Total Liab. & Equity	100,303	32,915	1,549

CAPITAL (000)			
Total Debt	29,336	3,621	750
Preferred Equity	0	0	0
Common Equity	59,284	26,175	447

Business:

GLOBAL STONE CORPORATION is involved in the lime and limestone business and is a major supplier of lime to Stelco Inc.

Date	EPS	DPS	Tot Rev	Inc Bex
Mar 95	0.04	0.00	21,652	832
Dec 94	0.06	0.00	15,982	1,087
Sep 94	0.11	0.00	16,877	2,054
Jun 94	0.06	0.00	11,463	1,088
Mar 94	0.04	0.00	10,433	627
Dec 93	0.04	0.00	8,633	487
Sep 93	0.10	0.00	4,522	711
Jun 93	0.04	0.00	4,580	372

Synopsis:

On April 24, 1995, Global Stone Corporation announced its purchase of the high purity calcium limestone quarries and associated processing plants owned by PenRoc Inc. and Delta Carbonate of New York. Details were not disclosed. The company said the purchase complements its existing businesses.

On January 1, 1995, Global Stone took control of Detroit Lime. In the three months following the purchase, operations have exceeded initial projections. Demand at Detroit Lime exceeds production capacity due to the highly active steel sector and emerging new lime markets.

On February 15, 1995, Global Stone announced it had completed a debt facility worth $55-million through a private placement. The placement was made with a group of leading North American life insurance companies. The debt was secured by issuing $30-million Series A 10.625% Secured Debentures with a seven year maturity. The proceeds from were used to pay down Global Stone's $23.3-million bank loan facilities and for capital expansion.

In the first quarter of 1995, Global Stone reported significantly higher sales, compared to the same period last year. The company attributes the rise to strong demand for lime and reasonable winter weather conditions. In the quarter, demand at times was so strong, Global Stone resorted to use external supplies to meet production requirements.

Relative strength to TSE300
Price
Volume (in 1000's of board lots)

Rank (Profit/Revenue/Assets)
451   560   485

Robert R. Stone
Chairman

David F. Singleton
President & C.E.O.

Michael A. Niblett
V.P. & C.F.O.

Herbert G.A. Wilson
Executive V.P. & C.O.O.

Address
Suite 306
251 North Service Road West
Oakville
ON
L6M 3E7
(905) 815-1050

Fax: (905) 815-1056
01003363/G/1.6

INCO LIMITED

Exchanges	Price (Jun29'95)	38 .25	Trailing P/E	21 .98	Stock Symbol
TMN	Trailing Yield (%)	1 .42	Trailing EPS	1 .28	**N**

Period Ending	Dec94	Dec93	Dec92	Dec91	Dec90
Yearly Statistics	US	US	US	US	US
Price-Close	40 .13	35 .50	28 .50	35 .25	29 .38
Price-High	42 .25	37 .00	39 .50	43 .88	36 .88
Price-Low	29 .63	23 .13	24 .50	27 .50	26 .00
P/E-Close	142 .89	96 .63	nm	36 .32	5 .16
Dividends per Share	0 .40	0 .40	0 .85	1 .00	1 .00
Dividend Yield (%)	1 .37	1 .46	3 .62	3 .25	3 .97
Sales per Share	21 .33	19 .41	23 .63	28 .48	29 .80
EPS before extra. item	0 .15	0 .22	(0 .21)	0 .74	4 .18
Cash Flow per Share	2 .27	2 .65	2 .96	3 .63	5 .16
Book Value per Share	15 .08	14 .57	14 .71	15 .70	15 .78
O/S Common Shares	117 ,183	110 ,270	109 ,292	106 ,247	104 ,438
Total Revenue	2 ,512 ,838	2 ,336 ,240	2 ,622 ,238	3 ,053 ,420	3 ,335 ,086
Income before extra.	21 ,659	28 ,182	(17 ,612)	82 ,648	441 ,217
Cash Flow	263 ,724	291 ,190	320 ,489	382 ,219	538 ,443
Debt/Equity	0 .55	0 .64	0 .68	0 .73	0 .59
Return on Capital (%)	2 .27	4 .15	3 .99	7 .57	30 .59
Ret. on Com. Equity (%)	1 .06	1 .50	(1 .36)	4 .68	0 .00
% Change Profit	(23 .1)	260 .0	(121 .3)	(81 .3)	(41 .4)
% Change Revenue	7 .6	(10 .9)	(14 .1)	(8 .4)	(17 .9)
% Change Assets	3 .2	(6 .5)	(7 .4)	10 .8	10 .7

Preferred Div. Coverage	5 .8	6 .8	0 .0
Total Div. Coverage	0 .4	0 .6	0 .0
Interest Coverage	0 .7	1 .2	1 .0
Current Ratio	2 .8	2 .4	2 .1
Operating Margin	2 .3	(3 .8)	2 .8
Asset Turnover	0 .6	0 .5	0 .6
5 YEAR RATIOS (%)			
Return on Capital	9 .7	23 .8	38 .2
Return on Com. Equity	7 .1	22 .0	38 .2
Profit Growth	(51 .1)	(48 .0)	na
Revenue Growth	(9 .2)	(7 .0)	7 .5
Asset Growth	1 .8	(1 .0)	6 .8
BALANCE SHEET (000)			
Cash	164 ,080	46 ,676	34 ,889
Current Assets	1 ,417 ,904	1 ,184 ,178	1 ,139 ,629
Net Fixed Assets	2 ,439 ,426	2 ,507 ,499	2 ,576 ,078
Invest's & Advances	21 ,356	33 ,740	240 ,889
Total Assets	4 ,016 ,206	3 ,890 ,313	4 ,161 ,278
Short Term Debt	71 ,856	112 ,834	60 ,076
Current Liabilities	498 ,389	491 ,940	541 ,973
Long Term Debt	921 ,548	946 ,096	1 ,081 ,038
Total Liabilities	2 ,193 ,267	2 ,223 ,991	2 ,490 ,638
Total Equity	1 ,822 ,939	1 ,666 ,322	1 ,670 ,640
Total Liab. & Equity	4 ,016 ,206	3 ,890 ,313	4 ,161 ,278
CAPITAL (000)			
Total Debt	993 ,404	1 ,058 ,930	1 ,141 ,114
Preferred Equity	56 ,224	59 ,644	62 ,592
Common Equity	1 ,766 ,715	1 ,606 ,678	1 ,608 ,048

Date		EPS	DPS	Tot Rev	Inc Bex
Mar 95	US	0 .60	0 .10	881 ,000	71 ,700
Dec 94	US	0 .73	0 .10	777 ,188	86 ,659
Sep 94	US	0 .02	0 .10	603 ,300	2 ,600
Jun 94	US	(0 .07)	0 .10	594 ,700	(7 ,600)
Mar 94	US	(0 .53)	0 .10	528 ,300	(60 ,000)
Dec 93	US	(0 .36)	0 .10	520 ,940	(38 ,218)
Sep 93	US	0 .83	0 .10	655 ,400	91 ,200
Jun 93	US	(0 .03)	0 .10	611 ,300	(2 ,200)

Business:

INCO LIMITED is a producer of nickel, copper, precious metals and cobalt. It also makes wrought and mechanically alloyed nickel alloys and manufactures blades, rings, discs and other forged and precision machined components. The company also produces sulphuric acid and liquid sulphur dioxide. The company has properties, operations and markets around the world.

Synopsis:

In June 1995, Inco ensured its control over the marketing of nickel worldwide by acquiring a 30% interest in Diamond Fields Resources Inc.'s rich base metals deposit at Voisey Bay, Labrador. The deal was worth $700-million. Voisey Bay, when developed, could capture 10% of the world's nickel market while becoming the second largest and lowest cost nickel producer in the Western world. The mine could be developed by the end of the decade. Annual production is forecast at 130 million pounds of nickel, 90 million pounds of copper and 3-5 million pounds of cobalt. The mine could cost $400-million and will be financed using bank debt.

Inco now has interests in three of the lowest cost nickel producing areas of the world, wholly owned Thompson, Manitoba, 58% owned PT Inco in Indonesia, and now Newfoundland. Inco currently delivers more than 500 million pounds of nickel annually. The company says global consumption of nickel is rising at a rate of over 50 million pounds per year. Boosting production at current and new sites by 20% by the end of the decade will ensure Inco's control of one-third of primary nickel demand worldwide.

Inco has lowered costs through productivity improvements, as well as increasing world-wide nickel production through the addition of new sources of low cost production. Nickel production costs at its Canadian operations have fallen by 13% over the past three years. Inco has strengthened its position in the growing Asian market, which accounted for 47% of 1994 primary nickel deliveries.

Stainless steel production is the largest single-use end market for nickel, accounting for more than 60% of the world-wide nickel consumption. Stainless steel production has nearly doubled since the early 1980s.

In 1994, nickel sales comprised 77% of primary metal revenues, with refined copper supplying most of the remainder. Primary metal sales generated 75% of total revenues of $2.484-billion (U.S.), with alloys and engineered products supplying one-fifth of sales.

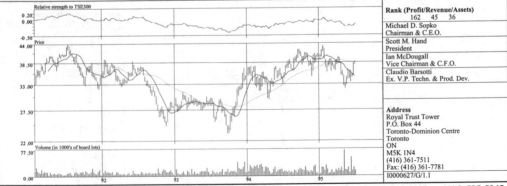

Rank (Profit/Revenue/Assets)
162   45   36

Michael D. Sopko
Chairman & C.E.O.
Scott M. Hand
President
Ian McDougall
Vice Chairman & C.F.O.
Claudio Barsotti
Ex. V.P. Techn. & Prod. Dev.

Address
Royal Trust Tower
P.O. Box 44
Toronto-Dominion Centre
Toronto
ON
M5K 1N4
(416) 361-7511
Fax: (416) 361-7781
I0000627/G/1.1

For further company information, call Globe Information Services 1-800-268-9128 or (416) 585-5345

INMET MINING CORPORATION

Exchanges	Price (Jun29'95)		9.62	Trailing P/E		19.25	Stock Symbol
TM	Trailing Yield (%)		0.00	Trailing EPS		0.50	**IMN**

Period Ending	Dec94	Dec93	Dec92	Dec91	Dec90
Yearly Statistics					
Price-Close	12.00	11.38	12.75	10.38	12.13
Price-High	13.88	13.00	14.25	13.13	15.25
Price-Low	10.13	10.00	10.38	10.00	10.88
P/E-Close	31.58	568.75	31.10	29.64	173.21
Dividends per Share	0.00	0.00	0.00	0.00	0.00
Dividend Yield (%)	0.00	0.00	0.00	0.00	0.00
Sales per Share	10.23	4.50	5.12	4.08	4.24
EPS before extra. item	0.38	0.02	0.41	0.35	0.07
Cash Flow per Share	0.08	(0.41)	0.72	0.11	0.09
Book Value per Share	13.25	12.46	12.96	12.36	11.94
O/S Common Shares	81,207	81,207	57,554	44,415	39,415
Total Revenue	929,745	336,407	312,786	215,515	190,744
Income before extra.	30,601	1,283	22,237	15,162	2,864
Cash Flow	6,460	(26,203)	38,937	4,665	3,711
Debt/Equity	0.31	0.28	0.36	0.35	0.48
Return on Capital (%)	4.38	1.37	5.99	4.65	3.73
Ret. on Com. Equity (%)	2.93	0.15	3.43	2.97	0.62
% Change Profit	2,285.1	(94.2)	46.7	429.4	(91.7)
% Change Revenue	176.4	7.6	45.1	13.0	44.6
% Change Assets	5.2	27.0	50.8	6.3	4.0

Preferred Div. Coverage	np	np	np
Total Div. Coverage	na	na	na
Interest Coverage	2.7	0.8	2.8
Current Ratio	2.1	1.9	2.0
Operating Margin	(5.5)	(12.4)	1.9
Asset Turnover	0.5	0.2	0.2
5 YEAR RATIOS (%)			
Return on Capital	4.0	4.9	6.5
Return on Com. Equity	2.0	3.0	4.5
Profit Growth	(2.1)	(47.5)	9.1
Revenue Growth	47.7	82.4	58.6
Asset Growth	17.3	25.9	22.2
BALANCE SHEET (000)			
Cash	212,700	246,729	174,536
Current Assets	473,127	507,004	288,927
Net Fixed Assets	762,832	649,561	413,815
Invest's & Advances	399,587	415,393	525,947
Total Assets	1,687,501	1,604,744	1,263,532
Short Term Debt	64,191	52,538	57,144
Current Liabilities	224,278	265,060	144,175
Long Term Debt	266,210	231,085	209,364
Total Liabilities	611,244	592,909	517,525
Total Equity	1,076,257	1,011,835	746,007
Total Liab. & Equity	1,687,501	1,604,744	1,263,532
CAPITAL (000)			
Total Debt	330,401	283,623	266,508
Preferred Equity	0	0	0
Common Equity	1,076,257	1,011,835	746,007

Business:

INMET MINING CORPORATION is an integrated mining company engaged in the exploration, development, mining and processing of base and precious metals. The company is primarily a copper producer, but also produces gold, zinc, silver and lead. The company's properties and joint ventures are located in Canada, the United States, Central America, the Pacific Rim, the European region and Africa.

Date	EPS	DPS	Tot Rev	Inc Bex
Mar 95	0.19	0.00	299,000	15,100
Dec 94	0.16	0.00	274,883	12,729
Sep 94	0.07	0.00	208,515	6,074
Jun 94	0.08	0.00	195,844	6,056
Mar 94	0.07	0.00	207,452	5,742
Dec 93	0.07	0.00	140,303	4,268
Sep 93	(0.09)	0.00	44,425	(5,913)
Jun 93	0.00	0.00	69,656	110

Synopsis:

In May 1995, Metall Mining Corp. changed its name to Inmet Mining Corp. after its former controlling shareholder Metallgesellschaft AG sold its Metall shares to raise cash.

Inmet's primary product is copper, but is also has significant interests in zinc and gold. Changing copper prices have the largest impact on Inmet's consolidated earnings and cash flows. Its most significant copper properties are Copper Range, Michigan, and Ok Tedi, Papua New Guinea.

During the three years ended December 1994, Inmet increased its production of copper by 2.5 times to 208,000 tonnes. It also doubled gold production to 252,000 ounces. Inmet intends to continue to advance its copper strategy. The strategy depends on the future of Copper Range, and on Inmet's efforts to acquire another significant copper property in order balance its production and smelting capacity.

The future of the high-cost Copper Range project remains uncertain. Inmet may turn the project into a small-scale solution mining operation by building a solvent extraction and electrowinning plant. Copper Range contains low grade ore, and it might take three years before the mine reaches full production using solution mining. If the solution mining idea fails, Copper range will likely be closed. In that case, Inmet would face up to $200-million in writedowns and cash costs necessary to close the mine. Copper Range contributes almost half of Inmet's copper production.

Throughout 1994 and the first half of 1995, Inmet recorded higher net earnings, in large part because of higher copper and zinc prices. Total revenues in 1994 tripled primarily from the inclusion of a full year's revenue from Norddueutsche Affinerie.

Rank (Profit/Revenue/Assets)
155   125   115

James M. Tory
Chairman
Dr. Klaus M. Zeitler
President & C.E.O.
H. Douglas Scharf
V.P. Finance & C.F.O.
Oliver R.E. Merton
V.P. Marketing

Address
Aetna Tower Suite 3400
79 Wellington Street West
P.O. Box 19
Toronto
ON
M5K 1A1
(416) 361-6400
Fax: (416) 368-4692
M0001406/G/1.1

KERR ADDISON MINES LIMITED

Exchanges	Price (Jun29'95)	25.00	Trailing P/E	23.58	Stock Symbol
T	Trailing Yield (%)	2.40	Trailing EPS	1.06	**KER**

Period Ending	Dec94	Dec93	Dec92	Dec91	Dec90
Yearly Statistics					
Price-Close	25.75	24.38	16.00	15.50	15.75
Price-High	26.00	24.38	19.25	17.38	21.00
Price-Low	22.13	15.00	14.50	13.50	14.38
P/E-Close	23.62	13.69	9.14	86.11	15.75
Dividends per Share	0.60	0.60	0.60	0.60	0.60
Dividend Yield (%)	2.33	2.46	3.75	3.87	3.81
Sales per Share	0.92	0.91	0.92	0.67	12.05
EPS before extra. item	1.09	1.78	1.75	0.18	1.00
Cash Flow per Share	1.22	1.02	(0.17)	(0.14)	4.99
Book Value per Share	22.76	22.27	21.09	19.94	20.37
O/S Common Shares	17,593	17,593	17,593	17,590	17,559
Total Revenue	38,709	58,970	20,226	29,980	252,017
Income before extra.	19,192	31,334	30,699	3,207	17,611
Cash Flow	21,433	17,881	(3,018)	(2,496)	87,543
Debt/Equity	nd	nd	nd	0.17	0.21
Return on Capital (%)	6.15	11.26	8.94	2.04	5.50
Ret. on Com. Equity (%)	4.85	8.22	8.51	0.91	4.97
% Change Profit	(38.8)	2.1	857.3	(81.8)	39.3
% Change Revenue	(34.4)	191.6	(32.5)	(88.1)	54.1
% Change Assets	1.0	2.5	(8.6)	(32.5)	(5.1)

Date	EPS	DPS	Tot Rev	Inc Bex
Mar 95	0.33	0.15	8,575	5,803
Dec 94	0.34	0.15	20,146	6,026
Sep 94	0.24	0.15	6,127	4,265
Jun 94	0.15	0.15	4,331	2,578
Mar 94	0.36	0.15	7,721	6,323
Dec 93	(0.01)	0.15	7,803	(148)
Sep 93	0.16	0.15	4,798	2,814
Jun 93	0.97	0.15	23,392	17,119

	Dec94	Dec93	Dec92
Preferred Div. Coverage	np	np	np
Total Div. Coverage	1.8	3.0	2.9
Interest Coverage	nd	nd	9.3
Current Ratio	170.5	509.5	79.3
Operating Margin	11.4	0.0	(10.1)
Asset Turnover	0.0	0.0	0.0
5 YEAR RATIOS (%)			
Return on Capital	6.8	6.4	5.2
Return on Com. Equity	5.5	5.2	4.2
Profit Growth	8.8	24.5	6.2
Revenue Growth	(25.1)	(15.3)	(31.0)
Asset Growth	(9.6)	(10.3)	(11.0)
BALANCE SHEET (000)			
Cash	240,134	215,135	73,850
Current Assets	250,473	224,668	173,103
Net Fixed Assets	25,452	25,683	25,889
Invest's & Advances	123,431	140,150	169,791
Total Assets	401,878	397,822	388,139
Short Term Debt	0	0	0
Current Liabilities	1,469	441	2,182
Long Term Debt	0	0	0
Total Liabilities	1,469	6,049	17,143
Total Equity	400,409	391,773	370,996
Total Liab. & Equity	401,878	397,822	388,139
CAPITAL (000)			
Total Debt	0	0	0
Preferred Equity	0	0	0
Common Equity	400,409	391,773	370,996

Business:

KERR ADDISON MINES LIMITED has interests in Canadian companies in the natural resources sector.

Synopsis:

Kerr Addison is no longer directly involved in the mining business. Its sensitivity to metal prices and fluctuations in the Canadian dollar exchange rates are limited to its 9.83% joint venture interest in the Canadian Electrolytic Zinc (CEZinc) reduction plant at Valleyfield, Quebec. Noranda Inc. is a major holder and operator of the plant.

Noranda Inc. is also Kerr Addison's majority shareholder. Noranda holds 48.3% of the shares and is considering making an offer to buy the remaining shares. Kerr Addison's affairs have been arranged to facilitate such a reorganization. The balance sheet at December 1994 had $250-million of cash and working capital, $150-million of long term investments, and no debt. The long term investments included 7.9 million shares of Noranda Inc. at a carrying cost of $13.97 per share, which is well below market value. Long term investments also included $25-million of fixed assets representing investment in the CEZinc plant, and $13-million invested in the Canadian Hunter oil and gas joint venture. Through the joint venture, Kerr Addison owns 13% of Canadian Hunter's Alberta properties.

Kerr Addison's income for 1995 will come primarily from Noranda dividends and interest on cash and short term investments. In addition, the company's share of CEZinc and the Canadian Hunter joint venture should provide earnings at or above last year's levels. Investment income should increase in 1995 for two reasons. The Noranda dividends, expected to be received in the total amount of $7.9-million, should qualify as earnings to Kerr Addison for the full year. And, interest income should increase based on a larger principal sum invested during a period of rising short term interest rates.

Relative strength to TSE300 / Price / Volume (in 1000's of board lots)

Rank (Profit/Revenue/Assets)
221   598   251

D.L. Bumstead
Chairman Of The Board
Jeffery Snow
President & C.E.O.

Address
Suite 2700
1 Adelaide Street East
Toronto
ON
M5C 2Z6
(416) 982-7270

Fax: (416) 982-7498
K0000647/G/1.2

For further company information, call Globe Information Services 1-800-268-9128 or (416) 585-5345

LYTTON MINERALS LIMITED

Exchanges						
TV	Price (Jun29'95)		2.34	Trailing P/E	nm	**Stock Symbol**
	Trailing Yield (%)		0.00	Trailing EPS	(0.01)	**LTL**

Period Ending	Dec94	Dec93	Dec92	Dec91	Dec90
Yearly Statistics					
Price-Close	2.17	3.85	2.08	0.06	0.26
Price-High	5.00	6.75	2.20	0.30	0.52
Price-Low	1.70	1.65	0.06	0.06	0.04
P/E-Close	nm	nm	nm	nm	nm
Dividends per Share	0.00	0.00	0.00	0.00	0.00
Dividend Yield (%)	0.00	0.00	0.00	0.00	0.00
Sales per Share	na	na	na	na	na
EPS before extra. item	(0.00)	(0.01)	(0.01)	(0.03)	(0.04)
Cash Flow per Share	(0.01)	(0.01)	(0.01)	(0.01)	(0.01)
Book Value per Share	0.45	0.26	0.09	0.01	0.03
O/S Common Shares	89,836	85,266	76,461	40,311	38,591
Total Revenue	1,882	412	(57)	113	50
Income before extra.	(276)	(876)	(798)	(1,274)	(1,532)
Cash Flow	(876)	(979)	(702)	(215)	(228)
Debt/Equity	0.00	0.01	0.04	0.68	0.29
Return on Capital (%)	(0.87)	(5.82)	(20.11)	(102.66)	(76.22)
Ret. on Com. Equity (%)	(0.88)	(5.95)	(21.99)	(152.02)	(96.49)
% Change Profit	68.4	(9.7)	37.3	16.8	(867.4)
% Change Revenue	357.3	816.3	(151.1)	126.1	(70.3)
% Change Assets	75.4	212.7	934.7	(60.6)	(17.3)

Date	EPS	DPS	Tot Rev	Inc Bex
Mar 95	(0.00)	0.00	10	(269)
Dec 94	(0.00)	0.00	1,684	600
Sep 94	(0.00)	0.00	21	(324)
Jun 94	(0.00)	0.00	130	(292)
Mar 94	(0.00)	0.00	47	(261)
Dec 93	(0.00)	0.00	266	(195)
Sep 93	(0.00)	0.00	11	(306)
Jun 93	(0.00)	0.00	84	(238)

	Dec94	Dec93	Dec92
Preferred Div. Coverage	na	na	na
Total Div. Coverage	na	na	na
Interest Coverage	na	na	na
Current Ratio	2.8	5.8	14.2
Operating Margin	na	na	na
Asset Turnover	na	na	na
5 YEAR RATIOS (%)			
Return on Capital	(41.1)	(42.3)	(44.6)
Return on Com. Equity	(55.5)	(56.9)	(60.4)
Profit Growth	na	na	na
Revenue Growth	62.2	13.4	na
Asset Growth	79.2	56.9	42.0
BALANCE SHEET (000)			
Cash	2,971	5,515	5,604
Current Assets	3,599	6,019	5,708
Net Fixed Assets	34,580	16,339	1,119
Invest's & Advances	3,557	1,436	781
Total Assets	41,736	23,795	7,609
Short Term Debt	60	60	63
Current Liabilities	1,281	1,045	403
Long Term Debt	119	179	239
Total Liabilities	1,400	1,224	642
Total Equity	40,336	22,571	6,967
Total Liab. & Equity	41,736	23,795	7,609
CAPITAL (000)			
Total Debt	179	239	302
Preferred Equity	36	40	52
Common Equity	40,300	22,530	6,915

Business:

LYTTON MINERALS LIMITED is engaged in the exploration for diamonds in Canada's Northwest Territories.

Synopsis:

In May 1995, the Northern Miner reported that Lytton Minerals released results pertaining to additional processing of core material from the original discovery hole on the land-based JD-OD-1 kimberlite deposit. Caustic dissolution of 218.57 kilograms of kimberlite material from hole JD-14 recovered 95 macros and 558 micros, or 29.88 diamonds per 10 kilogram. Lytton and partner New Indigo Resources plan to continue targeting additional kimberlite deposits. A 400-tonne bulk-sampling program of the JD-OD-1 pipe is proposed for the summer of 1995. The JD-OD claim block makes up part of Lytton and New Indigo's jointly held 3.6-million-hectare property in the Northwest Territories.

In late March 1995, Lytton's affiliate company, Glenmore Highlands, discovered diamonds about 50 kilometres southeast of the Lac de Gras diamond find. Glenmore said a 63.35-kilogram sample taken at the site and contained 986 diamonds, of which 176 were macrodiamonds. There are plans to make the Lac de Gras property Canada's first diamond mine.

In February 1995, Lytton completed, by private placement, the issue of $8-million in convertible subordinate debentures. Orvalor will purchase the bonds which bear interest of 4% and can be converted by Orvalor to common shares at any time until February 22, 2002, at a price of $1.75. Lytton can exercise the option at any time after February 22, 1999, until the bonds mature on February 22, 2002. If Orvalor were to convert all the convertible subordinate debentures, it would own 14.34% of Lytton Minerals.

Rank (Profit/Revenue/Assets)		
815	960	829

D.H.W. Dobson
Chairman

Desmond C.B. Alexander
President & C.E.O.

Address
Suite 501 - 700
West Pender Street
Vancouver
BC
V6C 1G8
(604) 689-7406

Fax: (604) 689-7401
L0002728/G/1.6

MINERA RAYROCK INC.

Exchanges	Price (Jun29'95)	1.67	Trailing P/E	nm	Stock Symbol
T	Trailing Yield (%)	0.00	Trailing EPS	(0.02)	**MRN.A**

Period Ending	Dec94	Dec93	Dec92	Dec91	Dec90
Yearly Statistics	US	US			
Price-Close	2.60	2.60	1.35	0.38	0.90
Price-High	3.10	3.15	1.35	1.40	2.50
Price-Low	2.10	1.17	0.32	0.35	0.90
P/E-Close	nm	nm	nm	nm	nm
Dividends per Share	0.00	0.01	0.00	0.00	0.00
Dividend Yield (%)	0.00	0.54	0.00	0.00	0.00
Sales per Share	na	na	na	na	na
EPS before extra. item	(0.02)	(0.08)	(0.20)	(0.15)	(0.13)
Cash Flow per Share	(0.03)	(0.08)	(0.14)	(0.11)	(0.11)
Book Value per Share	0.99	0.87	0.72	0.92	1.08
O/S Common Shares	50,993	41,930	14,656	14,656	14,656
Total Revenue	1,050	1,133	145	10	186
Income before extra.	(1,174)	(1,851)	(2,072)	(1,632)	(1,471)
Cash Flow	(1,174)	(1,851)	(2,072)	(1,632)	(1,464)
Debt/Equity	nd	nd	0.08	0.04	0.05
Return on Capital (%)	(2.71)	(6.79)	(9.25)	(7.57)	(7.20)
Ret. on Com. Equity (%)	(2.71)	(8.16)	(17.18)	(11.14)	(11.56)
% Change Profit	36.6	(15.6)	(26.9)	(10.9)	(5.9)
% Change Revenue	(7.3)	912.8	1,336.0	(94.6)	110.8
% Change Assets	120.2	113.8	2.5	7.5	24.1
Preferred Div. Coverage	np	np	na		
Total Div. Coverage	na	0.0	na		
Interest Coverage	nd	nd	na		
Current Ratio	3.7	15.8	0.5		
Operating Margin	na	na	na		
Asset Turnover	na	na	na		
5 YEAR RATIOS (%)					
Return on Capital	(6.7)	(8.2)	(8.5)		
Return on Com. Equity	(10.2)	(12.4)	(13.4)		
Profit Growth	(6.8)	(10.7)	na		
Revenue Growth	73.3	85.4	20.0		
Asset Growth	45.1	37.6	2.1		
BALANCE SHEET (000)					
Cash	5,381	14,977	225		
Current Assets	10,202	15,191	267		
Net Fixed Assets	57,312	21,113	22,035		
Invest's & Advances	12,900	0	0		
Total Assets	82,040	37,254	23,066		
Short Term Debt	0	0	0		
Current Liabilities	2,762	964	563		
Long Term Debt	0	0	1,705		
Total Liabilities	31,639	964	2,268		
Total Equity	50,401	36,290	20,798		
Total Liab. & Equity	82,040	37,254	23,066		
CAPITAL (000)					
Total Debt	0	0	1,705		
Preferred Equity	0	0	10,186		
Common Equity	50,401	36,290	10,612		

Business:

MINERA RAYROCK INC. is an exploration and mining development company focussing on Latin America.

Date		EPS	DPS	Tot Rev	Inc Bex
Mar 95	US	0.00	0.00	4,581	(191)
Dec 94	US	0.00	0.00	272	(161)
Sep 94	US	0.00	0.00	404	(100)
Jun 94	US	(0.02)	0.00	230	(912)
Mar 94	US	0.00	0.00	805	(1)
Dec 93	US	(0.01)	0.00	113	(830)
Sep 93	US	0.03	0.00	886	112
Jun 93	US	(0.05)	0.00	291	(592)

Synopsis:

Minera Rayrock is focusing its mining activities in Latin America. Before 1995, Minera Rayrock was a mining exploration company without a source of operating income or cash flow. The company's current priorities are to expand production at its 100% owned Ivan copper project in northern Chile, to complete the purchase of certain optioned properties near Ivan at Sierra Valenzuela, and to finance the capital cost of Sierra Valenzuela.

Minera Rayrock developed the Ivan copper project from mid-1993 through 1994. Ivan began commercially producing copper on January 1, 1995, and should achieve full capacity production during the third quarter of 1995. Plans to increase production by 20% above design capacity are under way, while demand for copper remains strong.

Costs incurred at Ivan since the start of construction in April 1993 to the end of 1994 total $32.6-million (U.S.). Minera Rayrock will spend an additional $2.5-million in 1995. Production will be 22 million pounds of copper cathode per year at a forecast cash operating cost between $0.50 (U.S.) and $0.60 (U.S.) per pound. Proven reserves are sufficient for 10 years of operation.

In addition, Minera Rayrock is exploring for copper at Sierra Valenzuela, 40 kilometres northeast of Ivan. Work done to date indicates a reserve potential of between 10 to 15 million metric tons grading 1.5 to 1.75% copper.

The results of the Rosario/Esperanza/Gorro deposit evaluation and mine plans should be available in the third quarter of 1995. Minera Rayrock is also completing a final feasibility study on its 100% owned Bellavista gold project in Costa Rica. Bellavista has at least 731,000 contained ounces of proven and probable mineable gold reserves. Further reserve determination and mine planning are in progress. Besides expanded open pit potential, there is potential for underground mining in the deeper and more northerly parts of the deposit. Results of these studies should be ready during the third quarter of 1995.

Rank (Profit/Revenue/Assets)
840   938   449

David R. Crombie
President & C.E.O.

C. Bruce Burton
V.P. & C.F.O.

Address
30 Soudan Avenue
Suite 500
Toronto
ON
M4S 1V6
(416) 489-0022

Fax: (416) 489-0096
M0028152/G/1.2

NOVICOURT INC.

Exchanges	Price (Jun29'95)	4.70	Trailing P/E	156.67	Stock Symbol
TM	Trailing Yield (%)	0.00	Trailing EPS	0.03	**NOV**

Period Ending	Dec94	Dec93	Dec92	Jun92
Yearly Statistics			24D	1D
Price-Close	4.40	4.80	n t	n t
Price-High	5.88	4.95	n t	n t
Price-Low	3.15	2.70	n t	n t
P/E-Close	nm	nm	n t	n t
Dividends per Share	0.00	0.00	0.00	0.00
Dividend Yield (%)	0.00	0.00	0.00	0.00
Sales per Share	0.00	0.00	0.00	0.00
EPS before extra. item	0.00	0.00	0.00	0.00
Cash Flow per Share	0.00	0.00	0.00	0.00
Book Value per Share	1.51	1.52	0.65	na
O/S Common Shares	38,882	38,837	20,297	0
Total Revenue	0	0	0	0
Income before extra.	0	0	0	0
Cash Flow	0	0	0	0
Debt/Equity	1.21	0.37	1.17	nd
Return on Capital (%)	na	na	na	na
Ret. on Com. Equity (%)	(0.80)	(1.28)	(0.26)	na
% Change Profit	na	na	na	na
% Change Revenue	na	na	na	na
% Change Assets	4,990.4	nm	9,890.9	na
Preferred Div. Coverage	0.0	0.0	0.0	
Total Div. Coverage	0.0	0.0	0.0	
Interest Coverage	na	na	na	
Current Ratio	3.1	0.7	0.5	
Operating Margin	na	na	na	
Asset Turnover	0.0	0.0	0.0	
5 YEAR RATIOS (%)				
Return on Capital	na	na	na	
Return on Com. Equity	na	na	na	
Profit Growth	na	na	na	
Revenue Growth	na	na	na	
Asset Growth	na	na	na	
BALANCE SHEET (000)				
Cash	3,373	4,306	230	
Current Assets	18,727	7,330	1,374	
Net Fixed Assets	124,015	86,540	39,107	
Invest's & Advances	0	0	0	
Total Assets	147,152	98,164	42,481	
Short Term Debt	0	0	0	
Current Liabilities	6,029	10,666	3,048	
Long Term Debt	77,393	23,406	21,284	
Total Liabilities	83,422	34,072	24,332	
Total Equity	63,730	64,092	18,149	
Total Liab. & Equity	147,152	98,164	42,481	
CAPITAL (000)				
Total Debt	77,393	23,406	21,284	
Preferred Equity	4,984	4,984	4,984	
Common Equity	58,746	59,108	13,165	

Business:

NOVICOURT INC. retains the 45% undivided interest that Louvem Mines Inc. had in the Louvicourt property. Novicourt will carry out the operation, development and business relating to base and precious metals.

Date	EPS	DPS	Tot Rev	Inc Bex
Mar 95	0.03	0.00	11,874	1,265
Dec 94	0.00	0.00	0	0
Sep 94	0.00	0.00	0	0
Jun 94	0.00	0.00	0	0
Mar 94	0.00	0.00	0	0
Dec 93	0.00	0.00	0	0
Sep 93	0.00	0.00	0	0
Jun 93	0.00	0.00	0	0

Synopsis:

Novicourt Inc. will receive most of its revenues [this year] from the sale of copper and zinc concentrates from future production at the Louvicourt mine. It holds a 45% interest in the $289-million Louvicourt copper, zinc, and precious metals development in Quebec. Novicourt's other partners are Aur Resources, which holds 30%, and Teck Corp., which holds 25%. Noranda Inc. owns equity in Novicourt and has guaranteed Novicourt's amount of the financing of the Louvicourt mine, which is $112-million.

Mine production began on January 1, 1995, in time to catch what should be cyclically strong copper markets for the next few years. Novicourt expects copper to remain between $1.25 (U.S.) to $1.35 (U.S.) per pound during the first half of 1995. However, longer term outlook is clouded by a series of impending copper mine projects.

In March 1994, the project discovered that the measured ore reserves at Louvicourt were lower than initially thought. There are only 14 million tonnes and not 24 million, with an ore reserve of 12 years and rather than 17. As well average copper grades were about 13% less than original estimates. Nevertheless, the company feels there is a significant quantity of high grade copper ore that can be mined to pay off debt and earn a profit.

The company expects to find additional reserves near the Louvicourt joint venture for exploration in 1995. In addition, Novicourt is a 45% partner with Aur Resources to explore for additional reserves in the Louvar properties that surround the deposit. Novicourt's share of this program will be $570,000.

Novicourt expects the mine to produce at the full rate of 4,000 tonnes per day on a continuous basis by mid-1995. During the first quarter of 1995, the mine operated at an average rate of 2,515 tonnes per calendar day. High quality copper and zinc concentrates were produced, containing 16 million pounds of payable copper and seven million pounds of zinc. Novicourt's share of these two programs generated a payable copper price of $1.25 (U.S.) per pound.

Rank (Profit/Revenue/Assets)

John C. White
President

Address
1 Adelaide Street East
Suite 2700
Toronto
ON
M5C 2Z6
(416) 982-7111

Fax: (416) 982-7498
01003304/G/1.2

PRINCETON MINING CORPORATION

Exchanges	Price (Jun29'95)	0.66	Trailing P/E	nm	Stock Symbol
T	Trailing Yield (%)	0.00	Trailing EPS	(0.03)	**PMC**

Period Ending	Dec94	Dec93	Dec92	Dec91	Dec90
Yearly Statistics					
Price-Close	1.06	0.48	1.45	0.85	3.25
Price-High	1.10	1.55	1.90	3.35	5.13
Price-Low	0.31	0.25	0.50	0.28	3.00
P/E-Close	nm	nm	nm	nm	6.92
Dividends per Share	0.00	0.00	0.00	0.00	0.16
Dividend Yield (%)	0.00	0.00	0.00	0.00	4.92
Sales per Share	0.30	1.26	1.98	1.24	2.70
EPS before extra. item	(0.09)	(0.67)	(0.04)	(3.58)	0.47
Cash Flow per Share	(0.05)	(0.28)	0.10	(0.41)	0.11
Book Value per Share	0.27	0.26	0.81	0.83	4.47
O/S Common Shares	74,970	58,767	31,079	31,079	23,404
Total Revenue	20,473	47,923	62,574	32,870	64,108
Income before extra.	(5,675)	(24,784)	(1,273)	(91,381)	10,808
Cash Flow	(3,012)	(10,450)	3,137	(10,400)	2,644
Debt/Equity	0.29	nd	0.62	0.61	0.39
Return on Capital (%)	(25.80)	(84.20)	0.28	(96.28)	8.07
Ret. on Com. Equity (%)	(32.20)	(122.94)	(4.98)	(140.17)	10.87
% Change Profit	77.1	(1,846.9)	98.6	(945.5)	(64.7)
% Change Revenue	(57.3)	(23.4)	90.4	(48.7)	(56.9)
% Change Assets	81.1	(51.7)	(3.6)	(73.3)	14.3

Business:

PRINCETON MINING CORP. is a mining company with one operating mine in British Columbia. The Similco mine produces copper with gold as a by-product. Princeton also owns Minera Princeton Chile Ltd. which is involved in copper and gold exploration in Chile.

Date	EPS	DPS	Tot Rev	Inc Bex
Mar 95	0.03	0.00	14,869	2,076
Dec 94	0.04	0.00	15,382	2,351
Sep 94	(0.07)	0.00	4,792	(4,230)
Jun 94	(0.03)	0.00	82	(2,041)
Mar 94	(0.03)	0.00	217	(1,755)
Dec 93	(0.28)	0.00	9,109	(12,172)
Sep 93	(0.09)	0.00	13,134	(3,410)
Jun 93	(0.17)	0.00	12,625	(5,269)

Preferred Div. Coverage	np	np	np
Total Div. Coverage	na	na	na
Interest Coverage	0.0	0.0	0.1
Current Ratio	2.3	1.4	2.4
Operating Margin	(22.2)	(28.0)	1.9
Asset Turnover	0.4	2.0	1.3
5 YEAR RATIOS (%)			
Return on Capital	(39.6)	(25.9)	0.5
Return on Com. Equity	(57.9)	(43.7)	(10.2)
Profit Growth	na	na	na
Revenue Growth	(32.8)	(15.7)	1.4
Asset Growth	(23.7)	(28.8)	(9.4)
BALANCE SHEET (000)			
Cash	12,430	2,173	3,591
Current Assets	27,203	7,992	16,119
Net Fixed Assets	11,932	9,476	28,067
Invest's & Advances	0	2,760	1,122
Total Assets	42,635	23,543	48,693
Short Term Debt	4,285	0	748
Current Liabilities	11,611	5,645	6,629
Long Term Debt	1,492	0	14,829
Total Liabilities	22,458	8,474	23,444
Total Equity	20,177	15,069	25,249
Total Liab. & Equity	42,635	23,543	48,693
CAPITAL (000)			
Total Debt	5,777	0	15,577
Preferred Equity	0	0	0
Common Equity	20,177	15,069	25,249

Synopsis:

Princeton Mining's strategy is to explore and develop copper or gold ore bodies in the Americas. Princeton prefers those bodies amenable to open pit mining. It uses low cost heap leach technology recover gold and copper on site. The company has one operating mine, Similco in British Columbia. The Similco open pit copper mine has a processing capacity greater than 25,000 tons per day. Its annual production is 50 million pounds of copper in concentrates that also contain over 15,000 ounces of gold and over 28,000 ounces of silver. During 1995 at the Similco mine site, Princeton will complete plans for the Ingerbelle pit, add reserves to the production plan, and complete definition drilling on the Alabama deposit.

Princeton suspended Similco operations from November 1993 until August 1994 due to a dramatic decline in copper prices. The average London Metal Exchange copper price was $0.812 (U.S.) per pound in 1993 and $1.047 (U.S.) in 1994, with a high of $1.40 (U.S.) in December 1994.

In early 1995, Princeton and Mitsubishi Materials Corp. formed an alliance to develop the Huckelberry Copper Project in northern British Columbia. Princeton obtained the Huckelberry project when it acquired New Canamin Resources Ltd. through an exchange of shares. Mitsubishi, which owns 40% of the project, is providing a long-term concentrate purchase agreement for the total production from the mine. It will also arrange a $60-million (U.S.) fixed term project loan. Mitsubishi also purchases all the copper concentrates from the Similco mine. Production from the Huckelberry deposit is should exceed 65 million pounds of copper annually, at a cash cost of $0.64 (U.S.) per pound for the first five years. The mine will cost about $135-million to put into production.

Princeton's Elenita oxide copper project in northern Chile is estimated to contain 9.1 million tonnes grading 1.57% copper. The company is evaluating the deposit for possible production of more than 25 million pounds of cathode copper annually by 1997. Princeton is also exploring the Rio Lluta and Nancagua projects in Chile.

Relative strength to TSE300 / Price / Volume (in 1000's of board lots)

Rank (Profit/Revenue/Assets)
914 710 676

James C. O'Rourke
President & C.E.O.

Mark D. Kucher
C.F.O. & Dir. Of Corp. Fin.

Address
Suite 2000
1055 West Hastings Street
Vancouver
BC
V6E 3V3
(604) 688-2511

Fax: (604) 688-4772
P0000482/G/1.2

RIO ALGOM LIMITED

Exchanges	Price (Jun29'95)			26 .50	Trailing P/E			13 .05	Stock Symbol
TMA	Trailing Yield (%)			2 .26	Trailing EPS			2 .03	ROM

Period Ending	Dec94	Dec93	Dec92	Dec91	Dec90
Yearly Statistics					
Price-Close	26 .75	22 .38	17 .38	16 .38	18 .50
Price-High	27 .13	22 .75	18 .50	22 .88	22 .88
Price-Low	21 .00	17 .00	15 .13	14 .25	16 .00
P/E-Close	18 .07	30 .66	20 .44	32 .12	9 .59
Dividends per Share	0 .60	0 .60	0 .70	7 .05	1 .05
Dividend Yield (%)	2 .24	2 .68	4 .03	43 .04	5 .68
Sales per Share	23 .93	21 .90	20 .69	23 .64	30 .19
EPS before extra. item	1 .48	0 .73	0 .85	0 .51	1 .93
Cash Flow per Share	3 .07	1 .47	1 .44	2 .09	4 .75
Book Value per Share	17 .37	14 .87	14 .46	13 .84	20 .24
O/S Common Shares	51 ,959	43 ,743	43 ,736	43 ,736	43 ,736
Total Revenue	1 ,237 ,019	995 ,156	919 ,397	1 ,059 ,592	1 ,377 ,970
Income before extra.	75 ,212	33 ,947	39 ,380	24 ,495	87 ,286
Cash Flow	155 ,379	63 ,961	63 ,156	91 ,346	207 ,893
Debt/Equity	0 .60	0 .78	0 .62	0 .73	0 .56
Return on Capital (%)	10 .41	5 .24	6 .45	5 .30	12 .37
Ret. on Com. Equity (%)	9 .66	4 .96	6 .02	3 .00	9 .67
% Change Profit	121 .6	(13 .8)	60 .8	(71 .9)	(16 .6)
% Change Revenue	24 .3	8 .2	(13 .2)	(23 .1)	(21 .4)
% Change Assets	17 .0	(0 .9)	7 .6	(19 .7)	(5 .0)

Date	EPS	DPS	Tot Rev	Inc Bex
Mar 95	0 .70	0 .00	400 ,491	36 ,145
Dec 94	0 .59	0 .30	368 ,530	29 ,979
Sep 94	0 .41	0 .00	322 ,720	21 ,206
Jun 94	0 .33	0 .30	287 ,116	17 ,022
Mar 94	0 .15	0 .00	256 ,810	7 ,005
Dec 93	0 .25	0 .30	255 ,433	11 ,206
Sep 93	0 .25	0 .00	258 ,105	11 ,615
Jun 93	0 .08	0 .30	242 ,975	4 ,108

Preferred Div. Coverage	np	16 .1	18 .6
Total Div. Coverage	2 .4	1 .2	1 .2
Interest Coverage	9 .1	12 .4	11 .3
Current Ratio	3 .1	2 .4	2 .4
Operating Margin	9 .6	3 .2	5 .6
Asset Turnover	0 .6	0 .6	0 .5
5 YEAR RATIOS (%)			
Return on Capital	8 .0	8 .6	11 .1
Return on Com. Equity	6 .7	7 .1	8 .9
Profit Growth	(6 .4)	(21 .7)	(15 .9)
Revenue Growth	(6 .8)	(13 .2)	(10 .2)
Asset Growth	(1 .0)	(4 .2)	(3 .9)
BALANCE SHEET (000)			
Cash	386 ,393	307 ,500	235 ,909
Current Assets	793 ,659	621 ,283	619 ,607
Net Fixed Assets	1 ,102 ,480	1 ,001 ,135	808 ,790
Invest's & Advances	17 ,105	13 ,805	8 ,735
Total Assets	1 ,983 ,472	1 ,694 ,985	1 ,711 ,163
Short Term Debt	4 ,955	20 ,661	23 ,558
Current Liabilities	256 ,894	263 ,674	258 ,725
Long Term Debt	536 ,344	508 ,206	381 ,692
Total Liabilities	1 ,081 ,105	1 ,018 ,141	1 ,052 ,593
Total Equity	902 ,367	676 ,844	658 ,570
Total Liab. & Equity	1 ,983 ,472	1 ,694 ,985	1 ,711 ,163
CAPITAL (000)			
Total Debt	541 ,299	528 ,867	405 ,250
Preferred Equity	0	26 ,203	26 ,384
Common Equity	902 ,367	650 ,641	632 ,186

Business:

RIO ALGOM LTD. is a diversified Canadian mining corporation with significant interests in the mining of uranium, copper, molybdenum, zinc and coal in North America and Chile. The corporation also operates metals distribution businesses in Canada, the United States and Australia.

Synopsis:

In April 1995, Rio Algom and North Limited of Australia jointly announced a $510-million offer for all the outstanding shares of International Musto Exploration Limited. Musto's principal asset is a 50% interest in the Bajo de la Alumbrera project in Argentina. Alumbrera is one of the world's largest undeveloped copper-gold porphyry deposits. Acquisition of this project would raise Rio's copper output to more than 350 million pounds annually, and add 160,000 ounces of gold.

Earlier in the year, Rio's North American Metals Distribution Group purchased the U.S. Metal Goods distribution business from Alcan Aluminium Limited for $110-million (U.S.). The acquisition expands Rio's geographic coverage and makes Rio a primary U.S. distributor of stainless steel and aluminum with sales of $900-million (U.S.). Financial results from this acquisition will be incorporated beginning in the second quarter of 1995.

Factors that had a positive impact on Rio Algom's first quarter of 1995 and 1994 financial results include: improvements in copper prices; higher copper volumes due to production contributions at Cerro Colorado in the second half of the year; growth in the metals distribution business; and the decline of the Canadian dollar.

Rio believes that copper prices will remain firm for the next quarter, however some weakening in copper, stainless steel, and aluminum prices is expected later in the year. Production from current mines and expansions at existing mines should increase copper inventories above current levels.

Rank (Profit/Revenue/Assets)
90   105   105

Gordon C. Gray
Chairman

Colin A. Macaulay
President & C.E.O.

Michael S. Parrett
V.P. C.F.O.

Address
120 Adelaide Street West
Suite 2600
Toronto
ON
M5H 1W5
(416) 367-4000

Fax: (416) 365-6870
R0001889/G/1.2

WESTMIN RESOURCES LIMITED

Exchanges	Price (Jun29'95)		6.25	Trailing P/E		nm		Stock Symbol
TV	Trailing Yield (%)		3.20	Trailing EPS		(0.52)		**WMI**

Period Ending	Dec94	Dec93	Dec92	Dec91	Dec90
Yearly Statistics					
Price-Close	6.13	5.63	5.50	3.35	2.10
Price-High	6.63	6.00	6.13	6.25	8.88
Price-Low	4.05	4.20	3.40	1.55	1.55
P/E-Close	nm	nm	nm	nm	nm
Dividends per Share	0.20	0.20	0.20	0.20	0.20
Dividend Yield (%)	3.27	3.56	3.64	5.97	9.52
Sales per Share	0.72	0.71	2.08	2.42	2.83
EPS before extra. item	(0.77)	(0.83)	(0.71)	(1.02)	(2.50)
Cash Flow per Share	(0.37)	(0.35)	0.16	(0.16)	0.45
Book Value per Share	(0.49)	(0.28)	0.69	1.44	2.52
O/S Common Shares	47,110	43,379	42,969	41,258	39,221
Total Revenue	34,239	36,962	105,724	122,768	139,631
Income before extra.	(24,786)	(27,021)	(18,108)	(26,286)	(80,841)
Cash Flow	(16,708)	(15,277)	6,655	(6,302)	17,838
Debt/Equity	2.61	0.90	1.11	0.75	0.42
Return on Capital (%)	(9.32)	(8.33)	(1.01)	(2.12)	(13.41)
Ret. on Com. Equity (%)	na	(405.79)	(67.39)	(51.93)	(64.96)
% Change Profit	8.3	(49.2)	31.1	67.5	(227.2)
% Change Revenue	(7.4)	(65.0)	(13.9)	(12.1)	22.8
% Change Assets	9.5	(39.2)	(33.3)	(4.3)	(30.6)

Date	EPS	DPS	Tot Rev	Inc Bex
Mar 95	0.08	0.05	31,075	5,251
Dec 94	(0.20)	0.05	16,734	(6,391)
Sep 94	(0.24)	0.05	5,428	(8,298)
Jun 94	(0.16)	0.05	6,948	(4,761)
Mar 94	(0.17)	0.05	5,129	(5,336)
Dec 93	(0.21)	0.05	4,260	(7,128)
Sep 93	(0.14)	0.05	5,326	(3,732)
Jun 93	(0.20)	0.05	8,426	(6,259)

	Dec94	Dec93	Dec92
Preferred Div. Coverage	0.0	0.0	0.0
Total Div. Coverage	0.0	0.0	0.0
Interest Coverage	0.0	0.0	0.0
Current Ratio	1.2	1.7	0.5
Operating Margin	(55.3)	(82.5)	(25.3)
Asset Turnover	0.2	0.2	0.3
5 YEAR RATIOS (%)			
Return on Capital	(6.8)	(2.7)	(0.2)
Return on Com. Equity	na	(113.0)	(31.8)
Profit Growth	na	na	na
Revenue Growth	(21.4)	(21.8)	(11.1)
Asset Growth	(21.7)	(26.4)	(18.2)
BALANCE SHEET (000)			
Cash	0	20	102
Current Assets	33,621	13,634	26,290
Net Fixed Assets	154,613	155,523	159,858
Invest's & Advances	6,857	8,310	109,582
Total Assets	202,097	184,578	303,357
Short Term Debt	11,344	1,101	37,661
Current Liabilities	28,332	8,164	49,142
Long Term Debt	119,571	81,745	114,992
Total Liabilities	151,919	92,643	165,918
Total Equity	50,178	91,935	137,439
Total Liab. & Equity	202,097	184,578	303,357
CAPITAL (000)			
Total Debt	130,915	82,846	152,653
Preferred Equity	73,048	103,851	107,804
Common Equity	(22,870)	(11,916)	29,635

Business:

WESTMIN RESOURCES LTD. is a mining company with two producing properties. Myra Falls produces copper and zinc concentrates, and the Premier Gold project produces gold and silver done.

Synopsis:

According to Westmin, the company's outlook for 1995 and beyond is much improved with the resumption of full production at Myra Falls and improvements in cost-cutting measures and productivity levels. The price of copper has steadily increased over the last year and zinc's price, while lagging, is starting to respond to declining stocks by increasing more than 20% from the lows in 1993. All these factors along with high zinc production from the New Gap/Battle Zone at Myra Falls should have a positive impact on the company's future cash flows. In addition, Westmin remains optimistic that extensive drillings during 1995 in the Yukon and at Johnson River in Alaska will yield significant new discoveries.

The company returned to profitability in the first quarter of 1995. During this period mill production at the Myra Falls operations averaged 3,366 tonnes per day. Total ore milled was 302,964 tonnes, at a grade of 2.23% copper and 2.86% zinc, which yielded 24,344 tonnes of copper concentrate and 8,355 tonnes of zinc concentrate. Activities to access and develop the zinc-rich Battle Zone deposits continued through the first quarter with the expectation that ore from this zone will start reaching the mill in the second quarter of 1995. The company's Premier Gold operations recorded a loss of $431,000 and the company's coal operations generated earnings of approximately $4-million. Revenues during this period included a one-time receipt of $2.5-million from an arbitration settlement under the company's long-term coal royalty contract.

Despite a slight improvement in total mining revenues in 1994, the company attributed its net loss to the labour disruption at Myra Falls which began in April 1993 and was finally resolved in August 1994. Revenues from Myra Falls should return to the $100-million plus range in 1995.

Relative strength to TSE300

Price

Volume (in 1000's of board lots)

Rank (Profit/Revenue/Assets)
977   623   355

Paul M. Marshall
Chairman Of The Board

Walter Segsworth
President

Address
P.O. Box 49066
1055 Dunsmuir Street
Suite 904
Vancouver
BC
V7X 1C4
(604) 681-2253
Fax: (604) 681-0357
W0002192/G/1.2

Page	Company		Fiscal year end	EARNINGS Last Year	Estim this ye	...year
27	Aber Resources		Jan-94	(0.17)	na	na
28	Agnico-Eagle Mines		Dec-94	0.38	0.51	0.55
29	Aur Resources		Dec-94	(0.01)	0.28	0.35
30	Barrick Gold	$US	Dec-94	0.81	0.86	0.99
31	Bema Gold		Dec-94	(0.06)	(0.03)	0.09
32	Breakwater Resources		Dec-94	(0.01)	na	na
33	Caledonia Mining		Dec-94	0.01	0.00	(0.03)
34	Cambior		Dec-94	0.39	0.46	0.59
35	Campbell Resources		Dec-94	0.05	0.07	0.05
36	Cornucopia Resources	$US	Dec-94	(0.09)	na	na
37	Dakota Mining	$US	Dec-94	(0.33)	na	na
38	Echo Bay Mines		Dec-94	0.07	(0.18)	(0.06)
39	Equity Silver Mines		Dec-94	0.14	na	na
40	Euro-Nevada Mining		Mar-95	0.60	0.68	0.97
41	Franco-Nevada Mining		Mar-95	3.10	3.44	3.65
42	Glamis Gold		Jun-94	0.32	0.17	0.29
43	Goldcorp		Dec-94	1.11	0.25	0.35
44	Golden Knight Resources		Dec-94	0.25	0.28	0.46
45	Golden Star Resources	$US	Dec-94	(0.42)	na	na
46	Granges Inc.		Dec-94	0.20	0.08	0.12
47	Hemlo Gold Mines		Dec-94	0.67	0.59	0.64
48	Kinross Gold		Dec-94	0.27	0.26	0.39
49	Miramar Mining		Dec-94	0.43	0.46	0.52
50	Muscocho Explorations		Dec-94	(0.04)	na	na
51	Northgate Exploration		Dec-94	0.05	na	na
52	Pegasus Gold	$US	Dec-94	(0.16)	(0.03)	0.10
53	Pioneer Metals		Dec-94	(0.00)	na	na
54	Placer Dome	$US	Dec-94	0.41	0.57	0.64
55	Prime Resources		Dec-94	0.10	0.42	0.65
56	QSR		Dec-94	(1.18)	na	na
57	Rayrock Yellowknife Resources		Dec-94	0.51	0.29	0.40
58	Rea Gold		Dec-94	0.02	0.21	0.14
59	Royal Oak Mines		Dec-94	0.22	0.28	0.40
60	Sonora Gold		Dec-94	0.26	na	na
61	TVX Gold		Dec-94	0.14	0.10	0.15
62	Teck Corporation		Dec-94	0.79	1.35	1.69
63	United Keno Hill Mines		Dec-94	(0.30)	na	na
64	Vengold		Dec-94	0.15	na	na
65	Viceroy Resource		Mar-95	0.50	0.54	0.47
66	Wharf Resources		Dec-94	0.53	0.44	0.52

Estimates from First Call Corporation, 22 Pittsburgh Street, Boston, MA 02210   (800) 366-9992   Fax (617) 261-5679

.ecious Metals

During 1994, minerals markets were strong in Canada as well as in the major western world economies. Minerals revenues increased during the year because of higher base and precious metal prices as well as a lower Canadian dollar. Economies in Asia, South America, and Europe were in a recovery phase throughout the year. This increased pressure on the supplies for both base and precious metals.

Gold prices for 1994 were very steady when compared to 1993. Previously gold traded in a range obetween $380 (U.S.) to $390 (U.S.) per ounce. The average price of gold in 1994 was $384 (U.S.) per ounce. In comparison, the average price of gold in 1993 was $360 (U.S.) per ounce.

The volatility of the bond and equity markets along with the large fluctuations in currency markets encouraged investment in gold. Upward price movements caused producer price hedging and selling by the central banks of several countries including Canada. Toward the end of 1994, there was growing concern about rising inflation. Gold has historically been regarded as an investment hedge against inflationary pressures.

Gold shares normally trade on the basis of the fundamental value of gold mining assets, augmented by a "blue-sky" premium. Investors hold the metal in the hope of a repeat of those three and one-half years when the price of gold went from $103.05 (U.S.) an ounce in August 1976 to an all-time high of $850 (U.S.) in January 1980. However, the price of gold crashed to $296.75 by mid-June 1982.

Another factor affecting the strength of metal prices in 1994 was the increased involvement of commodity funds in the markets. These huge pools of capital do not always reflect the fundamentals of supply and demand theory. These purchases or sales are, in many cases, prompted by movements in price trends rather than changes in inventory levels. During 1994, these types of purchases supported higher metal prices.

Although commodity funds have been around for some time, the current level of investment is unprecedented. The concern is how the commodity funds will react during a downward price trend. If their positions were liquidated in the short term, prices could be affected severely. However, the fundamentals of supply and demand should correct any unwarranted price declines within a short period of time. In an effort to manage the risk of commodity funds, companies participate in hedging activities. These include selling forward, buying put options, selling call options, and combinations of all three activities.

During 1994, West Africa continued to meet and exceed gold production targets for companies mining there. Analysts estimate annual gold production in West Africa at more than 250,000 ounces or an estimated $350,000 (U.S.) a day in revenues for the country. Many companies are becoming aware of properties like Ghana's second-largest gold-mining operation which ranks just behind Lonrho Corp.'s huge Ashanti Goldfields Co. Reserves contain about 6.7 million ounces of gold. Many mining companies from the United States, Canada, and Australia are exploring opportunities in West Africa.

U.S. reserves of gold bullion declined by 54 million ounces between 1970 and 1995, leaving 261.7 million ounces of gold at Fort Knox. Most Western nations, excluding Japan and Switzerland, have been major net sellers. Now, some governments have stopped selling. Canada basically has run out of gold. What remains of the former Soviet Union isn't doing much better. Given U.S. Federal Reserve chairman Alan Greenspan's recent mutterings about the validity of a gold standard to buttress the U.S dollar, perhaps U.S. selling is finally on the wane. If the price of bullion does break through $400 an ounce, the market will explode, as shares respond to the higher gold price combined with an immediate snapback of all that lost premium.

DIAMOND

ABER RESOURCES LTD.

Exchanges	Price (Jun29'95)			9.50	Trailing P/E		na	Stock Symbol
TQ	Trailing Yield (%)			na	Trailing EPS		na	**ABZ**

Period Ending	Jan95	Jan94	Jan93	Jan92	Jan91	**Business:**
Yearly Statistics						ABER RESOURCES LTD. is involved in the
Price-Close	6.50	4.35	1.97	1.25	0.40	acquisition, exploration and development of
Price-High	14.63	5.75	3.00	1.59	1.02	natural resource properties in the mining sector.
Price-Low	3.95	1.75	1.02	0.25	0.25	
P/E-Close	nm	nm	nm	nm	nm	
Dividends per Share	0.00	0.00	0.00	0.00	0.00	
Dividend Yield (%)	0.00	0.00	0.00	0.00	0.00	
Sales per Share	na	na	na	na	na	
EPS before extra. item	(0.25)	(0.17)	(0.16)	(0.08)	(0.09)	
Cash Flow per Share	(0.04)	(0.03)	(0.06)	(0.03)	(0.05)	
Book Value per Share	1.02	0.58	0.60	0.46	0.51	
O/S Common Shares	31,712	22,509	19,504	10,149	8,549	
Total Revenue	152	256	81	27	16	
Income before extra.	(7,306)	(3,711)	(2,568)	(742)	(754)	
Cash Flow	(1,242)	(633)	(950)	(295)	(435)	

Date	EPS	DPS	Tot Rev	Inc Bex
Jan 95	(0.21)	0.00	8	(6,079)
Oct 94	(0.01)	0.00	93	(406)
Jul 94	(0.01)	0.00	34	(451)
Apr 94	(0.02)	0.00	17	(370)
Jan 94	(0.15)	0.00	23	(3,252)
Oct 93	0.00	0.00	89	(120)
Jul 93	(0.01)	0.00	73	(201)
Apr 93	(0.01)	0.00	71	(138)

	Jan95	Jan94	Jan93	Jan92	Jan91
Debt/Equity	nd	0.01	0.02	0.02	0.02
Return on Capital (%)	(32.04)	(29.51)	(30.56)	(16.07)	(16.59)
Ret. on Com. Equity (%)	(32.29)	(29.99)	(31.23)	(16.36)	(16.73)
% Change Profit	(96.9)	(44.5)	(246.1)	1.5	(27.6)
% Change Revenue	(40.6)	216.6	194.4	75.5	(7.0)
% Change Assets	245.3	10.5	149.8	7.6	(3.9)

	Jan95	Jan94	Jan93
Preferred Div. Coverage	np	np	np
Total Div. Coverage	na	na	na
Interest Coverage	na	na	na
Current Ratio	9.1	5.0	16.3
Operating Margin	na	na	na
Asset Turnover	na	na	na
5 YEAR RATIOS (%)			
Return on Capital	(25.0)	(21.2)	(19.4)
Return on Com. Equity	(25.3)	(21.5)	(19.8)
Profit Growth	na	na	na
Revenue Growth	55.3	39.0	6.4
Asset Growth	58.0	25.3	19.6
BALANCE SHEET (000)			
Cash	3,845	1,854	5,445
Current Assets	5,196	2,122	5,658
Net Fixed Assets	27,056	5,607	6,461
Invest's & Advances	600	5,667	0
Total Assets	32,852	13,395	12,119
Short Term Debt	0	126	276
Current Liabilities	572	424	348
Long Term Debt	0	0	0
Total Liabilities	572	424	348
Total Equity	32,280	12,971	11,771
Total Liab. & Equity	32,852	13,395	12,119
CAPITAL (000)			
Total Debt	0	126	276
Preferred Equity	0	0	0
Common Equity	32,280	12,971	11,771

Synopsis:

In May 1995, Aber Resources announced the discovery of a new diamond bearing deposit in the Lac de Gras area of the Northwest Territories. The deposit covers an area that makes up the Diavik project, which is 60% owned by Aber and 40% owned by Kennecott Canada Inc. As of May 1995, 108 metres of kimberlite has been recovered, and a three millimetre clear and colourless diamond has been identified in a visual examination of kimberlite drill core. As a result of the discovery, Aber has planned a $20-million bulk sampling program at the site. Aber expects to release the results of the bulk sampling program upon completion.

In Aber's third quarter report, the company announced the discovery of a new diamond bearing kimberlite deposit on Aber's 40% owned Camsell Lake Block. The site is located about 100 kilometers south of the Lac de Gras in the Northwest Territories and covers about 560,000 acres. Two holes were drilled into the pipe with partial results being very positive. A 116 kilogram sample of split core analyzed contained 6 macros and 112 micros for a total of 118 diamonds. Further testing will continue at the site.

Also in its third quarter report, Aber announced the disappointing drilling results at the company's 15% interest in DHK, Wo and ATW properties in the Northwest Territories. Results were only 0.013 carats per tonne from the diatreme phase and 0.359 carats per tonne from the pyroclastic phase. Although drilling results have been disappointing, Kennecott Canada has informed participants of the venture that exploratory drilling will continue on the properties during 1995.

Aber expects to carry out an airborne geophysical survey to be carried out on the company's 100% interest in the Kuujua Nickel Project. The project covers over 2.6 million acres of claims and permits in the Victoria Islands of the Northwest Territories. The geological profile of the site is similar to a word class nickel, copper and platinum deposit in Siberia.

Relative strength to TSE300 / Price / Volume (in 1000's of board lots) charts

Rank (Profit/Revenue/Assets)
895   973   985

D. Grenville Thomas
President

Address
Suite 930
355 Burrard Street
Vancouver
BC
V6C 2G8
(604) 682-8555

Fax: (604) 685-8359
01002023/G/2.0

Globe Information Services (c) 1995

Precious Metals - 27

EAGLE MINES LIMITED

					Stock Symbol
Price (Jun29'95)	19.25	Trailing P/E		46.95	
Trailing Yield (%)	0.73	Trailing EPS		0.41	**AGE**

	Dec94	Dec93	Dec92	Dec91	Dec90
Yearly Statistics					
Price-Close	14.75	17.25	5.50	4.40	7.13
Price-High	19.75	21.25	6.75	7.50	12.88
Price-Low	11.25	4.70	3.95	4.00	5.13
P/E-Close	38.82	75.00	25.00	nm	nm
Dividends per Share	0.14	0.13	0.12	0.09	0.09
Dividend Yield (%)	0.95	0.77	2.09	1.96	1.24
Sales per Share	2.17	2.28	2.51	2.73	2.71
EPS before extra. item	0.38	0.23	0.22	(2.86)	(1.82)
Cash Flow per Share	0.84	0.52	0.51	0.28	0.40
Book Value per Share	3.89	3.88	1.40	1.16	4.45
O/S Common Shares	39,579	39,277	31,029	30,721	30,711
Total Revenue	111,782	90,888	71,675	58,779	62,699
Income before extra.	13,940	7,387	6,210	(81,904)	(47,687)
Cash Flow	30,862	16,638	14,215	7,988	10,383
Debt/Equity	0.97	nd	0.44	0.56	0.13
Return on Capital (%)	12.37	8.61	15.00	(76.84)	(27.92)
Ret. on Com. Equity (%)	9.10	7.56	15.74	(95.04)	(33.66)
% Change Profit	88.7	19.0	107.6	(71.8)	(373.5)
% Change Revenue	23.0	26.8	21.9	(6.3)	69.0
% Change Assets	88.4	85.6	9.7	(47.6)	(5.4)

Business:			

AGNICO-EAGLE MINES LTD. is a precious metals mining company. It has gold operations in Joutel and Cadillac, Quebec. Exploration activities are focused in Quebec and Ontario.

Date	EPS	DPS	Tot Rev	Inc Bex
Mar 95	0.15	0.00	24,303	5,410
Dec 94	0.06	0.14	19,788	2,339
Sep 94	0.10	0.00	23,217	3,565
Jun 94	0.10	0.00	23,326	3,641
Mar 94	0.12	0.00	23,052	4,395
Dec 93	0.13	0.00	23,212	4,421
Sep 93	0.01	0.00	20,119	228
Jun 93	0.08	0.10	20,152	2,394

	Dec94	Dec93	Dec92
Preferred Div. Coverage	np	np	np
Total Div. Coverage	2.7	1.5	1.7
Interest Coverage	3.1	9.1	5.5
Current Ratio	5.7	2.8	0.6
Operating Margin	16.0	9.7	12.0
Asset Turnover	0.2	0.4	0.7
5 YEAR RATIOS (%)			
Return on Capital	(13.8)	(18.7)	(21.8)
Return on Com. Equity	(19.3)	(22.9)	(25.9)
Profit Growth	na	na	(8.6)
Revenue Growth	24.6	14.5	4.7
Asset Growth	13.7	10.3	2.3
BALANCE SHEET (000)			
Cash	171,916	51,154	4,610
Current Assets	190,631	70,077	15,291
Net Fixed Assets	151,012	116,909	82,463
Invest's & Advances	4,093	3,563	4,032
Total Assets	359,415	190,821	102,826
Short Term Debt	0	0	6,100
Current Liabilities	33,558	24,869	25,551
Long Term Debt	149,680	0	12,929
Total Liabilities	205,379	38,633	59,496
Total Equity	154,036	152,188	43,330
Total Liab. & Equity	359,415	190,821	102,826
CAPITAL (000)			
Total Debt	149,680	0	19,029
Preferred Equity	0	0	0
Common Equity	154,036	152,188	43,330

Synopsis:

In May 1995, Agnico-Eagle announced that first quarter results improved significantly, compared to the same period last year. The company attributed the improvement to a 27% rise in the amount of ore processed during the period. During the quarter, Agnico-Eagle produced 40,250 ounces of gold, compared to 33,350 ounces in the first quarter of 1994. Agnico-Eagle also brought its cash operating costs to a new record low. The company's cash operating cost fell to $139 (U.S.) per ounce recovered compared to $195 (U.S.) in the first three months of 1994.

Because of the increase of processed ore during the first quarter, Agnico-Eagle reported sharp increases in copper production. Agnico-Eagle produced 3.4 million pounds in the first three months of 1995. This represents an increase of 1 million pounds over 1994.

In March 1995, the Northern Miner reported that Agnico-Eagle plans to expand three of its projects located in northwestern Quebec. The first expansion will be at Agnico-Eagle's No. 2 shaft at LaRonde, near Val d'Or, Quebec. Initial gold production there is expected in the second half of 1995. Reserves at LaRonde are estimated to contain 1 million ounces of gold in proven and probable ore. Also, there exits potential for an additional 3.3 million contained ounces of gold in the surrounding area.

In addition to expansion at the No. 2 shaft, work on the No. 1 shaft at LaRonde is being extended to reach its targeted depth of 4,200 feet by November 1995. Initial construction of Agnico-Eagle's No. 3 shaft is scheduled for July 1995.

Agnico-Eagle produced 144,584 ounces of gold during 1994. This was slightly lower than the 165,671 ounces produced in 1993. Although gold production dipped slightly in 1994, unit profit margins rose due to lower cash operating costs. In 1994, it cost Agnico-Eagle $174 (U.S.) per ounce of gold compared to $226 (U.S.) in 1993.

Rank (Profit/Revenue/Assets)
253 434 265

Paul Penna
Chairman & President

Sean Boyd
C.F.O. & Treasurer

Address
Suite 2302
401 Bay Street
P.O. Box 102
Toronto
ON
M5H 2Y4
(416) 947-1212
Fax: (416) 367-4681
A0000738/G/2.0

For further company information, call Globe Information Services 1-800-268-9128 or (416) 585-5345

AUR RESOURCES INC.

Exchanges	Price (Jun29'95)	5.00	Trailing P/E	nm	Stock Symbol
TM	Trailing Yield (%)	0.00	Trailing EPS	(0.10)	**AUR**

Period Ending	Dec94	Dec93	Sep93	Sep92	Sep91
Yearly Statistics		3M			
Price-Close	4.35	5.75	4.30	3.05	3.15
Price-High	7.88	6.00	4.85	3.45	4.30
Price-Low	3.60	4.20	2.60	1.95	2.90
P/E-Close	nm	nm	215.00	nm	nm
Dividends per Share	0.00	0.00	0.00	0.00	0.00
Dividend Yield (%)	0.00	0.00	0.00	0.00	0.00
Sales per Share	0.24	0.41	0.30	0.45	0.36
EPS before extra. item	(0.16)	(0.02)	0.02	(0.30)	(0.20)
Cash Flow per Share	(0.01)	(0.08)	0.08	(0.11)	(0.03)
Book Value per Share	1.46	0.92	0.83	0.88	1.12
O/S Common Shares	59,359	45,258	46,879	46,171	45,904
Total Revenue	17,612	5,355	19,756	22,043	21,911
Income before extra.	(8,495)	(959)	940	(13,383)	(8,921)
Cash Flow	(580)	(863)	3,434	(5,042)	(1,127)
Debt/Equity	0.33	0.25	nd	nd	nd
Return on Capital (%)	(6.28)	(8.12)	2.46	(29.69)	(20.62)
Ret. on Com. Equity (%)	(13.26)	(9.28)	2.36	(29.83)	(16.17)
% Change Profit	(121.6)	(507.7)	107.0	(50.0)	78.2
% Change Revenue	(17.8)	8.4	(10.4)	0.6	32.7
% Change Assets	94.2	21.4	21.1	(23.2)	(14.7)

	Dec94	Dec93	Sep93
Preferred Div. Coverage	np	np	np
Total Div. Coverage	na	na	na
Interest Coverage	0.0	na	nd
Current Ratio	1.4	2.9	3.0
Operating Margin	(54.9)	(24.8)	(23.4)
Asset Turnover	0.1	0.3	0.3
5 YEAR RATIOS (%)			
Return on Capital	(12.4)	(22.7)	(20.8)
Return on Com. Equity	(13.2)	(22.0)	(20.1)
Profit Growth	na	na	(3.1)
Revenue Growth	1.3	29.9	37.8
Asset Growth	13.3	(7.3)	(5.3)
BALANCE SHEET (000)			
Cash	39,648	28,917	27,708
Current Assets	51,235	34,655	34,927
Net Fixed Assets	47,844	28,673	17,167
Invest's & Advances	24,907	511	511
Total Assets	123,986	63,839	52,604
Short Term Debt	28,400	0	0
Current Liabilities	37,375	11,946	11,482
Long Term Debt	0	10,375	0
Total Liabilities	37,375	22,321	11,482
Total Equity	86,612	41,518	41,123
Total Liab. & Equity	123,986	63,839	52,604
CAPITAL (000)			
Total Debt	28,400	10,375	0
Preferred Equity	0	0	0
Common Equity	86,612	41,518	41,123

Date	EPS	DPS	Tot Rev	Inc Bex
Mar 95	0.08	0.00	14,555	4,655
Dec 94	(0.16)	0.00	2,857	(8,640)
Sep 94	(0.02)	0.00	3,103	(680)
Jun 94	0.00	0.00	4,870	(311)
Mar 94	0.02	0.00	6,783	1,135
Dec 93	(0.02)	0.00	5,355	(959)
Sep 93	0.04	0.00	6,576	1,727
Jun 93	(0.03)	0.00	3,131	(1,072)

Business:

AUR RESOURCES INC. is a mineral resources exploration, development and mining company which owns a 30% interest in and operates the Louvicourt property near Val d'or. Aur also holds an extensive portfolio of exploration properties and a 48.3% interest in Canada Tungsten Inc.

Synopsis:

In late April 1995, Aur Resources released initial production figures for the Louvicourt polymetallic mine near Val d'Or, Quebec. For the first three months of 1995, the Louvicourt mine produced 16.2 million pounds of payable copper, seven million pounds of zinc, 6,674 ounces of gold, and 119,924 ounces of silver. Since the mine began production on January 1, 1995, Aur Resources revenues have more than doubled compared to the same period last year. The Louvicourt mine is expected to be in full production by July 1995. Copper production is estimated to be 94 million pounds in 1995, approximately four million above initial projections. Aur Resources operates and owns 30% of the Louvicourt mine, with the remaining interest belonging to both Novicourt and Teck Corp.

Since the discovery of the Louvicourt deposit in 1989, plans to put the site into production have gone smoothly and under budget. Originally, Aur expected the mine to cost about $319-million. Now with the mine in production, actual costs will be fall between $285-million and $289-million. Reduced capital costs during construction in 1991 are partially responsible for the lower development costs at the mine.

In February 1995, the Northern Miner reported that Aur Resources plans to carry out two drilling programs on properties located southwest of Joutel, Quebec. Aur plans to target two holes with siginifant copper, zinc, and silver deposits.

Rank (Profit/Revenue/Assets)
937 734 436

James Gill
President & C.E.O.

Address
Suite 2501
1 Adelaide Street East
Toronto
ON
M5C 2V9
(416) 362-2614

Fax: (416) 367-0427
A0015314/G/2.0

BARRICK GOLD CORPORATION

Exchanges	Price (Jun29'95)	35.37	Trailing P/E	32.58	Stock Symbol
TMN	Trailing Yield (%)	0.38	Trailing EPS	0.80	ABX

Period Ending	Dec94	Dec93	Dec92	Dec91	Dec90
Yearly Statistics	US	US	US	US	US
Price-Close	31.38	37.63	19.63	16.00	12.69
Price-High	40.63	39.75	19.94	16.06	14.13
Price-Low	27.25	17.38	13.19	10.56	8.94
P/E-Close	28.29	38.79	26.06	41.08	48.33
Dividends per Share	0.10	0.08	0.07	0.06	0.04
Dividend Yield (%)	0.32	0.21	0.33	0.34	0.32
Sales per Share	3.03	2.34	1.91	1.26	0.97
EPS before extra. item	0.81	0.75	0.62	0.34	0.23
Cash Flow per Share	1.22	1.11	0.89	0.58	0.45
Book Value per Share	7.41	4.16	3.47	2.98	2.41
O/S Common Shares	353,300	286,514	283,779	281,837	267,987
Total Revenue	954,500	680,600	553,767	368,686	283,111
Income before extra.	250,500	213,400	174,940	92,440	58,205
Cash Flow	375,900	315,000	252,025	157,784	117,323
Debt/Equity	0.15	0.25	0.34	0.37	0.63
Return on Capital (%)	15.44	19.90	18.79	11.30	11.07
Ret. on Com. Equity (%)	13.16	19.62	19.17	12.45	10.24
% Change Profit	17.4	22.0	89.2	58.8	72.5
% Change Revenue	40.2	22.9	50.2	30.2	29.6
% Change Assets	112.4	9.1	14.7	13.9	13.0

Preferred Div. Coverage	np	np	np
Total Div. Coverage	7.8	9.4	9.5
Interest Coverage	30.5	31.4	25.0
Current Ratio	2.3	2.9	2.5
Operating Margin	35.1	39.9	40.5
Asset Turnover	0.3	0.4	0.4

5 YEAR RATIOS (%)

Return on Capital	15.3	14.3	12.4
Return on Com. Equity	14.9	13.8	11.6
Profit Growth	49.2	47.5	53.4
Revenue Growth	34.3	33.1	37.8
Asset Growth	27.8	18.4	17.2

BALANCE SHEET (000)

Cash	458,000	347,700	288,023
Current Assets	656,200	409,600	353,371
Net Fixed Assets	2,768,300	1,182,100	1,094,402
Invest's & Advances	0	0	0
Total Assets	3,472,000	1,634,500	1,498,667
Short Term Debt	112,500	82,200	77,185
Current Liabilities	288,800	139,900	143,821
Long Term Debt	283,300	211,100	260,098
Total Liabilities	854,800	443,600	514,478
Total Equity	2,617,200	1,190,900	984,189
Total Liab. & Equity	3,472,000	1,634,500	1,498,667

CAPITAL (000)

Total Debt	395,800	293,300	337,283
Preferred Equity	0	0	0
Common Equity	2,617,200	1,190,900	984,189

Business:

BARRICK GOLD CORPORATION is a gold mining company. Its principal producing mines are the Goldstrike mine in Nevada, the Mercur mine in Utah, and the Holt-McDermott mine in Ontario. It has a n interest in the Pinson Mine in Nevada. The company has exploration and development offices in Hermosillo, Mexico; Lima, Peru; Santiago, Chile; and Beijing, The People's Republic of China.

Date		EPS	DPS	Tot Rev	Inc Bex
Mar 95	US	0.20	0.00	307,200	71,100
Dec 94	US	0.18	0.00	330,002	66,443
Sep 94	US	0.20	0.05	222,846	61,257
Jun 94	US	0.22	0.05	211,841	62,376
Mar 94	US	0.21	0.00	189,811	60,424
Dec 93	US	0.18	0.00	173,963	51,811
Sep 93	US	0.21	0.04	180,284	58,343
Jun 93	US	0.20	0.00	178,393	57,156

Synopsis:

In early May 1995, Barrick Corporation appointed former United States President George Bush to its international advisory board. Barrick's international advisory board has several individuals with international connections and business experience. Other members include former Prime Minister of Canada, Brian Mulroney, U.S. Senator Howard Baker, and former president of the German central bank, Karl Otto Pohl. The advisory board will meet in May 1995 to help provide Barrick with strategic advice on geopolitical issues.

In late April 1995, Barrick sold the Macassa gold mine located near Kirkland Lake, Ontario. Kinross Gold will pay Barrick $42.5-million (U.S.) and 2.5 million warrants exercisable into Kinross shares at $10 a share before October 31, 1997.

For the first quarter ended March 31, 1995, Barrick produced more than 710,400 ounces of gold. This compares to 451,981 ounces produced during the same time last year. Barrick attributed increased production to the successful takeover of Lac Minerals. In the first quarter of 1995, Lac's operations contributed more than 220,000 ounces of gold to Barrick's total output. With the takeover of Lac Minerals, Barrick now has 11 operation mines and three mining projects in its portfolio. This makes Barrick the largest gold producer outside South Africa, and quite possibly the most profitable gold producer in the world.

At Barrick's annual meeting in April 1995, company chairman, Peter Munk, said continue growth for the company would have to come from exploration activities in Chile. Also, if continued growth was to continue, Barrick would have to spend billions of dollars to carry out such an aggressive exploration program. Barrick's area of interest is the El Indio gold belt high in the Andes.

Rank (Profit/Revenue/Assets)
17 100 44

Peter Munk
Chairman & C.E.O.

Robert M. Smith
President & C.O.O.

Randall Oliphant
Sr. V.P. & C.F.O.

Address
Suite 2700
200 Bay Street
P.O. Box 119
Toronto
ON
M5J 2J3
(416) 861-9911
Fax: (416) 861-2492
B0015879/G/2.0

For further company information, call Globe Information Services 1-800-268-9128 or (416) 585-5345

BEMA GOLD CORPORATION

Exchanges	Price (Jun29'95)		2.82	Trailing P/E		nm	Stock Symbol
TVA	Trailing Yield (%)		0.00	Trailing EPS		(0.10)	**BGO**

Period Ending	Dec94	Dec93	Dec92	Dec91	Dec90
Yearly Statistics					
Price-Close	2.50	3.10	0.85	1.56	2.95
Price-High	3.40	3.50	2.10	3.20	4.60
Price-Low	2.05	0.57	0.71	1.32	1.85
P/E-Close	nm	nm	nm	nm	nm
Dividends per Share	0.00	0.00	0.00	0.00	0.00
Dividend Yield (%)	0.00	0.00	0.00	0.00	0.00
Sales per Share	na	0.02	0.15	0.26	0.45
EPS before extra. item	(0.06)	(0.03)	(0.28)	(0.10)	(0.03)
Cash Flow per Share	0.00	(0.07)	(0.05)	(0.02)	0.01
Book Value per Share	1.84	0.97	0.71	0.98	1.00
O/S Common Shares	62,083	51,434	31,398	30,738	28,091
Total Revenue	6,615	6,510	5,609	7,792	11,539
Income before extra.	(3,500)	(1,103)	(8,605)	(3,030)	(726)
Cash Flow	5	(2,428)	(1,710)	(639)	234
Debt/Equity	0.01	0.17	1.10	0.88	0.44
Return on Capital (%)	(3.15)	(0.64)	(14.61)	(4.63)	(0.62)
Ret. on Com. Equity (%)	(4.27)	(3.06)	(32.84)	(10.42)	(2.93)
% Change Profit	(217.4)	87.2	(184.0)	(317.3)	68.2
% Change Revenue	1.6	16.0	(28.0)	(32.5)	254.6
% Change Assets	111.5	33.4	(15.9)	31.7	56.9
Preferred Div. Coverage	np	np	np		
Total Div. Coverage	na	na	na		
Interest Coverage	0.0	0.0	0.0		
Current Ratio	5.4	1.7	0.9		
Operating Margin	na	(865.3)	(123.4)		
Asset Turnover	na	0.0	0.1		
5 YEAR RATIOS (%)					
Return on Capital	(4.7)	(6.0)	(8.6)		
Return on Com. Equity	(10.7)	(12.2)	(14.3)		
Profit Growth	na	na	na		
Revenue Growth	15.2	88.9	84.1		
Asset Growth	37.4	28.8	34.2		
BALANCE SHEET (000)					
Cash	46,517	8,832	270		
Current Assets	49,998	11,675	2,914		
Net Fixed Assets	65,654	47,645	41,636		
Invest's & Advances	7,591	4,462	1,878		
Total Assets	140,414	66,401	49,790		
Short Term Debt	1,086	4,913	1,516		
Current Liabilities	9,302	6,811	3,279		
Long Term Debt	0	3,767	23,209		
Total Liabilities	26,099	16,635	27,371		
Total Equity	114,315	49,767	22,418		
Total Liab. & Equity	140,414	66,401	49,790		
CAPITAL (000)					
Total Debt	1,086	8,680	24,725		
Preferred Equity	0	0	0		
Common Equity	114,315	49,767	22,418		

Business:

BEMA GOLD CORPORATION is involved in the exploration and development of gold properties in South America. The company and 50/50 joint venture partner, Amax Gold Inc., have arranged project financing for the multi-million ounce Refugio Gold Project in Northern Chile.

Date	EPS	DPS	Tot Rev	Inc Bex
Mar 95	0.00	0.00	1,275	80
Dec 94	(0.08)	0.00	608	(4,780)
Sep 94	(0.01)	0.00	400	(295)
Jun 94	(0.01)	0.00	104	(758)
Mar 94	0.04	0.00	3,133	2,333
Dec 93	0.05	0.00	2,508	1,476
Sep 93	0.02	0.00	1,299	726
Jun 93	(0.08)	0.00	804	(2,562)

Synopsis:

In May 1995, the Northern Miner reported that initial drilling results at Bema Gold's joint venture in Chile are encouraging. The results relate to Bema's Aldebaran property, which is 50% owned by Arizona Star Resources. Five of the drill holes returned significant intersections highlighted by a 325-foot interval in hole eight, grading 0.033 ounces of gold per ton. The Bema-Arizona Gold partnership plans more drilling on the property.

Bema acquired its 49% interest in the Aldebaran gold project from Minera Anglo American Chile, in January 1995. Bema Gold will pay $4-million (U.S.) for the property, payable before March 30, 1996, and payable in cash or shares. Minable reserves at Aldebaran are estimated at 2.3 million contained ounces of gold.

In March 1995, Bema and partner Amax Gold reported that after six years of delays, the Refugio property will produce gold in February 1996. The project, located in Chile, will process ore at a rate of 30,000 tonnes per day when construction finishes. Refugio should produce 233,000 ounces of gold annually over its 9.4 year life.

For the year ended December 31, 1994, Bema had no gold or silver revenues. About 44.5% of Bema assets were in Chile at the end of 1994. Canadian assets accounted for another 28% of the company's assets. The remaining assets were in Venezuela, 15%; and the United States, 12%.

Relative strength to TSE300

Price

Volume (in 1000's of board lots)

Rank (Profit/Revenue/Assets)
891   834   410

Clive T. Johnson
Chairman, C.E.O. & President

Mark Corra
V.P. Finance

Address
Suite 1400
510 Burrard Street
P.O. Box 48
Vancouver
BC
V6C 3A8
(604) 681-8371
Fax: (604) 681-6209
01002528/G/2.0

BREAKWATER RESOURCES LTD.

Exchanges	Price (Jun29'95)	2.02	Trailing P/E	nm	Stock Symbol
TQ	Trailing Yield (%)	0.00	Trailing EPS	(0.02)	BWR

Period Ending	Dec94	Dec93	Dec92	Dec91	Dec90
Yearly Statistics					
Price-Close	2.20	3.40	5.80	4.20	14.00
Price-High	5.60	6.40	15.00	14.40	57.00
Price-Low	2.00	2.00	2.40	3.40	11.60
P/E-Close	nm	nm	nm	nm	nm
Dividends per Share	0.00	0.00	0.00	0.00	0.00
Dividend Yield (%)	0.00	0.00	0.00	0.00	0.00
Sales per Share	0.21	0.27	0.52	0.93	1.20
EPS before extra. item	(0.01)	(0.19)	(0.09)	(0.55)	(1.17)
Cash Flow per Share	0.00	(0.02)	(0.04)	(0.06)	0.23
Book Value per Share	0.07	(0.01)	0.16	0.20	0.77
O/S Common Shares	440,956	130,872	129,392	68,520	68,520
Total Revenue	44,562	35,255	76,480	64,581	81,747
Income before extra.	(2,532)	(24,106)	(8,442)	(37,383)	(75,391)
Cash Flow	719	(2,791)	(4,202)	(4,150)	14,621
Debt/Equity	0.28	8.63	1.00	5.10	1.15
Return on Capital (%)	2.22	(46.79)	(12.19)	(39.23)	(51.32)
Ret. on Com. Equity (%)	(16.43)	(250.28)	(49.22)	(112.54)	(87.16)
% Change Profit	89.5	(185.5)	77.4	50.4	(593.5)
% Change Revenue	26.4	(53.9)	18.4	(21.0)	(5.4)
% Change Assets	2.6	(15.7)	(20.5)	(28.3)	(17.5)

Preferred Div. Coverage	na	na	na
Total Div. Coverage	na	na	na
Interest Coverage	0.3	0.0	0.0
Current Ratio	1.3	0.4	0.5
Operating Margin	(6.6)	(68.6)	(52.2)
Asset Turnover	0.6	0.5	0.6
5 YEAR RATIOS (%)			
Return on Capital	(29.5)	(26.7)	(15.9)
Return on Com. Equity	(103.1)	(96.9)	(46.4)
Profit Growth	na	na	na
Revenue Growth	(12.4)	(0.4)	19.0
Asset Growth	(16.5)	(12.2)	(9.0)
BALANCE SHEET (000)			
Cash	6,958	3,583	3,731
Current Assets	34,309	22,068	24,274
Net Fixed Assets	39,442	39,997	51,459
Invest's & Advances	0	1,515	6,418
Total Assets	73,751	71,907	85,272
Short Term Debt	1,944	35,225	26,701
Current Liabilities	26,284	58,125	49,023
Long Term Debt	8,053	1,512	684
Total Liabilities	38,136	67,648	57,832
Total Equity	35,615	4,259	27,440
Total Liab. & Equity	73,751	71,907	85,272
CAPITAL (000)			
Total Debt	9,997	36,737	27,385
Preferred Equity	3,114	5,933	6,503
Common Equity	32,501	(1,674)	20,937

Date	EPS	DPS	Tot Rev	Inc Bex
Mar 95	(0.01)	0.00	6,159	(1,485)
Dec 94	(0.01)	0.00	13,196	(2,368)
Sep 94	0.00	0.00	12,016	481
Jun 94	0.00	0.00	9,330	511
Mar 94	(0.01)	0.00	10,240	(1,156)
Dec 93	(0.17)	0.00	2,874	(21,432)
Sep 93	(0.02)	0.00	9,137	(2,016)
Jun 93	(0.03)	0.00	8,362	(3,488)

Business:

BREAKWATER RESOURCES LTD. is a mining company which owns several mines of which the wholly-owned El Mochito Mine in Honduras is currently in production. The Caribou Mine in New Brunswick is being held on a care and maintenance program. The company also has a large portfolio of gold and base exploration properties in Canada and Central America.

Synopsis:

In April 1995, Breakwater Resources said that technological advancements may allow it to reopen a polymetallic mine near Bathurst, New Brunswick. The Caribou mine opened briefly in 1990, but closed due to the complex metallurgy of the lead-zinc-copper-silver-gold at the mine. Now, with new treatment technologies, able produce higher concentrates of metal, Caribou may be viable. Breakwater plans to test the new process at its Lakefield mill by using 150 tonnes of ore. The Lakefield results will determine if a final feasibility study at the Caribou property should take place. The Caribou mine has proven, probable, and possible reserves of 13 million tonnes averaging 8.18% zinc, 3.52% lead, 0.38% copper, 102 grams of silver and 1.4 grams of gold.

In March 1995, Breakwater said that reserves at its El Mochito mine have risen by 24%. Exploration work carried out in the second half of 1994 resulted in an additional 780,866 tonnes grading 7.8% zinc, 1.4% lead and 83 grams of silver. In total, reserves at El Mochito stand at 3.7 million tonnes grading 7.8% zinc, 1.4% lead and 83 grams of silver. Breakwater plans to continue exploration work on untested lands at El Mochito.

In March 1995, Breakwater completed a 10 hole drilling program at the O'Brian gold property in Cadillac, Quebec. The intersections resulted in assay values of between 0.03 0.88 ounces of gold per ton. Radisson Mining Resources has the option to buy a 50% interest in the property by spending $3-million on exploration and issuing Breakwater 500,000 class A Radisson shares before February 28, 1999.

As of December 31, 1994, Breakwater had assets in Latin America, the United States, and Canada. Almost 47% of Breakwater's assets are in Latin America. The remaining assets are in the United State (26.7%) and Canada (26.5%).

Rank (Profit/Revenue/Assets)
868 573 554
Garth A.C. MacRae
Chairman
Gordon F. Bub
President & C.E.O.
Rene R. Galipeau
V.P. & C.F.O.
Colin K. Benner
Exec. V.P. & C.O.O.

Address
Suite 2001
44 Victoria Street
Toronto
ON
M5C 1Y2
(416) 363-4798

Fax: (416) 363-9474

B0012021/G/2.0

CALEDONIA MINING CORPORATION

Exchanges	Price (Jun29'95)		8 .25	Trailing P/E		nm	Stock Symbol
TQ	Trailing Yield (%)		0 .00	Trailing EPS		(0 .01)	**CAL**

Period Ending	Dec94	Dec93	Dec92	Dec91	Sep91	Business:
Yearly Statistics						CALEDONIA MINING CORPORATION is
Price-Close	10 .50	0 .85	0 .25	0 .43	0 .67	involved directly or through subsidiaries in the
Price-High	13 .13	1 .17	0 .68	1 .15	na	exploration and production of various mineral
Price-Low	0 .82	0 .25	0 .21	0 .40	na	resources. The company operates in Canada, the
P/E-Close	1 ,050 .00	nm	nm	nm	nm	Unites States, the United Kingdom, Spain,
Dividends per Share	0 .00	0 .00	0 .00	0 .00	0 .00	Zimbabwe, Tanzania, Hungary and Slovakia.
Dividend Yield (%)	0 .00	0 .00	0 .00	0 .00	0 .00	

	Dec94	Dec93	Dec92	Dec91	Sep91
Sales per Share	0 .80	na	na	na	0 .00
EPS before extra. item	0 .01	(0 .13)	(0 .03)	(0 .09)	(0 .08)
Cash Flow per Share	0 .15	(0 .07)	(0 .13)	(0 .10)	(0 .04)
Book Value per Share	2 .28	1 .31	1 .52	0 .11	1 .86
O/S Common Shares	23 ,633	11 ,702	10 ,633	3 ,245	5 ,350
Total Revenue	14 ,442	42	1 ,543	98	505
Income before extra.	152	(1 ,531)	(327)	(198)	(402)
Cash Flow	2 ,691	(807)	(1 ,272)	(233)	(190)
Debt/Equity	0 .44	nd	0 .05	2 .35	nd
Return on Capital (%)	2 .34	(9 .46)	(2 .56)	(3 .04)	(3 .93)
Ret. on Com. Equity (%)	0 .44	(9 .72)	(3 .98)	(3 .84)	(3 .93)
% Change Profit	109 .9	(367 .7)	(65 .5)	50 .8	(946 .5)
% Change Revenue	nm	(97 .3)	1 ,482 .4	(80 .7)	(5 .8)
% Change Assets	600 .1	(8 .1)	1 ,266 .0	(87 .4)	(3 .4)

Date	EPS	DPS	Tot Rev	Inc Bex
Mar 95	0 .00	0 .00	9 ,469	24
Dec 94	0 .07	0 .00	6 ,405	1 ,245
Sep 94	(0 .06)	0 .00	3 ,441	(1 ,090)
Jun 94	(0 .02)	0 .00	88	(404)
Mar 94	(0 .02)	0 .00	92	(311)
Dec 93	(0 .03)	0 .00	(109)	(419)
Sep 93	(0 .02)	0 .00	125	(288)
Jun 93	(0 .04)	0 .00	56	(447)

	Dec94	Dec93	Dec92
Preferred Div. Coverage	np	np	np
Total Div. Coverage	na	na	na
Interest Coverage	2 .7	0 .0	0 .0
Current Ratio	3 .5	0 .7	2 .2
Operating Margin	15 .9	(127 .1)	(174 .5)
Asset Turnover	0 .1	na	na
5 YEAR RATIOS (%)			
Return on Capital	(3 .3)	(3 .7)	(2 .3)
Return on Com. Equity	(4 .2)	(4 .2)	(2 .7)
Profit Growth	26 .2	na	na
Revenue Growth	93 .2	(36 .8)	43 .5
Asset Growth	60 .7	10 .0	14 .8
BALANCE SHEET (000)			
Cash	27 ,063	121	2 ,155
Current Assets	33 ,577	447	2 ,492
Net Fixed Assets	70 ,452	6 ,649	5 ,575
Invest's & Advances	3 ,599	7 ,889	8 ,702
Total Assets	113 ,970	16 ,279	17 ,707
Short Term Debt	1 ,897	0	739
Current Liabilities	9 ,567	614	1 ,116
Long Term Debt	21 ,857	0	0
Total Liabilities	60 ,083	898	1 ,588
Total Equity	53 ,887	15 ,381	16 ,119
Total Liab. & Equity	113 ,970	16 ,279	17 ,707
CAPITAL (000)			
Total Debt	23 ,754	0	739
Preferred Equity	0	0	0
Common Equity	53 ,887	15 ,381	16 ,119

Synopsis:

In March 1995, Caledonia Mining Corp. and Holmer Gold Mines formed a partnership to explore mineral properties in Cuba. Caledonia can earn a 50% interest in the Cuban properties by spending $5-million over the next five years. Specifically, Caledonia must spend at least $1-million in the first year and may terminate the agreement after that time. If Caledonia elects to continue the alliance, it must spend an additional $1-million annually over the remaining four years of the agreement. Caledonia will earn a 10% interest in Holmer's share for every $1-million it spends on the Cuban properties. Holmer owns a 50% interest in the Cuban properties with the remaining interest being held by GeoMinera S.A., which is owned by the Cuban government. The reserves on the property are amenable to open-pit mining. Metallurgical tests indicate excellent deposits.

In February 1995, Caledonia announced that it found no diamonds in the Coronation Gulf area of the Arctic. A research vessel began a geophysical survey during the last two weeks of July 1994, but it found only a few areas with diamond mining potential. Caledonia will now focus its attention on diamond properties elsewhere in the Northwest Territories.

In February 1995, the Toronto Stock Exchange added Caledonia to the TSE 300 Composite Index. Caledonia replaced ISM Information System Management Corp.

In late January 1995, Caledonia bought an additional 15.2% interest in the Filon Sur gold mine in Spain for $1.3-million (U.S.). This raised Caledonia's interest in the producing mine to 98.4%. Forecast production on the property is estimated at 25,000 ounces of silver and 175,000 ounces of gold in 1995. Caledonia estimated the gold equivalent cash cost will be $176 (U.S.) per ounce. Proven and probable reserves on the property stand at 5.3 million tons, with an average grade of 0.058 ounces of gold and 0.84 ounces of silver per ton.

Relative strength to TSE300

Rank (Profit/Revenue/Assets)
739 764 454
D.S. MacLeod
Chairman
F.C. Harvey
President

Address
Suite 1
1775 Meyerside Drive
Mississauga
ON
L5T 1E2
(905) 564-5213
Fax: (905) 564-5214
G0023859/G/2.0

CAMBIOR INC.

Exchanges	Price (Jun29'95)		17.12	Trailing P/E		570.67	Stock Symbol
TM	Trailing Yield (%)		0.82	Trailing EPS		0.03	CBJ

Period Ending	Dec94	Dec93	Dec92	Dec91	Dec90
Yearly Statistics					
Price-Close	16.13	20.00	12.13	9.25	12.00
Price-High	23.75	20.88	12.75	11.88	20.50
Price-Low	14.13	10.75	7.00	8.25	9.75
P/E-Close	322.50	55.56	nm	20.56	15.39
Dividends per Share	0.14	0.14	0.14	0.14	0.13
Dividend Yield (%)	0.87	0.70	1.16	1.51	1.08
Sales per Share	6.09	6.67	5.45	5.32	4.53
EPS before extra. item	0.05	0.36	(0.13)	0.45	0.78
Cash Flow per Share	1.49	1.76	1.64	1.52	1.65
Book Value per Share	11.58	11.64	9.76	10.29	9.98
O/S Common Shares	49,011	48,961	36,877	30,711	30,711
Total Revenue	310,043	280,806	187,253	169,093	152,639
Income before extra.	2,454	14,952	(4,391)	13,920	23,991
Cash Flow	72,884	72,912	55,270	46,765	50,548
Debt/Equity	0.38	0.30	0.44	0.12	0.05
Return on Capital (%)	1.41	3.38	(0.80)	4.48	8.31
Ret. on Com. Equity (%)	0.43	3.22	(1.30)	4.47	8.22
% Change Profit	(83.6)	440.5	(131.5)	(42.0)	35.8
% Change Revenue	10.4	50.0	10.7	10.8	30.6
% Change Assets	7.1	33.8	49.2	12.0	6.5

	Dec94	Dec93	Dec92
Preferred Div. Coverage	np	np	np
Total Div. Coverage	0.4	2.5	0.0
Interest Coverage	1.5	2.5	0.0
Current Ratio	4.3	3.4	2.1
Operating Margin	(1.8)	3.8	(5.0)
Asset Turnover	0.3	0.3	0.3
5 YEAR RATIOS (%)			
Return on Capital	3.4	4.6	6.0
Return on Com. Equity	3.0	4.5	5.9
Profit Growth	(32.7)	(3.6)	na
Revenue Growth	21.4	20.6	15.1
Asset Growth	20.5	27.5	20.1
BALANCE SHEET (000)			
Cash	133,741	174,815	66,262
Current Assets	218,246	249,520	123,163
Net Fixed Assets	625,008	532,259	468,659
Invest's & Advances	4,260	647	1,096
Total Assets	863,654	806,632	603,052
Short Term Debt	5,351	40,793	23,791
Current Liabilities	50,198	73,098	58,979
Long Term Debt	209,888	128,659	135,452
Total Liabilities	295,977	236,666	243,326
Total Equity	567,677	569,966	359,726
Total Liab. & Equity	863,654	806,632	603,052
CAPITAL (000)			
Total Debt	215,239	169,452	159,243
Preferred Equity	0	0	0
Common Equity	567,677	569,966	359,726

Business:

CAMBIOR INC. is a major Canadian gold producer with interests in eight mines, three development projects and over one hundred exploration properties throughout North and South America.

Date	EPS	DPS	Tot Rev	Inc Bex
Mar 95	0.11	0.00	96,383	5,217
Dec 94	0.15	0.07	80,884	7,139
Sep 94	(0.31)	0.00	77,429	(15,383)
Jun 94	0.08	0.07	76,995	3,785
Mar 94	0.14	0.00	74,185	6,909
Dec 93	0.04	0.07	77,697	2,063
Sep 93	0.21	0.00	82,879	8,988
Jun 93	0.08	0.07	65,855	3,025

Synopsis:

In May 1995, Cambior Inc. and partner Gold Star Resources announced that reserves at the Omai mine, in Guyana, had risen by 446,000 ounces of gold. The gain was directly attributed to the results of the definition drilling program carried out at the eastern part of the Wenot pit. The new reserves total nine million tons grading 1.6 grams Au/tonne, containing 446,000 ounces of gold. Cambior's gold production is significantly higher than originally forecast. Mineable reserves on March 31, 1995, were 13% higher than on December 31, 1994, which in turn was 62% higher than when the Omai opened in January 1993. Cambior owns 65% of the project with the remaining interest belonging to Golden Star Resources. Cambior also operates the project.

In May 1995, Cambior announced that first quarter revenues were up 25%, compared to the same period last year. The increase was mainly attributed to the start up of commercial production at the company's Mobrun Mine in January 1995. Also, Cambior realized a successful gold hedging program that boosted its average gold selling price to $402 (U.S.) per ounce. This is approximately $23 (U.S.) per ounce higher than the average market value of gold during 1994.

Gold production for the year ended December 31, 1994, was slightly lower than in 1993. Cambior produced 126,452 ounces of gold in 1994 compared to 130,369 ounces in the previous year. Cambior attributed the drop mainly to the suspension of production activities at the Mouska Mine to allow for shaft deepening work. The results were also attributed to a lower milled grade at the Doyon Mine.

As of May 1995, the expansion work at Cambior's Omai mine was on schedule. The expansion, which started in the first quarter of 1995, includes foundation work as well as a new ore reclaim tunnel and the erection of the carbon-in-pulp and leaching tanks.

Rank (Profit/Revenue/Assets)		
541	253	168

Gilles Mercure
Chairman Of The Board

Louis P. Gignac
President & C.E.O.

Henry Roy
V.P. Finance & Administration

Address
Suite 850
800 Rene-Levesque Blvd. West
Montreal
PQ
H3B 1X9
(514) 878-3166

Fax: (514) 878-3324
C0000622/G/2.0

CAMPBELL RESOURCES INC.

Exchanges	Price (Jun29'95)	1 .03	Trailing P/E	14 .71	Stock Symbol
TMN	Trailing Yield (%)	0 .00	Trailing EPS	0 .07	**CCH**

Period Ending	Dec94	Dec93	Dec92	Dec91	Dec90
Yearly Statistics					
Price-Close	0 .77	0 .88	0 .38	0 .46	0 .42
Price-High	1 .03	1 .60	0 .63	0 .60	1 .25
Price-Low	0 .55	0 .33	0 .36	0 .33	0 .35
P/E-Close	15 .40	nm	nm	15 .33	nm
Dividends per Share	0 .00	0 .00	0 .00	0 .00	0 .00
Dividend Yield (%)	0 .00	0 .00	0 .00	0 .00	0 .00
Sales per Share	0 .40	0 .29	0 .35	0 .41	0 .48
EPS before extra. item	0 .05	(0 .03)	(0 .01)	0 .03	(0 .34)
Cash Flow per Share	0 .05	(0 .00)	0 .03	0 .24	0 .04
Book Value per Share	0 .72	0 .68	0 .69	0 .70	0 .66
O/S Common Shares	117 ,528	117 ,225	99 ,298	99 ,226	98 ,642
Total Revenue	50 ,923	31 ,227	35 ,625	44 ,562	45 ,557
Income before extra.	5 ,307	(3 ,493)	(910)	3 ,324	(26 ,965)
Cash Flow	5 ,970	(244)	3 ,005	23 ,891	3 ,509
Debt/Equity	0 .18	nd	0 .02	0 .10	0 .46
Return on Capital (%)	7 .06	(5 .36)	(0 .79)	5 .63	(23 .08)
Ret. on Com. Equity (%)	6 .47	(4 .74)	(1 .33)	4 .95	(36 .43)
% Change Profit	251 .9	(283 .8)	(127 .4)	112 .3	(998 .5)
% Change Revenue	63 .1	(12 .3)	(20 .1)	(2 .2)	(0 .5)
% Change Assets	20 .8	4 .3	(9 .6)	(11 .4)	(12 .0)

Business:
CAMPBELL RESOURCES INC. is a Canadian mining and natural resources company whose principal asset is the Joe Mann Mine, a gold producing mine near Chibougamau, Quebec. In addition the company holds an extensive exploration property inventory in northwest Mexico. During July 1994, the company acquired the Santa Gertridis Mine in Sonora, Mexico.

Date	EPS	DPS	Tot Rev	Inc Bex
Mar 95	0 .02	0 .00	16 ,493	2 ,010
Dec 94	0 .03	0 .00	17 ,403	3 ,542
Sep 94	0 .01	0 .00	12 ,347	747
Jun 94	0 .01	0 .00	10 ,565	866
Mar 94	(0 .00)	0 .00	10 ,150	152
Dec 93	(0 .01)	0 .00	8 ,522	(1 ,778)
Sep 93	(0 .01)	0 .00	6 ,820	(811)
Jun 93	(0 .01)	0 .00	7 ,788	(649)

	Dec94	Dec93	Dec92
Preferred Div. Coverage	np	np	np
Total Div. Coverage	na	na	na
Interest Coverage	10 .8	0 .0	0 .0
Current Ratio	5 .3	4 .1	1 .4
Operating Margin	6 .0	(9 .1)	(3 .5)
Asset Turnover	0 .4	0 .3	0 .4
5 YEAR RATIOS (%)			
Return on Capital	(3 .3)	(3 .4)	(13 .4)
Return on Com. Equity	(6 .2)	(6 .7)	(19 .9)
Profit Growth	12 .1	na	na
Revenue Growth	2 .2	(5 .6)	(5 .4)
Asset Growth	(2 .3)	(1 .8)	(10 .9)
BALANCE SHEET (000)			
Cash	24 ,242	17 ,795	4 ,593
Current Assets	36 ,841	22 ,687	10 ,508
Net Fixed Assets	70 ,223	66 ,536	70 ,648
Invest'& Advances	1 ,233	1 ,423	5 ,795
Total Assets	109 ,533	90 ,646	86 ,951
Short Term Debt	0	0	1 ,506
Current Liabilities	6 ,888	5 ,598	7 ,486
Long Term Debt	15 ,438	0	0
Total Liabilities	24 ,733	11 ,368	18 ,786
Total Equity	84 ,800	79 ,278	68 ,165
Total Liab. & Equity	109 ,533	90 ,646	86 ,951
CAPITAL (000)			
Total Debt	15 ,438	0	1 ,506
Preferred Equity	0	0	0
Common Equity	84 ,800	79 ,278	68 ,165

Synopsis:

Campbell Resources reported income for the first quarter of 1995 that was significantly higher than the corresponding period last year. Campbell attributed the higher profits to increased gold production and lower unit operation costs at the company's operating mines.

First quarter gold production climbed 62% to 28,000 ounces, versus the same period of 1994. Cash operating costs fell to $264 (U.S.) compared with $316 (U.S.) for the quarter ended March 31, 1994.

In February 1995, Campbell opted to acquire the Wildcat gold project in Nevada. Lac Minerals previously owned the property. Reverse-circulation drilling has revealed reserves totaling 72 million tons averaging 0.016 ounces of gold per ton. Campbell Resources believes there is potential to discover a smaller and higher grade deposit within the larger existing one.

Campbell operates producing mines in both Quebec and Mexico. The company also has exploration interests in Mexico and Nevada. As of December 31, 1994, Campbell's Mexican operations accounted for 16% of the company's total assets, and over 22% of the company's revenues.

On July 20, 1994, Campbell Resources acquired all the assets of the three companies that owned the Santa Gertrudis open pit leach gold mine in Sonora, Mexico. The companies were: Compania Minera Sante Gertrudis, S.A. de C.V.; Minera Tubac, S.A. de C.V.; and Minera Palo Verde, S.A. de C.V. Campbell paid $13.1-million in cash for the outstanding shares.

Rank (Profit/Revenue/Assets)
414   545   466

James C. McCartney
Chairman
John O. Kachmar
President & C.E.O.
Paul J. Ireland
V.P. Finance

Address
Suite 1910
120 Adelaide Street West
Toronto
ON
M5H 1T1
(416) 366-5201

Fax: (416) 367-3294
C0001051/G/2.0

CORNUCOPIA RESOURCES LTD.

Exchanges	Price (Jun29'95)		1.30	Trailing P/E		nm	Stock Symbol
TQ	Trailing Yield (%)		0.00	Trailing EPS		(0.09)	CNP

Period Ending	Dec94	Dec93	Dec92	Dec91	Dec90	Business:
Yearly Statistics	US	US	US	US	US	CORNUCOPIA RESOURCES LTD. is a
Price-Close	1.55	2.55	1.60	0.33	0.70	precious metals exploration company. Current
Price-High	3.05	4.00	1.60	0.82	2.40	operations centre on the Ivanhoe property
Price-Low	1.50	1.11	0.30	0.20	0.54	located on the Carlin Gold Trend in
P/E-Close	nm	nm	3.50	nm	nm	north-central Nevada and the Silver Peak
Dividends per Share	0.00	0.00	0.00	0.00	0.00	property in Nevada.
Dividend Yield (%)	0.00	0.00	0.00	0.00	0.00	
Sales per Share	0.01	0.04	0.06	na	na	
EPS before extra. item	(0.09)	(0.04)	0.31	(0.09)	(0.22)	
Cash Flow per Share	(0.07)	(0.40)	(0.04)	(0.04)	(0.05)	
Book Value per Share	0.55	0.41	0.44	0.14	0.23	
O/S Common Shares	21,535	21,275	20,230	19,371	19,371	
Total Revenue	266	1,322	8,237	212	94	
Income before extra.	(1,925)	(864)	6,004	(1,777)	(4,297)	
Cash Flow	(1,507)	(8,243)	(760)	(796)	(904)	

Date		EPS	DPS	Tot Rev	Inc Bex
Mar 95	US	(0.01)	0.00	298	(245)
Dec 94	US	(0.03)	0.00	40	(570)
Sep 94	US	(0.02)	0.00	7	(502)
Jun 94	US	(0.03)	0.00	150	(583)
Mar 94	US	(0.01)	0.00	69	(270)
Dec 93	US	0.01	0.00	241	64
Sep 93	US	(0.02)	0.00	403	(500)
Jun 93	US	(0.02)	0.00	121	(463)

	Dec94	Dec93	Dec92	Dec91	Dec90
Debt/Equity	0.02	0.01	nd	nd	nd
Return on Capital (%)	(18.48)	(14.77)	112.72	(49.99)	(65.18)
Ret. on Com. Equity (%)	(18.75)	(9.77)	103.60	(49.99)	(65.18)
% Change Profit	(122.7)	(114.4)	437.8	58.6	(6.3)
% Change Revenue	(79.8)	(83.9)	3,791.7	124.7	(69.2)
% Change Assets	42.0	(1.8)	247.4	(42.3)	(45.7)

Preferred Div. Coverage	np	np	np
Total Div. Coverage	na	na	na
Interest Coverage	na	na	nd
Current Ratio	10.9	35.9	16.1
Operating Margin	(728.2)	(186.4)	(35.4)
Asset Turnover	0.0	0.1	0.1
5 YEAR RATIOS (%)			
Return on Capital	(7.1)	(12.0)	(10.5)
Return on Com. Equity	(8.0)	(12.9)	(12.3)
Profit Growth	na	na	na
Revenue Growth	(2.9)	41.8	na
Asset Growth	8.7	(1.6)	(3.7)
BALANCE SHEET (000)			
Cash	4,156	5,368	7,405
Current Assets	6,989	6,036	8,311
Net Fixed Assets	5,764	2,764	1,278
Invest's & Advances	141	143	0
Total Assets	13,369	9,418	9,589
Short Term Debt	258	44	0
Current Liabilities	639	168	516
Long Term Debt	0	0	0
Total Liabilities	1,613	643	666
Total Equity	11,756	8,775	8,923
Total Liab. & Equity	13,369	9,418	9,589
CAPITAL (000)			
Total Debt	258	44	0
Preferred Equity	0	0	0
Common Equity	11,756	8,775	8,923

Synopsis:

In May 1995, Cornucopia Resources bought an additional 65 mining claims in the Philippines from Benguet Corp. The deal relates to nine patented and 55 unpatented claims on property continuous to the Mary/Drinkwater claims at Mineral Ridge. Previous exploration work on the property indicated resources of about 87,000 ounces of gold. Cornucopia intends to start an extensive exploration program on the property to increase reserves there. Combined with the reserves at the Mary/Drinkwater property, the total resources at the Mineral Ridge project now exceed 550,000 contained ounces of gold.

In 1995 and 1994, Cornucopia's main strategy has been to develop the mineable reserves at Mineral Ridge and put the operation into production. Cornucopia expects the capital costs associated with Mineral Ridge to be about $15-million. Once operational, Mineral Ridge will produce an ounce of gold with a direct operating cost of about $250 per ounce.

In February 1995, shareholders of Cornucopia announced they had authorized the issue of common shares on the exercise of share purchase warrants. The warrants relate to the $5-million (U.S.) private placement of four million Special Warrants completed in December 1994. Under that arrangement, the holder of a Special Warrant had the right to receive one common share of Cornucopia and one two-year Share Purchase Warrant.

Fundamentally, Cornucopia is a gold exploration and development company. The company has exploration and development activities in the United States, Ghana, and West Africa. Its strategy is to take known gold-bearing deposits to a stage were the company can develop the resources themselves or joint venture the project with other, larger companies.

Relative strength to TSE300 / Price / Volume (in 1000's of board lots)

Rank (Profit/Revenue/Assets)
869   965   884

Andrew F.B. Milligan
President & C.E.O.

Debbie Barfurth-Wood
Treasurer

Address
Suite 540
Marine Building
355 Burrard Street
Vancouver
BC
V6C 2G8
(604) 687-0619
Fax: (604) 681-4170
C0057738/G/2.0

DAKOTA MINING CORPORATION

Exchanges	Price (Jun29'95)	2.35	Trailing P/E	nm	Stock Symbol
TA	Trailing Yield (%)	0.00	Trailing EPS	(0.33)	**DKT**

Period Ending	Dec94	Dec93	Dec92	Dec91	Dec90
Yearly Statistics	US	US /107D	US	US	US
Price-Close	1.90	2.45	3.98	3.98	9.33
Price-High	4.35	3.75	9.33	13.18	49.74
Price-Low	1.50	1.80	3.11	3.73	6.59
P/E-Close	nm	nm	nm	nm	nm
Dividends per Share	0.00	0.00	0.00	0.00	0.00
Dividend Yield (%)	0.00	0.00	0.00	0.00	0.00
Sales per Share	0.48	0.22	9.90	11.51	16.36
EPS before extra. item	(0.33)	(0.10)	(2.74)	(12.19)	(1.37)
Cash Flow per Share	(0.19)	(0.18)	0.00	(0.30)	0.81
Book Value per Share	1.19	1.42	4.49	7.49	21.82
O/S Common Shares	21,360	13,973	3,819	2,998	2,324
Total Revenue	9,064	2,936	33,229	31,810	38,403
Income before extra.	(5,739)	(1,336)	(8,991)	(33,507)	(3,265)
Cash Flow	(3,331)	(2,286)	26	(819)	1,893
Debt/Equity	0.15	0.37	1.27	1.10	0.41
Return on Capital (%)	(17.84)	(2.55)	(14.99)	(55.31)	(3.86)
Ret. on Com. Equity (%)	(25.32)	(7.88)	(45.41)	(91.58)	(6.75)
% Change Profit	(293.9)	83.8	73.2	(926.2)	73.2
% Change Revenue	183.0	(90.4)	4.5	(17.2)	4.4
% Change Assets	(2.0)	(28.2)	(14.8)	(27.9)	17.4

Preferred Div. Coverage	np	np	np
Total Div. Coverage	na	na	na
Interest Coverage	0.0	0.0	0.0
Current Ratio	1.1	0.7	0.2
Operating Margin	(67.1)	(34.2)	(24.7)
Asset Turnover	0.2	0.1	0.7
5 YEAR RATIOS (%)			
Return on Capital	(18.9)	(19.7)	(19.1)
Return on Com. Equity	(35.4)	(35.0)	(33.4)
Profit Growth	na	na	na
Revenue Growth	(24.4)	(36.8)	(0.2)
Asset Growth	(12.7)	(17.3)	(1.5)
BALANCE SHEET (000)			
Cash	3,097	4,083	1,203
Current Assets	6,509	7,408	4,792
Net Fixed Assets	23,527	23,362	39,990
Invest's & Advances	0	0	0
Total Assets	34,344	35,036	48,804
Short Term Debt	2,982	4,878	20,494
Current Liabilities	6,111	11,120	27,938
Long Term Debt	898	2,416	1,333
Total Liabilities	8,859	15,185	31,661
Total Equity	25,485	19,852	17,143
Total Liab. & Equity	34,344	35,036	48,804
CAPITAL (000)			
Total Debt	3,880	7,294	21,827
Preferred Equity	0	0	0
Common Equity	25,485	19,852	17,143

Business:

DAKOTA MINING was formed in 1988 through the amalgamation of Brohm Resources Inc. and MFC Mining Finance Corp. The company has interests in gold mines located in Idaho, South Dakota and Colorado.

Date		EPS	DPS	Tot Rev	Inc Bex
Mar 95	US	(0.06)	0.00	2,034	1,224
Dec 94	US	(0.01)	0.00	2,576	(618)
Sep 94	US	(0.02)	0.00	2,550	(352)
Jun 94	US	(0.24)	0.00	2,424	(3,403)
Mar 94	US	(0.10)	0.00	1,569	(1,365)
Dec 93	US	(0.09)	0.00	2,491	(1,174)
Sep 93	US	(0.01)	0.00	445	(162)
Jun 93	US	(0.25)	0.00	2,745	(1,086)

Synopsis:

Dakota Mining Crop. announced that gold production was 4,488 ounces during the first quarter of 1995. Most of this gold was directly attributed to the company's 40% interest in the Golden Reward mine in South Dakota. Total production there was 10,245 ounces of gold in the first quarter of 1995. The remaining gold stems from Dakota's Gilt Edge mine in South Dakota and the Stibnite mine in Idaho.

During the first quarter of 1995, Dakota continued permitting and development of the Anchor Hill project at The Gilt Edge mine and completing permitting at the company's Stibnite mine. Both mines should begin gold production soon. As of the end of the first quarter of 1995, Dakota had submitted applications for the State of South Dakota mine permits necessary to start work. The company also expects to release an Environmental Impact Statement later in the second quarter that will be available for public comment.

On April 20, 1995, Dakota's common shares were listed on the Berlin Stock Exchange. The company will trade under the symbol DMC. The new listing should enhance the liquidity of Dakota Mining's common shares. Also, exposure in Berlin could help Dakota gain more international attention. This, in turn, could help Dakota expand its operations throughout the world.

In May 1995, Dakota appointed Martin Quick to the position of President and General Manager of the company.

Relative strength to TSE300

Price

Volume (in 1000's of board lots)

Rank (Profit/Revenue/Assets)
933   777   643
Paul A. Bailly
Chairman
Martin Quick
President and General Manager
Robert R. Gilmore
V.P. Fin., C.F.O. & Secretary

Address
Suite 2450
410 - 17th Street
Denver
CO
80202
(303) 573-0221

Fax: (303) 573-1012
C0059152/G/2.0

ECHO BAY MINES LTD.

Exchanges	Price (Jun29'95)		12.75	Trailing P/E		nm	Stock Symbol
TMA	Trailing Yield (%)		0.85	Trailing EPS		(0.13)	**ECO**

Period Ending	Dec94	Dec93	Dec92	Dec91	Dec90	Business:
Yearly Statistics	US	US	US	US	US	ECHO BAY MINES LTD. is a gold mining
Price-Close	15.13	17.13	6.25	8.63	10.38	company. It has 4 producing mines in the
Price-High	20.13	18.63	9.75	11.63	24.88	United States and Canada. The company has
Price-Low	13.38	5.13	5.38	7.63	8.25	mines in Ontario, the Northwest Territories,
P/E-Close	116.23	348.36	nm	94.10	nm	Washington and Nevada. It has other properties
Dividends per Share	0.08	0.08	0.08	0.08	0.08	in North America under development and is
Dividend Yield (%)	0.68	0.57	1.46	1.00	0.84	aggressively pursuing new growth opportunities
Sales per Share	3.36	3.39	2.97	3.12	3.42	outside North America.
EPS before extra. item	0.07	0.03	(0.30)	0.07	(0.60)	
Cash Flow per Share	0.96	0.99	0.73	0.87	0.91	
Book Value per Share	4.52	4.58	4.19	4.68	4.47	
O/S Common Shares	112,682	112,213	105,169	105,146	99,117	
Total Revenue	387,800	373,800	313,179	328,391	339,783	

Income before extra.	8,000	3,600	(31,721)	6,793	(59,670)	Date		EPS	DPS	Tot Rev	Inc Bex
Cash Flow	108,100	107,500	76,500	87,799	90,512	Mar 95	US	(0.10)	0.00	85,800	(11,700)
Debt/Equity	0.26	0.42	0.50	0.48	0.02	Dec 94	US	(0.05)	0.04	91,100	(5,200)
Return on Capital (%)	2.37	2.14	(3.76)	3.03	(11.49)	Sep 94	US	0.00	0.00	90,200	0
Ret. on Com. Equity (%)	1.56	0.76	(6.81)	1.45	(12.53)	Jun 94	US	0.02	0.04	96,858	3,893
% Change Profit	122.2	111.3	(567.0)	111.4	(472.5)	Mar 94	US	0.10	0.00	103,600	11,500
% Change Revenue	3.7	19.4	(4.6)	(3.4)	13.5	Dec 93	US	0.02	0.04	97,200	2,600
% Change Assets	(11.0)	5.8	7.0	(3.7)	(8.4)	Sep 93	US	0.00	0.00	92,000	100
						Jun 93	US	0.03	0.04	94,006	4,786

Preferred Div. Coverage	np	np	np	Synopsis:
Total Div. Coverage	0.9	0.4	0.0	
Interest Coverage	2.7	2.2	0.0	
Current Ratio	4.2	2.0	1.4	
Operating Margin	5.1	4.6	(0.3)	
Asset Turnover	0.4	0.4	0.3	

In early June 1995, Echo Bay and joint venture partner, TVI Pacific Inc., agreed with Benguet Corp. to buy the Kingking porphyry copper-gold project in the Philippines. Once the deal is complete, Echo Bay will own 75% of the Kingking project, and TVI Pacific will own 25%. Echo Bay, which will operate the project, and TVI Pacific will pay $2-million to Benguet and pay an additional $18-million (U.S.) when a definitive agreement has been completed. The final arrangement is expected by the end of August 1995. As well, the joint venture must spend at least $8-million (U.S.) on exploration activities relating to Kingking. Once a feasibility study is complete, the joint venture must pay $67-million (U.S.) for a 100% interest in Kingking. Benguet has retained an option, once the feasibility study is complete, to acquire a 20% in Kingking for the sum of $20-million (U.S.). This would leave Echo Bay with a 65% interest in Kingking and TVI Pacific with 15% of the project.

5 YEAR RATIOS (%)			
Return on Capital	(1.5)	(0.8)	1.9
Return on Com. Equity	(3.1)	(2.8)	(0.4)
Profit Growth	(13.0)	(41.9)	na
Revenue Growth	5.3	5.4	7.7
Asset Growth	(2.4)	2.7	10.0

Results from a pre-feasibility report prepared by Benguet in March 1994 revealed that Kingking has a substantial reserve base. The property has geologic resources of about 350 million short tons of minable ore. Within the ore there are approximately 5.3 million contained troy ounces of gold and 3.1 billion pounds of copper. The grade of the ore is 0.015 troy ounces of gold per ton and 0.44% copper per ton.

BALANCE SHEET (000)			
Cash	201,500	252,400	60,293
Current Assets	243,700	296,500	105,095
Net Fixed Assets	608,500	673,000	748,932
Invest's & Advances	29,400	21,000	74,699
Total Assets	881,600	990,500	936,585
Short Term Debt	10,800	86,200	9,388
Current Liabilities	57,500	147,600	73,986
Long Term Debt	121,900	131,200	210,696
Total Liabilities	372,000	476,800	496,292
Total Equity	509,600	513,700	440,293
Total Liab. & Equity	881,600	990,500	936,585

In May 1995, Echo Bay sold its 50% interest in the Kensington gold project to joint-venture partner, Coeur d'Alene. Echo-Bay will pay $32.5-million (U.S.) for the Kensington gold project in Alaska. Echo-Bay will also retain a scaled royalty on one million ounces of future gold production. The royalty ranges from 1% at a gold price of $400 (U.S.) per ounce to a maximum of 2.5% at prices above $475 (U.S.) per ounce. Kensington is estimated to hold upwards of 13.6 million tons of proven and probable ore reserves. The grade of the ore is about 0.143 ounces of gold per ton for a total of two million contained ounces of gold.

CAPITAL (000)			
Total Debt	132,700	217,400	220,084
Preferred Equity	0	0	0
Common Equity	509,600	513,700	440,293

Relative strength to TSE300 / Price / Volume (in 1000's of board lots)

Rank (Profit/Revenue/Assets)
283 191 139
Robert F. Calman
Chairman
Richard C. Kraus
President & C.E.O.
Peter Cheesbrough
Sr. V.P. Finance & C.F.O.
Robert C. Armstrong
Exec. V.P. & C.O.O.

Address
Suite 4050
370 - 17th Street
Denver
CO
80202
(303) 592-8000

Fax: (303) 592-8090
E0000405/G/2.0

EQUITY SILVER MINES LIMITED

Exchanges	Price (Jun29'95)		0 .83	Trailing P/E		5 .19	Stock Symbol
TV	Trailing Yield (%)		0 .00	Trailing EPS		0 .16	**EST.A**

Period Ending	Dec94	Dec93	Dec92	Dec91	Dec90
Yearly Statistics					
Price-Close	0 .55	1 .15	0 .75	1 .06	0 .84
Price-High	1 .20	1 .45	1 .13	1 .60	4 .40
Price-Low	0 .50	0 .70	0 .65	0 .63	0 .65
P/E-Close	3 .93	9 .58	nm	9 .64	2 .80
Dividends per Share	0 .00	0 .20	0 .20	0 .20	0 .20
Dividend Yield (%)	0 .00	17 .39	26 .67	18 .87	23 .81
Sales per Share	0 .27	0 .57	1 .05	1 .47	2 .63
EPS before extra. item	0 .14	0 .12	(0 .12)	0 .11	0 .30
Cash Flow per Share	0 .13	0 .07	0 .19	0 .39	0 .94
Book Value per Share	1 .46	1 .32	1 .41	1 .73	1 .81
O/S Common Shares	32 ,523	32 ,523	32 ,523	32 ,523	32 ,523
Total Revenue	12 ,836	23 ,344	39 ,509	54 ,069	91 ,573
Income before extra.	4 ,535	3 ,762	(3 ,881)	3 ,625	10 ,058
Cash Flow	4 ,239	2 ,243	6 ,089	12 ,543	30 ,596
Debt/Equity	nd	nd	nd	0 .00	0 .03
Return on Capital (%)	(0 .45)	4 .36	(11 .50)	6 .95	32 .00
Ret. on Com. Equity (%)	10 .02	8 .48	(7 .62)	6 .30	17 .10
% Change Profit	20 .5	196 .9	(207 .1)	(64 .0)	(54 .5)
% Change Revenue	(45 .0)	(40 .9)	(26 .9)	(41 .0)	(1 .9)
% Change Assets	8 .3	(7 .1)	(9 .0)	(8 .0)	(4 .7)
Preferred Div. Coverage	np	np	np		
Total Div. Coverage	na	0 .6	0 .0		
Interest Coverage	nd	nd	nd		
Current Ratio	2 .4	7 .8	7 .4		
Operating Margin	(49 .4)	(15 .7)	(33 .1)		
Asset Turnover	0 .1	0 .2	0 .4		
5 YEAR RATIOS (%)					
Return on Capital	6 .3	15 .7	20 .8		
Return on Com. Equity	6 .9	13 .2	16 .4		
Profit Growth	(27 .2)	(20 .9)	na		
Revenue Growth	(32 .8)	(22 .9)	(12 .0)		
Asset Growth	(4 .3)	(0 .6)	0 .3		
BALANCE SHEET (000)					
Cash	1 ,118	15 ,823	15 ,793		
Current Assets	10 ,241	32 ,432	36 ,650		
Net Fixed Assets	192	738	1 ,012		
Invest's & Advances	0	0	0		
Total Assets	81 ,380	75 ,133	80 ,911		
Short Term Debt	0	0	0		
Current Liabilities	4 ,330	4 ,156	4 ,939		
Long Term Debt	0	0	0		
Total Liabilities	33 ,848	32 ,136	35 ,171		
Total Equity	47 ,532	42 ,997	45 ,740		
Total Liab. & Equity	81 ,380	75 ,133	80 ,911		
CAPITAL (000)					
Total Debt	0	0	0		
Preferred Equity	0	0	0		
Common Equity	47 ,532	42 ,997	45 ,740		

Business:

EQUITY SILVER MINES LTD. is a natural resources company. Until January 1994, it operated a silver-gold-copper mine in British Columbia. The company is currently conducting a review of its strategic options. Placer Dome Canada Limited of Vancouver owns 58.8% cent of the company's common shares.

Date	EPS	DPS	Tot Rev	Inc Bex
Mar 95	0 .01	0 .00	1 ,458	253
Dec 94	0 .10	0 .00	541	3 ,085
Sep 94	0 .02	0 .00	1 ,230	719
Jun 94	0 .03	0 .00	9 ,520	1 ,049
Mar 94	(0 .01)	0 .00	1 ,545	(318)
Dec 93	0 .04	0 .05	8 ,771	1 ,084
Sep 93	0 .03	0 .05	4 ,706	902
Jun 93	0 .05	0 .05	4 ,446	1 ,599

Synopsis:

In late May 1995, Placer Dome Canada sweetened its offer to purchase the remaining interest in Equity Silver that it does not already own. Placer Dome has offered $0.85 cents per Equity Silver share, up from the original offer of $0.70 cents per share in April 1994. The offer applies to the minority 41.2% interest in Equity Silver. The bid from Placer Dome Canada represents a premium of about 77% above the late May 1995 trading price of Equity Silver.

Equity Silver does not have any ongoing mine operations. It is basically a shell company with 32.5 million common shares outstanding and $29-million in working capital. The company obtains revenue solely through investments. Equity Silver's gold production ceased in the first quarter of 1994, when the company's only mine closed.

Relative strength to TSE300

Price

Volume (in 1000's of board lots)

Rank (Profit/Revenue/Assets)
439 774 530

C. Henry Brehaut
Chairman

D.J. Fraser
President & C.E.O.

Address
P.O. Box 49305
Bentall Postal Station
Vancouver
BC
V7X 1L3
(604) 661-1991

Fax: (604) 661-3786
E0004172/G/2.0

Merged with Franco

EURO-NEVADA MINING CORPORATION LIMITED

Exchanges	Price (Jun29'95)	42.50	Trailing P/E	70.83	Stock Symbol
T	Trailing Yield (%)	0.00	Trailing EPS	0.60	**EN**

Period Ending	Mar95	Mar94	Mar93	Mar92	Mar91
Yearly Statistics					
Price-Close	37.00	43.00	22.63	15.50	12.00
Price-High	44.00	50.25	23.00	19.00	17.38
Price-Low	25.25	19.25	13.75	11.13	8.00
P/E-Close	61.67	86.00	75.42	59.62	70.59
Dividends per Share	0.09	0.07	0.05	0.06	0.02
Dividend Yield (%)	0.24	0.16	0.22	0.39	0.17
Sales per Share	na	na	na	na	na
EPS before extra. item	0.60	0.50	0.30	0.26	0.17
Cash Flow per Share	0.76	0.82	0.59	0.34	0.27
Book Value per Share	11.27	10.35	5.21	5.39	3.20
O/S Common Shares	20,339	19,586	15,569	14,056	13,854
Total Revenue	21,507	23,059	11,325	8,363	4,795
Income before extra.	11,719	9,103	4,609	3,613	2,205
Cash Flow	15,422	14,450	9,141	4,685	3,634
Debt/Equity	nd	nd	nd	0.13	0.22
Return on Capital (%)	8.34	10.77	8.83	7.90	7.43
Ret. on Com. Equity (%)	5.43	6.41	5.87	6.02	5.92
% Change Profit	28.7	97.5	27.6	63.9	128.3
% Change Revenue	(6.7)	103.6	35.4	74.4	39.8
% Change Assets	13.7	147.6	(2.6)	58.7	79.6
Preferred Div. Coverage	np	np	np		
Total Div. Coverage	6.4	6.6	5.9		
Interest Coverage	nd	nd	nd		
Current Ratio	35.9	35.5	37.4		
Operating Margin	64.3	31.1	47.1		
Asset Turnover	na	na	na		
5 YEAR RATIOS (%)					
Return on Capital	8.7	8.4	6.1		
Return on Com. Equity	5.9	5.7	3.1		
Profit Growth	64.7	99.3			
Revenue Growth	44.3	89.9	123.7		
Asset Growth	50.8	55.5	57.9		
BALANCE SHEET (000)					
Cash	171,972	164,358	46,770		
Current Assets	177,973	168,260	48,453		
Net Fixed Assets	62,003	42,824	36,790		
Invest's & Advances	0	0	0		
Total Assets	239,976	211,084	85,243		
Short Term Debt	0	0	0		
Current Liabilities	4,951	4,741	1,294		
Long Term Debt	0	0	0		
Total Liabilities	10,847	8,318	4,141		
Total Equity	229,129	202,766	81,102		
Total Liab. & Equity	239,976	211,084	85,243		
CAPITAL (000)					
Total Debt	0	0	0		
Preferred Equity	0	0	0		
Common Equity	229,129	202,766	81,102		

Business:

EURO-NEVADA MINING CORPORATION LIMITED's main objective is to seek out royalties on precious metal deposits world-wide. It holds royalties on 35 properties including a 4% NSR (Net Smelter Royalty) and a 5% NPI (Net Profit Interest) on the Meikle Mine in the Carlin Gold Belt of Nevada. The Company also holds royalties in Cuba, Venezuela, Yemen, and Australia.

Date	EPS	DPS	Tot Rev	Inc Bex
Mar 95	0.09	0.00	4,111	1,821
Dec 94	0.21	0.00	6,890	4,119
Sep 94	0.17	0.00	5,691	3,322
Jun 94	0.13	0.00	5,208	2,457
Mar 94	0.17	0.07	9,585	3,266
Dec 93	0.09	0.00	4,322	1,767
Sep 93	0.14	0.00	5,685	2,400
Jun 93	0.10	0.00	3,893	1,670

Synopsis:

Euro-Nevada Mining said in its fiscal 1995 annual report that it expects six new royalty properties to become operational over the next three years. One of the new properties is Eskay Creek in British Columbia. Gold production there began in January 1995. The first ore shipment went to smelters in Japan and Quebec. Proven reserves at Eskay Creek are estimated at 2.3 million ounces of gold, and more than 102 million ounces of silver.

Euro-Nevada expects to benefit from other properties, too, in the next three years. The Meekly Mine in the Carlin Trend is set to become the company's main asset for the next 20 years. Euro-Nevada has a 4% Net Smelter Return royalty on Barrick Gold's Meekly Mine. Reserves at Meekly total about 6.6 million contained ounces of gold. Production at Meekly is forecast at over 400,000 ounces of gold per year. Euro-Nevada expects royalties to be generated from other properties including the Rosebud property in Nevada, the Briggs property in California, and the Henty and Browns Creek properties in Australia.

Euro-Nevada will focus its acquisition strategy on Australia during 1995. Australia is the world's third largest gold producer. In an effort to capitalize on growth opportunities, Euro-Nevada will open an office in Sydney, Australia.

In February 1995, Euro-Nevada reached an agreement with the officers of Rendition Goldfields Consolidated to acquire Little River Goldfields. Rendition, which holds a 19.4% interest in Little River, will receive $0.48 per share for the 6.9 million outstanding common shares of Little River. Euro-Nevada will own over 85% of the Little River project once the transaction is completed.

Rank (Profit/Revenue/Assets)		
314	696	346

Seymour Schulich
Chairman Of The Board

Pierre Lassonde
President & C.E.O.

Ron W. Binns
V.P. Finance & C.F.O.

Address
20 Eglinton Avenue West
Suite 1900
P.O. Box 2005
Toronto
ON
M4R 1K8
(416) 480-6480
Fax: (416) 488-6598
01001620/G/2.0

For further company information, call Globe Information Services 1-800-268-9128 or (416) 585-5345

Handwritten at top: +$290 +15% 480m 2/4/0 clx 2175 R-22 5-18 → New Low 3days ago Chart Not fin

FRANCO-NEVADA MINING CORPORATION LIMITED

Exchanges	Price (Jun29'95)		72 .50	Trailing P/E		23 .39	Stock Symbol
T	Trailing Yield (%)		2.07	Trailing EPS		3.10	FN

Period Ending	Mar95	Mar94	Mar93	Mar92	Mar91
Yearly Statistics					
Price-Close	69 .50	80 .63	39 .88	24 .63	17 .25
Price-High	94 .75	95 .00	40 .00	28 .50	22 .75
Price-Low	67 .00	40 .25	23 .00	15 .38	12 .00
P/E-Close	22 .42	39 .33	31 .90	41 .04	43 .13
Dividends per Share	1 .50	0 .90	0 .60	0 .30	0 .20
Dividend Yield (%)	2 .16	1 .12	1 .51	1 .22	1 .16
Sales per Share	4 .25	na	na	na	na
EPS before extra. item	3 .10	2 .05	1 .25	0 .60	0 .40
Cash Flow per Share	3 .29	2 .04	1 .24	0 .59	0 .39
Book Value per Share	14 .90	12 .76	7 .20	4 .30	1 .79
O/S Common Shares	16 ,573	16 ,144	15 ,022	12 ,737	12 ,677
Total Revenue	77 ,553	48 ,483	25 ,491	11 ,685	7 ,881
Income before extra.	50 ,238	31 ,893	17 ,233	7 ,562	5 ,065
Cash Flow	53 ,381	31 ,772	17 ,056	7 ,489	4 ,864
Debt/Equity	nd	nd	nd	0 .05	0 .26
Return on Capital (%)	32 .27	29 .10	28 .78	24 .22	24 .44
Ret. on Com. Equity (%)	22 .19	20 .30	21 .15	19 .50	23 .55
% Change Profit	57 .5	85 .1	127 .9	49 .3	43 .9
% Change Revenue	60 .0	90 .2	118 .2	48 .3	32 .8
% Change Assets	20 .6	91 .2	89 .8	101 .0	(2 .6)

Preferred Div. Coverage	np	np	np
Total Div. Coverage	2 .0	2 .2	2 .0
Interest Coverage	nd	nd	nd
Current Ratio	35 .7	45 .4	43 .2
Operating Margin	93 .9	92 .3	92 .2
Asset Turnover	0 .3	na	na
5 YEAR RATIOS (%)			
Return on Capital	27 .8	26 .8	27 .1
Return on Com. Equity	21 .3	21 .8	21 .5
Profit Growth	70 .1	83 .8	165 .8
Revenue Growth	67 .1	72 .1	90 .2
Asset Growth	53 .6	61 .9	68 .8

BALANCE SHEET (000)			
Cash	169 ,654	159 ,849	81 ,922
Current Assets	187 ,203	164 ,767	84 ,273
Net Fixed Assets	35 ,269	31 ,050	16 ,517
Invest's & Advances	33 ,568	16 ,563	10 ,268
Total Assets	256 ,040	212 ,380	111 ,058
Short Term Debt	0	0	0
Current Liabilities	5 ,238	3 ,629	1 ,953
Long Term Debt	0	0	0
Total Liabilities	9 ,187	6 ,353	2 ,931
Total Equity	246 ,853	206 ,027	108 ,127
Total Liab. & Equity	256 ,040	212 ,380	111 ,058
CAPITAL (000)			
Total Debt	0	0	0
Preferred Equity	0	0	0
Common Equity	246 ,853	206 ,027	108 ,127

Business:

FRANCO-NEVADA MINING CORP. LTD. is a gold exploration and mining company. The company has interests in the Carlin Gold Belt in Nevada, including the Goldstrike Mine operated by Barrick Gold Corp. It owns 620 acres of land adjacent to the Williams and Golden Giant Mines near Hemlo, Ontario. It owns 36% of Redstone Resources Inc. of Toronto and a wholly-owned oil and gas division.

Date	EPS	DPS	Tot Rev	Inc Bex
Mar 95	0.60	1.50	17,190	9,974
Dec 94	0.88	0.00	21,551	14,184
Sep 94	0.80	0.00	21,871	12,859
Jun 94	0.82	0.00	19,794	13,223
Mar 94	0.49	0.90	13,648	7,767
Dec 93	0.54	0.00	12,274	8,291
Sep 93	0.62	0.00	14,414	9,882
Jun 93	0.40	0.00	8,724	5,953

Synopsis:

For the year ended March 31, 1995, Franco-Nevada reported that earnings were up 51% over the corresponding period last year. The company attributed most of the increase to improved gold production at the Goldstrike Mine. Goldstrike is Franco-Nevada's main asset. The company holds a 2% to 4% Net Smelter Return royalty on the property.

For the year ended 1994, Goldstrike produced a record 1.85 million ounces of gold. This represents an increase of 28% over the same time last year. The mine's operating cost was $151 (U.S.) per ounces of gold in 1994, down from $158 (U.S.) in 1993. Goldstrike's operator, Barrick Gold, says the mine is on target to produce 1,875,000 million ounces of gold in 1995. At the 1995 rate of production, Barrick expects the Goldstrike mine will operate for another 12 years.

Goldstrike has the largest reserve base on one property in North America. Barrick estimates the property contains upwards of 23 million contained ounces of gold within its ore. In an effort to develop the property fully, Barrick plans to expense $90-million (U.S.) in 1995 on the area. This is up from the $83.3-million (U.S.) spent in 1994. The money will be spent on expanding the processing facilities, adding new truck to the fleet, as well as water management and reserve development.

In the fall of 1994, Franco-Nevada acquired a 5% Net Profits Interest royalty in the 17,193 acre Pandora property. The property is in South Africa and is operated by Rustenburg Platinum. Pandora is estimated to contain 31 million ounces of proven and probable platinum. As a result of the purchase, Franco-Nevada's total gold equivalent reserves increased by more than 30% in 1994 to almost 5.7 million ounces.

Relative strength to TSE300 / Price / Volume (in 1000's of board lots) chart, 1992–1995.

Rank (Profit/Revenue/Assets)
148   556   344

Seymour Schulich
Chairman & C.E.O.

Pierre Lassonde
President & C.O.O.

Ronald W. Binns
V.P. Finance & C.F.O.

Address
20 Eglinton Ave. West
Suite 1900
P.O. Box 2005
Toronto
ON
M4R 1K8
(416) 480-6480
Fax: (416) 488-6598
F0007001/G/2.0

GLAMIS GOLD LTD.

Exchanges	Price (Jun29'95)			11.25	Trailing P/E		48.91	Stock Symbol
TN	Trailing Yield (%)			0.53	Trailing EPS		0.23	**GLG**

Period Ending	Jun94	Jun93	Jun92	Jun91	Jun90
Yearly Statistics					
Price-Close	9.50	10.50	3.55	3.45	2.62
Price-High	11.50	12.13	4.75	3.70	3.40
Price-Low	6.88	3.50	3.05	2.20	1.00
P/E-Close	29.69	210.00	50.71	11.13	8.45
Dividends per Share	0.60	0.06	0.06	0.04	0.00
Dividend Yield (%)	6.32	0.57	1.69	1.16	0.00
Sales per Share	2.10	1.63	1.91	1.73	1.19
EPS before extra. item	0.32	0.05	0.07	0.31	0.31
Cash Flow per Share	0.82	0.45	0.67	0.73	0.46
Book Value per Share	3.35	2.89	1.81	1.81	1.54
O/S Common Shares	25,896	22,955	17,350	16,816	16,380
Total Revenue	56,065	33,705	33,187	30,077	20,942
Income before extra.	7,914	864	1,138	5,176	4,991
Cash Flow	20,597	9,026	11,500	12,295	7,551
Debt/Equity	nd	0.15	0.61	0.30	0.22
Return on Capital (%)	11.96	3.71	7.25	19.36	28.68
Ret. on Com. Equity (%)	10.34	1.77	3.68	18.57	21.98
% Change Profit	816.0	(24.1)	(78.0)	3.7	195.7
% Change Revenue	66.3	1.6	10.3	43.6	35.9
% Change Assets	12.5	48.0	29.7	23.4	3.0

Business:

GLAMIS GOLD LTD. is a gold mining company. It has three producing open pit, heap leach gold mines in California: the Picacho, Yellow Aster, and Baltic. The company has an exploration property, the Imperial County Claims, located eight miles northeast of the Picacho Mine. Glamis is earning a 60% interest in the Cieneguita Gold Project in the State of Chihuahua, Mexico.

Date		EPS	DPS	Tot Rev	Inc Bex
Dec 94	US	0.00	0.00	9,014	95
Sep 94		0.04	0.06	10,981	1,109
Jun 94		0.07	0.00	16,930	1,718
Mar 94		0.12	0.00	15,868	3,144
Dec 93	US	0.08	0.00	13,814	1,880
Sep 93		0.01	0.06	6,438	335
Jun 93		(0.08)	0.00	7,979	(1,410)
Mar 93		0.01	0.00	7,629	223

Preferred Div. Coverage	np	np	np	
Total Div. Coverage	5.4	0.8	1.1	
Interest Coverage	54.1	4.5	2.6	
Current Ratio	8.7	7.6	4.8	
Operating Margin	11.7	4.5	9.4	
Asset Turnover	0.6	0.4	0.6	
5 YEAR RATIOS (%)				
Return on Capital	14.2	5.9	6.4	
Return on Com. Equity	11.3	4.6	5.1	
Profit Growth	36.2	(3.6)	(9.1)	
Revenue Growth	29.4	18.7	16.6	
Asset Growth	22.3	22.1	13.8	
BALANCE SHEET (000)				
Cash	17,714	22,443	6,142	
Current Assets	31,693	29,843	15,592	
Net Fixed Assets	59,642	49,915	37,179	
Invest's & Advances	450	1,326	1,242	
Total Assets	92,050	81,802	55,285	
Short Term Debt	0	139	80	
Current Liabilities	3,642	3,906	3,243	
Long Term Debt	0	9,725	19,044	
Total Liabilities	5,397	15,440	23,952	
Total Equity	86,653	66,362	31,333	
Total Liab. & Equity	92,050	81,802	55,285	
CAPITAL (000)				
Total Debt	0	9,864	19,124	
Preferred Equity	0	0	0	
Common Equity	86,653	66,362	31,333	

Synopsis:

For the three months ended December 31, 1994, Glamis reported that gold production was down 16%, compared to the same period last year. Glamis attributed the drop to two factors. Firstly, ore processed during the company's second quarter was of lower grade than the previous year. This resulted in lower production figures for Glamis during the quarter. Also, the company's pre-stripping operation adversely affected production. These conditions were partially offset by the slight increase in the price Glamis realized on its gold sale. The average price received for an ounce of gold in the second quarter of 1994 was $388 (U.S.), compared to $377 (U.S.) per ounce in the second quarter of 1993. Glamis also reported that the company is still on target to meet planned production of 100,000 ounces of gold by the company's fiscal year end.

During the second quarter ended December 31, 1994, Glamis reported that the average cash cost per ounce of gold climbed to $221 (U.S.) from $170 (U.S.) in the corresponding period last year. Glamis attributes the higher costs to lower grades of ore at the company's Yellow Aster and Baltic mines and pre-stripping at the Picacho mine.

In December 1995, Glamis agreed to merge with junior miner Golden Queen Mining. The deal, subject to regulatory and shareholder approval, will see Glamis issue one share of Glamis common stock for every five shares of Golden Queen. As a result of the merger, Glamis is expected to issue some 2.9 million common shares.

In January 1995, Glamis completed an exploration and drilling program on the Imperial project in California. The company expect to complete a preliminary study by April 1995. Initial indications were positive.

Rank (Profit/Revenue/Assets)
340   525   502
Chester F. Millar
Chairman
A. Dan Rovig
President & C.E.O.
Lorne B. Anderson
C.F.O. & Treasurer

Address
3324 - Four Bentall Centre
1055 Dunsmuir Street
P.O. Box 49287
Vancouver
BC
V7X 1L3
(604) 681-3541
Fax: (604) 681-9306
G0009788/G/2.0

For further company information, call Globe Information Services 1-800-268-9128 or (416) 585-5345

GOLDCORP INC.

Exchanges	Price (Jun29'95)		16.25	Trailing P/E		16.75	Stock Symbol
TM	Trailing Yield (%)		0.62	Trailing EPS		0.97	**G.A**

Period Ending	Dec94	Dec93	Dec92	Dec91	Dec90	Business:
Yearly Statistics						**GOLDCORP INC.** is an intermediate size
Price-Close	7.88	9.13	2.62	3.10	4.15	North American gold producer. The company
Price-High	13.25	9.50	3.70	4.45	6.50	controls three producing gold mines: its
Price-Low	6.13	2.30	2.55	2.97	3.85	wholly-owned, underground Red Lake Mine,
P/E-Close	7.10	11.41	21.83	nm	nm	situated in northwestern Ontario; and two open
Dividends per Share	0.10	0.00	0.00	0.00	0.00	pit mines located in the Black Hills area in the
Dividend Yield (%)	1.27	0.00	0.00	0.00	0.00	state of South Dakota, the Wharf Mine and the
Sales per Share	4.03	5.25	4.51	5.40	3.42	Golden Reward Mine. Goldcorp controls the 2
EPS before extra. item	1.11	0.80	0.12	(0.46)	(3.45)	U.S. mines through its 50.3% owned subsidiary
Cash Flow per Share	1.53	1.52	1.00	1.06	0.32	Wharf Res. Ltd.
Book Value per Share	5.95	7.16	6.29	6.02	6.46	

	Dec94	Dec93	Dec92	Dec91	Dec90
O/S Common Shares	31,125	17,412	17,428	17,428	17,541
Total Revenue	186,012	133,617	109,187	96,989	66,265
Income before extra.	30,587	13,885	2,079	(8,039)	(60,485)
Cash Flow	42,322	26,486	17,428	18,587	5,681

Date	EPS	DPS	Tot Rev	Inc Bex
Mar 95	0.07	0.00	37,227	2,110
Dec 94	0.03	0.00	35,728	1,938
Sep 94	0.15	0.10	44,666	4,585
Jun 94	0.72	0.00	73,289	22,380
Mar 94	0.10	0.00	32,329	1,684
Dec 93	0.19	0.00	34,101	3,333
Sep 93	0.07	0.00	33,382	1,214
Jun 93	0.13	0.00	33,714	2,183

	Dec94	Dec93	Dec92	Dec91	Dec90
Debt/Equity	0.22	0.48	0.60	0.49	0.44
Return on Capital (%)	28.10	12.18	4.14	(1.86)	(41.18)
Ret. on Com. Equity (%)	19.73	11.85	1.94	(7.37)	(44.03)
% Change Profit	120.3	567.9	125.9	86.7	(285.1)
% Change Revenue	39.2	22.4	12.6	46.4	85.3
% Change Assets	16.3	6.8	10.7	16.0	(29.4)

Preferred Div. Coverage	np	np	np
Total Div. Coverage	9.8	na	na
Interest Coverage	22.1	6.5	2.1
Current Ratio	2.9	2.4	2.0
Operating Margin	14.5	11.0	5.6
Asset Turnover	0.4	0.3	0.3

5 YEAR RATIOS (%)			
Return on Capital	0.3	(6.2)	(8.5)
Return on Com. Equity	(3.6)	(9.5)	(11.8)
Profit Growth	na	78.5	14.2
Revenue Growth	39.0	117.4	94.6
Asset Growth	2.3	11.3	2.3

BALANCE SHEET (000)			
Cash	107,022	71,679	51,503
Current Assets	137,443	99,163	78,880
Net Fixed Assets	166,406	158,085	164,418
Invest's & Advances	0	0	3,733
Total Assets	311,507	267,738	250,802
Short Term Debt	15,109	20,231	21,897
Current Liabilities	46,871	40,620	39,164
Long Term Debt	26,479	39,848	43,405
Total Liabilities	126,198	142,991	141,130
Total Equity	185,309	124,747	109,672
Total Liab. & Equity	311,507	267,738	250,802

CAPITAL (000)			
Total Debt	41,588	60,079	65,302
Preferred Equity	0	0	0
Common Equity	185,309	124,747	109,672

Synopsis:

In April 1995, Goldcorp Inc. purchased common shares and warrants of Wheaton River Minerals worth $2.5-million. As of April 1995, Goldcorp held 2,340,280 common shares and 823,540 warrants of Wheaton. The warrants entitle Goldcorp to buy Wheaton common shares on the basis of one share for every warrant held. The warrants are exerciseable at $1.30 each and expire on November 16, 1995.

In April 1995, Goldcorp Inc said would make a Small Shareholder Odd Lot Selling Program available to shareholders. The program would enable shareholders who held 99 or fewer shares of Goldcorp to sell their shares with no commissions. The program is conditional on each individual selling all of their shares before April 29, 1995. Goldcorp would not make any recommendation as to whether small shareholders should make use of the program.

In late March 1995, Goldcorp made two promising gold discoveries in northwestern Ontario. During a preliminary drill program carried out at the Red Lake mine, Goldcorp revealed a deposit with mineralization that is said to be good. Gold concentrations there are about 0.25 ounces of gold at widths of up to 30 feet. The exploration program at Red Lake is estimated at $6-million for the 1995-1996 exploration year.

For the year ended December 31, 1994, Goldcorp's consolidated share of gold production was 202,316 ounces. This gold is produced from three operating mines: the Red Lake mine; the Wharf mine; and the Golden Reward Mine. During the period, the average cash operating cost per ounce of gold recovered at these mines was $244 (U.S.), relatively unchanged from last year. As of December 31, 1994, Goldcorp's share of proven, probable and possible reserves at the three mines was over 2.2 million contained ounces of gold. In total, Goldcorp will spent $20-million in 1995 on the three mines.

Relative strength to TSE300

Price

Volume (in 1000's of board lots)

Rank (Profit/Revenue/Assets)
156   325   281
Robert R. McEwen
President Chairman & C.E.O.
Rolando C. Francisco
Sr. V.P. & C.F.O.

Address
Suite 2700
145 King Street West
Toronto
ON
M5H 1J8
(416) 865-0326

Fax: (416) 361-5741
G0017192/G/2.0

GOLDEN KNIGHT RESOURCES INC.

Exchanges	Price (Jun29'95)	8.87	Trailing P/E	68.27	Stock Symbol
TMVQ	Trailing Yield (%)	1.13	Trailing EPS	0.13	**GKR**

Period Ending	Dec94	Dec93	Dec92	Dec91	Dec90
Yearly Statistics					
Price-Close	8.25	10.75	6.75	9.38	11.75
Price-High	11.50	14.38	9.50	13.63	15.63
Price-Low	7.38	6.25	6.13	8.50	10.50
P/E-Close	34.38	63.24	67.50	28.41	39.17
Dividends per Share	0.10	0.10	0.00	0.00	0.00
Dividend Yield (%)	1.21	0.93	0.00	0.00	0.00
Sales per Share	1.71	1.34	1.12	1.62	1.27
EPS before extra. item	0.24	0.17	0.10	0.33	0.30
Cash Flow per Share	0.74	0.58	0.42	0.83	0.60
Book Value per Share	5.08	4.95	5.66	5.56	5.23
O/S Common Shares	12,393	12,387	12,167	12,167	12,167
Total Revenue	22,410	17,644	14,550	20,761	16,316
Income before extra.	2,936	2,026	1,181	4,015	3,577
Cash Flow	9,171	7,159	5,099	10,155	7,255
Debt/Equity	nd	nd	nd	nd	nd
Return on Capital (%)	7.91	5.50	2.90	8.84	8.52
Ret. on Com. Equity (%)	4.73	3.12	1.73	6.12	5.87
% Change Profit	44.9	71.6	(70.6)	12.2	43.9
% Change Revenue	27.0	21.3	(29.9)	27.2	39.9
% Change Assets	8.5	(7.2)	3.9	8.3	7.1

Date	EPS	DPS	Tot Rev	Inc Bex
Mar 95	(0.04)	0.00	3,729	(493)
Dec 94	0.09	0.10	6,762	1,087
Sep 94	0.05	0.00	5,125	639
Jun 94	0.03	0.00	4,891	399
Mar 94	0.07	0.00	5,632	811
Dec 93	0.00	0.10	3,562	(34)
Sep 93	0.06	0.00	4,707	734
Jun 93	0.02	0.00	3,833	271

	Dec94	Dec93	Dec92
Preferred Div. Coverage	np	np	np
Total Div. Coverage	2.4	1.6	na
Interest Coverage	nd	nd	nd
Current Ratio	7.4	17.6	15.2
Operating Margin	17.2	14.6	7.8
Asset Turnover	0.3	0.2	0.2
5 YEAR RATIOS (%)			
Return on Capital	6.7	6.5	5.9
Return on Com. Equity	4.3	4.3	3.9
Profit Growth	3.4	22.6	(0.6)
Revenue Growth	13.9	60.5	42.2
Asset Growth	3.9	5.1	7.4
BALANCE SHEET (000)			
Cash	20,729	23,394	17,514
Current Assets	32,062	30,507	23,095
Net Fixed Assets	46,594	42,008	55,012
Invest's & Advances	0	0	0
Total Assets	78,656	72,515	78,107
Short Term Debt	0	0	0
Current Liabilities	4,312	1,733	1,520
Long Term Debt	0	0	0
Total Liabilities	15,667	11,265	9,292
Total Equity	62,989	61,250	68,815
Total Liab. & Equity	78,656	72,515	78,107
CAPITAL (000)			
Total Debt	0	0	0
Preferred Equity	0	0	0
Common Equity	62,989	61,250	68,815

Business:

GOLDEN KNIGHT RESOURCES INC. is a gold mining company. It has a 40% interest in Les Mines Casa Berardi in northwestern Quebec. TVX Gold Inc. holds the remaining interest in the mines and is the operator. The Golden Knight/TVX joint venture also has other interests in the area.

Synopsis:

In May 1995, Golden Knight Resources agreed to a plan of arrangement that would merge the company with Mutual Resources of Vancouver. The deal will see Mutual shareholders receive one Golden Knight share for every seven shares held. Also, each Mutual shareholder will receive a warrant to buy one Golden Knight share for every four Golden Knight shares received. The warrants expire in 18 months and are exerciseable at $12 per share.

Following the merger, the new company will have approximately 15 million shares outstanding. The new entity will have no debt, and direct and indirect gold production of about 42,000 ounces of gold annually. The reserves will total 1.1 million contained ounces with a further potential reserve base at the Tarkwa and Casa Berardi properties in Quebec.

For the first quarter ended March 31, 1995, Golden Knight reported that gold production was down 37%, compared to the same period last year. The Casa Berardi mine, which Golden Knight has a 40% interest in, was responsible for the production slow-down. The operating performance of Casa Berardi was affected by underground development work carried out during the quarter. The development work left less time available for producing gold. The mine resumed normal operations in May, and Golden Knight expects year end production of gold to be about the same as last year, 100,000 ounces.

During the first quarter of 1995, Golden Knight was reviewing potential project opportunities in many areas. In North America, Golden Knight is review opportunities in Ontario, Quebec, and Mexico. Internationally, the company is exploring opportunities in Spain and Portugal.

In March 1995, Golden Knight appointed R. Davis as Chairman. It also appointed Robert Quartermain as President and Chief Executive Officer.

Relative strength to TSE300

Price

Volume (in 1000's of board lots)

Rank (Profit/Revenue/Assets)
514 702 534

R.E. Gordon Davis
Chairman

Robert A. Quartermain
President & C.E.O.

Address
Suite 1180
999 West Hastings Street
Vancouver
BC
V6C 2W2
(604) 689-3846

Fax: (604) 689-3847
G0017738/G/2.0

Being to Manipulate +53% 34M +77¢ 'Good Chart' NO

GOLDEN STAR RESOURCES LTD.

Exchanges	Price (Jun29'95)	10.25	Trailing P/E	nm	Stock Symbol
TA	Trailing Yield (%)	0.00	Trailing EPS	(0.41)	**GSC**

Period Ending	Dec94	Dec93	Dec92	Jun91	Jun90
Yearly Statistics	US	US	US/230D		
Price-Close	12.00	17.75	7.00	2.40	2.00
Price-High	22.88	19.75	7.00	2.40	3.90
Price-Low	10.63	6.50	2.15	0.71	0.80
P/E-Close	nm	nm	nm	nm	nm
Dividends per Share	0.00	0.00	0.00	0.00	0.00
Dividend Yield (%)	0.00	0.00	0.00	0.00	0.00
Sales per Share	0.03	na	na	na	na
EPS before extra. item	(0.42)	(0.10)	(1.14)	(0.24)	(0.90)
Cash Flow per Share	(0.14)	(0.17)	(0.21)	(0.14)	(0.19)
Book Value per Share	3.53	2.42	1.13	2.22	2.49
O/S Common Shares	22,570	19,210	14,763	6,663	6,273
Total Revenue	3,548	2,843	138	259	1,197
Income before extra.	(8,785)	(1,650)	(14,170)	(1,592)	(5,680)
Cash Flow	(2,926)	(2,840)	(1,871)	(915)	(1,096)
Debt/Equity	nd	nd	0.10	0.14	0.10
Return on Capital (%)	(13.93)	(5.00)	(115.45)	(9.28)	(28.40)
Ret. on Com. Equity (%)	(13.93)	(5.23)	(129.34)	(10.47)	(31.37)
% Change Profit	(432.4)	91.3	(1,362.4)	72.0	(21.0)
% Change Revenue	24.8	1,444.8	(12.5)	(78.3)	(60.2)
% Change Assets	80.8	146.1	34.9	(1.0)	(21.7)

Date		EPS	DPS	Tot Rev	Inc Bex
Mar 95	US	(0.01)	0.00	3,159	(317)
Dec 94	US	(0.35)	0.00	1,739	(7,286)
Sep 94	US	(0.01)	0.00	860	(374)
Jun 94	US	(0.04)	0.00	645	(653)
Mar 94	US	(0.02)	0.00	511	(472)
Dec 93	US	(0.06)	0.00	344	(960)
Sep 93	US	(0.07)	0.00	289	(1,224)
Jun 93	US	0.06	0.00	1,895	969

Preferred Div. Coverage	np	np	np	
Total Div. Coverage	na	na	na	
Interest Coverage	nd	0.0	0.0	
Current Ratio	10.5	20.9	1.6	
Operating Margin	(2,015.9)	na	na	
Asset Turnover	0.0	na	na	
5 YEAR RATIOS (%)				
Return on Capital	(34.4)	(35.4)	(34.0)	
Return on Com. Equity	(38.1)	(39.6)	(38.3)	
Profit Growth	na	na	na	
Revenue Growth	7.8	25.9	36.3	
Asset Growth	36.0	20.5	23.9	
BALANCE SHEET (000)				
Cash	34,387	17,074	3,793	
Current Assets	38,603	17,574	4,148	
Net Fixed Assets	41,890	24,921	9,681	
Invest's & Advances	4,346	4,804	5,391	
Total Assets	85,540	47,299	19,221	
Short Term Debt	0	0	1,663	
Current Liabilities	3,663	839	2,535	
Long Term Debt	0	0	0	
Total Liabilities	5,845	839	2,535	
Total Equity	79,695	46,460	16,686	
Total Liab. & Equity	85,540	47,299	19,221	
CAPITAL (000)				
Total Debt	0	0	1,663	
Preferred Equity	0	0	0	
Common Equity	79,695	46,460	16,686	

Business:

GOLDEN STAR RESOURCES LTD. is involved in the acquisition, exploration and development of precious metal, base metals and diamond properties in South America and Africa.

Synopsis:

In May 1995, Gold Star Resources and partner Cambior Inc. announced reserves at the Omai mine increased by 446,000 ounces of gold. The gain is directly attributed to the results of the definition drilling program carried out at the company's eastern part of the Wenot pit. The new reserves total nine million tons grading 1.6 grams of gold per ton, containing 446,000 ounces of gold. Cambior's gold production is significantly higher than originally forecast. Minable reserves at March 31, 1995, are 13% higher than on December 31, 1994, which in turn is 62% higher than when the Omai opened in January 1993. Cambior owns 65% of the project with the remainder belonging to Golden Star Resources. Cambior operates the project.

In early May 1995, Golden Star Resources entered into an agreement to obtain 90 exploration licenses covering an area of 1,800 square kilometers in Ethiopia. The licenses were granted by the Transitional Government of Ethiopia and cover the area called the Dul project. Each license expired in three years and covers a 20 square kilometer Area. Golden Star will spend $7.3-million (U.S.) to explore the Dul project. Golden Star will spend $2.15-million (U.S.) in the first year of exploration.

On March 14, 1995, Golden Star's 70% owned subsidiary, Guyanor Resources S.A., was listed on the Toronto Stock Exchange. Golden Star said the listing was to help focus attention on the special position and quality of the assets in French Guiana. Also, the listing will help raise new capital for Guyanor Resources. In Golden Star's 1995 first quarter report, the company said Guyanor had a market capitalization of about $72-million (U.S.).

As of the end of 1994, the breakdown of Golden Star's assets was: South America assets, 48.7%; corporate assets, 46.7%; and African assets, 4.6%.

Relative strength to TSE300

Price

Volume (in 1000's of board lots)

Rank (Profit/Revenue/Assets)
950 866 446

David K. Fagin
Chairman & C.E.O.

David A. Fennell
President & Secretary

Christopher W. Taylor
Vice President, Finance

Address
One Norwest Center
1700 Lincoln Street
Suite 1950
Denver
CO
80203
(303) 830-9000
Fax: (303) 830-9022
S0039081/G/2.0

GRANGES INC.

| Exchanges | Price (Jun29'95) | 2.44 | Trailing P/E | nm | Stock Symbol |
| TA | Trailing Yield (%) | 0.00 | Trailing EPS | (0.06) | GXL |

Period Ending	Dec94	Dec93	Dec92	Dec91	Dec90	Business:
Yearly Statistics						GRANGES INC. is a precious metals mining
Price-Close	2.45	3.90	1.80	1.20	1.44	company. Its principal mining operation and
Price-High	4.40	4.40	2.20	1.95	2.65	source of earnings is its interest in the
Price-Low	1.91	1.70	1.00	1.13	1.20	Crofoot/Lewis mine in the U.S. which produces
P/E-Close	12.25	48.75	nm	nm	nm	gold. Crofoot/Lewis is held through its 50.5%
Dividends per Share	0.00	0.00	0.00	0.00	0.00	owned subsidiary, Hycroft Resources &
Dividend Yield (%)	0.00	0.00	0.00	0.00	0.00	Development Corp.
Sales per Share	1.59	1.62	1.88	1.68	1.86	
EPS before extra. item	0.20	0.08	0.00	(0.79)	(0.05)	
Cash Flow per Share	0.05	(0.06)	0.19	0.13	0.34	
Book Value per Share	2.18	1.94	1.86	1.83	2.57	
O/S Common Shares	34,177	34,157	33,807	33,888	33,888	
Total Revenue	69,288	67,513	65,465	60,581	70,389	
Income before extra.	6,985	2,761	50	(26,689)	(1,603)	

Date	EPS	DPS	Tot Rev	Inc Bex
Mar 95	0.04	0.00	15,976	1,434
Dec 94	(0.05)	0.00	15,033	(1,593)
Sep 94	(0.03)	0.00	15,910	(1,148)
Jun 94	(0.02)	0.00	12,189	(751)
Mar 94	0.31	0.00	26,636	10,477
Dec 93	(0.05)	0.00	15,235	(1,626)
Sep 93	0.21	0.00	22,239	7,132
Jun 93	0.02	0.00	17,741	585

	Dec94	Dec93	Dec92	Dec91	Dec90
Cash Flow	1,594	(1,925)	6,445	4,350	11,584
Debt/Equity	0.01	0.09	0.25	0.17	0.23
Return on Capital (%)	10.28	4.41	1.42	(28.45)	0.36
Ret. on Com. Equity (%)	9.93	4.28	0.08	(35.79)	(1.51)
% Change Profit	153.0	5,422.0	100.2	(1,564.9)	80.3
% Change Revenue	2.6	3.1	8.1	(13.9)	0.8
% Change Assets	18.8	(3.6)	6.2	(31.1)	(32.6)

Preferred Div. Coverage	np	np	np
Total Div. Coverage	na	na	na
Interest Coverage	49.0	6.4	1.2
Current Ratio	3.1	3.3	2.5
Operating Margin	(12.0)	(16.1)	(0.4)
Asset Turnover	0.6	0.7	0.7
5 YEAR RATIOS (%)			
Return on Capital	(2.4)	(5.2)	(8.5)
Return on Com. Equity	(4.6)	(8.1)	(12.2)
Profit Growth	na	na	(49.1)
Revenue Growth	(0.2)	5.2	24.8
Asset Growth	(10.8)	(8.5)	(8.6)
BALANCE SHEET (000)			
Cash	45,440	27,056	35,885
Current Assets	62,239	41,659	51,324
Net Fixed Assets	36,587	41,550	34,977
Invest's & Advances	0	0	0
Total Assets	98,826	83,209	86,301
Short Term Debt	366	5,553	14,773
Current Liabilities	20,326	12,721	20,408
Long Term Debt	0	277	629
Total Liabilities	24,505	16,889	23,556
Total Equity	74,321	66,320	62,745
Total Liab. & Equity	98,826	83,209	86,301
CAPITAL (000)			
Total Debt	366	5,830	15,402
Preferred Equity	0	0	0
Common Equity	74,321	66,320	62,745

Synopsis:

Effective May 1, 1995, Granges Inc. and Hycroft Resources & Development Corporation amalgamated into one company. The amalgamated company should begin trading on the Toronto and American Stock Exchanges before the end of May. Until then, both Granges and Hycroft Resources will continue trading as separate companies on the two exchanges. Shareholders of the common stock of the two companies will receive Letters of Transmittal and also receive a new share certificate representing common shares of the amalgamated company.

In May 1995, Granges adopted a shareholders rights plan. The plan gives shareholders the right to purchase the company's common shares at half its market value. Granges said the purpose of the plan was to ensure the fair treatment of all shareholders in the event the company is subject to a hostile takeover. The rights plan takes effect when any party announces plans to buy more than 20% of Granges outstanding common shares.

For the first quarter ended March 31, 1995, Granges reported that consolidated gold production rose almost 20%, compared to the corresponding period last year. Also, the company's silver production rose over 36% over the period last year. Granges attributed the increases to good weather in the quarter, as well as the relatively fast leaching of crushed ore placed on the company's new leach pad.

In May 1995, Granges appointed Michael Richings as President and Chief Executive Officer of the company. Also, Granges appointed Paul Wright to as Vice-President of Operations and Project Development.

Granges' major producing asset is the Crofoot/Lewis mine in Nevada. Annual gold production at Crofoot/Lewis is about 100,000 ounces. The property has reserves containing 1.3 million ounces of gold.

Relative strength to TSE300 / Price / Volume (in 1000's of board lots)

Rank (Profit/Revenue/Assets)
370 483 487

David Sinclair
Chairman Of The Board

Michael Richings
President & C.E.O.

Address
Suite 2230
885 West Georgia Street
Vancouver
BC
V6C 3E8
(604) 687-2831

Fax: (604) 687-8699
G0025122/G/2.0

HEMLO GOLD MINES INC.

Exchanges	Price (Jun29'95)	14.87	Trailing P/E	23.23	Stock Symbol
TM	Trailing Yield (%)	2.35	Trailing EPS	0.64	HEM

Period Ending	Dec94	Dec93	Dec92	Dec91	Dec90
Yearly Statistics					
Price-Close	14.38	14.50	7.88	11.50	11.25
Price-High	15.75	15.50	11.75	12.00	20.38
Price-Low	11.50	6.75	7.38	7.38	9.00
P/E-Close	21.46	30.85	18.31	76.67	41.67
Dividends per Share	0.35	0.30	0.20	0.20	0.20
Dividend Yield (%)	2.44	2.07	2.54	1.74	1.78
Sales per Share	2.63	2.24	2.19	2.17	2.32
EPS before extra. item	0.67	0.47	0.43	0.15	0.27
Cash Flow per Share	0.99	0.83	0.72	0.76	0.87
Book Value per Share	3.52	2.92	2.75	2.50	2.16
O/S Common Shares	99,918	96,781	96,761	96,568	87,630
Total Revenue	268,166	226,409	220,825	202,866	215,832
Income before extra.	64,486	45,649	41,941	13,725	23,636
Cash Flow	96,363	80,333	69,370	71,013	75,797
Debt/Equity	0.08	0.17	0.26	0.34	0.53
Return on Capital (%)	30.18	22.90	21.78	10.37	23.10
Ret. on Com. Equity (%)	20.33	16.65	16.54	6.37	12.71
% Change Profit	41.3	8.8	205.6	(41.9)	(27.9)
% Change Revenue	18.4	2.5	8.9	(6.0)	8.4
% Change Assets	18.3	(3.6)	4.1	8.4	0.1

Preferred Div. Coverage	np	np	np
Total Div. Coverage	1.9	1.6	2.2
Interest Coverage	242.3	63.3	63.0
Current Ratio	2.0	2.3	1.8
Operating Margin	36.7	30.9	29.6
Asset Turnover	0.4	0.4	0.4

5 YEAR RATIOS (%)			
Return on Capital	21.7	22.2	28.3
Return on Com. Equity	14.5	14.2	16.6
Profit Growth	14.5	0.8	(6.1)
Revenue Growth	6.1	2.4	(0.3)
Asset Growth	5.1	2.2	4.3

BALANCE SHEET (000)			
Cash	131,965	65,006	92,658
Current Assets	215,302	137,023	142,106
Net Fixed Assets	345,584	309,317	312,017
Invest's & Advances	32,942	55,761	66,964
Total Assets	593,828	502,101	521,087
Short Term Debt	26,471	26,778	39,796
Current Liabilities	108,083	60,366	79,319
Long Term Debt	0	21,942	29,755
Total Liabilities	241,983	219,548	255,350
Total Equity	351,845	282,553	265,737
Total Liab. & Equity	593,828	502,101	521,087

CAPITAL (000)			
Total Debt	26,471	48,720	69,551
Preferred Equity	0	0	0
Common Equity	351,845	282,553	265,737

Business:

HEMLO GOLD MINES INC. is a gold mining, development and exploration company. It owns and operates the Golden Giant Mine in the Hemlo area of northeastern Ontario. It also owns 55% of, and is the operator of, Silider mine near Rouyn-Noranda, Quebec, 85% of the Holloway Joint venture in Ontario and a 60% placeholding in Crow Butte Resources in the development of the New World project in Montana.

Date	EPS	DPS	Tot Rev	Inc Bex
Mar 95	0.14	0.00	61,268	13,634
Dec 94	0.16	0.20	63,781	14,900
Sep 94	0.12	0.00	55,907	11,499
Jun 94	0.22	0.15	79,406	21,326
Mar 94	0.17	0.20	67,423	16,761
Dec 93	0.14	0.20	66,498	13,794
Sep 93	0.10	0.00	50,040	10,005
Jun 93	0.10	0.10	47,460	9,188

Synopsis:

In late May 1995, Hemlo Gold was granted an option from Birim Goldfields to acquire 72% of Birim's 90% stake in the 230 square kilometer Dunkwa property. Hemlo Gold can exercise the option on Dunkwa, in the Ashanti gold belt, by spending $5-million (U.S.) over a four year period. Hemlo Gold must spend $1-million during the first year.

In May 1995, Hemlo Gold said it intends to sell its 60% interest in the Hislop-Beatty gold mine joint venture. Glimmer Resources, 40% owner of the mine, said it will exercise its first right of refusal and buy the interest from Hemlo. Glimmer will pay Hemlo $150,000 before May 24, 1995, and another $2.8-million before September 30, 1995. Hemlo will retain a royalty on the Hislop-Beatty property. The royalty will range between 2% and 6%, depending on the price of gold.

For the first quarter ended March 31, 1995, Hemlo Gold produced 108,100 ounces of gold, down 14% over last the same period last year. The aggregated operating cost per ounce of gold recovered was $124 (U.S.) in the first three months of 1995, up slightly from last year. The company attributed the drop in gold production to normal quarterly fluctuations in the average head grade at the Golden Giant mine and to a temporary shortage of available working places at the Silidor miner. Although gold production is lower than last year's figure, Hemlo is above planned production for the quarter and should produce approximately 450,000 ounces of gold in 1995.

Over the next couple of years, Hemlo Gold expects to increase gold output with the completion of two new mines. The company expects that when the Holloway joint venture and the New World projects begin gold production in 1996 and 1997, each will provide between 10-15% of Hemlo's total annual gold production.

Rank (Profit/Revenue/Assets)
96   272   212

Alex G. Balogh
Chairman Of The Board

Ian D. Bayer
President & C.E.O.

Michael C. Proctor
V.P. Finance

John Keyes
Mine Manager Golden Giant

Address
Suite 2902
1 Adelaide Street East
Toronto
ON
M5C 2Z9
(416) 982-7116

Fax: (416) 982-7388
H0000930/G/2.0

KINROSS GOLD CORPORATION

Exchanges	Price (Jun29'95)	10.50	Trailing P/E	43.75	Stock Symbol
TN	Trailing Yield (%)	0.00	Trailing EPS	0.24	K

Period Ending	Dec94	Dec93	Dec92	Dec91	Dec90	Business:
Yearly Statistics				US	US/6M	KINROSS GOLD CORPORATION is a gold
Price-Close	7.25	4.20	1.50	1.10	1.30	mining company with operations in the United
Price-High	8.13	4.25	1.65	1.60	3.30	States, Canada and Zimbabwe. Production for
Price-Low	4.05	1.25	0.90	0.95	2.10	1994 was 245,002 gold and gold equivalent oz
P/E-Close	26.85	38.18	nm	32.35	nm	and is expected to increase to 305,000 and
Dividends per Share	0.00	0.00	0.00	0.00	0.00	413,000 gold equivalent oz. in 1995 and 1996.
Dividend Yield (%)	0.00	0.00	0.00	0.00	0.00	Kinross also has direct/ indirect exposure to
Sales per Share	1.37	0.72	0.37	0.70	0.65	gold exploration and development
EPS before extra. item	0.27	0.11	(0.04)	0.03	(0.07)	opportunitities in North & South America,the
Cash Flow per Share	0.46	0.18	0.15	0.18	0.05	Commonwealth Independent States & Africa.
Book Value per Share	2.31	1.47	0.95	1.38	1.35	

Period Ending	Dec94	Dec93	Dec92	Dec91	Dec90
O/S Common Shares	97,813	82,705	33,604	11,781	11,764
Total Revenue	134,555	47,064	12,965	8,930	3,834
Income before extra.	24,658	6,728	(1,143)	299	(819)
Cash Flow	42,039	10,368	4,569	2,162	287
Debt/Equity	0.03	0.09	0.38	0.70	0.60
Return on Capital (%)	17.43	10.32	(1.91)	2.62	(3.74)
Ret. on Com. Equity (%)	14.00	8.43	(4.52)	1.86	(10.02)
% Change Profit	266.5	688.6	(433.7)	118.3	(188.8)
% Change Revenue	185.9	263.0	26.7	16.5	171.0
% Change Assets	73.8	231.2	35.9	4.4	(1.0)

Date		EPS	DPS	Tot Rev	Inc Bex
Mar 95	US	0.03	0.00	24,420	3,343
Dec 94		0.07	0.00	35,958	6,506
Sep 94		0.08	0.00	38,028	7,021
Jun 94		0.06	0.00	33,735	6,397
Mar 94	US	0.04	0.00	19,697	3,057
Dec 93		0.07	0.00	30,443	4,781
Sep 93		0.02	0.00	10,418	1,179
Jun 93		0.01	0.00	3,960	804

	Dec94	Dec93	Dec92
Preferred Div. Coverage	65.6	23.9	np
Total Div. Coverage	65.6	23.9	na
Interest Coverage	103.3	15.2	0.0
Current Ratio	6.5	3.6	4.0
Operating Margin	19.0	9.3	17.4
Asset Turnover	0.5	0.3	0.2
5 YEAR RATIOS (%)			
Return on Capital	4.9	1.9	0.6
Return on Com. Equity	1.9	(1.5)	(4.4)
Profit Growth	na	na	na
Revenue Growth	110.6	71.6	73.8
Asset Growth	51.8	35.0	43.1
BALANCE SHEET (000)			
Cash	116,370	46,499	9,404
Current Assets	147,450	64,371	12,694
Net Fixed Assets	113,954	85,649	32,564
Invest's & Advances	5,420	2,631	400
Total Assets	268,445	154,463	46,631
Short Term Debt	2,203	3,123	1,849
Current Liabilities	22,640	17,727	3,196
Long Term Debt	5,148	8,048	10,136
Total Liabilities	38,175	28,522	14,857
Total Equity	230,270	125,941	31,774
Total Liab. & Equity	268,445	154,463	46,631
CAPITAL (000)			
Total Debt	7,351	11,171	11,985
Preferred Equity	4,700	4,700	0
Common Equity	225,570	121,241	31,774

Synopsis:

At the company's annual meeting in May 1995, Kinross Gold announced it expects future growth to come from mine expansion and acquisitions. Kinross expects gold production to reach 371,000 ounces in 1995 and to reach up to 500,000 ounces of gold-equivalent production by the end of 1996. Kinross has already started a major capital expenditures program in three areas. The three areas of expansion are the Hoyle Pond in northwestern Ontario, the QR area in British Columbia, and the Blanket operation in Zimbabwe.

In May 1995, Kinross agreed to purchase a 50% interest in the Goldbanks gold property located in Nevada. In exchange for the 50% interest, Kinross will pay Restoration Minerals $6-million (US) in cash and also issue 816,055 common shares of Kinross. The company estimates reserves at the property at 47 million tons grading; 0.027 ounces of gold per ton. The property also has an additional 36 million tons of ore grading; 0.007 ounces per ton of ore. Kinross, the operator of the property, classifies this ore deposit as lean. Once the property is operational, Kinross expects annual gold production to reach 150,000 ounces for its life of eight years.

In May 1995, a group of companies acquired 5 million common shares of Kinross Gold. Included in the group were Midland Walwyn Capital Inc., Nesbitt Thomson Inc., Goepel Shields & Partners, and Eagle & Partners. The five companies paid a total of $43.5-million ($8.70 a share) for the 5 million common shares.

In late April 1995, the company agreed to purchase the Macassa gold mine from Barrick Gold Corp. Kinross will pay $42.5-million (U.S.) in cash to Barrick as well as issue 2.5 million Kinross warrants. Each warrant entitles the holder to purchase Kinross shares for $10(CDN) until October 31, 1997. In April 1995, Kinross also acquired an additional 24.99% interest in the Denton-Rawhide gold mine in Nevada. Kinross will issue Kiewit Rawhide Corp. 4 million shares of Kinross for the interest.

Relative strength to TSE300 / Price / Volume (in 1000's of board lots)

Rank (Profit/Revenue/Assets)
188   376   304

Robert M. Buchan
Chairman President & C.E.O.

Brian W. Penny
V.P. Finance & C.F.O.

Arthur H. Ditto
Exec. V.P. & C.O.O.

Address
56th Floor
Scotia Plaza
40 King Street West
Toronto
ON
M5H 3Y2
(416) 365-5123
Fax: (416) 363-6622
P0007990/G/2.0

MIRAMAR MINING CORPORATION

Exchanges	Price (Jun29'95)		7.37	Trailing P/E		19.39	Stock Symbol
TVQ	Trailing Yield (%)		0.00	Trailing EPS		0.38	MAE

Period Ending	Dec94	Dec93	Nov92	Nov91	Nov90
Yearly Statistics		13M			
Price-Close	6.00	5.75	1.15	1.05	2.60
Price-High	7.88	6.00	1.99	2.70	3.90
Price-Low	4.85	5.50	0.75	0.55	2.52
P/E-Close	16.22	212.96	nm	nm	nm
Dividends per Share	0.00	0.00	0.00	0.00	0.00
Dividend Yield (%)	0.00	0.00	0.00	0.00	0.00
Sales per Share	1.97	1.31	0.11	0.05	0.08
EPS before extra. item	0.37	0.03	(0.13)	(0.10)	(0.14)
Cash Flow per Share	0.48	0.10	(0.10)	(0.09)	(0.11)
Book Value per Share	3.56	2.10	0.65	0.74	0.84
O/S Common Shares	41,435	26,797	9,454	7,917	7,563
Total Revenue	72,745	19,449	1,138	771	682
Income before extra.	12,968	435	(1,148)	(828)	(888)
Cash Flow	17,045	1,432	(841)	(727)	(690)
Debt/Equity	0.00	0.01	0.04	0.05	0.01
Return on Capital (%)	12.68	1.27	(18.40)	(13.22)	na
Ret. on Com. Equity (%)	12.72	1.29	(19.25)	(13.63)	na
% Change Profit	3,131.3	134.9	(38.7)	6.8	na
% Change Revenue	305.2	1,478.1	47.5	13.0	na
% Change Assets	139.4	932.0	7.6	(5.8)	na

Preferred Div. Coverage	np	np	np
Total Div. Coverage	na	na	na
Interest Coverage	na	na	na
Current Ratio	11.3	3.0	3.7
Operating Margin	13.9	0.3	(144.8)
Asset Turnover	0.4	0.3	0.1
5 YEAR RATIOS (%)			
Return on Capital	na	na	na
Return on Com. Equity	na	na	na
Profit Growth	na	na	na
Revenue Growth	na	na	na
Asset Growth	na	na	na
BALANCE SHEET (000)			
Cash	82,357	10,051	699
Current Assets	93,873	21,856	1,204
Net Fixed Assets	71,210	46,703	5,267
Invest's & Advances	490	590	229
Total Assets	165,573	69,148	6,700
Short Term Debt	44	194	41
Current Liabilities	8,286	7,302	323
Long Term Debt	208	243	203
Total Liabilities	17,938	12,872	594
Total Equity	147,635	56,277	6,106
Total Liab. & Equity	165,573	69,148	6,700
CAPITAL (000)			
Total Debt	253	437	244
Preferred Equity	0	0	0
Common Equity	147,635	56,277	6,106

Business:

MIRAMAR MINING CORPORATION is involved in the acquisition, exploration and development of precious metal properties. The company has operatio ns in Canada, the United States, Cuba, and Argentina including the Con Gold Mine in Yellowknife, N.W.T.

Date	EPS	DPS	Tot Rev	Inc Bex
Mar 95	0.14	0.00	61,268	13,634
Dec 94	0.05	0.00	16,036	2,457
Sep 94	0.12	0.00	20,531	4,397
Jun 94	0.07	0.00	18,241	2,724
Mar 94	0.13	0.00	17,937	3,390
Dec 93	0.13	0.00	18,790	1,422
Aug 93	(0.06)	0.00	(67)	(589)
Jun 93	(0.03)	0.00	317	(323)

Synopsis:

Miramar Mining produces gold and silver from the Con Mine in the Northwest Territories and the Golden Eagle Mine in Nevada. The company's operating results reflect the purchase of the Con Mine in October 1993. The Con Mine contributed $66.9-million of Miramar's total sales of $69.2-million in 1994.

During 1994, Miramar began two significant capital expansions at the Con Mine. The mill and the hydroelectric facility will be completed during the first half of 1995. This will increase mine production and further reduce costs. Miramar has reduced direct operating costs by more than $70 (U.S.) per ounce of gold produced to $282 (U.S.) since acquiring the Con Mine in 1993.

Miramar is also successfully exploring for reserves near the Con Mine. The company expects to continue to replace ore reserves within the mine limits for several years, ensuring the continued operation of the mine well after the current nine year life.

In January 1995, the company acquired the Talapoosa Project, a large open pit, heap leach operation under development near the company's Golden Eagle Mine in Nevada. Talapoosa contains resources of more than 1.4 million ounces of gold and 22 million ounces of silver.

Through its ownership in publicly held Northern Orion Explorations Ltd., Miramar has interests in more than 30 exploration projects throughout Argentina. The projects are principally located on known mineral occurrences and have potential for the discovery of gold, copper and base metal deposits. Northern Orion and its partners recognize the common geology Argentina shares with neighbouring Chile.

As at early 1995, Miramar had proven and probable reserves of 3,538,469 ounces of gold and 27,704,100 ounces of silver. The company's future growth can be measured by the continued production from its operations and from its development projects underway in Cuba and Argentina.

Rank (Profit/Revenue/Assets)		
265	474	379

Walter H. Berukoff
President & C.E.O.

Anthony P. Walsh
V.P. Finance & C.F.O.

Address
311 West First Street
North Vancouver
BC
V7M 1B5
(604) 985-2572

Fax: (604) 980-0731
M0029122/G/2.0

MUSCOCHO EXPLORATIONS LTD.

Exchanges	Price (Jun29'95)	0.36	Trailing P/E	nm	Stock Symbol
TQ	Trailing Yield (%)	0.00	Trailing EPS	0.00	**MUS**

Period Ending	Dec94	Dec93	Dec92	Dec91	Dec90
Yearly Statistics					
Price-Close	0.27	0.36	0.05	0.07	0.07
Price-High	0.40	0.65	0.09	0.11	1.90
Price-Low	0.24	0.04	0.03	0.03	0.02
P/E-Close	nm	nm	nm	nm	nm
Dividends per Share	0.00	0.00	0.00	0.00	0.00
Dividend Yield (%)	0.00	0.00	0.00	0.00	0.00
Sales per Share	na	na	0.08	0.17	0.20
EPS before extra. item	(0.04)	(0.02)	(0.06)	(0.32)	(1.09)
Cash Flow per Share	(0.03)	(0.02)	(0.03)	(0.07)	(1.06)
Book Value per Share	0.02	0.06	0.06	0.07	0.15
O/S Common Shares	46,675	45,847	43,634	41,045	31,406
Total Revenue	327	723	3,260	6,277	6,809
Income before extra.	(1,638)	(812)	(2,586)	(10,897)	(33,930)
Cash Flow	(1,584)	(798)	(1,410)	(2,343)	(33,210)
Debt/Equity	29.28	2.09	1.65	1.65	0.90
Return on Capital (%)	(5.42)	(5.96)	(26.69)	(124.37)	(131.28)
Ret. on Com. Equity (%)	(89.03)	(28.34)	(83.70)	(286.48)	(157.69)
% Change Profit	(101.7)	68.6	76.3	67.9	10.8
% Change Revenue	(54.8)	(77.8)	(48.1)	(7.8)	(55.7)
% Change Assets	341.3	(3.9)	(19.1)	(42.1)	(63.9)

Preferred Div. Coverage	np	np	np
Total Div. Coverage	na	na	na
Interest Coverage	0.0	0.0	0.0
Current Ratio	1.4	0.0	0.0
Operating Margin	(15,715.6)	(7,258.7)	(39.7)
Asset Turnover	na	na	0.4
5 YEAR RATIOS (%)			
Return on Capital	(58.7)	(70.5)	(69.9)
Return on Com. Equity	(129.0)	(124.6)	(119.5)
Profit Growth	na	na	na
Revenue Growth	(54.3)	(44.9)	(20.8)
Asset Growth	(6.4)	(36.8)	(30.2)
BALANCE SHEET (000)			
Cash	1,098	147	0
Current Assets	1,190	237	45
Net Fixed Assets	5,460	5,774	6,111
Invest's & Advances	2,555	2,503	2,704
Total Assets	37,567	8,514	8,860
Short Term Debt	35	5,343	5,228
Current Liabilities	873	5,956	5,686
Long Term Debt	32,828	0	0
Total Liabilities	36,445	5,956	5,686
Total Equity	1,123	2,558	3,173
Total Liab. & Equity	37,567	8,514	8,860
CAPITAL (000)			
Total Debt	32,863	5,343	5,228
Preferred Equity	0	0	0
Common Equity	1,123	2,558	3,173

Business:

MUSCOCHO EXPLORATIONS LTD. is principally engaged in the exploration, development and mining of gold properties. It operates the Magino Gold Mine and the Magnacon Gold Mine (which has recently closed) in Ontario. The company has other properties in Ontario, Quebec and Newfoundland. Muscocho has a 25% interest in MacMillan Gold Corp. of Vancouver.

Date	EPS	DPS	Tot Rev	Inc Bex
Mar 95	0.00	0.00	510	(215)
Jun 94	(0.01)	0.00	36	(266)
Mar 94	0.00	0.00	29	(211)
Dec 93	0.01	0.00	1,181	587
Sep 93	(0.01)	0.00	(160)	(586)
Jun 93	(0.01)	0.00	(95)	(375)
Mar 93	(0.01)	0.00	(203)	(439)
Dec 92	(0.02)	0.00	(66)	(948)

Synopsis:

In early March of 1995, a partnership in which Muscocho Exploration has a 38.8% stake and is operator, entered into an agreement whereby the Magnacon Joint Venture will lease the Magnacon Gold Mill to River Gold Mines Ltd. The agreement states the Magnacon Joint Venture reserves the right to process up to 100,000 tons per day of ore from its properties at the Magnacon mill. In exchange for processing the ore, the Magnacon Joint Ventures will receive a fee for every ton of River Gold ore processed through the mill. In turn, Magnacon Joint Ventures will pay the same fee to River Gold for Magnacon ore processed through the mill. Both companies expect the Magnacon Gold Mill to be operational sometime in September 1995.

After a difficult time in 1994, Muscocho Exploration is now ready to explore and develop its assets. During 1994, Muscocho Exploration not only survived but increased its investment from 25% of the Magnacon Joint Venture to 38.8%. Muschocho now plans to arrange further financing so the company can begin maximizing its assets.

In November 1994, Muscocho Exploration and its subsidiary ("608485") entered into a series of agreements with another company. Muscocho sold its interest (excluding the buildings and equipment) in the Magino Gold Mine to 608485, and the other company acquired 27,440 preferred shares of 608485 for cash proceeds of $2.74-million.

Rank (Profit/Revenue/Assets)
830 881 999

J.T. Flanagan
President

Address
Suite 1210
111 Richmond Street West
Toronto
ON
M5H 2G4
(416) 363-1124

Fax: (416) 360-0728
M0014546/G/2.0

NORTHGATE EXPLORATION LIMITED

Exchanges	Price (Jun29'95)		1 .30	Trailing P/E		18 .06	Stock Symbol
TMN	Trailing Yield (%)		0 .00	Trailing EPS		0 .07	**NGX**

Period Ending	Dec94	Dec93	Dec92	Dec91	Dec90
Yearly Statistics					
Price-Close	1 .00	1 .60	0 .64	0 .95	1 .42
Price-High	1 .80	2 .60	0 .95	2 .20	8 .63
Price-Low	0 .86	0 .55	0 .63	0 .85	1 .25
P/E-Close	20 .00	nm	nm	nm	nm
Dividends per Share	0 .00	0 .00	0 .00	0 .00	0 .00
Dividend Yield (%)	0 .00	0 .00	0 .00	0 .00	0 .00
Sales per Share	0 .08	na	na	0 .74	0 .78
EPS before extra. item	0 .05	(0 .26)	(0 .30)	(3 .17)	(5 .33)
Cash Flow per Share	0 .06	(0 .12)	(0 .11)	0 .06	0 .37
Book Value per Share	0 .61	0 .56	0 .78	1 .15	4 .26
O/S Common Shares	29 ,496	29 ,496	27 ,982	22 ,367	22 ,294
Total Revenue	3 ,972	2 ,517	8 ,253	22 ,364	26 ,615
Income before extra.	1 ,449	(7 ,528)	(8 ,261)	(70 ,724)	(118 ,233)
Cash Flow	1 ,806	(3 ,524)	(3 ,146)	1 ,434	8 ,095
Debt/Equity	0 .00	0 .13	1 .94	2 .10	0 .65
Return on Capital (%)	8 .12	(11 .66)	(5 .91)	(59 .01)	(45 .37)
Ret. on Com. Equity (%)	8 .38	(39 .35)	(34 .93)	(117 .27)	(79 .12)
% Change Profit	119 .2	8 .9	88 .3	40 .2	(1 ,352 .2)
% Change Revenue	57 .8	(69 .5)	(63 .1)	(16 .0)	26 .9
% Change Assets	(3 .8)	(58 .8)	(20 .9)	(48 .6)	(60 .4)

Preferred Div. Coverage	np	np	np
Total Div. Coverage	na	na	na
Interest Coverage	28 .8	0 .0	0 .0
Current Ratio	4 .4	11 .8	11 .2
Operating Margin	1 .0	na	na
Asset Turnover	0 .1	na	na
5 YEAR RATIOS (%)			
Return on Capital	(22 .8)	(23 .5)	(20 .3)
Return on Com. Equity	(52 .5)	(53 .2)	(45 .1)
Profit Growth	(31 .3)	na	na
Revenue Growth	(28 .5)	(34 .6)	(42 .5)
Asset Growth	(42 .5)	(38 .2)	(21 .5)
BALANCE SHEET (000)			
Cash	20 ,598	28 ,072	32 ,208
Current Assets	22 ,298	28 ,192	33 ,561
Net Fixed Assets	0	0	0
Invest's & Advances	5 ,867	1 ,085	37 ,503
Total Assets	28 ,165	29 ,277	71 ,064
Short Term Debt	0	0	0
Current Liabilities	5 ,075	2 ,396	3 ,004
Long Term Debt	59	2 ,157	42 ,157
Total Liabilities	10 ,138	12 ,699	49 ,381
Total Equity	18 ,027	16 ,578	21 ,683
Total Liab. & Equity	28 ,165	29 ,277	71 ,064
CAPITAL (000)			
Total Debt	59	2 ,157	42 ,157
Preferred Equity	0	0	0
Common Equity	18 ,027	16 ,578	21 ,683

Business:

NORTHGATE EXPLORATION LTD. is a gold mining company with mines in Califronia, Canada, and Chile. The company holds a 42% indirect interest in Sonora Gold Corp., which in turn through subsidiaries, own s a 100% interest in the Jamestown gold mine.

Date	EPS	DPS	Tot Rev	Inc Bex
Mar 95	0 .03	0 .00	2 ,273	778
Dec 94	0 .04	0 .00	2 ,406	1 ,089
Sep 94	0 .00	0 .00	256	24
Jun 94	0 .00	0 .00	358	39
Mar 94	0 .01	0 .00	732	297
Dec 93	(0 .18)	0 .00	(106)	(5 ,220)
Sep 93	0 .01	0 .00	1 ,194	236
Jun 93	(0 .03)	0 .00	868	(761)

Synopsis:

For the first quarter ended March 31, 1995, Northgate Exploration reported that revenues and profits were higher than last year. The company attributes the rise to their increased interest in the Choquelimpie mine located in Chile. In 1994, Nortgate Exploration increased its holding in the Choquelimpie mine from 35% to 100%.

The newly acquired interest in the Choquelimple helped Northgate Exploration obtain higher gold production figures in 1994. Gold production topped 19,000 ounces in 1994. Northgate Exploration expects 1995 production to be at least 10,000 ounces above last year's numbers. Silver production in the first quarter of 1995 was 261,000 ounces. Because of the Choquelimpie mine, Northgate Exploration expects to produce 150,000 more ounces of silver by year's end.

Northgate Exploration's Jamestown mine ceased production in July 1994. The company expects reclamation on the property to continue throughout 1996. Northgate Exploration is performing the ongoing reclamation while adhering to strict environmental and financial constraints.

In the future, the company will continue to search for new opportunities to increase the value of the company. Northgate expects the majority of future growth to stem from exploration activities in Chile. One of these exploration projects includes a joint venture that Northgate Exploration entered into with its Chilean subsidiary. The program, which is presently underway, entails the building of a $2-million exploration shaft at the Choquelimpie mine.

Northgate Exploration operates in Canada, the United States, and Chile. As of December 31, 1994, Canadian assets accounted for almost 88% of the company's total assets. Chilean assets comprise 9.4%, and assets in the United States accounted for the remaining assets in 1994.

Relative strength to TSE300 / Price / Volume (in 1000's of board lots)

Rank (Profit/Revenue/Assets)
616   880   785

John F. Kearney
Chairman Of The Board

Patrick D. Downey
President & C.E.O.

Address
1 First Canadian Place
Suite 2701
P.O. Box 143
Toronto
ON
M5X 1C7
(416) 362-6683
Fax: (416) 367-3250
N0003283/G/2.0

PEGASUS GOLD INC.

Exchanges	Price (Jun29'95)	14.00	Trailing P/E	nm	Stock Symbol
TMA	Trailing Yield (%)	0.00	Trailing EPS	(1.70)	PGU

Period Ending	Dec94	Dec93	Dec92	Dec91	Dec90	Business:
Yearly Statistics	US	US	US	US	US	PEGASUS GOLD INC. is a precious metals
Price-Close	16.13	29.00	18.75	14.25	14.88	mining company. It has gold, silver, zinc and
Price-High	32.75	36.00	22.75	16.13	18.50	lead mines in Montana, Idaho, Nevada and
Price-Low	14.75	16.25	13.50	11.00	10.88	Australia. The company has exploration
P/E-Close	nm	57.78	nm	29.40	nm	activities in the western United States, Chile
Dividends per Share	0.00	0.10	0.10	0.10	0.10	and Australia.
Dividend Yield (%)	0.00	0.45	0.65	0.80	0.78	
Sales per Share	6.73	6.38	6.29	5.95	6.95	
EPS before extra. item	(1.69)	0.30	(0.22)	0.37	(1.55)	
Cash Flow per Share	0.70	1.23	1.56	1.42	1.61	
Book Value per Share	8.44	9.90	9.31	8.82	8.04	
O/S Common Shares	34,630	34,556	31,473	27,857	24,701	
Total Revenue	236,878	230,294	184,574	158,034	155,871	
Income before extra.	(58,735)	9,993	(6,341)	9,599	(38,172)	
Cash Flow	24,287	41,442	45,139	37,235	39,800	

Date		EPS	DPS	Tot Rev	Inc Bex
Mar 95	US	(0.05)	0.00	56,336	(1,810)
Dec 94	US	(0.02)	0.00	67,453	(732)
Sep 94	US	0.02	0.00	66,563	832
Jun 94	US	(1.65)	0.00	61,738	(57,090)
Mar 94	US	(0.05)	0.10	42,653	(1,744)
Dec 93	US	0.16	0.10	73,785	5,482
Sep 93	US	0.01	0.00	60,697	381
Jun 93	US	0.14	0.00	63,391	4,579

	Dec94	Dec93	Dec92	Dec91	Dec90
Debt/Equity	0.20	0.20	0.22	0.29	0.24
Return on Capital (%)	(15.22)	3.78	(1.88)	5.21	(13.89)
Ret. on Com. Equity (%)	(18.52)	3.15	(2.35)	4.32	(17.69)
% Change Profit	(687.8)	257.6	(166.1)	125.1	(491.0)
% Change Revenue	2.9	24.8	16.8	1.4	(12.6)
% Change Assets	(8.5)	25.7	12.2	26.9	(4.5)

Preferred Div. Coverage	np	np	np
Total Div. Coverage	na	2.9	0.0
Interest Coverage	0.0	5.3	0.0
Current Ratio	2.3	4.4	3.8
Operating Margin	(26.1)	(0.6)	(5.9)
Asset Turnover	0.5	0.4	0.5
5 YEAR RATIOS (%)			
Return on Capital	(4.4)	na	1.2
Return on Com. Equity	(6.2)	(1.7)	(0.8)
Profit Growth	na	(8.5)	na
Revenue Growth	5.7	5.8	9.7
Asset Growth	9.4	11.8	8.0
BALANCE SHEET (000)			
Cash	89,316	149,313	109,753
Current Assets	168,278	212,962	168,569
Net Fixed Assets	259,448	261,908	175,242
Invest's & Advances	22,252	17,756	47,960
Total Assets	453,279	495,233	394,022
Short Term Debt	39,151	14,791	21,196
Current Liabilities	71,652	47,873	44,042
Long Term Debt	19,038	51,944	41,799
Total Liabilities	160,937	153,236	100,883
Total Equity	292,342	341,997	293,139
Total Liab. & Equity	453,279	495,233	394,022
CAPITAL (000)			
Total Debt	58,189	66,735	62,995
Preferred Equity	0	0	0
Common Equity	292,342	341,997	293,139

Synopsis:

In April 1995, Pegasus Gold made a takeover bid for the outstanding common shares of its Australian subsidiary company, Zapopan N.L. Currently, Pegasus owns 58% of the outstanding common shares of Zapopan, which owns the Mt. Todd mine. Pegasus offered notes, due April 2002 and carrying an interest rate of 6.25%, to shareholders of Zapopan. These notes can be converted by the holder into Pegasus common shares at a price of $14.92(US) per share. The total value of the bid is estimated at $99-million(US). In its first quarter report, Pegasus said that the bid, if completed, would raise significantly the company's ore reserves.

In April 1995 the Northern Miner reported that Pegasus' gold reserves had increased 14% since the start of 1995. Pegasus' gold reserves stand at about 5.3 million contained ounces of gold. The company attributes much of the increase to the Mt. Todd open pit mine located in Australia. Proven gold reserves have increased to 115.4 million tons grading 0.031 ounces of gold per ton. This represents about 3.6 million contained ounces of gold.

In the first quarter ended March 31, 1995, Pegasus' share of gold production totalled 116,039 ounces. This represents an increase of almost 40,000 ounces of gold over the corresponding period last year. The company attributes the increase to its US-based operations. Gold production in the U.S. was 37,000 ounces higher than last year. Pegasus' cash operating cost per ounce of gold in the quarter was virtually unchanged from last year's figure of $251(US).

Although gold production was higher in the first three months of 1995 compared to 1994, Pegasus still recorded a loss in that period. The company stated that income was negatively affected by the increased emphasis on international exploration activities. During the first quarter of 1995, Pegasus spent $5.2-million(US) in exploration and development activities. In comparison, the company spent $2.4-million(US) in the first quarter of 1994 on these activities.

Relative strength to TSE300

Price

Volume (in 1000's of board lots)

Rank (Profit/Revenue/Assets)
995   247   204

Werner G. Nennecker
President & C.E.O.

Phillips S. Baker
V.P. Finance & C.F.O.

Steven W. Banning
V.P. Operations

Address
Suite 400
North 9 Post Street
Spokane
WA
99201
(509) 624-4653

Fax: (509) 838-8317
P0001798/G/2.0

PIONEER METALS CORPORATION

| Exchanges | Price (Jun29'95) | 0.22 | Trailing P/E | nm | Stock Symbol |
| T | Trailing Yield (%) | 0.00 | Trailing EPS | 0.00 | PSM |

Period Ending	Dec94	Dec93	Dec92	Dec91	Dec90
Yearly Statistics					
Price-Close	0.25	0.30	0.12	0.18	0.13
Price-High	0.57	0.79	0.25	0.24	0.44
Price-Low	0.22	0.12	0.06	0.03	0.03
P/E-Close	nm	nm	nm	0.07	nm
Dividends per Share	0.00	0.00	0.00	0.00	0.00
Dividend Yield (%)	0.00	0.00	0.00	0.00	0.00
Sales per Share	na	na	na	na	na
EPS before extra. item	0.00	(0.01)	0.00	2.45	(0.98)
Cash Flow per Share	(0.01)	(0.01)	(0.01)	(0.03)	(0.29)
Book Value per Share	0.04	0.04	0.04	0.04	(2.20)
O/S Common Shares	47,517	47,479	45,179	43,079	23,392
Total Revenue	560	61	258	56,281	5,955
Income before extra.	19	(320)	(102)	55,854	(22,898)
Cash Flow	(521)	(365)	(264)	(627)	(6,816)
Debt/Equity	nd	nd	nd	nd	na
Return on Capital (%)	1.08	(18.38)	(5.80)	na	na
Ret. on Com. Equity (%)	1.08	(18.38)	(5.80)	na	na
% Change Profit	105.9	(213.7)	(100.2)	343.9	71.4
% Change Revenue	818.0	(76.3)	(99.5)	845.1	(20.2)
% Change Assets	6.8	(5.3)	3.5	(77.7)	(68.9)
Preferred Div. Coverage	np	np	np		
Total Div. Coverage	na	na	na		
Interest Coverage	nd	nd	nd		
Current Ratio	0.3	3.7	5.2		
Operating Margin	na	na	na		
Asset Turnover	na	na	na		
5 YEAR RATIOS (%)					
Return on Capital	na	na	na		
Return on Com. Equity	na	na	na		
Profit Growth	41.5	na	na		
Revenue Growth	293.4	(58.7)	(53.8)		
Asset Growth	(28.3)	(54.3)	(51.1)		
BALANCE SHEET					
Cash	22,420	309,110	158,810		
Current Assets	50,160	325,080	792,450		
Net Fixed Assets	1,835,370	1,424,530	1,077,670		
Invest's & Advances	0	0	0		
Total Assets	1,935,720	1,813,130	1,915,030		
Short Term Debt	0	0	0		
Current Liabilities	176,270	87,430	152,870		
Long Term Debt	0	0	0		
Total Liabilities	176,270	87,430	152,870		
Total Equity	1,759,450	1,725,700	1,762,160		
Total Liab. & Equity	1,935,720	1,813,130	1,915,030		
CAPITAL					
Total Debt	0	0	0		
Preferred Equity	0	0	0		
Common Equity	1,759,450	1,725,700	1,762,160		

Business:

PIONEER METALS CORP. is a gold-copper exploration company. It has properties in British Columbia and Manitoba and exploration activities in British Columbia and is re-activating the Pufty Lake Mine in Manitoba.

Date	EPS	DPS	Tot Rev	Inc Bex
Mar 95	0.00	0.00	5	(44)
Dec 94	0.00	0.00	5	(269)
Sep 94	(0.01)	0.00	5	(96)
Jun 94	0.01	0.00	427	328
Mar 94	0.00	0.00	123	56
Dec 93	0.00	0.00	12	(119)
Sep 93	(0.01)	0.00	5	(120)
Jun 93	0.00	0.00	44	(21)

Synopsis:

In April 1995, shareholders of Pioneer Metals Corp. approved a reorganization that will split the company into two separate entities. A new company, Scaffold Connection Corp., will trade on the Toronto Stock Exchange. The reorganized Pioneer Metals will retain all mining assets of the old company, while Scaffold will rent, lease, and sell scaffolding equipment, as well as make the company's new composite scaffolding material. Pioneer Metals expects to complete the reorganization in June 1995. Scaffold Connection is expected to undertake an initial public offering of at least $20-million.

In April 1995, Pioneer Metals committed to buy up to $5-million in convertible, secured, subordinated debenture of Scaffold Connection Inc. The debentures will pay interest of 9.75% per year, more than $121,000. Also, at the option of Pioneer Metals, the debentures can be converted into common shares of Scaffold Connection. The conversion price for the debentures will be 115% of the price of shares during Scaffold's initial public offering. The debentures mature in five years. The new debentures will help reduce the initial public offering that Scaffold had planned to make in the market.

Relative strength to TSE300 / Price / Volume (in 1000's of board lots)

Rank (Profit/Revenue/Assets)
902   620   893

Stephen H. Sorensen
Chairman President & C.E.O.

Graham C. Thody
C.F.O.

Address
Suite 1770
401 West Georgia St.
Vancouver
BC
V6B 5A1
(604) 669-3383

Fax: (604) 669-1240
P0025667/G/2.0

PLACER DOME INC.

Exchanges	Price (Jun29'95)	36 .62	Trailing P/E	61 .33	Stock Symbol
TMNN	Trailing Yield (%)	1 .04	Trailing EPS	0 .44	**PDG**

Period Ending	Dec94	Dec93	Dec92	Dec91	Dec90
Yearly Statistics	US	US	US	US	US
Price-Close	30 .38	32 .88	14 .75	12 .63	19 .75
Price-High	37 .13	34 .38	15 .50	19 .38	25 .00
Price-Low	25 .00	14 .38	10 .75	11 .13	15 .50
P/E-Close	50 .46	56 .49	25 .83	nm	24 .17
Dividends per Share	0 .27	0 .26	0 .26	0 .26	0 .30
Dividend Yield (%)	0 .89	0 .79	1 .76	2 .06	1 .52
Sales per Share	3 .77	3 .86	4 .31	4 .10	3 .96
EPS before extra. item	0 .44	0 .45	0 .47	(1 .00)	0 .70
Cash Flow per Share	1 .03	1 .15	1 .46	1 .25	1 .31
Book Value per Share	6 .41	6 .36	6 .15	6 .26	7 .45
O/S Common Shares	238 ,449	238 ,102	237 ,116	236 ,736	236 ,395
Total Revenue	966 ,000	996 ,000	1 ,090 ,000	1 ,030 ,000	1 ,031 ,300
Income before extra.	105 ,000	107 ,000	111 ,000	(236 ,000)	164 ,600
Cash Flow	246 ,000	272 ,000	345 ,000	295 ,000	308 ,200
Debt/Equity	0 .18	0 .17	0 .08	0 .21	0 .19
Return on Capital (%)	10 .22	8 .83	9 .21	(12 .22)	12 .29
Ret. on Com. Equity (%)	6 .90	7 .20	7 .55	(14 .56)	9 .71
% Change Profit	(1 .9)	(3 .6)	147 .0	(243 .4)	53 .6
% Change Revenue	(3 .0)	(8 .6)	5 .8	(0 .1)	19 .1
% Change Assets	0 .8	7 .8	(9 .8)	(14 .0)	9 .0

Date		EPS	DPS	Tot Rev	Inc Bex
Mar 95	US	0 .16	0 .07	255 ,000	37 ,000
Dec 94	US	0 .11	0 .07	246 ,000	26 ,000
Sep 94	US	0 .08	0 .07	227 ,000	18 ,000
Jun 94	US	0 .09	0 .07	255 ,000	24 ,000
Mar 94	US	0 .16	0 .07	238 ,000	37 ,000
Dec 93	US	0 .26	0 .07	297 ,000	62 ,000
Sep 93	US	0 .06	0 .07	229 ,000	13 ,000
Jun 93	US	0 .08	0 .07	242 ,000	21 ,000

Preferred Div. Coverage	np	np	np
Total Div. Coverage	1 .6	1 .7	1 .8
Interest Coverage	15 .3	6 .7	7 .8
Current Ratio	3 .2	6 .5	3 .8
Operating Margin	16 .7	11 .9	11 .8
Asset Turnover	0 .4	0 .4	0 .5
5 YEAR RATIOS (%)			
Return on Capital	5 .7	5 .7	7 .5
Return on Com. Equity	3 .4	3 .3	5 .0
Profit Growth	2 .8	(12 .0)	(3 .2)
Revenue Growth	2 .2	4 .7	4 .9
Asset Growth	(1 .7)	(0 .7)	2 .1
BALANCE SHEET (000)			
Cash	312 ,000	777 ,000	477 ,000
Current Assets	565 ,000	994 ,000	757 ,000
Net Fixed Assets	1 ,276 ,000	1 ,031 ,000	1 ,138 ,000
Invest's & Advances	265 ,000	91 ,000	86 ,000
Total Assets	2 ,246 ,000	2 ,228 ,000	2 ,067 ,000
Short Term Debt	51 ,000	21 ,000	46 ,000
Current Liabilities	177 ,000	153 ,000	201 ,000
Long Term Debt	225 ,000	243 ,000	69 ,000
Total Liabilities	717 ,000	714 ,000	608 ,000
Total Equity	1 ,529 ,000	1 ,514 ,000	1 ,459 ,000
Total Liab. & Equity	2 ,246 ,000	2 ,228 ,000	2 ,067 ,000
CAPITAL (000)			
Total Debt	276 ,000	264 ,000	115 ,000
Preferred Equity	0	0	0
Common Equity	1 ,529 ,000	1 ,514 ,000	1 ,459 ,000

Business:

PLACER DOME INC. is a gold mining company which also produces significant quantities of silver, copper and molybdenum. Through its subsidiaries, the company produces gold in Canada, the United States, Australia, Papua New Guinea and Chile. Exploration activities are underway in North and South America, Australia, Southeast Asia and Africa.

Synopsis:

In June, 1994. Placer Dome announced it had successfully won a litigation case brought against it by ECM Inc of Billings, Montana. Placer Dome stated that all but two charges of fraud brought against the company were dismissed by a jury in the United States. The original claim against Placer Dome's U.S. subsidiary, Placer Dome U.S., alleged the company negotiated a lease on a property that subsequent to closing, contained a large deposit, the South Pipeline deposit. Now that the case is settled, Placer Dome plans to develop the 60% owned South Pipeline Deposit.

In the first three months of 1995, Placer Dome produced 400,000 ounces of gold. This is down from 442,000 ounces last year. Placer Dome says lower gold production in the first quarter was the result of lower ore grades from its Campbell, Dome, and Porgera mines. During the period, Placer Dome's average cash cost was $235(US) per ounce of gold, compared to $200(US) per ounce in the corresponding period last year. The company blamed lower production in the period for the increase in cash production costs. Although gold production was lower than last year, Placer Dome fully expects to achieve its planned 1995 gold production of 1.9 million ounces of gold at an average cash cost of $200(US) per ounce.

In April of 1995, Placer Dome made a counter-offer bid of $14.99(CDN) for all the outstanding common stock of International Musto Exploration Ltd. The original offer of $12.50(CDN) per share was made in the first quarter of 1995. International Musto Exploration owns 50% of the Bajo de la Alumbrera gold-copper deposit in Argentina.

In the first quarter of 1995, Placer Dome came to an arrangement with the Government of Kazakhstan to purchase a 27.5% interest in the Vasilkovskoye gold deposit. As of the end of the first quarter of 1995, the property was in an advanced exploration stage with costs totalling $80-million(US) thus far.

Relative strength to TSE300 / Price / Volume (in 1000's of board lots)

Rank (Profit/Revenue/Assets)
48   99   66

Robert M. Franklin
Chairman
John M. Willson
President & C.E.O.
Ian G. Austin
Sr. V.P. Finance & C.F.O.

Address
1600 - 1055 Dunsmuir Street
P.O. Box 49330
Bentall Postal Station
Vancouver
BC
V7X 1P1
(604) 682-7082
Fax: (604) 682-7092
P0001699/G/2.0

PRIME RESOURCES GROUP INC.

Exchanges	Price (Jun29'95)		9.37	Trailing P/E		58.56	Stock Symbol
TV	Trailing Yield (%)		0.00	Trailing EPS		0.16	**PRU**

Period Ending	Dec94	Dec93	Dec92	Mar92	Mar91
Yearly Statistics			9M		
Price-Close	10.25	9.25	2.15	2.20	4.60
Price-High	11.38	9.50	2.70	4.65	9.38
Price-Low	8.13	5.75	1.85	1.85	3.00
P/E-Close	102.50	154.17	32.58	nm	nm
Dividends per Share	0.00	0.00	0.00	0.00	0.13
Dividend Yield (%)	0.00	0.00	0.00	0.00	2.83
Sales per Share	0.37	0.39	0.36	0.42	0.07
EPS before extra. item	0.10	0.06	0.05	(0.52)	(0.14)
Cash Flow per Share	0.17	0.09	0.16	0.13	(0.10)
Book Value per Share	2.85	2.32	2.27	3.05	3.41
O/S Common Shares	76,074	71,029	71,004	45,380	43,900
Total Revenue	28,626	32,792	20,484	20,034	8,929
Income before extra.	7,136	4,571	3,697	(23,917)	(5,823)
Cash Flow	12,443	6,363	8,302	6,089	(4,315)
Debt/Equity	0.04	0.01	0.18	0.18	0.11
Return on Capital (%)	4.63	3.12	3.53	(13.41)	(4.24)
Ret. on Com. Equity (%)	3.74	2.81	3.30	(16.61)	(5.31)
% Change Profit	56.1	(7.3)	120.6	(310.7)	87.6
% Change Revenue	(12.7)	20.1	36.3	124.4	4,973.3
% Change Assets	37.9	(11.7)	16.8	(3.2)	78.4

Preferred Div. Coverage	np	np	np
Total Div. Coverage	na	na	na
Interest Coverage	na	5.6	7.5
Current Ratio	0.9	2.1	0.5
Operating Margin	28.9	4.0	16.8
Asset Turnover	0.1	0.2	0.1
5 YEAR RATIOS (%)			
Return on Capital	(1.3)	(12.7)	(15.2)
Return on Com. Equity	(2.4)	(17.5)	(21.3)
Profit Growth	na	na	na
Revenue Growth	176.7	31.3	84.1
Asset Growth	19.7	10.0	9.8
BALANCE SHEET (000)			
Cash	693	2,956	8,143
Current Assets	14,978	9,867	13,677
Net Fixed Assets	214,094	160,348	157,725
Invest's & Advances	5,712	0	19,623
Total Assets	234,784	170,215	192,832
Short Term Debt	8,797	1,976	23,218
Current Liabilities	16,031	4,637	25,191
Long Term Debt	0	0	6,392
Total Liabilities	18,332	5,359	31,931
Total Equity	216,452	164,856	160,901
Total Liab. & Equity	234,784	170,215	192,832
CAPITAL (000)			
Total Debt	8,797	1,976	29,610
Preferred Equity	0	0	0
Common Equity	216,452	164,856	160,901

Business:

PRIME RESOURCES GROUP INC. is a gold mining company. It has a 40% joint venture interest in the Snip Mine. Production at Eskay Creek, one of North America's richest gold deposits, commenced in 1995. Prime's largest shareholder is Homestake Canada Inc. Homestake owns 50.6% of the company's shares.

Date	EPS	DPS	Tot Rev	Inc Bex
Mar 95	0.07	0.00	29,152	5,435
Dec 94	0.02	0.00	7,085	1,391
Sep 94	0.03	0.00	8,653	2,105
Jun 94	0.04	0.00	9,117	2,612
Mar 94	0.01	0.00	3,826	1,028
Dec 93	0.03	0.00	5,847	2,180
Sep 93	0.03	0.00	7,876	1,977
Jun 93	0.03	0.00	14,071	2,327

Synopsis:

In the first three months of 1995, Prime Resources reported that the start-up at its 100% owned Eskay Creek mine has met expectations. Ore shipments by the end of March 1995, totaled 20,400 tons. Prime Resources estimated the ore contained 43,000 ounces of gold equivalent. In the first quarter of 1995, the company's cash production cost at Eskay Creek was $186 (U.S.) per equivalent ounce of gold. Prime Resources projects that ore shipments will total 270,000 contained ounces of gold from Eskay Creek by the end of 1995.

During the first quarter of 1995, Prime Resources' 40% owned Snip mine produced 12,622 ounces of gold. This brought the company's total gold production to 77,849 ounces for the three months ended March 31, 1995. Cash production costs in the period were down 5% compared to last year at $162 (U.S.) per contained ounce.

In the first quarter of 1995, Prime Resources also announced it had entered into an agreement with Westmin Resources to sell all of Snip's production concentrate for the next two years. The two-year contract replaces a previous one-year contract that was less attractive to Prime Resources.

For the rest of 1995, Prime Resources will focus its efforts expanding the reserves of the Eskay Creek and Snip mines. The 1995 exploration budget for these two properties is expected to reach $3.3-million.

In May 1995, the Northern Miner reported that Prime Resources and Cominco intend to maintain their option on an area adjoining the southern boundary of the Snip mine located in British Columbia. Prime Resources owns 40% of the Snip mine. Cominco, who operates the mine, owns the other 60% interest.

Relative strength to TSE300 / Price / Volume (in 1000's of board lots)

Rank (Profit/Revenue/Assets)
361   656   329

Jack E. Thompson
Chairman

Ronald D. Parker
President & C.E.O.

Geoffrey A. Burns
C.F.O.

Address
Suite 1000
700 West Pender Street
Vancouver
BC
V6C 1G8
(604) 684-2345

Fax: (604) 684-9831
P0000136/G/2.0

QSR LIMITED

Exchanges	Price (Jun29'95)	0.61	Trailing P/E	nm	Stock Symbol
TQ	Trailing Yield (%)	0.00	Trailing EPS	(1.11)	QSR

Period Ending	Dec94	Dec93	Dec92	Dec91	Dec90	Business:
Yearly Statistics						QSR LIMITED is a gold exploration company.
Price-Close	0.85	2.15	1.15	1.15	2.35	The company has a 25.5% interest in St.
Price-High	2.75	4.50	3.50	2.50	7.75	Andrew Goldfields Ltd. of Toronto and a 100%
Price-Low	0.65	0.90	0.60	0.55	1.75	interest in Anglo Conodeon Exploration (ACE)
P/E-Close	nm	nm	nm	nm	nm	Limited of Wales.
Dividends per Share	0.00	0.00	0.00	0.00	0.00	
Dividend Yield (%)	0.00	0.00	0.00	0.00	0.00	
Sales per Share	na	na	6.61	4.73	6.51	
EPS before extra. item	(1.18)	(0.28)	(0.85)	(1.00)	(4.75)	
Cash Flow per Share	(0.08)	(0.04)	0.93	(0.50)	0.41	
Book Value per Share	0.63	1.82	2.16	3.06	2.05	

	Dec94	Dec93	Dec92	Dec91	Dec90
O/S Common Shares	3,426	3,399	1,992	1,930	1,870
Total Revenue	(1,998)	(159)	13,043	10,163	13,650
Income before extra.	(4,051)	(937)	(1,668)	(1,896)	(8,863)
Cash Flow	(269)	(143)	1,824	(948)	758
Debt/Equity	0.30	0.11	0.61	2.50	6.51
Return on Capital (%)	(83.28)	(12.15)	(10.02)	(5.87)	(22.34)
Ret. on Com. Equity (%)	(97.30)	(17.88)	(32.72)	(39.02)	(107.66)
% Change Profit	(332.4)	43.8	12.0	78.6	(329.7)
% Change Revenue	(1,156.6)	(101.2)	28.3	(25.5)	38.0
% Change Assets	(58.8)	1.8	(77.9)	(8.6)	(51.1)

Date	EPS	DPS	Tot Rev	Inc Bex
Mar 95	0.00	0.00	(220)	(260)
Dec 94	(0.86)	0.00	(1,160)	(2,971)
Sep 94	(0.10)	0.00	(238)	(312)
Jun 94	(0.15)	0.00	(464)	(540)
Mar 94	(0.07)	0.00	(136)	(228)
Dec 93	(0.10)	0.00	(270)	(330)
Sep 93	na	0.00	395	58
Jun 93	(0.20)	0.00	92	(316)

	Dec94	Dec93	Dec92
Preferred Div. Coverage	np	np	np
Total Div. Coverage	na	na	na
Interest Coverage	0.0	0.0	0.0
Current Ratio	0.1	0.2	0.0
Operating Margin	na	(1,232.8)	(6.5)
Asset Turnover	na	na	1.8
5 YEAR RATIOS (%)			
Return on Capital	(26.7)	(11.5)	(9.0)
Return on Com. Equity	(58.9)	(42.5)	(40.3)
Profit Growth	na	na	na
Revenue Growth	na	na	14.2
Asset Growth	(47.2)	(38.2)	(33.3)
BALANCE SHEET			
Cash	20,299	19,695	4,619
Current Assets	56,215	116,399	11,915
Net Fixed Assets	502,053	502,755	123,001
Invest's & Advances	2,388,328	6,537,373	6,898,413
Total Assets	2,946,596	7,156,527	7,033,329
Short Term Debt	337,775	387,831	861,325
Current Liabilities	493,705	682,612	949,061
Long Term Debt	300,000	300,000	1,781,744
Total Liabilities	793,705	982,612	2,730,805
Total Equity	2,152,891	6,173,915	4,302,524
Total Liab. & Equity	2,946,596	7,156,527	7,033,329
CAPITAL			
Total Debt	637,775	687,831	2,643,069
Preferred Equity	0	0	0
Common Equity	2,152,891	6,173,915	4,302,524

Synopsis:

Subsequent to QSR Limited's year end of December 31, 1994, the company arranged a private placement of 500,000 of its treasury shares at a price of $0.60 per share. QSR stated that out of the total proceeds of the private placement, $250,000, will be used to exercise the expected rights offering by St. Andrew Goldfields Ltd. The private placement should be completed sometime before the end of May 1995.

On November 16, 1994, St. Andrew Goldfields sought and was granted protection under the Companies' Creditors Arrangement Act. QSR is a significant holder of St. Andrew stock with almost $2.4-million invested in the company as of December 31, 1994. In March 1995, St. Andrew presented a plan of arrangement which if approved by creditors and debenture holders will be followed by a rights issue to its shareholders. QSR intends to exercise its right to purchase at least 1.25 million shares if prior creditor approval of the plan has been secured.

In August 1994, QSR entered into an option agreement with Stevan Resources Inc. The arrangement calls for Stevan Resources to explore and develop QSR's Pifher Township mining claims. Under the terms of the the deal QSR is required to make annual payments of $20,000. The deal also states that QSR will retain a 3% net smelter royalty on any future production on the property.

Relative strength to TSE300

Price

Volume (in 1000's of board lots)

Rank (Profit/Revenue/Assets)
747   699   627

G. Warren Armstrong
President

C.E. Peter Earl
V.P. Finance

Address
166 Pearl Street
Toronto
ON
M5H 1L3
(416) 597-0969

Fax: (416) 597-1776
Q0000425/G/2.0

RAYROCK YELLOWKNIFE RESOURCES INC.

Exchanges	Price (Jun29'95)	15 .00	Trailing P/E	166 .67	Stock Symbol
T	Trailing Yield (%)	0 .00	Trailing EPS	0 .09	**RAY**

Period Ending	Dec94	Dec93	Dec92	Dec91	Dec90
Yearly Statistics					
Price-Close	16 .63	15 .75	10 .13	4 .90	8 .88
Price-High	20 .25	16 .88	10 .25	8 .75	11 .00
Price-Low	13 .00	10 .00	4 .95	4 .70	7 .13
P/E-Close	32 .60	28 .13	38 .94	32 .67	26 .10
Dividends per Share	0 .00	0 .00	0 .00	0 .00	0 .00
Dividend Yield (%)	0 .00	0 .00	0 .00	0 .00	0 .00
Sales per Share	5 .44	5 .74	10 .60	8 .30	8 .73
EPS before extra. item	0 .51	0 .56	0 .26	0 .15	0 .34
Cash Flow per Share	0 .87	0 .84	2 .44	1 .54	1 .72
Book Value per Share	9 .70	7 .95	7 .86	7 .16	7 .03
O/S Common Shares	19 ,861	16 ,975	10 ,760	9 ,033	9 ,079
Total Revenue	97 ,550	94 ,026	102 ,869	76 ,348	84 ,845
Income before extra.	8 ,798	8 ,509	2 ,476	1 ,400	3 ,166
Cash Flow	15 ,132	12 ,804	22 ,447	13 ,982	15 ,572
Debt/Equity	0 .18	0 .10	0 .46	0 .62	0 .62
Return on Capital (%)	6 .22	8 .43	6 .45	4 .97	9 .12
Ret. on Com. Equity (%)	5 .34	7 .71	3 .30	2 .14	4 .86
% Change Profit	3 .4	243 .7	76 .9	(55 .8)	(0 .2)
% Change Revenue	3 .7	(8 .6)	34 .7	(10 .0)	46 .1
% Change Assets	55 .1	(9 .6)	28 .0	1 .0	31 .6
Preferred Div. Coverage	187 .2	193 .4	145 .6		
Total Div. Coverage	187 .2	193 .4	145 .6		
Interest Coverage	7 .6	11 .3	2 .6		
Current Ratio	4 .3	5 .2	2 .1		
Operating Margin	0 .7	(1 .7)	4 .2		
Asset Turnover	0 .3	0 .5	0 .5		
5 YEAR RATIOS (%)					
Return on Capital	7 .0	7 .5	8 .3		
Return on Com. Equity	4 .7	4 .6	5 .3		
Profit Growth	22 .7	5 .2	(18 .6)		
Revenue Growth	10 .9	19 .8	21 .1		
Asset Growth	18 .9	12 .9	17 .6		
BALANCE SHEET (000)					
Cash	47 ,902	43 ,180	22 ,164		
Current Assets	83 ,454	65 ,002	51 ,625		
Net Fixed Assets	184 ,356	100 ,931	156 ,279		
Invest's & Advances	27 ,081	24 ,144	2 ,366		
Total Assets	294 ,891	190 ,077	210 ,270		
Short Term Debt	2 ,243	2 ,115	5 ,052		
Current Liabilities	19 ,385	12 ,538	24 ,397		
Long Term Debt	33 ,234	11 ,202	34 ,284		
Total Liabilities	101 ,337	54 ,143	125 ,302		
Total Equity	193 ,554	135 ,934	84 ,968		
Total Liab. & Equity	294 ,891	190 ,077	210 ,270		
CAPITAL (000)					
Total Debt	35 ,477	13 ,317	39 ,336		
Preferred Equity	925	925	375		
Common Equity	192 ,629	135 ,009	84 ,593		

Business:

RAYROCK YELLOWKNIFE RESOURCES INC. is a gold mining company. It operates open-pit gold mines in Nevada and owns Western Ag-Minerals Co. of Houston, an agricultural mineral producer. It also has a 45% interest in Minera Rayrock Inc., a Central and South American gold and copper exploration company, and a 40.1% voting interest in Discovery West Corp., and oil and gas company.

Date	EPS	DPS	Tot Rev	Inc Bex
Mar 95	(0 .03)	0 .00	19 ,737	(492)
Dec 94	(0 .06)	0 .00	23 ,594	(838)
Sep 94	(0 .08)	0 .00	21 ,730	(863)
Jun 94	0 .26	0 .00	29 ,176	4 ,276
Mar 94	0 .39	0 .00	27 ,042	6 ,223
Dec 93	0 .44	0 .00	31 ,885	6 ,698
Sep 93	0 .10	0 .00	19 ,118	1 ,535
Jun 93	0 .11	0 .00	25 ,399	2 ,488

Synopsis:

In late May 1995, Rayrock Yellowknife Resources and Inter-Rock Gold announced that their Daisy gold project in Nevada should be operational by late 1996. Daisy is 25% owned and operated by Rayrock, with the remaining 75% interest belonging to Inter-Rock Gold, a subsidiary of Rayrock. As of May 1995, engineering work and permitting were under way at the Daisy. Also, mine construction should last six to seven months and cost $5.7-million (U.S.). The reserves surrounding the area total 49.1 million tons averaging 0.025 ounces of gold per ton at a cutoff grade of 0.005 ounces per ton.

The Daisy project is located in a 12.5 square kilometer area broken-down into four deposits: the Secret Pass, the Mother Lode; Sunday Night; and the West Zone. In the last year, Rayrock and Inter-Rock completed some infill drilling at the Secret Pass deposit. The two companies determined that a minable reserve of 17.9 million tons averaging 0.021 ounces of gold per ton was feasible, based on the results and a gold price of $400 (U.S.) per ounce. The Secret Pass deposit should produce 35,000 ounces of gold annually over an eight year period. The average cash operating cost will be about $294 (U.S.) per ounce of gold.

Rayrock and Inter-Rock plan to take a 10-ton bulk sample of the Mother Lode deposit to confirm recoveries. The sample should take six to seven months to complete. As of May 1995, reserves at Mother Lode were estimated at 9.4 million tons grading 0.046 ounces of gold per ton.

In the first quarter of 1995, Rayrock's share of gold production totalled 15,700 ounces, compared to 19,469 ounces in the first three months of 1994. The average cash cost per ounce of gold in the period was $389 (U.S.). Increased costs at the Dee mine were cited for Rayrock's higher cash costs. Rayrock expects its share of gold production in 1995 will total 87,000 ounces.

Relative strength to TSE300

Price

Volume (in 1000's of board lots)

Rank (Profit/Revenue/Assets)
317   425   288

David R. Crombie
Chairman & C.E.O.

C. Bruce Burton
V.P. & C.F.O.

Address
30 Soudan Avenue
Suite 500
Toronto
ON
M4S 1V6
(416) 489-0022

Fax: (416) 489-0096
R0000435/G/2.0

REA GOLD CORPORATION

Exchanges	Price (Jun29'95)	2.95	Trailing P/E		nm	Stock Symbol
TQ	Trailing Yield (%)	0.00	Trailing EPS		(0.01)	REO

Period Ending	Dec94	Dec93	Dec92	Dec91	Dec90
Yearly Statistics					
Price-Close	1.78	1.45	0.30	0.39	0.90
Price-High	2.45	1.85	0.55	1.28	3.20
Price-Low	1.40	0.28	0.25	0.35	0.75
P/E-Close	nm	nm	nm	nm	45.00
Dividends per Share	0.00	0.00	0.00	0.00	0.00
Dividend Yield (%)	0.00	0.00	0.00	0.00	0.00
Sales per Share	0.06	0.04	0.22	0.33	0.77
EPS before extra. item	(0.02)	(0.06)	(0.36)	(0.61)	0.02
Cash Flow per Share	0.01	(0.03)	(0.00)	(0.01)	0.28
Book Value per Share	1.15	0.77	0.75	1.05	1.86
O/S Common Shares	31,804	17,073	15,282	17,808	13,643
Total Revenue	2,209	1,184	4,983	6,374	12,021
Income before extra.	(428)	(801)	(6,226)	(10,030)	278
Cash Flow	236	(504)	(73)	(121)	3,827
Debt/Equity	0.51	nd	nd	nd	nd
Return on Capital (%)	(1.14)	(6.54)	(41.12)	(45.14)	2.33
Ret. on Com. Equity (%)	(1.72)	(6.50)	(41.31)	(45.58)	1.10
% Change Profit	46.5	87.1	37.9	(3,711.7)	113.8
% Change Revenue	86.5	(76.2)	(21.8)	(47.0)	145.7
% Change Assets	341.6	(43.0)	(25.5)	19.8	(6.8)

Preferred Div. Coverage	np	np	np
Total Div. Coverage	na	na	na
Interest Coverage	na	nd	nd
Current Ratio	1.1	7.1	6.0
Operating Margin	(76.6)	(197.2)	(172.0)
Asset Turnover	0.0	0.0	0.2
5 YEAR RATIOS (%)			
Return on Capital	(18.3)	(19.7)	na
Return on Com. Equity	(18.8)	(20.3)	na
Profit Growth	na	na	na
Revenue Growth	(14.8)	5.3	na
Asset Growth	16.0	(8.2)	na
BALANCE SHEET (000)			
Cash	5,010	2,023	2,409
Current Assets	7,364	2,965	3,084
Net Fixed Assets	51,518	10,355	8,662
Invest's & Advances	119	119	11,865
Total Assets	59,913	13,568	23,801
Short Term Debt	2,158	0	0
Current Liabilities	6,490	418	516
Long Term Debt	16,691	0	0
Total Liabilities	23,232	466	12,273
Total Equity	36,682	13,102	11,528
Total Liab. & Equity	59,913	13,568	23,801
CAPITAL (000)			
Total Debt	18,849	0	0
Preferred Equity	0	0	0
Common Equity	36,682	13,102	11,528

Business:

REA GOLD CORPORATION is a Canadian operating mining company with mineable reserves of just under 1.0 million ounces of gold on three main properties. Rea Gold has fast tracked two mines in the past two years into production and is aggressively pursuing additional acqui- sitions, while furthering the development work on the Bissett Gold Project in Manitoba.

Date	EPS	DPS	Tot Rev	Inc Bex
Mar 95	0.01	0.00	2,463	369
Dec 94	(0.02)	0.00	3	(368)
Sep 94	(0.01)	0.00	(90)	(177)
Jun 94	0.01	0.00	753	202
Mar 94	0.00	0.00	1,595	(86)
Dec 93	(0.04)	0.00	671	(483)
Sep 93	(0.01)	0.00	2	(198)
Jun 93	(0.01)	0.00	121	(114)

Synopsis:

In June 1995, Rea Gold began the initial stage of an exploration program on the Mt. Hamilton gold mine in Nevada. The $1-million program is intended to increase reserves in and around the NE Sheboygan deposit. Rea Gold purchased Mt. Hamilton in 1994 and within five months of construction of a mine, the project produced its first gold bar. Rea Gold expects to produce 54,000 ounces of gold from Mt. Hamilton in 1995.

Head grades at the Sheboygan property are doubled what was previously forecast in a feasibility study. When NE Sheboygan and the Coninential deposit were purchased, the reserves were estimated to contain 9.04 million tons grading 0.052 ounces of gold and 0.38 ounces of silver per ton. Since then, NE Sheboygan has realized an average head grade of 0.08 ounces of gold per ton.

Rea Gold also boosted reserves at the company's Bissett project near Winnipeg. Geological reserves now stand at three million tons grading 0.274 ounces of gold per ton.

For the first quarter ended March 31, 1995, Rea Gold reported a profit which was directly attributed to Mt. Hamilton gold mine. At the end of March 1995, Rea Gold had produced 7,906 ounces of gold at an average operating cost of $190 (U.S.) per ounce. The Mt. Hamilton mine should produce 54,500 ounces of gold and 141,000 ounces of silver annually for the life of the mine, about 7.5 years.

In May 1995, Rea Gold reported the closing of a $10-million special warrants offering through a private placement to institutional investors. Each special warrant, priced at $2.00, and entitles the holder to exchange it for one common share of Rea Gold. Proceeds from the private placement will go to general corporate uses and to fund ongoing activities at Rea Gold's Bissett Gold Project.

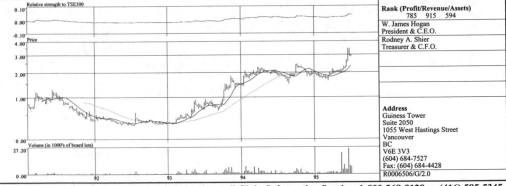

Rank (Profit/Revenue/Assets)
785 915 594

W. James Hogan
President & C.E.O.

Rodney A. Shier
Treasurer & C.F.O.

Address
Guiness Tower
Suite 2050
1055 West Hastings Street
Vancouver
BC
V6E 3V3
(604) 684-7527
Fax: (604) 684-4428
R0006506/G/2.0

ROYAL OAK MINES INC.

Exchanges	Price (Jun29'95)		4.30	Trailing P/E		25.29	Stock Symbol
TA	Trailing Yield (%)		0.00	Trailing EPS		0.17	**RYO**

Period Ending	Dec94	Dec93	Dec92	Dec91	Dec90
Yearly Statistics					
Price-Close	4.60	6.25	1.95	1.58	0.70
Price-High	7.13	8.88	2.62	1.70	1.32
Price-Low	4.00	1.80	1.41	0.66	0.40
P/E-Close	20.91	32.90	10.83	6.32	nm
Dividends per Share	0.00	0.00	0.00	0.00	0.00
Dividend Yield (%)	0.00	0.00	0.00	0.00	0.00
Sales per Share	1.60	1.61	1.81	2.79	2.08
EPS before extra. item	0.22	0.19	0.18	0.25	(0.17)
Cash Flow per Share	0.43	0.24	0.22	0.48	(0.09)
Book Value per Share	2.64	1.91	1.17	0.88	0.77
O/S Common Shares	114,495	96,956	69,947	56,118	20,599
Total Revenue	172,205	137,615	114,423	97,649	18,160
Income before extra.	22,166	15,623	11,437	8,641	(1,443)
Cash Flow	43,125	20,414	13,593	16,598	(788)
Debt/Equity	0.00	nd	nd	nd	1.24
Return on Capital (%)	9.32	11.85	17.60	26.65	(5.04)
Ret. on Com. Equity (%)	9.08	11.69	17.43	26.52	(16.19)
% Change Profit	41.9	36.6	32.4	698.8	(774.5)
% Change Revenue	25.1	20.3	17.2	437.7	nm
% Change Assets	76.8	94.5	49.9	(22.0)	4,740.5

Business:
ROYAL OAK MINES INC. is a gold mining and production company.

Date	EPS	DPS	Tot Rev	Inc Bex
Mar 95	0.03	0.00	53,164	3,503
Dec 94	(0.05)	0.00	48,462	(3,672)
Sep 94	0.08	0.00	42,010	7,775
Jun 94	0.11	0.00	44,444	11,011
Mar 94	0.07	0.00	37,289	7,051
Dec 93	0.08	0.00	39,562	7,090
Sep 93	0.05	0.00	34,829	4,386
Jun 93	0.04	0.00	33,488	2,911

Preferred Div. Coverage	np	np	np
Total Div. Coverage	na	na	na
Interest Coverage	na	nd	nd
Current Ratio	6.3	4.6	1.7
Operating Margin	17.3	11.1	12.5
Asset Turnover	0.4	0.6	1.0
5 YEAR RATIOS (%)			
Return on Capital	12.1	8.3	3.9
Return on Com. Equity	9.7	6.0	1.6
Profit Growth	na	na	na
Revenue Growth	307.1	347.3	392.5
Asset Growth	186.9	167.4	129.0
BALANCE SHEET (000)			
Cash	178,937	79,644	12,719
Current Assets	226,850	104,589	33,348
Net Fixed Assets	137,954	99,218	77,547
Invest's & Advances	19,270	13,419	775
Total Assets	384,074	217,226	111,670
Short Term Debt	0	0	0
Current Liabilities	35,800	22,708	19,433
Long Term Debt	1,037	0	0
Total Liabilities	81,343	31,864	29,735
Total Equity	302,731	185,362	81,935
Total Liab. & Equity	384,074	217,226	111,670
CAPITAL (000)			
Total Debt	1,037	0	0
Preferred Equity	0	0	0
Common Equity	302,731	185,362	81,935

Synopsis:
Although Royal Oak Mines was unsuccessful in its attempt to take over Lac Minerals in 1994, the company still hopes to acquire a gold property. A June 1995 report said Royal Oak had $189-million in its treasury account waiting for the right opportunity. The company said it will look to Australia, Bolivia, and Nevada as possible locations for acquisitions.

In the first quarter ended March 31, 1995, Royal Oak reported that declining gold production raised the average cash cost per ounce of gold during the period. Royal Oak produced 86,960 ounces of gold in the first quarter of 1995. This was up from the 66,273 ounces produced in the first quarter of 1994, but was 11% lower than was forecast. During the period, the average cash cost of gold rose to $360 (U.S.) per ounce from $317 (U.S.) in the first three months of 1994. Royal Oak attributed the lower production to lower head grades at the Giant mine in Yellowknife. The ore grades there were 13% below company expectations. Although Royal Oak did not achieve its production targets in the first quarter of 1995, the company should meet its production forecast of 425,000 ounces of gold by the end of 1995. Royal Oak also expects average cash costs to fall to between $300 (U.S.) and $310(US) per ounce of gold by the end of the year.

In May 1995, Royal Oak and subsidiary Geddes Resources walked away from the purchase of St. Philips Resources and El Condor Resources. Royal Oak and Geddes had offered $132-million for the two companies, which own 60% of the Kemess mine in British Columbia. Royal Oak said the deal fell through because the British Columbia government offered only $34-million instead of $150-million towards the purchase. The Kemess property is one of the largest gold deposits in British Columbia.

Relative strength to TSE300

Price

Volume (in 1000's of board lots)

Rank (Profit/Revenue/Assets)
203   335   257

Margaret K. Witte
Chairman President & C.E.O.

James H. Wood
C.F.O.

Address
5501 Lakeview Dr.
2nd Floor
Kirkland
WA
98033
(206) 822-8992

Fax: (206) 822-3552
H0002415/G/2.0

SONORA GOLD CORP.

Exchanges	Price (Jun29'95)	0.12	Trailing P/E	0.27	Stock Symbol
TV	Trailing Yield (%)	0.00	Trailing EPS	0.47	**SON**

Period Ending	Dec94	Dec93	Dec92	Dec91	Dec90
Yearly Statistics					
Price-Close	0.16	0.20	0.12	0.20	0.25
Price-High	0.33	0.41	0.25	0.45	1.85
Price-Low	0.12	0.12	0.08	0.15	0.15
P/E-Close	0.62	nm	nm	nm	nm
Dividends per Share	0.00	0.00	0.00	0.00	0.00
Dividend Yield (%)	0.00	0.00	0.00	0.00	0.00
Sales per Share	1.56	1.92	1.88	1.85	1.64
EPS before extra. item	0.26	(0.23)	(0.01)	(0.96)	(1.32)
Cash Flow per Share	0.28	(0.15)	0.21	0.18	(0.13)
Book Value per Share	(1.62)	(1.89)	(1.66)	(1.65)	(0.69)
O/S Common Shares	20,262	20,262	20,262	20,262	20,262
Total Revenue	31,507	38,992	38,093	37,970	33,900
Income before extra.	5,336	(4,578)	(276)	(19,366)	(26,662)
Cash Flow	5,773	(3,105)	4,161	3,656	(2,700)
Debt/Equity	na	na	na	na	na
Return on Capital (%)	116.09	(21.80)	30.53	(88.27)	(55.55)
Ret. on Com. Equity (%)	na	na	na	na	na
% Change Profit	216.6	(1,558.7)	98.6	27.4	(1,116.3)
% Change Revenue	(19.2)	2.4	0.3	12.0	(13.4)
% Change Assets	19.0	(25.2)	(14.9)	(46.5)	(38.0)

Date	EPS	DPS	Tot Rev	Inc Bex
Mar 95	0.21	0.00	5,026	4,335
Dec 94	(0.02)	0.00	508	(409)
Sep 94	0.21	0.00	8,771	4,385
Jun 94	0.07	0.00	11,278	1,330
Mar 94	0.00	0.00	10,555	30
Dec 93	(0.04)	0.00	11,701	(705)
Sep 93	(0.00)	0.00	12,318	(16)
Jun 93	(0.14)	0.00	6,678	(2,802)

Ratios			
Preferred Div. Coverage	np	np	np
Total Div. Coverage	na	na	na
Interest Coverage	3.3	0.0	0.9
Current Ratio	1.1	0.3	0.2
Operating Margin	25.4	(3.4)	8.0
Asset Turnover	1.9	2.8	2.1
5 YEAR RATIOS (%)			
Return on Capital	(3.8)	(26.4)	(35.1)
Return on Com. Equity	na	na	na
Profit Growth	na	na	na
Revenue Growth	(4.3)	0.6	44.3
Asset Growth	(24.2)	(27.5)	(30.1)
BALANCE SHEET (000)			
Cash	9,206	3,080	2,022
Current Assets	16,008	13,384	8,960
Net Fixed Assets	346	359	9,421
Invest's & Advances	0	0	0
Total Assets	16,354	13,743	18,381
Short Term Debt	7,941	38,071	38,709
Current Liabilities	14,487	48,358	45,781
Long Term Debt	34,757	3,611	6,108
Total Liabilities	49,244	51,969	52,029
Total Equity	(32,890)	(38,226)	(33,648)
Total Liab. & Equity	16,354	13,743	18,381
CAPITAL (000)			
Total Debt	42,698	41,682	44,817
Preferred Equity	0	0	0
Common Equity	(32,890)	(38,226)	(33,648)

Business:

SONORA GOLD CORP. is a gold mining company which owns the Jamestown mine, the third largest gold mine in the state of California. NorthWest Gold Corp., a subsidiary of Northgate Exploration Limited, owns 42% of the company.

Synopsis:

In the first quarter of 1995, Sonora Gold reported that earnings improved significantly over the corresponding period last year. Sonora said the higher earnings were the result of a gain on the sale of substantially all the freehold land at Jamestown. The company ceased operations at the Jamestown mine, and reclamation work is underway at the property. Sonora said the results in the first quarter of 1995 were not indicative of future earnings.

During the first three months of 1995, Sonora acquired the rights for $1.9-million (U.S.) plus a royalty on a potential future waste site. Sonora acquired the rights under a June 1993 purchase and sale agreement from the company's former 30% joint venture partner. The former joint venture partner had the right to receive the first $4.4-million (U.S.) of cash flow after all operating and reclamation obligations had been fulfilled and a further 30% of cash flow more than $4.4-million (U.S.).

In its 1994 annual report, Sonora Gold said that in its final year of production, the Jamestown mine produced 59,100 ounces of gold. This represents an increase of more than 14,000 ounces over planned production at the mine. The Jamestown mine closed in June 1994 because of depleted ore reserves. Sonora is now considering several future options for the site including the possibility of converting the tailings management facility to a landfill site. A decision is expected later in 1995.

Relative strength to TSE300 / Price / Volume (in 1000's of board lots) charts, 92–95

Rank (Profit/Revenue/Assets)
904   597   969

John F. Kearney
Chairman
Patrick D. Downey
President

Address
Suite 2701
P.O. Box 143
1 First Canadian Place
Toronto
ON
M5X 1C7
(416) 362-6683
Fax: (416) 367-3250
S0017384/G/2.0

TECK CORPORATION

Exchanges	Price (Jun29'95)	27.12	Trailing P/E		30.82	Stock Symbol
TMV	Trailing Yield (%)	0.74	Trailing EPS		0.88	**TEK.B**

Period Ending	Dec94	Dec93	Dec92	Dec91	Dec90
Yearly Statistics					
Price-Close	25.38	23.25	17.00	18.13	20.88
Price-High	27.50	24.25	22.13	23.00	28.50
Price-Low	21.50	15.75	16.38	17.00	19.38
P/E-Close	32.96	66.43	56.67	40.29	18.98
Dividends per Share	0.20	0.20	0.20	0.20	0.20
Dividend Yield (%)	0.79	0.86	1.18	1.10	0.96
Sales per Share	6.05	5.43	4.14	4.64	5.62
EPS before extra. item	0.77	0.35	0.30	0.45	1.10
Cash Flow per Share	1.36	1.37	1.40	1.50	2.06
Book Value per Share	11.45	10.87	9.97	9.81	8.86
O/S Common Shares	90,153	89,849	84,307	81,503	77,123
Total Revenue	551,416	492,136	377,576	396,365	474,060
Income before extra.	69,109	29,189	25,517	36,826	90,568
Cash Flow	121,507	114,808	114,817	118,517	158,723
Debt/Equity	0.48	0.26	0.31	0.09	0.09
Return on Capital (%)	6.96	4.77	5.88	8.42	19.41
Ret. on Com. Equity (%)	6.88	3.21	3.02	4.77	13.14
% Change Profit	136.8	14.4	(30.7)	(59.3)	(14.9)
% Change Revenue	12.0	30.3	(4.7)	(16.4)	14.4
% Change Assets	21.9	7.4	16.6	2.1	13.1

Preferred Div. Coverage	np	np	np
Total Div. Coverage	3.9	1.7	1.5
Interest Coverage	3.4	3.4	4.5
Current Ratio	2.6	4.3	4.9
Operating Margin	13.4	15.2	18.2
Asset Turnover	0.3	0.3	0.2
5 YEAR RATIOS (%)			
Return on Capital	9.1	12.4	16.7
Return on Com. Equity	6.2	8.4	12.7
Profit Growth	(8.3)	(22.7)	(5.4)
Revenue Growth	5.9	7.2	13.1
Asset Growth	11.9	7.6	16.7
BALANCE SHEET (000)			
Cash	131,682	253,129	214,762
Current Assets	226,760	347,576	288,532
Net Fixed Assets	893,538	765,799	724,841
Invest's & Advances	680,301	363,862	362,589
Total Assets	1,800,599	1,477,237	1,375,962
Short Term Debt	17,509	12,032	9,425
Current Liabilities	87,756	80,861	58,449
Long Term Debt	475,794	242,011	253,546
Total Liabilities	767,979	501,012	535,227
Total Equity	1,032,620	976,225	840,735
Total Liab. & Equity	1,800,599	1,477,237	1,375,962
CAPITAL (000)			
Total Debt	493,303	254,043	262,971
Preferred Equity	0	0	0
Common Equity	1,032,620	976,225	840,735

Business:

TECK CORP. is an international mining company which has interests in 12 mines producing gold, silver, copper, zinc, lead, niobium and coal. Investments include a 36% interest in Cominco Ltd., a 44% interest in Golden Knight Resources Inc. and a 10% interest in Aur Resources Inc.

Date	EPS	DPS	Tot Rev	Inc Bex
Mar 95	0.24	0.00	152,976	21,501
Dec 94	0.29	0.10	150,857	25,875
Sep 94	0.20	0.00	140,148	18,410
Jun 94	0.15	0.10	133,398	13,040
Mar 94	0.13	0.00	127,013	11,784
Dec 93	0.16	0.10	143,019	13,565
Sep 93	0.12	0.00	146,940	9,897
Jun 93	0.04	0.10	106,532	2,988

Synopsis:

In April 1995, Teck Corp acquired a 10.4% interest in Diamond Fields Resources for $108-million. Diamond Fields owns a massive nickel, copper, and cobalt deposit in remote Voisey Bay in northern Labrador. At the time of acquisition, Diamonds Fields' common shares were trading at around $35 per share on the TSE. As of June 21, 1995, the common shares of Diamond Fields traded at about $67 per share. The stock even reached the $80 mark previous to June 21, 1995. As it is, Teck made a substantial return on its investment in Diamond Fields in only a short period of time.

In February 1995, the Canadian Bond Rating Service revised its rating outlook regarding Teck Corp's long-term debt, commercial paper and convertible debentures. The rating agency raised its outlook of Teck's debt to stable from negative.

For the first quarter ended March 31, 1995, Teck's share of gold production totalled 74,000 ounces, down somewhat from the same period last year. Teck attributed the lower gold production to stope rescheduling at the Bell mine. Although gold production was lower in the first quarter, Teck still expects to produce 340,000 ounces of gold by year end.

Despite lower gold production in the first three months of 1995, Teck posted higher earnings and revenues than in the corresponding period last year. The improved revenues and earnings are due to the addition of the Louvicourt and Afton mines and the higher price received for copper in the first quarter of 1995. Teck owns 25% of the Louvicourt mine.

The Louvicourt mine operated at 63% capacity in the first three months of 1995. Total mineral production in the period reached 16.8 million pounds of copper, 147,360 ounces of silver, eight million pounds of zinc and 7,138 ounces of gold. Louvicourt should be operating at 100% capacity by July 1, 1995.

Relative strength to TSE300 / Price / Volume (in 1000's of board lots)

Rank (Profit/Revenue/Assets)
93 188 113

Robert J. Wright
Chairman

Norman B. Keevil
Chairman President & C.E.O.

John G. Taylor
V.P., C.F.O. & Treasurer

Address
6th Floor
200 Burrard Street
Vancouver
BC
V6C 3L9
(604) 687-1117

Fax: (604) 687-6100
T0000566/G/2.0

TVX GOLD INC.

Exchanges	Price (Jun29'95)	10.12	Trailing P/E	49.72	Stock Symbol
TM	Trailing Yield (%)	0.00	Trailing EPS	0.15	**TVX**

Period Ending	Dec94	Dec93	Dec92	Dec91	Jan91	Business:
Yearly Statistics	US	US	US	US /51W	US	
Price-Close	9.50	8.75	2.65	3.60	5.00	
Price-High	10.50	9.25	4.00	5.00	8.25	
Price-Low	7.00	2.45	2.30	3.05	3.80	
P/E-Close	49.74	56.45	27.32	63.16	28.74	
Dividends per Share	0.00	0.00	0.00	0.00	0.00	
Dividend Yield (%)	0.00	0.00	0.00	0.00	0.00	
Sales per Share	0.99	1.21	1.12	0.81	0.59	
EPS before extra. item	0.14	0.12	0.08	0.05	0.15	
Cash Flow per Share	0.43	0.43	0.36	0.36	0.27	
Book Value per Share	2.50	1.62	1.49	1.41	1.37	

TVX GOLD INC. is a Canadian based growth oriented international mining company with existing production of precious metals from interests in six producing mines located in North and South America. TVX maintains its head office in Toronto, Canada with major offices in Rio de Janeiro, Brazil and Santiago, Chile.

	Dec94	Dec93	Dec92	Dec91	Jan91
O/S Common Shares	160,023	135,288	134,032	134,032	134,038
Total Revenue	187,621	169,155	156,443	110,678	60,999
Income before extra.	22,779	15,725	10,402	6,405	12,786
Cash Flow	68,442	57,456	49,438	46,842	24,819
Debt/Equity	0.20	0.59	0.81	1.02	0.98
Return on Capital (%)	9.23	10.12	0.00	5.60	8.40
Ret. on Com. Equity (%)	7.35	7.50	5.34	3.51	10.28
% Change Profit	44.9	51.2	59.3	(48.9)	403.7
% Change Revenue	10.9	8.1	38.6	85.0	1,468.9
% Change Assets	37.4	(4.9)	(6.1)	7.5	432.7

Date		EPS	DPS	Tot Rev	Inc Bex
Mar 95	US	0.03	0.00	45,690	5,590
Dec 94	US	0.02	0.00	48,681	3,598
Sep 94	US	0.08	0.00	52,635	13,319
Jun 94	US	0.02	0.00	48,393	2,547
Mar 94	US	0.02	0.00	39,743	3,315
Dec 93	US	0.03	0.00	45,633	4,164
Sep 93	US	0.04	0.00	40,016	5,020
Jun 93	US	0.03	0.00	47,419	4,526

				Synopsis:
Preferred Div. Coverage	np	np	np	
Total Div. Coverage	na	na	na	
Interest Coverage	5.2	2.6	1.9	
Current Ratio	2.9	0.9	0.6	
Operating Margin	5.2	18.5	20.5	
Asset Turnover	0.3	0.4	0.4	
5 YEAR RATIOS (%)				
Return on Capital	8.6	5.6	5.3	
Return on Com. Equity	6.8	4.4	5.2	
Profit Growth	55.0	7.0	na	
Revenue Growth	117.1	48.1	111.0	
Asset Growth	47.6	11.2	33.6	
BALANCE SHEET (000)				
Cash	122,154	24,207	16,395	
Current Assets	182,749	60,360	49,938	
Net Fixed Assets	339,068	322,035	347,464	
Invest's & Advances	0	0	0	
Total Assets	540,398	393,418	413,862	
Short Term Debt	32,743	53,044	65,352	
Current Liabilities	63,865	70,025	86,522	
Long Term Debt	47,815	75,482	97,166	
Total Liabilities	140,090	173,860	213,932	
Total Equity	400,308	219,558	199,930	
Total Liab. & Equity	540,398	393,418	413,862	
CAPITAL (000)				
Total Debt	80,558	128,526	162,518	
Preferred Equity	0	0	0	
Common Equity	400,308	219,558	199,930	

Synopsis:

In May 1995, TVX Gold told shareholders at the company's annual meeting that gold production should reach one million ounces by 1998. TVX Gold expects this milestone to be achieved at a cash cost of $170 (U.S.) per ounce of gold recovered. The company said they expect to reach the one million level by expansion and acquisition of new resources worldwide.

In March 1995, TVX Gold completed the purchase of Greece-based Kassandra Mines. TVX paid $47-million (U.S.) for the 314 square kilometre concession and plans to spend another $180-million (U.S.) to construct a gold processing plant. Reserves at the time of the agreement totalled 14 million tonnes averaging 3% lead, 4% zinc, 6.3 grams gold and 100 grams silver. The property also has a stockpile of 250,000 tonnes of ore grading 22.65 grams gold and another stockpile with three million tonnes of tailings which average up to three grams gold. TVX Gold estimates that when the Kassandra project is operational, it should yield more than 190,000 ounces of gold in its first year of operation. Once capacity is maximized at Kassandra, the mine should produce 300,000 ounces of gold annually.

In February 1995, TVX Gold increased its investment in two separate projects. TVX Gold purchased a 10.3% interest in the Brasilia mine for $14-million (U.S.). The mine is located in Brazil. In 1994, gold production at Brasilia totalled 168,000 ounces at an average cash cost of $196 (U.S.) per ounce. TVX Gold also acquired a 9.5% equity interest in the Kasperske Hory project in the Czech Republic. TVX Gold now owns 100% of that project. Exploration and development activities are being carried out at the property.

For the first quarter ended March 31, 1995, TVX Gold produced 102,800 ounces of gold equivalent. This was down slightly from the 110,410 ounces it produced in the same period last year. The company's cash cost rose to $225 (U.S.) per ounce in the first quarter, up from $193 (U.S.) in 1994 quarter.

Relative strength to TSE300

Price

Volume (in 1000's of board lots)

Rank (Profit/Revenue/Assets)
152   281   181
Eike F. Batista Chairman & C.E.O.
John W.W. Hick President & C.F.O.
L. Rogerio Berto C.F.O.

Address
Suite 4300
161 Bay Street
Toronto
ON
M5J 2S1
(416) 366-8160

Fax: (416) 366-8163
T0009889/G/2.0

UNITED KENO HILL MINES LIMITED

Exchanges	Price (Jun29'95)		2.30	Trailing P/E		nm	Stock Symbol
T	Trailing Yield (%)		0.00	Trailing EPS		(0.27)	**UKH**

Period Ending	Dec94	Dec93	Dec92	Dec91	Dec90
Yearly Statistics					
Price-Close	2.00	3.70	0.45	0.55	1.00
Price-High	3.95	4.95	0.96	1.50	3.65
Price-Low	1.80	0.40	0.40	0.40	0.90
P/E-Close	nm	7.26	nm	nm	nm
Dividends per Share	0.00	0.00	0.00	0.00	0.00
Dividend Yield (%)	0.00	0.00	0.00	0.00	0.00
Sales per Share	na	na	na	na	na
EPS before extra. item	(0.30)	0.51	(0.20)	(0.05)	(0.43)
Cash Flow per Share	(0.23)	0.54	(0.23)	(0.29)	(0.36)
Book Value per Share	0.88	0.87	0.37	0.56	0.61
O/S Common Shares	10,296	7,129	7,129	7,129	7,129
Total Revenue	968	2,006	459	2,014	703
Income before extra.	(2,168)	3,629	(1,414)	(350)	(3,041)
Cash Flow	(2,039)	3,824	(1,637)	(2,069)	(2,564)
Debt/Equity	0.50	4.23	0.83	0.22	0.31
Return on Capital (%)	(4.15)	(2.89)	(26.70)	(6.59)	(46.31)
Ret. on Com. Equity (%)	(28.32)	82.21	(42.76)	(8.36)	(51.68)
% Change Profit	(159.7)	356.6	(304.0)	88.5	46.1
% Change Revenue	(51.7)	337.0	(77.2)	186.5	(70.8)
% Change Assets	(58.9)	609.0	(4.9)	(27.6)	4.0

	Date	EPS	DPS	Tot Rev	Inc Bex
	Mar 95	(0.05)	0.00	59	(493)
	Dec 94	0.35	0.00	442	2,452
	Sep 94	(0.38)	0.00	220	(2,729)
	Jun 94	(0.19)	0.00	630	(1,363)
	Mar 94	(0.06)	0.00	24	(404)
	Dec 93	0.46	0.00	38	3,264
	Sep 93	(0.09)	0.00	37	(612)
	Jun 93	0.20	0.00	1,914	1,389

Preferred Div. Coverage	na	na	np	
Total Div. Coverage	na	na	na	
Interest Coverage	0.0	0.0	0.0	
Current Ratio	4.8	1.3	0.2	
Operating Margin	na	na	na	
Asset Turnover	na	na	na	
5 YEAR RATIOS (%)				
Return on Capital	(17.3)	(33.8)	(61.1)	
Return on Com. Equity	(9.8)	(30.4)	(83.4)	
Profit Growth	na	na	na	
Revenue Growth	(16.7)	(35.8)	(53.8)	
Asset Growth	15.9	25.9	(17.7)	
BALANCE SHEET (000)				
Cash	2,930	3,868	0	
Current Assets	6,042	6,021	445	
Net Fixed Assets	8,844	4,814	5,015	
Invest's & Advances	918	28,530	0	
Total Assets	16,242	39,470	5,567	
Short Term Debt	0	3,301	2,169	
Current Liabilities	1,247	4,693	2,967	
Long Term Debt	5,000	27,500	0	
Total Liabilities	6,247	32,193	2,967	
Total Equity	9,995	7,277	2,600	
Total Liab. & Equity	16,242	39,470	5,567	
CAPITAL (000)				
Total Debt	5,000	30,801	2,169	
Preferred Equity	912	1,048	0	
Common Equity	9,083	6,229	2,600	

Business:

UNITED KENO HILL MINES LTD. is a silver and lead mining company. It has operations in the Mayo district of the Yukon. 44.9% of the company's common shares are owned by The Dominion Mineral Resources and Sterling Frontier Properties Company of Canada Limited.

Synopsis:

At its May 1995 annual meeting United Keno Mine released preliminary estimates for the Bellekeno, Silver King and Husky Southwest Mines. The results indicated that the Elsa Properties have advanced to 428,500 tons grading 34.1 ounces of silver per ton, 7.86% lead, and 5.27% zinc. As a result of exploration activities on the properties, total available, measured, indicated, and inferred mine resources present at the Elsa Properties now total over 640,000 tons grading 30.11 ounces of silver, 6% lead, and 6% zinc. These results indicate the highest concentration of minerals United Keno has ever explored.

At the end of 1994, United Keno issued 500 flow-through units as well as $5-million in convertible debentures. The debentures have a face value of 9% and are due December 1999. United Keno said the proceeds from the offering will be used to fund ongoing exploration activities in connection with United Keno's Reserve Development Strategy for its Elsa Properties.

During the 1994 and the first quarter of 1995, silver prices have risen. The average price of silver in 1994 was 22.5% higher than the average price in 1993. At the end of March 1995, the price of silver had climbed to over $5 (U.S.) an ounce with prices topping $6 (U.S.) per ounce of silver for a brief spell in mid-April. Recent statistics indicate demand for silver in the future should remain fundamentally strong in medium term.

United Keno's future depends on the future price of silver to sustain ongoing commercial silver production. The company's future is also contingent on United Keno's ability to locate and develop minable resources.

Rank (Profit/Revenue/Assets)
860   946   929

Stephen F. Powell
Chairman President & C.E.O.
J.W. Curran
V.P. C.F.O. & Treasurer

Address
196 Adelaide Street West
Toronto
ON
M5H 1W7
(416) 351-1762

Fax: (416) 351-1766
U0001293/G/2.0

VENGOLD INC.

Exchanges	Price (Jun29'95)	2.20	Trailing P/E	12.94	Stock Symbol
TVQ	Trailing Yield (%)	0.00	Trailing EPS	9.54	**VEN**

Period Ending	Dec94	Dec93	Dec92	Dec91
Yearly Statistics	US	US	US	
Price-Close	3.15	12.50	4.95	0.25
Price-High	15.00	15.00	5.00	0.65
Price-Low	2.26	6.50	0.19	0.21
P/E-Close	15.37	nm	nm	nm
Dividends per Share	0.00	0.00	0.00	0.00
Dividend Yield (%)	0.00	0.00	0.00	0.00
Sales per Share	na	na	na	0.00
EPS before extra. item	0.15	(0.35)	(0.09)	(0.00)
Cash Flow per Share	(0.35)	(0.35)	(0.09)	(0.00)
Book Value per Share	2.57	2.39	0.19	(0.01)
O/S Common Shares	21,867	20,816	7,183	3,952
Total Revenue	11,252	333	11	0
Income before extra.	3,359	(5,265)	(486)	(7)
Cash Flow	(7,610)	(5,265)	(486)	(7)
Debt/Equity	0.02	0.05	0.62	na
Return on Capital (%)	6.57	(18.23)	(42.65)	na
Ret. on Com. Equity (%)	6.34	(20.63)	(69.88)	na
% Change Profit	163.8	(983.3)	(8,422.9)	na
% Change Revenue	3,279.0	2,941.3	na	na
% Change Assets	10.1	2,142.0	nm	na
Preferred Div. Coverage	np	np	np	
Total Div. Coverage	na	na	na	
Interest Coverage	15.1	0.0	na	
Current Ratio	9.9	3.1	1.5	
Operating Margin	na	na	na	
Asset Turnover	na	na	na	
5 YEAR RATIOS (%)				
Return on Capital	na	na	na	
Return on Com. Equity	na	na	na	
Profit Growth	na	na	na	
Revenue Growth	na	na	na	
Asset Growth	na	na	na	
BALANCE SHEET (000)				
Cash	11,321	6,265	877	
Current Assets	11,402	6,370	891	
Net Fixed Assets	45,924	42,288	1,466	
Invest's & Advances	487	4,027	0	
Total Assets	58,179	52,847	2,357	
Short Term Debt	550	1,134	420	
Current Liabilities	1,152	2,049	591	
Long Term Debt	733	1,100	420	
Total Liabilities	1,885	3,149	1,011	
Total Equity	56,294	49,698	1,346	
Total Liab. & Equity	58,179	52,847	2,357	
CAPITAL (000)				
Total Debt	1,283	2,234	840	
Preferred Equity	0	0	0	
Common Equity	56,294	49,698	1,346	

Business:

VENGOLD INC. is involved in the acquisition, exploration and development of precious metal properties in Latin America and Papua New Guinea.

Date		EPS	DPS	Tot Rev	Inc Bex
Mar 95	US	(0.06)	0.00	88	(1,393)
Dec 94	US	(0.04)	0.00	155	(759)
Sep 94	US	(0.03)	0.00	1,860	(709)
Jun 94	US	0.30	0.00	9,213	6,520
Mar 94	US	(0.08)	0.00	25	(1,692)
Dec 93	US	(0.06)	0.00	248	(1,439)
Sep 93	US	(0.11)	0.00	18	(1,737)
Jun 93	US	(0.12)	0.00	(10)	(1,454)

Synopsis:

During the first quarter of 1995, Vengold Inc. signed an agreement to buy a 10% interest in the Lihir Gold project from RTZ Corporation PLC of London, England. Lihir is located on a tiny island in the Pacific Ocean, northeast of Papua New Guinea. Vengold paid $50-million (U.S.) for the 10% interest in the world's largest undeveloped gold deposit. There are plans to build a $671-million (U.S.) gold mine at Lihir with initial production scheduled for 1997. Lihir should produce 625,000 ounces of gold in its first three years of operation. Following that, an expansion program should increase annual production to about one million ounces of gold per year. Vengold expects that the Lihir project will have a cash production cost of approximately $211 (U.S.) per ounce of gold produced.

Reserves at Lihir are estimated at over 42 million contained ounces of gold. Twenty-one million ounces are classified as proven and probable reserves. Vengold expects that at 600,000 ounces of gold produced every year the new mine will have a life of 37 years. The size of the gold deposit compares to the Barrick mine in Nevada. Reserves at Barrick total 44 million contained ounces of gold.

In June 1995, a group of underwriters agreed to buy 26 million units from Vengold for $45-million (U.S.). Each unit consists of one common share and one-half share-purchase warrant. Each unit is priced at $1.75. The group included First Marathon Securities, Midland Walwyn Capital, Wood Gundy, Yorkton Securities, Goepel Shields and BZW Canada Ltd.

In April 1995, Vengold announced that preliminary results from the Bizkaitarra gold concession were positive. Five of six drill holes revealed significant intersections including one hole that graded 40 grams of gold per ton. Vengold has an option to earn a 65% interest in the property.

Rank (Profit/Revenue/Assets)
437 751 529

John Walton
Chairman

Ian W. Telfer
President & C.E.O.

Glenn A. Ives
V.P. Finance & C.F.O.

Address
Suite 1788
200 Burrard Street
Vancouver
BC
V6C 3L6
(604) 664-7050

Fax: (604) 681-9151
01003381/G/2.0

VICEROY RESOURCE CORPORATION

Exchanges	Price (Jun29'95)		7.00	Trailing P/E			14.00	Stock Symbol
TV	Trailing Yield (%)		0.00	Trailing EPS			0.50	VOY

Period Ending	Mar95	Mar94	Mar93	Mar92	Mar91
Yearly Statistics					
Price-Close	7.13	11.50	7.50	4.30	4.25
Price-High	11.88	13.00	7.63	5.50	6.00
Price-Low	6.13	6.13	3.75	2.90	3.55
P/E-Close	14.25	23.00	25.00	nm	nm
Dividends per Share	0.00	0.00	0.00	0.00	0.00
Dividend Yield (%)	0.00	0.00	0.00	0.00	0.00
Sales per Share	3.03	2.65	1.95	na	na
EPS before extra. item	0.50	0.50	0.30	(0.10)	(0.06)
Cash Flow per Share	1.49	0.99	0.68	(0.09)	(0.05)
Book Value per Share	4.48	3.98	2.68	2.14	2.01
O/S Common Shares	23,380	23,255	18,738	17,732	15,712
Total Revenue	72,970	61,147	36,166	504	585
Income before extra.	11,559	11,253	5,478	(1,688)	(909)
Cash Flow	34,950	22,050	12,352	(1,571)	(823)
Debt/Equity	0.02	0.33	0.66	0.83	nd
Return on Capital (%)	12.88	12.47	8.71	(3.36)	(2.22)
Ret. on Com. Equity (%)	11.72	15.77	12.45	(4.86)	(2.57)
% Change Profit	2.7	105.4	424.5	(85.7)	(500.6)
% Change Revenue	19.3	69.1	7,075.8	(13.8)	(44.9)
% Change Assets	(13.0)	44.9	21.2	121.7	(35.5)
Preferred Div. Coverage	np	np	np
Total Div. Coverage	na	na	na
Interest Coverage	31.9	11.8	7.2
Current Ratio	6.6	2.5	1.3
Operating Margin	21.1	18.4	16.8
Asset Turnover	0.6	0.5	0.4
5 YEAR RATIOS (%)			
Return on Capital	5.7	3.1	0.9
Return on Com. Equity	6.5	4.1	1.3
Profit Growth	na	69.7	64.1
Revenue Growth	133.1	108.3	98.7
Asset Growth	16.9	20.5	17.1
BALANCE SHEET (000)			
Cash	22,026	28,742	6,049
Current Assets	37,329	41,955	14,525
Net Fixed Assets	66,537	81,624	71,593
Invest's & Advances	6,871	3,679	0
Total Assets	111,552	128,192	88,495
Short Term Debt	1,831	12,594	6,428
Current Liabilities	5,698	16,929	11,226
Long Term Debt	0	17,930	26,798
Total Liabilities	6,885	35,615	38,344
Total Equity	104,667	92,577	50,151
Total Liab. & Equity	111,552	128,192	88,495
CAPITAL (000)			
Total Debt	1,831	30,524	33,226
Preferred Equity	0	0	0
Common Equity	104,667	92,577	50,151

Business:

VICEROY RESOURCE CORP. is a gold exploration and mining company. Its wholly owned subsidiary, Viceroy Gold Corp. of Las Vegas, is the operator of the Castle Mountain Gold Project in San Bernardino County, California. Output for the current fiscal year is forecast to exceed 160,000 ounces.

Date	EPS	DPS	Tot Rev	Inc Bex
Mar 95	0.09	0.00	19,463	1,949
Dec 94	0.14	0.00	18,849	3,417
Sep 94	0.13	0.00	17,470	2,877
Jun 94	0.14	0.00	17,188	3,316
Mar 94	0.14	0.00	18,756	3,319
Dec 93	0.12	0.00	14,775	2,642
Sep 93	0.12	0.00	14,468	2,764
Jun 93	0.12	0.00	13,148	2,528

Synopsis:

In April 1995, Viceroy Resources eliminated its gold loan 14 months ahead of schedule. Gold shipments from Viceroy's 75% interest in Castle Mountain were cited for the reason the company was able to reduce its debt so fast. Since the Castle Mountain mine opened in 1992, it has produced over 400,000 ounces of gold. This gold production has allowed Viceroy to pay back about $42-million (U.S.) in debt in three years. Viceroy has plans to develop the area surrounding Castle Mountain in an effort to expand the mine's life.

In early 1995, Viceroy Resources obtained the right to earn a 50% interest in a mine in Argentina. To earn the interest in Minas Argentinas, Viceroy must spend $3-million (U.S.) on exploration activities and additional property acquisitions by June 30, 1996. With the purchase of the property in Argentina, Viceroy gained a valuable foothold in a country where exploration activities are growing very rapidly.

As a result of higher grades of gold concentrate, Viceroy reported in the third quarter ended December 31, 1994, that gold production Castle Mountain was 20% higher than last year's figure. In the three month period, Castle Mountain produced 43,993 ounces of gold at a cash cost of $132 (U.S.) per ounce of gold. This represents a record low cash cost for Viceroy in the period and compares to $203 (U.S.) in the three month ended December 31, 1993.

In overseas exploration activities, Viceroy's 30% owned Channel Resources continues drill on the gold concession in Burkina Faso, West Africa. Through Viceroy's 26% owned Pacific Wildcat Resources, Viceroy is awaiting approval on two gold properties in Indonesia. Viceroy has also set up an office in Argentina to explore possible opportunities there.

Relative strength to TSE300

Price

Volume (in 1000's of board lots)

Rank (Profit/Revenue/Assets)
279   504   431

D. Ross Fitzpatrick
President & C.E.O.

Brian Flower
Senior Vice President

Address
Suite 880
999 West Hastings Street
Vancouver
BC
V6C 2W2
(604) 688-9780

Fax: (604) 682-3941
V0003263/G/2.0

WHARF RESOURCES LTD.

Exchanges	Price (Jun29'95)		11.25	Trailing P/E		17.64	Stock Symbol
TQ	Trailing Yield (%)		1.21	Trailing EPS		0.47	WFR

Period Ending	Dec94	Dec93	Dec92	Dec91	Dec90
Yearly Statistics	US	US	US	US	US
Price-Close	12.25	13.38	6.25	5.75	5.63
Price-High	13.75	14.25	6.75	6.38	7.25
Price-Low	9.50	5.50	5.00	4.75	5.00
P/E-Close	12.32	30.77	18.43	13.28	nm
Dividends per Share	0.10	0.10	0.10	0.30	0.00
Dividend Yield (%)	1.12	0.97	1.94	5.98	0.00
Sales per Share	2.88	2.31	1.93	1.90	1.56
EPS before extra. item	0.53	0.26	0.23	0.33	(0.33)
Cash Flow per Share	1.02	0.66	0.54	0.65	0.55
Book Value per Share	3.14	2.70	2.51	2.39	2.36
O/S Common Shares	19,229	19,229	18,951	18,941	18,941
Total Revenue	57,428	44,910	37,714	37,948	31,207
Income before extra.	10,378	5,246	4,643	6,641	(5,822)
Cash Flow	19,624	12,566	10,309	12,323	10,386
Debt/Equity	0.15	0.28	0.32	0.02	0.02
Return on Capital (%)	20.37	11.30	10.55	16.52	(7.96)
Ret. on Com. Equity (%)	18.22	9.82	9.20	13.89	(13.09)
% Change Profit	97.8	13.0	(30.1)	214.1	(197.5)
% Change Revenue	27.9	19.1	(0.6)	21.6	(1.5)
% Change Assets	1.0	0.6	41.0	2.5	(11.4)
Preferred Div. Coverage	69.2	14.9	12.5		
Total Div. Coverage	5.0	2.3	2.0		
Interest Coverage	14.6	7.1	30.3		
Current Ratio	3.6	1.8	1.2		
Operating Margin	22.4	16.0	14.2		
Asset Turnover	0.7	0.6	0.5		
5 YEAR RATIOS (%)					
Return on Capital	10.2	9.2	11.3		
Return on Com. Equity	7.6	6.4	8.5		
Profit Growth	11.7	(7.8)	1.7		
Revenue Growth	12.6	10.9	11.8		
Asset Growth	5.4	8.9	12.9		
BALANCE SHEET (000)					
Cash	19,831	12,367	7,615		
Current Assets	30,765	23,258	15,716		
Net Fixed Assets	46,443	52,008	56,166		
Invest's & Advances	0	0	3,731		
Total Assets	79,492	78,679	78,226		
Short Term Debt	3,575	6,023	5,908		
Current Liabilities	8,603	12,596	13,132		
Long Term Debt	5,649	9,206	10,619		
Total Liabilities	16,553	23,935	26,186		
Total Equity	62,939	54,744	52,040		
Total Liab. & Equity	79,492	78,679	78,226		
CAPITAL (000)					
Total Debt	9,224	15,229	16,527		
Preferred Equity	2,625	2,765	4,394		
Common Equity	60,314	51,979	47,646		

Business:

WHARF RESOURCES LTD. is engaged primarily in the business of gold exploration and mining in the western United States. Wharf operates two adjoining open pit, heap leach gold mines in South Dakota: the 100% owned Wharf Mine and the 60% owned Golden Reward Mine. Goldcorp Inc. owns 50.3% of its common shares.

Date		EPS	DPS	Tot Rev	Inc Bex
Mar 95	US	0.06	0.00	12,710	1,194
Dec 94	US	0.11	0.05	13,222	2,285
Sep 94	US	0.14	0.00	17,430	2,642
Jun 94	US	0.16	0.05	15,019	3,038
Mar 94	US	0.12	0.00	11,757	2,413
Dec 93	US	0.10	0.05	12,318	2,019
Sep 93	US	0.09	0.00	13,008	1,794
Jun 93	US	0.06	0.05	11,322	1,247

Synopsis:

For the first quarter ended March 31, 1995, Wharf Resources reported lower earnings despite an increase in the amount of gold produced. Wharf's share of gold production in first quarter 1995 was 29,278 ounces, up from 25,850 ounces in the same period last year. The lower earnings were due to an increase in the weighted average cash production of an ounce of gold. During the first quarter, the average cash production cost for an ounce of gold was $242 (U.S.), up $42 (U.S.) from the same period last year.

Wharf Resources has two operating mines, the Wharf mine and the Golden Reward mine. In the first quarter of 1995, the Wharf mine produced over 23,000 ounces of gold, an increase of about 2,500 ounces of gold over last year's total. However, higher costs at the mine nullified the effects of increased gold production. During the first quarter of 1995, the Wharf mine's cash production cost was $244 (U.S.), up from $181 (U.S.) in 1994. The company attributed the increased production costs to lower grade ore milled during the period. The Wharf mine should produce about 103,000 ounces of gold in 1995.

Production figures in the first quarter of 1995 at the Golden Reward mine improved. The production cost of an ounce of gold declined, too. Wharf has a 60% interest in the mine. During the quarter, Golden Reward produced 10,265 ounces of gold, a 16% increase over the first quarter of 1994. The cash production cost per ounce of gold dropped to $237 (U.S.) during the quarter from $289 (U.S.) in 1994. The Golden Reward mine should produce 45,000 ounces of gold in 1995.

Currently, Wharf Resources operates exclusively in the Untied States. Its operations include exploration, development and processing of precious metals.

Relative strength to TSE300 / Price / Volume (in 1000's of board lots)

Rank (Profit/Revenue/Assets)
250   459   460

Robert R. McEwen
Chairman President & C.E.O.
Rolando C. Francisco
Sr. V.P. & C.F.O.

Address
Suite 2700
145 King Street West
Toronto
ON
M5H 1J8
(416) 361-0402

Fax: (416) 361-5741
W0002465/G/2.0

Page	Company		Fiscal year end	EARNINGS] Last Year	Estim this yea	
71	Alberta Energy		Dec-94	1.34	1.44	1.50
72	Anderson Exploration		Sep-94	0.45	0.31	0.45
73	Archer Resources		Dec-94	0.50	0.05	0.23
74	Atcor Resources		Dec-94	0.12	0.09	0.12
75	Barrington Petroleum		Dec-94	0.29	0.23	0.36
76	Beau Canada Exploration		Dec-94	0.10	0.14	0.16
77	Cabre Exploration		Jul-94	0.60	0.62	0.90
78	Canada Southern Petroleum		Dec-94	(0.10)	na	na
79	Canadian Fracmaster		Dec-94	0.86	0.74	1.01
80	Canadian Natural Resources		Dec-94	0.85	0.76	1.01
81	Canadian Occidental Peteroleum		Dec-94	1.44	1.95	2.29
82	Chauvco Resources		Dec-94	0.65	0.79	0.91
83	Chieftain International	$US	Dec-94	(0.43)	(0.31)	0.04
84	Cimarron Petroleum		Dec-94	0.55	0.58	0.77
85	Coho Energy	$US	Dec-94	(0.12)	na	na
86	Computalog		Dec-94	1.10	1.06	1.33
87	Consolidated Ramrod Gold		Jun-94	(0.33)	na	na
88	Conwest Exploration		Dec-94	1.38	0.71	1.28
89	Crestar Energy		Dec-94	0.52	0.09	0.51
90	CS Resources		Dec-94	0.23	0.45	0.69
91	Czar Resources		Dec-94	0.22	0.11	0.15
92	Discovery West		Dec-94	0.52	0.27	0.36
93	Dorset Exploration		Dec-94	0.32	0.44	0.50
94	Dreco Energy Services		Aug-94	0.89	1.37	1.52
95	Elan Energy		Dec-94	0.21	0.42	0.55
96	Encal Energy		Dec-94	0.06	0.04	0.08
97	Enserv		Dec-94	1.60	1.30	1.41
98	Ensign Resource Service Group		Dec-94	1.06	0.95	1.06
99	Excel Energy		Dec-94	(0.91)	na	na
100	Grad & Walker Energy		Dec-94	0.28	0.17	0.41
101	Gulf Canada Resources		Dec-94	(1.36)	(0.19)	0.10
102	Home Oil		Dec-94	0.18	0.09	0.25
103	Horsham	$US	Dec-94	0.35	0.63	0.85
104	Imperial Oil		Dec-94	2.04	3.04	3.48
105	Intensity Resources		Dec-94	0.14	0.19	0.21
106	International Colin Energy		Dec-94	0.70	0.41	0.58
107	International Petroleum		Sep-94	0.12	0.39	0.19
108	Inverness Petroleum		Dec-94	0.33	0.14	0.44
109	Jordan Petroleum		Nov-94	0.41	0.39	0.52
110	Manville Oil & Gas		Dec-94	0.09	0.00	0.10
111	Mark Resources		Dec-94	0.25	0.22	0.27
112	Morgan Hydrocarbons		Dec-94	(0.47)	0.17	0.23
113	Morrison Petroleums		Dec-94	0.35	0.35	0.40
114	Norcen Engery Resources		Dec-94	0.28	0.39	0.54
115	Northrock Resources		Dec-94	0.36	0.41	0.60
116	Northstar Energy		Dec-94	0.61	0.49	0.70
117	Nowsco Well Services		Dec-94	1.41	0.90	1.07
118	Numac Oil & Gas		Dec-94	0.28	0.18	0.17
119	Ocelot Energy		Dec-94	0.50	0.61	0.68
120	Omega Hydrocarbons		Dec-94	0.02	na	na
121	PanCanadian Petroleum		Dec-94	2.30	2.59	3.01
122	Paramount Resources		Dec-94	0.73	0.46	0.61
124	Pe Ben Oilfield Services		Dec-94	0.39	na	na
123	Penn West Petroleum		Dec-94	0.28	0.28	0.42
125	Petro-Canada		Dec-94	0.90	0.89	1.13
126	Petromet Resources		Dec-94	0.04	0.25	0.36
127	Pinnacle Resources		Dec-94	0.58	0.56	0.78
128	Poco Petroleums		Dec-94	0.15	0.10	0.16
129	Precision Drilling		Apr-94	1.02	1.95	1.68
130	Ranchmen's Resources		Dec-94	0.09	0.33	0.47
131	Ranger Oil		Dec-94	0.06	0.12	0.22
132	Renaissance Energy		Dec-94	0.70	0.76	1.08
133	Rigel Energy		Dec-94	0.74	0.60	0.76
134	Rio Alto Exploration		Dec-94	0.41	0.34	0.48
135	Sceptre Resources		Dec-94	0.43	0.41	0.49
136	Serenpet		Dec-94	0.27	0.22	0.30
137	Shell Canada		Dec-94	2.85	3.79	3.84
138	Stampeder Exploration		Dec-94	0.23	0.38	0.42
139	Summit Resources		Dec-94	0.39	0.33	0.46
140	Suncor		Dec-94	2.22	2.74	3.19
141	Talisman Energy		Dec-94	0.74	0.66	0.90
142	Tarragon Oil and Gas		Dec-94	0.71	0.49	0.70
143	Total Petroleum (North America)	$US	Dec-94	0.44	0.35	0.92
144	Transwest Energy		Dec-94	0.11	0.02	0.09
145	Tri Link Resources		Mar-95	0.46	0.54	0.89
146	Ulster Petroleums		Dec-94	0.17	0.18	0.25
147	Wascana Energy		Dec-94	0.61	0.28	0.41

Estimates from First Call Corporation, 22 Pittsburgh Street, Boston, MA 02210   (800) 366-9992   Fax (617) 261-5679

.fter near-record levels of investment and exploration in 1994, the Toronto Stock Exchange's oil and gas services sub-index fell 40% between September 1994 and March 1995. Reasons cited for the decline included the warm 1994/95 North American winter and increased supplies resulting from the number of wells drilled in 1994.

Although companies have reduced capital spending plans for 1995, oil prices have rebound from mid-winter lows, and gas prices have also moved upwards.

Oil prices have been volatile recently due to labour tensions in a number of producing countries and to continuing U.S. led boycotts of Libya and Iran. Even though OPEC production currently is above its quota, there is speculation that the organization may remove or increase its quota over the next year to increase its share of total demand. This move would be aimed at non-OPEC producing countries because they have been meeting most of the recent increases in world demand. However, any subsequent drop in prices likely would regulate this trend.

Part of the Spring 1995 price increase in West Texas Intermediate was due to shrinking gasoline supplies. Analysts believe gasoline levels were leading crude prices upwards. There is a great deal of uncertainty in the gasoline refinement sector as the U.S. Clean Air Act amendment comes into effect. The act requires use of reformulated gasoline A number of states in the U.S. already have decided to opt out of the program, and this has stymied demand forecasts for gasoline production. Overall, the industry expects crude oil prices in real terms to remain relatively flat over the next two to three years.

Gas prices also suffered from the warm North American winter. While this affected quarterly performance, prices have partially recovered. There are several other factors that will improve the gas outlook. Despite record drilling levels in 1994, the Alberta Energy and Utilities Board reported that only 62% of the previous year's production was replaced. This bodes well for reduced levels of gas supply.

U.S. electric energy producers apparently are favouring the use of natural gas cogeneration power plants over purchases of hydraulically produced power from Canada. The industry expects several of the U.S. electric generating capacity additions over the next decade to be thermal plants using natural gas and coal.

Oil and gas distribution companies are expected to perform strongly in 1995, in the stock market and in terms of earnings. The National Energy Board, (NEB), recently ruled that Trans Canada Pipelines and Westcoast Energy may increase their rates of return as a percentage of their equities. It is allowing an average increase of 12.25%.

The NEB also is considering increasing the regulation time-frame from annual hearings to one hearing every third year, with the setting of yields each year. This will reduce significantly the regulatory costs for these companies and increase their earnings.

The TSE's oil and gas services index rebounded beginning in February although a number of listings have remained under-valued according to analysts.

Although the outlook for the Canadian oil and gas industry remains mixed, many companies currently have healthy balance sheets and should sustain their 1994 earnings' levels.

ALBERTA ENERGY COMPANY LTD.

Exchanges	Price (Jun29'95)		20.50	Trailing P/E		14.14	Stock Symbol
TMVZ	Trailing Yield (%)		1.95	Trailing EPS		1.45	**AEC**

Period Ending	Dec94	Dec93	Dec92	Dec91	Dec90
Yearly Statistics					
Price-Close	17.88	18.50	16.25	12.50	16.88
Price-High	22.75	23.63	17.00	16.88	20.25
Price-Low	17.50	15.50	9.75	11.50	15.50
P/E-Close	13.14	15.04	30.66	104.17	23.44
Dividends per Share	0.40	0.35	0.35	0.33	0.33
Dividend Yield (%)	2.24	1.89	2.15	2.64	1.96
Sales per Share	12.87	10.57	8.25	7.68	8.48
EPS before extra. item	1.36	1.23	0.53	0.12	0.72
Cash Flow per Share	4.11	3.61	3.27	2.46	3.08
Book Value per Share	14.26	12.93	11.99	11.74	11.94
O/S Common Shares	74,464	69,993	69,389	68,026	66,785
Total Revenue	931,600	751,600	570,300	519,600	565,400
Income before extra.	100,500	91,600	42,200	13,800	53,600
Cash Flow	294,800	251,400	225,300	165,800	204,000
Debt/Equity	0.56	0.57	0.50	0.72	0.73
Return on Capital (%)	13.08	12.38	6.13	4.65	9.73
Ret. on Com. Equity (%)	9.92	9.88	4.47	1.00	6.15
% Change Profit	9.7	117.1	205.8	(74.3)	43.7
% Change Revenue	23.9	31.8	9.8	(8.1)	10.6
% Change Assets	5.9	15.1	(6.3)	(0.9)	3.9

Date	EPS	DPS	Tot Rev	Inc Bex
Mar 95	0.32	0.00	236,600	24,200
Dec 94	0.25	0.00	398,800	19,400
Sep 94	0.59	0.00	194,000	41,600
Jun 94	0.29	0.40	177,300	22,300
Mar 94	0.23	0.00	224,100	17,200
Dec 93	0.50	0.00	321,000	36,200
Sep 93	0.31	0.00	160,700	23,200
Jun 93	0.29	0.35	140,800	21,600

Preferred Div. Coverage	np	15.8	7.3
Total Div. Coverage	3.2	3.0	1.4
Interest Coverage	5.8	6.4	2.5
Current Ratio	1.0	1.1	1.2
Operating Margin	25.6	23.2	20.8
Asset Turnover	0.4	0.3	0.3
5 YEAR RATIOS (%)			
Return on Capital	9.2	8.3	7.4
Return on Com. Equity	6.3	5.2	4.2
Profit Growth	21.9	20.5	(7.0)
Revenue Growth	12.7	9.2	3.8
Asset Growth	3.3	2.8	0.7
BALANCE SHEET (000)			
Cash	23,700	81,400	16,600
Current Assets	245,200	251,700	123,100
Net Fixed Assets	2,017,700	1,815,300	1,576,900
Invest's & Advances	63,200	111,200	194,200
Total Assets	2,357,600	2,225,500	1,932,900
Short Term Debt	34,200	28,100	2,900
Current Liabilities	240,500	232,200	104,900
Long Term Debt	561,800	528,200	449,600
Total Liabilities	1,295,700	1,245,800	1,025,800
Total Equity	1,061,900	979,700	907,100
Total Liab. & Equity	2,357,600	2,225,500	1,932,900
CAPITAL (000)			
Total Debt	596,000	556,300	452,500
Preferred Equity	0	75,000	75,000
Common Equity	1,061,900	904,700	832,100

Business:

ALBERTA ENERGY CO. LTD. participates in oil and gas exploration, production, marketing, storage and pipeline transportation.

Synopsis:

According to Alberta Energy Company Ltd.'s senior management, there will be continued rationalization in the oil and gas industry due to depressed natural gas prices. The past two years have seen rapid growth of equity investments in junior and intermediate companies, but management believes that the balance of this century will be dominated by high performance senior oil and gas producers.

The company's strong operating performance for the first quarter 1995, as compared to the same period in 1994, resulted from higher oil prices, higher lumber prices, and increases in daily crude oil and natural gas liquids sales volumes. The pipelines division contributed 21% of the company's operating income and the financial results of the forest products division showed improvement. These quarterly results were achieved despite a 24% decrease in its natural gas price. Reserve additions of more than 100 billion cubic feet equivalent resulted from an active first-quarter exploration and development drilling program.

Alberta Energy plans to spend $140-million in 1995 on exploration and development activities. About two-thirds of that amount will be dedicated to natural gas exploration and development with the balance invested in conventional oil. About $25-million will be invested in Syncrude, and another $25-million will be dedicated to higher-potential plays in Argentina. Alberta Energy continues to examine potential oil and gas and pipeline assets.

Rank (Profit/Revenue/Assets)
74   123   93

David E. Mitchell
Chairman

Gwyn Morgan
President & C.E.O.

John D. Watson
V.P. Finance & C.F.O.

Address
Suite 3900
421 - 7th Avenue S.W.
Calgary
AB
T2P 4K9
(403) 266-8111

Fax: (403) 266-8154
A0001293/G/3.2

ANDERSON EXPLORATION LTD.

Exchanges	Price (Jun29'95)	14.00	Trailing P/E	30.11	Stock Symbol
T	Trailing Yield (%)	0.00	Trailing EPS	0.47	AXL

Period Ending	Sep94	Sep93	Sep92	Sep91	Sep90	Business:
Yearly Statistics						ANDERSON EXPLORATION LTD. is an oil
Price-Close	15.38	16.50	6.44	5.63	9.19	and gas exploration and production company
Price-High	18.00	17.50	6.63	8.94	10.00	with emphasis placed on natural gas. It has
Price-Low	12.13	5.75	3.50	5.25	8.25	producing wells and exploration activities in
P/E-Close	34.17	50.00	80.47	38.79	25.52	western Canada, mainly Alberta.
Dividends per Share	0.00	0.00	0.00	0.00	0.00	
Dividend Yield (%)	0.00	0.00	0.00	0.00	0.00	
Sales per Share	3.87	3.02	2.38	2.29	2.27	
EPS before extra. item	0.45	0.33	0.08	0.15	0.36	
Cash Flow per Share	2.08	1.52	0.96	0.89	1.05	
Book Value per Share	7.22	5.59	4.74	4.66	4.98	
O/S Common Shares	56,920	49,374	41,409	41,129	36,666	

Total Revenue	209,169	136,791	95,599	94,377	88,837					
Income before extra.	24,167	14,965	3,208	5,971	13,209	**Date**	**EPS**	**DPS**	**Tot Rev**	**Inc Bex**
Cash Flow	112,243	68,828	38,661	36,264	38,188	Mar 95	0.05	0.00	58,436	2,840
Debt/Equity	0.22	0.33	0.78	0.38	0.41	Dec 94	0.10	0.00	59,848	5,544
Return on Capital (%)	12.21	9.85	6.13	10.08	15.35	Sep 94	0.27	0.00	53,911	4,936
Ret. on Com. Equity (%)	7.04	6.34	1.65	3.19	8.42	Jun 94	0.05	0.00	52,497	5,097
% Change Profit	61.5	366.5	(46.3)	(54.8)	20.2	Mar 94	0.14	0.00	53,193	7,527
% Change Revenue	52.9	43.1	1.3	6.2	26.8	Dec 93	0.14	0.00	50,344	6,607
% Change Assets	36.8	10.6	20.6	0.7	17.6	Sep 93	0.23	0.00	34,261	5,885
						Jun 93	0.04	0.00	36,157	3,955

				Synopsis:
Preferred Div. Coverage	np	np	np	
Total Div. Coverage	na	na	na	
Interest Coverage	6.3	3.5	1.7	
Current Ratio	0.6	0.7	1.2	
Operating Margin	25.3	25.7	19.4	
Asset Turnover	0.3	0.3	0.2	
5 YEAR RATIOS (%)				
Return on Capital	10.7	11.1	11.7	
Return on Com. Equity	5.3	5.7	5.7	
Profit Growth	17.1	15.5	(12.6)	
Revenue Growth	24.4	16.0	9.3	
Asset Growth	16.6	10.5	9.2	
BALANCE SHEET (000)				
Cash	137	671	0	
Current Assets	26,569	23,982	13,558	
Net Fixed Assets	659,805	477,573	439,777	
Invest's & Advances	0	0	0	
Total Assets	686,374	501,555	453,335	
Short Term Debt	0	0	205	
Current Liabilities	46,513	35,845	11,237	
Long Term Debt	90,972	91,000	153,000	
Total Liabilities	275,681	225,466	257,069	
Total Equity	410,693	276,089	196,266	
Total Liab. & Equity	686,374	501,555	453,335	
CAPITAL (000)				
Total Debt	90,972	91,000	153,205	
Preferred Equity	0	0	0	
Common Equity	410,693	276,089	196,266	

Synopsis:

In the first half of fiscal 1995, ending March 31, Anderson Exploration reported reduced earnings due primarily to lower gas prices. The company feels that increases in gas production in 1994 plus new efficiencies in the continental delivery system have created a slight supply-side surplus. That, coupled with a warm winter in the heavy consuming areas of the continent, resulted in weak gas prices. Because of the expectation of relatively low gas prices for the remainder of fiscal 1995, Anderson reduced its capital expenditure budget to $166-million from $196-million. It also deferred some gas projects until fiscal 1996, and is pursuing further development of the oil side of its business.

Anderson's cash flow from operations for the first half of fiscal 1995 increased 11% over 1994. The increase was production volume driven as the company continued to meet its natural gas and oil and liquids volume projections. Oil and liquids production increased to 10,330 barrels per day, while daily natural gas production increased to 297 million cubic feet. These increases resulted from development work on acquired properties and continuing start-up of newly completed projects.

1994 was highlighted by a $30-million acquisition of properties located in the Eaglesham area in the Peace River Arch region of Alberta. The properties, which include proven and probable reserves of seven million barrels of oil equivalent with 80% represented by gas, should replace 50% of the company's 1995 production.

During fiscal 1994 (1993), Anderson's average daily production consisted of 8,267 (5,957) barrels of oil and natural gas liquids, and 222 (160) million cubic feet of natural gas. At its September 1994 (1993) year-end, Anderson had 43.9 (28.4) million barrels of proven and probable oil and natural gas liquid reserves, and 1,378 (1,162) billion cubic feet of proven and probable natural gas reserves.

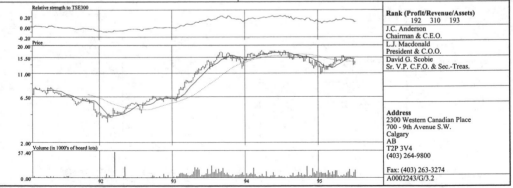

Rank (Profit/Revenue/Assets)
192   310   193

J.C. Anderson
Chairman & C.E.O.

L.J. Macdonald
President & C.O.O.

David G. Scobie
Sr. V.P. C.F.O. & Sec.-Treas.

Address
2300 Western Canadian Place
700 - 9th Avenue S.W.
Calgary
AB
T2P 3V4
(403) 264-9800

Fax: (403) 263-3274
A0002243/G/3.2

ARCHER RESOURCES LTD.

Exchanges	Price (Jun29'95)	5 .50	Trailing P/E	16 .67	Stock Symbol
T	Trailing Yield (%)	0 .00	Trailing EPS	0 .33	**ARC**

Period Ending	Dec94	Dec93	Dec92	Dec91
Yearly Statistics				
Price-Close	11 .88	16 .25	n t	n t
Price-High	23 .25	19 .50	n t	n t
Price-Low	11 .00	10 .50	n t	n t
P/E-Close	23 .75	35 .33	n t	n t
Dividends per Share	0 .00	0 .00	0 .00	0 .00
Dividend Yield (%)	0 .00	0 .00	0 .00	0 .00
Sales per Share	2 .97	2 .28	1 .65	1 .61
EPS before extra. item	0 .50	0 .46	0 .16	(0 .06)
Cash Flow per Share	1 .63	1 .24	0 .62	0 .33
Book Value per Share	5 .22	3 .46	1 .04	0 .26
O/S Common Shares	18 ,472	16 ,966	6 ,066	3 ,461
Total Revenue	53 ,111	31 ,066	8 ,588	5 ,180
Income before extra.	8 ,300	5 ,869	756	(182)
Cash Flow	27 ,771	15 ,812	2 ,887	1 ,002
Debt/Equity	0 .87	0 .16	2 .92	20 .22
Return on Capital (%)	14 .12	25 .72	12 .46	na
Ret. on Com. Equity (%)	10 .71	18 .07	20 .94	na
% Change Profit	41 .4	676 .0	515 .2	na
% Change Revenue	71 .0	261 .7	65 .8	na
% Change Assets	156 .7	191 .9	34 .5	na

Period Ending	Dec94	Dec93	Dec92
Preferred Div. Coverage	np	np	np
Total Div. Coverage	na	na	na
Interest Coverage	6 .2	7 .6	1 .7
Current Ratio	1 .0	0 .8	0 .7
Operating Margin	32 .9	38 .3	31 .7
Asset Turnover	0 .2	0 .3	0 .3
5 YEAR RATIOS (%)			
Return on Capital	na	na	na
Return on Com. Equity	na	na	na
Profit Growth	na	na	na
Revenue Growth	na	na	na
Asset Growth	na	na	na
BALANCE SHEET (000)			
Cash	0	0	1 ,124
Current Assets	29 ,516	11 ,516	3 ,817
Net Fixed Assets	188 ,746	73 ,512	25 ,316
Invest's & Advances	0	0	0
Total Assets	218 ,262	85 ,028	29 ,133
Short Term Debt	3 ,074	435	895
Current Liabilities	31 ,037	13 ,942	5 ,094
Long Term Debt	80 ,470	8 ,725	17 ,550
Total Liabilities	121 ,842	26 ,384	22 ,806
Total Equity	96 ,420	58 ,643	6 ,327
Total Liab. & Equity	218 ,262	85 ,028	29 ,133
CAPITAL (000)			
Total Debt	83 ,544	9 ,160	18 ,445
Preferred Equity	0	0	0
Common Equity	96 ,420	58 ,643	6 ,327

Business:

ARCHER RESOURCES LTD. is involved in the acquisition, exploitation, production, processing and marketing of natural gas in the Plains area of southeastern and east central Alberta.

Date	EPS	DPS	Tot Rev	Inc Bex
Mar 95	0 .00	0 .00	13 ,966	26
Dec 94	0 .03	0 .00	16 ,009	622
Sep 94	0 .14	0 .00	14 ,007	2 ,366
Jun 94	0 .16	0 .00	11 ,439	2 ,635
Mar 94	0 .17	0 .00	11 ,698	2 ,677
Dec 93	0 .13	0 .00	11 ,057	1 ,836
Sep 93	0 .06	0 .00	6 ,780	1 ,397
Jun 93	0 .11	0 .00	6 ,732	1 ,384

Synopsis:

Two important economic factors facing Archer Resources are its debt to cash flow ratio and low natural gas prices. Archer's short-term objective is to reduce debt, primarily through cash management activities and the rationalization of its natural gas gathering and processing systems. Another short-term objective is to maximize funds from operations by developing select natural gas projects, developing or rationalizing new oil discoveries, and reducing administrative and operating costs. Archer plans to maintain 1995 natural gas production with minimal capital expenditures by targeting only projects that generate the highest returns. The capital expenditure program for 1995 is not expected to exceed funds from operations.

Archers's growth in 1994 resulted from acquisitions, an aggressive drilling program, and an increase in the price of natural gas. Archer continued to strengthen its asset base in 1994. Thirty-two acquisitions, costing the company $52.3-million, added production, undeveloped reserves, land, and natural gas gathering and processing systems.

The increase in oil volumes and natural gas liquids during 1994 resulted from an effort to realize the potential in three of the company's oil-prone areas. Archer intends to exploit the potential of these and several other oil plays in the short term to generate funds flow for longer-term exploration programs for its core commodity, natural gas.

During fiscal 1994 (1993) average daily production of oil and natural gas liquids was 1,084 (454) barrels, and average daily production of natural gas was 64.2 (46.6) million cubic feet. At 1994 (1993) fiscal year end, Archer's proven and probable oil reserves totalled 4,406,000 (2,070,000) barrels, and natural gas reserves totalled 279.4 (225.2) billion cubic feet.

Relative strength to TSE300 / Price / Volume (in 1000's of board lots) chart

Rank (Profit/Revenue/Assets)
327   535   339

Grant A. Bartlett
President & C.E.O.

J. Peter H. Henry
Controller Treas. & C.F.O.

Gerald K. Tenove
C.O.O.

Address
Suite 2600
400 - 3rd Avenue S.W.
Calgary
AB
T2P 4H2
(403) 266-5522

Fax: (403) 232-6008
01003396/G/3.2

ATCOR RESOURCES LTD.

Exchanges	Price (Jun29'95)	3.40	Trailing P/E	18.88	Stock Symbol
T	Trailing Yield (%)	0.00	Trailing EPS	0.18	AKR.A

Period Ending	Dec94	Dec93	Dec92	Dec91	Dec90
Yearly Statistics					
Price-Close	2.75	4.90	3.75	3.45	2.50
Price-High	4.85	7.00	4.40	3.50	2.80
Price-Low	2.60	3.50	3.05	2.11	2.00
P/E-Close	18.33	18.85	16.30	24.64	14.71
Dividends per Share	0.00	0.00	0.00	0.00	0.05
Dividend Yield (%)	0.00	0.00	0.00	0.00	1.80
Sales per Share	6.45	5.57	4.64	3.80	4.12
EPS before extra. item	0.15	0.26	0.23	0.14	0.17
Cash Flow per Share	0.96	0.94	0.89	0.82	0.87
Book Value per Share	4.57	4.42	4.25	4.03	3.88
O/S Common Shares	38,108	38,108	29,765	29,766	29,765
Total Revenue	249,414	212,571	138,687	114,009	123,762
Income before extra.	5,756	10,238	7,473	5,431	6,449
Cash Flow	36,555	34,441	26,448	24,344	25,937
Debt/Equity	0.22	0.37	0.42	0.31	0.22
Return on Capital (%)	7.57	11.07	7.27	6.61	7.78
Ret. on Com. Equity (%)	3.36	6.54	5.46	3.66	3.18
% Change Profit	(43.8)	37.0	37.6	(15.8)	(0.1)
% Change Revenue	17.3	53.3	21.6	(7.9)	3.5
% Change Assets	(1.0)	19.5	14.2	8.4	(4.2)

Business:

ATCOR RESOURCES LTD. is engaged in the business of crude oil and gas exploration and production and in the processing and marketing of natural gas.

Date	EPS	DPS	Tot Rev	Inc Bex
Mar 95	0.05	0.00	62,883	1,978
Dec 94	0.09	0.00	79,111	3,281
Sep 94	0.02	0.00	63,092	869
Jun 94	0.02	0.00	47,912	777
Mar 94	0.02	0.00	39,944	829
Dec 93	0.13	0.00	87,926	4,997
Sep 93	0.04	0.00	41,586	1,436
Jun 93	0.04	0.00	40,345	1,762

Preferred Div. Coverage	np	np	10.0
Total Div. Coverage	na	17.3	10.0
Interest Coverage	4.2	5.1	93.9
Current Ratio	1.0	1.0	0.7
Operating Margin	5.3	7.8	9.4
Asset Turnover	0.8	0.7	0.5
5 YEAR RATIOS (%)			
Return on Capital	8.1	na	na
Return on Com. Equity	4.4	na	na
Profit Growth	(2.2)	na	na
Revenue Growth	15.8	na	na
Asset Growth	7.0	na	na
BALANCE SHEET (000)			
Cash	0	0	0
Current Assets	40,122	42,037	20,333
Net Fixed Assets	258,014	259,180	230,356
Invest's & Advances	4,985	4,985	5,520
Total Assets	303,121	306,202	256,209
Short Term Debt	5,000	15,250	6,147
Current Liabilities	41,547	41,205	27,137
Long Term Debt	34,005	46,251	51,697
Total Liabilities	129,057	137,894	117,583
Total Equity	174,064	168,308	138,626
Total Liab. & Equity	303,121	306,202	256,209
CAPITAL (000)			
Total Debt	39,005	61,501	57,844
Preferred Equity	0	0	12,000
Common Equity	174,064	168,308	126,626

Synopsis:

Throughout the past four years, one of Atcor Resource's principal business segments, Exploration-Production, has had an increasing impact on the company's cash flow. In 1990, 43% of operating cash flow (before corporate costs) was attributed to Atcor's Marketing and Processing unit. By 1994 year end, 81% of operating cash flow was generated by the Exploration-Production segment. This trend should continue in the future as Atcor continues to invest in exploration.

Of the $24-million 1995 exploration and development capital budget, $19-million will go for land acquisition, geophysics, and drilling, and $5-million will go for facility construction. Twenty-two exploration drilling prospects are planned during 1995. These prospects focus on the company's core areas in western Alberta and British Columbia. If they are successful, these pools should add significant reserves and future production volumes.

Increased earnings, cash flow, and revenue in the first quarter of 1995, were due to a 95% increase in gas marketing volumes, higher oil and natural gas production volumes, and a 56% increase in crude oil prices over the same period in 1994. Higher production volumes and gas prices accounted for the 14% increase in revenue for 1994 over the same period in 1993. In 1994, earnings include approximately $1.7-million received upon the amendment of a gas supply contract. In 1993, earnings included a net gain of about $3.7-million on the sale of one-third of Atcor's interest in an ethane extraction plant.

During fiscal 1994 (1993) average daily production of oil and natural gas liquids was 4,387 (3,927) barrels. Average daily production of natural gas was 44.9 (44.5) million cubic feet. At 1994 (1993) fiscal year end, Atcor's proven and probable oil reserves totalled 16.1 (18) million barrels. Natural gas reserves totalled 146.9 (181) billion cubic feet.

Relative strength to TSE300

Price

Volume (in 1000's of board lots)

Rank (Profit/Revenue/Assets)		
401	287	285

Ronald D. Southern
Chairman

Arthur C. Eastly
President & C.E.O.

Ronald E. Pratt
V.P. Finance

Address
Suite 600
800 - 6th Avenue S.W.
Calgary
AB
T2P 3G3
(403) 292-8000

Fax: (403) 261-7665
01003128/G/3.2

BARRINGTON PETROLEUM LTD.

Exchanges	Price (Jun29'95)	4 .50	Trailing P/E	18 .00	Stock Symbol
TM	Trailing Yield (%)	0 .00	Trailing EPS	0 .25	**BPL**

Period Ending	Dec94	Dec93	Dec92	Dec91	Dec90	Business:
Yearly Statistics						BARRINGTON PETROLEUM LTD. is
Price-Close	4 .75	6 .25	1 .48	1 .15	1 .75	involved in oil and gas exploration and
Price-High	7 .25	7 .25	1 .63	1 .75	2 .25	production.
Price-Low	4 .65	1 .50	0 .75	0 .85	1 .20	
P/E-Close	16 .38	28 .41	148 .00	nm	87 .50	
Dividends per Share	0 .00	0 .00	0 .00	0 .00	0 .00	
Dividend Yield (%)	0 .00	0 .00	0 .00	0 .00	0 .00	
Sales per Share	1 .47	0 .96	0 .43	0 .32	0 .19	
EPS before extra. item	0 .29	0 .22	0 .01	(0 .05)	0 .02	
Cash Flow per Share	0 .80	0 .58	0 .20	0 .09	0 .05	
Book Value per Share	2 .57	1 .56	0 .78	0 .64	0 .67	
O/S Common Shares	31 ,096	25 ,955	20 ,213	14 ,817	14 ,218	
Total Revenue	41 ,549	22 ,694	7 ,485	4 ,746	2 ,626	
Income before extra.	7 ,943	4 ,936	224	(784)	323	

Date	EPS	DPS	Tot Rev	Inc Bex
Mar 95	0 .02	0 .00	9 ,359	743
Dec 94	0 .10	0 .00	12 ,226	2 ,755
Sep 94	0 .08	0 .00	11 ,800	2 ,212
Jun 94	0 .05	0 .00	8 ,850	1 ,510
Mar 94	0 .06	0 .00	8 ,673	1 ,466
Dec 93	0 .05	0 .00	7 ,195	1 ,173
Sep 93	0 .08	0 .00	6 ,809	1 ,855
Jun 93	0 .05	0 .00	5 ,093	1 ,079

	Dec94	Dec93	Dec92	Dec91	Dec90
Cash Flow	22 ,154	13 ,236	3 ,207	1 ,337	689
Debt/Equity	0 .29	0 .09	0 .46	1 .23	0 .64
Return on Capital (%)	17 .88	23 .05	5 .40	0 .22	3 .20
Ret. on Com. Equity (%)	13 .18	17 .53	1 .78	(8 .28)	3 .70
% Change Profit	60 .9	2 ,108 .0	128 .5	(343 .0)	10 .5
% Change Revenue	83 .1	203 .2	57 .7	80 .7	24 .0
% Change Assets	134 .0	105 .6	16 .1	30 .3	54 .2

Preferred Div. Coverage	np	np	np
Total Div. Coverage	na	na	na
Interest Coverage	9 .4	20 .2	1 .2
Current Ratio	0 .7	0 .8	0 .8
Operating Margin	31 .6	34 .0	15 .9
Asset Turnover	0 .3	0 .4	0 .3
5 YEAR RATIOS (%)			
Return on Capital	9 .9	7 .5	2 .0
Return on Com. Equity	5 .6	3 .8	(0 .7)
Profit Growth	93 .6	na	na
Revenue Growth	81 .3	89 .3	56 .2
Asset Growth	62 .2	39 .8	32 .5
BALANCE SHEET (000)			
Cash	3	117	151
Current Assets	11 ,499	5 ,732	2 ,327
Net Fixed Assets	112 ,053	47 ,066	23 ,352
Invest's & Advances	0	0	0
Total Assets	123 ,552	52 ,798	25 ,679
Short Term Debt	286	260	131
Current Liabilities	15 ,484	7 ,176	2 ,808
Long Term Debt	22 ,716	3 ,226	7 ,107
Total Liabilities	43 ,548	12 ,223	9 ,952
Total Equity	80 ,004	40 ,575	15 ,727
Total Liab. & Equity	123 ,552	52 ,798	25 ,679
CAPITAL (000)			
Total Debt	23 ,002	3 ,486	7 ,238
Preferred Equity	0	0	0
Common Equity	80 ,004	40 ,575	15 ,727

Synopsis:

Barrington Petroleum expects a modest improvement in gas prices in 1995. According to the company, improved prices will result from storage drawdown and decreasing field output in the U.S. Barrington believes that the Canadian gas oversupply will be short lived in the face of reduced activity levels and high decline rates. Gas storage overhang is due to a moderate summer and mild winter during 1994 and early 1995, as well as a temporary increase in new field production in western Canada.

Barrington has continued its focus on gas development into 1995. Over the first half of this year, the company expects to bring onstream approximately 20-25 million cubic feet per day of new gas production, and anticipates average daily production for the year of 70 million cubic feet. During this same period, oil development drilling was renewed around successful exploration projects in western Saskatchewan and southern Alberta. Barrington plans to maintain oil volumes at a target of 35% of production.

Barrington invested $26-million in undeveloped land and reserve purchases in 1994 to consolidate working interests, increase control in the company's core areas, and provide future exploration inventory. Another $10-million was invested in gas plant infrastructure, which Barrington expects should lead to lower incremental on-stream costs in 1995 and 1996.

Average daily production in 1994 (1993) was: crude oil and natural gas liquids, 2,013 (1,675) barrels; and natural gas 39 (18) million cubic feet. Gross proven and probable reserves at the end of 1994 (1993) were: oil and natural gas liquids, 4.1 (3.6) million barrels; and natural gas 177.7 (93.8) billion cubic feet.

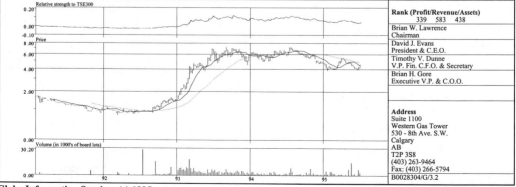

Rank (Profit/Revenue/Assets)
339   583   438

Brian W. Lawrence
Chairman

David J. Evans
President & C.E.O.

Timothy V. Dunne
V.P. Fin. C.F.O. & Secretary

Brian H. Gore
Executive V.P. & C.O.O.

Address
Suite 1100
Western Gas Tower
530 - 8th Ave. S.W.
Calgary
AB
T2P 3S8
(403) 263-9464
Fax: (403) 266-5794
B0028304/G/3.2

BEAU CANADA EXPLORATION LTD.

Exchanges	Price (Jun29'95)	1.81	Trailing P/E	18.10	Stock Symbol
TM	Trailing Yield (%)	0.00	Trailing EPS	0.10	**BAU**

Period Ending	Dec94	Dec93	Dec92	Dec91	Dec90
Yearly Statistics					
Price-Close	1.69	2.35	1.15	0.70	0.50
Price-High	2.59	3.20	1.30	0.85	0.70
Price-Low	1.65	0.92	0.50	0.30	0.27
P/E-Close	16.90	47.00	57.50	35.00	8.33
Dividends per Share	0.00	0.00	0.00	0.00	0.00
Dividend Yield (%)	0.00	0.00	0.00	0.00	0.00
Sales per Share	0.85	0.55	0.64	0.59	0.68
EPS before extra. item	0.10	0.05	0.02	0.02	0.06
Cash Flow per Share	0.41	0.22	0.19	0.15	0.18
Book Value per Share	1.35	1.20	0.47	0.21	0.19
O/S Common Shares	71,302	67,253	31,341	16,024	15,524
Total Revenue	60,201	25,241	10,542	9,390	10,707
Income before extra.	7,009	2,009	277	257	902
Cash Flow	28,512	9,546	3,054	2,330	2,727
Debt/Equity	0.56	0.51	0.86	4.36	4.84
Return on Capital (%)	11.31	6.28	7.02	10.87	27.05
Ret. on Com. Equity (%)	7.94	4.22	3.07	8.22	36.07
% Change Profit	248.8	624.3	7.9	(71.5)	491.5
% Change Revenue	138.5	139.4	12.3	(12.3)	1,673.7
% Change Assets	45.5	316.2	56.6	5.0	536.1

Date	EPS	DPS	Tot Rev	Inc Bex
Mar 95	0.02	0.00	16,505	1,446
Dec 94	0.02	0.00	15,256	1,258
Sep 94	0.03	0.00	19,044	2,653
Jun 94	0.03	0.00	14,757	1,656
Mar 94	0.02	0.00	11,235	1,442
Dec 93	0.02	0.00	11,757	1,097
Sep 93	0.02	0.00	6,769	559
Jun 93	0.00	0.00	3,911	197

Preferred Div. Coverage	np	np	np
Total Div. Coverage	na	na	na
Interest Coverage	3.9	1.8	1.2
Current Ratio	0.5	1.0	1.8
Operating Margin	24.9	15.2	12.9
Asset Turnover	0.3	0.2	0.3
5 YEAR RATIOS (%)			
Return on Capital	12.5	11.9	na
Return on Com. Equity	11.9	11.9	na
Profit Growth	115.2	107.1	na
Revenue Growth	151.1	224.1	na
Asset Growth	129.2	131.9	na
BALANCE SHEET (000)			
Cash	0	2,645	9,190
Current Assets	10,550	8,209	10,506
Net Fixed Assets	178,363	121,631	20,692
Invest's & Advances	0	0	0
Total Assets	188,913	129,840	31,198
Short Term Debt	1,115	1,245	2,525
Current Liabilities	22,679	8,367	5,922
Long Term Debt	52,949	39,586	10,142
Total Liabilities	92,852	49,422	16,448
Total Equity	96,061	80,418	14,749
Total Liab. & Equity	188,913	129,840	31,198
CAPITAL (000)			
Total Debt	54,064	40,831	12,667
Preferred Equity	0	0	0
Common Equity	96,061	80,418	14,749

Business:

BEAU CANADA EXPLORATION LTD. is engaged in oil and gas production and drilling.

Synopsis:

Beau Canada's operational objectives for 1995 include an emphasis on exploratory drilling and continued horizontal drilling. Oil exploration and development should continue in six of its traditional core properties in Alberta and Saskatchewan. Exploration for gas reserves will be concentrated in new areas such as the Peace River Arch area in Alberta and the Helmet area in Northeast B.C. Reasons behind the continued exploration for gas reserves in these areas are the multi-zone potential and the significant reserves associated with successful wells. Beau's gas development projects in 1995 will be limited to the tying-in of gas reserves in the Helmet and Alderson, Alberta, areas. Forecasted daily average production levels are 6,000 barrels of oil and 57 million cubic feet of gas. Beau's projections may vary if gas prices remain low as a certain portion of its gas will be voluntarily shut-in.

Beau Canada has established a capital budget of $45-million for 1995. About $25-million will be spent on drilling and facilities, $10-million on land and seismic, and the remaining $10-million spent on acquisitions and other items.

During 1994, Beau Canada achieved growth in revenue, earnings, and cash flow on the strength of higher production volumes and improved liquids and gas prices. Increased liquids production resulted from production coming onstream and the acquisition of Calex Resources Limited in August 1994. The gas production increase was largely a result of the tying-in of some shut-in gas reserves acquired in 1993.

In 1994 (1993), Beau's average daily production was: crude oil and natural gas liquids, 4,724 (2,167) barrels; and natural gas 44.2 (18.1) million cubic feet. At year-end total proven and probable reserves were: crude oil and natural gas liquids, 10.5 (10) million barrels; and natural gas, 216 (196) billion cubic feet.

Rank (Profit/Revenue/Assets)
368   509   362

Thomas Bugg
President & C.E.O.
Michael Lang
Treasurer & C.F.O.

Address
47th Floor
West Tower Petro Canada Ctr.
150 - 6th Ave. S.W.
Calgary
AB
T2P 3Y7
(403) 750-3400
Fax: (403) 233-2565
B0015980/G/3.2

CABRE EXPLORATION LTD.

Exchanges	Price (Jun29'95)		15 .00	Trailing P/E		23 .81	Stock Symbol
T	Trailing Yield (%)		0 .00	Trailing EPS		0 .63	CBE

Period Ending	Ju l94	Ju l93	Ju l92	Ju l91	Ju l90	Business:
Yearly Statistics						CABRE EXPLORATION LTD. is engaged in
Price-Close	15 .25	16 .63	11 .25	8 .25	8 .13	acquiring petroleum and natural gas rights and
Price-High	17 .00	19 .75	11 .25	9 .13	8 .63	in conducting exploration and development on
Price-Low	10 .75	10 .00	8 .25	7 .13	4 .05	those rights in Alberta, Saskatchewan and
P/E-Close	25 .85	27 .25	37 .50	27 .50	23 .90	British Columbia.
Dividends per Share	0 .00	0 .00	0 .00	0 .00	0 .00	
Dividend Yield (%)	0 .00	0 .00	0 .00	0 .00	0 .00	
Sales per Share	3 .98	3 .32	1 .88	1 .60	1 .27	
EPS before extra. item	0 .59	0 .61	0 .30	0 .30	0 .34	
Cash Flow per Share	2 .31	1 .92	1 .24	1 .22	1 .02	
Book Value per Share	7 .32	6 .68	5 .39	4 .79	3 .88	
O/S Common Shares	16 ,402	16 ,237	14 ,159	12 ,843	9 ,856	
Total Revenue	66 ,488	50 ,964	26 ,811	21 ,485	11 ,748	
Income before extra.	9 ,709	9 ,176	3 ,912	3 ,723	3 ,004	

	Date	EPS	DPS	Tot Rev	Inc Bex
Cash Flow	37 ,715	28 ,840	16 ,777	15 ,189	8 ,642
Debt/Equity	0 .21	0 .18	0 .20	nd	nd
Return on Capital (%)	11 .93	12 .21	7 .93	12 .66	14 .87
Ret. on Com. Equity (%)	8 .50	9 .93	5 .67	7 .46	10 .34
% Change Profit	5 .8	134 .6	5 .1	23 .9	181 .5
% Change Revenue	30 .5	90 .1	24 .8	82 .9	50 .9
% Change Assets	16 .8	40 .5	48 .8	60 .3	68 .9

Supplementary quarterly data:

Date	EPS	DPS	Tot Rev	Inc Bex
Apr 95	0 .15	0 .00	21 ,381	2 ,462
Jan 95	0 .11	0 .00	20 ,367	1 ,867
Oct 94	0 .18	0 .00	18 ,799	2 ,989
Jul 94	0 .19	0 .00	16 ,340	3 ,214
Apr 94	0 .10	0 .00	16 ,090	1 ,645
Jan 94	0 .13	0 .00	16 ,006	2 ,055
Oct 93	0 .17	0 .00	15 ,293	2 ,795
Jul 93	0 .10	0 .00	11 ,565	1 ,698

				Synopsis:
Preferred Div. Coverage	na	na	na	
Total Div. Coverage	na	na	na	
Interest Coverage	11 .0	14 .3	5 .1	
Current Ratio	0 .7	1 .1	0 .8	
Operating Margin	22 .7	24 .9	22 .7	
Asset Turnover	0 .4	0 .3	0 .2	
5 YEAR RATIOS (%)				
Return on Capital	11 .9	11 .1	9 .9	
Return on Com. Equity	8 .4	7 .7	6 .4	
Profit Growth	55 .5	64 .1	28 .0	
Revenue Growth	53 .5	55 .0	43 .2	
Asset Growth	45 .8	41 .9	36 .9	
BALANCE SHEET (000)				
Cash	1	648	721	
Current Assets	14 ,702	18 ,893	8 ,725	
Net Fixed Assets	165 ,476	134 ,775	97 ,763	
Invest's & Advances	0	0	5 ,400	
Total Assets	183 ,809	157 ,436	112 ,057	
Short Term Debt	0	0	0	
Current Liabilities	21 ,037	16 ,705	10 ,775	
Long Term Debt	25 ,125	19 ,807	15 ,297	
Total Liabilities	63 ,727	49 ,025	35 ,690	
Total Equity	120 ,082	108 ,411	76 ,367	
Total Liab. & Equity	183 ,809	157 ,436	112 ,057	
CAPITAL (000)				
Total Debt	25 ,125	19 ,807	15 ,297	
Preferred Equity	4	5	6	
Common Equity	120 ,078	108 ,406	76 ,361	

Synopsis:

While asset sales favoured the vendor in the oil and gas industry in 1994, soft equity markets and lower gas prices in 1995 may favour purchasers in 1995. Cabre intends to monitor purchase opportunities while focusing on further exploration and development of its predominantly oil-oriented land base.

Oil and gas sales in the second quarter ending January 31, 1995, were 8,476 barrels per day and 32.4 million cubic feet per day, up 20% and 9%, respectively from a year earlier. Cabre expects that the completion of waterflood and oil development projects will result in further oil production gains in the latter half of the company's fiscal year. Gas delivery capability should reach 45 million cubic feet per day. However, about eight million cubic feet of daily gas production may be shut-in due to low gas spot prices.

In November 1994, Cabre closed the purchase of Esso's interests at Joarcam, Alberta. Cabre was already a significant owner and operator of the gas cap unit and now also operates the two oil units. As operator of all three units, additional operating efficiencies are expected. The purchase price was $19.5-million effective May 1994. The purchase adds four million barrels of oil and equivalent natural gas, 1,050 barrels of oil and liquids, and one million cubic feet of daily gas production. As of October 1994, Joarcam was Cabre's largest producing property representing 22% of sales.

During fiscal 1994 (1993) average daily production by resource was: oil and natural gas liquids, 6,920 (5,727) barrels; natural gas, 28.4 (19.1) million cubic feet. At 1994 (1993) fiscal year end, proven and probable reserves were: oil, 20.3 (17.4) million barrels, natural gas, 131.8 (121) billion cubic feet.

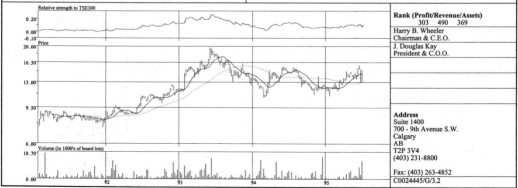

Rank (Profit/Revenue/Assets)	303 490 369
Harry B. Wheeler	Chairman & C.E.O.
J. Douglas Kay	President & C.O.O.

Address
Suite 1400
700 - 9th Avenue S.W.
Calgary
AB
T2P 3V4
(403) 231-8800

Fax: (403) 263-4852
C0024445/G/3.2

CANADA SOUTHERN PETROLEUM LTD.

Exchanges	Price (Jun29'95)		7.00	Trailing P/E		nm	Stock Symbol
T	Trailing Yield (%)		0.00	Trailing EPS		(0.12)	**CSW**

Period Ending	Dec94	Dec93	Jun93	Jun92	Jun91
Yearly Statistics		6M			
Price-Close	6.75	7.13	5.50	3.50	2.65
Price-High	9.00	10.50	7.00	5.38	4.00
Price-Low	5.75	5.13	3.15	2.31	2.05
P/E-Close	nm	nm	nm	nm	88.33
Dividends per Share	0.00	0.00	0.00	0.00	0.00
Dividend Yield (%)	0.00	0.00	0.00	0.00	0.00
Sales per Share	0.08	0.09	0.10	0.10	0.13
EPS before extra. item	(0.10)	(0.04)	(0.05)	(0.12)	0.03
Cash Flow per Share	(0.05)	(0.05)	(0.02)	(0.04)	0.06
Book Value per Share	1.01	1.11	1.11	1.15	1.27
O/S Common Shares	12,613	12,613	12,405	12,346	12,346
Total Revenue	2,000	1,090	2,525	1,894	3,146
Income before extra.	(1,210)	(553)	(613)	(1,431)	426
Cash Flow	(692)	(321)	(234)	(542)	791
Debt/Equity	nd	nd	nd	nd	nd
Return on Capital (%)	(9.06)	(7.98)	(4.39)	(9.59)	2.78
Ret. on Com. Equity (%)	(9.06)	(7.98)	(4.39)	(9.59)	2.78
% Change Profit	(9.4)	(80.4)	57.2	(436.0)	151.9
% Change Revenue	(8.2)	(13.7)	33.3	(39.8)	42.1
% Change Assets	(7.6)	2.7	(3.3)	(9.3)	3.2
Preferred Div. Coverage	np	np	np
Total Div. Coverage	na	na	na
Interest Coverage	nd	nd	nd
Current Ratio	7.9	13.6	19.9
Operating Margin	(89.9)	(69.3)	(52.3)
Asset Turnover	0.1	0.1	0.1
5 YEAR RATIOS (%)			
Return on Capital	(5.6)	(4.9)	(4.8)
Return on Com. Equity	(5.6)	(4.9)	(4.8)
Profit Growth	na	na	na
Revenue Growth	(2.0)	1.4	2.0
Asset Growth	(3.0)	(1.2)	(3.0)
BALANCE SHEET (000)			
Cash	2,226	3,556	3,496
Current Assets	2,766	4,199	3,948
Net Fixed Assets	10,625	9,975	9,826
Invest's & Advances	0	310	330
Total Assets	13,390	14,484	14,105
Short Term Debt	0	0	0
Current Liabilities	349	309	198
Long Term Debt	0	0	0
Total Liabilities	639	522	364
Total Equity	12,752	13,962	13,740
Total Liab. & Equity	13,390	14,484	14,105
CAPITAL (000)			
Total Debt	0	0	0
Preferred Equity	0	0	0
Common Equity	12,752	13,962	13,740

Business:

CANADA SOUTHERN PETROLEUM LTD. is a petroleum exploration and production company. The company has producing oil and gas wells in northeastern British Columbia. It has other properties in the Yukon, the Arctic Islands, Alberta and the Northern Territory, Australia.

Date	EPS	DPS	Tot Rev	Inc Bex
Mar 95	(0.04)	0.00	291	(537)
Dec 94	(0.03)	0.00	343	(354)
Sep 94	(0.02)	0.00	502	(214)
Jun 94	(0.03)	0.00	505	(345)
Mar 94	(0.02)	0.00	594	(297)
Dec 93	(0.02)	0.00	614	(338)
Sep 93	(0.02)	0.00	429	(215)
Jun 93	(0.03)	0.00	410	(319)

Synopsis:

Canada Southern Petroleum reported that its higher net loss for the period ending March 1995 was due principally to a temporary suspension of revenues from carried-interest properties. A major portion of Canada Southern's property interest is covered by carried-interest agreements, which provide that expenditures made by the operator are recouped solely out of revenue from production. The company expects that the increased capital expenditures made during the first quarter by the operators will result in increased revenues later this year. Other contributing factors to the first quarter loss were a 43% reduction in revenues from gas sales, due to lower wellhead prices and diminished sales volume, and the continuing litigation expenses involving the company's principal asset, the Kotaneelee gas field in the Yukon.

The lawsuit, filed in 1990, against the company's working interest partners, seeks the surrender of the partners' interests in the field as well as compensation for loss of income by Canada Southern as a result of the delay in marketing the gas. The gas field, which had been shut-in since 1980, began production in February 1991. According to government reports, the Kotaneelee field produced 16.8 billion cubic feet of gas from two wells during 1994. Canada Southern expects to receive income from Kotaneelee in about three and a half years, based upon present prices and assuming the payout period is not changed because of the litigation. Due to the volume of documentation and the number of companies involved, the court has scheduled a six-month trial to begin in September 1996.

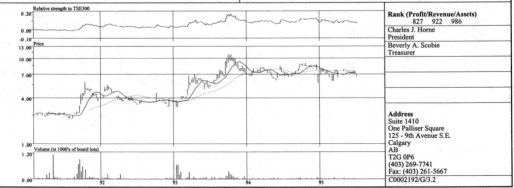

Rank (Profit/Revenue/Assets)
827 922 986

Charles J. Horne
President
Beverly A. Scobie
Treasurer

Address
Suite 1410
One Palliser Square
125 - 9th Avenue S.E.
Calgary
AB
T2G 0P6
(403) 269-7741
Fax: (403) 261-5667
C0002192/G/3.2

CANADIAN FRACMASTER LTD.

Exchanges	Price (Jun29'95)		5.87	Trailing P/E		11.99	Stock Symbol
TMZ	Trailing Yield (%)		0.00	Trailing EPS		0.49	**CFC**

Period Ending	Dec94	Jun94	Jun93	Jun92
Yearly Statistics	6M			
Price-Close	9.00	9.63	n t	n t
Price-High	12.00	16.88	n t	n t
Price-Low	7.50	9.25	n t	n t
P/E-Close	22.50	11.88	n t	n t
Dividends per Share	0.00	0.00	0.00	0.06
Dividend Yield (%)	0.00	0.00	0.00	na
Sales per Share	8.38	6.79	5.86	3.50
EPS before extra. item	0.20	0.81	1.13	0.87
Cash Flow per Share	1.65	1.63	1.91	1.18
Book Value per Share	4.25	4.08	2.98	1.71
O/S Common Shares	45,579	45,371	41,068	40,000
Total Revenue	180,937	290,995	240,289	154,051
Income before extra.	8,568	34,310	45,507	35,221
Cash Flow	35,497	69,144	76,890	47,174
Debt/Equity	0.12	0.12	0.50	0.61
Return on Capital (%)	15.24	24.45	38.71	na
Ret. on Com. Equity (%)	9.05	22.32	46.70	na
% Change Profit	(50.1)	(24.6)	29.2	na
% Change Revenue	24.4	21.1	56.0	na
% Change Assets	7.8	14.7	46.6	na
Preferred Div. Coverage	np	np	np	
Total Div. Coverage	na	na	47.2	
Interest Coverage	8.7	13.6	13.6	
Current Ratio	1.8	2.1	1.4	
Operating Margin	12.2	16.5	27.3	
Asset Turnover	1.3	1.1	1.0	
5 YEAR RATIOS (%)				
Return on Capital	na	na	na	
Return on Com. Equity	na	na	na	
Profit Growth	na	na	na	
Revenue Growth	na	na	na	
Asset Growth	na	na	na	
BALANCE SHEET (000)				
Cash	17,059	15,222	17,205	
Current Assets	127,697	121,921	114,745	
Net Fixed Assets	66,820	60,572	50,391	
Invest's & Advances	14,441	11,488	11,078	
Total Assets	288,627	267,631	233,417	
Short Term Debt	15,758	13,957	41,468	
Current Liabilities	69,501	58,464	82,431	
Long Term Debt	6,665	9,035	19,969	
Total Liabilities	94,854	82,513	111,027	
Total Equity	193,773	185,118	122,390	
Total Liab. & Equity	288,627	267,631	233,417	
CAPITAL (000)				
Total Debt	22,423	22,992	61,437	
Preferred Equity	0	0	0	
Common Equity	193,773	185,118	122,390	

Business:

CANADIAN FRACMASTER LTD. provides diversified, highly specialized services to the oil and gas industry around the world.

Date	EPS	DPS	Tot Rev	Inc Bex
Mar 95	0.16	0.00	92,349	7,021
Dec 94	0.07	0.00	92,410	2,948
Sep 94	0.13	0.00	90,112	5,620
Jun 94	0.13	0.00	73,101	5,489
Mar 94	0.13	0.00	68,394	5,501
Dec 93	0.24	0.00	77,669	10,102
Sep 93	0.32	0.00	71,854	13,218
Jun 93	0.21	0.00	74,775	8,478

Synopsis:

Canadian Fracmaster's has divided its business into three business segments and believes this will promote growth. The segments are downhole well service; "equity for service" or "joint venture production"; and emerging market ventures, a new segment.

Downhole well services includes Canadian operations and the Cuban operation. Canadian revenue accounted for 98% of revenues in this segment or $64.7-million, for the six months ended December 31, 1994. The results reflect increased oil and natural gas activity in Canada. Cuban operation revenue was $1.4-million and comes from a single customer. Fracmaster believes there are international opportunities in this segment, particularly in strategic alliances with local companies.

Fracmaster's joint enterprise services segment comprises the company's proportionate share of revenue in exporting oil from its Russian joint venture. Joint enterprise revenue for the period ended December 31, 1994, was $114.9-million. Revenue in this segment should grow as the Russian export tariff shrinks. It fell to approximately $5.30 per barrel from about $6.70 per barrel, in January 1995. The company conducted a demonstration program in China during 1994, and will investigate opportunities in Eastern Europe and Asia.

The company's new segment is traditional international production sharing ventures involving full field development or rehabilitation. Fracmaster feels there are opportunities for ventures and alliances with host governments and other companies where it can access markets and local expertise, and can apply its technology and operating expertise. Opportunities are under evaluation in Asia and the Middle East. Fracmaster will pursue similar opportunities in Russia once that country's new oil and gas legislation is established.

Relative strength to TSE300

Price

Volume (in 1000's of board lots)

Rank (Profit/Revenue/Assets)
231   229   292

Alfred H. Balm
Chairman

Robert G. Welty
President & C.E.O.

Jim M. Hill
Sr. V.P. & C.F.O.

Peter Kalutich
Sr. V.P.

Address
Suite 1700
355 - 4th Avenue S.W.
Calgary
AB
T2P 0J1
(403) 262-2222

Fax: (403) 265-4967
01003440/G/3.3

CANADIAN NATURAL RESOURCES LIMITED

Exchanges	Price (Jun29'95)	16.12	Trailing P/E	20.94	Stock Symbol
T	Trailing Yield (%)	0.00	Trailing EPS	0.77	CNQ

Period Ending	Dec94	Dec93	Dec92	Dec91	Dec90	Business:
Yearly Statistics						CANADIAN NATURAL RESOURCES
Price-Close	13.75	18.00	7.38	3.84	1.80	LIMITED is engaged in the exploration,
Price-High	22.75	25.00	7.50	4.38	2.20	development, and production of oil and gas.
Price-Low	13.38	7.25	3.63	1.63	0.95	The company has land holdings in Alberta,
P/E-Close	16.18	30.00	27.32	20.20	13.33	British Columbia, and Saskatchewan.
Dividends per Share	0.00	0.00	0.00	0.00	0.00	
Dividend Yield (%)	0.00	0.00	0.00	0.00	0.00	
Sales per Share	4.06	2.74	1.50	0.94	0.56	
EPS before extra. item	0.85	0.60	0.27	0.19	0.14	
Cash Flow per Share	2.39	1.64	0.81	0.50	0.30	
Book Value per Share	5.34	2.86	1.50	0.92	0.48	
O/S Common Shares	66,709	59,862	54,441	49,044	41,887	

Total Revenue	259,014	158,071	77,197	40,321	21,064	
Income before extra.	54,215	34,315	13,923	8,030	5,019	
Cash Flow	152,765	94,210	41,776	21,324	11,023	

Date	EPS	DPS	Tot Rev	Inc Bex
Mar 95	0.15	0.00	65,488	10,086
Dec 94	0.17	0.00	68,311	12,723
Sep 94	0.23	0.00	66,084	14,267
Jun 94	0.22	0.00	61,513	13,122
Mar 94	0.23	0.00	63,106	14,103
Dec 93	0.20	0.00	57,954	11,581
Sep 93	0.13	0.00	35,538	7,904
Jun 93	0.14	0.00	33,470	7,576

	Dec94	Dec93	Dec92	Dec91	Dec90
Debt/Equity	0.68	1.11	0.74	0.79	0.74
Return on Capital (%)	22.51	26.15	24.39	24.90	38.68
Ret. on Com. Equity (%)	20.56	27.16	21.98	24.58	37.98
% Change Profit	58.0	146.5	73.4	60.0	193.9
% Change Revenue	63.9	104.8	91.5	91.4	235.5
% Change Assets	68.9	152.3	73.6	111.6	202.2

				Synopsis:
Preferred Div. Coverage	np	np	np	
Total Div. Coverage	na	na	na	
Interest Coverage	8.8	10.1	7.1	
Current Ratio	1.1	1.1	0.8	
Operating Margin	41.7	41.5	35.0	
Asset Turnover	0.4	0.4	0.4	
5 YEAR RATIOS (%)				
Return on Capital	27.3	30.1	28.6	
Return on Com. Equity	26.5	33.2	na	
Profit Growth	99.6	181.2	181.8	
Revenue Growth	110.3	120.4	85.9	
Asset Growth	116.2	128.3	84.4	
BALANCE SHEET (000)				
Cash	13	25	9	
Current Assets	60,271	35,749	9,338	
Net Fixed Assets	677,528	401,116	163,848	
Invest'& Advances	0	0	0	
Total Assets	737,800	436,866	173,186	
Short Term Debt	0	0	0	
Current Liabilities	56,236	33,545	11,317	
Long Term Debt	242,856	189,165	60,478	
Total Liabilities	381,618	265,653	91,735	
Total Equity	356,182	171,213	81,451	
Total Liab. & Equity	737,800	436,866	173,186	
CAPITAL (000)				
Total Debt	242,856	189,165	60,478	
Preferred Equity	0	0	0	
Common Equity	356,182	171,213	81,451	

Canadian Natural Resources Limited continues to expand the productive asset base in each of its three core areas. A capital expenditure program of $215-million is slated for the company's ongoing property acquisition and exploration and development programs, which includes the drilling of up to 160 wells. The company has deferred the drilling of a portion of its natural gas wells and has targeted approximately 50% of its drilling program for oil prone areas. These expenditures are to be funded through cash flow and available bank financing.

Total daily sales in 1995 should reach 325 million cubic feet of natural gas and 17,200 barrels of crude oil and natural gas liquids. Canadian Natural forecasts a natural gas price of $1.55 per thousand cubic feet, and a West Texas Intermediate oil price of $18.25 per barrel in 1995. Based on this, the company expects cash flow to be between $165-million to $170-million.

1994 revenues increased by 64% over 1993 due to a 60% increase in oil and liquids sales volumes and a 44% increase in natural gas sales. Also contributing to revenue growth was a significant improvement in natural gas prices in 1994 compared to 1993. The fourth quarter of 1994 saw a decline in natural gas prices, and it is anticipated that gas prices will remain weak throughout 1995. Oil prices strengthened after the first quarter of 1994 and remained stable for the remainder of the year.

During fiscal 1994 (1993), Canadian Natural's average gross daily production by resource was: natural gas, 237.5 (164.8) million cubic feet, and oil and natural gas liquids, 12,820 (2,921.8) barrels. At its 1994 (1993) fiscal year-end, total proven and probable reserves were: natural gas, 1,069.4 (766.9) billion cubic feet and 57.5 (42.6) million barrels of oil. Contributions to revenue by commodity in 1994 were: natural gas, 67%; and oil and natural gas liquids, 33%.

Rank (Profit/Revenue/Assets)
109 280 183
Allan P. Markin
Chairman
John G. Langille
President
Keith A. J. Macphail
V.P. Operations & C.O.O.

Address
Suite 2000
425 - 1st Street S.W.
Calgary
AB
T2P 3L8
(403) 221-2100

Fax: (403) 233-8941
C0003899/G/3.2

CANADIAN OCCIDENTAL PETROLEUM LTD.

Exchanges	Price (Jun29'95)	42.37	Trailing P/E	24.35	Stock Symbol
TMA	Trailing Yield (%)	0.94	Trailing EPS	1.74	**CXY**

Period Ending	Dec94	Dec93	Dec92	Dec91	Dec90
Yearly Statistics					
Price-Close	31.75	29.75	25.13	27.13	14.50
Price-High	33.00	31.50	30.25	27.75	20.25
Price-Low	22.13	22.63	23.88	13.50	13.38
P/E-Close	22.05	297.50	96.64	77.50	30.85
Dividends per Share	0.40	0.40	0.40	0.40	0.40
Dividend Yield (%)	1.26	1.35	1.59	1.48	2.76
Sales per Share	15.13	9.33	7.78	8.42	8.80
EPS before extra. item	1.44	0.10	0.26	0.35	0.47
Cash Flow per Share	7.40	3.18	2.02	2.42	3.24
Book Value per Share	12.29	10.77	10.46	10.43	10.54
O/S Common Shares	67,155	67,032	66,933	66,696	66,628
Total Revenue	1,056,828	641,478	563,800	593,176	651,669
Income before extra.	96,305	6,750	17,267	23,101	31,573
Cash Flow	496,646	213,186	135,049	161,330	216,258
Debt/Equity	1.12	1.46	1.29	0.61	0.42
Return on Capital (%)	13.25	3.03	3.42	4.37	7.93
Ret. on Com. Equity (%)	12.45	0.95	2.47	3.30	4.55
% Change Profit	1,326.7	(60.9)	(25.3)	(26.8)	(18.5)
% Change Revenue	64.7	13.8	(5.0)	(9.0)	10.2
% Change Assets	0.4	10.6	34.3	5.1	3.3
Preferred Div. Coverage	np	np	np		
Total Div. Coverage	3.6	0.3	0.6		
Interest Coverage	3.2	1.5	1.1		
Current Ratio	1.5	0.8	1.8		
Operating Margin	18.9	5.5	0.5		
Asset Turnover	0.4	0.3	0.3		
5 YEAR RATIOS (%)					
Return on Capital	6.4	5.7	7.3		
Return on Com. Equity	4.7	3.4	4.3		
Profit Growth	20.0	(29.7)	(21.6)		
Revenue Growth	12.3	(2.8)	(1.2)		
Asset Growth	10.0	10.7	6.7		
BALANCE SHEET (000)					
Cash	66,212	34,522	285,045		
Current Assets	267,058	172,593	453,313		
Net Fixed Assets	1,945,047	2,020,075	1,530,812		
Invest's & Advances	0	0	0		
Total Assets	2,271,315	2,261,996	2,045,065		
Short Term Debt	7,533	19,102	79,476		
Current Liabilities	182,497	222,466	248,740		
Long Term Debt	919,024	1,035,898	819,612		
Total Liabilities	1,446,279	1,540,008	1,345,115		
Total Equity	825,036	721,988	699,950		
Total Liab. & Equity	2,271,315	2,261,996	2,045,065		
CAPITAL (000)					
Total Debt	926,557	1,055,000	899,088		
Preferred Equity	0	0	0		
Common Equity	825,036	721,988	699,950		

Business:

CANADIAN OCCIDENTAL PETROLUEM LTD. is an energy and chemicals company. It has oil and gas and sulphur operations in North America, South America, the North Sea, and the Middle East. It has oil sands interests in Alberta. The company also supplies bleaching agents to the pulp and paper industry and thermoset plastics and polyvinyl chloride film to markets in North America.

Date	EPS	DPS	Tot Rev	Inc Bex
Mar 95	0.45	0.10	285,784	30,305
Dec 94	0.44	0.10	294,235	29,398
Sep 94	0.51	0.10	281,409	33,932
Jun 94	0.34	0.10	256,645	22,843
Mar 94	0.15	0.10	224,539	10,132
Dec 93	(0.10)	0.10	209,624	(6,577)
Sep 93	0.12	0.10	155,714	8,025
Jun 93	0.05	0.10	142,632	3,319

Synopsis:

In 1994 CanOxy saw improvements in virtually all divisions despite lower average oil prices. Production from the Republic of Yemen provided the greatest contribution to CanOxy's financial results, despite the political turmoil in the spring of 1994. Net crude oil production was 78,100 barrels per day. Both the Alternative Fuels and Chemicals Divisions showed improvements in operating results due to price improvements and reduced operating costs. Consistent with CanOxy's desire to grow its international production base, new exploration and exploitation interests were acquired in Kazakhstan, Vietnam, and the North Sea. In Canada, CanOxy sold certain non-core assets.

Growing reserves and production will remain the focus for CanOxy in 1995. Capital and exploration spending should total $400-million, an increase of 52% over 1994. Approximately 90% will be spent by the oil and gas divisions, of which 33% will be invested in exploration projects. Oil and gas expenditures should be split equally between the International and North American Divisions. The North American Division's exploration activities are targeted primarily at increasing natural gas reserves, while development activities will focus on increasing production from existing properties. International Division spending will be directed primarily at exploration and development activities in the Republic of Yemen, the North Sea, Kazakhstan, Vietnam, Romania, and Indonesia.

During 1994 (1993), average gross daily production by resource was: natural gas, 241 (225) million cubic feet; oil and gas liquids, 105 (41.1) thousand barrels; and 13.8 (13.3) thousand barrels of synthetic oil. At its 1994 (1993) year-end total proven and probable reserves by resource were: 827.4 (919.1) billion cubic feet of natural gas; 408.1 (370.3) million barrels of oil and gas liquids; and 179.7 (127.9) million barrels of synthetic oil. In 1994, revenue contributions to total revenue by business unit were: International Oil and Gas, 45%; North American Oil and Gas, 28% Alternate Fuels, 10%, and Chemicals, 17%.

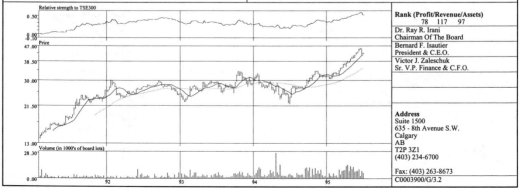

Rank (Profit/Revenue/Assets)
78   117   97

Dr. Ray R. Irani
Chairman Of The Board

Bernard F. Isautier
President & C.E.O.

Victor J. Zaleschuk
Sr. V.P. Finance & C.F.O.

Address
Suite 1500
635 - 8th Avenue S.W.
Calgary
AB
T2P 3Z1
(403) 234-6700

Fax: (403) 263-8673
C0003900/G/3.2

CHAUVCO RESOURCES LTD.

Exchanges	Price (Jun29'95)		16.00	Trailing P/E		25.81	Stock Symbol
TMZ	Trailing Yield (%)		0.00	Trailing EPS		0.62	CHA

Period Ending	Dec94	Dec93	Dec92	Dec91	Dec90	Business:
Yearly Statistics						CHAUVCO RESOURCES LTD. is an oil and
Price-Close	18.50	17.25	12.88	11.00	8.25	gas exploration and production company. The
Price-High	22.00	19.25	14.13	12.25	9.13	Corporation's activities are concentrated on the
Price-Low	15.50	12.75	9.88	8.13	5.25	acquisition, exploration, development and
P/E-Close	28.46	26.95	24.29	29.33	17.74	production of petroleum and natural gas
Dividends per Share	0.00	0.00	0.00	0.00	0.00	reserves in Canada (primarily in Alberta,
Dividend Yield (%)	0.00	0.00	0.00	0.00	0.00	British Columbia, Saskatchewan and Manitoba)
Sales per Share	4.25	3.61	3.36	2.95	2.35	and in Argentina in the provinces of Tierra del
EPS before extra. item	0.65	0.64	0.53	0.38	0.47	Feugo and Neuquen.
Cash Flow per Share	2.19	1.89	1.84	1.69	1.29	
Book Value per Share	6.32	5.66	5.03	3.84	3.06	
O/S Common Shares	44,538	44,232	43,745	39,034	36,141	
Total Revenue	194,342	160,989	144,380	114,561	81,115	
Income before extra.	29,052	28,220	22,614	14,402	15,715	
Cash Flow	97,362	83,259	78,253	64,622	43,697	

Date	EPS	DPS	Tot Rev	Inc Bex
Mar 95	0.10	0.00	51,767	4,394
Dec 94	0.15	0.00	50,881	6,776
Sep 94	0.17	0.00	53,209	7,429
Jun 94	0.20	0.00	51,736	9,129
Mar 94	0.13	0.00	39,387	5,718
Dec 93	0.16	0.00	41,507	7,136
Sep 93	0.17	0.00	41,754	7,627
Jun 93	0.18	0.00	40,939	7,769

Debt/Equity	0.66	0.21	0.24	0.36	0.35
Return on Capital (%)	13.08	13.17	15.44	18.18	27.12
Ret. on Com. Equity (%)	10.93	12.00	12.23	11.05	19.78
% Change Profit	2.9	24.8	57.0	(8.4)	253.1
% Change Revenue	20.7	11.5	26.0	41.2	200.8
% Change Assets	46.8	15.8	29.9	36.0	100.6

Preferred Div. Coverage	np	np	np
Total Div. Coverage	na	na	na
Interest Coverage	4.9	8.3	6.8
Current Ratio	1.0	0.6	1.0
Operating Margin	24.5	23.3	24.6
Asset Turnover	0.3	0.4	0.4
5 YEAR RATIOS (%)			
Return on Capital	17.4	17.5	16.1
Return on Com. Equity	13.2	13.0	11.5
Profit Growth	45.5	71.3	42.6
Revenue Growth	48.4	55.7	57.1
Asset Growth	43.2	37.3	38.6
BALANCE SHEET (000)			
Cash	1,180	2,040	471
Current Assets	39,892	16,342	17,309
Net Fixed Assets	523,282	366,716	314,628
Invest's & Advances	1,478	1,545	115
Total Assets	564,652	384,603	332,052
Short Term Debt	4,685	1,930	1,452
Current Liabilities	40,641	28,214	16,678
Long Term Debt	180,715	51,405	50,303
Total Liabilities	283,210	134,326	112,094
Total Equity	281,442	250,277	219,958
Total Liab. & Equity	564,652	384,603	332,052
CAPITAL (000)			
Total Debt	185,400	53,335	51,755
Preferred Equity	0	0	0
Common Equity	281,442	250,277	219,958

Synopsis:

Chauvco feels that the company is on the threshold of major growth, primarily in Argentina where Chauvco expects to witness substantial increases in both oil and gas production in 1995 and beyond. The company estimates that sometime during 1996, 50% of its cash flow will come from Argentina, as a result of prospects currently under development. Initiatives taken by the Argentine government to deregulate the oil and gas industry have led to increased activity, efficiency improvements, increased investment opportunities, growing demand, and production gains. A pipeline to Chile expected within two to three years and the possibility of pipeline construction from Bolivia to Brazil towards the year 2000, will enable Argentina to serve major consuming countries and open new markets for Argentine natural gas.

Continued exploitation of the company's asset base in Canada and Argentina should maintain daily oil production relatively constant at 21,000 barrels. Natural gas production should grow to 115-125 million cubic feet per day. This level of production should generate cash flow of $110-million and earnings of $32-million in 1995.

Planned capital expenditures in 1995 will consist of $120-million for exploration and development, of which Canadian operations will account for $53-million and Argentine operations for $67-million. The portion of capital expenditures in Argentina for 1995 has increased relative to the previous year in order to develop 1994 discoveries, construct facilities, and develop recently acquired properties. The capital budget will be funded by cash flow with a modest increase in debt.

Average gross daily production in 1994 (1993) was: crude oil and natural gas liquids 20,754 (19,689) barrels; and natural gas, 84.9 (55) million cubic feet. Gross proven and probable reserves in 1994 (1993) were: crude oil and natural gas liquids, 65.7 (52.3) million barrels; and natural gas, 682.4 (571.8) billion cubic feet.

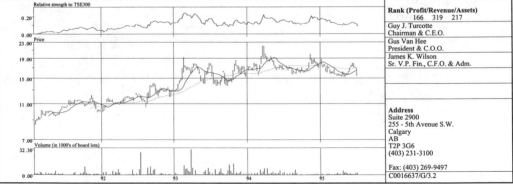

Rank (Profit/Revenue/Assets)
166   319   217

Guy J. Turcotte
Chairman & C.E.O.
Gus Van Hee
President & C.O.O.
James K. Wilson
Sr. V.P. Fin., C.F.O. & Adm.

Address
Suite 2900
255 - 5th Avenue S.W.
Calgary
AB
T2P 3G6
(403) 231-3100

Fax: (403) 269-9497
C0016637/G/3.2

CHIEFTAIN INTERNATIONAL, INC.

Exchanges	Price (Jun29'95)	18.62	Trailing P/E	nm	Stock Symbol
TZA	Trailing Yield (%)	0.00	Trailing EPS	(1.35)	**CID**

Period Ending	Dec94	Dec93	Dec92	Dec91	Dec90
Yearly Statistics	US	US	US	US	US
Price-Close	14.63	21.88	22.00	16.25	22.00
Price-High	24.75	28.00	23.75	22.13	28.25
Price-Low	14.00	18.25	14.25	13.25	20.75
P/E-Close	nm	nm	377.17	nm	20.98
Dividends per Share	0.00	0.00	0.00	0.00	0.00
Dividend Yield (%)	0.00	0.00	0.00	0.00	0.00
Sales per Share	3.27	4.31	4.01	3.47	4.62
EPS before extra. item	(1.32)	(0.01)	0.04	(0.58)	0.77
Cash Flow per Share	1.61	2.45	2.21	2.21	3.38
Book Value per Share	12.59	13.90	13.90	13.40	13.98
O/S Common Shares	10,912	10,993	10,988	9,488	9,488
Total Revenue	40,717	51,050	40,592	35,429	46,972
Income before extra.	(14,470)	(59)	437	(5,492)	7,324
Cash Flow	17,647	26,894	22,601	20,948	32,073
Debt/Equity	nd	nd	nd	nd	nd
Return on Capital (%)	(13.28)	2.03	1.10	(6.22)	9.02
Ret. on Com. Equity (%)	(9.98)	(0.04)	0.31	(4.23)	5.68
% Change Profit	nm	(113.5)	108.0	(175.0)	784.5
% Change Revenue	(20.2)	25.8	14.6	(24.6)	152.3
% Change Assets	(8.0)	0.8	71.0	(8.8)	11.0

Business:

CHIEFTAIN INTERNATIONAL, INC. is an oil and gas exploration and development company. It is active in the United States, the North Sea, Libya, and Peru.

Date		EPS	DPS	Tot Rev	Inc Bex
Mar 95	US	(0.12)	0.00	6,558	(1,290)
Dec 94	US	(1.03)	0.00	13,519	(11,269)
Sep 94	US	(0.08)	0.00	8,434	(877)
Jun 94	US	(0.12)	0.00	9,178	(1,292)
Mar 94	US	(0.09)	0.00	9,586	(1,032)
Dec 93	US	(0.02)	0.00	10,170	(186)
Sep 93	US	0.02	0.00	11,932	191
Jun 93	US	0.03	0.00	10,964	412

Preferred Div. Coverage	np	np	np	
Total Div. Coverage	na	na	na	
Interest Coverage	nd	nd	nd	
Current Ratio	23.0	26.6	22.1	
Operating Margin	(53.1)	9.3	2.1	
Asset Turnover	0.2	0.2	0.2	
5 YEAR RATIOS (%)				
Return on Capital	(1.5)	na	na	
Return on Com. Equity	(1.7)	na	na	
Profit Growth	na	na	na	
Revenue Growth	16.9	na	na	
Asset Growth	9.9	na	na	
BALANCE SHEET (000)				
Cash	102,151	112,808	114,750	
Current Assets	107,915	119,556	122,672	
Net Fixed Assets	95,036	103,443	98,341	
Invest's & Advances	0	0	0	
Total Assets	208,516	226,738	225,050	
Short Term Debt	0	0	0	
Current Liabilities	4,690	4,491	5,555	
Long Term Debt	0	0	0	
Total Liabilities	71,165	73,984	72,308	
Total Equity	137,351	152,754	152,742	
Total Liab. & Equity	208,516	226,738	225,050	
CAPITAL (000)				
Total Debt	0	0	0	
Preferred Equity	0	0	0	
Common Equity	137,351	152,754	152,742	

Synopsis:

According to Chieftain International, the weakness in natural gas prices that began last summer and continued into 1995 will force further restructuring in the natural gas production sector. Producers are experiencing significant reductions in cash flow, and for some producers higher interest rates coupled with increased debt/equity ratios could result in asset sales. Chieftain views this current environment as one of increasing opportunity to acquire reserves at competitive prices.

Chieftain's 1995 $35-million (U.S.) exploration and development budget will be directed towards its interests in the U.S., the North Sea, Libya, and Peru. Gas and oil development programs have been approved for areas in the Gulf of Mexico and oil production units in Utah. In the North Sea, Chieftain is participating with a 17.8% interest in the development of a gas field. The gas field should begin production in November 1995. It should produce an average of nine million cubic feet of gas per day net to Chieftain. In addition, Chieftain plans to participate in 12 to 14 exploration wells in the Gulf of Mexico, Libya, and the North Sea. The remaining $60-million (U.S.) of the company's capital budget is allocated towards the acquisition of gas and oil producing properties in the U.S.

The 24% decline in production revenue in 1994 resulted almost entirely from a 29% decrease in the volume of natural gas sales. Lower production levels resulted from voluntary curtailments during periods of low gas prices, from interruptions during development and pipeline activities, and from some reduction in deliverability.

During 1994 (1993) average daily gross production by resource was: oil and natural gas liquids, 1,895 (1,830) barrels; and natural gas, 34.5 (48.4) million cubic feet. At the end of 1994 (1993), gross proven and probable oil reserves totalled 7.3 (6) million barrels, natural gas reserves totalled 79.5 (79.1) billion cubic feet. Chieftain's 1994 (1993) revenues by resource were: natural gas, 59% (77%); oil and natural gas liquids, 27% (23%) and interest and other sources, 14%(0%).

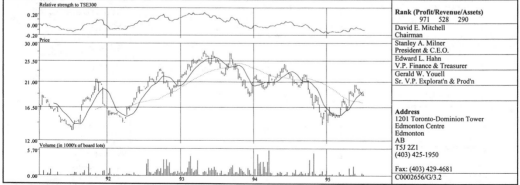

Rank (Profit/Revenue/Assets)
971   528   290
David E. Mitchell
Chairman
Stanley A. Milner
President & C.E.O.
Edward L. Hahn
V.P. Finance & Treasurer
Gerald W. Youell
Sr. V.P. Explorat'n & Prod'n

Address
1201 Toronto-Dominion Tower
Edmonton Centre
Edmonton
AB
T5J 2Z1
(403) 425-1950

Fax: (403) 429-4681
C0002656/G/3.2

CIMARRON PETROLEUM LTD.

Exchanges		Price (Jun29'95)		12.00	Trailing P/E		19.67	Stock Symbol
T		Trailing Yield (%)		0.00	Trailing EPS		0.61	CIR

Period Ending	Dec94	Apr94	Apr93	Apr92	Apr91
Yearly Statistics	8M				
Price-Close	11.50	9.63	8.38	9.50	12.00
Price-High	12.88	10.25	10.75	14.25	13.50
Price-Low	9.13	7.50	6.75	9.50	8.63
P/E-Close	24.73	31.05	nm	950.00	150.00
Dividends per Share	0.00	0.00	0.00	0.00	0.10
Dividend Yield (%)	0.00	0.00	0.00	0.00	0.83
Sales per Share	4.19	2.91	2.07	1.98	2.52
EPS before extra. item	0.31	0.31	(0.19)	0.01	0.08
Cash Flow per Share	2.33	1.47	0.97	0.96	1.39
Book Value per Share	5.60	5.29	4.99	5.18	5.17
O/S Common Shares	7,914	7,884	7,681	7,674	7,661
Total Revenue	21,266	23,331	15,871	15,169	19,967
Income before extra.	2,412	2,381	(1,478)	45	564
Cash Flow	12,271	11,269	7,447	7,374	10,339
Debt/Equity	0.38	0.31	0.24	0.14	0.00
Return on Capital (%)	10.59	7.98	(6.12)	(0.26)	1.04
Ret. on Com. Equity (%)	8.41	5.95	(3.79)	0.11	1.60
% Change Profit	52.0	261.1	(3,384.4)	(92.0)	(56.8)
% Change Revenue	36.7	47.0	4.6	(24.0)	40.5
% Change Assets	17.3	20.4	0.0	3.4	23.7

Business:

CIMARRON PETROLEUM LTD. is engaged in the exploration for and development of oil and gas properties in Canada.

Date	EPS	DPS	Tot Rev	Inc Bex
Mar 95	0.17	0.00	8,521	1,316
Dec 94	0.04	0.00	9,224	407
Sep 94	0.19	0.00	8,544	1,410
Apr 94	0.21	0.00	8,611	1,595
Jan 94	0.07	0.00	5,806	568
Oct 93	0.04	0.00	4,922	275
Jul 93	(0.01)	0.00	3,992	(57)
Apr 93	(0.23)	0.00	4,073	(1,778)

Preferred Div. Coverage	np	np	np
Total Div. Coverage	na	na	na
Interest Coverage	6.5	5.2	0.0
Current Ratio	0.7	0.9	0.9
Operating Margin	22.0	13.8	(17.7)
Asset Turnover	0.4	0.3	0.3
5 YEAR RATIOS (%)			
Return on Capital	2.6	2.1	1.4
Return on Com. Equity	2.5	1.9	1.4
Profit Growth	22.6	29.1	na
Revenue Growth	17.5	19.9	12.2
Asset Growth	12.5	12.3	12.4
BALANCE SHEET (000)			
Cash	0	0	0
Current Assets	6,716	5,711	3,327
Net Fixed Assets	68,749	58,642	50,118
Invest's & Advances	0	0	0
Total Assets	75,465	64,353	53,445
Short Term Debt	0	0	0
Current Liabilities	9,572	6,319	3,540
Long Term Debt	16,779	12,735	9,091
Total Liabilities	31,136	22,687	15,136
Total Equity	44,329	41,666	38,309
Total Liab. & Equity	75,465	64,353	53,445
CAPITAL (000)			
Total Debt	16,779	12,735	9,091
Preferred Equity	0	0	0
Common Equity	44,329	41,666	38,309

Synopsis:

Historically, Cimarron Petroleum has tried to maintain an equitable balance between oil and gas production. This mix changes occasionally if one commodity becomes more profitable in the short term as evidenced by the company's 37% increase in gas production in 1994. Cimarron expects that this momentum will continue into 1995, despite the soft gas price environment. The gas that the company has placed on stream in the last two years incurs very low operating costs, thus Cimarron remains confident that this production will continue to produce a profitable netback. To capitalize on current oil prices and to match the pace of gas volume growth, Cimarron intends to focus on raising its oil production volumes. According to the company this should become evident late in 1995 with new development at Valhalla and Lymburn, both situated in Alberta. A combination of increases in gas and liquids production volumes and oil prices contributed to the 41% increase in revenue for the eight month period ending December 1994.

Cimarron's capital expenditure program in the calendar year totalled $27.8 million. Land expenditures and seismic represented 9%, and 2% respectively. An even split of exploratory and development drilling accounted for 39%, development for 34% and acquisitions 16%. Dispositions, which included a package of several non-core properties, produced $6-million and reduced Cimarron's net capital outlay to $21.8-million. The company's budget for capital reinvestment in 1995 remains unchanged at $27-million.

During the eight-month period ending December 31, 1994, (year ending April 30, 1994), average daily production by resource was: oil and natural gas liquids, 2,318 (1,710) barrels; and natural gas, 23.1, (16.1) million cubic feet. At December 1994 (April 1994), total gross proven and probable reserves by resource were: 6.4 (6.3) million barrels of crude oil and liquids; and 107 (95) billion cubic feet of natural gas.

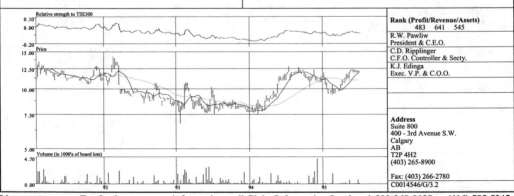

Rank (Profit/Revenue/Assets)		
483	641	545

R.W. Pawliw
President & C.E.O.

C.D. Ripplinger
C.F.O. Controller & Secty.

K.J. Edinga
Exec. V.P. & C.O.O.

Address
Suite 800
400 - 3rd Avenue S.W.
Calgary
AB
T2P 4H2
(403) 265-8900

Fax: (403) 266-2780
C0014546/G/3.2

COHO ENERGY INC.

Exchanges	Price (Jun29'95)		6.87	Trailing P/E		nm	Stock Symbol
TQ	Trailing Yield (%)		0.00	Trailing EPS		(0.13)	**CEE**

Period Ending	Dec94	Dec93	Dec92	Dec91	Dec90
Yearly Statistics	US	US			
Price-Close	7.25	6.00	6.54	4.43	13.67
Price-High	7.50	8.50	9.62	13.86	28.87
Price-Low	5.00	5.25	3.66	4.23	12.70
P/E-Close	nm	nm	17.36	nm	10.44
Dividends per Share	0.00	0.00	0.00	0.00	0.00
Dividend Yield (%)	0.00	0.00	0.00	0.00	0.00
Sales per Share	1.57	2.35	2.27	6.12	6.78
EPS before extra. item	(0.12)	(1.12)	0.31	(7.13)	1.31
Cash Flow per Share	0.56	1.02	1.21	1.92	2.69
Book Value per Share	3.36	3.16	4.15	3.00	10.82
O/S Common Shares	16,783	14,007	11,847	7,357	7,357
Total Revenue	34,647	28,350	27,039	47,631	63,257
Income before extra.	(1,654)	(13,449)	3,637	(53,712)	10,053
Cash Flow	7,928	12,248	14,352	14,100	19,787
Debt/Equity	1.26	1.22	1.06	3.36	0.66
Return on Capital (%)	1.17	(15.14)	9.75	(42.21)	17.45
Ret. on Com. Equity (%)	(3.45)	(28.79)	10.46	(106.36)	13.14
% Change Profit	87.7	(469.8)	108.2	(634.3)	291.3
% Change Revenue	22.2	4.9	(31.0)	(24.7)	65.6
% Change Assets	88.9	(6.3)	8.9	(27.8)	20.5
Preferred Div. Coverage	0.0	np	np
Total Div. Coverage	0.0	na	na
Interest Coverage	0.4	0.0	2.8
Current Ratio	0.9	1.1	1.4
Operating Margin	11.9	(53.7)	33.9
Asset Turnover	0.2	0.3	0.2
5 YEAR RATIOS (%)			
Return on Capital	(5.8)	(4.2)	0.1
Return on Com. Equity	(23.0)	(21.9)	(16.8)
Profit Growth	na	na	na
Revenue Growth	4.9	7.2	17.5
Asset Growth	13.1	1.1	6.4
BALANCE SHEET (000)			
Cash	1,613	3,936	3,258
Current Assets	22,852	6,878	6,705
Net Fixed Assets	171,524	96,317	103,581
Invest's & Advances	0	0	0
Total Assets	196,970	104,286	111,292
Short Term Debt	0	0	0
Current Liabilities	25,231	6,007	4,915
Long Term Debt	86,311	54,000	52,000
Total Liabilities	124,429	60,007	62,134
Total Equity	72,541	44,279	49,158
Total Liab. & Equity	196,970	104,286	111,292
CAPITAL (000)			
Total Debt	91,567	54,000	52,000
Preferred Equity	16,125	0	0
Common Equity	56,416	44,279	49,158

Business:

COHO ENERGY INC. is an oil and gas company whose major asset is a 68% ownership in Coho Resources, Inc., an active United States oil and gas company. Effective October 5, 1993, Coho Resources Limited amalgamated with Coho Resources, Inc. to form Coho Energy Inc. The company was reincorporated at that time in the United States.

Date		EPS	DPS	Tot Rev	Inc Bex
Mar 95	US	(0.01)	0.00	31,328	177
Dec 94	US	(0.11)	0.00	15,904	(1,613)
Sep 94	US	(0.01)	0.00	6,495	(85)
Jun 94	US	0.00	0.00	6,295	(24)
Mar 94	US	0.00	0.00	5,953	68
Dec 93	US	(1.24)	0.00	6,255	(14,932)
Sep 93	US	0.06	0.00	7,262	709
Jun 93	US	(0.01)	0.00	7,524	(173)

Synopsis:

Coho Energy, Inc. bought the privately owned Interstate Natural Gas Company in December 1994. Coho paid approximately $55-million, made up of $20-million in cash, 2.78 million shares of its common stock, shares of a newly created series of preferred stock valued at $16.3-million, and the assumption of a working capital deficiency of about $5-million. The acquisition of Interstate Natural Gas, a producer, gatherer. and pipeline company, increased Coho's asset base, reserves, and production capability by 50%. In addition, Interstate diversified Coho's asset base from its existing oil orientation.

The company attributed the largest component in increased gas production volumes during the first quarter of 1995 to Interstate. Gas production quarter over quarter increased from less than 300,000 cubic feet per day in 1994 to 20.2 million cubic feet in 1995. Daily oil production, of 5,616 barrels for the same period declined slightly from the fourth quarter of 1994 as a result of temporary interruptions in operations at two of its reservoirs near Laurel, Mississippi. First quarter net earnings, prior to the provision for preferred share dividends, was $177,000.

Although oil and gas volumes increased in 1994 over 1993, lower realized commodity prices, particularly in the first half of the year, offset production increases. Included in operating revenues is $7.9-million derived from Interstate's marketing and transportation facilities for the month of December. In addition, a $2.5-million non-recurring restructuring charge relating to the integration of Interstate into existing operations, is included in net earnings for the period.

Average daily crude oil and natural gas liquids production in 1994 (1993) was 5,416 (4,988) barrels. Natural gas production figures were unavailable at time of writing. Net proven reserves in 1994 (1993) were: crude oil and natural gas liquids, 27.5 (24.9) million barrels; and natural gas, 100.1 (14) billion cubic feet.

Relative strength to TSE300 / Price / Volume (in 1000's of board lots)

Rank (Profit/Revenue/Assets)
373   502   369

Jeffrey Clark
Chairman, President & C.E.O.

Eddie M. LeBlanc III
Sr. V.P. & C.F.O.

Address
Suite 860
14785 Preston Road
Dallas
TX
75240
(214) 991-9493

Fax: (214) 991-8514

C0009031/G/3.2

COMPUTALOG LTD.

Exchanges	Price (Jun29'95)	7.75	Trailing P/E	4.61	Stock Symbol
TQ	Trailing Yield (%)	0.00	Trailing EPS	1.68	**CGH**

Period Ending	Dec94	Dec93	Dec92	Dec91	Dec90	Business:
Yearly Statistics						COMPUTALOG LTD. provides oil and gas
Price-Close	7.25	12.00	1.76	3.72	14.00	field services to the Canadian, United States
Price-High	12.00	15.00	4.40	14.80	20.00	and international markets. Services include
Price-Low	6.88	1.68	1.40	3.00	11.20	logging of oil and gas wells to determine
P/E-Close	4.29	9.09	nm	nm	nm	quality and quantity of hydrocarbons present
Dividends per Share	0.00	0.00	0.00	0.00	0.00	and the provision of directional drilling
Dividend Yield (%)	0.00	0.00	0.00	0.00	0.00	services. The company also manufactures
Sales per Share	15.30	13.06	8.57	11.46	14.10	specialized downhole tools and surface
EPS before extra. item	1.69	1.32	(1.28)	(4.28)	(3.72)	computer systems for its own operations and
Cash Flow per Share	2.43	2.04	(0.26)	(0.98)	0.22	other clients.
Book Value per Share	8.51	7.24	6.00	7.25	11.63	
O/S Common Shares	7,518	6,902	6,733	6,733	6,728	
Total Revenue	114,395	89,942	58,434	84,840	86,125	
Income before extra.	12,611	9,161	(8,617)	(28,780)	(23,739)	
Cash Flow	18,166	13,875	(1,746)	(6,628)	1,401	

Date	EPS	DPS	Tot Rev	Inc Bex
Mar 95	0.74	0.00	37,242	5,575
Dec 94	0.32	0.00	31,296	2,424
Sep 94	0.43	0.00	29,937	3,175
Jun 94	0.19	0.00	22,054	1,438
Mar 94	0.76	0.00	31,051	5,573
Dec 93	0.32	0.00	26,725	2,425
Sep 93	0.28	0.00	22,297	1,999
Jun 93	0.00	0.00	16,572	24

	Dec94	Dec93	Dec92	Dec91	Dec90
Debt/Equity	nd	0.19	0.37	0.23	0.30
Return on Capital (%)	25.59	18.08	(12.68)	(28.13)	(22.92)
Ret. on Com. Equity (%)	22.12	20.28	(19.33)	(45.31)	(28.80)
% Change Profit	37.7	206.3	70.1	(21.2)	(61.9)
% Change Revenue	27.2	53.9	(31.1)	(1.5)	24.3
% Change Assets	18.5	9.6	(6.7)	(39.0)	(2.2)

	Dec94	Dec93	Dec92	Synopsis:
Preferred Div. Coverage	np	np	np	Computalog expects 1995 capital spending to rise to $15-million, with
Total Div. Coverage	na	na	na	$7.7-million to be spend on equipment constructed at the company's
Interest Coverage	24.1	8.4	0.0	manufacturing facility. Capital spending will be primarily for the replacement of
Current Ratio	2.2	2.4	2.0	wireline units, additional surface systems, downhole tools and measurement while
Operating Margin	13.7	10.6	(12.0)	drilling systems. The company will finance capital expenditures from operating
Asset Turnover	1.3	1.2	0.9	cash flow and will adjust spending downwards should operating performance or
5 YEAR RATIOS (%)				the market decline. Computalog plans to grow earnings through further market
Return on Capital	(4.0)	(12.6)	(15.4)	penetration, selected alliances, and strategic acquisitions. Computalog expects
Return on Com. Equity	(10.2)	(17.8)	(21.4)	continued growth in Venezuela, Russia, and other countries with favorable market
Profit Growth	16.6	33.0	na	conditions.
Revenue Growth	10.5	2.8	(4.3)	
Asset Growth	(6.3)	(9.4)	(11.2)	The company's 1994 results were primarily due to the strong Canadian market.
BALANCE SHEET (000)				The strength of the Canadian market is shown by average rig count, which
Cash	4,751	332	1,592	reached 331 rigs last year versus 244 in 1993. In the United States, Computalog
Current Assets	45,066	37,196	32,938	completed improvements in wireline technology and services in a better market
Net Fixed Assets	38,212	32,984	31,074	where an average of 774 rigs were active in 1994, against 753 in 1993. The
Invest's & Advances	1,841	1,340	616	company also improved its United States presence in directional drilling market
Total Assets	85,119	71,850	65,578	through alliances with a number of directional drilling companies. Internationally,
Short Term Debt	0	3,629	6,999	Computalog realized a profit in Venezuela. It made its first sale of equipment
Current Liabilities	20,409	15,642	16,865	in the Russia through a joint stock company, and made other sales in India, China,
Long Term Debt	0	6,026	8,000	Egypt, and Europe.
Total Liabilities	21,110	21,855	25,218	
Total Equity	64,009	49,995	40,360	In 1994 revenues (net income) by geographic location were: Canada, 69% (95%);
Total Liab. & Equity	85,119	71,850	65,578	United States, 23% (6%); and international, 8% (-1%). Revenue distribution by
CAPITAL (000)				type of customer in 1994 was: independent oil companies, 68%; major oil
Total Debt	0	9,655	14,999	companies, 13%; national oil companies, 5%; and other companies, 14%.
Preferred Equity	0	0	0	Revenue distribution by product line was: cased hole service, 42%; open hole
Common Equity	64,009	49,995	40,360	services, 26%; drilling services, 24%; and wireline and drilling products, 8%.

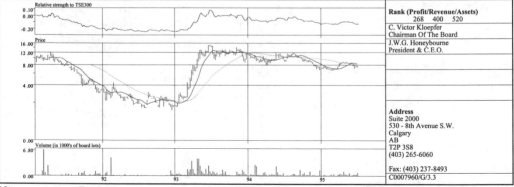

Rank (Profit/Revenue/Assets)
268   400   520

C. Victor Kloepfer
Chairman Of The Board

J.W.G. Honeybourne
President & C.E.O.

Address
Suite 2000
530 - 8th Avenue S.W.
Calgary
AB
T2P 3S8
(403) 265-6060

Fax: (403) 237-8493
C0007960/G/3.3

CONSOLIDATED RAMROD GOLD CORPORATION

Exchanges	Price (Jun29'95)	4.30	Trailing P/E	nm	Stock Symbol
TQ	Trailing Yield (%)	0.00	Trailing EPS	(0.35)	CYN

Period Ending	Jun94	Jun93	Jun92	Jun91	Jun90
Yearly Statistics					4M
Price-Close	6.75	4.20	3.30	3.25	n t
Price-High	10.50	4.60	3.40	4.00	n t
Price-Low	3.55	2.85	1.00	2.50	n t
P/E-Close	nm	nm	nm	nm	n t
Dividends per Share	0.00	0.00	0.00	0.00	0.00
Dividend Yield (%)	0.00	0.00	0.00	0.00	0.00
Sales per Share	0.01	0.00	na	na	na
EPS before extra. item	(0.33)	(0.24)	(0.29)	(0.30)	(0.06)
Cash Flow per Share	(0.09)	(0.08)	(0.09)	(0.11)	(0.13)
Book Value per Share	0.78	0.61	0.43	0.61	0.50
O/S Common Shares	23,958	20,342	16,039	8,419	6,492
Total Revenue	386	189	104	(164)	(1)
Income before extra.	(7,094)	(4,160)	(2,531)	(2,131)	(417)
Cash Flow	(1,875)	(1,373)	(790)	(769)	(282)
Debt/Equity	0.09	0.00	nd	0.01	0.09
Return on Capital (%)	(42.94)	(42.95)	(41.74)	(47.98)	(37.46)
Ret. on Com. Equity (%)	(45.43)	(42.99)	(41.92)	(50.74)	(41.92)
% Change Profit	(70.5)	(64.4)	(18.8)	(70.4)	(16.2)
% Change Revenue	104.5	80.9	163.6	(4,644.2)	(102.6)
% Change Assets	75.0	81.2	31.7	46.1	23.2

Date	EPS	DPS	Tot Rev	Inc Bex
Mar 95	(0.09)	0.00	(280)	(2,279)
Dec 94	(0.05)	0.00	888	(1,232)
Sep 94	(0.04)	0.00	61	(951)
Jun 94	(0.17)	0.00	177	(3,779)
Mar 94	(0.11)	0.00	90	(2,271)
Dec 93	(0.02)	0.00	51	(497)
Sep 93	(0.03)	0.00	67	(548)
Jun 93	(0.04)	0.00	13	(805)

Preferred Div. Coverage	np	np	np
Total Div. Coverage	na	na	na
Interest Coverage	0.0	0.0	0.0
Current Ratio	0.5	8.0	4.8
Operating Margin	(3,575.4)	(66,449.4)	na
Asset Turnover	0.0	0.0	na
5 YEAR RATIOS (%)			
Return on Capital	(42.6)	(41.3)	(37.6)
Return on Com. Equity	(44.6)	(43.3)	(40.2)
Profit Growth	(54.3)	na	na
Revenue Growth	23.6	17.7	54.9
Asset Growth	49.6	34.0	63.3
BALANCE SHEET (000)			
Cash	371	4,785	735
Current Assets	1,932	5,186	1,517
Net Fixed Assets	18,420	6,969	5,075
Invest's & Advances	900	850	538
Total Assets	22,914	13,094	7,227
Short Term Debt	1,768	1	0
Current Liabilities	4,128	649	315
Long Term Debt	0	0	0
Total Liabilities	4,128	649	315
Total Equity	18,786	12,445	6,912
Total Liab. & Equity	22,914	13,094	7,227
CAPITAL (000)			
Total Debt	1,768	1	0
Preferred Equity	0	0	0
Common Equity	18,786	12,445	6,912

Business:

CONSOLIDATED RAMROD GOLD CORPORATION is engaged in the acquisition and exploration of natural resource properties in the United States, Canada and Central and South America. The Company has an extensive portfolio of precious and base metals properties as well as oil and gas projects.

Synopsis:

Consolidated Ramrod Gold Corp. is engaged in the mineral resource industry at the exploration stage. At the exploration stage, a mineral resource company has not determined whether its mineral properties contain ore reserves that are economically recoverable. Nor has it achieved revenue from production. Cumulative losses, cash flows, and mineral property costs deferred are measured from inception of the exploration stage, which was March 1, 1985, after substantial reorganization of the company. As at June 30, 1994, the company had $12.9-million in mineral properties, mostly in Canada and the United States, with some in Latin America and Europe.

In October 1993, Consolidated Ramrod entered the oil and gas industry by purchasing Ramrod Oil and Gas Limited, formerly Grant Energy Ltd., in consideration for the issue of 65,000 shares. Ramrod Oil and Gas is active in exploration for oil and gas and the development and management of oil and gas wells in western Canada and Texas. Revenues for 1994 included $203,269 that were derived from oil and gas activities with the balance derived from investment income and gain on investments.

The company has financed the purchases of properties primarily through the issue of shares. Subsequent to the company's June 1994 year end, it realized $11.5-million from the sale of shares, the exercise of warrants and stock options, and the sale of convertible debentures. A portion of the funding was applied to the working capital deficiency of $2.2-million which existed at June 30, 1994. The balance went towards the company's mineral exploration and oil and gas exploration and development activities. Management expects to raise additional debt and equity financing for 1995.

Consolidated Ramrod is exploring for gold, and to a lesser degree, zinc, lead, silver, diamonds, and copper. Acquisitions in the company's new oil and gas division are underway in concessions in Ecuador and Guatemala. During 1994, the company bought Westmount Gold Inc. Its assets include several prospects in the Carlin Trend in Nevada.

Relative strength to TSE300 / Price / Volume (in 1000's of board lots)

Rank (Profit/Revenue/Assets)
926   964   841

Karl Rollke
President

Address
Suite 1440
625 Howe Street
Vancouver
BC
V6C 2T6
(604) 682-6477

Fax: (604) 683-5912
01002441/G/3.2

CONWEST EXPLORATION COMPANY LIMITED

Exchanges	Price (Jun29'95)		25.75	Trailing P/E		20.12	Stock Symbol
TMQ	Trailing Yield (%)		0.93	Trailing EPS		1.28	**CEX**

Period Ending	Dec94	Dec93	Dec92	Dec91	Dec90
Yearly Statistics					
Price-Close	21.75	21.13	10.00	9.13	13.75
Price-High	26.50	26.50	11.50	14.63	15.38
Price-Low	20.50	9.75	8.00	8.88	11.50
P/E-Close	15.76	28.94	13.89	nm	38.19
Dividends per Share	0.24	0.24	0.24	0.48	0.46
Dividend Yield (%)	1.10	1.14	2.40	5.26	3.35
Sales per Share	4.39	3.99	4.51	4.46	6.25
EPS before extra. item	1.38	0.73	0.72	(0.86)	0.36
Cash Flow per Share	3.10	2.13	2.13	1.41	2.35
Book Value per Share	14.24	13.04	10.43	9.96	11.15
O/S Common Shares	26,339	26,048	19,906	19,706	19,702
Total Revenue	158,659	121,309	108,850	75,145	103,110
Income before extra.	36,441	17,161	13,971	(15,852)	6,129
Cash Flow	81,186	49,277	40,174	26,427	37,860
Debt/Equity	0.42	0.20	0.70	0.75	0.56
Return on Capital (%)	12.51	9.26	8.20	(2.85)	6.61
Ret. on Com. Equity (%)	10.12	6.19	6.73	(7.80)	3.03
% Change Profit	112.3	22.8	188.1	(358.6)	(40.5)
% Change Revenue	30.8	11.4	44.9	(27.1)	(0.1)
% Change Assets	35.5	13.3	3.4	(0.8)	7.8
Preferred Div. Coverage	138.6	74.3	36.7		
Total Div. Coverage	5.6	2.9	2.7		
Interest Coverage	6.3	3.9	2.4		
Current Ratio	1.9	3.0	3.4		
Operating Margin	18.2	11.9	10.6		
Asset Turnover	0.2	0.2	0.2		
5 YEAR RATIOS (%)					
Return on Capital	6.7	6.4	7.1		
Return on Com. Equity	3.7	2.9	3.3		
Profit Growth	28.7	6.2	(16.3)		
Revenue Growth	8.9	4.4	0.5		
Asset Growth	11.1	6.4	6.7		
BALANCE SHEET (000)					
Cash	27,493	17,670	24,309		
Current Assets	88,898	62,970	55,556		
Net Fixed Assets	476,220	351,605	300,457		
Invest's & Advances	82,178	62,827	63,586		
Total Assets	647,759	477,891	421,618		
Short Term Debt	430	390	353		
Current Liabilities	46,563	20,703	16,242		
Long Term Debt	157,960	69,119	149,129		
Total Liabilities	265,763	136,790	207,661		
Total Equity	381,996	341,101	213,957		
Total Liab. & Equity	647,759	477,891	421,618		
CAPITAL (000)					
Total Debt	158,390	69,509	149,482		
Preferred Equity	7,005	1,400	6,299		
Common Equity	374,991	339,701	207,658		

Business:

CONWEST EXPLORATION CO. LTD. is a resource company engaged in the exploration and development of natural gas in western Canada. The company also owns a low-cost zinc mine in Canada's high Arctic, a small hydro business and a portfolio of securities in the mining and oil and gas sectors.

Date	EPS	DPS	Tot Rev	Inc Bex
Mar 95	0.17	0.06	38,189	4,464
Dec 94	0.23	0.06	39,236	6,226
Sep 94	0.67	0.06	51,046	17,559
Jun 94	0.21	0.06	34,170	5,616
Mar 94	0.27	0.06	34,207	7,040
Dec 93	0.17	0.06	31,619	4,448
Sep 93	0.08	0.06	29,137	2,707
Jun 93	0.26	0.06	31,351	5,796

Synopsis:

During 1995, Conwest's efforts will focus on the construction and tie-in of its major natural gas and condensate discovery in the Sexsmith/Valhalla region of the Peace River Arch. Facilities design and construction are being timed to bring this production onstream by October 1995. It is estimated that when fully onstream, Sexsmith's daily production will add 75 million cubic feet of gas and 2,900 barrels of natural gas liquids to the company's production.

Conwest's 1995 development, exploration, and land acquisition expenditures will exceed $135-million. About $40-million is committed to the Sexsmith project. Capital required to fund the proposed capital budget and further acquisitions will be provided by operating cash flow, bank borrowings, and possible asset dispositions. Anticipated production levels during 1995 will average 100 million cubic feet of gas per day, and oil and natural gas liquids will average 10,000 barrels per day.

Oil and gas revenue in 1994 was $74.1-million, representing a 13% increase over 1993 revenues. This improvement was due to increases in production volumes and average prices for both oil and gas.

Despite a modest increase in the price of zinc, Nanisivik, the company's Arctic zinc mine, made a substantial contribution to operating income in 1994. The improvement resulted from both higher prices and a further reduction in operating costs. Nanisivik more than replaced ore mined in 1994 with new ore reserve additions.

During 1994 (1993) average daily production was: oil and natural gas liquids, 7,000 (6,200) barrels, and natural gas, 59.7 (50.4) million cubic feet. At the end of 1994 (1993), the company's total proven and probable reserves were: oil and natural gas liquids, 47.6 (36.2) million barrels and natural gas, 704.3 (519.5) billion cubic feet.

Relative strength to TSE300

Price

Volume (in 1000's of board lots)

Rank (Profit/Revenue/Assets)
137 349 202

M.P. Connell
Chairman Of The Board

John C. Lamacraft
President & C.E.O.

J.A. Patterson
V.P. & Secretary, C.F.O.

Address
Suite 2000
95 Wellington Street West
Toronto
ON
M5J 2N7
(416) 362-6721

Fax: (416) 362-0069
C0010506/G/3.2

CRESTAR ENERGY INC.

Exchanges	Price (Jun29'95)		14 .25	Trailing P/E		52 .78	Stock Symbol
TM	Trailing Yield (%)		0 .00	Trailing EPS		0 .27	**CRS**

Period Ending	Dec94	Dec93	Dec92
Yearly Statistics			10M
Price-Close	14 .50	14 .38	n t
Price-High	18 .00	17 .63	n t
Price-Low	14 .13	12 .75	n t
P/E-Close	27 .89	102 .68	n t
Dividends per Share	0 .00	0 .00	0 .00
Dividend Yield (%)	0 .00	0 .00	0 .00
Sales per Share	8 .32	7 .07	5 .94
EPS before extra. item	0 .52	0 .14	(0 .17)
Cash Flow per Share	3 .81	3 .39	2 .66
Book Value per Share	5 .00	4 .47	4 .67
O/S Common Shares	40 ,055	40 ,000	40 ,000
Total Revenue	336 ,873	288 ,098	201 ,010
Income before extra.	20 ,730	5 ,719	(6 ,942)
Cash Flow	152 ,669	135 ,633	88 ,547
Debt/Equity	1 .02	1 .08	1 .19
Return on Capital (%)	12 .58	7 .45	na
Ret. on Com. Equity (%)	10 .93	3 .13	na
% Change Profit	262 .5	168 .7	na
% Change Revenue	16 .9	19 .4	na
% Change Assets	4 .8	(3 .2)	na
Preferred Div. Coverage	np	np	np
Total Div. Coverage	na	na	na
Interest Coverage	4 .4	3 .0	0 .4
Current Ratio	0 .8	1 .0	1 .6
Operating Margin	14 .8	10 .3	2 .4
Asset Turnover	0 .5	0 .4	0 .3
5 YEAR RATIOS (%)			
Return on Capital	na	na	na
Return on Com. Equity	na	na	na
Profit Growth	na	na	na
Revenue Growth	na	na	na
Asset Growth	na	na	na
BALANCE SHEET (000)			
Cash	2 ,331	2 ,218	10 ,429
Current Assets	59 ,359	55 ,751	46 ,350
Net Fixed Assets	649 ,342	625 ,044	663 ,527
Invest's & Advances	0	0	0
Total Assets	734 ,324	700 ,519	723 ,556
Short Term Debt	0	0	0
Current Liabilities	72 ,578	54 ,542	28 ,965
Long Term Debt	204 ,651	193 ,734	222 ,443
Total Liabilities	533 ,979	521 ,681	536 ,711
Total Equity	200 ,345	178 ,838	186 ,845
Total Liab. & Equity	734 ,324	700 ,519	723 ,556
CAPITAL (000)			
Total Debt	204 ,651	193 ,734	222 ,443
Preferred Equity	0	0	0
Common Equity	200 ,345	178 ,838	186 ,845

Business:

CRESTAR ENERGY INC. is engaged in upstream oil and gas exploration, production and marketing.

Date	EPS	DPS	Tot Rev	Inc Bex
Mar 95	(0 .24)	0 .00	84 ,245	(9 ,704)
Sep 94	0 .14	0 .00	81 ,940	5 ,757
Jun 94	0 .20	0 .00	87 ,583	7 ,996
Mar 94	0 .17	0 .00	81 ,295	6 ,839
Dec 93	0 .13	0 .00	76 ,229	5 ,297
Sep 93	0 .02	0 .00	67 ,509	985
Jun 93	0 .06	0 .00	77 ,160	2 ,300
Mar 93	(0 .07)	0 .00	67 ,199	(2 ,863)

Synopsis:

In January 1995, Crestar Energy's two largest shareholders, Amoco Canada Petroleum Company Ltd. and Dow Chemical Canada Inc., agreed with Investment Canada to restructure and extend their commitment to sell their interests in Crestar. Each company owns approximately 17.5% of Crestar's common shares. Under the agreement, the two companies have until December 31, 1998, to reduce their holdings in Crestar, independently of the other. Dow may continue to hold an interest in Crestar after 1998 equal to the greater of the largest interest owned by a single Canadian shareholder (up to 15%), or 10% of Crestar's outstanding common shares. Crestar expects that the extended period will reduce the negative effect of the sale obligation on the trading value of the company's shares.

Despite strong operational results in the first quarter of 1995, Crestar's cash flow declined by 12% from 1994 levels. Higher oil prices were more than offset by lower natural gas prices. Earnings were also affected by a non-recurring foreign exchange charge and a disproportionately high exploration expense related to spending in winter access areas. In view of current low natural gas prices, the drilling and tie-in of some shorter reserve life and higher operating cost projects have been deferred. Crestar continues to maintain its liquids development and exploration programs. During Crestar's first full year as a public company, it achieved growth in earnings and cash flow on the strength of higher production volumes, improved gas and liquids prices, and continued cost control.

In 1994 (1993), Crestar's average daily production was: crude oil and natural gas liquids, 24,400 (23,200) barrels; and natural gas 253 (241) million cubic feet. At year-end total proven and probable reserves were: crude oil and natural gas liquids, 69.2 (62.5) million barrels; and natural gas, 777 (773) billion cubic feet.

Relative strength to TSE300 / Price / Volume (in 1000's of board lots)

Rank (Profit/Revenue/Assets)		
210	242	184

T.D. Stacy
Chairman
S. Barry Jackson
President & C.E.O.
James Smith
V.P. Fin. & Adm. & C.F.O.

Address
Suite 1900
700 - 2nd Street S.W.
Calgary
AB
T2P 2W1
(403) 231-6700

Fax: (403) 231-3801
01003243/G/3.2

CS RESOURCES LIMITED

Exchanges	Price (Jun29'95)	8.37	Trailing P/E	22.03	Stock Symbol
TM	Trailing Yield (%)	0.00	Trailing EPS	0.38	**CRZ**

Period Ending	Dec94	Dec93	Dec92	Dec91	Dec90
Yearly Statistics					
Price-Close	6.75	6.50	5.88	4.10	6.00
Price-High	7.88	10.00	6.38	6.00	6.50
Price-Low	5.25	5.63	3.15	3.75	3.85
P/E-Close	29.35	25.00	19.58	34.17	15.39
Dividends per Share	0.00	0.00	0.00	0.00	0.00
Dividend Yield (%)	0.00	0.00	0.00	0.00	0.00
Sales per Share	2.82	2.46	2.23	1.74	2.58
EPS before extra. item	0.23	0.26	0.30	0.12	0.39
Cash Flow per Share	1.52	1.27	1.10	0.73	0.90
Book Value per Share	5.21	4.98	3.24	2.94	2.81
O/S Common Shares	19,996	19,754	12,171	12,134	12,104
Total Revenue	60,576	43,912	30,834	23,989	26,396
Income before extra.	4,491	4,205	3,625	1,505	3,375
Cash Flow	30,198	20,206	13,337	8,877	7,809
Debt/Equity	0.17	0.23	0.10	0.20	0.15
Return on Capital (%)	9.12	11.24	18.48	9.57	34.86
Ret. on Com. Equity (%)	4.43	6.10	9.66	4.32	15.05
% Change Profit	6.8	16.0	140.9	(55.4)	6,342.0
% Change Revenue	37.9	42.4	28.5	(9.1)	1,167.6
% Change Assets	7.0	149.6	11.0	20.7	233.6

Preferred Div. Coverage	np	np	np
Total Div. Coverage	na	na	na
Interest Coverage	6.4	8.6	10.6
Current Ratio	1.0	0.7	1.1
Operating Margin	17.3	18.2	23.2
Asset Turnover	0.4	0.3	0.5

5 YEAR RATIOS (%)			
Return on Capital	16.7	14.8	5.9
Return on Com. Equity	7.9	6.8	(2.8)
Profit Growth	143.5	173.5	135.9
Revenue Growth	96.2	129.6	472.0
Asset Growth	64.1	145.2	93.5

BALANCE SHEET (000)			
Cash	0	0	8
Current Assets	17,121	9,325	9,196
Net Fixed Assets	130,500	127,875	41,800
Invest's & Advances	6,922	7,264	6,873
Total Assets	154,543	144,464	57,869
Short Term Debt	0	0	0
Current Liabilities	17,155	13,019	8,584
Long Term Debt	17,918	22,380	4,035
Total Liabilities	50,363	46,030	18,439
Total Equity	104,180	98,434	39,430
Total Liab. & Equity	154,543	144,464	57,869

CAPITAL (000)			
Total Debt	17,918	22,380	4,035
Preferred Equity	0	0	0
Common Equity	104,180	98,434	39,430

Business:

CS RESOURCES LIMITED is involved in resources exploration using horizontal production technologies.

Date	EPS	DPS	Tot Rev	Inc Bex
Mar 95	0.12	0.00	18,157	2,501
Dec 94	0.08	0.00	15,557	1,560
Sep 94	0.11	0.00	17,521	2,229
Jun 94	0.07	0.00	15,598	1,368
Mar 94	(0.03)	0.00	11,905	(666)
Dec 93	(0.05)	0.00	13,300	(388)
Sep 93	0.07	0.00	11,750	1,535
Jun 93	0.14	0.00	10,152	1,772

Synopsis:

Traditionally, CS Resources has pursued the development and implementation of horizontal drilling and completion technologies for the exploitation of heavy oil. Recent joint venture agreements with Gulf Canada and the acquisition of American Eagle in 1993 have increased the company's exposure to opportunities for natural gas and light crude oil.

In 1994 the Lateral Tie-Back System, (LTBS) evolved from a prototype to a commercial tool. LTBS, developed in collaboration with Sperry-Sun Drilling Services of Canada, enables a series of lateral wellbores to be drilled from a horizontal well with each lateral connected to the main horizontal wellbore. Using LTBS, the wellbore can be cost effectively taken to the oil. This method increases reservoir exposure, reduces operating costs and minimizes surface environmental exposure. The company expects to begin drilling using this new system in the first quarter of 1995.

Higher volumes of crude oil and natural gas combined with increases in commodity prices resulted in the company's strong performance in 1994. Although production figures did increase over 1993 volumes, they were lower than projected. This was the result of a deferral of drilling activity in the first quarter when oil prices were weak and the effect of swaps and disposals of producing properties that took place throughout the year. The company estimates that crude oil production will average 12,000 barrels per day in 1995, and natural gas volumes should average 25 million cubic feet per day.

During 1994 (1993) average daily production by resource was: oil, 9,853 (8,116) barrels; and natural gas, 14,250 (5,027) thousand cubic feet. At the end of 1994 (1992), gross proven and probable oil reserves totalled 61 (62.7) million barrels, natural gas reserves totalled 56.3 (62.4) billion cubic feet.

Relative strength to TSE300 / Price / Volume (in 1000's of board lots)

Rank (Profit/Revenue/Assets)
441 507 388

Richard J. Renaud
Chairman

Dennis A. Sharp
President & C.E.O.

George A. Crookshank
Vice President Finance

Address
29th Floor
645 - 7th Avenue S.W.
Calgary
AB
T2P 4G8
(403) 260-6100

Fax: (403) 260-6191
L0002637/G/3.2

CZAR RESOURCES LTD.

Exchanges	Price (Jun29'95)	1.05	Trailing P/E	5.83	Stock Symbol
T	Trailing Yield (%)	0.00	Trailing EPS	0.18	**CZR**

Period Ending	Dec94	Dec93	Dec92	Dec91	Dec90
Yearly Statistics					
Price-Close	1.28	1.70	0.94	0.53	1.13
Price-High	2.24	2.45	1.29	1.20	1.50
Price-Low	1.17	0.90	0.40	0.41	0.93
P/E-Close	5.82	9.44	9.40	nm	22.60
Dividends per Share	0.00	0.00	0.00	0.00	0.00
Dividend Yield (%)	0.00	0.00	0.00	0.00	0.00
Sales per Share	0.54	0.60	0.80	0.73	0.72
EPS before extra. item	0.22	0.18	0.10	(0.01)	0.05
Cash Flow per Share	0.40	0.35	0.31	0.18	0.21
Book Value per Share	1.10	0.89	0.45	0.25	0.26
O/S Common Shares	68,846	63,987	42,817	36,445	36,280
Total Revenue	40,420	34,437	29,923	27,243	26,916
Income before extra.	14,027	9,504	3,701	(387)	1,637
Cash Flow	25,923	18,729	11,466	6,693	7,669
Debt/Equity	0.14	0.02	1.92	4.92	4.88
Return on Capital (%)	19.47	20.77	14.25	10.53	13.68
Ret. on Com. Equity (%)	21.12	24.97	26.18	(4.25)	20.46
% Change Profit	47.6	156.8	1,056.3	(123.6)	25.8
% Change Revenue	17.4	15.1	9.8	1.2	10.7
% Change Assets	25.4	20.1	8.6	(1.1)	7.8
Preferred Div. Coverage	np	np	np		
Total Div. Coverage	na	na	na		
Interest Coverage	502.0	5.0	1.9		
Current Ratio	0.9	0.6	0.9		
Operating Margin	34.8	34.4	26.0		
Asset Turnover	0.3	0.4	0.4		
5 YEAR RATIOS (%)					
Return on Capital	15.7	16.2	49.1		
Return on Com. Equity	17.7	46.1	na		
Profit Growth	60.9	45.2	610.1		
Revenue Growth	10.6	12.8	14.3		
Asset Growth	11.7	9.5	11.1		
BALANCE SHEET (000)					
Cash	1,895	5,172	4,974		
Current Assets	17,230	16,837	12,691		
Net Fixed Assets	89,725	68,463	58,047		
Invest's & Advances	0	0	0		
Total Assets	106,955	85,300	71,006		
Short Term Debt	462	648	948		
Current Liabilities	18,887	26,519	14,655		
Long Term Debt	10,000	462	36,044		
Total Liabilities	30,957	28,479	51,717		
Total Equity	75,998	56,821	19,289		
Total Liab. & Equity	106,955	85,300	71,006		
CAPITAL (000)					
Total Debt	10,462	1,110	36,992		
Preferred Equity	0	0	0		
Common Equity	75,998	56,821	19,289		

Business:

CZAR RESOURCES LTD. is a natural gas exploration and production company. The company has producing wells in Alberta and British Columbia. It also has exploration activities in the two provinces. The company markets gas to industrial customers in Alberta, British Columbia and the United States.

Date	EPS	DPS	Tot Rev	Inc Bex
Mar 95	0.01	0.00	6,417	686
Dec 94	0.02	0.00	6,818	1,359
Sep 94	0.11	0.00	14,285	6,886
Jun 94	0.04	0.00	10,251	2,370
Mar 94	0.05	0.00	10,087	3,412
Dec 93	0.08	0.00	8,851	4,475
Sep 93	0.02	0.00	8,228	1,409
Jun 93	0.04	0.00	8,647	1,811

Synopsis:

As a result of the 1994 downturn in natural gas prices, industry focus has switched from an exploration to a new phase of asset rationalization. Consequently, Czar Resources is actively pursuing land and reserve purchases, principally in its core areas, to position itself for the anticipated rebound in gas prices.

Czar's reaction to low gas prices was to curtail its planned capital program starting in the summer of 1994. In addition, the company accelerated the restructuring of its gas contract portfolio with a focus on marketing new volumes of gas to purchasers outside Alberta and British Columbia. It also began to base the price of its new gas contracts on U.S. indices, primarily NYMEX. By doing so, Czar will be able to optimize the gas price it receives in both Canadian and U.S. markets.

In 1994, revenue rose by 18% over the previous year as a result of increases in product prices, production, and natural gas decontracting fees received. The revenue increase was the major contributor to the growth in funds flow. However, reduced interest expenses were also a key contributor.

Czar's average daily gross production in 1994 (1993) was: crude oil and natural gas liquids, 570.7 (483.9) barrels; and natural gas, 48.5 (46.5) million cubic feet. Gross proven and probable reserves at the end of 1994 (1993) were: oil and natural gas liquids, 1,735.5 (1,551.7) thousand million stock tank barrels; and natural gas, 203.6 (186.5) billion cubic feet.

Natural gas accounts for approximately 90% of total revenue. The distribution of 1994 gas sales was: B.C. 29%; U.S. Northeast 22%; U.S. Mid West 17%; Eastern Canada 13%; Alberta 10%; U.S. Pacific Northwest 7%, and California 2%.

Rank (Profit/Revenue/Assets)
251   587   471

Robert W. Lamond
Chairman President & C.E.O.

Charles A. Teare
Exec. V.P. & C.F.O.

P. Richard Ewacha
Vice President Production

Address
Suite 2100
144 - 4th Avenue S.W.
Calgary
AB
T2P 3N4
(403) 750-4400

Fax: (403) 263-2341
C0012102/G/3.2

DISCOVERY WEST CORP.

Exchanges	Price (Jun29'95)	4 .00	Trailing P/E		8 .89	Stock Symbol
T	Trailing Yield (%)	0 .00	Trailing EPS		0 .45	**DSW**

Period Ending	Dec94	Dec93	Dec92	Dec91	Dec90
Yearly Statistics					
Price-Close	4 .95	5 .88	5 .00	1 .55	1 .55
Price-High	6 .13	7 .88	5 .88	2 .00	2 .40
Price-Low	4 .55	4 .40	1 .50	1 .35	1 .35
P/E-Close	9 .52	17 .80	29 .41	17 .22	4 .43
Dividends per Share	0 .00	0 .00	0 .00	0 .00	0 .00
Dividend Yield (%)	0 .00	0 .00	0 .00	0 .00	0 .00
Sales per Share	1 .30	1 .06	0 .87	0 .66	0 .65
EPS before extra. item	0 .52	0 .33	0 .17	0 .09	0 .35
Cash Flow per Share	0 .84	0 .72	0 .54	0 .37	0 .37
Book Value per Share	2 .93	2 .45	2 .13	1 .90	1 .83
O/S Common Shares	31 ,340	31 ,244	31 ,054	23 ,021	23 ,100
Total Revenue	45 ,486	32 ,012	20 ,774	13 ,671	12 ,499
Income before extra.	14 ,989	9 ,491	4 ,258	1 ,775	6 ,306
Cash Flow	24 ,146	20 ,641	12 ,597	7 ,430	6 ,596
Debt/Equity	0 .05	nd	nd	0 .18	0 .18
Return on Capital (%)	21 .71	18 .09	10 .60	5 .66	18 .15
Ret. on Com. Equity (%)	17 .80	13 .27	7 .68	4 .01	17 .86
% Change Profit	57 .9	122 .9	139 .9	(71 .9)	390 .0
% Change Revenue	42 .1	54 .1	52 .0	9 .4	51 .4
% Change Assets	23 .5	16 .5	28 .0	2 .1	24 .4

Date	EPS	DPS	Tot Rev	Inc Bex
Mar 95	0 .04	0 .00	8 ,189	1 ,203
Dec 94	0 .01	0 .00	9 ,084	170
Sep 94	0 .04	0 .00	9 ,231	1 ,322
Jun 94	0 .36	0 .00	16 ,806	10 ,280
Mar 94	0 .11	0 .00	9 ,010	3 ,217
Dec 93	0 .13	0 .00	8 ,926	3 ,810
Sep 93	0 .07	0 .00	7 ,692	2 ,040
Jun 93	0 .08	0 .00	7 ,365	2 ,247

Preferred Div. Coverage	499 .6	316 .4	118 .3
Total Div. Coverage	499 .6	316 .4	118 .3
Interest Coverage	174 .5	nd	16 .5
Current Ratio	0 .7	1 .4	1 .8
Operating Margin	29 .3	34 .3	27 .6
Asset Turnover	0 .3	0 .3	0 .2
5 YEAR RATIOS (%)			
Return on Capital	14 .8	11 .4	8 .5
Return on Com. Equity	12 .1	9 .5	7 .6
Profit Growth	63 .4	50 .3	36 .3
Revenue Growth	40 .6	34 .4	21 .0
Asset Growth	18 .5	13 .5	10 .9
BALANCE SHEET (000)			
Cash	250	5 ,032	9 ,126
Current Assets	5 ,015	9 ,641	12 ,558
Net Fixed Assets	87 ,830	71 ,407	56 ,793
Invest's & Advances	29 ,377	18 ,035	15 ,740
Total Assets	122 ,722	99 ,344	85 ,256
Short Term Debt	0	0	0
Current Liabilities	6 ,867	7 ,114	7 ,079
Long Term Debt	4 ,500	0	0
Total Liabilities	30 ,532	22 ,413	18 ,558
Total Equity	92 ,190	76 ,931	66 ,698
Total Liab. & Equity	122 ,722	99 ,344	85 ,256
CAPITAL (000)			
Total Debt	4 ,500	0	0
Preferred Equity	500	500	500
Common Equity	91 ,690	76 ,431	66 ,198

Business:

DISCOVERY WEST CORP. is an independent Canadian oil and natural gas company. In addition to its oil and gas assets, Discovery has a significant ownership position in Rayrock Yellowknife Resources Inc., a mineral exploration, development and operating company.

Synopsis:

Discovery West's capital spending on oil and gas interests in 1994 reached $28.9-million. Funds went towards exploration activity, seismic activity, land acquisition, and facilities and pipeline construction. Major increases in productive capacity for natural gas were developed and an aggressive drilling program undertaken late in the year resulted in three new oil discoveries. These oil discoveries, combined with an infill drilling program in existing fields, reversed the recent trend of declining production.

During 1995, Discovery West expects to maintain an active exploration and development program with approximately 70 company operated, high interest wells planned. About 40 wells will be exploratory. Approximately $20.6-million has been budgeted for exploration and development programs, excluding land acquisitions. Activity will again be mainly in east central and southern Alberta, with about 70% of spending directed toward oil prospects. The company expects to maintain current debt levels by matching capital programs to cash flow through the year.

In an attempt to forecast 1995 volumes of oil and gas, Discovery West believes that gas prices will stay depressed through the year. The revised gas sales forecast average of approximately 26 million cubic feet per day is based on the premise that some company gas will remain shut-in and new gas discoveries will be delayed. Oil production should average 3,500 barrels per day.

During fiscal 1994 (1993), average daily production by resource was: oil and natural gas liquids, 3,049 (3,428) barrels; and natural gas, 21,221 (11,210) thousand cubic feet. In 1994 (1993) total gross proven and probable reserves by resource were: 7.4 (6.8) million barrels of crude oil and natural gas liquids; and 72.8 (60.8) billion cubic feet of natural gas.

Relative strength to TSE300

Price

Volume (in 1000's of board lots)

Rank (Profit/Revenue/Assets)
245   569   442

David R. Crombie
Chairman & C.E.O.

O. Michael Isaac
President & C.O.O.

C. Bruce Burton
V.P. & C.F.O.

Address
30 Soudan Avenue
Suite 500
Toronto
ON
M4S 1V6
(416) 489-0022

Fax: (416) 489-0096
D0001223/G/3.2

For further company information, call Globe Information Services 1-800-268-9128 or (416) 585-5345

DORSET EXPLORATION LTD.

Exchanges	Price (Jun29'95)	6.25	Trailing P/E	16.02	Stock Symbol
T	Trailing Yield (%)	0.00	Trailing EPS	0.39	**DXL**

Period Ending	Dec94	Dec93	Dec92	Dec91	Dec90
Yearly Statistics					
Price-Close	7.63	13.25	10.50	3.80	0.95
Price-High	14.00	19.50	11.13	4.20	1.15
Price-Low	5.75	10.38	3.55	0.70	0.55
P/E-Close	23.84	36.81	38.89	63.33	nm
Dividends per Share	0.00	0.00	0.00	0.00	0.00
Dividend Yield (%)	0.00	0.00	0.00	0.00	0.00
Sales per Share	2.25	1.49	1.05	0.58	0.54
EPS before extra. item	0.32	0.36	0.27	0.06	(1.07)
Cash Flow per Share	1.45	1.09	0.74	0.32	0.25
Book Value per Share	3.51	3.23	1.88	1.55	1.98
O/S Common Shares	27,896	27,359	24,859	24,422	13,790
Total Revenue	62,880	39,582	26,090	13,373	7,438
Income before extra.	9,005	9,524	6,764	1,363	(14,528)
Cash Flow	40,465	29,008	18,344	7,263	3,452
Debt/Equity	0.68	0.31	0.38	0.24	0.31
Return on Capital (%)	13.57	17.05	22.05	9.24	(34.61)
Ret. on Com. Equity (%)	9.67	14.09	15.97	4.18	(45.94)
% Change Profit	(5.4)	40.8	396.3	109.4	(1,605.2)
% Change Revenue	58.9	51.7	95.1	79.8	34.1
% Change Assets	38.0	84.9	42.0	31.2	(13.1)

Business:
DORSET EXPLORATION LTD. is engaged in the exploration for and development of oil and gas reserves.

Date	EPS	DPS	Tot Rev	Inc Bex
Mar 95	0.06	0.00	14,478	1,770
Dec 94	(0.01)	0.00	15,185	(181)
Sep 94	0.11	0.00	17,150	3,085
Jun 94	0.13	0.00	17,093	3,752
Mar 94	0.09	0.00	13,452	2,349
Dec 93	0.08	0.00	11,965	2,276
Sep 93	0.08	0.00	9,346	2,062
Jun 93	0.10	0.00	9,702	2,757

	Dec94	Dec93	Dec92
Preferred Div. Coverage	np	np	np
Total Div. Coverage	na	na	na
Interest Coverage	5.8	20.0	13.5
Current Ratio	0.5	0.4	0.7
Operating Margin	30.3	38.8	47.1
Asset Turnover	0.3	0.3	0.3
5 YEAR RATIOS (%)			
Return on Capital	5.5	2.8	na
Return on Com. Equity	(0.4)	(2.8)	na
Profit Growth	na	na	na
Revenue Growth	62.4	46.6	na
Asset Growth	32.8	22.6	na
BALANCE SHEET (000)			
Cash	0	0	0
Current Assets	6,831	5,771	3,672
Net Fixed Assets	191,352	137,789	71,941
Invest's & Advances	0	0	2,040
Total Assets	198,183	143,560	77,653
Short Term Debt	0	0	0
Current Liabilities	13,649	14,119	5,042
Long Term Debt	66,979	27,113	17,779
Total Liabilities	100,233	55,198	30,834
Total Equity	97,950	88,362	46,819
Total Liab. & Equity	198,183	143,560	77,653
CAPITAL (000)			
Total Debt	66,979	27,113	17,779
Preferred Equity	0	0	0
Common Equity	97,950	88,362	46,819

Synopsis:

In contrast to markets one year ago, oil prices have steadily improved since April 1994. Aided by a weaker Canadian dollar and strong differentials for heavy crude, Dorset Exploration's wellhead oil price rose by $1.14 a barrel to average $18.51 a barrel for the year. This upward trend continued in the first quarter of 1995, with Dorset's wellhead price averaging $20.50 a barrel, largely due to stronger demand and improved pricing for heavy crude.

Natural gas prices also improved during 1994, averaging $1.84 per thousand cubic feet, an increase of $0.24 over 1993. However, the year ended with a downward slide in gas prices that continued into 1995. The slide stems from milder winter weather, lower demand throughout North America, and export constraints in Alberta. Due to soft gas markets most of Dorset's new gas discoveries will not reach markets until the spring of 1996.

Capital expenditures in 1995 are projected to be $36-million. Dorset expects to finance the capital program through cash flow and debt financing. The program will involve the drilling of 60-65 wells, associated facilities, land, and geophysical data. Over half the wells will be horizontal development wells with the remainder being exploratory, appraisal, and development drilling wells.

Dorset reported improved oil and gas revenues and cash flow for fiscal 1994. This was due to stronger production volumes and higher average prices for both oil and gas.

During fiscal 1994 (1993), average daily production by resource was: oil and natural gas liquids, 7,769 (4,574) barrels; and natural gas, 29.7 (27.5) million cubic feet. At its 1994 (1993) fiscal year end, Dorset's gross proven and probable reserves by resource were: 21.5 (17.2) million barrels of crude oil and natural gas liquids; and 81.6 (93.5) billion cubic feet of natural gas. Contributions to Dorset's total revenue in 1994 by resource were: light oil, 46%; natural gas, 27%; heavy oil, 17%; and medium oil and other, 10%.

Relative strength to TSE300

Price

Volume (in 1000's of board lots)

Rank (Profit/Revenue/Assets)
315   497   358
Edward L. Molnar
Chairman, President & C.E.O.
R. James Brown
C.F.O.

Address
205 - 5th Avenue S.W.
Suite 3600
Calgary
AB
T2P 2V7
(403) 267-0700

Fax: (403) 267-0777
01002510/G/3.2

DRECO ENERGY SERVICES LTD.

Exchanges	Price (Jun29'95)	20.00	Trailing P/E	10.92	Stock Symbol
TQ	Trailing Yield (%)	0.00	Trailing EPS	1.35	**DRE.A**

Period Ending	Aug94	Aug93	Aug92	Aug91	Aug90
Yearly Statistics	US	US	US	US	US
Price-Close	12.50	30.63	14.38	12.00	10.25
Price-High	30.88	33.00	17.50	19.25	11.25
Price-Low	9.50	14.38	8.75	8.25	2.05
P/E-Close	nm	14.37	9.94	6.88	11.19
Dividends per Share	0.00	0.00	0.00	0.00	0.00
Dividend Yield (%)	0.00	0.00	0.00	0.00	0.00
Sales per Share	12.98	15.36	10.91	13.76	10.16
EPS before extra. item	(1.05)	1.32	1.05	1.31	0.67
Cash Flow per Share	1.56	2.68	1.43	1.88	1.17
Book Value per Share	6.30	7.60	6.76	5.94	4.23
O/S Common Shares	6,139	6,139	6,089	6,085	4,695
Total Revenue	71,137	91,296	69,465	78,854	49,064
Income before extra.	(6,467)	8,284	6,452	7,402	3,218
Cash Flow	9,553	16,379	8,674	10,635	5,615
Debt/Equity	0.08	0.10	0.07	0.08	0.47
Return on Capital (%)	(13.90)	13.77	16.49	23.58	16.45
Ret. on Com. Equity (%)	(15.16)	18.87	16.69	26.43	17.78
% Change Profit	(178.1)	28.4	(12.8)	130.0	98.5
% Change Revenue	(22.1)	31.4	(11.9)	60.7	15.8
% Change Assets	(6.4)	35.6	15.6	28.2	24.9

Preferred Div. Coverage	np	np	np
Total Div. Coverage	na	na	na
Interest Coverage	0.0	13.0	21.6
Current Ratio	1.6	2.1	3.4
Operating Margin	3.8	10.9	6.9
Asset Turnover	1.1	1.3	1.2
5 YEAR RATIOS (%)			
Return on Capital	11.3	16.4	14.6
Return on Com. Equity	12.9	18.1	14.4
Profit Growth	na	162.0	186.7
Revenue Growth	10.9	25.9	21.3
Asset Growth	18.6	19.3	9.9
BALANCE SHEET (000)			
Cash	20,016	21,272	6,980
Current Assets	47,485	52,289	36,437
Net Fixed Assets	19,232	19,404	17,370
Invest's & Advances	0	0	785
Total Assets	69,323	74,047	54,592
Short Term Debt	1,818	2,004	130
Current Liabilities	29,193	24,564	10,843
Long Term Debt	1,440	2,857	2,579
Total Liabilities	30,633	27,421	13,422
Total Equity	38,690	46,626	41,170
Total Liab. & Equity	69,323	74,047	54,592
CAPITAL (000)			
Total Debt	3,258	4,861	2,709
Preferred Equity	0	0	0
Common Equity	38,690	46,626	41,170

Business:

DRECO ENERGY SERVICES LTD. participates in two principal business segments: drilling and well servicing equipment; and downhole drilling products.

Date		EPS	DPS	Tot Rev	Inc Bex
May 95	US	0.23	0.00	18,401	1,509
Feb 95	US	0.35	0.00	21,577	2,283
Nov 94	US	0.51	0.00	24,827	3,312
Aug 94	US	0.26	0.00	19,815	1,590
May 94	US	0.14	0.00	18,099	924
Feb 94	US	(1.78)	0.00	4,330	(10,902)
Nov 93	US	0.31	0.00	28,678	1,921
Aug 93	US	0.38	0.00	23,898	2,391

Synopsis:

In fiscal 1995, the Drilling and Well Servicing Equipment segment of Dreco Energy Services expects to see opportunities for its products and services in the offshore drilling markets in the North Sea and elsewhere. It also expects to do well in the specialized drilling and well servicing rig markets in the Middle East, South America and Russia and the former Soviet republics. Dreco's Downhole Products segment intends to increase its market share in the U.S. Gulf Coast, the North Sea, North Africa and Venezuela.

Dreco's Norwegian joint venture, Hitec-Dreco A.S., continued to incur losses on its contract with A.S. Norske Shell. During fiscal 1994 the company's joint venture recognized losses of $12.4-million ($7.2-million in 1993). The company recognized $218,000 in revenues in fiscal 1992, $14-million in 1993, and $8.8-million in 1994 from the Troll Project. Excluding the Troll project, Dreco's Drilling and Well Servicing segment generated revenues of $52.1-million and operating profits of $2.2-million, in fiscal 1994. The Downhole Products segment generated revenues of $18.7-million and operating profit of $6.3-million.

Dreco, Hitec-Dreco A.S., and A.S. Norske Shell signed an amendment to the contract, effective March 1, 1994, that essentially converted the remainder of the contract for the Troll Project to a cost-reimbursable format. In return, Hitec-Dreco had to waive all of its outstanding claims for additional costs incurred to that date. Under the terms of the contract for the Troll Project, Hitec- Dreco may be liable for late delivery penalties. Dreco is not able to determine if A.S. Norske Shell will assess liquidated damages for late delivery and whether or to what extent such assessment will be valid.

Fiscal 1994 total revenues (operating profit) by segment were: drilling and well servicing equipment, 76% (23%); and downhole products, 24% (77%). Total revenues (operating profit) by geographic area of operation were: United States, 23% (10%); Canada, 67% (93%); and International, 10% (-3%).

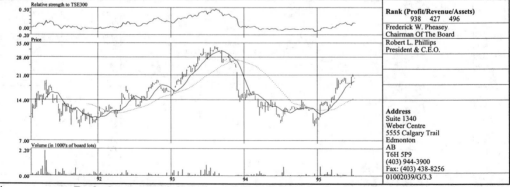

Rank (Profit/Revenue/Assets)
938   427   496

Frederick W. Pheasey
Chairman Of The Board

Robert L. Phillips
President & C.E.O.

Address
Suite 1340
Weber Centre
5555 Calgary Trail
Edmonton
AB
T6H 5P9
(403) 944-3900
Fax: (403) 438-8256
01002039/G/3.3

ELAN ENERGY INC.

Exchanges	Price (Jun29'95)			11.50	Trailing P/E		42.59	Stock Symbol
TM	Trailing Yield (%)			0.00	Trailing EPS		0.27	**ELN**

Period Ending	Dec94	Dec93	Dec92	Dec91	Dec90
Yearly Statistics					
Price-Close	7.75	10.63	10.88	8.50	4.30
Price-High	12.13	18.13	11.63	9.50	5.25
Price-Low	6.25	9.13	7.75	3.75	3.35
P/E-Close	43.06	29.51	24.72	50.00	9.56
Dividends per Share	0.00	0.00	0.00	0.00	0.00
Dividend Yield (%)	0.00	0.00	0.00	0.00	0.00
Sales per Share	3.17	2.97	2.19	2.02	1.78
EPS before extra. item	0.18	0.36	0.44	0.17	0.45
Cash Flow per Share	2.06	1.91	1.39	0.98	0.99
Book Value per Share	6.42	6.25	4.50	4.18	3.61
O/S Common Shares	46,103	45,933	36,849	29,964	24,935
Total Revenue	146,037	134,094	78,962	52,465	40,795
Income before extra.	8,073	16,384	16,053	4,483	10,340
Cash Flow	94,647	86,133	50,236	25,493	22,681
Debt/Equity	0.31	0.36	0.38	0.61	1.00
Return on Capital (%)	10.09	12.67	9.84	7.15	12.08
Ret. on Com. Equity (%)	2.77	7.23	11.03	4.16	13.35
% Change Profit	(50.7)	2.1	258.1	(56.6)	146.0
% Change Revenue	8.9	69.8	50.5	28.6	52.0
% Change Assets	5.6	73.1	12.6	16.8	57.1

Preferred Div. Coverage	na	na	na
Total Div. Coverage	na	na	na
Interest Coverage	6.4	7.6	5.2
Current Ratio	1.0	0.7	0.6
Operating Margin	26.9	29.2	26.9
Asset Turnover	0.3	0.3	0.3
5 YEAR RATIOS (%)			
Return on Capital	10.4	10.3	1.4
Return on Com. Equity	7.7	8.5	(0.5)
Profit Growth	13.9	52.9	84.6
Revenue Growth	40.3	53.1	40.1
Asset Growth	30.3	40.1	17.9
BALANCE SHEET (000)			
Cash	34	158	122
Current Assets	21,788	15,398	9,791
Net Fixed Assets	429,333	411,844	237,020
Invest's & Advances	0	0	0
Total Assets	451,121	427,242	246,811
Short Term Debt	0	0	0
Current Liabilities	21,802	21,520	16,728
Long Term Debt	92,700	102,100	62,700
Total Liabilities	154,927	139,745	80,778
Total Equity	296,194	287,497	166,033
Total Liab. & Equity	451,121	427,242	246,811
CAPITAL (000)			
Total Debt	92,700	102,100	62,700
Preferred Equity	209	214	217
Common Equity	295,985	287,283	165,816

Business:

ELAN ENERGY INC. is an oil and gas exploration and production company. It has operations and exploration activities in Alberta and Saskatchewan.

Date	EPS	DPS	Tot Rev	Inc Bex
Mar 95	0.10	0.00	42,756	4,583
Dec 94	0.03	0.00	36,912	1,337
Sep 94	0.04	0.00	37,998	1,329
Jun 94	0.10	0.00	40,105	5,029
Mar 94	0.01	0.00	29,138	378
Dec 93	0.06	0.00	34,909	2,795
Sep 93	0.05	0.00	33,525	2,605
Jun 93	0.05	0.00	33,500	2,539

Synopsis:

Commodity pricing continues to be the most volatile component of the oil and gas industry. Oil prices recovered over the course of 1994. Natural gas prices were strong throughout the winter of 1993/1994; then began to slide during the latter half of 1994. Elan Energy expects that the current supply and demand balance for oil will remain. This will result in a relatively stable pricing environment. Natural gas prices are expected to remain low, at least for the coming year. However, the impact on Elan will be minimal as the company's principal product is oil. The company has strategically positioned itself to maximize its profitability under any oil pricing scenario.

Elan altered its asset mix by acquiring Amoco Canada Petroleum Co. Ltd.'s interest in the Elk Point/Lindbergh area of Alberta in March 1995. As a result of the acquisition, the company's proforma reserve base constitutes 49% heavy oil, 43% light and medium oil, and 8% natural gas. The acquisition adds 43.9 million barrels of heavy oil reserves, production of 7,500 barrels of oil per day, and undeveloped land of approximately 60,000 net acres. During the remainder of 1995, Elan plans to engage in a recompletion program on a number of wells in the area.

Elan expects to repay the incremental debt incurred to finance the $126-million Elk Point/Lindbergh acquisition within the next three years. To meet this objective, the company has reduced its 1995 capital program to $60-million. The company plans to dedicate cash flow, estimated at $50-million, in excess of this program, to debt repayment.

During fiscal 1994 (1993), average daily production by resource was: oil and natural gas liquids, 24,500 (23,000) barrels and natural gas, 20.0 (21.0) million cubic feet. At 1994 (1993) fiscal year end, gross proven and probable reserves by resource were: 66.1 (70.8) million barrels of crude oil and natural gas liquids and 100.4 (112.5) billion cubic feet of natural gas.

Rank (Profit/Revenue/Assets)
331   366   238

Dennis G. Flanagan
Chairman

Verne G. Johnson
President & C.E.O.

Curtis W. Hicks
V.P. Finance

Victor M. Luhowy
Sr. V.P. & C.O.O.

Address
Suite 4100
150 - 6th Avenue S.W.
Calgary
AB
T2P 3Y7
(403) 266-8500

Fax: (403) 262-7337
O0000950/G/3.2

ENCAL ENERGY LTD.

Exchanges	Price (Jun29'95)	3.00	Trailing P/E	75.00	Stock Symbol
T	Trailing Yield (%)	0.00	Trailing EPS	0.04	ENL

Period Ending	Dec94	Dec93	Dec92	Dec91	Dec90	Business:
Yearly Statistics						ENCAL ENERGY LTD. is involved in the
Price-Close	3.00	4.55	1.90	0.43	0.36	acquisition, exploration and development of oil
Price-High	4.70	7.50	2.08	1.50	0.45	and natural gas properties.
Price-Low	2.50	1.47	0.90	0.20	0.10	
P/E-Close	50.00	41.36	47.50	107.50	18.00	
Dividends per Share	0.00	0.00	0.00	0.00	0.00	
Dividend Yield (%)	0.00	0.00	0.00	0.00	0.00	
Sales per Share	1.02	1.15	0.32	0.27	0.14	
EPS before extra. item	0.06	0.11	0.04	0.00	0.02	
Cash Flow per Share	0.51	0.59	0.16	0.09	0.06	
Book Value per Share	2.42	2.05	0.32	0.17	0.17	
O/S Common Shares	103,458	59,147	25,417	19,135	18,935	
Total Revenue	82,870	48,399	6,659	5,058	2,229	
Income before extra.	4,480	4,757	880	156	304	
Cash Flow	41,483	24,719	3,247	1,789	922	

Date	EPS	DPS	Tot Rev	Inc Bex
Mar 95	0.00	0.00	24,175	9
Dec 94	0.00	0.00	25,349	21
Sep 94	0.02	0.00	27,578	1,688
Jun 94	0.02	0.00	15,730	1,242
Mar 94	0.03	0.00	14,481	1,529
Dec 93	0.03	0.00	15,254	1,916
Sep 93	0.02	0.00	13,403	751
Jun 93	0.04	0.00	16,269	1,449

	Dec94	Dec93	Dec92	Dec91	Dec90
Debt/Equity	0.10	0.05	0.65	1.88	2.03
Return on Capital (%)	5.32	16.64	17.63	11.51	12.03
Ret. on Com. Equity (%)	2.41	7.15	15.72	2.35	12.56
% Change Profit	(5.8)	440.6	463.9	(48.7)	170.5
% Change Revenue	71.2	626.8	31.7	126.9	315.5
% Change Assets	136.9	674.7	34.6	(0.7)	280.2

Synopsis:

Historically, Encal had specialized in acquisitions and exploitation within the oil and gas industry. However, through a deal with Luscar Oil and Gas Ltd. in July 1994, Encal has evolved into a full cycle exploration and production company. The transaction was completed through the exchange of one common share of Encal for each 2.65 common shares of Luscar. At closing, Luscar management assumed responsibility for the operation of the combined entity.

During the remainder of 1995, Encal Energy will focus on larger reserve potential, high impact natural gas prospects, and the ongoing pursuit of light to medium gravity crude oil prospects. An asset rationalization program has been initiated to reduce the number of smaller or non-core properties acquired through the merger. Proceeds from asset sales, which could reach $25-million, and the $51-million capital budget will be reinvested in the further development of core properties.

Production increases brought about by successful drilling, the contribution from the Luscar acquisition, changes in both natural gas and crude oil pricing were just some of the factors affecting the company's financial performance in 1994.

During 1994 (1993) average daily production by resource was: oil and natural gas liquids, 4,680 (2,605) barrels, and natural gas, 76.3 (49.7) million cubic feet. At 1994 (1993) year end, proven and probable reserves were: oil, 23.1 (12.5) million barrels, and natural gas, 478 (256) billion cubic feet.

	Dec94	Dec93	Dec92
Preferred Div. Coverage	np	np	na
Total Div. Coverage	na	33.3	na
Interest Coverage	9.6	4.4	3.9
Current Ratio	0.7	0.8	0.5
Operating Margin	12.9	24.3	35.3
Asset Turnover	0.2	0.3	0.3
5 YEAR RATIOS (%)			
Return on Capital	12.6	13.4	9.9
Return on Com. Equity	8.0	9.0	7.4
Profit Growth	109.0	273.5	413.7
Revenue Growth	173.9	308.5	292.3
Asset Growth	147.7	136.9	100.3
BALANCE SHEET (000)			
Cash	0	313	187
Current Assets	27,460	13,098	1,502
Net Fixed Assets	320,783	133,929	17,343
Invest's & Advances	0	0	0
Total Assets	348,243	147,027	18,979
Short Term Debt	0	0	250
Current Liabilities	41,757	15,682	3,295
Long Term Debt	25,678	5,560	5,542
Total Liabilities	97,795	25,943	10,029
Total Equity	250,448	121,084	8,950
Total Liab. & Equity	348,243	147,027	18,979
CAPITAL (000)			
Total Debt	25,678	5,560	5,792
Preferred Equity	0	0	953
Common Equity	250,448	121,084	7,997

Relative strength to TSE300

Price

Volume (in 1000's of board lots)

Rank (Profit/Revenue/Assets)
443   448   273

Gordon D. Ulrich
Chairman

David D. Johnson
President

Steven A. Allaire
V.P. Finance

Address
P.O. Box 2310
Postal Station 'M'
Calgary
AB
T2P 2M6
(403) 750-3300

Fax: (403) 266-1072
01001768/G/3.2

For further company information, call Globe Information Services 1-800-268-9128 or (416) 585-5345

ENSERV CORPORATION

Exchanges	Price (Jun29'95)	9.50	Trailing P/E	6.74	Stock Symbol
T	Trailing Yield (%)	0.00	Trailing EPS	1.41	**ESV**

Period Ending	Dec94	Dec93	Dec92	Dec91	Dec90	Business:
Yearly Statistics						ENSERV CORPORATION is a diversified oil
Price-Close	11.38	11.25	6.25	5.25	5.00	field services company. Activities include well
Price-High	14.50	17.25	6.50	6.50	5.38	serving and snubbing operations, rental of
Price-Low	10.50	5.50	4.70	4.50	3.20	production equipment, natural gas compressor
P/E-Close	6.58	13.24	62.50	18.75	20.00	packaging, design, sales, rentals and service,
Dividends per Share	0.00	0.00	0.00	0.00	0.00	provision of specialized plant maintenance and
Dividend Yield (%)	0.00	0.00	0.00	0.00	0.00	changeover services, provision of
Sales per Share	17.28	11.07	6.21	7.81	7.39	environmental services and equipment.
EPS before extra. item	1.73	0.85	0.10	0.28	0.25	
Cash Flow per Share	2.31	1.81	0.64	1.07	0.81	
Book Value per Share	9.27	7.55	5.39	5.30	5.13	
O/S Common Shares	11,673	11,667	8,553	8,513	8,140	
Total Revenue	201,629	116,171	51,328	63,476	54,132	
Income before extra.	20,140	8,901	827	2,276	1,625	

	Date	EPS	DPS	Tot Rev	Inc Bex
Cash Flow	26,931	18,984	5,317	8,677	5,917

Date	EPS	DPS	Tot Rev	Inc Bex
Mar 95	0.29	0.00	44,717	3,401
Dec 94	0.19	0.00	51,995	2,141
Sep 94	0.43	0.00	54,029	5,048
Jun 94	0.50	0.00	55,636	5,883
Mar 94	0.61	0.00	39,969	7,068
Dec 93	0.25	0.00	39,789	2,833
Sep 93	0.27	0.00	39,917	2,918
Jun 93	0.09	0.00	16,231	940

	Dec94	Dec93	Dec92	Dec91	Dec90
Debt/Equity	0.01	0.14	0.42	0.42	0.34
Return on Capital (%)	32.93	19.43	4.67	9.75	9.02
Ret. on Com. Equity (%)	20.52	13.27	1.81	5.24	4.38
% Change Profit	126.3	976.3	(63.7)	40.1	1,628.7
% Change Revenue	73.6	126.3	(19.1)	17.3	80.8
% Change Assets	9.2	63.4	6.7	9.6	61.0

				Synopsis:
Preferred Div. Coverage	np	np	np	
Total Div. Coverage	na	na	na	
Interest Coverage	94.1	21.8	2.0	
Current Ratio	2.3	1.5	1.2	
Operating Margin	15.7	13.4	5.9	
Asset Turnover	1.4	0.9	0.6	
5 YEAR RATIOS (%)				
Return on Capital	15.2	9.0	5.4	
Return on Com. Equity	9.0	5.0	2.4	
Profit Growth	192.6	133.7	(0.2)	
Revenue Growth	46.4	36.3	16.9	
Asset Growth	27.3	30.7	21.5	
BALANCE SHEET (000)				
Cash	8,378	0	16,039	
Current Assets	63,962	52,011	27,659	
Net Fixed Assets	74,033	73,286	49,854	
Invest's & Advances	0	0	0	
Total Assets	145,773	133,443	81,671	
Short Term Debt	426	11,845	13,412	
Current Liabilities	27,696	34,700	23,875	
Long Term Debt	199	428	6,103	
Total Liabilities	37,525	45,366	35,565	
Total Equity	108,248	88,077	46,106	
Total Liab. & Equity	145,773	133,443	81,671	
CAPITAL (000)				
Total Debt	625	12,273	19,515	
Preferred Equity	0	0	0	
Common Equity	108,248	88,077	46,106	

Synopsis:

EnServ Corp. will continue to add to its current businesses with smaller acquisitions that either improve efficiency, or establish geographic and product diversity. The company plans to continue to build by acquisitions, as it has in the past.

During 1994, as part of its objective of achieving a more stable and sustainable earnings base, EnServ sold its drilling business. The sale resulted in gross proceeds of $21-million, which included the recovery of working capital.

Also, in March 1994, EnServ bought the assets and business of Certified Rentals Ltd. for $13.2-million. This, together with the CEDA acquisition in 1993, balanced EnServ's presence in the energy services sector. Over 40% of Enserv's revenue and earnings come from outside the exploration and production sector.

In 1994, EnServ's fleet of production rental equipment grew by 7%. Well services grew from 11 to 18 snubbing units. This was partly due to the December acquisition of Live Well Service, Inc., a snubbing contractor based in Wyoming. Also, the Certified Rentals fleet grew by about 20%.

EnServ's revenue by sector (percentage increase) in 1994 was: natural gas compressors (sale and rental), $73-million (33%); well servicing, $28-million (37%); equipment rentals, (118%); and services to the processing industry (CEDA), $66-million (20%). Assets, revenues, and earnings derived from within the United States account for less than 10% consolidated totals.

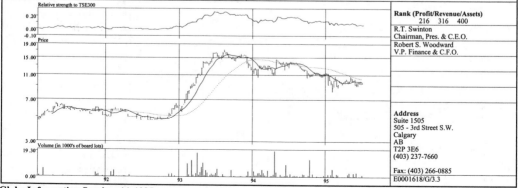

Rank (Profit/Revenue/Assets)
216 316 400

R.T. Swinton
Chairman, Pres. & C.E.O.
Robert S. Woodward
V.P. Finance & C.F.O.

Address
Suite 1505
505 - 3rd Street S.W.
Calgary
AB
T2P 3E6
(403) 237-7660

Fax: (403) 266-0885
E0001618/G/3.3

ENSIGN RESOURCE SERVICE GROUP INC.

Exchanges	Price (Jun29'95)	4 .40	Trailing P/E	3 .61	Stock Symbol
T	Trailing Yield (%)	0 .00	Trailing EPS	1 .22	**ESI**

Period Ending	Dec94	Dec93	Dec92	Dec91	Dec90
Yearly Statistics					
Price-Close	5 .00	5 .63	1 .45	1 .00	na
Price-High	7 .38	8 .50	1 .62	1 .50	n t
Price-Low	4 .20	4 .80	0 .70	0 .60	n t
P/E-Close	4 .72	11 .48	6 .30	10 .00	n t
Dividends per Share	0 .00	0 .00	0 .00	0 .00	0 .00
Dividend Yield (%)	0 .00	0 .00	0 .00	0 .00	0 .00
Sales per Share	9 .79	5 .62	2 .99	2 .44	1 .98
EPS before extra. item	1 .06	0 .49	0 .23	0 .10	(0 .24)
Cash Flow per Share	1 .44	0 .82	0 .34	0 .21	(0 .06)
Book Value per Share	2 .48	1 .44	0 .90	0 .66	0 .58
O/S Common Shares	18 ,039	17 ,614	16 ,007	13 ,754	13 ,719
Total Revenue	174 ,940	94 ,040	41 ,741	33 ,503	16 ,884
Income before extra.	19 ,165	8 ,258	3 ,438	1 ,361	(2 ,096)
Cash Flow	25 ,703	13 ,554	4 ,710	2 ,879	(551)
Debt/Equity	0 .35	0 .63	0 .96	1 .03	0 .81
Return on Capital (%)	66 .51	34 .95	16 .15	11 .78	(13 .04)
Ret. on Com. Equity (%)	54 .04	40 .37	27 .30	13 .27	(41 .96)
% Change Profit	132 .1	140 .2	152 .6	164 .9	(139 .1)
% Change Revenue	86 .0	125 .3	24 .6	98 .4	364 .9
% Change Assets	65 .9	62 .1	41 .3	40 .9	340 .4

Date	EPS	DPS	Tot Rev	Inc Bex
Mar 95	0 .40	0 .00	63 ,170	7 ,306
Dec 94	0 .40	0 .00	58 ,474	7 ,116
Sep 94	0 .30	0 .00	47 ,171	5 ,575
Jun 94	0 .12	0 .00	28 ,788	2 ,044
Mar 94	0 .24	0 .00	40 ,507	4 ,430
Dec 93	0 .09	0 .00	35 ,305	1 ,492
Sep 93	0 .13	0 .00	20 ,581	2 ,162
Jun 93	0 .50	0 .00	14 ,793	1 ,656

Preferred Div. Coverage	82 .6	35 .5	14 .4
Total Div. Coverage	82 .6	35 .5	14 .4
Interest Coverage	23 .2	11 .9	4 .0
Current Ratio	1 .0	1 .0	1 .0
Operating Margin	20 .7	13 .4	10 .1
Asset Turnover	1 .5	1 .4	1 .0
5 YEAR RATIOS (%)			
Return on Capital	23 .3	7 .7	(0 .4)
Return on Com. Equity	18 .6	(0 .9)	(14 .8)
Profit Growth	na	na	na
Revenue Growth	117 .0	67 .0	60 .3
Asset Growth	88 .1	60 .8	44 .7
BALANCE SHEET (000)			
Cash	742	704	0
Current Assets	51 ,215	31 ,158	16 ,417
Net Fixed Assets	61 ,563	36 ,516	25 ,154
Invest's & Advances	0	0	0
Total Assets	113 ,679	68 ,515	42 ,270
Short Term Debt	9 ,638	11 ,439	7 ,933
Current Liabilities	52 ,264	30 ,144	16 ,979
Long Term Debt	6 ,876	6 ,139	8 ,343
Total Liabilities	66 ,854	40 ,765	25 ,322
Total Equity	46 ,825	27 ,749	16 ,948
Total Liab. & Equity	113 ,679	68 ,515	42 ,270
CAPITAL (000)			
Total Debt	16 ,514	17 ,579	16 ,275
Preferred Equity	2 ,100	2 ,400	2 ,537
Common Equity	44 ,725	25 ,349	14 ,411

Business:

ENSIGN RESOURCE SERVICE GROUP INC. is a contract drilling and well servicing company.

Synopsis:

Ensign Resource Service Group continued its course of expansion in 1994. In March, the company acquired the drilling assets of Derrick Drilling Ltd., a Calgary based contractor and operator of 11 drilling rigs. The Ensign Drilling division operates seven of the rigs. The remaining rigs are operated by the Tri-City Drilling division.

In September 1994, Ensign formed an alliance with a United States drilling contractor. The alliance resulted in a long-term lease giving Ensign the use of all of the drilling assets of the contractor. Ensign moved two rigs to Canada. It refurbished and prepared for the western Canadian market.

Also in September, Ensign made its first entry into foreign markets when it established a subsidiary in the United States and bought the assets of Caza Drilling Company of Denver. Caza operates in the U.S. Rocky Mountain region and has five drilling rigs. Ensign Drilling leases three rigs in the U.S. In December 1994, Caza Drilling bought 11 rigs from Veco Drilling, Inc. Caza now operates a fleet of 19 drilling rigs.

The Rockwell Servicing rig fleet expanded in September 1994, when four well servicing rigs were acquired from Trophy Well Service Ltd. Rockwell is a subsidiary of Ensign.

Ensign Group operated an average of 56 drilling rigs and 55 well servicing rigs in 1994. As of December 31, 1994, Ensign had a fleet of 78 drilling rigs and 62 well servicing rigs.

In the first quarter of 1995, The Ensign Drilling and Tri-City Drilling divisions together recorded 36% more drilling days than in the first quarter of 1994. The company's well servicing fleet recorded operating hours of 33,461 in the quarter, an 11% increase over the same period in 1994.

Relative strength to TSE300

Price

Volume (in 1000's of board lots)

Rank (Profit/Revenue/Assets)
222   332   455
N. Murray Edwards
Chairman
George Ward
President
Glenn Dagenais
Vice President Finance

Address
Suite 900
400 - 5th Avenue S.W.
Calgary
AB
T2P 0L6
(403) 262-1361

Fax: (406) 266-3596
01002026/G/3.3

EXCEL ENERGY INC.

Exchanges	Price (Jun29'95)	1.35	Trailing P/E	nm	Stock Symbol
T	Trailing Yield (%)	0.00	Trailing EPS	(0.91)	EEI

Period Ending	Dec94	Dec93	Dec92	Dec91	Dec90
Yearly Statistics					
Price-Close	2.55	5.50	2.43	0.80	1.00
Price-High	6.63	10.38	2.58	1.30	1.55
Price-Low	2.00	2.40	0.55	0.80	0.80
P/E-Close	nm	39.29	60.75	nm	6.67
Dividends per Share	0.00	0.00	0.00	0.00	0.00
Dividend Yield (%)	0.00	0.00	0.00	0.00	0.00
Sales per Share	0.86	0.84	0.62	0.54	0.49
EPS before extra. item	(0.91)	0.14	0.04	(0.60)	0.15
Cash Flow per Share	0.44	0.44	0.28	0.17	0.30
Book Value per Share	2.13	3.04	1.25	1.26	1.88
O/S Common Shares	25,625	25,483	14,751	10,210	9,821
Total Revenue	21,957	14,883	6,976	5,329	5,225
Income before extra.	(23,222)	2,395	456	(5,920)	1,521
Cash Flow	11,228	7,817	3,095	1,631	2,978
Debt/Equity	0.42	0.13	0.19	0.40	0.26
Return on Capital (%)	(25.38)	5.86	5.38	(25.56)	7.68
Ret. on Com. Equity (%)	(35.16)	4.99	2.91	(37.88)	8.61
% Change Profit	(1,069.6)	425.2	107.7	(489.2)	102.0
% Change Revenue	47.5	113.3	30.9	2.0	25.1
% Change Assets	(18.4)	317.6	26.6	(18.2)	32.7
Preferred Div. Coverage	np	np	np		
Total Div. Coverage	na	na	na		
Interest Coverage	0.0	14.2	2.9		
Current Ratio	0.6	0.5	1.1		
Operating Margin	18.5	21.6	15.4		
Asset Turnover	0.3	0.1	0.3		
5 YEAR RATIOS (%)					
Return on Capital	(6.4)	(0.4)	(1.3)		
Return on Com. Equity	(11.3)	(3.4)	(4.2)		
Profit Growth	na	86.2	(40.6)		
Revenue Growth	39.3	31.5	22.9		
Asset Growth	36.2	43.6	8.9		
BALANCE SHEET (000)					
Cash	1,164	2,418	2,994		
Current Assets	5,679	8,062	5,259		
Net Fixed Assets	79,061	95,842	19,625		
Invest's & Advances	0	0	0		
Total Assets	84,740	103,904	24,884		
Short Term Debt	3,060	0	1,800		
Current Liabilities	10,180	16,059	4,780		
Long Term Debt	19,700	10,199	1,620		
Total Liabilities	30,152	26,396	6,400		
Total Equity	54,588	77,508	18,484		
Total Liab. & Equity	84,740	103,904	24,884		
CAPITAL (000)					
Total Debt	22,760	10,199	3,420		
Preferred Equity	0	0	0		
Common Equity	54,588	77,508	18,484		

Business:

EXCEL ENERGY INC. is an oil and gas exploration and production company. It has producing oil and gas assets in Canada with land holdings in Alberta, British Columbia and Saskatchewan.

Date	EPS	DPS	Tot Rev	Inc Bex
Dec 94	(1.07)	0.00	3,444	(27,344)
Sep 94	0.03	0.00	6,004	917
Jun 94	0.06	0.00	6,867	1,399
Mar 94	0.07	0.00	5,642	1,806
Dec 93	0.04	0.00	4,753	778
Sep 93	0.01	0.00	4,196	174
Jun 93	0.02	0.00	2,952	367
Mar 93	0.07	0.00	2,982	1,076

Synopsis:

In June 1995, Excel Energy Inc. and Ranchmen's Resources Ltd. agreed to merge. Under the agreement, Excel will exchange 3.3 of its common shares for every one common share of Ranchmen's. According to both companies, Excel's operations in northwestern Alberta and northeastern B.C. provide a good base for Ranchmen's new thrust in these areas.

1994 was a difficult year for Excel. The company spent a significant amount of capital and effort in the Birch area of B.C. based on its belief in the potential for the area. Although the area remains economical, production and cash flow fell short of projections and resulted in curtailed expansion in other areas. The result of reserve reductions, declining natural gas prices, and unavailable funding to develop reserves in other core areas contributed to a significant adjustment to Excel's reserves, and a writedown of its oil and gas assets in 1994.

During fiscal 1994 (1993), average daily production by resource was: oil and natural gas liquids, 1,345 (904) barrels; and natural gas, 18.9 (14.1) million cubic feet. At its 1994 (1993) fiscal year end, the company's gross proven and probable reserves by resource were: 3.9 (11.6) million barrels of crude oil and natural gas liquids; and 63.7 (66.4) billion cubic feet of natural gas.

Relative strength to TSE300

Rank (Profit/Revenue/Assets)
973   706   521

John J. Fleming
Chairman & C.E.O.
John Andriuk
President & C.O.O.
Richard K. Jaggard
Secretary & V.P. Finance

Address
Suite 1400
340 - 12th Avenue S.W.
Calgary
AB
T2R 1L5
(403) 269-8850

Fax: (403) 264-1088
D0003192/G/3.2

GRAD & WALKER ENERGY CORPORATION

Exchanges	Price (Jun29'95)	6.62	Trailing P/E	33.13	Stock Symbol
T	Trailing Yield (%)	0.00	Trailing EPS	0.20	GWE

Period Ending	Dec94	Dec93	May93
Yearly Statistics		4M	1D
Price-Close	6.13	12.50	n t
Price-High	15.50	14.75	n t
Price-Low	6.13	11.13	n t
P/E-Close	21.12	27.78	n t
Dividends per Share	0.00	0.00	0.00
Dividend Yield (%)	0.00	0.00	0.00
Sales per Share	2.72	2.10	0.00
EPS before extra. item	0.29	0.15	0.00
Cash Flow per Share	1.54	1.32	0.00
Book Value per Share	4.76	3.18	1.00
O/S Common Shares	16,116	12,000	0
Total Revenue	34,893	8,747	0
Income before extra.	3,584	1,786	0
Cash Flow	19,234	5,266	0
Debt/Equity	1.29	0.41	nd
Return on Capital (%)	7.62	39.60	na
Ret. on Com. Equity (%)	6.24	28.06	na
% Change Profit	(33.1)	na	na
% Change Revenue	33.0	na	na
% Change Assets	231.7	nm	na

Date	EPS	DPS	Tot Rev	Inc Bex
Mar 95	0.01	0.00	15,348	224
Dec 94	(0.04)	0.00	10,874	(331)
Sep 94	0.08	0.00	9,237	919
Jun 94	0.15	0.00	8,180	1,844
Mar 94	0.10	0.00	6,602	1,152
Dec 93	0.15	0.00	8,747	1,786

Preferred Div. Coverage	np	np	np
Total Div. Coverage	na	na	na
Interest Coverage	4.3	12.0	nd
Current Ratio	0.4	0.5	na
Operating Margin	25.0	40.5	na
Asset Turnover	0.2	0.4	0.0
5 YEAR RATIOS (%)			
Return on Capital	na	na	na
Return on Com. Equity	na	na	na
Profit Growth	na	na	na
Revenue Growth	na	na	na
Asset Growth	na	na	na
BALANCE SHEET (000)			
Cash	0	0	0
Current Assets	10,609	3,967	0
Net Fixed Assets	191,824	57,062	0
Invest's & Advances	0	0	0
Total Assets	202,433	61,029	1
Short Term Debt	11,436	586	0
Current Liabilities	30,343	7,600	0
Long Term Debt	87,622	14,889	0
Total Liabilities	125,671	22,832	0
Total Equity	76,762	38,197	0
Total Liab. & Equity	202,433	61,029	1
CAPITAL (000)			
Total Debt	99,058	15,475	0
Preferred Equity	0	0	0
Common Equity	76,762	38,197	0

Business:
GRAD & WALKER ENERGY CORPORATION is involved in the acquisition, exploration and development of oil and gas properties.

Synopsis:
Investment in 1995 will focus on Grad & Walker's core areas and on the newly acquired Atlantis lands. The acquisition of Atlantis Resources Ltd. in November 1994 provided the company with another core area with gas reserves of 73.3 billion cubic feet, and operatorship of gas plants and related facilities. The acquisition also included land and production in southeast Saskatchewan that complements Grad & Walker's existing operations.

During 1995, Grad & Walker will conduct a smaller capital program because of the higher priority being placed on retiring a portion of debt. To further re-allocate its capital, the company plans to sell various non-core assets and perhaps all or a part interest in a large heavy oil discovery made in 1994 in the Montario area, in west central Saskatchewan.

The company expects 1995 to generate moderate growth in its gas projects, particularly with low natural gas price levels realized in the first quarter of 1995. The current strength of crude oil prices help to mitigate the impact of gas price levels and led the company to place a priority on crude oil development projects in the near future.

In 1994 (1993), average daily production was: crude oil and natural gas liquids, 2,123 (744) barrels; and natural gas 34 (29) million cubic feet. At year-end total proven and probable reserves were: crude oil and natural gas liquids, 29.9 (9.4) million barrels; and natural gas, 178 (85) billion cubic feet.

Relative strength to TSE300

Price

Volume (in 1000's of board lots)

Rank (Profit/Revenue/Assets)
486 618 354

Stan G.P. Grad
Chairman, President & C.E.O.

Bradley Hurtubise
V.P., Finance, C.F.O. & Secret

Clifford W. Demetrick
Executive V.P. & C.O.O.

Address
Suite 1600
700 - 9th Avenue S.W.
Calgary
AB
T2P 4K7
(403) 262-5622

01003420/G/3.2

For further company information, call Globe Information Services 1-800-268-9128 or (416) 585-5345

GULF CANADA RESOURCES LIMITED

Exchanges	Price (Jun29'95)	5.50	Trailing P/E	nm	Stock Symbol
TMA	Trailing Yield (%)	0.00	Trailing EPS	(1.53)	**GOU**

Period Ending	Dec94	Dec93	Dec92	Dec91	Dec90
Yearly Statistics					
Price-Close	4.30	4.20	4.15	10.25	10.63
Price-High	6.25	6.00	10.88	10.63	17.38
Price-Low	3.75	2.85	3.60	6.00	10.00
P/E-Close	nm	nm	nm	nm	nm
Dividends per Share	0.00	0.00	0.10	0.40	0.40
Dividend Yield (%)	0.00	0.00	2.41	3.90	3.77
Sales per Share	4.00	4.31	4.31	5.01	5.59
EPS before extra. item	(1.39)	(0.37)	(2.16)	(0.84)	(0.82)
Cash Flow per Share	1.42	1.67	2.09	2.09	3.25
Book Value per Share	2.59	3.68	3.89	5.97	7.19
O/S Common Shares	163,768	163,236	162,748	158,623	155,876
Total Revenue	763,000	858,000	928,000	1,057,000	956,000
Income before extra.	(197,000)	(32,000)	(302,000)	(63,000)	(23,000)
Cash Flow	232,000	272,000	339,000	328,000	507,000
Debt/Equity	1.43	1.39	1.42	1.17	0.44
Return on Capital (%)	(3.55)	2.37	(8.19)	1.92	2.03
Ret. on Com. Equity (%)	(49.02)	(10.06)	(50.38)	(12.68)	(10.54)
% Change Profit	(515.6)	89.4	(379.4)	(173.9)	(150.0)
% Change Revenue	(11.1)	(7.5)	(12.2)	10.6	(0.3)
% Change Assets	(11.4)	(4.1)	(13.8)	4.2	13.4

Date	EPS	DPS	Tot Rev	Inc Bex
Mar 95	(0.30)	0.00	167,000	(51,000)
Dec 94	(0.85)	0.00	180,000	(132,000)
Sep 94	(0.15)	0.00	184,000	(16,000)
Jun 94	(0.23)	0.00	183,000	(29,000)
Mar 94	(0.16)	0.00	172,000	(20,000)
Dec 93	(0.08)	0.00	194,000	(8,000)
Sep 93	0.06	0.00	220,000	17,000
Jun 93	(0.01)	0.00	228,000	6,000

	Dec94	Dec93	Dec92
Preferred Div. Coverage	na	0.0	0.0
Total Div. Coverage	na	0.0	0.0
Interest Coverage	0.0	0.8	0.0
Current Ratio	2.3	3.4	1.7
Operating Margin	5.7	14.3	8.2
Asset Turnover	0.2	0.2	0.2
5 YEAR RATIOS (%)			
Return on Capital	(1.1)	0.6	1.0
Return on Com. Equity	(26.5)	(17.5)	(15.6)
Profit Growth	na	na	na
Revenue Growth	(4.5)	(1.4)	1.8
Asset Growth	(2.9)	(2.7)	0.5
BALANCE SHEET (000)			
Cash	496,000	685,000	396,000
Current Assets	707,000	926,000	656,000
Net Fixed Assets	1,939,000	2,086,000	2,360,000
Invest's & Advances	6,000	6,000	185,000
Total Assets	2,876,000	3,245,000	3,384,000
Short Term Debt	58,000	55,000	147,000
Current Liabilities	314,000	274,000	382,000
Long Term Debt	1,372,000	1,577,000	1,570,000
Total Liabilities	1,875,000	2,068,000	2,174,000
Total Equity	1,001,000	1,177,000	1,210,000
Total Liab. & Equity	2,876,000	3,245,000	3,384,000
CAPITAL (000)			
Total Debt	1,430,000	1,632,000	1,717,000
Preferred Equity	577,000	577,000	577,000
Common Equity	424,000	600,000	633,000

Business:

GULF CANADA RESOURCES LTD. is an oil and gas production and exploration company. The company is a producer of crude oil, natural gas liquids and natural gas in western Canada. It also has producing oil wells in Indonesia. The company has exploration activities in western Canada and Southeast Asia. It also holds lands in Algeria, Africa and the Canadian frontier.

Synopsis:

Despite a loss in the first quarter of 1995, Gulf Canada Resources expects a return to profitability as early as the second quarter of this year. Management remains optimistic that recent acquisitions and higher capital spending in 1995 will translate into increases in production and revenues. Results include a $27-million provision related to the reduction of 40% of its staff plus a $36-million charge associated with debts connected to foreign exchange losses in the first quarter.

In June 1995, Gulf Canada Resources Limited announced that holders of 29,619,504 shares or 93% of the common shares of Mannville Oil and Gas Ltd. have tendered their shares to Gulf's offer of $4.50 cash per common share that expires on June 30, 1995. Upon expiry of the takeover bid, Gulf will proceed to acquire all the remaining common shares and take Mannville private. In the meantime, Gulf has met with the officers and staff of Mannville and begun a transition program that includes a review of personnel and assets.

Gulf completed another strategic acquisition during the same month. It acquired Archer Resources Ltd.'s properties in the Richdale area near Drumheller, Alberta for $53-million. The properties provide Gulf with 102,000 net acres of developed land, 135 net acres of undeveloped land, and current daily production of approximately 25 million cubic feet of gas and 550 barrels of liquids. The acquisition also includes nine gas processing facilities with under-utilized capacity which the company plans to operate. Gulf is also farming 74,000 acres adjacent to the purchased properties.

Cash generated from continuing operations dropped in 1994. This primarily was a result of lower volumes from 1993 asset sales, lower liquids prices, and restructuring charges accrued in the year. An upswing in the natural gas price, the lower Canadian dollar's positive impact on U.S. dollar-denominated sales, and reduced operating expenses mitigated these negative factors.

Relative strength to TSE300 / Price / Volume (in 1000's of board lots)

Rank (Profit/Revenue/Assets)		
1000	145	73

H.E. Joudrie
Chairman

J.P. Bryan
President & C.E.O.

A.B. Wiswell
Sr. V.P. & C.F.O.

Address
401 - 9th Avenue S.W.
P.O. Box 130
Calgary
AB
T2P 2H7
(403) 233-4000

Fax: (403) 233-5143
G0003506/G/3.2

HOME OIL COMPANY LIMITED

Exchanges	Price (Jun29'95)		17.62	Trailing P/E		135.58	Stock Symbol
TA	Trailing Yield (%)		0.00	Trailing EPS		0.13	**HOC**

Period Ending	Dec94	Dec93	Dec92	Dec91	Dec90
Yearly Statistics					
Price-Close	14.88	17.25	15.00	15.00	n t
Price-High	21.25	23.25	16.63	18.38	n t
Price-Low	14.00	13.00	13.75	14.13	n t
P/E-Close	82.64	57.50	88.24	nm	n t
Dividends per Share	0.00	0.00	0.00	0.06	0.25
Dividend Yield (%)	0.00	0.00	0.00	0.40	na
Sales per Share	7.99	8.31	6.89	6.71	8.22
EPS before extra. item	0.18	0.30	0.17	(0.01)	1.68
Cash Flow per Share	3.84	3.68	3.48	2.93	4.61
Book Value per Share	11.75	10.57	10.09	9.91	15.64
O/S Common Shares	45,863	40,360	39,644	39,644	39,637
Total Revenue	345,700	341,700	281,200	273,100	333,600
Income before extra.	7,500	12,000	6,900	(400)	66,400
Cash Flow	163,000	146,500	138,000	116,000	182,500
Debt/Equity	0.67	0.92	1.07	1.35	0.48
Return on Capital (%)	6.59	8.26	7.28	5.90	15.42
Ret. on Com. Equity (%)	1.55	2.90	1.74	(0.16)	14.28
% Change Profit	(37.5)	73.9	1,825.0	(100.6)	51.9
% Change Revenue	1.2	21.5	3.0	(18.1)	20.1
% Change Assets	5.8	(2.6)	(6.8)	(0.8)	5.1

Preferred Div. Coverage	np	np	np
Total Div. Coverage	na	na	na
Interest Coverage	1.4	1.6	1.4
Current Ratio	1.0	0.8	0.8
Operating Margin	14.7	17.4	20.9
Asset Turnover	0.2	0.2	0.2
5 YEAR RATIOS (%)			
Return on Capital	8.7	na	na
Return on Com. Equity	4.1	na	na
Profit Growth	(29.8)	na	na
Revenue Growth	4.4	na	na
Asset Growth	(0.0)	na	na
BALANCE SHEET (000)			
Cash	0	0	0
Current Assets	67,400	60,400	63,300
Net Fixed Assets	1,348,400	1,275,500	1,304,700
Invest's & Advances	14,100	14,900	13,300
Total Assets	1,433,100	1,355,000	1,390,500
Short Term Debt	0	0	1,700
Current Liabilities	70,800	80,400	74,600
Long Term Debt	360,000	390,100	426,500
Total Liabilities	894,300	928,500	990,600
Total Equity	538,800	426,500	399,900
Total Liab. & Equity	1,433,100	1,355,000	1,390,500
CAPITAL (000)			
Total Debt	360,000	390,100	428,200
Preferred Equity	0	0	0
Common Equity	538,800	426,500	399,900

Business:

HOME OIL COMPANY LIMITED is an upstream petroleum company. With properties and facilities across western Canada, Home Oil operates 25 of its 45 core areas, including 13 natural gas processing plants, a markets natural gas, crude oil and natural gas liquids. It operates and owns 50% of Federated Pipe Lines Ltd.

Date	EPS	DPS	Tot Rev	Inc Bex
Mar 95	(0.02)	0.00	67,900	(900)
Dec 94	0.05	0.00	70,500	2,000
Sep 94	0.02	0.00	70,400	900
Jun 94	0.08	0.00	74,900	3,600
Mar 94	0.03	0.00	75,800	1,000
Dec 93	0.03	0.00	68,900	1,400
Sep 93	0.03	0.00	67,100	1,000
Jun 93	0.11	0.00	72,400	4,600

Synopsis:

Home Oil expects that recent initiatives and the completion of its exploration and development program in 1994 will positively affect future operating results. Home's lack of success with its deep drilling program in 1994 and development in northeastern B.C. this past winter reinforces the company's commitment to shallow gas development. Proceeds from the sale of non-strategic assets will be used to acquire two producing oil properties and adjoining exploration acreage in Argentina, and to reduce debt.

Weak natural gas prices, lower gas volumes and lower liquids production were partially offset by higher crude oil prices during the first quarter of 1995. During this period, average daily natural gas sales averaged 213 million cubic feet, (mmcf), about 24 mmcf below the first quarter of 1994, and well below productive capacity of about 260 mmcf per day. This decline reflects Home's decision to shut in uncontracted gas volumes from fields having high operating costs until gas prices improve. Gas sales and volumes should climb by more than 30 mmcf per day during the second quarter as new lower cost production comes on stream. Daily crude oil production of 17,287 barrels during the first quarter of 1995, was 2,265 barrels lower than the same period in 1994. Production from a new field in B.C. and an additional working interest was more than offset by natural declines in several mature fields and property dispositions.

Despite the 11% increase in cash flow from operations in fiscal 1994 due to higher operating revenues and lower current taxes, cash flow from operations per share increased only 4%. In August 1994, Home issued 5.5 million common shares. The share issue provided the company net proceeds of $103-million.

In 1994 (1993), Home's average daily production was: crude oil and natural gas liquids, 25,481 (27,547) barrels; and natural gas 236 (229) million cubic feet. At year-end total proven and probable reserves were: crude oil and natural gas liquids, 120 (116) million barrels; and natural gas, 1,491 (1,375) billion cubic feet.

Relative strength to TSE300

Price

Volume (in 1000's of board lots)

Rank (Profit/Revenue/Assets)
353 236 131

David E. Powell
President & C.E.O.

Allen R. Hagerman
Vice President & C.F.O.

Bruce W. Sherley
Vice President Production

Address
1600 Home Oil Tower
324 - 8th Avenue S.W.
Calgary
AB
T2P 2Z5
(403) 232-7100

Fax: (403) 232-7678
01003209/G/3.2

HORSHAM CORPORATION (THE)

Exchanges	Price (Jun29'95)		18.62	Trailing P/E		7.73	Stock Symbol
TMN	Trailing Yield (%)		0.44	Trailing EPS		1.77	**HSM**

Period Ending	Dec94	Dec93	Dec92	Dec91	Dec90	Business:
Yearly Statistics	US	US	US	US	US	THE HORSHAM CORPORATION is a
Price-Close	17.75	19.38	11.13	10.50	9.13	Canadian-based management company which
Price-High	22.13	20.25	11.63	11.88	12.38	owns a controlling interest (20%) in American
Price-Low	16.88	10.50	8.00	8.00	6.75	Barrick Resources Corporation, a major gold
P/E-Close	7.16	36.56	22.34	13.11	11.34	company, Clark Refining and Marketing, Inc., a
Dividends per Share	0.06	0.05	0.00	0.00	0.00	Fortune 500 company, and Horsham Properties
Dividend Yield (%)	0.34	0.26	0.00	0.00	0.00	GmbH, a property management company
Sales per Share	25.21	23.85	25.49	27.83	32.93	operating in Berlin, Germany.
EPS before extra. item	1.81	0.41	0.41	0.70	0.69	
Cash Flow per Share	0.57	0.74	0.36	1.05	0.81	
Book Value per Share	7.55	5.74	5.07	4.92	4.24	
O/S Common Shares	102,309	98,582	89,407	87,861	84,703	
Total Revenue	2,727,443	2,340,381	2,311,124	2,482,789	2,832,007	
Income before extra.	178,740	39,261	36,245	61,442	58,157	
Cash Flow	56,413	70,261	31,803	91,636	68,787	

Date		EPS	DPS	Tot Rev	Inc Bex
Mar 95	US	0.16	0.00	873,300	16,500
Dec 94	US	(0.09)	0.00	638,130	(8,831)
Sep 94	US	1.54	0.00	850,353	152,228
Jun 94	US	0.16	0.06	607,490	15,794
Mar 94	US	0.20	0.00	596,022	19,549
Dec 93	US	0.02	0.00	555,586	2,758
Sep 93	US	0.16	0.00	564,050	15,731
Jun 93	US	0.15	0.05	596,929	13,948

	Dec94	Dec93	Dec92	Dec91	Dec90
Debt/Equity	1.52	2.04	1.07	0.99	0.84
Return on Capital (%)	14.47	6.29	7.23	15.25	19.49
Ret. on Com. Equity (%)	26.73	7.71	8.19	15.54	17.62
% Change Profit	355.3	8.3	(41.0)	5.6	(3.2)
% Change Revenue	16.5	1.3	(6.9)	(12.3)	35.0
% Change Assets	12.1	69.2	2.8	23.8	15.2

				Synopsis:
Preferred Div. Coverage	np	np	np	
Total Div. Coverage	30.1	7.9	na	
Interest Coverage	3.4	1.6	1.4	
Current Ratio	2.7	5.4	1.9	
Operating Margin	2.7	0.7	1.1	
Asset Turnover	1.1	1.2	1.9	
5 YEAR RATIOS (%)				
Return on Capital	12.5	14.5	14.8	
Return on Com. Equity	15.2	14.9	15.2	
Profit Growth	24.4	27.3	52.4	
Revenue Growth	5.3	65.0	235.8	
Asset Growth	22.6	24.5	60.6	
BALANCE SHEET (000)				
Cash	425,520	970,382	285,187	
Current Assets	679,506	1,209,242	516,175	
Net Fixed Assets	550,110	474,147	401,550	
Invest's & Advances	938,307	245,992	224,280	
Total Assets	2,207,379	1,968,910	1,163,530	
Short Term Debt	37	317	85,000	
Current Liabilities	249,310	224,907	271,751	
Long Term Debt	1,171,404	1,154,942	401,514	
Total Liabilities	1,435,204	1,403,483	710,254	
Total Equity	772,175	565,427	453,276	
Total Liab. & Equity	2,207,379	1,968,910	1,163,530	
CAPITAL (000)				
Total Debt	1,171,441	1,155,259	486,514	
Preferred Equity	0	0	0	
Common Equity	772,175	565,427	453,276	

Synopsis:

The Horsham Corporation acquired a 46.5% interest in Trizec Corporation Ltd. in July 1994. Horsham bought 46,508,690 common shares of Trizec, 5,416,775 rights to purchase common shares, and 6,066,684 class B warrants to purchase common shares of Trizec. Horsham paid 19,399 Horsham shares and about $428.6-million in cash. Horsham paid an additional $48.1-million in October 1994 in connection with the exercise of the acquired rights. Horsham's 51,925,465 shares of Trizec represent approximately 48% of the common shares outstanding. The warrants expire July 25, 1996, and are exercisable at $12.86 per share. Horsham uses the equity method to account for he investment in Trizec.

American Barrick acquired Lac Minerals Ltd. in September 1994 at a cost of $1.36-billion through a combination of cash and common shares. As a result of the transaction Horsham's interest in American Barrick dropped to 16.5% from 20%, and resulted in a dilution gain of $136-million. The 3.25% Exchangeable Debentures issued by Horsham last year are exchangeable into Barrick shares. Horsham had placed 21,428,580 Barrick shares with a trustee as collateral for the obligation, representing the maximum number of shares required to be pledged as collateral. Horsham's obligation can be satisfied by the Barrick shares, cash equivalent of the current market value of the shares, or a combination of the two.

Clark USA, Inc. sold $120-million of common shares in a private placement, reducing Horsham's interest to 60% and creating a dilution gain for Horsham of $24-million. Clark used the proceeds from the private placement to finance the purchase of Chevron's Port Arthur, Texas refinery. The acquisition of the 200,000 barrel per day refinery has more than doubled the oil refining capacity of Clark USA. Clark contributed a $20.4-million loss to the net earnings of Horsham for the first quarter of 1995, compared to a $9.2-million profit for the first three months of 1994. Warm weather and the transition to reformulated gasoline in the United States led to unusually weak refining margins. The margins showed a recovery during the second quarter.

Relative strength to TSE300

Rank (Profit/Revenue/Assets)
23   40   67
Peter Munk
Chairman & C.E.O.
Gregory C. Wilkins
President
Robert B. Wickham
V.P. Finance

Address
BCE Place, 181 Bay Street
Suite 3900
P.O. Box 768
Toronto
ON
M5J 2T3
(416) 682-8600
Fax: (416) 364-1504
U0001475/G/3.1

IMPERIAL OIL LIMITED

Exchanges	Price (Jun29'95)	50.37	Trailing P/E	24.69	Stock Symbol
TMA	Trailing Yield (%)	9.53	Trailing EPS	2.04	**IMO**

Period Ending	Dec94	Dec93	Dec92	Dec91	Dec90
Yearly Statistics					
Price-Close	46.25	44.75	40.63	40.00	58.63
Price-High	48.75	50.25	48.13	61.13	67.63
Price-Low	40.13	40.13	37.75	38.75	53.25
P/E-Close	25.00	31.08	40.22	47.62	43.75
Dividends per Share	4.80	1.80	1.80	1.80	1.80
Dividend Yield (%)	10.38	4.02	4.43	4.50	3.07
Sales per Share	45.97	45.37	46.29	48.84	58.81
EPS before extra. item	1.85	1.44	1.01	0.84	1.34
Cash Flow per Share	5.50	6.02	5.92	5.14	3.53
Book Value per Share	30.93	33.87	34.23	35.03	35.80
O/S Common Shares	194	194	194	194	192
Total Revenue	8,988	8,876	9,046	9,592	11,674
Income before extra.	359	279	195	162	256
Cash Flow	1,067	1,166	1,148	993	673
Debt/Equity	0.33	0.31	0.34	0.36	0.57
Return on Capital (%)	9.96	8.54	6.85	5.04	7.11
Ret. on Com. Equity (%)	5.72	4.23	2.91	2.37	3.65
% Change Profit	28.7	43.1	20.4	(36.7)	(43.9)
% Change Revenue	1.3	(1.9)	(5.7)	(17.8)	15.3
% Change Assets	(7.3)	(2.1)	(2.9)	(6.7)	(6.9)

Preferred Div. Coverage	np	np	np
Total Div. Coverage	0.4	0.8	0.6
Interest Coverage	4.8	4.2	3.7
Current Ratio	1.8	1.8	1.7
Operating Margin	9.2	8.9	6.1
Asset Turnover	0.7	0.7	0.7
5 YEAR RATIOS (%)			
Return on Capital	7.5	8.1	9.2
Return on Com. Equity	3.8	4.0	5.0
Profit Growth	(4.7)	(11.1)	(23.6)
Revenue Growth	(2.4)	4.3	3.3
Asset Growth	(5.2)	5.9	6.7
BALANCE SHEET (mil)			
Cash	1,268	1,479	1,022
Current Assets	2,797	2,964	2,638
Net Fixed Assets	8,538	9,389	9,965
Invest's & Advances	264	152	159
Total Assets	11,928	12,861	13,135
Short Term Debt	0	0	0
Current Liabilities	1,581	1,658	1,563
Long Term Debt	1,977	2,030	2,222
Total Liabilities	5,933	6,295	6,499
Total Equity	5,995	6,566	6,636
Total Liab. & Equity	11,928	12,861	13,135
CAPITAL (mil)			
Total Debt	1,977	2,030	2,222
Preferred Equity	0	0	0
Common Equity	5,995	6,566	6,636

Business:

IMPERIAL OIL LTD. is an integrated oil company. Its diversified activities fall into three groups. The resource division engages in the exploration and production of crude oil and natural gas. The petroleum-product division refines, markets and distributes refined products. The chemicals division makes and markets various chemicals. Exxon Corp. owns 69% of the company.

Date	EPS	DPS	Tot Rev	Inc Bex
Mar 95	0.66	0.45	2,227,000	127,000
Dec 94	0.52	0.45	2,347,000	101,000
Sep 94	0.88	0.45	2,333,000	171,000
Jun 94	(0.02)	3.45	2,231,000	(5,000)
Mar 94	0.47	0.45	2,087,000	92,000
Dec 93	0.28	0.45	2,207,000	54,000
Sep 93	0.43	0.45	2,231,000	84,000
Jun 93	0.35	0.45	2,272,000	68,000

Synopsis:

1994 proved to be another year of sustained growth for Imperial Oil. Earnings in the natural resources segment were $167-million on the strength of improved prices for heavy crude oil and natural gas. Demand for heavy crude oil was strong in North America and elsewhere. Refiners sought to reduce costs by turning to heavier feedstocks. This increased international demand for heavy oil boosted its price relative to lighter grades of crude.

While the recovering economy in 1994 increased demand for petroleum products, there was no improvement in the slim margins that have prevailed in this segment of the industry for several years. Low margins are largely the result of the surplus capacity that exists throughout Canada, particularly in the retail area. Despite the decline in contribution to earnings, 1994 earnings from the company's petroleum products segment were $212-million. Imperial continues to take initiatives to improve its refining margins by introducing higher-value new products, shedding low-margin sales, and streamlining its retail network.

Despite a revenue decline in the company's chemical operations, net earnings from these operations rose by nearly 50% to $52-million in 1994. Strong markets for petrochemicals more than offset the absence of earnings from the company's fertilizer operations that were sold earlier in the year.

Imperial wants to reduce production costs in the oil and gas segment by $100-million by the end of 1995. It will continue to develop the Cold Lake project. In addition Imperial is continuing the rationalization of its service-station network by closing or consolidating less productive stations and upgrading 200 existing high-potential outlets.

The company's capital spending program for 1995 is set at about $650-million. About $400-million is allocated to the natural resources segment.

Relative strength to TSE300

Price

Volume (in 1000's of board lots)

Rank (Profit/Revenue/Assets)
15 12 26

R.B. Peterson
Chairman, C.E.O. & Pres.

Address
111 St. Clair Avenue West
Toronto
ON
M5W 1K3
(416) 968-4111

Fax: (416) 968-5228
I0000445/G/3.1

For further company information, call Globe Information Services 1-800-268-9128 or (416) 585-5345

INTENSITY RESOURCES LTD.

Exchanges		Price (Jun29'95)		3.05	Trailing P/E		17.94	Stock Symbol
T		Trailing Yield (%)		0.00	Trailing EPS		0.17	ITY

Period Ending	Dec94	Dec93	Dec92	Dec91	Dec90
Yearly Statistics					
Price-Close	2.32	2.70	1.85	0.85	1.00
Price-High	3.35	4.70	1.99	1.15	1.06
Price-Low	2.15	1.80	0.65	0.80	0.52
P/E-Close	16.57	33.75	46.25	nm	100.00
Dividends per Share	0.00	0.00	0.00	0.00	0.00
Dividend Yield (%)	0.00	0.00	0.00	0.00	0.00
Sales per Share	0.72	0.44	0.32	0.30	0.33
EPS before extra. item	0.14	0.08	0.04	0.00	0.01
Cash Flow per Share	0.52	0.30	0.20	0.15	0.16
Book Value per Share	1.24	1.10	0.70	0.67	0.65
O/S Common Shares	51,307	51,120	45,278	45,191	39,941
Total Revenue	36,796	21,472	14,573	12,761	11,465
Income before extra.	6,941	3,593	1,920	282	650
Cash Flow	26,455	14,556	9,116	6,491	5,637
Debt/Equity	0.38	0.00	0.25	0.24	0.28
Return on Capital (%)	14.90	11.86	9.43	3.81	8.33
Ret. on Com. Equity (%)	11.59	7.67	5.44	0.11	1.91
% Change Profit	93.2	87.1	580.9	(56.6)	1,811.8
% Change Revenue	71.4	47.3	14.2	11.3	106.7
% Change Assets	44.0	44.6	5.5	9.2	53.4

Preferred Div. Coverage	na	16.9	8.0
Total Div. Coverage	na	16.9	8.0
Interest Coverage	16.1	11.4	6.9
Current Ratio	1.1	0.8	1.0
Operating Margin	29.8	27.0	27.1
Asset Turnover	0.3	0.3	0.3
5 YEAR RATIOS (%)			
Return on Capital	9.7	6.7	(3.9)
Return on Com. Equity	5.3	3.0	(7.6)
Profit Growth	0.0	191.9	82.8
Revenue Growth	46.0	40.9	30.6
Asset Growth	29.7	27.0	13.2
BALANCE SHEET (000)			
Cash	2,995	3,866	1,767
Current Assets	9,549	8,998	4,881
Net Fixed Assets	99,561	66,755	47,499
Invest's & Advances	0	0	0
Total Assets	109,110	75,753	52,380
Short Term Debt	0	6	32
Current Liabilities	9,005	10,810	4,994
Long Term Debt	24,957	0	8,277
Total Liabilities	44,160	17,898	18,915
Total Equity	64,950	57,855	33,465
Total Liab. & Equity	109,110	75,753	52,380
CAPITAL (000)			
Total Debt	24,957	6	8,309
Preferred Equity	1,502	1,502	1,693
Common Equity	63,448	56,353	31,772

Business:

INTENSITY RESOURCES LTD. is an oil and gas exploration and development company with properties in Alberta.

Date	EPS	DPS	Tot Rev	Inc Bex
Mar 95	0.06	0.00	12,297	2,875
Dec 94	0.03	0.00	11,029	1,513
Sep 94	0.03	0.00	10,064	1,200
Jun 94	0.05	0.00	8,719	2,925
Mar 94	0.03	0.00	6,984	1,303
Dec 93	0.03	0.00	6,940	1,426
Sep 93	0.02	0.00	4,904	726
Jun 93	0.02	0.00	5,506	872

Synopsis:

Intensity Resources experienced another year of significant growth in 1994. During this period, Intensity undertook an aggressive exploration and development program that focused on oil opportunities. Its biggest success happened at Cessford, Alberta, where the Kirkpatrick Lake field was discovered in July. Kirkpatrick was one of the three pools discovered in the area. Further expansion of all three pools is planned, with a 1995 exploration program in place to drill 19 exploratory wells in the Cessford area.

As a result of the weak natural gas prices, Intensity does not intend to drill on its inventory of gas prospects, other than honouring existing drilling commitments. The timing of further development of gas prospects will depend on natural gas prices. As of April 1995, the company had not shut-in any gas production.

During 1995, Intensity plans to continue to increase its land base, by expanding existing core areas and reviewing potential acquisitions. Intensity's $30-million current base capital budget will be partially funded by internally generated cash flow. About $14-million is allocated for exploration, and $16-million for development and facilities enhancement.

Intensity's financial performance in 1994 was achieved through higher production volumes and greater operating efficiencies resulting in lower per unit costs.

During fiscal 1994 (1993) average daily production of oil and natural gas liquids was 5,366 (3,476) barrels, and average daily production of natural gas was 14.79 (8.21) million cubic feet. At 1994 (1993) fiscal year end, the company's proven and probable oil reserves totalled 13.9 (12) million barrels, and natural gas reserves totalled 46.6 (53.7) billion cubic feet.

Relative strength to TSE300

Price

Volume (in 1000's of board lots)

Rank (Profit/Revenue/Assets)
373   609   467

Daniel U. Pekarsky
Chairman

Ronald Wickwire
President & C.E.O.

Address
Suite 2500
425 - 1st Street S.W.
Calgary
AB
T2P 3L8
(403) 263-3440

Fax: (403) 262-8508
01001470/G/3.2

INTERNATIONAL COLIN ENERGY CORPORATION

Exchanges	Price (Jun29'95)	6 .87	Trailing P/E	10 .42	Stock Symbol
TA	Trailing Yield (%)	0 .00	Trailing EPS	0 .66	**KCN**

Period Ending	Dec94	Dec93	Jun93	Jun92	Jun91	Business:
Yearly Statistics						INTERNATIONAL COLIN ENERGY
Price-Close	9 .13	16 .75	23 .63	9 .75	3 .35	CORPORATION is involved in oil and gas
Price-High	21 .75	26 .63	26 .63	10 .00	3 .65	exploration and development in Western
Price-Low	8 .38	14 .13	9 .75	3 .55	1 .50	Canada.
P/E-Close	13 .04	13 .62	24 .11	19 .12	14 .57	
Dividends per Share	0 .00	0 .00	0 .00	0 .00	0 .00	
Dividend Yield (%)	0 .00	0 .00	0 .00	0 .00	0 .00	
Sales per Share	5 .50	5 .11	3 .94	2 .24	1 .77	
EPS before extra. item	0 .70	1 .23	0 .98	0 .51	0 .23	
Cash Flow per Share	3 .27	3 .58	2 .78	1 .53	1 .00	
Book Value per Share	8 .87	8 .13	8 .41	3 .26	1 .93	

						Date	EPS	DPS	Tot Rev	Inc Bex
O/S Common Shares	12 ,866	12 ,832	12 ,879	7 ,335	3 ,118					
Total Revenue	71 ,164	57 ,717	37 ,433	11 ,893	5 ,613					
Income before extra.	9 ,106	13 ,886	9 ,170	2 ,772	904	Mar 95	0 .12	0 .00	17 ,129	1 ,487
Cash Flow	42 ,228	40 ,490	25 ,986	8 ,054	3 ,100	Dec 94	0 .07	0 .00	16 ,175	941
Debt/Equity	0 .80	0 .65	0 .65	0 .67	1 .26	Sep 94	0 .21	0 .00	20 ,066	2 ,787
Return on Capital (%)	12 .05	15 .20	16 .15	17 .24	13 .73	Jun 94	0 .26	0 .00	19 ,306	3 ,374
Ret. on Com. Equity (%)	8 .34	13 .06	13 .87	17 .88	12 .40	Mar 94	0 .16	0 .00	15 ,617	2 ,003
% Change Profit	(34 .4)	51 .4	230 .8	206 .8	30 .3	Dec 93	0 .31	0 .00	18 ,900	4 ,006
% Change Revenue	23 .3	54 .2	214 .8	111 .9	59 .8	Sep 93	0 .30	0 .00	16 ,071	3 ,862
% Change Assets	19 .4	(2 .6)	367 .9	115 .3	36 .8	Jun 93	0 .36	0 .00	12 ,520	3 ,491

				Synopsis:
Preferred Div. Coverage	np	np	np	
Total Div. Coverage	na	na	na	
Interest Coverage	3 .9	9 .3	7 .6	
Current Ratio	1 .0	0 .8	1 .6	
Operating Margin	32 .0	46 .3	47 .2	
Asset Turnover	0 .3	0 .3	0 .2	

International Colin Energy plans to focus its 1995 capital program on projects that will generate immediate cash flow and provide the basis for an expanded drilling program in 1996. The 1994 capital program of $64-million exceeded cash flow by $22-million increasing year end debt to over $91-million.

5 YEAR RATIOS (%)			
Return on Capital	14 .9	14 .3	14 .2
Return on Com. Equity	13 .1	14 .2	16 .7
Profit Growth	67 .3	106 .1	180 .2
Revenue Growth	82 .4	52 .1	82 .2
Asset Growth	74 .1	89 .6	123 .9

International Colin completed the issue of $40-million (U.S.) worth of senior secured notes in August 1994. The proceeds went to reduce existing bank debt. International Colin has also targeted selected assets for disposition to reduce debt by $15-million to $20-million in 1995. It's expected that the company will also reduce debt during the first half of 1995 from internal cash flow. Cash flow should exceed capital requirements in the first half of the year.

BALANCE SHEET (000)			
Cash	148	1 ,246	4 ,326
Current Assets	13 ,322	13 ,159	34 ,991
Net Fixed Assets	224 ,248	187 ,052	171 ,230
Invest's & Advances	0	0	0
Total Assets	239 ,682	200 ,810	206 ,220
Short Term Debt	33	150	143
Current Liabilities	13 ,171	16 ,145	21 ,268
Long Term Debt	91 ,749	67 ,900	70 ,543
Total Liabilities	125 ,588	96 ,484	97 ,898
Total Equity	114 ,094	104 ,326	108 ,323
Total Liab. & Equity	239 ,682	200 ,810	206 ,220

International Colin had mixed results with its 1994 drilling program, leading to slower than expected production and reserve growth. The company participated in drilling 49 wells resulting in 25 oil wells and 12 gas wells. Daily average production increased 25% on a barrel of oil equivalent (BOE) basis, production was replaced by a factor of 147%, and proven and probable reserves climbed 18% in 1994.

In 1994 revenues were $48.5-million in oil sales, $17.8-million in gas sales, and $4.9-million in processing, pipeline, and marketing. The production mix was 76% oil and 24% gas on a BOE basis. The increased revenue resulted from increased production compared to the previous year.

CAPITAL (000)			
Total Debt	91 ,782	68 ,050	70 ,685
Preferred Equity	0	0	0
Common Equity	114 ,094	104 ,326	108 ,323

Average daily production in 1994 before royalties was: crude oil, 7,773 barrels and natural gas, 25.1 million cubic feet. As of December 1994, the company reported gross proven and probable oil reserves totalling 17,953,000 barrels and 185.9 million cubic feet of natural gas reserves.

Relative strength to TSE300

Price

Volume (in 1000's of board lots)

Rank (Profit/Revenue/Assets)
313   478   327
P. David Williams
Chairman & C.E.O.
Lloyd Mann
President & C.O.O.
Paul D. Wright
V.P. Finance & C.F.O.
Lloyd Mann
President & C.O.O.

Address
Suite 1210
333 - 11th Avenue S.W.
Calgary
AB
T2R 1L9
(403) 269-6822

Fax: (403) 263-1410
D0001132/G/3.2

For further company information, call Globe Information Services 1-800-268-9128 or (416) 585-5345

INTERNATIONAL PETROLEUM CORPORATION

Exchanges	Price (Jun29'95)		4.25	Trailing P/E		19.57	Stock Symbol
TQ	Trailing Yield (%)		0.00	Trailing EPS		0.16	IRP

Period Ending	Sep94	Sep93	Sep92	Sep91	Sep90	Business:
Yearly Statistics	US	US	US	US	US	INTERNATIONAL PETROLEUM CORP. is
Price-Close	1.60	2.22	3.70	5.63	2.40	involved in the acquisition, exploration and
Price-High	2.45	3.95	7.25	6.25	3.00	development of oil and gas properties.
Price-Low	1.20	1.82	3.50	1.60	1.80	Properties are located in Europe, Africa, the
P/E-Close	9.88	nm	nm	nm	nm	Middle East and Asia.
Dividends per Share	0.00	0.00	0.00	0.00	0.00	
Dividend Yield (%)	0.00	0.00	0.00	0.00	0.00	
Sales per Share	0.69	0.15	na	na	0.07	
EPS before extra. item	0.12	(0.28)	(0.10)	(0.32)	(0.31)	
Cash Flow per Share	0.32	(0.08)	(0.07)	(0.07)	(0.02)	
Book Value per Share	1.31	1.20	1.58	1.65	1.29	
O/S Common Shares	40,087	40,049	31,704	23,933	23,483	
Total Revenue	27,363	8,125	3,298	2,753	(100)	
Income before extra.	4,408	(9,181)	(2,856)	(7,439)	(5,628)	
Cash Flow	11,500	(2,776)	(1,967)	(1,676)	(278)	

Date		EPS	DPS	Tot Rev	Inc Bex
Mar 95	US	0.02	0.00	8,711	1,261
Dec 94	US	0.05	0.00	8,660	1,684
Sep 94	US	0.05	0.00	9,046	1,456
Jun 94	US	0.05	0.00	7,069	1,928
Mar 94	US	0.00	0.00	4,896	(184)
Dec 93	US	0.03	0.00	6,608	1,208
Sep 93	US	(0.27)	0.00	4,230	(8,886)
Jun 93	US	0.05	0.00	3,722	1,785

Debt/Equity	0.87	0.60	0.01	0.02	0.02
Return on Capital (%)	7.62	(13.91)	(6.22)	(20.92)	(20.60)
Ret. on Com. Equity (%)	8.75	(18.69)	(6.39)	(21.36)	(21.27)
% Change Profit	148.0	(221.4)	61.6	(32.2)	(78.4)
% Change Revenue	236.8	146.4	19.8	2,856.0	(102.4)
% Change Assets	33.4	52.6	22.4	29.3	39.3

Preferred Div. Coverage	np	np	np
Total Div. Coverage	na	na	na
Interest Coverage	2.9	0.0	0.0
Current Ratio	1.2	1.2	6.6
Operating Margin	20.2	(146.1)	(241.6)
Asset Turnover	0.2	0.1	na
5 YEAR RATIOS (%)			
Return on Capital	(10.8)	(15.0)	(21.8)
Return on Com. Equity	(11.8)	(16.3)	(22.8)
Profit Growth	na	na	na
Revenue Growth	46.2	(4.8)	(23.4)
Asset Growth	34.9	25.9	17.0
BALANCE SHEET (000)			
Cash	14,852	8,165	16,017
Current Assets	25,120	15,673	22,981
Net Fixed Assets	95,101	73,906	36,174
Invest's & Advances	0	0	0
Total Assets	121,677	91,197	59,764
Short Term Debt	11,653	3,834	405
Current Liabilities	21,704	12,690	3,486
Long Term Debt	34,001	24,953	0
Total Liabilities	69,055	43,033	9,678
Total Equity	52,622	48,164	50,086
Total Liab. & Equity	121,677	91,197	59,764
CAPITAL (000)			
Total Debt	45,654	28,788	405
Preferred Equity	0	0	0
Common Equity	52,622	48,164	50,086

Synopsis:

In 1995, International Petroleum Corporation (IPC) expects additional revenue and net profit growth as the Bukha field in Oman enters its first full year of production. The company's Malaysian properties should start to contribute to corporate earnings in 1996. Selling excess Bukha natural gas to consumers in the United Arab Emirates may also provide additional growth. IPC will continue to focus on exploration as it drills in Malaysia, Libya, Eritrea and the Sudan.

1994 was a busy year for IPC. The Welton field and satellites in the United Kingdom provided their first full year of production. The Bukha field came on stream in April. IPC made two additional oil and gas discoveries off the coast of Malaysia. The most recent produced more than 10,000 barrels per day of crude oil and 179 million cubic feet per day of gas. IPC's total production in 1994 was 1,466,000 barrels, net liquid hydrocarbon reserves ended up at 29.6 million barrels, and IPC's gas reserves were 527.5 billion cubic feet.

In April and May 1995, IPC sold its U.K. Welton field as part of the sale of IPC Expro (UK) Limited and its subsidiaries to Morrison Middlefield Resources. IPC also sold a 10% interest in the Bukha field, and its shareholdings in Sands Petroleum AB. The three sales generated about $60.7-million. The money will allow IPC to implement the first phase of the Malaysian field development, and begin drilling wildcat wells in Libya and Sudan later this year.

Rank (Profit/Revenue/Assets)
395   607   381

Adolf H. Lundin
Chairman

Ian H. Lundin
President

Nigel R. McCue
Chief Financial Officer

Address
Suite 1320
885 West Georgia Street
Vancouver
BC
V6C 3E8
(604) 689-7842

Fax: (604) 689-4250
01000209/G/3.2

INVERNESS PETROLEUM LTD.

Exchanges	Price (Jun29'95)	7.62	Trailing P/E	25.42	Stock Symbol
TM	Trailing Yield (%)	0.00	Trailing EPS	0.30	IES

Period Ending	Dec94	Dec93	Dec92	Dec91	Dec90
Yearly Statistics					6M
Price-Close	8.50	9.75	7.75	5.88	6.25
Price-High	12.00	14.38	8.25	7.25	7.50
Price-Low	8.25	7.50	4.75	5.00	5.75
P/E-Close	25.76	37.50	59.62	nm	10.42
Dividends per Share	0.00	0.00	0.00	0.00	0.00
Dividend Yield (%)	0.00	0.00	0.00	0.00	0.00
Sales per Share	3.74	2.81	2.45	2.48	3.55
EPS before extra. item	0.33	0.26	0.13	(1.79)	0.30
Cash Flow per Share	2.05	1.51	1.22	1.19	2.10
Book Value per Share	5.02	4.69	3.77	3.39	3.77
O/S Common Shares	31,063	30,928	27,786	24,842	10,681
Total Revenue	115,957	83,237	63,374	43,867	19,023
Income before extra.	10,168	8,265	4,282	(30,062)	3,658
Cash Flow	63,471	44,885	31,394	20,814	11,193
Debt/Equity	0.78	0.37	0.37	0.59	0.77
Return on Capital (%)	10.64	9.25	6.74	(19.27)	19.07
Ret. on Com. Equity (%)	6.76	3.48	3.48	(50.26)	16.55
% Change Profit	23.0	93.0	114.2	(510.9)	240.0
% Change Revenue	39.3	31.3	44.5	15.3	52.8
% Change Assets	40.4	25.6	0.6	79.2	26.1

Date	EPS	DPS	Tot Rev	Inc Bex
Mar 95	0.02	0.00	29,955	637
Dec 94	0.04	0.00	30,601	1,066
Sep 94	0.11	0.00	29,071	3,334
Jun 94	0.13	0.00	29,915	4,055
Mar 94	0.06	0.00	26,370	1,713
Dec 93	0.09	0.00	23,896	2,898
Sep 93	0.04	0.00	21,001	1,192
Jun 93	0.08	0.00	20,325	2,584

Preferred Div. Coverage	np	np	4.3
Total Div. Coverage	na	15.9	4.3
Interest Coverage	5.1	6.4	3.2
Current Ratio	0.7	0.8	0.8
Operating Margin	22.2	20.2	16.7
Asset Turnover	0.3	0.3	0.3
5 YEAR RATIOS (%)			
Return on Capital	5.3	4.9	4.0
Return on Com. Equity	(3.5)	(4.2)	(5.8)
Profit Growth	36.4	66.4	15.9
Revenue Growth	36.0	33.3	24.3
Asset Growth	32.0	23.4	18.1
BALANCE SHEET (000)			
Cash	0	0	0
Current Assets	22,677	18,647	14,200
Net Fixed Assets	329,429	232,080	185,466
Invest's & Advances	0	0	0
Total Assets	352,106	250,727	199,666
Short Term Debt	0	0	0
Current Liabilities	34,577	22,107	17,654
Long Term Debt	121,214	54,241	42,923
Total Liabilities	196,242	105,604	84,656
Total Equity	155,864	145,123	115,010
Total Liab. & Equity	352,106	250,727	199,666
CAPITAL (000)			
Total Debt	121,214	54,241	42,923
Preferred Equity	0	0	10,393
Common Equity	155,864	145,123	104,617

Business:

INVERNESS PETROLEUM LTD. is involved in the acquisition, exploration and development of oil and gas properties.

Synopsis:

The 1995 capital program at Inverness Petroleum will not exceed operating cash flow. Inverness does not want to substantially increase its current level of debt. Due to an aggressive capital program in 1994, including the $25.8-million net purchase of Anadarko, bank debt climbed to $123-million at year end. During 1994, Inverness spent $104-million on exploration and development and made acquisitions totalling $38-million. These actions resulted in Inverness having the largest inventory of undeveloped land in its history.

Average daily production levels should increase to 9,000 barrels of liquids and between 93 and 100 million cubic feet of natural gas per day in 1995. Gas volumes will depend on pricing. Low prices have already reduced production and deferred gas projects in 1995.

In June 1994, Inverness completed a swap/purchase transaction, which resulted in the sale of the majority of its Provost area properties plus $9.8-million cash. In exchange Inverness received working interests in two oil units in southwest Saskatchewan. The Saskatchewan properties provide Inverness with long-term oil reserves in a rapidly expanding area of operations.

In the final quarter of 1994, Inverness completed the purchase of Anadarko Petroleum of Canada Ltd. Anadarko provides Inverness with expansion opportunities with in its existing Peace River Arch core area, in B.C. and Alberta. The purchase added reserves of 45 billion cubic feet of natural gas and 2 million barrels of oil. A total of 10.8 million cubic feet of gas and 560 barrels of liquids were added to daily production levels.

During 1994 (1993), average daily production was: natural gas, 85.9 (63.1) million cubic feet; and crude oil and natural gas liquids, 7,819 (6,515) barrels. Total gross proven and probable reserves at 1994 (1993) year-end were: 324.9 (242.9) billion cubic feet of natural gas; and 26.3 (16.9) million barrels of crude oil and liquids.

Rank (Profit/Revenue/Assets)
297   396   269

William J. Anderson
Chairman & C.E.O.

Murray M. Frame
President & C.O.O.

R. Ross Liland
V.P. Finance & C.F.O.

Address
Suite 2200
400 - 3rd Avenue S.W.
Calgary
AB
T2P 4H2
(403) 294-3800

Fax: (403) 264-1810
I0001899/G/3.2

JORDAN PETROLEUM LTD.

Exchanges	Price (Jun29'95)	8.75	Trailing P/E	22.44	Stock Symbol
TMZ	Trailing Yield (%)	0.00	Trailing EPS	0.39	**JDN**

Period Ending	Nov94	Nov93	Nov92	Nov91	Nov90	Business:
Yearly Statistics						JORDAN PETROLEUM LTD. is an oil and gas
Price-Close	9.13	8.00	3.50	2.50	3.00	exploration and development company which
Price-High	10.75	11.38	3.60	3.30	4.40	conducts operations in western Canada.
Price-Low	7.25	3.40	1.95	2.22	2.50	
P/E-Close	22.26	32.00	20.59	12.50	11.54	
Dividends per Share	0.00	0.00	0.00	0.00	0.00	
Dividend Yield (%)	0.00	0.00	0.00	0.00	0.00	
Sales per Share	2.49	1.98	1.45	1.29	1.61	
EPS before extra. item	0.41	0.25	0.17	0.20	0.26	
Cash Flow per Share	1.40	0.98	0.57	0.51	0.76	
Book Value per Share	4.22	3.72	2.77	2.70	2.12	
O/S Common Shares	18,315	17,793	14,215	11,889	14,555	

Total Revenue	44,747	30,610	18,978	15,547	11,190
Income before extra.	7,402	3,852	1,946	2,377	1,811

Date	EPS	DPS	Tot Rev	Inc Bex
Feb 95	0.07	0.00	10,912	1,289
Nov 94	0.07	0.00	10,596	1,277
Aug 94	0.13	0.00	12,248	2,268
May 94	0.12	0.00	11,539	2,161
Feb 94	0.10	0.00	10,364	1,696
Nov 93	0.08	0.00	9,368	1,234
Aug 93	0.05	0.00	8,231	749
May 93	0.06	0.00	6,892	843

	Nov94	Nov93	Nov92	Nov91	Nov90
Cash Flow	25,129	15,163	7,475	6,202	5,181
Debt/Equity	0.40	0.18	0.51	0.44	0.25
Return on Capital (%)	15.17	11.76	7.63	9.60	13.55
Ret. on Com. Equity (%)	10.31	7.29	5.44	7.55	9.38
% Change Profit	92.2	97.9	(18.1)	31.2	156.3
% Change Revenue	46.2	61.3	22.1	38.9	74.5
% Change Assets	58.3	39.6	29.4	13.6	169.0

Preferred Div. Coverage	np	np	np
Total Div. Coverage	na	na	na
Interest Coverage	8.5	7.1	3.2
Current Ratio	0.8	0.8	3.4
Operating Margin	31.6	26.4	21.2
Asset Turnover	0.3	0.3	0.3
5 YEAR RATIOS (%)			
Return on Capital	11.5	10.9	9.7
Return on Com. Equity	8.0	7.9	6.8
Profit Growth	59.9	98.6	40.4
Revenue Growth	47.4	46.3	48.4
Asset Growth	54.2	50.0	38.2
BALANCE SHEET (000)			
Cash	15	203	78
Current Assets	10,194	5,531	9,790
Net Fixed Assets	131,838	84,092	54,098
Invest's & Advances	0	0	632
Total Assets	142,615	90,080	64,520
Short Term Debt	0	0	0
Current Liabilities	13,525	6,981	2,865
Long Term Debt	31,220	11,884	19,941
Total Liabilities	65,275	23,836	25,110
Total Equity	77,340	66,244	39,409
Total Liab. & Equity	142,615	90,080	64,520
CAPITAL (000)			
Total Debt	31,220	11,884	19,941
Preferred Equity	0	0	0
Common Equity	77,340	66,244	39,409

Synopsis:

Jordan Petroleum set its 1995 capital budget at $35-million, excluding acquisitions. Jordan will fund capital spending from an expected cash flow of $28-million, a $3-million flow-through share issue, and $4-million of additional bank borrowing. The company will only spend capital on projects with near-term cash flow potential. Jordan will emphasize oil projects, until natural gas prices improve.

Jordan plans to participate in the drilling of 75 wells in 1995, with an average working interest of 65%. The majority of the wells will be drilled in the company's five core areas, and will target both oil and gas reservoirs. Gas wells will be drilled where the company has an existing infrastructure of gas processing facilities and pipelines.

In 1994, spending for land, seismic, and drilling amounted to $32.3-million. Facility, equipment, and pipeline costs amounted to $15.4-million. Jordan participated in 88 gross wells (51.6 net) in 1994, including 43 exploratory wells and 45 development wells. The bulk of drilling took place in Jordan's core holdings. Jordan's core holdings include Thorsby in central Alberta, Primrose in western Saskatchewan, Ante Creek in western Alberta, and Little Horse in north-central Alberta.

During fiscal 1994 (1993) Jordan's average daily production of oil and natural gas liquids was 2,353 (1,675) barrels. Its average daily production of natural gas was 40.1 (28.4) million cubic feet. At its 1994 (1993) fiscal year end, the Jordan's proven and probable oil reserves totalled 9.5 (7) million barrels. Natural gas reserves totalled 163 (139.7) billion cubic feet.

Relative strength to TSE300 / Price / Volume (in 1000's of board lots) chart

Rank (Profit/Revenue/Assets)
354   572   406

Harold V. Pedersen
President

Glenn R. Ruttan
V.P. Finance

Address
Suite 850
Bow Valley Square III
255 - 5th Avenue S.W.
Calgary
AB
T2P 3G6
(403) 266-1024
Fax: (403) 266-4325
L0003172/G/3.2

MANNVILLE OIL & GAS LTD.

Exchanges	Price (Jun29'95)	4.55	Trailing P/E	227.50	Stock Symbol
TZ	Trailing Yield (%)	0.00	Trailing EPS	0.02	MOG

Period Ending	Dec94	Dec93	Dec92	Dec91	Dec90
Yearly Statistics					
Price-Close	4.25	6.50	2.05	2.36	2.50
Price-High	7.38	8.50	2.75	2.80	3.20
Price-Low	4.10	1.75	1.60	2.15	2.50
P/E-Close	47.22	81.25	51.25	nm	25.00
Dividends per Share	0.00	0.00	0.00	0.00	0.00
Dividend Yield (%)	0.00	0.00	0.00	0.00	0.00
Sales per Share	1.75	1.52	0.84	0.94	1.28
EPS before extra. item	0.09	0.08	0.04	(0.47)	0.10
Cash Flow per Share	0.90	0.72	0.38	0.41	0.70
Book Value per Share	5.04	4.96	2.72	2.66	3.29
O/S Common Shares	30,440	30,253	11,899	11,899	7,938
Total Revenue	54,338	28,519	11,058	8,105	10,213
Income before extra.	2,731	1,414	468	(4,074)	796
Cash Flow	27,151	13,398	4,510	3,583	5,560
Debt/Equity	0.46	0.20	0.15	0.16	0.08
Return on Capital (%)	3.76	2.81	2.43	(19.20)	6.65
Ret. on Com. Equity (%)	1.80	1.55	1.46	(14.11)	3.10
% Change Profit	93.1	202.1	111.5	(611.8)	736.8
% Change Revenue	90.5	157.9	36.4	(20.6)	19.1
% Change Assets	28.3	359.9	(3.0)	26.0	(1.5)

Date	EPS	DPS	Tot Rev	Inc Bex
Mar 95	(0.02)	0.00	13,571	(579)
Dec 94	(0.03)	0.00	12,475	(1,003)
Sep 94	0.04	0.00	14,224	1,201
Jun 94	0.03	0.00	13,658	1,116
Mar 94	0.05	0.00	13,981	1,417
Dec 93	0.01	0.00	12,928	321
Sep 93	(0.01)	0.00	7,213	188
Jun 93	0.06	0.00	5,396	724

	Dec94	Dec93	Dec92
Preferred Div. Coverage	np	np	np
Total Div. Coverage	na	na	na
Interest Coverage	2.9	3.2	2.4
Current Ratio	0.7	0.8	0.9
Operating Margin	14.0	11.6	(1.7)
Asset Turnover	0.2	0.1	0.2
5 YEAR RATIOS (%)			
Return on Capital	(0.7)	(1.3)	(1.4)
Return on Com. Equity	(1.2)	(1.7)	(1.7)
Profit Growth	na	28.0	(12.5)
Revenue Growth	44.7	30.4	10.8
Asset Growth	48.0	40.4	6.1
BALANCE SHEET (000)			
Cash	326	107	0
Current Assets	14,976	9,947	2,694
Net Fixed Assets	236,698	178,335	37,310
Invest's & Advances	0	7,877	2,648
Total Assets	251,674	196,159	42,652
Short Term Debt	1,725	825	0
Current Liabilities	20,909	11,889	3,050
Long Term Debt	69,207	29,489	4,896
Total Liabilities	98,341	46,057	10,293
Total Equity	153,333	150,102	32,359
Total Liab. & Equity	251,674	196,159	42,652
CAPITAL (000)			
Total Debt	70,932	30,314	4,896
Preferred Equity	0	0	0
Common Equity	153,333	150,102	32,359

Business:

MANNVILLE OIL & GAS LTD. is an independent, active oil and gas exploration company with producing properties in both Alberta and Saskatchewan. The company also owns petroleum and natural gas leases and production facilities in both provinces.

Synopsis:

Sales volumes should increase in 1995 for Mannville Oil & Gas as reserves added in late 1994 come into production. The company expects average production to be 25% higher in 1995, but lower gas prices should limit cash flow growth to approximately 10%. Mannville will continue to sell non-core assets. About $10-million worth of assets will be sold. Proceeds from the sale will reduce long-term debt. The capital budget for 1995 has been set at 90% of expected cash flow. Mannville has also deferred its natural gas projects, as it expects low gas prices to continue. It will concentrate on drilling and developing existing prospects and properties.

Exploration and development added reserves of 300% of 1994 natural gas production, and 200% of 1994 liquids production. Drilling resulted in 70 successful wells, with a 65% success rate.

In August 1994, Mannville purchased Exchange Resources Ltd. for $34.7-million. The deal was part of Mannville's rationalization program. The key property holdings for Mannville were Exchange's natural gas holdings in southwestern Alberta, in which the two companies were partners. The transaction also included other properties in western Alberta next to Mannville lands.

As another part of its rationalization process, Mannville spent $15.7-million to boost its working interest in existing properties and supplement land positions in core areas. As well, Mannville sold $20.6-million worth of non-core properties, several of which were part of the Exchange purchase. Mannville participated in more than $70-million worth of aggregate asset rationalization transactions.

Average daily production in 1994 (1993) was: crude oil and natural gas liquids, 2,947 (1,601) barrels; and natural gas, 47.2 (29.1) million cubic feet. Proven and probable reserves in 1994 (1993) were: crude oil and natural gas liquids, 11.8 (9.3) million barrels; and natural gas, 226.9 (179.6) billion cubic feet.

Rank (Profit/Revenue/Assets)
524   532   316

S. Douglas Martin
Chairman Of The Board

Victor J. Stobbe
President & C.E.O.

Wayne E. Larosee
Treasurer & C.F.O.

William G. Crossley
V.P. Finance

Address
Suite 2400
425 - First Street S.W.
Calgary
AB
T2P 3L8
(403) 231-7800

Fax: (403) 237-6955
M0001384/G/3.2

MARK RESOURCES INC.

Exchanges	Price (Jun29'95)	6.50	Trailing P/E	46.43	Stock Symbol
TM	Trailing Yield (%)	0.00	Trailing EPS	0.14	MKC

Period Ending	Dec94	Dec93	Dec92	Dec91	Dec90
Yearly Statistics					
Price-Close	7.00	8.88	5.25	6.25	9.50
Price-High	9.75	11.88	6.25	9.75	12.75
Price-Low	6.50	4.60	4.50	5.75	9.00
P/E-Close	41.18	68.27	nm	nm	67.86
Dividends per Share	0.00	0.00	0.00	0.00	0.00
Dividend Yield (%)	0.00	0.00	0.00	0.00	0.00
Sales per Share	3.44	3.45	4.13	4.04	4.16
EPS before extra. item	0.17	0.13	(0.29)	(2.65)	0.14
Cash Flow per Share	1.52	1.49	1.31	1.48	1.73
Book Value per Share	6.59	6.17	5.59	5.88	8.53
O/S Common Shares	38,985	33,585	26,634	26,539	26,465
Total Revenue	126,761	104,205	109,863	107,193	109,639
Income before extra.	6,366	3,857	(7,611)	(70,260)	3,570
Cash Flow	55,657	44,914	34,832	39,131	45,711
Debt/Equity	0.42	0.48	1.14	1.11	0.69
Return on Capital (%)	6.78	6.20	3.07	(26.93)	5.89
Ret. on Com. Equity (%)	2.74	2.17	(4.99)	(36.81)	1.60
% Change Profit	65.1	150.7	89.2	(2,068.1)	677.8
% Change Revenue	21.6	(5.2)	2.5	(2.2)	58.4
% Change Assets	20.0	(2.3)	(1.8)	(20.0)	4.6

Preferred Div. Coverage	np	np	np
Total Div. Coverage	na	na	na
Interest Coverage	2.7	2.0	0.7
Current Ratio	0.5	1.6	0.9
Operating Margin	17.2	18.4	12.3
Asset Turnover	0.3	0.3	0.3
5 YEAR RATIOS (%)			
Return on Capital	(1.0)	(1.4)	(1.9)
Return on Com. Equity	(7.1)	(7.6)	(8.0)
Profit Growth	69.2	62.7	na
Revenue Growth	12.8	14.5	16.6
Asset Growth	(0.8)	(2.0)	1.3
BALANCE SHEET (000)			
Cash	0	25,102	0
Current Assets	22,606	36,911	61,706
Net Fixed Assets	458,011	363,297	347,837
Invest's & Advances	0	0	0
Total Assets	482,328	401,925	411,396
Short Term Debt	8,912	0	51,321
Current Liabilities	43,534	23,678	69,797
Long Term Debt	100,000	100,000	118,490
Total Liabilities	225,353	194,558	262,472
Total Equity	256,975	207,367	148,924
Total Liab. & Equity	482,328	401,925	411,396
CAPITAL (000)			
Total Debt	108,912	100,000	169,811
Preferred Equity	0	0	0
Common Equity	256,975	207,367	148,924

Business:

MARK RESOURCES INC. is an oil and gas exploration, development and production company. It has producing wells and exploration activities primarily in Western Canada.

Date	EPS	DPS	Tot Rev	Inc Bex
Mar 95	0.02	0.00	33,689	725
Dec 94	(0.01)	0.00	34,964	(156)
Sep 94	0.06	0.00	32,666	2,393
Jun 94	0.07	0.00	31,405	2,449
Mar 94	0.05	0.00	27,726	1,196
Dec 93	0.03	0.00	26,797	972
Sep 93	0.03	0.00	24,100	1,084
Jun 93	0.02	0.00	25,423	532

Synopsis:

Mark Resources has set its 1995 capital budget at $70-million to reflect current commodity prices. Mark will be drilling approximately 90 exploratory and development wells, focusing in its core areas. Mark will increase its capital expenditure programs when natural gas prices rise. The largest source of funding for Mark's capital programs is cash flow, which is directly affected by commodity pricing. Mark has targeted production and cash flow to grow by 15% to 20%. During 1995, capital will be primarily allocated to projects that generate immediate cash flow.

During 1995, Mark will continue to increase production volumes. It expects to average 14,500 barrels per day of oil and natural gas liquids, and 70 million cubic feet per day (mmcf/d) of gas. This represents a 23% increase. The company had shut-in approximately 5 mmcf/d of gas production at the end of 1994. Mark has deferred exploiting some gas projects, due to low spot gas prices.

In April 1995, Mark announced the takeover of Hillcrest Resources Limited. Mark offered Hillcrest shareholders the choice of either 0.8 Mark shares or $4.50 for each Hillcrest share. By the end of April, 20,029,685 Hillcrest shares, about 97.8%, were tendered.

The board of directors of Mark Resources approved a shareholders' rights plan in December 1994. The plan states that if any person or group seeks to acquire 20% or more of Mark's outstanding common shares, that person or group must either make a "permitted bid" or negotiate with Mark's board. A "permitted bid" is one that must be made to all common shareholders, and must be open for at least 60 days.

Average daily production during 1994 (1993) was: oil, 11,321 (9,714) barrels; and natural gas, 62.1 (60.3) million cubic feet. Gross proven and probable reserves in 1994 (1993) totalled: 51.6 (43.6) million barrels of oil, and 443.5 (450.4) billion cubic feet of natural gas.

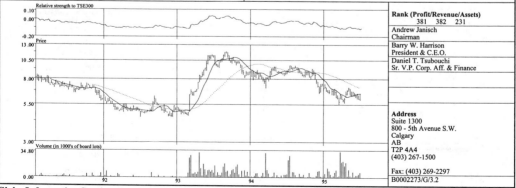

Rank (Profit/Revenue/Assets)
381 382 231

Andrew Janisch
Chairman

Barry W. Harrison
President & C.E.O.

Daniel T. Tsubouchi
Sr. V.P. Corp. Aff. & Finance

Address
Suite 1300
800 - 5th Avenue S.W.
Calgary
AB
T2P 4A4
(403) 267-1500

Fax: (403) 269-2297
B0002273/G/3.2

MORGAN HYDROCARBONS INC.

Exchanges	Price (Jun29'95)	4.10	Trailing P/E	nm	Stock Symbol
TMZ	Trailing Yield (%)	0.00	Trailing EPS	(0.46)	**MHI**

Period Ending	Dec94	Dec93	Dec92	Dec91	Dec90
Yearly Statistics					
Price-Close	4.15	4.40	5.25	5.25	6.50
Price-High	6.00	7.00	5.75	6.63	7.88
Price-Low	3.55	4.15	3.90	4.40	3.70
P/E-Close	nm	88.00	47.73	nm	27.08
Dividends per Share	0.00	0.00	0.00	0.00	0.00
Dividend Yield (%)	0.00	0.00	0.00	0.00	0.00
Sales per Share	2.01	1.72	1.91	1.92	1.94
EPS before extra. item	(0.47)	0.05	0.11	(0.06)	0.24
Cash Flow per Share	1.11	0.92	0.78	0.49	0.85
Book Value per Share	3.24	3.65	3.17	3.26	2.94
O/S Common Shares	42,426	40,274	32,611	24,555	20,593
Total Revenue	85,639	70,847	57,075	43,663	39,801
Income before extra.	(19,391)	2,001	3,406	(1,318)	4,901
Cash Flow	45,350	33,522	23,386	11,119	17,467
Debt/Equity	0.51	0.41	0.57	0.64	0.75
Return on Capital (%)	(13.17)	4.93	6.39	1.10	10.25
Ret. on Com. Equity (%)	(13.63)	1.60	3.71	(1.88)	8.44
% Change Profit	(1,069.1)	(41.3)	358.4	(126.9)	25.6
% Change Revenue	20.9	24.1	30.7	9.7	22.6
% Change Assets	0.5	29.4	34.1	14.2	22.2

Preferred Div. Coverage	np	np	np
Total Div. Coverage	na	na	na
Interest Coverage	0.0	2.3	1.8
Current Ratio	0.7	1.2	1.1
Operating Margin	(31.9)	12.9	16.4
Asset Turnover	0.3	0.3	0.3
5 YEAR RATIOS (%)			
Return on Capital	1.9	6.3	6.5
Return on Com. Equity	(0.4)	3.8	4.3
Profit Growth	na	(3.3)	(1.2)
Revenue Growth	21.4	22.7	20.8
Asset Growth	19.4	24.7	23.8
BALANCE SHEET (000)			
Cash	1,360	8,640	5,714
Current Assets	23,919	27,576	13,058
Net Fixed Assets	225,835	220,694	178,500
Invest's & Advances	250	250	250
Total Assets	250,102	248,766	192,241
Short Term Debt	0	0	0
Current Liabilities	33,512	22,879	11,942
Long Term Debt	69,400	60,900	59,411
Total Liabilities	112,558	101,726	88,768
Total Equity	137,544	147,040	103,472
Total Liab. & Equity	250,102	248,766	192,241
CAPITAL (000)			
Total Debt	69,400	60,900	59,411
Preferred Equity	0	0	0
Common Equity	137,544	147,040	103,472

Business:

MORGAN HYDROCARBONS INC. is an oil and gas exploration and production company. It has producing wells and exploration activities in Alberta and Saskatchewan. The company markets natural gas in Canada and the United States.

Date	EPS	DPS	Tot Rev	Inc Bex
Mar 95	0.03	0.00	21,436	1,388
Dec 94	0.03	0.00	19,693	682
Sep 94	(0.53)	0.00	17,976	(21,379)
Jun 94	0.01	0.00	19,381	664
Mar 94	0.02	0.00	17,844	642
Dec 93	0.01	0.00	18,775	538
Sep 93	0.01	0.00	15,752	437
Jun 93	0.01	0.00	14,915	482

Synopsis:

In 1995, Morgan Hydrocarbons plans to continue its pattern of increasing reserves and production, with further development of core assets and new exploration of the company's undeveloped lands. Morgan will maintain a balanced mix of light oil, heavy oil, and natural gas production and reserves. It forecasts 15% to 20% growth in cash flow, and 20% to 25% growth in production compared to 1994. Cash flow from operations should exceed $60-million in 1995.

Natural gas production should increase slightly in 1995 as certain gas prospects will either be shut-in or deferred until gas prices improve. Natural gas production should average 75 million cubic feet per day and crude oil and natural gas liquids production should be 12,500 barrels per day in 1995, reflecting new production from assets acquired in Saskatchewan.

In the first quarter of 1995, Morgan purchased undeveloped land and producing properties previously owned by the Canadian National Railway and operated by CN Exploration Inc. The properties were bought from Smart On Resources, a privately owned Hong Kong company. As a result of this transaction, Smart On became a 20% shareholder of Morgan. The $80-million deal should close in the second quarter. It will be financed by equity and bank debt. The acquisition includes 900,000 acres of undeveloped land near Morgan's southwestern Saskatchewan core area, and reserves of 11 million barrels of oil equivalent. Production from these reserves amounts to 3,750 barrels of oil per day, and 2.5 million cubic feet of natural gas per day. Morgan's capital spending budget for 1995 is approximately $140-million, including the Smart On purchase.

Daily production in 1994 (1993) was: crude oil and natural gas liquids, 8,675 (7,758) barrels; and natural gas, 44.2 (30.5) million cubic feet. Proven and probable reserves in 1994 (1993) were: oil and natural gas liquids, 18.7 (15.8) million barrels; and natural gas, 138.8 (136.3) billion cubic feet. In 1994 production revenues by product were: light oil and gas liquids, 30%; natural gas, 35%; and heavy oil, 35%.

Relative strength to TSE300 / Price / Volume (in 1000's of board lots) charts

Rank (Profit/Revenue/Assets)	
968 444 318	
Vernon L. Horte	
Chairman	
William A. Trickett	
President & C.E.O.	
Allen Emes	
V.P. Finance & C.F.O.	
John D. Wright	
Ex. V.P. & C.O.O.	

Address
2200 Bow Valley Square II
205 - 5th Avenue S.W.
Calgary
AB
T2P 2V7
(403) 298-8300

Fax: (403) 298-8390

M0015445/G/3.2

MORRISON PETROLEUMS LTD.

Exchanges	Price (Jun29'95)	9.75	Trailing P/E	23.78	Stock Symbol
T	Trailing Yield (%)	0.41	Trailing EPS	0.41	**MRP**

Period Ending	Dec94	Dec93	Dec92	Dec91	Dec90
Yearly Statistics					
Price-Close	7.00	9.88	8.50	4.13	3.58
Price-High	11.50	14.38	8.79	4.33	4.33
Price-Low	6.38	7.25	4.00	3.17	2.71
P/E-Close	19.44	21.47	27.42	17.19	12.80
Dividends per Share	0.04	0.04	0.03	0.03	0.00
Dividend Yield (%)	0.57	0.41	0.35	0.81	0.00
Sales per Share	2.18	2.01	1.46	0.96	0.87
EPS before extra. item	0.36	0.46	0.31	0.24	0.28
Cash Flow per Share	1.42	1.40	0.89	0.64	0.60
Book Value per Share	5.01	3.78	2.47	2.00	1.79
O/S Common Shares	62,669	52,877	47,147	40,930	40,749
Total Revenue	138,352	106,993	68,807	41,518	36,559
Income before extra.	21,034	23,041	14,024	9,839	11,344
Cash Flow	82,306	70,018	40,483	25,968	24,367
Debt/Equity	0.05	0.16	0.27	0.01	0.01
Return on Capital (%)	13.40	19.88	21.53	19.76	22.32
Ret. on Com. Equity (%)	8.18	14.57	14.15	12.71	16.96
% Change Profit	(8.7)	64.3	42.5	(13.3)	87.7
% Change Revenue	29.3	55.5	65.7	13.6	56.1
% Change Assets	41.5	59.1	73.1	12.8	23.8

Preferred Div. Coverage	np	np	np
Total Div. Coverage	9.9	12.2	10.3
Interest Coverage	29.1	21.1	11.6
Current Ratio	1.1	1.0	1.2
Operating Margin	19.9	31.0	33.3
Asset Turnover	0.3	0.3	0.3
5 YEAR RATIOS (%)			
Return on Capital	19.4	20.0	17.7
Return on Com. Equity	13.3	14.1	12.6
Profit Growth	28.3	54.0	32.5
Revenue Growth	42.6	53.8	42.9
Asset Growth	40.2	41.2	31.4
BALANCE SHEET (000)			
Cash	17,370	2,968	3,415
Current Assets	52,874	36,112	23,032
Net Fixed Assets	367,412	259,754	164,438
Invest's & Advances	15,854	13,683	7,038
Total Assets	437,980	309,549	194,508
Short Term Debt	2,432	2,215	1,090
Current Liabilities	47,491	36,665	19,228
Long Term Debt	12,293	29,441	30,004
Total Liabilities	123,823	109,709	78,006
Total Equity	314,157	199,840	116,502
Total Liab. & Equity	437,980	309,549	194,508
CAPITAL (000)			
Total Debt	14,725	31,656	31,094
Preferred Equity	0	0	0
Common Equity	314,157	199,840	116,502

Business:

MORRISON PETROLEUMS LTD. is an independent petroleum explorer and producer whose main area of activity is in Alberta and northeastern British Columbia. Most of the company's revenues result from the sale of light and medium crude oil.

Date	EPS	DPS	Tot Rev	Inc Bex
Mar 95	0.10	0.00	38,174	6,128
Dec 94	0.10	0.00	38,435	6,424
Sep 94	0.11	0.00	37,577	6,671
Jun 94	0.10	0.04	35,943	5,223
Mar 94	0.05	0.00	26,170	2,716
Dec 93	0.09	0.00	27,749	4,854
Sep 93	0.12	0.00	28,543	6,397
Jun 93	0.14	0.00	27,315	6,708

Synopsis:

During 1995, Morrison Petroleums will continue an aggressive exploration and development program. The bulk of exploratory wells will be drilled on natural gas prospects in the company's five core areas. The program includes drilling approximately 100 high working interest wells, with 40% of the wells designated exploratory.

The 1995 capital expenditures for exploration and development are budgeted at $90-million. About 60% of the spending will go to natural gas prospects. The capital program will be primarily financed from cash flow. Morrison forecasts its cash flow to be $90-million in 1995. Morrison feels that by participating with its investment partners, it has the necessary capital available for property acquisitions without resorting to debt financing.

Morrison's 1995 production levels should average 16,000 barrels per day of crude oil and natural gas liquids, and 81 million cubic feet per day of natural gas. The company may delay production in certain areas, if natural gas prices remained depressed.

Morrison's primary focus in 1994 was on exploration. The company believed reasonably priced acquisitions were scarce due to the overheated pace of the Canadian industry. Morrison operated 149 new drilling locations in 1994, and drilled 207 wells including non-operated wells. This represented 41 exploratory wells, and 166 wells drilled to develop previously discovered crude oil and natural gas deposits, with a 85% success rate.

Morrison produces 75% of its revenue from the sale of crude oil. In 1994 (1993) daily production was: crude oil and natural gas liquids, 14,626 (12,214) barrels; and natural gas, 40.8 (35.5) million cubic feet. The 1994 (1993) total gross proven and probable reserves were: crude oil and natural gas liquids, 25.9 (23) million barrels; and natural gas, 269.1 (147.4) billion cubic feet.

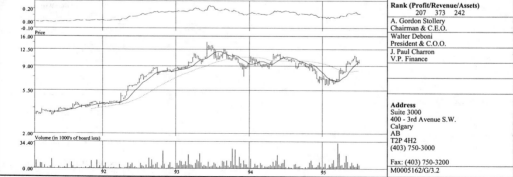

Rank (Profit/Revenue/Assets)		
207	373	242

A. Gordon Stollery
Chairman & C.E.O.

Walter Deboni
President & C.O.O.

J. Paul Charron
V.P. Finance

Address
Suite 3000
400 - 3rd Avenue S.W.
Calgary
AB
T2P 4H2
(403) 750-3000

Fax: (403) 750-3200
M0005162/G/3.2

NORCEN ENERGY RESOURCES LIMITED

Exchanges	Price (Jun29'95)	18.37	Trailing P/E	nm	Stock Symbol
TMA	Trailing Yield (%)	3.27	Trailing EPS	(1.35)	**NCN**

Period Ending	Dec94	Dec93	Dec92	Dec91	Dec90
Yearly Statistics					
Price-Close	16.63	15.88	17.50	23.50	22.88
Price-High	18.75	22.50	23.75	26.63	25.38
Price-Low	13.63	14.75	16.50	19.88	16.88
P/E-Close	nm	54.74	35.71	47.96	12.04
Dividends per Share	0.60	0.60	0.60	0.60	0.55
Dividend Yield (%)	3.61	3.78	3.43	2.55	2.40
Sales per Share	15.73	14.39	14.42	15.33	16.60
EPS before extra. item	(1.39)	0.29	0.49	0.49	1.90
Cash Flow per Share	4.78	4.65	4.84	4.66	6.01
Book Value per Share	14.92	16.92	17.23	17.66	17.77
O/S Common Shares	82,603	82,357	69,653	60,100	59,412
Total Revenue	1,409,000	1,195,300	1,009,090	978,497	1,050,297
Income before extra.	(114,000)	24,400	38,857	44,064	129,188
Cash Flow	394,500	368,100	316,775	279,212	356,143
Debt/Equity	1.24	1.10	0.92	0.90	1.00
Return on Capital (%)	(0.25)	5.44	7.14	7.30	13.49
Ret. on Com. Equity (%)	(8.74)	1.75	2.82	2.76	11.09
% Change Profit	(567.2)	(37.2)	(11.8)	(65.9)	17.2
% Change Revenue	17.9	18.5	3.1	(6.8)	24.3
% Change Assets	(12.7)	31.7	4.9	1.6	15.0
Preferred Div. Coverage	0.0	14.4	5.6		
Total Div. Coverage	0.0	0.5	0.8		
Interest Coverage	0.0	1.4	1.9		
Current Ratio	0.9	1.0	1.5		
Operating Margin	(8.3)	7.4	16.0		
Asset Turnover	0.4	0.3	0.3		
5 YEAR RATIOS (%)					
Return on Capital	6.6	9.4	10.7		
Return on Com. Equity	1.9	5.9	7.5		
Profit Growth	na	(23.3)	(17.2)		
Revenue Growth	10.7	10.1	6.5		
Asset Growth	7.1	12.6	7.4		
BALANCE SHEET (000)					
Cash	11,100	51,500	90,850		
Current Assets	418,200	430,000	335,261		
Net Fixed Assets	3,025,700	3,281,400	2,457,521		
Invest's & Advances	137,400	365,700	269,093		
Total Assets	3,679,400	4,214,500	3,200,853		
Short Term Debt	184,500	122,200	63,874		
Current Liabilities	480,000	421,500	225,497		
Long Term Debt	1,358,100	1,422,400	1,143,381		
Total Liabilities	2,437,100	2,811,200	1,890,500		
Total Equity	1,242,300	1,403,300	1,310,353		
Total Liab. & Equity	3,679,400	4,214,500	3,200,853		
CAPITAL (000)					
Total Debt	1,542,600	1,544,600	1,207,255		
Preferred Equity	9,800	10,000	110,099		
Common Equity	1,232,500	1,393,300	1,200,254		

Business:

NORCEN ENERGY RESOURCES LTD. is a major resource enterprise with three business segments: oil and gas; propane marketing; and mineral resources. In its core oil and gas business, Norcen exlores, develops, and produces in Canada, the U.S., Australia, and Argentina. Superior Propane distributes propane across Canada and the U.S. Norcen holds an 11% equity interest in Iron Ore Company of Canada.

Date	EPS	DPS	Tot Rev	Inc Bex
Mar 95	0.22	0.15	367,100	18,200
Dec 94	(1.84)	0.15	98,037	(151,929)
Sep 94	0.10	0.15	363,825	8,676
Jun 94	0.17	0.15	378,109	13,826
Mar 94	0.18	0.15	357,200	15,400
Dec 93	(0.07)	0.15	169,790	(5,361)
Sep 93	0.06	0.15	311,562	4,965
Jun 93	0.01	0.15	361,129	695

Synopsis:

Norcen Energy Resources identified 12 core areas, nine in western Canada; the others in the Gulf of Mexico, Venezuela, and Argentina. It also designated its propane marketing operation as a core business. The 1995 capital program is expected to be approximately $400-million. Norcen has allocated $375-million to its core oil and gas areas and $25-million to its propane marketing operations. It identified non-core assets aggregating $700-million to $800-million of carrying value to sell over the next two to three years, with between $200 and $300-million to be marketed in 1995. This includes properties determined not to be core holdings. It also includes its equity and royalty interest in the Iron Ore Company of Canada and its investment portfolio. Proceeds will be applied to reduce debt.

In 1994, Norcen's capital expenditures, (excluding acquisitions) were $382-million. Of the $348-million spent on oil and gas activities, 66% was spent in western Canada. Asset dispositions included the sale of almost all of the company's cogeneration business and its Polaris Mine net profits interest. Also included were its industrial gas system and a significant portion of its investment portfolio. These, plus oil and gas property sales of $171-million, generated net proceeds of $497-million. Norcen used this amount mainly to acquire the minority interests of the North Canadian Oils Limited (NCO).

At the end of 1994, Norcen acquired all the common and preferred shares of NCO, which it did not own for $318-million. In early 1995, Norcen offered and received approval to buy the minority equity interests in 66% owned Prairie Oil Royalties Company, Ltd. at a cost of about $45.5-million.

Average daily production in 1994 (1993) was: oil and gas liquids, 68.7 (59.5) thousand barrels and natural gas, 554 (481) million cubic feet. Proved reserves in 1994 (1993) were: oil and gas liquids, 181 (231) million barrels and natural gas, 1,977 (2,344) billion cubic feet. Sale of propane in 1994 (1993) was 1,869 (1,559) millions of litres.

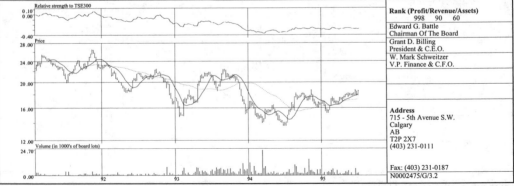

Rank (Profit/Revenue/Assets)
998   90   60

Edward G. Battle
Chairman Of The Board

Grant D. Billing
President & C.E.O.

W. Mark Schweitzer
V.P. Finance & C.F.O.

Address
715 - 5th Avenue S.W.
Calgary
AB
T2P 2X7
(403) 231-0111

Fax: (403) 231-0187
N0002475/G/3.2

   For further company information, call Globe Information Services 1-800-268-9128 or (416) 585-5345

NORTHROCK RESOURCES LTD.

Exchanges	Price (Jun29'95)	8.37	Trailing P/E	23.93	Stock Symbol
T	Trailing Yield (%)	0.00	Trailing EPS	0.35	NRK

Period Ending	Dec94	Dec93	Dec92	Dec91	Dec90	Business:
Yearly Statistics						NORTHROCK RESOURCES LTD. is
Price-Close	9.25	7.63	4.00	0.85	0.49	involved in the acquisition, exploration and
Price-High	12.50	11.50	4.00	1.00	0.50	development of petroleum and natural gas.
Price-Low	7.25	3.60	0.80	0.40	0.25	
P/E-Close	25.69	38.13	40.00	42.50	35.00	
Dividends per Share	0.00	0.00	0.00	0.00	0.00	
Dividend Yield (%)	0.00	0.00	0.00	0.00	0.00	
Sales per Share	3.13	1.30	0.61	0.22	0.07	
EPS before extra. item	0.36	0.20	0.10	0.02	0.01	
Cash Flow per Share	1.44	0.62	0.29	0.11	0.03	
Book Value per Share	3.49	1.74	0.63	0.27	0.20	

							Date	EPS	DPS	Tot Rev	Inc Bex
O/S Common Shares	17,086	13,809	12,164	10,409	7,859		Mar 95	0.06	0.00	13,002	985
Total Revenue	44,481	16,300	6,430	2,108	535		Dec 94	0.10	0.00	13,918	1,522
Income before extra.	5,165	2,449	1,013	193	104		Sep 94	0.09	0.00	12,182	1,255
Cash Flow	20,467	7,795	3,072	1,068	263		Jun 94	0.10	0.00	10,577	1,460
Debt/Equity	0.61	1.03	0.19	0.74	1.28		Mar 94	0.07	0.00	7,803	928
Return on Capital (%)	16.54	16.12	25.29	12.13	5.82		Dec 93	0.07	0.00	7,566	845
Ret. on Com. Equity (%)	12.34	15.43	19.27	8.76	6.97		Sep 93	0.06	0.00	4,527	786
% Change Profit	110.9	141.6	424.5	85.2	168.3		Jun 93	0.04	0.00	2,108	417
% Change Revenue	172.9	153.5	205.0	294.0	74.9						
% Change Assets	105.9	403.6	114.4	38.4	147.5						

					Synopsis:
Preferred Div. Coverage	np	np	np		Northrock Resources is planning a $40-million exploration and development
Total Div. Coverage	na	na	na		program for 1995. It will direct $13-million towards exploration, more than
Interest Coverage	5.1	7.7	9.5		double the 1994 level. With no significant changes in production volumes, prices,
Current Ratio	0.6	0.9	0.9		or costs, Northrock expects anticipated cash flow from operations will finance the
Operating Margin	27.0	28.7	27.7		majority of its exploration and development capital expenditure program. The
Asset Turnover	0.4	0.3	0.6		company expects to finish 1995 with production levels in excess of 10,000 barrels
5 YEAR RATIOS (%)					of oil equivalent per day.
Return on Capital	15.2	na	na		Gross production revenue jumped 173%, in 1994. This was attributed to
Return on Com. Equity	12.6	na	na		significant development activity in southeast Saskatchewan and at Red Rock in
Profit Growth	165.8	na	na		Northwest Alberta. In addition, the full-year impact of the 1993 acquisitions of
Revenue Growth	170.6	na	na		natural gas producing properties in the Medicine Hat area and several oil
Asset Growth	137.8	na	na		producing properties in southeast Saskatchewan also contributed to rising
BALANCE SHEET (000)					revenues.
Cash	41	4	748		Northrock plans to drill 70 gross wells in 1995. In 1994, the company participated
Current Assets	6,812	3,856	2,017		in the drilling of 60 gross (42.0 net) wells up from 30 gross (11.3 net) in 1993. Its
Net Fixed Assets	107,883	51,857	8,938		overall success rate was 85%.
Invest's & Advances	0	0	108		The proportion of total reserves at 1994 year end by location were: southeast
Total Assets	114,695	55,713	11,063		Saskatchewan, 35%; southeast/central Alberta, 30%; northwest Alberta, 27%; and
Short Term Debt	0	0	975		northeast Alberta, 8%. Daily production in 1994 (1993) was: crude oil and natural
Current Liabilities	11,624	4,315	2,280		gas liquids, 3,940 (1,711) barrels; and natural gas 21.4 (8.1) million cubic feet.
Long Term Debt	36,594	24,768	494		Proven and probable reserves at the end of 1994 (1993) were: oil and natural gas
Total Liabilities	55,068	31,631	3,399		liquids, 14.8 (11.9) million barrels; and natural gas 118.3 (50.8) billion cubic feet.
Total Equity	59,627	24,082	7,664		
Total Liab. & Equity	114,695	55,713	11,063		
CAPITAL (000)					
Total Debt	36,594	24,768	1,469		
Preferred Equity	0	0	0		
Common Equity	59,627	24,082	7,664		

Relative strength to TSE300

Price

Volume (in 1000's of board lots)

Rank (Profit/Revenue/Assets)
416   574   450

V.W. Sutherland
Executive Chairman

Donald Hansen
President & C.E.O.

Address
Suite 3500
700 - 2nd Street S.W.
Calgary
AB
T2P 2W2
(403) 269-3100

Fax: (403) 232-4650
01001173/G/3.2

NORTHSTAR ENERGY CORPORATION

Exchanges	Price (Jun29'95)	11.25	Trailing P/E	20.45	Stock Symbol
TZ	Trailing Yield (%)	0.00	Trailing EPS	0.55	NEN

Period Ending	Dec94	Dec93	Dec92	Dec91	Dec90
Yearly Statistics					
Price-Close	12.00	13.00	5.56	2.38	2.30
Price-High	17.50	15.75	5.56	2.50	3.38
Price-Low	11.38	5.50	2.25	2.05	2.30
P/E-Close	19.67	31.71	35.89	33.93	25.56
Dividends per Share	0.00	0.00	0.00	0.00	0.00
Dividend Yield (%)	0.00	0.00	0.00	0.00	0.00
Sales per Share	2.36	2.33	0.90	0.59	0.61
EPS before extra. item	0.61	0.41	0.16	0.07	0.09
Cash Flow per Share	1.75	1.77	0.65	0.43	0.48
Book Value per Share	4.48	3.88	2.37	2.13	2.07
O/S Common Shares	36,685	36,166	31,787	28,341	28,354
Total Revenue	95,787	65,713	35,297	25,062	24,843
Income before extra.	22,411	13,874	4,699	2,061	3,158
Cash Flow	63,813	42,488	19,494	12,128	13,188
Debt/Equity	0.05	0.06	0.12	0.09	0.11
Return on Capital (%)	24.09	21.08	11.06	6.06	9.18
Ret. on Com. Equity (%)	14.73	12.89	6.93	3.22	4.56
% Change Profit	61.5	195.3	128.0	(34.7)	89.1
% Change Revenue	45.8	86.2	40.8	0.9	15.1
% Change Assets	18.5	72.8	24.2	(12.5)	21.0

Date	EPS	DPS	Tot Rev	Inc Bex
Mar 95	0.09	0.00	28,447	3,470
Dec 94	0.15	0.00	23,534	5,545
Sep 94	0.14	0.00	23,098	5,132
Jun 94	0.17	0.00	28,067	6,490
Mar 94	0.15	0.00	21,186	5,244
Dec 93	0.13	0.00	19,144	4,624
Sep 93	0.10	0.00	16,651	3,517
Jun 93	0.10	0.00	15,819	3,237

Preferred Div. Coverage	np	np	np
Total Div. Coverage	na	na	na
Interest Coverage	41.0	19.7	13.4
Current Ratio	0.8	2.2	0.8
Operating Margin	39.3	36.5	23.0
Asset Turnover	0.4	0.3	0.2
5 YEAR RATIOS (%)			
Return on Capital	14.3	11.2	8.2
Return on Com. Equity	8.5	6.0	3.8
Profit Growth	68.1	56.3	29.8
Revenue Growth	34.7	30.5	20.7
Asset Growth	21.9	20.9	12.3
BALANCE SHEET (000)			
Cash	5,463	42,301	121
Current Assets	25,019	61,123	9,103
Net Fixed Assets	211,205	140,594	107,059
Invest's & Advances	9,558	5,646	3,865
Total Assets	245,782	207,363	120,027
Short Term Debt	1,147	1,051	1,087
Current Liabilities	29,701	27,883	11,585
Long Term Debt	6,254	7,401	7,608
Total Liabilities	81,614	67,213	44,829
Total Equity	164,168	140,150	75,198
Total Liab. & Equity	245,782	207,363	120,027
CAPITAL (000)			
Total Debt	7,401	8,452	8,695
Preferred Equity	0	0	0
Common Equity	164,168	140,150	75,198

Business:

NORTHSTAR ENERGY CORP. is engaged in petroleum and natural gas exploration, production, processing, marketing and cogeneration. The company's principal reserves and land holdings are in Alberta.

Synopsis:

In January 1995, Northstar Energy completed the acquisition of oil and gas properties from Deminex (Canada) Limited. The $64.1-million purchase also included over $100-million of income tax pools. The current production from the properties includes 3,500 barrels per day of oil and natural gas liquids, and 10 million cubic feet per day of natural gas, with reserves of about 9.5 million barrels of oil equivalent. The acquisition was financed with bank debt. Northstar's 1995 capital budget, including the Deminex purchase is expected to be around $150-million.

Total capital investment in 1994 was $100.3-million, including $95.6-million relating to oil and gas activities. The capital expenditures were financed by $64-million from operating cash flow and $37-million reduction in cash reserves. Exploration and development costs included the drilling of 87 wells (65.9 net) with an overall success rate of 85%. Northstar continued to emphasize natural gas. Drilling resulted in 61 gas wells, 13 oil wells, and 13 dry holes. In the first quarter of 1995, Northstar drilled 55 wells including 44 gas, two oil, and nine dry holes.

Northstar, through its PowerLink Canada Corp. and PLC-Windsor Ltd. subsidiaries, owns a 50% interest in West Windsor Power, an Ontario partnership which owns a cogeneration project in Windsor. As of March 1995, construction of the 102 megawatt cogeneration plant was approximately 75% complete. Construction should be finished by July. The plant should generate $7-million of annual cash flow and $3-million of net earnings for Northstar.

Average daily production before royalties in 1994 (1993) was: oil and natural gas liquids, 3,233 (2,405) barrels; and natural gas, 90 (61.4) million cubic feet. At 1994 (1993) year end, the company reported gross proven and probable oil reserves totalling 12 (7.8) million barrels; and 331.8 (280.1) billion cubic feet of natural gas reserves.

Relative strength to TSE300 / Price / Volume (in 1000's of board lots) chart, 1992–1995

Rank (Profit/Revenue/Assets)
201   428   321

John A. Hagg
Chairman, President & C.E.O.
Brian K. Lemke
V.P. Finance

Address
Suite 300
535 - 7th Avenue S.W.
Calgary
AB
T2P 0Y4
(403) 298-0500

Fax: (403) 298-0579
G0012859/G/3.2

NOWSCO WELL SERVICE LTD.

Exchanges	Price (Jun29'95)		13.75	Trailing P/E		11.09	Stock Symbol
TQ	Trailing Yield (%)		2.62	Trailing EPS		1.24	NWS

Period Ending	Dec94	Dec93	Dec92	Dec91	Dec90
Yearly Statistics					
Price-Close	15.25	19.00	11.00	10.25	14.63
Price-High	24.50	22.50	11.75	16.00	18.50
Price-Low	14.00	10.13	7.00	9.50	13.25
P/E-Close	10.82	13.77	16.92	nm	38.49
Dividends per Share	0.36	0.26	0.15	0.14	0.14
Dividend Yield (%)	2.36	1.37	1.36	1.37	0.96
Sales per Share	19.09	15.01	12.88	12.77	12.35
EPS before extra. item	1.41	1.38	0.65	(0.35)	0.38
Cash Flow per Share	2.82	2.64	1.94	0.42	1.14
Book Value per Share	13.33	12.12	9.51	9.22	9.80
O/S Common Shares	20,770	20,707	16,418	16,272	16,124
Total Revenue	401,485	294,513	223,482	223,558	220,059
Income before extra.	29,282	26,436	10,707	(5,636)	6,165
Cash Flow	58,541	50,403	31,774	6,783	18,401
Debt/Equity	0.01	0.15	0.32	1.02	1.00
Return on Capital (%)	11.30	13.80	7.94	3.94	10.16
Ret. on Com. Equity (%)	11.09	12.99	7.00	(3.66)	4.04
% Change Profit	10.8	146.9	290.0	(191.4)	315.2
% Change Revenue	36.3	31.8	(0.0)	1.6	28.6
% Change Assets	3.5	41.3	(29.3)	(2.4)	4.8
Preferred Div. Coverage	np	np	np		
Total Div. Coverage	3.9	4.9	4.3		
Interest Coverage	21.1	6.6	2.2		
Current Ratio	1.8	2.1	2.0		
Operating Margin	6.9	9.2	5.6		
Asset Turnover	1.1	0.8	0.9		
5 YEAR RATIOS (%)					
Return on Capital	9.4	8.1	7.0		
Return on Com. Equity	6.3	4.3	3.6		
Profit Growth	81.5	11.9	(5.1)		
Revenue Growth	18.5	10.9	7.9		
Asset Growth	1.1	0.5	0.1		
BALANCE SHEET (000)					
Cash	7,291	83,898	23,622		
Current Assets	136,880	184,103	101,696		
Net Fixed Assets	190,158	128,325	111,556		
Invest's & Advances	12,510	11,830	11,136		
Total Assets	356,670	344,636	243,838		
Short Term Debt	2,739	34,757	15,142		
Current Liabilities	77,366	87,720	50,467		
Long Term Debt	0	2,757	35,081		
Total Liabilities	79,811	93,598	87,718		
Total Equity	276,859	251,038	156,120		
Total Liab. & Equity	356,670	344,636	243,838		
CAPITAL (000)					
Total Debt	2,739	37,514	50,223		
Preferred Equity	0	0	0		
Common Equity	276,859	251,038	156,120		

Business:

NOWSCO WELL SERVICE LTD. is an oil and gas service company. It provides specialized products, equipment and technology to the oil and gas industry and to the pipeline, mining and industrial sectors. The company has operations in North America, United Kingdom Europe, Middle East, North Africa, Russia, Argentina, and Southeast Asia.

Date	EPS	DPS	Tot Rev	Inc Bex
Mar 95	0.22	0.00	120,287	4,652
Dec 94	0.26	0.18	113,506	5,231
Sep 94	0.70	0.00	113,591	14,586
Jun 94	0.06	0.18	81,039	1,246
Mar 94	0.40	0.00	93,349	8,208
Dec 93	0.29	0.07	94,297	6,132
Sep 93	0.57	0.04	79,078	11,296
Jun 93	0.22	0.16	60,066	3,995

Synopsis:

Nowsco Well Service expects its core business of cementing and stimulation to continue to generate most of its revenue. It also plans to continue its expansion in coiled tubing and pipeline services. Nowsco anticipates 1995 to be a year of consolidation and cost management.

The company expects that the Canadian energy industry will continue to be an important source of revenue. Now that it has established itself in key United States locations, Nowsco's goal is to double market share in the U.S. over the next three to five years. Internationally, the company has undertaken projects in Russia and China. It believes both countries offer potential for additional business. Through broad geographic coverage, Nowsco believes it can take advantage of growing and emerging markets world-wide to hedge against downturns in other regions.

During 1994, Nowsco spent $54.4-million on capital expenditures which were aimed at diversification and expansion of the company's operations. Capital expenditures are expected to be $28-million in 1995.

Expansion into the United States continued in 1994, with the acquisition of Service Fracturing Company a provider of well stimulation services. Nowsco also bought Pipeline Dehydrators, Inc., a company specializing in air drying of pipelines. Over the past two years the company has spent $72-million on acquisitions.

Revenue in 1994 (1993) by geographic segment was: Canada, 41% (44%); the U.S., 28% (16%); and international, 31% (40%). Percentage of operating revenue in 1994 (1993) by segment was: pipeline service, 8% (12%); cementing, stimulation and coiled tubing, 77% (65%); and other, 15% (23%). Operating income from Canada represented 96% of the total.

Rank (Profit/Revenue/Assets)
163   219   266

S. Patrick Shouldice
Chairman & C.E.O.

R.F. Simard
President & C.O.O.

A.J. Robertson
V.P. Treasurer & C.F.O.

Address
Suite 2750
801 - 6th Avenue S.W.
Calgary
AB
T2P 4L8
(403) 531-5151

Fax: (403) 262-8066
N0003809/G/3.3

NUMAC ENERGY INC.

Exchanges	Price (Jun29'95)		6.50	Trailing P/E		22.41	Stock Symbol
TMA	Trailing Yield (%)		0.00	Trailing EPS		0.29	**NMC**

Period Ending	Dec94	Dec93	Dec92	Dec91	Dec90	Business:
Yearly Statistics						NUMAC ENERGY INC. is involved in the
Price-Close	8.00	8.00	6.00	n t	n t	exploration, development, production and
Price-High	9.50	9.13	6.38	n t	n t	marketing of crude oil, natural gas liquids and
Price-Low	7.13	5.63	4.70	n t	n t	natural gas.
P/E-Close	28.57	44.44	nm	n t	n t	
Dividends per Share	0.00	0.00	0.85	0.58	0.37	
Dividend Yield (%)	0.00	0.00	14.17	na	na	
Sales per Share	2.66	2.62	2.81	2.33	2.99	
EPS before extra. item	0.28	0.18	(2.56)	0.44	0.72	
Cash Flow per Share	1.56	1.54	1.28	1.62	2.10	
Book Value per Share	5.66	5.37	4.91	10.93	12.59	

						Date	EPS	DPS	Tot Rev	Inc Bex
O/S Common Shares	93,385	92,731	50,436	49,137	48,860					
Total Revenue	270,495	178,098	151,122	139,289	145,638					
Income before extra.	26,460	11,503	(126,052)	21,714	32,996	Mar 95	0.03	0.00	65,092	3,138
Cash Flow	144,818	97,782	63,015	79,347	95,716	Dec 94	(0.02)	0.00	63,751	(1,307)
Debt/Equity	0.39	0.39	0.62	0.12	0.02	Sep 94	0.20	0.00	83,507	18,395
Return on Capital (%)	10.13	5.71	(38.43)	5.77	8.72	Jun 94	0.08	0.00	66,538	7,369
Ret. on Com. Equity (%)	5.16	3.09	(32.14)	3.77	5.75	Mar 94	0.02	0.00	56,730	2,003
% Change Profit	130.0	109.1	(680.5)	(34.2)	26.6	Dec 93	0.05	0.00	58,479	4,523
% Change Revenue	51.9	17.9	8.5	(4.4)	14.7	Sep 93	0.00	0.00	44,544	121
% Change Assets	6.0	40.8	(33.9)	(2.3)	3.1	Jun 93	na	0.00	38,090	5,023

				Synopsis:
Preferred Div. Coverage	np	np	np	
Total Div. Coverage	na	na	0.0	
Interest Coverage	6.4	3.7	0.0	
Current Ratio	2.0	2.0	1.7	
Operating Margin	21.5	16.5	(131.8)	
Asset Turnover	0.3	0.2	0.2	
5 YEAR RATIOS (%)				
Return on Capital	(1.6)	(2.1)	na	
Return on Com. Equity	(2.9)	(2.9)	na	
Profit Growth	0.3	(8.4)	na	
Revenue Growth	16.3	10.2	na	
Asset Growth	(0.1)	0.6	na	
BALANCE SHEET (000)				
Cash	44,135	57,628	1,960	
Current Assets	88,735	90,224	48,063	
Net Fixed Assets	740,747	692,026	507,708	
Invest's & Advances	0	0	0	
Total Assets	829,482	782,250	555,771	
Short Term Debt	0	0	0	
Current Liabilities	45,023	45,030	28,861	
Long Term Debt	205,668	195,708	152,177	
Total Liabilities	300,823	284,554	308,271	
Total Equity	528,659	497,696	247,500	
Total Liab. & Equity	829,482	782,250	555,771	
CAPITAL (000)				
Total Debt	205,668	195,708	152,177	
Preferred Equity	0	0	0	
Common Equity	528,659	497,696	247,500	

Synopsis:

Numac Energy's major exploration focus in 1995 will be on natural gas, although it will pursue selective higher-risk, higher-reward oil opportunities in west-central Alberta. Numac will also continue to sell non-strategic assets, and explore company or property acquisitions. About 120 properties are for sale. Proceeds from the asset rationalization program along with $44-million worth year-end cash resources and a $79-million unused line of credit will finance future acquisitions.

Numac's 1995 exploration and development capital budget will be $120-million, excluding $65-million for acquisitions. The company plans to invest up to $8-million, or 7%, of the capital budget internationally. Numac will continue its long-term focus on natural gas exploration. Approximately 80% (or $40-million) of the planned 1995 Western Canada Basin exploration program will be directed to natural gas. Up to $30-million will be spent on exploration and development activities in northeastern British Columbia, the company's prime focus area for natural gas. Numac believes that there is potential in the Western Canadian Basin for significant oil discoveries, and will target about 20% to 25% of its domestic capital budget to oil prospects. In 1995, average daily production of crude oil and natural gas liquids should be about 20,500 barrels. Average daily production of natural gas should be 185 million cubic feet.

In January 1995, Numac Energy, Canadian Occidental Petroleum Ltd., and New Zealand's Fletcher Challenge Ltd. formed a company to explore and develop oil fields in Venezuela. The new company, based in Caracas, is CXY International Venezuela SA.

During fiscal 1994 (1993), average daily production consisted of 20,536 (15,698) barrels of oil and natural gas liquids, and 138.7 (99.8) million cubic feet of natural gas. In 1994 (1993) gross proven reserves at year end were: 51,216 (50,957) thousand barrels of oil and natural gas liquids, and 490.3 (494.8) billion cubic feet of natural gas.

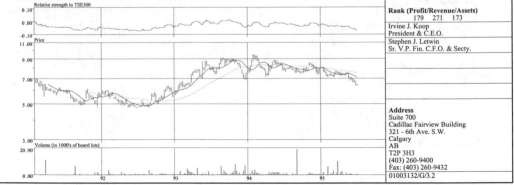

Rank (Profit/Revenue/Assets)
179   271   173

Irvine J. Koop
President & C.E.O.

Stephen J. Letwin
Sr. V.P. Fin. C.F.O. & Secty.

Address
Suite 700
Cadillac Fairview Building
321 - 6th Ave. S.W.
Calgary
AB
T2P 3H3
(403) 260-9400
Fax: (403) 260-9432
01003132/G/3.2

For further company information, call Globe Information Services 1-800-268-9128 or (416) 585-5345

OCELOT ENERGY INC.

Exchanges	Price (Jun29'95)	10 .50	Trailing P/E	15 .91	Stock Symbol
TM	Trailing Yield (%)	0 .00	Trailing EPS	0 .66	**OCE.B**

Period Ending	Dec94	Dec93	Dec92	Dec91
Yearly Statistics				14W
Price-Close	9 .88	10 .13	7 .00	3 .95
Price-High	13 .50	15 .63	7 .25	4 .50
Price-Low	8 .88	6 .75	3 .80	3 .70
P/E-Close	19 .75	20 .25	35 .00	1 .69
Dividends per Share	0 .00	0 .00	0 .00	0 .00
Dividend Yield (%)	0 .00	0 .00	0 .00	0 .00
Sales per Share	3 .58	6 .14	3 .99	12 .78
EPS before extra. item	0 .50	0 .50	0 .20	0 .63
Cash Flow per Share	1 .46	1 .40	0 .92	3 .63
Book Value per Share	3 .98	3 .43	3 .96	3 .65
O/S Common Shares	29 ,428	28 ,588	26 ,426	15 ,702
Total Revenue	104 ,579	168 ,860	95 ,887	57 ,753
Income before extra.	14 ,644	13 ,828	4 ,745	10 ,491
Cash Flow	42 ,574	38 ,458	21 ,847	16 ,355
Debt/Equity	0 .68	0 .87	0 .60	2 .00
Return on Capital (%)	17 .02	18 .35	11 .35	na
Ret. on Com. Equity (%)	13 .61	13 .63	5 .86	na
% Change Profit	5 .9	191 .4	(87 .8)	na
% Change Revenue	(38 .1)	76 .1	(55 .3)	na
% Change Assets	8 .2	20 .1	(5 .2)	na
Preferred Div. Coverage	np	np	np	
Total Div. Coverage	na	na	na	
Interest Coverage	5 .1	4 .2	2 .0	
Current Ratio	1 .0	1 .1	1 .2	
Operating Margin	30 .9	19 .1	22 .4	
Asset Turnover	0 .4	0 .7	0 .5	
5 YEAR RATIOS (%)				
Return on Capital	na	na	na	
Return on Com. Equity	na	na	na	
Profit Growth	na	na	na	
Revenue Growth	na	na	na	
Asset Growth	na	na	na	
BALANCE SHEET (000)				
Cash	9 ,579	9 ,056	6 ,196	
Current Assets	28 ,132	36 ,387	28 ,608	
Net Fixed Assets	216 ,046	189 ,048	124 ,394	
Invest's & Advances	0	0	0	
Total Assets	244 ,856	226 ,369	188 ,430	
Short Term Debt	1 ,101	2 ,297	2 ,705	
Current Liabilities	27 ,311	34 ,380	23 ,528	
Long Term Debt	78 ,396	82 ,971	59 ,774	
Total Liabilities	127 ,865	128 ,189	83 ,694	
Total Equity	116 ,991	98 ,180	104 ,736	
Total Liab. & Equity	244 ,856	226 ,369	188 ,430	
CAPITAL (000)				
Total Debt	79 ,497	85 ,268	62 ,479	
Preferred Equity	0	0	0	
Common Equity	116 ,991	98 ,180	104 ,736	

Business:

OCELOT ENERGY INC. is engaged in the exploration, production and marketing of oil and natural gas. The company operates in British Columbia, Alberta and Saskatchewan. Through wholly-owned subsidiary O.J. Pipelines, the company offers contract services in large-diameter pipeline projects.

Date	EPS	DPS	Tot Rev	Inc Bex
Mar 95	0 .37	0 .00	42 ,088	10 ,873
Dec 94	0 .10	0 .00	20 ,877	2 ,912
Sep 94	0 .10	0 .00	24 ,618	2 ,898
Jun 94	0 .09	0 .00	12 ,496	2 ,931
Mar 94	0 .21	0 .00	46 ,588	5 ,903
Dec 93	0 .06	0 .00	15 ,139	1 ,841
Sep 93	0 .15	0 .00	49 ,239	3 ,999
Jun 93	0 .04	0 .00	16 ,818	1 ,080

Synopsis:

In 1994, Ocelot Energy focused on the exploration and development of its core areas. It will continue this strategy in 1995. Ocelot plans to drill approximately 93 (32.3 net) wells in 1995. Capital spending in 1995 should be $54.3-million funded mainly from cash flow. During 1994, capital spending totalled $64.6-million. Net expenditures were $43.3-million after deducting $21.3-million from disposal of property interests, related facilities, and pipeline construction equipment.

The Sylvan Lake property acquired by Ocelot in early 1993 has proved exceptional. Ocelot's optimization efforts more than doubled liquids production from 1,900 barrels of oil and natural gas liquids (NGLs) per day in January 1993 to over 4,300 barrels per day by the end of 1994. Ocelot also had successful drilling at Sukunka in the British Columbia foothills, where 25 million cubic feet per day of new gas deliverability was added in 1994. By the end of 1995, Ocelot expects its gas equivalent production to approach 150 million cubic feet per day.

In October 1994, Ocelot disposed of the Nig Creek property in northeastern British Columbia. The disposition represented 5% of corporate proven natural gas reserves and netted $19.8-million. The proceeds will be redeployed into corporate projects that should yield a higher return.

In 1994 (1993), Ocelot's average daily production was: crude oil and NGLs, 3,105 (2,144) barrels; and natural gas 53.5 (57.8) million cubic feet. At year-end total proven and probable reserves were: crude oil and NGLs, 16,365 (10,542) thousand barrels; and natural gas, 418.4 (478.9) billion cubic feet.

Relative strength to TSE300

Price

Volume (in 1000's of board lots)

Rank (Profit/Revenue/Assets)
246   418   323

W. David Lyons
President & C.E.O.

Glenn D. Gradeen
Exec. V.P. & C.O.O.

Address
30th Floor, West Tower
Petro-Canada Centre
150-6th Avenue S.W.
Calgary
AB
T2P 3Y7
(403) 299-5700
Fax: (403) 299-5750
01003210/G/3.2

OMEGA HYDROCARBONS LTD.

Exchanges	Price(Jun29'95)	2.00	Trailing P/E		50.00	Stock Symbol
T	Trailing Yield (%)	0.00	Trailing EPS		0.04	**OMH**

Period Ending	Dec94	Dec93	Dec92	Dec91	Dec90
Yearly Statistics					
Price-Close	2.14	3.00	2.90	2.75	2.95
Price-High	3.25	4.50	3.70	3.70	4.35
Price-Low	2.10	2.60	2.10	2.45	2.75
P/E-Close	107.00	42.86	41.43	nm	11.80
Dividends per Share	0.00	0.00	0.00	0.00	0.00
Dividend Yield (%)	0.00	0.00	0.00	0.00	0.00
Sales per Share	1.58	1.73	1.62	1.60	2.03
EPS before extra. item	0.02	0.07	0.07	(0.98)	0.25
Cash Flow per Share	0.53	0.61	0.67	0.61	0.97
Book Value per Share	3.48	3.46	3.38	3.31	4.28
O/S Common Shares	14,005	14,005	13,485	13,492	13,195
Total Revenue	22,530	23,905	22,213	22,242	27,418
Income before extra.	306	909	953	(13,211)	3,218
Cash Flow	7,489	8,256	9,085	8,170	12,711
Debt/Equity	0.31	0.43	0.42	0.47	0.34
Return on Capital (%)	2.90	4.46	5.66	(32.09)	10.43
Ret. on Com. Equity (%)	0.63	1.93	2.11	(26.11)	5.90
% Change Profit	(66.3)	(4.6)	107.2	(510.5)	718.8
% Change Revenue	(5.8)	7.6	(0.1)	(18.9)	32.0
% Change Assets	0.1	7.8	(0.6)	(20.8)	2.4

Date	EPS	DPS	Tot Rev	Inc Bex
Mar 95	0.01	0.00	5,500	79
Dec 94	(0.01)	0.00	4,978	(116)
Sep 94	0.01	0.00	4,708	210
Jun 94	0.03	0.00	5,266	362
Mar 94	(0.01)	0.00	4,561	(150)
Dec 93	0.01	0.00	5,376	144
Sep 93	0.01	0.00	5,007	135
Jun 93	0.03	0.00	5,421	382

Preferred Div. Coverage	np	np	np
Total Div. Coverage	na	na	na
Interest Coverage	1.5	2.2	2.2
Current Ratio	0.5	0.7	0.8
Operating Margin	8.6	12.5	15.0
Asset Turnover	0.3	0.3	0.3
5 YEAR RATIOS (%)			
Return on Capital	(1.7)	(1.4)	(8.7)
Return on Com. Equity	(3.1)	(3.1)	(8.4)
Profit Growth	(4.9)	na	(16.4)
Revenue Growth	1.6	5.7	(2.6)
Asset Growth	(2.8)	(2.7)	(8.8)
BALANCE SHEET (000)			
Cash	0	0	0
Current Assets	5,152	3,157	2,835
Net Fixed Assets	80,797	82,703	76,831
Invest's & Advances	0	0	0
Total Assets	85,949	85,860	79,666
Short Term Debt	0	0	0
Current Liabilities	9,720	4,816	3,733
Long Term Debt	14,966	20,718	19,227
Total Liabilities	37,167	37,375	34,033
Total Equity	48,782	48,485	45,633
Total Liab. & Equity	85,949	85,860	79,666
CAPITAL (000)			
Total Debt	14,966	20,718	19,227
Preferred Equity	0	0	0
Common Equity	48,782	48,485	45,633

Business:

OMEGA HYDROCARBONS LTD. is an oil and gas exploration and production company. It has wells and exploration activities in Alberta, Saskatchewan, and Manitoba.

Synopsis:

Omega Hydrocarbons has allocated $10-million for capital spending in 1995. The capital budget is expected to be funded from cash flow. Omega plans to direct its spending towards light oil. It also plans to take advantage of reduced land prices. The near term price of natural gas prices is forcing gas producers to reduce their exploration and development budgets. Omega wants to achieve a balance between light oil and natural gas production.

In June 1994, Omega sold oil and gas properties in the Worsley area of Alberta for $8-million. The bulk of the proceeds went to reduce bank debt. A portion of the proceeds went to offset production sold by successful horizontal drilling, and connecting the second phase of the shallow gas project on the Siksika Nation in southern Alberta.

In 1994, shallow gas development of the Medicine Hat zone on the Siksika Nation lands continued. Omega drilled 19 (6.3 net) wells during the second half of the year. This area represents more than half of Omega's total production of natural gas.

Capital spending in 1994 totalled $13.7-million. Omega drilled 49 gross wells (26.6 net) drilled during the year. The 8.7 net oil, 17.1 net gas, and 0.8 net dry and abandoned wells contributed a success rate of 97%.

Average daily production before royalties in 1994 (1993) was: oil and natural gas liquids, 2,287 (2,905) barrels; and natural gas, 8.1 (5.1) million cubic feet. Gross proven and probable reserves in 1994 (1993) were: oil and natural gas liquids, 10 (11.9) million barrels; and natural gas, 76.4 (81.2) billion cubic feet. Contributions to production revenues in 1994 were: crude oil and natural gas liquids, 75%; and natural gas, 25%.

Rank (Profit/Revenue/Assets)		
725	700	515

Thomas J. (Jack) Hall
Chairman
Dennis E. Hall
President & C.E.O.
Robert A. Maitland
V.P. Finance

Address
Suite 1300
Sun Life Plaza III
112 - 4th Avenue S.W.
Calgary
AB
T2P 0H3
(403) 294-7200
Fax: (403) 294-7222
O0000778/G/3.2

PANCANADIAN PETROLEUM LIMITED

Exchanges							Stock Symbol
TMZ	Price (Jun29'95)		47 .25	Trailing P/E		18 .98	
	Trailing Yield (%)		1 .69	Trailing EPS		2 .49	**PCP**

Period Ending	Dec94	Dec93	Dec92	Dec91	Dec90
Yearly Statistics					
Price-Close	40 .25	38 .13	33 .50	24 .50	30 .38
Price-High	44 .75	48 .38	33 .50	34 .00	32 .00
Price-Low	37 .00	33 .13	23 .00	22 .38	25 .25
P/E-Close	17 .50	20 .61	24 .45	64 .47	17 .97
Dividends per Share	0 .80	0 .75	0 .60	0 .60	0 .60
Dividend Yield (%)	1 .99	1 .97	1 .79	2 .45	1 .98
Sales per Share	10 .40	8 .88	7 .57	6 .77	7 .58
EPS before extra. item	2 .30	1 .85	1 .37	0 .38	1 .69
Cash Flow per Share	6 .10	4 .95	3 .92	3 .38	3 .95
Book Value per Share	16 .03	14 .53	13 .41	12 .64	12 .86
O/S Common Shares	125 ,238	125 ,172	124 ,920	124 ,910	124 ,910
Total Revenue	1 ,478 ,200	1 ,124 ,200	951 ,100	852 ,700	951 ,800
Income before extra.	287 ,300	231 ,000	170 ,600	47 ,500	211 ,600
Cash Flow	763 ,400	619 ,200	490 ,300	422 ,400	493 ,100
Debt/Equity	0 .24	0 .16	0 .21	0 .20	0 .17
Return on Capital (%)	18 .56	15 .89	14 .97	7 .14	19 .94
Ret. on Com. Equity (%)	15 .02	13 .22	10 .49	2 .98	13 .76
% Change Profit	24 .4	35 .4	259 .2	(77 .6)	59 .1
% Change Revenue	31 .5	18 .2	11 .5	(10 .4)	20 .9
% Change Assets	16 .7	4 .1	5 .5	0 .9	6 .0

Preferred Div. Coverage	np	np	np	
Total Div. Coverage	2 .9	2 .5	2 .3	
Interest Coverage	11 .9	10 .9	10 .4	
Current Ratio	1 .1	1 .4	1 .5	
Operating Margin	28 .1	28 .3	30 .8	
Asset Turnover	0 .3	0 .3	0 .3	
5 YEAR RATIOS (%)				
Return on Capital	15 .3	14 .3	13 .7	
Return on Com. Equity	11 .1	9 .9	9 .1	
Profit Growth	16 .7	13 .2	(1 .2)	
Revenue Growth	13 .4	10 .2	6 .3	
Asset Growth	6 .4	3 .7	5 .5	
BALANCE SHEET (000)				
Cash	40 ,500	93 ,800	64 ,000	
Current Assets	341 ,400	296 ,400	290 ,400	
Net Fixed Assets	3 ,338 ,400	2 ,877 ,700	2 ,739 ,100	
Invest's & Advances	4 ,100	7 ,900	16 ,100	
Total Assets	3 ,751 ,100	3 ,214 ,500	3 ,086 ,500	
Short Term Debt	0	0	0	
Current Liabilities	301 ,400	209 ,300	190 ,800	
Long Term Debt	472 ,300	283 ,000	352 ,800	
Total Liabilities	1 ,743 ,200	1 ,395 ,600	1 ,411 ,800	
Total Equity	2 ,007 ,900	1 ,818 ,900	1 ,674 ,700	
Total Liab. & Equity	3 ,751 ,100	3 ,214 ,500	3 ,086 ,500	
CAPITAL (000)				
Total Debt	472 ,300	283 ,000	352 ,800	
Preferred Equity	0	0	0	
Common Equity	2 ,007 ,900	1 ,818 ,900	1 ,674 ,700	

Business:

PANCANADIAN PETROLEUM LIMITED is engaged, directly and through subsidiaries, in the exploration for and development, production and marketing of crude oil, natural gas, natural gas liquids and sulphur. It is a major producer of crude oil and natural gas in Canada and augments its conventional and synthetic crude oil operations with international projects.

Date	EPS	DPS	Tot Rev	Inc Bex
Mar 95	0 .62	0 .20	389 ,600	77 ,700
Dec 94	0 .52	0 .20	396 ,900	64 ,000
Sep 94	0 .73	0 .20	401 ,800	91 ,400
Jun 94	0 .62	0 .20	365 ,000	77 ,800
Mar 94	0 .43	0 .20	316 ,800	54 ,100
Dec 93	0 .44	0 .20	304 ,500	55 ,100
Sep 93	0 .43	0 .20	271 ,000	53 ,400
Jun 93	0 .49	0 .20	282 ,500	61 ,200

Synopsis:

PanCanadian Petroleum expects 1995 capital expenditures to be about $850-million and to drill over 1,200 wells. The company will focus on lower risk oil and shallow gas projects as well as heavy oil programs. PanCanadian plans to drill approximately 600 oil wells in 1995, 200 in the heavy oil areas of east-central Alberta. Natural gas reserves will remain a key growth target. However, additional production volumes not contracted early in 1995 may be shut-in if spot market prices remain unattractive.

In 1994, capital spending, excluding acquisitions and dispositions, was $854-million. In 1994, PanCanadian participated in the drilling of 1,129 interest wells, of which 606 were natural gas and 378 were oil. This contributed to the addition of 136 million barrels of oil equivalent to proven reserves. In addition, 925 wells in which PanCanadian holds a royalty interest were drilled, for a total participation in 2,054 wells. As a result of this drilling activity and an extensive gas program, PanCanadian's natural gas production is expected to grow substantially in 1995.

PanCanadian is also participating in the construction of a major new natural gas liquids extraction facility at Empress, Alberta which PanCanadian will operate. This investment is expected to increase its natural gas liquids supply and revenue.

Gross daily production in 1994 (1993) was: conventional crude oil, 108,308 (96,037) barrels; field natural gas liquids, 10,692 (9,683) barrels; synthetic crude oil, 19,069 (17,779) barrels; Empress Plants, 13,490 (16,715) barrels; and natural gas, 603 (562) million cubic feet. Gross proven and probable reserves in 1994 (1993) were: conventional crude oil, 289.4 (277.4) million barrels; natural gas liquids, 39.8 (36.7) million barrels; natural gas, 3,172 (2,860) billion cubic feet; synthetic crude oil, 245.8 (157.3) million barrels. Contributions to total revenues in 1994 by product segment were: crude oil, 42%; synthetic crude oil, 10%; natural gas liquids, 8%; natural gas, 27%; and marketing & other, 13%.

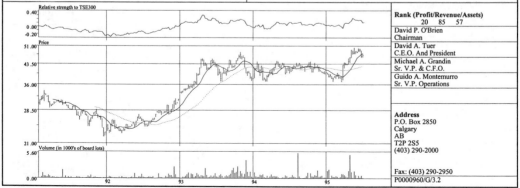

Rank (Profit/Revenue/Assets)		
20	85	57

David P. O'Brien
Chairman

David A. Tuer
C.E.O. And President

Michael A. Grandin
Sr. V.P. & C.F.O.

Guido A. Montemurro
Sr. V.P. Operations

Address
P.O. Box 2850
Calgary
AB
T2P 2S5
(403) 290-2000

Fax: (403) 290-2950
P0000960/G/3.2

PARAMOUNT RESOURCES LTD.

Exchanges	Price (Jun29'95)	15 .00	Trailing P/E		25 .64	Stock Symbol
T	Trailing Yield (%)	0 .67	Trailing EPS		0 .59	**POU**

Period Ending	Dec94	Dec93	Dec92	Dec91	Dec90
Yearly Statistics					
Price-Close	13 .25	19 .63	10 .75	7 .25	9 .75
Price-High	23 .50	26 .38	11 .00	11 .00	10 .25
Price-Low	12 .50	10 .50	5 .00	6 .38	7 .50
P/E-Close	18 .15	22 .30	53 .75	45 .31	23 .21
Dividends per Share	0 .10	0 .10	0 .10	0 .10	0 .20
Dividend Yield (%)	0 .76	0 .51	0 .93	1 .38	2 .05
Sales per Share	4 .57	4 .36	2 .78	2 .40	2 .69
EPS before extra. item	0 .73	0 .88	0 .20	0 .16	0 .42
Cash Flow per Share	2 .23	2 .37	1 .36	1 .24	1 .42
Book Value per Share	5 .31	4 .67	2 .35	2 .05	1 .97
O/S Common Shares	15 ,901	15 ,772	14 ,363	11 ,900	11 ,754
Total Revenue	85 ,049	66 ,967	38 ,978	30 ,049	33 ,151
Income before extra.	11 ,504	12 ,982	2 ,821	1 ,880	4 ,972
Cash Flow	35 ,213	35 ,076	19 ,275	14 ,708	16 ,613
Debt/Equity	1 .30	0 .77	1 .30	1 .57	1 .31
Return on Capital (%)	16 .65	22 .66	13 .08	9 .51	23 .38
Ret. on Com. Equity (%)	14 .56	24 .16	0 .00	7 .90	22 .86
% Change Profit	(11 .4)	360 .2	50 .1	(62 .2)	21 .0
% Change Revenue	27 .0	71 .8	29 .7	(9 .4)	18 .0
% Change Assets	36 .2	71 .0	19 .8	2 .8	8 .4

Period Ending				
Preferred Div. Coverage	np	np	np	
Total Div. Coverage	7 .2	8 .3	2 .0	
Interest Coverage	4 .6	7 .2	2 .4	
Current Ratio	1 .2	1 .0	0 .8	
Operating Margin	23 .9	32 .8	24 .4	
Asset Turnover	0 .3	0 .3	0 .4	
5 YEAR RATIOS (%)				
Return on Capital	17 .1	17 .6	16 .7	
Return on Com. Equity	15 .8	17 .0	15 .6	
Profit Growth	22 .9	31 .7	(2 .7)	
Revenue Growth	24 .8	26 .4	17 .2	
Asset Growth	25 .4	20 .1	14 .1	
BALANCE SHEET (000)				
Cash	60	3	2	
Current Assets	32 ,697	33 ,586	11 ,147	
Net Fixed Assets	189 ,546	148 ,937	95 ,583	
Invest's & Advances	31 ,750	4 ,440	2 ,856	
Total Assets	256 ,668	188 ,446	110 ,202	
Short Term Debt	0	0	0	
Current Liabilities	28 ,117	33 ,060	13 ,923	
Long Term Debt	110 ,063	57 ,006	43 ,818	
Total Liabilities	172 ,273	114 ,762	76 ,420	
Total Equity	84 ,395	73 ,684	33 ,782	
Total Liab. & Equity	256 ,668	188 ,446	110 ,202	
CAPITAL (000)				
Total Debt	110 ,063	57 ,006	43 ,818	
Preferred Equity	0	0	0	
Common Equity	84 ,395	73 ,684	33 ,782	

Business:

PARAMOUNT RESOURCES LTD. is a public Canadian resource company engaged in the exploration for and the development and production of petroleum and natural gas, principally in Western Canada.

Date	EPS	DPS	Tot Rev	Inc Bex
Mar 95	0 .05	0 .00	17 ,723	712
Dec 94	0 .12	0 .10	27 ,661	1 ,891
Sep 94	0 .21	0 .00	18 ,226	3 ,300
Jun 94	0 .21	0 .00	17 ,688	3 ,381
Mar 94	0 .19	0 .00	21 ,471	2 ,932
Dec 93	0 .35	0 .10	21 ,857	5 ,359
Sep 93	0 .21	0 .00	14 ,502	2 ,952
Jun 93	0 .19	0 .00	15 ,187	2 ,825

Synopsis:

Paramount Resources expected capital budget for 1995 is between $35 to $40-million, with cash flow (after tax) budgeted the same. The company predicts production levels for 1995 at 140 to 145 million cubic feet per day of natural and 1000 to 1200 barrels per day of crude oil and natural gas liquids.

In 1994, Paramount constructed three new gas plants at Corner and Leismer in northeastern Alberta and at Kaybob in west central Alberta. The three plants cost Paramount $19.97-million. In addition, the company upgraded its three pre-existing plants (purchased in November 1993, at Liege) with additional compression. New wells were drilled at a net cost of $3.94-million. The three new plants plus the three upgrades added 44 million cubic feet per day net sales capacity compared to the first quarter of 1994. Total capital expenditures in 1994 were $85.3-million.

During the first quarter of 1995, Paramount constructed one new gas plant at South Leismer and expanded the Corner gas plant by 50%. The Company upgraded the Legend gas plant and began building a new oil production facility at Alder Flats. These projects, when fully operational in mid-1995, are expected to net 15 to 20 million cubic feet per day of gas and 700 to 800 barrels per day of oil.

In 1994, Paramount drilled 81 natural gas wells (51 net), seven oil wells (6.7 net), and one (100%) oil and natural gas well representing a 90% success rate on a total of 99 wells (65.6 net). During the first three months of 1995, drilling resulted in 76 natural gas wells (39.8 net) and one oil well (0.6 net) for a 82% success rate on 94 total wells (48.4 net).

Average gross daily production in 1994 (1993) was: crude oil and natural gas liquids, 313 (161) barrels and natural gas, 116.1 (98.7) million cubic feet. Gross proven and probable reserves in 1994 (1993) were: oil and natural gas liquids, 2,164,000 (1,176,000) barrels and natural gas, 435 (414) billion cubic feet. Paramount generates 97% of its revenue from the sale of natural gas sales.

Rank (Profit/Revenue/Assets)
276   446   314

C.H. Riddell
Chairman & President

G.B. Padley
Chief Financial Officer

Address
4000 First Canadian Centre
350 - 7th Avenue S.W.
Calgary
AB
T2P 3W5
(403) 266-2047

Fax: (403) 262-7994
P0004728/G/3.2

PE BEN OILFIELD SERVICES LTD.

Exchanges	Price (Jun29'95)	2.40	Trailing P/E	4.80	Stock Symbol
T	Trailing Yield (%)	0.00	Trailing EPS	0.50	**PBN**

Period Ending	Dec94	Dec93	Dec92	Dec91	Dec90
Yearly Statistics					
Price-Close	1.80	3.50	0.55	1.25	0.55
Price-High	4.15	6.00	1.25	1.40	1.20
Price-Low	1.80	0.50	0.48	0.25	0.45
P/E-Close	4.62	5.56	nm	7.81	nm
Dividends per Share	0.00	0.00	0.00	0.00	0.00
Dividend Yield (%)	0.00	0.00	0.00	0.00	0.00
Sales per Share	8.72	7.60	4.35	5.92	3.79
EPS before extra. item	0.39	0.63	(0.03)	0.16	(0.82)
Cash Flow per Share	0.61	0.70	0.04	0.52	0.11
Book Value per Share	1.74	1.36	0.73	0.76	0.60
O/S Common Shares	3,066	3,020	3,020	3,020	3,020
Total Revenue	26,717	22,988	13,142	17,909	11,450
Income before extra.	1,195	1,915	(100)	488	(2,472)
Cash Flow	1,878	2,115	116	1,576	318
Debt/Equity	0.25	0.15	0.41	0.60	2.32
Return on Capital (%)	29.21	50.40	(1.62)	23.78	(32.18)
Ret. on Com. Equity (%)	25.29	60.75	(4.46)	23.81	(81.27)
% Change Profit	(37.6)	2,012.4	(120.5)	119.7	(1,057.3)
% Change Revenue	16.2	74.9	(26.6)	56.4	(64.5)
% Change Assets	62.2	53.1	(10.1)	(34.4)	(44.9)

Preferred Div. Coverage	np	np	np
Total Div. Coverage	na	na	na
Interest Coverage	24.9	36.7	0.0
Current Ratio	1.7	2.2	1.7
Operating Margin	6.4	8.4	(0.5)
Asset Turnover	2.3	3.2	2.8
5 YEAR RATIOS (%)			
Return on Capital	13.9	8.9	(1.6)
Return on Com. Equity	4.8	1.0	(13.0)
Profit Growth	35.8	na	na
Revenue Growth	(3.7)	(3.7)	(5.6)
Asset Growth	(4.2)	(8.3)	(11.0)
BALANCE SHEET (000)			
Cash	2,461	2,020	503
Current Assets	8,894	5,908	3,223
Net Fixed Assets	2,254	1,275	1,381
Invest's & Advances	0	0	57
Total Assets	11,652	7,183	4,690
Short Term Debt	293	179	307
Current Liabilities	5,209	2,644	1,904
Long Term Debt	1,025	430	592
Total Liabilities	6,314	3,074	2,496
Total Equity	5,338	4,109	2,194
Total Liab. & Equity	11,652	7,183	4,690
CAPITAL (000)			
Total Debt	1,318	609	899
Preferred Equity	0	0	0
Common Equity	5,338	4,109	2,194

Business:

PE BEN OILFIELD SERVICES LTD. is engaged in the transportation and field warehousing of drill pipe and casing for the petroleum industry. It also is engaged in the transportation and stockpiling of pipeline material for the oil and gas transmission industry. The company operates in Western and Central Canada.

Date	EPS	DPS	Tot Rev	Inc Bex
Mar 95	0.27	0.00	11,384	828
Dec 94	0.07	0.00	8,469	208
Sep 94	0.16	0.00	6,992	515
Jun 94	0.00	0.00	4,207	(17)
Mar 94	0.16	0.00	7,049	489
Dec 93	0.11	0.00	4,830	343
Sep 93	0.18	0.00	7,399	538
Jun 93	0.11	0.00	5,143	337

Synopsis:

Activity levels in the oilfield services segment of Pe Ben Oilfield Services climbed in 1994 as a result of increased oil and gas industry drilling activity. Revenue generated from transportation, material handling, and fieldwarehousing jumped by 46%. Oilfield activity levels remained strong in the first quarter of 1995, and with decreased gas prices some curtailment of drilling is expected in the second and third quarters. Pe Ben expects declining gas activity will be offset by increased oil exploration. The bulk of the company's transportation work occurred in central and northern Alberta, and north eastern B.C. In July 1994, Pe Ben expanded into southern Alberta through an arrangement with a major oil company to use the company's Calgary warehouse and distribution centre.

In August 1994, Pe Ben bought the oilfield operations and selected assets of Northwest Oilfield Services Inc. of Fort St. John, B.C. This acquisition enhanced the company's viability of this segment and increased its participation in the development of a region which accounts for 12% of Canada's total gas supply. The acquisition also contributed to the company's 21% increase in volume of oil country tubular goods stored on behalf of clients, with the Fort St. John facility more than doubling the quantity of oilfield goods in stock.

Pe Ben's light oilfield, hotshot, and specialty transportation service revenues rose by 23.6% in 1994. Revenue from pipeline subcontracting operations dipped by $2-million from 1993. The decline in pipeline subcontracting happened despite increased activity levels. This was due to differences in the scope, complexity, and risk associated with projects undertaken in the respective periods.

In June 1995, subsidiary Pe Ben Industries Co. signed an agreement to take over operations of Mannion Transportation Ltd., and buy the operating assets of the company. Mannion is an Edmonton based carrier engaged in the transportation of bulk petroleum products throughout Western Canada, Yukon, and the Northwest Territories.

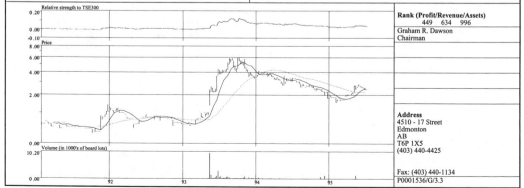

Rank (Profit/Revenue/Assets)
449   634   996

Graham R. Dawson
Chairman

Address
4510 - 17 Street
Edmonton
AB
T6P 1X5
(403) 440-4425

Fax: (403) 440-1134
P0001536/G/3.3

PENN WEST PETROLEUM LTD.

Exchanges	Price (Jun29'95)	6.25	Trailing P/E	24.03	Stock Symbol
T	Trailing Yield (%)	0.00	Trailing EPS	0.26	PWT

Period Ending	Dec94	Dec93	Dec92	Dec91	Dec90
Yearly Statistics					
Price-Close	5.88	5.00	3.00	1.30	2.65
Price-High	9.25	10.65	3.30	3.10	3.25
Price-Low	4.50	2.60	0.35	1.20	1.75
P/E-Close	20.98	19.23	nm	nm	53.00
Dividends per Share	0.00	0.00	0.00	0.00	0.00
Dividend Yield (%)	0.00	0.00	0.00	0.00	0.00
Sales per Share	3.54	1.20	0.90	1.00	1.20
EPS before extra. item	0.28	0.26	(0.20)	(1.80)	0.05
Cash Flow per Share	1.64	0.56	0.17	0.25	0.48
Book Value per Share	4.06	1.81	1.21	2.20	4.00
O/S Common Shares	30,312	17,876	13,974	7,374	7,427
Total Revenue	89,538	20,123	7,135	7,479	7,786
Income before extra.	7,123	4,398	(1,544)	(13,353)	246
Cash Flow	41,483	9,445	1,338	1,872	3,094
Debt/Equity	1.02	0.77	0.72	0.72	0.26
Return on Capital (%)	16.15	12.64	(1.73)	(37.41)	3.81
Ret. on Com. Equity (%)	9.17	17.90	(9.34)	(58.17)	0.90
% Change Profit	62.0	384.8	88.4	(5,528.0)	137.7
% Change Revenue	345.0	182.0	(4.6)	(3.9)	24.3
% Change Assets	355.7	113.0	1.3	(26.3)	10.8
Preferred Div. Coverage	np	np	np		
Total Div. Coverage	na	na	na		
Interest Coverage	4.1	6.0	0.0		
Current Ratio	1.1	0.5	1.9		
Operating Margin	27.6	27.0	(9.4)		
Asset Turnover	0.3	0.3	0.2		
5 YEAR RATIOS (%)					
Return on Capital	(1.3)	(4.1)	(10.0)		
Return on Com. Equity	(7.9)	(10.3)	(18.7)		
Profit Growth	na	na	na		
Revenue Growth	70.2	35.5	5.1		
Asset Growth	51.6	11.5	(8.7)		
BALANCE SHEET (000)					
Cash	0	0	2,200		
Current Assets	43,814	3,951	2,979		
Net Fixed Assets	256,907	62,043	28,000		
Invest's & Advances	0	0	0		
Total Assets	300,721	65,994	30,979		
Short Term Debt	0	0	0		
Current Liabilities	40,607	7,867	1,579		
Long Term Debt	125,992	24,800	12,100		
Total Liabilities	177,657	33,709	14,119		
Total Equity	123,064	32,285	16,860		
Total Liab. & Equity	300,721	65,994	30,979		
CAPITAL (000)					
Total Debt	125,992	24,800	12,100		
Preferred Equity	0	0	0		
Common Equity	123,064	32,285	16,860		

Business:

PENN WEST PETROLEUM LTD. is a Canadian energy company engaged in the acquisition, exploration, development and production of oil and natural gas in Canada and the United States. Operations in the United States are carried out through a wholly owned subsidiary, Penn West Petroleum, Inc., and those in Australia through Penn West Petroleum, Ltd., and Springwest-Page Petroleum N.L.

Date	EPS	DPS	Tot Rev	Inc Bex
Mar 95	0.07	0.00	28,833	2,040
Dec 94	0.03	0.00	31,251	1,286
Sep 94	0.07	0.00	28,057	1,994
Jun 94	0.09	0.00	22,333	1,845
Mar 94	0.11	0.00	7,897	1,998
Dec 93	0.13	0.00	7,695	2,222
Sep 93	0.05	0.00	4,593	829
Jun 93	0.04	0.00	4,610	730

Synopsis:

Penn West Petroleum's 1995 capital spending should equal its expected $55-million cash flow for the year. The company forecasts new production of about 4,400 barrels of oil equivalent per day. The 1995 exit rate should be about 20,000 barrels per day. Penn West feels its balanced resource base will allow it to switch between oil and natural gas, if price advantages occur in a specific commodity.

In May 1994, Penn West bought TroCana Resources for $171.2-million. The deal added daily production of 6,600 barrels of oil, 41 million cubic feet of natural gas, proven and probable reserves of 26.3 million barrels of oil and natural gas liquids, 137 billion cubic feet of natural gas, and 500,000 acres of undeveloped land.

Penn West completed 58 asset transactions in 1994. The company sold 30 properties for total value of $35.9-million. It purchased properties totalling $191.6-million, and bought $9.2-million worth of undeveloped Crown land. The company also cleared rights of first refusal on 120 TroCana properties. In 1995, Penn West plans to continue swapping, buying and selling properties, as it moves toward greater consolidation.

Penn West's net capital spending in 1994 was $217-million. Spending was funded by cash flow of $41.5-million, an equity offering of $82.5-million, and the draw down of $93-million against bank lines. Year end debt was $123-million, net of working capital.

The company's 1994 average daily production was equally balanced between oil and natural gas. Production finished the year at 17,300 barrels of oil equivalent. Average daily production in 1994 (1993) was: crude oil and liquids, 6,934 (1,753) barrels; and natural gas, 58.2 (13) million cubic feet. Proven and probable reserves in 1994 (1993) were: crude oil and liquids, 30.5 (9.6) million barrels; and natural gas, 328.7 (108.6) billion cubic feet.

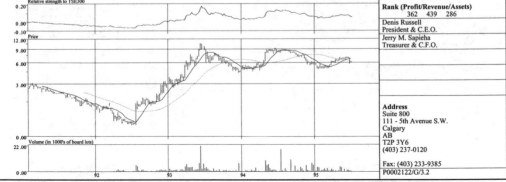

Rank (Profit/Revenue/Assets)
362   439   286

Denis Russell
President & C.E.O.

Jerry M. Sapieha
Treasurer & C.F.O.

Address
Suite 800
111 - 5th Avenue S.W.
Calgary
AB
T2P 3Y6
(403) 237-0120

Fax: (403) 233-9385
P0002122/G/3.2

PETRO-CANADA

Exchanges	Price(Jun29'95)	13 .00	Trailing P/E	17 .57	Stock Symbol
TMVZW	Trailing Yield (%)	1 .40	Trailing EPS	0 .74	**PCA**

Period Ending	Dec94	Dec93	Dec92	Dec91	Dec90
Yearly Statistics					
Price-Close	11 .38	12 .00	8 .13	9 .50	n t
Price-High	14 .88	14 .00	10 .88	13 .25	n t
Price-Low	10 .75	7 .25	7 .88	9 .00	n t
P/E-Close	10 .73	18 .46	203 .13	nm	n t
Dividends per Share	0 .15	0 .13	0 .13	0 .20	0 .26
Dividend Yield (%)	1 .29	1 .08	1 .60	2 .11	na
Sales per Share	18 .57	18 .28	20 .96	24 .76	33 .78
EPS before extra. item	1 .06	0 .65	0 .04	(3 .08)	1 .02
Cash Flow per Share	2 .83	2 .56	2 .38	1 .41	3 .57
Book Value per Share	11 .94	11 .04	10 .72	11 .58	15 .03
O/S Common Shares	246 ,667	246 ,526	246 ,463	215 ,295	171 ,831
Total Revenue	4 ,730 ,000	4 ,603 ,000	4 ,710 ,000	4 ,984 ,000	5 ,873 ,000
Income before extra.	262 ,000	160 ,000	9 ,000	(598 ,000)	176 ,000
Cash Flow	698 ,000	630 ,000	517 ,000	274 ,000	601 ,000
Debt/Equity	0 .38	0 .39	0 .40	0 .68	0 .89
Return on Capital (%)	14 .65	11 .21	4 .50	(16 .91)	13 .20
Ret. on Com. Equity (%)	9 .25	5 .97	0 .35	(23 .57)	7 .10
% Change Profit	63 .8	1 ,677 .8	101 .5	(439 .8)	780 .0
% Change Revenue	2 .8	(2 .3)	(5 .5)	(15 .1)	16 .9
% Change Assets	6 .9	3 .4	(11 .3)	(17 .1)	7 .9
Preferred Div. Coverage	np	np	np		
Total Div. Coverage	6 .4	5 .0	0 .3		
Interest Coverage	5 .5	4 .1	1 .5		
Current Ratio	1 .3	1 .2	1 .0		
Operating Margin	8 .1	7 .1	2 .9		
Asset Turnover	0 .8	0 .8	0 .9		
5 YEAR RATIOS (%)					
Return on Capital	5 .3	3 .7	2 .1		
Return on Com. Equity	(0 .2)	(1 .8)	(3 .2)		
Profit Growth	67 .3	na	(47 .0)		
Revenue Growth	(1 .2)	(0 .9)	(1 .5)		
Asset Growth	(2 .6)	(3 .9)	(8 .7)		
BALANCE SHEET (000)					
Cash	95 ,000	129 ,000	82 ,000		
Current Assets	1 ,331 ,000	1 ,141 ,000	1 ,156 ,000		
Net Fixed Assets	4 ,183 ,000	4 ,027 ,000	3 ,865 ,000		
Invest's & Advances	81 ,000	88 ,000	80 ,000		
Total Assets	5 ,912 ,000	5 ,532 ,000	5 ,350 ,000		
Short Term Debt	0	0	175 ,000		
Current Liabilities	995 ,000	972 ,000	1 ,108 ,000		
Long Term Debt	1 ,106 ,000	1 ,052 ,000	868 ,000		
Total Liabilities	2 ,967 ,000	2 ,810 ,000	2 ,707 ,000		
Total Equity	2 ,945 ,000	2 ,722 ,000	2 ,643 ,000		
Total Liab. & Equity	5 ,912 ,000	5 ,532 ,000	5 ,350 ,000		
CAPITAL (000)					
Total Debt	1 ,106 ,000	1 ,052 ,000	1 ,043 ,000		
Preferred Equity	0	0	0		
Common Equity	2 ,945 ,000	2 ,722 ,000	2 ,643 ,000		

Business:

PETRO-CANADA is the largest Canadian controlled integrated oil and gas company. It is involved in the exploration, development, production and marketing of crude oil, natural gas, natural gas liquids, synthetic oil, bitumen and sulphur. The company refines and produces a broad range of fuels and other petroluem products. It markets petroleum products through its retail and wholesale network.

Date	EPS	DPS	Tot Rev	Inc Bex
Mar 95	(0 .03)	0 .05	1 ,169 ,000	(8 ,000)
Dec 94	0 .22	0 .05	1 ,247 ,000	54 ,000
Sep 94	0 .30	0 .05	1 ,254 ,000	76 ,000
Jun 94	0 .25	0 .03	1 ,177 ,000	60 ,000
Mar 94	0 .29	0 .03	1 ,111 ,000	72 ,000
Dec 93	0 .14	0 .03	1 ,155 ,000	35 ,000
Sep 93	0 .22	0 .03	1 ,175 ,000	55 ,000
Jun 93	0 .13	0 .03	1 ,102 ,000	30 ,000

Synopsis:

Since 1992, Petro-Canada has achieved a dramatic turnaround in financial and operational performance by selling assets, closing service stations, and reducing staff. Continued aggressive cost management is the company's focus as it embarks on further restructuring in 1995. The current plan is to merge the company's existing three divisions and establish "strategic business units" made up of a pool of workers to provide management and support services. As a result, 700 jobs will be cut including 250 from the Calgary-based ICG Propane subsidiary.

Uncertainty over the timing of Petrocan's imminent privatization has affected share value. In this year's Budget Speech, the federal government said it would sell its shares when market conditions improve. The government finds itself in a paradoxical situation. It wants the stock price to increase before it sells its shares, but the stock price will not increase until the government sells its shares. In the meantime, the government is examining alternatives to maximize any gain on the eventual sale of Petro-Canada.

A $900-million capital expenditure program was approved for 1995. Some $230-million, net of grants, will be spent on the company's 25% share of expenditures related to the Hibernia offshore oil field. Approximately $340-million will be allocated to other conventional oil and gas development and exploration projects, and strategic property acquisitions in western Canada. About $180-million will be invested to enhance refinery reliability and efficiency and further upgrade the marketing network, while some $45-million will be directed to the lubricants plant expansion announced in December 1994.

During 1994 (1993), average daily production consisted of 73.3 (79.8) thousand barrels of oil and natural gas liquids, and 540 (562) million cubic feet of natural gas. At its 1994 (1993) year end, Petrocan had 411 (389) million barrels of gross proven oil and natural gas liquid reserves, and 2.1 (2.3) trillion cubic feet of gross proven natural gas reserves.

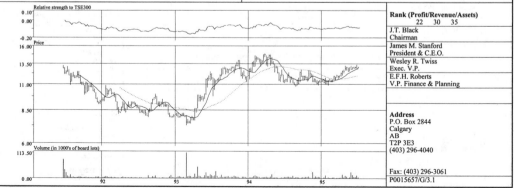

Rank (Profit/Revenue/Assets)		
22	30	35

J.T. Black
Chairman

James M. Stanford
President & C.E.O.

Wesley R. Twiss
Exec. V.P.

E.F.H. Roberts
V.P. Finance & Planning

Address
P.O. Box 2844
Calgary
AB
T2P 3E3
(403) 296-4040

Fax: (403) 296-3061
P0015657/G/3.1

PETROMET RESOURCES LIMITED

Period Ending	Dec94	Dec93	Dec92	Jan92	Jan91	Business:
Yearly Statistics			11M			PETROMET RESOURCES LIMITED is a
Price-Close	6.00	6.25	0.95	0.25	0.25	natural gas exploration, development and
Price-High	10.13	7.00	0.95	na	na	production company concentrating its activities
Price-Low	5.88	0.93	0.23	na	na	in west central Alberta. Its strategy is to own
P/E-Close	150.00	56.82	nm	nm	nm	and operate its production facilities, generate
Dividends per Share	0.00	0.00	0.00	0.00	0.00	prospects internally and to maintain high
Dividend Yield (%)	0.00	0.00	0.00	0.00	0.00	working interests.
Sales per Share	0.36	0.32	0.17	0.08	0.06	
EPS before extra. item	0.04	0.11	(0.07)	(0.05)	(0.03)	
Cash Flow per Share	0.17	0.21	0.08	0.00	0.00	
Book Value per Share	1.24	1.26	0.40	0.41	0.46	
O/S Common Shares	26,932	23,787	17,732	12,238	12,238	
Total Revenue	9,665	8,267	3,068	969	1,190	
Income before extra.	1,096	2,636	(933)	(667)	(418)	

Date	EPS	DPS	Tot Rev	Inc Bex
Mar 95	0.01	0.00	4,214	360
Dec 94	0.00	0.00	3,189	105
Sep 94	0.01	0.00	2,297	261
Jun 94	0.01	0.00	2,054	268
Mar 94	0.02	0.00	2,141	462
Dec 93	0.00	0.00	2,592	35
Sep 93	0.05	0.00	2,023	1,021
Jun 93	0.03	0.00	1,818	791

	Dec94	Dec93	Dec92	Jan92	Jan91
Cash Flow	4,620	4,735	1,019	49	19
Debt/Equity	1.23	nd	nd	0.10	0.05
Return on Capital (%)	6.69	19.17	(15.46)	(11.00)	(6.94)
Ret. on Com. Equity (%)	3.47	14.22	(16.79)	(12.50)	(7.11)
% Change Profit	(58.4)	358.9	(52.6)	(59.5)	48.6
% Change Revenue	16.9	147.0	245.5	(18.6)	136.2
% Change Assets	129.3	407.0	30.0	(6.9)	2.9

Preferred Div. Coverage	np	np	np
Total Div. Coverage	na	na	na
Interest Coverage	2.2	41.1	0.0
Current Ratio	0.8	1.4	2.7
Operating Margin	35.4	35.2	11.0
Asset Turnover	0.1	0.2	0.3
5 YEAR RATIOS (%)			
Return on Capital	(1.5)	(5.6)	(17.6)
Return on Com. Equity	(3.7)	(7.2)	(18.3)
Profit Growth	(11.5)	17.0	(30.9)
Revenue Growth	80.5	70.0	40.1
Asset Growth	70.6	37.0	(1.3)
BALANCE SHEET (000)			
Cash	2,536	9,039	1,593
Current Assets	12,620	14,487	2,176
Net Fixed Assets	80,056	25,922	5,794
Invest's & Advances	0	0	0
Total Assets	92,675	40,408	7,970
Short Term Debt	0	0	0
Current Liabilities	15,230	10,004	814
Long Term Debt	41,142	0	0
Total Liabilities	59,340	10,450	846
Total Equity	33,335	29,958	7,124
Total Liab. & Equity	92,675	40,408	7,970
CAPITAL (000)			
Total Debt	41,142	0	0
Preferred Equity	0	0	0
Common Equity	33,335	29,958	7,124

Synopsis:

Petromet Resources expects 1995 will be a year of ongoing exploration and development. Petromet will add more pipeline infrastructure to complement production growth where processing facilities are now in place. The 1995 capital budget should be about $35-million.

Petromet, in early 1995, entered into an agreement to issue seven million common shares for gross proceeds of $29.8-million. The funds will go to eliminate bank debt and finance 1995 capital programs.

Spending totalled $57-million in 1994, with facilities and undeveloped land purchases accounting for $25-million. Petromet built three new gas plants in 1994, which added more than 40 million cubic feet per day of natural gas processing capacity.

Petromet participated in the drilling of 40 wells (24 net) during 1994. Drilling resulted in 24 natural gas wells, eight oil wells and eight dry holes for an overall success rate of 80%.

Average daily production in 1994 (1993) was: crude oil, 188.2 (71) barrels; and natural gas, 12.5 (13) million cubic feet. Proven and probable reserves in 1994 (1993) were: crude oil & natural gas liquids, 3.9 (2.8) million barrels; and natural gas, 159.5 (119.6) billion cubic feet.

Relative strength to TSE300

Price

Volume (in 1000's of board lots)

Rank (Profit/Revenue/Assets)
649   807   501
P. Gren Schoch
Chairman
Laurie J. Smith
President & C.E.O.
Sharon A. Supple
C.F.O.

Address
Suite 350
839 - 5th Avenue S.W.
Calgary
AB
T2P 3C8
(403) 269-2627

Fax: (403) 266-4150
P0018001/G/3.2

PINNACLE RESOURCES LTD.

Exchanges	Price (Jun29'95)	14.62	Trailing P/E	28.68	Stock Symbol
TM	Trailing Yield (%)	0.00	Trailing EPS	0.51	PNN

Period Ending	Dec94	Dec93	Dec92	Dec91	Dec90
Yearly Statistics					
Price-Close	16.75	18.00	15.25	7.00	4.00
Price-High	22.75	23.75	16.38	8.00	5.25
Price-Low	14.50	15.25	6.63	2.65	3.40
P/E-Close	28.88	25.71	28.77	35.00	14.29
Dividends per Share	0.00	0.00	0.00	0.00	0.00
Dividend Yield (%)	0.00	0.00	0.00	0.00	0.00
Sales per Share	4.97	3.61	2.43	1.47	1.39
EPS before extra. item	0.58	0.70	0.53	0.20	0.28
Cash Flow per Share	2.81	2.22	1.54	0.82	0.92
Book Value per Share	8.17	4.96	4.26	2.44	1.46
O/S Common Shares	18,787	15,068	14,620	12,823	9,209
Total Revenue	86,394	54,606	33,642	17,605	12,528
Income before extra.	10,001	10,437	6,933	2,327	2,297
Cash Flow	48,893	33,297	20,113	8,870	7,415
Debt/Equity	0.37	0.26	nd	nd	nd
Return on Capital (%)	11.99	20.09	21.31	15.86	25.23
Ret. on Com. Equity (%)	8.77	15.23	14.63	9.73	23.71
% Change Profit	(4.2)	50.5	198.0	1.3	104.3
% Change Revenue	58.2	62.3	91.1	40.5	70.5
% Change Assets	109.1	49.8	92.6	38.9	66.1

Preferred Div. Coverage	np	np	np
Total Div. Coverage	na	na	82.5
Interest Coverage	9.8	37.1	108.4
Current Ratio	0.5	0.5	2.1
Operating Margin	21.1	28.1	26.0
Asset Turnover	0.3	0.4	0.4
5 YEAR RATIOS (%)			
Return on Capital	18.9	19.9	15.6
Return on Com. Equity	14.4	18.5	14.6
Profit Growth	54.8	183.8	na
Revenue Growth	63.7	86.1	na
Asset Growth	69.3	54.4	72.7
BALANCE SHEET (000)			
Cash	0	0	21,821
Current Assets	14,680	7,832	27,043
Net Fixed Assets	249,827	118,687	57,440
Invest's & Advances	0	0	0
Total Assets	264,507	126,519	84,483
Short Term Debt	0	0	0
Current Liabilities	29,634	16,675	12,768
Long Term Debt	56,738	19,155	0
Total Liabilities	111,055	51,809	22,158
Total Equity	153,452	74,710	62,325
Total Liab. & Equity	264,507	126,519	84,483
CAPITAL (000)			
Total Debt	56,738	19,155	0
Preferred Equity	0	0	0
Common Equity	153,452	74,710	62,325

Business:

PINNACLE RESOURCES LTD. is involved in oil and gas exploration and development prospects in Alberta and Saskatchewan.

Date	EPS	DPS	Tot Rev	Inc Bex
Mar 95	0.12	0.00	24,381	2,290
Dec 94	0.01	0.00	23,565	377
Sep 94	0.13	0.00	24,045	2,500
Jun 94	0.25	0.00	21,006	4,044
Mar 94	0.20	0.00	17,778	3,080
Dec 93	0.17	0.00	16,971	2,576
Sep 93	0.16	0.00	12,919	2,329
Jun 93	0.20	0.00	13,153	3,024

Synopsis:

During 1995, Pinnacle Resources plans to direct 70% of its capital spending towards oil exploration and development activities in the Provost and Saskatchewan areas. The remaining 30% will go towards natural gas. It will be used to maximize existing facility capacity at the Northern Gas Project during the first quarter, and expand Edmonton area prospects during the balance of the year. Pinnacle set its capital budget for 1995, at $85-million, to be financed with $58-million of cash flow, $22-million of new equity proceeds and an increase in bank borrowings of $5-million. This will result in year end estimated debt of $76-million. The company plans to drill 206 wells, with a minimum of 40% of the wells to be exploratory. Expected 1995 average daily production is 9,500 barrels of crude oil and 75 million cubic feet of natural gas.

In June 1994, Pinnacle acquired all the common shares of ResoQuest Resources Ltd. The $64.2-million takeover was financed with the issue of 2.1 million Pinnacle common shares at $20.30, for total consideration of $43.5-million plus cash of $7.7-million for the remaining ResoQuest common shares, the assumption of $12.3-million in debt, and acquisition costs of $675,000. The ResoQuest purchase increased Pinnacle's presence in southwest Saskatchewan, and included nine million barrels of reserves, 1,450 barrels of daily crude oil production, and 40,000 acres of undeveloped land. Pinnacle expects to realize significant gains from the deal as the Shaunavon oil trend develops into a major new core area in 1995.

In January 1995, Pinnacle announced a deal to issue 1.05 million shares to investment dealers at $15.75 a share. The proceeds will be used to finance Pinnacle's capital spending during 1995.

Average daily production in 1994 (1993) was: crude oil, 7,713 (6,280) barrels; natural gas, 49 (21) million cubic feet. Proven and probable reserves in 1994 (1993) were: crude oil, 22.1 (9.4) million barrels; natural gas, 190.5 (146.2) billion cubic feet. Sales in 1994 (1993) by product were: oil, 61% (73%); and natural gas, 39% (27%).

Relative strength to TSE300 / Price / Volume (in 1000's of board lots) chart, 1992–1995

Rank (Profit/Revenue/Assets)
300 443 308

Richard J.S. Wigington
Chairman

Matthew J. Brister
President & C.E.O.

Stuart G. Clark
Exec. V.P. C.F.O. & Treasurer

Address
P.O. Box 20067
Calgary Place Postal Outlet
Calgary
AB
T2P 4J2
(403) 232-9100

Fax: (403) 232-9200
01000587/G/3.2

POCO PETROLEUMS LTD.

Exchanges	Price (Jun29'95)	9.37	Trailing P/E	49.34	Stock Symbol
TMZ	Trailing Yield (%)	0.00	Trailing EPS	0.19	**POC**

Period Ending	Dec94	Dec93	Dec92	Dec91	Dec90
Yearly Statistics					
Price-Close	7.50	8.88	4.60	5.63	8.13
Price-High	11.00	10.75	5.88	8.63	8.88
Price-Low	6.63	4.35	3.50	5.00	5.75
P/E-Close	50.00	147.92	nm	140.63	38.69
Dividends per Share	0.00	0.00	0.10	0.13	0.00
Dividend Yield (%)	0.00	0.00	2.17	2.31	0.00
Sales per Share	3.02	2.94	3.21	3.62	3.72
EPS before extra. item	0.15	0.06	(1.55)	0.04	0.21
Cash Flow per Share	1.58	1.36	1.26	1.54	1.92
Book Value per Share	6.14	5.51	5.35	7.39	7.37
O/S Common Shares	93,938	82,693	77,924	60,352	41,587
Total Revenue	277,685	234,483	204,783	190,787	154,218
Income before extra.	13,471	5,435	(97,512)	127	11,205
Cash Flow	145,188	108,017	80,386	80,559	79,490
Debt/Equity	0.36	0.54	0.51	0.65	0.34
Return on Capital (%)	6.35	4.94	(19.03)	5.29	9.32
Ret. on Com. Equity (%)	2.61	1.07	(22.91)	(0.50)	2.83
% Change Profit	147.9	105.6	nm	(98.9)	37.1
% Change Revenue	18.4	14.5	7.3	23.7	48.7
% Change Assets	16.6	8.1	(19.7)	67.0	16.3

Preferred Div. Coverage	np	np	0.0
Total Div. Coverage	na	6.9	0.0
Interest Coverage	3.0	1.8	0.0
Current Ratio	1.0	1.1	0.9
Operating Margin	18.6	15.1	(65.0)
Asset Turnover	0.3	0.3	0.3
5 YEAR RATIOS (%)			
Return on Capital	1.4	1.3	0.7
Return on Com. Equity	(3.4)	(3.4)	(4.9)
Profit Growth	10.5	na	na
Revenue Growth	21.7	19.2	22.4
Asset Growth	14.4	11.8	13.8
BALANCE SHEET (000)			
Cash	0	0	0
Current Assets	59,306	37,007	32,128
Net Fixed Assets	799,597	699,176	649,659
Invest's & Advances	0	0	0
Total Assets	876,952	752,396	696,121
Short Term Debt	722	654	8,391
Current Liabilities	58,536	33,172	34,688
Long Term Debt	208,645	245,860	209,887
Total Liabilities	300,065	296,829	266,347
Total Equity	576,887	455,567	429,774
Total Liab. & Equity	876,952	752,396	696,121
CAPITAL (000)			
Total Debt	209,367	246,514	218,278
Preferred Equity	0	0	13,084
Common Equity	576,887	455,567	416,690

Business:

POCO PETROLEUMS LTD. is an oil and gas exploration development and production company. It has producing wells and land holdings in Alberta, Saskatchewan and northeastern British Columbia. The company markets natural gas to customers in Canada and the United States.

Date	EPS	DPS	Tot Rev	Inc Bex
Mar 95	0.05	0.00	75,245	4,312
Dec 94	0.05	0.00	72,287	4,149
Sep 94	0.04	0.00	71,868	4,070
Jun 94	0.05	0.00	70,117	3,974
Mar 94	0.01	0.00	63,413	1,278
Dec 93	0.02	0.00	64,954	1,276
Sep 93	0.01	0.00	59,603	1,523
Jun 93	0.01	0.00	53,563	1,092

Synopsis:

In the first quarter of 1995, Poco Petroleums reported that due to a successful first quarter, it would increase its 1995 capital budget from $131-million to $170-million. On the basis of first quarter exploration, Poco expects 1995 exit rates to be 275 million cubic ft per day of natural gas and 21,000 barrels per day of liquids. The company's winter drilling program cost $44.0-million and consisted of 63 (44.4 net) wells, including 39 (31.0 net) natural gas wells and 17 (8.8 net) oil wells.

In 1994, net capital expenditures were $209.4-million. These included $112.6-million (exploration and development projects), $15.3-million (net property acquisitions), $25.3 million (land), $53.8-million (facilities), and $2.4-million (corporate assets). Drilling in 1994 resulted in 64 (49.9 net) exploration wells and 100 (60.0 net) development wells. Of the 182 wells drilled, there were 121(90.2 net) natural gas wells, 43(19.7 net) oil wells, and 18(13.3 net) dry & abandoned; for a success ratio of 90% (89% net).

During 1994, Poco shifted its operations from its Eastern Region (eastern Alberta and southeastern Saskatchewan), to its Western Region (west central Alberta) and its Northern Region (northwestern Alberta and northeastern British Columbia). This change occurred because the Western and Northern Regions contain larger and longer life reserves. The company expects significant production from the Fort Nelson area to be onstream in 1995 as well as production increases in the Western Region. By the end of 1995, Poco plans to leverage its stable production base in the Eastern Region into a portfolio of producing properties across its three regions.

Average daily sales in 1994 (1993) were: crude oil and natural gas liquids, 20,265 (18,264) barrels and natural gas, 191.5 (160.3) million cubic feet. Gross proven and probable reserves in 1994 (1993) were: oil and gas liquids, 52.0 (50.8) million barrels and natural gas, 866.4 (714.5) billion cubic feet. Contributions to net revenue in 1994 by product were: crude oil and natural gas liquids, 46%; natural gas 51%; and marketing and other 3%.

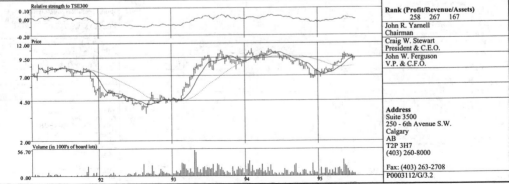

Rank (Profit/Revenue/Assets)
258   267   167

John R. Yarnell
Chairman

Craig W. Stewart
President & C.E.O.

John W. Ferguson
V.P. & C.F.O.

Address
Suite 3500
250 - 6th Avenue S.W.
Calgary
AB
T2P 3H7
(403) 260-8000

Fax: (403) 263-2708
P0003112/G/3.2

PRECISION DRILLING CORP.

Exchanges	Price (Jun29'95)	14.62	Trailing P/E		7.09	Stock Symbol
T	Trailing Yield (%)	0.00	Trailing EPS		2.06	**PD.A**

Period Ending	Apr94	Apr93	Apr92	Apr91	Apr90
Yearly Statistics					
Price-Close	16.38	10.13	2.25	2.50	2.75
Price-High	18.50	10.25	3.25	3.80	3.65
Price-Low	10.00	2.10	2.25	2.00	1.40
P/E-Close	16.05	16.08	9.78	10.42	17.19
Dividends per Share	0.00	0.00	0.00	0.00	0.00
Dividend Yield (%)	0.00	0.00	0.00	0.00	0.00
Sales per Share	12.40	7.42	5.45	6.97	5.65
EPS before extra. item	1.02	0.63	0.23	0.24	0.16
Cash Flow per Share	2.08	1.25	0.60	0.70	1.27
Book Value per Share	6.13	3.40	2.69	2.47	2.23
O/S Common Shares	8,183	6,494	5,626	5,787	5,695
Total Revenue	97,550	44,623	31,519	40,075	36,836
Income before extra.	8,001	3,741	1,294	1,386	886
Cash Flow	16,331	7,475	3,413	4,012	7,113
Debt/Equity	0.48	0.11	0.41	0.63	0.70
Return on Capital (%)	31.78	31.17	12.84	14.43	8.51
Ret. on Com. Equity (%)	22.16	20.13	8.81	10.27	7.26
% Change Profit	113.9	189.1	(6.6)	56.4	59.1
% Change Revenue	118.6	41.6	(21.4)	8.8	(0.7)
% Change Assets	160.9	34.6	(8.8)	14.6	(12.2)

Date	EPS	DPS	Tot Rev	Inc Bex
Apr 95	0.39	0.00	40,503	3,202
Jan 95	0.93	0.00	56,090	7,657
Oct 94	0.42	0.00	45,781	3,378
Jul 94	0.32	0.00	36,941	2,649
Apr 94	0.26	0.00	27,842	2,116
Jan 94	0.44	0.00	32,168	3,430
Oct 93	0.20	0.00	21,711	1,537
Jul 93	0.12	0.00	15,829	918

	Apr94	Apr93	Apr92
Preferred Div. Coverage	np	np	np
Total Div. Coverage	na	na	na
Interest Coverage	29.3	18.3	4.6
Current Ratio	1.1	1.7	2.0
Operating Margin	16.1	15.5	7.6
Asset Turnover	1.0	1.1	1.1
5 YEAR RATIOS (%)			
Return on Capital	19.7	16.6	32.6
Return on Com. Equity	13.7	10.5	17.2
Profit Growth	70.4	16.0	30.0
Revenue Growth	21.3	12.0	24.9
Asset Growth	26.4	30.9	48.3
BALANCE SHEET (000)			
Cash	259	2,101	1,054
Current Assets	33,599	15,123	8,893
Net Fixed Assets	64,776	22,266	19,050
Invest's & Advances	2,254	1,175	718
Total Assets	100,629	38,564	28,661
Short Term Debt	13,308	1,041	1,074
Current Liabilities	30,264	8,950	4,446
Long Term Debt	10,688	1,366	5,096
Total Liabilities	50,483	16,499	13,550
Total Equity	50,146	22,065	15,111
Total Liab. & Equity	100,629	38,564	28,661
CAPITAL (000)			
Total Debt	23,996	2,407	6,170
Preferred Equity	0	0	0
Common Equity	50,146	22,065	15,111

Business:

PRECISION DRILLING CORPORATION is engaged in providing contract well drilling and other services to the oil and gas industry in western Canada.

Synopsis:

Precision Drilling, with the completion of 2,788 wells, continued to be Canada's most active drilling contractor during 1994. This was the sixth consecutive year that Precision was ranked number one based on total number of wells drilled. Precision was responsible for 24% of all wells drilled by members of the Canadian Association of Oilwell Drilling Contractors. Precision had all of its 84 drilling rigs under contract through to break-up and about 70% of its fleet is contracted until the end of 1995. The rig utilization rate for fiscal 1994 (1993) was: Precision Drilling, 56.1 (42.1); with the industry average, 54.7 (32.9).

In fiscal 1995 Precision has entered into three letters of intent with two major oil companies to provide three additional slant drilling rigs. The rigs will be owned by Precision and contracted for a minimum of four years with the option to extend the terms to a maximum of ten years. These rigs will generate additional gross revenue of approximately $8-million per year, and will increase its slant rig fleet in Canada to seven.

On January 31, 1995, Precision purchased a 20% interest in Alberta based ECL group of companies, which carries on a variety of businesses in the trucking industry. Its core business Economy Carriers Limited is a bulk liquid's transporter of fuels and liquefied petroleum gases. ECL Group owns and operates 270 trucks and 500 trailers and had consolidated gross revenues of approximately $60-million in 1994.

During fiscal 1994 Precision acquired all of the shares of Arrowstar Drilling Corporation, Duranco Drilling Ltd., and Geosearch Drilling Ltd., all of which have been or will be wound up. Precision also acquired LRG Oilfield Services Ltd. and a 50% interest in the Taro Drilling Partnership, now Arrowstar Drilling Partnership. The total cost of these purchases was $37.9-million.

Rank (Profit/Revenue/Assets)
338 425 484

Hank Swartout
Chairman President & C.E.O.

Dale Tremblay
V.P. Finance & Corp. Secretary

Address
Suite 700
112 - 4th Avenue S.W.
Calgary
AB
T2P 0H3
(403) 264-4882

Fax: (403) 266-1480
01000333/G/3.3

RANCHMEN'S RESOURCES LTD.

Exchanges	Price (Jun29'95)		4.55	Trailing P/E		50.56	Stock Symbol
TZ	Trailing Yield (%)		0.00	Trailing EPS		0.09	RRL

Period Ending	Dec94	Dec93	Dec92	Dec91	Dec90
Yearly Statistics					
Price-Close	6.00	5.38	4.00	4.70	8.38
Price-High	8.00	6.88	5.63	8.37	9.25
Price-Low	5.00	3.80	3.70	4.40	7.12
P/E-Close	66.67	44.79	nm	nm	167.50
Dividends per Share	0.00	0.00	0.00	0.00	0.23
Dividend Yield (%)	0.00	0.00	0.00	0.00	2.75
Sales per Share	3.06	2.48	3.01	3.15	3.35
EPS before extra. item	0.09	0.12	(0.07)	(0.95)	0.05
Cash Flow per Share	1.47	1.20	1.28	0.86	1.53
Book Value per Share	3.74	3.60	3.46	3.42	4.24
O/S Common Shares	21,045	20,558	20,235	15,985	15,487
Total Revenue	64,791	50,561	51,746	49,043	51,692
Income before extra.	1,918	3,355	265	(13,228)	2,773
Cash Flow	30,672	24,402	22,412	13,492	23,482
Debt/Equity	0.55	0.44	0.29	0.71	0.48
Return on Capital (%)	4.11	4.59	2.33	(7.18)	3.87
Ret. on Com. Equity (%)	2.51	3.35	(1.93)	(24.79)	1.14
% Change Profit	(42.8)	1,166.0	102.0	(577.0)	123.8
% Change Revenue	28.1	(2.3)	5.5	(5.1)	28.5
% Change Assets	14.2	0.2	(6.8)	(6.2)	40.4

Business:

RANCHMEN'S RESOURCES LTD. explores for and produces oil and gas and is exploring in new areas in Alberta and northeastern British Columbia.

Date	EPS	DPS	Tot Rev	Inc Bex
Mar 95	0.08	0.00	16,300	1,800
Dec 94	(0.24)	0.00	16,291	(4,882)
Sep 94	0.17	0.00	19,200	3,400
Jun 94	0.08	0.00	15,400	1,800
Mar 94	0.08	0.00	14,100	1,800
Dec 93	0.00	0.00	12,461	(45)
Sep 93	0.09	0.00	12,500	2,100
Jun 93	0.01	0.00	13,300	500

Preferred Div. Coverage	np	np	0.2
Total Div. Coverage	na	3.5	0.2
Interest Coverage	1.9	3.6	1.3
Current Ratio	0.5	0.5	0.9
Operating Margin	5.7	11.5	6.8
Asset Turnover	0.4	0.4	0.4
5 YEAR RATIOS (%)			
Return on Capital	1.5	1.0	0.5
Return on Com. Equity	(3.9)	(4.7)	(5.6)
Profit Growth	9.1	20.2	(42.5)
Revenue Growth	10.0	9.6	16.4
Asset Growth	7.0	2.0	8.8
BALANCE SHEET (000)			
Cash	268	148	35
Current Assets	9,768	8,893	10,878
Net Fixed Assets	136,307	119,467	117,823
Invest's & Advances	0	0	11
Total Assets	147,563	129,177	128,961
Short Term Debt	107	105	0
Current Liabilities	19,850	16,416	11,943
Long Term Debt	43,353	32,569	24,790
Total Liabilities	68,818	55,195	44,305
Total Equity	78,745	73,982	84,656
Total Liab. & Equity	147,563	129,177	128,961
CAPITAL (000)			
Total Debt	43,460	32,674	24,790
Preferred Equity	0	0	14,730
Common Equity	78,745	73,982	69,926

Synopsis:

In 1995, Ranchmen's Resources expects its capital budget to be about $35-million. The budget would be limited to 1995 cash flow. The capital budget does not apply to acquisitions which will be financed with a combination of debt, equity, and property dispositions. One-third of the capital budget will be spent on exploration drilling, seismic, and land acquisition. The goal is to establish new core areas that would add reserves greater than 30 billion cubic feet of gas, or more than three million barrels of oil. To fund acquisitions, Ranchmen's is prepared to sell or swap up to $20-million of non-core properties. In 1995 oil production should be 7,000 barrels per day. Natural gas production should be 40 million cubic feet per day.

In June, Ranchmen's entered a formal merger agreement with Excel Energy Inc. Each Excel common share will be exchanged for 0.30 of a Ranchmen's common share. Excel has operations in northwestern Alberta and northeastern British Columbia.

Net capital expenditures in 1994 were $45.2-million. This included $5.9-million for land, $4.4-million for seismic, $21.6-million for drilling, and $10.5-million for facilities. Drilling expenditures included $5.4-million on exploration wells and $16.2-million on development wells. The company drilled a total of 163 wells (52.7 net), which resulted in 54 (28.1 net) oil wells, 80 (9.1 net) gas wells, one (0.5 net) service well, and 28 (15.0 net) dry holes. The overall success rate was 83% (72% net).

Average daily production in 1994 (1993) was: crude oil and natural gas liquids, 6,088 (5,306) barrels; and natural gas, 37.4 (33.5) million cubic feet. Gross proven and probable reserves in 1994 (1993) were: crude oil and natural gas liquids, 14.7 (14) million barrels; and natural gas, 128.4 (140) billion cubic feet.

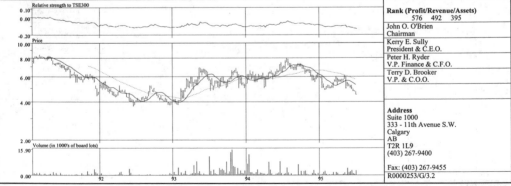

Rank (Profit/Revenue/Assets)
576   492   395

John O. O'Brien
Chairman

Kerry E. Sully
President & C.E.O.

Peter H. Ryder
V.P. Finance & C.F.O.

Terry D. Brooker
V.P. & C.O.O.

Address
Suite 1000
333 - 11th Avenue S.W.
Calgary
AB
T2R 1L9
(403) 267-9400

Fax: (403) 267-9455
R0000253/G/3.2

RANGER OIL LIMITED

Exchanges	Price (Jun29'95)	8.50	Trailing P/E	104.40	Stock Symbol
TMN	Trailing Yield (%)	1.28	Trailing EPS	0.06	**RGO**

Period Ending	Dec94	Dec93	Dec92	Dec91	Dec90
Yearly Statistics	US	US	US	US	US
Price-Close	8.38	6.75	7.00	8.75	8.00
Price-High	9.88	7.88	9.38	10.00	9.63
Price-Low	6.38	5.38	6.38	7.00	6.63
P/E-Close	74.56	19.25	19.80	112.31	12.76
Dividends per Share	0.08	0.08	0.08	0.08	0.06
Dividend Yield (%)	1.31	1.53	1.39	1.05	0.88
Sales per Share	1.55	1.50	1.53	1.22	1.81
EPS before extra. item	0.06	0.21	0.24	0.06	0.46
Cash Flow per Share	0.93	0.93	1.22	0.82	1.07
Book Value per Share	4.66	4.67	4.55	4.39	4.36
O/S Common Shares	98,590	98,494	98,486	98,461	97,118
Total Revenue	176,772	171,363	170,505	135,812	185,538
Income before extra.	6,074	20,197	23,486	5,794	42,445
Cash Flow	91,196	91,852	120,018	80,047	94,452
Debt/Equity	0.24	0.11	0.08	0.01	0.03
Return on Capital (%)	3.21	5.27	3.85	1.43	10.80
Ret. on Com. Equity (%)	1.32	4.45	5.34	1.27	11.16
% Change Profit	(69.9)	(14.0)	305.4	(86.3)	82.7
% Change Revenue	3.2	0.5	25.5	(26.8)	24.0
% Change Assets	10.7	6.0	8.7	0.2	4.2

Preferred Div. Coverage	np	np	np
Total Div. Coverage	0.8	2.6	3.0
Interest Coverage	3.2	13.2	14.0
Current Ratio	0.7	1.5	2.0
Operating Margin	8.3	10.8	6.0
Asset Turnover	0.2	0.2	0.2
5 YEAR RATIOS (%)			
Return on Capital	4.9	6.4	6.8
Return on Com. Equity	4.7	6.1	6.2
Profit Growth	(23.6)	14.7	7.4
Revenue Growth	3.3	9.8	8.9
Asset Growth	5.8	8.1	6.3
BALANCE SHEET (000)			
Cash	46,451	21,325	12,729
Current Assets	77,178	54,472	56,550
Net Fixed Assets	675,124	618,388	577,578
Invest's & Advances	0	6,726	7,199
Total Assets	752,302	679,586	641,327
Short Term Debt	62,050	0	1,695
Current Liabilities	104,088	36,046	28,712
Long Term Debt	50,000	50,000	33,000
Total Liabilities	293,410	219,394	193,497
Total Equity	458,892	460,192	447,830
Total Liab. & Equity	752,302	679,586	641,327
CAPITAL (000)			
Total Debt	112,050	50,000	34,695
Preferred Equity	0	0	0
Common Equity	458,892	460,192	447,830

Business:

RANGER OIL LTD. is an oil and gas exploration and production company. The company has producing wells in North America and the North Sea. Exploration areas include North America, the United Kingdom, Angola, Namibia, Algeria and Peru.

Date		EPS	DPS	Tot Rev	Inc Bex
Mar 95	US	0.04	0.08	53,770	4,284
Dec 94	US	0.00	0.00	58,033	(20)
Sep 94	US	0.02	0.00	41,119	1,814
Jun 94	US	0.00	0.00	36,741	390
Mar 94	US	0.04	0.08	40,553	3,890
Dec 93	US	0.06	0.00	45,034	5,612
Sep 93	US	0.03	0.00	35,965	2,814
Jun 93	US	0.05	0.00	42,336	4,662

Synopsis:

Ranger Oil expects capital spending to be $160-million in 1995, depending on oil and gas prices. Planned capital spending in the North Sea will amount to about $50-million. Completion of the Harding oil field development will be Ranger's major project. Capital spending in North America and other international areas will be $75-million and $30-million, respectively. Ranger's diversified exploration program will cover five countries in the first half of 1995. The countries are Canada, the United Kingdom, Peru, Namibia, and Angola. Ranger's daily production for 1995 is forecast at 36,000 barrels of oil equivalent.

In 1994, capital spending amounted to $128.1-million. Half of the spending went to North American exploration and development program. The remainder went to North Sea development activity. Ranger has reduced its exploration activity in the North Sea over the past two years. In 1994, it drilled only one exploration well and two appraisal wells, compared to one exploration well and one appraisal well in 1993, and 11 wells in 1992. Exploration spending increased in North America in 1994. Ranger drilled 63 exploration wells. This included 51 in Western Canada and 12 in the Gulf of Mexico. In 1993 Ranger drilled 48 wells, and in 1992 it drilled 26 wells. International exploration in 1994 and 1993 took place mainly in Angola, Algeria; and Namibia. Ranger's first offshore exploration well in Angola led to the discovery of the Kiame oil field.

Average daily production in 1994 (1993) in the North Sea was: oil and natural gas liquids, 10,600 (9,000) barrels; and natural gas, 25.9 (29.9) million cubic feet. Average daily production in 1994 (1993) in North America was: oil and natural gas liquids, 4,400 (4,800) barrels; natural gas, 80.3 (83) million cubic feet. Gross proved and probable reserves in 1994 (1993) were: crude oil and natural gas liquids, 62 (44.7) million barrels; natural gas, 425.1 (408.4) billion cubic feet. Oil and gas revenues in 1994 (1993) by geographic segment were: the North Sea, 65.5% (61.9%) and North America, 34.5% (38.1%).

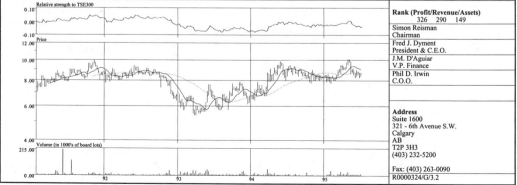

Rank (Profit/Revenue/Assets)		
326	290	149

Simon Reisman
Chairman

Fred J. Dyment
President & C.E.O.

J.M. D'Aguiar
V.P. Finance

Phil D. Irwin
C.O.O.

Address
Suite 1600
321 - 6th Avenue S.W.
Calgary
AB
T2P 3H3
(403) 232-5200

Fax: (403) 263-0090
R0000324/G/3.2

RENAISSANCE ENERGY LTD.

Exchanges	Price (Jun29'95)	28.25	Trailing P/E	39.79	Stock Symbol
TM	Trailing Yield (%)	0.00	Trailing EPS	0.71	RES

Period Ending	Dec94	Dec93	Dec92	Dec91	Dec90
Yearly Statistics					
Price-Close	27.13	28.25	18.63	13.13	15.75
Price-High	32.00	36.00	19.75	17.13	16.50
Price-Low	26.50	18.25	12.25	11.88	12.00
P/E-Close	38.20	46.31	53.21	41.03	41.45
Dividends per Share	0.00	0.00	0.00	0.00	0.00
Dividend Yield (%)	0.00	0.00	0.00	0.00	0.00
Sales per Share	5.85	4.76	3.76	3.21	3.00
EPS before extra. item	0.71	0.61	0.35	0.32	0.38
Cash Flow per Share	3.31	2.67	1.91	1.67	1.43
Book Value per Share	11.19	8.55	6.04	4.78	3.84
O/S Common Shares	93,708	83,457	74,668	65,046	60,330
Total Revenue	522,418	381,740	266,071	206,679	179,961
Income before extra.	63,071	48,992	24,552	20,805	22,812
Cash Flow	295,870	214,304	135,152	107,005	86,012
Debt/Equity	0.34	0.24	0.43	0.55	0.54
Return on Capital (%)	11.44	12.17	9.45	11.58	14.56
Ret. on Com. Equity (%)	7.16	8.41	6.44	7.67	10.51
% Change Profit	28.7	99.5	18.0	(8.8)	27.3
% Change Revenue	36.9	43.5	28.7	14.8	37.8
% Change Assets	57.8	39.7	35.7	34.0	25.6

Business:
RENAISSANCE ENERGY LTD. is an oil and gas exploration, development and production company. It has producing wells in Alberta, and sells natural gas to markets in Alberta, eastern Canada, and the United States. Exploration activities focus on the plains area of western Canada.

Date	EPS	DPS	Tot Rev	Inc Bex
Mar 95	0.16	0.00	143,133	15,219
Dec 94	0.14	0.00	139,525	12,254
Sep 94	0.20	0.00	140,889	19,105
Jun 94	0.21	0.00	127,318	18,162
Mar 94	0.16	0.00	114,686	13,550
Dec 93	0.18	0.00	111,633	14,668
Sep 93	0.13	0.00	93,143	11,046
Jun 93	0.17	0.00	92,923	13,228

Preferred Div. Coverage	np	np	np
Total Div. Coverage	na	na	na
Interest Coverage	8.9	10.3	4.6
Current Ratio	0.7	0.7	0.6
Operating Margin	26.7	25.3	20.5
Asset Turnover	0.3	0.4	0.4
5 YEAR RATIOS (%)			
Return on Capital	11.8	12.2	11.3
Return on Com. Equity	8.0	8.5	7.7
Profit Growth	28.6	43.9	17.8
Revenue Growth	31.9	34.6	36.3
Asset Growth	38.1	29.4	31.2
BALANCE SHEET (000)			
Cash	1,810	65	120
Current Assets	55,358	45,244	25,619
Net Fixed Assets	1,584,954	991,966	714,339
Invest's & Advances	0	0	0
Total Assets	1,655,440	1,048,851	750,525
Short Term Debt	0	0	0
Current Liabilities	82,147	68,036	41,599
Long Term Debt	358,616	167,687	193,310
Total Liabilities	606,673	335,309	299,375
Total Equity	1,048,767	713,542	451,150
Total Liab. & Equity	1,655,440	1,048,851	750,525
CAPITAL (000)			
Total Debt	358,616	167,687	193,310
Preferred Equity	0	0	0
Common Equity	1,048,767	713,542	451,150

Synopsis:

Renaissance Energy has earmarked $500-million for its 1995 capital expenditure budget. About half of the budget will be used to replace production during 1995 and to meet year end objectives. The remainder will go to projects providing longer term growth. The budget will be funded by cash flow by drawing from company credit facilities. Renaissance's 1995 drilling program includes 1,400 wells. The wells will be balanced between oil and natural gas prospects, and half of the wells will be exploratory.

Total spending in 1994 came to $761.4-million, with $753.3-million spent on finding and onstream costs. Capital spending focused on adding to Renaissance's undeveloped land inventory in Alberta and Saskatchewan, strengthening its position in Southern Alberta through acquisitions, drilling a high number of wells to develop existing fields, and increasing production volumes. Drilling activity included 1,251 (1,218 net) wells. This resulted in 440 (424 net) oil wells, 329 (320 net) natural gas wells, and 482 (474 net) dry wells.

At the end of the first quarter of 1995, Renaissance's daily production volumes averaged 53,000 barrels of oil and 375 million cubic feet of natural gas. Oil volumes should increase during the second half of the year as new production comes on stream. Approximately 65 million cubic feet of natural gas production will remain shut-in until natural gas prices improve. Renaissance drilled 400 net wells during the quarter. Most were exploratory wells for natural gas.

Average daily production in 1994 (1993) was: oil, 42,979 (34,086) barrels; and natural gas, 362 (300) million cubic feet. Gross proven and probable reserves in 1994 (1993) were: oil, 247 (165) million barrels; and natural gas, 1,325 (1,057) billion cubic feet.

Rank (Profit/Revenue/Assets)
98 194 120
Ronald G. Greene
Chairman
Clayton H. Woitas
President & C.E.O.
John A. Thomson
Sr. V.P., C.F.O. & Secretary

Address
Suite 3000
425 First Street S.W.
Calgary
AB
T2P 3L8
(403) 750-1400

Fax: (403) 750-1468
R0012081/G/3.2

RIGEL ENERGY CORPORATION

Exchanges	Price (Jun29'95)	13.12	Trailing P/E	19.30	Stock Symbol
TMA	Trailing Yield (%)	0.00	Trailing EPS	0.68	**RJL**

Period Ending	Dec94	Dec93	Dec92	Dec91	Dec90
Yearly Statistics					
Price-Close	14.13	18.00	10.25	6.13	na
Price-High	23.00	24.50	10.50	7.25	na
Price-Low	13.50	9.63	4.80	5.25	na
P/E-Close	19.09	28.13	36.61	32.26	n t
Dividends per Share	0.00	0.00	0.00	0.00	0.00
Dividend Yield (%)	0.00	0.00	0.00	0.00	0.00
Sales per Share	3.71	3.16	2.71	2.61	2.66
EPS before extra. item	0.74	0.64	0.28	0.19	0.43
Cash Flow per Share	2.22	1.89	1.40	1.21	1.45
Book Value per Share	4.68	3.94	3.29	3.01	4.58
O/S Common Shares	35,543	35,463	35,352	35,251	35,251
Total Revenue	133,286	115,947	97,498	94,391	98,077
Income before extra.	26,228	22,548	9,843	6,831	15,333
Cash Flow	78,939	67,004	49,230	42,759	51,182
Debt/Equity	0.14	0.12	0.19	0.27	nd
Return on Capital (%)	20.86	20.98	13.92	10.12	na
Ret. on Com. Equity (%)	17.14	17.62	8.86	5.11	na
% Change Profit	16.3	129.1	44.1	(55.4)	na
% Change Revenue	15.0	18.9	3.3	(3.8)	na
% Change Assets	16.5	10.8	(3.8)	(11.3)	na

	Date	EPS	DPS	Tot Rev	Inc Bex
	Mar 95	0.09	0.00	31,248	3,186
	Dec 94	0.12	0.00	31,699	4,155
	Sep 94	0.23	0.00	35,068	8,101
	Jun 94	0.24	0.00	34,419	8,406
	Mar 94	0.16	0.00	32,207	5,566
	Dec 93	0.15	0.00	32,046	5,077
	Sep 93	0.16	0.00	27,428	5,692
	Jun 93	0.18	0.00	28,799	6,445

	Dec94	Dec93	Dec92
Preferred Div. Coverage	np	np	np
Total Div. Coverage	na	na	na
Interest Coverage	19.9	15.2	11.1
Current Ratio	1.2	1.3	1.3
Operating Margin	26.1	24.0	18.1
Asset Turnover	0.5	0.5	0.5
5 YEAR RATIOS (%)			
Return on Capital	na	na	na
Return on Com. Equity	na	na	na
Profit Growth	na	na	na
Revenue Growth	na	na	na
Asset Growth	na	na	na
BALANCE SHEET (000)			
Cash	3,093	4,770	2,691
Current Assets	19,773	19,368	14,590
Net Fixed Assets	251,467	213,992	196,602
Invest's & Advances	0	0	0
Total Assets	272,813	234,111	211,386
Short Term Debt	0	0	0
Current Liabilities	17,063	14,872	11,602
Long Term Debt	22,429	16,786	22,140
Total Liabilities	106,331	94,515	95,087
Total Equity	166,482	139,596	116,299
Total Liab. & Equity	272,813	234,111	211,386
CAPITAL (000)			
Total Debt	22,429	16,786	22,140
Preferred Equity	0	0	0
Common Equity	166,482	139,596	116,299

Business:

RIGEL ENERGY CORPORATION is in the business of exploration, development, production and marketing of oil and natural gas in Canada.

Synopsis:

In 1995, Rigel Energy plans to spend $90-million on its capital program. This includes $49-million for drilling and completions, and $12-million for gas plants and facilities. Rigel expects to fund the capital program with funds from operations and by drawing from available committed credit facilities.

Rigel plans several projects for 1995. It plans to explore horizontally drilled, light oil reservoirs in the Williston Basin, extending into the U.S. It also plans crude oil and natural gas projects in Peace River Arch area, as well as higher risk ventures in the foothills of Alberta and British Columbia. In 1995, Rigel will emphasize crude oil development, because of oil's current price advantage over natural gas. Rigel's goal is to balance revenues between crude oil and natural gas, even with the current depressed natural gas prices.

During 1994, Rigel's capital expenditures before dispositions was $92.2-million. Proceeds from the sale of non-core oil and gas assets and other capital assets were $8.0-million. The company had bank commitments worth $37.6-million of unutilized term credit and for an additional $5-million operating facility at year end. In March 1995, Rigel negotiated an additional $20-million term credit facility.

In the first quarter Rigel acquired 2.6 million barrels of light oil reserves in southeast Saskatchewan. The reserves will produce approximately 500 barrels per day beginning in June 1995.

Average daily production in 1994 (1993) was: crude oil and natural gas liquids, 12,570 (11,123) barrels; and natural gas, 64.9 (63.1) million cubic feet. Gross proven and probable reserves in 1994 (1993) were: crude oil, condensate and natural gas liquids, 38.2 (36.8) million barrels; and natural gas, 319.6 (331.6) billion cubic feet. Contributions to gross production revenues in 1994 (1993) by product were: crude oil and condensate, 59% (55%); natural gas, 36% (37%); and natural gas liquids, 5% (8%).

Relative strength to TSE300 / Price / Volume (in 1000's of board lots) chart

Rank (Profit/Revenue/Assets)
182   377   301

Richard S. Aberg
Chairman

Donald T. West
President & C.E.O.

Donald R. Gardner
V.P. Finance C.F.O. & Secty.

Address
1900 Bow Valley Square 3
255 - 5th Avenue S.W.
Calgary
AB
T2P 3G6
(403) 267-3000

Fax: (403) 267-3006
01003159/G/3.2

RIO ALTO EXPLORATION LTD.

Exchanges	Price (Jun29'95)	4.35	Trailing P/E	13.18	Stock Symbol
T	Trailing Yield (%)	0.00	Trailing EPS	0.33	**RAX**

Period Ending	Dec94	Dec93	Dec92	Dec91	Dec90
Yearly Statistics					
Price-Close	5.25	8.25	3.45	0.92	0.42
Price-High	10.13	11.75	3.55	1.30	0.60
Price-Low	5.00	3.30	0.80	0.31	0.12
P/E-Close	12.81	21.71	31.36	306.67	nm
Dividends per Share	0.00	0.00	0.00	0.00	0.00
Dividend Yield (%)	0.00	0.00	0.00	0.00	0.00
Sales per Share	1.80	1.31	0.32	0.05	0.09
EPS before extra. item	0.41	0.38	0.11	0.00	(0.11)
Cash Flow per Share	1.12	0.85	0.23	0.02	0.03
Book Value per Share	2.30	1.19	0.54	0.40	0.29
O/S Common Shares	44,009	38,619	35,997	34,303	15,770
Total Revenue	74,215	49,545	11,117	1,167	(128)
Income before extra.	16,866	14,237	3,876	59	(1,411)
Cash Flow	46,051	32,166	7,962	303	356
Debt/Equity	0.84	0.79	1.20	0.05	0.19
Return on Capital (%)	25.65	37.53	16.65	1.70	(21.31)
Ret. on Com. Equity (%)	22.95	43.74	23.48	0.65	(28.80)
% Change Profit	18.5	267.3	6,438.7	104.2	(387.1)
% Change Revenue	49.8	345.7	852.6	1,014.3	(110.4)
% Change Assets	131.2	102.5	137.9	255.8	(25.8)

Date	EPS	DPS	Tot Rev	Inc Bex
Mar 95	0.05	0.00	17,027	2,026
Dec 94	0.08	0.00	16,220	3,391
Sep 94	0.08	0.00	16,125	3,783
Jun 94	0.12	0.00	16,840	4,569
Mar 94	0.13	0.00	17,119	5,122
Dec 93	0.11	0.00	11,826	3,953
Sep 93	0.05	0.00	10,125	2,093
Jun 93	0.13	0.00	10,794	5,052

Preferred Div. Coverage	np	np	np
Total Div. Coverage	na	na	na
Interest Coverage	6.9	13.1	5.5
Current Ratio	1.0	1.3	1.0
Operating Margin	46.3	47.2	42.5
Asset Turnover	0.3	0.5	0.2
5 YEAR RATIOS (%)			
Return on Capital	12.0	6.5	(3.8)
Return on Com. Equity	12.4	6.7	(5.6)
Profit Growth	na	na	95.8
Revenue Growth	127.1	106.4	42.8
Asset Growth	96.7	66.1	41.4
BALANCE SHEET (000)			
Cash	64	3	2,307
Current Assets	18,133	12,069	7,069
Net Fixed Assets	199,666	85,804	41,253
Invest's & Advances	0	0	0
Total Assets	226,260	97,873	48,322
Short Term Debt	973	973	984
Current Liabilities	18,241	9,528	6,879
Long Term Debt	83,870	35,312	22,169
Total Liabilities	125,083	52,053	29,048
Total Equity	101,177	45,820	19,274
Total Liab. & Equity	226,260	97,873	48,322
CAPITAL (000)			
Total Debt	84,843	36,285	23,153
Preferred Equity	0	0	0
Common Equity	101,177	45,820	19,274

Business:

RIO ALTO EXPLORATION LTD. is an oil and gas exploration and production company.

Synopsis:

Rio Alto Exploration's capital spending in 1994 was $130.9-million. Rio Alto financed spending from cash flow, bank debt, and the proceeds from a share issue. The 1995 capital spending program is should total $60-million. This is down from last year due to soft natural gas market conditions. Rio Alto will finance 1995 spending through cash flow and existing bank debt capacity.

Overall company production should average over 14,000 barrels of oil equivalent per day in 1995. Land acquisitions will continue to be a priority. Rio Alto plans to drill 80 wells (72 net) in its northeast Alberta core region in the first quarter of 1995. It will drill development wells, as well as a significant number of "set up" locations for future 1995-96 development. At Ante Creek, development activity will be balanced between oil and gas. Drilling at Ante Creek will be concentrated in the last quarter of the year, with five to eight wells being drilled.

In 1994, Rio Alto brought three new compression facilities on- stream. It also continued building up its land position through both acquisitions as well as Crown purchase activities. Rio Alto increased its property inventory by 65% to 1,052,000 net acres.

Average daily production in 1994 (1993) was: oil and natural gas liquids, 1,158 (953) barrels; and natural gas, 98.9 (66.5) million cubic feet. Gross proven and probable reserves in 1994 (1993) were: oil and gas liquids, 3,948,000 (3,014,000) barrels; and natural gas, 333 (204) billion cubic feet.

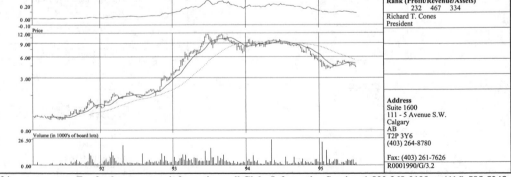

Rank (Profit/Revenue/Assets)		
232	467	334

Richard T. Cones
President

Address
Suite 1600
111 - 5 Avenue S.W.
Calgary
AB
T2P 3Y6
(403) 264-8780

Fax: (403) 261-7626
R0001990/G/3.2

SCEPTRE RESOURCES LIMITED

Exchanges	Price (Jun29'95)	8.37	Trailing P/E	21.47	Stock Symbol
TMA	Trailing Yield (%)	0.00	Trailing EPS	0.39	**SRL**

Period Ending	Dec94	Dec93	Dec92	Dec91	Dec90
Yearly Statistics					
Price-Close	9.13	12.75	5.63	17.00	37.00
Price-High	14.88	15.50	17.50	41.50	51.25
Price-Low	8.63	5.13	4.40	15.50	32.00
P/E-Close	21.22	29.65	nm	nm	46.25
Dividends per Share	0.00	0.00	0.00	0.00	0.00
Dividend Yield (%)	0.00	0.00	0.00	0.00	0.00
Sales per Share	4.48	3.98	11.30	20.92	27.15
EPS before extra. item	0.43	0.43	(0.04)	(22.89)	0.80
Cash Flow per Share	2.31	1.91	3.75	5.61	10.05
Book Value per Share	6.31	5.47	5.05	7.49	30.31
O/S Common Shares	56,686	53,031	52,321	9,358	9,358
Total Revenue	251,419	211,093	181,755	198,516	246,445
Income before extra.	23,947	22,748	307	(210,502)	11,309
Cash Flow	127,951	100,286	60,262	52,458	91,098
Debt/Equity	0.48	0.63	0.60	2.88	1.05
Return on Capital (%)	10.39	9.33	6.33	(30.98)	7.58
Ret. on Com. Equity (%)	7.39	8.21	(0.36)	(121.13)	3.25
% Change Profit	5.3	7,309.8	100.1	(1,961.4)	146.8
% Change Revenue	19.1	16.1	(8.4)	(19.4)	23.4
% Change Assets	15.4	15.0	(9.5)	(30.2)	(3.7)

Date	EPS	DPS	Tot Rev	Inc Bex
Mar 95	0.09	0.00	64,359	4,955
Dec 94	0.02	0.00	67,288	1,711
Sep 94	0.15	0.00	65,689	8,540
Jun 94	0.13	0.00	63,485	7,117
Mar 94	0.12	0.00	54,957	6,519
Dec 93	0.08	0.00	61,131	4,566
Sep 93	0.10	0.00	51,442	5,117
Jun 93	0.14	0.00	53,318	7,341

	Dec94	Dec93	Dec92
Preferred Div. Coverage	np	np	np
Total Div. Coverage	na	na	0.3
Interest Coverage	5.1	4.3	1.0
Current Ratio	0.9	0.7	0.8
Operating Margin	19.5	19.1	15.1
Asset Turnover	0.4	0.4	0.4
5 YEAR RATIOS (%)			
Return on Capital	0.5	(0.9)	(1.9)
Return on Com. Equity	(20.5)	(25.2)	(26.6)
Profit Growth	na	29.3	(48.3)
Revenue Growth	4.7	13.7	17.4
Asset Growth	(4.2)	2.5	0.4
BALANCE SHEET (000)			
Cash	259	299	519
Current Assets	46,639	32,011	28,470
Net Fixed Assets	576,700	508,018	440,938
Invest's & Advances	0	0	0
Total Assets	623,339	540,029	469,408
Short Term Debt	0	0	0
Current Liabilities	52,306	44,904	33,925
Long Term Debt	171,942	182,233	157,628
Total Liabilities	265,528	250,015	205,095
Total Equity	357,811	290,014	264,313
Total Liab. & Equity	623,339	540,029	469,408
CAPITAL (000)			
Total Debt	171,942	182,233	157,628
Preferred Equity	0	0	0
Common Equity	357,811	290,014	264,313

Business:

SCEPTRE RESOURCES LTD. is an oil and gas exploration and production company. The company has producing wells in Western Canada. It has exploration activities in Western Canada. The company sells its production in the North American market.

Synopsis:

Sceptre Resources originally expected its 1995 capital budget to be $150-million, excluding acquisitions. During the 1995 first quarter, Sceptre lowered the budget to $135-million. Low natural gas prices caused Sceptre to shut-in some natural gas wells, defer certain gas projects, and accelerate natural gas plant maintenance.

During the first quarter of 1995, Sceptre participated in drilling 54 gross (43.2 net) wells. This resulted in 19 gross (14.9 net) oil wells, 15 gross (13.1 net) gas wells, 15 gross (13.8 net) abandonments, and five gross (1.4 net) farmouts. Exploration and development expenditures totalled $30.8-million during the period.

In 1994, total capital spending was $181.1-million, with emphasis placed on exploration and development, which had total costs of $148.9-million. Drilling activity in 1994 totalled 295 gross wells (222 net). This resulted in 75 (47 net) oil wells, 180 (149 net) gas wells, 38 (25 net) dry and abandoned, and 2 (1 net) service wells. Property dispositions during 1994 totalled $29.9-million. Dispositions comprised 45 billion cubic feet of natural gas reserves and 1.2 million barrels of crude oil and natural gas liquids reserves.

Average daily production in 1994 (1993) was: crude oil and natural gas liquids, 22,503 (20,628) barrels; natural gas, 147 (122) million cubic feet. Proven and probable reserves in 1994 (1993) were: crude oil and natural gas liquids, 74 (82) million barrels; natural gas, 630 (640) billion cubic feet. Gross revenue in 1994 (1993) by product was: crude oil liquids, 56.1% (56.8%); and natural gas and liquids, 43.9% (43.2%).

Relative strength to TSE300 / Price / Volume (in 1000's of board lots)

Rank (Profit/Revenue/Assets)
193   285   207

Maurice J. Leclair
Chairman

Michael Grandin
President & C.E.O.

Stanley G. Weber
V.P. Fin. C.F.O. & Corp. Sec.

Address
Suite 2000
400 - 3rd Avenue S.W.
Calgary
AB
T2P 4H2
(403) 298-9800

Fax: (403) 290-1106
S0000627/G/3.2

SERENPET INC.

Exchanges	Price (Jun29'95)		3.95	Trailing P/E		nm	Stock Symbol
TA	Trailing Yield (%)		0.00	Trailing EPS		(1.12)	**SPY**

Period Ending	Dec94	Dec93	Dec92	Dec91	Dec90
Yearly Statistics					
Price-Close	3.50	7.88	5.88	n t	n t
Price-High	9.50	15.75	6.50	n t	n t
Price-Low	3.10	6.00	4.50	n t	n t
P/E-Close	nm	23.16	20.98	n t	n t
Dividends per Share	0.00	0.00	0.00	0.01	0.00
Dividend Yield (%)	0.00	0.00	0.00	n t	0.00
Sales per Share	2.42	2.40	1.41	0.64	0.18
EPS before extra. item	(1.03)	0.34	0.28	0.00	(0.05)
Cash Flow per Share	1.40	1.59	0.82	0.24	0.03
Book Value per Share	4.15	3.94	2.24	0.99	0.34
O/S Common Shares	22,779	12,343	9,406	6,055	5,932
Total Revenue	41,744	28,447	10,413	2,157	638
Income before extra.	(17,335)	3,693	2,025	5	(176)
Cash Flow	23,435	17,537	5,996	748	104
Debt/Equity	0.48	0.42	0.10	0.52	0.24
Return on Capital (%)	(21.18)	17.07	24.08	6.05	na
Ret. on Com. Equity (%)	(24.21)	10.59	14.96	0.12	na
% Change Profit	(569.4)	82.4	nm	102.7	na
% Change Revenue	46.7	173.2	382.9	238.2	na
% Change Assets	91.7	197.9	129.1	339.2	na
Preferred Div. Coverage	np	np	np		
Total Div. Coverage	na	na	na		
Interest Coverage	0.0	6.9	7.1		
Current Ratio	0.8	0.5	0.3		
Operating Margin	11.7	27.7	37.3		
Asset Turnover	0.3	0.3	0.4		
5 YEAR RATIOS (%)					
Return on Capital	na	na	na		
Return on Com. Equity	na	na	na		
Profit Growth	na	na	na		
Revenue Growth	na	na	na		
Asset Growth	na	na	na		
BALANCE SHEET (000)					
Cash	0	0	0		
Current Assets	15,695	7,519	1,763		
Net Fixed Assets	145,836	76,607	26,291		
Invest's & Advances	328	296	282		
Total Assets	161,859	84,422	28,336		
Short Term Debt	3,958	3,075	2,028		
Current Liabilities	20,090	14,084	6,288		
Long Term Debt	41,000	17,560	0		
Total Liabilities	67,290	35,771	7,234		
Total Equity	94,569	48,651	21,102		
Total Liab. & Equity	161,859	84,422	28,336		
CAPITAL (000)					
Total Debt	44,958	20,635	2,028		
Preferred Equity	0	0	0		
Common Equity	94,569	48,651	21,102		

Business:

SERENPET INC. is involved in the exploration, development and production of petroleum and natural gas in western Canada.

Date	EPS	DPS	Tot Rev	Inc Bex
Mar 95	0.01	0.00	13,063	333
Dec 94	(1.21)	0.00	11,343	(20,011)
Sep 94	0.01	0.00	11,854	579
Jun 94	0.07	0.00	9,247	851
Mar 94	0.10	0.00	9,300	1,245
Dec 93	0.17	0.00	10,491	1,867
Sep 93	0.03	0.00	7,944	400
Jun 93	0.04	0.00	5,852	499

Synopsis:

Serenpet Inc. expects average 1995 production to be 5,200 barrels of oil per day and 39 million cubic feet of natural gas per day. In 1995, Serenpet plans to drill at least 50 gross wells, including 25 exploratory wells. It plans to increase the company's drilling success rate to 70%. Drilling activity in 1995 will concentrate on those areas that offer low finding costs, ready access to markets and, a high return on investment.

In August 1994, it completed a Plan of Arrangement with Lakewood Energy Inc. for an exchange of shares. Serenpet issued 10,453,062 shares and exchanged them for all of the outstanding shares of Lakewood. The transaction almost doubled the size of Serenpet and included additional production of 2,399 barrels of oil per day and 5.5 million cubic feet of natural gas per day. In October, Serenpet sold non-core properties owned by Lakewood, which reduced debt by $26.4-million.

Capital spending in 1994 totalled $116.4-million, with the acquisition of Lakewood Energy Inc. and other property accounting for $72.8-million. Serenpet participated in the drilling of 60 gross (42.9 net) wells, of which 53 wells were operated by Serenpet. The results from the drilling program were 20 (11.1 net) oil wells, 18 (13.9 net) gas wells, and 22 (17.9 net) dry holes, with a success ratio of 63%. Production in 1994 was lower than expected due to timing delays in production, reduced exploration success, production declines in existing properties, the sale of some non-core producing properties, and lower than expected production from the Lakewood properties.

Average daily production in 1994 (1993) was: crude oil and natural gas liquids, 3,956 (2,949) barrels; and natural gas, 29.60 (17.33) million cubic feet. Proven and probable reserves in 1994 (1993) were: crude oil and natural gas liquids, 12 (7.6) million barrels; and natural gas, 204.5 (139) billion cubic feet.

Rank (Profit/Revenue/Assets)
963   582   383

Gerald D. Sutton
Chairman

E. Keith Conrad
President & C.E.O.

Douglas E. Allen
V.P., Finance & C.F.O.

Address
Suite 2300
421 - 7th Avenue S.W.
Calgary
AB
T2P 4K9
(403) 231-3000

Fax: (403) 231-3099
01001793/G/3.2

SHELL CANADA LIMITED

Exchanges	Price (Jun29'95)		42.37	Trailing P/E		10.46	Stock Symbol
TM	Trailing Yield (%)		2.36	Trailing EPS		4.05	**SHC**

Period Ending	Dec94	Dec93	Dec92	Dec91	Dec90
Yearly Statistics					
Price-Close	42.75	38.38	34.63	38.50	37.00
Price-High	46.00	44.00	46.00	45.50	42.75
Price-Low	37.25	31.50	34.00	34.50	34.38
P/E-Close	15.00	255.83	48.09	nm	13.41
Dividends per Share	1.00	0.90	0.90	0.90	0.90
Dividend Yield (%)	2.34	2.35	2.60	2.34	2.43
Sales per Share	44.89	41.94	40.08	42.23	48.00
EPS before extra. item	2.85	0.15	0.72	(1.12)	2.76
Cash Flow per Share	7.04	4.97	3.54	3.22	6.87
Book Value per Share	27.54	25.68	26.73	26.91	28.94
O/S Common Shares	112,188	112,109	112,092	112,078	112,048
Total Revenue	5,060,000	4,789,000	4,664,000	4,844,000	5,441,000
Income before extra.	320,000	16,000	80,000	(126,000)	309,000
Cash Flow	790,000	557,000	397,000	361,000	770,000
Debt/Equity	0.35	0.50	0.48	0.43	0.32
Return on Capital (%)	14.99	3.68	4.38	(0.72)	14.17
Ret. on Com. Equity (%)	10.72	0.55	2.66	(4.03)	9.78
% Change Profit	1,900.0	(80.0)	163.5	(140.8)	45.8
% Change Revenue	5.7	2.7	(3.7)	(11.0)	10.7
% Change Assets	2.2	(0.7)	1.9	(3.9)	8.5

Preferred Div. Coverage	na	na	na
Total Div. Coverage	2.9	0.2	0.8
Interest Coverage	5.6	1.3	1.5
Current Ratio	1.4	1.2	1.8
Operating Margin	12.1	4.0	2.6
Asset Turnover	0.8	0.8	0.7
5 YEAR RATIOS (%)			
Return on Capital	7.3	6.6	10.1
Return on Com. Equity	3.9	3.2	6.1
Profit Growth	8.6	(48.3)	(25.6)
Revenue Growth	0.5	(1.1)	(0.9)
Asset Growth	1.5	1.2	1.8
BALANCE SHEET (000)			
Cash	256,000	(34,000)	128,000
Current Assets	1,674,000	1,306,000	1,516,000
Net Fixed Assets	4,200,000	4,428,000	4,349,000
Invest's & Advances	239,000	245,000	159,000
Total Assets	6,113,000	5,979,000	6,024,000
Short Term Debt	228,000	388,000	147,000
Current Liabilities	1,211,000	1,071,000	849,000
Long Term Debt	849,000	1,064,000	1,279,000
Total Liabilities	3,022,000	3,099,000	3,027,000
Total Equity	3,091,000	2,880,000	2,997,000
Total Liab. & Equity	6,113,000	5,979,000	6,024,000
CAPITAL (000)			
Total Debt	1,077,000	1,452,000	1,426,000
Preferred Equity	1,000	1,000	1,000
Common Equity	3,090,000	2,879,000	2,996,000

Business:

SHELL CANADA LTD. is an integrated oil company. It has oil and gas exploration and production operations in Western Canada. The oil products division operates refineries and a network of service stations. The chemicals division produces petrochemicals for markets worldwide. Shell Investments Ltd., a wholly owned subsidiary of Shell Petroleum NV of the Netherlands, is the major shareholder.

Date	EPS	DPS	Tot Rev	Inc Bex
Mar 95	1.97	0.00	1,422,000	221,000
Dec 94	0.92	0.55	1,361,000	103,000
Sep 94	0.79	0.00	1,354,000	89,000
Jun 94	0.37	0.45	1,186,000	42,000
Mar 94	0.77	0.00	1,098,000	86,000
Dec 93	0.04	0.45	1,293,000	3,000
Sep 93	0.01	0.00	1,171,000	1,000
Jun 93	(0.03)	0.45	1,166,000	(3,000)

Synopsis:

In 1994, earnings for Shell Canada increased to $320-million from $16-million. Higher margins and volumes in the chemicals division, increases in commodity prices and production volumes in the resources division, and an overall improvement in the company's refinery operations contributed to earnings growth. Operating costs fell significantly from 1993, but are comparable to 1992 levels as the cost of additional business activity offset cost reduction measures.

For 1995, the Resources division's capital and exploration program will total $230-million. About $70-million is to be spent on exploration, focused on Western Canadian Sedimentary Basin gas, while $145-million has been allocated to development projects. Operations and marketing infrastructure projects should account for $15-million. Shell will spend $115-million on the company's refinery business, and $5-million on the Chemicals division. Shell's capital and exploration expenditures will be funded from cash flow.

During 1994 (1993), average daily production was: 77,400 (71,100) barrels of oil, bitumen and natural gas liquids; 731 (706) million cubic feet of natural gas; and 6,306 (5,528) tons of sulphur. At its 1994 (1993) year end, Shell had 290 (298) million barrels of net proven oil and condensate reserves, and 2,494 (2,588) billion cubic feet of net proven natural gas reserves. Contributions to revenue by division in 1994, before inter-segment sales were: petroleum products, 67%; resources, 17%, and chemicals, 14%.

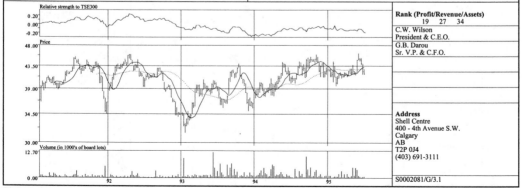

Rank (Profit/Revenue/Assets)
19   27   34
C.W. Wilson
President & C.E.O.
G.B. Darou
Sr. V.P. & C.F.O.

Address
Shell Centre
400 - 4th Avenue S.W.
Calgary
AB
T2P 0J4
(403) 691-3111

S0002081/G/3.1

STAMPEDER EXPLORATION LTD.

Exchanges	Price (Jun29'95)	4.45	Trailing P/E	14.35	Stock Symbol
T	Trailing Yield (%)	0.00	Trailing EPS	0.31	SDX

Period Ending	Dec94	May94	May93	May92	May91
Yearly Statistics	7M				
Price-Close	4.90	5.75	5.25	n t	n t
Price-High	6.38	7.63	5.25	n t	n t
Price-Low	4.50	4.15	1.45	n t	n t
P/E-Close	12.44	95.83	175.00	n t	n t
Dividends per Share	0.00	0.00	0.00	0.00	0.00
Dividend Yield (%)	0.00	0.00	0.00	0.00	0.00
Sales per Share	1.61	1.21	0.67	0.01	0.00
EPS before extra. item	0.23	0.06	0.03	(0.02)	0.00
Cash Flow per Share	0.82	0.54	0.24	(0.02)	0.01
Book Value per Share	2.43	1.89	1.47	0.04	0.05
O/S Common Shares	37,791	32,923	18,523	9,523	9,105
Total Revenue	69,823	41,354	8,744	95	158
Income before extra.	8,182	1,744	388	(198)	31
Cash Flow	18,067	15,797	3,089	(145)	61
Debt/Equity	0.70	0.97	1.10	2.78	0.51
Return on Capital (%)	12.87	4.88	5.85	(15.98)	na
Ret. on Com. Equity (%)	18.22	3.90	2.81	(49.87)	na
% Change Profit	704.3	349.5	296.0	(740.2)	na
% Change Revenue	189.4	372.9	9,114.8	(39.9)	na
% Change Assets	33.2	121.8	4,300.6	99.7	na
Preferred Div. Coverage	np	np	np		
Total Div. Coverage	na	na	na		
Interest Coverage	4.6	1.7	1.9		
Current Ratio	0.7	0.8	0.6		
Operating Margin	14.7	10.2	18.4		
Asset Turnover	0.3	0.3	0.1		
5 YEAR RATIOS (%)					
Return on Capital	na	na	na		
Return on Com. Equity	na	na	na		
Profit Growth	na	na	na		
Revenue Growth	na	na	na		
Asset Growth	na	na	na		
BALANCE SHEET (000)					
Cash	270	178	0		
Current Assets	19,233	11,398	3,107		
Net Fixed Assets	166,436	126,252	57,654		
Invest's & Advances	0	2,000	2,000		
Total Assets	186,055	139,692	62,969		
Short Term Debt	0	0	0		
Current Liabilities	26,700	14,117	4,935		
Long Term Debt	63,853	60,044	29,987		
Total Liabilities	94,337	77,438	35,718		
Total Equity	91,718	62,254	27,251		
Total Liab. & Equity	186,055	139,692	62,969		
CAPITAL (000)					
Total Debt	63,853	60,044	29,987		
Preferred Equity	0	0	0		
Common Equity	91,718	62,254	27,251		

Business:

STAMPEDER EXPLORATION LTD. is involved in the exploration, development and production of crude oil and natural gas in Alberta, Saskatchewan and British Columbia. The company's subsidiary, Stamp Gas Inc. is engaged in the business of natural gas marketing.

Date	EPS	DPS	Tot Rev	Inc Bex
Mar 95	0.09	0.00	42,331	3,353
Dec 94	0.16	0.00	41,249	5,879
Sep 94	0.07	0.00	28,574	2,303
May 94	(0.01)	0.00	16,435	(257)
Feb 94	0.02	0.00	8,671	714
Nov 93	0.02	0.00	9,212	593
Aug 93	0.03	0.00	7,036	694
May 93	(0.01)	0.00	3,378	(140)

Synopsis:

Stampeder Exploration has budgeted approximately $58-million for capital expenditures in 1995. This should include $33-million for current development projects, $23-million for future land accumulation and exploration, and $2-million on miscellaneous capital items. The budget will be financed primarily from 1995 cash flow.

During 1994, the major portion of Stampeder's capital resources went to exploration and development activities. Total capital spending in the period was $50.8-million, including $14.3-million on the acquisition of an additional working interest in the company's core oil producing field at Nipisi. Spending on exploration and development activities during the period amounted to $36.1-million, with the major focus being the Nipisi oil field. Stampeder successfully discovered or extended several natural gas plays in Alberta and Saskatchewan and an oil play in Alberta.

Approximately 91% of Stampeder's total operating sales in 1994 came from oil and natural gas liquids. About 5% came from natural gas, and 4% came from oil and currency hedging, royalties and processing fees. Stampeder plans to continue its emphasis on oil reserves and production during 1995, but gas reserves should increase, too. During 1994 Stampeder drilled 40 (35.6 net) wells, including 18 (13.6 net) oil wells, 10 (10 net) natural gas wells, and 12 (12 net) dry wells. Its success ratio was 70% (66% net). In the first quarter of 1995, Stampeder drilled 41 (35.6 net) wells, with a success ratio of 86%. The drilling resulted in 20 (19.7 net) oil wells, 16 (10.9 net) gas wells, and 5 (5 net) dry and abandoned wells.

Average daily production in the period ended December 31, 1994, (May 31, 1994) was: oil, 6,610 (4,246) barrels; natural gas, 5.2 (4.5) million cubic feet; and natural gas liquids, 146 (123) barrels. Proven and probable reserves at December 1994 (May 1994) were: oil, 29.1 (19.6) million barrels; natural gas, 87.8 (40) billion cubic feet; and gas liquids, 2.7 (1.3) million barrels.

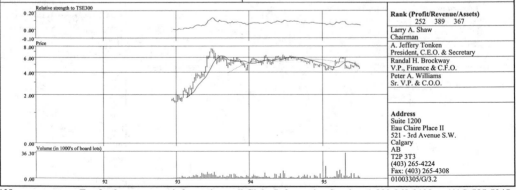

Rank (Profit/Revenue/Assets)
252 389 367

Larry A. Shaw
Chairman

A. Jeffery Tonken
President, C.E.O. & Secretary

Randal H. Brockway
V.P., Finance & C.F.O.

Peter A. Williams
Sr. V.P. & C.O.O.

Address
Suite 1200
Eau Claire Place II
521 - 3rd Avenue S.W.
Calgary
AB
T2P 3T3
(403) 265-4224
Fax: (403) 265-4308
01003305/G/3.2

SUMMIT RESOURCES LIMITED

Exchanges	Price (Jun29'95)	16.12	Trailing P/E	41.35	Stock Symbol
TZ	Trailing Yield (%)	0.25	Trailing EPS	0.39	SUI

Period Ending	Dec94	Dec93	Dec92	Dec91	Dec90	Business:
Yearly Statistics						SUMMIT RESOURCES LIMITED explores
Price-Close	8.63	8.63	4.69	3.25	4.38	for, develops, produces and markets crude oil
Price-High	11.25	12.50	4.75	4.38	6.13	and natural gas in Western Canada and the
Price-Low	8.13	4.00	2.25	3.00	3.88	Northern United States.
P/E-Close	22.12	26.95	24.04	nm	27.34	
Dividends per Share	0.04	0.04	0.02	0.00	0.00	
Dividend Yield (%)	0.46	0.46	0.32	0.00	0.00	
Sales per Share	2.91	2.13	1.35	1.18	1.55	
EPS before extra. item	0.39	0.32	0.20	(0.88)	0.16	
Cash Flow per Share	1.59	1.18	0.64	0.50	0.72	
Book Value per Share	4.07	3.69	2.41	2.23	3.10	
O/S Common Shares	28,301	28,004	21,443	21,408	21,454	
Total Revenue	81,558	52,289	28,873	25,294	30,666	
Income before extra.	10,807	7,960	4,209	(18,704)	3,183	

	Date	EPS	DPS	Tot Rev	Inc Bex
Cash Flow	44,565	29,044	13,755	10,598	14,198
	Mar 95	0.06	0.00	21,399	1,825
Debt/Equity	0.75	0.35	0.63	0.58	0.28
	Dec 94	0.10	0.02	22,740	2,668

	Dec94	Dec93	Dec92	Dec91	Dec90
Cash Flow	44,565	29,044	13,755	10,598	14,198
Debt/Equity	0.75	0.35	0.63	0.58	0.28
Return on Capital (%)	13.10	13.07	7.58	(30.67)	10.61
Ret. on Com. Equity (%)	9.89	10.28	8.48	(32.77)	5.60
% Change Profit	35.8	89.1	122.5	(687.6)	82.0
% Change Revenue	56.0	81.1	14.2	(17.5)	33.2
% Change Assets	49.7	73.4	13.0	(19.0)	16.8

Date	EPS	DPS	Tot Rev	Inc Bex
Mar 95	0.06	0.00	21,399	1,825
Dec 94	0.10	0.02	22,740	2,668
Sep 94	0.12	0.00	21,539	3,284
Jun 94	0.11	0.02	20,073	3,044
Mar 94	0.06	0.00	17,323	1,811
Dec 93	0.10	0.02	15,705	2,641
Sep 93	0.06	0.00	13,662	1,746
Jun 93	0.08	0.03	11,987	1,922

	Dec94	Dec93	Dec92
Preferred Div. Coverage	na	na	na
Total Div. Coverage	8.6	8.4	13.1
Interest Coverage	5.7	7.5	4.8
Current Ratio	0.8	1.0	1.7
Operating Margin	27.9	30.2	28.2
Asset Turnover	0.3	0.3	0.3
5 YEAR RATIOS (%)			
Return on Capital	2.7	1.7	0.9
Return on Com. Equity	0.3	(0.9)	(1.7)
Profit Growth	43.9	28.5	18.7
Revenue Growth	28.8	25.8	26.4
Asset Growth	22.6	21.4	14.7
BALANCE SHEET (000)			
Cash	656	5,452	5,189
Current Assets	17,504	13,880	9,910
Net Fixed Assets	220,279	145,013	81,734
Invest's & Advances	0	0	0
Total Assets	237,783	158,893	91,644
Short Term Debt	0	0	0
Current Liabilities	21,942	13,603	5,816
Long Term Debt	85,882	35,939	32,591
Total Liabilities	122,469	55,651	39,872
Total Equity	115,314	103,242	51,772
Total Liab. & Equity	237,783	158,893	91,644
CAPITAL (000)			
Total Debt	85,882	35,939	32,591
Preferred Equity	22	29	149
Common Equity	115,292	103,213	51,623

Synopsis:

Summit Resources plans a $50-million capital budget in 1995. The budget includes $40-million for exploration and development activities in core areas, and $10-million for select property acquisitions. Its 1995 drilling program will be split between exploration and development, with an early focus on gas projects followed by oil projects beginning in the second quarter. Summit expects to drill 60 gross (40 net) wells. Oil production in 1995 should average 7,000 barrels per day, and gas production should average 70 million cubic feet per day.

Summit's spent $100-million on capital expenditures in 1994. Exploration and development expenses were $63.5-million. This included the drilling of 82 gross wells (65.9 net) and an extensive seismic and land acquisition program. Drilling resulted in 24 gross (19.6 net) oil wells, 34 gross (25.1 net) gas wells, one gross (one net) service wells, and 23 gross (20.2 net) dry holes. The company spent $24.3-million on expanding and installing equipment and facilities, including the construction of two new gas plants and expanding two natural gas facilities. Acquisitions net of dispositions were $11.8-million and were focused on increasing interests in core areas.

In the first quarter, Summit made discoveries at Sturgeon Lake and Ante Creek Alberta. The company also increased its land holdings on the Lodgepole light oil play in North Dakota. In April 1995, Summit entered a bought deal financing agreement with five investment dealers to issue 2.5 million common shares at a price of $9.95 per share. The $23.9-million deal closed on May 16, 1995. The proceeds were applied against bank lines of credit and may be drawn down as required for exploration and development.

Average daily production in 1994 (1993) was: crude oil and natural gas liquids, 5,960 (4,619) barrels; and natural gas, 53.6 (34.1) million cubic feet. Proven and probable reserves in 1994 (1993) were: crude oil and natural gas liquids, 15 (11.2) million barrels; and natural gas, 238.0 (171.5) billion cubic feet.

Relative strength to TSE300 / Price / Volume (in 1000's of board lots)

Rank (Profit/Revenue/Assets)		
285	451	328

Ernest S. Rady
Chairman

Larry B. Krause
President & C.E.O.

Barry J. Stobo
Sr. V.P. & C.O.O.

Address
Suite 2300
144 - 4th Avenue S.W.
Calgary
AB
T2P 3N4
(403) 269-4400

Fax: (403) 269-4444
S0008354/G/3.2

SUNCOR INC.

Exchanges	Price (Jun29'95)	38.37	Trailing P/E	15.35	Stock Symbol
TMVZA	Trailing Yield (%)	2.79	Trailing EPS	2.50	**SU**

Period Ending	Dec94	Dec93	Dec92	Dec91	Dec90
Yearly Statistics					
Price-Close	32.00	30.88	n t	n t	n t
Price-High	35.50	34.88	n t	n t	n t
Price-Low	27.13	23.38	n t	n t	n t
P/E-Close	14.41	22.37	n t	16.99	10.57
Dividends per Share	1.06	1.04	1.04	1.05	0.40
Dividend Yield (%)	3.31	3.37	n t	n t	n t
Sales per Share	30.01	28.40	28.65	28.76	32.29
EPS before extra. item	2.22	1.38	(4.19)	1.42	2.27
Cash Flow per Share	6.08	4.11	3.14	6.11	6.31
Book Value per Share	18.98	17.82	17.49	22.44	22.07
O/S Common Shares	54,522	54,447	54,428	54,374	54,374
Total Revenue	1,637,000	1,549,000	1,562,000	1,566,000	1,759,000
Income before extra.	121,000	75,000	(228,000)	77,000	124,000
Cash Flow	331,000	224,000	171,000	332,000	343,000
Debt/Equity	0.22	0.23	0.21	0.12	0.20
Return on Capital (%)	16.48	11.11	(24.85)	9.97	14.27
Ret. on Com. Equity (%)	12.07	7.80	(20.99)	6.28	10.71
% Change Profit	61.3	132.9	(396.1)	(37.9)	117.5
% Change Revenue	5.7	(0.8)	(0.3)	(11.0)	18.2
% Change Assets	8.8	2.5	(11.8)	(0.9)	9.4
Preferred Div. Coverage	np	np	np		
Total Div. Coverage	2.1	1.3	0.0		
Interest Coverage	10.6	7.6	0.0		
Current Ratio	1.0	1.0	1.1		
Operating Margin	12.2	8.7	2.8		
Asset Turnover	0.7	0.8	0.8		
5 YEAR RATIOS (%)					
Return on Capital	5.4	3.8	1.1		
Return on Com. Equity	3.2	1.8	(0.7)		
Profit Growth	16.2	na	na		
Revenue Growth	1.9	2.9	2.7		
Asset Growth	1.2	(0.1)	(1.1)		
BALANCE SHEET (000)					
Cash	36,000	0	0		
Current Assets	417,000	355,000	399,000		
Net Fixed Assets	1,560,000	1,412,000	1,342,000		
Invest's & Advances	38,000	40,000	30,000		
Total Assets	2,201,000	2,023,000	1,973,000		
Short Term Debt	36,000	30,000	26,000		
Current Liabilities	420,000	340,000	350,000		
Long Term Debt	190,000	191,000	171,000		
Total Liabilities	1,166,000	1,053,000	1,021,000		
Total Equity	1,035,000	970,000	952,000		
Total Liab. & Equity	2,201,000	2,023,000	1,973,000		
CAPITAL (000)					
Total Debt	226,000	221,000	197,000		
Preferred Equity	0	0	0		
Common Equity	1,035,000	970,000	952,000		

Business:

SUNCOR INC. is a Canadian integrated oil and gas company. It explores for and produces conventional crude oil and natural gas in Western Canada where it also operates the world's first commercial oil sands plant. Suncor markets natural gas in Canada and the U.S. It has a refinery in Sarnia, Ontario, and manufactures and distributes fuels, petrochemicals, and heating oil under the Sunoco and Sunchem brands.

Date	EPS	DPS	Tot Rev	Inc Bex
Mar 95	0.68	0.27	453,000	37,000
Dec 94	0.60	0.27	430,000	33,000
Sep 94	0.78	0.27	444,000	42,000
Jun 94	0.44	0.26	389,000	24,000
Mar 94	0.40	0.26	374,000	22,000
Dec 93	0.42	0.26	388,000	23,000
Sep 93	0.53	0.26	390,000	29,000
Jun 93	0.19	0.26	397,000	10,000

Synopsis:

From 1995 to 1997, Suncor plans to reinvest in its upstream business where it sees the greatest potential for profitable growth. The company's goal is to increase cash flow by 10% per year over the next three years through a combination of higher production volumes and lower costs. Suncor anticipates total oil and natural gas production to increase to 105,000 barrels of oil equivalent (boe) in 1995, and reach 120,000 boe per day in 1998.

The Oil Sands Group plans to spend $250-million over the next three years to increase its production to more than 80,000 barrels per day in 1998. At the same time, this investment should lower unit costs and create the infrastructure for future growth. Suncor believes that past performance of this business segment has proven that mining for oil is an economical alternative to conventional exploration and development. Over the next five years, the company plans to spend up to $200-million to develop a new mine site on a recently acquired lease.

The Resources Group plans to spend $300-million over the next two years to increase reserves through focused exploration and development. Suncor plans to raise production to 40,000 boe per day in 1998, and replace 150% of production each year with new reserve additions.

Cost-cutting initiatives implemented during 1994 in the company's refineries and retail marketing business began to show positive results. The segment's 1994 cash flow increased to $93-million from $67-million in 1993.

During 1994 (1993), average daily production consisted of 70.7 (60.5) thousand barrels of synthetic crude oil, 13.8 (13) thousand barrels of oil and liquids, and 155 (148) million cubic feet of natural gas. Gross proven reserves at end of 1994 (1993) were, 52 (44) million barrels of synthetic crude oil, 205 (231) million barrels of oil and natural gas liquids, and 748 (632) billion cubic feet of natural gas reserves.

Relative strength to TSE300 / Price / Volume (in 1000's of board lots)

Rank (Profit/Revenue/Assets)
64 78 99

Richard L. George
President & C.E.O.

David W. Byler
Senior Vice President Finance

Address
36 York Mills Road
North York
ON
M2P 2C5
(416) 733-7300

Fax: (416) 733-0958
S0005839/G/3.1

TALISMAN ENERGY INC.

Exchanges	Price (Jun29'95)			25 .62	Trailing P/E		32 .03	Stock Symbol
TMV	Trailing Yield (%)			0 .00	Trailing EPS		0 .80	**TLM**

Period Ending	Dec94	Dec93	Dec92	Dec91	Dec90
Yearly Statistics					
Price-Close	23 .50	29 .00	15 .38	12 .00	16 .63
Price-High	33 .75	35 .25	15 .50	18 .00	22 .00
Price-Low	23 .00	14 .25	10 .50	11 .50	15 .38
P/E-Close	28 .66	67 .44	69 .89	nm	30 .79
Dividends per Share	0 .00	0 .00	0 .00	0 .19	0 .19
Dividend Yield (%)	0 .00	0 .00	0 .00	1 .58	1 .14
Sales per Share	9 .23	6 .53	4 .50	3 .97	5 .33
EPS before extra. item	0 .82	0 .43	0 .22	(3 .40)	0 .54
Cash Flow per Share	4 .63	3 .17	1 .72	1 .10	1 .94
Book Value per Share	16 .41	9 .28	6 .25	6 .02	9 .61
O/S Common Shares	96 ,282	66 ,169	50 ,466	50 ,466	50 ,462
Total Revenue	760 ,696	408 ,950	243 ,044	106 ,887	285 ,308
Income before extra.	64 ,041	25 ,829	11 ,178	(171 ,539)	27 ,434
Cash Flow	361 ,517	189 ,391	86 ,590	55 ,622	98 ,056
Debt/Equity	0 .76	0 .40	0 .01	0 .60	0 .22
Return on Capital (%)	8 .80	11 .85	8 .29	(40 .45)	7 .55
Ret. on Com. Equity (%)	5 .84	5 .56	3 .61	(43 .48)	5 .68
% Change Profit	147 .9	131 .1	106 .5	(725 .3)	53 .0
% Change Revenue	86 .0	68 .3	127 .4	(62 .5)	(28 .9)
% Change Assets	201 .4	142 .2	(25 .3)	(26 .6)	(9 .2)

Preferred Div. Coverage	np	np	np
Total Div. Coverage	na	na	na
Interest Coverage	3 .9	6 .0	2 .5
Current Ratio	1 .8	1 .0	1 .0
Operating Margin	15 .3	9 .5	6 .6
Asset Turnover	0 .2	0 .4	0 .5
5 YEAR RATIOS (%)			
Return on Capital	(0 .8)	(1 .7)	(3 .8)
Return on Com. Equity	(4 .6)	(5 .0)	(5 .8)
Profit Growth	29 .0	36 .1	(24 .2)
Revenue Growth	13 .7	3 .3	(7 .4)
Asset Growth	29 .4	4 .2	(12 .0)
BALANCE SHEET (000)			
Cash	34 ,303	542	7 ,528
Current Assets	425 ,979	130 ,462	55 ,477
Net Fixed Assets	2 ,772 ,076	908 ,531	325 ,392
Invest's & Advances	0	0	11 ,098
Total Assets	3 ,259 ,259	1 ,081 ,298	446 ,390
Short Term Debt	0	0	0
Current Liabilities	241 ,349	130 ,110	58 ,325
Long Term Debt	1 ,202 ,556	245 ,839	1 ,503
Total Liabilities	1 ,678 ,941	466 ,961	131 ,237
Total Equity	1 ,580 ,318	614 ,337	315 ,153
Total Liab. & Equity	3 ,259 ,259	1 ,081 ,298	446 ,390
CAPITAL (000)			
Total Debt	1 ,202 ,556	245 ,839	1 ,503
Preferred Equity	0	0	0
Common Equity	1 ,580 ,318	614 ,337	315 ,153

Business:

TALISMAN ENERGY INC. is a senior oil and gas explorer and producer, active both domestically and internationally. The company is the third largest natural gas producer in Canada.

Date	EPS	DPS	Tot Rev	Inc Bex
Mar 95	0 .25	0 .00	288 ,540	23 ,672
Dec 94	0 .21	0 .00	272 ,954	19 ,957
Sep 94	0 .18	0 .00	207 ,705	15 ,197
Jun 94	0 .16	0 .00	143 ,285	15 ,566
Mar 94	0 .20	0 .00	136 ,614	13 ,321
Dec 93	0 .10	0 .00	140 ,881	6 ,604
Sep 93	0 .07	0 .00	118 ,512	4 ,341
Jun 93	0 .10	0 .00	88 ,360	7 ,015

Synopsis:

In 1995, Talisman Energy plans to spend between $400-million and $500-million on exploration and development projects. In Canada, the company will invest primarily on operated gas properties and on operated oil properties. Internationally, Talisman will divide capital spending between the North Sea and Indonesia. The company will reduce investment in the event of sustained low natural gas prices and may defer spending on some natural gas facilities and well tie-ins. Some natural gas development programs may be slowed, or Talisman will divert the money to oil projects.

In August 1994, Talisman bought Bow Valley Energy Inc. This added $1.9-million of property, plant, and equipment to the company's balance sheet. The purchase brought Talisman strategic positions in the North Sea and Indonesia.

Total capital expenditures in 1994 were $429.3-million, including $327.4-million for exploration and development, $98.2-million for resource property acquisitions, and $3.7-million for corporate expenditures. Exploration and development spending in Canada were 76% of total, with the remainder spent internationally.

During the first quarter of 1995, Talisman participated in 19 (12.9 net) exploration wells, resulting in 10 (6.7 net) gas wells, 4 (3 net) oil wells, and 5 (3.2 net) dry holes. The company also participated in 140 (50.5 net) development wells, resulting in 77 (22.1 net) gas wells, 48 (21 net) oil wells, and 15 (7.4 net) dry holes.

Average daily production in 1994 (1993) was: crude oil, natural gas liquids, and synthetic oil; 51,782 (28,985) barrels and natural gas, 496 (338) million cubic feet. Proven and probable reserves in 1994 (1993) were: oil, gas liquids, and synthetic oil; 314.7 (162.2) million barrels, natural gas; 3,142.4 (1,810.9) billion cubic feet, and sulphur, 3.8 (2.4) million tons. Contributions to gross sales in 1994 by resource product were: oil, natural gas liquids, and synthetic oil; 52% and natural gas; 48%.

Relative strength to TSE300 / Price / Volume (in 1000's of board lots) chart

Rank (Profit/Revenue/Assets)		
97	146	65

S. Keith McWalter
Chairman

James Buckee
President & C.E.O.

Wayne Bobye
V.P. Finance & C.F.O.

Address
Suite 2400
855 - 2nd Street S.W.
Calgary
AB
T2P 4J9
(403) 237-1234

Fax: (403) 237-1902
B0016718/G/3.2

TARRAGON OIL AND GAS LIMITED

Exchanges	Price (Jun29'95)	14.00	Trailing P/E		20.59	Stock Symbol
TM	Trailing Yield (%)	0.00	Trailing EPS		0.68	**TN**

Period Ending	Dec94	Dec93	Dec92	Dec91	Dec90
Yearly Statistics					
Price-Close	14.25	17.25	8.25	4.06	2.40
Price-High	19.00	22.50	8.38	4.25	3.80
Price-Low	13.63	8.25	3.63	2.00	2.00
P/E-Close	20.07	37.50	29.46	45.14	nm
Dividends per Share	0.00	0.00	0.00	0.00	0.00
Dividend Yield (%)	0.00	0.00	0.00	0.00	0.00
Sales per Share	3.74	2.53	1.20	0.90	0.42
EPS before extra. item	0.71	0.46	0.28	0.09	0.00
Cash Flow per Share	2.25	1.54	0.75	0.45	0.21
Book Value per Share	6.58	5.01	3.02	2.25	2.08
O/S Common Shares	37,827	34,541	24,295	20,705	17,432
Total Revenue	143,718	78,227	29,130	17,454	7,768
Income before extra.	26,336	14,076	6,503	2,078	428
Cash Flow	83,331	47,284	17,635	8,595	3,527
Debt/Equity	0.47	0.52	0.36	0.41	0.19
Return on Capital (%)	15.54	14.40	13.28	8.69	3.99
Ret. on Com. Equity (%)	12.48	11.42	10.83	4.15	(1.47)
% Change Profit	87.1	116.5	212.9	385.5	224.2
% Change Revenue	83.7	168.5	66.9	124.7	32.8
% Change Assets	41.5	162.6	51.5	52.7	28.6

Date	EPS	DPS	Tot Rev	Inc Bex
Mar 95	0.07	0.00	36,908	2,690
Dec 94	0.17	0.00	35,884	6,384
Sep 94	0.22	0.00	42,574	8,322
Jun 94	0.22	0.00	36,380	8,242
Mar 94	0.10	0.00	28,880	3,388
Dec 93	0.09	0.00	25,731	3,191
Sep 93	0.16	0.00	26,810	5,267
Jun 93	0.12	0.00	14,532	3,302

Preferred Div. Coverage	np	np	np
Total Div. Coverage	na	na	na
Interest Coverage	7.2	7.4	8.4
Current Ratio	0.6	0.6	4.0
Operating Margin	31.5	32.9	36.3
Asset Turnover	0.3	0.2	0.2
5 YEAR RATIOS (%)			
Return on Capital	11.2	8.8	5.8
Return on Com. Equity	7.5	(816.5)	(827.6)
Profit Growth	188.3	196.0	138.4
Revenue Growth	89.7	81.9	89.4
Asset Growth	61.6	59.8	30.2
BALANCE SHEET (000)			
Cash	92	252	650
Current Assets	26,155	18,379	26,593
Net Fixed Assets	422,147	298,504	92,395
Invest's & Advances	0	0	1,680
Total Assets	448,302	316,883	120,668
Short Term Debt	0	0	0
Current Liabilities	43,399	29,811	6,648
Long Term Debt	115,934	89,672	26,392
Total Liabilities	199,418	143,815	47,213
Total Equity	248,884	173,068	73,455
Total Liab. & Equity	448,302	316,883	120,668
CAPITAL (000)			
Total Debt	115,934	89,672	26,392
Preferred Equity	0	0	0
Common Equity	248,884	173,068	73,455

Business:

TARRAGON OIL AND GAS LIMITED is involved in the acquisition, exploration and development of petroleum and natural gas properties.

Synopsis:

Tarragon Oil and Gas set its capital budget at $140-million and allocated $50-million to property purchases in 1995. The budget reflects deteriorating gas prices and increasing interest rates. Tarragon does not believe its reduced capital budget will affect projected production volumes.

Tarragon is anticipating combined production growth of nearly 20% over 1994. Crude oil production should average 12,000 barrels per day, while natural gas should average 125 million cubic feet per day, after accounting for voluntary curtailment. The increase will come from various tie-ins throughout southern and central Alberta, together with the startup of new facilities in northeast British Columbia during the first half of 1995. The company's natural gas curtailment in 1995 is estimated at 25 million cubic feet per day. This is the result of development projects being delayed and reduced spot market sales from existing properties.

In March 1995, Tarragon issued four million treasury shares at $12.00 per share on a bought deal basis. The issue raised net proceeds of $46-million net, which went to reduce bank debt. This allows the company to go ahead with its 1995 capital expenditures with only a minor increase in bank debt. Tarragon will fund the 1995 capital program primarily from cash flow.

Average daily production in 1994 (1994) was: oil, 9,433 (6,706) barrels; and natural gas, 111.6 (54) million cubic feet. Proven and probable reserves in 1994 (1993) were: oil, 35.4 (28.5) million barrels; and natural gas, 518.5 (492.7) billion cubic feet.

Rank (Profit/Revenue/Assets)
181 368 239

Joseph L. Rotman
Chairman

Ed Chwyl
President & C.E.O.

Raymond T. Chan
V.P. Finance & Secretary

Address
500 - 4th Avenue S.W.
Suite 2500
Calgary
AB
T2P 2V6
(403) 974-7500

Fax: (403) 262-5324
N0000940/G/3.2

TOTAL PETROLEUM (NORTH AMERICA) LTD.

Exchanges	Price (Jun29'95)	14.75	Trailing P/E	nm	Stock Symbol
TMA	Trailing Yield (%)	1.25	Trailing EPS	(0.13)	**TPN**

Period Ending	Dec94	Dec93	Dec92	Dec91	Dec90
Yearly Statistics	US	US	US	US	US
Price-Close	17.38	14.25	7.50	12.63	23.25
Price-High	25.00	17.25	13.38	29.50	33.75
Price-Low	14.25	7.13	5.13	12.50	22.75
P/E-Close	14.72	12.00	171.44	nm	14.71
Dividends per Share	0.23	0.05	0.30	0.80	0.80
Dividend Yield (%)	1.77	0.45	4.86	7.26	4.02
Sales per Share	58.40	62.25	65.04	73.92	87.09
EPS before extra. item	0.63	0.71	0.03	(0.45)	1.16
Cash Flow per Share	2.47	2.76	1.60	1.64	3.49
Book Value per Share	12.38	11.97	11.28	11.68	14.30
O/S Common Shares	38,005	37,459	37,422	36,288	30,983
Total Revenue	2,204,600	2,330,500	2,397,000	2,486,200	2,657,700
Income before extra.	23,800	27,500	2,100	(11,500)	42,000
Cash Flow	93,200	103,500	58,800	55,000	106,600
Debt/Equity	0.92	0.96	0.61	0.41	0.22
Return on Capital (%)	6.83	7.64	2.33	(0.63)	11.36
Ret. on Com. Equity (%)	5.18	6.16	0.33	(3.01)	8.24
% Change Profit	(13.5)	1,209.5	118.3	(127.4)	(12.9)
% Change Revenue	(5.4)	(2.8)	(3.6)	(6.5)	22.4
% Change Assets	8.1	16.7	3.9	(9.6)	(0.4)

Preferred Div. Coverage	np	np	3.0
Total Div. Coverage	2.8	11.0	0.2
Interest Coverage	2.7	5.4	1.3
Current Ratio	1.2	1.2	1.2
Operating Margin	2.8	2.6	0.6
Asset Turnover	1.6	1.8	2.2
5 YEAR RATIOS (%)			
Return on Capital	5.5	6.9	9.7
Return on Com. Equity	3.4	4.8	9.2
Profit Growth	(13.2)	(17.7)	na
Revenue Growth	0.3	4.9	6.5
Asset Growth	3.3	5.5	1.2
BALANCE SHEET (000)			
Cash	8,500	6,200	17,700
Current Assets	437,700	368,600	368,000
Net Fixed Assets	904,700	882,200	702,800
Invest's & Advances	0	0	0
Total Assets	1,363,700	1,261,400	1,080,900
Short Term Debt	0	0	0
Current Liabilities	351,400	304,000	316,700
Long Term Debt	433,800	428,200	264,200
Total Liabilities	893,100	813,000	645,800
Total Equity	470,600	448,400	435,100
Total Liab. & Equity	1,363,700	1,261,400	1,080,900
CAPITAL (000)			
Total Debt	433,800	428,200	264,200
Preferred Equity	0	0	13,100
Common Equity	470,600	448,400	422,000

Business:

TOTAL PETROLEUM (NORTH AMERICA) LTD. is an independent petroleum company with refinery and marketing operations in the central United States. The company markets its petroleum products under the brand name Total in twelve states in the Central United States. Total S.A., which is headquartered in France owns 54% of the company's voting shares.

Date		EPS	DPS	Tot Rev	Inc Bex
Mar 95	US	(0.42)	0.08	475,200	(16,000)
Dec 94	US	(0.12)	0.06	572,300	(4,700)
Sep 94	US	0.40	0.05	622,600	15,200
Jun 94	US	0.01	0.00	542,000	400
Mar 94	US	0.34	0.05	467,700	12,900
Dec 93	US	0.19	0.05	558,700	7,400
Sep 93	US	0.35	0.00	628,300	13,300
Jun 93	US	0.32	0.00	628,700	12,100

Synopsis:

Over the next three years, Total Petroleum plans to increase its branded marketing business by 50%. This growth will occur through construction of new retail stores, an expanded branded distributor network, and selected acquisitions. By 1997, the company plans to grow its branded marketing activities to a point where 100% of all gasoline and diesel fuels produced in its refineries will be sold through its network, as opposed to the current 65%.

Continued efforts are being made to enhance operational flexibility and profitability. Total Petroleum plans to build new proprietary pipelines in the mid-continent, enhance its storage and distribution capabilities in central Michigan, the mid-continent, and the western slope of Colorado, and further reduce transpiration costs. Further reductions in raw material, power, and operating material costs are expected to improve the refining operations' profit margins. At the same time, the company will increase production of higher value products, such as aviation gasoline, solvents, premium gasoline, and premium diesel.

Weak market conditions and a scheduled turnaround in one of the company's refineries in the first quarter of 1995, resulted in a decline in its refining and wholesale operations' gross margin. Market conditions that prevailed resulted from the combined impact of unseasonably mild weather keeping distillate supplies high, unstable gasoline markets due to the introduction of reformulated gasoline, and a continued squeeze on the differential between sweet and sour crude oil prices. Retail marketing operations income improved to $5.1-million during this same period, despite the operation of 6% fewer stores. While growing sales per store, the company was able to maintain strong fuel and merchandise margins.

Relative strength to TSE300 / Price / Volume (in 1000's of board lots)

Rank (Profit/Revenue/Assets)
147 50 108
Jean-Paul Veltier Chairman
C. Gary Jones President & C.E.O.
Richard E. Dana C.F.O.

Address
Total Tower
900 19th Street
Denver
CO
80202
(303) 291-2000

Fax: (303) 291-2113
T0002162/G/3.1

TRANSWEST ENERGY INC.

Exchanges	Price (Jun29'95)	1.22	Trailing P/E		17.43	Stock Symbol
TMZ	Trailing Yield (%)	0.00	Trailing EPS		0.07	**TWE**

Period Ending	Dec94	Dec93	May93	May92	May91
Yearly Statistics		7M			
Price-Close	1.80	2.45	2.05	0.65	0.75
Price-High	2.95	3.70	2.15	0.90	2.00
Price-Low	1.45	0.44	0.37	0.30	0.60
P/E-Close	16.36	72.06	nm	nm	nm
Dividends per Share	0.00	0.00	0.00	0.00	0.00
Dividend Yield (%)	0.00	0.00	0.00	0.00	0.00
Sales per Share	0.86	0.83	0.73	1.05	1.40
EPS before extra. item	0.11	0.02	(0.03)	(0.39)	(0.14)
Cash Flow per Share	0.53	0.39	0.23	0.16	0.32
Book Value per Share	1.07	1.00	0.65	0.67	1.11
O/S Common Shares	50,380	49,985	40,235	39,790	23,905
Total Revenue	50,660	24,605	31,500	31,675	38,080
Income before extra.	6,860	2,065	(7,705)	(645)	
Cash Flow	26,280	10,465	9,370	3,925	7,755
Debt/Equity	0.55	0.53	0.48	0.41	0.58
Return on Capital (%)	13.67	12.10	4.60	(10.74)	4.45
Ret. on Com. Equity (%)	10.67	3.49	(4.82)	(36.75)	(11.92)
% Change Profit	93.8	440.5	108.5	(1,094.6)	(114.6)
% Change Revenue	20.1	33.9	(0.6)	(16.8)	(27.0)
% Change Assets	13.1	39.0	5.1	(14.8)	(4.8)

Date	EPS	DPS	Tot Rev	Inc Bex
Mar 95	0.00	0.00	8,684	563
Dec 94	0.02	0.00	10,324	1,411
Sep 94	0.02	0.00	9,877	1,274
Jun 94	0.03	0.00	10,068	1,684
Mar 94	0.04	0.00	10,581	2,491
Dec 93	0.02	0.00	10,549	1,298
Nov 93	0.01	0.00	7,741	961
Sep 93	0.01	0.00	7,852	912

Preferred Div. Coverage	5.1	1.6	0.3
Total Div. Coverage	5.1	1.6	0.3
Interest Coverage	5.5	3.9	2.0
Current Ratio	0.5	0.8	0.8
Operating Margin	26.0	21.3	1.6
Asset Turnover	0.3	0.3	0.4
5 YEAR RATIOS (%)			
Return on Capital	4.8	4.9	2.9
Return on Com. Equity	(7.9)	(9.0)	(13.1)
Profit Growth	9.2	na	26.8
Revenue Growth	(0.6)	(2.7)	(7.9)
Asset Growth	6.0	(1.0)	(9.1)
BALANCE SHEET (000)			
Cash	0	0	0
Current Assets	5,815	8,360	4,920
Net Fixed Assets	124,230	106,490	61,260
Invest's & Advances	0	0	16,515
Total Assets	130,240	115,175	82,835
Short Term Debt	245	395	365
Current Liabilities	10,915	10,305	5,833
Long Term Debt	37,060	32,265	20,355
Total Liabilities	62,380	52,980	39,545
Total Equity	67,860	62,195	43,290
Total Liab. & Equity	130,240	115,175	82,835
CAPITAL (000)			
Total Debt	37,305	32,660	20,720
Preferred Equity	14,185	12,445	17,355
Common Equity	53,675	49,750	25,935

Business:

TRANSWEST ENERGY INC. is an oil and gas exploration and production company. It also markets and gathers natural gas. The company has producing wells and exploration activities in western Canada.

Synopsis:

Transwest Energy's capital spending for 1995 is forcast to be about $18.5-million. The bulk of it will be spent on developing the Cold Lake property. The capital budget should not exceed internally generated cash flows. All capital spending in 1994 was funded by cash flow, except the Cold Lake purchase. It was funded principally with debt.

In June 1994, Transwest bought gas properties adjacent to its gathering system in the Cold Lake area of Alberta for $8.5-million plus a limited net profits interest. This acquisition included five producing and 11 shut-in gas wells with an estimated 14 billion cubic feet of proven reserves, seven billion cubic feet of probable reserves, and 12,000 acres of undeveloped land.

Transwest participated in 52 gross (26.5 net) wells in 1994. The 44 working interest wells resulted in 14 oil and 16 gas wells. The nine farm-out wells (drilled at no cost to Transwest) resulted in five oil wells and three gas wells.

In the fourth quarter of 1994, Transwest participated at a 25% working interest in its first well in northeast British Columbia. This resulted in a new pool gas discovery on a large Debolt structure at the company's Sikanni prospect.

Average daily production in 1994 (1993) before royalties was: gas, 45.6 (45.2) million cubic feet; and oil, 1,440 (1,323) barrels. Total reserves before royalties in 1994 (1993) were: gas, 112.8 (108.4) billion cubic feet; and oil, 4.4 (4.3) million barrels.

Rank (Profit/Revenue/Assets)
376   546   428

Edward W. Best
Chairman
J. Joseph Ciavarra Jr.
President & C.E.O.

Address
4th Floor
Bow Valley Square III
255 - 5th Avenue S.W.
Calgary
AB
T2P 3G6
(403) 261-5500
Fax: (403) 264-3013
C0029839/G/3.2

TRI LINK RESOURCES LTD.

Exchanges	Price (Jun29'95)	14.75	Trailing P/E	24.70	Stock Symbol
T	Trailing Yield (%)	0.00	Trailing EPS	0.44	**TLR**

Period Ending	Mar94	Mar93	Mar92	Mar91	Mar90	Business:
Yearly Statistics						TRI LINK RESOURCES LTD. is an
Price-Close	14.13	14.38	5.88	4.95	nt	independent oil and natural gas exploration,
Price-High	16.00	14.75	6.75	6.50	nt	development and production company
Price-Low	11.25	5.50	5.00	4.20	nt	operating primarily in Saskatchewan and
P/E-Close	100.89	49.57	53.41	12.07	nt	Alberta.
Dividends per Share	0.00	0.00	0.00	0.00	0.02	
Dividend Yield (%)	0.00	0.00	0.00	0.00	nt	
Sales per Share	1.81	2.01	1.43	2.28	1.91	
EPS before extra. item	0.14	0.29	0.11	0.41	0.17	
Cash Flow per Share	0.99	1.11	0.66	1.33	0.93	
Book Value per Share	6.69	4.83	3.77	3.18	2.11	
O/S Common Shares	18,805	14,368	11,094	8,089	4,345	
Total Revenue	30,098	25,634	13,682	14,172	8,309	
Income before extra.	2,208	3,897	1,165	2,859	1,167	

Date	EPS	DPS	Tot Rev	Inc Bex
Mar 95	0.09	0.00	14,447	1,670
Dec 94	0.12	0.00	13,075	2,214
Sep 94	0.11	0.00	12,168	2,165
Jun 94	0.12	0.00	10,959	2,217
Mar 94	0.00	0.00	7,976	(16)
Dec 93	0.04	0.00	7,870	658
Sep 93	0.03	0.00	6,963	428
Jun 93	0.07	0.00	7,603	1,138

	Mar94	Mar93	Mar92	Mar91	Mar90
Cash Flow	16,363	14,115	6,349	8,255	4,028
Debt/Equity	0.07	0.15	0.30	0.44	0.67
Return on Capital (%)	4.60	12.47	5.14	17.17	10.42
Ret. on Com. Equity (%)	2.26	7.01	3.45	15.16	8.38
% Change Profit	(43.3)	234.4	(59.2)	145.0	142.2
% Change Revenue	17.4	87.4	(3.5)	70.6	43.8
% Change Assets	32.3	63.1	49.6	37.8	27.9

				Synopsis:
Preferred Div. Coverage	np	np	np	
Total Div. Coverage	na	na	na	
Interest Coverage	62.2	13.0	3.5	
Current Ratio	0.9	0.4	1.1	
Operating Margin	16.3	32.6	17.2	
Asset Turnover	0.2	0.2	0.2	
5 YEAR RATIOS (%)				
Return on Capital	10.0	10.1	na	
Return on Com. Equity	7.3	7.0	na	
Profit Growth	35.6	32.4	na	
Revenue Growth	39.1	36.7	na	
Asset Growth	41.5	37.4	na	
BALANCE SHEET (000)				
Cash	0	0	266	
Current Assets	8,293	3,929	3,114	
Net Fixed Assets	145,013	91,939	59,922	
Invest's & Advances	0	0	0	
Total Assets	153,306	115,869	71,036	
Short Term Debt	1,069	2,215	0	
Current Liabilities	9,536	9,613	2,797	
Long Term Debt	7,230	8,150	12,550	
Total Liabilities	27,463	46,518	29,188	
Total Equity	125,843	69,351	41,848	
Total Liab. & Equity	153,306	115,869	71,036	
CAPITAL (000)				
Total Debt	8,299	10,365	12,550	
Preferred Equity	0	0	0	
Common Equity	125,843	69,351	41,848	

Synopsis:

Tri Link Resources capital program's focus will be on growing its light and medium gravity oil production base through continued development of properties discovered in its core Hazelwood project area over the last two years. The capital program for fiscal 1996 consists of $65-million, with $50-million used for development drilling, facilities construction, and workovers. The development program involves drilling 80 wells, with at least 75 vertical and horizontal wells focused in the Hazelwood oil producing area.

Exploration expenditures of $15-million are allocated to land acquisition, seismic and exploration drilling, for fiscal 1996. The program includes drilling five new exploratory gas prospects and 10 new exploratory oil prospects in the Hazelwood area. The company will defer extensive development of natural gas for one to three years, pending stabilization of demand, supply and price.

Tri Link's drilling program for the year ended March 1995 consisted of 75 wells (74 net), resulting in 47 oil wells, 7 gas wells, three saltwater disposal wells, 11 wells cased for horizontal re-entry and seven dry holes. During the year its exploration program was focused on the Hazelwood/White Bear project in southeast Saskatchewan and the Seal gas area of north central Alberta. Approximately 65% of Tri Link's $69-million capital expenditures in fiscal 1995 were directed to development, primarily allocated to new, light gravity reserves at Hazelwood "G" and White Bear.

About 90% of Tri Link's production is composed of light and medium gravity oil. Average daily production in fiscal 1995 (1994) was: oil, 7,692 (6,170); and natural gas 7.8 (3.8) million cubic feet. For the year ending March 31, 1995, (1994) proven and probable reserves were: oil, 46.6 (36.6) million barrels; and natural gas 60.2 (46.1) billion cubic feet.

Relative strength to TSE300 / Price / Volume (in 1000's of board lots)

Rank (Profit/Revenue/Assets)
556 649 390
Gary W. Burns
President & C.E.O.
James B. McCashin
V.P., Corp. Affairs & C.F.O.
Dennis R. Goruk
C.O.O.

Address
10th Floor
550 - 6th Avenue S.W.
Calgary
AB
T2P 0S2
(403) 262-4601

Fax: (403) 265-0892
01003045/G/3.2

ULSTER PETROLEUMS LTD.

Exchanges	Price (Jun29'95)	5 .12	Trailing P/E	30 .15	Stock Symbol
T	Trailing Yield (%)	0 .00	Trailing EPS	0 .17	**ULP**

Period Ending	Dec94	Dec93	Dec92	Dec91	Dec90
Yearly Statistics					
Price-Close	4 .60	4 .75	3 .30	2 .70	3 .30
Price-High	4 .85	6 .63	3 .40	3 .45	3 .95
Price-Low	3 .90	3 .15	1 .85	2 .45	2 .40
P/E-Close	27 .06	95 .00	47 .14	67 .50	22 .00
Dividends per Share	0 .00	0 .00	0 .00	0 .00	0 .00
Dividend Yield (%)	0 .00	0 .00	0 .00	0 .00	0 .00
Sales per Share	1 .21	0 .80	0 .69	0 .55	0 .61
EPS before extra. item	0 .17	0 .05	0 .07	0 .04	0 .15
Cash Flow per Share	0 .85	0 .54	0 .42	0 .32	0 .42
Book Value per Share	3 .27	3 .12	2 .60	2 .54	2 .54
O/S Common Shares	50 ,992	50 ,743	33 ,954	33 ,942	33 ,389
Total Revenue	61 ,701	35 ,092	23 ,267	18 ,784	19 ,905
Income before extra.	8 ,700	2 ,040	2 ,350	1 ,310	4 ,757
Cash Flow	43 ,360	23 ,586	14 ,425	10 ,781	13 ,561
Debt/Equity	0 .90	0 .33	0 .44	0 .31	0 .13
Return on Capital (%)	7 .11	4 .28	4 .88	3 .98	9 .13
Ret. on Com. Equity (%)	5 .35	1 .65	2 .69	1 .53	6 .17
% Change Profit	326 .5	(13 .2)	79 .4	(72 .5)	41 .7
% Change Revenue	75 .8	50 .8	23 .9	(5 .6)	21 .3
% Change Assets	54 .3	63 .8	12 .4	16 .8	17 .1

Business:

ULSTER PETROLEUMS LTD. is an oil and gas exploration and production company. Its producing wells and exploration activities are located in Alberta. The company sells natural gas to customers in Alberta and the United States.

Date	EPS	DPS	Tot Rev	Inc Bex
Mar 95	0 .04	0 .00	17 ,088	1 ,831
Dec 94	0 .04	0 .00	15 ,097	2 ,317
Sep 94	0 .04	0 .00	17 ,460	2 ,176
Jun 94	0 .05	0 .00	16 ,703	2 ,428
Mar 94	0 .04	0 .00	12 ,441	1 ,779
Dec 93	(0 .02)	0 .00	9 ,497	(851)
Sep 93	0 .01	0 .00	11 ,573	307
Jun 93	0 .03	0 .00	7 ,066	1 ,352

Preferred Div. Coverage	np	np	np
Total Div. Coverage	na	na	na
Interest Coverage	3 .7	3 .1	2 .2
Current Ratio	1 .0	4 .9	0 .6
Operating Margin	30 .4	21 .9	25 .2
Asset Turnover	0 .2	0 .2	0 .2
5 YEAR RATIOS (%)			
Return on Capital	5 .9	6 .0	6 .0
Return on Com. Equity	3 .5	3 .4	3 .6
Profit Growth	21 .0	3 .4	(1 .6)
Revenue Growth	30 .3	25 .0	17 .6
Asset Growth	31 .1	24 .1	13 .0
BALANCE SHEET (000)			
Cash	7	31 ,536	8
Current Assets	69 ,626	42 ,782	2 ,977
Net Fixed Assets	283 ,857	186 ,338	136 ,869
Invest's & Advances	0	0	0
Total Assets	353 ,483	229 ,120	139 ,846
Short Term Debt	55 ,371	0	0
Current Liabilities	69 ,187	8 ,650	4 ,969
Long Term Debt	95 ,384	52 ,217	39 ,107
Total Liabilities	186 ,581	70 ,690	51 ,438
Total Equity	166 ,902	158 ,430	88 ,408
Total Liab. & Equity	353 ,483	229 ,120	139 ,846
CAPITAL (000)			
Total Debt	150 ,755	52 ,217	39 ,107
Preferred Equity	0	0	0
Common Equity	166 ,902	158 ,430	88 ,408

Synopsis:

In the first quarter of 1995, Ulster Petroleums' average daily production of crude oil was 7,000 barrels per day and natural gas was 51.7 million cubic feet. During its winter drilling, Ulster drilled 39 gross wells (22.2 net), including 13 gross (7.5 net) successful exploratory wells. The 14 development wells drilled, resulted in six gross (4.7 net) oil wells and eight gross (4.2 net) natural gas wells. Total drilling in 1995 should see 100 wells, with a 70/30 split between natural gas and crude oil, and 60/40 split between exploration and development.

Ulster's drilling activity in 1994 totalled 70 gross wells, with a success ratio of 80%. The company drilled 38 gross (16.4 net) development wells, resulting in 27 gross (10.3 net) oil wells, six gross (3.2 net) natural gas, and five gross (2.9 net) dry holes. There were 32 gross (18.2 net) exploratory wells drilled, including five gross (3.5 net) oil wells, 18 gross (8.9 net) natural gas wells and nine gross (5.8 net) dry holes.

Ulster's capital expenditures in 1994 amounted to $141.5-million. This total was broken down into $24.2-million for drilling and completion, $8-million for undeveloped lands, $7.5-million for geological and geophysical expenditures, $82.4-million for reserve acquisitions, and $19.4-million for production facilities and equipment. Reserve dispositions during the period resulted in $15.1-million.

Average daily production in 1994 (1993) totalled: crude oil and natural gas liquids, 5,200 (3,100) barrels; and natural gas, 52.4 (33.1) million cubic feet. Gross proven and probable reserves in 1994 (1993) were: crude oil and natural gas liquids, 25.6 (13.3) million barrels; and natural gas, 217.2 (135.1) billion cubic feet.

Relative strength to TSE300

Price

Volume (in 1000's of board lots)

Rank (Profit/Revenue/Assets)
318   502   267
Donne C. Traxel
President
Judy Stripling
V.P. Finance & C.F.O.

Address
Suite 1400
144 - 4th Avenue S.W.
Sun Life Plaza I
Calgary
AB
T2P 3N4
(403) 269-0400
Fax: (403) 264-5835
U0000283/G/3.2

For further company information, call Globe Information Services 1-800-268-9128 or (416) 585-5345

WASCANA ENERGY INC.

Exchanges	Price (Jun29'95)	12.12	Trailing P/E	50.50	Stock Symbol
TM	Trailing Yield (%)	0.00	Trailing EPS	0.24	WE

Period Ending	Dec94	Dec93	Dec92	Dec91	Dec90	Business:
Yearly Statistics						WASCANA ENERGY INC. is an oil and gas
Price-Close	10.00	8.25	4.85	6.63	13.00	exploration and production company. It has
Price-High	12.00	11.50	6.25	13.00	16.13	producing wells and exploration activities in
Price-Low	7.75	4.10	4.25	6.00	12.38	western Canada. The company markets its
P/E-Close	16.13	nm	nm	nm	61.91	production across North America. The
Dividends per Share	0.00	0.00	0.00	0.00	0.00	Saskatchewan Oil and Gas Corporation
Dividend Yield (%)	0.00	0.00	0.00	0.00	0.00	Amendment Act, 1992, allows ownership of the
Sales per Share	5.52	5.26	5.68	4.68	5.52	voting shares of the company to a maximum of
EPS before extra. item	0.62	(0.46)	(0.57)	(1.10)	0.21	35% for non-citizens of Canada. Maximum
Cash Flow per Share	2.32	1.76	1.71	1.21	2.09	individual ownership is 10%.
Book Value per Share	7.22	6.60	6.68	7.27	10.85	
O/S Common Shares	79,500	79,200	68,800	68,364	68,146	
Total Revenue	475,400	384,900	389,200	319,900	346,691	
Income before extra.	49,000	(33,700)	(39,000)	(74,900)	14,723	
Cash Flow	183,700	130,300	117,400	82,600	130,363	
Debt/Equity	0.30	0.50	0.89	0.91	0.48	
Return on Capital (%)	8.99	0.58	0.78	(2.80)	7.29	
Ret. on Com. Equity (%)	8.94	(6.86)	(8.16)	(12.12)	1.96	
% Change Profit	245.4	13.6	47.9	(608.7)	90.2	
% Change Revenue	23.5	(1.1)	21.7	(7.7)	51.4	
% Change Assets	(11.4)	(1.0)	(4.3)	(10.8)	10.3	

Date	EPS	DPS	Tot Rev	Inc Bex
Mar 95	0.02	0.00	115,100	1,800
Dec 94	0.07	0.00	110,900	5,100
Sep 94	0.09	0.00	126,700	6,900
Jun 94	0.06	0.00	110,000	4,500
Mar 94	0.41	0.00	127,200	32,500
Dec 93	0.01	0.00	111,900	600
Sep 93	(0.26)	0.00	86,100	(20,100)
Jun 93	(0.10)	0.00	98,800	(6,500)

Preferred Div. Coverage	np	np	np	**Synopsis:**
Total Div. Coverage	na	na	na	
Interest Coverage	4.2	0.2	0.2	
Current Ratio	1.1	1.3	0.9	
Operating Margin	7.5	2.5	2.1	
Asset Turnover	0.5	0.4	0.4	
5 YEAR RATIOS (%)				
Return on Capital	3.0	2.1	2.1	
Return on Com. Equity	(3.2)	(4.9)	(4.5)	
Profit Growth	44.6	na	na	
Revenue Growth	15.7	27.1	26.3	
Asset Growth	(3.7)	9.4	23.7	
BALANCE SHEET (000)				
Cash	0	0	0	
Current Assets	187,800	232,800	132,700	
Net Fixed Assets	757,200	833,300	943,800	
Invest's & Advances	0	0	0	
Total Assets	945,000	1,066,100	1,076,500	
Short Term Debt	5,600	10,900	11,100	
Current Liabilities	178,400	174,400	155,000	
Long Term Debt	165,900	249,100	396,600	
Total Liabilities	371,100	543,700	617,000	
Total Equity	573,900	522,400	459,500	
Total Liab. & Equity	945,000	1,066,100	1,076,500	
CAPITAL (000)				
Total Debt	171,500	260,000	407,700	
Preferred Equity	0	0	0	
Common Equity	573,900	522,400	459,500	

Wascana Energy has set its capital budget at $185-million, in order to operate and grow within its cash flow. The company has identified and prioritized additional projects totalling $50- million to be pursued as cash flow permits during the year. Wascana's drilling program is should expand in 1995, with the company participating in the drilling of 200 net exploration and development wells. Production for 1995 should average 45,000 barrels of oil per day and 205 million cubic feet per day of natural gas.

Production and development spending, including development drilling, waterflooding, enhanced oil recovery, production maintenance, and environmental restoration will total $89-million in 1995. The exploration program will cost $70-million with about 90% going to domestic activities. Capital for pipelines, transportation, and other activities is budgeted at $26-million. Continued asset management activities will complement exploration and development activities by consolidating company interests in core areas and divesting marginal properties.

Drilling activity in 1994 totalled 33 (24.1 net) exploration wells and 260 (132.7 net) development wells. This activity resulted in 92 (70.5 net) vertical oil wells, 96 (24.4 net) horizontal oil wells, 59 (29.3 net) gas wells, 44 (31.1 net) dry and abandoned wells, and two (1.5 net) service wells, with a success rate of 84.9 (80.2 net).

Average daily sales in 1994 (1993) were: crude oil and natural gas liquids, 41,900 (41,200) barrels; and natural gas, 195 (231) million cubic feet. Proven and probable reserves in 1994 (1993) were: crude oil and natural gas liquids, 168.6 (210.2) million barrels; and natural gas, 634.7 (1,022.7) billion cubic feet.

Relative strength to TSE300 / Price / Volume (in 1000's of board lots)

Rank (Profit/Revenue/Assets)
114 199 159

Theodore M. Hanlon
Chairman

Frank W. Proto
President & C.E.O.

C.J. Byrne McNamara
V.P. Finance & C.F.O.

Address
1777 Victoria Avenue
P.O. Box 1550
Regina
SK
S4P 3C4
(306) 781-8200

Fax: (306) 781-8364
S0038455/G/3.2

Volume too Low (handwritten)

Page	Company			Fiscal year end	EARNINGS PER SHARE		
		Price VTL 3/8/2 Symbol			Last Year	Estimate this year	Estimate next year
151	Abitibi-Price *Consolidated* $14⁷⁸ -A-			Dec-94	$15⁰³ (0.45) $9⁴¹	2.42	3.53
152	Ainsworth Lubmer *(VTL)*		ANS	Dec-94	1.65	1.92	1.84
153	Alliance Forest Products ?			Dec-94	1.71	4.37	5.80
154	Avenor ?	$10⁸⁵ CAS		Dec-94	(1.42)	4.83	5.84
155	Canfor	13⁹⁰ -CFP-		Dec-94	12⁶⁶(1.42) 8⁰⁸ 2.18 6⁴⁵	4.83 2.10	5.84 2.57
156	Cascades			Dec-94	13⁹⁹ 0.42	1.47	1.82
157	Crestbrook Forest ?			Dec-94	(0.03)	3.25	5.20
158	Doman Industries *Insider Trading*			Dec-94	1.42	1.55	1.65
159	Domtar	18⁴⁵ DTC		Dec-94	18⁹⁹ 0.22 11¹⁵	2.31	2.72
160	Donohue ?			Dec-94	1.47	2.76	3.44
161	Fletcher Challenge Canada *Bought by NS*			Jun-94	5⁷⁵(0.19)	0.91	2.94
162	International Forest Products 5⁰⁰ -IFP-			Dec-94	1.68 3⁰¹	1.68	2.24
163	MacMillan Bloedel *Bought out.*			Dec-94	1.22	2.37	3.03
164	Mallette ?			Sep-94	0.85	(1.95)	(2.50)
165	Mallette Quebec ?			Sep-94	(0.64)	0.15	0.45
166	Noranda Forest *consolidated into 1?*			Dec-94	0.75	1.74	2.13
167	Pacific Forest Products ?			Dec-94	1.18	2.14	2.27
168	Quno Corporation ?			Dec-94	0.52	3.40	5.06
169	Rainy River Forest Products ?			Dec-94	(1.81)	2.33	3.49
170	Repap Enterprises ?			Dec-94	⁰⁰(0.75)	1.77	2.39
171	Riverside Forest Products	14⁵⁰ RFP		Sep-94	15 4.25 9⁰⁰	2.99	2.92
172	Rolland ?			Dec-94	14²⁵0.82	1.00	1.45
173	Slocan Forest Productss	10⁶⁹ SFP.		Dec-94	2.03 7⁴⁵	2.68	3.09
174	Stone-Consolidated *Bought out by Abitibi-Price.*			Dec-94	14⁸⁵(0.12) 9⁴⁰	2.49	3.61
175	Tembec 13⁴⁵			Sep-94	0.25	2.19	2.68
176	Timberwest Forest Limited 13³¹			Jun-94	13⁵⁷ 1.07 10⁶⁹	2.03	2.14
177	Weldwood of Canada ?			Dec-94	2.81	5.15	5.09
178	West Fraser Timber *(VTL)* 41⁰⁰			Dec-94	45⁰⁰ 5.19 28⁷⁵ 4.78	5.15 4.78	5.09 5.84

NEXFOR 8⁸⁸ ↳(Large portion owned by Brascan) 8⁹³ 6³⁰ (handwritten)

Estimates from First Call Corporation, 22 Pittsburgh Street, Boston, MA 02210   (800) 366-9992   Fax (617) 261-5679

Forestry

Industry officials expect that the Canadian forest industry will make at least $3-billion in profit during 1995 and perhaps surpass the $3.36-billion record set in 1987. While the country's lumber producers have faced softer markets this year, the much bigger pulp and paper sector is seeing prices for its products soar world-wide. With growth in new markets emerging in Asia and Latin America and low inflation in most industrialized countries, the supply and demand fundamentals should benefit pulp and paper producers for the next few years.

A report on Canada's forest industry released by Price Waterhouse in June 1995, shows that the industry posted record sales of $44.3-billion in 1994, up 18% from $37.6-billion in 1993. The industry also generated a profit of almost $2.5-billion in 1994 after three years of losses that totalled more than $4-billion.

In addition to selling more pulp, paper, and lumber at higher prices, last year the industry benefited from more favourable exchange rates and the return of countervailing duties collected by the U.S. government on Canadian softwood imports. The industry expects a $900-million refund from duties collected between March 1992 and the beginning of 1994.

The pulp and paper sector expects an even better year in 1995 because demand continues to grow and little new capacity will enter the market. However, the lumber and panel sector expects to do less well. The sawmills are facing lower housing starts in the United States and higher logging costs. However, Price Waterhouse expects the lumber sector to earn a profit of at least $500-million in 1995. The lumber sector earned more than $2-billion in 1994.

Little new pulp and paper capacity will be built in Canada because most of the commercial forest land has already been allocated. Industry officials remember that the last building binge in the late 1980s led to the industry's worst recession in 60 years. Instead, many companies expect to use their profits to buy capacity and fibre, especially because Canadian companies are relatively small compared with international rivals. For example, Tembec Inc. of Montreal recently launched a $300-million bid for Timmins-based Malette Inc. West Fraser Timber Co. Ltd. of Vancouver agreed to pay $385-million for the forest products division of Calgary-based Alberta Energy Co. Ltd. Canfor Corp. attempted to purchase Slocan Forest Products in early 1995 in order to access Slocan's fibre supply.

Because announced capacity additions have been limited, many pulp and paper companies expect the current upswing to extend beyond 1996. The severe downturn from 1991 through mid 1994 left their balance sheets in terrible shape. Instead of investing in additional capacity, companies will use the enormous cash flow to pay down debt, comply with stricter environmental regulation, and invest in mill improvements. The forest industry expects to devote more money to capital projects in 1995 after spending $3-billion in 1994. As a result of this and customer demands for higher grade papers, the industry is focussing on higher margins generated through higher product grades and profitability, rather than capacity upgrades.

Also, the current shortage of fibre and recycled materials necessary for production will not ease. This will limit capacity additions and support higher paper prices. Demand for paper, especially newsprint, with high recycled-fibre content is increasing steadily, in tandem with regulatory requirements in Canada and the U.S. Publishers and printers in the western U.S. must use paper with a recycled content rate of 25%. This will increase to 50% by the year 2000.

Margins for lumber producers are being squeezed by higher log costs, which they have been unable to pass on to retailers carrying lighter inventories. Log costs have increased due to environmental legislation in recent year. The new laws have limited timber harvesting in the western regions of the United States and British Columbia. Meanwhile, lumber capacity in the southern United States has grown considerably.

Although Canadian lumber producers are receiving refunds of $900-million in duties collected from 1992 to 1994 from the U.S. government, American producers are again pressuring for more countervailing duties or other trade actions. Anger in the U.S. is being fuelled by market conditions. Lumber prices have fallen to four year lows, and many U.S. mills are experiencing financial difficulties. Canadian mills are being targeted, since they have been selling their lumber into some U.S. markets for the first time. Canadian producers now supply about 35% of the $33-billion (U.S.) market in the United States, up from 27% four years ago.

The paper companies did not expect the sudden recovery of paper prices from the middle of 1994. Prices for pulp and linerboard, which bottomed in late 1993 and have now climbed to record highs, led the rebound. The strength in the pulp market spilled over into commodity board and paper grades in 1994 as improved North American and European economies absorbed the large capacity brought on line in the early 1990s. Late cycle paper products, such as coated free sheet and coated groundwood, experienced price increases in early 1995. Most companies expect these grades, as well as uncoated free sheet and newsprint, will show the largest price gains in 1995.

Analysts expect the positive market situation for both pulp and coated paper to continue for the balance of the decade. There is growing demand for coated paper. This is likely to translate into coated paper producer rates continuing to operate at practical maximum capacity. The tight market conditions throughout 1995 and 1996 should lead to higher prices. In July 1995, the coated groundwood paper price was $1,200 (U.S.) a tonne, up from $440 (U.S.) a tonne in July 1994.

ABITIBI-PRICE INC.

Exchanges	Price (Jun29'95)	22.12	Trailing P/E	221.20	Stock Symbol
TMVN	Trailing Yield (%)	0.00	Trailing EPS	0.10	A

Period Ending	Dec94	Dec93	Dec92	Dec91	Dec90
Yearly Statistics					
Price-Close	19.38	15.63	14.50	14.63	12.00
Price-High	20.63	16.00	16.63	16.75	16.25
Price-Low	15.25	10.75	13.13	11.25	12.00
P/E-Close	nm	nm	nm	nm	nm
Dividends per Share	0.00	0.13	0.50	0.50	0.50
Dividend Yield (%)	0.00	0.80	3.45	3.42	4.17
Sales per Share	25.01	26.03	23.11	23.89	44.58
EPS before extra. item	(0.66)	(1.56)	(3.19)	(1.12)	(0.76)
Cash Flow per Share	0.81	(0.22)	(1.17)	0.33	0.95
Book Value per Share	9.59	9.37	10.76	14.45	16.07
O/S Common Shares	87,415	77,283	69,267	69,267	69,267
Total Revenue	2,089,000	1,833,000	1,558,300	1,667,000	3,092,400
Income before extra.	(55,000)	(111,000)	(219,300)	(75,900)	(50,400)
Cash Flow	68,000	(16,000)	(81,100)	22,600	65,700
Debt/Equity	0.62	0.66	0.52	0.43	0.49
Return on Capital (%)	(3.39)	(10.22)	(22.27)	(4.91)	(1.33)
Ret. on Com. Equity (%)	(7.17)	(15.25)	(25.30)	(7.34)	(4.55)
% Change Profit	50.5	49.4	(188.9)	(50.6)	(193.0)
% Change Revenue	14.0	17.6	(6.5)	(46.1)	(5.6)
% Change Assets	8.7	(1.6)	(21.1)	(12.7)	(3.2)
Preferred Div. Coverage	0.0	0.0	0.0		
Total Div. Coverage	0.0	0.0	0.0		
Interest Coverage	0.0	0.0	0.0		
Current Ratio	1.6	1.5	1.1		
Operating Margin	1.2	(2.1)	(8.6)		
Asset Turnover	1.2	1.1	0.9		
5 YEAR RATIOS (%)					
Return on Capital	(8.4)	(6.2)	(0.1)		
Return on Com. Equity	(11.9)	(9.7)	(3.5)		
Profit Growth	na	na	na		
Revenue Growth	(8.6)	(11.2)	(12.3)		
Asset Growth	(6.6)	(8.6)	(7.7)		
BALANCE SHEET (000)					
Cash	250,000	138,000	120,000		
Current Assets	605,000	457,000	388,500		
Net Fixed Assets	906,000	865,000	917,000		
Invest's & Advances	135,000	175,000	233,600		
Total Assets	1,821,000	1,676,000	1,703,600		
Short Term Debt	44,000	13,000	12,200		
Current Liabilities	381,000	311,000	343,800		
Long Term Debt	479,000	474,000	382,500		
Total Liabilities	972,000	935,000	938,800		
Total Equity	849,000	741,000	764,800		
Total Liab. & Equity	1,821,000	1,676,000	1,703,600		
CAPITAL (000)					
Total Debt	523,000	487,000	394,700		
Preferred Equity	11,000	17,000	19,500		
Common Equity	838,000	724,000	745,300		

Business:

ABITIBI-PRICE INC., a Canadian-based forest products company, manufactures newsprint and value-added papers at ten mills in North America and markets these products to customers around the world. The company is also a major distributor of office products in North America and Western Europe.

Date	EPS	DPS	Tot Rev	Inc Bex
Mar 95	0.34	0.00	611,000	30,000
Dec 94	0.01	0.00	561,900	12,300
Sep 94	(0.06)	0.00	548,700	(5,700)
Jun 94	(0.19)	0.00	512,100	(17,700)
Mar 94	(0.52)	0.00	471,000	(40,000)
Dec 93	(0.47)	0.00	472,400	(35,600)
Sep 93	(0.38)	0.00	456,600	(26,800)
Jun 93	(0.29)	0.00	456,400	(19,800)

Synopsis:

Since December 1994, the turnaround in the newsprint market has been dramatic. Prices hit a 60 year low of $411 (U.S.) a tonne in early 1994, but rebounded by 34% by the end of the year. Abitibi-Price is set for strong newsprint pricing until the third quarter of 1996, with prices set to rise to $825 (U.S.) at the beginning of 1996.

The fourth quarter of 1994 was Abitibi's first quarterly net profit in five years. During this period, Canadian producers lost about $2.4-billion, and Abitibi lost more than $500-million, due to weak demand and overcapacity. The turnaround has resulted from significantly improved volume, higher newsprint prices, and favorable exchange rates, coupled with reduced costs. These factors were partially offset by increased costs for raw materials, such as kraft pulp, old newsprint, and old magazine grade papers.

Abitibi is one of the world's largest newsprint manufacturers, with a 5.8% share of the world newsprint market. It supplies about 10.5% of all North American newsprint. In 1994, Abitibi sold about 68% of its newsprint in North America, and 32% to international markets. Its principal market for newsprint is the United States. For the remainder of 1995, Abitibi expects North American newsprint consumption to equal available supply, and offshore markets to demonstrate continued strong demand. Abitibi will focus on increasing international sales as the company believes future growth will come primarily from these markets. The newsprint and valued-added papers generated 67% of 1994 sales. Office products generated 21% of sales, and other activities generated 12%.

Abitibi has taken a sharp look at each of its operations since the 1989-1994 slump. It has been assessing what needs to be done at each mill to bring its costs down to the lowest quartile among newsprint producers. This is to ensure that the mills will produce cash at the bottom of the business cycle. New capacity must also be able to supply international markets or value-added paper markets. Otherwise assets will be sold.

Relative strength to TSE300 / Price / Volume (in 1000's of board lots)

Rank (Profit/Revenue/Assets)
990 65 112

Bernd K. Koken
Chairman Of The Board

Ronald Y. Oberlander
President & C.E.O.

Patrick G. Crowley
C.F.O. & V.P.

Address
207 Queens Quay West
Suite 680
P.O. Box 102
Toronto
ON
M5J 2P5
(416) 203-5000
Fax: (416) 203-5094
A0000192/G/4.1

AINSWORTH LUMBER CO. LTD.

Exchanges		Price (Jun29'95)	9.12	Trailing P/E	6.91	Stock Symbol
TV		Trailing Yield (%)	0.00	Trailing EPS	1.32	**ANS**

Period Ending	Dec94	Oct93	Oct92	Oct91
Yearly Statistics	14M			
Price-Close	13.75	15.13	nt	nt
Price-High	18.75	15.38	nt	nt
Price-Low	11.00	9.88	nt	nt
P/E-Close	8.58	10.22	nt	nt
Dividends per Share	0.00	0.00	0.00	0.00
Dividend Yield (%)	0.00	0.00	0.00	0.00
Sales per Share	13.58	13.28	12.01	9.10
EPS before extra. item	1.87	1.48	0.48	(0.37)
Cash Flow per Share	2.54	1.88	1.04	0.65
Book Value per Share	7.53	5.45	1.03	0.55
O/S Common Shares	14,560	14,551	9,000	9,000
Total Revenue	237,388	154,327	108,520	83,012
Income before extra.	27,425	16,981	4,361	(3,331)
Cash Flow	43,077	21,596	9,394	5,846
Debt/Equity	1.12	0.16	1.93	5.07
Return on Capital (%)	26.25	47.51	33.11	na
Ret. on Com. Equity (%)	24.74	38.37	61.41	na
% Change Profit	38.4	289.4	230.9	na
% Change Revenue	31.8	42.2	30.7	na
% Change Assets	128.0	117.3	(0.6)	na

Date	EPS	DPS	Tot Rev	Inc Bex
Mar 95	0.24	0.00	62,400	3,500
Dec 94	0.38	0.00	63,933	5,769
Sep 94	0.35	0.00	49,154	5,164
Jun 94	0.35	0.00	47,733	5,121
Mar 94	0.56	0.00	49,685	8,171
Dec 93	0.13	0.00	36,272	1,900
Sep 93	0.54	0.00	45,126	6,235
Jun 93	0.63	0.00	38,822	5,647

	Dec94	Oct93	Oct92
Preferred Div. Coverage	np	na	np
Total Div. Coverage	152.4	na	na
Interest Coverage	10.1	18.4	3.6
Current Ratio	2.0	3.0	1.2
Operating Margin	18.8	18.1	8.3
Asset Turnover	0.7	1.3	1.9
5 YEAR RATIOS (%)			
Return on Capital	na	na	na
Return on Com. Equity	na	na	na
Profit Growth	na	na	na
Revenue Growth	na	na	na
Asset Growth	na	na	na
BALANCE SHEET (000)			
Cash	44,302	24,605	4,239
Current Assets	106,725	59,372	27,134
Net Fixed Assets	168,248	61,917	29,124
Invest's & Advances	3,078	934	0
Total Assets	278,703	122,223	56,258
Short Term Debt	21,323	0	2,093
Current Liabilities	53,535	19,657	22,145
Long Term Debt	101,028	13,488	15,773
Total Liabilities	169,125	39,982	46,976
Total Equity	109,578	82,241	9,282
Total Liab. & Equity	278,703	122,223	56,258
CAPITAL (000)			
Total Debt	122,351	13,488	17,866
Preferred Equity	0	3,000	0
Common Equity	109,578	79,241	9,282

Business:

AINSWORTH LUMBER CO. LTD. is engaged in harvesting timber and producing lumber, specialty plywood, veneer, pulp chips, and oriented strand board (OSB).

Synopsis:

Earnings for Ainsworth Lumber in the first quarter of 1995 were negatively affected by weak North American lumber markets and increased costs. Delivered log costs rose significantly over those in the same period in 1994. This was due to increased stumpage charges related to the B.C. Government's Forest Renewal Plan and delays in cutting permit approvals arising from the implementation of the Forest Practices Code.

Ainsworth, as all B.C. based forestry companies, is having to deal with increased stumpage rates, effective May 1994, and a more restricted supply of timber. As a result, the company is moving to produce premium quality products, while focusing on maximum recovery and value from each log harvested.

Ainsworth expects North American lumber and oriented strand board (OSB) prices will improve in the second quarter of 1995 as home building activity increases. Even though home building activity in the United States is expected to be lower in 1995 than 1994, prices for lumber should receive a boost from further timber shortages in B.C. and the Pacific Northwest. With improved pulp markets, woodchip prices have more than doubled in the past year, and further woodchip price increases are expected during 1995. Japan is a premium market for both lumber and OSB. Ainsworth will continue to focus on the emerging and growing OSB market in the Pacific Rim.

The company's OSB plant at 100 Mile House, B.C., should reach its annual rated capacity of 365 million square feet (3/8 inch basis) by mid 1995. A second OSB plant near Grande Prairie, Alberta, should begin production in December 1995. This facility will produce 540 million square feet (3/8 inch basis) of OSB along with wood I-beams and finger-jointed lumber. The project will cost $143-million.

The company's sales of $230.6-million in 1994 by product line were: lumber, 58%; veneer, 6%; plywood, 21%; chips, 9%; and OSB, 6%. Sales by major markets were: Canada, 44%; United States, 43%; and Japan and other, 13%.

Relative strength to TSE300

Price

Volume (in 1000's of board lots)

Rank (Profit/Revenue/Assets)
196   312   296

Brian E. Ainsworth
Chairman & C.E.O.

D. Allen Ainsworth
President & C.O.O.

Catherine E. Ainsworth
C.F.O. & Secretary

Address
Exeter Road
P.O. Box 67
100 Mile House
BC
V0K 2E0
(604) 395-6200

Fax: (604) 395-6201
01003368/G/4.2

ALLIANCE FOREST PRODUCTS INC.

Exchanges	Price (Jun29'95)	24.87	Trailing P/E	9.28	Stock Symbol
TM	Trailing Yield (%)	0.00	Trailing EPS	2.68	ALP

Period Ending	Dec94	Dec93	Dec92
Yearly Statistics	233D		
Price-Close	24.00	n t	n t
Price-High	24.00	n t	n t
Price-Low	16.25	n t	n t
P/E-Close	10.53	n t	n t
Dividends per Share	0.00	0.00	0.00
Dividend Yield (%)	0.00	0.00	0.00
Sales per Share	13.80	0.00	0.00
EPS before extra. item	1.71	na	na
Cash Flow per Share	3.49	0.00	0.00
Book Value per Share	12.56	na	na
O/S Common Shares	17,850	0	0
Total Revenue	185,000	259,200	217,600
Income before extra.	30,400	26,800	700
Cash Flow	46,700	43,000	16,800
Debt/Equity	nd	nd	nd
Return on Capital (%)	23.40	13.58	na
Ret. on Com. Equity (%)	19.44	13.58	na
% Change Profit	51.2	3,728.6	na
% Change Revenue	(4.8)	19.1	na
% Change Assets	14.3	(4.0)	na

Date	EPS	DPS	Tot Rev	Inc Bex
Mar 95	0.97	0.00	83,200	17,300
Dec 94	0.74	0.00	76,300	13,300
Sep 94	0.69	0.00	74,600	12,300
Jun 94	0.28	0.00	34,200	4,800

Preferred Div. Coverage	np	np	np
Total Div. Coverage	na	na	na
Interest Coverage	nd	nd	nd
Current Ratio	2.7	2.4	2.4
Operating Margin	19.7	10.3	0.3
Asset Turnover	0.9	1.1	0.9
5 YEAR RATIOS (%)			
Return on Capital	na	na	na
Return on Com. Equity	na	na	na
Profit Growth	na	na	na
Revenue Growth	na	na	na
Asset Growth	na	na	na
BALANCE SHEET (000)			
Cash	34,100	0	0
Current Assets	102,600	67,400	66,700
Net Fixed Assets	170,000	171,000	181,600
Invest's & Advances	0	0	0
Total Assets	272,600	238,400	248,300
Short Term Debt	0	0	0
Current Liabilities	38,100	28,000	28,300
Long Term Debt	0	0	0
Total Liabilities	48,400	45,500	46,500
Total Equity	224,200	192,900	201,800
Total Liab. & Equity	272,600	238,400	248,300
CAPITAL (000)			
Total Debt	0	0	0
Preferred Equity	0	0	0
Common Equity	224,200	192,900	201,800

Business:

ALLIANCE FOREST PRODUCTS INC. has acquired the newsprint, uncoated groundwood papers and related lumber business of Domtar Inc.

Synopsis:

Alliance Forest Products was formed in early 1994 to acquire assets earmarked for disposal by Domtar Inc. On May 12, 1994, Alliance acquired the newsprint and uncoated groundwood paper activities as well as a portion of the related lumber business of Domtar. Shares were issued at $17. The issue raised $303-million, $14.4-million of which went to working capital and the remainder was paid to Domtar.

The company's results since inception reflect the favourable economic conditions relating to lumber and paper prices, the weakness of the Canadian dollar, and higher levels of production at Alliance's four mills. Paper sales in 1994 totalled $121.3-million, representing 66% of total sales. Alliance exported 90% of its production, including 85% to the United States. Lumber sales generated $63.5-million during 1994, representing 34% of total sales. The United States accounted for 83% of lumber sales.

Alliance has implemented a cost control and productivity improvement program. Since 1989, while total paper production rose by 14% and lumber production by 8%, the workforce shrank by 21%. Alliance is undertaking a three year, $117-million investment plan. The plan will require compliance with environmental regulations and enhanced productivity in the mills. The Quebec government, in early 1995, announced a 31% increase in stumpage fees. Alliance will attempt to control other production costs to offset this fee increase.

Alliance plans to acquire recycled-fibre production capacity. Demand for paper with high recycled-fibre content, especially newsprint, is increasing steadily in tandem with regulatory requirements in Canada and the United States.

Market conditions are expected to be favourable in 1995. Certain paper mills having announced price increases of 41% during the year. This may increase newsprint prices to $780 (U.S.) per tonne. The demand for uncoated groundwood papers generally increase at a greater rate than demand for newsprint. Wood prices should remain stable.

Rank (Profit/Revenue/Assets)	117 263 302
Robert Despres	Chairman
Michel Gervais	Administrator

Address
1000 De La Gauchetiere West
Suite 2820
Montreal
PQ
H3B 4W5
(514) 954-2100

01003642/G/4.1

AVENOR INC.

Exchanges	Price (Jun29'95)	29.12	Trailing P/E	30.98	Stock Symbol
TM	Trailing Yield (%)	0.00	Trailing EPS	0.94	AVR

Period Ending	Dec94	Dec93	Dec92	Dec91	Dec90
Yearly Statistics					
Price-Close	27.75	19.38	22.50	24.25	28.00
Price-High	28.25	23.50	28.50	35.00	40.00
Price-Low	19.00	15.00	20.00	22.00	27.50
P/E-Close	nm	nm	nm	nm	nm
Dividends per Share	0.00	0.00	0.40	0.40	1.15
Dividend Yield (%)	0.00	0.00	1.78	1.65	4.11
Sales per Share	28.56	26.03	35.47	45.03	47.74
EPS before extra. item	(1.07)	(4.88)	(4.82)	(13.00)	(0.21)
Cash Flow per Share	0.52	(2.57)	(2.86)	(5.16)	5.14
Book Value per Share	13.60	14.25	19.05	23.83	37.23
O/S Common Shares	67,124	60,483	52,459	43,959	43,959
Total Revenue	1,879,300	1,367,500	1,749,700	1,926,900	2,051,200
Income before extra.	(71,000)	(285,600)	(248,000)	(571,500)	(9,400)
Cash Flow	34,500	(150,600)	(147,900)	(226,800)	226,000
Debt/Equity	1.86	1.75	1.48	1.20	0.51
Return on Capital (%)	2.78	(13.03)	(11.09)	(32.08)	1.50
Ret. on Com. Equity (%)	(8.00)	(30.69)	(24.23)	(42.58)	(0.56)
% Change Profit	75.1	(15.2)	56.6	(5,979.8)	(104.3)
% Change Revenue	37.4	(21.8)	(9.2)	(6.1)	(28.9)
% Change Assets	6.4	(5.3)	1.2	(9.1)	6.3

Preferred Div. Coverage	np	np	np
Total Div. Coverage	na	na	0.0
Interest Coverage	0.4	0.0	0.0
Current Ratio	2.9	2.3	1.6
Operating Margin	4.7	(8.6)	(10.4)
Asset Turnover	0.6	0.5	0.6

5 YEAR RATIOS (%)

Return on Capital	(10.4)	(7.3)	1.5
Return on Com. Equity	(21.2)	(16.9)	(6.4)
Profit Growth	na	na	na
Revenue Growth	(8.2)	(14.6)	(8.8)
Asset Growth	(0.3)	0.5	2.3

BALANCE SHEET (000)

Cash	106,600	0	0
Current Assets	901,100	688,700	601,200
Net Fixed Assets	1,887,400	1,980,800	2,117,800
Invest's & Advances	19,700	26,000	160,500
Total Assets	3,023,700	2,842,500	3,000,800
Short Term Debt	23,300	39,300	88,000
Current Liabilities	307,600	293,900	378,400
Long Term Debt	1,672,300	1,468,500	1,392,200
Total Liabilities	2,110,900	1,980,400	2,001,600
Total Equity	912,800	862,100	999,200
Total Liab. & Equity	3,023,700	2,842,500	3,000,800

CAPITAL (000)

Total Debt	1,695,600	1,507,800	1,480,200
Preferred Equity	0	0	0
Common Equity	912,800	862,100	999,200

Business:

AVENOR INC. is an integrated forest products company. Products include newsprint, white paper, and pulp; and lumber through its subsidiary, Pacific Forest Products Limited in British Columbia. The Company has customers in 40 countries and has offices in North America, Europe and Asia.

Date	EPS	DPS	Tot Rev	Inc Bex
Mar 95	0.99	0.00	675,300	66,400
Dec 94	(0.14)	0.00	499,100	(9,700)
Sep 94	0.25	0.00	483,300	(16,600)
Jun 94	(0.16)	0.00	468,000	(10,600)
Mar 94	(0.53)	0.00	459,400	(34,100)
Dec 93	(2.65)	0.00	224,200	(160,500)
Sep 93	(0.20)	0.00	394,400	(12,300)
Jun 93	(0.79)	0.00	391,500	(48,000)

Synopsis:

The improved economic conditions in Avenors major markets in 1994 created favourable market conditions for its newsprint, pulp, white paper and wood products. Prices recovered to levels not seen for five years, although they were still lower than the pre-recession peaks. The wood products business benefited from continuing strong demand. The white paper sector reported higher shipments amid recovering prices.

A sustained economic recovery world-wide should increase prices and shipments in Avenor's business units during 1995. Substantial newsprint and pulp prices have been announced through to the beginning of 1996. Productivity improvements should cover the increased material costs.

The company's improved operating results since the beginning of 1994 were due to improved performance in its newsprint and pulp sectors. Productivity improvements in all operations and a stronger U.S. dollar also contributed to the turnaround. The company has spent more than $2-billion over the past several years to upgrade and modernize both Avenor and joint venture operations. In 1995, Avenor will spend $250-million, mainly for the Dalhousie newsprint mill renewal program and cost reduction programs at its pulp and newsprint mills.

The company sold its paperboard business in June 1994. This was the last step in the company's restructuring. This will allow it to focus on its core business units of newsprint, pulp, white paper and wood products.

In 1994, sales by business segment were: newsprint, 38%; pulp, 28%; white paper, 15%; wood products, 16%; and other, 3%. In 1994, the newsprint and pulp groups exported about 95% of production, mainly to the United States. The company is a major supplier of white paper to the Canadian market, where it sells 55% of its production. The wood products group, Pacific Forest Products Limited, exports two-thirds of its production to Japan.

Rank (Profit/Revenue/Assets)		
994	72	70

Michel Belanger, Chairman
Paul E. Gagne, President & C.E.O.
Denis Aubin, V.P. & C.F.O.

Address
1250 Rene-Levesque Blvd. West
Montreal
PQ
H3B 4Y3
(514) 846-5061

Fax: (514) 846-5071
G0002394/G/4.1

CANFOR CORPORATION

Exchanges	Price (Jun29'95)	14.50	Trailing P/E	3.94	Stock Symbol
TV	Trailing Yield (%)	3.59	Trailing EPS	3.68	CFP

Period Ending	Dec94	Dec93	Dec92	Dec91	Dec90
Yearly Statistics					
Price-Close	18.50	20.75	13.50	12.69	10.88
Price-High	24.63	21.75	14.88	14.88	14.94
Price-Low	16.00	12.88	12.00	9.69	10.00
P/E-Close	8.49	30.07	nm	nm	310.71
Dividends per Share	0.26	0.26	0.26	0.23	0.28
Dividend Yield (%)	1.41	1.25	1.91	1.77	2.53
Sales per Share	24.70	20.50	17.72	17.35	19.37
EPS before extra. item	2.18	0.69	(0.95)	(2.09)	0.04
Cash Flow per Share	4.11	3.00	0.64	(0.67)	2.16
Book Value per Share	12.26	10.33	9.89	10.85	12.95
O/S Common Shares	56,945	56,917	56,872	51,737	45,689
Total Revenue	1,395,324	1,145,701	948,656	767,548	922,379
Income before extra.	124,487	41,250	(49,894)	(99,053)	3,798
Cash Flow	233,839	170,474	35,446	(31,705)	98,563
Debt/Equity	0.70	0.81	0.68	0.63	0.41
Return on Capital (%)	23.30	12.16	(2.18)	(14.73)	4.66
Ret. on Com. Equity (%)	19.28	6.81	(9.26)	(17.57)	0.26
% Change Profit	201.8	182.7	49.6	(2,708.0)	(96.1)
% Change Revenue	21.8	20.8	23.6	(16.8)	(5.9)
% Change Assets	14.1	14.4	4.2	0.9	(4.8)

Preferred Div. Coverage	np	19.7	0.0
Total Div. Coverage	8.1	2.4	0.0
Interest Coverage	7.7	4.4	0.0
Current Ratio	1.2	1.5	1.4
Operating Margin	20.3	12.7	2.0
Asset Turnover	0.8	0.8	0.8
5 YEAR RATIOS (%)			
Return on Capital	4.6	4.4	7.0
Return on Com. Equity	(0.1)	(0.7)	2.2
Profit Growth	5.3	(16.5)	na
Revenue Growth	7.3	0.2	(5.4)
Asset Growth	5.4	4.5	6.5
BALANCE SHEET (000)			
Cash	15,309	100,732	8,470
Current Assets	596,207	475,984	337,694
Net Fixed Assets	657,366	624,452	572,123
Invest's & Advances	335,855	296,660	324,570
Total Assets	1,657,634	1,453,158	1,270,358
Short Term Debt	227,496	145,631	100,912
Current Liabilities	509,987	311,473	236,729
Long Term Debt	264,027	348,594	298,611
Total Liabilities	959,410	842,147	684,288
Total Equity	698,224	611,011	586,070
Total Liab. & Equity	1,657,634	1,453,158	1,270,358
CAPITAL (000)			
Total Debt	491,523	494,225	399,523
Preferred Equity	0	23,170	23,500
Common Equity	698,224	587,841	562,570

Business:

CANFOR CORP. is an integrated forest products company. It produces kraft pulp and sack kraft paper, lumber and other wood and wood fibre products. Canfor has facilities in British Columbia, northern Alberta and northwestern United States. It has pulp sales offices in Canada, Europe and Japan. The company owns 50% of a pulp and newsprint company and 50% of a Canadian building materials distribution company.

Date	EPS	DPS	Tot Rev	Inc Bex
Mar 95	0.26	0.00	488,600	14,700
Dec 94	1.64	0.26	419,943	46,787
Sep 94	1.02	0.00	380,200	28,700
Jun 94	0.76	0.26	363,400	21,400
Mar 94	0.47	0.00	420,300	27,600
Dec 93	0.50	0.26	315,993	14,750
Sep 93	(0.29)	0.00	263,300	(7,900)
Jun 93	0.60	0.26	298,700	17,600

Synopsis:

For Canfor Corp., the first quarter of 1995 marked a break from declining quarterly earnings in 1994, if the $2.5-million expense in the first quarter of 1995 relating to the unsuccessful bid to acquire Slocan Forest Products Ltd., and the refund of countervailing duties in the third and fourth quarters of 1994 are excluded. The turnaround is the result of improved markets for pulp, kraft paper, and newsprint in combination with the weaker Canadian dollar. These positive factors overcame declining lumber prices and increased stumpage, log, and wood chip costs. Offshore lumber markets are reasonably strong and the company believes North American lumber prices are near the bottom of their decline.

Stumpage paid to British Columbia and Alberta for the timber the company harvested off crown land rose by $88.8-million in 1994 over 1993, an increase of 114% while the volume harvested was down by 8%. The cost of chips to pulp mills also rose substantially in 1994, reflecting the shortage of chips that has developed in British Columbia. Pulp mills are boosting their operating levels in response to the improved demand for pulp, while at the same time sawmills are emphasizing lumber recovery and timber harvests are being reduced by the provincial government. To gain greater control over its wood chip supply, the company bid for Slocan and its wood chip assets. The company is scouring its own sawmills for additional wood scraps and signing up supply from other sources, such as Ainsworth Lumber.

Sales in 1994 (including the company's equity in sales of affiliates) by segment were: wood and wood products (mostly lumber), 61%; pulp and paper, 26%; and building materials distribution, 13%. Sales by market were: Canada, 11%; United States, 57%; Europe, 14%; Far East, 17%; and other, 1%.

In April 1995, Peter Bentley turned over the chief executive reigns to Arild Nielssen, Canfor's president and chief operating officer for the past three years. Mr. Bentley will remain company chairman.

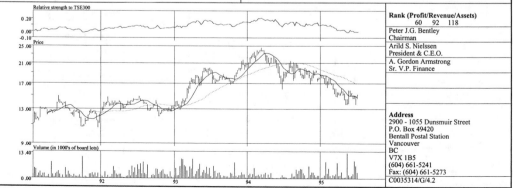

Rank (Profit/Revenue/Assets)
60 92 118

Peter J.G. Bentley
Chairman

Arild S. Nielssen
President & C.E.O.

A. Gordon Armstrong
Sr. V.P. Finance

Address
2900 - 1055 Dunsmuir Street
P.O. Box 49420
Bentall Postal Station
Vancouver
BC
V7X 1B5
(604) 661-5241
Fax: (604) 661-5273
C0035314/G/4.2

CASCADES INC.

Exchanges	Price (Jun29'95)	7.50	Trailing P/E	10.14	Stock Symbol
TM	Trailing Yield (%)	0.00	Trailing EPS	0.74	CAS

Period Ending	Dec94	Dec93	Dec92	Dec91	Dec90
Yearly Statistics					
Price-Close	7.38	6.88	6.75	6.00	4.10
Price-High	8.88	7.00	8.50	6.50	5.38
Price-Low	6.38	5.00	5.25	3.80	3.13
P/E-Close	16.39	nm	13.78	nm	9.76
Dividends per Share	0.00	0.00	0.00	0.00	0.00
Dividend Yield (%)	0.00	0.00	0.00	0.00	0.00
Sales per Share	29.86	29.75	16.50	15.67	16.94
EPS before extra. item	0.45	(1.21)	0.49	(0.03)	0.42
Cash Flow per Share	1.75	0.66	0.68	1.02	1.27
Book Value per Share	5.18	4.48	5.70	5.14	5.22
O/S Common Shares	57,774	57,773	54,749	54,637	48,288
Total Revenue	1,740,865	1,628,461	939,292	818,392	833,227
Income before extra.	33,891	(59,120)	28,235	(1,559)	20,126
Cash Flow	101,291	36,881	37,351	52,449	61,541
Debt/Equity	1.75	1.82	1.85	1.47	1.69
Return on Capital (%)	10.42	3.75	7.89	7.59	12.92
Ret. on Com. Equity (%)	10.52	(22.28)	9.01	(0.59)	8.52
% Change Profit	157.3	(309.4)	1,911.1	(107.7)	(32.7)
% Change Revenue	6.9	73.4	14.8	(1.8)	20.4
% Change Assets	12.1	(15.2)	84.0	3.0	29.1
Preferred Div. Coverage	7.5	0.0	18.3		
Total Div. Coverage	7.5	0.0	18.3		
Interest Coverage	1.8	0.5	1.7		
Current Ratio	1.3	1.4	1.3		
Operating Margin	6.1	3.7	3.8		
Asset Turnover	1.1	1.2	0.5		
5 YEAR RATIOS (%)					
Return on Capital	8.5	9.3	12.2		
Return on Com. Equity	1.0	1.9	10.3		
Profit Growth	2.5	na	5.6		
Revenue Growth	20.2	22.3	12.0		
Asset Growth	18.4	21.6	29.4		
BALANCE SHEET (000)					
Cash	34,816	73,274	54,405		
Current Assets	597,126	493,279	566,530		
Net Fixed Assets	943,802	887,887	1,057,048		
Invest's & Advances	0	0	50,259		
Total Assets	1,629,302	1,453,048	1,713,312		
Short Term Debt	173,499	136,078	178,846		
Current Liabilities	458,238	350,741	429,531		
Long Term Debt	558,445	550,590	616,985		
Total Liabilities	1,211,784	1,075,754	1,283,089		
Total Equity	417,518	377,294	430,223		
Total Liab. & Equity	1,629,302	1,453,048	1,713,312		
CAPITAL (000)					
Total Debt	731,944	686,668	795,831		
Preferred Equity	118,397	118,397	118,397		
Common Equity	299,121	258,897	311,826		

Business:

CASCADES INC. is a pulp and paper company. It also operates in the packaging and building materials industry. The company has operations in Canada, the United States, France, Belgium and Sweden. Its products include deinked pulp, coated folding boxboard, corrugated containers, linerboard and corregating medium fine papers, and kraft paper. The company has markets in Canada, the U.S., Europe and Sweden.

Date	EPS	DPS	Tot Rev	Inc Bex
Mar 95	0.37	0.00	561,759	23,213
Dec 94	0.26	0.00	551,022	18,862
Sep 94	0.10	0.00	422,933	7,290
Jun 94	0.01	0.00	394,121	2,525
Mar 94	0.06	0.00	388,833	5,214
Dec 93	(1.04)	0.00	387,550	(54,849)
Sep 93	(0.09)	0.00	402,370	(3,167)
Jun 93	(0.07)	0.00	417,366	(1,951)

Synopsis:

During 1994 the pulp and paper industry shifted into one of the most favourable growth cycles in the past 30 years. Demand exceeds supply, the worldwide trend towards recycled products is gaining ground, and the selling prices for Cascades products are rising.

In 1995, Cascades expects to surpass $2-billion in sales as a result of stronger demand for its products, and efforts in 1994 to boost productivity at its plants. Cascades' boxboard, fine papers, and containerboard groups are also benefiting from the growing demand for products with recycled content and high operational rates in their industries, especially since no additional capacity is expected. Increased sales are being offset by the significant increase in raw materials costs. Both waste papers and virgin pulp prices began to soar in 1994 and into 1995, with costs tripling in some waste paper categories.

Productivity gains in its plants and the streamlining of the European operations over the past three years continue to benefit Cascades. The company also integrated its 50% joint venture in the French fluff pulp mill (boxboard group), Tartas S.A. (a joint venture with Tembec Inc.) in July 1994. In 1994, revenues rose 3.1%, despite the sale and shutdown of several Cascades Paperboard International plants in 1993.

Cascades expects its financial position and cash flow to improve, with the improved profits and debt repayments. Cascades would like to increase its presence in the U.S. by acquiring mills specializing in the converting of boxboard and the production of fine papers and tissue paper. The company will also build a linerboard mill in Kingsey Falls, Quebec.

In 1994, sales by group were: boxboard, 42%; fine papers (headed by subsidiary Rolland Inc.), 22%; containerboard, 14%; and others, 22%. Canadian plants generated 68% of sales; U.S. plants, 12%; and European plants, 20%. The company's largest markets are Canada and the U.S., with Europe accounting for 41% of the boxboard sales.

Relative strength to TSE300

Price

Volume (in 1000's of board lots)

Rank (Profit/Revenue/Assets)
141 75 122

Bernard Lemaire
Chairman Of The Board

Laurent Lemaire
President & C.E.O.

Andre Belzile
V.P. Finance

Martin Pelletier
V.P. Operations

Address
404 Rue Marie-Victorin
C.P. 30
Kingsey-Falls
PQ
J0A 1B0
(819) 363-5100

Fax: (819) 363-5155
C0027546/G/4.1

CRESTBROOK FOREST INDUSTRIES LTD.

Exchanges	Price (Jun29'95)	24 .50	Trailing P/E	37 .69	Stock Symbol
TV	Trailing Yield (%)	0 .61	Trailing EPS	0 .65	CFI

Period Ending	Dec94	Dec93	Dec92	Dec91	Dec90
Yearly Statistics					
Price-Close	19 .38	15 .63	12 .00	13 .75	17 .50
Price-High	26 .50	17 .25	15 .75	21 .00	22 .00
Price-Low	15 .50	12 .00	10 .25	12 .00	14 .75
P/E-Close	31 .25	28 .41	nm	nm	12 .41
Dividends per Share	0 .15	0 .15	0 .15	0 .60	0 .60
Dividend Yield (%)	0 .77	0 .96	1 .25	4 .36	3 .43
Sales per Share	22 .17	20 .24	15 .46	17 .23	28 .83
EPS before extra. item	0 .62	0 .55	(0 .69)	(1 .84)	1 .41
Cash Flow per Share	5 .86	3 .12	1 .69	(1 .74)	2 .18
Book Value per Share	14 .64	12 .52	12 .13	13 .73	16 .31
O/S Common Shares	15 ,634	11 ,570	11 ,560	11 ,560	7 ,639
Total Revenue	318 ,169	239 ,428	180 ,984	173 ,517	224 ,071
Income before extra.	7 ,568	6 ,315	(8 ,018)	(15 ,014)	10 ,776
Cash Flow	79 ,674	36 ,099	19 ,594	(16 ,690)	16 ,619
Debt/Equity	1 .27	2 .39	0 .57	0 .11	0 .17
Return on Capital (%)	9 .50	5 .74	(4 .37)	(15 .51)	13 .65
Ret. on Com. Equity (%)	4 .05	4 .43	(5 .37)	(10 .60)	8 .87
% Change Profit	19 .8	178 .8	46 .6	(239 .3)	(66 .5)
% Change Revenue	32 .9	32 .3	4 .3	(22 .6)	(16 .0)
% Change Assets	7 .2	101 .8	19 .3	17 .1	2 .7
Preferred Div. Coverage	np	np	np		
Total Div. Coverage	4 .3	3 .6	0 .0		
Interest Coverage	2 .0	1 .9	0 .0		
Current Ratio	1 .4	1 .4	2 .3		
Operating Margin	20 .6	7 .5	(5 .7)		
Asset Turnover	0 .5	0 .4	0 .6		
5 YEAR RATIOS (%)					
Return on Capital	1 .8	8 .6	17 .8		
Return on Com. Equity	0 .3	5 .6	12 .7		
Profit Growth	(25 .1)	(27 .2)	na		
Revenue Growth	3 .6	(1 .2)	(5 .5)		
Asset Growth	25 .3	26 .3	14 .7		
BALANCE SHEET (000)					
Cash	0	9 ,563	7 ,440		
Current Assets	125 ,415	86 ,252	75 ,601		
Net Fixed Assets	379 ,866	369 ,052	128 ,457		
Invest's & Advances	115 ,004	129 ,821	83 ,937		
Total Assets	640 ,239	597 ,276	296 ,014		
Short Term Debt	46 ,909	15 ,542	3 ,050		
Current Liabilities	89 ,670	62 ,119	32 ,518		
Long Term Debt	244 ,033	330 ,067	77 ,335		
Total Liabilities	411 ,309	452 ,380	155 ,798		
Total Equity	228 ,930	144 ,896	140 ,216		
Total Liab. & Equity	640 ,239	597 ,276	296 ,014		
CAPITAL (000)					
Total Debt	290 ,942	345 ,609	80 ,385		
Preferred Equity	0	0	0		
Common Equity	228 ,930	144 ,896	140 ,216		

Business:

CRESTBROOK FOREST INDUSTRIES LTD. is a vertically integrated forest products company. The company has operations in British Columbia and Alberta. Products, including lumber and bleached kraft pulp, are sold to markets in the United States, Canada, Japan, Mexico and Europe. Honshu Paper Co. Ltd. owns 20.44% of the company's common shares and Mitsubishi Corp. owns 30.68%.

Date	EPS	DPS	Tot Rev	Inc Bex
Mar 95	0 .27	0 .15	131 ,499	4 ,168
Dec 94	0 .74	0 .00	111 ,815	8 ,967
Sep 94	0 .13	0 .00	76 ,647	1 ,490
Jun 94	(0 .49)	0 .00	57 ,658	(5 ,663)
Mar 94	0 .24	0 .15	71 ,586	2 ,774
Dec 93	(0 .08)	0 .00	70 ,014	(964)
Sep 93	0 .00	0 .00	61 ,728	32
Jun 93	0 .30	0 .00	55 ,192	3 ,411

Synopsis:

Crestbrook Forest Industries expanded into Alberta. This improved its geographic diversification and balanced its product profile with a greater emphasis on pulp. Pulp production increased significantly in 1994 with the addition of its 40% share in the Al-Pac Joint Venture.

Rebounding pulp markets drove the company's improved results in 1994 and 1995. World demand for paper products grew quickly in 1994 in response to improving world economies. Prices for NBSK pulp have risen steadily from $430 (U.S.) per tonne in January 1994 to $700 (U.S.) in December 1994 and $925 (U.S.) in June 1995. With the industry operating at capacity and no major increases in world capacity expected in 1995, higher prices are expected in 1996. The company expects pulp production to reach capacity of 410,000 air dried metric tonnes (ADt) in 1995. Further cost reductions are forecast as the new facilities are fine-tuned.

Lumber markets were strong in 1994, with prices and demand similar to 1993. However, the lumber market weakened in the first half of 1995 with a gradual decline in pricing. Slower economic activity in North America has affected housing starts and higher lumber inventories have resulted. The company's three sawmills continue to balance the higher cost of fibre by increasing production of value added lumber products and by improving recovery levels of fibre.

The company's 20-year Forest Management Agreement with Alberta supplies 100% of Al-Pac's requirements with secure, low cost fibre. However, the company expects some reduction in fibre supply in B.C. in 1995 and beyond. The company is pursuing all potential fibre sources, as a result of the government's forest management policies.

Crestbrook sells all its pulp at market prices to its majority shareholders, Honshu Paper Co. and Mitsubishi Corp. Sales in 1994 were $301.6-million. Sales by product were: wood products, 62%; and pulp, 38%. Sales by geographic area were: United States, 85%; Japan, 10%; Canada, 2%; and other, 3%.

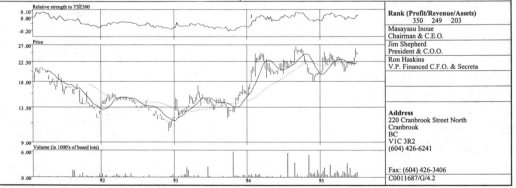

Rank (Profit/Revenue/Assets)
350   249   203

Masayasu Inoue
Chairman & C.E.O.

Jim Shepherd
President & C.O.O.

Ron Haskins
V.P. Financed C.F.O. & Secreta

Address
220 Cranbrook Street North
Cranbrook
BC
V1C 3R2
(604) 426-6241

Fax: (604) 426-3406
C0011687/G/4.2

DOMAN INDUSTRIES LIMITED

Exchanges	Price (Jun29'95)	10.00	Trailing P/E	6.71	Stock Symbol
TV	Trailing Yield (%)	2.00	Trailing EPS	1.49	**DOM.B**

Period Ending	Dec94	Dec93	Dec92	Dec91	Dec90	Business:
Yearly Statistics						DOMAN INDUSTRIES Ltd. is a forest
Price-Close	11.75	18.63	8.50	5.75	5.38	products company with logging, pulp and
Price-High	19.50	19.00	8.50	8.50	11.38	sawmill operations along the coast of British
Price-Low	10.38	8.13	5.50	4.50	4.95	Columbia. The main products are kraft pulp,
P/E-Close	8.28	16.48	10.00	nm	23.37	sulphite pulp and lumber, which the company
Dividends per Share	0.20	0.24	0.27	0.30	0.28	markets worldwide. Doman also sells logs and
Dividend Yield (%)	1.70	1.27	3.18	5.18	5.12	pulp chips.
Sales per Share	21.22	21.69	21.45	25.60	30.74	
EPS before extra. item	1.42	1.13	0.85	(2.34)	0.23	
Cash Flow per Share	4.37	4.15	2.07	(0.95)	3.48	
Book Value per Share	7.72	6.47	3.75	1.72	4.46	
O/S Common Shares	36,566	34,767	27,316	19,385	19,139	
Total Revenue	779,705	673,534	582,061	514,240	615,756	

Income before extra.	55,794	40,199	27,213	(46,537)	5,376
Cash Flow	156,064	126,552	53,171	(18,529)	66,032

Date	EPS	DPS	Tot Rev	Inc Bex
Mar 95	0.35	0.05	208,268	13,858
Dec 94	0.64	0.05	212,992	24,256
Sep 94	0.17	0.05	193,355	7,448
Jun 94	0.33	0.05	199,488	13,001
Mar 94	0.28	0.05	171,355	11,089
Dec 93	(0.01)	0.05	164,839	1,477
Sep 93	0.30	0.05	166,196	11,157
Jun 93	0.50	0.14	165,137	16,590

	Dec94	Dec93	Dec92	Dec91	Dec90
Debt/Equity	1.52	1.80	3.12	14.45	6.61
Return on Capital (%)	16.59	13.58	11.26	(0.95)	12.84
Ret. on Com. Equity (%)	19.94	20.28	34.44	(80.08)	5.08
% Change Profit	38.8	47.7	158.5	(965.6)	(83.1)
% Change Revenue	15.8	15.7	13.2	(16.5)	24.7
% Change Assets	6.5	6.5	5.5	(4.0)	0.2
Preferred Div. Coverage	10.7	5.7	7.1		
Total Div. Coverage	4.5	2.8	2.6		
Interest Coverage	2.6	2.3	1.5		
Current Ratio	3.5	4.1	1.5		
Operating Margin	19.1	18.0	11.5		
Asset Turnover	0.6	0.6	0.5		
5 YEAR RATIOS (%)					
Return on Capital	10.7	11.8	15.1		
Return on Com. Equity	(0.1)	4.9	9.5		
Profit Growth	11.8	14.7	2.1		
Revenue Growth	9.5	17.2	12.5		
Asset Growth	2.8	39.2	42.6		
BALANCE SHEET (000)					
Cash	36,573	8,826	0		
Current Assets	370,599	344,719	257,519		
Net Fixed Assets	747,417	732,444	749,415		
Invest's & Advances	11,786	11,692	19,889		
Total Assets	1,224,380	1,149,738	1,079,690		
Short Term Debt	1,668	5,093	104,731		
Current Liabilities	105,389	84,586	175,564		
Long Term Debt	598,335	625,130	609,917		
Total Liabilities	829,661	798,542	850,672		
Total Equity	394,719	351,196	229,018		
Total Liab. & Equity	1,224,380	1,149,738	1,079,690		
CAPITAL (000)					
Total Debt	600,003	630,223	714,648		
Preferred Equity	112,309	126,212	126,648		
Common Equity	282,410	224,984	102,370		

Synopsis:

Since the beginning of 1993, Doman Industries has achieved record sales, earnings, and cash flow. In 1993, the company benefited from a very strong lumber market. Prices and markets in the pulp segment improved dramatically in 1994. List prices for kraft pulp increased from $390 (U.S.) per tonne at the end of 1993 to $700 (U.S.) at the end of 1994. Prices increased to $925 (U.S.) in June 1995. Lumber prices were marginally higher in 1994 on slightly lower volumes than in 1993.

Results in the first half of 1995 reflected higher volumes and sharply higher pulp prices. This compensated Doman for lower volumes and prices for lumber. As in 1994, the pulp segment has compensated for increases in fibre costs that were driven upward by both shortages and by sharply higher stumpage and royalty rates.

In 1994, the company's sales by product were: lumber, 50%; pulp, 36%; logs, 12%; and sawmill by-products, 2%. Sales by market were: Canada, 25%; United States, 36%; Europe, 15%; Far East, 22%; and other, 2%. Doman's U.S. dollar based sales of lumber and pulp represented approximately 71% of its 1994 sales. The U.S. is the primary market for Doman's lumber. The Far East and Europe are its main markets for pulp. Doman's production capacity at its six sawmills totals 900 million board feet of lumber and the annual production capacity at two pulp mills totals 400,000 tonnes of pulp.

As a result of volatile and depressed wood and paper markets in the early 1990s, and the increased costs of fibre, Doman is continuing to emphasize value-added manufacturing in both the solid wood and the pulp segments. The company's log merchandizer at Nanaimo creates added value from low grade logs by extracting the lumber portion contained in pulp logs and then processing what is left over into pulp chips. The lumber processed at Chemainus is used in the manufacture of items where appearance is important. The pulp segment produces northern bleached softwood kraft or NBSK at Squamish. It also produces specialty chemical cellulose products from low quality timber at the dissolving sulphite mill at Port Alice.

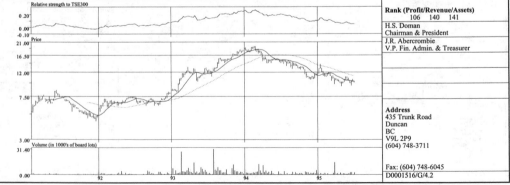

Rank (Profit/Revenue/Assets)
106   140   141

H.S. Doman
Chairman & President

J.R. Abercrombie
V.P. Fin. Admin. & Treasurer

Address
435 Trunk Road
Duncan
BC
V9L 2P9
(604) 748-3711

Fax: (604) 748-6045
D0001516/G/4.2

DOMTAR INC.

Exchanges	Price (Jun29'95)	12.87	Trailing P/E	13.14	Stock Symbol
TMVN	Trailing Yield (%)	0.00	Trailing EPS	0.98	DTC

Period Ending	Dec94	Dec93	Dec92	Dec91	Dec90
Yearly Statistics					
Price-Close	9.63	8.38	5.25	7.75	9.50
Price-High	10.13	9.25	8.38	10.00	13.50
Price-Low	6.50	4.90	4.25	7.00	9.00
P/E-Close	17.19	nm	nm	nm	nm
Dividends per Share	0.00	0.00	0.00	0.21	0.31
Dividend Yield (%)	0.00	0.00	0.00	2.66	3.21
Sales per Share	16.82	13.44	15.56	19.05	26.64
EPS before extra. item	0.56	(0.90)	(1.36)	(1.69)	(3.44)
Cash Flow per Share	1.67	(0.31)	(0.59)	(0.48)	(0.14)
Book Value per Share	5.23	4.68	5.58	7.12	8.94
O/S Common Shares	127,448	127,077	126,235	100,892	87,036
Total Revenue	2,180,000	1,709,000	1,884,000	1,805,000	2,314,000
Income before extra.	75,000	(111,000)	(159,000)	(148,000)	(294,000)
Cash Flow	212,000	(39,000)	(72,000)	(45,000)	(12,000)
Debt/Equity	1.52	1.61	1.23	1.40	1.17
Return on Capital (%)	10.17	(2.19)	(7.14)	(6.08)	(15.60)
Ret. on Com. Equity (%)	11.41	(17.55)	(23.07)	(21.39)	(32.45)
% Change Profit	167.6	30.2	(7.4)	49.7	(990.9)
% Change Revenue	27.6	(9.3)	4.4	(22.0)	(8.1)
% Change Assets	5.6	0.8	(2.6)	2.9	(13.9)
Preferred Div. Coverage	25.0	0.0	0.0		
Total Div. Coverage	25.0	0.0	0.0		
Interest Coverage	1.6	0.0	0.0		
Current Ratio	2.5	2.0	1.3		
Operating Margin	8.4	(2.5)	(6.6)		
Asset Turnover	0.8	0.6	0.7		
5 YEAR RATIOS (%)					
Return on Capital	(4.2)	(5.3)	(2.9)		
Return on Com. Equity	(16.6)	(18.5)	(13.2)		
Profit Growth	17.8	na	na		
Revenue Growth	(2.9)	(7.3)	(6.1)		
Asset Growth	(2.9)	(3.4)	(1.8)		
BALANCE SHEET (000)					
Cash	87,000	115,000	42,000		
Current Assets	888,000	663,000	599,000		
Net Fixed Assets	1,809,000	1,898,000	1,955,000		
Invest's & Advances	24,000	27,000	19,000		
Total Assets	2,841,000	2,691,000	2,670,000		
Short Term Debt	25,000	21,000	169,000		
Current Liabilities	353,000	331,000	465,000		
Long Term Debt	1,318,000	1,298,000	976,000		
Total Liabilities	1,955,000	1,874,000	1,741,000		
Total Equity	886,000	817,000	929,000		
Total Liab. & Equity	2,841,000	2,691,000	2,670,000		
CAPITAL (000)					
Total Debt	1,343,000	1,319,000	1,145,000		
Preferred Equity	219,000	222,000	225,000		
Common Equity	667,000	595,000	704,000		

Business:

DOMTAR INC is a North American manufacturer of pulp and paper products and construction materials. The Company manufactures and markets printing and writing papers and produces containerboard and corrugated containers and is an Eastern Canadian lumber producer. The Company also manufactures decorative panels and gypsum products.

Date	EPS	DPS	Tot Rev	Inc Bex
Mar 95	0.58	0.00	679,000	75,000
Dec 94	0.26	0.00	609,000	34,000
Sep 94	0.16	0.00	573,000	22,000
Jun 94	(0.02)	0.00	511,000	34,000
Mar 94	(0.12)	0.00	460,000	(15,000)
Dec 93	(0.21)	0.00	447,000	(26,000)
Sep 93	(0.18)	0.00	438,000	(22,000)
Jun 93	(0.26)	0.00	421,000	(28,000)

Synopsis:

Domtar feels it is well positioned to benefit from the current economic recovery following four years of productivity improvements and substantial cost reductions in all businesses. Domtar's markets began to improve in 1994, particularly in the second half of the year. Selling prices, which had dropped to historically low levels in 1993, recovered in 1994 and in some businesses, like lumber, reached historic high levels.

Sales in 1994 were 26% higher than in 1993, primarily because of higher sales volumes, improved pricing due to increased demand for Domtar's products, and the weakening of the Canadian dollar. Manufacturing costs rose due to price increases for raw materials, in particular purchased recycled fibre, reflecting a rapid increase in industry demand. A significant portion of the raw material cost increases was offset by cost reductions and productivity improvement programs.

Domtar has continued to narrow its focus and concentrate on businesses in which it feels it has a discernible competitive advantage. In 1994, Domtar sold its Newsprint and Uncoated Groundwood Papers division and related lumber business to Alliance Forest Products Inc. for $289-million.

In 1994, Domtar's sales (operating earnings) by industry segment were: pulp and forest products, 14% (43%); fine papers, 40% (21%); construction materials, 25% (22%); and packaging, 21% (14%). In 1994, 52% of sales were to the United States, 46% were to Canadian customers, and 2% were overseas.

For 1995, Domtar expects attractive pricing for its products to continue, as demand should remain strong. Prices, which recovered faster than anticipated in the second half of 1994, should continue to improve.

Rank (Profit/Revenue/Assets)
91 64 75

Gilles Blondeau
Chairman

Stephen C. Larson
President & C.O.O.

Pierre Fitzgibbon
Sr. V.P. & C.F.O.

Address
395 De Maisonneuve Blvd. W.
Montreal
PQ
H3A 1L6
(514) 848-5400

Fax: (514) 848-6850
D0002748/G/4.1

DONOHUE INC.

Exchanges	Price (Jun29'95)	20.00	Trailing P/E	10.20	Stock Symbol
TM	Trailing Yield (%)	1.60	Trailing EPS	1.96	**DHC.A**

Period Ending	Dec94	Dec93	Dec92	Dec91	Dec90
Yearly Statistics					
Price-Close	15.13	11.50	7.00	6.00	5.75
Price-High	15.75	11.69	7.00	7.63	6.25
Price-Low	11.00	6.75	6.50	5.38	4.75
P/E-Close	9.51	50.00	nm	nm	12.92
Dividends per Share	0.24	0.02	0.00	0.09	0.24
Dividend Yield (%)	1.59	0.17	0.00	1.50	4.17
Sales per Share	11.30	8.16	8.05	7.30	9.50
EPS before extra. item	1.59	0.23	(0.24)	(0.91)	0.45
Cash Flow per Share	2.68	1.27	0.47	0.84	1.60
Book Value per Share	6.80	5.29	5.08	5.16	6.16
O/S Common Shares	78,454	70,405	70,363	64,325	64,326
Total Revenue	810,852	576,268	523,228	482,203	629,744
Income before extra.	114,239	16,805	(14,712)	(58,013)	29,088
Cash Flow	191,905	89,512	30,464	54,114	102,950
Debt/Equity	0.50	0.49	0.64	0.95	0.51
Return on Capital (%)	27.99	6.85	0.49	(8.79)	12.99
Ret. on Com. Equity (%)	25.12	4.48	(4.41)	(16.10)	7.33
% Change Profit	579.8	214.2	74.6	(299.4)	(34.3)
% Change Revenue	40.7	10.1	8.5	(23.4)	(4.8)
% Change Assets	46.6	(3.7)	(9.5)	(2.6)	(3.6)

Date	EPS	DPS	Tot Rev	Inc Bex
Mar 95	0.59	0.12	247,638	46,238
Dec 94	0.66	0.12	228,805	48,198
Sep 94	0.43	0.06	213,292	30,880
Jun 94	0.28	0.02	206,474	19,429
Mar 94	0.22	0.02	157,122	15,732
Dec 93	0.10	0.02	155,396	7,127
Sep 93	0.02	0.00	132,313	1,334
Jun 93	0.03	0.00	150,974	1,996

	Dec94	Dec93	Dec92
Preferred Div. Coverage	270.7	37.2	0.0
Total Div. Coverage	6.3	9.0	0.0
Interest Coverage	13.7	3.3	0.2
Current Ratio	2.5	2.8	2.1
Operating Margin	24.5	8.5	1.6
Asset Turnover	0.7	0.7	0.7
5 YEAR RATIOS (%)			
Return on Capital	7.9	5.9	9.4
Return on Com. Equity	3.3	0.6	4.1
Profit Growth	20.9	(24.6)	na
Revenue Growth	4.1	(3.0)	0.0
Asset Growth	3.7	(3.3)	(1.7)
BALANCE SHEET (000)			
Cash	156,722	28,998	28,682
Current Assets	428,570	237,951	226,034
Net Fixed Assets	674,432	508,217	545,758
Invest's & Advances	6,665	3,254	3,517
Total Assets	1,123,374	766,169	795,377
Short Term Debt	22,350	13,641	41,107
Current Liabilities	171,985	84,503	105,625
Long Term Debt	246,394	170,605	191,180
Total Liabilities	585,383	386,577	430,463
Total Equity	537,991	379,592	364,914
Total Liab. & Equity	1,123,374	766,169	795,377
CAPITAL (000)			
Total Debt	268,744	184,246	232,287
Preferred Equity	4,578	6,912	7,578
Common Equity	533,413	372,680	357,336

Business:

DONOHUE INC. is an integrated forest products company. The company produces newsprint, market pulp and lumber at its operations in the province of Quebec. The company markets its products to customers in the United States, Canada, Europe, Asia and South America. Through its subsidiaries, it has arrangements with Normick Perron Inc. and The New York Times Company.

Synopsis:

Market conditions for newsprint and market pulp have been difficult in recent years. However, 1994 showed an upswing in demand and selling prices. Lumber prices reached record highs. Donohue expects world demand for its products to remain firm at least until 1997. The company expects the improved prices to lead to record sales and shipments in 1995. Donohue will also be looking for acquisitions that will allow it to broaden the range of value-added products and boost sales to offshore markets.

Excess newsprint and market pulp from 1990 through mid-1994 caused prices to tumble for the entire industry. Only strong lumber prices helped Donohue to mitigate its losses. This severe period forced Donohue to reduce production costs, improve its facilities and optimize shipments.

The 41% increase in sales in 1994 to $807-million was due to more productive and lower cost operations. There were also higher selling prices for all products, increased lumber and newsprint shipments, the weaker Canadian dollar, and the acquisition of Finlay Forest Industries. Costs rose, too, as a result of increased shipments, the inclusion of Finlay's results, and extra costs incurred in producing more value-added lumber products.

Donohue aims to reduce the impact of a downturn in this cyclical industry. It wants to be one of the most profitable companies and not fall into the trap of overestimating demand and bringing too much capacity on-stream. The company is focusing on maintaining its manufacturing costs at a level among the lowest in the industry, adding value-added products, and obtaining ISO 9002 quality assurance accreditation for its mills.

In 1994, the company's sales by country were: Canada, 25%; United States, 58%; and overseas, 17%. Sales by product were: newsprint, 35%; kraft pulp, 25%; and lumber 40%. The lumber group was responsible for two-thirds of operating earnings.

Rank (Profit/Revenue/Assets)
71   136   147

Charles-Albert Poissant
Chairman

Michel Desbiens
President & C.E.O.

Claude Helie
V.P. & C.F.O.

Address
801 Chemin Saint-Louis
Quebec
PQ
GIS 4W3
(418) 684-7700

Fax: (418) 684-7707
D0004980/G/4.1

For further company information, call Globe Information Services 1-800-268-9128 or (416) 585-5345

FLETCHER CHALLENGE CANADA LIMITED

Exchanges	Price (Jun29'95)	21.87	Trailing P/E	49.70	Stock Symbol
TMV	Trailing Yield (%)	1.28	Trailing EPS	0.44	**FCC.A**

Period Ending	Jun94	Jun93	Jun92	Dec91	Jun91
Yearly Statistics					
Price-Close	16.88	21.25	15.38	16.88	18.00
Price-High	23.25	22.13	18.63	18.63	18.50
Price-Low	16.00	14.25	14.00	14.00	12.25
P/E-Close	80.36	nm	nm	nm	nm
Dividends per Share	0.28	0.26	0.00	0.23	0.40
Dividend Yield (%)	1.66	1.22	0.00	1.36	2.22
Sales per Share	13.49	13.08	15.43	17.27	18.59
EPS before extra. item	0.21	(0.26)	(0.70)	(0.44)	(0.42)
Cash Flow per Share	1.16	0.95	(0.79)	(0.70)	0.18
Book Value per Share	14.23	13.95	14.30	14.81	14.77
O/S Common Shares	124,189	90,730	77,058	60,186	60,086
Total Revenue	1,737,600	1,235,200	1,020,000	1,116,316	1,162,800
Income before extra.	26,400	(24,200)	(43,500)	(26,317)	(25,000)
Cash Flow	144,200	88,900	(49,200)	(42,300)	10,700
Debt/Equity	0.25	0.24	0.40	0.69	0.74
Return on Capital (%)	3.49	1.00	(1.57)	0.12	0.13
Ret. on Com. Equity (%)	1.74	(2.05)	(4.36)	(2.96)	(2.76)
% Change Profit	209.1	44.4	(65.3)	(5.3)	(145.5)
% Change Revenue	40.7	21.1	(8.6)	(4.0)	(7.3)
% Change Assets	1.7	48.5	0.5	(4.7)	3.1

Preferred Div. Coverage	np	na	np	
Total Div. Coverage	0.8	0.0	na	
Interest Coverage	1.6	0.4	0.0	
Current Ratio	1.4	1.6	1.6	
Operating Margin	2.6	0.8	(9.0)	
Asset Turnover	0.6	0.4	0.5	
5 YEAR RATIOS (%)				
Return on Capital	0.6	1.5	3.8	
Return on Com. Equity	(2.1)	(1.2)	1.4	
Profit Growth	(13.7)	na	na	
Revenue Growth	6.7	(3.2)	(7.7)	
Asset Growth	8.3	8.4	2.2	
BALANCE SHEET (000)				
Cash	35,700	74,400	4,500	
Current Assets	485,200	452,500	340,500	
Net Fixed Assets	2,248,700	2,278,000	1,470,200	
Invest's & Advances	18,500	14,600	35,900	
Total Assets	2,818,700	2,770,400	1,866,100	
Short Term Debt	52,600	48,000	21,300	
Current Liabilities	351,600	289,500	213,100	
Long Term Debt	391,500	367,700	413,700	
Total Liabilities	1,051,900	1,055,200	764,200	
Total Equity	1,766,800	1,715,200	1,101,900	
Total Liab. & Equity	2,818,700	2,770,400	1,866,100	
CAPITAL (000)				
Total Debt	444,100	415,700	435,000	
Preferred Equity	0	450,000	0	
Common Equity	1,766,800	1,265,200	1,101,900	

Business:

FLETCHER CHALLENGE CANADA LIMITED, is a forest products company. Its operations are in Western Canada and the United States. Products include newsprint and ground wood specialties, lightweight coated paper, market pulp, draft paper and lumber. The company has markets worldwide. As at December 31, 1993, Fletcher Challenge Ltd. of New Zealand owns a 51% interest.

Date	EPS	DPS	Tot Rev	Inc Bex
Mar 95	0.16	0.00	431,300	20,200
Dec 94	0.20	0.00	527,700	23,900
Sep 94	0.00	0.00	490,700	500
Jun 94	0.08	0.28	459,000	10,400
Mar 94	(0.07)	0.00	421,900	(8,900)
Dec 93	0.31	0.00	413,900	37,800
Sep 93	(0.11)	0.00	381,800	(12,900)
Jun 93	0.10	0.26	439,100	6,100

Synopsis:

Fletcher Challenge Canada is benefiting from improved markets in all of its products, especially pulp and paper. Sales in the nine months ended March 1995 reflect prices well above last year's levels. This improvement was offset by significantly lower volumes during the third quarter resulting from the strike. Prices began improving in 1994 and have increased substantially in 1995. List prices for kraft pulp increased from $390 (U.S.) per ton at the end of 1993 to $700 (U.S.) at the end of 1994 and to $925 (U.S.) in June 1995. Prices in 1995 have already increased more than $100 (U.S.) per ton for newsprint and $185 (U.S.) per short ton for coated paper.

The Dominion Bond Rating Service believes the company will have significantly improved sales, earnings, and cash flow throughout the remainder of 1995 and 1996. This is a result of sustained strength in the pulp and paper markets. Demand is strong globally and little new capacity is expected over the next two to three years, particularly in North America. Asia and Latin America are experiencing dramatic increases in paper consumption. The limited availability of fibre in these regions, and the lead time required to construct new facilities will constrain capacity growth.

In the nine months ended March 1995, net sales by segment were: newsprint and specialty papers, 28%; coated paper, 24%; market pulp, 20%; and wood products, 28%. Sales in the year ended June 1994 by market were: Canada, 23%; United States, 51%; Pacific Rim, 18%; and other offshore, 8%. The United States is the major market for newsprint and specialties and coated paper. Canada accounts for over half of wood product sales. Fletcher exports pulp to the Pacific Rim and other offshore countries.

There is an increase in the cost of wood chips and pulp wood in B.C. This is a result of reduced timber harvest levels, substantially higher stumpage and royalty rates, increased pulp and paper operating rates, and higher utilization of available fibre for structural wood end uses. The availability of recycled pulp for newsprint is also shrinking, as demand is growing.

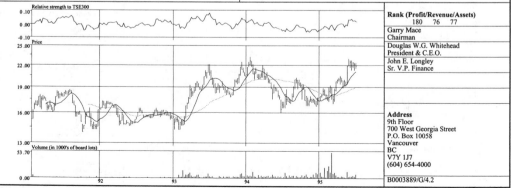

Rank (Profit/Revenue/Assets)		
180	76	77

Garry Mace
Chairman

Douglas W.G. Whitehead
President & C.E.O.

John E. Longley
Sr. V.P. Finance

Address
9th Floor
700 West Georgia Street
P.O. Box 10058
Vancouver
BC
V7Y 1J7
(604) 654-4000

B0003889/G/4.2

INTERNATIONAL FOREST PRODUCTS LIMITED

Exchanges	Price (Jun29'95)		12.25	Trailing P/E		8.22	Stock Symbol
T	Trailing Yield (%)		0.00	Trailing EPS		1.49	**IFP.A**

Period Ending	Dec94	Dec93	Dec92	Dec91	Dec90
Yearly Statistics					
Price-Close	13.00	21.50	10.75	8.50	6.50
Price-High	22.00	22.00	10.88	9.00	9.38
Price-Low	10.63	10.50	7.38	5.50	5.25
P/E-Close	7.74	9.82	97.73	nm	nm
Dividends per Share	0.00	0.00	0.00	0.22	0.23
Dividend Yield (%)	0.00	0.00	0.00	2.55	3.54
Sales per Share	23.82	20.02	14.55	11.05	16.85
EPS before extra. item	1.68	2.19	0.11	(0.94)	(0.69)
Cash Flow per Share	3.27	3.91	1.41	(0.72)	0.21
Book Value per Share	9.78	8.10	5.91	5.47	6.04
O/S Common Shares	32,577	32,566	32,444	29,884	18,972
Total Revenue	775,774	653,823	465,478	254,948	319,159
Income before extra.	54,770	71,294	3,517	(21,672)	(13,031)
Cash Flow	106,545	127,368	45,101	(16,602)	3,990
Debt/Equity	0.27	0.20	0.58	0.75	0.98
Return on Capital (%)	26.72	38.54	5.11	(10.81)	(4.76)
Ret. on Com. Equity (%)	18.82	31.32	1.98	(15.59)	(10.76)
% Change Profit	(23.2)	1,927.1	116.2	(66.3)	(168.1)
% Change Revenue	18.7	40.5	82.6	(20.1)	(15.6)
% Change Assets	19.5	20.7	13.3	15.7	1.3

Preferred Div. Coverage	np	np	np
Total Div. Coverage	na	na	na
Interest Coverage	23.0	32.3	1.7
Current Ratio	1.9	1.9	2.2
Operating Margin	12.4	18.0	4.0
Asset Turnover	1.5	1.5	1.3
5 YEAR RATIOS (%)			
Return on Capital	11.0	9.2	2.9
Return on Com. Equity	5.2	4.6	(1.7)
Profit Growth	23.4	147.0	(30.1)
Revenue Growth	15.4	10.1	3.9
Asset Growth	13.9	6.2	2.7
BALANCE SHEET (000)			
Cash	0	0	0
Current Assets	270,636	226,013	151,705
Net Fixed Assets	221,176	192,016	189,920
Invest's & Advances	14,901	5,625	9,050
Total Assets	507,406	424,491	351,656
Short Term Debt	70,869	31,851	28,222
Current Liabilities	143,996	117,175	69,611
Long Term Debt	16,000	22,000	83,342
Total Liabilities	188,913	160,840	160,030
Total Equity	318,493	263,651	191,626
Total Liab. & Equity	507,406	424,491	351,656
CAPITAL (000)			
Total Debt	86,869	53,851	111,564
Preferred Equity	0	0	0
Common Equity	318,493	263,651	191,626

Business:

INTERNATIONAL FOREST PRODUCTS LTD. is a logging and sawmilling company producing a diversified range of wood products for sale to world markets. It harvests timber and manufactures and markets lumber products, logs, and wood chips. The Company has 58 logging operations and eight sawmills in the southern coastal region of British Columbia and has one logging operation and sawmill in the central interior.

Date	EPS	DPS	Tot Rev	Inc Bex
Mar 95	0.24	0.00	207,228	8,416
Dec 94	0.38	0.00	196,357	12,289
Sep 94	0.40	0.00	208,945	13,231
Jun 94	0.47	0.00	202,554	15,300
Mar 94	0.43	0.00	170,492	13,950
Dec 93	0.36	0.00	164,001	11,611
Sep 93	0.50	0.00	187,066	16,577
Jun 93	0.77	0.00	157,595	25,059

Synopsis:

International Forest Products (Interfor) is primarily a lumber company with the Pacific Rim as its main market. In 1994, the company generated 71% of its revenue from lumber, 23% from log sales, with the remainder from wood chips and other by-products. Sales by market were: Pacific Rim, 42%; United States, 24%; Canada, 21%; U.K. and Europe, 11%; and other, 2%.

Lumber prices increased very little in 1994, and fell in the first half of 1995. However, Interfor's average selling price increased 13% to $808 per thousand board feet in 1994 and increased again by 6% in the first quarter of 1995. This reflected the company's increased value-added production, redirection of products to Asian markets, and the continuing softening of the Canadian dollar against the U.S. Dollar and the Japanese Yen. The revenue improvements were sufficient to offset Interfor's increased costs of logging, as the B.C. government changed logging practices and doubled stumpage fees.

Sawmill by-products used in the manufacturing of pulp continue to increase in price, the price of which doubled from late 1994 to March 1995. Profit margins should also improve, partly due to further price increases for lumber and wood chips, but primarily due to logging cost decreases. Log production volumes should double in the second quarter, which should result in further unit cost decreases and reduced log purchases.

In the first quarter of 1995, lumber sales volumes rose by 18%, due to the acquisition in late February of the coastal operations of Weldwood of Canada Limited. The acquisition will provide cost savings and improve revenues at Interfor's sawmills by narrowing the range of products produced at each mill and allowing log supplies to match more closely the needs of each sawmill. The logging operations are being integrated with Interfor's existing operations to reduce logging costs and improve production scheduling. The acquisition will increase Interfor's lumber production to 915 million board feet in 1995 from 672 million board feet in 1994.

Rank (Profit/Revenue/Assets)
107   141   224

William L. Sauder
Chairman & C.E.O.

R.M. Sitter
President & C.O.O.

G.J. Friesen
V.P. Finance & Secretary

Address
P.O. Box 49114
Bentall Postal Station
3500 - 1055 Dunsmuir Street
Vancouver
BC
V7X 1H7
(604) 689-6800
Fax: (604) 688-0313
W0002647/G/4.2

For further company information, call Globe Information Services 1-800-268-9128 or (416) 585-5345

MACMILLAN BLOEDEL LIMITED

Exchanges	Price (Jun29'95)	19 .12	Trailing P/E	10 .51	Stock Symbol
TMVQ	Trailing Yield (%)	3 .14	Trailing EPS	1 .82	**MB**

Period Ending	Dec94	Dec93	Dec92	Dec91	Dec90
Yearly Statistics					
Price-Close	17 .63	21 .25	16 .88	18 .50	16 .75
Price-High	23 .50	23 .63	21 .13	22 .63	18 .87
Price-Low	15 .50	16 .13	15 .63	15 .50	14 .25
P/E-Close	12 .41	50 .60	nm	nm	45 .27
Dividends per Share	0 .60	0 .60	0 .60	0 .60	0 .80
Dividend Yield (%)	3 .40	2 .82	3 .56	3 .24	4 .78
Sales per Share	31 .91	28 .88	26 .99	25 .48	29 .26
EPS before extra. item	1 .42	0 .42	(0 .52)	(0 .98)	0 .37
Cash Flow per Share	2 .72	2 .34	1 .85	(0 .27)	1 .75
Book Value per Share	13 .76	12 .56	12 .01	13 .37	14 .39
O/S Common Shares	123 ,754	123 ,732	112 ,629	111 ,302	102 ,650
Total Revenue	3 ,976 ,600	3 ,424 ,500	3 ,066 ,600	2 ,754 ,600	3 ,014 ,500
Income before extra.	180 ,200	53 ,200	(48 ,800)	(93 ,400)	50 ,800
Cash Flow	336 ,200	270 ,900	208 ,600	(29 ,000)	179 ,600
Debt/Equity	1 .06	1 .13	1 .27	0 .96	0 .78
Return on Capital (%)	11 .16	6 .28	1 .90	(3 .07)	4 .43
Ret. on Com. Equity (%)	10 .80	3 .35	(4 .25)	(7 .30)	2 .36
% Change Profit	238 .7	209 .0	47 .8	(283 .9)	(79 .4)
% Change Revenue	16 .1	11 .7	11 .3	(8 .6)	(8 .2)
% Change Assets	7 .3	7 .1	2 .1	6 .9	9 .2
Preferred Div. Coverage	41 .0	11 .8	0 .0		
Total Div. Coverage	2 .3	0 .7	0 .0		
Interest Coverage	2 .7	1 .5	0 .4		
Current Ratio	1 .6	2 .4	2 .6		
Operating Margin	7 .8	5 .3	1 .6		
Asset Turnover	0 .9	0 .8	0 .8		
5 YEAR RATIOS (%)					
Return on Capital	4 .1	5 .5	9 .5		
Return on Com. Equity	1 .0	2 .0	6 .2		
Profit Growth	(6 .1)	(30 .6)	na		
Revenue Growth	3 .9	0 .8	(0 .6)		
Asset Growth	6 .4	8 .6	9 .1		
BALANCE SHEET (000)					
Cash	324 ,800	260 ,500	142 ,700		
Current Assets	1 ,636 ,200	1 ,407 ,500	1 ,193 ,000		
Net Fixed Assets	1 ,887 ,800	1 ,825 ,600	2 ,034 ,600		
Invest'& Advances	904 ,900	667 ,400	656 ,500		
Total Assets	4 ,481 ,100	4 ,177 ,700	3 ,899 ,600		
Short Term Debt	489 ,400	193 ,000	102 ,100		
Current Liabilities	1 ,013 ,500	584 ,500	460 ,800		
Long Term Debt	1 ,384 ,600	1 ,640 ,200	1 ,738 ,200		
Total Liabilities	2 ,704 ,300	2 ,547 ,800	2 ,451 ,000		
Total Equity	1 ,776 ,800	1 ,629 ,900	1 ,448 ,600		
Total Liab. & Equity	4 ,481 ,100	4 ,177 ,700	3 ,899 ,600		
CAPITAL (000)					
Total Debt	1 ,874 ,000	1 ,833 ,200	1 ,840 ,300		
Preferred Equity	73 ,800	75 ,700	96 ,200		
Common Equity	1 ,703 ,000	1 ,554 ,200	1 ,352 ,400		

Business:

MACMILLAN BLOEDEL LTD. is the largest forest products company in Canada and has integrated operations in Canada and the United States as well as major investments in Canada, the United States and Europe. The products of the Company and its affiliated companies are marketed throughout the world and include lumber, panelboards, engineered wood, cement-fiber roofing, newsprint, and groundwood printing papers.

Date	EPS	DPS	Tot Rev	Inc Bex
Mar 95	0 .51	0 .15	1 ,253 ,000	65 ,300
Dec 94	0 .47	0 .15	1 ,058 ,300	59 ,900
Sep 94	0 .46	0 .15	1 ,040 ,500	58 ,100
Jun 94	0 .38	0 .15	1 ,048 ,500	48 ,300
Mar 94	0 .11	0 .15	985 ,000	13 ,900
Dec 93	0 .03	0 .15	854 ,000	5 ,100
Sep 93	(0 .19)	0 .15	835 ,300	(20 ,700)
Jun 93	0 .19	0 .15	904 ,800	22 ,500

Synopsis:

There is increasingly intense global competition in forest product commodities, and diminishing availability of high value fibre throughout North America. MacMillan Bloedel is responding by increasing its supply of high quality, value-added products through its world-wide marketing network. It is also focusing on three core businesses: building materials, 64% of sales; packaging, 16% of sales; and paper, 16% of sales. The majority of the company's lumber is sold to Japan and the United States. Over half of the company's newsprint and other groundwood printing papers are sold in the U.S.

The company has diversified geographically and expanded product lines. In 1994, the company acquired a combination particleboard, laminated beam and re-manufacturing plant in Mexico, which will be expanded in 1995 to add a second particleboard machine. It also invested in two new oriented strand board mills, one in Ontario and one in Quebec. In early 1995 it acquired Ontario-based Green Forest Lumber Corp. and invested in modern, cost-efficient facilities including two proposed medium density fibreboard mills, one in Pennsylvania and one in Ontario. Construction is continuing on the Nexgen project at Port Alberni to convert a standard newsprint machine to lightweight coated paper, which will use less fibre. The company is also building a recycled lightweight linerboard mini-mill in Kentucky.

The B.C. government reduced timber cutting allowances and increased stumpage and royalty fees. To recover the increasing log harvesting costs, the company is taking steps to increase fibre recovery and add value through improved harvesting techniques, refined log sorting, and re-manufacturing. Programs are in place to improve the cost competitiveness of its two paper mills.

Most of the improved performance in 1994 was a result of increased volumes and prices of the company's lumber and packaging. Prices for standard newsprint and other groundwood printing papers continued to recover in 1995. Prices and demand for the company's other products continued stable.

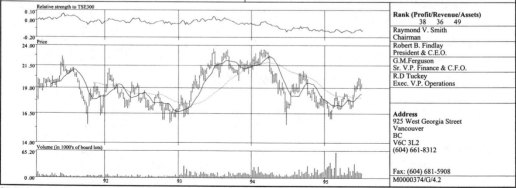

Rank (Profit/Revenue/Assets)		
38	36	49

Raymond V. Smith
Chairman

Robert B. Findlay
President & C.E.O.

G.M.Ferguson
Sr. V.P. Finance & C.F.O.

R.D Tuckey
Exec. V.P. Operations

Address
925 West Georgia Street
Vancouver
BC
V6C 3L2
(604) 661-8312

Fax: (604) 681-5908
M0000374/G/4.2

MALETTE INC.

Exchanges	Price (Jun29'95)	16.00	Trailing P/E	11.03	Stock Symbol
TM	Trailing Yield (%)	3.16	Trailing EPS	1.45	MTI

Period Ending	Sep94	Sep93	Sep92	Sep91	Sep90	Business:
Yearly Statistics						MALETTE INC. is an integrated forest
Price-Close	10.75	9.63	6.75	6.33	6.33	products company. The company is involved in
Price-High	11.38	13.00	6.75	7.67	na	the management and development of forest
Price-Low	8.68	7.75	4.75	5.67	na	resources and the production of lumber, wood
P/E-Close	12.65	nm	nm	nm	2.76	chips, oriented stand board and bleached kraft
Dividends per Share	0.30	0.30	0.20	0.20	0.33	pulp and paper.
Dividend Yield (%)	2.79	3.12	2.96	3.16	5.26	
Sales per Share	12.96	11.41	11.08	10.77	16.37	
EPS before extra. item	0.85	(0.47)	(1.04)	(0.56)	2.29	
Cash Flow per Share	2.37	0.25	(0.20)	0.96	2.54	
Book Value per Share	8.83	7.99	8.42	9.83	10.67	
O/S Common Shares	17,049	13,709	10,194	9,860	9,737	
Total Revenue	203,097	141,031	114,964	108,710	167,244	
Income before extra.	13,131	(5,494)	(11,108)	(5,667)	22,040	
Cash Flow	36,538	2,989	(2,009)	9,449	23,792	
Debt/Equity	1.31	1.74	2.05	1.30	0.58	
Return on Capital (%)	11.30	0.07	(4.15)	(2.13)	26.14	
Ret. on Com. Equity (%)	10.10	(5.62)	(12.16)	(5.65)	23.83	
% Change Profit	339.0	50.5	(96.0)	(125.7)	18.7	
% Change Revenue	44.0	22.7	5.8	(35.0)	19.0	
% Change Assets	18.8	8.9	12.5	23.2	41.8	

Date	EPS	DPS	Tot Rev	Inc Bex
Mar 95	0.47	0.20	69,868	10,081
Dec 94	0.44	0.31	60,831	7,555
Sep 94	0.41	0.00	58,998	6,576
Jun 94	0.13	0.00	50,217	2,211
Mar 94	0.28	0.00	50,647	3,991
Dec 93	0.03	0.00	43,189	353
Sep 93	(0.44)	0.00	35,649	(5,145)
Jun 93	(0.25)	0.00	31,814	(2,814)

				Synopsis:
Preferred Div. Coverage	np	np	np	Malette Inc. returned to profitability in fiscal 1994, after sustaining losses for
Total Div. Coverage	3.2	0.0	0.0	three consecutive years. The turnaround, which should continue into 1996, is due
Interest Coverage	2.4	0.0	0.0	to the economic recovery and the substantial investments made during the
Current Ratio	3.3	1.7	1.2	recession to renovate and improve its facilities at the lowest possible cost. Sales
Operating Margin	18.2	(0.2)	(7.3)	increased in fiscal 1994 and 1995 due to increased sales volumes and better prices
Asset Turnover	0.5	0.4	0.3	for lumber and oriented structural board (OSB). This resulted from an improved
5 YEAR RATIOS (%)				North American economy, increased housing starts, and increased exports to
Return on Capital	6.2	10.6	17.2	Europe. While logging restrictions in the U.S. northwest and British Columbia
Return on Com. Equity	2.1	5.2	11.9	resulted in lumber and plywood shortages, demand drove selling prices up more
Profit Growth	(6.7)	na	na	than 50% higher than those of 1992. OSB panel markets have also increased
Revenue Growth	7.6	0.3	(1.6)	substantially, as OSB continues to replace plywood in home construction.
Asset Growth	20.4	19.4	18.4	
BALANCE SHEET (000)				Strong demand for kraft pulp, especially in Europe, led increased pulp prices.
Cash	26,333	0	0	Kraft pulp prices increased four times in fiscal 1994 to reach $630 (U.S.) per
Current Assets	85,010	41,399	44,032	metric tonne at September 30, 1994. They reached $700 (U.S.) in October and
Net Fixed Assets	292,237	278,845	252,191	steadily rose to $925 (U.S.) by June 1995. Sales were $200.1-million in fiscal
Invest's & Advances	32,149	28,683	23,730	1994. By product, sales were: lumber, 37%; logs and by-products, 2%; oriented
Total Assets	424,356	357,323	327,997	structural board, 21%; pulp, 40%. Solid wood segment sales were split between
Short Term Debt	18	7,421	12,013	Canada and the United States. Canadian customers purchased 76% of pulp sales
Current Liabilities	25,598	24,872	35,786	and American customers, 20%.
Long Term Debt	196,591	183,116	163,802	Mallette is taking advantage of the economic upturn to restructure its debt, reduce
Total Liabilities	273,801	247,738	242,181	production costs further and improve productivity and capacity, while maintaining
Total Equity	150,555	109,585	85,816	high standards of quality. The expansion at Malette Timmins OSB is an example.
Total Liab. & Equity	424,356	357,323	327,997	The expansion, expected at $65-million, will almost triple the plant's capacity to
CAPITAL (000)				supply growing demand, while lowering production costs.
Total Debt	196,609	190,537	175,815	In June 1995, Tembec launched a $300-million takeover bid for Malette Inc.
Preferred Equity	0	0	0	Malette would provide ready access to an abundant, cheap supply of wood chips
Common Equity	150,555	109,585	85,816	for Tembec's 41% owned Spruce Falls newsprint and sawmill operation in
				Kapuskasing, Ontario.

Rank (Profit/Revenue/Assets)
263   313   246

Gaston Malette
Chairman & C.E.O.

Fred Burrows
President & C.O.O.

Gerald Brousseau
V.P. Finance

Address
Highway 101 West
P.O. Box 1100
Timmins
ON
P4N 7H9
(705) 268-1462

Fax: (705) 268-5065
W0000112/G/4.1

MALETTE QUEBEC INC.

Exchanges	Price (Jun29'95)		4.75	Trailing P/E		nm	Stock Symbol
TM	Trailing Yield (%)		0.00	Trailing EPS		(0.12)	**MQI**

Period Ending	Sep94	Sep93	Sep92	Sep91
Yearly Statistics				
Price-Close	3.10	n t	n t	n t
Price-High	4.75	n t	n t	n t
Price-Low	2.45	n t	n t	n t
P/E-Close	nm	n t	n t	n t
Dividends per Share	0.00	0.00	0.00	0.00
Dividend Yield (%)	0.00	0.00	0.00	0.00
Sales per Share	4.95	4.29	1.97	528.95
EPS before extra. item	(0.64)	0.04	(0.29)	(0.30)
Cash Flow per Share	(0.27)	0.70	0.06	(27.60)
Book Value per Share	3.69	4.32	4.27	917.01
O/S Common Shares	13,138	10,938	10,938	55
Total Revenue	59,947	47,182	21,878	29,029
Income before extra.	(8,286)	492	(3,164)	(3,331)
Cash Flow	(3,306)	7,609	674	(1,509)
Debt/Equity	1.77	1.82	2.10	0.88
Return on Capital (%)	(1.59)	2.74	(1.71)	na
Ret. on Com. Equity (%)	(17.33)	1.05	(6.53)	na
% Change Profit	(1,784.1)	115.6	5.0	na
% Change Revenue	27.1	115.7	(24.6)	na
% Change Assets	(0.8)	11.1	26.3	na

Business:

MALETTE QUEBEC INC. is a forest products company involved in the production of oriented structural board, machine finishd coated paper and high brightness printing paper and logging.

Date	EPS	DPS	Tot Rev	Inc Bex
Mar 95	0.22	0.00	27,231	2,814
Dec 94	0.03	0.00	19,227	428
Sep 94	(0.25)	0.00	17,422	(1,767)
Jun 94	(0.12)	0.00	15,324	1,560
Mar 94	(0.13)	0.00	12,471	(1,756)
Dec 93	(0.14)	0.00	14,431	(1,767)
Sep 93	(0.04)	0.00	9,987	(1,904)
Jun 93	0.06	0.00	11,983	645

Preferred Div. Coverage	na	na	na	
Total Div. Coverage	na	na	na	
Interest Coverage	0.0	2.7	0.0	
Current Ratio	1.8	1.1	1.2	
Operating Margin	(1.0)	9.9	(11.2)	
Asset Turnover	0.3	0.3	0.1	
5 YEAR RATIOS (%)				
Return on Capital	na	na	na	
Return on Com. Equity	na	na	na	
Profit Growth	na	na	na	
Revenue Growth	na	na	na	
Asset Growth	na	na	na	
BALANCE SHEET (000)				
Cash	1,361	0	2,019	
Current Assets	15,398	14,274	9,930	
Net Fixed Assets	149,709	149,913	143,731	
Invest's & Advances	0	0	0	
Total Assets	178,323	179,767	161,810	
Short Term Debt	3,396	8,191	1,377	
Current Liabilities	8,558	13,586	8,436	
Long Term Debt	104,157	99,739	101,437	
Total Liabilities	117,670	120,371	112,906	
Total Equity	60,653	59,396	48,904	
Total Liab. & Equity	178,323	179,767	161,810	
CAPITAL (000)				
Total Debt	107,553	107,930	102,814	
Preferred Equity	12,200	12,200	2,200	
Common Equity	48,453	47,196	46,704	

Synopsis:

Malette Quebec produces oriented structural board (OSB) through its Panneaux Malette OSB plant. It produces machine coated finished paper (MFC) and high brightness printing paper at the Papiers Malette paper mill. Currently, the OSB sector is booming. There is a short supply of logs in western Canada and the U.S. Northwest, rising housing starts and renovations, and rapidly expanding markets in Europe and Asia. However, through 1994 and 1995 Malette experienced substantial improvements in OSB panel prices and reduced sales volumes.

During fiscal 1994, bad weather and aging equipment slowed down production, so Malette undertook a modernization and expansion program for its OSB plant. The bulk of the $13.4-million project will be completed by September 1995. This should reduce unit production costs and increase the plant's annual capacity by 40% to 1.3 billion square feet of 1/16-inch base OSB. Panneaux Malette OSB's main markets are in Quebec, Ontario, the United States, Europe and Asia. Its sales accounted for 51% of Malette Quebec's sales in fiscal 1994.

In the paper sector, sales volumes and selling prices have also increased dramatically. The addition of a top former to a number one paper machine in fiscal 1994 substantially improved both paper quality and grade. This combined with increased production and additional clients boosted prices and sales. However, the significant increase in operating costs of Papier Malette caused the company to lose $8.3-million in fiscal 1994. The increased costs were due to the depreciation and interest that were capitalized during pre-production.

In fiscal 1994, Papiers Malette's production figures rose by 36% to reach 38,300 metric tonnes. The division has an annual production capacity of 67,000 metric tonnes. The new plant should be at capacity by September 1995. Papiers Malette generated 49% of Malette Quebec's sales in fiscal 1994. This figure should be higher in 1995 with the lower production of OSB, coupled with higher paper prices and sales volumes.

Rank (Profit/Revenue/Assets)
936   511   371

Gaston Malette
Chairman President & C.E.O.

Address
625 Ouest Blvd Rene Levesque
Montreal
PQ
H3B 1R2
(514) 397-1434

Fax: (514) 397-0735
01003464/G/4.1

NORANDA FOREST INC.

Exchanges	Price (Jun29'95)		11 .50	Trailing P/E		9 .74	Stock Symbol
TMV	Trailing Yield (%)		3 .48	Trailing EPS		1 .18	**NF**

Period Ending	Dec94	Dec93	Dec92	Dec91	Dec90
Yearly Statistics					
Price-Close	11 .13	12 .00	7 .60	8 .75	8 .00
Price-High	14 .25	12 .50	9 .50	10 .50	14 .50
Price-Low	9 .88	7 .25	6 .38	6 .88	7 .13
P/E-Close	11 .02	nm	nm	nm	nm
Dividends per Share	0 .40	0 .40	0 .40	0 .40	0 .70
Dividend Yield (%)	3 .59	3 .33	5 .26	4 .57	8 .75
Sales per Share	13 .66	11 .96	11 .06	36 .79	45 .80
EPS before extra. item	1 .01	(0 .87)	(0 .77)	(2 .01)	(1 .16)
Cash Flow per Share	2 .00	1 .01	0 .36	(0 .88)	1 .06
Book Value per Share	6 .79	6 .05	7 .03	8 .31	11 .16
O/S Common Shares	133 ,073	132 ,903	132 ,692	127 ,283	101 ,964
Total Revenue	1 ,879 ,000	1 ,538 ,000	1 ,400 ,000	4 ,133 ,000	4 ,565 ,000
Income before extra.	146 ,000	(104 ,000)	(88 ,000)	(209 ,000)	(95 ,000)
Cash Flow	264 ,000	132 ,000	47 ,000	(99 ,000)	105 ,000
Debt/Equity	0 .75	1 .05	1 .27	2 .31	1 .97
Return on Capital (%)	15 .93	(2 .07)	(0 .27)	(3 .76)	1 .80
Ret. on Com. Equity (%)	15 .58	(13 .13)	(10 .05)	(20 .49)	(9 .50)
% Change Profit	240 .4	(18 .2)	57 .9	(120 .0)	(150 .3)
% Change Revenue	22 .2	9 .9	(66 .1)	(9 .5)	(7 .4)
% Change Assets	(2 .3)	(16 .2)	(53 .3)	1 .1	6 .9
Preferred Div. Coverage	11 .2	0 .0	0 .0		
Total Div. Coverage	2 .2	0 .0	0 .0		
Interest Coverage	4 .7	0 .0	0 .0		
Current Ratio	2 .1	1 .9	1 .2		
Operating Margin	13 .3	7 .1	1 .6		
Asset Turnover	0 .8	0 .7	0 .5		
5 YEAR RATIOS (%)					
Return on Capital	2 .3	2 .5	7 .7		
Return on Com. Equity	(7 .5)	(7 .9)	(0 .8)		
Profit Growth	(5 .0)	na	na		
Revenue Growth	(17 .6)	(20 .3)	(21 .0)		
Asset Growth	(16 .3)	(12 .4)	(7 .5)		
BALANCE SHEET (000)					
Cash	84 ,000	0	0		
Current Assets	861 ,000	738 ,000	464 ,000		
Net Fixed Assets	1 ,260 ,000	1 ,096 ,000	1 ,287 ,000		
Invest's & Advances	125 ,000	135 ,000	1 ,033 ,000		
Total Assets	2 ,302 ,000	2 ,356 ,000	2 ,810 ,000		
Short Term Debt	81 ,000	129 ,000	175 ,000		
Current Liabilities	406 ,000	384 ,000	384 ,000		
Long Term Debt	746 ,000	929 ,000	1 ,262 ,000		
Total Liabilities	1 ,199 ,000	1 ,352 ,000	1 ,677 ,000		
Total Equity	1 ,103 ,000	1 ,004 ,000	1 ,133 ,000		
Total Liab. & Equity	2 ,302 ,000	2 ,356 ,000	2 ,810 ,000		
CAPITAL (000)					
Total Debt	827 ,000	1 ,058 ,000	1 ,437 ,000		
Preferred Equity	200 ,000	200 ,000	200 ,000		
Common Equity	903 ,000	804 ,000	933 ,000		

Business:

NORANDA FOREST INC. is one of Canada's largest forest products companies with operations across North America and in the United Kingdom. Products include lumber and building materials, paper and pulp. The company markets its products worldwide. Noranda Inc. of Toronto holds 74% of the company's outstanding common shares (66% of outstanding common shares on a fully diluted basis).

Date	EPS	DPS	Tot Rev	Inc Bex
Mar 95	0 .39	0 .10	511 ,000	56 ,000
Dec 94	0 .46	0 .10	534 ,000	64 ,000
Sep 94	0 .18	0 .10	467 ,000	28 ,000
Jun 94	0 .15	0 .10	461 ,000	22 ,000
Mar 94	0 .22	0 .10	418 ,000	32 ,000
Dec 93	(0 .49)	0 .10	444 ,000	(62 ,000)
Sep 93	0 .02	0 .10	391 ,000	6 ,000
Jun 93	0 .01	0 .10	391 ,000	4 ,000

Synopsis:

Noranda Forest operates in three segments: building materials (lumber and panel), papers (newsprint, woodfree and groundwood paper, and boxboard), and market kraft pulp (softwood and hardwood). Sales in 1994 were: building materials, 53%; papers, 33%; market pulp, 13%; and other, 1%. Sales by geographic segment were: Canada, 66%; United States, 30%; and United Kingdom, 4%. About 61% of Canadian sales were exported.

Improved results for 1994 and the first half of 1995 were due to recovering economies world-wide and higher U.S. dollar denominated prices for building materials and newsprint. A weak Canadian dollar relative to the U.S. dollar, productivity improvements, and continuing reductions in costs also were factors. Shipments of lumber, OSB, medium density fibreboard (MDF), boxboard, and newsprint all were at record levels in 1994.

The pulp segment reported the most dramatic improvement over 1993 due to the sharp escalation in prices, especially in the fourth quarter. The building materials segment remained strong, posting record-breaking operating earnings of $242-million, up 35% from 1993.

Noranda Forest expects earnings in 1995 to exceed the near record earnings of 1989. Paper and pulp prices should provide major improvements in earnings. However, rising interest rates, which slow construction, could decrease the record earnings levels of 1994 in the building materials segment.

In February 1995, the company more than doubled its capacity to make fine papers by acquiring Minnesota-based Cross Pointe Paper Corp. for about $200-million (U.S.). Cross Pointe, with sales worth $320-million (Canadian) in 1994, will increase 1995 sales by 15%. Noranda Forest has been looking for acquisitions that can smooth out the boom-bust tendencies of its industry. Cross Point remained profitable throughout the cyclical downturn. It makes a wide range of specialty printing and writing papers that provide better margins.

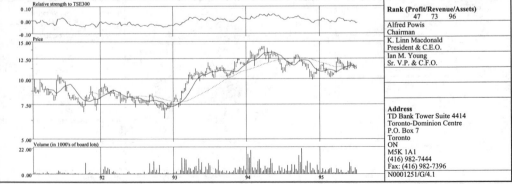

Rank (Profit/Revenue/Assets)		
47	73	96

Alfred Powis
Chairman

K. Linn Macdonald
President & C.E.O.

Ian M. Young
Sr. V.P. & C.F.O.

Address
TD Bank Tower Suite 4414
Toronto-Dominion Centre
P.O. Box 7
Toronto
ON
M5K 1A1
(416) 982-7444
Fax: (416) 982-7396
N0001251/G/4.1

PACIFIC FOREST PRODUCTS LIMITED

Exchanges	Price (Jun29'95)		15.62	Trailing P/E		8.58	Stock Symbol
TMV	Trailing Yield (%)		0.00	Trailing EPS		1.82	**PFF**

Period Ending	Dec94	Dec93	Dec92	Dec91
Yearly Statistics		5M		
Price-Close	12.38	20.75	nt	nt
Price-High	21.50	21.13	nt	nt
Price-Low	9.75	13.38	nt	nt
P/E-Close	10.49	13.95	nt	nt
Dividends per Share	0.00	0.00	0.00	0.00
Dividend Yield (%)	0.00	0.00	0.00	0.00
Sales per Share	12.88	11.73	0.00	0.00
EPS before extra. item	1.18	0.62	na	na
Cash Flow per Share	2.26	2.16	0.00	0.00
Book Value per Share	8.26	7.64	na	na
O/S Common Shares	20,408	20,408	0	0
Total Revenue	266,652	100,513	174,941	134,671
Income before extra.	28,079	14,749	20,294	(10,269)
Cash Flow	46,030	18,376	37,259	899
Debt/Equity	0.07	0.09	0.03	0.03
Return on Capital (%)	21.43	25.38	10.07	na
Ret. on Com. Equity (%)	14.83	16.74	9.55	na
% Change Profit	(20.7)	74.4	297.6	na
% Change Revenue	10.5	37.9	29.9	na
% Change Assets	0.5	9.6	0.4	na
Preferred Div. Coverage	7.0	7.4	np	
Total Div. Coverage	7.0	7.4	na	
Interest Coverage	41.5	67.4	97.6	
Current Ratio	1.8	1.7	2.4	
Operating Margin	16.5	22.7	13.2	
Asset Turnover	0.9	0.9	0.7	
5 YEAR RATIOS (%)				
Return on Capital	na	na	na	
Return on Com. Equity	na	na	na	
Profit Growth	na	na	na	
Revenue Growth	na	na	na	
Asset Growth	na	na	na	
BALANCE SHEET (000)				
Cash	0	0	0	
Current Assets	95,560	89,234	75,663	
Net Fixed Assets	180,555	180,521	175,020	
Invest's & Advances	1,134	1,714	664	
Total Assets	277,249	275,756	251,630	
Short Term Debt	1,069	19,679	3,518	
Current Liabilities	52,317	53,187	31,073	
Long Term Debt	12,839	60	2,800	
Total Liabilities	74,155	60,090	42,125	
Total Equity	203,094	215,666	209,505	
Total Liab. & Equity	277,249	275,756	251,630	
CAPITAL (000)				
Total Debt	13,908	19,739	6,318	
Preferred Equity	34,545	59,847	0	
Common Equity	168,549	155,819	209,505	

Business:

PACIFIC FOREST PRODUCTS LIMITED has been in the business of producing lumber products for over 40 years through its predecessors Tahsis Company Ltd. and Pacific Logging Company Limited. These companies were acquired from Canadian Pacific Forest Products Wood Products Group on July 29, 1993.

Date	EPS	DPS	Tot Rev	Inc Bex
Mar 95	0.89	0.00	108,534	18,208
Dec 94	0.31	0.00	61,318	7,135
Sep 94	0.21	0.00	63,413	5,120
Jun 94	0.41	0.00	81,096	9,607
Mar 94	0.25	0.00	88,880	5,094
Dec 93	0.35	0.00	66,706	8,311
Sep 93	0.27	0.00	33,807	6,438

Synopsis:

Pacific Forest Products became a public company on July 29, 1993. It is 51%-owned by Avenor. The company feels it is a preeminent supplier of high-valued, high-quality wood products to Japan and other world markets. In 1994, 71% of its lumber sales were to Japan, with 7% to the U.K., 4% to northwest Europe, 5% to Australia, and 13% to other countries. About 60% of its sales were denominated in United States dollars and 26% in Japanese Yen. The company recorded net sales of $262.9-million, producing 320,000 thousand feet board of lumber from its sawmills. Net earnings attributable to common shares amounted to $24.1-million or $1.18 per share. cash flow from operations was $49.1-million and operating earnings were $43.3-million.

In the first quarter of 1995, Pacific Forest generated higher sales and net earnings over the same period in 1994, as a result of higher sales volumes and dramatically increased prices for logs and wood chips. Lumber shipments to Japan remained steady and prices were firm, while offshore markets were active and prices rose. Pacific expects 1995 to follow this pattern. Sales totalled $108.5-million compared with $88.9-million in the 1994 first quarter. Profit was $18.2-million or 89 cents a share, up from $5.1-million or 25 cents.

Pacific has enjoyed buoyant product markets. However, stumpage and royalty rates payable on timber harvested from Crown tenures increased by 55% in May 1994. This increased Pacific's costs by $16.7-million over the prior year. The company's single greatest asset is its private forest land. It has 20 million cubic metres of standing timber of harvestable age. It has increased its annual rate of harvest on private lands by 33% to 800,000 cubic metres.

In response to customer requests, and the higher costs of fibre, the company is increasing the processing of its lumber into semi-finished and finished products, to be remanufactured and customized. Since 1993, the amount of lumber production being kiln-dried has increased by 104%. This is increasing Pacific's sales volume of lumber and broadening its customer base. Pacific Forest is also extracting more value through log sorting, sales, and trades.

Relative strength to TSE300 / Price / Volume (in 1000's of board lots)

Rank (Profit/Revenue/Assets)
170   274   298

Paul E. Gagne
Chairman

Sandy M. Fulton
President & C.E.O.

James Logan
V.P. Finance & C.F.O.

Address
Suite 1000
1040 West Georgia Street
Vancouver
BC
V6E 4K4
(604) 640-3400

Fax: (604) 640-3480
01003417/G/4.2

QUNO CORPORATION

Exchanges	Price (Jun29'95)		24.50	Trailing P/E		10.34	Stock Symbol
TM	Trailing Yield (%)		0.00	Trailing EPS		2.37	**QNO**

Period Ending	Dec94	Dec93	Dec92	Dec91
Yearly Statistics				
Price-Close	25.88	23.00	n t	n t
Price-High	29.00	24.75	n t	n t
Price-Low	22.00	16.25	n t	n t
P/E-Close	25.37	nm	n t	n t
Dividends per Share	0.00	0.00	0.00	0.00
Dividend Yield (%)	0.00	0.00	0.00	0.00
Sales per Share	25.12	24.76	54.64	60.57
EPS before extra. item	1.02	(2.16)	(10.39)	(3.14)
Cash Flow per Share	2.48	1.55	(10.57)	(0.40)
Book Value per Share	12.05	10.96	9.98	20.38
O/S Common Shares	22,452	22,047	8,000	8,000
Total Revenue	561,193	497,925	436,120	494,847
Income before extra.	22,769	(43,450)	(83,148)	(25,140)
Cash Flow	55,413	31,038	(84,522)	(3,239)
Debt/Equity	1.59	1.75	7.23	2.79
Return on Capital (%)	4.44	(3.33)	(12.42)	na
Ret. on Com. Equity (%)	8.89	(27.03)	(68.48)	na
% Change Profit	152.4	47.7	(230.7)	na
% Change Revenue	12.7	14.2	(11.9)	na
% Change Assets	5.6	0.5	(1.4)	na

Date	EPS	DPS	Tot Rev	Inc Bex
Mar 95	0.82	0.00	182,700	18,400
Dec 94	1.21	0.00	152,563	26,869
Sep 94	0.31	0.00	148,900	6,900
Jun 94	0.03	0.00	134,100	600
Mar 94	(0.52)	0.00	126,500	(11,600)
Dec 93	(1.76)	0.00	120,575	(35,550)
Sep 93	(0.20)	0.00	115,600	(4,400)
Jun 93	0.04	0.00	134,400	800

	Dec94	Dec93	Dec92
Preferred Div. Coverage	np	np	np
Total Div. Coverage	na	na	na
Interest Coverage	1.6	0.0	0.0
Current Ratio	2.4	2.8	2.4
Operating Margin	5.8	(1.1)	(11.2)
Asset Turnover	0.7	0.7	0.6
5 YEAR RATIOS (%)			
Return on Capital	na	na	na
Return on Com. Equity	na	na	na
Profit Growth	na	na	na
Revenue Growth	na	na	na
Asset Growth	na	na	na
BALANCE SHEET (000)			
Cash	168	436	3,519
Current Assets	167,380	170,890	159,959
Net Fixed Assets	519,098	514,744	534,681
Invest's & Advances	0	0	0
Total Assets	781,097	739,998	736,313
Short Term Debt	0	0	0
Current Liabilities	68,546	61,954	66,805
Long Term Debt	429,279	423,027	577,681
Total Liabilities	510,498	498,358	656,461
Total Equity	270,599	241,640	79,852
Total Liab. & Equity	781,097	739,998	736,313
CAPITAL (000)			
Total Debt	429,279	423,027	577,681
Preferred Equity	0	0	0
Common Equity	270,599	241,640	79,852

Business:

QUNO CORPORATION is an integrated forest products company. The company operates pulp and newsprint mills in Thorold, Ontario and Baie-Comeau, Quebec and owns and operates a sawmill near Baie-Comeau. It is active in the development and application of recycling technology.

Synopsis:

The next few years should be profitable for the North American newsprint industry and for QUNO Corporation. The supply and demand balance should remain tight through the end of 1996, with no significant industry capacity increases expected and demand growing faster than supply. With two low-cost newsprint operations, QUNO feels it is in position to prosper from the improved market conditions.

Rebounding prices in 1994 boosted QUNO's transaction prices by about 31% since the end of the first quarter. Prices were up only 4% over the year as a result of the low first quarter prices. Price increases announced for March and May of 1995 restored newsprint prices to 1988 levels, representing a further increase of approximately 23%. Higher newsprint volumes, higher average Canadian dollar transaction prices, and higher lumber revenues contributed to QUNO's improved revenues and earnings in 1994 and 1995 are. Operating expenses in 1994 were higher primarily as a result of higher newsprint and lumber sales volumes.

During 1995, the company plans to increase annual newsprint capacity by 40,000 tonnes, increase recycling capacity, continue to contain costs, and develop its export sales. QUNO, and the rest of the industry, is currently absorbing the impact of three main cost factors: regional increases in virgin fibre prices; increases in recycled fibre prices; and a changing Canadian dollar exchange rate.

QUNO's principal shareholder, Tribune Company, reduced its basic equity interest in QUNO from 59% to 34% during 1994. Tribune Company remains the company's largest customer, with sales to Tribune newspapers to about 33% of the total volume.

Operating revenues by product in 1994 were: newsprint, 86%; lumber, 9%; and recycling, power and other, 5%. The company exported 75% of sales to the United States, 9% to other foreign countries, and sold 15% to Canadian customers. The company sold 787,000 tonnes of newsprint in 1994, 6% more than in 1993.

Relative strength to TSE300

Price

Volume (in 1000's of board lots)

Rank (Profit/Revenue/Assets)
200   184   178

John E. Houghton
Chairman

William J. McNally
President & C.E.O.

James G. Lawn
V.P. & C.F.O.

Address
80 King Street
St. Catharines
ON
L2R 7G1
(905) 688-5030

Fax: (905) 688-6005
01003345/G/4.1

For further company information, call Globe Information Services 1-800-268-9128 or (416) 585-5345

RAINY RIVER FOREST PRODUCTS INC.

Exchanges	Price (Jun29'95)	13.75	Trailing P/E	16.37	Stock Symbol
TM	Trailing Yield (%)	0.00	Trailing EPS	0.84	**RRF**

Period Ending	Dec94	Dec93	Dec92
Yearly Statistics			
Price-Close	12.75	nt	nt
Price-High	14.25	nt	nt
Price-Low	11.13	nt	nt
P/E-Close	nm	nt	nt
Dividends per Share	0.00	0.00	0.00
Dividend Yield (%)	0.00	0.00	0.00
Sales per Share	15.89	21.62	20.51
EPS before extra. item	(1.81)	(1.92)	(2.09)
Cash Flow per Share	(0.39)	(0.83)	(0.28)
Book Value per Share	12.34	16.80	16.86
O/S Common Shares	34,704	20,704	20,730
Total Revenue	555,968	450,663	432,003
Income before extra.	(43,875)	(39,783)	(43,370)
Cash Flow	(13,427)	(17,099)	(5,858)
Debt/Equity	0.93	0.55	0.42
Return on Capital (%)	(7.02)	(10.27)	na
Ret. on Com. Equity (%)	(11.31)	(11.41)	na
% Change Profit	(10.3)	8.3	na
% Change Revenue	23.4	4.3	na
% Change Assets	39.9	3.6	na
Preferred Div. Coverage	np	np	np
Total Div. Coverage	na	na	na
Interest Coverage	0.0	0.0	0.0
Current Ratio	1.9	1.6	1.7
Operating Margin	(7.4)	(11.6)	(15.3)
Asset Turnover	0.6	0.6	0.6
5 YEAR RATIOS (%)			
Return on Capital	na	na	na
Return on Com. Equity	na	na	na
Profit Growth	na	na	na
Revenue Growth	na	na	na
Asset Growth	na	na	na
BALANCE SHEET (000)			
Cash	71,547	5,371	4,185
Current Assets	234,942	107,743	115,209
Net Fixed Assets	708,177	556,057	535,161
Invest's & Advances	0	6,753	3,800
Total Assets	992,732	709,590	685,114
Short Term Debt	32,744	3,307	4,448
Current Liabilities	122,886	68,774	67,658
Long Term Debt	364,301	187,526	143,897
Total Liabilities	564,651	361,685	335,542
Total Equity	428,081	347,905	349,572
Total Liab. & Equity	992,732	709,590	685,114
CAPITAL (000)			
Total Debt	397,045	190,833	148,345
Preferred Equity	0	0	0
Common Equity	428,081	347,905	349,572

Business:

RAINY RIVER FOREST PRODUCTS INC. is a manufacturer and seller of uncoated groundwood papers and newsprint. The Company also produces and sells market pulp. The Company has also entered into an exclusive newsprint marketing agreement with Boise Cascade Corporation under which the company will purchase, at a brokerage discount for resale to customers, all of the newsprint produced at the mill in Louisiana.

Date	EPS	DPS	Tot Rev	Inc Bex
Jun 95	0.73	0.00	271,469	25,382
Mar 95	0.30	0.00	240,478	10,490
Dec 94	(0.10)	0.00	199,647	(3,316)
Sep 94	(0.09)	0.00	133,820	(3,055)
Jun 94	(0.42)	0.00	117,390	(8,623)
Mar 94	(1.39)	0.00	107,410	(28,881)
Dec 93	(0.53)	0.00	108,148	(10,928)
Sep 93	(0.23)	0.00	115,959	(7,851)

Synopsis:

Rainy River was incorporated in April 1994 and shares were issued to the public on October 13, 1994, as Boise Cascade Corp. disposed 51% of its interest in its subsidiary, Boise Cascade Canada. The company issued $420-million worth of units composed of equal amounts of common shares and convertible subordinated debentures. It also issued $110-million (U.S.) of seven year secured notes.

Rainy River owns and operates three integrated pulp and paper mills that have an annual capacity of approximately 870,000 metric tonnes of newsprint, uncoated groundwood papers, and market pulp. It also markets an additional 387,000 metric tonnes per year of newsprint produced by a Boise Cascade Corp. mill in DeRidder, Louisiana.

Rainy River incurred a net loss of $43.9-million in 1994 as prices did not recover from a deep trough until late in the second quarter for newsprint and late in the third quarter for uncoated groundwood papers. Prices for both products were falling for most of the first half of the year.

Rainy River expects its financial performance to improve throughout 1995 due to its focus on cost control, productivity improvements, and price increases for all its products. When the company's major capital projects are completed in late 1995 and 1996, Rainy River expects further improvements in all three of its pulp and paper mills.

The company expects prices to increase beyond the increases of at least $100 (U.S.) per tonne in the first half of 1995. There is increased demand for such products and there is no significant new uncoated groundwood paper or newsprint production capacity currently under construction in North America.

Sales in 1994 of products by segment were: uncoated groundwood papers, 41%; newsprint, 45%; market pulp, 12%; and other, 2%. The company only sold newsprint from the DeRidder mill for the fourth quarter, generating $55-million. The U.S. is the company's main market.

Rank (Profit/Revenue/Assets)		
986	185	155

George V. Harad
Chairman

Martin J. O'Brien
President & C.E.O.

David G. Gadda
Ex. V.P. Fin. & Admin.

Address
Suite 2000
P.O. Box 759 BCE Place
181 Bay Street
Toronto
ON
M5J 2T3
(416) 956-7588
Fax: (416) 956-4844
B0016445/G/4.1

REPAP ENTERPRISES INC.

Exchanges	Price (Jun29'95)	10.75	Trailing P/E	nm	Stock Symbol
TMVQ	Trailing Yield (%)	0.00	Trailing EPS	(0.06)	RPP

Period Ending	Dec94	Dec93	Dec92	Dec91	Dec90
Yearly Statistics					
Price-Close	7.25	3.20	2.10	5.25	5.13
Price-High	7.75	5.63	6.88	8.75	10.00
Price-Low	3.25	1.96	1.51	3.80	4.90
P/E-Close	nm	nm	nm	nm	85.42
Dividends per Share	0.00	0.00	0.00	0.00	0.21
Dividend Yield (%)	0.00	0.00	0.00	0.00	4.10
Sales per Share	13.17	14.10	13.40	18.08	21.19
EPS before extra. item	(0.75)	(2.50)	(2.77)	(3.47)	0.06
Cash Flow per Share	0.19	(0.54)	(1.95)	(2.49)	1.89
Book Value per Share	1.09	0.88	3.27	6.20	9.69
O/S Common Shares	121,940	84,394	84,394	51,949	51,949
Total Revenue	1,564,800	1,193,200	1,014,100	939,800	1,117,900
Income before extra.	(88,400)	(211,100)	(209,900)	(180,200)	3,100
Cash Flow	21,900	(45,900)	(147,800)	(129,500)	98,100
Debt/Equity	8.90	10.40	5.01	3.99	2.62
Return on Capital (%)	4.32	(2.02)	(5.50)	(5.96)	4.65
Ret. on Com. Equity (%)	(85.62)	(120.59)	(70.15)	(43.66)	0.61
% Change Profit	58.1	(0.6)	(16.5)	(5,912.9)	(96.7)
% Change Revenue	31.1	17.7	7.9	(15.9)	(0.1)
% Change Assets	4.5	1.4	6.8	0.4	10.7

Preferred Div. Coverage	na	na	na
Total Div. Coverage	na	na	na
Interest Coverage	0.6	0.0	0.0
Current Ratio	1.1	1.0	1.3
Operating Margin	8.3	1.9	(7.1)
Asset Turnover	0.4	0.4	0.3
5 YEAR RATIOS (%)			
Return on Capital	(0.9)	0.4	4.1
Return on Com. Equity	(63.9)	(42.8)	(14.1)
Profit Growth	na	na	na
Revenue Growth	6.9	4.7	3.6
Asset Growth	4.6	8.1	16.5
BALANCE SHEET (000)			
Cash	27,200	6,600	26,600
Current Assets	440,300	423,100	422,700
Net Fixed Assets	2,477,100	2,448,400	2,474,100
Invest's & Advances	32,200	28,900	28,400
Total Assets	3,506,700	3,355,400	3,308,600
Short Term Debt	89,000	104,400	58,100
Current Liabilities	416,800	403,800	336,000
Long Term Debt	2,315,700	2,095,700	2,016,500
Total Liabilities	3,236,500	3,143,900	2,894,800
Total Equity	270,200	211,500	413,800
Total Liab. & Equity	3,506,700	3,355,400	3,308,600
CAPITAL (000)			
Total Debt	2,404,700	2,200,100	2,074,600
Preferred Equity	137,600	137,600	137,600
Common Equity	132,600	73,900	276,200

Business:

REPAP ENTERPRISES INC. is a forest products company. Its products include high-quality coated paper for magazines, catalogues, inserts, coupons and brochures, unbleached kraft paper and lumber, and northern bleached softwood kraft pulp used for quality fine papers. Repap has operations in Wisconsin, Manitoba, New Brunswick and B.C. and markets in North America, Europe and Asia.

Date	EPS	DPS	Tot Rev	Inc Bex
Mar 95	0.27	0.00	482,600	32,400
Dec 94	0.11	0.00	465,600	12,200
Sep 94	(0.25)	0.00	400,300	(30,300)
Jun 94	(0.29)	0.00	369,500	(35,800)
Mar 94	(0.33)	0.00	325,800	(34,500)
Dec 93	(0.49)	0.00	285,300	(41,400)
Sep 93	(0.32)	0.00	329,700	(26,800)
Jun 93	(0.64)	0.00	274,500	(54,200)

Synopsis:

Repap has benefited from the strong recovery in coated paper and pulp markets world-wide. Repap returned to profitability in the fourth quarter of 1994. The turnaround in coated paper and pulp markets is reflected in a 31% increase in revenues to $1.7-billion in 1994.

With new growth in emerging in Asian and Latin American markets and low inflation in most industrialized countries, markets will be in Repap's favour for the next few years. There should be continued demand for the company's coated paper, kraft paper, market pulp products, and lumber.

Strong markets for pulp and coated paper should persist over the balance of the decade. There is growing coated paper demand while only limited new capacity is scheduled to come on stream. The tight market conditions throughout 1995 and 1996 are expected to lead to higher prices. In July, the price of coated groundwood paper (two-thirds of Repap's coated paper business) will be $1,200 (U.S.) a tonne, up $440 (U.S.) a tonne from July 1994.

Repap has no plans to invest in a new coated paper machine. Instead, it will optimize its coated paper operations and use the substantial cash flow expected to be generated from operations to reduce debt. The company has invested $2.8-billion during the past four years to capitalize on the market recovery that is now underway. By the end of 1995, coated paper productivity will increase by 35% over 1990. Further fine-tuning will enable the new equipment to exceed the one million ton rated capacity within the next few years.

Repap's revenues by product in 1994 were: coated papers, 62%; pulp, 18%; lumber, 13%; and kraft paper, 7%. Revenues by country were: North America, 74%; Europe, 10%; Asia, 15%; and other, 1%.

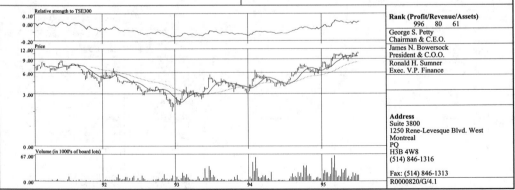

Rank (Profit/Revenue/Assets)		
996	80	61

George S. Petty
Chairman & C.E.O.

James N. Bowersock
President & C.O.O.

Ronald H. Sumner
Exec. V.P. Finance

Address
Suite 3800
1250 Rene-Levesque Blvd. West
Montreal
PQ
H3B 4W8
(514) 846-1316

Fax: (514) 846-1313
R0000820/G/4.1

RIVERSIDE FOREST PRODUCTS LIMITED

Exchanges	Price (Jun29'95)		17.25	Trailing P/E		4.20	Stock Symbol
TV	Trailing Yield (%)		1.74	Trailing EPS		4.11	RFP

Period Ending	Sep94	Sep93	Sep92	Oct91	Oct90
Yearly Statistics			11M		
Price-Close	24.00	22.25	nt	nt	nt
Price-High	30.00	22.88	nt	nt	nt
Price-Low	20.50	9.50	nt	nt	nt
P/E-Close	5.65	7.84	nt	nt	nt
Dividends per Share	0.22	0.08	0.78	0.00	0.00
Dividend Yield (%)	0.92	0.36	na	0.00	0.00
Sales per Share	42.73	32.10	20.53	13.66	16.05
EPS before extra. item	4.25	2.84	1.22	(1.65)	(0.81)
Cash Flow per Share	6.26	4.36	1.67	(0.64)	0.02
Book Value per Share	13.93	7.83	1.35	0.91	2.56
O/S Common Shares	7,599	6,599	2,016	2,016	2,016
Total Revenue	309,221	197,075	39,750	27,457	32,416
Income before extra.	30,184	17,359	2,452	(3,317)	(1,635)
Cash Flow	44,494	26,620	3,083	(1,291)	39
Debt/Equity	0.47	0.43	3.75	6.75	1.62
Return on Capital (%)	46.73	73.34	30.23	(16.33)	na
Ret. on Com. Equity (%)	38.33	63.84	117.13	(94.71)	na
% Change Profit	73.9	549.0	180.6	(102.9)	na
% Change Revenue	56.9	354.5	57.9	(15.3)	na
% Change Assets	94.4	486.5	(1.3)	4.3	na

Date	EPS	DPS	Tot Rev	Inc Bex
Mar 95	0.61	0.06	99,366	4,675
Dec 94	1.38	0.06	96,901	10,474
Sep 94	0.97	0.06	91,840	7,449
Jun 94	1.15	0.12	91,446	8,710
Mar 94	1.46	0.06	69,897	9,607
Dec 93	0.67	0.06	55,717	4,418
Sep 93	0.79	0.04	51,670	3,842
Jun 93	0.74	0.04	57,819	4,872

	Sep94	Sep93	Sep92
Preferred Div. Coverage	np	np	np
Total Div. Coverage	19.2	32.9	1.6
Interest Coverage	15.1	11.4	4.3
Current Ratio	1.4	1.3	1.1
Operating Margin	15.8	15.7	5.2
Asset Turnover	1.3	1.7	2.0
5 YEAR RATIOS (%)			
Return on Capital	na	na	na
Return on Com. Equity	na	na	na
Profit Growth	na	na	na
Revenue Growth	na	na	na
Asset Growth	na	na	na
BALANCE SHEET (000)			
Cash	5,256	11,288	0
Current Assets	89,222	54,051	10,128
Net Fixed Assets	135,941	59,682	6,919
Invest's & Advances	1,318	1,807	2,249
Total Assets	230,884	118,742	20,247
Short Term Debt	0	2,350	4,396
Current Liabilities	63,581	40,214	9,112
Long Term Debt	50,000	19,583	5,820
Total Liabilities	125,028	67,084	17,524
Total Equity	105,856	51,657	2,723
Total Liab. & Equity	230,884	118,742	20,247
CAPITAL (000)			
Total Debt	50,000	21,933	10,216
Preferred Equity	0	0	0
Common Equity	105,856	51,657	2,723

Business:

RIVERSIDE FOREST PRODUCTS LIMITED is in the business of harvesting timber and producing lumber, plywood, veneer and wood chips.

Synopsis:

In the six months ended in March 1995, sales for Riverside Forest Products almost doubled over the same period in fiscal 1994. Net earnings declined because lumber prices fell and the costs incurred due to increased volume outweighed the jump in sales. Even though the lumber market is at its lowest level in two years, the plywood market remains strong. As well, the company's continued penetration of the Japanese and European markets has provided excellent returns. Value added product lines have increased as a result of the capital expenditure programs. They also have helped offset the higher stumpage fees charged by the B.C. government.

Since September 1992, the company invested $36-million primarily to expand and upgrade the Kelowna and Armstrong plywood plants. Its objective was to reduce manufacturing costs, and position its plywood product profile away from the new competition coming from oriented stranded board production in North America. New equipment has doubled Riverside's production of specialized ULAY panels and increased its ability to produce panels of different thicknesses and plys. In addition, its plywood can now be manufactured from solid core, enhancing sales to the quality conscious Japanese.

The major emphasis in 1995 is the $25-million upgrade of the Williams Lake Sawmill. The upgrade should increase fibre recovery by 25% while reducing production costs substantially. This project will be completed in two phases with completion expected in December 1996. This sawmill has an annual production capacity of 180 million fbm (foot board measure). This operation's production increased the company's lumber volume by 65%.

Sales in 1994 by product were: studs, 39%; plywood, 32%; dimension, 12%; chips, 9%; veneer, 7%; and bins, 1%. Canada is Riverside's primary market for plywood. Americans buy the majority of the company's lumber. The company has been gaining access to the Japanese market, and in fiscal 1994 increased plywood shipments to Japan by 25%. The company is also beginning to sell its plywood to Europe and the U.S.

Relative strength to TSE300 / Price / Volume (in 1000's of board lots)

Rank (Profit/Revenue/Assets)		
159	254	330

Gordon W. Steele
President & C.E.O.

Michael E. Moore
C.F.O. & Secretary-Treasurer

Gerald E. Raboch
C.O.O.

Address
820 Guy Street
Kelowna
BC
V1Y 7R5
(604) 762-3411

Fax: (604) 762-6888
01003313/G/4.2

ROLLAND INC.

Exchanges	Price (Jun29'95)	10.00	Trailing P/E	7.69	Stock Symbol
TM	Trailing Yield (%)	0.00	Trailing EPS	1.30	RL

Period Ending	Dec94	Dec93	Dec92	Dec91	Dec90
Yearly Statistics					
Price-Close	7.13	6.50	5.00	7.63	8.38
Price-High	9.50	7.50	8.00	11.50	11.00
Price-Low	6.38	4.80	4.25	7.50	6.75
P/E-Close	8.69	65.00	nm	nm	22.04
Dividends per Share	0.00	0.00	0.00	0.05	0.00
Dividend Yield (%)	0.00	0.00	0.00	0.66	0.00
Sales per Share	47.78	38.03	45.86	81.98	108.83
EPS before extra. item	0.82	0.10	(2.60)	(2.09)	0.38
Cash Flow per Share	2.14	1.09	(1.24)	(1.89)	(1.10)
Book Value per Share	7.58	6.73	6.59	11.04	13.20
O/S Common Shares	7,628	7,628	7,629	3,695	3,695
Total Revenue	365,951	291,498	261,641	305,692	415,739
Income before extra.	6,312	796	(9,877)	(7,726)	1,461
Cash Flow	16,330	8,320	(7,020)	(6,994)	(4,052)
Debt/Equity	1.17	1.41	1.41	1.28	1.11
Return on Capital (%)	13.44	5.42	(7.36)	(3.23)	4.62
Ret. on Com. Equity (%)	11.46	1.45	(21.82)	(17.38)	2.90
% Change Profit	693.0	108.1	(27.8)	(628.8)	115.1
% Change Revenue	25.5	11.4	(14.4)	(26.5)	(5.8)
% Change Assets	11.6	3.6	23.9	(15.5)	(9.4)

Date	EPS	DPS	Tot Rev	Inc Bex
Mar 95	0.62	0.00	114,952	4,736
Dec 94	0.47	0.00	110,628	3,579
Sep 94	0.12	0.00	91,469	917
Jun 94	0.09	0.00	83,114	697
Mar 94	0.14	0.00	80,877	1,119
Dec 93	0.14	0.00	75,103	1,025
Sep 93	(0.05)	0.00	72,411	(384)
Jun 93	0.00	0.00	71,393	12

Preferred Div. Coverage	107.0	13.5	0.0
Total Div. Coverage	107.0	13.5	0.0
Interest Coverage	3.1	1.4	0.0
Current Ratio	1.6	1.0	0.9
Operating Margin	4.6	2.5	(2.0)
Asset Turnover	2.1	1.9	1.8
5 YEAR RATIOS (%)			
Return on Capital	2.6	(1.3)	0.3
Return on Com. Equity	(4.7)	(10.6)	(8.8)
Profit Growth	na	(33.3)	na
Revenue Growth	(3.7)	(8.3)	(7.7)
Asset Growth	1.8	(1.7)	(0.1)
BALANCE SHEET (000)			
Cash	0	0	0
Current Assets	101,507	79,837	68,332
Net Fixed Assets	56,174	58,019	59,957
Invest's & Advances	0	2,281	7,189
Total Assets	171,174	153,402	148,141
Short Term Debt	27,827	57,111	55,691
Current Liabilities	61,893	79,564	76,826
Long Term Debt	41,367	17,112	17,241
Total Liabilities	111,988	100,684	96,478
Total Equity	59,186	52,718	51,663
Total Liab. & Equity	171,174	153,402	148,141
CAPITAL (000)			
Total Debt	69,194	74,223	72,932
Preferred Equity	1,399	1,399	1,399
Common Equity	57,787	51,319	50,264

Business:

ROLLAND INC. is engaged in the manufacturing and distribution of fine and specialty papers. The company makes well over 100 grades of high quality fine papers from all-cotton to chemical pulp grades and to recycled grades used for commercial printing, reprography, business forms, envelopes and special applications. Rolland has paper distribution operations in Canada.

Synopsis:

In keeping with the trend set in the last quarter of 1994, Rolland expects its sales, net earnings, and cash flow from operations to continue to rise substantially in 1995. The increase will be sustained by the steady growth in demand for the company's products and higher selling prices. The positive climate for the Fine Papers division should prevail until at least 1997.

In 1994, the Fine Papers division boosted its market share in Canada and the United States in uncoated recycled fine papers. The Distribution division increased its Canadian market share by enhancing its line of recycled paper products and graphic arts supplies after signing exclusive marketing franchises with several major North American and European producers. To focus on being a leading Canadian distributor of fine paper products, Rolland sold its U.S. subsidiary Select Robinson Inc. for $3.6-million (U.S.) in January 1995.

Nearly a third of the products from Rolland's de-inking kraft pulp mill were sold to the Fine Papers division. This integration ensured the Fine Papers mill with a reliable supply of de-inked pulp. By late 1994, nearly 95% of the Fine Papers division's production contained recycled fibres, and 70% consisted of value-added papers. Most of the products contained 20% post-consumer fibres, in keeping with new U.S. standards that will take effect in September 1995.

In 1994, both divisions increased revenues by 25% to $364.5-million and Rolland's operating profit rose 127% to $16-million. The pulp and paper manufacturing division generated 37% of revenues. The Distribution division generated 63%. Sales outside Canada were $86.9-million, mostly to the U.S.

The company plans to use its increased cash flow to implement environmental protection measures at the Saint-Jerome mill. As well it Rolland will investment in its mills and Distribution division. It also expects to repay $3.5-million in long term debt in 1995.

Relative strength to TSE300

Price

Volume (in 1000's of board lots)

92	93	94	95

Rank (Profit/Revenue/Assets)
385 228 377

Lucien G. Rolland
Chairman
Alain Lemaire
President

Address
2000 McGill College Avenue
Suite 1400
Montreal
PQ
H3A 3H3
(514) 289-1779

Fax: (514) 289-9349
R0002304/G/4.1

SLOCAN FOREST PRODUCTS LTD.

Exchanges	Price (Jun29'95)	12 .50	Trailing P/E	4 .98	Stock Symbol
T	Trailing Yield (%)	1 .80	Trailing EPS	2 .51	SFF

Period Ending	Dec94	Dec93	Dec92	Dec91	Dec90
Yearly Statistics					
Price-Close	16 .00	16 .69	5 .94	2 .94	2 .35
Price-High	17 .75	17 .25	6 .00	3 .63	4 .25
Price-Low	11 .50	5 .88	2 .94	2 .20	2 .23
P/E-Close	6 .25	8 .56	25 .27	nm	nm
Dividends per Share	0 .20	0 .12	0 .05	0 .05	0 .09
Dividend Yield (%)	1 .25	0 .72	0 .84	1 .53	3 .83
Sales per Share	19 .13	14 .35	9 .52	7 .72	9 .18
EPS before extra. item	2 .56	1 .95	0 .24	(0 .57)	(0 .06)
Cash Flow per Share	5 .09	3 .19	1 .77	0 .51	0 .86
Book Value per Share	7 .72	5 .38	2 .29	2 .11	2 .73
O/S Common Shares	38 ,221	37 ,933	27 ,067	26 ,973	21 ,658
Total Revenue	773 ,356	498 ,797	257 ,574	192 ,826	199 ,346
Income before extra.	97 ,744	61 ,519	6 ,369	(14 ,234)	(1 ,319)
Cash Flow	193 ,673	103 ,628	47 ,888	12 ,790	18 ,591
Debt/Equity	0 .79	0 .86	1 .32	1 .91	1 .44
Return on Capital (%)	39 .33	46 .93	15 .54	(5 .71)	4 .48
Ret. on Com. Equity (%)	39 .17	46 .25	10 .71	(24 .56)	(2 .18)
% Change Profit	58 .9	865 .9	144 .7	(979 .2)	(112 .7)
% Change Revenue	55 .0	93 .7	33 .6	(3 .3)	0 .4
% Change Assets	47 .2	138 .6	3 .5	9 .6	12 .4

Preferred Div. Coverage	np	np	np
Total Div. Coverage	12 .8	15 .1	4 .7
Interest Coverage	9 .9	7 .1	3 .7
Current Ratio	1 .5	1 .6	1 .0
Operating Margin	18 .2	19 .5	12 .9
Asset Turnover	0 .9	0 .9	1 .2
5 YEAR RATIOS (%)			
Return on Capital	20 .1	16 .5	13 .6
Return on Com. Equity	13 .9	9 .7	5 .3
Profit Growth	56 .5	38 .9	(11 .7)
Revenue Growth	31 .2	21 .9	11 .4
Asset Growth	34 .9	37 .1	17 .1
BALANCE SHEET (000)			
Cash	0	0	0
Current Assets	282 ,625	153 ,870	72 ,700
Net Fixed Assets	0	355 ,408	101 ,012
Invest's & Advances	0	8 ,134	43 ,736
Total Assets	766 ,741	520 ,994	218 ,371
Short Term Debt	61 ,664	19 ,992	33 ,743
Current Liabilities	192 ,451	96 ,908	74 ,422
Long Term Debt	171 ,832	155 ,548	48 ,152
Total Liabilities	471 ,667	317 ,039	156 ,290
Total Equity	295 ,074	203 ,955	62 ,081
Total Liab. & Equity	766 ,741	520 ,994	218 ,371
CAPITAL (000)			
Total Debt	233 ,496	175 ,540	81 ,895
Preferred Equity	0	0	0
Common Equity	295 ,074	203 ,955	62 ,081

Business:

SLOCAN FOREST PRODUCTS LTD., through its subsidiary and affiliated companies, participates in the harvesting, manufacturing and marketing of wood products which are sold throughout the world. The principal markets for these products are North America, Asia and Europe. Slocan has a 50% interest in a plywood plant, 85.8% interest in a pulp mill, and a 49.9% interest in a paper mill and two sawmills, all in B.C.

Date	EPS	DPS	Tot Rev	Inc Bex
Mar 95	0 .42	0 .08	214 ,937	15 ,012
Dec 94	0 .96	0 .05	239 ,720	36 ,522
Sep 94	0 .67	0 .05	201 ,271	25 ,517
Jun 94	0 .46	0 .05	190 ,268	17 ,411
Mar 94	0 .48	0 .05	131 ,575	18 ,294
Dec 93	0 .86	0 .03	173 ,399	28 ,491
Sep 93	0 .30	0 .03	130 ,412	10 ,043
Jun 93	0 .37	0 .03	97 ,600	11 ,006

Synopsis:

Slocan achieved record sales for the past two years as a result of strong lumber markets. Net sales in 1994 were $728.3-million, up from $466.4-million in 1993, primarily as a result in an increase in lumber shipments from 664 million board feet (mmfbm) to 941 mmfbm in 1994. In 1994, Slocan generated 85% of its sales from wood products, most of which was from lumber. Sales by market were: the United States, 57%; Canada, 26%; and other, 17%.

In 1995 sales continue to increase, even though lumber prices have weakened with demand due to higher interest rates. Plywood prices remained strong due to demand from offshore markets, wood chip prices doubled in the past year in accordance with the strong pulp market, and newsprint prices are strengthening. Pulp prices have risen due to reduced capacity and increased demand.

Earnings are under pressure because of lower demand for lumber resulting in lower lumber prices, reduced shipment volumes, and higher log costs chiefly due to a 150% increase in stumpage rates introduced in April 1994. Finlay's newsprint operation is facing sharp increases in costs for the purchase of kraft pulp, a situation that will be eliminated with the completion of the pulp project.

Slocan is expanding its product mix to balance the cyclical nature of lumber markets. In April 1994 it purchased Finlay Forest Industries along with Donohue Inc. The paper mill modernization and sawmill upgrading project at Finlay should be completed in December 1995. It is constructing an oriented strand board plant at Fort Nelson, B.C., which should begin producing 395 million square feet of panelling a year in 1996. It also plans to invest $60-million to nearly double the production of its chlorine-free pulp mill at Taylor, B.C. To remain a strong lumber producer, Slocan completed a $21-million technical upgrading of its sawmills in 1994.

In early 1995, Slocan fended off a take-over attempt by Canfor Corp. Slocan bought back eight million, or 21%, of its shares for $20 per share, with significant debt.

Rank (Profit/Revenue/Assets)
77   142   179

Irving K. Barber
Chairman President & C.E.O.

Ronald D. Price
Sr. V.P. C.F.O. & Secretary

George A. Edgson
Sr. V.P. Operations

Address
240 - 10451 Shellbridge Way
Richmond
BC
V6X 2W8
(604) 278-7311

Fax: (604) 278-7316
01000475/G/4.2

STONE-CONSOLIDATED CORPORATION

Exchanges	Price (Jun29'95)	19.00	Trailing P/E		52.78	Stock Symbol
TM	Trailing Yield (%)	0.00	Trailing EPS		0.36	**SO**

Period Ending	Dec94	Dec93	Dec92	Dec91
Yearly Statistics				
Price-Close	16.50	15.00	nt	nt
Price-High	20.00	15.50	nt	nt
Price-Low	14.38	14.50	nt	nt
P/E-Close	nm	nm	nt	nt
Dividends per Share	0.00	0.00	0.00	0.00
Dividend Yield (%)	0.00	0.00	0.00	0.00
Sales per Share	16.79	14.28	0.00	0.00
EPS before extra. item	(0.12)	(1.06)	na	na
Cash Flow per Share	1.25	(0.08)	0.00	0.00
Book Value per Share	19.75	19.43	na	na
O/S Common Shares	65,000	65,000	0	0
Total Revenue	1,115,476	929,233	842,155	952,773
Income before extra.	(7,842)	(68,652)	(110,200)	(13,721)
Cash Flow	80,992	(5,246)	(71,712)	56,938
Debt/Equity	0.43	0.44	0.65	0.68
Return on Capital (%)	2.76	(1.40)	(5.00)	na
Ret. on Com. Equity (%)	(0.62)	na	na	na
% Change Profit	88.6	37.7	(703.1)	na
% Change Revenue	20.0	10.3	(11.6)	na
% Change Assets	2.2	4.1	(4.2)	na

Date	EPS	DPS	Tot Rev	Inc Bex
Mar 95	0.33	0.00	328,398	22,163
Dec 94	0.23	0.00	322,610	14,908
Sep 94	(0.07)	0.00	284,154	(4,546)
Jun 94	(0.13)	0.00	274,709	(8,228)
Mar 94	(0.15)	0.00	237,897	(9,976)
Dec 93	(0.33)	0.00	244,694	(21,687)
Sep 93	na	0.00	226,894	(11,739)
Jun 93	na	0.00	229,249	(11,852)

	Dec94	Dec93	Dec92
Preferred Div. Coverage	np	np	np
Total Div. Coverage	na	na	na
Interest Coverage	0.9	0.0	0.0
Current Ratio	2.4	2.5	1.7
Operating Margin	3.4	(2.8)	(10.5)
Asset Turnover	0.5	0.5	0.4
5 YEAR RATIOS (%)			
Return on Capital	na	na	na
Return on Com. Equity	na	na	na
Profit Growth	na	na	na
Revenue Growth	na	na	na
Asset Growth	na	na	na
BALANCE SHEET (000)			
Cash	104,816	197,530	244
Current Assets	440,042	443,017	312,241
Net Fixed Assets	1,069,911	1,037,484	1,091,251
Invest's & Advances	12,285	11,492	10,675
Total Assets	2,099,671	2,054,857	1,973,610
Short Term Debt	934	29,529	27,040
Current Liabilities	186,560	178,123	180,950
Long Term Debt	546,641	528,935	647,727
Total Liabilities	816,125	791,650	939,757
Total Equity	1,283,546	1,263,207	1,033,853
Total Liab. & Equity	2,099,671	2,054,857	1,973,610
CAPITAL (000)			
Total Debt	547,575	558,464	674,767
Preferred Equity	0	0	0
Common Equity	1,283,546	1,263,207	1,033,853

Business:

STONE-CONSOLIDATED CORPORATION manufactures newsprint and uncoated groundwood papers, with production facilities in Quebec and the United Kingdom and lumber production with Sawmills in the province of Quebec.

Synopsis:

Stone-Consolidated Corp. issued its initial public offering in December 1993. The offering raised $462-million in common shares and convertible debentures. The company's primary business is newsprint and uncoated groundwood papers. In 1994, sales were $1.1-billion, with 57% from newsprint, 32% from uncoated groundwood papers, 8% from lumber, and 3% from bag and kraft tissue paper. The overall volume of recycled content newsprint marketed by the company reached 39% at the end of 1994. De-inking capacity at the Bridgewater and Belgo mills are being expanded, and the Snowflake mill will be reconfigured in 1996. As a result of these changes, the recycled content proportion of total newsprint marketed by the company will climb to 47% in 1996.

A new pricing momentum that began in the latter half of 1994 is the result of increased consumption and strong demand, reduced inventories, limited capacity additions, and full operating rates. Further price increases have been implemented in 1995 for newsprint and uncoated groundwood papers.

In 1994, newsprint demand was especially strong in Europe, Latin America, and Asia (excluding Japan). The company ships 11% of its newsprint to Canada, 46% to the United States, 28% to Europe, and 15% to other overseas markets, mostly Asia and Latin America. Newsprint demand in the key U.S. market has rebounded strongly. Since a decline of 7% in 1991, U.S. newsprint consumption has been climbing, with a gain of 2.6% in 1994.

The company is continually upgrading its production of value-added uncoated groundwood paper. Projected capacity increases for groundwood papers to 1997 amount to 2.3% per year, for North America and Western Europe, much less than the expected growth in demand. The United States is the company's largest market for uncoated groundwood papers, accounting for 83% of company sales of that product in 1994. Market demand has been very strong for two years, growing 7.4% in 1993 and 6.7% in 1994. These increases were due to growth in the printing and writing sector as well as a switch away from newsprint.

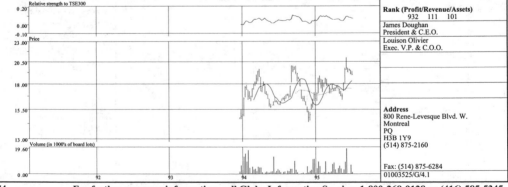

Rank (Profit/Revenue/Assets)		
932	111	101

James Doughan
President & C.E.O.

Louison Olivier
Exec. V.P. & C.O.O.

Address
800 Rene-Levesque Blvd. W.
Montreal
PQ
H3B 1Y9
(514) 875-2160

Fax: (514) 875-6284
01003525/G/4.1

TEMBEC INC.

Period Ending	Sep94	Sep93	Sep92	Sep91	Sep90
Yearly Statistics					
Price-Close	13.13	8.63	10.88	9.25	9.00
Price-High	13.13	11.00	11.25	10.63	10.50
Price-Low	8.00	7.25	8.00	8.75	8.75
P/E-Close	5.86	nm	nm	nm	8.33
Dividends per Share	0.00	0.00	0.00	0.00	0.00
Dividend Yield (%)	0.00	0.00	0.00	0.00	0.00
Sales per Share	14.95	13.18	14.42	14.52	16.24
EPS before extra. item	2.24	(1.73)	(1.36)	(1.98)	1.08
Cash Flow per Share	1.21	(0.61)	0.12	0.98	2.37
Book Value per Share	9.55	7.01	8.75	10.06	12.10
O/S Common Shares	38,420	28,167	28,022	17,767	17,581
Total Revenue	555,946	377,230	311,776	262,790	277,866
Income before extra.	72,731	(48,616)	(28,821)	(34,997)	18,374
Cash Flow	39,317	(17,224)	2,483	17,319	39,104
Debt/Equity	0.98	1.76	1.51	1.22	0.70
Return on Capital (%)	14.86	(4.93)	(3.50)	(6.23)	10.77
Ret. on Com. Equity (%)	25.78	(21.96)	(13.64)	(17.88)	9.62
% Change Profit	249.6	(68.7)	17.6	(290.5)	(46.3)
% Change Revenue	47.4	21.0	18.6	(5.4)	(3.3)
% Change Assets	1.7	(7.8)	75.4	16.5	17.2

Date	EPS	DPS	Tot Rev	Inc Bex
Mar 95	0.69	0.00	194,133	26,617
Dec 94	0.53	0.00	151,714	20,472
Sep 94	2.22	0.00	199,239	72,077
Jun 94	0.18	0.00	134,542	5,324
Mar 94	(0.07)	0.00	115,181	(2,071)
Dec 93	(0.09)	0.00	101,834	(2,599)
Sep 93	(0.52)	0.00	100,607	(14,528)
Jun 93	(0.23)	0.00	94,408	(6,675)

Preferred Div. Coverage	na	na	0.0
Total Div. Coverage	na	na	0.0
Interest Coverage	3.3	0.0	0.0
Current Ratio	2.0	1.5	2.5
Operating Margin	7.8	(5.3)	(2.9)
Asset Turnover	0.5	0.4	0.3
5 YEAR RATIOS (%)			
Return on Capital	2.2	3.8	9.2
Return on Com. Equity	(3.6)	(4.3)	4.8
Profit Growth	16.3	na	na
Revenue Growth	14.1	7.9	11.2
Asset Growth	17.5	22.1	29.4
BALANCE SHEET (000)			
Cash	25,887	40,000	21,466
Current Assets	206,960	206,030	234,559
Net Fixed Assets	716,361	707,786	750,674
Invest's & Advances	58,508	50,538	40,054
Total Assets	991,066	974,702	1,057,304
Short Term Debt	32,989	76,267	30,406
Current Liabilities	102,239	140,022	92,225
Long Term Debt	393,621	335,162	393,783
Total Liabilities	557,684	740,541	777,048
Total Equity	433,382	234,161	280,256
Total Liab. & Equity	991,066	974,702	1,057,304
CAPITAL (000)			
Total Debt	426,610	411,429	424,189
Preferred Equity	66,628	36,628	34,965
Common Equity	366,754	197,533	245,291

Business:

TEMBEC INC. is a fully integrated forest products company. Tembec's products are sold in over 50 countries and include softwood and hardwood lumber, specialty alpha and dissolving cellulose pulp, high yield chlorine-free market pulps, coated paperboard, lignosulfonates, resins, ethanol and newsprint.

Synopsis:

In June 1995, Tembec launched a $300-million takeover bid for Malette Inc. Tembec is offering either $16.50 in cash or 1.138 Tembec class A shares for each Malette share, tendered to a maximum of $202-million cash and 7.5 million Tembec shares. The acquisition would transform Tembec into a larger, more diversified forest products firm. Tembec would also be able to sell other value-added products, such as bleached kraft pulp, lumber, oriented structural board, machine finish coated paper, and high brightness paper. More importantly, the deal would provide ready access to an abundant, cheap supply of wood chips for Tembec's 41% owned Spruce Falls newsprint and sawmill operation in Kapuskasing, Ontario.

Tembec's improved performance since September 1993 is due to the sharp turnaround in the pulp market, particularly high yield pulp, and continued strength in the wood products division. The company expects further pulp price increases and sustained demand for lumber for the remainder of 1995.

Cash generation continues to be the company's primary focus. By 1994 Tembec had modern assets, efficient, low cost operations, and one of the industry's best fibre resources. Tembec began to reduce unit costs, increase production, and maximize the full potential of fibre resources. The company expanded its pulp grade mix and increased yields at its sawmills. Analysts expect the company to generate cash flow from operations of $200-million by September 1996.

Gross sales of $574.4-million by industry segment in fiscal 1994 were: pulp, 36%; wood products, 36%; paperboard products, 24%; and chemical products, 4%. Spruce Falls generated $141.1-million in net sales, $35.2-million in cash flow from operations. Net earnings were $16.7-million, of which Tembec's share was $6.9-million. The primary markets for pulp are the U.K. and Europe, and the Pacific Rim and India. The wood products are primarily sold in Canada and the United States. The U.S. accounts for over half of paperboard sales. Sales by country were: Canada, 30%; United States, 35%; Pacific Rim and India, 13%; and United Kingdom, Europe and other, 22%.

Rank (Profit/Revenue/Assets)		
92	186	156

Jacques Giasson
Chairman Of The Board

Frank A. Dottori
President & C.E.O.

Thomas W. Laberge
V.P. Finance & C.F.O.

Address
800 Rene-Levesque Blvd. West
27th Floor
Montreal
PQ
H3B 1X9
(514) 871-0137

Fax: (514) 397-0896
T0013617/G/4.1

TIMBERWEST FOREST LIMITED

Exchanges	Price (Jun29'95)	13.62	Trailing P/E	6.65	Stock Symbol
TV	Trailing Yield (%)	0.00	Trailing EPS	2.05	TFL

Period Ending	Jun94	Jun93	Jun92
Yearly Statistics	28W		
Price-Close	11.88	n t	n t
Price-High	17.75	n t	n t
Price-Low	10.75	n t	n t
P/E-Close	5.98	n t	n t
Dividends per Share	0.00	0.00	0.00
Dividend Yield (%)	0.00	0.00	0.00
Sales per Share	18.58	0.00	0.00
EPS before extra. item	1.07	na	na
Cash Flow per Share	5.47	0.00	0.00
Book Value per Share	9.44	na	na
O/S Common Shares	31,020	0	0
Total Revenue	232,800	329,854	207,882
Income before extra.	35,900	55,842	(33,361)
Cash Flow	68,100	69,846	(18,389)
Debt/Equity	nd	nd	nd
Return on Capital (%)	30.20	18.43	na
Ret. on Com. Equity (%)	19.42	18.43	na
% Change Profit	19.4	267.4	na
% Change Revenue	31.1	58.7	na
% Change Assets	21.8	34.3	na

Preferred Div. Coverage	13.3	np	np
Total Div. Coverage	13.3	na	na
Interest Coverage	nd	nd	nd
Current Ratio	1.9	1.6	2.1
Operating Margin	25.9	16.0	(17.5)
Asset Turnover	0.9	0.8	0.7

5 YEAR RATIOS (%)			
Return on Capital	na	na	na
Return on Com. Equity	na	na	na
Profit Growth	na	na	na
Revenue Growth	na	na	na
Asset Growth	na	na	na

BALANCE SHEET (000)			
Cash	39,400	0	0
Current Assets	135,400	85,230	66,348
Net Fixed Assets	313,500	313,456	233,666
Invest's & Advances	0	4,370	0
Total Assets	491,500	403,446	300,366
Short Term Debt	0	0	0
Current Liabilities	71,600	54,318	32,012
Long Term Debt	0	0	0
Total Liabilities	83,800	61,009	36,715
Total Equity	407,700	342,437	263,651
Total Liab. & Equity	491,500	403,446	300,366

CAPITAL (000)			
Total Debt	0	0	0
Preferred Equity	115,000	0	0
Common Equity	292,700	342,437	263,651

Business:

TIMBERWEST FOREST LIMITED is involved in the lumber and logging segment of the forest industry. Its logging operations are located in the coastal and interior regions of British Columbia. It produces specialty and dimension lumber products at two coastal sawmill complexes on Vancouver Island and stud lumber and railway ties at a sawmill complex in the interior of British Columbia.

Date	EPS	DPS	Tot Rev	Inc Bex
Mar 95	0.46	0.00	108,100	14,200
Dec 94	0.55	0.00	122,000	17,200
Sep 94	0.51	0.00	125,700	16,700
Jun 94	0.53	0.00	124,600	18,000
Mar 94	0.54	0.00	108,300	17,900

Synopsis:

TimberWest Forest is a solid wood products firm with all its operations located in British Columbia. Fletcher Challenge Limited and Fletcher Challenge Canada Limited own 51% of the company's outstanding common shares and 100% of its preferred shares.

Sales for the nine months ended March 31, 1995, were $340.3-million, benefiting from strong demand in coastal logs and Japanese lumber markets. Prices for both chips and coastal logs have been steadily improving over the past year. This trend, driven by an overall log shortage attributable to harvest reductions and significantly improved markets for pulp and paper, should continue throughout 1995. The Japanese lumber market has been strong and should improve modestly in the coming months. The North American lumber market, however, remains soft and is not expected to improve significantly in 1995.

The pressure on earnings is coming from increased stumpage and royalty costs, and unfavourable weather for logging in early 1995. In addition, during the quarter ended in March 1995, there were lower shipments of logs and lumber and lower lumber prices, partly offset by higher sales prices for logs and chips. The B.C. government is also reviewing harvest levels on all-long term tenures to ensure that cutting rates do not exceed long-term sustainable levels. Some cut reductions have already been implemented.

TimberWest owns 210,000 hectares of private forest lands comprising 32% of B.C.'s total private managed forest lands. These lands provide 29% of the coastal harvest. The 12 million cubic metres of harvestable, mature timber on its private lands is a hedge against government reductions in annual allowable cuts on public lands.

Sales of $231.2-million in the company's first fiscal year ended June 30, 1994, by product were: logs, 53%; lumber, 37%; and other, 10%. Total sales by market were: Canada, 71%; United States, 11%; Japan, 17%; and other, 1%. The market distribution of lumber was: Japan, 45%; United States, 30%; Canada, 21%; and other, 4%.

Relative strength to TSE300

Price

Volume (in 1000's of board lots)

Rank (Profit/Revenue/Assets)
95 207 226

Douglas W.G. Whitehead
Chairman

R. Keith Purchase
President & C.E.O.

Keith E. Winrow
V.P. Finance & C.F.O.

Address
700 West Georgia Street
7th Floor
P.O Box 10017 Pacific Centre
Vancouver
BC
V7Y 1A1
(604) 654-4400
Fax: (604) 654-4960
01003523/G/4.2

WELDWOOD OF CANADA LIMITED

Exchanges	Price (Jun29'95)	31.50	Trailing P/E	5.84	Stock Symbol
T	Trailing Yield (%)	0.56	Trailing EPS	5.39	WLW

Period Ending	Dec94	Dec93	Dec92	Dec91	Dec90
Yearly Statistics					
Price-Close	24.75	24.50	17.50	11.00	16.00
Price-High	25.63	24.75	17.50	16.00	18.50
Price-Low	17.00	15.50	11.00	9.50	13.25
P/E-Close	7.22	25.79	37.23	nm	106.67
Dividends per Share	0.22	0.20	0.20	0.20	0.40
Dividend Yield (%)	0.89	0.82	1.14	1.82	2.50
Sales per Share	28.31	23.27	19.75	18.06	19.29
EPS before extra. item	3.43	0.95	0.47	(0.89)	0.15
Cash Flow per Share	5.61	2.91	2.33	0.14	1.93
Book Value per Share	14.93	11.72	10.94	10.62	11.70
O/S Common Shares	37,649	37,584	37,361	36,844	36,450
Total Revenue	1,107,737	880,020	737,993	666,467	694,466
Income before extra.	129,107	35,817	17,511	(33,097)	5,396
Cash Flow	211,154	109,232	86,574	5,091	68,389
Debt/Equity	0.23	0.57	0.61	0.75	0.69
Return on Capital (%)	31.44	10.29	7.26	(3.83)	5.19
Ret. on Com. Equity (%)	25.75	8.43	4.38	(8.10)	1.25
% Change Profit	260.5	104.5	152.9	(713.4)	(91.7)
% Change Revenue	25.9	19.2	10.7	(4.0)	(11.1)
% Change Assets	8.6	6.2	0.5	(5.0)	5.2

Business:

WELDWOOD OF CANADA LIMITED is an integrated forest products company with operations in British Columbia, Alberta, and Ontario. Products include plywood, waferboard, lumber, and pulp. It has markets in the United States, Canada, Japan, the United Kingdom, Europe, Australia, New Zealand and South-East Asia. At December 1994, 84.1% of the company's common shares were owned by Champion International Corp.

Date	EPS	DPS	Tot Rev	Inc Bex
Mar 95	2.45	0.07	390,100	92,300
Dec 94	1.45	0.06	316,415	54,707
Sep 94	0.87	0.00	294,900	32,500
Jun 94	0.62	0.05	261,000	23,400
Mar 94	0.49	0.05	234,200	18,500
Dec 93	0.10	0.05	233,454	3,717
Sep 93	0.02	0.05	204,800	1,100
Jun 93	0.38	0.10	211,000	14,100

	Dec94	Dec93	Dec92
Preferred Div. Coverage	np	np	np
Total Div. Coverage	15.6	4.8	2.4
Interest Coverage	21.2	5.1	2.7
Current Ratio	1.4	1.1	2.0
Operating Margin	19.5	7.5	6.1
Asset Turnover	1.0	0.9	0.8
5 YEAR RATIOS (%)			
Return on Capital	10.1	7.7	12.1
Return on Com. Equity	6.3	4.4	7.2
Profit Growth	14.6	(12.2)	(18.2)
Revenue Growth	7.2	(0.5)	(0.3)
Asset Growth	2.9	6.5	17.0
BALANCE SHEET (000)			
Cash	8,059	1,915	4,854
Current Assets	386,143	275,300	260,233
Net Fixed Assets	621,264	640,124	596,731
Invest's & Advances	23,993	24,171	20,588
Total Assets	1,057,737	974,049	917,363
Short Term Debt	94,729	124,783	16,788
Current Liabilities	277,037	243,579	129,235
Long Term Debt	35,000	126,680	233,497
Total Liabilities	495,470	533,576	508,531
Total Equity	562,267	440,473	408,832
Total Liab. & Equity	1,057,737	974,049	917,363
CAPITAL (000)			
Total Debt	129,729	251,463	250,285
Preferred Equity	0	0	0
Common Equity	562,267	440,473	408,832

Synopsis:

Sales and earnings for Weldwood continued to rise in the first half of 1995, primarily due to rising pulp markets. Prices for northern bleached softwood kraft pulp have risen steadily from $430 (U.S.) per tonne in January 1994 to $750 (U.S.) in January 1995 and $925 (U.S.) in June 1995. Prices have now moved beyond 1989's all-time high. The price increases are supported by strong paper markets and low pulp inventories. The weak U.S. dollar in relation to other major currencies is mitigating the effect of these increases to European and Asian customers. The higher pulp prices were not fully translated into increases in earnings since the cost of purchased chips has also escalated significantly. Prices in the North American lumber market retreated in the first quarter. However, panelboard prices remain strong. Offshore demand for plywood has supported strong domestic pricing.

Weldwood completed the sale of its B.C. coastal assets, consisting of the Squamish and Port Moody sawmills and related timber licences and logging operations in late February 1995. International Forest Products Ltd. bought the assets for $177-million. The 13,000 hectares of timberland located on the eastern side of Vancouver Island were sold in May 1995 to a unit of John Hancock Mutual Life for $40-million. Weldwood is focusing on its core pulp, lumber and softwood plywood businesses in western Canada.

Reductions in B.C.'s allowable annual cuts, new pulp capacity in the early 1990's, higher pulp operating rates, and efforts to increase lumber recoveries in sawmills have contributed to a chip shortage. Weldwood has responded by increasing recovery of fibre in its lumber operations. It is also purchasing pulpwood fibre. The company feels its fibre supply is secure, with about 80% of its requirements coming from long-term tenures on Crown land.

Sales of $1.065-billion in 1994 by product were: pulp, 31%; softwood lumber, 43%; softwood plywood, 11%; hardwood plywood, 4%; waferboard, 4%; and logs, 7%. It sold 27% of its product in Canada, 46% in the United States and 27% to other countries.

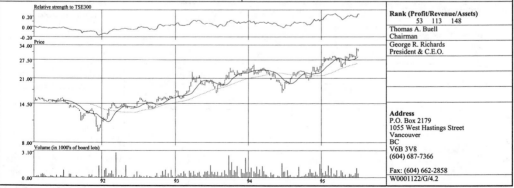

Rank (Profit/Revenue/Assets)
53   113   148

Thomas A. Buell
Chairman

George R. Richards
President & C.E.O.

Address
P.O. Box 2179
1055 West Hastings Street
Vancouver
BC
V6B 3V8
(604) 687-7366

Fax: (604) 662-2858
W0001122/G/4.2

WEST FRASER TIMBER CO. LTD.

Exchanges	Price (Jun29'95)	33.62	Trailing P/E	6.89	Stock Symbol
TV	Trailing Yield (%)	1.11	Trailing EPS	4.88	WFT

Period Ending	Dec94	Dec93	Dec92	Dec91	Dec90
Yearly Statistics					
Price-Close	38.88	48.00	28.64	16.74	13.84
Price-High	48.25	49.75	28.64	18.60	17.36
Price-Low	33.00	28.75	18.18	14.05	13.64
P/E-Close	7.49	19.12	57.27	nm	76.14
Dividends per Share	0.40	0.40	0.36	0.33	0.33
Dividend Yield (%)	1.03	0.83	1.27	1.98	2.39
Sales per Share	57.80	46.70	36.14	27.22	28.84
EPS before extra. item	5.19	2.51	0.50	(0.84)	0.18
Cash Flow per Share	9.86	6.54	3.31	1.96	4.17
Book Value per Share	22.58	18.98	14.73	13.22	14.11
O/S Common Shares	23,565	20,741	18,741	20,615	18,800
Total Revenue	1,342,067	905,683	677,027	537,730	542,084
Income before extra.	118,478	53,433	10,226	(16,532)	3,407
Cash Flow	218,385	126,645	62,026	38,502	78,212
Debt/Equity	1.04	1.14	1.35	1.33	1.44
Return on Capital (%)	23.35	15.95	6.47	(1.99)	3.52
Ret. on Com. Equity (%)	25.60	15.96	3.73	(6.15)	1.28
% Change Profit	121.7	422.5	161.9	(585.2)	(88.0)
% Change Revenue	48.2	33.8	25.9	(0.8)	(1.8)
% Change Assets	27.4	30.6	3.8	(1.3)	19.0

Preferred Div. Coverage	np	np	np
Total Div. Coverage	13.0	6.8	1.5
Interest Coverage	6.5	4.8	1.8
Current Ratio	1.5	1.6	2.1
Operating Margin	13.8	13.7	6.6
Asset Turnover	0.9	0.8	0.8
5 YEAR RATIOS (%)			
Return on Capital	9.5	7.4	8.6
Return on Com. Equity	8.1	5.2	5.6
Profit Growth	33.1	5.8	(26.4)
Revenue Growth	19.4	14.2	10.4
Asset Growth	15.2	16.1	16.1
BALANCE SHEET (000)			
Cash	3,636	3,877	63,923
Current Assets	493,375	333,282	273,619
Net Fixed Assets	875,648	743,894	567,187
Invest's & Advances	14,875	9,749	7,120
Total Assets	1,415,403	1,110,668	850,422
Short Term Debt	129,218	63,157	39,248
Current Liabilities	328,510	207,612	129,997
Long Term Debt	422,555	385,445	333,387
Total Liabilities	883,217	717,083	574,373
Total Equity	532,186	393,585	276,049
Total Liab. & Equity	1,415,403	1,110,668	850,422
CAPITAL (000)			
Total Debt	551,773	448,602	372,635
Preferred Equity	0	0	0
Common Equity	532,186	393,585	276,049

Business:

WEST FRASER TIMBER CO. LTD. is a forest products and building supplies company. The company produces lumber, linerboard, kraft paper, newsprint and bleached CTMP pulp at its operations in British Columbia and Alberta. It has markets in North America, Europe, and the Far East. Revelstoke Home Centres Ltd., a 100% subsidiary, operates a chain of building supply stores in Western Canada.

Date	EPS	DPS	Tot Rev	Inc Bex
Mar 95	0.90	0.10	343,800	23,300
Dec 94	1.76	0.09	368,767	44,378
Sep 94	1.18	0.09	350,700	29,600
Jun 94	1.04	0.09	352,600	25,900
Mar 94	0.74	0.09	270,000	18,600
Dec 93	0.74	0.08	284,383	18,133
Sep 93	0.44	0.08	227,800	10,100
Jun 93	0.42	0.09	205,200	9,500

Synopsis:

Sales and earnings have increased for West Fraser Timber since the beginning of 1992, primarily from rising prices and volumes for lumber. Strong demand and advancing prices in the first half of 1994 were partly reversed by rising interest rates in the second half of the year and an overall increase in North American lumber production. Increased interest rates continued to reduce housing starts in the United States during 1995. By April 1995, lumber prices were close to their lowest level in three years.

In contrast to the lumber market, pulp and paper markets are strong. By March 1995, export linerboard prices had virtually doubled since early 1994. Kraft markets began to improve in late 1994 and show strength. Newsprint prices are also strong. As a result, all production facilities are operating well and near capacity.

To deal with increased fibre costs, and market demands, the company introduced more value-added products. It also increased lumber recovery and operational efficiencies through major capital projects. A new sawmill producing high-value lumber, primarily on a custom-cut basis for export, began production in February 1995. Construction of a medium density fibreboard mill at Quesnel, B.C., expected to cost $100-million, began in April 1995. In 1994, production began at the value-added plant, built adjacent to its sawmill in Terrace, B.C. This plant recycles shop-grade lumber from its Terrace sawmill into higher-value specialty products.

West Fraser expanded its Revelstoke Home Centres division. The company wants to be a major player both in the traditional building supply sector and in the large warehouse format retail business.

Sales of $1.28-billion in 1994 by product were: lumber and wood chips, 52%; pulp and paper, 27%; and building supplies, 21%. Lumber and wood chips generated 89% of the operating earnings. Sales by market were: United States, 45%; Canada, 36%; Europe, 6%; Far East, 11%; and other, 2%.

Relative strength to TSE300 / Price / Volume (in 1000's of board lots)

Rank (Profit/Revenue/Assets)
67 97 133

Henry H. Ketcham Jr.
Chairman Of The Board

Henry H. Ketcham III
President & C.E.O.

Martti Solin
V.P. Finance & C.F.O.

Gary W. Townsend
V.P. Lumber Operations

Address
Suite 1000
1100 Melville Street
Vancouver
BC
V6E 4A6
(604) 895-2700

Fax: (604) 681-6061
W0000488/G/4.2

Page	Company	Fiscal year end	EARNINGS PER SHARE		
			Last Year	Estimate this year	Estimate next year
183	Andres Wines	Mar-95	0.90	na	na
184	Ault Foods	Apr-95	1.37	1.62	1.73
185	BC Sugar Refinery	Sep-94	0.44.	0.39	0.50
186	Canada Malting	Dec-94	1.20	1.42	1.55
187	Coca-Cola Beverages	Dec-94	(0.47)	(0.02)	0.42
188	Corby Distillers	Feb-95	4.05	3.60	na
189	Corporate Foods	Dec-94	1.06	1.19	1.33
190	Cott Corporation	Jan-95	0.69	0.83	1.00
191	Dover Industries	Dec-94	1.58	na	na
192	FPI Limited	Dec-94	0.85	0.86	1.01
193	Maple Leaf Foods	Dec-94	0.94	0.59	0.63
194	Molson Companies	Jun-94	1.87	1.20	1.66
195	National Sea Products	Dec-94	0.17	na	na
196	Noble China	Dec-94	0.51	1.15	1.35
197	Rothmans	Dec-94	10.64	11.02	11.03
198	Schneider Corporation	Oct-94	1.35	1.41	1.57

Estimates from First Call Corporation, 22 Pittsburgh Street, Boston, MA 02210   (800) 366-9992   Fax (617) 261-5679

Food, Beverages & Tobacco

Soft Drink Industry - Industry Report [May-4-95] PAINEWEBBER INC., reported by Goldman, E. The Soft Drink Industry Q1 domestic soft drink sales slowed by mid-single-digit price increases; diet drinks underperform

This report provides a brief description of volume and pricing trends within the domestic soft drink industry for the four-week and twelve-week periods ending March 26. In a nutshell, higher prices slowed the volume growth of the industry to a plus 1% rate for the first quarter and a minus 1% rate for March, as price (as measured by revenue per case) was up 6% for both periods.

The Coca-Cola Company: The growth rate of Coke Classic in March was above the industry's, while Diet Coke's was below. KO's flagship brand, Coke Classic, grew 2% in the first quarter, while Diet Coke's sales were down 2%. This compares to industry growth of 1%. Sprite's sales were up a solid 10% in the quarter, concurrent with a 2% decline in Diet Sprite's volume. In March, KO's sales were off 1%, in line with the industry's 1% decline. For the first quarter, KO's sales were up 1%, in line with the industry's 1% increase. KO's revenue per case was up 7% in both the four-week period and the quarter.

Private label: First quarter volume increase of 4% fueled by below-industry-level pricing within the drug store and mass merchandiser channels. While private label's supermarket sales suffered declines in March and the first quarter (off 7% and 2%, respectively), drug stores and mass merchandisers continued to be areas of growth for the private label sector. Private label sales in mass merchandisers, being over six times as large as those in drug stores, appear to be seeing more aggressive price discounting than in the other channels.

Beverage/Tobacco Market Share Analysis - Industry Report [May-1-95] DEAN WITTER REYNOLDS, reported by Adelman, L., et al. Beverage/Tobacco Market Share Analysis Carbonated Beverages: For the 12- and 4-week periods ending March 26, 1995, the most noteworthy market development in the market-share analysis continues to be carbonated beverage pricing, which after relatively flat pricing in 1994 experienced 12- and 4- week price increases of 5.9% and 6.2%, respectively. These price increases were implemented to offset higher metal container costs. Coca-Cola (KO, Accumulate, $58 1/8, (o)) and private label (including mix shifts) have registered the most aggressive price increases, with four-week increases of 6.7% and 9.3%, respectively. Until recently, these price increases have had only a modest effect on volume trends. However, industry four-week volume, which was down 0.4%, suggests that price increases are beginning to temporarily affect category growth. Finally, of special interest, private-label soft-drink volume continues to register significant declines with 12- and 4- week volume falling 2.1% and 7.2%, respectively.

Tobacco: We also feel it is important to highlight 12- and 4-week cigarette price increases of 0.7% and 0.8%, respectively, due to mix change and the exclusion of "Marlboro Friday" price reductions from the year-ago period data. We feel these trends reinforce our moderate overweighting recommendation in the beverage sector and our belief that tobacco fundamentals are improving. Also of significance is the continued share gain registered by Philip Morris (MO, Accumulate, $67 3/4, (o)) during the 12- and 4-week periods of 1.8 and 1.5 share points, respectively. This share gain is largely at the expense of RJR Nabisco (RN, Neutral, $26 1/4, m,o), which continues to register significant volume declines.

Packaged-Food Market Share Analysis - Industry Report [Apr-12-95] DEAN WITTER REYNOLDS, reported by Adelman, L., et al. Consumer Group, Industry Periodical #690, April 12, 1995. Packaged-Food Market Share Analysis Cold Cereal - We feel it is important to highlight the continued share erosion experienced by Kellogg and General Mills in the cold cereal category. Kellogg and General Mills have lost 1.0 and 2.4 volume share points for the 4-week period, respectively. This share loss is largely due to the reduction in "buy-one-get-one-free" promotions by both companies as well as strong 4-week volume growth by private label, Quaker Oats, and Malt-O-Meal, which recorded volume growth of 8.2%, 16.8%, and 43.0%, respectively. (Malt-O-Meal is a small manufacturer whose products are priced slightly above private label.) We believe that the elimination of these costly "buy-one-get-one-free" promotions will benefit long-term category profitability.

Private Label - Volume share during the 12- and 4-week periods remained flat to up slightly in most packaged food categories except for chips and snacks (down 0.6 share points during the 4-week period) and Mexican food (down 2.4 share points during the 4-week period). Cold cereal continues to be the fastest-growing packaged food private label category registering 8.9% and 8.2% volume gains during the respective 12- and 4-week periods compared to industry tonnage declines of 0.3% and 0.4% during the same periods. This above-industry growth resulted in 12- and 4-week market share gains of 0.8 share points.

ANDRES WINES LTD.

Exchanges	Price (Jun29'95)	11.25	Trailing P/E	12.50	Stock Symbol
TMV	Trailing Yield (%)	5.29	Trailing EPS	0.90	ADW.A

Period Ending	Mar95	Mar94	Mar93	Mar92	Mar91
Yearly Statistics					
Price-Close	11.25	11.38	13.00	14.00	9.63
Price-High	11.88	15.00	14.25	15.00	9.63
Price-Low	10.00	10.38	12.25	9.50	8.00
P/E-Close	12.50	12.93	13.13	13.59	9.63
Dividends per Share	0.60	2.90	0.60	0.60	0.60
Dividend Yield (%)	5.33	25.47	4.60	4.27	6.21
Sales per Share	15.31	12.20	12.59	12.51	11.78
EPS before extra. item	0.90	0.88	0.99	1.03	1.00
Cash Flow per Share	1.64	1.10	1.25	1.26	1.26
Book Value per Share	9.16	8.85	10.83	10.44	9.99
O/S Common Shares	4,629	4,593	4,492	4,462	4,462
Total Revenue	70,601	55,835	56,360	55,803	52,634
Income before extra.	4,166	4,048	4,426	4,616	4,467
Cash Flow	7,557	5,034	5,607	5,623	5,621
Debt/Equity	0.10	0.03	0.03	0.03	0.04
Return on Capital (%)	17.38	14.63	15.45	16.90	17.04
Ret. on Com. Equity (%)	9.99	9.02	9.26	10.09	10.19
% Change Profit	2.9	(8.5)	(4.1)	3.3	(2.0)
% Change Revenue	26.4	(0.9)	1.0	6.0	(1.3)
% Change Assets	9.1	(12.7)	3.1	2.3	5.4
Preferred Div. Coverage	np	202.5	221.5		
Total Div. Coverage	1.5	0.3	1.7		
Interest Coverage	20.0	47.0	47.0		
Current Ratio	2.9	6.1	9.0		
Operating Margin	11.0	12.2	13.6		
Asset Turnover	1.3	1.1	1.0		
5 YEAR RATIOS (%)					
Return on Capital	16.3	16.3	16.7		
Return on Com. Equity	9.7	9.9	10.1		
Profit Growth	0.1	0.1	2.0		
Revenue Growth	1.1	(0.1)	(0.2)		
Asset Growth	0.0	(0.1)	3.4		
BALANCE SHEET (000)					
Cash	0	11,995	20,262		
Current Assets	32,927	38,143	46,270		
Net Fixed Assets	18,179	11,787	10,938		
Invest's & Advances	0	0	0		
Total Assets	54,486	49,930	57,208		
Short Term Debt	4,181	175	175		
Current Liabilities	11,251	6,281	5,122		
Long Term Debt	0	1,091	1,301		
Total Liabilities	12,071	8,940	8,227		
Total Equity	42,415	40,990	48,981		
Total Liab. & Equity	54,486	49,930	57,208		
CAPITAL (000)					
Total Debt	4,181	1,266	1,476		
Preferred Equity	0	333	333		
Common Equity	42,415	40,656	48,648		

Business:

ANDRES WINES LTD. operates wineries in British Columbia, Alberta, Ontario, Quebec and Nova Scotia. The company sells wine across Canada and exports wine internationally.

Date	EPS	DPS	Tot Rev	Inc Bex
Mar 95	(0.02)	0.15	14,035	(84)
Dec 94	0.44	0.15	23,785	2,040
Sep 94	0.22	0.15	18,580	999
Jun 94	0.26	0.15	14,201	1,211
Mar 94	(0.06)	0.15	9,839	(239)
Dec 93	0.49	0.15	18,194	2,237
Sep 93	0.19	2.51	13,862	896
Jun 93	0.26	0.15	13,940	1,154

Synopsis:

According to Andres, total volume of wine sales in Canada, including wine coolers and cider, fell by 1.4% in the year ending March 1994. However, the decline does not reflect the growth of wine sales through the untaxed "black" market, or the lower taxed "make your own" wine establishments. Increased sales through these channels have a negative impact on wineries such as Andres.

Total volume of imported wine sales rose by 1.8%, while sales of Canadian wines fell by 5.6% during the same period. According to Andres, the increase in imported wines has occurred as a result of the popularity of New World wines, and growing popularity of red wine where imports have traditionally maintained a high market share. As a result, Canadian wines share of market fell to 41.9% from 43.8% the year before. Within these market conditions, Andres sales volume declined 5.5%, resulting in a 9% share of total market. Despite these trends, the company increased its market share in the premium, red, and cider categories.

While market conditions remain somewhat uncertain, the forecast for 1995 is for lower sales volumes of white table wines, wine coolers, and sparkling wines. Andres' objective is to capitalize on its strength and position in the premium wine segment to achieve increases in both sales and market share.

In June 1994, Andres acquired Hillebrand Estates Winery Ltd. of Niagara-on-the-Lake, Ontario, for $10.75-million. Hillebrand is the largest producer of VQA wines and premium wines in Canada and has annual sales of $14-million. The purchase should strengthen Andres' commitment to the premium wine market.

Rank (Profit/Revenue/Assets)
462   527   630

Joseph A. Peller
Chairman
John E. Peller
President & C.E.O.

Address
P.O. Box 10550
Winona
ON
L8E 5S4
(905) 643-4131

Fax: (905) 643-4944
A0002263/G/5.3.3

AULT FOODS INC.

Exchanges	Price (Jun29'95)		17.00	Trailing P/E		21.25	Stock Symbol
TM	Trailing Yield (%)		4.88	Trailing EPS		0.80	**AUL**

Period Ending	Apr94	Apr93	Apr92	Apr91
Yearly Statistics				
Price-Close	16.75	nt	nt	nt
Price-High	18.88	nt	nt	nt
Price-Low	14.88	nt	nt	nt
P/E-Close	11.76	nt	nt	nt
Dividends per Share	0.45	0.00	0.00	0.00
Dividend Yield (%)	2.83	0.00	0.00	0.00
Sales per Share	67.70	64.23	64.69	59.45
EPS before extra. item	1.35	0.82	1.74	1.75
Cash Flow per Share	3.61	2.77	3.37	2.47
Book Value per Share	15.41	20.45	20.95	20.22
O/S Common Shares	18,297	18,297	18,380	18,250
Total Revenue	1,240,055	1,177,038	1,189,000	1,085,000
Income before extra.	24,646	15,000	32,000	32,000
Cash Flow	66,106	50,701	62,000	45,000
Debt/Equity	0.44	0.00	nd	nd
Return on Capital (%)	11.92	8.57	14.06	na
Ret. on Com. Equity (%)	7.51	3.95	8.49	na
% Change Profit	64.3	(53.1)	na	na
% Change Revenue	5.4	(1.0)	9.6	na
% Change Assets	4.8	5.4	10.7	na

Date	EPS	DPS	Tot Rev	Inc Bex
Apr 95	0.03	0.17	326,306	522
Jan 95	0.14	0.17	298,402	2,543
Oct 94	0.36	0.32	321,777	6,644
Jul 94	0.27	0.17	347,221	4,900
Apr 94	0.43	0.15	325,372	7,795
Jan 94	0.12	0.15	284,231	2,174
Oct 93	0.34	0.15	306,521	6,338
Jul 93	0.46	0.00	322,568	8,339

	Apr94	Apr93	Apr92
Preferred Div. Coverage	np	np	np
Total Div. Coverage	3.0	na	na
Interest Coverage	8.0	4.0	nd
Current Ratio	1.3	1.3	1.4
Operating Margin	3.9	3.8	5.7
Asset Turnover	2.1	2.1	2.2
5 YEAR RATIOS (%)			
Return on Capital	na	na	na
Return on Com. Equity	na	na	na
Profit Growth	na	na	na
Revenue Growth	na	na	na
Asset Growth	na	na	na
BALANCE SHEET (000)			
Cash	872	22,626	14,000
Current Assets	219,581	199,480	213,000
Net Fixed Assets	234,836	227,099	209,000
Invest's & Advances	39,791	42,005	21,000
Total Assets	596,521	569,137	540,000
Short Term Debt	23,311	225	0
Current Liabilities	166,535	147,830	155,000
Long Term Debt	100,894	760	0
Total Liabilities	314,599	194,960	155,000
Total Equity	281,922	374,177	385,000
Total Liab. & Equity	596,521	569,137	540,000
CAPITAL (000)			
Total Debt	124,205	985	0
Preferred Equity	0	0	0
Common Equity	281,922	374,177	385,000

Business:

AULT FOODS INC. is Canada's largest fully integrated dairy processor. Operations include 15 plants and 41 distribution centres in Ontario and Quebec. Ault employs 2,800 and is publicly traded on the Toronto and Montreal Stock exchanges (AUL). Well known brand names are Sealtest, Lactantia, Black Diamond, Parlour, and Light n' Lively.

Synopsis:

In May 1995, Ault Foods Inc. announced plans to combine three of its divisions along with earmarking $2-million for a potential liability at a Mexican dairy. Plans call for the divisions to be merged into one national business unit solely responsible for the manufacture, marketing, and distribution of milk, yogurt, sour cream, drinks, and other refrigerated products. This strategy aims at improving business effectiveness.

Ault's alternative milk product "PurFiltre", with a shelf life double that of conventional milk, has been introduced in Ontario and Quebec. Ault has plans to license PurFiltre in other provinces, the U.S. and Europe. Ault is very confident of sales in the Quebec market because PurFiltre is being marketed under the Lactantia label, a strong brand in that province. Ault expects this premium priced milk to boost its profit margin despite declining milk sales in Canada. In Ontario, Ault has as yet been unable to market PurFiltre in Loblaw stores. There is opposition to Ault's claims that the milk holds "92 times less bacteria" than regular milk. Competitors fear the success of this product will negatively affect sales of regular milk products.

In March, Ault lost a $25-million contract to sell its Sealtest milk through 43 Canadian Miracle Food Mart stores. This adversely affected fiscal 1995 profits by eight cents a share. The loss may be partially offset by a new agreement with Great Atlantic & Pacific Tea Co., Miracle Mart's parent.

In fiscal 1994, Ault weathered selling price deflation, partially offset by major cost reductions, improvements in the branded products businesses, and lower short-term interest rates. During the year, Ault acquired Lovell & Christmas, an import-export and trading business for $11.1-million cash. This gave Ault a major presence in the cheese importing business. In fiscal 1994, sales of Ault's Refrigerated and Frozen Products represented 55% of total sales versus 45% for its Cheese and Butter Products division.

Relative strength to TSE300 / Price / Volume (in 1000's of board lots)

Rank (Profit/Revenue/Assets)
189   104   211

Donald Loadman
Chairman

Graham P.M. Freeman
President & C.E.O.

Douglas. G. Shields
V.P. Finance

Address
10th Floor
405 The West Mall
Etobicoke
ON
M9C 5J1
(416) 626-1973

Fax: (416) 620-3123
01003366/G/5.1

For further company information, call Globe Information Services 1-800-268-9128 or (416) 585-5345

BC SUGAR REFINERY, LIMITED

Exchanges	Price (Jun29'95)	8.50	Trailing P/E	9.14	Stock Symbol
T	Trailing Yield (%)	4.71	Trailing EPS	0.93	BCS.A

Period Ending	Sep94	Sep93	Sep92	Sep91	Sep90
Yearly Statistics					
Price-Close	8.13	9.50	9.00	15.00	14.13
Price-High	11.75	11.63	15.75	16.25	18.38
Price-Low	7.50	8.25	8.13	13.63	13.50
P/E-Close	7.59	15.08	12.68	nm	17.23
Dividends per Share	0.40	0.40	0.60	0.80	0.80
Dividend Yield (%)	4.92	4.21	6.67	5.33	5.66
Sales per Share	32.13	29.77	17.09	11.29	13.04
EPS before extra. item	1.07	0.63	0.71	(0.60)	0.82
Cash Flow per Share	1.50	1.27	0.97	0.66	1.14
Book Value per Share	8.11	7.59	6.77	5.18	6.59
O/S Common Shares	24,722	24,722	22,722	14,271	14,176
Total Revenue	808,992	706,173	281,445	161,187	184,261
Income before extra.	26,536	15,023	11,694	(8,554)	11,603
Cash Flow	36,970	30,053	16,009	9,450	16,091
Debt/Equity	0.84	1.33	2.03	2.27	0.52
Return on Capital (%)	15.28	11.70	9.05	5.81	18.32
Ret. on Com. Equity (%)	13.67	8.76	10.20	(10.32)	12.76
% Change Profit	76.6	28.5	236.7	(173.7)	(50.5)
% Change Revenue	14.6	150.9	74.6	(12.5)	(36.3)
% Change Assets	(10.6)	(1.9)	112.9	60.6	(11.6)

Date	EPS	DPS	Tot Rev	Inc Bex
Mar 95	(0.11)	0.10	192,381	(2,707)
Dec 94	0.21	0.10	219,000	5,290
Sep 94	0.26	0.10	219,178	6,387
Jun 94	0.57	0.10	204,726	14,183
Mar 94	0.03	0.10	187,102	885
Dec 93	0.21	0.10	183,522	5,081
Sep 93	0.16	0.10	197,638	4,055
Jun 93	0.13	0.10	178,489	3,178

Preferred Div. Coverage	na	190.2	148.0
Total Div. Coverage	2.7	1.6	1.2
Interest Coverage	2.8	2.1	1.8
Current Ratio	1.8	1.5	1.6
Operating Margin	6.0	7.5	10.8
Asset Turnover	1.6	1.3	0.5
5 YEAR RATIOS (%)			
Return on Capital	12.0	16.6	23.0
Return on Com. Equity	7.0	10.1	15.3
Profit Growth	2.5	(8.6)	(8.3)
Revenue Growth	22.8	21.9	5.9
Asset Growth	21.6	28.3	28.6
BALANCE SHEET (000)			
Cash	592	1,105	28,447
Current Assets	182,737	191,118	202,284
Net Fixed Assets	144,484	196,694	191,247
Invest's & Advances	8,738	0	2,183
Total Assets	489,468	547,235	557,631
Short Term Debt	28,668	44,647	64,207
Current Liabilities	99,249	125,362	125,334
Long Term Debt	140,203	206,148	250,432
Total Liabilities	287,302	358,109	402,228
Total Equity	202,166	189,126	155,403
Total Liab. & Equity	489,468	547,235	557,631
CAPITAL (000)			
Total Debt	168,871	250,795	314,639
Preferred Equity	1,570	1,570	1,570
Common Equity	200,596	187,556	153,833

Business:

BC SUGAR is involved in the production, distribution and marketing of sugar products. The company has sugar facilites in Canada and the United States.

Synopsis:

Fiscal 1994 was a key year for BC Sugar Refinery Limited. The company sold its chemical division to concentrate on its core sugar operations. The $82-million proceeds from the sale of Kalama Chemical will go to reduce debt and associated interest costs. With renewed emphasis on sugar operations, BC Sugar's sugar revenues hit record levels. The increase was attributed mainly to increased sales volumes and to a rise in the average world price of raw sugar.

However, problems persist between Canada and U.S. regarding sugar and sugar-containing products. The U.S. domestic sugar price support program in the U.S. continues to affect BC Sugar's U.S. operations. Sales margins in both countries continue to be affected by excess U.S. beet sugar production. The establishment of marketing allotments by the U.S. government for domestic beet and raw cane sugar in October 1994 may affect BC Sugar's future operations in the U.S. and Canada. Finally, as of October 1, 1995, the new U.S. GATT tariff is expected to restrict world sugar quotas for refined sugar imports to 22,000 tonnes, from which Canada must compete for its share. According to BC Sugar, the resolution of trade matters with the U.S. remains the key issue facing the company.

During fiscal 1994, sales at BC Sugar's Western operations achieved record levels. The Eastern Canadian operations faced a very competitive market due to U.S. sugar imports. To compete, BC will focus on cost reduction and control. In the U.S., BC Sugar faced strong competitive pressures in both the industrial and grocery sectors. During fiscal 1994, Canada was responsible for 63% of sales, versus 37% for the U.S.

In November 1994, Balaclava Enterprises, through its wholly owned subsidiary 338446 British Columbia, increased its holdings of BC Sugar's Class A shares to 10.6%. Balaclava said the purchase was for investment purposes only. This purchase followed on the heels of Jimmy Pattison's doubling his stake in BC Sugar to 18.5%. According to the Pattison group, the purchase was for investment purposes only.

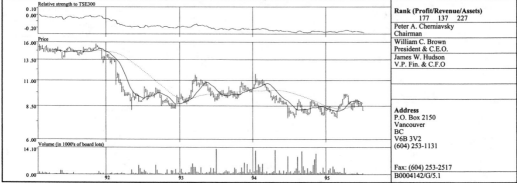

Rank (Profit/Revenue/Assets)	177 137 227
Peter A. Cherniavsky	Chairman
William C. Brown	President & C.E.O.
James W. Hudson	V.P. Fin. & C.F.O

Address
P.O. Box 2150
Vancouver
BC
V6B 3V2
(604) 253-1131

Fax: (604) 253-2517
B0004142/G/5.1

CANADA MALTING CO. LIMITED

Exchanges	Price (Jun29'95)		17.25	Trailing P/E		12.06	Stock Symbol
TM	Trailing Yield (%)		2.09	Trailing EPS		1.43	**CMG**

Period Ending	Dec94	Dec93	Dec92	Dec91	Dec90
Yearly Statistics					
Price-Close	14.00	16.00	13.63	15.33	9.67
Price-High	17.25	17.88	17.50	15.33	11.33
Price-Low	13.00	13.13	12.88	8.67	8.67
P/E-Close	10.45	12.90	17.03	12.85	6.84
Dividends per Share	0.36	0.36	0.35	0.33	0.32
Dividend Yield (%)	2.57	2.25	2.57	2.17	3.31
Sales per Share	19.08	19.57	18.86	19.15	22.72
EPS before extra. item	1.34	1.24	0.80	1.19	1.41
Cash Flow per Share	1.79	2.10	1.77	1.73	1.54
Book Value per Share	14.18	12.45	11.41	11.51	10.79
O/S Common Shares	19,291	19,196	19,156	19,105	19,087
Total Revenue	371,964	375,490	361,120	366,147	407,901
Income before extra.	25,797	23,801	15,268	22,781	24,888
Cash Flow	34,465	40,234	33,781	33,100	27,181
Debt/Equity	0.53	0.56	0.72	0.59	0.65
Return on Capital (%)	12.35	11.72	8.40	12.23	15.00
Ret. on Com. Equity (%)	10.07	10.40	6.96	10.70	15.18
% Change Profit	8.4	55.9	(33.0)	(8.5)	23.9
% Change Revenue	(0.9)	4.0	(1.4)	(10.2)	22.6
% Change Assets	12.9	6.3	6.8	3.8	4.1

Preferred Div. Coverage	np	np	np
Total Div. Coverage	3.7	3.4	2.3
Interest Coverage	4.8	4.2	2.7
Current Ratio	2.1	0.8	1.4
Operating Margin	12.1	12.0	11.3
Asset Turnover	0.7	0.8	0.8
5 YEAR RATIOS (%)			
Return on Capital	11.9	13.4	15.7
Return on Com. Equity	10.7	12.2	13.1
Profit Growth	5.1	9.8	10.0
Revenue Growth	2.2	16.8	18.0
Asset Growth	6.7	29.5	28.1
BALANCE SHEET (000)			
Cash	29,691	21,896	8,663
Current Assets	149,334	124,853	154,910
Net Fixed Assets	343,860	310,526	272,210
Invest's & Advances	20,139	19,236	0
Total Assets	521,720	462,232	434,817
Short Term Debt	14,794	110,031	72,595
Current Liabilities	72,859	153,245	108,354
Long Term Debt	129,661	23,133	84,394
Total Liabilities	248,200	223,344	216,183
Total Equity	273,520	238,888	218,634
Total Liab. & Equity	521,720	462,232	434,817
CAPITAL (000)			
Total Debt	144,455	133,164	156,989
Preferred Equity	0	0	0
Common Equity	273,520	238,888	218,634

Business:

CANADA MALTING CO. LTD. is a producer and exporter of barley malt for sale to brewers, distillers and food manufacturers. Export markets include Japan and other Pacific Rim countries. Canada Malting is Canada's leading malt producer and exporter. Subsidiary companies include Great Western Malting Co. in the western United States and Hugh Baird & Sons in England.

Date	EPS	DPS	Tot Rev	Inc Bex
Mar 95	0.29	0.09	98,632	5,687
Dec 94	0.37	0.09	94,108	7,062
Sep 94	0.31	0.09	97,727	6,103
Jun 94	0.46	0.09	103,163	8,818
Mar 94	0.20	0.09	76,966	3,814
Dec 93	0.31	0.09	89,228	5,895
Sep 93	0.30	0.09	100,540	5,783
Jun 93	0.37	0.09	101,258	7,130

Synopsis:

Canada Malting Co. Limited seeks to become a supplier to major brewers entering virgin markets. With mature markets in North America and Western Europe, the company is continuing to explore opportunities in South America, China, and India. Canada Malting plans to increase its stake in Argentina-based Malteria Pampa to 33.33% from 20%. Malteria is the largest malt producer in South America. Canada Malting has established a new international development team, Canada Malting International, to pursue international ventures.

During fiscal 1994, declining sales revenues offset rising sales volumes. The decline resulted from lower export pricing, reduced European Union subsidies received by subsidiary Hugh Baird on export sales, and a higher proportion of tolling business. Total malt shipments rose 6.7% from a year ago. Canada Malting's domestic markets in Canada, the U.S., and the U.K. accounted for 68% of consolidated malt shipments. Export sales jumped 16% and represented 32% of total shipments. Export markets include Mexico, Korea, South Africa and the Philippines, while markets in Japan and Brazil showed particularly strong results. Capital spending was $35.3-million in 1994. A further $50-million will be spent in 1995. Canada Malting expects its plants to run at or near full capacity during 1995.

International trade agreements will affect Canada Malting's future. The Canada/U.S. Free Trade Agreement will eliminate restrictions on barley and malt imports from the U.S. to Canada when subsidies to U.S. barley farmers fall to the same level or lower than Canadian subsidies. Furthermore, the North American Free Trade Agreement will allow 120,000 tonnes of barley and/or malt from the U.S. and 30,000 tonnes from Canada into Mexico duty free during the first year of the agreement. This amount will rise annually for ten years until the removal of Mexican import restrictions.

Sales revenues at subsidiary Leaver Mushrooms jumped 13% mainly due to higher selling prices. Leaver represents less than 10% of Canada Malting's total sales.

Relative strength to TSE300

Price

Volume (in 1000's of board lots)

Rank (Profit/Revenue/Assets)
184   226   223

Ronald W. Eden
President & C.E.O.
W. Wesley De Shane
V.P. C.F.O. & Secretary

Address
10 Four Seasons Place
Suite 600
Toronto
ON
M9B 6H7
(416) 622-6151

Fax: (416) 620-4182
C0001506/G/5.1

COCA-COLA BEVERAGES LTD.

Exchanges	Price (Jun29'95)	6.87	Trailing P/E	nm	Stock Symbol
TM	Trailing Yield (%)	0.00	Trailing EPS	(0.43)	KOC

Period Ending	Dec94	Dec93	Dec92	Dec91	Dec90
Yearly Statistics					
Price-Close	4.30	6.63	4.30	7.88	9.25
Price-High	6.63	6.75	8.50	11.38	13.00
Price-Low	4.15	3.90	3.10	6.38	8.63
P/E-Close	nm	nm	nm	787.50	44.05
Dividends per Share	0.00	0.04	0.05	0.05	0.05
Dividend Yield (%)	0.00	0.60	1.16	0.64	0.54
Sales per Share	21.32	22.00	22.32	25.10	25.14
EPS before extra. item	(0.47)	(3.56)	(1.25)	0.01	0.21
Cash Flow per Share	0.55	0.31	(0.13)	1.03	1.68
Book Value per Share	1.07	1.53	5.04	6.34	6.38
O/S Common Shares	40,114	40,103	40,103	40,103	40,008
Total Revenue	855,181	882,257	894,967	1,005,399	1,005,646
Income before extra.	(15,992)	(139,033)	(45,049)	5,300	13,215
Cash Flow	22,086	12,310	(5,360)	41,249	67,167
Debt/Equity	5.19	3.93	1.54	1.10	1.01
Return on Capital (%)	3.99	(24.16)	(3.90)	8.56	10.76
Ret. on Com. Equity (%)	(35.99)	(108.49)	(21.91)	0.14	3.29
% Change Profit	88.5	(208.6)	(950.0)	(59.9)	(16.7)
% Change Revenue	(3.1)	(1.4)	(11.0)	(0.0)	7.3
% Change Assets	(1.7)	(14.2)	(2.6)	8.0	5.6

Date	EPS	DPS	Tot Rev	Inc Bex
Apr 95	(0.23)	0.00	172,544	(8,365)
Dec 94	(0.15)	0.00	211,084	(5,001)
Oct 94	0.01	0.00	237,774	1,308
Jul 94	(0.06)	0.00	235,062	(1,792)
Apr 94	(0.28)	0.00	170,676	(10,507)
Dec 93	(3.09)	0.00	202,884	(123,049)
Oct 93	(0.06)	0.01	243,926	(1,409)
Jul 93	(0.08)	0.01	248,534	(2,188)

	Dec94	Dec93	Dec92
Preferred Div. Coverage	0.0	0.0	0.0
Total Div. Coverage	0.0	0.0	0.0
Interest Coverage	0.6	0.0	0.0
Current Ratio	0.9	0.8	1.5
Operating Margin	3.4	3.0	(1.7)
Asset Turnover	1.2	1.2	1.1
5 YEAR RATIOS (%)			
Return on Capital	(0.9)	(0.7)	5.1
Return on Com. Equity	(32.6)	(24.1)	(1.4)
Profit Growth	na	na	na
Revenue Growth	(1.8)	1.4	4.3
Asset Growth	(1.3)	2.1	9.6
BALANCE SHEET (000)			
Cash	509	13,480	13,681
Current Assets	160,178	148,046	200,840
Net Fixed Assets	268,633	283,072	393,162
Invest's & Advances	0	0	0
Total Assets	695,870	707,549	824,707
Short Term Debt	51,449	24,643	20,035
Current Liabilities	175,463	184,955	136,944
Long Term Debt	428,000	411,512	386,412
Total Liabilities	603,463	596,467	560,361
Total Equity	92,407	111,082	264,346
Total Liab. & Equity	695,870	707,549	824,707
CAPITAL (000)			
Total Debt	479,449	436,155	406,447
Preferred Equity	49,702	49,702	62,202
Common Equity	42,705	61,380	202,144

Business:

COCA-COLA BEVERAGES LTD., through its subsidiary Coca-Cola Bottling Ltd., cans, bottles, packages and distributes Coca-Cola soft drink products, as well as various products under Canada Dry, Schweppes and A & W trademarks. The Company operates in all ten provinces. The Coca-Cola Company of Atlanta, Georgia, through Coca-Cola Ltd., holds approximately 49% of the outstanding common shares.

Synopsis:

Coca-Cola Beverages Ltd. after a first quarter 1995 loss, launched a new marketing plan for the second and third quarter 1995. The plan will focus in bottle design and new packaging initiatives. The company re-examined its packaging represents as part of an overall strategy to boost demand through brand loyalty not price cuts. The company will emphasize commercials instead of price wars. In prior quarters, the company found itself embroiled in price wars with Pepsi-Cola and Cott Corp.

In fiscal 1994, Coca-Cola refocused its marketing strategy, developed key alliances with customers, and improved its production and distribution. The restructuring program saved $29-million in 1994 and should save another $12-million in 1995. Production plants were pared to 8 from 16, and storage warehouses were cut to 29 from 68. The labour force saw a 13%. To offer a more attractive product, the company initiated a number of new packaging formats. Marketing strategies were refocused on life stages rather than brand lines.

This jump was related to innovative product differentiation resulting from new packaging. Coca-Cola also continued to focus on its non-carbonated beverage opportunities, which offer higher margins. According to the company, non-carbonated beverages afford "a significant opportunity to enhance long-term growth and profitability." Capital expenditures in 1994 totalled $29.4-million, a 34% drop from the prior year. Spending in 1995 should fall within the $30-million range.

In 1995, Coca-Cola plans to be market-driven, while focusing on revenue and cost control. The company plans to add new products, and rejuvenate existing products in response to changing consumer demands.

Rank (Profit/Revenue/Assets)
959   128   190

Joseph R. Gladden
Chairman

William P. Casey
President & C.E.O.

Shaun B. Higgins
Sr. V.P. & C.F.O.

William T. Highberger
Sr. V.P. & C.O.O.

Address
42 Overlea Boulevard
Toronto
ON
M4H 1B8
(416) 424-6000

Fax: (416) 424-6079
T0001589/G/5.1

CORBY DISTILLERIES LIMITED

Exchanges	Price (Jun29'95)		36.75	Trailing P/E		8.94	Stock Symbol
TMVZ	Trailing Yield (%)		3.05	Trailing EPS		4.11	**CDL.A**

Period Ending	Feb95	Feb94	Feb93	Feb92	Feb91
Yearly Statistics					
Price-Close	37.13	48.25	48.25	51.00	36.25
Price-High	58.13	54.00	54.00	56.00	37.00
Price-Low	37.13	42.00	42.00	35.00	28.75
P/E-Close	9.17	11.30	9.77	22.97	11.96
Dividends per Share	1.12	17.62	1.07	0.88	0.76
Dividend Yield (%)	3.02	36.52	2.22	1.73	2.10
Sales per Share	10.53	11.34	12.08	12.67	13.99
EPS before extra. item	4.05	4.27	4.94	2.22	3.03
Cash Flow per Share	3.15	4.33	4.89	2.46	3.37
Book Value per Share	14.76	11.54	24.67	21.01	19.74
O/S Common Shares	7,058	7,057	7,024	7,009	6,968
Total Revenue	98,124	106,524	114,059	109,064	112,325
Income before extra.	28,601	30,025	34,664	15,518	21,111
Cash Flow	22,261	30,470	34,307	17,181	23,443
Debt/Equity	0.03	0.03	0.01	0.01	0.01
Return on Capital (%)	45.20	37.66	35.20	17.55	27.51
Ret. on Com. Equity (%)	30.82	23.57	21.63	10.90	16.33
% Change Profit	(4.7)	(13.4)	123.4	(26.5)	35.6
% Change Revenue	(7.9)	(6.6)	4.6	(2.9)	(4.7)
% Change Assets	(44.8)	9.4	14.6	3.0	15.5

Preferred Div. Coverage	np	np	np
Total Div. Coverage	3.5	0.2	4.6
Interest Coverage	na	na	na
Current Ratio	7.3	1.4	9.2
Operating Margin	37.8	41.2	42.6
Asset Turnover	0.6	0.4	0.4
5 YEAR RATIOS (%)			
Return on Capital	32.6	28.1	24.7
Return on Com. Equity	20.7	17.3	15.4
Profit Growth	13.0	17.2	28.2
Revenue Growth	(3.6)	(0.7)	5.6
Asset Growth	(3.9)	9.2	8.8
BALANCE SHEET (000)			
Cash	21,645	122,175	111,447
Current Assets	72,801	175,860	164,769
Net Fixed Assets	1,486	942	2,039
Invest's & Advances	32,143	22,767	15,880
Total Assets	115,542	209,458	191,445
Short Term Debt	3,006	2,382	1,525
Current Liabilities	10,002	126,653	17,857
Long Term Debt	0	0	0
Total Liabilities	11,395	128,014	18,155
Total Equity	104,147	81,444	173,290
Total Liab. & Equity	115,542	209,458	191,445
CAPITAL (000)			
Total Debt	3,006	2,382	1,525
Preferred Equity	0	0	0
Common Equity	104,147	81,444	173,290

Business:

CORBY DISTILLERIES LTD. markets a full range of domestically produced distilled spirits and liqueurs as well as imported cognac, scotch, gin, liqueurs and aperitifs and a wide range of quality imported wines.

Date	EPS	DPS	Tot Rev	Inc Bex
May 95	0.70	0.28	16,248	4,941
Feb 95	0.96	0.28	21,660	6,773
Nov 94	1.54	0.28	32,483	10,857
Aug 94	0.91	0.28	23,862	6,486
May 94	0.64	0.28	17,934	4,485
Feb 94	0.56	16.78	22,586	3,933
Nov 93	1.85	0.28	36,764	12,991
Aug 93	1.05	0.28	25,459	7,391

Synopsis:

Although Corby maintained its market share in fiscal 1995, gross operating revenues declined by 5.4% from the previous year. Of this decline, 4% relates to reduced pricing due to strong competitive pressure and 1.4% to a volume decline resulting from reduced consumption and increased smuggling in the Canadian marketplace.

Continuing high liquor taxation is the principal cause of the underground economy. As the most highly taxed commodity in the country at 83%, the Canadian spirits market remains vulnerable to illegally imported U.S. products. The Association of Canadian Distillers and its member companies, in an effort to adjust the current tax practice on spirits, have been actively lobbying government representatives and sensitizing the public to the seriousness of the issue. With the exception of Alberta, governments remain reticent to the idea of taking corrective measures. Corby feels the privitization of the Alberta Liquor Control Board retail system in September 1993 set a trend towards deregulation and privatization of provincial liquor jurisdictions. Faced with increased pressure to control costs and generate additional revenues, the issues of modernization and privitization will become a part of the political agenda in other provinces.

During the first quarter ending May 1995, Corby concluded the purchase of the remaining 60% outstanding shares of The Upper Canada Brewing Company Limited and shortly afterwards sold this investment. The sale generated a gain of $1.3-million ($0.9-million after tax).

Corby maintains a broad portfolio of brands in all segments of the market and is less vulnerable to consumer shifts. The company's success with lead entries of pre-mixed cocktails such as Long Island Iced Tea, Kahlua Combos, and Sauza Margarita looks promising for the future.

Rank (Profit/Revenue/Assets)
161   415   348

John Giffen
Chairman

Martin A. Jones
President & C.E.O.

Alastair K. Symers
Sr. V.P. & C.F.O.

Address
1002 Rue Sherbrooke Ouest
Suite 2300
Montreal
PQ
H3A 3L6
(514) 288-4181

Fax: (514) 288-0749
C0010839/G/5.3.2

CORPORATE FOODS LIMITED

Exchanges	Price (Jun29'95)		16.87	Trailing P/E		15.34	Stock Symbol
T	Trailing Yield (%)		1.42	Trailing EPS		1.10	CFL

Period Ending	Dec94	Dec93	Dec92	Dec91	Dec90	Business:
Yearly Statistics						CORPORATE FOODS LIMITED is a
Price-Close	14.63	18.25	16.50	17.88	11.75	diversified bakery and specialty food company
Price-High	19.88	18.63	19.75	19.75	12.00	operating within the North American food
Price-Low	13.00	13.25	14.75	10.00	8.75	industry. It is the leading national baker of fresh
P/E-Close	13.80	17.89	20.63	19.02	14.33	bread and rolls with facilities coast to coast in
Dividends per Share	0.24	0.24	0.24	0.21	0.20	Canada.
Dividend Yield (%)	1.64	1.32	1.46	1.18	1.70	
Sales per Share	20.25	17.21	10.07	10.83	11.00	
EPS before extra. item	1.06	1.02	0.80	0.94	0.82	
Cash Flow per Share	1.66	1.45	0.80	0.96	0.92	
Book Value per Share	7.79	6.95	6.15	4.84	4.08	
O/S Common Shares	21,003	20,955	20,902	19,283	19,144	
Total Revenue	424,848	361,736	203,563	209,387	217,018	

Income before extra.	22,338	21,415	15,502	18,103	15,700		Date	EPS	DPS	Tot Rev	Inc Bex
Cash Flow	34,774	30,270	16,126	18,504	17,621		Mar 95	0.17	0.06	95,403	3,487
Debt/Equity	0.27	0.24	0.01	0.01	0.01		Dec 94	0.37	0.06	134,582	7,915
Return on Capital (%)	18.46	21.00	19.03	30.02	31.41		Sep 94	0.29	0.06	100,503	5,962
Ret. on Com. Equity (%)	14.46	15.62	13.94	21.05	21.79		Jun 94	0.27	0.06	98,282	5,709
% Change Profit	4.3	38.1	(14.4)	15.3	23.2		Mar 94	0.13	0.06	91,481	2,752
% Change Revenue	17.4	77.7	(2.8)	(3.5)	6.7		Dec 93	0.36	0.06	126,746	7,588
% Change Assets	8.8	54.5	35.8	14.2	14.3		Sep 93	0.29	0.06	93,954	6,110
							Jun 93	0.22	0.06	74,006	4,559

Preferred Div. Coverage	np	np	np	**Synopsis:**
Total Div. Coverage	4.4	4.3	3.3	In the first quarter of 1995, improvements in all product areas combined to
Interest Coverage	17.7	76.8	na	increase earnings at Corporate Foods Limited. Corporate Food's strategy was to
Current Ratio	0.7	0.5	1.8	increase volumes, improve production efficiencies, and reduce costs. According
Operating Margin	7.1	6.8	6.7	to the company, overall volume increases along with added capacity in late 1994
Asset Turnover	1.5	1.4	1.2	and early 1995 were enough to offset competitive pricing pressures in some of its
5 YEAR RATIOS (%)				markets. The Ontario facility rationalization last year was a key factor in the
Return on Capital	24.0	26.3	29.0	improvements. Intense competition in the Quebec market depressed equity
Return on Com. Equity	17.4	18.7	20.7	earnings in the quarter, but the situation should improve later in the year.
Profit Growth	11.9	13.7	16.8	
Revenue Growth	15.9	12.8	8.3	Wallace McCain recently acquired Maple Leaf Foods, the parent company of
Asset Growth	24.3	25.1	22.8	Corporate Foods. A new set of directors at Corporate Foods reflects the
BALANCE SHEET (000)				ownership change. New directors, all officers of Maple Leaf, include Wallace
Cash	0	0	3,471	McCain, Archie McLean, Scott McCain, and Michael McCain. Corporate Foods
Current Assets	46,962	45,776	52,742	President and C.E.O., David Lees, was the only existing director to remain on the
Net Fixed Assets	119,258	100,784	58,452	board.
Invest's & Advances	37,818	34,393	43,745	Fiscal 1994 was a year of growth and record financial performance. Acquisitions
Total Assets	278,553	255,977	165,637	in 1993, higher sales volumes, increased sales of higher margin value added
Short Term Debt	8,513	24,928	1,817	products, successful new products, and increased productivity and cost reductions
Current Liabilities	62,674	86,634	30,116	across the companies contributed to the 18% jump in sales. The frozen bakery
Long Term Debt	36,022	9,900	0	companies -- Dough Delight Ltd., Brooklyn Bagel Boys Inc. and Circlet Foods
Total Liabilities	115,051	110,437	37,048	Inc. -- had strong performances in 1994. Olivieri Foods successfully expanded
Total Equity	163,502	145,540	128,589	into Quebec, Ontario, and new U.S. markets. In the fresh bakeries division, cost
Total Liab. & Equity	278,553	255,977	165,637	control programs and productivity optimization programs were successful.
CAPITAL (000)				However, high Canadian flour prices remain a concern for the company. Flour
Total Debt	44,535	34,828	1,817	prices are being affected by volatile U.S. and world markets.
Preferred Equity	0	0	0	
Common Equity	163,502	145,540	128,589	

Relative strength to TSE300

Price

Volume (in 1000's of board lots)

Rank (Profit/Revenue/Assets)
202 210 297
Norman T. Currie
Chairman
David Lees
President & C.E.O.
K.A. Welsh
V.P. Finance & C.F.O.

Address
10 Four Seasons Place
Etobicoke
ON
M9B 6H7
(416) 622-2040

Fax: (416) 622-8954
C0010940/G/5.1

COTT CORPORATION

Exchanges	Price (Jun29'95)		16 .00	Trailing P/E		27 .59	Stock Symbol
TMQ	Trailing Yield (%)		0 .68	Trailing EPS		0 .58	**BCB**

Period Ending	Jan95	Jan94	Jan93	Jan92	Jan91
Yearly Statistics					
Price-Close	12 .38	35 .50	16 .00	4 .62	0 .33
Price-High	42 .38	49 .63	20 .44	5 .22	0 .39
Price-Low	12 .00	14 .25	9 .38	0 .32	0 .33
P/E-Close	21 .34	57 .26	64 .00	22 .02	13 .33
Dividends per Share	0 .09	0 .06	0 .04	0 .03	0 .01
Dividend Yield (%)	0 .73	0 .17	0 .25	0 .76	2 .48
Sales per Share	18 .39	12 .01	6 .85	3 .61	1 .74
EPS before extra. item	0 .58	0 .62	0 .25	0 .21	0 .02
Cash Flow per Share	1 .12	1 .01	0 .41	0 .30	0 .01
Book Value per Share	5 .35	4 .79	1 .45	0 .65	0 .28
O/S Common Shares	59 ,667	59 ,176	52 ,256	44 ,588	37 ,292
Total Revenue	1 ,094 ,669	687 ,740	331 ,551	137 ,427	68 ,208
Income before extra.	34 ,827	35 ,376	12 ,796	8 ,094	958
Cash Flow	66 ,279	57 ,618	19 ,787	11 ,509	400
Debt/Equity	0 .44	0 .07	0 .38	0 .71	2 .15
Return on Capital (%)	16 .11	30 .72	31 .62	32 .08	3 .14
Ret. on Com. Equity (%)	11 .56	19 .68	24 .38	40 .90	9 .33
% Change Profit	(1 .6)	176 .5	58 .1	744 .9	130 .8
% Change Revenue	59 .2	107 .4	141 .3	101 .5	59 .2
% Change Assets	64 .9	92 .2	153 .6	71 .9	42 .9

	Jan95	Jan94	Jan93
Preferred Div. Coverage	np	np	np
Total Div. Coverage	6 .5	10 .5	6 .5
Interest Coverage	9 .2	24 .4	10 .0
Current Ratio	1 .6	2 .7	1 .2
Operating Margin	6 .1	9 .7	8 .0
Asset Turnover	1 .6	1 .7	1 .6
5 YEAR RATIOS (%)			
Return on Capital	22 .7	20 .8	14 .9
Return on Com. Equity	21 .2	19 .7	14 .7
Profit Growth	142 .5	197 .6	89 .1
Revenue Growth	91 .1	87 .1	59 .8
Asset Growth	81 .5	89 .0	57 .0
BALANCE SHEET (000)			
Cash	43 ,911	79 ,436	7 ,894
Current Assets	349 ,709	250 ,574	117 ,073
Net Fixed Assets	191 ,828	78 ,423	48 ,178
Invest's & Advances	12 ,026	12 ,229	10 ,303
Total Assets	671 ,382	407 ,255	211 ,870
Short Term Debt	32 ,889	4 ,288	5 ,727
Current Liabilities	217 ,303	94 ,135	101 ,183
Long Term Debt	106 ,082	15 ,014	23 ,145
Total Liabilities	352 ,316	123 ,571	135 ,955
Total Equity	319 ,066	283 ,684	75 ,915
Total Liab. & Equity	671 ,382	407 ,255	211 ,870
CAPITAL (000)			
Total Debt	138 ,971	19 ,302	28 ,872
Preferred Equity	0	0	0
Common Equity	319 ,066	283 ,684	75 ,915

Business:

COTT CORPORATION produces a wide selection of bottled and canned carbonated beverages which are sold under private label, under its own brand names and under licensed brand names.

Date	EPS	DPS	Tot Rev	Inc Bex
Apr 95	0.16	0.03	287 ,130	9 ,812
Jan 95	(0.02)	0.03	294 ,498	(607)
Oct 94	0.17	0.03	260 ,714	9 ,890
Jul 94	0.27	0.02	320 ,148	15 ,930
Apr 94	0.16	0.02	217 ,644	9 ,614
Jan 94	0.15	0.02	183 ,607	9 ,138
Oct 93	0.17	0.02	174 ,848	9 ,835
Jul 93	0.19	0.01	198 ,084	10 ,652

Synopsis:

In June 1995, Cott Corporation filed a preliminary prospectus related to a proposed public offering in the United States. The offering concerns $100-million (U.S.) of unsecured Senior Notes due 2005. The net proceeds of the offering are earmarked to reduce debt, and for working capital and other general corporate purposes. Standard & Poor's assigned a rating of double-B minus to the proposed issue.

Cott expects further growth in the U.S. where it currently derives over 50% of its revenues and operating income. The key for Cott in the U.S. is its relation and sales agreement with major retailers, such as Wal-Mart. There are plans to develop markets outside North America. This should minimize dependence on any given region.

In the first quarter of 1995, despite a 13% increase in case sales, Canadian volumes fell 16%. This was offset by a 15% rise in the U.S. and 60% in Britain. Cott is battling an intense price war with Coke and Pepsi in Canada. Selling, general, and administrative expenses climbed 7.8%, but are expected to decline as a percentage of sales as the year progresses. Cost control will remain key as Cott tries to reduce the company's operating and financial costs while boosting operating efficiencies and customer service. In June 1995, Cott completed its acquisition of the 49% minority interest of Benjamin Shaw (Pontefract) Ltd. of Britain for about $9.4-million in cash.

For fiscal 1994, Cott's margins were negatively affected by higher commodity prices and intense price discounting by the major brands. Late in 1994, Cott began to deliver shipments of soft drinks under the new Preferred Selection label to SUPERVALU, a leading U.S. food distribution and retailing company. Cott also disclosed that its 90% owned Lakeport Brewing Corporation lost the contract to brew Loblaws PC regular strength beer. The PC brand represented about 28% of Lakeport case sales.

Relative strength to TSE300

Price

Volume (in 1000's of board lots)

Rank (Profit/Revenue/Assets)
140   160   249

Gerald N. Pencer
Chairman & C.E.O.

David A. Nichol
President

Paul Henderson
V.P. Fin. & Admin. Secretary

Fraser Latta
Vice Chairman & C.O.O.

Address
207 Queens Quay West
Suite 800
Toronto
ON
M5J 1A7
(416) 203-3898

01000795/G/5.1

DOVER INDUSTRIES LIMITED

Exchanges	Price (Jun29'95)	17.12	Trailing P/E	10.84	Stock Symbol
T	Trailing Yield (%)	3.39	Trailing EPS	1.58	DVI

Period Ending	Dec94	Dec93	Dec92	Dec91	Dec90
Yearly Statistics					
Price-Close	16.50	16.00	15.25	18.00	13.38
Price-High	18.50	17.50	18.50	18.50	18.75
Price-Low	14.75	14.50	14.00	13.25	13.00
P/E-Close	10.44	10.96	11.91	12.77	9.29
Dividends per Share	0.56	0.56	0.56	0.56	0.56
Dividend Yield (%)	3.39	3.50	3.67	3.11	4.19
Sales per Share	34.63	32.83	30.46	30.98	31.63
EPS before extra. item	1.58	1.46	1.28	1.41	1.44
Cash Flow per Share	2.30	2.18	2.09	2.09	2.10
Book Value per Share	13.64	12.63	11.74	11.02	10.17
O/S Common Shares	3,428	3,428	3,428	3,428	3,428
Total Revenue	119,348	112,624	104,501	106,313	108,406
Income before extra.	5,488	5,063	4,443	4,882	5,012
Cash Flow	7,889	7,481	7,176	7,147	7,191
Debt/Equity	0.09	0.05	0.05	0.05	0.25
Return on Capital (%)	17.19	18.36	17.33	19.40	21.87
Ret. on Com. Equity (%)	12.05	11.97	11.24	13.27	14.85
% Change Profit	8.4	14.0	(9.0)	(2.6)	(5.5)
% Change Revenue	6.0	7.8	(1.7)	(1.9)	(0.4)
% Change Assets	9.8	5.2	2.7	(1.4)	16.3
Preferred Div. Coverage	88.5	81.7	71.7		
Total Div. Coverage	2.7	2.6	2.2		
Interest Coverage	na	257.7	90.2		
Current Ratio	3.2	3.5	3.0		
Operating Margin	6.6	7.2	6.9		
Asset Turnover	1.9	2.0	1.9		
5 YEAR RATIOS (%)					
Return on Capital	18.8	20.7	22.4		
Return on Com. Equity	12.7	13.8	15.1		
Profit Growth	0.7	0.2	2.3		
Revenue Growth	1.8	0.1	0.1		
Asset Growth	6.3	4.6	4.2		
BALANCE SHEET (000)					
Cash	0	0	0		
Current Assets	37,149	33,559	30,294		
Net Fixed Assets	24,860	22,987	23,506		
Invest's & Advances	0	0	0		
Total Assets	63,032	57,410	54,559		
Short Term Debt	4,478	2,012	2,223		
Current Liabilities	11,433	9,672	9,980		
Long Term Debt	0	0	0		
Total Liabilities	15,262	13,078	13,309		
Total Equity	47,770	44,332	41,250		
Total Liab. & Equity	63,032	57,410	54,559		
CAPITAL (000)					
Total Debt	4,478	2,012	2,223		
Preferred Equity	1,026	1,026	1,026		
Common Equity	46,744	43,306	40,224		

Business:

DOVER INDUSTRIES LTD. is a food products and packaging company. Operations and products include flour milling for domestic and export markets, disposable paper food containers, folding cartons, plastic drinking straws and ice cream cones. It has facilities in Ontario and Nova Scotia. Operations include Bondware, Dover Flour Mills, Dover Mills Limited, Howell Packaging and Robinson Cone.

Date	EPS	DPS	Tot Rev	Inc Bex
Mar 95	0.29	0.15	27,144	1,039
Dec 94	0.42	0.14	28,863	1,476
Sep 94	0.37	0.15	28,814	1,284
Jun 94	0.50	0.14	31,880	1,718
Mar 94	0.29	0.14	29,779	1,010
Dec 93	0.48	0.14	31,330	1,673
Sep 93	0.32	0.14	28,015	1,111
Jun 93	0.40	0.14	28,398	1,341

Synopsis:

Export sales for Dover Industries Limited jumped 81.3% in fiscal 1994 versus the prior year. In fiscal 1994, export sales represented 15.8% of total sales. This increase benefited from the company's aggressive entry into the U.S. and Central American markets, along with the weak Canadian dollar. Capital spending during fiscal 1994 amounted to $4.8-million, up 145% from 1993. The paper and plastic products segments accounted for 55% of spending, with the remaining 45% allocated primarily to Dover Flour Mills. Capital spending will be $10-million in 1995, with 90% earmarked for the paper and plastic division. Dover expects the spending will reduce production costs and increase productivity.

The food products division, responsible for 55% of total sales, had a 2% increase in sales in 1994. Sales increased despite the sale of Taylor Grain in April 1994. Dover sold the four grain elevators of its Taylor Grain division for $750,000. Food products operating profit fell 12%, due to continued losses at the Robinson Cone division and general weakness in the remaining food divisions. Robinson Cone suffered higher raw material costs and major competition from U.S. companies providing low price imports, despite a 16% increase in unit sales. In August 1995, the removal of freight subsidies should positively affect its Halifax operation. At the Dover Mills division, new export opportunities developed in the U.S. and the Caribbean.

In the paper and plastic products division, the Bondware and Howell Packaging divisions accounted for 93.3% of total sales. Operating profit increased 8.4%. Export markets continued to grow to include Europe and Asia, which together make up about 5% of Bondware's sales volume. Howell Packaging had a 8% increase in sales, mainly due to a 65% jump in export sales to the U.S. and Mexico. However, this division struggled with higher raw material costs and competition. Howell will undergo a major expansion in 1995.

Relative strength to TSE300 / Price / Volume (in 1000's of board lots) chart

Rank (Profit/Revenue/Assets)
409   392   584
Mrs. Kenneth L. Campbell
Chairman & President
Brian J. Short
V.P. Finance & Admin.

Address
P.O. Box 10
4350 Harvester Road
Burlington
ON
L7R 3X8
(905) 333-1515

Fax: (905) 333-1584
D0002819/G/5.1

FPI LIMITED

Exchanges	Price (Jun29'95)	8.50	Trailing P/E	10.12	Stock Symbol
TM	Trailing Yield (%)	0.00	Trailing EPS	0.84	**FPL**

Period Ending	Dec94	Dec93	Dec92	Dec91	Dec90
Yearly Statistics					
Price-Close	7.25	3.50	3.10	6.38	4.80
Price-High	7.75	4.40	7.38	8.63	7.00
Price-Low	3.25	3.05	2.65	4.85	4.00
P/E-Close	8.53	nm	nm	nm	6.67
Dividends per Share	0.00	0.00	0.00	0.00	0.00
Dividend Yield (%)	0.00	0.00	0.00	0.00	0.00
Sales per Share	40.49	36.63	35.98	33.10	32.63
EPS before extra. item	0.85	(0.94)	(4.10)	(0.02)	0.72
Cash Flow per Share	1.45	0.83	0.74	1.05	1.44
Book Value per Share	8.97	8.01	8.96	13.04	13.07
O/S Common Shares	16,421	16,415	16,411	16,407	16,402
Total Revenue	669,156	604,905	598,583	553,066	552,589
Income before extra.	13,881	(15,367)	(67,299)	(288)	11,771
Cash Flow	23,736	13,636	12,148	17,199	23,584
Debt/Equity	0.61	0.64	0.69	0.29	0.31
Return on Capital (%)	9.38	(3.43)	(22.91)	2.34	6.84
Ret. on Com. Equity (%)	9.96	(11.03)	(37.29)	(0.13)	5.64
% Change Profit	190.3	77.2	nm	(102.4)	153.0
% Change Revenue	10.6	1.1	8.2	0.1	55.5
% Change Assets	5.5	(14.3)	(3.8)	(1.3)	0.1

Preferred Div. Coverage	np	np	np
Total Div. Coverage	na	na	na
Interest Coverage	3.6	0.0	0.0
Current Ratio	1.9	1.7	1.6
Operating Margin	3.2	1.8	0.5
Asset Turnover	2.4	2.2	1.9
5 YEAR RATIOS (%)			
Return on Capital	(1.6)	(4.6)	(2.4)
Return on Com. Equity	(6.6)	(10.6)	(6.9)
Profit Growth	na	na	na
Revenue Growth	13.4	10.3	8.5
Asset Growth	(3.0)	(2.8)	2.3
BALANCE SHEET (000)			
Cash	1,628	7,256	3,595
Current Assets	195,038	179,728	206,036
Net Fixed Assets	71,448	76,694	95,907
Invest's & Advances	3,244	0	0
Total Assets	282,715	267,930	312,772
Short Term Debt	57,767	54,935	64,291
Current Liabilities	103,237	104,008	128,336
Long Term Debt	32,244	28,540	37,414
Total Liabilities	135,481	136,423	165,750
Total Equity	147,234	131,507	147,022
Total Liab. & Equity	282,715	267,930	312,772
CAPITAL (000)			
Total Debt	90,011	83,475	101,705
Preferred Equity	0	0	0
Common Equity	147,234	131,507	147,022

Business:

FPI LTD. is an international seafood harvasting, processing and marketing company. It operates a fleet of deep sea vessels and processing plants in Newfoundland, Nova Scotia and Massachusetts. It procures seafood products worldwide, particularly through its Clouston Foods division. FPI sells fresh and frozen seafood to food service and retail markets in the U.S., Canada, Europe and Japan.

Date	EPS	DPS	Tot Rev	Inc Bex
Dec 94	0.22	0.00	174,374	3,658
Oct 94	0.20	0.00	170,792	3,265
Jul 94	0.24	0.00	160,332	4,015
Apr 94	0.18	0.00	163,643	2,943
Dec 93	0.13	0.00	152,079	2,214
Oct 93	(1.10)	0.00	157,491	(18,078)
Jul 93	0.05	0.00	143,198	809
Apr 93	(0.02)	0.00	152,076	(312)

Synopsis:

In 1994, FPI Limited returned to profitability after struggling with the dramatic changes in the North Atlantic fishing industry over the past years. FPI repositioned itself as a seafood marketer with over 200 products. FPI now buys much of its seafood from foreign sources. The company markets its products in North America, Germany and England. The U.S. markets account for 66% of total sales, Canada 25%, and Europe and Japan 8%. FPI diversified its product line with the purchase of Clouston Foods in 1989, and the purchase of the U.S. food service operations of National Sea Products in 1992. FPI is now well regarded in the seafood business, with a very efficient broker and distribution system.

During fiscal 1994, FPI derived 48% of total sales from the FPI division and 52% from the Clouston division. Improved sales performance stemmed from higher gross profit from the FPI division product categories of value-added seafood, cold water shrimp, crab, and scallops. Also helping was the increased gross profit on the Clouston division trading sales. However, the FPI division suffered reduced profits due to lower sales of primary processed ground-fish. As a result of the declining ground-fish quotas and FPI's entry into value-added shrimp processing, FPI has steadily increased its buying from foreign sources. The Clouston division will continue to focus on earnings growth by expanding its base of world-wide partners.

For 1995, FPI plans to increase volume in value-added ground-fish and shrimp products to offset the impact of quota cuts on scallops and redfish. Furthermore, the company's vessel divestiture program should conclude this year. The Clouston division expects to add new supplies of shrimp from Mexico and sea bass from Chile. Overall, FPI plans to add new species, develop new products, and expand value added sales.

Relative strength to TSE300 / Price / Volume (in 1000's of board lots)

Rank (Profit/Revenue/Assets)
254 159 294

Victor L. Young
Chairman & C.E.O.

David G. Norris
Exec. V.P. Fin. & Bus. Dev.

Address
70 O'Leary Avenue
P.O. Box 550
St. John'S
NF
A1C 5L1
(709) 570-0000

Fax: (709) 570-0479
F0001100/G/5.1

MAPLE LEAF FOODS INC.

Exchanges	Price (Jun29'95)	7.25	Trailing P/E	7.47	Stock Symbol
TM	Trailing Yield (%)	5.51	Trailing EPS	0.97	**MFI**

Period Ending	Dec94	Dec93	Dec92	Dec91	Dec90
Yearly Statistics					
Price-Close	12.25	12.88	14.63	17.00	10.88
Price-High	13.13	14.63	17.50	17.50	18.50
Price-Low	10.75	12.25	13.13	10.75	9.00
P/E-Close	13.03	14.80	16.25	17.53	17.26
Dividends per Share	0.38	0.38	0.38	0.38	0.38
Dividend Yield (%)	3.10	2.95	2.60	2.24	3.49
Sales per Share	39.38	37.53	34.03	43.89	54.68
EPS before extra. item	0.94	0.87	0.90	0.97	0.63
Cash Flow per Share	1.93	1.58	1.60	1.92	1.27
Book Value per Share	12.80	12.19	11.68	11.12	9.67
O/S Common Shares	80,873	80,873	80,856	80,800	65,621
Total Revenue	3,200,470	3,054,030	2,772,112	3,043,311	3,582,008
Income before extra.	75,729	70,121	72,493	67,228	41,102
Cash Flow	156,417	127,779	129,625	133,035	83,235
Debt/Equity	0.04	0.05	0.05	0.09	0.28
Return on Capital (%)	12.85	11.65	12.40	13.60	15.38
Ret. on Com. Equity (%)	7.50	7.26	7.87	8.77	8.04
% Change Profit	8.0	(3.3)	7.8	63.6	226.4
% Change Revenue	4.8	10.2	(8.9)	(15.0)	15.7
% Change Assets	7.1	5.8	(0.8)	13.3	61.7

Preferred Div. Coverage	np	np	np
Total Div. Coverage	2.5	2.3	2.4
Interest Coverage	55.6	45.1	36.9
Current Ratio	1.7	1.8	2.0
Operating Margin	4.2	3.7	4.0
Asset Turnover	2.0	2.0	1.9
5 YEAR RATIOS (%)			
Return on Capital	13.2	11.9	12.1
Return on Com. Equity	7.9	6.9	6.8
Profit Growth	43.1	15.1	23.5
Revenue Growth	0.6	(5.1)	(1.9)
Asset Growth	15.5	2.5	11.9
BALANCE SHEET (000)			
Cash	222,143	204,993	253,118
Current Assets	712,810	654,361	678,567
Net Fixed Assets	596,834	562,433	521,832
Invest's & Advances	51,937	49,268	58,528
Total Assets	1,607,324	1,500,703	1,419,018
Short Term Debt	4,114	4,627	2,299
Current Liabilities	409,282	373,851	343,066
Long Term Debt	34,151	47,553	46,089
Total Liabilities	572,250	514,764	474,390
Total Equity	1,034,952	985,939	944,628
Total Liab. & Equity	1,607,324	1,500,703	1,419,018
CAPITAL (000)			
Total Debt	38,265	52,180	48,388
Preferred Equity	0	0	0
Common Equity	1,034,952	985,939	944,628

Business:

MAPLE LEAF FOODS INC. operates a diverse portfolio of food businesses. The company has operations in Canada, the United States, Europe and Asia. Its products include fresh and prepared meats, poultry, flour, fresh and frozen bakery products, seafood and animal feeds. Maple Leaf sells to retail, wholesale, industrial and foodservice customers worldwide.

Date	EPS	DPS	Tot Rev	Inc Bex
Mar 95	0.13	0.10	748,605	10,187
Dec 94	0.33	0.10	935,371	26,777
Sep 94	0.29	0.10	799,709	23,077
Jun 94	0.22	0.10	800,239	17,859
Mar 94	0.10	0.10	662,710	8,016
Dec 93	0.28	0.10	884,653	22,260
Sep 93	0.26	0.10	782,779	20,814
Jun 93	0.20	0.10	746,481	16,858

Synopsis:

For the first quarter of 1995, Maple Leaf Foods Inc's increased earnings were attributed to the sale of property and improved investment income. However, operating income declined by 4.9% due to poor poultry sales and higher costs in the prepared meats division, caused by the relocation of a prepared meats plant. The Shur-Gain livestock feed, real estate, and corporate foods divisions saw improved profits. Maple Leaf also bought the remaining shares in its Buns Master franchise, increasing its ownership to 100%. Buns Master will be merged with the Country Style Donuts unit. In May 1995, Maple Leaf sold its Monarch Added Touch dessert and baking mix business to Mississauga-based Oetker Ltd.

Maple Leaf elected Michael and Scott McCain as President and Executive Vice-President, respectively. This followed the April 1995 takeover of Maple Leaf by Wallace McCain, the former president of McCain Foods Ltd., and the Ontario Teachers Pension Plan Board in a deal valued at $1.23-billion. The deal will add about $575-million worth of long-term debt and other obligations.

With the takeover of Maple Leaf, Wallace McCain plans to expand and improve the company. Maple Leaf is the only Canadian food processing company large enough to rival McCain Foods. No significant changes are anticipated in the near term, but it is expected that Maple Leaf will concentrate on the meat and grocery products businesses.

In fiscal 1994, increased earnings were attributed to strong performances of the agribusiness and milling and baking business, along with cost control. Consumer foods earnings declined due to the restructuring under way in the prepared meats division. During 1994, segmented sales were as follows: consumer foods, 18%; milling and baking, 21%; agribusiness, 60%; and Corporate, 1%. Exports sales were 17% of total sales.

Relative strength to TSE300

Price

Volume (in 1000's of board lots)

Rank (Profit/Revenue/Assets)
89   47   123

Wallace Mccain
Chairman Of The Board

Gorden Brent Ballantyne
President & C.E.O.

Address
30 St. Clair Avenue West
Suite 1500
Toronto
ON
M4V 3A2
(416) 926-2000

Fax: (416) 926-2018
C0001677/G/5.1

MOLSON COMPANIES LIMITED (THE)

Exchanges	Price (Jun29'95)	22.50	Trailing P/E	15.10	Stock Symbol
TMV	Trailing Yield (%)	3.20	Trailing EPS	1.49	MOL.A

Period Ending	Mar94	Mar93	Mar92	Mar91	Mar90
Yearly Statistics					
Price-Close	24.88	25.50	34.75	28.83	25.17
Price-High	29.88	36.00	35.25	29.09	26.83
Price-Low	22.13	25.38	27.00	18.83	21.08
P/E-Close	11.68	9.24	15.44	nm	11.62
Dividends per Share	0.72	0.72	0.72	0.67	0.61
Dividend Yield (%)	2.89	2.82	2.07	2.32	2.44
Sales per Share	50.19	51.52	45.53	39.78	42.79
EPS before extra. item	2.13	2.76	2.25	(0.72)	2.17
Cash Flow per Share	3.19	3.18	4.08	3.42	3.36
Book Value per Share	22.22	19.68	16.32	14.41	14.71
O/S Common Shares	58,896	59,382	56,588	55,637	49,333
Total Revenue	3,037,101	3,268,465	2,577,840	2,053,176	2,134,975
Income before extra.	125,669	164,694	126,223	(38,667)	106,696
Cash Flow	188,245	190,117	229,067	183,511	165,867
Debt/Equity	0.43	0.59	0.68	1.16	0.47
Return on Capital (%)	11.75	13.56	15.59	9.04	20.89
Ret. on Com. Equity (%)	10.15	15.75	14.63	(5.06)	15.69
% Change Profit	(23.7)	30.5	426.4	(136.2)	22.5
% Change Revenue	(7.1)	26.8	25.6	(3.8)	0.0
% Change Assets	1.2	14.7	(8.0)	39.7	30.0

Preferred Div. Coverage	np	np	np
Total Div. Coverage	3.0	3.8	3.1
Interest Coverage	4.7	3.9	3.6
Current Ratio	1.4	1.3	1.3
Operating Margin	6.2	6.5	9.2
Asset Turnover	1.1	1.1	1.1
5 YEAR RATIOS (%)			
Return on Capital	14.2	15.5	16.5
Return on Com. Equity	10.2	11.0	10.7
Profit Growth	7.6	15.9	19.3
Revenue Growth	7.3	10.0	6.7
Asset Growth	14.1	14.7	13.8
BALANCE SHEET (000)			
Cash	224,344	208,590	97,559
Current Assets	1,039,856	1,130,456	881,827
Net Fixed Assets	885,063	782,601	784,337
Invest's & Advances	285,213	342,415	270,861
Total Assets	2,748,198	2,715,627	2,368,087
Short Term Debt	51,080	275,366	139,325
Current Liabilities	756,901	901,223	676,716
Long Term Debt	505,670	412,415	484,250
Total Liabilities	1,439,690	1,547,292	1,444,397
Total Equity	1,308,508	1,168,335	923,690
Total Liab. & Equity	2,748,198	2,715,627	2,368,087
CAPITAL (000)			
Total Debt	556,750	687,781	623,575
Preferred Equity	0	0	0
Common Equity	1,308,508	1,168,335	923,690

Business:

THE MOLSON COMPANIES LIMITED operates in the brewing, cleaning and sanitizing, retail merchandising, and sports and entertainment industries in Canada, the United States and around the world. Subsidiaries include Molson Breweries(40%), Diversey Corp., Beaver Lumber Company, The Home Depot Canada (25%) and the Montreal. Canadians. Molson also owns 19.8% of Canada Malting Co. Limited.

Date	EPS	DPS	Tot Rev	Inc Bex
Mar 95	(0.04)	0.18	888,397	(2,705)
Dec 94	0.13	0.18	627,902	7,598
Sep 94	0.56	0.18	688,127	32,669
Jun 94	0.84	0.18	681,174	49,238
Mar 94	0.45	0.18	677,050	26,351
Dec 93	0.43	0.18	687,223	25,367
Sep 93	0.63	0.18	694,256	37,193
Jun 93	0.62	0.18	699,600	36,758

Synopsis:

Molson Companies cited lower operating profits from Diversey and the four month National Hockey League work stoppage as reasons for a sharp drop in earnings for fiscal 1995. Net earnings for fiscal 1995 were $86.8-million compared to $125.7-million for 1994. The 1994/95 National Hockey League work stoppage resulted in a one time decline in revenue for the Montreal Canadiens hockey club of 38.8%.

The corporation has announced plans to sell its non-core businesses and concentrate on two core segments, brewing and chemical specialities. Wholly owned subsidiaries to be affected include Beaver Lumber, Home Depot Canada, Groupe Val Royal and some of the sports interests.

Brewing profits were down by $6.5-million to $111.5-million for fiscal 1995 despite a 14% increase in sales volume of beer to Miller for sale in the U.S. Part of the decline in profits was due to accounting for the 1994 closure of the company's Calgary brewery.

The Diversey U.S. operations continued to operate at a loss of $37.7-million compared to loss of $13-million for 1994. However, some turn-around was evident in the fourth quarter. Price increases for raw materials as well as a major expansion of the field sales and support infrastructure accounted for much of this loss. Continued positive performance in international markets resulted in overall profits of $42.2-million for fiscal 1995. Novamax, Diversey's metal finishing treatment business realized increased profits by 37.3% to $16.4-million, due to increased sales revenue.

As a result of consumer trends towards warehouse merchandising stores such as Home Depot, Beaver Lumber is now focussing on the contractor business. By the end of fiscal 1995 Beaver plans to operate only building centres.

Rank (Profit/Revenue/Assets)
59   49   81

Eric H. Molson
Chairman of the Board

Marshall Cohen
President & C.E.O.

S.L. Hartley
Exec. V.P. & C.F.O.

Address
40 King Street West
Suite 3600 Scotia Plaza
Toronto
ON
M5H 3Z5
(416) 360-1786

Fax: (416) 360-4345
M0004536/G/5.3.1

NATIONAL SEA PRODUCTS LIMITED

Period Ending	Dec94	Jan94	Jan93	Dec91	Dec90
Yearly Statistics					
Price-Close	8.00	5.80	8.60	17.00	22.00
Price-High	10.00	9.60	23.00	29.00	30.00
Price-Low	5.04	4.00	6.00	15.60	16.00
P/E-Close	11.77	nm	nm	nm	nm
Dividends per Share	0.00	0.00	0.00	0.00	0.00
Dividend Yield (%)	0.00	0.00	0.00	0.00	0.00
Sales per Share	34.04	38.00	47.88	66.80	97.12
EPS before extra. item	0.68	(6.08)	(4.72)	(6.80)	(0.88)
Cash Flow per Share	1.92	1.92	1.28	0.64	1.28
Book Value per Share	(1.48)	(2.32)	3.64	8.08	12.20
O/S Common Shares	7,213	7,213	7,351	7,337	4,946
Total Revenue	246,805	278,664	351,492	372,361	467,506
Income before extra.	6,318	(42,515)	(32,525)	(35,873)	(2,201)
Cash Flow	13,809	13,772	9,397	3,568	6,111
Debt/Equity	8.04	16.36	2.07	1.51	2.14
Return on Capital (%)	15.14	(29.76)	(11.89)	(9.02)	6.73
Ret. on Com. Equity (%)	na	(868.53)	(76.00)	(64.25)	(3.86)
% Change Profit	114.9	(30.7)	9.3	(1,529.9)	93.2
% Change Revenue	(11.4)	(20.7)	(5.6)	(20.4)	(23.8)
% Change Assets	2.0	(28.5)	(22.4)	20.3	(18.5)

Preferred Div. Coverage	59.6	0.0	0.0
Total Div. Coverage	59.6	0.0	0.0
Interest Coverage	1.8	0.0	0.0
Current Ratio	1.3	1.2	1.2
Operating Margin	5.7	4.0	2.2
Asset Turnover	1.8	2.0	1.8
5 YEAR RATIOS (%)			
Return on Capital	(5.8)	(10.1)	(3.6)
Return on Com. Equity	na	(213.5)	(44.6)
Profit Growth	na	na	na
Revenue Growth	(16.7)	(13.1)	(8.6)
Asset Growth	(18.2)	(19.6)	(8.7)
BALANCE SHEET (000)			
Cash	51	1,315	1,850
Current Assets	70,631	58,890	78,667
Net Fixed Assets	57,137	60,514	87,907
Invest's & Advances	8,966	7,994	2,260
Total Assets	139,735	137,023	191,526
Short Term Debt	20,071	9,132	21,014
Current Liabilities	54,598	48,330	63,101
Long Term Debt	70,165	77,108	79,772
Total Liabilities	128,511	131,750	142,873
Total Equity	11,224	5,273	48,653
Total Liab. & Equity	139,735	137,023	191,526
CAPITAL (000)			
Total Debt	90,236	86,240	100,786
Preferred Equity	21,929	21,929	21,929
Common Equity	(10,705)	(16,656)	26,724

Business:

NATIONAL SEA PRODUCTS LTD. is a harvester, procurer, processor and marketer of fish and seafood. The company's operations are concentrated in North America.

Date	EPS	DPS	Tot Rev	Inc Bex
Apr 95	0.52	0.00	78,619	4,120
Dec 94	0.00	0.00	68,379	469
Oct 94	0.24	0.00	57,428	2,102
Jul 94	0.04	0.00	51,731	515
Apr 94	0.40	0.00	71,589	3,231
Jan 94	(5.84)	0.00	67,182	(41,701)
Oct 93	(0.44)	0.00	66,665	(2,947)
Jul 93	(0.16)	0.00	66,410	(805)

Synopsis:

During fiscal 1994, National Sea Products Limited posted its first annual profit in seven years. Responding to the collapse of the North Atlantic cod fishery, National Sea sold inactive trawlers and processing plants, and reorganized its operations. The company also began buying fish from foreign sources. The turnaround continued in the first quarter of 1995. Strong fish markets in the U.S. and higher prices for redfish and scallops contributed to rising profits. Growing sales of value-added products and improved operating efficiencies added to the strong performance of the Canadian retail division. New marketing strategies new product introductions were successful. However, U.S. operations faced an extremely competitive market.

During 1994, National Sea sold 13 vessels, a fish processing plant in France, and a shrimp processing plant in Florida. These sales raised $7.8-million. National Sea is now positioned as a seafood processor. It buys 90% of its fish from foreign fisheries. National Sea expects to increase foreign fish purchases in 1995 by 10% to about $35-million (U.S.). It has also invested about $6-million in a scallop aquaculture operation. The scallop farm should be functional by 1997, producing about two million pounds of scallops a year. The farm is National Sea's response to a 36% cut in the domestic scallop quota. Forecast cuts to perch and scallop quotas should reduce sales in 1994 by $4-million or $5-million. To counter this shortfall, the company plans to increase purchases of headless and gutted fish, and control costs.

In April 1995, National Sea completed the sale of its idle North Sydney plant as part of its Nova Scotia rationalization program. In February, it signed a deal to sell a plant in La Scie, which completed the restructuring of Newfoundland operations. In March, the company approved a $1-million private placement of convertible debentures, a one-for-four common stock consolidation, and a resolution to reduce the book value of common share capital. The three actions are subject to regulatory and shareholder approval.

Rank (Profit/Revenue/Assets)	
384 288 411	
W.O. Morrow	
Chairman	
H.E. Demone	
President & C.E.O.	
K.L. Nelson	
V.P. Finance & Admin.	

Address
P.O. Box 910
Lunenburg
NS
B0J 2C0
(902) 634-8811

Fax: (902) 634-4785
N0000495/G/5.1

NOBLE CHINA INC.

Exchanges	Price (Jun29'95)	4.90	Trailing P/E	7.54	Stock Symbol
T	Trailing Yield (%)	0.00	Trailing EPS	0.65	**NMO**

Period Ending	Dec94	Dec93	Dec92	Dec91	Dec90
Yearly Statistics					
Price-Close	6.50	11.50	0.50	0.24	0.40
Price-High	11.38	13.00	0.52	0.40	0.80
Price-Low	4.75	0.22	0.24	0.10	0.40
P/E-Close	12.75	88.46	nm	nm	nm
Dividends per Share	0.00	0.00	0.00	0.00	0.00
Dividend Yield (%)	0.00	0.00	0.00	0.00	0.00
Sales per Share	3.23	1.14	na	0.28	0.33
EPS before extra. item	0.51	0.13	(0.02)	(0.06)	(0.02)
Cash Flow per Share	0.68	0.19	0.13	0.07	0.10
Book Value per Share	6.62	13.79	0.80	0.84	0.90
O/S Common Shares	16,638	6,923	2,148	2,053	2,053
Total Revenue	54,372	6,288	589	582	678
Income before extra.	8,482	669	(26)	(125)	(23)
Cash Flow	11,370	1,004	274	149	202
Debt/Equity	0.38	0.04	0.03	0.11	0.16
Return on Capital (%)	7.06	1.33	(0.62)	(4.64)	(0.27)
Ret. on Com. Equity (%)	8.26	1.38	(1.52)	(7.01)	(1.21)
% Change Profit	1,168.8	2,655.6	79.1	(454.5)	nm
% Change Revenue	764.7	966.9	1.3	(14.2)	136.3
% Change Assets	92.5	5,669.8	(9.5)	(7.6)	(13.2)

Date	EPS	DPS	Tot Rev	Inc Bex
Dec 94	0.06	0.00	19,788	933
Sep 94	0.16	0.00	20,953	2,712
Jun 94	0.29	0.00	36,073	4,777
Mar 94	0.14	0.00	17,045	2,273
Dec 93	0.24	0.00	6,240	921
Sep 93	(0.03)	0.00	20	(83)
Jun 93	(0.06)	0.00	19	(86)
Mar 93	(0.02)	0.00	9	(83)

Preferred Div. Coverage	np	np	np	
Total Div. Coverage	na	na	na	
Interest Coverage	22.8	na	0.0	
Current Ratio	1.2	2.1	2.6	
Operating Margin	17.7	10.4	(2.6)	
Asset Turnover	0.3	0.1	na	
5 YEAR RATIOS (%)				
Return on Capital	0.6	(0.8)	(2.5)	
Return on Com. Equity	(0.0)	(1.7)	(3.3)	
Profit Growth	836.1	na	na	
Revenue Growth	185.4	89.6	12.2	
Asset Growth	140.8	154.7	11.7	
BALANCE SHEET (000)				
Cash	8,508	2,938	0	
Current Assets	44,229	17,992	214	
Net Fixed Assets	109,848	38,171	1,592	
Invest's & Advances	6,110	2,986	0	
Total Assets	200,571	104,183	1,806	
Short Term Debt	11,157	3,531	49	
Current Liabilities	35,826	8,653	82	
Long Term Debt	30,861	90	0	
Total Liabilities	90,497	8,742	82	
Total Equity	110,074	95,441	1,724	
Total Liab. & Equity	200,571	104,183	1,806	
CAPITAL (000)				
Total Debt	42,017	3,621	49	
Preferred Equity	0	0	0	
Common Equity	110,074	95,441	1,724	

Business:

NOBLE CHINA INC. has a 60% equity interest in a Sino-foreign equity joint venture enterprise, Zhaoqing Blue Ribbon Brewery Noble Ltd. Zhaoqing Blue Ribbon Brewery is engaged in the sale and production of beer and is located in the City of Zhaqing in the Guangdong Province in The People's Republic of China.

Synopsis:

Recently, a settlement agreement was reached between Noble China and its partners in China, following the resignation of Lei Kat Cheong, the company's former chairman, president and C.E.O. in April 1995. According to Noble, Mr. Lei had, without approval or knowledge of the board of directors, entered into several agreements in the name and on behalf of Noble with Zhaoqing Brewery Co., the 40% minority shareholder in the Noble Zhaoqing Brewery. Under this agreement with Zhaoqing Brewery and the Municipality of Zhaoqing, Noble will retain its 60% ownership in the brewery and this interest will not be subject to dilution. In addition, the brewery will be permitted to produce and sell up to 100,000 tonnes of Pabst Blue Ribbon beer annually at an existing brewery adjacent to the Noble Brewery. Noble will have the right to acquire up to 40% of that brewery for cash in 1996. Noble will also honour a commitment made by Mr. Lei to contribute $3-million in capital to the Noble Zhaoqing Brewery.

Noble filed suit in the Ontario Court in June 1995, seeking damages from Mr. Lei for breach of his duties owed to Noble resulting from his unauthorized actions and for other relief. In the meantime, Mr. Lei's interest in Noble, approximately 4.8 million common shares, has been placed in a trust controlled by the company's board. Mr. Lei has informed Noble that he disputes the validity of the trust.

The company's financial results for the first quarter of 1995 include only operating results of the Zhaoqing Noble Brewery and do not include the results of Noble's two other breweries, namely its newly acquired interests in the Shouguang and Shanhaiguan Breweries. As part of the ongoing dispute with Mr. Lei, these breweries have been instructed to withhold financial information.

Noble's products are produced and sold almost exclusively in China. They include local market brands of beers such as "Aolei" and a foreign premium brand, "Pabst Blue Ribbon". The strongest growth in demand has been the foreign premium category which still only constitutes 8% of beer consumed in China.

Relative strength to TSE300 / Price / Volume (in 1000's of board lots)

Rank (Profit/Revenue/Assets)		
680	799	425

Lei Kat Cheong
Chairman & President

Address
1 First Canadian Place
Suite 6930
Box 465
Toronto
ON
M5X 1E5
(416) 956-4906
Fax: (416) 956-4907
N0001950/G/5.3.1

For further company information, call Globe Information Services 1-800-268-9128 or (416) 585-5345

ROTHMANS INC.

Exchanges	Price (Jun29'95)	91.00	Trailing P/E	8.26	Stock Symbol
TMV	Trailing Yield (%)	4.40	Trailing EPS	11.02	**ROC**

Period Ending	Mar95	Mar94	Mar93	Mar92	Mar91
Yearly Statistics					
Price-Close	91.00	83.50	101.00	94.00	55.00
Price-High	100.00	110.00	104.00	97.00	69.50
Price-Low	66.00	83.00	85.00	54.00	42.00
P/E-Close	8.26	7.85	10.06	10.86	7.26
Dividends per Share	4.00	22.00	4.00	3.70	18.40
Dividend Yield (%)	4.40	26.35	3.96	3.94	33.46
Sales per Share	83.39	82.76	84.96	80.67	75.74
EPS before extra. item	11.02	10.64	10.04	8.66	7.58
Cash Flow per Share	21.96	17.36	17.57	15.67	13.00
Book Value per Share	27.89	20.87	32.23	26.19	21.24
O/S Common Shares	5,511	5,511	5,511	5,511	5,511
Total Revenue	463,193	461,770	472,453	448,517	428,960
Income before extra.	60,701	58,654	55,327	49,305	43,318
Cash Flow	121,011	95,680	96,824	86,342	71,652
Debt/Equity	0.31	0.49	0.24	0.37	0.39
Return on Capital (%)	71.76	61.34	53.60	50.26	41.22
Ret. on Com. Equity (%)	45.18	40.09	34.37	36.54	28.46
% Change Profit	3.5	6.0	12.2	13.8	7.2
% Change Revenue	0.3	(2.3)	5.3	4.6	7.1
% Change Assets	(6.7)	(8.3)	4.1	10.0	(17.9)

Date	EPS	DPS	Tot Rev	Inc Bex
Mar 95	2.37	1.00	103,512	13,033
Dec 94	2.72	1.00	119,235	14,985
Sep 94	2.98	1.00	120,235	16,402
Jun 94	2.95	1.00	119,848	16,281
Mar 94	2.06	19.00	108,203	11,357
Dec 93	2.90	1.00	109,332	16,000
Sep 93	2.81	1.00	102,921	15,486
Jun 93	2.87	1.00	141,006	15,812

	Mar95	Mar94	Mar93
Preferred Div. Coverage	np	np	np
Total Div. Coverage	2.8	0.5	2.5
Interest Coverage	223.5	390.5	134.9
Current Ratio	2.4	1.6	2.3
Operating Margin	37.0	33.4	30.7
Asset Turnover	1.3	1.2	1.2
5 YEAR RATIOS (%)			
Return on Capital	55.6	48.1	43.4
Return on Com. Equity	36.9	32.7	29.3
Profit Growth	8.4	11.7	12.7
Revenue Growth	2.9	1.9	2.2
Asset Growth	(4.3)	(1.4)	0.3
BALANCE SHEET (000)			
Cash	53,177	101,467	86,241
Current Assets	295,447	304,177	343,981
Net Fixed Assets	36,451	37,915	43,718
Invest's & Advances	707	943	1,179
Total Assets	347,609	372,452	406,358
Short Term Debt	47,018	56,797	42,742
Current Liabilities	123,941	187,512	151,170
Long Term Debt	0	0	0
Total Liabilities	193,926	257,427	228,752
Total Equity	153,683	115,025	177,606
Total Liab. & Equity	347,609	372,452	406,358
CAPITAL (000)			
Total Debt	47,018	56,797	42,742
Preferred Equity	0	0	0
Common Equity	153,683	115,025	177,606

Business:

ROTHMANS INC. is a holding company. It produces and sells tobacco products through its 60% owned subsidiary Rothmans Bensons & Hedges Inc. Rothmans International plc of the United Kingdom owns 71.2% of the company's common shares.

Synopsis:

For fiscal 1994, Rothmans Inc. attributed improved earnings from its tobacco operations to a combination of higher prices and cost control measures. The improvement came despite the negative effect of federal and Quebec surtaxes, and government anti-smoking measures. Government tax and regulatory initiatives continue to be a major influence on the Canadian tobacco industry. The possible imposition of plain packaging remains a key issue. Rothmans believes plain packaging would not affect tobacco consumption, but might boost the supply of foreign products in Canada.

In the past, taxes imposed by provincial and federal governments on tobacco widened the price gap between Canadian and U.S. tobacco products. However in 1994, many governments substantially reduced tobacco taxes to curtail the illegal smuggling of cigarettes into Canada. Health message packaging requirements were another government measure to affect the Canadian tobacco industry. These requirements will add major costs to operations. Other government measures included the re-imposition of an export tax, and continued tobacco advertising restrictions.

Rothmans declared a special dividend of $8.00 per share in 1994. This followed two prior payments made in 1987 and 1991, amounting to $40.00 and $16.00 per share. Rothmans regularly makes special distributions from its surplus funds in the absence of attractive investment alternatives. Rothmans maintains its strategy of investing in new product development to broaden future prospects. It also invests in capital equipment and distribution facilities to maintain its cost competitiveness.

According to Rothmans, the company currently controls a 22% share of the Canadian tobacco market.

Rank (Profit/Revenue/Assets)
101   202   261

Hon. William M. Kelly
Chairman

Joseph J. Heffernan
President & C.E.O.

Dennis Robertson
V.P. Finance

Address
1500 Don Mills Road
North York
ON
M3B 3L1
(416) 449-5525

R0002697/G/5.2

SCHNEIDER CORPORATION

Exchanges	Price (Jun29'95)	13.50	Trailing P/E	10.23	Stock Symbol
T	Trailing Yield (%)	2.37	Trailing EPS	1.32	SCD.A

Period Ending	Oct94	Oct93	Oct92	Oct91	Oct90
Yearly Statistics					
Price-Close	12.50	13.88	14.50	12.13	8.25
Price-High	18.00	16.25	16.44	12.25	13.50
Price-Low	12.25	12.00	11.88	8.00	8.25
P/E-Close	9.26	10.59	12.95	13.04	nm
Dividends per Share	0.31	0.27	0.23	0.22	0.22
Dividend Yield (%)	2.48	1.95	1.59	1.81	2.67
Sales per Share	127.71	123.58	116.43	115.88	117.45
EPS before extra. item	1.35	1.31	1.12	0.93	(0.31)
Cash Flow per Share	2.82	3.43	2.77	2.26	1.56
Book Value per Share	15.14	14.03	12.88	11.99	11.28
O/S Common Shares	6,138	5,881	5,585	5,585	5,430
Total Revenue	767,462	725,279	649,877	630,966	627,797
Income before extra.	8,019	7,688	6,279	5,064	(1,677)
Cash Flow	16,960	20,157	15,445	12,285	8,327
Debt/Equity	1.00	0.95	0.75	0.90	1.06
Return on Capital (%)	12.65	13.48	13.43	12.63	4.76
Ret. on Com. Equity (%)	9.14	9.96	9.04	7.90	(2.70)
% Change Profit	4.3	22.4	24.0	402.0	(8,485.0)
% Change Revenue	5.8	11.6	3.0	0.5	1.4
% Change Assets	14.2	24.8	(2.2)	5.4	(3.0)

Business:

SCHNEIDER CORP., through its subsidiaries, J.M. Schneider Inc., Mother Jackson's Open Kitchens Limited, Charcuterie Roy Inc., Horizon Poultry Products Inc., and Fleetwood Sausage Ltd., and its 50% owned joint venture National Meats Inc., produces and distributes meat, poultry, cheese and baked goods across Canada. The companies have retail and food service markets in Canada, the U.S. and Japan.

Date	EPS	DPS	Tot Rev	Inc Bex
May 95	0.09	0.08	186,817	585
Feb 95	0.38	0.08	240,856	2,311
Oct 94	0.44	0.08	184,119	2,625
Aug 94	0.41	0.08	182,521	2,451
May 94	0.27	0.08	178,170	1,608
Feb 94	0.23	0.07	222,652	1,335
Oct 93	0.36	0.06	175,353	2,109
Aug 93	0.46	0.07	177,270	2,673

Preferred Div. Coverage	np	np	np	
Total Div. Coverage	4.3	4.8	4.8	
Interest Coverage	2.8	2.7	2.8	
Current Ratio	1.3	1.5	1.5	
Operating Margin	2.8	2.8	2.6	
Asset Turnover	3.1	3.4	3.8	
5 YEAR RATIOS (%)				
Return on Capital	11.4	9.8	8.6	
Return on Com. Equity	6.7	4.8	3.5	
Profit Growth	231.6	30.8	2.3	
Revenue Growth	4.3	3.8	(1.1)	
Asset Growth	7.3	8.1	3.1	
BALANCE SHEET (000)				
Cash	0	0	0	
Current Assets	108,890	92,018	76,352	
Net Fixed Assets	110,488	103,382	83,872	
Invest's & Advances	2,368	2,496	2,666	
Total Assets	244,550	214,086	171,561	
Short Term Debt	37,261	18,698	11,479	
Current Liabilities	84,760	61,847	49,682	
Long Term Debt	55,900	59,514	42,171	
Total Liabilities	151,635	131,550	99,648	
Total Equity	92,915	82,536	71,913	
Total Liab. & Equity	244,550	214,086	171,561	
CAPITAL (000)				
Total Debt	93,161	78,212	53,650	
Preferred Equity	0	0	0	
Common Equity	92,915	82,536	71,913	

Synopsis:

During the first quarter 1995, Schneider Corporation continued its winning ways after a successful fiscal 1994. The 8.2% increase in sales resulted from exceptional performance in its fresh pork business, caused by low hog costs and strong sales in both domestic and export markets. The processed meats sector saw strong returns from the Fleetwood Sausage division and the Prince Group joint venture. Schneider's baked goods sector achieved both sales and earnings growth. The cheese business produced satisfactory returns.

Two divisions were less successful during the quarter. The processed meat unit continued to face strong pressures in the Ontario retail market. And the poultry division accumulated losses despite increased sales. Notwithstanding these difficulties, Schneider raised its quarterly dividend to $.09 per share, from $.08 per share.

During fiscal 1994, red meat sales jumped 6.5% and poultry sales rose 10.9%. Export sales were up 15% due to favourable currency exchange rates on sales to Japan and the U.S. However, consolidated gross margins dipped 0.8% due to strong competition in the Ontario retail market, and low selling prices for poultry products. Capital spending remained stable at about $12.5-million. The majority of funds went to upgrade manufacturing technology in the red meats and poultry processing units. Spending in 1995 will be $15.6-million. The poultry unit will receive 45% of these funds to increase its value added production capabilities. Another 32% of the funds will go to expand deli and sliced meat production capabilities.

Key events during 1994 included the acquisition of the remaining minority interest in Mother Jackson's Open Kitchens, and the formation of a new joint venture with the Prince Group. The Prince Group was formed to produce retail and foodservice side bacon products, and to be a competitor in the company's core business. In 1995 Schneider plans to focus on geographic expansion, private label business growth, new products, low-cost production, and customer service enhancements.

Relative strength to TSE300

Price

Volume (in 1000's of board lots)

Rank (Profit/Revenue/Assets)
335 143 324

Herbert J. Schneider
Chairman

Douglas W. Dodds
President & C.E.O.

Gerald A. Hooper
V.P. & C.F.O.

Address
321 Courtland Avenue East
P.O. Box 130
Kitchener
ON
N2G 3X8
(519) 885-8259

Fax: (519) 885-8918
H0001263/G/5.1

Page	Company	Fiscal year end	EARNINGS PER SHARE		
			Last Year	Estimate this year	Estimate next year
203	Algo Group	Dec-94	(0.55)	na	na
204	Camco	Dec-94	0.18	0.00	0.50
205	Canadian Manoir Industries	Aug-94	(0.05)	na	na
206	Consoltex	Dec-94	0.01	0.13	0.44
207	Dominion Textile	Jun-94	0.65	0.88	1.02
208	Irwin Toy	Jan-95	1.15	na	na
209	Peerless Carpet	Dec-94	0.36	na	na
210	Semi-Tech	Dec-94	(0.14)	0.24	0.33

Estimates from First Call Corporation, 22 Pittsburgh Street, Boston, MA 02210   (800) 366-9992   Fax (617) 261-5679

Household & Leisure Goods

Both the U.S. and Canadian economies slowed dramatically during the first quarter of 1995 and it appears both contracted during the second quarter. Canada sells about one-quarter of all its goods to the U.S. The slow-down south of the border knocked out the Canadian economy's major source of growth at a time when higher Canadian interest rates and weak employment curbed consumer spending at home. Statistics Canada's figures for the first quarter of 1995 also reflect the negative impact of the rail strike and work stoppages that occurred earlier in the year at the ports of Montreal and Vancouver. In its March report on domestic demand, StatsCan also reported that spending on furniture and household appliances continued to slump, as consumers remained reluctant to spend.

Economists debated whether the two countries entered a new recession or simply experienced a short-lived pause before embarking on long term growth. Prospects for Canada have improved considerably according to U.S. statistics released for the month of June and Canadian statistics on domestic activity for the same period. In June, U.S. consumer spending rose and industrial production advanced slightly, while inflation moderated. Canadian statistics revealed an increase in sales of existing homes and new housing starts in June. This growth in housing activity was an indication that the recent declines in both the prime lending rate and mortgage rates were beginning to have a positive effect. Declines in rates are expected to spur consumer purchases of big-ticket items such as cars, appliances, and home renovations. (Consumer spending accounts for 60% of economic activity.) Canadian rates are likely to fall further only if the dollar strengthens considerably. However, the referendum in Quebec this fall creates uncertainty in the Canadian financial market.

According to a joint study on consumer attitudes by the Royal Bank of Canada and Environics Research Group Ltd. released in July 1995, shoppers now are cautious. Consumers are concentrating on family needs and expressing a desire for durability in an uncertain economic climate. The survey gauged attitudes toward 12 large purchases that included cars, furniture, appliances, vacations, home renovations and RRSPs. Among its findings: 58% of Canadians plan to take a vacation in the next year; 51% will buy an RRSP; 35% will purchase furniture or a major appliance; 29% will invest in stocks, bonds and GICs; 24% will purchase an automobile, and 11% plan to purchase a home computer system. Of those surveyed 11% plan to spend on home renovations, and 7% intend to buy a boat or other recreational vehicle. Factors that explain prudence in spending include the evolution of consumer attitudes that began during the last recession and an aging population. Baby boomers, the largest demographic group, are adjusting their spending to meet the economic realities of this decade as they cope with the demands and responsibilities of children and aging parents.

The aging boomer population also has changed its spending pattern on sports and leisure activities. The National Sporting Goods Association, (NSGA), which tracks industry sales in the U.S., noted a decline in aerobic gear sales and an increase in sporting goods equipment that offers a more relaxed route to fitness. Industry experts say that the trends are similar in Canada. According to the NSGA, sales of tennis equipment will fall another 5% in 1995. The sales of aerobic apparel and shoes also are declining. Camping is attracting aging athletes, and the NSGA projects an 8% jump, to $1.02-billion (U.S.), in sales of tents, canteens, and other camping gear.

According to Sportmart Inc., a U.S. sporting goods chain that recently expanded into Canada, a fashion trend has evolved from this relaxed attitude to sports. Sportmart calls it the "rugged outdoor look". The look consists of a flannel shirt and thick-soled boots or the sports sandal. Forzani Group Ltd. of Calgary, a sporting retailer which owns chains such as Collegiate and Sports Experts, claims that more people are gliding instead of running. In-line skates continue to be a top-selling product across Canada and year-over year sales have doubled in volume. Although many are shying away from physical exertion, sales of hockey and soccer gear are expected to rise significantly according to the NSGA. The NSGA also believes that a promotional push by Nike Inc. will popularize street hockey in the near future.

ALGO GROUP INC.

Exchanges	Price (Jun29'95)		0.43	Trailing P/E		nm	Stock Symbol
TM	Trailing Yield (%)		0.00	Trailing EPS		(0.67)	**AO.A**

Period Ending	Dec94	Dec93	Dec92	Dec91	Dec90	Business:
Yearly Statistics						ALGO GROUP INC. operates in the fashion
Price-Close	0.75	2.20	2.00	1.95	2.00	apparel field, and its activities include the
Price-High	2.50	3.20	2.55	3.00	4.50	designing, manufacturing, marketing and
Price-Low	0.68	2.00	1.45	1.70	1.80	importing of ladies, mens and childrens apparel.
P/E-Close	nm	22.00	nm	97.50	25.00	The company is a converter of fashion fabrics
Dividends per Share	0.00	0.00	0.00	0.00	0.25	and operates two chains of ladies retail stores.
Dividend Yield (%)	0.00	0.00	0.00	0.00	12.50	Its operations are conducted in both Canada and
Sales per Share	15.70	17.53	16.37	15.24	15.24	the United States.
EPS before extra. item	(0.55)	0.10	0.00	0.02	0.08	
Cash Flow per Share	(0.34)	0.30	0.18	0.16	0.28	
Book Value per Share	1.72	2.24	2.21	2.21	2.19	

						Date	EPS	DPS	Tot Rev	Inc Bex
O/S Common Shares	20,261	20,261	18,813	18,813	18,813					
Total Revenue	317,932	338,294	308,161	287,072	286,607					
Income before extra.	(11,087)	2,012	74	418	1,539	Mar 95	0.03	0.00	70,756	588
Cash Flow	(6,983)	5,833	3,360	3,054	5,303	Dec 94	(0.59)	0.00	67,952	(11,813)
Debt/Equity	1.90	1.42	1.52	1.29	1.16	Sep 94	0.04	0.00	249,980	726
Return on Capital (%)	(1.30)	8.99	6.10	7.72	10.95	Jun 94	(0.15)	0.00	66,945	(2,954)
Ret. on Com. Equity (%)	(27.65)	4.63	0.18	1.01	3.60	Mar 94	0.04	0.00	80,049	898
% Change Profit	(651.0)	2,618.9	(82.3)	(72.8)	(77.8)	Dec 93	(0.16)	0.00	76,550	(2,988)
% Change Revenue	(6.0)	9.8	7.3	0.2	(6.2)	Sep 93	0.26	0.00	261,744	5,000
% Change Assets	(6.6)	(1.0)	10.6	2.7	(0.1)	Jun 93	(0.10)	0.00	69,528	(1,863)

Preferred Div. Coverage	na	na	na	**Synopsis:**
Total Div. Coverage	na	na	na	Algo Group reported net earnings declined in the first quarter ended March 31,
Interest Coverage	0.0	1.6	1.0	1995, to $588,000 from $898,000 for the first quarter of 1994. The decrease in
Current Ratio	1.2	1.3	1.3	earnings and sales reflects the decision to discontinue the operations of certain
Operating Margin	(0.4)	2.9	2.2	Algo divisions in 1994. Although the operations had contributed to Algo's
Asset Turnover	2.5	2.5	2.2	profitability in the first quarter of 1994, they accounted for significant losses
5 YEAR RATIOS (%)				during the remainder of 1994. Net earnings before minority interests were
Return on Capital	6.5	10.6	12.2	$191,000 for the first quarter of 1995 compared to $684,000 the previous year.
Return on Com. Equity	(3.6)	5.1	7.0	Minority interest in earnings increased net earnings by $397,000 for first quarter
Profit Growth	na	(18.9)	(61.0)	1995 compared to $214,000 for the first three months of 1994.
Revenue Growth	0.8	6.2	8.6	
Asset Growth	0.9	2.3	11.8	In November 1994, Algo closed an additional five non-performing divisions, after
BALANCE SHEET (000)				it closed three divisions that were not performing to expectations earlier in 1994.
Cash	0	0	0	The closures were part of a continuing rationalization. The five divisions were
Current Assets	102,705	110,395	109,738	estimated to account for 10% of 1994 sales, but no material charges against
Net Fixed Assets	15,336	15,957	17,031	earnings in 1994 were anticipated. Leasehold costs were written off and it was
Invest's & Advances	0	0	0	expected that inventory could be disposed of in the usual manner. Algo will focus
Total Assets	128,098	137,132	138,524	on its dresses, children's apparel, and textiles segments to enhance future
Short Term Debt	58,502	56,282	58,916	profitability. Algo entered into a joint venture to market North American made
Current Liabilities	84,335	82,650	84,504	women's dresses in Europe.
Long Term Debt	8,075	8,137	8,617	
Total Liabilities	93,139	91,736	94,118	Algo filed a preliminary prospectus in relation to a proposed rights offering on
Total Equity	34,959	45,396	44,406	May 10, 1995. One right will be issued for each class A subordinate voting share
Total Liab. & Equity	128,098	137,132	138,524	and class B multiple voting share. Fifteen rights entitle the holder to subscribe for
CAPITAL (000)				one unit at a unit price of $5.25. Each unit will consist of one 6% Cumulative
Total Debt	66,577	64,419	67,533	Redeemable Convertible Second Preferred Share, Series I of Algo, convertible
Preferred Equity	76	86	2,782	into class A shares, and two warrants to purchase class A shares. Proceeds will be
Common Equity	34,883	45,310	41,624	used to improve working capital and strengthen the capital base of Algo.

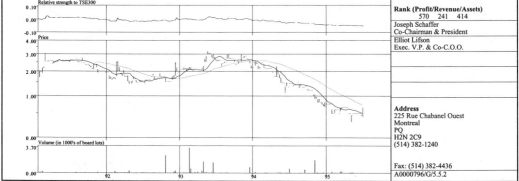

Rank (Profit/Revenue/Assets)
570   241   414
Joseph Schaffer
Co-Chairman & President
Elliot Lifson
Exec. V.P. & Co-C.O.O.

Address
225 Rue Chabanel Ouest
Montreal
PQ
H2N 2C9
(514) 382-1240

Fax: (514) 382-4436
A0000796/G/5.5.2

CAMCO INC.

Exchanges	Price (Jun29'95)	4.65	Trailing P/E	93.00	Stock Symbol
TM	Trailing Yield (%)	1.51	Trailing EPS	0.05	COC

Period Ending	Dec94	Dec93	Dec92	Dec91	Dec90
Yearly Statistics					
Price-Close	5.75	7.00	6.00	8.75	8.13
Price-High	10.50	8.25	10.38	10.25	9.00
Price-Low	5.25	5.13	4.55	6.25	4.75
P/E-Close	31.94	87.50	75.00	175.00	13.11
Dividends per Share	2.78	0.03	0.02	0.24	0.36
Dividend Yield (%)	48.35	0.43	0.33	2.74	4.43
Sales per Share	23.52	22.35	21.01	20.96	23.39
EPS before extra. item	0.18	0.08	0.08	0.05	0.62
Cash Flow per Share	0.67	0.59	0.55	0.45	0.93
Book Value per Share	3.75	6.35	6.30	6.24	6.43
O/S Common Shares	20,000	20,000	20,000	20,000	20,000
Total Revenue	470,753	449,819	422,527	422,293	469,624
Income before extra.	3,679	1,598	1,518	985	12,461
Cash Flow	13,458	11,756	11,026	9,050	18,553
Debt/Equity	0.04	0.02	0.02	nd	nd
Return on Capital (%)	5.72	1.75	2.26	1.16	16.75
Ret. on Com. Equity (%)	3.64	1.26	1.21	0.78	9.93
% Change Profit	130.2	5.3	54.1	(92.1)	(32.8)
% Change Revenue	4.7	6.5	0.1	(10.1)	(9.7)
% Change Assets	(23.9)	(3.0)	0.3	(3.2)	(6.7)

Preferred Div. Coverage	np	np	np
Total Div. Coverage	0.1	2.7	3.8
Interest Coverage	na	na	na
Current Ratio	1.6	2.7	2.5
Operating Margin	1.2	0.3	0.1
Asset Turnover	3.3	2.4	2.2
5 YEAR RATIOS (%)			
Return on Capital	5.5	9.8	17.7
Return on Com. Equity	3.4	5.7	11.0
Profit Growth	(27.5)	(44.6)	(41.8)
Revenue Growth	(2.0)	(4.3)	(4.4)
Asset Growth	(7.8)	(4.8)	(3.3)
BALANCE SHEET (000)			
Cash	6,436	60,269	50,242
Current Assets	98,355	141,581	139,619
Net Fixed Assets	43,523	44,825	50,442
Invest's & Advances	0	0	0
Total Assets	141,878	186,406	192,129
Short Term Debt	50	0	0
Current Liabilities	60,135	51,676	55,499
Long Term Debt	2,850	2,900	2,900
Total Liabilities	66,827	59,434	66,155
Total Equity	75,051	126,972	125,974
Total Liab. & Equity	141,878	186,406	192,129
CAPITAL (000)			
Total Debt	2,900	2,900	2,900
Preferred Equity	0	0	0
Common Equity	75,051	126,972	125,974

Business:

CAMCO INC. is a manufacturer and distributor of major home appliances in Canada. Its products include such brands as GE, Hotpoint, Moffat and McClary, and private brands for leading department stores. The company produces refrigerators, ranges, dishwashers, and automatic washers and dryers. Its production facilities are in Montreal and Hamilton.

Date	EPS	DPS	Tot Rev	Inc Bex
Mar 95	(0.13)	0.07	85,847	(2,679)
Dec 94	0.16	0.00	127,911	3,319
Sep 94	0.00	0.00	123,747	(119)
Jun 94	0.02	0.00	126,575	454
Mar 94	0.00	2.78	92,704	25
Dec 93	0.06	0.00	135,296	1,252
Sep 93	0.01	0.00	118,913	177
Jun 93	0.05	0.00	111,972	961

Synopsis:

The decline in first quarter net income for Camco, from a net profit of $25,000 in 1994 to a net loss of $2,679,000 in 1995, was attributed to lower sales volume and higher prices for key components and materials. Loss from operations in the first quarter of 1995 totaled $4,424,000 compared to $571,000 in 1994. The lower domestic market, and a short term decline in domestic market share as Camco raised prices during the first quarter, offset the growth in export sales. The price increases were required to counteract the significant increases in global commodity prices. Camco will introduce a new line of washers and dryers in the second half of the year. Camco believes the 1995 results will benefit from the introduction of the new range line introduced in the fall of 1994, which enjoyed a very positive response from consumer groups and dealers.

The $25-million investment in the Montreal plant to produce a large capacity dryer is on schedule. The dryer will be sold domestically and will be exported to General Electric and GE's Mexican affiliate. Electric range products, manufactured in Hamilton, underwent a complete redesign of appearance and features in 1994. Key elements of its Strategic Vision are Camco remaining a major marketer of a full line of major appliances in Canada, manufacturing products in which it can be competitive in the North American market and sourcing products it does not manufacture from the best global sources. Camco will also continue to seek out export opportunities. Its goal is to have exports exceed imports.

Contributions to total sales by segment in 1994 (1993) were: kitchen products, 62% (59%); laundry products, 30% (32%); and consumer service, 8% (9%). In 1994, export revenues amounted to $60.7-million, an increase of 16% from 1993, due to increased dryer and dishwasher exports. Export sales are anticipated to exceed $100-million in 1995. Export sales are primarily through General Electric Company.

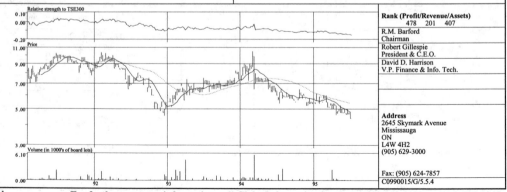

Rank (Profit/Revenue/Assets)
478   201   407
R.M. Barford
Chairman
Robert Gillespie
President & C.E.O.
David D. Harrison
V.P. Finance & Info. Tech.

Address
2645 Skymark Avenue
Mississauga
ON
L4W 4H2
(905) 629-3000

Fax: (905) 624-7857
C0990015/G/5.5.4

For further company information, call Globe Information Services 1-800-268-9128 or (416) 585-5345

CANADIAN MANOIR INDUSTRIES LIMITED

Exchanges	Price (Jun29'95)	0.55	Trailing P/E	nm	Stock Symbol
T	Trailing Yield (%)	0.00	Trailing EPS	(0.02)	**CMQ**

Period Ending	Aug94	Aug93	Aug92	Dec91	Dec90	Business:
Yearly Statistics			8M			CANADIAN MANOIR INDUSTRIES LTD.
Price-Close	0.50	0.50	0.30	0.25	1.40	operates two businesses, DMO Industries and
Price-High	0.95	1.25	0.45	1.50	2.60	Air Heat Supplies, that manufacture and
Price-Low	0.30	0.25	0.26	0.20	1.40	distribute residential heating, ventilation and
P/E-Close	nm	nm	nm	nm	nm	cooling equipment. Its markets are in Toronto
Dividends per Share	0.00	0.00	0.00	0.00	0.00	and Southwestern Ontario, the northeastern
Dividend Yield (%)	0.00	0.00	0.00	0.00	0.00	United States and Western Canada.
Sales per Share	22.43	6.46	5.77	6.40	7.14	
EPS before extra. item	(0.05)	(0.36)	(0.34)	(0.83)	(1.30)	
Cash Flow per Share	0.35	(0.19)	(0.32)	(0.47)	(1.02)	
Book Value per Share	4.92	1.59	1.95	2.29	3.12	
O/S Common Shares	1,600	5,092	5,092	5,092	5,092	
Total Revenue	35,896	32,872	19,576	32,587	36,355	
Income before extra.	(230)	(1,812)	(1,736)	(4,240)	(6,632)	

Date	EPS	DPS	Tot Rev	Inc Bex
Feb 95	(0.16)	0.00	8,277	(821)
Nov 94	0.27	0.00	15,280	1,389
Aug 94	(0.03)	0.00	9,151	(113)
May 94	(0.20)	0.00	5,011	(1,018)
Feb 94	(0.06)	0.00	8,143	(324)
Nov 93	0.24	0.00	13,586	1,225
Aug 93	(0.18)	0.00	7,660	(920)
May 93	(0.23)	0.00	5,157	(1,192)

	Aug94	Aug93	Aug92	Dec91	Dec90
Cash Flow	565	(970)	(1,073)	(2,399)	(5,207)
Debt/Equity	0.59	0.71	0.63	0.46	0.51
Return on Capital (%)	2.32	(8.62)	(10.32)	(17.40)	(16.78)
Ret. on Com. Equity (%)	(2.88)	(20.12)	(24.16)	(30.80)	(34.54)
% Change Profit	87.3	30.4	38.6	36.1	(2,542.2)
% Change Revenue	9.2	11.9	0.0	(10.4)	(33.6)
% Change Assets	0.2	(20.0)	1.2	(27.8)	(24.9)

Preferred Div. Coverage	np	np	np
Total Div. Coverage	na	na	na
Interest Coverage	0.6	0.0	0.0
Current Ratio	1.7	2.3	2.0
Operating Margin	0.8	(3.9)	(5.8)
Asset Turnover	2.0	1.9	1.3
5 YEAR RATIOS (%)			
Return on Capital	(10.2)	(10.5)	(9.3)
Return on Com. Equity	(22.5)	(22.1)	(19.3)
Profit Growth	na	na	na
Revenue Growth	(8.1)	(10.0)	(18.9)
Asset Growth	(15.2)	(17.0)	(14.1)
BALANCE SHEET (000)			
Cash	1,392	24	28
Current Assets	11,524	11,032	14,684
Net Fixed Assets	6,055	6,505	7,250
Invest's & Advances	0	0	0
Total Assets	17,579	17,537	21,934
Short Term Debt	1,629	1,099	1,482
Current Liabilities	6,701	4,813	7,276
Long Term Debt	3,009	4,625	4,747
Total Liabilities	9,710	9,438	12,023
Total Equity	7,869	8,099	9,911
Total Liab. & Equity	17,579	17,537	21,934
CAPITAL (000)			
Total Debt	4,638	5,724	6,229
Preferred Equity	0	0	0
Common Equity	7,869	8,099	9,911

Synopsis:

The first half of fiscal 1995, ending February 28, 1995, can be divided into two distinct phases. During the traditional heating season, from September to December, demand for furnaces was relatively strong and sales exceeded last year's levels. Increasing interest rates and a relatively warm winter combined to dampen demand in January and February, and sales for DMO Industries fell below last year's totals. The $1.8-million increase in sales for the first half of fiscal 1995, compared to the first half of fiscal 1994, can be attributed to the contribution made by the new Hunter Comfort business. Net income for the first half of 1995 was $568,000, compared to $901,000 recorded last year. The reduction was due to an increase in selling expenses to meet the increasing competitive pressures and maintain present sales volumes being partially offset by a slight gross profit improvement in 1995. Management is addressing increased inventories in February due to the sharp drop in demand. Demand remains sluggish.

In September 1994, Canadian Manoir and Hunter Energy and Technologies Inc. formed Hunter Comfort, a strategic alliance to further develop and expand Hunter's oil furnace business in North America. DMO Industries' Wallaceburg plant will manufacture the Hunter line of oil furnaces that will be sold through Hunter Comfort. The partnership will allow Canadian Manoir to better use its available manufacturing capacity and will lead to increased sales.

In January 1995, CFM International Inc. announced it would not purchase all the outstanding shares of Canadian Manoir. CFM's initial offer in October 1994 was rejected by the Board of Directors of Canadian Manoir as inadequate. On December 23, 1994, Canadian Manoir and CFM International entered into negotiations and CFM performed due diligence investigations. From its investigations CFM found that the two companies were not a match.

Rank (Profit/Revenue/Assets)
776 615 902

Geraldine Clever
Chairman & President

Address
2 Glengrove Avenue West
Toronto
ON
M4R 1N4
(416) 487-5363

Fax: (416) 487-7290
C0003637/G/5.5.4

CONSOLTEX GROUP INC.

Exchanges	Price (Jun29'95)	1.80	Trailing P/E	180.00	Stock Symbol
TM	Trailing Yield (%)	0.00	Trailing EPS	0.01	CTX

Period Ending	Dec94	Dec93	Jun93	Jun92
Yearly Statistics		6M		
Price-Close	4.25	6.75	6.38	n t
Price-High	6.75	7.13	6.50	n t
Price-Low	4.15	5.63	4.90	n t
P/E-Close	425.00	nm	9.81	n t
Dividends per Share	0.00	0.00	0.00	0.00
Dividend Yield (%)	0.00	0.00	0.00	0.00
Sales per Share	28.35	21.44	35.33	35.53
EPS before extra. item	0.01	(0.36)	0.65	0.47
Cash Flow per Share	1.37	0.78	1.70	2.24
Book Value per Share	4.72	6.21	6.53	1.04
O/S Common Shares	13,625	13,565	13,565	31,500
Total Revenue	385,923	146,639	226,964	145,111
Income before extra.	60	(4,868)	4,150	1,898
Cash Flow	18,587	5,287	10,884	8,945
Debt/Equity	3.63	1.88	0.46	2.05
Return on Capital (%)	10.37	3.79	12.75	na
Ret. on Com. Equity (%)	0.08	(11.27)	6.85	na
% Change Profit	100.6	(334.6)	118.7	na
% Change Revenue	31.6	29.2	56.4	na
% Change Assets	29.1	77.4	37.3	na

Business:

CONSOLTEX GROUP INC. is a North American textile company which perform s all stages of fabric manufacturing from production of yarn through to weaving, dyeing, printing, finishing and coating. CONSOLTEX also conducts its own research and development and maintains its own sales and marketing networks. The company has: 6 manufacturing plants in PQ & ON, 1 in South Carolina, 3 in Mexico, and 1 in Costa Rica.

Date	EPS	DPS	Tot Rev	Inc Bex
Dec 94	(0.34)	0.00	107,588	(4,769)
Sep 94	0.11	0.00	101,238	1,564
Jun 94	0.21	0.00	97,915	2,816
Mar 94	0.03	0.00	79,182	449
Dec 93	(0.21)	0.00	72,267	(2,894)
Sep 93	(0.15)	0.00	73,129	(1,974)
Jun 93	0.15	0.00	69,484	2,043
Mar 93	0.16	0.00	61,397	640

Preferred Div. Coverage	np	np	np
Total Div. Coverage	na	na	na
Interest Coverage	1.3	0.4	2.2
Current Ratio	1.5	2.5	1.7
Operating Margin	8.7	5.6	7.2
Asset Turnover	1.0	0.9	1.3
5 YEAR RATIOS (%)			
Return on Capital	na	na	na
Return on Com. Equity	na	na	na
Profit Growth	na	na	na
Revenue Growth	na	na	na
Asset Growth	na	na	na
BALANCE SHEET (000)			
Cash	0	2,839	0
Current Assets	154,066	122,067	95,489
Net Fixed Assets	170,055	119,622	58,325
Invest's & Advances	0	0	0
Total Assets	396,641	307,297	173,179
Short Term Debt	30,841	0	19,830
Current Liabilities	100,565	48,154	55,986
Long Term Debt	202,444	158,604	20,593
Total Liabilities	332,333	223,096	84,665
Total Equity	64,308	84,201	88,514
Total Liab. & Equity	396,641	307,297	173,179
CAPITAL (000)			
Total Debt	233,285	158,604	40,423
Preferred Equity	0	0	0
Common Equity	64,308	84,201	88,514

Synopsis:

Consoltex Group Inc. had mixed results for the first quarter of 1995. The Apparel operations' export sales to the United States continued to improve and its profitability continued to grow due to increased market penetration, productivity gains, and the weak Canadian dollar. The Polypropylene operations experienced difficulties as a result of the increased cost of polypropylene resin and the weak Mexican economy which affected Consoltex's Mexican subsidiary, Rafytek.

Sales for the first quarter of 1995 rose by 53% to $121.4-million from $79.2-million in the comparable period of 1994. The increase was attributed to the additional sales contributed by the four acquisitions made in 1994, totalling $25.3-million, and the internal growth of the Apparel operations. Earnings from operations rose from $6.6-million in the first quarter of 1994 to $10.4- million for the first three months of 1995. Consoltex expects the mixed results to continue for the remainder of 1995 as the benefits from internal factors could be offset by external factors, such as the cost of polypropylene resins.

Consoltex acquired, through LINQ, the assets of the Exxon Geotextiles Marketing Division of Exxon Chemical Company on May 1, 1994, for $3.3-million (U.S.). The transaction was financed through LINQ's working capital line of credit. Geotextiles sells and distributes woven and non-woven industrial fabrics for the U.S. market. John King, Inc. was acquired, through Balson-Hercules, on July 1, 1994, for $4-million (U.S.). John King is a textile converter and importer of nylon and polyester fabrics located in California. Rafytek, S.A. de C.V. was acquired in August 1994 for $27.5-million (U.S.). Rafytek is a Mexican polypropylene-based textile company that manufactures and sells small bags for the Mexican market. Consoltex paid $1-million (U.S.) for Rafytica, S.A., a Cost Rica-based manufacturer of polypropylene textile bags for sale to the Costa Rican market.

Relative strength to TSE300 / Price / Volume (in 1000's of board lots)

Rank (Profit/Revenue/Assets)
747 222 253

Richard H. Willett
Chairman President & C.E.O.

Paul J. Bamatter
V.P. Finance & C.F.O.

Address
125 Chabanel Street West
Montreal
PQ
H2N 1E4
(514) 382-1811

Fax: (514) 382-1022
01003354/G/5.5.2

DOMINION TEXTILE INC.

Exchanges	Price (Jun29'95)	8.75	Trailing P/E	8.33	Stock Symbol
TM	Trailing Yield (%)	0.57	Trailing EPS	1.05	**DTX**

Period Ending	Jun94	Jun93	Jun92	Jun91	Jun90
Yearly Statistics					
Price-Close	6.13	11.25	6.25	7.75	11.88
Price-High	11.88	11.63	9.50	12.00	18.31
Price-Low	5.88	5.50	5.63	5.00	10.79
P/E-Close	8.75	16.54	nm	nm	62.50
Dividends per Share	0.00	0.00	0.00	0.22	0.60
Dividend Yield (%)	0.00	0.00	0.00	2.84	5.05
Sales per Share	32.49	36.05	39.71	38.52	47.33
EPS before extra. item	0.70	0.68	(2.31)	(4.07)	0.19
Cash Flow per Share	2.80	3.32	3.89	1.20	4.05
Book Value per Share	10.59	0.00	8.82	10.51	16.11
O/S Common Shares	41,037	40,863	34,588	34,571	30,524
Total Revenue	1,343,903	1,339,001	1,378,763	1,281,000	1,400,155
Income before extra.	33,535	30,334	(74,823)	(128,827)	11,043
Cash Flow	114,789	122,861	134,462	39,600	118,012
Debt/Equity	1.13	1.17	1.54	1.41	0.97
Return on Capital (%)	11.30	13.17	0.86	(7.85)	6.42
Ret. on Com. Equity (%)	7.07	7.44	(23.94)	(31.39)	1.16
% Change Profit	10.6	140.5	41.9	(1,266.6)	19.0
% Change Revenue	0.4	(2.9)	7.6	(8.5)	(1.1)
% Change Assets	6.3	0.5	(2.6)	(5.5)	5.0
Preferred Div. Coverage	6.8	6.1	0.0		
Total Div. Coverage	6.8	6.1	0.0		
Interest Coverage	1.9	2.1	0.1		
Current Ratio	2.0	1.6	1.8		
Operating Margin	7.9	9.6	6.3		
Asset Turnover	0.9	1.0	1.0		
5 YEAR RATIOS (%)					
Return on Capital	4.8	3.7	3.2		
Return on Com. Equity	(7.9)	(9.2)	(8.9)		
Profit Growth	29.3	(6.8)	na		
Revenue Growth	(1.1)	1.8	5.5		
Asset Growth	0.6	(3.0)	10.1		
BALANCE SHEET (000)					
Cash	105,313	156,674	46,956		
Current Assets	619,673	598,147	527,440		
Net Fixed Assets	603,145	556,358	627,021		
Invest's & Advances	30,978	32,799	28,748		
Total Assets	1,412,583	1,329,112	1,323,155		
Short Term Debt	69,873	162,560	66,261		
Current Liabilities	306,535	376,208	295,364		
Long Term Debt	501,833	361,616	517,380		
Total Liabilities	908,267	882,154	945,067		
Total Equity	504,316	446,958	378,088		
Total Liab. & Equity	1,412,583	1,329,112	1,323,155		
CAPITAL (000)					
Total Debt	571,706	524,176	583,641		
Preferred Equity	69,841	71,441	73,041		
Common Equity	434,475	375,517	305,047		

Business:

DOMINION TEXTILE INC. is a producer and marketer of textiles and textile-related products on five continents. The corporation has 33 manufacturing facilities - 8 in Canada, 11 in the U.S., 11 in Europe, one in South America and 2 in the Far East - and does business in 50 countries through subsidiaries and associated companies. The company produces and distributes denim, workware apparel fabrics, yarns, etc.

Date	EPS	DPS	Tot Rev	Inc Bex
Mar 95	0.22	0.05	424,245	10,142
Dec 94	0.18	0.00	399,081	8,649
Sep 94	0.13	0.00	359,040	6,482
Jun 94	0.52	0.00	399,725	22,397
Mar 94	0.05	0.00	318,175	3,315
Dec 93	0.05	0.00	324,414	3,360
Sep 93	0.08	0.00	302,942	4,463
Jun 93	0.25	0.00	361,834	11,267

Synopsis:

Dominion Textile Inc. reported income from operations for the three months ended March 31, 1995, of $26.9-million compared to last year's corresponding figure of $17.2-million. Denim sales for the quarter were up 41.2% over last year. Swift's facilities operated at full capacity as shipments and sales revenue reached record levels in the quarter ended March 31, 1995. Higher sales, due to increased demand, and exports contributed to the improved results. Strong demand and improving selling prices contributed to the improved results in the North American commodity yarn division. Volumes were higher as a result of capacity expansions and new capacity was coming on stream for the fourth quarter ended June 1995. The strength of the yarns market should continue.

In May 1995, Dominion concluded the sale of its interlining business carried out under the name DHJ Industries to Chargeurs Textiles of France. Net proceeds were estimated to be $65-million (U.S.) and will be used by Domtex to reduce debt and for general corporate purposes. Dominion's nonwovens subsidiary, Nordlys S.A., and Chargeurs subsidiary, Intissel S.A., agreed to exchange businesses. Nordlys will take over Intissel's nonwoven business in exchange for its interlinings business and a small cash payment to be determined. In March 1995, Domtex announced a $37-million investment at its Swift Textiles denim manufacturing facilities in Drummondville, Quebec, and Erwin, North Carolina. The money will be used to add new looms and increase capcity. The additions should be completed by the third quarter of fiscal 1996. Domtex announced in October 1994 that its was investing $12-million (U.S.) in its nonwovens subsidiary Poly-Bond Inc. to convert a nonwoven fabric line in its factory.

Total sales in fiscal 1994 by business were: denim, 39%; yarns, 21%; technical fabrics, 17%; apparel fabrics, 13%; industrial products, 8%; other, 1%.

Rank (Profit/Revenue/Assets)
142   96   134

Charles H. Hantho
Chairman

John A. Boland III
President & C.E.O.

Milo Smith
C.F.O.

Address
1950 Sherbrooke Street West
Montreal
PQ
H3H 1E7
(514) 989-6000

Fax: (514) 989-6214
D0002586/G/5.5.2

IRWIN TOY LIMITED

Exchanges	Price (Jun29'95)	8 .50	Trailing P/E	7 .39	Stock Symbol
TM	Trailing Yield (%)	2 .35	Trailing EPS	1 .15	IWT

Period Ending	Jan95	Jan94	Jan93	Jan92	Jan91	Business:
Yearly Statistics						IRWIN TOY LTD. manufactures and
Price-Close	6 .63	6 .25	5 .50	7 .50	4 .50	distributes a broad range of leisure products in
Price-High	8 .38	7 .25	7 .00	7 .50	7 .00	Canada. The main business of the company is
Price-Low	5 .25	4 .75	5 .25	4 .50	4 .05	toys and games. The company also distributes
P/E-Close	5 .76	52 .08	16 .67	16 .67	22 .50	souvenir items, furniture and other leisure
Dividends per Share	0 .20	0 .20	0 .22	0 .20	0 .20	goods. It markets Winnwell hockey and Cooper
Dividend Yield (%)	3 .02	3 .20	4 .00	2 .67	4 .44	baseball equipment. Irwin also distributes the
Sales per Share	21 .38	14 .57	23 .49	20 .72	17 .91	products of foriegn toy companies and develops
EPS before extra. item	1 .15	0 .12	0 .33	0 .45	0 .20	its own products.
Cash Flow per Share	1 .51	0 .43	0 .61	0 .71	0 .46	
Book Value per Share	4 .97	4 .00	4 .08	4 .16	3 .91	
O/S Common Shares	5 ,230	5 ,190	5 ,170	5 ,124	5 ,105	
Total Revenue	111 ,403	75 ,489	120 ,857	105 ,973	91 ,333	
Income before extra.	6 ,019	617	1 ,705	2 ,296	1 ,015	
Cash Flow	7 ,875	2 ,244	3 ,159	3 ,609	2 ,338	

Date	EPS	DPS	Tot Rev	Inc Bex
Jan 95	0 .33	0 .10	27 ,332	1 ,711
Oct 94	0 .45	0 .00	42 ,969	2 ,403
Jul 94	0 .26	0 .10	24 ,003	1 ,321
Apr 94	0 .11	0 .00	17 ,099	584
Jan 94	0 .04	0 .10	17 ,791	206
Oct 93	0 .08	0 .00	29 ,594	401
Jul 93	0 .02	0 .10	15 ,413	123
Apr 93	(0 .02)	0 .00	12 ,691	(113)

	Jan95	Jan94	Jan93	Jan92	Jan91
Debt/Equity	0 .34	0 .67	0 .80	0 .64	0 .85
Return on Capital (%)	34 .99	7 .91	15 .20	21 .35	14 .31
Ret. on Com. Equity (%)	25 .75	2 .95	8 .04	11 .13	5 .09
% Change Profit	875 .5	(63 .8)	(25 .7)	126 .2	(55 .6)
% Change Revenue	47 .6	(37 .5)	14 .0	16 .0	(3 .8)
% Change Assets	22 .1	(25 .6)	10 .8	4 .9	6 .7

				Synopsis:
Preferred Div. Coverage	np	np	np	Irwin Toy reported a decline in net earnings to $189,000 for the first quarter
Total Div. Coverage	5 .8	0 .6	1 .5	ended April 30, 1995, compared to $584,000 from the first quarter of the previous
Interest Coverage	9 .5	1 .8	2 .7	year. The first quarter results are not indicative of the full year's results due to the
Current Ratio	2 .2	2 .7	1 .8	seasonal nature of Irwin's business. Irwin had an unusually good quarter in the
Operating Margin	10 .9	3 .8	4 .6	first quarter of 1994 due to retailers stocking all the Power Ranger products they
Asset Turnover	2 .0	1 .6	1 .9	could get their hands. Pent up unfulfilled demand and a fear of product shortages
5 YEAR RATIOS (%)				led to the increase in sales. Irwin was able to catch up with demand by the end of
Return on Capital	18 .8	15 .8	17 .3	1994. While Power Rangers continue to be the best selling action figures, demand
Return on Com. Equity	10 .6	7 .8	8 .9	has cooled. Many retailers are delaying deliveries of toys. Most toys will not be
Profit Growth	21 .4	(16 .5)	1 .1	sold by retailers until the fourth quarter. As a result there has been an even greater
Revenue Growth	3 .2	(4 .3)	8 .1	shift of Irwin's deliveries to the second half of the year. Irwin believes that results
Asset Growth	2 .4	(2 .1)	6 .6	for the company will improve as the year progresses.
BALANCE SHEET (000)				Consolidated net sales were of $11,403,000 for the year ended January 31, 1995,
Cash	10 ,000	5 ,000	7 ,000	or 48% higher than the previous year. Net earnings for the year ended January 31,
Current Assets	49 ,905	39 ,597	55 ,373	1995, were $6,019,000 compared with $617,000 for the previous year. Sales to
Net Fixed Assets	7 ,125	7 ,114	7 ,406	the United States were 11.2% of total revenues for the year ended January 31,
Invest's & Advances	0	0	0	1995. Irwin expects the percentage to be higher in the current year as it continues
Total Assets	57 ,030	46 ,711	62 ,779	to develop its business in the U.S. by introducing toys and sporting goods which
Short Term Debt	1 ,386	3 ,361	6 ,041	have been successful in Canada. The strength of the sales of the Mighty Morphin
Current Liabilities	23 ,101	14 ,876	30 ,370	Power Rangers toy line and the Mighty Max line are the primary reasons for the
Long Term Debt	7 ,519	10 ,604	10 ,757	higher sales and earnings.
Total Liabilities	31 ,062	25 ,928	41 ,666	In 1994 the Suzie Stretch doll, a soft-bodied doll which stretches up to 60 inches
Total Equity	25 ,968	20 ,783	21 ,113	tall, was the number one selling doll in Canada. The doll is being launched in the
Total Liab. & Equity	57 ,030	46 ,711	62 ,779	United States in 1995 and initial sales indications were positive. Irwin is
CAPITAL (000)				launching a line of action figures based on the TV show ReBoot in North America
Total Debt	8 ,905	13 ,965	16 ,798	in 1995. Irwin shipped new Power Ranger movie figures just prior to the release
Preferred Equity	0	0	0	of the movie in June 1995.
Common Equity	25 ,968	20 ,783	21 ,113	

Relative strength to TSE300

Rank (Profit/Revenue/Assets)
393   404   601

Arnold B. Irwin
Co-Chairman

George M. Irwin
President & C.E.O.

Address
43 Hanna Avenue
Toronto
ON
M6K 1X6
(416) 533-3521

Fax: (416) 533-3257
I0002152/G/5.5.3

PEERLESS CARPET CORPORATION

Exchanges	Price (Jun29'95)	3.00	Trailing P/E	18.75	Stock Symbol
TM	Trailing Yield (%)	0.00	Trailing EPS	0.16	**PRG**

Period Ending	Dec94	Feb94	Feb93	Feb92	Feb91
Yearly Statistics	10M				
Price-Close	4.15	3.08	5.00	3.30	3.00
Price-High	6.00	6.25	6.00	4.50	7.25
Price-Low	3.75	3.85	2.55	2.75	3.00
P/E-Close	9.61	nm	nm	nm	nm
Dividends per Share	0.00	0.00	0.00	0.00	0.04
Dividend Yield (%)	0.00	0.00	0.00	0.00	1.33
Sales per Share	44.08	45.33	48.11	46.69	58.47
EPS before extra. item	0.36	(0.35)	(0.52)	(1.18)	(1.67)
Cash Flow per Share	1.31	0.71	0.61	0.19	(0.09)
Book Value per Share	4.47	4.07	4.22	4.74	6.18
O/S Common Shares	12,606	12,576	9,977	9,977	8,799
Total Revenue	462,468	493,391	480,066	438,402	510,378
Income before extra.	4,521	(3,964)	(5,221)	(10,944)	(14,577)
Cash Flow	13,794	8,126	6,142	1,818	(844)
Debt/Equity	2.25	3.84	4.51	3.91	3.30
Return on Capital (%)	10.60	4.22	3.47	3.00	0.47
Ret. on Com. Equity (%)	10.09	(8.49)	(11.68)	(21.51)	(23.64)
% Change Profit	236.9	24.1	52.3	24.9	(428.8)
% Change Revenue	12.5	2.8	9.5	(14.1)	11.7
% Change Assets	(28.2)	4.0	3.9	(4.1)	(9.1)

Date	EPS	DPS	Tot Rev	Inc Bex
Mar 95	(0.20)	0.00	62,274	(2,501)
Dec 94	0.24	0.00	176,379	2,990
Aug 94	0.04	0.00	140,347	511
May 94	0.08	0.00	145,742	1,020
Feb 94	(0.20)	0.00	120,597	(2,570)
Aug 93	(0.06)	0.00	134,314	(250)
May 93	(0.66)	0.00	112,514	(2,167)
Feb 93	(1.05)	0.00	119,584	(3,489)

Preferred Div. Coverage	np	np	np	
Total Div. Coverage	na	na	na	
Interest Coverage	1.7	0.8	0.6	
Current Ratio	1.5	1.3	1.4	
Operating Margin	4.2	2.1	1.7	
Asset Turnover	2.5	1.6	1.6	
5 YEAR RATIOS (%)				
Return on Capital	4.4	5.1	10.2	
Return on Com. Equity	(11.0)	(11.8)	(6.0)	
Profit Growth	4.1	na	na	
Revenue Growth	3.9	14.2	15.0	
Asset Growth	(7.5)	19.6	17.8	
BALANCE SHEET (000)				
Cash	0	0	0	
Current Assets	184,801	228,532	212,517	
Net Fixed Assets	36,555	78,412	82,760	
Invest's & Advances	0	0	0	
Total Assets	221,624	308,712	296,966	
Short Term Debt	93,007	123,273	95,901	
Current Liabilities	125,689	176,767	153,076	
Long Term Debt	33,685	73,408	94,052	
Total Liabilities	165,321	257,466	254,854	
Total Equity	56,303	51,246	42,112	
Total Liab. & Equity	221,624	308,712	296,966	
CAPITAL (000)				
Total Debt	126,692	196,681	189,953	
Preferred Equity	0	0	0	
Common Equity	56,303	51,246	42,112	

Business:

PEERLESS CARPET CORPORATION directly and with its subsidiaries, manufactures broadloom carpet and bathroom broadloom sets. Peerless also distributes other related products. The company is represented in the United States, United Kingdom and Australia through subsidiaries.

Synopsis:

The economic climate during the first quarter of 1995 was very difficult for Peerless Carpet Corporation. Residential resale activity declined by 35.6% from 83,263 units for 1994 compared to 53,642 units for the first quarter of 1995, and Canadian housing starts declined by 19%. Peerless was able to increase sales in Canada but consumers concentrated their purchases on lower priced items, which placed significant pressure on gross margin rates. The results for the first quarter ended February 1994 included the assets of Galaxy Carpet Mills Inc., which was sold in December 1994. The Galaxy sale reduced consolidated debt by $130-million.

Peerless developed a strategic plan in late 1993 that is designed to take the company to the year 2000. The first part of the plan involved the company taking advantage of several opportunities available to its carpet operations. There are fewer domestic manufacturers in Canada, where there has been a slowly increasing demand for carpet. Although the number of imports has increased, the company found that it could improve its domestic market share, particularly by selling to independent distributors. Peerless is also able to take advantage of the lower Canadian dollar, increasing competitiveness in foreign markets, and manufacturing assets that allow it to be vertically integrated. The purchase of the spinning and yarn preparation assets of Soreltex International in June 1994 and movement of the assets to Peerless' own buildings, substantially increased its yarn processing capacities.

With the purchase in February 1995 of the assets of Ramca Tiles Limited, Peerless built on its position as leading floor covering products distributor in Canada. This is the second part of its strategic plan. Peerless Carpet added wood flooring to its product offering and launched a line of area rugs in the summer of 1995.

Trade sales (operating profit) by geographic area for the ten months ended December 31, 1994, were: Canada, 46% (61%); United States and other, 54% (39%).

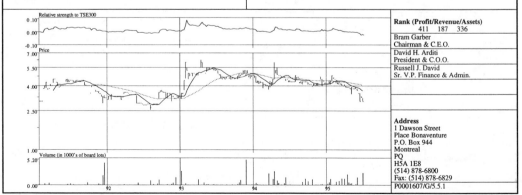

Relative strength to TSE300 — Price — Volume (in 1000's of board lots)

Rank (Profit/Revenue/Assets)
411   187   336

Bram Garber
Chairman & C.E.O.

David H. Arditi
President & C.O.O.

Russell J. David
Sr. V.P. Finance & Admin.

Address
1 Dawson Street
Place Bonaventure
P.O. Box 944
Montreal
PQ
H5A 1E8
(514) 878-6800
Fax: (514) 878-6829
P0001607/G/5.5.1

SEMI-TECH CORPORATION

Exchanges	Price (Jun29'95)	11.12	Trailing P/E	nm	Stock Symbol
TM	Trailing Yield (%)	3.60	Trailing EPS	(0.14)	SEM.A

Period Ending	Mar94	Apr93	Apr92	Jan92	Apr91
Yearly Statistics	11M				
Price-Close	18.00	21.50	16.88	16.00	9.50
Price-High	22.25	22.25	17.00	16.50	9.88
Price-Low	16.13	15.88	9.13	3.65	3.25
P/E-Close	56.96	5.67	3.89	3.43	27.14
Dividends per Share	0.20	0.00	0.00	0.00	0.00
Dividend Yield (%)	1.11	0.00	0.00	0.00	0.00
Sales per Share	14.03	0.23	na	na	na
EPS before extra. item	0.29	3.79	4.34	4.66	0.35
Cash Flow per Share	2.25	0.55	0.36	0.43	(0.08)
Book Value per Share	16.71	15.31	9.15	9.05	3.92
O/S Common Shares	66,587	23,674	16,584	13,147	12,893
Total Revenue	626,900	96,900	54,902	53,504	36,029
Income before extra.	14,700	80,600	60,048	60,463	4,530
Cash Flow	93,000	11,700	4,952	5,602	(1,083)
Debt/Equity	0.86	0.10	0.72	0.88	1.79
Return on Capital (%)	6.27	25.33	25.41	31.43	7.32
Ret. on Com. Equity (%)	2.17	31.36	44.37	71.33	8.87
% Change Profit	(80.1)	34.2	(0.7)	1,234.7	(17.2)
% Change Revenue	605.8	76.5	2.6	48.5	2.8
% Change Assets	510.7	48.2	13.2	36.6	0.1

Date	EPS	DPS	Tot Rev	Inc Bex
Dec 94	0.00	0.10	356,000	400
Sep 94	0.03	0.10	380,300	1,700
Jun 94	(0.02)	0.10	363,100	(1,200)
Mar 94	(0.15)	0.10	11,512	(5,475)
Dec 93	0.20	0.10	424,580	10,790
Oct 93	0.12	0.10	180,500	6,500
Jul 93	0.12	0.00	2,900	2,900
Apr 93	0.19	0.00	12,359	6,734

	Mar94	Apr93	Apr92
Preferred Div. Coverage	na	na	na
Total Div. Coverage	1.1	na	na
Interest Coverage	1.4	14.2	8.7
Current Ratio	1.9	0.6	1.6
Operating Margin	13.1	(85.7)	(36.0)
Asset Turnover	0.2	0.0	na
5 YEAR RATIOS (%)			
Return on Capital	19.2	19.6	16.5
Return on Com. Equity	31.6	33.0	31.9
Profit Growth	24.0	43.3	56.2
Revenue Growth	81.1	30.9	(33.0)
Asset Growth	69.5	23.6	(1.4)
BALANCE SHEET (000)			
Cash	356,100	24,600	26,282
Current Assets	1,099,700	46,400	40,110
Net Fixed Assets	300,800	27,200	28,127
Invest's & Advances	465,400	379,900	235,769
Total Assets	2,774,300	454,300	306,543
Short Term Debt	300,000	38,300	2,570
Current Liabilities	574,900	80,000	24,439
Long Term Debt	661,000	0	114,435
Total Liabilities	1,649,800	80,000	142,934
Total Equity	1,124,500	374,300	163,609
Total Liab. & Equity	2,774,300	454,300	306,543
CAPITAL (000)			
Total Debt	961,000	38,300	117,005
Preferred Equity	11,900	11,900	11,912
Common Equity	1,112,600	362,400	151,697

Business:

SEMI-TECH CORPORATION is a multinational company with interests in the retailing and distribution of consumer durables and sewing related products principally through the company's 51% ownership in Singer Co. N.V., 39% investment in Semi-Tech. The principal operating units are Singer Co. N.V., a 72% interest in G.M. Pfaff, and a 44% interest in Sansui Electric Co.

Synopsis:

In June 1995, Semi-Tech Corporation made a $320-million bid for Kong Wah Holdings Ltd., a thriving TV manufacturer based in China with headquarters in Bermuda. The purchase concluded a three month global search to find a new supply of televisions for Akai Electric Co., Ltd. Akai had been purchasing TV sets from Kong Wah and selling them under the Akai label for five years, but Semi-Tech decided it needed to increase the number of sets sold. Kong Wah has three plants in China and one each in Britain and Malaysia. Akai will offer $0.21 a share for 81% of Kong Wah. The remaining 19% will be held by Kong Wah's two founders. Semi-Tech will provide a short-term loan to Akai to close the deal. Akai will then raise additional funding through bank loans or a bond issue. Semi-Tech will make its loan permanent, and increase its equity in Akai, if Akai cannot come up with the financing.

Semi-Tech Global purchased a 55% share in Akai Electric Co., Ltd. for $172-million (U.S.) in early 1995. Akai issued new shares to Semi-Tech Global. Akai is a Japanese public company engaged in the manufacture and sale of quality video and audio equipment, electronic musical instruments, and electronic parts. Akai bought a 17.5% interest in Sansui Electric Co., Ltd. from Semi-Tech Global for $97-million. Akai's main export markets are Europe, South East Asia, the Middle East, and Africa. Akai will have access to Singer's global distribution network, which should enhance Akai's sales.

Semi-Tech Global sold its 12% stake in Tomei International (Holdings) Ltd. to Sansui for $26-million. Tomei and Sansui had jointly invested in a manufacturing facility in China so that Sansui could shift production of its lower-end products there.

Semi-Tech Corporation changed its name from International Semi-Tech Microelectronics Inc. at the annual meeting in September 1994.

Relative strength to TSE300

Price

Volume (in 1000's of board lots)

Rank (Profit/Revenue/Assets)
237 156 78

James H. Ting
Chairman President & C.E.O.

Chuck C.H. Tam
Exec. V.P. & C.F.O.

Address
131 McNabb Street
Markham
ON
L3R 5V7
(905) 475-2670

Fax: (905) 475-3652
S0001900/G/5.5.4

Page	Company		Fiscal year end	EARNINGS PER SHARE		
				Last Year	Estimate this year	Estimate next year
215	Budd Canada		Sep-94	(2.03)	na	na
216	Enscor	$US	Jul-94	0.02	na	na
217	Ford Motor Company of Canada		Dec-94	(4.21)	na	na
218	Magna International		Jul-94	3.87	4.95	5.85
219	Meridian Technologies		Mar-95	(0.33)	0.14	0.36
220	South China Industries (Canada)		Dec-94	0.15	0.18	0.25
221	TCG International		Dec-94	0.04	na	na
222	Western Star Truck Holdings		Jun-94	2.61	3.26	2.21

Automotive

The world automotive industry achieved a significant breakthrough in June 1995 as the United States and Japan avoided a trade war by agreeing to open Japan's auto and auto parts sector. The agreement includes three key areas: increasing access for U.S. car companies to the Japanese dealer network; raising sales of U.S. auto parts to Japanese car makers; and boosting U.S. auto parts sales to Japanese repair shops. Currently, due to Japan's protectionist automotive industry, only 2.5% of auto parts sold in Japan are foreign-made versus 32.5% in the United States. Andrew Card, president of the American Automobile Manufacturers Association, states, "Chrysler, Ford, and General Motors are committed to the Japanese market for the long haul." Japanese purchases of foreign-made auto parts are expected to increase by about 50% or $9-billion within three years. Analysts expect major Japanese automotive dealers to increase foreign purchases. Manufacturers also plan to increase U.S. production of their cars and the amount of North American parts in Japanese autos.

The North American automotive market continued its recovery in 1994. Total light vehicle production volumes for the model year from all the Original Equipment Manufacturers (OEMs) increased by over 12% compared to 1993. This represented the best showings for OEM's in the past five years. Economists and industry analysts expect this trend to continue into 1995 in an environment characterized by relatively low inflation, lower interest rates, and improving consumer confidence. All the various vehicle market segments are improving, especially the light truck group, where sales over the past two years have jumped by 32% in the U.S. market.

In 1994, car and truck sales increased by 5.5%, the first year by year increase in six years. In Canada, the industry expects overall economic activity to improve in 1995 with export growth to the United States being the key factor. It expects sales of cars and trucks in Canada to increase in 1995, with truck sales representing the majority of the increase. Analysts expect vehicle production to increase in Canada in 1995.

Automobile Industry: Industry Report [May-5-95] Zero To Sixty Automotive Monthly: April. Donaldson, Lufkin & Jenrette Securities

April's new light vehicle selling rate came in at a very disappointing 13.9 million (14.2 million including heavy-duty vehicles), which was at the low end of expectations and well below the 15.1 million light vehicle rate of the first quarter. Moreover, industry sources report that the final 10 days of April were weaker than the first 20, which does not bode well for May. (When the industry used to report 10-day sales, the final period of the month was typically the strongest.) Total vehicle sales fell 6.1% (calculated on a daily selling rate), the fourth consecutive monthly decline. The total seasonally adjusted annual selling rate (SAAR) was 13.9 million, down from 15.1 million in March and 15.2 million in April of 1994. It was the lowest SAAR since the capacity-constrained rate of 13.8 million recorded in July 1994. The industry has solved most of its capacity problems in the subsequent nine months, so April 1995's weak sales were not so easily explained away. Light truck sales fell only 1.2% in April, with domestics down 1.9% and imports up 5.9%. (Toyota's large pickup and Land Cruiser, the Range Rover products, and the Honda Odyssey accounted for most of that gain.) The SAAR for domestic trucks was a weak 5.4 million, again the worst since last July. While some products are capacity constrained (automatic transmission pickups at GM, for example), others are not. There is plenty of minivan capacity, and an increasing amount of sport utility vehicle (SUV) capacity. The SAAR, thus, is suggesting a general slowing in truck demand. The import truck SAAR was 0.37 million, also the lowest since last July. Total car sales fell 8.2%, with domestics down 8.3% and imports off 13.2%. The domestic car SAAR was 6.6 million, while the import selling rate fell to an anaemic 1.5 million.

BUDD CANADA INC.

Exchanges	Price (Jun29'95)		19.37	Trailing P/E		nm	Stock Symbol
T	Trailing Yield (%)		5.16	Trailing EPS		(1.48)	**BUD**

Period Ending	Sep94	Sep93	Sep92	Sep91	Sep90	Business:
Yearly Statistics						BUDD CANADA INC. is an automotive parts
Price-Close	18.75	27.75	32.00	31.00	29.00	manufacturer, specializing in the production of
Price-High	27.75	32.50	39.00	39.50	37.00	chassis component parts and light truck frames.
Price-Low	17.50	22.63	29.75	28.25	28.00	Its production facilities are located in Kitchner.
P/E-Close	nm	38.54	33.68	70.46	5.89	Budcan Holdings Inc., a wholly owned
Dividends per Share	1.00	2.50	3.50	6.00	6.00	subsidiary of the Budd Company of Michigan,
Dividend Yield (%)	5.33	9.01	10.94	19.36	20.69	owns 77.3% of the outstanding shares of the
Sales per Share	72.89	61.93	50.57	46.54	61.02	company.
EPS before extra. item	(2.03)	0.72	0.95	0.44	4.92	
Cash Flow per Share	0.16	2.82	2.83	2.34	6.70	
Book Value per Share	19.08	22.12	23.90	26.45	32.00	
O/S Common Shares	3,767	3,767	3,767	3,767	3,767	
Total Revenue	275,386	235,743	194,253	191,409	250,967	
Income before extra.	(7,653)	2,701	3,587	1,675	18,518	

Date	EPS	DPS	Tot Rev	Inc Bex
Mar 95	0.10	0.25	81,700	348
Dec 94	0.11	0.25	85,690	427
Sep 94	(0.92)	0.25	67,472	(3,476)
Jun 94	(0.77)	0.25	63,951	(2,912)
Mar 94	(0.07)	0.25	83,040	(236)
Dec 93	(0.27)	0.25	61,083	(1,029)
Sep 93	(0.24)	1.75	45,648	(925)
Jun 93	0.21	0.25	53,965	812

Cash Flow	601	10,641	10,669	8,802	25,233
Debt/Equity	nd	0.05	0.04	0.00	0.00
Return on Capital (%)	(14.60)	5.24	6.75	3.15	25.84
Ret. on Com. Equity (%)	(9.86)	3.12	3.78	1.52	15.11
% Change Profit	(383.3)	(24.7)	114.1	(91.0)	(33.0)
% Change Revenue	16.8	21.4	1.5	(23.7)	(16.0)
% Change Assets	(9.1)	5.2	(11.1)	(10.3)	(5.4)

				Synopsis:
Preferred Div. Coverage	np	np	np	
Total Div. Coverage	0.0	0.3	0.3	
Interest Coverage	nd	15.8	na	
Current Ratio	1.7	2.1	3.0	
Operating Margin	(4.0)	1.2	1.5	
Asset Turnover	2.4	1.8	1.6	

Synopsis:

The first quarter results for Budd Canada Inc. included a gain of 18 cents a share related to research and development tax credits. The increase in net earnings was attributed mainly to the increase in sales volume, offset partly by the higher costs of introducing two new frame assembly lines.

In the November 1994, Budd sold its Temro Division to its majority shareholder, Budcan Holdings Inc., in a deal valued at $8.87-million. Budcan Holdings is a unit of Budd Co. of Troy, Michigan. According to Budd Canada, the transaction will allow it to focus on its core business of manufacturing automotive component chassis assemblies and light-truck frames. The deal will have no material effect on Budd's core business. Temro manufacturers and distributes cold-weather starting aids and exhaust silencers.

In fiscal 1994, Budd faced problems related to the launch of a new product. The company completed the installation of its second highly automated assembly line. This added to overall costs due to machinery problems. Budd also received the replacement business for the new 1996 Jeep Wrangler. The bulk of increased sales in the year was due to the tooling and prototype sales and the weaker Canadian dollar. The Kitchener plant made sales to General Motors, Ford, and Chrysler. For fiscal 1995, Budd expects the North American automotive sector to remain strong. Budd also plans to continue to focus on more efficient methods of production by way of technology advances, and cost reductions through overall improvements.

In August 1994, Budd Co. of Troy, Michigan, was named as supplier of frames for the new Mercedes-Benz activity vehicle to be built starting in 1997. Consequently, Budd Canada's Kitchener plant will produce frame assemblies and parts.

5 YEAR RATIOS (%)			
Return on Capital	5.3	16.3	21.7
Return on Com. Equity	2.7	9.4	12.4
Profit Growth	na	(32.8)	(32.9)
Revenue Growth	(1.7)	(2.1)	(5.8)
Asset Growth	(6.4)	(3.5)	(3.0)

BALANCE SHEET (000)			
Cash	6,237	22,181	26,546
Current Assets	63,257	81,190	73,995
Net Fixed Assets	45,939	40,857	43,681
Invest's & Advances	0	0	0
Total Assets	115,135	126,686	120,433
Short Term Debt	0	4,318	3,698
Current Liabilities	38,090	38,409	25,037
Long Term Debt	0	0	0
Total Liabilities	43,251	43,382	30,413
Total Equity	71,884	83,304	90,020
Total Liab. & Equity	115,135	126,686	120,433

CAPITAL (000)			
Total Debt	0	4,318	3,698
Preferred Equity	0	0	0
Common Equity	71,884	83,304	90,020

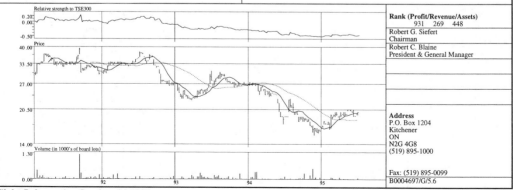

Rank (Profit/Revenue/Assets)
931   269   448
Robert G. Siefert
Chairman
Robert C. Blaine
President & General Manager

Address
P.O. Box 1204
Kitchener
ON
N2G 4G8
(519) 895-1000

Fax: (519) 895-0099
B0004697/G/5.6

ENSCOR INC.

Exchanges	Price (Jun29'95)	1.60	Trailing P/E		nm	Stock Symbol
TQ	Trailing Yield (%)	0.00	Trailing EPS		(0.03)	ENZ

Period Ending	Ju l94	Ju l93	Dec92	Dec91	Dec90
Yearly Statistics	US	US /7M	US		
Price-Close	1.25	1.35	1.35	0.50	0.35
Price-High	1.65	1.85	1.35	1.10	2.00
Price-Low	1.20	1.15	0.50	0.40	0.35
P/E-Close	46.30	nm	nm	nm	nm
Dividends per Share	0.00	0.00	0.00	0.00	0.00
Dividend Yield (%)	0.00	0.00	0.00	0.00	0.00
Sales per Share	5.23	2.60	na	na	na
EPS before extra. item	0.02	(0.04)	(0.12)	(0.17)	(0.56)
Cash Flow per Share	0.34	0.15	0.22	0.06	1.19
Book Value per Share	0.92	0.91	0.92	1.30	1.71
O/S Common Shares	23,446	23,430	16,195	16,195	10,887
Total Revenue	124,586	30,879	29,348	21,010	74,261
Income before extra.	998	(470)	(1,716)	(1,960)	(5,830)
Cash Flow	7,892	1,689	3,616	819	12,956
Debt/Equity	1.30	1.33	0.63	1.23	2.60
Return on Capital (%)	7.11	1.75	(7.18)	(4.89)	(12.26)
Ret. on Com. Equity (%)	2.58	(6.41)	(12.27)	(11.42)	(28.10)
% Change Profit	223.9	53.0	(6.4)	66.4	(202.3)
% Change Revenue	135.4	80.4	69.7	(71.7)	60.7
% Change Assets	3.7	155.2	(29.0)	(28.1)	(19.3)

Date		EPS	DPS	Tot Rev	Inc Bex
Apr 95	US	(0.01)	0.00	36,000	(116)
Jan 95	US	(0.05)	0.00	32,271	(854)
Oct 94	US	(0.01)	0.00	33,729	(231)
Jul 94	US	0.04	0.00	35,149	1,127
Apr 94		0.03	0.00	33,793	751
Jan 94		(0.02)	0.00	28,628	(312)
Oct 93		(0.03)	0.00	27,372	(568)
Jul 93		0.00	0.00	29,785	171

Preferred Div. Coverage	2.3	0.0	0.0
Total Div. Coverage	2.3	0.0	0.0
Interest Coverage	1.5	0.5	0.0
Current Ratio	2.4	1.9	2.7
Operating Margin	3.2	(1.7)	(14.9)
Asset Turnover	1.3	0.6	na
5 YEAR RATIOS (%)			
Return on Capital	(3.1)	(0.9)	1.7
Return on Com. Equity	(11.1)	(6.7)	(1.7)
Profit Growth	(25.1)	na	na
Revenue Growth	26.7	17.4	2.2
Asset Growth	1.8	12.0	2.7
BALANCE SHEET (000)			
Cash	4,405	8,260	14,051
Current Assets	54,776	52,256	14,315
Net Fixed Assets	21,815	21,004	14,720
Invest's & Advances	0	0	5,655
Total Assets	93,635	90,264	35,373
Short Term Debt	4,558	9,700	0
Current Liabilities	22,707	27,602	5,382
Long Term Debt	29,930	25,394	11,633
Total Liabilities	67,073	63,966	17,015
Total Equity	26,562	26,298	18,358
Total Liab. & Equity	93,635	90,264	35,373
CAPITAL (000)			
Total Debt	34,488	35,094	11,633
Preferred Equity	4,896	4,896	3,400
Common Equity	21,666	21,402	14,958

Business:

ENSCOR INC. is involved in the U.S. automotive industry and also maintains residual operations in the Canadian real estate industry, previously its principal business. The company's principal operating business is carried on through The Equion Corp. which manufactures and distributes vehicle systems and components.

Synopsis:

In April 1995, Enscor Inc. announced that its 70% owned subsidiary, Equion Corp., plans to sell the business and assets of its Signet Systems division to Modine Manufacturing Co. of Racine, Wisconsin. The deal is valued at about $54-million (U.S.), net of the assumption of certain liabilities by Modine. Signet, based in Kentucky, is a full-service supplier of climate control systems and components to the North American and European automotive markets.

For the first half of fiscal 1995, the bulk of Enscor's revenues were attributable to the automotive sector. The increase in sales was due to the strong performance of the Hayden division. However, margins were negatively affected by a combination of factors including an unfavourable product mix, labour and pricing variances related to production cutbacks and unscheduled parts shortages, and lower margins related to start-up at Signet AutoAir. There were no property sales recorded in this period. Enscor's hotel operations had a 11% increase in revenues, with strong advance bookings in December and January tempered by cancellations due to unfavorable weather conditions. In November 1994, Enscor sold last remaining oil and gas assets, with no impact on earnings.

Enscor bought Equion in July 1994. The Equion purchase transformed Enscor from a real estate developer to a major player in the automotive aftermarket. Enscor initiated its departure from the real estate business in late 1991. Currently it owns only residual operations. For fiscal 1994, Enscor's revenues by industry segment were: automotive, 97.8%; hotel, 1.4%; and real estate and other, 0.08%.

Enscor believes that business developments at Equion are on target. The company's start-up costs related to its European operations continue to exceed plan, but Enscor is expecting long-term market opportunities. Plans called for additional sales of non-core holdings, including hotel operations, when an attractive deal can be negotiated.

Relative strength to TSE300

Price

Volume (in 1000's of board lots)

Rank (Profit/Revenue/Assets)
622 339 430

Sam Reisman
Chairman & C.E.O.

Stephen Morrison
President

Martin Simon
C.O.O. & C.F.O.

Address
156 Duncan Mill Road
Unit 12
Don Mills
ON
M3B 3N2
(416) 449-3535

Fax: (416) 449-9887

E0002667/G/5.6

FORD MOTOR COMPANY OF CANADA, LIMITED

Exchanges	Price (Jun29'95)	185.00	Trailing P/E	67.52	Stock Symbol
TA	Trailing Yield (%)	0.00	Trailing EPS	2.74	**FMC**

Period Ending	Dec94	Dec93	Dec92	Dec91	Dec90
Yearly Statistics					
Price-Close	139.00	132.00	110.00	140.00	120.00
Price-High	165.00	134.50	150.00	146.00	185.00
Price-Low	129.00	108.00	108.00	113.00	110.00
P/E-Close	nm	nm	nm	nm	nm
Dividends per Share	0.00	0.00	0.00	0.00	11.00
Dividend Yield (%)	0.00	0.00	0.00	0.00	9.17
Sales per Share	2,424.35	1,919.93	1,741.99	1,468.33	1,653.12
EPS before extra. item	(4.21)	(29.76)	(43.87)	(26.67)	(6.89)
Cash Flow per Share	48.97	(0.86)	10.90	13.48	23.69
Book Value per Share	59.17	52.85	81.61	125.83	172.73
O/S Common Shares (mil)	8	8	8	8	8
Total Revenue ($mil)	20,139	15,954	14,474	12,248	13,798
Income before extra. ($mil)	(35)	(247)	(364)	(221)	(57)
Cash Flow ($mil)	406	(7)	90	112	196
Debt/Equity	0.52	0.78	0.64	0.50	0.34
Return on Capital (%)	(2.35)	(41.06)	(38.23)	(12.59)	(1.66)
Ret. on Com. Equity (%)	(7.52)	(44.26)	(42.31)	(17.86)	(3.78)
% Change Profit	85.9	32.2	(64.5)	(287.2)	(118.2)
% Change Revenue	26.2	10.2	18.2	(11.2)	(10.4)
% Change Assets	19.3	8.6	9.3	(0.3)	1.0

	Dec94	Dec93	Dec92
Preferred Div. Coverage	np	np	np
Total Div. Coverage	na	na	na
Interest Coverage	0.0	0.0	0.0
Current Ratio	0.6	0.6	0.9
Operating Margin	0.4	(2.3)	(2.9)
Asset Turnover	4.0	3.8	3.7
5 YEAR RATIOS (%)			
Return on Capital	(19.2)	(12.0)	2.7
Return on Com. Equity	(23.1)	(17.5)	(4.4)
Profit Growth	na	na	na
Revenue Growth	5.5	(0.2)	0.5
Asset Growth	7.3	3.1	1.3
BALANCE SHEET (000)			
Cash	223,900	221,600	375,500
Current Assets	1,886,500	1,647,600	1,690,800
Net Fixed Assets	2,566,000	2,194,300	1,895,600
Invest's & Advances	54,500	44,500	44,200
Total Assets	5,029,000	4,216,100	3,881,900
Short Term Debt	170,000	221,200	93,100
Current Liabilities	3,392,600	2,743,100	1,973,000
Long Term Debt	86,200	120,300	340,400
Total Liabilities	4,538,400	3,777,900	3,205,300
Total Equity	490,600	438,200	676,600
Total Liab. & Equity	5,029,000	4,216,100	3,881,900
CAPITAL (000)			
Total Debt	256,200	341,500	433,500
Preferred Equity	0	0	0
Common Equity	490,600	438,200	676,600

Business:

FORD MOTOR CO. OF CANADA LTD. is a major automotive manufacturer and distributor. The company operates assembly plants in Oakville and St. Thomas, ON, and casting plants in Windsor. Cars and trucks are sold through a national network of dealers. The company has subsidiaries in Australia and New Zealand. Ford Motor Co. of Michigan owns 94% of the company's shares.

Date	EPS	DPS	Tot Rev	Inc Bex
Mar 95	(4.46)	0.00	5,380,000	(37,060)
Dec 94	(1.93)	0.00	5,630,400	(16,000)
Sep 94	0.67	0.00	4,603,100	5,500
Jun 94	8.46	0.00	5,962,300	70,200
Mar 94	(11.41)	0.00	3,905,200	(94,600)
Dec 93	(19.43)	0.00	4,071,700	(161,100)
Sep 93	(13.73)	0.00	3,615,600	(113,800)
Jun 93	1.66	0.00	4,607,900	13,700

Synopsis:

In May 1995, Ford Motor Company of Canada Limited announced plans to invest an additional $500-million at its Ontario Truck Plant. Ford Canada will build and equip a 400,000 square foot body shop, and modify the existing plant. A $423-million paint facility under construction at the same plant will be completed early next year. The Ontario Truck Plant manufactures the F-Series pickup truck, the best selling vehicle in Canada last year.

In April 1995, Ford Canada's parent company said it will buy the remaining shares of Ford Canada. It plans to merge Ford Canada with a wholly owned Canadian subsidiary, Ford Ensite International Inc.

Despite a 28% jump in total sales in the fourth quarter, Ford Canada still recorded a net loss. Vehicle sales were 217,600 units, up 42,800 from 1994. This improvement was attributed to increased export sales to Ford U.S., higher sales to dealers, and an improved mix of sales. The higher sales were offset by unfavourable exchange rate costs resulting from a weak Canadian dollar. Combined car and truck sales rose by 8% while its market share hit 21.7%, up from 21.3%. In 1994, Ford cars accounted for 17% of industry retail sales versus 28.7% for trucks.

Fiscal 1994 represented the best sales performance for Ford Canada since 1989. The success was attributed to sales of the F-Series pickup trucks, its minivans, Mustangs, and Escorts. During the year, truck sales were up 17.9% versus 38.7% for car sales. During 1994, sales by geographic segment at Ford Canada were: Canada, 84%; Australia, 14%; and New Zealand, 2%. Canadian sales included export sales of $10.79-billion.

In 1995, Ford Canada expects strong exports to the U.S. and increased sales of cars and trucks. The profitability of the Canadian operations will again be affected by the Canadian dollar. Ford Canada also expects improvements in the Australian and New Zealand economies in the year.

Relative strength to TSE300

Price

Volume (in 1000's of board lots)

Rank (Profit/Revenue/Assets)
981 2 39

Mark W. Hutchins
President & C.E.O.

Address
The Canadian Road
Oakville
ON
L6J 5E4
(905) 845-2511

Fax: (905) 844-8085
F0001536/G/5.6

MAGNA INTERNATIONAL INC.

Exchanges	Price (Jun29'95)		58 .75	Trailing P/E		11 .82	Stock Symbol
TMN	Trailing Yield (%)		1 .82	Trailing EPS		4 .91	**MG.A**

Period Ending	Ju l94	Ju l93	Ju l92	Ju l91	Ju l90
Yearly Statistics					
Price-Close	57 .50	50 .50	30 .38	12 .88	3 .60
Price-High	73 .75	52 .13	35 .25	14 .25	13 .38
Price-Low	46 .75	22 .00	12 .13	2 .10	3 .15
P/E-Close	13 .76	16 .34	10 .44	21 .82	nm
Dividends per Share	0 .93	0 .60	0 .20	0 .00	0 .24
Dividend Yield (%)	1 .62	1 .19	0 .66	0 .00	6 .67
Sales per Share	63 .75	57 .36	70 .15	72 .50	69 .28
EPS before extra. item	4 .18	3 .09	2 .91	0 .59	(8 .06)
Cash Flow per Share	6 .46	5 .77	7 .30	5 .46	2 .62
Book Value per Share	21 .72	16 .91	14 .74	9 .63	8 .31
O/S Common Shares	60 ,777	49 ,936	40 ,044	27 ,849	27 ,819
Total Revenue	3 ,601 ,600	2 ,625 ,000	2 ,360 ,400	2 ,014 ,500	1 ,930 ,700
Income before extra.	234 ,400	140 ,400	98 ,000	16 ,500	(224 ,200)
Cash Flow	361 ,500	262 ,100	245 ,300	151 ,800	72 ,800
Debt/Equity	0 .07	0 .12	0 .55	2 .82	nd
Return on Capital (%)	31 .33	23 .43	20 .37	20 .03	(14 .21)
Ret. on Com. Equity (%)	21 .66	19 .57	22 .83	6 .61	(64 .48)
% Change Profit	67 .0	43 .3	493 .9	107 .4	(767 .0)
% Change Revenue	37 .2	11 .2	17 .2	4 .3	(3 .6)
% Change Assets	49 .0	10 .7	(4 .6)	(18 .3)	(3 .5)

Preferred Div. Coverage	np	np	np
Total Div. Coverage	5 .1	5 .6	13 .2
Interest Coverage	65 .9	12 .7	4 .0
Current Ratio	1 .4	1 .4	1 .2
Operating Margin	9 .9	8 .4	9 .0
Asset Turnover	1 .5	1 .7	1 .7
5 YEAR RATIOS (%)			
Return on Capital	16 .2	11 .8	8 .6
Return on Com. Equity	1 .2	(1 .6)	(4 .7)
Profit Growth	47 .5	48 .3	19 .4
Revenue Growth	12 .4	12 .2	15 .1
Asset Growth	4 .4	(1 .5)	1 .7
BALANCE SHEET (000)			
Cash	205 ,000	105 ,000	51 ,600
Current Assets	1 ,063 ,800	626 ,600	500 ,200
Net Fixed Assets	925 ,600	707 ,200	706 ,200
Invest's & Advances	183 ,100	103 ,900	80 ,300
Total Assets	2 ,310 ,600	1 ,551 ,100	1 ,401 ,400
Short Term Debt	44 ,100	7 ,600	79 ,700
Current Liabilities	750 ,200	438 ,000	413 ,300
Long Term Debt	43 ,700	94 ,800	245 ,700
Total Liabilities	990 ,800	706 ,700	811 ,100
Total Equity	1 ,319 ,800	844 ,400	590 ,300
Total Liab. & Equity	2 ,310 ,600	1 ,551 ,100	1 ,401 ,400
CAPITAL (000)			
Total Debt	87 ,800	102 ,400	325 ,400
Preferred Equity	0	0	0
Common Equity	1 ,319 ,800	844 ,400	590 ,300

Business:

MAGNA INTERNATIONAL INC. designs and manufactures a broad range of automotive components and systems for the North American facilities of the major automobile manufacturers. The company has plants across North America and also in Europe. Products include exterior and interior decorative products, seating systems, airbags, electronic devices, formed and welded metal parts, and sunroofs.

Date		EPS	DPS	Tot Rev	Inc Bex
Apr	95	1 .31	0 .27	1 ,230 ,000	79 ,800
Jan	95	1 .20	0 .27	1 ,111 ,800	73 ,400
Oct	94	1 .33	0 .27	1 ,052 ,000	80 ,800
Jul	94	1 .07	0 .26	1 ,048 ,500	65 ,200
Apr	94	1 .28	0 .20	1 ,024 ,100	72 ,400
Jan	94	0 .89	0 .20	784 ,900	49 ,700
Oct	93	0 .93	0 .15	744 ,100	47 ,100
Jul	93	0 .75	0 .15	654 ,800	39 ,600

Synopsis:

Magna International Inc.'s strong fiscal 1995 third quarter was attributed to increased North American car and light truck production, increased equity income, and lower interest costs and income taxes. Magna believes that the North American market should remain strong for the next few years. The European economy should continue its recovery, and costs related to Magna's European operations should fall. As well, the dollar value of Magna content in North American cars should increase over the next two years.

During the third quarter, problems associated with Chrysler minivan production led to the temporary closing of several plants. There was also a sales-related shut-down at Chrysler's sedan assembly plant in Bramalea, Ontario. Magna is endeavouring to increase sales to customers other than Chrysler. These efforts were recently rewarded when General Motors chose Magna as its worldwide supplier of the year.

Also in the quarter, Magna closed the previously announced acquisition of a 90% interest in EYBL Durmont AG. EYBL supplies interior components to several European auto manufacturers, and has annual sales of about $175-million. The deal is part of Magna's strategy to expand operations in Europe and strengthen its position in the global automotive market. Magna's European operations are active in Germany, Austria, the United Kingdom, Spain, and the Czech and Slovak Republics. They have annualized sales worth $1-billion.

In January 1995, Magna received a $500-million a year contract from General Motors. Magna's Cosma Body & Chassis Systems Group signed a deal with GM to produce frames for GM's 1997 light-duty trucks. Magna has refined technology that will reduce costs and cut up to 25% of the weight of a vehicle. Magna also has agreements to supply radiator supports for Ford and engine cradles for Chrysler Corp. In December 1994, Ford elected Magna as its "general contractor" for a new 1998 model. This is first such deal with an automotive parts supplier. Magna will design, develop, and engineer the new model.

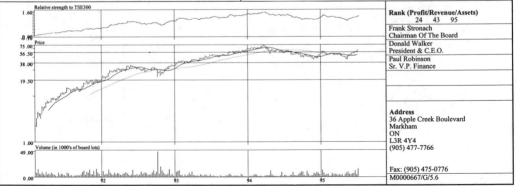

Rank (Profit/Revenue/Assets)
24   43   95
Frank Stronach
Chairman Of The Board
Donald Walker
President & C.E.O.
Paul Robinson
Sr. V.P. Finance

Address
36 Apple Creek Boulevard
Markham
ON
L3R 4Y4
(905) 477-7766

Fax: (905) 475-0776
M0000667/G/5.6

MERIDIAN TECHNOLOGIES INC.

Exchanges	Price (Jun29'95)		6.25	Trailing P/E		nm	Stock Symbol
T	Trailing Yield (%)		0.00	Trailing EPS		(0.33)	**MNI**

Period Ending	Mar95	Mar94	Mar93	Mar92	Mar91
Yearly Statistics					
Price-Close	5.75	9.50	6.75	1.50	1.50
Price-High	10.38	11.88	7.38	4.50	2.70
Price-Low	4.30	6.38	3.50	1.45	1.45
P/E-Close	nm	50.00	28.13	7.50	nm
Dividends per Share	0.00	0.00	0.00	0.00	0.05
Dividend Yield (%)	0.00	0.00	0.00	0.00	3.33
Sales per Share	8.60	8.39	9.47	11.63	12.22
EPS before extra. item	(0.33)	0.19	0.24	0.20	(0.34)
Cash Flow per Share	(0.03)	0.45	0.69	0.70	0.26
Book Value per Share	5.21	5.08	3.80	3.00	2.76
O/S Common Shares	26,257	21,028	16,297	12,500	8,349
Total Revenue	199,372	147,806	126,312	105,153	101,714
Income before extra.	(7,743)	3,306	3,173	1,766	(2,858)
Cash Flow	(795)	7,950	9,176	6,369	2,202
Debt/Equity	0.35	0.19	0.43	0.81	1.74
Return on Capital (%)	(4.77)	6.46	10.02	9.74	5.14
Ret. on Com. Equity (%)	(6.36)	3.92	6.38	5.84	(11.60)
% Change Profit	(334.2)	4.2	79.7	161.8	(205.2)
% Change Revenue	34.9	17.0	20.1	3.4	27.3
% Change Assets	49.2	40.7	34.3	11.7	(9.6)

Business:
MERIDIAN TECHNOLOGIES INC. is a Canadian company whose principal business is the manufacture of aluminum and magnesium high pressure die cast original equipment components for the North American automotive industry.

Date	EPS	DPS	Tot Rev	Inc Bex
Mar 95	(0.04)	0.00	61,195	(1,333)
Dec 94	(0.11)	0.00	49,275	(2,544)
Sep 94	(0.12)	0.00	42,495	(2,520)
Jun 94	(0.06)	0.00	46,407	(1,346)
Mar 94	0.04	0.00	42,395	721
Dec 93	0.05	0.00	37,470	1,002
Sep 93	0.02	0.00	31,686	348
Jun 93	0.08	0.00	35,988	1,235

Preferred Div. Coverage	np	np	np
Total Div. Coverage	na	na	na
Interest Coverage	0.0	4.8	4.0
Current Ratio	1.7	2.1	2.5
Operating Margin	(3.7)	4.5	6.0
Asset Turnover	0.9	1.0	1.1
5 YEAR RATIOS (%)			
Return on Capital	5.3	9.0	11.7
Return on Com. Equity	(0.4)	3.1	4.7
Profit Growth	na	4.6	6.6
Revenue Growth	20.0	13.8	19.4
Asset Growth	23.2	25.1	18.6
BALANCE SHEET (000)			
Cash	3,979	4,591	18,485
Current Assets	83,234	56,729	59,574
Net Fixed Assets	126,512	92,956	43,257
Invest's & Advances	220	1,322	3,263
Total Assets	230,184	154,309	109,677
Short Term Debt	3,914	2,006	4,934
Current Liabilities	49,233	27,511	24,209
Long Term Debt	44,163	18,394	21,565
Total Liabilities	93,396	47,535	47,754
Total Equity	136,788	106,774	61,923
Total Liab. & Equity	230,184	154,309	109,677
CAPITAL (000)			
Total Debt	48,077	20,400	26,499
Preferred Equity	0	0	0
Common Equity	136,788	106,774	61,923

Synopsis:

In the first quarter 1995, Meridian Technologies announced that its Eaton Rapid's started commercial operation with 10 of the 14 planned die cast machines installed. The plant makes products for three of Meridian's six customers, including Chrysler Corp.

In November 1994, Italy-based Teksid S.P.A. completed the acquisition of about 4.36-million common shares of Meridian pursuant to a private placement for about $28.5-million. Consequently, Teksid controls a 16.7% stake in Meridian before dilution and is now one of the largest single shareholders of Meridian. Further to the deal, Teksid sold its joint venture interest in Meridian Magnesium N.V. to Meridian. Meridian now controls 100% of Meridian Magnesium N.V. Meridian Magnesium N.V. is in the process of building a plant in Italy to manufacture magnesium die cast components for the automotive industry. The purchase by Teksid is said to be for investment purposes only.

In October 1994, Meridian said it would build a third magnesium casting plant in North America for about $60-million. This plant will handle new auto parts orders from General Motors Corp. The company has two other magnesium casting plants in Strathroy, Ontario, and Eaton Rapids, Michigan. The new plant will be completed by the end of 1996. Two GM light-truck orders will account for 70% of the plant's capacity. The GM deal represents annual revenues of $70-million. Meridian also has three aluminum casting plants in Canada.

In August 1994, GM nominated Meridian as supplier of magnesium instrument panels for the GMT 800 series of light trucks. This deal is worth about $35-million annually. The deal will start in the 1998 model year and is expected to continue over 10 years. Meridian believes that this deal signifies the importance of magnesium in the automotive industry.

Relative strength to TSE300

Rank (Profit/Revenue/Assets)
500   361   389
Anthony F. Griffiths
Chairman
Scott Griffin
President & C.E.O.
Gary S. Love
Vice President & C.F.O.

Address
Suite 1700
2 St. Clair Avenue West
Toronto
ON
M4V 1L5
(416) 922-2050

Fax: (416) 922-4282
M0015718/G/5.6

SOUTH CHINA INDUSTRIES (CANADA) INC.

Exchanges	Price (Jun29'95)		1.00	Trailing P/E		8.33	Stock Symbol
T	Trailing Yield (%)		0.00	Trailing EPS		0.12	**SGC**

Period Ending	Dec94	Dec93	Dec92
Yearly Statistics			
Price-Close	1.59	5.75	n t
Price-High	6.38	6.38	n t
Price-Low	1.16	5.00	n t
P/E-Close	10.60	287.50	n t
Dividends per Share	0.00	0.00	0.00
Dividend Yield (%)	0.00	0.00	0.00
Sales per Share	2.39	0.23	0.00
EPS before extra. item	0.15	0.02	(0.03)
Cash Flow per Share	0.24	0.04	(0.03)
Book Value per Share	3.09	2.79	(0.08)
O/S Common Shares	27,502	28,026	707
Total Revenue	68,198	5,325	0
Income before extra.	4,203	548	(20)
Cash Flow	6,738	796	(20)
Debt/Equity	0.09	nd	na
Return on Capital (%)	5.54	1.40	na
Ret. on Com. Equity (%)	5.16	1.40	na
% Change Profit	667.1	2,888.8	na
% Change Revenue	1,180.8	na	na
% Change Assets	32.1	nm	na
Preferred Div. Coverage	np	np	np
Total Div. Coverage	na	na	na
Interest Coverage	9.0	nd	na
Current Ratio	3.4	19.5	0.0
Operating Margin	6.5	11.4	na
Asset Turnover	0.5	0.1	0.0
5 YEAR RATIOS (%)			
Return on Capital	na	na	na
Return on Com. Equity	na	na	na
Profit Growth	na	na	na
Revenue Growth	na	na	na
Asset Growth	na	na	na
BALANCE SHEET (000)			
Cash	31,507	56,558	0
Current Assets	85,263	73,914	0
Net Fixed Assets	34,552	19,668	0
Invest's & Advances	1,868	0	0
Total Assets	123,590	93,582	0
Short Term Debt	7,633	0	50
Current Liabilities	25,217	3,793	54
Long Term Debt	0	0	0
Total Liabilities	38,683	15,458	54
Total Equity	84,906	78,124	(54)
Total Liab. & Equity	123,590	93,582	0
CAPITAL (000)			
Total Debt	7,633	0	50
Preferred Equity	0	0	0
Common Equity	84,906	78,124	(54)

Business:

SOUTH CHINA INDUSTRIES (CANADA) INC. is a holding company whose major asset is an 80% interest in Guilin South Rubber International Corporation, a Sino-foreign equity joint venture enterprise located in the People's Republic of China. Guilin South Rubber International Corporation manufactures tires for engineering machinery, loading vehicles, light trucks, automobiles and agriculture equipment.

Date	EPS	DPS	Tot Rev	Inc Bex
Mar 95	0.02	0.00	17,473	531
Dec 94	0.00	0.00	20,994	(121)
Sep 94	0.05	0.00	19,561	1,537
Jun 94	0.05	0.00	15,665	1,374
Mar 94	0.05	0.00	11,978	1,413

Synopsis:

In January 1995, South China Industries (Canada) Inc. announced changes to its management team. Ivy Chan was named Deputy Chairman. John Pennal was named President and C.E.O. Anthony Tam was named C.F.O.

South China Industries operates its business in a precarious economic and political environment. Despite strong results, fiscal 1994 proved to be challenging as the Chinese government continued to control inflation through credit tightening measures, slowing growth in the industrial sector. Consequently, fewer funds were available to the clients of South China Industries. This affected the company's accounts receivable. Furthermore, costs associated with raw materials increased significantly, especially the price of natural rubber. To reduce its dependence on the Chinese domestic market, South China Industries initiated an export sales strategy. It opened a new export sales office in Guangzhou. Several export sales to North America, South America, Asia-Pacific, South Africa, and Europe were carried out or negotiated in the first quarter 1995. The company aims to increase exports to 30% of total sales by early 1996.

To improve its distribution network in China, South China Industries formed a new tire distribution company with Singapore-based Stamford Tires. The new venture will develop wholesale and retail tire distribution centres in China. The company postponed planned expansion into the passenger car radial tire market due to competition. It will concentrate on its specialties, off-the-road (OTR) light truck, truck, and agricultural bias tire segments. South China Industries believes that capacity utilization and economies of scale are the key issues for achieving long-term profitability. The company will concentrate on the non-passenger car bias tire market, and expand production in this area. Contingent on obtaining a business license, South China Industries agreed to buy a 90% equity interest in Wuhan S.C.I. Tire Co., a China-foreign equity joint venture, for $6-million. The assets of this company consist mainly of land use rights, buildings, and machinery tire production.

Rank (Profit/Revenue/Assets)		
454	486	437

Shan Ho
Chairman

Ivy Chan
Deputy Chairman

John Pennal
President & C.E.O.

Address
Suite 7028
1 First Canadian Place
Toronto
ON
M5X 1E5
(416) 956-4926

Fax: (416) 956-4930
01003517/G/5.6

TCG INTERNATIONAL INC.

Exchanges	Price (Jun29'95)		4.20	Trailing P/E		22.11	Stock Symbol
TMV	Trailing Yield (%)		2.14	Trailing EPS		0.19	**TCG.A**

Period Ending	Dec94	Dec93	Dec92	Dec91	Dec90	Business:
Yearly Statistics						TCG INTERNATIONAL INC. is a retail and
Price-Close	4.95	6.00	4.15	3.50	3.65	wholesale distributor of automotive glass in
Price-High	7.25	7.38	5.00	5.75	9.75	Canada and the United States. The Company is
Price-Low	4.75	2.50	3.30	3.20	3.00	also active in the retail sales and distribution of
P/E-Close	123.75	6.00	3.43	nm	nm	automotive parts such as mufflers, brakes, tires
Dividends per Share	0.62	0.37	0.10	0.10	0.10	and audio systems through its majority
Dividend Yield (%)	12.53	6.17	2.41	2.86	2.74	ownership in Autostock Inc. Through its
Sales per Share	16.35	16.12	16.17	16.07	21.30	majority interest in Glentel Inc., the Company
EPS before extra. item	0.04	1.00	1.21	(0.22)	(1.63)	is involved in the mobile communications
Cash Flow per Share	0.47	(0.09)	(0.17)	0.16	0.70	industry.
Book Value per Share	3.08	3.67	3.08	2.00	2.31	
O/S Common Shares	23,718	23,370	23,263	23,253	23,253	

Period Ending	Dec94	Dec93	Dec92	Dec91	Dec90
Total Revenue	394,639	425,595	389,339	374,735	496,523
Income before extra.	1,043	23,490	28,074	(5,069)	(37,868)
Cash Flow	11,051	(2,011)	(3,967)	3,835	16,338

Date	EPS	DPS	Tot Rev	Inc Bex
Mar 95	0.07	0.03	93,918	1,644
Dec 94	(0.02)	0.03	99,781	(451)
Sep 94	0.03	0.03	102,077	734
Jun 94	0.11	0.00	106,230	2,586
Mar 94	(0.08)	0.55	85,363	(1,826)
Dec 93	0.94	0.03	134,160	22,027
Sep 93	(0.01)	0.09	98,490	(143)
Jun 93	0.10	0.28	104,347	2,377

Period Ending	Dec94	Dec93	Dec92	Dec91	Dec90
Debt/Equity	1.44	0.97	0.85	3.62	3.22
Return on Capital (%)	6.57	28.83	24.13	3.50	(2.55)
Ret. on Com. Equity (%)	1.31	29.85	47.59	(10.11)	(51.48)
% Change Profit	(95.6)	(16.3)	653.8	86.6	(462.8)
% Change Revenue	(7.3)	9.3	3.9	(24.5)	19.4
% Change Assets	3.4	18.8	(29.2)	(6.1)	(20.3)

Preferred Div. Coverage	np	np	np
Total Div. Coverage	0.1	2.7	11.8
Interest Coverage	1.9	8.5	5.6
Current Ratio	2.3	2.5	2.0
Operating Margin	2.3	0.9	(1.0)
Asset Turnover	1.4	1.4	1.7
5 YEAR RATIOS (%)			
Return on Capital	12.1	14.3	12.7
Return on Com. Equity	3.4	6.0	2.6
Profit Growth	(37.0)	29.8	42.0
Revenue Growth	(1.1)	9.6	11.9
Asset Growth	(8.3)	11.8	12.0
BALANCE SHEET (000)			
Cash	14,593	42,073	9,920
Current Assets	138,878	147,563	123,124
Net Fixed Assets	79,781	72,344	68,736
Invest's & Advances	32,169	25,397	18,995
Total Assets	275,046	266,049	224,035
Short Term Debt	1,988	1,164	4,741
Current Liabilities	59,319	57,959	62,646
Long Term Debt	103,206	82,090	56,167
Total Liabilities	201,897	180,193	152,501
Total Equity	73,149	85,856	71,534
Total Liab. & Equity	275,046	266,049	224,035
CAPITAL (000)			
Total Debt	105,194	83,254	60,908
Preferred Equity	0	0	0
Common Equity	73,149	85,856	71,534

Synopsis:

In the first quarter of 1995, TCG International Inc., reported a pre-tax gain on the sale of shares in Glenayre Technologies, Inc. worth $9.8-million. Also during the quarter, franchise sales were $25.5-million, up 67% from 1994.

In fiscal 1994, TCG reached its goal of becoming a vertically integrated, automotive glass business. It bought a 30% interest in a new manufacturing plant in Spain. The Spanish plant will be an additional source of supply for TCG's European and North American retail and distribution operations. Responding to intense competition, TCG has expanded the products and services offered at its retail locations. To improve the operational efficiency of its Canadian distribution operations, TCG combined three Toronto distribution centres into one major hub. TCG expects to add distribution centres in strategic locations in the U.S.

TCG's 58%owned communications subsidiary, Glentel Inc., signed an agreement in 1994 to be the first national satellite full-service provider for TMI Communications, a subsidiary of BCE Inc. Glentel has committed to purchase $9-million worth of satellite airtime services over a three year period beginning in 1995.

Also in fiscal 1994, TCG acquired the assets of seven automotive aftermarket businesses in Canada and the U.S. TCG also bought about 60% of the outstanding shares of an automotive parts distributor in Western Europe. TCG sold 450,000 shares of Glentel Inc. and 1.5 million shares of Autostock Inc. during fiscal 1994. This reduced its equity interests to 58% and 65% respectively at year end. TCG also sold 50,000 shares of Glenayre Technologies.

In 1994 TCG's sales by geographic segment were: Canada, 83.5%; the U.S., 16%; and other, 0.5%. Sales by operating segment were: automotive, 90%; and communication, 10%.

Relative strength to TSE300
Price
Volume (in 1000's of board lots)

Rank (Profit/Revenue/Assets)
197 211 307

Arthur Skidmore
Chairman Of The Board & C.E.O.

Ronald E. Sowerby
Exec. V.P. Fin. C.F.O. & Sec.

A. Allan Skidmore
Vice Chairman Operations

Address
28th Floor
4710 Kingsway
Burnaby
BC
V5H 4M2
(604) 431-2300

Fax: (604) 438-7414

T0002435/G/5.6

WESTERN STAR TRUCK HOLDINGS LTD.

Exchanges	Price (Jun29'95)	20.50	Trailing P/E	5.94	Stock Symbol
TM	Trailing Yield (%)	1.12	Trailing EPS	3.45	**WS**

Period Ending	Jun94	Jun93
Yearly Statistics		
Price-Close	10.50	n t
Price-High	11.38	n t
Price-Low	10.25	n t
P/E-Close	4.02	n t
Dividends per Share	0.00	0.00
Dividend Yield (%)	0.00	0.00
Sales per Share	52.76	26.76
EPS before extra. item	2.61	0.32
Cash Flow per Share	2.98	0.61
Book Value per Share	4.02	(0.68)
O/S Common Shares	11,131	7,731
Total Revenue	426,974	206,872
Income before extra.	21,122	2,509
Cash Flow	24,127	4,743
Debt/Equity	0.43	na
Return on Capital (%)	68.03	na
Ret. on Com. Equity (%)	107.01	na
% Change Profit	741.8	na
% Change Revenue	106.4	na
% Change Assets	137.1	na

Preferred Div. Coverage	np	np
Total Div. Coverage	na	na
Interest Coverage	57.3	4.5
Current Ratio	1.3	0.9
Operating Margin	6.5	1.9
Asset Turnover	2.6	3.0
5 YEAR RATIOS (%)		
Return on Capital	na	na
Return on Com. Equity	na	na
Profit Growth	na	na
Revenue Growth	na	na
Asset Growth	na	na
BALANCE SHEET (000)		
Cash	20,863	423
Current Assets	136,742	50,263
Net Fixed Assets	10,967	8,869
Invest's & Advances	0	0
Total Assets	161,913	68,291
Short Term Debt	5,683	11,052
Current Liabilities	103,900	57,172
Long Term Debt	13,318	7,386
Total Liabilities	117,218	73,508
Total Equity	44,695	(5,217)
Total Liab. & Equity	161,913	68,291
CAPITAL (000)		
Total Debt	19,001	18,438
Preferred Equity	0	0
Common Equity	44,695	(5,217)

Business:

WESTERN STAR TRUCK HOLDINGS LTD. custom designs and builds heavy duty trucks with a gross vehicle weight in excess of 33,000 lbs., primarily for use in highway freight haulage and in construction, logging, oilfield service and mining industries. The company also assembles light support vehicles in a variety of configurations for specified military and defense purposes.

Date	EPS	DPS	Tot Rev	Inc Bex
Mar 95	0.99	0.10	205,813	11,042
Dec 94	0.86	0.10	176,952	9,576
Sep 94	1.07	0.03	152,373	11,868
Jun 94	0.99	0.00	146,248	8,653
Mar 94	0.73	0.00	118,674	5,629
Dec 93	0.53	0.00	91,019	4,080
Sep 93	0.36	0.00	71,033	2,760

Synopsis:

For the third quarter of fiscal 1995, Western Star Trucks Holdings Ltd. continued its strong performance. During the quarter, demand for Western Star's heavy duty trucks remained high, with the order backlog jumping 21.2%. To keep pace with demand, the company made upgraded its manufacturing and paint lines.

Western Star's dealer network expanded its Middle East segment with the signing of new dealer arrangements in Oman and the United Arab Emirates. The company also received a $2.6-million order for custom built trucks from a Lebanon company.

In April 1994, Western Star signed a letter of intent with the Ontario government to buy certain assets of Ontario Bus Industries Inc. and its U.S. subsidiary, Bus Industries of America. Ontario Bus has about $200-million worth of contracts to supply buses to 38 transit organizations in North America. Western Star will pay about $35-million, subject to certain closing adjustments. Western Star will invest $15-million from available cash in a new wholly owned subsidiary that will acquire assets from Ontario Bus. An additional $20-million will come from other non-reimbursable sources. The Ontario government will also invest $15-million in preferred shares of the new company.

Fiscal 1994 was a tremendous year for Western Star as revenues jumped 106%. This was due to the robust North American economy, and the pent-up demand for heavy duty trucks. Western Star is experiencing steady diversification into international markets, a strong aftermarket parts business, and success as a supplier of military vehicles. The company is pursuing joint venture manufacturing opportunities in Mexico and China. It plans to continue expanding its dealer networks domestically and internationally. Sales in Australia, Indonesia, and the Middle East rose in the past year due to the expanded international dealer network. In 1994, sales by geographic segment were: Canada, 41%; the U.S., 42%; and international, 17%.

Relative strength to TSE300 / Price / Volume (in 1000's of board lots)

Rank (Profit/Revenue/Assets)		
205	209	382

Terrence E. Peabody
Chairman President & C.E.O.

Gerard J. McParland
Exec. V.P. & C.O.O

Address
2076 Enterprise Way
Kelowna
BC
V1Y 6H8
(604) 860-3319

Fax: (604) 860-1252
01003652/G/5.6

| | | | EARNINGS PER SHARE | | |
| | | Fiscal | Last | Estimate | Estimate |
Page	Company	year end	Year	this year	next year
227	Biochem Pharmaceuticals	Dec-94	(0.30)	(0.18)	0.38
228	Biomira	Dec-94	(1.27)	(0.88)	(0.95)
229	Draxis Health	Dec-94	0.06	0.05	0.06
230	International Murex Technologies	Dec-94	0.30	0.32	0.49
231	Quadra Logic Technologies	Dec-94	(0.63)	(0.47)	(0.26)
232	Spectral Diagnostics	Mar-94	(0.64)	(1.20)	0.00

Estimates from First Call Corporation, 22 Pittsburgh Street, Boston, MA 02210   (800) 366-9992   Fax (617) 261-5679

Biotechnology & Pharmaceuticals

The Biotechnology and Pharmaceutical sector constantly undergoes ups and downs from the initial discovery of a drug or process, through in-depth product testing, and finally, to federal approval for release.

In July 1995, major drug manufacturers initiated a pre-emptive strike against a British Columbia proposal known as reference-based pricing. This is an attempt by the B.C. government to significantly reduce health care costs. The proposal would allow Pharmacare, the provincial drug plan, to only pay for the lowest-priced treatment found to be effective. The Patent Medicine Prices Review Board released findings which showed that in 1993, only eight of 42 new drugs were breakthroughs or new treatments. The other 34 offered little or no improvement over existing treatments, according to Pharmacare officials.

In 1994, the price of patented-drugs dropped for the first time since 1987 when the federal government moved to extend the patents of drug companies. According to Ottawa's drug price watchdog, the Patented Medicine Prices Review Board, the drop proves that the government is keeping excessive price hikes by manufacturers in check.

The patented medicines price index declined 0.42% in 1994 compared to 1993. Since 1987, patented drug prices have increased an average of 2.1% annually. From 1983 to 1987, drug prices increased 7.5% annually. The board can require drug manufacturers to keep annual wholesale price hikes for patented drugs in line with the Consumer Price Index. However, Canadian drug prices were 55% more than world prices in 1993.

Manufacturers in Canada have lengthy patent protection. Drug companies have increased spending on research and development since the federal government extended the length of patent protection by passing law C-91. In 1994, according to the Board, drug companies spent $561-million on R&D, up from $503-million in 1993. The ratio of R&D to sales was 11.3%, up from 10.6% in 1993. The companies had pledged to spend 10% of total sales on R&D if C-91 won approval. Furthermore, companies are spending less on basic research and more on field and clinical trials. Spending on basic research fell for the first time since 1987 and represents 22% of total R&D spending by the industry. The volume of patented drugs sold increased 5.7% in 1994, the smallest increase since 1990.

Brand-name and generic drug companies have joined forces to push the federal government to speed up the approval process for new drugs.

The industry believes that Canada's drug-approval system is among the slowest and most inefficient among drug-producing countries. The groups involved include the Pharmaceutical Manufacturers Association of Canada, which represents the brand-name drug companies, and the CDMA, representing generic manufacturers. At present, according to the groups, it takes up to four years to get a generic drug approved in Canada and nearly three years for a brand-name or innovator drug.

Britain, which has an independent drug approval agency, reviews nearly 89% of generic drugs in 60 days or less, according to figures from the CDMA. In the United States, the review process for generics and brand-name drugs takes about two years.

In the U.S., health maintenance organizations (HMOs) and other managed health care plans often use the less expensive generics. According to some analysts, generics could represent about 50% of the prescription drug market by the year 2000. However, generic drug manufacturers face some tough hurdles. HMOs are demanding larger price reductions and a broader selection. As well, the drug companies must deal with the U.S. Food and Drug Administration, a strict regulator.

BIOCHEM PHARMA INC.

Exchanges	Price (Jun29'95)		29 .50	Trailing P/E		nm	Stock Symbol
TM	Trailing Yield (%)		0 .00	Trailing EPS		(0 .25)	BCH

Period Ending	Dec94	Jan94	Jan93	Jan92	Jan91	Business:
Yearly Statistics	11M					BIOCHEM PHARMA INC. is a
Price-Close	17 .25	17 .00	19 .75	30 .50	6 .50	Canadian-based pharmaceutical company
Price-High	18 .25	19 .63	35 .50	30 .88	7 .00	engaged in the research, development and
Price-Low	11 .50	11 .13	12 .68	6 .38	2 .50	commercialization of high quality prodcuts for
P/E-Close	nm	nm	nm	82 .43	nm	the diagnosis, treatment and prevention of
Dividends per Share	0 .00	0 .00	0 .00	0 .00	0 .00	human diseases.
Dividend Yield (%)	0 .00	0 .00	0 .00	0 .00	0 .00	
Sales per Share	2 .29	0 .69	0 .69	0 .59	0 .31	
EPS before extra. item	(0 .30)	(0 .21)	(0 .32)	0 .37	(0 .03)	
Cash Flow per Share	0 .01	(0 .00)	(0 .12)	0 .05	0 .03	
Book Value per Share	2 .10	2 .25	2 .45	2 .12	1 .18	
O/S Common Shares	47 ,313	46 ,968	46 ,653	39 ,700	33 ,599	

Total Revenue	109 ,721	42 ,196	36 ,568	47 ,359	16 ,461	
Income before extra.	(14 ,156)	(9 ,712)	(13 ,147)	12 ,674	(925)	

Date	EPS	DPS	Tot Rev	Inc Bex
Cash Flow	541	(181)	(4 ,929)	1 ,562	863	Mar 95	(0 .02)	0 .00	48 ,820	(996)
Debt/Equity	0 .94	0 .19	0 .08	0 .14	0 .13	Dec 94	(0 .09)	0 .00	27 ,409	(4 ,184)
Return on Capital (%)	(4 .53)	(5 .95)	(10 .54)	18 .72	(1 .52)	Oct 94	(0 .12)	0 .00	42 ,715	(5 ,364)
Ret. on Com. Equity (%)	(15 .06)	(8 .83)	(13 .27)	20 .49	(2 .83)	Jul 94	(0 .02)	0 .00	29 ,357	(922)
% Change Profit	(59 .0)	26 .1	(203 .7)	1 ,469 .9	(510 .9)	Apr 94	(0 .08)	0 .00	10 ,158	(3 ,686)
% Change Revenue	183 .7	15 .4	(22 .8)	187 .7	165 .2	Jan 94	(0 .08)	0 .00	9 ,582	(3 ,559)
% Change Assets	69 .3	4 .7	27 .1	109 .6	79 .3	Oct 93	(0 .02)	0 .00	13 ,550	(897)
						Jul 93	(0 .06)	0 .00	10 ,431	(2 ,757)

						Synopsis:
Preferred Div. Coverage	np	np	np			In June 1995, BioChem Pharma Inc. shareholders adopted a rights plan to counter
Total Div. Coverage	na	na	na			the possibility of a hostile takeover. BioChem claimed to be unaware of any
Interest Coverage	0 .0	0 .0	0 .0			specific bidder for the company. Glaxo Wellcome PLC of Britain owns 17 % of
Current Ratio	2 .3	3 .8	4 .6			BioChem. Glaxo has an agreement with BioChem to bring to market 3TC, a
Operating Margin	(1 .2)	(9 .7)	(17 .3)			AIDS treatment. BioChem will receive 12% of all future drug sales. BioChem
Asset Turnover	0 .4	0 .2	0 .2			plans to file for regulatory approval to sell 3TC in Canada, the U.S., and Europe.

The drug should be available commercially by the end of 1995 or early 1996.
BioChem will apply for approval to administer 3TC together with another AIDS
drug, Burroughs Wellcome's AZT. BioChem said clinical trials show that in
combination the two drugs reduced the amount of HIV in a person's blood by up
to 90%. Current world-wide sales of AZT are about $450-million. Regulatory
approval depends upon whether 3TC is significantly better than rival products,
some of which are already being sold for use with AZT.

5 YEAR RATIOS (%)			
Return on Capital	(0 .8)	0 .8	0 .7
Return on Com. Equity	(3 .9)	(0 .7)	(0 .4)
Profit Growth	na	na	na
Revenue Growth	80 .7	67 .9	87 .0
Asset Growth	53 .2	52 .7	60 .6

BioChem also plans to market Lamivudine, a drug used to treat hepatitis B.
Lamivudine should be available by late 1997. The drug could prove quite
profitable for BioChem as the market for hepatitis B treatment is estimated at ten
times larger than the market for AIDS treatment. BioChem considers Asia to be a
large potential market for Lamivudine.

BALANCE SHEET (000)			
Cash	31 ,934	56 ,822	60 ,248
Current Assets	132 ,300	82 ,210	82 ,350
Net Fixed Assets	65 ,700	35 ,474	20 ,918
Invest's & Advances	19 ,947	16 ,687	20 ,854
Total Assets	245 ,240	144 ,892	138 ,373

For the first quarter of 1995, BioChem revenue was up mainly due primarily to
increased sales of the company's diagnostic products. In fiscal 1995, BioChem
expects sales of $180-million. The diagnostics unit, BioChem ImmunoSystems,
will earn $10-million in pretax profit. However, the company as a whole will
remain only close to profitable. Results will depend on the performance of
BioChem's 37.4% stake in Maryland-based North American Vaccine Inc.
BioChem expects strong revenue growth and earnings as it begins to market 3TC
and Lamivudine, expand the diagnostics and vaccines operations, and bring other
drugs to commercial development. BioChem said that while research and
development will remain the cornerstone of future growth, the company will
become more commercially focused. R&D costs were $16-million in 1994,
excluding amortization.

Short Term Debt	13 ,136	6 ,541	5 ,776
Current Liabilities	58 ,158	21 ,362	17 ,759
Long Term Debt	80 ,126	14 ,003	2 ,895
Total Liabilities	145 ,897	39 ,201	24 ,151
Total Equity	99 ,343	105 ,691	114 ,222
Total Liab. & Equity	245 ,240	144 ,892	138 ,373
CAPITAL (000)			
Total Debt	93 ,262	20 ,544	8 ,671
Preferred Equity	0	0	0
Common Equity	99 ,343	105 ,691	114 ,222

Relative strength to TSE300

Price

Volume (in 1000's of board lots)

Rank (Profit/Revenue/Assets)
956   390   322
Jean-Louis Fontaine
Chairman
Francesco Bellini
President & C.E.O.
Francois Legault
Sr. V.P. Fin. & Treasurer
Gervais Dionne
Exec. V.P.

Address
275 Armand-Frappier Blvd.
Laval
PQ
H7V 4A7
(514) 681-1744

Fax: (514) 978-7755
I0000852/G/5.7

BIOMIRA INC.

Exchanges	Price (Jun29'95)	3.40	Trailing P/E	nm	Stock Symbol
TMQ	Trailing Yield (%)	0.00	Trailing EPS	(1.31)	**BRA**

Period Ending	Dec94	Dec93	Dec92	Dec91	Dec90
Yearly Statistics					
Price-Close	5.00	9.00	11.25	13.38	2.10
Price-High	9.88	15.68	31.00	17.38	3.60
Price-Low	4.65	7.50	7.13	2.05	1.30
P/E-Close	nm	nm	nm	nm	nm
Dividends per Share	0.00	0.00	0.00	0.00	0.00
Dividend Yield (%)	0.00	0.00	0.00	0.00	0.00
Sales per Share	0.17	0.01	0.04	0.42	0.18
EPS before extra. item	(0.77)	(1.09)	(1.25)	(0.70)	(0.61)
Cash Flow per Share	(0.90)	(0.58)	(0.33)	(0.36)	(0.43)
Book Value per Share	1.54	2.09	2.38	3.36	0.88
O/S Common Shares	22,523	21,323	18,979	18,001	11,242
Total Revenue	17,632	2,976	8,424	17,524	7,552
Income before extra.	(17,011)	(21,032)	(22,674)	(9,240)	(6,004)
Cash Flow	(19,942)	(11,199)	(5,924)	(4,744)	(4,170)
Debt/Equity	0.01	0.01	0.01	0.01	0.06
Return on Capital (%)	(42.42)	(46.49)	(42.41)	(25.49)	(55.75)
Ret. on Com. Equity (%)	(43.00)	(46.94)	(42.93)	(26.38)	(57.86)
% Change Profit	19.1	7.2	(145.4)	(53.9)	(48.7)
% Change Revenue	492.5	(64.7)	(51.9)	132.0	192.2
% Change Assets	(17.1)	(2.2)	(31.9)	324.3	39.5

Date	EPS	DPS	Tot Rev	Inc Bex
Mar 95	(0.24)	0.00	1,722	(5,436)
Dec 94	(0.34)	0.00	2,004	(7,454)
Sep 94	(0.25)	0.00	1,867	(5,689)
Jun 94	(0.48)	0.00	1,981	(10,532)
Mar 94	0.28	0.00	1,097	6,039
Dec 93	(0.40)	0.00	782	(7,721)
Sep 93	(0.26)	0.00	(179)	(5,051)
Jun 93	(0.20)	0.00	782	(4,130)

	Dec94	Dec93	Dec92
Preferred Div. Coverage	na	na	na
Total Div. Coverage	na	na	na
Interest Coverage	0.0	0.0	0.0
Current Ratio	8.8	23.0	19.4
Operating Margin	(593.9)	(537.1)	(343.5)
Asset Turnover	0.1	0.0	0.0
5 YEAR RATIOS (%)			
Return on Capital	(42.5)	(40.2)	(34.6)
Return on Com. Equity	(43.4)	(41.1)	(35.4)
Profit Growth	na	na	na
Revenue Growth	46.9	7.3	51.0
Asset Growth	26.7	24.6	20.7
BALANCE SHEET (000)			
Cash	28,050	35,237	34,175
Current Assets	31,265	38,878	40,296
Net Fixed Assets	5,433	4,255	3,886
Invest's & Advances	471	3,412	3,387
Total Assets	38,600	46,545	47,570
Short Term Debt	0	0	0
Current Liabilities	3,534	1,689	2,074
Long Term Debt	390	354	322
Total Liabilities	3,924	2,043	2,396
Total Equity	34,676	44,502	45,174
Total Liab. & Equity	38,600	46,545	47,570
CAPITAL (000)			
Total Debt	390	354	322
Preferred Equity	30	30	30
Common Equity	34,646	44,472	45,144

Business:

BIOMIRA is a biotechnology company formed to conduct research and to develop and market products in the fields of cancer diagnostics and therapeutics. The components to cancer management include inexpensive blood tests as well as imaging agents and innovative, non-toxic approaches to therapy.

Synopsis:

Biomira Inc. aims to bring to market an integrated line of cost effective and value-added cancer products. The products include in vitro diagnostics, in vivo diagnostics, and immunotherapy products. Highlights in fiscal 1994 include the sale of Biomira's majority interest in a hospital information systems software business. Biomira sold the firm to focus on its core business and expertise. Also in 1994, a subsidiary of Hoechst AG of Germany licensed Biomira's antibody for breast cancer. Before Hoechst AG, both Tosoh Corp. of Japan and Ciba Corning Diagnostics of the U.S. licensed Biomira's antibodies for automated cancer diagnostic systems. During 1994, Biomira changed the name of wholly owned ADI Diagnostics to Biomira Diagnostics, reflecting its commitment to in vitro cancer management.

Product sales at Biomira Diagnostics rose 8.6% in 1994 versus 1993. These numbers should continue to rise as the in vitro business adds market share. The U.S. should grant approval for TRUQUANT in early 1996. This should develop into a major revenue stream. Royalty income from the first of Biomira's in vitro licensees is expected in 1995. In 1994 licensing revenue was $100,000, while research and development expenses were $18.3-million.

Currently, Biomira derives its financing from revenues from product sales by Biomira Diagnostics, royalties from licensing agreements, and fees from contract manufacturing. It also raises funds through the capital market. In June 1995, Biomira Inc. raised $26.6-million through a rights offering. Almiria Capital Corp., the venture capital arm of the Montreal-based Altamira group, bought five million units for $18-million. Almiria now has a 16.7% interest in Biomira's common shares.

In December 1994, Biomira adopted a plan to protect shareholders should any party attempt to purchase more than 20% of the company.

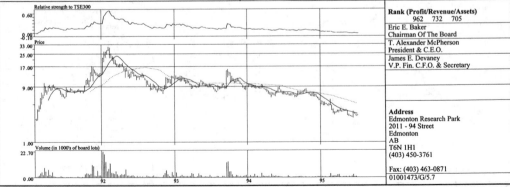

Rank (Profit/Revenue/Assets)
962   732   705

Eric E. Baker
Chairman Of The Board

T. Alexander McPherson
President & C.E.O.

James E. Devaney
V.P. Fin. C.F.O. & Secretary

Address
Edmonton Research Park
2011 - 94 Street
Edmonton
AB
T6N 1H1
(403) 450-3761

Fax: (403) 463-0871
01001473/G/5.7

DRAXIS HEALTH INC.

Exchanges						Business:
TQ	Price (Jun29'95)		2.21	Trailing P/E	73.67	**Stock Symbol**
	Trailing Yield (%)		0.00	Trailing EPS	0.03	**DAX**

Period Ending	Dec94	Dec93	Dec92	Dec91	Dec90	Business:
Yearly Statistics						DRAXIS HEALTH INC. is a Canadian
Price-Close	1.85	2.40	7.00	20.88	5.94	pharmaceutical company. In addition to its
Price-High	2.35	7.25	23.50	21.38	7.18	Canadian pharmaceutical marketing operations
Price-Low	1.35	2.28	3.75	5.25	4.75	it operates a dermatology research division
P/E-Close	30.83	nm	20.00	50.92	22.84	(Lipopharm) and has significant interest in two
Dividends per Share	0.00	0.00	0.46	0.43	0.12	development-stage, publicly-traded affilates. It
Dividend Yield (%)	0.00	0.00	6.57	2.06	2.02	holds approximately 20% of the common shares
Sales per Share	0.81	0.83	1.02	0.86	0.77	of DUSA Pharmaceuticals, Inc. and
EPS before extra. item	0.06	(0.11)	0.35	0.41	0.26	approximately 36% of the common shares of
Cash Flow per Share	0.20	0.14	0.14	0.24	0.26	Deprenyl Animal Health.
Book Value per Share	1.36	1.31	1.17	1.53	2.09	
O/S Common Shares	20,019	19,836	17,042	17,144	7,394	
Total Revenue	17,279	12,985	24,537	22,375	13,494	
Income before extra.	1,099	(2,079)	6,007	6,552	3,771	
Cash Flow	3,906	2,530	2,380	3,799	3,763	

Date	EPS	DPS	Tot Rev	Inc Bex
Mar 95	0.00	0.00	3,583	14
Dec 94	0.01	0.00	4,246	148
Sep 94	0.01	0.00	4,285	178
Jun 94	0.01	0.00	5,330	257
Mar 94	0.03	0.00	3,839	517
Dec 93	0.00	0.00	3,596	(91)
Sep 93	0.03	0.00	4,714	482
Jun 93	0.01	0.00	4,172	202

	Dec94	Dec93	Dec92	Dec91	Dec90
Debt/Equity	nd	nd	nd	nd	nd
Return on Capital (%)	10.68	(13.27)	43.94	51.57	43.44
Ret. on Com. Equity (%)	4.13	(9.06)	26.09	31.44	26.89
% Change Profit	152.9	(134.6)	(8.3)	73.8	22.2
% Change Revenue	33.1	(47.1)	9.7	65.8	105.8
% Change Assets	3.4	13.8	(30.6)	51.5	67.6

Preferred Div. Coverage	np	np	np
Total Div. Coverage	na	na	0.8
Interest Coverage	nd	nd	nd
Current Ratio	3.9	4.0	2.2
Operating Margin	25.3	5.3	17.2
Asset Turnover	0.5	0.5	0.6
5 YEAR RATIOS (%)			
Return on Capital	27.3	32.2	35.0
Return on Com. Equity	15.9	20.7	22.6
Profit Growth	(18.7)	na	423.7
Revenue Growth	21.3	82.2	na
Asset Growth	15.6	26.7	177.8
BALANCE SHEET (000)			
Cash	12,458	15,018	8,299
Current Assets	16,845	20,082	15,036
Net Fixed Assets	453	449	605
Invest's & Advances	8,776	7,221	7,805
Total Assets	33,062	31,986	28,097
Short Term Debt	0	0	0
Current Liabilities	4,333	4,990	6,789
Long Term Debt	0	0	0
Total Liabilities	5,904	5,950	8,238
Total Equity	27,159	26,036	19,859
Total Liab. & Equity	33,062	31,986	28,097
CAPITAL (000)			
Total Debt	0	0	0
Preferred Equity	0	0	0
Common Equity	27,159	26,036	19,859

Synopsis:

In June 1995, Draxis Health Inc. acquired a 50% interest in Indianapolis-based Innovative Health Systems (IHS). IHS develops and distributes science-based health related nutritional products through independent distributors. The IHS product line includes O2T, an exclusive anti-oxidant product, BLD, a nutritional supplement and meal replacement product, and No Diet, a weight reduction program. IHS has sales of $1.9-million (U.S.) annually. Draxis plans to provide marketing support and scientific and regulatory assistance. Draxis will also provide IHS with access to its consumer dermatology product line, new product development guidance, and $450,000 (U.S.) of working capital. This deal is the initial phase of Draxis' strategy to enter the U.S. market by way of a joint venture with an American distribution company. Draxis plans to aggressively expand in the U.S.

In February, Draxis acquired the Canadian marketing rights to the anti-osteoporosis drug ipriflavone from Tampa-based Somerset Pharmaceuticals Inc. The company will provide scientific and regulatory assistance to Somerset relating to Canadian regulatory approvals for ipriflavone, and certain R&D activities in Canada. Draxis also markets its anti-Parkinson's disease drug, Eldepryl(R), under license from Somerset. Somerset will assume overall responsibility, activity through the regulatory approval process in the U.S. and Canada. Draxis and Somerset will split profits equally from marketing and selling of Ipriflavone in Canada. Ipriflavone is currently in Phase II development in the U.S. and Canadian markets.

For the first quarter 1995, pharmaceutical revenues increased 15.5%, as income from the sale of Permax, and to Draxis's continuing cost reduction program. Losses relating to it Dermatology operations declined 40% to $347-thousand. Draxis expects related income from Eldepryl to decline in 1995. Novopharm, as part of a strategic alliance with Draxis, produces a generic version of Eldepryl. As the cheaper generic drug increases its market share, Eldepryl sales will fall.

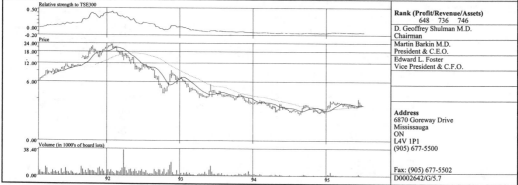

Rank (Profit/Revenue/Assets)
648   736   746
D. Geoffrey Shulman M.D.
Chairman
Martin Barkin M.D.
President & C.E.O.
Edward L. Foster
Vice President & C.F.O.

Address
6870 Goreway Drive
Mississauga
ON
L4V 1P1
(905) 677-5500

Fax: (905) 677-5502
D0002642/G/5.7

INTERNATIONAL MUREX TECHNOLOGIES CORPORATION

Exchanges	Price (Jun29'95)		3.40	Trailing P/E		3.80	Stock Symbol
Q	Trailing Yield (%)		0.00	Trailing EPS		0.66	MXX

Period Ending	Dec94	Dec93	Dec92	Dec91	Dec90	Business:
Yearly Statistics	US	US	US	US	US	INTERNATIONAL MUREX
Price-Close	5.38	6.75	9.75	15.38	5.38	TECHNOLOGIES CORPORATION develops,
Price-High	8.63	10.00	19.75	16.00	7.70	manufactures and markets medical diagnostic
Price-Low	4.69	4.40	5.83	4.00	3.99	products and services for the diagnosis and
P/E-Close	3.37	25.33	nm	nm	nm	monitoring of infectious diseases and other
Dividends per Share	0.00	0.00	0.00	0.00	0.00	medical conditions.
Dividend Yield (%)	0.00	0.00	0.00	0.00	0.00	
Sales per Share	5.57	4.88	4.81	0.23	0.37	
EPS before extra. item	0.85	0.16	(1.17)	(0.62)	(1.31)	
Cash Flow per Share	1.10	0.35	(0.73)	(0.56)	(1.17)	
Book Value per Share	3.37	2.40	2.17	3.02	0.89	

O/S Common Shares	16,779	16,645	16,040	13,934	9,395	
Total Revenue	103,376	80,064	73,359	3,137	1,891	
Income before extra.	14,224	2,674	(17,597)	(6,201)	(6,646)	

Date		EPS	DPS	Tot Rev	Inc Bex
Mar 95	US	(0.13)	0.00	23,500	(2,200)
Dec 94	US	0.11	0.00	27,211	1,783
Sep 94	US	0.09	0.00	23,314	1,523
Jun 94	US	0.59	0.00	32,050	9,947
Mar 94	US	0.06	0.00	20,716	971
Dec 93	US	0.10	0.00	18,689	1,772
Sep 93	US	0.08	0.00	20,073	1,331
Jun 93	US	0.00	0.00	20,989	(18)

Cash Flow	18,469	5,799	(10,934)	(5,633)	(5,921)	
Debt/Equity	0.02	0.02	0.06	0.05	0.22	
Return on Capital (%)	33.72	10.55	(41.14)	(21.62)	(77.09)	
Ret. on Com. Equity (%)	29.52	7.16	(45.75)	(24.55)	(155.95)	
% Change Profit	431.9	115.2	(183.8)	6.7	(16.3)	
% Change Revenue	29.1	9.1	2,238.5	65.9	839.5	
% Change Assets	45.2	(1.5)	26.9	280.1	92.9	

				Synopsis:
Preferred Div. Coverage	np	np	np	
Total Div. Coverage	na	na	na	
Interest Coverage	26.1	4.5	0.0	
Current Ratio	2.4	2.7	2.2	
Operating Margin	15.7	6.1	(12.6)	
Asset Turnover	1.1	1.4	1.2	
5 YEAR RATIOS (%)				
Return on Capital	(19.1)	na	na	
Return on Com. Equity	(37.9)	na	na	
Profit Growth	na	na	na	
Revenue Growth	248.3	na	na	
Asset Growth	67.8	na	na	
BALANCE SHEET (000)				
Cash	19,213	13,726	8,449	
Current Assets	69,581	50,470	49,764	
Net Fixed Assets	8,540	7,064	9,576	
Invest's & Advances	0	0	0	
Total Assets	85,643	58,966	59,844	
Short Term Debt	249	252	1,333	
Current Liabilities	28,413	18,374	23,012	
Long Term Debt	586	505	599	
Total Liabilities	29,139	19,090	24,982	
Total Equity	56,504	39,876	34,862	
Total Liab. & Equity	85,643	58,966	59,844	
CAPITAL (000)				
Total Debt	835	757	1,932	
Preferred Equity	0	0	0	
Common Equity	56,504	39,876	34,862	

In February 1995, International Murex Technologies Corp. launched the Murex Hybrid Capture DNA test for cytomegalovirus in European markets. Murex said the product is the "first commercial DNA probe based diagnostic product and the first to meet customer need for same-day CMV diagnosis." The product resulted from a collaborative research, development, and marketing agreement between Murex and Digene Diagnostics Inc. Murex expects to initially market the DNA test for research use only. It plans to register the product for sale outside North America. Murex manufactures and markets more than 600 products world-wide. It markets and distributes in more than 100 countries, and has local representatives in 34 leading markets.

In May 1995, Murex said it would begin trading on NASDAQ effective June 1, 1995. Murex believes that the multiple market maker system will help it gain exposure within the investment community and offer shareholders greater liquidity.

First quarter 1995 results included a gain of $9.3-million (U.S.), or 51 cents (U.S.) a share, derived from Murex's licensing agreement with Abbott Laboratories. The results also included a charge of $3.1-million related to litigation settlements of 1992 class action suits and the Allen F. Campbell actions. In December 1994, the German Infringement Court ruled that the hepatitis patent held by Chiron Corp. was valid as it relates to diagnostic tests. Murex must stop the sale in Germany of the Murex anti-HCV tests to detect hepatitis C. Murex plans to appeal the ruling. Murex will continue to supply other European and international customers with anti-HCV tests. Previously, Murex was ordered to discontinue in the U.K. the manufacture and sale of Murex anti-HCV tests. Murex plans to appeal this ruling. Murex still has pending legal action in the U.K. and Australia concerning Chiron Corp.

Research & development spending rose slightly due to the introduction of the Murex DNA probe. Murex also boosted development spending on the Immune Capture Enzyme Immunoassay technology scheduled for launch in late 1995.

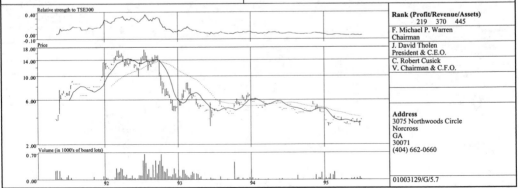

Rank (Profit/Revenue/Assets)
219   370   445
F. Michael P. Warren
Chairman
J. David Tholen
President & C.E.O.
C. Robert Cusick
V. Chairman & C.F.O.

Address
3075 Northwoods Circle
Norcross
GA
30071
(404) 662-0660

01003129/G/5.7

QUADRA LOGIC TECHNOLOGIES INC.

Exchanges	Price (Jun29'95)	7 .50	Trailing P/E	nm	Stock Symbol
TQ	Trailing Yield (%)	0 .00	Trailing EPS	(0 .72)	QLT

Period Ending	Dec94	Dec93	Dec92	Dec91	Dec90
Yearly Statistics					
Price-Close	8 .00	10 .63	9 .88	8 .50	8 .00
Price-High	11 .13	13 .13	10 .63	11 .75	14 .25
Price-Low	7 .25	9 .13	4 .70	5 .38	7 .00
P/E-Close	nm	nm	nm	nm	nm
Dividends per Share	0 .00	0 .00	0 .00	0 .00	0 .00
Dividend Yield (%)	0 .00	0 .00	0 .00	0 .00	0 .00
Sales per Share	na	na	na	na	0 .03
EPS before extra. item	(0 .72)	(0 .75)	(0 .69)	(0 .88)	(0 .81)
Cash Flow per Share	(0 .73)	(0 .69)	(0 .62)	(0 .79)	(0 .73)
Book Value per Share	1 .41	2 .11	1 .23	0 .91	1 .78
O/S Common Shares	19,741	19,661	15,622	12,703	12,667
Total Revenue	3,776	1,169	1,282	1,567	3,463
Income before extra.	(14,276)	(12,730)	(9,788)	(11,176)	(10,196)
Cash Flow	(14,291)	(11,723)	(8,825)	(10,019)	(9,222)
Debt/Equity	0 .05	0 .10	0 .29	0 .38	0 .11
Return on Capital (%)	(32 .53)	(30 .02)	(31 .48)	(37 .63)	(29 .33)
Ret. on Com. Equity (%)	(41 .16)	(41 .90)	(63 .49)	(65 .54)	(37 .40)
% Change Profit	(12 .1)	(30 .1)	12 .4	(9 .6)	(18 .4)
% Change Revenue	223 .1	(8 .8)	(18 .2)	(54 .7)	(8 .0)
% Change Assets	(31 .4)	61 .8	33 .5	(29 .3)	(19 .6)
Preferred Div. Coverage	na	na	na		
Total Div. Coverage	na	na	na		
Interest Coverage	na	na	0 .0		
Current Ratio	7 .4	18 .0	19 .6		
Operating Margin	na	na	na		
Asset Turnover	na	na	na		
5 YEAR RATIOS (%)					
Return on Capital	(32 .2)	(30 .1)	(30 .2)		
Return on Com. Equity	(49 .9)	(47 .1)	(46 .9)		
Profit Growth	(12 .6)	(9 .5)	(3 .1)		
Revenue Growth	0 .1	(18 .0)	(4 .0)		
Asset Growth	(3 .4)	4 .4	7 .0		
BALANCE SHEET (000)					
Cash	26,220	47,873	26,680		
Current Assets	27,808	48,610	27,176		
Net Fixed Assets	1,922	1,398	1,332		
Invest's & Advances	4,295	0	0		
Total Assets	37,513	54,660	33,781		
Short Term Debt	1,710	330	129		
Current Liabilities	3,749	2,706	1,386		
Long Term Debt	0	4,553	7,226		
Total Liabilities	3,749	7,259	8,613		
Total Equity	33,765	47,401	25,169		
Total Liab. & Equity	37,513	54,660	33,781		
CAPITAL (000)					
Total Debt	1,710	4,883	7,356		
Preferred Equity	5,900	5,900	5,900		
Common Equity	27,865	41,501	19,269		

Date	EPS	DPS	Tot Rev	Inc Bex
Dec 94	(0 .24)	0 .00	1,032	(4,734)
Sep 94	(0 .17)	0 .00	947	(3,465)
Jun 94	(0 .17)	0 .00	913	(3,365)
Mar 94	(0 .14)	0 .00	884	(2,712)
Dec 93	(0 .21)	0 .00	217	(4,068)
Sep 93	(0 .18)	0 .00	356	(3,027)
Jun 93	(0 .18)	0 .00	221	(2,821)
Mar 93	(0 .18)	0 .00	375	(2,816)

Business:

QUADRA LOGIC TECHNOLOGIES is a pharmaceutical corporation engaged in the development of new drugs and applications for photodynamic therapy, an emerging medical field that uses light-activated drugs in the treatment of cancer and other diseases.

Synopsis:

At its May 1995 annual meeting, Quadra Logic Technologies Inc. changed the name of the company to QLT Phototherapeutics Inc. For 1995, QLT forecasts that revenues from initial Photofrin sales in Japan and Holland will be between $2-million and $4-million. QLT attributed its weak revenue stream to slow regulatory approvals in Japan and elsewhere, and to problems related to the recent takeover of QLT's former partner, American Cyanamid Co. In September 1994, QLT re-acquired North American rights to market and distribute Photofrin from Cyanamid. Cyanamid will remain the contract manufacturer for Photofrin for commercial distribution in Canada and the U.S.

In March 1995, QLT entered into a 10-year agreement with Ligand Pharmaceuticals Inc. of San Diego. Ligand will have the exclusive right to market and sell Photofrin in Canada. QLT is still searching for a new strategic partner for the U.S. market. Canada approved Photofrin for the treatment of superficial bladder cancer. Canadian authorities are currently reviewing QLT's request to market the product as a treatment for esophageal cancer. QLT expects to receive more than 32.5% of the gross revenues from sales of Photofrin. Photofrin has receive regulatory approval in Holland for lung and esophageal cancers, and in Japan for gastric and cervical cancer. Japan represents the second-largest pharmaceutical market in the world. QLT has also applied in the U.S. to treat esophageal cancer with Photophrin. QLT plans to launch its own clinical and development activities in Canada in late 1995.

In February 1995, Belgium rejected QLT's submission for Photofrin regulatory approval. As well, QLT and Ciba Vision Ophthalmics signed an agreement to jointly pursue world-wide development and commercialization of photodynamic therapy as a treatment for eye diseases. Ciba will fund 60% of the development costs, but profits will be divided evenly after deductions for marketing costs, manufacturing costs, and third-party royalties.

Relative strength to TSE300

Price

Volume (in 1000's of board lots)

Rank (Profit/Revenue/Assets)
955   882   709

E. Duff Scott
Chairman

Randal D. Chase
President & C.E.O.

Kenneth H. Galbraith
V.P. Fin. C.F.O. & Secretary

Address
520 West 6th Avenue
Suite 200
Vancouver
BC
V5Z 4H5
(604) 872-7881

Fax: (604) 875-0001

Q0001711/G/5.7

SPECTRAL DIAGNOSTICS INC.

Exchanges	Price (Jun29'95)	28.00	Trailing P/E	nm	Stock Symbol
T	Trailing Yield (%)	0.00	Trailing EPS	(1.12)	SDI

Period Ending	Mar94	Mar93	Mar92
Yearly Statistics			8M
Price-Close	nt	nt	nt
Price-High	nt	nt	nt
Price-Low	nt	nt	nt
P/E-Close	nt	nt	nt
Dividends per Share	0.00	0.00	0.00
Dividend Yield (%)	0.00	0.00	0.00
Sales per Share	0.04	na	na
EPS before extra. item	(0.64)	(0.79)	(0.39)
Cash Flow per Share	(0.56)	(0.49)	(0.13)
Book Value per Share	2.69	0.79	0.32
O/S Common Shares	5,911,823	4,781,527	3,111,278
Total Revenue	1,869,659	982,213	277,049
Income before extra.	(3,368,787)	(3,232,804)	(375,199)
Cash Flow	(2,996,412)	(2,223,503)	(342,649)
Debt/Equity	0.01	0.03	0.15
Return on Capital (%)	(33.54)	(128.36)	na
Ret. on Com. Equity (%)	(34.29)	(135.96)	na
% Change Profit	(4.2)	(474.4)	na
% Change Revenue	90.4	136.4	na
% Change Assets	271.2	230.5	na

Business:

SPECTRAL DIAGNOSTICS INC. is a development stage biotechnology company engaged in the development and commercialization of its proprietary in-vitro rapid format cardiac diagnostic test kits and reagents.

Date	EPS	DPS	Tot Rev	Inc Bex
Dec 94	(0.27)	0.00	584	(1,858)
Sep 94	(0.36)	0.00	834	(2,498)
Jun 94	(0.28)	0.00	438	(1,645)
Dec 93	(0.21)	0.00	272	(1,200)
Sep 93	(0.22)	0.00	245	(1,083)
Jun 93	(0.11)	0.00	225	(530)

	Mar94	Mar93	Mar92
Preferred Div. Coverage	np	np	np
Total Div. Coverage	na	na	na
Interest Coverage	0.0	0.0	0.0
Current Ratio	14.2	5.4	2.9
Operating Margin	(2,453.4)	na	na
Asset Turnover	0.0	na	na
5 YEAR RATIOS (%)			
Return on Capital	na	na	na
Return on Com. Equity	na	na	na
Profit Growth	na	na	na
Revenue Growth	na	na	na
Asset Growth	na	na	na
BALANCE SHEET (000)			
Cash	9,941	2,911	511
Current Assets	10,967	3,728	797
Net Fixed Assets	5,786	785	442
Invest's & Advances	0	0	0
Total Assets	16,753	4,513	1,366
Short Term Debt	129	52	47
Current Liabilities	770	693	271
Long Term Debt	101	53	106
Total Liabilities	871	746	377
Total Equity	15,882	3,767	989
Total Liab. & Equity	16,753	4,513	1,366
CAPITAL (000)			
Total Debt	230	106	153
Preferred Equity	0	0	0
Common Equity	15,882	3,767	989

Synopsis:

In March 1995, Spectral Diagnostics Inc. announced that its cardiac test kit received marketing approval from the U.S. Food and Drug Administration. This represents a significant step towards profitability for the kit. Spectral's U.S. partner, Princeton BioMeditech Corp., will market the kit.

In May 1995, Spectral acquired patent pending technology as part of a collaborative research agreement with The Toronto Hospital. The venture will develop a new technique to rapidly diagnose the cause of septic shock. If commercial production of the technique can be achieved, the Toronto Hospital will receive a royalty on sales. Septic shock is a life threatening manifestation of bacterial and viral infections. It affects approximately 400,000 Americans each year.

In December 1994, Spectral's shares were listed on NASDAQ. Spectral believes the listing will be important because of its growing U.S. shareholder roster. This should increase the liquidity of Spectral's shares. As well, the U.S. market is important to Spectral's goal of becoming a leader in cardiac diagnostic research.

In November 1994, Spectral acquired an exclusive human cardiac gene bank as part of a three year research agreement with the University of Toronto. Spectral believes the gene bank will provide a reliable commercial supply of specific cardiac proteins and antibodies.

Spectral is investigating possible expansion, and has opened an office in Europe. The company is pursuing regulatory approval in Europe.

Rank (Profit/Revenue/Assets)
888   929   922

Douglas C. Ball
Chairman & C.E.O.

George Jackowski
President

Christoper R. Plaxton
Ex. V.P. & C.F.O.

Address
135 - 2 The West Mall
Toronto
ON
M9C 1C2
(416) 626-3233

Fax: (416) 626-7383
01003655/G/5.7

			EARNINGS PER SHARE		
Page	Company	Fiscal year end	Last Year	Estimate this year	Estimate next year
237	Algoma Steel	Dec-94	4.85	4.00	1.65
238	BICC Phillips	Dec-94	(0.04)	na	na
239	Canam Manac Group	Dec-94	0.31	0.49	0.69
240	Co-Steel	Dec-94	1.74	2.66	3.49
241	Dofasco	Dec-94	1.28	1.99	2.63
242	Emco	Dec-94	0.54	0.97	1.06
243	Harris Steel Group	Dec-94	2.37	1.55	1.50
244	Hawker Siddeley Canada	Dec-94	(6.53)	na	na
245	IPSCO	Dec-94	2.13	2.68	2.63
246	Ivaco	Dec-94	0.13	0.83	0.78
247	Samuel Manu-Tech	Dec-94	2.37	2.75	2.65
248	Slater Industries	Dec-94	2.23	2.85	2.25
249	Stelco	Dec-94	0.89	1.64	1.40
250	Toromont Industries	Dec-94	2.40	na	na
251	Varity	Jan-95	3.24	na	na

Estimates from First Call Corporation, 22 Pittsburgh Street, Boston, MA 02210   (800) 366-9992   Fax (617) 261-5679

Globe Information Services © 1995

Steel, Metal & Machinery

In 1994, the demand for all steel products in Canada grew, with the exception of tinplate, which experienced a decline of 5% primarily due to the loss of beverage can business to aluminum in Ontario. Flat rolled steel grew by 20% to 10.8 million tons, almost 15% above the previous peak achieved in 1988. The demand for hot rolled increased by 25%, cold rolled by 20% and galvanized by 11%. A record was also set for imports as almost 2.5 million tons of flat rolled steel was imported in 1994, which accounted for 23% of total Canadian demand.

Steel has found a new market in residential housing, which is now the fastest-growing market for steel in North America. The product has been used in framing, interior walls and roofing. Builders who have switched to steel framing have indicated in a recent survey that they had done so because it is faster to erect, results in a better overall quality house, eliminates nail pops in the drywall, and results in fewer builder callbacks. Superior performance has been demonstrated by steel under extreme weather conditions such as hurricanes and tornadoes. Steel has also proven to be cost-effective and environmentally friendly.

North America faced a tight supply situation early in 1994, for hot rolled wire rods resulting in a flood of imports of commodity grade products, particularly in the southeastern U.S. However, increased economic activity in Europe and Asia is now beginning to absorb much excess production capacity from newly exporting countries. Market conditions have stabilized significantly in early 1995, particularly for premium grades.

The outlook for energy related tubulars in western Canada shows overall line pipe demand should be relatively strong due to higher levels of drilling that occurred in 1994. Oil drilling is expected to be stronger in 1995 while gas drilling will move to lower levels due to weaker gas prices. This is not expected to have any significant difference in the total metres drilled. In 1994, there were 5,369 gas wells and 3,853 oil wells drilled in western Canada. However, there was no significant difference, the total metres drilled for gas was 5.27 million, while oil totalled 5.16 million metres. Due to the greater average depth of oil wells, a decline in overall wells drilled will be somewhat mitigated by the increased mix towards oil drilling in 1995.

In 1994, the commercial and industrial construction markets posted a recovery in Canada. Non-residential construction starts increased by 5.5% in terms of square footage. In Ontario, non-residential construction starts rose by 21.6%, but Quebec saw a decline of 1.8%. The United States saw construction starts climb by 16.8%. This confirms that the economic recovery is fully under way in that country, and that the United States presents major potential for Canadian steel fabricators who could further benefit from a favourable exchange rate.

While Canadian Armed Forces contracts were at a reduced level of defence spending in 1994, the aerospace industry view these contracts positively. They provide a solid foundation for their operations at the same time as they are using their skills to expand the business and utilize the inherent fixed costs for more efficient operation. The specialized component re-manufacturing process which have been developed in conjunction with the Canadian Armed Forces is an example of the above. Re-manufactured components can be supplied at quality levels comparable to or better than new parts, at a much lower price to aircraft engine users.

Demand for diesel engines in the agricultural, construction, industrial and power generation segment improved in 1994, particularly in the United States and Europe. The difficult economic conditions in continental Europe were offset by higher sales in the United Kingdom, the United States, Middle East, and Asia/Pacific.

ALGOMA STEEL INC.

Exchanges	Price (Jun29'95)	6.87	Trailing P/E	1.15	Stock Symbol
T	Trailing Yield (%)	0.00	Trailing EPS	5.96	**ALG**

Period Ending	Dec94	Dec93	Dec92	Jun92	Dec91	Business:
Yearly Statistics			7M	1D		ALGOMA STEEL INC. is an integrated steel
Price-Close	n t	n t	n t	n t	0.55	producer. It produces sheet and strip, plate,
Price-High	n t	n t	n t	n t	14.75	seamless tubular steel, structural shapes and
Price-Low	n t	n t	n t	n t	0.50	steel rails at its steelworks in Sault Ste. Marie.
P/E-Close	n t	n t	n t	n t	nm	The principal markets for Algoma's products
Dividends per Share	0.00	0.00	0.00	0.00	0.00	are steel service centres, the automotiv
Dividend Yield (%)	0.00	0.00	0.00	0.00	0.00	industry, steel fabricators and manufacturing,
Sales per Share	41.56	33.87	27.68	0.00	50.22	pipe and tube manufacturers, and the oil and
EPS before extra. item	4.85	0.27	(2.96)	na	(11.58)	gas exploration industry.
Cash Flow per Share	6.31	2.39	(1.64)	0.00	(6.95)	
Book Value per Share	(0.79)	(5.64)	(5.91)	(3.24)	(19.86)	
O/S Common Shares	26,250	26,250	26,250	25,000	17,283	
Total Revenue	1,095,797	893,906	416,065	0	961,857	
Income before extra.	127,288	7,140	(74,065)	0	(189,708)	
Cash Flow	165,556	62,729	(24,801)	0	(120,086)	

	Date	EPS	DPS	Tot Rev	Inc Bex
Debt/Equity	na	na	na	na	na	Mar 95	1.72	0.00	318,400	45,100
Return on Capital (%)	654.65	na	na	na	(19.92)	Dec 94	1.82	0.00	285,500	47,700
Ret. on Com. Equity (%)	na	na	na	na	na	Sep 94	1.16	0.00	277,000	30,300
% Change Profit	1,682.7	105.6	na	nm	73.0	Jun 94	1.26	0.00	266,600	33,200
% Change Revenue	22.6	25.3	na	(100.0)	16.9	Mar 94	0.61	0.00	266,700	16,000
% Change Assets	12.7	(3.3)	(3.1)	(1.9)	(13.7)	Dec 93	0.93	0.00	250,900	24,500
						Sep 93	0.19	0.00	207,600	4,900
						Jun 93	(0.17)	0.00	225,900	(4,500)

Preferred Div. Coverage	np	np	np
Total Div. Coverage	na	na	na
Interest Coverage	22.0	1.7	0.0
Current Ratio	1.9	1.7	1.7
Operating Margin	14.8	3.5	(12.2)
Asset Turnover	1.3	1.2	0.9

Synopsis:

Algoma Steel Inc.'s earnings rose in the first quarter of 1995, ending March 31, to $45.1-million from $16-million a year earlier. The increase was due in part to higher selling prices for most products. The company expects its production facilities to operate at capacity beyond the second quarter. Demand for steel products remained relatively strong during the first quarter.

5 YEAR RATIOS (%)			
Return on Capital	na	na	na
Return on Com. Equity	na	na	na
Profit Growth	na	(3.2)	na
Revenue Growth	5.9	(8.4)	(13.3)
Asset Growth	(2.3)	(16.4)	(16.0)

Algoma Steel plans to go ahead with a $500-million plant modernization. The company says the modernization will make it one of the most efficient and lowest cost steel producers in North America. The modernization could only be started after the company and its 5,000 employees agreed on substantial concessions. This included lowering employee ownership to below 57%. The plan provides for approximately $500-million of capital spending, the cornerstone of which is the construction of a thin-slab caster linked to a new hot strip mill. An important first step in this process was the listing of Algoma's common shares on the Toronto Stock Exchange on February 13, 1995. The company expects to finance the expansion through the issue of $150-million worth of common shares, in Canada and the United States, and a public offering in the United States of $250-million (U.S.) worth of first-mortgage notes. Internally generated funds will also help pay for the expansion.

BALANCE SHEET (000)			
Cash	0	0	0
Current Assets	508,918	408,177	398,813
Net Fixed Assets	322,529	319,631	340,432
Invest's & Advances	0	10,000	20,000
Total Assets	831,447	737,808	763,058
Short Term Debt	69,458	104,827	111,540
Current Liabilities	266,125	240,052	238,061
Long Term Debt	17,083	23,077	23,720
Total Liabilities	852,181	885,830	918,220
Total Equity	(20,734)	(148,022)	(155,162)
Total Liab. & Equity	831,447	737,808	763,058

Total sales revenue for Algoma Steel Inc. rose by 23% to $11-billion or $541 per ton shipped in 1994, compared to $889-million or $447 per ton shipped on 1992. The increase was principally the result of price increases and improved product mix. The average selling price for the company's products was 15% higher than in 1993. This improvement was achieved by buying slabs and tube rounds from outside sources for conversion by Algoma, resulting in higher shipments of plate, structural products, and seamless tube. Strong market conditions in 1994 accelerated the rebuilding of the company's core business. By the fourth quarter, welded tubular and automotive customers grew to represent 53% of Algoma's total sheet sales compared with just 40% in the fourth quarter of 1992.

CAPITAL (000)			
Total Debt	86,541	127,904	135,260
Preferred Equity	0	0	0
Common Equity	(20,734)	(148,022)	(155,162)

Relative strength to TSE300

Price

Volume (in 1000's of board lots)

Rank (Profit/Revenue/Assets)
56 114 172
H. Earl Joudrie
Chairman
W. Allan Hopkins
President & C.E.O.

Address
105 West Street
Sault Ste Marie
ON
P6A 5P2
(705) 945-2351

Fax: (705) 945-2203
A0001586/G/6.1

BICC PHILLIPS INC.

Exchanges	Price (Jun29'95)	9.75	Trailing P/E	nm	Stock Symbol
TM	Trailing Yield (%)	0.00	Trailing EPS	(0.04)	**BPP**

Period Ending	Dec94	Dec93	Dec92	Dec91	Dec90
Yearly Statistics					
Price-Close	9.00	8.50	10.25	9.75	12.00
Price-High	11.00	11.00	11.50	14.00	16.50
Price-Low	8.50	8.00	9.00	8.25	10.50
P/E-Close	nm	nm	nm	nm	10.00
Dividends per Share	0.00	0.00	0.00	0.20	1.00
Dividend Yield (%)	0.00	0.00	0.00	2.05	8.33
Sales per Share	35.73	33.03	31.04	30.68	37.26
EPS before extra. item	(0.04)	(0.52)	(0.39)	(0.36)	1.20
Cash Flow per Share	0.18	0.06	0.18	0.34	1.82
Book Value per Share	8.48	8.52	9.33	9.72	10.27
O/S Common Shares	8,104	8,104	8,104	8,104	8,103
Total Revenue	291,348	268,453	251,567	248,642	300,629
Income before extra.	(322)	(4,234)	(3,138)	(2,890)	9,658
Cash Flow	1,463	475	1,465	2,778	14,711
Debt/Equity	0.36	0.21	0.06	nd	0.04
Return on Capital (%)	2.41	(6.16)	(5.66)	(5.43)	19.03
Ret. on Com. Equity (%)	(0.47)	(5.85)	(4.07)	(3.57)	11.76
% Change Profit	92.4	(34.9)	(8.6)	(129.9)	(42.1)
% Change Revenue	8.5	6.7	1.2	(17.3)	(13.7)
% Change Assets	9.9	(0.5)	12.1	(8.6)	2.8

Business:

BICC PHILLIPS INC. with its seven factories across Canada, designs, engineers, manufactures and markets wire and cable for the transmission and distribution of electrical energy and telecommunications signals. It has customers in Canada, the United States and worldwide.

Date	EPS	DPS	Tot Rev	Inc Bex
Dec 94	(0.11)	0.00	74,242	(882)
Sep 94	(0.12)	0.00	71,710	(1,014)
Jun 94	0.05	0.00	74,717	466
Mar 94	0.14	0.00	68,860	1,108
Dec 93	0.07	0.00	77,752	550
Sep 93	(0.23)	0.00	62,347	(1,905)
Jun 93	(0.08)	0.00	67,577	(582)
Mar 93	(0.28)	0.00	59,979	(2,298)

Preferred Div. Coverage	np	np	np		
Total Div. Coverage	na	na	na		
Interest Coverage	0.8	0.0	0.0		
Current Ratio	1.3	1.4	1.5		
Operating Margin	0.4	0.0	(0.2)		
Asset Turnover	1.9	2.0	1.8		
5 YEAR RATIOS (%)					
Return on Capital	0.8	7.5	14.4		
Return on Com. Equity	(0.4)	4.1	8.8		
Profit Growth	na	na	na		
Revenue Growth	(3.6)	(2.8)	(0.3)		
Asset Growth	2.8	(0.4)	1.1		
BALANCE SHEET (000)					
Cash	0	1,305	6,661		
Current Assets	101,188	87,140	85,273		
Net Fixed Assets	42,251	44,763	47,664		
Invest's & Advances	3,164	2,705	2,838		
Total Assets	150,572	137,071	137,714		
Short Term Debt	24,372	14,654	4,580		
Current Liabilities	79,642	63,013	57,060		
Long Term Debt	0	0	0		
Total Liabilities	81,832	68,009	62,110		
Total Equity	68,740	69,062	75,604		
Total Liab. & Equity	150,572	137,071	137,714		
CAPITAL (000)					
Total Debt	24,372	14,654	4,580		
Preferred Equity	0	0	0		
Common Equity	68,740	69,062	75,604		

Synopsis:

Phillips Cables announced on May 11, 1995, that it was entering into an agreement with BICC Industrial Cable Company, the industrial cables business unit of BICC Cable Corporation. The agreement combines the management of the Phillips industrial and construction business, including the Brockville, Ontario, plant, with BICC Industrial's operation. This merger forms an integrated North American industrial and construction cable business. BICC Phillips will be managed from headquarters in York, Pennsylvania.

Sales for the first quarter ended March 31, 1995, were $75-million, 5% higher than the first quarter of 1994. The volume of physical product was lower during this quarter than the previous first quarter. Higher metal and other raw material costs resulted in higher selling prices which in turn inflated the sales revenue. Domestic sales were higher for the first quarter, sales to the U.S.A. were also higher, while sales outside North America continued to suffer from weaknesses in the Russian market and input and currency restrictions in China.

In 1994, BICC Phillips closed its plant in Dartmouth, Nova Scotia, because of the excess capacity for the telecom market. Although the plant has been a productive and cost efficient operation, customers converting to fibre optics made it necessary to focus efforts on Phillips' larger Vancouver operation.

In the company's joint venture with Furukawa Electric of Japan, BICC Phillips has had a very satisfactory level of progress and profit. The specialized facility in Rimouski, Quebec, achieved success in the growing North American and world markets for optical ground wire. BICC Phillips had positive growth in its specialty Mineral Insulated cable market, with increased penetration in the U.S. There has been a growing demand for the unequalled fire performance of these cables because of the concern for public safety.

Rank (Profit/Revenue/Assets)
780   262   393

D.L. Torrey
Chairman

M.J. Stagg
President & C.E.O.

D. Kong
V.P. Finance

Address
Suite 200
300 Consilium Place
Scarborough
ON
M1H 3G2
(416) 296-0250

Fax: (416) 296-0262
P0002677/G/6.2

CANAM MANAC GROUP INC. (THE)

Exchanges	Price (Jun29'95)	4.85	Trailing P/E	11.83	Stock Symbol
TM	Trailing Yield (%)	0.00	Trailing EPS	0.41	**CAM.A**

Period Ending	Dec94	Dec93	Dec92	Dec91	Dec90
Yearly Statistics					
Price-Close	3.85	4.75	1.90	2.80	3.25
Price-High	5.38	5.00	3.00	4.30	5.50
Price-Low	3.30	1.70	1.17	2.00	2.65
P/E-Close	12.42	158.33	nm	nm	nm
Dividends per Share	0.00	0.00	0.00	0.13	0.20
Dividend Yield (%)	0.00	0.00	0.00	4.46	6.15
Sales per Share	16.38	12.37	11.32	9.72	10.91
EPS before extra. item	0.31	0.03	(0.60)	(0.73)	(2.05)
Cash Flow per Share	0.90	0.51	0.19	(1.28)	(0.20)
Book Value per Share	3.32	3.51	2.86	3.51	4.35
O/S Common Shares	42,152	30,898	30,892	23,821	23,820
Total Revenue	570,425	382,773	285,797	246,956	254,656
Income before extra.	10,833	825	(14,941)	(17,272)	(48,851)
Cash Flow	31,325	15,860	4,743	(30,462)	(4,860)
Debt/Equity	1.56	1.95	2.30	2.52	4.31
Return on Capital (%)	9.49	5.64	(1.03)	(1.60)	(7.71)
Ret. on Com. Equity (%)	8.72	0.84	(17.38)	(18.45)	(37.65)
% Change Profit	1,213.1	105.5	13.5	64.6	(2,398.8)
% Change Revenue	49.0	33.9	15.7	(3.0)	(18.2)
% Change Assets	23.4	12.3	(0.2)	(42.5)	(5.5)

Date	EPS	DPS	Tot Rev	Inc Bex
Mar 95	0.09	0.00	165,304	3,921
Dec 94	0.15	0.00	182,393	5,263
Sep 94	0.12	0.00	171,130	4,104
Jun 94	0.05	0.00	120,948	1,862
Mar 94	(0.01)	0.00	95,954	(396)
Dec 93	0.09	0.00	116,419	2,792
Sep 93	0.05	0.00	115,351	1,682
Jun 93	(0.03)	0.00	80,626	(1,022)

Preferred Div. Coverage	na	na	na
Total Div. Coverage	na	na	na
Interest Coverage	2.1	1.2	0.0
Current Ratio	2.2	1.3	1.2
Operating Margin	5.8	4.8	(2.2)
Asset Turnover	1.2	1.0	0.8
5 YEAR RATIOS (%)			
Return on Capital	1.0	(0.7)	(0.2)
Return on Com. Equity	(12.8)	(14.8)	(12.1)
Profit Growth	na	(48.0)	na
Revenue Growth	12.8	(0.1)	(9.1)
Asset Growth	(5.6)	(10.0)	(3.1)
BALANCE SHEET (000)			
Cash	2,766	32,693	12,508
Current Assets	252,187	193,396	143,940
Net Fixed Assets	154,453	125,633	130,212
Invest's & Advances	28,226	25,896	26,237
Total Assets	481,808	390,585	347,766
Short Term Debt	4,907	85,593	75,076
Current Liabilities	117,096	148,077	121,685
Long Term Debt	217,181	128,043	131,141
Total Liabilities	339,682	280,788	258,158
Total Equity	142,126	109,797	89,608
Total Liab. & Equity	481,808	390,585	347,766
CAPITAL (000)			
Total Debt	222,088	213,636	206,217
Preferred Equity	2,105	1,445	1,270
Common Equity	140,021	108,352	88,338

Business:

CANAM MANAC GROUP INC. makes and markets structural steel components products in Canada and the United States, and manufactures semitrailers for the transport industries.

Synopsis:

Canam Manac reported consolidated sales increased by 72% in the first quarter ended March 31, 1995, over the same period last year. All subsidiaries and divisions contributed to the higher sales. The Manac division recorded the strongest increase, with sales up 99% during the quarter. This was mainly as a result of the start-up of a new semitrailer plant in Orangeville, Ontario, in the fourth quarter of 1994. Sales in the steel sector showed an increase of 69% over the first quarter of 1994. Bookings were up in all Groups, 41% in the metal construction components sector, 88% for semitrailers, and 75% for MRM Steel.

In the first quarter of 1995, the company agreed to sell the assets of MRM Steel of Selkirk, Manitoba, to Gerdau Empreemdimentos Ltda. of Brazil. The transaction closed on June 20, 1995. Canam Manac consolidated the results of MRM Steel until May 31, 1995. The company sees this sale as confirmation of the group's policy to return to its core business, the fabrication of metal construction components and semitrailers. Proceeds from the sale, which should be about $160-million will be used to reduce debt. The assets of the Group mill will total $364-million following the transaction compared with $482-million at year end.

Canam Manac announced its continuing expansion in the U.S. by establishing two new metal construction components plants in Jacksonville, Florida, and Columbus, Ohio. These facilities will require an investment of more than $14-million. The company said the new plant in Jacksonville will begin production in July 1995. Production should begin at the Columbus plant in November.

Canam Manac, which had shown a small profit in 1993 after four consecutive years of loses, reported consolidated sales in 1994 of $549-million, an increase of 49% over 1993. While this was a significant improvement the company views 1994 as an ordinary year for profitability and believes it can do better in future years. The steel production segment accounted for 79% of sales while the transportation and forestry equipment segment accounted for 21%.

Relative strength to TSE300 / Price / Volume (in 1000's of board lots)

Rank (Profit/Revenue/Assets)		
284	180	232

Marcel Dutil
Chairman President & C.E.O.
Andre Marsann
V.P. Finance

Address
11535 - 1re Avenue
Bureau 500
Ville De St-Georges
PQ
G5Y 7H5
(418) 228-8031

Fax: (418) 228-1750
C0055041/G/6.2

CO-STEEL INC.

Exchanges	Price (Jun29'95)	25 .62	Trailing P/E	11 .05	Stock Symbol
TM	Trailing Yield (%)	1 .40	Trailing EPS	2.32	**CEI**

Period Ending	Dec94	Dec93	Dec92	Dec91	Dec90
Yearly Statistics					
Price-Close	29 .00	28 .50	17 .50	18 .00	15 .75
Price-High	30 .25	28 .50	19 .38	20 .75	17 .50
Price-Low	27 .00	19 .63	15 .50	15 .75	14 .63
P/E-Close	12.78	32.76	159 .09	81 .82	3 .97
Dividends per Share	0 .34	0 .32	0 .32	0 .48	0 .60
Dividend Yield (%)	1 .17	1 .12	1 .83	2 .67	3 .81
Sales per Share	41 .44	35 .00	30 .36	34 .10	35 .99
EPS before extra. item	2 .27	0 .87	0 .11	0 .22	3 .97
Cash Flow per Share	3 .48	2 .50	1 .51	1 .93	2 .94
Book Value per Share	19 .65	16 .79	16 .01	16 .56	16 .78
O/S Common Shares	30 ,413	30 ,299	30 ,162	24 ,455	24 ,312
Total Revenue	1 ,284 ,096	1 ,060 ,260	873 ,507	848 ,476	882 ,474
Income before extra.	68 ,879	26 ,409	3 ,153	5 ,461	96 ,470
Cash Flow	105 ,736	75 ,585	43 ,566	47 ,911	71 ,456
Debt/Equity	0 .43	0 .24	0 .29	0 .38	0 .40
Return on Capital (%)	14 .14	8 .00	2 .37	4 .50	27 .11
Ret. on Com. Equity (%)	12 .45	5 .33	0 .71	1 .34	26 .81
% Change Profit	160 .8	737 .6	(42 .3)	(94 .3)	113 .7
% Change Revenue	21 .1	21 .4	3 .0	(3 .9)	(9 .0)
% Change Assets	29 .6	9 .4	7 .0	(2 .0)	16 .6

Date	EPS	DPS	Tot Rev	Inc Bex
Mar 95	0 .73	0 .10	382 ,646	22 ,053
Dec 94	0 .64	0 .10	336 ,293	19 ,354
Sep 94	0 .51	0 .08	314 ,179	15 ,487
Jun 94	0 .44	0 .08	333 ,465	13 ,302
Mar 94	0 .68	0 .08	300 ,270	20 ,736
Dec 93	0 .24	0 .08	283 ,521	7 ,446
Sep 93	0 .29	0 .08	262 ,685	8 ,805
Jun 93	0 .27	0 .08	270 ,143	8 ,051

Preferred Div. Coverage	np	np	np
Total Div. Coverage	6 .7	2 .7	0 .3
Interest Coverage	11 .1	4 .9	1 .3
Current Ratio	1 .8	1 .5	1 .8
Operating Margin	6 .8	4 .7	1 .6
Asset Turnover	1 .1	1 .2	1 .1
5 YEAR RATIOS (%)			
Return on Capital	11 .2	12 .8	16 .3
Return on Com. Equity	9 .3	9 .8	12 .7
Profit Growth	9 .0	(12 .8)	(36 .3)
Revenue Growth	5 .7	1 .6	1 .2
Asset Growth	11 .6	5 .8	5 .0
BALANCE SHEET (000)			
Cash	85 ,083	14 ,873	69 ,006
Current Assets	448 ,373	324 ,828	317 ,621
Net Fixed Assets	600 ,681	438 ,998	370 ,730
Invest's & Advances	28 ,900	64 ,905	64 ,905
Total Assets	1 ,172 ,461	904 ,972	827 ,035
Short Term Debt	34 ,478	22 ,040	46 ,263
Current Liabilities	248 ,534	210 ,552	175 ,530
Long Term Debt	222 ,839	99 ,398	91 ,911
Total Liabilities	574 ,780	396 ,380	344 ,006
Total Equity	597 ,681	508 ,592	483 ,029
Total Liab. & Equity	1 ,172 ,461	904 ,972	827 ,035
CAPITAL (000)			
Total Debt	257 ,317	121 ,438	138 ,174
Preferred Equity	0	0	0
Common Equity	597 ,681	508 ,592	483 ,029

Business:

CO-STEEL INC. manufactures and markets steel products including special quality bar and rod, concrete reinforcing bar and rod and other structural shapes. Its products are used in the construction, automotive, appliance, machinery and equipment industries in North America and Europe. The company has facilities in Ontario, New Jersey and the United Kingdom.

Synopsis:

For the first three months ended March 31, 1995, Co-Steel Inc. reported earnings from operations of $22.1-million. This was a significant increase over the $4.5-million reported in 1994. The improved first quarter reflected strong markets in both North America and Europe, and increased selling prices and currency translations. Co-Steel is optimistic about 1995, given its record first quarter. It also has a full order-book for the second quarter at its North American and European mini-mills. With the U.S. economy approaching a plateau and Canada following suit, Co-Steel anticipates reduced North American demand during the second half of the year. The upturn in the European economy is more recent, and Co- Steel does not expect market conditions there to weaken.

A $40-million, three-year program to rebuild Co-Steel's Lasco structural mill is underway. It is scheduled to be completed by the end of 1997. The program will achieve two main objectives, increasing production by about 10% to an annual capacity of one million tons, and broadening Lasco's product range. The wider range of finished products will allow for greater market penetration by Co-Steel Lasco. Reduced production cost will also result from improvements to the mill.

In 1994 Co-Steel posted sales of just over $1.26-billion on shipments of 2.4 million tons. This was its strongest performance ever with record earnings, sales and shipments. All Co-Steel units recorded improved sales and earnings over 1993. The improvement was due in part to reduced operating costs. Manpower reductions over the last four years and programs to improve productivity led to the lower operating costs. Automotive and construction demand drove the strong U.S. steel market during 1994.

Sales (shipments) by geographic region in 1994 were: Canada, 18% (26%); the United States, 48% (35%); and Europe, 34% (39%). Shipments in 1994 by product were: concrete reinforcing bar and rod, 31%; special bar and rod quality, 28%; structural shapes, 26%; and other, 15%.

Rank (Profit/Revenue/Assets)
94 101 144

William J. Shields
President & C.E.O.
Edward G. Reilly
V.P. & C.F.O.
Ronald P. Fournier
Exec. V.P. & Deputy C.E.O.

Address
P.O. Box 130
40 King Street West
Scotia Plaza
Toronto
ON
M5H 3Y2
(416) 366-4500
Fax: (416) 366-4616
C0000523/G/6.1

DOFASCO INC.

Exchanges	Price (Jun29'95)	17.25	Trailing P/E	5.83	Stock Symbol
TM	Trailing Yield (%)	2.32	Trailing EPS	2.96	DFS

Period Ending	Dec94	Dec93	Dec92	Dec91	Dec90
Yearly Statistics					
Price-Close	18.88	23.25	10.25	16.50	16.25
Price-High	26.38	23.50	19.00	23.50	24.75
Price-Low	17.13	9.50	7.25	15.00	16.25
P/E-Close	8.10	16.49	nm	nm	nm
Dividends per Share	0.30	0.00	0.15	0.80	1.28
Dividend Yield (%)	1.59	0.00	1.46	4.85	7.88
Sales per Share	27.11	26.49	24.81	29.03	35.49
EPS before extra. item	2.33	1.41	(2.96)	(0.73)	(10.64)
Cash Flow per Share	4.22	3.22	1.68	1.80	3.92
Book Value per Share	16.80	14.39	12.98	16.19	17.34
O/S Common Shares	84,891	79,461	79,276	78,290	67,018
Total Revenue	2,356,200	2,195,000	1,978,800	2,064,200	2,363,100
Income before extra.	220,900	138,600	(207,100)	(25,000)	(679,200)
Cash Flow	352,500	255,300	132,200	127,300	259,200
Debt/Equity	0.47	0.57	0.70	0.55	0.56
Return on Capital (%)	13.64	9.68	(11.73)	0.53	(18.50)
Ret. on Com. Equity (%)	15.11	10.30	(20.36)	(4.26)	(45.83)
% Change Profit	59.4	166.9	(728.4)	96.3	(411.7)
% Change Revenue	7.3	10.9	(4.1)	(12.6)	(40.1)
% Change Assets	8.4	(1.5)	(5.3)	1.5	(33.2)
Preferred Div. Coverage	8.3	5.2	0.0		
Total Div. Coverage	4.2	5.2	0.0		
Interest Coverage	4.2	2.5	0.0		
Current Ratio	4.2	3.9	2.9		
Operating Margin	10.3	6.6	2.1		
Asset Turnover	0.6	0.7	0.6		
5 YEAR RATIOS (%)					
Return on Capital	(1.3)	(1.4)	(0.4)		
Return on Com. Equity	(9.0)	(10.0)	(9.6)		
Profit Growth	0.3	(9.0)	na		
Revenue Growth	(9.8)	(6.1)	(2.1)		
Asset Growth	(7.3)	(8.0)	1.3		
BALANCE SHEET (000)					
Cash	532,000	227,800	214,900		
Current Assets	1,454,000	1,158,100	1,111,200		
Net Fixed Assets	1,887,400	1,916,700	2,003,800		
Invest's & Advances	147,500	132,300	139,600		
Total Assets	3,488,900	3,218,300	3,266,900		
Short Term Debt	51,200	11,400	26,600		
Current Liabilities	342,900	295,300	381,600		
Long Term Debt	780,900	833,100	927,600		
Total Liabilities	1,724,500	1,735,700	1,897,900		
Total Equity	1,764,400	1,482,600	1,369,000		
Total Liab. & Equity	3,488,900	3,218,300	3,266,900		
CAPITAL (000)					
Total Debt	832,100	844,500	954,200		
Preferred Equity	338,100	339,100	339,700		
Common Equity	1,426,300	1,143,500	1,029,300		

Business:

DOFASCO INC. is a fully integrated steel maker specializing in a broad range of high quality flat rolled products. These include cold rolled, hot rolled and plate, galvanized, Galvalume, prepainted, tinplate and chromium coated, all in coils and cut lengths. Dofasco's products serve major North American markets including: automotive, construction, energy, manufacturing, container and steel distribution.

Date	EPS	DPS	Tot Rev	Inc Bex
Mar 95	0.52	0.20	662,500	50,700
Dec 94	0.67	0.10	619,200	63,400
Sep 94	0.56	0.10	574,000	53,800
Jun 94	1.21	0.00	634,000	105,900
Mar 94	(0.11)	0.00	568,500	(2,200)
Dec 93	0.95	0.00	615,100	82,400
Sep 93	0.70	0.00	509,400	62,000
Jun 93	0.00	0.00	544,500	6,700

Synopsis:

In April 1995, Dofasco announced a $200-million expansion that will marry mini-mill technology with the company's blast furnaces in Hamilton. Scheduled for completion late next year, the expansion consists of an electric arc furnace that melts scrap steel and a new continuous slab caster that flattens 8.5 inch thick slabs of hot steel. From the company's existing work force of about 7,000, 240 people will be taken and employed at the mill. The additional steel from the expansion, which is approximately 1.35 million tons of cast slab-steel per year, will replace Dofasco's practice of purchasing approximately 900,000 tons of cast slab steel annually for further processing at the Hamilton plant. The net increase per year in hot rolling capability is about 450,000 tons over the 3.55 million tons currently produced at the Hot Strip Mill. The purchased slab program was initiated when its older ingot production facilities were downsized and closed in 1993.

When the new facilities come on stream in 1996, Dofasco expects to have one of the most modern low cost steel production facilities with full capabilities for producing high quality flat rolled steel in North America. The new electric furnace will be capable of using 70% scrap fed with 30% liquid iron mix, using Dofasco's existing coke oven and blast furnace capability. This in turn reduces dependency on scrap. The expansion will be financed out of Dofasco's cash reserves, which were $532-million at year-end.

Dofasco forecasts that demand for flat rolled steel, on a North American basis, will decline by 2% to 3%, reflecting the larger inventory built up in the United States than in Canada. A reduction in the current high level of imports should allow producers to operate at near-capcity levels throughout 1995. In the past two years Dofasco has shifted to higher value-added steel products, capitalizing on the modern finishing technology in Hamilton. Product mix in 1994 (1993) was: Hot rolled, 31%(50%); Cold rolled, 20%(17%); Galvanized, 39%(25%); and Tinplate, 10% (8%).

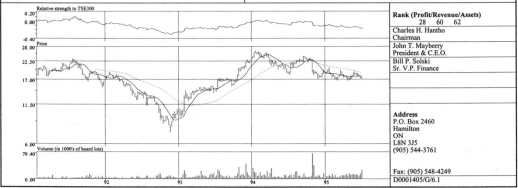

Rank (Profit/Revenue/Assets)
28 60 62

Charles H. Hantho
Chairman

John T. Mayberry
President & C.E.O.

Bill P. Solski
Sr. V.P. Finance

Address
P.O. Box 2460
Hamilton
ON
L8N 3J5
(905) 544-3761

Fax: (905) 548-4249
D0001405/G/6.1

EMCO LIMITED

Exchanges	Price (Jun29'95)	7.87	Trailing P/E	27.14	Stock Symbol
TM	Trailing Yield (%)	0.00	Trailing EPS	0.29	EML

Period Ending	Dec94	Dec93	Dec92	Dec91	Dec90
Yearly Statistics					
Price-Close	7.50	8.75	5.38	4.85	4.75
Price-High	10.63	9.50	8.00	8.00	11.25
Price-Low	7.50	5.50	4.25	3.60	4.00
P/E-Close	50.00	175.00	nm	nm	nm
Dividends per Share	0.00	0.00	0.00	0.00	0.35
Dividend Yield (%)	0.00	0.00	0.00	0.00	7.37
Sales per Share	46.63	42.69	73.25	70.38	80.68
EPS before extra. item	0.15	0.05	(0.67)	(1.37)	(2.11)
Cash Flow per Share	1.14	1.11	0.49	(0.50)	(1.04)
Book Value per Share	5.39	5.23	4.63	5.30	6.36
O/S Common Shares	23,163	23,080	14,167	14,167	14,167
Total Revenue	1,078,246	940,624	1,038,983	1,004,774	1,139,916
Income before extra.	3,451	1,101	(9,504)	(19,394)	(29,957)
Cash Flow	26,377	24,492	6,945	(7,142)	(14,666)
Debt/Equity	2.37	2.32	4.71	4.41	3.58
Return on Capital (%)	6.74	6.22	5.92	3.80	(0.15)
Ret. on Com. Equity (%)	2.81	1.18	(13.52)	(23.49)	(28.27)
% Change Profit	213.4	111.6	51.0	35.3	(211.5)
% Change Revenue	14.6	(9.5)	3.4	(11.9)	(5.9)
% Change Assets	9.0	6.2	(4.6)	1.5	(10.7)

Preferred Div. Coverage	np	np	np
Total Div. Coverage	na	na	na
Interest Coverage	1.2	1.1	0.8
Current Ratio	2.3	2.5	1.9
Operating Margin	3.4	3.5	2.2
Asset Turnover	1.8	1.7	2.0
5 YEAR RATIOS (%)			
Return on Capital	4.5	4.2	5.3
Return on Com. Equity	(12.3)	(14.3)	(12.5)
Profit Growth	na	(40.4)	na
Revenue Growth	(2.3)	(4.5)	4.3
Asset Growth	(0.0)	(4.4)	(3.8)
BALANCE SHEET (000)			
Cash	1,278	1,146	2,749
Current Assets	393,615	358,001	329,454
Net Fixed Assets	157,039	144,424	141,605
Invest'& Advances	6,790	6,922	7,081
Total Assets	586,215	537,949	506,341
Short Term Debt	9,151	8,573	41,834
Current Liabilities	172,991	143,558	171,912
Long Term Debt	286,292	271,369	266,983
Total Liabilities	461,329	417,174	440,780
Total Equity	124,886	120,775	65,561
Total Liab. & Equity	586,215	537,949	506,341
CAPITAL (000)			
Total Debt	295,443	279,942	308,817
Preferred Equity	0	0	0
Common Equity	124,886	120,775	65,561

Business:

EMCO LTD. is a manufacturer and distributor of building and home improvement products and is a major distributor of plumbing and related products. In addition, Emco manufactures and distributes worldwide, fluid handling equipment for the petroleum and petrochemical industries, and produces custom components including brass and aluminum forgings.

Date	EPS	DPS	Tot Rev	Inc Bex
Mar 95	(0.17)	0.00	241,919	(3,948)
Dec 94	(0.21)	0.00	156,229	(4,980)
Sep 94	0.51	0.00	370,932	11,696
Jun 94	0.16	0.00	323,667	3,665
Mar 94	(0.30)	0.00	227,420	(6,930)
Dec 93	(0.04)	0.00	129,615	(848)
Sep 93	0.30	0.00	317,934	7,024
Jun 93	0.09	0.00	287,969	2,186

Synopsis:

Emco Limited reported increased sales in the first quarter ended March 1995 of 22%, $241.9-million from $197.5-million in 1994. The company credits approximately 25% of this increase to a special winter promotion in roofing. The promotion generated sales that typically would not occur in the first quarter. Sales in the Distribution Group increased 16%; 9% when 1994 acquisitions are excluded. Emco believes part of this increase reflected a strengthening in the Ontario market. There were, however, signs of weakening demand in other regions of the country. Emco sold its Vinyl Siding Division in May 1995 to ABT Corporation of Neenah, Wisconsin for $45-million. Emco will use proceeds from the sale of the business to pay down debt. The company had plans to dispose of this division as well as the Environmental Products division and had designated both groups as discontinued in 1994.

The Emco Distribution Group intends to emphasize industrial and consumer products to reduce its dependence on the cyclical residential construction industry. The Group reported record sales in 1994 with an increase of 17.9% over 1993. This was a result of continued market share gains across Canada and the acquisition of the operations of Ideal Plumbing in Atlantic Canada. The company expects the Group's sales will continue to experience a strong growth trend in 1995.

For certain manufacturing divisions in the Building Products Group, 1994 was a disappointing year. Early in the year this business saw rising raw material costs and downward competitive pressures on pricing. Subsequently, several manufacturing problems combined with lower prices and higher costs produced results that were far below the results for 1993 and previous years. Sales for the group improved by 8.6%, but gross margins declined by 3.8% from 1993, despite improved margins for the Wood Fibre and Kindred Industries divisions. Management believes it has taken effective steps to overcome the production inefficiencies in roofing and expects that the margins will return to normal levels in 1995.

Relative strength to TSE300

Price

Volume (in 1000's of board lots)

Rank (Profit/Revenue/Assets)
491   116   214

Wayne B. Lyon
Chairman Of The Board

Frank Mittennessey
President & C.E.O.

Richard B. Grogan
V.P. Fin. & C.F.O.

Address
620 Richmond Street
London
ON
N6A 5J9
(519) 645-3900

Fax: (519) 645-2465
E0001142/G/6.2

For further company information, call Globe Information Services 1-800-268-9128 or (416) 585-5345

HARRIS STEEL GROUP INC.

Exchanges	Price (Jun29'95)	9 .00	Trailing P/E	3 .81	Stock Symbol
T	Trailing Yield (%)	2 .67	Trailing EPS	2 .36	HSG.A

Period Ending	Dec94	Dec93	Dec92	Dec91	Dec90
Yearly Statistics					
Price-Close	11 .00	10 .50	5 .25	6 .00	4 .30
Price-High	14 .25	12 .50	7 .75	7 .00	6 .00
Price-Low	9 .25	5 .00	5 .00	4 .00	3 .80
P/E-Close	4 .89	26 .25	nm	33 .33	9 .77
Dividends per Share	0 .21	0 .13	0 .13	0 .13	0 .24
Dividend Yield (%)	1 .93	1 .24	2 .48	2 .08	5 .58
Sales per Share	26 .91	17 .73	16 .52	17 .18	19 .53
EPS before extra. item	2 .25	0 .40	(0 .03)	0 .18	0 .44
Cash Flow per Share	2 .56	0 .71	0 .19	0 .47	0 .95
Book Value per Share	6 .97	4 .93	4 .67	4 .83	4 .78
O/S Common Shares	11 ,351	11 ,351	11 ,521	11 ,568	11 ,591
Total Revenue	305 ,402	201 ,377	191 ,110	198 ,777	235 ,862
Income before extra.	25 ,559	4 ,544	(377)	2 ,092	5 ,325
Cash Flow	29 ,056	8 ,018	2 ,245	5 ,473	11 ,541
Debt/Equity	0 .49	0 .63	0 .33	0 .01	0 .07
Return on Capital (%)	37 .42	11 .32	3 .52	9 .09	21 .51
Ret. on Com. Equity (%)	37 .83	8 .28	(0 .69)	3 .76	9 .56
% Change Profit	462 .5	1 ,306 .6	(118 .0)	(60 .7)	nm
% Change Revenue	51 .7	5 .4	(3 .9)	(15 .7)	(1 .4)
% Change Assets	39 .1	10 .5	19 .8	(11 .2)	(7 .8)

Preferred Div. Coverage	np	np	np
Total Div. Coverage	10 .6	3 .1	0 .0
Interest Coverage	17 .5	7 .5	6 .3
Current Ratio	1 .7	1 .6	1 .6
Operating Margin	13 .3	5 .2	1 .4
Asset Turnover	1 .9	1 .7	1 .8
5 YEAR RATIOS (%)			
Return on Capital	16 .6	10 .8	10 .3
Return on Com. Equity	11 .7	4 .2	3 .8
Profit Growth	na	3 .3	na
Revenue Growth	5 .0	(1 .3)	na
Asset Growth	8 .5	(8 .3)	(12 .2)
BALANCE SHEET (000)			
Cash	0	0	0
Current Assets	141 ,123	95 ,265	82 ,380
Net Fixed Assets	21 ,852	21 ,451	21 ,877
Invest's & Advances	0	0	0
Total Assets	164 ,573	118 ,314	107 ,051
Short Term Debt	39 ,063	35 ,067	17 ,652
Current Liabilities	83 ,647	60 ,326	51 ,184
Long Term Debt	0	0	0
Total Liabilities	85 ,428	62 ,316	53 ,264
Total Equity	79 ,145	55 ,998	53 ,786
Total Liab. & Equity	164 ,573	118 ,314	107 ,051
CAPITAL (000)			
Total Debt	39 ,063	35 ,067	17 ,652
Preferred Equity	0	0	0
Common Equity	79 ,145	55 ,998	53 ,786

Business:

HARRIS STEEL GROUP INC. is engaged in the fabrication and installation of concrete reinforcing steel and the production and marketing of epoxy-coated reinforcing steel. The company also manufactures and distributes wire and wired products, welded wire mesh, cold finished bar and heavy industrial steel and aluminum grating. The Company serves Canada and the North Eastern, Central and Western U.S.

Date	EPS	DPS	Tot Rev	Inc Bex
Mar 95	0 .34	0 .06	75 ,459	3 ,820
Dec 94	0 .77	0 .06	86 ,019	8 ,772
Sep 94	0 .74	0 .06	90 ,881	8 ,443
Jun 94	0 .51	0 .06	74 ,721	5 ,750
Mar 94	0 .23	0 .03	53 ,780	2 ,594
Dec 93	0 .14	0 .03	57 ,052	1 ,577
Sep 93	0 .14	0 .03	54 ,154	1 ,556
Jun 93	0 .11	0 .03	52 ,381	1 ,317

Synopsis:

Harris Steel reported a strong quarter for the period ended March 31, 1995. The company continued to benefit from large inventories acquired below current replacement costs. Current prices from its steel mill suppliers are increasing faster than its ability to recover from the marketplace. This will lead to substantially reduced margins in the latter half of the year. The company's earnings are now fully taxable, as Harris Steel used up all U.S. tax loss carry forwards in 1994.

Harris Steel began 1995 with large inventories priced below replacement costs in all of its divisions. This will help performance in the first half of the year. Harris Rebar has an excellent order backlog in Ontario. Spending is slowing in some key markets in the U.S. Boston's massive Central Artery project has been slow to come to tender, and little shipping activity is expected this year. Phoenix and Oakland continue to build profitable backlogs, but the Seattle market continues to be plagued with uneconomic fabricator pricing.

Harris Steel, after carefully assessing the whole American northeast, has decided to relocate its epoxy-coating facility and some fabrication equipment from Boston to Bethlehem, Pennsylvania. Harris feels that in this location it can be competitive from Maine to the Virginias, and from Western New York to Tennessee. However, Harris Steel will keep Boston as a fully equipped branch facility.

In 1994 all divisions performed well. Harris Rebar entered the year with a large backlog of profitable jobs in the U.S. The Canadian backlog was sparse because the company would not accept low margin work in the face of rapidly increasing steel costs. As the year progressed, pricing started to reflect steel market conditions. Laurel Steel saw strong demand for its industrial products coupled with the tightening of supplies of raw steel materials. However, aided by a lower Canadian dollar, Laurel recovered cost increases from its suppliers.

Relative strength to TSE300 / Price / Volume (in 1000's of board lots)

Rank (Profit/Revenue/Assets)
185 256 380

Milton E. Harris
Chairman President & C.E.O.

John Harris
President & C.O.O.

Bruce J. Timmerman
V.P. Finance & Secretary

Address
4120 Yonge Street
Suite 604
Toronto
ON
M2P 2B8
(416) 590-9549

H0000617/G/6.2

HAWKER SIDDELEY CANADA INC.

Exchanges	Price (Jun29'95)	13.87	Trailing P/E	nm	Stock Symbol
TMV	Trailing Yield (%)	7.78	Trailing EPS	(6.19)	HSC

Period Ending	Dec94	Dec93	Dec92	Dec91	Dec90
Yearly Statistics					
Price-Close	19.00	25.50	20.25	26.00	22.50
Price-High	27.00	28.00	26.00	28.00	26.50
Price-Low	16.50	18.75	20.00	22.00	20.00
P/E-Close	nm	nm	11.38	20.16	8.04
Dividends per Share	1.08	1.08	1.08	1.08	1.08
Dividend Yield (%)	5.68	4.24	5.33	4.15	4.80
Sales per Share	38.77	40.54	41.34	47.89	50.33
EPS before extra. item	(6.53)	(0.49)	1.78	1.29	2.80
Cash Flow per Share	1.52	6.23	5.64	4.31	5.84
Book Value per Share	21.32	28.00	29.27	28.67	28.80
O/S Common Shares	8,205	8,200	8,200	8,184	8,157
Total Revenue	318,500	332,800	340,000	392,700	413,000
Income before extra.	(52,800)	(3,200)	15,400	11,300	23,700
Cash Flow	12,500	51,100	46,200	35,200	47,600
Debt/Equity	0.56	0.50	0.40	0.47	0.26
Return on Capital (%)	(9.55)	6.02	10.82	8.46	13.96
Ret. on Com. Equity (%)	(26.50)	(1.70)	6.15	4.47	10.24
% Change Profit	(1,550.0)	(120.8)	36.3	(52.3)	73.0
% Change Revenue	(4.3)	(2.1)	(13.4)	(4.9)	12.7
% Change Assets	(14.1)	3.8	0.6	12.9	3.7
Preferred Div. Coverage	0.0	0.0	19.3		
Total Div. Coverage	0.0	0.0	1.6		
Interest Coverage	0.0	2.1	4.3		
Current Ratio	1.3	1.5	1.3		
Operating Margin	1.2	15.9	12.9		
Asset Turnover	0.7	0.6	0.6		
5 YEAR RATIOS (%)					
Return on Capital	5.9	10.2	11.6		
Return on Com. Equity	(1.5)	5.0	6.9		
Profit Growth	na	na	(6.3)		
Revenue Growth	(2.8)	(3.5)	(3.3)		
Asset Growth	1.0	3.3	4.1		
BALANCE SHEET (000)					
Cash	8,900	19,400	21,800		
Current Assets	115,800	166,400	158,300		
Net Fixed Assets	327,900	345,600	332,400		
Invest's & Advances	0	0	0		
Total Assets	475,200	553,100	532,700		
Short Term Debt	9,700	23,400	39,700		
Current Liabilities	86,700	111,800	120,700		
Long Term Debt	96,900	99,100	61,700		
Total Liabilities	286,300	309,500	278,700		
Total Equity	188,900	243,600	254,000		
Total Liab. & Equity	475,200	553,100	532,700		
CAPITAL (000)					
Total Debt	106,600	122,500	101,400		
Preferred Equity	14,000	14,000	14,000		
Common Equity	174,900	229,600	240,000		

Business:

HAWKER SIDDELEY CANADA INC. manufactures components for repairs and overhauls aero and industrial gas turbine engines; manufactures sawmill and mining equipment; leases railcars; and provides for PRK vision correction.

Date	EPS	DPS	Tot Rev	Inc Bex
Mar 95	(0.04)	0.27	88,400	(200)
Dec 94	(4.46)	0.27	79,000	(36,400)
Sep 94	(0.54)	0.27	79,500	(4,300)
Jun 94	(1.15)	0.27	81,300	(9,200)
Mar 94	(0.38)	0.27	78,200	(2,900)
Dec 93	(1.76)	0.27	73,000	(14,200)
Sep 93	0.27	0.27	86,100	2,400
Jun 93	0.65	0.27	88,400	5,500

Synopsis:

Hawker Siddeley reported sales of $88.4-million for the first quarter ended March 31, 1995, compared to sales of $76.4-million in 1994. Aerospace operations sales were higher with both Orenda and Middleton Aerospace making a contribution. CGTX continued to post increased sales and the mining-related companies increased their overall contribution.

In 1994, Specialty Consumer Services created a U.S. subsidiary, Beacon Eye Institute, and a Canadian subsidiary, Beacon Eye Centre Inc., to provide facilities and services for eye care professionals performing laser-PRK vision correction. The company believes the market potential for refractive surgery is enormous. About120 million people in North America are potential clients. If, over the next 10 years, only 10% of these people elected to have this procedure performed the market potential could be $40-billion. By using the laser centre in Toronto, Beacon Eye Institute hopes to tap the vast U.S. market, subject to FDA approval of the laser equipment.

In 1995, the company expects improvement from its Sawmill Equipment operations. Performance in 1994 was marred by complications during recovery from a poorly executed plant relocation and new plant start-up in the previous year. The installation of a new management team has led to the recovery from the significant loss position of a year ago. The order book at the end of April 1995 was more than 50% higher than a year ago. The company feels sales for 1995 could exceed 1994 by as much as 15 to 20%.

Aerospace Operations are an area in which the company expects it will be able to increase sales. Canadian Armed Forces contracts have been awarded for 1995 and 1996. The acquisition of the assets of A-R Technologies provides an opportunity to commercialize the specialized component re-manufacturing process currently in place. These products can be supplied at quality levels comparable or better than new parts, at a much lower price.

Rank (Profit/Revenue/Assets)
989   248   234

John F. Howard
Chairman

Keith F. Moore
President & C.E.O.

A.M. Gordon Turnbull
Sr. V.P. Finance & C.F.O.

Address
3 Robert Speck Parkway
#700
Mississauga
ON
L4Z 2G5
(905) 897-7161

Fax: (905) 897-1466
H0000980/G/6.3

For further company information, call Globe Information Services 1-800-268-9128 or (416) 585-5345

IPSCO INC.

Exchanges	Price (Jun29'95)	25.00	Trailing P/E	10.00	Stock Symbol
TZQ	Trailing Yield (%)	1.92	Trailing EPS	2.50	**ISP**

Period Ending	Dec94	Dec93	Dec92	Dec91	Dec90
Yearly Statistics					
Price-Close	25.25	26.00	20.25	22.63	18.25
Price-High	27.75	28.00	24.25	25.25	19.00
Price-Low	21.75	19.25	15.88	17.75	13.25
P/E-Close	11.85	18.31	20.66	8.94	nm
Dividends per Share	0.48	0.48	0.48	0.48	0.48
Dividend Yield (%)	1.90	1.85	2.37	2.12	2.63
Sales per Share	31.33	28.36	30.35	37.49	32.92
EPS before extra. item	2.13	1.42	0.98	2.53	(0.34)
Cash Flow per Share	2.79	2.28	1.72	3.96	0.89
Book Value per Share	24.46	22.14	19.01	18.61	16.62
O/S Common Shares	27,081	27,055	16,874	14,464	14,240
Total Revenue	847,916	573,224	480,359	538,657	462,105
Income before extra.	57,715	28,697	15,512	36,348	(4,772)
Cash Flow	75,496	46,109	27,254	56,935	12,506
Debt/Equity	0.52	0.16	0.18	0.21	0.32
Return on Capital (%)	12.49	9.60	8.86	20.75	0.54
Ret. on Com. Equity (%)	9.15	6.24	5.26	14.37	(1.97)
% Change Profit	101.1	85.0	(57.3)	861.7	(124.7)
% Change Revenue	47.9	19.3	(10.8)	16.6	0.3
% Change Assets	47.3	65.8	10.4	3.3	0.4
Preferred Div. Coverage	np	np	np		
Total Div. Coverage	4.4	2.7	2.0		
Interest Coverage	5.2	8.5	5.5		
Current Ratio	1.9	4.4	3.0		
Operating Margin	12.5	9.0	6.5		
Asset Turnover	0.7	0.7	1.0		
5 YEAR RATIOS (%)					
Return on Capital	10.4	10.5	12.6		
Return on Com. Equity	6.6	6.4	7.7		
Profit Growth	24.4	(0.1)	13.3		
Revenue Growth	12.9	5.8	9.9		
Asset Growth	22.8	13.1	5.1		
BALANCE SHEET (000)					
Cash	81,098	283,753	66,728		
Current Assets	341,863	556,928	248,268		
Net Fixed Assets	496,339	276,364	256,113		
Invest's & Advances	390,645	0	0		
Total Assets	1,234,575	838,023	505,415		
Short Term Debt	0	39,312	0		
Current Liabilities	182,729	127,927	82,317		
Long Term Debt	340,801	57,953	57,787		
Total Liabilities	572,293	238,958	184,656		
Total Equity	662,282	599,065	320,759		
Total Liab. & Equity	1,234,575	838,023	505,415		
CAPITAL (000)					
Total Debt	340,801	97,265	57,787		
Preferred Equity	0	0	0		
Common Equity	662,282	599,065	320,759		

Business:

IPSCO INC. manufactures a diverse range of steel and steel products. Products include steel coil, sheet, plate, bar, tubular products, and alloy steel and line pipe. It operates facilities in Saskatchewan, Alberta, British Columbia, Iowa, Minnesota, and Nebraska. IPSCO markets its products across Canada and the United States.

Date	EPS	DPS	Tot Rev	Inc Bex
Mar 95	0.85	0.12	204,327	23,119
Dec 94	0.77	0.12	227,169	20,925
Sep 94	0.53	0.12	227,280	14,385
Jun 94	0.35	0.12	211,378	9,394
Mar 94	0.48	0.12	201,536	13,011
Dec 93	0.39	0.12	165,025	9,084
Sep 93	0.28	0.12	139,518	6,441
Jun 93	0.21	0.12	121,299	4,087

Synopsis:

IPSCO plans a 25% increase in capacity at a mini-mill being built in Iowa and may expand again after operation begins in the second quarter of 1996. Capacity can be boosted to 1.25 million tons by spending another $15-million during the construction of the mill. The flat-rolled mill, budgeted at $360 million (U.S.), was originally scheduled to produce one million tons of steel plate a year. The mill can be expanded to allow production of 1.5-million tons within a year of start-up. Iowa provided $73-million (U.S.) worth of incentives to IPSCO to locate the mini-mill in Muscatine County, about 50 kilometres from the company's pipe mill at Comanche, Iowa.

Sales revenue of $198.4-million for the first quarter ended March 31, 1995, was 3% higher than the first quarter a year earlier. Tonnage shipped fell 10% below the first quarter of last year and 12% below the fourth quarter. The lack of competitively priced steel to supplement IPSCO's own record levels of production rather than a drop in demand reduced sales and shipments. IPSCO bought an average of 62,000 tons of steel per quarter for conversion to further fabricated goods. The company's ability to make profitable use of available imports in the first quarter of 1995 was sharply restricted by the rising cost of offshore hot-rolled coil. As a result, the company reduced its use of bought material to 49,000 tons.

IPSCO shipped 1,350,300 tons in 1994, a 35% increase over the previous company high of 999,200 tons. IPSCO supplemented its own production by buying flat rolled steel from third parties, making possible above average growth. IPSCO bought steel from other producers because steel needed for its further fabrication operations falls within specifications not produced by the company. In 1994, IPSCO adopted a strategy to buy some grades that it normally produces but for which it lacked production capacity. Using this strategy increased its market share and established a valuable buffer in the event of a downturn. The potential demand for production from the U.S. mill also has grown due to this strategy.

Relative strength to TSE300

Price

Volume (in 1000's of board lots)

92	93	94	95

Rank (Profit/Revenue/Assets)
104   130   140

Thomas Kierans
Chairman Of The Board

Roger Phillips
President & C.E.O.

Mario J. Dalla-Vicenza
Sr. V.P. & C.F.O.

Address
P.O. Box 1670
Regina
SK
S4P 3C7
(306) 924-7700

Fax: (306) 924-7500
I0001728/G/6.1

IVACO INC.

Exchanges	Price (Jun29'95)	5.75	Trailing P/E	12.78	Stock Symbol
TM	Trailing Yield (%)	0.00	Trailing EPS	0.45	**IVA.A**

Period Ending	Dec94	Dec93	Dec92	Dec91	Dec90
Yearly Statistics					
Price-Close	5.25	6.00	2.30	3.60	6.75
Price-High	8.75	7.50	5.13	8.00	11.50
Price-Low	4.60	1.60	2.00	3.00	6.13
P/E-Close	nm	nm	nm	nm	nm
Dividends per Share	0.00	0.00	0.00	0.32	0.60
Dividend Yield (%)	0.00	0.00	0.00	8.89	8.89
Sales per Share	53.01	55.57	52.16	55.06	98.31
EPS before extra. item	(0.25)	(0.63)	(1.71)	(3.86)	(0.25)
Cash Flow per Share	3.08	2.28	(0.06)	(1.78)	2.67
Book Value per Share	9.18	8.97	9.28	10.32	14.38
O/S Common Shares	28,642	24,866	21,833	20,584	19,950
Total Revenue	1,423,768	1,226,610	1,091,367	1,120,592	1,883,878
Income before extra.	8,054	321	(19,565)	(59,396)	16,966
Cash Flow	82,296	50,186	(1,161)	(36,048)	50,707
Debt/Equity	1.06	1.18	1.32	1.36	1.13
Return on Capital (%)	7.39	5.34	1.29	(2.47)	7.47
Ret. on Com. Equity (%)	2.61	(0.66)	(10.77)	(28.53)	(1.66)
% Change Profit	2,409.0	101.6	67.1	(450.1)	32.0
% Change Revenue	16.1	12.4	(2.6)	(40.5)	(6.2)
% Change Assets	8.8	1.8	(8.8)	(8.2)	(23.2)

Preferred Div. Coverage	4.7	0.2	0.0
Total Div. Coverage	4.7	0.2	0.0
Interest Coverage	1.9	1.4	0.3
Current Ratio	1.9	1.8	1.4
Operating Margin	5.5	4.0	(0.1)
Asset Turnover	1.1	1.0	0.9
5 YEAR RATIOS (%)			
Return on Capital	3.8	3.8	5.0
Return on Com. Equity	(7.8)	(9.0)	(7.6)
Profit Growth	(8.9)	(62.9)	na
Revenue Growth	(6.7)	(9.6)	(12.6)
Asset Growth	(6.6)	(8.3)	(7.7)
BALANCE SHEET (000)			
Cash	18,573	12,000	0
Current Assets	571,465	484,868	453,356
Net Fixed Assets	472,106	469,683	484,661
Invest's & Advances	205,908	199,192	191,559
Total Assets	1,309,237	1,203,395	1,182,633
Short Term Debt	65,222	71,711	153,214
Current Liabilities	308,428	264,237	325,833
Long Term Debt	448,141	450,701	404,653
Total Liabilities	826,520	760,616	760,359
Total Equity	482,717	442,779	422,274
Total Liab. & Equity	1,309,237	1,203,395	1,182,633
CAPITAL (000)			
Total Debt	513,363	522,412	557,867
Preferred Equity	219,711	219,711	219,724
Common Equity	263,006	223,068	202,550

Business:

IVACO is a steel producer with annual steelmaking and rolling capacity in excess of two million tons. Ivaco produces steel billets, hot rolled bars and shapes, wire rod, wire, welded wire fabric, nails, fasteners, precision machined components, forgings, wire ropes, and cables. Ivaco has 51 plants: 33 in Canada, and 18 in the United States.

Date	EPS	DPS	Tot Rev	Inc Bex
Mar 95	0.37	0.00	409,665	14,482
Sep 94	0.02	0.00	370,607	4,040
Jun 94	0.08	0.00	365,412	5,825
Mar 94	(0.02)	0.00	309,541	3,113
Dec 93	(0.09)	0.00	312,015	1,434
Sep 93	0.04	0.00	313,235	4,520
Jun 93	(0.01)	0.00	319,273	3,247
Mar 93	(0.57)	0.00	282,744	(8,880)

Synopsis:

Ivaco's sales for the first quarter, ended March 31, 1995, were $407.4-million, up from $308.7-million in the first quarter of 1994. With this improvement, and some dividends back in place, the company expects a strong second quarter, and an impressive year for sales and earnings. In 1994, Ivaco's profit was $8.1-million on sales of $1.4-billion. With the exception of Canron's structural steel unit, and Atlantic Steel, all of the company's operating groups delivered profits from ongoing operations for the year.

Laclede Steel, of which Ivaco owns 49.8%, made significant progress in 1994. Continuous weld pipe and electric resistance weld tubing are among the company's main products, yet most of the growth was in the steel tubular business. Laclede modified its continuous caster to produce larger slabs for efficient rolling of skelp used to make steel pipe. It is the only mill to make its own steel skelp. Laclede is one of North America's largest steel pipe manufacturers, making it a leader in low cost production. Special Bar Quality steels, wire, and oil tempered wire and chain are also manufactured at Laclede. Laclede's operating results continue to show improvement for 1995.

Ivaco's surplus lands are attracting prospective buyers. Ivaco expects to sell these land holdings, including a 40 acre redevelopment site in Metropolitan Toronto and a 125 acre site near downtown Atlanta. Ivaco is waiting for an appropriate price to sell these locations. High levels of production are expected throughout the year and the order backlog at most units is substantial. With the combination of low unit cost production, strong product demand, and the more appropriate level of the Canadian dollar, Ivaco hopes to have a strong year.

Rank (Profit/Revenue/Assets)		
333	89	138

Paul Ivanier
President & C.E.O.

Albert A. Kassab
Sr. V.P. & C.F.O.

Address
Place Mercantile
770 Rue Sherbrooke Ouest
Suite 2000
Montreal
PQ
H3A 1G1
(514) 288-4545
Fax: (514) 288-7814
I0002425/G/6.1

246   **For further company information, call Globe Information Services 1-800-268-9128 or (416) 585-5345**

SAMUEL MANU-TECH INC.

Exchanges	Price (Jun29'95)		9 .75	Trailing P/E		8 .71	Stock Symbol
T	Trailing Yield (%)		1 .74	Trailing EPS		1 .12	**SMT**

Period Ending	Dec94	Dec93	Dec92	Dec91	Dec90
Yearly Statistics					
Price-Close	12 .00	10 .63	7 .32	7 .00	5 .75
Price-High	12 .75	10 .63	8 .00	7 .00	6 .63
Price-Low	9 .32	7 .25	6 .88	5 .63	4 .75
P/E-Close	10 .13	14 .76	30 .47	21 .21	10 .55
Dividends per Share	0 .20	0 .12	0 .12	0 .17	0 .24
Dividend Yield (%)	1 .67	1 .13	1 .64	2 .36	4 .17
Sales per Share	18 .37	14 .03	10 .95	9 .74	11 .24
EPS before extra. item	1 .19	0 .72	0 .24	0 .33	0 .55
Cash Flow per Share	1 .64	0 .99	0 .81	0 .59	0 .79
Book Value per Share	6 .55	5 .47	4 .86	4 .70	4 .54
O/S Common Shares	17 ,294	17 ,294	17 ,444	17 ,444	17 ,638
Total Revenue	317 ,777	243 ,284	191 ,427	170 ,705	199 ,173
Income before extra.	20 ,455	12 ,482	4 ,232	5 ,759	9 ,660
Cash Flow	28 ,355	17 ,170	14 ,072	10 ,233	13 ,902
Debt/Equity	0 .26	0 .11	0 .17	0 .11	0 .10
Return on Capital (%)	27 .30	20 .25	11 .30	12 .10	20 .99
Ret. on Com. Equity (%)	19 .70	13 .92	5 .08	7 .11	12 .47
% Change Profit	63 .9	195 .0	(26 .5)	(40 .4)	(20 .5)
% Change Revenue	30 .6	27 .1	12 .1	(14 .3)	(9 .8)
% Change Assets	42 .8	7 .1	11 .0	2 .9	(1 .7)

Preferred Div. Coverage	np	np	np
Total Div. Coverage	7 .4	6 .0	2 .0
Interest Coverage	36 .8	30 .9	16 .3
Current Ratio	1 .8	2 .6	2 .4
Operating Margin	10 .6	8 .4	7 .7
Asset Turnover	1 .6	1 .8	1 .5
5 YEAR RATIOS (%)			
Return on Capital	18 .4	18 .8	23 .4
Return on Com. Equity	11 .7	11 .4	14 .4
Profit Growth	11 .0	(3 .0)	(17 .8)
Revenue Growth	7 .6	6 .3	8 .4
Asset Growth	11 .4	5 .5	13 .3
BALANCE SHEET (000)			
Cash	234	1 ,116	7 ,811
Current Assets	122 ,692	89 ,775	78 ,364
Net Fixed Assets	71 ,925	47 ,563	49 ,422
Invest's & Advances	0	0	0
Total Assets	197 ,510	138 ,357	129 ,210
Short Term Debt	15 ,387	4 ,962	6 ,760
Current Liabilities	66 ,521	34 ,819	32 ,280
Long Term Debt	14 ,324	5 ,773	7 ,278
Total Liabilities	84 ,298	43 ,847	44 ,437
Total Equity	113 ,212	94 ,510	84 ,774
Total Liab. & Equity	197 ,510	138 ,357	129 ,210
CAPITAL (000)			
Total Debt	29 ,711	10 ,735	14 ,039
Preferred Equity	0	0	0
Common Equity	113 ,212	94 ,510	84 ,774

Business:

SAMUEL MANU-TECH INC. processes steel and manufactures steel products. Products include stainless steel pipe and tube, pickled flat rolled coil steel, steel and plastic packaging systems, steel tanks and wire rope and chain. The company markets products to the automotive, urban transit, mining and construction industries in Canada, the United States and Europe.

Date	EPS	DPS	Tot Rev	Inc Bex
Mar 95	0 .38	0 .08	98 ,879	6 ,487
Jun 94	0 .34	0 .03	80 ,430	5 ,854
Mar 94	0 .23	0 .03	64 ,506	3 ,986
Dec 93	0 .17	0 .03	65 ,130	2 ,964
Sep 93	0 .20	0 .03	60 ,950	3 ,403
Jun 93	0 .18	0 .03	60 ,534	3 ,056
Mar 93	0 .18	0 .03	56 ,670	3 ,059
Dec 92	0 .11	0 .03	49 ,839	1 ,926

Synopsis:

Samuel Manu-Tech reported first quarter sales of $98.8-million, an increase of 53% compared to the first quarter of last year. Included in the first quarter results were the sales of Delta Shipping Corporation, Brockhouse Canada, and Roll Formed Specialty and Equipment Limited which were acquired in April 1994, August 1994, and November 1994 respectively. If these operations were excluded, sales for the first quarter were ahead 32% compared to the previous year.

The company acquired the assets of RH Strapping on March 17, 1995. Located in Rock Hill, South Carolina, the facility makes standard duty and high tensile steel strapping. The acquisition complements the activities of the Samuel Strapping Group and helps strengthen the division's market position, particularly in the southern and southeastern United States.

The steel trade is optimistic that 1995 will see the establishment of common steel trade rules under the North American Free Trade Agreement to address anti-dumping actions between Canada and the U.S. A number of duties are currently in effect on various steel products traded between the two countries. While these duties do not materially restrict the company's cross-border business opportunities, in the future the company hopes that these disputes can be settled in a less punitive manner. Samuel Manu-Tech, in addition to its ongoing fostering of internal growth opportunities, continues to be interested in adding value to its operations through acquisition. As 1995 began a number of negotiations were underway.

Samuel Manu-Tech enjoyed the best year of its history in 1994. This was shared on both sides of the border, as all divisions contributed to record sales and profitability. In 1994, the company derived more than half of its total sales from the U.S. market. The company sees it as a strength in having this balance of exposure between the two economies.

Relative strength to TSE300 / Price / Volume (in 1000's of board lots)

Rank (Profit/Revenue/Assets)
213 250 359

Ernest L. Samuel
Chairman

Mark C. Samuel
President

Wallace H. Rayner
V.P. Finance & Secretary

Address
191 The West Mall
Suite 418
Etobicoke
ON
M9C 5K8
(416) 626-2190

Fax: (416) 656-5969
S0000269/G/6.2

SLATER INDUSTRIES INC.

Exchanges	Price (Jun29'95)	12.75	Trailing P/E	4.53	Stock Symbol
T	Trailing Yield (%)	0.00	Trailing EPS	2.81	SSI

Period Ending	Dec94	Dec93	Dec92	Dec91	Dec90
Yearly Statistics					
Price-Close	10.88	5.63	3.00	4.00	4.00
Price-High	12.88	7.00	4.45	6.25	6.25
Price-Low	6.00	2.65	2.45	3.90	3.80
P/E-Close	4.65	nm	nm	nm	25.00
Dividends per Share	0.00	0.00	0.00	0.00	0.00
Dividend Yield (%)	0.00	0.00	0.00	0.00	0.00
Sales per Share	48.58	49.79	45.06	43.34	47.45
EPS before extra. item	2.34	(0.93)	(0.72)	(1.16)	0.16
Cash Flow per Share	4.21	1.32	0.59	(0.81)	1.04
Book Value per Share	13.38	13.21	14.17	14.71	15.85
O/S Common Shares	11,490	8,190	8,100	8,100	8,100
Total Revenue	494,589	404,616	364,951	351,028	384,347
Income before extra.	24,056	(7,357)	(5,643)	(9,210)	1,507
Cash Flow	42,877	10,696	4,755	(6,537)	8,427
Debt/Equity	0.51	0.93	0.95	0.92	0.85
Return on Capital (%)	18.33	(0.59)	(0.47)	(2.53)	4.80
Ret. on Com. Equity (%)	18.22	(6.78)	(4.99)	(7.61)	1.01
% Change Profit	427.0	(30.4)	38.7	(711.1)	(81.0)
% Change Revenue	22.2	10.9	4.0	(8.7)	(2.4)
% Change Assets	18.2	(3.7)	(0.3)	(8.7)	5.2

Preferred Div. Coverage	121.5	0.0	0.0
Total Div. Coverage	121.5	0.0	0.0
Interest Coverage	6.8	0.0	0.0
Current Ratio	2.2	2.2	2.5
Operating Margin	8.4	2.5	(0.3)
Asset Turnover	1.6	1.5	1.3

5 YEAR RATIOS (%)			
Return on Capital	3.9	2.2	4.2
Return on Com. Equity	(0.0)	(2.4)	(0.0)
Profit Growth	24.9	na	na
Revenue Growth	4.6	0.9	2.4
Asset Growth	1.7	(1.0)	2.2

BALANCE SHEET (000)			
Cash	13,241	0	0
Current Assets	178,197	132,265	126,906
Net Fixed Assets	110,708	108,780	116,085
Invest's & Advances	0	598	1,267
Total Assets	314,164	265,732	275,813
Short Term Debt	17,150	13,469	11,191
Current Liabilities	82,110	59,732	51,034
Long Term Debt	63,243	89,619	99,850
Total Liabilities	157,704	154,829	158,304
Total Equity	156,460	110,903	117,509
Total Liab. & Equity	314,164	265,732	275,813

CAPITAL (000)			
Total Debt	80,393	103,088	111,041
Preferred Equity	2,750	2,750	2,750
Common Equity	153,710	108,153	114,759

Business:

SLATER INDUSTRIES INC. is primarily a specialty steel company with mini-mills in Fort Wayne, Indiana, Hamilton, Ontario, and Sorel, Quebec. Slater has ancillary operations in the steel service centre, electrical and telecommunication, transmission, hardware and trucking industries.

Date	EPS	DPS	Tot Rev	Inc Bex
Mar 95	0.84	0.00	161,100	9,800
Dec 94	0.69	0.00	125,178	7,879
Sep 94	0.58	0.00	121,088	6,711
Jun 94	0.70	0.00	130,722	6,665
Mar 94	0.34	0.00	117,601	2,801
Dec 93	(1.13)	0.00	99,399	(9,157)
Sep 93	(0.03)	0.00	93,508	(134)
Jun 93	0.12	0.00	102,670	976

Synopsis:

Slater Industries reported net sales of $161-million for the first quarter ended March 31, 1995, compared to $117.6-million in the same period in 1993. The company credited the increase on higher selling prices and the increased utilization of capacity at all the major divisions. When combined with a favourable Canadian currency value and ongoing cost cutting initiatives, performance improved over 1994 levels.

Through a combination of increased prices, volumes, and productivity, Fort Wayne Specialty Alloys had a much improved performance in 1994. It generated earnings of $15.1-million compared to a loss of $1.4-million in 1993. Fort Wayne's strategy of focusing on large national distributors, who market directly to end users proved successful, as it is now the dominant and preferred supplier of stainless bars to the major service centres. The favourable ruling, received in January 1995, on the stainless bar industry's anti-dumping action, will further stem the flow of unfairly priced foreign bar into the U.S.

Hamilton Specialty Bar's improved performance came from its ability to pass along increased scrap prices, price increases, and producing a higher value added product mix. With the installation of Hamilton's proposed new electric arc furnace, its production could increase to 400,000 tons per year, from the current level of 330,000 tons. By upgrading other components of the facility, substantial additional capacity could be achieved. Hamilton's prospects for 1995 look promising as it produces spring flat steels for the light truck and sport utility market. This sector grew by 16.8% in 1994.

The improved performance at Sorel Forge Inc. was accounted for by both a strong automotive sector and the successful introduction of a direct sales program in the United States. A modernization program aimed at upgrading the capability and capacity of the operations at Sorel began in 1994.

Rank (Profit/Revenue/Assets)		
929	216	306

Benjamin Swirsky
President & C.E.O.

Teddy Chien
V.P. & C.F.O.

Address
Yonge Corporate Centre
4100 Yonge Street
Suite 410
Toronto
ON
M2P 2B2
(416) 733-4400
Fax: (416) 733-4429
S0003304/G/6.1

STELCO INC.

Exchanges	Price (Jun29'95)	6.50	Trailing P/E	4.11	Stock Symbol
TMV	Trailing Yield (%)	0.00	Trailing EPS	1.58	**STE.A**

Period Ending	Dec94	Dec93	Dec92	Dec91	Dec90
Yearly Statistics					
Price-Close	8.00	8.75	1.40	6.38	12.13
Price-High	9.88	8.88	6.63	12.38	21.38
Price-Low	7.13	1.17	0.90	5.00	11.00
P/E-Close	7.92	nm	nm	nm	nm
Dividends per Share	0.00	0.00	0.00	0.00	0.75
Dividend Yield (%)	0.00	0.00	0.00	0.00	6.18
Sales per Share	27.94	30.91	27.43	44.47	59.25
EPS before extra. item	1.01	(0.62)	(1.76)	(3.05)	(5.96)
Cash Flow per Share	2.52	1.43	(1.02)	(1.17)	(4.40)
Book Value per Share	9.37	9.27	9.81	11.42	22.71
O/S Common Shares	104,836	81,041	80,436	80,094	35,492
Total Revenue	2,818,000	2,500,000	2,221,000	1,959,000	2,092,000
Income before extra.	115,000	(36,000)	(127,000)	(136,000)	(197,000)
Cash Flow	252,000	115,000	(82,000)	(52,000)	(156,000)
Debt/Equity	0.61	0.99	1.02	0.81	0.99
Return on Capital (%)	11.57	2.90	(5.13)	(6.76)	(11.90)
Ret. on Com. Equity (%)	11.31	(10.00)	(14.91)	(15.81)	(26.20)
% Change Profit	419.4	71.7	6.6	31.0	(309.9)
% Change Revenue	12.7	12.6	13.4	(6.4)	(24.2)
% Change Assets	5.7	(2.4)	(2.3)	(1.6)	(18.1)

Preferred Div. Coverage	6.8	0.0	na	
Total Div. Coverage	6.8	0.0	na	
Interest Coverage	3.3	0.6	0.0	
Current Ratio	1.7	1.5	1.5	
Operating Margin	6.8	1.8	(5.4)	
Asset Turnover	1.1	1.1	0.9	
5 YEAR RATIOS (%)				
Return on Capital	(1.9)	(2.2)	(0.6)	
Return on Com. Equity	(11.1)	(11.6)	(8.2)	
Profit Growth	4.1	na	na	
Revenue Growth	0.4	(1.9)	(2.9)	
Asset Growth	(4.1)	(3.7)	(2.9)	
BALANCE SHEET (000)				
Cash	262,000	111,000	68,000	
Current Assets	1,174,000	927,000	867,000	
Net Fixed Assets	1,061,000	1,194,000	1,309,000	
Invest's & Advances	172,000	193,000	193,000	
Total Assets	2,499,000	2,364,000	2,423,000	
Short Term Debt	181,000	224,000	216,000	
Current Liabilities	672,000	628,000	588,000	
Long Term Debt	528,000	695,000	767,000	
Total Liabilities	1,339,000	1,435,000	1,456,000	
Total Equity	1,160,000	929,000	967,000	
Total Liab. & Equity	2,499,000	2,364,000	2,423,000	
CAPITAL (000)				
Total Debt	709,000	919,000	983,000	
Preferred Equity	178,000	178,000	178,000	
Common Equity	982,000	751,000	789,000	

Business:

STELCO INC. is composed of a group of businesses which include two integrated steel businesses, two minimills, and a number of steel fabricating businesses. Revenue exceeds $2.8 billion.

Date	EPS	DPS	Tot Rev	Inc Bex
Mar 95	0.45	0.00	783,000	51,000
Dec 94	0.44	0.00	759,000	49,000
Sep 94	0.48	0.00	690,000	53,000
Jun 94	0.21	0.00	730,000	26,000
Mar 94	(0.19)	0.00	674,000	(13,000)
Dec 93	0.12	0.00	676,000	13,000
Sep 93	(0.02)	0.00	615,000	2,000
Jun 93	(0.21)	0.00	636,000	(13,000)

Synopsis:

Stelco reported that strong markets helped its various businesses achieve significantly improved financial results in the first quarter of 1995 compared to the first quarter of 1994. Sales revenue jumped by $106-million over 1994 to $780-million. Product shipments were 1.1 million tons, an increase of 62,000 tons over the same period last year. Consolidated revenue per ton shipped was $681 per ton compared to $623 per ton in 1994. The company reported that order books remained relatively strong through to the middle of the year, although the market is increasingly volatile and uncertain.

Stelco plans to cut corporate debt to zero and build up a cash and credit cushion. The first priority in paying down the debt is the $150-million worth of convertible debentures due in 1998 and the $125-million worth of retractable debentures due in 1999. Stelco paid down about $186-million in debt last year. Stelco made payment of the dividend arrears on its Series A, B and C Preferred Shares, but will not restore common dividends until a sufficient reserve is in place.

Hilton Works and Mitsubishi Corporation of Japan plan to form a joint venture company to install a $60-million pulverized coal injection facility. The facility will supply pulverized coal to both Hilton Works blast furnaces. The introduction of coal injection will greatly improve the competitive position of the Hilton Works. Both companies are already partners in a zinc-coating line in Hamilton. The facility will open at the end of 1995.

Further progress was made in realizing value from non-core assets in 1994 with the sale of Steltech, the 50% ownership in ME International, the 50% of Jannock Steel Fabricating of Oakville, and Jannock Steel Fabricating Inc. of Kentucky. Also during 1994, Page-Hersey Works and Welland Tube Works were incorporated as separate, wholly owned subsidiary companies Stelpipe Ltd. and Welland Pipe Ltd. This change should provide them with enhanced operational and marketing flexibility.

Relative strength to TSE300 / Price / Volume (in 1000's of board lots)

Rank (Profit/Revenue/Assets)
70 55 88

Frederick H. Telmer
Chairman & C.E.O.

Robert J. Milbourne
President & C.O.O.

R. Eric Rogan
Exec. V.P. & C.F.O.

Address
Stelco Tower
100 King Street West
P.O. Box 2030
Hamilton
ON
L8N 3T1
(905) 528-2511
Fax: (905) 577-4575
S0004667/G/6.1

TOROMONT INDUSTRIES LTD.

Exchanges	Price (Jun29'95)	31.50	Trailing P/E	12.07	Stock Symbol
T	Trailing Yield (%)	1.11	Trailing EPS	2.61	**TIH**

Period Ending	Dec94	Dec93	Dec92	Dec91	Dec90
Yearly Statistics					
Price-Close	26.75	33.50	8.00	6.25	0.45
Price-High	26.75	34.38	8.00	6.94	6.25
Price-Low	16.38	15.75	6.25	5.13	4.50
P/E-Close	11.15	27.92	13.68	11.16	0.76
Dividends per Share	0.32	0.52	0.49	0.22	0.21
Dividend Yield (%)	1.20	1.55	6.06	3.52	46.67
Sales per Share	57.65	43.11	31.10	31.29	32.20
EPS before extra. item	2.40	1.20	0.59	0.56	0.59
Cash Flow per Share	2.62	2.05	1.42	1.40	1.34
Book Value per Share	8.92	6.77	4.38	4.18	3.84
O/S Common Shares	7,225	7,225	5,925	5,929	5,909
Total Revenue	416,489	282,961	184,285	185,629	192,083
Income before extra.	17,336	7,762	3,454	3,322	3,520
Cash Flow	18,951	13,262	8,407	8,324	7,982
Debt/Equity	0.75	0.84	0.81	0.75	1.04
Return on Capital (%)	30.51	29.13	21.39	22.96	25.68
Ret. on Com. Equity (%)	30.58	20.74	13.61	13.99	16.17
% Change Profit	123.3	124.7	4.0	(5.6)	18.0
% Change Revenue	47.2	53.5	(0.7)	(3.4)	7.7
% Change Assets	44.3	69.3	13.4	(10.4)	8.1

Preferred Div. Coverage	np	np	np
Total Div. Coverage	7.5	4.6	1.2
Interest Coverage	8.5	5.9	3.9
Current Ratio	1.6	2.2	1.8
Operating Margin	6.2	6.3	6.0
Asset Turnover	2.0	1.9	2.1
5 YEAR RATIOS (%)			
Return on Capital	25.9	23.8	21.3
Return on Com. Equity	19.0	15.9	14.2
Profit Growth	42.2	25.9	14.7
Revenue Growth	18.4	18.0	24.3
Asset Growth	21.8	11.8	11.8
BALANCE SHEET (000)			
Cash	0	6,470	0
Current Assets	164,879	118,452	53,549
Net Fixed Assets	31,772	16,960	22,737
Invest's & Advances	14,880	11,173	848
Total Assets	211,531	146,585	86,562
Short Term Debt	5,933	1,233	3,497
Current Liabilities	101,219	55,051	30,121
Long Term Debt	42,625	40,000	17,614
Total Liabilities	147,071	97,676	60,604
Total Equity	64,460	48,909	25,958
Total Liab. & Equity	211,531	146,585	86,562
CAPITAL (000)			
Total Debt	48,558	41,233	21,111
Preferred Equity	0	0	0
Common Equity	64,460	48,909	25,958

Business:

TOROMONT INDUSTRIES LTD. is a Canadian company with operations in Canada and the United States. Its major operations are in industrial, commercial and process refrigeration, and gas compression. The company is also the Caterpillar dealer for most of Ontario.

Date	EPS	DPS	Tot Rev	Inc Bex
Mar 95	0.63	0.11	114,872	4,534
Dec 94	0.75	0.08	119,002	5,403
Sep 94	0.68	0.08	113,755	4,936
Jun 94	0.55	0.08	95,674	3,930
Mar 94	0.42	0.08	88,058	3,067
Dec 93	0.44	0.07	81,383	3,010
Sep 93	0.46	0.06	94,866	2,986
Jun 93	0.24	0.06	56,761	1,431

Synopsis:

Toromont Industries reported revenue of $114.9-million in the first quarter of 1995, an increase of 30% over the same period last year. Dealership revenues were 28% higher as the demand for equipment remained very strong. Operating income in the group increased from $3-million to $4-million. The Refrigeration Group reported a 34% increase in revenue, from $37.1-million to $49.9-million. Operating income for the group rose 85%, from $1.2-million to $2.2-million.

Fiscal 1994 was the first full year that the Caterpillar Dealership operated under the Toromont banner. Using the full year 1993 for comparison, revenues were up 52%. The company credits a 75% increase in equipment revenues to a general recovery in the Ontario economy, and active mining, forestry and road building sectors. Sales of power systems saw large growth, and product support revenues were up 15%.

Toromont should benefit from increased road building in Ontario. The company secured a major equipment order for delivery in the spring of 1995, to the Highway 407 project. This project will extend over the next three to four years. With improved prices for paper and lumber, forestry has been strong. The recent unveiling of a new grapple skidder by Caterpillar will round out the forestry product line.

Toromont's refrigeration group had significant growth in 1994. The business has been very strong for the recreational group as the demand for quality and efficient ice facilities grows across Canada and the United States. The company is currently involved in projects with various hockey leagues as well as community, private, and municipal skating facilities across North America. This market will continue to grow in 1995. Some of the key projects for 1995 include the new Montreal Forum, the new Spectrum II in Philadelphia, and a new twin pad facility in Anaheim, for the Walt Disney Company.

Relative strength to TSE300 / Price / Volume (in 1000's of board lots) chart

Rank (Profit/Revenue/Assets)
230 213 345

Robert M. Ogilvie
Chairman President & C.E.O.
Wayne S. Hill
V.P. Fin. C.F.O. & Sec.-Treas.

Address
One Crothers Drive
P.O. Box 20011
Concord
ON
L4K 4T1
(905) 667-5662

Fax: (905) 667-5555
T0001738/G/6.3

For further company information, call Globe Information Services 1-800-268-9128 or (416) 585-5345

VARITY CORPORATION

Exchanges	Price (Jun29'95)	58.87	Trailing P/E	12.76	Stock Symbol
TMN	Trailing Yield (%)	0.00	Trailing EPS	3.40	**VAT**

Period Ending	Jan95	Jan94	Jan93	Jan92	Jan91
Yearly Statistics	US	US	US	US	US
Price-Close	49.50	59.00	36.88	17.75	24.00
Price-High	67.25	62.88	38.00	33.50	40.50
Price-Low	46.00	32.25	14.13	12.13	19.00
P/E-Close	8.06	nm	44.08	nm	5.77
Dividends per Share	0.00	0.00	0.00	0.00	0.00
Dividend Yield (%)	0.00	0.00	0.00	0.00	0.00
Sales per Share	51.54	49.79	128.48	126.99	145.08
EPS before extra. item	3.24	(2.18)	0.56	(7.87)	3.06
Cash Flow per Share	4.28	3.77	6.10	2.02	9.07
Book Value per Share	18.65	14.19	10.53	10.93	19.96
O/S Common Shares	41,661	43,957	30,999	24,988	24,930
Total Revenue	2,276,300	1,838,200	3,403,400	3,190,300	3,681,600
Income before extra.	144,700	(69,800)	33,400	(178,000)	94,400
Cash Flow	188,200	138,200	160,200	50,500	226,000
Debt/Equity	0.22	0.41	0.84	2.56	1.73
Return on Capital (%)	21.21	(2.09)	14.08	0.14	6.45
Ret. on Com. Equity (%)	20.32	(16.88)	4.97	(50.99)	16.22
% Change Profit	307.3	(309.0)	118.8	(288.6)	2.5
% Change Revenue	23.8	(46.0)	6.7	(13.3)	50.9
% Change Assets	3.6	(15.7)	(34.4)	(8.4)	16.3
Preferred Div. Coverage	60.3	0.0	1.8		
Total Div. Coverage	60.3	0.0	1.8		
Interest Coverage	7.2	0.0	1.3		
Current Ratio	1.3	1.4	1.1		
Operating Margin	6.5	5.3	5.7		
Asset Turnover	1.2	1.0	1.6		
5 YEAR RATIOS (%)					
Return on Capital	8.0	7.1	11.7		
Return on Com. Equity	(5.3)	(5.3)	3.9		
Profit Growth	9.5	na	(8.0)		
Revenue Growth	(1.4)	(4.7)	10.5		
Asset Growth	(9.4)	1.6	5.1		
BALANCE SHEET (000)					
Cash	189,700	109,200	153,600		
Current Assets	733,700	807,300	1,008,500		
Net Fixed Assets	624,900	522,200	597,100		
Invest's & Advances	103,100	93,500	130,500		
Total Assets	1,823,500	1,759,600	2,086,500		
Short Term Debt	5,300	73,600	156,800		
Current Liabilities	555,800	563,700	915,100		
Long Term Debt	163,400	185,500	305,200		
Total Liabilities	1,039,800	1,128,900	1,538,000		
Total Equity	783,700	630,700	548,500		
Total Liab. & Equity	1,823,500	1,759,600	2,086,500		
CAPITAL (000)					
Total Debt	168,700	259,100	462,000		
Preferred Equity	6,800	6,800	222,100		
Common Equity	776,900	623,900	326,400		

Business:

VARITY CORP. is an industrial management company. Its businesses design, manufacture, and distribute automotive components, diesel engines and heavy duty truck and tractor components at facilities in Norht America and Europe. Subsidiaries are Kelsey-Hayes, Perkins Engines, Dayton Walther and 46% owned affiliate Hayes Wheels Inc. The company markets its product internationally through distributors.

Date		EPS	DPS	Tot Rev	Inc Bex
Apr 95	US	0.81	0.00	595,300	34,200
Jan 95	US	0.84	0.00	642,400	36,600
Oct 94	US	0.73	0.00	605,000	32,700
Jul 94	US	1.02	0.00	518,300	46,000
Apr 94	US	0.65	0.00	494,100	29,400
Jan 94	US	0.94	0.00	490,100	27,000
Oct 93	US	0.58	0.00	463,200	22,200
Jul 93	US	0.34	0.00	424,100	16,100

Synopsis:

Varity Corporation reported sales of $595-million (U.S.) for the first quarter ended April 30, a 20% increase from the $494-million (U.S.) reported last year. Operating income increased by 30% from $40-million (U.S.) to $52-million (U.S.). This was due to the continued strength of the European markets for the Perkins engine systems and higher margin sales for Kelsey-Hayes' anti-lock braking systems.

The operations of Pacoma Hydraulik GmbH, a Germany-based hydraulic cylinder manufacturer, were discontinued during the first quarter. The company has not recognized a gain or a loss on the planned sale of Pacoma, expected to be completed within the year. Kelsey-Hayes sold, for book value, its non-ABS sensor business during the first quarter. In an agreement valued at $550-million (U.S.), Perkins will provide Linde AG, a German fork-lift truck maker, with an engine to power trucks. Perkins and Halla Business Group, located in South Korea, have formed a partnership to make and market engines in Korea. Production is planned to start in late 1996.

The Kelsey-Hayes brake systems segment had sales of $1.2-billion (U.S.) for the year ended January 31, 1995, a 21% increase over the previous year. During the year ended January 1995, sales of vehicles (both automobile and light truck) in the United States increased by 10%. North American production of light trucks, vans and sport utility vehicles increased by 16% over the year ended January 1995. Over 70% of Kelsey-Hayes sales of braking systems are generated from these three types of vehicles. Operating earnings for the brake systems segment grew by 39%, from $87-million (U.S.) to $121-million (U.S.).

The Perkins engines segment had sales of $861-million (U.S.) for the year ended January 1995, a 23% increase over the $702-million (U.S.) recorded the previous year. The increase could be attributed to an increase in demand for diesel engines in the United States and Europe. Operating income for the segment grew 50%, from $46-million (U.S.) the previous year to $69-million (U.S.).

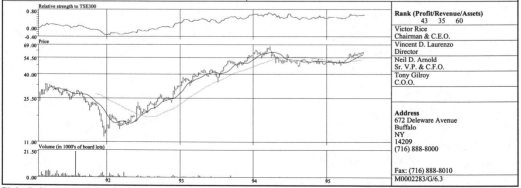

Rank (Profit/Revenue/Assets)
43   35   60

Victor Rice
Chairman & C.E.O.

Vincent D. Laurenzo
Director

Neil D. Arnold
Sr. V.P. & C.F.O.

Tony Gilroy
C.O.O.

Address
672 Deleware Avenue
Buffalo
NY
14209
(716) 888-8000

Fax: (716) 888-8010
M0002283/G/6.3

Page	Company		Fiscal year end	EARNINGS PER SHARE		
				Last Year	Estimate this year	Estimate next year
255	Bombardier		Jan-95	1.39	1.87	2.29
256	C-MAC Industries		Dec-94	0.20	0.36	0.40
257	CAE Industries		Mar-95	0.44	0.52	0.61
258	Canadian Marconi		Mar-94	1.31	0.20	0.73
259	Circo Craft		Dec-94	0.45	0.69	0.86
260	Develcon Electronics		Aug-94	0.02	na	na
261	Dy 4 Systems		Sep-94	0.55	0.65	0.80
262	Electrohome		Aug-94	1.68	1.27	1.38
263	Fleet Aerospace		Sep-94	(0.57)	na	na
264	Gandalf Technologies	$US	Mar-95	(0.03)	0.14	0.22
265	Gennum		Nov-94	1.15	1.20	na
266	Glentel		Dec-94	0.22	na	na
267	Haley Industries		Dec-94	(0.09)	na	na
268	Helix Circuits		Dec-94	(0.28)	na	na
269	International Verifact		Mar-95	(3.20)	0.45	na
270	Linamar		Dec-94	1.44	1.71	2.02
271	NBS Technologies		Sep-94	0.50	na	na
272	Newbridge Networks		Apr-95	2.22	2.79	3.35
273	Noma		Dec-94	0.23	0.44	0.58
274	Qsound Labs		Dec-94	(0.22)	na	na
275	SR Telecom		Dec-94	0.42	0.57	0.79
276	Spar Aerospace		Dec-94	0.53	0.81	0.98
277	Tee-Comm Electronics		Dec-94	0.07	na	na
278	Xerox Canada		Dec-94	2.51	na	na

Estimates from First Call Corporation, 22 Pittsburgh Street, Boston, MA 02210   (800) 366-9992   Fax (617) 261-5679

Electrical & Electronic

Statistics Canada reported that the Canadian electrical and electronic industries operated at 84.8% of capacity in the fourth quarter of 1994, up from a revised 83.9% in the third quarter. The fourth quarter was the third consecutive one when producers increased their use of productive facilities. Capacity utilization rates in the fourth quarter (third quarter), for machinery were 80% (78.3%); transportation equipment 85.2% (83%); and electrical and electronic products 88% (82.9%). Statscan said, "boosted by robust profits, industries are investing heavily in new technology, which in turn will ease pressure on capacity and leave room for continued economic growth".

In the first quarter of 1995, utilization of available capacity remained unchanged at 84.8% from the fourth quarter of 1994. This was up from 80.5% in the first quarter of 1994. Industrial production increased 0.6%, but didn't increase capacity utilization because of new capacity being brought on stream. Companies have spent heavily on new machinery and equipment in the past few years, which added to their production capabilities.

Sales of Canadian manufactured goods to Japan in 1994 remained relatively low despite continued growth. Telecommunications equipment sales increased 38.8% to $66.6-million.

The Canadian computer industry is growing faster than the computer industry in the United States according to some estimates. Industry Canada estimates show that the top 100 Canadian computer companies grew 30% from 1992 to 1993, while the top 100 U.S. computer companies grew only 19% in the same period.

The Information Technology sector in Canada is worth between $19-billion and $49-billion a year. IDC Canada Ltd., a Toronto based market research firm, estimates the figure at $19.04-billion, based on an industry defined by computer hardware, telecommunications equipment, and packaged software and services. Industry Canada puts the figure at $49.5-billion but also includes activity in the consumer electronics, electronic components, and office equipment areas. The information technology industry grew by 6.7% in 1994, according to IDC. Industry Canada estimates that the IT industry employs 342,000 Canadians.

BOMBARDIER INC.

Exchanges	Price (Jun29'95)	16.63	Trailing P/E	22.02	Stock Symbol
TM	Trailing Yield (%)	0.96	Trailing EPS	0.76	BBD.B

Period Ending	Jan95	Jan94	Jan93	Jan92	Jan91
Yearly Statistics					
Price-Close	11.38	10.57	5.83	8.57	3.94
Price-High	12.63	10.94	8.63	8.63	5.16
Price-Low	8.88	4.82	5.19	3.88	3.22
P/E-Close	15.69	18.86	13.68	23.46	11.10
Dividends per Share	0.16	0.11	0.11	0.09	0.09
Dividend Yield (%)	1.37	1.01	1.83	1.01	2.18
Sales per Share	17.66	15.12	14.32	10.42	10.42
EPS before extra. item	0.73	0.56	0.43	0.37	0.36
Cash Flow per Share	1.43	0.91	0.69	0.67	0.69
Book Value per Share	4.86	4.09	3.08	2.84	2.32
O/S Common Shares	331,426	329,948	308,560	304,674	282,886
Total Revenue	5,969,400	4,782,200	4,448,000	3,054,300	2,894,400
Income before extra.	241,900	175,600	132,800	107,700	100,100
Cash Flow	470,200	279,600	210,200	191,400	185,800
Debt/Equity	1.20	1.21	1.82	1.35	1.40
Return on Capital (%)	14.48	12.08	9.40	9.21	13.90
Ret. on Com. Equity (%)	16.17	15.05	14.36	13.79	17.13
% Change Profit	37.8	32.2	23.3	7.6	9.4
% Change Revenue	24.8	7.5	45.6	5.5	37.9
% Change Assets	22.4	5.2	39.1	19.8	67.9

	Jan95	Jan94	Jan93
Preferred Div. Coverage	96.8	70.2	51.1
Total Div. Coverage	4.5	5.0	3.8
Interest Coverage	3.5	2.4	2.9
Current Ratio	1.2	1.6	1.1
Operating Margin	7.7	7.1	5.2
Asset Turnover	1.1	1.0	1.0
5 YEAR RATIOS (%)			
Return on Capital	11.8	12.7	14.3
Return on Com. Equity	15.3	16.3	17.0
Profit Growth	21.4	20.7	20.5
Revenue Growth	23.2	27.5	25.8
Asset Growth	29.1	38.8	41.4
BALANCE SHEET (000)			
Cash	425,100	633,100	235,100
Current Assets	3,053,100	2,740,400	2,438,200
Net Fixed Assets	974,700	874,200	834,500
Invest's & Advances	1,401,800	776,600	942,100
Total Assets	5,500,400	4,493,300	4,270,000
Short Term Debt	764,300	423,600	884,900
Current Liabilities	2,480,800	1,745,600	2,265,800
Long Term Debt	1,199,100	1,254,000	908,100
Total Liabilities	3,858,500	3,110,200	3,285,900
Total Equity	1,641,900	1,383,100	984,100
Total Liab. & Equity	5,500,400	4,493,300	4,270,000
CAPITAL (000)			
Total Debt	1,963,400	1,677,600	1,793,000
Preferred Equity	31,500	33,100	34,100
Common Equity	1,610,400	1,350,000	950,000

Business:

BOMBARDIER INC. is engaged in design, development, manufacturing and marketing activities in the fields of transportation equipment, civil and military aerospace, motorized consumer products and real estate and financial services. The Company has production facilities in North America and Europe and nearly 90% of sales are made in markets outside of Canada.

Date	EPS	DPS	Tot Rev	Inc Bex
Apr 95	0.19	0.04	1,360,000	62,400
Jan 95	0.23	0.04	2,308,300	77,100
Oct 94	0.18	0.04	1,301,100	57,900
Jul 94	0.17	0.04	1,169,900	54,500
Apr 94	0.16	0.03	1,169,000	52,400
Jan 94	0.19	0.03	1,521,100	57,700
Oct 93	0.13	0.03	1,149,000	39,500
Jul 93	0.13	0.03	1,105,800	39,200

Synopsis:

In April 1995, Bombardier Inc.'s motorized consumer products group announced the signing of an agreement in principle to buy the assets of its supplier-partner, Le Groupe AMT Marine Inc. (AMT), located in St. Antoine de Tilly, Quebec. It also signed an agreement to purchase the assets related to boat designing, manufacturing, and selling of Celebrity Boats Inc. The company will continue to produce a variety of models, including the Sea-Doo jet boat. The Celebrity facilities, located in Benton, Illinois, also will produce part of the Sea-Doo jet boat models, and will continue to manufacture and market the Celebrity line of power boats. The company expects to complete these transactions by the end of July 1995. Bombardier will continue to produce the Sea-Doo watercraft in its plant in Valcourt, Quebec.

In early 1995, the Short Brothers PLC unit of Bombardier Inc. agreed to sell Belfast City Airport Ltd. as well as an adjoining site to Sarcon Diamond Ltd. of Northern Ireland. The sale price was approximately $52-million. The final transaction will be completed by June, subject to due diligence procedures. As well, Bombardier signed a letter of intent with Power Corp. of Canada and China National Railway Locomotive and Rolling Stock Industry Corporation (LORIC). This is to create a joint venture in the Republic of China, giving the company access to the Chinese market for urban and intercity rail transportation equipment.

In February 1995, Bombardier entered into an agreement with the Talbot and Capellmann families to acquire all shares of Waggonfabrik Talbot KG of Aachen, Germany, a transportation equipment manufacturer. The transaction, worth about $130-million, was completed at the end of March 1995. The facility, with annual sales in the range of $300-million, is near the border between the Netherlands and Belgium. Bombardier Eurorail received an initial order for the supply of articulated GLT 2000 vehicles in the city Caen, France.

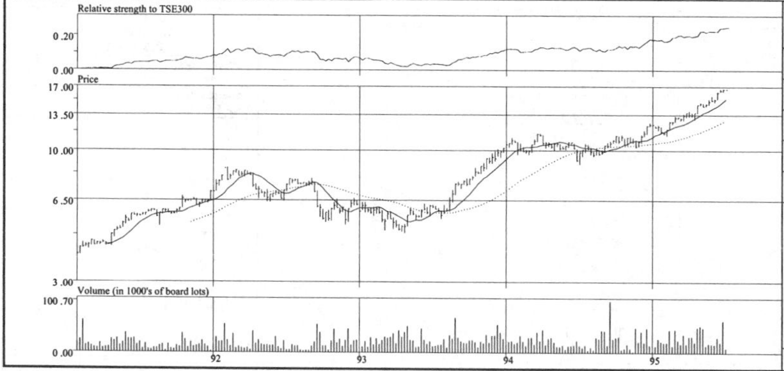

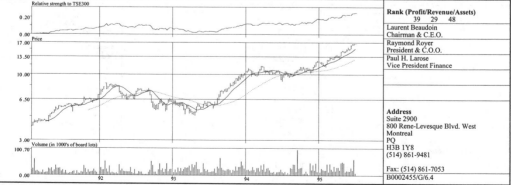

Rank (Profit/Revenue/Assets)
39 29 48

Laurent Beaudoin
Chairman & C.E.O.

Raymond Royer
President & C.O.O.

Paul H. Larose
Vice President Finance

Address
Suite 2900
800 Rene-Levesque Blvd. West
Montreal
PQ
H3B 1Y8
(514) 861-9481

Fax: (514) 861-7053

B0002455/G/6.4

C-MAC INDUSTRIES INC.

Exchanges	Price (Jun29'95)	3.60	Trailing P/E	200.00	Stock Symbol
TM	Trailing Yield (%)	0.00	Trailing EPS	0.02	CMS

Period Ending	Dec94	Dec93	Dec92	Dec91	Dec90
Yearly Statistics					
Price-Close	3.00	9.50	4.63	n t	n t
Price-High	9.37	9.75	5.50	n t	n t
Price-Low	2.85	4.30	4.19	n t	n t
P/E-Close	15.00	21.59	16.23	n t	n t
Dividends per Share	0.00	0.00	0.00	0.00	0.00
Dividend Yield (%)	0.00	0.00	0.00	0.00	0.00
Sales per Share	10.09	8.08	10.48	3.92	3.03
EPS before extra. item	0.20	0.44	0.57	0.24	0.28
Cash Flow per Share	0.68	0.72	0.87	0.43	0.54
Book Value per Share	4.05	3.76	1.96	0.64	0.50
O/S Common Shares	25,862	25,862	19,452	10,147	6,432
Total Revenue	263,007	172,640	117,751	31,015	19,673
Income before extra.	5,150	9,392	6,378	1,841	1,750
Cash Flow	17,689	15,337	9,681	3,338	3,430
Debt/Equity	0.51	0.48	0.80	1.98	1.23
Return on Capital (%)	8.06	16.22	23.91	18.89	na
Ret. on Com. Equity (%)	5.10	13.88	28.64	38.09	na
% Change Profit	(45.2)	47.3	246.4	5.2	na
% Change Revenue	52.3	46.6	279.7	57.7	na
% Change Assets	27.0	91.9	162.4	97.3	na

Date	EPS	DPS	Tot Rev	Inc Bex
Apr 95	0.06	0.00	76,930	1,451
Dec 94	(0.05)	0.00	65,762	(1,389)
Oct 94	0.02	0.00	61,063	576
Jul 94	(0.01)	0.00	67,449	(371)
Apr 94	0.13	0.00	68,733	3,350
Dec 93	0.08	0.00	42,017	2,316
Oct 93	0.10	0.00	42,120	2,018
Jul 93	0.14	0.00	45,661	2,775

	Dec94	Dec93	Dec92
Preferred Div. Coverage	np	np	na
Total Div. Coverage	na	na	na
Interest Coverage	3.1	7.7	6.9
Current Ratio	1.9	2.1	2.0
Operating Margin	4.5	9.7	10.0
Asset Turnover	1.2	1.0	1.3
5 YEAR RATIOS (%)			
Return on Capital	na	na	na
Return on Com. Equity	na	na	na
Profit Growth	na	na	na
Revenue Growth	na	na	na
Asset Growth	na	na	na
BALANCE SHEET (000)			
Cash	24,100	43,112	15,637
Current Assets	124,315	108,659	59,392
Net Fixed Assets	67,895	57,764	26,154
Invest's & Advances	936	437	157
Total Assets	217,871	171,487	89,378
Short Term Debt	24,142	23,155	9,809
Current Liabilities	64,793	50,725	29,652
Long Term Debt	29,135	23,529	21,168
Total Liabilities	113,197	74,254	50,820
Total Equity	104,674	97,233	38,558
Total Liab. & Equity	217,871	171,487	89,378
CAPITAL (000)			
Total Debt	53,277	46,684	30,977
Preferred Equity	0	0	500
Common Equity	104,674	97,233	38,058

Business:

C-MAC INDUSTRIES INC. manufactures micro-electronic products and components destined primarily for the electronic systems manufacturers for use in telecommunications, data processing, military, medical and automotive applications. The company operates in Canada, the United States, Great Britain and France. C-Mac also holds 51.2% of Memotec shares, a leader in the communications networking industry.

Synopsis:

The consolidated revenues of C-MAC Industries were $76.9-million for the first quarter ended April 1, 1995, compared to $68.7-million in the corresponding period of 1994. The company reported satisfaction with revenues and net earnings. Both exceeded forecast levels for the first quarter of 1995. C-MAC believes with the level of activities and an order backlog, it will achieve a very good performance in 1995. The order backlog was $125-million compared to $92-million in the first quarter of 1994.

In July 1994, C-MAC called off the merger with Memotec. C-MAC has owned a controlling 51.2% stake in Memotec since December 1993. The company began talks with Memotec on April 1, 1994, to buy the remaining 48.8%. In July 1994, C-MAC dropped the merger proposal as it was dissatisfied with certain conditions in the agreement between the two companies. C-MAC felt it did not possess all the information needed to evaluate the fairness of the offer, and felt it best not to proceed with the proposal. The company decided to keep the shares they already had.

C-MAC intends to place greater emphasis on research and development in 1995, feeling this will lead to marketing products with superior added value. The company expects to achieve this by greater investment in R&D, partnerships with companies that have the technology required in C-MAC's targeted areas, and acquisitions that would provide it with technology and expand its customer network. The company believes that half of its revenue in 1997 should come from products whose intellectual property or exclusive manufacturing rights are held by C-MAC or one of its subsidiaries.

In 1993 a single customer accounted for 53% of C-MAC's total revenue. Feeling that such reliance on a single customer may constitute a risk, C-MAC reduced this percentage to 38% and intends to lower it further in 1995.

Rank (Profit/Revenue/Assets)
417   276   341

Dennis Wood
Chairman

Isabelle Lanoue
Vice President Finance

Address
3000 Industrial Boulevard
Sherbrooke
PQ
J1L 1V8
(819) 821-4524

Fax: (819) 563-1167
01003312/G/6.5

For further company information, call Globe Information Services 1-800-268-9128 or (416) 585-5345

CAE INC.

Exchanges	Price (Jun29'95)	9.75	Trailing P/E	69.64	Stock Symbol
TM	Trailing Yield (%)	1.64	Trailing EPS	0.14	**CAE**

Period Ending	Mar95	Mar94	Mar93	Mar92	Mar91
Yearly Statistics					
Price-Close	7.50	6.88	4.90	6.00	6.25
Price-High	8.00	7.25	6.63	7.75	8.13
Price-Low	5.63	4.75	4.75	5.75	3.90
P/E-Close	53.57	nm	16.33	19.36	25.00
Dividends per Share	0.16	0.16	0.16	0.16	0.16
Dividend Yield (%)	2.13	2.33	3.27	2.67	2.56
Sales per Share	6.05	5.44	9.23	9.75	11.40
EPS before extra. item	0.14	(3.64)	0.30	0.31	0.25
Cash Flow per Share	0.61	0.53	0.69	0.70	0.62
Book Value per Share	1.27	1.61	5.53	5.14	4.74
O/S Common Shares	108,947	108,627	108,565	108,510	96,330
Total Revenue	674,540	609,416	1,003,237	1,045,952	1,097,728
Income before extra.	15,631	(394,960)	32,244	32,785	24,157
Cash Flow	65,779	57,592	74,422	74,879	59,749
Debt/Equity	0.42	1.16	0.38	0.37	0.67
Return on Capital (%)	16.73	(60.64)	7.88	9.36	8.78
Ret. on Com. Equity (%)	9.97	(102.00)	5.57	6.46	5.37
% Change Profit	104.0	(1,324.9)	(1.7)	35.7	798.4
% Change Revenue	10.7	(39.3)	(4.1)	(4.7)	(2.7)
% Change Assets	(32.9)	(33.4)	3.9	(4.7)	(4.4)

Preferred Div. Coverage	np	np	np
Total Div. Coverage	0.9	0.0	1.9
Interest Coverage	2.8	0.0	3.5
Current Ratio	1.0	1.6	0.9
Operating Margin	9.5	7.9	6.1
Asset Turnover	1.2	0.7	0.8
5 YEAR RATIOS (%)			
Return on Capital	(3.6)	(5.3)	10.1
Return on Com. Equity	(14.9)	(16.8)	7.6
Profit Growth	42.2	na	3.7
Revenue Growth	(9.8)	(6.3)	23.8
Asset Growth	(15.8)	(7.1)	29.5
BALANCE SHEET (000)			
Cash	43,040	10,752	31,786
Current Assets	313,083	601,641	339,048
Net Fixed Assets	141,680	125,226	169,937
Invest's & Advances	0	0	0
Total Assets	540,235	804,692	1,208,142
Short Term Debt	1,421	1,241	19,218
Current Liabilities	302,217	386,419	370,726
Long Term Debt	56,336	200,995	207,503
Total Liabilities	401,396	630,106	608,280
Total Equity	138,839	174,586	599,862
Total Liab. & Equity	540,235	804,692	1,208,142
CAPITAL (000)			
Total Debt	57,757	202,236	226,721
Preferred Equity	0	0	0
Common Equity	138,839	174,586	599,862

Business:

CAE INC. is the world leader in commercial, military and manned space-flight simulation and training. CAE is also engaged in a number of other aerospace, electronics and industrial product activities globally. It has facilities throughout Canada, the United States and Europe.

Date	EPS	DPS	Tot Rev	Inc Bex
Mar 95	0.09	0.04	173,000	10,635
Dec 94	(0.15)	0.04	175,016	(16,224)
Sep 94	0.10	0.04	264,570	10,872
Jun 94	0.10	0.04	246,367	10,348
Mar 94	0.09	0.04	153,952	10,124
Dec 93	(3.86)	0.04	154,050	(418,083)
Sep 93	0.06	0.04	251,321	5,986
Jun 93	0.07	0.04	252,965	7,613

Synopsis:

Under a $134.9-million contract with the Department of National Defence, CAE Inc. will design and install a modern avionics package in 30 Hercules aircraft. CAE, the prime contractor, will work closely with Collins Avionics and Communications, a division of Rockwell International Corporation.

The Royal Malaysian Airforce awarded CAE a $48-million contract involving simulator and training support. CAE acquired Inverton Simulated Systems Ltd., a British company, from Alvis PLC for approximately $13.4-million. Inverton designs and builds artillery and armoured fighting vehicle simulators. Inverton will become a part of the CAE Electronics group of companies and will be renamed CAE Inverton Limited.

CAE sold CAE-Link Corporation, its U.S. defense simulation and training company, in early 1995 for $155-million (U.S.). The proceeds were used to reduce debt. Long term debt was reduced from about $201-million to $56-million. CAE won 14 out of 18 full flight simulator and 5 out of 8 flight training contracts that were awarded worldwide during fiscal year 1995, increasing its share from 50% to 73% of the market. An expected increase in the amount of new aircraft over the next few years, due to the recovering airline industry, should boost demand for aircraft simulation products.

CAE's net earnings rose 36% in fiscal 1995, from $34.7-million to $47.3-million. After accounting for a loss from discontinued operations, CAE's net earnings were $15.6-million. Revenues by product line for the year ended March 31, 1995, were: Commercial Simulation, 36%; Military and Space Simulation, 24%; Other Aerospace and Electronics, 20%; and Industrial Technologies, 20%. Revenues by geographic distribution were: Asia/Africa, 26%; Canada, 26%; United States, 24%; Europe, 23%; and Other, 1%. CAE spent approximately $100-million, or 15% of revenues, on research and development in fiscal 1995.

Relative strength to TSE300 / Price / Volume (in 1000's of board lots)

Rank (Profit/Revenue/Assets)
239   157   221

David H. Race
Chairman Of The Board

John E. Caldwell
Executive Vice President

Paul G. Renaud
V.P. Finance & Secretary

Address
Suite 3060
P.O. Box 30
Royal Bank Plaza
Toronto
ON
M5J 2J1
(416) 865-0070
Fax: (416) 865-0337
C0000203/G/6.4

CANADIAN MARCONI COMPANY

Exchanges	Price (Jun29'95)		12.25	Trailing P/E		61.25	Stock Symbol
TMA	Trailing Yield (%)		2.29	Trailing EPS		0.20	**CMW**

Period Ending	Mar95	Mar94	Mar93	Mar92	Mar91
Yearly Statistics					
Price-Close	15.00	16.13	14.25	15.88	12.75
Price-High	17.50	17.25	16.88	18.00	13.63
Price-Low	13.50	13.00	12.75	11.75	8.88
P/E-Close	75.00	12.31	14.11	13.45	24.06
Dividends per Share	0.28	0.28	0.28	0.21	0.21
Dividend Yield (%)	1.87	1.97	1.32	1.65	2.61
Sales per Share	10.47	12.15	12.37	13.70	12.21
EPS before extra. item	0.20	1.31	1.01	1.18	0.53
Cash Flow per Share	0.74	1.77	1.73	1.90	1.64
Book Value per Share	14.41	14.39	13.10	12.23	11.20
O/S Common Shares	23,938	23,912	23,779	23,773	23,773
Total Revenue	261,676	298,075	299,741	338,810	303,949
Income before extra.	4,695	31,219	23,971	27,955	12,715
Cash Flow	17,891	42,320	41,172	45,279	39,011
Debt/Equity	0.02	0.02	0.02	0.02	0.02
Return on Capital (%)	2.47	12.11	9.40	10.97	5.49
Ret. on Com. Equity (%)	2.41	9.52	7.96	10.04	4.84
% Change Profit	(85.0)	30.2	(14.3)	119.9	(32.5)
% Change Revenue	(14.9)	(0.6)	(11.5)	11.5	(2.9)
% Change Assets	(0.6)	8.6	4.3	4.8	4.8

Preferred Div. Coverage	np	np	np
Total Div. Coverage	0.9	4.7	3.6
Interest Coverage	19.5	125.7	75.0
Current Ratio	4.3	4.9	4.7
Operating Margin	12.3	11.2	7.9
Asset Turnover	0.6	0.7	0.8
5 YEAR RATIOS (%)			
Return on Capital	8.1	9.3	9.1
Return on Com. Equity	7.9	8.0	8.1
Profit Growth	(24.3)	5.1	1.7
Revenue Growth	(3.5)	(1.2)	6.1
Asset Growth	(4.9)	3.6	5.0
BALANCE SHEET (000)			
Cash	208,076	226,686	212,098
Current Assets	340,578	345,002	327,753
Net Fixed Assets	71,386	67,244	51,262
Invest's & Advances	0	0	0
Total Assets	435,278	425,875	392,203
Short Term Debt	0	0	0
Current Liabilities	78,839	70,450	69,605
Long Term Debt	8,107	7,869	7,014
Total Liabilities	80,443	81,769	80,696
Total Equity	344,835	344,106	311,507
Total Liab. & Equity	435,278	425,875	392,203
CAPITAL (000)			
Total Debt	8,107	7,869	7,014
Preferred Equity	0	0	0
Common Equity	344,835	344,106	311,507

Business:

CANADIAN MARCONI CO. is a designer and manufacturer of electronics systems and components in the fields of avionics, communications and radar. Customers include military and government agencies and commercial companies worldwide. It has plants in Quebec and Ontario, in addition to subsidiaries in Nova Scotia, New Jersey, Massachusetts, and Ohio. GEC plc of the U.K. owns 51.3% of the company.

Date	EPS	DPS	Tot Rev	Inc Bex
Mar 95	0.16	0.00	93,761	3,851
Dec 94	0.39	0.14	70,128	9,253
Sep 94	(0.18)	0.00	46,716	(4,273)
Jun 94	(0.17)	0.14	51,071	(4,136)
Mar 94	0.83	0.00	94,180	19,795
Dec 93	0.19	0.14	62,811	4,621
Sep 93	0.17	0.00	93,992	4,008
Jun 93	0.12	0.14	47,092	2,795

Synopsis:

Canadian Marconi's sales fell from $290-million in fiscal 1994 to $250.3-million in the fiscal year ended March 1995. The company went through a difficult year in which it had additional costs associated with restructuring to position itself for the competitive environment in which it operates. As well, the company suffered from reduced revenues in the defence sector, reduced government assistance on research and development, and costs associated with the closure of surplus facilities and provisions for obsolete inventory.

In its continued thrust to diversify into commercial markets, Canadian Marconi acquired the assets and technology of the facsimile products line of NetExpress Inc. of Foster City, California. Marconi has for the past five years been distributing the Enhanced Facsimile Switching System for twenty-four value-added service providers at multiple sites in 16 countries.

Canadian Marconi has established a strong foundation for growth in the commercial aviation sector. The company has achieved a dominant position in Global Positioning System (GPS) technology in the airborne transportation section. This was accomplished through solid market positioning of its new satellite navigation and satellite communication products. Its 12 channel GPS receiver has a substantial share of the air transport market. This product was type approved by the Federal Aviation Administration and Transport Canada. As well it was selected as a standard option on new Boeing 777 aircraft, and as an option on all Airbus aircraft models.

The company's new-generation Satcom antenna that was approved for service, and is the first multi-channel system to be commissioned, has been very well received by both airlines and aircraft manufacturers. This product was chosen by McDonnell Douglas as a standard option on the MD-11 aircraft. The antenna has also been chosen by a large number of International airlines for installation on their existing aircraft.

Rank (Profit/Revenue/Assets)
151   258   244

Dr. J.E. Soos
President & C.E.O.

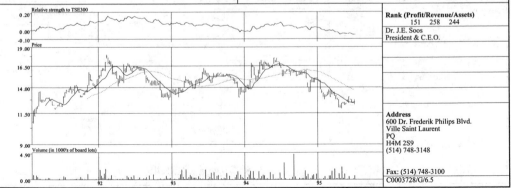

Address
600 Dr. Frederik Philips Blvd.
Ville Saint Laurent
PQ
H4M 2S9
(514) 748-3148

Fax: (514) 748-3100
C0003728/G/6.5

For further company information, call Globe Information Services 1-800-268-9128 or (416) 585-5345

CIRCO CRAFT CO. INC.

Exchanges	Price (Jun29'95)		8 .75	Trailing P/E		12 .32	Stock Symbol
TM	Trailing Yield (%)		0 .00	Trailing EPS		0 .71	CCC

Period Ending	Dec94	Dec93	Dec92	Dec91	Dec90
Yearly Statistics					
Price-Close	4 .20	5 .63	6 .50	1 .75	2 .10
Price-High	5 .75	7 .50	6 .75	2 .25	4 .25
Price-Low	4 .20	5 .00	1 .80	1 .45	1 .25
P/E-Close	9 .33	563 .00	26 .00	nm	nm
Dividends per Share	0 .00	0 .00	0 .00	0 .00	0 .00
Dividend Yield (%)	0 .00	0 .00	0 .00	0 .00	0 .00
Sales per Share	10 .79	7 .89	7 .79	6 .63	6 .73
EPS before extra. item	0 .45	0 .01	0 .25	(0 .49)	(0 .19)
Cash Flow per Share	1 .10	0 .53	0 .81	0 .12	0 .31
Book Value per Share	4 .35	3 .89	3 .55	3 .30	3 .79
O/S Common Shares	14 ,073	14 ,073	12 ,073	12 ,073	12 ,073
Total Revenue	151 ,825	106 ,244	94 ,010	80 ,068	81 ,301
Income before extra.	6 ,384	70	3 ,037	(5 ,878)	(2 ,374)
Cash Flow	15 ,519	7 ,087	9 ,758	1 ,432	3 ,687
Debt/Equity	0 .23	0 .12	0 .23	0 .43	0 .18
Return on Capital (%)	14 .07	3 .97	9 .70	(13 .14)	(5 .98)
Ret. on Com. Equity (%)	11 .01	0 .14	7 .35	(13 .75)	(5 .12)
% Change Profit	9 ,020 .0	(97 .7)	151 .7	(147 .6)	(145 .5)
% Change Revenue	42 .9	13 .0	17 .4	(1 .5)	(10 .6)
% Change Assets	25 .1	16 .6	(1 .0)	0 .4	9 .1

Date	EPS	DPS	Tot Rev	Inc Bex
Mar 95	0.19	0 .00	42 ,144	2 ,644
Dec 94	0.41	0 .00	46 ,843	5 ,813
Sep 94	0.01	0 .00	34 ,538	179
Jun 94	0.10	0 .00	37 ,427	1 ,468
Mar 94	(0 .08)	0 .00	33 ,023	(1 ,076)
Dec 93	(0 .07)	0 .00	30 ,328	(951)
Sep 93	(0 .07)	0 .00	25 ,255	(964)
Jun 93	0 .07	0 .00	26 ,660	979

Preferred Div. Coverage	np	np	np
Total Div. Coverage	na	na	na
Interest Coverage	18 .7	6 .7	6 .2
Current Ratio	2 .5	2 .1	2 .2
Operating Margin	8 .1	2 .7	5 .7
Asset Turnover	1 .5	1 .3	1 .4
5 YEAR RATIOS (%)			
Return on Capital	1 .7	2 .4	4 .4
Return on Com. Equity	(0 .1)	(0 .0)	1 .9
Profit Growth	4 .1	(56 .3)	3 .3
Revenue Growth	10 .8	3 .0	6 .0
Asset Growth	9 .5	2 .4	(1 .0)
BALANCE SHEET (000)			
Cash	7 ,202	0	1 ,083
Current Assets	57 ,609	34 ,054	27 ,505
Net Fixed Assets	43 ,566	44 ,533	41 ,972
Invest's & Advances	0	0	0
Total Assets	101 ,313	81 ,003	69 ,477
Short Term Debt	2 ,856	2 ,179	351
Current Liabilities	23 ,349	16 ,185	12 ,572
Long Term Debt	11 ,383	4 ,325	9 ,467
Total Liabilities	40 ,148	26 ,223	26 ,615
Total Equity	61 ,165	54 ,780	42 ,862
Total Liab. & Equity	101 ,313	81 ,003	69 ,477
CAPITAL (000)			
Total Debt	14 ,239	6 ,504	9 ,818
Preferred Equity	0	0	0
Common Equity	61 ,165	54 ,780	42 ,862

Business:

CIRCO CRAFT CO. INC. is a manufacturer of sophisticated printed circuits for telecommunications, computers and automotive and other electronic Systems. The company has manufacturing facilities in Quebec and Puerto Rico. Circo Craft supplies its products to the telecommunications, computer, and automotive industries in Canada and the United States.

Synopsis:

Circo Craft reported all-time record revenue and earnings for the first quarter ended March 26, 1995. Consolidated revenues increased 27% to $41.9-million. The most improved subsidiary was Circo Caribe, which more than doubled its revenue to $6.5-million from $3-million in the first quarter of 1994. Circo Caribe continued the improvement started in 1994 with net earnings of $3,000 compared with a net loss of $2.2-million for the first quarter of 1994.

At the end of March, the company received official certification for ISO 9002 standards. This international recognition was granted by the Quality Management Institute. In May 1995, Circo Craft signed, on behalf of Circo Caribe, a major supply agreement with Intel Corp. of Santa Clara, California. The company said the total value of the supply award represents the single largest manufacturing award ever for its Puerto Rican subsidiary. The agreement is for the manufacture and supply of select, advance multilayer product structures.

Circo Craft believes its strategy to diversify its markets and establish longer-term alliances with key customers has been reflected in the strong revenue growth over the past few years. The company expects 1995 to be another good year with value-added products and services in strong demand. Circo Craft is very solid financially, entering 1995 with sound balance sheets and robust cash flow generated from their Canadian operations. Working capital totaled $34.2 million at March 26, 1995. Circo's main priorities will be to make further headway in areas of the business already showing prime opportunities for solid improvement.

Circo Craft enjoyed one of its best years ever in 1994, as consolidated revenues increased by 43% to $151.8-million. Canadian revenues were up by 25% to $127.5-million. Circo Caribe posted revenue of $24.3-million. This was helped by an out of court settlement in the United States worth $5.6-million.

Rank (Profit/Revenue/Assets)
379 358 482

Hans-Karl Muhlegg
President & C.E.O.
Normand Potvin
Director Of Finances

Address
17600 Trans Canada Highway
Kirkland
PQ
H9J 3A3
(514) 694-8000

Fax: (514) 694-8604
C0056940/G/6.5

DEVELCON ELECTRONICS LTD.

Exchanges	Price (Jun29'95)	0.75	Trailing P/E		nm	Stock Symbol
T	Trailing Yield (%)	0.00	Trailing EPS		0.00	**DLC**

Period Ending	Aug94	Aug93	Aug92	Aug91	Aug90
Yearly Statistics					
Price-Close	0.60	0.77	0.11	0.40	0.60
Price-High	1.20	1.00	0.40	0.50	0.90
Price-Low	0.52	0.05	0.10	0.10	0.20
P/E-Close	30.00	77.00	nm	nm	nm
Dividends per Share	0.00	0.00	0.00	0.00	0.00
Dividend Yield (%)	0.00	0.00	0.00	0.00	0.00
Sales per Share	0.71	0.74	1.12	1.19	1.35
EPS before extra. item	0.02	0.01	(0.17)	(0.17)	(0.36)
Cash Flow per Share	0.04	0.04	(0.12)	(0.05)	(0.19)
Book Value per Share	0.17	0.14	0.06	0.40	0.58
O/S Common Shares	20,329	19,870	7,730	7,730	7,678
Total Revenue	14,186	10,940	8,931	10,005	10,671
Income before extra.	415	166	(1,340)	(1,319)	(2,072)
Cash Flow	813	562	(933)	(377)	(1,054)
Debt/Equity	0.87	0.86	9.68	1.58	0.97
Return on Capital (%)	8.46	4.63	(13.65)	(8.96)	(18.27)
Ret. on Com. Equity (%)	13.37	10.18	(74.92)	(34.97)	(83.85)
% Change Profit	150.0	112.4	(1.6)	36.3	30.1
% Change Revenue	29.7	22.5	(10.7)	(6.2)	(20.7)
% Change Assets	21.9	9.1	(31.4)	(6.9)	(17.3)

Preferred Div. Coverage	np	np	np
Total Div. Coverage	na	na	na
Interest Coverage	6.6	3.4	0.0
Current Ratio	2.0	2.5	1.1
Operating Margin	3.1	1.7	(13.6)
Asset Turnover	1.6	1.5	1.3
5 YEAR RATIOS (%)			
Return on Capital	(5.6)	(12.4)	(25.9)
Return on Com. Equity	(34.0)	(71.9)	(96.7)
Profit Growth	56.1	44.1	19.1
Revenue Growth	1.0	2.2	(12.4)
Asset Growth	(6.9)	(12.7)	(18.7)
BALANCE SHEET			
Cash	749,000	1,197,000	550,000
Current Assets	5,704,000	5,179,000	4,562,000
Net Fixed Assets	2,348,000	1,934,000	1,955,000
Invest's & Advances	0	0	0
Total Assets	8,670,000	7,113,000	6,517,000
Short Term Debt	520,000	185,000	2,729,000
Current Liabilities	2,823,000	2,104,000	4,292,000
Long Term Debt	2,437,000	2,211,000	1,761,000
Total Liabilities	5,260,000	4,315,000	6,053,000
Total Equity	3,410,000	2,798,000	464,000
Total Liab. & Equity	8,670,000	7,113,000	6,517,000
CAPITAL			
Total Debt	2,957,000	2,396,000	4,490,000
Preferred Equity	0	0	0
Common Equity	3,410,000	2,798,000	464,000

Business:

DEVELCON ELECTRONICS LTD. designs and manufactures sophisticated electronic data communications equipment. Its network products, under the trademark DevelNet, allow for the transmission of information among mainframe computers, minicomputers, microcomputers, terminals and other equipment. The company has operations in Canada and the United States.

Date	EPS	DPS	Tot Rev	Inc Bex
Feb 95	(0.02)	0.00	3,204	(369)
Nov 94	0.01	0.00	3,659	100
Aug 94	0.01	0.00	3,699	141
May 94	0.00	0.00	3,676	10
Feb 94	0.01	0.00	3,221	173
Nov 93	0.01	0.00	3,590	91
Aug 93	(0.01)	0.00	2,812	(31)
May 93	0.01	0.00	2,780	64

Synopsis:

Develcon Electronics Ltd. saw a slight increase of $100,000 in revenue for the six months ended February 1995 compared to February 1994. For the three months ended November 30, 1994, sales increased by 2% versus a year ago. Develcon had increased product revenues in the U.S. and Asia Pacific regions, but had decreased sales in Europe and the Middle East.

Develcon completed matters related to acquiring Sphere Tech Electronics, a contract manufacturer to the Canadian electronics industry, and acquired the operations of GlobalNet Communications. GlobalNet is a designer of ethernet stackable hubs, rounding out Develcon's LAN product line. Develcon anticipates that these products to contribute over 15% to revenues in 1995. Its research and development staff has increased by 30% in part due to this acquisition. Due to terms imposed by the related funding agencies, the percentage of total expenditures recovered under various grant programs fell from 40% in 1993 to 25% in 1994. Develcon introduced ISDN capable products in 1994, and the development and release of Frame Relay products is scheduled for 1995. The company does not expect to deploy ATM networks in the remote access market, but will monitor the progress of ATM, and provide ATM support for its products as this market evolves. Develcon hopes to improve on-time delivery of projects and work will continue on core data communications products.

Through the increase of world-wide sales channels and expanding its LAN internet working product line, Develcon saw an increase of 30% in revenues. Total revenues were $14.1-million at the end of August 1994 compared to $10.9-million in 1993. Develcon saw improved net earnings with an increase in sales and decrease in operating expenses. Sales of LAN products were 56% in 1993 but now account for 61% of company revenues. With the opening of new offices in the United Kingdom and Singapore, the company hopes to expand its presence in the international market place.

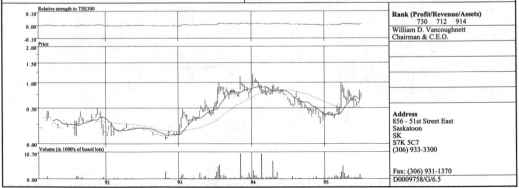

Rank (Profit/Revenue/Assets)
730   712   914

William D. Vancoughnett
Chairman & C.E.O.

Address
856 - 51st Street East
Saskatoon
SK
S7K 5C7
(306) 933-3300

Fax: (306) 931-1370
D0009758/G/6.5

For further company information, call Globe Information Services 1-800-268-9128 or (416) 585-5345

DY 4 SYSTEMS INC.

Exchanges	Price (Jun29'95)		12.75	Trailing P/E		17.46	Stock Symbol
T	Trailing Yield (%)		0.00	Trailing EPS		0.73	DYF

Period Ending	Sep94	Sep93	Sep92	Sep91
Yearly Statistics				
Price-Close	10.00	2.72	n t	n t
Price-High	12.75	2.89	n t	n t
Price-Low	7.83	1.32	n t	n t
P/E-Close	15.39	11.84	n t	n t
Dividends per Share	0.00	0.00	0.00	0.00
Dividend Yield (%)	0.00	0.00	0.00	0.00
Sales per Share	3.81	1.51	5.03	4.50
EPS before extra. item	0.65	0.23	0.59	0.45
Cash Flow per Share	0.80	0.24	0.66	0.60
Book Value per Share	2.84	0.74	0.99	0.39
O/S Common Shares	12,045	34,469	5,354	5,324
Total Revenue	49,419	38,475	26,897	22,260
Income before extra.	7,577	5,835	3,129	2,252
Cash Flow	10,094	5,964	3,547	2,981
Debt/Equity	nd	nd	1.30	3.43
Return on Capital (%)	37.83	35.37	38.56	na
Ret. on Com. Equity (%)	25.43	37.98	84.63	na
% Change Profit	29.9	86.5	38.9	na
% Change Revenue	28.4	43.0	20.8	na
% Change Assets	47.9	73.4	54.7	na
Preferred Div. Coverage	np	np	np	
Total Div. Coverage	na	na	na	
Interest Coverage	nd	18.3	5.7	
Current Ratio	3.3	3.7	1.3	
Operating Margin	21.1	16.6	15.3	
Asset Turnover	1.0	1.2	1.4	
5 YEAR RATIOS (%)				
Return on Capital	na	na	na	
Return on Com. Equity	na	na	na	
Profit Growth	na	na	na	
Revenue Growth	na	na	na	
Asset Growth	na	na	na	
BALANCE SHEET (000)				
Cash	27,644	15,456	1,966	
Current Assets	43,817	27,119	14,398	
Net Fixed Assets	4,579	4,324	4,067	
Invest's & Advances	0	0	0	
Total Assets	48,396	32,727	18,872	
Short Term Debt	0	0	4,294	
Current Liabilities	13,222	7,306	10,989	
Long Term Debt	0	0	2,577	
Total Liabilities	14,222	7,306	13,566	
Total Equity	34,174	25,421	5,306	
Total Liab. & Equity	48,396	32,727	18,872	
CAPITAL (000)				
Total Debt	0	0	6,871	
Preferred Equity	0	0	0	
Common Equity	34,174	25,421	5,306	

Business:

DY 4 SYSTEMS INC. is involved in the design and manufacture of off the shelf high end open architecture computer systems. These systems are used in applications that require high reliability when operating in rugged or harsh environments. Primary applications for DY 4's systems include defence, surveillance, space and aerospace.

Date	EPS	DPS	Tot Rev	Inc Bex
Mar 95	0.16	0.00	11,010	2,025
Dec 94	0.22	0.00	13,132	2,605
Sep 94	0.19	0.00	12,204	2,164
Jun 94	0.16	0.00	14,076	1,918
Mar 94	0.12	0.00	10,583	1,371
Dec 93	0.18	0.00	12,556	2,125
Sep 93	0.16	0.00	10,916	1,883
Jun 93	0.17	0.00	9,761	1,772

Synopsis:

In the first six months of fiscal 1995, sales for DY 4 Systems Inc. were $23.7-million, compared to $22.8-million for the same period last year. Earnings rose due to the combined effect of improved gross margins and interest income, the realization into income of prior years' investment tax credits, and flat overall expenses compared to the same period last year. The nature of DY 4 Systems business can cause quarterly shipments to fluctuate. Quarterly results do not necessarily forecast accurate annual results.

DY 4 recently introduced the PowerPC 603 SVME/DMV 170, the first in a new family of RISC-based single board computers. It is the company's first product to incorporate major new ease of use features and provides improved performance to cost opportunity. These features simplify the integration of DY 4 hardware with other systems. For the first six months of fiscal 1995, gross research and development expenses were $3.8-million including $1.5-million of customer funded development, compared to $3.2-million with $816,000 of customer funded development for the same period last year.

DY 4's ongoing emphasis on its emerging markets and its focus on differentiating itself is reflected in the growth and geographical results for the first six months. DY 4, known mostly as a hardware vendor, is now putting a major effort into developing software libraries and tools to help customers get their applications running quickly. Research and development expenditures for software were 25% in 1994, up from 10% in 1993. DY 4's product support and software staff doubled. Part of DY 4's R&D in 1995 will focus on component technology and packaging.

Relative strength to TSE300 / Price / Volume (in 1000's of board lots)

Rank (Profit/Revenue/Assets)
348 551 639

Danny B. Osadca
Chairman President & C.E.O.

Address
21 Fitzgerald Road
Nepean
ON
K2H 9J4
(613) 596-9091

Fax: (613) 596-0574
01003355/G/6.5

ELECTROHOME LIMITED

Period Ending	Aug94	Aug93	Dec92	Aug92	Dec91
Yearly Statistics					
Price-Close	8.75	7.63	7.75	6.50	6.25
Price-High	9.75	9.88	8.63	8.75	7.50
Price-Low	7.00	5.00	5.00	4.50	4.40
P/E-Close	5.00	4.98	6.86	nm	nm
Dividends per Share	0.11	0.00	0.00	0.00	0.00
Dividend Yield (%)	1.26	0.00	0.00	0.00	0.00
Sales per Share	22.54	23.43	22.85	22.87	20.92
EPS before extra. item	1.75	1.53	1.13	(0.27)	(1.58)
Cash Flow per Share	2.27	1.41	1.49	1.07	0.56
Book Value per Share	6.64	4.32	3.96	3.06	2.83
O/S Common Shares	7,841	5,567	5,526	5,508	5,508
Total Revenue	152,110	131,840	127,464	125,643	116,376
Income before extra.	12,078	8,500	6,253	(1,446)	(8,663)
Cash Flow	15,246	7,819	8,197	5,800	3,095
Debt/Equity	0.55	2.19	2.74	3.51	4.65
Return on Capital (%)	20.01	17.51	16.10	7.04	(0.85)
Ret. on Com. Equity (%)	31.65	36.86	32.14	(9.07)	(43.66)
% Change Profit	42.1	35.9	532.4	83.3	(145.8)
% Change Revenue	15.4	3.4	1.4	8.0	(1.4)
% Change Assets	9.7	(6.7)	12.6	(16.0)	(6.2)
Preferred Div. Coverage	402.6	283.3	240.5		
Total Div. Coverage	16.2	283.3	240.5		
Interest Coverage	4.3	2.4	1.9		
Current Ratio	1.6	1.1	1.3		
Operating Margin	11.8	9.3	9.5		
Asset Turnover	1.4	1.3	1.2		
5 YEAR RATIOS (%)					
Return on Capital	12.0	8.7	6.6		
Return on Com. Equity	9.6	0.5	(6.8)		
Profit Growth	na	163.4	na		
Revenue Growth	5.2	(0.8)	0.2		
Asset Growth	(1.9)	(5.9)	(3.8)		
BALANCE SHEET (000)					
Cash	0	0	0		
Current Assets	48,467	42,994	48,884		
Net Fixed Assets	25,937	23,875	25,265		
Invest's & Advances	2,384	2,493	519		
Total Assets	110,378	100,621	107,892		
Short Term Debt	4,384	20,426	14,425		
Current Liabilities	29,730	40,330	37,872		
Long Term Debt	24,633	33,407	46,982		
Total Liabilities	57,795	76,018	85,448		
Total Equity	52,583	24,603	22,444		
Total Liab. & Equity	110,378	100,621	107,892		
CAPITAL (000)					
Total Debt	29,017	53,833	61,407		
Preferred Equity	506	537	550		
Common Equity	52,077	24,066	21,894		

Business:

ELECTROHOME LIMITED operates in two business segments in Canada. The electronics group designs, manufactures and markets internationally a wide range of video display and projection oriented products. The broadcast group operates a number of radio and television stations in Alberta and Ontario.

Date	EPS	DPS	Tot Rev	Inc Bex
May 95	0.36	0.00	46,505	2,845
Feb 95	0.21	0.00	41,410	3,209
Nov 94	0.48	0.00	46,372	3,793
Aug 94	0.22	0.00	37,444	1,222
May 94	0.56	0.00	40,971	4,375
Feb 94	0.12	0.00	35,422	775
Nov 93	0.94	0.00	37,594	5,219
Aug 93	0.39	0.00	29,631	(1,362)

Synopsis:

Electrohome Limited's revenue for the six months ended February 28, 1995, was $87.6-million up from the $72.7-million a year ago. The revenue at the end of 1994 was $151.1-million, or 17% ahead of the $129.6-million achieved in 1993. Through new product introductions and expanded market coverage, two divisions, Projection Systems and Display Systems, achieved sales increases. The Projection Systems division saw an unprecedented 47% year over year growth in 1994, with more than 90% of these revenues generated outside of Canada. For all Display Systems' Markets, the total year over year revenue growth was 27% with over 90% of the sales to customers in the Americas. Both divisions are part of the company's Electronic Group. In 1994 the Electronic Group saw an over 30% increase in sales, with $93.5-million. The Broadcast Group, television stations CFRN-TV in Edmonton and CKCO-TV in Kitchener, had sales slightly lower than the previous year, at $57.6-million.

In May 1995, Electrohome said the Display Technologies Incorporated (DTI) acquisition, is proceeding through the due diligence phase. The company estimated that this acquisition will add $42-million to first year revenues, doubling its participation in the direct view display field. DTI manufactures high-resolution monochrome displays and participates in the low to medium resolution colour field, supplying monitors to the North American document imaging industry. This is the technology of choice in the growing medical field of filmless x-ray. Electrohome will have DTI operate as the Electronic Group's third division, along with the Display and Projection divisions.

In July 1995, Electrohome Limited's Display Systems began supplying customized display monitors to be installed in Dynapro Systems. Dynapro specializes in interface technology, helping companies manage processes and information. By December 1995, Electrohome expects final delivery of current display monitor products to its customer Bloomberg L.P.

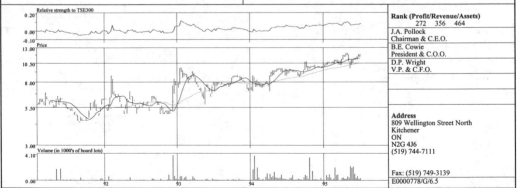

Rank (Profit/Revenue/Assets)		
272	356	464

J.A. Pollock
Chairman & C.E.O.

B.E. Cowie
President & C.O.O.

D.P. Wright
V.P. & C.F.O.

Address
809 Wellington Street North
Kitchener
ON
N2G 4J6
(519) 744-7111

Fax: (519) 749-3139
E0000778/G/6.5

FLEET AEROSPACE CORPORATION

Exchanges	Price (Jun29'95)	0.23	Trailing P/E		nm	Stock Symbol
T	Trailing Yield (%)	0.00	Trailing EPS		(0.52)	**FLT**

Period Ending	Sep94	Sep93	Sep92	Sep91	Sep90
Yearly Statistics					
Price-Close	0.27	0.40	0.32	0.75	1.00
Price-High	0.62	0.85	1.85	2.00	2.90
Price-Low	0.25	0.21	0.30	0.50	0.75
P/E-Close	nm	nm	nm	nm	nm
Dividends per Share	0.00	0.00	0.00	0.00	0.00
Dividend Yield (%)	0.00	0.00	0.00	0.00	0.00
Sales per Share	3.23	4.43	4.53	15.25	17.04
EPS before extra. item	(0.57)	(0.32)	(0.11)	(0.65)	(1.42)
Cash Flow per Share	(0.47)	(0.19)	0.03	0.15	(0.37)
Book Value per Share	(0.25)	0.31	0.56	(4.15)	(3.78)
O/S Common Shares	23,304	22,613	22,314	7,891	7,811
Total Revenue	73,755	98,333	96,494	120,932	134,260
Income before extra.	(12,971)	(7,285)	(2,345)	(2,699)	(8,613)
Cash Flow	(10,750)	(4,320)	636	1,165	(2,876)
Debt/Equity	na	9.32	5.38	4.94	4.20
Return on Capital (%)	(21.57)	(6.62)	2.54	4.16	(1.96)
Ret. on Com. Equity (%)	(2,017.26)	(74.37)	na	na	na
% Change Profit	(78.1)	(210.7)	13.1	68.7	(39.1)
% Change Revenue	(25.0)	1.9	(20.2)	(9.9)	(0.8)
% Change Assets	(21.7)	(10.9)	7.6	(8.6)	(28.7)

Preferred Div. Coverage	np	np	np
Total Div. Coverage	na	na	na
Interest Coverage	0.0	0.0	0.3
Current Ratio	0.6	1.3	1.3
Operating Margin	(15.3)	0.6	2.9
Asset Turnover	1.0	1.0	0.9
5 YEAR RATIOS (%)			
Return on Capital	(4.7)	(0.5)	1.7
Return on Com. Equity	na	na	na
Profit Growth	na	na	na
Revenue Growth	(11.4)	(13.3)	(9.3)
Asset Growth	(13.3)	(10.9)	(8.0)
BALANCE SHEET (000)			
Cash	0	0	0
Current Assets	42,579	61,689	78,588
Net Fixed Assets	12,918	13,717	13,768
Invest's & Advances	0	0	0
Total Assets	75,908	96,906	108,763
Short Term Debt	25,467	29,122	36,096
Current Liabilities	66,583	47,694	59,265
Long Term Debt	9,785	36,226	31,619
Total Liabilities	81,637	89,891	96,187
Total Equity	(5,729)	7,015	12,576
Total Liab. & Equity	75,908	96,906	108,763
CAPITAL (000)			
Total Debt	35,252	65,348	67,715
Preferred Equity	0	0	0
Common Equity	(5,729)	7,015	12,576

Business:

FLEET AEROSPACE CORP., through its subsidiaries and divisions manufactures products for the commercial aerospace and defence markets. The company has facilities and markets in Canada and the United States. Products include commercial and military aircraft components.

Date	EPS	DPS	Tot Rev	Inc Bex
Mar 95	(0.08)	0.00	17,169	(1,585)
Dec 94	(0.07)	0.00	15,801	(1,382)
Sep 94	(0.26)	0.00	14,137	(5,617)
Jun 94	(0.11)	0.00	19,132	(2,296)
Mar 94	(0.19)	0.00	20,117	(3,754)
Dec 93	(0.01)	0.00	21,726	10
Sep 93	(0.10)	0.00	24,824	(2,049)
Jun 93	(0.06)	0.00	25,178	(1,007)

Synopsis:

Fleet Aerospace Corporation announced on January 18, 1995, that its shareholders overwhelmingly had endorsed its capital restructuring proposal. Under the terms of the reorganization, the company received $5.0-million in new cash and eliminated $29.15-million of debt and related financing costs. As a result, Fleet's permanent equity increases by a minimum of $34.15-million. The company now has the capital base to pursue and to finance growth as the aerospace sector recovers from the worst recession in its history.

Fleet announced sales contracts that exceed $31-million during the first few months of 1995. Southwest Airlines, McDonnell Douglas, and DeHavilland all signed contracts that have long-term potential. Additional sales are likely as a result of expected contract extensions and renewals. Under the terms of the contract with Southwest Airlines to build engine fan cowl doors, Fleet retained the ownership of the tooling and data rights. These included FAA certification which is required to build these parts. The initial Southwest order is for the retrofit of 150 Boeing 737's. The potential market includes over 1,200 of the applicable series of Boeing 737's in service worldwide. In early March 1995, the company delivered the first fuselage produced for the Bell 430 helicopter program, achieved on schedule, despite aggressive lead times. Fleet expects this program to translate into average annual sales in excess of $10-million.

Fleet feels the outlook is promising for the rest of 1995. The bid opportunities for new programs has increased substantially, owing to several factors. These include the number of competitors in North America and the advantage of exchange rates. The emphasis by the prime aircraft manufacturers in final assembly, which leads to more outsourcing of details parts and sub-assemblies, and the strengths of the commuter aircraft market also contribute. With some of the world's major airlines returning to profitability, there is a reasonable expectation that the aerospace industry is in the early stages of recovery.

Rank (Profit/Revenue/Assets)
953   469   542

William A. Dimma
Chairman
Donald C. Lowe
President & C.E.O.
Bruce W. Gowan
V.P. Finance & Sec.-Treasurer

Address
Suite 1450
55 York Street
Toronto
ON
M5J 1R7
(416) 365-0565

Fax: (416) 365-2131
F0007334/G/6.4

GANDALF TECHNOLOGIES INC.

Exchanges	Price (Jun29'95)	12.37	Trailing P/E	175.46	Stock Symbol
TQ	Trailing Yield (%)	0.00	Trailing EPS	0.05	GAN

Period Ending	Mar94	Mar93	Mar92	Ju191	Ju190	Business:
Yearly Statistics	US	US	US/8M	US		GANDALF TECHNOLOGIES INC. designs,
Price-Close	1.41	4.30	3.25	2.85	3.50	manufactures, markets and services a line of
Price-High	4.60	5.50	3.90	4.30	7.75	computerized communications systems,
Price-Low	0.95	1.85	1.50	2.10	2.90	software and hardware products that permit
P/E-Close	nm	nm	nm	nm	nm	users to communicate between computers and
Dividends per Share	0.00	0.00	0.00	0.00	0.00	terminals of various types in local and wide
Dividend Yield (%)	0.00	0.00	0.00	0.00	0.00	area networks. The company has operations in
Sales per Share	4.37	7.25	8.46	8.55	11.28	North America and Europe and markets its
EPS before extra. item	(2.27)	(1.24)	(0.63)	(0.48)	(0.87)	products and services worldwide.
Cash Flow per Share	(0.67)	(0.20)	(0.23)	(0.10)	0.11	
Book Value per Share	0.68	2.16	3.54	4.87	6.40	
O/S Common Shares	28,072	15,865	15,672	12,195	12,195	
Total Revenue	132,314	161,349	119,691	129,827	164,364	
Income before extra.	(47,238)	(19,507)	(9,912)	(5,869)	(10,583)	
Cash Flow	(13,925)	(3,083)	(2,376)	(1,254)	1,342	
Debt/Equity	1.82	1.68	0.83	0.34	0.25	
Return on Capital (%)	(57.58)	(15.38)	(11.94)	(5.04)	(6.80)	
Ret. on Com. Equity (%)	(176.87)	(43.45)	(25.89)	(9.27)	(12.89)	
% Change Profit	(142.2)	(31.2)	(153.3)	35.9	(2,907.2)	
% Change Revenue	(18.0)	(10.1)	38.3	(8.7)	(3.7)	
% Change Assets	(31.2)	(8.3)	37.3	(7.0)	(4.5)	

Date		EPS	DPS	Tot Rev	Inc Bex
Mar 95	US	0.01	0.00	30,382	209
Dec 94	US	0.08	0.00	29,751	2,154
Oct 94	US	0.02	0.00	30,748	602
Jul 94	US	(0.06)	0.00	29,775	(1,559)
Mar 94	US	(1.67)	0.00	31,994	(36,156)
Jan 94	US	(0.29)	0.00	30,783	(6,788)
Oct 93	US	(0.15)	0.00	35,190	(2,347)
Jul 93	US	(0.12)	0.00	34,347	(1,947)

Preferred Div. Coverage	np	np	np
Total Div. Coverage	na	na	na
Interest Coverage	0.0	0.0	0.0
Current Ratio	1.3	1.5	1.3
Operating Margin	(32.7)	(6.1)	(3.4)
Asset Turnover	1.0	0.9	0.9
5 YEAR RATIOS (%)			
Return on Capital	(19.3)	(7.1)	(1.0)
Return on Com. Equity	(53.7)	(18.2)	(7.8)
Profit Growth	na	na	na
Revenue Growth	(2.2)	2.4	9.3
Asset Growth	(5.1)	3.1	10.2
BALANCE SHEET (000)			
Cash	5,273	9,737	3,832
Current Assets	60,354	74,049	81,464
Net Fixed Assets	20,214	30,768	38,416
Invest's & Advances	0	0	3,019
Total Assets	89,186	129,603	141,408
Short Term Debt	11,098	10,719	22,102
Current Liabilities	46,376	48,453	62,188
Long Term Debt	23,701	46,842	23,729
Total Liabilities	70,077	95,295	85,917
Total Equity	19,109	34,308	55,491
Total Liab. & Equity	89,186	129,603	141,408
CAPITAL (000)			
Total Debt	34,799	57,561	45,831
Preferred Equity	0	0	0
Common Equity	19,109	34,308	55,491

Synopsis:

Gandalf Technologies Inc. announced its financial results for the year ended March 31, 1995, closing the fiscal year by reporting profitable results and positive cash flow for a third consecutive quarter. Revenue for the fiscal year ended March 31, 1995, was $120.5-million (U.S.).Due to a reduction in the company's operations in February 1994, these figures can not be compared to fiscal 1994. This restructuring apparently worked as the company reported a net income of $1.4-million (U.S.) compared to a net loss of $47.2-million (U.S.) in fiscal 1994.

The company credits the improvement in financial performance to the combined effect of significant growth in new products and a reduced cost infrastructure. This led to substantially lower operating costs and improved gross margins. The majority of new product introductions and enhancements in 1995 were in the remote access and feeder/concentrator lines of business. Gandalf continued its commitment to research and development spending more than 12% of product revenue.

The company announced the launch of the last product, Xpress Stack*TM, in the Xpress group of products. This is a new family of products designed to expand the range of Gandalf's remote access solutions. This product joins XpressConnect*TM, a family of compact inter-networking access devices. These devices operate at the edge of the network. XpressStack is a family of modular, stackable, concentration, and inter-networking devices. XpressWay*TM is a family of chassis-based, high density concentration, and inter- networking devices.

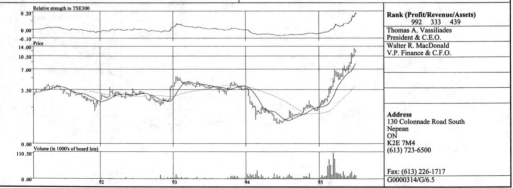

Rank (Profit/Revenue/Assets)
992 333 439

Thomas A. Vassiliades
President & C.E.O.

Walter R. MacDonald
V.P. Finance & C.F.O.

Address
130 Colonnade Road South
Nepean
ON
K2E 7M4
(613) 723-6500

Fax: (613) 226-1717
G0000314/G/6.5

GENNUM CORPORATION

Exchanges	Price (Jun29'95)	22 .50	Trailing P/E	16 .92	Stock Symbol
T	Trailing Yield (%)	1 .00	Trailing EPS	1 .33	**GND**

Period Ending	Nov94	Nov93	Nov92	Nov91	Nov90
Yearly Statistics					
Price-Close	19 .13	15 .75	13 .75	8 .75	5 .00
Price-High	20 .38	19 .00	13 .75	10 .75	9 .75
Price-Low	15 .63	13 .50	8 .50	4 .38	4 .75
P/E-Close	14 .94	14 .86	13 .48	8 .75	nm
Dividends per Share	0 .23	0 .50	1 .00	1 .00	0 .00
Dividend Yield (%)	1 .18	3 .18	7 .27	34 .29	0 .00
Sales per Share	8 .31	6 .85	6 .61	6 .10	4 .74
EPS before extra. item	1 .28	1 .06	1 .02	1 .00	(0 .59)
Cash Flow per Share	1 .88	1 .63	1 .57	1 .38	0 .93
Book Value per Share	5 .65	4 .74	4 .05	3 .93	5 .88
O/S Common Shares	3 ,963	4 ,008	3 ,960	3 ,904	3 ,889
Total Revenue	33 ,466	27 ,740	26 ,238	24 ,410	19 ,588
Income before extra.	5 ,113	4 ,257	4 ,018	3 ,907	(2 ,338)
Cash Flow	7 ,523	6 ,555	6 ,195	5 ,391	3 ,642
Debt/Equity	nd	nd	nd	nd	nd
Return on Capital (%)	38 .66	38 .10	41 .68	32 .73	(3 .98)
Ret. on Com. Equity (%)	24 .70	24 .31	25 .62	20 .47	(9 .69)
% Change Profit	20 .1	5 .9	2 .8	267 .1	(185 .6)
% Change Revenue	20 .6	5 .7	7 .5	24 .6	0 .1
% Change Assets	17 .2	12 .4	14 .9	(27 .4)	(7 .0)
Preferred Div. Coverage	np	np	np		
Total Div. Coverage	5 .7	2 .1	1 .0		
Interest Coverage	nd	nd	nd		
Current Ratio	3 .0	2 .9	2 .3		
Operating Margin	23 .3	23 .4	24 .4		
Asset Turnover	1 .1	1 .1	1 .1		
5 YEAR RATIOS (%)					
Return on Capital	29 .4	25 .5	23 .9		
Return on Com. Equity	17 .1	14 .4	13 .0		
Profit Growth	13 .4	4 .0	7 .9		
Revenue Growth	11 .3	3 .7	8 .5		
Asset Growth	0 .4	(2 .4)	(0 .9)		
BALANCE SHEET (000)					
Cash	7 ,950	4 ,609	3 ,894		
Current Assets	20 ,677	16 ,550	13 ,087		
Net Fixed Assets	9 ,786	9 ,441	10 ,040		
Invest's & Advances	0	0	0		
Total Assets	30 ,463	25 ,991	23 ,127		
Short Term Debt	0	0	0		
Current Liabilities	6 ,946	5 ,707	5 ,657		
Long Term Debt	0	0	0		
Total Liabilities	8 ,064	6 ,994	7 ,097		
Total Equity	22 ,399	18 ,997	16 ,030		
Total Liab. & Equity	30 ,463	25 ,991	23 ,127		
CAPITAL (000)					
Total Debt	0	0	0		
Preferred Equity	0	0	0		
Common Equity	22 ,399	18 ,997	16 ,030		

Business:

GENNUM CORPORATION is a high-technology company engaged in the design and manufacture of silicon integrated circuits and thick-film hybrid circuits. Its operations are in Ontario. The company markets its products to the hearing instrument industry, professional video and broadcast markets and to other specialized applications where information is being conditioned transmitted or interpreted.

Date	EPS	DPS	Tot Rev	Inc Bex
Feb 95	0 .38	0 .00	9 ,480	1 ,501
Nov 94	0 .23	0 .08	7 ,781	921
Aug 94	0 .34	0 .08	8 ,699	1 ,329
May 94	0 .38	0 .08	9 ,169	1 ,546
Feb 94	0 .33	0 .00	7 ,860	1 ,317
Nov 93	0 .30	0 .50	7 ,465	1 ,201
Aug 93	0 .26	0 .00	7 ,064	1 ,066
May 93	0 .26	0 .00	7 ,063	1 ,020

Synopsis:

For the three months ended February 28, 1995, Gennum Corporation reported record revenues of approximately $9.3-million. This represents an increase of approximately 20% over revenues last year. There was significant growth for the Video and Broadcast Products Group resulting from a growing demand for the company's GENLINX*TM product line as well as increased demand for its analog crosspoint switches. Acceptance of Gennum's proprietary DynamEQ components continued to grow among hearing instrument manufacturers.

To support growth through new products and to prepare Gennums's manufacturing processes for new developments in the miniaturization of electronic components, spending in research and development continues. Research and development also supports Gennum's adaptation of existing technologies to its customer's needs. Gennum expects that it will have to invest more in research and development as support from both levels of government is being reduced. Government support fell from 33.7% of spending in 1993 to 26% of similar spending in 1994. It continues to work with all levels of government to ensure that there is adequate support for research and development. Gennum expects moderate growth in hearing instrument products and believes that there will be continued strong demand for its video and broadcast products. About 25% of their total revenues are from sales of these products.

The company saw record revenues in 1994, with $33.2-million in sales, a 21% increase over 1993. An important role in expanding business in global markets and in meeting increasing competition, is quality in all areas of business. Gennum has programs for continuous improvement to implement and enhance quality actions throughout the organization. In October 1994, the company was registered to ISO 9001, the highest level in international quality standards.

Rank (Profit/Revenue/Assets)
419   629   769

H. Patrick Thode
Chairman

H. Douglas Barber
President & C.E.O.

C. Timothy Zahavich
V.P. Fin. Admin. & C.F.O.

Address
P.O. Box 489
Station A
Burlington
ON
L7R 3Y3
(905) 632-2996

Fax: (905) 632-2055
L0003627/G/6.5

GLENTEL INC.

Exchanges	Price (Jun29'95)		8.37	Trailing P/E		9.10	Stock Symbol
T	Trailing Yield (%)		14.93	Trailing EPS		0.92	**GLN**

Period Ending	Dec94	Dec93	Dec92	Dec91	Dec90
Yearly Statistics					3M
Price-Close	5.75	7.63	1.70	4.85	3.20
Price-High	10.25	9.63	7.00	5.50	5.38
Price-Low	4.85	1.25	1.00	3.00	3.00
P/E-Close	26.14	2.53	0.28	nm	nm
Dividends per Share	3.00	0.00	0.04	0.05	0.00
Dividend Yield (%)	52.17	0.00	2.53	0.99	0.00
Sales per Share	3.07	2.40	2.47	2.83	16.30
EPS before extra. item	0.22	3.02	6.12	(1.63)	(0.47)
Cash Flow per Share	(0.07)	(0.54)	(0.94)	(1.05)	(0.86)
Book Value per Share	4.44	7.34	4.42	1.67	3.28
O/S Common Shares	8,402	8,339	8,721	8,708	8,507
Total Revenue	30,230	53,125	23,861	21,309	34,669
Income before extra.	1,861	26,001	53,994	(13,581)	(3,964)
Cash Flow	(616)	(4,646)	(8,150)	(9,012)	(1,822)
Debt/Equity	nd	nd	nd	3.71	2.72
Return on Capital (%)	4.27	70.94	83.78	(10.81)	(11.38)
Ret. on Com. Equity (%)	3.78	52.15	203.28	(63.91)	na
% Change Profit	(92.8)	(51.8)	497.6	14.3	64.7
% Change Revenue	(43.1)	122.6	12.0	(84.6)	(23.4)
% Change Assets	(30.1)	50.8	(63.7)	(22.0)	(6.2)

Business:

GLENTEL INC. designs, manufactures and sells advanced wireless communications products and systems worldwide for radio paging, voice processing, computer assisted telephone message management, radio telephone, mobile data and transportation communications.

Date	EPS	DPS	Tot Rev	Inc Bex
Mar 95	0.74	1.25	19,593	6,243
Dec 94	0.25	0.00	11,810	2,126
Sep 94	(0.05)	0.00	6,342	(436)
Jun 94	(0.02)	0.00	6,128	(194)
Mar 94	0.04	3.00	6,018	365
Dec 93	2.98	0.00	36,927	25,649
Sep 93	(0.02)	0.00	5,330	(158)
Jun 93	0.05	0.00	5,474	427

Preferred Div. Coverage	np	np	np	
Total Div. Coverage	0.1	na	144.8	
Interest Coverage	nd	na	38.6	
Current Ratio	3.3	8.5	3.2	
Operating Margin	(9.2)	(3.2)	(42.1)	
Asset Turnover	0.5	0.3	0.5	
5 YEAR RATIOS (%)				
Return on Capital	27.4	22.2	7.9	
Return on Com. Equity	na	na	na	
Profit Growth	(17.5)	na	81.0	
Revenue Growth	(30.2)	(11.9)	(16.7)	
Asset Growth	(22.5)	(19.9)	(11.3)	
BALANCE SHEET (000)				
Cash	14,593	42,073	9,920	
Current Assets	29,380	51,408	21,944	
Net Fixed Assets	7,104	6,009	7,345	
Invest's & Advances	9,588	9,893	15,013	
Total Assets	47,767	68,354	45,342	
Short Term Debt	0	0	0	
Current Liabilities	8,881	6,080	6,795	
Long Term Debt	0	0	0	
Total Liabilities	10,434	7,179	6,795	
Total Equity	37,333	61,175	38,547	
Total Liab. & Equity	47,767	68,354	45,342	
CAPITAL (000)				
Total Debt	0	0	0	
Preferred Equity	0	0	0	
Common Equity	37,333	61,175	38,547	

Synopsis:

Glentel reports revenue of $9.5-million for the first quarter of 1995, an increase of 65.4% over sales of $5.7-million for the same period of 1994. The company's wireless division increased sales 13.3% in 1995 with $6.0-million as compared to $5.3-million in 1994. Glentel attributes this gain to increased retail activity by the wireless retail operations. Long distance air time sales represented 95.5% or $3.3-million of the total sales reported by the company's consumer division. First quarter operating results for 1995 resulted in a loss of $707,000 compared to income of $404,000 in 1994. Glentel feels the main reason for this decrease was non-operational. Foreign exchange gains attributed to the holding of U.S. dollar-denominated investments decreased from gains of $907,000 in 1994 to a loss of $14,000 in 1995. Overall the company's wireless division achieved improved operating results. However, this result was offset by higher corporate costs as well as greater losses generated by the consumer division.

The company's goal for 1994 was to establish a foundation for sustained growth in the years ahead. Glentel based growth on increasing profits in established sectors combined with development and growth in new fields of communication. Glentel established a network of 150 dealers with the intent to market satellite phones and air time to individuals and businesses across Canada. The company sells and services cellular phones, two-way radios, and paging systems. It provides corporate and independent retailers with wireless communications products. The company also resells long distance services to residential and small business customers through its network marketing company.

In 1994, the company achieved its primary goal of becoming a national full service provider of satellite services. The MSAT satellite, owned and operated by TMI Communications, provides the company with seamless access to communications from anywhere in North America and 400 kilometres offshore.

Relative strength to TSE300 / Price / Volume (in 1000's of board lots)

Rank (Profit/Revenue/Assets)
183   536   569
Thomas E. Skidmore
Chairman President & C.E.O.
Ronald E. Sowerby
C.F.O. Secretary-Treasurer

Address
Suite 2600
4710 Kingsway
Burnaby
BC
V5H 4M2
(604) 431-2300

Fax: (604) 438-7414
G0013950/G/6.5

HALEY INDUSTRIES LIMITED

Exchanges	Price (Jun29'95)		2.55	Trailing P/E		nm	Stock Symbol
T	Trailing Yield (%)		0.00	Trailing EPS		(0.03)	**HLY**

Period Ending	Dec94	Dec93	Dec92	Sep92	Sep91
Yearly Statistics			15M		
Price-Close	1.70	1.75	1.50	2.00	3.70
Price-High	1.95	2.53	3.50	3.70	4.80
Price-Low	1.25	1.00	1.20	2.00	2.10
P/E-Close	nm	nm	nm	nm	11.94
Dividends per Share	0.00	0.00	0.05	0.05	0.05
Dividend Yield (%)	0.00	0.00	3.33	2.50	1.35
Sales per Share	2.77	2.69	2.46	2.46	4.01
EPS before extra. item	(0.09)	(0.18)	(0.24)	(0.21)	0.31
Cash Flow per Share	0.05	0.04	0.05	(0.02)	0.47
Book Value per Share	1.47	1.51	1.67	1.66	1.84
O/S Common Shares	10,334	10,334	10,334	10,334	10,334
Total Revenue	28,918	28,009	32,168	25,790	41,785
Income before extra.	(949)	(1,908)	(2,429)	(2,138)	3,202
Cash Flow	544	437	642	(203)	4,859
Debt/Equity	1.37	1.26	1.09	1.08	0.91
Return on Capital (%)	0.34	(4.30)	(5.21)	(6.20)	17.00
Ret. on Com. Equity (%)	(6.16)	(11.61)	(11.29)	(11.82)	18.08
% Change Profit	50.3	1.8	9.1	(166.8)	140.7
% Change Revenue	3.2	8.8	(0.2)	(38.3)	14.8
% Change Assets	2.0	(3.9)	(0.4)	(1.4)	0.1

Date	EPS	DPS	Tot Rev	Inc Bex
Mar 95	0.01	0.00	8,606	63
Dec 94	0.01	0.00	11,604	77
Sep 94	(0.04)	0.00	5,645	(458)
Jun 94	(0.01)	0.00	6,699	(120)
Mar 94	(0.04)	0.00	5,317	(448)
Dec 93	(0.13)	0.00	8,448	(1,357)
Sep 93	(0.05)	0.00	4,920	(545)
Jun 93	0.00	0.00	7,209	(33)

Preferred Div. Coverage	np	np	np
Total Div. Coverage	na	na	0.0
Interest Coverage	0.1	0.0	0.0
Current Ratio	5.1	6.8	6.4
Operating Margin	(0.5)	(4.1)	(3.4)
Asset Turnover	0.7	0.7	0.6
5 YEAR RATIOS (%)			
Return on Capital	0.3	(2.3)	1.8
Return on Com. Equity	(4.6)	(10.9)	(5.9)
Profit Growth	na	na	na
Revenue Growth	(4.6)	(7.7)	(8.8)
Asset Growth	(0.8)	(4.4)	3.1
BALANCE SHEET (000)			
Cash	6,942	9,433	6,350
Current Assets	20,400	20,228	21,167
Net Fixed Assets	16,405	16,205	17,053
Invest's & Advances	675	508	525
Total Assets	41,319	40,505	42,153
Short Term Debt	0	0	0
Current Liabilities	4,022	2,989	3,322
Long Term Debt	20,749	19,771	18,822
Total Liabilities	26,146	24,855	24,920
Total Equity	15,173	15,650	17,233
Total Liab. & Equity	41,319	40,505	42,153
CAPITAL (000)			
Total Debt	20,749	19,771	18,822
Preferred Equity	0	0	0
Common Equity	15,173	15,650	17,233

Business:

HALEY INDUSTRIES LTD. makes and markets light alloy sand castings for the international aerospace industry. The company's main facility is located near Haley, west of Ottawa. The company has an American subsidiary, Presto Casting Co. of Arizona, which is a high-tech aerospace industry supplier.

Synopsis:

Haley Industries Limited increased sales for the first quarter in 1995 to $8-million compared to $6.5-million for the same period last year. This gain reflects improved aerospace sales levels which the company expects will continue. At the end of March 1995, sales order backlog was 30% higher than at the end of March 1994.

In November 1994, Haley Industries signed a letter of intent to enter into a joint venture agreement with Amcan Castings Limited, a subsidiary of Haley's largest shareholder. Haley is responsible for the manufacturing, while Amcan is responsible for the marketing, product design, and technology requirements. The company expects the market to grow from 32 million pounds per year to 100 million pounds per year by 1997. The name of this 50/50 joint venture between Haley and Amcan is Trimag.

In April 1995, General Motors Corporation's Small Truck Division awarded a contract to Trimag. The contract is for five years and worth an estimated $85-million. Trimag is to design, develop, and supply a new die-cast magnesium column support bracket. General Motors will use the bracket in all GMC and Chevy S-10 pick-up trucks as well as in all small utility trucks beginning with the 1998 model year. The company expects annual sales volume to total approximately $17-million per year beginning in 1997. The company will locate manufacturing operations at Haley's Renfrew facility. Trimag has recently ordered two new state-of-the-art die-casting machines.

Haley succeeded in securing orders for tooling on new programs in 1994, with production commencing in 1995. Five parts that utilize a new magnesium alloy, WE43, which has superior corrosion resistance and higher operating temperature capabilities were awarded to the Renfrew plant. These parts are for the F22 fighter aircraft's new PW-F119 jet engine. This plant also secured the intermediate case casting on a turbofan engine for commuter aircraft, the BW500. Pratt & Whitney, Canada developed the engine.

Rank (Profit/Revenue/Assets)
817   654   686

James D. Meekison
Chairman Of The Board

David Gorman
President & C.E.O.

James C. Lemenchick
V.P. Finance

Address
Haley
ON
K0J 1Y0
(613) 432-8841

Fax: (613) 432-9456
H0000162/G/6.4

HELIX CIRCUITS INC.

Exchanges	Price (Jun29'95)	0.15	Trailing P/E	0.33	Stock Symbol
TM	Trailing Yield (%)	0.00	Trailing EPS	0.45	**HLX**

Period Ending	Dec94	Dec93	Dec92	Dec91	Dec90
Yearly Statistics					
Price-Close	0.11	0.87	0.38	0.15	0.09
Price-High	1.08	1.42	0.58	0.20	0.25
Price-Low	0.11	0.32	0.14	0.03	0.05
P/E-Close	nm	nm	nm	nm	nm
Dividends per Share	0.00	0.00	0.00	0.00	0.00
Dividend Yield (%)	0.00	0.00	0.00	0.00	0.00
Sales per Share	0.70	2.01	2.00	2.91	3.54
EPS before extra. item	(0.28)	(0.16)	(0.11)	(0.42)	(0.99)
Cash Flow per Share	(0.11)	0.26	0.17	(0.12)	(0.02)
Book Value per Share	(0.26)	0.02	(1.76)	(1.75)	(1.43)
O/S Common Shares	35,115	35,115	10,601	10,601	10,611
Total Revenue	24,561	32,814	21,232	30,838	37,543
Income before extra.	(9,793)	(2,340)	39	(3,238)	(9,475)
Cash Flow	(3,756)	3,789	1,800	(1,276)	(181)
Debt/Equity	na	8.50	na	na	na
Return on Capital (%)	(264.88)	(21.40)	20.27	(18.39)	(44.27)
Ret. on Com. Equity (%)	na	na	na	na	na
% Change Profit	(318.5)	(6,100.0)	101.2	65.8	(180.6)
% Change Revenue	(25.2)	54.6	(31.2)	(17.9)	(21.4)
% Change Assets	(53.7)	8.5	21.5	(22.7)	(41.5)

Preferred Div. Coverage	np	np
Total Div. Coverage	na	na
Interest Coverage	0.0	0.0
Current Ratio	0.3	1.1
Operating Margin	(9.3)	12.3
Asset Turnover	3.1	1.7

5 YEAR RATIOS (%)			
Return on Capital	(65.7)	(14.5)	(8.7)
Return on Com. Equity	na	na	na
Profit Growth	na	na	na
Revenue Growth	(12.4)	(8.5)	(12.9)
Asset Growth	(22.7)	(12.9)	(21.2)

BALANCE SHEET (000)			
Cash	5	2,489	0
Current Assets	5,195	11,138	11,672
Net Fixed Assets	2,553	2,018	1,754
Invest's & Advances	1	0	0
Total Assets	7,816	16,876	15,552
Short Term Debt	7,665	560	818
Current Liabilities	15,764	10,085	9,450
Long Term Debt	1,071	6,017	17,583
Total Liabilities	16,835	16,102	27,033
Total Equity	(9,019)	774	(11,481)
Total Liab. & Equity	7,816	16,876	15,552

CAPITAL (000)			
Total Debt	8,736	6,577	18,401
Preferred Equity	0	0	7,164
Common Equity	(9,019)	774	(18,645)

Business:

HELIX CIRCUITS INC. designs and manufactures printed circuit boards. It has operations in Ontario. The company markets its products to computer industry, military and telecommunications customers in Canada and in the United States. The company's controlling shareholder is Helix Investments, which owns 47% of the common stock.

Date	EPS	DPS	Tot Rev	Inc Bex
Apr 95	(0.02)	0.00	4,506	(760)
Dec 94	(0.02)	0.00	7,313	(730)
Apr 94	(0.01)	0.00	6,998	(242)
Dec 93	0.50	0.00	10,412	3,795
Sep 93	0.04	0.00	7,394	732
Jun 93	(0.69)	0.00	7,695	(7,030)
Apr 93	(0.01)	0.00	7,427	163
Dec 92	(0.02)	0.00	5,993	77

Synopsis:

Helix Circuits Inc. faced a year of challenge in 1994. Net sales of $24.6-million in 1994 were down 16.3% from sales of $29.3-million in 1993. Cost of goods sold rose to 97.8% of sales in 1994 from 81.2% in 1993. The loss from continuing operations, which included a $2-million restructuring charge in 1994, was $4.7-million compared to income of $2.8-million in 1993.

Helix suffered losses from discontinued operations in both years. In 1994 the loss was $5.1-million, this related to the company's wholly owned subsidiary, Myrand Electronic Systems (1993) Ltd (Myrand). The loss in 1993 was $8.6-million and related to the company's facility in Irvine California. Net loss for 1994 was $9.8-million compared to a loss of $2.3-million in 1993.

Myrand's operations were primarily intended to service the needs of one particular customer who required the manufacture of high volume long-run orders for circuit boards. During the year Myrand lost this customer and was petitioned into bankruptcy in March 1995 and a trustee was appointed to administer the liquidation. As a result of the loss of control over Myrand, Helix stopped consolidating Myrand's operation, classified it as discontinued, and wrote down the investment to a nominal value of $1,000.

Before the end of 1994 Helix began discussions regarding a restructuring with its various stakeholders. The company filed a Notice of Intention to Make a Proposal Under the Bankruptcy Act on March 13, 1995. Helix reported that its unsecured creditors had approved its proposal, which is still subject to court approval.

The company's reorganization requires obtaining additional financing to fund the initial payments to creditors under the proposal, and to facilitate the recapitalization of the company. Under the terms of the proposal, Helix is obligated to raise between $5-million to $10-million through the private placement of senior secured convertible debentures, or through other means.

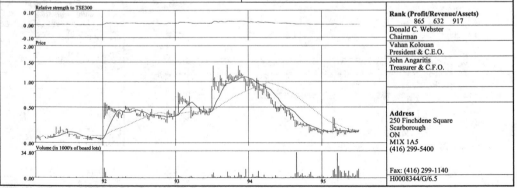

Rank (Profit/Revenue/Assets)		
865	632	917

Donald C. Webster
Chairman

Vahan Kolouan
President & C.E.O.

John Angaritis
Treasurer & C.F.O.

Address
250 Finchdene Square
Scarborough
ON
M1X 1A5
(416) 299-5400

Fax: (416) 299-1140
H0008344/G/6.5

INTERNATIONAL VERIFACT INC.

Exchanges								Stock Symbol
T	Price (Jun29'95)			5.75	Trailing P/E		nm	
	Trailing Yield (%)			0.00	Trailing EPS		(3.07)	**IVI**

Period Ending	Dec94	Mar94	Mar93	Mar92	Mar91
Yearly Statistics	9M				
Price-Close	7.80	18.60	33.00	16.70	3.05
Price-High	22.00	43.50	35.00	19.70	4.70
Price-Low	6.00	18.00	9.50	2.70	2.70
P/E-Close	nm	37.20	33.00	167.00	nm
Dividends per Share	0.00	0.00	0.00	0.00	0.00
Dividend Yield (%)	0.00	0.00	0.00	0.00	0.00
Sales per Share	7.68	8.34	7.43	4.15	4.70
EPS before extra. item	(3.20)	0.50	1.00	0.10	(0.60)
Cash Flow per Share	(1.94)	0.83	1.17	0.34	(0.27)
Book Value per Share	3.80	5.41	4.69	1.77	(0.97)
O/S Common Shares	6,555	4,228	3,950	3,122	2,174
Total Revenue	31,056	34,445	26,716	11,009	8,928
Income before extra.	(14,223)	2,061	3,558	433	(934)
Cash Flow	(7,839)	3,428	4,218	904	(519)
Debt/Equity	0.01	0.01	0.00	0.00	0.52
Return on Capital (%)	(76.11)	9.07	24.15	10.61	(11.13)
Ret. on Com. Equity (%)	(79.52)	8.77	28.65	25.31	na
% Change Profit	(1,020.1)	(42.1)	721.7	146.4	49.2
% Change Revenue	20.2	28.9	142.7	23.3	16.2
% Change Assets	14.1	17.7	145.3	141.3	(35.3)

Preferred Div. Coverage	np	8.4	32.4
Total Div. Coverage	0.0	8.4	32.4
Interest Coverage	0.0	na	na
Current Ratio	1.9	3.3	3.6
Operating Margin	(26.9)	8.6	12.9
Asset Turnover	1.1	1.1	1.0
5 YEAR RATIOS (%)			
Return on Capital	(8.7)	1.2	(0.5)
Return on Com. Equity	na	na	na
Profit Growth	na	25.9	58.0
Revenue Growth	40.0	29.6	75.6
Asset Growth	38.8	38.2	43.8
BALANCE SHEET (000)			
Cash	4,111	4,911	7,925
Current Assets	21,470	23,808	22,522
Net Fixed Assets	2,006	1,236	761
Invest's & Advances	0	1,116	1,116
Total Assets	36,345	31,850	27,052
Short Term Debt	44	60	34
Current Liabilities	11,361	7,282	6,283
Long Term Debt	83	69	34
Total Liabilities	11,444	7,351	6,317
Total Equity	24,901	24,499	20,735
Total Liab. & Equity	36,345	31,850	27,052
CAPITAL (000)			
Total Debt	127	129	67
Preferred Equity	0	1,635	2,197
Common Equity	24,901	22,864	18,538

Business:

INTERNATIONAL VERIFACT INC. is a publicly-owned corporation engaged in the design, development, manufacture and marketing of terminals and related products for use in electronic funds transfer and point of sale applications (EFT/POS). These applications include credit card authorization and verification, direct debit transactions and electronic draft capture.

Date	EPS	DPS	Tot Rev	Inc Bex
Mar 95	0.12	0.00	15,509	795
Dec 94	(3.22)	0.00	9,268	(15,340)
Sep 94	0.02	0.00	11,563	669
Jun 94	0.01	0.00	10,227	448
Mar 94	0.00	0.00	7,418	49
Dec 93	(0.01)	0.00	7,280	(422)
Sep 93	0.03	0.00	9,203	1,080
Jun 93	0.03	0.00	8,300	1,213

Synopsis:

International Verifact in the first quarter of 1995 rationalized its U.S. operations with those of Soricon Corporation, the company it acquired on December 30, 1994. Verifact's U.S. office in Scottsdale, Arizona, was rolled into the former head office of Soricon in Boulder, Colorado. The Soricon trade name has been phased out. Verifact reported revenue of $15.5-million in the first quarter ended March 31, 1995, an increase of about $5-million over the same period in 1994. The company had success overseas in the first quarter with additional orders from Saudi Arabia and Korea.

Now that the company has established a solid base in the important U.S. market, it intends to take the opportunity to build on this base. Verifact wants to be identified in the U.S., as well as Canada, as a leader in service and innovation regarding electronic payment solutions. The acceptance of the debit payment system in Canada has continued to exceed expectations. INTERAC, the Canadian association of banks and other financial institutions, became the largest debit processor in North America during 1994. The number of debit transactions more than doubled reaching 185.2-million.

Verifact introduced a new cheque processing unit, Power Encoder, in February 1995. The Power Encoder reads the magnetic ink character recognition lines from cheques and compares this information with data captured at the point-of-sale (POS) for authorization. Using the information from the POS data base, the Power Encoder automatically encodes the cheque with the dollar amount, endorses the back of each cheque with the first bank of deposit information, and prints batch reports and deposit slips. By eliminating the need for manual cheque encoding it reduces the labour involved in deposit preparation. The Power Encoder can process over 700 cheques an hour.

Relative strength to TSE300

Price

Volume (in 1000's of board lots)

Rank (Profit/Revenue/Assets)
965   584   724

George Whitton
Chairman President & C.E.O.

L. Barry Thomson
President & C.O.O.

Address
79 Torbarrie Road
Downsview
ON
M3L 1G5
(416) 245-6700

Fax: (416) 245-6701
01000241/G/6.5

LINAMAR CORPORATION

Exchanges	Price (Jun29'95)	19.37	Trailing P/E	13.09	Stock Symbol
T	Trailing Yield (%)	0.00	Trailing EPS	1.48	LNR

Period Ending	Dec94	Dec93	Jun93	Jun92	Jun91
Yearly Statistics		6M			
Price-Close	19.50	19.13	14.63	8.13	3.56
Price-High	25.00	20.50	14.63	8.38	3.75
Price-Low	15.63	12.13	8.00	3.50	2.00
P/E-Close	13.54	18.75	19.76	15.19	11.13
Dividends per Share	0.00	0.00	0.00	0.00	0.00
Dividend Yield (%)	0.00	0.00	0.00	0.00	0.00
Sales per Share	19.89	17.78	13.88	10.95	10.82
EPS before extra. item	1.44	0.51	0.74	0.54	0.32
Cash Flow per Share	2.66	1.74	1.43	0.99	0.95
Book Value per Share	7.01	5.61	3.97	3.26	2.44
O/S Common Shares	21,694	21,476	18,274	17,772	15,838
Total Revenue	432,479	184,744	251,316	179,998	171,007
Income before extra.	31,091	10,530	13,357	8,730	5,069
Cash Flow	57,661	18,013	25,799	16,167	14,950
Debt/Equity	0.21	0.27	0.90	0.60	0.90
Return on Capital (%)	29.23	22.70	20.65	19.47	15.90
Ret. on Com. Equity (%)	22.81	21.82	20.49	18.10	14.07
% Change Profit	47.6	57.7	53.0	72.2	55.4
% Change Revenue	17.0	47.0	39.6	5.3	32.6
% Change Assets	19.7	8.2	45.5	21.7	4.6

	Date	EPS	DPS	Tot Rev	Inc Bex
	Mar 95	0.35	0.00	121,100	7,700
	Dec 94	0.31	0.00	109,459	6,719
	Sep 94	0.40	0.00	121,110	8,607
	Jun 94	0.42	0.00	111,124	9,046
	Mar 94	0.31	0.00	90,786	6,719
	Dec 93	0.03	0.00	82,711	5,718
	Sep 93	0.24	0.00	102,033	4,812
	Jun 93	0.27	0.00	76,707	4,910

Preferred Div. Coverage	np	np	np
Total Div. Coverage	na	na	na
Interest Coverage	18.2	9.1	8.0
Current Ratio	1.5	1.5	1.0
Operating Margin	11.2	8.1	9.1
Asset Turnover	1.7	1.8	1.3
5 YEAR RATIOS (%)			
Return on Capital	21.6	18.7	16.6
Return on Com. Equity	19.5	16.9	13.9
Profit Growth	56.9	59.4	23.9
Revenue Growth	27.3	26.3	17.1
Asset Growth	19.0	19.5	17.4
BALANCE SHEET (000)			
Cash	0	0	0
Current Assets	123,847	107,006	100,785
Net Fixed Assets	125,263	100,818	90,852
Invest's & Advances	261	66	0
Total Assets	250,650	209,443	193,581
Short Term Debt	18,448	15,138	44,251
Current Liabilities	83,512	70,905	97,905
Long Term Debt	12,890	17,459	20,715
Total Liabilities	98,485	88,937	121,047
Total Equity	152,165	120,506	72,534
Total Liab. & Equity	250,650	209,443	193,581
CAPITAL (000)			
Total Debt	31,338	32,597	64,966
Preferred Equity	0	0	0
Common Equity	152,165	120,506	72,534

Business:

LINAMAR CORPORATION operates in two industry segments. The precision machining segment consists primarily of the manufacturing and assembly of automotive, components for original equipment manufactures and their suppliers. The agricultural equipment segment assembles and sells rotary combines, corn heads, grain dryers, and other harvesting equipment.

Synopsis:

Linamar Corporation reported sales of $121.1-million for the first quarter of 1995, an increase over the $90.7-million in the same period of 1994. The company credits the increased results to the continued growth in their automotive group, which realized an additional $30-million in revenues, when compared to 1994. In May 1995, Linamar reported it had been awarded contracts from General Motors totalling over $250-million for the production of transmission components and assemblies.

In June 1995, Linamar agreed to purchase the remaining 10% equity interest in Western Combine from FPM Holdings Ltd., making Western Combine a wholly owned subsidiary. Western Combine assembles and sells harvesting equipment to the agricultural industry in North America and Europe. Linamar also agreed to buy FPM's equity interest in Portage Manufacturing Inc., increasing Linamar's equity interest to 75%.

Linamar's sales reached a record level in 1994, showing an increase of 34% over 1993. The automotive component of the precision machining segment was responsible for the bulk of the improvement. Volumes continued to increase in the car and truck markets, as well as the successful launching of the new ABS projects. In August 1994, Linamar completed the formation of the Jiayuan Grain Drying Engineering and Equipment Company, to produce grain drying equipment in Shenyang, China. Linamar will be a minority shareholder and will limit its investment primarily to technology transfer and support.

In 1994, 87.2% of the company's consolidated sales were accounted for by the precision machining equipment. Consolidated sales by customer were: General Motors, 33.9%; Ford Motor, 14.1%; and Detroit Diesel, 12.8%. No single product sold to any of these customers constituted more than 10% of the company's consolidated sales.

Relative strength to TSE300

Rank (Profit/Revenue/Assets)
153   206   317

Frank J. Hasenfratz
Chairman & C.E.O.

Larry J. Pearson
President C.O.O. & Treasurer

Address
301 Massey Road
Guelph
ON
N1K 1B2
(519) 836-7550

Fax: (519) 824-8479

L0000441/G/6.4

NBS TECHNOLOGIES INC.

Exchanges	Price (Jun29'95)		4.35	Trailing P/E		4.18	Stock Symbol
T	Trailing Yield (%)		0.00	Trailing EPS		1.04	NBS

Period Ending	Sep94	Sep93	Sep92	Sep91	Sep90
Yearly Statistics					
Price-Close	1.70	1.45	2.70	0.43	0.62
Price-High	3.10	3.25	3.70	0.85	7.40
Price-Low	1.25	1.25	0.60	0.43	0.60
P/E-Close	3.40	nm	nm	nm	nm
Dividends per Share	0.00	0.00	0.00	0.00	0.00
Dividend Yield (%)	0.00	0.00	0.00	0.00	0.00
Sales per Share	89.07	79.05	73.47	77.95	81.20
EPS before extra. item	0.50	(0.58)	(3.29)	(12.36)	(28.51)
Cash Flow per Share	7.96	7.13	3.34	(6.07)	(14.45)
Book Value per Share	(72.68)	(73.51)	(73.26)	(70.26)	(58.01)
O/S Common Shares	1,600	1,600	1,600	1,600	1,600
Total Revenue	142,502	126,462	117,534	124,708	132,706
Income before extra.	1,333	(397)	(4,808)	(19,601)	(45,602)
Cash Flow	12,735	11,403	5,340	(9,711)	(23,123)
Debt/Equity	na	na	na	na	na
Return on Capital (%)	56.86	50.86	30.25	(14.59)	(47.14)
Ret. on Com. Equity (%)	na	na	na	na	na
% Change Profit	435.8	91.7	75.5	57.0	(22.1)
% Change Revenue	12.7	7.6	(5.8)	(6.0)	4.9
% Change Assets	(4.6)	(6.7)	(15.3)	(17.2)	(28.9)

Date	EPS	DPS	Tot Rev	Inc Bex
Mar 95	(0.01)	0.00	43,488	(98)
Dec 94	(0.04)	0.00	38,006	74
Sep 94	1.53	0.00	40,869	2,584
Jun 94	(0.44)	0.00	35,908	(562)
Mar 94	0.11	0.00	33,832	300
Dec 93	(0.70)	0.00	31,893	(989)
Sep 93	2.05	0.00	38,708	3,412
Jun 93	(0.35)	0.00	34,716	(431)

	Sep94	Sep93	Sep92
Preferred Div. Coverage	na	na	na
Total Div. Coverage	na	na	na
Interest Coverage	1.2	1.0	0.6
Current Ratio	0.2	0.5	0.6
Operating Margin	11.3	10.3	7.2
Asset Turnover	2.4	2.1	1.8
5 YEAR RATIOS (%)			
Return on Capital	15.3	0.0	(16.0)
Return on Com. Equity	na	na	na
Profit Growth	85.6	43.8	na
Revenue Growth	2.3	0.8	(3.9)
Asset Growth	(15.0)	(19.9)	(25.0)
BALANCE SHEET (000)			
Cash	0	0	0
Current Assets	33,142	37,866	40,046
Net Fixed Assets	25,472	23,576	25,842
Invest's & Advances	0	0	0
Total Assets	58,614	61,442	65,888
Short Term Debt	111,609	38,976	30,761
Current Liabilities	138,387	75,744	70,146
Long Term Debt	29,904	96,708	106,355
Total Liabilities	168,291	172,452	176,501
Total Equity	(109,677)	(111,010)	(110,613)
Total Liab. & Equity	58,614	61,442	65,888
CAPITAL (000)			
Total Debt	141,513	135,684	137,116
Preferred Equity	6,593	6,593	6,593
Common Equity	(116,270)	(117,603)	(117,206)

Business:

NBS TECHNOLOGIES supplies equipment and related services to issuers of plastic transcation cards. The company sells card embossers, encoders, imprinters, benefits and credit authorization terminals, and non-impact printers to banks, oil companies, retailers, hospitals, universities, and government agencies.

Synopsis:

NBS Technologies Inc. reported sales for the six months ending March 31, 1995, increased 24% over the prior year to $81.5-million compared with $65.7-million in 1994. The company attributes the growth to a significant increase in demand for many of its products.

On January 19, 1995, shareholders approved a recapitalization plan that included the issue of 25.5 million shares at $3.00 per share for gross proceeds of $76.5-million. The plan also included the exchange of approximately $8.5-million worth of Class AAA preferred shares and accumulated dividends into common equity at $3.00 per share for 2.8 million shares. In addition, NBS Technologies Inc. will issue $18.5-million of junior notes bearing interest of 8% annually. NBS will base repayment of these notes on a percentage of net income from future equity issues. NBS will repay short-term and long-term debt totalling $95-million using total proceeds from these transactions. This will reduce short-term and long-term debt significantly and will lead to lower interest costs in the future.

NBS reported its POS Systems maintained its position as the leading stand alone point of sale system in Canada with the successful rollout of the direct payment card program across the country. The transaction volume of the Interac Direct Payment System is far ahead of original projections. The company expects continued expansion as the financial institutions who support the Interac Network offer debit and credit applications using NBS hardware and software solutions. Since the majority of point of sale systems installed today can only handle credit card purchases, the company believes the market potential for their system is significant. NBS also expanded its product line with the addition of the Advantage ImageMaster*TM graphics printer. It developed this product in response to the growing market for custom graphics and photo images on plastic cards. High growth markets such as gaming, prepaid phone cards, and healthcare have responded well to this development.

Rank (Profit/Revenue/Assets)
625   369   596

Timothy W. Casgrain
President & C.E.O.

J. Kenneth Rutherford
V.P. C.F.O. & Secretary

Address
3220 Orlando Drive
Mississauga
ON
L4V 1R5
(905) 671-3334

Fax: (905) 671-0690
N0024728/G/6.5

NEWBRIDGE NETWORKS CORPORATION

Exchanges	Price (Jun29'95)	48.62	Trailing P/E	21.33	Stock Symbol
TN	Trailing Yield (%)	0.00	Trailing EPS	2.28	NNC

Period Ending	Apr94	Apr93	Apr92	Apr91	Apr90
Yearly Statistics					
Price-Close	69.50	38.94	8.56	4.19	5.50
Price-High	97.50	39.50	10.63	5.56	10.69
Price-Low	38.00	8.25	3.13	1.78	4.00
P/E-Close	35.10	48.07	61.16	nm	84.61
Dividends per Share	0.00	0.00	0.00	0.00	0.00
Dividend Yield (%)	0.00	0.00	0.00	0.00	0.00
Sales per Share	6.93	4.17	2.63	2.21	1.95
EPS before extra. item	1.98	0.81	0.14	(0.27)	0.07
Cash Flow per Share	2.31	1.13	0.39	(0.09)	0.17
Book Value per Share	5.86	3.65	1.56	1.37	1.63
O/S Common Shares	80,782	78,916	70,308	68,291	67,040
Total Revenue	564,221	312,285	181,735	150,280	122,457
Income before extra.	157,811	60,022	9,777	(17,913)	3,889
Cash Flow	184,325	83,043	27,170	(6,041)	10,361
Debt/Equity	0.03	0.12	0.31	0.40	0.52
Return on Capital (%)	58.74	38.17	14.20	(6.85)	7.59
Ret. on Com. Equity (%)	41.44	30.17	9.62	(17.65)	5.25
% Change Profit	162.9	513.9	154.6	(560.6)	(57.5)
% Change Revenue	80.7	71.8	20.9	22.7	81.7
% Change Assets	52.3	115.6	9.7	(8.6)	104.7

Preferred Div. Coverage	np	np	np
Total Div. Coverage	na	na	na
Interest Coverage	59.9	19.6	2.2
Current Ratio	4.5	3.8	2.8
Operating Margin	41.0	28.2	12.6
Asset Turnover	0.9	0.8	1.0
5 YEAR RATIOS (%)			
Return on Capital	22.4	16.7	na
Return on Com. Equity	13.8	13.9	na
Profit Growth	76.7	na	na
Revenue Growth	52.9	77.6	na
Asset Growth	46.4	64.8	na
BALANCE SHEET (000)			
Cash	275,785	199,855	17,019
Current Assets	452,279	299,095	101,012
Net Fixed Assets	92,895	66,472	62,037
Invest's & Advances	20,087	487	3,923
Total Assets	584,764	383,877	178,069
Short Term Debt	7,272	18,731	6,482
Current Liabilities	100,821	79,131	36,040
Long Term Debt	7,767	14,447	27,525
Total Liabilities	111,192	95,723	68,339
Total Equity	473,572	288,154	109,730
Total Liab. & Equity	584,764	383,877	178,069
CAPITAL (000)			
Total Debt	15,039	33,178	34,007
Preferred Equity	0	0	0
Common Equity	473,572	288,154	109,730

Business:

NEWBRIDGE NETWORKS CORPORATION designs, manufactures and markets integrated digital networking products. The company distributes and services its products in over 50 countries either through its direct sales force or through authorized dealers, distributors, common carriers, original equipment manufacturers and value added resellers. Products are manufactured in Canada, the U.S., and the U.K.

Date	EPS	DPS	Tot Rev	Inc Bex
Feb 95	0.61	0.00	214,370	49,398
Nov 94	0.56	0.00	195,465	45,260
Jul 94	0.52	0.00	175,078	41,910
Apr 94	0.59	0.00	167,479	47,316
Jan 94	0.52	0.00	148,046	41,381
Oct 93	0.47	0.00	130,931	37,079
Jul 93	0.41	0.00	117,924	32,035
Apr 93	0.33	0.00	102,778	25,515

Synopsis:

Due in part to an increased demand for its communications network products, Newbridge Networks Corporation saw a revenue increase of 45% from the previous year's sales of $552.5-million, to a new high of $800-million for the year ended April 30, 1995. The company expects continued growth in sales in 1996 because of a substantial increase of its product lines. These products have been delivered to organizations in more than 100 countries throughout the world and have doubled Newbridge's market, leading to major expansion overseas.

In May 1995, Newbridge announced a number of important initiatives related to its product business units (PBUs), which form a key element of Action 95, a plan designed to strengthen its ability to continued innovation and success. The principal objectives of organizational changes within the PBUs are to continue to focus on market growth, solidify the business units, and reinforce total business accountability within these units.

Newbridge Networks, in June 1995, announced a formal joint agreement with GTE telephone operations to launch the first nationwide Asynchronous Transfer Mode (ATM) network. The project, initially focused on the U.K., is designed specifically for manufacturing and marketing advanced interactive communications services. Newbridge handles more than 800 of the 36150 MainStreet ATMnet switches deployed in 22 countries around the world. Scheduled to begin in 1995, the first jointly developed ATM products will be available in 1996.

In 1994, the company secured many contracts including a nationwide digital network for CANTV, the Venezuelan carrier. Newbridge signed deals with the Chinese government for the National Public Data Network backbone, and with Deutsche Telekom for the IDN Plus (Integrated Data Network) in Germany. Other sales include a nationwide business network for Swiss Telecom, and a contract with Siemens Albis AG of Switzerland for the supply of ATM products.

Relative strength to TSE300

Price

Volume (in 1000's of board lots)

Rank (Profit/Revenue/Assets)
43 182 215

Terence H. Matthews
Chairman & C.E.O.

Peter Sommerer
President & C.O.O.

Peter D. Charbonneau
Exec. V.P. Finance & C.F.O.

Address
P.O. Box 13600
600 March Road
Kanata
ON
K2K 2E6
(613) 591-3600

Fax: (613) 591-3680
N0002769/G/6.5

NOMA INDUSTRIES LIMITED

Exchanges	Price (Jun29'95)	5.25	Trailing P/E	nm	Stock Symbol
T	Trailing Yield (%)	2.29	Trailing EPS	(0.44)	NMA.A

Period Ending	Dec94	Dec93	Dec92	Dec91	Dec90
Yearly Statistics					
Price-Close	4.35	7.00	5.50	5.50	4.65
Price-High	7.50	7.75	7.50	8.50	13.00
Price-Low	4.10	4.50	4.75	4.20	4.10
P/E-Close	nm	nm	137.50	nm	nm
Dividends per Share	0.12	0.12	0.12	0.15	0.24
Dividend Yield (%)	2.76	1.71	2.18	2.73	5.16
Sales per Share	12.75	10.34	10.39	17.91	18.25
EPS before extra. item	(0.49)	(0.85)	0.04	(0.36)	(0.01)
Cash Flow per Share	(0.16)	0.49	0.41	0.45	0.67
Book Value per Share	3.19	3.73	4.61	4.36	4.89
O/S Common Shares	34,139	33,919	33,870	30,210	30,210
Total Revenue	435,056	350,604	336,574	541,201	551,191
Income before extra.	(16,843)	(28,673)	1,288	(10,837)	(474)
Cash Flow	(5,316)	16,673	13,429	13,605	20,191
Debt/Equity	0.54	0.88	0.62	0.98	1.17
Return on Capital (%)	(2.08)	(7.62)	4.45	(0.10)	6.86
Ret. on Com. Equity (%)	(14.30)	(20.28)	0.89	(7.76)	(0.31)
% Change Profit	41.3	(2,326.2)	111.9	(2,186.3)	(106.4)
% Change Revenue	24.1	4.2	(37.8)	(1.8)	(13.8)
% Change Assets	(26.0)	2.6	6.6	(16.0)	(5.7)

	Dec94	Dec93	Dec92
Preferred Div. Coverage	np	np	np
Total Div. Coverage	0.0	0.0	0.3
Interest Coverage	0.0	0.0	1.6
Current Ratio	1.8	1.6	2.0
Operating Margin	5.1	5.3	5.5
Asset Turnover	1.7	1.0	1.0
5 YEAR RATIOS (%)			
Return on Capital	0.3	2.9	9.2
Return on Com. Equity	(8.4)	(4.5)	3.4
Profit Growth	na	na	(45.1)
Revenue Growth	(7.5)	(11.1)	(8.7)
Asset Growth	(8.5)	(1.0)	0.4
BALANCE SHEET (000)			
Cash	0	0	0
Current Assets	159,424	283,803	270,881
Net Fixed Assets	65,598	51,704	53,233
Invest's & Advances	0	0	0
Total Assets	257,783	348,120	339,414
Short Term Debt	14,324	68,928	51,447
Current Liabilities	88,152	179,512	137,789
Long Term Debt	45,012	42,093	45,349
Total Liabilities	148,764	221,605	183,138
Total Equity	109,019	126,515	156,276
Total Liab. & Equity	257,783	348,120	339,414
CAPITAL (000)			
Total Debt	59,336	111,021	96,796
Preferred Equity	0	0	0
Common Equity	109,019	126,515	156,276

Business:

NOMA INDUSTRIES LTD. is a group of companies with operations in Canada and the United States. The company specializes in the manufacturing and marketing of electrical products for consumer and industrial markets. Products include electrical wire and components for other manufacturers and Christmas ornaments and consumer extension cords.

Date	EPS	DPS	Tot Rev	Inc Bex
Mar 95	0.13	0.03	96,700	4,500
Dec 94	(0.66)	0.03	153,443	(22,750)
Sep 94	0.07	0.03	164,355	2,592
Jun 94	0.02	0.03	63,290	728
Mar 94	0.08	0.03	53,968	2,587
Dec 93	(0.91)	0.03	(102,292)	(30,547)
Sep 93	(0.03)	0.03	184,217	(1,236)
Jun 93	0.00	0.03	53,432	36

Synopsis:

Noma decided to place all its companies into one of three core business groups where it feels they will have a long term competitive edge. To accomplish this, many of the independent but similar companies that were part of Noma in previous years were consolidated. As well, Noma completely left some businesses. The three core groups are the Electric Wire and Components Group, the Christmas Products Group, and the Consumer Electrical Products Group.

The first move in Nomads new plan was the sale of its Outdoor Power Equipment Group for $106-million. This allowed Noma to reduce debt, and significantly strengthen its balance sheet. In a move to strengthen its Electrical Wire and Components Group, Noma bought Fleck Manufacturing, Inc. for $22-million. Noma felt that Fleck, which had embarked on a similar strategy to Noma and was an increasingly profitable operation, was very complementary to its own operations. The added bonus was Fleck's strong presence in the U.S. appliance harness industry and its low cost Mexican manufacturing facilities. This gave Noma additional strength in the automotive industry and in its profitable Canadian manufacturing facilities.

In the first quarter ended March 31, 1995, Noma reported an increase in sales to $96.7-million from $54-million in the same period last year. The sales and earnings for the Electrical Wire and Components Division were ahead of 1993 and plan, excluding the Fleck acquisition. The Fleck Division is performing to plan. Due to a slower than expected retail market, the Consumer Electrical Products Division results were somewhat under plan.

The company priorities are: the growth of its Electrical Wire and Components Business on a North American basis through acquisitions and export sales; the successful implementation of the restructuring of the Christmas Products Group; and development of a longer term strategy to allow it to profitably grow in the U.S. market.

Relative strength to TSE300 — Price — Volume (in 1000's of board lots)

Rank (Profit/Revenue/Assets)		
961	205	313

H. Thomas Beck
Chairman

Stephen G. Snyder
President & C.E.O.

Norman S. Eckler
Secretary & C.F.O.

W. David Wrende
Exec. V.P.

Address
4100 Yonge Street
Toronto
ON
M2P 2B5
(416) 222-6662

Fax: (416) 222-9165
N0002031/G/6.5

QSOUND LABS, INC.

Exchanges	Price (Jun29'95)	4.70	Trailing P/E	nm	Stock Symbol
TQ	Trailing Yield (%)	0.00	Trailing EPS	(0.22)	**QSL**

Period Ending	Dec94	Dec93	Dec92	Dec91	Dec90
Yearly Statistics					
Price-Close	4.20	5.25	2.75	2.35	12.00
Price-High	6.00	7.00	3.55	14.50	26.00
Price-Low	2.65	2.75	0.75	2.15	10.50
P/E-Close	nm	nm	nm	nm	nm
Dividends per Share	0.00	0.00	0.00	0.00	0.00
Dividend Yield (%)	0.00	0.00	0.00	0.00	0.00
Sales per Share	0.18	0.28	0.22	0.22	na
EPS before extra. item	(0.22)	(0.14)	(0.34)	(0.56)	(0.43)
Cash Flow per Share	(0.20)	(0.08)	(0.23)	(0.50)	(0.18)
Book Value per Share	0.06	0.12	(0.04)	0.26	0.48
O/S Common Shares	16,853	14,997	12,734	12,516	11,737
Total Revenue	3,010	3,958	2,848	2,742	265
Income before extra.	(3,408)	(1,954)	(4,270)	(6,775)	(4,976)
Cash Flow	(3,449)	(1,168)	(2,855)	(6,087)	(2,028)
Debt/Equity	3.91	2.69	na	0.61	0.07
Return on Capital (%)	(50.04)	(22.70)	(67.13)	(109.06)	(74.84)
Ret. on Com. Equity (%)	(233.21)	(281.52)	(311.01)	(153.94)	(82.19)
% Change Profit	(74.4)	54.3	37.0	(36.2)	(89.3)
% Change Revenue	(24.0)	39.0	3.9	935.1	19.5
% Change Assets	(29.0)	3.6	16.5	(15.3)	9.8

Preferred Div. Coverage	np	np	np
Total Div. Coverage	na	na	na
Interest Coverage	0.0	0.0	0.0
Current Ratio	1.8	1.6	0.7
Operating Margin	(104.3)	(37.1)	(127.9)
Asset Turnover	0.4	0.4	0.3
5 YEAR RATIOS (%)			
Return on Capital	(64.8)	(63.1)	(65.2)
Return on Com. Equity	(213.8)	(175.0)	(128.0)
Profit Growth	na	na	na
Revenue Growth	168.4	179.9	393.6
Asset Growth	na	12.4	50.8
BALANCE SHEET (000)			
Cash	1,127	1,180	234
Current Assets	3,118	3,943	1,305
Net Fixed Assets	1,623	1,835	2,227
Invest's & Advances	577	1,458	2,209
Total Assets	7,150	10,063	9,715
Short Term Debt	995	1,796	869
Current Liabilities	1,750	2,424	1,788
Long Term Debt	3,098	3,182	5,021
Total Liabilities	6,076	8,214	10,176
Total Equity	1,074	1,849	(461)
Total Liab. & Equity	7,150	10,063	9,715
CAPITAL (000)			
Total Debt	4,093	4,978	5,890
Preferred Equity	0	0	0
Common Equity	1,074	1,849	(461)

Business:

QSOUND LABS, INC. has patent status for its QSound enhancement and audio imaging technology. Primary markets include computer, home entertainment and consumer electronics industries. The music industry, film and television are secondary markets for QSound.

Date	EPS	DPS	Tot Rev	Inc Bex
Dec 94	(0.02)	0.00	1,311	584
Sep 94	(0.06)	0.00	594	(950)
Jun 94	(0.08)	0.00	539	(1,147)
Mar 94	(0.06)	0.00	471	(937)
Dec 93	(0.01)	0.00	976	(282)
Sep 93	(0.04)	0.00	1,013	(491)
Jun 93	(0.05)	0.00	951	(698)
Mar 93	(0.04)	0.00	899	(482)

Synopsis:

QSound Labs, Inc. announced on May 15, 1995, that Sega of America will produce the first game in QSound that will conform to Intel's Native Signal Processing (NSP) design specifications. The initial offering of the PC version will be as software bundled with NSP capable pentium processor-based computers. QSound is incorporated in the Intel NSP architecture and the company believes that with companies such as Sega writing games for NSP the platform will be successful. QSound is currently involved in joint ventures with two companies, Capcom and Spectrum. Both of these companies have shown confidence in QSound and have advanced funds either in the form of loans or the purchase of QSound shares.

QSound established a U.S. based subsidiary on January 10, 1995. QSound Electronics Inc. will market and distribute its consumer products. QSound Electronics, based in Newport Beach, California, has already established a distribution network for QSound consumer products, which should reach markets by the middle of 1995. Earlier in December 1994 the company had announced the opening of a European based sales, marketing, and technical support office. An important component to game developers worldwide is 3D audio. The company intends to aggressively pursue this untapped market in Europe, as it is the base for a majority of prominent software developers.

QSound, although it has not yet achieved profitability, maintained a positive working capital position during 1994 and continues to enter into new licensing arrangements, and new arrangements for product sales. With a working capital at December 31, 1994, of $1,368,608 combined with proceeds from the exercise of share purchase warrants and other financing sources, the company can meet its obligations as they come due.

Rank (Profit/Revenue/Assets)
808   861   963

Danny D. Lowe
Chairman

David Gallagher
President & C.E.O.

Address
2748 - 37th Avenue N.E.
Calgary
AB
T1Y 5L3
(403) 291-2492

Fax: (403) 250-1521
01000068/G/6.5

SPAR AEROSPACE LIMITED

Exchanges	Price (Jun29'95)		13 .37	Trailing P/E		24 .31		Stock Symbol
TM	Trailing Yield (%)		1 .79	Trailing EPS		0 .55		**SPZ**

Period Ending	Dec94	Dec93	Dec92	Dec91	Dec90
Yearly Statistics					
Price-Close	9 .75	18 .13	15 .88	16 .00	10 .88
Price-High	20 .50	18 .50	20 .00	16 .25	11 .38
Price-Low	8 .38	13 .25	14 .63	10 .50	7 .88
P/E-Close	18 .40	453 .13	32 .40	16 .33	45 .31
Dividends per Share	0 .24	0 .24	0 .24	0 .12	0 .12
Dividend Yield (%)	2 .46	1 .32	1 .51	0 .75	1 .10
Sales per Share	38 .79	35 .83	38 .91	35 .01	27 .06
EPS before extra. item	0 .53	0 .04	0 .49	0 .98	0 .24
Cash Flow per Share	2 .64	2 .00	3 .32	2 .20	1 .31
Book Value per Share	10 .76	10 .46	8 .44	8 .17	7 .29
O/S Common Shares	14 ,770	14 ,712	12 ,497	12 ,394	12 ,420
Total Revenue	577 ,949	527 ,526	485 ,500	434 ,339	335 ,691
Income before extra.	7 ,841	595	5 ,684	11 ,245	2 ,715
Cash Flow	38 ,951	29 ,389	41 ,322	27 ,252	16 ,257
Debt/Equity	0 .35	0 .28	0 .83	0 .11	0 .24
Return on Capital (%)	11 .86	1 .83	10 .53	17 .03	3 .34
Ret. on Com. Equity (%)	5 .02	0 .46	5 .50	11 .72	3 .03
% Change Profit	1 ,217 .8	(89 .5)	(49 .5)	314 .2	123 .0
% Change Revenue	9 .6	8 .7	11 .8	29 .4	44 .0
% Change Assets	11 .0	(7 .3)	49 .7	17 .9	(22 .5)

Preferred Div. Coverage	np	np	np
Total Div. Coverage	2 .2	0 .2	2 .1
Interest Coverage	6 .3	1 .3	16 .2
Current Ratio	1 .4	1 .2	1 .0
Operating Margin	4 .2	4 .0	5 .1
Asset Turnover	1 .6	1 .6	1 .4
5 YEAR RATIOS (%)			
Return on Capital	8 .9	4 .4	5 .3
Return on Com. Equity	5 .1	1 .6	2 .8
Profit Growth	45 .2	(37 .4)	7 .1
Revenue Growth	19 .8	14 .2	15 .3
Asset Growth	7 .1	5 .0	9 .1
BALANCE SHEET (000)			
Cash	40 ,822	4 ,349	0
Current Assets	215 ,936	159 ,438	183 ,700
Net Fixed Assets	49 ,459	54 ,842	72 ,178
Invest's & Advances	11 ,073	11 ,073	9 ,869
Total Assets	363 ,323	327 ,337	353 ,062
Short Term Debt	1 ,048	4 ,522	23 ,722
Current Liabilities	150 ,164	133 ,059	182 ,434
Long Term Debt	54 ,029	38 ,848	63 ,566
Total Liabilities	204 ,452	173 ,480	247 ,622
Total Equity	158 ,871	153 ,857	105 ,440
Total Liab. & Equity	363 ,323	327 ,337	353 ,062
CAPITAL (000)			
Total Debt	55 ,077	43 ,370	87 ,288
Preferred Equity	0	0	0
Common Equity	158 ,871	153 ,857	105 ,440

Business:

SPAR AEROSPACE LTD. is engaged in the design, development, manufacture and servicing of systems for the space, robotics, communications, remote sensing, electro-optics and aviation markets. Products include satellites and satellite subsystems, and the Shuttle Remote Manipulator System. The company markets its products in Canada and internationally.

Date	EPS	DPS	Tot Rev	Inc Bex
Mar 95	0 .10	0 .06	144 ,000	1 ,550
Dec 94	0 .42	0 .06	181 ,326	6 ,173
Sep 94	0 .02	0 .06	131 ,191	290
Jun 94	0 .01	0 .06	130 ,279	168
Mar 94	0 .08	0 .06	128 ,973	1 ,210
Dec 93	(0 .48)	0 .06	153 ,543	(6 ,727)
Sep 93	0 .13	0 .06	128 ,764	1 ,940
Jun 93	0 .17	0 .06	128 ,474	2 ,502

Synopsis:

Spar Aerospace reported an increase in revenues for the first quarter ended March 31, 1995, with revenues of $144.7-million compared to $129-million in the same period of 1994. The company's four business units all had operating profits. Spar credits the company-wide operational improvements started last September, with the increase in both revenue and earnings.

One of the highlights of the first quarter was the final preparations for the successful launch in early April for the first of two MSAT mobile communications satellites. Onboard testing was satisfactory and the satellite was accepted by the customer. The launch of the second satellite later in 1995, is on-schedule, as is the RADARSAT remote sensing satellite. Spar was also pleased with the performance of ComStream who after experiencing strong sales growth in 1994, made solid progress in the first quarter, especially in its High Media and Broadcast business. The explosive growth experienced by ComStream in 1994 should slow somewhat in 1995, but profit performance should improve.

The late 1993 re-alignment of the company into four core business areas, Space, Communications, Aviation and Defence and Informatics, was fully realized in 1994. The last step was the reconfiguration of Spar's headquarters operations. Consequently the company's headquarters is now half its original size. The result is that Spar has evolved from operating as a single company doing business in many markets to operating as several semi-autonomous enterprises, each functioning according to the needs of its customers and markets.

Spar finds that research and advanced technologies now account for an increasing proportion the activities of it 2,500 employees. Communications and Informatics now accounts for nearly 40% of total revenue, and 22% of sales are made to customers outside North America.

Relative strength to TSE300

Price

Volume (in 1000's of board lots)

Rank (Profit/Revenue/Assets)
342   175   263

Earl H. Orser
Chairman

John D. Macnaughton
President & C.E.O.

Chris W. Jamieson
V.P. Finance & Administration

Karsten J. Westphal
V.P. International Operations

Address
Suite 900
5090 Explorer Drive
Mississauga
ON
L4W 4X6
(905) 629-7727

Fax: (905) 629-0854
S0004041/G/6.5

SR TELECOM INC.

Exchanges	Price (Jun29'95)	14.25	Trailing P/E	37.50	Stock Symbol
TM	Trailing Yield (%)	0.74	Trailing EPS	0.38	**SRX**

Period Ending	Dec94	Dec93	Dec92	Dec91	Dec90
Yearly Statistics					
Price-Close	14.00	12.00	3.63	1.65	1.05
Price-High	15.50	13.75	4.00	2.00	1.33
Price-Low	10.25	3.45	1.62	0.93	0.80
P/E-Close	33.33	37.50	21.32	16.50	22.50
Dividends per Share	0.10	0.10	0.04	0.01	0.00
Dividend Yield (%)	0.71	0.83	1.10	0.61	0.00
Sales per Share	3.13	2.84	1.99	1.50	1.21
EPS before extra. item	0.42	0.32	0.17	0.10	0.05
Cash Flow per Share	0.53	0.47	0.27	0.16	0.11
Book Value per Share	2.37	1.04	0.81	0.67	0.58
O/S Common Shares	35,477	32,205	31,980	31,654	31,423
Total Revenue	109,543	91,492	63,285	47,150	37,866
Income before extra.	14,533	10,226	5,343	3,154	1,415
Cash Flow	18,442	15,223	8,596	4,933	3,315
Debt/Equity	0.12	0.27	0.14	0.13	0.50
Return on Capital (%)	31.64	44.70	29.19	16.53	9.29
Ret. on Com. Equity (%)	24.76	34.46	22.62	15.95	8.12
% Change Profit	42.1	91.4	69.4	122.8	752.5
% Change Revenue	19.7	44.6	34.2	24.5	31.8
% Change Assets	96.8	46.4	16.1	16.7	3.0

Preferred Div. Coverage	np	np	np		
Total Div. Coverage	4.2	3.2	3.9		
Interest Coverage	26.6	16.0	14.7		
Current Ratio	2.8	2.1	2.1		
Operating Margin	18.7	17.6	12.8		
Asset Turnover	0.9	1.4	1.4		
5 YEAR RATIOS (%)					
Return on Capital	26.3	20.7	7.7		
Return on Com. Equity	21.2	16.4	4.5		
Profit Growth	144.5	162.7	142.6		
Revenue Growth	30.6	35.0	18.3		
Asset Growth	32.1	19.4	7.7		
BALANCE SHEET (000)					
Cash	988	0	2,518		
Current Assets	108,309	50,459	29,200		
Net Fixed Assets	16,354	12,220	7,603		
Invest's & Advances	0	0	531		
Total Assets	126,058	64,054	43,746		
Short Term Debt	10,187	6,443	1,023		
Current Liabilities	38,593	24,542	13,823		
Long Term Debt	0	2,536	2,621		
Total Liabilities	42,164	30,578	17,863		
Total Equity	83,894	33,476	25,883		
Total Liab. & Equity	126,058	64,054	43,746		
CAPITAL (000)					
Total Debt	10,187	8,979	3,644		
Preferred Equity	0	0	0		
Common Equity	83,894	33,476	25,883		

Business:

SR TELECOM INC. designs, manufactures and sells point-to-multipoint microwave radio systems for use by public and private telephone networks worldwide. The company sells primarily to telephone companies which use its systems as part of their telephone networks. A second group of customers consists of private users, including power utilities and resource companies.

Date	EPS	DPS	Tot Rev	Inc Bex
Mar 95	0.07	0.03	30,416	2,445
Dec 94	0.12	0.03	37,975	4,408
Sep 94	0.07	0.03	20,460	2,457
Jun 94	0.12	0.02	27,211	4,161
Mar 94	0.11	0.02	23,989	3,507
Dec 93	0.11	0.03	27,043	3,366
Sep 93	0.08	0.02	22,779	2,455
Jun 93	0.07	0.02	20,235	2,183

Synopsis:

SR Telecom Inc. reported sales were up 26% at $30.3-million in the first quarter ended March 31, 1995, compared to the first quarter of 1994. The sales figures which showed a significant growth did not translate into a corresponding growth in profits. The company expects a similar pattern to be seen in the second quarter with most of the growth in profits being achieved in the third and fourth quarters of 1995. Although this pattern differs from 1994, the company had anticipated it, considering the additional expenses incurred in sales, marketing, and R&D in preparation for the growth ahead.

SR Telecom's backlog reached $146-million at March 31, 1995, of which some $55-million is scheduled for delivery this year. This backlog includes the $75-million contract with AT&T for Saudi Arabia signed in January. The backlog does not include $35-million in awards from China and Vietnam announced in late 1994 as the financing arrangements between these countries and the Canadian Export Development Corporation are still in negotiation. When financing arrangements are 100% complete these orders will be added to the backlog. The company feels, based on the volume of backlog, overall results for 1995 will be in line with the average year over year sales growth of approximately 30% and earnings will be within range of their current expectations.

SR Telecom, to provide greater ability to take advantage of emerging project opportunities, decided to organize around three geographical sectors: North & South America and the Caribbean; Asia, Australasia and the Pacific region; and Europe, the Middle East and Africa. The three regions will have their own sales, project management, technical support, and installation functions. This geographic focus allows for much closer contact with their customers, better communication and quicker response to their needs.

Relative strength to TSE300
Price
Volume (in 1000's of board lots)

Rank (Profit/Revenue/Assets)
247   408   434

Paul Dickie
Chairman

W. Ronald Couchman
President & C.E.O.

Darcy Leddy
C.F.O.

Address
8150 Trans Canada Highway
St-Laurent
PQ
H4S 1M5
(514) 335-1210

Fax: (514) 334-7783
01000533/G/6.5

TEE-COMM ELECTRONICS INC.

Exchanges	Price (Jun29'95)		9.12	Trailing P/E		304.00	Stock Symbol
T	Trailing Yield (%)		0.00	Trailing EPS		0.03	TEN

Period Ending	Dec94	Dec93	Dec92	Dec91	Dec90
Yearly Statistics					
Price-Close	6.75	4.15	3.20	1.97	0.57
Price-High	6.75	5.68	4.15	2.30	0.73
Price-Low	2.75	3.05	1.90	0.51	0.25
P/E-Close	96.43	207.50	nm	10.94	3.17
Dividends per Share	0.00	0.00	0.00	0.00	0.00
Dividend Yield (%)	0.00	0.00	0.00	0.00	0.00
Sales per Share	3.07	2.28	2.54	2.96	3.75
EPS before extra. item	0.07	0.02	(0.03)	0.18	0.18
Cash Flow per Share	0.19	0.06	0.01	0.17	0.23
Book Value per Share	2.04	1.98	1.36	1.13	1.01
O/S Common Shares	22,695	22,504	16,879	14,451	13,345
Total Revenue	69,533	44,979	37,424	41,833	47,133
Income before extra.	1,568	271	(437)	2,503	2,248
Cash Flow	4,400	1,191	117	2,358	2,862
Debt/Equity	0.06	0.05	0.28	0.29	0.40
Return on Capital (%)	5.55	1.95	(2.14)	18.39	20.19
Ret. on Com. Equity (%)	3.46	0.81	(2.23)	16.81	19.19
% Change Profit	478.6	162.1	(117.4)	11.3	179.9
% Change Revenue	54.6	20.2	(10.5)	(11.2)	18.1
% Change Assets	1.4	60.3	35.1	6.2	6.8
Preferred Div. Coverage	np	np	np		
Total Div. Coverage	na	na	na		
Interest Coverage	5.9	0.7	0.0		
Current Ratio	4.3	4.2	1.9		
Operating Margin	3.5	2.7	(0.5)		
Asset Turnover	1.3	0.9	1.2		
5 YEAR RATIOS (%)					
Return on Capital	8.8	5.8	3.4		
Return on Com. Equity	7.6	2.0	(2.1)		
Profit Growth	na	na	na		
Revenue Growth	11.7	1.0	(2.3)		
Asset Growth	19.9	16.7	1.8		
BALANCE SHEET (000)					
Cash	0	0	0		
Current Assets	24,946	28,659	17,444		
Net Fixed Assets	17,118	15,574	8,964		
Invest's & Advances	2,459	978	1,007		
Total Assets	52,037	51,305	31,996		
Short Term Debt	2,741	2,055	6,329		
Current Liabilities	5,856	6,868	9,087		
Long Term Debt	0	0	0		
Total Liabilities	5,856	6,868	9,087		
Total Equity	46,180	44,437	22,910		
Total Liab. & Equity	52,037	51,305	31,996		
CAPITAL (000)					
Total Debt	2,741	2,055	6,329		
Preferred Equity	0	0	0		
Common Equity	46,180	44,437	22,910		

Business:

TEE-COMM ELECTRONICS INC. is primarily a manufacturer and distributor of satellite television receiving systems for private homeowners use. The company also sells cable-like television programming from coast to coast in Canada through its extensive branch network. Tee-Comm also distributes ceiling fans, lighting and other consumer products.

Date	EPS	DPS	Tot Rev	Inc Bex
Mar 95	(0.01)	0.00	12,779	(324)
Dec 94	0.00	0.00	16,558	38
Sep 94	0.02	0.00	19,668	473
Jun 94	0.02	0.00	17,298	426
Mar 94	0.03	0.00	16,009	631
Dec 93	0.02	0.00	13,711	261
Sep 93	0.01	0.00	12,380	245
Jun 93	0.01	0.00	11,389	119

Synopsis:

Tee-Comm underwent significant changes in 1994. The number of TCI Home Entertainment subscribers increased during 1994 from 30,000 to nearly 45,000. During this time Tee-Comm moved away from renting to selling systems. This has allowed the company to place a cap on its rental assets and increase equipment sales by 59%. The company also made attempts to establish a more efficient dealer sales system in Canada by reducing the overall number of preferred dealers and distribution branches. These changes have enhanced efficiency and led to larger, fewer and more profitable product shipments. The introduction of a new distribution software system has also enhanced productivity by connecting all distribution branches with the head office. This has established better information exchange and improvement in financial trading, inventory control and communications.

During the past year the company also made changes in the United States by establishing a network of nine distributors with designated territories. This change was made to enhance sales and Tee-Comm receivers are now the third highest selling brand in the U.S. market. Tee-Comm also continues to build sales in Asia, Mexico, South America, and the Middle East, capitalizing on the global expansion in satellite television programming.

On September 1, 1995, service is scheduled to start on Expressvu, Canada's leader in digital direct-to-home entertainment. Expressvu was formed to provide a Canadian DBS system to offer digital television via a 24 inch satellite dish. Tee-Comm Electronics holds 33.3% of this service with BCE Inc. and Cancom holding an equal percentage of the remaining shares. Tee-Comm has committed an additional $16.7-million towards the future operating capital resources will be required when the company begins to manufacture the satellite reception equipment. The exact resources required will depend on the overall success achieved by the launch of the product.

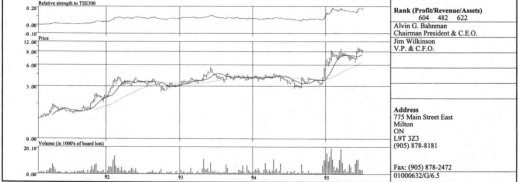

Rank (Profit/Revenue/Assets)
604   482   622

Alvin G. Bahnman
Chairman President & C.E.O.

Jim Wilkinson
V.P. & C.F.O.

Address
775 Main Street East
Milton
ON
L9T 3Z3
(905) 878-8181

Fax: (905) 878-2472
01000632/G/6.5

XEROX CANADA INC.

Exchanges	Price (Jun29'95)	52.00	Trailing P/E	20.00	Stock Symbol
TM	Trailing Yield (%)	2.70	Trailing EPS	2.60	**XXC.B**

Period Ending	Dec94	Dec93	Dec92	Dec91	Dec90
Yearly Statistics					
Price-Close	46.88	40.00	33.38	25.75	13.50
Price-High	51.00	40.00	34.00	25.75	22.50
Price-Low	38.25	30.50	25.00	14.50	12.00
P/E-Close	18.68	55.56	19.18	23.62	13.92
Dividends per Share	1.37	1.28	1.21	1.14	1.17
Dividend Yield (%)	2.92	3.19	3.63	4.43	8.67
Sales per Share	21.60	21.21	19.06	18.64	18.15
EPS before extra. item	2.51	0.72	1.74	1.09	0.97
Cash Flow per Share	3.63	2.89	2.62	2.14	2.11
Book Value per Share	18.93	18.12	17.44	16.16	15.67
O/S Common Shares	34,586	36,448	34,115	34,777	35,313
Total Revenue	1,171,669	1,144,715	1,079,301	1,051,390	1,040,681
Income before extra.	88,849	25,777	61,125	39,504	35,664
Cash Flow	128,922	98,531	90,122	74,796	74,610
Debt/Equity	0.60	0.71	0.97	0.97	1.44
Return on Capital (%)	15.81	6.26	11.61	8.65	8.34
Ret. on Com. Equity (%)	12.31	3.90	10.35	6.85	6.35
% Change Profit	244.7	(57.8)	54.7	10.8	(43.7)
% Change Revenue	2.4	6.1	2.7	1.0	(2.2)
% Change Assets	(6.2)	(0.6)	1.8	(11.4)	(2.1)

Preferred Div. Coverage	11.2	20.1	47.8
Total Div. Coverage	11.2	4.0	9.2
Interest Coverage	9.4	3.2	5.2
Current Ratio	1.0	0.7	0.7
Operating Margin	7.5	3.4	2.2
Asset Turnover	0.5	0.4	0.4
5 YEAR RATIOS (%)			
Return on Capital	10.1	9.1	11.2
Return on Com. Equity	8.0	7.8	10.0
Profit Growth	7.0	(19.2)	(1.0)
Revenue Growth	1.9	0.2	1.5
Asset Growth	(3.8)	(1.9)	1.3
BALANCE SHEET (000)			
Cash	455	410	6,397
Current Assets	228,667	214,639	238,496
Net Fixed Assets	103,176	117,366	116,019
Invest's & Advances	841,135	802,128	740,080
Total Assets	1,601,321	1,706,759	1,717,519
Short Term Debt	33,786	93,685	187,602
Current Liabilities	240,067	323,544	339,819
Long Term Debt	371,600	383,152	403,132
Total Liabilities	930,664	1,030,444	1,106,611
Total Equity	670,657	676,315	610,908
Total Liab. & Equity	1,601,321	1,706,759	1,717,519
CAPITAL (000)			
Total Debt	405,386	476,837	590,734
Preferred Equity	16,000	16,000	16,000
Common Equity	654,657	660,315	594,908

Business:

XEROX CANADA INC. operates in the document processing solutions industry. Its primary operations are the development, manufacture, marketing, financing, servicing, distribution and administration of Xerox equipment. It provides supplies for office systems and also provides related professional consulting services in document management.

Date	EPS	DPS	Tot Rev	Inc Bex
Mar 95	0.43	0.35	264,113	15,225
Dec 94	1.19	0.35	372,121	41,736
Sep 94	0.49	0.35	260,613	17,233
Jun 94	0.49	0.34	275,143	17,478
Mar 94	0.34	0.33	263,792	12,402
Dec 93	(0.42)	0.32	365,383	(13,868)
Sep 93	0.46	0.33	270,491	16,094
Jun 93	0.44	0.31	266,311	15,310

Synopsis:

Xerox Canada slightly increased revenues, to $264.1-million for the first quarter of 1995 compared to $259.4-million for the comparable 1994 period. Digital products, mid-volume printers, personal and convenience copiers, and colour toner exports contributed significantly to the revenue. Lower sales of other equipment product lines and declines in rental fleet sales offset this growth.

Revenue rose slightly in 1994 due to growth in non-paper supply revenues and higher export sales. In 1994, revenues from export sales amounted to $246-million compared to $213-million in 1993. The total cost of sales as a percentage of sales revenue also increased marginally in 1994 as the net result of several factors. There was a shift towards newer products with higher costs. In addition the lower Canadian dollar negatively impacted on the cost of foreign-sourced inventories. However, favourable prices partially mitigated the effect of increased paper costs on margins.

Net earnings were $89-million in 1994 compared with $26-million in 1993. The 1993 result includes a $81-million before tax charge related to the Document Processing Productivity Restructuring Program. The 1994 results also include a $4-million before tax charge to cover additional costs in the same program. The program should be completed during 1996.

Xerox Canada expects the current economic recovery to provide reasonable sales growth prospects in 1995. The company plans to continue developing new revenue sources through expanded channels of distribution and new product and service offerings. Interest costs should be matched against income from leasing transactions and the profit streams from service, finance and supplies businesses are anticipated to remain healthy. It is also anticipated that the impact of the restructuring program will assist the company in maintaining a reasonable level of profit.

Rank (Profit/Revenue/Assets)		
82	109	125

Diane E. McGarry
President & C.E.O.

Richard Ragazzo
V.P. & Controller

Address
5650 Yonge Street
North York
ON
M2M 4G7
(416) 229-3769

Fax: (416) 229-6826
X0000213/G/6.5

For further company information, call Globe Information Services 1-800-268-9128 or (416) 585-5345

Page	Company		Fiscal year end	EARNINGS PER SHARE		
				Last Year	Estimate this year	Estimate next year
283	Agrium		Dec-94	4.16	7.48	6.44
284	AT Plastics		Dec-94	1.29	1.97	1.81
285	Celanese Canada		Dec-94	2.46	3.18	2.47
286	DuPont Canada		Dec-94	1.64	1.97	2.21
287	Methanex	$US	Dec-94	2.24	1.59	0.91
288	Potash Corp. of Saskatchewan		Dec-94	2.98	5.07	5.96
289	Sico		Dec-94	0.94	1.25	1.40

Estimates from First Call Corporation, 22 Pittsburgh Street, Boston, MA 02210   (800) 366-9992   Fax (617) 261-5679

Chemicals

Future prospects for basic chemical manufacturing companies appear promising. Many companies have increased shipments as worldwide economic activity continues to gather momentum. Manufacturers are substituting chemical feedstocks, (used to manufacture plastics), more frequently for conventional materials such as wood and metals. In particular, there is more demand for caustic soda, ethylene, styrene, acrylonitrile, polymers, and agricultural products. The supply of these products is tight. Manufacturers are operating plants at higher output levels to meet the increasing demand and to realize economies of scale.

Chemical prices began their latest climb in the second half of 1994, as industry operating rates reached about 90%. This level usually is the inflection point for pricing. Analysts feel that once capacity utilization rates for the industry reach maximum levels, these companies gain the ability to raise prices. Specialty chemical companies compete through the production of proprietary goods that have customized applications. In contrast, basic chemical producers compete largely on a price basis and are more sensitive to broad economic trends.

Commodity cycles typically end when supply exceeds demand which is often the result of capacity additions. However, according to analysts, global chemicals capacity expansion will be limited at least through 1997, while demand continues to grow. They forecast demand in the U.S. and the Far East to increase by 5% in the next two years. European economies' demand for chemicals is expected to grow by 3%. For operating rates to decrease and prices to fall, both European and American economies would have to slow to a 1.5% growth rate.

Most specialty chemical companies have increased product prices to avoid narrowing their profit margins. Many continue to streamline operations through plant modifications and cost-cutting measures. Specialty companies with exposure to the domestic auto, housing, and apparel/textile industries witnessed a softening of customer demand through early 1995 that followed the economic decline in North America. However, many companies remain optimistic about an ongoing economic recovery. Some specialty companies with extensive foreign operations have been able to capitalize on expanding overseas economies, with the possible exception of Japan and Latin America. Some companies have benefitted from foreign exchange rates relative to a weakening Canadian dollar.

Market demand remains strong for hydrogen peroxide due to the global recovery of the pulp and paper market. Demand also remains strong because of peroxide's recognized advantage as an environmentally friendly bleaching agent. Demand for chlorofluorochemical (CFC) alternatives used in air conditioning and refrigeration markets continues to grow steadily. Growth also continues in export markets for more environmentally friendly fluorochemicals.

Amendments to the U.S. Clean Air Act require the use of reformulated gasoline in certain states that are in non-attainment of clean air standards. As a result, markets for methyl tertiary butyl ether (MTBE), a major component of reformulated gasoline and an octane enhancer, should show significant growth. MTBE is a gasoline derivative produced from methanol. There also is potential for market growth in many European countries for MTBE. MMT (a metal additive), which has replaced lead as an octane enhancer in gasoline, may degrade emission control systems in vehicles. If MMT is banned, MTBE could play an expanded role in gasoline products.

According to a study completed by Roskill Information Services of London, demand for potash continues to grow in Asia, the Middle East, and South America. Fueling this demand is population growth and strengthening economies. Companies are planning capacity expansions despite what appears to be overcapacity in the world potash industry. The number of producing countries probably will increase to 19 from 15 before the end of the decade. South American projects are a response to expanding fertilizer requirements and the need to reduce regional dependence on North American imports. Meanwhile, consumption of potash fertilizers likely will decline in both Western and Eastern Europe until the end of the century. However, the rate of decline is expected to stabilize in 1996. In addition, Roskill expects strong growth in the use of potassium chemicals in glass and ceramics, particularly potassium carbonate which is produced from caustic potash.

AGRIUM INC.

Exchanges	Price (Jun29'95)	45 .62	Trailing P/E	9 .58	Stock Symbol
T	Trailing Yield (%)	0 .99	Trailing EPS	4 .76	**AGU**

Period Ending	Dec94	Dec93	Jan93	Dec91
Yearly Statistics				
Price-Close	31 .75	22 .38	n t	n t
Price-High	32 .50	22 .50	n t	n t
Price-Low	22 .50	11 .13	n t	n t
P/E-Close	7 .63	15 .54	n t	n t
Dividends per Share	0 .45	0 .45	0 .00	0 .00
Dividend Yield (%)	1 .42	2 .01	0 .00	0 .00
Sales per Share	51 .20	29 .17	24 .20	0 .00
EPS before extra. item	4 .16	1 .44	0 .73	na
Cash Flow per Share	6 .29	2 .81	2 .55	0 .00
Book Value per Share	17 .91	11 .91	6 .10	na
O/S Common Shares	22 ,260	18 ,000	17 ,999	0
Total Revenue	1 ,080 ,909	529 ,113	438 ,717	384 ,704
Income before extra.	87 ,045	25 ,855	13 ,073	20 ,313
Cash Flow	131 ,540	50 ,570	45 ,953	44 ,552
Debt/Equity	0 .18	0 .81	1 .73	na
Return on Capital (%)	31 .92	12 .60	21 .57	na
Ret. on Com. Equity (%)	28 .40	15 .95	23 .83	na
% Change Profit	236 .7	97 .8	(35 .6)	na
% Change Revenue	104 .3	20 .6	14 .0	na
% Change Assets	23 .8	46 .3	na	na
Preferred Div. Coverage	np	np	np	
Total Div. Coverage	8 .7	3 .2	na	
Interest Coverage	16 .8	7 .3	3 .6	
Current Ratio	2 .5	2 .4	3 .2	
Operating Margin	11 .8	7 .4	6 .7	
Asset Turnover	1 .6	1 .0	1 .2	
5 YEAR RATIOS (%)				
Return on Capital	na	na	na	
Return on Com. Equity	na	na	na	
Profit Growth	na	na	na	
Revenue Growth	na	na	na	
Asset Growth	na	na	na	
BALANCE SHEET (000)				
Cash	89 ,762	4 ,524	4 ,102	
Current Assets	376 ,685	270 ,322	144 ,901	
Net Fixed Assets	264 ,465	252 ,878	200 ,296	
Invest's & Advances	0	0	16 ,388	
Total Assets	656 ,489	530 ,070	362 ,280	
Short Term Debt	5 ,419	1 ,941	0	
Current Liabilities	153 ,732	110 ,678	45 ,384	
Long Term Debt	64 ,274	172 ,649	190 ,000	
Total Liabilities	257 ,680	315 ,679	252 ,548	
Total Equity	398 ,689	214 ,391	109 ,732	
Total Liab. & Equity	656 ,489	530 ,070	362 ,280	
CAPITAL (000)				
Total Debt	69 ,693	174 ,590	190 ,000	
Preferred Equity	0	0	0	
Common Equity	398 ,689	214 ,391	109 ,732	

Business:

AGRIUM INC. is an integrated fertilizer production and marketing company. It produces both nitrogen-based fertilizers and potash, and markets four primary nutriests vital to plant growth: nitrogen, phosphorus, potassium and sulphur.

Date	EPS	DPS	Tot Rev	Inc Bex
Mar 95	0 .49	0 .23	278 ,735	11 ,534
Dec 94	0 .92	0 .00	239 ,016	20 ,493
Sep 94	0 .36	0 .23	215 ,543	9 ,457
Jun 94	2 .99	0 .00	466 ,987	59 ,109
Mar 94	(0 .11)	0 .23	159 ,363	(2 ,014)
Dec 93	0 .16	0 .23	188 ,004	2 ,770
Sep 93	0 .00	0 .00	70 ,795	(50)
Jun 93	1 .30	0 .23	197 ,174	23 ,335

Synopsis:

Agrium Inc., formerly Cominco Fertilizers Ltd., on January 6, 1995, formally completed its acquisition of Western Farmco Holdings Inc. Farmco is the parent company of Western Farm Services Inc., a major western U.S. retailer of crop production inputs headquartered in Fresno, California. Western Farm operates retail agricultural outlets and has 79 stores in Arizona, California, and the Pacific Northwest. It is a major distributor of Agrium products throughout western North America. With annual sales of $300-million (U.S.), the acquisition nearly doubles Agrium's retail sales in the United States.

During the three years ended December 1994, domestic producers satisfied the North American demand for fertilizers. On average, North American ammonia and urea fertilizer producers operated in excess of rated capacity. Canadian potash producers, who produce a majority of North American requirement, operated at 65% of capacity. Due to an increase in global demand Canadian potash production increased significantly. Agrium's 1994 potash production increased by 33% to 1.2 million tonnes, an increase from approximately 64% to 85% of rated capacity.

Agrium expects continued strong fertilizer demand in North America in 1995. Natural gas prices declined significantly in Canada and to a lesser extent in the United States, in the last quarter of 1994. If current strength in demand and pricing for nitrogen fertilizer and lower natural gas costs continue through 1995, Agrium should realize a higher gross profit on nitrogen fertilizer. Demand for fertilizers is growing in developing countries. This will lead to higher sales of fertilizers. Agrium believes it is ideally positioned to meet the anticipated demand.

Rank (Profit/Revenue/Assets)
84   115   201

G. Woody Maclaren
Chairman

John M. Van Brunt
President & C.E.O.

Larry B. Thiessen
V.P. Finance & C.F.O.

Address
Suite 426
10333 Southport Road S.W.
Calgary
AB
T2W 3X6
(403) 258-4600

Fax: (403) 258-4692
01003358/G/6.7

AT PLASTICS INC.

Exchanges	Price (Jun29'95)	13.37	Trailing P/E	8.52	Stock Symbol
T	Trailing Yield (%)	1.50	Trailing EPS	1.57	**ATP**

Period Ending	Dec94	Dec93	Dec92	Dec91
Yearly Statistics				
Price-Close	11.50	n t	n t	n t
Price-High	12.25	n t	n t	n t
Price-Low	6.50	n t	n t	n t
P/E-Close	8.91	n t	n t	n t
Dividends per Share	0.14	0.00	0.00	0.00
Dividend Yield (%)	1.17	0.00	0.00	0.00
Sales per Share	15.80	40.10	76.24	72.81
EPS before extra. item	1.29	(1.97)	(1.48)	(3.43)
Cash Flow per Share	1.98	1.49	3.22	1.38
Book Value per Share	6.52	(1.66)	0.59	3.43
O/S Common Shares	12,668	3,928	2,048	2,048
Total Revenue	186,903	157,494	156,130	149,108
Income before extra.	15,035	(7,719)	(5,807)	(13,325)
Cash Flow	23,123	5,859	6,600	2,818
Debt/Equity	1.23	na	40.43	18.04
Return on Capital (%)	14.96	8.65	0.00	na
Ret. on Com. Equity (%)	39.50	na	(141.07)	na
% Change Profit	294.8	(32.9)	56.4	na
% Change Revenue	18.7	0.9	4.7	na
% Change Assets	5.2	(3.6)	(1.2)	na
Preferred Div. Coverage	na	na	na	
Total Div. Coverage	8.8	na	na	
Interest Coverage	2.3	0.7	0.8	
Current Ratio	1.8	0.2	1.1	
Operating Margin	14.1	10.9	11.6	
Asset Turnover	0.8	0.8	0.7	
5 YEAR RATIOS (%)				
Return on Capital	na	na	na	
Return on Com. Equity	na	na	na	
Profit Growth	na	na	na	
Revenue Growth	na	na	na	
Asset Growth	na	na	na	
BALANCE SHEET (000)				
Cash	1,357	0	0	
Current Assets	55,090	44,617	46,222	
Net Fixed Assets	151,201	152,762	158,123	
Invest's & Advances	0	665	660	
Total Assets	217,646	206,931	214,559	
Short Term Debt	5,729	173,788	22,576	
Current Liabilities	29,888	192,407	41,870	
Long Term Debt	99,713	17,530	167,976	
Total Liabilities	132,015	209,937	209,846	
Total Equity	85,631	(3,006)	4,713	
Total Liab. & Equity	217,646	206,931	214,559	
CAPITAL (000)				
Total Debt	105,442	191,318	190,552	
Preferred Equity	3,000	3,500	3,500	
Common Equity	82,631	(6,506)	1,213	

Business:

AT PLASTICS INC. develops and manufactures specialty plastics raw materials and fabricated products. The Polymers business focuses on specialty resins and compounds in pellet form. The Films business focuses on specialty products for the agricultural, horticultural and construction industries. The Packaging business focuses on specialty shipping sacks for a wide range of industrial products.

Date	EPS	DPS	Tot Rev	Inc Bex
Mar 95	0.51	0.05	48,557	6,477
Dec 94	0.47	0.05	50,952	5,760
Sep 94	0.40	0.05	49,761	5,014
Jun 94	0.19	0.05	44,749	2,425
Mar 94	0.21	0.00	39,096	1,836
Dec 93	(0.56)	0.00	39,821	(2,161)
Sep 93	(0.27)	0.00	40,110	(1,078)
Jun 93	(0.25)	0.00	41,269	(979)

Synopsis:

AT Plastics Inc. reported higher consolidated sales in the first quarter of 1995. This was due to higher selling prices in all three strategic business units. In the Polymers business, sales volumes in the United States increased, but were constrained in other markets due to the need to rebuild inventories. AT withdrew from some commodity markets in the Films business leading to a decline in overall sales volume, although sales of silage films increased. Higher sales of shipping sacks and performance films increased sales volumes in the Packaging business. While sales climbed 24% from $39.1-million to $48.6-million in the first quarter, cost of sales and other expenses climbed by only 11%, from $32.9-million to $36.2-million.

AT issued 8.6 million shares during the first quarter of 1994 for net proceeds of $72-million. It also issued senior secured notes worth $70.6-million (U.S.) and $4-million Canadian. Part of the proceeds from the equity and debt issues was used to repay the Class B and C Debentures, which had higher interest rates than the senior secured notes. As the company pursues its growth strategy it expects a significant increase in capital expenditures over the next year. Capital spending will be funded through internally generated funds, but the company may find it necessary to use capital markets.

Sales from the Polymers business accounted for approximately 65% of AT's sales in 1994. The higher sales for Polymers in 1994 were due to the tight supply and increased demand for most plastic products after a number of years of oversupply. A planned shutdown to upgrade and refurbish a large compressor led to a loss of about 2,400 tonnes of production in 1994. Some inventories were depleted due to the shutdown, leading to some inventory rebuilding in 1995. Export sales accounted for roughly 62% of sales in 1994 compared to 57% of sales in 1993. Export sales to the United States accounted for 53% of total sales in 1994 compared to 46% in 1993.

Relative strength to TSE300

Price

Volume (in 1000's of board lots)

Rank (Profit/Revenue/Assets)
244   323   342

John G. Clarke
President & C.E.O.

James B. Donaghy
V.P. Fin. C.F.O. & Secretary

Address
134 Kennedy Road South
Brampton
ON
L6W 3G5
(905) 451-1630

Fax: (905) 451-0039
01003591/G/6.7

CELANESE CANADA INC.

Exchanges	Price (Jun29'95)	23.87	Trailing P/E	7.08	Stock Symbol
TM	Trailing Yield (%)	5.32	Trailing EPS	3.37	**CCL**

Period Ending	Dec94	Dec93	Dec92	Dec91	Dec90
Yearly Statistics					
Price-Close	24.38	20.83	13.33	13.75	10.75
Price-High	26.00	20.83	15.92	14.00	10.92
Price-Low	20.00	13.25	12.67	10.25	8.92
P/E-Close	9.91	14.07	16.06	16.91	10.86
Dividends per Share	1.26	0.80	0.50	0.50	0.62
Dividend Yield (%)	5.17	3.84	3.75	3.64	5.74
Sales per Share	15.43	11.98	11.01	10.33	8.95
EPS before extra. item	2.46	1.48	0.83	0.81	0.99
Cash Flow per Share	4.41	2.15	2.00	1.52	1.58
Book Value per Share	7.54	6.47	5.93	5.36	5.04
O/S Common Shares	40,734	40,734	40,734	40,734	40,733
Total Revenue	641,284	497,178	456,006	421,701	379,509
Income before extra.	100,158	60,613	34,815	34,142	41,273
Cash Flow	179,588	87,739	81,450	62,055	64,294
Debt/Equity	nd	nd	nd	nd	nd
Return on Capital (%)	54.88	36.95	25.18	24.07	31.34
Ret. on Com. Equity (%)	35.12	23.91	14.72	15.66	20.37
% Change Profit	65.2	74.1	2.0	(17.3)	(14.6)
% Change Revenue	29.0	9.0	8.1	11.1	(7.5)
% Change Assets	21.3	5.8	0.5	19.3	0.6
Preferred Div. Coverage	np	np	35.6		
Total Div. Coverage	2.0	1.8	1.6		
Interest Coverage	nd	nd	nd		
Current Ratio	3.9	3.3	3.5		
Operating Margin	32.5	19.6	13.9		
Asset Turnover	1.4	1.3	1.3		
5 YEAR RATIOS (%)					
Return on Capital	34.5	31.3	32.9		
Return on Com. Equity	22.0	20.2	21.4		
Profit Growth	15.7	4.4	4.1		
Revenue Growth	9.3	3.8	4.9		
Asset Growth	9.0	4.1	6.4		
BALANCE SHEET (000)					
Cash	171,639	119,001	122,192		
Current Assets	317,791	238,747	226,939		
Net Fixed Assets	117,864	120,286	117,026		
Invest's & Advances	0	0	0		
Total Assets	454,662	374,786	354,293		
Short Term Debt	0	0	0		
Current Liabilities	81,688	71,479	63,960		
Long Term Debt	0	0	0		
Total Liabilities	147,682	111,412	100,314		
Total Equity	306,980	263,374	253,979		
Total Liab. & Equity	454,662	374,786	354,293		
CAPITAL (000)					
Total Debt	0	0	0		
Preferred Equity	0	0	12,363		
Common Equity	306,980	263,374	241,616		

Date	EPS	DPS	Tot Rev	Inc Bex
Mar 95	1.28	0.13	226,650	52,317
Dec 94	0.94	0.88	203,499	38,264
Sep 94	0.66	0.13	148,811	26,771
Jun 94	0.49	0.13	145,319	20,031
Mar 94	0.37	0.12	143,655	15,092
Dec 93	0.43	0.45	160,725	17,400
Sep 93	0.36	0.12	118,947	15,001
Jun 93	0.38	0.12	112,996	15,464

Business:

CELANESE CANADA INC. is a diversified manufacturer of fibres, chemicals and industrial products. The company's textile group makes polyester and acetate yarns. The chemicals group makes petrochemicals and cellulose products. The company serves Canadian and international markets. Hoechst AG of Frankfurt, Germany, through Hoechst, controls the majority of the company's common shares.

Synopsis:

Celanese, a manufacturer of fibres, chemicals and industrial products, had earnings of $100.2-million in 1994, up 65% over 1993. The net income for the first quarter ended March 31, 1995, was $52.3-million, compared to $15.1-million in 1994. These high earnings were due to the high methanol prices compared to early 1994. Due to a more favourable market mix following the expiration of low fixed price contracts, there was a significant increase in methanol earnings. The improved market in the United States for MTBC also added to the rise in methanol earnings.

Celanese believes the material called polyethylene terephthalate (PET) resin will be the latest money making product over the next decade. Celanese will invest $190-million in its Millhaven polyester plant in Ontario. This facility can produce the material used in shatter-resistant plastic containers such as pop bottles. Resin sales were $250-million in the first year, and Celanese forecasts the plant will produce 160 million kilograms of the resin by the end of 1996. The company plans to expand the plant. Celanese states this will be the only operation producing resin in Canada.

Both sales volumes and prices in the Chemical and Industrial Products Group were higher, mostly for vinyl acetate monomer and pentaerythritol. Demand for formaldehyde and pentaerythritol was strong throughout the year, allowing both units in the chemical area to run at full capacity. Record volumes were reached in each unit. Overall, the industrial products area performed well, with production of cellulose acetate tow at 31,800 tonnes, mostly for Far East markets. This area continues to be an excellent contributor to the Group's profitability, despite operation income falling by about 3% for the combined cellulose acetate and cigarette tow lines.

Rank (Profit/Revenue/Assets)
75   168   236

Pierre Cote
Chairman Of The Board
Alban W. Schuele
President
Mary Weiner
Corp. Controller

Address
800 Rene-Levesque Blvd. W.
Montreal
PQ
H3B 1Z1
(514) 871-5511

Fax: (514) 871-5635
C0005980/G/6.7

DUPONT CANADA INC.

Exchanges	Price (Jun29'95)	19 .62	Trailing P/E	10.38	Stock Symbol
TM	Trailing Yield (%)	1 .63	Trailing EPS	1 .89	**DUP.A**

Period Ending	Dec94	Dec93	Dec92	Dec91	Dec90
Yearly Statistics					
Price-Close	18 .75	16 .42	13 .67	13 .50	8 .17
Price-High	20 .13	17 .00	16 .00	13 .83	10 .00
Price-Low	14 .75	13 .17	13 .33	7 .92	7 .25
P/E-Close	11 .16	23 .23	15 .53	22 .38	12 .13
Dividends per Share	0 .32	0 .23	0 .23	0 .23	0 .23
Dividend Yield (%)	1 .68	1 .42	1 .71	1 .73	2 .86
Sales per Share	18 .11	16 .97	15 .29	14 .31	15 .26
EPS before extra. item	1 .68	0 .71	0 .88	0 .60	0 .67
Cash Flow per Share	2 .53	2 .07	2 .00	1 .56	1 .50
Book Value per Share	9 .07	7 .76	7 .28	6 .74	6 .38
O/S Common Shares	92 ,288	92 ,635	92 ,219	92 ,947	92 ,351
Total Revenue	1 ,683 ,206	1 ,598 ,605	1 ,453 ,019	1 ,341 ,153	1 ,439 ,063
Income before extra.	155 ,243	65 ,632	81 ,779	56 ,165	62 ,433
Cash Flow	233 ,875	191 ,574	185 ,434	144 ,531	138 ,351
Debt/Equity	0 .13	0 .16	0 .17	0 .21	0 .29
Return on Capital (%)	29 .00	14 .50	18 .32	14 .16	15 .79
Ret. on Com. Equity (%)	19 .94	9 .42	12 .58	9 .21	10 .94
% Change Profit	136 .5	(19 .7)	45 .6	(10 .0)	(27 .8)
% Change Revenue	5 .3	10 .0	8 .3	(6 .8)	0 .5
% Change Assets	10 .9	5 .2	8 .9	1 .5	8 .0

Date	EPS	DPS	Tot Rev	Inc Bex
Mar 95	0 .57	0 .09	488 ,085	52 ,823
Dec 94	0 .42	0 .08	397 ,703	38 ,739
Sep 94	0 .41	0 .08	397 ,825	37 ,493
Jun 94	0 .49	0 .08	509 ,342	45 ,249
Mar 94	0 .36	0 .07	383 ,811	33 ,762
Dec 93	(0 .02)	0 .06	546 ,594	2 ,872
Sep 93	0 .16	0 .06	329 ,342	15 ,462
Jun 93	0 .31	0 .06	389 ,882	28 ,638

Preferred Div. Coverage	897 .4	377 .2	470 .0
Total Div. Coverage	5 .3	3 .0	3 .8
Interest Coverage	18 .2	8 .1	8 .6
Current Ratio	2 .2	1 .8	1 .7
Operating Margin	15 .0	10 .4	8 .4
Asset Turnover	1 .2	1 .3	1 .2
5 YEAR RATIOS (%)			
Return on Capital	18 .4	17 .0	21 .1
Return on Com. Equity	12 .4	11 .7	14 .2
Profit Growth	12 .4	(8 .1)	(2 .0)
Revenue Growth	3 .2	2 .7	1 .4
Asset Growth	6 .8	9 .8	8 .3
BALANCE SHEET (000)			
Cash	299 ,571	205 ,890	88 ,559
Current Assets	726 ,462	529 ,403	437 ,296
Net Fixed Assets	597 ,985	631 ,875	660 ,786
Invest's & Advances	16 ,442	43 ,214	45 ,663
Total Assets	1 ,353 ,943	1 ,220 ,752	1 ,160 ,881
Short Term Debt	12 ,379	15 ,325	10 ,743
Current Liabilities	329 ,638	294 ,863	256 ,214
Long Term Debt	94 ,782	98 ,569	105 ,885
Total Liabilities	517 ,026	499 ,733	487 ,579
Total Equity	836 ,917	721 ,019	673 ,302
Total Liab. & Equity	1 ,353 ,943	1 ,220 ,752	1 ,160 ,881
CAPITAL (000)			
Total Debt	107 ,161	113 ,894	116 ,628
Preferred Equity	70	2 ,325	2 ,325
Common Equity	836 ,847	718 ,694	670 ,977

Business:

DUPONT CANADA INC. makes and markets specialty products and chemicals for use by customers in the manufacturing, resource and service sectors in over 60 countries. Products include fall into three main categories: fibres and intermediates; specialty chemicals and materials; and specialty plastics and films. E.I. du Pont de Nemours & Company of Delaware owns about 75% of DuPont Canada.

Synopsis:

DuPont Canada saw its second highest quarterly sales on record, at the end of March 31, 1995, with the revenues of $482-million. It also had the highest level ever of net earnings at $52.8-million. This compares to $382-million of revenue and $33.8-million of net earnings at the same time last year. Strong earning gains were posted by many of the company's business units, including Furnishings, Agricultural Products, Engineering Polymers, Finishes, Apparel and Auto products. Domestic and export shipments were substantially higher than last year.

DuPont Canada announced a project worth $70-million to expand hydrogen peroxide production at Gibbons, Alberta, in December 1994. The company will shift to environmentally-sound bleaching methods, incorporate more recycled material and adapt to produce higher grade papers to support the major changes taking place in the North American pulp and paper industry. Summer of 1996 is the expected start-up date.

All business units performed well the past year. Liquid packaging won a contract to supply milk pouch packaging machines to Leche Industrializada Conasupo S.A. de C.V., Mexico's leading dairy. The company's Kingston, Ontario, site expanded capacity to spin high quality industrial nylon yarn for automotive air-bag applications. To produce both automotive air-bag yarns and carpet yarn, Kingston converted some bulked continuous filament nylon facilities.

In 1994, there were record earnings of $155.2-million, more than double last year's net earnings of $65.6-million. Sales revenue increased 7% from $1.57-billion in 1993 to $1.676-billion in 1994, setting a new record. Underlying revenue from ongoing operations rose 21%, more than offsetting sales lost from discontinued operations, underlying revenue from ongoing operations rose 21%. export sales increased 5%. Representing 67% of manufactured revenue. This was due to higher shipments to DuPont world-wide, particularly to the United States.

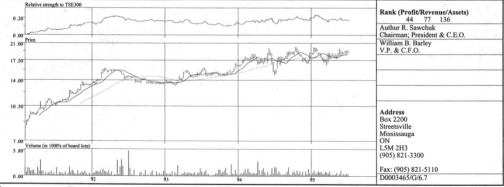

Rank (Profit/Revenue/Assets)
44   77   136

Authur R. Sawchuk
Chairman; President & C.E.O.

William B. Barley
V.P. & C.F.O.

Address
Box 2200
Streetsville
Mississauga
ON
L5M 2H3
(905) 821-3300

Fax: (905) 821-5110
D0003465/G/6.7

METHANEX CORPORATION

Exchanges	Price (Jun29'95)	11.62	Trailing P/E	2.88	Stock Symbol
TM	Trailing Yield (%)	0.00	Trailing EPS	2.97	MX

Period Ending	Dec94	Dec93	Dec92	Dec91	Dec90
Yearly Statistics	US	US	US	US	US
Price-Close	18.00	10.38	9.50	8.63	6.00
Price-High	24.50	12.63	14.88	8.75	10.50
Price-Low	10.25	7.13	7.50	4.50	5.25
P/E-Close	5.87	134.74	48.97	62.96	nm
Dividends per Share	0.00	0.00	0.00	0.00	0.00
Dividend Yield (%)	0.00	0.00	0.00	0.00	0.00
Sales per Share	7.53	3.13	2.74	3.62	3.44
EPS before extra. item	2.24	0.06	0.16	0.12	(1.95)
Cash Flow per Share	2.80	0.42	0.41	0.30	(1.14)
Book Value per Share	5.17	2.51	2.42	(0.93)	(4.71)
O/S Common Shares	194,798	171,294	170,183	35,367	16,320
Total Revenue	1,493,225	536,381	442,929	75,266	55,762
Income before extra.	442,671	10,726	26,071	2,505	(31,734)
Cash Flow	552,812	71,507	65,226	6,076	(18,601)
Debt/Equity	0.41	1.03	0.94	na	na
Return on Capital (%)	47.44	4.68	9.92	17.39	(35.95)
Ret. on Com. Equity (%)	61.58	2.55	13.77	na	na
% Change Profit	4,027.1	(58.9)	940.8	107.9	(4.2)
% Change Revenue	178.4	21.1	488.5	35.0	(62.5)
% Change Assets	74.1	6.2	549.3	(25.2)	(7.6)

Preferred Div. Coverage	np	np	np
Total Div. Coverage	na	na	na
Interest Coverage	15.0	1.4	2.8
Current Ratio	2.7	1.8	1.5
Operating Margin	36.1	6.8	10.3
Asset Turnover	0.9	0.6	0.5
5 YEAR RATIOS (%)			
Return on Capital	8.7	(1.3)	2.4
Return on Com. Equity	na	na	na
Profit Growth	223.1	28.9	na
Revenue Growth	58.6	20.6	32.8
Asset Growth	52.7	33.5	19.6
BALANCE SHEET (000)			
Cash	192,225	85,306	95,342
Current Assets	651,893	221,427	185,874
Net Fixed Assets	974,647	698,447	686,900
Invest's & Advances	16,803	18,100	18,207
Total Assets	1,688,293	969,785	912,760
Short Term Debt	9,451	32,269	19,626
Current Liabilities	240,785	120,256	125,046
Long Term Debt	398,350	409,069	368,808
Total Liabilities	680,543	539,821	501,022
Total Equity	1,007,750	429,964	411,738
Total Liab. & Equity	1,688,293	969,785	912,760
CAPITAL (000)			
Total Debt	407,801	441,338	388,434
Preferred Equity	0	0	0
Common Equity	1,007,750	429,964	411,738

Business:

METHANEX CORPORATION is engaged in the production and marketing of methanol and ammonia. The company operates or has interests in production facilities in British Columbia, Alberta, the United States, Trinidad, Chile and New Zealand.

Date		EPS	DPS	Tot Rev	Inc Bex
Mar 95	US	0.83	0.00	544,900	160,300
Dec 94	US	1.19	0.00	613,225	236,271
Sep 94	US	0.70	0.00	393,000	137,900
Jun 94	US	0.25	0.00	267,100	48,900
Mar 94	US	0.10	0.00	219,800	19,600
Dec 93	US	0.03	0.00	143,536	5,926
Sep 93	US	0.02	0.00	140,000	2,600
Jun 93	US	0.01	0.00	126,100	100

Synopsis:

Methanex generated revenue of $525-million from methanol during the first quarter of 1995, an increase from $199.1-million in 1994. During the first three months of 1995, there was a sharp decline in methanol prices. The U.S. Gulf Coast Transaction price was $506 per ton in January, declining to $185 per ton in April. This decline was a result of lower MTBE (methyl tertiary butyl ether) production. Reformed gasoline in the U.S. caused a lower demand for MTBE as an octane source.

In January 1994, Methanex acquired a three-plant methanol facility for NOVA Corp. in Medicine Hat, Alberta. In September 1994, the company converted a facility near New Orleans, Louisiana to a 570,000 ton methanol facility. This facility was producing methanol before the end of the third quarter. Methanex owns a 70% interest in Fortier Methanol Company, allowing them to market 400,000 tonnes of methanol. Of the 143,009 tons of methanol produced by Fortier in 1994, 100,107 represented Methanex's share of production.

Methanex accounts for about 40% of the world market of methanol sales. By the end of 1996, the company hopes to have an operating facility adjacent to its plant at Punta Arenas, Chile. Construction began in late October 1994, at a cost of $245-million. Methanex hopes to take advantage of low operating and construction costs to build Chile II. It will use the existing infrastructure and new pipeline to be installed at the Argentina-Chile border to supply the gas from both Argentina and Chile. The nominal capacity in Chile will rise to 1.7 million tons when both plants are on stream. In New Zealand, a 700,000 ton third column within the company's Motunui Facility, Distillation III, came on stream on December 23, 1994. In late October 1994, construction began on a twin of DIII with a completion date of mid-1995. With these two on stream, the swing capacity will increase to 1.85 million tons annually, representing 10% of the global merchant market. With the new plants in Chile and New Zealand, Methanex's global capacity will increase to 6.4 million tons at the start of 1997.

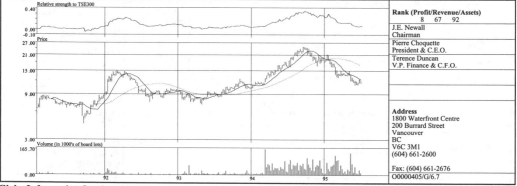

Rank (Profit/Revenue/Assets)
8   67   92

J.E. Newall
Chairman

Pierre Choquette
President & C.E.O.

Terence Duncan
V.P. Finance & C.F.O.

Address
1800 Waterfront Centre
200 Burrard Street
Vancouver
BC
V6C 3M1
(604) 661-2600

Fax: (604) 661-2676
O0000405/G/6.7

POTASH CORPORATION OF SASKATCHEWAN INC.

Exchanges	Price (Jun29'95)	74.62	Trailing P/E	16.85	Stock Symbol
TMN	Trailing Yield (%)	1.69	Trailing EPS	4.43	**POT**

Period Ending	Dec94	Dec93	Dec92	Dec91	Dec90
Yearly Statistics					
Price-Close	47.63	33.38	25.75	21.13	15.88
Price-High	56.38	33.38	27.38	21.25	16.63
Price-Low	31.13	23.13	21.00	15.38	13.00
P/E-Close	15.98	21.12	17.17	18.06	23.01
Dividends per Share	1.08	0.72	0.72	0.72	0.72
Dividend Yield (%)	2.27	2.16	2.80	3.41	4.54
Sales per Share	13.92	9.41	9.56	7.92	7.66
EPS before extra. item	2.98	1.58	1.50	1.17	0.69
Cash Flow per Share	4.28	2.64	2.58	2.18	1.72
Book Value per Share	31.47	29.63	29.58	28.82	28.37
O/S Common Shares	42,988	42,781	38,737	38,674	38,669
Total Revenue	613,560	414,938	382,836	311,840	288,750
Income before extra.	127,962	62,701	58,176	45,183	25,443
Cash Flow	183,606	104,884	99,921	84,313	63,362
Debt/Equity	0.00	0.10	0.08	0.10	0.13
Return on Capital (%)	10.04	6.05	5.83	4.55	4.01
Ret. on Com. Equity (%)	9.77	5.20	5.15	4.09	2.37
% Change Profit	104.1	7.8	28.8	77.6	(69.5)
% Change Revenue	47.9	8.4	22.8	8.0	(13.8)
% Change Assets	(0.8)	13.3	1.8	(1.8)	(0.1)

Business:

POTASH CORPORATION OF SASKATCHEWAN INC. along with its subsidiary PCS Sales, is a leading publicly owned North American company engaged in the mining, production and sale of potash to agricultural and industrial markets in North America and around the world. The company represents 8% to 10% of world potash production, 15% of world capacity and 40% of the world's excess capacity.

Date	EPS	DPS	Tot Rev	Inc Bex
Mar 95	1.68	0.36	226,267	72,353
Dec 94	0.75	0.36	131,063	32,310
Sep 94	0.77	0.36	142,808	33,327
Jun 94	1.23	0.18	213,051	52,270
Mar 94	0.23	0.18	126,638	10,055
Dec 93	0.06	0.18	97,648	3,887
Sep 93	0.78	0.18	100,169	30,146
Jun 93	0.53	0.18	121,835	20,665

Preferred Div. Coverage	np	np	np
Total Div. Coverage	2.8	2.1	2.1
Interest Coverage	26.1	6.5	6.1
Current Ratio	2.7	1.3	2.6
Operating Margin	22.5	19.2	18.8
Asset Turnover	0.4	0.3	0.3
5 YEAR RATIOS (%)			
Return on Capital	6.1	5.6	6.2
Return on Com. Equity	5.3	4.8	na
Profit Growth	8.9	(10.0)	31.4
Revenue Growth	12.8	2.2	7.8
Asset Growth	2.3	1.6	(0.5)
BALANCE SHEET (000)			
Cash	23,253	0	9,460
Current Assets	231,060	209,899	178,998
Net Fixed Assets	1,197,553	1,229,117	1,091,309
Invest's & Advances	4,486	3,948	4,178
Total Assets	1,441,750	1,453,988	1,283,631
Short Term Debt	779	99,475	25,756
Current Liabilities	86,177	158,016	69,404
Long Term Debt	2,806	28,235	68,597
Total Liabilities	88,983	186,251	138,001
Total Equity	1,352,767	1,267,737	1,145,630
Total Liab. & Equity	1,441,750	1,453,988	1,283,631
CAPITAL (000)			
Total Debt	3,585	127,710	94,353
Preferred Equity	0	0	0
Common Equity	1,352,767	1,267,737	1,145,630

Synopsis:

Potash Corporation closed a deal on April 10, 1995, to buy 100% of Texasgulf, a leading phosphate producer, from Elf Aquitaine, France's petrochemical giant, and an associated firm, for a total of $810-million (U.S.). The company borrowed $760-million to purchase Texasgulf. Potash Corp., however, expects the phosphate acquisition to make a positive contribution to net income and earnings per share, following the recovery of the phosphate market in 1994. The same trends are expected by the company in phosphate as in potash. With this acquisition Potash Corp. has essentially doubled in size.

For the first quarter of 1995, the company had record sales and production. Prices were up 15% over the first quarter of 1994. Potash reported strong export sales in the first quarter mainly to purchases by China, with 62% of total sales destined for offshore customers. Export sales of 1,235,590 metric tonnes were 143% higher than 1994. The weaker Canadian dollar helped in part to raise prices 18% when compared to the similar period last year. Domestic sales also climbed to 1,753,366 metric tonnes, 16% over the same period in 1994.

With the purchase of Texasgulf, renamed PCS Phosphate, Potash Corp. is the second largest miner of phosphate rock by capacity in the United States. The new subsidiary has reserves to permit mining at current rates for about 75 years. It also has the world's largest integrated phosphate mine and processing complex at one site, which minimizes transportation and reclamation costs.

For the first year since 1988, world consumption of potash increased in 1994, over the levels of the previous year. The problem of declining consumption in Eastern Europe and the Former Soviet Union, which began in 1989 was made worse by the drop in China and India in 1992 and 1993. Both China and India increased orders, while the closing of inefficient mines in Europe has led to greater demand.

Rank (Profit/Revenue/Assets)		
55	171	130

Charles E. Childers
Chairman President & C.E.O.

Barry E. Humphreys
Sr. V.P. Finance & Treasurer

Address
PCS Tower
Suite 500
122 - 1st Avenue South
Saskatoon
SK
S7K 7G3
(306) 933-8500
Fax: (306) 652-2699
P0014021/G/6.7

For further company information, call Globe Information Services 1-800-268-9128 or (416) 585-5345

SICO INC.

Exchanges	Price (Jun29'95)	9 .00	Trailing P/E	9 .47	Stock Symbol
TM	Trailing Yield (%)	3 .56	Trailing EPS	0 .95	**SIC**

Period Ending	Dec94	Dec93	Dec92	Dec91	Dec90
Yearly Statistics					
Price-Close	9 .88	13 .00	13 .75	9 .00	7 .50
Price-High	14 .25	14 .50	14 .00	9 .63	12 .00
Price-Low	6 .00	10 .75	8 .75	7 .25	6 .50
P/E-Close	10 .51	19 .70	11 .65	nm	18 .29
Dividends per Share	0 .32	0 .32	0 .30	0 .28	0 .44
Dividend Yield (%)	3 .24	2 .46	2 .18	3 .11	5 .87
Sales per Share	32 .07	28 .72	30 .77	31 .76	29 .91
EPS before extra. item	0 .94	0 .66	1 .18	(0 .85)	0 .41
Cash Flow per Share	1 .43	1 .12	1 .68	1 .23	1 .25
Book Value per Share	7 .23	6 .62	6 .24	5 .31	6 .10
O/S Common Shares	5 ,061	5 ,082	5 ,027	4 ,961	4 ,936
Total Revenue	162 ,755	144 ,713	152 ,959	156 ,799	146 ,915
Income before extra.	5 ,143	3 ,708	6 ,239	(3 ,832)	2 ,404
Cash Flow	7 ,248	5 ,666	8 ,352	6 ,082	6 ,137
Debt/Equity	0 .91	0 .54	0 .54	0 .89	1 .28
Return on Capital (%)	14 .57	13 .81	20 .89	1 .25	9 .27
Ret. on Com. Equity (%)	13 .57	10 .24	20 .30	(14 .91)	6 .72
% Change Profit	38 .7	(40 .6)	262 .8	(259 .4)	(54 .8)
% Change Revenue	12 .5	(5 .4)	(2 .4)	6 .7	(27 .8)
% Change Assets	28 .0	4 .3	(7 .4)	(14 .0)	(9 .1)

Preferred Div. Coverage	13 .5	9 .8	16 .4
Total Div. Coverage	2 .6	1 .9	3 .3
Interest Coverage	4 .2	4 .1	6 .3
Current Ratio	1 .6	1 .7	1 .8
Operating Margin	6 .2	7 .5	7 .7
Asset Turnover	1 .5	1 .8	1 .9
5 YEAR RATIOS (%)			
Return on Capital	12 .0	12 .0	12 .9
Return on Com. Equity	7 .2	7 .9	11 .5
Profit Growth	(0 .7)	(13 .1)	(1 .5)
Revenue Growth	(4 .4)	(6 .9)	(3 .4)
Asset Growth	(0 .7)	(5 .6)	(4 .3)
BALANCE SHEET (000)			
Cash	781	63	216
Current Assets	61 ,890	50 ,295	50 ,534
Net Fixed Assets	31 ,878	27 ,406	24 ,992
Invest's & Advances	1 ,608	2 ,230	2 ,672
Total Assets	105 ,282	82 ,227	78 ,859
Short Term Debt	13 ,376	8 ,054	7 ,106
Current Liabilities	38 ,310	29 ,361	28 ,257
Long Term Debt	23 ,156	12 ,000	12 ,000
Total Liabilities	64 ,909	44 ,778	43 ,692
Total Equity	40 ,373	37 ,449	35 ,167
Total Liab. & Equity	105 ,282	82 ,227	78 ,859
CAPITAL (000)			
Total Debt	36 ,532	20 ,054	19 ,106
Preferred Equity	3 ,800	3 ,800	3 ,800
Common Equity	36 ,573	33 ,649	31 ,367

Business:

SICO INC. manufactures and distributes trade, industrial, and specialty paints and coatings across Canada. Products include paint, varnish, stains, caulkings and adhesives under the brand names Sico, Crown Diamond, and Mulco. The company has operations in Quebec, Ontario and Massachusetts.

Date	EPS	DPS	Tot Rev	Inc Bex
Mar 95	(0.02)	0.08	39,666	(21)
Dec 94	(0.12)	0.08	31,181	(531)
Sep 94	0.43	0.08	45,976	2,293
Jul 94	0.66	0.08	53,468	3,456
Apr 94	(0.03)	0.08	31,984	(75)
Dec 93	(0.47)	0.08	24,533	(2,251)
Oct 93	0.44	0.08	38,909	2,305
Jul 93	0.80	0.08	50,946	4,140

Synopsis:

Sico continued its administrative and industrial restructuring in 1994, due to the fierce competition within the North American Market. Efforts were made to streamline organizational structure and management methods. This included reducing the number of administrative layers in the organization. A new information system was created as part of a $4-million, three-year program. This system will allow managers to monitor the development of the company's units and serve to simplify decision making in the organization. Due to the rationalization program begun at the end of 1993, the ratio of operating costs to sales fell by 2.3%, despite the large sums spent on updating management systems.

In September 1994, Sico made two strategic acquisitions by purchasing Chateau Paints and Hancock Paint. Chateau gave Sico the ability to offer Quebec consumers a third major paint brand. It also gave Sico exclusive distribution rights for the Sikkens line of products in eastern Canada. By purchasing Boston-based Hancock Paint, Sico broadened its presence beyond Quebec. These two companies contributed $6.3-million to total sales in 1994. To acquire Hancock and Chateau, Sico paid $11.195-million. Sico negotiated a loan under a $25-million revolving term agreement, and a $4-million (U.S.) loan to finance these acquisitions.

Although the company's consumer paint products are distributed across Canada and other countries, 64% of the sales are in Quebec. The company has established business dealings in Russia, France, Germany, and Cuba as part of its market diversification strategy. Sico's sales rose from $38.9-million to $45.976-million for the third quarter, an 18% increase over the same period last year.

Relative strength to TSE300

Price

Volume (in 1000's of board lots)

Rank (Profit/Revenue/Assets)
418   345   474

Jean-Paul Lortie
Chairman

Pierre Dupuis
President & C.E.O.

Gilles Laurin
V.P. Finance

Address
2505 De La Metropole
Longueuil
PQ
J4G 1E5
(514) 527-5111

Fax: (514) 651-1257
S0000449/G/6.7

Page	Company	Fiscal year end	EARNINGS PER SHARE		
			Last Year	Estimate this year	Estimate next year
293	Bonar	Dec-94	2.68	na	na
294	Cascades Paperboard International	Aug-94	(0.22)	0.69	1.03
295	CCL Industries	Dec-94	0.85	1.11	1.31
296	Consumers Packaging	Dec-94	1.09	0.72	2.10
297	Great Pacific Enterprises	Dec-94	1.83	na	na
298	Intertape Polymer Group	Dec-94	1.41	1.90	2.46
299	Winpak	Dec-94	1.64	1.80	2.00

Estimates from First Call Corporation, 22 Pittsburgh Street, Boston, MA 02210   (800) 366-9992   Fax (617) 261-5679

Packaging & Containers

For some companies in this industry, price increases on raw materials have hurt margins. The first half of 1994 was characterized by stable raw material prices and a weak demand within the market, leading to lower selling prices. During the last half of 1994 raw materiasl costs increased, affecting margins. A tightening of supply in the last half of 1994 lead to an increase in selling prices, so that average selling prices for the year were similar to 1993 levels.

A continuation of the higher selling prices into the first quarter of 1995, combined with the weaker Canadian dollar, led to improved revenues. Prebuying of raw materials have benefited some companies as they protect themselves from the price increases that continue within the industry. Aluminum price increases and increases in the prices of products offered by paper suppliers will have a negative effect on the margins within the industry. Options available to combat the price increases include hedging through prepaying of raw materials and increasing prices, when possible, to cover raw material price increases.

Capital investments have been made to increase capacity and improve production technology. The capital investments give the companies the ability to produce a higher quality of product as well as giving the companies a low cost production capability. The increase in prices for raw materials can be offset by improvements in production capabilities for some of the companies. The amount of capital investment required remains an important decision.

The creation of a global presence through acquisition and the development of joint ventures and other arrangements is another strategy that has been adopted within the industry. The maturation of the North American market leads companies to look for specialty and niche markets within this market or to look at the markets outside of North America. One company within the industry has taken over some of its customers' production and component supply requirements and expects the number of companies it does this for to increase as the North American market matures.

BONAR INC.

Exchnges	Price (Jun29'95)	21.00	Trailing P/E	6.58	Stock Symbol
T	Trailing Yield (%)	0.95	Trailing EPS	3.19	**BON**

Period Ending	Dec94	Nov93	Nov92	Nov91	Dec90
Yearly Statistics					
Price-Close	22.00	22.50	20.00	22.00	23.50
Price-High	25.50	24.25	26.00	26.13	24.50
Price-Low	22.00	21.00	16.00	22.00	22.00
P/E-Close	8.21	10.71	nm	21.78	11.41
Dividends per Share	0.20	0.20	0.20	0.35	0.40
Dividend Yield (%)	0.91	0.89	1.00	1.59	1.70
Sales per Share	48.93	41.13	39.63	41.84	41.54
EPS before extra. item	2.68	2.10	(1.49)	1.01	2.06
Cash Flow per Share	4.56	3.74	(0.94)	2.89	3.28
Book Value per Share	22.87	20.31	18.31	19.64	19.08
O/S Common Shares	4,898	4,898	4,898	4,898	4,898
Total Revenue	239,668	201,442	194,081	204,942	203,460
Income before extra.	13,116	10,277	(7,301)	4,916	10,074
Cash Flow	22,345	18,296	(4,595)	14,165	16,071
Debt/Equity	0.29	0.30	0.35	0.13	0.11
Return on Capital (%)	15.90	12.16	(7.33)	9.03	17.01
Ret. on Com. Equity (%)	12.40	10.87	(7.86)	5.18	11.29
% Change Profit	27.6	240.8	(248.5)	(51.2)	29.7
% Change Revenue	19.0	3.8	(5.3)	0.7	(12.6)
% Change Assets	18.6	5.1	13.5	6.4	1.7

Preferred Div. Coverage	np	np	np
Total Div. Coverage	13.4	10.5	0.0
Interest Coverage	42.9	40.8	na
Current Ratio	1.3	1.3	1.2
Operating Margin	9.1	7.5	5.0
Asset Turnover	1.2	1.2	1.2
5 YEAR RATIOS (%)			
Return on Capital	9.4	9.0	10.9
Return on Com. Equity	6.4	5.8	6.5
Profit Growth	11.0	(1.8)	na
Revenue Growth	0.5	(2.5)	(0.7)
Asset Growth	8.8	3.9	7.0
BALANCE SHEET (000)			
Cash	26,045	23,691	12,768
Current Assets	103,975	88,314	81,748
Net Fixed Assets	83,185	80,933	79,629
Invest's & Advances	0	0	0
Total Assets	207,018	174,577	166,172
Short Term Debt	32,171	29,482	31,119
Current Liabilities	82,739	65,612	68,120
Long Term Debt	0	0	0
Total Liabilities	94,984	75,127	76,495
Total Equity	112,034	99,450	89,677
Total Liab. & Equity	207,018	174,577	166,172
CAPITAL (000)			
Total Debt	32,171	29,482	31,119
Preferred Equity	0	0	0
Common Equity	112,034	99,450	89,677

Business:

BONAR INC. is a manufacturer of flexible packaging, plastic films and bags and rotationally molded plastics. The company operates in Canada and the United States. It supplies products to many industries in the United States and Canada, including food processing, fishing, chemicals, construction, and agribusiness.

Date	EPS	DPS	Tot Rev	Inc Bex
Mar 95	0.94	0.05	69,231	4,626
Dec 94	0.83	0.05	73,122	4,068
Aug 94	0.65	0.05	58,002	3,168
May 94	0.77	0.05	58,753	3,781
Feb 94	0.43	0.05	49,791	2,099
Nov 93	0.91	0.05	52,462	4,452
Aug 93	0.34	0.05	49,382	1,642
May 93	0.51	0.05	52,175	2,499

Synopsis:

Bonar Inc. reported sales of $69.2-million for the first quarter ended March 4, 1995. This was an increase over the $49.8-million reported in the same period in 1994. The company believes this reflects its continued underlying growth and the recovery of the higher cost of raw materials. Sales also benefited from the completion of initial stocking orders, the Twinpac acquisition in the second quarter of 1994, and from several new accounts. Bonar anticipates further progress, helped by its continued focus on improving spending efficiencies.

In early 1994, Bonar had the large task of integrating Twinpac into its operation. The company accomplished this in record time with a minimum of disruption. The company began enjoying the benefits of this investment as early as the second half of the year. To date, the acquisition has met all of its expectations and has improved its ability to compete in Bonar's core packaging business throughout the North American marketplace.

Supply and demand swung prices in favour of raw material producers. The year, 1994, saw a rampant increase in raw material prices, doubling the cost of polyethylene resins, and increasing their basic natural kraft paper cost by 28%. These increases were accompanied by some shortages in supply which hampered Bonar's ability to properly plan the company's production and satisfy all its customers' needs in a timely fashion. Bonar, thanks to understanding customers and hard work, got through these difficult times. The company hopes that as stability returns to raw material supply, it can provide uninterrupted service to its customers. In the rigid plastic operation, Bonar reported a volume growth of 37%, led by the Chicago facility. The plant in Chicago was able to develop significant new accounts for custom products while also showing growth in the company's principal proprietary product line. Bonar continues to invest in this business adding space and a new moulding machine. The company also added a new machine to its Atlanta facility.

Rank (Profit/Revenue/Assets)
264   292   351

J.W. Leng
Chairman

J.L. Heilig
C.E.O. & President

Todd D.G. Eby
V.P. Finance & C.F.O.

Address
2380 McDowell Road
Burlington
ON
L7R 4A1
(905) 637-5611

Fax: (905) 637-9954
B0021687/G/6.8

CASCADES PAPERBOARD INTERNATIONAL INC.

Exchanges	Price (Jun29'95)		5.87	Trailing P/E		53.36	Stock Symbol
TM	Trailing Yield (%)		0.00	Trailing EPS		0.11	CAP

Period Ending	Dec94	Dec93	Dec92	Dec91
Yearly Statistics				
Price-Close	5.50	7.13	7.88	nt
Price-High	8.00	8.63	8.00	nt
Price-Low	5.00	5.25	7.75	nt
P/E-Close	nm	nm	nm	nt
Dividends per Share	0.00	0.00	0.00	0.00
Dividend Yield (%)	0.00	0.00	0.00	0.00
Sales per Share	15.61	18.79	15.47	16.57
EPS before extra. item	(0.09)	(2.68)	(0.32)	0.36
Cash Flow per Share	0.52	(0.12)	0.35	1.12
Book Value per Share	3.92	3.61	6.54	na
O/S Common Shares	46,440	46,440	46,424	0
Total Revenue	738,763	876,708	435,573	445,951
Income before extra.	318	(120,063)	(8,661)	9,592
Cash Flow	24,253	(5,461)	9,774	29,962
Debt/Equity	1.51	1.40	1.35	1.53
Return on Capital (%)	5.41	(7.05)	1.74	na
Ret. on Com. Equity (%)	(0.84)	(51.70)	(4.00)	na
% Change Profit	100.3	(1,286.2)	(190.3)	na
% Change Revenue	(15.7)	101.3	(2.3)	na
% Change Assets	12.7	(31.1)	122.1	na

	Dec94	Dec93	Dec92
Preferred Div. Coverage	0.2	0.0	0.0
Total Div. Coverage	0.2	0.0	0.0
Interest Coverage	1.0	0.0	0.5
Current Ratio	1.2	1.4	1.5
Operating Margin	3.4	2.0	0.8
Asset Turnover	0.8	1.1	0.4
5 YEAR RATIOS (%)			
Return on Capital	na	na	na
Return on Com. Equity	na	na	na
Profit Growth	na	na	na
Revenue Growth	na	na	na
Asset Growth	na	na	na
BALANCE SHEET (000)			
Cash	27,481	33,928	48,578
Current Assets	334,308	257,325	374,093
Net Fixed Assets	516,977	505,979	754,318
Invest's & Advances	0	0	0
Total Assets	902,685	800,960	1,162,280
Short Term Debt	115,739	59,087	91,012
Current Liabilities	278,930	182,015	257,498
Long Term Debt	305,257	311,527	449,019
Total Liabilities	623,132	535,890	761,375
Total Equity	279,553	265,070	400,905
Total Liab. & Equity	902,685	800,960	1,162,280
CAPITAL (000)			
Total Debt	420,996	370,614	540,031
Preferred Equity	97,500	97,500	97,500
Common Equity	182,053	167,570	303,405

Business:

CASCADES PAPERBOARD INTERNATIONAL INC. is involved in the manufacturing of boxboard and containerboard. The company integrates the production of these boards with the conversion of these products into folding cartons and corrugated containers. Operations are in Canada, the United States, France, Belgium and Sweden. Cascades Inc. owns 63.4% of the company.

Date	EPS	DPS	Tot Rev	Inc Bex
Mar 95	0.17	0.00	253,833	9,062
Dec 94	0.09	0.00	226,258	4,526
Sep 94	0.02	0.00	177,238	682
Jun 94	(0.17)	0.00	166,740	(6,602)
Mar 94	0.01	0.00	168,527	1,712
Dec 93	(2.14)	0.00	195,716	(98,031)
Sep 93	(0.25)	0.00	211,592	(10,606)
Jun 93	(0.16)	0.00	231,218	(6,256)

Synopsis:

Cascades Paperboard International Inc. reported highly improved results in the first quarter of 1995. Sales were $253.1-million compared to $161.1-million for the same period in 1994. Favourable market conditions for boxboard and containerboard plus strong raw material price increases, led to successive price increases, especially since the third quarter of 1994. The increased price of raw materials also resulted in price increases for converted products, folding cartons, and corrugated containers. Productivity gains and successful marketing strategies enabled the company to boost shipments for most of its business groups.

The company acquired a 50% interest in an Ontario-based wastepaper collection enterprise, on April 3, 1995. This acquisition generates 150,000 tonnes of wastepaper annually and will improve the security of supply for the company's North American mills. The purchase should also have a favourable impact on the consolidated results starting with the third quarter.

In 1994, Cascades Paperboard focused its efforts on improving production process and implementing its management style throughout its network. This entailed decentralizing operations management and the strengthening the sales organization to ensure effective coverage of the North American market.

Cascades Paperboard believes between now and 1998, world-wide demand for boxboard and containerboard packaging products will continue to grow, given the law of supply and demand. The company's efforts in 1995 will be focused on profitability and capital expenditures designed to increase operational efficiency. As well, the company plans to expand its converting operations and secure a greater share of its raw material supplies.

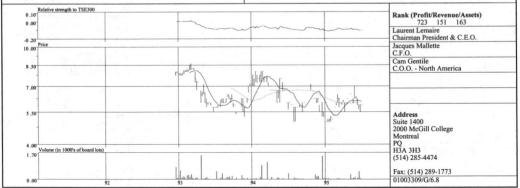

Rank (Profit/Revenue/Assets)
723 151 163
Laurent Lemaire
Chairman President & C.E.O.
Jacques Mallette
C.F.O.
Cam Gentile
C.O.O. - North America

Address
Suite 1400
2000 McGill College
Montreal
PQ
H3A 3H3
(514) 285-4474

Fax: (514) 289-1773
01003309/G/6.8

CCL INDUSTRIES INC.

Exchanges	Price (Jun29'95)		13.75	Trailing P/E		14.78	Stock Symbol
TM	Trailing Yield (%)		2.04	Trailing EPS		0.93	**CCQ.B**

Period Ending	Dec94	Dec93	Dec92	Dec91	Dec90
Yearly Statistics					
Price-Close	9.75	10.50	9.38	9.50	8.00
Price-High	11.68	11.00	10.38	11.88	10.13
Price-Low	8.00	8.25	7.50	8.00	7.00
P/E-Close	11.47	55.26	6.84	950.00	13.56
Dividends per Share	0.28	0.28	0.28	0.28	0.28
Dividend Yield (%)	2.87	2.67	2.99	2.95	3.50
Sales per Share	28.01	24.97	21.58	18.19	14.52
EPS before extra. item	0.85	0.19	1.37	0.01	0.59
Cash Flow per Share	2.07	0.83	1.28	0.97	1.46
Book Value per Share	10.18	9.26	9.21	7.82	8.13
O/S Common Shares	32,929	33,852	32,907	32,870	32,695
Total Revenue	934,640	897,113	758,854	621,711	476,678
Income before extra.	28,035	6,103	44,708	185	18,982
Cash Flow	68,971	27,632	41,958	31,674	47,714
Debt/Equity	0.43	0.44	0.82	0.77	0.75
Return on Capital (%)	11.83	5.90	16.59	4.81	8.95
Ret. on Com. Equity (%)	8.40	1.98	15.96	0.07	7.36
% Change Profit	359.4	(86.3)	nm	(99.0)	(75.8)
% Change Revenue	4.2	18.2	22.1	30.4	23.5
% Change Assets	0.6	(10.4)	23.3	5.2	(5.2)

Preferred Div. Coverage	np	np	np	
Total Div. Coverage	3.1	0.7	5.0	
Interest Coverage	5.4	2.5	5.0	
Current Ratio	1.1	1.2	1.3	
Operating Margin	6.2	4.5	5.6	
Asset Turnover	1.4	1.3	1.0	
5 YEAR RATIOS (%)				
Return on Capital	9.6	11.1	11.8	
Return on Com. Equity	6.8	12.4	14.7	
Profit Growth	(18.6)	(22.7)	na	
Revenue Growth	19.3	20.1	0.2	
Asset Growth	2.0	7.6	4.4	
BALANCE SHEET (000)				
Cash	10,906	72,178	0	
Current Assets	261,420	297,670	314,651	
Net Fixed Assets	302,640	259,882	248,227	
Invest's & Advances	0	0	50,000	
Total Assets	664,760	660,919	737,442	
Short Term Debt	64,161	57,427	60,670	
Current Liabilities	229,609	246,265	239,583	
Long Term Debt	80,620	81,490	188,122	
Total Liabilities	329,473	347,298	434,517	
Total Equity	335,287	313,621	302,925	
Total Liab. & Equity	664,760	660,919	737,442	
CAPITAL (000)				
Total Debt	144,781	138,917	248,792	
Preferred Equity	0	0	0	
Common Equity	335,287	313,621	302,925	

Business:

CCL INDUSTRIES INC. is active in three major business segments. The Custom Manufacturing Division produces many household, personal care and cosmetic products. The Container Division manufactures aluminum spray containers and tubes. The Label Division produces the labels used in a broad spectrum of products.

Date	EPS	DPS	Tot Rev	Inc Bex
Mar 95	0.26	0.07	254,464	8,709
Dec 94	0.19	0.07	232,956	6,147
Sep 94	0.25	0.07	244,143	8,017
Jun 94	0.23	0.07	235,121	7,699
Mar 94	0.18	0.07	221,006	6,172
Dec 93	(1.32)	0.07	208,975	(44,007)
Sep 93	1.29	0.07	276,512	43,043
Jun 93	0.13	0.07	206,866	4,179

Synopsis:

Through strategic acquisitions in the United States and the United Kingdom, CCL Industries Inc. has broadened its markets and become a company with an international presence. As the North American matures the company will take on more of its customers' production and component supply requirements. CCL will also look for specialty and niche markets within the North America. Outside North America, markets are still developing and CCL will try to develop strategic alliances with its current customers, as well as looking at joint ventures with partners in the foreign markets.

In the first quarter of 1995, sales rose by 15% to $254.5-million from $221-million the previous year. Net income jumped from only $6.2-million in 1994 to $8.7-million in the first quarter of 1995, an increase of 40%. The Custom Manufacturing Division, along with the Kolmar Cosmetics Division, reported a 14.5% increase in sales over the first quarter of 1994. Kolmar reported operating income in the first quarter of 1995 compared to a loss in 1994. The Container Manufacturing Division had sales increase by 18.4% over the first quarter of last year. High aluminium prices are affecting the margins in this division but the operating earnings still improved over the first quarter of 1994. The Container Division has hedged approximately 65% of aluminium purchases for 1995 and has tied them to specific customer contracts. The Label Manufacturing Division's sales improved by 15.6% and operating income improved from the first quarter of 1994. This division is affected by cost increases from paper suppliers. It is looking at options to offset the increases, including its own price increase.

In 1994, contributions to sales (operating income) by industry segment were: Custom Manufacturing, 75% (50%); Container Manufacturing, 12% (32%); and Label Manufacturing, 13% (18%). In 1994 contributions to sales (operating income) by geographic segment were: United States, 62% (50%); Canada, 26% (45%); United Kingdom, 12% (5%).

Relative strength to TSE300 / Price / Volume (in 1000's of board lots)

Rank (Profit/Revenue/Assets)
171 121 197

Gordon S. Lang
Chairman

Wayne M.E. McLeod
President & C.E.O.

Mel H. Snider
Sr. V.P. Finance & Admin.

Address
105 Gordon Baker Road
Suite 800
Willowdale
ON
M2H 3P8
(416) 756-8500

Fax: (416) 756-8555
C0005879/G/6.8

CONSUMERS PACKAGING INC.

Exchanges	Price (Jun29'95)	13.25	Trailing P/E		10.86	Stock Symbol
T	Trailing Yield (%)	0.00	Trailing EPS		1.22	CGC

Period Ending	Dec94	Dec93	Dec92	Dec91	Dec90	Business:
Yearly Statistics						CONSUMERS PACKAGING INC. makes and
Price-Close	9.50	3.15	1.90	2.90	4.00	markets glass containers. Customers include the
Price-High	10.00	3.40	4.50	5.25	18.00	food, beverage, pharmaceutical, household
Price-Low	1.65	0.80	0.40	1.95	3.90	product, toiletries and cosmetics industries in
P/E-Close	8.33	nm	nm	nm	nm	Canada and the United States. G & G
Dividends per Share	0.00	0.00	0.00	0.00	0.38	INVESTMENT has a 57.6% equity interest in
Dividend Yield (%)	0.00	0.00	0.00	0.00	9.50	the company.
Sales per Share	15.86	15.37	15.81	15.73	25.20	
EPS before extra. item	1.14	(1.03)	(1.35)	(2.76)	(3.01)	
Cash Flow per Share	2.00	0.71	0.16	(0.69)	(0.80)	
Book Value per Share	2.42	1.16	2.20	3.55	6.31	
O/S Common Shares	27,094	25,980	25,948	25,948	25,948	
Total Revenue	420,801	400,162	414,236	419,417	579,642	
Income before extra.	30,079	(26,647)	(35,149)	(71,563)	(69,037)	
Cash Flow	53,061	18,476	4,022	(17,851)	(18,481)	

Date	EPS	DPS	Tot Rev	Inc Bex
Mar 95	0.13	0.00	98,591	3,393
Dec 94	0.13	0.00	97,211	3,753
Sep 94	0.41	0.00	115,624	10,820
Jun 94	0.55	0.00	118,465	14,246
Mar 94	0.05	0.00	89,177	1,260
Dec 93	(1.16)	0.00	101,377	(29,914)
Sep 93	(0.04)	0.00	102,683	(1,115)
Jun 93	0.19	0.00	109,266	4,803

	Dec94	Dec93	Dec92	Dec91	Dec90
Debt/Equity	2.72	6.29	4.57	2.85	1.73
Return on Capital (%)	20.54	(3.02)	(4.48)	(12.20)	(7.15)
Ret. on Com. Equity (%)	62.87	(61.35)	(47.19)	(55.95)	na
% Change Profit	212.9	24.2	50.9	(3.7)	(529.9)
% Change Revenue	5.2	(3.4)	(1.2)	(27.6)	1.0
% Change Assets	9.8	(25.4)	(11.3)	(16.6)	(3.8)

	Dec94	Dec93	Dec92
Preferred Div. Coverage	1,114.0	0.0	0.0
Total Div. Coverage	1,114.0	0.0	0.0
Interest Coverage	2.7	0.0	0.0
Current Ratio	0.9	0.4	0.8
Operating Margin	11.1	3.7	(1.0)
Asset Turnover	1.3	1.3	1.0
5 YEAR RATIOS (%)			
Return on Capital	(1.3)	(5.3)	(9.1)
Return on Com. Equity	na	na	na
Profit Growth	na	na	na
Revenue Growth	(6.0)	0.4	0.5
Asset Growth	(10.2)	(2.3)	7.4
BALANCE SHEET (000)			
Cash	0	0	0
Current Assets	108,199	99,470	169,223
Net Fixed Assets	214,467	198,926	231,467
Invest's & Advances	0	0	0
Total Assets	329,011	299,665	401,435
Short Term Debt	44,330	182,645	138,450
Current Liabilities	122,085	255,201	212,003
Long Term Debt	135,551	9,534	124,325
Total Liabilities	262,856	269,101	343,923
Total Equity	66,155	30,564	57,512
Total Liab. & Equity	329,011	299,665	401,435
CAPITAL (000)			
Total Debt	179,881	192,179	262,775
Preferred Equity	558	558	558
Common Equity	65,597	30,006	56,954

Synopsis:

Consumers Packaging confirmed that the previously announced offering of 14,706,659 special warrants at a price of $12 per special warrant was completed on June 1, 1995. Pending satisfaction of certain conditions the proceeds of the offering will be held in escrow. The proceeds will fund a portion of the proposed purchase of one of the largest United States glass manufacturers, to reduce debt, and for other purposes. Proceeds of the offering will be returned if the proposed acquisition is not carried through.

A new Canadian holding company will issue these special warrants. It is proposed that a reorganization would be processed after which this company would exchange its common shares for outstanding Consumers shares on a one for one basis. Holders of special warrants and existing shareholders of Consumers will then become the shareholders of a new public entity. All of the common shares of Consumers would be owned by the new holding company after the reorganization is completed. Under the same terms, G & G Investments Inc., the majority shareholder of Consumers, has agreed to subscribe for 1,810,008 special warrants.

Consumers reported it was negotiating a $600-million (U.S.) acquisition that would make it the second-largest glass manufacturing company in North America. The proposed target is believed to be Foster-Forbes of Marion, Indiana, the fourth largest manufacturer of glass containers in the U.S. Foster-Forbes is a division of American National Can Co. of Chicago, which is a unit of Paris-based Pechiney Intenational SA. Pechiney said in mid-April that it plans to put Foster-Forbes on the block. While the unit had been a consistent profit spinner, the company plans to focus on its core aluminum business. Consumers believe the company needs to move into the U.S. market to boost sales if it hopes to get any bigger. Foster-Forbes had sales of about $650-million (U.S.) in 1994 and controls about 16% of the U.S. market for soft-drink, wine, beer and glass food containers.

Relative strength to TSE300

Price

Volume (in 1000's of board lots)

Rank (Profit/Revenue/Assets)
160 212 276

John Ghaznavi
Chairman Of The Board & C.E.O.

Charles Rhodes
President & C.O.O.

Address
401 The West Mall
Suite 900
Etobicoke
ON
M9C 5J7
(416) 232-3000

Fax: (416) 232-3314
C0009364/G/6.8

GREAT PACIFIC ENTERPRISES INC.

Exchanges	Price (Jun29'95)	22.00	Trailing P/E	8.66	Stock Symbol
T	Trailing Yield (%)	0.00	Trailing EPS	2.54	**GPN**

Period Ending	Dec94	Dec93	Dec92	Dec91	Dec90	Business:
Yearly Statistics					16M	GREAT PACIFIC ENTERPRISES is a
Price-Close	22.50	17.00	13.00	10.63	6.75	diversified packaging company with
Price-High	24.00	19.25	13.63	11.13	23.00	manufacturing plants in Canada and the United
Price-Low	16.00	13.00	10.25	5.00	6.75	States.
P/E-Close	12.30	nm	nm	nm	nm	
Dividends per Share	0.00	0.00	0.00	0.00	1.20	
Dividend Yield (%)	0.00	0.00	0.00	0.00	17.78	
Sales per Share	90.25	76.03	69.21	89.79	104.90	
EPS before extra. item	1.83	(0.60)	(2.50)	(4.16)	(6.11)	
Cash Flow per Share	9.49	6.23	4.20	4.45	4.36	
Book Value per Share	26.77	23.84	23.73	24.19	32.94	
O/S Common Shares	3,449	3,449	3,449	3,449	2,759	
Total Revenue	311,230	262,193	238,681	260,949	386,175	

						Date	EPS	DPS	Tot Rev	Inc Bex
Income before extra.	6,320	(2,067)	(8,609)	(12,081)	(16,881)					
Cash Flow	32,739	21,497	14,477	12,912	16,026	Mar 95	0.67	0.00	88,079	2,299
Debt/Equity	0.83	0.76	0.93	1.23	1.34	Dec 94	0.47	0.00	83,853	1,621
Return on Capital (%)	11.77	5.73	1.54	0.49	(0.07)	Sep 94	0.70	0.00	78,721	2,417
Ret. on Com. Equity (%)	7.24	(2.52)	(10.42)	(13.86)	(13.65)	Jun 94	0.70	0.00	79,391	2,415
% Change Profit	405.8	76.0	28.7	4.6	(0.8)	Mar 94	(0.04)	0.00	69,265	(133)
% Change Revenue	18.7	9.9	(8.5)	(9.9)	2.4	Dec 93	(0.45)	0.00	69,363	(1,564)
% Change Assets	19.9	(4.0)	(10.5)	(11.2)	(3.1)	Sep 93	0.20	0.00	66,243	696
						Jun 93	0.26	0.00	66,054	891

Preferred Div. Coverage	np	np	np	**Synopsis:**
Total Div. Coverage	na	na	na	Great Pacific Enterprises reported sales of $311-million, an increase of 18.7%
Interest Coverage	3.0	1.2	0.3	over 1993. The company's net income for the year ended December 31, 1994, was
Current Ratio	1.8	1.7	1.8	$6.3-million compared to a net loss of $2.1-million in 1993. The company credits
Operating Margin	5.9	3.3	1.7	the improved results to the containment of costs and a continuing increase in sales
Asset Turnover	1.4	1.4	1.2	performance. A number of the company's operating divisions had improved gross
5 YEAR RATIOS (%)				margins, although virtually all the divisions felt pressure from increased raw
Return on Capital	3.9	1.6	1.6	material and packaging costs in the latter part of 1994 and in the first weeks of
Return on Com. Equity	(6.6)	(10.5)	(9.5)	1995. The company will have to pass on the increase in the cost of sales to the
Profit Growth	64.0	na	na	prices of its products, to maintain similar gross margin levels in 1995.
Revenue Growth	1.9	(2.2)	(1.3)	Progressive Packaging's new plant in Lancaster, South Carolina, began production
Asset Growth	(2.4)	(7.4)	(2.7)	in December 1994 and has been building volume during 1995. During 1994,
BALANCE SHEET (000)				Purity Packaging moved all its creamer cup manufacturing from Peterborough to
Cash	14,916	1,186	2,972	Genpak's facility in Longview, Texas. A new plant is under construction for
Current Assets	99,116	61,457	61,211	Genpak in Cedar City, Utah, which should be in operation in the second quarter of
Net Fixed Assets	98,716	96,969	101,177	1995. The acquisition of new machinery is on order or under review for certain
Invest's & Advances	0	0	0	divisions of the company that are currently feeling production constraints. In
Total Assets	221,134	184,497	192,207	1995, increased spending on capital equipment is anticipated.
Short Term Debt	6,315	450	2,790	The company will continue its ongoing program of reducing long-term debt,
Current Liabilities	54,314	36,376	33,820	subject to the capital requirements of its operating divisions to improve their
Long Term Debt	70,229	62,368	73,126	competitive positions.
Total Liabilities	128,822	102,281	110,367	
Total Equity	92,312	82,216	81,840	
Total Liab. & Equity	221,134	184,497	192,207	
CAPITAL (000)				
Total Debt	76,544	62,818	75,916	
Preferred Equity	0	0	0	
Common Equity	92,312	82,216	81,840	

Relative strength to TSE300

Price

Volume (in 1000's of board lots)

Rank (Profit/Revenue/Assets)
383   252   337

Jim Pattison
President & C.E.O.

Kirk Henderson
C.O.O.

Address
Suite 1600
1055 West Hastings Street
Vancouver
BC
V6E 2H2
(604) 688-6764

Fax: (604) 687-2601
I0010637/G/6.8

INTERTAPE POLYMER GROUP INC.

Exchanges	Price (Jun29'95)	31.00	Trailing P/E	19.02	Stock Symbol
TA	Trailing Yield (%)	0.45	Trailing EPS	1.63	**ITP**

Period Ending	Dec94	Dec93	Dec92	Dec91	Dec90
Yearly Statistics					
Price-Close	22.25	17.50	n t	n t	n t
Price-High	24.50	18.38	n t	n t	n t
Price-Low	17.00	11.38	n t	n t	n t
P/E-Close	15.78	18.42	n t	n t	n t
Dividends per Share	0.12	0.10	0.00	0.00	0.00
Dividend Yield (%)	0.54	0.57	0.00	0.00	0.00
Sales per Share	17.43	13.25	11.65	15.97	15.49
EPS before extra. item	1.41	0.95	0.59	0.62	0.82
Cash Flow per Share	2.81	2.22	1.71	1.94	1.87
Book Value per Share	11.03	9.63	8.76	7.85	6.76
O/S Common Shares	10,256	10,161	10,152	7,392	6,390
Total Revenue	176,973	134,521	112,360	115,026	102,674
Income before extra.	14,369	9,623	5,721	4,358	5,243
Cash Flow	28,559	22,540	16,678	13,964	12,325
Debt/Equity	0.52	0.44	0.48	0.97	1.63
Return on Capital (%)	17.08	14.19	10.52	12.43	na
Ret. on Com. Equity (%)	13.62	10.30	7.79	8.61	na
% Change Profit	49.3	68.2	31.3	(16.9)	na
% Change Revenue	31.6	19.7	(2.3)	12.0	na
% Change Assets	25.3	7.7	13.6	(0.7)	na

Business:

INTERTAPE POLYMER GROUP INC. develops, manufactures and sells a variety of specialized polyolefin plastic packaging products for industrial use.

Date	EPS	DPS	Tot Rev	Inc Bex
Mar 95	0.47	0.14	54,656	4,835
Dec 94	0.43	0.00	50,319	4,355
Sep 94	0.38	0.00	45,167	3,920
Jun 94	0.35	0.00	43,034	3,589
Mar 94	0.25	0.12	38,720	2,505
Dec 93	0.28	0.00	36,556	2,801
Sep 93	0.27	0.00	34,206	2,725
Jun 93	0.21	0.00	33,068	2,116

	Dec94	Dec93	Dec92
Preferred Div. Coverage	np	np	np
Total Div. Coverage	11.8	9.5	na
Interest Coverage	8.1	6.5	4.8
Current Ratio	2.4	1.9	1.8
Operating Margin	15.9	15.7	14.5
Asset Turnover	0.9	0.8	0.7
5 YEAR RATIOS (%)			
Return on Capital	na	na	na
Return on Com. Equity	na	na	na
Profit Growth	na	na	na
Revenue Growth	na	na	na
Asset Growth	na	na	na
BALANCE SHEET (000)			
Cash	10,252	197	329
Current Assets	76,440	49,892	48,452
Net Fixed Assets	78,851	63,413	57,545
Invest's & Advances	584	745	566
Total Assets	207,572	165,693	153,784
Short Term Debt	6,994	10,835	9,343
Current Liabilities	32,050	26,677	26,485
Long Term Debt	51,667	32,294	32,848
Total Liabilities	94,491	67,801	64,897
Total Equity	113,081	97,892	88,887
Total Liab. & Equity	207,572	165,693	153,784
CAPITAL (000)			
Total Debt	58,661	43,129	42,191
Preferred Equity	0	0	0
Common Equity	113,081	97,892	88,887

Synopsis:

Intertape Polymer Group Inc. reported record sales of $54.7-million in the first quarter ended March 31, 1995. This was an increase of 41.2% over the same quarter in 1994. The company's distribution and end user products had a high level of demand world-wide, and pricing has kept pace with rising material costs. Intertape expects this demand to remain strong throughout the year and expects no significant deterioration in finished goods pricing.

While Intertape investigated a number of companies 1994, it did not find a suitable match to its requirements. However, Intertape did negotiate joint ventures in two areas, both of which were finalized in early 1995. The first is with FIBOPE Portuguesa in Portugal, and the transfer of imformation-technology to enable the company to manufacture and market shrink wrap in Europe has already started. The second was with Schoeller International and Intertape is currently test marketing various returnable cases in the produce areas. The product has proven to be extremely successful for Intertape's new German partners.

The company's Industrial Distribution Group saw record sales in 1994 mostly from the sale of shrink wrap. Sales of this product more than doubled, as Intertape acquired a significant number of new customer accounts. A new technical sales support team was formed to ensure the continued growth in this area. Intertape's market for carton sealing tape continued to expand by over 8% per year. The continued development of its automatic equipment lines through the 1993 acquisition of Interpack Machinery Co. and the addition of an acrylic coater, will further broaden this product line. The End User Products Group had continued growth in 1994 in all sectors. Demand for woven products was exceptionally strong.

Rank (Profit/Revenue/Assets)
249   328   350

Melbourne F. Yull
Chairman

Andrew M. Archibald
V.P. Finance & Secretary

H. Dale McSween
Sr. V.P. & C.O.O

Address
110 E Montee De Liesse
St-Laurent
PQ
H4T 1N4
(514) 731-0731

Fax: (514) 731-5039
01003315/G/6.8

For further company information, call Globe Information Services 1-800-268-9128 or (416) 585-5345

WINPAK LTD.

Exchanges	Price (Jun29'95)	26.25	Trailing P/E	14.50	Stock Symbol
TW	Trailing Yield (%)	1.52	Trailing EPS	1.81	WPK

Period Ending	Dec94	Dec93	Dec92	Dec91	Dec90
Yearly Statistics					
Price-Close	22.00	25.75	16.50	12.00	10.00
Price-High	26.50	25.75	16.63	12.00	11.63
Price-Low	20.00	16.50	11.75	9.25	10.00
P/E-Close	13.42	17.17	14.87	13.79	9.90
Dividends per Share	0.40	0.40	0.40	0.40	0.20
Dividend Yield (%)	1.82	1.55	2.42	3.33	2.00
Sales per Share	38.56	40.32	21.57	15.28	15.82
EPS before extra. item	1.64	1.50	1.11	0.87	1.01
Cash Flow per Share	3.79	3.80	1.56	1.44	1.64
Book Value per Share	13.39	11.80	9.49	8.35	7.88
O/S Common Shares	6,500	6,500	5,359	5,359	5,359
Total Revenue	250,852	235,287	115,829	82,277	86,625
Income before extra.	10,658	8,726	5,947	4,645	5,399
Cash Flow	24,603	22,155	8,363	7,725	8,771
Debt/Equity	0.49	0.55	0.12	0.10	0.28
Return on Capital (%)	16.87	20.50	19.19	16.09	16.27
Ret. on Com. Equity (%)	13.02	13.68	12.44	10.68	13.49
% Change Profit	22.1	46.7	28.0	(14.0)	25.4
% Change Revenue	6.6	103.1	40.8	(5.0)	(2.8)
% Change Assets	14.1	79.4	23.8	(5.0)	1.7

Date	EPS	DPS	Tot Rev	Inc Bex
Mar 95	0.46	0.10	67,228	2,977
Dec 94	0.47	0.10	64,789	3,084
Sep 94	0.42	0.10	64,086	2,670
Jun 94	0.46	0.10	64,720	3,018
Mar 94	0.29	0.10	57,257	1,886
Dec 93	0.36	0.10	60,818	2,363
Sep 93	0.42	0.10	58,522	2,490
Jun 93	0.43	0.10	59,147	2,336

Preferred Div. Coverage	np	np	np	
Total Div. Coverage	4.1	3.7	2.8	
Interest Coverage	9.5	6.1	28.3	
Current Ratio	1.6	1.8	1.6	
Operating Margin	8.7	8.1	8.8	
Asset Turnover	1.5	1.5	1.4	
5 YEAR RATIOS (%)				
Return on Capital	17.8	17.7	18.2	
Return on Com. Equity	12.7	12.6	12.9	
Profit Growth	19.9	14.9	9.4	
Revenue Growth	23.0	21.7	19.2	
Asset Growth	19.6	17.2	13.2	
BALANCE SHEET (000)				
Cash	0	0	0	
Current Assets	76,603	59,782	43,353	
Net Fixed Assets	73,823	68,389	27,039	
Invest's & Advances	0	0	0	
Total Assets	172,833	151,513	84,477	
Short Term Debt	11,588	6,715	3,635	
Current Liabilities	46,996	32,885	26,943	
Long Term Debt	30,916	35,199	2,381	
Total Liabilities	85,833	74,802	33,620	
Total Equity	87,000	76,711	50,857	
Total Liab. & Equity	172,833	151,513	84,477	
CAPITAL (000)				
Total Debt	42,504	41,914	6,016	
Preferred Equity	0	0	0	
Common Equity	87,000	76,711	50,857	

Business:

WINPAK LTD. is committed to the production of high-quality packaging materials for the protection of perishable foods, beverage and dairy products, and for non-food markets such as pharmaceutical and complex industrial applications.

Synopsis:

Winpak marginally improved its first quarter revenue results to $67.2-million in 1995 from $57.2-million during the comparable 1994 period. A combination of higher selling prices and the weaker Canadian dollar accounted for the majority of this increase. The other contributing factors include a combination of market growth, pre-buying to avoid price increases, and gains in market share.

Selling prices and demand fluctuated dramatically during 1994. Weak demand forced selling prices lower early in the year while raw material prices were stable. Through the third and fourth quarters raw material prices began to rise, supply tightened, lead times extended, and prices rose sharply upward. Consequently, average selling prices for the year were at about the same levels as in 1993.

During the past three years the company invested $32.6-million towards increasing capacity and improved production technology in order to enhance quality and low-cost production capability. In 1994, the company's $14.8-million capital expenditures included $2.5-million for the purchase of a property and building in Toronto. The company's capital plan includes a $10-million expenditure to expand and upgrade the production capabilities of this location.

Winpak's 1995 capital program will spend approximately $17-million to expand capacity, install filling equipment at customer locations, and enhance productivity at all plant sites. The capital program includes a new production line and expansion of its Chicago facility. Commercial production from the new line is expected in the second quarter and will increase sales capacity to approximately $330-million.

Rank (Profit/Revenue/Assets)		
288	286	375

A. Aarnio-Wihuri
Chairman

J. Robert Lavery
President & C.E.O.

Olav Lindstrom
V.P. Operations

Address
100 Saulteaux Crescent
Winnipeg
MB
R3J 3T3
(204) 889-1015

Fax: (204) 832-7781
W0000645/G/6.8

| Page | Company | Fiscal year end | EARNINGS PER SHARE | | |
			Last Year	Estimate this year	Estimate next year
303	Cambridge Shopping Centres	Mar-94	0.58	0.24	0.31
304	Camdev	Jan-95	(1.06)	na	na
305	Carena Developments	Oct-94	(0.94)	(0.15)	0.00
306	Centrefund Realty	Dec-94	0.27	0.50	0.55
307	Consolidated Carma	Dec-94	0.37	0.25	0.40
308	Consolidated HCI Holdings	Sep-94	0.08	na	na
309	Coscan Development	Dec-94	(0.52)	(0.39)	(0.19)
310	Intrawest	Sep-94	0.70	0.72	0.89
311	Markborough Properties	Jan-95	0.05	0.05	0.08
312	Melcor Developments	Dec-94	1.98	0.45	0.65
313	Monarch Development	Dec-94	0.42	0.49	0.56
314	Revenue Properties Company	Dec-94	0.03	0.12	0.16
315	Royal LePage	Dec-94	(0.34)	(0.62)	(0.01)
316	Trizec	Dec-94	0.40	0.40	0.43
317	Wall Financial	Jan-95	0.03	na	na

Estimates from First Call Corporation, 22 Pittsburgh Street, Boston, MA 02210   (800) 366-9992   Fax (617) 261-5679

Real Estate Developers & Managers

The real estate market continued to plummet at the beginning of 1995. Housing sales fell 20% nationally in January and 38% in February. While last year's overall sales were down only 1% from 1993, this was due to an increase in sales in the first half of 1994. The numbers have decreased ever since. The last half of 1994 was the most brutal on record, with sales falling significantly.

Low consumer confidence is the main reason for the decline in housing starts to their lowest level since the early 1960s, according to a survey of home builders and renovators across Canada. The Canadian Home Builders Association said the issue of consumer confidence was cited by more than 50% of the 409 builders who responded, compared with less than 30% in previous polls. As a result, builders are predicting that housing starts will plunge 21% this year to 122,400 dwellings from 154,057 in 1994. In January, Canada Mortgage and Housing Corp. estimated housing starts at 141,000 for 1995, but slashed its forecast to 128,500 in May.

The renovation sector is the industry's one bright spot. Almost 45% of renovators expect the level of their activity to be higher in the next 12 months than in the past year according to the Canadian Home Builders Association. The survey found that builders expect to continue erecting smaller houses next year to attract cost-conscious buyers. Builders also plan to include more energy efficient features in new homes next year.

Market conditions have started to recover in the second half of 1995. Interest rates have fallen due to sluggish economic growth. One-year closed mortgages were trimmed twice in June and again in July, falling to 7.63%, compared with a high of 10% in January. The five-year rate in July is 8.5%, down from 10.75% at the start of the year.

Falling mortgage rates propelled construction of new homes in Canada in June, setting the stage for the much anticipated housing recovery in the second half of the year. According, Canada Mortgage and Housing Corp., construction of houses, condominiums, and apartments rose 12.9% in June to an annual rate of 114,600 from a 13-year low of 101,500 in May.

CMHC reported that June housing starts increased 39% in Ontario and 15.5% in British Columbia, with both single-detached and multiple dwellings contributing to the rise. Activity in the Greater Toronto Area accelerated markedly, according to the report. However, housing starts fell in Montreal, extending a trend that has lasted for more than a year. CMHC predicts a housing start count below 10,000 this year. This would be the lowest activity level in the Montreal metropolitan area since 1960.

Although performance improved in June, a turnaround in the real estate development market is unlikely. Traditionally, housing starts lag behind a recovery in the resale market by anywhere from three to seven months. Resale activity bottomed in April and began to improve in May, so it will take a few months to prove that housing starts are consistently higher. Moreover, CMHC has found that housing construction generally picks up four to six months after an interest rate peak. This points to a summer recovery in home building.

In June, Statistics Canada reported that new house prices declined further in May, led by a fall on the West Coast. CMHC's index of new house prices fell to 134.9 in May, down 0.2% from April and 0.8% from a year earlier. May was the 11th consecutive month new house prices dipped from year-earlier levels. Victoria led the slump, with new home prices in May falling 1.4% and 8.4% from a year earlier. New house prices in Toronto in May were down 0.1% from April but up 1.4% from a year earlier.

CAMBRIDGE SHOPPING CENTRES LIMITED

Exchanges	Price (Jun29'95)	10.75	Trailing P/E		nm	Stock Symbol
TM	Trailing Yield (%)	2.98	Trailing EPS		(0.54)	CBG

Period Ending	Mar95	Mar94	Mar93	Mar92	Mar91
Yearly Statistics					
Price-Close	12.00	16.38	15.75	18.50	27.75
Price-High	16.38	20.50	19.25	28.50	29.75
Price-Low	10.75	14.38	10.13	18.25	20.25
P/E-Close	nm	28.23	nm	28.03	396.43
Dividends per Share	0.32	0.32	0.46	0.60	0.60
Dividend Yield (%)	2.67	1.95	2.92	3.24	2.16
Sales per Share	5.88	7.72	10.04	10.84	10.59
EPS before extra. item	(0.54)	0.58	(2.42)	0.66	0.07
Cash Flow per Share	1.06	1.18	1.67	2.06	2.16
Book Value per Share	14.09	14.95	15.05	18.43	14.23
O/S Common Shares	50,326	50,275	32,066	27,932	25,833
Total Revenue	308,971	341,071	354,659	308,421	280,364
Income before extra.	(27,437)	23,532	(77,547)	18,483	1,701
Cash Flow	53,643	47,782	53,488	57,278	55,730
Debt/Equity	2.08	1.96	3.95	3.27	3.54
Return on Capital (%)	4.37	7.36	1.41	7.43	7.00
Ret. on Com. Equity (%)	(3.76)	3.81	(15.55)	na	0.42
% Change Profit	(216.6)	130.3	(519.6)	986.6	(93.2)
% Change Revenue	(9.4)	(3.8)	15.0	10.0	9.8
% Change Assets	(1.3)	(6.1)	(3.7)	24.4	6.0

Preferred Div. Coverage	np	np	np		
Total Div. Coverage	0.0	2.0	0.0		
Income prop.(% tot. prop.)	91.1	90.4	92.4		
Develop. prop.(% tot. prop.)	8.9	9.6	7.6		
5 YEAR RATIOS (%)					
Return on Capital	5.5	6.3	6.5		
Return on Com. Equity	na	na	na		
Profit Growth	na	0.1	na		
Revenue Growth	3.8	8.6	12.3		
Asset Growth	3.3	5.4	9.6		
BALANCE SHEET (000)					
Cash	60,204	127,227	66,105		
Total Real Estate Assets	2,206,542	2,182,710	2,396,955		
Invest's & Advances	33,995	35,834	54,234		
Total Assets	2,388,353	2,420,921	2,577,445		
Bank Indebtedness	19,019	4,844	213,962		
Long Term Debt	1,456,105	1,467,041	1,693,900		
Total Liabilities	1,679,344	1,669,223	2,094,777		
Total Equity	709,009	751,698	482,668		
Total Liab. & Equity	2,388,353	2,420,921	2,577,445		
CAPITAL (000)					
Total Debt	1,475,124	1,471,885	1,907,862		
Preferred Equity	0	0	0		
Common Equity	709,009	751,698	482,668		

Business:

CAMBRIDGE SHOPPING CENTRES LTD. is a manager and developer of commercial real estate across Canada. The company's properties include shopping centres, urban mixed-use properties and self-storage facilities. The company also has a 50% interest in Donahue Schriber, a California corporation involved in the management and development of shopping centres in the southwestern United States.

Date	EPS	DPS	Tot Rev	Inc Bex
Mar 95	(0.68)	0.08	86,481	(34,301)
Dec 94	0.04	0.08	75,810	1,662
Sep 94	0.05	0.08	73,811	2,848
Jun 94	0.05	0.08	73,094	2,354
Mar 94	0.13	0.08	91,081	6,871
Dec 93	0.30	0.08	84,975	11,689
Sep 93	0.08	0.08	81,722	2,600
Jun 93	0.07	0.08	83,671	2,372

Synopsis:

Cambridge Shopping Centres posted a loss of $27.4-million for the fiscal year ended March 31, 1995. It had to take a $40-million provision against land held for future development due to the lack of development prospects in the near term. Provisions were taken against land in London, Ontario, Surrey, British Columbia, and expansion lands next to several of the company's existing shopping centres. Cambridge has about 500 acres of land in its portfolio at an average "written down" value of $150,000 an acre. In fiscal 1995, rental revenue dipped 5.1% to $297.4-million from $313.2-million a year earlier because of the sale of property interests. However, cash flow rose 12.3% to $53.6-million from $47.8-million the year before. The company cited higher property operating income and lower interest costs for the improved cash flow.

In May 1895, Donald Priddle, Cambridge's C.F.O., said the company is "interested in and looking at" some shopping malls formerly owned by Bramalea Inc. Bramalea went bankrupt in early 1995.

In February 1995, Cadillac Fairview Inc. rejected Cambridge's bid to acquire the company. Cadillac owns or has interests in some of the best shopping malls in Canada, including Pacific Centre in Vancouver, and Eaton Centre and Fairview Mall in Toronto. It also has several U.S. shopping mall interests.

In September 1994, Cambridge and the Ontario Teachers Pension Plan Board said they would spend $42-million to expand the Intercity Shopping Centre in Thunder Bay, Ontario. Intercity is a 402,500 square-foot regional shopping centre. Cambridge said the expansion will take two years and will see the relocation of the Sears department store to a new, two-level, 137,000-square-foot store. An additional 105,000 square feet of ancillary tenants comprising 65 new stores will connect the new Sears store to the existing shopping centre.

Relative strength to TSE300

Price

Volume (in 1000's of board lots)

Rank (Profit/Revenue/Assets)
195 238 91

J. Lorne Braithwaite
President & C.E.O.

Donald F. Priddle
Exec. V.P. & C.F.O.

Address
Suite 300
95 Wellington Street West
Toronto
ON
M5J 2R2
(416) 369-1200

Fax: (416) 369-1328
C0040576/R/7.2

CAMDEV CORPORATION

Exchanges	Price (Jun29'95)		4.25	Trailing P/E		nm	Stock Symbol
TM	Trailing Yield (%)		0.00	Trailing EPS		(1.77)	**CVO**

Period Ending	Jan95	Jan94	Jan93	Jan92	Jan91
Yearly Statistics					
Price-Close	4.00	5.38	2.80	24.00	21.50
Price-High	5.88	6.25	18.75	72.50	150.00
Price-Low	4.00	2.75	2.40	18.50	17.50
P/E-Close	nm	nm	nm	63.16	nm
Dividends per Share	0.00	0.00	0.00	0.00	0.00
Dividend Yield (%)	0.00	0.00	0.00	0.00	0.00
Sales per Share	13.43	12.91	13.21	32.43	288.75
EPS before extra. item	(1.06)	(0.24)	(2.16)	0.38	(605.71)
Cash Flow per Share	0.07	0.78	(0.45)	(13.06)	(103.77)
Book Value per Share	19.27	20.33	20.57	22.67	(2,959.72)
O/S Common Shares	6,354	6,354	6,353	6,353	887
Total Revenue	86,887	81,999	83,937	465,000	312,000
Income before extra.	(6,726)	(1,524)	(13,693)	2,470,000	(525,000)
Cash Flow	444	4,939	(2,890)	(83,000)	(92,000)
Debt/Equity	3.68	3.50	3.50	3.29	na
Return on Capital (%)	5.27	5.13	4.48	1,720.52	na
Ret. on Com. Equity (%)	(5.35)	(1.17)	(9.97)	na	na
% Change Profit	(341.3)	88.9	(100.6)	570.5	74.0
% Change Revenue	6.0	(2.3)	(81.9)	49.0	119.6
% Change Assets	(1.3)	(0.1)	(5.1)	(49.3)	(14.0)

Preferred Div. Coverage	np	np	np
Total Div. Coverage	na	na	na
Income prop.(% tot. prop.)	96.9	94.8	93.5
Develop. prop.(% tot. prop.)	3.1	5.2	6.5
5 YEAR RATIOS (%)			
Return on Capital	na	na	na
Return on Com. Equity	na	na	na
Profit Growth	na	na	na
Revenue Growth	(9.4)	(62.9)	(54.7)
Asset Growth	(16.4)	(48.6)	(38.5)
BALANCE SHEET (000)			
Cash	7,743	14,820	13,247
Total Real Estate Assets	511,261	507,425	497,235
Invest's & Advances	72,556	72,556	93,029
Total Assets	602,855	610,725	611,391
Bank Indebtedness	0	0	0
Long Term Debt	450,935	452,154	457,935
Total Liabilities	480,423	481,567	480,711
Total Equity	122,432	129,158	130,680
Total Liab. & Equity	602,855	610,725	611,391
CAPITAL (000)			
Total Debt	450,935	452,154	457,935
Preferred Equity	0	0	0
Common Equity	122,432	129,158	130,680

Business:

CAMDEV CORPORATION is an owner and manager of real estate properties, which include more than 3.1 million square feet of commercial and retail space. Approximately 2.3 million square feet is located in the National Capital Region.

Date	EPS	DPS	Tot Rev	Inc Bex
Apr 95	(0.67)	0.00	19,459	(4,233)
Jan 95	(0.31)	0.00	19,052	(1,941)
Oct 94	(0.37)	0.00	31,295	(2,341)
Jul 94	(0.42)	0.00	17,080	(2,681)
Apr 94	0.04	0.00	19,460	237
Jan 94	(0.01)	0.00	17,470	(58)
Oct 93	(0.09)	0.00	17,755	(582)
Jul 93	(0.11)	0.00	27,360	(673)

Synopsis:

During the fiscal year ended January 31, 1995, Camdev had several accomplishments. It concluded an agreement to sell Talphs Grocery Company as part of a merger with the Food 4 Less grocery chain. This sale should close in June 1995. Camdev also sold the south Keys regional shopping centre site.

During fiscal 1995, Camdev entered into new or renewed leases for approximately 180,000 square feet of space in its office and retail properties. The vacancy rate at its core downtown Ottawa office properties is less than 2%. Camdev managed the $90-million retrofit programs in Tower "C" and Podium of Place de Ville II, as well as in Journal Towers. Both programs are on time, under budget, and nearing completing. Place de Ville I and II and Journal Towers consist of 1,974,000 square feet, of which 1,680,000 square feet is office space with the remainder used for retail and storage purposes. Camdev upgraded the concourse level retail shopping area of Place de Ville to provide new services to building occupants and more meeting space for office and hotel tenants.

For the 12 months ended January 31, 1995, Camdev reported a net loss of $6.7-million or $1.06 per share on $86.9-million of revenue. Camdev said its floating rate debt makes the company vulnerable to interest rate fluctuations. Currently, Camdev is unprofitable when the prime rate rises over 6.25%.

Relative strength to TSE300

Price

Volume (in 1000's of board lots)

Rank (Profit/Revenue/Assets)
923   442   209

Stanley H. Hartt
Chairman President & C.E.O.

Dale Kearns
Sr. V.P. Finance & C.F.O.

Address
Suite 2700
40 King Street West
Toronto
ON
M5H 3Y2
(416) 365-2050

Fax: (416) 365-2510

C0001122/R/7.2

CARENA DEVELOPMENTS LTD.

Exchanges	Price (Jun29'95)	0.80	Trailing P/E		nm	Stock Symbol
TM	Trailing Yield (%)	0.00	Trailing EPS		(1.14)	**CDN**

Period Ending	Dec94	Oct93	Oct92	Oct91	Oct90	Business:
Yearly Statistics	14M					
Price-Close	1.10	1.25	3.10	10.75	10.38	
Price-High	2.95	3.05	12.00	15.63	28.25	
Price-Low	0.65	1.05	3.00	9.00	10.38	
P/E-Close	nm	nm	nm	17.62	18.86	
Dividends per Share	0.00	0.09	0.42	0.50	0.50	
Dividend Yield (%)	0.00	6.80	13.55	4.65	4.82	
Sales per Share	12.42	24.65	22.00	38.85	44.23	
EPS before extra. item	(1.03)	(2.79)	(4.55)	0.61	0.55	
Cash Flow per Share	7.92	7.10	8.61	16.42	22.18	
Book Value per Share	1.73	2.30	5.18	10.27	9.93	
O/S Common Shares	156,732	56,732	56,732	56,149	50,844	
Total Revenue	882,409	1,487,934	1,343,984	2,269,181	2,447,440	
Income before extra.	(35,215)	(141,384)	(245,468)	45,000	42,052	
Cash Flow	530,422	402,761	487,934	883,829	1,127,627	
Debt/Equity	5.42	9.42	6.05	15.17	16.04	
Return on Capital (%)	2.61	7.68	(0.66)	5.73	6.47	
Ret. on Com. Equity (%)	(25.21)	(74.72)	(59.25)	6.02	5.55	
% Change Profit	78.7	42.4	(645.5)	7.0	(22.2)	
% Change Revenue	(49.2)	10.7	(40.8)	(7.3)	(3.5)	
% Change Assets	6.8	(9.4)	(66.9)	3.2	15.3	

CARENA DEVELOPMENTS LTD. is a diversified North American real estate development company owning rental properties concentrated in major urban centres in the United States and Canada.

Date	EPS	DPS	Tot Rev	Inc Bex
Mar 95	(0.06)	0.00	165,464	(1,925)
Dec 94	(0.18)	0.00	383,399	(2,831)
Jul 94	(0.87)	0.00	186,173	(43,605)
Apr 94	(0.03)	0.00	149,954	4,282
Jan 94	0.05	0.00	162,883	6,939
Oct 93	(2.59)	0.00	384,795	(142,698)
Jul 93	(0.14)	0.00	378,382	(3,957)
Apr 93	(0.12)	0.09	344,985	(2,293)

Preferred Div. Coverage	0.0	0.0	0.0
Total Div. Coverage	0.0	0.0	0.0
Income prop.(% tot. prop.)	59.0	39.9	29.8
Develop. prop.(% tot. prop.)	41.0	60.1	70.2
5 YEAR RATIOS (%)			
Return on Capital	4.4	5.2	5.0
Return on Com. Equity	(29.5)	(22.7)	(5.9)
Profit Growth	na	na	na
Revenue Growth	(21.5)	3.2	2.7
Asset Growth	(17.6)	(15.7)	(11.3)
BALANCE SHEET (000)			
Cash	0	0	0
Total Real Estate Assets	4,164,200	3,664,955	3,497,951
Invest's & Advances	202,033	397,391	809,442
Total Assets	4,522,155	4,233,502	4,673,784
Bank Indebtedness	141,241	278,338	394,543
Long Term Debt	3,313,240	2,982,817	2,687,989
Total Liabilities	3,884,802	3,887,342	4,164,405
Total Equity	637,353	346,160	509,379
Total Liab. & Equity	4,522,155	4,233,502	4,673,784
CAPITAL (000)			
Total Debt	3,454,481	3,261,155	3,082,532
Preferred Equity	365,780	215,780	215,780
Common Equity	271,573	130,380	293,599

Synopsis:

In May 1995, Carena Developments said it is still negotiating to acquire a stake in the U.S. arm of Olympia & York Developments Ltd. Carena currently holds a 35% interest in the World Financial Center in Manhattan, majority-owned by O&Y. Carena has participated in talks with a consortium of creditors vying for a chunk of the restructured Olympia & York Cos. (USA), tentatively called O&Y America. The proposed deal would see Carena swap its stake in the Financial Center for equity in the newly formed company. Under one proposal, Carena could also be required to inject new capital into the new structure.

At its shareholders meeting, Carena said it expects to break even this year, after posting a $35-million (Canadian) loss in fiscal 1994. Improved results are due in part to better leasing terms at its commercial properties. The company said commercial space rentals were 90%, up from 83% a year earlier. Over the next year, and into the longer term, Carena is likely to benefit from a stronger U.S. housing market that hasn't been hit as hard as Canada's, the company said. About 80% of the company's commercial and housing assets are in the United States.

On April 26, 1995, Carena sold its holding of Consolidated Carma Corporation's Class AAA Participating Non-Voting Series 2 Shares as part of Carma's purchase offer. The transaction resulted in Carena receiving about $92-million in cash and 18.2 million common shares of Carma. This increased Carena's shares of Carma to about 67% from 50%. As part of the offer, Carena lend Carma $75-million under a revolving term credit facility.

On January 20, 1995, Carena issued formal demand letters and notices stipulating that it will enforce its rights to all the shares of BF Realty's sole operating subsidiary, Brookfield Development Corp. The shares had been pledged indirectly to Carena for a loan. A group of BF Realty debenture holders has amended a 1993 statement of claim to complain that Carena was not entitled to seize BF Realty's shares in Brookfield.

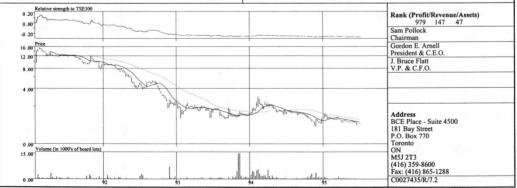

Rank (Profit/Revenue/Assets)
979   147   47

Sam Pollock
Chairman

Gordon E. Arnell
President & C.E.O.

J. Bruce Flatt
V.P. & C.F.O.

Address
BCE Place - Suite 4500
181 Bay Street
P.O. Box 770
Toronto
ON
M5J 2T3
(416) 359-8600
Fax: (416) 865-1288
C0027435/R/7.2

CENTREFUND REALTY CORPORATION

Exchanges	Price (Jun29'95)	9.75	Trailing P/E	24.38	Stock Symbol
T	Trailing Yield (%)	6.15	Trailing EPS	0.40	**CFE**

Period Ending	Dec94	Dec93
Yearly Statistics	9M	
Price-Close	9.00	n t
Price-High	10.00	n t
Price-Low	8.00	n t
P/E-Close	25.00	n t
Dividends per Share	0.48	0.00
Dividend Yield (%)	5.33	0.00
Sales per Share	4.14	3.96
EPS before extra. item	0.27	0.02
Cash Flow per Share	0.71	0.34
Book Value per Share	9.28	9.01
O/S Common Shares	4,672	3,408
Total Revenue	10,629	13,520
Income before extra.	933	61
Cash Flow	1,807	1,149
Debt/Equity	3.89	3.03
Return on Capital (%)	4.99	na
Ret. on Com. Equity (%)	3.36	na
% Change Profit	1,939.3	na
% Change Revenue	4.8	na
% Change Assets	74.0	na

Preferred Div. Coverage	np	np
Total Div. Coverage	0.6	na
Income prop.(% tot. prop.)	100.0	100.0
Develop. prop.(% tot. prop.)	na	na
5 YEAR RATIOS (%)		
Return on Capital	na	na
Return on Com. Equity	na	na
Profit Growth	na	na
Revenue Growth	na	na
Asset Growth	na	na
BALANCE SHEET (000)		
Cash	1,310	961
Total Real Estate Assets	210,443	122,675
Invest's & Advances	0	0
Total Assets	215,082	123,636
Bank Indebtedness	0	0
Long Term Debt	168,547	92,916
Total Liabilities	171,733	92,916
Total Equity	43,349	30,720
Total Liab. & Equity	215,082	123,636
CAPITAL (000)		
Total Debt	168,547	92,916
Preferred Equity	0	0
Common Equity	43,349	30,720

Business:

CENTREFUND REALTY CORPORATION has been created to assemble, by the acquisition of existing properties, a portfolio of well located neighbourhood/community shopping centres in Canada and the United States to be managed by real estate professionals.

Date	EPS	DPS	Tot Rev	Inc Bex
Mar 95	0.13	0.15	6,941	597
Dec 94	0.14	0.15	3,668	486
Sep 94	0.06	0.15	3,536	200
Jun 94	0.07	0.15	na	247

Synopsis:

On March 29, 1994, Centrefund Realty Corporation began operations with the acquisition of a portfolio of five shopping centres. The centres contained a total of 933,000 square feet. They were financed in part from the net proceeds of a $57-million initial public offering. During 1994, Centrefund grew through acquisitions and expansion.

It entered the U.S. market with the acquisition of North American Realty Corporation. Centrefund issued common shares and securities convertible or exchangeable into common shares. The deal expanded Centrefund's capital base by $38-million. North American Realty owns six shopping centres in Florida with 630,000 square feet of leaseable area.

Centrefund bought seven shopping centers, including those owned by North American, containing a total of 780,000 square feet of gross leaseable area. Centrefund expanded three shopping centers. On completion, this expansion will increase gross leaseable area by 132,000 square feet.

It entered into contracts, during the second quarter of 1995, for an additional 445,000 square feet in two projects. On April 5, 1995, it closed a private placement of 2,941,180 special warrants, exchangeable into common shares. The placement raised $25-million before issue costs. The proceeds will be used to fund the equity component of its expansion and acquisition activities. At last report, Centrefund had 4,672,301 common shares outstanding, and will have 7,613,481 common shares outstanding after the exercise of all special warrants issued.

Rank (Profit/Revenue/Assets)

Peter F. Cohen
President & C.E.O.

Percy A. Fink
Chief Financial Officer

Address
Suite 1400
30 St. Clair Avenue West
Toronto
ON
M4V 3A1
(416) 515-1400

Fax: (416) 515-1401
01003638/R/7.2

For further company information, call Globe Information Services 1-800-268-9128 or (416) 585-5345

CONSOLIDATED CARMA CORPORATION

Exchanges	Price (Jun29'95)		2 .60	Trailing P/E		9 .63	Stock Symbol
TZ	Trailing Yield (%)		0 .00	Trailing EPS		0 .27	**CVP.A**

Period Ending	Dec94	Dec93	Dec92	Dec91	Dec90
Yearly Statistics					
Price-Close	2 .95	3 .30	1 .95	2 .10	1 .80
Price-High	4 .50	3 .75	2 .70	2 .55	2 .70
Price-Low	2 .60	1 .80	1 .65	1 .67	1 .55
P/E-Close	7 .97	7 .86	3 .20	4 .38	4 .00
Dividends per Share	0 .00	0 .00	0 .00	0 .00	0 .00
Dividend Yield (%)	0 .00	0 .00	0 .00	0 .00	0 .00
Sales per Share	4 .52	4 .90	5 .88	3 .66	4 .79
EPS before extra. item	0 .37	0 .42	0 .61	0 .48	0 .45
Cash Flow per Share	4 .62	4 .98	1 .95	1 .81	1 .74
Book Value per Share	6 .88	6 .17	5 .32	3 .85	2 .80
O/S Common Shares	20 ,797	20 ,797	20 ,797	20 ,797	20 ,797
Total Revenue	106 ,183	112 ,850	142 ,675	110 ,552	143 ,608
Income before extra.	24 ,310	27 ,248	39 ,905	37 ,082	35 ,643
Cash Flow	96 ,159	103 ,508	40 ,589	37 ,654	36 ,164
Debt/Equity	0 .12	0 .10	0 .06	0 .51	0 .78
Return on Capital (%)	9 .37	11 .18	17 .21	14 .16	12 .60
Ret. on Com. Equity (%)	10 .91	14 .86	31 .88	31 .66	0 .00
% Change Profit	(10 .8)	(31 .7)	7 .6	4 .0	73 .0
% Change Revenue	(5 .9)	(20 .9)	29 .1	(23 .0)	1 .1
% Change Assets	13 .7	2 .2	(13 .1)	(32 .5)	2 .9

Date	EPS	DPS	Tot Rev	Inc Bex
Mar 95	0 .07	0 .00	17 ,268	3 ,906
Dec 94	0 .05	0 .00	22 ,437	5 ,521
Sep 94	0 .06	0 .00	25 ,613	6 ,779
Jun 94	0 .09	0 .00	32 ,944	6 ,158
Mar 94	0 .17	0 .00	25 ,189	5 ,852
Dec 93	0 .13	0 .00	34 ,481	10 ,375
Sep 93	0 .06	0 .00	25 ,341	6 ,529
Jun 93	0 .06	0 .00	27 ,930	4 ,471

	Dec94	Dec93	Dec92
Preferred Div. Coverage	2 .6	2 .9	4 .2
Total Div. Coverage	2 .6	2 .9	4 .2
Income prop.(% tot. prop.)	19 .7	13 .6	13 .5
Develop. prop.(% tot. prop.)	80 .3	86 .4	86 .5
5 YEAR RATIOS (%)			
Return on Capital	12 .9	12 .7	12 .3
Return on Com. Equity	25 .8	27 .6	26 .4
Profit Growth	3 .3	18 .8	55 .7
Revenue Growth	(5 .7)	16 .2	33 .6
Asset Growth	(6 .9)	5 .6	24 .0
BALANCE SHEET (000)			
Cash	80 ,602	10 ,167	14 ,991
Total Real Estate Assets	188 ,487	156 ,447	143 ,948
Invest's & Advances	79 ,646	135 ,277	82 ,026
Total Assets	350 ,040	307 ,846	301 ,130
Bank Indebtedness	0	0	0
Long Term Debt	31 ,907	24 ,539	14 ,156
Total Liabilities	88 ,360	60 ,970	71 ,996
Total Equity	261 ,680	246 ,876	229 ,134
Total Liab. & Equity	350 ,040	307 ,846	301 ,130
CAPITAL (000)			
Total Debt	31 ,907	24 ,539	14 ,156
Preferred Equity	118 ,575	118 ,575	118 ,575
Common Equity	143 ,105	128 ,301	110 ,559

Business:

CONSOLIDATED CARMA CORP. is a Western Canadian public real estate company active in the development of master-planned residential communities. Carma also builds homes for sale and develops commercial lands and income properties for investment and sale. Carma maintains offices in Calgary, Edmonton, Regina, Winnipeg, and Fort Lauderdale.

Synopsis:

In April 1995, Consolidated Carma Corp. completed the purchase of all of its Class AAA Participating Non-Voting Series 1 Shares and Class AAA Participating Non-Voting Series 2 Shares. The company said Carena Developments Ltd. of Toronto owns 99% of the series 1 shares, 40% of the series 2 shares and 10.4 million common shares. Coscan Development Corp. owns 59% of the series 2 shares. Both Carena and Coscan have agreed to exercise an option that includes both cash and common shares in exchange for their class AAA shares. This will result in Carena receiving about $92-million in cash and 18.2 million common shares, and Coscan $26-million and 3.7 million shares. Upon completion of the offer, Carena's stake in the common shares of Carma would increase to about 67% from 50%, while Coscan would hold about 9%. As part of the offer, Carena would lend Carma $75-million under a revolving term credit facility. Carma said the acquisition of the Class AAA will provide it with a more efficient long-term financing structure. Its shareholders' equity would be comprised of only common shares. This should improve the return to all shareholders.

During 1995, Carma will launch two new communities in Calgary, Tuscany and McKenzie Towne. These communities, of which the company owns 950 acres and 1,500 acres respectively, are Carma's first new major master-planned communities in Calgary since the early 1980s. The company is planning a 400-acre master-planned community in Edmonton called Terwillegar Towne. Carma hopes to receive municipal approval for this project later in 1995.

In 1994, sales were down from 1993 in all segments in which Carma operates due to a combination of declining overall residential markets and increased competition. During 1994, Carma sold 1,300 lots compared with 11,476 in 1993. Revenue from lot sales declined $5-million from 1993. Housing sales during 1994 totalled 260 units with revenues of $34.4-million, compared with sales of 270 units and revenues of $35.7-million in 1993. Sales of land parcels totalled 16 acres and produced revenues of $2.1-million, a drop of $1.8-million from 1993.

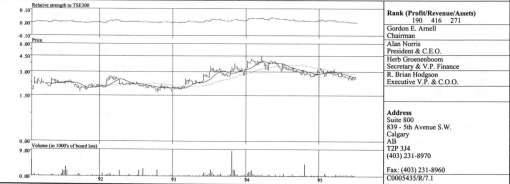

Rank (Profit/Revenue/Assets)
190   416   271
Gordon E. Arnell Chairman
Alan Norris President & C.E.O.
Herb Groenenboom Secretary & V.P. Finance
R. Brian Hodgson Executive V.P. & C.O.O.

Address
Suite 800
839 - 5th Avenue S.W.
Calgary
AB
T2P 3J4
(403) 231-8970

Fax: (403) 231-8960
C0005435/R/7.1

CONSOLIDATED HCI HOLDINGS CORPORATION

Exchanges	Price (Jun29'95)	0.68	Trailing P/E	13.60	Stock Symbol
T	Trailing Yield (%)	0.00	Trailing EPS	0.05	**CXA.A**

Period Ending	Sep94	Sep93	Sep92	Sep91	Sep90
Yearly Statistics					
Price-Close	1.34	0.85	0.86	3.80	7.00
Price-High	2.25	1.15	4.00	8.50	13.50
Price-Low	0.40	0.50	0.55	3.80	7.00
P/E-Close	16.75	nm	nm	nm	nm
Dividends per Share	0.00	0.00	0.00	0.00	0.00
Dividend Yield (%)	0.00	0.00	0.00	0.00	0.00
Sales per Share	3.52	1.35	1.86	4.31	3.68
EPS before extra. item	0.08	(0.10)	(0.95)	(1.82)	(1.35)
Cash Flow per Share	0.22	(0.02)	0.04	0.09	(0.83)
Book Value per Share	2.31	2.23	2.33	3.27	4.89
O/S Common Shares	19,368	19,368	19,368	19,368	16,766
Total Revenue	70,237	27,563	38,101	83,095	64,033
Income before extra.	1,482	(1,852)	(18,385)	(34,079)	(22,599)
Cash Flow	4,256	(446)	725	1,618	(13,970)
Debt/Equity	4.47	4.47	4.05	2.85	3.33
Return on Capital (%)	5.40	1.96	(9.62)	(16.85)	(7.81)
Ret. on Com. Equity (%)	3.37	(4.20)	(33.91)	(46.86)	(24.21)
% Change Profit	180.0	89.9	46.1	(50.8)	(251.2)
% Change Revenue	154.8	(27.7)	(54.1)	29.8	(34.1)
% Change Assets	4.8	(0.8)	(4.5)	(31.5)	0.0

Preferred Div. Coverage	np	np	np
Total Div. Coverage	na	na	na
Income prop.(% tot. prop.)	30.4	28.3	29.4
Develop. prop.(% tot. prop.)	69.6	71.7	70.6
5 YEAR RATIOS (%)			
Return on Capital	(5.4)	(4.2)	(1.0)
Return on Com. Equity	(21.2)	(18.8)	(12.7)
Profit Growth	(37.0)	na	na
Revenue Growth	(6.3)	(24.5)	(16.6)
Asset Growth	(7.4)	(5.3)	(2.5)
BALANCE SHEET (000)			
Cash	6,250	9,422	8,084
Total Real Estate Assets	234,475	246,166	237,179
Invest's & Advances	1,127	1,317	1,654
Total Assets	289,716	276,491	278,625
Bank Indebtedness	76,009	64,983	69,352
Long Term Debt	123,413	127,903	113,140
Total Liabilities	245,055	233,312	233,594
Total Equity	44,661	43,179	45,031
Total Liab. & Equity	289,716	276,491	278,625
CAPITAL (000)			
Total Debt	199,422	192,886	182,492
Preferred Equity	0	0	0
Common Equity	44,661	43,179	45,031

Business:

CONSOLIDATED HCI HOLDINGS CORP. is a real estate company based in Ontario. The company develops residential, industrial and commercial land in the Greater Toronto Area. In addition it both builds and leases industrial and commercial properties. Through various joint ventures, Cosolidated HCI is involved in housing sales. The company maintains significant land holdings in the Toronto area.

Date	EPS	DPS	Tot Rev	Inc Bex
Mar 95	(0.01)	0.00	6,074	(112)
Dec 94	0.06	0.00	21,068	1,155
Sep 94	0.02	0.00	26,110	291
Jun 94	(0.02)	0.00	7,335	(358)
Mar 94	0.10	0.00	28,278	1,884
Dec 93	(0.02)	0.00	8,514	(335)
Sep 93	(0.11)	0.00	8,689	(2,141)
Jun 93	(0.02)	0.00	6,829	(337)

Synopsis:

During the first quarter of 1995, Consolidated HCL obtained land in Mississauga. The land was in settlement of a claim arising from the default of a note receivable. The company also received back the original underlying security for the note. This settlement resulted in after tax income of $ 1,215,000 or six cents per share.

In fiscal 1994, HCI's total revenues increased to $70.2-million or 154% from a year earlier. The largest component of this increase relates to the sale of land. The revenue is comprised of specific projects as the marketplace dictates and buyers become available. During the year the company sold the first phase of 193 lots of the subdivision in Markham, 167 street townhouse lots and land for 108 condominium townhouse units in Woodbridge, and 21 lots in a small subdivision in Kleinburg.

The portion of revenue recorded as real estate land sales was $42.8-million for 1994 compared to $2.9-million for 1993. The revenue from housing sales as recorded by its joint ventures increased to $15.2-million for 1994 from the previous year's $13.8- million.

Rental revenue showed an increase for the year of $0.5-million over the two previous years which reflected a combination of lower vacancy rates, a variation in renewal rates, and the addition of two properties during the year. Interest and other income showed an increase of $0.7-million. This included the $1.1-million of deemed interest on sales.

Income-producing properties increased in 1994 by $2.4-million (15,000 square feet) with the completion of a Saturn dealership and a Dairy Queen outlet in Woodbridge, Ontario. At September 30, 1994, the company's portfolio of wholly owned income producing properties was comprised of 1.5 million square feet of industrial space and 97,000 square feet of office space. Vacancy rates by segment at September 30, 1994, were: industrial, 4.2%; office, 68%; and commercial, 7.8%.

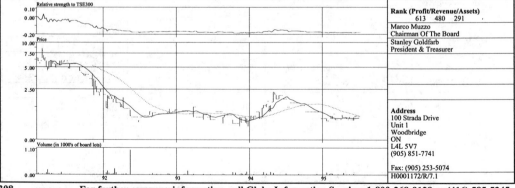

Rank (Profit/Revenue/Assets)
613   480   291

Marco Muzzo
Chairman Of The Board

Stanley Goldfarb
President & Treasurer

Address
100 Strada Drive
Unit 1
Woodbridge
ON
L4L 5V7
(905) 851-7741

Fax: (905) 253-5074
H0001172/R/7.1

COSCAN DEVELOPMENT CORPORATION

Period Ending	Dec94	Dec93	Dec92	Dec91	Dec90
Yearly Statistics					
Price-Close	1.20	2.80	1.50	8.50	5.00
Price-High	3.00	3.60	9.00	9.38	12.25
Price-Low	1.00	0.45	1.40	4.75	5.00
P/E-Close	nm	nm	nm	13.93	4.43
Dividends per Share	0.00	0.00	0.00	0.30	0.30
Dividend Yield (%)	0.00	0.00	0.00	3.53	6.00
Sales per Share	14.45	14.12	10.81	15.59	18.62
EPS before extra. item	(0.52)	(4.74)	(4.78)	0.61	1.13
Cash Flow per Share	(0.18)	(0.91)	(2.53)	13.96	16.46
Book Value per Share	2.47	3.64	8.12	12.11	13.69
O/S Common Shares	77,300	19,746	19,740	20,449	14,772
Total Revenue	350,645	308,046	249,455	319,097	331,017
Income before extra.	(1,976)	(85,089)	(94,747)	15,038	22,813
Cash Flow	(3,969)	(17,956)	(49,978)	240,335	243,160
Debt/Equity	3.72	4.59	3.04	2.85	3.49
Return on Capital (%)	2.11	(5.18)	(10.89)	5.27	7.86
Ret. on Com. Equity (%)	(8.82)	(80.60)	(48.07)	4.66	8.51
% Change Profit	97.7	10.2	(730.1)	(34.1)	(17.1)
% Change Revenue	13.8	23.5	(21.8)	(3.6)	(19.9)
% Change Assets	35.0	(2.9)	(3.4)	(0.1)	5.7

Preferred Div. Coverage	0.0	0.0	0.0
Total Div. Coverage	0.0	0.0	0.0
Income prop.(% tot. prop.)	19.4	30.6	32.2
Develop. prop.(% tot. prop.)	80.6	69.4	67.8
5 YEAR RATIOS (%)			
Return on Capital	(0.2)	1.6	4.5
Return on Com. Equity	(24.9)	(20.6)	(2.3)
Profit Growth	na	na	na
Revenue Growth	(3.3)	(8.0)	(6.2)
Asset Growth	6.0	8.2	9.7
BALANCE SHEET (000)			
Cash	1,946	975	
Total Real Estate Assets	1,447,088	806,653	681,403
Invest's & Advances	58,045	98,812	432,532
Total Assets	1,607,286	1,190,416	1,226,109
Bank Indebtedness	9,639	75,366	219,047
Long Term Debt	1,185,253	853,074	663,752
Total Liabilities	1,286,085	987,966	935,337
Total Equity	321,201	202,450	290,772
Total Liab. & Equity	1,607,286	1,190,416	1,226,109
CAPITAL (000)			
Total Debt	1,194,892	928,440	882,799
Preferred Equity	130,558	130,558	130,574
Common Equity	190,643	71,892	160,198

Business:

COSCAN DEVELOPMENT CORP. is a real estate development company that operates in major market areas in North America. The Company develops land for sale and builds and markets single family, multiple and condominium housing units and acquires and manages commercial properties.

Date	EPS	DPS	Tot Rev	Inc Bex
Mar 95	(0.08)	0.00	63,961	(3,981)
Dec 94	(0.28)	0.00	95,518	(4,299)
Sep 94	(0.16)	0.00	94,901	(737)
Jun 94	(0.07)	0.00	95,681	575
Mar 94	0.01	0.00	64,545	2,485
Dec 93	(4.61)	0.00	32,268	(88,695)
Sep 93	(0.06)	0.00	101,494	1,234
Jun 93	(0.05)	0.00	100,213	1,330

Synopsis:

In May 1995, Coscan Development Corp. outlined an ambitious strategy to improve its debt-laden balance sheet and nearly triple its housing operations over the next few years. William Pringle, President and C.E.O., said the company will build about 1,200 homes across North America this year, unchanged from 1994. However, he expects that total to climb to 2,000 in 1996 and 3,000 by 1998. Sales of lots are running at forecast levels. So far this year, 283 house sales have closed with a further 481 sold for closing later in the year.

Mr. Pringle said Coscan finished 1994 with a debt-to-equity ratio of four-to-one, a level considered too high. By developing and selling land, and selling non-core assets, Coscan expects to reduce debt by $500-million over the next few years so that at current equity levels, its debt-to-equity ratio would fall to 2.5-to-one.

Coscan also plans to improve the productivity of its housing assets. Last year, housing generated sales of $247-million against assets of $224-million, indicating that assets turn over 1.1 times a year. Coscan's goal is to turn its housing assets twice per year and increase volume to 3,000 houses per year. Instead of buying undeveloped land as it did in the past, Coscan now will focus on buying finished or nearly finished lots for its housing program.

In April 1995, Coscan redeemed its holding on Consolidated Carma's series 2 class AAA participating non-voting shares. Coscan was paid $30 in cash and 4.29 common shares of Carma, for each series 2 share. Coscan owned about 59% of the series 2 shares. The transaction saw Coscan receive about $26-million and 3.7 million common shares of Carma.

Rank (Profit/Revenue/Assets)
853   233   124

L. Ross Cullingworth
Chairman
W.J. (Bill) Pringle
President & C.E.O.
John P. Barratt
Exec. V.P. & C.O.O.
Robert Visentin
Sr. V.P. & C.F.O.

Address
BCE Place - Suite 4200
181 Bay Street
P.O. Box 763
Toronto
ON
M5J 2T3
(416) 369-8200
Fax: (416) 369-0973
C0011223/R/7.1

INTRAWEST CORPORATION

Exchanges	Price (Jun29'95)	11.75	Trailing P/E	19.91	Stock Symbol
TMV	Trailing Yield (%)	1.36	Trailing EPS	0.59	**ITW**

Period Ending	Sep94	Sep93	Sep92	Sep91	Sep90	Business:
Yearly Statistics						INTRAWEST CORPORATION operates in
Price-Close	13.25	12.50	10.88	10.50	6.38	two businesses: resorts and real estate. The
Price-High	19.00	12.75	9.50	12.00	10.00	company owns and operates ski resorts at
Price-Low	12.00	8.75	11.50	6.00	6.38	Blackcomb in Whistler, B.C., Panoramam,
P/E-Close	18.93	16.67	10.56	nm	9.24	B.C., Mont Tremblant in Quebec, and Stratto n
Dividends per Share	0.16	0.16	0.16	0.16	0.00	Mountain Resort in Vermont. The company is
Dividend Yield (%)	1.21	1.28	1.47	1.52	0.00	also developing the real estate at Keystone
Sales per Share	11.70	4.63	2.46	2.31	7.02	Resort in Colorado in partnership with its
EPS before extra. item	0.70	0.75	1.03	(0.20)	0.69	owner.
Cash Flow per Share	1.37	1.26	0.91	0.67	1.89	
Book Value per Share	11.63	10.66	10.00	9.00	9.34	
O/S Common Shares	22,827	20,316	20,016	17,281	14,111	
Total Revenue	332,106	156,040	122,271	76,915	118,992	
Income before extra.	15,055	15,178	19,631	(3,186)	8,504	

Date	EPS	DPS	Tot Rev	Inc Bex
Mar 95	0.61	0.08	149,700	14,000
Dec 94	0.09	0.00	58,500	2,000
Sep 94	(0.10)	0.00	49,141	(1,714)
Jun 94	(0.01)	0.00	146,144	35
Mar 94	0.62	0.08	84,859	12,715
Dec 93	0.19	0.00	51,962	4,019
Sep 93	0.25	0.08	13,372	5,231
Jun 93	0.11	0.00	40,020	2,054

Cash Flow	29,427	25,400	17,405	10,561	23,310
Debt/Equity	1.13	1.60	1.27	1.41	1.27
Return on Capital (%)	5.47	4.42	6.95	0.86	6.33
Ret. on Com. Equity (%)	6.25	7.29	11.04	(2.22)	7.66
% Change Profit	(0.8)	(22.7)	716.2	(137.5)	(29.8)
% Change Revenue	112.8	27.6	59.0	(35.4)	87.2
% Change Assets	2.3	22.5	21.2	21.6	27.1

Preferred Div. Coverage	np	np	np
Total Div. Coverage	4.3	4.7	6.6
Income prop.(% tot. prop.)	24.1	21.9	26.2
Develop. prop.(% tot. prop.)	75.9	78.1	73.8
5 YEAR RATIOS (%)			
Return on Capital	4.8	5.7	na
Return on Com. Equity	6.0	7.6	na
Profit Growth	4.4	18.4	na
Revenue Growth	39.2	25.8	na
Asset Growth	18.5	23.8	na
BALANCE SHEET (000)			
Cash	37,596	37,349	43,240
Total Real Estate Assets	325,037	371,726	304,775
Invest's & Advances	1,790	2,125	26,678
Total Assets	629,002	614,692	501,618
Bank Indebtedness	0	0	254,714
Long Term Debt	300,629	346,316	0
Total Liabilities	363,463	398,212	301,505
Total Equity	265,539	216,480	200,113
Total Liab. & Equity	629,002	614,692	501,618
CAPITAL (000)			
Total Debt	300,629	346,316	254,714
Preferred Equity	0	0	0
Common Equity	265,539	216,480	200,113

Synopsis:

Intrawest Corporation's revenue for the first six months ended March 31, 1995, was $149.7-million compared with $118.6-million in 1994. Ski and resort operations revenue climbed to $88.2-million from $58.6-million, a 50% increase. Record results at Blackcomb and Panorama contributed to this increase as well as revenue from the new Stratton operation. Revenue from resort real estate sales jumped from $19.1-million to $28.2-million. Sales during the second quarter principally comprised units of The Aspens at Blackcomb, Le Chalumeau at Mont Tremblant, and the sale of ownership points at The Resort Club at Blackcomb.

Skier visits were approximately 14% higher than the previous year due mainly to an earlier than normal opening at Blackcomb. In keeping with Intrawest's growth strategy in the ski business, the company is investing $26-million this summer across its resorts to further enhance the ski visitor experience.

Intrawest will invest $17-million to build a new luxury condominium hotel at Mont Tremblant. With construction scheduled to begin in May 1995, this new hotel will carry the name Residence Inn by Marriott. Demand for this type of resort accomodation has grown dramatically at Mont Tremblant. Previous Intrawest developments at Mont Tremblant include Le St-Bernard, completed in the winter of 1994, and the Le Johannsen and Le Deslauriers hotel condominiums that will be completed this summer.

In October 1994, Intrawest announced the acquisition of 100 percent of the shares of Stratton Mountain Resort in Vermont. Stratton Mountain Resort is a four-season resort consisting of the Stratton Mountain ski area and village, a 27-hole championship golf course, a 22-acre golf school, an extensive sports and tennis complex, and numerous other indoor and outdoor recreational facilities, together with about 1,500 acres of land. With the addition of Stratton Mountain, Intrawest expects to host over two million skier visits in the 1994-95 season.

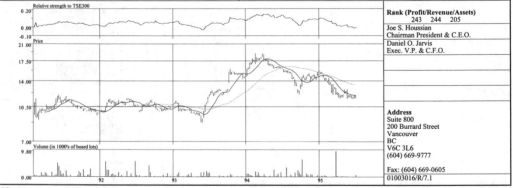

Rank (Profit/Revenue/Assets)
243   244   205

Joe S. Houssian
Chairman President & C.E.O.

Daniel O. Jarvis
Exec. V.P. & C.F.O.

Address
Suite 800
200 Burrard Street
Vancouver
BC
V6C 3L6
(604) 669-9777

Fax: (604) 669-0605
01003016/R/7.1

MARKBOROUGH PROPERTIES INC.

Exchanges	Price (Jun29'95)	1.94	Trailing P/E	48.50	Stock Symbol
TM	Trailing Yield (%)	0.00	Trailing EPS	0.04	MKP

Period Ending	Jan95	Jan94	Jan93	Jan92	Jan91
Yearly Statistics					
Price-Close	2.15	3.25	2.50	7.38	7.50
Price-High	3.65	4.00	8.00	10.50	9.75
Price-Low	1.90	2.40	2.25	6.13	5.75
P/E-Close	43.00	nm	nm	49.17	24.19
Dividends per Share	0.00	0.00	0.00	0.00	0.00
Dividend Yield (%)	0.00	0.00	0.00	0.00	0.00
Sales per Share	1.10	1.34	2.89	3.07	9.27
EPS before extra. item	0.05	(0.64)	(6.98)	0.15	0.31
Cash Flow per Share	0.13	0.15	0.79	0.82	4.37
Book Value per Share	1.98	1.84	2.04	8.38	8.43
O/S Common Shares	217,401	217,401	153,248	72,018	45,011
Total Revenue	259,163	240,324	220,435	209,139	260,852
Income before extra.	10,426	(112,504)	(507,522)	10,031	14,021
Cash Flow	28,677	25,774	57,337	54,424	120,679
Debt/Equity	3.39	3.48	4.84	2.52	4.67
Return on Capital (%)	5.73	(5.40)	(22.17)	3.77	4.92
Ret. on Com. Equity (%)	2.51	(31.57)	(110.86)	2.04	3.77
% Change Profit	109.3	77.8	(5,159.5)	(28.5)	(47.0)
% Change Revenue	7.8	9.0	5.4	(19.8)	(4.1)
% Change Assets	4.7	(11.7)	(14.3)	8.0	20.3

Business:

MARKBOROUGH PROPERTIES INC. is a real estate development company that carries on business primarily in Canada and also in the U.S. and the U.K. The company's principal business is the development, ownership and management of income producing properties. The company also develops land for sale for residential, retail, office and industrial uses.

Date	EPS	DPS	Tot Rev	Inc Bex
Apr 95	0.00	0.00	59,800	0
Jan 95	0.02	0.00	67,100	4,100
Oct 94	0.01	0.00	65,900	2,700
Jul 94	0.01	0.00	53,530	576
Apr 94	0.01	0.00	57,853	2,998
Jan 94	(0.11)	0.00	64,876	(23,904)
Oct 93	(0.56)	0.00	62,923	(92,775)
Jul 93	0.02	0.00	53,766	1,749

	Jan95	Jan94	Jan93
Preferred Div. Coverage	np	np	np
Total Div. Coverage	na	na	na
Income prop.(% tot. prop.)	54.8	57.7	54.5
Develop. prop.(% tot. prop.)	45.2	42.3	45.5
5 YEAR RATIOS (%)			
Return on Capital	(2.6)	(2.2)	0.4
Return on Com. Equity	(26.8)	(25.8)	(18.6)
Profit Growth	(17.0)	na	na
Revenue Growth	(1.0)	(1.5)	(2.9)
Asset Growth	0.5	3.6	7.4
BALANCE SHEET (000)			
Cash	0	0	0
Total Real Estate Assets	1,839,493	1,766,562	1,870,261
Invest's & Advances	0	0	0
Total Assets	1,964,382	1,876,330	2,125,251
Bank Indebtedness	0	115,386	178,501
Long Term Debt	1,458,129	1,276,661	1,332,709
Total Liabilities	1,533,615	1,475,751	1,813,147
Total Equity	430,767	400,579	312,104
Total Liab. & Equity	1,964,382	1,876,330	2,125,251
CAPITAL (000)			
Total Debt	1,458,129	1,392,047	1,511,210
Preferred Equity	0	0	0
Common Equity	430,767	400,579	312,104

Synopsis:

In 1994, Markborough Properties Inc. had a net income of $10,426,000, compared to a loss of $112,504,000 in 1993. Part of this improvement came from profit on the sale of some small income properties. Markborough sold substantial land parcels from its commercial property portfolio in 1994. The land sales in Ajax, Ontario, St. Albert, Alberta, and St. John's, Newfoundland raised a total of $11,686,000. Markborough sold its office buildings in Las Vegas, and its 50% interest in 273 Bay Street, a small 70 year old office building in Toronto. The company also sold Eastwood Square, a small shopping centre in Kitchener. As well during 1994, Markborough sold 14 industrial buildings in Greater Toronto and Arizona, totalling 654,000 square feet. Its 50% interest in the Calhoun Outlet Centre in Georgia was also sold. Markborough renovated its mall in St. Albert. Completed leases in effect at its renovated Chicago Wacker Drive office building increased from 63% to 87%.

In 1994, rental income increased by 6% to $112,630,000, while the vacancy rate remained at 2.8%. Sales productivity in company malls rose by 4.6%. Markborough's residential land operation in Calgary sold 189 lots in 1994, for an annual profit of $4,223,000.

During 1995, Markborough expects to start construction of retail facilities on shopping centre sites in both Ajax and Bowmanville, Ontario. Action is also being taken to exploit potential retail opportunities in several other locations.

In London, England, Markborough owns a one acre site in the City of London, on the Thames river. It plans future development of an office building with approximately 220,000 rentable square feet. The company said a number of potential tenants have expressed interest in the proposed building.

Relative strength to TSE300 / Price / Volume (in 1000's of board lots) chart, 1992–1995

Rank (Profit/Revenue/Assets)		
294	279	106

Kenneth R. Thomson
Chairman

Neil R. Wood
President & C.E.O.

John A. Brough
Sr. V.P. & C.F.O.

Address
1 Dundas Street West
Suite 2800
Toronto
ON
M5G 2J2
(416) 591-7660

Fax: (416) 591-8942
M0016728/R/7.1

MELCOR DEVELOPMENTS LTD.

Exchanges	Price (Jun29'95)	10.00	Trailing P/E	4.88	Stock Symbol
T	Trailing Yield (%)	3.00	Trailing EPS	2.05	**MRD**

Period Ending	Dec94	Dec93	Dec92	Dec91	Dec90
Yearly Statistics					
Price-Close	10.00	12.00	11.00	11.25	9.25
Price-High	12.50	14.00	11.50	12.75	10.50
Price-Low	9.25	10.00	9.75	9.00	7.88
P/E-Close	5.05	8.22	6.71	18.44	2.96
Dividends per Share	0.30	0.25	0.25	0.20	0.10
Dividend Yield (%)	3.00	2.08	2.27	1.78	1.08
Sales per Share	13.71	13.09	17.26	12.78	14.26
EPS before extra. item	1.98	1.46	1.64	0.61	3.13
Cash Flow per Share	1.37	2.86	3.65	1.94	2.38
Book Value per Share	19.73	18.25	16.76	14.68	14.38
O/S Common Shares	3,197	3,131	3,016	2,996	2,958
Total Revenue	48,763	43,340	55,226	42,091	57,413
Income before extra.	6,277	4,495	4,995	1,854	9,279
Cash Flow	4,352	8,741	10,977	5,823	7,043
Debt/Equity	0.47	0.58	0.81	0.87	1.02
Return on Capital (%)	13.63	11.16	12.80	7.64	18.09
Ret. on Com. Equity (%)	10.13	8.29	10.48	4.19	24.66
% Change Profit	39.6	(10.0)	169.4	(80.0)	0.4
% Change Revenue	12.5	(21.5)	31.2	(26.7)	(34.9)
% Change Assets	8.2	(6.5)	8.4	2.4	(21.9)
Preferred Div. Coverage	33.4	149.8	124.9		
Total Div. Coverage	5.5	5.5	6.3		
Income prop.(% tot. prop.)	15.8	17.6	22.1		
Develop. prop.(% tot. prop.)	84.2	82.4	77.9		
5 YEAR RATIOS (%)					
Return on Capital	12.7	13.0	12.5		
Return on Com. Equity	11.6	16.1	16.5		
Profit Growth	(7.5)	13.3	35.3		
Revenue Growth	(11.2)	(8.4)	(7.8)		
Asset Growth	(2.7)	(5.8)	(6.6)		
BALANCE SHEET (000)					
Cash	8,072	1,740	1,558		
Total Real Estate Assets	94,888	91,317	95,925		
Invest's & Advances	453	814	1,542		
Total Assets	123,356	114,057	121,979		
Bank Indebtedness	3,557	6,904	0		
Long Term Debt	26,464	26,704	42,417		
Total Liabilities	59,811	56,056	69,801		
Total Equity	63,545	58,001	52,178		
Total Liab. & Equity	123,356	114,057	121,979		
CAPITAL (000)					
Total Debt	30,021	33,608	42,417		
Preferred Equity	477	856	1,618		
Common Equity	63,068	57,145	50,560		

Business:

MELCOR DEVELOPMENTS LTD. is a real estate development company. It acquires land for the development and sale of residential and industrial subdivisions. It also builds and markets single-family housing and develops and acquires income-producing properties. Current activities are located in Alberta and Tucson, Arizona.

Date	EPS	DPS	Tot Rev	Inc Bex
Mar 95	0.12	0.00	5,644	395
Dec 94	1.55	0.15	22,017	4,910
Sep 94	0.16	0.00	7,629	501
Jun 94	0.22	0.15	9,540	701
Mar 94	0.05	0.00	6,088	165
Dec 93	0.81	0.15	14,922	2,479
Sep 93	0.26	0.00	9,067	824
Jun 93	0.33	0.10	10,951	1,021

Synopsis:

In fiscal 1994, Melcor's net earnings increased 39.6% over 1993. The increase in earnings is due to the sales of a 68,730 square foot commercial retail centre and part of a 50 acre commercial site in northwest Calgary. Earnings from land and housing were lower than the prior year due to competitive real estate markets in Alberta, especially in the Edmonton region.

In 1994, revenues from land operation grew by 4% primarily due to higher single family lot sales in Calgary and Red Deer and to expansion into Lethbridge, Alberta. Total lot sales increased by 20% during the period. Income from joint venture management fees were $92,000 in 1994 compared to $476,000 in 1993. The land sales, primarily commercial sites, were 22.9 acres ($2,566,000) compared to 25.2 acres ($2,997,000) in 1993. In 1994, Melcor developed 22 new residential subdivisions.

During fiscal 1994, the company developed two new condominium projects with 94 units under Melcor's 2/3 owned partnership, Melcor Homes. Three projects with 201 units are possible starts for 1995. To reduce the risk associated with residential construction, the Partnership limits its inventory of unsold units. Generally, Melcor Homes also does not start construction of condominium projects until it has refundable deposits and has obtained a project loan for the development.

During 1994, Melcor purchased a commercial property for $1,200,000 that was financed with a $900,000 mortgage. Vacancy rates in office buildings remain at a high level. Only a minimal reduction is projected in the short term.

In 1994, Melcor purchased 93 acres of land in Alberta and Arizona. The company bought 61 acres in Arbour Lake in northwest Calgary in 1995. All of these can be developed over the short term. In 1994, the company acquired a 66,600 square foot warehouse, and other investments are currently being considered.

Relative strength to TSE300

Price

Volume (in 1000's of board lots)

Rank (Profit/Revenue/Assets)
387 555 441

T.C. Melton
President

W.G. Holmes
V.P. Fin. & Sec.-Treasurer

Address
Suite 900
10310 Jasper Avenue
Edmonton
AB
T5J 1Y8
(403) 423-6931

Fax: (403) 426-1796

M0003182/R/7.1

For further company information, call Globe Information Services 1-800-268-9128 or (416) 585-5345

MONARCH DEVELOPMENT CORPORATION

Exchanges	Price (Jun29'95)		7 .50	Trailing P/E		16 .30	Stock Symbol
T	Trailing Yield (%)		1.07	Trailing EPS		0 .46	**MON**

Period Ending	Dec94	Dec93	Dec92	Dec91	Dec90
Yearly Statistics					
Price-Close	7 .00	5 .25	3 .50	3 .42	3 .22
Price-High	7 .25	5 .25	3 .67	4 .00	5 .35
Price-Low	5 .25	3 .29	3 .42	2 .75	3 .22
P/E-Close	16 .28	14 .58	10 .29	11 .14	9 .12
Dividends per Share	0 .07	0 .05	0 .05	0 .05	0 .04
Dividend Yield (%)	1 .00	0 .95	1 .52	1 .43	1 .10
Sales per Share	5 .54	4 .64	3 .47	3 .30	5 .01
EPS before extra. item	0 .43	0 .36	0 .34	0 .31	0 .35
Cash Flow per Share	0 .52	0 .44	0 .42	0 .37	0 .38
Book Value per Share	5 .16	4 .53	4 .18	3 .83	3 .57
O/S Common Shares	37 ,145	34 ,145	33 ,944	34 ,035	34 ,088
Total Revenue	202 ,234	158 ,628	118 ,713	113 ,356	171 ,563
Income before extra.	15 ,558	12 ,206	11 ,536	10 ,476	12 ,038
Cash Flow	18 ,805	14 ,960	14 ,175	12 ,721	12 ,906
Debt/Equity	0 .37	0 .45	0 .48	0 .56	0 .59
Return on Capital (%)	13 .81	12 .66	12 .35	12 .45	17 .08
Ret. on Com. Equity (%)	8 .98	8 .23	8 .47	8 .31	10 .31
% Change Profit	27 .5	5 .8	10 .1	(13 .0)	(29 .3)
% Change Revenue	27 .5	33 .6	4 .7	(33 .9)	(2 .6)
% Change Assets	20 .3	7 .5	1 .8	4 .4	2 .2

Preferred Div. Coverage	np	np	np	
Total Div. Coverage	5 .8	6 .7	6 .4	
Income prop.(% tot. prop.)	27 .7	31 .7	31 .5	
Develop. prop.(% tot. prop.)	72 .3	68 .3	68 .5	
5 YEAR RATIOS (%)				
Return on Capital	13 .7	15 .6	18 .3	
Return on Com. Equity	8 .9	10 .4	12 .5	
Profit Growth	(1 .8)	(6 .0)	1 .0	
Revenue Growth	2 .8	(1 .8)	(4 .3)	
Asset Growth	6 .9	7 .8	8 .6	
BALANCE SHEET (000)				
Cash	0	0	0	
Total Real Estate Assets	279 ,098	237 ,713	222 ,159	
Invest's & Advances	7 ,205	2 ,288	0	
Total Assets	299 ,710	249 ,037	231 ,614	
Bank Indebtedness	10 ,894	13 ,150	8 ,075	
Long Term Debt	60 ,472	56 ,690	59 ,898	
Total Liabilities	107 ,878	94 ,519	89 ,664	
Total Equity	191 ,832	154 ,518	141 ,950	
Total Liab. & Equity	299 ,710	249 ,037	231 ,614	
CAPITAL (000)				
Total Debt	71 ,366	69 ,840	67 ,973	
Preferred Equity	0	0	0	
Common Equity	191 ,832	154 ,518	141 ,950	

Business:

MONARCH DEVELOPMENT CORP. is engaged in land development, residential construction and investment in rental properties. The operations are currently being conducted in two main geographical areas, Canada and the United States.

Date	EPS	DPS	Tot Rev	Inc Bex
Mar 95	0 .09	0 .02	41 ,068	3 ,425
Dec 94	0 .13	0 .02	59 ,542	4 ,752
Sep 94	0 .14	0 .02	67 ,749	5 ,182
Jun 94	0 .10	0 .02	40 ,574	3 ,447
Mar 94	0 .06	0 .02	34 ,369	2 ,177
Dec 93	0 .11	0 .01	42 ,412	3 ,740
Sep 93	0 .11	0 .01	44 ,849	3 ,836
Jun 93	0 .09	0 .01	38 ,853	2 ,822

Synopsis:

In May 1995, Monarch Development said it is planning a $100-million expansion of its Eglinton Square Shopping Centre in Scarborough, Ontario, that would double the size of the mall. Construction should begin in 1997 and will be completed in 2000.

Monarch is negotiating with Trizec Corp. Ltd. to purchase about 100 acres of land in Meadowvale, Ontario, that Trizec received from bankrupt Bramalea Inc. earlier this year. Bramalea bought the land for about $35-million. The land is now worth about $60,000 an acre or $6-million. Monarch is in discussions with Bramalea's bankers on several properties.

In October 1994, Monarch acquired a 50% interest in a 799-lot golf course community in Naples, Florida, for $8.5-million (U.S.). This transaction was the company's second major golf course community purchase in Florida in two months. Monarch said the Naples development was acquired by a 50-50 partnership between itself and Taylor Woodrow Homes Florida Inc., an affiliated company.

In September 1994, Monarch Development purchased an interest in a 653-acre golf course community in the Boca Raton area of Florida for $20-million (U.S.). The company said the property consists of land with development approvals for up to 1,500 houses. The property is being acquired by a 50-50 partnership between Monarch, with an associated company, and a local land developer. Monarch has plans are to build an 18-hole golf course, a tennis centre, a clubhouse, and up to 1,500 houses. House prices will range between $150,000 and $1-million.

For fiscal 1994 (1993) revenues by segment were: real estate sales, $175,511,000 ($132,964,000); investment properties operations, $25,327,000 ($25,028,000); and interest and sundry, $1,396,000 ($636,000).

Relative strength to TSE300

Price

Volume (in 1000's of board lots)

Rank (Profit/Revenue/Assets)		
240	315	287

C.J. Parsons
Chairman

E.J. Latimer
President

B. Johnston
C.F.O.

Address
Heron's Hill
2025 Sheppard Ave East
Suite 1201
Willowdale
ON
M2J 1V7
(416) 491-7440
Fax: (416) 491-7216
M0004607/R/7.1

REVENUE PROPERTIES COMPANY LIMITED

Exchanges	Price (Jun29'95)	3.10	Trailing P/E	62.00	Stock Symbol
TQ	Trailing Yield (%)	3.55	Trailing EPS	0.05	**RPC**

Period Ending	Dec94	Dec93	Dec92	Dec91	Dec90
Yearly Statistics					
Price-Close	2.75	3.90	2.85	3.95	3.75
Price-High	4.30	4.20	4.00	4.55	6.38
Price-Low	2.50	2.25	2.50	3.50	3.25
P/E-Close	91.67	nm	nm	197.50	9.38
Dividends per Share	0.05	0.00	0.00	0.00	0.00
Dividend Yield (%)	1.82	0.00	0.00	0.00	0.00
Sales per Share	1.25	2.82	2.49	1.19	2.49
EPS before extra. item	0.03	(0.76)	(0.68)	0.02	0.40
Cash Flow per Share	0.14	0.01	(0.09)	0.10	0.41
Book Value per Share	1.72	2.09	1.44	1.64	1.67
O/S Common Shares	67,630	57,090	44,022	37,074	37,162
Total Revenue	89,825	139,674	105,860	46,499	103,104
Income before extra.	2,110	(37,212)	(28,860)	773	14,819
Cash Flow	9,391	490	(3,777)	3,670	15,095
Debt/Equity	3.67	3.06	6.23	1.93	1.66
Return on Capital (%)	6.48	(1.10)	(1.27)	6.50	23.35
Ret. on Com. Equity (%)	1.79	(40.73)	(46.51)	1.26	37.28
% Change Profit	105.7	(28.9)	(3,833.5)	(94.8)	267.9
% Change Revenue	(35.7)	31.9	127.7	(54.9)	276.5
% Change Assets	9.9	(4.4)	154.0	4.5	99.8

Date	EPS	DPS	Tot Rev	Inc Bex
Mar 95	0.02	0.06	23,245	1,183
Dec 94	0.00	0.00	22,574	(182)
Sep 94	0.01	0.00	21,672	707
Jun 94	0.02	0.05	27,189	1,196
Mar 94	0.01	0.00	19,992	389
Dec 93	(0.65)	0.00	70,056	(32,260)
Sep 93	(0.05)	0.00	21,584	(2,742)
Jun 93	(0.02)	0.00	20,391	(759)

Preferred Div. Coverage	np	np	na
Total Div. Coverage	0.6	na	na
Income prop.(% tot. prop.)	91.8	91.2	91.8
Develop. prop.(% tot. prop.)	8.2	8.8	8.2
5 YEAR RATIOS (%)			
Return on Capital	6.8	7.8	10.4
Return on Com. Equity	(9.4)	(4.6)	8.3
Profit Growth	(12.2)	na	na
Revenue Growth	26.8	35.1	22.1
Asset Growth	40.9	40.4	44.7
BALANCE SHEET (000)			
Cash	29,277	48,030	15,123
Total Real Estate Assets	482,400	431,364	490,610
Invest's & Advances	38,387	19,293	800
Total Assets	561,806	511,169	534,718
Bank Indebtedness	2,522	5,570	30,455
Long Term Debt	424,010	360,045	382,983
Total Liabilities	445,620	391,710	468,340
Total Equity	116,186	119,459	66,378
Total Liab. & Equity	561,806	511,169	534,718
CAPITAL (000)			
Total Debt	426,532	365,615	413,438
Preferred Equity	0	0	3,095
Common Equity	116,186	119,459	63,283

Business:

REVENUE PROPERTIES COMPANY LIMITED is involved in the acquisition, development and management of income producing properties. Properties are located in Toronto, ON, Grande Prairie, Alberta, Saint John, N.B., Washington, Oregon, California, Nevada, Florida, Tennessee, Kentucky, New Mexico and Connecticut.

Synopsis:

In June 1995 RPC Gaming Inc., a subsidiary of Revenue Properties Company Limited, agreed to provide loans to McGoo's, a casino, tavern, and restaurant chain in Las Vegas. This ended RPC's nearly year-long search for an entry into the gaming industry. RPC and McGoo's also plan to form a limited liability corporation as a joint venture to hold all of McGoo's properties, pending approval of RPC as a casino owner by Nevada's gaming commission. Revenue Properties is still looking at other potential casino acquisitions.

At its annual meeting, Revenue Properties said that wants to increase the current 4% return on about $95-million of low-yielding assets. The assets consist of land and development projects, cash, mortgages and accounts receivable. Revenue Properties is determined to raise the return on these funds to more than 12%, improving net profits and cash flow by $8-million or 12 cents per share.

In November 1995, a $51-million mortgage on the company's Centerpoint and East York Town Centre malls matures. Revenue Properties is negotiating to renew the mortgage at a lower interest rate. The company faces about $68-million in mortgages maturing next year.

During 1995, Revenue Properties will start construction of two community centres in Seattle, Washington, and Sacramento, California. Expansion of Centerpoint Mall in Toronto is on schedule. The mall will have approximately 11,000 square feet of additional retail space.

In 1994, rental income rose by 14% compared to 1993. This was due to four factors: higher occupancy rates; improved rental rates; additional rental properties; and favourable currency exchange rates. The company's total portfolio had an occupancy rate of 96.2% at 1994 year end, compared to 94.1% at December 31, 1993.

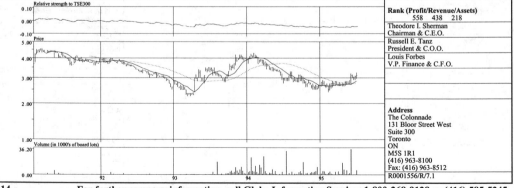

Rank (Profit/Revenue/Assets)		
558	438	218

Theodore I. Sherman
Chairman & C.E.O.

Russell E. Tanz
President & C.O.O.

Louis Forbes
V.P. Finance & C.F.O.

Address
The Colonnade
131 Bloor Street West
Suite 300
Toronto
ON
M5S 1R1
(416) 963-8100
Fax: (416) 963-8512
R0001556/R/7.1

ROYAL LEPAGE LIMITED

Exchanges	Price (Jun29'95)	2.60	Trailing P/E	nm	Stock Symbol
TMV	Trailing Yield (%)	0.00	Trailing EPS	(0.45)	RLG

Period Ending	Dec94	Dec93	Dec92	Dec91	Dec90
Yearly Statistics					
Price-Close	2.90	3.00	5.00	8.00	7.63
Price-High	4.95	5.88	10.50	10.13	12.13
Price-Low	2.75	2.20	4.25	6.75	6.00
P/E-Close	nm	nm	nm	160.00	nm
Dividends per Share	0.00	0.00	0.38	0.70	0.70
Dividend Yield (%)	0.00	0.00	7.50	8.75	9.18
Sales per Share	na	na	na	na	na
EPS before extra. item	(0.42)	(2.43)	(1.18)	0.05	(0.50)
Cash Flow per Share	(0.27)	(2.12)	(0.79)	0.97	(0.95)
Book Value per Share	1.41	1.81	3.99	5.43	6.71
O/S Common Shares	32,013	31,890	15,944	15,242	14,220
Total Revenue	390,527	392,978	480,274	498,963	466,877
Income before extra.	(12,931)	(38,847)	(16,275)	756	(6,988)
Cash Flow	(8,491)	(33,813)	(10,889)	14,638	(13,248)
Debt/Equity	0.84	0.27	1.76	2.11	2.30
Return on Capital (%)	(16.05)	(28.66)	(4.62)	4.21	1.72
Ret. on Com. Equity (%)	(25.15)	(64.02)	(22.23)	0.85	(6.88)
% Change Profit	66.7	(138.7)	(2,252.8)	110.8	(124.9)
% Change Revenue	(0.6)	(18.2)	(3.7)	6.9	(27.0)
% Change Assets	(3.4)	(37.0)	(27.2)	(13.9)	(30.6)

Preferred Div. Coverage	np	np	np
Total Div. Coverage	na	na	0.0
Income prop.(% tot. prop.)	na	na	na
Develop. prop.(% tot. prop.)	na	na	na
5 YEAR RATIOS (%)			
Return on Capital	(8.7)	(2.2)	7.8
Return on Com. Equity	(23.5)	(12.6)	7.3
Profit Growth	na	na	na
Revenue Growth	(9.4)	(9.7)	(3.4)
Asset Growth	(23.4)	(20.6)	(6.1)
BALANCE SHEET (000)			
Cash	0	0	0
Total Real Estate Assets	0	0	0
Invest's & Advances	33,780	33,781	110,091
Total Assets	146,066	151,176	240,067
Bank Indebtedness	30,425	8,320	108,529
Long Term Debt	7,385	7,425	3,294
Total Liabilities	100,939	93,459	176,433
Total Equity	45,127	57,717	63,634
Total Liab. & Equity	146,066	151,176	240,067
CAPITAL (000)			
Total Debt	37,810	15,745	111,823
Preferred Equity	0	0	0
Common Equity	45,127	57,717	63,634

Business:

ROYAL LEPAGE LIMITED is a diversified real estate services company. It has residential, commercial and professional services offices in Canada. International affiliates further augment the company's service network. Trilon Financial Corp. of Toronto is a major shareholder of the company.

Date	EPS	DPS	Tot Rev	Inc Bex
Mar 95	(0.40)	0.00	61,416	(12,372)
Dec 94	(0.36)	0.00	78,575	(11,194)
Sep 94	(0.10)	0.00	88,733	(2,833)
Jun 94	0.05	0.00	121,945	1,447
Mar 94	(0.01)	0.00	101,274	(351)
Dec 93	(0.11)	0.00	85,867	(4,962)
Sep 93	(1.43)	0.00	100,137	(20,921)
Jun 93	(0.33)	0.00	119,004	(4,813)

Synopsis:

During the first quarter in 1995, Royal LePage was hard-hit by the steep decline in residential sales activity. Royal LePage said it will continue to cut costs to survive in these lower market conditions. In 1994, the company cut its overhead expenses by $11-million to $20.2-million, or about half the level of 1992, as it weeded out 1,500 underperforming sales agents.

On the other hand, in 1994, the company recruited 1,200 new sales agents, together with two acquisitions which added 500 sales representatives, bringing its residential sales force to 5,203. Last year, the company revamped its operating structure so that agents keep a higher proportion of gross commissions but pay a larger share of overhead expenses. The move was aimed at reversing its sliding market share. In September 1994, Royal LePage acquired two residential brokerages, Johnston & Daniel and Alec Murray Real Estate. The merge boosted its market share to 17% in Metropolitan Toronto, and gave it a dominant position in the Muskoka vacation area.

Commercial brokerage and professional services areas showed strong performance in 1994. The Commercial Division increased its contribution to consolidated net incomes by almost 50%. Revenue in 1994 exceeded that in 1993 by more than 13% with gains recorded in most markets. In alliance with Johnson Controls World Services of Florida, Royal LePage secured a five-year $160-million contract to manage Canada Post facilities across the country. With Cushman and Wakefield of New York, Royal LePage signed agreements with AT&T, Westinghouse and Wang/Bull to serve the Canadian real estate holdings of these firms.

In 1995, the company will speed the decentralization of critical sales support functions. As part of decentralization, branch managers have become more fully accountable for cost containment and sales agent recruitment and retention. The company has implemented new training initiatives to enhance the skills of managers to support the development of their agents.

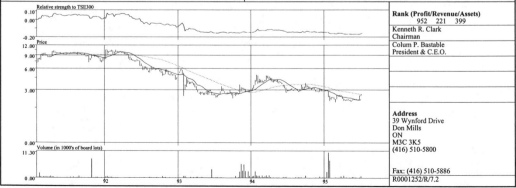

Rank (Profit/Revenue/Assets)	952 221 399
Kenneth R. Clark	Chairman
Colum P. Bastable	President & C.E.O.

Address
39 Wynford Drive
Don Mills
ON
M3C 3K5
(416) 510-5800

Fax: (416) 510-5886
R0001252/R/7.2

TRIZEC CORPORATION LTD.

Exchanges	Price (Jun29'95)	10.00	Trailing P/E	27.03	Stock Symbol
TM	Trailing Yield (%)	0.00	Trailing EPS	0.27	TZC.A

Period Ending	Dec94	Ju l94	Oc t93	Oc t92	Oc t91
Yearly Statistics	US /5M	US /9M			
Price-Close	9.50	0.17	0.88	3.00	12.13
Price-High	11.50	1.30	3.05	13.38	17.25
Price-Low	9.00	0.17	0.69	2.90	10.00
P/E-Close	17.15	nm	nm	nm	73.49
Dividends per Share	0.00	0.00	0.05	0.30	0.36
Dividend Yield (%)	0.00	0.00	5.68	10.00	2.97
Sales per Share	5.49	2.84	4.86	5.23	11.56
EPS before extra. item	0.17	(0.12)	(1.57)	(3.28)	0.17
Cash Flow per Share	0.84	0.15	0.32	0.84	1.49
Book Value per Share	9.42	9.37	0.79	2.36	5.42
O/S Common Shares	108,357	100,000	214,039	214,039	152,928
Total Revenue	242,900	468,200	1,091,700	925,500	1,761,600
Income before extra.	17,400	(14,300)	(312,100)	(544,100)	62,100
Cash Flow	36,300	23,800	67,500	146,800	222,000
Debt/Equity	2.25	2.51	7.91	5.43	7.34
Return on Capital (%)	8.45	6.77	0.91	(6.78)	4.79
Ret. on Com. Equity (%)	4.27	(5.76)	(98.11)	(85.71)	2.98
% Change Profit	319.0	91.7	42.6	(976.2)	25.7
% Change Revenue	(6.6)	(22.1)	18.0	(47.5)	(3.7)
% Change Assets	0.9	(16.3)	(10.3)	(46.1)	4.0

Preferred Div. Coverage	np	np	0.0
Total Div. Coverage	na	na	0.0
Income prop.(% tot. prop.)	95.5	95.4	91.9
Develop. prop.(% tot. prop.)	4.5	4.6	8.1
5 YEAR RATIOS (%)			
Return on Capital	2.8	2.2	2.2
Return on Com. Equity	(36.5)	(37.2)	(34.1)
Profit Growth	2.9	na	na
Revenue Growth	(15.4)	(15.3)	(1.8)
Asset Growth	(15.8)	(13.9)	(7.8)
BALANCE SHEET (000)			
Cash	69,600	19,400	0
Total Real Estate Assets	3,279,700	3,240,800	4,894,900
Invest's & Advances	0	0	180,200
Total Assets	3,510,400	3,479,600	5,748,400
Bank Indebtedness	0	0	0
Long Term Debt	2,294,500	2,351,900	4,812,700
Total Liabilities	2,489,200	2,543,100	5,140,000
Total Equity	1,021,200	936,500	608,400
Total Liab. & Equity	3,510,400	3,479,600	5,748,400
CAPITAL (000)			
Total Debt	2,294,500	2,351,900	4,812,700
Preferred Equity	0	0	440,300
Common Equity	1,021,200	936,500	168,100

Business:

TRIZEC CORP. LTD. is a North American real estate development company. Through wholly-owned subsidiaries in Canada and the United States, Trizec has interests in 85 income properties, principally office buildings and regional shopping centres. Trizec's properties contain approximate 54 million square feet of commercial space, of which 77% is in the United States and 23% in Canada.

Date		EPS	DPS	Tot Rev	Inc Bex
Mar 95	US	0.09	0.00	131,000	10,100
Dec 94	US	0.06	0.00	136,800	6,700
Sep 94	US	0.11	0.00	100,100	10,700
Jul 94		0.01	0.00	225,400	7,900
Apr 94		(0.10)	0.00	199,900	(15,000)
Jan 94		(0.09)	0.00	209,500	(13,400)
Oct 93		(1.43)	0.00	274,600	(299,400)
Jul 93		(0.11)	0.00	261,700	(17,700)

Synopsis:

During its May 1995 annual meeting, Trizec said it has raised about $250-million (U.S.) in new capital so far this year to finance its construction projects. Not all of that financing is on the balance sheet because it relates to projects that are coming on stream. Trizec raised $132-million for Park Meadows. The $160-million, 1.5 million square foot mall is scheduled to open in late 1996. The company also has raised $27-million for its Oakridge Mall in San Jose, California, and $26-million for the University Place Town Centre mall in San Diego. Trizec also received a $66-million loan from TD Bank in the second quarter 1995.

Trizec sold three office buildings, one mid-market mall, and certain financial assets for proceeds totaling more than $60-million as part of its strategy to sell $400-million of non-strategic assets over the next two to three years. The proceeds from these sales will be used to retire debt as it comes due and for new acquisitions of individual properties and real estate portfolios.

In January 1995, Primaris Corporate Services Ltd., an equal partnership between Trizec and Trammell Crow Corporate Services in Dallas, began operations. Trizec said the market for the new company's service is significant, and will include more than 200 of Canada's largest companies whose real estate activities aren't part of its core business. In May 1995, Trizec said Primaris will take over the facility management responsibilities of Triax Infrastructure Management Corp., a unit of Toronto-based Ainsworth Electric Co. Primaris is responsible for all Triax accounts, including the IBM Canada Ltd. portfolio, which consists of about 2.5 million square feet.

Trizec has assets of $3.5-billion, including a portfolio of 78 office buildings and shopping malls totaling 52 million square feet across North America. The company emerged from bankruptcy court protection in July 1994, after Horsham Corp. of Toronto and Argo Partnership LP of New York injected $750-million of new equity into Trizec.

Relative strength to TSE300

Price

Volume (in 1000's of board lots)

Rank (Profit/Revenue/Assets)
105 138 43

Peter Munk
Chairman

Willard J. L'Heureux
President & C.E.O.

Gregory W. Sullivan
Exec. V.P. & C.F.O.

Address
181 Bay Street
Suite 3900
P.O. Box 800
Toronto
ON
M5J 2T3
(416) 361-7200
Fax: (416) 361-7205
T0003152/R/7.2

WALL FINANCIAL CORPORATION

Exchanges	Price (Jun29'95)	2.40	Trailing P/E	48.00	Stock Symbol
TV	Trailing Yield (%)	0.00	Trailing EPS	0.05	WFC

Period Ending	Jan95	Jan94	Jan93	Jan92	Jan91
Yearly Statistics					
Price-Close	3.10	3.95	2.25	1.80	2.00
Price-High	3.85	8.25	2.40	2.90	2.75
Price-Low	2.05	3.80	1.57	1.65	1.30
P/E-Close	103.33	26.33	22.50	16.36	14.29
Dividends per Share	0.17	0.00	0.00	0.11	0.00
Dividend Yield (%)	5.48	0.00	0.00	6.11	0.00
Sales per Share	1.50	1.67	1.15	0.89	0.75
EPS before extra. item	0.03	0.15	0.10	0.11	0.14
Cash Flow per Share	0.05	0.24	0.14	0.13	0.03
Book Value per Share	0.63	0.76	0.62	0.54	0.52
O/S Common Shares	33,996	34,011	33,561	33,457	33,047
Total Revenue	53,649	57,816	41,137	29,783	28,401
Income before extra.	1,145	5,035	3,470	3,555	4,767
Cash Flow	1,859	8,070	4,783	4,266	999
Debt/Equity	7.20	3.75	3.84	3.11	4.30
Return on Capital (%)	7.90	13.43	15.13	14.57	15.61
Ret. on Com. Equity (%)	4.85	21.71	17.93	20.13	31.98
% Change Profit	(77.3)	45.1	(2.4)	(25.4)	(19.2)
% Change Revenue	(7.2)	40.5	38.1	4.9	(22.9)
% Change Assets	40.1	25.7	29.5	(15.1)	9.8

Preferred Div. Coverage	np	np	np	
Total Div. Coverage	0.2	na	na	
Income prop.(% tot. prop.)	86.7	30.6	41.8	
Develop. prop.(% tot. prop.)	13.3	69.4	58.2	
5 YEAR RATIOS (%)				
Return on Capital	13.3	16.4	16.7	
Return on Com. Equity	19.3	30.7	36.1	
Profit Growth	(28.0)	14.1	34.1	
Revenue Growth	7.8	18.2	11.6	
Asset Growth	16.2	6.6	4.9	
BALANCE SHEET (000)				
Cash	0	0	0	
Total Real Estate Assets	161,316	133,699	99,713	
Invest's & Advances	26,836	3,200	10,710	
Total Assets	203,821	145,490	115,763	
Bank Indebtedness	60,032	66,714	45,268	
Long Term Debt	94,667	29,601	34,033	
Total Liabilities	182,337	119,774	95,083	
Total Equity	21,483	25,716	20,680	
Total Liab. & Equity	203,821	145,490	115,763	
CAPITAL (000)				
Total Debt	154,699	96,315	79,301	
Preferred Equity	0	0	0	
Common Equity	21,483	25,716	20,680	

Business:

WALL FINANCIAL CORPORATION is involved in real estate development, investment in revenue producing properties and real estate sales.

Date	EPS	DPS	Tot Rev	Inc Bex
Apr 95	0.02	0.00	14,432	621
Jan 95	(0.03)	0.00	13,275	(955)
Oct 94	0.04	0.00	15,258	1,235
Jul 94	0.02	0.00	13,395	624
Apr 94	0.03	0.00	11,834	834
Jan 94	0.05	0.00	15,778	2,821
Oct 93	0.04	0.00	22,022	2,982
Jul 93	0.03	0.00	10,847	872

Synopsis:

In the fiscal 1995, Wall Financial completed the successful placement of $65,000,000 worth of new fixed term mortgage financing at an average rate of about 8%. The company opened the Suite & Wall Centre. This 216 unit residential property opened in March 1994, and enjoys a 99% occupancy rate. The 391 room Wall Centre Garden Hotel opened in August 1994. This property represents a significant diversification of the company's portfolio of income-producing assets into the tourism sector of the economy.

By managing hotel construction and opening with its own team of executives, the company has benefited from significant cost savings. It has also reduced its inventory of land held for development. By aggressively marketing the bulk of its inventory of residential units, Wall Financial has been able to reduce bank indebtedness and reduce carrying cost expenses.

Revenue from the company's rental apartment portfolio jumped 15% in 1995 from 1994. The improvement in 1995 was due to increases from its existing portfolio of residential properties plus the revenue generated by the new Suite & Wall Centre. The Suite & Wall Centre reached the required occupancy rate of 80% by June 1, 1994. Over fiscal 1996, the company expects a 2% to 3% increase in its rental revenue due to stable occupancy rates and increased demand for rental accommodation.

During fiscal 1995, Wall Financial sold 141 units of condominiums and townhouses compared with over 200 in 1994. Profit margins on sales were reduced in order to encourage sales. Sales from its feed operations continue to improve from $9,455,050 in 1994 to $11,351,175 in 1995. Margins on sales were lower due to the lower Canadian dollar and the competitive nature of the market. During 1995, the company sold two revenue producing properties totaling 92 units resulting in a gain of $1,146,4000.

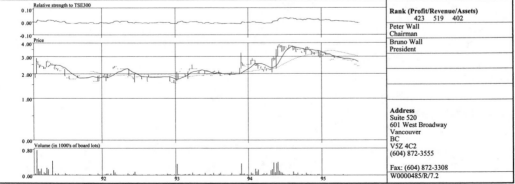

Rank (Profit/Revenue/Assets)
423   519   402

Peter Wall
Chairman
Bruno Wall
President

Address
Suite 520
601 West Broadway
Vancouver
BC
V5Z 4C2
(604) 872-3555

Fax: (604) 872-3308
W0000485/R/7.2

| Page | Company | Fiscal year end | EARNINGS PER SHARE | | |
			Last Year	Estimate this year	Estimate next year
321	Air Canada	Dec-94	0.97	0.77	0.94
322	Algoma Central	Dec-94	3.53	na	na
323	Canadian Airlines	Dec-94	(0.05)	0.44	1.05
324	CHC Helicopter	Apr-95	(0.09)	0.60	0.75
325	Greyhound Lines of Canada	Dec-94	1.12	1.25	1.50
326	Newfoundland Capital	Dec-94	0.65	na	na
327	Royal Aviation	Apr-94	0.66	0.70	0.80
328	Trimac	Dec-94	1.07	0.94	1.06
329	Westar Group	Dec-94	0.06	na	na

Estimates from First Call Corporation, 22 Pittsburgh Street, Boston, MA 02210   (800) 366-9992   Fax (617) 261-5679

Transportation

The Canada-U.S. Open Skies Agreement expands the air travel market dramatically. It opens the U.S. market for Canadian airline companies and provides a much larger customer base in a market worth $1-billion a year in gross sales for scheduled passenger airlines. Before the agreement, Air Canada had laid off 243 pilots, and had several pilots on furlough for up to three years. With the new agreement, the airline recalled all of those pilots and also hired another one hundred pilots. Now it is contemplating adding 600 more pilots to its roster.

The negotiations preceding the Open Skies treaty were protracted because of their complexity, and because Canadian officials were fearful that U.S. deregulation would jeopardize Canada's excellent record of airline safety. Changes at the executive level of government in the United States and in Canada also caused delays. The frustrating and fruitless quibbling over details lasted 20 years before a real desire to reach an agreement emerged.

Under the treaty, U.S. carriers may fly as often as they like between any cities in the United States and Canada except Toronto, Montreal (Dorval), and Vancouver. U.S. carriers will phase in new services over two years at Dorval and Vancouver. As well, the airlines will offer new flights to Toronto.

The two major airlines in Canada have launched services on the new routes created by Open Skies. Both of them have scheduled flights between major cities in the U.S. and Canada. For example, beginning May 1, 1995, Air Canada offered direct flights between Ottawa and Washington. Canadian Airlines International Ltd. will add more than 50 daily transborder flights, using its own aircraft and those of American Airlines Inc., its partner and holder of 25% of its common shares. By mid-1995, it will offer 64 daily transborder flights to New York, Dallas, Chicago, Miami, and other U.S. destinations.

The partnership of Canadian Airlines International and American Airlines provided the Canadian company with a foundation to compete in the new situation. A code-sharing arrangement allows the two airline companies to share their resources more efficiently. In code-sharing, participating airlines use identical flight numbers for aircraft of either airline. Thus a Canadian Airlines flight may fly in a plane with the American Airlines name on the tail or vice-versa. The partnership will offer new flights from Canadian points to Atlanta and Philadelphia as well as Las Vegas, Reno, Miami, and smaller Florida cities.

There will be losers under the deal. Business passengers, who accumulated large amounts of frequent flier points by covering extra miles before Open Skies, will no longer accumulate such large amounts. Hoteliers with rooms to rent may find that fewer cross-border travellers must stay overnight before finding a flight home. Increased travel and demand for hotel space likely will offset those losses.

Among those benefitting from the agreement are the travelling public. More flights will mean more choice in reaching a desired destination, more competitive ticket prices, less time wasted in travel, and more business done as the travel markets of Canada and the United States merge into one.

AIR CANADA

TMVZW

Exchanges	Price (Jun29'95)	6.00	Trailing P/E	9.84	Stock Symbol	
	Trailing Yield (%)	0.00	Trailing EPS	0.61	**AC**	

Period Ending	Dec94	Dec93	Dec92	Dec91	Dec90
Yearly Statistics					
Price-Close	8.38	5.00	2.75	8.00	8.50
Price-High	8.63	6.63	8.38	10.38	11.38
Price-Low	5.00	2.20	2.20	6.63	7.25
P/E-Close	7.68	nm	nm	nm	nm
Dividends per Share	0.00	0.00	0.00	0.00	0.00
Dividend Yield (%)	0.00	0.00	0.00	0.00	0.00
Sales per Share	29.62	39.45	42.62	42.81	48.38
EPS before extra. item	1.09	(4.23)	(6.13)	(2.94)	(1.01)
Cash Flow per Share	2.42	(0.55)	(2.61)	(1.81)	1.32
Book Value per Share	3.08	1.96	4.27	10.40	13.35
O/S Common Shares	118,469	117,534	74,034	74,034	74,027
Total Revenue	4,210,000	3,668,000	3,495,000	3,529,000	4,032,000
Income before extra.	129,000	(326,000)	(454,000)	(218,000)	(74,000)
Cash Flow	286,000	(44,000)	(193,000)	(134,000)	97,000
Debt/Equity	9.30	15.53	10.68	3.92	2.25
Return on Capital (%)	10.37	(2.38)	(6.34)	(5.43)	0.72
Ret. on Com. Equity (%)	43.36	(119.41)	(83.61)	(24.80)	(7.22)
% Change Profit	139.6	28.2	(108.3)	(194.6)	(149.7)
% Change Revenue	14.8	5.0	(1.0)	(12.5)	2.8
% Change Assets	(0.8)	4.8	(2.3)	7.5	11.1

Date	EPS	DPS	Tot Rev	Inc Bex
Mar 95	(0.74)	0.00	1,027,000	(88,000)
Dec 94	0.03	0.00	1,094,000	4,000
Sep 94	1.10	0.00	1,202,000	130,000
Jun 94	0.22	0.00	1,002,000	27,000
Mar 94	(0.27)	0.00	946,000	(32,000)
Dec 93	(1.03)	0.00	897,000	(90,000)
Sep 93	0.57	0.00	1,042,000	43,000
Jun 93	0.19	0.00	918,000	14,000

Preferred Div. Coverage	np	np	np
Total Div. Coverage	na	na	na
Interest Coverage	1.6	0.0	0.0
Current Ratio	1.3	1.4	1.1
Operating Margin	6.1	0.0	(5.6)
Asset Turnover	0.7	0.6	0.7
5 YEAR RATIOS (%)			
Return on Capital	(0.6)	(0.3)	2.3
Return on Com. Equity	(38.3)	(44.0)	(17.8)
Profit Growth	(2.9)	na	na
Revenue Growth	1.4	0.6	1.7
Asset Growth	3.9	7.9	9.3
BALANCE SHEET (000)			
Cash	599,000	845,000	418,000
Current Assets	1,206,000	1,373,000	925,000
Net Fixed Assets	2,617,000	2,687,000	2,949,000
Invest's & Advances	244,000	241,000	186,000
Total Assets	4,997,000	5,039,000	4,810,000
Short Term Debt	55,000	136,000	45,000
Current Liabilities	897,000	1,007,000	851,000
Long Term Debt	3,340,000	3,435,000	3,330,000
Total Liabilities	4,632,000	4,809,000	4,494,000
Total Equity	365,000	230,000	316,000
Total Liab. & Equity	4,997,000	5,039,000	4,810,000
CAPITAL (000)			
Total Debt	3,395,000	3,571,000	3,375,000
Preferred Equity	0	0	0
Common Equity	365,000	230,000	316,000

Business:

AIR CANADA is an international air carrier providing scheduled and chartered air transportation for passengers and cargo. The company also provides computer services, maintenance and other ground services to other airlines. It holds equity interest in five Canadian regional airlines. The airline's diversification includes Air Canada Vacations, a tour operator.

Synopsis:

Air Canada carried revenue paying passengers a total of 1.27 billion miles (RPMs) in May 1995, a 10.3% increase from the same period in 1994. According to the airline, domestic traffic rose 8.4% to 531 million RPMs while international traffic increased 11.8% to 739 million RPMS. The year-to-date travel statistics show similar trends. The airline has 5.9 billion RPMs between January 1 and May 30, up 8.8% from the same period last year. Domestic traffic rose 7.9% year-to-date, while international traffic climbed 9.4%.

On June 16, 1995, Air Canada took delivery of its first Airbus A340 aircraft. The eight A340s to be added to Air Canada's fleet will give the company one of the youngest fleets in the world by 1998. Air Canada began service to Osaka, Japan, from Toronto and Vancouver on September 21, 1994, with Boeing 747 aircraft. The new additions to the fleet will allow the airline to extend daily service to Osaka starting June 30.

In May 1995, Air Canada signed a deal with United Airlines Inc. that will double its transborder revenue over the next three years. The two airlines said they will expand the marketing agreement over time to give their passengers one-stop access to the 275 cities served by the two airlines. Transborder services accounted for 20% of Air Canada's total world-wide revenue of $4-billion in 1994.

To meet the challenge of Open Skies, the airline plans to raise $500-million to finance ambitious expansion plans. It is now beginning to take delivery of 24 Canadair regional jets, 35 A-319s, and five 767-300 aircraft in a restructuring of its fleet to meet new needs. The airline has announced the introduction of 20 new services to the United States over the next 18 months, from Orlando to Honolulu. Also planned are expanded services to Chicago and New York and new daily service between Ottawa and Chicago and Halifax and Chicago.

Relative strength to TSE300 / Price / Volume (in 1000's of board lots)

Rank (Profit/Revenue/Assets)
54   32   40

Hollis L. Harris
Chairman President & C.E.O.

M.R. Peterson
V.P. Finance & C.F.O.

Jean-Jacques Bourgeault
Exec. V.P. & C.O.O.

Lamar Durrett
Exec. V.P. Technical Ops.

Address
P.O. Box 14000
Saint-Laurent
PQ
H4Y 1H4
(514) 422-5000

A0015425/G/8.0

ALGOMA CENTRAL CORPORATION

Exchanges	Price (Jun29'95)	27.75	Trailing P/E	6.92	Stock Symbol
T	Trailing Yield (%)	0.00	Trailing EPS	4.01	**ALC**

Period Ending	Dec94	Dec93	Dec92	Dec91	Dec90
Yearly Statistics					
Price-Close	20.50	15.50	12.50	8.38	10.00
Price-High	22.00	15.50	12.75	8.38	15.25
Price-Low	13.00	9.00	8.00	7.75	7.00
P/E-Close	5.81	8.81	6.76	9.74	7.81
Dividends per Share	0.00	0.00	0.00	0.00	0.15
Dividend Yield (%)	0.00	0.00	0.00	0.00	1.50
Sales per Share	42.14	33.49	40.81	42.60	41.68
EPS before extra. item	3.53	1.76	1.85	0.86	1.28
Cash Flow per Share	9.10	4.96	5.75	5.63	5.98
Book Value per Share	20.37	16.84	15.08	13.17	12.29
O/S Common Shares	3,891	3,891	3,891	3,891	3,891
Total Revenue	163,965	133,868	161,416	166,342	167,804
Income before extra.	13,726	6,861	7,181	3,346	4,982
Cash Flow	35,406	19,284	22,358	21,918	23,268
Debt/Equity	0.50	0.90	1.23	1.69	3.48
Return on Capital (%)	21.35	13.67	13.22	10.80	14.15
Ret. on Com. Equity (%)	18.96	11.05	13.07	6.76	10.93
% Change Profit	100.1	(4.5)	114.6	(32.8)	6.6
% Change Revenue	22.5	(17.1)	(3.0)	(0.9)	7.9
% Change Assets	1.7	1.8	(6.9)	(22.1)	3.3

Date	EPS	DPS	Tot Rev	Inc Bex
Mar 95	(0.02)	0.00	11,248	(67)
Dec 94	2.08	0.00	34,431	8,066
Sep 94	1.10	0.00	61,645	4,280
Jun 94	0.85	0.00	55,828	3,319
Mar 94	(0.50)	0.00	5,987	(1,939)
Dec 93	0.30	0.00	21,456	1,161
Sep 93	0.69	0.00	48,411	2,710
Jun 93	0.80	0.00	49,778	3,090

	Dec94	Dec93	Dec92
Preferred Div. Coverage	np	np	np
Total Div. Coverage	na	na	na
Interest Coverage	5.8	3.1	2.3
Current Ratio	1.3	0.7	0.8
Operating Margin	14.9	14.1	12.8
Asset Turnover	0.7	0.5	0.7
5 YEAR RATIOS (%)			
Return on Capital	14.6	12.1	11.6
Return on Com. Equity	12.2	9.5	8.6
Profit Growth	24.1	(2.1)	0.2
Revenue Growth	1.0	(1.7)	(2.3)
Asset Growth	(5.0)	(4.5)	(3.9)
BALANCE SHEET (000)			
Cash	0	10,205	(50)
Current Assets	79,915	45,248	29,910
Net Fixed Assets	162,811	158,784	204,925
Invest's & Advances	0	0	0
Total Assets	243,571	239,555	235,304
Short Term Debt	9,139	9,096	11,097
Current Liabilities	61,388	60,824	39,830
Long Term Debt	30,163	49,986	61,317
Total Liabilities	164,309	174,019	176,629
Total Equity	79,262	65,536	58,675
Total Liab. & Equity	243,571	239,555	235,304
CAPITAL (000)			
Total Debt	39,302	59,082	72,414
Preferred Equity	0	0	0
Common Equity	79,262	65,536	58,675

Business:

ALGOMA CENTRAL CORPORATION primarily transports cargo by ship. It owns and operates a fleet of 24 dry-bulk-cargo vessels mainly within the Great Lakes and St. Lawrence Seaway but with operating limits along the East coast of North America and in the Gulf of Mexico. It also owns commerical real estate in Sault Ste. Marie and Elliot Lake, Ontario and 850,000 acres of land, in the District of Algoma.

Synopsis:

On January 31, 1995, Algoma Central Corp. sold its rail division, Algoma Central Railway, to various subsidiaries of Wisconsin Central Transportation Corp. for $8.4-million (U.S.). The Government of Ontario acted as a facilitator to the transaction by providing $11.5-million in financing through the Northern Ontario Heritage Fund Corp. The deal includes 500 kilometres of rail line between Sault Ste. Marie and Hearst, Ontario. In a related transaction, Wisconsin Central's WCL Railcars Inc. unit will buy Algoma's 966 rail cars and 23 locomotives for $11.3-million. Wisconsin Central is also buying Algoma's existing communications system, maintenance and shop equipment, inventory, and miscellaneous assets for $4.7-million.

Algoma Central's total revenues for the year of 1994 jumped 28% from 1993, and the total tonnes carried rose 18%. The fleet of 12 self-unloaders generated revenues in 1994 that were 5% above 1993 levels. The 12 bulkers generated revenues that were 105% above 1993 levels. Algoma attributed the improvement to the effect of Seaway Self Unloaders, and the net addition of six bulkers. Seaway Self Unloaders is a joint-venture between Algoma Central and ULS Corporation. It began operations in 1994. Seaway is responsible for the traffic and marketing functions for 11 self-unloaders owned by Algoma Central, and six self-unloaders owned by ULS Corporation. The combined Seaway Bulk Carrier and Seaway Self Unloader fleet now totals 47 vessels, and has a combined carrying capacity of 1,175,000 tonnes.

In 1994, Algoma spent $2,989,000 on the vessel modernization program and $781,000 on the onboard computerization program. In 1995, an additional $4,065,000 and $689,000 will be spent on vessel modernization and computerization, respectively.

The three marine labour unions that represent Algoma's shipboard personnel are operating under contracts that expire on May 31, 1996. Algoma began discussions with the unions in 1995. It hopes to negotiate satisfactory new agreements before the old ones expire.

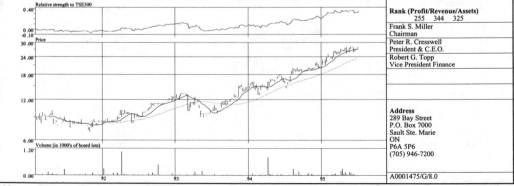

Rank (Profit/Revenue/Assets)
255 344 325

Frank S. Miller
Chairman

Peter R. Cresswell
President & C.E.O.

Robert G. Topp
Vice President Finance

Address
289 Bay Street
P.O. Box 7000
Sault Ste. Marie
ON
P6A 5P6
(705) 946-7200

A0001475/G/8.0

CANADIAN AIRLINES CORPORATION

Exchanges	Price (Jun29'95)	7.25	Trailing P/E	nm	Stock Symbol
TZV	Trailing Yield (%)	0.00	Trailing EPS	(0.10)	**CA**

Period Ending	Dec94	Dec93	Dec92	Dec91	Dec90
Yearly Statistics					
Price-Close	0.42	1.12	0.80	5.63	7.50
Price-High	1.75	2.00	6.25	9.38	13.00
Price-Low	0.36	0.31	0.54	4.00	6.75
P/E-Close	nm	nm	nm	nm	nm
Dividends per Share	0.00	0.00	0.00	0.00	0.00
Dividend Yield (%)	0.00	0.00	0.00	0.00	0.00
Sales per Share	3.73	55.68	58.51	61.93	87.07
EPS before extra. item	(0.05)	(6.13)	(11.37)	(3.66)	(0.60)
Cash Flow per Share	0.22	(0.65)	(3.94)	(2.74)	(1.36)
Book Value per Share	0.37	(6.40)	(0.35)	10.99	17.67
O/S Common Shares	804,200	48,241	48,248	48,009	31,815
Total Revenue	2,963,400	2,773,900	2,902,000	2,904,200	2,831,400
Income before extra.	(37,800)	(291,800)	(543,300)	(161,700)	(14,600)
Cash Flow	173,100	(31,300)	(189,800)	(124,000)	(43,000)
Debt/Equity	3.74	na	67.40	2.71	2.56
Return on Capital (%)	3.63	(10.85)	(21.81)	(3.72)	3.50
Ret. on Com. Equity (%)	na	na	(214.38)	(30.44)	(3.32)
% Change Profit	87.0	46.3	(236.0)	(1,007.5)	73.9
% Change Revenue	6.8	(4.4)	(0.1)	2.6	4.2
% Change Assets	3.8	(8.0)	(12.4)	(5.2)	1.8

Date	EPS	DPS	Tot Rev	Inc Bex
Mar 95	(0.13)	0.00	709,700	(108,600)
Dec 94	(0.08)	0.00	693,500	(57,300)
Sep 94	0.11	0.00	859,100	85,400
Jun 94	0.00	0.00	727,400	1,500
Mar 94	(0.10)	0.00	674,000	(67,400)
Dec 93	(1.94)	0.00	647,400	(92,600)
Sep 93	0.11	0.00	826,200	86,500
Jun 93	(2.73)	0.00	683,800	(130,600)

Preferred Div. Coverage	np	na	0.0
Total Div. Coverage	na	na	0.0
Interest Coverage	0.6	0.0	0.0
Current Ratio	0.6	0.5	0.9
Operating Margin	2.4	(2.4)	(3.8)
Asset Turnover	1.2	1.2	1.1
5 YEAR RATIOS (%)			
Return on Capital	(5.9)	(6.8)	(3.0)
Return on Com. Equity	na	na	(51.0)
Profit Growth	na	na	na
Revenue Growth	1.7	3.4	8.8
Asset Growth	(4.2)	1.2	4.3
BALANCE SHEET (000)			
Cash	105,800	108,800	107,600
Current Assets	550,800	501,500	510,600
Net Fixed Assets	1,682,200	1,592,400	1,783,700
Invest's & Advances	16,500	18,000	20,200
Total Assets	2,352,300	2,265,400	2,461,900
Short Term Debt	238,600	0	9,700
Current Liabilities	921,400	950,300	573,600
Long Term Debt	876,500	1,566,100	1,675,200
Total Liabilities	2,054,400	2,532,200	2,436,900
Total Equity	297,900	(266,800)	25,000
Total Liab. & Equity	2,352,300	2,265,400	2,461,900
CAPITAL (000)			
Total Debt	1,115,100	1,566,100	1,684,900
Preferred Equity	0	41,800	41,800
Common Equity	297,900	(308,600)	(16,800)

Business:

CANADIAN AIRLINES CORPORATION holds investments in the airline industry. It owns 100% of both Canadian Airlines International Ltd. (CAI) and Canadian Holidays. PWA also has significant investments in regional air carriers. CAI provides scheduled transportation for passengers and cargo to 145 destinations on five continents.

Synopsis:

In April 1995, Canadian Airlines Corp. (CA) announced a massive increase in its flights to the United States. This was the airline's response to the recently signed Canada-U.S. open skies treaty. Starting in June, CA will add more than 50 daily transborder flights, allowing its passengers to fly directly to New York, Chicago and Miami. Additional cities will be added in the summer Until open skies, CA was limited to just two transborder routes, Vancouver-San Francisco and Vancouver-Los Angeles. The new agreement allows CA to compete directly with Air Canada on North American routes for the first time. It also opens up many new destinations for Canadia and U.S. travellers. Canadian Airlinesdoes not have the resources to operate all the flights on its own. It will be helped by its minority shareholder, American Airlines Inc. of Fort Worth, Texas, under a marketing agreement that allows the airlines to carry each other's passengers. The agreement with American Airlines will give Canadian Airlines passengers direct access to 213 destinations in the U.S. American Airlines passengers will be able to fly directly to 113 domestic airports served by CAI and its affiliates. The two airlines intend to merge their overseas destinations later this year, allowing passengers to fly directly from South America to Bangkok, for example, on one ticket. The airlines use similar jet airplanes on domestic flights, largely Boeing 727s, 737s and 757s, and McDonnell-Douglas MD-80s.

Canadian Airlines posted a lost of $37.8-million in fiscal 1994, compared to the original projected loss of $11-million. The company said the loss grew because of the decline in the Canadian dollar, a pilots' strike at a subsidiary, and the grounding of its fleet of 15 ATR regional aircraft over Christmas. But the airline believes an extensive cost-cutting program and more efficient fleet management can help it steer a profitable course in 1995. Canadian Airlines projects a net profit for 1995 of $52.1-million, $89.9-million higher than 1994 and $22.9-millio lower than the previous projection, largely due to a weaker Canadian dollar.

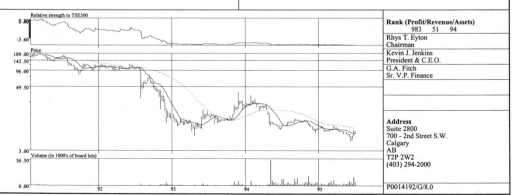

Rank (Profit/Revenue/Assets)
983 51 94

Rhys T. Eyton
Chairman

Kevin J. Jenkins
President & C.E.O.

G.A. Fitch
Sr. V.P. Finance

Address
Suite 2800
700 - 2nd Street S.W.
Calgary
AB
T2P 2W2
(403) 294-2000

P0014192/G/8.0

CHC HELICOPTER CORPORATION

| Exchanges | Price (Jun 29'95) | 5.25 | Trailing P/E | nm | Stock Symbol |
| T | Trailing Yield (%) | 1.90 | Trailing EPS | (0.35) | FLY.A |

Period Ending	Apr94	Apr93	Apr92	Apr91	Apr90
Yearly Statistics					6M
Price-Close	11.75	4.75	4.00	4.90	4.50
Price-High	12.88	5.38	5.70	na	na
Price-Low	4.10	3.80	4.00	na	na
P/E-Close	nm	22.62	15.39	5.16	nm
Dividends per Share	0.10	0.10	0.20	0.00	0.20
Dividend Yield (%)	0.85	2.11	5.00	0.00	4.44
Sales per Share	17.84	12.42	14.08	21.28	14.99
EPS before extra. item	(0.41)	0.21	0.26	0.95	(1.41)
Cash Flow per Share	1.46	1.00	1.23	1.75	(4.41)
Book Value per Share	6.63	6.71	6.60	6.88	5.94
O/S Common Shares	11,602	9,493	9,461	7,436	7,426
Total Revenue	233,789	163,867	143,567	164,840	57,287
Income before extra.	(3,947)	2,038	2,259	7,030	(10,403)
Cash Flow	14,133	9,521	10,585	12,982	(16,246)
Debt/Equity	3.19	2.09	1.78	2.20	2.81
Return on Capital (%)	4.02	7.99	8.93	14.82	(12.52)
Ret. on Com. Equity (%)	(5.62)	3.23	3.98	14.76	(41.74)
% Change Profit	(293.7)	(9.8)	(67.9)	133.8	(394.6)
% Change Revenue	42.7	14.1	(12.9)	43.9	(28.3)
% Change Assets	67.3	14.0	7.0	(0.9)	(8.4)

Preferred Div. Coverage	na	np	np
Total Div. Coverage	0.0	2.1	1.5
Interest Coverage	0.7	1.4	1.5
Current Ratio	1.9	1.7	2.3
Operating Margin	8.2	6.8	9.1
Asset Turnover	0.4	0.5	0.5
5 YEAR RATIOS (%)			
Return on Capital	4.6	6.8	7.4
Return on Com. Equity	(5.1)	(1.3)	(0.3)
Profit Growth	na	(12.7)	na
Revenue Growth	7.9	6.7	25.3
Asset Growth	13.1	6.6	6.1
BALANCE SHEET (000)			
Cash	0	0	0
Current Assets	139,658	76,081	70,600
Net Fixed Assets	249,126	136,374	125,070
Invest's & Advances	1,381	15,542	2,285
Total Assets	425,740	254,468	223,180
Short Term Debt	21,563	25,654	17,832
Current Liabilities	73,399	45,282	31,155
Long Term Debt	231,684	107,301	93,362
Total Liabilities	346,240	190,817	160,700
Total Equity	79,500	63,651	62,480
Total Liab. & Equity	425,740	254,468	223,180
CAPITAL (000)			
Total Debt	253,247	132,955	111,194
Preferred Equity	2,575	0	0
Common Equity	76,925	63,651	62,480

Business:

CHC HELICOPTER CORPORATION, through its operating subsidiaries, owns, operates or leases approximately 250 aircraft in nine countries around the world. It offers repair and overhaul facilities in Richmond, British Columbia, and in Summerside, Prince Edward Island. CHC also operates two flight training schools in Canada, one in Ontario and one in British Columbia.

Date	EPS	DPS	Tot Rev	Inc Bex
Jan 95	(0.59)	0.00	78,146	(6,848)
Oct 94	0.28	0.10	103,457	3,308
Jul 94	0.52	0.00	105,119	6,035
Apr 94	(0.56)	0.00	74,000	(4,800)
Jan 94	(0.67)	0.00	50,413	(6,437)
Oct 93	0.42	0.10	58,660	4,029
Jul 93	0.42	0.00	50,106	4,000
Apr 93	0.12	0.00	36,800	1,000

Synopsis:

In April 1995, CHC Helicopter's subsidiary, Brintel Helicopters Ltd., secured two long-term contracts to provide offshore helicopter services in the North Sea. The contracts are potentially worth more than 125 million British pounds ($275-million). The contracts are for three-year periods, but may be extended. The largest contract, for service to East Shetland Basin installations, calls for up to eight heavy-capacity helicopters. The other contract involves a single helicopter from Aberdeen to support Shell Expro's Central North Sea operations. This contract complements an existing service operated by British International Helicopters from Aberdeen for the same area.

In October 1994, CHC disclosed problems in Mozambique, where it operates six Super Puma helicopters on behalf of UN peace-keeping forces in the area. There have been so many difficulties with the Super Pumas that CHC ran up a pretax loss of $6-million on the contract. To resolve the problems, CHC appointed Sylvain Allard as interim president of the international division. Allard will try to improve the profitability of all UN contracts, especially in Mozambique.

In August 1994, Canadian Helicopters Ltd. unit won a $44-million five-year contract to provide helicopters for the Ontario government's air ambulance program. Canadian Helicopters is a subsidiary of CHC.

In 1994, CHC's revenues by geographic segments were: domestic, 63%; United Kingdom, 15%; and international, 22 %. During 1994, revenues generated by business units other than domestic operations soared by 131%. Revenues by industrial segments in 1994 were: helicopter operations, 74.4%; and repair and overhaul, 25.6%.

Relative strength to TSE300

Rank (Profit/Revenue/Assets)
899 295 245
Craig L. Dobbin
Chairman & C.E.O.
Rudy Palladina
President & C.E.O.
Christopher P. Lloyd
C.F.O. & Secretary

Address
Hangar #1
St. John's Airport
P.O. Box 5188
St. John's
NF
A1C 5V5
(709) 570-0700
Fax: (709) 570-0506
01001466/G/8.0

GREYHOUND LINES OF CANADA LTD.

Exchanges	Price (Jun29'95)	12.25	Trailing P/E	11.24	Stock Symbol
T	Trailing Yield (%)	5.71	Trailing EPS	1.09	**GHL**

Period Ending	Dec94	Dec93	Dec92	Dec91	Dec90
Yearly Statistics					
Price-Close	13.00	22.00	27.25	34.00	31.50
Price-High	25.00	29.50	36.25	37.38	33.50
Price-Low	12.00	16.50	25.25	31.25	28.75
P/E-Close	11.61	14.10	13.36	17.71	11.05
Dividends per Share	5.70	0.70	1.20	1.20	1.20
Dividend Yield (%)	43.85	3.18	4.40	3.53	3.81
Sales per Share	25.37	24.49	22.08	23.27	35.45
EPS before extra. item	1.12	1.56	2.04	1.92	2.85
Cash Flow per Share	2.43	2.54	2.13	2.31	3.86
Book Value per Share	11.06	15.63	21.32	20.48	19.73
O/S Common Shares	8,408	8,405	8,398	8,392	8,349
Total Revenue	213,337	205,749	185,507	194,626	305,345
Income before extra.	9,432	13,136	17,091	16,106	24,066
Cash Flow	20,429	21,319	17,862	19,278	32,623
Debt/Equity	0.36	nd	0.00	0.01	0.00
Return on Capital (%)	13.08	14.44	14.19	14.34	26.08
Ret. on Com. Equity (%)	8.41	8.47	9.74	9.57	15.03
% Change Profit	(28.2)	(23.1)	6.1	(33.1)	8.9
% Change Revenue	3.7	10.9	(4.7)	(36.3)	10.4
% Change Assets	1.7	(25.1)	2.8	1.5	2.7
Preferred Div. Coverage	np	np	np		
Total Div. Coverage	0.2	1.9	1.7		
Interest Coverage	na	nd	65.2		
Current Ratio	0.7	1.2	1.9		
Operating Margin	9.3	9.6	8.6		
Asset Turnover	1.2	1.1	0.8		
5 YEAR RATIOS (%)					
Return on Capital	16.4	19.0	21.9		
Return on Com. Equity	10.2	11.5	13.1		
Profit Growth	(15.7)	(10.3)	(0.7)		
Revenue Growth	(5.1)	(5.2)	(5.5)		
Asset Growth	(4.1)	(2.2)	4.7		
BALANCE SHEET (000)					
Cash	2,039	76	86		
Current Assets	20,458	31,020	75,808		
Net Fixed Assets	144,216	142,550	152,191		
Invest's & Advances	1,946	2,138	6,337		
Total Assets	182,823	179,725	240,024		
Short Term Debt	0	0	458		
Current Liabilities	31,267	26,643	40,932		
Long Term Debt	33,757	0	0		
Total Liabilities	89,864	48,363	61,012		
Total Equity	92,959	131,362	179,012		
Total Liab. & Equity	182,823	179,725	240,024		
CAPITAL (000)					
Total Debt	33,757	0	458		
Preferred Equity	0	0	0		
Common Equity	92,959	131,362	179,012		

Business:

GREYHOUND LINES OF CANADA LTD. is a motor coach transportation company operating in five Canadian provinces and the two territories. In addition to offering scheduled passenger services, the company provides courier express services and is involved in a variety of tourism related businesses through its wholly-owned subsidiary, Brewster Transport Company Limited.

Date	EPS	DPS	Tot Rev	Inc Bex
Mar 95	(0.18)	0.18	42,710	(1,512)
Dec 94	0.08	0.18	52,811	711
Sep 94	1.06	0.18	71,932	8,914
Jun 94	0.13	0.18	48,738	1,053
Mar 94	(0.15)	5.18	40,267	(1,246)
Dec 93	0.13	0.18	47,817	1,170
Sep 93	1.01	0.18	67,158	8,405
Jun 93	0.38	0.18	50,372	3,237

Synopsis:

In March 1995, Greyhound Lines of Canada Ltd. bought 35 new coaches for $13.5-million. The company bought 33 coaches from MCI Industries Ltd. of Winnipeg, Manitoba, and two from Prevost Car Inc. of St-Clair, Quebec. Greyhound expects the coaches to arrive by June.

Greyhound wants to start a new budget airline that would compete head to head with Air Canada and Canadian Airlines International Ltd. The company said the new airline would provide "a low-cost, low-frill, long-haul service across Canada." As such, the proposed airline would bear many similarities to Southwest Airlines Co. of Dallas, a highly successful and profitable operation that is shaking up traditional airlines in the United States. Under Canadian federal law, foreign investors cannot own more than 25% of a Canadian airline. That presents problems for Greyhound because 69% of its shares are held by Dial Corp., a consumer products company based in Phoenix, Arizona. The remaining 31% of Greyhound shares trade on the Toronto Stock Exchange. Dial is considering a variety of ways to restructure its operations to meet the requirements of Canadian law. Under one option, it could sell a minimum of 75% of the proposed airline to Canadian citizens, and keep up to 25% for itself. Another option would see Dial sell the entire Greyhound bus business to a Canadian partner, and be a silent partner in the airline division.

In September 1994, Greyhound agreed to buy six Southern Ontario routes from Ottawa-based Voyageur-Colonial Lines. The deal includes the Toronto-Peterborough-Ottawa, Toronto-Ottawa, and Ottawa-North Bay routes and involves 87 Voyageur employees. With the $10-million purchase, the Ontario market accounts for 30% of Greyhound Canada's overall revenue.

Relative strength to TSE300 / Price / Volume (in 1000's of board lots)

Rank (Profit/Revenue/Assets)
305   306   370

Dick Huisman
President & C.E.O.

Bruce J. Elmore
Senior V.P. Fin. & C.F.O.

Address
877 Greyhound Way S.W.
Calgary
AB
T3C 3V8
(403) 260-0877

Fax: (403) 260-0742
G0003122/G/8.0

NEWFOUNDLAND CAPITAL CORPORATION LIMITED

Exchanges	Price (Jun29'95)		4.50	Trailing P/E		7.76	Stock Symbol
TM	Trailing Yield (%)		0.00	Trailing EPS		0.58	NCC.A

Period Ending	Dec94	Dec93	Dec92	Dec91	Dec90
Yearly Statistics					
Price-Close	4.75	3.90	1.25	2.50	3.60
Price-High	5.88	4.15	2.65	4.00	6.75
Price-Low	3.75	1.05	1.00	2.10	3.25
P/E-Close	7.31	9.29	nm	nm	nm
Dividends per Share	0.00	0.00	0.00	0.00	0.00
Dividend Yield (%)	0.00	0.00	0.00	0.00	0.00
Sales per Share	22.24	21.22	41.94	42.15	37.52
EPS before extra. item	0.65	0.42	(1.27)	(0.90)	(4.69)
Cash Flow per Share	1.17	1.18	1.08	1.00	(1.08)
Book Value per Share	3.65	3.01	2.56	3.83	4.73
O/S Common Shares	11,865	11,845	4,953	4,953	4,953
Total Revenue	263,733	215,867	208,114	210,233	187,639
Income before extra.	7,667	4,279	(6,305)	(4,458)	(23,229)
Cash Flow	13,834	11,970	5,357	4,949	(5,343)
Debt/Equity	1.28	1.66	7.46	5.62	4.85
Return on Capital (%)	12.83	9.66	1.30	5.26	(8.28)
Ret. on Com. Equity (%)	19.42	17.72	(39.82)	(21.01)	(66.26)
% Change Profit	79.2	167.9	(41.4)	80.8	nm
% Change Revenue	22.2	3.7	(1.0)	12.0	1.6
% Change Assets	7.7	(7.3)	(14.1)	(3.7)	(0.8)

Preferred Div. Coverage	np	np	np
Total Div. Coverage	na	na	na
Interest Coverage	2.7	1.7	0.2
Current Ratio	0.9	0.8	0.6
Operating Margin	4.7	4.0	2.4
Asset Turnover	2.0	1.7	1.6
5 YEAR RATIOS (%)			
Return on Capital	4.2	3.3	4.2
Return on Com. Equity	(18.0)	(21.9)	(23.2)
Profit Growth	258.2	(3.2)	na
Revenue Growth	7.3	1.9	4.7
Asset Growth	(3.9)	(4.5)	3.9
BALANCE SHEET (000)			
Cash	613	913	336
Current Assets	43,421	35,552	37,426
Net Fixed Assets	44,590	46,669	53,780
Invest's & Advances	2,114	1,983	0
Total Assets	133,828	124,269	134,010
Short Term Debt	14,905	13,736	34,406
Current Liabilities	49,945	43,285	60,752
Long Term Debt	40,540	45,376	60,230
Total Liabilities	90,485	88,661	121,328
Total Equity	43,343	35,608	12,682
Total Liab. & Equity	133,828	124,269	134,010
CAPITAL (000)			
Total Debt	55,445	59,112	94,636
Preferred Equity	0	0	0
Common Equity	43,343	35,608	12,682

Business:

NEWFOUNDLAND CAPITAL CORP. LTD. is a transportation and communications company. Operating transportation divisions include rail pool cars, trucking, container shipping and marine container terminal services and a vehicle and passenger ferry service. Communications operations include radio stations across Canada, publishing and printing in Newfoundland, Nova Scotia and Southwestern Ontario.

Date	EPS	DPS	Tot Rev	Inc Bex
Mar 95	(0.15)	0.00	61,439	(1,791)
Dec 94	0.22	0.00	66,896	2,623
Sep 94	0.20	0.00	68,496	2,342
Jun 94	0.31	0.00	73,520	3,673
Mar 94	(0.08)	0.00	55,312	(971)
Dec 93	0.10	0.00	56,262	1,245
Sep 93	0.16	0.00	55,593	1,858
Jun 93	0.23	0.00	55,243	2,715

Synopsis:

In early May 1995, Newfoundland Capital bought back 531,075 class A subordinate voting shares and 63,500 class B common shares. The company said the buy-back represents up to 5% of the outstanding shares in each class.

In early 1994, subsidiary Clarke Transport installed a computerized dispatch system. The new on-line tracking, automated rating and billing, and pick-up and delivery system have improved the timely and error-free delivery of goods. In 1995, Clarke will enhance its electronic data interchange capabilities by introducing data imaging systems to manage shipping documents.

The company's net incomes rose 79.2% and revenues grew 22.8% in 1994. The improvement is largely due to the acquisition of Sunac International. Sunac accounted for 83% of the increase in revenues. Since it was acquired in March 1994, Sunac has shown annual revenue gains of 23%. Through its Clarke Transport and Sunac America Divisions, Newfoundland Capital is the largest facilitator of inter modal transportation in Canada and one of the largest in North America.

In 1994, revenues from transportation represented 79.8% of total company revenues, with the rest contributed by the communication business. The transportation division contributed operating earnings of $14.5-million, while communications and other corporate operations experienced a loss of $2.07-million.

Relative strength to TSE300

Price

Volume (in 1000's of board lots)

Rank (Profit/Revenue/Assets)
347   275   419

Harry R. Steele
Chairman & C.E.O.

Roy P. Rideout
President & C.O.O.

Address
Suite 302
800 Windmill Road
Dartmouth
NS
B3B 1L1
(902) 468-7557

Fax: (902) 468-7558
N0001132/G/8.0

ROYAL AVIATION INC.

Exchanges	Price (Jun29'95)	3.95	Trailing P/E	6.27	Stock Symbol
TM	Trailing Yield (%)	0.00	Trailing EPS	0.63	**ROY**

Period Ending	Apr94	Apr93	Apr92
Yearly Statistics			
Price-Close	4.75	nt	nt
Price-High	4.95	nt	nt
Price-Low	4.00	nt	nt
P/E-Close	7.20	nt	nt
Dividends per Share	0.00	0.05	0.00
Dividend Yield (%)	0.00	nt	0.00
Sales per Share	10.92	4.41	0.91
EPS before extra. item	0.66	0.29	0.01
Cash Flow per Share	1.25	0.66	0.17
Book Value per Share	1.89	0.54	0.39
O/S Common Shares	13,850	10,000	8,000
Total Revenue	124,131	35,675	7,402
Income before extra.	7,402	2,363	70
Cash Flow	14,086	5,306	1,398
Debt/Equity	1.28	5.28	2.81
Return on Capital (%)	29.71	21.19	na
Ret. on Com. Equity (%)	46.75	55.55	na
% Change Profit	213.2	3,275.7	na
% Change Revenue	248.0	382.0	na
% Change Assets	101.9	176.8	na

Preferred Div. Coverage	np	np	na
Total Div. Coverage	na	4.7	0.1
Interest Coverage	6.6	4.2	1.2
Current Ratio	0.9	0.7	0.6
Operating Margin	10.6	13.2	10.5
Asset Turnover	1.4	0.8	0.5
5 YEAR RATIOS (%)			
Return on Capital	na	na	na
Return on Com. Equity	na	na	na
Profit Growth	na	na	na
Revenue Growth	na	na	na
Asset Growth	na	na	na

BALANCE SHEET (000)			
Cash	24,833	4,779	100
Current Assets	35,312	9,220	1,735
Net Fixed Assets	51,022	33,967	13,016
Invest's & Advances	523	0	0
Total Assets	90,010	44,572	16,100
Short Term Debt	13,087	5,192	1,272
Current Liabilities	39,936	13,682	2,850
Long Term Debt	20,566	23,486	8,795
Total Liabilities	63,773	39,142	12,523
Total Equity	26,237	5,430	3,577
Total Liab. & Equity	90,010	44,572	16,100
CAPITAL (000)			
Total Debt	33,653	28,678	10,067
Preferred Equity	0	0	500
Common Equity	26,237	5,430	3,077

Business:

ROYAL AVIATION INC. is engaged in the airline passenger carrier industry and specializes in charter airline services for passengers in Canada. The company also operates aerial spraying services, aircraft maintenance services and passenger and cargo services to certain hunting areas in Quebec.

Date	EPS	DPS	Tot Rev	Inc Bex
Apr 95	0.21	0.00	49,919	2,946
Jan 95	0.14	0.00	42,534	1,834
Oct 94	0.10	0.00	40,948	1,403
Jul 94	0.18	0.00	42,533	2,540
Apr 94	0.23	0.00	46,931	3,019
Jan 94	0.20	0.00	36,795	2,134
Oct 93	0.13	0.00	20,107	1,258
Jul 93	0.10	0.00	20,163	991

Synopsis:

For the fiscal year ended April 30, 1995, Royal Aviations's net earnings increased 18% over the previous year. The airline's revenues increased 42% compared with fiscal 1994. The cash flow amounted to $17.7-million which represents a 26% increase over the previous fiscal year's cash flow, which stood at $14.1-million. Despite the fact that the exchange rate had a negative impact on the portion of its expenses which is paid in U.S. dollars, Royal posted a net profit margin of 5% and a return on average shareholders' equity of 29%. This makes Royal one of the most profitable charter airlines in North America. In fiscal 1995, Royal reduced its interest payments, after having paid back the debt related to three of its aircraft. As at April 30, 1995, Royal had a long-term debt of $15.2-million. Its long-term debt to equity ratio was 0.43:1. This compares favourably with $20.6-million of debt and a ratio of 0.78:1 the previous year.

During the last year, Royal successfully established a presence in the Ottawa market and developed its operating base in Quebec City. It also substantially increased its services to Europe, as well as its domestic services and those to sun spot destinations. Royal introduced various improvements to its management processes. It finalized a new computerized payload management system, which will improve its management and facilitate the work of its tour operator clients. Royal was also the first in the industry to test and offer advance seat selection to its passengers on flights to Florida.

In the coming years, Royal expects its revenues to grow through the development of certain markets, such as Western Canada. It has established an operating base in Vancouver. It will also closely evaluate the opportunities resulting from the new "Open Skies" agreement recently signed between Canada and the U.S. Finally, Royal plans to continue to improve its balance sheet through the growth of its cash flow and by paying back long-term debt. In December 1995, Royal will have fully paid back the debt related to a fourth Boeing 727.

Rank (Profit/Revenue/Assets)
354   386   506

Michel Leblanc
Chairman, President & C.E.O.
Nicole Simard-Laurin
V.P.; Finance, Sec. & C.F.O.

Address
6700 Cote De Liesse
Suite 503
St-Laurent
PQ
H4T 1E3
(514) 739-7000

Fax: (514) 739-8819
01003536/G/8.0

TRIMAC LIMITED

Exchanges	Price (Jun29'95)		12.75	Trailing P/E		12.62	Stock Symbol
TM	Trailing Yield (%)		1.41	Trailing EPS		1.01	TMA

Period Ending	Dec94	Dec93	Dec92	Dec91	Dec90
Yearly Statistics					
Price-Close	12.88	15.75	9.38	8.50	6.63
Price-High	18.00	19.00	9.38	9.88	8.63
Price-Low	11.50	9.00	7.25	6.13	6.13
P/E-Close	12.62	22.83	13.02	13.93	19.50
Dividends per Share	0.15	0.12	0.12	0.10	0.20
Dividend Yield (%)	1.17	0.76	1.28	1.18	3.02
Sales per Share	17.02	16.03	13.01	12.21	13.04
EPS before extra. item	1.02	0.69	0.72	0.61	0.34
Cash Flow per Share	2.54	2.20	1.53	1.32	1.38
Book Value per Share	7.81	6.91	5.66	4.97	4.63
O/S Common Shares	40,217	40,527	36,683	36,515	36,177
Total Revenue	704,696	632,497	503,837	473,759	459,798
Income before extra.	42,980	27,380	26,823	22,715	13,183
Cash Flow	102,492	85,053	56,039	48,576	47,284
Debt/Equity	0.75	0.91	1.01	0.76	0.91
Return on Capital (%)	11.39	10.12	11.99	12.93	11.17
Ret. on Com. Equity (%)	14.47	11.14	13.63	12.83	7.75
% Change Profit	57.0	2.1	18.1	72.3	52.5
% Change Revenue	11.4	25.5	6.3	3.0	28.0
% Change Assets	0.1	23.8	33.6	1.4	4.3

Business:
TRIMAC LIMITED is involved in bulk commodity transportation, contract drilling, truck leasing and rentals, and environmental services. Its core businesses are carried on through wholly owned subsidiaries including: Trimac Transportation, Kenting Energy Services, Rentway and TriWaste and through associated companies including: Bovar, Bantrel, Chauvco, Banister, Intera Information and Taro Industries.

Date	EPS	DPS	Tot Rev	Inc Bex
Mar 95	0.17	0.18	183,829	13,932
Dec 94	0.25	0.00	197,723	11,691
Sep 94	0.36	0.00	183,148	14,478
Jun 94	0.23	0.00	157,546	9,323
Mar 94	0.18	0.15	166,439	7,488
Dec 93	0.29	0.00	176,660	11,045
Sep 93	0.24	0.00	166,069	9,703
Jun 93	0.10	0.00	144,356	3,795

	Dec94	Dec93	Dec92
Preferred Div. Coverage	np	np	81.0
Total Div. Coverage	7.1	5.9	5.7
Interest Coverage	4.6	3.3	3.5
Current Ratio	1.3	1.1	1.0
Operating Margin	6.5	5.7	3.7
Asset Turnover	1.0	0.9	0.9
5 YEAR RATIOS (%)			
Return on Capital	11.5	11.6	11.4
Return on Com. Equity	12.0	10.1	8.5
Profit Growth	37.7	48.4	27.5
Revenue Growth	14.4	13.4	11.1
Asset Growth	11.8	10.9	5.0
BALANCE SHEET (000)			
Cash	14,525	14,558	10,143
Current Assets	159,338	153,432	138,686
Net Fixed Assets	387,592	408,704	310,582
Invest's & Advances	102,726	84,239	70,778
Total Assets	658,098	657,213	531,005
Short Term Debt	28,056	33,927	36,860
Current Liabilities	126,328	143,753	133,918
Long Term Debt	208,809	221,503	176,777
Total Liabilities	344,023	377,336	319,951
Total Equity	314,075	279,877	211,054
Total Liab. & Equity	658,098	657,213	531,005
CAPITAL (000)			
Total Debt	236,865	255,430	213,637
Preferred Equity	0	0	3,612
Common Equity	314,075	279,877	207,442

Synopsis:

In May 1995, Trimac subsidiary Kenting Energy Services Ltd. purchased Cadesa Compania Argentina de Servicios Sociedad Anonima, a drilling company in Argentina. Kenting Energy paid approximately $11.3-million (U.S.) for Cadesa. Cadesa had revenues of $30-million (U.S.) in 1994. It currently owns and operates 13 drilling and work-over rigs in Argentina. All of its rigs are currently under contract to YPF, Argentina's national oil and gas producer.

In March 1995, Trimac Transportation Services (Western), Inc. said it would resume transporting nickel ore from Glenbrook Nickel Company's import terminal in Coos Bay, Oregon, to the Glenbrook smelter in Riddle, Oregon. Revenues from the deal should be more than $4-million annually.

Trimac Transportation Services (Western), Inc. will expand its business with Rohm and Haas Company of Philadelphia. Trimac will supply transportation services for a Rohm and Haas facility in La Mirada, California. Revenues should exceed $3-million (U.S.) annually by mid-1995.

In October 1994, Trimac Transportation System won two contracts worth $14.5-million. One contract, valued at $11-million over five years, makes Trimac the exclusive carrier at Geon Co.'s Niagara Falls, Ontario, plant. Trimac said it will invest $750,000 in new specially designed trailers. The contract also appoints Trimac Transportation as Geon's exclusive carrier at the CN Cargo Flo intermodal facilities in Toronto and Montreal. The second contract, valued at $3.5-million over three years, was awarded by Marsulex Inc. of Toronto.

In March 1995, Trimac agreed to buy an additional 400,000 common shares of Chauvco Resources Ltd. of Calgary. Trimac agreed to pay $15.75 per share. Trimac is Chauvco's major shareholder.

Relative strength to TSE300

Price

Volume (in 1000's of board lots)

Rank (Profit/Revenue/Assets)
129 153 199
J.R. McCaig
Chairman
Jeffrey J. McCaig
President & C.E.O.
T.J. Jackson
V.P. Finance & C.F.O.

Address
Suite 2100
800 - 5th Avenue S.W.
P.O. Box 3500
Calgary
AB
T2P 2P9
(403) 298-5100
Fax: (403) 298-5258
T0002980/G/8.0

WESTAR GROUP LTD.

Exchanges	Price (Jun29'95)		27.50	Trailing P/E		126.15	Stock Symbol
TV	Trailing Yield (%)		0.00	Trailing EPS		0.22	WGL

Period Ending	Dec94	Dec93	Dec92	Dec91	Dec90	Business:
Yearly Statistics						WESTAR GROUP LTD. operates a shipping
Price-Close	0.14	0.22	0.18	0.53	0.60	terminal near Vancouver serving coal producers
Price-High	0.34	0.30	0.72	0.88	1.15	in Western Canada and the United States,
Price-Low	0.08	0.10	0.08	0.41	0.50	through Westshore Terminals.
P/E-Close	2.33	0.60	nm	nm	nm	
Dividends per Share	0.00	0.00	0.00	0.00	0.00	
Dividend Yield (%)	0.00	0.00	0.00	0.00	0.00	
Sales per Share	0.29	0.43	0.38	0.57	0.69	
EPS before extra. item	0.06	0.37	(0.58)	(0.04)	(0.11)	
Cash Flow per Share	0.09	0.08	(0.04)	0.33	0.39	
Book Value per Share	(0.25)	(0.68)	(1.18)	(0.61)	(0.57)	

	Dec94	Dec93	Dec92	Dec91	Dec90
O/S Common Shares	447,444	192,994	192,994	192,994	192,994
Total Revenue	98,677	83,422	72,500	110,700	99,600
Income before extra.	20,444	71,133	(110,300)	(7,800)	(19,200)
Cash Flow	30,349	14,479	(8,600)	63,600	57,100

Date	EPS	DPS	Tot Rev	Inc Bex
Mar 95	0.02	0.00	28,429	11,314
Dec 94	0.01	0.00	23,877	9,144
Sep 94	0.05	0.00	30,300	10,400
Jun 94	0.14	0.00	25,900	1,400
Mar 94	(0.00)	0.00	18,558	(559)
Dec 93	0.03	0.00	21,322	4,933
Sep 93	0.04	0.00	23,600	9,000
Jun 93	0.33	0.00	22,300	62,100

	Dec94	Dec93	Dec92	Dec91	Dec90
Debt/Equity	na	na	na	na	na
Return on Capital (%)	19.84	50.01	(17.73)	16.02	12.71
Ret. on Com. Equity (%)	na	na	na	na	na
% Change Profit	(71.3)	164.5	(1,314.1)	59.4	(173.3)
% Change Revenue	18.3	15.1	(34.5)	11.1	(74.5)
% Change Assets	(7.7)	(10.2)	(29.5)	(10.7)	(21.7)

				Synopsis:
Preferred Div. Coverage	np	np	np	
Total Div. Coverage	na	na	na	
Interest Coverage	2.4	4.3	0.0	
Current Ratio	1.3	0.1	0.1	
Operating Margin	35.5	31.5	14.8	
Asset Turnover	0.5	0.4	0.3	
5 YEAR RATIOS (%)				
Return on Capital	16.2	18.2	12.5	
Return on Com. Equity	na	na	na	
Profit Growth	(4.8)	32.7	na	
Revenue Growth	(24.2)	(25.0)	(23.9)	
Asset Growth	(16.4)	(15.8)	(13.4)	
BALANCE SHEET (000)				
Cash	23,390	31,139	15,300	
Current Assets	33,506	41,862	57,800	
Net Fixed Assets	150,608	158,757	167,800	
Invest's & Advances	0	0	0	
Total Assets	187,008	202,514	225,600	
Short Term Debt	11,204	319,111	413,400	
Current Liabilities	26,295	331,310	425,200	
Long Term Debt	269,065	0	0	
Total Liabilities	297,441	333,391	454,200	
Total Equity	(110,433)	(130,877)	(228,600)	
Total Liab. & Equity	187,008	202,514	225,600	
CAPITAL (000)				
Total Debt	280,269	319,111	413,400	
Preferred Equity	0	0	0	
Common Equity	(110,433)	(130,877)	(228,600)	

Synopsis:

In June 1994, shareholders of Westar Group Ltd. approved the restructuring of the company. On September 2, 1994, the company issued an additional 450.3 million shares, 254.5 million of which are voting common shares. The remaining 195.9 million are convertible, non-voting common shares. The debt owed by Westar Group, acquired in January 1994 by 461847 British Columbia Ltd. (a company owned by Jim Pattison and the CIBC), was restated on July 15, 1994, as adjusting balance notes. Interest was waived for a five-year period. The adjusting balance notes require repayment of principal quarterly. They depend upon the cash flow from the operations of the company. At the end of 1994, the bank indebtedness owed by Westshore Terminals also was refinanced at a lower interest cost by a consortium of three banks.

In April 1995, Westar Group announced consolidation of the company's common shares and non-voting shares on a 125 for one basis. The company also announced that in accordance with the terms of the Amended and Restated Trust Indenture, the company will pay $8,720,000 to Montreal Trust on June 15, 1995. (The terms govern the company's repayment obligations regarding the adjusting balance notes which have a current outstanding principal of approximately $205-million.)

After the consolidation, Westar Group closed at $28.125 on May 4, 1995. The company believes that this figure should give it new appeal with large institutional investors. This is crucial if the company needs to raise new equity to finance future growth. The company says the exchange may remove many of the small investors among 88,000 shareholders who now hold 640 million shares. However, it will produce large savings in administrative costs.

During 1994, Westshore Terminals shipped 17.5 million tons of metallurgical and thermal coal. This compared to 15.4 million tons in the previous year, resulting in an 18% increase in sales revenue.

Rank (Profit/Revenue/Assets)
214   424   365

Nicholas Geer
Chairman & President

Address
Suite 1600
1055 West Hastings Street
Vancouver
BC
V6E 2H2
(604) 488-5295

Fax: (604) 688-6776
B0004071/G/8.0

| | | | EARNINGS PER SHARE | | |
| | | Fiscal | Last | Estimate | Estimate |
Page	Company	year end	Year	this year	next year
333	Gaz Metropolitain	Sep-94	1.24	1.33	1.30
334	IPL Energy	Dec-94	1.09	2.47	2.75
335	Nova Corporation	Dec-94	0.96	1.78	1.73
336	TransCanada PipeLines	Dec-94	1.60	1.73	1.81
337	Westcoast Energy	Dec-94	1.83	1.97	2.14

Estimates from First Call Corporation, 22 Pittsburgh Street, Boston, MA 02210   (800) 366-9992   Fax (617) 261-5679

Pipelines

Expansion has slowed for many of the pipeline companies as demand for natural gas and the ability to meet it are more in balance. Expansion plans are developed after consultation with shippers, and a plan only proceeds if it meets the transmission requirements of both producers and consumers. Expansion in the near future will be as a result of increased gas shipments to the United States.

An integral part of long-term growth for many of the pipeline companies is the pursuit of international opportunities. Trans-Canada PipeLines Limited (TCPL) is involved in three global projects. An oil pipeline in Colombia will carry oil from the Cusiana and Cupiagua fields to the Caribbean port of Covenas. The second project, the Mariquita to Cali natural gas pipeline, is part of Colombia's national gasification plan. Construction of the pipeline will start in 1995, with operations expected to begin in late 1996. The third global initiative is the Songo Songo Gas Development Project in Tanzania. A pipeline that will transport natural gas from Qatar to Pakistan is still in the planning stage.

On April 1, 1995 the National Energy Board approved the tolls negotiated under the incentive tolling agreement with IPL System shippers were approved by the National Energy Board and were put into effect.

This is the first time in Canada that a regulated company arrived at a multi-year incentive agreement with its customers. The ability to achieve higher earnings is based on maximizing system utilization and increasing operating efficiency, which is different from the traditional cost based regulation where earnings are based on the level of capital investment.

Pipeline companies are searching for opportunities in international markets where they can make use of the expertise that exists within the organization. For many of the companies the international sales presently account for a small percentage of their total revenues and net income, but it is hoped that in the future the percentage will increase as domestic markets mature.

Pipeline companies have adopted a corporate structure that places their regulated operations and non-regulated operations into different companies. This simplifies the regulation of pipeline operations and gives all operations greater flexibility to develop and finance business opportunities.

GAZ METROPOLITAIN AND COMPANY, LIMITED PARTNERSHIP

Exchanges	Price (Jun29'95)	13.87	Trailing P/E	11.76	Stock Symbol
TM	Trailing Yield (%)	8.81	Trailing EPS	1.18	**GZM.UN**

Period Ending	Sep94	Sep93	Sep92	Sep91
Yearly Statistics				
Price-Close	12.38	11.88	n t	n t
Price-High	14.50	12.75	n t	n t
Price-Low	11.13	10.00	n t	n t
P/E-Close	9.98	9.90	n t	n t
Dividends per Share	1.22	1.86	1.02	n t
Dividend Yield (%)	9.86	15.66	n t	n t
Sales per Share	12.33	11.55	12.76	0.00
EPS before extra. item	1.24	1.20	1.30	na
Cash Flow per Share	2.54	2.38	2.46	0.00
Book Value per Share	6.50	6.21	6.50	na
O/S Common Shares	100,708	96,509	85,519	0
Total Revenue	1,224,868	1,070,844	1,091,396	1,007,655
Income before extra.	123,613	111,368	111,043	111,935
Cash Flow	252,769	220,508	210,679	196,138
Debt/Equity	1.29	1.06	1.01	1.17
Return on Capital (%)	15.09	15.40	16.10	na
Ret. on Com. Equity (%)	19.73	19.29	20.41	na
% Change Profit	11.0	0.3	(0.8)	na
% Change Revenue	14.4	(1.9)	8.3	na
% Change Assets	19.6	8.5	(0.1)	na

Preferred Div. Coverage	np	np	np
Total Div. Coverage	1.0	0.6	1.3
Interest Coverage	2.5	2.6	2.5
Current Ratio	0.7	0.9	0.7
Operating Margin	19.9	19.4	19.5
Asset Turnover	0.7	0.8	0.9
5 YEAR RATIOS (%)			
Return on Capital	na	na	na
Return on Com. Equity	na	na	na
Profit Growth	na	na	na
Revenue Growth	na	na	na
Asset Growth	na	na	na
BALANCE SHEET (000)			
Cash	7,306	9,670	0
Current Assets	179,144	143,606	148,996
Net Fixed Assets	1,300,483	1,090,457	1,003,224
Invest's & Advances	20,118	10,806	9,593
Total Assets	1,647,436	1,376,981	1,269,039
Short Term Debt	101,820	19,023	51,354
Current Liabilities	254,116	162,951	200,792
Long Term Debt	738,861	615,132	512,235
Total Liabilities	993,021	778,120	713,067
Total Equity	654,415	598,861	555,972
Total Liab. & Equity	1,647,436	1,376,981	1,269,039
CAPITAL (000)			
Total Debt	840,681	634,155	563,589
Preferred Equity	0	0	0
Common Equity	654,415	598,861	555,972

Business:

GAZ METROPOLITAIN AND COMPANY, LIMITED PARTNERSHIP is a natural gas distribution company. With a system that covers more than 7,500 km, the Partnership accounts for 95% of the natural gas distributed in Quebec to approximately 150,000 customers.

Date	EPS	DPS	Tot Rev	Inc Bex
Mar 95	0.77	0.00	404,035	79,497
Dec 94	0.50	0.00	320,618	50,788
Sep 94	(0.22)	0.35	183,217	(20,621)
Jun 94	0.13	0.29	245,090	13,186
Mar 94	0.83	0.29	461,643	82,194
Dec 93	0.51	0.29	337,423	48,854
Sep 93	(0.27)	0.29	159,183	(23,226)
Jun 93	0.16	0.19	207,546	15,347

Synopsis:

Gaz Metropolitain's revenue for the first half of fiscal 1995 fell by $74.3-million, compared to the first half of fiscal 1994. The full pass-through to customers of lower natural gas commodity prices accounted for a large part of this amount, about $56.2- million. The pass-through had no effect on the gross margin. The gross margin fell by approximately $8.4-million during the first half of fiscal 1995 compared to the first half of fiscal 1994. The decline in gross margin was the result of the warmer weather, partially offset by the rate stabilization account. The rate stabilization accounts alleviate the unpredictable effects of certain factors, mainly annual temperature fluctuations. Income before the net effect of rate stabilization accounts was $118.9- million for the six months ended March 31, 1995, and about $140- million for the six months ended March 31, 1994. Sales volumes rose to 3,762 million cubic metres from 3,724 million cubic metres due mainly to a significant increase in deliveries in Quebec offset by the temperature impact.

On March 13, 1995, Gaz Metropolitain issued 1,760,000 partnership units to an underwriting syndicate at a price of $12.75 per unit for total proceeds of $22.44-million. In May, Gaz Metropolitain entered into an agreement for the sale of one million units with an option for an additional 100,000 units at a price of $13.50 per unit. Proceeds from the issues went to repay long-term debt.

Gaz Metropolitain acquired a 50% ownership interest in TQM Pipeline Partnership, a company involved in natural gas transmission in Quebec, $52.8-million including acquisition costs. Gaz issued 4.2 million shares for net proceeds of $52,688,000, on January 27, 1994. The proceeds were used to repay the amount borrowed to finance the acquisition of 50% of TQM. Natural gas deliveries in Quebec by the partnership for the fiscal year ended September 30, 1994, totalled 5,579 million cubic metres. Deliveries to the industrial sector declined by 5.3% and rose by 8.3% in the commercial and residential sectors.

Relative strength to TSE300 / Price / Volume (in 1000's of board lots)

Rank (Profit/Revenue/Assets)
61 106 121

Yves Rheault
Chairman
Andre Caille
President & C.E.O.
Robert Normand
V.P. Finance
Robert Vincent
V.P., Operations
Hung Bui-Quang
V.P., Marketing & Sales

Address
1717 Du Havre Street
Montreal
PQ
H2K 2X3
(514) 598-3324

Fax: (514) 521-8168
01003495/G/9.2

IPL ENERGY INC.

Exchanges	Price (Jun29'95)	30.25	Trailing P/E	27.25	Stock Symbol
TMQ	Trailing Yield (%)	6.61	Trailing EPS	1.11	**IPL**

Period Ending	Dec94	Dec93	Dec92	Dec91	Dec90
Yearly Statistics					
Price-Close	28.50	32.25	23.00	32.38	47.75
Price-High	34.25	33.00	34.88	49.50	50.50
Price-Low	26.88	22.38	21.88	28.50	42.75
P/E-Close	26.15	15.89	12.11	3.81	13.12
Dividends per Share	2.00	2.00	2.00	9.00	2.00
Dividend Yield (%)	7.02	6.20	8.70	27.80	4.19
Sales per Share	14.23	9.91	9.86	15.80	15.70
EPS before extra. item	1.09	2.03	1.90	8.50	3.64
Cash Flow per Share	3.14	4.23	2.96	4.57	5.05
Book Value per Share	11.00	11.60	11.53	11.55	27.89
O/S Common Shares	40,583	39,932	39,816	39,699	39,637
Total Revenue	663,600	445,400	438,900	1,010,200	625,100
Income before extra.	43,600	80,800	75,500	337,200	144,000
Cash Flow	126,000	168,600	117,900	181,200	200,200
Debt/Equity	8.72	1.62	1.67	1.52	0.55
Return on Capital (%)	6.85	15.33	15.15	41.86	15.13
Ret. on Com. Equity (%)	9.59	17.53	16.46	43.12	13.43
% Change Profit	(46.0)	7.0	(77.6)	134.2	23.9
% Change Revenue	49.0	1.5	(56.6)	61.6	(29.1)
% Change Assets	220.8	0.2	(12.2)	(8.9)	(33.2)

Preferred Div. Coverage	np	np	np
Total Div. Coverage	0.5	1.0	0.9
Interest Coverage	1.2	2.7	2.4
Current Ratio	1.2	4.4	2.5
Operating Margin	19.7	34.5	34.0
Asset Turnover	0.1	0.2	0.2
5 YEAR RATIOS (%)			
Return on Capital	18.9	20.4	20.3
Return on Com. Equity	20.0	20.4	19.0
Profit Growth	(17.9)	(4.9)	(9.2)
Revenue Growth	(5.6)	(12.6)	(12.6)
Asset Growth	11.4	(11.2)	(10.9)
BALANCE SHEET (000)			
Cash	48,800	274,900	358,300
Current Assets	977,300	344,500	395,000
Net Fixed Assets	4,051,900	1,127,000	1,113,400
Invest's & Advances	162,400	142,400	138,600
Total Assets	5,346,100	1,666,600	1,663,900
Short Term Debt	432,700	26,100	104,400
Current Liabilities	796,600	78,800	160,100
Long Term Debt	3,458,400	722,100	660,400
Total Liabilities	4,899,700	1,203,400	1,205,000
Total Equity	446,400	463,200	458,900
Total Liab. & Equity	5,346,100	1,666,600	1,663,900
CAPITAL (000)			
Total Debt	3,891,100	748,200	764,800
Preferred Equity	0	0	0
Common Equity	446,400	463,200	458,900

Business:

IPL ENERGY INC. transports liquid hydrocarbons and the distribution of natural gas. In Canada, the petroleum pipeline business is conducted through the wholly owned subsidiary Interprovincial Pipe Line Inc. Wholly owned Lakehead Pipe Line Co. Inc. holds an 18% int. in the portion of the pipeline in the United States. The natural gas distribution is conducted through 85% owned Consumers' Gas Company.

Date	EPS	DPS	Tot Rev	Inc Bex
Mar 95	0.53	0.50	108,900	25,700
Dec 94	(0.34)	0.50	308,100	(13,600)
Sep 94	0.49	0.50	126,700	19,800
Jun 94	0.43	0.50	112,800	17,100
Mar 94	0.51	0.50	116,000	20,300
Dec 93	0.30	0.50	105,000	12,100
Sep 93	0.79	0.50	121,800	31,300
Jun 93	0.59	0.50	114,400	23,500

Synopsis:

IPL Energy reported earnings of $25.7-million for the first quarter of 1995, a 27% increase over earnings achieved during the first quarter of 1994. The increase was due to improved earnings of the crude oil pipeline operations, and a positive contribution from gas distribution activities, as a result of the acquisition of Consumers' Gas. Deliveries of crude oil and liquids averaged 1,589,000 barrels per day for the first quarter as a result of the capacity expansion. Power costs for the first quarter of 1995 were less than the comparable period in 1994 as less horsepower was required to ship similar volumes on the expanded system. Earnings for the segment improved by $3.2-million to $21.7-million. Earnings from the gas distribution activities, adversely affected by warmer weather, contributed $13.5-million to consolidated earnings.

On April 1, 1995, the tolls negotiated under the incentive tolling agreement with IPL System shippers were put into effect, retroactive to January, following approval by the National Energy Board. This is the first time in Canada that a regulated company arrived at a multi-year incentive agreement with its customers. The ability to achieve higher earnings is based on maximizing system utilization and increasing operating efficiency, which is different from the traditional cost based regulation where earnings are based on the level of capital investment.

During the first quarter, IPL acquired Producers Pipelines Inc. for $50-million. Producers operates crude oil trunk and gathering lines in Saskatchewan and Manitoba which connect with the IPL System in Manitoba. Construction on the Colombian crude oil pipeline project is scheduled to begin in the second half of 1995, with completion expected in early 1997. IPL has a 17.5% equity interest in Oleoducto Central S.A., a new Colombian pipeline company that will own, expand, and operate the crude oil pipeline.

In May, IPL Energy entered into an agreement with underwriters to sell 4,170,000 treasury common shares at $30 each for distribution to the public.

Rank (Profit/Revenue/Assets)
128 162 38

H. Gordon MacNeill
Chairman

Brian F. MacNeill
President & C.E.O.

Derek P. Truswell
V.P. Finance

Address
3100 205 - 5th Ave. S.W.
Calgary
AB
T2P 2V7
(403) 231-3900

Fax: (403) 231-3920

I0001637/G/9.1

NOVA CORPORATION

Period Ending	Dec94	Dec93	Dec92	Dec91	Dec90
Yearly Statistics					
Price-Close	13.00	9.38	8.75	7.25	8.63
Price-High	15.00	10.13	9.13	9.50	9.38
Price-Low	9.13	8.38	6.88	6.38	6.63
P/E-Close	10.48	19.95	22.44	nm	15.40
Dividends per Share	0.24	0.24	0.24	0.45	0.52
Dividend Yield (%)	1.85	2.56	2.74	6.21	6.03
Sales per Share	8.03	8.04	7.80	9.82	13.31
EPS before extra. item	1.24	0.47	0.39	(2.99)	0.56
Cash Flow per Share	1.44	1.11	1.16	0.71	1.70
Book Value per Share	6.99	5.23	4.98	4.18	7.40
O/S Common Shares	478,172	406,725	406,280	325,661	299,625
Total Revenue	4,094,000	3,371,000	3,085,000	3,161,000	4,098,000
Income before extra.	575,000	191,000	164,000	(923,000)	185,000
Cash Flow	668,000	450,000	451,000	223,000	509,000
Debt/Equity	1.18	1.82	1.48	2.30	1.40
Return on Capital (%)	15.96	9.64	10.31	(11.37)	11.20
Ret. on Com. Equity (%)	21.04	9.21	8.98	(52.35)	7.55
% Change Profit	201.0	16.5	117.8	(598.9)	(0.5)
% Change Revenue	21.4	9.3	(2.4)	(22.9)	(15.5)
% Change Assets	19.3	11.9	6.7	(13.2)	(15.5)

Date	EPS	DPS	Tot Rev	Inc Bex
Mar 95	0.53	0.06	1,288,000	253,000
Dec 94	0.43	0.06	1,178,000	203,000
Sep 94	0.29	0.06	1,021,000	136,000
Jun 94	0.15	0.06	900,000	69,000
Mar 94	0.37	0.06	1,004,000	166,000
Dec 93	0.10	0.06	869,000	40,000
Sep 93	0.10	0.06	844,000	42,000
Jun 93	0.16	0.06	848,000	66,000

	Dec94	Dec93	Dec92
Preferred Div. Coverage	np	np	13.7
Total Div. Coverage	5.1	1.9	1.5
Interest Coverage	3.2	1.7	1.6
Current Ratio	0.8	0.9	0.9
Operating Margin	18.7	14.2	16.1
Asset Turnover	0.5	0.5	0.5
5 YEAR RATIOS (%)			
Return on Capital	7.1	6.3	8.1
Return on Com. Equity	(1.1)	(3.6)	(0.2)
Profit Growth	25.3	(13.6)	(1.7)
Revenue Growth	(3.3)	(3.3)	5.8
Asset Growth	0.8	(3.2)	5.7
BALANCE SHEET (000)			
Cash	14,000	14,000	17,000
Current Assets	929,000	992,000	750,000
Net Fixed Assets	6,121,000	5,481,000	5,096,000
Invest's & Advances	1,176,000	421,000	306,000
Total Assets	8,257,000	6,923,000	6,189,000
Short Term Debt	491,000	585,000	303,000
Current Liabilities	1,103,000	1,151,000	841,000
Long Term Debt	3,449,000	3,281,000	2,956,000
Total Liabilities	4,916,000	4,798,000	3,985,000
Total Equity	3,341,000	2,125,000	2,204,000
Total Liab. & Equity	8,257,000	6,923,000	6,189,000
CAPITAL (000)			
Total Debt	3,940,000	3,866,000	3,259,000
Preferred Equity	0	0	182,000
Common Equity	3,341,000	2,125,000	2,022,000

Business:

NOVA CORP. is a Canadian corporation. Its principal business segments are natural gas services, including transmission and marketing of natural gas and related activities and the production and marketing of petrochemicals.

Synopsis:

The increase in the earnings of Nova Corporation for the first quarter of 1995, compared to the first quarter of 1994, were due to the strength of chemical prices that have carried over from the second half of 1994. In the first quarter of 1995, the chemical operations had a net income of $206-million, compared to about $124-million in the first quarter of 1994 and $173-million in the fourth quarter of 1994. The Alberta natural gas pipeline system had a net income of $46-million, which was influenced by high levels of investment in new facilities to meet customers' needs. NOVA spent $310-million on property, plant, and equipment additions during the first quarter. Expansion of the NOVA Gas Transmission pipeline system accounts for 91% of the spending. NOVA invested $95-million to complete the combination of Natural Gas Clearinghouse and Trident.

Natural Gas Clearinghouse merged its operations with Trident NGL Holding, Inc., a fully integrated U.S. based natural gas liquids company, during the first quarter. NOVA's share of the new company, NGC Corporation, is approximately 34%. NGC Corporation is the largest independent energy commodity marketer in North America. NOVA announced the combination of Pan-Alberta Gas Ltd., a wholly owned subsidiary, and Novagas Clearinghouse Limited Partnership. Novagas is a joint venture of NOVA and NGC Corporation in which NOVA has a 50.1% direct investment. The combination creates a strong strategic linkage and operational coordination among NOVA's North American gas marketing activities.

Novacor Chemicals Inc. will sell its polypropylene business to Huntsman Chemical Corp. of Utah for $44-million (U.S.). The agreement also includes a provision for Hunstman to pay an estimated $9-million for the working capital of the polypropylene business. The deal is part of a plan to concentrate on core strengths in the chemical business and in businesses big enough to develop and spinning off areas such as polypropylene, whose assets were too small to continue to hold.

Rank (Profit/Revenue/Assets)
10   33   30

Richard F. Haskayne
Chairman

J.E. Newall
C.E.O. & Vice Chairman

Jeffrey M. Lipton
President & C.O.O.

A.T. (Terry) Poole
Sr. V.P. & C.F.O.

Address
P.O. Box 2535
Postal Station M
Calgary
AB
T2P 2N6
(403) 290-6000

Fax: (403) 290-6379
N0003576/G/9.2

Relative strength to TSE300 / Price / Volume (in 1000's of board lots)

TRANSCANADA PIPELINES LIMITED

Exchanges	Price (Jun29'95)	18.37	Trailing P/E	11.48	Stock Symbol
TMZVN	Trailing Yield (%)	5.22	Trailing EPS	1.60	**TRP**

Period Ending	Dec94	Dec93	Dec92	Dec91	Dec90
Yearly Statistics					
Price-Close	17.13	20.13	17.63	17.50	17.00
Price-High	20.88	21.88	18.50	18.00	17.50
Price-Low	16.00	16.13	16.00	16.00	15.12
P/E-Close	10.70	12.42	11.30	13.06	13.82
Dividends per Share	0.94	0.86	0.78	0.73	0.69
Dividend Yield (%)	5.49	4.27	4.43	4.17	4.06
Sales per Share	26.69	23.69	20.46	18.40	19.17
EPS before extra. item	1.60	1.62	1.56	1.34	1.23
Cash Flow per Share	3.32	3.15	2.69	2.06	1.97
Book Value per Share	12.86	12.02	11.13	9.68	8.30
O/S Common Shares	197,311	192,510	188,512	171,377	154,187
Total Revenue	5,242,500	4,573,900	4,007,600	3,308,100	3,242,800
Income before extra.	358,600	355,600	328,700	251,200	214,900
Cash Flow	647,300	600,700	486,900	337,100	302,300
Debt/Equity	1.84	1.90	1.78	1.66	1.81
Return on Capital (%)	12.08	12.65	13.77	14.26	14.64
Ret. on Com. Equity (%)	12.86	14.01	14.91	14.93	15.47
% Change Profit	0.8	8.2	30.9	16.9	9.3
% Change Revenue	14.6	14.1	21.1	2.0	(0.4)
% Change Assets	6.6	13.1	24.7	26.0	13.3
Preferred Div. Coverage	7.7	7.6	6.8		
Total Div. Coverage	1.5	1.6	1.7		
Interest Coverage	1.8	1.8	2.0		
Current Ratio	0.7	0.6	0.8		
Operating Margin	19.4	21.0	18.2		
Asset Turnover	0.5	0.5	0.4		
5 YEAR RATIOS (%)					
Return on Capital	13.5	13.7	13.1		
Return on Com. Equity	14.4	14.1	10.8		
Profit Growth	12.7	113.9	15.5		
Revenue Growth	10.0	6.2	3.9		
Asset Growth	16.4	13.1	9.0		
BALANCE SHEET (000)					
Cash	113,300	90,000	598,900		
Current Assets	861,000	670,100	1,180,200		
Net Fixed Assets	8,760,200	8,376,100	6,000,600		
Invest's & Advances	153,900	149,600	879,500		
Total Assets	9,926,400	9,312,800	8,236,600		
Short Term Debt	479,100	286,400	741,500		
Current Liabilities	1,320,600	1,035,900	1,409,700		
Long Term Debt	5,310,200	5,209,100	4,044,800		
Total Liabilities	6,777,400	6,415,700	5,550,100		
Total Equity	3,149,000	2,897,100	2,686,500		
Total Liab. & Equity	9,926,400	9,312,800	8,236,600		
CAPITAL (000)					
Total Debt	5,789,300	5,495,500	4,786,300		
Preferred Equity	612,600	582,800	588,300		
Common Equity	2,536,400	2,314,300	2,098,200		

Business:

TRANSCANADA PIPELINES LTD. transports and markets natural gas. The company owns and manages a pipeline system from Alberta to Quebec, and has investments in other pipeline systems in Canada, United States and Internationally. Its subsidiary, Western Gas Marketing Ltd., buys and sells natural gas from Western Canada.

Date	EPS	DPS	Tot Rev	Inc Bex
Mar 95	0.43	0.25	1,701,400	97,100
Dec 94	0.40	0.25	1,726,300	90,400
Sep 94	0.39	0.23	1,097,600	88,000
Jun 94	0.38	0.23	1,131,800	85,500
Mar 94	0.43	0.23	1,320,500	94,700
Dec 93	0.40	0.23	1,330,800	88,800
Sep 93	0.40	0.21	1,047,600	87,800
Jun 93	0.42	0.21	1,027,600	91,700

Synopsis:

TransCanada PipeLines Limited is involved in three global projects. Phase One expansion of the Cusiana oil pipeline in Colombia will be operational in 1995 and Phase Two will be operational by late 1997. In March, all shareholder, operating and transportation agreements for Oleoducto Central S.A. (OCENSA), a new Colombian pipeline company, were substantially completed. The pipeline will carry oil from the Cusiana and Cupiagua fields to the Caribbean port of Covenas. TransCanada has a 17.5% interest in OCENSA. The second project, the Mariquita to Cali natural gas pipeline, is part of Colombia's national gasification plan. Construction of the pipeline will start in 1995, with operations expected to begin in late 1996. Contributions to TransCanada's earnings should start in 1997. The third global initiative is the Songo Songo Gas Development Project in Tanzania. In 1994, TransCanada and Ocelot Energy were chosen to develop the Songo Songo gas field for power generation. The main project is currently under negotiation.

In March 1995, TransCanada notified holders of all 12.5 million Cumulative Equity Second Preferred Shares, Series B that the shares will be converted to common shares on August 1, 1995. The 1995 first quarter results reflect a growth in all of TransCanada's business activities. A higher rate base helped pipeline operations, while the contribution of the Northridge group of companies, partially offset by lower natural gas prices, helped the Energy Marketing segment. TransCanada bought the marketing businesses of Northridge Canada Inc. in late 1994. The acquisition expanded TransCanada's marketing base to include crude oil, gas liquids, and other associated products.

Annual gas transmission volumes for 1994 (1993) in billions of cubic feet were: domestic, 1,203 (1,205); and export, 1,017 (923). Revenues (operating income) by segment were: gas transmission, 36% (97%); energy marketing, 61% (2%); power generation and other, 3% (1%).

Relative strength to TSE300 / Price / Volume (in 1000's of board lots) charts

Rank (Profit/Revenue/Assets)
16   26   29

Gerald J. Maier
Chairman

George W. Watson
President & C.E.O.

Robert Hodgins
Sr. V.P. & C.F.O.

George M. Hugh
Chief Operating Officer

Address
P.O. Box 1000
Station M
Calgary
AB
T2P 4K5
(403) 267-6100

Fax: (403) 267-6444

T0002546/G/9.2

WESTCOAST ENERGY INC.

Exchanges	Price (Jun29'95)	20 .12	Trailing P/E	12 .20	Stock Symbol
TMVN	Trailing Yield (%)	4 .47	Trailing EPS	1 .65	W

Period Ending	Dec94	Dec93	Dec92	Dec91	Dec90
Yearly Statistics					
Price-Close	22 .25	22 .00	17 .25	20 .63	21 .50
Price-High	24 .63	22 .63	21 .13	21 .50	22 .25
Price-Low	19 .63	16 .25	15 .00	19 .00	19 .63
P/E-Close	12 .16	12 .09	nm	15 .17	15 .25
Dividends per Share	0 .89	0 .82	0 .80	0 .80	0 .80
Dividend Yield (%)	4 .00	3 .73	4 .64	3 .88	3 .72
Sales per Share	34 .63	37 .28	21 .50	20 .26	24 .82
EPS before extra. item	1 .83	1 .82	(1 .31)	1 .36	1 .41
Cash Flow per Share	3 .86	4 .63	3 .65	3 .11	4 .23
Book Value per Share	16 .75	15 .76	14 .05	15 .78	15 .18
O/S Common Shares	86 ,445	85 ,319	72 ,679	57 ,255	56 ,487
Total Revenue	3 ,789 ,000	3 ,672 ,000	1 ,825 ,949	1 ,499 ,273	1 ,648 ,599
Income before extra.	173 ,000	158 ,000	(64 ,272)	86 ,028	86 ,250
Cash Flow	332 ,000	361 ,000	219 ,277	176 ,777	232 ,104
Debt/Equity	2 .50	2 .45	3 .01	2 .07	1 .92
Return on Capital (%)	10 .94	10 .80	4 .59	9 .52	13 .69
Ret. on Com. Equity (%)	11 .24	12 .00	(8 .15)	8 .76	10 .01
% Change Profit	9 .5	345 .8	(174 .7)	(0 .3)	22 .8
% Change Revenue	3 .2	101 .1	21 .8	(9 .1)	95 .3
% Change Assets	13 .1	(0 .5)	68 .5	8 .3	66 .8
Preferred Div. Coverage	10 .8	9 .9	0 .0		
Total Div. Coverage	1 .9	2 .0	0 .0		
Interest Coverage	1 .8	1 .7	0 .9		
Current Ratio	0 .6	0 .7	0 .6		
Operating Margin	15 .4	15 .2	18 .6		
Asset Turnover	0 .4	0 .4	0 .2		
5 YEAR RATIOS (%)					
Return on Capital	9 .9	9 .9	10 .1		
Return on Com. Equity	6 .8	6 .4	5 .6		
Profit Growth	19 .7	20 .6	na		
Revenue Growth	35 .0	34 .1	16 .2		
Asset Growth	27 .9	24 .8	24 .7		
BALANCE SHEET (000)					
Cash	0	0	0		
Current Assets	1 ,018 ,000	949 ,000	845 ,738		
Net Fixed Assets	6 ,022 ,000	5 ,306 ,000	5 ,517 ,620		
Invest's & Advances	251 ,000	207 ,000	169 ,351		
Total Assets	7 ,422 ,000	6 ,562 ,000	6 ,594 ,924		
Short Term Debt	1 ,192 ,000	805 ,000	783 ,578		
Current Liabilities	1 ,757 ,000	1 ,383 ,000	1 ,326 ,292		
Long Term Debt	3 ,119 ,000	2 ,867 ,000	2 ,977 ,684		
Total Liabilities	5 ,694 ,000	5 ,062 ,000	5 ,344 ,037		
Total Equity	1 ,728 ,000	1 ,500 ,000	1 ,250 ,887		
Total Liab. & Equity	7 ,422 ,000	6 ,562 ,000	6 ,594 ,924		
CAPITAL (000)					
Total Debt	4 ,311 ,000	3 ,672 ,000	3 ,761 ,262		
Preferred Equity	280 ,000	155 ,000	229 ,969		
Common Equity	1 ,448 ,000	1 ,345 ,000	1 ,020 ,918		

Business:

WESTCOAST ENERGY INC. operates in Canada's natural gas industry. Company interests include natural gas pipelines, processing, storage, distribution, power generation and gas services businesses. Westcoast has expanded and diversified its energy business activities throughout Canada and the United States, and has recently begun the process of establishing joint venture businesses in international markets.

Date	EPS	DPS	Tot Rev	Inc Bex
Mar 95	1 .25	0 .23	1 ,276 ,000	114 ,000
Dec 94	0 .48	0 .23	1 ,024 ,000	47 ,000
Sep 94	(0 .17)	0 .22	693 ,000	(10 ,000)
Jun 94	0 .09	0 .22	791 ,000	11 ,000
Mar 94	1 .43	0 .22	1 ,301 ,000	125 ,000
Dec 93	0 .64	0 .22	1 ,101 ,000	56 ,000
Sep 93	(0 .21)	0 .20	678 ,029	(8 ,688)
Jun 93	0 .13	0 .20	752 ,424	14 ,626

Synopsis:

Westcoast Energy Inc. abandoned plans to build a $672-million gas processing plant in Tumbler Ridge in northeastern British Columbia. Falling natural gas prices and uncertainty over future market demand led to the decision made by Westcoast. A $400-million expansion of Westcoast's Pine River plant is an alternative way to meet the gas producers' reduced demand, which dropped from 313 million cubic feet per day to 230 cubic feet per day.

Foothills Pipe Lines Ltd. received conditional approval from the National Energy Board in January, to build a 134-mile pipeline from Wild Horse, Alberta, to Princess, Alberta. The cost of the proposed project is estimated at $140-million. The pipeline would connect with NOVA and run to the Canada-U.S. border and transport 737 million cubic feet of gas per day, primarily to U.S. markets.

Westcoast anticipates expenditures in excess of $1-billion to Union Gas' facilities over the next four years as the integration of Canadian and U.S. markets leads to a steady rise in volumes transported by Union Gas. The Centra companies expect to spend about $600-million on capital expenditures over the next four years.

The decline in net income for the first quarter of 1995, compared to the first three months of 1994, is primarily due to the weather conditions in Ontario. The first quarter of 1995 had warmer weather than normal while the first quarter of 1994 had considerably colder weather than normal. The warmer weather negatively affected the operating revenues and net income of the Gas Distribution segment. Earnings increases during the first quarter of 1995 from higher rate bases and rates of return on common equity were partially offset by higher short-term interest rates. Revenues (operating income) by segment in 1994 were: pipeline, 11% (25%); gas distribution, 66% (75%); gas services, 22% (1%); power generation, 1% (1%); other activities, less than 1% (-2%).

Rank (Profit/Revenue/Assets)
40   39   31

Michael E.J. Phelps
Chairman & C.E.O.

Arthur H. Willms
President & C.O.O.

Graham M. Wilson
Exec. V.P. & C.F.O.

Address
Suite 3400
Park Place
666 Burrard Street
Vancouver
BC
V6C 3M8
(604) 488-8000
Fax: (604) 488-8099

W0001495/G/9.2

Page	Company	Fiscal year end	EARNINGS PER SHARE		
			Last Year	Estimate this year	Estimate next year
341	Anglo-Canadian Telephone	Dec-94	99.64	na	na
342	BC Gas	Dec-94	0.97	1.22	1.35
343	BC Gas Utility	Dec-94	0.88	na	na
344	BC Tel	Dec-94	1.69	na	na
345	BC Telecom	Dec-94	1.88	1.99	2.12
346	BCE Inc.	Dec-94	3.03	2.34	3.19
347	Bruncor	Sep-94	1.68	1.60	1.70
348	Canadian Utilities	Dec-94	2.22	2.25	2.41
349	Canadian Western Natural Gas	Dec-94	7.36	na	na
350	Centra Gas Ontario	Dec-94	1.87	na	na
351	Consumers' Gas Company	Sep-94	1.82	1.57	1.71
352	Fortis	Dec-94	2.46	2.62	2.66
353	Island Telephone	Dec-94	1.87	1.86	1.98
354	Maritime Telegraph and Telephone	Dec-94	1.61	1.63	1.77
355	Newfoundland Light & Power	Dec-94	2.70	na	na
356	Newtel Enterprises	Dec-94	1.89	1.96	2.05
357	Northwestern Utilities	Dec-94	11.35	na	na
358	Nova Scotia Power	Dec-94	1.10	1.15	1.20
359	Pacific Northern Gas	Dec-94	1.77	1.88	1.94
360	Quebec-Telephone	Dec-94	1.75	1.80	1.88
361	Telus Corporation	Dec-94	1.52	1.45	1.66
362	TransAlta Corporation	Dec-94	1.18	1.18	1.23
363	TransAlta Utilities	Dec-94	1.07	na	na
364	Unicorp Energy	Dec-94	2.47	na	na

Estimates from First Call Corporation, 22 Pittsburgh Street, Boston, MA 02210   (800) 366-9992   Fax (617) 261-5679

Utilities

Telephone Utilities

On September 16, 1994, the CRTC set out a regulation framework for telephone companies. The framework will change earnings regulations to price caps by January 1, 1998. It will split the rate base into utility and competitive segments. Effective January 1, 1995, only the utility segment will be subject to earnings regulation. The framework implemented a Carrier Access Tariff (CAT) applicable to both the telephone companies and their competitors in long distance services. CAT consists of a contribution component applied on a per-minute basis, a component to cover the cost of switching and aggregation, and a component for the recovery of start-up costs. The new framework allows each telephone company to increase monthly basic local service rates by up to $2 in each of 1995, 1996, and 1997 and reduce basic toll rates by a corresponding amount. It requires that competitive network services offered by the telephone companies be subject to the CAT.

After the proposal was released, various interest group filed a number of appeals to the Cabinet and to the CRTC against Decision 94-19. As a result of these appeals, the Federal Cabinet requested the CRTC to reconsider the rate rebalancing program contained in Decision 94-19, and to undertake a comparison of telephone company costs with external U.S. benchmarks as part of that process. The Cabinet also requested the CRTC to look at the need for rate rebalancing on an individual telephone company basis and to ensure that the principle of affordable telephone service is not compromised.

The CRTC put a hold on its decision to make alternative long distance service providers subject to a per-minute contribution mechanism instead of the existing per-trunk contribution mechanism. Acknowledging that a uniform per-minute rate might adversely affect competitors' willingness to compete in the off-peak market, the CRTC suggested a "de-averaging" of the per-minute contribution mechanism into two rate components, one rate for peak minutes and another, at 50% less, for off-peak minutes. Public hearings have been initiated to consider this alternative proposal and the timing of its implementation .

Other parts of Decision 94-19 have proceeded as planned since. The CRTC has initiated proceedings to split the rate base of the telephone companies into Utility and Competitive segments. A process to determine 1995 contribution rates for long distance services under the resulting split rate base has been proceeding. The split rate base proceeding was subsequently expanded to address Canada/U.S. cost comparisons for both local and long distance telephone services. It examined the telephone companies' broadband initiatives (including Beacon) to determine how much of that investment should be allocated to the Utility segment.

Gas Utilities

The milder winter in 1995 had a negative effect on revenues within the gas utilities industry. The warmer weather led to lower gas volumes being shipped, which led to lower revenues. Some companies were able to offset the declines through an increase in the customer base or through an increase in the allowed rate of return or a combination of the two. The higher gas prices caused record drilling activity which in turn produced a large oversupply of natural gas within Alberta in 1994. During the latter part of 1994, the oversupply combined with other factors and led to a decline in the cost of gas at the wellhead. Short term gas was selling for less than $1 per Gigajoule (GJ) in December, 1994 compared to more than $2 per GJ in December 1993.

Sources for customer growth include residential conversions, to natural gas from oil and electricity, and new home construction. One company is reducing the time required to install natural gas service to a customer's home to less than three weeks from an average of six to eight weeks. Some companies within this industry are either the regulated portion of its parent's holdings or have holdings that consist of regulated and non-regulated companies.

Electic Utilities

With new price cap regulations, Maritime Electric base rates are falling. To combat this, the company undertook measures to reduce operating costs. Other sources for energy, including oil and gas, remain as competition for the electrical utilities. Competitive rates and controlling costs are methods dor the companies to remain competitive. The deregulation of Alberta's electricity market, which continues to unfold, will lead to increased competition for TransAlta Utilities Corporation. Cost cutting and searching for opportunities both inside and outside the Alberta market are methods being used by TransAlta to combat this.

ANGLO-CANADIAN TELEPHONE COMPANY

Exchanges	Price (Jun29'95)	40.00	Trailing P/E	nc	Stock Symbol
TM	Trailing Yield (%)	nc	Trailing EPS	107.11	**ACT.PR.C**

Period Ending	Dec94	Dec93	Dec92	Dec91	Dec90
Yearly Statistics					
Price-Close	40.00	41.50	38.00	35.25	29.75
Price-High	44.00	43.00	40.50	36.00	32.25
Price-Low	38.00	36.50	33.00	30.25	28.75
P/E-Close	nc	nc	nc	nc	nc
Dividends per Share	nc	nc	nc	nc	nc
Dividend Yield (%)	nc	nc	nc	nc	nc
Sales per Share	1,633.21	1,598.93	1,480.81	1,422.14	1,603.59
EPS before extra. item	99.64	96.91	93.42	91.53	83.24
Cash Flow per Share	494.13	452.84	396.41	391.18	358.14
Book Value per Share	872.26	815.86	721.33	669.79	612.16
O/S Common Shares	1,284	1,284	1,284	1,284	1,284
Total Revenue	2,565,400	2,504,700	2,302,456	2,223,351	2,106,112
Income before extra.	129,900	126,400	119,926	117,500	108,541
Cash Flow	634,300	581,300	508,859	502,142	466,992
Debt/Equity	1.56	1.51	1.81	1.84	1.98
Return on Capital (%)	18.19	19.34	18.47	18.28	11.10
Ret. on Com. Equity (%)	11.80	12.61	13.20	14.03	14.04
% Change Profit	2.8	5.4	2.1	8.3	(21.2)
% Change Revenue	2.4	8.8	3.6	5.6	10.0
% Change Assets	6.0	4.5	4.8	4.3	4.1
Preferred Div. Coverage	65.0	63.2	58.3		
Total Div. Coverage	2.3	63.2	2.2		
Interest Coverage	3.3	3.0	3.0		
Current Ratio	0.7	0.8	0.6		
Operating Margin	24.9	25.0	25.9		
Asset Turnover	0.4	0.4	0.4		
5 YEAR RATIOS (%)					
Return on Capital	17.1	17.3	18.2		
Return on Com. Equity	13.1	14.6	17.7		
Profit Growth	(1.2)	(8.2)	2.1		
Revenue Growth	5.9	5.9	5.0		
Asset Growth	4.6	4.7	4.7		
BALANCE SHEET (000)					
Cash	33,800	39,000	35,993		
Current Assets	606,900	513,900	457,231		
Net Fixed Assets	4,232,000	4,026,700	3,861,426		
Invest's & Advances	71,100	93,400	103,255		
Total Assets	4,965,000	4,684,800	4,485,137		
Short Term Debt	372,200	169,400	368,134		
Current Liabilities	917,700	681,800	762,577		
Long Term Debt	1,434,900	1,466,600	1,372,820		
Total Liabilities	3,807,800	3,600,000	3,521,692		
Total Equity	1,157,200	1,084,800	963,445		
Total Liab. & Equity	4,965,000	4,684,800	4,485,137		
CAPITAL (000)					
Total Debt	1,807,100	1,636,000	1,740,954		
Preferred Equity	37,500	37,500	37,500		
Common Equity	1,119,700	1,047,300	925,945		

Business:

ANGLO-CANADIAN TELEPHONE CO. operates, through subsidiaries, telecommunications services in British Columbia and Quebec. The company owns 50.46% of British Columbia Telephone Co. and 50.31% of Quebec-Telephone. Dominion Directories is an operating division. GTE Corp. of Stamford, CT, is the major shareholder of the company.

Date	EPS	DPS	Tot Rev	Inc Bex
Dec 94	23.29	nc	664,800	29,900
Sep 94	30.07	nc	659,100	38,600
Jun 94	26.95	nc	628,100	34,600
Mar 94	26.80	nc	612,800	217,600
Dec 93	26.31	nc	649,500	33,700
Sep 93	30.29	nc	632,054	38,885
Jun 93	25.36	nc	630,651	32,557
Mar 93	26.80	nc	581,800	21,200

Synopsis:

In 1994, Anglo-Canadian Telephone's long-distance service revenues dipped $66.3-million to $1.048-billion, or 5.9% from a year ago. The number of calls completed by the company during 1994 rose by approximately 7%. However, this was offset by a drop in average revenue per minute. Discount calling packages introduced for both business and residential customers were partly responsible for the revenue drop. Also contributing to the decrease in this revenue category was a $38-million decline in BC Tel's portion of long-distance revenues shared with other Canadian telephone companies. This was mainly the result of a non-recurring recovery of $34-million worth of shared long-distance revenues in 1993.

In 1994, local service revenues rose 11.8% or $110.3-million to $1.048-billion in 1994. The number of customer access lines grew by about 4%. The cellular phone customer base continued to grow. As well, additional revenues flowed from the expanded use of customer calling features. About two thirds of local service revenue was earned by providing network access services and renting equipment to business and residential customers.

Directory advertising, equipment sales and other revenues rose by 9%, or $37.2-million, to $453.5-million in 1994. This increase was mainly due to higher revenues in non-regulated businesses, excluding cellular business that was reflected in local service revenues.

Spending on property, plant, and equipment came to $678.5-million, an increase of $112.1-million from 1993. Investment included the installation of digital central office switches, remote switches connected to the central office by fibre optic links, and additional facilities connecting subscribers to local switching offices. Spending on long-distance facilities also rose due to spending on additional fibre optic routes.

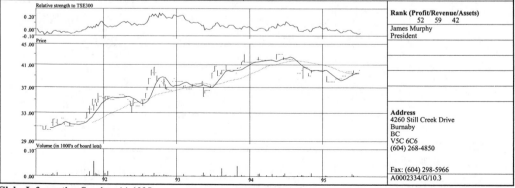

Rank (Profit/Revenue/Assets)
52   59   42

James Murphy
President

Address
4260 Still Creek Drive
Burnaby
BC
V5C 6C6
(604) 268-4850

Fax: (604) 298-5966
A0002334/G/10.3

BC GAS INC.

Exchanges	Price (Jun29'95)	14 .62	Trailing P/E	13 .42	Stock Symbol
TMV	Trailing Yield (%)	6 .15	Trailing EPS	1 .09	**BCG**

Period Ending	Dec94	Dec93	Dec92	Dec91	Dec90
Yearly Statistics					
Price-Close	13 .50	16 .63	14 .75	17 .13	14 .75
Price-High	17 .25	17 .00	17 .88	17 .38	15 .75
Price-Low	13 .13	13 .75	13 .88	14 .25	13 .75
P/E-Close	13 .92	11 .63	42 .14	8 .83	8 .24
Dividends per Share	0 .90	0 .90	0 .90	0 .90	0 .82
Dividend Yield (%)	6 .67	5 .41	6 .10	5 .26	5 .56
Sales per Share	17 .23	18 .09	16 .53	31 .37	35 .96
EPS before extra. item	0 .97	1 .43	0 .35	1 .94	1 .79
Cash Flow per Share	2 .98	3 .46	2 .80	5 .52	5 .51
Book Value per Share	12 .11	11 .95	11 .42	11 .85	11 .42
O/S Common Shares	45 ,075	40 ,468	39 ,388	38 ,495	16 ,338
Total Revenue	853 ,968	794 ,699	591 ,588	707 ,746	690 ,944
Income before extra.	37 ,336	55 ,564	26 ,153	50 ,882	42 ,547
Cash Flow	115 ,250	122 ,829	97 ,178	103 ,538	89 ,725
Debt/Equity	2 .43	2 .43	1 .61	1 .34	3 .07
Return on Capital (%)	8 .42	9 .41	6 .49	11 .98	11 .94
Ret. on Com. Equity (%)	7 .26	10 .80	3 .48	12 .60	18 .62
% Change Profit	(32 .8)	112 .5	(48 .6)	0 .0	20 .7
% Change Revenue	7 .5	34 .3	(16 .4)	2 .4	4 .6
% Change Assets	9 .3	20 .6	9 .7	7 .3	7 .9

Date	EPS	DPS	Tot Rev	Inc Bex
Mar 95	1 .45	0 .23	321 ,520	58 ,791
Dec 94	0 .92	0 .23	289 ,063	35 ,601
Sep 94	(0 .63)	0 .23	119 ,993	(23 ,720)
Jun 94	(0 .65)	0 .23	134 ,011	(22 ,514)
Mar 94	1 .33	0 .23	311 ,264	47 ,969
Dec 93	0 .98	0 .23	271 ,162	34 ,751
Sep 93	(0 .49)	0 .23	112 ,991	(17 ,396)
Jun 93	(0 .16)	0 .23	135 ,087	(2 ,378)

Preferred Div. Coverage	np	np	2 .5	
Total Div. Coverage	1 .1	1 .5	0 .6	
Interest Coverage	1 .4	1 .7	1 .4	
Current Ratio	0 .3	0 .4	0 .3	
Operating Margin	18 .8	19 .9	15 .5	
Asset Turnover	0 .3	0 .3	0 .3	
5 YEAR RATIOS (%)				
Return on Capital	9 .6	10 .4	10 .3	
Return on Com. Equity	10 .5	12 .9	12 .3	
Profit Growth	1 .1	43 .6	53 .7	
Revenue Growth	5 .2	18 .5	23 .1	
Asset Growth	10 .8	10 .9	34 .4	
BALANCE SHEET (000)				
Cash	955	10 ,814	0	
Current Assets	203 ,852	197 ,990	138 ,541	
Net Fixed Assets	1 ,949 ,724	1 ,761 ,639	1 ,515 ,448	
Invest's & Advances	11 ,412	13 ,717	14 ,246	
Total Assets	2 ,225 ,896	2 ,035 ,818	1 ,687 ,386	
Short Term Debt	412 ,572	312 ,437	332 ,279	
Current Liabilities	597 ,590	484 ,192	463 ,642	
Long Term Debt	911 ,478	862 ,095	583 ,154	
Total Liabilities	1 ,680 ,105	1 ,552 ,367	1 ,117 ,713	
Total Equity	545 ,791	483 ,451	569 ,673	
Total Liab. & Equity	2 ,225 ,896	2 ,035 ,818	1 ,687 ,386	
CAPITAL (000)				
Total Debt	1 ,324 ,050	1 ,174 ,532	915 ,433	
Preferred Equity	0	0	120 ,000	
Common Equity	545 ,791	483 ,451	449 ,673	

Business:

BC GAS INC. operates principally in two business segments: gas utility operations, primarily involving the transmission and distribution of natural gas; and oil pipeline operations, primarily involving the transportation of crude oil and refines products.

Synopsis:

In the first quarter ended March 31, 1995, B.C. Gas Inc. reported increased revenues of $167.8-million compared to $149.1-million over the same period in 1994. The first quarter results were helped by the increase in the allowed rate of return on common equity from 10.65% in 1994 to 12% in 1995, following a decision by the British Columbia Utilities commission on June 10, 1994. Customer growth remained strong with BC Gas Utility serving 684,552 customers as of March 31, 1995, a one year increase of 21,347 new customers.

The company has expressed an interest in selling its share of FuelMaker Corp. of Toronto. FuelMaker was formed six years ago when BC Gas joined Questar Corp. of Salt Lake City and Sulzer Bros. Ltd. of Switzerland to produce equipment that could be leased to homeowners to provide convenient, overnight refuelling of natural gas tanks. FuelMaker cost BC Gas $2.5-million for its one-third losses this year, and the company decided to write down its entire $4.1-million investment in the venture. Sales of home refuellers have not met expectations as consumers failed to embrace natural gas-powered cars the way the partners had hoped. BC Gas will make a decision on Inland Gas & Oil Ltd., its production and exploration subsidiary based in Calgary. Options that include selling Inland outright, taking it public, or finding a joint venture partner to help take it public.

In late 1994, BC Gas bought all the outstanding shares of Trans Mountain. This helped simplify the corporate structure, representing a sound long-term investment and provide regulatory diversification. The 1995 future of Trans Mountain continues the growth of the past few years. The diminishing production from the Alaska oil fields has resulted in increased shipments to the Washington state refineries they serve. With the increase of crude oil in Alberta and the increased capacity of the Trans Mountain pipeline this growth can be accommodated. The Stage II expansion of this pipeline will be completed in 1995.

Rank (Profit/Revenue/Assets)
134 129 98

Ronald L. Cliff
Chairman

Robert E. Kadlec
President & C.E.O.

Address
1111 West Georgia Street
Vancouver
BC
V6E 4M4
(604) 443-6500

Fax: (604) 443-6929
01003623/G/10.1

For further company information, call Globe Information Services 1-800-268-9128 or (416) 585-5345

BC GAS UTILITY LTD.

Exchanges **TMV**   Stock Symbol **BCG.PR.A**

	Price (Jun29'95)	7.62	Trailing P/E	nc
	Trailing Yield (%)	nc	Trailing EPS	1.08

Period Ending	Dec94	Dec93	Dec92	Dec91	Dec90
Yearly Statistics					
Price-Close	25.38	16.50	14.75	17.13	14.75
Price-High	25.63	17.00	17.88	17.38	15.75
Price-Low	25.00	13.75	13.88	14.25	13.75
P/E-Close	nc	nc	nc	nc	nc
Dividends per Share	nc	nc	nc	nc	nc
Dividend Yield (%)	nc	nc	nc	nc	nc
Sales per Share	15.95	17.10	16.53	31.37	35.96
EPS before extra. item	0.88	1.34	0.35	1.94	1.79
Cash Flow per Share	1.98	2.55	2.80	5.52	5.51
Book Value per Share	11.33	11.28	11.42	11.85	11.42
O/S Common Shares	43,182	39,937	39,388	38,495	16,338
Total Revenue	704,434	675,852	591,588	707,746	690,944
Income before extra.	43,627	59,492	26,153	50,882	42,547
Cash Flow	82,324	95,128	97,178	103,538	89,725
Debt/Equity	1.49	1.44	1.61	1.34	3.07
Return on Capital (%)	7.84	8.88	6.49	11.98	11.94
Ret. on Com. Equity (%)	7.13	10.91	3.48	12.60	18.62
% Change Profit	(26.7)	127.5	(48.6)	0.0	20.7
% Change Revenue	4.2	14.2	(16.4)	2.4	4.6
% Change Assets	9.2	(9.1)	9.7	7.3	7.9
Preferred Div. Coverage	4.3	5.7	2.5		
Total Div. Coverage	0.9	1.3	0.6		
Interest Coverage	1.6	1.8	1.4		
Current Ratio	0.4	0.5	0.3		
Operating Margin	16.0	18.3	15.5		
Asset Turnover	0.4	0.4	0.3		
5 YEAR RATIOS (%)					
Return on Capital	9.4	10.3	10.3		
Return on Com. Equity	10.5	13.0	12.3		
Profit Growth	4.3	45.6	53.7		
Revenue Growth	1.2	14.7	23.1		
Asset Growth	4.7	4.8	34.4		
BALANCE SHEET (000)					
Cash	0	18	0		
Current Assets	167,435	156,677	138,541		
Net Fixed Assets	1,476,469	1,347,350	1,515,448		
Invest's & Advances	12,594	10,210	14,246		
Total Assets	1,675,072	1,533,845	1,687,386		
Short Term Debt	235,752	202,318	332,279		
Current Liabilities	384,748	329,547	463,642		
Long Term Debt	670,570	618,364	583,154		
Total Liabilities	1,065,974	963,386	1,117,713		
Total Equity	609,098	570,459	569,673		
Total Liab. & Equity	1,675,072	1,533,845	1,687,386		
CAPITAL (000)					
Total Debt	906,322	820,682	915,433		
Preferred Equity	120,000	120,000	120,000		
Common Equity	489,098	450,459	449,673		

Business:

BC GAS UTILITY LTD., is a publicly-traded, integrated energy company involved in the regulated businesses of natural gas distribution and petroleum transportation and the non-regulated areas of energy marketing, project development and international consulting services.

Date	EPS	DPS	Tot Rev	Inc Bex
Mar 95	1.45	nc	167,897	58,791
Dec 94	0.92	nc	251,044	37,473
Sep 94	(0.72)	nc	77,549	(24,516)
Jun 94	(0.57)	nc	103,085	(19,953)
Mar 94	1.22	nc	272,756	50,623
Dec 93	0.93	nc	233,867	38,562
Sep 93	(0.49)	nc	83,741	(17,279)
Jun 93	(0.16)	nc	111,060	(2,378)

Synopsis:

B.C. Gas Utility Inc. reported increased revenues in the first quarter ended March 31, 1995. Revenue was $269-million compared to $261.2-million over the same period in 1994. The first quarter results were helped by the increase in the allowed rate of return on common equity from 10.65% in 1994 to 12% in 1995 following a decision by the British Columbia Utilities commission on June 10, 1994. Customer growth remained strong with B.C. Gas Utility serving 684,552 B.C. customers as of March 31, 1995, a one year increase of 21,347 new customers.

The implementation of a Revenue Stabilization Adjustment Mechanism (RSAM) in accordance with the Commission's decision has removed weather related volume risk experienced by the utility during the five winter months from November through March. The weather was warmer than normal by 6% in the coastal region and 2% in the interior region during the three months ended March 31, 1995. The contribution from RSAM for this period was $3.6-million.

British Columbia has a steady population growth, adding to the demand for service and increasing B.C. Gas' already large and stable customer base. As the utility prepares for a more competitive environment, changes are appearing in the concept of what constitutes suitable expansion within a local distribution company. For many years the pipeline system was routinely extended to serve communities and businesses as they expanded. Today when the company is faced with growing pressure on the system, it examines a much broader array of demand management and alternative supply options. Plans for the expansion are then aggressively analyzed to ensure that they are economic and do not place an unrealistic rate burden on customers while nor expose shareholders to undue risk.

Relative strength to TSE300 / Price / Volume (in 1000's of board lots)

Rank (Profit/Revenue/Assets)
127   154   117

Robert E. Kadlec
Chairman Of The Board

Stephen T. Bellringer
President

John M. Reid
Exec. V.P. Finance & C.F.O.

Patrick D. Lloyd
Exec. V.P. Operations

Address
1111 West Georgia Street
Vancouver
BC
V6E 4M4
(604) 443-6500

Fax: (604) 443-6614
I0001011/G/10.1

BC TEL

Exchanges	Price (Jun29'95)	63.00	Trailing P/E	nc	Stock Symbol
TMV	Trailing Yield (%)	nc	Trailing EPS	1.61	BT.PR.A

Period Ending	Dec94	Dec93	Dec92	Dec91	Dec90
Yearly Statistics					
Price-Close	65.00	62.00	19.63	23.00	19.25
Price-High	66.00	65.00	23.88	23.00	19.50
Price-Low	60.00	56.00	18.75	18.63	16.25
P/E-Close	nc	nc	nc	nc	nc
Dividends per Share	nc	nc	nc	nc	nc
Dividend Yield (%)	nc	nc	nc	nc	nc
Sales per Share	16.52	17.09	17.51	17.99	17.67
EPS before extra. item	1.69	1.68	1.78	1.78	1.72
Cash Flow per Share	4.41	4.57	4.08	4.53	4.45
Book Value per Share	14.91	14.19	14.22	13.42	12.59
O/S Common Shares	121,380	121,380	111,596	108,746	105,698
Total Revenue	2,020,900	2,012,900	1,949,200	1,969,700	1,877,700
Income before extra.	204,700	204,000	205,700	201,000	193,200
Cash Flow	535,200	532,500	451,200	487,900	466,400
Debt/Equity	0.74	0.67	0.81	0.91	0.97
Return on Capital (%)	16.06	16.56	16.19	17.08	16.77
Ret. on Com. Equity (%)	11.32	11.80	12.91	13.71	14.15
% Change Profit	0.3	(0.8)	2.3	4.0	8.8
% Change Revenue	0.4	3.3	(1.0)	4.9	10.4
% Change Assets	5.0	(0.3)	0.3	4.6	4.1

Preferred Div. Coverage	43.6	23.2	22.9
Total Div. Coverage	1.8	0.8	1.5
Interest Coverage	4.0	3.8	3.6
Current Ratio	0.6	0.8	0.8
Operating Margin	24.6	24.3	24.2
Asset Turnover	0.5	0.5	0.5
5 YEAR RATIOS (%)			
Return on Capital	16.5	16.6	16.7
Return on Com. Equity	12.8	13.3	13.6
Profit Growth	2.8	4.8	6.9
Revenue Growth	3.5	4.1	3.5
Asset Growth	2.6	3.2	3.8
BALANCE SHEET (000)			
Cash	3,500	0	0
Current Assets	410,500	354,100	424,000
Net Fixed Assets	3,464,400	3,313,100	3,242,300
Invest's & Advances	29,700	51,600	48,500
Total Assets	3,933,500	3,745,900	3,758,500
Short Term Debt	311,100	103,100	247,800
Current Liabilities	661,800	432,900	561,800
Long Term Debt	1,082,800	1,137,800	1,165,200
Total Liabilities	2,052,500	1,884,700	2,025,400
Total Equity	1,881,000	1,861,200	1,733,100
Total Liab. & Equity	3,933,500	3,745,900	3,758,500
CAPITAL (000)			
Total Debt	1,393,900	1,240,900	1,413,000
Preferred Equity	70,700	138,400	146,400
Common Equity	1,810,300	1,722,800	1,586,700

Date	EPS	DPS	Tot Rev	Inc Bex
Mar 95	0.33	nc	487,000	41,000
Dec 94	0.41	nc	521,300	50,800
Sep 94	0.42	nc	505,900	51,800
Jun 94	0.45	nc	480,100	55,900
Mar 94	0.37	nc	493,400	46,200
Dec 93	0.42	nc	520,600	53,500
Sep 93	0.54	nc	500,800	59,000
Jun 93	0.49	nc	494,700	55,700

Business:

BC TEL provides telecommunication services in British Columbia through its operating divisions and with its affiliated companies. In addition, BC TEL is a member of a number of strategic alliances, and directly or indirectly holds all of the shares of subsidiaries such as Canadian Telephones and Supplies Ltd., and Microtel Limited.

Synopsis:

In June 1995, the Supreme Court of Canada said BC Tel must allow Shaw Communications Inc. access to phone company facilities. The court restored a Canadian Radio-Television and Telecommunications Commission decision that granted Shaw the right to install its own cable on BC Tel support structures. Shaw pays the phone company for the right to lay the wires along the structures.

Sprint Canada Inc. and its sister company, Lightel Inc., are suing BC Tel and Bell Canada for $60-million. They claim to have lost long-distance business because of anti-competitive commissions paid to hotels. The lawsuit follows Sprint Canada's successful challenge at the CRTC against Bell's and BC Tel's so-called hotel-motel commission plan. Sprint applied to the CRTC three years ago for an order to either force the phone companies to offer the same discounts to all customers (including competitors) or to strike down the plan as anti-competitive. The CRTC ruled in favour of Sprint last February on the grounds that the payment of commissions was contrary to the Telecommunications Act and conferred an undue benefit on the phone companies. Under the Act, parties also may launch a civil action for damages from any carrier that violates any provision of that law.

In May 1995, BC Tel submitted an application for rate increases. In the first year, the average increase would be $4 a month for most residential and business customers. The company wants to cut the number of different rate groups in the province to seven from 21. This would result in an average residential rate increase of 75 cents a month and $1.35 a month for businesses starting in July.

In March 1995, BC Tel Mobility plans to spend over $6-million to bring cellular phone service to the West and East Kootenay regions of B.C. The expansion will mean cellular service for both residents and travellers in areas never serviced before. The plan aims to have full cellular service up and running in Nelson, Castlegar, and Trail as early as June 15; the Columbia Valley between Cranbrook and Radium Hot Springs by mid-summer; and Creston by late summer.

Relative strength to TSE300 / Price / Volume (in 1000's of board lots)

Rank (Profit/Revenue/Assets)
33 68 55

Brian A. Canfield
Chairman & C.E.O.

E. Lynn Patterson
Sales And Services

Leo J. Dooling
V.P. Finance & Administration

Address
3777 Kingsway
Burnaby
BC
V5H 3Z7
(604) 432-2151

Fax: (604) 434-6616
B0004233/G/10.3

For further company information, call Globe Information Services 1-800-268-9128 or (416) 585-5345

BC TELECOM INC.

Exchanges	Price (Jun29'95)	23.37	Trailing P/E	12.37	Stock Symbol
TMV	Trailing Yield (%)	5.26	Trailing EPS	1.89	BCT

Period Ending	Dec94	Dec93	Dec92	Dec91	Dec90
Yearly Statistics					
Price-Close	24.00	25.38	19.63	23.00	19.25
Price-High	27.38	25.38	23.88	23.00	19.50
Price-Low	21.50	18.63	18.75	18.63	16.25
P/E-Close	12.77	14.02	11.03	12.92	11.19
Dividends per Share	1.23	1.19	1.15	1.10	1.02
Dividend Yield (%)	5.13	4.69	5.86	4.78	5.30
Sales per Share	19.61	19.42	18.44	17.99	17.67
EPS before extra. item	1.88	1.81	1.78	1.78	1.72
Cash Flow per Share	5.24	5.33	4.58	4.53	4.45
Book Value per Share	15.84	14.99	14.22	13.42	12.59
O/S Common Shares	118,036	114,986	111,596	108,746	105,698
Total Revenue	2,319,600	2,242,600	2,063,400	1,969,700	1,877,700
Income before extra.	224,500	214,600	205,700	201,000	193,200
Cash Flow	613,800	606,400	505,900	487,900	466,400
Debt/Equity	0.84	0.79	0.89	0.91	0.97
Return on Capital (%)	16.76	17.32	17.05	17.08	16.77
Ret. on Com. Equity (%)	12.24	12.43	12.91	13.71	14.15
% Change Profit	4.6	4.3	2.3	4.0	8.8
% Change Revenue	3.4	8.7	4.8	4.9	10.4
% Change Assets	6.4	4.6	5.0	4.6	4.1

Preferred Div. Coverage	47.8	24.4	22.9
Total Div. Coverage	1.5	1.5	1.5
Interest Coverage	3.9	3.6	3.5
Current Ratio	0.6	0.7	0.6
Operating Margin	24.7	24.8	25.7
Asset Turnover	0.5	0.5	0.5
5 YEAR RATIOS (%)			
Return on Capital	17.0	17.0	16.9
Return on Com. Equity	13.1	13.4	13.6
Profit Growth	4.7	5.9	6.9
Revenue Growth	6.3	6.3	4.7
Asset Growth	4.8	5.2	4.7
BALANCE SHEET (000)			
Cash	6,000	0	0
Current Assets	521,300	424,700	379,700
Net Fixed Assets	3,742,800	3,553,700	3,398,900
Invest's & Advances	63,000	86,500	94,300
Total Assets	4,377,000	4,114,500	3,934,900
Short Term Debt	367,600	140,000	312,600
Current Liabilities	850,500	583,300	673,300
Long Term Debt	1,264,400	1,335,100	1,221,900
Total Liabilities	2,437,200	2,252,400	2,201,800
Total Equity	1,939,800	1,862,100	1,733,100
Total Liab. & Equity	4,377,000	4,114,500	3,934,900
CAPITAL (000)			
Total Debt	1,632,000	1,475,100	1,534,500
Preferred Equity	70,600	138,400	146,400
Common Equity	1,869,200	1,723,700	1,586,700

Business:

BC TELECOM INC. is a management corporation. The company will provide strategic direction to BC Tel, BC Tel Services and their respective subsidiaries with respect to financing matters.

Date	EPS	DPS	Tot Rev	Inc Bex
Mar 95	0.43	0.31	571,800	51,700
Dec 94	0.45	0.31	606,000	53,300
Sep 94	0.52	0.31	586,500	62,900
Jun 94	0.49	0.30	562,900	57,800
Mar 94	0.42	0.30	551,900	50,500
Dec 93	0.48	0.30	580,900	56,600
Sep 93	0.54	0.30	558,700	64,700
Jun 93	0.49	0.30	560,800	57,500

Synopsis:

In April 1995, BC Telecom took a major step in restructuring when its board of directs approved the creation of a retail division to complement the wholesale division that was formed in January. The Communication Services Division positions BC Telecom to respond quickly, effectively, and aggressively to meet the needs of residential and business customers throughout the province. The new division will be organized along seven distinct lines of business: local services; long-distance services; personal communications services; terminal equipment; data and integrated networks; interactive multimedia; and systems support services. These business units will be supported by sales and field services. Each one will have its own customers, products, competitors, resources, business strategies, and measures of success.

BC Tel estimates that capital expenditures will be $650-million in 1995. For 1996 through 1999, planned annual investment is expected to range from $655-million to $670-million. Approximately 75% of BC Telecom's future spending is needed to meet the growth in demand for basic telecommunications, cellular and paging services. Growth in the company's transport network will be provided almost exclusively on fibre. New fibre links are being deployed throughout the province and reach to areas outside British Columbia. Project spending for system modernization is over $50-million in 1995. Annual amounts ranging from $25-million to $75-million during the 1996-1999 period will provide for installation of digital switches and facilities.

In 1994, BC Telecom's business lines increased by 38,000 or 5.6%. Residential lines increased by 54,000 or 3.7%. Cellular telephone customers grew 39% to more than 148,000 at the end of 1994. That resulted in a $29-million increase in local cellular revenues.

For fiscal 1994 (1993) revenues by segment were: Local service, $970.7-million ($867-million); Long-distance, $915.3-million ($977.4-million); and Other, $409.4-million ($365.2-million).

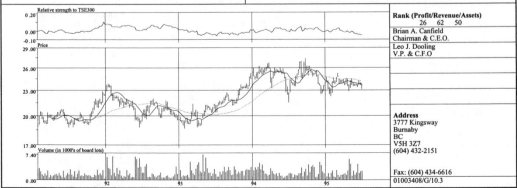

Rank (Profit/Revenue/Assets)
26 62 50
Brian A. Canfield
Chairman & C.E.O.
Leo J. Dooling
V.P. & C.F.O

Address
3777 Kingsway
Burnaby
BC
V5H 3Z7
(604) 432-2151

Fax: (604) 434-6616
01003408/G/10.3

BCE INC.

Exchanges	Price (Jun29'95)	44.00	Trailing P/E	13.75	Stock Symbol
TMVN	Trailing Yield (%)	6.11	Trailing EPS	3.20	**B**

Period Ending	Dec94	Dec93	Dec92	Dec91	Dec90
Yearly Statistics					
Price-Close	45.13	46.25	41.50	47.63	39.50
Price-High	52.88	47.00	50.00	48.25	46.50
Price-Low	43.75	40.75	40.88	38.25	34.75
P/E-Close	12.82	nm	9.86	11.88	11.29
Dividends per Share	2.69	2.65	2.61	2.57	2.53
Dividend Yield (%)	5.96	5.73	6.29	5.40	6.41
Sales per Share	70.17	64.58	63.23	59.42	53.71
EPS before extra. item	3.52	(2.44)	4.21	4.01	3.50
Cash Flow per Share	12.83	11.99	13.81	13.12	11.72
Book Value per Share	32.73	31.46	36.28	34.57	33.04
O/S Common Shares (mil)	309	308	305	310	305
Total Revenue ($mil)	22,362	20,015	20,058	20,194	18,846
Income before extra. ($mil)	1,178	(656)	1,390	1,329	1,147
Cash Flow ($mil)	3,961	3,681	4,247	4,036	3,562
Debt/Equity	1.19	1.19	0.93	0.85	0.82
Return on Capital (%)	12.95	4.01	15.32	14.94	13.50
Ret. on Com. Equity (%)	10.96	(7.22)	11.88	11.87	10.82
% Change Profit	279.6	(147.2)	4.6	15.9	50.7
% Change Revenue	11.7	(0.2)	(0.7)	7.2	10.3
% Change Assets	3.8	0.1	(19.8)	8.9	6.9

Preferred Div. Coverage	12.8	0.0	14.6
Total Div. Coverage	1.3	0.0	1.6
Interest Coverage	2.6	0.8	3.2
Current Ratio	1.1	0.9	0.8
Operating Margin	13.0	13.3	18.1
Asset Turnover	0.6	0.5	0.5
5 YEAR RATIOS (%)			
Return on Capital	12.1	12.1	13.7
Return on Com. Equity	7.7	7.0	10.3
Profit Growth	9.1	na	5.0
Revenue Growth	5.5	6.2	5.9
Asset Growth	(0.6)	7.1	6.9
BALANCE SHEET (mil)			
Cash	1,367	121	237
Current Assets	8,797	7,680	6,753
Net Fixed Assets	22,157	22,308	21,384
Invest's & Advances	4,627	3,984	5,218
Total Assets	38,092	36,708	36,656
Short Term Debt	2,019	2,591	2,832
Current Liabilities	8,305	8,972	8,700
Long Term Debt	11,434	10,449	8,613
Total Liabilities	26,740	25,785	24,349
Total Equity	11,352	10,923	12,307
Total Liab. & Equity	38,092	36,708	36,656
CAPITAL (mil)			
Total Debt	13,453	13,040	11,445
Preferred Equity	1,229	1,229	1,229
Common Equity	10,123	9,694	11,078

Business:

BCE INC. is Canada's largest telecommunications company. Its subsidiaries and affiliated companies, including wholly owned Bell Canada, provide telecommunications services to some 70% of the Canadian population. Its subsidairy Northern Telecom Limited, 52.1% owned, is a world leader in the manufacture of telecommunications equipment.

Date	EPS	DPS	Tot Rev	Inc Bex
Mar 95	0.42	0.68	5,500,000	155,000
Dec 94	0.96	0.68	6,335,000	318,000
Sep 94	1.17	0.67	5,473,000	386,000
Jun 94	0.65	0.67	5,378,000	223,000
Mar 94	0.74	0.67	5,176,000	251,000
Dec 93	(1.73)	0.67	5,679,000	(509,000)
Sep 93	0.42	0.66	4,843,000	152,000
Jun 93	(1.77)	0.66	4,701,000	(520,000)

Synopsis:

In May 1995, BCE business unit Bell Canada said that it is considering the possibility of entering the U.S. market. Bell has no immediate plans or announcements to make about the U.S. market. However, Bell is analyzing its strategic position in the whole North American marketplace.

In April 1995, Bell Canada International (BCI) announced it will buy 51% of Canbras TVA of Sao Paulo, Brazil. Canbras is cable television company. BCI will invest $26.25-million into Canbras through the purchase of a convertible debenture issued by a subsidiary of Canbras Communications of Vancouver. The debenture is convertible into at least 51% of the shares of either the subsidiary or Canbras Communications. BCI said the deal will close after regulators grant approval.

BCE's profit for the first quarter ended March 31, 1995, fell 38% to $155-million from $251-million a year earlier. The drop was due to the lackluster performance at flagship Bell Canada. Bell Canada's poor performance is being linked to long-distance competition. Bell Canada intends to seek an increase later this year for rates paid by its seven million customers in Ontario and Quebec. It also has a three-year plan to eliminate 10,000 jobs, about 20% of the utility's payroll. Although Bell Canada's revenue for the first quarter was flat at $1.9-billion, its profit contribution to BCE for the period just ended was $98-million, down from $180-million a year ago. Profit from BCE's entire domestic telecommunications group, including investments in several phone companies in the Maritimes and the Arctic, fell to $122-million in the quarter from $202-million a year ago.

In April 1995, BCE said it would not increase its 1995 dividend, nor would not it recommend an increase next year. This marks only the second time in more than 25 years that BCE will not increase its dividend. BCE linked the decision to the financial performance of Bell Canada.

Relative strength to TSE300

Price

Volume (in 1000's of board lots)

Rank (Profit/Revenue/Assets)
1   1   10

Lynton R. Wilson
Chairman President & C.E.O.

Ronald W. Osborne
Exec. V.P. & C.F.O.

Address
1000 Rue De La Gauchetiere O.
Bureau 3700
Montreal
PQ
H3B 4Y7
(514) 397-7000

Fax: (514) 397-7057
B0018061/G/10.3

BRUNCOR INC.

Exchanges	Price (Jun29'95)	21.37	Trailing P/E	10.18	Stock Symbol
TM	Trailing Yield (%)	5.99	Trailing EPS	2.10	**BRR**

Period Ending	Dec94	Dec93	Dec92	Dec91	Dec90	Business:
Yearly Statistics						BRUNCOR INC. is a management holding
Price-Close	24.25	24.13	20.25	18.63	17.88	company. Its main interests are in
Price-High	27.25	24.13	21.00	19.00	18.13	telecommunications. The bulk of the company's
Price-Low	18.63	18.68	18.00	16.63	15.25	business is in New Brunswick. The company's
P/E-Close	11.33	68.93	11.51	11.36	11.53	principal subsidiary is wholly owned New
Dividends per Share	1.28	1.28	1.27	1.24	1.21	Brunswick Telephone Co. Ltd.
Dividend Yield (%)	5.28	5.31	6.27	6.66	6.77	
Sales per Share	17.01	17.10	17.37	18.66	18.13	
EPS before extra. item	2.14	0.35	1.76	1.64	1.55	
Cash Flow per Share	5.17	4.87	5.65	5.06	5.26	
Book Value per Share	14.85	13.98	14.83	14.02	13.48	
O/S Common Shares	21,699	21,692	21,374	20,138	19,282	
Total Revenue	377,658	374,519	370,944	373,739	354,888	

						Date	EPS	DPS	Tot Rev	Inc Bex
Income before extra.	47,438	9,383	38,494	34,017	31,643	Mar 95	0.32	0.32	93,413	7,011
Cash Flow	112,217	104,915	117,740	99,543	101,462	Dec 94	0.56	0.32	98,114	12,280
Debt/Equity	1.07	1.13	1.04	1.38	1.37	Sep 94	0.39	0.32	93,427	8,377
Return on Capital (%)	16.07	9.95	14.76	15.27	15.73	Jun 94	0.83	0.32	93,160	18,585
Ret. on Com. Equity (%)	14.88	2.44	12.24	11.88	11.62	Mar 94	0.36	0.32	92,957	8,196
% Change Profit	405.6	(75.6)	13.2	7.5	479.1	Dec 93	(0.90)	0.32	97,163	(19,118)
% Change Revenue	0.8	1.0	(0.7)	5.3	7.7	Sep 93	0.43	0.32	93,902	9,936
% Change Assets	(10.2)	(0.1)	4.3	6.6	10.7	Jun 93	0.41	0.32	93,283	9,302

Preferred Div. Coverage	np	5.2	21.2		
Total Div. Coverage	1.7	0.3	1.4		
Interest Coverage	3.3	2.2	3.0		
Current Ratio	0.6	0.6	0.7		
Operating Margin	24.6	24.9	26.5		
Asset Turnover	0.5	0.4	0.4		
5 YEAR RATIOS (%)					
Return on Capital	14.4	13.4	14.1		
Return on Com. Equity	10.6	7.9	9.7		
Profit Growth	54.0	(21.7)	3.8		
Revenue Growth	2.7	4.7	1.6		
Asset Growth	1.9	5.6	(0.3)		
BALANCE SHEET (000)					
Cash	0	0	0		
Current Assets	81,848	78,154	66,024		
Net Fixed Assets	665,245	664,972	657,871		
Invest's & Advances	37,391	31,698	29,673		
Total Assets	813,610	906,314	907,067		
Short Term Debt	72,229	66,409	41,405		
Current Liabilities	135,665	125,356	98,253		
Long Term Debt	271,056	303,616	312,695		
Total Liabilities	491,406	577,972	565,056		
Total Equity	322,204	328,342	342,011		
Total Liab. & Equity	813,610	906,314	907,067		
CAPITAL (000)					
Total Debt	343,285	370,025	354,100		
Preferred Equity	0	25,000	25,000		
Common Equity	322,204	303,342	317,011		

Synopsis:

In August 1994, Bruncor's New Brunswick Telephone Co. Ltd. spun off its interactive CallMall business into a new company, New North Media. New North offers display-based marketing and services such as home shopping and banking through a screen-display telephone. In the fourth quarter of 1994, Bruncor sold a 49% interest in New North to Northern Telecom as part of a plan to offer New North's services in markets outside New Brunswick. Bruncor recognized an after-tax dilution gain of $3.2-million. NBTel said it expects the new company to expand to 50 employees by the end of 1995 and 100 employees by the end of 1996. The CallMall operations currently employ 15 people. NB Tel expects the total investment in the company over the next two years to be $40-million.

Bruncor's principal operating subsidiary, NBTel, reported operating revenues of $354.7-million for 1994, compared to $355.2-million for the preceding year. NBTel continues to experience strong gains in local service revenues for the year, up 8.4% to $170.9-million. This is due mainly to an access line increase of 22,270, up 4.6% over last year, as well as continuing strong demand from customers for enhanced services. In addition, revenues from cellular services totalled $14.9-million, an increase of 39.3% over the same period last year. However, total long-distance revenues declined 7.4% to $174.1-million. This decrease was the result of lower revenues received for the Stentor revenue settlement plan. Revenues for long-distance calls made within the province were virtually the same as last year.

As a result of Bruncor's decision to focus its strategic direction and future growth on telecommunications in eastern Canada, Bruncor reclassified two undeveloped cable television/telephone franchises in the United Kingdom as discontinued operations in 1994. In the second quarter of 1994, Bruncor recognized a $11.5-million gain on divestment of the UK franchises.

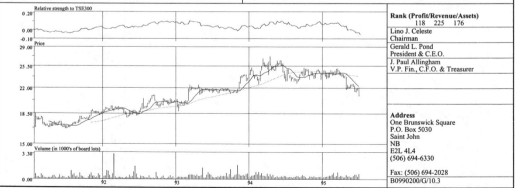

Rank (Profit/Revenue/Assets)		
118	225	176

Lino J. Celeste
Chairman
Gerald L. Pond
President & C.E.O.
J. Paul Allingham
V.P. Fin., C.F.O. & Treasurer

Address
One Brunswick Square
P.O. Box 5030
Saint John
NB
E2L 4L4
(506) 694-6330

Fax: (506) 694-2028
B0990200/G/10.3

CANADIAN UTILITIES LIMITED

Exchanges	Price (Jun29'95)	24.25	Trailing P/E	11.07	Stock Symbol
TMZ	Trailing Yield (%)	7.44	Trailing EPS	2.19	**CU**

Period Ending	Dec94	Dec93	Dec92	Dec91	Dec90
Yearly Statistics					
Price-Close	24.00	25.63	20.50	21.38	20.38
Price-High	27.00	26.88	23.00	21.75	22.00
Price-Low	21.88	20.25	18.75	18.63	18.25
P/E-Close	10.81	12.38	10.25	11.94	11.71
Dividends per Share	1.44	1.42	1.40	1.38	1.37
Dividend Yield (%)	6.00	5.54	6.83	6.46	6.70
Sales per Share	25.37	22.32	19.91	18.87	20.27
EPS before extra. item	2.22	2.07	2.00	1.79	1.74
Cash Flow per Share	4.55	4.19	3.96	3.59	3.66
Book Value per Share	16.62	15.83	15.18	14.48	14.08
O/S Common Shares	62,132	62,121	62,091	60,825	60,818
Total Revenue	1,602,400	1,413,087	1,256,636	1,192,621	1,243,832
Income before extra.	182,400	180,674	175,077	157,388	145,412
Cash Flow	282,800	259,968	241,114	218,244	218,290
Debt/Equity	0.85	0.84	0.80	0.76	0.87
Return on Capital (%)	15.39	15.14	14.67	13.89	14.52
Ret. on Com. Equity (%)	13.71	13.37	13.34	12.51	11.91
% Change Profit	1.0	3.2	11.2	8.2	(1.8)
% Change Revenue	13.4	12.5	5.4	(4.1)	1.9
% Change Assets	2.5	5.0	5.2	(1.7)	2.4
Preferred Div. Coverage	4.1	3.5	3.3		
Total Div. Coverage	1.4	1.3	1.3		
Interest Coverage	3.3	3.2	3.1		
Current Ratio	1.3	1.2	1.3		
Operating Margin	28.7	30.9	31.3		
Asset Turnover	0.5	0.4	0.4		
5 YEAR RATIOS (%)					
Return on Capital	14.7	14.6	14.7		
Return on Com. Equity	13.0	12.7	12.6		
Profit Growth	4.2	4.4	2.6		
Revenue Growth	5.5	3.6	1.1		
Asset Growth	2.5	3.7	3.6		
BALANCE SHEET (000)					
Cash	9,700	20,347	18,099		
Current Assets	297,900	301,418	262,401		
Net Fixed Assets	2,916,800	2,876,374	2,767,981		
Invest's & Advances	131,100	98,925	96,637		
Total Assets	3,387,100	3,305,077	3,148,257		
Short Term Debt	17,700	21,456	16,542		
Current Liabilities	225,900	248,062	198,748		
Long Term Debt	1,423,500	1,379,303	1,291,546		
Total Liabilities	1,685,800	1,641,557	1,506,603		
Total Equity	1,701,300	1,663,520	1,641,654		
Total Liab. & Equity	3,387,100	3,305,077	3,148,257		
CAPITAL (000)					
Total Debt	1,441,200	1,400,759	1,308,088		
Preferred Equity	669,000	680,093	699,277		
Common Equity	1,032,300	983,427	942,377		

Business:

CANADIAN UTILITIES LTD., through subsidiaries, is primarily in the business of generating, transmitting, distributing and selling electric power and natural gas. The Company also engages in complimentary businesses related to its utility operations including independent power generation and natural gas transmission and storage.

Date	EPS	DPS	Tot Rev	Inc Bex
Mar 95	0.90	0.37	492,800	68,800
Dec 94	0.69	0.36	466,247	53,063
Sep 94	0.27	0.36	284,654	27,246
Jun 94	0.33	0.72	315,891	32,057
Mar 94	0.93	0.36	550,000	70,000
Dec 93	0.67	0.35	434,196	54,248
Sep 93	0.27	0.36	261,039	29,898
Jun 93	0.32	0.36	284,055	33,167

Synopsis:

Canadian Utilities Limited, a member of the ATCO group of companies, operates in three segments: electrical utility; natural gas utility; and complementary operations. In fiscal 1994, company earnings rose more than 7% over 1993. Alberta's relatively strong economy and growth in oil, gas, forestry, and the province's energy-intensive manufacturing industries boosted the company's utility sales. Also, 1994 marked the first full-year of operations at Northland Utilities (Yellowknife) and Northland Utilities (Northwest Territories). Canadian Utilities gained controlling in interest both companies in late 1993.

Earnings from the electric utility segment rose by 2.7% in 1994 to $78-million, representing 56.4% of company earnings. Earnings from the natural gas segment rose 12% in 1994 to $55-million, representing 40% of company earnings.

Canadian Utilities' complementary operations, which consist of gas and electricity-related businesses, represent only 3.6% of the company's consolidated earnings. However, the company intends to enhance its core utility profits with earnings from complementary operations. It expects the complementary arm to contribute in a significant way to earnings by 1997. In 1995, CU Power International Ltd. should finish building the 1000 megawatt Barking Power Station in London, England, for which it has a 15-year contract to operate. Also, in January 1995, Canadian Utilities bought 100% of Frontec, a group of affiliated companies providing facilities management, technical operations, and maintenance services for government and industry.

Through its complementary operations, Canadian Utilities is pursuing independent power projects, natural gas gathering, processing and storing, and facilities management in Canada, the United States, and internationally.

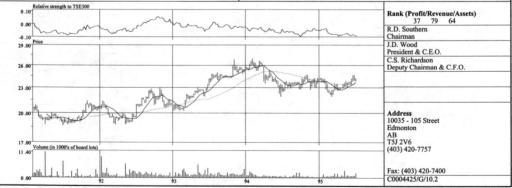

Rank (Profit/Revenue/Assets)
37 79 64

R.D. Southern
Chairman

J.D. Wood
President & C.E.O.

C.S. Richardson
Deputy Chairman & C.F.O.

Address
10035 - 105 Street
Edmonton
AB
T5J 2V6
(403) 420-7757

Fax: (403) 420-7400
C0004425/G/10.2

CANADIAN WESTERN NATURAL GAS COMPANY LIMITED

Exchanges	Price (Jun29'95)	10.87	Trailing P/E	nc	Stock Symbol
TZ	Trailing Yield (%)	nc	Trailing EPS	9.03	CWN.PR.A

Period Ending	Dec94	Dec93	Dec92	Dec91	Dec90
Yearly Statistics					
Price-Close	10.25	11.75	10.00	9.50	8.50
Price-High	12.75	12.50	11.00	9.50	9.25
Price-Low	10.00	9.88	9.00	8.25	8.50
P/E-Close	nc	nc	nc	nc	nc
Dividends per Share	nc	nc	nc	nc	nc
Dividend Yield (%)	nc	nc	nc	nc	nc
Sales per Share	153.68	138.03	120.38	119.64	127.36
EPS before extra. item	7.36	7.38	5.51	6.08	6.43
Cash Flow per Share	15.67	15.61	13.87	13.56	13.04
Book Value per Share	56.15	53.97	50.49	47.02	45.13
O/S Common Shares	2,637	2,637	2,456	2,456	2,456
Total Revenue	406,353	353,202	297,138	296,585	297,448
Income before extra.	24,210	24,284	19,268	19,929	19,271
Cash Flow	41,326	39,752	34,075	33,313	30,361
Debt/Equity	0.87	0.92	0.96	0.73	0.82
Return on Capital (%)	16.09	15.81	13.74	14.68	16.51
Ret. on Com. Equity (%)	13.36	14.12	11.30	13.20	14.56
% Change Profit	(0.3)	26.0	(3.3)	3.4	17.0
% Change Revenue	15.0	18.9	0.2	(0.3)	2.3
% Change Assets	2.7	7.9	13.4	(12.1)	8.1

Preferred Div. Coverage	5.0	4.4	3.4
Total Div. Coverage	1.3	1.2	1.8
Interest Coverage	3.3	3.1	2.8
Current Ratio	0.9	1.0	1.2
Operating Margin	16.5	17.9	16.7
Asset Turnover	0.8	0.7	0.7
5 YEAR RATIOS (%)			
Return on Capital	15.4	15.2	15.6
Return on Com. Equity	13.3	13.2	13.8
Profit Growth	8.0	4.3	0.6
Revenue Growth	6.9	3.4	(0.9)
Asset Growth	3.6	3.6	3.0
BALANCE SHEET (000)			
Cash	0	0	0
Current Assets	65,719	79,305	73,643
Net Fixed Assets	415,717	393,374	365,559
Invest's & Advances	0	0	0
Total Assets	489,011	476,383	441,605
Short Term Debt	12,440	22,998	18,850
Current Liabilities	69,830	80,001	60,103
Long Term Debt	184,858	177,519	176,291
Total Liabilities	261,283	258,986	238,330
Total Equity	227,728	217,397	203,275
Total Liab. & Equity	489,011	476,383	441,605
CAPITAL (000)			
Total Debt	197,298	200,517	195,141
Preferred Equity	79,633	75,065	79,265
Common Equity	148,095	142,332	124,010

Business:

CANADIAN WESTERN NATURAL GAS CO. LTD. distributes natural gas to 115 communities in southern Alberta. The company serves industrial, commercial and residential customers. Canadian Utilities Ltd. is the corporation's parent company.

Date	EPS	DPS	Tot Rev	Inc Bex
Dec 94	3.21	nc	128,980	8,452
Sep 94	(0.36)	nc	53,113	(949)
Jun 94	1.20	nc	69,976	3,161
Mar 94	4.98	nc	154,284	13,546
Dec 93	2.73	nc	116,522	8,242
Sep 93	(0.22)	nc	51,555	812
Jun 93	0.29	nc	61,059	2,120
Mar 93	4.76	nc	124,066	13,110

Synopsis:

During the year, Canadian Western Natural Gas launched the "Wired for Gas" program. This program is designed to increase the use of natural gas for cooking and clothes drying in new and renovated houses. The program promotes the advantages of new labour saving flexible house piping and a recently approved gas "quick connect" for indoor use. This program has been well received by builders and renovators.

During 1994 capital expenditures to provide for customer growth and meet existing customer needs totalled $52.9-million. The company's largest individual project in 1994 was the replacement of bare steel pipe originally installed in urban areas in the 1920's and 1930's. Spending during the fourth year for the replacement program amounted to $6.9-million. Also in 1994 a sixth compressor and additional equipment costing $6.4-million were added at Carbon, increasing the plant's capacity by 5 petajoules. Canadian Western reduced financing costs by redeeming $26.5-million of debentures and second preferred shares and replacing them with $40.8-million at lower rates. The net proceeds were used to finance the capital program.

Record drilling activity, spurred on by higher natural gas prices, produced a large oversupply of natural gas within Alberta in 1994. This oversupply, in combination with the increased storage capability in the province and milder weather in November and December, led to declines in the cost of gas at the wellhead during the latter part of the year. For example, short term gas was selling for less than $1 per gigajoule (GJ) in December 1994, compared to more than $2 per GJ in December 1993. The lower prices were passed on to customers early in 1995.

In 1994, the company increased its customer lease by 18,789 over the previous year. At the year end the company was providing natural gas service to 340,914 in 115 communities in southern Alberta. Total systems throughput was 166.6 petajoules (PJ) in 1994, an increase of 5.3% or 8.4 PJ over 1993.

Relative strength to TSE300 / Price / Volume (in 1000's of board lots)

Rank (Profit/Revenue/Assets)
191 215 228

J.D. Wood
Chairman & C.E.O.

J.D. Graham
President

B.M. Andrews
V.P. & Controller

Address
909 - 11th Avenue S.W.
Calgary
AB
T2R 1L8
(403) 245-7110

Fax: (403) 245-7488

C0004536/G/10.1

CENTRA GAS ONTARIO INC.

Exchanges	Price (Jun29'95)	25.00	Trailing P/E	nc	Stock Symbol
TM	Trailing Yield (%)	nc	Trailing EPS	1.87	**CGE.PR.C**

Period Ending	Dec94	Dec93	Dec92	Dec91	Dec90
Yearly Statistics					
Price-Close	25.00	25.50	23.75	23.13	19.00
Price-High	26.00	26.00	25.00	23.13	23.88
Price-Low	24.75	25.50	22.00	20.00	19.00
P/E-Close	nc	nc	nc	nc	nc
Dividends per Share	nc	nc	nc	nc	nc
Dividend Yield (%)	nc	nc	nc	nc	nc
Sales per Share	40.68	36.42	34.72	32.28	32.54
EPS before extra. item	1.87	2.13	2.10	1.54	1.74
Cash Flow per Share	4.33	4.26	4.71	4.46	4.27
Book Value per Share	17.64	17.17	16.44	15.94	15.65
O/S Common Shares	14,283	14,283	14,283	14,283	14,283
Total Revenue	652,800	594,800	561,637	513,303	491,098
Income before extra.	28,100	31,900	31,563	23,704	26,792
Cash Flow	61,900	60,900	67,294	63,772	61,025
Debt/Equity	1.86	1.68	1.56	1.61	1.75
Return on Capital (%)	11.39	12.27	13.29	10.39	11.04
Ret. on Com. Equity (%)	10.74	12.70	12.97	9.76	11.24
% Change Profit	(11.9)	1.1	33.2	(11.5)	(28.7)
% Change Revenue	9.8	5.9	9.4	4.5	(5.0)
% Change Assets	6.2	8.5	2.9	(2.0)	15.8
Preferred Div. Coverage	20.1	22.8	20.1		
Total Div. Coverage	1.3	1.5	1.3		
Interest Coverage	2.0	2.2	2.3		
Current Ratio	0.6	1.0	0.9		
Operating Margin	12.4	13.5	15.0		
Asset Turnover	0.6	0.6	0.6		
5 YEAR RATIOS (%)					
Return on Capital	11.7	12.2	12.5		
Return on Com. Equity	11.5	12.3	12.4		
Profit Growth	(5.7)	(2.7)	3.7		
Revenue Growth	4.7	5.3	(1.9)		
Asset Growth	6.1	3.9	1.2		
BALANCE SHEET (000)					
Cash	0	0	0		
Current Assets	150,200	139,800	123,481		
Net Fixed Assets	699,300	652,700	602,121		
Invest's & Advances	37,900	39,400	45,682		
Total Assets	905,700	852,500	785,903		
Short Term Debt	139,800	26,100	36,430		
Current Liabilities	242,600	137,100	130,836		
Long Term Debt	362,400	417,800	361,621		
Total Liabilities	636,000	587,900	530,244		
Total Equity	269,700	264,600	255,659		
Total Liab. & Equity	905,700	852,500	785,903		
CAPITAL (000)					
Total Debt	502,200	443,900	398,051		
Preferred Equity	17,800	19,300	20,807		
Common Equity	251,900	245,300	234,852		

Business:

CENTRA GAS ONTARIO INC. owns and operates natural gas distribution facilities in Ontario, serving about 160 communities in northwestern, northern and eastern Ontario. It sells to industrial, commercial and residential customers. The company's common shares are held by Westcoast Energy Inc.

Date	EPS	DPS	Tot Rev	Inc Bex
Dec 94	0.77	nc	175,858	11,315
Sep 94	(0.60)	nc	110,797	(8,217)
Jun 94	(0.13)	nc	130,527	(1,445)
Mar 94	1.83	nc	236,273	26,447
Dec 93	0.94	nc	183,932	13,836
Sep 93	(0.80)	nc	79,943	(11,022)
Jun 93	0.06	nc	117,180	1,213
Mar 93	1.93	nc	214,011	27,873

Synopsis:

Centra Gas in association with Westcoast Power participated in the development of a cogeneration plant at Lake Superior Power in Sault Ste. Marie. It also took part in building facilities to serve Cardinal Power in Cardinal, Ontario. Both plants became operational in 1994 and Centra's industrial and transportation volumes were significantly increased. Two new facilities owned by TransCanada PipeLines in North Bay and Kapuskasing, scheduled for completion in 1996, will also be supplied by Centra. Also coming on line for 1996 are new industrial cogeneration installations in Iroquois Falls and Kingston. This activity plays an important role in the expansion of the Company's gas distribution business.

Centra reported revenue of $77.7-million for the first quarter of 1995 down from $82.6-million for the same period in 1994. The weather in 1995 was 14.7% warmer than in 1994. This was partly offset by an increase in power and steam sales at the company's Fort Frances cogeneration facility and higher industrial gas sales. On March 23, 1995, the Ontario Energy Board (OEB) set Centra's allowed rate of return on common equity at 12.125%.

During 1994 Centra, Union Gas Ltd. and their common shareholder, Westcoast Energy Inc. sought and received OEB approval for the implementation of a shared service arrangement between Centra and Union. The company feels that the sharing of certain management and administrative functions of the two utilities would result in operating efficiencies and cost savings for customers of approximately $16-million after a two year transition period. In February 1995 the OEB held a hearing to review this proposal. The decision is expected in the second quarter.

Centra reported 1994 as a year of growth and continued strong performance. Customers increased by 11,800 bringing the total number to more than 226,000. Throughput was up by 6% from 1993 6% from 1993 to four billion cubic metres. Volumes increased by more than 8% in the important industrial market, as Ontario's economy regained momentum.

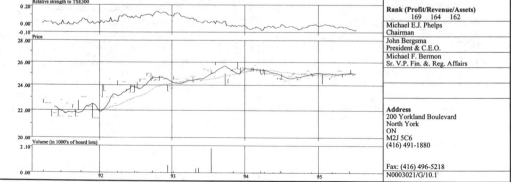

Rank (Profit/Revenue/Assets)
169 164 162

Michael E.J. Phelps
Chairman

John Bergsma
President & C.E.O.

Michael F. Bermon
Sr. V.P. Fin. &. Reg. Affairs

Address
200 Yorkland Boulevard
North York
ON
M2J 5C6
(416) 491-1880

Fax: (416) 496-5218
N0003021/G/10.1

CONSUMERS' GAS COMPANY LTD. (THE)

Exchanges	Price (Jun29'95)		17.62	Trailing P/E		11.60	Stock Symbol
TM	Trailing Yield (%)		5.48	Trailing EPS		1.52	**CGT**

Period Ending	Sep94	Sep93	Sep92	Sep91	Sep90
Yearly Statistics					
Price-Close	17.13	17.25	n t	12.50	12.25
Price-High	20.00	18.13	n t	17.31	12.44
Price-Low	16.00	6.50	n t	14.25	12.00
P/E-Close	9.41	9.80	n t	11.16	13.46
Dividends per Share	0.96	0.94	0.94	0.94	0.94
Dividend Yield (%)	5.58	5.45	na	7.52	7.67
Sales per Share	27.85	24.99	25.61	23.63	24.73
EPS before extra. item	1.82	1.76	1.50	1.12	0.91
Cash Flow per Share	3.54	3.37	2.92	2.49	2.69
Book Value per Share	12.32	11.43	10.60	9.37	9.13
O/S Common Shares	66,228	66,124	66,124	66,124	65,218
Total Revenue	1,948,882	1,748,569	1,801,349	1,692,472	1,771,963
Income before extra.	126,758	124,174	107,501	81,990	67,487
Cash Flow	234,452	222,694	192,945	164,569	175,120
Debt/Equity	1.77	1.65	1.62	1.99	1.79
Return on Capital (%)	13.55	14.49	13.09	12.09	12.62
Ret. on Com. Equity (%)	15.37	15.97	15.07	12.17	9.96
% Change Profit	2.1	15.5	31.1	21.5	(34.4)
% Change Revenue	11.5	(2.9)	6.4	(4.5)	(1.6)
% Change Assets	10.3	8.2	(3.8)	9.9	8.6

Business:

CONSUMERS' GAS CO. LTD. is a natural gas distribution utility serving over one million residential, commercial and industrial customers in central and eastern Ontario and northern New York State. At September 30, 1994, IPL Energy Inc. held indirectly 85 per cent of the common shares of the company.

Date	EPS	DPS	Tot Rev	Inc Bex
Mar 95	1.43	0.25	850,798	96,565
Dec 94	0.28	0.24	452,154	19,830
Sep 94	(0.27)	0.24	193,088	(15,997)
Jun 94	0.08	0.24	378,715	6,260
Mar 94	1.62	0.24	940,541	108,774
Dec 93	0.39	0.24	451,195	27,721
Sep 93	(0.25)	0.24	168,003	(14,431)
Jun 93	0.16	0.24	334,532	12,286

	Sep94	Sep93	Sep92
Preferred Div. Coverage	21.0	15.8	13.4
Total Div. Coverage	1.8	1.8	1.5
Interest Coverage	2.5	2.4	2.2
Current Ratio	0.8	0.8	0.8
Operating Margin	12.5	13.8	10.5
Asset Turnover	0.7	0.6	0.7
5 YEAR RATIOS (%)			
Return on Capital	13.2	13.6	13.8
Return on Com. Equity	13.7	13.8	13.9
Profit Growth	4.2	4.2	5.3
Revenue Growth	1.6	(0.7)	1.6
Asset Growth	6.4	4.7	4.7
BALANCE SHEET (000)			
Cash	1,563	3,810	1,844
Current Assets	549,820	461,170	444,302
Net Fixed Assets	2,216,595	2,046,091	1,872,927
Invest's & Advances	0	0	0
Total Assets	2,825,568	2,561,481	2,368,258
Short Term Debt	422,562	344,917	319,235
Current Liabilities	688,651	612,454	570,053
Long Term Debt	1,209,655	1,080,930	987,826
Total Liabilities	1,903,735	1,698,800	1,560,754
Total Equity	921,833	862,681	807,504
Total Liab. & Equity	2,825,568	2,561,481	2,368,258
CAPITAL (000)			
Total Debt	1,632,217	1,425,847	1,307,061
Preferred Equity	106,258	106,766	106,867
Common Equity	815,575	755,915	700,637

Synopsis:

Consumers' Gas reported income of $113.2-million for the six months ended March 31, 1995, compared to $133-million for the same period in 1993. A drop in total distribution volume of 757 million cubic metres, or 9.3% less than the same period in 1993, caused lower earnings. The weather in the first six months of 1995 was 16.2% warmer than last year and 7.7% warmer than normal. The company's growing customer base partially offset the weather related decline in distribution volume. Consumers' had over 1,241,000 customers at March 31, 1995.

An agreement with ANR Pipeline Company of Michigan to pursue a new pipeline project was reached by Consumers' Gas in November 1994. The new facilities will have an initial capacity of 150 million cubic feet of gas per day and with no delay in regulatory approvals is expected to be in service on November 1, 1995. The Consumers' Link will be constructed from the border south of Sarnia to the company's Tecumseh storage complex in southwestern Ontario. The cost of the 9.4 kilometre line will be approximately $10-million. The company's link will connect with ANR at the U.S. border. The company feels that it will give greater security to supplying its customers by being able to draw on these extensive storage capabilities.

With residential conversions leading the way, 1994 was another year of solid customer growth. Consumer's added the second highest number of conversion customers, to natural gas from oil and electricity, in its history. The number of customers added as a result of new construction slightly increased in 1994 over 1993. In 1994, the company brought gas for the first time to three unserved areas in Ontario, and to three previously all-electric subdivisions in the greater Toronto area. Although still in the testing phase, The Distribution Plant Lifecycle project, reduces the time of installing natural gas service to a customers home to less than three weeks from an average of six to eight weeks. This creates the potential for cost savings through the streamlining of the process.

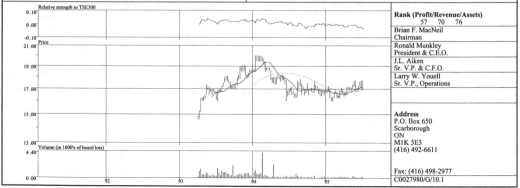

Rank (Profit/Revenue/Assets)
57   70   76

Brian F. MacNeil
Chairman

Ronald Munkley
President & C.E.O.

J.L. Aiken
Sr. V.P. & C.F.O.

Larry W. Youell
Sr. V.P., Operations

Address
P.O. Box 650
Scarborough
ON
M1K 5E3
(416) 492-6611

Fax: (416) 498-2977
C0027980/G/10.1

FORTIS INC.

Exchanges	Price (Jun29'95)	26.12	Trailing P/E	10.89	Stock Symbol
TM	Trailing Yield (%)	6.28	Trailing EPS	2.40	**FTS**

Period Ending	Dec94	Dec93	Dec92	Dec91	Dec90
Yearly Statistics					
Price-Close	25.75	28.75	24.50	23.88	21.63
Price-High	30.00	29.25	25.38	24.25	22.75
Price-Low	23.75	23.50	21.38	21.00	19.38
P/E-Close	10.47	11.23	9.61	9.91	8.79
Dividends per Share	1.68	1.54	1.49	1.48	1.45
Dividend Yield (%)	6.52	5.36	6.08	6.20	6.71
Sales per Share	34.88	33.42	34.69	33.75	33.35
EPS before extra. item	2.46	2.56	2.55	2.41	2.46
Cash Flow per Share	5.39	5.75	5.57	5.62	5.44
Book Value per Share	23.29	22.13	21.10	20.04	18.82
O/S Common Shares	11,799	10,340	10,191	10,071	9,291
Total Revenue	384,634	345,377	353,615	335,902	310,409
Income before extra.	31,313	30,633	30,162	28,192	23,998
Cash Flow	59,016	59,016	56,394	55,674	50,313
Debt/Equity	1.15	1.02	0.98	0.87	0.97
Return on Capital (%)	13.50	14.11	14.68	14.96	15.48
Ret. on Com. Equity (%)	10.71	11.84	12.39	12.66	13.49
% Change Profit	2.2	1.6	7.0	17.5	12.2
% Change Revenue	11.4	(2.3)	5.3	8.2	11.1
% Change Assets	26.7	2.7	6.4	9.2	16.2
Preferred Div. Coverage	7.2	7.0	6.9		
Total Div. Coverage	1.4	1.5	1.5		
Interest Coverage	2.8	2.8	2.7		
Current Ratio	0.5	0.6	0.6		
Operating Margin	21.8	21.7	20.1		
Asset Turnover	0.5	0.5	0.5		
5 YEAR RATIOS (%)					
Return on Capital	14.5	14.8	15.3		
Return on Com. Equity	12.2	12.9	13.3		
Profit Growth	7.8	9.6	11.2		
Revenue Growth	6.5	5.1	7.0		
Asset Growth	11.9	9.3	10.4		
BALANCE SHEET (000)					
Cash	9,866	9,366	9,465		
Current Assets	77,921	57,504	62,176		
Net Fixed Assets	650,551	508,213	493,631		
Invest's & Advances	14,652	36,574	73,696		
Total Assets	836,018	659,689	642,220		
Short Term Debt	89,602	42,817	39,678		
Current Liabilities	160,628	102,660	96,638		
Long Term Debt	282,871	241,671	218,906		
Total Liabilities	511,231	380,857	377,177		
Total Equity	324,787	278,832	265,043		
Total Liab. & Equity	836,018	659,689	642,220		
CAPITAL (000)					
Total Debt	372,473	284,488	258,584		
Preferred Equity	50,000	50,000	50,000		
Common Equity	274,787	228,832	215,043		

Business:

FORTIS INC. is a holding company with investments in two electric utilities, Newfoundland Power and Maritime Electric, principal distributors of electricity in Newfoundland and Prince Edward Island respectively. Its other subsidiaries are Fortis Trust Corporation, dealing principally in residential mortgages, and Fortis Properties Corp. holding a 50% interest in Unitel Newfoundland.

Date	EPS	DPS	Tot Rev	Inc Bex
Mar 95	0.94	0.42	131,033	12,320
Dec 94	0.20	0.42	108,820	3,889
Sep 94	0.34	0.40	78,062	5,291
Jun 94	0.92	0.40	87,622	10,693
Mar 94	1.00	0.40	110,130	11,440
Dec 93	0.26	0.39	89,308	3,753
Sep 93	0.31	0.38	63,241	4,311
Jun 93	0.96	0.38	85,392	10,930

Synopsis:

In 1994, Fortis Inc., which already owned a 32% stake in Maritime Electric, finalized a deal to buy all the remaining common shares of the company. The $65-million takeover came after Fortis rejected an offer by the Prince Edward Island government to nationalize Maritime Electric and sell it to New Brunswick Power.

In May 1994, the P.E.I. proclaimed new electricity price-cap regulations, resulting in Maritime Electric's base rates falling by 7% on July 1, 1994. Rates will continue to decline by 1% every six months until such time as they reach a level 10% above rates offered for similar service by New Brunswick Power. Maritime Electric has undertaken measures to reduce operating costs in order to remain financially successful under the new regime.

Despite a weak Newfoundland economy, Newfoundland Power's revenue rose from $329-million in 1993 to $334.2-million in 1994, reflecting a 2.1% increase in residential sales and a 1.9% increase in industrial sales. Newfoundland Power expects the province's economy to remain unchanged, in 1995.

Fortis Properties, which owns and manages commercial real estate, did not buy any new properties in 1994, but made capital improvements to existing properties totaling $4.3-million. Fortis Properties plans to expand into the Maritime Provinces in 1995, but expects earnings to be tempered by low demand for office space in Newfoundland.

Fortis Properties also holds a 50% interest in Unitel Newfoundland, with the remaining interest held by Unitel Communications. In 1995, Fortis expects Unitel Newfoundland to gain access to new customers and to earn greater market share. However, any changes to Unitel at the national level will likely effect Unitel Newfoundland.

Relative strength to TSE300

Price

Volume (in 1000's of board lots)

Rank (Profit/Revenue/Assets)
150   223   171

Angus A. Bruneau
Chairman President & C.E.O.

G. Wayne Watson
V.P. Finance & C.F.O.

Address
139 Water Street
P.O. Box 8837
St. John'S
NF
A1B 3T2
(709) 737-2800

Fax: (709) 737-5307
01002187/G/10.2

For further company information, call Globe Information Services 1-800-268-9128 or (416) 585-5345

ISLAND TELEPHONE COMPANY LIMITED (THE)

Exchanges	Price (Jun29'95)	19.75	Trailing P/E	10.97	Stock Symbol
TM	Trailing Yield (%)	6.08	Trailing EPS	1.80	**IT**

Period Ending	Dec94	Dec93	Dec92	Dec91	Dec90
Yearly Statistics					
Price-Close	21.25	24.75	18.75	20.25	15.00
Price-High	26.25	25.75	20.25	20.50	16.75
Price-Low	21.25	17.50	17.00	14.50	14.00
P/E-Close	11.36	12.89	9.52	10.60	8.52
Dividends per Share	1.20	1.17	1.13	1.09	1.05
Dividend Yield (%)	5.65	4.73	6.03	5.38	7.00
Sales per Share	16.40	15.66	15.09	14.78	16.11
EPS before extra. item	1.87	1.92	1.97	1.91	1.76
Cash Flow per Share	6.23	5.31	5.62	5.28	5.55
Book Value per Share	17.20	16.58	15.82	14.99	14.07
O/S Common Shares	3,469	3,469	3,469	3,466	3,144
Total Revenue	60,381	57,774	55,746	53,029	51,998
Income before extra.	6,911	7,097	7,246	6,922	5,814
Cash Flow	21,617	18,308	19,234	17,760	16,788
Debt/Equity	0.90	0.89	0.87	0.87	1.05
Return on Capital (%)	15.26	15.95	16.72	15.64	15.67
Ret. on Com. Equity (%)	10.97	11.77	12.66	13.39	12.73
% Change Profit	(2.6)	(2.1)	4.7	19.1	6.3
% Change Revenue	4.5	3.6	5.1	2.0	7.3
% Change Assets	3.5	5.5	3.8	3.5	7.0

Business:
THE ISLAND TELEPHONE COMAPNY LTD. is the telecommunications company serving Prince Edward Island. It provides telephone and telecommunications services. Maritime Telegraph and Telephone Company Ltd. of Halifax has a 52% interest in the company.

Date	EPS	DPS	Tot Rev	Inc Bex
Mar 95	0.25	0.30	14,172	958
Dec 94	0.44	0.30	14,647	1,617
Sep 94	0.53	0.30	15,236	1,968
Jun 94	0.58	0.30	16,719	2,107
Mar 94	0.32	0.30	13,726	1,220
Dec 93	0.46	0.30	14,819	1,684
Sep 93	0.53	0.29	14,536	1,969
Jun 93	0.58	0.29	15,392	2,135

Preferred Div. Coverage	14.3	14.7	15.0
Total Div. Coverage	1.5	1.6	1.7
Interest Coverage	3.1	3.2	3.4
Current Ratio	1.0	1.0	0.6
Operating Margin	30.8	31.5	32.9
Asset Turnover	0.4	0.4	0.4
5 YEAR RATIOS (%)			
Return on Capital	15.8	16.2	16.5
Return on Com. Equity	12.3	12.7	13.1
Profit Growth	4.7	6.4	8.2
Revenue Growth	4.4	5.1	6.4
Asset Growth	4.5	5.7	6.7
BALANCE SHEET (000)			
Cash	51	103	44
Current Assets	12,604	11,936	9,783
Net Fixed Assets	129,305	126,115	120,885
Invest's & Advances	719	563	474
Total Assets	146,716	141,815	134,395
Short Term Debt	5,286	3,866	10,099
Current Liabilities	12,930	12,509	17,281
Long Term Debt	53,835	52,937	43,000
Total Liabilities	80,808	78,066	73,271
Total Equity	65,908	63,750	61,123
Total Liab. & Equity	146,716	141,815	134,395
CAPITAL (000)			
Total Debt	59,121	56,803	53,099
Preferred Equity	6,250	6,250	6,250
Common Equity	59,658	57,500	54,873

Synopsis:

In April 1995, Island Telephone signed a deal with the Government of Prince Edward Island committing $150-million over five years to upgrade the province's information services. Island Tel plans to have complete digital services available across the province, install fibre optics, and add phone features like call answer and call display. The technical expansion will eventually allow Islanders access to home shopping, banking, and video-on-demand through the information highway.

On February 14, 1995, Island Tel redeemed its 12.75% series P bonds due January 31, 2000. Island Tel redeemed $5-million of outstanding bonds at 12.75% of principal plus accrued interest to the redemption date. It received a total of $1,032.40 for each $1,000 principal amount.

Total revenues during the first quarter of 1995 were 3% above last year. Revenue growth was due in large part to increased local revenues, which jumped by 21% to $8.5-million. Robust basic and cellular service demand, a local rate increase that came into effect in April 1994, and increased demand for custom calling features fuelled local revenue growth. Local revenues were offset by declining long-distance revenues due to price reductions and market share losses.

The cellular market showed particularly strong growth. Island Tel Mobility experienced a 52% increase in the number of cellular access services compared to the end of the first quarter of 1994.

During the first quarter of 1995, Island Tel invested $3.8-million to expand and modernize the telecommunications network across Prince Edward Island. The value of Island Tel's telecommunications assets in Prince Edward Island now exceeds $200-million.

Relative strength to TSE300

Price

Volume (in 1000's of board lots)

Rank (Profit/Revenue/Assets)
374   508   396
Ivan E.H. Duvar
Chairman Of The Board
Frederick D. Morash
President & C.E.O.
A. Douglas Hartt
V.P. Finance

Address
69 Belvedere Avenue
P.O. Box 820
Charlottetown
PE
C1A 7M1
(902) 566-0131
Fax: (902) 429-8755
I0002243/G/10.3

MARITIME TELEGRAPH AND TELEPHONE COMPANY, LIMITED

Exchanges		Price (Jun29'95)	19.75	Trailing P/E	12.91	Stock Symbol
TM		Trailing Yield (%)	6.48	Trailing EPS	1.53	**MTT**

Period Ending	Dec94	Dec93	Dec92	Dec91	Dec90
Yearly Statistics					
Price-Close	22.50	24.50	21.13	21.00	18.25
Price-High	26.38	25.75	22.38	21.75	19.00
Price-Low	21.63	18.88	18.50	17.88	16.00
P/E-Close	13.98	12.76	10.41	11.23	9.61
Dividends per Share	1.28	1.25	1.21	1.17	1.12
Dividend Yield (%)	5.69	5.10	5.73	5.57	6.14
Sales per Share	18.68	18.59	18.21	18.07	17.58
EPS before extra. item	1.61	1.92	2.03	1.87	1.90
Cash Flow per Share	6.80	6.63	6.44	6.23	5.80
Book Value per Share	17.49	17.24	16.54	15.72	14.89
O/S Common Shares	28,047	28,040	28,040	27,929	27,060
Total Revenue	550,049	549,506	548,397	533,440	501,023
Income before extra.	48,181	59,832	64,028	59,259	57,114
Cash Flow	188,194	183,200	178,325	170,050	152,893
Debt/Equity	1.29	1.06	0.98	0.94	0.96
Return on Capital (%)	13.08	14.96	16.27	16.12	15.25
Ret. on Com. Equity (%)	9.12	11.20	12.43	12.11	13.06
% Change Profit	(19.5)	(6.6)	8.0	3.8	16.7
% Change Revenue	0.1	0.2	2.8	6.5	9.4
% Change Assets	5.7	5.6	4.4	5.0	9.1
Preferred Div. Coverage	12.8	8.8	8.1		
Total Div. Coverage	1.2	1.5	1.5		
Interest Coverage	2.5	3.1	3.3		
Current Ratio	0.7	0.7	0.7		
Operating Margin	28.3	30.7	31.8		
Asset Turnover	0.3	0.4	0.4		
5 YEAR RATIOS (%)					
Return on Capital	15.1	16.0	16.4		
Return on Com. Equity	11.6	12.4	12.7		
Profit Growth	(0.4)	7.2	10.2		
Revenue Growth	3.7	7.1	8.5		
Asset Growth	5.9	9.2	10.4		
BALANCE SHEET (000)					
Cash	3,459	568	1,361		
Current Assets	147,445	138,121	125,116		
Net Fixed Assets	1,309,332	1,261,113	1,214,772		
Invest's & Advances	16,597	13,978	12,602		
Total Assets	1,520,437	1,438,611	1,362,233		
Short Term Debt	124,398	118,813	99,571		
Current Liabilities	200,175	190,391	171,163		
Long Term Debt	562,703	482,047	447,351		
Total Liabilities	988,362	873,727	802,632		
Total Equity	532,075	564,884	559,601		
Total Liab. & Equity	1,520,437	1,438,611	1,362,233		
CAPITAL (000)					
Total Debt	687,101	600,860	546,922		
Preferred Equity	41,500	81,500	95,884		
Common Equity	490,575	483,384	463,717		

Business:

MARITIME TELEGRAPH AND TELEPHONE CO. LTD. (MT&T) and its operating subsidiaries are the principal suppliers of telecommunications services in Nova Scotia and Prince Edward Island, providing a wide range of telecommuncations products and services.

Date	EPS	DPS	Tot Rev	Inc Bex
Mar 95	0.17	0.32	133,114	5,625
Dec 94	0.29	0.32	135,864	8,767
Sep 94	0.62	0.32	138,670	17,995
Jun 94	0.45	0.32	144,672	13,481
Mar 94	0.25	0.32	130,843	7,938
Dec 93	0.53	0.32	137,564	16,276
Sep 93	0.55	0.31	138,762	16,771
Jun 93	0.53	0.31	143,433	16,350

Synopsis:

On May 1, 1995, the CRTC granted part of Maritime Tel's request for higher basic residential and business rates, on an interim basis. The company can now raise residential rates by $2.10, business single-line services by $6, and business multi-line services by $9.70. The rate increases will ease the pain of falling long distance revenue. Long distance revenue fell by almost $30-million in 1994, to $253-million. The drop cut company profit by more than 16% to $44-million.

In May 1995, Unitel Communications Inc. laid charges in the Nova Scotia Provincial Court against Maritime Tel and one of its officers, Ronald Smith. Unitel alleged that Maritime Tel violated the Telecommunications Act. The company could be fined up to $500,000 for a first offense, while the officer could be fined $50,000. In March 1994, Unitel won a contract to provide the Government of Nova Scotia with long distance service. After Maritime Tel offered the province concessions, the government switched back to Maritime Tel. The government suspended Maritime Tel's contract after Unitel lodged a complaint with the CRTC. The CRTC said Maritime Tel offered illegal and anti-competitive concessions to woo the Nova Scotia account away from Unitel.

Maritime Tel experienced a 3.3% rise in the volume of long distance calls placed by customers, despite a loss of just under 10% in long distance market share over the past year. Over 35 million long distance messages were carried over the company's network during the first quarter of this year. During the first three months of 1995, the sale of new cellular services grew by 70% compared to the same period last year. The total number of cellular customers on the company's network grew to about 50,000, a growth rate of 50% since March 1994.

During the first quarter of 1995, a voluntary separation offer to its employees reduced Maritime Tel's work force by 240 positions.

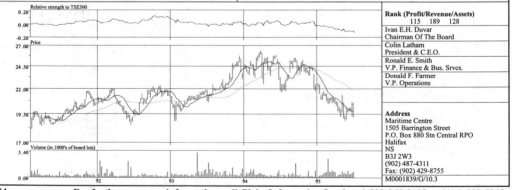

Rank (Profit/Revenue/Assets)		
115	189	128

Ivan E.H. Duvar
Chairman Of The Board

Colin Latham
President & C.E.O.

Ronald E. Smith
V.P. Finance & Bus. Srvcs.

Donald F. Farmer
V.P. Operations

Address
Maritime Centre
1505 Barrington Street
P.O. Box 880 Stn Central RPO
Halifax
NS
B3J 2W3
(902) 487-4311
Fax: (902) 429-8755
M0001839/G/10.3

NEWFOUNDLAND LIGHT & POWER CO. LIMITED

Exchanges						Stock Symbol
M	Price (Jun29'95)	7.00	Trailing P/E	nc		**NFL.PR.H**
	Trailing Yield (%)	nc	Trailing EPS	2.60		

Period Ending	Dec94	Dec93	Dec92	Dec91	Dec90
Yearly Statistics					
Price-Close	7.00	7.00	10.13	9.50	9.88
Price-High	7.75	7.75	10.38	10.00	9.88
Price-Low	6.75	6.25	9.88	9.50	9.00
P/E-Close	nc	nc	nc	nc	nc
Dividends per Share	nc	nc	nc	nc	nc
Dividend Yield (%)	nc	nc	nc	nc	nc
Sales per Share	32.46	32.14	33.88	32.56	31.71
EPS before extra. item	2.70	2.71	2.73	2.52	2.36
Cash Flow per Share	5.34	5.62	5.42	5.32	5.29
Book Value per Share	21.81	22.01	20.87	19.67	18.65
O/S Common Shares	10,320	10,271	10,200	10,121	10,071
Total Revenue	340,031	335,694	346,431	330,271	307,632
Income before extra.	27,802	29,182	29,662	27,799	26,235
Cash Flow	55,024	57,480	55,105	53,683	51,055
Debt/Equity	0.98	0.97	0.98	0.95	0.95
Return on Capital (%)	15.36	15.45	15.07	14.99	15.49
Ret. on Com. Equity (%)	12.01	12.62	13.46	13.17	13.59
% Change Profit	(4.7)	(1.6)	6.7	6.0	7.3
% Change Revenue	1.3	(3.1)	4.9	7.4	10.5
% Change Assets	0.7	0.4	4.8	4.4	9.8

Preferred Div. Coverage	39.0	19.7	15.4
Total Div. Coverage	0.9	1.6	1.7
Interest Coverage	2.9	2.9	2.9
Current Ratio	0.6	0.8	0.9
Operating Margin	19.9	20.0	19.4
Asset Turnover	0.6	0.6	0.6

5 YEAR RATIOS (%)			
Return on Capital	15.3	15.1	15.2
Return on Com. Equity	13.0	13.4	13.6
Profit Growth	2.5	5.5	7.6
Revenue Growth	4.0	4.5	6.6
Asset Growth	3.9	5.5	6.9

BALANCE SHEET (000)			
Cash	2,080	9,543	7,610
Current Assets	50,368	54,127	57,930
Net Fixed Assets	489,400	483,220	477,711
Invest's & Advances	0	0	0
Total Assets	552,972	549,164	547,034
Short Term Debt	24,351	12,288	11,275
Current Liabilities	84,020	70,304	67,324
Long Term Debt	207,706	216,631	218,906
Total Liabilities	316,972	312,205	311,834
Total Equity	236,000	236,959	235,200
Total Liab. & Equity	552,972	549,164	547,034

CAPITAL (000)			
Total Debt	232,057	228,919	230,181
Preferred Equity	10,902	10,905	22,296
Common Equity	225,098	226,054	212,904

Business:

NEWFOUNDLAND LIGHT & POWER CO. LTD. is an electrical utility serving the province of Newfoundland. Fortis Inc. of St. John's is the company's major shareholder.

Date	EPS	DPS	Tot Rev	Inc Bex
Mar 95	1.00	nc	108,297	10,530
Dec 94	0.18	nc	83,472	1,906
Sep 94	0.38	nc	61,936	4,078
Jun 94	1.04	nc	85,166	10,828
Mar 94	1.05	nc	107,793	10,990
Dec 93	0.33	nc	83,609	3,388
Sep 93	0.32	nc	60,818	3,592
Jun 93	1.02	nc	83,547	10,810

Synopsis:

Despite a weak Newfoundland economy, Newfoundland Light & Power Co. Ltd.'s revenue grew from $329-million in 1993 to $334.2-million in 1994, reflecting a 2.1% increase in residential sales and a 1.9% rise in industrial sales.

Newfoundland Power, 100% owned by Fortis Inc., provides service to more than 205,000 customers, or approximately 85% of the population of the province. The company generates about 10% of the energy sold to its customers and purchases the balance from Newfoundland and Labrador Hydro. Because energy consumption is sensitive to temperature variations, sales are reported on a weather-adjusted basis. In 1994, weather adjusted sales were 4,371 Gwh, an increase of almost 2% over 1993. Actual sales were 4,393 Gwh, a decrease of .59% from the previous year.

In December 1994, a major winter storm with winds up to 168 kilometres an hour, caused damage to the transmission and distribution systems in Eastern Newfoundland. Power was interrupted for 100,000 customers, affecting Newfoundland Power's revenues. Year-end costs for system damage were in excess of $2.2-million. Operating expenses for the three months ended March 1995, reflect these costs. However, the company expects to recover some of the costs from insurance.

Newfoundland Light & Power faces increased competition from oil companies that are targeting the heating market in Newfoundland. Therefore, the company is focusing on controlling costs and keeping its rates competitive. It is also boosting its customer service through new technology and implementing a more structured approach to marketing.

In 1995, Newfoundland Power expects only a modest sales growth. It predicts the province's economy to remain unchanged and anticipates increased competition in the heating market.

Relative strength to TSE300

Rank (Profit/Revenue/Assets)
172 239 219

Angus A. Bruneau
Chairman

Aidan F. Ryan
President & C.E.O.

Kevin S. Warr
V.P. Fin. Treasurer & C.F.O.

Address
55 Kenmount Rd.
P.O. Box 8910
St. John's
NF
A1B 3P6
(709) 737-5600

Fax: (709) 737-5832
N0001223/G/10.2

NEWTEL ENTERPRISES LIMITED

Exchanges	Price (Jun29'95)	20.00	Trailing P/E	10.70	Stock Symbol
TM	Trailing Yield (%)	6.80	Trailing EPS	1.87	**NEL**

Period Ending	Dec94	Dec93	Dec92	Dec91	Dec90	Business:
Yearly Statistics						NEWTEL ENTERPRISES LTD. is a
Price-Close	19.75	23.50	19.38	19.50	17.38	telecommunications company with operations
Price-High	24.50	24.13	20.88	20.25	19.50	in telecommunications, information technology
Price-Low	19.00	18.38	17.25	17.00	14.50	and electroni cs manufacturing. The company's
P/E-Close	10.29	13.74	11.20	12.04	13.37	wholly owned subsidiary, Newfoundland
Dividends per Share	1.36	1.36	1.36	1.36	1.36	Telephone Co. Ltd., supplies
Dividend Yield (%)	6.89	5.79	7.02	6.97	7.83	telecommunications and information handling
Sales per Share	15.94	17.00	17.21	19.29	19.77	services to Newfoundland and Labrador. Six
EPS before extra. item	1.92	1.71	1.73	1.62	1.30	smaller, owned subsidiaries, make up the
Cash Flow per Share	5.97	6.54	6.37	7.28	7.06	balance of NewTel's business.
Book Value per Share	17.76	17.04	16.56	16.11	15.41	

	Dec94	Dec93	Dec92	Dec91	Dec90
O/S Common Shares	17,500	16,801	16,187	15,464	13,321
Total Revenue	297,086	297,583	287,662	280,242	268,294
Income before extra.	32,826	31,602	30,958	25,817	20,366
Cash Flow	102,362	108,092	101,104	100,203	91,786
Debt/Equity	0.93	1.14	0.94	1.00	1.34
Return on Capital (%)	14.34	14.78	14.69	14.60	13.89
Ret. on Com. Equity (%)	11.00	10.18	10.60	9.80	8.45
% Change Profit	3.9	2.1	19.9	26.8	(20.4)
% Change Revenue	(0.2)	3.4	2.6	4.5	3.7
% Change Assets	0.2	0.7	4.6	3.3	6.1

Date	EPS	DPS	Tot Rev	Inc Bex
Mar 95	0.40	0.34	82,252	7,017
Dec 94	0.55	0.34	78,590	9,580
Sep 94	0.43	0.34	71,525	7,370
Jun 94	0.49	0.34	73,906	8,248
Mar 94	0.45	0.34	73,065	7,628
Dec 93	0.40	0.34	75,505	7,373
Sep 93	0.50	0.34	76,422	9,141
Jun 93	0.49	0.34	74,206	8,876

						Synopsis:
Preferred Div. Coverage	np	np	8.7			In October 1994, NewTel Enterprises and its two consortium partners purchased
Total Div. Coverage	1.4	1.2	1.2			all the shares of Newfoundland and Labrador Computer Services Ltd. (NLCS)
Interest Coverage	3.2	3.2	3.0			from the Government of Newfoundland. Terms of the deal were not disclosed.
Current Ratio	0.6	0.3	0.7			NLCS will be 80% owned by NewTel and 10% owned by each of its partners,
Operating Margin	28.7	30.4	30.2			Bell Sygma Inc. and Andersen Consulting Canada of Toronto. Bell Sygma is a
Asset Turnover	0.4	0.4	0.4			subsidiary of BCE Inc. NewTel said it will transfer the operations and staff of the
5 YEAR RATIOS (%)						Information Technology division of Newfoundland Telephone to NLCS. In
Return on Capital	14.5	14.7	14.7			addition to a seven year contract to provide information technology services to the
Return on Com. Equity	10.0	10.3	10.8			Newfoundland government and Memorial University, NLCS will provide services
Profit Growth	5.0	9.0	10.0			to Newfoundland Telephone. It also has firm commitments for $35-million of
Revenue Growth	2.7	8.7	11.3			business from outside the province.
Asset Growth	2.9	4.4	13.4			Revenues for NewTel's principal subsidiary, Newfoundland Telephone, fell by
BALANCE SHEET (000)						$11.1-million in 1994 compared to 1993. In 1994, the number of long-distance
Cash	1,767	117	1,423			calls increased 8%. However, rate reductions and discount pricing resulted in
Current Assets	36,000	27,445	51,442			long-distance revenues declining by 11.3% compared to 1993, a drop of
Net Fixed Assets	668,051	652,884	631,399			$18.1-million. During fiscal 1994, the number of network access lines increased
Invest's & Advances	6,402	22,857	24,901			to 271,963 compared to 262,856 a year earlier.
Total Assets	730,019	728,581	723,660			Cost control, restructured financing arrangements, and strong local service
Short Term Debt	6,447	57,867	37,777			revenue enabled NewTel to offset this decline. Net earnings in 1994 were
Current Liabilities	57,115	97,170	76,474			$32.1-million, a slight drop from the $32.4-million posted in 1993. Non-regulated
Long Term Debt	281,284	267,225	257,052			subsidiaries expanded rapidly in 1994. With an aggregate net income contribution
Total Liabilities	419,186	442,377	410,613			of $1.9-million from these subsidiaries, consolidated net income rose 16.4% to
Total Equity	310,833	286,204	313,047			$32.8-million in 1994, compared to $28.2-million in 1993.
Total Liab. & Equity	730,019	728,581	723,660			
CAPITAL (000)						
Total Debt	287,731	325,092	294,829			
Preferred Equity	0	0	45,000			
Common Equity	310,833	286,204	268,047			

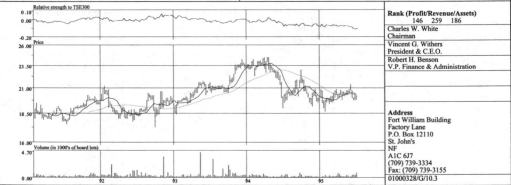

Rank (Profit/Revenue/Assets)	146 259 186
Charles W. White	Chairman
Vincent G. Withers	President & C.E.O.
Robert H. Benson	V.P. Finance & Administration

Address
Fort William Building
Factory Lane
P.O. Box 12110
St. John's
NF
A1C 6J7
(709) 739-3334
Fax: (709) 739-3155
01000328/G/10.3

For further company information, call Globe Information Services 1-800-268-9128 or (416) 585-5345

NORTHWESTERN UTILITIES LIMITED

Exchanges	Price (Jun29'95)	56 .50	Trailing P/E	nc	Stock Symbol
TZ	Trailing Yield (%)	nc	Trailing EPS	(0 .37)	**NWT.PR.A**

Period Ending	Dec94	Dec93	Dec92	Dec91	Dec90
Yearly Statistics					
Price-Close	57 .00	59 .00	49 .00	42 .75	40 .50
Price-High	60 .00	59 .00	50 .00	42 .88	45 .00
Price-Low	53 .00	47 .00	43 .25	39 .00	40 .50
P/E-Close	nc	nc	nc	nc	nc
Dividends per Share	nc	nc	nc	nc	nc
Dividend Yield (%)	nc	nc	nc	nc	nc
Sales per Share	153 .90	133 .60	114 .83	123 .59	123 .26
EPS before extra. item	11 .35	9 .65	8 .58	8 .55	7 .66
Cash Flow per Share	23 .78	18 .92	18 .07	18 .16	15 .96
Book Value per Share	73 .50	71 .11	67 .72	63 .63	62 .72
O/S Common Shares	3 ,167	3 ,167	3 ,167	2 ,941	2 ,901
Total Revenue	488 ,638	426 ,813	353 ,985	366 ,357	363 ,902
Income before extra.	44 ,323	40 ,481	36 ,625	34 ,579	30 ,607
Cash Flow	75 ,332	59 ,915	55 ,288	53 ,396	46 ,612
Debt/Equity	0 .80	0 .82	0 .73	0 .76	0 .79
Return on Capital (%)	16 .25	15 .37	14 .64	14 .90	15 .12
Ret. on Com. Equity (%)	15 .69	13 .90	13 .07	13 .64	12 .54
% Change Profit	9 .5	10 .5	5 .9	13 .0	(10 .6)
% Change Revenue	14 .5	20 .6	(3 .4)	0 .7	0 .3
% Change Assets	5 .3	6 .4	6 .2	(6 .2)	5 .5

Preferred Div. Coverage	5 .3	4 .1	3 .5	
Total Div. Coverage	1 .2	1 .4	1 .3	
Interest Coverage	3 .7	3 .4	3 .1	
Current Ratio	0 .9	0 .9	1 .0	
Operating Margin	21 .7	22 .1	24 .1	
Asset Turnover	0 .7	0 .6	0 .5	
5 YEAR RATIOS (%)				
Return on Capital	15 .3	15 .3	15 .7	
Return on Com. Equity	13 .8	13 .7	13 .9	
Profit Growth	5 .2	4 .2	6 .8	
Revenue Growth	6 .1	5 .1	1 .4	
Asset Growth	3 .2	3 .2	1 .9	
BALANCE SHEET (000)				
Cash	0	0	0	
Current Assets	93 ,318	83 ,966	69 ,347	
Net Fixed Assets	641 ,688	620 ,203	592 ,270	
Invest's & Advances	0	0	0	
Total Assets	746 ,852	709 ,508	666 ,599	
Short Term Debt	27 ,008	31 ,291	18 ,757	
Current Liabilities	102 ,092	92 ,481	68 ,405	
Long Term Debt	271 ,188	260 ,282	241 ,405	
Total Liabilities	374 ,284	353 ,474	312 ,371	
Total Equity	372 ,568	356 ,034	354 ,228	
Total Liab. & Equity	746 ,852	709 ,508	666 ,599	
CAPITAL (000)				
Total Debt	298 ,196	291 ,573	260 ,162	
Preferred Equity	139 ,769	130 ,795	139 ,719	
Common Equity	232 ,799	225 ,239	214 ,509	

Business:

NORTHWESTERN UTILITIES LIMITED is a natural gas utility, serving customers in north-central Alberta. The company is a subsidiary of Canadian Utilities Limited of Edmonton.

Date	EPS	DPS	Tot Rev	Inc Bex
Mar 95	(5 .53)	nc	150 ,836	19 ,717
Dec 94	4 .89	nc	155 ,505	17 ,496
Sep 94	(0 .13)	nc	58 ,715	(410)
Jun 94	0 .40	nc	74 ,926	3 ,347
Mar 94	6 .80	nc	199 ,630	23 ,890
Dec 93	4 .18	nc	147 ,292	15 ,617
Sep 93	(0 .50)	nc	57 ,017	829
Jun 93	0 .78	nc	74 ,778	5 ,019

Synopsis:

Northwestern Utilities Limited reported an increase in revenues in 1994, to $487.5-million from $423.2-million in 1993. The increase was due to higher gas cost recovery rates ($28.9-million), colder weather ($20-million), changes in cost of service ($9.1-million), franchise taxes ($3.9-million), and transportation ($39-million). The company continued to increase its customer base by adding an additional 6,142 in 1994. Natural gas service was provided to 372,541 customers in 175 communities in north-central Alberta by Northwesten Utilities, at year end.

The company incurred capital expenditures of $61.9-million in 1994, which was used to provide for customer growth and to meet existing customers needs. The largest individual project was the replacement of bare steel pipe originally installed in urban areas in the 1920s and 1930s. The company spent $9-million on this project, now in its 8th year of a 10 year time period. A sixth salt cavern was placed in service, resulting in increased peak capacity for the 1994/95 winter season and ensuring a secure supply for Northwestern's sales and transportation customers during extremely cold weather.

The higher gas prices caused record drilling activity which in turn produced a large oversupply of natural gas within Alberta in 1994. During the latter part of the year, this oversupply combined with the increased storage capability in the province led to significant declines in the cost of gas at the wellhead. Short term gas was selling for less than $1 per Gigajoule (GJ) in December 1994 compared to more than $2 per GJ in December 1993.

The company redeemed $103.8-million of debentures and second preferred shares. Taking advantage of lower interest rates to reduce financing costs, it replaced them with $129.5-million at lower rates. The net proceeds went to finance the capital program. Northwestern also replaced preferred shares with the issue of two new series paying lower dividend rates.

Rank (Profit/Revenue/Assets)
123   196   182

J.D. Wood
Chairman & C.E.O.

R.G. Lock
President

D.M. Ellard
Sr. V.P. & General Manager

Address
10035 - 105 Street
Edmonton
AB
T5J 2V6
(403) 420-7211

Fax: (403) 420-7400
N0003465/G/10.1

NOVA SCOTIA POWER INC.

Exchanges	Price (Jun29'95)	11.62	Trailing P/E	11.29	Stock Symbol
TM	Trailing Yield (%)	6.58	Trailing EPS	1.03	**NSI**

Period Ending	Dec94	Dec93	Dec92	Mar92	Mar91	Business:
Yearly Statistics			9M			NOVA SCOTIA POWER INC. generates,
Price-Close	11.13	13.00	10.75	nt	nt	transmits and distributes electricity in Nova
Price-High	13.38	13.13	11.63	nt	nt	Scotia.
Price-Low	10.63	10.38	10.50	nt	nt	
P/E-Close	10.11	12.15	23.73	nt	nt	
Dividends per Share	0.76	0.75	0.19	0.00	0.00	
Dividend Yield (%)	6.83	5.77	1.74	0.00	0.00	
Sales per Share	8.30	8.22	7.70	0.00	0.00	
EPS before extra. item	1.10	1.07	0.34	na	na	
Cash Flow per Share	2.11	1.99	1.53	0.00	0.00	
Book Value per Share	9.43	9.08	8.80	na	na	
O/S Common Shares	85,400	85,200	85,135	0	0	
Total Revenue	765,500	814,200	573,200	770,600	677,200	
Income before extra.	110,800	95,400	38,000	46,300	24,000	
Cash Flow	180,300	169,200	97,800	125,000	98,200	

Date	EPS	DPS	Tot Rev	Inc Bex
Mar 95	0.45	0.20	209,500	42,800
Dec 94	0.36	0.19	185,000	34,700
Sep 94	0.05	0.19	162,900	8,600
Jun 94	0.17	0.19	174,400	20,200
Mar 94	0.52	0.19	220,200	47,300
Dec 93	0.32	0.19	196,300	31,800
Sep 93	(0.06)	0.19	167,600	(5,400)
Jun 93	0.34	0.19	179,300	28,800

Debt/Equity	1.60	1.61	2.14	18.11	27.40
Return on Capital (%)	11.11	12.50	12.86	15.23	12.71
Ret. on Com. Equity (%)	11.90	12.02	11.78	52.47	45.20
% Change Profit	16.1	88.3	9.4	92.9	14.3
% Change Revenue	(6.0)	6.5	(0.8)	13.8	4.9
% Change Assets	3.0	7.1	7.7	17.0	15.7

				Synopsis:
Preferred Div. Coverage	6.6	24.5	np	Nova Scotia Power Inc. reported revenue for 1994 of $715.6-million, compared
Total Div. Coverage	1.4	1.4	2.4	with $709.1-million in 1993. For the period ended December 31, 1994, the
Interest Coverage	1.6	1.5	1.2	company had earnings available to common shareholders of $94-million or $1.10
Current Ratio	0.3	0.6	0.9	a share, up from $91.5-million or $1.07 a year earlier.
Operating Margin	32.1	30.3	29.3	
Asset Turnover	0.3	0.3	0.3	In August 1994, Nova Scotia Power issued $100-million 25-year debentures and

5 YEAR RATIOS (%)

Return on Capital	12.9	13.4	13.1	two mid-term notes totalling $100-million. The company's long-term debt carries a credit rating of A (Low).
Return on Com. Equity	26.7	38.0	26.8	
Profit Growth	39.4	77.0	71.1	The Point Aconi generating station became fully operational in 1994. The new
Revenue Growth	3.4	6.8	7.1	165 megawatt station uses the largest circulating fluidized bed boiler in the world.
Asset Growth	9.9	10.9	10.5	This technology reduces sulphur dioxide emissions by 90%, and produces lower

BALANCE SHEET (000)

				levels of nitrogen oxide. In the first quarter of 1995, Nova Scotia Power's revenue
Cash	100	2,300	0	and net profit declined due to the company's increase in deferred depreciation
Current Assets	212,900	234,200	201,100	costs for Point Aconi.
Net Fixed Assets	2,275,600	2,264,000	2,208,700	
Invest's & Advances	0	0	0	Nova Scotia Power did not apply for a rate increase in 1994, but still saw
Total Assets	2,760,600	2,679,000	2,500,700	residential revenue grow 2.5% from 1993. Commercial revenue grew by 0.4%.
Short Term Debt	511,300	264,800	67,800	Industrial electric revenue dipped 0.9% from 1993. For 1995, the company
Current Liabilities	653,800	405,600	213,900	expects sales volume to grow by 1% or 2%. This reflects improving economic
Long Term Debt	1,101,200	1,299,700	1,537,700	conditions in Nova Scotia.
Total Liabilities	1,755,000	1,705,300	1,751,600	
Total Equity	1,005,600	973,700	749,100	Coal represents three-quarters of Nova Scotia Power's fuel supply and more than
Total Liab. & Equity	2,760,600	2,679,000	2,500,700	one-third of its costs. The company buys about two-thirds of its coal from the

CAPITAL (000)

				Cape Breton Development Corporation (CBDC), under a 33-year contract that is
Total Debt	1,612,500	1,564,500	1,605,500	reviewed every five years. When the contract was reviewed in March 1995, Nova
Preferred Equity	200,000	200,000	0	Scotia Power stated it would terminate the contract unless CBDC reduced coal
Common Equity	805,600	773,700	749,100	prices. CBDC took Nova Scotia Power to court.

In April 1995, Nova Scotia Power President and C.E.O. Louis Comeau announced he will step down in 1996, after 13 years with the company.

Relative strength to TSE300

Price

Volume (in 1000's of board lots)

Rank (Profit/Revenue/Assets)
73   144   79

J.A.F. Macdonald
Chairman

Louis R. Comeau
President & C.E.O.

Gary Kendall Oickle
Vice President & C.F.O.

Address
P.O. Box 910
Halifax
NS
B3J 2W5
(902) 428-6230

Fax: (902) 428-6112
N0990033/G/10.2

PACIFIC NORTHERN GAS LTD.

Exchanges	Price (Jun29'95)	19.75	Trailing P/E	10.34	Stock Symbol
TV	Trailing Yield (%)	4.46	Trailing EPS	1.91	PNG.A

Period Ending	Dec94	Dec93	Dec92	Dec91	Dec90
Yearly Statistics					
Price-Close	20.25	22.00	16.50	13.63	11.25
Price-High	23.50	22.00	16.50	14.56	12.50
Price-Low	17.75	14.50	13.00	10.75	10.63
P/E-Close	11.25	13.50	11.15	8.39	7.01
Dividends per Share	0.88	0.88	0.80	0.78	0.75
Dividend Yield (%)	4.35	4.00	4.85	5.69	6.67
Sales per Share	17.91	16.67	14.42	20.18	22.64
EPS before extra. item	1.80	1.63	1.48	1.63	1.61
Cash Flow per Share	3.36	3.04	2.73	2.95	3.22
Book Value per Share	13.84	12.95	12.22	11.58	10.76
O/S Common Shares	3,499	3,459	3,439	3,401	3,361
Total Revenue	62,468	57,662	49,459	68,529	76,380
Income before extra.	6,601	5,963	5,403	5,828	5,726
Cash Flow	11,704	10,498	9,339	9,996	10,781
Debt/Equity	1.62	1.60	1.50	1.50	1.70
Return on Capital (%)	13.87	13.53	13.08	15.14	15.14
Ret. on Com. Equity (%)	13.44	12.96	12.45	14.54	15.55
% Change Profit	10.7	10.4	(7.3)	1.8	11.2
% Change Revenue	8.3	16.6	(27.8)	(10.3)	2.9
% Change Assets	6.6	14.5	3.9	2.7	7.6
Preferred Div. Coverage	19.6	17.7	16.0		
Total Div. Coverage	1.9	1.8	1.8		
Interest Coverage	2.3	2.1	2.0		
Current Ratio	0.4	0.6	0.5		
Operating Margin	29.8	28.7	30.0		
Asset Turnover	0.4	0.4	0.3		
5 YEAR RATIOS (%)					
Return on Capital	14.2	14.5	14.8		
Return on Com. Equity	13.8	14.1	14.5		
Profit Growth	5.0	4.4	3.1		
Revenue Growth	(3.5)	(5.6)	(8.1)		
Asset Growth	6.9	5.7	3.3		
BALANCE SHEET (000)					
Cash	0	0	0		
Current Assets	12,478	12,228	11,927		
Net Fixed Assets	156,593	146,090	127,640		
Invest's & Advances	0	0	0		
Total Assets	174,161	163,441	142,765		
Short Term Debt	22,542	11,872	18,535		
Current Liabilities	32,052	20,900	25,380		
Long Term Debt	63,990	67,937	51,875		
Total Liabilities	120,729	113,654	95,745		
Total Equity	53,432	49,787	47,020		
Total Liab. & Equity	174,161	163,441	142,765		
CAPITAL (000)					
Total Debt	86,532	79,809	70,410		
Preferred Equity	5,000	5,000	5,000		
Common Equity	48,432	44,787	42,020		

Business:

PACIFIC NORTHERN GAS LTD. is a natural gas utility. It supplies natural gas to industry in Prince Rupert, Kitimat, and northwestern B.C. The company's east-west pipeline connects with the north-south pipeline of its parent company, Westcoast Energy Inc. of Vancouver. Pacific Northern Gas (N.E.) Ltd., a subsidiary, supplies natural gas to Dawson Creek and Tumbler Ridge in northeastern B.C.

Date	EPS	DPS	Tot Rev	Inc Bex
Mar 95	0.88	0.22	19,790	3,162
Dec 94	0.67	0.22	16,888	2,408
Sep 94	0.00	0.22	11,723	91
Jun 94	0.36	0.22	14,988	1,332
Mar 94	0.77	0.22	18,869	2,770
Dec 93	0.51	0.22	14,747	1,854
Sep 93	(0.06)	0.22	11,070	(113)
Jun 93	0.37	0.22	13,378	1,342

Synopsis:

For the second consecutive year, Pacific Northern Gas Ltd. has reached a negotiated settlement and avoided the added cost and time of a public hearing. The B.C. Utilities Commission approved the settlement proposals agreed to by the company, its customers, and other interested parties. The company's application related to its three operating divisions. To recover its forecast 1995 cost of service requirements, the PNG-West settlement allows PNG a 2.67% increase. Due to general increases in operating and maintenance costs, the Dawson Creek division 1995 forecast rose by 4.55%. The 1995 forecast costs of service requirements for the Tumbler Ridge division have declined by 5.05%.

From the almost 26,000 customers Pacific Northern serves, a few large industrial customers account for more than 80% of the natural gas the company delivers. The largest single customer is Methanex, taking more than 60% of all the gas delivered on the company's system. In addition to its own plant in Kitimat, Methanex is a joint owner of an ammonia plant nearby. The ammonia plant was expanded during 1994 to 700 tonnes from 500 tonnes. To meet this plant's need for additional natural gas PNG added 21 miles of pipeline loop and upgraded a turbine compressor unit. The gas is delivered under a new transportation agreement that came into effect September 1, 1994. Under this agreement PNG delivers an additional seven million cubic feet of gas per day. These are firm, as opposed to interruptible, gas sales.

In 1994, PNG reported the best year in its 26-year history. Net income exceeded $6.6-million, an increase of 10% over 1993. The company credits this increase to a number of factors, but mainly from increased sales to its major customers, which reflects the continuing growth of the British Columbia economy and the strong performance of its main industrial customers. The company feels its business prospects are promising, as their main system is located in a region of the province well suited for industrial growth.

Rank (Profit/Revenue/Assets)
377   499   374

Richard D. Walker
Chairman

Roy G. Dyce
C.E.O. & President

Address
Suite 1400
1185 West Georgia Street
Vancouver
BC
V6E 4E6
(604) 691-5680

Fax: (604) 691-5863
P0000304/G/10.1

QUEBEC-TELEPHONE

Exchanges	Price (Jun29'95)	19.00	Trailing P/E	10.80	Stock Symbol
TM	Trailing Yield (%)	6.61	Trailing EPS	1.76	QT

Period Ending	Dec94	Dec93	Dec92	Dec91	Dec90
Yearly Statistics					
Price-Close	18.13	21.50	16.75	18.50	14.38
Price-High	24.25	22.00	19.38	18.75	16.00
Price-Low	17.50	16.00	16.00	14.13	13.75
P/E-Close	10.36	12.72	9.85	11.64	9.91
Dividends per Share	1.25	1.21	1.17	1.12	1.06
Dividend Yield (%)	6.89	5.63	6.99	6.03	7.34
Sales per Share	12.32	12.32	12.78	12.51	12.17
EPS before extra. item	1.75	1.69	1.70	1.59	1.45
Cash Flow per Share	4.70	4.38	4.24	4.02	3.69
Book Value per Share	13.03	12.50	11.97	11.40	10.90
O/S Common Shares	17,082	16,917	16,700	16,525	16,364
Total Revenue	254,316	246,250	245,091	235,577	226,544
Income before extra.	30,222	28,971	28,849	26,716	24,072
Cash Flow	79,848	73,605	70,469	66,198	60,052
Debt/Equity	0.75	0.77	0.79	0.83	0.88
Return on Capital (%)	16.66	16.83	17.51	16.64	16.13
Ret. on Com. Equity (%)	13.67	13.82	14.57	14.26	13.50
% Change Profit	4.3	0.4	8.0	11.0	6.4
% Change Revenue	3.3	0.5	4.0	4.0	5.1
% Change Assets	5.5	2.2	0.8	1.6	1.5
Preferred Div. Coverage	54.8	52.4	51.6		
Total Div. Coverage	1.4	1.4	1.4		
Interest Coverage	4.0	3.8	3.7		
Current Ratio	0.6	0.3	0.5		
Operating Margin	25.2	25.1	25.7		
Asset Turnover	0.4	0.4	0.5		
5 YEAR RATIOS (%)					
Return on Capital	16.8	16.7	16.6		
Return on Com. Equity	14.0	13.9	13.8		
Profit Growth	5.9	6.2	7.0		
Revenue Growth	3.3	3.8	5.2		
Asset Growth	2.3	2.3	3.6		
BALANCE SHEET (000)					
Cash	0	0	0		
Current Assets	34,547	27,396	26,686		
Net Fixed Assets	442,261	425,438	415,972		
Invest's & Advances	8,058	7,238	7,028		
Total Assets	488,442	463,060	453,060		
Short Term Debt	4,364	39,744	15,688		
Current Liabilities	56,650	79,033	55,690		
Long Term Debt	170,000	130,000	150,000		
Total Liabilities	255,532	241,320	242,798		
Total Equity	232,910	221,740	210,262		
Total Liab. & Equity	488,442	463,060	453,060		
CAPITAL (000)					
Total Debt	174,364	169,744	165,688		
Preferred Equity	10,318	10,362	10,380		
Common Equity	222,592	211,378	199,882		

Business:

QUEBEC-TELEPHONE is a telecommunications company. Its network serves clients on the outskirts of Quebec City and in the Lower St. Lawrence, Gaspe and North Shore regions of Quebec. The company provides voice, data, image and cellular transmission services. Anglo Canadian Telephone Co. of Montreal holds 50.6% of the company's outstanding common shares.

Date	EPS	DPS	Tot Rev	Inc Bex
Mar 95	0.36	0.32	63,389	6,224
Dec 94	0.49	0.32	66,129	8,401
Sep 94	0.48	0.31	64,286	8,262
Jun 94	0.43	0.31	63,831	7,443
Mar 94	0.35	0.31	60,070	6,116
Dec 93	0.46	0.31	62,857	7,940
Sep 93	0.45	0.30	61,844	7,708
Jun 93	0.43	0.30	62,576	7,338

Synopsis:

In May 1995, Dominion Bond Rating Service Ltd. downgraded the debt rating of Quebec-Telephone. DBRS said the cuts reflect the effect of intense competition for long-distance market share, which has reduced revenues. DBRS also concerned about the impact of pending regulatory changes and whether the CRTC will allow local telephone rates to rise to offset declining long-distance revenue. The rating on Quebec-Telephone's first mortgage bonds was lowered to single-A (low) from single-A. Its unsecured debentures were unchanged at single-A (low), and its preferred shares were unchanged at pfd-2.

In 1994, Quebec-Telephone deployed a second 300 kilometre fibre optic route between Rimouski and Laurier-Station, to ensure more reliable transmissions between central Canada and the Maritimes. This network is part of the information highway that will enable a broad range of advanced applications including video-on-demand, interactive games, video shopping, home banking, telecommuting, and access to data banks, videophones, and electronic mail. The company said building the information highway over Quebec-Telephone's territory will require an investment of $200-million by the year 2005.

During fiscal 1994, the company invested $4-million to upgrade and expand its cellular network. This increased the percentage of the population having access to the service from 77% to 87%. New cells were installed in Gaspesie to extend service to Tourelle, 90 kilometres east of Matane. The quality of transmission was also improved in the areas of Mont-Joli, Amqui, Causapscal, and Gaspe.

For fiscal 1994, Quebec-Telephone revenues by segment were: Local service, 30.7%; Long distance, 52.8%; and Other, 16.5%.

Rank (Profit/Revenue/Assets)
158   282   229

Gilles Laroche
Chairman, President & C.E.O.

Yvon Gendron
V.P. Finance & Treasurer

Address
6 Rue Jules-A-Brillant
Rimouski
PQ
G5L 7E4
(418) 723-2271

Fax: (418) 722-2059
Q0000536/G/10.3

TELUS CORPORATION

Exchanges	Price (Jun29'95)	16.75	Trailing P/E	11.47	Stock Symbol
TMZ	Trailing Yield (%)	5.49	Trailing EPS	1.46	**AGT**

Period Ending	Dec94	Dec93	Dec92	Dec91	Dec90
Yearly Statistics					3M
Price-Close	15.88	16.00	13.00	15.75	13.25
Price-High	18.00	16.25	16.38	15.75	13.50
Price-Low	14.38	12.13	13.00	12.88	11.88
P/E-Close	10.44	12.31	10.16	11.84	6.37
Dividends per Share	0.92	0.92	0.92	0.89	0.22
Dividend Yield (%)	5.80	5.75	7.08	5.65	1.66
Sales per Share	8.94	8.35	7.88	8.34	8.05
EPS before extra. item	1.52	1.30	1.28	1.33	0.52
Cash Flow per Share	3.77	3.25	2.63	2.56	2.67
Book Value per Share	12.63	11.97	11.61	11.31	10.93
O/S Common Shares	139,340	139,247	139,195	138,416	137,626
Total Revenue	1,387,345	1,280,975	1,251,955	1,289,730	298,690
Income before extra.	211,733	180,544	177,768	183,379	71,718
Cash Flow	524,932	452,017	363,926	353,380	91,954
Debt/Equity	0.69	0.65	0.63	0.61	0.74
Return on Capital (%)	11.65	11.16	11.66	12.33	na
Ret. on Com. Equity (%)	12.36	11.00	11.18	11.95	na
% Change Profit	17.3	1.6	(3.1)	(36.1)	na
% Change Revenue	8.3	2.3	(2.9)	7.9	na
% Change Assets	7.4	1.5	5.3	(2.8)	na

Preferred Div. Coverage	np	np	np
Total Div. Coverage	1.7	1.4	1.4
Interest Coverage	2.9	2.6	2.5
Current Ratio	0.7	0.6	0.9
Operating Margin	22.4	22.9	19.9
Asset Turnover	0.4	0.4	0.3
5 YEAR RATIOS (%)			
Return on Capital	na	na	na
Return on Com. Equity	na	na	na
Profit Growth	na	na	na
Revenue Growth	na	na	na
Asset Growth	na	na	na
BALANCE SHEET (000)			
Cash	66,567	20,261	114,247
Current Assets	351,187	278,373	361,154
Net Fixed Assets	2,908,716	2,798,326	2,728,588
Invest's & Advances	53,790	49,519	41,241
Total Assets	3,483,722	3,244,200	3,195,164
Short Term Debt	107,250	78,546	983
Current Liabilities	491,240	431,062	402,877
Long Term Debt	1,098,215	997,257	1,009,863
Total Liabilities	1,724,218	1,576,940	1,579,602
Total Equity	1,759,504	1,667,260	1,615,562
Total Liab. & Equity	3,483,722	3,244,200	3,195,164
CAPITAL (000)			
Total Debt	1,205,465	1,075,803	1,010,846
Preferred Equity	0	0	0
Common Equity	1,759,504	1,667,260	1,615,562

Date	EPS	DPS	Tot Rev	Inc Bex
Mar 95	0.38	0.23	372,704	53,310
Dec 94	0.42	0.23	359,784	58,646
Sep 94	0.33	0.23	335,031	45,389
Jun 94	0.33	0.23	334,892	47,070
Mar 94	0.44	0.23	340,487	60,628
Dec 93	0.47	0.23	332,987	65,656
Sep 93	0.33	0.23	317,662	44,945
Jun 93	0.29	0.23	313,966	41,239

Business:

TELUS CORPORATION is a management holding company serving as a corporate umbrella for AGT Limited, AGT Mobility and AGT Directory.

Synopsis:

In May 1995, Telus Corp. announced the creation of a new subsidiary that will specialize in high-speed data communications services. This is one of the fastest-growing segments of the telecommunications market. AGT Advanced Communications will offer high-speed access to the Internet, improved service for local computer networks, and desktop video conferencing, which allows users to communicate between offices by video.

In March 1995, Telus acquired Edmonton Telephones (Ed Tel) from the City of Edmonton. The deal included cash proceeds of $465-million and a debt of $170-million. Telus will expand Edmonton based research and development by $12-million and invest $27-million in an Ed Tel capital expenditure program. Considering all features of the deal, the total cost of the package is $720-million. With the addition of Ed Tel, Telus remains Canada's third largest telecommunications company with total assets of $ 4-billion and operating revenues greater than $ 1.6 billion.

After introducing a variety of price plans and promotions, AGT mobility surpassed the 100,000 customer mark in October 1994. Total customers grew over 58% in 1994. The paging business enjoyed good customer growth at 28%. AGT Mobility's successful one-day pager delivery system was enhanced with a retail distribution option. AGT Mobility also introduced an exclusive new two-way paging service.

In December 1994, ISM (Alberta), a joint-venture of Telus and ISM Information Systems Management Corporation, formed a corporation with the Alberta Government. The company will deliver accounts payable and payroll services to governments, public sector organizations, and private sector clients. New features will be added to satisfy private sector requirements. The new corporation will employ the Alberta Government's advanced payroll system, which is uniquely suited to the public sector. The corporation began making its financial services package commercially available in February 1995.

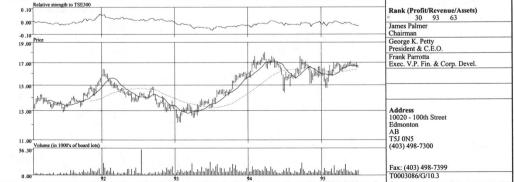

Rank (Profit/Revenue/Assets)
30   93   63

James Palmer
Chairman

George K. Petty
President & C.E.O.

Frank Parrotta
Exec. V.P. Fin. & Corp. Devel.

Address
10020 - 100th Street
Edmonton
AB
T5J 0N5
(403) 498-7300

Fax: (403) 498-7399
T0003086/G/10.3

TRANSALTA CORPORATION

Exchanges	Price (Jun29'95)	14.37	Trailing P/E	12.39	Stock Symbol
TMZ	Trailing Yield (%)	6.82	Trailing EPS	1.16	**TA**

Period Ending	Dec94	Dec93	Dec92	Dec91	Dec90
Yearly Statistics					
Price-Close	14.50	15.25	13.75	n t	n t
Price-High	16.25	15.50	13.75	n t	n t
Price-Low	13.13	12.63	13.50	n t	n t
P/E-Close	12.29	13.15	11.65	n t	45.69
Dividends per Share	0.98	0.98	0.98	0.98	0.98
Dividend Yield (%)	6.76	6.43	7.13	n t	n t
Sales per Share	9.29	8.75	8.26	8.21	7.83
EPS before extra. item	1.18	1.16	1.18	1.12	0.26
Cash Flow per Share	2.64	2.66	2.50	2.42	2.35
Book Value per Share	9.54	9.31	9.12	8.71	8.42
O/S Common Shares	158,800	158,700	158,500	144,000	137,300
Total Revenue	1,498,700	1,407,500	1,318,200	1,211,500	1,111,500
Income before extra.	186,900	183,800	182,500	158,300	87,300
Cash Flow	419,200	422,200	388,100	341,900	319,700
Debt/Equity	1.14	1.16	1.04	1.23	0.88
Return on Capital (%)	16.53	17.06	17.48	14.92	11.85
Ret. on Com. Equity (%)	12.49	12.57	13.52	13.14	2.96
% Change Profit	1.7	0.7	15.3	81.3	(53.9)
% Change Revenue	6.5	6.8	8.8	9.0	11.4
% Change Assets	(0.0)	(0.1)	5.1	3.3	(1.2)
Preferred Div. Coverage	np	np	np		
Total Div. Coverage	1.2	1.2	1.2		
Interest Coverage	3.4	3.4	3.4		
Current Ratio	0.9	0.9	0.6		
Operating Margin	37.1	39.9	40.9		
Asset Turnover	0.4	0.3	0.3		
5 YEAR RATIOS (%)					
Return on Capital	15.6	15.2	14.9		
Return on Com. Equity	10.9	10.7	10.0		
Profit Growth	(0.3)	0.8	(6.0)		
Revenue Growth	8.4	7.9	6.2		
Asset Growth	1.4	2.3	2.5		
BALANCE SHEET (000)					
Cash	58,000	32,800	25,600		
Current Assets	328,400	287,600	270,500		
Net Fixed Assets	3,618,600	3,725,200	3,852,300		
Invest's & Advances	176,600	117,700	15,600		
Total Assets	4,170,500	4,171,700	4,176,100		
Short Term Debt	157,400	127,700	211,600		
Current Liabilities	381,300	332,900	459,000		
Long Term Debt	1,569,900	1,580,800	1,290,800		
Total Liabilities	2,655,500	2,694,100	2,730,100		
Total Equity	1,515,000	1,477,600	1,446,000		
Total Liab. & Equity	4,170,500	4,171,700	4,176,100		
CAPITAL (000)					
Total Debt	1,727,300	1,708,500	1,502,400		
Preferred Equity	0	0	0		
Common Equity	1,515,000	1,477,600	1,446,000		

Business:

TRANSALTA CORPORATION is a management holding company with principal operations in the electrical utility industry. The company's two principal subsidiaries are: TransAlta Utilities Corporation which conducts regulated electrical utility operations in Alberta; and TransAlta Energy Corporation which conducts non-regulated operations, including the operation of independent power facilities.

Date	EPS	DPS	Tot Rev	Inc Bex
Mar 95	0.38	0.25	358,100	68,900
Dec 94	0.34	0.25	391,600	53,100
Sep 94	0.24	0.25	364,500	38,800
Jun 94	0.20	0.25	354,900	31,200
Mar 94	0.40	0.25	342,400	74,300
Dec 93	0.34	0.25	370,300	54,200
Sep 93	0.24	0.25	338,800	37,400
Jun 93	0.23	0.25	335,300	36,100

Synopsis:

TransAlta Corporation recorded revenue and earnings gains in both its energy and utilities sectors in 1994. TransAlta Utilities saw earnings rise to $170-million from $168.7-million in 1993, or $1.07 per share compared with $1.06 in 1993. Sales totaled 27,450 million kilowatt-hours in 1994, an increase of 6.3% from 1993. The strong Alberta economy, with growth in the energy-intensive oil, gas, forestry, and manufacturing industries contributed to gains in the company's industrial sales.

TransAlta Energy contributed $0.11 earnings per share, compared to $0.10 cents per share in 1993. Revenues reached $84-million, compared to 1993's $75-million. In 1994, TransAlta Energy completed the construction of its hydroelectric facility in Argentina, which has a capacity of 1,400 megawatts, and supplies 10% of Argentina's electricity needs. In January 1995, TransAlta Energy purchased 49% of the common shares of Capital Energy Ltd., owners of New Zealand's fourth largest electric distribution company. TransAlta Energy continues to look for growth opportunities in Latin America, New Zealand, Australia, China, and India.

TransAlta Utilities' largest 10 customers, all wholesale and industrial customers, represented 43% of its electric revenue in 1994. About 30% of its electric revenue is from the oil and gas, petrochemical and forestry sectors. The company is forecasting industrial sales to increase by 1.2% in 1995, led by the oil and gas export activities in Alberta.

TransAlta Utilities is poised for increased competition as the deregulation of Alberta's electricity market unfolds. The company intends to remain competitive by seeking growth opportunities both inside and outside Alberta. It is continuing cost-cutting initiatives, which in 1994 included a reduction of 400 employees.

TransAlta Corporation's dividend declared on common shares was $0.98 cents per share in 1994, the same as in 1993.

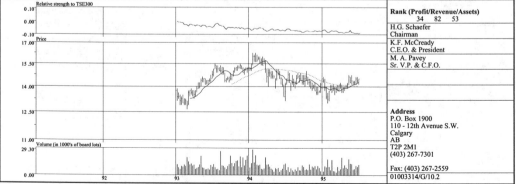

Rank (Profit/Revenue/Assets)		
34	82	53

H.G. Schaefer
Chairman

K.F. McCready
C.E.O. & President

M. A. Pavey
Sr. V.P. & C.F.O.

Address
P.O. Box 1900
110 - 12th Avenue S.W.
Calgary
AB
T2P 2M1
(403) 267-7301

Fax: (403) 267-2559
01003314/G/10.2

TRANSALTA UTILITIES CORPORATION

Exchanges	Price (Jun29'95)		26.00	Trailing P/E		nc	Stock Symbol
TMZ	Trailing Yield (%)		nc	Trailing EPS		1.08	**TAU.PR.T**

Period Ending	Dec94	Dec93	Dec92	Dec91	Dec90
Yearly Statistics					
Price-Close	26.25	26.75	13.75	13.50	11.88
Price-High	27.00	27.25	14.50	13.88	14.38
Price-Low	25.00	25.50	12.00	11.88	11.13
P/E-Close	nc	nc	nc	nc	nc
Dividends per Share	nc	nc	nc	nc	nc
Dividend Yield (%)	nc	nc	nc	nc	nc
Sales per Share	8.76	8.27	8.23	8.21	7.83
EPS before extra. item	1.07	1.06	1.12	1.16	0.26
Cash Flow per Share	2.54	2.51	2.45	2.46	2.35
Book Value per Share	8.66	8.66	8.65	8.47	8.42
O/S Common Shares	158,800	158,700	158,500	144,000	137,300
Total Revenue	1,398,400	1,322,500	1,305,200	1,208,600	1,111,500
Income before extra.	209,200	218,800	233,100	220,800	87,300
Cash Flow	402,600	398,000	379,600	348,100	319,700
Debt/Equity	0.78	0.77	0.64	0.75	0.88
Return on Capital (%)	16.15	15.85	15.85	15.20	11.85
Ret. on Com. Equity (%)	12.38	12.29	13.44	13.78	2.96
% Change Profit	(4.4)	(6.1)	5.6	152.9	(53.9)
% Change Revenue	5.7	1.3	8.0	8.7	11.4
% Change Assets	(2.0)	(3.0)	1.4	1.1	(1.2)

Business:

TRANSALTA UTILITIES CORP. is an electric utility operating in Alberta. The company develops, owns and operates hydro and thermal power plants and electric transmission and distribution systems.

Date	EPS	DPS	Tot Rev	Inc Bex
Mar 95	0.34	nc	308,300	63,200
Dec 94	0.32	nc	364,400	59,600
Sep 94	0.23	nc	344,100	46,100
Jun 94	0.18	nc	333,300	39,400
Mar 94	0.34	nc	304,900	64,100
Dec 93	0.30	nc	343,500	58,900
Sep 93	0.22	nc	320,900	45,200
Jun 93	0.21	nc	316,800	48,300

	Dec94	Dec93	Dec92
Preferred Div. Coverage	5.4	4.4	4.0
Total Div. Coverage	1.0	1.0	1.0
Interest Coverage	3.8	3.9	3.8
Current Ratio	0.7	0.8	0.5
Operating Margin	38.2	40.8	40.9
Asset Turnover	0.4	0.3	0.3
5 YEAR RATIOS (%)			
Return on Capital	15.0	14.7	14.6
Return on Com. Equity	11.0	10.7	10.1
Profit Growth	2.0	4.4	(1.3)
Revenue Growth	6.9	6.6	6.0
Asset Growth	(0.8)	0.6	1.3
BALANCE SHEET (000)			
Cash	0	0	0
Current Assets	269,500	242,600	230,200
Net Fixed Assets	3,450,700	3,558,400	3,683,200
Invest's & Advances	0	0	0
Total Assets	3,745,000	3,821,400	3,939,000
Short Term Debt	152,800	123,500	208,300
Current Liabilities	379,800	319,100	440,100
Long Term Debt	1,285,900	1,348,000	1,148,000
Total Liabilities	1,907,200	1,898,500	1,814,000
Total Equity	1,837,800	1,922,900	2,125,000
Total Liab. & Equity	3,745,000	3,821,400	3,939,000
CAPITAL (000)			
Total Debt	1,438,700	1,471,500	1,356,300
Preferred Equity	462,800	549,000	754,400
Common Equity	1,375,000	1,373,900	1,370,600

Synopsis:

In 1994, TransAlta Utilities saw earnings climb to $170-million from $168.7-million in 1993. Energy sales in 1994 were 27,450 million kilowatt-hours, an increase of 6.3% from 1993. Industrial customers were responsible for a large portion of the increase, due to an overall strong Alberta economy. Growth came from the energy-intensive oil, gas, forestry, and manufacturing industries.

TransAlta Utilities is poised for increased competition in the coming years as the deregulation of Alberta's electricity market unfolds. The company has been vocal in its insistence that new players on the energy field, such as the city-owned Edmonton Power, be subject to the same taxation regulations as the publicly traded companies. Meanwhile, TransAlta Utilities intends to remain competitive by seeking growth opportunities both inside and outside of Alberta and continuing its cost-cutting initiatives. In 1994 it laid off 400 employees.

In its 1995 budget, the federal government announced the elimination of the Public Utilities Income Tax Transfer Act (PUITTA) rebate. The rebate was established in 1947 so that customers of investor-owned electric and natural gas utilities were on a level playing field with customers of government-owned utilities, which do not pay federal income taxes. TransAlta Utilities is lobbying for a reversal of the federal decision, which will result in up to 7% increased cost for residential and industrial utilities consumers in Alberta.

TransAlta Utilities' largest 10 customers, all wholesale and industrial customers, represented 43% of its electric revenue in 1994. About 30% of the company's electric revenue is from the oil and gas, petrochemical and forestry sectors. TransAlta Utilities is forecasting industrial sales to increase by 1.2% in 1995, led again by the oil and gas export-related activities in Alberta. It also expects some load growth from the chemical and forestry sectors in 1995, driven by the export markets.

Relative strength to TSE300 / Price / Volume (in 1000's of board lots) charts

Rank (Profit/Revenue/Assets)
32 91 58

H.G. Schaefer
Chairman

K.F. McCready
C.E.O.

W. Saponja
President & C.O.O.

Michael A. Pavey
C.F.O.

Address
P.O. Box 1900
110 - 12th Avenue S.W.
Calgary
AB
T2P 2M1
(403) 267-7301

Fax: (403) 267-2559

T0002324/G/10.2

UNICORP ENERGY CORPORATION

Exchanges	Price (Jun29'95)	1.95	Trailing P/E	nm	Stock Symbol
T	Trailing Yield (%)	0.00	Trailing EPS	2.53	UNI.A

Period Ending	Dec94	Dec93	Dec92	Dec91	Dec90
Yearly Statistics					
Price-Close	1.95	0.55	0.26	0.46	2.55
Price-High	2.25	0.90	2.30	0.87	15.00
Price-Low	0.60	0.33	0.26	0.25	2.25
P/E-Close	0.79	0.97	0.25	nm	nm
Dividends per Share	0.00	0.00	0.00	0.00	0.15
Dividend Yield (%)	0.00	0.00	0.00	0.00	5.88
Sales per Share	na	na	na	164.34	166.58
EPS before extra. item	2.47	0.57	1.03	(2.80)	(1.62)
Cash Flow per Share	0.20	0.07	(1.30)	17.21	18.28
Book Value per Share	3.74	1.27	0.69	0.10	2.91
O/S Common Shares	10,727	10,735	10,735	10,735	10,735
Total Revenue	26,884	6,255	38,419	1,764,154	1,759,700
Income before extra.	26,579	6,150	11,057	(11,890)	1,000
Cash Flow	2,123	763	(13,972)	184,776	193,000
Debt/Equity	0.46	0.13	nd	0.58	5.69
Return on Capital (%)	72.28	53.93	22.05	(0.08)	11.49
Ret. on Com. Equity (%)	98.87	58.43	151.06	(186.53)	(124.19)
% Change Profit	332.2	(44.4)	193.0	(1,289.0)	100.7
% Change Revenue	329.8	(83.7)	(97.8)	0.3	(4.0)
% Change Assets	16.2	(0.8)	(98.0)	2.0	4.8

Date	EPS	DPS	Tot Rev	Inc Bex
Mar 95	0.08	0.00	na	819
Dec 94	0.10	0.00	1,414	1,160
Sep 94	2.33	0.00	489	25,908
Jun 94	0.02	0.00	302	286
Mar 94	0.02	0.00	223	205
Dec 93	0.51	0.00	5,546	5,479
Sep 93	0.03	0.00	331	319
Jun 93	0.01	0.00	172	161

	Dec94	Dec93	Dec92
Preferred Div. Coverage	np	np	np
Total Div. Coverage	na	na	2.4
Interest Coverage	178.2	na	1.4
Current Ratio	6.9	12.2	8.3
Operating Margin	41.9	na	na
Asset Turnover	na	na	na
5 YEAR RATIOS (%)			
Return on Capital	31.9	17.8	9.4
Return on Com. Equity	(0.5)	(60.7)	(69.9)
Profit Growth	na	(30.2)	(19.5)
Revenue Growth	(57.4)	(71.1)	(51.8)
Asset Growth	(52.2)	(54.3)	(61.0)
BALANCE SHEET (000)			
Cash	43,358	10,721	13,206
Current Assets	43,358	10,721	13,206
Net Fixed Assets	0	0	0
Invest's & Advances	20,269	3,050	0
Total Assets	64,912	55,851	56,300
Short Term Debt	0	0	0
Current Liabilities	6,307	880	1,584
Long Term Debt	18,439	1,757	0
Total Liabilities	24,746	42,250	48,849
Total Equity	40,166	13,601	7,451
Total Liab. & Equity	64,912	55,851	56,300
CAPITAL (000)			
Total Debt	18,439	1,757	0
Preferred Equity	0	0	0
Common Equity	40,166	13,601	7,451

Business:

UNICORP ENERGY CORPORATION is a Canadian-owned company conducting financing and investment activities in the power generating and real estate sectors in North America.

Synopsis:

Unicorp closed the sale of The Lincoln Savings Bank in August 1994. Unicorp's share from the sale, after repayment of related debt, was $26.8-million and resulted in a gain of $24.5-million being recognized in income from discontinued operations. This allowed Unicorp to achieve its principal objective of recent years, which has been to solidify its financial position. Unicorp can now turn its attention to investing the company's capital for the future. The current operating assets are in power generation and real estate sectors and include a recently developed power project in northwestern Ontario, and an effective 50% interest in seven commercial real estate properties in the United States. To produce growth over the medium to longer-term Unicorp will focus on building a solid earnings base from its power generation operations and real estate assets.

Construction of the nine megawatt hydro-electric power station was completed in October 1994 and delivery of power has begun. The facility at Valerie Falls is near Atikokan in northwestern Ontario. Unicorp holds a 31.9% participation in this project with Great Lakes Power and a local partner. The company is presently seeking additional investment opportunities in this sector.

Unicorp filed and subsequently received regulatory approval to make a normal course issuer bid, pursuant to which Unicorp may purchase up to 482,700 of its Class A non-voting shares and 53,900 of its Class B voting shares over a 12 month period. These shares represent about 5% of the Class A and Class B issued shares. Unicorp believes that its outstanding common shares represent an attractive investment and an appropriate use of its available funds.

Relative strength to TSE300 / Price / Volume (in 1000's of board lots)

Rank (Profit/Revenue/Assets)
176 664 575

Robert A. Dunford
Chairman
Ian G. Cockwell
President

Address
Suite 2320
161 Bay Street
Toronto
ON
M5J 2S1
(416) 867-9370

Fax: (416) 867-1961
U0000465/G/10.1

Page	Company		Fiscal year end	EARNINGS PER SHARE		
				Last Year	Estimate this year	Estimate next year
369	Baton Broadcasting		Aug-94	0.12	0.20	0.42
370	BCE Mobile Communications		Dec-94	0.53	0.84	1.29
371	Call-Net Enterprises		Dec-94	(1.62)	(1.42)	(0.46)
372	Canadian Satellite		Aug-94	0.61	0.79	0.84
373	CanWest Global Communications		Aug-94	1.17	1.53	1.64
374	CFCF Inc.		Aug-94	0.48	0.43	0.57
375	CHUM Limited		Aug-94	0.66	0.83	1.09
376	Cogeco Cable		Aug-94	0.82	0.73	0.79
377	Cogeco		Aug-94	0.60	0.55	0.65
378	Fundy Cable		Aug-94	(0.13)	(0.22)	(0.05)
379	Groupe Videotron		Aug-94	0.11	0.03	0.11
380	G.T.C. Transcontinental Group		Oct-94	0.60	0.71	0.83
381	Hollinger		Dec-94	0.53	0.73	1.05
382	Mitel		Mar-95	0.27	0.38	0.47
383	Moffat Communications		Aug-94	1.49	1.68	1.92
384	Northern Telecom	$US	Dec-94	1.20	1.89	2.34
385	Petersburgh Long Distance		Dec-94	(0.89)	0.30	0.60
386	Quebecor Inc.		Dec-94	1.31	1.78	1.99
387	Quebecor Printing	$US	Dec-94	0.87	1.01	1.19
388	Rogers Cantel Mobile		Dec-94	(0.02)	0.33	0.69
389	Rogers Communications		Dec-94	(0.91)	(0.67)	(0.31)
390	Shaw Communications		Aug-94	0.59	0.47	0.52
391	Southam		Dec-94	0.58	0.65	0.86
392	Tele-Metropole		Aug-94	0.89	0.81	1.00
393	Telemedia		Aug-94	0.22	0.39	0.49
394	Thomson Corporation		Dec-94	0.71	0.83	0.95
395	Toronto Sun Publishing		Dec-94	0.38	0.35	0.47
396	Torstar		Dec-94	1.09	1.03	1.33
397	WIC Western Internationa Communications		Aug-94	0.40	0.74	0.89

Estimates from First Call Corporation, 22 Pittsburgh Street, Boston, MA 02210   (800) 366-9992   Fax (617) 261-5679

Communications & Media

The media and communications industry is in the midst of rapid change. The latest technologies or soon-to-be-available technologies have spawned new ways of transmitting information. They are blurring the lines between television, cable, telecommunications, broadcasting, and home computer capabilities. As a result, competition is stiff, and companies in the industry are scrambling to keep their respective market shares.

The cable industry will offer the first Canadian direct-to-home (DTH) satellite television service beginning in September 1995. Expressvu Inc. of Mississauga, Ontario received Canadian Radio-Television Telecommunications Commission approval for the service in July 1995. The service will offer subscribers as many as 100 channels plus pay-per-view movies. It also will allow consumers to customize the package of channels they wish to receive. Consumers will pay $1,000 for a 60-centimetre in-home satellite dish and a set-top decoder box. Direct broadcast satellite company DirecTv Inc. of Los Angeles, which already offers 150-channel satellite service in the United States, has joined with Power Corp. of Montreal to form Power DirecTv. This company plans to launch a competing DTH service in November 1995. Other DTH services probably will appear in 1996.

The telephone industry soon will be competing in the video and entertainment arena. A CRTC statement in May 1995 recommended that telephone companies be licenced to offer home television and electronic services, thereby competing with cable companies. Cable companies have requested a waiting period so that they can prepare for the onslaught, pointing to the large revenue base telephone companies have. A federal ruling is expected in the fall of 1995. A consortium of cable companies is testing a new service that will allow personal computer users to connect their equipment to cable TV and gain access to the Internet and other on-line services. This service should be fully operational by 1996 and will provide online access at a much faster rate than telephone lines.

In wireless communications, competition for customers, particularly the growing personal-use customer, is fierce. However, personal-use customers are light users of wireless products. Companies such as Cantel and Bell Mobility are experiencing shrinking profit margins as this category of customer grows.

In television broadcasting, advertising revenues in 1994-95 recovered somewhat from recessionary drops in the early 1990s, but national and retail advertising remains sluggish in most markets. In 1994, the CRTC granted seven new specialty channel licences. The new channels that debuted in January 1995 are: the Women's Television Network (WTN), Bravo!, Showcase, the Discovery Channel, Life Network, New Country and RDI, a French-language news service. The new channels reflect a preference in the broadcasting industry for channels that focus on a narrow market and carry advertising targeted to particular niches rather than mass audiences. At the same time, specialty channels rely less than standard networks on the volatile advertising market, with a substantial part of their revenues being derived from cable subscription fees.

However, the number of viewers for the seven new specialty channels is much lower than projected. The CRTC licenced most of the channels on the assumption that the cable companies would ensure that 90% or more of their subscribers would adopt the channels. However, the plan for capturing a large audience failed when consumers rebelled against negative-option billing in early 1995. In July 1995, Rogers Cable reported that only 52% of its cable subscribers ordered the six new English-language channels in its Toronto and Vancouver markets. Ratings for the channels are low. Only about 69,000 viewers, aged 18-to-49, watch all six channels in an average minute between 6:00 a.m. and midnight. This figure is well below 1% of the country's 7.2-million cabled households. Fewer viewers translates into lower revenues from advertising and cable fees.

New specialty channels in Canada and the United States, the opening of Europe, and general globalization have a positive impact on independent entertainment producers like Alliance Communications and Atlantis Communications. The increased number of channels creates a rise in demand for original productions. Television broadcasting in Australia, New Zealand, South America, and China has just begun to expand, creating demand for more programming from international sources. To a lesser extent, broadcasters such as Baton Broadcasting and CanWest Global Communications Corp., which produce some of their own product and also secure rights to movies and programs for distribution, also benefit from globalization.

In the publishing industry, soaring newsprint prices are a major concern for newspapers. Prices, spurred by world-wide demand, increased 75% as of April 1995 compared to the rock-bottom prices of late 1993. The increases prompted several newspapers to shave a few centimetres off the size of their papers to save costs. Meanwhile, a recovering classified and retail advertising market is effecting the profits of most newspapers. Several publishers have responded to the competition from television as a source of news and information by offering their newspaper packages online. Also, companies such as Quebecor Inc. and G.T.C. Transcontinental have acquired CD and CD-ROM production facilities to broaden their revenue base and obtain a foothold in the computer-related market.

Generally, every segment of the media and communications industry is in flux. The unfolding of multimedia has implications for all areas of communications. However, those implications are not clearly defined, causing uncertainty in the industry.

BATON BROADCASTING INCORPORATED

Exchanges	Price (Jun29'95)	7.50	Trailing P/E	53.57	Stock Symbol
TM	Trailing Yield (%)	0.00	Trailing EPS	0.14	**BNB**

Period Ending	Aug94	Aug93	Aug92	Aug91	Aug90
Yearly Statistics					
Price-Close	6.88	6.00	7.00	6.13	7.13
Price-High	8.38	7.00	9.00	7.25	15.25
Price-Low	5.75	5.25	5.50	5.25	7.00
P/E-Close	57.29	100.00	700.00	nm	64.77
Dividends per Share	0.00	0.00	0.00	0.00	0.24
Dividend Yield (%)	0.00	0.00	0.00	0.00	3.37
Sales per Share	9.01	8.01	7.13	6.56	6.27
EPS before extra. item	0.12	0.06	0.01	(1.25)	0.11
Cash Flow per Share	0.88	0.73	0.59	0.21	0.44
Book Value per Share	4.16	4.04	3.98	3.97	5.43
O/S Common Shares	28,122	28,122	28,122	28,122	28,122
Total Revenue	253,346	225,318	200,439	184,426	175,719
Income before extra.	3,411	1,704	290	(35,062)	3,131
Cash Flow	24,748	20,492	16,592	5,879	12,332
Debt/Equity	1.46	1.46	1.22	1.32	0.57
Return on Capital (%)	7.12	6.17	6.62	(12.86)	7.10
Ret. on Com. Equity (%)	2.96	1.51	0.26	(26.53)	2.04
% Change Profit	100.2	487.6	100.8	(1,219.8)	(82.6)
% Change Revenue	12.4	12.4	8.7	5.0	0.0
% Change Assets	3.3	13.9	(2.5)	7.5	1.2

Preferred Div. Coverage	np	np	np
Total Div. Coverage	na	na	na
Interest Coverage	1.7	1.5	1.1
Current Ratio	1.7	1.8	1.7
Operating Margin	8.0	7.2	8.4
Asset Turnover	0.8	0.7	0.7
5 YEAR RATIOS (%)			
Return on Capital	2.8	4.7	7.3
Return on Com. Equity	(4.0)	(2.1)	0.6
Profit Growth	(28.3)	(38.6)	(56.3)
Revenue Growth	7.5	8.8	(2.2)
Asset Growth	4.4	1.9	6.5
BALANCE SHEET (000)			
Cash	0	0	0
Current Assets	79,633	73,367	56,687
Net Fixed Assets	94,786	88,410	74,774
Invest's & Advances	2,576	2,576	7,287
Total Assets	323,918	313,649	275,281
Short Term Debt	10,681	5,986	6,773
Current Liabilities	46,953	40,095	33,431
Long Term Debt	160,000	160,000	130,000
Total Liabilities	206,953	200,095	163,431
Total Equity	116,965	113,554	111,850
Total Liab. & Equity	323,918	313,649	275,281
CAPITAL (000)			
Total Debt	170,681	165,986	136,773
Preferred Equity	0	0	0
Common Equity	116,965	113,554	111,850

Business:

BATON BROADCASTING INC. is a communications company operating television stations serving Ontario and Saskatchewan. The Company has extensive facilities in Toronto and Ottawa for the production of television programming and is involved in the syndication of television programming in Canada and the United States.

Date	EPS	DPS	Tot Rev	Inc Bex
May 95	0.20	0.00	75,209	5,761
Feb 95	(0.20)	0.00	57,074	(5,838)
Nov 94	0.22	0.00	75,322	6,342
Aug 94	(0.08)	0.00	57,335	(2,407)
May 94	0.12	0.00	70,371	3,376
Feb 94	(0.14)	0.00	53,096	(3,862)
Nov 93	0.22	0.00	72,544	6,304
Aug 93	(0.07)	0.00	53,523	(2,034)

Synopsis:

Baton is responding to the increasingly competitive television broadcasting environment by continuing to expand its reach into both mass audiences and specific local markets. At the same time, it continues to secure the rights to Canadian and non-Canadian entertainment and sports programming, which it plans to supply to other TV outlets, notably the emerging cable specialty channels.

Baton Broadcasting's primary source of revenue is consumer advertising on its television stations. Advertising revenues are significantly affected by the level of general economic activity in Canada.

Baton's net income for the six months ended February 1995 was $504,000, or two cents per share. This represents a drop of almost $2-million from net income of $2.4-million, or eight cents per share, earned during the same period last year. During the fiscal 1995 second quarter, a reorganization and layoffs cost Baton approximately $7.8-million, significantly effecting its net income for the quarter. Excluding reorganization costs, Baton posted a $3.5-million improvement in income before income taxes during the second quarter, compared with the same period in 1994. Baton expects to save more than $7.5-million annually as a result of the reorganization.

Baton reported net income of $3.4-million for the fiscal year ended August 31, 1994, compared to $1.7-million in 1993. However, results for fiscal 1994 are not directly comparable to fiscal 1993. Fiscal 1994 results take into account full-year operations at CFPL-TV London and CKNX-TV Wingham. Both stations were acquired in March 1993.

Relative strength to TSE300 / Price / Volume (in 1000's of board lots) chart

Rank (Profit/Revenue/Assets)
494   283   278

Allan L. Beattie
Chairman

Douglas G. Bassett
President & C.E.O.

Robin A. Fillingham
Sr. V.P. Admin. & C.F.O.

Ivan Fecan
Ex. V.P. & C.O.O.

Address
9 Channel Nine Court
Scarborough
ON
M1S 4B5
(416) 299-2000

Fax: (416) 299-2220
B0001041/G/11.1

BCE MOBILE COMMUNICATIONS INC.

Exchanges	Price (Jun29'95)		45.00	Trailing P/E		78.95		Stock Symbol
TM	Trailing Yield (%)		0.00	Trailing EPS		0.57		**BCX**

Period Ending	Dec94	Dec93	Dec92	Dec91	Dec90
Yearly Statistics					
Price-Close	44.50	41.38	32.00	29.63	18.38
Price-High	45.25	43.00	33.25	30.00	34.00
Price-Low	35.00	31.50	24.25	18.00	14.75
P/E-Close	83.96	827.50	nm	nm	nm
Dividends per Share	0.00	0.00	0.00	0.00	0.00
Dividend Yield (%)	0.00	0.00	0.00	0.00	0.00
Sales per Share	9.18	7.40	6.50	5.67	5.34
EPS before extra. item	0.53	0.05	(0.06)	(0.27)	(0.34)
Cash Flow per Share	2.66	1.95	1.44	0.89	0.83
Book Value per Share	6.22	5.68	5.60	5.65	4.95
O/S Common Shares	69,281	69,248	69,153	69,106	64,994
Total Revenue	651,558	511,816	449,744	391,433	337,027
Income before extra.	36,625	3,580	(3,873)	(17,901)	(21,320)
Cash Flow	183,934	134,749	99,469	59,341	52,460
Debt/Equity	0.72	0.96	0.87	0.86	1.24
Return on Capital (%)	13.37	8.21	5.62	3.60	3.29
Ret. on Com. Equity (%)	8.89	0.92	(1.00)	(5.03)	(7.11)
% Change Profit	923.0	192.4	78.4	16.0	(207.6)
% Change Revenue	27.3	13.8	14.9	16.1	39.4
% Change Assets	3.7	4.9	1.5	1.5	30.8

Preferred Div. Coverage	np	np	np
Total Div. Coverage	na	na	na
Interest Coverage	2.9	1.8	1.0
Current Ratio	1.0	1.1	0.9
Operating Margin	16.0	12.9	10.4
Asset Turnover	0.7	0.6	0.5
5 YEAR RATIOS (%)			
Return on Capital	6.8	4.7	4.1
Return on Com. Equity	(0.7)	(3.0)	(3.0)
Profit Growth	na	12.1	na
Revenue Growth	21.9	23.8	29.4
Asset Growth	7.9	17.3	23.1
BALANCE SHEET (000)			
Cash	0	360	1,052
Current Assets	163,867	107,831	103,468
Net Fixed Assets	644,004	647,389	592,205
Invest's & Advances	26,975	19,899	38,414
Total Assets	895,137	863,135	822,515
Short Term Debt	12,968	5,432	19,951
Current Liabilities	161,659	95,417	113,907
Long Term Debt	298,932	372,026	318,517
Total Liabilities	464,210	469,706	434,969
Total Equity	430,927	393,429	387,546
Total Liab. & Equity	895,137	863,135	822,515
CAPITAL (000)			
Total Debt	311,900	377,458	338,468
Preferred Equity	0	0	0
Common Equity	430,927	393,429	387,546

Business:

BCE MOBILE COMMUNICATIONS INC. is a mobile communications holding company. It provides cellular telecommunications through Bell Mobility Cellular, paging data and air-to-ground communications through Bell Mobility Paging and Skytel Communications. BCE Inc. of Montreal owns 65% of the company's common shares.

Date	EPS	DPS	Tot Rev	Inc Bex
Mar 95	0.11	0.00	170,100	7,300
Dec 94	0.13	0.00	175,942	9,006
Sep 94	0.18	0.00	168,262	12,123
Jun 94	0.15	0.00	153,244	10,728
Mar 94	0.07	0.00	138,914	4,768
Dec 93	(0.06)	0.00	139,843	(3,857)
Sep 93	0.07	0.00	130,984	4,742
Jun 93	0.07	0.00	127,621	5,019

Synopsis:

Strong demand for mobility services had a positive impact on BCE Mobile Communications Inc.'s revenues in 1994. The company's cellular telephone subscribers increased from 421,000 in 1993 to 592,000 in 1994, a rise of 41%. Pagers in service stood at 220,000 at fiscal year end, a 22% jump from 181,000 a year earlier. In 1994, 88% of the company's operating income was derived from cellular service, 9% from paging, data and airline passenger, and 3% stemming from product sales and other sources.

BCE Mobile, which operates under the Bell Mobility banner, aims to grow its customer base by 35% each year for the next three years. The company estimates that by 1997, more than five million Quebec and Ontario residents will have the means and the need for some form of wireless communications. To meet these needs, it plans to forge alliances with value-adding innovators and re-work its business processes to lower cost, remove inefficiencies and speed up the time it takes to bring new products to market. In 1994, Bell Mobility launched Liberti, a new family of boxed cellular phone and service combinations made available through retail outlets. The product is designed for the growing number of personal-use customers.

In 1994, Bell Mobility launched several other new services including: voice-activated dialing; a 411 Direct program which allows cellular telephone users to be connected directly to the number attained from directory assistance; and a two-way Personal Communications Services (PCS) system trial, operating in the 1.9 GHz range of the spectrum. Through an alliance with Quebec-based AVEL-TECH, Inc., Bell Mobility signed a deal to launch real-time vehicle management. Cellular technology provides data transfers between a central dispatch office and vehicles so that, for example, customers can locate and remain in contact with its fleet of trucks. The company also began equipping Air Canada's regional jet fleet with air-to-ground terminals.

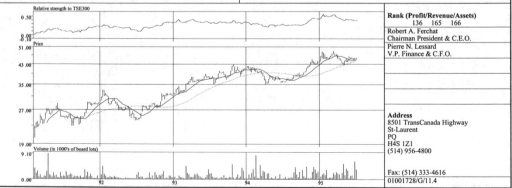

Rank (Profit/Revenue/Assets)
136   165   166

Robert A. Ferchat
Chairman President & C.E.O.

Pierre N. Lessard
V.P. Finance & C.F.O.

Address
8501 TransCanada Highway
St-Laurent
PQ
H4S 1Z1
(514) 956-4800

Fax: (514) 333-4616
01001728/G/11.4

For further company information, call Globe Information Services 1-800-268-9128 or (416) 585-5345

CALL-NET ENTERPRISES INC.

Exchanges	Price (Jun29'95)	9.25	Trailing P/E	nm	Stock Symbol
TM	Trailing Yield (%)	0.00	Trailing EPS	(2.44)	**CN**

Period Ending	Dec94	Dec93	Dec92	Dec91
Yearly Statistics				
Price-Close	5.50	11.68	7.50	n t
Price-High	13.25	12.63	8.25	n t
Price-Low	5.00	7.88	7.31	n t
P/E-Close	nm	nm	42.86	n t
Dividends per Share	0.00	0.00	0.00	0.00
Dividend Yield (%)	0.00	0.00	0.00	0.00
Sales per Share	5.16	6.94	9.66	8.98
EPS before extra. item	(1.62)	(0.16)	0.18	(0.66)
Cash Flow per Share	(0.85)	0.44	0.68	0.09
Book Value per Share	5.19	6.65	3.01	0.69
O/S Common Shares	39,388	33,535	14,342	7,921
Total Revenue	180,257	134,966	82,824	68,745
Income before extra.	(55,359)	(3,095)	1,705	(5,007)
Cash Flow	(29,029)	8,458	5,822	725
Debt/Equity	0.70	0.06	0.34	3.50
Return on Capital (%)	(17.70)	(1.09)	10.38	na
Ret. on Com. Equity (%)	(25.92)	(2.33)	6.18	na
% Change Profit	(1,688.7)	(281.5)	134.1	na
% Change Revenue	33.6	63.0	20.5	na
% Change Assets	57.0	288.2	63.2	na

Date	EPS	DPS	Tot Rev	Inc Bex
Jun 95	(0.48)	0.00	101,541	(18,887)
Mar 95	(0.53)	0.00	86,000	(20,900)
Dec 94	(0.94)	0.00	64,463	(32,557)
Sep 94	(0.49)	0.00	41,877	(16,467)
Jun 94	(0.11)	0.00	37,576	(3,529)
Mar 94	(0.08)	0.00	36,341	(2,806)
Dec 93	(0.08)	0.00	34,417	(1,668)
Sep 93	(0.05)	0.00	35,114	(956)

Preferred Div. Coverage	np	np	np	
Total Div. Coverage	na	na	8.4	
Interest Coverage	0.0	0.0	1.7	
Current Ratio	3.6	5.5	3.6	
Operating Margin	(31.5)	(2.0)	5.2	
Asset Turnover	0.4	0.5	1.3	
5 YEAR RATIOS (%)				
Return on Capital	na	na	na	
Return on Com. Equity	na	na	na	
Profit Growth	na	na	na	
Revenue Growth	na	na	na	
Asset Growth	na	na	na	
BALANCE SHEET (000)				
Cash	157,730	90,472	27,267	
Current Assets	199,237	115,131	38,558	
Net Fixed Assets	85,290	44,532	24,286	
Invest's & Advances	4,255	663	0	
Total Assets	399,973	254,774	65,630	
Short Term Debt	1,292	2,699	2,851	
Current Liabilities	54,790	21,125	10,693	
Long Term Debt	140,929	10,767	11,724	
Total Liabilities	195,719	31,892	22,417	
Total Equity	204,254	222,882	43,213	
Total Liab. & Equity	399,973	254,774	65,630	
CAPITAL (000)				
Total Debt	142,221	13,466	14,575	
Preferred Equity	0	0	0	
Common Equity	204,254	222,882	43,213	

Business:

CALL-NET ENTERPRISES INC. is involved in providing long distance and data telecommunications services to business customers in the provinces of Ontario, Quebec and British Columbia.

Synopsis:

Call-Net Enterprises Inc., the parent company of Sprint Canada, made inroads into the fiercely competitive long-distance market in 1994 through acquisitions and expansion of its services. The company's strategy is to focus on long-term gains by gradually acquiring a larger share of Canada's $8-billion long-distance voice and data sector.

In 1994, Call-Net bought Integrated Network Services Inc. (INSINC), a Vancouver-based data communications reseller and integrator. INSINC will operate as an independent division of Sprint Canada. Call-Net also obtained a 21% interest in MicroCell, developers of a new digital cordless telephone. As well, it invested in In-flight Phone Canada, a carrier licensed to provide air-to-ground communications.

Call-Net had $157.7-million in cash and $144-million of working capital for fiscal 1994. At year end, shareholder's equity amounted to $204-million and long-term debt was $139-million, resulting in a debt-to-equity ratio of 0.70:1, compared with 0.06:1 in 1993.

In 1994 and 1995, Sprint Canada began targeting big corporations and government, while continuing to focus on building its existing strength in the small- and medium-sized business market. In mid 1994, Sprint launched a residential market campaign. By year end it had won approximately 225,000 customers, due at least in part to strong advertising and marketing support.

Call-Net expects to break even in 1995 and return to profitability in 1996. It is striving to earn a 10% share of the long-distance market by 1998. Ultimately Call-Net aims to be the number one alternative to local telephone companies.

Sprint U.S., based in Kansas City, bought a 25% equity interest in Call-Net in 1993. The deal gave Call-Net exclusive Canadian rights to the trademarks, technologies and marketing expertise of Sprint U.S.

Relative strength to TSE300 / Price / Volume (in 1000's of board lots)

Rank (Profit/Revenue/Assets)
991 326 252

Juri Koor
President & C.E.O.
Gerald Throop
Vice President & C.F.O.

Address
7th Floor
105 Gordon Baker Road
Willowdale
ON
M2H 3S1
(416) 496-1644

Fax: (416) 496-0975
01003306/G/11.4

CANADIAN SATELLITE COMMUNICATIONS INC.

Exchanges	Price (Jun29'95)	7.00	Trailing P/E	10.29	Stock Symbol
TM	Trailing Yield (%)	2.86	Trailing EPS	0.68	SAT

Period Ending	Aug94	Aug93	Aug92	Aug91	Aug90
Yearly Statistics					
Price-Close	8.75	9.50	13.38	11.63	13.50
Price-High	10.50	13.50	14.50	13.75	17.00
Price-Low	8.00	9.00	10.50	11.00	12.25
P/E-Close	17.16	25.00	19.67	15.50	16.88
Dividends per Share	0.20	0.20	0.20	0.10	0.00
Dividend Yield (%)	2.29	2.11	1.50	0.86	0.00
Sales per Share	7.06	6.18	4.67	4.16	3.90
EPS before extra. item	0.51	0.38	0.68	0.75	0.80
Cash Flow per Share	1.16	1.13	1.26	1.16	1.20
Book Value per Share	3.61	3.30	3.36	2.88	2.22
O/S Common Shares	10,006	10,006	10,317	10,318	10,305
Total Revenue	70,635	62,617	48,135	42,662	40,082
Income before extra.	5,089	3,890	7,034	7,708	8,193
Cash Flow	11,590	11,416	13,036	11,910	12,330
Debt/Equity	0.07	nd	0.01	0.02	0.37
Return on Capital (%)	30.56	26.05	25.58	26.28	30.05
Ret. on Com. Equity (%)	14.72	11.50	21.87	29.32	43.79
% Change Profit	30.8	(44.7)	(8.7)	(5.9)	105.8
% Change Revenue	12.8	30.1	12.8	6.4	10.0
% Change Assets	(6.3)	16.0	24.3	3.4	(7.2)

Preferred Div. Coverage	np	np	np
Total Div. Coverage	2.6	1.9	3.4
Interest Coverage	31.4	129.9	na
Current Ratio	1.5	1.3	2.4
Operating Margin	17.9	17.3	17.5
Asset Turnover	1.5	1.2	1.1
5 YEAR RATIOS (%)			
Return on Capital	27.7	26.6	25.2
Return on Com. Equity	24.2	28.1	30.6
Profit Growth	5.1	17.5	37.7
Revenue Growth	14.1	15.4	14.3
Asset Growth	5.3	7.8	4.8
BALANCE SHEET (000)			
Cash	0	862	5,493
Current Assets	17,151	22,701	18,235
Net Fixed Assets	27,703	23,319	21,111
Invest's & Advances	1,030	2,755	3,480
Total Assets	47,579	50,756	43,742
Short Term Debt	2,344	0	175
Current Liabilities	11,465	17,017	7,752
Long Term Debt	0	0	0
Total Liabilities	11,465	17,742	9,090
Total Equity	36,114	33,014	34,652
Total Liab. & Equity	47,579	50,756	43,742
CAPITAL (000)			
Total Debt	2,344	0	175
Preferred Equity	0	0	0
Common Equity	36,114	33,014	34,652

Business:

CANADIAN SATELLITE COMMUNICATIONS INC. (Cancom) provides radio and television signals to Canadian households, through cable companies and direct to home services, via satellite. Cancom's Business Division and Television Unit offer digital networks for data and voice through VSAT technology and end-to-end BTV services. The Mobile unit provides two-way data messaging and tracking for the transportaiton industry.

Date	EPS	DPS	Tot Rev	Inc Bex
May 95	0.19	0.00	20,403	1,923
Feb 95	0.17	0.10	19,074	1,720
Nov 94	0.18	0.00	18,923	1,757
Aug 94	0.14	0.10	18,487	1,402
May 94	0.02	0.00	17,739	198
Feb 94	0.20	0.10	16,997	1,968
Nov 93	0.15	0.00	17,412	1,521
Aug 93	0.18	0.10	17,323	1,902

Synopsis:

Canadian Satellite Communications (Cancom) operates two divisions. The broadcast division uses satellites to deliver mainstream television and radio signals to cable systems and users of home receiving dishes. The business division creates satellite networks for a variety of business uses.

The broadcast division's cable services is Cancom's principal source of income. In fiscal 1994 the cable services unit distributed TV and radio signals to 2,422 affiliated cable systems. Channel subscribers (number of households multiplied by the number of signals per household) reached a level of nine million, an increase of 223,000 over 1993. More than 2.9 million households now receive one or more satellite signals from Cancom.

Cancom's Direct-to-Home (DTH) is Canada's largest provider of satellite-to-home television signals, serving primarily households beyond the reach of cable systems. Cancom DTH will move to digital video compression technology in 1995, opening the way for more signals. Cancom has joined Astral, BCE, Labatt Communications Inc., Tee-Comm and Western International Communications in a direct-to-home consortium that will eventually offer more than 100 network and specialty channels, pay TV, pay-per-view and information services to individual dish owners.

Cancom now delivers about a dozen signals to cable companies, mostly in remote or small communities. Its strategy for the coming few years will be to increase the number of signals it carries to 22.

Within the first half of fiscal 1995, Cancom's business division achieved a 49% increase in revenues over the same period in 1994. Cancom Mobile, a two-way tracking service used by the trucking industry, was the major growth contributor. Using all Canadian satellites, the service allows constant communications between dispatcher and driver anywhere in North America.

Relative strength to TSE300

Price

Volume (in 1000's of board lots)

Rank (Profit/Revenue/Assets)
421 479 649

Douglas M. Holtby
Chairman Of The Board

Alain Gourd
President & C.E.O.

Colley Clarke
V.P. Fin. Adm. & Hum. Res.

Address
50 Burnhamthorpe Road West
10th Floor
Mississauga
ON
L5B 3C2
(905) 272-4960

Fax: (905) 272-3399
C0039192/G/11.4

For further company information, call Globe Information Services 1-800-268-9128 or (416) 585-5345

CANWEST GLOBAL COMMUNICATIONS CORP.

Exchanges	Price (Jun29'95)	22 .00	Trailing P/E	13 .09	Stock Symbol
T	Trailing Yield (%)	0 .81	Trailing EPS	1 .68	**CWW**

Period Ending	Aug94	Aug93	Aug92	Aug91	Aug90
Yearly Statistics					
Price-Close	31 .00	20 .88	13 .00	n t	n t
Price-High	36 .00	22 .00	14 .75	n t	n t
Price-Low	19 .38	12 .75	10 .75	n t	n t
P/E-Close	13 .25	14 .40	15 .12	n t	n t
Dividends per Share	0 .30	0 .20	0 .10	0 .30	2 .61
Dividend Yield (%)	0 .97	0 .96	0 .77	na	na
Sales per Share	14 .20	15 .03	13 .57	17 .12	14 .91
EPS before extra. item	2 .34	1 .45	0 .86	0 .69	0 .39
Cash Flow per Share	2 .13	1 .77	1 .88	1 .84	0 .81
Book Value per Share	9 .41	5 .90	4 .42	0 .48	0 .53
O/S Common Shares	20 ,463	18 ,055	17 ,896	13 ,160	13 ,160
Total Revenue	273 ,396	270 ,236	235 ,162	225 ,872	196 ,181
Income before extra.	44 ,716	25 ,956	14 ,860	9 ,023	6 ,024
Cash Flow	40 ,986	31 ,814	32 ,513	24 ,173	10 ,633
Debt/Equity	1 .17	2 .15	2 .22	40 .20	39 .66
Return on Capital (%)	21 .94	22 .75	20 .28	18 .05	16 .28
Ret. on Com. Equity (%)	29 .92	27 .98	34 .80	136 .26	23 .77
% Change Profit	72 .3	74 .7	64 .7	49 .8	(21 .2)
% Change Revenue	1 .2	14 .9	4 .1	15 .1	41 .8
% Change Assets	20 .2	21 .7	3 .7	1 .9	68 .6

Preferred Div. Coverage	np	np	np
Total Div. Coverage	6 .7	7 .2	8 .3
Interest Coverage	4 .7	3 .1	2 .7
Current Ratio	1 .1	1 .1	1 .0
Operating Margin	21 .8	22 .0	25 .1
Asset Turnover	0 .4	0 .5	0 .6
5 YEAR RATIOS (%)			
Return on Capital	19 .9	na	na
Return on Com. Equity	50 .5	na	na
Profit Growth	42 .3	na	na
Revenue Growth	14 .5	na	na
Asset Growth	21 .0	na	na
BALANCE SHEET (000)			
Cash	11 ,206	1 ,431	809
Current Assets	210 ,392	170 ,285	145 ,970
Net Fixed Assets	58 ,414	52 ,419	39 ,853
Invest's & Advances	85 ,103	54 ,532	32 ,681
Total Assets	625 ,496	520 ,317	427 ,524
Short Term Debt	31 ,358	10 ,450	7 ,268
Current Liabilities	195 ,815	160 ,058	146 ,005
Long Term Debt	192 ,887	218 ,067	167 ,907
Total Liabilities	433 ,005	413 ,878	348 ,431
Total Equity	192 ,491	106 ,439	79 ,093
Total Liab. & Equity	625 ,496	520 ,317	427 ,524
CAPITAL (000)			
Total Debt	224 ,245	228 ,517	175 ,175
Preferred Equity	0	0	0
Common Equity	192 ,491	106 ,439	79 ,093

Business:

CANWEST GLOBAL COMMUNICATIONS CORP. through its principal broadcasting subsidiaries is licensed to provide over-the-air English language television broadcasting services using independent television stations with signals originating across Canada. Canwest, through its subsidiary CanWest International, owns 20% of New Zealand's TV3 network and 15% of Australia's Channel Ten television.

Date	EPS	DPS	Tot Rev	Inc Bex
May 95	0 .33	0 .10	93 ,118	13 ,284
Feb 95	0 .37	0 .00	84 ,044	14 ,989
Nov 94	0 .72	0 .08	94 ,243	29 ,355
Aug 94	0 .26	0 .00	75 ,674	10 ,879
May 94	0 .28	0 .08	66 ,712	10 ,974
Feb 94	0 .15	0 .08	67 ,580	5 ,496
Nov 93	0 .48	0 .00	78 ,722	17 ,367
Aug 93	0 .15	0 .05	72 ,146	5 ,224

Synopsis:

With a successful fiscal 1994 and a promising six-month period ended February 1995, CanWest Global Communications Corp. continued its aim of expanding current operations and acquiring new business both in Canada and internationally.

CanWest Global made four major acquisitions in 1994-95. It bought MITV, a regional New Brunswick and Nova Scotia television network, for $24.6-million. It also bought 25% of the newly licensed radio network Talk Radio for $3.4-million. This was CanWest Global's first entry into the United Kingdom market. CanWest Global also bought 50% of the La Red television network in Chile, and a 20% stake in Television and Media Services Ltd., Australia's largest independent supplier of television production services. In June 1995, CanWest Global submitted a $79.5-million bid to obtain the licence for Britain's Channel 5, a new national television network.

In 1994, the CRTC refused CanWest Global's application for licences to start a new regional network in Alberta and three new national specialty channels. However, the company plans to continue efforts to broaden its markets in Alberta and in English-speaking Montreal.

Revenue from Canadian operations totalled $155-million, an 18% jump for the six months ended February 1995. The increase was aided by the prolonged baseball and hockey strikes, which negatively affected competitors. As well, increased automobile and telecommunications advertising campaigns, and a highly rated program schedule contributed to revenue.

In 1994, revenues (operating profit) for CanWest Global's consolidated operations by segment were: Canada, 90% (93%); New Zealand, 10% (4%); and corporate, 0% (3%). The operations of Network 10 in Australia, of which CanWest Global owns a 57.5% interest, are not consolidated. Network 10 produced $340.6-million in revenue and $87-million in profit.

Rank (Profit/Revenue/Assets)
121   270   206

I.H. Asper
Chairman & C.E.O.

Thomas C. Strike
Ex. V.P. Bus. Devel. & C.F.O.

Address
31st Floor
TD Centre
201 Portage Avenue
Winnipeg
MB
R3B 3L7
(204) 956-2025
Fax: (204) 947-9841
01003215/G/11.1

CFCF INC.

Exchanges	Price (Jun29'95)	10.87	Trailing P/E	77.64	Stock Symbol
TM	Trailing Yield (%)	1.84	Trailing EPS	0.14	CF

Period Ending	Aug94	Aug93	Aug92	Aug91	Aug90
Yearly Statistics					
Price-Close	13.00	13.63	8.75	6.50	9.50
Price-High	19.50	14.63	10.50	11.00	18.13
Price-Low	12.75	7.13	7.63	6.25	8.13
P/E-Close	22.41	13.10	35.00	nm	nm
Dividends per Share	0.18	0.08	0.00	0.00	0.15
Dividend Yield (%)	1.35	0.55	0.00	0.00	1.58
Sales per Share	12.73	14.04	13.97	14.63	14.73
EPS before extra. item	0.58	1.04	0.25	(2.13)	(1.54)
Cash Flow per Share	2.62	2.65	2.11	(1.02)	(0.31)
Book Value per Share	7.37	6.83	4.58	4.30	6.36
O/S Common Shares	13,898	13,629	11,040	11,040	11,040
Total Revenue	175,642	161,338	154,252	161,521	162,572
Income before extra.	8,019	12,014	2,802	(23,566)	(16,987)
Cash Flow	36,171	30,396	23,327	(11,212)	(3,454)
Debt/Equity	1.57	1.00	2.31	2.84	1.75
Return on Capital (%)	11.97	12.73	10.95	(6.54)	(3.60)
Ret. on Com. Equity (%)	8.20	16.72	5.72	(40.06)	(21.23)
% Change Profit	(33.3)	328.8	111.9	(38.7)	(635.4)
% Change Revenue	8.9	4.6	(4.5)	(0.6)	29.9
% Change Assets	33.8	8.3	(4.4)	(12.6)	10.4
Preferred Div. Coverage	np	np	np		
Total Div. Coverage	3.3	13.4	na		
Interest Coverage	2.1	2.0	1.3		
Current Ratio	1.0	1.0	0.9		
Operating Margin	17.5	15.6	14.2		
Asset Turnover	0.5	0.6	0.6		
5 YEAR RATIOS (%)					
Return on Capital	5.1	4.3	5.2		
Return on Com. Equity	(6.1)	(7.0)	(7.0)		
Profit Growth	20.4	(1.8)	(22.3)		
Revenue Growth	6.9	9.1	10.8		
Asset Growth	5.9	2.8	4.8		
BALANCE SHEET (000)					
Cash	8,806	2,490	0		
Current Assets	72,085	63,692	58,071		
Net Fixed Assets	104,736	84,411	86,386		
Invest's & Advances	25,717	20,058	931		
Total Assets	352,352	263,427	243,275		
Short Term Debt	189	118	803		
Current Liabilities	69,891	64,104	62,597		
Long Term Debt	160,176	93,034	116,152		
Total Liabilities	249,963	170,289	192,741		
Total Equity	102,389	93,138	50,534		
Total Liab. & Equity	352,352	263,427	243,275		
CAPITAL (000)					
Total Debt	160,365	93,152	116,955		
Preferred Equity	0	0	0		
Common Equity	102,389	93,138	50,534		

Business:

CFCF INC. is a diversified communications company active in television broadcasting, cable television and production. Broadcasting includes two TV divisions, CFCF 12 and Television Quatre Saisons, and two production units, Champlain Productions and R.S.Video Consultants Ltd. Cable includes CF Cable TV, Laurentien Cable TV, Maniwaki Television, Northern Cable Holding, and Sudbury Cable System.

Date	EPS	DPS	Tot Rev	Inc Bex
May 95	0.15	0.05	68,869	2,157
Feb 95	(0.20)	0.05	56,321	(2,830)
Nov 94	0.29	0.05	63,318	4,073
Aug 94	(0.10)	0.05	37,099	(1,353)
May 94	0.32	0.05	49,526	4,377
Feb 94	(0.03)	0.05	43,085	(287)
Nov 93	0.39	0.03	49,362	5,282
Aug 93	(0.15)	0.03	33,305	(1,179)

Synopsis:

In 1994, CFCF Inc. restructured to officially create two distinct operations: broadcast and cable. The Broadcast Group includes Montreal's CFCF-12 CTV affiliate, the Television Quatre Saisons (TQS), and two production facilities, Champlain Productions Inc., and R.S. Video Consultants. With an emphasis on synergy, the broadcast group is focused on improving performance at its existing companies and actively seeking new business opportunities.

The Cable Group, representing about two-thirds of earnings, consists of CF Cable Inc., Laurentien Cable TV, acquired in September 1993, and Northern Cable, acquired in September 1994. The goal of the cable arm is to apply new technologies such as direct broadcast satellites and strong customer service to build its base of subscribers, now at 420,000.

In 1994, broadcast group operating income fell 11%, with CFCF-12's poor showing cancelling out the 6% increase in revenues at TQS. On the other hand, in the first and second quarter of 1995, revenues climbed at CFCF-12 while falling at TQS, due in large part to the hockey strike.

Financial objectives for 1995 call for an increase in operating income from $49.1-million to $59.7-million. This was due to higher interest expense and amortization resulting from the acquisition of Northern Cable and a one-time increase in cable operation expenses relating to the introduction of an extended basic tier in the CF Cable division and Laurentien Cable. Net income for fiscal 1995 should drop $8-million to $4.1-million, or 58 cents per share to 29 cents per share in 1995.

Long-term debt surged in 1994 to $160-million from $93-million in 1993. This was due in part to the Laurentien acquisition, as well as a $20-million investment in convertible debentures in Regional Cablesystems. In May 1994, CFCF issued $50-million of convertible subordinate debentures to strengthen its financial base.

Rank (Profit/Revenue/Assets)
335   330   268

J.A. Pouliot
Chairman Of The Board

A.D. Pouliot
President & C.E.O.

Address
405 Ogilvy Avenue
Montreal
PQ
H3N 1M4
(514) 273-6311

Fax: (514) 276-9399
C0000044/G/11.1

For further company information, call Globe Information Services 1-800-268-9128 or (416) 585-5345

CHUM LIMITED

Exchanges	Price (Jun29'95)	16.50	Trailing P/E	23.24	Stock Symbol
T	Trailing Yield (%)	1.78	Trailing EPS	0.71	**CHM.B**

Period Ending	Aug94	Aug93	Aug92	Aug91	Aug90
Yearly Statistics					
Price-Close	17.75	19.63	25.13	21.38	19.00
Price-High	22.50	25.50	26.25	27.50	26.75
Price-Low	17.50	18.50	20.50	17.00	16.88
P/E-Close	26.89	16.92	17.95	17.81	13.87
Dividends per Share	0.17	0.17	0.08	0.17	0.17
Dividend Yield (%)	0.96	0.87	0.32	0.80	0.90
Sales per Share	15.60	15.80	15.57	14.63	14.10
EPS before extra. item	0.66	1.16	1.40	1.20	1.37
Cash Flow per Share	1.32	1.78	2.03	1.80	1.97
Book Value per Share	14.19	13.76	12.77	11.60	10.57
O/S Common Shares	12,711	12,815	12,815	12,878	12,878
Total Revenue	202,585	205,427	203,047	192,150	183,564
Income before extra.	8,448	14,863	18,013	15,504	17,683
Cash Flow	16,882	22,840	26,089	23,222	25,412
Debt/Equity	nd	nd	nd	0.00	0.00
Return on Capital (%)	9.15	16.34	21.18	20.70	25.20
Ret. on Com. Equity (%)	4.74	8.74	11.51	10.86	13.69
% Change Profit	(43.2)	(17.5)	16.2	(12.3)	5.7
% Change Revenue	(1.4)	1.2	5.7	4.7	7.3
% Change Assets	2.7	6.4	10.4	8.9	10.7

Preferred Div. Coverage	np	np	np	
Total Div. Coverage	3.9	6.8	8.2	
Interest Coverage	nd	nd	352.7	
Current Ratio	5.3	5.5	4.7	
Operating Margin	7.1	12.8	15.8	
Asset Turnover	1.0	1.0	1.1	
5 YEAR RATIOS (%)				
Return on Capital	18.5	22.0	24.4	
Return on Com. Equity	9.9	11.9	12.7	
Profit Growth	(12.8)	1.8	13.0	
Revenue Growth	3.4	5.0	7.0	
Asset Growth	7.7	8.3	9.4	
BALANCE SHEET (000)				
Cash	37,240	42,031	38,116	
Current Assets	92,535	91,410	82,217	
Net Fixed Assets	59,743	55,762	53,851	
Invest's & Advances	3,054	3,004	1,351	
Total Assets	199,591	194,360	182,674	
Short Term Debt	0	0	0	
Current Liabilities	17,599	16,572	17,559	
Long Term Debt	0	0	0	
Total Liabilities	19,252	18,052	19,050	
Total Equity	180,339	176,308	163,624	
Total Liab. & Equity	199,591	194,360	182,674	
CAPITAL (000)				
Total Debt	0	0	0	
Preferred Equity	0	0	0	
Common Equity	180,339	176,308	163,624	

Business:

CHUM LTD. is involved in broadcasting through ownership and operation of radio stations, television stations, the MuchMusic Network across Canada and via satellite to the U.S., the Atlantic Satellite Network throughout Atlantic Canada, and BRAVO! a specialty television service from Canada and abroad. The Company is also engaged in environmental background music and owns a 50% interest in MusiquePlus Inc.

Date	EPS	DPS	Tot Rev	Inc Bex
Feb 95	0.02	0.01	47,925	189
Nov 94	0.32	0.11	60,244	4,074
Aug 94	0.24	0.15	49,042	3,059
May 94	0.13	0.02	51,490	1,683
Feb 94	0.00	0.02	43,425	(58)
Nov 93	0.29	0.04	58,628	3,764
Aug 93	0.51	0.11	51,567	6,538
May 93	0.23	0.02	53,963	2,874

Synopsis:

Results for the six-month period ended February 1995 saw a 5.7% increase in revenue over the same period in 1994 at CHUM Limited. Revenue was $106-million compared with $101-million in 1993. Net earnings were up 15%, at $4.2-million compared with $3.7-million. These results came after a disappointing fiscal 1994, which CHUM attributes to an increasingly competitive broadcasting environment and a stagnant advertising market. Revenue dipped from $202-million in 1993 to $199-million at the fiscal year ended August 1994. Company revenue was strengthened in the early part of 1995 by advertising revenue from Bravo!, CHUM's new cable channel which began broadcasting in January 1995.

CHUM's CKVR television station in Barrie, Ontario, will cut its ties as a CBC affiliate in September 1995, and become a fully independent station. CKVR has signed a contract to air 41 Raptors games, when the National Basketball Association expansion team begins play in the fall. CKVR reaches southern and central Ontario markets. CHUM's Toronto-based CITY-TV will air 25 Raptors games.

CHUM made its first overseas investment in November 1994, acquiring a 26% interest in Canal Joven SA, an Argentine television station.

In 1994, as part of the Canadian Radio-Television and Telecommunications Commission's call for new cable channels, CHUM's CITY-TV/MuchMusic division submitted seven applications with only one (Bravo!) getting a license. CHUM has reassessed its unsuccessful applications and will reapply for specialty channel licenses during the CRTC's second licensing phase in June 1995.

CHUM Limited has paid dividends every year since becoming a public company in 1967. Total dividends paid in 1994 were to $2.2-million, or 17 cents per Class B and common share.

Rank (Profit/Revenue/Assets)
324   314   356

Allan Waters
President

Fred Sherratt
Exec. V.P. & C.O.O.

Address
1331 Yonge Street
Toronto
ON
M4T 1Y1
(416) 925-6666

Fax: (416) 926-4026
C0007071/G/11.1

COGECO CABLE INC.

Exchanges	Price (Jun29'95)	8.87	Trailing P/E	11.52	Stock Symbol
TM	Trailing Yield (%)	1.13	Trailing EPS	0.77	CCA

Period Ending	Aug94	Aug93	Aug92	Aug91
Yearly Statistics				
Price-Close	10.50	10.75	n t	n t
Price-High	13.13	11.50	n t	n t
Price-Low	10.13	10.00	n t	n t
P/E-Close	12.81	24.43	n t	n t
Dividends per Share	0.75	0.00	0.00	na
Dividend Yield (%)	7.14	0.00	0.00	na
Sales per Share	5.88	7.14	6.99	(94,852.85)
EPS before extra. item	0.82	0.44	0.11	na
Cash Flow per Share	1.63	1.40	0.96	(7,349.35)
Book Value per Share	7.78	7.73	(1.05)	na
O/S Common Shares	21,268	21,366	15,691	(1)
Total Revenue	125,468	118,823	110,660	94,592
Income before extra.	17,494	7,279	1,803	(1,865)
Cash Flow	34,706	23,220	15,074	7,342
Debt/Equity	1.00	0.99	2.44	3.02
Return on Capital (%)	12.03	11.41	9.18	na
Ret. on Com. Equity (%)	10.58	9.80	na	na
% Change Profit	140.3	303.7	196.7	na
% Change Revenue	5.6	7.4	17.0	na
% Change Assets	3.1	1.7	6.1	na

Preferred Div. Coverage	np	np	na
Total Div. Coverage	1.1	na	1.5
Interest Coverage	2.5	1.6	1.1
Current Ratio	0.3	0.6	0.4
Operating Margin	32.2	31.8	26.3
Asset Turnover	0.3	0.3	0.3
5 YEAR RATIOS (%)			
Return on Capital	na	na	na
Return on Com. Equity	na	na	na
Profit Growth	na	na	na
Revenue Growth	na	na	na
Asset Growth	na	na	na
BALANCE SHEET (000)			
Cash	2,828	6,751	3,799
Current Assets	8,471	11,631	9,226
Net Fixed Assets	112,007	94,327	91,544
Invest's & Advances	115	148	148
Total Assets	378,479	367,041	360,765
Short Term Debt	0	0	0
Current Liabilities	26,024	20,618	21,149
Long Term Debt	164,912	164,057	234,979
Total Liabilities	212,982	201,892	264,364
Total Equity	165,497	165,149	96,401
Total Liab. & Equity	378,479	367,041	360,765
CAPITAL (000)			
Total Debt	164,912	164,057	234,979
Preferred Equity	0	0	112,928
Common Equity	165,497	165,149	(16,527)

Business:

COGECO CABLE INC. is a cable television company. The Company's cable systems serve subscribers in five provinces.

Date	EPS	DPS	Tot Rev	Inc Bex
Feb 95	0.17	0.03	33,338	3,677
Nov 94	0.18	0.03	32,623	3,857
Aug 94	0.15	0.03	31,649	3,168
May 94	0.27	0.03	31,573	5,751
Feb 94	0.25	0.03	31,334	5,432
Nov 93	0.15	0.03	30,912	3,143
Aug 93	0.13	0.00	30,266	2,439
May 93	0.12	0.00	29,904	1,931

Synopsis:

Cogeco Cable completed its first full fiscal year as a public company in fiscal 1994. With 460,000 subscribers, Cogeco Cable's net income more than doubled compared to 1993. Cash flow from operations went from $23-million in 1993 to $34.7-million in fiscal 1994, a jump of 49.5%. The increases are attributed to continuing basic cable growth in both the Quebec division and the Cablenet Division in Ontario, Saskatchewan, Alberta and British Columbia. Cogeco also saw its discretionary services, such as pay-per-view, grow in 1994.

With the CRTC's recent decision that telephone companies can enter the entertainment business, cable companies are preparing for increased competition. Phone companies may be able to deliver movies into homes using phone lines in two to five years. Cogeco also anticipates competition from direct broadcast satellite services. In response, the company is upgrading its cable system using fibre optics to provide better reception and service, and to lay a strong foundation to support multimedia and interactive services. Cogeco continues to expand its customer base through acquisitions such as Cable Laurentides of Ste-Agathe and Telediffusion Sainte-Adele Inc. Cogeco bought both Quebec companies in 1994. It also applied to the CRTC in 1995 to offer a video game service to subscribers.

In 1995, Cogeco launched an "information highway" test project in Quebec, whereby 600 volunteers have their personal computers connected to the cable network. This enables subscribers to access video programs and a range of interactive and multimedia services.

In August 1995, Cogeco issued a special dividend of 65 cents per share to shareholders. The dividend is the result of the company's substantial growth.

Relative strength to TSE300

Price

Volume (in 1000's of board lots)

Rank (Profit/Revenue/Assets)
228 385 258

Henri Audet
Chairman

Louis Audet
President & C.E.O.

Michel J. Carter
V.P. Finance

Address
Suite 3636
1 Place Ville-Marie
Montreal
PQ
H3B 3P2
(514) 874-2600

Fax: (514) 874-2625
01003400/G/11.2

For further company information, call Globe Information Services 1-800-268-9128 or (416) 585-5345

COGECO INC.

Exchanges	Price (Jun29'95)	6.62	Trailing P/E	11.83	Stock Symbol
TM	Trailing Yield (%)	1.58	Trailing EPS	0.56	CGO

Period Ending	Aug94	Aug93	Aug92	Aug91	Aug90	Business:
Yearly Statistics						COGECO INC. is a diversified communications
Price-Close	9.38	9.38	5.75	4.10	2.85	company. Operating through subsidiaries, the
Price-High	13.50	9.50	5.75	4.34	8.38	company is involved in: cable television,
Price-Low	9.38	5.38	3.40	2.09	2.69	television, radio and weekly newspaper
P/E-Close	15.37	5.33	143.75	nm	8.38	publishing.
Dividends per Share	0.10	0.08	0.08	0.08	0.11	
Dividend Yield (%)	1.07	0.85	1.39	1.95	3.86	
Sales per Share	11.46	16.28	19.54	18.09	12.66	
EPS before extra. item	0.61	1.76	0.04	(0.14)	0.34	
Cash Flow per Share	2.15	2.51	2.25	1.79	1.39	
Book Value per Share	9.56	9.18	6.20	6.24	6.41	
O/S Common Shares	17,767	14,329	9,083	9,092	9,161	

Total Revenue	194,612	208,500	177,956	164,731	116,296	Date	EPS	DPS	Tot Rev	Inc Bex
Income before extra.	10,712	22,323	2,114	500	4,816	Feb 95	0.08	0.03	48,816	1,362
Cash Flow	36,349	29,380	20,482	16,338	12,732	Nov 94	0.17	0.03	51,636	3,053
Debt/Equity	1.23	1.50	2.01	2.05	1.99	Aug 94	0.01	0.03	45,479	215
Return on Capital (%)	9.84	14.27	8.78	8.01	6.31	May 94	0.30	0.03	51,973	5,048
Ret. on Com. Equity (%)	6.83	21.91	0.81	(2.25)	6.19	Feb 94	0.17	0.03	46,006	2,697
% Change Profit	(52.0)	956.0	322.8	(89.6)	24.7	Nov 93	0.16	0.03	51,103	2,752
% Change Revenue	(6.7)	17.2	8.0	41.6	13.8	Aug 93	1.38	0.02	61,513	16,813
% Change Assets	2.5	(0.5)	(0.9)	3.2	139.1	May 93	0.25	0.02	51,295	3,142

Preferred Div. Coverage	np	12.8	1.3	**Synopsis:**
Total Div. Coverage	5.0	8.3	0.9	Cogeco Inc. is a diversified communications company. It serves 460,000 cable
Interest Coverage	1.8	2.0	1.1	television subscribers across the country through its Cogeco Cable division,
Current Ratio	0.6	0.9	1.0	making it the fourth largest cable company in the country. Cogeco also operates
Operating Margin	22.3	22.2	21.7	four television stations and five radio stations in Quebec, and publishes 33 weekly
Asset Turnover	0.4	0.4	0.4	newspapers in Ontario and Quebec. Cogeco's strong financial performance in
5 YEAR RATIOS (%)				fiscal 1994 was due to its cable sector. Cogeco Cable's 1994 net income more
Return on Capital	9.4	10.0	9.8	than doubled over 1993. Cash flow from operations jumped from $23-million in
Return on Com. Equity	6.7	6.6	4.6	1993 to $34.7-million in fiscal 1994, an increase of 49.5%. The increases were
Profit Growth	22.7	38.8	(8.5)	due to continuing basic cable growth in both its Quebec division and its Cablenet
Revenue Growth	13.7	33.5	44.3	Division in Ontario, Saskatchewan, Alberta, and British Columbia. Cogeco also
Asset Growth	20.0	30.3	53.3	saw growth in 1994 in its discretionary services, such as pay-per-view.
BALANCE SHEET (000)				
Cash	0	864	2,717	Cogeco's cable division anticipates increased competition with the arrival of
Current Assets	19,383	19,600	20,475	direct broadcast satellite services and phone companies' involvement in the
Net Fixed Assets	122,135	105,271	103,299	cable-television business. Both are expected within the next few years. In
Invest's & Advances	3,636	4,130	4,238	response, Cogeco is upgrading its cable system using fibre optics to provide better
Total Assets	476,639	465,029	467,235	service and to lay a strong foundation to support multimedia and interactive
Short Term Debt	1,232	0	0	services. Cogeco is continuing to expand its customer base through acquisitions
Current Liabilities	32,479	22,593	20,358	such as Cable Laurentides of Ste-Agathe and Telediffusion Sainte-Adele Inc.
Long Term Debt	207,674	227,481	288,981	Cogeco bought the Quebec companies in 1994.
Total Liabilities	306,835	313,298	323,567	
Total Equity	169,804	151,731	143,668	Both Cogeco's radio stations and its publishing arm saw declines in revenue in
Total Liab. & Equity	476,639	465,029	467,235	1994 and the first quarter of 1995. Television showed some revenue growth, but
CAPITAL (000)				its profit margin declined. Cogeco is responding to the tight advertising market by
Total Debt	208,906	227,481	288,981	implementing strict cost controls. It has begun computerizing its pre-press
Preferred Equity	0	20,234	87,369	activities in the newspaper division, which should generate significant cost
Common Equity	169,804	131,497	56,299	savings.

In 1994, approximately 35% of revenues and 7% of operating income came from Cogeco's media sector. The cable division was responsible for 65% of the revenues and approximately 93% of operating income.

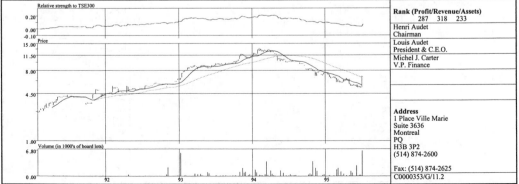

Rank (Profit/Revenue/Assets)
287   318   233

Henri Audet
Chairman

Louis Audet
President & C.E.O.

Michel J. Carter
V.P. Finance

Address
1 Place Ville Marie
Suite 3636
Montreal
PQ
H3B 3P2
(514) 874-2600

Fax: (514) 874-2625
C0000353/G/11.2

FUNDY CABLE LTD.

Exchanges	Price (Jun29'95)	6.37	Trailing P/E	nm	Stock Symbol
T	Trailing Yield (%)	0.00	Trailing EPS	(0.23)	**FDY**

Period Ending	Aug94	Aug93	Sep92
Yearly Statistics			
Price-Close	9.25	n t	n t
Price-High	12.00	n t	n t
Price-Low	8.63	n t	n t
P/E-Close	nm	n t	n t
Dividends per Share	0.00	0.00	0.10
Dividend Yield (%)	0.00	0.00	n t
Sales per Share	11.01	11.84	11.17
EPS before extra. item	(0.13)	(0.30)	(0.06)
Cash Flow per Share	1.93	1.93	1.37
Book Value per Share	3.01	(2.57)	(2.27)
O/S Common Shares	5,224	2,929	2,929
Total Revenue	44,380	35,455	32,709
Income before extra.	(223)	(539)	(99)
Cash Flow	7,589	5,658	4,012
Debt/Equity	4.86	na	na
Return on Capital (%)	9.89	9.19	na
Ret. on Com. Equity (%)	(12.77)	na	na
% Change Profit	58.6	(444.4)	na
% Change Revenue	25.2	8.4	na
% Change Assets	88.0	2.2	na
Preferred Div. Coverage	0.0	0.0	0.0
Total Div. Coverage	0.0	0.0	0.0
Interest Coverage	1.1	0.9	1.0
Current Ratio	0.3	0.4	0.7
Operating Margin	18.9	16.8	15.1
Asset Turnover	0.4	0.6	0.6
5 YEAR RATIOS (%)			
Return on Capital	na	na	na
Return on Com. Equity	na	na	na
Profit Growth	na	na	na
Revenue Growth	na	na	na
Asset Growth	na	na	na
BALANCE SHEET (000)			
Cash	0	0	0
Current Assets	3,762	3,402	3,423
Net Fixed Assets	31,392	23,197	22,529
Invest's & Advances	10,167	9,513	9,916
Total Assets	100,920	53,685	52,550
Short Term Debt	6,260	4,422	297
Current Liabilities	14,616	9,674	4,975
Long Term Debt	70,069	49,613	51,762
Total Liabilities	85,202	60,416	58,041
Total Equity	15,718	(6,731)	(5,491)
Total Liab. & Equity	100,920	53,685	52,550
CAPITAL (000)			
Total Debt	76,329	54,035	52,059
Preferred Equity	4	794	1,152
Common Equity	15,714	(7,525)	(6,643)

Business:

FUNDY CABLE LTD. is involved in the provision of cable television services including basic cable, extended basic and community programming.

Date	EPS	DPS	Tot Rev	Inc Bex
Feb 95	(0.06)	0.00	12,577	(240)
Nov 94	(0.08)	0.00	12,726	(360)
Aug 94	(0.08)	0.00	12,387	(283)
May 94	(0.04)	0.00	12,124	(128)
Feb 94	(0.01)	0.00	10,378	57
Nov 93	0.02	0.00	9,184	131
Aug 93	(0.18)	0.00	9,190	(454)
May 93	0.08	0.00	9,144	321

Synopsis:

Fundy Cable is Atlantic Canada's largest cable television operator, now reaching about 98% of the province's cable market. Fundy owns two radio stations in Saint John, New Brunswick, and two in Sydney, Nova Scotia. It also owns a 23% equity interest in LCL Cable Communications Limited (LCL) in Leicester, England.

Fundy invests in industry research and development through its NCA Microelectronics sector. In recent years, NCA developed a new scrambling system, called the "Chameleon", in response to lost revenues occurring where pay-TV reception was available illegally. In 1994, Fundy began marketing the scrambler world-wide. The scrambler sells in Canada, the United States, Brazil and South Korea.

In January 1994, Fundy completed the $32-million purchase of the outstanding shares of Cable Services Ltd. (CSL). CSL serves approximately 36,000 customers in the Moncton region. Fundy also committed $50-million to the purchase of Cable 2000 Inc., which operates systems mainly in northern New Brunswick. The Canadian Radio-Television and Telecommunications Commission application included an agreement by which Fundy will provide for the rebuilding of the province's cable system using fibre optics. The company says fibre optics will enhance quality of service and lead Fundy into new sectors such as data transmission, multi-media interconnects, and telephony.

In 1994, Fundy's cable television operations accounted for over 88% of total revenues and 96% of operating income. At August 1994 year end, operating income for Canadian cable operations climbed to $13.7-million representing an increase of 32.3% over 1993. This was mainly due to the acquisition of Moncton's CSL. Fundy's U.K. operation, LCL, is still in the development stage and incurred a $2.4-million loss in 1994, and a $1.7-million loss for the first six months of 1995. However, Fundy predicts LCL will generate positive cash flow by the end of fiscal 1995.

Relative strength to TSE300 / Price / Volume (in 1000's of board lots) chart, 1992–1995

Rank (Profit/Revenue/Assets)
775   575   483

James A. MacMurray
Chairman

C. William Stanley
President & C.E.O.

Alexander A. MacLellan
Ex. V.P. & C.F.O.

Address
199 Chesley Drive
Saint John
NB
E2K 4S9
(506) 634-5800

Fax: (506) 634-5019
01003624/G/11.2

G.T.C. TRANSCONTINENTAL GROUP LTD.

Exchanges	Price (Jun29'95)	9 .00	Trailing P/E	7 .20	Stock Symbol
TM	Trailing Yield (%)	1 .33	Trailing EPS	1 .25	**GRT.B**

Period Ending	Oc t94	Oc t93	Oc t92	Oc t91	Oc t90
Yearly Statistics					
Price-Close	7 .75	11 .50	8 .63	3 .80	2 .80
Price-High	12 .38	12 .25	9 .00	4 .90	5 .25
Price-Low	6 .00	7 .38	4 .85	3 .45	2 .50
P/E-Close	12 .92	18 .55	20 .07	190 .00	23 .33
Dividends per Share	0 .12	0 .17	0 .00	0 .00	0 .00
Dividend Yield (%)	1 .55	1 .48	0 .00	0 .00	0 .00
Sales per Share	22 .70	22 .31	42 .91	20 .28	20 .45
EPS before extra. item	0 .60	0 .62	0 .43	0 .02	0 .12
Cash Flow per Share	2 .19	2 .13	3 .34	1 .58	1 .31
Book Value per Share	7 .58	7 .12	5 .60	4 .89	4 .92
O/S Common Shares	34 ,827	34 ,784	23 ,432	20 ,257	20 ,324
Total Revenue	790 ,336	638 ,162	544 ,566	411 ,901	415 ,631
Income before extra.	20 ,956	18 ,277	11 ,466	1 ,987	2 ,750
Cash Flow	76 ,405	61 ,047	42 ,421	32 ,163	26 ,677
Debt/Equity	0 .55	0 .75	0 .64	0 .92	0 .70
Return on Capital (%)	12 .37	12 .42	13 .26	6 .64	8 .73
Ret. on Com. Equity (%)	8 .13	9 .34	8 .08	0 .33	2 .36
% Change Profit	14 .7	59 .4	477 .1	(27 .7)	(63 .1)
% Change Revenue	23 .8	17 .2	32 .2	(0 .9)	13 .4
% Change Assets	7 .7	46 .4	35 .0	8 .1	0 .0

Period Ending			
Preferred Div. Coverage	134 .3	np	5 .3
Total Div. Coverage	4 .8	3 .4	5 .3
Interest Coverage	3 .2	4 .0	2 .6
Current Ratio	1 .3	1 .5	1 .2
Operating Margin	7 .9	7 .5	6 .4
Asset Turnover	1 .2	1 .0	1 .3
5 YEAR RATIOS (%)			
Return on Capital	10 .7	10 .4	10 .0
Return on Com. Equity	5 .6	5 .6	5 .1
Profit Growth	23 .0	24 .9	0 .7
Revenue Growth	16 .6	14 .3	15 .8
Asset Growth	18 .1	22 .8	14 .3
BALANCE SHEET (000)			
Cash	9 ,716	3 ,617	0
Current Assets	216 ,158	209 ,564	142 ,556
Net Fixed Assets	328 ,415	317 ,173	239 ,331
Invest's & Advances	32 ,339	2 ,798	617
Total Assets	663 ,322	616 ,122	420 ,771
Short Term Debt	30 ,256	7 ,627	13 ,204
Current Liabilities	160 ,776	138 ,089	116 ,075
Long Term Debt	135 ,357	178 ,146	95 ,450
Total Liabilities	359 ,501	368 ,379	250 ,638
Total Equity	303 ,821	247 ,743	170 ,133
Total Liab. & Equity	663 ,322	616 ,122	420 ,771
CAPITAL (000)			
Total Debt	165 ,613	185 ,773	108 ,654
Preferred Equity	40 ,000	0	39 ,000
Common Equity	263 ,821	247 ,743	131 ,133

Business:

G.T.C. TRANSCONTINENTAL GROUP LTD. is a corporate head office which through its subsidiaries and a joint venture, carries on business in the printing, publishing, distribution, and compact disc industries.

Date	EPS	DPS	Tot Rev	Inc Bex
Apr 95	0 .22	0 .03	240 ,362	8 ,375
Jan 95	0 .07	0 .03	196 ,756	3 ,292
Oct 94	0 .90	0 .03	220 ,926	10 ,566
Jul 94	0 .06	0 .03	181 ,881	2 ,176
Apr 94	0 .19	0 .03	196 ,765	6 ,586
Jan 94	0 .05	0 .03	191 ,375	1 ,628
Oct 93	0 .34	0 .03	201 ,352	10 ,285
Jul 93	0 .05	0 .03	139 ,482	1 ,566

Synopsis:

In 1994 G.T.C. Transcontinental Group pursued an "integrated growth" strategy, by which it is building the company through synergy between its constituent companies. This strategy led the company to conclude a deal in November 1994 with Ross-Ellis, a specialist in printing booklets for audio CD and CD-ROM packages. Ross-Ellis complements Americ Disc, a manufacturer of CDs and CD-ROMs that Transcontinental bought in 1993.

In 1994, Transcontinental opened new printing plants in Vancouver, Boucherville, and Montreal. It also opened an Americ Disc plant in Miami, to better serve the southern United States, Mexico, and South America. Transcontinental also bought Yorkville Printing Group Ltd. Yorkville operates two printing plants in the Toronto area with a total revenue of $60-million. The Yorkville plants give Continental the ability to serve the direct mail industry in Ontario, a capacity it already has in Quebec.

In June 1993, Transcontinental acquired BABN Technologies, a lottery ticket printer for $43.5-million. However, the company did not satisfy Transcontinental's objectives. It was re-sold in 1994.

In 1994, Transcontinental arranged for public financing through a preferred share issue in the amount of $40-million of permanent capital. The financing will strengthen the corporation's ability to manage future development.

Transcontinental sees the growth in electronic communications as compatible with its newspaper and printing divisions. The company hopes to break new ground in 1995 with direct-to-plate printing. This allows for the electronic gathering of information that can be directly transmitted to the printing press. Transcontinental also believes that the volume of printed material will continue to grow along-side electronic media, and plans to explore further opportunities like the Ross-Ellis acquisition.

Rank (Profit/Revenue/Assets)
208   139   198

Remi Marcoux
Chairman President & C.E.O.

Luc Sicotte
V.P. Finance & Treasurer

Address
1 Place Ville Marie
Suite 3315
Montreal
PQ
H3B 3N2
(514) 954-4000

Fax: (514) 954-4016

G0025506/G/11.3

GROUPE VIDEOTRON LTEE (LE)

Exchanges	Price (Jun29'95)	11.00	Trailing P/E	30.55	Stock Symbol
TM	Trailing Yield (%)	0.55	Trailing EPS	0.36	**VDO**

Period Ending	Aug94	Aug93	Aug92	Aug91	Aug90
Yearly Statistics					
Price-Close	14.00	12.38	8.13	6.94	4.88
Price-High	16.63	12.56	9.00	7.50	9.75
Price-Low	11.50	7.25	6.13	4.75	4.81
P/E-Close	127.27	82.50	325.00	nm	34.82
Dividends per Share	0.06	0.06	0.06	0.06	0.06
Dividend Yield (%)	0.43	0.49	0.74	0.87	1.23
Sales per Share	6.20	6.16	6.28	5.32	5.47
EPS before extra. item	0.11	0.15	0.03	(0.06)	0.14
Cash Flow per Share	1.26	1.47	1.20	0.77	0.81
Book Value per Share	4.18	3.33	3.68	2.38	2.59
O/S Common Shares	107,710	94,848	94,589	76,844	76,728
Total Revenue	646,340	598,680	546,458	481,950	431,306
Income before extra.	20,462	25,093	12,594	5,341	18,070
Cash Flow	130,588	138,970	103,252	58,983	62,317
Debt/Equity	1.85	1.71	1.68	2.29	1.63
Return on Capital (%)	6.29	8.21	7.67	6.45	0.00
Ret. on Com. Equity (%)	3.00	4.38	0.76	(2.48)	5.16
% Change Profit	(18.5)	99.2	135.8	(70.4)	(26.5)
% Change Revenue	8.0	9.6	13.4	11.7	24.3
% Change Assets	34.3	(5.4)	27.6	22.6	35.6
Preferred Div. Coverage	2.3	2.4	1.2		
Total Div. Coverage	1.3	1.5	0.8		
Interest Coverage	1.2	1.4	1.2		
Current Ratio	1.7	0.8	1.5		
Operating Margin	13.4	17.5	14.6		
Asset Turnover	0.3	0.4	0.3		
5 YEAR RATIOS (%)					
Return on Capital	7.7	9.1	10.4		
Return on Com. Equity	2.2	4.2	6.1		
Profit Growth	(3.6)	3.6	(7.1)		
Revenue Growth	13.2	14.1	13.2		
Asset Growth	21.9	21.9	25.9		
BALANCE SHEET (000)					
Cash	224,671	19,189	141,856		
Current Assets	346,953	119,034	258,440		
Net Fixed Assets	1,245,751	1,012,898	932,874		
Invest's & Advances	21,267	16,290	35,893		
Total Assets	2,082,455	1,551,010	1,639,894		
Short Term Debt	46,276	26,336	35,069		
Current Liabilities	200,392	148,075	167,365		
Long Term Debt	969,069	685,121	719,644		
Total Liabilities	1,532,195	1,135,233	1,191,369		
Total Equity	550,260	415,777	448,525		
Total Liab. & Equity	2,082,455	1,551,010	1,639,894		
CAPITAL (000)					
Total Debt	1,015,345	711,457	754,713		
Preferred Equity	100,000	100,003	100,003		
Common Equity	450,260	315,774	348,522		

Business:

GROUPE VIDEOTRON LTEE is a communications company. The Company's core business is cable television with its cable network located mainly in Quebec. The Company controls Tele-Metropole Inc., the largest private French-language television broadcaster in Quebec. It also develops and operates cable and telephone services in England and has recently entered the wireless cable and private cable industries in the U.S.

Date	EPS	DPS	Tot Rev	Inc Bex
May 95	0.35	0.02	245,700	41,800
Feb 95	0.00	0.02	129,600	200
Nov 94	0.02	0.02	182,600	4,000
Aug 94	(0.01)	0.02	155,043	1,418
May 94	0.07	0.02	171,594	9,268
Feb 94	0.01	0.02	156,562	3,621
Nov 93	0.04	0.02	159,662	6,155
Aug 93	0.00	0.02	137,979	2,985

Synopsis:

Large investments in foreign operations during 1994 contributed to a lower profit for Le Groupe Videotron Ltee. in the three-month period ended November 30, 1994. Videotron recovered in the second quarter of 1995 due to growth in its United Kingdom operation. Videotron Holdings PLC in the U.K. began fibre optic network construction in 1988. By the end of 1994, the company had completed 35% of the network.

In 1994, Le Groupe Videotron's revenues (income before depreciation and amortization) by segment and geographical location before inter-segment items were: cable television Canada, 56% (82%); broadcasting Canada, 25% (11%); other services Canada, 14% (7%); United Kingdom cable television and telecommunications, 11% (2%).

In 1995, the Canadian Radio-Television Telecommunications Commission (CRTC) recommended that telephone companies be allowed to compete with cable companies to provide home entertainment services. During hearings on the Information Highway, Videotron recommended to the CRTC that there be a transition period in order to prepare for full competition and a stable regulatory framework. The federal government expects to announce its regulatory policy in the fall of 1995.

In order to counter the potential strength of telephone companies, Videotron has joined other cable companies to create a Canada-wide network. The network, expected in 1996, will enable personal computer users to connect to cable TV and gain access to the Internet and other services.

The European Union has decided that national telephone monopolies must end by 1998. A market of about 350 million people will open at a time when telephone, television, and computer technologies are merging. Opportunities will arise for a range of telecommunications companies. Videotron's U.K. operation is positioned to take advantage of these emerging European markets.

Rank (Profit/Revenue/Assets)
212 166 103

Andre Chagnon
Chairman & C.E.O.

Serge Gouin
President & C.O.O.

Alain Michel
Sr. V.P. & C.F.O.

Address
300 Viger Avenue East
Montreal
PQ
H2X 3W4
(514) 281-1232

Fax: (514) 985-8431
G0000447/G/11.2

HOLLINGER INC.

Exchanges	Price (Jun29'95)	12.37	Trailing P/E	6.55	Stock Symbol
TMV	Trailing Yield (%)	4.44	Trailing EPS	1.89	HLG

Period Ending	Dec94	Dec93	Dec92	Dec91	Dec90
Yearly Statistics					
Price-Close	12.63	13.75	10.63	11.63	11.38
Price-High	17.50	14.38	13.50	14.50	14.00
Price-Low	12.13	8.50	9.75	9.88	10.00
P/E-Close	6.44	44.36	9.32	38.75	47.40
Dividends per Share	0.50	0.40	0.70	0.40	0.70
Dividend Yield (%)	3.96	2.91	6.59	3.44	6.15
Sales per Share	22.38	15.96	15.50	13.84	14.05
EPS before extra. item	1.96	0.31	1.14	0.30	0.24
Cash Flow per Share	3.27	2.42	2.10	1.89	1.43
Book Value per Share	6.43	4.23	3.96	4.15	4.38
O/S Common Shares	55,643	55,952	54,892	55,353	55,158
Total Revenue	1,450,519	949,671	925,110	808,888	809,999
Income before extra.	118,343	25,305	73,971	31,427	34,201
Cash Flow	185,763	134,067	116,127	104,463	79,077
Debt/Equity	2.38	2.24	1.34	1.94	1.58
Return on Capital (%)	16.02	11.51	14.90	9.56	10.02
Ret. on Com. Equity (%)	37.47	7.68	28.27	7.01	5.87
% Change Profit	367.7	(65.8)	135.4	(8.1)	(53.2)
% Change Revenue	52.7	2.7	14.4	(0.1)	7.3
% Change Assets	38.6	35.4	(6.2)	8.8	19.1

Preferred Div. Coverage	17.2	3.2	6.9
Total Div. Coverage	3.3	0.8	1.5
Interest Coverage	3.7	2.2	3.3
Current Ratio	1.1	1.1	1.3
Operating Margin	12.7	17.1	15.9
Asset Turnover	0.5	0.4	0.6
5 YEAR RATIOS (%)			
Return on Capital	12.4	11.9	12.0
Return on Com. Equity	17.3	15.3	17.1
Profit Growth	10.1	(8.9)	41.4
Revenue Growth	13.9	6.4	12.0
Asset Growth	17.9	12.3	9.3
BALANCE SHEET (000)			
Cash	171,460	39,992	70,523
Current Assets	399,377	206,295	220,427
Net Fixed Assets	1,356,904	935,595	187,112
Invest's & Advances	823,921	727,391	421,889
Total Assets	2,750,103	1,984,803	1,465,409
Short Term Debt	126,531	38,260	55,602
Current Liabilities	373,627	194,599	168,892
Long Term Debt	1,159,938	950,522	520,397
Total Liabilities	2,208,821	1,543,000	1,034,664
Total Equity	541,282	441,803	430,745
Total Liab. & Equity	2,750,103	1,984,803	1,465,409
CAPITAL (000)			
Total Debt	1,286,469	988,782	575,999
Preferred Equity	183,282	204,937	213,381
Common Equity	358,000	236,866	217,364

Business:

HOLLINGER INC., through its subsidiaries, is engaged in the printing, publishing, and distribution of newspapers and magazines in Canada, the U.K., and the U.S. Publications include Saturday Night, The Daily Telegraph and Sunday Telegraph, Chicago Sun Times and the Jerusalem Post in Israel. The Company holds an interest in Southam Inc.

Date	EPS	DPS	Tot Rev	Inc Bex
Mar 95	0.13	0.15	390,785	9,122
Dec 94	0.04	0.15	396,610	4,526
Sep 94	0.05	0.15	333,281	4,648
Jun 94	1.67	0.10	462,240	96,592
Mar 94	0.20	0.10	256,766	12,577
Dec 93	(0.14)	0.10	255,578	(6,130)
Sep 93	0.09	0.10	225,291	6,790
Jun 93	0.16	0.10	229,992	10,950

Synopsis:

The board of directors of Hollinger Inc. and its subsidiary, American Publishing Company (APC), proposed a reorganization of international newspaper operations in February 1995. The reorganization would involve the transfer of Hollinger's interests in both The Telegraph, including its investments in Australia's John Fairfax Holdings Limited and Southam Inc., and Southam to APC. However as of May 1995, the independent directors of The Telegraph were unable to agree on the terms of the deal with APC, and discussions ceased.

The proposal was part of Hollinger's plan to strengthen and diversify its newspaper portfolio and facilitate future expansion. Hollinger feels such a reorganization would insulate the group as a whole from the vagaries of temporary market and competitive conditions in individual countries. This last consideration comes after a year of volatile price wars between The Telegraph and The Times of London, which in September 1993 reduced its cover price from 45 pence to 30 pence. By May 1994, The Times reported strong gains in circulation, while The Telegraph's circulation dipped below one million. After The Telegraph reduced its own cover price, its weekly circulation recovered to more than one million. Despite the price wars, The Telegraph remained profitable in 1994.

Hollinger's American Publishing division, which includes the Chicago Sun-Times, produced record sales and profits in 1994. This contribution assisted Hollinger in achieving its objective of making the United States its largest source of cash flow.

In 1995, Hollinger will continue its attempt to raise the level of permitted ownership in Fairfax, publishers of Australia's Sydney Morning Herald, from 25% to 35%. Hollinger believes an increase in its ownership will make the company less vulnerable to a takeover.

Relative strength to TSE300 / Price / Volume (in 1000's of board lots)

Rank (Profit/Revenue/Assets)
68 87 80
Conrad M. Black — Chairman & C.E.O.
F. David Radler — President & C.O.O.
J.A. Boultbee — V.P. Finance & Treasury
Charles G. Gowan — V.P. & Secretary

Address
10 Toronto Street
Toronto
ON
M5C 2B7
(416) 363-8721

Fax: (416) 364-0832
A0033243/G/11.3

MITEL CORPORATION

Exchanges	Price (Jun29'95)		7.12	Trailing P/E		26.37	Stock Symbol
TMN	Trailing Yield (%)		0.00	Trailing EPS		0.27	**MLT**

Period Ending	Mar94	Mar93	Mar92	Mar91	Mar90
Yearly Statistics					
Price-Close	6.75	2.78	1.55	1.55	2.55
Price-High	12.00	2.98	2.24	2.83	4.25
Price-Low	2.45	1.35	0.70	0.98	2.20
P/E-Close	42.19	nm	nm	nm	28.33
Dividends per Share	0.00	0.00	0.00	0.00	0.00
Dividend Yield (%)	0.00	0.00	0.00	0.00	0.00
Sales per Share	4.72	5.28	5.14	5.46	5.41
EPS before extra. item	0.16	(0.01)	(0.12)	(1.41)	0.09
Cash Flow per Share	0.39	0.32	0.21	(0.62)	0.44
Book Value per Share	1.81	1.55	1.50	1.60	2.98
O/S Common Shares	105,516	104,478	79,019	79,019	79,019
Total Revenue	500,500	426,200	411,000	441,500	441,300
Income before extra.	20,700	2,600	(5,700)	(107,000)	12,100
Cash Flow	40,600	25,400	16,700	(49,300)	34,400
Debt/Equity	0.14	0.13	0.11	0.03	0.04
Return on Capital (%)	10.57	0.88	(1.78)	(44.37)	5.12
Ret. on Com. Equity (%)	9.71	(0.86)	(7.92)	(61.40)	3.00
% Change Profit	696.2	145.6	94.7	(984.3)	(45.5)
% Change Revenue	17.4	3.7	(6.9)	0.0	(1.9)
% Change Assets	16.4	5.0	(3.6)	(19.9)	(8.4)

Date	EPS	DPS	Tot Rev	Inc Bex
Mar 95	0.13	0.00	165,500	14,400
Dec 94	0.09	0.00	149,900	10,500
Sep 94	0.02	0.00	145,200	2,900
Jul 94	0.03	0.00	132,100	4,000
Mar 94	0.03	0.00	146,200	4,800
Dec 93	0.07	0.00	130,000	7,900
Sep 93	0.04	0.00	115,800	5,000
Jun 93	0.02	0.00	108,500	3,000

Preferred Div. Coverage	5.8	0.7	0.0
Total Div. Coverage	5.8	0.7	0.0
Interest Coverage	26.1	3.0	0.0
Current Ratio	2.6	2.5	1.6
Operating Margin	4.4	(0.2)	(2.0)
Asset Turnover	1.3	1.3	1.3
5 YEAR RATIOS (%)			
Return on Capital	(5.9)	(6.4)	(7.2)
Return on Com. Equity	(11.5)	(12.0)	(15.0)
Profit Growth	(1.4)	na	na
Revenue Growth	2.1	(0.8)	(3.4)
Asset Growth	(2.9)	(6.3)	(13.7)
BALANCE SHEET (000)			
Cash	101,100	82,800	49,900
Current Assets	286,300	232,700	206,700
Net Fixed Assets	78,800	78,700	90,100
Invest's & Advances	1,400	2,700	2,800
Total Assets	376,400	323,400	308,000
Short Term Debt	3,900	2,800	4,000
Current Liabilities	111,900	93,300	131,000
Long Term Debt	27,800	23,200	13,400
Total Liabilities	144,700	119,100	144,400
Total Equity	231,700	204,300	163,600
Total Liab. & Equity	376,400	323,400	308,000
CAPITAL (000)			
Total Debt	31,700	26,000	17,400
Preferred Equity	40,800	42,800	44,800
Common Equity	190,900	161,500	118,800

Business:

MITEL CORP. is a Canadian-based international telecommunications solutions supplier. Mitel provides Customer Premise Equipment including PBX systems, consoles and telephone sets and manufactures semiconductor products for sale to world markets. The company is also active in wireless applications, computer telephone integration and emerging technology system.

Synopsis:

Mitel Corporation saw revenue rise by 19% and earnings by 54% in the year ended March 25, 1995. Sales in the United States rose 27%, primarily due to the higher levels of new Private Branch Exchange (PBX) system installations. European sales rose by 16% chiefly as a result of favourable exchange rates and PBX sales. In Canada, sales fell by 9% due to lower demand for dialers. New long-distance carriers can connect to end users without dialers. Mitel saw increased demand for its SX-2000 switching system in Hong Kong and China, and higher semiconductor sales in Korea and South America.

In Mitel's semiconductor division, revenue from custom wafers, integrated circuits, and thick film hybrid circuits jumped by 24% to $88-million, from $71-million a year earlier. Revenue gains came from the increased international sales of traditional telecom components and from the expansion into new markets such as China. Research and development funding in the semiconductor segment was directed to products for use in multimedia networks. The new integrated circuits will allow real-time voice and video traffic to be combined with data traffic. The first major circuit of this sort will be launched in fiscal 1996.

In March 1995, Mitel signed a joint development agreement with Digital Equipment Corporation of Massachusetts to develop a family of computer telephony integration products that integrate computing and communications on a client/server platform.

Revenues for the period ended March 1995 by location of end customers were: United States, 52%; Europe, 26%; Canada, 9%; and Other regions, 13%. In fiscal 1996, Mitel will focus on enhancing its PBX portfolio and simplifying the use of its fibre-optic switching series systems. Mitel is also focusing on its wireless communications equipment for use in offices.

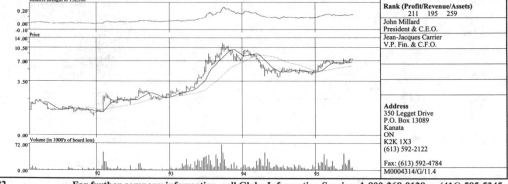

Rank (Profit/Revenue/Assets)
211   195   259

John Millard
President & C.E.O.
Jean-Jacques Carrier
V.P. Fin. & C.F.O.

Address
350 Legget Drive
P.O. Box 13089
Kanata
ON
K2K 1X3
(613) 592-2122

Fax: (613) 592-4784
M0004314/G/11.4

MOFFAT COMMUNICATIONS LIMITED

Exchanges	Price (Jun29'95)	24.50	Trailing P/E	13.69	Stock Symbol
T	Trailing Yield (%)	1.55	Trailing EPS	1.79	MOF

Period Ending	Aug94	Aug93	Aug92	Aug91	Aug90
Yearly Statistics					
Price-Close	24.25	20.38	15.50	11.63	10.50
Price-High	28.00	20.38	15.88	12.00	25.50
Price-Low	20.00	15.50	11.00	8.25	9.50
P/E-Close	16.28	7.49	29.25	55.36	23.33
Dividends per Share	0.30	0.15	0.00	0.11	0.42
Dividend Yield (%)	1.24	0.74	0.00	0.90	4.00
Sales per Share	14.99	14.25	11.94	10.77	15.58
EPS before extra. item	1.49	2.72	0.53	0.21	0.45
Cash Flow per Share	3.26	3.11	2.22	2.03	2.17
Book Value per Share	15.03	13.84	11.32	10.79	10.68
O/S Common Shares	4,862	4,862	4,862	4,862	4,862
Total Revenue	72,905	69,267	58,051	52,367	75,742
Income before extra.	7,245	13,226	2,577	1,021	2,188
Cash Flow	15,870	15,100	10,797	9,865	10,532
Debt/Equity	0.59	0.49	1.08	1.06	1.06
Return on Capital (%)	15.91	19.69	10.14	7.54	10.20
Ret. on Com. Equity (%)	10.32	21.63	4.80	1.96	4.22
% Change Profit	(45.2)	413.2	152.4	(53.3)	(49.4)
% Change Revenue	5.3	19.3	10.9	(30.9)	7.5
% Change Assets	8.4	(5.5)	6.3	0.9	28.2
Preferred Div. Coverage	np	np	np		
Total Div. Coverage	5.0	18.1	na		
Interest Coverage	3.9	5.0	2.1		
Current Ratio	0.4	0.4	0.8		
Operating Margin	24.4	23.1	22.1		
Asset Turnover	0.5	0.5	0.4		
5 YEAR RATIOS (%)					
Return on Capital	12.7	12.3	12.1		
Return on Com. Equity	8.6	8.2	6.0		
Profit Growth	10.9	21.3	(12.9)		
Revenue Growth	0.6	0.4	(2.0)		
Asset Growth	7.0	7.3	10.6		
BALANCE SHEET (000)					
Cash	0	0	0		
Current Assets	9,671	8,962	13,887		
Net Fixed Assets	82,636	73,347	76,974		
Invest's & Advances	2,663	2,820	824		
Total Assets	138,919	128,117	135,525		
Short Term Debt	17,407	5,849	8,411		
Current Liabilities	27,110	21,852	17,483		
Long Term Debt	25,500	27,000	51,132		
Total Liabilities	65,852	60,836	80,489		
Total Equity	73,067	67,281	55,036		
Total Liab. & Equity	138,919	128,117	135,525		
CAPITAL (000)					
Total Debt	42,907	32,849	59,543		
Preferred Equity	0	0	0		
Common Equity	73,067	67,281	55,036		

Business:

MOFFAT COMMUNICATIONS LTD. is a communications company. It has cable operations in Winnipeg, Houston and Tampa. It owns the Winnipeg CTV affiliate and 14 per cent of CTV, as well as 68.4 per cent of WTN, Women's Television Network. Moffat has a 10 per cent interest in the Winnipeg Jets Hockey Club.

Date	EPS	DPS	Tot Rev	Inc Bex
May 95	0.58	0.10	26,480	2,820
Feb 95	0.43	0.10	21,522	2,091
Nov 94	0.54	0.10	19,505	2,626
Aug 94	0.24	0.08	17,703	1,167
May 94	0.48	0.08	18,999	2,334
Feb 94	0.32	0.08	17,930	1,556
Nov 93	0.45	0.08	18,273	2,188
Aug 93	0.04	0.05	16,974	218

Synopsis:

Moffat Communications Inc. saw financial improvement in 1994. It realized record earnings of $7.2-million, 24% higher than previous record earnings in 1982 of $5.9-million.

Moffat's Canadian cable division was responsible for the improved earnings. Wholly owned Videon Incorporated of Winnipeg had a 1994 fiscal income of $14.8-million, a 6% boost over 1993. Cable earnings were offset by declines in broadcasting revenues. Winnipeg CTV affiliate, CKY-TV, faced low advertising revenues. Its income after operating expenses declining by 23%.

In 1994, cable operators in Manitoba purchased their respective distribution systems from Manitoba Telephone System, which they had previously leased. Videon bought cable distribution systems in Flin Flon, Winnipeg and Thompson, making a $5.2-million investment that should increase Videon's income after direct operating expenses by $1.3-million in 1995. Videon, along with other cable operators, is also committed to modernizing existing cable TV networks in Manitoba. It will deliver wireless cable TV service to a potential 50,000 rural households by building a new digital microwave system.

In fiscal 1994, the Canadian Radio-television and Telecommunications granted a six-year licence to Lifestyle Television to operate WTN, Women's Television Network, a new specialty channel. Moffat holds a 68.4% interest in Lifestyle. Based in Winnipeg, WTN is distributed nationally via cable systems. Through advertising and subscription revenues from cable systems, WTN should contribute moderately to Moffat revenues for the year ending August 1995.

Moffat also owns two cable companies in Houston, Texas, and owns 81.5% of a Pasco County, Florida, system. In 1994, $51.9-million of Moffat's revenue came from Canada, while $21-million came from the United States.

Rank (Profit/Revenue/Assets)		
360	471	412

Randall L. Moffat
President & Chairman

William A. Davis
V.P. Finance & Treasurer

Address
CKY Building
Polo Park
Winnipeg
MB
R3G 0L7
(204) 788-3440

Fax: (204) 956-2710
M0004425/G/11.2

NORTHERN TELECOM LIMITED

Exchanges	Price (Jun29'95)		50 .50	Trailing P/E		24 .98	Stock Symbol
TMVN	Trailing Yield (%)		0 .97	Trailing EPS		1 .49	NTL

Period Ending	Dec94	Dec93	Dec92	Dec91	Dec90
Yearly Statistics	US	US	US	US	US
Price-Close	46 .75	40 .88	55 .00	52 .00	32 .50
Price-High	51 .00	58 .38	58 .50	52 .50	34 .63
Price-Low	36 .13	27 .50	37 .88	30 .25	25 .63
P/E-Close	.15 .58	nm	17 .17	19 .52	13 .25
Dividends per Share	0 .36	0 .36	0 .34	0 .32	0 .30
Dividend Yield (%)	1 .05	1 .14	0 .75	0 .70	1 .08
Sales per Share	35 .21	32 .59	34 .04	33 .45	27 .91
EPS before extra. item	1 .60	(3 .54)	2 .17	2 .03	1 .80
Cash Flow per Share	2 .90	2 .00	3 .74	4 .13	3 .52
Book Value per Share	13 .24	12 .00	15 .97	14 .97	13 .24
O/S Common Shares	253 ,354	251 ,266	248 ,414	245 ,619	243 ,516
Total Revenue	9 ,247 ,000	8 ,230 ,000	8 ,521 ,000	8 ,284 ,400	6 ,835 ,400
Income before extra.	408 ,000	(878 ,000)	548 ,000	514 ,900	460 ,200
Cash Flow	731 ,000	499 ,000	923 ,000	1 ,011 ,200	853 ,500
Debt/Equity	0 .45	0 .84	0 .47	0 .53	0 .38
Return on Capital (%)	14 .24	(13 .93)	17 .24	17 .30	15 .20
Ret. on Com. Equity (%)	12 .69	(25 .33)	14 .03	14 .39	14 .73
% Change Profit	146 .5	(260 .2)	6 .4	11 .9	22 .2
% Change Revenue	12 .4	(3 .4)	2 .9	21 .2	10 .4
% Change Assets	(7 .4)	1 .1	(1 .6)	39 .3	8 .4

Preferred Div. Coverage	102 .0	0 .0	45 .7
Total Div. Coverage	4 .3	0 .0	5 .8
Interest Coverage	4 .0	0 .0	4 .8
Current Ratio	1 .7	1 .2	1 .2
Operating Margin	4 .9	(10 .8)	11 .8
Asset Turnover	1 .0	0 .9	0 .9

5 YEAR RATIOS (%)			
Return on Capital	10 .0	10 .1	14 .5
Return on Com. Equity	6 .1	6 .3	12 .8
Profit Growth	1 .6	na	9 .5
Revenue Growth	8 .3	8 .2	11 .3
Asset Growth	6 .8	10 .0	13 .3

BALANCE SHEET (000)			
Cash	1 ,059 ,000	138 ,000	90 ,000
Current Assets	5 ,355 ,000	4 ,812 ,000	4 ,155 ,000
Net Fixed Assets	1 ,705 ,000	1 ,899 ,000	1 ,930 ,000
Invest's & Advances	596 ,000	1 ,093 ,000	1 ,149 ,000
Total Assets	8 ,785 ,000	9 ,485 ,000	9 ,379 ,000
Short Term Debt	31 ,000	1 ,066 ,000	794 ,000
Current Liabilities	3 ,195 ,000	4 ,147 ,000	3 ,409 ,000
Long Term Debt	1 ,507 ,000	1 ,512 ,000	1 ,147 ,000
Total Liabilities	5 ,357 ,000	6 ,398 ,000	5 ,258 ,000
Total Equity	3 ,428 ,000	3 ,087 ,000	4 ,121 ,000
Total Liab. & Equity	8 ,785 ,000	9 ,485 ,000	9 ,379 ,000

CAPITAL (000)			
Total Debt	1 ,538 ,000	2 ,578 ,000	1 ,941 ,000
Preferred Equity	73 ,000	73 ,000	154 ,000
Common Equity	3 ,355 ,000	3 ,014 ,000	3 ,967 ,000

Business:

NORTHERN TELECOM LTD. is a global supplier of fully digital telecommunications systems. The company has a presence in more than 90 countries and operates 48 manufacuturing facilities worldwide. It conducts research principally through its subsidiary Bell-Northern Research Ltd. in Canada, the United States, the United Kingdom and Japan. BCE Inc. is the company's major shareholder.

Date		EPS	DPS	Tot Rev	Inc Bex
Mar 95	US	0 .24	0 .09	2 ,306 ,000	62 ,000
Dec 94	US	0 .88	0 .09	2 ,851 ,000	225 ,000
Sep 94	US	0 .22	0 .09	2 ,073 ,000	57 ,000
Jun 94	US	0 .15	0 .09	2 ,158 ,000	38 ,000
Mar 94	US	0 .35	0 .09	2 ,134 ,000	88 ,000
Dec 93	US	0 .42	0 .09	2 ,511 ,000	106 ,000
Sep 93	US	(0 .13)	0 .09	1 ,907 ,000	(33 ,000)
Jun 93	US	(4 .13)	0 .09	1 ,865 ,000	(1027000)

Synopsis:

Northern Telecom (Nortel) posted a 1994 profit of $408-million on revenue of almost $8.9-billion, in contrast to its 1993 loss of $884-million on revenue of $8.1-billion. The results were attributed to cost-cutting and restructuring that began in mid 1993 and an increase in international business. Markets outside North America accounted for 31% of the company's revenue in 1994, with particular growth seen in Latin America and China. The U.S. market reported some growth, while the European market remained flat. In Canada, sales fell almost one-third. According to Nortel, this mainly was due to decreased spending by Canadian telephone companies. These businesses are in the midst of a competitive and uncertain environment. In 1994, revenues increased in the company's wireless, multimedia communications, transmission, and central office switching products. Revenues were partly offset by lower cable revenues.

In 1994, segmented revenues, based on the geographical location of the customer, were as follows: United States, $4.85-billion (55%); Europe (including Africa, the Commonwealth of Independent States and the Middle East), $1.54-billion (17%); Canada, $1.14-billion (13%). Other international markets (including the Caribbean, Latin America and the Asia Pacific market), $1.34-billion (15%).

Nortel sees tremendous growth possibilities outside North America. It estimates that by 1996-97, the company may do about 40% of its business outside the continent. In 1995, Nortel bid on a vast new European telecommunication network containing 25,000 kilometres of fibre-optic cable. Since the 15-country European Union has decided that national telephone monopolies must end by 1998, Nortel expects expanding opportunities in the coming years.

In June 1995, Nortel eliminated manufacturing at its flagship Brampton, Ontario factory. It cut 580 jobs and announced its plan to convert the facility into its headquarters by the end of the year.

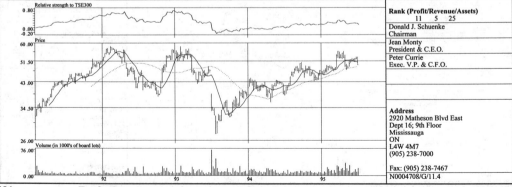

Rank (Profit/Revenue/Assets)		
11	5	25

Donald J. Schuenke
Chairman

Jean Monty
President & C.E.O.

Peter Currie
Exec. V.P. & C.F.O.

Address
2920 Matheson Blvd East
Dept 16; 9th Floor
Mississauga
ON
L4W 4M7
(905) 238-7000

Fax: (905) 238-7467
N0004708/G/11.4

PETERSBURG LONG DISTANCE INC.

Exchanges	Price (Jun29'95)	8.50	Trailing P/E	nm	Stock Symbol
T	Trailing Yield (%)	0.00	Trailing EPS	(0.73)	**PLD**

Period Ending	Dec94	Dec93	Dec92	Dec91	Dec90
Yearly Statistics			9M		
Price-Close	8.88	15.50	8.88	4.40	6.00
Price-High	16.25	17.00	9.50	12.30	19.50
Price-Low	8.75	7.25	3.50	4.00	5.00
P/E-Close	nm	nm	nm	nm	nm
Dividends per Share	0.00	0.00	0.00	0.00	0.00
Dividend Yield (%)	0.00	0.00	0.00	0.00	0.00
Sales per Share	0.70	na	na	1.06	0.00
EPS before extra. item	(0.89)	(1.26)	(1.02)	(0.01)	(12.20)
Cash Flow per Share	(0.36)	(0.34)	(0.72)	0.04	(0.43)
Book Value per Share	12.43	2.42	3.36	(1.32)	(21.96)
O/S Common Shares	30,012	8,562	7,867	2,996	1,870
Total Revenue	8,761	46	5,950	2,375	0
Income before extra.	(10,892)	(9,645)	(5,301)	(40)	(22,635)
Cash Flow	4,457	(2,755)	(3,866)	93	(792)
Debt/Equity	0.04	0.28	0.28	na	na
Return on Capital (%)	(5.66)	(23.02)	(17.61)	1.86	(17.75)
Ret. on Com. Equity (%)	(7.34)	(41.97)	(47.25)	na	na
% Change Profit	(51.7)	(82.0)	(9,839.4)	99.8	28.7
% Change Revenue	25,767.0	(99.2)	87.9	na	(100.0)
% Change Assets	430.5	(15.6)	279.5	(92.9)	(6.5)

Preferred Div. Coverage	0.0	0.0	na
Total Div. Coverage	0.0	0.0	na
Interest Coverage	na	na	0.0
Current Ratio	2.8	0.3	0.9
Operating Margin	62.7	na	na
Asset Turnover	0.1	na	na
5 YEAR RATIOS (%)			
Return on Capital	(12.4)	(13.2)	(12.4)
Return on Com. Equity	na	na	na
Profit Growth	na	na	na
Revenue Growth	(45.7)	(100.0)	(43.8)
Asset Growth	(3.5)	(33.5)	(13.8)
BALANCE SHEET (000)			
Cash	56,710	1,187	7,873
Current Assets	61,319	2,613	10,318
Net Fixed Assets	21,718	8,322	5,993
Invest's & Advances	31,778	0	0
Total Assets	174,562	43,892	51,984
Short Term Debt	6,637	2,810	4,348
Current Liabilities	22,315	8,299	10,926
Long Term Debt	0	5,471	5,678
Total Liabilities	22,404	13,770	16,604
Total Equity	152,158	30,122	35,380
Total Liab. & Equity	174,562	43,892	51,984
CAPITAL (000)			
Total Debt	6,637	8,281	10,026
Preferred Equity	4,917	9,376	8,980
Common Equity	147,241	20,746	26,400

Business:

PETERSBURG LONG DISTANCE INC., through its investment in Peterstar Company Limited, is a provider of modern international and domestic telecommunications services to the city of St. Petersburg, Russia.

Date	EPS	DPS	Tot Rev	Inc Bex
Mar 95	(0.06)	0.00	4,640	(1,808)
Dec 94	(0.26)	0.00	3,099	(4,884)
Sep 94	(0.39)	0.00	3,848	(4,803)
Jun 94	(0.19)	0.00	2,408	(2,144)
Mar 94	(0.17)	0.00	1,670	(1,464)
Dec 93	(1.02)	0.00	303	(7,977)
Sep 93	(0.21)	0.00	12	(1,163)
Jun 93	(0.06)	0.00	42	(509)

Synopsis:

Petersburg Long Distance provides telecommunication services to emerging markets. Its current key operations are in Russia and the Commonwealth of Independent States through its investments in PeterStar Company Limited and BECET International.

In March 1994, the company acquired an additional 9% interest in PeterStar for $5-million (U.S.). This raised its total stake to 59%. Also in March, Petersburg acquired a 50% interest in BECET International, a joint venture with the Ministry of Communications in Kazakhstan. BECET is licensed for 15 years, exclusive for the first 5 years, to install and operate the first nationwide cellular telephone network in Kazakhstan. BECET will invest $20-million (U.S.) in developing the network over the next three years.

Also in March, Cable and Wireless PLC acquired a 25% interest in Petersburg Long Distance. This will allow Petersburg to draw upon the support and expertise of Cable and Wireless, which operates in over 50 countries.

In November 1994, Petersburg agreed to acquire a 51% interest in Technocom Limited for $15-million (U.S.). Technocom's main asset is a 41.83% interest in Teleport-TP, a Russian company. Teleport-TP operates a telecommunications network consisting of an earth station, a gateway switch, and a fibre optic cable network in Moscow.

Petersburg believes the recovery of its investments in PeterStar and BECET is dependent upon both attaining profitable operations. Risks and uncertainties include the economic and political environment in the C.I.S., the ability to maintain the necessary telecommunication licences, and the ability to obtain adequate financing.

Rank (Profit/Revenue/Assets)
942   988   668

Rupert Galliers-Pratt
Executive Chairman
James Hatt
Chief Executive Officer
Clayton A. Waite
Sr. V.P. & C.F.O.

Address
166 Pearl Street
Ground Floor
Toronto
ON
M5H 1L3
(416) 593-4989

Fax: (416) 597-1776
01000505/G/11.4

QUEBECOR INC.

Exchanges	Price (Jun29'95)		19.87	Trailing P/E		13.71	Stock Symbol
TMA	Trailing Yield (%)		0.86	Trailing EPS		1.45	**QBR.A**

Period Ending	Dec94	Dec93	Dec92	Dec91	Dec90
Yearly Statistics					
Price-Close	17.75	18.00	16.63	10.88	7.62
Price-High	21.75	21.00	17.00	10.88	7.75
Price-Low	15.50	16.75	10.50	7.63	5.50
P/E-Close	13.25	15.65	11.63	27.89	4.61
Dividends per Share	0.24	0.20	0.15	0.13	0.12
Dividend Yield (%)	1.35	1.11	0.90	1.20	1.57
Sales per Share	59.91	47.52	41.38	49.35	51.63
EPS before extra. item	1.34	1.15	1.43	0.39	1.65
Cash Flow per Share	7.67	5.14	3.92	4.32	4.92
Book Value per Share	12.54	11.17	10.01	7.76	7.22
O/S Common Shares	66,077	66,435	64,282	53,579	47,131
Total Revenue	3,980,629	3,094,834	2,612,196	2,390,312	2,521,196
Income before extra.	88,636	74,566	87,339	18,516	77,945
Cash Flow	508,765	334,691	240,254	207,668	232,000
Debt/Equity	1.55	0.93	1.12	2.88	3.45
Return on Capital (%)	16.60	14.65	16.33	8.97	21.59
Ret. on Com. Equity (%)	11.29	10.76	16.49	4.90	25.47
% Change Profit	18.9	(14.6)	371.7	(76.2)	320.4
% Change Revenue	28.6	18.5	9.3	(5.2)	41.7
% Change Assets	39.7	13.8	(0.5)	(3.3)	45.1
Preferred Div. Coverage	np	np	np		
Total Div. Coverage	5.6	5.7	9.5		
Interest Coverage	5.0	4.7	2.9		
Current Ratio	1.8	1.6	1.6		
Operating Margin	11.5	8.3	8.0		
Asset Turnover	1.0	1.0	1.0		
5 YEAR RATIOS (%)					
Return on Capital	15.6	15.7	16.7		
Return on Com. Equity	13.8	13.2	15.1		
Profit Growth	36.8	17.8	30.3		
Revenue Growth	17.4	18.8	30.5		
Asset Growth	17.3	15.7	14.0		
BALANCE SHEET (000)					
Cash	198,508	43,769	51,341		
Current Assets	1,274,361	805,419	669,320		
Net Fixed Assets	2,395,791	1,810,171	1,593,377		
Invest's & Advances	19,303	15,097	15,147		
Total Assets	4,171,315	2,986,574	2,623,869		
Short Term Debt	63,933	67,184	48,593		
Current Liabilities	723,206	512,586	413,699		
Long Term Debt	1,220,416	621,378	671,624		
Total Liabilities	3,342,895	2,244,233	1,980,260		
Total Equity	828,420	742,341	643,609		
Total Liab. & Equity	4,171,315	2,986,574	2,623,869		
CAPITAL (000)					
Total Debt	1,284,349	688,562	720,217		
Preferred Equity	0	0	0		
Common Equity	828,420	742,341	643,609		

Business:

QUEBECOR INC. is a publishing and distribution, printing, and forest products company. It publishes four dailies, 55 weeklies, 5 monthlies, 11 magazines and numerous specials as well as books. It has printing and specialized plants in Canada, the United States, France, India, Mexico, and the U.K. Donohue Inc. is one subsidiary of the company.

Date	EPS	DPS	Tot Rev	Inc Bex
Mar 95	0.37	0.00	1,277,725	24,191
Dec 94	0.49	0.06	1,172,171	32,370
Sep 94	0.41	0.00	1,071,920	27,238
Jun 94	0.18	0.11	908,058	11,804
Mar 94	0.26	0.00	820,089	17,224
Dec 93	0.34	0.04	878,840	22,405
Sep 93	0.27	0.00	792,610	17,485
Jun 93	0.30	0.10	742,697	19,269

Synopsis:

Quebecor Inc. showed growth in revenue and income for both fiscal 1994 and the first quarter of 1995. The printing segment, Quebecor Printing Inc., contributed 73% of the company's revenues and 53% of its operating income in 1994. Its forest products segment was responsible for 20% of the revenues and 41% of its operating income. In the first quarter 1995, forestry earnings before interest and taxes jumped to $76-million, compared to $26-million in the first quarter of 1994. The results were due to significant increases in market prices for pulp and newsprint.

Quebecor's printing segment is one of the world's largest commercial printers with 84 printing and related services facilities in Canada, the United States, France, the United Kingdom, Mexico and India. For 1994, 76% of Quebecor Printing's revenues originated in the United States. The segment's growth in 1994 is attributable to the businesses bought in 1994 and the full-year contribution of businesses bought during 1993. In 1994, the printing division acquired Arcata Corporation, making Quebecor Printing the second largest book manufacturer in North America, and marking its entry into the CD-ROM market. In 1995, the company completed the acquisition of Groupe Jean Didier, the largest commercial printer in France. It also bought four Maclean Hunter printing facilities and purchased HunterPrint Group PLC, a U.K. company with annual revenue of about $100-million.

In 1994, Quebecor founded a new subsidiary, Quebecor Multimedia Inc., aimed at enriching its current assets through digital and interactive forms. In June 1995, the subsidiary acquired Les Logiciels Educatifs Auba, a major Quebec distributor of interactive software and CD-ROMs.

In 1995, Quebecor is planning to continue expansion in its forestry, publishing and distribution activities, while, in its printing sector, it will focus on its existing assets and increasing their efficiency.

Relative strength to TSE300 / Price / Volume (in 1000's of board lots) chart, 92–95

Rank (Profit/Revenue/Assets)		
83	35	52

Pierre Peladeau
Chairman President & C.E.O.

Francois R. Roy
V.P. Finance & Treasurer

Address
612 Rue St-Jacques
Montreal
PQ
H3C 4M8
(514) 877-9777

Fax: (514) 877-9757
Q0001162/G/11.3

For further company information, call Globe Information Services 1-800-268-9128 or (416) 585-5345

QUEBECOR PRINTING INC.

Exchanges	Price (Jun29'95)	17 .62	Trailing P/E	14 .92	Stock Symbol
TM	Trailing Yield (%)	1 .08	Trailing EPS	0 .87	**IQI**

Period Ending	Dec94	Dec93	Dec92	Dec91	Dec90
Yearly Statistics	US	US	US	US	US
Price-Close	14 .88	16 .50	14 .58	n t	n t
Price-High	19 .13	18 .68	14 .75	n t	n t
Price-Low	13 .13	13 .63	10 .50	n t	n t
P/E-Close	12 .49	15 .57	16 .67	n t	n t
Dividends per Share	0 .13	0 .10	0 .16	0 .09	0 .11
Dividend Yield (%)	0 .87	0 .62	1 .10	n t	n t
Sales per Share	21 .17	19 .02	19 .16	23 .13	22 .02
EPS before extra. item	0 .87	0 .82	0 .72	0 .55	0 .38
Cash Flow per Share	2 .14	1 .89	2 .07	1 .97	1 .64
Book Value per Share	7 .08	6 .43	5 .79	4 .06	3 .55
O/S Common Shares	99 ,950	99 ,950	82 ,448	58 ,875	58 ,125
Total Revenue	2 ,115 ,867	1 ,743 ,120	1 ,444 ,426	1 ,386 ,852	1 ,264 ,937
Income before extra.	87 ,240	75 ,210	54 ,491	33 ,223	21 ,643
Cash Flow	213 ,677	172 ,796	156 ,206	118 ,206	94 ,510
Debt/Equity	1 .02	0 .64	0 .79	2 .51	3 .07
Return on Capital (%)	14 .05	15 .63	15 .11	13 .28	16 .83
Ret. on Com. Equity (%)	12 .93	13 .43	15 .14	14 .67	14 .56
% Change Profit	16 .0	38 .0	64 .0	53 .5	196 .9
% Change Revenue	21 .4	20 .7	4 .2	9 .6	94 .9
% Change Assets	33 .0	20 .6	3 .6	(1 .2)	151 .1

Preferred Div. Coverage	np	np	np
Total Div. Coverage	6 .7	7 .9	4 .4
Interest Coverage	6 .2	7 .8	3 .8
Current Ratio	1 .7	1 .4	1 .4
Operating Margin	8 .8	9 .2	9 .8
Asset Turnover	1 .1	1 .2	1 .2
5 YEAR RATIOS (%)			
Return on Capital	15 .0	na	na
Return on Com. Equity	14 .1	na	na
Profit Growth	64 .2	na	na
Revenue Growth	26 .6	na	na
Asset Growth	32 .7	na	na
BALANCE SHEET (000)			
Cash	0	0	0
Current Assets	535 ,786	380 ,387	290 ,419
Net Fixed Assets	1 ,158 ,872	927 ,453	771 ,772
Invest's & Advances	2 ,273	0	0
Total Assets	1 ,955 ,942	1 ,471 ,070	1 ,219 ,512
Short Term Debt	9 ,157	39 ,295	7 ,232
Current Liabilities	315 ,673	275 ,504	203 ,908
Long Term Debt	712 ,279	373 ,280	369 ,184
Total Liabilities	1 ,248 ,756	828 ,637	742 ,067
Total Equity	707 ,186	642 ,433	477 ,445
Total Liab. & Equity	1 ,955 ,942	1 ,471 ,070	1 ,219 ,512
CAPITAL (000)			
Total Debt	721 ,436	412 ,575	376 ,416
Preferred Equity	0	0	0
Common Equity	707 ,186	642 ,433	477 ,445

Business:

QUEBECOR PRINTING INC., a subsidiary of Quebecor Inc., is the largest commercial printer in Canada and the second largest in North America. It has 22,700 employees working in 84 international printing and related services plants. It is a leader in web offset, gravure and sheetfed printing for the magazine, retail insert, catalogue, book, newspaper, directory, cheque, and other commercial printing markets.

Date		EPS	DPS	Tot Rev	Inc Bex
Mar 95	US	0 .17	0 .00	687 ,324	17 ,271
Dec 94	US	0 .27	0 .07	634 ,311	27 ,163
Sep 94	US	0 .22	0 .00	580 ,205	22 ,416
Jun 94	US	0 .21	0 .07	455 ,863	20 ,530
Mar 94	US	0 .17	0 .00	445 ,488	17 ,131
Dec 93	US	0 .21	0 .06	493 ,104	21 ,360
Sep 93	US	0 .21	0 .00	460 ,182	20 ,777
Jun 93	US	0 .22	0 .05	411 ,935	18 ,244

Synopsis:

Quebecor Printing Inc. is one of the world's largest commercial printers with 84 printing and related services facilities in Canada, the United States, France, the United Kingdom, Mexico, and India. It prints inserts, magazines, books, catalogues, directories, cheques, bonds and banknotes and newspapers. Revenues and operating income increased both in fiscal 1994 and for the three months ended March 31, 1995.

The company's growth was due to the businesses acquired in 1994 and the full-year contribution of businesses acquired during 1993. In 1994, the printing division acquired Arcata Corporation, making Quebecor Printing the second largest book manufacturer in North America, and marking its entry into the CD-ROM market. In 1995, the company bought Groupe Jean Didier, the largest commercial printer in France. It acquired four Maclean Hunter printing facilities and the contracts to print magazines like Chatelaine, Maclean's and L'actualite. Quebecor Printing also purchased HunterPrint Group PLC, a U.K. company with annual revenue of about $100-million.

Pro forma revenues in 1994 by region, resulting from acquisitions up to February 1995, were: Canada, 21%; United States, 62%; Europe 16%; and other, 1%.

The company has been retooling its North American plants over the past two years in efforts to reach the highest levels of efficiency. Capital expenditures in 1994 were $178.3-million (U.S.) compared to $104.5-million (U.S.) in 1993, and are expected to reach $200- million (U.S.) in 1995. In its North American operations, rather than acquiring more assets, Quebecor Printing plans to focus in 1995 primarily on its existing assets and increasing their efficiency. However, Quebecor Printing is poised to seek opportunities overseas, as the expanding European Union takes shape.

Rank (Profit/Revenue/Assets)
66   54   82

Jean Neveu
Chairman & C.E.O.
Charles G. Cavell
President & C.O.O.
Pierre L. Royr
V.P. & C.F.O.

Address
612 St-Jacques
Montreal
PQ
H3C 4M8
(514) 954-0101

Fax: (514) 954-9624
01003273/G/11.3

ROGERS CANTEL MOBILE COMMUNICATIONS INC.

Exchanges	Price (Jun29'95)		32 .25	Trailing P/E		1 ,075 .00	Stock Symbol
TMVZQ	Trailing Yield (%)		0 .00	Trailing EPS		0 .03	RCM.B

Period Ending	Dec94	Dec93	Dec92	Dec91	Dec90
Yearly Statistics					4M
Price-Close	40 .75	35 .50	24 .50	26 .38	n t
Price-High	43 .50	41 .50	30 .00	26 .38	n t
Price-Low	30 .88	24 .00	19 .75	18 .13	n t
P/E-Close	nm	nm	nm	nm	n t
Dividends per Share	0 .00	0 .00	0 .00	0 .00	0 .00
Dividend Yield (%)	0 .00	0 .00	0 .00	0 .00	0 .00
Sales per Share	7 .99	6 .45	5 .51	4 .24	3 .99
EPS before extra. item	(0 .02)	(1 .61)	(1 .86)	(0 .45)	(0 .46)
Cash Flow per Share	1 .91	0 .96	0 .41	0 .28	(0 .40)
Book Value per Share	(0 .67)	(0 .65)	0 .96	2 .81	1 .77
O/S Common Shares	93 ,894	93 ,894	93 ,894	93 ,894	93 ,851
Total Revenue	750 ,672	603 ,388	518 ,088	439 ,764	125 ,956
Income before extra.	(1 ,972)	(151 ,170)	(174 ,279)	(42 ,022)	(43 ,152)
Cash Flow	178 ,875	89 ,961	38 ,523	25 ,991	(12 ,380)
Debt/Equity	na	na	10 .51	2 .58	3 .76
Return on Capital (%)	10 .02	(5 .15)	(9 .07)	3 .11	(1 .81)
Ret. on Com. Equity (%)	na	(1 ,060 .69)	(98 .48)	(19 .55)	(150 .93)
% Change Profit	98 .7	13 .3	(314 .7)	67 .5	(30 .2)
% Change Revenue	24 .4	16 .5	17 .8	16 .4	32 .0
% Change Assets	4 .0	(2 .6)	13 .9	18 .0	11 .3

Preferred Div. Coverage	np	np	np
Total Div. Coverage	na	na	na
Interest Coverage	1 .0	0 .0	0 .0
Current Ratio	0 .4	0 .3	0 .7
Operating Margin	13 .6	4 .4	(4 .4)
Asset Turnover	0 .6	0 .5	0 .4

5 YEAR RATIOS (%)			
Return on Capital	(0 .6)	(3 .4)	na
Return on Com. Equity	na	(555 .6)	na
Profit Growth	na	na	na
Revenue Growth	21 .2	28 .4	na
Asset Growth	8 .6	20 .9	na

BALANCE SHEET (000)			
Cash	0	0	34 ,901
Current Assets	116 ,851	99 ,511	126 ,686
Net Fixed Assets	964 ,212	969 ,895	930 ,034
Invest's & Advances	17 ,509	12 ,046	11 ,420
Total Assets	1 ,219 ,467	1 ,173 ,028	1 ,204 ,022
Short Term Debt	153 ,011	201 ,529	6 ,710
Current Liabilities	327 ,143	392 ,574	177 ,063
Long Term Debt	955 ,629	841 ,787	937 ,122
Total Liabilities	1 ,282 ,772	1 ,234 ,361	1 ,114 ,185
Total Equity	(63 ,305)	(61 ,333)	89 ,837
Total Liab. & Equity	1 ,219 ,467	1 ,173 ,028	1 ,204 ,022

CAPITAL (000)			
Total Debt	1 ,108 ,640	1 ,043 ,316	943 ,832
Preferred Equity	0	0	0
Common Equity	(63 ,305)	(61 ,333)	89 ,837

Business:

ROGERS CANTEL MOBILE COMMUNICATIONS INC. through its subsidiaries Rogers Cantel Mobile Inc. and Rogers Cantel Inc., operates the largest integrated cellular telephone network in Canada and is the only company authorized to provide cellular telephone service on a nation-wide basis. Cantel also operates retail service centres, a national paging system, and a mobile data communications service.

Date	EPS	DPS	Tot Rev	Inc Bex
Mar 95	(0 .05)	0 .00	192 ,145	(5 ,136)
Dec 94	0 .03	0 .00	206 ,138	3 ,159
Sep 94	0 .05	0 .00	202 ,736	4 ,807
Jun 94	0 .00	0 .00	183 ,355	414
Mar 94	(0 .11)	0 .00	158 ,553	(10 ,352)
Dec 93	(0 .13)	0 .00	161 ,677	(12 ,603)
Sep 93	(0 .90)	0 .00	159 ,156	(84 ,524)
Jun 93	(0 .21)	0 .00	151 ,890	(19 ,782)

Synopsis:

Rogers Cantel Mobile Communications Inc. saw strong cellular telephone subscription growth in fiscal 1994 and during the first quarter of 1995. The number of cellular subscribers rose 35.1% to a total of 820,455 for the quarter ended March 31, 1995. The quarterly average monthly revenue per subscriber, however was $69, down 8% from $75 in the prior year. Cantel attributes the decline to the lower usage profile of the growing number of personal-use subscribers.

In June 1994, Cantel launched its new consumer-targeted Amigo phones, made available nationally in large retail stores. As a result, as of December 31, 1994, 30% of Cantel's cumulative subscriber base was in the consumer and safety segment, compared to 20% in 1993 and 11% in 1992. For the same period, the small business segment made up 47% of subscribers and corporate and large business 23%.

Cantel realized a 50.3% increase in its paging service revenue for the quarter, a direct result of the company's acquisition of Maclean Hunter Paging for $33-million in April 1994.

The company continues its efforts to cut the cost of supporting its subscriber base, reporting an 18% decline in operating expenses excluding sales and marketing costs for the period ending March 1995. However sales and marketing costs, which reached $472 per gross addition, rose sharply in the quarter compared to the last quarter of 1994. Cantel estimates that, due to aggressive competition in the industry, marketing and sales costs will continue at this level. This may affect the rate of growth in operating cash flow. Cantel's strategy for 1995-1996 is to continue to expand its consumer segment. It will do this by increasing the speed-to-market of its products and keeping operating costs low.

Rank (Profit/Revenue/Assets)		
852	148	142

Edward S. Rogers
Chairman

David S. Gergacz
President & C.E.O.

William W. Linton
V.P. Finance & C.F.O.

Address
10 York Mills Road
North York
ON
M2P 2C9
(416) 229-1400

Fax: (416) 250-4902
01003181/G/11.4

For further company information, call Globe Information Services 1-800-268-9128 or (416) 585-5345

ROGERS COMMUNICATIONS INC.

Exchanges	Price (Jun29'95)	15.62	Trailing P/E	nm	Stock Symbol
TMZV	Trailing Yield (%)	0.00	Trailing EPS	(1.33)	**RCI.B**

Period Ending	Dec94	Dec93	Dec92	Dec91	Dec90
Yearly Statistics					16M
Price-Close	18.75	21.88	14.50	14.00	5.88
Price-High	24.00	24.88	15.13	14.38	16.86
Price-Low	17.25	14.50	11.75	5.86	5.25
P/E-Close	nm	nm	nm	nm	nm
Dividends per Share	0.00	0.00	0.00	0.00	0.00
Dividend Yield (%)	0.00	0.00	0.00	0.00	0.00
Sales per Share	9.04	8.32	7.67	7.64	7.30
EPS before extra. item	(1.16)	(1.89)	(1.30)	(0.76)	(1.51)
Cash Flow per Share	1.59	1.12	0.73	0.77	0.68
Book Value per Share	0.25	0.59	1.07	0.93	2.28
O/S Common Shares	287,204	279,990	265,331	242,322	128,232
Total Revenue	1,482,755	1,182,537	1,222,788	1,115,153	1,130,779
Income before extra.	(168,013)	(287,049)	(180,317)	(59,994)	(113,122)
Cash Flow	274,817	180,069	111,240	99,890	105,534
Debt/Equity	5.66	4.75	3.97	2.96	2.38
Return on Capital (%)	4.18	(2.47)	2.91	7.35	3.46
Ret. on Com. Equity (%)	(168.49)	(135.58)	(79.00)	(36.03)	(35.14)
% Change Profit	41.5	(59.2)	(200.6)	29.3	(228.3)
% Change Revenue	25.4	(3.3)	9.7	31.5	35.5
% Change Assets	54.3	(3.0)	22.3	4.3	60.3

Preferred Div. Coverage	0.0	0.0	0.0
Total Div. Coverage	0.0	0.0	0.0
Interest Coverage	0.5	0.0	0.3
Current Ratio	0.7	1.2	1.7
Operating Margin	16.2	11.3	6.4
Asset Turnover	0.3	0.3	0.3
5 YEAR RATIOS (%)			
Return on Capital	3.1	3.7	6.8
Return on Com. Equity	(90.8)	(67.5)	na
Profit Growth	na	na	na
Revenue Growth	18.7	26.3	34.5
Asset Growth	25.0	28.9	44.3
BALANCE SHEET (000)			
Cash	125,918	265,964	419,840
Current Assets	492,151	456,011	610,735
Net Fixed Assets	2,380,114	1,900,932	1,835,005
Invest's & Advances	513,498	549,601	516,001
Total Assets	6,128,627	3,970,877	4,094,998
Short Term Debt	77,810	0	0
Current Liabilities	732,613	371,611	364,027
Long Term Debt	4,174,922	2,773,721	2,696,286
Total Liabilities	5,377,856	3,386,398	3,415,847
Total Equity	750,771	584,479	679,151
Total Liab. & Equity	6,128,627	3,970,877	4,094,998
CAPITAL (000)			
Total Debt	4,252,732	2,773,721	2,696,286
Preferred Equity	680,274	418,709	395,748
Common Equity	70,497	165,770	283,403

Business:

ROGERS COMMUNICATIONS has operations in cable television, broadcasting, mobile communications and telecommunications. Rogers operates cable systems across Canada. It owns radio stations and a TV station in Toronto, in B.C. and Alberta. It has interests in the YTV and CHSN cable channels. It owns 40% of Unitel Communications Inc. and 80% of Rogers Cantel Mobile Communications.

Date	EPS	DPS	Tot Rev	Inc Bex
Mar 95	(0.38)	0.00	595,364	(57,416)
Dec 94	(0.49)	0.00	375,210	(76,378)
Sep 94	(0.21)	0.00	393,811	(27,715)
Jun 94	(0.25)	0.00	364,655	(33,644)
Mar 94	(0.26)	0.00	346,747	(38,810)
Dec 93	(1.02)	0.00	224,022	(163,319)
Sep 93	(0.87)	0.00	330,853	(132,844)
Jun 93	(0.25)	0.00	325,234	(35,279)

Synopsis:

Rogers Communications Inc. reported record revenues for the quarter ended March 31, 1995, due mainly to operations acquired from Maclean Hunter Limited in 1994. Subsequent to the acquisition, Rogers sold off some Maclean Hunter properties, but retained the cable, newspaper, periodical and broadcasting segments and a 62% interest in the Toronto Sun. In 1994, Rogers also acquired some cable systems from Shaw Communications.

Rogers wireless communications operations, Rogers Cantel, saw strong cellular telephone subscription growth in fiscal 1994 and during the first quarter of 1995. The number of cellular subscribers rose 35.1% to a total of 820,455 for the quarter ended March 31, 1995. The quarterly average monthly revenue per subscriber, however was $69, down 8% from $75 in the prior year. Cantel attributes the decline to the lower usage profile of the growing number of personal-use subscribers. Cantel realized a 50.3% increase in its paging service revenue for the quarter, a direct result of the company's acquisition of Maclean Hunter Paging.

Rogers currently holds a 29% stake in Unitel Communications, and for the first quarter of fiscal 1995, it took a $29.3-million loss for its share in the debt-ridden company. In April 1995, Rogers turned down its right to acquire an addition 48% stake in the company. In May, a group of six banks extended a $650-million loan to Unitel until the end of June 1995. If Unitel is unable to survive, Rogers expects to write off $130-million.

For the remainder of 1995, Rogers intends to focus on current businesses rather than further acquisitions. The company is preparing for potential competition in cable from telephone companies. It has joined Le Groupe Videotron Ltee. and Shaw Communications to set up a Canada-wide network, expected to be operational in 1996. The network will enable personal computer users to hook their equipment to cable TV and gain access to the Internet and other online services.

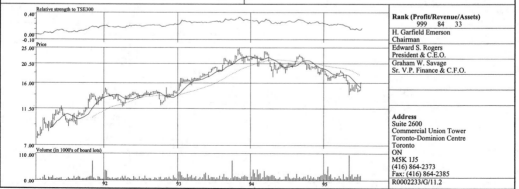

Rank (Profit/Revenue/Assets)
999   84   33

H. Garfield Emerson
Chairman

Edward S. Rogers
President & C.E.O.

Graham W. Savage
Sr. V.P. Finance & C.F.O.

Address
Suite 2600
Commercial Union Tower
Toronto-Dominion Centre
Toronto
ON
M5K 1J5
(416) 864-2373
Fax: (416) 864-2385
R0002233/G/11.2

SHAW COMMUNICATIONS INC.

Exchanges	Price (Jun29'95)	8 .37	Trailing P/E	14 .19	Stock Symbol
TZ	Trailing Yield (%)	0 .84	Trailing EPS	0 .59	SCL.B

Period Ending	Aug94	Aug93	Aug92	Aug91	Aug90
Yearly Statistics					
Price-Close	10 .25	20 .25	8 .38	6 .50	4 .38
Price-High	14 .75	20 .25	9 .25	7 .13	6 .75
Price-Low	10 .13	16 .75	6 .13	4 .00	4 .19
P/E-Close	17 .37	43 .09	20 .43	20 .00	7 .96
Dividends per Share	0 .07	0 .12	0 .04	0 .05	0 .05
Dividend Yield (%)	0 .68	0 .59	0 .51	0 .77	1 .14
Sales per Share	4 .99	9 .10	3 .81	3 .30	2 .54
EPS before extra. item	0 .59	0 .47	0 .41	0 .33	0 .55
Cash Flow per Share	1 .39	2 .21	0 .99	0 .83	0 .65
Book Value per Share	6 .73	8 .55	3 .87	2 .60	2 .36
O/S Common Shares	63 ,716	25 ,640	51 ,151	42 ,373	43 ,229
Total Revenue	288 ,789	233 ,800	166 ,088	143 ,959	134 ,740
Income before extra.	33 ,280	24 ,586	18 ,754	15 ,086	24 ,853
Cash Flow	79 ,811	56 ,556	42 ,912	35 ,414	28 ,522
Debt/Equity	0 .68	1 .87	0 .65	1 .32	1 .18
Return on Capital (%)	14 .93	15 .78	16 .63	17 .14	22 .93
Ret. on Com. Equity (%)	10 .23	11 .56	11 .49	12 .76	24 .80
% Change Profit	35 .4	31 .1	24 .3	(39 .3)	150 .3
% Change Revenue	23 .5	40 .8	15 .4	6 .8	54 .0
% Change Assets	10 .7	82 .1	18 .0	25 .1	7 .2

Business:

SHAW COMMUNICATIONS INC. currently operates cable television systems in British Columbia, Alberta, Saskatchewan, Manitoba, Ontario and Nova Scotia, serving approximately 1,100,000 subscribers. Shaw operates two radio stations in B.C., four in Alberta, and three in Ontario.

Date	EPS	DPS	Tot Rev	Inc Bex
Feb 95	0.12	0.04	90 ,529	7 ,660
Nov 94	0.16	0.00	77 ,660	10 ,084
Aug 94	0.15	0.04	73 ,951	9 ,762
May 94	0.16	0.00	73 ,680	9 ,036
Feb 94	0.14	0.04	70 ,471	7 ,030
Nov 93	0.15	0.00	70 ,554	7 ,452
Aug 93	0.14	0.03	68 ,328	7 ,320
May 93	0.12	0.00	67 ,781	6 ,146

Preferred Div. Coverage	234 .4	52 .3	18 .2
Total Div. Coverage	8 .7	6 .9	5 .7
Interest Coverage	2 .7	2 .6	2 .9
Current Ratio	0 .3	0 .2	0 .8
Operating Margin	35 .2	33 .2	32 .0
Asset Turnover	0 .3	0 .3	0 .4
5 YEAR RATIOS (%)			
Return on Capital	17 .5	17 .2	17 .8
Return on Com. Equity	14 .2	14 .3	14 .4
Profit Growth	27 .3	19 .4	18 .5
Revenue Growth	26 .9	27 .6	25 .0
Asset Growth	26 .0	34 .1	25 .3
BALANCE SHEET (000)			
Cash	0	0	47 ,289
Current Assets	18 ,407	17 ,059	56 ,104
Net Fixed Assets	314 ,380	257 ,357	168 ,356
Invest's & Advances	44 ,419	23 ,124	8 ,357
Total Assets	825 ,163	745 ,262	409 ,351
Short Term Debt	16 ,375	8 ,644	47 ,515
Current Liabilities	72 ,616	69 ,905	73 ,946
Long Term Debt	275 ,687	409 ,950	89 ,125
Total Liabilities	394 ,010	521 ,906	198 ,800
Total Equity	431 ,153	223 ,356	210 ,551
Total Liab. & Equity	825 ,163	745 ,262	409 ,351
CAPITAL (000)			
Total Debt	292 ,062	418 ,594	136 ,640
Preferred Equity	2 ,451	4 ,160	12 ,385
Common Equity	428 ,702	219 ,196	198 ,166

Synopsis:

After a 1994 deal with Rogers Communications, Shaw Communications Inc. obtained full cable coverage in Victoria and Calgary, giving the company a total of 1.6 million subscribers across the four western provinces, Ontario and Nova Scotia. Calgary is now Shaw's largest individual system with 250,000 subscribers. To centralize operations and take advantage of economies of scale, Shaw moved its head office from Edmonton to Calgary in mid-1995.

Shaw bought Classic Communications Ltd. of Richmond Hill, Ontario, and its subsidiary, Suburban Communications, in 1995 for a record breaking $240-million. The purchase price works out to $2,352 per subscriber, or roughly 12 times operating cash flow. Although the price was steep, Shaw said that Classic's customer base made the transaction worthwhile. Class, serving areas north of Toronto, is located in one of the most affluent and fastest-growing communities in Canada.

In 1995, Shaw sold its stake in a British cable service it had acquired in 1994 when it bought CUC Broadcasting. Shaw said it will now focus strictly on its expanding Canadian operations. Shaw retained CUC's 34% stake in the youth channel YTV Canada Inc.

Shaw, along with Rogers Cablesystems and CF Cable TV, plans to invest $19-million in a new company called CableSat. CableSat will deliver 16 pay-per-view channels by beaming signals via satellite to the cable companies. Shaw also joined with Rogers and Videotron Ltd. to set up a Canada-wide network, expected to be operational in 1996, that will enable personal computer users to hook their equipment to cable TV and gain access to the Internet and other on-line services.

Total cable revenue for the six months ended February 28, 1995, was $156-million compared to $134-million for the same period in 1994. In the radio division, revenue reached almost $11-million in the first half of fiscal 1995, up from $9.2-million in 1994. This was due in large part to Shaw's new ownership of Toronto's CFNY-FM, acquired as part of the Rogers deal.

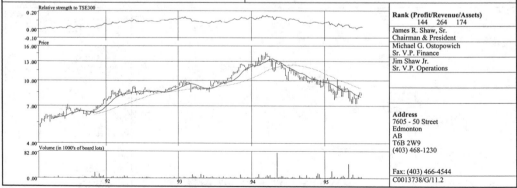

Rank (Profit/Revenue/Assets)
144   264   174

James R. Shaw, Sr.
Chairman & President

Michael G. Ostopowich
Sr. V.P. Finance

Jim Shaw Jr.
Sr. V.P. Operations

Address
7605 - 50 Street
Edmonton
AB
T6B 2W9
(403) 468-1230

Fax: (403) 466-4544
C0013738/G/11.2

For further company information, call Globe Information Services 1-800-268-9128 or (416) 585-5345

SOUTHAM INC.

Exchanges					Stock Symbol
TM	Price (Jun29'95)	14.50	Trailing P/E	24.57	**STM**
	Trailing Yield (%)	1.38	Trailing EPS	0.59	

Period Ending	Dec94	Dec93	Dec92	Dec91	Dec90
Yearly Statistics					
Price-Close	15.50	17.63	15.38	16.38	18.75
Price-High	21.00	19.25	20.38	20.88	32.88
Price-Low	14.25	13.00	14.75	14.75	17.25
P/E-Close	26.72	60.78	nm	nm	625.00
Dividends per Share	0.20	0.20	0.40	0.40	0.80
Dividend Yield (%)	1.29	1.14	2.60	2.44	4.27
Sales per Share	15.73	16.02	19.20	20.01	21.35
EPS before extra. item	0.58	0.29	(4.26)	(2.60)	0.03
Cash Flow per Share	1.46	1.03	0.85	0.28	1.13
Book Value per Share	5.95	5.57	3.74	7.11	9.85
O/S Common Shares	76,443	76,426	63,503	63,278	62,892
Total Revenue	1,202,526	1,176,251	1,171,385	1,179,021	1,227,000
Income before extra.	44,008	21,568	(262,851)	(153,157)	1,403
Cash Flow	111,698	75,953	52,625	16,628	64,885
Debt/Equity	0.27	0.39	1.32	1.48	0.93
Return on Capital (%)	14.22	9.45	(32.01)	(11.09)	4.50
Ret. on Com. Equity (%)	10.00	6.50	(76.44)	(28.65)	0.22
% Change Profit	104.0	108.2	(71.6)	nm	(98.4)
% Change Revenue	2.2	0.4	(0.6)	(3.9)	(26.9)
% Change Assets	(1.7)	2.2	(35.3)	(9.7)	8.6
Preferred Div. Coverage	np	na	np		
Total Div. Coverage	2.9	1.5	0.0		
Interest Coverage	6.2	2.7	0.0		
Current Ratio	1.0	1.0	1.2		
Operating Margin	7.7	5.4	3.1		
Asset Turnover	1.3	1.3	1.3		
5 YEAR RATIOS (%)					
Return on Capital	(3.0)	(2.4)	(0.9)		
Return on Com. Equity	(17.7)	(17.0)	(15.8)		
Profit Growth	(13.0)	(21.7)	na		
Revenue Growth	(6.5)	(5.7)	(4.2)		
Asset Growth	(8.7)	(6.0)	(4.9)		
BALANCE SHEET (000)					
Cash	2,358	51,399	20,823		
Current Assets	293,953	309,303	307,078		
Net Fixed Assets	328,366	318,065	316,542		
Invest's & Advances	18,106	27,051	10,811		
Total Assets	898,933	914,241	894,359		
Short Term Debt	0	51,626	0		
Current Liabilities	288,889	323,778	262,749		
Long Term Debt	124,500	117,922	312,883		
Total Liabilities	444,130	480,844	656,639		
Total Equity	454,803	433,397	237,720		
Total Liab. & Equity	898,933	914,241	894,359		
CAPITAL (000)					
Total Debt	124,500	169,548	312,883		
Preferred Equity	0	7,720	0		
Common Equity	454,803	425,677	237,720		

Business:

SOUTHAM INC. is a leading Canadian information company. It operates daily newspapers in major cities across Canada as well as community papers. The company publishes business information in print and electronic mediums, and produces and manages trade and consumer shows in Canada and the United States.

Date	EPS	DPS	Tot Rev	Inc Bex
Mar 95	0.04	0.05	na	3,400
Dec 94	0.40	0.05	362,914	30,264
Sep 94	0.01	0.05	274,133	502
Jun 94	0.14	0.05	292,425	10,995
Mar 94	0.03	0.05	272,887	2,247
Dec 93	0.40	0.05	348,398	29,284
Sep 93	(0.05)	0.05	266,878	(3,713)
Jun 93	0.04	0.05	288,354	3,164

Synopsis:

For the first quarter of fiscal 1995, Southam Inc.'s newspaper group segment earnings were $13-million, 55.4% higher than in 1994. A recovering advertising market and increased circulation revenues offset soaring newsprint prices. In fiscal 1994, the company saw a slight decline in its newspaper revenue due to the sale of its interest in the Angus Reid Group, but segment income improved by 57% due to lower operating costs.

In daily newspapers, advertising and circulation represented 78% and 22% of revenues respectively. In the volatile advertising market, Southam saw an increase in national advertising, but a decline in both retail and classified advertising. This resulted in an overall decline of 3.9% in advertising linage. Southam is committed to investing $200-million over the next three years to upgrade the Montreal, Vancouver and Windsor printing facilities.

Southam finalized its sale of Coles Book Stores to Smith Books in April 1995. Southam received $35-million in cash, a $17.5-million 8.5% secured note due 1999, and a continuing ownership stake of 12.5% in the combined Smith-Coles entity.

The business communications segment, which includes trade publications in Canada and the United States and a trade and consumer show division, registered segment income of $14.5-million, up 39% from 1993. The assets of three home shows in the U.S. were acquired as were the assets of a construction information centre in Arizona.

Southam expects to improve profitability in 1995 through a more buoyant advertising environment and lower operational costs. Rising newspaper prices will offset some of the gains. Revenues (segment income) by segment in 1994 were: newspaper group, 68% (78%); business communications, 14% (15%); and book retailing, 18% (7%). Canadian operations accounted for 93% of revenues and 94% of segment income.

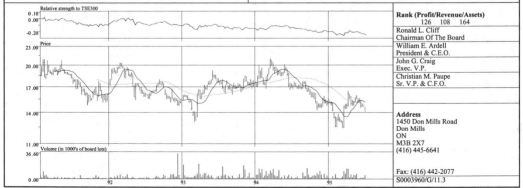

Rank (Profit/Revenue/Assets)
126 108 164

Ronald L. Cliff
Chairman Of The Board

William E. Ardell
President & C.E.O.

John G. Craig
Exec. V.P.

Christian M. Paupe
Sr. V.P. & C.F.O.

Address
1450 Don Mills Road
Don Mills
ON
M3B 2X7
(416) 445-6641

Fax: (416) 442-2077
S0003960/G/11.3

TELE-METROPOLE INC.

Exchanges	Price (Jun29'95)	10.75	Trailing P/E	16.80	Stock Symbol
TM	Trailing Yield (%)	0.00	Trailing EPS	0.64	TM.B

Period Ending	Aug94	Aug93	Aug92	Aug91	Aug90
Yearly Statistics			371D		
Price-Close	9.88	13.25	12.50	11.25	12.75
Price-High	15.25	13.50	14.00	11.75	24.00
Price-Low	8.75	9.25	12.50	8.50	12.00
P/E-Close	329.17	15.06	49.41	nm	nm
Dividends per Share	0.00	0.00	0.00	0.00	0.00
Dividend Yield (%)	0.00	0.00	0.00	0.00	0.00
Sales per Share	20.87	21.22	28.35	19.74	17.53
EPS before extra. item	0.03	0.88	0.19	(1.75)	(1.33)
Cash Flow per Share	1.18	2.53	1.95	(1.50)	(1.38)
Book Value per Share	9.51	9.48	8.80	8.93	10.69
O/S Common Shares	7,944	7,910	7,877	7,835	7,804
Total Revenue	165,929	168,277	167,504	154,901	137,725
Income before extra.	218	6,948	1,502	(13,729)	(10,415)
Cash Flow	9,385	19,994	11,473	(11,692)	(10,737)
Debt/Equity	1.58	1.49	1.70	1.79	1.35
Return on Capital (%)	6.15	12.04	11.43	(3.29)	(4.13)
Ret. on Com. Equity (%)	0.29	9.63	2.88	(17.90)	(11.75)
% Change Profit	(96.9)	246.9	114.6	(31.8)	(959.3)
% Change Revenue	(1.4)	(24.7)	44.2	12.5	22.0
% Change Assets	2.6	(2.8)	(1.9)	(1.9)	28.3

Business:

TELE-METROPOLE INC. is a television broadcasting and production company. It operates French-language television stations in Montreal, Quebec City, Sherbrooke, Rimouski, Trois-Rivieres, and Chicoutimi, Quebec. Through subsidiaries, it supplies production services to advertising agencies, producers, and film makers. Groupe Videotron is the company's major shareholder.

Date	EPS	DPS	Tot Rev	Inc Bex
Feb 95	(0.05)	0.00	38,281	(338)
Nov 94	0.63	0.00	52,731	5,002
Aug 94	(0.52)	0.00	27,052	(4,118)
May 94	0.58	0.00	49,159	4,555
Feb 94	(0.36)	0.00	40,182	(2,842)
Nov 93	0.33	0.00	47,464	2,623
Aug 93	(0.48)	0.00	28,052	(3,780)
May 93	0.74	0.00	50,272	5,815

	Aug94	Aug93	Aug92
Preferred Div. Coverage	np	np	np
Total Div. Coverage	na	na	na
Interest Coverage	1.1	2.0	1.2
Current Ratio	1.0	1.3	1.1
Operating Margin	6.9	12.9	9.4
Asset Turnover	0.7	0.8	1.0
5 YEAR RATIOS (%)			
Return on Capital	4.4	3.9	1.7
Return on Com. Equity	(3.4)	(3.2)	(5.0)
Profit Growth	(29.1)	78.7	(24.5)
Revenue Growth	8.0	10.3	18.0
Asset Growth	4.2	11.8	11.7
BALANCE SHEET (000)			
Cash	0	0	0
Current Assets	60,154	54,890	61,712
Net Fixed Assets	60,897	59,116	62,628
Invest's & Advances	2,999	2,990	3,191
Total Assets	226,321	220,642	226,975
Short Term Debt	28,158	9,166	17,990
Current Liabilities	59,896	43,427	57,800
Long Term Debt	90,853	102,258	99,864
Total Liabilities	150,749	145,685	157,664
Total Equity	75,572	74,957	69,311
Total Liab. & Equity	226,321	220,642	226,975
CAPITAL (000)			
Total Debt	119,011	111,424	117,854
Preferred Equity	0	0	0
Common Equity	75,572	74,957	69,311

Synopsis:

Tele-Metropole Inc. reported a profit of only $218,000 for 1994. This was due in part to the cost overruns incurred by the TVA network's coverage of the Lillehammer Winter Olympics, and the loss of advertising revenue caused by the National Hockey League lockout. Due to stagnant advertising markets and low audience ratings in 1992 and the first half of 1993, Tele-Metropole began its fiscal 1994 in September 1993 with advance advertising sales lagging several million dollars behind the previous year. However, Tele-Metropole began a turnaround in the first half of fiscal 1995, with substantial increases in net income and in cash flow from operations.

The broadcasting sector, made up of six TVA television stations across Quebec, posted revenues almost 7% higher in 1995 than for the same six-month period ending February 1994. Fiscal 1995 revenues were stronger even with the inclusion of the Olympic revenues generated in February 1994.

In February 1995, the Canadian Radio-television and Telecommunications Commission renewed Tele-Metropole's broadcasting licence for its Quebec City station CFCM-TV for only two years, from September 1995 until August 1997. The CRTC denied Tele-Metropole's request to reduce the station's local production from 21 hours to 17 hours 23 minutes a week. The CRTC cited the importance of indigenous programming and Tele-Metropole's failure to honour that obligation in the past.

Tele-Metropole, along with other Quebec companies, plans to apply to the CRTC in 1995 for a French-language pay-per-view channel. The company applied for a similar channel in 1994, but was denied a licence.

In 1995, while keeping strict budgetary limits, Tele-Metropole plans to increase the appeal and quality of its programming and explore new opportunities in communications.

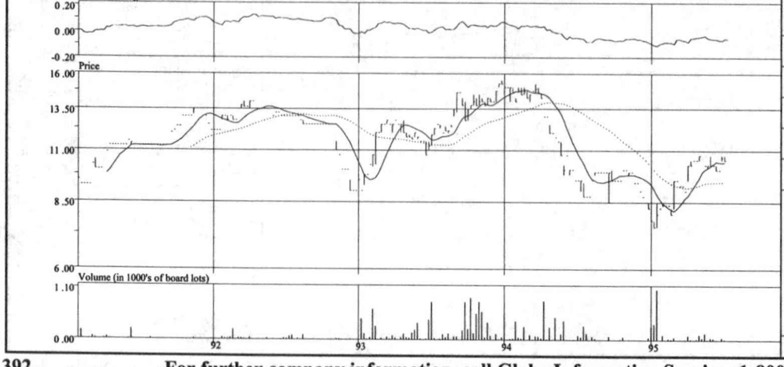

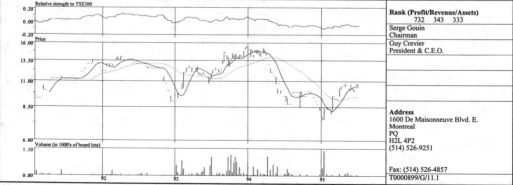

Rank (Profit/Revenue/Assets)
732 343 333

Serge Gouin
Chairman

Guy Crevier
President & C.E.O.

Address
1600 De Maisonneuve Blvd. E.
Montreal
PQ
H2L 4P2
(514) 526-9251

Fax: (514) 526-4857

T0000899/G/11.1

TELEMEDIA INC.

Exchanges	Price (Jun29'95)	3.75	Trailing P/E	13.39	Stock Symbol
TM	Trailing Yield (%)	0.00	Trailing EPS	0.28	**TMD.A**

Period Ending	Aug94	Aug93	Aug92	Aug91	Aug90	Business:
Yearly Statistics						TELEMEDIA INC. is engaged in broadcasting
Price-Close	4.90	4.70	5.00	3.50	2.89	and publishing. It operates radio stations in
Price-High	6.50	5.00	5.00	4.55	6.00	Quebec and Ontario. It publishes and distributes
Price-Low	4.50	3.50	3.15	2.75	2.75	consumer magazines, weekly newspapers,
P/E-Close	49.00	17.41	33.33	nm	nm	books, and consumer coupons.
Dividends per Share	0.00	0.00	0.00	0.00	0.00	
Dividend Yield (%)	0.00	0.00	0.00	0.00	0.00	
Sales per Share	19.70	19.90	20.73	19.38	20.40	
EPS before extra. item	0.10	0.27	0.15	(0.23)	(0.33)	
Cash Flow per Share	0.91	1.06	0.97	0.58	0.55	
Book Value per Share	3.62	3.52	3.24	3.09	3.33	
O/S Common Shares	11,248	11,238	11,121	11,111	11,112	
Total Revenue	220,799	223,163	231,633	215,198	221,553	
Income before extra.	1,081	3,052	1,705	(2,600)	(3,630)	
Cash Flow	10,216	11,873	10,813	6,391	6,059	

Date	EPS	DPS	Tot Rev	Inc Bex
Feb 95	(0.18)	0.00	45,500	(2,000)
Nov 94	0.18	0.00	63,682	1,982
Aug 94	0.03	0.00	52,421	270
May 94	0.25	0.00	60,451	2,822
Feb 94	(0.23)	0.00	44,764	(2,537)
Nov 93	0.05	0.00	64,456	526
Aug 93	0.08	0.00	53,548	860
May 93	0.21	0.00	60,000	2,361

	Aug94	Aug93	Aug92	
Debt/Equity	1.16	1.42	1.66	
Return on Capital (%)	6.96	10.62	10.32	
Ret. on Com. Equity (%)	2.69	8.07	4.84	
% Change Profit	(64.6)	79.0	165.6	
% Change Revenue	(1.1)	(3.7)	7.6	
% Change Assets	(2.2)	3.3	(0.6)	

				Synopsis:
Preferred Div. Coverage	np	np	np	
Total Div. Coverage	na	na	na	
Interest Coverage	1.6	2.3	2.5	
Current Ratio	1.2	1.2	1.4	
Operating Margin	4.3	4.5	5.7	
Asset Turnover	1.4	1.4	1.5	
5 YEAR RATIOS (%)				
Return on Capital	7.0	8.1	10.6	
Return on Com. Equity	(0.2)	0.4	2.0	
Profit Growth	(13.7)	(11.2)	(19.5)	
Revenue Growth	0.5	4.1	10.8	
Asset Growth	1.6	3.2	11.5	
BALANCE SHEET (000)				
Cash	0	0	0	
Current Assets	42,961	47,507	43,849	
Net Fixed Assets	19,981	18,324	17,748	
Invest's & Advances	4,684	4,985	4,293	
Total Assets	158,180	161,799	156,705	
Short Term Debt	4,461	6,275	464	
Current Liabilities	36,426	40,003	31,178	
Long Term Debt	42,774	49,945	59,283	
Total Liabilities	117,478	122,221	120,623	
Total Equity	40,702	39,578	36,082	
Total Liab. & Equity	158,180	161,799	156,705	
CAPITAL (000)				
Total Debt	47,235	56,220	59,747	
Preferred Equity	0	0	0	
Common Equity	40,702	39,578	36,082	

Synopsis:

Telemedia Inc. participated in several major transactions in 1994 and early 1995. In February 1995, Telemedia concluded the purchase of CJEZ-FM 97.3 in Toronto for $16.9-million. The deal gave the company a strong entry in Canada's largest radio market. In December 1994, Telemedia bought CKYC-AM 590 in Toronto for $5-million, and switched The Fan 1430, its all-sports radio station, to the 590 frequency. The new frequency offers the station a much stronger signal and wider coverage of the Toronto market, and is expected to generate improved revenues.

To counter the nearly $4-million loss it incurs annually through its Quebec AM radio operation, Telemedia concluded a 50-50 joint venture with Radiomutuel Inc. The joint venture created an AM radio network in Quebec called Radiomedia. Under the new agreement, Telemedia owns 50% of the leading AM stations in Montreal and Quebec City.

For the second quarter ended February 28, 1995, typically a slow period for the industry, Telemedia's net loss was $2-million, compared to a loss of $2.5-million for the same period last year. For the six-month period ended February 28, 1995, net income was $20,000, compared to a loss of $2-million for the same period last year.

In publishing, revenues for 1994 fell more than 10% from the previous year, reflecting a still-weak market for national advertising. Telemedia acquired the American magazine 'Harrowsmith Country Life' in 1994 and discontinued 'Sportif' and 'Qui Hebdo'.

In January 1995, Telemedia sold its Coupon Clipper free-standing insert business. The company indicated the free-standing insert business no longer fit its strategic plan. Telemedia plans to concentrate on major market radio in Canada, and consumer media properties in Canada and the United States.

Rank (Profit/Revenue/Assets)
650   299   387

Philippe De Gaspe Beaubien
Chairman

R. James McCoubrey
President & C.E.O.

Stephen J. Weir
Exec. V.P. & C.F.O.

Address
Suite 500
1411 Peel Street
Montreal
PQ
H3A 1S5
(514) 845-6291

Fax: (514) 845-3628

T0000750/G/11.3

THOMSON CORPORATION (THE)

Exchanges	Price (Jun29'95)	18.75	Trailing P/E	18.93	Stock Symbol
TM	Trailing Yield (%)	3.47	Trailing EPS	0.73	**TOC**

Period Ending	Dec94	Dec93	Dec92	Dec91	Dec90
Yearly Statistics	US	US	US	US	US
Price-Close	17.25	16.25	14.50	16.00	17.00
Price-High	19.00	16.88	17.63	18.25	17.00
Price-Low	14.75	13.75	12.13	14.00	12.50
P/E-Close	17.03	26.21	39.84	26.36	20.81
Dividends per Share	0.46	0.45	0.45	0.45	0.44
Dividend Yield (%)	2.69	2.78	3.12	2.83	2.59
Sales per Share	10.95	10.24	10.63	10.06	9.80
EPS before extra. item	0.74	0.48	0.30	0.53	0.70
Cash Flow per Share	1.52	1.32	1.32	1.24	1.10
Book Value per Share	5.37	5.00	4.91	5.36	5.24
O/S Common Shares	585,488	576,929	567,250	559,459	552,843
Total Revenue	6,401,000	5,880,000	6,033,000	5,654,000	5,461,000
Income before extra.	437,000	294,000	185,000	320,000	420,000
Cash Flow	884,000	752,000	740,000	688,000	604,000
Debt/Equity	1.11	1.07	1.02	0.69	0.61
Return on Capital (%)	11.24	8.71	7.61	11.30	14.62
Ret. on Com. Equity (%)	14.18	9.78	5.74	9.91	14.02
% Change Profit	48.6	58.9	(42.2)	(23.8)	(7.5)
% Change Revenue	8.9	(2.5)	6.7	3.5	4.2
% Change Assets	13.9	3.9	(3.2)	3.9	13.0

Preferred Div. Coverage	43.7	17.3	9.7
Total Div. Coverage	1.6	1.1	0.7
Interest Coverage	3.6	2.8	2.2
Current Ratio	1.0	1.1	1.1
Operating Margin	12.9	12.5	11.5
Asset Turnover	0.7	0.7	0.8
5 YEAR RATIOS (%)			
Return on Capital	10.7	11.6	15.0
Return on Com. Equity	10.7	11.6	15.4
Profit Growth	(0.8)	(8.8)	(2.4)
Revenue Growth	4.0	4.1	13.9
Asset Growth	6.1	0.0	18.2
BALANCE SHEET (000)			
Cash	514,000	496,000	315,000
Current Assets	1,945,000	1,770,000	1,491,000
Net Fixed Assets	2,215,000	2,059,000	1,940,000
Invest's & Advances	0	0	0
Total Assets	9,358,000	8,213,000	7,907,000
Short Term Debt	232,000	193,000	70,000
Current Liabilities	2,006,000	1,659,000	1,381,000
Long Term Debt	3,376,000	2,993,000	2,983,000
Total Liabilities	6,106,000	5,221,000	4,900,000
Total Equity	3,252,000	2,992,000	3,007,000
Total Liab. & Equity	9,358,000	8,213,000	7,907,000
CAPITAL (000)			
Total Debt	3,608,000	3,186,000	3,053,000
Preferred Equity	110,000	110,000	223,000
Common Equity	3,142,000	2,882,000	2,784,000

Business:

THOMSON CORP. is a diversified communications and travel company. Its principal activities are specialized information publishing, newspaper publishing, and leisure travel. Thomson operates primarily in the United Kingdom, the United States, and Canada.

Date		EPS	DPS	Tot Rev	Inc Bex
Mar 95	US	(0.12)	0.13	1,339,000	(73,000)
Dec 94	US	0.22	0.13	1,632,000	123,000
Sep 94	US	0.45	0.11	2,033,000	263,000
Jun 94	US	0.18	0.11	1,582,000	104,000
Mar 94	US	(0.11)	0.11	1,138,000	(63,000)
Dec 93	US	0.06	0.11	1,446,000	38,000
Sep 93	US	0.39	0.11	1,863,000	223,000
Jun 93	US	0.13	0.11	1,474,000	75,000

Synopsis:

The Thomson Corporation went through a year of reorganizing and restructuring, particularly in its Thomson Newspapers (TN) division. In the United States, Thomson began linking many of its newspapers into strategic marketing groups (SMGs) serving regional markets. The new structure allows newspapers to share services such as administration staff, technology, and financial management. The strategy provides opportunities for the newspapers to support or expand their businesses by developing and launching new broad-based products. These include additional niche publications, database publishing, advertising products, distribution services, and commercial printing.

Although Canada's low population density doesn't allow for as many SMGs, Thomson's Canadian approach is similar. By gathering and distributing information and linking readers with advertisers, Thomson intends to develop its newspapers into broader regional marketing and communications businesses. Thomson decided in 1994 to sell 25 U.S. daily papers. The company also decided to sell 14 daily and seven non-daily Canadian papers that don't fit with its new strategy. Thomson plans to continue with a high level of capital expenditures, especially on technology, such as computer hardware and software and electronic publishing equipment.

In 1994, Thomson Corporations's operating profit by business segment was: Thomson Corporation Publishing International, 39%; Newspapers, 23%; Thomson Financial & Professional Publishing Group, 21%; and U.K.-based Thomson Travel Group, 17%. Thomson's operating profit by geographical segment was: United States, 59%; United Kingdom, 30%; Canada, 8%; and other countries, 3%.

Thomson paid a $0.12 per share dividend in December 1994. This was a 10.6% increase over the previous year.

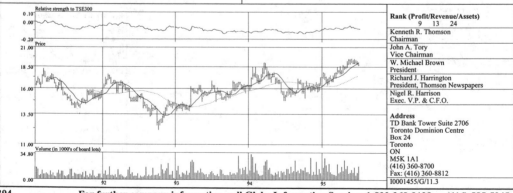

Rank (Profit/Revenue/Assets)
9   13   24
Kenneth R. Thomson
Chairman
John A. Tory
Vice Chairman
W. Michael Brown
President
Richard J. Harrington
President, Thomson Newspapers
Nigel R. Harrison
Exec. V.P. & C.F.O.

Address
TD Bank Tower Suite 2706
Toronto Dominion Centre
Box 24
Toronto
ON
M5K 1A1
(416) 360-8700
Fax: (416) 360-8812
I0001455/G/11.3

For further company information, call Globe Information Services 1-800-268-9128 or (416) 585-5345

TORONTO SUN PUBLISHING CORPORATION

Exchanges	Price (Jun29'95)	11.25	Trailing P/E	28.13	Stock Symbol
T	Trailing Yield (%)	1.78	Trailing EPS	0.40	TSP

Period Ending	Dec94	Dec93	Dec92	Dec91	Dec90
Yearly Statistics					
Price-Close	15.38	13.00	12.00	14.00	16.75
Price-High	16.50	15.50	17.00	18.50	26.13
Price-Low	12.50	12.00	12.00	12.87	16.50
P/E-Close	40.46	nm	120.00	466.67	nm
Dividends per Share	0.20	0.20	0.20	0.20	0.20
Dividend Yield (%)	1.30	1.54	1.67	1.43	1.19
Sales per Share	12.63	12.08	12.35	12.34	12.69
EPS before extra. item	0.38	(2.14)	0.10	0.03	(0.95)
Cash Flow per Share	1.13	0.93	0.89	0.67	0.69
Book Value per Share	9.75	9.49	11.82	11.73	11.87
O/S Common Shares	24,601	24,215	23,811	23,418	23,078
Total Revenue	348,896	328,725	330,510	322,462	323,298
Income before extra.	9,214	(51,163)	2,358	593	(21,637)
Cash Flow	27,602	22,185	21,001	15,440	15,728
Debt/Equity	0.07	0.06	0.06	0.11	0.12
Return on Capital (%)	7.05	(18.61)	2.34	2.05	(9.96)
Ret. on Com. Equity (%)	3.93	(20.02)	0.85	0.22	(7.60)
% Change Profit	118.0	(2,269.8)	297.6	102.7	(202.8)
% Change Revenue	6.1	(0.5)	2.5	(0.3)	(0.3)
% Change Assets	5.2	(12.5)	(1.3)	0.2	(7.9)

Preferred Div. Coverage	np	np	np
Total Div. Coverage	1.9	0.0	0.5
Interest Coverage	69.3	0.0	7.0
Current Ratio	1.1	1.0	1.1
Operating Margin	5.2	1.8	1.6
Asset Turnover	0.9	0.9	0.8
5 YEAR RATIOS (%)			
Return on Capital	(3.4)	(2.9)	4.6
Return on Com. Equity	(4.5)	(3.8)	2.0
Profit Growth	(15.3)	na	(33.7)
Revenue Growth	1.4	2.7	12.0
Asset Growth	(3.5)	(3.2)	7.1
BALANCE SHEET (000)			
Cash	13,044	5,859	6,790
Current Assets	78,277	65,223	62,572
Net Fixed Assets	147,629	149,021	151,076
Invest's & Advances	9,282	4,866	34,098
Total Assets	326,818	310,588	355,115
Short Term Debt	16,410	13,939	16,442
Current Liabilities	68,644	67,209	56,882
Long Term Debt	0	0	0
Total Liabilities	87,009	80,881	73,772
Total Equity	239,809	229,707	281,343
Total Liab. & Equity	326,818	310,588	355,115
CAPITAL (000)			
Total Debt	16,410	13,939	16,442
Preferred Equity	0	0	0
Common Equity	239,809	229,707	281,343

Business:

TORONTO SUN PUBLISHING CORP. is a newspaper publishing company. It operates daily newspapers in Toronto, Ottawa, Calgary, and Edmonton. It owns a 60% interest in Financial Post Co., and a 100% interest in Bowes Publishing, which publishes newspapers and magazines in smaller cities across Canada. The company owns community newspapers in Florida, and commercial printing operations near Washington, D.C.

Date	EPS	DPS	Tot Rev	Inc Bex
Apr 95	0.03	0.00	85,198	716
Dec 94	0.22	0.10	101,542	5,289
Sep 94	0.01	0.00	79,363	202
Jun 94	0.14	0.10	88,986	3,596
Mar 94	0.01	0.00	78,967	127
Dec 93	(2.07)	0.10	90,334	(49,412)
Sep 93	(0.08)	0.00	76,637	(1,951)
Jun 93	0.09	0.10	86,084	2,182

Synopsis:

The Toronto Sun Publishing Corporation was in the black at the end of December 1994. It posted a profit of $9.2-million. For the first quarter ended April 1, 1995, the company reported profit of $716,000 on revenue of $85.2-million, compared with a profit of $127,000 on revenue of $79-million a year earlier.

The Toronto Sun Corporation's stronger performance in 1994 was attributed to benefits from cost-cutting and increased advertising sales. Growth was strong at The Financial Post and The Ottawa Sun, where revenue increased 14% and 10% respectively. The Financial Post, which has yet to make a profit since it moved to daily publication seven years ago, cut its losses in half in 1994 compared to 1993. The Calgary and Edmonton Suns also posted revenue gains.

The biggest threat to Sun Publishing's profits in 1995 is rising newsprint prices. Demand for newsprint particularly in the United States and Asia has dramatically pushed up newsprint prices in Canada. As of April 1995, newsprint prices had risen more than 75% from the rock-bottom levels they reached in late 1993. A new rate hike is expected for the fall of 1995. Sun Publishing reacted by shaving 1.25 inches off the top of its tabloids as of July 1995. The company has budgeted for a 33% or $19-million jump in newsprint expenses for 1995.

Sun Publishing has looked into American urban markets with a view to launching a Sun-style daily newspaper in an American city. It also expects further acquisition opportunities in Canada as rising newsprint prices may force the sale of some papers.

As a step into the new world of multi-media, The Toronto Sun plans to launch an on-line service on the Internet this year. Sun Publishing is also considering possible ventures with its new controlling shareholder, Rogers Communications Inc. Rogers acquired a 62% stake when it bought Maclean Hunter in 1994.

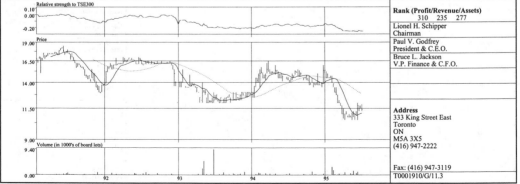

Rank (Profit/Revenue/Assets)		
310	235	277

Lionel H. Schipper
Chairman

Paul V. Godfrey
President & C.E.O.

Bruce L. Jackson
V.P. Finance & C.F.O.

Address
333 King Street East
Toronto
ON
M5A 3X5
(416) 947-2222

Fax: (416) 947-3119
T0001910/G/11.3

TORSTAR CORPORATION

Exchanges	Price (Jun29'95)	21.50	Trailing P/E	19.37	Stock Symbol
TM	Trailing Yield (%)	3.91	Trailing EPS	1.11	**TS.B**

Period Ending	Dec94	Dec93	Dec92	Dec91	Dec90
Yearly Statistics					
Price-Close	23.13	24.25	22.75	22.00	24.00
Price-High	27.50	25.00	25.88	27.25	35.00
Price-Low	21.25	21.13	20.00	20.00	20.00
P/E-Close	21.22	nm	18.80	nm	22.02
Dividends per Share	0.84	0.84	0.84	0.84	0.84
Dividend Yield (%)	3.63	3.46	3.69	3.82	3.50
Sales per Share	26.21	24.23	22.86	23.06	24.29
EPS before extra. item	1.09	(0.24)	1.21	(0.09)	1.09
Cash Flow per Share	2.40	0.34	1.95	1.99	2.40
Book Value per Share	14.14	13.67	14.84	13.32	14.13
O/S Common Shares	40,323	40,127	40,762	41,607	41,481
Total Revenue	1,054,910	981,424	982,606	893,513	938,861
Income before extra.	44,013	(9,602)	48,828	(3,425)	42,212
Cash Flow	96,399	13,725	78,762	76,971	92,430
Debt/Equity	0.43	0.49	0.72	0.60	0.29
Return on Capital (%)	10.85	0.44	8.68	3.06	12.28
Ret. on Com. Equity (%)	7.86	(1.67)	8.42	(0.61)	7.24
% Change Profit	558.4	(119.7)	1,525.6	(108.1)	(55.4)
% Change Revenue	7.5	(0.1)	10.0	(4.8)	(0.7)
% Change Assets	(1.4)	(17.4)	17.5	17.1	6.0

Date	EPS	DPS	Tot Rev	Inc Bex
Mar 95	0.24	0.21	274,573	9,792
Dec 94	0.42	0.21	304,112	17,203
Sep 94	0.12	0.21	262,221	4,901
Jun 94	0.33	0.21	248,771	13,369
Mar 94	0.21	0.21	247,436	8,540
Dec 93	(0.39)	0.21	276,509	(15,753)
Sep 93	(0.05)	0.21	239,124	(1,913)
Jun 93	0.06	0.21	228,838	2,595

Preferred Div. Coverage	978.1	0.0	1,220.7	
Total Div. Coverage	1.3	0.0	1.4	
Interest Coverage	5.9	0.2	2.9	
Current Ratio	1.4	1.2	3.1	
Operating Margin	8.3	3.0	8.9	
Asset Turnover	1.0	0.9	0.7	
5 YEAR RATIOS (%)				
Return on Capital	7.1	9.7	14.2	
Return on Com. Equity	4.2	6.0	9.7	
Profit Growth	(14.2)	na	(9.6)	
Revenue Growth	2.2	0.4	1.6	
Asset Growth	3.5	4.5	9.0	
BALANCE SHEET (000)				
Cash	30,565	98,747	40,004	
Current Assets	289,356	334,221	550,356	
Net Fixed Assets	449,682	475,621	470,081	
Invest's & Advances	29,644	33,002	26,167	
Total Assets	1,018,441	1,032,395	1,250,328	
Short Term Debt	11,424	78,940	13,133	
Current Liabilities	201,336	281,188	180,072	
Long Term Debt	236,206	190,460	424,465	
Total Liabilities	444,003	479,539	641,700	
Total Equity	574,438	552,856	608,628	
Total Liab. & Equity	1,018,441	1,032,395	1,250,328	
CAPITAL (000)				
Total Debt	247,630	269,400	437,598	
Preferred Equity	4,485	4,234	3,786	
Common Equity	569,953	548,622	604,842	

Business:

TORSTAR CORP. is a broadly based information and entertainment communications company. Its operations include The Toronto Star newspaper; Metroland Printing, commercial printers, publishers of community newspapers and distributors of advertising materials; Harlequin Enterprises; and Miles Kimball, a direct catalogue marketer. Torstar owns 50% of Hebdo Mag Inc.

Synopsis:

Torstar's net income for the three months ended March 31, 1995, rose to $9.8-million or 24 cents per share, up from $8.5-million or 21 cents per share for the same period in 1994. Higher profits in the Harlequin book publishing division and the May 1994 acquisition of Frank Schaffer Publications Inc. accounted for the improvement. Frank Schaffer is a leading American publisher of teaching aids and educational products. Torstar expects Frank Schaffer to become its third major operating division after newspapers and book publishing.

Despite competition for advertising dollars and a tight economy, Torstar's four-year decline in revenues for its newspaper segment halted in 1994. Toronto Star advertising volume in 1994 was up 61.1 million lines or 3% from 59.1 lines in 1993. Torstar's Metroland community newspaper division saw linage fall 3% in 1994, mostly due to lower real estate and retail advertising. In the 1995 first quarter, advertising linage in the Toronto Star was up by 2.4%, but down in Metroland papers by 2.7%.

Torstar's revenue increases for the period ended March 31, 1995, up by $11-million from the same period in 1994, were offset by newsprint price increases, up 33% in the first quarter of 1995. Newsprint prices should continue rising in 1995. Torstar's newspaper segment expects the price hikes to increase its costs by $35-million for fiscal 1995.

In 1994, Harlequin Enterprises recorded the best year in its history with operating profits of $70.7-million, up 13% from 1993. Its strategy for future growth is to develop new markets, including China, Russia, the republics of the former Soviet Union, Central and South America, India, and South East Asia. In January 1995, Harlequin published Chinese-language romance novels in China for the first time.

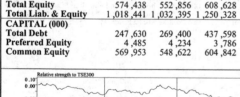

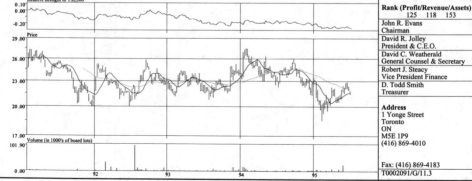

Rank (Profit/Revenue/Assets)
125 118 153

John R. Evans
Chairman

David R. Jolley
President & C.E.O.

David C. Weatherald
General Counsel & Secretary

Robert J. Steacy
Vice President Finance

D. Todd Smith
Treasurer

Address
1 Yonge Street
Toronto
ON
M5E 1P9
(416) 869-4010

Fax: (416) 869-4183
T0002091/G/11.3

For further company information, call Globe Information Services 1-800-268-9128 or (416) 585-5345

WIC WESTERN INTERNATIONAL COMMUNICATIONS LTD.

Exchanges	Price (Jun29'95)		17.37	Trailing P/E		27.15	Stock Symbol
TV	Trailing Yield (%)		2.79	Trailing EPS		0.64	**WIC.B**

Period Ending	Aug94	Aug93	Aug92	Aug91	Aug90
Yearly Statistics					
Price-Close	17.25	15.00	14.25	12.63	11.25
Price-High	19.75	16.88	15.00	14.88	15.75
Price-Low	14.88	14.25	10.00	10.63	10.25
P/E-Close	43.13	107.14	71.25	20.04	12.78
Dividends per Share	0.55	0.55	0.50	0.50	0.50
Dividend Yield (%)	3.19	3.67	3.51	3.96	4.44
Sales per Share	16.04	16.05	15.31	15.49	18.26
EPS before extra. item	0.40	0.14	0.20	0.63	0.88
Cash Flow per Share	2.57	2.39	2.44	2.28	2.45
Book Value per Share	12.28	12.39	12.22	12.64	12.46
O/S Common Shares	24,461	24,231	19,581	17,483	13,598
Total Revenue	393,028	343,983	298,181	240,116	207,463
Income before extra.	9,807	2,995	3,775	9,675	9,810
Cash Flow	62,777	51,179	47,183	34,928	27,390
Debt/Equity	0.87	0.93	1.19	1.52	1.36
Return on Capital (%)	9.87	8.85	8.60	9.98	14.08
Ret. on Com. Equity (%)	3.27	1.11	1.64	4.96	7.33
% Change Profit	227.4	(20.7)	(61.0)	(1.4)	(43.1)
% Change Revenue	14.3	15.4	24.2	15.7	25.9
% Change Assets	(1.1)	10.9	(3.2)	40.9	94.7

Preferred Div. Coverage	np	np	np
Total Div. Coverage	0.7	0.3	0.4
Interest Coverage	2.1	1.6	1.4
Current Ratio	0.9	0.9	1.0
Operating Margin	21.0	20.3	19.6
Asset Turnover	0.6	0.5	0.5
5 YEAR RATIOS (%)			
Return on Capital	10.3	12.3	13.1
Return on Com. Equity	3.7	6.9	8.3
Profit Growth	(10.6)	(14.7)	(2.3)
Revenue Growth	18.9	25.5	25.2
Asset Growth	23.8	25.7	26.6
BALANCE SHEET (000)			
Cash	0	0	0
Current Assets	107,099	101,024	78,971
Net Fixed Assets	126,306	125,210	109,761
Invest's & Advances	32,536	35,261	27,456
Total Assets	691,868	699,524	630,499
Short Term Debt	43,281	42,733	19,223
Current Liabilities	115,188	114,865	77,516
Long Term Debt	218,863	235,995	265,161
Total Liabilities	391,437	399,299	391,198
Total Equity	300,431	300,225	239,301
Total Liab. & Equity	691,868	699,524	630,499
CAPITAL (000)			
Total Debt	262,144	278,728	284,384
Preferred Equity	0	0	0
Common Equity	300,431	300,225	239,301

Business:

WIC WESTERN INTERNATIONAL COMMUNICATIONS LTD. is a broadcasting company. It owns radio stations in Western Canada and Ontario, and has eight television stations in Western Canada and Ontario. The company owns 53.7% of Canadian Satellite Communications Inc. (Cancom), 100% of Allarcom Pay Television Ltd., known as Pay Service Superchannel Moviemax and Home Theatre, and 50% of the Family Channel.

Date	EPS	DPS	Tot Rev	Inc Bex
Feb 95	0.01	0.07	99,165	221
Nov 94	0.47	0.14	116,965	11,425
Aug 94	(0.06)	0.14	90,427	(1,341)
May 94	0.22	0.14	107,357	5,371
Feb 94	(0.08)	0.14	85,373	(1,885)
Nov 93	0.32	0.14	109,871	7,662
Aug 93	(0.08)	0.14	81,366	(1,424)
May 93	0.20	0.14	94,868	4,078

Synopsis:

In 1994, WIC Western International Communications Ltd. revenues came from four segments: television (60%) satellite network services (18%), radio (15%) and pay television. Television revenues amounted to $234-million, an increase of 15% over fiscal 1993.

The Canadian television industry's advertising revenues rose by 2.1% in 1994. The largest increase came in British Columbia at 6.6%. WIC benefited from B.C.'s buoyant economy through its three B.C. stations -- Vancouver's BCTV, Victoria's CHEK, and Kelowna's CHBC. WIC also owns four stations in Alberta, and CHCH in Hamilton, Ontario.

Despite an improved advertising market in 1994, WIC recognizes advertising revenue as sensitive to economic conditions. It is diversifying its revenue sources within broadcasting, increasing its activities in film and video production and post-production, and expanding its subscription revenue base. In 1994, in line with this strategy, WIC launched MovieMax!, a subscriber-based movie pay-TV service in Western Canada. WIC currently owns Edmonton-based Superchannel.

In satellite network services, WIC owns 53.7% of Canadian Satellite Communications Inc. (Cancom). Cancom gives the WIC another source of subscriber-based revenue.

WIC has acquired rights to an innovative cellular distribution technology that could be more cost-effective than cable in delivering television and other communications signals. WIC hopes CellularVision, currently in the experimental stage, will be a source of future revenue.

In radio, WIC owns nine stations in Western Canada, two in Ontario, and three radio networks. Combined operating income from radio was $4.2-million in 1994, compared with $789,000 in 1993.

Rank (Profit/Revenue/Assets)
301   220   192

Frank A. Griffiths
Co-Chairman
Harold A. Roozen
Co-Chairman
Douglas M. Holtby
President & C.E.O.
William F. Ramsey
V.P. & C.F.O.

Address
Suite 1960
One Bentall Centre
505 Burrard Street
Vancouver
BC
V7X 1M6
(604) 687-2844
Fax: (604) 687-4118
W0007859/G/11.1

Page	Company	Fiscal year end	EARNINGS PER SHARE		
			Last Year	Estimate this year	Estimate next year
401	Acklands	Dec-94	1.22	1.40	1.36
402	Beamscope Canada	Dec-94	0.75	na	na
403	EMJ Data Systems	Jul-94	0.41	na	na
404	Finning	Dec-94	1.58	1.92	2.24
405	Marshall Steel	Dec-94	0.26	na	na
406	UAP Inc.	Dec-94	1.37	1.45	1.60
407	Wajax	Dec-94	0.66	1.00	1.20
408	Westburne	Dec-94	0.58	0.94	1.40

Estimates from First Call Corporation, 22 Pittsburgh Street, Boston, MA 02210   (800) 366-9992   Fax (617) 261-5679

Wholesale Distributors

Canadian wholesalers had sales of $20.85-billion in March 1995, a decrease of 0.1% from February and up 12.9% from a year earlier, according to Statistics Canada. Analysts attributed the decline in wholesale activity to higher interest rates. In March, wholesaling of lumber and building materials dropped 1.9% for the month, and machinery, equipment, and supplies dipped 0.7%. Inventories as of March 31, 1995, were $30.29-billion, an increase of 0.6% in the month and 13.1% over last March. The inventories-to-sales ratio at March 31, 1995, increased to 1.45:1 from 1.44:1 at the end of February. Statistics Canada's industrial product price index was 127.7 in May 1995, unchanged from April and up 8.4% from a year earlier. The raw materials price index in May 1995, was 132.4, down 1.1% from April, but up 8.9% from a year earlier.

The new auto deal between Japan and United States may decrease Japanese auto production in Canada and in turn affect the Canadian auto parts industry. Increased Japanese investment in United States assembly plants and a $9-billion (U.S.) increase in parts purchases (50% increase) might mean the end of the Japanese expansion of auto plants in Canada. This would damage Canadian parts makers attempts to do more business with Japanese companies. It also is likely that Japanese parts companies might follow the auto makers and set up plants here, especially considering the close relationships between the makers and suppliers.

While Canadian imports of Japanese-made cars have declined since 1991, imports of vehicle engines, engine parts, and other parts have increased. On a customs basis, the value of engines imported increased to $742-million in 1994 from $345-million in 1991. The value of parts, excluding engines, increased in the same period from $755-million to $1-billion. Exports to Japan of engines and engine parts dropped from $3.3-million in 1991 to a little more than $3-million in 1994. From 1991 to 1994, other parts increased from $38.3-million to $56.2-million. Of auto parts sold to Japanese auto makers, 3.7% go to Japan, about 49% go to Japanese auto makers operating in Canada, and 47% to Japanese auto makers operating in the United States according to an Automotive Parts Manufactures Association survey. Also according to the survey, sales during the period 1992 to 1994 increased 30% overall, while sales to Japanese-based industry increased 55%. The association estimates that sales to the Japanese industry operating in Canada and Japan were worth about $1.5-billion in 1994.

Canadian primary steel production totalled 292,642 tonnes in the week ended March 25, 1995. This was up 4.4% from the previous week and 23.1% from the same week a year ago, when production totalled 237,667 tonnes according to Statistics Canada. Production for the year to date March 25, 1995, totalled 3,377,137 tonnes, an increase of 9.9% from 3,072,949 a year earlier.

ACKLANDS LIMITED

Exchanges	Price (Jun29'95)	11.25	Trailing P/E	9.45	Stock Symbol
TW	Trailing Yield (%)	0.00	Trailing EPS	1.19	ACK

Period Ending	Jan95	Jan94	Jan93	Jan92	Jan91
Yearly Statistics					
Price-Close	11.00	14.25	5.00	4.80	5.88
Price-High	15.00	15.00	6.00	6.00	12.00
Price-Low	10.88	4.75	4.50	4.00	4.90
P/E-Close	8.80	11.59	13.51	21.82	nm
Dividends per Share	0.00	0.00	0.00	0.00	0.00
Dividend Yield (%)	0.00	0.00	0.00	0.00	0.00
Sales per Share	37.27	34.60	23.27	22.77	36.98
EPS before extra. item	1.25	1.23	0.37	0.22	(1.04)
Cash Flow per Share	1.67	1.68	0.73	0.61	(0.44)
Book Value per Share	11.05	9.82	8.20	7.85	7.62
O/S Common Shares	17,337	17,282	13,690	13,630	13,630
Total Revenue	645,747	536,272	315,654	310,713	344,288
Income before extra.	21,645	18,414	5,012	3,048	(9,024)
Cash Flow	28,919	26,012	9,895	8,330	(4,050)
Debt/Equity	0.36	0.24	0.29	0.20	0.24
Return on Capital (%)	12.59	13.14	5.02	4.25	(1.33)
Ret. on Com. Equity (%)	11.98	13.06	4.57	2.89	(10.42)
% Change Profit	17.5	267.4	64.4	133.8	(5.4)
% Change Revenue	20.4	69.9	1.6	(9.8)	(3.7)
% Change Assets	25.2	44.5	14.6	(0.4)	(11.2)
Preferred Div. Coverage	np	np	np		
Total Div. Coverage	na	na	na		
Interest Coverage	7.7	4.9	2.9		
Current Ratio	1.8	2.3	2.0		
Operating Margin	4.5	4.3	2.0		
Asset Turnover	1.8	1.9	1.6		
5 YEAR RATIOS (%)					
Return on Capital	6.7	4.3	0.8		
Return on Com. Equity	4.4	(0.3)	(5.8)		
Profit Growth	73.4	78.4	9.7		
Revenue Growth	12.5	9.0	(4.5)		
Asset Growth	12.9	6.2	(3.3)		
BALANCE SHEET (000)					
Cash	0	0	0		
Current Assets	271,271	218,755	149,388		
Net Fixed Assets	65,918	51,563	38,468		
Invest's & Advances	5,688	5,736	1,660		
Total Assets	352,078	281,123	194,595		
Short Term Debt	60,955	24,387	24,976		
Current Liabilities	149,186	93,553	73,260		
Long Term Debt	7,882	15,814	7,358		
Total Liabilities	160,454	111,419	82,368		
Total Equity	191,624	169,704	112,227		
Total Liab. & Equity	352,078	281,123	194,595		
CAPITAL (000)					
Total Debt	68,837	40,201	32,334		
Preferred Equity	0	0	0		
Common Equity	191,624	169,704	112,227		

Business:

ACKLANDS LTD. distributes automotive after-market parts and industrial supplies and equipment, and occupational health and safety supplies. It supplies wholesalers and industrial, commericial and retail customers across Canada through 19 distribution centres, 318 corporate stores and 334 associate stores across Canada.

Date	EPS	DPS	Tot Rev	Inc Bex
Apr 95	0.18	0.00	179,389	3,060
Jan 95	0.31	0.00	173,303	5,423
Oct 94	0.34	0.00	166,014	5,795
Jul 94	0.36	0.00	158,013	6,277
Apr 94	0.24	0.00	148,417	4,150
Jan 94	0.42	0.00	140,427	7,245
Oct 93	0.46	0.00	150,740	6,363
Jul 93	0.21	0.00	139,903	2,946

Synopsis:

Earnings for Acklands Limited for year ended January 31, 1995, were $21.6-million or $1.25 per share. This was up from $18.4-million or $1.23 per share, an increase of 17% over 1994. The improvement was due to the earnings of companies acquired in 1993 and 1994 and reduced operating costs.

The automotive division distributes replacement parts, accessories, and paint to the mechanic/installer market and the do-it-yourself market. During 1994-95, Acklands acquired a number of regional distributors of auto parts, paint, and supplies, giving the company coast-to-coast coverage in this segment. In October 1994, Acklands also acquired shares of Rose Auto Stores, a retailer in southern Florida. This marked the company's first entry into the United States and into retail, which Acklands feels is a natural and profitable extension of its business. In fiscal 1995, the new acquisitions boosted sales by $46-million.

The demand for industrial segment products, such as welding supplies, maintenance supplies, power tools and fasteners, and workplace safety supplies is driven by industrial activity particularly in the forestry, construction and pipeline, mining and oil and gas. With a slowly expanding North American economy, Acklands feels demand for its products will grow 1-2% in the coming year. It also expects to benefit from the full year impact of its 1995 acquisitions.

In 1995 sales (net earnings) by geographical segment were: Canada, 95% (99.5%); and the U.S., 5% (0.5%). Figures from the U.S. segment represent the period beginning October 2, 1994, the date of the Rose Auto acquisition.

Relative strength to TSE300

Price

Volume (in 1000's of board lots)

Rank (Profit/Revenue/Assets)
204   167   270

K. (Rai) Sahi
Chairman & C.E.O.
Don Turple
V.P. Finance

Address
945 Wilson Avenue
North York
ON
M3K 1E8
(416) 631-5200

Fax: (416) 635-9549
A0000283/G/12.1

BEAMSCOPE CANADA INC.

Exchanges	Price (Jun29'95)	13.75	Trailing P/E	18.33	Stock Symbol
T	Trailing Yield (%)	0.00	Trailing EPS	0.75	BSP

Period Ending	Dec94	Dec93	Dec92	Dec91
Yearly Statistics				
Price-Close	14.25	9.38	n t	n t
Price-High	14.50	10.88	n t	n t
Price-Low	9.00	6.63	n t	n t
P/E-Close	19.00	13.02	n t	n t
Dividends per Share	0.00	0.24	0.00	0.00
Dividend Yield (%)	0.00	2.56	0.00	0.00
Sales per Share	27.62	22.83	18.29	14.81
EPS before extra. item	0.75	0.72	0.03	0.02
Cash Flow per Share	0.83	0.74	0.05	0.03
Book Value per Share	3.65	2.78	0.38	0.35
O/S Common Shares	7,205	6,960	4,575	4,575
Total Revenue	195,886	111,804	83,899	68,098
Income before extra.	5,276	3,520	157	77
Cash Flow	5,894	3,621	226	150
Debt/Equity	0.33	nd	nd	nd
Return on Capital (%)	35.42	59.10	12.12	na
Ret. on Com. Equity (%)	23.12	33.38	9.38	na
% Change Profit	49.9	2,142.0	103.9	na
% Change Revenue	75.2	33.3	23.2	na
% Change Assets	47.9	93.9	30.0	na

Date	EPS	DPS	Tot Rev	Inc Bex
Mar 95	0.16	0.00	51,963	1,147
Dec 94	0.34	0.00	80,267	2,403
Sep 94	0.18	0.00	47,283	1,252
Jun 94	0.07	0.00	33,334	499
Mar 94	0.16	0.00	35,002	1,122
Dec 93	0.29	0.00	50,273	1,741
Sep 93	0.15	0.00	25,607	697
Jun 93	0.05	0.00	14,964	246

	Dec94	Dec93	Dec92
Preferred Div. Coverage	np	np	np
Total Div. Coverage	na	3.0	na
Interest Coverage	na	nd	nd
Current Ratio	1.4	1.4	1.1
Operating Margin	4.7	5.4	4.9
Asset Turnover	2.2	1.8	2.6
5 YEAR RATIOS (%)			
Return on Capital	na	na	na
Return on Com. Equity	na	na	na
Profit Growth	na	na	na
Revenue Growth	na	na	na
Asset Growth	na	na	na
BALANCE SHEET (000)			
Cash	5,488	18,762	10,447
Current Assets	87,080	59,968	31,467
Net Fixed Assets	3,214	736	226
Invest's & Advances	0	0	0
Total Assets	90,886	61,438	31,693
Short Term Debt	8,540	0	0
Current Liabilities	64,224	42,101	29,940
Long Term Debt	0	0	0
Total Liabilities	64,575	42,101	29,940
Total Equity	26,311	19,337	1,753
Total Liab. & Equity	90,886	61,438	31,693
CAPITAL (000)			
Total Debt	8,540	0	0
Preferred Equity	0	0	0
Common Equity	26,311	19,337	1,753

Business:

BEAMSCOPE CANADA INC. sells, markets, and distributes brand name home office products, consumer software, and video entertainment products.

Synopsis:

Beamscope Canada Inc.'s revenues soared 75% and net income climbed 50% in fiscal 1994, as a result of the high demand for home computers, computer software, and video games. In 1994, Beamscope entered into two new ventures. Beamscope Chile S.A., the company's first subsidiary, opened in October 1994 and will distribute similar products as Beamscope in Canada. Beamscope hopes to add $10-million to its revenue in 1995 from its new Chilean operation and is investigating opportunities in other developing countries, where markets tend to be less competitive. A/B Interactive Distribution Inc. is a multimedia product development joint venture with Astral communications Inc. In June 1995, Beamscope entered into an agreement with Advantis Canada and Magder Entertainment to create a video and CD-ROM on how to use the Internet. The product is being launched in the fall of 1995.

In 1994, sales by product category were: home office, 58%; computer software, 23%; video entertainment, 19%. The figures mark a 5% increase over total sales in 1993 in the home office category, and a 2% and 3% drop in software and video respectively. Within the home office category, sales in 1994 were 92% higher than in 1993, the result of increased consumer demand and more affordable home computers. Many of the latest versions of home computers, however, are equipped with built-in CD-ROM drives and multimedia capabilities. These newer functions raise the average selling price of home computers and are expected to contribute to Beamscope's future sales in the category.

Beamscope is continuing to focus on the retail channel, which is expanding. New venues, such as music stores and bookstores, are now selling software, hardware, and video entertainment products. The company expects sales in 1995 will be further enhanced by the launch of such software as IBM's OS/2 Warp and Microsoft Windows '95.

Rank (Profit/Revenue/Assets)
415   317   504

Larry Wasser
President & C.E.O.

Morey Chaplick
Exec. V.P. C.F.O. & Secretary

Address
35 Ironside Crescent
Scarborough
ON
M1X 1G5
(416) 291-0000

Fax: (416) 291-5721
01003507/G/12.1

EMJ DATA SYSTEMS LTD.

Exchanges	Price (Jun29'95)	5.12	Trailing P/E	10.67	Stock Symbol
T	Trailing Yield (%)	0.00	Trailing EPS	0.48	EMJ

Period Ending	Ju l94	Ju l93	Ju l92
Yearly Statistics			
Price-Close	4.10	n t	n t
Price-High	4.50	n t	n t
Price-Low	4.00	n t	n t
P/E-Close	10.00	n t	n t
Dividends per Share	0.00	0.00	0.00
Dividend Yield (%)	0.00	0.00	0.00
Sales per Share	11.89	9.52	7.08
EPS before extra. item	0.41	0.18	0.19
Cash Flow per Share	0.44	0.23	0.23
Book Value per Share	1.90	1.19	1.02
O/S Common Shares	6,794	5,685	5,633
Total Revenue	68,064	53,710	39,909
Income before extra.	2,368	987	1,090
Cash Flow	2,492	1,307	1,321
Debt/Equity	0.42	1.06	0.94
Return on Capital (%)	27.94	17.90	na
Ret. on Com. Equity (%)	24.09	15.77	na
% Change Profit	139.9	(9.4)	na
% Change Revenue	26.7	34.6	na
% Change Assets	38.1	28.4	na
Preferred Div. Coverage	np	np	np
Total Div. Coverage	na	na	na
Interest Coverage	10.4	5.7	6.5
Current Ratio	2.0	1.7	2.1
Operating Margin	6.6	5.9	5.7
Asset Turnover	3.0	3.2	3.1
5 YEAR RATIOS (%)			
Return on Capital	na	na	na
Return on Com. Equity	na	na	na
Profit Growth	na	na	na
Revenue Growth	na	na	na
Asset Growth	na	na	na
BALANCE SHEET (000)			
Cash	0	0	0
Current Assets	20,054	14,116	10,541
Net Fixed Assets	2,384	2,382	2,407
Invest's & Advances	238	146	10
Total Assets	22,993	16,644	12,958
Short Term Debt	5,430	5,723	3,298
Current Liabilities	10,113	8,380	5,119
Long Term Debt	0	1,484	2,104
Total Liabilities	10,113	9,864	7,223
Total Equity	12,880	6,780	5,735
Total Liab. & Equity	22,993	16,644	12,958
CAPITAL (000)			
Total Debt	5,430	7,207	5,402
Preferred Equity	0	0	0
Common Equity	12,880	6,780	5,735

Business:

EMJ DATA SYSTEMS LTD. is a Canadian distributor of computers specializing in Apple, UNIX, Point of Sale and Computer Aided Design Products.

Date	EPS	DPS	Tot Rev	Inc Bex
Apr 95	0.14	0.00	27,127	954
Jan 95	0.13	0.00	24,700	905
Oct 94	0.09	0.00	20,839	608
Jul 94	0.12	0.00	17,690	697
Apr 94	0.12	0.00	19,465	689
Jan 94	0.09	0.00	16,205	535
Oct 93	0.08	0.00	14,704	447

Synopsis:

EMJ Data Systems currently serves more than 15,000 Canadian resellers with products and peripherals for DOS, Windows, Unix, and Apple microcomputers. It also sells CAD and retail point-of-sale products and telephony applications. In 1994, EMJ became a public company.

Net earnings for the company in fiscal 1994 rose 139% to $2.4-million from approximately $1-million in 1993. As of the nine months ended April 1995, earnings grew to $2.5-million, compared to $1.7-million in 1993. EMJ reported especially strong sales growth in the Apple, Point of Sale, and Unix markets.

EMJ plans to continue to focus on offering specialty, high performance products and in-depth technical service. The company's sales increases are largely driven by increased purchases of information technology by corporations. EMJ feels improved corporate profits over the early 1990s and corporate downsizing will continue to drive the need for new technology. In addition, new products and services such as bar coding, the Internet, and new generations of microprocessors create new needs that EMJ feels will provide growth for the company.

In June 1994, EMJ bought all the issued and outstanding shares of TCR Technologies Limited, a manufacturer and distributor of computer equipment. While EMJ is focusing on reducing costs due to the competitive nature of its business and the resulting declines in gross margins, it plans to continue to consider other acquisitions of regional distributors.

EMJ has five offices in Canada and three in the United States. It plans to open a European office in 1995. In 1994, sales amounted to $58-million in Canada and $10-million in the U.S. EMJ reported a 38% increase in sales in 1994 for the U.S., and a 25% sales growth in Canada.

Relative strength to TSE300 / Price / Volume (in 1000's of board lots) — chart 1992–1995

Rank (Profit/Revenue/Assets)
548 487 839

James A. Estill
President & C.E.O.
Glen R. Estill
V.P. & C.F.O.

Address
P.O. Box 1012
Guelph
ON
N1H 6N1
(519) 837-2444

Fax: (519) 836-1914
01003701/G/12.1

FINNING LTD.

| Exchanges | Price (Jun29'95) | 21.25 | Trailing P/E | 1.97 | Stock Symbol |
| TM | Trailing Yield (%) | 8.38 | Trailing EPS | 10.76 | FTT |

Period Ending	Dec94	Dec93	Dec92	Dec91	Dec90
Yearly Statistics					
Price-Close	19.50	19.00	12.00	13.50	12.25
Price-High	24.13	21.75	14.50	15.63	17.00
Price-Low	18.38	11.75	10.50	11.75	10.25
P/E-Close	12.19	31.67	200.00	135.00	13.92
Dividends per Share	0.08	0.18	0.15	0.21	0.46
Dividend Yield (%)	0.41	0.95	1.25	1.52	3.76
Sales per Share	37.98	28.69	24.78	25.47	32.84
EPS before extra. item	1.60	0.60	0.06	0.10	0.88
Cash Flow per Share	4.61	3.20	2.81	3.06	3.44
Book Value per Share	11.58	9.90	8.78	9.11	9.28
O/S Common Shares	38,513	38,133	33,685	33,528	33,320
Total Revenue	1,457,538	1,042,957	832,737	851,370	1,091,217
Income before extra.	61,421	22,271	2,878	4,612	30,283
Cash Flow	176,764	116,371	94,546	102,180	114,467
Debt/Equity	1.35	1.23	1.59	1.47	1.63
Return on Capital (%)	14.38	8.64	5.91	6.77	13.48
Ret. on Com. Equity (%)	14.88	6.53	0.67	1.12	9.80
% Change Profit	175.8	673.8	(37.6)	(84.8)	(28.2)
% Change Revenue	39.8	25.2	(2.2)	(22.0)	20.7
% Change Assets	25.7	12.9	(1.6)	(3.2)	10.8

Preferred Div. Coverage	404.1	76.3	3.3
Total Div. Coverage	6.1	3.2	0.5
Interest Coverage	3.3	2.0	1.0
Current Ratio	1.7	1.4	1.3
Operating Margin	9.4	6.8	5.6
Asset Turnover	1.1	1.0	0.9
5 YEAR RATIOS (%)			
Return on Capital	9.8	10.6	12.6
Return on Com. Equity	6.6	7.1	10.3
Profit Growth	7.9	(9.6)	(36.0)
Revenue Growth	10.0	5.5	4.7
Asset Growth	8.4	10.7	9.8
BALANCE SHEET (000)			
Cash	0	0	0
Current Assets	1,003,763	675,808	587,329
Net Fixed Assets	324,023	146,023	123,505
Invest's & Advances	0	223,080	223,001
Total Assets	1,376,883	1,095,296	970,007
Short Term Debt	287,474	280,176	314,805
Current Liabilities	577,260	499,027	452,414
Long Term Debt	316,614	188,067	175,458
Total Liabilities	928,364	713,847	661,295
Total Equity	448,519	381,449	308,712
Total Liab. & Equity	1,376,883	1,095,296	970,007
CAPITAL (000)			
Total Debt	604,088	468,243	490,263
Preferred Equity	2,661	3,858	13,050
Common Equity	445,858	377,591	295,662

Business:

FINNING LTD. sells, services and finances Caterpillar heavy equipment and complementary equipment in western and northern Canada and through a wholly owned subsidiary, Finning Limited, in the southwest and Industrial Midlands of England, Wales, Scotland and Poland and through Gildemeister S.A.C., in Chile.

Date	EPS	DPS	Tot Rev	Inc Bex
Mar 95	0.52	0.10	448,838	20,010
Dec 94	3.28	0.64	380,052	15,581
Sep 94	3.52	0.64	341,248	17,168
Jun 94	3.44	0.40	390,762	16,393
Mar 94	2.56	0.40	345,476	12,279
Dec 93	1.76	1.04	338,835	8,436
Sep 93	1.20	0.24	253,261	5,519
Jun 93	1.12	0.24	232,880	4,992

Synopsis:

Sparked by a resurgence in all the markets it serves, Finning Ltd. realized record results both in 1994 and the first quarter of fiscal 1995. Finning derives more than 85% of revenues from the sale, financing, and customer support for Caterpillar mobile equipment and engines. The company, which operates in Western Canada, the United Kingdom, Poland, and Chile, benefited from growth in the mining, forestry, pipeline and natural gas, and construction sectors. Finning reported a 21% increase in equipment and service volume in 1994.

For the first quarter of 1995, revenue from the company's Canadian operations jumped 30%. All markets served in Western Canada showed an increase over 1994, with particular strength shown in the forestry industry. Revenue for the quarter from the European operations increased 18%, with notable gains in revenue from construction and quarrying. In addition, due to higher volumes and lower costs, net income for the quarter rose 70%.

In 1994, Finning benefited from the first full year of its Chilean operation, Gildemeister S.A.C. Revenues for the year were around $241-million. In the first quarter of 1995, revenues increased 43% and net income 223% over the same three-month period in 1994.

Revenues from Finning's geographical segments in 1994 were: Canada, 60%; Europe, 23%; Chile, 17%. Finning's equipment sales accounted for 62% of revenues, while customer support services contributed 38% to revenues. In Canada, 1994 product deliveries by market in terms of sales dollars were: forestry, 33%; mining 25%; construction, 20%; pipeline, 13%; government, 6%; other, 3%.

In February 1995, Finning announced a regular dividend of $0.10 per share on the outstanding common shares without par value. The dividend is double the amount paid in the same quarter in 1994.

Rank (Profit/Revenue/Assets)		
100	86	135

W.R. Wyman
Chairman

James F. Shepard
President & C.E.O.

Richard T. Mahler
V.P. & C.F.O.

Address
555 Great Northern Way
Vancouver
BC
V5T 1E2
(604) 872-4444

Fax: (604) 872-2994
F0000788/G/12.1

MARSHALL STEEL LIMITED

Exchanges		Price (Jun29'95)	2.50	Trailing P/E		6.94	Stock Symbol
M		Trailing Yield (%)	20.00	Trailing EPS		0.36	**MS.A**

Period Ending	Dec94	Dec93	Dec92	Dec91	Dec90
Yearly Statistics					
Price-Close	1.95	1.65	0.75	1.65	2.65
Price-High	2.50	2.50	1.65	2.50	3.70
Price-Low	1.50	1.50	0.75	1.50	2.20
P/E-Close	7.50	3.51	nm	nm	nm
Dividends per Share	0.50	0.00	0.00	0.08	0.15
Dividend Yield (%)	25.64	0.00	0.00	4.55	5.66
Sales per Share	5.20	3.77	5.13	8.38	14.05
EPS before extra. item	0.26	0.47	(0.92)	(1.99)	(0.12)
Cash Flow per Share	0.37	0.24	0.05	(1.37)	1.09
Book Value per Share	2.96	3.19	2.70	3.35	5.42
O/S Common Shares	8,199	8,294	8,536	8,536	8,530
Total Revenue	45,051	40,881	45,177	71,933	121,761
Income before extra.	2,138	3,967	(7,878)	(16,981)	(1,053)
Cash Flow	3,024	2,018	408	(11,699)	9,332
Debt/Equity	0.38	0.10	nd	0.36	0.25
Return on Capital (%)	18.94	20.88	(35.34)	(48.07)	3.76
Ret. on Com. Equity (%)	8.43	16.04	(35.35)	(45.41)	(2.20)
% Change Profit	(46.1)	150.4	53.6	(1,512.6)	61.5
% Change Revenue	10.2	(9.5)	(37.2)	(40.9)	(8.5)
% Change Assets	10.0	31.3	(36.1)	(40.4)	(18.1)
Preferred Div. Coverage	na	na	0.0		
Total Div. Coverage	0.5	na	0.0		
Interest Coverage	2.2	30.5	0.0		
Current Ratio	1.8	2.3	1.9		
Operating Margin	(1.4)	(3.6)	1.1		
Asset Turnover	0.9	0.7	1.3		
5 YEAR RATIOS (%)					
Return on Capital	(8.0)	(11.7)	(13.1)		
Return on Com. Equity	(58.5)	(14.6)	(16.2)		
Profit Growth	na	1.6	na		
Revenue Growth	(19.5)	(22.4)	(18.1)		
Asset Growth	(14.7)	(13.2)	(13.4)		
BALANCE SHEET (000)					
Cash	0	7,439	4,077		
Current Assets	26,364	25,597	18,549		
Net Fixed Assets	18,443	15,113	11,932		
Invest's & Advances	1,232	856	0		
Total Assets	48,564	44,161	33,628		
Short Term Debt	3,309	483	0		
Current Liabilities	14,730	11,380	9,930		
Long Term Debt	5,905	2,269	0		
Total Liabilities	24,261	17,695	10,617		
Total Equity	24,303	26,466	23,011		
Total Liab. & Equity	48,564	44,161	33,628		
CAPITAL (000)					
Total Debt	9,214	2,752	0		
Preferred Equity	10	10	10		
Common Equity	24,293	26,456	23,001		

Business:

MARSHALL STEEL LTD. operates as a distributor, processor, fabricator and erector of structural steel products primarily in Canada and the United States. It has operations in Ontario, Quebec, Massachusetts, and Tennessee.

Date	EPS	DPS	Tot Rev	Inc Bex
Mar 95	0.15	0.00	18,194	1,234
Dec 94	0.16	0.00	16,786	1,350
Sep 94	(0.01)	0.50	10,104	(108)
Jun 94	0.06	0.00	9,041	504
Mar 94	0.05	0.00	9,120	392
Dec 93	(0.26)	0.00	17,700	(2,278)
Sep 93	0.16	0.00	4,706	1,339
Jun 93	0.48	0.00	9,810	4,124

Synopsis:

In 1994, Marshall Steel continued its diversification program. The company launched the program after losses in the depressed structural steel market during the late 1980s and early 1990s. As a result, Marshall Steel shut down its Henderson operations in Montreal in 1993. In 1994, the corporation entered into purchase and sale agreements to sell two of the five Montreal properties. The closing of these properties occurred over 1994-1995. Marshall continues to market the remaining three surplus properties.

As part of its diversification, Marshall has acquired steel businesses in related fields that cater to their existing customers. Its wholly owned pipe fitting operation, Henderson Barwick Inc., acquired the assets of CE Pipe and all the shares of Alloytec Mechanical Limited in mid-1994. These acquisitions added to the product range and the pipe fitting capabilities of the corporation. The 1994 pipe and fittings revenues were more than double that of 1993, mainly due to the acquisitions.

In 1993, Marshall acquired control of Falvo, which manufactures tank heads through its Conrex Steel Limited subsidiary. In June 1994, Conrex acquired CE Macpherson, expanding the size range of the tank heads Conrex can produce. Revenues from tank heads, including those of CE Macpherson for six months, were $6-million. This compares to $1.4-million in 1993.

Marshall's wholly owned Norsteel Ltd. carries on a structural steel distribution operation based in Laval, Quebec. Sales from the continuing operations of the division increased by 35% in 1994 over 1993. Sales from Marshall's structural steel fabrication operation, on the other hand, declined by 43% in 1994. This was due to a stagnant market in fabricated structural steel in Quebec over the past several years.

In 1994, Marshall paid its shareholders dividends of $0.50 per share, its first dividend payment since 1991.

Rank (Profit/Revenue/Assets)
467 585 666

Stanley R. Hawkins
Chairman & President

Cecil S. Hawkins
Chief Executive Officer

Lucien Melancon
Senior Vice President

Address
807 Marshall Street
Laval
PQ
H7S 1S9

M0021233/G/12.1

UAP INC.

Exchanges	Price (Jun29'95)	16.25	Trailing P/E	12.04	Stock Symbol
TM	Trailing Yield (%)	2.18	Trailing EPS	1.35	**UAP.A**

Period Ending	Dec94	Dec93	Dec92	Dec91	Dec90	**Business:**
Yearly Statistics						UAP INC. is a manufacturer and wholesaler of
Price-Close	14.50	15.33	12.00	11.00	10.67	automotive parts and accessories. It imports,
Price-High	17.50	16.00	12.00	12.17	12.67	sells and distributes auto parts and accessories
Price-Low	13.25	11.00	10.00	10.17	9.42	and rebuilds all parts, accessories and
P/E-Close	10.58	15.65	16.36	16.02	14.68	equipment vital to maintenance and repair of
Dividends per Share	0.34	0.31	0.31	0.31	0.31	vehicles. It operates 14 distribution centres and
Dividend Yield (%)	2.35	2.00	2.56	2.79	2.88	a network of more than 3,500 corporate,
Sales per Share	39.71	34.71	32.90	32.35	29.33	associate and bannered outlets in Canada.
EPS before extra. item	1.37	0.98	0.73	0.69	0.73	
Cash Flow per Share	2.06	1.61	1.31	1.35	1.26	
Book Value per Share	12.26	11.23	10.62	10.20	9.82	
O/S Common Shares	14,716	14,701	14,275	14,080	14,075	
Total Revenue	583,865	502,288	464,435	455,391	412,761	
Income before extra.	20,047	14,115	10,208	9,560	10,126	
Cash Flow	30,244	23,339	18,449	18,947	17,699	

Date	EPS	DPS	Tot Rev	Inc Bex
Mar 95	0.19	0.10	160,140	2,714
Dec 94	0.35	0.09	150,140	5,175
Sep 94	0.41	0.09	153,033	5,861
Jun 94	0.40	0.09	153,246	5,966
Mar 94	0.21	0.09	127,446	3,045
Dec 93	0.24	0.08	126,548	3,488
Sep 93	0.29	0.08	131,723	4,271
Jun 93	0.36	0.08	134,512	5,094

	Dec94	Dec93	Dec92	
Debt/Equity	0.55	0.30	0.35	
Return on Capital (%)	16.30	13.59	11.79	
Ret. on Com. Equity (%)	11.60	8.91	6.92	
% Change Profit	42.0	38.3	6.8	
% Change Revenue	16.2	8.2	2.0	
% Change Assets	32.2	6.5	6.0	

				Dec91	Dec90
Debt/Equity				0.37	0.39
Return on Capital (%)				12.43	14.15
Ret. on Com. Equity (%)				6.79	7.49
% Change Profit				(5.6)	(22.2)
% Change Revenue				10.3	1.2
% Change Assets				11.7	2.9

	Dec94	Dec93	Dec92
Preferred Div. Coverage	np	np	np
Total Div. Coverage	4.1	3.3	2.4
Interest Coverage	9.9	9.1	4.4
Current Ratio	2.3	3.6	3.6
Operating Margin	7.2	6.0	5.2
Asset Turnover	1.4	1.6	1.6
5 YEAR RATIOS (%)			
Return on Capital	13.7	13.7	13.8
Return on Com. Equity	8.3	8.3	8.6
Profit Growth	9.0	9.2	4.9
Revenue Growth	7.4	7.3	7.4
Asset Growth	11.3	9.2	10.4
BALANCE SHEET (000)			
Cash	3,778	3,735	3,379
Current Assets	318,833	233,647	216,144
Net Fixed Assets	67,347	62,325	63,012
Invest's & Advances	4,601	2,331	1,458
Total Assets	404,797	306,187	287,400
Short Term Debt	58,211	10,859	10,924
Current Liabilities	139,052	65,329	60,789
Long Term Debt	40,766	39,401	41,394
Total Liabilities	224,325	141,058	135,778
Total Equity	180,472	165,129	151,622
Total Liab. & Equity	404,797	306,187	287,400
CAPITAL (000)			
Total Debt	98,977	50,260	52,318
Preferred Equity	0	0	0
Common Equity	180,472	165,129	151,622

Synopsis:

In 1994, UAP Inc. focused on expanding its geographical base particularly in Ontario, Manitoba, and Saskatchewan. As of December 1994, UAP's network of corporate and associate wholesalers had 68 more outlets than in 1993, due to recruitment of new affiliates and 26 new acquisitions. UAP's sales rose by 16.2% in fiscal 1994. Its net earnings of $20-million marked a 42% increase over 1993, and set a record for the company.

Of the 26 acquisitions made by the automotive group in 1994, the most significant was Fort Ignition Limited of Winnipeg, which added 36 new points of sale to UAP's wholesalers network, all in Central and Western Canada. On an annual basis, the acquisition is expected to add $57-million in sales volume. In 1994, UAP also developed commercial banners, such as Autopro Mechanical and Autopro Collision, UAP/NAPA Member Installer, and UAP/NAPA Certified Bodyshop. NAPA is an arm of Genuine Parts Co. of Atlanta, which has an interest in UAP. The banners are used by garages and collision repair shops to promote their use of UAP services and products.

UAP reorganized its industrial division in 1994 into three groups. Its Cadel, Premium Industrial, and CHV Hydraulics divisions were placed under the Industrial Group banner. The group supplies parts and equipment for production lines, railways, manufacturing and agricultural and industrial machinery. The Heavy Vehicle Parts Group gained market share in 1994 from its 1993 acquisition of Wheel & Rim Company of Canada, which operates nine branches in Ontario and one in Quebec. The Diesel and Rebuilding Group provides parts and services for diesel engines.

UAP's capital expenditure budget for 1995 is $17-million. It will be used to increase productivity by expanding the capacity and performance of its computer systems, and by modernizing its distribution facilities.

In early 1995, UAP increased its dividends from $0.085 to $0.10 per Class A Share and from $0.0746 to $0.09 per Class B Share.

Rank (Profit/Revenue/Assets)		
217	174	248

Jean Douville
Chairman & C.E.O.

Robert Martin
V.P. Finance & Secretary

Address
7025 Ontario Street East
Montreal
PQ
H1N 2B3
(514) 256-5031

Fax: (514) 256-8469

U0000192/G/12.1

For further company information, call Globe Information Services 1-800-268-9128 or (416) 585-5345

WAJAX LIMITED

Exchanges	Price (Jun29'95)	9.37	Trailing P/E		15.89	Stock Symbol
TM	Trailing Yield (%)	0.00	Trailing EPS		0.59	WJX.A

Period Ending	Dec94	Dec93	Dec92	Dec91	Dec90	Business:
Yearly Statistics						WAJAX LTD. is the controlling entity in a
Price-Close	9.00	9.38	6.38	7.00	6.75	family of subsidiary companies engaged in the
Price-High	9.88	9.75	7.75	8.75	11.50	distribution and servicing of industrial
Price-Low	7.75	5.50	5.50	6.00	6.25	equipment and heavy machinery in the forestry,
P/E-Close	19.57	72.11	91.07	50.00	51.92	mining, steel, construction, oil and gas, and
Dividends per Share	0.00	0.00	0.00	0.28	0.50	utility sectors.
Dividend Yield (%)	0.00	0.00	0.00	4.00	7.41	
Sales per Share	36.34	33.51	28.91	30.13	34.61	
EPS before extra. item	0.46	0.13	0.07	0.14	0.13	
Cash Flow per Share	1.15	0.63	0.48	0.72	0.37	
Book Value per Share	8.05	9.93	7.56	7.47	7.61	
O/S Common Shares	11,287	8,628	8,545	8,573	8,571	
Total Revenue	404,519	287,398	247,865	258,266	296,913	
Income before extra.	5,091	1,088	574	1,170	1,083	
Cash Flow	12,847	5,407	4,121	6,169	3,170	

Date	EPS	DPS	Tot Rev	Inc Bex
Mar 95	0.19	0.00	119,066	2,115
Dec 94	0.03	0.00	126,709	268
Sep 94	0.21	0.00	103,103	2,415
Jun 94	0.16	0.00	94,379	1,793
Mar 94	0.06	0.00	80,328	615
Dec 93	0.07	0.00	88,760	582
Sep 93	0.05	0.00	72,455	442
Jun 93	0.05	0.00	67,187	440

	Dec94	Dec93	Dec92	Dec91	Dec90
Debt/Equity	0.76	0.87	0.95	1.01	1.24
Return on Capital (%)	9.76	5.67	5.87	6.60	8.95
Ret. on Com. Equity (%)	5.77	1.45	0.89	1.81	1.62
% Change Profit	367.9	89.5	(50.9)	8.0	69.2
% Change Revenue	40.8	15.9	(4.0)	(13.0)	(5.9)
% Change Assets	11.6	34.5	(0.1)	(12.7)	(11.1)

				Synopsis:
Preferred Div. Coverage	np	np	np	Wajax Limited benefited in 1994 from a growing economy, particularly in
Total Div. Coverage	na	na	na	Alberta and Saskatchewan where forestry, oil and gas and construction markets
Interest Coverage	2.8	1.5	1.3	are expanding. Wajax's growth in the West was also helped by the first full year
Current Ratio	2.3	1.6	2.1	of operation for its British Columbia Cypress Equipment.
Operating Margin	5.0	2.8	3.0	In July 1994, Wajax bought Eastern Hydraulic Group, which includes Teris
Asset Turnover	1.6	1.3	1.5	Hydraulics in Alberta and A.E. Hydraulique in Quebec. The new business was
5 YEAR RATIOS (%)				amalgamated with the company's existing Affiliated Dynesco business to form
Return on Capital	7.4	7.3	7.8	Wajax Fluid Power division. This will develop into a long-term core business for
Return on Com. Equity	2.3	1.3	0.7	Wajax.
Profit Growth	51.4	32.7	(38.9)	Western Canada now generates more than half of the company's gross revenues,
Revenue Growth	5.0	(0.7)	(1.4)	while approximately 20% comes from Quebec and another 20% from the
Asset Growth	3.1	2.9	(2.5)	Maritimes and Ontario combined. Wajax sees a lack in its business base in
BALANCE SHEET (000)				Central and Eastern Canada, and aims to correct this deficiency. Thus in 1995, the
Cash	0	0	0	company bought Hydrofor Inc., a Quebec distributor of forestry and construction
Current Assets	211,831	168,421	135,761	equipment. Wajax also announced its intention to acquire Detroit Diesel-Allison
Net Fixed Assets	24,913	26,005	20,065	Canada East, which distributes and services Detroit Diesel, Perkins and Volvo
Invest's & Advances	0	0	0	Penta engines, Allison transmissions and Spectrum electrical generators in
Total Assets	245,986	220,342	163,858	Quebec and the Maritimes. These acquisitions, financed through the company's
Short Term Debt	8,168	42,769	27,167	bank facilities, are part of the company's strategy of strengthening its core
Current Liabilities	94,057	102,550	65,228	businesses while reducing its exposure to localized business cycles.
Long Term Debt	60,845	32,127	34,064	As a result of its regional growth, Wajax decided in 1994 to create a more
Total Liabilities	155,146	134,677	99,292	decentralized structure. It downsized the corporate executive office, relocated
Total Equity	90,840	85,665	64,566	senior operational managers closer to their operation sites, and moved C.E.O. and
Total Liab. & Equity	245,986	220,342	163,858	C.F.O offices to Vancouver.
CAPITAL (000)				
Total Debt	69,013	74,896	61,231	
Preferred Equity	0	0	0	
Common Equity	90,840	85,665	64,566	

Rank (Profit/Revenue/Assets)
420 217 320

H. Gordon MacNeill
Chairman

John Powell
President & C.E.O.

Laurence G. Sellyn
V.P. Fin. & C.F.O. & Treas.

Address
Place Mercantile Suite 1750
Suite 1750
770 Sherbrooke Street West
Montreal
PQ
H3A 1G1
(514) 849-0583
Fax: (514) 849-8493
W0000203/G/12.1

WESTBURNE INC.

Exchanges	Price (Jun29'95)		10.87	Trailing P/E		17.26	Stock Symbol
TM	Trailing Yield (%)		0.00	Trailing EPS		0.63	**WBI**

Period Ending	Dec94	Dec93	Dec92	Dec91	Dec90
Yearly Statistics					
Price-Close	11.63	8.13	4.30	7.13	7.50
Price-High	11.63	8.13	9.13	9.63	10.38
Price-Low	8.00	4.20	4.00	6.88	5.50
P/E-Close	20.04	nm	nm	nm	15.31
Dividends per Share	0.00	0.00	0.12	0.26	0.26
Dividend Yield (%)	0.00	0.00	2.79	3.65	3.47
Sales per Share	53.66	57.60	56.62	57.17	63.23
EPS before extra. item	0.58	(0.80)	(0.29)	(0.73)	0.49
Cash Flow per Share	1.19	0.55	0.39	0.12	1.15
Book Value per Share	9.03	8.63	9.45	9.76	10.71
O/S Common Shares	46,936	37,351	37,403	37,367	37,331
Total Revenue	2,277,318	2,165,456	2,130,914	2,152,441	2,371,653
Income before extra.	25,400	(29,783)	(10,828)	(27,350)	18,197
Cash Flow	50,206	20,624	14,726	4,339	42,836
Debt/Equity	0.80	1.53	1.42	1.43	1.46
Return on Capital (%)	9.50	0.99	3.81	2.17	10.72
Ret. on Com. Equity (%)	6.81	(8.82)	(3.02)	(7.16)	4.59
% Change Profit	185.3	(175.1)	60.4	(250.3)	(54.7)
% Change Revenue	5.2	1.6	(1.0)	(9.2)	(11.3)
% Change Assets	(8.0)	0.2	(1.9)	(5.7)	(5.1)

Business:

WESTBURNE INC. devotes its resources to the wholesale distribution of plumbing, heating, water works, PVF air conditioning, refrigeration, electrical and electronic supplies. Its major markets are the residential, commercial and industrial building and renovation industry, engineering construction, and the replacement market for electrical and mechanical machinery.

Date	EPS	DPS	Tot Rev	Inc Bex
Mar 95	0.03	0.00	486,567	1,301
Dec 94	0.17	0.00	571,936	7,658
Sep 94	0.27	0.00	623,960	12,121
Jun 94	0.16	0.00	574,660	6,466
Mar 94	(0.02)	0.00	506,762	(845)
Dec 93	(0.74)	0.00	554,806	(27,434)
Sep 93	0.09	0.00	607,629	3,511
Jun 93	0.02	0.00	535,764	861

Preferred Div. Coverage	np	np	np
Total Div. Coverage	na	na	0.0
Interest Coverage	2.2	0.2	0.7
Current Ratio	2.8	2.6	2.2
Operating Margin	2.8	1.6	1.5
Asset Turnover	2.2	2.0	1.9
5 YEAR RATIOS (%)			
Return on Capital	5.4	6.6	9.7
Return on Com. Equity	(1.5)	(0.3)	5.3
Profit Growth	(8.8)	na	na
Revenue Growth	(3.2)	(1.0)	4.1
Asset Growth	(4.2)	(1.2)	6.7
BALANCE SHEET (000)			
Cash	0	9,590	17,140
Current Assets	726,815	788,703	776,491
Net Fixed Assets	89,530	111,495	113,832
Invest's & Advances	3,643	2,225	2,405
Total Assets	1,009,924	1,097,150	1,095,077
Short Term Debt	17,219	28,585	113,448
Current Liabilities	258,558	302,020	348,936
Long Term Debt	323,506	464,563	386,645
Total Liabilities	586,132	774,792	741,710
Total Equity	423,792	322,358	353,367
Total Liab. & Equity	1,009,924	1,097,150	1,095,077
CAPITAL (000)			
Total Debt	340,725	493,148	500,093
Preferred Equity	0	0	0
Common Equity	423,792	322,358	353,367

Synopsis:

United Westburne Inc. underwent a dramatic turnaround in 1994. Sales grew 5% to $2.3-billion. Net earnings rose to $25.4-million, a dramatic 185% swing from 1993's loss of $29.8-million. This made Westburne the largest distribution company in Canada and the third largest in North America, by sales volume. Cash flow from operations grew seven-fold to $87-million, and the company's overall debt level fell 30% to $341-million. This was due to its strong cash flow and proceeds from a $77-million share issue.

The profitable results of 1994 came after a rigorous strategy of cost-cutting measures began in 1993. Under the guidance of President and Chief Executive Officer Robert Chevrier, hired in late 1993, the company focused on profitability rather than sales volume as it had done in the past. In 1994, the workforce was cut by 452 employees, several superfluous warehouses were shut down, inventories were reduced, and administrative operations centralized. The numerous initiatives reduced operating costs by about $15.5-million and should generate cost savings of over $30-million on an annualized basis.

Beginning in 1995, Westburne's second phase of restructuring will examine all aspects of its customer service and business processes. The company plans to develop a branch model for its network of distribution centres. It will open some small branches that target specific niches or regional markets.

Western Canada is Westburne's largest market (28.8% of revenues), followed by Ontario (26.6%), Eastern Canada (18.5%), United States Pacific (15.8%) and U.S. Central and East (10.3%). More than 58% of its customers are residential, industrial, and commercial contractors, while industries accounts for 26% of its market, and institutions, utilities, and others make up 15.5%.

Rank (Profit/Revenue/Assets)
186   63   154

Guy De Panafieu
Chairman Of The Board

Robert Chevrier
Vice Chair President & C.E.O.

John A. Hanna
Sr. V.P. Fin. Admin. & C.F.O.

Address
6333 Decarie Boulevard
Suite 400
Montreal
PQ
H3W 3E1
(514) 342-5181

Fax: (514) 342-9838
U0001657/G/12.1

Page	Company	Fiscal year end	EARNINGS PER SHARE		
			Last Year	Estimate this year	Estimate next year
413	Becker Milk Company	Apr-94	(1.74)	na	na
414	Canadian Tire Corporation	Dec-94	1.30	1.31	1.41
415	Cara Operations	Mar-95	0.30	0.33	0.36
416	Chateau Stores	Jan-95	1.18	1.58	1.00
417	Dalmys (Canada)	Feb-95	(0.53)	na	na
418	Dylex	Jan-95	(3.65)	na	na
419	Empire Company	Apr-94	0.95	1.05	1.19
420	Future Shop	Mar-95	1.31	1.77	2.28
421	Gendis	Jan-95	0.76	0.80	1.02
422	George Weston	Dec-94	2.48	3.98	4.81
423	Hudson's Bay Company	Jan-95	3.23	2.54	2.86
424	Jean Coutu Group (PJC)	May-94	0.69	0.86	0.94
425	Leon's Funiture	Dec-94	0.85	na	na
426	Loblaw Companies	Dec-94	1.51	1.75	2.05
427	Metro-Richelieu	Sep-94	1.09	1.45	1.65
428	North West Company	Dec-94	1.00	1.08	1.23
429	Oshawa Group	Jan-95	1.52	1.72	1.92
430	Provigo	Jan-95	0.56	0.66	0.76
431	Reitmans (Canada)	Jan-95	1.34	1.78	1.95
432	Sears Canada	Dec-94	0.47	0.61	0.74
433	Silcorp	Dec-94	1.60	1.60	1.71
434	Sodisco-Howden Group	Dec-94	0.18	na	na
435	Speedy Muffler King	Dec-94	1.37	1.34	1.63
436	Westfair Foods	Dec-94	na	na	na
437	White Rose Crafts	July-94	0.40	0.29	0.38

Estimates from First Call Corporation, 22 Pittsburgh Street, Boston, MA 02210   (800) 366-9992   Fax (617) 261-5679

Retailing

The retail industry continues to feel pressure due to intense competition, particularly from mass merchandise stores and a new entrant, Wal-Mart Canada. Consumers continued to be cautious in 1994 and the first half of 1995, and analysts expect conditions in the second half to remain unchanged. Following three months of declines, total retail sales for the month of April 1995 increased a scant .2%. Major department store (The Bay, Eaton's, Sears) sales were down 1.4% for 1994, compared to a drop of 4.7% in 1993. However, discount department store (Zellers, K-Mart, Wal-Mart) sales rose 9.7% in 1994. The trend continued in the first five months of 1995. Overall, department store sales were up for March, April, and May of 1995. Major stores reported a 1% decline in sales while discount store sales rose a whopping 18.7%. The figures reflect an increasingly demanding consumer who places high value on low prices and convenience.

As a result of the competitive environment in 1994 and 1995, many retailers, particularly department stores and food stores, continued to restructure and/or downsize. Retailers who are attempting to compete in the discount store arena are seeing reduced margins due to discount pricing. In 1994 and 1995, apparel sales continued to be soft. Due to a pullback in the real estate market, sales of appliances and furniture declined as well. In the electronics and appliance markets, retailers are bracing themselves for the arrival of Incredible Universe, a subsidiary of Texas-based Tandy Corp. The chain plans to open two superstores in the Toronto area.

Wal-Mart's advantage over many other retailers is its ability to sell a wide range of products and services, catering to the busy shopper in search of one-stop shopping. It is able to offer consumers low prices because of its super-efficient and continent-wide electronic inventory and distribution system, massive volume buying, and non-union workforce.

Further squeezing of retail margins stems from rising shrinkage rates. According to the Retail Council of Canada, Canadian retailers lost $3-billion to shrinkage in 1994. Stealing accounted for 80% of this amount. Customer theft accounts for 50% of shrinkage, employee theft accounts for 30%, and paperwork errors account for 20%.

In the tough retail merchandise climate, companies are searching for new and creative ways to expand or at least maintain their market share. Sears, facing stiff competition in sporting goods from mega-stores, has eliminated all but the most basic sporting goods from its stores. It will focus on expanding its selection of fashion apparel. It also plans to open new stand-alone furniture and housewares stores to compete with IKEA and the Brick. Some retail operations, like Dalmys, are expanding their number of discount, warehouse-style stores.

Several retail food chains are expanding their wholesale and "super-store" format to compete with Wal-Mart, K-Mart, and Zellers. In some cases, they are turning supermarkets into one-stop shopping outlets for food as well as videos, books, film processing, dry cleaning, and pharmaceuticals. Another growing trend in food retailing is private label or store brands. These should deliver about a 30% increase in net income for supermarket chains over the next 10 years. Manufacturers produce the private label products for a low cost and sell directly to retailers — circumventing the usual food brokers. Therefore, private label products, like Masters Choice, Our Compliments and President's Choice, have high profit margins. They also enhance customer loyalty which is highly desirable.

The retail food industry has organized the Efficient Consumer Response (ECR) initiative, whereby the industry is gradually adopting practices and technology to create a more efficient distribution of products from manufacturer to store shelves. The goal of ECR is to distribute products based on the "pull" of consumer demand rather than the "push" of manufacturers. With ECR, product categories are managed like individual businesses. Disruptive and expensive inventory peaks and valleys are eliminated through continuous replenishment. Electronic data interchange is used to link suppliers and customers, and transportation and storage activities are streamlined. The system relies on up-to-the-minute sharing of sales and cost information amongst retailers, distributors, brokers, and manufacturers. In the short term, adopting ECR is costly as retailers must restructure operations and obtain the new technologies. In the long term, the initiative will result in efficiencies and cost savings. The stores will pass cost savings to the consumer in the form of lower pricing.

In February 1994, convenience stores began benefiting from the federal and provincial governments' decision to lower the amount of taxes added to cigarette prices. Gradually cigarette sales returned to the legitimate retail market. Previously, organized crime and smuggling captured 40% of the cigarette market. Meanwhile, sales for drugstores decreased due to the federal ruling in late 1994 prohibiting the sale of tobacco in drugstores.

BECKER MILK COMPANY LIMITED (THE)

Exchanges	Price (Jun29'95)	9.25	Trailing P/E	nm	Stock Symbol
T	Trailing Yield (%)	0.00	Trailing EPS	(1.19)	BEK.B

Period Ending	Apr94	Apr93	Apr92	Apr91	Apr90
Yearly Statistics					
Price-Close	11.00	12.00	29.00	36.00	nt
Price-High	16.00	31.50	36.00	45.00	nt
Price-Low	5.00	12.00	29.00	34.00	nt
P/E-Close	nm	nm	nm	38.71	nt
Dividends per Share	0.00	0.00	0.75	0.75	0.75
Dividend Yield (%)	0.00	0.00	2.59	2.08	nt
Sales per Share	219.66	235.16	249.48	248.29	246.60
EPS before extra. item	(1.74)	(3.10)	(0.48)	0.93	1.01
Cash Flow per Share	1.06	0.67	3.63	5.45	5.12
Book Value per Share	25.60	27.34	30.44	31.67	31.49
O/S Common Shares	1,728	1,728	1,728	1,728	1,728
Total Revenue	379,647	406,443	431,196	429,135	426,214
Income before extra.	(2,970)	(5,317)	(802)	1,640	1,781
Cash Flow	1,833	1,152	6,274	9,420	8,846
Debt/Equity	0.79	0.87	0.81	0.53	0.60
Return on Capital (%)	(1.91)	(6.43)	2.65	8.48	8.44
Ret. on Com. Equity (%)	(6.57)	(10.72)	(1.56)	2.94	3.22
% Change Profit	44.1	(563.1)	(148.9)	(7.9)	16.4
% Change Revenue	(6.6)	(5.7)	0.5	0.7	7.7
% Change Assets	(11.8)	(6.6)	9.2	(1.8)	(1.6)

Preferred Div. Coverage	0.0	0.0	0.0
Total Div. Coverage	0.0	0.0	0.0
Interest Coverage	0.0	0.0	0.7
Current Ratio	1.0	1.1	1.2
Operating Margin	(0.4)	(1.5)	0.6
Asset Turnover	3.7	3.5	3.5
5 YEAR RATIOS (%)			
Return on Capital	2.2	3.7	7.8
Return on Com. Equity	(2.5)	(0.7)	3.3
Profit Growth	na	na	na
Revenue Growth	(0.9)	1.3	5.0
Asset Growth	(2.8)	(0.3)	4.3
BALANCE SHEET (000)			
Cash	80	84	86
Current Assets	39,343	47,153	51,792
Net Fixed Assets	57,770	64,184	69,092
Invest's & Advances	700	700	116
Total Assets	102,138	115,805	124,050
Short Term Debt	16,899	19,070	17,003
Current Liabilities	37,932	44,394	44,868
Long Term Debt	18,442	22,585	26,012
Total Liabilities	57,322	67,985	70,880
Total Equity	44,816	47,820	53,171
Total Liab. & Equity	102,138	115,805	124,050
CAPITAL (000)			
Total Debt	35,341	41,656	43,015
Preferred Equity	568	568	568
Common Equity	44,248	47,253	52,603

Business:

THE BECKER MILK COMPANY LIMITED operates convenience stores in Ontario, a portion of which are under franchise. The Company processes milk and dairy products and has a fully automated blow-molding plant to manufacture plastic one, two and four litre milk jugs.

Date	EPS	DPS	Tot Rev	Inc Bex
Jan 95	(0.38)	0.00	82,754	(658)
Oct 94	0.26	0.00	93,806	469
Jul 94	0.22	0.00	97,851	381
Apr 94	(1.29)	0.00	80,679	(2,209)
Jan 94	(0.61)	0.00	89,349	(1,046)
Oct 93	(0.03)	0.00	102,627	(58)
Jul 93	0.19	0.00	106,992	343

Synopsis:

After bleak financial returns in 1993, The Becker's Milk Company underwent a year of re-organization and cost-cutting. In 1994, it shut down 58 unprofitable corporate stores. As a result, sales declined by 6.6% from $406.4-million in 1993 to $379.6-million in 1994. However, due to reduced expenses, the $3-million net loss for the year compared favourably to 1993's net loss of $5.3-million. Becker's showed gains in fiscal 1995, reporting a net income of $191,000 for the nine month period ending January 31, 1995, compared to a net loss over the same period in 1994 of $762,000.

In February 1994, Becker's began benefiting from the federal and provincial government's response to the 40% share of the cigarette market that had been captured by smugglers. After the government lowered cigarette taxes, sales returned to the retail market, benefiting Becker's and other retailers.

Becker's strategy is to continue its cost-cutting efforts by closing marginal and unprofitable stores. It hopes to achieve a network of higher volume locations through aggressive marketing campaigns and expanding the services offered by its stores.

In 1994, Becker's converted nine gas bars attached to its stores to the Becker's brand. This brought the total number of these sites to 23, almost a third of the locations selling gasoline. The Becker branded sites provide opportunities to cross merchandise with in store promotions. As of April 1994, Becker's had opened four Subway fast food franchises in its stores. It plans to escalate fast food service, offering an additional 25 to 30 Subway sandwich shop franchises in 1995, and experimenting with other branded fast food offerings.

Rank (Profit/Revenue/Assets)
879   224   479

Geoffrey W.J. Pottow
President
John Juhasz
Dir. Of Finance

Address
671 Warden Avenue
Scarborough
ON
M1L 3Z7
(416) 698-2591

Fax: (416) 698-2907
B0001374/G/12.2

CANADIAN TIRE CORPORATION, LIMITED

Exchanges	Price (Jun29'95)	14.62	Trailing P/E	121.88	Stock Symbol
TM	Trailing Yield (%)	2.74	Trailing EPS	0.12	**CTR.A**

Period Ending	Dec94	Jan94	Jan93	Dec91	Dec90
Yearly Statistics					
Price-Close	12.50	17.50	15.75	22.38	20.50
Price-High	17.63	18.88	23.38	27.50	24.88
Price-Low	10.00	11.63	14.75	22.25	19.25
P/E-Close	208.33	19.44	19.69	15.87	12.81
Dividends per Share	0.40	0.40	0.40	0.40	0.38
Dividend Yield (%)	3.20	2.29	2.54	1.79	1.85
Sales per Share	40.72	37.69	35.75	33.10	33.88
EPS before extra. item	0.06	0.90	0.80	1.41	1.60
Cash Flow per Share	1.77	1.67	1.75	1.96	2.05
Book Value per Share	13.03	13.40	12.87	12.15	11.44
O/S Common Shares	88,431	90,189	89,826	91,674	89,793
Total Revenue	3,603,966	3,420,566	3,232,836	3,008,050	3,091,214
Income before extra.	5,492	81,405	72,293	127,076	144,366
Cash Flow	156,667	151,773	157,666	176,690	185,025
Debt/Equity	0.62	0.41	0.50	0.47	0.44
Return on Capital (%)	7.89	12.03	10.86	16.78	20.97
Ret. on Com. Equity (%)	0.47	6.89	6.37	11.87	14.82
% Change Profit	(93.3)	12.6	(43.1)	(12.0)	(3.5)
% Change Revenue	5.4	5.8	7.5	(2.7)	3.8
% Change Assets	11.2	2.3	5.6	11.8	14.7

Business:

CANADIAN TIRE CORP. LTD. is engaged in the retail merchandising of automotive products, sporting goods, housewares and hardware products. Its stores, auto parts depots and gas bars are located across Canada. The company's financial services division operates the Canadian Tire credit card and auto club. It also operates a national emergency road service.

Date	EPS	DPS	Tot Rev	Inc Bex
Apr 95	0.26	0.10	838,828	22,851
Dec 94	(0.81)	0.10	926,967	(72,004)
Oct 94	0.37	0.10	938,010	32,720
Jul 94	0.30	0.10	951,080	26,557
Apr 94	0.20	0.10	771,833	18,219
Jan 94	0.13	0.10	812,161	12,022
Oct 93	0.32	0.10	902,154	28,957
Jul 93	0.27	0.10	928,158	23,890

Preferred Div. Coverage	np	np	np	
Total Div. Coverage	0.1	1.7	2.0	
Interest Coverage	2.2	3.3	2.8	
Current Ratio	1.6	2.0	1.9	
Operating Margin	6.8	6.5	5.3	
Asset Turnover	1.3	1.4	1.4	
5 YEAR RATIOS (%)				
Return on Capital	13.7	17.0	19.5	
Return on Com. Equity	8.1	11.4	13.3	
Profit Growth	(48.9)	(8.3)	(6.1)	
Revenue Growth	3.9	5.1	5.5	
Asset Growth	9.0	9.3	10.6	
BALANCE SHEET (000)				
Cash	156,038	139,519	163,624	
Current Assets	1,655,445	1,388,091	1,308,082	
Net Fixed Assets	972,007	945,719	1,009,046	
Invest's & Advances	12,934	13,871	15,054	
Total Assets	2,668,863	2,400,279	2,345,230	
Short Term Debt	244,345	20,045	124,678	
Current Liabilities	1,044,418	691,610	698,755	
Long Term Debt	465,027	474,555	449,331	
Total Liabilities	1,516,757	1,191,947	1,189,490	
Total Equity	1,152,106	1,208,332	1,155,740	
Total Liab. & Equity	2,668,863	2,400,279	2,345,230	
CAPITAL (000)				
Total Debt	709,372	494,600	574,009	
Preferred Equity	0	0	0	
Common Equity	1,152,106	1,208,332	1,155,740	

Synopsis:

For the first quarter of 1995, Canadian Tire Corporation, Limited saw improvement in all divisions. Revenues from Canadian Tire Retail rose 5.9%. Revenues from Financial Services rose 24.2% and revenues from Canadian Tire Petroleum rose 15.2%. Retail's performance was mainly due to increased revenue which resulted in increased margins. However, this increase was partially offset by increased operating expenses. Retail sales for the quarter rose 1.5% on a comparable store basis. Canadian Tire believes to further increase sales it must expand or replace existing stores across the country. This strategy was initiated in 1994. In 1994, Canadian Tire planned 18 new format stores in existing markets, and opened eight stores. In 1995, the company plans to start construction on 40 new stores, and open 30 new stores. Furthermore, plans call for building 60 new stores in each of the following three years, bringing the number of new format stores to 240. The new stores will provide customers with increased floor space, greater convenience, and a higher level of customer service. According to Canadian Tire, the eight stores opened in 1994 exceeded the company's expectations for traffic counts, average transaction amounts, and average store sales. Store sales increased more than 60%.

Petroleum's strong revenue performance in the quarter was due to a 8.6% volume increase in gasoline sales. However, earnings were affected by the impact of lower gasoline margins. Financial Services' strong revenue numbers were due to a substantial increase in credit card sales, resulting from the new Options Bonus Points program introduced in 1994.

In the fourth quarter, Canadian Tire closed Auto Source, a new warehouse concept for auto parts retailing and service. The closing resulted in a 1994 loss from discontinued operations of $1.24 per share.

Relative strength to TSE300
Price
Volume (in 1000's of board lots)

Rank (Profit/Revenue/Assets)
408   42   85

Earl Joudrie
Chairman Of The Board

Stephen E. Bachand
President, C.E.O. & C.O.O.

Gerald S. Kishner
Ex. V.P. Fin. & Adm. & C.F.O.

Address
2180 Yonge Street
P.O. Box 770
Station K
Toronto
ON
M4P 2V8
(416) 480-3000
Fax: (416) 480-3746
C0004314/G/12.5

CARA OPERATIONS LIMITED

Exchanges	Price (Jun29'95)	3.70	Trailing P/E	16.16	Stock Symbol
TM	Trailing Yield (%)	2.16	Trailing EPS	0.23	**CAO.A**

Period Ending	Apr95	Apr94	Mar93	Mar92	Mar91
Yearly Statistics					
Price-Close	3.55	4.30	4.45	5.50	5.50
Price-High	4.30	4.55	5.38	6.63	6.00
Price-Low	2.95	3.65	4.15	5.25	4.50
P/E-Close	15.50	16.41	17.12	20.91	17.74
Dividends per Share	0.08	0.08	0.08	0.08	0.08
Dividend Yield (%)	2.25	1.86	1.80	1.51	1.52
Sales per Share	7.74	7.00	6.66	6.51	4.88
EPS before extra. item	0.23	0.26	0.26	0.26	0.31
Cash Flow per Share	0.44	0.44	0.44	0.44	0.46
Book Value per Share	2.48	2.33	2.15	1.97	1.79
O/S Common Shares	117,432	117,432	117,432	117,432	117,430
Total Revenue	909,747	822,988	783,229	765,904	567,834
Income before extra.	26,844	30,754	30,492	30,835	35,624
Cash Flow	51,994	51,584	51,170	51,571	53,724
Debt/Equity	0.32	0.37	0.37	0.60	0.70
Return on Capital (%)	14.12	17.10	18.01	17.89	27.29
Ret. on Com. Equity (%)	9.50	11.69	12.60	13.96	18.72
% Change Profit	(12.7)	0.9	(1.1)	(13.4)	(6.7)
% Change Revenue	10.5	5.1	2.3	34.9	75.0
% Change Assets	3.9	8.9	(4.4)	4.3	96.7

Preferred Div. Coverage	np	np	np
Total Div. Coverage	2.9	3.3	3.2
Interest Coverage	5.8	7.2	6.1
Current Ratio	1.0	1.0	1.2
Operating Margin	6.3	7.8	8.5
Asset Turnover	1.8	1.7	1.7
5 YEAR RATIOS (%)			
Return on Capital	18.9	24.0	29.1
Return on Com. Equity	13.3	16.3	19.1
Profit Growth	(6.8)	(1.0)	2.7
Revenue Growth	22.8	21.5	22.1
Asset Growth	17.2	19.6	18.4
BALANCE SHEET (000)			
Cash	1,079	7,287	10,355
Current Assets	138,632	128,054	115,080
Net Fixed Assets	224,756	218,084	200,577
Invest's & Advances	24,222	24,070	23,008
Total Assets	507,191	488,324	448,256
Short Term Debt	30,899	26,770	1,690
Current Liabilities	145,843	127,353	93,048
Long Term Debt	61,749	75,105	90,787
Total Liabilities	215,874	214,456	195,747
Total Equity	291,317	273,868	252,509
Total Liab. & Equity	507,191	488,324	448,256
CAPITAL (000)			
Total Debt	92,648	101,875	92,477
Preferred Equity	0	0	0
Common Equity	291,317	273,868	252,509

Business:

CARA OPERATIONS LIMITED is in the food services and office products industries. It operates and is the franchisor of Swiss Chalet and Harvey's restaurants. Catering and support services are provided to educational and health institutions through Beaver Foods and to major airlines through the Airport Services Division. Cara distributes office products through Grand & Toy.

Date	EPS	DPS	Tot Rev	Inc Bex
Apr 95	0.04	0.00	285,460	5,098
Dec 94	0.08	0.04	227,445	9,491
Sep 94	0.07	0.00	199,026	7,662
Jun 94	0.04	0.04	196,958	4,593
Apr 94	0.09	0.04	271,705	10,283
Dec 93	0.07	0.04	198,362	9,159
Sep 93	0.06	0.00	174,231	7,576
Jun 93	0.04	0.04	177,608	4,282

Synopsis:

During fiscal 1994, Cara Operations Limited undertook a rationalization program. It closed a number of marginal Grand & Toy stores, along with most of its non-productive Steak & Burger restaurants. Cara took a restructuring charge of $13.6-million on a pre-tax basis to account for changes at Grand & Toy, Steak & Burger, Swiss Chalet, and Harvey's. The restructuring will allow the divisions to focus on the growth segments of their businesses.

All core divisions experienced sales growth was in fiscal 1994. Cara attributed the growth to price and volume increases and expansion due to new units and new contracts. In fiscal 1995, Cara will continue to investigate strategic alliances for its core businesses, and invest capital as needed to strengthen the divisions. Cara forecasts capital expenditures of $30-million in fiscal 1995.

In March 1995, the Dominion Bond Rating Service Ltd. lowered its rating on Cara's senior debt to triple-B (high) from single-A (low). DBRS said the rating trend on Cara's senior debt is stable. Competition in the restaurant and office products industries continues to hurt Cara's operating profit. DBRS expects that earnings and cash flow will show only moderate improvement in fiscal 1996. Furthermore, Cara's Grand & Toy operations continue to suffer from competition from office supply warehouse stores.

In August 1994, Cara was re-awarded a Canada-wide contract to be Air Canada's primary in-flight caterer until the year 2000. According to Cara, the contract is "the largest agreement of its kind in the Canadian airline industry." It represents the exclusive supply of all in-flight catering services for Air Canada flights using major Canadian airports. Cara also provides Air Canada with duty-free boutique products, wine and bar supplies, daily news videos, and headsets.

In fiscal 1994, sales by division were: Beaver Foods, 17.3%; Harvey's, 17.8%; Grand & Toy, 22.3%; Swiss Chalet, 22.7%; Airport Services, 12.5%; Summit, 4.%; and other, 3.4%.

Relative strength to TSE300

Price

Volume (in 1000's of board lots)

Rank (Profit/Revenue/Assets)
154   133   230

M. Bernard Syron
Chairman & C.E.O.

Gunter B. Otto
President & C.O.O.

Michael Nahirny
Ex. V.P. Fin. Admin. & C.F.O.

Address
230 Bloor Street West
Toronto
ON
M5S 1T8
(416) 962-4571

Fax: (416) 969-2547
C0005253/G/12.6

CHATEAU STORES OF CANADA LTD.

Exchanges	Price (Jun29'95)		6 .50	Trailing P/E		8 .78	Stock Symbol
TM	Trailing Yield (%)		4 .92	Trailing EPS		0 .74	CTU.A

Period Ending	Jan95	Jan94	Jan93	Jan92	Jan91	Business:
Yearly Statistics						CHATEAU STORES OF CANADA LTD.
Price-Close	7 .00	13 .00	7 .25	3 .05	5 .38	operates retail stores across Canada and the
Price-High	14 .25	17 .00	7 .75	10 .50	10 .25	United States under the name Le Chateau. The
Price-Low	6 .00	6 .50	2 .15	2 .90	2 .05	stores sell full lines of men's and women's
P/E-Close	6 .93	8 .18	6 .97	nm	5 .43	fashionable clothing, footwear and accessories
Dividends per Share	0 .30	0 .08	0 .00	0 .00	0 .00	at medium prices. The company designs and
Dividend Yield (%)	4 .29	0 .58	0 .00	0 .00	0 .00	manufactures many of the products sold.
Sales per Share	35 .49	34 .13	36 .24	35 .22	34 .83	
EPS before extra. item	1 .01	1 .59	1 .04	(1 .25)	0 .99	
Cash Flow per Share	1 .91	2 .34	2 .25	(0 .13)	2 .20	
Book Value per Share	7 .89	7 .18	5 .69	4 .81	6 .09	
O/S Common Shares	4 ,535	4 ,432	4 ,382	4 ,312	4 ,234	
Total Revenue	159 ,768	150 ,282	156 ,900	150 ,775	147 ,456	

Income before extra.	4 ,565	7 ,009	4 ,509	(5 ,349)	4 ,199	Date	EPS	DPS	Tot Rev	Inc Bex
Cash Flow	8 ,618	10 ,293	9 ,761	(567)	9 ,298	Apr 95	(0 .09)	0 .08	30 ,520	(410)
Debt/Equity	0 .01	0 .01	0 .02	0 .33	0 .12	Jan 95	0 .06	0 .08	43 ,100	281
Return on Capital (%)	23 .23	40 .98	36 .80	(16 .93)	31 .29	Oct 94	0 .47	0 .08	44 ,152	2 ,126
Ret. on Com. Equity (%)	13 .51	24 .70	19 .74	(22 .99)	17 .36	Jul 94	0 .30	0 .08	38 ,593	1 ,353
% Change Profit	(34 .9)	55 .4	184 .3	(227 .4)	215 .2	Apr 94	0 .18	0 .08	34 ,188	805
% Change Revenue	6 .3	(4 .2)	4 .1	2 .3	16 .7	Jan 94	0 .60	0 .08	44 ,560	2 ,659
% Change Assets	8 .2	11 .3	(8 .6)	4 .7	13 .6	Oct 93	0 .51	0 .00	38 ,573	2 ,258
						Jul 93	0 .39	0 .00	36 ,299	1 ,720

Preferred Div. Coverage	np	np	np	**Synopsis:**
Total Div. Coverage	3 .4	21 .1	na	
Interest Coverage	66 .8	140 .9	8 .0	
Current Ratio	2 .7	2 .5	1 .7	
Operating Margin	5 .0	7 .9	8 .3	
Asset Turnover	3 .3	3 .4	3 .9	
5 YEAR RATIOS (%)				
Return on Capital	23 .1	21 .4	12 .1	
Return on Com. Equity	10 .5	9 .0	0 .5	
Profit Growth	27 .9	na	na	
Revenue Growth	4 .7	5 .1	5 .4	
Asset Growth	5 .5	1 .9	(1 .0)	
BALANCE SHEET (000)				
Cash	10 ,244	13 ,749	10 ,751	
Current Assets	31 ,563	30 ,936	24 ,978	
Net Fixed Assets	15 ,596	13 ,098	14 ,071	
Invest's & Advances	898	389	881	
Total Assets	48 ,057	44 ,423	39 ,930	
Short Term Debt	146	114	187	
Current Liabilities	11 ,549	12 ,300	14 ,567	
Long Term Debt	222	307	422	
Total Liabilities	12 ,276	12 ,607	14 ,989	
Total Equity	35 ,781	31 ,816	24 ,941	
Total Liab. & Equity	48 ,057	44 ,423	39 ,930	
CAPITAL (000)				
Total Debt	368	421	609	
Preferred Equity	0	0	0	
Common Equity	35 ,781	31 ,816	24 ,941	

Synopsis:

In fiscal 1994, Chateau Stores of Canada Ltd. despite recording a 6.3% jump in sales, saw earnings decline by 34%. Comparable store sales rose 7.9% compared to 1993. The weaker earnings were attributed primarily to soft apparel sales in the fourth quarter that made necessary promotional pricing and increased markdown activity. For the first quarter of fiscal 1995, the company reported that comparable store sales fell by 8.4% over the same period last year.

Chateau Stores is a vertically integrated retailer of the moderately priced fashion apparel. The company adapts mainly European designs of clothing, accessories, and footwear for the North American market. The store caters primarily to clients between 15 and 30 years of age.

There are currently 155 stores in operation averaging 3,000 square feet in size. Major stores average between 5,000 and 6,000 square feet. Most stores are in Canada, but Chateau operates four U.S. stores. The company's Le Chateau brand name clothing is also distributed in two complementary retail formats. There are 56 boutiques in Sears stores cross Canada. As well, the company operates three Le Chateau outlet centres with about 20,000 square feet each. The company plans to increase the number of Sears outlets to 118.

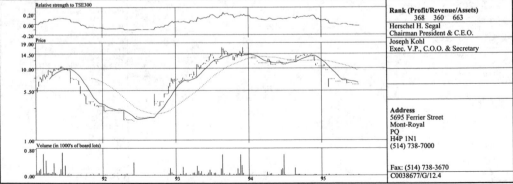

Rank (Profit/Revenue/Assets)
368   360   663

Herschel H. Segal
Chairman President & C.E.O.

Joseph Kohl
Exec. V.P., C.O.O. & Secretary

Address
5695 Ferrier Street
Mont-Royal
PQ
H4P 1N1
(514) 738-7000

Fax: (514) 738-3670
C0038677/G/12.4

DALMYS (CANADA) LIMITED

Exchanges	Price (Jun29'95)	0.70	Trailing P/E	nm	Stock Symbol
TM	Trailing Yield (%)	0.00	Trailing EPS	(0.56)	**DYC**

Period Ending	Feb95	Feb94	Feb93	Feb92	Feb91
Yearly Statistics					
Price-Close	0.60	1.65	3.00	1.25	6.25
Price-High	1.75	3.90	4.00	4.25	8.38
Price-Low	0.56	1.40	1.00	1.10	5.50
P/E-Close	nm	nm	10.00	nm	nm
Dividends per Share	0.00	0.00	0.00	0.00	0.06
Dividend Yield (%)	0.00	0.00	0.00	0.00	0.96
Sales per Share	19.88	22.86	27.80	25.53	29.04
EPS before extra. item	(0.53)	(0.17)	0.30	(3.95)	(0.63)
Cash Flow per Share	0.03	0.50	1.17	(0.98)	1.09
Book Value per Share	2.21	2.74	3.02	2.71	6.66
O/S Common Shares	5,580	5,580	4,180	4,180	4,180
Total Revenue	111,058	111,827	116,209	106,735	121,383
Income before extra.	(2,937)	(862)	1,271	(16,495)	(2,627)
Cash Flow	160	2,434	4,890	(4,108)	4,544
Debt/Equity	0.08	0.07	0.10	1.06	0.36
Return on Capital (%)	(18.82)	(4.63)	9.53	(50.41)	(3.99)
Ret. on Com. Equity (%)	(21.24)	(6.18)	10.62	(84.22)	(8.97)
% Change Profit	(240.7)	(167.8)	107.7	(527.9)	(2,474.2)
% Change Revenue	(0.7)	(3.8)	8.9	(12.1)	(23.0)
% Change Assets	(11.5)	(1.0)	(16.9)	(25.4)	(13.0)

Date	EPS	DPS	Tot Rev	Inc Bex
May 95	(0.02)	0.00	25,668	(92)
Feb 95	(0.25)	0.00	27,658	(1,381)
Nov 94	0.14	0.00	29,204	815
Aug 94	(0.43)	0.00	28,292	(2,417)
May 94	0.01	0.00	25,904	46
Feb 94	(0.03)	0.00	27,058	(202)
Nov 93	0.41	0.00	30,944	1,765
Aug 93	(0.51)	0.00	27,810	(2,239)

	Feb95	Feb94	Feb93
Preferred Div. Coverage	np	np	np
Total Div. Coverage	na	na	na
Interest Coverage	0.0	0.0	3.5
Current Ratio	1.1	1.2	1.0
Operating Margin	(2.6)	(0.9)	1.5
Asset Turnover	4.0	3.6	3.7
5 YEAR RATIOS (%)			
Return on Capital	(13.7)	(9.0)	(7.2)
Return on Com. Equity	(22.0)	(17.7)	(16.2)
Profit Growth	na	na	18.5
Revenue Growth	(6.8)	(6.1)	(4.5)
Asset Growth	(13.9)	(13.1)	(12.9)
BALANCE SHEET (000)			
Cash	3,011	7,385	5,111
Current Assets	15,188	18,377	16,947
Net Fixed Assets	11,643	12,144	14,033
Invest's & Advances	0	0	0
Total Assets	27,408	30,964	31,278
Short Term Debt	266	232	204
Current Liabilities	14,154	14,735	17,574
Long Term Debt	728	863	1,095
Total Liabilities	15,052	15,671	18,669
Total Equity	12,356	15,293	12,609
Total Liab. & Equity	27,408	30,964	31,278
CAPITAL (000)			
Total Debt	994	1,095	1,299
Preferred Equity	0	0	0
Common Equity	12,356	15,293	12,609

Business:

DALMYS (CANADA) LTD. is in the business of marketing women's apparel through company-operated retail stores in Canada. Serving a wide range of market types, the Canadian stores operate under the names Dalmys, Gazebo, Cactus and Antels. The stores offer dresses, outerwear, sportswear and accessories.

Synopsis:

In June 1995, Dalmys (Canada) Ltd. announced the planned closing of about 35 under-performing stores to restore profitability in 1995. Dalmys has closed 17 stores since the restructuring began in late 1994. Most of the closings are in the Dalmys division and will occur as leases expire. The recent closings are expected to save Dalmys approximately $1.7-million annually. The company has plans to build additional Entrepot warehouse outlets, which are about five times the size of an average store. The company also plans to examine its merchandise mix. The downsizing will bring the total number of Dalmys-owned stores to 160 at year end. According to the company, there will be virtually no writeoffs of fixed assets or termination charges.

In the first quarter of 1995, despite a marginal drop in sales, sales on a comparable store-to-store basis increased by 0.5%. This was due to the lower number of stores in operation this year.

Hit by the tough operating climate in the retail merchandise industry, clothing companies like Dalmys are looking for new and creative ways of retailing. The company will expand its stores and opening large warehouse-style stores. The first large warehouse store opened in late 1994 in Montreal. Warehouse merchandise costs at least 30% less than in the company's other clothing stores. The company's store names in Canada include Dalmys, Cactus, Gazebo and Antels.

The success of the Montreal warehouse store will dictate whether similar stores will be built in other major Canadian cities. Each Dalmys Warehouse costs about $250,000 to build, which is about the same cost as opening a smaller store. Dalmys has plans to build eight more warehouse stores.

Relative strength to TSE300 / Price / Volume (in 1000's of board lots) chart

Rank (Profit/Revenue/Assets)
814   403   762

Fred Perlman
President
Fred Hutchinson
V.P. Finance

Address
9475 Meilleur Street
Montreal
PQ
H2N 2C6
(514) 384-1030

D0000384/G/12.4

DYLEX LIMITED

Exchanges	Price (Jun29'95)	2.45	Trailing P/E	nm	Stock Symbol
TM	Trailing Yield (%)	0.00	Trailing EPS	(3.67)	**DLX**

Period Ending	Jan95	Jan94	Jan93	Feb92	Feb91
Yearly Statistics					
Price-Close	nm	nm	nm	nm	nm
Price-High	nm	nm	nm	nm	nm
Price-Low	nm	nm	nm	nm	nm
P/E-Close	nm	nm	nm	nm	nm
Dividends per Share	0.00	0.00	0.01	0.01	0.10
Dividend Yield (%)	0.00	0.00	nm	nm	nm
Sales per Share	24.49	25.80	27.44	35.36	36.83
EPS before extra. item	(3.65)	(0.02)	(0.35)	(1.07)	(0.07)
Cash Flow per Share	(0.70)	0.22	0.13	(0.09)	0.61
Book Value per Share	3.56	1.43	1.36	1.31	1.93
O/S Common Shares	27,000	71,380	71,380	63,379	47,378
Total Revenue	1,692,348	1,880,963	1,940,627	1,840,391	1,757,109
Income before extra.	(260,303)	1,232	(21,945)	(55,430)	(3,223)
Cash Flow	(50,282)	15,497	8,854	(4,801)	28,876
Debt/Equity	2.12	1.56	1.94	2.49	2.80
Return on Capital (%)	(68.65)	6.78	0.38	(6.25)	5.59
Ret. on Com. Equity (%)	(262.57)	1.24	(27.21)	(63.49)	(3.33)
% Change Profit	na	105.6	60.4	(1,619.8)	94.7
% Change Revenue	(10.0)	(3.1)	5.5	4.7	1.6
% Change Assets	(33.4)	(8.2)	(3.3)	0.3	5.3

Preferred Div. Coverage	0.0	na	0.0
Total Div. Coverage	0.0	na	0.0
Interest Coverage	0.0	1.1	0.0
Current Ratio	1.2	1.3	1.5
Operating Margin	0.7	(0.3)	0.3
Asset Turnover	3.8	2.7	2.6
5 YEAR RATIOS (%)			
Return on Capital	(12.4)	1.4	3.8
Return on Com. Equity	(71.1)	(27.6)	(24.1)
Profit Growth	na	(47.2)	na
Revenue Growth	(0.4)	5.2	8.0
Asset Growth	(9.0)	(1.4)	1.4
BALANCE SHEET (000)			
Cash	73,417	94,795	111,579
Current Assets	311,946	376,849	401,159
Net Fixed Assets	75,030	171,115	215,118
Invest's & Advances	34,448	20,345	16,028
Total Assets	462,731	694,671	756,793
Short Term Debt	129,586	70,871	47,162
Current Liabilities	259,905	287,261	265,789
Long Term Debt	74,354	167,777	240,735
Total Liabilities	366,465	541,168	608,175
Total Equity	96,266	153,503	148,618
Total Liab. & Equity	462,731	694,671	756,793
CAPITAL (000)			
Total Debt	203,940	238,648	287,897
Preferred Equity	0	51,495	51,495
Common Equity	96,266	102,008	97,123

Business:

DYLEX Ltd. is a specialty fashion retailer and manufacturer. The company is represented in major markets through chains of women's, men's and family clothing stores across North America. Store names in Canada include Fairweather, Braemar, TipTop, Harry Rosen, Biway, Thriftys, Club Monaco. U.S. stores include NBO and Club Monaco U.S.

Date	EPS	DPS	Tot Rev	Inc Bex
Apr 95	(0.21)	0.00	271,604	(8,616)
Jan 95	(1.80)	0.00	547,449	(128,405)
Oct 94	(1.55)	0.00	435,687	(110,154)
Jul 94	(0.11)	0.00	406,714	(7,516)
Apr 94	(0.21)	0.00	358,012	(14,228)
Jan 94	0.14	0.00	550,188	10,706
Oct 93	(0.04)	0.00	458,634	(2,502)
Jul 93	0.13	0.00	472,381	10,430

Synopsis:

In June 1995, Dylex Limited emerged from court protection. Dylex successfully implemented its plan of arrangement and reorganization of share capital under the Companies' Creditors Arrangement Act (CCAA) and the Canada Business Corporations Act. Dylex believes that as a result of the restructuring, its various divisions are now financially secure. Company management will be able to focus on improving Dylex's competitive position. In May 1995, Dylex reached an agreement in principle with its two principal bankers, Royal Bank and Bank of Montreal. The agreement allowed Dylex to go ahead with the restructuring plan under the CCAA.

In the fourth quarter of fiscal 1994, Dylex was affected by disrupted shipments from vendors, the need to generate cash, and activities related to the subsequent closure of about 190 stores. Earnings for the year were affected by numerous write-downs and provisions that contributed to a large net loss for the year. In the fourth quarter of 1994, Dylex recorded an aggregate provision of $140-million. This accounted for store closings and other CCAA charges, losses from operations, writedowns of assets during the plan of arrangement period, disposed operations, and the writeoff of tax loss carry forward benefits. The 1994 and comparative 1993 sales from ongoing operations exclude the results of NBO Stores. Dylex sold NBO in December 1994. Effective January 1, 1995, Wet Seal is being accounted for as an equity investment. The 1993 and 1994 sales also exclude Suzy Shier, Steel, and National Knitting.

In the future, Dylex plans to work with each of its operating units to further refine operations and to investigate and develop new retailing concepts. In fiscal 1994, Dylex's retail unit accounted for 97% of all sales. Sales in Canada accounted for 84% of total sales versus 16% in the U.S.

Rank (Profit/Revenue/Assets)
636   71   191

Wilfred Posluns
Chairman & C.E.O.

Lionel Robins
President & C.O.O.

David Posluns
C.F.O. Sr. V.P. & Sec.-Treas.

Address
637 Lake Shore Boulevard West
Toronto
ON
M5V 1A8
(416) 586-7000

Fax: (416) 586-7056
D0003576/G/12.4

For further company information, call Globe Information Services 1-800-268-9128 or (416) 585-5345

EMPIRE COMPANY LIMITED

Exchanges	Price (Jun29'95)	15.50	Trailing P/E	15.50	Stock Symbol
TM	Trailing Yield (%)	1.29	Trailing EPS	1.00	**EMP.A**

Period Ending	Apr94	Apr93	Apr92	Apr91	Apr90	Business:
Yearly Statistics						EMPIRE COMPANY LIMITED is a
Price-Close	16.13	14.25	12.63	11.88	12.50	diversified operating and investment company.
Price-High	17.75	14.75	13.75	13.50	17.50	Operating companies include Sobeys Inc. (food
Price-Low	12.25	10.00	11.00	8.75	12.25	retailer in Atlantic Canada, Quebec and
P/E-Close	14.79	27.40	45.09	1,187.50	nm	Ontario), Atlantic Shopping Centres Limited
Dividends per Share	0.20	0.18	0.16	0.16	0.16	(real estate) and Lawton's Drug Stores Limited
Dividend Yield (%)	1.24	1.26	1.27	1.35	1.28	(pharmaceutical retailer). Investments include
Sales per Share	73.89	68.99	64.96	60.66	53.68	Hannaford Bros. Co. (25%), Univa Inc. (25%),
EPS before extra. item	1.09	0.52	0.28	0.01	(0.17)	Jannock Limited (12%) and Wajax Limited
Cash Flow per Share	2.61	2.42	1.90	1.73	1.60	(47%).
Book Value per Share	9.24	7.66	7.53	7.41	7.42	
O/S Common Shares	37,048	34,051	34,461	34,484	34,434	
Total Revenue	2,591,241	2,363,312	2,238,835	2,092,935	1,809,280	

Income before extra.	47,915	28,494	20,950	14,425	8,568	Date	EPS	DPS	Tot Rev	Inc Bex
Cash Flow	91,297	82,967	65,508	59,783	54,078	Jan 95	0.17	0.05	670,072	7,977
Debt/Equity	2.05	1.87	1.85	1.70	1.46	Oct 94	0.28	0.05	672,100	12,114
Return on Capital (%)	12.00	10.19	9.61	9.73	8.76	Jul 94	0.28	0.05	684,740	11,933
Ret. on Com. Equity (%)	12.64	6.88	3.70	0.10	(2.33)	Apr 94	0.27	0.05	684,742	12,427
% Change Profit	68.2	36.0	45.2	68.4	(77.1)	Jan 94	0.22	0.05	629,653	10,218
% Change Revenue	9.6	5.6	7.0	15.7	13.4	Oct 93	0.36	0.05	642,524	14,650
% Change Assets	18.0	0.3	1.4	8.6	5.4	Jul 93	0.24	0.05	634,324	10,620
						Apr 93	(0.05)	0.03	578,078	791

Preferred Div. Coverage	4.9	2.7	1.8
Total Div. Coverage	3.1	1.9	1.4
Interest Coverage	1.8	1.6	1.4
Current Ratio	1.0	0.7	0.7
Operating Margin	4.8	4.5	4.3
Asset Turnover	1.5	1.7	1.6
5 YEAR RATIOS (%)			
Return on Capital	10.1	10.0	10.8
Return on Com. Equity	4.2	3.8	5.9
Profit Growth	5.1	(5.1)	(9.1)
Revenue Growth	10.1	10.9	13.3
Asset Growth	6.5	6.5	12.6
BALANCE SHEET (000)			
Cash	288,025	103,979	95,831
Current Assets	551,532	324,831	321,876
Net Fixed Assets	909,920	714,538	720,298
Invest's & Advances	195,653	373,703	366,651
Total Assets	1,683,893	1,426,471	1,421,909
Short Term Debt	257,778	235,188	277,002
Current Liabilities	552,421	453,141	486,413
Long Term Debt	633,622	514,856	472,635
Total Liabilities	1,248,943	1,024,889	1,016,922
Total Equity	434,950	401,582	404,987
Total Liab. & Equity	1,683,893	1,426,471	1,421,909
CAPITAL (000)			
Total Debt	891,400	750,044	749,637
Preferred Equity	92,571	140,864	145,458
Common Equity	342,379	260,718	259,529

Synopsis:

In 1995, Empire Company Limited had 119 retail stores in Atlantic Canada, Quebec, and Ontario, as well as wholesale, food service and industrial groups under its Sobeys Inc. subsidiary. Among its investments, it has 80 retail drugstores under the Lawton's banner, a 25% share of New England food retailer Hannaford Bros., and a 24% interest in Provigo Inc. The retail and wholesale distribution of food, through Sobeys Inc., accounts for over 85% of Empire's operating revenue, almost 45% of the consolidated income from operations, and over 60% of cash flow.

For the nine months ended January 31, 1995, earnings declined about 10%, due to lower margins at the retail level, where ongoing competition and competitive pricing from other retail outlets continues. The entry of Wal-Mart stores into the market in 1994 added to the competition for both Sobeys and Lawton's. Empire, however, receives offsetting benefits to Wal-Mart penetration. About 10% of Empire's Real Estate Group's retail portfolio is leased by Wal-Mart.

Empire's strategy is to cut distribution costs and continue geographical diversification of food distribution through direct investment in Central Canada and by equity investments in North American companies. In Quebec, where Empire currently has nine stores, it intends to expand its presence, resulting in competition for Provigo stores. In 1995, this move raised the issue of conflict of interest because of Empire's stake in Provigo. As a result, two members of Provigo's board of directors, David and Donald Sobey, left the Provigo board.

Empire's operating cash flow rose from $72.4-million to $81.5-million in fiscal 1994. Its 1994 capital expenditure of $98.1- million reflected new store and expansion and renovation program of Sobeys Inc., and the acquisitions of the Atlantic Canada food service division of Maple Leaf Foods and Judson's Foods. Empire is planning $91-million of capital expenditure for fiscal 1995.

Relative strength to TSE300 / Price / Volume (in 1000's of board lots)

Rank (Profit/Revenue/Assets)
116 58 116
Donald R. Sobey
Chairman
James W. Gogan
President & C.E.O.
Jon N. Hagan
Exec. V.P., Fin. & Corp. Dev.

Address
115 King Street
Stellarton
NS
B0K 1S0
(902) 755-4440

Fax: (902) 755-6477
E0001788/G/12.2

FUTURE SHOP LTD.

Exchanges	Price (Jun29'95)	17.87	Trailing P/E	13.64	Stock Symbol
TV	Trailing Yield (%)	0.00	Trailing EPS	1.31	FSS

Period Ending	Mar95	Mar94	Mar93	Mar92
Yearly Statistics				
Price-Close	19.75	23.75	nt	nt
Price-High	30.00	33.00	nt	nt
Price-Low	16.25	10.38	nt	nt
P/E-Close	15.07	20.65	nt	nt
Dividends per Share	0.00	0.00	0.00	0.00
Dividend Yield (%)	0.00	0.00	0.00	0.00
Sales per Share	85.45	51.32	35.82	26.67
EPS before extra. item	1.31	1.15	0.72	0.45
Cash Flow per Share	3.28	2.10	1.16	1.32
Book Value per Share	5.02	3.72	0.54	na
O/S Common Shares	12,670	12,670	9,334	0
Total Revenue	1,083,672	594,975	334,824	249,981
Income before extra.	16,544	13,337	6,712	4,230
Cash Flow	41,590	24,327	10,802	12,334
Debt/Equity	0.04	0.05	1.96	nd
Return on Capital (%)	52.62	77.52	87.20	na
Ret. on Com. Equity (%)	29.87	51.14	69.65	na
% Change Profit	24.0	98.7	58.7	na
% Change Revenue	82.3	77.7	33.9	na
% Change Assets	42.1	112.1	45.9	na

Date	EPS	DPS	Tot Rev	Inc Bex
Mar 95	0.14	0.00	277,200	1,700
Dec 94	0.76	0.00	394,500	9,627
Sep 94	0.32	0.00	248,878	4,030
Jun 94	0.09	0.00	163,379	1,152
Mar 94	0.23	0.00	151,600	3,000
Dec 93	0.53	0.00	220,200	6,224
Sep 93	0.37	0.00	134,058	3,841
Jun 93	0.02	0.00	88,946	227

Preferred Div. Coverage	np	np	np
Total Div. Coverage	na	na	na
Interest Coverage	na	na	na
Current Ratio	1.3	1.4	1.3
Operating Margin	2.7	4.1	3.7
Asset Turnover	4.2	3.5	4.2
5 YEAR RATIOS (%)			
Return on Capital	na	na	na
Return on Com. Equity	na	na	na
Profit Growth	na	na	na
Revenue Growth	na	na	na
Asset Growth	na	na	na
BALANCE SHEET (000)			
Cash	12,380	42,799	8,271
Current Assets	209,864	147,658	68,449
Net Fixed Assets	47,155	20,049	10,608
Invest's & Advances	0	0	0
Total Assets	257,019	167,707	79,057
Short Term Debt	0	0	0
Current Liabilities	162,329	103,193	52,531
Long Term Debt	2,364	2,364	9,864
Total Liabilities	193,364	120,596	74,013
Total Equity	63,655	47,111	5,044
Total Liab. & Equity	257,019	167,707	79,057
CAPITAL (000)			
Total Debt	2,364	2,364	9,864
Preferred Equity	0	0	0
Common Equity	63,655	47,111	5,044

Business:

FUTURE SHOP LTD. is a large volume retailer of computers, consumer electronics products and appliances. Recently the company commenced selling music software including compact discs and audio cassettes.

Synopsis:

In April 1995, Future Shop Ltd. said it would not proceed with the acquisition of Digital Discs Inc., a chain of four music and video stores based in Bellevue, Washington. In February, Future Shop had agreed in principle to buy the outstanding shares of Digital Discs for about $5-million (U.S.).

For fiscal 1995, Future Shop plans to open eight new stores in the Pacific Northwest, and 10 new stores in Canada, bringing the total number of North American outlets to 65. The company said its goal is to double the number of stores to 125, over the next two to three years, with 90 stores in Canada.

The Canadian electronic and appliance retail market including Future will be even more crowded with the planned arrival of Incredible Universe. Incredible Universe, a subsidiary of Texas-based Tandy Corp., plans to start with at least two superstores in the Toronto area.

For the third quarter of 1994, same store sales at Future Shop jumped 28%. The company launched the sale of music software in 20 stores across Canada. It also opened three stores in Montreal. This was the company's first venture into Quebec. Plans call for the possible opening of 20 Quebec stores. As well, seven new stores were opened across Canada during the quarter.

In August 1994, Future Shop agreed in principal to acquire all the outstanding shares of Toronto-based Granada Canada. It will pay about $3-million in cash. Future Shop bought six Granada stores and certain tax benefits. The remaining Granada stores will being transferred to Granada Canada Holdings Ltd. The acquisition gives Future Shop the ability serve customers who want to rent merchandise.

Relative strength to TSE300 / Price / Volume (in 1000's of board lots) chart, 1992–1995

Rank (Profit/Revenue/Assets)
259   172   378

Hassan Khosrowshahi
Chairman

Mohammad Ziabakhsh
President & C.E.O.

Gary A. Patterson
C.F.O.

Address
Suite 1400
1111 West Georgia Street
Vancouver
BC
V6E 4M3
(604) 689-1804

Fax: (604) 681-9258
01003415/G/12.5

GENDIS INC.

Exchanges	Price (Jun29'95)	15.00	Trailing P/E	2.22	Stock Symbol
T	Trailing Yield (%)	3.60	Trailing EPS	6.75	GDS.A

Period Ending	Jan95	Jan94	Jan93	Jan92	Jan91
Yearly Statistics					
Price-Close	16.13	19.25	17.00	22.50	19.50
Price-High	19.25	22.25	23.25	25.50	22.63
Price-Low	14.00	16.50	16.00	18.25	18.88
P/E-Close	21.22	17.99	21.52	24.46	11.82
Dividends per Share	0.54	0.54	0.54	0.54	0.52
Dividend Yield (%)	3.35	2.81	3.18	2.40	2.67
Sales per Share	49.54	48.46	47.10	44.89	46.18
EPS before extra. item	0.76	1.07	0.79	0.92	1.65
Cash Flow per Share	0.71	1.41	1.12	1.40	1.97
Book Value per Share	12.05	11.81	11.28	11.03	10.65
O/S Common Shares	16,936	16,853	16,838	16,835	16,825
Total Revenue	836,996	816,264	793,126	755,561	776,962
Income before extra.	12,803	18,054	13,279	15,436	27,757
Cash Flow	11,954	23,736	18,928	23,516	33,083
Debt/Equity	0.94	0.86	0.68	0.62	0.58
Return on Capital (%)	7.48	10.36	9.56	12.26	22.29
Ret. on Com. Equity (%)	6.35	9.28	7.07	8.46	16.36
% Change Profit	(29.1)	36.0	(14.0)	(44.4)	10.3
% Change Revenue	2.5	2.9	5.0	(2.8)	3.9
% Change Assets	5.2	12.5	5.6	6.9	(4.5)

Preferred Div. Coverage	np	np	np
Total Div. Coverage	1.4	2.0	1.5
Interest Coverage	2.2	3.5	2.4
Current Ratio	1.2	1.3	1.3
Operating Margin	2.1	3.3	2.7
Asset Turnover	1.8	1.9	2.0
5 YEAR RATIOS (%)			
Return on Capital	12.4	15.5	18.6
Return on Com. Equity	9.5	11.6	13.3
Profit Growth	(12.6)	(7.1)	(10.0)
Revenue Growth	2.2	3.7	5.4
Asset Growth	4.9	6.9	7.2
BALANCE SHEET (000)			
Cash	2,570	3,970	7,927
Current Assets	223,235	219,096	188,832
Net Fixed Assets	126,338	121,381	111,357
Invest's & Advances	107,339	94,347	85,858
Total Assets	462,806	440,079	391,253
Short Term Debt	121,230	111,676	84,344
Current Liabilities	187,569	173,525	147,967
Long Term Debt	70,000	60,000	45,000
Total Liabilities	258,775	240,970	201,329
Total Equity	204,031	199,109	189,924
Total Liab. & Equity	462,806	440,079	391,253
CAPITAL (000)			
Total Debt	191,230	171,676	129,344
Preferred Equity	0	0	0
Common Equity	204,031	199,109	189,924

Business:

GENDIS INC. is a holding company with interests in merchandising, real estate and oil and gas. The company wholly owns Metropolitan Stores of Canada Ltd., which operates junior department and clothing stores under the names Greenberg, Saan and Metropolitan. It also owns 31% of Chauvco Resources Ltd., and 50% of Tundra Diland Gas Ltd.

Date	EPS	DPS	Tot Rev	Inc Bex
Apr 95	5.91	0.14	102,140	100,088
Jan 95	0.27	0.14	249,782	4,541
Oct 94	0.35	0.14	225,566	5,838
Jul 94	0.22	0.14	193,922	3,717
Apr 94	(0.08)	0.14	106,596	(1,293)
Jan 94	0.51	0.14	245,888	8,677
Oct 93	0.45	0.14	221,672	7,534
Jul 93	0.13	0.14	188,614	2,106

Synopsis:

In March 1995 Gendis sold its 51% interest in Sony of Canada to Japan-based Sony Corp. for $207-million. The sale ended a 40 year business relationship between the two parties. The agreement calls for Gendis to not compete with Sony for five years. Sony of Canada had sales of about $600-million last year. Gendis will use the money from the sale to stock its retail stores, reduce corporate debt levels, and strengthen its General Merchandising division. The company also does not rule out possible acquisitions. The sale transforms Gendis business into a retailing operation, with significant investments in oil & gas and real estate. In March 1995, Gendis was committed to subscribe for 900,000 shares of Chauvco Resources for about $14.2-million.

For fiscal 1994, Gendis recorded its lowest earnings in seven years. Despite record sales, the drop in net earnings was attributed to Canada's sluggish retail recovery and a major restructuring of the company's retail holdings, specifically Metropolitan and Greenberg. Gendis plans to open nine new Saan stores in 1995 and renovate 19 others. This follows the 1994 purchase of 26 Wise-Peoples outlets. Gendis believes the additional revenue streams from the acquired and new stores should add an additional $50-million in sales to the group. Gendis is also banking on new technologies and the standardization of its retail stores to improve its operating position. In 1994, Gendis also was involved in financing the expansion of a restaurant chain. Sales in 1994 by segment were: General Merchandising, 63.7%; Electronics, 35.9%; and Real Estate 0.4%.

In April 1995, MMG Management Group, a division of Gendis Inc., signed leases for 23 former locations of the bankrupt Peoples department store chain in Quebec, New Brunswick, Newfoundland, and Ontario. The majority of the stores will reopen under the Metropolitan banner.

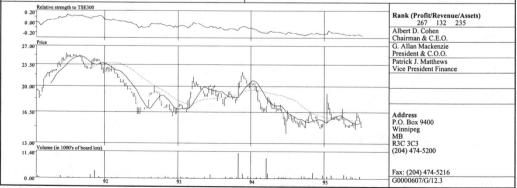

Rank (Profit/Revenue/Assets)
267   132   235

Albert D. Cohen
Chairman & C.E.O.

G. Allan Mackenzie
President & C.O.O.

Patrick J. Matthews
Vice President Finance

Address
P.O. Box 9400
Winnipeg
MB
R3C 3C3
(204) 474-5200

Fax: (204) 474-5216
G0000607/G/12.3

GEORGE WESTON LIMITED

Exchanges	Price (Jun29'95)		45.75	Trailing P/E		16.22	Stock Symbol
TMV	Trailing Yield (%)		1.53	Trailing EPS		2.82	**WN**

Period Ending	Dec94	Dec93	Dec92	Dec91	Dec90
Yearly Statistics					
Price-Close	42.25	39.00	36.75	36.75	41.75
Price-High	44.00	45.50	40.00	46.50	43.75
Price-Low	35.00	34.00	33.00	35.50	36.75
P/E-Close	17.04	32.23	43.24	20.30	16.57
Dividends per Share	0.70	0.70	0.70	0.70	0.70
Dividend Yield (%)	1.66	1.80	1.91	1.91	1.68
Sales per Share	276.88	254.63	248.86	232.07	234.87
EPS before extra. item	2.48	1.21	0.85	1.81	2.52
Cash Flow per Share	9.35	7.06	6.69	6.21	7.70
Book Value per Share	29.75	27.42	27.08	26.24	25.35
O/S Common Shares (mil)	47	47	47	47	46
Total Revenue ($mil)	13,002	11,931	11,599	10,770	10,869
Income before extra. ($mil)	117	57	48	92	125
Cash Flow ($mil)	439	331	312	288	356
Debt/Equity	0.84	0.89	0.69	0.63	0.63
Return on Capital (%)	13.29	8.99	8.22	11.37	15.99
Ret. on Com. Equity (%)	8.72	4.48	3.22	7.02	10.37
% Change Profit	105.3	18.8	(47.8)	(26.4)	(16.7)
% Change Revenue	9.0	2.9	7.7	(0.9)	3.8
% Change Assets	6.4	12.5	3.6	3.3	4.4

	Dec94	Dec93	Dec92
Preferred Div. Coverage	na	na	6.0
Total Div. Coverage	3.5	1.7	1.2
Interest Coverage	3.0	2.3	1.9
Current Ratio	1.0	1.0	1.1
Operating Margin	2.9	2.0	1.8
Asset Turnover	2.7	2.7	2.9
5 YEAR RATIOS (%)			
Return on Capital	11.6	12.6	14.1
Return on Com. Equity	6.8	7.8	9.6
Profit Growth	(4.9)	(16.2)	(18.6)
Revenue Growth	4.3	1.9	0.9
Asset Growth	5.8	5.0	2.2
BALANCE SHEET (mil)			
Cash	251	296	211
Current Assets	1,754	1,697	1,564
Net Fixed Assets	2,704	2,462	2,129
Invest's & Advances	108	113	125
Total Assets	4,744	4,459	3,965
Short Term Debt	176	287	148
Current Liabilities	1,753	1,653	1,388
Long Term Debt	1,008	861	730
Total Liabilities	3,340	3,170	2,699
Total Equity	1,404	1,289	1,266
Total Liab. & Equity	4,744	4,459	3,965
CAPITAL (mil)			
Total Debt	1,184	1,148	878
Preferred Equity	4	4	4
Common Equity	1,400	1,285	1,262

Business:

GEORGE WESTON LTD. is a diversified company with interests in food processing, food distribution and resources in North America. Loblaw Cos. Ltd. is a wholesale and retail food distributor. Weston Foods Ltd. makes baked goods. Weston Resources Ltd. is a forest products and fisheries company.

Date	EPS	DPS	Tot Rev	Inc Bex
Mar 95	0.64	0.18	3,066,300	30,200
Dec 94	0.96	0.18	3,199,500	45,400
Sep 94	0.74	0.18	3,854,500	34,700
Jun 94	0.48	0.18	3,102,700	22,600
Mar 94	0.30	0.17	2,845,500	14,300
Dec 93	0.13	0.18	2,873,800	6,400
Sep 93	0.45	0.18	3,550,320	21,200
Jun 93	0.39	0.18	2,792,400	18,300

Synopsis:

In 1994, George Weston Limited's earnings improved substantially to $117-million with earnings per share up to $2.48. Shareholder equity was up $115-million to $1.4-billion. George Weston's capital investment of $552-million in 1994 included nine cookie and frozen dough baking lines, two million square feet of retail space, and the rebuild of a fine paper machine.

In 1994, both Loblaw's Eastern and Western Canadian divisions saw record sales. In the East, the company's unprofitable Hasty Market convenience store business was sold in 1994, and the company plans to focus on its core supermarket business. To that end, Loblaw's will continue expanding its product categories and services to reflect its view of its stores as one-stop shops for everyday household needs, rather than simply food.

In the West, as an effort to compete with the entry of Wal-Mart into the marketplace and the competitive reaction of other mass merchandise stores, five new Real Canadian Superstores opened in 1994 and several more are planned for 1995. Loblaw's Western Canada wholesale business underwent a rationalization beginning in 1993 that saw wholesale sales decline 11.9% in 1994.

Weston Foods saw a sales growth of 10% in 1994, but operating income declined to $6-million from $22-million in 1993, due mostly to margin pressure in the fresh bread business in the United States. To improve the long-term performance of in this business, Weston withdrew from certain markets and closed some production lines and distribution centres.

Weston Resources saw a 28% increase in sales, due to the acquisition of Island Paper Mills in 1993. Prices for pulp and wood products jumped 41% and 20% respectively.

Sales (operating income) by group in 1994 were: Loblaw Companies, 74% (71%); Weston Resources, 11% (27%); Weston Foods, 15% (1%).

Rank (Profit/Revenue/Assets)
69   4   46

W. Galen Weston
Chairman & President

Earl R. Pearce
Sr. V.P. & C.F.O.

Address
22 St. Clair Avenue East
Suite 1901
Toronto
ON
M4T 2S7
(416) 922-2500

Fax: (416) 922-4395
W0002354/G/12.2

HUDSON'S BAY COMPANY

Exchanges	Price (Jun29'95)	27 .12	Trailing P/E	9 .29	Stock Symbol
TM	Trailing Yield (%)	3 .39	Trailing EPS	2 .92	HBC

Period Ending	Jan95	Jan94	Jan93	Jan92	Jan91
Yearly Statistics					
Price-Close	23 .75	32 .38	29 .38	29 .25	24 .00
Price-High	32 .63	41 .13	32 .25	37 .00	34 .00
Price-Low	22 .88	29 .25	25 .50	23 .88	16 .00
P/E-Close	7 .35	11 .90	12 .66	18 .17	6 .94
Dividends per Share	0 .92	0 .80	0 .80	0 .80	0 .80
Dividend Yield (%)	3 .87	2 .47	2 .72	2 .74	3 .33
Sales per Share	102 .31	100 .31	102 .51	102 .79	110 .19
EPS before extra. item	3 .23	2 .72	2 .32	1 .61	3 .46
Cash Flow per Share	6 .07	5 .98	4 .57	3 .46	4 .51
Book Value per Share	30 .76	28 .56	25 .92	24 .43	23 .56
O/S Common Shares	57 ,635	56 ,523	50 ,756	49 ,828	45 ,598
Total Revenue	5 ,829 ,243	5 ,441 ,498	5 ,164 ,482	5 ,049 ,963	4 ,969 ,978
Income before extra.	184 ,320	147 ,701	116 ,723	82 ,780	163 ,282
Cash Flow	345 ,991	324 ,509	229 ,803	169 ,548	203 ,227
Debt/Equity	0 .81	0 .78	0 .99	1 .13	1 .10
Return on Capital (%)	13 .25	13 .24	12 .43	11 .28	13 .73
Ret. on Com. Equity (%)	10 .88	10 .08	9 .19	6 .79	15 .42
% Change Profit	24 .8	26 .5	41 .0	(49 .3)	(2 .9)
% Change Revenue	7 .1	5 .4	2 .3	1 .6	8 .0
% Change Assets	9 .3	12 .0	0 .2	5 .6	12 .3

Preferred Div. Coverage	np	np	np
Total Div. Coverage	3 .5	3 .4	2 .9
Interest Coverage	4 .0	3 .7	2 .6
Current Ratio	2 .7	2 .7	2 .2
Operating Margin	6 .3	6 .7	6 .4
Asset Turnover	1 .5	1 .5	1 .6
5 YEAR RATIOS (%)			
Return on Capital	12 .8	12 .7	11 .9
Return on Com. Equity	10 .5	11 .8	10 .4
Profit Growth	1 .8	24 .5	44 .1
Revenue Growth	4 .7	3 .0	1 .3
Asset Growth	7 .7	1 .0	(2 .0)
BALANCE SHEET (000)			
Cash	6 ,704	17 ,018	14 ,620
Current Assets	2 ,674 ,971	2 ,452 ,707	2 ,170 ,593
Net Fixed Assets	862 ,768	773 ,160	705 ,571
Invest's & Advances	122 ,041	96 ,383	83 ,843
Total Assets	4 ,016 ,624	3 ,674 ,722	3 ,279 ,679
Short Term Debt	300 ,329	179 ,241	426 ,514
Current Liabilities	979 ,294	893 ,161	1 ,007 ,462
Long Term Debt	1 ,126 ,048	1 ,084 ,232	874 ,792
Total Liabilities	2 ,243 ,734	2 ,060 ,270	1 ,964 ,226
Total Equity	1 ,772 ,890	1 ,614 ,452	1 ,315 ,453
Total Liab. & Equity	4 ,016 ,624	3 ,674 ,722	3 ,279 ,679
CAPITAL (000)			
Total Debt	1 ,426 ,377	1 ,263 ,473	1 ,301 ,306
Preferred Equity	0	0	0
Common Equity	1 ,772 ,890	1 ,614 ,452	1 ,315 ,453

Business:

HUDSON'S BAY CO. is a merchandising company. Through its three operating divisions, The Bay, Zellers, and Fields, the company covers the Canadian retail market across all price zones and from coast to coast. On a combined basis, it accounts for about 7.6% of Canadian retail sales, excluding food and automobiles. The Thomson family holds 23.9% of the company's shares.

Date	EPS	DPS	Tot Rev	Inc Bex
Apr 95	(0 .25)	0 .23	1 ,230 ,000	(14 ,703)
Jan 95	1 .81	0 .23	1 ,880 ,000	103 ,530
Oct 94	0 .64	0 .23	1 ,440 ,000	36 ,463
Jul 94	0 .72	0 .23	1 ,310 ,125	40 ,985
Apr 94	0 .06	0 .23	1 ,194 ,999	3 ,342
Jan 94	1 .90	0 .20	1 ,778 ,491	103 ,779
Oct 93	0 .59	0 .20	1 ,372 ,331	31 ,828
Jul 93	0 .32	0 .20	1 ,185 ,786	16 ,526

Synopsis:

In June 1995, the Canadian Bond Rating Service assigned a rating of A (low) to Hudson's Bay Company (HBC) $500-million shelf registration. The proceeds of the issue were earmarked primarily for capital expenditures and general corporate purposes. The rating agency said that a combination of lower margins and increased financing charges could weaken HBC's financial position in fiscal 1996, but it expects the financial performance to remain within the A (low) rating category.

The weak results from the 1996 first quarter were attributed to slow sales, increased price competition, rising interest charges. Revenues at the Zellers stores rose 4.9% to $734.8-million, while revenue at The Bay dipped 0.9% to $469.9-million. However, profits at The Bay fell by $4.2-million as a result of lower sales. At Zellers, the $14.6-million drop in profits was due to reduced margins resulting from competition with Wal-Mart Canada Inc. HBC believe that the disappointing performance will turn around in the next few quarters as HBC earns only 20% of its sales and revenue in the first quarter, compared to 33% in the fourth quarter.

HBC has earmarked $250-million for capital expenditures in 1995, including $23-million for new technology. Zellers plans to open 18 stores, close nine stores, and expand five stores in 1995. The Bay plans to open three stores, close two, and renovate 16.

In May 1995, the Dominion Bond Rating Service confirmed its ratings on the notes and debentures of HBC. The agency said HBC performed fairly well in 1994 in face of competition, and that an increase in borrowing is likely in 1995 to finance Zellers accelerated store expansion program and planned new store openings. The modernization is expected to affect near-term profitability but will allow HBC to remain competitive in the future. Also in May, shareholders approved a rights protection plan.

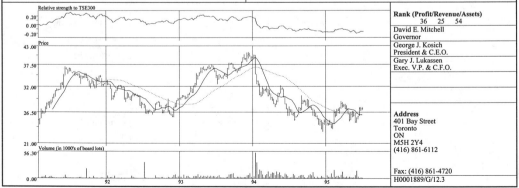

Rank (Profit/Revenue/Assets)
36   25   54
David E. Mitchell Governor
George J. Kosich President & C.E.O.
Gary J. Lukassen Exec. V.P. & C.F.O.

Address
401 Bay Street
Toronto
ON
M5H 2Y4
(416) 861-6112

Fax: (416) 861-4720
H0001889/G/12.3

JEAN COUTU GROUP (PJC) INC. (THE)

Exchanges	Price (Jun29'95)	8.75	Trailing P/E	11.08	Stock Symbol
TM	Trailing Yield (%)	1.37	Trailing EPS	0.79	**PJC.A**

Period Ending	May94	May93	May92	May91	May90
Yearly Statistics					
Price-Close	8.13	14.00	14.00	11.31	6.56
Price-High	15.88	18.25	15.25	11.88	7.25
Price-Low	7.25	13.00	11.31	6.56	5.88
P/E-Close	18.06	18.92	20.29	nm	12.15
Dividends per Share	0.12	0.12	0.10	0.10	0.07
Dividend Yield (%)	1.48	0.86	0.71	0.88	0.99
Sales per Share	14.90	13.51	12.59	10.78	8.68
EPS before extra. item	0.45	0.74	0.69	(0.58)	0.54
Cash Flow per Share	0.70	0.96	0.89	0.73	0.62
Book Value per Share	4.69	4.32	3.69	3.06	2.59
O/S Common Shares	52,522	52,487	52,464	52,411	52,111
Total Revenue	893,549	814,554	755,002	644,718	522,678
Income before extra.	23,845	38,865	35,945	30,410	28,028
Cash Flow	36,571	50,119	46,645	38,300	32,206
Debt/Equity	0.16	0.27	0.34	0.32	0.03
Return on Capital (%)	15.31	24.91	25.96	29.22	33.88
Ret. on Com. Equity (%)	10.08	18.51	20.31	20.56	22.80
% Change Profit	(38.6)	8.1	18.2	8.5	51.5
% Change Revenue	9.7	7.9	17.1	23.3	10.8
% Change Assets	(3.2)	14.9	13.0	53.6	18.3

Preferred Div. Coverage	np	np	np
Total Div. Coverage	3.8	6.2	6.9
Interest Coverage	9.6	13.3	9.6
Current Ratio	1.7	1.3	1.5
Operating Margin	7.9	9.0	7.4
Asset Turnover	2.2	1.9	2.0
5 YEAR RATIOS (%)			
Return on Capital	25.9	28.3	29.4
Return on Com. Equity	18.5	20.0	19.8
Profit Growth	5.1	20.2	26.4
Revenue Growth	13.6	15.8	22.2
Asset Growth	17.9	21.3	24.4
BALANCE SHEET (000)			
Cash	0	0	0
Current Assets	153,043	155,063	152,255
Net Fixed Assets	148,632	139,969	121,661
Invest's & Advances	19,587	38,612	16,244
Total Assets	361,845	373,748	325,172
Short Term Debt	13,159	34,261	33,422
Current Liabilities	88,238	119,066	99,091
Long Term Debt	26,514	27,158	31,803
Total Liabilities	115,359	147,093	131,811
Total Equity	246,486	226,655	193,361
Total Liab. & Equity	361,845	373,748	325,172
CAPITAL (000)			
Total Debt	39,673	61,419	65,225
Preferred Equity	0	0	0
Common Equity	246,486	226,655	193,361

Business:

JEAN COUTU GROUP (PJC) INC. oversees the operation of 210 retail franchises in Canada and 21 company stores in the United States. The drug stores sell pharmaceuticals, health products, cosmetics, snacks and other products. It operates under the names PJC Jean Coutu, Super Escomptes Jean Coutu, Pharmacie Jean Coutu Pharmacy, Maxi Drug, and Douglas Maxi Drug.

Date	EPS	DPS	Tot Rev	Inc Bex
Feb 95	0.27	0.03	384,556	14,131
Nov 94	0.19	0.03	276,837	9,863
Aug 94	0.17	0.03	217,202	9,119
May 94	0.16	0.03	216,242	8,626
Feb 94	(0.07)	0.03	215,229	(3,876)
Nov 93	0.18	0.03	239,529	9,616
Aug 93	0.18	0.03	222,549	9,479
May 93	0.20	0.03	219,159	10,329

Synopsis:

In June 1995, Jean Coutu Group Inc. (JCG) acquired 10 additional U.S. drugstores in a bid to expand further in the U.S. This acquisition for $2.5-million (U.S.) followed the September 1994 purchase of 221 small New England Brooks Drugstores by JCG for $147.5-million (U.S.). The Brooks stores have combined sales of $425.8-million (U.S.). JCG plans to acquire up to 100 more stores in the same area over the next few years. The 10 stores in this deal were all independent operations with total annual revenues of about $20-million. The stores will operate under the Brooks banner. The company is also in the midst of negotiating to buy 10 more U.S. drugstores. JCG now has 248 corporate-owned stores in the U.S. and 227 pharmacies in Canada. Many of the stores in Ontario, Quebec, and New Brunswick are franchised.

The plans for U.S. expansion come from the company's belief that Canada currently offers little in terms of expansion opportunity. JCG is eyeing existing independent pharmacies or smaller regional chains. In 1994, its Maxi stores operated under competitive pressures from other drugstore chains, grocery stores, discount buying clubs, and mail-order outlets. JCG has successfully integrated the Brooks network in the U.S. and has brought its new Dayville, Connecticut distribution centre on stream.

The third quarter 1995 results include a provision of $18-million for losses on receivables from franchisees, and a $1.9-million provision for obsolete inventories and other items. The company has been operating in a retail climate characterized by intense price competition with supermarkets and mega-retailers such as Wal-Mart. Despite this, revenues jumped 78.7% in the quarter, with the U.S. subsidiary contributing to most of this growth. Retail sales of the franchise network in Canada was $1.049-billion, a jump of 4.8%. With the expansion in the U.S., JCG's long-term debt has increased from about $26-million in the first quarter to about $117-million in this quarter with a decline from the second quarter. For the nine months ended February 1995, sales derived from Canadian operations were 66% versus 34% for the U.S. operations.

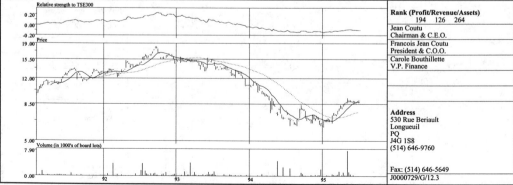

Rank (Profit/Revenue/Assets)
194 126 264

Jean Coutu
Chairman & C.E.O.
Francois Jean Coutu
President & C.O.O.
Carole Bouthillette
V.P. Finance

Address
530 Rue Beriault
Longueuil
PQ
J4G 1S8
(514) 646-9760

Fax: (514) 646-5649
J0000729/G/12.3

For further company information, call Globe Information Services 1-800-268-9128 or (416) 585-5345

LEON'S FURNITURE LIMITED

Period Ending	Dec94	Dec93	Dec92	Dec91	Dec90
Yearly Statistics					
Price-Close	11.50	12.25	10.75	10.63	7.13
Price-High	14.00	13.50	11.25	10.88	7.75
Price-Low	10.00	10.50	10.50	6.88	6.25
P/E-Close	13.53	14.94	20.28	15.68	11.18
Dividends per Share	0.18	0.16	0.15	1.15	0.15
Dividend Yield (%)	1.57	1.27	1.40	10.85	2.15
Sales per Share	13.60	13.77	13.14	13.09	14.36
EPS before extra. item	0.85	0.82	0.53	0.68	0.64
Cash Flow per Share	1.12	1.09	0.83	0.83	0.86
Book Value per Share	5.89	4.98	4.32	4.23	4.69
O/S Common Shares	19,758	20,553	20,572	20,627	20,674
Total Revenue	278,093	277,975	266,320	266,551	284,570
Income before extra.	16,769	16,188	10,412	13,437	12,615
Cash Flow	22,168	21,502	16,361	16,442	17,065
Debt/Equity	0.02	0.02	0.10	0.13	0.12
Return on Capital (%)	25.63	28.12	20.13	24.72	24.25
Ret. on Com. Equity (%)	15.34	16.94	11.83	14.59	14.20
% Change Profit	3.6	55.5	(22.5)	6.5	(12.8)
% Change Revenue	0.0	4.4	(0.1)	(6.3)	14.6
% Change Assets	9.9	9.4	(13.4)	4.1	19.1

	Preferred Div. Coverage	Total Div. Coverage	Interest Coverage	Current Ratio	Operating Margin	Asset Turnover
	np	5.5	144.2	2.3	7.1	1.7
	np	5.2	122.7	1.9	8.3	1.8
	np	3.4	16.3	1.5	5.0	1.9

Date	EPS	DPS	Tot Rev	Inc Bex
Mar 95	0.09	0.05	58,203	1,746
Dec 94	0.39	0.05	93,680	7,591
Sep 94	0.26	0.05	76,806	5,202
Jun 94	0.14	0.00	59,662	2,841
Mar 94	0.06	0.08	47,945	1,135
Dec 93	0.33	0.00	84,766	6,558
Sep 93	0.27	0.08	78,817	5,357
Jun 93	0.13	0.00	63,213	3,074

Business:

LEON'S FURNITURE LIMITED sells home furniture, appliances, and electronics through a chain of retail facilities and franchises located across Canada and the United States.

5 YEAR RATIOS (%)

	Return on Capital	Return on Com. Equity	Profit Growth	Revenue Growth	Asset Growth
	24.6	14.6	3.0	2.3	5.2
	25.9	15.4	1.8	3.3	4.5
	28.3	16.6	(3.5)	3.8	4.5

BALANCE SHEET (000)			
Cash	51,757	37,499	19,012
Current Assets	100,595	81,537	67,368
Net Fixed Assets	58,017	61,323	63,803
Invest's & Advances	0	0	0
Total Assets	161,856	147,219	134,573
Short Term Debt	292	267	6,874
Current Liabilities	43,912	42,947	43,485
Long Term Debt	1,587	1,962	2,226
Total Liabilities	45,499	44,909	45,711
Total Equity	116,357	102,310	88,862
Total Liab. & Equity	161,856	147,219	134,573
CAPITAL (000)			
Total Debt	1,879	2,229	9,100
Preferred Equity	1,138	0	0
Common Equity	115,219	102,310	88,862

Synopsis:

Fiscal 1994 for Leon's Furniture Limited was highlighted by the successful implementation of its new computer system throughout the company. The new system will provide access to more accurate information on a timely basis. The system integrates inventory, sales, merchandising, and customer data. Leon's will absorb the cost of computer system in the short-term.

During fiscal 1994, 22% of Leon's total sales came from franchises. The marginal decline in corporate sales was partly due to a difficult retail environment. Sales from franchises totalled $76-million, an increase of 8.5%. Two new franchise stores were added in Thunder Bay, Ontario, and Hinton, Alberta. At the end of 1994, Leon's had 21 franchise stores. In foreign operations, sales at the Arizona branch declined 8.4% in the year. The Arizona operation remains a concern to Leon's. It has added a major appliance area and new store management in Arizona.

In November 1994, Leon's announced plans for a $50-million expansion including eight new facilities in Canada. Leon's will finance the expansion using internal funds. Phase one will include large new warehouse showrooms in Ottawa, Kitchener, and Mississauga, Ontario. Leon's also plans to add to its Calgary operation to meet growing demand in that market. Phase two of the expansion includes new warehouse showrooms in London and Oshawa in Ontario, and in Quebec City. The second phase should be completed by the close of 1996.

Rank (Profit/Revenue/Assets)
234   266   384
Anthony T. Leon
Chairman
Mark J. Leon
President & C.E.O.
Terrence T. Leon
V.P. & Secretary & C.E.O.

Address
88 Gordon Mackay Rd.
P.O. Box 1100
Station "B"
Weston
ON
M9L 2R8
(416) 243-7880
Fax: (416) 243-7890
L0001667/G/12.5

LOBLAW COMPANIES LIMITED

Exchanges	Price (Jun29'95)		27.75	Trailing P/E		17.90	Stock Symbol
TMV	Trailing Yield (%)		0.97	Trailing EPS		1.55	L

Period Ending	Dec94	Jan94	Jan93	Dec91	Dec90	Business:
Yearly Statistics						LOBLAW COS. LTD. is a food distribution
Price-Close	23.88	23.63	19.50	17.88	18.38	company with operations across Canada and in
Price-High	26.00	24.00	20.50	22.50	18.88	the United States. The company operates
Price-Low	19.50	18.50	16.38	16.38	13.63	grocery stores under various banners including
P/E-Close	15.81	22.08	22.16	15.28	16.71	Loblaws, Zehrs, Save-Easy, OK! Economy and
Dividends per Share	0.26	0.24	0.24	0.24	0.20	The Real Canadian Superstore. George Weston
Dividend Yield (%)	1.09	1.02	1.23	1.34	1.09	Limited of Toronto owns 70% of the company's
Sales per Share	125.83	118.47	117.75	112.55	116.19	common shares.
EPS before extra. item	1.51	1.07	0.88	1.17	1.10	
Cash Flow per Share	3.44	2.91	2.61	2.72	2.73	
Book Value per Share	12.92	11.48	10.67	9.63	8.11	
O/S Common Shares (mil)	80	79	79	78	73	

Date	EPS	DPS	Tot Rev	Inc Bex
Mar 95	0.30	0.07	2,302,700	24,300
Dec 94	0.51	0.07	2,404,800	42,400
Oct 94	0.39	0.07	3,092,400	33,500
Jun 94	0.35	0.06	2,334,100	29,400
Mar 94	0.26	0.06	2,176,300	21,400
Jan 94	0.31	0.06	2,188,100	26,100
Oct 93	0.27	0.06	2,893,700	24,400
Jun 93	0.28	0.06	2,162,900	24,300

	Dec94	Jan94	Jan93	Dec91	Dec90
Total Revenue ($mil)	10,008	9,360	9,266	8,539	8,417
Income before extra. ($mil)	127	93	80	105	96
Cash Flow ($mil)	274	230	205	206	198
Debt/Equity	0.65	0.76	0.59	0.63	0.58
Return on Capital (%)	15.52	12.32	12.16	16.00	16.62
Ret. on Com. Equity (%)	12.36	9.64	8.65	13.20	14.35
% Change Profit	35.7	17.0	(23.8)	9.1	36.8
% Change Revenue	6.9	1.0	8.5	1.5	6.1
% Change Assets	7.5	10.9	4.8	12.3	3.1

Preferred Div. Coverage	18.9	10.5	7.5
Total Div. Coverage	4.6	3.3	2.7
Interest Coverage	3.7	3.4	3.0
Current Ratio	1.0	1.2	1.2
Operating Margin	2.7	2.1	2.1
Asset Turnover	3.4	3.4	3.7
5 YEAR RATIOS (%)			
Return on Capital	14.5	14.4	13.9
Return on Com. Equity	11.6	11.5	10.7
Profit Growth	12.5	18.0	1.6
Revenue Growth	4.7	2.4	1.4
Asset Growth	7.5	6.4	2.2
BALANCE SHEET (000)			
Cash	215,500	271,900	208,000
Current Assets	1,118,700	1,116,800	1,051,900
Net Fixed Assets	1,603,400	1,413,700	1,231,400
Invest's & Advances	94,300	84,100	94,100
Total Assets	2,947,200	2,742,700	2,474,100
Short Term Debt	56,900	37,800	5,600
Current Liabilities	1,089,100	968,300	868,400
Long Term Debt	666,400	722,300	572,000
Total Liabilities	1,825,300	1,739,900	1,501,900
Total Equity	1,121,900	1,002,800	972,200
Total Liab. & Equity	2,947,200	2,742,700	2,474,100
CAPITAL (000)			
Total Debt	723,300	760,100	577,600
Preferred Equity	90,900	91,300	129,700
Common Equity	1,031,000	911,500	842,500

Synopsis:

In 1994, Loblaw Companies Limited's Eastern and Western Canadian divisions produced record sales. In the East, Loblaw's saw a shift in growth as retail sales grew almost twice as much as wholesale sales. Loblaws continues to expand its product categories and services. This reflects its view of its stores as one-stop shops for everyday household needs, rather than simply food stores. Loblaws anticipates growth by competing with the new mass merchandise stores. It offers such non-food services such as pharmaceuticals, music, books, clothing, videos, photofinishing, and dry cleaning. The company sold its unprofitable Hasty Market convenience stores.

In the West, The Real Canadian Superstores performed well despite stiff competition from Wal-Mart beginning in 1994 and the competitive reaction of other mass merchandise stores. Five new Superstores opened in 1994, and several more are planned for 1995. The company also plans to open three new Real Canadian Wholesale Club stores. Loblaw's Western Canada wholesale business underwent a rationalization beginning in 1993 that resulted in wholesale sales declining 11.9% in 1994. For 1995, the company's objective includes focusing on the produce section of the business, integrating its brokerage affiliates, located in Florida, Texas, and California into operations.

In its United States division, Loblaw's primary focus was in rebuilding its business in New Orleans. There a 1993 strike cost the company $25-million in lost profits and costs related to the strike. In 1995, the company sold all the assets of its 85 National Tea Co. supermarkets.

The percentages of 1994 sales (operating income) by region were: Eastern Canada, 56% (44%); Western Canada, 29% (40%); United States, 15% (15%).

Loblaw's debt-to-equity ratio was 0.45:1 in 1994, and its cash flow from operations was $329-million, up from $281.8-million in 1993.

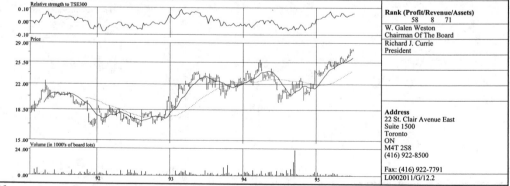

Rank (Profit/Revenue/Assets)	58 8 71
W. Galen Weston	Chairman Of The Board
Richard J. Currie	President

Address
22 St. Clair Avenue East
Suite 1500
Toronto
ON
M4T 2S8
(416) 922-8500

Fax: (416) 922-7791
L000201I/G/12.2

METRO-RICHELIEU INC.

Exchanges	Price (Jun29'95)	16 .25	Trailing P/E	11 .86	Stock Symbol
TM	Trailing Yield (%)	0 .25	Trailing EPS	1 .37	**MRU.A**

Period Ending	Sep94	Sep93	Sep92	Sep91	Sep90
Yearly Statistics					
Price-Close	11 .38	10 .38	7 .75	7 .63	2 .95
Price-High	12 .38	11 .00	8 .38	7 .63	4 .00
Price-Low	10 .38	7 .63	5 .00	2 .80	2 .50
P/E-Close	9 .98	12 .35	15 .82	20 .61	nm
Dividends per Share	0 .00	0 .00	0 .00	0 .00	0 .00
Dividend Yield (%)	0 .00	0 .00	0 .00	0 .00	0 .00
Sales per Share	89 .15	88 .84	98 .04	115 .70	119 .35
EPS before extra. item	1 .14	0 .84	0 .49	0 .37	(0 .63)
Cash Flow per Share	2 .36	2 .10	1 .89	2 .15	0 .96
Book Value per Share	8 .46	7 .39	6 .53	6 .25	5 .85
O/S Common Shares	32 ,680	32 ,666	28 ,664	19 ,406	18 ,668
Total Revenue	2 ,909 ,000	2 ,772 ,700	2 ,308 ,600	2 ,219 ,914	2 ,187 ,879
Income before extra.	37 ,200	26 ,200	13 ,100	9 ,409	(9 ,002)
Cash Flow	77 ,100	65 ,500	44 ,500	41 ,159	17 ,698
Debt/Equity	0 .27	0 .47	1 .07	1 .32	1 .75
Return on Capital (%)	21 .26	16 .00	10 .68	10 .45	4 .20
Ret. on Com. Equity (%)	14 .36	12 .22	5 .45	5 .50	(10 .27)
% Change Profit	42 .0	100 .0	39 .2	204 .5	2 .5
% Change Revenue	4 .9	20 .1	4 .0	1 .5	(4 .7)
% Change Assets	2 .2	(3 .2)	22 .3	(1 .5)	(9 .4)

Preferred Div. Coverage	np	na	2 .8
Total Div. Coverage	na	na	2 .8
Interest Coverage	6 .9	3 .9	2 .3
Current Ratio	1 .0	1 .0	1 .0
Operating Margin	3 .0	2 .6	2 .0
Asset Turnover	4 .8	4 .7	3 .8
5 YEAR RATIOS (%)			
Return on Capital	12 .5	9 .3	8 .4
Return on Com. Equity	5 .5	0 .6	(0 .0)
Profit Growth	65 .2	15 .0	8 .4
Revenue Growth	4 .8	5 .1	3 .7
Asset Growth	1 .5	0 .9	2 .6
BALANCE SHEET (000)			
Cash	0	0	0
Current Assets	259 ,300	242 ,800	234 ,900
Net Fixed Assets	148 ,400	146 ,600	161 ,200
Invest's & Advances	14 ,900	14 ,500	17 ,400
Total Assets	600 ,100	587 ,400	606 ,700
Short Term Debt	27 ,200	34 ,100	31 ,400
Current Liabilities	264 ,000	251 ,500	238 ,900
Long Term Debt	46 ,700	79 ,400	168 ,600
Total Liabilities	323 ,500	345 ,800	419 ,100
Total Equity	276 ,600	241 ,400	187 ,600
Total Liab. & Equity	600 ,100	587 ,400	606 ,700
CAPITAL (000)			
Total Debt	73 ,900	113 ,500	200 ,000
Preferred Equity	0	200	300
Common Equity	276 ,600	241 ,400	187 ,300

Business:

METRO-RICHELIEU INC. is engaged primarily in the purchase and wholesale distribution of food products and general merchandise. Its operating territory extends throughout Quebec and Northern Ontario.

Date	EPS	DPS	Tot Rev	Inc Bex
Mar 95	0 .33	0 .04	683 ,000	10 ,100
Dec 94	0 .36	0 .00	717 ,400	11 ,600
Sep 94	0 .28	0 .00	698 ,500	9 ,200
Jul 94	0 .40	0 .00	898 ,900	12 ,900
Mar 94	0 .22	0 .00	634 ,800	7 ,100
Dec 93	0 .24	0 .00	676 ,800	8 ,000
Sep 93	0 .21	0 .00	641 ,200	7 ,100
Jul 93	0 .29	0 .00	861 ,169	9 ,002

Synopsis:

Metro-Richelieu had strong results in the six months ended March 1995. Net earnings for the period climbed to $21.7-million, up from $15-million for the same period in 1993, an increase of 43.7%. Earnings per share for the period amounted to $0.67 per share, up 52% from the previous year. Metro-Richelieu has gradually increased its market share in Quebec, which was at 32% in January 1995. At March 1995, long-term debt stood at $61.8-million and shareholders' equity at $272.5-million.

Metro-Richelieu divides its food operations into three sections. In wholesaling, Metro-Richelieu supplies grocery, produce and meat products to customers operating stores under the Metro, Marche Richelieu, Super C, Les 5 Saisons, Ami and Gem banners, as well as independent grocers. In food retailing it operates 25 Super C discount stores. In food services, it supplies institutions, restaurants, hotels, and convenience stores. Metro-Richelieu's subsidiary, McMahon-Essaim Inc., is a pharmaceutical distributor that acts as the franchiser of the Brunet drugstores chain. Segmented revenues for the food sector in 1995 were: wholesaling, 71%; food services, 7%; and retailing, 21%. Pharmaceutical revenues were 6% of the company's overall revenues.

Operations during the year generated cash flow of $78.7-million. A large part of that amount was used to buy assets. Nearly $5-million was earmarked for expansion and modernization of the meat division's Boeuf Merite, while more than $16-million was spent on converting and remodelling 17 supermarkets and opening new stores. The company also invested in its computer system and in a warehouse. In 1995, the company will invest nearly $32-million in fixed assets.

In November 1994, the company bought back from the Caisse de depot et placement du Quebec two million of its first preferred shares, series 2, for $25-million.

Relative strength to TSE300

Price

Volume (in 1000's of board lots)

Rank (Profit/Revenue/Assets)
135 53 210

Bernard Belair
Chairman

Pierre H. Lessard
President & C.E.O.

Address
11011 Boul. Maurice Duplessis
Montreal
PQ
H1C 1V6
(514) 643-1055

Fax: (514) 643-1215
E0013203/G/12.2

NORTH WEST COMPANY INC. (THE)

Exchanges	Price (Jun29'95)	10.37	Trailing P/E	11.52	Stock Symbol
TW	Trailing Yield (%)	3.86	Trailing EPS	0.90	NWC

Period Ending	Jan95	Jan94	Jan93	Jan92	Jan91
Yearly Statistics					
Price-Close	9.88	17.25	15.13	16.13	7.00
Price-High	18.00	20.25	16.13	16.50	8.75
Price-Low	9.75	14.75	13.25	5.25	6.13
P/E-Close	9.88	16.27	14.27	16.62	20.00
Dividends per Share	0.40	0.36	0.36	0.30	0.32
Dividend Yield (%)	4.05	2.09	2.38	1.86	4.57
Sales per Share	36.27	34.02	33.66	28.90	28.87
EPS before extra. item	1.00	1.06	1.06	0.97	0.35
Cash Flow per Share	1.62	1.82	1.78	1.47	1.46
Book Value per Share	9.90	9.14	8.41	6.89	6.29
O/S Common Shares	16,164	16,164	16,097	13,673	13,290
Total Revenue	586,242	548,679	472,710	390,446	377,413
Income before extra.	16,239	17,162	14,954	12,923	4,575
Cash Flow	26,173	29,283	25,060	19,841	19,071
Debt/Equity	1.11	0.85	0.79	1.05	1.63
Return on Capital (%)	12.71	14.77	15.44	16.06	12.03
Ret. on Com. Equity (%)	10.56	12.13	13.03	14.54	5.54
% Change Profit	(5.4)	14.8	15.7	182.5	(61.9)
% Change Revenue	6.8	16.1	21.1	3.5	2.5
% Change Assets	18.5	10.9	23.2	(5.4)	10.4

Preferred Div. Coverage	np	np	np
Total Div. Coverage	2.5	3.0	2.9
Interest Coverage	3.6	4.5	3.7
Current Ratio	1.5	2.2	2.0
Operating Margin	6.6	6.9	7.1
Asset Turnover	1.5	1.7	1.6
5 YEAR RATIOS (%)			
Return on Capital	14.2	15.2	15.7
Return on Com. Equity	11.2	12.5	14.4
Profit Growth	6.2	11.2	19.1
Revenue Growth	9.6	5.2	3.4
Asset Growth	11.1	7.9	6.2
BALANCE SHEET (000)			
Cash	6,453	7,136	13,385
Current Assets	204,253	182,735	174,486
Net Fixed Assets	179,822	145,255	122,024
Invest's & Advances	4,399	0	0
Total Assets	392,434	331,055	298,412
Short Term Debt	90,809	36,640	40,933
Current Liabilities	135,591	83,285	87,142
Long Term Debt	85,939	88,336	66,382
Total Liabilities	232,460	183,403	163,066
Total Equity	159,974	147,652	135,346
Total Liab. & Equity	392,434	331,055	298,412
CAPITAL (000)			
Total Debt	176,748	124,976	107,315
Preferred Equity	0	0	0
Common Equity	159,974	147,652	135,346

Business:

THE NORTHWEST COMPANY INC., operating under the names Northern and AC Value Centre, is the leading retailer of food, family apparel and general merchandise in small, northern communities. It also operates complementary businesses which draw upon the company's unique heritage and knowledge of the North.

Date	EPS	DPS	Tot Rev	Inc Bex
Apr 95	0.02	0.10	139,682	362
Jan 95	0.31	0.10	162,093	5,150
Oct 94	0.32	0.10	148,500	5,153
Jul 94	0.25	0.10	143,275	4,010
Apr 94	0.12	0.10	133,286	1,926
Jan 94	0.39	0.09	153,885	6,309
Oct 93	0.31	0.09	137,034	5,011
Jul 93	0.28	0.09	134,196	4,575

Synopsis:

Fiscal 1994 was a busy year for The North West Company Inc. North West added 115,000 square feet of selling space. Its Northern stores division opened two new stores and eight replacement stores, and completed major renovations in five stores. As well, 16 Quickstop food courts and four Quickstop convenience stores were opened. The Alaska Commercial Company opened three replacement stores and bought eight stores in the Kodiak Island region.

The company undertook an extensive store expansion and renovation program in 1994 as a means of securing its place as the leading retailer in the North. A new management structure contributed to the success of its Canadian operations. Debt loss in fiscal 1994 declined by 45% and food margins improved as a result of an increased direct buy program through the company's new food distribution facility in Winnipeg. Performance at the Alaskan operations was up despite margin erosion, competition in key markets, and a one time charge associated with store expansion and remodeling. Operating profit from the Diversified Business Group soared 120%. Capital spending for 1995 is earmarked at $28-million, a drop of 35%. Spending will focus on 10 new or replacement stores, along with renovations. North West has spent more than $93-million since 1992 to acquire, build, and renovate stores. The company also plans to continue evaluating its product mix. It will initiate changes as necessary.

In 1995, North West plans to reduce administration and distribution costs by 5% or $1.5-million in Canada as a result of cost reductions in all support functions. Alaskan operations should also achieve comparative cost reductions. Furthermore, the full impact of the Winnipeg food facility should generate positive results.

Sales by segment in 1994 were: food, 54%; general merchandise, 44%; and other, 2%. Northern operations in Canada accounted for 78.8% of total revenue in 1994. Alaskan operations accounted for 19.7% of revenue, with the remaining 1.5% coming from the Diversified Business and Shipping division.

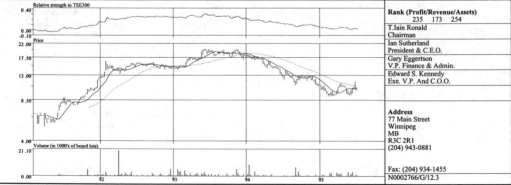

Rank (Profit/Revenue/Assets)
235 173 254

T.Iain Ronald
Chairman

Ian Sutherland
President & C.E.O.

Gary Eggertson
V.P. Finance & Admin.

Edward S. Kennedy
Exe. V.P. And C.O.O.

Address
77 Main Street
Winnipeg
MB
R3C 2R1
(204) 943-0881

Fax: (204) 934-1455
N0002766/G/12.3

OSHAWA GROUP LIMITED (THE)

Exchanges	Price (Jun29'95)	21.25	Trailing P/E	14.66	Stock Symbol
TM	Trailing Yield (%)	1.76	Trailing EPS	1.45	**OSH.A**

Period Ending	Jan95	Jan94	Jan93	Jan92	Jan91
Yearly Statistics					
Price-Close	18.63	23.38	21.63	18.88	33.75
Price-High	24.25	25.25	24.13	35.63	33.75
Price-Low	17.13	20.13	17.00	19.25	27.25
P/E-Close	13.21	17.32	18.97	19.66	20.09
Dividends per Share	0.50	0.48	0.46	0.46	0.43
Dividend Yield (%)	2.66	2.03	2.13	2.41	1.27
Sales per Share	160.74	153.83	136.18	126.57	127.64
EPS before extra. item	1.41	1.35	1.14	0.96	1.68
Cash Flow per Share	3.10	2.74	2.29	2.03	3.09
Book Value per Share	19.77	17.90	17.98	17.29	16.70
O/S Common Shares	37,993	39,510	36,987	36,618	36,346
Total Revenue	6,073,100	5,730,600	5,016,900	4,635,600	4,609,500
Income before extra.	53,200	50,200	41,800	35,100	60,400
Cash Flow	117,000	101,900	84,400	74,000	111,500
Debt/Equity	0.24	0.23	0.16	0.07	0.10
Return on Capital (%)	10.41	10.66	9.63	8.90	17.05
Ret. on Com. Equity (%)	7.30	7.32	6.44	5.66	10.42
% Change Profit	6.0	20.1	19.1	(41.9)	(13.2)
% Change Revenue	6.0	14.2	8.2	0.6	5.0
% Change Assets	4.3	8.8	15.1	1.2	9.8

Preferred Div. Coverage	np	np	np
Total Div. Coverage	2.8	2.9	2.5
Interest Coverage	8.4	9.3	13.1
Current Ratio	1.8	1.7	1.4
Operating Margin	1.5	1.5	1.3
Asset Turnover	4.6	4.5	4.3
5 YEAR RATIOS (%)			
Return on Capital	11.3	13.7	16.2
Return on Com. Equity	7.4	8.9	10.6
Profit Growth	(5.3)	(2.5)	(3.5)
Revenue Growth	6.6	5.9	5.6
Asset Growth	7.6	9.6	11.4
BALANCE SHEET (000)			
Cash	54,600	35,100	5,200
Current Assets	662,500	627,300	566,100
Net Fixed Assets	470,600	473,900	466,500
Invest's & Advances	58,700	45,600	34,700
Total Assets	1,313,700	1,259,700	1,158,100
Short Term Debt	57,000	36,500	80,900
Current Liabilities	376,600	371,100	411,000
Long Term Debt	123,500	124,200	23,700
Total Liabilities	562,700	552,400	493,200
Total Equity	751,000	707,300	664,900
Total Liab. & Equity	1,313,700	1,259,700	1,158,100
CAPITAL (000)			
Total Debt	180,500	160,700	104,600
Preferred Equity	0	0	0
Common Equity	751,000	707,300	664,900

Business:

THE OSHAWA GROUP LIMITED markets groceries and pharmaceuticals through a network of distribution centres and retail stores in nine provinces across Canada. The company supplies IGA markets across Canada. It operates Food City and IGA supermarkets and Pharma Plus drug stores. The company also has real estate holdings.

Date	EPS	DPS	Tot Rev	Inc Bex
Apr 95	0.28	0.13	1,363,900	10,600
Jan 95	0.35	0.00	1,483,400	13,200
Oct 94	0.28	0.13	1,387,900	10,700
Aug 94	0.54	0.13	1,869,100	20,400
Apr 94	0.24	0.13	1,329,400	8,900
Jan 94	0.41	0.12	1,334,600	15,400
Oct 93	0.25	0.12	1,333,000	9,300
Aug 93	0.48	0.12	1,788,300	17,900

Synopsis:

The Oshawa Group Limited posted gains in both revenue and earnings for the year ended January 1995. Revenues grew 6% mainly due to the food distribution operations. Sales by segmented were: Wholesale and retail food, 86% (Eastern region, 41%; Central, 40%; Western, 19%); Foodservice, 7%; Drugstore, 6.7%; and Real Estate, 0.3%.

Results for fiscal 1994 were adversely affected by a fourth quarter charge of $7.2-million. This was incurred to finance a staff restructuring, including a wage rollback program in the Ontario corporate stores. The revamping will lower the operating costs of the stores and help offset the continued margin pressure from new entrants into the Ontario retail food market.

For the period ending April 1995, Oshawa foods posted a $10-million profit, up almost 20% from the year before. Again, the food division results accounted for the gains. Drugstore earnings from Pharma Plus declined due to a federal ruling in late 1994 prohibiting the sale of tobacco in drugstores.

In June 1995, following on the 1994 success of its Price Chopper discount stores in Central Canada, Oshawa said it would convert 10 more supermarkets into the no-frills Price Chopper format.

Oshawa Foods is at the forefront of the industry-wide Efficient Consumer Response (ECR) initiative, whereby the industry is gradually adopting practices and technology to create a more efficient distribution of products from manufacturer to store shelves. In ECR, product categories are managed like individual businesses. Disruptive and expensive inventory peaks and valleys are eliminated through continuous replenishment. Electronic data interchange is used to link suppliers and customers, and transportation and storage activities are streamlined. In fiscal 1995, Oshawa Foods invested $17-million in ECR-related computer technology alone.

Rank (Profit/Revenue/Assets)
110 21 137

Allister P. Graham
Chairman & C.E.O.

Jonathan A. Wolfe
President & C.O.O.

Robert E. Boyd
Exec. V.P. & C.F.O.

Address
302 The East Mall
Etobicoke
ON
M9B 6B8
(416) 236-1971

Fax: (416) 236-2071
O0001142/G/12.2

PROVIGO INC.

Exchanges						Stock Symbol
TM	Price (Jun29'95)	8.25	Trailing P/E		nm	
	Trailing Yield (%)	0.73	Trailing EPS		(1.19)	**PGV**

Period Ending	Jan95	Jan94	Jan93	Jan92	Jan91
Yearly Statistics					
Price-Close	5.13	7.50	7.75	8.38	10.40
Price-High	7.63	10.63	9.13	13.00	10.50
Price-Low	4.85	7.00	6.50	8.13	8.25
P/E-Close	nm	nm	25.83	14.69	1,040.00
Dividends per Share	0.06	0.28	0.28	0.25	0.24
Dividend Yield (%)	1.17	3.73	3.61	2.97	2.31
Sales per Share	71.29	71.71	78.06	77.64	76.01
EPS before extra. item	(1.22)	(1.33)	0.30	0.57	0.01
Cash Flow per Share	1.38	0.20	0.58	1.55	1.38
Book Value per Share	1.14	2.42	4.02	3.94	3.59
O/S Common Shares	86,670	86,624	86,538	86,442	86,024
Total Revenue	6,036,500	6,213,700	6,809,100	6,714,600	6,540,700
Income before extra.	(98,300)	(108,200)	32,500	49,300	700
Cash Flow	119,200	17,200	50,200	134,100	118,200
Debt/Equity	2.60	1.81	1.38	2.10	2.22
Return on Capital (%)	(3.31)	(8.77)	11.00	13.80	11.31
Ret. on Com. Equity (%)	(68.05)	(41.26)	7.76	15.19	0.22
% Change Profit	9.2	(432.9)	(34.1)	6,942.9	101.4
% Change Revenue	(2.9)	(8.7)	1.4	2.7	6.3
% Change Assets	(21.2)	(11.2)	(4.1)	2.3	3.4

Preferred Div. Coverage	0.0	0.0	5.6			
Total Div. Coverage	0.0	0.0	1.1			
Interest Coverage	0.0	0.0	1.9			
Current Ratio	0.9	0.7	1.2			
Operating Margin	2.2	1.8	1.6			
Asset Turnover	6.0	4.8	4.6			
5 YEAR RATIOS (%)						
Return on Capital	4.8	6.4	11.2			
Return on Com. Equity	(17.2)	(6.4)	5.0			
Profit Growth	na	na	(13.5)			
Revenue Growth	(0.4)	2.9	1.6			
Asset Growth	(6.6)	(0.6)	(0.2)			
BALANCE SHEET (000)						
Cash	22,100	40,900	27,000			
Current Assets	399,300	521,100	602,100			
Net Fixed Assets	387,500	491,000	510,400			
Invest's & Advances	81,000	74,100	169,000			
Total Assets	1,026,000	1,302,000	1,465,600			
Short Term Debt	50,200	231,000	92,300			
Current Liabilities	422,100	711,000	516,500			
Long Term Debt	421,300	298,700	500,300			
Total Liabilities	844,600	1,009,700	1,035,600			
Total Equity	181,400	292,300	430,000			
Total Liab. & Equity	1,026,000	1,302,000	1,465,600			
CAPITAL (000)						
Total Debt	471,500	529,700	592,600			
Preferred Equity	82,400	82,400	82,400			
Common Equity	99,000	209,900	347,600			

Business:

PROVIGO INC. is a retailer and distributor in the food sector operating in Canada. The Company operates through three subsidiaries: Provigo Distribution Inc.; Loeb Inc.; and C. Corp Inc.

Date	EPS	DPS	Tot Rev	Inc Bex
Apr 95	0.13	0.00	1,260,000	13,400
Jan 95	0.15	0.00	1,261,700	14,900
Nov 94	(1.62)	0.02	1,422,900	(138,700)
Aug 94	0.15	0.02	1,949,200	15,200
Apr 94	0.10	0.02	1,402,700	10,300
Jan 94	(0.58)	0.07	1,438,300	(49,100)
Nov 93	(0.88)	0.07	1,435,000	(74,100)
Aug 93	0.11	0.07	1,943,700	11,500

Synopsis:

After a decade of diversification efforts, Provigo Inc. is refocusing on its Canadian retail food business. Provigo is in the midst of a $250-million, three-year plan to renovate existing stores and to open 30 new ones in Quebec and Ontario (under the Loeb banner).

Before 1995, Provigo divested itself of Sports Experts, Consumers Distributing, and some unprofitable Canadian food outlets. In 1995, the company also rid itself of its money-losing California operation, Provigo Corp., in a share deal worth $16-million (U.S.). Although the sale boosts earnings long-term, the company took a $147-million after-tax writedown on the unit. As a result, the Canadian Bond Rating Service downgraded Provigo's debt in January 1995. As of April 1995, Provigo's debt stood at $364-million.

In Canada, 74% of Provigo's revenues come from its supermarkets and discount stores. The remaining 26% in revenues stems from convenience stores, cash and carry operations, smaller independent food stores, its food service segment, and gas marts. Provigo stores in Quebec are subject to unrelenting competition from other food stores, including Sobeys which is stepping up its presence with new store openings. Sobeys holds a 24% interest in Provigo.

Results for the three months ending April 1995, showed improvements for Provigo. Net income amounted to $13.4-million, 24% better than it achieved (in its Canadian operations) a year earlier. Operating activities generated a net cash inflow of $22.8-million, compared with a net cash outflow of $4.5-million a year earlier. Six supermarkets and discount stores were renovated during the period. In addition to strengthening its competitive position in Ontario and Quebec, Provigo's overall strategy is to employ new grocery industry technologies to reduce distribution, receiving, and inventory expenses.

Rank (Profit/Revenue/Assets)
997   24   151

Pierre Michaud
Chairman

Pierre L. Mignault
President & C.E.O.

Roland Harel
Ex. V.P. & C.F.O.

Address
1611 Cremazie Blvd. East
Montreal
PQ
H2M 2R9
(514) 383-3000

Fax: (514) 383-3088
P0004273/G/12.2

REITMANS (CANADA) LIMITED

Exchanges	Price (Jun29'95)		16 .50	Trailing P/E		13 .87	Stock Symbol
TM	Trailing Yield (%)		3 .15	Trailing EPS		1 .19	RET.A

Period Ending	Jan95	Jan94	Jan93	Feb92	Feb91	Business:
Yearly Statistics						REITMANS (CANADA) LTD. operates a
Price-Close	16 .50	21 .00	19 .25	20 .00	13 .25	network of clothing stores specializing in
Price-High	22 .00	25 .25	20 .50	20 .00	17 .25	women's fashions and accessories. The
Price-Low	15 .00	18 .00	15 .00	14 .00	11 .25	company operates stores under the names
P/E-Close	12 .31	13 .55	9 .82	18 .18	nm	Reitmans, Smart Set, Un-Deux-Trois and
Dividends per Share	0 .52	0 .52	0 .52	0 .52	0 .52	Pennington's.
Dividend Yield (%)	3 .15	2 .48	2 .70	2 .60	3 .93	
Sales per Share	35 .47	36 .27	34 .08	32 .01	32 .29	
EPS before extra. item	1 .34	1 .55	1 .96	1 .10	(3 .18)	
Cash Flow per Share	1 .01	1 .36	1 .66	1 .41	0 .87	
Book Value per Share	15 .26	14 .44	13 .41	11 .97	11 .38	
O/S Common Shares	9 ,401	9 ,393	9 ,330	9 ,324	9 ,314	
Total Revenue	341 ,888	346 ,442	324 ,150	303 ,651	308 ,176	

Income before extra.	12 ,548	14 ,510	18 ,273	10 ,260	(29 ,647)	Date	EPS	DPS	Tot Rev	Inc Bex
Cash Flow	9 ,482	12 ,705	15 ,439	13 ,105	8 ,059	Apr 95	(0.17)	0 .13	67 ,704	(1 ,572)
Debt/Equity	nd	nd	nd	0 .03	0 .04	Jan 95	0 .54	0 .13	102 ,058	5 ,035
Return on Capital (%)	12 .14	16 .06	20 .27	13 .47	(19 .59)	Oct 94	0 .07	0 .13	76 ,160	618
Ret. on Com. Equity (%)	8 .99	11 .13	15 .44	9 .43	(23 .96)	Jul 94	0 .75	0 .13	98 ,015	7 ,075
% Change Profit	(13 .5)	(20 .6)	78 .1	134 .6	(525 .0)	Apr 94	(0.02)	0 .13	65 ,655	(180)
% Change Revenue	(1 .3)	6 .9	6 .8	(1 .5)	5 .1	Jan 94	0 .67	0 .13	105 ,462	6 ,219
% Change Assets	1 .4	8 .5	11 .7	(1 .5)	(21 .0)	Oct 93	0 .33	0 .13	81 ,710	3 ,177
						Jul 93	0 .54	0 .13	93 ,603	4 ,978

Preferred Div. Coverage	np	np	np	**Synopsis:**
Total Div. Coverage	2 .6	3 .0	3 .8	
Interest Coverage	74 .6	180 .5	91 .0	
Current Ratio	1 .8	1 .6	1 .8	
Operating Margin	2 .5	4 .1	4 .5	
Asset Turnover	1 .9	1 .9	2 .0	
5 YEAR RATIOS (%)				
Return on Capital	8 .5	8 .2	6 .3	
Return on Com. Equity	4 .2	3 .4	2 .4	
Profit Growth	12 .5	12 .3	14 .1	
Revenue Growth	3 .1	(0 .9)	(2 .0)	
Asset Growth	(0 .9)	0 .0	(1 .4)	
BALANCE SHEET (000)				
Cash	28 ,306	29 ,382	29 ,679	
Current Assets	55 ,885	57 ,092	60 ,409	
Net Fixed Assets	23 ,244	23 ,717	22 ,978	
Invest's & Advances	94 ,148	90 ,550	74 ,931	
Total Assets	178 ,085	175 ,617	161 ,788	
Short Term Debt	0	0	0	
Current Liabilities	31 ,884	36 ,505	33 ,811	
Long Term Debt	0	0	0	
Total Liabilities	34 ,643	39 ,953	36 ,684	
Total Equity	143 ,442	135 ,664	125 ,104	
Total Liab. & Equity	178 ,085	175 ,617	161 ,788	
CAPITAL (000)				
Total Debt	0	0	0	
Preferred Equity	0	0	0	
Common Equity	143 ,442	135 ,664	125 ,104	

Synopsis:

In April 1995, Reitmans (Canada) Ltd. announced the planned repurchase of up to 600,000 of its class A non-voting shares, representing about 9.6% of the public float.

In February 1995, Reitmans acquired 10 Pennington stores situated in shopping malls, along with 30 Wearhouse stores from bankrupt Pennington's Stores Ltd. Reitmans paid $1.5-million. Reitmans plans to use the stores as a platform to expand into large-size women's clothing, where Reitmans has had success. The Pennington's banner will be kept by Reitmans. Furthermore, the company may also go after some Pennington's and Liz Porter shopping centre stores which are available. According to Reitmans, the shopping centre stores had the greatest negative impact on Pennington's operations, but the Wearhouse division was profitable. The Wearhouse division offers a wide selection of value-priced merchandise, in stores averaging 5,500 square feet in high traffic strip or off-price shopping centres. Reitmans plans to open 12 Wearouse and four mall stores in 1995.

The weaker sales and earnings figures relating to fiscal 1995 were attributed to poor consumer confidence and unseasonable weather. Gross margins at both Reitmans and Smart Set increased 5% and 11% respectively for the first half of fiscal 1995. This was attributed to a generally improving Canadian economy, low and stable interest rates, along with an excellent product mix in the stores of both divisions. However, in the second half, weakening consumer confidence along with rising interest rates were blamed for the weaker performances. Overall, comparable store sales fell 4% in the Reitmans division and 7% in the Smart Set division. In the year, 10 Reitmans and one Smart Set store opened, but 11 other Reitmans and 11 Smart Set stores closed for a net closure of 11 stores. In fiscal 1995, Reitman's plans to continue to close underperforming stores and open new profitable stores. For fiscal 1996, it will spend $7-million on store development and $800,000 on new management information systems.

Relative strength to TSE300

Price

Volume (in 1000's of board lots)

Rank (Profit/Revenue/Assets)
269   237   372
Jack Reitman
Chairman Of The Board
Jeremy H. Reitman
President
Richard Wait
V.P. & Comptroller

Address
250 Sauve Street West
Montreal
PQ
H3L 1Z2
(514) 384-1140

Fax: (514) 385-2636
R0001263/G/12.4

SEARS CANADA INC.

	Exchanges	Price (Jun29'95)	7.00	Trailing P/E	14.29	Stock Symbol
TM		Trailing Yield (%)	3.43	Trailing EPS	0.49	**SCC**

Period Ending	Dec94	Dec93	Dec92	Dec91	Dec90
Yearly Statistics					
Price-Close	7.75	9.88	7.00	10.88	10.00
Price-High	10.00	10.00	10.50	14.25	12.50
Price-Low	6.50	5.38	5.50	9.38	10.00
P/E-Close	16.49	197.50	nm	nm	40.00
Dividends per Share	0.24	0.24	0.24	0.24	0.24
Dividend Yield (%)	3.10	2.43	3.43	2.21	2.40
Sales per Share	42.18	41.50	45.23	48.51	53.84
EPS before extra. item	0.47	0.05	(1.04)	(0.34)	0.25
Cash Flow per Share	1.33	(0.07)	(1.26)	0.16	0.66
Book Value per Share	9.13	8.90	9.10	10.67	11.25
O/S Common Shares	94,943	94,936	94,866	84,383	84,260
Total Revenue	4,009,300	4,009,100	3,974,600	4,089,200	4,590,000
Income before extra.	44,700	4,400	(90,900)	(28,800)	21,300
Cash Flow	126,300	(6,700)	(110,500)	13,500	55,800
Debt/Equity	1.16	1.09	1.06	1.18	1.77
Return on Capital (%)	10.99	7.14	(1.62)	5.16	8.03
Ret. on Com. Equity (%)	5.22	0.52	(10.31)	(3.12)	2.22
% Change Profit	915.9	104.8	(215.6)	(235.2)	(79.9)
% Change Revenue	0.0	0.9	(2.8)	(10.9)	0.6
% Change Assets	8.1	1.7	(9.2)	(17.7)	2.6

Business:

SEARS CANADA INC. is a retailer of general merchandise. It operates department stores across Canada. The company also operates a Canada-wide network of catalogue sales offices. Sears, Roebuck and Co. of Chicago, Illinois, is the company's major shareholder.

Date	EPS	DPS	Tot Rev	Inc Bex
Apr 95	(0.12)	0.06	839,126	(11,241)
Dec 94	0.50	0.06	1,302,756	47,976
Oct 94	0.07	0.06	932,558	6,534
Jul 94	0.04	0.06	932,822	3,204
Apr 94	(0.14)	0.06	852,128	(13,014)
Dec 93	0.54	0.06	1,312,709	50,596
Sep 93	(0.06)	0.06	961,849	(5,473)
Jun 93	(0.20)	0.06	891,677	(18,961)

Preferred Div. Coverage	np	np	np
Total Div. Coverage	2.0	0.2	0.0
Interest Coverage	1.7	1.0	0.0
Current Ratio	2.3	2.1	2.1
Operating Margin	5.0	3.1	0.2
Asset Turnover	1.5	1.6	1.6
5 YEAR RATIOS (%)			
Return on Capital	5.9	6.6	8.1
Return on Com. Equity	(1.1)	0.2	2.3
Profit Growth	(15.9)	(46.2)	na
Revenue Growth	(2.6)	(1.6)	(0.3)
Asset Growth	(3.4)	(2.9)	(1.5)
BALANCE SHEET (000)			
Cash	41,600	54,400	57,600
Current Assets	1,993,100	1,793,700	1,704,800
Net Fixed Assets	516,200	531,900	565,100
Invest's & Advances	20,600	24,300	35,100
Total Assets	2,672,800	2,473,400	2,431,400
Short Term Debt	124,500	183,100	183,700
Current Liabilities	875,600	866,400	806,800
Long Term Debt	877,800	734,300	732,400
Total Liabilities	1,805,800	1,628,300	1,568,300
Total Equity	867,000	845,100	863,100
Total Liab. & Equity	2,672,800	2,473,400	2,431,400
CAPITAL (000)			
Total Debt	1,002,300	917,400	916,100
Preferred Equity	0	0	0
Common Equity	867,000	845,100	863,100

Synopsis:

Sears Canada Inc. is limiting its exposure to the sporting goods retail market by reducing product lines to a small selection of athletic shoes and licensed apparel. This is a response to stiff competition from sporting goods superstores. Sears may eventually eliminate sporting goods from all its outlets. Currently, Sears generates about 2% of its sales from sports merchandise. Sears will continue to emphasize the sale and promotion of fashions. In April, Sears announced a strategy to expand and enhance its selection of fashion apparel, soft home fashions, and appliances and electronics. Sears plans to boost capital spending to $90-million in 1995, an increase of 76% or $39-million from 1994. The spending will include $29-million for a new point-of-sale system, and $19-million for store renovations.

Despite a slow real estate market, causing the sales of appliances and furniture to decline, in April 1995 Sears said it would launch a chain of stand-alone furniture stores to compete with the Brick and IKEA. The first Sears Homelife Furniture store should open in August 1995 in Kitchener, Ontario. It will have about three times as much retail furniture space as a typical Sears department store. There are plans to open up to 40 possible furniture-only stores across Canada in the next five years, depending on future performance.

In the first quarter, traditionally the weakest in the retail, Sears saw improved results versus the same quarter last year. This was due to its continuing emphasis on inventory management and cost reductions. In fiscal 1994, year-on-year sales increased for the first time since 1990. Highlights from 1994 include the launch of a new Electronic Data Interchange system with suppliers, new point of sale terminals, a new target marketing programs, and expanded services for its catalogue customers. In 1994, Sears trimmed its full-time payroll by 10.8%, or 1,220 employees. Sears also let go 545 part-time employees.

Rank (Profit/Revenue/Assets)
122   34   84

C. Richard Sharpe
Chairman Of The Board

Donald S. Shaffer
President & C.E.O.

Larry E. Ginther
V.P. C.F.O. & Treasurer

Address
222 Jarvis Street
Toronto
ON
M5B 2B8
(416) 362-1711

Fax: (416) 941-4793
S0003142/G/12.3

432   **For further company information, call Globe Information Services 1-800-268-9128 or (416) 585-5345**

SILCORP LIMITED

Exchanges	Price (Jun29'95)	11.00	Trailing P/E	6.01	Stock Symbol
TM	Trailing Yield (%)	0.00	Trailing EPS	1.83	**SIL**

Period Ending	Dec94	Dec93	Dec92	Dec91	Dec90
Yearly Statistics					
Price-Close	10.13	10.75	2.50	24.00	25.00
Price-High	11.88	13.50	27.50	45.00	127.50
Price-Low	7.50	1.80	1.00	17.50	22.50
P/E-Close	5.92	13.78	nm	nm	nm
Dividends per Share	0.00	0.00	0.00	0.00	1.40
Dividend Yield (%)	0.00	0.00	0.00	0.00	5.60
Sales per Share	164.22	209.60	232.98	2,630.82	2,727.81
EPS before extra. item	1.71	0.78	(21.02)	(105.60)	(25.90)
Cash Flow per Share	4.33	4.87	1.11	18.21	15.86
Book Value per Share	8.81	4.93	3.80	(15.74)	89.56
O/S Common Shares	4,120	2,870	2,870	287	287
Total Revenue	574,618	599,046	671,767	755,732	783,618
Income before extra.	6,870	2,242	(63,739)	(30,312)	(7,428)
Cash Flow	15,137	13,982	3,199	5,227	4,552
Debt/Equity	0.57	2.67	4.41	na	4.21
Return on Capital (%)	17.21	7.96	(69.31)	(17.64)	0.35
Ret. on Com. Equity (%)	27.24	17.88	(1,993.40)	(286.17)	(25.11)
% Change Profit	206.4	103.5	(110.3)	(308.1)	(29.7)
% Change Revenue	(4.1)	(10.8)	(11.1)	(3.6)	(8.2)
% Change Assets	3.7	(7.3)	(38.1)	(14.5)	(12.1)

Preferred Div. Coverage	np	np	np
Total Div. Coverage	na	na	na
Interest Coverage	3.7	2.0	0.0
Current Ratio	1.0	1.0	0.9
Operating Margin	1.5	1.2	(0.3)
Asset Turnover	5.3	5.8	6.0
5 YEAR RATIOS (%)			
Return on Capital	(12.3)	(15.0)	(14.9)
Return on Com. Equity	(451.9)	(460.1)	(462.9)
Profit Growth	na	1.5	na
Revenue Growth	(7.6)	(3.7)	(0.1)
Asset Growth	(14.9)	(15.1)	(10.2)
BALANCE SHEET (000)			
Cash	4,833	0	0
Current Assets	60,602	54,964	53,008
Net Fixed Assets	37,944	36,849	41,051
Invest's & Advances	1,506	5,186	7,055
Total Assets	107,909	104,037	112,170
Short Term Debt	12,141	7,214	12,111
Current Liabilities	59,026	53,582	58,326
Long Term Debt	8,449	30,633	36,014
Total Liabilities	71,625	89,875	101,258
Total Equity	36,284	14,162	10,912
Total Liab. & Equity	107,909	104,037	112,170
CAPITAL (000)			
Total Debt	20,590	37,847	48,125
Preferred Equity	0	0	0
Common Equity	36,284	14,162	10,912

Business:

SILCORP LTD. operates convenience stores across Canada under the names Mac's and Mike's Mart. In Michigan, Hop-In Food Stores operate in the convenience store/gas bar sector. Gal Corp. distributes gasoline, home fuel oil and related products.

Date	EPS	DPS	Tot Rev	Inc Bex
Mar 95	(0.32)	0.00	111,254	(1,315)
Dec 94	0.58	0.00	176,524	2,380
Sep 94	1.08	0.00	147,980	4,458
Jun 94	0.49	0.00	131,887	2,022
Mar 94	(0.54)	0.00	117,595	(1,990)
Dec 93	0.01	0.00	181,966	23
Sep 93	0.39	0.00	152,676	1,128
Jun 93	0.65	0.00	142,754	1,874

Synopsis:

The first quarter of 1995 saw improved results for Silcorp Limited. The net loss of $1.3-million was better than the almost $2-million net loss for the same period in 1994. The improvement was the result of several factors principally the increase in tobacco and service sales in Ontario, lower interest costs, the absence of a tobacco inventory charge in the first quarter of 1994, and the realization of a foreign exchange gain.

Under the Companies' Creditors Arrangement Act, Silcorp continues to reduce its indebtedness. In 1994, the company paid $5.5-million to unsecured creditors. In 1995, Silcorp is required to pay $5.2-million under the restructuring plan. As well an additional amount of up to $4.6-million is payable if there is sufficient available cash flow. The final mandatory payment of $1.5-million is due in June 1996.

In February 1994, Mac's and Mike's Mart began benefiting from the government's response to the 40% share of the cigarette market that had fallen to smugglers. The government lowered the level of taxes slapped on cigarettes, and cigarette buyers returned to the retail market.

Management continues its efforts to reduce the company's dependence on tobacco sales by boosting the sales of snack foods, hot and cold beverages, and food services. During 1994, the company entered into master franchise agreements with Subway and Pizza Hut, which allows Silcorp to open branded food kiosks in its stores.

Silcorp operates 528 stores under the Mac's and Mike's Mart names in Ontario and Western Canada, and 51 Hop-In convenience stores in Michigan. Canadian operations account for approximately 68% of sales and operating income result, with the U.S. accounting for 32%.

Relative strength to TSE300 / Price / Volume (in 1000's of board lots)

Rank (Profit/Revenue/Assets)
375   177   469

Robert W. Martin
Chairman

Derek M. Ridout
President & C.E.O.

Michael S. Rousseau
V.P. & C.F.O.

Joseph E. Lewis
Sr. V.P. & C.O.O.

Address
10 Commander Boulevard
Scarborough
ON
M1S 3T2
(416) 291-4441

Fax: (416) 291-4947
S0002970/G/12.2

SODISCO-HOWDEN GROUP INC.

Exchanges	Price (Jun29'95)	0.30	Trailing P/E	nm	Stock Symbol
TM	Trailing Yield (%)	0.00	Trailing EPS	na	SOD

Period Ending	Dec94	Mar94	Mar93	Mar92	Mar91
Yearly Statistics	9M				
Price-Close	0.38	0.79	0.80	2.11	3.25
Price-High	0.39	1.64	2.15	3.30	3.75
Price-Low	0.30	0.71	0.70	2.02	1.90
P/E-Close	1.58	nm	nm	nm	n t
Dividends per Share	0.00	0.00	0.00	0.14	0.14
Dividend Yield (%)	0.00	0.00	0.00	6.64	na
Sales per Share	9.32	15.37	19.63	18.67	13.95
EPS before extra. item	0.18	(1.37)	(1.29)	(0.10)	(0.82)
Cash Flow per Share	0.16	0.29	0.50	0.49	(0.20)
Book Value per Share	0.71	0.64	2.02	3.19	3.43
O/S Common Shares	80,893	26,309	26,309	26,200	26,157
Total Revenue	354,410	404,334	517,456	492,706	380,237
Income before extra.	8,915	(35,978)	(33,854)	(899)	(19,726)
Cash Flow	6,103	7,642	13,198	12,747	(5,298)
Debt/Equity	1.68	8.97	6.36	3.04	2.63
Return on Capital (%)	13.54	(9.27)	(3.97)	4.04	0.37
Ret. on Com. Equity (%)	31.92	(102.98)	(49.53)	(3.02)	(20.64)
% Change Profit	133.0	(6.3)	(3,665.7)	95.4	(229.4)
% Change Revenue	16.9	(21.9)	5.0	29.6	(23.5)
% Change Assets	(24.8)	(46.8)	(3.3)	7.4	(4.9)

Preferred Div. Coverage	117.3	na	na
Total Div. Coverage	117.3	na	na
Interest Coverage	2.4	0.0	0.0
Current Ratio	1.4	0.7	0.7
Operating Margin	3.2	3.1	2.9
Asset Turnover	2.4	1.5	1.0

5 YEAR RATIOS (%)			
Return on Capital	0.9	(0.4)	2.7
Return on Com. Equity	(28.8)	(36.4)	(14.7)
Profit Growth	na	na	na
Revenue Growth	(1.1)	27.1	64.8
Asset Growth	(17.0)	(2.6)	17.8

BALANCE SHEET (000)			
Cash	0	0	0
Current Assets	109,000	127,506	321,077
Net Fixed Assets	34,854	65,273	65,312
Invest's & Advances	3,262	3,358	4,156
Total Assets	198,531	264,143	496,941
Short Term Debt	39,626	109,808	337,097
Current Liabilities	76,217	181,118	431,763
Long Term Debt	61,774	56,445	9,762
Total Liabilities	137,991	245,612	442,432
Total Equity	60,540	18,531	54,509
Total Liab. & Equity	198,531	264,143	496,941

CAPITAL (000)			
Total Debt	101,400	166,253	346,859
Preferred Equity	3,514	1,703	1,464
Common Equity	57,026	16,828	53,045

Business:

SODISCO-HOWDEN GROUP INC. oversees a retail network of traditional hardware stores and renovation centres. The dealer owned stores offer consumers a comprehensive selection of hardware products and building materials, product and project expertise, and personalized service.

Date	EPS	DPS	Tot Rev	Inc Bex
Mar 95	(0.02)	0.00	87,951	(2,328)
Dec 94	na	0.00	na	na
Sep 94	0.11	0.00	119,128	5,413
Jun 94	0.17	0.00	135,853	4,492
Mar 94	(1.24)	0.00	109,666	(32,662)
Dec 93	(0.15)	0.00	119,305	(4,026)
Sep 93	(0.03)	0.00	131,017	(735)
Jun 93	0.05	0.00	126,228	1,445

Synopsis:

In the first quarter of 1995, Sodisco-Howden Group Inc.'s results included $4.4-million related to a change in the provision for swap facilities, along with a reduction of $35-million in the value of goodwill. Operations were affected by the change to regionally dedicated distribution centres, along with the implementation of new warehouse management software in Victoriaville.

In February 1995, the company issued Montreal-based CAI Capital 25 million shares at 40 cents each, for a total of $10-million in cash. CAI Capital and related parties owned about 23.6% of Sodisco's outstanding common shares after the transaction. Proceeds from the deal will go to reduce of bank debt. CAI Capital is a private equity fund established to invest in North America, with an emphasis on Canada.

In 1994, the company completed a reorganization that converted the old holding company, Unigesco Inc., into Sodisco-Howden Group Inc., the operating company. The transformation involved the sale of unrelated Unigesco divisions, the relocation of its head office to St-Bruno, and the streamlining of retail distribution and store support operations. Sodisco-Howden expensed all costs related to the restructuring of the company. Furthermore, it reimbursed more than $47-million worth of debts and reduced its future commitments by $18-million. Despite a jump in sales, operating revenues were relatively flat compared to 1993. This was due to costs related to its investment in marketing programs to support the development of its bannered dealers, along with the company's intent to deal with some long standing credit issues in the Ontario market.

In November 1994, Sodisco-Howden sold the operating assets of the La Cantiniere division to a new company formed by the current management. The deal was valued at about $10.33-million. The La Cantiniere sale completes the corporate reorganization. The company has sold all assets not related to the distribution of hardware and renovation products.

Rank (Profit/Revenue/Assets)
273   200   357

Douglass G. McDougall
President & C.E.O.

Address
1800 Marie-Victorin
St. Bruno
PQ
J3V 6B9
(514) 441-6001

Fax: (514) 441-6758
U0002263/G/12.5

SPEEDY MUFFLER KING INC.

Exchanges	Price (Jun29'95)	11 .87	Trailing P/E	8 .79	Stock Symbol
T	Trailing Yield (%)	0 .00	Trailing EPS	1 .35	**SMK**

Period Ending	Dec94	Jan94	Jan93	Dec91
Yearly Statistics				
Price-Close	16 .25	18 .25	n t	n t
Price-High	23 .88	20 .13	n t	n t
Price-Low	15 .00	13 .00	n t	n t
P/E-Close	11 .86	30 .42	n t	n t
Dividends per Share	0 .00	0 .00	0 .00	0 .00
Dividend Yield (%)	0 .00	0 .00	0 .00	0 .00
Sales per Share	44 .52	42 .24	42 .43	35 .96
EPS before extra. item	1 .37	0 .60	0 .87	(0 .09)
Cash Flow per Share	2 .85	2 .61	2 .38	1 .57
Book Value per Share	7 .41	5 .26	3 .62	2 .64
O/S Common Shares	12 ,628	12 ,598	10 ,000	10 ,000
Total Revenue	561 ,476	477 ,311	424 ,304	359 ,586
Income before extra.	17 ,346	6 ,738	8 ,714	(892)
Cash Flow	35 ,992	29 ,492	23 ,794	15 ,696
Debt/Equity	1 .72	2 .37	5 .01	6 .83
Return on Capital (%)	15 .82	10 .90	14 .03	na
Ret. on Com. Equity (%)	21 .71	13 .16	27 .86	na
% Change Profit	157 .4	(22 .7)	1 ,076 .9	na
% Change Revenue	17 .6	12 .5	18 .0	na
% Change Assets	15 .6	4 .3	2 .8	na
Preferred Div. Coverage	np	np	np	
Total Div. Coverage	na	na	na	
Interest Coverage	3 .1	1 .4	1 .4	
Current Ratio	1 .0	1 .1	0 .9	
Operating Margin	6 .7	7 .3	7 .0	
Asset Turnover	1 .8	1 .7	1 .6	
5 YEAR RATIOS (%)				
Return on Capital	na	na	na	
Return on Com. Equity	na	na	na	
Profit Growth	na	na	na	
Revenue Growth	na	na	na	
Asset Growth	na	na	na	
BALANCE SHEET (000)				
Cash	2 ,419	11 ,278	4 ,392	
Current Assets	86 ,221	76 ,021	59 ,060	
Net Fixed Assets	216 ,858	184 ,296	186 ,700	
Invest's & Advances	0	0	0	
Total Assets	317 ,174	274 ,411	263 ,180	
Short Term Debt	28 ,251	27 ,422	25 ,429	
Current Liabilities	86 ,009	71 ,079	66 ,842	
Long Term Debt	132 ,460	129 ,783	155 ,967	
Total Liabilities	223 ,597	208 ,175	226 ,972	
Total Equity	93 ,577	66 ,236	36 ,208	
Total Liab. & Equity	317 ,174	274 ,411	263 ,180	
CAPITAL (000)				
Total Debt	160 ,711	157 ,205	181 ,396	
Preferred Equity	0	0	0	
Common Equity	93 ,577	66 ,236	36 ,208	

Business:

SPEEDY MUFFLER KING INC. is an "under-the-car" repair specialist in North America and continental Europe, specializing in the maintenance, repair and replacement of exhaust systems, brakes and road handling systems of cars and light trucks.

Date	EPS	DPS	Tot Rev	Inc Bex
Mar 95	0 .03	0 .00	133 ,762	(368)
Dec 94	0 .08	0 .00	131 ,100	1 ,072
Oct 94	0 .72	0 .00	159 ,079	9 ,094
Jul 94	0 .52	0 .00	153 ,746	6 ,544
Apr 94	0 .05	0 .00	117 ,551	636
Jan 94	(0 .45)	0 .00	109 ,431	(5 ,681)
Oct 93	0 .70	0 .00	136 ,614	8 ,644
Jul 93	0 .51	0 .00	132 ,485	5 ,113

Synopsis:

In the first quarter of 1995, Speedy Muffler King Inc.'s operating profit from European operations rose $600,000, while profits from North American operations fell $1.7-million. Total revenues jumped 13.8% (with 10.2% due to exchange rate shifts). European revenues grew 32.1%, while North American revenues dipped 1.2%. Same store revenues were flat in 1995 with 5.4% growth in Europe offset by a 2.6% drop in North America. Overall, revenues were affected by soft North American retail sales, and by falling exhaust sales attributed to longer-lasting systems. Sales increases in brakes, tires, steering and alignment mitigated the decline in exhaust sales. Speedy plans to expand by 50-60 new shops in 1995, with the bulk of growth in Europe. At the end of the quarter, it had 907 shops: 370 shops in the U.S.; 258 in France; 154 in Canada; 104 in Germany; and 21 in Belgium. Speedy aims to have 1,000 shops by the end of 1996.

In fiscal 1994, Speedy opened 45 new shops while closing 13. Disregarding foreign currency exchange rate changes, revenues jumped 10.8%, with same store sales up 9.3%. European and North American revenues rose 19.2% and 4.2% respectively. The effect of expansion related costs and higher training costs caused operating margins to decline. Speedy's decision to concentrate on European growth resulted in revenue gains of over 30%. The European denominated debt refinancing was completed in the year and will provide the company with additional financing opportunities in target growth areas. International operations represented 82% of total sales in the year. The company's product diversification strategy achieved a 27% increase in non-exhaust sales. Non-exhaust sales represented 54% of total revenues.

Speedy's strategy is to become an international brand name, with strong product diversification. It seeks to grow its business in both existing and new markets. The company has also formed strategic alliances with companies such as Castrol, Mobil, and Michelin/B.F. Goodrich.

Relative strength to TSE300

Price

Volume (in 1000's of board lots)

Rank (Profit/Revenue/Assets)
229   183   280

Martin Goldfarb
Chairman

Fred L. Karp
President & C.E.O.

Robert Von Der Porten
Sen. V.P. & C.F.O.

Address
Suite 1200
365 Bloor Street East
Toronto
ON
M4W 3M7
(416) 961-1133

Fax: (416) 960-7964
01003398/G/12.5

WESTFAIR FOODS LTD.

Exchanges	Price (Jun29'95)	25.87	Trailing P/E	nm	Stock Symbol
W	Trailing Yield (%)	2.94	Trailing EPS	0.00	**WF.A**

Period Ending	Dec94	Jan94	Jan93	Dec91	Dec90
Yearly Statistics					
Price-Close	na	na	na	na	na
Price-High	na	na	na	na	na
Price-Low	na	na	na	na	na
P/E-Close	na	na	na	na	na
Dividends per Share	1.56	0.00	0.00	0.00	43.52
Dividend Yield (%)	na	0.00	0.00	0.00	na
Sales per Share	31,580.52	29,815.39	27,864.72	26,049.10	25,339.90
EPS before extra. item	na	na	na	343.90	274.76
Cash Flow per Share	802.59	547.23	646.08	566.40	472.89
Book Value per Share	3,196.08	2,617.45	2,131.15	1,667.29	1,323.39
O/S Common Shares	87	87	87	87	87
Total Revenue	2,736,705	2,583,742	2,414,701	2,257,363	2,195,905
Income before extra.	50,278	42,277	40,332	29,937	23,946
Cash Flow	69,551	47,422	55,988	49,083	40,980
Debt/Equity	0.68	0.84	1.03	1.26	1.50
Return on Capital (%)	24.32	22.62	25.28	24.08	24.77
Ret. on Com. Equity (%)	19.96	20.48	24.42	23.00	22.75
% Change Profit	18.9	4.8	34.7	25.0	33.3
% Change Revenue	5.9	7.0	7.0	2.8	16.6
% Change Assets	9.9	10.5	21.6	10.9	11.9
Preferred Div. Coverage	na	313.2	298.8		
Total Div. Coverage	372.4	313.2	298.8		
Interest Coverage	7.3	6.6	5.0		
Current Ratio	1.0	0.9	1.0		
Operating Margin	3.9	3.5	3.7		
Asset Turnover	3.4	3.5	3.6		
5 YEAR RATIOS (%)					
Return on Capital	24.2	23.7	23.4		
Return on Com. Equity	22.1	21.9	21.4		
Profit Growth	22.8	20.7	21.8		
Revenue Growth	7.7	9.9	10.7		
Asset Growth	12.8	13.6	14.9		
BALANCE SHEET (000)					
Cash	11,416	19,069	12,964		
Current Assets	340,257	298,112	292,882		
Net Fixed Assets	454,577	423,753	371,307		
Invest's & Advances	973	1,289	1,623		
Total Assets	814,280	740,840	670,507		
Short Term Debt	7,657	2,017	376		
Current Liabilities	353,705	322,580	291,426		
Long Term Debt	180,986	188,582	191,116		
Total Liabilities	536,729	513,432	485,241		
Total Equity	277,551	227,408	185,266		
Total Liab. & Equity	814,280	740,840	670,507		
CAPITAL (000)					
Total Debt	188,643	190,599	191,492		
Preferred Equity	585	585	585		
Common Equity	276,966	226,823	184,681		

Business:

WESTFAIR FOODS is a major wholesaler and retailer of food products in Western Canada. It is a wholly owned subsidiary of Loblaw Companies Limited.

Date	EPS	DPS	Tot Rev	Inc Bex
Mar 95	na	0.38	644,885	9,479
Dec 94	na	0.38	692,940	19,726
Oct 94	na	0.00	856,579	10,966
Jun 94	na	0.00	612,400	11,131
Mar 94	96.01	0.00	575,329	8,455
Jan 94	na	0.00	617,793	15,433
Oct 93	na	0.00	815,655	12,154
Jun 93	89.46	0.00	596,405	7,752

Synopsis:

Westfair Foods Ltd., a wholly owned subsidiary of Loblaws Inc., operates from broad geographic base of food stores in Western Canada. It offers a variety of store formats and sizes to appeal to as wide a demographic as possible. The retail segment of the business accounted for 81% of its sales in 1994, with 19% attributed to wholesale operations.

Retail sales growth exceed 10% in 1994, reflecting the operations of both its conventional store group and its Real Canadian Superstores. The latter have been subject to unrelenting competition, with the 1994 entry into the marketplace of Wal-Mart and the competitive reactions of other mass merchandise stores. Westfair's Alberta stores faced price wars in 1994. The company responded by taking short-term earnings reductions, with a view to building long-term strength.

Five new Superstores opened in 1994 and several more are planned for 1995. The company plans three new openings for its Real Canadian Wholesale Club stores. Westfair's wholesale business underwent a rationalization beginning in 1993 that saw small, less profitable independent accounts discontinued. As well, the product listing base was reduced. The warehouse network was realigned and some warehouses closed. As a result, wholesale sales declined by 11.9% in 1994 after a 3.3% decline in 1993. For 1995, the company's plan for its wholesale division includes improving transportation, focusing on the produce section of the business, and integrating its U.S. brokerage affiliate into operations.

Westfair will invest approximately $57-million in new fixed assets in 1995. Of this amount, about 98% will be spent on corporate stores, compared to 88% in 1994. The cash required will be generated through operations, parent company borrowings, and bank financing.

Rank (Profit/Revenue/Assets)
113   57   175

Serge K. Darkazanli
President
John S. Zeller
Sr. V.P. Finance & C.F.O.

Address
3225 - 12th Street N.E.
Calgary
AB
T2E 7S9
(403) 291-7700

Fax: (403) 291-7899
W0001506/G/12.2

WHITE ROSE CRAFTS AND NURSERY SALES LIMITED

Exchanges	Price (Jun29'95)		3.35	Trailing P/E		18.61	Stock Symbol
T	Trailing Yield (%)		0.00	Trailing EPS		0.18	WRL

Period Ending	Ju 194	Ju 193	Ju 192	Aug91
Yearly Statistics			11M	
Price-Close	5.25	7.50	n t	n t
Price-High	9.75	12.38	n t	n t
Price-Low	4.75	7.50	n t	n t
P/E-Close	13.13	24.19	n t	n t
Dividends per Share	0.00	0.00	0.00	0.00
Dividend Yield (%)	0.00	0.00	0.00	0.00
Sales per Share	14.76	14.92	14.82	0.00
EPS before extra. item	0.40	0.31	0.57	na
Cash Flow per Share	0.80	0.85	0.99	0.00
Book Value per Share	5.10	4.70	na	na
O/S Common Shares	11,330	11,330	0	0
Total Revenue	167,237	146,148	124,293	108,552
Income before extra.	4,532	3,062	5,264	1,845
Cash Flow	9,120	8,372	8,264	2,390
Debt/Equity	0.56	0.60	1.97	0.23
Return on Capital (%)	13.95	12.55	31.95	na
Ret. on Com. Equity (%)	8.16	7.69	na	na
% Change Profit	48.0	(46.7)	211.2	na
% Change Revenue	14.4	7.8	24.9	na
% Change Assets	9.6	11.0	373.8	na

Preferred Div. Coverage	np	np	np
Total Div. Coverage	na	na	na
Interest Coverage	3.5	2.4	4.0
Current Ratio	2.6	2.7	1.7
Operating Margin	7.3	7.0	10.3
Asset Turnover	1.5	1.4	1.5
5 YEAR RATIOS (%)			
Return on Capital	na	na	na
Return on Com. Equity	na	na	na
Profit Growth	na	na	na
Revenue Growth	na	na	na
Asset Growth	na	na	na
BALANCE SHEET (000)			
Cash	9,897	9,661	3,195
Current Assets	52,421	44,596	33,745
Net Fixed Assets	16,199	14,646	13,558
Invest's & Advances	0	0	0
Total Assets	111,368	101,592	91,557
Short Term Debt	839	144	6,000
Current Liabilities	19,945	16,326	19,400
Long Term Debt	31,681	31,556	45,809
Total Liabilities	53,575	48,331	65,209
Total Equity	57,793	53,261	26,348
Total Liab. & Equity	111,368	101,592	91,557
CAPITAL (000)			
Total Debt	32,520	31,700	51,809
Preferred Equity	0	0	0
Common Equity	57,793	53,261	26,348

Business:

WHITE ROSE CRAFTS AND NURSERY SALES LIMITED is a specialty retailer of nursery and crafts products. The company operates in Ontario and with the July 1, 1994, acquisition of W.H. Perron, in Quebec.

Date	EPS	DPS	Tot Rev	Inc Bex
Apr 95	(0.11)	0.00	39,397	(1,243)
Jan 95	0.16	0.00	53,778	1,789
Oct 94	(0.09)	0.00	40,028	(992)
Jul 94	0.22	0.00	54,919	2,446
Apr 94	(0.04)	0.00	33,342	(402)
Jan 94	0.24	0.00	46,418	2,736
Oct 93	(0.02)	0.00	32,558	(248)
Jul 93	0.21	0.00	49,202	2,115

Synopsis:

For the first half of fiscal 1995, same-store sales to date at White Rose Crafts and Nursery Sales Limited were flat versus the same period last year, despite a 13% increase in sales. This was primarily due to severe winter weather conditions in January. The sales increase was attributed to successful store openings in Sudbury and Peterborough, Ontario, and Gatineau, Quebec. However, the net earnings decline during the period reflects the additional costs of venturing into the Quebec market, increased competition for crafts business, and lower than expected revenues. New competiton in the crafts business stems from a rapidly expanding new chain, and enhanced crafts departments in major department stores.

In December 1994, White Rose bought a 130-acre nursery farm site near Trenton, Ontario. The facility will produce perennials and flowering shrubs. In 1995, the company plans to open new stores in Guelph, Ontario, and Anjou, Quebec, and plans to open as many as six more stores by the end of 1996. White Rose had 36 stores as of March 1995. Company policy is to expand by three to four new stores each year. Currently, the majority of stores are found in major centres in Ontario.

Fiscal 1994 saw the launch of a major expansion into Quebec with the purchase of established Montreal based nursery retailer, W.H. Perron. White Rose paid $3.08-million for two stores. White Rose views the highly fragmented Quebec market as providing vast opportunities. The company plans to open 18 to 20 new stores in Quebec over the next few years, operating under the W.H. Perron name. The stores will follow White Rose's prototype, featuring crafts and nursery goods. Plans also call for further expansion in Ontario, and possible expansion into the rest of Canada.

White Rose supplies a large portion of its goods from internal sourcing, but also purchases about 40% of its goods from suppliers outside Canada, mainly the U.S., Asia, and Europe.

Relative strength to TSE300 / Price / Volume (in 1000's of board lots) charts (1992–1995)

Rank (Profit/Revenue/Assets)		
440	341	461

Ron MacLean
President & C.E.O.

Marlene Oilgisser
V.P. C.F.O. & Secretary

Address
4038 Highway No. 7
Unionville
ON
L3R 2L5
(905) 477-3330

Fax: (905) 477-3902
01003352/G/12.5

			EARNINGS PER SHARE		
Page	Company	Fiscal year end	Last Year	Estimate this year	Estimate next year
441	B.C. Bancorp	Dec-94	(0.03)	na	na
442	Bank of Montreal	Oct-94	2.97	3.23	3.56
443	Bank of Nova Scotia	Oct-94	3.15	3.37	3.69
444	Canada Trustco Mortgage	Dec-94	3.51	na	na
445	Canadian Imperial Bank of Commerce	Oct-94	3.52	3.69	4.29
446	Canadian Western Bank	Oct-94	1.14	1.33	1.49
447	CT Financial Services	Dec-94	1.64	1.86	2.08
448	Genecan Financial	Dec-94	(0.43)	na	na
449	Gentra Inc.	Dec-94	(0.23)	(0.25)	0.00
450	Laurentian Bank of Canada	Oct-94	1.84	2.10	2.32
451	Montreal Trustco	Dec-94	(0.04)	na	na
452	National Bank of Canada	Oct-94	1.12	1.25	1.48
453	National Trustco	Oct-94	1.64	1.49	1.77
454	Royal Bank of Canada	Oct-94	3.19	3.51	3.93
456	Surrey Metro Savings Credit Union	Dec-94	na	1.60	1.80
456	Toronto-Dominion Bank	Oct-94	2.14	2.24	2.62

Estimates from First Call Corporation, 22 Pittsburgh Street, Boston, MA 02210   (800) 366-9992   Fax (617) 261-5679

Banks & Trusts

Fiscal 1994 was an incredible operating year for the Big Six banks as they earned record profits of $4.2-billion. The Royal Bank of Canada alone recorded net earnings of more than $1-billion. The industry is transforming itself as the banks began a foray into the insurance industry and the high risk area of derivative trading.

The Bank and Trust Index was up 13% for the year ending June 1995. The total return index stood at 10775.60 in May. The average bank price-earnings ratio (P/E) was 9.18 for the month of May 1995. The average indicated dividend yield was 4.24% for May. In the options market, specifically LEAPS, three banks (The Royal Bank, Toronto-Dominion Bank, and The Bank of Nova Scotia) together had 1,306 call contracts and only 36 put contracts.

According to data from Globe Information Service's Reportline as at July 13, 1995, the average P/E of all banks was 16.4, the average Price to Book value was 1.3, the average return on equity was 8.2%, the average Debt to Equity ratio was 0.50, the average Earnings per share was 1.81, and the average dividend paid was $0.73.

The federal government has decided not to deal with several key issues regarding an overhaul of the financial services industry. The issues involve its plans to reform deposit insurance and the status of the life insurance industry's consumer plan. Other issues include the Office of the Superintendent of Financial Institutions (OSFI) dealings with financial institutions in trouble, the initiation of new power under the Winding Up Act to shut down companies while they still have positive capital, and increased financial disclosure requirements.

In the arena of high finance, derivative trading has become a major focus of the major chartered banks. This type of transaction often is used as a hedge for other investments held by the banks. The federal government has not proceeded with decisions regarding the disclosure of derivatives trading activity. The questions concern the amount and type of information disclosed regarding derivative trading revenues and losses.

The banks also have decided to become more entrenched in the insurance business. Currently, The Canadian Imperial Bank of Commerce markets car insurance via the phone. It also plans to compete in auto insurance markets in provinces without public car insurance. The CIBC purchased Personal Insurance Co. of Canada and then established CIBC General Insurance Co., a wholly owned subsidiary, selling auto insurance to consumers over the phone. The Bank of Nova Scotia purchased Glacier National Life Assurance Company and renamed it Scotia Life Insurance Co. Currently, banks may not solicit business from clients but only may respond to requests. Under Ontario's Registered Insurance Brokers Act, insurance sales are restricted to licenced brokers. CIBC plans to sell in the general home and commercial insurance market nationwide.

Other financial institutions are expected to follow CIBC's lead into the several billion dollar insurance business. The insurance industry plans to actively fight the invasion of banks into their stronghold. It believes that the invasion of banks into insurance retailing will lead to the demise of marginal companies. Others believe the opening up of this pillar will allow increased competition and ultimately benefit consumers. Further, some institutions are entering the business by the takeover of insurance companies. In 1992, reforms to legislation for financial institutions allowed banks to purchase insurance companies and set up subsidiaries to sell insurance. The Finance Department plans to enact further reforms by in the fall of 1996.

The government has given the six major chartered banks a temporary surcharge on capital tax along with the suspension of the banks right to collect federal R&D tax credits for software development.

The era of troubled loan losses for the banks appears to be over. In the past, the losses were a result of Third World debt, business failures related to the recession, and major debt crises of large companies such as Olympia and York Developments. The Big Six banks will benefit from lower loan-loss charges compared to the prior year.

The effect of rising interest rates has created a temporary environment of weaker credit demand and intense price competition in certain financial services such as mortgages and investment accounts. The average net interest rate spread has declined to 3.13 percentage points in the first quarter of 1995 from 3.40 percentage points in prior years.

B.C. BANCORP

Exchanges	Price (Jun29'95)	0.17	Trailing P/E	nm	Stock Symbol
TV	Trailing Yield (%)	0.00	Trailing EPS	(0.42)	BBC

Period Ending	Oct94	Oct93	Oct92	Oct91	Oct90
Yearly Statistics					
Price-Close	0.72	1.33	1.25	2.02	1.71
Price-High	1.40	1.81	2.34	2.20	1.80
Price-Low	0.61	1.17	1.22	1.69	1.37
P/E-Close	nm	26.60	10.42	10.10	6.58
Dividends per Share	0.00	0.00	0.00	0.00	0.00
Dividend Yield (%)	0.00	0.00	0.00	0.00	0.00
Sales per Share	0.03	0.07	0.21	0.30	0.31
EPS before extra. item	(0.03)	0.05	0.12	0.20	0.26
Cash Flow per Share	(0.03)	0.05	0.19	0.30	0.36
Book Value per Share	0.53	0.56	1.02	1.92	1.74
O/S Common Shares	33,964	33,964	33,964	33,964	33,964
Total Revenue	952	2,445	7,207	10,662	12,870
Income before extra.	(1,040)	1,692	6,412	10,089	12,077
Cash Flow	(1,040)	1,692	6,412	10,089	12,077
Debt/Equity	nd	nd	nd	nd	nd
Return on Capital (%)	(5.23)	6.04	9.82	10.43	12.80
Ret. on Com. Equity (%)	(5.58)	6.31	6.75	8.32	(2.57)
% Change Profit	(161.5)	(73.6)	(36.4)	(16.5)	20.0
% Change Revenue	(61.1)	(66.1)	(32.4)	(17.2)	38.6
% Change Assets	(2.6)	(45.0)	(65.5)	5.7	(2.0)

Business:

B.C. BANCORP, formerly the Bank of British Columbia, has since Nov. 27, 1986, restricted its activities to those incidental to the winding-up of its affairs.

Date	EPS	DPS	Tot Rev	Inc Bex
Apr 95	(0.43)	0.00	320	(14,750)
Jan 95	0.01	0.00	241	170
Oct 94	0.00	0.00	847	(114)
Jul 94	0.00	0.00	215	138
Apr 94	(0.04)	0.00	(404)	(1,252)
Jan 94	0.01	0.00	294	188
Oct 93	0.01	0.00	548	263
Jul 93	0.02	0.00	586	511

	Oct94	Oct93	Oct92
Preferred Div. Coverage	np	np	np
Total Div. Coverage	na	na	2.1
Capital Ratio	1.1	1.0	1.0
Operat. Costs/$100 of Assets	6.5	2.0	1.3
5 YEAR RATIOS			
Return on Capital	6.8	10.1	10.6
Return on Com. Equity	2.6	3.7	2.3
Profit Growth	(36.8)	(14.1)	24.8
Revenue Growth	(36.8)	(21.1)	6.5
Asset Growth	(28.2)	(27.0)	(16.1)
BALANCE SHEET (000)			
Cash	547	5,553	11,505
Total Loans	0	0	4,307
Net Fixed Assets	0	0	0
Total Assets	19,039	19,540	35,549
Total Deposits	0	0	0
Subordinated Debt	0	0	0
Total Liabilities	905	366	1,085
Total Equity	18,134	19,174	34,464
Total Liab. & Equity	19,039	19,540	35,549
CAPITAL (000)			
Total External Debt	0	0	0
Preferred Equity	0	0	0
Common Equity	18,134	19,174	34,464

Synopsis:

In March 1995, B.C. Bancorp announced that the B.C. Court of Appeal varied the 1993 Supreme Court of B.C. ruling and determined that the B.C. Bancorp was not entitled to any part of the pension plan surplus. The court also required B.C. Bancorp to make further contributions to the pension plan of approximately $5-million, to make up for contributions that were not made from 1983 to 1986. B.C. Bancorp originally won the pension surplus litigation case in August 1993, but the decision was appealed. The plaintiff was seeking the entire $40-million pension surplus. The B.C. Bancorp will seek leave to appeal to the Supreme Court of Canada. If B.C. Bancorp is ultimately directed to make such payments, the amount required, together with any interest that may be awarded, would reduce substantially or possibly eliminate entirely any further distributions. The surplus represents approximately $1.15 per share and the liquidation value of the B.C. Bancorp's other remaining assets would represent approximately $0.54 per share.

The net loss for fiscal 1994 totalled $1.04-million, or 3 cents a share, due to adjustments for litigation costs and revaluation of a repossessed property. That compares with a profit of $1.69-million, or 5 cents a share, for the previous year. For the three months ended April 30, 1995, B.C. Bancorp lost $14.75-million or 43.4 cents per share, compared to a loss of $1.25-million or 3.7 cents a share for the same period last year. The increased loss was a result of the company providing $15-million for the judgement arising from the March 1995 ruling of the B.C. Court of Appeal in the pension surplus litigation. Book value per common share dropped to 10.5 cents as of April 30, 1995, compared to 53.8 cents at January 31, 1995. Capital and reserves declined sharply to $3.55-million from $18.3-million a year ago.

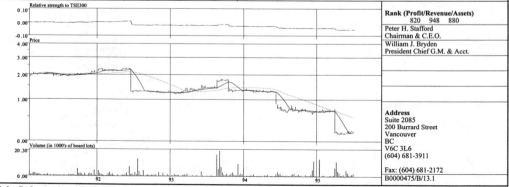

Rank (Profit/Revenue/Assets)
820   948   880

Peter H. Stafford
Chairman & C.E.O.
William J. Bryden
President Chief G.M. & Acct.

Address
Suite 2085
200 Burrard Street
Vancouver
BC
V6C 3L6
(604) 681-3911

Fax: (604) 681-2172
B0000475/B/13.1

BANK OF MONTREAL

Exchanges	Price (Jun29'95)	28.75	Trailing P/E	9.07	Stock Symbol
TMVZW	Trailing Yield (%)	4.38	Trailing EPS	3.17	**BMO**

Period Ending	Oc t94	Oc t93	Oc t92	Oc t91	Oc t90
Yearly Statistics					
Price-Close	25.13	26.88	23.56	18.69	13.50
Price-High	30.75	27.38	24.13	19.19	17.25
Price-Low	22.00	21.31	18.56	13.25	12.25
P/E-Close	8.35	10.38	9.90	8.07	6.43
Dividends per Share	1.20	1.12	1.06	1.06	1.06
Dividend Yield (%)	4.78	4.17	4.50	5.67	7.85
Sales per Share	29.28	28.76	30.91	37.18	42.18
EPS before extra. item	3.01	2.59	2.38	2.32	2.10
Cash Flow per Share	0.13	0.44	5.76	2.53	2.34
Book Value per Share	21.39	19.41	17.70	16.05	15.00
O/S Common Shares (mil)	265	249	245	239	230
Total Revenue ($mil)	9,108	8,706	8,847	9,960	10,581
Income before extra. ($mil)	825	709	640	595	522
Cash Flow ($mil)	32	110	1,394	595	529
Debt/Equity	0.76	0.72	0.53	0.51	0.55
Return on Capital (%)	18.76	20.31	18.50	19.89	20.68
Ret. on Com. Equity (%)	14.38	13.99	14.11	14.94	14.49
% Change Profit	16.4	10.8	7.6	13.9	1,453.5
% Change Revenue	4.6	(1.6)	(11.2)	(5.9)	(0.9)
% Change Assets	18.2	7.2	10.4	13.0	10.7

Preferred Div. Coverage	12.0	10.4	10.0		
Total Div. Coverage	2.2	2.0	2.0		
Capital Ratio	21.1	20.6	21.1		
Operat. Costs/$100 of Assets	2.3	2.5	2.5		
5 YEAR RATIOS					
Return on Capital	19.6	16.9	16.8		
Return on Com. Equity	14.4	11.0	11.4		
Profit Growth	89.5	5.1	na		
Revenue Growth	(3.1)	(1.0)	2.0		
Asset Growth	11.8	8.1	5.3		
BALANCE SHEET (mil)					
Cash	14,659	12,081	11,288		
Total Loans	88,634	74,028	68,251		
Net Fixed Assets	1,575	1,458	1,327		
Total Assets	138,175	116,869	109,035		
Total Deposits	98,241	87,859	90,747		
Subordinated Debt	2,218	2,363	1,666		
Total Liabilities	131,637	111,183	103,871		
Total Equity	6,538	5,686	5,164		
Total Liab. & Equity	138,175	116,869	109,035		
CAPITAL (mil)					
Total External Debt	4,994	4,076	2,733		
Preferred Equity	860	852	832		
Common Equity	5,678	4,834	4,332		

Business:

BANK OF MONTREAL is chartered under the Bank Act of Canada. The bank provides a full range of banking services to individuals, small business, corporations and governments through its network of branches and offices across Canada and around the world. Subsidiaries of the bank include Harris Bankcorp Inc., a Chicago-area bank, and Nesbitt Burns Inc., a full-service investment dealer.

Date	EPS	DPS	Tot Rev	Inc Bex
Apr 95	0.78	0.33	2,972,000	225,000
Jan 95	0.79	0.33	2,731,000	228,000
Oct 94	0.99	0.30	2,546,000	268,000
Jul 94	0.61	0.30	2,318,000	172,000
Apr 94	0.69	0.30	2,100,000	188,000
Jan 94	0.72	0.30	2,144,000	197,000
Oct 93	0.74	0.28	2,125,000	201,000
Jul 93	0.66	0.28	2,166,000	180,000

Synopsis:

For the second quarter ending April 30, 1995, Bank of Montreal reported net income of $225-million, up 19% from the $188-million for the same quarter last year. Return on equity was 14.5% for the quarter, compared to 14% a year ago. Market share growth in small- and medium-sized business contributed to strong results in Personal and Commercial banking. U.S. operations continued to show strong growth as loans at Harris Bank grew 20% over last year. For the three months ended March 31, 1995, Harris Bank reported a profit of $38.1-million (U.S.), up 24% from a year ago.

Strong business growth was partially offset by higher and unusually volatile interest rates. This resulted in lower money market trading revenues, lower margins from customers shifting to higher cost deposits, and lower gains on the sale of other securities. The Bank of Montreal's net interest spread for the quarter dipped to 2.49% from 2.81% one year ago.

In 1994 Bank of Montreal aggressively advanced its U.S. expansion program. The bank bought Suburban Bancorp Inc., a prestigious Chicago-area bank, and merged it with subsidiary Harris Bancorp under the Harris name. This brought Harris significantly closer to its goal of tripling the size of its network by 2002. In May 1995, Bank of Montreal launched a program called "Your U.S. Connection", designed to allow Canadian customers to do their banking while in the United States. Bank of Montreal also became the first Canadian bank to have a listing on the New York Stock Exchange.

In Fall 1994, bank subsidiary Nesbitt Thomson joined forces with Burns Fry to form Nesbitt Burns, Canada's leading investment bank. The merger combines a powerful domestic base with strength in U.S. and international markets. The creation of Nesbitt Burns reinforces the bank's long-standing presence in European financial markets. Bank of Montreal is also vigorously expanding its presence in China, a major focus of the bank's Asian strategy.

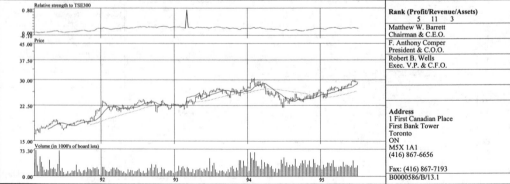

Rank (Profit/Revenue/Assets)		
5	11	3

Matthew W. Barrett
Chairman & C.E.O.

F. Anthony Comper
President & C.O.O.

Robert B. Wells
Exec. V.P. & C.F.O.

Address
1 First Canadian Place
First Bank Tower
Toronto
ON
M5X 1A1
(416) 867-6656

Fax: (416) 867-7193
B0000586/B/13.1

BANK OF NOVA SCOTIA (THE)

Exchanges	Price (Jun29'95)	29 .62	Trailing P/E	9 .12	Stock Symbol
TMZVW	Trailing Yield (%)	4 .05	Trailing EPS	3 .25	**BNS**

Period Ending	Oc t94	Oc t93	Oc t92	Oc t91	Oc t90
Yearly Statistics					
Price-Close	27 .50	29 .00	24 .00	19 .75	11 .00
Price-High	33 .25	29 .50	24 .75	20 .00	18 .13
Price-Low	23 .13	21 .88	19 .00	10 .50	11 .00
P/E-Close	15 .63	9 .73	8 .16	7 .03	4 .72
Dividends per Share	1 .16	1 .12	1 .04	1 .00	1 .00
Dividend Yield (%)	4 .22	3 .86	4 .33	5 .06	9 .09
Sales per Share	36 .18	34 .32	36 .84	42 .71	43 .76
EPS before extra. item	1 .76	2 .98	2 .94	2 .81	2 .33
Cash Flow per Share	6 .78	5 .85	4 .30	7 .77	4 .34
Book Value per Share	22 .72	21 .79	19 .78	17 .59	16 .94
O/S Common Shares	226 ,259	211 ,272	206 ,187	201 ,061	190 ,198
Total Revenue	9 ,376 ,000	8 ,318 ,000	8 ,483 ,000	9 ,315 ,176	9 ,353 ,990
Income before extra.	482 ,000	714 ,000	676 ,000	633 ,015	511 ,989
Cash Flow	1 ,482 ,000	1 ,219 ,000	873 ,000	1 ,534 ,395	845 ,104
Debt/Equity	0 .48	0 .54	0 .66	0 .68	0 .77
Return on Capital (%)	17 .43	20 .23	20 .63	22 .55	22 .68
Ret. on Com. Equity (%)	7 .90	14 .33	15 .68	16 .42	14 .49
% Change Profit	(32 .5)	5 .6	6 .8	23 .6	130 .8
% Change Revenue	12 .7	(1 .9)	(8 .9)	(0 .4)	7 .5
% Change Assets	24 .8	8 .5	10 .7	1 .7	7 .7
Preferred Div. Coverage	5 .0	7 .8	8 .6		
Total Div. Coverage	1 .4	2 .2	2 .3		
Capital Ratio	21 .3	18 .0	19 .3		
Operat. Costs/$100 of Assets	2 .3	2 .2	2 .2		
5 YEAR RATIOS					
Return on Capital	20 .7	20 .2	20 .7		
Return on Com. Equity	13 .8	13 .5	14 .3		
Profit Growth	16 .7	7 .0	42 .2		
Revenue Growth	1 .5	3 .4	6 .9		
Asset Growth	10 .3	7 .3	6 .5		
BALANCE SHEET (mil)					
Cash	11 ,388	8 ,634	8 ,337		
Total Loans	86 ,779	72 ,204	68 ,052		
Net Fixed Assets	1 ,200	1 ,099	1 ,110		
Total Assets	132 ,928	106 ,510	98 ,210		
Total Deposits	99 ,755	77 ,748	76 ,627		
Subordinated Debt	3 ,016	3 ,156	2 ,128		
Total Liabilities	126 ,687	100 ,606	93 ,131		
Total Equity	6 ,241	5 ,904	5 ,079		
Total Liab. & Equity	132 ,928	106 ,510	98 ,210		
CAPITAL (mil)					
Total External Debt	3 ,016	3 ,156	3 ,367		
Preferred Equity	1 ,100	1 ,300	1 ,000		
Common Equity	5 ,141	4 ,604	4 ,079		

Business:

THE BANK OF NOVA SCOTIA is chartered under the Bank Act. The bank offers a full range of retail, commercial, corporate, investment and wholesale banking and other related financial services through its network of branches and offices across Canada and around the world. ScotiaMcLeod, a 100% owned subsidiary of the bank, provides full service brokerage and underwriting services.

Date	EPS	DPS	Tot Rev	Inc Bex
Apr 95	0.82	0.31	3 ,011 ,000	211 ,000
Jan 95	0.82	0.31	2 ,807 ,000	210 ,000
Oct 94	0.81	0.29	2 ,636 ,000	205 ,000
Jul 94	0.80	0.29	2 ,544 ,000	198 ,000
Apr 94	(0.67)	0.29	2 ,079 ,000	(118 ,000)
Jan 94	0.82	0.29	2 ,117 ,000	197 ,000
Oct 93	0.80	0.28	2 ,093 ,000	194 ,000
Jul 93	0.77	0.28	2 ,067 ,000	183 ,000

Synopsis:

The Bank of Nova Scotia's profit for the three months ended April 30, 1995, was up 12.7% to $211-million from last year's second quarter. However, the comparison excludes one-time charges worth $305-million relating to the acquisition of Montreal Trust and goodwill write-offs from ScotiaMcLeod. Net interest income for the quarter was $817-million, an increase of 14.5% year over year. This increase was achieved through a combination of higher loan origination fees, increased gains from the sale of securities, and the inclusion of Montreal Trust's net interest income. Despite strong loan growth in the quarter in both its domestic and foreign lending markets, total assets declined by 1.3% to $135.1-billion as at April 31, 1995. This was due in part to reduced securities holdings and the effects of foreign currency translation. The market value of the bank's securities portfolio was $400-million below book value as at April 30, 1995. The deficiency was mainly due to the reduction in the value of the bank's Mexican assets, which includes Mexican Brady bonds and an investment in Grupo Financiero Inverlat.

In May 1995, to boost capital, Scotiabank issued $250-million worth of 6.75% non-cumulative preferred shares and another $250-million of 8.9% subordinated debentures. In June, the bank announced that it was shutting 22 of the 62 Montreal Trust branches it acquired when it bought parent Montreal Trustco Inc. from BCE Inc. in March 1994. Scotiabank will keep the Montreal Trust name for the corporate services division, but will combine the retail branches with its own Canadian branch network.

During the past year, Scotiabank bought Glacier National Life Assurance Company and renamed it Scotia Life Insurance Co. As well, the bank continued its international expansion, with an agreement to purchase a 25% interest in Banco Quilmes in Argentina. It also converted its representative office in Guangzhou into a branch, establishing it as the first Canadian bank branch in southern China. New branches were also opened in the U.S. Virgin Islands, Puerto Rico, and Trinidad and Tobago.

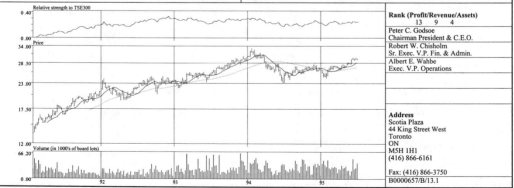

Rank (Profit/Revenue/Assets)
13 9 4

Peter C. Godsoe
Chairman President & C.E.O.

Robert W. Chisholm
Sr. Exec. V.P. Fin. & Admin.

Albert E. Wahbe
Exec. V.P. Operations

Address
Scotia Plaza
44 King Street West
Toronto
ON
M5H 1H1
(416) 866-6161

Fax: (416) 866-3750
B0000657/B/13.1

CANADA TRUSTCO MORTGAGE COMPANY

Exchanges	Price (Jun29'95)		17.37	Trailing P/E		nc	Stock Symbol
T	Trailing Yield (%)		nc	Trailing EPS		3.65	**CT.PR.C**

Period Ending	Dec94	Dec93	Dec92	Dec91	Dec90
Yearly Statistics					
Price-Close	17.00	18.25	17.00	16.50	18.75
Price-High	19.00	19.00	18.75	19.50	20.50
Price-Low	16.75	16.25	15.00	16.25	17.50
P/E-Close	nc	nc	nc	nc	nc
Dividends per Share	nc	nc	nc	nc	nc
Dividend Yield (%)	nc	nc	nc	nc	nc
Sales per Share	79.57	79.62	87.64	102.22	108.48
EPS before extra. item	3.51	2.32	3.48	4.75	4.89
Cash Flow per Share	8.35	8.81	10.69	9.53	7.73
Book Value per Share	36.30	35.08	35.18	40.47	35.57
O/S Common Shares	43,583	39,287	39,287	39,287	39,287
Total Revenue	3,127,000	3,154,000	3,453,000	4,018,115	4,267,666
Income before extra.	154,000	109,000	155,000	196,403	205,155
Cash Flow	328,000	346,000	420,000	374,517	303,776
Debt/Equity	0.42	0.33	0.30	0.27	0.30
Return on Capital (%)	14.72	11.72	10.44	13.91	15.89
Ret. on Com. Equity (%)	9.32	6.59	9.22	12.50	14.52
% Change Profit	41.3	(29.7)	(21.1)	(4.3)	(15.8)
% Change Revenue	(0.9)	(8.7)	(14.1)	(5.8)	8.0
% Change Assets	4.7	1.6	3.2	3.6	6.5

Preferred Div. Coverage	9.6	6.1	8.6
Total Div. Coverage	1.5	1.0	0.7

5 YEAR RATIOS (%)			
Return on Capital	13.3	14.5	17.2
Return on Com. Equity	10.4	12.6	15.9
Profit Growth	(8.7)	(14.8)	(6.5)
Revenue Growth	(4.6)	(0.7)	3.4
Asset Growth	3.9	5.2	7.7

BALANCE SHEET (mil)			
Cash	3,054	2,596	2,679
Total Loans	30,058	28,845	28,300
Net Fixed Assets	1,326	1,342	1,250
Invest's & Advances	4,912	4,788	4,728
Total Assets	39,359	37,582	36,984
Total Deposits	36,827	35,215	34,582
Insurance Liability	0	0	0
Long Term Debt	718	552	500
Total Liabilities	37,652	35,927	35,323
Total Equity	1,707	1,655	1,661
Total Liab. & Equity	39,359	37,582	36,984

CAPITAL (mil)			
Total Debt	718	552	500
Preferred Equity	125	277	279
Common Equity	1,582	1,378	1,382

Business:

CANADA TRUSTCO MORTGAGE CO. and its wholly owned subsidiary, Canada Trust Co., are completely integrated for operating purposes. The companies offer a range of savings, loans and trust services through a Canada-wide branch network. Residential real estate brokerage services are also available. Imasco Ltd. of Montreal, has a major interest in the company, through CT Financial Services Inc.

Date	EPS	DPS	Tot Rev	Inc Bex
Mar 95	0.97	nc	890,000	44,000
Dec 94	0.77	nc	820,000	35,000
Sep 94	0.92	nc	796,000	40,000
Jun 94	0.99	nc	765,000	42,000
Mar 94	0.83	nc	741,000	37,000
Dec 93	0.52	nc	744,000	25,000
Sep 93	0.72	nc	778,026	32,541
Jun 93	0.55	nc	798,000	26,000

Synopsis:

Canada Trustco Mortgage Company reported for the first quarter ended March 31, 1995, revenues of $779-million, a 19% increase over the $652-million from the first quarter of 1994. Net earnings also rose 19% to $44-million from $37-million in the same period the previous year. Total assets increased to $40.3-billion from $37.2-billion.

In May 1995, the company file a short form prospectus for a public offering of $200-million Capital debentures, due May 26, 2025. This follows the $150-million in subordinated capital debentures issued in August 1994.

For the year ended December 31, 1994, the company reported a 41% increase in net earnings to $154-million from $109-million, as a result of rising revenues, expense control and lower provision for investment losses. As lending activities focused on the residential segment of the mortgage market, residential mortgages grew 6% and commercial mortgages declined 18% during the period. All other loans and leases grew 9% over 1993. Mutual fund fees earned in 1994 were 97% higher than fees earned in 1993 and fund assets under administration grew 23%. During fiscal 1994, total revenue from investment properties was $124-million. The vacancy rate at year end was 10.1%, up from 9.8% at year end 1993.

In March 1994, the Canada trust announced the creation of a new subsidiary, CT Private Portfolio Management Inc. CT Private will offer services for personal trust and retail financial services customers, as well as provide asset allocation services for the 14 Everest mutual funds.

In 1994, Beverly L. Topping and Joseph Y.K. Wong were appointed directors of the company. Late in 1994, Canada Trust launched new sales and service technology in 41 Ontario branches and opened a second EasyLine telephone banking centre, this one in New Brunswick. Canada Trustco also added 21 net new branches and 217 new automatic banking machines, including 50 drive-throughs.

Relative strength to TSE300 / Price / Volume (in 1000's of board lots) chart, 1992–1995

Rank (Profit/Revenue/Assets)
46   48   9
Purdy Crawford Chairman
W. Edmund Clark President & C.E.O.
Paul W. Derksen Sr. V.P. & C.F.O.

Address
161 Bay Street
34th Floor
Toronto
ON
M5J 2T2
(416) 361-8002

Fax: (416) 361-8202
C0002283/F/13.2

CANADIAN IMPERIAL BANK OF COMMERCE

Exchanges	Price (Jun29'95)	33 .00	Trailing P/E	9 .19	Stock Symbol
TMVZ	Trailing Yield (%)	4 .24	Trailing EPS	3 .59	**CM**

Period Ending	Oc t94	Oc t93	Oc t92	Oc t91	Oc t90
Yearly Statistics					
Price-Close	32 .00	31 .63	28 .75	30 .88	22 .25
Price-High	36 .25	33 .63	37 .00	33 .00	33 .63
Price-Low	28 .00	23 .63	25 .13	21 .63	21 .63
P/E-Close	9 .09	10 .58	nm	7 .86	5 .52
Dividends per Share	1 .32	1 .32	1 .32	1 .32	1 .32
Dividend Yield (%)	4 .13	4 .17	4 .59	4 .28	5 .93
Sales per Share	42 .33	44 .74	51 .96	62 .64	66 .01
EPS before extra. item	3 .52	2 .99	(0 .59)	3 .93	4 .03
Cash Flow per Share	9 .33	6 .89	5 .97	8 .77	4 .55
Book Value per Share	31 .18	28 .90	27 .44	29 .41	26 .90
O/S Common Shares (mil)	216	210	189	184	179
Total Revenue ($mil)	11 ,214	10 ,844	11 ,375	12 ,912	13 ,005
Income before extra. ($mil)	890	730	12	811	802
Cash Flow ($mil)	1 ,984	1 ,383	1 ,107	1 ,587	802
Debt/Equity	0 .41	0 .38	0 .43	0 .37	0 .46
Return on Capital (%)	14 .79	13 .60	2 .06	17 .67	19 .70
Ret. on Com. Equity (%)	11 .69	10 .65	(2 .04)	13 .89	15 .66
% Change Profit	21 .9	5 ,983 .3	(98 .5)	1 .1	78 .3
% Change Revenue	3 .4	(4 .7)	(11 .9)	(0 .7)	15 .2
% Change Assets	6 .9	6 .9	9 .2	6 .0	14 .0

Preferred Div. Coverage	6 .3	5 .6	0 .1
Total Div. Coverage	2 .1	1 .9	0 .0
Capital Ratio	17 .9	17 .8	19 .9
Operat. Costs/$100 of Assets	2 .6	2 .5	2 .6
5 YEAR RATIOS			
Return on Capital	13 .6	13 .3	14 .1
Return on Com. Equity	10 .0	9 .5	10 .3
Profit Growth	14 .9	4 .6	(7 .6)
Revenue Growth	(0 .2)	3 .4	7 .2
Asset Growth	8 .4	8 .2	8 .3
BALANCE SHEET (mil)			
Cash	9 ,436	7 ,880	6 ,245
Total Loans	99 ,938	97 ,181	94 ,927
Net Fixed Assets	1 ,995	1 ,951	1 ,754
Total Assets	151 ,033	141 ,299	132 ,212
Total Deposits	115 ,462	110 ,905	107 ,018
Subordinated Debt	3 ,441	3 ,003	2 ,848
Total Liabilities	142 ,598	133 ,345	125 ,574
Total Equity	8 ,435	7 ,954	6 ,638
Total Liab. & Equity	151 ,033	141 ,299	132 ,212
CAPITAL (mil)			
Total External Debt	3 ,441	3 ,003	2 ,848
Preferred Equity	1 ,691	1 ,878	1 ,460
Common Equity	6 ,744	6 ,076	5 ,178

Business:

CANADIAN IMPERIAL BANK OF COMMERCE is a diversified financial institution governed by the Bank Act of Canada. CIBC comprises two main business units: the Personal and Commercial Bank provides financial services to individuals, small business and farms. The Investment and Corporate Bank serves institutional investors and corporate clients.

Date	EPS	DPS	Tot Rev	Inc Bex
Apr 95	0 .76	0 .37	3 ,216 ,000	192 ,000
Jan 95	1 .03	0 .37	3 ,082 ,000	255 ,000
Oct 94	0 .93	0 .33	3 ,041 ,000	236 ,000
Jul 94	0 .87	0 .33	2 ,886 ,000	223 ,000
Apr 94	0 .86	0 .33	2 ,638 ,000	217 ,000
Jan 94	0 .86	0 .33	2 ,649 ,000	214 ,000
Oct 93	0 .75	0 .33	2 ,661 ,000	191 ,000
Jul 93	0 .75	0 .33	2 ,676 ,000	190 ,000

Synopsis:

In the second quarter of 1995, CIBC reported disappointing results, due mainly to its losses in the global derivatives and junk bond businesses. Net income for the second quarter ended April 30, 1995, amounted to $192-million compared with $217-million for the same quarter last year and $255-million in the first quarter. The level of net non-performing loans increased by $135-million over the quarter to $1.5-billion, mainly because of the failure of the Bramalea Inc. restructuring. The provision for credit losses remained unchanged from the first quarter at $170-million. Besides the continued weakness in financial markets and adverse movements in interest rates, profits in the second quarter were affected by continued strategic investments in core businesses. In April, CIBC announced that its U.S. investment dealer subsidiary, Wood Gundy Corp., would buy New York junk bond dealer The Argosy Group for an undisclosed amount. The deal with Argosy, which last year in the United States placed $500-million (U.S.) in junk bonds, will be an important part of the bank's ambitious strategy to becoming a global provider of credit and capital market services.

During 1994, CIBC bought The Personal Insurance Company of Canada to accompany the launch of its insurance subsidiaries. CIBC Insurance expects to gain about 1% of the $6-billion Canadian individual life insurance market over the next three years. Also in 1994, CIBC reorganized its Caribbean operations by consolidating them into CIBC West Indies Holdings Ltd. with the objective of being the leading bank in the Caribbean and contributing to the region's growing economic development. In June 1995, CIBC sold its Hyperion family of mutual funds to affiliate Talvest Fund Management Inc. CIBC owns 55% of Talvest's parent, TAL Investment Counsel, one of the country's largest money managers with more than $20-billion in assets. TAL, in turn, owns 75% of Talvest. CIBC currently manages more than $6-billion in mutual fund assets, ranking it fifth in the country.

The geographic distribution of major assets in 1994 was: Canada, 72.9%; the U.S., 14.2%; Europe, 4.5%; and other, 8.4%.

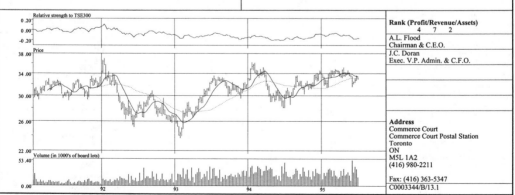

Rank (Profit/Revenue/Assets)
4 7 2

A.L. Flood
Chairman & C.E.O.

J.C. Doran
Exec. V.P. Admin. & C.F.O.

Address
Commerce Court
Commerce Court Postal Station
Toronto
ON
M5L 1A2
(416) 980-2211

Fax: (416) 363-5347
C0003344/B/13.1

CANADIAN WESTERN BANK

Exchanges	Price (Jun29'95)	11 .00	Trailing P/E	7.91	Stock Symbol
TVZ	Trailing Yield (%)	0.91	Trailing EPS	1 .39	**CWB**

Period Ending	Oct94	Oct93	Oct92	Oct91	Oct90
Yearly Statistics					
Price-Close	9 .50	6 .25	3 .95	4 .10	4 .00
Price-High	10 .00	6 .75	4 .60	5 .85	5 .00
Price-Low	6.13	3 .90	3 .75	3 .70	3 .90
P/E-Close	7 .54	13 .59	12 .34	13 .23	11 .43
Dividends per Share	0.07	0 .05	0 .00	0 .00	0 .00
Dividend Yield (%)	0.74	0 .80	0 .00	0 .00	0 .00
Sales per Share	13 .49	11 .94	11 .84	13 .03	12 .04
EPS before extra. item	1 .26	0 .46	0 .32	0 .31	0 .35
Cash Flow per Share	2 .14	1 .25	0 .88	1 .62	2 .21
Book Value per Share	12 .39	11 .20	10 .79	10 .47	10 .16
O/S Common Shares	3 ,944	3 ,944	3 ,944	3 ,944	3 ,944
Total Revenue	57 ,614	51 ,044	50 ,267	54 ,086	49 ,775
Income before extra.	4 ,967	1 ,805	1 ,266	1 ,233	1 ,378
Cash Flow	8 ,456	4 ,935	3 ,465	6 ,383	8 ,703
Debt/Equity	0.16	0 .09	0.05	0 .05	0 .05
Return on Capital (%)	10 .09	4 .06	3 .06	2 .87	3 .43
Ret. on Com. Equity (%)	10 .68	4 .16	3 .02	3 .03	3 .50
% Change Profit	175 .2	42 .6	2 .7	(10 .5)	(19 .1)
% Change Revenue	12 .9	1 .5	(7 .1)	8 .7	25 .2
% Change Assets	18 .2	10 .1	11 .8	16 .2	22 .5

Preferred Div. Coverage	np	np	np
Total Div. Coverage	18 .0	9 .2	na
Capital Ratio	14 .5	13 .5	12 .8
Operat. Costs/$100 of Assets	2 .2	2 .2	2 .2
5 YEAR RATIOS			
Return on Capital	4 .7	3 .5	1 .6
Return on Com. Equity	4 .9	3 .6	1 .6
Profit Growth	23 .9	23 .6	22 .2
Revenue Growth	7 .6	10 .9	30 .9
Asset Growth	15 .6	16 .6	32 .2
BALANCE SHEET (000)			
Cash	41 ,936	27 ,162	39 ,520
Total Loans	600 ,543	511 ,341	447 ,970
Net Fixed Assets	5 ,638	5 ,299	4 ,820
Total Assets	706 ,338	597 ,559	542 ,803
Total Deposits	634 ,379	535 ,053	484 ,949
Subordinated Debt	8 ,000	4 ,000	2 ,000
Total Liabilities	657 ,468	553 ,380	500 ,232
Total Equity	48 ,870	44 ,179	42 ,571
Total Liab. & Equity	706 ,338	597 ,559	542 ,803
CAPITAL (000)			
Total External Debt	8 ,000	4 ,000	2 ,000
Preferred Equity	0	0	0
Common Equity	48 ,870	44 ,179	42 ,571

Business:

CANADIAN WESTERN BANK provides loan and deposit services for individuals and business customers. The bank is a Schedule I bank. It was formed by the amalgamation of the Bank of Alberta and Western Pacific Bank on April 29, 1988.

Date	EPS	DPS	Tot Rev	Inc Bex
Apr 95	0.34	0 .00	32 ,516	2 ,757
Jan 95	0.34	0 .10	21 ,875	1 ,833
Oct 94	0.34	0 .00	15 ,706	1 ,344
Jul 94	0.37	0 .00	15 ,093	1 ,452
Apr 94	0.33	0 .00	13 ,571	1 ,296
Jan 94	0.22	0 .07	13 ,244	875
Oct 93	0.20	0 .00	13 ,239	783
Jul 93	0.11	0 .00	12 ,704	421

Synopsis:

Net income of Canadian Western Bank for the three months ended April 30, 1995, was $2.8-million or 34 cents per share. In the second quarter of 1994, income was $1.3-million or 33 cents per share. Year to date income rose to $4.6-million from $2.2-million for the same period last year. Net interest income was $9-million for the second quarter, double the $4.5-million recorded a year ago. The increase was primarily due to greater interest earning assets resulting from the impact of North West Trust's portfolio. Total assets grew to $1.3-billion from $633-million last year. Loans originated from North West Trust accounted for 79% of the growth. Total deposits were $1.2-billion compared to $571-million one year ago, with deposits originating from North West Trust branches contributing approximately $292-million of the growth. Also contributing to the Canadian Western Bank's solid growth was its continued expansion during 1994. It opened new branches in Nanaimo, Red Deer, and Vancouver. In July 1994, Crown Life became an investor in the bank with the purchase of a $4-million debenture. Crown Life will play a key role in the bank's future position within the Canadian insurance industry.

Effective December 31, 1994, Canadian Western Bank amalgamated with North West Trust Company. This gives the bank exposure to other marketplaces, as well as the benefit of North West's tax loss carry forwards during the next two to three years. The bank later issued 4.1-million special warrants for gross proceeds of $34.9-million to finance part of the $93-million deal with North West. In February 1995, 70,232 additional common shares of the bank were issued for $697,000 upon the deemed conversion of any remaining North West shares then outstanding.

The bank's affiliation with Charlton Securities, a full service securities dealer in Western Canada, has broadened its ability to provide retail investment services. The relationship the bank has with the Hokkaido Takushoku Bank gives the bank the ability to provide services to both Canadian and Japanese businesses.

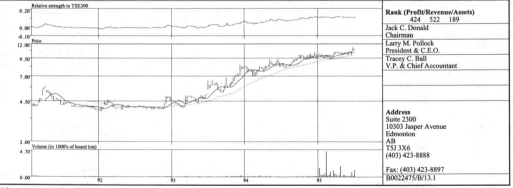

Rank (Profit/Revenue/Assets)
424 522 189

Jack C. Donald
Chairman
Larry M. Pollock
President & C.E.O.
Tracey C. Ball
V.P. & Chief Accountant

Address
Suite 2300
10303 Jasper Avenue
Edmonton
AB
T5J 3X6
(403) 423-8888

Fax: (403) 423-8897
B0022475/B/13.1

CT FINANCIAL SERVICES INC.

Exchanges	Price (Jun29'95)	20.50	Trailing P/E	11.71	Stock Symbol
TM	Trailing Yield (%)	3.90	Trailing EPS	1.75	CFS

Period Ending	Dec94	Dec93	Dec92	Dec91	Dec90
Yearly Statistics					
Price-Close	19.00	19.75	17.50	19.75	15.00
Price-High	20.50	20.00	21.25	20.75	25.00
Price-Low	17.13	16.00	17.00	14.50	14.25
P/E-Close	11.59	16.19	11.51	11.22	8.82
Dividends per Share	0.80	0.80	0.80	0.80	0.80
Dividend Yield (%)	4.21	4.05	4.57	4.05	5.33
Sales per Share	32.04	30.85	33.24	37.03	36.62
EPS before extra. item	1.64	1.22	1.52	1.76	1.70
Cash Flow per Share	3.84	3.76	4.32	3.49	2.62
Book Value per Share	16.59	15.57	15.05	14.11	13.15
O/S Common Shares	119,361	119,235	119,036	118,890	118,706
Total Revenue	3,825,000	3,703,000	3,999,000	4,412,600	4,347,508
Income before extra.	222,000	166,000	193,000	221,574	212,424
Cash Flow	458,000	448,000	514,000	415,151	310,156
Debt/Equity	1.67	1.43	1.47	1.35	0.37
Return on Capital (%)	10.17	8.78	8.87	13.15	16.11
Ret. on Com. Equity (%)	10.22	7.95	10.44	12.94	13.38
% Change Profit	33.7	(14.0)	(12.9)	4.3	(13.6)
% Change Revenue	3.3	(7.4)	(9.4)	1.5	8.3
% Change Assets	6.3	4.2	4.9	20.2	7.4

Preferred Div. Coverage	8.5	7.9	16.1
Total Div. Coverage	1.8	1.4	1.8

5 YEAR RATIOS (%)			
Return on Capital	11.4	13.5	17.0
Return on Com. Equity	11.0	12.4	14.7
Profit Growth	(2.0)	(6.5)	(0.8)
Revenue Growth	(1.0)	2.7	6.5
Asset Growth	8.4	9.5	11.6

BALANCE SHEET (mil)			
Cash	3,626	3,153	3,092
Total Loans	36,012	33,600	32,249
Net Fixed Assets	1,421	1,436	1,358
Invest's & Advances	6,892	7,003	6,666
Total Assets	49,036	46,132	44,265
Total Deposits	42,499	40,420	39,181
Insurance Liability	0	0	0
Long Term Debt	1,782	1,304	1,126
Total Liabilities	46,693	43,912	42,324
Total Equity	2,343	2,220	1,941
Total Liab. & Equity	49,036	46,132	44,265

CAPITAL (mil)			
Total Debt	3,906	3,173	2,845
Preferred Equity	363	363	150
Common Equity	1,980	1,857	1,791

Business:

CT FINANCIAL SERVICES INC. is the parent holding company of Canada Trustco Mortgage Co. Its operations consist of the following segments: intermediary; fiduciary; real estate sales; and real estate investments.

Date	EPS	DPS	Tot Rev	Inc Bex
Mar 95	0.45	0.20	1,076,000	61,000
Dec 94	0.43	0.20	1,000,000	59,000
Sep 94	0.43	0.20	962,000	57,000
Jun 94	0.44	0.20	916,000	58,000
Mar 94	0.34	0.20	881,000	48,000
Dec 93	0.32	0.20	911,000	45,000
Sep 93	0.36	0.20	912,000	49,000
Jun 93	0.27	0.20	936,000	36,000

Synopsis:

CT Financial Services reported a 27% increase in earnings for the quarter ended March 31, 1995, to $61-million from $48-million in the same period last year. During the quarter revenues also rose 22% to $947-million from $777-million. These results were mainly due to a 20% increase in fee-based product revenues and a 14% reduction in the provision for investment losses. For the period, corporate assets reached $50-billion, an increase of 8% since March 31, 1994.

During the quarter, the company acquired First Canada Securities. This acquisition, in combination with Meridian Securities, gives Canada Trust the resources to offer a complete discount brokerage service later in the year. Canada Trust Pensions also launched CTconnect, a software package that allows pension customers to access information through their own PC. First Federal also introduced telephone banking capabilities to their operations.

For the year ended December 31, 1994, CT Financial posted a 34% increase in earnings to $222-million from $166-million in 1993. Total income was $1.4-billion, a 15% increase over the $1.2-billion earned in the previous year. Assets under management increased to $182-billion from $160-billion, as a result of continued growth in the Everest Mutual Funds and CT's pension and institutional groups. Net non-performing investments dropped substantially during 1994 to $137-million compared to $284-million in 1993.

In fiscal 1994, the company introduced an array of new products and services. Four new MasterCard cards, a family of new GIC products, several new mortgage initiatives, and two new mutual funds were launched in 1994. New services introduced in the year included a Chinese telephone language service, automated teller, and customer service platforms in 81 First Federal branches, and MortgageSelect USA, a computer service package for real estate brokers and builders. During 1994, Canada Trust added 21 branches, 217 automatic banking machines, 50 drive-thru locations, and created CT Private Portfolio Management. The company's EasyLine telephone banking service registered over 6.7 million calls in 1994, up from 1.9 million.

Relative strength to TSE300 / Price / Volume (in 1000's of board lots) chart

Rank (Profit/Revenue/Assets)
27 38 7

Purdy Crawford
Chairman
Ed W. Clark
President & C.E.O.
Paul W. Derksen
Sr. V.P. & C.F.O.

Address
161 Bay Street
34th Floor
Toronto
ON
M5J 2T2
(416) 361-8002

Fax: (416) 361-8202
C0001730/F/13.2

GENECAN FINANCIAL CORPORATION

Exchanges	Price (Jun29'95)	19.87	Trailing P/E		nm	Stock Symbol
TM	Trailing Yield (%)	0.00	Trailing EPS		(0.41)	**GNF**

Period Ending	Dec94	Dec93	Dec92	Dec91	Dec90
Yearly Statistics					
Price-Close	0.02	0.02	2.50	2.75	5.13
Price-High	0.25	1.70	3.00	5.75	7.63
Price-Low	0.01	0.02	2.00	2.75	4.85
P/E-Close	nm	nm	nm	nm	256.25
Dividends per Share	0.00	0.00	0.00	0.13	0.32
Dividend Yield (%)	0.00	0.00	0.00	4.55	6.24
Sales per Share	0.45	0.52	0.49	0.82	20.61
EPS before extra. item	(0.43)	(1.32)	(3.90)	(1.84)	0.02
Cash Flow per Share	(0.24)	(0.17)	(0.50)	(0.27)	0.60
Book Value per Share	(2.11)	(1.68)	(0.35)	3.28	5.24
O/S Common Shares	45,073	45,073	45,073	35,012	34,893
Total Revenue	20,329	22,427	13,783	16,233	719,241
Income before extra.	(19,393)	(59,710)	(157,781)	(59,946)	5,473
Cash Flow	(10,902)	(7,836)	(19,881)	(9,520)	21,019
Debt/Equity	na	na	7.96	1.55	1.04
Return on Capital (%)	(2.54)	(16.80)	(36.55)	(13.35)	0.09
Ret. on Com. Equity (%)	na	na	(325.05)	(43.09)	0.29
% Change Profit	67.5	62.2	(163.2)	(1,195.3)	0.0
% Change Revenue	(9.4)	62.7	(15.1)	(97.7)	11.5
% Change Assets	(6.4)	(95.0)	(34.0)	(5.3)	4.3

Preferred Div. Coverage	na	0.0	0.0
Total Div. Coverage	na	0.0	0.0

Date	EPS	DPS	Tot Rev	Inc Bex
Mar 95	(0.06)	0.00	4,717	(2,865)
Dec 94	(0.24)	0.00	6,070	(10,716)
Sep 94	(0.03)	0.00	4,628	(1,246)
Jun 94	(0.08)	0.00	4,530	(3,935)
Mar 94	(0.08)	0.00	5,103	(3,496)
Dec 93	(1.14)	0.00	5,350	(51,684)
Sep 93	(0.02)	0.00	5,791	(731)
Jun 93	(0.09)	0.00	5,488	(3,994)

5 YEAR RATIOS (%)			
Return on Capital	(13.8)	(12.1)	(7.3)
Return on Com. Equity	na	na	(68.9)
Profit Growth	na	na	na
Revenue Growth	(50.1)	(47.5)	(51.4)
Asset Growth	(50.7)	(48.6)	(2.3)

BALANCE SHEET (000)			
Cash	613	887	300,508
Total Loans	5,584	5,833	2,607,633
Net Fixed Assets	79,314	81,473	186,304
Invest's & Advances	82,955	83,119	509,930
Total Assets	172,332	184,079	3,701,992
Total Deposits	0	0	3,369,227
Insurance Liability	0	0	0
Long Term Debt	211,578	203,556	271,714
Total Liabilities	217,397	209,751	3,667,835
Total Equity	(45,065)	(25,672)	34,157
Total Liab. & Equity	172,332	184,079	3,701,992

CAPITAL (000)			
Total Debt	215,178	207,156	271,714
Preferred Equity	50,000	50,000	50,000
Common Equity	(95,065)	(75,672)	(15,843)

Business:

GENECAN FINANCIAL CORPORATION decided to discontinue its financial intermediary operations and those related to real estae development in 1992. As a result, Genecan sold its subsidiaries, General Trust of Canada, Sherbrooke Trust, Gentrust Investment Counsellors and General Trust Corporation of Canada. It continues to hold and manage its real estate portfolio.

Synopsis:

For the first quarter ended March 31, 1995, Genecan Financial Corp. reported a net loss of $2.9-million, or $0.06 per share, compared to a net loss of $3.5-million, or $0.08 per share, for the same period last year. Total revenue for the period amounted to $4.7-million compared to $5.1-million in 1994. The loss includes accrued interest totalling $2.1-million on its debentures, payable in 1997.

The company reported for the fiscal year ended December 31, 1994, a loss of $19.4-million, or $0.43 per share, compared to a loss of $59.7-million, or $1.32 per share, in the previous year. Income from investments totalled $2.6-million, down $5.5-million. Rental income increased $2.4-million to $17.7-million from 1993.

In 1994, Genecan closed the sale of its trust and financial intermediaries' services in Quebec to the National Bank. Genecan, the National Bank, and the Regie de L'Assurance-Depots created a new company called Immobiliere Natgen Inc. to acquire non-performing loans and properties transferred to the National Bank. Genecan finalized the funding terms of the newly formed company in an agreement completed in February 1995.

The company also finalized the sale of General Trust Corporation shares to the Laurentian Bank of Canada. In addition, the Laurentian Bank transferred certain loans to Genecan and returned $700,000 in debentures. The effect of these transactions and the costs and fees incurred accounted for a loss of $5.7-million.

During the year, Genecan continued to gradually withdraw from its real estate investments in Ontario. It developed its properties in Quebec and Alberta by concentrating on leasing vacant space in office buildings. The occupancy rate at three residences for the elderly owned by the company stood at 96%.

In fiscal 1994, Genecan exercised its repurchasing right vis-à-vis its minority partner, Le Clair Matin, in Longueuil, increasing its interest by $1.1-million. The company acquired this interest against sums owed to it by the partner.

Rank (Profit/Revenue/Assets)
969 713 376

Yvon Cote
Chairman

Hubert Marceau
President & C.E.O.

Address
Suite 700
2000 McGill College Avenue
Montreal
PQ
H3A 3H3
(514) 499-2912

Fax: (514) 282-9904
G0990080/F/13.2

GENTRA INC.

Exchanges	Price (Jun29'95)	0.99	Trailing P/E	nm	Stock Symbol
TMVZ	Trailing Yield (%)	0.00	Trailing EPS	(0.12)	**GTA**

Period Ending	Dec94	Dec93	Dec92	Dec91	Dec90
Yearly Statistics					
Price-Close	0.55	0.43	2.94	8.00	9.50
Price-High	0.70	3.25	9.38	11.25	18.25
Price-Low	0.33	0.23	2.40	6.38	8.13
P/E-Close	nm	nm	nm	32.00	nm
Dividends per Share	0.00	0.00	0.52	0.74	0.74
Dividend Yield (%)	0.00	0.00	17.69	9.25	7.79
Sales per Share	1.34	9.41	18.47	25.44	40.02
EPS before extra. item	(0.23)	(1.53)	(5.93)	0.25	(1.20)
Cash Flow per Share	(0.10)	(0.26)	(0.31)	1.89	1.87
Book Value per Share	0.97	0.91	1.32	7.74	8.87
O/S Common Shares	162,241	162,241	153,446	152,667	125,982
Total Revenue	217,000	1,625,000	2,827,000	3,706,000	5,025,000
Income before extra.	(19,000)	(214,000)	(852,000)	107,000	(65,000)
Cash Flow	(16,000)	(40,000)	(47,000)	274,000	235,000
Debt/Equity	2.12	3.54	2.97	2.96	3.05
Return on Capital (%)	(0.76)	(6.40)	(11.02)	1.63	(2.47)
Ret. on Com. Equity (%)	(12.50)	(129.51)	(131.16)	2.96	(10.94)
% Change Profit	91.1	74.9	(896.3)	264.6	(124.5)
% Change Revenue	(86.6)	(42.5)	(23.7)	(26.2)	33.5
% Change Assets	(33.7)	(87.5)	(33.1)	(8.4)	2.8

Preferred Div. Coverage	na	0.0	0.0
Total Div. Coverage	na	0.0	0.0

5 YEAR RATIOS (%)			
Return on Capital	(3.8)	(2.0)	1.2
Return on Com. Equity	(56.2)	(50.3)	(20.9)
Profit Growth	na	na	na
Revenue Growth	(43.8)	(10.6)	4.5
Asset Growth	(44.9)	(35.7)	0.4

BALANCE SHEET (mil)			
Cash	395	197	3,131
Total Loans	1,427	2,512	17,614
Net Fixed Assets	138	87	108
Invest'% & Advances	97	252	2,973
Total Assets	2,083	3,143	25,114
Total Deposits	0	0	21,048
Insurance Liability	0	0	0
Long Term Debt	1,337	2,364	2,878
Total Liabilities	1,451	2,476	24,146
Total Equity	632	667	968
Total Liab. & Equity	2,083	3,143	25,114

CAPITAL (mil)			
Total Debt	1,337	2,364	2,878
Preferred Equity	475	520	766
Common Equity	157	147	202

Business:

GENTRA INC. is engaged in the management and collection of its loans, real estate and other investments. Gentra's assets are comprised primarily of loans secured by real estate and direct real estate holdings located in three principal markets, Canada, the west coast of the United States and southern England.

Date	EPS	DPS	Tot Rev	Inc Bex
Mar 95	0.01	0.00	45,000	8,000
Dec 94	0.01	0.00	51,000	6,000
Sep 94	(0.06)	0.00	49,000	(5,000)
Jun 94	(0.08)	0.00	68,000	(8,000)
Mar 94	(0.10)	0.00	49,000	(12,000)
Dec 93	(0.13)	0.00	75,000	(20,000)
Sep 93	(0.26)	0.00	488,000	(42,000)
Jun 93	(0.57)	0.00	510,000	(77,000)

Synopsis:

In May 1995, Gentra was negotiating with its remaining semi-secured creditors to let management turn the one-time Canadian financial corporation into an active real estate company. To achieve this, Gentra must either repay its remaining $870-million in subordinated debt or re-negotiate the 1993 debt plan. Under the 1993 plan, which approved the sale of subsidiary Royal Trust and related financial services assets to the Royal Bank, management was instructed to liquidate loans and repay all senior and subordinated debenture debt by May 29, 1998.

In 1994, Gentra trimmed its losses by more than 90%. It reported a loss of $19-million, or $0.23 per share, compared to a 1993 loss of $214-million, or $1.53 per share. During the fourth quarter, Gentra recorded a profit of $6-million, or $0.01 per share, compared with a loss of $20-million, or $0.13 per share, for the same period in 1993. This was the first quarterly profit since the first quarter of 1992. The Dominion Bond Rating Service acknowledged Gentra's improved financial performance by upgrading the subordinated debt to BB from CCC during the year. Subsequent to Gentra's 1994 year end, the company repurchased a further $150-million in subordinated debt.

In October 1994, Gentra's common and preferred shareholders approved a mini-restructuring of approximately $280-million of the financial obligations owed to investors in the former Royal Trust. Gentra asked all preferred shareholders, except parent company Trilon Financial Corp., to accept new priority preferred shares that are better secured but worth less money. These priority shares will be convertible into a new form of junior subordinated debenture once Gentra has finished repaying about $1.35-billion in existing obligations of this type.

In November 1994, Gentra announced the appointment of James B. Walker as Vice-Chairman, with the primary responsibility for Canadian operations. Michael W. Freund was appointed President and Chief Financial Officer. His responsibilities will include international operations.

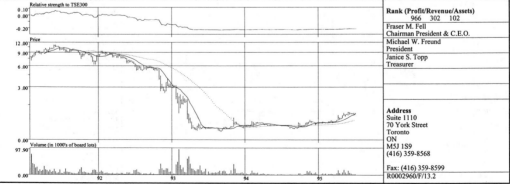

Rank (Profit/Revenue/Assets)
966   302   102

Fraser M. Fell
Chairman President & C.E.O.

Michael W. Freund
President

Janice S. Topp
Treasurer

Address
Suite 1110
70 York Street
Toronto
ON
M5J 1S9
(416) 359-8568

Fax: (416) 359-8599
R0002960/F/13.2

LAURENTIAN BANK OF CANADA

Exchanges	Price (Jun29'95)	15.87	Trailing P/E	34.51	Stock Symbol
TM	Trailing Yield (%)	4.79	Trailing EPS	0.46	**LB**

Period Ending	Oc t94	Oc t93	Oc t92	Oc t91	Oc t90
Yearly Statistics					
Price-Close	14.50	18.38	18.00	20.25	13.63
Price-High	19.25	20.25	22.75	20.63	17.00
Price-Low	14.00	16.25	17.00	13.38	13.00
P/E-Close	35.37	11.20	8.82	9.88	6.71
Dividends per Share	0.76	0.76	0.60	0.68	0.60
Dividend Yield (%)	5.24	4.14	3.33	3.36	4.40
Sales per Share	42.79	46.48	52.58	46.21	42.27
EPS before extra. item	0.41	1.64	2.04	2.05	2.03
Cash Flow per Share	1.25	7.23	(4.21)	4.05	2.27
Book Value per Share	19.24	19.58	18.66	17.39	16.11
O/S Common Shares	18,000	18,000	15,500	15,500	15,500
Total Revenue	837,338	856,068	865,014	758,665	693,952
Income before extra.	13,177	35,594	38,675	34,159	35,154
Cash Flow	22,438	124,557	(65,233)	62,773	35,154
Debt/Equity	0.45	0.28	0.20	0.21	nd
Return on Capital (%)	4.76	11.50	13.55	12.83	16.42
Ret. on Com. Equity (%)	2.21	8.80	11.35	12.22	13.12
% Change Profit	(63.0)	(8.0)	13.2	(2.8)	2.1
% Change Revenue	(2.2)	(1.0)	14.0	9.3	19.2
% Change Assets	8.3	16.3	18.9	15.4	15.2

Preferred Div. Coverage	2.4	4.8	5.5
Total Div. Coverage	0.7	1.7	2.1
Capital Ratio	25.7	21.8	21.9
Operat. Costs/$100 of Assets	2.6	2.5	2.6
5 YEAR RATIOS			
Return on Capital	11.8	13.9	13.3
Return on Com. Equity	9.5	11.7	11.5
Profit Growth	(17.5)	9.6	10.1
Revenue Growth	7.5	11.3	16.8
Asset Growth	14.7	14.7	16.1
BALANCE SHEET (mil)			
Cash	285	357	296
Total Loans	8,834	7,821	6,730
Net Fixed Assets	100	96	91
Total Assets	10,468	9,662	8,308
Total Deposits	9,576	8,778	7,570
Subordinated Debt	185	125	75
Total Liabilities	10,061	9,220	7,929
Total Equity	407	442	379
Total Liab. & Equity	10,468	9,662	8,308
CAPITAL (mil)			
Total External Debt	185	125	75
Preferred Equity	60	90	90
Common Equity	346	352	289

Business:

LAURENTIAN BANK OF CANADA is chartered under the Bank Act of Canada. The bank offers a full range of banking and financial services responding to the needs of individuals and small and medium-sized businesses through branches across Quebec, Ontario, Manitoba, Alberta, Nova Scotia, Saskatchewan and British Columbia. The bank is a member of the Desjardins-Laurentian Financial Corportation.

Date	EPS	DPS	Tot Rev	Inc Bex
Apr 95	0.44	0.19	233,324	9,187
Jan 95	0.49	0.19	229,815	10,211
Oct 94	(0.96)	0.19	213,387	(15,730)
Jul 94	0.49	0.19	212,810	10,173
Apr 94	0.44	0.19	204,888	9,304
Jan 94	0.44	0.19	206,253	9,430
Oct 93	0.42	0.19	211,744	9,471
Jul 93	0.48	0.19	227,641	10,360

Synopsis:

In March 1995, Laurentian Bank began negotiations to acquire the troubled North American Trust Co., a subsidiary of North American Life Assurance Co. The deal was contingent on the insurers ability to unload approximately $1-billion in troubled loans and other real estate assets on the trust's books. The trust company has 30 branches, mostly in Ontario and the West, which are precisely the regions Laurentian intends to expand its network of about 250 branches. The deal would give the bank the opportunity to continue its strategy of diversifying outside Quebec. Laurentian had the exclusive right to negotiate with the trust up until April 30, 1995, but that pact has expired. National Bank began negotiations with the trust, and a deal is expected this summer.

For the second quarter of 1995 net income totalled $9.2-million, compared to $9.3-million for the same quarter of 1994. Reduced net interest income was offset by reduced loan losses, accompanied by a significant reduction of $17.5-million in non-accrual loans. The bank's loan portfolio was $8.8-billion as at April 31, 1995, up $449-million from the previous year. The growth was mainly from the October 31, 1994, acquisition of the retail operations of Manulife Bank. Net interest income fell 8.5% to $64.4-million from the corresponding quarter of 1994. Contributing factors were volatile interest rates and a shift in customer preference to shorter-term loans and longer-term deposits. Provisions for credit losses narrowed to $7.3-million from $11.7-million a year ago. Tier 1 capital and total capital were 6.9% and 9.9% of risk-weighted assets, compared to 7.2% and 9.8% the previous year.

During fiscal 1994 the bank began a strategy of expanding and geographically diversifying its branch network. On January 1, 1994, the bank acquired $559-million in assets from Prenor Trust Co., along with 13 branches and deposits of more than $800-million. On October 31, 1994, the bank purchased 12 retail branches from Manulife Bank, along with $530-million in assets, primarily superior-quality residential mortgages.

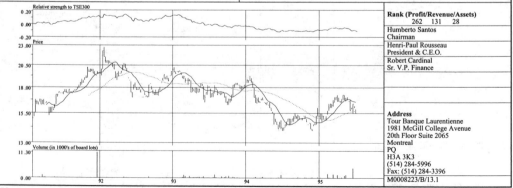

Rank (Profit/Revenue/Assets)		
262	131	28

Humberto Santos
Chairman
Henri-Paul Rousseau
President & C.E.O.
Robert Cardinal
Sr. V.P. Finance

Address
Tour Banque Laurentienne
1981 McGill College Avenue
20th Floor Suite 2065
Montreal
PQ
H3A 3K3
(514) 284-5996
Fax: (514) 284-3396
M0008223/B/13.1

MONTREAL TRUSTCO INC.

Exchanges	Price (Jun29'95)	21.75	Trailing P/E	nm	Stock Symbol
TM	Trailing Yield (%)		Trailing EPS	nm	**MTU.PR.A**

Period Ending	Dec94	Dec93	Dec92	Dec91	Dec90
Yearly Statistics					
Price-Close	20.50	20.25	15.50	20.25	19.50
Price-High	23.00	28.13	20.38	22.00	23.00
Price-Low	19.50	19.13	15.00	18.13	18.00
P/E-Close	nc	nc	nc	nc	nc
Dividends per Share	nc	nc	nc	nc	nc
Dividend Yield (%)	nc	nc	nc	nc	nc
Sales per Share	31.71	26.01	30.76	37.86	42.25
EPS before extra. item	(0.04)	(1.17)	(1.98)	0.87	1.50
Cash Flow per Share	8.59	1.31	1.04	2.12	2.52
Book Value per Share	10.81	10.57	11.74	12.54	11.83
O/S Common Shares	45,240	45,240	45,240	39,675	37,327
Total Revenue	1,385,383	1,176,788	1,308,397	1,491,251	1,577,248
Income before extra.	3,474	(48,696)	(78,867)	41,580	64,760
Cash Flow	388,471	59,279	44,380	83,309	93,938
Debt/Equity	27.19	15.61	16.36	17.92	19.78
Return on Capital (%)	0.62	(0.92)	7.29	10.46	12.03
Ret. on Com. Equity (%)	(0.33)	(10.48)	(16.35)	7.26	13.08
% Change Profit	107.1	38.3	(289.7)	(35.8)	(9.1)
% Change Revenue	17.7	(10.1)	(12.3)	(5.5)	13.3
% Change Assets	61.9	(8.5)	(2.9)	1.3	12.3
Preferred Div. Coverage	0.7	0.0	0.0		
Total Div. Coverage	0.1	0.0	0.0		

Business:

MONTREAL TRUSTCO INC. is a diversified marketer of financial and trust services to individuals, businesses and other types of organizations. Incorporated in 1889, the company operates throughout Canada from more than 109 branches and offices. Montreal Trustco Inc. is a wholly owned subsidiary of The Bank of Nova Scotia.

Date	EPS	DPS	Tot Rev	Inc Bex
Dec 94	3.04	0.16	606,585	139,221
Sep 94	2.10	0.00	406,938	96,599
Jun 94	(5.13)	0.24	321,731	(231,032)
Mar 94	(0.05)	0.00	246,079	(1,230)
Dec 93	(0.38)	0.00	298,242	(16,101)
Sep 93	(0.25)	0.00	273,023	(10,365)
Jun 93	(0.53)	0.00	288,807	(22,845)
Mar 93	(0.01)	0.00	303,822	616

5 YEAR RATIOS (%)			
Return on Capital	5.9	8.1	11.9
Return on Com. Equity	(1.4)	1.9	7.4
Profit Growth	(45.5)	na	na
Revenue Growth	(0.1)	1.2	7.8
Asset Growth	10.3	1.7	9.7

BALANCE SHEET (mil)			
Cash	2,848	1,305	1,073
Total Loans	14,161	8,828	9,480
Net Fixed Assets	42	113	119
Invest's & Advances	796	509	1,177
Total Assets	18,044	11,149	12,187
Total Deposits	1,262	1,474	1,144
Insurance Liability	0	0	0
Long Term Debt	16,012	9,029	10,329
Total Liabilities	17,455	10,570	11,555
Total Equity	589	578	631
Total Liab. & Equity	18,044	11,149	12,187

CAPITAL (mil)			
Total Debt	16,012	9,029	10,329
Preferred Equity	100	100	100
Common Equity	489	478	531

Synopsis:

On April 11, 1994, The Bank of Nova Scotia acquired all of the common shares of Montreal Trustco from BCE Inc. During 1994, RoyNat Inc., which was previously a wholly owned subsidiary of Montreal Trust Co. of Canada, became a wholly owned subsidiary of Montreal Trustco.

For the year ended December 31, 1994, the company posted net income of $3.5-million compared to a loss of $48.7-million a year ago. Special charges of $277.4-million were taken in the second quarter to cover adjustments made to Montreal Trust's assets and liabilities, and the expenses associated with restructuring. Excluding these charges, net income for the year would have been $280.9-million. The improvement in income over last year was primarily due to an increase in revenues generated by the purchase of mortgages and loans from the Bank totalling $6.7-billion. Corporate assets increased to $18-billion compared to $11.1-billion in 1993.

In 1994, Pension and Investment Fund Services division strengthened its alliance with Morgan Stanley Trust Company of New York. This affiliation was established to capitalize on relaxed foreign content limits for pension plans and to meet increased demands for global custody services. In addition, the Pension and Investment Fund Services division saw assets under administration grow from several clients such as University of Toronto and Gulf Canada.

During 1994, Montreal Trust's Stock Transfer Services entered into 214 new agency agreements representing approximately 60% of all new business listed on the major Canadian stock exchanges. Currently, Montreal Trust acts on behalf of 65% of all publicly-traded companies in Canada. The company's Corporate Trust operation was also appointed registrar and fiscal agent for Ontario Hydro's debt administration. Among the accounts added to the Stock Transfer Services were Irwin Toys and BC Telecom.

In April 1995, the company announced that the Board of Directors has elected to change the ending date of its financial year from December 31 to October 31 to coincide with the Bank of Nova Scotia's year end.

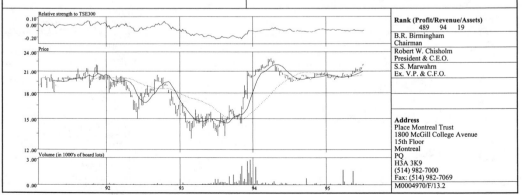

Rank (Profit/Revenue/Assets)
489   94   19

B.R. Birmingham
Chairman

Robert W. Chisholm
President & C.E.O.

S.S. Marwahrn
Ex. V.P. & C.F.O.

Address
Place Montreal Trust
1800 McGill College Avenue
15th Floor
Montreal
PQ
H3A 3K9
(514) 982-7000
Fax: (514) 982-7069
M0004970/F/13.2

NATIONAL BANK OF CANADA

Exchanges	Price (Jun29'95)	11.25	Trailing P/E	9.53	Stock Symbol
TMV	Trailing Yield (%)	3.56	Trailing EPS	1.18	**NA**

Period Ending	Oc t94	Oc t93	Oc t92	Oc t91	Oc t90
Yearly Statistics					
Price-Close	9.38	10.63	8.13	11.13	7.13
Price-High	11.63	10.75	12.75	11.38	14.00
Price-Low	8.25	7.25	7.38	7.00	7.13
P/E-Close	8.37	10.52	nm	9.27	6.36
Dividends per Share	0.40	0.40	0.70	0.80	0.80
Dividend Yield (%)	4.27	3.77	8.62	7.19	11.23
Sales per Share	17.98	19.98	24.97	29.13	32.90
EPS before extra. item	1.12	1.01	(0.29)	1.20	1.12
Cash Flow per Share	2.43	3.81	3.67	4.07	4.00
Book Value per Share	11.09	10.41	10.11	11.18	10.78
O/S Common Shares	160,976	148,474	127,152	127,031	126,875
Total Revenue	3,591,230	3,418,993	3,713,168	4,170,559	4,382,345
Income before extra.	217,172	174,565	1,016	185,971	170,323
Cash Flow	387,676	531,397	466,216	517,273	479,142
Debt/Equity	0.59	0.69	0.79	0.85	0.78
Return on Capital (%)	12.33	9.87	2.97	11.74	11.88
Ret. on Com. Equity (%)	10.76	9.95	(2.69)	10.95	10.19
% Change Profit	24.4	nm	(99.5)	9.2	436.7
% Change Revenue	5.0	(7.9)	(11.0)	(4.8)	16.1
% Change Assets	4.8	6.7	9.8	1.5	5.9
Preferred Div. Coverage	5.7	5.2	0.0		
Total Div. Coverage	2.1	2.0	0.0		
Capital Ratio	19.3	21.7	22.8		
Operat. Costs/$100 of Assets	2.6	2.4	2.5		
5 YEAR RATIOS					
Return on Capital	9.8	8.8	10.2		
Return on Com. Equity	7.8	5.8	7.1		
Profit Growth	46.9	(5.1)	(51.4)		
Revenue Growth	(1.0)	1.7	5.9		
Asset Growth	5.6	6.6	5.9		
BALANCE SHEET (mil)					
Cash	3,765	3,204	3,693		
Total Loans	32,227	30,693	30,003		
Net Fixed Assets	319	381	374		
Total Assets	44,774	42,734	40,035		
Total Deposits	36,850	35,113	33,433		
Subordinated Debt	1,354	1,157	969		
Total Liabilities	42,457	40,762	38,281		
Total Equity	2,317	1,972	1,754		
Total Liab. & Equity	44,774	42,734	40,035		
CAPITAL (mil)					
Total External Debt	1,363	1,364	1,392		
Preferred Equity	532	427	468		
Common Equity	1,785	1,545	1,286		

Business:

NATIONAL BANK OF CANADA is chartered under the Bank Act of Canada. The bank offers retail, commercial, corporate, international and treasury banking services through its branches and offices in Canada and around the world. Levesque Beaubien Geoffrion of Montreal, a subsidiary of the bank, is an investment dealer. General Trust, a subsidiary, provides trust and assets management services.

Date	EPS	DPS	Tot Rev	Inc Bex
Apr 95	0.29	0.10	na	57,200
Jan 95	0.31	0.10	983,599	60,635
Oct 94	0.29	0.10	951,230	57,272
Jul 94	0.29	0.10	920,259	57,400
Apr 94	0.27	0.10	842,870	51,910
Jan 94	0.27	0.10	876,871	50,589
Oct 93	0.23	0.10	869,908	42,195
Jul 93	0.27	0.10	821,861	47,267

Synopsis:

In June 1995, National Bank of Canada strengthened its ties with Mexico by signing a cooperation agreement with the Mexican bank Confia, a subsidiary of Abaco Grupo Financiero. Under the terms of this agreement, the two banks will promote the development of commercial operations between Mexico and Canada by making their vast networks of services and business contacts available to clients of both institutions, not only in their own countries but around the world. This agreement is further proof that NAFTA is helping to bring the Canadian and Mexican business communities together. National Bank also has a major interest in Banco Osorno, one of the largest banks in Chile.

In the second quarter of 1995, National Bank posted earnings of $57.2-million compared with $51.9-million for the corresponding quarter of 1994. The improvement was largely due to the $2-billion volume increase in business with individuals and small businesses. Net interest income for the quarter grew to $299.7-million from $264.2-million a year ago. Higher business volumes enabled the bank to raise its income from intermediation services by $3.7-million. However, this growth was more than offset by the $10.6-million decline in income from brokerage activities. On April 30, 1995, assets totalled $46.8-billion compared to $42.8-billion the previous year. Over half of the increase came from cash resources and securities, the remainder being attributed to residential mortgages and loans to independent businesses. Non-performing loans were down to $566-million in the second quarter, a $62-million drop from the previous quarter.

On April 28, 1995, the bank purchased Canassurance Life Insurance Co., a subsidiary of Quebec Blue Cross. This agreement provides for a partnership with Blue Cross to develop group life and disability insurance, and a 40% stake in Canassistance, another subsidiary. In June, the National Bank jumped into the ring along with Laurentian Bank, tabling an offer to purchase North American Trust Co.

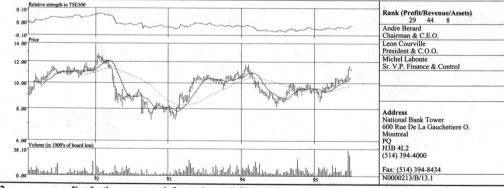

Rank (Profit/Revenue/Assets)
29   44   8

Andre Berard
Chairman & C.E.O.

Leon Courville
President & C.O.O.

Michel Labonte
Sr. V.P. Finance & Control

Address
National Bank Tower
600 Rue De La Gauchetiere O.
Montreal
PQ
H3B 4L2
(514) 394-4000

Fax: (514) 394-8434
N0000213/B/13.1

NATIONAL TRUSTCO INC.

Exchanges	Price (Jun29'95)	19 .12	Trailing P/E	14 .94	Stock Symbol
T	Trailing Yield (%)	4 .60	Trailing EPS	1 .28	NT

Period Ending	Oc t94	Oc t93	Oc t92	Oc t91	Oc t90
Yearly Statistics					
Price-Close	22 .25	23 .00	15 .25	23 .00	20 .25
Price-High	26 .25	24 .13	24 .00	24 .75	27 .50
Price-Low	18 .50	14 .25	15 .25	19 .38	19 .00
P/E-Close	13 .57	16 .91	13 .38	11 .50	9 .60
Dividends per Share	0 .88	0 .88	0 .88	0 .88	0 .88
Dividend Yield (%)	3 .96	3 .83	5 .77	3 .83	4 .35
Sales per Share	38 .00	41 .91	48 .44	54 .84	53 .20
EPS before extra. item	1 .64	1 .36	1 .14	2 .00	2 .11
Cash Flow per Share	3 .42	1 .79	2 .51	5 .30	5 .10
Book Value per Share	21 .76	21 .03	20 .58	20 .34	19 .20
O/S Common Shares	35 ,655	35 ,073	34 ,763	34 ,338	33 ,926
Total Revenue	1 ,365 ,864	1 ,490 ,136	1 ,684 ,608	1 ,871 ,224	1 ,795 ,859
Income before extra.	57 ,734	47 ,597	39 ,287	68 ,109	71 ,688
Cash Flow	120 ,664	62 ,454	86 ,902	180 ,532	172 ,871
Debt/Equity	0 .24	0 .26	0 .26	0 .27	0 .17
Return on Capital (%)	11 .29	9 .70	6 .53	11 .81	12 .65
Ret. on Com. Equity (%)	7 .63	6 .55	5 .56	10 .09	11 .37
% Change Profit	21 .3	21 .2	(42 .3)	(5 .0)	(8 .3)
% Change Revenue	(8 .3)	(11 .5)	(10 .0)	4 .2	18 .5
% Change Assets	0 .4	(4 .5)	(0 .2)	6 .0	11 .4

Preferred Div. Coverage	np	np	np
Total Div. Coverage	1 .9	1 .6	1 .3

5 YEAR RATIOS (%)			
Return on Capital	10 .4	10 .6	11 .2
Return on Com. Equity	8 .2	0 .0	10 .6
Profit Growth	(5 .9)	(7 .1)	(10 .4)
Revenue Growth	(2 .1)	3 .4	8 .4
Asset Growth	2 .4	5 .3	8 .6

BALANCE SHEET (mil)			
Cash	1 ,885	1 ,770	1 ,672
Total Loans	13 ,045	13 ,193	13 ,957
Net Fixed Assets	123	110	101
Invest's & Advances	735	671	760
Total Assets	15 ,888	15 ,825	16 ,567
Total Deposits	14 ,744	14 ,817	15 ,619
Insurance Liability	0	0	0
Long Term Debt	188	188	188
Total Liabilities	15 ,112	15 ,087	15 ,851
Total Equity	776	738	715
Total Liab. & Equity	15 ,888	15 ,825	16 ,567

CAPITAL (mil)			
Total Debt	188	188	188
Preferred Equity	0	0	0
Common Equity	776	738	715

Business:

NATIONAL TRUSTCO INC. is a public holding company for a group of trust and loan corporations. National Trust Company is the principal operating subsidiary of National Trustco. National Trust provides personal trust and investment management services, retail banking, custody and pension investment services and commercial lending through more than 190 branches across Canada.

Date	EPS	DPS	Tot Rev	Inc Bex
Apr 95	0 .23	0 .22	350 ,146	8 ,432
Jan 95	0 .31	0 .22	346 ,786	11 ,060
Oct 94	0 .37	0 .22	344 ,709	13 ,109
Jul 94	0 .37	0 .22	341 ,402	12 ,917
Apr 94	0 .43	0 .22	330 ,056	15 ,058
Jan 94	0 .47	0 .22	349 ,697	16 ,650
Oct 93	0 .37	0 .22	355 ,008	13 ,002
Jul 93	0 .28	0 .22	365 ,194	9 ,770

Synopsis:

National Trustco reported for the quarter ended January 31, 1995, net income of $11.1-million compared with $16.7-million for the same period last year. The company reported net investment income declined 6.1% to $80.6-million. This was due to declining interest margins and a slowdown in the housing market. Operating expenses rose due to implementing new computer systems and configuring the branch network.

For the year ended October 31, 1994, the company's net income increased 21.3% to $57.7-million, or $1.64 per share, compared to $47.6-million, or $1.36 per share, in 1993.

Over the year, the mutual fund client base doubled, assets increased 51%, and three new mutual funds were introduced. National integrated the Commercial Real Estate, Automotive Finance and Smaller Enterprise Banking operations into the newly formed Business Banking Group.

In 1994, the company filed an application with the Ontario Securities Commission to register the investment management operations of Cassels Blaikie within a new entity, Cassels Blaikie Investment Management Limited, to provide portfolio management to the trust business within National Trust. The company also merged the operations of the wholly owned subsidiaries, Victoria and Grey Mortgage Corp., and Premier Trust, and continued operations under the name of Victoria and Grey Mortgage Corporation.

During 1994, National Trust opened new branches in Kelowna and Port Coquitlam, British Columbia; London and Burlington, Ontario; and Hull, Quebec. The company also acquired certain assets and liabilities of The Dominion Trust Company and Inland Trust and Savings Corporation Limited.

In September 1994, Chrysler Canada filed a $200-million claim against National Trust for pension fund losses incurred in 1991 and 1992.

In April 1995, Paul Cantor was named National's President and C.E.O., replacing Christopher Barron, interim president and C.E.O. after Rowland Fleming left unexpectedly last June.

Relative strength to TSE300 / Price / Volume (in 1000's of board lots) chart, 92–95

Rank (Profit/Revenue/Assets)
103   95   22

Paul Cantor
President & C.E.O.

B.E. Wilson
Sr. V.P. & C.F.O.

Address
1 Adelaide St E.
3rd Floor
1 Financial Place
Toronto
ON
M5C 2W8
(416) 361-3611
Fax: (416) 361-4037
N0023112/F/13.2

ROYAL BANK OF CANADA

Exchanges	Price (Jun29'95)	30.75	Trailing P/E	9.21	Stock Symbol
TMVZW	Trailing Yield (%)	3.77	Trailing EPS	3.34	RY

Period Ending	Oc t94	Oc t93	Oc t92	Oc t91	Oc t90
Yearly Statistics					
Price-Close	28.38	27.25	24.13	27.00	20.75
Price-High	31.88	28.88	29.00	27.50	25.69
Price-Low	25.13	22.00	21.50	20.50	19.75
P/E-Close	8.90	59.24	nm	9.25	6.92
Dividends per Share	1.16	1.16	1.16	1.16	1.16
Dividend Yield (%)	4.09	4.26	4.81	4.30	5.59
Sales per Share	34.18	30.78	33.03	40.44	44.70
EPS before extra. item	3.19	0.46	(0.05)	2.92	3.00
Cash Flow per Share	5.68	5.01	4.47	6.64	3.32
Book Value per Share	20.13	18.09	18.82	19.91	18.10
O/S Common Shares (mil)	314	314	314	306	293
Total Revenue ($mil)	13,434	11,767	12,199	13,954	14,628
Income before extra. ($mil)	1,169	300	107	983	965
Cash Flow ($mil)	1,783	1,573	1,388	2,004	965
Debt/Equity	0.67	0.82	0.53	0.52	0.48
Return on Capital (%)	16.49	5.01	3.25	16.92	19.45
Ret. on Com. Equity (%)	16.68	2.52	(0.27)	15.43	17.49
% Change Profit	289.7	180.4	(89.1)	1.9	82.4
% Change Revenue	14.2	(3.5)	(12.6)	(4.6)	10.6
% Change Assets	4.9	19.3	4.5	5.1	9.8

Preferred Div. Coverage	7.0	1.9	0.9
Total Div. Coverage	2.2	0.6	0.2
Capital Ratio	20.2	20.8	18.4
Operat. Costs/$100 of Assets	2.7	2.7	2.8
5 YEAR RATIOS			
Return on Capital	12.2	11.5	14.4
Return on Com. Equity	10.4	9.2	12.0
Profit Growth	17.2	(16.0)	(7.9)
Revenue Growth	0.3	2.1	5.1
Asset Growth	8.5	8.3	6.2

BALANCE SHEET (mil)					
Cash	16,449	10,874	10,938		
Total Loans	115,386	116,469	99,530		
Net Fixed Assets	1,975	2,057	1,914		
Total Assets	173,079	164,941	138,293		
Total Deposits	135,815	130,399	112,222		
Subordinated Debt	3,477	3,442	3,127		
Total Liabilities	164,490	157,011	130,787		
Total Equity	8,589	7,930	7,506		
Total Liab. & Equity	173,079	164,941	138,293		
CAPITAL (mil)					
Total External Debt	5,724	6,529	3,954		
Preferred Equity	2,266	2,248	1,594		
Common Equity	6,323	5,682	5,912		

Business:

THE ROYAL BANK OF CANADA is chartered under the Bank Act of Canada. The Royal provides a full range of banking services for individuals, businesses and communities through its Canada-wide branch network. It also offers corporate, investment and treasury banking through its offices around the world. The bank has a 74% interest in RBC Dominion Securities Ltd., an investment dealer.

Date	EPS	DPS	Tot Rev	Inc Bex
Apr 95	0.83	0.29	3,788,000	304,000
Jan 95	0.88	0.29	3,586,000	319,000
Oct 94	0.83	0.29	3,531,000	302,000
Jul 94	0.80	0.29	3,354,000	294,000
Apr 94	0.74	0.29	3,127,000	273,000
Jan 94	0.82	0.29	3,400,000	300,000
Oct 93	(1.47)	0.29	3,030,000	(420,000)
Jul 93	0.58	0.29	2,845,000	223,000

Synopsis:

Royal Bank's net income in the second quarter of 1995 was a record $304-million, up 11% from the comparative period of 1994. Lower provisions for credit losses and reduced non-interest expenses more than offset a reduction in other income which stemmed from weak securities market conditions in the quarter. The second quarter brought profit for the first half of the year to $623-million, up 9% year over year. The strong performance resulted partly from tight cost controls. However, the main reason was that the bank was able to cut loan-loss estimates for the second time this year to $140-million from $205-million last year, a feat that none of its competitors could match. Excluding RBC Dominion Securities, whose expenses are closely tied to its revenues, the bank's productivity ratio improved to 60.9% from 62.6% last year. At April 30, 1995, Royal's assets totalled $175.5-billion, an increase of $146-million from the first quarter, as larger holdings of securities more than compensated for lower volumes of loans and cash resources.

In May 1995, Royal signed on as a Canadian franchisee for Mondex International, a smart card system developed by Britain's National Westminster Bank. The smart card is like a credit card with a computer chip embedded in it in place of the magnetic strip. Consumers will be able to download money from their accounts, via automated teller, telephone or computer modem, to the card and use it instead of cash, credit, or debit cards. The Mondex system will be tested over the summer.

At the end of May, the bank opened a representative office in Santiago, its first in Chile, and a third Chinese office in Guangzhou. The Chile office will provide multinational banking services for mainly Canadian clients with investments in Chile. In June, Royal Bank acquired two million common shares of Timminco Ltd. in a private placement. The acquisition was part of a deal in which the bank agreed to a full settlement of Timminco's debt to the bank for a cash payment and the issue of the shares.

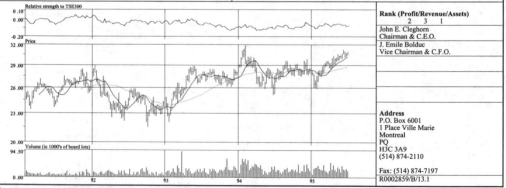

Rank (Profit/Revenue/Assets)		
2	3	1

John E. Cleghorn
Chairman & C.E.O.

J. Emile Bolduc
Vice Chairman & C.F.O.

Address
P.O. Box 6001
1 Place Ville Marie
Montreal
PQ
H3C 3A9
(514) 874-2110

Fax: (514) 874-7197
R0002859/B/13.1

SURREY METRO SAVINGS CREDIT UNION

Exchanges	Price (Jun29'95)	9 .62	Trailing P/E	5 .90	Stock Symbol
T	Trailing Yield (%)	4 .16	Trailing EPS	1 .63	**SMS**

Period Ending	Dec94	Dec93	Dec92	Dec91	Dec90
Yearly Statistics					
Price-Close	12 .25	9 .13	7 .38	n t	n t
Price-High	15 .00	10 .25	8 .00	n t	n t
Price-Low	9 .25	7 .25	7 .00	n t	n t
P/E-Close	6 .62	4 .93	3 .91	n t	n t
Dividends per Share	0 .40	0 .30	0 .15	0 .00	0 .00
Dividend Yield (%)	3 .27	3 .29	2 .03	0 .00	0 .00
Sales per Share	20 .69	19 .82	20 .46	20 .24	22 .17
EPS before extra. item	1 .85	1 .85	1 .89	1 .47	1 .15
Cash Flow per Share	2 .37	2 .31	2 .73	1 .80	1 .45
Book Value per Share	10 .10	9 .14	5 .33	3 .92	
O/S Common Shares	5 ,640	5 ,640	5 ,631	5 ,686	5 ,606
Total Revenue	116 ,672	111 ,597	115 ,753	114 ,283	112 ,427
Income before extra.	10 ,434	10 ,412	10 ,608	8 ,288	5 ,841
Cash Flow	13 ,351	12 ,988	15 ,461	10 ,158	7 ,363
Debt/Equity	1 .46	0 .93	1 .12	1 .09	0 .28
Return on Capital (%)	15 .48	19 .55	24 .00	26 .77	29 .93
Ret. on Com. Equity (%)	19 .23	22 .73	30 .16	31 .69	31 .07
% Change Profit	0 .2	(1 .8)	28 .0	41 .9	11 .0
% Change Revenue	4 .5	(3 .6)	1 .3	1 .7	23 .2
% Change Assets	17 .1	7 .1	13 .9	12 .3	9 .2

Preferred Div. Coverage	na	np	na
Total Div. Coverage	4 .6	6 .2	12 .6

5 YEAR RATIOS (%)			
Return on Capital	23 .1	26 .9	31 .5
Return on Com. Equity	27 .0	31 .3	36 .5
Profit Growth	14 .6	21 .9	31 .2
Revenue Growth	5 .0	10 .9	16 .0
Asset Growth	11 .8	13 .4	16 .2

BALANCE SHEET (000)			
Cash	149 ,428	149 ,692	161 ,400
Total Loans	1 ,221 ,162	1 ,056 ,657	964 ,559
Net Fixed Assets	18 ,471	15 ,412	14 ,499
Invest's & Advances	56 ,083	12 ,693	12 ,186
Total Assets	1 ,449 ,071	1 ,237 ,122	1 ,155 ,166
Total Deposits	1 ,295 ,530	1 ,131 ,246	1 ,054 ,630
Insurance Liability	0	0	0
Long Term Debt	87 ,000	48 ,000	48 ,000
Total Liabilities	1 ,389 ,531	1 ,185 ,555	1 ,112 ,266
Total Equity	59 ,540	51 ,567	42 ,900
Total Liab. & Equity	1 ,449 ,071	1 ,237 ,122	1 ,155 ,166

CAPITAL (000)			
Total Debt	87 ,000	48 ,000	48 ,000
Preferred Equity	2 ,564	0	2 ,870
Common Equity	56 ,976	51 ,567	40 ,030

Business:

SURREY METRO SAVINGS CREDIT UNION provides a full range of retail banking services. The Company provides its services through 15 retail branches serving the South Fraser Valley region. The Company also operates three insurance agencies and a property development subsidiar subsidiary.

Date	EPS	DPS	Tot Rev	Inc Bex
Mar 95	0 .30	0 .20	33 ,972	1 ,689
Dec 94	0 .33	0 .00	30 ,848	1 ,888
Sep 94	0 .47	0 .20	29 ,686	2 ,663
Jun 94	0 .53	0 .00	29 ,038	3 ,020
Mar 94	0 .51	0 .20	27 ,100	2 ,863
Dec 93	0 .54	0 .30	27 ,487	3 ,050
Sep 93	0 .53	0 .00	28 ,079	2 ,983
Jun 93	0 .43	0 .00	28 ,271	2 ,418

Synopsis:

Surrey Metro Savings Credit Union has grown to become Canada's second largest credit union. It holds more than $1.5-billion in assets, and serves more than 100,000 customers in British Columbia's Fraser Valley. Besides providing a full range of retail banking services, Surrey Metro owns a property development subsidiary, and Metro Insurance Services Ltd. Metro Insurance operates three insurance agencies.

Net income for 1994 was $10.4-million, matching 1993 results. Earnings per share was unchanged at $1.85. Growth was flat despite strong deposit and asset growth due to a combination of rising interest rates and lower pre-payment penalty income. Loans climbed 15.6% to $1.22-billion, while deposits grew 14.5% to $1.29-billion. At December 31, 1994, Surrey Metro's portfolio of residential mortgage loans granted to individuals totalled $966.6-million, or 79% of total loans outstanding. Non interest income from items such as commissions, service fees and foreign exchange income rose 9.3% to $11.6-million in 1994.

Surrey Metro is committed to a program of rapid growth. This includes opening two new branches in 1995, upgrading computer equipment, launching platform automation, and developing a call centre for telephone banking. The increased overhead has already adversely affected earnings growth. In the first quarter of 1995, earnings per share dipped to $0.30 from $0.51 a year ago. Besides overhead, profit drop in profits can be attributed to continued interest rate hikes. The hikes lowered Surrey Metro's net interest income and reduced new mortgage business by slowing the real estate market. Loan loss provisions fell to $85,000 for the three months ending March 31, 1995, compared to $119,000 a year ago.

In 1994, Surrey Metro boosted its annual dividend, paid semiannually, from $0.30 to $0.40 per share. Surrey Metro, the only credit union trading on the stock market, undertook a two-for-one stock split of its non-voting shares on April 29, 1994.

Relative strength to TSE300

Price

Volume (in 1000's of board lots)

Rank (Profit/Revenue/Assets)
293   395   129

Tom R. Kirstein
Chairman

Lloyd M. Craig
President & C.E.O.

William F. Keen
Sr. V.P. Finance

Address
15117 - 101 Avenue
Fourth Floor
Surrey
BC
V3R 8P7
(604) 581-2661

Fax: (604) 588-3855
S0990072/F/13.8

TORONTO-DOMINION BANK (THE)

Exchanges	Price (Jun29'95)	21 .12	Trailing P/E	9 .60	Stock Symbol
TMVZ	Trailing Yield (%)	3 .98	Trailing EPS	2 .20	TD

Period Ending	Oc t94	Oc t93	Oc t92	Oc t91	Oc t90
Yearly Statistics					
Price-Close	20 .50	21 .00	18 .13	18 .50	15 .38
Price-High	23 .38	21 .38	19 .75	19 .75	21 .63
Price-Low	18 .88	14 .88	15 .75	14 .88	14 .50
P/E-Close	9 .58	25 .61	14 .50	12 .25	8 .54
Dividends per Share	0 .79	0 .76	0 .76	0 .76	0 .76
Dividend Yield (%)	3 .85	3 .62	4 .19	4 .11	4 .94
Sales per Share	19 .41	17 .69	17 .37	21 .06	22 .80
EPS before extra. item	2 .14	0 .82	1 .25	1 .51	1 .80
Cash Flow per Share	2 .47	2 .14	3 .64	3 .77	3 .45
Book Value per Share	16 .74	15 .30	15 .14	14 .55	13 .82
O/S Common Shares	301 ,201	301 ,090	301 ,090	301 ,090	301 ,090
Total Revenue	6 ,993 ,000	6 ,325 ,000	6 ,121 ,000	7 ,199 ,000	7 ,756 ,198
Income before extra.	683 ,000	275 ,000	408 ,000	497 ,000	595 ,674
Cash Flow	745 ,000	644 ,000	1 ,096 ,000	1 ,135 ,000	1 ,038 ,867
Debt/Equity	0 .49	0 .45	0 .34	0 .21	0 .21
Return on Capital (%)	16 .74	8 .37	11 .94	14 .52	17 .84
Ret. on Com. Equity (%)	13 .33	5 .37	8 .41	10 .60	13 .57
% Change Profit	148 .4	(32 .6)	(17 .9)	(16 .6)	(14 .2)
% Change Revenue	10 .6	3 .3	(15 .0)	(7 .2)	6 .5
% Change Assets	17 .3	14 .7	7 .6	3 .0	6 .1

Preferred Div. Coverage	17 .1	9 .5	12 .8
Total Div. Coverage	2 .5	1 .1	1 .6
Capital Ratio	18 .3	16 .9	14 .8
Operat. Costs/$100 of Assets	2 .2	2 .5	2 .4
5 YEAR RATIOS			
Return on Capital	13 .9	15 .2	19 .3
Return on Com. Equity	10 .3	11 .2	14 .1
Profit Growth	(0 .3)	(16 .3)	22 .8
Revenue Growth	(0 .9)	1 .5	3 .5
Asset Growth	9 .5	7 .3	6 .2
BALANCE SHEET (mil)			
Cash	3 ,148	1 ,791	2 ,523
Total Loans	68 ,861	62 ,580	54 ,236
Net Fixed Assets	911	880	845
Total Assets	99 ,759	85 ,011	74 ,133
Total Deposits	80 ,463	67 ,739	59 ,691
Subordinated Debt	2 ,510	2 ,179	1 ,560
Total Liabilities	94 ,320	79 ,995	69 ,118
Total Equity	5 ,439	5 ,016	5 ,015
Total Liab. & Equity	99 ,759	85 ,011	74 ,133
CAPITAL (mil)			
Total External Debt	2 ,643	2 ,276	1 ,723
Preferred Equity	397	408	456
Common Equity	5 ,042	4 ,608	4 ,559

Business:

THE TORONTO-DOMINION BANK is a chartered bank, serving individuals, businesses, financial institutions and governments through its network of Canadian branches. The bank also offers a range of credit, non-credit and financial advisory services to businesses, governments and correspondent banks through offices worldwide. Subsidiaries offer discount brokerage services and a full range of trust services.

Date	EPS	DPS	Tot Rev	Inc Bex
Apr 95	0 .52	0 .22	2 ,159 ,000	164 ,000
Jan 95	0 .56	0 .22	2 ,010 ,000	179 ,000
Oct 94	0 .62	0 .20	1 ,871 ,000	195 ,000
Jul 94	0 .50	0 .20	1 ,796 ,000	162 ,000
Apr 94	0 .50	0 .20	1 ,656 ,000	158 ,000
Jan 94	0 .52	0 .19	1 ,670 ,000	168 ,000
Oct 93	0 .25	0 .19	1 ,609 ,000	82 ,000
Jul 93	0 .32	0 .19	1 ,566 ,000	102 ,000

Synopsis:

In the second quarter of 1995, total revenue at TD Bank reached its highest level since the record first quarter of 1994. This was due to a 25 basis point improvement in TD's interest rate margins, strong securities gains, and lower provisions for credit losses. TD showed a profit of $164-million of 52 cents a share for the three months ended April 30, 1995. This was a modest increase of 4% over the $158-million the bank reported a year ago. Net interest income increased to $636-million, while loan loss provisions declined to $60-million from $112-million a year ago. TD's net interest margin rose during the quarter to 2.77%, as a result of higher interest recoveries and improved spreads on personal deposits. At April 30, 1995, TD's total assets rose 11% from a year ago to $103.7-billion, due to higher levels of trading securities and loans to all segments.

Near the end of the quarter, TD scrapped its plans to enter the Ontario car insurance market. Initially, TD and Continental Insurance were said to have struck a deal that would have Continental underwrite a portion of the insurance risk and provide the bank with actuarial backing. TD felt that it couldn't make money in the current volatile marketplace. With the acquisition of Lancaster Financial Holdings in December of 1994 and its integration with TD Securities, financial advisory services and mergers and acquisition capabilities have been strengthened. Earlier in the year, the Bank began transforming some of its key branches to TD Bank & Trust, becoming the first Canadian financial institution to combine bank and trust operations within branches. By the end of 1995, TD expects to have redesigned 180 of its 966 branches across the country. TD Trust now has about $55-billion in assets, and ranks third behind Canada Trust and Royal Trust.

In June, Green Line Investor Services Inc. opened its first U.S. office, which will offer a full range of discount brokerage services. TD Bank also opted out of the revamped Canada Student Loans Program and will launch its own program for university and college students.

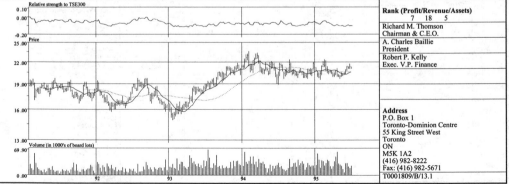

Rank (Profit/Revenue/Assets)
7   18   5

Richard M. Thomson
Chairman & C.E.O.

A. Charles Baillie
President

Robert P. Kelly
Exec. V.P. Finance

Address
P.O. Box 1
Toronto-Dominion Centre
55 King Street West
Toronto
ON
M5K 1A2
(416) 982-8222
Fax: (416) 982-5671
T0001809/B/13.1

Page	Company		Fiscal year end	EARNINGS PER SHARE		
				Last Year	Estimate this year	Estimate next year
461	BGR Precious Metals		Jan-95	1.32	1.33	0.90
462	Canada Trust Income Investments		Dec-94	0.69	na	na
463	Canadian General Investments		Dec-94	0.51	na	na
464	Central Capital		Dec-94	0.29	na	na
465	Central Fund of Canada	$US	Oct-94	(0.05)	na	na
466	Consolidated Canadian Express		Dec-94	(0.25)	na	na
467	Desjardins Laurentian Financial		Dec-94	(0.43)	na	na
468	Dundee Bancorp		Dec-94	1.76	na	na
469	Edper Group		Dec-94	0.42	na	na
470	Fahnestock Viner Holdings	$US	Dec-94	0.96	na	na
471	First Marathon		Dec-94	1.03	na	na
472	Greyvest Capital		Dec-94	0.25	na	na
473	Hees International Bancorp		Dec-94	1.10	1.50	1.50
474	Home Capital Group		Dec-94	0.04	na	na
475	Investors Group		Dec-94	0.80	0.96	1.13
476	Mackenzie Financial		Mar-95	0.49	0.70	0.85
477	Marleau, Lemire		Dec-94	0.69	na	na
478	Merchant Private		Dec-94	0.38	na	na
479	MFP Technology Services		Mar-94	1.01	1.20	1.41
480	Midland Walwyn		Dec-94	0.88	na	na
481	Municipal Financial		Oct-94	0.46	0.50	0.65
482	Newcourt Credit Group		Dec-94	1.19	1.41	1.70
483	Newgrowth Corp		Jun-94	1.92	na	na
484	Ondaatje Corporation		Mar-94	0.21	na	na
485	Power Corporation		Dec-94	1.46	1.57	1.72
486	Power Financial		Dec-94	2.99	3.21	3.53
487	Trilon Financial		Dec-94	0.25	0.39	0.44
488	Trimark Financial		Mar-95	1.36	1.77	2.50
489	United Corporations		Mar-95	1.02	na	na

Estimates from First Call Corporation, 22 Pittsburgh Street, Boston, MA 02210   (800) 366-9992   Fax (617) 261-5679

Investing, Financing & Leasing

As of July 1995, interest rates continued to fall in Canada as a result of falling rates in the United States and the slowing of the economy in Canada. The lowering of interest rates in both countries should help boost the economy. Lower interest rates act like an insurance policy against a recession, they help the economy to grow. On the other hand, lowering interest rates has a tendency to increase inflation. The issue becomes more complicated when one looks at the political implications.

With governments in the U.S. and Canada under pressure to reduce deficits, political decisions sometimes override economic ones. Each government knows its political future depends on how effective it is at reducing its deficit. This leads government officials to overlook the effects of inflation in order to achieve high growth which increases revenue for the government. Achieving higher revenue gives the government a better chance of cutting the deficit.

During the spring and the beginning of the summer of 1995, stock markets in the United States experienced tremendous growth. The investment community says that high levels in the stock market represent a new era of low inflation in the face of massive earnings and global competition. Analysts want to reassess productivity and profits because of the enormous success of companies doing business in the information markets. Wall Street endorses the idea, reflected by the soaring prices of software companies on the Nasdaq Stock Exchange.

The consensus regarding the current slowdown in North America markets is that the slowdown is temporary. With falling interest rates, the economy should pick up again. Analysts believe there is a risk in the market, and they point to Japan and Mexico as examples. In Japan, the world's second largest economy, economic conditions present difficulties. Since the late 1980s, the Japanese market has lost 60% of its value. Worsening of the markets could lead to widespread deflation and falling stock prices. This could further damage the positions of banks and insurance companies and force them to liquidate their positions or to withdraw from foreign markets. The fear is that if there is a financial collapse in Japan, there will be consequences throughout the world.

Lower interest rates in Canada (as of July 1995) should spark consumer spending later in the year. Recent cuts in the prime rate should convince people who have been on the sidelines to invest in cars, appliances, houses, and renovations. Once consumer spending begins to rise, Canada's economy will improve, because consumer spending accounts for 60% of the economic activity in Canada.

The Federal Reserve Board in the U.S. is planning to make it easier for consumers to compare the costs of leasing a car with those of financing the purchase. The new disclosure will apply to auto leasing companies as well as banks. The move is a response to the need to educate consumers on the differences between leasing and financing a purchase.

BGR PRECIOUS METALS INC.

Exchanges	Price (Jun29'95)	14 .50	Trailing P/E	14 .80	Stock Symbol
TM	Trailing Yield (%)	0 .00	Trailing EPS	0 .98	**BPT.A**

Period Ending	Jan95	Jan94	Jan93	Jan92	Jan91
Yearly Statistics					
Price-Close	12 .50	15 .00	5 .88	7 .63	7 .38
Price-High	16 .38	16 .50	8 .00	8 .63	11 .75
Price-Low	12 .50	5 .75	5 .25	7 .00	7 .00
P/E-Close	9 .47	8 .52	16 .79	40 .13	32 .07
Dividends per Share	0 .00	0 .00	0 .00	1 .00	1 .00
Dividend Yield (%)	0 .00	0 .00	0 .00	13 .12	13 .55
Sales per Share	0 .23	0 .18	0 .16	0 .14	0 .15
EPS before extra. item	1 .32	1 .76	0 .35	0 .19	0 .23
Cash Flow per Share	(0 .85)	(1 .20)	(0 .16)	(0 .22)	(0 .13)
Book Value per Share	16 .10	16 .68	8 .21	8 .25	8 .42
O/S Common Shares	7 ,837	5 ,605	5 ,665	5 ,957	5 ,957
Total Revenue	17 ,740	17 ,619	3 ,886	3 ,286	3 ,030
Income before extra.	10 ,494	9 ,860	2 ,045	1 ,130	1 ,382
Cash Flow	(5 ,714)	(6 ,738)	(910)	(1 ,306)	(771)
Debt/Equity	nd	nd	nd	nd	nd
Return on Capital (%)	14 .11	20 .50	6 .25	2 .88	3 .13
Ret. on Com. Equity (%)	9 .56	14 .14	4 .30	2 .28	2 .23
% Change Profit	6 .4	382 .2	81 .0	(18 .2)	119 .3
% Change Revenue	0 .7	353 .4	18 .3	8 .4	140 .5
% Change Assets	17 .2	150 .4	(5 .0)	0 .5	(35 .9)

Preferred Div. Coverage	np	np	np
Total Div. Coverage	na	na	na

5 YEAR RATIOS (%)			
Return on Capital	9 .4	3 .9	(1 .2)
Return on Com. Equity	6 .5	2 .6	(1 .1)
Profit Growth	75 .5	na	(39 .4)
Revenue Growth	69 .6	na	(35 .5)
Asset Growth	12 .5	11 .2	(12 .4)

BALANCE SHEET (000)			
Cash	8 ,835	3 ,381	2 ,148
Total Loans	0	0	0
Net Fixed Assets	0	0	0
Invest's & Advances	131 ,636	116 ,837	43 ,768
Total Assets	140 ,940	120 ,304	48 ,043
Total Deposits	0	0	0
Insurance Liability	0	0	0
Long Term Debt	0	0	0
Total Liabilities	14 ,750	26 ,828	2 ,040
Total Equity	126 ,190	93 ,476	46 ,003
Total Liab. & Equity	140 ,940	120 ,304	48 ,043

CAPITAL (000)			
Total Debt	0	0	0
Preferred Equity	0	0	0
Common Equity	126 ,190	93 ,476	46 ,003

Business:

BGR PRECIOUS METALS INC. is a closed-end investment company that invests primarily in precious metals and shares of precious metals companies. The company invests in North American and overseas equities and precious metals using a flexible asset-mix policy. The company may make use of options and futures contracts but will not make uncovered sales or deal in put options.

Date	EPS	DPS	Tot Rev	Inc Bex
Apr 95	(0 .04)	0 .00	276	(337)
Jan 95	0 .19	0 .00	1 ,548	1 ,506
Oct 94	0 .42	0 .00	6 ,455	3 ,355
Jul 94	0 .41	0 .00	5 ,731	3 ,368
Apr 94	0 .30	0 .00	4 ,006	2 ,265
Jan 94	1 .11	0 .00	10 ,154	6 ,207
Oct 93	0 .24	0 .00	2 ,760	1 ,384
Jul 93	0 .26	0 .00	2 ,969	1 ,432

Synopsis:

For the year ended January 31, 1995, the total net assets of BGR Precious Metals increased significantly as a result of an equity issue which netted $43.6-million. The issue comprised 2,520,000 units at $17.85 per unit, which was $1.00 higher than the company's net asset value at the time. Each unit consisted of one Class A share and one Class A purchase warrant exerciseable at $25.00 per share to February 20, 2004.

The net asset value of the company at year end was $126.19-million, or $16.10 per share, compared with $93.48-million, or $16.68 per share, at the end of the previous year, a drop of 3%. Due to the weak gold market, the market value of investments net of deferred taxes fell by $17.4-million during the year. This drop was partially offset by increased net income for the year of $10.5-million compared with $9.9-million in the previous year. During the year BGR bought 287,500 Class A shares under its normal course issuer bid for $4-million in an attempt to increase shareholder value.

In 1994, the company added its first Latin American listed equity by acquiring what was originally a 5% portfolio position in Peruvian listed Buenaventura Ciap de Minas. BGR bought the stock at the equivalent of $3.20 per share, traded as high as $6.71 in November, and closed the year at $5.17.

The portfolio is managed by Goodman & Company Ltd., a wholly owned subsidiary of Dundee Bancorp Inc. At year end the portfolio consisted of North American equities (51%), Australian equities (19%), Latin American equities (9%), African equities (8%), and gold and platinum holdings (13%). BGR has cash and precious metals holdings in excess of $25-million that will be used to increase equity investments.

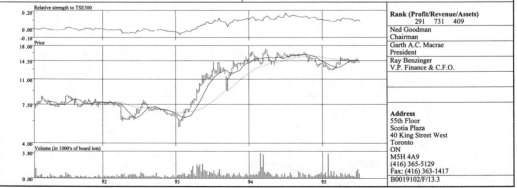

Rank (Profit/Revenue/Assets)
291   731   409

Ned Goodman
Chairman

Garth A.C. Macrae
President

Ray Benzinger
V.P. Finance & C.F.O.

Address
55th Floor
Scotia Plaza
40 King Street West
Toronto
ON
M5H 4A9
(416) 365-5129
Fax: (416) 363-1417
B0019102/F/13.3

CANADA TRUST INCOME INVESTMENTS

Exchanges	Price (Jun29'95)	8 .62	Trailing P/E	12 .55	Stock Symbol
TM	Trailing Yield (%)	7 .98	Trailing EPS	0 .69	**CNN.UN**

Period Ending	Dec94	Dec93	Dec92	Dec91	Dec90
Yearly Statistics					
Price-Close	8 .25	9 .63	8 .13	9 .13	7 .63
Price-High	10 .00	9 .88	9 .38	9 .50	8 .63
Price-Low	7 .75	7 .88	8 .13	8 .13	7 .00
P/E-Close	11 .97	13 .44	11 .67	11 .14	8 .85
Dividends per Share	0 .69	0 .72	0 .70	0 .82	0 .86
Dividend Yield (%)	8 .34	7 .44	8 .57	8 .98	11 .31
Sales per Share	0 .79	0 .82	0 .80	0 .92	0 .96
EPS before extra. item	0 .69	0 .72	0 .70	0 .82	0 .86
Cash Flow per Share	0 .69	0 .72	0 .70	0 .82	0 .86
Book Value per Share	8 .80	9 .88	9 .08	9 .40	8 .53
O/S Common Shares	4 ,435	4 ,435	4 ,435	4 ,435	4 ,423
Total Revenue	3 ,507	3 ,631	3 ,533	4 ,085	4 ,225
Income before extra.	3 ,056	3 ,174	3 ,085	3 ,631	3 ,814
Cash Flow	3 ,056	3 ,174	3 ,085	3 ,631	3 ,814
Debt/Equity	nd	nd	nd	nd	nd
Return on Capital (%)	7 .38	7 .55	7 .53	9 .15	9 .94
Ret. on Com. Equity (%)	7 .38	7 .55	7 .53	9 .15	9 .94
% Change Profit	(3 .7)	2 .9	(15 .0)	(4 .8)	(1 .2)
% Change Revenue	(3 .4)	2 .8	(13 .5)	(3 .3)	(1 .5)
% Change Assets	(10 .9)	9 .0	(3 .5)	10 .2	(8 .0)

Preferred Div. Coverage	np	np	np
Total Div. Coverage	1 .0	1 .0	1 .0

Business:

CANADA TRUST INCOME INVESTMENTS is a closed-end investment trust. Its portfolio contains fixed-income securities. Income from the trust is paid to unit holders on a monthly basis.

Date	EPS	DPS	Tot Rev	Inc Bex
Mar 95	0.17	0.11	865	753
Dec 94	0.17	0.24	871	759
Sep 94	0.17	0.17	881	768
Jun 94	0.17	0.17	882	769
Mar 94	0.17	0.17	874	760
Dec 93	0.17	0.21	874	759
Sep 93	0.17	0.19	869	754
Jun 93	0.17	0.17	869	755

5 YEAR RATIOS (%)			
Return on Capital	8 .3	8 .8	9 .2
Return on Com. Equity	8 .3	8 .8	9 .2
Profit Growth	(4 .6)	(3 .2)	(3 .7)
Revenue Growth	(4 .0)	(2 .7)	(3 .2)
Asset Growth	(1 .0)	2 .4	0 .4
BALANCE SHEET (000)			
Cash	1 ,575	272	4 ,459
Total Loans	0	0	0
Net Fixed Assets	0	0	0
Invest's & Advances	37 ,182	43 ,264	35 ,563
Total Assets	39 ,426	44 ,225	40 ,565
Total Deposits	0	0	0
Insurance Liability	0	0	0
Long Term Debt	0	0	0
Total Liabilities	377	410	297
Total Equity	39 ,050	43 ,815	40 ,267
Total Liab. & Equity	39 ,426	44 ,225	40 ,565
CAPITAL (000)			
Total Debt	0	0	0
Preferred Equity	0	0	0
Common Equity	39 ,050	43 ,815	40 ,267

Synopsis:

In early 1995, Canada Trust appointed Mulvihill Capital Management Inc. to provide investment advisory services to the Trust. Mulvihill Capital was formerly CT Investment Counsel Inc., a subsidiary of Canada Trust. In February 1995, Canada Trust sold its interest in CT Investment Council.

For the first quarter ended March 31, 1995, Canada Trust Income Investments generated improved results as the fund produced a 5% return in the quarter based on opening and closing unit values and income distributed. Mulvihill Capital Management feels optimistic about future performance with the average term of the portfolio at the longer end of its policy range at 8.7 years. This allows the fund to lock in the previously high interest rates for a longer period of time.

In fiscal 1994, the Canadian bond market as a whole produced its worst performance since 1956. The only major asset class to post a positive return for the year was Treasury Bills. Canada Trust Income Investment's fund generated an overall return of -3.9%, compared to the ScotiaMcLeod Universal Bond Index which produced a total return of -4.3%. Income distributed during the year was $0.69 per unit, down slightly from $0.72 in 1993. The decline was due to rolling over maturing securities at lower yields. Averaging the opening and closing TSE market values in 1994, the units generated a 7.72% return compared with a 5.45% return on Treasury Bills, and the 7.1% average yield on GIC investments.

In the second half of 1994 and the first half of 1995, the fund plans to slowly increase the average term of the portfolio. This lock in high yields for a longer period of time.

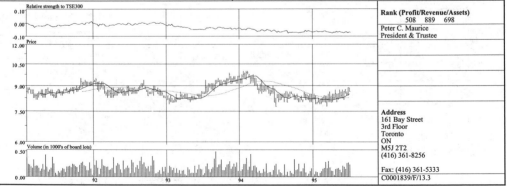

Rank (Profit/Revenue/Assets)		
508	889	698

Peter C. Maurice
President & Trustee

Address
161 Bay Street
3rd Floor
Toronto
ON
M5J 2T2
(416) 361-8256

Fax: (416) 361-5333
C0001839/F/13.3

CANADIAN GENERAL INVESTMENTS LIMITED

Exchanges	Price (Jun29'95)	29 .00	Trailing P/E	61 .70	Stock Symbol
T	Trailing Yield (%)	3 .31	Trailing EPS	0 .47	**CGI**

Period Ending	Dec94	Dec93	Dec92	Dec91	Dec90
Yearly Statistics					
Price-Close	28 .00	34 .50	27 .50	21 .50	19 .50
Price-High	39 .00	36 .00	32 .00	23 .75	23 .50
Price-Low	27 .50	26 .00	21 .50	18 .00	17 .57
P/E-Close	54 .90	36 .70	30 .22	19 .11	15 .29
Dividends per Share	4 .05	1 .03	1 .03	1 .03	1 .03
Dividend Yield (%)	14 .46	2 .97	3 .73	4 .77	5 .26
Sales per Share	1 .05	1 .38	1 .35	1 .33	1 .46
EPS before extra. item	0 .51	0 .94	0 .91	1 .13	1 .28
Cash Flow per Share	0 .51	0 .94	0 .91	1 .12	1 .27
Book Value per Share	39 .08	42 .44	33 .34	34 .25	31 .12
O/S Common Shares	4 ,760	7 ,561	7 ,561	7 ,561	7 ,561
Total Revenue	5 ,510	10 ,443	10 ,231	10 ,080	11 ,012
Income before extra.	2 ,635	7 ,133	6 ,905	8 ,496	9 ,631
Cash Flow	2 ,635	7 ,133	6 ,905	8 ,496	9 ,631
Debt/Equity	nd	nd	nd	nd	0 .01
Return on Capital (%)	0 .69	2 .32	2 .39	3 .45	3 .78
Ret. on Com. Equity (%)	1 .04	2 .49	2 .70	3 .44	3 .88
% Change Profit	(63 .1)	3 .3	(18 .7)	(11 .8)	(8 .1)
% Change Revenue	(47 .2)	2 .1	1 .5	(8 .5)	(7 .4)
% Change Assets	(45 .1)	23 .1	(2 .2)	13 .6	(12 .6)

Preferred Div. Coverage	np	np	np
Total Div. Coverage	0 .1	0 .9	0 .9

5 YEAR RATIOS (%)			
Return on Capital	2 .5	3 .2	3 .5
Return on Com. Equity	2 .7	3 .3	3 .5
Profit Growth	(24 .2)	(3 .2)	(1 .3)
Revenue Growth	(14 .3)	0 .1	1 .0
Asset Growth	(8 .1)	5 .9	2 .4

BALANCE SHEET (000)			
Cash	3 ,040	7 ,773	2 ,071
Total Loans	0	0	0
Net Fixed Assets	0	0	0
Invest's & Advances	182 ,884	332 ,701	272 ,640
Total Assets	188 ,352	342 ,846	278 ,418
Total Deposits	0	0	0
Insurance Liability	0	0	0
Long Term Debt	0	0	0
Total Liabilities	2 ,312	21 ,965	26 ,336
Total Equity	186 ,040	320 ,881	252 ,082
Total Liab. & Equity	188 ,352	342 ,846	278 ,418

CAPITAL (000)			
Total Debt	0	0	0
Preferred Equity	0	0	0
Common Equity	186 ,040	320 ,881	252 ,082

Business:

CANADIAN GENERAL INVESTMENTS LTD. is a closed-end investment company. Substantially all its portfolio is comprised of Canadian quoted securities. Industries in the portfolio include: oil & gas, financial services, technology, consumer products, metals & minerals, forest products, manufacturing, utilities, merchandising, and communications.

Date	EPS	DPS	Tot Rev	Inc Bex
Mar 95	0 .12	0 .23	1 ,249	559
Dec 94	0 .05	0 .29	1 ,153	179
Sep 94	0 .14	0 .23	1 ,076	647
Jun 94	0 .16	0 .23	1 ,329	771
Mar 94	0 .16	3 .38	1 ,953	1 ,037
Dec 93	0 .32	0 .26	3 ,032	2 ,472
Sep 93	0 .23	0 .23	2 ,478	1 ,723
Jun 93	0 .18	0 .23	2 ,673	1 ,373

Synopsis:

Canadian General Investments reported for the quarter ended March 31, 1995, total income was down 36.02%, to $1.2-million, compared with the first quarter of 1994. Net income was down 46.11%, to $559,000, for the same period. The declines were due to the reduction of income earning assets by the completion of the February 1994 Offer to Purchase agreement. This was only partly offset by a 23.6% reduction in expenses. Earnings per share dipped only 25% as a result of the reduced number of common shares outstanding.

In February 1995, the company issued, at no cost, long term warrants to shareholders of record on February 21, 1995. Each shareholder received one warrant for each five common shares held. The warrants were listed on the Toronto and London Stock Exchanges on February 27, 1995, and are exercisable on the 30th of June in the years 2000 to 2007.

On April 3, 1995, the Ontario Court decided that Canadian General pay a further sum of $2.40 per share, or $6,725,000, together with prejudgement interest to certain shareholders. The shareholders affected by the decision are those who made applications for additional payment for their shares purchased pursuant to the Offer to Purchase dated February 2, 1994, and to all other shareholders for their shares also purchased. Since management believes that $42.50 per share is fair value for their purchased shares, the company has appealed the court's decision.

For the year ended December 31, 1994, Canadian General reported that net income fell to $2.1-million from $7.1-million in 1993. Total net assets declined to $186-million from $320.9-million after tendering $119.1-million of common shares in the Offer to Purchase mentioned above. Net asset value per share stood at $39.08 at year end versus $42.44 the previous year. For shareholders who retained shares in the Canadian World Fund Ltd., which were distributed by the company in March 1994, the value of net assets was maintained.

During the year, Canadian General shares were listed on the London Stock Exchange. This made Canadian General the only general Canadian fund trading on a foreign stock exchange.

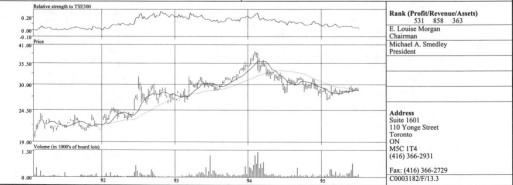

Rank (Profit/Revenue/Assets)
531   858   363
E. Louise Morgan
Chairman
Michael A. Smedley
President

Address
Suite 1601
110 Yonge Street
Toronto
ON
M5C 1T4
(416) 366-2931

Fax: (416) 366-2729
C0003182/F/13.3

CENTRAL CAPITAL CORPORATION

Exchanges	Price (Jun29'95)	0.45	Trailing P/E	1.96	Stock Symbol
TM	Trailing Yield (%)	0.00	Trailing EPS	0.13	**CEH**

Period Ending	Dec94	Dec93	Dec92	Dec91	Dec90
Yearly Statistics					
Price-Close	0.35	0.38	0.03	28.39	433.67
Price-High	0.80	1.75	0.50	75.69	717.52
Price-Low	0.15	0.04	0.01	17.66	354.82
P/E-Close	1.20	nm	nm	nm	nm
Dividends per Share	0.00	0.00	0.00	15.77	44.16
Dividend Yield (%)	0.00	0.00	0.00	55.56	10.18
Sales per Share	0.08	0.18	3.85	23.53	28.76
EPS before extra. item	0.29	(1.88)	na	(1,578.24)	(58.03)
Cash Flow per Share	0.07	(0.31)	(13.23)	(156.18)	(144.64)
Book Value per Share	0.70	0.99	20.50	(925.05)	661.95
O/S Common Shares	14,733	7,154	1,000	1,000	998
Total Revenue	6,077	2,280	208,951	(1,077,978)	146,066
Income before extra.	3,192	(13,439)	117,374	(1,561,482)	(43,786)
Cash Flow	811	(2,221)	(13,229)	(156,068)	(146,804)
Debt/Equity	1.38	2.97	1.02	na	1.19
Return on Capital (%)	16.86	(34.38)	56.51	(130.92)	(4.74)
Ret. on Com. Equity (%)	36.87	(97.52)	na	na	(8.16)
% Change Profit	123.8	(111.5)	107.5	(3,466.2)	(147.5)
% Change Revenue	166.5	(98.9)	119.4	(838.0)	(93.4)
% Change Assets	(18.9)	(30.7)	(89.7)	(75.2)	(89.0)

Preferred Div. Coverage	np	np	np
Total Div. Coverage	na	na	na

5 YEAR RATIOS (%)			
Return on Capital	(19.3)	(22.3)	(14.8)
Return on Com. Equity	na	na	na
Profit Growth	(49.1)	na	18.5
Revenue Growth	(71.1)	(74.9)	(27.5)
Asset Growth	(74.9)	(74.9)	(71.1)

BALANCE SHEET (000)			
Cash	12,161	13,763	5,554
Total Loans	836	2,310	23,964
Net Fixed Assets	4,693	4,643	4,890
Invest's & Advances	9,224	12,342	12,065
Total Assets	27,681	34,142	49,260
Total Deposits	0	0	0
Insurance Liability	0	0	0
Long Term Debt	14,137	21,000	21,000
Total Liabilities	17,428	27,081	28,760
Total Equity	10,253	7,061	20,500
Total Liab. & Equity	27,681	34,142	49,260

CAPITAL (000)			
Total Debt	14,137	21,000	21,000
Preferred Equity	0	0	0
Common Equity	10,253	7,061	20,500

Business:

CENTRAL CAPITAL CORP is a financial services industry holding company. On July 9, 1992, an Order in the Ontario Court of Justice was made under which some assets of the company are to be transferred to a new company owned by the company's creditors. The company is authorized to file with the Court a Plan of Arrangement under the Companies' Creditors Arrangment Act and the Canada Business Corporations Act.

Date	EPS	DPS	Tot Rev	Inc Bex
Mar 95	0.07	0.00	1,486	988
Dec 94	0.06	0.00	1,876	899
Sep 94	0.01	0.00	674	145
Jun 94	(0.01)	0.00	484	(185)
Mar 94	0.23	0.00	3,043	2,333
Dec 93	(0.90)	0.00	636	(6,436)
Sep 93	(0.60)	0.00	441	(4,318)
Jun 93	(0.07)	0.00	491	(499)

Synopsis:

Central Capital Corp. recorded revenues of $1.5-million and net income of $988,000 for the first quarter ended March 31, 1995, compared to revenues and net income of $2.3-million in the same period last year. In 1994, Central had revenues of $5-million with net income of $3.2-million, compared with revenues of $2.3-million and a loss of $13.4-million in 1993. During 1994 expenses fell to $1.8-million from $15.7-million, which included $9.7-million in loan losses, the prior year. The main sources of the 1994 revenues were gains on disposal of assets, income from non-consolidated subsidiaries, and interest income.

As of December 31, 1994, Central reduced its liabilities by almost $10-million to $17.4-million, due to the repayment of $6.9-million in notes payable and a $2.8-million reduction in accounts payable. On March 1, 1995, Central announced plans to repay $6.6-million of First Secured Notes and a pro rata interest payment of $1-million.

Central Capital ended 1994 with total assets of $27.7-million, including $12.1-million in cash. This was down from $34.1-million at the prior year end. As at December 31, 1994, the securities portfolio had a market value of $10.4-million and a book value of $7.4-million. The portfolio was comprised of publicly traded and private securities.

There are still several unresolved claim disputes relating to Central's restructuring plan that was implemented January 1, 1993. The largest group of claims relate to preferred shareholders and they were dismissed in court on January 9, 1995. An appeal has been launched and will be heard by a higher court on August 17, 1995.

Central's major objective is to conclude the implementation of the restructuring plan through the distribution of notes, cash, and shares. The company will continue to monetize the securities portfolio and to the manage other assets to maximize value and liquidity.

Relative strength to TSE300 / Price / Volume (in 1000's of board lots) charts (1992–1995)

Rank (Profit/Revenue/Assets)		
505	842	793

Stanley M. Beck
Chairman

Richard C. Hazell
President & C.E.O.

Richard A. Howard
V.P. Finance

Valerie K. Pettipas
V.P. Admin. & Corp. Sec.

Address
20 Queen Street West
35th Floor
Toronto
ON
M5H 3C8
(416) 214-2200

Fax: (416) 214-2212

C0000635/F/13.3

CENTRAL FUND OF CANADA LIMITED

Exchanges	Price (Jun29'95)	6.75	Trailing P/E		nm	Stock Symbol
TA	Trailing Yield (%)	0.00	Trailing EPS		(0.06)	CEF.A

Period Ending	Oc t94	Oc t93	Oc t92	Oc t91	Oc t90
Yearly Statistics	US	US			
Price-Close	6.75	6.38	4.80	4.40	5.13
Price-High	8.50	7.50	5.25	5.50	7.25
Price-Low	6.25	4.40	4.25	4.30	4.80
P/E-Close	nm	nm	nm	nm	nm
Dividends per Share	0.01	0.01	0.01	0.01	0.01
Dividend Yield (%)	0.10	0.11	0.21	0.23	0.20
Sales per Share	0.00	0.00	0.01	0.01	0.02
EPS before extra. item	(0.05)	(0.04)	(0.04)	(0.05)	(0.06)
Cash Flow per Share	(0.05)	(0.05)	(0.05)	(0.05)	(0.05)
Book Value per Share	4.92	4.52	5.05	4.94	5.45
O/S Common Shares	18,139	18,139	16,864	16,864	16,864
Total Revenue	25	104	154	188	162
Income before extra.	(956)	(744)	(759)	(823)	(939)
Cash Flow	(881)	(812)	(826)	(773)	(803)
Debt/Equity	nd	nd	nd	nd	nd
Return on Capital (%)	(0.93)	(0.79)	(0.73)	(0.78)	(0.83)
Ret. on Com. Equity (%)	(1.12)	(0.99)	(0.90)	(0.94)	(0.98)
% Change Profit	(28.5)	(26.0)	7.8	12.4	5.5
% Change Revenue	(76.3)	(13.1)	(18.0)	16.1	(55.2)
% Change Assets	8.9	27.2	2.3	(9.3)	(8.9)

Preferred Div. Coverage	np	np	np
Total Div. Coverage	0.0	0.0	0.0

5 YEAR RATIOS (%)			
Return on Capital	(0.8)	(0.8)	(0.8)
Return on Com. Equity	(1.0)	(0.9)	(0.9)
Profit Growth	(7.6)	2.4	na
Revenue Growth	(38.8)	(16.7)	(25.9)
Asset Growth	3.2	(2.3)	(10.8)

BALANCE SHEET (000)			
Cash	63	847	805
Total Loans	0	0	0
Net Fixed Assets	0	0	0
Invest's & Advances	89,505	81,362	84,685
Total Assets	89,610	82,257	85,490
Total Deposits	0	0	0
Insurance Liability	0	0	0
Long Term Debt	0	0	0
Total Liabilities	377	354	310
Total Equity	89,233	81,903	85,181
Total Liab. & Equity	89,610	82,257	85,490

CAPITAL (000)			
Total Debt	0	0	0
Preferred Equity	0	0	0
Common Equity	89,233	81,903	85,181

Business:

CENTRAL FUND OF CANADA LTD. is a specialized closed-end investment holding company. The company provides a vehicle for investors interested in holding marketable gold and silver related investments. The company invests primarily in long-term holdings of gold and silver bullion. It holds a minimum of 90% of its non-cash assets in gold and silver bullion, primarily in bar form.

Date		EPS	DPS	Tot Rev	Inc Bex
Apr 95	US	(0.01)	0.00	5	(234)
Jan 95	US	(0.03)	0.00	(348)	(577)
Oct 94	US	(0.01)	0.00	(8)	(226)
Jul 94	US	(0.01)	0.00	4	(237)
Apr 94	US	(0.01)	0.00	18	(220)
Jan 94	US	(0.02)	0.00	11	(273)
Oct 93	US	0.00	0.00	97	(85)
Jul 93	US	(0.02)	0.00	10	(292)

Synopsis:

For the quarter ended January 31, 1995, Central Fund Corp. reported a 6.7% drop in net assets per Class A share, from $6.48 to $4.60. This was due to the mix of gold which dropped in value by 2.3%, and silver which dropped by 12.1%. The net loss for the period was $576,734 compared with a loss of $272,694 in the first quarter of 1994. The company realized losses of approximately $344,000 on the sales of gold certificates representing 1,288 fine ounces, and silver certificates representing 65,457 ounces. At the same time, operating expenses were 21.7% lower than in the comparable period of 1994 due to reduced foreign currency exchange losses. All amounts expressed in this profile are in U.S. dollars.

At January 31, 1995, Central Fund was 99.2% invested in gold and silver bullion. Gold holdings were 123,788 ounces of physical bullion and 11,712 ounces of gold bullion certificates. Silver holdings were 6,138,707 ounces of physical bullion and 636,293 ounces of silver certificates.

At October 31, 1994, the company's year end, the Class A shares of Central Fund were backed by 99.8% of gold and silver bullion investments. During fiscal 1994, net assets per Class A share increased by 9.1% from $4.52 to $4.93. Gold and silver prices rose by 3.9% and 21.4%, respectively. In Canadian dollar terms, net assets were further increased as the U.S. dollar increased by 2.3% relative to the Canadian dollar during the year.

The net loss for fiscal 1994 rose 28.5% from $744,070 to $956,009. The reasons for the results include a decrease in the gain on sale of investments, declining interest income, and an increase in administration fees. Though operating expenses increased during the year, they still represented only 0.9% of net assets compared with 0.8% of net assets in 1993.

During the second quarter of 1994, the company began presenting its financial statements in United States dollars, with net asset value per share also being presented in Canadian dollars.

Relative strength to TSE300 / Price / Volume (in 1000's of board lots)

Rank (Profit/Revenue/Assets)
829   991   444

Philip M. Spicer
President & C.E.O.

Michael A. Parente
Vice President Finance

Address
Hallmark Estates
Suite 805
1323 - 15th Avenue S.W.
Calgary
AB
T3C 0X8
(403) 228-5861
Fax: (403) 228-2222
C0006172/F/13.3

CONSOLIDATED CANADIAN EXPRESS LIMITED

Exchanges	Price (Jun29'95)	0.85	Trailing P/E	nm	Stock Symbol
T	Trailing Yield (%)	0.00	Trailing EPS	(0.25)	CXE

Period Ending	Dec94	Dec93	Dec92	Dec91	Dec90
Yearly Statistics					
Price-Close	0.90	0.85	0.69	1.80	2.10
Price-High	1.35	1.15	2.40	3.75	14.40
Price-Low	0.51	0.40	0.40	1.20	1.60
P/E-Close	nm	nm	nm	nm	nm
Dividends per Share	0.00	0.00	0.00	0.00	0.00
Dividend Yield (%)	0.00	0.00	0.00	0.00	0.00
Sales per Share	2.74	2.21	2.85	3.06	4.16
EPS before extra. item	(0.25)	(1.05)	(2.35)	(9.82)	(2.07)
Cash Flow per Share	1.97	1.52	2.17	1.61	2.55
Book Value per Share	1.30	1.55	2.60	4.95	14.77
O/S Common Shares	8,829	8,829	8,829	8,829	8,829
Total Revenue	24,176	19,233	7,819	(26,434)	13,490
Income before extra.	20,296	13,196	1,854	(62,452)	7,950
Cash Flow	17,402	13,457	19,177	14,227	22,544
Debt/Equity	0.19	0.20	0.18	0.17	nd
Return on Capital (%)	7.58	5.90	2.12	(16.61)	2.59
Ret. on Com. Equity (%)	(17.35)	(50.67)	(62.20)	(99.60)	(13.09)
% Change Profit	53.8	611.8	103.0	(885.6)	122.2
% Change Revenue	25.7	146.0	129.6	(296.0)	(64.7)
% Change Assets	1.4	1.6	(5.3)	(16.4)	(8.3)

Preferred Div. Coverage	0.9	0.6	0.1
Total Div. Coverage	0.9	0.6	0.1

Date	EPS	DPS	Tot Rev	Inc Bex
Mar 95	(0.10)	0.00	6,119	5,001
Dec 94	0.07	0.00	7,343	6,297
Sep 94	(0.32)	0.00	3,720	2,797
Jun 94	0.01	0.00	6,862	5,674
Mar 94	(0.01)	0.00	6,251	5,528
Dec 93	(0.35)	0.00	7,673	6,265
Sep 93	(0.41)	0.00	3,951	2,065
Jun 93	(0.32)	0.00	4,326	2,758

5 YEAR RATIOS (%)			
Return on Capital	0.3	(1.8)	(9.9)
Return on Com. Equity	(48.6)	(52.7)	(57.5)
Profit Growth	na	na	(36.8)
Revenue Growth	(8.7)	(1.0)	(21.3)
Asset Growth	(5.6)	(6.6)	(6.6)

BALANCE SHEET (000)			
Cash	1,801	74,111	31,375
Total Loans	76,286	13,394	17,731
Net Fixed Assets	0	0	0
Invest's & Advances	270,299	255,944	288,838
Total Assets	348,386	343,449	337,944
Total Deposits	35,697		
Insurance Liability	0	0	0
Long Term Debt	0	0	0
Total Liabilities	93,389	86,268	71,479
Total Equity	254,997	257,181	266,465
Total Liab. & Equity	348,386	343,449	337,944

CAPITAL (000)			
Total Debt	48,865	52,172	48,986
Preferred Equity	243,500	243,500	243,500
Common Equity	11,497	13,681	22,965

Business:

CONSOLIDATED CANADIAN EXPRESS has investment interests in the manufacturing and financial services industries.

Synopsis:

Consolidated Canadian Express reported that net income for the three months ended March 31, 1995, was $5-million compared with net income of $5.5-million for the same period in 1994. After providing for preferred dividends, the net loss per common share was $0.10 compared with a net loss of $0.01 per common share during the three months ended March 31, 1994.

During 1995, Complax Corporation, a subsidiary of Canadian Express, recovered its $4-million debenture interest in Complax Components Corp. It sold its property interest in Cobourg for $5.1-million. This completes the restructuring of Complax's automotive interests. In 1994, Complax realized a gain of $2.4-million from the sale of 400,000 shares of The Tarxien Corporation. The company also entered into an agreement to sell its Windsor manufacturing facility for $7.4-million. The transaction finished in February 1995.

Canadian Express reported net income of $20.3-million in 1994, on revenue of $24.2-million, compared with earnings of $13.2-million, on revenue of $19.2-million in 1993. After preferred share dividends, the company reported a loss of $0.25 per common share compared with a loss of $1.05 per share in 1993. Canadian Express earns $8.1-million in dividends annually from its 9% common share investment in Hees International.

Canadian Express is an investment holding company and its two principal investments are a 99% interest in the American Resource Corporation Ltd., a Bermuda-based merchant finance company, and a 9% fully diluted equity interest in Hees International Bancorp Inc., a Canadian-based merchant bank. Canadian Express holds a 49% interest in the Complax Corporation, and in Consolidated Enfield Corporation, which holds the remaining 51% interest in Complax.

The company and other parties are subject to a lawsuit brought in 1990 by Renegade Capital Corporation, the personal holding company of the former president of Enfield. The company has counterclaimed against the plaintiff and other parties.

Relative strength to TSE300

Price

Volume (in 1000's of board lots)

Rank (Profit/Revenue/Assets)
215   686   272

Manfred J. Walt
Chairman

Brian D. Lawson
President & Secretary

Address
Suite 4501
BCE Place
181 Bay Street
Toronto
ON
M5J 2V1
(416) 359-8620
Fax: (416) 865-1288
C0000761/F/13.3

For further company information, call Globe Information Services 1-800-268-9128 or (416) 585-5345

DESJARDINS LAURENTIAN FINANCIAL CORPORATION

Exchanges	Price (Jun29'95)		7.87	Trailing P/E		nm	Stock Symbol
TM	Trailing Yield (%)		0.00	Trailing EPS		(0.41)	**DJN.A**

Period Ending	Dec94	Dec93	Dec92
Yearly Statistics			
Price-Close	5.25	n t	n t
Price-High	9.00	n t	n t
Price-Low	5.00	n t	n t
P/E-Close	nm	n t	n t
Dividends per Share	0.00	0.00	0.00
Dividend Yield (%)	0.00	0.00	0.00
Sales per Share	96.92	64.07	97.21
EPS before extra. item	(0.43)	1.60	1.07
Cash Flow per Share	20.74	16.24	2.91
Book Value per Share	16.21	13.68	15.57
O/S Common Shares	40,968	27,533	40,983
Total Revenue	3,970,818	1,607,073	3,984,063
Income before extra.	(7,385)	40,201	48,975
Cash Flow	849,696	407,307	119,250
Debt/Equity	0.98	0.41	nd
Return on Capital (%)	4.51	9.61	na
Ret. on Com. Equity (%)	(2.78)	7.93	na
% Change Profit	(118.4)	(17.9)	na
% Change Revenue	147.1	(59.7)	na
% Change Assets	267.0	(68.9)	na

Preferred Div. Coverage	0.0	np	na
Total Div. Coverage	0.0	na	na

5 YEAR RATIOS (%)			
Return on Capital	na	na	na
Return on Com. Equity	na	na	na
Profit Growth	na	na	na
Revenue Growth	na	na	na
Asset Growth	na	na	na

BALANCE SHEET (mil)			
Cash	1,494	268	886
Total Loans	13,889	3,041	0
Net Fixed Assets	571	94	0
Invest's & Advances	5,451	2,309	17,708
Total Assets	22,471	6,122	19,672
Total Deposits	11,888	2,535	0
Insurance Liability	7,288	2,516	0
Long Term Debt	808	154	0
Total Liabilities	21,646	5,746	18,877
Total Equity	825	377	795
Total Liab. & Equity	22,471	6,122	19,672

CAPITAL (mil)			
Total Debt	808	154	0
Preferred Equity	161	0	157
Common Equity	664	377	638

Business:

DESJARDINS LAURENTIAL FINANCIAL CORPORATION is a holding company in the casualty insurance, life insurance, financial and trust services and securities sectors.

Date	EPS	DPS	Tot Rev	Inc Bex
Mar 95	0.36	0.00	1,100,000	17,200
Dec 94	0.33	0.00	1,023,456	15,994
Sep 94	(1.13)	0.00	991,337	(43,875)
Jun 94	0.21	0.00	972,673	11,251
Mar 94	0.16	0.00	983,352	9,245
Dec 93	0.40	0.00	408,576	10,190
Sep 93	1.13	0.00	401,481	28,438
Jun 93	0.01	0.00	377,751	301

Synopsis:

On January 1, 1994, Desjardins-Laurentian Financial Corp. (DLFC) completed a major regrouping of Societe financiere des caisses Desjardins and The Laurentian Group Corporation. This resulted in DLFC becoming the only major holding company in Canada active in all five pillars of the financial industry: life insurance; general insurance; trust services; securities brokerage; and banking.

For the quarter ended March 31, 1995, revenues were $1.1-billion and earnings were $17.2-million compared to revenues of $983.4-million and earnings of $9.2-million as at March 31, 1994. The increases were due mainly to the regrouping and acquisitions made in 1994.

During 1994, the company posted a net loss of $7.4-million compared with consolidated net earnings of $40.2-million in 1993, due mainly to a $73.4-million operating loss reported by Desjardins Trustco. Revenues for the period totalled $4-billion, a 147% increase over 1993. Assets totalled $22.5-billion, up almost $16.4-billion from December 31, 1993.

In 1994, Laurentian Bank acquired Manulife Bank of Canada and Prenor Trust Company of Canada. During the year DLFC acquired, through The Laurentian Group, 362,000 common shares of Laurentian Bank, raising its interest to 57.5%. In 1994, Desjardins-Laurentian Life Group acquired Aeterna Life and negotiated one of its largest group insurance contracts with 35,000 members from nine unions. Also during the period Laurentian Fund Management launched three new international mutual funds.

On December 31, 1994, DLFC formed Desjardins-Laurentian Life Assurance by merging Desjardins Life Assurance and Laurentian Life. In addition, The Imperial Life Assurance Company acquired Laurentian Financial Services.

On April 25, 1995, DLFC sold its interest in Laurentian Financial Group PLC and its subsidiaries to Lincoln National (U.K.) PLC., for $320-million. Lincoln is the U.K. subsidiary of U.S.-based Lincoln National Corp.

Rank (Profit/Revenue/Assets)
930 37 15

Claude Beland	Chairman
Humberto Santos	President & C.E.O.
Jocelyn Proteau	Vice Chairman
Guy Rivard	Sr. V.P. Finance & Admin.

Address
1 Complexe Desjardins
P.O. Box 7; Desjardins Station
South Tower; 28th Floor
Montreal
PQ
H5B 1B2
(514) 281-7061
Fax: (514) 281-7745
01003537/F/13.3

DUNDEE BANCORP INC.

Exchanges	Price (Jun29'95)	13.00	Trailing P/E	7.43	Stock Symbol
TM	Trailing Yield (%)	0.00	Trailing EPS	1.75	DBC.A

Period Ending	Dec94	Dec93	Dec92	Dec91
Yearly Statistics				3M
Price-Close	9.63	9.13	3.15	3.05
Price-High	11.63	9.50	3.55	6.50
Price-Low	8.50	3.00	2.25	2.90
P/E-Close	5.47	9.04	nm	nm
Dividends per Share	0.00	0.00	0.00	0.00
Dividend Yield (%)	0.00	0.00	0.00	0.00
Sales per Share	1.98	0.97	0.71	1.10
EPS before extra. item	1.76	1.01	(0.06)	(6.76)
Cash Flow per Share	0.46	(0.09)	(0.48)	0.12
Book Value per Share	10.68	8.95	7.70	7.80
O/S Common Shares	21,636	23,202	25,412	25,057
Total Revenue	85,179	56,688	53,785	7,790
Income before extra.	40,992	26,418	626	(168,949)
Cash Flow	10,364	(2,230)	(12,089)	774
Debt/Equity	0.07	0.11	0.22	0.60
Return on Capital (%)	16.69	11.47	4.61	na
Ret. on Com. Equity (%)	18.00	11.92	(0.78)	na
% Change Profit	55.2	4,120.1	100.1	na
% Change Revenue	50.3	5.4	72.6	na
% Change Assets	(1.0)	(13.6)	(28.6)	na
Preferred Div. Coverage	27.5	11.1	0.3	
Total Div. Coverage	27.5	11.1	0.3	

Business:

DUNDEE BANCORP INC.'s principal business activities are the provision of investment management and administrative services to the 18 Dynamic Mutual Funds, BGR Precious Metals Inc., pension and other institutional clients, private clients and the management of its own corporate investment portfolio.

Date	EPS	DPS	Tot Rev	Inc Bex
Mar 95	0.40	0.00	19,793	8,969
Dec 94	0.49	0.00	24,679	11,092
Sep 94	0.55	0.00	22,001	12,640
Jun 94	0.31	0.00	17,640	7,247
Mar 94	0.41	0.00	21,972	10,013
Dec 93	0.14	0.00	15,629	3,769
Sep 93	0.38	0.00	15,290	9,223
Jun 93	0.30	0.00	13,867	8,355

Synopsis:

Dundee Bancorp reported revenue of $19.8-million and net income of $9-million for the first quarter of 1995, compared with revenue of $22-million and net income of $10-million for the same period in 1994. Net investment gains generated from the corporate portfolio were $5.8-million. The bulk of this came from the sale of the balance of the company's Homestake Mining shares.

In 1994, revenue totalled $85.2-million compared with $56.7-million for 1993. Net income rose to $41-million, a 55% increase over the $26.4-million earned in 1993. Management fee income doubled to $40.5-million from $20.3-million, while assets under management increased to $3.2-billion from $2.5-billion at the end of 1993. However, asset growth resulted in increased selling, marketing and service expenses. Expenses amounted to $15.3-million, more than double those of the previous year.

In 1994, Dundee had more than $1-billion of mutual fund sales. The publication "Top Funds 1995" named Dynamic "Fund Company of the Year". The Dynamic Israel Growth Fund was launched in 1994 and Dundee is working on a joint venture to distribute its mutual funds in Israel. Dundee also opened Eagles & Partners Inc., an institutional investment dealer subsidiary, and the Mid Ocean Trust Company in Bermuda was recently licensed.

During 1994 Goodman & Company, Investment Counsel, achieved acceptance as a pension fund manager in Canada. As well, Goodman's U.S. operations were registered with the Securities and Exchange Commission as an investment counsel.

Dundee's corporate portfolio is valued at $40.7-million. It has significant holdings in Kinross Gold Corporation, 10%; Zemex Corporation, 30%; Breakwater Resources Ltd., 40%; as well as several other resource companies and real estate holdings.

5 YEAR RATIOS (%)			
Return on Capital	na	na	na
Return on Com. Equity	na	na	na
Profit Growth	na	na	na
Revenue Growth	na	na	na
Asset Growth	na	na	na
BALANCE SHEET (000)			
Cash	5,244	6,261	24,992
Total Loans	35,890	17,969	14,036
Net Fixed Assets	3,966	1,219	1,379
Invest's & Advances	163,081	212,299	267,644
Total Assets	275,157	277,976	321,765
Total Deposits	0	0	0
Insurance Liability	0	0	0
Long Term Debt	16,062	26,693	49,008
Total Liabilities	26,450	42,372	102,900
Total Equity	248,707	235,604	218,865
Total Liab. & Equity	275,157	277,976	321,765
CAPITAL (000)			
Total Debt	16,062	26,693	49,008
Preferred Equity	17,565	27,865	23,279
Common Equity	231,142	207,739	195,586

Rank (Profit/Revenue/Assets)		
131	445	300

Ned Goodman
Chairman President & C.E.O.

Ray Benzinger
V.P. Finance And C.F.O.

Address
55th Floor
Scotia Plaza
40 King Street West
Toronto
ON
M5H 4A9
(416) 863-6990
Fax: (416) 363-4536
01003229/F/13.6

For further company information, call Globe Information Services 1-800-268-9128 or (416) 585-5345

EDPER GROUP LIMITED (THE)

Exchanges	Price (Jun29'95)	4.35	Trailing P/E	10.12	Stock Symbol
T	Trailing Yield (%)	6.90	Trailing EPS	0.43	**EPR.A**

Period Ending	Dec94	Dec93	Dec92	Dec91	Dec90	Business:
Yearly Statistics						THE EDPER GROUP LIMITED is an
Price-Close	4.65	3.55	2.30	5.25	6.00	investment company with significant direct and
Price-High	4.90	3.80	5.63	7.25	8.75	indirect shareholdings in Hees International
Price-Low	3.15	1.15	2.22	4.10	5.75	Bancorp Inc.
P/E-Close	11.07	11.09	6.97	10.29	9.68	
Dividends per Share	0.30	0.30	0.60	0.60	0.60	
Dividend Yield (%)	6.45	8.45	26.09	11.43	10.00	
Sales per Share	0.09	0.12	0.08	0.17	0.29	
EPS before extra. item	0.42	0.32	0.33	0.51	0.62	
Cash Flow per Share	0.30	0.42	0.37	0.50	0.59	
Book Value per Share	8.51	8.42	8.43	8.71	8.80	
O/S Common Shares	92,517	91,865	91,395	91,307	91,307	
Total Revenue	49,177	39,965	37,203	56,485	68,875	
Income before extra.	38,415	29,404	30,190	46,535	56,597	

Cash Flow	27,294	38,210	33,543	45,504	53,892
Debt/Equity	0.12	0.12	0.12	0.12	0.12
Return on Capital (%)	5.56	4.54	4.18	6.27	7.57
Ret. on Com. Equity (%)	4.92	3.81	3.86	5.82	7.06
% Change Profit	30.6	(2.6)	(35.1)	(17.8)	19.7
% Change Revenue	23.1	7.4	(34.1)	(18.0)	(3.7)
% Change Assets	1.4	0.9	(2.5)	(0.9)	(2.7)

Date	EPS	DPS	Tot Rev	Inc Bex
Mar 95	0.15	0.08	15,297	13,555
Dec 94	0.04	0.08	9,420	3,750
Sep 94	0.12	0.08	12,863	11,106
Jun 94	0.12	0.08	13,240	11,030
Mar 94	0.14	0.08	13,654	12,529
Dec 93	(0.05)	0.08	1,381	(4,477)
Sep 93	0.12	0.08	11,758	10,819
Jun 93	0.06	0.08	7,429	5,344

	Dec94	Dec93	Dec92
Preferred Div. Coverage	np	np	np
Total Div. Coverage	1.4	1.1	0.6

Synopsis:

At the recent shareholders meeting the company changed its name from The Pagurian Corporation Limited to The Edper Group Limited. This better reflects its ownership of Edper Enterprises Ltd. and its commitment to the group's ongoing development.

5 YEAR RATIOS (%)			
Return on Capital	5.6	6.6	10.4
Return on Com. Equity	5.1	5.6	9.1
Profit Growth	(4.1)	(19.9)	(19.4)
Revenue Growth	(7.2)	(5.5)	(18.0)
Asset Growth	(0.8)	14.1	17.5

For the quarter of 1995, Edper Group earned $13.6-million on income of $15.3-million compared with earnings of $12.5-million on income of $13.9-million for the same period in 1994.

During the quarter, the company exchanged $252-million preferred shares of Edper Enterprises for an equivalent number of preferred shares of Edper Holdings Inc., enabling the company to hold all of its holdings in Edper Enterprises through Edper Holdings Inc. In addition, an agreement was reached with Peter F. Bronfman, whereby he can elect to exchange his stake in Edper Holdings for shares of Edper Group at any point, up until February 1997. The company has the right to trigger the transaction at anytime after that date.

BALANCE SHEET (000)			
Cash	0	0	0
Total Loans	124,062	96,106	77,984
Net Fixed Assets	0	0	0
Invest's & Advances	763,721	777,542	789,348
Total Assets	896,535	883,824	875,563
Total Deposits	0	0	0
Insurance Liability	0	0	0
Long Term Debt	0	0	0
Total Liabilities	109,661	110,186	105,017
Total Equity	786,874	773,638	770,546
Total Liab. & Equity	896,535	883,824	875,563
CAPITAL (000)			
Total Debt	90,912	94,923	94,186
Preferred Equity	0	0	0
Common Equity	786,874	773,638	770,546

During fiscal 1994, the company earned $38.4-million compared with $29.4-million in 1993. The increase in earnings reflects continued improvement in the financial performance of its affiliates in the natural resources, power generation, real estate, and financial services sectors.

For 1994, Edper Enterprises reported net income of $19.6-million compared with a loss of $5.7-million in 1993. This resulted from reduced debt levels and increased earnings by Hees International. During the year, Trilon completed the restructuring of its operations by selling its fleet vehicle leasing business and its investment in Eurobrokers for proceeds of $295-million and raised $66-million from a public right offering. London Insurance Group and Great Lakes Power also reported increased earnings in 1994.

In 1994, the Edper Group simplified its corporate structure by eliminating Brascan Holdings Inc., Carena Holdings Inc., and Hees Holdings Inc. Noranda also completed the merger of Norcen Energy and North Canadian Oils.

Relative strength to TSE300

Price

Volume (in 1000's of board lots)

Rank (Profit/Revenue/Assets)
132 554 165
Timothy W. Casgrain
Chairman
Manfred Walt
President
Brian D. Lawson
V.P. Finance & Secretary

Address
Suite 4440 BCE Place
181 Bay Street
P.O. Box 770
Toronto
ON
M5J 2T3
(416) 359-8615
Fax: (416) 865-1288
P0000526/F/13.3

FAHNESTOCK VINER HOLDINGS INC.

Exchanges	Price (Jun29'95)	10.00	Trailing P/E	8 .57	Stock Symbol
T	Trailing Yield (%)	2 .03	Trailing EPS	0 .86	**FHV.A**

Period Ending	Dec94	Dec93	Dec92	Dec91	Dec90
Yearly Statistics	US	US	US	US	US
Price-Close	9 .13	11 .75	9 .00	8 .13	1 .63
Price-High	12 .75	12 .63	12 .13	8 .75	2 .45
Price-Low	8 .13	7 .38	6 .75	1 .42	1 .40
P/E-Close	5 .07	4 .42	5 .12	7 .47	7 .98
Dividends per Share	0 .15	0 .10	0 .00	0 .00	0 .00
Dividend Yield (%)	2 .25	1 .10	0 .00	0 .00	0 .00
Sales per Share	12 .87	13 .54	12 .00	10 .29	7 .47
EPS before extra. item	0 .96	1 .59	1 .19	0 .83	0 .15
Cash Flow per Share	1 .01	1 .64	1 .24	0 .90	0 .26
Book Value per Share	7 .34	6 .54	5 .06	3 .88	3 .05
O/S Common Shares	12 ,098	11 ,998	11 ,828	11 ,441	11 ,251
Total Revenue	157 ,253	161 ,985	139 ,156	116 ,176	84 ,036
Income before extra.	11 ,780	19 ,022	13 ,823	9 ,401	1 ,668
Cash Flow	12 ,370	19 ,657	14 ,344	10 ,132	2 ,879
Debt/Equity	4 .36	2 .86	2 .37	0 .50	0 .20
Return on Capital (%)	8 .41	16 .00	21 .73	39 .55	10 .83
Ret. on Com. Equity (%)	14 .09	27 .51	26 .54	23 .92	4 .99
% Change Profit	(38 .1)	37 .6	47 .0	463 .6	(32 .5)
% Change Revenue	(2 .9)	16 .4	19 .8	38 .2	1 .1
% Change Assets	19 .2	34 .4	34 .7	13 .1	(2 .5)

Business:

FAHNESTOCK VINER HOLDINGS INC. is engaged in the stock brokerage business. Substantially all of the company's revenues are derived from or identifiable assets are applicable to operations in the United States.

Date		EPS	DPS	Tot Rev	Inc Bex
Mar 95	US	0 .26	0 .15	40 ,748	3 ,144
Dec 94	US	0 .08	0 .00	35 ,993	1 ,024
Sep 94	US	0 .29	0 .00	37 ,237	3 ,509
Jun 94	US	0 .23	0 .00	38 ,350	2 ,779
Mar 94	US	0 .37	0 .00	45 ,673	4 ,468
Dec 93	US	0 .40	0 .10	44 ,196	4 ,856
Sep 93	US	0 .34	0 .00	38 ,404	4 ,028
Jun 93	US	0 .37	0 .00	38 ,515	4 ,378

Preferred Div. Coverage	np	np	np
Total Div. Coverage	6 .4	15 .9	na

Synopsis:

Fahnestock reported for the three months ended March 31, 1995, net profit was $3.1-million compared to $4.5-million for the comparable period of 1994. Revenue for the 1995 first quarter was $40.7- million, a 10% decline compared to $45.7-million in the first quarter of 1994. However, revenue rose by 13% over the 1994 fourth quarter, and profit before taxes rose by 15%. All amounts in this profile are in U.S. dollars. Fahnestock's results were not as poor as those of other Canadian publicly traded brokerage houses because the company operates only in the U.S. where market conditions were better.

In the first quarter of 1995, Fahnestock purchased 140,865 Class A non-voting shares through the Toronto Stock Exchange via a normal course issuer bid bringing the total number of shares cancelled to 400,965. The company intends to buy up to 800,000 Class A non-voting shares prior to May 4, 1996.

During 1994 earnings were $11.8-million, a drop of 38% compared to $19-million in 1993. Total revenue in 1994 was $157.3-million. This represents a drop of 3% compared to record revenue of $162-million. The decline was due to poor market conditions, high interest rates, and increased costs as a result of the Reich & Co. acquisition in late 1993.

In 1994 Fahnestock participated in the creation of a minority-owned investment advisory business, Niagara Investment Advisors, located in Buffalo, New York. Also during the year, its public finance departments raised over $1.2-billion (U.S.) from the issue of municipal bonds for 104 issuers in 12 states, managed three initial public offerings, and co-managed offerings totalling over $1.9-billion.

5 YEAR RATIOS (%)			
Return on Capital	19 .3	19 .3	17 .4
Return on Com. Equity	19 .4	18 .2	13 .1
Profit Growth	36 .7	101 .3	121 .3
Revenue Growth	13 .5	15 .2	30 .8
Asset Growth	18 .8	10 .8	18 .6

BALANCE SHEET (000)			
Cash	11 ,043	7 ,437	5 ,628
Total Loans	0	0	0
Net Fixed Assets	1 ,355	1 ,071	877
Invest's & Advances	30 ,197	37 ,712	31 ,345
Total Assets	510 ,636	428 ,315	318 ,799
Total Deposits	0	0	0
Insurance Liability	0	0	0
Long Term Debt	338 ,509	191 ,453	118 ,038
Total Liabilities	421 ,848	349 ,855	258 ,982
Total Equity	88 ,788	78 ,460	59 ,817
Total Liab. & Equity	510 ,636	428 ,315	318 ,799

CAPITAL (000)			
Total Debt	387 ,253	224 ,064	141 ,660
Preferred Equity	0	0	0
Common Equity	88 ,788	78 ,460	59 ,817

Fahnestock brokerage subsidiaries operate throughout the eastern and midwestern United States under such names as Fahnestock & Co., Hudson Capital Advisors, Pace Securities, Reich & Co., B.C. Christopher, W.H. Newbold, and Fahnestock Asset Management.

Relative strength to TSE300

Price

Volume (in 1000's of board lots)

Rank (Profit/Revenue/Assets)
236   304   188
A.G. Lowenthal
Chairman & C.E.O.
E.K. Roberts
President & Treasurer

Address
P.O. Box 16
Suite 1204
181 University Avenue
Toronto
ON
M5H 3M7
(416) 364-3397
Fax: (416) 364-9717
G0001708/F/13.7

For further company information, call Globe Information Services 1-800-268-9128 or (416) 585-5345

FIRST MARATHON INC.

Exchanges
TMV

					Stock Symbol
Price (Jun29'95)		14.75	Trailing P/E	17.15	**FMS.A**
Trailing Yield (%)		7.39	Trailing EPS	0.86	

Period Ending	Dec94	Dec93	Dec92	Dec91	Dec90
Yearly Statistics					
Price-Close	13.00	17.25	10.75	11.00	6.25
Price-High	19.50	18.00	12.88	11.00	9.00
Price-Low	11.00	10.50	8.88	6.00	6.13
P/E-Close	12.62	5.58	11.94	13.75	10.78
Dividends per Share	1.08	0.48	0.43	0.40	0.40
Dividend Yield (%)	8.31	2.78	4.00	3.64	6.40
Sales per Share	6.44	7.71	3.53	3.55	2.76
EPS before extra. item	1.03	3.09	0.90	0.80	0.58
Cash Flow per Share	0.75	1.38	0.80	(0.79)	0.80
Book Value per Share	10.43	10.49	7.90	7.42	6.78
O/S Common Shares	24,470	24,282	23,745	23,466	21,462
Total Revenue	160,532	187,458	84,967	78,866	59,874
Income before extra.	25,196	74,211	21,178	17,385	12,328
Cash Flow	18,404	33,186	18,776	(17,163)	17,016
Debt/Equity	3.74	1.99	1.02	1.49	1.44
Return on Capital (%)	3.70	18.66	6.79	5.67	5.40
Ret. on Com. Equity (%)	9.88	33.55	11.71	10.88	8.70
% Change Profit	(66.0)	250.4	21.8	41.0	(26.1)
% Change Revenue	(14.4)	120.6	7.7	31.7	(14.4)
% Change Assets	80.0	17.9	55.4	16.7	39.7

Date	EPS	DPS	Tot Rev	Inc Bex
Mar 95	0.27	0.10	39,556	6,617
Dec 94	0.12	0.09	32,741	3,060
Sep 94	0.25	0.09	37,316	6,051
Jun 94	0.22	0.81	35,659	5,324
Mar 94	0.44	0.09	54,816	10,761
Dec 93	1.75	0.08	53,593	42,032
Sep 93	0.46	0.08	46,830	11,089
Jun 93	0.51	0.25	49,473	12,253

Preferred Div. Coverage	np	np	np
Total Div. Coverage	1.0	6.3	2.0

5 YEAR RATIOS (%)			
Return on Capital	8.0	9.1	8.1
Return on Com. Equity	14.9	15.5	11.6
Profit Growth	8.6	33.8	(1.8)
Revenue Growth	18.1	20.1	(2.3)
Asset Growth	39.9	33.3	22.1

BALANCE SHEET (000)			
Cash	11,731	1,449	1,421
Total Loans	46,880	32,000	0
Net Fixed Assets	12,086	4,577	3,600
Invest'S & Advances	1,787,229	663,922	531,052
Total Assets	2,572,048	1,429,005	1,211,870
Total Deposits	0	0	0
Insurance Liability	0	0	0
Long Term Debt	746,874	415,987	191,539
Total Liabilities	2,316,769	1,174,217	1,024,277
Total Equity	255,279	254,788	187,593
Total Liab. & Equity	2,572,048	1,429,005	1,211,870

CAPITAL (000)			
Total Debt	954,114	506,844	191,766
Preferred Equity	0	0	0
Common Equity	255,279	254,788	187,593

Business:

FIRST MARATHON INC. is a financial services company. Its principal subsidiary is First Marathon Securities Limited, a securities dealer and member of the Toronto, Montreal, Vancouver and Alberta stock exchanges.

Synopsis:

For the first quarter ended March 31, 1995, revenues at First Marathon fell 28% to $39.6-million from $54.8-million in the first quarter of 1994. Final earnings for the period were $6.6-million, compared to $10.8-million for the same period in 1994, which represents a decline of 39%. Poor market conditions and a higher effective tax rate were the main reasons for the drop. For the remainder of 1995, First Marathon will focus on trading in its own accounts where the margins are higher, and on derivatives trading.

First Marathon reported for the year ended December 31, 1994, a 14% decline in revenues to $161-million. Net income from continuing operations of $25.2-million was 39% lower than the $41.6-million earned in 1993.

In fiscal 1994, First Marathon again achieved the number one ranking in Toronto Stock Exchange block trading and began operations of First Marathon Bank GmbH in Frankfurt, Germany. During the year the company acted as lead manager or co-underwriter in 125 public financings and as an agent in 76 private placements, raising over $4.9-billion. First Marathon's Correspondent Network maintained its position as the leading supplier of Canadian correspondent brokerage services. With 35 associated operations encompassing over 325 registered representatives, the total value of securities traded by the group was nearly $9-billion.

During 1994, First Marathon purchased a minority interest in Maplehaven, N.V., an international hedge trading firm based in the Netherlands Antilles. The company also acquired remaining interests in Bridgebrown International Capital Corp. and Marathon Arbitrage C.V., international hedge trading firms based in Barbados.

First Marathon's wholly owned operating subsidiaries include First Marathon Securities Ltd., First Marathon Capital Corp., First Marathon Bank GmbH, First Marathon (U.S.A.) Inc., First Marathon America Inc., Marathon Arbitrage C.V., First Marathon (U.K.) Ltd. and Bridgebrown International Capital Corp.

Rank (Profit/Revenue/Assets)
187   348   86

Thomas A. Kierans
Chairman

Lawrence S. Bloomberg
President & C.E.O.

Stuart W. Henry
Secretary

Address
2 First Canadian Place
Exchange Tower Suite 3200
P.O. Box 21
Toronto
ON
M5X 1J9
(416) 869-3707
Fax: (416) 869-0089
F0007263/F/13.7

GREYVEST CAPITAL INC.

Exchanges	Price (Jun29'95)	2.65	Trailing P/E	10.19	Stock Symbol
T	Trailing Yield (%)	4.72	Trailing EPS	0.26	**GFI**

Period Ending	Dec94	Dec93	Dec92	Dec91	Dec90
Yearly Statistics					
Price-Close	2.40	2.90	2.64	2.32	2.40
Price-High	2.95	3.40	2.80	2.80	3.80
Price-Low	2.40	2.20	2.12	2.16	2.40
P/E-Close	9.60	nm	10.65	12.61	10.00
Dividends per Share	0.13	0.11	0.11	0.11	0.14
Dividend Yield (%)	5.42	3.79	4.24	4.83	5.67
Sales per Share	2.67	2.19	2.34	2.31	2.31
EPS before extra. item	0.25	(0.03)	0.25	0.18	0.24
Cash Flow per Share	1.08	0.66	0.72	0.58	0.55
Book Value per Share	2.48	2.36	2.51	2.37	2.28
O/S Common Shares	18,378	18,390	18,340	18,568	18,191
Total Revenue	49,179	40,748	43,127	42,206	42,020
Income before extra.	4,600	(615)	4,531	3,364	4,433
Cash Flow	19,941	12,342	13,363	10,684	10,026
Debt/Equity	2.09	3.88	3.28	3.99	4.34
Return on Capital (%)	7.12	5.43	9.84	10.21	11.65
Ret. on Com. Equity (%)	10.34	(1.38)	10.07	7.87	10.92
% Change Profit	848.4	(113.6)	34.7	(24.1)	(25.0)
% Change Revenue	20.7	(5.5)	2.2	0.4	(3.3)
% Change Assets	(34.5)	4.4	(9.6)	(0.0)	(12.2)

Preferred Div. Coverage	np	np	np
Total Div. Coverage	1.9	0.0	2.2

5 YEAR RATIOS (%)			
Return on Capital	8.9	10.0	11.7
Return on Com. Equity	7.6	8.6	11.9
Profit Growth	(4.9)	na	3.5
Revenue Growth	2.4	6.3	16.6
Asset Growth	(11.5)	(2.8)	17.2

BALANCE SHEET (000)			
Cash	1,451	2,092	1,311
Total Loans	74,490	171,261	162,049
Net Fixed Assets	52,314	45,910	30,564
Invest's & Advances	21,127	16,049	25,144
Total Assets	158,993	242,736	232,602
Total Deposits	0	0	0
Insurance Liability	0	0	0
Long Term Debt	95,376	168,322	150,910
Total Liabilities	113,429	199,324	186,639
Total Equity	45,563	43,412	45,963
Total Liab. & Equity	158,993	242,736	232,602

CAPITAL (000)			
Total Debt	95,376	168,322	150,910
Preferred Equity	0	0	0
Common Equity	45,563	43,412	45,963

Business:

GREYVEST CAPITAL INC. and its subsidiaries provide commercial equipment financing through direct finance leases, conditional sales contracts and secured loans. The company is actively engaged in the short and long-term rental of PCs and microcomputer systems. Greyvest has branch offices across Canada and in the northeastern United States.

Date	EPS	DPS	Tot Rev	Inc Bex
Mar 95	0.05	0.00	16,300	897
Dec 94	0.09	0.07	13,357	1,697
Sep 94	0.06	0.00	11,441	1,105
Jun 94	0.06	0.06	10,864	1,032
Mar 94	0.04	0.00	13,516	766
Dec 93	(0.26)	0.81	12,352	(4,042)
Sep 93	0.08	0.00	9,028	1,131
Jun 93	0.08	0.06	9,902	1,372

Synopsis:

Revenues for Greyvest Capital in the first quarter ended March 31, 1995, rose by 21% to $16.3-million from $13.5-million for the corresponding period in 1994. Net income for the quarter rose to $897,000, or $0.05 per share, compared with $766,000, or $0.04 per share, for the same period in the previous year. The increases were due to the consolidation of the former LDI Canada Inc. and the acquisition of Princeton Credit Corporation.

Greyvest reported for the year ended December 31, 1994, net income of $4.6-million, or $0.25 per share, compared with a net loss of $615,000, or $0.03 per share in 1993. During the year revenues rose by 21% to $49.2-million from $40.7-million a year ago. Total assets for the period amounted to $159-million, down 34% from a year ago due to the sale of the capital leasing portfolio in early 1994. More importantly, the business focus has changed dramatically towards an emphasis on computer leasing and rental revenues. At the end of 1994 shareholders approved changing the company's name from Greyvest Financial Services Inc. to Greyvest Capital Inc. The stock symbol on the Toronto Stock Exchange remained unchanged.

Effective April 1995, Greyvest acquired Princeton Credit Corp., a New Jersey based computer leasing company. Princeton will contribute $75-million in assets and $35-million in annual revenue. This acquisition will strongly compliment Greyvest's existing U.S. and Canadian computer leasing operations. The company stated that 1995 represents the first year in which its U.S. revenue and asset base will exceed 50% of the company's total revenues and assets.

In July 1994, Greyvest acquired the Toronto based computer leasing operations of Leasing Dynamics Inc. from its U.S. parent and renamed the operation Greyvest Technology Inc.

Greyvest's Canadian subsidiaries include Greyvest Leasing Inc., Greyvest Canada Inc., Vernon Rentals & Leasing Inc. and Greyvest Technology Inc. Subsidiaries of Greyvest (U.S.) Inc. are Vernon Computer Leasing Inc. (U.S.) and Frank Orlando Jr. & Co. Inc.

Rank (Profit/Revenue/Assets)
438   553   386

Lou Elmaleh
Chairman President & C.E.O.

Address
Suite 1300
20 Adelaide Street East
Toronto
ON
M5C 2T6
(416) 366-1513

Fax: (416) 366-2021
G0003051/F/13.6

HEES INTERNATIONAL BANCORP INC.

Exchanges	Price (Jun29'95)	15.00	Trailing P/E	13.51	Stock Symbol
TM	Trailing Yield (%)	6.53	Trailing EPS	1.11	**HIL**

Period Ending	Dec94	Dec93	Dec92	Dec91	Dec90
Yearly Statistics					
Price-Close	12.00	15.50	8.00	14.88	16.63
Price-High	17.13	15.50	18.13	20.38	30.38
Price-Low	12.00	5.00	7.75	13.75	13.25
P/E-Close	10.91	28.18	80.00	8.60	7.26
Dividends per Share	0.98	0.98	0.98	0.98	0.94
Dividend Yield (%)	8.17	6.32	12.25	6.59	5.65
Sales per Share	4.67	4.45	5.04	6.02	7.31
EPS before extra. item	1.10	0.55	0.10	1.73	2.29
Cash Flow per Share	2.77	2.77	2.63	2.60	3.10
Book Value per Share	19.95	19.76	20.13	21.01	20.49
O/S Common Shares	81,210	80,887	80,436	80,363	79,901
Total Revenue	449,070	377,751	405,011	482,984	667,717
Income before extra.	112,063	67,013	36,255	178,358	232,828
Cash Flow	224,391	223,042	211,451	208,471	246,497
Debt/Equity	0.99	1.12	1.23	1.16	1.29
Return on Capital (%)	5.90	5.29	4.73	8.62	11.25
Ret. on Com. Equity (%)	5.53	2.77	0.50	8.35	11.55
% Change Profit	67.2	84.8	(79.7)	(23.4)	(6.4)
% Change Revenue	18.9	(6.7)	(16.1)	(27.7)	9.6
% Change Assets	2.1	0.7	0.8	(4.4)	0.7

Preferred Div. Coverage	4.8	3.0	1.3
Total Div. Coverage	1.1	0.7	0.3

5 YEAR RATIOS (%)			
Return on Capital	7.2	8.2	9.2
Return on Com. Equity	5.7	7.7	10.2
Profit Growth	(14.7)	(18.9)	(24.9)
Revenue Growth	(5.9)	(4.6)	8.5
Asset Growth	(0.1)	4.3	6.7

BALANCE SHEET (000)			
Cash	0	0	0
Total Loans	1,296,101	1,701,258	1,458,642
Net Fixed Assets	753,036	735,372	643,667
Invest's & Advances	3,420,090	2,918,490	3,213,880
Total Assets	5,469,227	5,355,120	5,316,189
Total Deposits	0	0	0
Insurance Liability	0	0	0
Long Term Debt	1,635,409	1,406,907	1,275,841
Total Liabilities	3,276,283	3,271,280	3,211,712
Total Equity	2,192,944	2,083,840	2,104,477
Total Liab. & Equity	5,469,227	5,355,120	5,316,189

CAPITAL (000)			
Total Debt	2,177,913	2,336,100	2,580,900
Preferred Equity	573,000	485,500	485,500
Common Equity	1,619,944	1,598,340	1,618,977

Business:

HEES INTERNATIONAL BANCORP INC. is a North American merchant bank. The company provides financial and management services to affiliates, other corporations and individual clients. Hees owns interests in a diversified group of companies including: Brascan Ltd., Trilon Financial Corp., Noranda Inc., Carena Developments Ltd. and Great Lakes Group Inc.

Date	EPS	DPS	Tot Rev	Inc Bex
Mar 95	0.38	0.25	137,293	39,665
Dec 94	0.21	0.25	111,453	23,385
Sep 94	0.13	0.25	94,010	17,150
Jun 94	0.39	0.25	129,367	37,778
Mar 94	0.36	0.25	114,240	33,750
Dec 93	(0.80)	0.25	36,568	(61,062)
Sep 93	0.36	0.25	111,217	34,003
Jun 93	0.39	0.25	100,319	36,349

Synopsis:

Hees reported increased earnings for the three months ended March 31, 1995, of $39.7-million compared with $33.7-million for the same period in 1994. Revenues rose at Hees' 15 power generating stations, and in the natural resource and financial services affiliates. Returns from interests in the real estate sector remained stable.

During the quarter, the financial restructuring of NBS Technologies Inc. was completed, adding $85-million to the NBS equity base. This allowed Hees to withdraw $42.5-million while still retaining a 45% interest in NBS.

For 1994, net income totalled $112.1-million, a 67% increase from the $67-million reported in 1993. Revenues for the period rose to $449-million from $378-million. During the year, Hees' ownership of Brascan and Carena Developments was significantly increased through the acquisition of Edper Enterprises' remaining economic interest in Brascan Holdings and Carena Holdings. Hees now holds 100% of the holding companies, increased from 49.9%, and will receive full benefit of their growth.

In 1994, Great Lakes Power opened two new power plants increasing revenues by 20%. Great Lakes issued $410-million worth of long term debentures. The capital base of the real'estate sector increased in 1994 by Hees converting $350-million of loans receivable into common and preferred shares of Carena Developments, raising its ownership to 87%.

Early in 1994, Hees completed the acquisition of BCE Inc.'s remaining economic interest in Brookfield Development Corporation. The final step in the restructuring of Unicorp Energy was completed with the sale of its interests in Lincoln Savings Bank in the summer of 1994. As a result, Unicorp repaid all of its liabilities. In the forest products sector, a new Scottish panelboard plant began production, and construction began on another plant in Mississippi. In the mining and metals sector, Falconbridge was re-established as a public company.

Relative strength to TSE300 / Price / Volume (in 1000's of board lots)

Rank (Profit/Revenue/Assets)		
72	204	37

Timothy R. Price
Chairman

Robert J. Harding
President & C.E.O.

J. Bruce Flatt
Managing Partner Finance

Timothy W. Casgrain
Managing Partner Operations

Address
Suite 4500
BCE Place
181 Bay Street
Toronto
ON
M5J 2T3
(416) 865-0430
Fax: (416) 865-1288
H0007738/F/13.6

HOME CAPITAL GROUP INC.

Exchanges		Price (Jun29'95)		0.55	Trailing P/E		18.33	Stock Symbol
T		Trailing Yield (%)		0.00	Trailing EPS		0.03	**HCG.B**

Period Ending	Dec94	Dec93	Dec92	Dec91	Dec90	Business:
Yearly Statistics						HOME CAPITAL operates through one
Price-Close	0.65	0.65	0.70	1.25	1.20	subsidiary, Home Savings & Loan Corp., to
Price-High	0.86	1.05	1.30	1.70	2.25	provide mortgage lending and deposit services
Price-Low	0.55	0.50	0.55	1.06	0.95	in the Greater Metropolitan Toronto, Hamilton
P/E-Close	16.25	nm	nm	nm	8.00	and St. Catharines regions.
Dividends per Share	0.00	0.00	0.00	0.03	0.05	
Dividend Yield (%)	0.00	0.00	0.00	2.00	4.17	
Sales per Share	2.94	3.37	4.15	4.85	5.31	
EPS before extra. item	0.04	(0.03)	(0.31)	(0.07)	0.15	
Cash Flow per Share	0.41	0.43	0.82	0.66	1.32	
Book Value per Share	1.79	1.76	1.79	2.08	2.18	
O/S Common Shares	10,781	10,781	10,781	10,656	10,698	

						Date	EPS	DPS	Tot Rev	Inc Bex
Total Revenue	32,088	36,312	44,484	51,359	57,658					
Income before extra.	409	(344)	(3,297)	(771)	1,630	Mar 95	0.01	0.00	8,565	105
Cash Flow	4,405	4,633	8,804	7,071	14,314	Dec 94	(0.01)	0.00	8,206	(102)
Debt/Equity	0.34	0.32	0.34	0.29	0.32	Sep 94	0.01	0.00	8,109	96
Return on Capital (%)	1.67	(4.96)	(25.51)	(9.46)	5.58	Jun 94	0.02	0.00	7,669	223
Ret. on Com. Equity (%)	2.14	(1.80)	(15.89)	(3.39)	6.99	Mar 94	0.02	0.00	8,104	192
% Change Profit	218.7	89.6	(327.7)	(147.3)	(69.1)	Dec 93	0.01	0.00	8,232	97
% Change Revenue	(11.6)	(18.4)	(13.4)	(10.9)	23.3	Sep 93	(0.08)	0.00	8,833	(818)
% Change Assets	0.9	(11.5)	(0.2)	(2.6)	13.4	Jun 93	0.01	0.00	9,300	72

Preferred Div. Coverage	np	np	np			**Synopsis:**
Total Div. Coverage	na	na	na			Home Capital Group reported net earnings for the three months ended March 31, 1995, were $105,314 on revenue of $8,565,077. This compares to earnings of $192,058 on revenue of $8,103,761 recorded during the same period in 1994. These results were due in part to the impact of interest rate fluctuations, a soft residential real estate market, and short term pressure on interest spreads. The long standing strategic objective to decrease mortgage loans as a percentage of the company's portfolio and avoid potential losses is on track. At the end of the quarter, non-performing loans represented less than 2% of the overall portfolio.

5 YEAR RATIOS (%)						
Return on Capital	(6.5)	(0.1)	4.2			
Return on Com. Equity	(2.4)	2.1	4.5			
Profit Growth	(40.1)	na	na			For the year ending December 31, 1994, Home Capital reported revenue of $32.1-million and net earnings of $408,738 compared with revenue of $36.3-million and a net loss of $344,319 in the previous year. Revenues fell 11.6% due to a decline in the average yield on investments from 9.6% in 1993 to 8.8% in 1994, and a decline in fee income. The main reason for the improved earnings was a decline in mortgage arrears and a corresponding reduction in loss provisions from $5.73-million in 1993 to $4.15-million in 1994. The company continued its efforts to collect from guarantors of mortgages for which there were shortfalls.
Revenue Growth	(7.3)	0.0	17.5			
Asset Growth	(0.3)	8.3	27.0			

BALANCE SHEET (000)						
Cash	6,658	12,284	41,028			
Total Loans	337,090	321,813	350,413			During 1994, commercial loans represented 3.4% of the mortgage portfolio, down from 4.5% in 1993 and significantly lower than the 9% recorded in 1990. The percentage of second residential mortgages in the portfolio fell to 2%, down from 4% in 1993 and far below the 15% reported in 1989. Reserves taken against known and potential non-performing loans totalled $4.6-million, down from $6.2-million in 1993.
Net Fixed Assets	405	1,154	2,084			
Invest's & Advances	23,895	29,823	16,252			
Total Assets	373,629	370,268	418,172			
Total Deposits	347,109	344,580	391,388			
Insurance Liability	0	0	0			
Long Term Debt	2,250	1,000	0			In fiscal 1994, Home Capital completed a private issue of an additional $1.25-million of convertible subordinated debentures. The company's liquidity position continued to strengthen and exceed regulatory requirements.
Total Liabilities	354,283	351,331	398,891			
Total Equity	19,346	18,937	19,282			
Total Liab. & Equity	373,629	370,268	418,172			

CAPITAL (000)			
Total Debt	6,583	6,055	6,500
Preferred Equity	0	0	0
Common Equity	19,346	18,937	19,282

Relative strength to TSE300

Price

Volume (in 1000's of board lots)

Rank (Profit/Revenue/Assets)
711   638   260

William A. Dimma
Chairman

Gerald M. Soloway
President & C.E.O.

W. Roy Vincent
Sr. V.P. & C.O.O.

Address
Suite 1910
145 King Street West
Toronto
ON
M5H 1J8
(416) 360-4663

Fax: (416) 363-7611
S0003859/F/13.6

INVESTORS GROUP INC.

Exchanges	Price (Jun29'95)	18 .87	Trailing P/E	23 .02	Stock Symbol
TMW	Trailing Yield (%)	1 .64	Trailing EPS	0 .82	**IGI**

Period Ending	Dec94	Dec93	Dec92	Dec91	Dec90
Yearly Statistics					
Price-Close	17.38	22.75	12.94	10.66	6.38
Price-High	23.63	23.88	14.00	10.66	6.41
Price-Low	14.63	12.88	10.38	6.31	5.25
P/E-Close	21.72	33.96	22.70	20.11	12.88
Dividends per Share	0.32	0.24	0.22	0.21	0.20
Dividend Yield (%)	1.84	1.03	1.70	1.92	3.14
Sales per Share	5.14	4.79	4.59	4.52	4.03
EPS before extra. item	0.80	0.67	0.57	0.53	0.50
Cash Flow per Share	(0.45)	0.96	0.91	0.86	0.89
Book Value per Share	5.11	4.62	4.20	3.02	2.70
O/S Common Shares	105,685	105,685	105,685	95,685	95,828
Total Revenue	543,225	505,812	468,103	432,486	387,095
Income before extra.	84,603	70,303	58,333	50,715	47,620
Cash Flow	(47,810)	101,482	93,128	82,728	85,089
Debt/Equity	0.27	0.30	0.34	0.53	0.59
Return on Capital (%)	18.21	17.91	18.02	18.61	13.02
Ret. on Com. Equity (%)	16.47	15.09	15.93	18.53	19.23
% Change Profit	20.3	20.5	15.0	6.5	(5.4)
% Change Revenue	7.4	8.1	8.2	11.7	7.9
% Change Assets	(4.4)	(7.2)	(1.7)	(4.0)	2.4

Business:

INVESTORS GROUP INC. is a financial services holding company. Through subsidiaries, it offers mutual funds, investment certificates, insurance programs, pension plans, annuities and tax-shelter plans. Subsidiaries include Investors Group Financial Services Inc., Les Services Investors Limitee and Investors Group Trust Co. Ltd. Power Financial Corp. of Montreal owns 67% of the company.

Date	EPS	DPS	Tot Rev	Inc Bex
Mar 95	0.19	0.08	135,198	20,529
Dec 94	0.22	0.08	129,124	23,210
Sep 94	0.22	0.08	129,053	23,168
Jun 94	0.19	0.07	133,558	20,212
Mar 94	0.17	0.07	151,490	18,013
Dec 93	0.21	0.07	138,215	21,532
Sep 93	0.18	0.06	126,866	18,763
Jun 93	0.16	0.06	120,954	16,353

Preferred Div. Coverage	np	np	np	
Total Div. Coverage	2.6	2.7	2.6	

Synopsis:

Investors Group's net income for the three months ended March 31, 1995, was $20.5-million on revenues of $135.2-million compared with net income of $18-million and revenue of $151.5-million in the first quarter of 1994. Revenues fell as a result of decreased sales and the removal of most front-end loads in 1994. Sales of financial products and services for the period totalled $1.34-billion. This was $500-million or 27% lower than the first quarter of 1994. Mutual fund sales reached $1.04-billion, 37% below the prior year.

5 YEAR RATIOS (%)			
Return on Capital	17.2	16.9	16.9
Return on Com. Equity	17.1	18.2	19.3
Profit Growth	10.9	10.9	4.8
Revenue Growth	8.5	11.2	9.2
Asset Growth	(3.0)	0.7	7.0

Assets under administration totalled $25.2-billion at March 31, 1995, an increase of $2-billion above March 31, 1994. Mutual fund assets reached $18.2-billion at the end of the quarter, a year over year increase of $1.5-billion. Redemption rates, excluding money market funds, were well below industry norms. The Board of Directors increased the quarterly dividend to $0.09 payable May 1, 1995.

BALANCE SHEET (000)			
Cash	239,205	170,368	78,722
Total Loans	832,012	958,225	1,139,469
Net Fixed Assets	79,465	80,267	78,680
Invest's & Advances	632,030	671,172	724,800
Total Assets	1,865,851	1,951,008	2,102,367
Total Deposits	1,093,271	1,247,700	1,435,993
Insurance Liability	0	0	0
Long Term Debt	145,067	147,831	150,381
Total Liabilities	1,326,211	1,463,210	1,658,451
Total Equity	539,640	487,798	443,916
Total Liab. & Equity	1,865,851	1,951,008	2,102,367
CAPITAL (000)			
Total Debt	145,067	147,831	150,381
Preferred Equity	0	0	0
Common Equity	539,640	487,798	443,916

During fiscal 1994, net income grew by 20.3% to $84.6-million, up from $70.3-million in 1993. This was mostly due to the growth of fund management fees. Sales reached a record $4.24-billion, an increase of 7.4% from the prior year. Assets under administration grew $24.3-billion, up 7.7% during the year from $22.6-billion. Mutual fund assets grew 11.2% to $17.6-billion. Ten new regional sales offices in Canada were set up and the sales force grew by 12.5%.

In 1994, the company introduced the Investors Group Flex Plan and launched the Investors Corporate Bond Fund. The number of Investors funds climbed to 26.

The company initiated a Normal Course Issuer Bid on February 15, 1995, to buy up to 5,284,242 common shares by February 14, 1996. This represents 5% of the outstanding common shares. The company said that on June 1, 1995, it will launch I.G. Insurance Services in collaboration with Great-West Life. The operation will provide a new system to deliver insurance products.

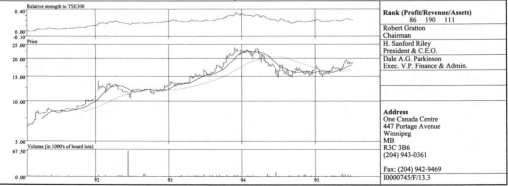

Rank (Profit/Revenue/Assets)
86 190 111

Robert Gratton
Chairman

H. Sanford Riley
President & C.E.O.

Dale A.G. Parkinson
Exec. V.P. Finance & Admin.

Address
One Canada Centre
447 Portage Avenue
Winnipeg
MB
R3C 3B6
(204) 943-0361

Fax: (204) 942-9469

I0000745/F/13.3

MACKENZIE FINANCIAL CORPORATION

Exchanges	Price (Jun29'95)	10.62	Trailing P/E	21.24	Stock Symbol
TM	Trailing Yield (%)	1.13	Trailing EPS	0.50	MKF

Period Ending	Mar94	Mar93	Mar92	Mar91	Mar90
Yearly Statistics					
Price-Close	10.38	6.63	5.88	8.13	7.88
Price-High	12.38	7.00	8.38	8.63	9.25
Price-Low	6.50	4.70	5.25	5.50	5.13
P/E-Close	17.01	21.37	11.30	14.77	10.79
Dividends per Share	0.11	0.10	0.09	0.08	0.07
Dividend Yield (%)	1.06	1.51	1.53	0.99	0.89
Sales per Share	3.17	2.31	2.51	2.75	2.79
EPS before extra. item	0.61	0.31	0.52	0.55	0.73
Cash Flow per Share	1.05	0.44	0.68	0.73	1.00
Book Value per Share	3.91	3.39	3.18	2.73	1.99
O/S Common Shares	59,254	58,128	57,872	57,100	54,075
Total Revenue	186,499	133,490	144,229	151,515	150,888
Income before extra.	36,061	17,863	30,026	30,630	39,434
Cash Flow	61,665	25,637	39,169	40,050	54,220
Debt/Equity	0.24	nd	nd	nd	nd
Return on Capital (%)	23.12	16.83	34.17	46.35	84.24
Ret. on Com. Equity (%)	16.82	9.38	17.67	23.22	44.04
% Change Profit	101.9	(40.5)	(2.0)	(22.3)	71.3
% Change Revenue	39.7	(7.4)	(4.8)	0.4	43.1
% Change Assets	39.2	14.1	22.2	23.7	62.4

Preferred Div. Coverage	np	np	np
Total Div. Coverage	5.6	3.1	5.8

5 YEAR RATIOS (%)			
Return on Capital	40.9	52.3	65.9
Return on Com. Equity	22.2	26.5	32.4
Profit Growth	9.4	2.1	20.5
Revenue Growth	12.0	9.0	18.4
Asset Growth	31.2	33.6	36.0

BALANCE SHEET (000)			
Cash	4,608	409	3,047
Total Loans	152,881	149,127	120,953
Net Fixed Assets	16,760	12,768	14,546
Invest's & Advances	171,142	144,256	135,848
Total Assets	526,956	378,622	331,974
Total Deposits	179,345	147,661	121,541
Insurance Liability	0	0	0
Long Term Debt	50,000	0	0
Total Liabilities	295,131	181,672	148,071
Total Equity	231,825	196,950	183,903
Total Liab. & Equity	526,956	378,622	331,974

CAPITAL (000)			
Total Debt	54,909	0	0
Preferred Equity	0	0	0
Common Equity	231,825	196,950	183,903

Business:

MACKENZIE FINANCIAL CORPORATION is engaged in the management of common stock and bond portfolios. Clients include public mutual funds, pension funds, national associations, and high net worth individuals and estates. The company markets and sponsors mutual funds in Canada and the United States. The company owns 22.6% of brokerage house Midland Walwyn Inc.

Date	EPS	DPS	Tot Rev	Inc Bex
Mar 95	0.13	0.00	58,845	7,342
Dec 94	0.14	0.06	54,903	8,564
Sep 94	0.14	0.00	55,399	8,101
Jun 94	0.09	0.06	51,749	5,443
Mar 94	0.20	0.00	54,014	12,150
Dec 93	0.17	0.06	47,879	9,901
Sep 93	0.12	0.00	43,974	6,874
Jun 93	0.12	0.05	41,423	7,136

Synopsis:

Mackenzie Financial reported revenue of $58.845-million and earnings of $7.342-million in the quarter ending March 31, 1995. In the same period in 1994, revenue was $54.395-million and earnings were $12.15-million.

For the year ending March 31, 1995, the company posted total revenue of $220.896-million up from $187.671-million in the previous year. The increase of $33.225-million was primarily due to higher management and administration fee income. Net earnings for the period were $29.5-million compared to $36.1-million in the year ended March 31, 1994, attributed to a decrease in earnings contributed by Midland Walwyn Inc. Gross mutual fund sales in Canada and the United States amounted to $4.3-billion compared to $1.8-billion. Net sales increased by $2.1-billion.

During the year, Alexander Christ was named president and chief executive officer of Mackenzie Financial Corp. The Board of Directors expanded to seven members. In 1994, M.R.S. Trust Company began sourcing mortgages and providing administrative services to Mackenzie's new N.H.A. Mortgage fund and to the increasingly popular mortgage-backed securities market. The company's shares were also listed on NASDAQ and the Montreal Stock Exchange.

Mackenzie launched a total of nine new mutual funds in 1994/95 in Canada and the United States. The company also expanded the international adviser affiliations with the addition of Thornton Management (Asia) Limited and Cursitor-Eaton Asset Management Company.

The company launched the Star Asset Allocation program in January 1995 to help dealers ensure the optimal allocation of investment dollars. As of May 25, 1995, fund sales within the program have exceeded $115-million. In May 1995, a proposed consolidation of all of the Industrial Partnerships into the Mackenzie Master Limited Partnership was overwhelmingly approved.

Rank (Profit/Revenue/Assets)		
139	324	222

William G. Crerar
Chairman

Alexander Christ
President

James T. Dryburgh
V.P. Finance

Address
150 Bloor Street West
Suite M111
Toronto
ON
M5S 3B5
(416) 922-5322

Fax: (416) 922-7062
M0000112/F/13.3

For further company information, call Globe Information Services 1-800-268-9128 or (416) 585-5345

MARLEAU, LEMIRE INC.

Exchanges	Price (Jun29'95)	5 .62	Trailing P/E	17 .03	Stock Symbol
T	Trailing Yield (%)	4 .27	Trailing EPS	0 .33	MRM

Period Ending	Dec94	Dec93	Dec92	Jan92
Yearly Statistics			11M	9M
Price-Close	8 .85	13 .65	n t	n t
Price-High	15 .75	17 .25	n t	n t
Price-Low	7 .44	13 .35	n t	n t
P/E-Close	12 .83	7 .34	n t	n t
Dividends per Share	0 .33	0 .21	0 .00	0 .00
Dividend Yield (%)	3 .73	1 .54	0 .00	0 .00
Sales per Share	5 .97	10 .44	14 .73	6 .99
EPS before extra. item	0 .69	1 .86	1 .80	(0 .18)
Cash Flow per Share	0 .78	2 .25	2 .61	0 .60
Book Value per Share	9 .81	9 .48	6 .36	5 .31
O/S Common Shares	6 ,079	6 ,160	2 ,139	833
Total Revenue	36 ,465	36 ,855	13 ,025	4 ,371
Income before extra.	4 ,253	6 ,569	1 ,735	(143)
Cash Flow	4 ,777	7 ,984	2 ,309	368
Debt/Equity	2 .00	0 .80	0 .05	2 .91
Return on Capital (%)	5 .56	20 .66	22 .91	na
Ret. on Com. Equity (%)	7 .21	18 .24	20 .98	na
% Change Profit	(35 .3)	247 .1	1 ,092 .6	na
% Change Revenue	(1 .1)	159 .4	143 .8	na
% Change Assets	94 .3	341 .7	39 .1	na

	Dec94	Dec93	Dec92
Preferred Div. Coverage	np	np	np
Total Div. Coverage	2 .1	2 .1	na

5 YEAR RATIOS (%)			
Return on Capital	na	na	na
Return on Com. Equity	na	na	na
Profit Growth	na	na	na
Revenue Growth	na	na	na
Asset Growth	na	na	na

BALANCE SHEET (000)			
Cash	8 ,522	0	1 ,491
Total Loans	27 ,071	0	3 ,622
Net Fixed Assets	2 ,196	1 ,045	389
Invest's & Advances	70 ,574	33 ,475	4 ,470
Total Assets	224 ,916	115 ,771	26 ,209
Total Deposits	0	0	0
Insurance Liability	0	0	0
Long Term Debt	87 ,348	39 ,704	0
Total Liabilities	165 ,288	57 ,337	12 ,601
Total Equity	59 ,628	58 ,434	13 ,608
Total Liab. & Equity	224 ,916	115 ,771	26 ,209

CAPITAL (000)			
Total Debt	119 ,451	46 ,533	731
Preferred Equity	0	0	0
Common Equity	59 ,628	58 ,434	13 ,608

Business:

MARLEAU, LEMIRE INC. is a full-service investment dealer which engages in securities brokerage and trading, corproate finance and other financial services.

Date	EPS	DPS	Tot Rev	Inc Bex
Mar 95	(0 .06)	0 .00	7 ,830	(338)
Dec 94	0 .03	0 .06	8 ,998	124
Sep 94	0 .18	0 .06	9 ,164	1 ,126
Jun 94	0 .18	0 .12	7 ,943	1 ,005
Mar 94	0 .33	0 .12	10 ,360	2 ,000
Dec 93	0 .30	0 .06	13 ,462	2 ,162
Sep 93	0 .51	0 .00	8 ,715	1 ,872
Jun 93	0 .42	0 .00	7 ,914	1 ,036

Synopsis:

For the quarter ended March 31, 1995, revenues at Marleau, Lemire were $7.8-million compared with $10.4-million in the first quarter of 1994, representing a decrease of 25%. The company realized a net loss of $338,000 compared with a net profit of $2-million for the comparable period of 1994. During the quarter, Marleau, Lemire made a normal course issuer bid through the Toronto and Montreal stock exchanges to buy up to 546,130 common shares, or 3% of the total shares outstanding. The firm also announced plans to open an office in New York. About 10% to 15% of Marleau, Lemire's revenue comes from U.S. activities.

For the year ended December 31, 1994, total revenue remained fairly stable, dipping 1% to $36.5-million from $36.9-million. Expenses rose 27% to $29.9-million from $23.5-million. The company's net income fell 35% to $4.25-million from $6.57-million in 1993, but total assets jumped 94% from $115.8-million to $224.9-million.

In 1994, Marleau, Lemire bought the net assets of Bekhor Securities Canada Ltd., a futures and commodities broker. Marleau, Lemire also entered into a joint venture with a Texas based mutual fund company, United Services Advisors Inc. and its offshore fund business in Guernsey. The deal includes a joint venture to distribute three of United Services' no-load mutual funds across Canada. During the year, Marleau, Lemire formed a strategic alliance with Polaris Securities Inc., an Asian broker based in Taiwan.

During fiscal 1994, the corporate finance group participated in 48 small and mid-cap financing transactions that raised $1.3-billion. It also opened an office in Calgary. The company also increased its interest in Aureus Capital Corp., its fixed income subsidiary, and Marleau, Lemire Clearing to 100%. The assets of Aureus were transferred to the parent company. Marleau, Lemire also increased its interest in TFH, an insurance concern, for strategic investment purposes. Marleau, Lemire will maintain its focus on the small and mid-cap market while expanding activities in the U.S., Europe and the Pacific Rim.

Relative strength to TSE300

Price

Volume (in 1000's of board lots)

Rank (Profit/Revenue/Assets)
453   612   335

Hubert R. Marleau
Chairman & C.E.O.

Andre Lemire
Co-Chairman

Joanne S. Ferstman
V.P.& C.F.O.

Address
Suite 3601
1 Place Ville-Marie
Montreal
PQ
H3B 3P2
(514) 877-3800

Fax: (514) 875-0398
01003489/F/13.7

MERCHANT PRIVATE LIMITED

Exchanges	Price (Jun29'95)	6.37	Trailing P/E	15.92	Stock Symbol
T	Trailing Yield (%)	1.88	Trailing EPS	0.40	**MPL.A**

Period Ending	Dec94	Dec93	Mar93	Mar92	Mar91
Yearly Statistics		9M			
Price-Close	4.70	3.75	3.30	3.90	4.15
Price-High	5.00	3.75	3.90	4.30	5.50
Price-Low	3.75	3.00	3.30	3.90	3.35
P/E-Close	12.37	16.59	nm	18.57	nm
Dividends per Share	0.12	0.12	0.12	0.12	0.12
Dividend Yield (%)	2.55	3.20	3.64	3.08	2.89
Sales per Share	2.52	2.34	1.49	1.59	3.43
EPS before extra. item	0.38	0.17	(0.76)	0.21	(0.69)
Cash Flow per Share	0.45	0.39	(0.01)	0.18	0.33
Book Value per Share	3.56	2.81	2.73	3.62	3.49
O/S Common Shares	13,591	10,650	10,650	10,550	8,423
Total Revenue	30,606	18,693	9,487	16,611	24,346
Income before extra.	4,624	1,790	(8,055)	2,180	(4,928)
Cash Flow	5,411	3,113	(144)	1,892	2,350
Debt/Equity	0.02	0.75	0.80	0.52	1.05
Return on Capital (%)	9.93	0.20	(16.68)	0.91	(10.49)
Ret. on Com. Equity (%)	11.81	8.10	(23.95)	6.45	(18.78)
% Change Profit	93.7	129.6	(469.5)	144.2	(310.6)
% Change Revenue	22.8	162.7	(42.9)	(31.8)	7.4
% Change Assets	2.3	24.1	26.0	22.0	(23.1)

Preferred Div. Coverage	np	np	np
Total Div. Coverage	3.2	1.9	0.0

Business:						

MERCHANT PRIVATE LIMITED is a financial services company whose principal activity is the management of financial assets for its own account and for the accounts of others. Financial assets consist of investment and mortgage loan portfolios.

Date	EPS	DPS	Tot Rev	Inc Bex
Mar 95	0.17	0.03	8,895	2,302
Dec 94	0.04	0.03	6,069	623
Sep 94	0.14	0.03	9,465	1,830
Jun 94	0.05	0.03	6,999	528
Mar 94	0.15	0.03	8,073	1,643
Dec 93	0.10	0.03	8,680	1,061
Sep 93	0.03	0.03	4,397	292
Jun 93	0.04	0.03	5,616	437

5 YEAR RATIOS (%)			
Return on Capital	(3.2)	(1.8)	0.6
Return on Com. Equity	(3.3)	(3.5)	(2.8)
Profit Growth	14.6	1.1	na
Revenue Growth	6.2	6.0	(9.5)
Asset Growth	8.4	17.3	16.9

BALANCE SHEET (000)			
Cash	8,684	14,445	3,892
Total Loans	128,435	127,195	123,065
Net Fixed Assets	2,476	2,024	2,117
Invest's & Advances	99,897	88,480	57,554
Total Assets	246,475	241,018	194,180
Total Deposits	161,139	149,426	132,687
Insurance Liability	20,241	19,542	0
Long Term Debt	684	17,241	15,551
Total Liabilities	198,039	211,122	165,116
Total Equity	48,436	29,896	29,064
Total Liab. & Equity	246,475	241,018	194,180

CAPITAL (000)			
Total Debt	1,084	22,391	23,376
Preferred Equity	0	0	0
Common Equity	48,436	29,896	29,064

Synopsis:

For the quarter ended March 31, 1995, Merchant Private Limited reported revenues of $8.895-million compared with $8.073-million in the first quarter of 1994. Net income was $2.3-million compared with $1.6-million during the same period last year.

In 1993 Merchant Private moved its year-end to December from March. The comparative 1993 figures represent a nine month period. For the year ended December 31, 1994, earnings rose by $2.8-million, or 158%, to $4.624-million from $1.790-million in 1993. Revenue rose to $30.606-million from $18.693-million. Assets under management rose to $159.2-million from $122.4-million, a 30% increase.

In November 1994, the directors of Merchant Private approved a dividend reinvestment and share repurchase plan. Under the plan, quarterly dividends can be reinvested in Class A non-voting shares. Also in 1994, the residual income from Merchant Private's equipment leasing operations were all but eliminated by year-end. Other than a preferred share interest in Tuckahoe Leasing Inc., Merchant no longer has any stake in the equipment leasing industry.

During fiscal 1994, the company reduced its interest in Connor, Clark from 21.3% to 18.4%. Also in 1994, Merchant Investors (MI) sold its 21.4% interest in Arbor Memorial Services Inc. to The Loewen Group Inc. for a total consideration of $30.9-million. Arbor represented more than 70% of MI's net assets. Following the sale, MI was liquidated. This left about $13-millionl in cash and liquid securities to expand the core businesses. With the funds from the asset sales, a private placement of 1.5 million Class A shares, and the conversion of $7.7-million debenture into common shares, Merchant Private paid off all of its debt.

In 1994 Merchant Private increased its interest in Halton Reinsurance Company Limited from 50.3% to 57%. During the year Halton acquired the future income stream of Alexander Touche Inc., an investment management firm in Barbados. In January 1995, the company acquired additional preferred shares of Halton.

Relative strength to TSE300 / Price / Volume (in 1000's of board lots)

Rank (Profit/Revenue/Assets)		
436	648	319

John C. Clark
Chairman & C.E.O.

Mark Damelin
President

Bryan Krikst
Chief Financial Officer

Address
Scotia Plaza
40 King Street West
Suite 4714
Toronto
ON
M5H 3Y2
(416) 867-1716
Fax: (416) 867-9771
01000162/F/13.3

For further company information, call Globe Information Services 1-800-268-9128 or (416) 585-5345

MFP TECHNOLOGY SERVICES LTD.

Exchanges	Price (Jun29'95)	10 .75	Trailing P/E	8 .60	Stock Symbol
T	Trailing Yield (%)	0 .93	Trailing EPS	1 .25	**MFP**

Period Ending	Ma r94	Ma r93	Ma r92
Yearly Statistics			8M
Price-Close	10 .00	n t	n t
Price-High	11 .38	n t	n t
Price-Low	8 .50	n t	n t
P/E-Close	8 .55	n t	n t
Dividends per Share	0 .15	0 .00	0 .00
Dividend Yield (%)	1 .50	0 .00	0 .00
Sales per Share	53 .28	55 .34	27 .54
EPS before extra. item	1 .17	1 .00	0 .50
Cash Flow per Share	28 .74	28 .84	14 .16
Book Value per Share	8 .32	6 .35	6 .64
O/S Common Shares	9 ,263	5 ,848	5 ,912
Total Revenue	415 ,139	324 ,431	109 ,539
Income before extra.	10 ,052	6 ,257	2 ,975
Cash Flow	223 ,845	168 ,632	56 ,156
Debt/Equity	6 .95	11 .36	10 .21
Return on Capital (%)	10 .01	11 .56	na
Ret. on Com. Equity (%)	16 .15	16 .38	na
% Change Profit	60 .7	40 .2	na
% Change Revenue	28 .0	97 .5	na
% Change Assets	18 .6	21 .9	na
Preferred Div. Coverage	12 .1	na	np
Total Div. Coverage	4 .5	na	na

5 YEAR RATIOS (%)

Return on Capital	na	na	na
Return on Com. Equity	na	na	na
Profit Growth	na	na	na
Revenue Growth	na	na	na
Asset Growth	na	na	na
BALANCE SHEET (000)			
Cash	3 ,915	435	2 ,708
Total Loans	215 ,963	100 ,337	56 ,761
Net Fixed Assets	521 ,985	521 ,674	454 ,253
Invest's & Advances	4 ,529	186	171
Total Assets	765 ,411	645 ,173	529 ,167
Total Deposits	0	0	0
Insurance Liability	0	0	0
Long Term Debt	582 ,469	485 ,440	367 ,691
Total Liabilities	678 ,925	599 ,289	489 ,906
Total Equity	86 ,486	45 ,884	39 ,261
Total Liab. & Equity	765 ,411	645 ,173	529 ,167
CAPITAL (000)			
Total Debt	601 ,134	521 ,006	400 ,816
Preferred Equity	9 ,444	8 ,750	0
Common Equity	77 ,042	37 ,134	39 ,261

Business:

MFP TECHNOLOGY SERVICES LTD. is a computer leasing and remarketing company. The company is engaged in the leasing and remarketing of new and used equipment from major manufacturers, including mainframe hardware, minicomputers, personal computers and workstations and related peripheral equipment such as printers and storage and communications devices.

Date	EPS	DPS	Tot Rev	Inc Bex
Mar 95	0.37	0.00	133 ,357	4 ,040
Dec 94	0.32	0.00	119 ,560	3 ,755
Sep 94	0.28	0.05	105 ,260	3 ,123
Jun 94	0.28	0.05	116 ,214	3 ,007
Mar 94	0.26	0.05	104 ,289	2 ,702
Dec 93	0.29	0.05	105 ,468	2 ,833
Sep 93	0.29	0.05	102 ,259	2 ,442
Jun 93	0.33	0.00	103 ,123	2 ,075

Synopsis:

MFP Technology Services Ltd. reported record financial results, as net earnings increased 38% to $13.9-million in the year ended March 31, 1995, from $10.1-million in fiscal 1994. Earnings per share on a fully diluted basis rose to $1.15 from $1.01, notwithstanding an increase in the number of shares outstanding to 12.2 million from 10.3 million. Total revenue rose 14% to $474.4-million in fiscal 1995 from $415.1-million in fiscal 1994. While leasing volumes remained steady year over year, the re-marketing business showed outstanding growth. Total assets on lease rose 6% to $755.8-million at March 31, 1995, from $711.9-million at fiscal 1994 year end. New lease volumes during fiscal 1995 were $403-million.

While U.S. lease volumes declined significantly on a year-over-year basis, volumes improved sharply in the second half of the year, with the final two quarters accounting for about 70% of the total. Overall, U.S. revenues were up more than 25% in fiscal 1995 compared to fiscal 1994. During fiscal 1995, MFP set up offices in five additional U.S. cities: Minneapolis; Stratford, Connecticut; Cleveland; Miami; and San Francisco.

In 1994, MFP acquired 39% of Onyx Corporation, a Toronto-based computer sales and distribution company with a significant foothold in China. Also during 1994, as part of its U.S. growth strategy, MFP purchased a $65-million lease portfolio of Unisys equipment, representing over 300 customer relationships.

MFP has offices throughout Canada, the United States, South America, Mexico and Europe. The company has also gained access to mainland China through its investment in Onyx. Major distribution facilities are located in Mississauga and Atlanta. MPF's client base includes Huntington National Bank, Prudential Securities, and Sears Canada.

Relative strength to TSE300

Price

Volume (in 1000's of board lots)

Rank (Profit/Revenue/Assets)
299   214   180

Peter Wolfraim
Chairman & President

Gary Wade
Sr. V.P. & C.F.O.

Address
2281 North Sheridan Way
Mississauga
ON
L5K 2S3
(905) 855-2500

Fax: (905) 855-2725
01003411/F/13.6

MIDLAND WALWYN INC.

Exchanges	Price (Jun29'95)	11.00	Trailing P/E	52.38	Stock Symbol
TM	Trailing Yield (%)	1.09	Trailing EPS	0.21	MWI

Period Ending	Dec94	Dec93	Dec92	Dec91	Dec90
Yearly Statistics					
Price-Close	7.63	14.00	7.25	5.75	2.25
Price-High	15.38	14.13	9.25	7.50	6.50
Price-Low	7.13	5.75	5.25	2.00	2.00
P/E-Close	8.66	6.97	8.24	287.50	nm
Dividends per Share	0.12	0.00	0.00	0.00	0.00
Dividend Yield (%)	1.57	0.00	0.00	0.00	0.00
Sales per Share	14.55	15.81	10.65	13.14	24.28
EPS before extra. item	0.88	2.01	0.88	0.02	(7.11)
Cash Flow per Share	1.21	2.36	1.14	0.29	(6.44)
Book Value per Share	6.13	5.36	3.12	2.22	1.00
O/S Common Shares	33,179	32,548	31,178	30,998	7,580
Total Revenue	480,840	495,999	332,069	242,840	135,500
Income before extra.	29,077	63,040	27,518	370	(39,685)
Cash Flow	40,052	73,862	35,652	5,381	(35,962)
Debt/Equity	8.95	6.32	6.92	7.50	16.67
Return on Capital (%)	3.38	8.00	6.62	5.89	(26.73)
Ret. on Com. Equity (%)	15.40	46.43	33.15	0.97	(287.95)
% Change Profit	(53.9)	129.1	7,337.3	100.9	(642.7)
% Change Revenue	(3.1)	49.4	36.7	79.2	77.9
% Change Assets	63.7	82.1	55.1	41.4	156.4

Preferred Div. Coverage	np	np	np
Total Div. Coverage	7.4	na	na

5 YEAR RATIOS (%)			
Return on Capital	(0.6)	na	na
Return on Com. Equity	(38.4)	na	na
Profit Growth	na	na	na
Revenue Growth	44.5	na	na
Asset Growth	75.7	na	na

BALANCE SHEET (000)			
Cash	13,130	2,462	5,003
Total Loans	54,056	38,724	50,067
Net Fixed Assets	27,340	24,015	24,954
Invest's & Advances	1,009,324	581,433	251,553
Total Assets	3,087,907	1,885,946	1,035,735
Total Deposits	0	0	0
Insurance Liability	0	0	0
Long Term Debt	1,819,353	1,102,928	672,147
Total Liabilities	2,884,641	1,711,554	938,547
Total Equity	203,266	174,392	97,188
Total Liab. & Equity	3,087,907	1,885,946	1,035,735

CAPITAL (000)			
Total Debt	1,819,353	1,102,928	672,147
Preferred Equity	0	0	0
Common Equity	203,266	174,392	97,188

Business:

MIDLAND WALWYN INC. is a financial services holding company. Its operating subsidiary, Midland Walwyn Capital Inc., is Canada's largest financial services organization. Through its subsidiaries, the company serves clients through 135 offices across Canada and seven international offices. Midland Walwyn Capital is a full service investment dealer, serving individuals and institutions.

Date	EPS	DPS	Tot Rev	Inc Bex
Mar 95	0.04	0.03	126,764	1,479
Dec 94	0.01	0.03	110,045	420
Sep 94	0.04	0.03	106,671	1,602
Jun 94	0.12	0.03	104,550	3,737
Mar 94	0.71	0.00	159,574	23,318
Dec 93	0.57	0.00	141,510	18,035
Sep 93	0.46	0.00	121,875	14,237
Jun 93	0.50	0.00	120,357	15,755

Synopsis:

Midland Walwyn reported for the three months ended March 31, 1995, earnings of $1.5-million on revenue of $126.8-million. This compares with earnings of $23.3-million on revenue of $159.6-million during the same period last year. Included in the latest earnings was a restructuring provision of $5.5-million related to severances. Assets under administration grew in the quarter by $2.5-billion and totalled $23.1-billion.

For the year ended December 31, 1994, earnings decreased 54% to $29.1-million compared to earnings of $63-million for 1993. Revenues decreased 3% to $480.8-million in 1994 from $496-million. Capital totalled $269.9-million, a net increase of $28.9-million, or 12%, from 1993. Assets under administration climbed 29%, from $16-billion to $20.6-billion.

In 1994, the company purchased a majority interest in Toronto-based Financial Concept Group and acquired J.A. Gifford Associates of Ottawa and First Investments Ltd. of Sudbury. During the year, the Atlas Capital Group was formed to manage client portfolios. Midland also formed the Financial Services Clearing Group to provide clearing services for external and related companies. During 1994, Peter Wallace, President of Midland Walwyn Capital Inc. resigned and was replaced by Robert B. Schultz.

In early 1995, one of Midland's subsidiary companies, Financial Concepts Group, acquired Winnipeg-based Pro-fund Distributors Ltd., a leading Western Canadian financial planning firm. The company also purchased Halmac & Associates of Regina and opened an office in New York to serve U.S. institutional investors.

In March 1995, the company announced an agreement in principle to form a joint-venture securities firm with the Credit Union Central of Canada. Upon regulatory approval, the Canadian Credit Union would own 80% of the firm and Midland the remaining 20%. This initiative would give Midland access to more than four million members of the 1,010 associated Credit Unions across the country.

Relative strength to TSE300 / Price / Volume (in 1000's of board lots)

Rank (Profit/Revenue/Assets)		
165	198	68

John A. Rhind
Chairman

Robert B. Schultz
President & C.E.O.

William R.J. Fulton
Chief Financial Officer

William D. Packham
Chief Operating Officer

Address
Suite 400
181 Bay Street
Toronto
ON
M5J 2V8
(416) 369-7400

Fax: (416) 369-7517
01003046/F/13.7

MUNICIPAL FINANCIAL CORPORATION

Exchanges	Price (Jun29'95)	2.90	Trailing P/E	32.22	Stock Symbol
T	Trailing Yield (%)	0.00	Trailing EPS	0.09	MFC.A

Period Ending	Oc t94	Oc t93	Oc t92	Oc t91	Oc t90
Yearly Statistics					
Price-Close	3.90	3.15	3.10	8.00	7.50
Price-High	5.25	3.50	8.13	10.50	17.88
Price-Low	2.60	2.10	3.10	4.90	7.00
P/E-Close	8.67	nm	38.75	15.39	11.72
Dividends per Share	0.00	0.00	0.23	0.60	0.60
Dividend Yield (%)	0.00	0.00	7.42	7.50	8.00
Sales per Share	21.08	23.05	25.96	30.73	32.26
EPS before extra. item	0.45	(1.68)	0.08	0.52	0.64
Cash Flow per Share	3.19	1.38	4.81	3.40	3.98
Book Value per Share	7.40	6.96	9.69	9.82	9.78
O/S Common Shares	5,573	5,573	5,573	5,569	5,569
Total Revenue	117,496	128,470	144,671	177,201	173,637
Income before extra.	2,724	(9,110)	693	3,055	4,351
Cash Flow	17,755	7,677	26,790	18,915	22,139
Debt/Equity	1.57	2.30	2.27	2.20	2.15
Return on Capital (%)	8.95	(3.10)	4.67	6.73	6.31
Ret. on Com. Equity (%)	6.21	(20.16)	0.82	5.14	6.44
% Change Profit	129.9	(1,413.9)	(77.3)	(29.8)	(63.9)
% Change Revenue	(8.5)	(11.2)	(18.4)	2.1	15.9
% Change Assets	(3.8)	(6.7)	(0.5)	(7.6)	14.7

Preferred Div. Coverage	11.3	0.0	2.8		
Total Div. Coverage	11.3	0.0	0.5		

5 YEAR RATIOS (%)			
Return on Capital	4.7	6.6	11.1
Return on Com. Equity	(0.3)	3.1	11.3
Profit Growth	(25.7)	na	(35.6)
Revenue Growth	(4.8)	3.0	11.2
Asset Growth	(1.1)	5.6	11.0

BALANCE SHEET (000)			
Cash	55,839	78,773	81,258
Total Loans	939,267	1,010,456	991,672
Net Fixed Assets	36,663	36,801	43,719
Invest's & Advances	132,209	79,376	181,780
Total Assets	1,191,686	1,239,077	1,328,596
Total Deposits	1,055,640	1,078,626	1,118,076
Insurance Liability	0	0	0
Long Term Debt	508	41,374	47,295
Total Liabilities	1,148,231	1,198,108	1,272,377
Total Equity	43,455	40,969	56,219
Total Liab. & Equity	1,191,686	1,239,077	1,328,596
CAPITAL (000)			
Total Debt	68,400	94,021	127,755
Preferred Equity	2,198	2,198	2,219
Common Equity	41,257	38,771	54,000

Business:

MUNICIPAL FINANCIAL CORP. is involved in financial and real estate services in communities across Ontario through five subsidiaries. Municipal Savings & Loan and Municipal Trust offer deposit and lending services; Municipal Financial Leasing finances office equipment and cars; MSL Properties develops and operates real estate holdings; and Municipal Securities operates in the mutual fund market.

Date	EPS	DPS	Tot Rev	Inc Bex
Apr 95	(0.09)	0.00	25,995	(438)
Jan 95	0.03	0.00	26,286	205
Oct 94	0.14	0.00	28,716	828
Jul 94	0.01	0.00	27,817	95
Apr 94	0.13	0.00	27,944	790
Jan 94	0.18	0.00	29,354	1,011
Oct 93	(1.15)	0.00	30,629	(6,209)
Jul 93	(0.32)	0.00	30,584	(1,701)

Synopsis:

Municipal Financial reported earnings of $205,392 on revenues of $26.132-million for the three months ending January 31, 1995. This compares with earnings of $1,011,233 on revenues of $29.354-million for the same period in the previous year. The decrease in earnings stemmed from write-offs and provisions totalling $1.2-million.

For the year ending October 31, 1994, net earnings increased to $2.7-million after a loss of $9.1-million in 1993. Revenues rose to $32.165-million from $17.349-million in the previous year. The increases were primarily a result of improved net interest earnings and reduced loan losses. A reduction in net non-performing loans and controlling operating expenses also contributed to the rise. Earnings per share for the Class A and common shares were $0.46 and $0.42 respectively compared with losses of $1.72 and $1.57 per share in 1993.

The company recorded a prior period adjustment in 1994 totalling $5.9-million relating to real estate development activities in 1990 and 1991. A 1992 litigation ruling in favour of the company was reversed in mid-1994 by the Ontario Court of Appeal.

During the year, Municipal Trust introduced several new products including an Adjustable Rate Mortgage and TrustLease. TrustLease is the first major partnership between Municipal Trust and the Municipal Leasing divisions. For the year, new product sales totalled $5.3-million. Municipal Trust opened two new branches in Orillia and in North York, Ontario in May 1994.

In November 1994, Municipal Securities Inc. was incorporated as a wholly owned subsidiary of The Municipal Savings & Loan Corp. to facilitate Municipal Financial's entry into the mutual fund market. Registration as a mutual fund dealer was granted effective February 1, 1995. Municipal intends to sell funds administered by independent fund managers through its 29 branches. The company has entered into a distribution relationship with the Templeton Group.

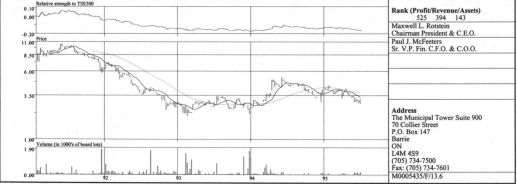

Rank (Profit/Revenue/Assets)		
525	394	143

Maxwell L. Rotstein
Chairman President & C.E.O.

Paul J. McFeeters
Sr. V.P. Fin. C.F.O. & C.O.O.

Address
The Municipal Tower Suite 900
70 Collier Street
P.O. Box 147
Barrie
ON
L4M 4S9
(705) 734-7500
Fax: (705) 734-7601
M0005435/F/13.6

NEWCOURT CREDIT GROUP INC.

Exchanges	Price (Jun29'95)		18.25	Trailing P/E		15.47	Stock Symbol
TM	Trailing Yield (%)		1.10	Trailing EPS		1.18	NCT

Period Ending	Dec94	Dec93	Dec92	Dec91
Yearly Statistics				
Price-Close	15.50	nt	nt	nt
Price-High	17.88	nt	nt	nt
Price-Low	13.75	nt	nt	nt
P/E-Close	12.92	nt	nt	nt
Dividends per Share	0.20	1.25	0.00	0.00
Dividend Yield (%)	1.29	na	0.00	0.00
Sales per Share	5.18	4.76	6.96	5.14
EPS before extra. item	1.20	1.33	0.97	0.55
Cash Flow per Share	1.14	2.06	1.14	0.70
Book Value per Share	9.70	2.19	4.01	2.36
O/S Common Shares	16,026	10,306	10,306	8,929
Total Revenue	92,058	73,803	73,701	50,227
Income before extra.	18,737	14,268	9,654	5,127
Cash Flow	15,057	21,233	11,152	6,280
Debt/Equity	3.36	15.74	13.01	22.28
Return on Capital (%)	9.86	9.17	9.82	na
Ret. on Com. Equity (%)	20.70	42.93	30.28	na
% Change Profit	31.3	47.8	88.3	na
% Change Revenue	24.7	0.1	46.7	na
% Change Assets	34.1	(24.9)	18.7	na

Business:

NEWCOURT CREDIT GROUP INC. is a financial services company which manages and sells asset-based financings comprised of secured loan, conditional sales contracts and leases.

Date	EPS	DPS	Tot Rev	Inc Bex
Mar 95	0.28	0.05	18,313	5,295
Dec 94	0.32	0.05	16,434	5,676
Sep 94	0.33	0.05	15,327	4,885
Jun 94	0.25	0.05	63,778	4,142
Mar 94	0.30	0.05	12,953	4,034
Dec 93	0.59	0.18	17,150	6,158
Sep 93	0.36	0.00	12,103	3,707

	Dec94	Dec93	Dec92	Dec91
Preferred Div. Coverage	60.2	26.2	49.3	
Total Div. Coverage	6.9	1.1	49.3	

5 YEAR RATIOS (%)			
Return on Capital	na	na	na
Return on Com. Equity	na	na	na
Profit Growth	na	na	na
Revenue Growth	na	na	na
Asset Growth	na	na	na

BALANCE SHEET (000)			
Cash	0	0	0
Total Loans	605,747	482,174	651,461
Net Fixed Assets	15,566	8,094	6,327
Invest's & Advances	75,067	39,906	56,026
Total Assets	733,970	547,423	729,220
Total Deposits	0	0	0
Insurance Liability	0	0	0
Long Term Debt	536,703	438,673	600,282
Total Liabilities	573,006	519,412	682,402
Total Equity	160,964	28,011	46,818
Total Liab. & Equity	733,970	547,423	729,220

CAPITAL (000)			
Total Debt	540,381	440,809	609,129
Preferred Equity	5,450	5,450	5,450
Common Equity	155,514	22,561	41,368

Synopsis:

For the first three months ended March 31, 1995, Newcourt Credit Group posted net income of $5.3-million, representing an increase of 31% over the $4-million reported for the same period last year. Total asset finance income for the quarter rose to $18.3-million from $13-million in the prior period last year. The increase in fee based and affiliate income from $9.1-million to $11.8-million accounted for 50% of the revenue increase.

During the first quarter of 1995, Newcourt's portfolio of owned and managed assets grew by over $180-million, surpassing the $3-billion mark through acquisition and internal growth. With nine new vendor finance programs added during the period, including relationships with Dallas-based EDS, Newcourt Financial now has over 100 vendor programs in place. In addition, the existing program with Sharp Electronics was expanded, allowing the company to offer services directly from Sharp's head office. Also during the period, Newcourt Capital completed a $51-million (U.S.) interim funding arrangement with Bombardier Inc. for the acquisition of six Dash 8 aircraft by Mesa Airlines.

In fiscal 1994, net income jumped by 31% to $18.7-million from $14.2-million in 1993. For the year, Newcourt's total asset finance income increased to $58.96-million from $44.17-million. Growth in 1994 was powered by a 197% increase in new asset financing.

In February 1994, Newcourt raised $77-million in equity through an initial public offering. This was followed in December with an additional equity issue of $44-million. In December 1994, William D. Douglas resigned as the chairman of the Board of Directors and was replaced by Ronald A. McKinlay.

In April 1995, Newcourt Credit Group Inc. was added to TSE 300 composite index and the TSE 200 index. It replaced Bramalea Ltd. Newcourt will be added to TSE 300's financial management subgroup and Bramalea will be dropped from the real estate group.

Relative strength to TSE300

Price

Volume (in 1000's of board lots)

Rank (Profit/Revenue/Assets)
223   435   185

Ronald A. McKinlay
Chairman

Steven K. Hudson
President & C.E.O.

Colin A. Grant
C.F.O.

Address
Bce Place
181 Bay Street
Suite 3500 P.O. Box 827
Toronto
ON
M5J 2T3
(416) 594-2400

01003599/F/13.6

NEWGROWTH CORP.

Exchanges	Price (Jun29'95)	9.87	Trailing P/E	5.06	Stock Symbol
T	Trailing Yield (%)	19.78	Trailing EPS	1.95	**NEW**

Period Ending	Jun94	Jun93	Jun92
Yearly Statistics			1D
Price-Close	25.25	26.50	n t
Price-High	28.75	26.88	n t
Price-Low	26.25	25.25	n t
P/E-Close	13.15	12.93	n t
Dividends per Share	1.94	1.71	0.00
Dividend Yield (%)	7.68	6.46	0.00
Sales per Share	1.99	2.12	0.00
EPS before extra. item	1.92	2.05	0.00
Cash Flow per Share	1.92	2.05	0.00
Book Value per Share	25.05	27.61	(6,595.00)
O/S Common Shares	4,512	5,501	1
Total Revenue	10,913	11,642	0
Income before extra.	10,534	11,261	0
Cash Flow	10,534	11,261	0
Debt/Equity	nd	nd	nd
Return on Capital (%)	6.03	6.12	na
Ret. on Com. Equity (%)	7.91	15.42	na
% Change Profit	(6.5)	na	na
% Change Revenue	(6.3)	na	na
% Change Assets	(4.0)	12.1	na

Preferred Div. Coverage	192.2	204.7	na
Total Div. Coverage	1.0	1.2	na

5 YEAR RATIOS (%)			
Return on Capital	na	na	na
Return on Com. Equity	na	na	na
Profit Growth	na	na	na
Revenue Growth	na	na	na
Asset Growth	na	na	na

BALANCE SHEET (000)			
Cash	709	1,096	1,124
Total Loans	31,677	0	0
Net Fixed Assets	0	0	0
Invest's & Advances	152,648	191,542	172,296
Total Assets	186,709	194,422	173,420
Total Deposits	0	0	0
Insurance Liability	0	0	0
Long Term Debt	0	0	0
Total Liabilities	31,677	0	0
Total Equity	155,031	194,422	173,420
Total Liab. & Equity	186,709	194,422	173,420

CAPITAL (000)			
Total Debt	0	0	0
Preferred Equity	42,020	42,515	180,015
Common Equity	113,011	151,907	(6,595)

Business:

NEWGROWTH CORP. is involved in investing in a portfolio of publicly listed common shares of selected Canadian chartered banks and utilities. The company is a mutual fund but does not generally operate in accordance with policies of the Canadian securities regulators applicable to conventional mutual funds.

Date	EPS	DPS	Tot Rev	Inc Bex
Mar 95	0.45	0.49	2,228	2,144
Dec 94	0.52	0.49	2,412	2,326
Sep 94	0.49	0.49	2,303	2,219
Jun 94	0.49	0.48	2,761	2,665
Mar 94	0.46	0.48	2,642	2,537
Dec 93	0.49	0.48	2,763	2,674
Sep 93	0.48	0.48	2,748	2,658
Jun 93	0.49	0.48	2,756	2,659

Synopsis:

Newgrowth Corporation's net investment income for the quarter ended March 26, 1995, was $2.144-million, which was less than distributable income by $90,905. A change in the ex-dividend date of one of the portfolios and an increase in dividend income earned but not yet received by the company was the reason for the difference.

During the quarter, 5,000 units of capital shares and equity dividend shares were retracted jointly in accordance with the company's provisions. To fund the retractions, Newgrowth sold portfolio securities in the same proportions as in the original portfolio.

For the nine months ended March 26, 1995, Newgrowth reported net investment income of $6.689-million. This was $1.179-million less than 1994, mainly due to a decrease in dividends earned as a result of portfolio securities being sold to fund the retractions. At the close of March 26, 1995, the unit value was $36.95 and net asset value was $37.26. This represents an increase of $2.95 and $2.89 per unit respectively.

For the year ended June 26, 1994, Newgrowth reported net investment income of $10.534-million, $726,938 less than 1993. In fiscal 1994, the stated capital of the capital shares and equity dividend shares of Newgrowth were reduced by $7.644-million and $24.722-million respectively for repayment of shares surrendered for retraction. Newgrowth's portfolio will be liquidated prior to the redemption of all capital shares and equity dividend shares on June 26, 1998.

During the year, the company declared and paid dividends of $0.01 per capital share and $1.9269 per equity share. Dividend payments totalled $10.613 million and were substantially equal to distributable earnings. Also during the year ended June 26, 1994, 988,886 units of capital shares and equity dividend shares were retracted jointly in accordance with the company's share provisions. To fund the retractions, Newgrowth sold portfolio securities the same proportions as in the original portfolio.

Rank (Profit/Revenue/Assets)
290 790 366

Donald W. Paterson
Chairman

Robert C. Williams
President & C.E.O.

Jeffrey C. Heath
C.F.O. & Secretary

Address
40 King St W
66th Floor
Scotia Plaza
Toronto
ON
M5W 1X6
(416) 863-7411
Fax: (416) 863-7751
01003287/F/13.3

ONDAATJE CORPORATION (THE)

Exchanges	Price (Jun29'95)	1.78	Trailing P/E	7.74	Stock Symbol
TMV	Trailing Yield (%)	0.00	Trailing EPS	0.23	VOC

Period Ending	Mar94	Mar93	Mar92	Mar91	Mar90
Yearly Statistics					
Price-Close	3.15	2.00	1.75	3.05	4.75
Price-High	4.00	3.90	3.10	4.85	7.13
Price-Low	1.85	1.35	1.50	1.90	4.13
P/E-Close	15.00	nm	nm	nm	nm
Dividends per Share	0.00	0.00	0.00	0.00	0.05
Dividend Yield (%)	0.00	0.00	0.00	0.00	1.05
Sales per Share	0.52	0.47	5.00	4.89	6.46
EPS before extra. item	0.21	(1.00)	(0.61)	(0.91)	(0.89)
Cash Flow per Share	0.21	(0.48)	(0.34)	(0.68)	(0.77)
Book Value per Share	2.13	1.52	2.61	3.23	4.14
O/S Common Shares	57,832	39,974	12,207	13,055	13,055
Total Revenue	23,647	12,217	65,189	63,527	75,752
Income before extra.	9,335	(12,992)	(7,952)	(11,824)	(10,751)
Cash Flow	9,632	(12,644)	(4,496)	(8,782)	(9,011)
Debt/Equity	nd	nd	0.69	0.34	0.74
Return on Capital (%)	11.17	(22.46)	(3.83)	(1.90)	(3.05)
Ret. on Com. Equity (%)	10.15	(28.07)	(21.47)	(24.58)	(20.27)
% Change Profit	171.9	(63.4)	32.7	(10.0)	(1,142.0)
% Change Revenue	93.6	(81.3)	2.6	(16.1)	220.9
% Change Assets	120.1	(64.7)	4.5	(29.5)	132.7

Preferred Div. Coverage	np	np	np
Total Div. Coverage	na	na	na

Date	EPS	DPS	Tot Rev	Inc Bex
Mar 95	0.11	0.00	43,267	6,179
Dec 94	0.00	0.00	8,129	256
Sep 94	0.08	0.00	14,834	4,238
Jun 94	0.04	0.00	7,875	2,543
Mar 94	0.21	0.00	23,647	9,335
Dec 93	0.05	0.00	9,977	2,362
Sep 93	0.05	0.00	2,801	1,802
Jun 93	0.04	0.00	2,519	1,693

5 YEAR RATIOS (%)			
Return on Capital	(4.0)	(7.9)	(1.2)
Return on Com. Equity	(16.8)	(19.2)	(10.2)
Profit Growth	na	na	na
Revenue Growth	0.0	(27.8)	1.3
Asset Growth	5.8	(10.3)	0.2

BALANCE SHEET (000)			
Cash	71,308	10,254	42,229
Total Loans	6,300	0	0
Net Fixed Assets	9,229	26	4,301
Invest's & Advances	29,292	7,150	8,142
Total Assets	141,443	64,249	182,176
Total Deposits	0	0	0
Insurance Liability	0	0	0
Long Term Debt	0	0	0
Total Liabilities	18,099	3,566	150,280
Total Equity	123,344	60,683	31,896
Total Liab. & Equity	141,443	64,249	182,176

CAPITAL (000)			
Total Debt	0	0	22,078
Preferred Equity	0	0	0
Common Equity	123,344	60,683	31,896

Business:

ONDAATJE CORPORATION is an investment banking company which, through its subsidiaries and associated companies, has established and/or acquired international operations that include investment banking in North America and South East Asia, commodities broking, exports and export finance, as well as other operating businesses.

Synopsis:

The Ondaatje Corporation has transformed from an unprofitable stock brokerage company to a management and investment company developing businesses in South East Asia. The company purchased 100% of Forbes & Walker Limited, a commodities and stock brokerage firm in Sri Lanka, for $8.4-million. Forbes & Walker was restructured and a new Sri Lankan company called Forbes Ceylon Limited bought selected assets and businesses from Forbes & Walker for about $26-million. The Ondaatje Corp. invested $33-million in Forbes Ceylon and a further $33-million was invested by a group of international institutional and Sri Lankan investors.

Forbes Ceylon concentrates on four businesses in Sri Lanka: tea producing and exports; managing the Government's tea estates; tourism; and managing the food assets acquired from Forbes & Walker. The company is listed on the Colombo Stock Exchange in Sri Lanka.

In June 1995, the company announced that Anthony Griffiths, the President and Chief Executive Officer for the past four months, resigned and was replaced by chairman Christopher Ondaatje. Mr. Ondaatje is the company's largest single shareholder, holding 37.5% of the outstanding shares.

In March 1995, the Ondaatje Corp. negotiated an agreement to buy 50% of Amalgamated Bean Coffee Trading Company for $21-million. The acquisition will be assigned to Forbes Capital International Limited, which is 50% owned by the Ondaatje Corp.

The company reported for the year ended March 31, 1994, revenues of $23.6-million, representing an increase of 94% from 1993. Earnings rose to $9.3-million compared with a loss of $13-million in fiscal 1993. On a per share basis, the loss of $1.00 per share in fiscal 1993 was replaced by earnings of $0.21 per share in fiscal 1994.

In December 1993, the company privately placed 15 million common shares through a Special Warrant indenture at $3.20 per share for total proceeds of $44-million.

Relative strength to TSE300

Price

Volume (in 1000's of board lots)

Rank (Profit/Revenue/Assets)
307   692   408

Christopher Ondaatje
Chairman President & C.E.O.

James P. Mcglone
V.P. C.F.O. & Secretary

Address
30a Hazelton Avenue
4th Floor
Toronto
ON
M5R 2E2
(416) 925-3555

Fax: (416) 925-5633
01000497/F/13.7

POWER CORPORATION OF CANADA

Exchanges	Price (Jun29'95)	21.25	Trailing P/E	14.17	Stock Symbol
TMV	Trailing Yield (%)	3.29	Trailing EPS	1.50	POW

Period Ending	Dec94	Dec93	Dec92	Dec91	Dec90
Yearly Statistics					
Price-Close	19.38	21.25	15.50	15.00	16.00
Price-High	23.63	22.13	16.25	18.13	16.50
Price-Low	17.75	15.00	13.88	13.38	14.00
P/E-Close	13.27	18.16	13.36	14.71	11.43
Dividends per Share	0.70	0.70	0.70	0.70	0.68
Dividend Yield (%)	3.61	3.29	4.52	4.67	4.22
Sales per Share	55.27	48.74	48.75	46.52	0.66
EPS before extra. item	1.46	1.17	1.16	1.02	1.40
Cash Flow per Share	8.73	4.49	7.99	11.96	0.82
Book Value per Share	19.23	17.63	17.14	15.93	15.89
O/S Common Shares	125,326	125,049	124,892	126,919	126,904
Total Revenue	7,034,867	6,209,826	6,286,140	5,987,301	217,433
Income before extra.	186,354	150,236	152,258	136,275	186,293
Cash Flow	1,093,343	561,343	1,013,596	1,518,094	104,670
Debt/Equity	0.29	0.25	0.29	0.32	nd
Return on Capital (%)	10.83	10.15	15.33	7.79	9.68
Ret. on Com. Equity (%)	7.90	6.73	7.07	6.39	9.13
% Change Profit	24.0	(1.3)	11.7	(26.8)	(15.8)
% Change Revenue	13.3	(1.2)	5.0	2,653.6	(19.0)
% Change Assets	6.5	6.7	11.1	1,055.0	(4.7)
Preferred Div. Coverage	46.2	36.9	29.5		
Total Div. Coverage	2.0	1.6	1.6		

Business:

POWER CORP. OF CANADA is a management holding company. Its principal subsidiaries are Power Financial Corp., Gesca Ltee and Power Broadcasting Inc. Subsidiaries of Power Financial include Great-West Lifeco Inc. and Investors Group Inc., both of Winnipeg, and its affiliate Pargesa Holdings SA of Switzerland.

Date	EPS	DPS	Tot Rev	Inc Bex
Mar 95	0.40	0.18	1,781,344	51,647
Dec 94	0.44	0.18	2,060,956	55,278
Sep 94	0.29	0.18	1,741,975	37,988
Jun 94	0.37	0.18	1,544,766	46,969
Mar 94	0.36	0.18	1,611,150	46,119
Dec 93	0.38	0.18	1,536,795	48,331
Sep 93	0.25	0.18	1,437,800	32,600
Jun 93	0.31	0.18	1,541,689	39,617

5 YEAR RATIOS (%)			
Return on Capital	10.8	11.4	12.1
Return on Com. Equity	7.4	8.4	9.9
Profit Growth	(3.4)	(7.2)	(3.5)
Revenue Growth	92.1	93.2	100.0
Asset Growth	69.2	78.9	78.4

BALANCE SHEET (mil)			
Cash	931	901	999
Total Loans	9,015	8,740	8,929
Net Fixed Assets	876	850	829
Invest's & Advances	19,627	18,170	16,142
Total Assets	31,526	29,593	27,746
Total Deposits	1,708	1,848	1,989
Insurance Liability	21,886	20,395	19,606
Long Term Debt	577	548	654
Total Liabilities	29,031	27,298	25,509
Total Equity	2,495	2,296	2,237
Total Liab. & Equity	31,526	29,593	27,746

CAPITAL (mil)			
Total Debt	713	580	654
Preferred Equity	86	91	96
Common Equity	2,410	2,205	2,140

Synopsis:

For the three months ended March 31, 1995, Power Corp. reported net earnings increased 12% to $51.6-million from $46.1-million for the same period in 1994. Revenues for the quarter rose to $1.771-billion from $1.599-billion in the first quarter of 1994. Due to improved results from Power Financial, the company's share of earnings in subsidiaries was $43.3-million, an increase of $41.8-million from March 31, 1994.

For the year ended December 31, 1994, the company posted revenues of $6.904-billion and net earnings of $186.4-million compared with revenues of $6.082-billion and earnings of $150.2-million in 1993. These results were due mainly to earnings growth in Power Financial, The Great-West Life Assurance Company, and Investors Group Inc.

In September 1994, Power Broadcasting and the Canadian Broadcasting Corp. launched two new television programming services in the U.S. During the year, Power's DirecTv venture with Hughes Aircraft Canada Ltd. proposed to offer direct-to-home television service in Canada, subject to approval. Power also purchased an additional two million shares in Southam Inc., raising its interest to 21.4%.

In November 1994, Power Corp. entered an agreement with AIG Asian Infrastructure Fund, Pacific Infrastructure Development Ltd., and the China International Trust and Investment Corp. to invest in projects in Asia. Power Corp. holds a 51% controlling interest in the new entity named Power Asia Capital Limited. In the same month, Power Corp., Bombardier Inc., and China National Railway Locomotive and Rolling Stock Industry Corp. announced the intention of forming a company to manufacture passenger rail cars in China.

In 1994, Power Pacific Corp. opened offices in Hong Kong and entered into a joint venture with Barrick Gold Corp. studying properties in China in cooperation with the China National Gold Corp. The Asia Power Group is also reviewing possible power generation projects in China, India, and Indonesia. In addition, Power Asia Capital Ltd. has made a $12-million investment for 10% interest in the Shi-Tai toll highway in China. The highway will open in January, 1996.

Relative strength to TSE300

Price

Volume (in 1000's of board lots)

Rank (Profit/Revenue/Assets)
35   17   13

Paul Desmarais Sr.
Chairman & C.E.O.

Andre Desmarais
President & C.O.O.

Michel Plessis-Belair
Executive V.P. & C.F.O.

Address
751 Square Victoria
Montreal
PQ
H2Y 2J3
(514) 286-7400

Fax: (514) 286-7424
P0003758/F/13.6

POWER FINANCIAL CORPORATION

Exchanges	Price (Jun29'95)	33.25	Trailing P/E	11.01	Stock Symbol
TMW	Trailing Yield (%)	3.28	Trailing EPS	3.02	**PWF**

Period Ending	Dec94	Dec93	Dec92	Dec91	Dec90
Yearly Statistics					
Price-Close	28.00	34.00	20.88	20.00	18.25
Price-High	35.75	34.25	22.25	23.13	21.50
Price-Low	27.00	19.50	18.00	17.50	16.25
P/E-Close	9.30	15.18	9.99	11.30	9.04
Dividends per Share	1.06	0.79	0.70	0.70	0.68
Dividend Yield (%)	3.79	2.32	3.35	3.50	3.70
Sales per Share	78.43	68.69	68.92	66.71	0.69
EPS before extra. item	3.01	2.24	2.09	1.77	2.02
Cash Flow per Share	12.57	6.20	12.09	17.49	0.88
Book Value per Share	25.48	21.75	20.27	17.80	16.89
O/S Common Shares	85,180	84,946	84,552	84,341	84,253
Total Revenue	6,778,659	5,943,276	5,973,005	5,707,472	241,061
Income before extra.	273,081	200,541	184,884	159,695	184,653
Cash Flow	1,069,427	525,752	1,021,768	1,474,765	74,232
Debt/Equity	0.77	0.83	0.63	0.41	0.33
Return on Capital (%)	10.25	9.75	16.62	8.95	9.10
Ret. on Com. Equity (%)	12.76	10.67	10.99	10.19	12.78
% Change Profit	36.2	8.5	15.8	(13.5)	(8.7)
% Change Revenue	14.1	(0.5)	4.7	2,267.6	(6.2)
% Change Assets	6.8	7.1	11.9	966.5	8.1

Preferred Div. Coverage	16.2	19.1	22.6
Total Div. Coverage	2.6	2.6	2.7

5 YEAR RATIOS (%)			
Return on Capital	10.9	11.4	11.7
Return on Com. Equity	11.5	12.1	12.8
Profit Growth	6.2	4.3	4.9
Revenue Growth	92.4	99.1	103.2
Asset Growth	71.2	81.0	78.6

BALANCE SHEET (mil)			
Cash	777	649	420
Total Loans	9,015	8,740	8,929
Net Fixed Assets	712	693	676
Invest's & Advances	18,981	17,603	15,854
Total Assets	30,453	28,522	26,622
Total Deposits	1,708	1,848	1,989
Insurance Liability	21,886	20,395	19,606
Long Term Debt	1,887	1,771	1,174
Total Liabilities	28,001	26,392	24,754
Total Equity	2,452	2,130	1,868
Total Liab. & Equity	30,453	28,522	26,622

CAPITAL (mil)			
Total Debt	1,887	1,771	1,174
Preferred Equity	282	282	154
Common Equity	2,170	1,847	1,714

Business:

POWER FINANCIAL CORP. is a holding and management company. Its operations provide a range of individual and corporate financial and fiduciary services in North America and Europe. Subsidiaries include Great-West Lifeco Inc. and Investors Group Inc., both of Winnipeg, and major affiliate, Pargesa Holding SA of Switzerland. Power Corp. of Canada is the company's main shareholder.

Date	EPS	DPS	Tot Rev	Inc Bex
Mar 95	0.73	0.29	1,708,779	66,639
Dec 94	0.87	0.29	1,976,771	78,362
Sep 94	0.68	0.27	1,691,538	62,144
Jun 94	0.74	0.24	1,485,463	67,703
Mar 94	0.72	0.24	1,548,867	64,872
Dec 93	0.63	0.24	1,452,318	57,934
Sep 93	0.56	0.20	1,377,546	50,268
Jun 93	0.60	0.18	1,473,646	52,775

Synopsis:

Power Financial reported for the first quarter 1995 consolidated net earnings were $66.6-million compared with $64.9-million in the same quarter in 1994. Its share of earnings from its subsidiaries and affiliate increased to $62.6-million from $59.5-million due to improvements in the earnings of Great-West Lifeco and Investors Group. Other income of a non-recurring nature consisted of about $1.3-million of net gains on the sale of long term holdings by companies in the Pargesa group.

For the year ended December 31, 1994, the company posted consolidated revenues of $6.7-billion compared with $5.8-billion in 1993, due primarily to a $797-million increase in premium income during the year. Net earnings were $273.1-million, or $3.01 per share, compared with $200.5-million, or $2.24 per share, in 1993. Newcourt's share of earnings from its subsidiaries and affiliate rose to $259.4-million from $217.8-million in 1993, as a result of significant earnings growth by Great-West Lifeco and Investors Group. Parjointco N.V., which holds Power Financial's interest in Pargesa Holding S.A., contributed $45.4-million to Power's earnings in 1994, as against $40.8-million in 1993.

During 1994, Great West Lifeco U.S. acquired a block of 1,500 group life and health insurance cases, representing an 11% increase in business. In 1995, the company's first Health Management Organization will begin operation in California.

In 1994, Investors Group achieved a 7.6% increase in mutual fund sales to $4.24-billion and net income rose by 20.3% to $84.6- million. In addition, Investors introduced the Flex Plan to hold RRSP accounts and launched two new funds, Investors Asset Allocation Fund and Investors Corporate Bond Fund.

During fiscal 1994, total dividends declared on common shares were increased twice and amounted to $1.06 per share compared with $0.79 in 1993. In April 1995, the company filed notice of a normal course issuer bid to buy back up to 4,260,000 of its common shares by April 5, 1996.

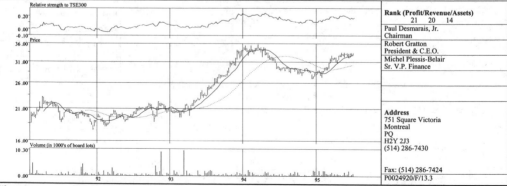

Rank (Profit/Revenue/Assets)		
21	20	14

Paul Desmarais, Jr.
Chairman

Robert Gratton
President & C.E.O.

Michel Plessis-Belair
Sr. V.P. Finance

Address
751 Square Victoria
Montreal
PQ
H2Y 2J3
(514) 286-7430

Fax: (514) 286-7424
P0024920/F/13.3

TRILON FINANCIAL CORPORATION

Exchanges	Price (Jun29'95)	4.30	Trailing P/E	16.54	Stock Symbol
TMV	Trailing Yield (%)	6.98	Trailing EPS	0.26	TFC.A

Period Ending	Dec94	Dec93	Dec92	Dec91	Dec90
Yearly Statistics					
Price-Close	3.85	3.55	4.40	10.75	12.38
Price-High	5.25	4.40	11.13	13.12	21.00
Price-Low	3.50	1.65	3.15	9.12	11.00
P/E-Close	15.40	nm	nm	14.93	176.79
Dividends per Share	0.30	0.30	0.76	0.90	0.90
Dividend Yield (%)	7.79	8.45	17.27	8.37	7.27
Sales per Share	45.56	51.62	49.25	48.82	76.54
EPS before extra. item	0.25	(0.74)	(3.90)	0.72	0.07
Cash Flow per Share	13.03	14.36	2.35	16.68	4.71
Book Value per Share	5.87	7.10	9.56	14.22	15.21
O/S Common Shares	151,054	96,376	93,643	93,300	80,281
Total Revenue	5,026,000	4,603,000	4,610,000	4,264,000	6,223,000
Income before extra.	58,000	(38,000)	(331,000)	107,000	59,000
Cash Flow	1,440,000	1,309,000	220,000	1,457,000	378,000
Debt/Equity	0.88	1.44	1.46	4.45	0.93
Return on Capital (%)	6.38	4.37	(4.59)	2.30	(0.67)
Ret. on Com. Equity (%)	3.44	(8.74)	(32.85)	4.87	0.41
% Change Profit	252.6	88.5	(409.3)	81.4	(72.9)
% Change Revenue	0.0	(0.2)	8.1	(31.5)	23.0
% Change Assets	1.7	4.1	(66.4)	19.9	1.3

Preferred Div. Coverage	1.9	0.0	0.0
Total Div. Coverage	0.9	0.0	0.0

5 YEAR RATIOS (%)			
Return on Capital	1.6	2.1	3.9
Return on Com. Equity	(6.6)	(4.2)	0.3
Profit Growth	(23.3)	na	na
Revenue Growth	(0.2)	3.4	8.0
Asset Growth	(15.5)	(10.0)	(8.0)

BALANCE SHEET (mil)			
Cash	692	903	690
Total Loans	6,171	6,767	7,103
Net Fixed Assets	1,374	1,402	1,489
Invest's & Advances	9,419	8,421	7,865
Total Assets	19,178	18,859	18,110
Total Deposits	0	0	0
Insurance Liability	14,163	12,846	12,625
Long Term Debt	1,214	1,854	2,017
Total Liabilities	17,805	17,567	16,732
Total Equity	1,373	1,292	1,378
Total Liab. & Equity	19,178	18,859	18,110

CAPITAL (mil)			
Total Debt	1,214	1,854	2,017
Preferred Equity	487	608	483
Common Equity	886	684	895

Business:

TRILON FINANCIAL CORP. is a diversified financial services company. It provides insurance services, investment banking, real estate brokerage, and commercial financing services. Subsidiaries include London Insurance Group Inc., Royal LePage Ltd. and Trilon Securities Corp. of Toronto. It also has a 46% interest in Gentra Inc., formerly Royal Trustco Ltd.

Date	EPS	DPS	Tot Rev	Inc Bex
Mar 95	0.06	0.08	1,280,000	17,000
Dec 94	0.02	0.08	966,000	11,000
Sep 94	0.09	0.08	1,422,000	18,000
Jun 94	0.09	0.08	1,393,000	17,000
Mar 94	0.05	0.08	1,160,000	12,000
Dec 93	(0.05)	0.08	1,141,000	3,000
Sep 93	(0.06)	0.08	1,149,000	2,000
Jun 93	(0.30)	0.08	1,171,000	(22,000)

Synopsis:

Trilon Financial's net income for the three months ended March 31, 1995, was $17-million on revenue of $1.28-billion compared to net income of $12-million on revenue of $1.16-billion last year. Earnings from the insurance and commercial finance operations and Trilon's share of Gentra's earnings all increased in the quarter.

For 1994, net income was $58-million compared with $38-million loss in 1993. Revenues for the period increased to $5.026-billion from $4.603-billion in the previous year. The main reason for the improvement is the turnaround at Gentra and Royal LePage.

During the year, London Insurance Group acquired the remaining shares of The Holden Group, which conducts the company's U.S. insurance operations in the retirement products market. London Insurance also disposed of the personal and business property and casualty lines of business of Wellington Insurance. London Insurance will continue to operate the fidelity and surety business of Wellington and will rename it London Guarantee Insurance Company.

In September 1994, London Insurance created London Life International Corporation. Located in Malaysia, it focuses on supporting existing operations at Shin Fu Life in Taiwan and the recently opened representative office in Beijing, as well as, expanding the business base in Asia. In October 1994, Trilon completed a $190-million common share rights offering.

During 1994, Royal LePage acquired the residential real estate brokerage business of Johnson & Daniel and Alec Murray. Also during the year, Trilon's vehicle and equipment financing subsidiary, Triathlon Leasing Inc., sold the majority of its assets and late in the year Trilon sold its remaining equipment lease investments, recording a small loss.

Trilon's share of Gentra's loss in 1994 plunged to $10-million compared to a loss of $107-million last year. In 1994, Gentra repaid all of its senior debt through purchases and redemptions.

Relative strength to TSE300

Price

Volume (in 1000's of board lots)

Rank (Profit/Revenue/Assets)
102   28   16

J. Trevor Eyton
Chairman

George E. Myhal
President & C.E.O.

Frank N.C. Lochan
Sr. V.P. & C.F.O.

Address
BCE Place
4420 - 181 Bay Street
P.O. Box 771
Toronto
ON
M5J 2T3
(416) 363-0061
Fax: (416) 365-9642
T0011819/F/13.6

TRIMARK FINANCIAL CORPORATION

Exchanges	Price (Jun29'95)	30.00	Trailing P/E	44.12	Stock Symbol
TM	Trailing Yield (%)	0.37	Trailing EPS	0.68	**TMF**

Period Ending	Mar95	Mar94	Mar93	Mar92	Mar91
Yearly Statistics					
Price-Close	21.50	18.00	12.88	nt	nt
Price-High	21.63	22.50	13.31	nt	nt
Price-Low	14.75	11.25	6.07	nt	nt
P/E-Close	31.62	35.64	103.00	nt	nt
Dividends per Share	0.12	0.10	0.10	0.05	0.11
Dividend Yield (%)	0.56	0.56	0.78	na	na
Sales per Share	8.22	6.18	4.20	2.88	2.12
EPS before extra. item	0.68	0.50	0.13	0.12	0.14
Cash Flow per Share	4.40	3.14	1.81	1.29	0.13
Book Value per Share	4.86	4.25	2.32	1.18	0.89
O/S Common Shares	22,732	22,374	20,270	15,270	15,090
Total Revenue	185,565	131,910	74,751	43,742	31,574
Income before extra.	15,341	10,424	2,469	1,746	1,997
Cash Flow	99,356	67,013	32,135	19,553	1,901
Debt/Equity	0.06	0.08	0.37	1.03	nd
Return on Capital (%)	27.23	24.92	10.20	14.29	29.03
Ret. on Com. Equity (%)	14.92	14.66	7.57	11.07	15.63
% Change Profit	47.2	322.3	41.4	(12.6)	(35.3)
% Change Revenue	40.7	76.5	70.9	38.5	15.3
% Change Assets	20.3	66.0	43.2	161.3	22.0

Preferred Div. Coverage	np	np	np
Total Div. Coverage	5.9	5.0	1.2

Date	EPS	DPS	Tot Rev	Inc Bex
Mar 95	0.15	0.03	52,406	3,407
Dec 94	0.16	0.03	46,655	3,525
Sep 94	0.18	0.03	43,814	4,131
Jun 94	0.19	0.03	42,690	4,278
Mar 94	0.12	0.03	39,820	2,639
Dec 93	0.11	0.03	34,568	2,365
Sep 93	0.16	0.03	30,738	3,207
Jun 93	0.11	0.03	26,785	2,213

5 YEAR RATIOS (%)			
Return on Capital	21.1	na	na
Return on Com. Equity	12.8	na	na
Profit Growth	37.8	na	na
Revenue Growth	46.5	na	na
Asset Growth	55.5	na	na

BALANCE SHEET (000)			
Cash	12,214	18,471	5,336
Total Loans	0	0	0
Net Fixed Assets	11,419	9,050	6,212
Invest's & Advances	3,727	3,361	4,677
Total Assets	165,728	137,804	83,001
Total Deposits	0	0	0
Insurance Liability	0	0	0
Long Term Debt	7,000	0	17,300
Total Liabilities	55,168	42,718	35,849
Total Equity	110,560	95,085	47,152
Total Liab. & Equity	165,728	137,804	83,001

CAPITAL (000)			
Total Debt	7,000	7,200	17,300
Preferred Equity	0	0	0
Common Equity	110,560	95,085	47,152

Business:

TRIMARK FINANCIAL CORPORATION, through its wholly owned subsidiary Trimark Investment Management Inc., is a mutual fund company. It is a sponsor, manager and distributor of mutual funds, with an emphasis on equity portfolios.

Synopsis:

During fiscal 1995, mutual fund assets under management at Trimark Financial Corp. grew from $7.6-billion to $10.5-billion, an increase of 38%. Overall sales, net of transfers, jumped by 25%. The Trimark Group of Funds experienced their strongest sales growth ever, showing an increase of 67%. As a result of increased assets, management fees climbed 41% and revenues from other sources rose 33%. Net income for the period increased 47% from $10.4-million to $15.3-million, while Trimark's expenses grew at a lower rate than revenues. Earnings per share rose 35%, slightly less than the increase in net income, due to a full year's dilution effect resulting from the additional one million shares issued late in fiscal 1994. Total redemptions, net of transfers, also grew from $719-million to $890-million, but declined as a percentage of average assets under management.

During fiscal 1995, Trimark's share of the Canadian mutual fund market exceeded 8%, up from less than 6% in the previous year. Trimark introduced a single, toll-free general inquiry phone number for its clients.

Near the end of 1994, Trimark introduced three new mutual funds to the Select Fund group. The funds were the Indo-Pacific Fund, the Advantage Bond Fund, and the Canadian Bond Fund. Trimark also took a small ownership interest in Lloyd George Management Limited of Hong Kong, an Investment Advisor for the new Trimark Indo-Pacific Fund.

In May 1995, Trimark announced that it would boost its quarterly dividend by 33% to eight cents. The company said it would also ask shareholders to approve a two-for-one stock split to lower the equity market price and make the shares available to a larger number of investors.

Relative strength to TSE300

Rank (Profit/Revenue/Assets)
295 379 413

Robert C. Krembil
Chairman

Arthur S. Labatt
President

Brad J. Badeau
Sr. V.P. C.F.O. & Corp. Sec.

David Stewart
C.O.O. & Exec. V.P.

Address
Suite 5600
One First Canadian Place
P.O. Box 487
Toronto
ON
M5X 1E5
(416) 362-7181
Fax: (416) 362-8515
01003272/F/13.3

UNITED CORPORATIONS LIMITED

Exchanges	Price (Jun29'95)	33.00	Trailing P/E	32.87	Stock Symbol
T	Trailing Yield (%)	15.53	Trailing EPS	1.00	UNC

Period Ending	Mar95	Mar94	Mar93	Mar92	Mar91	Business:
Yearly Statistics						UNITED CORPORATIONS LTD. is an
Price-Close	32.00	35.88	28.24	26.12	31.53	investment company. Its portfolio includes
Price-High	39.75	37.41	28.24	31.06	32.00	companies in a wide range of Canadian
Price-Low	29.75	24.94	24.00	24.00	23.65	businesses including financial services,
P/E-Close	31.37	39.30	29.13	25.23	25.77	precious metals mining, real estate and
Dividends per Share	5.30	0.89	1.93	0.99	1.27	construction, communications, transportation,
Dividend Yield (%)	16.56	2.49	6.83	3.78	4.03	and consumer and industrial goods
Sales per Share	1.23	1.12	1.21	1.33	1.76	manufacturing.
EPS before extra. item	1.02	0.91	0.97	1.04	1.22	
Cash Flow per Share	1.06	0.96	1.04	1.08	1.31	
Book Value per Share	44.55	45.06	39.32	39.52	39.96	
O/S Common Shares	7,833	7,846	7,846	7,645	7,645	
Total Revenue	9,600	8,831	9,300	10,164	13,058	

						Date	EPS	DPS	Tot Rev	Inc Bex
Income before extra.	8,341	7,570	7,995	8,258	9,717					
Cash Flow	8,341	7,570	7,995	8,258	9,717	Mar 95	0.24	0.25	2,269	1,931
Debt/Equity	nd	nd	nd	nd	nd	Dec 94	0.23	0.19	2,304	2,013
Return on Capital (%)	2.38	2.29	2.66	2.91	3.58	Sep 94	0.23	0.20	2,202	1,877
Ret. on Com. Equity (%)	2.27	2.17	2.50	2.59	2.92	Jun 94	0.31	4.49	2,825	2,520
% Change Profit	10.2	(5.3)	(3.2)	(15.0)	(44.1)	Mar 94	0.24	0.19	2,223	1,931
% Change Revenue	8.7	(5.0)	(8.5)	(22.2)	(33.8)	Dec 93	0.23	0.19	2,268	2,008
% Change Assets	(2.2)	16.2	2.6	(2.0)	(9.7)	Sep 93	0.22	0.19	2,060	1,781
						Jun 93	0.23	0.19	2,280	1,850

Preferred Div. Coverage	22.1	20.0	21.2
Total Div. Coverage	1.0	1.0	0.5

Synopsis:

United Corporations reported March 31, 1995, year end net income of $8.30-million, or $1.02 per share, compared to $7.6-million, or $0.92 per share, in fiscal 1994. Canadian dividend income rose 4.6% from $7.5-million in 1994 to $7.9-million. Due to an increase in foreign securities with higher capital appreciation potential, the foreign dividend income fell by 9.3% from $728,000 in 1994 to $660,000 in 1995. During the year the company realized net gains on investments of $13.3-million down from $30.6-million.

5 YEAR RATIOS (%)			
Return on Capital	2.8	3.4	3.6
Return on Com. Equity	2.5	3.1	3.2
Profit Growth	(13.7)	(3.8)	2.2
Revenue Growth	(13.4)	(6.4)	(2.9)
Asset Growth	0.6	2.1	(1.0)

Total assets in 1994 fell 2.2% from $370.6-million to $362.5-million. The cost of investments in Canadian securities in 1995 climbed to $260.8-million from $260.5-million in 1994. The cost of foreign securities at March 31, 1995, was $40.1-million, an increase of 21.5%, from $33-million in 1994.

BALANCE SHEET (000)			
Cash	10,550	7,810	11,949
Total Loans	0	0	0
Net Fixed Assets	0	0	0
Invest's & Advances	350,137	357,233	304,019
Total Assets	362,515	370,556	318,913
Total Deposits	0	0	0
Insurance Liability	0	0	0
Long Term Debt	0	0	0
Total Liabilities	7,465	10,883	4,310
Total Equity	355,050	359,673	314,603
Total Liab. & Equity	362,515	370,556	318,913

According to the Income Tax Act, the company is required to distribute 85% of the aggregate of taxable Canadian dividends received and 66.6% of taxable income excluding taxable capital gains. Regular quarterly dividends on the first and second preferred shares totalled $1.00 per share for the year compared with $0.90 during 1994. On April 26, 1995, the Department of Finance proposed amendments to the Act that would affect United's income tax status. As a result, United intends to delay payment of the capital gains dividend until the impact of the proposed amendments are fully known.

CAPITAL (000)			
Total Debt	0	0	0
Preferred Equity	6,119	6,119	6,119
Common Equity	348,931	353,554	308,484

The company retains the National Trust Company to manage certain investments. E-L Financial Corporation Limited provides clerical, statistical and accounting services.

Relative strength to TSE300 / Price / Volume (in 1000's of board lots) chart, 92–95

Rank (Profit/Revenue/Assets)
349   814   262

J.C.C. Wansbrough
Chairman & President

Address
10th Floor
165 University Avenue
Toronto
ON
M5H 3B8
(416) 947-2578

Fax: (416) 868-6199
U0001031/F/13.3

Page	Company	Fiscal year end	EARNINGS PER SHARE		
			Last Year	Estimate this year	Estimate next year
493	Crown Life Insurance	Dec-94	7.82	na	na
494	E-L Financial Corporation	Dec-94	10.69	na	na
495	Fairfax Financial Holdings	Dec-94	4.66	6.00	6.58
496	FT Capital	Dec-94	(3.56)	na	na
497	Goran Capital	Dec-94	1.10	na	na
498	Great-West Life Assurance	Dec-94	99.39	na	na
499	Great-West Lifeco	Dec-94	2.38	2.58	2.95
500	Imperial Life Assurance	Dec-94	(0.69)	na	na
501	KRG Management	Jul-94	(0.01)	na	na
502	London Insurance Group	Dec-94	2.69	2.95	3.13
503	MICC Investments	Dec-94	0.32	na	na

Estimates from First Call Corporation, 22 Pittsburgh Street, Boston, MA 02210   (800) 366-9992   Fax (617) 261-5679

Insurance

The Canadian life insurance industry has modified the Canadian Life and Health Insurance Compensation Corp. (CompCorp) to help strengthen it. The changes are required to meet the federal government's conditions for allowing the industry to keep control of CompCorp., the industry-run consumer protection plan designed to pay claimants if a company fails. The failure of Confederation Life Insurance Co. prompted the government action. The government first proposed replacing CompCorp with an independent federal Policy Holder Protection Board. Then it decided to allow the industry to continue to run CompCorp, provided the industry took steps to strengthen it. Three life insurers, including Confederation, have failed in the past three years. The changes to CompCorp include selecting independent directors and increasing the amount allowed a company to borrow from members from $200-million to $600-million. Also, CompCorp now has the power to become involved with federal or Quebec regulators in restructuring "soft-landing" solutions for companies in financial trouble, rather than allowing failures to happen before acting. CompCorp also has the power to levy a temporary, supplementary assessment if it doesn't have the financial resources to handle the effect of a number of failures. Under the change, annual assessments can be increased by up to 70% for up to seven years. Assessments are based on members annual premium income and currently generate $100-million a year.

Canadian life insurance companies have asked to join the Canadian Payments Association (CPA) so they can issue credit and debit cards. The life insurers want to expand the financial services they can offer in an increasingly competitive market. Currently life insurers can't offer these payment services, because they are not members of CPA. The matter will become tied up in the 1997 review and reform of financial services legislation.

Life insurance sales in Canada dropped in 1994. The number of life polices sold in Canada dropped 7%, while annualized premiums (policies are assumed to be sold on January 1) were down 4%, according to a survey by Life Insurance Marketing and Research Association Inc., of Hartford, Connecticut. The survey found that sale of whole life polices (in force until death with fixed annual premiums) fell 30% last year and all other permanent insurance sales dropped 2%. Universal life sales declined 9%. Increased interest rates made other bank savings products more competitive. The annualized premium sales of term insurance products (protection for a predetermined time period) increased 12% in 1994.

Canadian life insurers are still facing the fall-out from the real estate boom of the 1980s. The companies find they must sell many of their real estate and mortgage holdings or must take further write downs in their value.

The federal government introduced new legislation in June to beef up the powers of the Office of the Superintendent of Financial Institutions (OSFI). The legislation is aimed at making it easier for regulators to rescue troubled financial institutions. Under the new legislation, the OSFI may close a company and begin wind-up proceedings before it loses all of its capital. As well, the OSFI can veto the appointment of directors and executives of companies in financial trouble. The legislation also calls on the OFSI and financial institutions to increase public disclosure on the health of financial institutions. Amendments to the Winding-Up Act that would give the liquidator of a life insurer power to conduct reinsurance transactions to improve the resale value of assets.

Property and casualty insurance companies may expect continued consolidation in an industry that has seen 104 companies disappear in the past 15 years. Since 1990, 53 companies have ceased business or left Canada, compared to a total of 51 during the 1980s. Probably, foreign companies will lead the rationalization by closing branches in a market where one property and casualty insurer exists to serve 100,000 Canadians. Currently, there are 240 federally licensed property and casualty insurers and hundreds more mutual and provincially regulated companies. These represent assets of $37-billion compared to the health and life insurance sector with $177.1-billion in assets. New technology is altering methods of distribution, placing a heavy competitive burden on smaller insurers. Banks are probably less of a threat than first thought, despite relaxed rules regarding insurance subsidiaries, because the average return on equity for property and casualty products is much lower than the return on most banking products.

In the first quarter of 1995, Canadian property and casualty insurers' earnings increased 105% compared to the same period a year ago. This reflected a recovery from poor results in 1994. Property and casualty companies reported net investment income of $597-million, down 13.6%, during the first quarter and a loss on underwriting activities of $190-million, down from $522-million, in the same period last year. Insurers reported almost $10-billion in underwriting losses over the past seven years.

CROWN LIFE INSURANCE COMPANY

Exchanges	Price (Jun29'95)	55.00	Trailing P/E	6.51	Stock Symbol
TM	Trailing Yield (%)	0.00	Trailing EPS	8.45	CLA

Period Ending	Dec94	Dec93	Dec92	Dec91	Dec90
Yearly Statistics					
Price-Close	45.00	48.50	60.00	60.00	140.00
Price-High	57.00	55.00	60.00	90.13	180.00
Price-Low	40.00	45.00	31.00	60.00	100.00
P/E-Close	5.75	nm	nm	nm	311.11
Dividends per Share	0.00	0.00	0.00	0.00	6.40
Dividend Yield (%)	0.00	0.00	0.00	0.00	4.57
Sales per Share	431.39	797.18	832.27	982.35	1,235.89
EPS before extra. item	7.82	(0.78)	0.00	(86.66)	0.45
Cash Flow per Share	(266.48)	(438.50)	(196.13)	36.20	271.67
Book Value per Share	99.23	(16.71)	4.05	136.16	178.71
O/S Common Shares	3,455	2,000	2,000	2,000	2,000
Total Revenue	1,507,780	1,627,068	1,664,544	1,964,707	2,471,771
Income before extra.	36,233	6,838	(44,098)	(170,550)	18,788
Cash Flow	(912,224)	(876,992)	(392,268)	72,402	543,346
Debt/Equity	0.48	0.27	0.19	0.13	0.43
Return on Capital (%)	8.70	3.75	(1.98)	(24.16)	2.09
Ret. on Com. Equity (%)	17.45	na	(38.33)	(58.54)	0.24
% Change Profit	429.9	115.5	74.1	(1,007.8)	(62.8)
% Change Revenue	(7.3)	(2.3)	(15.3)	(20.5)	(19.4)
% Change Assets	(9.7)	(11.4)	2.1	(18.4)	5.0
Preferred Div. Coverage	3.9	0.7	0.0		
Total Div. Coverage	3.9	0.7	0.0		
5 YEAR RATIOS (%)					
Return on Capital	(2.3)	(2.9)	(3.2)		
Return on Com. Equity	na	na	(17.3)		
Profit Growth	(6.4)	(19.5)	na		
Revenue Growth	(13.3)	(11.0)	(12.4)		
Asset Growth	(6.9)	(3.7)	(1.2)		
BALANCE SHEET (000)					
Cash	74,494	157,702	203,930		
Total Loans	3,084,940	3,367,931	3,632,326		
Net Fixed Assets	518,628	555,858	555,093		
Invest's & Advances	2,697,791	3,000,543	3,452,595		
Total Assets	6,745,669	7,473,168	8,433,144		
Total Deposits	0	0	0		
Insurance Liability	5,824,618	6,601,200	7,407,687		
Long Term Debt	0	0	0		
Total Liabilities	6,311,022	7,089,083	8,038,512		
Total Equity	434,647	384,085	394,632		
Total Liab. & Equity	6,745,669	7,473,168	8,433,144		
CAPITAL (000)					
Total Debt	206,761	105,112	73,468		
Preferred Equity	91,847	417,500	386,528		
Common Equity	342,800	(33,415)	8,104		

Business:

CROWN LIFE INSURANCE CO. offers a range of life and health insurance and pensions to individuals and groups. It also offers reinsurance services to other insurance companies. Offices are located in Canada, the United Kingdom, the Caribbean Islands, Hong Kong and Macau. Extendicare Inc. of Toronto owns 32% of the Company's common equity and Haro Financial Corporation of Regina owns 64%.

Date	EPS	DPS	Tot Rev	Inc Bex
Mar 95	1.49	0.00	345,206	8,914
Dec 94	3.07	0.00	377,194	12,886
Sep 94	2.24	0.00	367,309	10,066
Jun 94	1.65	0.00	370,234	8,006
Mar 94	0.86	0.00	372,093	5,275
Dec 93	(2.81)	0.00	383,611	(7,049)
Sep 93	0.69	0.00	410,070	4,717
Jun 93	0.73	0.00	397,848	4,765

Synopsis:

Crown Life's operating results for the first three months of 1995 reflect a consistent trend of improving profitability, asset quality, and capital strength. Earnings per share after payment of preferred share dividends were $1.49 in 1995, compared with $0.86 in 1994. Premium income in fiscal 1994 was 4% lower than in 1993, mainly because of lower deposits from Canadian group pension business. The 12% drop in investment income can be attributed to the North American real estate crash that began in 1990. Total consolidated assets were $6.7-billion, compared with $7.5-billion at December 31, 1993. The asset drop primarily results from maturities of U.S. guaranteed interest contracts. GIC sales stopped in 1990 and significant maturities were scheduled for each year since.

In early 1995, Crown Life sold two subsidiaries, Crown Financial Management Ltd. and American Crown Life Insurance Company. The sales are part of Crown Life's plan to focus on core businesses, which are in the North American life and health business, as well as Canadian group life and health and pensions. In January 1995, Crown Life opened a new sales office in Toronto to serve individual insurance clients. In May 1995, Crown Life opened a group sales office in Edmonton.

On March 24, 1995, Crown Life announced a rights offering, which will entitle holders of common shares to subscribe for subordinated convertible debentures of Crown Life. Crown Life will receive a minimum of $150-million from the offering. It will use the addition capital to improve its regulatory capital structure, provide for business growth and increase confidence in the financial strength of the company. Moody's Investors Service is considering upgrading its rating on Crown Life, which currently is the lowest of the 10 largest Canadian insurers. Moody's currently has Crown Life rated below its investment-grade category. This bars institutional clients by their own rules from investing with Crown Life.

Rank (Profit/Revenue/Assets)		
138	81	32

Paul J. Hill
Chairman

Brian A. Johnson
President & C.E.O.

Alan M. Rowe
Sr. V.P. & C.F.O.

Address
1901 Scarth Street
P.O. Box 827
Regina
SK
S4P 3B1
(306) 751-6000

Fax: (306) 751-6001
C0011778/F/13.5.2

E-L FINANCIAL CORPORATION LIMITED

Exchanges	Price (Jun29'95)	79.00	Trailing P/E	7.32	Stock Symbol
T	Trailing Yield (%)	0.63	Trailing EPS	10.79	**ELF**

Period Ending	Dec94	Dec93	Dec92	Dec91	Dec90
Yearly Statistics					
Price-Close	75.00	80.00	38.00	54.38	50.00
Price-High	80.00	80.00	57.00	54.50	75.00
Price-Low	65.00	36.50	35.00	45.00	43.00
P/E-Close	7.02	7.38	7.80	6.35	26.60
Dividends per Share	0.50	0.50	0.50	0.50	0.50
Dividend Yield (%)	0.67	0.63	1.32	0.92	1.00
Sales per Share	206.66	218.96	238.19	232.07	169.10
EPS before extra. item	10.69	10.84	4.87	8.56	1.88
Cash Flow per Share	(3.09)	5.60	4.87	8.56	16.85
Book Value per Share	104.87	94.51	84.04	79.47	64.24
O/S Common Shares	3,840	3,840	3,840	3,840	3,840
Total Revenue	812,062	860,867	935,074	908,680	649,325
Income before extra.	41,055	41,619	18,700	32,875	7,208
Cash Flow	(11,852)	21,518	18,700	32,875	64,689
Debt/Equity	0.02	0.05	0.09	0.14	nd
Return on Capital (%)	14.13	13.70	4.85	12.84	2.28
Ret. on Com. Equity (%)	10.72	12.14	5.96	11.92	2.90
% Change Profit	(1.4)	122.6	(43.1)	356.1	(82.1)
% Change Revenue	(5.7)	(7.9)	2.9	39.9	(6.8)
% Change Assets	3.2	5.5	6.7	35.4	2.5

Preferred Div. Coverage	na	na	na
Total Div. Coverage	21.4	21.7	9.7

Business:

E-L FINANCIAL CORPORATION LIMITED is a financial services holding company. Its subsidiaries are engaged in underwriting all types of insurance. Subsidiaries include The Dominion of Canada General Insurance Company E-L Financial Services Ltd. and The Empire Life Insurance Company.

Date	EPS	DPS	Tot Rev	Inc Bex
Mar 95	1.81	0.13	239,071	6,934
Dec 94	3.33	0.13	166,430	12,801
Sep 94	3.07	0.13	217,763	11,786
Jun 94	2.58	0.13	198,911	9,888
Mar 94	1.71	0.13	230,958	6,580
Dec 93	3.41	0.13	238,006	13,065
Sep 93	2.24	0.13	224,669	8,629
Jun 93	2.43	0.13	217,882	9,338

5 YEAR RATIOS (%)			
Return on Capital	9.6	10.0	10.5
Return on Com. Equity	8.7	10.0	11.1
Profit Growth	0.5	3.0	(3.0)
Revenue Growth	3.1	7.0	9.1
Asset Growth	9.9	11.9	12.4

BALANCE SHEET (000)			
Cash	159,776	75,420	172,074
Total Loans	20,954	22,027	301,819
Net Fixed Assets	11,202	10,338	31,901
Invest's & Advances	1,615,993	1,714,292	1,693,850
Total Assets	3,029,425	2,935,581	2,783,297
Total Deposits	0	0	0
Insurance Liability	1,432,515	1,467,123	1,621,842
Long Term Debt	0	0	0
Total Liabilities	2,626,691	2,572,655	2,460,591
Total Equity	402,734	362,926	322,706
Total Liab. & Equity	3,029,425	2,935,581	2,783,297

CAPITAL (000)			
Total Debt	9,697	18,632	29,042
Preferred Equity	1	1	1
Common Equity	402,733	362,925	322,705

Synopsis:

For the second year in a row, shareholder Richard Holbrook, a partner in pension fund managers Knight Bain Seath & Holbrook Capital Management, unsuccessfully challenged E-L Financial's board of directors to improve the marketability of the company's shares. The board considered raising the annual dividend, now 50 cents per share, but decided to continue investing most of its earnings into the firm. E-L controls, directly or indirectly, Dominion of Canada General Insurance Co. and Empire Life Insurance Co. It owns about 12% of National Trustco Inc., and is part of the group of private and public businesses controlled by Ontario Lieutenant-Governor Hal Jackman. Its largest shareholders are Dominion and Anglo Investment Corp. (35%) and Economic Investment Trust Ltd. (8.5%), both controlled by Jackman and his family.

E-L's first quarter net earnings were up 5% from the same period last year to $6.9-million or $1.81 a share, due in part from higher annuity premiums and a reduction in commissions paid. In 1994, it earned $41.1-million or $10.69 per share, down slightly from the record earnings of $41.6-million or $10.84 per share in 1993. Included in 1994 earnings was a small gain on the sale of Empire Life's U.S. subsidiary, Connecticut National Life. The sale was completed so that E-L could focus on opportunities being created by the industry consolidation taking place in Canada. Gross written premiums dropped $14.2-million to $528-million for fiscal 1994. Underwriting losses declined to $30.2-million from $37.3-million in 1993. Ongoing planned broker management and the aggressive action on deductibles and rates were cited as the cause for the decline. About 62% of premium income in 1994 came from individual insurance, while 38% resulted from group insurance.

George Cooke, who runs the firm's car insurance arm, said the entry of Canadian Imperial Bank of Commerce into the business has not directly affected E-L. However, the move produced consolidation and prompted some insurers to re-evaluate how they do business. E-L will not follow CIBC's approach of direct selling by telephone and will continue to focus on selling through independent brokers.

Relative strength to TSE300

Price

Volume (in 1000's of board lots)

Rank (Profit/Revenue/Assets)
130 135 69

E. Kendall Cork
Chairman & President

Address
10th Floor
165 University Avenue
Toronto
ON
M5H 3B8
(416) 947-2578

Fax: (416) 868-6199
E0000950/F/13.5.1

For further company information, call Globe Information Services 1-800-268-9128 or (416) 585-5345

FAIRFAX FINANCIAL HOLDINGS LIMITED

Exchanges	Price (Jun29'95)	79.00	Trailing P/E	14.60	Stock Symbol
T	Trailing Yield (%)	0.00	Trailing EPS	5.41	**FFH**

Period Ending	Dec94	Dec93	Dec92	Dec91	Dec90	Business:
Yearly Statistics						FAIRFAX FINANCIAL HOLDINGS
Price-Close	67.00	61.25	25.00	21.25	11.00	LIMITED is a financial services holding
Price-High	76.00	61.25	30.00	22.50	21.63	company, involved in the insurance of
Price-Low	50.00	24.00	21.75	10.75	8.88	commercial property, oil and gas casualty and
P/E-Close	14.38	11.30	14.21	5.17	3.68	life risks, investment management, and the
Dividends per Share	0.00	0.00	0.00	0.00	0.00	provision of claims adjusting and appraisal and
Dividend Yield (%)	0.00	0.00	0.00	0.00	0.00	loss management services in Canada and the
Sales per Share	75.22	51.38	49.13	43.79	22.09	United States. Its main subsidiaries are Ranger
EPS before extra. item	4.66	5.42	1.76	4.11	2.99	Insurance, Commonwealth Insurance,
Cash Flow per Share	3.94	(0.51)	2.29	6.10	(1.80)	Federated Insurance and Morden & Helwig
Book Value per Share	43.77	35.14	23.75	21.41	17.29	Group.
O/S Common Shares	8,955	7,955	6,055	5,455	5,477	
Total Revenue	634,897	344,022	286,830	250,353	195,430	
Income before extra.	38,105	33,340	10,045	22,515	21,306	

Date	EPS	DPS	Tot Rev	Inc Bex
Mar 95	1.50	0.00	266,000	13,400
Dec 94	1.85	0.00	184,592	15,717
Sep 94	1.05	0.00	152,204	8,378
Jun 94	1.01	0.00	153,319	8,083
Mar 94	0.75	0.00	145,085	5,927
Dec 93	2.05	0.00	96,924	13,260
Sep 93	1.36	0.00	88,632	8,110
Jun 93	1.31	0.00	83,926	7,797

	Dec94	Dec93	Dec92	Dec91	Dec90
Cash Flow	32,234	(3,109)	13,172	33,417	(12,791)
Debt/Equity	0.64	0.56	0.60	0.62	1.02
Return on Capital (%)	10.88	15.79	6.83	16.99	14.18
Ret. on Com. Equity (%)	11.35	15.75	7.71	21.30	22.97
% Change Profit	14.3	231.9	(55.4)	5.7	27.3
% Change Revenue	84.6	19.9	14.6	28.1	55.4
% Change Assets	81.1	103.2	14.3	(3.6)	116.1

Preferred Div. Coverage	np	np	np
Total Div. Coverage	na	na	na

5 YEAR RATIOS (%)

Return on Capital	12.9	14.0	15.3
Return on Com. Equity	15.8	17.6	18.7
Profit Growth	17.9	18.3	(6.9)
Revenue Growth	38.2	20.8	20.4
Asset Growth	54.3	37.2	26.0

BALANCE SHEET (000)

Cash	271,026	287,880	83,495
Total Loans	0	0	0
Net Fixed Assets	29,832	24,919	21,882
Invest's & Advances	1,280,317	560,894	308,286
Total Assets	2,173,411	1,200,275	590,548
Total Deposits	7,541	5,664	5,844
Insurance Liability	921,674	444,846	208,816
Long Term Debt	240,494	146,750	81,937
Total Liabilities	1,781,462	920,796	446,730
Total Equity	391,949	279,479	143,818
Total Liab. & Equity	2,173,411	1,200,275	590,548

CAPITAL (000)

Total Debt	249,369	157,213	86,729
Preferred Equity	0	0	0
Common Equity	391,949	279,479	143,818

Synopsis:

In the first quarter of 1995, Fairfax's earnings increased 127% to $13.4-million from $5.9-million last year. Revenues increased to $266-million from $145-million as a result of increased premium and investment income. This mainly was related to the November 30, 1994, acquisition of Continental Insurance. The combined ratio dropped to 102% due to better weather and improved underwriting. In its annual report, Fairfax's Chairman and CEO, V. Prem Watsa, stated "It happened again! For the second time since we began in 1985, we did not earn a return on equity in excess of 20%." In fact, the company earned 12.1% on shareholders' equity in 1994, compared to 9.5% for the TSE300. Underwriting performance in 1994 was dismal, but the company is expecting Continental to achieve consistent profitability in the future. Book value increased from $2.08 in 1985 to $43.77 in 1994. This represents a compound rate of 40.3%.

Late in 1994, Fairfax bought Continental Canada, which consists of The Continental Insurance Company of Canada and The Dominion Insurance Corp. The purchase price was $155-million. Fairfax issued a 7.75% note due December 15, 2003, for $25-million of the purchase price. The balance was financed by a $60-million unsecured, five year bank loan, and the issue of one million treasury shares through a planned private placement at $76 a share. The Ontario Municipal Employees Retirement Board purchased 600,000 of the shares, increasing their stake in Fairfax to 14.4%.

With the purchase of Continental, along with the 1993 acquisition of Ranger Insurance, Fairfax's increased its total assets to over $2.1-billion. The company will benefit from industry consolidation. Many international companies are looking to sell. Most Canadian companies, other than Fairfax, don't have the financial strength to take advantage of the sell off. The company focuses on niche markets, a worthwhile strategy, since those sectors are less likely to suffer direct competition. The Commonwealth subsidiary specializes in oil and gas. Markel handles trucking, Federated deals with farm equipment, and Morden & Helwig is one of the largest adjustment and appraisal companies in North America.

Rank (Profit/Revenue/Assets)
133   170   100

V. Prem Watsa
Chairman & C.E.O.

John C. Varnell
Vice President & C.F.O.

Address
95 Wellington Street West
Suite 800
Toronto
ON
M5J 2N7
(416) 367-4941

M0001940/F/13.5.1

FT CAPITAL LTD.

Exchanges	Price (Jun29'95)	0.04	Trailing P/E	nm	Stock Symbol
TZ	Trailing Yield (%)	0.00	Trailing EPS	(1.84)	FTC

Period Ending	Dec94	Dec93	Dec92	Dec91	Dec90
Yearly Statistics					
Price-Close	0.06	0.06	0.02	0.03	0.04
Price-High	0.17	0.30	0.08	0.06	0.20
Price-Low	0.04	0.01	0.02	0.02	0.02
P/E-Close	nm	nm	nm	nm	nm
Dividends per Share	0.00	0.00	0.00	0.00	0.00
Dividend Yield (%)	0.00	0.00	0.00	0.00	0.00
Sales per Share	0.44	0.94	0.81	12.02	9.15
EPS before extra. item	(3.56)	(2.34)	(3.95)	(2.12)	(3.21)
Cash Flow per Share	(3.72)	(2.48)	(3.64)	3.12	0.58
Book Value per Share	(30.91)	(27.35)	(25.01)	(21.06)	(19.16)
O/S Common Shares	10,200	10,200	10,200	10,199	10,199
Total Revenue	6,063	10,976	5,107	132,619	95,349
Income before extra.	(36,314)	(23,880)	(40,268)	(18,477)	(29,514)
Cash Flow	(37,929)	(25,318)	(37,119)	31,862	5,870
Debt/Equity	na	na	na	na	na
Return on Capital (%)	(9.76)	0.32	(51.85)	na	na
Ret. on Com. Equity (%)	na	na	na	na	na
% Change Profit	(52.1)	40.7	(117.9)	37.4	14.4
% Change Revenue	(44.8)	114.9	(96.1)	39.1	17.3
% Change Assets	185.6	(21.8)	(76.1)	35.4	7.1

Business:
FT CAPITAL LTD., formerly Financial Trustco Ltd., is an insurance holding company. Its subsidiary, Morgan Financial Corp. of Toronto, operates Westbury Canadian Life Insurance Co. and MECI Properties Inc.

Date	EPS	DPS	Tot Rev	Inc Bex
Mar 95	(0.53)	0.00	7,279	(4,632)
Dec 94	(0.96)	0.00	(4,199)	(39,689)
Sep 94	0.25	0.00	10,262	3,375
Jun 94	(0.60)	0.00	1,535	(4,556)
Mar 94	(1.75)	0.00	1,290	(17,022)
Dec 93	(0.19)	0.00	(999)	(1,889)
Sep 93	(1.52)	0.00	1,440	(14,932)
Jun 93	(0.65)	0.00	3,035	(7,625)

Preferred Div. Coverage	na	na	na
Total Div. Coverage	na	na	na

5 YEAR RATIOS (%)			
Return on Capital	na	na	na
Return on Com. Equity	na	na	na
Profit Growth	na	na	na
Revenue Growth	(40.8)	(14.6)	(49.1)
Asset Growth	(4.9)	(25.5)	(38.4)

BALANCE SHEET (000)			
Cash	1,279	0	2,349
Total Loans	96,128	51,894	48,398
Net Fixed Assets	0	0	0
Invest's & Advances	66,798	5,572	22,614
Total Assets	164,223	57,494	73,511
Total Deposits	0	0	0
Insurance Liability	0	0	0
Long Term Debt	423,830	305,162	297,302
Total Liabilities	448,481	305,438	297,575
Total Equity	(284,258)	(247,944)	(224,064)
Total Liab. & Equity	164,223	57,494	73,511

CAPITAL (000)			
Total Debt	435,614	305,162	297,302
Preferred Equity	31,039	31,039	31,039
Common Equity	(315,297)	(278,983)	(255,103)

Synopsis:

For the first quarter of 1995, FT Capital Ltd. posted a loss of $4.6-million or $0.53 per share, compared to a loss of $17-million or $1.75 per share for the same period in 1994. The reduced loss was due to increased revenue from realization on assets of Triathlon Leasing. Increased interest expenses were offset by substantially reduced foreign exchange losses due to stabilization of the Canadian dollar reflected in the company's U.S. dollar subordinated debentures.

In November 1994 FT Capital bought 100% of Triathlon Leasing Inc., which was formally in the leasing business and has disposed of a substantial portion of its assets. FT Capital intends to work with Triathlon towards a profitable liquidation of the remaining assets. FT Capital has a 29.5% interest in Morgan Financial Corporation, whose only significant liability is its guarantee to Canada Deposit Insurance Corp., which grew to $62.2-million at the end of 1994. Because Morgan is in default of certain commitments made in support of the guarantee, the liability is in effect on a demand basis, although CDIC has extended the term of the debt to July 1996.

At March 31, 1995, FT Capital had outstanding $154-million of principal and $144-million of accrued interest on its debentures. In June 1995, FT Capital said that it wouldn't be able to retract the outstanding 3,159,027 first preferred shares, series I by the final retraction date of June 30. FT Capital continues to be unable to meet its debt obligations, which rank ahead of the obligations to preferred shareholders and, as a result, is unable to retract the preferred shares. Edper Bronfman group's Trilon Financial Corp., which owns 98% of FT Capital's debentures, will not allow the company to restructure its preferred and common shares unless various targets are met. These include paying preferred shareholders at least $1.4-million or 45 cents on the dollar for their principal. As well FT Capital must find at least $400,000 to reimburse common shareholders, including B.C. Pacific Capital Corp., which owns 35% of the common stock. FT Capital will continue to work with B.C. Pacific and Trilon to develop a comprehensive restructuring plan.

Relative strength to TSE300

Price

Volume (in 1000's of board lots)

Rank (Profit/Revenue/Assets)
975   788   600

Terrence A. Lyons
President & C.E.O.

Address
Royal Centre Suite 1632
1055 West Georgia Street
P.O. Box 11179
Vancouver
BC
V6E 3R5
(604) 669-3141
Fax: (604) 687-3419
F0005910/F/13.5.2

GORAN CAPITAL INC.

Exchanges	Price (Jun29'95)	7.50	Trailing P/E	6.82	Stock Symbol
TQ	Trailing Yield (%)	0.00	Trailing EPS	1.10	GNC

Period Ending	Dec94	Dec93	Dec92	Dec91	Dec90
Yearly Statistics					
Price-Close	7.38	4.70	2.65	0.30	0.30
Price-High	8.00	7.00	2.98	0.70	4.15
Price-Low	3.70	2.30	0.30	0.20	0.30
P/E-Close	6.71	12.70	2.33	0.37	nm
Dividends per Share	0.00	0.00	0.00	0.00	0.00
Dividend Yield (%)	0.00	0.00	0.00	0.00	0.00
Sales per Share	17.03	14.94	15.31	11.97	9.38
EPS before extra. item	1.10	0.37	1.14	0.81	(2.16)
Cash Flow per Share	3.11	(0.07)	0.37	6.51	(0.74)
Book Value per Share	1.44	0.30	(0.20)	(1.41)	(2.22)
O/S Common Shares	4,934	4,883	4,802	4,670	4,670
Total Revenue	84,137	73,947	76,558	56,559	43,810
Income before extra.	5,382	1,803	5,334	3,787	(10,075)
Cash Flow	15,275	(342)	1,747	30,384	(3,446)
Debt/Equity	3.48	17.50	na	na	na
Return on Capital (%)	27.90	13.37	32.07	30.02	(18.97)
Ret. on Com. Equity (%)	125.89	717.84	na	na	na
% Change Profit	198.5	(66.2)	40.9	137.6	30.2
% Change Revenue	13.8	(3.4)	35.4	29.1	(46.0)
% Change Assets	15.5	(8.1)	(6.8)	44.2	(8.5)

Preferred Div. Coverage	np	np	np
Total Div. Coverage	na	na	na

5 YEAR RATIOS (%)			
Return on Capital	16.9	7.1	7.0
Return on Com. Equity	na	na	na
Profit Growth	34.4	(0.2)	58.9
Revenue Growth	0.7	(1.4)	4.0
Asset Growth	5.5	(5.9)	(2.7)

BALANCE SHEET (000)			
Cash	10,645	10,877	16,984
Total Loans	7,908	5,809	6,886
Net Fixed Assets	6,695	11,533	10,136
Invest's & Advances	40,949	40,215	53,412
Total Assets	130,373	112,852	122,735
Total Deposits	0	0	0
Insurance Liability	58,196	52,700	57,258
Long Term Debt	17,128	18,597	19,540
Total Liabilities	123,265	111,411	123,674
Total Equity	7,108	1,441	(939)
Total Liab. & Equity	130,373	112,852	122,735
CAPITAL (000)			
Total Debt	24,761	25,217	28,182
Preferred Equity	0	0	0
Common Equity	7,108	1,441	(939)

Business:

GORAN CAPITAL INC. is the holding company of Granite Insurance Company of Toronto, Pafco General Insurance Company of Indianapolis, IGF Insurance Company of Des Moines and Granite Reinsurance Company Ltd. of Barbados. The Companies operate in all provinces of Canada, 25 states in the United States and Barbados.

Date	EPS	DPS	Tot Rev	Inc Bex
Dec 94	0.23	0.00	28,082	1,150
Sep 94	0.25	0.00	17,123	1,190
Jun 94	0.32	0.00	21,571	1,588
Mar 94	0.30	0.00	17,308	1,454
Dec 93	(0.42)	0.00	21,224	(1,978)
Sep 93	0.23	0.00	17,784	1,053
Jun 93	0.30	0.00	18,917	1,490
Mar 93	0.26	0.00	15,803	1,238

Synopsis:

Goran Capital Inc. reported its net income in the first quarter of 1995 was $1.76-million, up 21% from $1.45-million in the same quarter last year. Gross premium revenue rose 10% to $41.2-million from $37.7-million a year ago. The increase in sales and net income were due to higher volumes in Goran's crop insurance subsidiary, IGF Insurance Co. of Des Moines, Iowa, and improved profitability in Goran's surcharged auto insurer, Pafco General Insurance Co. of Indiana. IGF should see higher sales and earnings in the first quarter of 1995, due to the positive impact of the U.S. Crop Insurance Reform Act signed in October 1994. As a result of the legislation, IGF's 1995 sales should show unprecedented growth, while expenses should rise at a much slower rate.

During 1994, Goran improved its financial condition by substantially strengthening its balance sheet and enhancing prospects for long-term growth. Shareholders' equity jumped to $7.1-million in 1994 from $1.4-million in 1993. Long-term debt fell to $18.5-million from $22.6-million last year. Changes were made to IGF's reinsurance structure following the 1993 crop year to minimize its exposure to extreme weather patterns. Another subsidiary, Granite Reinsurance Co. of Barbados, had a strong year in 1994, posting profits of $1.89-million. The Canadian subsidiary, Granite Insurance Co. of Toronto, limits its business to servicing its investment portfolio and outstanding claims. It has been in a run-off position for several years. Granite stopped writing business on December 31, 1989. It sold its book of Canadian business in June 1990.

In 1994, Goran Capital's 1994 gross written premiums were split as follows: Auto, $62.2-million; Crop, $58-million; Finite Reinsurance, $32.6-million; and Miscellaneous, $4.3-million. Goran derives more than 75% of its gross revenue from the United States.

Relative strength to TSE300

Price

Volume (in 1000's of board lots)

Rank (Profit/Revenue/Assets)
413 447 426
G. Gordon Symons
Chairman & C.E.O.
Alan G. Symons
President & Secretary
Douglas H. Symons
V.P. & C.O.O.

Address
Suite 1101
181 University Avenue
Box 11
Toronto
ON
M5H 3M7
(416) 594-1155
Fax: (416) 594-0711
01000494/F/13.5.1

GREAT-WEST LIFE ASSURANCE COMPANY (THE)

Exchanges	Price (Jun29'95)		26.25	Trailing P/E		nc	Stock Symbol
TMW	Trailing Yield (%)		nc	Trailing EPS		101.37	**GWL.PR.A**

Period Ending	Dec94	Dec93	Dec92	Dec91	Dec90
Yearly Statistics					
Price-Close	26.00	27.25	25.50	25.00	24.50
Price-High	29.00	29.00	26.00	25.00	25.25
Price-Low	25.00	23.00	24.00	21.50	24.13
P/E-Close	nc	nc	nc	nc	nc
Dividends per Share	nc	nc	nc	nc	nc
Dividend Yield (%)	nc	nc	nc	nc	nc
Sales per Share	3,034.00	2,637.94	2,677.30	2,560.09	2,849.90
EPS before extra. item	0.00	81.10	43.60	58.40	58.58
Cash Flow per Share	509.03	313.10	535.04	723.26	1,005.72
Book Value per Share	903.60	799.01	722.08	659.11	612.45
O/S Common Shares	2,000	2,000	2,000	2,000	2,000
Total Revenue	6,067,996	5,275,882	5,354,592	5,120,173	5,596,174
Income before extra.	229,854	195,056	116,850	139,588	155,936
Cash Flow	1,018,069	626,203	1,070,079	1,446,517	2,011,447
Debt/Equity	0.06	0.02	0.02	0.04	0.04
Return on Capital (%)	16.26	15.70	9.51	10.46	11.52
Ret. on Com. Equity (%)	11.68	10.66	6.32	9.19	11.59
% Change Profit	17.8	66.9	(16.3)	(10.5)	3.0
% Change Revenue	15.0	(1.5)	4.6	(8.5)	5.6
% Change Assets	12.7	31.0	13.9	(2.6)	10.7

Preferred Div. Coverage	7.4	5.9	3.9
Total Div. Coverage	2.2	2.3	1.7

5 YEAR RATIOS (%)			
Return on Capital	12.7	12.1	11.0
Return on Com. Equity	9.9	10.0	10.1
Profit Growth	8.7	8.9	4.8
Revenue Growth	2.7	1.2	2.0
Asset Growth	12.6	11.9	8.3

BALANCE SHEET (mil)			
Cash	271	197	136
Total Loans	8,183	7,781	7,789
Net Fixed Assets	624	604	588
Invest's & Advances	17,148	15,907	14,080
Total Assets	34,295	30,431	23,226
Total Deposits	0	0	0
Insurance Liability	21,886	20,395	20,159
Long Term Debt	5	32	36
Total Liabilities	32,062	28,406	21,381
Total Equity	2,233	2,024	1,845
Total Liab. & Equity	34,295	30,431	23,226

CAPITAL (mil)			
Total Debt	136	32	36
Preferred Equity	426	426	401
Common Equity	1,807	1,598	1,444

Business:

GREAT-WEST LIFE ASSURANCE CO. offers a range of insurance, retirement and investment products and services for individuals, businesses and organizations. The company has marketing, benefit payment and property investment offices across the United States and Canada. The company is a subsidiary of Great-West Lifeco Inc. of Winnipeg.

Date	EPS	DPS	Tot Rev	Inc Bex
Mar 95	25.35	nc	1,552,776	58,867
Dec 94	25.47	nc	1,820,444	58,761
Sep 94	24.99	nc	1,547,452	57,736
Jun 94	25.56	nc	1,327,855	58,911
Mar 94	23.37	nc	1,372,245	54,446
Dec 93	23.02	nc	1,295,511	54,374
Sep 93	20.82	nc	1,238,122	49,920
Jun 93	19.98	nc	1,327,282	48,181

Synopsis:

The Great-West Life Assurance Company, Canada's third largest life insurer, reported a first quarter profit of $50.7-million, up 8% from a year ago. Despite higher death claims, earnings improved due to lower expenses in Canada and improved interest rate spreads in its U.S. operations. Fiscal 1994 turned out to be an outstanding year for Great-West. Life insurance sales grew 30%, annuity revenue was up 38%, and health insurance premiums were up 25% over last year. Company profitability is strong and has allowed Great-West to absorb mortgage loss provisions totalling $413-million since 1989. Segregated fund assets grew to $3.6-billion in 1994, up by more than 22%. This represents the opposite of what members of the Investment Funds Institute of Canada experienced. IFIC members reported a decline in assets during 1994. In the U.S., growth was aided by the acquisition of Confederation Life's U.S. life and health business.

Great-West ranks among the top 25 largest insurers in North America with $35.0-billion in assets and $2.3-billion in capital and surplus. Great-West's U.S. subsidiary, Great-West Life & Annuity Insurance Co., made up 66% of the company's year end 1994 consolidated assets and 57% of net income. The subsidiary concentrates on employee benefits and financial services, where it has created a niche in public non-profit defined-contribution plans. The Canadian operation's strongest strategic position is in group life and health, where it is the number one player with over 12% of the premiums in a $10-billion market. Great-West Canada is also strong in individual disability income, individual life insurance, and retirement and investment services. Canadian operations produced 43% of consolidated net income in 1994. During 1995, Great-West's focus will remain on expense management and stabilization in the Canadian and U.S. mortgage loan portfolio.

Relative strength to TSE300

Price

Volume (in 1000's of board lots)

Rank (Profit/Revenue/Assets)
25   23   12

James W. Burns
Chairman Of The Board
Raymond L. McFeetors
President & C.E.O.
Mitchell T.G. Graye
Sr. V.P. & C.F.O.

Address
100 Osborne Street North
Winnipeg
MB
R3C 3A5
(204) 946-1190

Fax: (204) 946-7133
G0002778/F/13.5.2

GREAT-WEST LIFECO INC.

Period Ending	Dec94	Dec93	Dec92	Dec91	Dec90
Yearly Statistics					
Price-Close	22.13	23.00	14.75	14.00	12.25
Price-High	25.50	23.25	15.25	16.38	17.13
Price-Low	19.25	14.00	13.00	11.25	9.75
P/E-Close	9.30	11.92	13.80	9.50	8.28
Dividends per Share	0.80	0.58	0.50	0.50	0.50
Dividend Yield (%)	3.62	2.52	3.39	3.57	4.08
Sales per Share	76.97	66.92	67.94	64.93	72.30
EPS before extra. item	2.38	1.93	1.07	1.47	1.48
Cash Flow per Share	12.91	7.00	13.00	18.34	25.51
Book Value per Share	16.61	14.38	12.68	11.02	10.03
O/S Common Shares	78,845	78,841	78,834	78,826	78,813
Total Revenue	6,068,319	5,276,169	5,356,045	5,120,725	5,597,004
Income before extra.	209,842	173,312	89,822	116,173	116,682
Cash Flow	1,018,136	551,693	1,024,609	1,446,616	2,011,675
Debt/Equity	0.08	0.02	0.03	0.07	0.08
Return on Capital (%)	21.16	21.27	13.43	16.72	16.32
Ret. on Com. Equity (%)	15.34	14.26	9.02	14.01	15.47
% Change Profit	21.1	93.0	(22.7)	(0.4)	7.3
% Change Revenue	15.0	(1.5)	4.6	(8.5)	5.6
% Change Assets	12.7	31.0	14.0	(2.6)	10.7

Preferred Div. Coverage	9.3	8.2	16.2
Total Div. Coverage	2.5	2.6	2.0

5 YEAR RATIOS (%)			
Return on Capital	17.8	17.4	16.0
Return on Com. Equity	13.6	13.8	14.0
Profit Growth	14.0	12.6	7.0
Revenue Growth	2.7	1.2	2.0
Asset Growth	12.6	12.0	8.4

BALANCE SHEET (mil)			
Cash	271	197	137
Total Loans	8,183	7,781	7,789
Net Fixed Assets	624	604	588
Invest's & Advances	17,148	15,907	14,083
Total Assets	34,297	30,432	23,229
Total Deposits	0	0	0
Insurance Liability	21,886	20,995	20,159
Long Term Debt	5	32	36
Total Liabilities	32,688	28,998	22,030
Total Equity	1,609	1,434	1,199
Total Liab. & Equity	34,297	30,432	23,229

CAPITAL (mil)			
Total Debt	136	32	36
Preferred Equity	300	300	200
Common Equity	1,309	1,134	999

Business:

GREAT-WEST LIFECO INC. is a holding company. It owns 99.4% of the outstanding common shares of Great-West Life Assurance Co. of Winnipeg. In turn, Power Financial Corp. of Montreal owns 86.4% of Great-West Lifeco Inc.'s issued and outstanding common shares.

Date	EPS	DPS	Tot Rev	Inc Bex
Mar 95	0.59	0.22	1,552,966	53,462
Dec 94	0.61	0.22	1,820,539	53,715
Sep 94	0.60	0.20	1,547,538	52,790
Jun 94	0.61	0.20	1,327,945	53,815
Mar 94	0.56	0.18	1,372,297	49,522
Dec 93	0.55	0.18	1,295,572	48,835
Sep 93	0.49	0.15	1,238,181	44,445
Jun 93	0.47	0.13	1,327,358	42,576

Synopsis:

In May 1995, the President of Power Financial Corp, Robert Gratton, called on the federal government to level the playing field between banks and other financial institutions. Power Financial is the parent company of Great-West Lifeco Inc. Currently, the federal government provides funds to protect consumers against bank and trust company failures through the Canada Deposit Insurance Corp., while insurance companies have to fund their own consumer protection plan, called CompCorp. In 1994, Great-West Life and its U.S. counterparts kicked in a total of $23-million to CompCorp. There are also concerns that Ottawa may amend legislation to let banks sell insurance through their branches. This could create a conflict of interest, as confidential information customers provide when they apply for products, such as loans and mortgages, could be used by the banks to sell them insurance. This would give the banks a competitive advantage. In its brief to the Senate Committee on Banking, Trade and Commerce, Great-West Life proposed that a single crown corporation, providing financial risk insurance to both deposit-taking and insurance institutions, would be the best means of effectively addressing these concerns. It would also ensure that all consumers are equally protected when a financial institution fails.

In February 1995 Great-West Lifeco completed the sale of a new series of preferred shares worth $100-million. The investment may be used to increase the capital base of Lifeco's subsidiaries, Great West Life Assurance Co. and Great-West Life and Annuity Insurance Co., and permit them to expand their existing business activities and pursue new business opportunities. It may also be used to redeem certain of their outstanding preferred shares. Great-West Lifeco enjoys superior ratings for financial strength and claims paying ability with four out of five public rating agencies awarding them the highest rating available.

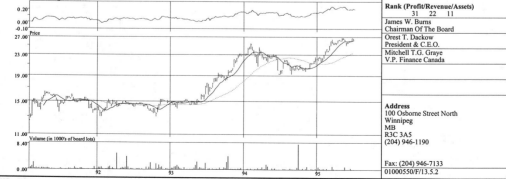

Rank (Profit/Revenue/Assets)		
31	22	11

James W. Burns
Chairman Of The Board

Orest T. Dackow
President & C.E.O.

Mitchell T.G. Graye
V.P. Finance Canada

Address
100 Osborne Street North
Winnipeg
MB
R3C 3A5
(204) 946-1190

Fax: (204) 946-7133
01000550/F/13.5.2

IMPERIAL LIFE ASSURANCE COMPANY OF CANADA (THE)

Exchanges	Price (Jun29'95)	25.00	Trailing P/E	nc	Stock Symbol
TM	Trailing Yield (%)	nc	Trailing EPS	(0.36)	IL.PR.D

Period Ending	Dec94	Dec93	Dec92	Dec91	Dec90
Yearly Statistics					
Price-Close	23.88	24.75	24.75	24.00	22.25
Price-High	26.00	26.00	25.25	24.38	23.88
Price-Low	21.75	20.13	23.25	21.75	21.00
P/E-Close	nc	nc	nc	nc	nc
Dividends per Share	nc	nc	nc	nc	nc
Dividend Yield (%)	nc	nc	nc	nc	nc
Sales per Share	614.33	620.32	691.84	695.79	786.17
EPS before extra. item	(0.69)	14.14	8.04	16.31	2.77
Cash Flow per Share	19.20	50.97	81.19	150.23	116.44
Book Value per Share	242.13	229.25	221.73	163.68	116.62
O/S Common Shares	1,813	1,813	1,634	1,634	1,634
Total Revenue	1,113,732	1,124,592	1,130,303	1,136,757	1,157,686
Income before extra.	1,694	32,758	18,393	32,394	11,346
Cash Flow	34,811	92,402	132,640	245,443	171,460
Debt/Equity	0.33	0.31	0.34	0.45	0.69
Return on Capital (%)	2.38	8.07	6.13	7.27	3.38
Ret. on Com. Equity (%)	(0.61)	6.94	4.18	11.64	2.39
% Change Profit	(94.8)	78.1	(43.2)	185.5	(55.5)
% Change Revenue	(1.0)	(0.5)	(0.6)	(1.8)	5.1
% Change Assets	3.5	3.3	3.2	(33.1)	5.1

Preferred Div. Coverage	0.4	5.7	3.5
Total Div. Coverage	0.2	3.4	1.9

5 YEAR RATIOS (%)			
Return on Capital	5.4	5.8	5.0
Return on Com. Equity	4.9	6.9	6.7
Profit Growth	(42.1)	8.9	(16.3)
Revenue Growth	0.2	(1.2)	1.4
Asset Growth	(5.0)	(5.3)	(5.9)

BALANCE SHEET (000)			
Cash	183,339	158,156	204,808
Total Loans	1,569,178	1,642,477	1,533,932
Net Fixed Assets	296,567	324,618	310,453
Invest's & Advances	2,374,010	2,165,069	2,126,253
Total Assets	4,752,076	4,591,321	4,442,623
Total Deposits	0	0	0
Insurance Liability	3,632,161	3,547,103	3,440,994
Long Term Debt	165,117	147,934	158,581
Total Liabilities	4,253,117	4,115,702	3,968,776
Total Equity	498,959	475,619	473,847
Total Liab. & Equity	4,752,076	4,591,321	4,442,623

CAPITAL (000)			
Total Debt	165,117	147,934	158,581
Preferred Equity	60,000	60,000	111,600
Common Equity	438,959	415,619	362,247

Business:

IMPERIAL LIFE ASSURANCE CO. OF CANADA issues a comprehensive line of life insurance and other financial products. As of January 1, 1994, Imperial is an indirect subsidiary of Desjardins Laurentian Financial Corporation based in Montreal. Through subsidiaries the company has offices across Canada and in the United States, the Bahamas, the United Kingdom and Hong Kong.

Date	EPS	DPS	Tot Rev	Inc Bex
Mar 95	0.51	nc	328,819	2,115
Dec 94	(1.51)	nc	577,597	(390)
Sep 94	(0.76)	nc	267,696	(141)
Jun 94	1.40	nc	265,512	2,025
Mar 94	0.44	nc	279,712	1,814
Dec 93	8.25	nc	555,657	18,641
Sep 93	2.04	nc	249,987	4,659
Jun 93	4.19	nc	268,043	8,493

Synopsis:

As a result of the 1994 merger of the member companies of The Laurentian Group with those of the Societe financiere des caisses Desjardins, Imperial Life became part of the Desjardins-Laurentian Life Group (DL Life). The DL Life will administer the Movement Desjardins' interests in the life insurance and investment management sectors. Its life insurance operations are ranked as the fifth largest in Canada. Effective December 31, 1994, Imperial Life acquired control of Laurentian Financial Services Inc. and its wholly owned subsidiary, Laurentian Funds Management Inc. Both companies operate in the Canadian mutual funds industry. In April 1995, Imperial Life sold its British unit, Laurentian Financial Group PLC, for $320-million to Lincoln National UK. In May 1995, Imperial sold its U.S. subsidiary, Laurentian Capital Corp., to American Annuity Group Inc. for $105.6-million. The sales put Imperial in a much stronger financial position. Its profits plunged to $1.7-million in 1994 from $32.8-million the previous year because of troubled commercial real estate loans. The British operation was a big drain on profits, losing $9-million in 1994, while the U.S. operation had a profit of $4-million. Movement Desjardins was to inject $35-million in capital into Imperial at the end of last year to cover losses, but the capital was unnecessary once a buyer was found for the British operation. Now with the sale of the U.S. arm, Imperial has the capital needed to expand its domestic insurance business.

Imperial Life reported net income of $2.1-million for the three months ended March 31, 1995, compared to $1.8-million a year ago. Canadian operations were mainly responsible for the $1-million decline in the consolidated net operating income, despite a significant increase in premiums. Consolidated premiums were up 26% over last year, exceeding $213-million. Canadian operations were negatively influenced by fluctuations in mortality and long-term disability experience, as well as restructuring costs. Total assets owned and under administration climbed to $10-billion at March 31, 1995.

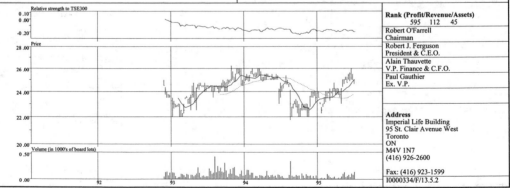

Rank (Profit/Revenue/Assets)
595   112   45

Robert O'Farrell
Chairman

Robert J. Ferguson
President & C.E.O.

Alain Thauvette
V.P. Finance & C.F.O.

Paul Gauthier
Ex. V.P.

Address
Imperial Life Building
95 St. Clair Avenue West
Toronto
ON
M4V 1N7
(416) 926-2600

Fax: (416) 923-1599
I0000334/F/13.5.2

For further company information, call Globe Information Services 1-800-268-9128 or (416) 585-5345

KRG MANAGEMENT INC.

Exchanges	Price (Jun29'95)	0.80	Trailing P/E		nm	Stock Symbol
T	Trailing Yield (%)	0.00	Trailing EPS		0.00	**KRG**

Period Ending	Ju l94	Ju l93	Ju l92	Ju l91	Ju l90
Yearly Statistics					
Price-Close	1.20	0.75	1.00	1.30	1.60
Price-High	1.67	0.90	1.70	2.25	3.75
Price-Low	0.70	0.60	0.70	1.00	1.25
P/E-Close	nm	75.00	7.14	10.00	nm
Dividends per Share	0.00	0.00	0.00	0.00	0.10
Dividend Yield (%)	0.00	0.00	0.00	0.00	6.25
Sales per Share	1.50	1.54	1.60	1.75	2.24
EPS before extra. item	(0.01)	0.01	0.14	0.13	(0.52)
Cash Flow per Share	(0.01)	0.03	0.12	0.12	(0.04)
Book Value per Share	0.76	0.77	0.77	0.68	0.50
O/S Common Shares	2,696,494	2,748,494	2,838,194	2,812,944	3,465,984
Total Revenue	4,112,259	4,344,473	4,533,319	4,960,812	6,445,142
Income before extra.	(18,028)	14,540	398,499	353,382	(1,521,469)
Cash Flow	(36,525)	96,818	334,161	330,052	(106,944)
Debt/Equity	nd	nd	0.09	0.37	0.56
Return on Capital (%)	(9.55)	(8.75)	12.37	9.18	(52.32)
Ret. on Com. Equity (%)	(0.86)	0.68	0.00	19.36	(61.32)
% Change Profit	(224.0)	(96.4)	12.8	123.2	(611.6)
% Change Revenue	(5.3)	(4.2)	(8.6)	(23.0)	(23.3)
% Change Assets	2.5	2.1	(3.9)	(17.0)	(19.7)

Preferred Div. Coverage	np	np	np
Total Div. Coverage	na	na	na

5 YEAR RATIOS (%)			
Return on Capital	(9.8)	(5.0)	7.1
Return on Com. Equity	(4.5)	(2.6)	3.2
Profit Growth	na	(52.6)	(19.7)
Revenue Growth	(13.3)	(9.5)	(7.2)
Asset Growth	(7.7)	(8.6)	5.3

BALANCE SHEET			
Cash	3,358,192	4,025,534	3,769,145
Total Loans	0	0	583,555
Net Fixed Assets	751,576	830,007	870,704
Invest's & Advances	1,003,955	1,065,486	632,752
Total Assets	9,644,288	9,410,179	9,219,162
Total Deposits	0	0	0
Insurance Liability	0	0	0
Long Term Debt	0	0	200,000
Total Liabilities	7,584,559	7,292,782	7,046,253
Total Equity	2,059,729	2,117,397	2,172,909
Total Liab. & Equity	9,644,288	9,410,179	9,219,162
CAPITAL			
Total Debt	0	0	200,000
Preferred Equity	0	0	0
Common Equity	2,059,729	2,117,397	2,172,909

Business:

KRG MANAGEMENT INC., through wholly owned KRG Insurance Brokers Inc. and 50% owned KRG Life Insurance Agency Inc., provides professional advice and the related services necessary to implement that advice in the areas of general insurance, life insurance, and employee benefits to clients throughout Canada.

Date	EPS	DPS	Tot Rev	Inc Bex
Apr 95	0.02	0.00	1,475	55
Jan 95	0.00	0.00	1,109	3
Oct 94	0.01	0.00	1,038	18
Jul 94	(0.03)	0.00	1,080	(61)
Apr 94	0.00	0.00	1,030	3
Jan 94	0.01	0.00	993	21
Oct 93	0.01	0.00	1,009	19
Jul 93	0.00	0.00	1,179	(14)

Synopsis:

In KRG Management Inc.'s 1995 second quarter report, C.E.O. Steven Wise said that over the next several months, KRG Management would add to its asset and revenue base through acquisitions in the commercial, personal and group lines of business. One month later, in April 1995, KRG Management agreed to buy the remaining 50% interest in KRG Life Insurance Agency. A total of 512,000 common shares will be issued at 60 cents per share to a group controlled by KRG Management insiders. Executive vice president and chief executive Martin Shaw and his wife would each receive 185,000 common shares, chief information officer Sheldon Robinson would receive 117,500 shares, and corporate controller Roderick MacDonald would receive 25,000 shares. All have agreed to vote their shares as directed by Mr. Shaw, pursuant to a voting trust agreement. This would give Mr. Shaw control of more than 17.8% of the 2.7 million outstanding shares of KRG Management. He currently holds 2.2%.

In the interim, KRG Life formed a technology company, Data Capture Systems Inc., to develop turnkey systems for the group insurance industry. This new venture will benefit KRG, which is continuing to forge directions in its automation services. During the past four years, KRG has invested significant amounts of time and resources into the development of automation, for which it has applied for investment tax credits in the amount of $108,000.

For the three months ended January 1995, gross revenues climbed to $1.1-million compared to $1-million a year ago. Net income before income taxes rose to $3,094 from a $17,067 loss a year earlier. Gross premiums at wholly owned KRG Insurance Brokers Inc. amounted to $6.21-million during the second quarter, compared to $5.53-million for the same period last year. On a combined basis, KRG Brokers and KRG Life recorded six month premium income of $19.82-million compared to $18.27-million a year ago.

KRG Management's current mission is growth. It currently supplies and consults on the products of more than 40 general insurance companies and 20 life insurance companies around the world.

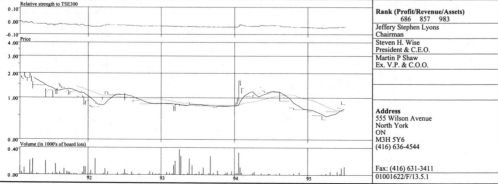

Rank (Profit/Revenue/Assets)
686   857   983

Jeffery Stephen Lyons
Chairman

Steven H. Wise
President & C.E.O.

Martin P Shaw
Ex. V.P. & C.O.O.

Address
555 Wilson Avenue
North York
ON
M3H 5Y6
(416) 636-4544

Fax: (416) 631-3411
01001622/F/13.5.1

LONDON INSURANCE GROUP INC.

Exchanges	Price (Jun29'95)	26 .25	Trailing P/E	10 .29	Stock Symbol
TMV	Trailing Yield (%)	4 .99	Trailing EPS	2 .55	LON

Period Ending	Dec94	Dec93	Dec92	Dec91	Dec90
Yearly Statistics					
Price-Close	23 .00	25 .38	21 .25	25 .00	19 .63
Price-High	27 .00	26 .50	26 .25	25 .50	22 .88
Price-Low	22 .00	19 .00	18 .50	19 .25	18 .00
P/E-Close	9 .20	9 .40	7 .99	10 .25	8 .08
Dividends per Share	1 .30	1 .30	1 .26	1 .20	1 .10
Dividend Yield (%)	5 .65	5 .12	5 .93	4 .80	5 .61
Sales per Share	115 .73	102 .15	98 .52	90 .29	97 .40
EPS before extra. item	2 .50	2 .70	2 .66	2 .44	2 .43
Cash Flow per Share	37 .10	32 .73	35 .40	26 .47	26 .12
Book Value per Share	25 .90	24 .50	23 .09	21 .74	20 .20
O/S Common Shares	39 ,660	41 ,560	41 ,834	41 ,730	36 ,432
Total Revenue	4 ,721 ,000	4 ,301 ,000	4 ,151 ,000	3 ,605 ,000	3 ,487 ,000
Income before extra.	121 ,000	132 ,000	126 ,000	116 ,000	114 ,000
Cash Flow	1 ,512 ,000	1 ,362 ,000	1 ,480 ,000	1 ,057 ,000	935 ,000
Debt/Equity	0 .50	0 .53	0 .56	0 .57	0 .56
Return on Capital (%)	7 .18	8 .34	12 .37	8 .79	8 .98
Ret. on Com. Equity (%)	9 .98	11 .39	11 .85	11 .81	12 .42
% Change Profit	(8 .3)	4 .8	8 .6	1 .8	17 .5
% Change Revenue	9 .8	3 .6	15 .1	3 .4	5 .3
% Change Assets	7 .3	5 .7	11 .1	8 .9	5 .8
Preferred Div. Coverage	6 .4	6 .9	8 .4		
Total Div. Coverage	1 .7	1 .8	1 .9		
5 YEAR RATIOS (%)					
Return on Capital	9 .1	9 .4	9 .9		
Return on Com. Equity	11 .5	12 .0	12 .1		
Profit Growth	4 .5	8 .9	10 .5		
Revenue Growth	7 .3	6 .9	9 .0		
Asset Growth	7 .7	7 .5	8 .4		
BALANCE SHEET (mil)					
Cash	579	583	505		
Total Loans	5 ,943	5 ,985	6 ,312		
Net Fixed Assets	1 ,536	1 ,525	1 ,422		
Invest's & Advances	7 ,774	7 ,247	6 ,569		
Total Assets	17 ,816	16 ,610	15 ,707		
Total Deposits	0	0	0		
Insurance Liability	14 ,092	12 ,781	12 ,625		
Long Term Debt	387	335	286		
Total Liabilities	16 ,414	15 ,217	14 ,366		
Total Equity	1 ,402	1 ,393	1 ,341		
Total Liab. & Equity	17 ,816	16 ,610	15 ,707		
CAPITAL (mil)					
Total Debt	707	734	755		
Preferred Equity	375	375	375		
Common Equity	1 ,027	1 ,018	966		

Business:

LONDON INSURANCE GROUP INC. is a life and general insurance company. It offers a full line of insurance products to individuals and groups in Canada and the United States. Operations include London Life Insurance Co., Holden Group Inc., Wellington Insurance and Meloche Monnex Inc. Trilon Financial Corporation owns 55% of the company.

Date	EPS	DPS	Tot Rev	Inc Bex
Mar 95	0 .65	0 .34	1 ,198 ,000	32 ,000
Dec 94	0 .26	0 .33	912 ,000	15 ,000
Sep 94	0 .81	0 .33	1 ,332 ,000	38 ,000
Jun 94	0 .83	0 .33	1 ,268 ,000	39 ,000
Mar 94	0 .60	0 .33	1 ,056 ,000	29 ,000
Dec 93	0 .53	0 .33	1 ,130 ,000	27 ,000
Sep 93	0 .79	0 .33	1 ,011 ,000	37 ,000
Jun 93	0 .79	0 .33	1 ,044 ,000	38 ,000

Synopsis:

Rumours that the Hees Edper conglomerate is willing to part with London Insurance Group have plagued the company for two years. Hees Edper controls London Insurance through Trilon Financial Corp. The most likely buyer for London Insurance would be one of the larger Canadian banks. Over the past few years, the banks have broadened their presence in the insurance market. The chartered banks may begin to act more aggressively by acquiring existing life insurance companies. The 1997 review of federal financial services legislation may give the banks additional powers. London Life Insurance Co., the main subsidiary of London Insurance, is vulnerable if the banks begin to sell life insurance directly due to its large sales force, which is costly to maintain. With approximately 2,500 agents, London Life holds about 15% of the individual life insurance market.

Following the February 1995 sale of general insurer Wellington Insurance Co., London Insurance now owns 98% of London Life. London Insurance continues to be profitable, but a $210-million loss on the sale of Wellington reduced 1994 profits to $121-million from $132-million a year ago. For the three months ended March 31, 1995, profits totalled $32-million compared with $29.3-million a year ago. Earnings in the life insurance segment rose 22% reflecting increased contributions from individual insurance operations, U.S. retirement products, and the international reinsurance operations. Investment earnings were enhanced by higher than anticipated bond yields. However this was offset by lower returns from the real estate and stock portfolios. Sales of retirement savings products slowed, as a result of funds being shifted to fixed rate products during the 1995 RRSP season.

In April 1995, London Life launched a new national advertising campaign, building on its Freedom 55 commercials. That campaign found success by focusing on the dreams of Canadians for the future.

Rank (Profit/Revenue/Assets)
64 31 20

Melvin M. Hawkrigg
Chairman.

Gordon R. Cunningham
President & C.E.O.

Douglas S. Alexander
Sr. V.P. & C.F.O.

Address
255 Dufferin Avenue
London
ON
N6A 4K1
(519) 432-5281

Fax: (519) 661-0479
L0000064/F/13.5.2

MICC INVESTMENTS LIMITED

Exchanges	Price (Jun29'95)	0.75	Trailing P/E	2.34	Stock Symbol
T	Trailing Yield (%)	0.00	Trailing EPS	0.32	**MIV**

Period Ending	Dec94	Dec93	Dec92	Dec91	Dec90
Yearly Statistics					
Price-Close	0.50	1.00	2.50	4.00	12.63
Price-High	1.55	3.00	6.25	16.00	14.75
Price-Low	0.50	1.00	1.90	4.00	12.00
P/E-Close	1.56	nm	nm	nm	5.56
Dividends per Share	0.00	0.00	0.00	0.40	0.80
Dividend Yield (%)	0.00	0.00	0.00	10.00	6.34
Sales per Share	1.44	1.70	2.29	2.67	2.73
EPS before extra. item	0.32	(1.43)	(3.27)	(3.83)	2.27
Cash Flow per Share	(0.71)	(1.61)	(2.14)	(3.40)	0.69
Book Value per Share	(0.07)	(0.43)	0.97	4.13	8.48
O/S Common Shares	35,445	35,445	35,444	35,444	35,361
Total Revenue	63,279	55,728	50,810	76,942	131,282
Income before extra.	12,816	(49,426)	(114,443)	(134,085)	82,152
Cash Flow	(25,192)	(57,211)	(75,649)	(120,282)	24,383
Debt/Equity	nd	13.59	0.86	0.27	0.16
Return on Capital (%)	52.76	(57.79)	(70.52)	(45.51)	18.03
Ret. on Com. Equity (%)	na	(515.47)	(127.15)	(60.79)	29.44
% Change Profit	125.9	56.8	14.6	(263.2)	(2.1)
% Change Revenue	13.6	9.7	(34.0)	(41.4)	(12.5)
% Change Assets	(11.6)	(22.3)	(16.5)	(22.8)	(32.9)

Business:

MICC INVESTMENTS LTD. operates principally through its subsidiary, The Mortgage Insurance Company of Canada (MICC). MICC provides mortgage default insurance to regulated lenders. It also provides surety bonding, excess condominium deposit and new home warranty program insurance.

Date	EPS	DPS	Tot Rev	Inc Bex
Mar 95	(0.04)	0.00	8,178	(1,070)
Dec 94	0.36	0.00	10,461	13,202
Sep 94	(0.01)	0.00	13,597	298
Jun 94	0.01	0.00	10,100	400
Mar 94	(0.04)	0.00	14,332	(1,118)
Dec 93	(0.02)	0.00	13,923	(436)
Sep 93	(0.84)	0.00	14,624	(29,549)
Jun 93	(0.44)	0.00	10,501	(15,092)

Preferred Div. Coverage	na	na	0.0		
Total Div. Coverage	na	na	0.0		

5 YEAR RATIOS (%)			
Return on Capital	(20.6)	(26.9)	(10.4)
Return on Com. Equity	na	(127.3)	(18.5)
Profit Growth	(31.4)	na	na
Revenue Growth	(15.9)	(13.1)	(10.2)
Asset Growth	(21.6)	(14.3)	(4.6)

BALANCE SHEET (000)			
Cash	9,899	9,712	12,002
Total Loans	15,211	15,813	16,350
Net Fixed Assets	1,104	1,980	2,604
Invest's & Advances	166,403	193,116	255,052
Total Assets	265,979	300,784	386,876
Total Deposits	54,743	0	0
Insurance Liability	84,793	97,944	104,674
Long Term Debt	0	49,890	45,813
Total Liabilities	249,492	297,113	333,784
Total Equity	16,487	3,671	53,092
Total Liab. & Equity	265,979	300,784	386,876

CAPITAL (000)			
Total Debt	0	49,890	45,813
Preferred Equity	18,793	18,793	18,793
Common Equity	(2,306)	(15,122)	34,299

Synopsis:

For the first quarter ended March 31, 1995, MICC reported a loss of $1.07-million or 4 cents a share. In the same period last year, the company reported a loss of $1.12-million (also 4 cents per share). Lower claims activity in all lines of The Mortgage Insurance Company of Canada resulted in losses on claims of $5.5-million in 1995 compared to $9.7-million in 1994. The decrease in investment income from $4.6-million in 1994 to $1.8-million stemmed from a $2.4-million decline in gains on sales of investments. On May 3, 1993, the insurance company suspended writing new insurance business due to a regulatory capital deficiency. Since then, its operations are funded primarily by the disposition of common and preferred share investments. The portfolio holdings in these types of investments were $93.5-million at December 31, 1994, down from $146.4-million at the end of 1993. MICC had $18.3-billion of mortgage insurance in-force at December 31, 1994, and remains responsible for the run-off of its existing in-force portfolio.

On April 6, 1994, the insurance company signed an agreement with GE Capital Mortgage Corporation for the sale of certain non-financial assets related to its residential mortgage insurance business. On January 17, 1995, the sale was completed. The selling price was $15.25-million plus $1-million as compensation for a delayed closing. The company received $8.25-million and a deferred amount of $8-million. Interest accrued at 8.44% will be received when MICC can meet its policy obligations and its minimum acid test. The insurance company has an obligation to the Canadian Insurance Group Limited, its parent company to repay notes payable on September 30, 1995. The outstanding balance at March 31, 1995, was $56.3-million and likely will require restructuring in order to deal with this maturing note obligation.

MICC's principal line of business has been homeownership mortgage insurance coverage in Canada offered to regulated lenders. At December 31, 1994, 89% of the insurance company's insurance in force consisted of mortgage insurance.

Relative strength to TSE300

Price

Volume (in 1000's of board lots)

Rank (Profit/Revenue/Assets)
266   496   305

David A. Rattee
Chairman President & C.E.O.

Address
141 Adelaide Street West
Suite 1810
Toronto
ON
M5H 3L5
(416) 977-6254

Fax: (416) 598-1967
M0003899/F/13.5.1

Page	Company		Fiscal year end	EARNINGS PER SHARE		
				Last Year	Estimate this year	Estimate next year
507	Alberta Natural Gas		Dec-94	1.23	1.50	1.62
508	Atco Ltd.		Dec-94	1.73	1.80	1.93
509	Brascade Resources		Dec-94	0.57	na	na
510	Brascan		Dec-94	1.17	2.22	2.23
511	BRL Enterprises		Dec-94	0.35	na	na
512	Canadian Pacific		Dec-94	0.95	1.39	2.02
513	Consolidated Enfield		Dec-94	0.01	na	na
514	Counsel Corporation		Dec-94	0.28	na	na
515	Dexleigh		Jun-94	0.14	na	na
516	Great Lakes Power		Dec-94	1.92	na	na
517	Harrowston		Dec-94	1.17	na	na
518	HIL Corporation		Nov-94	0.20	na	na
519	Imasco		Dec-94	4.18	4.82	5.38
520	Jannock		Dec-94	0.88	1.31	1.85
521	John Labatt		Apr-94	1.53	1.60	1.78
522	Laidlaw	$US	Aug-94	0.39	0.46	0.58
523	Noranda Inc.		Dec-94	1.33	2.37	2.77
524	Onex Corporation		Mar-94	4.42	1.37	0.90
525	Roman Corporation		Dec-94	0.24	na	na
526	Russel Metals		Dec-94	(0.25)	0.60	0.78
527	Scott's Hospitality		Apr-94	0.49	0.55	0.65
528	SeagramCompany	$US	Jan-95	2.42	1.47	1.66
529	Sherrit		Dec-94	1.07	1.89	2.14
530	United Dominion Industries	$US	Dec-94	1.52	2.05	2.44

Estimates from First Call Corporation, 22 Pittsburgh Street, Boston, MA 02210   (800) 366-9992   Fax (617) 261-5679

Management Companies

During 1994, many management companies initiated strategies to consolidate their operations, choosing to stay in only the few industries in which they remain competitive. By engaging in only a few industries, companies can focus their attention and put all their effort and resources into making their operations successful.

Most of the management companies have achieved their objective of reducing the number of industries in which they are involved. Some companies have used acquisitions to strengthen the industries in which they have chosen to remain, while a few others have made equity investments in companies that they believe will strengthen their organizations. Proceeds have been used to reduce debt and have also been used to fund acquisitions. Until likely candidates are found, some companies are holding funds in short-term investments, taking time to decide rather than make quick purchases.

Some of the management companies have simplified the organizational structure of their group of related companies, reducing levels of cross ownership among the companies. Shareholders now have a better idea of the complete holdings of an individual company as well as the share ownership of subsidiaries. A few companies changed their corporate names to better reflect their operations.

ALBERTA NATURAL GAS COMPANY LTD

Exchanges	Price (Jun29'95)	20.62	Trailing P/E	14.84	Stock Symbol
TMZV	Trailing Yield (%)	3.30	Trailing EPS	1.39	ANG

Period Ending	Dec94	Dec93	Dec92	Dec91	Dec90
Yearly Statistics					
Price-Close	15.25	16.50	15.75	13.88	12.88
Price-High	17.63	18.50	16.00	17.25	19.50
Price-Low	13.25	14.50	12.00	12.38	11.50
P/E-Close	12.40	12.41	nm	nm	10.64
Dividends per Share	0.68	0.68	0.68	0.68	0.68
Dividend Yield (%)	4.46	4.12	4.32	4.90	5.28
Sales per Share	26.40	25.81	24.18	21.39	17.70
EPS before extra. item	1.23	1.33	(0.10)	(2.00)	1.21
Cash Flow per Share	2.55	2.29	1.87	1.81	2.97
Book Value per Share	8.78	7.95	6.61	5.02	7.94
O/S Common Shares	25,705	25,698	25,654	20,990	21,233
Total Revenue	688,291	676,398	532,503	453,383	382,594
Income before extra.	31,491	34,188	(2,276)	(42,130)	25,728
Cash Flow	65,461	58,767	40,837	38,020	63,166
Debt/Equity	1.21	1.23	1.14	2.36	1.16
Return on Capital (%)	13.93	19.36	9.07	(2.62)	18.57
Ret. on Com. Equity (%)	14.65	18.30	(1.66)	(30.76)	16.02
% Change Profit	(7.9)	1,602.1	94.6	(263.8)	8.9
% Change Revenue	1.8	27.0	17.5	18.5	4.0
% Change Assets	7.0	25.8	15.2	(3.1)	18.1

Date	EPS	DPS	Tot Rev	Inc Bex
Mar 95	0.45	0.17	168,872	11,566
Dec 94	0.30	0.17	156,629	7,658
Sep 94	0.31	0.17	148,864	7,921
Jun 94	0.33	0.17	193,476	8,350
Mar 94	0.29	0.17	189,322	7,562
Dec 93	0.31	0.17	195,999	7,804
Sep 93	0.29	0.17	165,652	7,584
Jun 93	0.53	0.17	154,625	13,774

Preferred Div. Coverage	np	np	np
Total Div. Coverage	1.8	2.0	0.0
Interest Coverage	3.7	4.8	1.7
Current Ratio	1.0	1.0	1.0
Operating Margin	8.3	9.8	9.1
Asset Turnover	1.0	1.0	1.0
5 YEAR RATIOS (%)			
Return on Capital	11.7	12.6	11.4
Return on Com. Equity	3.3	3.6	2.3
Profit Growth	5.9	15.0	na
Revenue Growth	13.3	14.4	10.3
Asset Growth	12.1	11.1	5.6
BALANCE SHEET (000)			
Cash	52,120	13,668	39,501
Current Assets	199,314	191,246	179,010
Net Fixed Assets	428,230	376,474	289,752
Invest's & Advances	39,926	38,532	18,489
Total Assets	685,529	640,616	509,272
Short Term Debt	97,609	79,445	82,009
Current Liabilities	200,711	197,839	184,833
Long Term Debt	175,990	170,978	111,813
Total Liabilities	459,880	436,343	339,796
Total Equity	225,649	204,273	169,476
Total Liab. & Equity	685,529	640,616	509,272
CAPITAL (000)			
Total Debt	273,599	250,423	193,822
Preferred Equity	0	0	0
Common Equity	225,649	204,273	169,476

Business:

ALBERTA NATURAL GAS CO. LTD. operates in four business segments: pipelines; extraction; marketing; and chemicals. ANG owns and operates gas pipelines in Alberta and British Columbia. The extraction plant is located near Cochrane, Alberta. Subsidiary, Angus Chemical Company, makes and markets nitorparrafin products. TransCanada PipeLines owns 49.00% of the of ANG's shares.

Synopsis:

Alberta Natural Gas Company Ltd. (ANG) saw a 53% increase in net income from the $7.6-million reported in the first quarter of 1994 to $11.6-million reported in the first quarter of 1995. ANG's revenue declined when compared to the first three months of 1994, but this was offset by the decline in operating expenses. The decline in revenue and operating expenses was mainly due to lower natural gas prices. ANGUS Chemical generated higher sales world-wide and across all product lines due to better market conditions and market penetration. This partially offset the decline in revenue from lower natural gas prices. The completion of the Cochrane Recommissioning Project, which increased natural gas liquids production capacity by over 40%, resulted in a higher operating income being reported by the Extraction segment. The higher production of gas liquids resulted in higher sales volumes for the marketing segment. With continued strong prices for gas liquids, the marketing segment reported a higher operating income. All segments reported higher operating incomes.

The Cochrane Recommissioning project was completed and in service by November 1, 1994, at a cost of $53-million. An additional $3-million was spent during 1995. The Extraction segment has budgeted a further $3-million for sustaining capital expenditures in 1995. ANGUS will spend $23-million on capital expenditures for 1995. The major projects include the construction of a pilot plant at its Sterlington, Louisiana, facility. The plant will facilitate new market and product development and provide processing scale-up data. ANGUS spends approximately 4% of sales revenue on research and development, as part of a long-term strategy to develop nitroparaffin products. A pipeline expansion may be required in 1996 or 1997 as market demand is growing again. The budgeted capital expenditures totalling $45-million for 1995 will primarily be financed through cash flow from operations.

Contributions to operating revenue (operating income) for 1994 by industry segment were: Extraction, 24% (33%); Marketing and Services, 42% (16%); Chemicals, 24% (27%); Pipeline, 10% (24%).

Relative strength to TSE300

Price

Volume (in 1000's of board lots)

Rank (Profit/Revenue/Assets)
149   155   194

Gerald J. Maier
Chairman

Wayne E. Lunt
President & C.E.O.

Address
Suite 2900
240 - 4th Avenue S.W.
Calgary
AB
T2P 4L7
(403) 691-7777

Fax: (403) 691-7893
A0004223/G/14.0

ATCO LTD.

Exchanges	Price (Jun29'95)	16.75	Trailing P/E	9.15	Stock Symbol
TMZ	Trailing Yield (%)	1.79	Trailing EPS	1.83	**ACO.X**

Period Ending	Dec94	Dec93	Dec92	Dec91	Dec90
Yearly Statistics					
Price-Close	15.00	16.75	12.25	12.00	12.00
Price-High	16.75	17.00	12.63	14.25	12.25
Price-Low	12.00	11.50	10.50	11.00	9.38
P/E-Close	8.67	10.67	8.57	9.16	10.00
Dividends per Share	0.27	0.24	0.24	0.24	0.24
Dividend Yield (%)	1.80	1.43	1.96	2.00	2.00
Sales per Share	66.50	59.08	51.51	47.99	47.63
EPS before extra. item	1.73	1.57	1.43	1.31	1.20
Cash Flow per Share	12.88	12.55	11.67	10.02	9.49
Book Value per Share	15.12	13.71	13.03	11.80	10.78
O/S Common Shares	30,425	30,415	30,297	30,297	30,275
Total Revenue	2,058,000	1,807,600	1,595,327	1,497,968	1,489,698
Income before extra.	52,600	47,600	43,386	39,738	41,542
Cash Flow	392,000	380,800	353,580	303,676	287,351
Debt/Equity	3.21	3.63	3.67	3.79	4.08
Return on Capital (%)	19.21	18.25	17.21	16.09	17.32
Ret. on Com. Equity (%)	12.00	11.73	11.53	11.57	11.63
% Change Profit	10.5	9.7	9.2	(4.3)	(28.4)
% Change Revenue	13.9	13.3	6.5	0.6	5.3
% Change Assets	1.7	5.0	5.0	(1.5)	4.5

Preferred Div. Coverage	np	np	np
Total Div. Coverage	6.4	6.5	6.0
Interest Coverage	2.4	2.3	2.1
Current Ratio	1.5	1.2	1.2
Operating Margin	24.4	26.6	26.8
Asset Turnover	0.5	0.5	0.4
5 YEAR RATIOS (%)			
Return on Capital	17.6	17.6	17.1
Return on Com. Equity	11.7	11.4	6.9
Profit Growth	(1.9)	83.4	100.6
Revenue Growth	7.7	5.4	2.7
Asset Growth	2.8	4.0	3.7
BALANCE SHEET (000)			
Cash	99,700	35,000	14,437
Current Assets	468,700	383,900	330,837
Net Fixed Assets	3,193,100	3,245,600	3,125,540
Invest's & Advances	71,400	50,400	38,749
Total Assets	3,879,900	3,814,800	3,633,460
Short Term Debt	7,200	38,300	26,353
Current Liabilities	302,600	316,800	272,442
Long Term Debt	1,469,600	1,475,500	1,420,573
Total Liabilities	3,419,900	3,397,900	3,238,613
Total Equity	460,000	416,900	394,847
Total Liab. & Equity	3,879,900	3,814,800	3,633,460
CAPITAL (000)			
Total Debt	1,476,800	1,513,800	1,446,926
Preferred Equity	0	0	0
Common Equity	460,000	416,900	394,847

Business:

ATCO LTD. is a diversified company with four operating groups. Canadian Utilities is a gas and electric utility. Frontec Logistics Corp. provides management, operation, maintenance and technical services. ATCO Structures Inc. manufactures, sells and leases industri al workforce housing. ATCOR Resources is engaged in oil and gas exploration, production and in marketing and processing natural gas.

Date	EPS	DPS	Tot Rev	Inc Bex
Mar 95	0.85	0.09	563,500	31,200
Dec 94	0.71	0.07	604,716	21,645
Sep 94	0.10	0.07	399,329	8,840
Jun 94	0.17	0.07	414,994	11,029
Mar 94	0.75	0.06	611,400	28,500
Dec 93	0.46	0.06	528,132	13,959
Sep 93	0.22	0.06	368,214	12,449
Jun 93	0.19	0.06	382,667	11,704

Synopsis:

ATCO Ltd.'s reported improved results for the first quarter of 1995, compared to the same period in 1994. These were attributed to a number of factors including higher earnings from ATCO structures Inc. and ATCOR Resources Ltd. plus increased investment income in ATCO Ltd. Results for the first three quarters may not be compared with the prior year. They also are not indicative of the full year results due to seasonal factors as well as the timing of general rate applications for ATCO's utility subsidiaries.

The Barking Power Plant in London, England, is complete, and the official opening is October 1995. The ATCO Group has a 25.5% equity interest in the plant with a 15-year contract to operate the plant after commissioning. ATCO Ltd. sold its 50% interest in Frontec Logistics Corp. and its property management operations to Canadian Utilities for $35.7-million. The company issued 935,679 Class A non-voting shares and 599,756 Class B common shares of CanUtilities to make the payment. CU purchased ATCO's property management operations on Frontec's behalf. Frontec became a wholly owned subsidiary of CU as a result of the purchase.

ATCO Enterprises Inc. sold its North American space rentals business to GE Capital Modular Space for $103.6-million in November 1994. The gain on sale before income taxes was $17.2-million. The proceeds allowed ATCO to reduce debt by $49.3-million and increase cash reserves by $44.1-million. Increasing competition and diminishing returns in the near future led to the decision to sell. ATCO will use the reserve to redeem CanUtilities Holdings Ltd. preferred shares. ATCO Enterprises amalgamated with ATCO and ATCO Enterprises transferred its Workforce Housing and Noise Management operations to ATCO Structures Inc., a new subsidiary.

Contributions to revenues (operating profit) in 1994 by industry were: Electric Power 32% (54%), Natural Gas 44% (33%), Manufacturing and Leasing 5% (2%), Oil and Gas 13% (7%), and Other, 6% (4%).

Rank (Profit/Revenue/Assets)
112 66 56

R.D. Southern
Chairman & C.E.O.
J.D. Wood
President & C.O.O.
C.S. Richardson
Sr. V.P. Finance & C.F.O.

Address
1600 Canadian Western Centre
909 - 11th Avenue S.W.
Calgary
AB
T2R 1N6
(403) 292-7500

Fax: (403) 292-7507
A0015607/G/14.0

BRASCADE RESOURCES INC.

Exchanges	Price (Jun29'95)	38.62	Trailing P/E	nc	Stock Symbol
TV	Trailing Yield (%)	nc	Trailing EPS	1.25	BCA.PR.A

Period Ending	Dec94	Dec93	Dec92	Dec91	Dec90
Yearly Statistics					
Price-Close	38.50	38.50	35.00	36.00	38.00
Price-High	40.50	39.25	37.38	39.13	40.50
Price-Low	37.00	32.00	30.00	29.00	32.00
P/E-Close	nc	nc	nc	nc	nc
Dividends per Share	nc	nc	nc	nc	nc
Dividend Yield (%)	nc	nc	nc	nc	nc
Sales per Share	0.49	0.46	1.30	1.66	2.19
EPS before extra. item	0.57	(1.47)	(1.15)	(3.34)	(1.89)
Cash Flow per Share	0.98	0.99	1.39	1.03	1.79
Book Value per Share	10.74	10.17	11.64	12.78	17.24
O/S Common Shares	66,998	66,998	66,998	66,999	51,407
Total Revenue	157,000	22,200	120,200	83,400	183,000
Income before extra.	93,900	(42,500)	(20,500)	(123,500)	(36,300)
Cash Flow	65,800	66,000	93,000	60,800	92,200
Debt/Equity	0.07	0.06	0.13	0.33	0.27
Return on Capital (%)	6.94	(2.26)	0.20	(3.15)	(0.78)
Ret. on Com. Equity (%)	5.48	(13.46)	(9.38)	(20.67)	(10.41)
% Change Profit	320.9	(107.3)	83.4	(240.2)	(128.5)
% Change Revenue	607.2	(81.5)	44.1	(54.4)	(51.6)
% Change Assets	3.5	(13.1)	(23.7)	(0.3)	(8.8)

Date	EPS	DPS	Tot Rev	Inc Bex
Mar 95	0.55	nc	78,600	50,700
Dec 94	0.54	nc	76,700	50,100
Sep 94	0.02	nc	28,400	15,300
Jun 94	0.14	nc	35,400	23,500
Mar 94	(0.13)	nc	16,500	5,000
Dec 93	(0.12)	nc	16,800	6,900
Sep 93	(0.36)	nc	(800)	(11,200)
Jun 93	(0.39)	nc	3,600	(11,600)

Preferred Div. Coverage	1.7	0.0	0.0
Total Div. Coverage	1.7	0.0	0.0
Interest Coverage	14.5	0.0	0.2
Current Ratio	1.8	3.2	1.0
Operating Margin	(59.9)	(87.1)	(26.2)
Asset Turnover	0.0	0.0	0.0
5 YEAR RATIOS (%)			
Return on Capital	0.2	0.5	1.9
Return on Com. Equity	(9.7)	(9.3)	(6.4)
Profit Growth	(5.9)	na	na
Revenue Growth	(16.1)	(44.2)	(17.8)
Asset Growth	(9.1)	(10.0)	(6.3)
BALANCE SHEET (000)			
Cash	7,600	12,100	45,400
Current Assets	55,000	38,000	83,600
Net Fixed Assets	167,400	169,600	173,700
Invest's & Advances	1,434,800	1,393,300	1,585,500
Total Assets	1,657,200	1,600,900	1,842,800
Short Term Debt	6,300	4,700	65,000
Current Liabilities	31,300	11,900	86,600
Long Term Debt	90,300	78,500	125,700
Total Liabilities	263,000	242,200	377,800
Total Equity	1,394,200	1,358,700	1,465,000
Total Liab. & Equity	1,657,200	1,600,900	1,842,800
CAPITAL (000)			
Total Debt	96,600	83,200	190,700
Preferred Equity	674,500	677,400	685,400
Common Equity	719,700	681,300	779,600

Business:

BRASCADE RESOURCES INC. is a natural resources investment company which owns a 31% interest in Noranda Inc. and a 76% interest in Westmin Resources Limited.

Synopsis:

Brascade reported a net income of $94-million in 1994, compared to a loss of $43-million in 1993. The results were mainly due to improved productivity, higher prices for base metals and forest products, and more favourable currency exchange rates. Noranda reported net income of $330-million in 1994, which included net investment gains of $27-million on the sale of Norandex and Central Canada Potash as well as the dilution of its ownership interest in Falconbridge. Operating earnings increased from $116-million in 1993 to $314-million due to higher prices and continued strength in the lumber and panelboard markets. The Mining and Metals operating earnings had the greatest increase, to $229-million in 1994 from $212-million in 1993. However, oil and gas operations had a loss of $25-million in 1994 as a result of lower natural gas prices, higher depletion taxes, and a $61-million charge associated with the restructuring of Norcen Energy Resources.

Westmin recorded a loss of $25-million in 1994 compared to a loss of $27-million in 1993. The shut-down of the mine at Myra Falls, following the labour reduction that began in 1993, reduced its operating losses. Lower operating results from Premier Gold and lower investment income partly offset the relative improvement at Myra Falls. The Myra Falls labour dispute was settled by arbitration in 1994, and mine operations commenced in October on a significantly improved basis. Premier Gold obtained custom milling contracts for its mill in British Columbia.

Brascade expects prices to be higher, on average, than in 1994 for most of the company's natural resources. Noranda is well positioned to benefit from this improvement. The company expects Westmin to return to increased profitability due to higher base metal prices and improved mining and work methods at Myra Falls. The higher operating results expected in most operations should lead to improved results for Brascade in 1995.

Rank (Profit/Revenue/Assets)
80   350   119

Paul M. Marshall
Chairman & President

Edward C. Kress
Vice President Finance

Address
BCE Place - Suite 4400
P.O. Box 762
181 Bay Street
Toronto
ON
M5J 2T3
(416) 363-9491
Fax: (416) 363-2856
B0003263/G/14.0

BRASCAN LIMITED

Exchanges	Price (Jun29'95)	21.62	Trailing P/E	13.86	Stock Symbol
TMA	Trailing Yield (%)	4.81	Trailing EPS	1.56	**BL.A**

Period Ending	Dec94	Dec93	Dec92	Dec91	Dec90
Yearly Statistics					
Price-Close	20.38	16.00	13.75	18.25	15.63
Price-High	21.00	16.75	20.00	20.38	26.25
Price-Low	16.13	8.25	12.50	14.25	14.00
P/E-Close	17.42	15.84	nm	nm	39.06
Dividends per Share	1.04	1.04	1.04	1.04	1.04
Dividend Yield (%)	5.10	6.50	7.56	5.70	6.66
Sales per Share	na	na	na	na	na
EPS before extra. item	1.17	1.01	(1.56)	(0.60)	0.40
Cash Flow per Share	1.76	2.23	2.30	2.06	2.77
Book Value per Share	18.63	18.51	18.51	21.20	23.08
O/S Common Shares	87,861	87,790	87,773	87,658	81,213
Total Revenue	275,600	48,100	107,700	249,200	373,100
Income before extra.	121,300	109,300	(113,400)	(17,700)	80,300
Cash Flow	154,300	195,400	201,700	173,700	225,200
Debt/Equity	0.54	0.61	0.67	0.60	0.58
Return on Capital (%)	5.96	4.52	(1.15)	2.78	5.48
Ret. on Com. Equity (%)	6.29	5.44	(7.86)	(2.74)	1.69
% Change Profit	11.0	196.4	(540.7)	(122.0)	(71.4)
% Change Revenue	473.0	(55.3)	(56.8)	(33.2)	(39.6)
% Change Assets	(3.2)	(10.8)	(6.2)	(8.3)	(4.6)
Preferred Div. Coverage	6.5	5.2	0.0		
Total Div. Coverage	1.1	1.0	0.0		
Interest Coverage	3.2	2.4	0.0		
Current Ratio	2.2	8.7	6.3		
Operating Margin	na	na	na		
Asset Turnover	na	na	na		
5 YEAR RATIOS (%)					
Return on Capital	3.5	4.6	5.9		
Return on Com. Equity	0.6	1.8	3.4		
Profit Growth	(15.5)	(16.1)	na		
Revenue Growth	(14.9)	(40.4)	(24.8)		
Asset Growth	(6.7)	(2.0)	(0.9)		
BALANCE SHEET (000)					
Cash	30,900	28,800	323,800		
Current Assets	136,000	362,900	346,800		
Net Fixed Assets	167,400	169,600	173,800		
Invest's & Advances	3,911,100	3,838,800	4,383,300		
Total Assets	4,244,800	4,386,900	4,920,300		
Short Term Debt	3,800	0	1,700		
Current Liabilities	63,100	41,600	54,800		
Long Term Debt	1,077,200	1,166,800	1,340,600		
Total Liabilities	2,229,300	2,483,100	2,918,500		
Total Equity	2,015,500	1,903,800	2,001,800		
Total Liab. & Equity	4,244,800	4,386,900	4,920,300		
CAPITAL (000)					
Total Debt	1,081,000	1,166,800	1,342,300		
Preferred Equity	378,700	278,900	377,300		
Common Equity	1,636,800	1,624,900	1,624,500		

Business:

BRASCAN LTD. is a diversified company operating primarily in the mining and metals, forest products, oil and gas, financial services and power generating sectors. The company has equity interests in Noranda Inc., Westmin Resources Ltd., Trilon Financial Corp., and Great Lakes Power Inc.

Date	EPS	DPS	Tot Rev	Inc Bex
Mar 95	0.53	0.26	109,700	55,000
Dec 94	0.36	0.26	77,100	39,500
Sep 94	0.31	0.26	72,000	31,000
Jun 94	0.36	0.26	71,400	35,600
Mar 94	0.14	0.26	57,100	15,200
Dec 93	0.02	0.26	35,400	6,500
Sep 93	(0.20)	0.26	17,100	(19,000)
Jun 93	(0.23)	0.26	17,200	(14,900)

Synopsis:

Brascan reported net income of $55-million for the first quarter of 1995 compared to $15.2-million for the comparative period in 1994. The improvement was due, in part, to the continued strength of natural resource products' prices. Base metal and natural gas prices were down, but pulp and newsprint and oil prices were higher.

Brascan received $200-million from Great Lakes Power, $66-million from Trilon, and $250-million from its John Labatt installment receipts. The funds were used to reduce short-term debt, acquire $174-million of minority interests, and to increase ownership in some of its corporate investments. Brascan increased its interest in Great Lakes Power from 34% to 45% through the purchase of common shares. Brascan increased its ownership in Westmin from 74% to 76% by participating in the company's dividend reinvestment program and converting preferred shares into common shares. Trilon completed a common share rights offering that resulted in Brascan's ownership increasing to 56% from 48%.

Brascan's improvement in net income for 1994 reflects higher base metal prices and more favourable exchange rates. Natural resources operations were also helped by improved forest product results. Gentra's return to a profitable situation in the fourth quarter of 1994 and the steady results from insurance operations created the positive contribution from the financial services operations. Noranda Minerals was split into two new companies, Noranda Mining and Exploration and Noranda Metallurgy, to better pursue the individual business goals of both companies. Brascan Brazil's results continued to improve; equity capital had increased to $331- million at the end of 1994 but was being carried at $103-million on Brascan's consolidated accounts.

Brascan's unaudited share of group revenues (operating income before unallocated expenses) by industry segment in 1994 was: Natural resources, 48% (51%); Financial services, 42% (12%); Power generation, 2% (18%); Brazilian operations, 7% (3%); Investment and other income, 1% (16%).

Rank (Profit/Revenue/Assets)
63   268   51

J. Trevor Eyton
Chairman

Jack L. Cockwell
President & C.E.O.

Aaron W. Regent
C.F.O. & Sr. V.P.

Address
BCE Place - Suite 4400
P.O. Box 762
181 Bay Street
Toronto
ON
M5J 2T3
(416) 363-9491
Fax: (416) 363-2856
B0003334/G/14.0

BRL ENTERPRISES INC.

Exchanges	Price (Jun29'95)	3.80	Trailing P/E	9.50	Stock Symbol
TQ	Trailing Yield (%)	0.00	Trailing EPS	0.40	BRL

Period Ending	Dec94	Dec93	Dec92	Dec91	Dec90
Yearly Statistics					
Price-Close	4.10	3.50	2.60	2.85	3.00
Price-High	4.45	3.95	3.10	3.25	12.50
Price-Low	3.15	2.40	2.45	2.50	1.75
P/E-Close	11.71	13.46	7.43	9.83	nm
Dividends per Share	0.00	0.00	0.00	0.00	0.00
Dividend Yield (%)	0.00	0.00	0.00	0.00	0.00
Sales per Share	na	na	na	na	1.49
EPS before extra. item	0.35	0.26	0.35	0.29	(1.83)
Cash Flow per Share	0.35	0.26	0.25	0.38	1.23
Book Value per Share	5.99	5.65	5.38	5.03	4.73
O/S Common Shares	5,806	5,806	5,806	5,806	5,806
Total Revenue	2,234	1,882	2,799	3,081	741
Income before extra.	2,010	1,530	2,054	2,212	(8,661)
Cash Flow	2,010	1,530	1,441	2,212	6,668
Debt/Equity	nd	nd	nd	nd	nd
Return on Capital (%)	6.01	4.88	7.10	5.42	(13.09)
Ret. on Com. Equity (%)	5.95	4.78	6.80	6.04	(41.99)
% Change Profit	31.4	(25.5)	(7.1)	125.5	(3,819.0)
% Change Revenue	18.7	(32.8)	(9.2)	315.8	(94.5)
% Change Assets	5.9	4.5	6.0	(44.3)	(33.2)
Preferred Div. Coverage	np	np	np		
Total Div. Coverage	na	na	na		
Interest Coverage	nd	nd	nd		
Current Ratio	17.1	9.9	5.3		
Operating Margin	na	na	na		
Asset Turnover	na	na	na		
5 YEAR RATIOS (%)					
Return on Capital	2.1	1.0	(5.8)		
Return on Com. Equity	(3.7)	na	na		
Profit Growth	na	na	na		
Revenue Growth	(30.0)	(28.5)	(25.1)		
Asset Growth	(15.3)	(20.8)	(27.8)		
BALANCE SHEET (000)					
Cash	5,751	3,740	2,248		
Current Assets	6,196	4,044	2,611		
Net Fixed Assets	0	0	0		
Invest's & Advances	28,957	29,009	29,009		
Total Assets	35,153	33,188	31,747		
Short Term Debt	0	0	0		
Current Liabilities	363	408	497		
Long Term Debt	0	0	0		
Total Liabilities	363	408	497		
Total Equity	34,790	32,780	31,250		
Total Liab. & Equity	35,153	33,188	31,747		
CAPITAL (000)					
Total Debt	0	0	0		
Preferred Equity	0	0	0		
Common Equity	34,790	32,780	31,250		

Business:

BRL ENTERPRISES INC., formerly Bralorne Resources Ltd., is primarily an investment company. The company's major shareholder is B.C. Pacific Capital Corp. of Vancouver.

Date	EPS	DPS	Tot Rev	Inc Bex
Mar 95	0.12	0.00	759	685
Dec 94	0.10	0.00	632	552
Sep 94	0.09	0.00	602	548
Jun 94	0.09	0.00	561	511
Mar 94	0.07	0.00	439	399
Dec 93	0.06	0.00	502	375
Sep 93	0.06	0.00	420	365
Jun 93	0.06	0.00	430	339

Synopsis:

BRL Enterprises reviewed a number of profitable investment opportunities in 1994 that would establish a new industry focus and long-term direction for the company. However, the company found it would not be appropriate to pursue them at this time. The operations either were not attractive, or the transaction prices were in excess of what BRL considered to be reasonable. BRL prefers to take a conservative approach with its capital and continues to maintain its portfolio of preferred shares. However, the company continues to search for new investment or acquisition opportunities that meet its investment criteria. BRL also will examine other strategies that will enhance shareholder value.

BRL held an investment portfolio at December 31, 1994, that consisted of 797,900 Noranda Forest Class A Series 1 Preferred Shares, 73,000 Canadian Imperial Bank of Commerce Class A Series 4 Preferred Shares and 72,000 Brascade Resources Class B Retractable Preferred Shares.

Higher interest rates increased revenues in the investment portfolio as some of the preferred share dividends are adjusted to movements in the bank prime rate. Administration expenses of $196,000 in 1994 were 38% lower than the $319,000 recorded in 1993. The 1994 amount included one time pension costs, of $47,000 for former employees. The cash flow from operations was approximately $2,010,000 in 1994 compared to $1,530,000 in 1993. Investments included $22.8-million in securities of related parties. Revenues for 1994 included $1,489,800 received from related parties.

Rank (Profit/Revenue/Assets)
605   928   745

Brian G. Kenning
President
Terrence A. Lyons
V.P. Finance & Secretary

Address
1632 - 1055 West Georgia St.
Box 11179
Royal Centre
Vancouver
BC
V6E 3R5
(604) 669-3141
Fax: (604) 687-3419
B0003001/G/14.0

CANADIAN PACIFIC LIMITED

Exchanges	Price (Jun29'95)	23 .62	Trailing P/E	19 .85	Stock Symbol
TMVZN	Trailing Yield (%)	1 .35	Trailing EPS	1 .19	**CP**

Period Ending	Dec94	Dec93	Dec92	Dec91	Dec90	Business:
Yearly Statistics						CANADIAN PACIFIC Ltd. is a diversified
Price-Close	20 .88	21 .63	16 .13	18 .00	19 .75	company. It is active in transportation (CP Rail
Price-High	24 .75	23 .13	19 .38	23 .25	26 .63	System, CP Ships); energy (PanCanadian
Price-Low	19 .25	15 .88	13 .50	16 .38	17 .25	Petroleum and Fording Coal); real estate and
P/E-Close	18 .00	nm	nm	nm	17 .79	hotels (Marathon Realty and Canadian Pacific
Dividends per Share	0 .32	0 .32	0 .32	0 .63	0 .92	Hotels & Resorts); telecommunications
Dividend Yield (%)	1 .53	1 .48	1 .98	3 .50	4 .66	(Unitel); and waste and passenger services
Sales per Share	20 .90	19 .85	22 .51	31 .62	32 .75	(Laidlaw Inc.).
EPS before extra. item	1 .16	(0 .60)	(1 .50)	(2 .87)	1 .11	
Cash Flow per Share	3 .85	3 .41	2 .42	2 .36	3 .95	
Book Value per Share	19 .89	18 .84	19 .74	21 .02	24 .55	
O/S Common Shares	342	319	319	319	318	
Total Revenue	7 ,249	6 ,477	7 ,285	10 ,370	10 ,620	
Income before extra.	393	(191)	(478)	(914)	355	
Cash Flow	1 ,301	1 ,089	771	752	1 ,259	

Date	EPS	DPS	Tot Rev	Inc Bex
Mar 95	0 .08	0 .08	1 ,722 ,000	27 ,400
Dec 94	0 .29	0 .08	1 ,884 ,000	100 ,000
Sep 94	0 .22	0 .08	1 ,786 ,800	77 ,500
Jun 94	0 .60	0 .08	2 ,003 ,100	198 ,400
Mar 94	0 .05	0 .08	1 ,593 ,300	17 ,200
Dec 93	(0 .37)	0 .08	1 ,724 ,500	(117 ,500)
Sep 93	(0 .33)	0 .08	1 ,628 ,000	(106 ,800)
Jun 93	0 .03	0 .08	1 ,665 ,200	12 ,000

	Dec94	Dec93	Dec92	
Debt/Equity	0 .75	1 .04	1 .27	1 .16	0 .78
Return on Capital (%)	8 .69	3 .18	(0 .29)	(3 .67)	8 .75
Ret. on Com. Equity (%)	6 .13	(3 .10)	(7 .37)	(12 .60)	4 .55
% Change Profit	306 .2	60 .2	47 .7	(357 .2)	(52 .3)
% Change Revenue	11 .9	(11 .1)	(29 .8)	(2 .4)	(5 .2)
% Change Assets	(1 .3)	(15 .5)	(1 .5)	1 .8	6 .2

				Synopsis:
Preferred Div. Coverage	786 .2	0 .0	0 .0	
Total Div. Coverage	3 .6	0 .0	0 .0	
Interest Coverage	2 .1	0 .7	0 .0	
Current Ratio	1 .2	0 .9	1 .1	
Operating Margin	15 .8	14 .7	2 .3	
Asset Turnover	0 .4	0 .4	0 .4	
5 YEAR RATIOS (%)				
Return on Capital	3 .3	4 .3	6 .6	
Return on Com. Equity	(2 .5)	(1 .7)	1 .3	
Profit Growth	(12 .0)	na	na	
Revenue Growth	(8 .4)	(10 .0)	(9 .8)	
Asset Growth	(2 .4)	(0 .6)	2 .3	
BALANCE SHEET (mil)				
Cash	1 ,287	1 ,668	1 ,387	
Current Assets	2 ,619	2 ,690	3 ,090	
Net Fixed Assets	12 ,678	12 ,193	15 ,094	
Invest's & Advances	1 ,134	1 ,380	1 ,107	
Total Assets	16 ,912	17 ,134	20 ,275	
Short Term Debt	378	1 ,403	844	
Current Liabilities	2 ,162	2 ,990	2 ,824	
Long Term Debt	4 ,748	4 ,869	7 ,194	
Total Liabilities	10 ,098	11 ,104	13 ,962	
Total Equity	6 ,814	6 ,031	6 ,313	
Total Liab. & Equity	16 ,912	17 ,134	20 ,275	
CAPITAL (mil)				
Total Debt	5 ,126	6 ,272	8 ,038	
Preferred Equity	15	15	15	
Common Equity	6 ,799	6 ,016	6 ,299	

Synopsis:

Canadian Pacific granted Rogers Communications an option to buy its 48% interest in Unitel for $200-million, but by the deadline of April 28, 1995, the option had not been exercised. Canadian Pacific will not invest any more money in Unitel because it is a non-core asset. Unitel and Canadian Pacific continue to look for a buyer for the 48% interest.

The federal government rejected CP Rail System's offer to purchase Canadian National's eastern rail operations. CP Rail's plan would have privatized CN's eastern operation and made it possible to privatize the western operations in the near term. CP supports the privatization of CN but does not want to see a recapitalized CN gain an unfair advantage over CP Rail. The fundamental issue of overcapacity in the eastern rail network remains unresolved.

Canadian Pacific bought Cast's container business, its brand name, and its operating assets for an undisclosed sum in March 1995. The purchase strengthened CP's position in the North Atlantic container trade, where it was already a significant force with Canadian Maritime. Canadian Maritime, the wholly owned shipping unit of Canadian Pacific, said it would invest $50-million in Cast. The two companies will be run separately. By operating the companies separately, CP will be able to maximize opportunities for shippers in the highly competitive routes between Europe and North America.

Operating income was slightly lower for the first quarter of 1995, at $222.9-million, compared to the first quarter of 1994, at $229.1-million. This was due mainly to labour disruptions affecting CP Rail Systems and CP Ships. The Transportation segment's operating income dropped from $95.8-million in first quarter 1994 to $58-million in first quarter 1995 due in part to the 19-day industry wide rail strike-lockout, and 17-day longshoremen strike. The Energy segment had operating earnings rise from $100.9-million to $139.4-million, due mostly to PanCanadian's $34-million increase.

Relative strength to TSE300

Price

Volume (in 1000's of board lots)

Rank (Profit/Revenue/Assets)
14   16   21
W.W. Stinson
Chairman & C.E.O.
D. O'Brien
President & C.O.O.
W.R. Fatt
Exec. V.P. & C.F.O.

Address
Suite 800, Place Du Canada
P.O. Box 6042
Station Centre-Ville
Montreal
PQ
H3C 3E4
(514) 395-6691
Fax: (514) 395-7306
C0004081/G/14.0

CONSOLIDATED ENFIELD CORP. LTD.

Exchanges	Price (Jun29'95)	0.28	Trailing P/E		nm	Stock Symbol
T	Trailing Yield (%)	0.00	Trailing EPS		(0.10)	CEZ

Period Ending	Dec94	Dec93	Dec92	Dec91	Dec90	Business:
Yearly Statistics						CONSOLIDATED ENFIELD CORP. LTD. is a
Price-Close	0.27	0.33	0.41	1.10	2.30	holding company with interests in the
Price-High	0.65	0.65	1.50	3.30	25.50	manufacturing sector.
Price-Low	0.22	0.16	0.15	0.81	1.90	
P/E-Close	27.00	nm	nm	nm	nm	
Dividends per Share	0.00	0.00	0.00	0.00	0.00	
Dividend Yield (%)	0.00	0.00	0.00	0.00	0.00	
Sales per Share	na	na	na	40.81	62.70	
EPS before extra. item	0.01	(1.28)	(3.71)	(14.53)	(1.78)	
Cash Flow per Share	(0.06)	0.06	(0.18)	(3.08)	(2.22)	
Book Value per Share	(3.82)	(4.09)	(3.08)	0.36	14.84	
O/S Common Shares	10,927	10,926	10,926	10,926	10,926	
Total Revenue	3,372	5,184	5,999	445,863	636,035	

Income before extra.	2,968	(11,055)	(37,608)	(155,856)	(14,864)		Date	EPS	DPS	Tot Rev	Inc Bex
Cash Flow	(690)	661	(2,017)	(33,627)	(22,224)		Mar 95	0.08	0.00	2,662	1,602
Debt/Equity	146.98	na	6.98	8.54	2.18		Dec 94	0.00	0.00	684	644
Return on Capital (%)	15.83	(17.55)	(12.75)	(23.05)	4.43		Sep 94	(0.09)	0.00	993	(214)
Ret. on Com. Equity (%)	na	na	na	(190.36)	(11.27)		Jun 94	(0.09)	0.00	885	(182)
% Change Profit	126.8	70.6	75.9	(948.5)	52.3		Mar 94	0.19	0.00	3,331	2,720
% Change Revenue	(35.0)	(13.6)	(98.7)	(29.9)	(0.2)		Dec 93	0.76	0.00	819	9,076
% Change Assets	(25.0)	(39.9)	(83.5)	(29.0)	(4.8)		Sep 93	0.17	0.00	2,104	2,533
							Jun 93	(2.11)	0.00	1,120	(22,321)

				Synopsis:
Preferred Div. Coverage	na	na	na	
Total Div. Coverage	na	na	na	
Interest Coverage	2.4	0.0	0.0	
Current Ratio	na	0.2	0.9	
Operating Margin	na	na	na	
Asset Turnover	na	na	na	
5 YEAR RATIOS (%)				
Return on Capital	(6.6)	(10.0)	(6.6)	
Return on Com. Equity	na	na	na	
Profit Growth	na	na	na	
Revenue Growth	(68.7)	(62.9)	(60.2)	
Asset Growth	(45.3)	(41.2)	(35.5)	
BALANCE SHEET (000)				
Cash	0	7,166	40,254	
Current Assets	0	7,166	52,444	
Net Fixed Assets	0	0	17,349	
Invest's & Advances	38,066	43,237	33,938	
Total Assets	46,764	62,315	103,731	
Short Term Debt	2,291	16,931	32,989	
Current Liabilities	10,479	29,583	59,460	
Long Term Debt	22,990	24,626	24,819	
Total Liabilities	46,592	65,111	95,451	
Total Equity	172	(2,796)	8,280	
Total Liab. & Equity	46,764	62,315	103,731	
CAPITAL (000)				
Total Debt	25,281	41,557	57,808	
Preferred Equity	41,899	41,924	41,924	
Common Equity	(41,727)	(44,720)	(33,644)	

Synopsis:

Consolidated Enfield Corporation's 51% owned subsidiary, The Complax Corporation, completed the sale of its remaining assets in the automotive parts sector during 1994 and early 1995. In early 1995, Complax closed the sale of land and buildings located in Windsor, Ontario, for $7.4-million. Complax sold land and building located in Cobourg, Ontario, for $5.1-million and recovered its debenture interest in Complax Components Corporation during 1995. Proceeds went to repay debt at both Complax and Consolidated Enfield and invested in money market instruments as a decision is made about deployment of the funds in the future.

Consolidated Enfield reported investment income of $3.4-million in 1994, compared with $5.2-million in 1993. The decline was attributed to a lower average balance of invested funds. Enfield's interest expense declined from $3.4-million to $2.1-million as a result of lower debt levels. Enfield's remaining long-term debt consists of $23-million 8% subordinated debentures due in 2002 which are convertible into common shares of Enfield at $65.90 per Enfield common share. At December 31, 1994, Enfield had a portfolio of securities totalling $32.5-million. The portfolio consisted of a $13.6-million investment in 9% preferred shares of Brascade Resources Inc., a $10,295,000 investment in senior notes of Great Lakes Power Inc., an $8.5-million investment in debentures of Coscan Development Corporation, and $125,000 invested in other securities.

Increased operating expenditures have been resulted from litigation, as the company tries to recover payments it made in 1989 in one action and defends itself in another. Enfield expects to be successful in the recovery of funds. Enfield expects to report a profit in 1995 as a result of gains from the sale of assets by Complax Corporation, which will be partially offset by litigation costs.

Relative strength to TSE300

Price

Volume (in 1000's of board lots)

Rank (Profit/Revenue/Assets)
513 891 652

Manfred J. Walt
Chairman

Brian D. Lawson
President & Secretary

Address
Suite 4501
BCE Place
181 Bay Street
Toronto
ON
M5J 2T3
(416) 359-8625
Fax: (416) 865-1288
E0000495/G/14.0

COUNSEL CORPORATION

Exchanges	Price (Jun29'95)	7.37	Trailing P/E	13.41	Stock Symbol
T	Trailing Yield (%)	0.00	Trailing EPS	0.55	**CXS**

Period Ending	Dec94	Dec93	Dec92	Dec91	Dec90
Yearly Statistics					
Price-Close	4.65	2.65	4.05	7.00	5.63
Price-High	5.50	4.15	7.75	8.38	12.50
Price-Low	2.75	1.30	3.30	4.60	5.38
P/E-Close	16.61	nm	nm	6.48	2.25
Dividends per Share	0.00	0.00	0.13	0.26	0.24
Dividend Yield (%)	0.00	0.00	3.21	3.71	4.27
Sales per Share	9.80	12.10	9.65	6.81	13.13
EPS before extra. item	0.28	(0.67)	(6.78)	1.08	2.50
Cash Flow per Share	0.29	0.98	0.44	1.60	0.46
Book Value per Share	3.22	3.24	3.54	10.25	12.58
O/S Common Shares	21,437	15,138	15,138	14,952	14,952
Total Revenue	225,680	210,871	179,556	135,976	267,763
Income before extra.	9,350	(6,180)	(98,921)	20,318	36,334
Cash Flow	5,523	14,852	6,717	23,897	6,586
Debt/Equity	1.03	1.73	4.35	1.04	2.69
Return on Capital (%)	11.52	0.31	(20.34)	7.29	10.97
Ret. on Com. Equity (%)	0.06	(12.05)	(99.47)	9.46	21.63
% Change Profit	251.3	93.8	(586.9)	(44.1)	125.9
% Change Revenue	7.0	17.4	32.1	(49.2)	0.2
% Change Assets	1.7	(50.7)	42.1	(42.7)	7.6

Period Ending	Dec94	Dec93	Dec92
Preferred Div. Coverage	1.0	na	0.0
Total Div. Coverage	1.0	na	0.0
Interest Coverage	2.9	0.1	0.0
Current Ratio	1.5	1.6	0.7
Operating Margin	9.1	4.1	6.4
Asset Turnover	0.6	0.6	0.2
5 YEAR RATIOS (%)			
Return on Capital	1.9	1.6	9.1
Return on Com. Equity	(16.1)	(13.7)	(9.4)
Profit Growth	(10.3)	na	na
Revenue Growth	(3.4)	(9.8)	(1.7)
Asset Growth	(15.2)	(30.9)	(14.3)
BALANCE SHEET (000)			
Cash	16,643	10,525	15,522
Current Assets	124,475	157,989	62,546
Net Fixed Assets	91,276	85,790	422,509
Invest's & Advances	19,170	26,491	111,392
Total Assets	307,412	302,263	612,924
Short Term Debt	47,584	70,696	18,056
Current Liabilities	83,673	98,058	90,622
Long Term Debt	69,877	91,527	409,581
Total Liabilities	193,640	208,397	514,498
Total Equity	113,772	93,866	98,426
Total Liab. & Equity	307,412	302,263	612,924
CAPITAL (000)			
Total Debt	117,461	162,223	427,637
Preferred Equity	44,780	44,830	44,855
Common Equity	68,992	49,036	53,571

Business:

COUNSEL CORPORATION operates in two areas of business: real estate asset and property management in Canada through Management Services Inc.; and Health Care in the U.S. through American Homepatient Inc. and Choice Drug Systems Inc.

Date	EPS	DPS	Tot Rev	Inc Bex
Mar 95	0.35	0.00	65,600	8,559
Dec 94	0.01	0.00	49,010	1,348
Sep 94	0.04	0.00	56,135	1,614
Jun 94	0.15	0.00	59,530	4,136
Mar 94	0.08	0.00	56,451	2,252
Dec 93	(0.77)	0.00	60,292	(10,712)
Sep 93	0.00	0.00	64,035	1,033
Jun 93	0.05	0.00	52,020	1,691

Synopsis:

Counsel Corporation registered its common stock under U.S. securities laws when it filed form 40-F in February 1995. Its shares were approved for listing on the Nasdaq Stock Market in April. A public offering of 2.415 million common shares of American HomePatient was announced in April 1995. AHOM Holdings Inc., a subsidiary of Counsel, was offering 600,000 shares while American HomePatient was offering 1.815-million shares. After the sale of the 600,000 shares AHOM, and indirectly Counsel, held a 41.4% interest in American HomePatient. The proceeds from American HomePatient's offering were used to reduce its existing acquisition line of credit. Increasing HomePatients liquidity and making it attractive to institutional investors were some of the reasons given for Counsel selling its 600,000 shares.

In June 1995, a division of Counsel Corporation, Counsel Management Services Inc., announced that Counsel Real Estate Investment Trust acquired the Wellington Woods shopping centre in London, Ontario, for $5.5-million. Counsel sold the Palmer Club, a retirement centre in Florida, for $6.6-million (U.S.) in April. Counsel purchased a 25% interest in Choice Drug Systems Inc., a New York based pharmaceutical supplier, in December. Counsel increased its ownership of Choice Drug to 27% in May. Choice Drug acquired Premier Pharmacy, a provider of pharmacy services to nursing homes and hospitals, in May for $4.25-million (U.S.).

American HomePatient entered into a four-year management contract with Coronado, an Arizona based home health care company, in January. American HomePatient has the right to acquire Coronado for a pre-determined price. American HomePatient bought ConPharma Home Healthcare Inc., based in the U.S., from Continental Pharma Cryosan Inc. for $42-million. ConPharma operates 32 home health care centres in seven states and has annual sales of $23-million (U.S.). The purchase will help Counsel expand throughout the United States. American HomePatient acquired Procare, a Missouri home medical equipment company, and Medical Solutions, based in Phoenix.

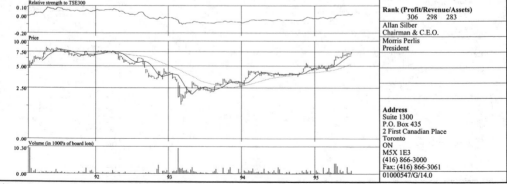

Rank (Profit/Revenue/Assets)
306 298 283

Allan Silber
Chairman & C.E.O.

Morris Perlis
President

Address
Suite 1300
P.O. Box 435
2 First Canadian Place
Toronto
ON
M5X 1E3
(416) 866-3000
Fax: (416) 866-3061
01000547/G/14.0

DEXLEIGH CORPORATION

Exchanges		Price (Jun29'95)	0.70	Trailing P/E	5.00	Stock Symbol
T		Trailing Yield (%)	0.00	Trailing EPS	0.14	**DXH**

Period Ending	Jun94	Jun93	Jun92	Jun91	Jun90
Yearly Statistics					
Price-Close	0.72	0.62	0.85	1.10	2.01
Price-High	1.20	0.85	1.48	2.05	2.40
Price-Low	0.60	0.51	0.85	1.05	1.98
P/E-Close	5.14	3.88	5.31	6.11	8.74
Dividends per Share	0.00	0.00	0.00	0.00	0.00
Dividend Yield (%)	0.00	0.00	0.00	0.00	0.00
Sales per Share	0.35	0.36	0.37	0.35	0.58
EPS before extra. item	0.14	0.16	0.16	0.18	0.23
Cash Flow per Share	1.01	1.12	1.03	1.09	1.18
Book Value per Share	2.81	2.67	2.50	2.34	2.16
O/S Common Shares	12,078	12,078	12,078	12,078	12,078
Total Revenue	17,997	19,413	22,809	32,552	27,212
Income before extra.	12,427	12,838	13,025	13,901	14,758
Cash Flow	12,168	13,552	12,481	13,190	14,219
Debt/Equity	0.18	0.18	0.30	0.47	0.37
Return on Capital (%)	7.46	7.76	8.71	13.17	10.15
Ret. on Com. Equity (%)	5.10	6.35	6.71	8.09	11.38
% Change Profit	(3.2)	(1.4)	(6.3)	(5.8)	7.6
% Change Revenue	(7.3)	(14.9)	(29.9)	19.6	(40.8)
% Change Assets	10.9	(8.1)	(10.4)	9.3	(34.6)
Preferred Div. Coverage	1.2	1.2	1.2		
Total Div. Coverage	1.2	1.2	1.2		
Interest Coverage	9.4	6.8	3.3		
Current Ratio	3.2	226.2	7.4		
Operating Margin	3.3	(0.9)	8.0		
Asset Turnover	0.0	0.0	0.0		
5 YEAR RATIOS (%)					
Return on Capital	9.4	9.6	10.6		
Return on Com. Equity	7.5	8.5	8.8		
Profit Growth	(2.0)	2.1			
Revenue Growth	(17.1)	(26.3)	(18.5)		
Asset Growth	(8.2)	(10.3)	(7.2)		
BALANCE SHEET (000)					
Cash	119,797	127,293	132,492		
Current Assets	153,267	176,693	140,723		
Net Fixed Assets	5,692	3,331	3,520		
Invest's & Advances	47,900	6,473	58,600		
Total Assets	206,859	186,497	202,843		
Short Term Debt	28,500	0	18,442		
Current Liabilities	47,957	781	19,109		
Long Term Debt	0	28,500	28,500		
Total Liabilities	47,957	29,281	47,609		
Total Equity	158,902	157,216	155,234		
Total Liab. & Equity	206,859	186,497	202,843		
CAPITAL (000)					
Total Debt	28,500	28,500	46,942		
Preferred Equity	125,000	125,000	125,000		
Common Equity	33,902	32,216	30,234		

Business:

DEXLEIGH CORPORATION invests for the long term in real estate and other assets where value can be enhanced through an orderly restructuring.

Date	EPS	DPS	Tot Rev	Inc Bex
Mar 95	0.03	0.00	5,685	3,059
Dec 94	0.04	0.00	5,057	3,290
Sep 94	0.03	0.00	4,897	3,098
Jun 93	0.04	0.00	3,849	3,143
Mar 94	0.03	0.00	4,616	3,034
Dec 93	0.04	0.00	4,316	3,204
Sep 93	0.03	0.00	5,216	3,046
Jun 93	0.05	0.00	3,928	3,253

Synopsis:

Dexleigh Corporation's total assets increased from $186.5-million for the year ended June 30, 1993, to $206.9-million for the year ended June 30, 1994. The increase in total assets was due to an increase in the loans receivable portfolio, partially offset by the continued disposal of dividend yielding securities as target sales levels were reached. Investments on the balance sheet fell from $127.3-million to $119.8-million for the year ended June 30, 1994. Dexleigh's investment in the natural resource based sector increased from 31.5% to 53.3% of the portfolio year over year, as the company takes advantage of the growing recovery in commodities. The increase is due to a combination of an increase in investments in the sector combined with a reduction in the portfolio in total. Investment in the natural resources sector rose by $23.8-million to $63.8-million.

The investments in the natural resources sector was funded through the sale of investments in the management companies sector. The investment in management companies as a percentage of the total portfolio decreased from 36.1% in fiscal 1993 to 17.5% in fiscal 1994. The investment in the management companies sector fell by $25-million to $21-million at June 30, 1994. Utilities and real estate remained relatively consistent contributors to earnings and as a percentage of the total portfolio remained relatively the same from fiscal 1993 to fiscal 1994. The banking and insurance sector remained a relatively consistent contributor but the investment as a percentage of the total portfolio dipped from 12.6% to 9.7% at June 30, 1994.

Dexleigh's investment activities are based on research performed to determine the underlying values and potential for appreciation for each of the securities in the investment portfolio. The company tries to invest in companies when market values are perceived as being substantially less than underlying values. Dexleigh continues to look for opportunities to dispose of its restaurant properties, which totalled 35 at June 30, 1994.

Relative strength to TSE300 / Price / Volume (in 1000's of board lots) chart

Rank (Profit/Revenue/Assets)
270 728 352

Timothy W. Gasgrain
President

Address
P.O. Box 770
Suite 4500
BCE Place, 181 Bay St.
Toronto
ON
M5J 2T3
(416) 359-8630
Fax: (416) 865-1288
D0014718/G/14.0

GREAT LAKES POWER INC.

Exchanges	Price (Jun29'95)	20 .50	Trailing P/E	10 .62	Stock Symbol
T	Trailing Yield (%)	5 .86	Trailing EPS	1 .93	**GLZ**

Period Ending	Dec94	Dec93	Dec92	Dec91	Dec90
Yearly Statistics					
Price-Close	18.50	16.00	18.38	22.75	21.75
Price-High	19.50	21.13	21.50	22.75	22.00
Price-Low	15.88	13.00	14.75	19.00	16.00
P/E-Close	9.64	8.33	9.77	12.30	11.45
Dividends per Share	1.13	5.92	0.88	0.84	0.84
Dividend Yield (%)	6.11	37.00	4.79	3.69	3.86
Sales per Share	2.86	2.39	2.17	2.21	1.89
EPS before extra. item	1.92	1.92	1.88	1.85	1.90
Cash Flow per Share	2.25	2.44	2.33	2.36	2.92
Book Value per Share	16.60	15.80	19.80	18.79	17.79
O/S Common Shares	50,007	50,007	49,889	49,889	49,889
Total Revenue	261,100	235,600	226,400	255,800	278,000
Income before extra.	96,100	95,800	93,900	92,900	97,100
Cash Flow	112,700	122,100	116,200	117,500	145,900
Debt/Equity	1.11	1.15	0.90	0.86	0.89
Return on Capital (%)	10.07	9.83	9.07	10.16	11.54
Ret. on Com. Equity (%)	11.86	10.78	9.75	10.09	11.02
% Change Profit	0.3	2.0	1.1	(4.3)	(6.5)
% Change Revenue	10.8	4.1	(11.5)	(8.0)	3.1
% Change Assets	4.3	(8.6)	2.6	(3.4)	7.0

Preferred Div. Coverage	np	np	np
Total Div. Coverage	1.7	0.3	2.1
Interest Coverage	2.7	3.0	2.8
Current Ratio	17.6	29.3	4.7
Operating Margin	45.6	57.4	53.8
Asset Turnover	0.1	0.1	0.1
5 YEAR RATIOS (%)			
Return on Capital	10.1	10.6	10.8
Return on Com. Equity	10.7	10.9	11.2
Profit Growth	(1.6)	(0.1)	2.4
Revenue Growth	(0.7)	1.4	2.6
Asset Growth	0.2	2.7	8.8
BALANCE SHEET (000)			
Cash	643,800	576,900	680,600
Current Assets	717,900	688,400	713,200
Net Fixed Assets	603,200	581,200	532,300
Invest's & Advances	680,000	649,000	854,600
Total Assets	2,001,100	1,918,600	2,100,100
Short Term Debt	0	0	129,000
Current Liabilities	40,900	23,500	153,100
Long Term Debt	921,700	905,500	762,800
Total Liabilities	1,171,200	1,128,400	1,112,300
Total Equity	829,900	790,200	987,800
Total Liab. & Equity	2,001,100	1,918,600	2,100,100
CAPITAL (000)			
Total Debt	921,700	905,500	891,800
Preferred Equity	0	0	0
Common Equity	829,900	790,200	987,800

Business:

GREAT LAKES POWER INC. is a Canadian-based power company which generates and distributes electric energy in the Algoma District of Northern Ontario and has interests in and operates other power generating facilities in Canada and the United States. The company also holds a portfolio of investments.

Date	EPS	DPS	Tot Rev	Inc Bex
Mar 95	0.48	0.30	75,000	24,000
Dec 94	0.45	0.30	64,600	22,300
Sep 94	0.50	0.30	60,900	25,100
Jun 94	0.50	0.30	67,500	24,800
Mar 94	0.48	0.23	72,800	23,900
Dec 93	0.48	5.23	63,200	23,600
Sep 93	0.49	0.23	55,800	25,000
Jun 93	0.48	0.23	54,200	23,800

Synopsis:

Income from power operations decreased slightly for Great Lakes Power Inc. from $47.5-million for the first quarter of 1994 to $43.7-million for the same period in 1995. Investment income increased in the first quarter of 1995 compared to the same period in 1994. This offset the lower contribution from power operations and the higher interest expense. Gigawatt hour sales volume in the Northern Ontario operations decreased by 4% due to warmer weather during the first quarter of 1995 compared to the same period in 1994. The percentage of electricity generated by the company's power plants dropped from 65% in 1994 to 61% in 1995 due to lower water levels. The Louisiana HydroElectric generating facility produced 271.5 gigawatt hours (GWh) of energy in the first quarter, compared to 325.8 GWh for the first three months of 1994. Lake Superior Power's co-generation plant in Sault Ste. Marie produced 209.8 GWh of energy as it continued to exceed expectations.

Great Lakes Power raised the rates charged for power supplied to its major customers by 3%. The increase went into effect on April 3, 1995, and was the first increase in over three years. Great Lakes acquired Western Pacific Powergen Corporation during the first quarter of 1995. Western Pacific completed development work on seven potential sites for hydro-electric plants in British Columbia. Great Lakes and Western Pacific plan three separate projects in British Columbia in response to B.C. Hydro's Request for Proposals for up to 300 megawatts of power.

Great Lakes Power issued $300-million (U.S.) worth of debentures during 1994. The company sold $125-million (U.S.) of 9% notes maturing August 1, 2004, in August and $175-million (U.S.) of 8.9% notes maturing December 1, 1999, in November. Lake Superior Power's co-generation plant produced 819 GWh of electricity during its first full year of operations in 1994. Louisiana HydroElectric Power produced 943 GWh during 1994. Great Lakes Power's 12 stations generated 1,352 GWh, down from 1,733 GWh the previous year; internal power generation represented 62.9% of the electricity sales of those 12 stations.

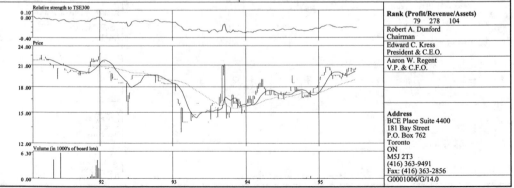

Rank (Profit/Revenue/Assets)
79   278   104

Robert A. Dunford
Chairman

Edward C. Kress
President & C.E.O.

Aaron W. Regent
V.P. & C.F.O.

Address
BCE Place Suite 4400
181 Bay Street
P.O. Box 762
Toronto
ON
M5J 2T3
(416) 363-9491
Fax: (416) 363-2856
G0001006/G/14.0

For further company information, call Globe Information Services 1-800-268-9128 or (416) 585-5345

HARROWSTON INC.

Exchanges						Stock Symbol
T	Price (Jun29'95)		3.10	Trailing P/E	3.65	
	Trailing Yield (%)		0.00	Trailing EPS	0.85	**HRW.A**

Period Ending	Dec94	Dec93	Dec92	Dec91	Dec90
Yearly Statistics					
Price-Close	2.35	2.20	2.00	34.00	900.00
Price-High	3.25	4.40	35.00	940.00	2,300.00
Price-Low	2.15	1.50	0.80	20.00	720.00
P/E-Close	2.01	0.53	nm	nm	nm
Dividends per Share	0.00	0.00	0.00	2.00	28.00
Dividend Yield (%)	0.00	0.00	0.00	5.88	3.11
Sales per Share	8.50	na	na	na	na
EPS before extra. item	1.17	4.13	(20.53)	(1,227.60)	(869.60)
Cash Flow per Share	1.47	1.70	8.42	809.36	1,517.16
Book Value per Share	3.01	1.84	(41.44)	(15.18)	988.54
O/S Common Shares	22,810	22,596	946	1,104	262
Total Revenue	210,158	47,728	6,784	(186,492)	(130,771)
Income before extra.	26,471	39,816	(22,428)	(324,495)	(228,064)
Cash Flow	33,210	16,418	9,200	213,941	397,873
Debt/Equity	2.05	0.00	na	na	2.14
Return on Capital (%)	29.42	111.49	(20.94)	(51.44)	(12.23)
Ret. on Com. Equity (%)	48.02	3,338.87	na	(267.89)	(62.99)
% Change Profit	(33.5)	277.5	93.1	(42.3)	(473.7)
% Change Revenue	340.3	603.5	103.6	(42.6)	(113.5)
% Change Assets	149.2	9.7	(29.7)	(77.6)	(85.0)

Preferred Div. Coverage	np	np	np
Total Div. Coverage	na	na	na
Interest Coverage	4.8	18.6	0.0
Current Ratio	2.2	6.2	3.4
Operating Margin	6.0	na	(117.0)
Asset Turnover	0.5	na	na
5 YEAR RATIOS (%)			
Return on Capital	11.3	10.7	(6.9)
Return on Com. Equity	na	na	na
Profit Growth	(15.4)	0.4	na
Revenue Growth	(26.4)	(43.8)	(61.0)
Asset Growth	(42.3)	(51.1)	(51.1)
BALANCE SHEET (000)			
Cash	65,231	53,101	33,855
Current Assets	133,040	53,906	34,685
Net Fixed Assets	94,043	13	0
Invest's & Advances	2,631	7,892	18,968
Total Assets	388,769	155,994	142,219
Short Term Debt	5,719	0	0
Current Liabilities	59,948	8,672	10,282
Long Term Debt	134,899	45	72,897
Total Liabilities	320,087	114,418	181,410
Total Equity	68,682	41,576	(39,191)
Total Liab. & Equity	388,769	155,994	142,219
CAPITAL (000)			
Total Debt	140,618	45	72,897
Preferred Equity	0	0	0
Common Equity	68,682	41,576	(39,191)

Business:

HARROWSTON INC. is essentially a new company which currently has two distinct business segments. One segment is new business acquisitions. Although the company has not yet completed its initial acquisition, many proposals have been received and reviewed. The other segment involves managing the orderly disposition of the assets of Harrowston Corporation, now a company 100% owned by Harrowston Inc.

Date	EPS	DPS	Tot Rev	Inc Bex
Mar 95	0.17	0.00	88,313	3,992
Dec 94	0.42	0.00	86,771	9,603
Mar 94	0.23	0.00	2,565	5,311
Dec 93	0.03	0.00	1,471	704
Sep 93	0.46	0.00	6,450	10,443
Jun 93	(0.02)	0.00	3,746	(1,290)
Mar 93	30.88	0.00	33,703	29,959
Dec 92	5.37	0.00	6,196	6,177

Synopsis:

For the first quarter of 1995, net sales for Harrowston Inc. of $85.6-million represented a 7% increase over the fourth quarter ended December 31, 1994. Marsulex and SPI Polyols met their earnings targets for the first quarter, while Principal Marques had nominal results in a period that usually is its weakest. The company attributes the increase in cash and cash equivalents of approximately $6.9-million to the $7.3-million increase in the cash balances of Marsulex in the first quarter. Marsulex continues to search for expansion opportunities to diversify its business. It also seeks to temper the effects of the potential loss of any one customer with the maturation of some historical contracts. By the end of April, Harrowston Developments had sold substantially all of the Electra residential condominium units. Harrowston Developments used proceeds from the sales, plus a tax refund of $7.3-million, to reduce its total indebtedness by $45-million to about $73-million.

Harrowston had indirectly owned Marsulex since 1989 through Talborne Capital Corporation, a non-consolidated subsidiary. It purchased 54% of Marsulex in May 1994. Marsulex used part of its proceeds from a debt refinancing in 1994 to finance a buyback of capital stock from certain institutional shareholders. Harrowston's ownership of Marsulex increased from 54% to 65% as a result of the buyback. As a result of the refinancing, Marsulex was provided with long-term fixed rate financing with reduced repayment obligations and interest expense.

In July 1994, Harrowston and two large U.S. institutions acquired the polyols business of ICI Americas, Inc. Harrowston owns 47.5% of SPI Polyols and exercises control over the company. SPI was operating at near capacity at the time of acquisition, which resulted in capital improvements that increased volumes by the middle of 1995. Harrowston reached a long-term agreement with TOWA Chemical Industry Co. Ltd., Mitsubishi Corporation, and Mitsubishi International Corporation to provide SPI with the exclusive North American rights to sell crystalline malitol, a sugar substitute.

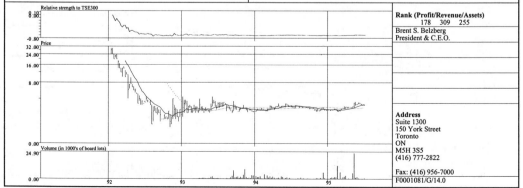

Rank (Profit/Revenue/Assets)
178 309 255

Brent S. Belzberg
President & C.E.O.

Address
Suite 1300
150 York Street
Toronto
ON
M5H 3S5
(416) 777-2822

Fax: (416) 956-7000
F0001081/G/14.0

HIL CORPORATION LTD.

Exchanges	Price (Jun29'95)	5.25	Trailing P/E	15.91	Stock Symbol
T	Trailing Yield (%)	7.62	Trailing EPS	0.33	**HCO.A**

Period Ending	Nov94	Nov93	Nov92	Nov91	Nov90
Yearly Statistics					
Price-Close	5.38	4.50	4.40	8.00	11.50
Price-High	6.00	4.75	9.75	17.50	27.50
Price-Low	4.50	1.75	3.90	8.00	10.13
P/E-Close	26.88	nm	nm	19.51	13.22
Dividends per Share	0.40	0.40	0.80	0.80	0.80
Dividend Yield (%)	7.44	8.89	18.18	10.00	6.96
Sales per Share	na	na	na	na	na
EPS before extra. item	0.20	(0.13)	(5.77)	0.41	0.87
Cash Flow per Share	0.23	0.17	0.17	0.38	(0.20)
Book Value per Share	8.29	8.74	9.90	14.81	19.76
O/S Common Shares	64,175	59,584	53,480	58,025	40,130
Total Revenue	52,199	32,848	(117,926)	71,526	103,076
Income before extra.	19,609	(5,656)	(298,571)	19,370	38,186
Cash Flow	14,355	9,440	8,818	15,676	(7,909)
Debt/Equity	0.10	0.19	0.31	0.18	0.26
Return on Capital (%)	3.15	0.62	(31.66)	4.20	6.75
Ret. on Com. Equity (%)	2.40	(1.41)	(43.28)	2.02	4.40
% Change Profit	446.7	98.1	(1,641.4)	(49.3)	(50.7)
% Change Revenue	58.9	127.9	(264.9)	(30.6)	(24.2)
% Change Assets	(2.4)	(2.8)	(24.7)	(0.5)	7.4

Preferred Div. Coverage	2.8	0.0	0.0
Total Div. Coverage	0.6	0.0	0.0
Interest Coverage	4.8	0.4	0.0
Current Ratio	na	na	na
Operating Margin	na	na	na
Asset Turnover	na	na	na
5 YEAR RATIOS (%)			
Return on Capital	(3.4)	(1.5)	0.8
Return on Com. Equity	(7.2)	(5.1)	(1.7)
Profit Growth	(24.0)	na	na
Revenue Growth	(17.4)	(20.4)	na
Asset Growth	(5.3)	2.5	6.1
BALANCE SHEET (000)			
Cash	0	0	0
Current Assets	0	0	0
Net Fixed Assets	0	0	0
Invest's & Advances	1,033,946	1,059,086	1,090,109
Total Assets	1,034,283	1,059,421	1,090,441
Short Term Debt	0	0	0
Current Liabilities	2,362	2,391	956
Long Term Debt	82,792	105,781	174,391
Total Liabilities	208,307	496,588	518,790
Total Equity	825,976	562,833	571,651
Total Liab. & Equity	1,034,283	1,059,421	1,090,441
CAPITAL (000)			
Total Debt	82,792	105,781	174,391
Preferred Equity	293,925	42,000	42,000
Common Equity	532,051	520,833	529,651

Business:

HIL CORPORATION LTD. is a diversified Canadian company with interests in the natural resources, real estate, financial services and consumer products sectors. Its principal corporate investments include direct and indirect equity interests in Hees International Bancorp Inc., Brascan Limited and Carena Developments Limited.

Date	EPS	DPS	Tot Rev	Inc Bex
Feb 95	0.13	0.20	18,659	14,546
Nov 94	0.06	0.00	5,861	2,427
Aug 94	0.07	0.20	14,676	4,968
May 94	0.07	0.00	14,922	5,053
Feb 94	0.12	0.20	16,740	7,161
Nov 93	(0.59)	0.00	(25,712)	(32,452)
Aug 93	0.08	0.20	14,658	4,835
May 93	(0.08)	0.00	7,501	(2,583)

Synopsis:

Edper Enterprises Ltd. announced in June 1995 that it would seek shareholder approval on July 18 to change the company name to HIL Corporation Ltd. The name change would distinguish the company from its parent company Edper Group Ltd., formerly The Pagurian Corporation Limited, and reflect the 48% ownership in Hees International Bancorp Inc. Edper Enterprises started trading under the symbol HCO.A in June 1995. Management intends to merge Edper Group and HIL, either in 1995 or 1996, although no discussions had taken place by the time of the 1995 annual meeting.

The Edper group simplified its corporate structure during 1994. Pagurian sold its preferred share and 25% common share interests in Hees Holdings Inc. to Edper Enterprises for $252-million of retractable preferred shares of Edper. Approximately $100-million worth of the preferred shares is convertible into common shares of Edper. Edper had a 48% equity interest in Hees International Bancorp Inc. at November 30, 1994. Edper's interest in Hees International is held principally through Hees Holdings Inc.

Edper transferred its remaining economic interests in Brascan Holdings Inc. and Carena Holdings Inc. to Hees International for net proceeds of $87.5-million of convertible preferred shares of Hees. Edper continues to hold voting share interests in Brascan Holdings Inc. of 50.1%. It holds voting share interests in Carena Holdings Inc. of 49.9%. However, Hees effectively holds 100% of the common share equity in both companies through non-voting common shares. Edper's carrying values for both holding companies are nil due to the common equity ownership.

The improved results for Edper for the year ended November 30, 1994, could be attributed to the improved domestic and international markets for many of the products and services of Edper's operating affiliates. Edper expects to report higher earnings in 1995 than in 1994. This is because of the expected growth in the earnings of its operating affiliates; especially the natural resources sector due to the price recovery, cost reductions, and productivity improvements.

Rank (Profit/Revenue/Assets)
218   539   150

Peter F. Bronfman
Chairman

M.J. Walt
President

Address
Suite 4500
BCE Place
181 Bay Street
Toronto
ON
M5J 2T3
(416) 359-8605
Fax: (416) 865-9845
E0002767/G/14.0

For further company information, call Globe Information Services 1-800-268-9128 or (416) 585-5345

IMASCO LIMITED

Exchanges

TMV

	Price (Jun29'95)		24 .00	**Trailing P/E**		10 .86	Stock Symbol
	Trailing Yield (%)		3 .50	**Trailing EPS**		2 .21	**IMS**

Period Ending	Dec94	Dec93	Dec92	Dec91	Dec90
Yearly Statistics					
Price-Close	19 .88	20 .00	20 .63	18 .25	13 .81
Price-High	22 .13	20 .81	20 .69	18 .38	19 .13
Price-Low	16 .00	17 .13	15 .75	13 .31	12 .75
P/E-Close	9 .51	12 .27	13 .89	14 .26	12 .28
Dividends per Share	0 .78	0 .74	0 .68	0 .64	0 .64
Dividend Yield (%)	3 .93	3 .70	3 .30	3 .51	4 .63
Sales per Share	34 .34	33 .46	33 .33	33 .40	33 .11
EPS before extra. item	2 .09	1 .63	1 .49	1 .28	1 .13
Cash Flow per Share	4 .22	3 .97	4 .01	3 .01	2 .42
Book Value per Share	13 .72	12 .35	11 .35	10 .32	9 .75
O/S Common Shares	58 ,371	59 ,594	59 ,550	59 ,557	59 ,557
Total Revenue	8 ,135 ,000	7 ,978 ,000	7 ,941 ,000	7 ,957 ,700	7 ,902 ,000
Income before extra.	506 ,000	409 ,000	380 ,000	331 ,600	295 ,100
Cash Flow	1 ,000 ,000	946 ,000	955 ,000	716 ,000	575 ,800
Debt/Equity	1 .77	1 .67	1 .58	1 .63	13 .28
Return on Capital (%)	35 .96	36 .77	9 .80	3 .80	18 .19
Ret. on Com. Equity (%)	16 .11	13 .78	13 .68	12 .75	11 .72
% Change Profit	23 .7	7 .6	14 .6	12 .4	(19 .4)
% Change Revenue	2 .0	0 .5	(0 .2)	0 .7	147 .6
% Change Assets	6 .1	3 .9	4 .5	17 .3	635 .8
Preferred Div. Coverage	46 .0	20 .5	14 .1		
Total Div. Coverage	2 .6	2 .1	2 .0		
Interest Coverage	1 .4	1 .3	4 .0		
Current Ratio	1 .4	1 .5	1 .5		
Operating Margin	40 .8	39 .3	10 .5		
Asset Turnover	0 .2	0 .2	0 .2		
5 YEAR RATIOS (%)					
Return on Capital	20 .9	16 .6	11 .9		
Return on Com. Equity	13 .6	13 .6	13 .7		
Profit Growth	6 .6	5 .4	3 .0		
Revenue Growth	20 .5	9 .8	9 .0		
Asset Growth	58 .2	56 .7	53 .6		
BALANCE SHEET (mil)					
Cash	148	221	111		
Current Assets	1 ,333	1 ,332	1 ,241		
Net Fixed Assets	1 ,731	1 ,595	1 ,655		
Invest's & Advances	48 ,665	45 ,713	43 ,890		
Total Assets	53 ,482	50 ,407	48 ,519		
Short Term Debt	71	92	27		
Current Liabilities	970	904	813		
Long Term Debt	5 ,833	5 ,069	4 ,804		
Total Liabilities	50 ,145	47 ,307	45 ,461		
Total Equity	3 ,337	3 ,100	3 ,058		
Total Liab. & Equity	53 ,482	50 ,407	48 ,519		
CAPITAL (mil)					
Total Debt	5 ,904	5 ,161	4 ,831		
Preferred Equity	135	156	356		
Common Equity	3 ,202	2 ,944	2 ,702		

Business:

IMASCO LTD. is a diversified consumer products and services company with operations in Canada and the United States. Operations include Imperial Tobacco, Shoppers Drug Mart/Pharmaprix, Hardee's Food System, Genstar Development Co. and The UCS Group. Imasco operates in the financial services sector, by ownership of 98% of CT Financial Service s Inc., the holding company of the Canada Trust group of companies.

Date	EPS	DPS	Tot Rev	Inc Bex
Mar 95	0 .41	0 .24	2 ,354 ,000	98 ,000
Dec 94	0 .63	0 .20	2 ,096 ,000	150 ,000
Sep 94	0 .64	0 .20	2 ,102 ,000	153 ,000
Jun 94	0 .53	0 .20	2 ,393 ,000	128 ,000
Mar 94	0 .30	0 .20	2 ,176 ,000	75 ,000
Dec 93	0 .51	0 .19	2 ,035 ,000	125 ,000
Sep 93	0 .50	0 .19	2 ,049 ,000	123 ,000
Jun 93	0 .37	0 .19	2 ,467 ,000	95 ,000

Synopsis:

Imasco split its shares on a two for one basis on Tuesday, May 9, 1995. Although Imperial Tobacco Ltd. and CT Financial Services Inc. will generate the bulk of Imasco's earnings in 1995, Imasco expects Shoppers Drug Mart/Pharmaprix and Genstar Development Co. to take over that role in two years. Shoppers has been hurt in the short term by the ban on tobacco sales in drugstores. However, it will benefit in the long term by buying the more vulnerable smaller independents that were hit harder by the ban. The acquisitions will help Shoppers increase its market share.

Imasco's first quarter earnings rose by 31%, to $98-million, compared to the first quarter 1994 earnings of $75-million. Revenues increased from $1.86-billion in first quarter 1994 to $2.07-billion for the first three months of 1995. Imperial benefited from reduced federal and provincial taxes as its revenues, after tobacco taxes and duties, rose 7% to $311-million and operating earnings rose 16% to $132-million. Imperial's share of Canada's cigarette market rose 1.1%, from the first quarter of 1994, to stand at 65.8% at the end of the first quarter of 1995. CT Financial had a 29% rise in operating profits to $94-million, due in part to a smaller loan loss provision. Shoppers operating earnings fell 7% to $18-million for the first quarter of 1995.

Shoppers Drug Mart acquired Bi-Rite Drug in Saskatchewan, which includes 26 stores in Saskatchewan, from Bi-Rite Drugs Ltd. of Regina. Bi-Rite Drugs, which had been in Saskatchewan for over 30 years, will increase Shoppers' presence in Saskatchewan as it brings the total number of Shoppers stores in Saskatchewan to 42. Under the federal Trust and Loan Companies Act, Imasco will have to reduce its ownership in CT Financial's voting shares, from its current 97.7%, to 65% by June 1, 1997. Hardee's Food Systems started a strategic review of its competitive positioning and unit economics during 1994. The review resulted in better defined consumer segments, the image it wants those segments to perceive, and the specific actions required to establish that image.

Rank (Profit/Revenue/Assets)
12   14   6

Purdy Crawford
Chairman

Brian M. Levitt
President & C.E.O.

Raymond E. Guyatt
Exec. V.P. & C.F.O.

Address
600 De Maisonneuve Blvd. West
20th Floor
Montreal
PQ
H3A 3K7
(514) 982-9111

Fax: (514) 982-9369
I0000263/G/14.0

JANNOCK LIMITED

Exchanges					
TM	Price (Jun29'95)	15.37	Trailing P/E	15.07	Stock Symbol
	Trailing Yield (%)	5.20	Trailing EPS	1.02	**JN**

Period Ending	Dec94	Dec93	Dec92	Dec91	Dec90
Yearly Statistics					
Price-Close	16.13	19.88	14.00	17.00	13.00
Price-High	22.88	20.00	18.50	17.88	19.75
Price-Low	14.13	13.63	12.13	12.50	11.38
P/E-Close	18.32	nm	12.96	nm	30.95
Dividends per Share	0.80	0.80	0.80	0.80	0.80
Dividend Yield (%)	4.96	4.03	5.71	4.71	6.15
Sales per Share	30.80	23.40	11.85	10.52	11.55
EPS before extra. item	0.88	(0.05)	1.08	(1.25)	0.42
Cash Flow per Share	1.92	1.46	0.26	0.12	1.26
Book Value per Share	9.85	9.50	9.16	9.60	11.02
O/S Common Shares	30,258	30,258	27,258	27,258	27,158
Total Revenue	932,000	666,800	370,700	279,100	319,100
Income before extra.	27,700	300	30,300	(32,400)	13,100
Cash Flow	58,000	41,500	7,100	3,300	34,300
Debt/Equity	0.58	0.44	0.22	0.42	0.64
Return on Capital (%)	12.59	6.65	14.46	(6.18)	7.63
Ret. on Com. Equity (%)	1.20	(0.45)	11.60	(12.49)	3.78
% Change Profit	9,133.3	(99.0)	193.5	(347.3)	(73.3)
% Change Revenue	39.8	79.9	32.8	(12.5)	(15.2)
% Change Assets	19.0	39.8	(8.8)	(28.1)	31.0

Preferred Div. Coverage	1.1	0.2	18.9
Total Div. Coverage	1.1	0.0	1.3
Interest Coverage	4.4	2.4	8.0
Current Ratio	1.8	1.9	2.8
Operating Margin	6.4	5.0	3.7
Asset Turnover	1.4	1.2	0.8
5 YEAR RATIOS (%)			
Return on Capital	7.0	9.1	13.3
Return on Com. Equity	0.7	3.7	7.4
Profit Growth	(10.8)	(65.3)	(15.0)
Revenue Growth	19.9	14.8	(2.7)
Asset Growth	7.4	6.8	(0.5)
BALANCE SHEET (000)			
Cash	6,600	33,900	29,200
Current Assets	312,400	262,900	170,700
Net Fixed Assets	285,200	248,700	171,300
Invest's & Advances	13,700	11,000	45,300
Total Assets	656,700	551,900	394,900
Short Term Debt	35,500	45,900	1,700
Current Liabilities	177,800	141,000	62,000
Long Term Debt	148,600	89,100	57,800
Total Liabilities	339,900	245,400	126,100
Total Equity	316,800	306,500	268,800
Total Liab. & Equity	656,700	551,900	394,900
CAPITAL (000)			
Total Debt	184,100	135,000	59,500
Preferred Equity	18,900	19,100	19,200
Common Equity	297,900	287,400	249,600

Business:

JANNOCK LTD. manufactures and distributes building products for the North American construction industry through its Brick, Vinyl and Metal Fabricating Groups. These Groups operate their businesses out of more than 60 manufacturing plants and 35 distribution centres across North America. Key among these product offerings are clay brick, vinyl siding, insulation, metal cladding, roofing & decking, & metal tubing.

Date	EPS	DPS	Tot Rev	Inc Bex
Mar 95	(0.13)	0.20	227,400	(3,400)
Dec 94	0.30	0.20	585,800	9,300
Sep 94	0.50	0.20	142,100	15,300
Jun 94	0.35	0.20	132,700	10,800
Mar 94	(0.27)	0.20	134,800	(7,700)
Dec 93	(0.28)	0.20	374,700	(7,000)
Sep 93	0.29	0.20	117,800	8,000
Jun 93	0.19	0.20	108,800	5,300

Synopsis:

Jannock's Vinyl Group bought the business and assets of a Kentucky vinyl siding plant from Bird Corp. for $42.5-million (U.S.), in March 1995. Jannock also exercised its option to purchase Bird's vinyl window business for $2.8-million (U.S.) in June. The acquired business, operating Leechburg, Pennsylvania, makes and markets high-performance, energy-efficient, vinyl windows for use primarily in the residential replacement market. The business, which will operate under the name Kensington Windows Inc., had 1994 sales of $24-million but has the capacity to generate sales of $50-million. The acquisition gives Jannock an entry point into a new product line that could strengthen its position in the less cyclical residential replacement market sector.

The net loss of $3.4-million for the first quarter of 1995 represents an improvement over the results from the first quarter of 1994, when Jannock recorded a $7.7-million loss. The unseasonably mild winter and better business conditions led to improved sales in all groups. Earnings from operations increased from a loss of $4.7-million in the first quarter of 1994 to earnings of $2-million for the first three months of 1995, due to the gains made by the Metal Fabricating Group. The increase in earnings was partially offset by the increase in interest expense, of $3-million, in the first quarter of 1995 over the first quarter of 1994.

Effective October 31, 1994, Jannock bought its partner's 50% interest in Jannock Steel Fabricating Inc. for $16.5-million (U.S.). Effective March 31, 1994, Jannock bought its partner's 50% interest in Jannock Steel Fabricating Company, for $51.7-million. To finance the deals, Jannock assumed bank debt of $44.4-million, but the debt was not guaranteed by Jannock. The results of the two companies during 1994 were better than had been projected. Results for 1995 show continued improvement.

Rank (Profit/Revenue/Assets)
173 122 200

H. Gordon MacNeill
Chairman

R. Jay Atkinson
President & C.E.O.

Brian W. Jamieson
V.P. Finance & C.F.O.

Address
Suite 5205, Scotia Plaza
P.O. Box 1012
40 King Street West
Toronto
ON
M5H 3Y2
(416) 364-8586
Fax: (416) 364-9342
J0000182/G/14.0

JOHN LABATT LIMITED

Exchanges	Price (Jun29'95)		27.87	Trailing P/E		16.69	Stock Symbol
TMV	Trailing Yield (%)		2.94	Trailing EPS		1.67	**LBT**

Period Ending	Apr94	Apr93	Apr92	Apr91	Apr90
Yearly Statistics					
Price-Close	21.00	25.00	25.75	23.13	20.63
Price-High	26.25	30.38	27.88	26.00	27.50
Price-Low	20.50	24.25	22.25	18.38	20.50
P/E-Close	13.13	nm	24.76	21.02	10.31
Dividends per Share	0.82	0.81	0.80	0.77	0.73
Dividend Yield (%)	3.91	3.26	3.09	3.33	3.54
Sales per Share	26.90	26.79	22.27	47.23	62.34
EPS before extra. item	1.60	(1.12)	1.04	1.10	2.00
Cash Flow per Share	3.15	3.38	2.14	3.10	3.73
Book Value per Share	8.34	10.60	15.23	14.42	14.08
O/S Common Shares	87,340	85,460	78,350	76,560	75,790
Total Revenue	2,332,000	2,169,000	1,757,000	3,626,000	4,718,000
Income before extra.	155,000	(70,000)	101,000	109,000	169,000
Cash Flow	272,000	269,000	166,000	236,000	280,000
Debt/Equity	0.78	0.70	0.63	0.75	0.65
Return on Capital (%)	15.40	2.41	7.07	8.10	14.26
Ret. on Com. Equity (%)	16.89	(8.48)	6.97	7.74	14.91
% Change Profit	321.4	(169.3)	(7.3)	(35.5)	25.2
% Change Revenue	7.5	23.4	(51.5)	(23.1)	(3.3)
% Change Assets	(16.0)	(10.9)	11.2	3.4	6.9

Preferred Div. Coverage	9.1	0.0	4.8
Total Div. Coverage	1.8	0.0	1.2
Interest Coverage	5.1	0.9	4.2
Current Ratio	1.5	1.3	1.9
Operating Margin	12.2	12.4	13.4
Asset Turnover	0.9	0.7	0.5
5 YEAR RATIOS (%)			
Return on Capital	9.4	9.1	11.8
Return on Com. Equity	7.6	7.2	12.3
Profit Growth	2.8	na	(4.3)
Revenue Growth	(13.7)	(14.1)	(14.4)
Asset Growth	(1.7)	3.5	7.5
BALANCE SHEET (000)			
Cash	368,000	276,000	740,000
Current Assets	1,102,000	1,187,000	1,736,000
Net Fixed Assets	813,000	784,000	684,000
Invest's & Advances	370,000	430,000	180,000
Total Assets	2,536,000	3,020,000	3,388,000
Short Term Debt	104,000	102,000	41,000
Current Liabilities	721,000	932,000	904,000
Long Term Debt	701,000	741,000	901,000
Total Liabilities	1,508,000	1,814,000	1,895,000
Total Equity	1,028,000	1,206,000	1,493,000
Total Liab. & Equity	2,536,000	3,020,000	3,388,000
CAPITAL (000)			
Total Debt	805,000	843,000	942,000
Preferred Equity	300,000	300,000	300,000
Common Equity	728,000	906,000	1,193,000

Business:

JOHN LABATT LTD. operates internationally in two core businesses. The Brewing segment is a major competitor in North America and Europe and produces many leading brands. The Broadcast segment consists of Labatt Communications Inc. whose major businesses are TSN, the Discovery Channel, Dome Productions, The Blue Jays, The Argonauts, and an equity interest in SkyDome.

Date	EPS	DPS	Tot Rev	Inc Bex
Jan 95	0.26	0.21	751,000	27,000
Oct 94	0.47	0.21	845,000	45,000
Jul 94	0.67	0.21	924,000	62,000
Apr 94	0.27	0.21	516,000	28,000
Jan 94	0.21	0.21	486,000	23,000
Oct 93	0.51	0.21	637,000	47,000
Jul 93	0.61	0.21	682,000	57,000
Apr 93	(2.64)	0.21	446,000	(204,000)

Synopsis:

Interbrew S.A. purchased John Labatt Limited's common shares for approximately $2.7-billion. The combined operations of Labatt and Interbrew make it the fourth largest brewery in the world. Interbrew is contributing a minimum of $730-million of its own funds to fund the offer while a bank syndicate led by CIBC is providing bank financing for the offer. The broadcasting assets of John Labatt will be held in a trust while Interbrew seeks the required approvals for the sale of the assets to an eligible Canadian buyer.

Labatt Communications's principal broadcast businesses include the following ventures. TSN is an all-sports specialty television service, with RDS being its French-language counterpart. Labatt has a 25% interest in Viewer's Choice Canada, a pay-per-view service in Eastern Canada, and an 80% interest in Discovery Channel, a Canadian non-fiction specialty channel. Labatt's broadcast-related businesses include Dome Productions, a television event-production facility at the SkyDome, and LCI Enterprises, the operator of real time closed-captioning services and TSN SportsRadio. The sports and sports-related businesses of LCI include the Toronto Blue Jays (90%), The Toronto Argonauts Football Club 100%, and an 41.6% equity interest in the SkyDome.

Supercorp/Skyvision includes Partners Canada (100%) and Partners USA (80%) producers of television commercials in Canada and the United States, respectively. Skyvision creates, develops, and produces episodic television programming for domestic and foreign markets. Labatt holds a 75% interest in BCL Entertainment, a live event promoter and merchandiser of related apparel. Labatt has a 50% interest in International Talent Group, which represents contemporary and rock music artists, as well as film and television artists, in North America and the United Kingdom.

Rank (Profit/Revenue/Assets)
45 61 87

Samuel Pollock
Chairman Of The Board

G.S. Taylor
President & C.E.O.

R.G. Vaux
Sr. V.P. Fin. & Corp. Dev.

Address
Labatt House, BCE Place
181 Bay Street
Suite 200, P.O. Box 811
Toronto
ON
M5J 2T3
(416) 865-6000
Fax: (416) 865-6074
L0000102/G/14.0

LAIDLAW INC.

Exchanges	Price (Jun29'95)	12.75	Trailing P/E	31.10	Stock Symbol
TMQ	Trailing Yield (%)	1.25	Trailing EPS	0.41	**LDM.B**

Period Ending	Aug94	Aug93	Aug92	Aug91	Aug90
Yearly Statistics	US	US	US	US	US
Price-Close	11.13	9.25	10.00	13.13	21.25
Price-High	11.50	12.25	13.25	23.50	28.38
Price-Low	7.13	7.75	8.25	11.25	19.00
P/E-Close	24.89	nm	16.39	nm	17.83
Dividends per Share	0.16	0.13	0.14	0.27	0.23
Dividend Yield (%)	1.44	1.36	1.37	2.04	1.09
Sales per Share	9.37	7.19	7.24	7.63	7.44
EPS before extra. item	0.33	(1.05)	0.52	(1.41)	1.02
Cash Flow per Share	1.56	1.26	1.37	1.64	1.75
Book Value per Share	5.69	5.57	7.04	6.60	7.98
O/S Common Shares	277,188	277,188	277,188	253,336	239,056
Total Revenue	2,158,400	2,046,940	1,978,927	1,925,890	1,868,158
Income before extra.	90,800	(291,572)	138,492	(344,361)	247,928
Cash Flow	354,100	348,685	364,301	404,488	409,440
Debt/Equity	0.91	0.91	0.67	0.92	0.72
Return on Capital (%)	7.91	(6.79)	8.96	(5.50)	13.60
Ret. on Com. Equity (%)	5.79	(16.72)	7.62	(19.50)	14.86
% Change Profit	131.1	(310.5)	140.2	(238.9)	17.6
% Change Revenue	5.4	3.4	2.8	3.1	30.9
% Change Assets	1.6	(4.2)	3.8	(7.7)	46.9

Date		EPS	DPS	Tot Rev	Inc Bex
May 95	US	0.18	0.04	733,400	50,300
Feb 95	US	0.10	0.04	597,000	27,200
Nov 94	US	0.14	0.04	569,700	38,200
Aug 94	US	(0.01)	0.04	488,760	(3,154)
May 94	US	0.14	0.04	584,174	38,942
Feb 94	US	0.06	0.04	526,708	16,967
Nov 93	US	0.14	0.04	558,758	38,045
Aug 93	US	(1.21)	0.03	481,184	(334,946)

Preferred Div. Coverage	181.6	0.0	248.2		
Total Div. Coverage	2.7	3.8			
Interest Coverage	2.0	0.0	2.4		
Current Ratio	1.6	1.6	1.8		
Operating Margin	10.5	10.2	12.3		
Asset Turnover	0.6	0.6	0.5		
5 YEAR RATIOS (%)					
Return on Capital	3.6	5.4	10.4		
Return on Com. Equity	(1.6)	1.2	8.4		
Profit Growth	(15.5)	na	8.4		
Revenue Growth	8.5	11.1	16.6		
Asset Growth	6.5	16.9	24.3		
BALANCE SHEET (000)					
Cash	199,600	212,170	163,226		
Current Assets	613,700	653,747	555,209		
Net Fixed Assets	1,775,200	1,715,104	1,795,073		
Invest's & Advances	725,800	711,167	910,905		
Total Assets	3,633,200	3,575,082	3,731,449		
Short Term Debt	41,300	43,381	45,878		
Current Liabilities	391,900	407,326	316,234		
Long Term Debt	1,403,200	1,377,086	1,260,892		
Total Liabilities	2,047,300	2,021,772	1,771,495		
Total Equity	1,585,900	1,553,310	1,959,954		
Total Liab. & Equity	3,633,200	3,575,082	3,731,449		
CAPITAL (000)					
Total Debt	1,444,500	1,420,467	1,306,770		
Preferred Equity	9,600	9,609	9,609		
Common Equity	1,576,300	1,543,701	1,950,345		

Business:

LAIDLAW INC. is a waste disposal and passenger services company. The company provides chemical waste services and solid waste services to residential, commercial and industrial customers in the United States and Canada. Laidlaw also provides contract school busing, healthcare transportation, and public transit system management.

Synopsis:

Laidlaw reported a 14.7% increase in net revenues to $597-million (U.S.) for the second quarter ended February 28, 1995, from the $520.4-million (U.S.) reported for the second quarter of 1994. The 15% revenue increase was due mainly to the acquisition of USPCI and acquisitions in the transportation business. A 4.4% increase in revenues was caused by price and volume changes while a revenue reduction of 3.6% was caused by the sale of Laidlaw's European hazardous waste management interests. A decline in the Canadian dollar caused a 1.1% decrease in revenues. Operating income grew by 49%, to $64.4-million (U.S.) from $43.3-million (U.S.) in last year's second quarter, as income from operations increased in each of its businesses. For the six months ended February 1995, Laidlaw experienced revenue growth of 9.9% and operating income growth of 30%, compared to the same period last year.

Laidlaw bought Mayflower Contract Services at the end of March 1995, for $157-million (U.S.). Mayflower has school bus operations primarily in the Mid-West and Pacific Northwest. The second-largest student transportation company in the United States is not expected to have a meaningful impact on earnings until the start of the school year in September. The acquisition increases Laidlaw's market share of the private sector school bus business by 5% to 20%, and extends its operations into seven states previously not served by the company.

Laidlaw bought United States Pollution Control Inc. (USPCI), the waste management assets of Union Pacific Railroad, for $225-million (U.S.) plus the assumption of $38-million (U.S.) in debt and associated environmental guarantees. With more than $300-million (U.S.) in annual revenue from USPCI, Laidlaw Environmental Services becomes the largest company in the North American hazardous waste industry. USPCI has facilities in the western states east of the Rockies, an area previously unserved by Laidlaw.

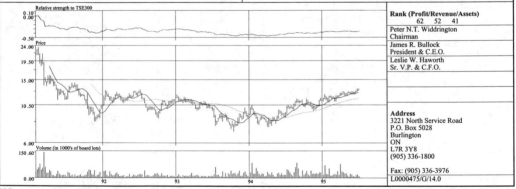

Rank (Profit/Revenue/Assets)		
62	52	41

Peter N.T. Widdrington
Chairman

James R. Bullock
President & C.E.O.

Leslie W. Haworth
Sr. V.P. & C.F.O.

Address
3221 North Service Road
P.O. Box 5028
Burlington
ON
L7R 3Y8
(905) 336-1800

Fax: (905) 336-3976
L0000475/G/14.0

NORANDA INC.

Exchanges						Stock Symbol
TMV	Price (Jun29'95)	27.00	Trailing P/E	13.71		
	Trailing Yield (%)	3.70	Trailing EPS	1.97		**NOR**

Period Ending	Dec94	Dec93	Dec92	Dec91	Dec90
Yearly Statistics					
Price-Close	26.50	25.88	18.50	18.63	16.75
Price-High	27.88	26.13	20.75	20.38	24.50
Price-Low	22.38	14.88	16.38	15.50	14.13
P/E-Close	18.28	nm	185.00	nm	46.53
Dividends per Share	1.00	1.00	1.00	1.00	1.00
Dividend Yield (%)	3.77	3.87	5.41	5.37	5.97
Sales per Share	31.58	25.99	29.16	44.05	50.86
EPS before extra. item	1.45	(0.41)	0.10	(1.04)	0.36
Cash Flow per Share	5.67	2.76	3.98	2.72	5.41
Book Value per Share	17.69	16.54	17.04	18.29	20.12
O/S Common Shares	223,392	211,944	192,473	187,166	190,292
Total Revenue	6,924,000	5,302,000	5,562,000	8,476,000	9,565,000
Income before extra.	330,000	(37,000)	79,000	(133,000)	120,000
Cash Flow	1,191,000	559,000	748,000	509,000	1,003,000
Debt/Equity	0.81	0.84	0.95	1.29	1.15
Return on Capital (%)	12.31	1.65	4.81	1.74	2.13
Ret. on Com. Equity (%)	8.13	(2.42)	0.54	(5.35)	1.72
% Change Profit	991.9	(146.8)	159.4	(210.8)	(72.9)
% Change Revenue	30.6	(4.7)	(34.4)	(11.4)	2.1
% Change Assets	21.3	(12.1)	(23.6)	(2.7)	6.2
Preferred Div. Coverage	12.2	0.0	1.3
Total Div. Coverage	1.4	0.0	0.3
Interest Coverage	4.1	0.7	1.6
Current Ratio	2.1	2.0	1.8
Operating Margin	13.4	3.9	7.1
Asset Turnover	0.6	0.5	0.5
5 YEAR RATIOS (%)			
Return on Capital	4.5	5.0	9.4
Return on Com. Equity	0.5	1.0	4.9
Profit Growth	(5.7)	na	(25.5)
Revenue Growth	(5.9)	(9.9)	(5.5)
Asset Growth	(3.4)	(2.6)	2.9
BALANCE SHEET (mil)			
Cash	1,390	896	361
Current Assets	4,385	2,837	2,532
Net Fixed Assets	6,046	5,063	6,218
Invest's & Advances	1,317	1,787	2,295
Total Assets	11,836	9,756	11,097
Short Term Debt	351	331	379
Current Liabilities	2,061	1,448	1,435
Long Term Debt	2,941	2,968	3,526
Total Liabilities	7,751	5,813	6,974
Total Equity	4,085	3,943	4,123
Total Liab. & Equity	11,836	9,756	11,097
CAPITAL (mil)			
Total Debt	3,292	3,299	3,905
Preferred Equity	134	437	844
Common Equity	3,951	3,506	3,279

Business:

NORANDA INC. is a diversified natural resources company operating in three groups: mining and metals, forest products, and oil and gas. Major assets are in North America, but Noranda operates worldwide. Metals include copper, zinc, nickel, aluminum and gold. Noranda has significant interests in Brunswick Mining & Smelting, Hemlo Gold, Falconbridge, Noranda Forest, and Norcen Energy.

Date	EPS	DPS	Tot Rev	Inc Bex
Mar 95	0.70	0.25	2,115,000	158,000
Dec 94	0.57	0.25	1,979,000	127,000
Sep 94	0.35	0.25	1,804,000	78,000
Jun 94	0.35	0.25	1,573,000	81,000
Mar 94	0.18	0.25	1,400,000	44,000
Dec 93	(0.01)	0.25	1,433,000	1,000
Sep 93	(0.08)	0.25	1,287,000	(8,000)
Jun 93	(0.07)	0.25	1,314,000	1,000

Synopsis:

During the first quarter of 1995 Falconbridge, a Noranda subsidiary, said it would increase its ownership in the Collahuasi copper deposit in Chile to 50% with the purchase of an additional one-sixth interest. Falconbridge will pay about $98-million (U.S.) for the one-sixth interest. Minorco owns the other half interest in the project. The development of the Raglan nickel deposit in Northern Quebec was approved with capital expenditures estimated at $486-million. The spending is needed to bring the property into production at an annual rate of 20,000 tonnes of refined nickel. A capital budget of $84-million has been set for the development of a zinc ore body located in the Matagami camp. Production would begin in 1998 and the mine would extend the life of Matagami to the year 2002.

Noranda Forest acquired Cross Pointe Paper Corporation of Minnesota for $200-million (U.S.), effective April 1, 1995.

In late 1994 Noranda Minerals Inc. was reorganized into two companies, Noranda Mining and Exploration Inc., and Noranda Metallurgy Inc., to better focus on its core strategies and competencies. Researchers at the Noranda Technology Centre in Pointe Claire, Quebec developed a proprietary process to extract magnesium out of the tailing hills near Thetford Mines, Quebec. Noranda could become one of the lowest cost producers of magnesium in the world because of its technology, the grade of tailings and the competitive electricity prices in Quebec.

Contributions to total sales (segment earnings) for the first quarter of 1995 by industry segment were: mining and minerals, 74% (72%); forest products, 24% (26%); oil and gas, 2% (4%); and corporate and inter-segment, -% (-2%). Contributions to segment earnings for 1994 by industry segment were: mining and minerals, 77%; forest products, 37%; oil and gas, -8%; and corporate and inter-segment, -6%. Canadian operations had export sales of about $3-billion and sales from U.S. operations were $2.4-billion.

Relative strength to TSE300
Price
Volume (in 1000's of board lots)

Rank (Profit/Revenue/Assets)
18   19   27

David W. Kerr
Chairman & C.E.O.

E. Courtney Pratt
President

Alan R. Thomas
Sr. V.P., C.F.O. & Treasurer

Address
BCE Place Suite 4100
181 Bay Street
P.O. Box 755
Toronto
ON
M5J 2T3
(416) 982-7111
Fax: (416) 982-7423
N0002293/G/14.0

ONEX CORPORATION

Exchanges	Price (Jun29'95)	14.50	Trailing P/E	3.78	Stock Symbol
TM	Trailing Yield (%)	2.86	Trailing EPS	3.84	**OCX**

Period Ending	Dec94	Dec93	Dec92	Dec91	Dec90
Yearly Statistics					
Price-Close	13.25	17.25	7.88	7.00	6.38
Price-High	18.38	19.00	8.88	13.25	14.50
Price-Low	12.50	7.25	5.63	5.88	4.75
P/E-Close	2.98	5.37	17.90	3.54	nm
Dividends per Share	0.42	0.40	0.40	3.89	0.34
Dividend Yield (%)	3.13	2.32	5.08	55.57	5.33
Sales per Share	96.07	146.91	116.71	78.58	58.61
EPS before extra. item	4.45	3.21	0.44	1.98	(1.69)
Cash Flow per Share	2.47	4.14	3.92	3.42	1.27
Book Value per Share	15.37	11.41	11.57	12.74	15.06
O/S Common Shares	41,124	35,601	28,485	22,139	23,257
Total Revenue	3,663,256	4,098,750	2,832,938	1,680,182	1,355,547
Income before extra.	162,530	90,097	13,538	63,410	(19,310)
Cash Flow	90,108	113,361	94,664	72,591	29,024
Debt/Equity	0.57	0.80	1.93	1.91	2.21
Return on Capital (%)	28.22	24.22	11.33	13.96	2.51
Ret. on Com. Equity (%)	31.31	24.49	4.43	20.06	(5.25)
% Change Profit	80.4	565.5	(78.7)	428.4	(152.8)
% Change Revenue	(10.6)	44.7	68.6	23.9	(20.6)
% Change Assets	26.0	(16.2)	26.3	(22.1)	(22.0)

Date	EPS	DPS	Tot Rev	Inc Bex
Mar 95	0.69	0.11	998,700	25,700
Dec 94	0.13	0.10	997,056	5,830
Sep 94	0.72	0.11	907,900	27,300
Jun 94	2.30	0.10	915,500	84,300
Mar 94	1.30	0.10	842,800	45,100
Dec 93	1.28	0.10	999,750	37,897
Sep 93	1.29	0.10	1,033,800	35,200
Jun 93	0.51	0.10	1,108,000	13,200

Preferred Div. Coverage	np	np	np
Total Div. Coverage	10.5	0.6	1.0
Interest Coverage	8.4	3.4	1.6
Current Ratio	1.5	1.2	1.0
Operating Margin	2.8	3.7	4.0
Asset Turnover	2.1	3.0	1.7
5 YEAR RATIOS (%)			
Return on Capital	16.0	11.9	9.4
Return on Com. Equity	15.0	10.7	7.8
Profit Growth	34.7	20.3	(11.4)
Revenue Growth	16.5	22.0	18.5
Asset Growth	(4.1)	(6.3)	(4.8)
BALANCE SHEET (000)			
Cash	186,618	229,644	83,550
Current Assets	701,976	659,450	575,546
Net Fixed Assets	338,035	296,211	450,501
Invest's & Advances	230,775	90,569	0
Total Assets	1,703,745	1,351,694	1,613,729
Short Term Debt	37,073	112,457	129,834
Current Liabilities	467,098	529,913	570,310
Long Term Debt	322,926	212,973	507,584
Total Liabilities	1,071,880	945,435	1,284,170
Total Equity	631,865	406,259	329,559
Total Liab. & Equity	1,703,745	1,351,694	1,613,729
CAPITAL (000)			
Total Debt	359,999	325,430	637,418
Preferred Equity	0	0	0
Common Equity	631,865	406,259	329,559

Business:

ONEX CORP. is a diversified holding company. Its companies operate as autonomous businesses in the airline catering, courier services, foodservice distribution, automotive products, foodservice equipment and industrial manufacturing industries. Operating companies include Sky Chefs Inc., ProSource Distribution Services Inc., Automotive Industries, and The Delfield Company.

Synopsis:

Onex Corporation entered into an agreement for Onex Food Services to acquire the international operations and lease the U.S. assets of Caterair International for $700-million. ProSource acquired the National Accounts Division of Martin-Brower Company, which had annual revenues of $2.8-billion, for approximately $197-million. Onex provided about $60-million to ProSource through an investment in a combination of equity and subordinated debt of ProSource. With the acquisition, Prosource became the largest foodservice distributor to restaurant chains in North America. It will take two to three years to restructure the distribution network and integrate the two companies.

During 1994, Tower Automotive completed two acquisitions in the metal-stamping business. This allowed the company to become large enough to make an Initial Public Offering of Tower Treasury shares. The offering reduced Onex's ownership from 74% to approximately 33%. It also established a value for the holdings, at the offering price, of $56-million. In October 1994, Onex purchased a 6.5% convertible debenture of Alliance Communications Corporation for $16.5-million, maturing April 5, 2002. At the conversion price of $19 per share, Onex would own 8.2% of Alliance's common equity. Onex formed a partnership with Tom Garvin of G.G. Products, located in Chicago, to acquire and develop companies in the food-processing industry. The company formed a partnership with Tom Gibson, Asbury Automotive Group, based in Philadelphia and will acquire automobile mega-dealerships. Onex sold 250,000 shares of Automotive Industries for proceeds of $9.7-million and a gain of $6.2-million in August 1994.

Revenues for 1994 (earnings before income taxes and non-controlling interest) by industry segment were: airline catering, 18%(23%); foodservice distribution, 62%(-2%); automotive products 14%(15%); industrial manufacturing 4%(12%); other, 2%(2%); parent company, less than 1%(50%). The parent company's contribution to earnings includes a gain on the sale of shares of subsidiaries totalling approximately $106.3-million.

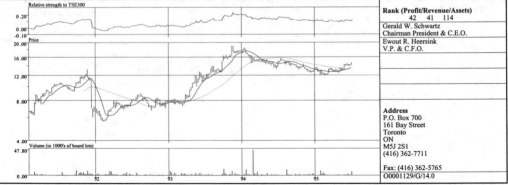

Rank (Profit/Revenue/Assets)
42 41 114

Gerald W. Schwartz
Chairman President & C.E.O.

Ewout R. Heersink
V.P. & C.F.O.

Address
P.O. Box 700
161 Bay Street
Toronto
ON
M5J 2S1
(416) 362-7711

Fax: (416) 362-5765
O0001129/G/14.0

ROMAN CORPORATION LIMITED

Exchanges	Price (Jun29'95)	1 .45	Trailing P/E	6 .59	Stock Symbol
T	Trailing Yield (%)	0 .00	Trailing EPS	0 .22	**RMN**

Period Ending	Dec94	Dec93	Dec92	Dec91	Dec90
Yearly Statistics					
Price-Close	1 .60	2 .70	1 .75	1 .70	2 .50
Price-High	3 .00	3 .25	2 .55	4 .60	9 .63
Price-Low	1 .00	1 .45	1 .25	1 .00	2 .00
P/E-Close	6 .67	9 .64	7 .96	6 .80	nm
Dividends per Share	0 .00	0 .10	0 .10	0 .00	0 .00
Dividend Yield (%)	0 .00	3 .70	5 .71	0 .00	0 .00
Sales per Share	5 .10	4 .70	4 .52	4 .34	4 .27
EPS before extra. item	0 .24	0 .28	0 .22	0 .25	(14 .41)
Cash Flow per Share	0 .39	0 .44	0 .55	0 .69	0 .45
Book Value per Share	1 .26	1 .02	0 .84	0 .74	0 .48
O/S Common Shares	10 ,306	10 ,306	10 ,306	10 ,306	10 ,306
Total Revenue	52 ,566	49 ,256	46 ,532	44 ,709	43 ,957
Income before extra.	2 ,455	2 ,911	2 ,506	4 ,052	(142 ,471)
Cash Flow	4 ,043	4 ,582	5 ,644	7 ,076	4 ,677
Debt/Equity	0 .71	0 .96	1 .24	0 .09	4 .81
Return on Capital (%)	22 .30	26 .34	26 .70	11 .53	(87 .14)
Ret. on Com. Equity (%)	20 .90	30 .38	27 .61	45 .40	(187 .04)
% Change Profit	(15 .6)	16 .2	(38 .2)	102 .8	(6 ,154 .2)
% Change Revenue	6 .7	5 .9	4 .1	1 .7	1 .5
% Change Assets	7 .1	8 .7	4 .5	(72 .6)	(60 .4)

Business:
ROMAN CORP. LTD. is a management company. Its main investment is in 100% owned Strathcona Paper Co. Strathcona is a paper recycling company.

Date	EPS	DPS	Tot Rev	Inc Bex
Mar 95	0 .01	0 .00	15 ,802	79
Dec 94	0 .12	0 .00	15 ,308	1 ,192
Sep 94	0 .05	0 .00	14 ,708	575
Jun 94	0 .04	0 .00	11 ,428	397
Mar 94	0 .03	0 .00	11 ,121	291
Dec 93	0 .10	0 .00	14 ,495	1 ,025
Sep 93	0 .04	0 .10	10 ,648	400
Jun 93	0 .12	0 .00	12 ,289	1 ,269

	Dec94	Dec93	Dec92
Preferred Div. Coverage	np	np	np
Total Div. Coverage	na	2 .8	1 .9
Interest Coverage	4 .2	4 .3	5 .0
Current Ratio	1 .9	2 .0	1 .9
Operating Margin	9 .1	9 .3	11 .3
Asset Turnover	1 .7	1 .7	1 .7
5 YEAR RATIOS (%)			
Return on Capital	(0 .1)	(4 .0)	(8 .9)
Return on Com. Equity	(12 .5)	(16 .4)	(22 .7)
Profit Growth	0 .8	na	(21 .8)
Revenue Growth	3 .9	2 .5	(1 .0)
Asset Growth	(33 .4)	(34 .0)	(30 .5)
BALANCE SHEET (000)			
Cash	265	1 ,640	90
Current Assets	11 ,441	10 ,476	8 ,785
Net Fixed Assets	17 ,227	16 ,834	16 ,694
Invest's & Advances	300	250	0
Total Assets	31 ,001	28 ,956	26 ,637
Short Term Debt	1 ,125	875	625
Current Liabilities	5 ,893	5 ,155	4 ,603
Long Term Debt	8 ,125	9 ,250	10 ,125
Total Liabilities	18 ,025	18 ,435	17 ,996
Total Equity	12 ,976	10 ,521	8 ,641
Total Liab. & Equity	31 ,001	28 ,956	26 ,637
CAPITAL (000)			
Total Debt	9 ,250	10 ,125	10 ,750
Preferred Equity	0	0	0
Common Equity	12 ,976	10 ,521	8 ,641

Synopsis:

Roman Corporation Limited reported a decrease in net earnings for the first quarter of 1995 when compared to the first three months of 1994. The decrease in earnings, from $291,000 to $79,000, reflects the rise in waste paper fibre costs experienced by Strathcona Paper Company. Revenues for first quarter increased, from $11.1-million for first quarter 1994 to $15.8-million for first quarter 1995, as production and shipments increased year over year and selling prices were up over 1994 levels. Increased demand for waste-paper fibre and the recovery of paper prices is leading to the rising costs for the fibre. Strathcona will continue initiatives to counter the price increase, and resulting margin squeeze, throughout the year.

Strathcona achieved a record level of sales and production in 1994. Revenue of $52.5-million represented a increase of 8.5% over the previous year. The increase was due to a 5% increase in production tonnage available for sale and by selling price increases recorded in July and October. The increases were offset by the increase in raw material costs as total fibre costs increased by 36% over 1993 levels. The company changed its fibre mix during 1994 to reduce overall raw material costs and as one way to combat the price increases. Export sales increased from $14.3-million in 1993 to $14.7-million in 1994 but as a percentage of production tonnage, it decreased from 34% of tonnage to 32%. As demand tightened with the changing market conditions, the business base served by Strathcona in the U.S. market contracted in 1994.

Roman purchased 207,408 shares of Exall Resources Limited during 1994, increasing its holdings to 1,325,394 shares, or less than 10% of the outstanding shares. On March 14, 1995, the company completed a transaction to provide new credit facilities. The transaction included a $3-million revolving credit facility, a $5-million revolving term credit facility, and a $10-million non-revolving term loan. Part of the non-revolving term loan was used to refinance the outstanding long-term debt.

Rank (Profit/Revenue/Assets)
540   538   764

Helen Roman-Barber
Chairman & C.E.O.

P. Gael Mourant
V.P. & C.F.O.

Address
Suite 1315
200 King Street West
Box 82
Toronto
ON
M5H 3T4
(416) 971-3330
Fax: (416) 971-9181
R0002415/G/14.0

RUSSEL METALS INC.

Exchanges	Price (Jun29'95)	5.12	Trailing P/E	nm	Stock Symbol
TW	Trailing Yield (%)	0.00	Trailing EPS	(0.04)	**RUS.A**

Period Ending	Dec94	Dec93	Dec92	Dec91	Dec90
Yearly Statistics					
Price-Close	5.88	8.50	4.10	7.50	6.38
Price-High	9.75	8.88	8.75	10.50	14.25
Price-Low	5.38	3.50	3.19	6.00	5.75
P/E-Close	nm	nm	nm	nm	79.69
Dividends per Share	0.00	0.00	0.10	0.20	0.35
Dividend Yield (%)	0.00	0.00	2.44	2.67	5.49
Sales per Share	27.09	27.33	43.58	47.53	64.80
EPS before extra. item	(0.25)	(0.23)	(2.08)	(4.86)	0.08
Cash Flow per Share	1.17	0.49	(0.37)	0.06	1.83
Book Value per Share	5.44	5.17	5.15	7.10	14.04
O/S Common Shares	51,008	40,963	33,263	33,134	23,372
Total Revenue	1,336,170	968,229	1,450,776	1,390,626	1,540,169
Income before extra.	(8,803)	(1,915)	(62,714)	(134,277)	8,372
Cash Flow	57,572	17,258	(12,276)	1,681	43,087
Debt/Equity	1.25	1.04	1.20	0.98	1.12
Return on Capital (%)	6.61	5.47	(7.04)	(16.01)	5.79
Ret. on Com. Equity (%)	(5.02)	(4.33)	(34.00)	(49.98)	0.57
% Change Profit	(359.7)	96.9	53.3	(1,703.9)	(81.7)
% Change Revenue	38.0	(33.3)	4.3	(9.7)	(32.8)
% Change Assets	9.4	0.7	(8.9)	(16.8)	(9.7)

Preferred Div. Coverage	0.0	0.0	0.0
Total Div. Coverage	0.0	0.0	0.0
Interest Coverage	1.2	0.9	0.0
Current Ratio	1.6	1.7	1.1
Operating Margin	5.4	3.5	1.0
Asset Turnover	1.4	1.1	1.7
5 YEAR RATIOS (%)			
Return on Capital	(1.0)	1.0	3.7
Return on Com. Equity	(18.6)	(14.4)	(9.3)
Profit Growth	na	na	na
Revenue Growth	(10.3)	(12.8)	(2.4)
Asset Growth	(5.5)	(2.4)	(1.8)
BALANCE SHEET (000)			
Cash	0	37,372	0
Current Assets	564,087	490,015	433,619
Net Fixed Assets	153,309	143,014	213,912
Invest's & Advances	45,503	30,616	23,934
Total Assets	922,418	842,908	836,990
Short Term Debt	116,107	49,544	117,124
Current Liabilities	348,800	287,339	389,813
Long Term Debt	266,388	258,954	190,735
Total Liabilities	615,188	546,293	580,548
Total Equity	307,230	296,615	256,442
Total Liab. & Equity	922,418	842,908	836,990
CAPITAL (000)			
Total Debt	382,495	308,498	307,859
Preferred Equity	30,000	85,000	85,000
Common Equity	277,230	211,615	171,442

Business:

RUSSEL METALS INC. is a metals processing and distribution organization, with a network of 43 Canadian and 12 U.S. service centers, which provide and process a wide range of carbon steel and alloy metal products. It also operates an international metals trading company which exports North American steel products to international customers and imports foreign steel products into Canada & the U.S.

Date	EPS	DPS	Tot Rev	Inc Bex
Mar 95	0.08	0.00	397,701	4,416
Dec 94	(0.30)	0.00	130,407	(13,980)
Sep 94	0.14	0.00	443,630	7,171
Jun 94	0.04	0.00	412,842	2,464
Mar 94	(0.15)	0.00	283,237	(4,458)
Dec 93	0.03	0.00	(78,728)	1,927
Sep 93	0.00	0.00	364,046	1,708
Jun 93	(0.03)	0.00	382,802	714

Synopsis:

Federal Industries Ltd.'s shareholders, at the May Annual and Special Meeting, approved a prospective change in the name of the company to Russel Metals Inc., reflecting the company's focus on its metals operations. In the first quarter report, the company stated that the name change would occur at the same time as the formal merging of Federal Industries and its wholly owned subsidiary, Fedmet. Federal spent $44.4-million in 1994 to acquire three pipe distributors; two in the United States and one in Canada. The company acquired several small Canadian companies during the first quarter of 1995, expanding its capabilities in pre-assembly processing of metals for the manufacturing industry.

During 1994, Federal decided to classify its consumer operations as discontinued. The loss of $25.5-million from discontinued operations for 1994 includes a net provision of $13.8-million to cover all foreseeable cost or losses associated with the disposal of these interests. The company did not allocate any of its interest expense to discontinued operations but chose to reflect all of it on the income statement. Cashway Building Centres remained the sole active business in discontinued operations at the end of the first quarter of 1995.

Revenues from continuing operations for the first quarter of 1995 were $397.7-million, a 41% increase over the $282.9-million for the same period in 1994. The 56% increase in the Metals segment revenues, to $350.1-million in 1995, was offset by the drop in aggregate Transport sales, from $58-million to $47.5-million, due to the sale of the Poolcar operations in 1994. The operating margins for the first quarter of 1995 were up 83% compared with 1994. Both segments contributed to the improvement, with the Metals segment showing an increase in operating earnings. The Transport segment reported operating earnings in 1995 compared to an operating loss of $300,000 for the first quarter of 1994. Two-thirds of the growth in revenues and three-quarters of the operating margin growth derived from the increased volumes and prices in the existing service center operations for the Metals segment.

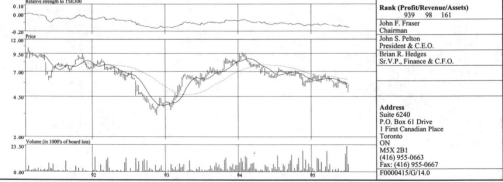

Rank (Profit/Revenue/Assets)
939 98 161

John F. Fraser
Chairman

John S. Pelton
President & C.E.O.

Brian R. Hedges
Sr.V.P., Finance & C.F.O.

Address
Suite 6240
P.O. Box 61 Drive
1 First Canadian Place
Toronto
ON
M5X 2B1
(416) 955-0663
Fax: (416) 955-0667
F0000415/G/14.0

SCOTT'S HOSPITALITY INC.

Exchanges	Price (Jun29'95)	8 .00	Trailing P/E	15 .09	Stock Symbol
TM	Trailing Yield (%)	3 .25	Trailing EPS	0 .53	**SRC**

Period Ending	Apr94	Apr93	Apr92	Apr91	Apr90
Yearly Statistics					
Price-Close	7 .00	9 .25	15 .00	18 .75	15 .00
Price-High	11 .13	15 .00	19 .88	19 .50	21 .50
Price-Low	6 .88	8 .50	15 .00	13 .00	13 .38
P/E-Close	14 .29	nm	16 .67	18 .56	14 .42
Dividends per Share	0 .26	0 .26	0 .26	0 .26	3 .25
Dividend Yield (%)	3 .71	2 .81	1 .73	1 .39	21 .67
Sales per Share	13 .55	13 .15	12 .53	14 .27	15 .60
EPS before extra. item	0 .49	0 .00	0 .90	1 .01	1 .04
Cash Flow per Share	1 .64	1 .58	1 .62	2 .18	2 .06
Book Value per Share	6 .55	6 .20	6 .64	5 .80	5 .09
O/S Common Shares	59 ,725	59 ,730	59 ,730	59 ,717	59 ,697
Total Revenue	814 ,497	792 ,688	800 ,792	1 ,017 ,550	943 ,488
Income before extra.	29 ,225	7	53 ,530	60 ,308	61 ,933
Cash Flow	97 ,690	94 ,527	96 ,766	129 ,923	122 ,577
Debt/Equity	1 .19	1 .33	1 .10	1 .27	0 .97
Return on Capital (%)	7 .97	4 .20	12 .57	17 .21	19 .14
Ret. on Com. Equity (%)	7 .68	0 .00	14 .41	18 .54	19 .12
% Change Profit	nm	(100 .0)	(11 .2)	(2 .6)	15 .9
% Change Revenue	2 .8	(1 .0)	(21 .3)	7 .9	9 .5
% Change Assets	(0 .1)	2 .2	3 .7	15 .7	2 .4

Preferred Div. Coverage	np	np	np
Total Div. Coverage	1 .9	0 .0	3 .4
Interest Coverage	1 .9	1 .0	2 .5
Current Ratio	2 .3	1 .8	1 .7
Operating Margin	7 .9	7 .6	9 .6
Asset Turnover	0 .8	0 .8	0 .8
5 YEAR RATIOS (%)			
Return on Capital	12 .2	13 .9	16 .7
Return on Com. Equity	12 .0	13 .6	16 .6
Profit Growth	(11 .4)	(100 .0)	6 .4
Revenue Growth	(1 .2)	(5 .9)	(1 .8)
Asset Growth	4 .6	2 .6	4 .8
BALANCE SHEET (000)			
Cash	124 ,346	74 ,099	12 ,582
Current Assets	229 ,985	172 ,364	152 ,763
Net Fixed Assets	629 ,902	652 ,681	622 ,178
Invest's & Advances	6 ,488	4 ,461	13 ,230
Total Assets	976 ,701	977 ,680	956 ,291
Short Term Debt	1 ,449	1 ,389	137
Current Liabilities	101 ,763	98 ,315	91 ,390
Long Term Debt	464 ,704	491 ,709	436 ,441
Total Liabilities	585 ,636	607 ,521	559 ,713
Total Equity	391 ,065	370 ,159	396 ,578
Total Liab. & Equity	976 ,701	977 ,680	956 ,291
CAPITAL (000)			
Total Debt	466 ,153	493 ,098	436 ,578
Preferred Equity	0	0	0
Common Equity	391 ,065	370 ,159	396 ,578

Business:

SCOTT'S HOSPITALITY INC. is an international consumer service company with interests in the food service, hotels, and transportation industries. The company operates in Canada, the United States, and the United Kingdom. Subsidiaries of the company include Scott's Food Services, Scott's Hotels Limited, Charterways Transportation Ltd. and National School Bus Services, Inc.

Date		EPS	DPS	Tot Rev	Inc Bex
Jan	95	0 .11	0 .13	214 ,779	9 ,286
Oct	94	0 .13	0 .00	204 ,067	7 ,760
Jul	94	0 .16	0 .13	206 ,914	9 ,333
Apr	94	0 .13	0 .00	201 ,646	7 ,798
Jan	94	0 .10	0 .13	209 ,284	6 ,162
Oct	93	0 .11	0 .00	199 ,609	6 ,544
Jul	93	0 .15	0 .13	203 ,013	8 ,721
Apr	93	(0 .41)	0 .00	201 ,325	(24 ,389)

Synopsis:

Scott's Hospitality reported higher operating earnings for the nine months ended January 31, 1995, compared to the same period ended January 31, 1994. The higher earnings and sales were due to the stronger comparable sales and operating earnings experienced by all three of Scott's divisions. The Food Services Division reported improved earnings for both the three and nine month periods. This was due mostly to successful promotional activities and cost reductions at Scott's KFC. The Manchu Wok and Perfect Pizza brands still require work. Sales for the division were down slightly for both the three and nine month periods. The operating earnings of the transportation division increased by 8% for the three month period ended January 1995 over the comparable period in 1994. The 11% increase in Transportation's earnings in the United States was offset by a slight decline in Canadian earnings. The Hotel Division's operating earnings for the nine month period more than doubled the results from the nine months ended January 31, 1994. The improvement came from higher occupancies and higher average room rates.

A major reorganization of the Food Services Division occurred in 1994. This should streamline operations, allow management to respond more quickly to competition, and reduce divisional overhead by 15%. In 1994, a computerized Demand Forecast System, which forecasts likely occupancy demand based on historical data, was introduced as an integral part of the Marriot reservation system. The two test hotels increased revenues as a result of the information provided, and expect to add more incremental business as management's familiarity with the program increases.

Sales (operating earnings) by geographic segment in fiscal 1994 were: Canada, 58% (51%); United States, 24% (37%); and Great Britain, 18% (12%). All three of Scott's business segments had operating earnings in fiscal 1994. Hotels went from a loss in fiscal 1993 to a profit in fiscal 1994.

Relative strength to TSE300 / Price / Volume (in 1000's of board lots) charts

Rank (Profit/Revenue/Assets)
164   134   157

Patrick W.E. Hodgson
Chairman

John S. Lacey
President & C.E.O.

Bonita J. Then
Sr. V.P. & C.F.O.

Address
BCE Place 181 Bay Street
Suite 1500
Box 810
Toronto
ON
M5J 2T3
(416) 369-9050
Fax: (416) 369-2500

S0001182/G/14.0

Split 4 for 1 92

Split '83 3 for 1.

SEAGRAM COMPANY LTD. (THE)

Exchanges	Price (Jun29'95)	45.62	Trailing P/E	18.57	Stock Symbol
TMVN	Trailing Yield (%)	1.29	Trailing EPS	10.48	**VO**

Period Ending	Jan95	Jan94	Jan93	Jan92	Jan91
Yearly Statistics	US	US	US	US	US
Price-Close	40.50	40.63	32.00	35.06	25.81
Price-High	44.63	40.88	36.50	36.25	26.06
Price-Low	37.25	31.38	31.25	25.50	21.12
P/E-Close	9.81	23.63	16.98	13.75	9.46
Dividends per Share	0.58	0.56	0.55	0.50	0.46
Dividend Yield (%)	1.97	1.79	2.08	1.64	2.09
Sales per Share	17.18	16.19	13.87	13.82	13.35
EPS before extra. item	2.18	1.02	1.26	1.94	2.01
Cash Flow per Share	1.79	1.88	1.81	2.61	1.73
Book Value per Share	14.79	13.43	13.19	17.11	15.87
O/S Common Shares	372,537	372,489	373,690	378,841	374,972
Total Revenue	6,727,000	6,344,000	5,510,000	5,448,000	5,029,000
Income before extra.	811,000	379,000	474,000	727,000	756,000
Cash Flow	665,000	700,000	680,000	992,000	650,000
Debt/Equity	0.97	0.98	0.69	0.55	0.65
Return on Capital (%)	13.57	9.87	10.72	12.80	13.39
Ret. on Com. Equity (%)	15.43	7.63	8.31	11.69	13.37
% Change Profit	114.0	(20.0)	(34.8)	(3.8)	6.4
% Change Revenue	6.0	15.1	1.1	8.3	12.0
% Change Assets	10.6	16.0	(14.9)	3.5	12.4

Preferred Div. Coverage	np	np	np
Total Div. Coverage	3.8	1.8	2.3
Interest Coverage	3.4	2.6	2.9
Current Ratio	1.0	1.3	1.9
Operating Margin	11.3	12.5	14.6
Asset Turnover	0.5	0.5	0.5
5 YEAR RATIOS (%)			
Return on Capital	12.1	12.1	12.7
Return on Com. Equity	11.3	11.0	11.9
Profit Growth	2.6	(8.5)	(1.9)
Revenue Growth	8.4	9.7	13.9
Asset Growth	4.8	3.8	5.9
BALANCE SHEET (mil)			
Cash	157	131	116
Current Assets	4,176	3,794	3,836
Net Fixed Assets	1,267	1,220	1,215
Invest's & Advances	5,713	4,923	3,315
Total Assets	12,956	11,718	10,104
Short Term Debt	2,475	1,844	851
Current Liabilities	4,091	2,996	2,003
Long Term Debt	2,841	3,053	2,559
Total Liabilities	7,447	6,717	5,174
Total Equity	5,509	5,001	4,930
Total Liab. & Equity	12,956	11,718	10,104
CAPITAL (mil)			
Total Debt	5,316	4,897	3,410
Preferred Equity	0	0	0
Common Equity	5,509	5,001	4,930

Business:

THE SEAGRAM COMPANY LTD. produces and markets distilled spirits, wines, soft drinks and fruit juices. Brands include Chivas, Martell, Glenlivet, Barton & Guestier, Crown Royal, Paul Masson, and Tropicana. Seagram owns 80% of the outstanding common shares of MCA Inc., an entertainment company.

Date		EPS	DPS	Tot Rev	Inc Bex
Apr 95	US	8.83	0.15	1,280,000	3299,000
Jan 95	US	0.52	0.15	2,319,000	191,000
Oct 94	US	0.53	0.15	1,596,000	199,000
Jul 94	US	0.60	0.14	1,525,000	224,000
Apr 94	US	0.53	0.14	1,210,000	122,000
Jan 94	US	0.40	0.14	2,060,000	147,000
Oct 93	US	(0.27)	0.14	1,543,000	(100,000)
Jul 93	US	0.46	0.14	1,515,000	170,000

Synopsis:

In April 1995, Seagram Company Ltd. redeemed most of its position in DuPont stock. Seagram sold 156 million DuPont shares, comprising 95% of its total holdings, back to the company for $1-billion (U.S.) in cash, $7.3-billion (U.S.) in 90 day DuPont notes, and equity warrants valued at $440-million (U.S.). Seagram used the proceeds to buy an 80% interest in MCA Inc. from Matsushita Electric Industrial Co., Ltd. for $5.7-billion (U.S.) in cash. Matsushita will retain a 20% interest in MCA. MCA Motion Picture Group runs Universal Pictures, which produces, finances, and distributes movies. Universal has a film relationship with Steven Spielberg and his production company, Amblin Entertainment.

Among MCA Television Group's best-known products are Murder, She Wrote, Coach and SeaQuest. MCA Music Entertainment Group includes MCA Records, Geffen Records, Chess and Uptown. The group has a market value of between $2-billion (U.S.) and $3-billion (U.S.), and had a profit of around $220-million (U.S.) in 1994. MCA owns Putnam Publishing Group Inc., a publisher of authors such as Tom Clancy and Robin Cook. It owns Universal Studios in California and has a 50% stake in the park in Orlando, Florida. MCA is a controlling shareholder in Cineplex Odeon Corp., an operator of one of the largest theatre chains in the world. MCA signed a 10 year strategic alliance with DreamWorks SKG that gives MCA key distribution rights to DreamWorks' movies, home videos, and music, and the right to use its characters and concepts in MCA theme parks.

In May 1995, Seagram completed the acquisition of the Dole global juice business from Dole Food Co. Inc. for $240-million (U.S.). The transaction excludes Dole's joint venture in Japan. Seagram formed two new operating units, one to direct its North American juice operations and the other to direct international juice operations.

Relative strength to TSE300

Rank (Profit/Revenue/Assets)
3 10 18

Edgar M. Bronfman
Chairman

Edgar Bronfman, Jr.
President & C.E.O.

Address
1430 Peel Street
Montreal
PQ
H3A 1S9
(514) 849-5271

S0001344/G/14.0

SHERRITT INC.

Exchanges	Price (Jun29'95)	14.00	Trailing P/E	8.19	Stock Symbol
T	Trailing Yield (%)	0.00	Trailing EPS	1.71	SE

Period Ending	Dec94	Dec93	Dec92	Dec91	Dec90	Business:
Yearly Statistics						SHERRITT INC. is engaged in the production
Price-Close	13.50	10.75	6.63	7.50	6.50	and marketing of fertilizer and chemicals, the
Price-High	15.38	11.38	9.38	8.38	11.00	mining, refining and sale of nickel and cobalt,
Price-Low	10.50	5.75	5.88	5.75	5.25	the production and sale of oil and natural gas,
P/E-Close	10.39	nm	110.42	187.50	nm	and the development and marketing of
Dividends per Share	0.00	0.00	0.00	0.14	0.13	advanced industrial materials and metallurgical
Dividend Yield (%)	0.00	0.00	0.00	1.87	2.00	technologies.
Sales per Share	14.93	9.61	11.85	12.77	13.76	
EPS before extra. item	1.30	(0.97)	0.06	0.04	(1.29)	
Cash Flow per Share	3.35	1.21	1.74	1.34	0.78	
Book Value per Share	9.46	6.84	7.82	7.76	8.14	
O/S Common Shares	67,580	43,271	42,625	35,033	25,118	
Total Revenue	930,942	421,358	439,929	389,160	345,250	

Income before extra.	79,976	(41,461)	2,274	1,150	(32,387)	Date	EPS	DPS	Tot Rev	Inc Bex
Cash Flow	206,697	51,778	63,965	40,232	19,600	Mar 95	0.44	0.00	255,895	29,734
Debt/Equity	0.83	1.31	0.90	1.22	0.79	Dec 94	0.46	0.00	299,021	29,921
Return on Capital (%)	19.95	(3.93)	3.25	4.01	(10.32)	Sep 94	0.06	0.00	173,129	5,129
Ret. on Com. Equity (%)	17.10	(13.18)	0.75	0.48	(14.58)	Jun 94	0.75	0.00	328,353	43,170
% Change Profit	292.9	(1,923.3)	97.7	103.6	(200.6)	Mar 94	0.03	0.00	127,112	1,756
% Change Revenue	120.9	(4.2)	13.0	12.7	(36.8)	Dec 93	(0.54)	0.00	110,662	(23,277)
% Change Assets	72.6	2.2	3.1	53.3	(6.6)	Sep 93	(0.20)	0.00	80,190	(8,463)
						Jun 93	0.05	0.00	128,171	2,203

				Synopsis:
Preferred Div. Coverage	np	np	np	
Total Div. Coverage	na	na	na	Sherritt reported increased revenues for the first quarter of 1995 from
Interest Coverage	3.2	0.0	1.1	$127.1-million to $255.9-million. Net earnings also rose from $1.8-million to
Current Ratio	3.2	1.9	1.3	$29.7-million. Earnings before R&D, corporate, and financing expenses rose from
Operating Margin	19.4	(5.7)	5.1	$14.4-million in 1994 to $64.9-million during the first quarter. The increases were
Asset Turnover	0.6	0.5	0.5	due to the performance of Sherritt Fertilizers, where earnings rose to
5 YEAR RATIOS (%)				$45.3-million from $474,000, and revenue grew to $119.5-million in first quarter
Return on Capital	2.6	1.5	6.6	1995 from $29.3-million one year ago. The results reflected the larger production
Return on Com. Equity	(1.9)	(2.7)	5.8	base, due to the acquisition of the Redwater facilities on March 1994, and strong
Profit Growth	20.0	na	(17.3)	market demand for both nitrogen and phosphate products.
Revenue Growth	11.3	(5.1)	7.5	
Asset Growth	21.0	6.6	8.6	Strong market demand during the first quarter and increased production at its
BALANCE SHEET (000)				operations led to an increase in the Commodity Metals division's earnings. The
Cash	128,553	67,834	62,595	Specialty Products division had earnings increase by 80% from $3-million to
Current Assets	591,290	310,739	300,991	$5.4-million. This was due to the contribution from Specialty Materials, which
Net Fixed Assets	891,072	545,574	540,203	includes value-added cobalt and nickel powders. Earnings from Specialty
Invest's & Advances	32,353	22,262	24,842	Materials nearly tripling to $4.6-million for first quarter 1995 compared to 1994.
Total Assets	1,528,035	885,194	866,036	
Short Term Debt	0	75,708	139,500	An increase in the demand for fertilizer in Western Canada and the Pacific
Current Liabilities	186,690	160,345	239,789	Northwest and upper Midwest is expected for the fifth consecutive year. Prices
Long Term Debt	532,697	310,724	160,059	should remain ahead of last spring's level. The higher productivity rates should
Total Liabilities	888,931	589,130	532,764	continue during the year, leading to increased production levels and lower unit
Total Equity	639,104	296,064	333,272	operating costs.
Total Liab. & Equity	1,528,035	885,194	866,036	
CAPITAL (000)				The acquisition of the Redwater plant from Imperial Oil allowed Sherritt
Total Debt	532,697	386,432	299,559	Fertilizers to produce and sell a wider range of fertilizer products. The Western
Preferred Equity	0	0	0	Canadian market accounted for approximately 65% of total sales and the United
Common Equity	639,104	296,064	333,272	States Pacific Northwest accounted for about 25% of sales. In January, Sherritt

Inc. acquired Talisman Energy Inc.'s oil and gas interests in Cuba for $10-million (U.S.). Sherritt and Talisman had operated the Cuban joint venture since December 1992.

Rank (Profit/Revenue/Assets)
88   124   127

Ian W. Delaney
Chairman & C.E.O.

Michael McKibbon
Sr. V.P. Finance & C.F.O.

Michael G. Weedon
Executive V.P. & C.O.O.

Address
Bag 9
Fort Saskatchewan
AB
T8L 2P2
(403) 998-6911

Fax: (403) 998-6568
S0002425/G/14.0

UNITED DOMINION INDUSTRIES LIMITED

Exchanges	Price (Jun29'95)	31.00	Trailing P/E	12.97	Stock Symbol
TMN	Trailing Yield (%)	0.88	Trailing EPS	1.76	**UDI**

Period Ending	Dec94	Dec93	Dec92	Dec91	Dec90
Yearly Statistics	US	US	US	US	US
Price-Close	27.00	25.13	10.50	10.50	10.00
Price-High	28.75	26.00	13.00	14.00	21.25
Price-Low	23.75	10.13	9.75	9.25	7.75
P/E-Close	9.28	15.49	11.66	10.13	30.59
Dividends per Share	0.20	0.20	0.20	0.51	0.58
Dividend Yield (%)	1.02	1.03	2.31	5.56	6.77
Sales per Share	54.76	50.93	45.87	46.05	50.46
EPS before extra. item	1.55	0.97	0.61	0.79	0.24
Cash Flow per Share	3.80	2.27	1.66	0.88	1.77
Book Value per Share	13.37	11.50	11.12	11.54	11.38
O/S Common Shares	39,443	35,901	35,826	29,325	28,489
Total Revenue	2,046,536	1,829,789	1,531,208	1,391,862	1,448,624
Income before extra.	62,143	39,811	25,684	37,010	26,381
Cash Flow	141,133	81,285	55,182	25,687	50,333
Debt/Equity	0.55	0.98	0.55	0.58	0.46
Return on Capital (%)	14.45	9.56	8.77	9.40	7.97
Ret. on Com. Equity (%)	12.24	8.59	5.50	6.99	2.14
% Change Profit	56.1	55.0	(30.6)	40.3	(64.0)
% Change Revenue	11.8	19.5	10.0	(3.9)	1.9
% Change Assets	4.0	28.6	16.4	(9.5)	(5.3)

Date		EPS	DPS	Tot Rev	Inc Bex
Mar 95	US	0.30	0.05	530,994	12,741
Dec 94	US	0.41	0.05	548,726	17,135
Sep 94	US	0.62	0.05	558,017	23,966
Jun 94	US	0.43	0.05	510,616	16,843
Mar 94	US	0.08	0.05	426,068	4,199
Dec 93	US	0.45	0.05	498,228	17,436
Sep 93	US	0.35	0.05	496,881	13,774
Jun 93	US	0.20	0.05	449,592	8,472

	Dec94	Dec93	Dec92
Preferred Div. Coverage	13.5	8.0	4.7
Total Div. Coverage	5.2	3.3	2.1
Interest Coverage	4.9	3.8	3.0
Current Ratio	1.7	1.8	1.7
Operating Margin	5.9	4.3	3.2
Asset Turnover	1.5	1.4	1.5
5 YEAR RATIOS (%)			
Return on Capital	10.0	10.0	9.9
Return on Com. Equity	7.1	7.7	6.2
Profit Growth	(3.2)	9.4	61.1
Revenue Growth	7.5	7.1	6.2
Asset Growth	5.9	2.0	1.2
BALANCE SHEET (000)			
Cash	101,839	63,305	72,576
Current Assets	660,466	597,103	554,996
Net Fixed Assets	222,148	232,132	166,827
Invest's & Advances	0	0	0
Total Assets	1,359,356	1,307,459	1,016,416
Short Term Debt	9,234	20,457	26,040
Current Liabilities	396,659	335,409	325,753
Long Term Debt	309,768	433,135	219,164
Total Liabilities	783,348	842,826	566,266
Total Equity	576,008	464,633	450,150
Total Liab. & Equity	1,359,356	1,307,459	1,016,416
CAPITAL (000)			
Total Debt	319,002	453,592	245,204
Preferred Equity	48,816	51,746	51,784
Common Equity	527,192	412,887	398,366

Business:

UNITED DOMINION INDUSTRIES LIMITED provides manufactured products, engineering services, and construction products and services to industrial, energy and construction markets worldwide.

Synopsis:

In the first quarter of 1995, United Dominion saw net income of $12.7-million compared to $4.2-million in the first quarter of 1994. This reflected United Dominion's growing manufacturing orientation, more stable earnings, and the continuing strong operating momentum that started in 1994. The first quarter has traditionally been United Dominion's weakest due to seasonal factors. Sales in the first quarter increased 25% to $531-million compared to the first quarter a year ago. Bookings of $529-million were up 13% from the first quarter of 1994, with especially strong activity in the company's compaction business. Most units experienced volume or pricing gains during the first quarter of 1995.

United Dominion has developed a new five-year strategic plan, VISION '99. The strategic growth and profit improvement plan consists of two major action plans. The margin improvement initiative has the ultimate objective of improving operating margins on sales from the 7% achieved in 1994, to 10% over a three year period. The second plan is the Investment Program. United Dominion anticipates spending about $600-million for acquisitions over the next four to five years while it maintains a satisfactory debt-to-capital ratio of 40% net debt to capital. The acquisitions would fit its strategic profile of manufacturing operations that complement and expand existing product lines and produce proprietary, engineered products.

In June 1995, United Dominion signed a definitive agreement to sell the assets of The Litwin Companies to Raytheon Engineers & Constructors, Inc. for $58-million. This is the approximate book value of Litwin. Litwin was the petroleum and petrochemical engineering services segment of United Dominion. The company purchased 95.6% of the outstanding shares of Flair Corp., a manufacturer of equipment used to dehydrate, filter and purify air, gas and fluids, for $125-million (U.S.).

Rank (Profit/Revenue/Assets)
85   56   110

William R. Holland
Chairman & C.E.O.

Jan K. Ver Hagen
President & C.O.O.

Robert Drury
Sr. V.P. & C.F.O.

Address
2300 - 1 First Union Center
301 S. College St.
Charlotte
NC
28202
(704) 347-6800

Fax: (704) 347-6900
A0001819/G/14.0

Page	Company		Fiscal year end	EARNINGS PER SHARE		
				Last Year	Estimate this year	Estimate next year
535	ATI Technologies		Aug-94	(0.06)	0.40	0.58
536	Cognos		Feb-95	0.86	1.30	1.70
537	Corel	$US	Nov-94	0.63	0.67	0.97
538	Delrina		Jun-94	0.68	0.70	1.23
539	Eicon Technology		Jun-94	0.63	0.58	0.96
540	Geac Computer		Apr-94	0.81	1.10	1.37
541	Hummingbird Communications		Sep-94	0.96	1.42	1.78
542	I.S.G. Technologies		Jun-94	(0.17)	0.00	(0.19)
543	OCS Technologies		Apr-94	0.14	0.18	0.25
544	SHL Systemhous		Aug-94	0.29	0.39	0.68
545	Softkey Software		Dec-93	(1.52)	na	na
546	Systems Excellence		Feb-95	0.33	na	na
547	Teleglobe		Dec-94	1.25	1.37	1.54

Estimates from First Call Corporation, 22 Pittsburgh Street, Boston, MA 02210   (800) 366-9992   Fax (617) 261-5679

Computer Software & Processing

Recently, the computer software industry experienced a rash of mergers and takeovers while at the same time enjoying booming business. This led to spectacular gains in the stock market for computer software companies during the last 18 months. However, many Canadian software companies were victims of the maturing of the industry. To position themselves in the huge and growing software industry, large U.S. software companies are acquiring small companies. With the growth of the computer software industry, it makes sense to merge products and distribution networks to achieve synergy and efficiencies. Given the recent run-up in share prices of U.S. technology stocks — which have propelled markets to record highs — many companies are cash rich. They are seeking to purchase smaller businesses that will give them a bigger piece of the growing and enormous global market for software products.

The acquisition by Symantec Corp. of Cupertino, California, of Toronto-based Delrina Corp. in a $415-million (U.S.) deal is an example. Analysts expect takeover and merger activity will increase markedly as the maturing software industry rushes to position itself for future growth.

Cognos Inc. and Corel Corp. are among the last big players in the Canadian software industry that have not yet been swallowed up by U.S. software giants. Recently, Silicon Graphics Inc. of Mountain View California, purchased Toronto's Alias Research Inc. Microsoft Corp. of Redmond, Washington acquired Montreal-based Softimage Inc.

One analyst at Midland Walwyn in Toronto, referring to potential Canadian takeover candidates, says there are a number of companies with key technologies desired by other high tech companies. This is particularly true for companies that create software for the Internet. Among the possible targets are: Fulcrum Technologies Inc. of Ottawa; Hummingbird Communications Ltd. of Markham, Ontario; and Softquad International Inc. of Toronto. All of these companies are experiencing rapid growth and are possible takeover targets.

Industry sources claim Novell Inc. of Provo, Utah, and International Business Machines Corp. of Armonk, New York are looking for acquisition opportunities. IBM has approximately $7-billion to spend on acquisitions.

The largest deal the computer software industry has ever seen was the purchase of Lotus Development Corp. for $3.52-billion (U.S.) by International Business Machines Corp. The two companies agreed on a $64 per share purchase price. This was $4 per share or $220-million higher than an initial offer of $3.3-billion by IBM. IBM's initial offer of $60 a share was twice the market value of Lotus shares at the time. The final arrangement turned IBM's first hostile takeover bid into a friendly one. The deal has the potential to realign the personal computer software industry by putting IBM of Armonk, New York in a strong position to challenge Microsoft Corp. Microsoft leads the industry by dominating operating system programs that run the basic functions of personal computers.

ATI TECHNOLOGIES INC.

Exchanges	Price (Jun29'95)	10.62	Trailing P/E	53.10	Stock Symbol
T	Trailing Yield (%)	0.00	Trailing EPS	0.20	**ATY**

Period Ending	Aug94	Aug93	Aug92
Yearly Statistics			
Price-Close	5.13	n t	n t
Price-High	19.88	n t	n t
Price-Low	5.00	n t	n t
P/E-Close	nm	n t	n t
Dividends per Share	0.00	0.00	0.00
Dividend Yield (%)	0.00	0.00	0.00
Sales per Share	5.32	5.54	3.97
EPS before extra. item	(0.06)	0.07	(0.02)
Cash Flow per Share	(0.16)	0.17	0.03
Book Value per Share	2.19	0.20	0.38
O/S Common Shares	47,250	40,000	40,000
Total Revenue	234,508	222,445	159,072
Income before extra.	(2,691)	2,729	(940)
Cash Flow	(6,772)	6,635	1,137
Debt/Equity	0.23	5.62	1.21
Return on Capital (%)	(3.23)	11.00	na
Ret. on Com. Equity (%)	(4.83)	23.57	na
% Change Profit	(198.6)	390.3	na
% Change Revenue	5.4	39.8	na
% Change Assets	82.5	45.2	na

Preferred Div. Coverage	np	np	np
Total Div. Coverage	na	na	na
Interest Coverage	0.0	7.0	0.0
Current Ratio	2.8	1.0	1.2
Operating Margin	(2.2)	1.8	(0.4)
Asset Turnover	1.6	2.8	2.9
5 YEAR RATIOS (%)			
Return on Capital	na	na	na
Return on Com. Equity	na	na	na
Profit Growth	na	na	na
Revenue Growth	na	na	na
Asset Growth	na	na	na
BALANCE SHEET (000)			
Cash	29,275	0	0
Current Assets	119,357	64,901	48,461
Net Fixed Assets	19,479	15,480	5,943
Invest's & Advances	0	0	0
Total Assets	146,700	80,381	55,340
Short Term Debt	23,734	41,912	18,235
Current Liabilities	43,397	67,158	39,662
Long Term Debt	0	3,300	0
Total Liabilities	43,397	72,336	40,224
Total Equity	103,303	8,045	15,116
Total Liab. & Equity	146,700	80,381	55,340
CAPITAL (000)			
Total Debt	23,734	45,212	18,235
Preferred Equity	0	0	0
Common Equity	103,303	8,045	15,116

Business:

ATI TECHNOLOGIES INC. manufactures graphic enhancement products for personal computers. The company's main product lines are component and board level graphics accelerators. ATI supplies leading original equipment manufacturers and distributors. It is also engaged in joint technology development projects.

Date	EPS	DPS	Tot Rev	Inc Bex
May 95	0.06	0.00	95,594	2,765
Feb 95	0.12	0.00	93,217	5,919
Nov 94	0.09	0.00	73,358	4,122
Aug 94	(0.07)	0.00	61,400	(2,906)
May 94	(0.16)	0.00	52,130	(7,373)
Feb 94	0.14	0.00	78,181	6,561
Nov 93	0.03	0.00	41,925	1,027
Aug 93	na	0.00	36,572	(16,337)

Synopsis:

In June 1995, ATI Technologies announced its first product for Apple's peripheral component interconnect-based systems (PCI). ATI will produce the XCLAIM GA graphics accelerator board for Apple Computers. The XCLAIM GA uses ATI's highly regarded mach64 controller on a PCI local bus board. This brings affordable performance to the Power Macintosh market with a graphics accelerator board specifically designed for Macintosh design and publishing professionals.

In June 1995, ATI had made a similar announcement to produce graphics accelerator boards for Apple computers. ATI announced it had won an original equipment manufacturer contract to supply Apple Computers with PCI graphics accelerator boards for Apple's new PCI Power Macintosh(TM) 9500/120 system. The is the first time an Apple personal computer incorporates the industry standard PCI bus into it. By incorporating the new PCI technology into Macintosh computers, significant performance gains of up to three times faster have been realized by users.

In late May 1995, ATI announced cut prices across the board on its 64-bit PC graphics accelerator cards. The suggested retail price of ATI's Graphic Pro Turbo and Win Turbo boards were reduced by 5% to 20%.

With the introduction of the PCI-based graphics boards, ATI has positioned itself as an industry leader in the PCI-based local bus technology market. PCI-based graphics accelerator boards are becoming so widely used that there seems little doubt that PCI technology will be the industry standard. Local bus technology makes the graphic cards in personal computers faster by giving the cards a direct line to the computer processor.

Relative strength to TSE300 / Price / Volume (in 1000's of board lots) charts

Rank (Profit/Revenue/Assets)
870   294   397

Kwok Yuen Ho
President & C.E.O.

Lance McIntosh
V.P. Finance & Admin.

Address
33 Commerce Valley Drive East
Thornhill
ON
L3T 7N6
(905) 882-2600

Fax: (905) 882-2620
01003511/G/15.2

COGNOS INCORPORATED

Period Ending	Feb95	Feb94	Feb93	Feb92	Feb91
Yearly Statistics					
Price-Close	29.50	13.50	8.00	12.00	19.00
Price-High	30.50	18.38	na	24.00	19.00
Price-Low	13.50	7.75	na	8.50	5.13
P/E-Close	34.30	43.55	nm	27.91	52.78
Dividends per Share	0.00	0.00	0.00	0.00	0.00
Dividend Yield (%)	0.00	0.00	0.00	0.00	0.00
Sales per Share	11.38	10.52	10.23	11.91	12.93
EPS before extra. item	0.86	0.31	(0.62)	0.43	0.36
Cash Flow per Share	1.80	1.16	0.15	1.12	1.16
Book Value per Share	5.72	4.74	4.40	4.99	3.05
O/S Common Shares	13,444	12,910	12,851	12,682	10,692
Total Revenue	171,230	152,163	150,666	147,759	137,477
Income before extra.	11,365	3,981	(7,914)	5,244	3,823
Cash Flow	23,722	14,811	1,962	13,643	12,285
Debt/Equity	0.05	0.07	0.08	0.08	0.17
Return on Capital (%)	22.76	11.54	(8.28)	16.00	18.11
Ret. on Com. Equity (%)	16.47	6.76	(13.21)	10.94	10.05
% Change Profit	185.5	150.3	(250.9)	37.2	122.3
% Change Revenue	12.5	1.0	2.0	7.5	21.1
% Change Assets	19.5	10.4	(5.5)	44.7	15.5

Preferred Div. Coverage	np	np	np
Total Div. Coverage	na	na	na
Interest Coverage	27.5	11.7	0.0
Current Ratio	1.8	1.6	1.6
Operating Margin	8.1	3.5	(5.7)
Asset Turnover	1.0	1.1	1.1
5 YEAR RATIOS (%)			
Return on Capital	12.0	2.9	4.2
Return on Com. Equity	6.2	(3.7)	(2.8)
Profit Growth	na	(8.9)	na
Revenue Growth	8.5	6.5	12.0
Asset Growth	15.7	7.7	8.3
BALANCE SHEET (000)			
Cash	74,984	47,139	42,332
Current Assets	121,131	98,154	87,348
Net Fixed Assets	20,295	19,282	19,630
Invest's & Advances	0	0	0
Total Assets	150,740	126,103	114,258
Short Term Debt	164	221	551
Current Liabilities	67,653	60,341	53,669
Long Term Debt	3,770	3,800	4,014
Total Liabilities	73,880	64,931	57,683
Total Equity	76,860	61,172	56,575
Total Liab. & Equity	150,740	126,103	114,258
CAPITAL (000)			
Total Debt	3,934	4,021	4,565
Preferred Equity	0	0	0
Common Equity	76,860	61,172	56,575

Business:

COGNOS INCORPORATED develops, markets and supports, both directly and through resellers worldwide, advanced client/server development tools and reporting applications on a wide range of open and proprietary platforms. Cognos has dual headquarters in Ottawa, Ontario, and Burlington, Massachusetts.

Date	EPS	DPS	Tot Rev	Inc Bex
Feb 95	0.40	0.00	47,513	4,390
Nov 94	0.20	0.00	42,861	2,645
Aug 94	0.16	0.00	41,224	2,080
May 94	0.10	0.00	38,678	1,250
Feb 94	0.18	0.00	40,014	2,262
Nov 93	0.05	0.00	38,254	674
Aug 93	0.07	0.00	37,229	915
May 93	0.01	0.00	36,666	130

Synopsis:

In June 1995, Cognos released its first quarter report ended May 31, 1995. The company reported that total revenue increased 135% over the corresponding period last year. Cognos attributed the increase in revenue to a 33% increase in software license revenues, compared to Cognos' 1994 first quarter results. Cognos said the success of the company in the quarter was a result of the company's business intellectual products, including PowerPlay and Impromptu. PowerPlay and Inpromptu allow users to easily access and retrieve information from large databases. The software also gives clients the ability to bundle and create new value added features for their databases.

In March 1995, Cognos began shipping a Macintosh version of PowerPlay, the company's database manipulation and retrieval software. As of the end of March 1995, the software program had a list price of $795.

In May 1995, Cognos announced it has developed a fourth generation language for Axiant, a client-server application. The software, which works with Cognos' Axiant Developers' Workbench, offers users a solution for deploying complex client-server applications. Developers can choose from five topologies including mobile, client with data server, client with application server, functionally distributed, or server only. The suggested price for a single PC version is $3955.

In April 1995, New York brokerage house Alex Brown and Sons Inc. gave Cognos stock an improved rating. Alex Brown gave a new rating of buy. The company's improved rating was the result of the positive good reception of new data base management products from Cognos.

Rank (Profit/Revenue/Assets)		
278	337	392

Michael U. Potter
Chairman & C.E.O.

Renato Zambonini
President & C.O.O.

Donnie M. Moore
Sr. V.P. Fin. Admin. & C.F.O

Address
3755 Riverside Drive
P.O. Box 9707
Ottawa
ON
K1G 3Z4
(613) 738-1440

Fax: (613) 738-0002
C0041586/G/15.2

COREL CORPORATION

Exchanges	Price (Jun29'95)	23.12	Trailing P/E	23.02	Stock Symbol
TQ	Trailing Yield (%)	0.00	Trailing EPS	0.74	**COS**

Period Ending	Nov94	Nov93	Nov92	Nov91	Nov90	Business:
Yearly Statistics	US	US				COREL CORPORATION is a software
Price-Close	19.00	17.25	7.08	6.33	3.96	development and marketing company
Price-High	22.75	18.17	8.29	9.83	5.37	specializing in graphics and SCSI (small
Price-Low	14.13	4.88	4.92	3.62	1.32	computer systems interface) software.
P/E-Close	19.92	27.34	20.43	18.63	17.99	
Dividends per Share	0.00	0.00	0.00	0.00	0.00	
Dividend Yield (%)	0.00	0.00	0.00	0.00	0.00	
Sales per Share	3.53	2.49	2.54	1.56	0.91	
EPS before extra. item	0.70	0.49	0.35	0.34	0.22	
Cash Flow per Share	0.97	0.68	0.48	0.41	0.25	
Book Value per Share	3.45	2.47	2.41	1.47	1.05	
O/S Common Shares	47,829	45,051	41,025	33,954	32,118	
Total Revenue	167,174	107,896	94,940	54,851	31,905	
Income before extra.	32,503	20,853	11,186	11,357	6,990	
Cash Flow	45,040	28,518	16,871	13,790	7,878	

Date		EPS	DPS	Tot Rev	Inc Bex
May 95	US	0.00	0.00	35,213	24
Feb 95	US	0.03	0.00	38,336	1,253
Nov 94		0.24	0.00	49,797	11,186
Aug 94		0.35	0.00	67,242	16,444
May 94	US	0.12	0.00	38,973	5,748
Feb 94	US	0.06	0.00	28,798	2,655
Nov 93		0.20	0.00	38,618	9,150
Aug 93		0.23	0.00	43,260	9,588

	Nov94	Nov93	Nov92	Nov91	Nov90
Debt/Equity	nd	nd	nd	nd	nd
Return on Capital (%)	34.35	36.12	25.73	46.66	38.53
Ret. on Com. Equity (%)	23.54	21.73	15.06	27.15	23.08
% Change Profit	55.9	140.3	(1.5)	62.5	173.2
% Change Revenue	54.9	46.5	73.1	71.9	45.7
% Change Assets	44.7	67.9	77.4	41.8	35.8

				Synopsis:
Preferred Div. Coverage	np	np	np	
Total Div. Coverage	na	na	na	
Interest Coverage	nd	nd	nd	
Current Ratio	6.3	5.5	13.3	
Operating Margin	28.1	30.3	17.1	
Asset Turnover	0.9	0.8	0.9	

Synopsis:

During the first quarter of 1995, Corel's multimedia division continued to show strong results. Unit sales of Corel Professional Photos on CD-ROM were 31% higher than the corresponding period last year. Along with the success of Corel Professional Photos, Corel continues to branch out into the home computing side with its line of CD-ROMs. In the first quarter, Corel introduced a number of new CD-ROM products which focus on teaching and entertaining kids. Including all the CD-ROM products Corel presently has on the market, the company expects to have up to 50 CD-ROM titles by the end of 1995.

5 YEAR RATIOS (%)

Return on Capital	36.3	35.6	29.9
Return on Com. Equity	22.1	20.9	17.6
Profit Growth	74.9	193.4	185.4
Revenue Growth	57.9	83.9	77.5
Asset Growth	52.6	117.1	108.7

In May 1995, Corel started shipping its new CD-ROM product "Adventures with Edison". The CD-ROM includes three games that teach children science, music, and logic skills. The new product carries a suggested retail price of $39.95 (U.S.)

BALANCE SHEET (000)

	Nov94	Nov93	Nov92
Cash	85,618	57,000	49,720
Current Assets	153,233	103,685	86,481
Net Fixed Assets	38,189	28,605	18,832
Invest's & Advances	0	0	0
Total Assets	191,422	132,290	105,313
Short Term Debt	0	0	0
Current Liabilities	24,139	18,864	6,520
Long Term Debt	0	0	0
Total Liabilities	26,469	21,056	6,520
Total Equity	164,953	111,234	98,793
Total Liab. & Equity	191,422	132,290	105,313

In June 1995, Corel signed a book publishing agreement with Osborne/McGraw-Hill. The agreement states Osborne/McGraw-Hill will develop books that focus on Corel's family of software products. Over the next year and a half, Osborne/MaGraw-Hill will publish five to eight books for Corel. These include a new book on Corel Software and Windows 95 as well as an official guide to the company's Corel VENTURA 6.0 software program.

CAPITAL (000)

Total Debt	0	0	0
Preferred Equity	0	0	0
Common Equity	164,953	111,234	98,793

In May 1995, Corel began shipping copies of "Corel CD Office Companion". This software package combines various software programs targeted towards personal computer workstations. Features include extensive libraries, business utilities, an Internet browser, and multimedia utilities as well as system diagnostic and fax software. The package includes an extensive collection of fonts and clipart. The CD has a suggested retail price of $199.

During the year ended November 30, 1994, Corel carried on operations in Ireland and Canada. During 1994, 63% of Corel's products were shipped around the world from Ireland with the remainder coming from Canada.

Relative strength to TSE300

Rank (Profit/Revenue/Assets)
124 296 309

Michael C.J. Cowpland
Chairman President & C.E.O.

Charles A. Norris
Director Of Finance & C.F.O.

Address
1600 Carling Avenue
Ottawa
ON
K1Z 8R7
(613) 728-8200

Fax: (613) 728-9790
C0002878/G/15.2

DELRINA CORPORATION

Exchanges	Price (Jun29'95)	18.62	Trailing P/E	19.81	Stock Symbol
TQ	Trailing Yield (%)	0.00	Trailing EPS	0.94	DC

Period Ending	Jun94	Jun93	Jun92	Jun91	Jun90
Yearly Statistics					
Price-Close	17.25	12.50	2.95	3.70	1.55
Price-High	31.25	12.50	4.75	na	na
Price-Low	11.13	2.75	2.65	na	na
P/E-Close	21.04	nm	nm	nm	nm
Dividends per Share	0.00	0.00	0.00	0.00	0.00
Dividend Yield (%)	0.00	0.00	0.00	0.00	0.00
Sales per Share	4.94	2.79	1.24	1.00	0.91
EPS before extra. item	0.82	(0.57)	(0.14)	(0.15)	(0.23)
Cash Flow per Share	1.11	(0.33)	0.10	0.09	0.08
Book Value per Share	4.10	1.56	1.03	1.44	0.65
O/S Common Shares	21,793	17,944	15,333	11,130	10,982
Total Revenue	105,262	48,584	19,208	11,885	8,232
Income before extra.	16,818	(9,711)	(2,002)	(1,750)	(2,113)
Cash Flow	22,621	(5,760)	1,475	1,066	759
Debt/Equity	nd	nd	nd	nd	nd
Return on Capital (%)	46.37	(30.34)	(11.46)	(12.18)	(33.43)
Ret. on Com. Equity (%)	28.67	(44.30)	(12.60)	(15.11)	(37.91)
% Change Profit	273.2	(385.1)	(14.4)	17.2	(201.8)
% Change Revenue	116.7	152.9	61.6	44.4	58.5
% Change Assets	180.1	92.6	(3.4)	89.7	100.0

Date	EPS	DPS	Tot Rev	Inc Bex
Mar 95	0.18	0.00	38,512	3,905
Dec 94	0.39	0.00	42,638	8,566
Sep 94	0.14	0.00	31,323	3,028
Jun 94	0.23	0.00	32,545	4,891
Mar 94	0.25	0.00	29,909	5,218
Dec 93	0.25	0.00	27,307	4,870
Sep 93	0.09	0.00	15,824	1,840
Jun 93	(0.19)	0.00	13,654	(3,333)

Preferred Div. Coverage	np	np	np
Total Div. Coverage	na	na	na
Interest Coverage	nd	nd	nd
Current Ratio	5.4	3.3	3.9
Operating Margin	24.3	(12.6)	0.6
Asset Turnover	0.9	1.3	0.9
5 YEAR RATIOS (%)			
Return on Capital	(8.2)	(22.8)	(12.0)
Return on Com. Equity	(16.2)	(25.4)	(14.2)
Profit Growth	na	na	na
Revenue Growth	82.5	62.9	47.6
Asset Growth	81.6	47.4	37.9
BALANCE SHEET (000)			
Cash	62,449	18,415	7,995
Current Assets	89,893	28,382	15,506
Net Fixed Assets	7,579	2,843	1,534
Invest's & Advances	709	676	0
Total Assets	106,525	38,029	19,747
Short Term Debt	0	0	0
Current Liabilities	16,634	8,635	3,958
Long Term Debt	0	0	0
Total Liabilities	17,275	9,972	3,958
Total Equity	89,250	28,057	15,789
Total Liab. & Equity	106,525	38,029	19,747
CAPITAL (000)			
Total Debt	0	0	0
Preferred Equity	0	0	0
Common Equity	89,250	28,057	15,789

Business:

DELRINA CORPORATION is a software publisher that designs, develops, markets and supports software products for use on personal computers. Delrina's products include software in several categories: forms processing; fax communications; electronic daily planners and content publishing. Delrina is recognized as the technical and market leader for PC forms and fax software sold worldwide.

Synopsis:

In July 1995, Symantec Corp. of California bought Delrina Corp. for $415-million (U.S.). Symantec will offer Delrina shareholders 0.61 of a Symantec share for each Delrina share held. Approximately 25% of the 730 people employed by Delrina will lose their jobs as a result of the merger. The deal is conditional upon shareholder and regulatory approval.

In May 1995, Delrina Corporation bought a 20% interest in Ex Machina Inc. Delrina said the Ex Machina purchase advances its goal of providing software that combines voice, fax, data, and paging capabilities for personal computers.

In April 1995, Delrina introduced its new line of fax scanning machines. Scanners give users the ability to scan documents directly into personal computers. A document could then be faxed out directly from the PC. Delrina hopes the new scanning machine will replace both the traditional fax machine and the photocopier. The fax scanning machine will have a suggested retail price of $399 in Canada. Customers will also receive a copy of Delrina's WinFax software with the scanner.

Delrina announced in its March 1995, third quarter report, that the company has released its new product, CommSuite for Networks. CommSuite for Networks is the only product on the market that allows workgroups to access and share fax modems across a local area network. The software also allows network access to Delrina's Fax Broadcasting service, which lets users broadcast faxes to large groups without tying up their computer networks.

During the 1995 third quarter, Delrina's profits were down despite a 35% increase in revenues. Delrina said higher revenues were more than offset by increased costs. During the quarter, Delrina's research and development costs more than doubled, when compared to the third quarter of 1994. Delrina reported that sales and marketing, as well as administrative expenses, rose 51% and 37% respectively.

Rank (Profit/Revenue/Assets)
233   417   472

Dennis Bennie
Chairman & C.E.O.
Mark Skapinker
President
Michael Cooperman
C.F.O. & Sec.-Treasurer

Address
895 Don Mills Road
500 - 2 Park Centre
Toronto
ON
M3C 1W3
(416) 441-3676

Fax: (416) 441-0333
01000456/G/15.2

EICON TECHNOLOGY CORPORATION

Exchanges	Price (Jun29'95)	15 .00	Trailing P/E	29 .41	Stock Symbol
TM	Trailing Yield (%)	0 .00	Trailing EPS	0 .51	**EIC**

Period Ending	Jun94	Jun93	Jun92
Yearly Statistics			
Price-Close	12 .00	na	na
Price-High	na	na	na
Price-Low	na	na	na
P/E-Close	19 .05	n t	n t
Dividends per Share	0 .46	0 .07	0 .08
Dividend Yield (%)	3 .83	na	na
Sales per Share	2 .58	2 .35	1 .88
EPS before extra. item	0 .63	0 .39	0 .31
Cash Flow per Share	0 .75	0 .63	0 .45
Book Value per Share	2 .91	1 .26	0 .95
O/S Common Shares	32 ,144	26 ,376	26 ,276
Total Revenue	80 ,812	62 ,832	47 ,602
Income before extra.	19 ,252	10 ,283	8 ,077
Cash Flow	22 ,793	16 ,601	11 ,720
Debt/Equity	nd	nd	0 .00
Return on Capital (%)	40 .71	58 .97	na
Ret. on Com. Equity (%)	30 .34	35 .35	na
% Change Profit	87 .2	27 .3	na
% Change Revenue	28 .6	32 .0	na
% Change Assets	143 .0	38 .8	na
Preferred Div. Coverage	np	np	np
Total Div. Coverage	1 .4	5 .6	3 .8
Interest Coverage	140 .4	104 .8	156 .7
Current Ratio	9 .0	4 .8	6 .4
Operating Margin	29 .9	32 .5	34 .3
Asset Turnover	0 .8	1 .5	1 .7
5 YEAR RATIOS (%)			
Return on Capital	na	na	na
Return on Com. Equity	na	na	na
Profit Growth	na	na	na
Revenue Growth	na	na	na
Asset Growth	na	na	na
BALANCE SHEET (000)			
Cash	37 ,138	18 ,111	8 ,616
Current Assets	58 ,864	36 ,980	25 ,502
Net Fixed Assets	5 ,490	4 ,200	4 ,157
Invest's & Advances	34 ,855	0	0
Total Assets	100 ,069	41 ,180	29 ,659
Short Term Debt	0	0	0
Current Liabilities	6 ,507	7 ,628	3 ,990
Long Term Debt	0	0	92
Total Liabilities	6 ,507	7 ,852	4 ,803
Total Equity	93 ,562	33 ,328	24 ,856
Total Liab. & Equity	100 ,069	41 ,180	29 ,659
CAPITAL (000)			
Total Debt	0	0	92
Preferred Equity	0	0	0
Common Equity	93 ,562	33 ,328	24 ,856

Business:

EICON TECHNOLOGY CORPORATION designs, manufactures, markets and supports high performance, integrated hardware and software products for PCs and LANs for customers in more than 70 countries.

Date	EPS	DPS	Tot Rev	Inc Bex
Mar 95	0 .14	0 .00	29 ,769	4 ,750
Dec 94	0 .15	0 .00	24 ,541	4 ,883
Sep 94	0 .09	0 .00	20 ,102	2 ,884
Jun 94	0 .13	0 .00	21 ,973	4 ,089
Mar 94	0 .21	0 .00	21 ,972	6 ,394
Dec 93	0 .14	0 .00	19 ,739	4 ,750
Sep 93	0 .15	0 .53	16 ,944	4 ,019
Jun 93	0 .10	0 .07	18 ,099	2 ,770

Synopsis:

In May 1995, Eicon Technology launched its new line of integrated hardware and software-based remote local area network products. The products give users the ability to connect from remote local area networks and servers over ISDN or PPP wide area network services. Included as part of these new products are the MPR PacketBlaster/ISDN, and MPR PacketBlaster software packages. Users of these products can take advantage of value-added routing features like data compression, NLSP, and SAP filtering to reduce wide area network costs. The systems also provide OSPF, network scaling, and fast convergence around network link failures. As of May 1995, the retail price of the MPR PacketBlaster was $1,595. The suggested price of MPR PacketBlaster/ISDN starts at $1,995.

On February 1, 1995, Eicon Technologies made its first acquisition since the company's initial public offering in October 1993. Eicon paid $34.3-million for Diehl ISDN GmbH, a German firm that manufactures ISDN products for personal computers. With this purchase, Eicon strengthened its position in the ISDN manufacturing market for personnel computers. Along with Eicon's existing products, the purchase will allow the company to address four different ISDN markets: remote dial-in/dial-out over ISDN; office, home and mobile users of ISDN; server-to-server internetworking over ISDN; and high-speed server-integrated communications for emerging applications like video-conferencing. ISDN technology has been around for some time but only recently has the technology increased in popularity. New applications like the Internet have significantly increased the interest in ISDN technology. The Internet allows the user the ability to access multi-media demonstrations through the World Wide Web. ISND is important because these multi-media sites are very large in size and bandwidth speed is critical.

Rank (Profit/Revenue/Assets)
220   453   486

Peter Brojde
President & C.E.O.

Francois Campeau
V.P. Finance & C.F.O.

Address
2196 - 32 Avenue
Lachine
PQ
H8T 3H7
(514) 631-2592

Fax: (514) 631-3092
01003431/G/15.2

GEAC COMPUTER CORPORATION LIMITED

Exchanges	Price (Jun29'95)	17 .50	Trailing P/E	16 .99	Stock Symbol
T	Trailing Yield (%)	0 .00	Trailing EPS	1 .03	**GAC**

Period Ending	Apr94	Apr93	Apr92	Apr91	Apr90
Yearly Statistics					
Price-Close	13 .63	10 .25	5 .13	1 .45	1 .10
Price-High	18 .25	12 .50	5 .63	2 .00	3 .20
Price-Low	10 .00	4 .35	1 .45	1 .10	1 .10
P/E-Close	16 .82	60 .29	10 .25	nm	2 .90
Dividends per Share	0 .00	0 .00	0 .00	0 .00	0 .00
Dividend Yield (%)	0 .00	0 .00	0 .00	0 .00	0 .00
Sales per Share	5 .30	3 .92	3 .74	3 .65	3 .39
EPS before extra. item	0 .81	0 .17	0 .50	(0 .25)	0 .38
Cash Flow per Share	1 .10	0 .74	0 .62	(0 .15)	0 .18
Book Value per Share	3 .37	2 .52	2 .19	1 .68	1 .94
O/S Common Shares	28 ,745	27 ,948	22 ,472	22 ,361	21 ,530
Total Revenue	152 ,156	105 ,074	85 ,322	82 ,165	81 ,186
Income before extra.	22 ,932	4 ,453	11 ,101	(5 ,507)	8 ,150
Cash Flow	31 ,047	19 ,413	13 ,916	(3 ,352)	3 ,891
Debt/Equity	nd	nd	nd	0 .02	0 .00
Return on Capital (%)	32 .23	12 .18	27 .09	(10 .07)	22 .47
Ret. on Com. Equity (%)	27 .41	7 .44	25 .59	(13 .90)	21 .99
% Change Profit	415 .0	(59 .9)	301 .6	(167 .6)	80 .3
% Change Revenue	44 .8	23 .2	3 .8	1 .2	7 .9
% Change Assets	26 .4	63 .2	7 .1	1 .9	13 .6

Business:

GEAC COMPUTER CORP. LTD. is engaged in the design, manufacture, sale, rental and service of computer systems and software. A client-server applications software provider, the company supplys total automation solutions to selected vertical markets, principally libraries, leasing and asset finance companies, and the property management, hospitality construction, manufacturing and distribution industries.

Date		EPS	DPS	Tot Rev	Inc Bex
Jan	95	0 .30	0 .00	49 ,177	8 ,533
Oct	94	0 .28	0 .00	44 ,691	8 ,044
Jul	94	0 .24	0 .00	43 ,167	6 ,794
Apr	94	0 .21	0 .00	39 ,719	6 ,008
Jan	94	0 .20	0 .00	38 ,873	5 ,803
Oct	93	0 .21	0 .00	38 ,040	5 ,888
Jul	93	0 .19	0 .00	35 ,524	5 ,233
Apr	93	0 .18	0 .00	32 ,017	4 ,782

Preferred Div. Coverage	np	na	na	
Total Div. Coverage	na	na	na	
Interest Coverage	341 .9	56 .8	143 .7	
Current Ratio	2 .1	1 .9	2 .8	
Operating Margin	16 .8	15 .2	13 .5	
Asset Turnover	1 .0	0 .9	1 .2	
5 YEAR RATIOS (%)				
Return on Capital	16 .8	13 .2	6 .7	
Return on Com. Equity	13 .7	11 .2	0 .6	
Profit Growth	38 .4	na	na	
Revenue Growth	15 .1	8 .8	5 .8	
Asset Growth	20 .6	14 .5	4 .1	
BALANCE SHEET (000)				
Cash	53 ,327	40 ,943	32 ,027	
Current Assets	108 ,300	88 ,511	62 ,139	
Net Fixed Assets	16 ,083	15 ,196	10 ,098	
Invest's & Advances	0	0	0	
Total Assets	149 ,028	117 ,872	72 ,237	
Short Term Debt	0	0	0	
Current Liabilities	52 ,084	47 ,194	22 ,554	
Long Term Debt	0	0	0	
Total Liabilities	52 ,084	47 ,194	22 ,554	
Total Equity	96 ,944	70 ,678	49 ,683	
Total Liab. & Equity	149 ,028	117 ,872	72 ,237	
CAPITAL (000)				
Total Debt	0	0	0	
Preferred Equity	0	269	398	
Common Equity	96 ,944	70 ,409	49 ,285	

Synopsis:

Geac Computer Corp.'s fiscal year ends April 30, and analysts have forecasted net income of about $30-million on revenues of about $180-million. In fiscal 1994, Geac earned $22.9-million or 81 cents a share, on revenues of $152.2-million. The company says growth will come from all of the company's businesses and from acquisitions. Geac doesn't have a specific acquisitions budget for the year. However, it has $50-million cash in the bank and no debt. Geac usually finances acquisitions internally through cash flow. Geac has operations in Canada, the U.S., Europe, and Australasia. The U.S. portion of sales is around 50%, up from 44% at the end of fiscal 1994. The Canadian portion has declined to about 10% from 14% a year ago.

Geac sells software systems to libraries, financial institutions, hotels, clubs, and other businesses. Over the past couple of years, the company has expanded its business into other markets. In September 1994, Geac purchased Collier-Jackson Inc. which produces software used by newspapers to automate circulation records. Later in the year, the company bought Fasfax Corp. a company the provides hardware and software systems used in over 9,000 U.S. fast-food restaurants. In June 1995, Geac entered into a business alliance with IBM Corp. Geac's Fasfax division will become a value-added remarketer and national solution provider for IBM's retail point of sale restaurant systems. Also in June, the company announced that its Australian subsidiary signed two significant deals for the licensing of its TIMS manufacturing software. These contracts have a value of about $500,000(Aust.). The TIMS software product is one of the leading products used by various industries in the Australian marketplace to provide software solutions to the manufacturing and distribution industry.

In 1987 Geac was rescued from bankruptcy by Helix Investments Inc., a technology venture capital fund. Helix currently owns 2.3 million of Geac's shares which are presently listed on the Toronto Stock Exchange. Geac will be exploring a U.S. listing on NASDAQ within a year.

Rank (Profit/Revenue/Assets)
199   355   394

Donald C. Webster
Chairman

Stephen J. Sadler
President & C.E.O.

David G. B. Scott
V.P. Finance & Administration

Address
11 Allstate Parkway
Suite 300
Markham
ON
L3R 9T8
(905) 475-0525

Fax: (905) 475-3847
G0014748/G/15.2

For further company information, call Globe Information Services 1-800-268-9128 or (416) 585-5345

HUMMINGBIRD COMMUNICATIONS LTD.

Exchanges	Price (Jun29'95)	37 .62	Trailing P/E	31 .35	Stock Symbol
TQ	Trailing Yield (%)	0 .00	Trailing EPS	1 .20	**HUM**

Period Ending	Sep94	Sep93	Sep92	Sep91
Yearly Statistics				
Price-Close	19 .50	19 .88	na	na
Price-High	23 .75	22 .25	na	na
Price-Low	16 .75	16 .00	na	na
P/E-Close	20 .31	30 .11	n t	n t
Dividends per Share	0 .00	0 .00	0 .00	0 .00
Dividend Yield (%)	0 .00	0 .00	0 .00	0 .00
Sales per Share	2 .77	1 .76	0 .66	0 .21
EPS before extra. item	0 .96	0 .66	0 .02	0 .01
Cash Flow per Share	0 .97	0 .67	0 .03	0 .01
Book Value per Share	3 .68	2 .72	0 .10	0 .09
O/S Common Shares	11 ,938	11 ,932	9 ,900	8 ,610
Total Revenue	34 ,576	18 ,706	6 ,650	1 ,787
Income before extra.	11 ,430	6 ,774	213	81
Cash Flow	11 ,567	6 ,825	266	95
Debt/Equity	nd	nd	nd	nd
Return on Capital (%)	52 .94	70 .09	18 .00	na
Ret. on Com. Equity (%)	29 .94	40 .52	23 .52	na
% Change Profit	68 .7	3 ,080 .3	163 .0	na
% Change Revenue	84 .8	181 .3	272 .1	na
% Change Assets	28 .1	635 .3	187 .6	na
Preferred Div. Coverage	np	np	na	
Total Div. Coverage	na	na	na	
Interest Coverage	nd	nd	nd	
Current Ratio	8 .4	6 .0	1 .4	
Operating Margin	56 .5	62 .4	2 .7	
Asset Turnover	0 .7	0 .5	1 .2	
5 YEAR RATIOS (%)				
Return on Capital	na	na	na	
Return on Com. Equity	na	na	na	
Profit Growth	na	na	na	
Revenue Growth	na	na	na	
Asset Growth	na	na	na	
BALANCE SHEET (000)				
Cash	40 ,905	33 ,583	3 ,269	
Current Assets	49 ,067	38 ,532	5 ,062	
Net Fixed Assets	739	359	134	
Invest's & Advances	0	0	93	
Total Assets	49 ,806	38 ,891	5 ,289	
Short Term Debt	0	0	0	
Current Liabilities	5 ,867	6 ,472	3 ,659	
Long Term Debt	0	0	0	
Total Liabilities	5 ,867	6 ,472	3 ,659	
Total Equity	43 ,939	32 ,419	1 ,630	
Total Liab. & Equity	49 ,806	38 ,891	5 ,289	
CAPITAL (000)				
Total Debt	0	0	0	
Preferred Equity	0	0	617	
Common Equity	43 ,939	32 ,419	1 ,013	

Business:

HUMMINGBIRD COMMUNICATIONS LTD. is a computer software development company that designs, manufactures and markets a complete line of PC X server software products, as well as X development tools for various computer platforms.

Date	EPS	DPS	Tot Rev	Inc Bex
Mar 95	0.35	0 .00	12,506	4 ,222
Dec 94	0.32	0 .00	12,409	3 ,884
Sep 94	0.30	0 .00	11 ,110	3 ,566
Jun 94	0.23	0 .00	8 ,940	2 ,779
Mar 94	0.22	0 .00	7 ,604	2 ,617
Dec 93	0.21	0 .00	6 ,922	2 ,468
Sep 93	0.25	0 .00	6 ,859	2 ,664
Jun 93	0.19	0 .00	5 ,184	1 ,877

Synopsis:

In the second quarter of 1995, Hummingbird Communications Ltd. had sales of $12.5-million, an increase of 78% over sales of $7-million in the second quarter of 1994. Sales increases were seen across all geographic market segments. Net income for the quarter rose 61% to $4.2-million, compared to $2.6-million last year. About 78% of sales during the first half of the fiscal year were attributed to products that work with Microsoft Corp's Windows software. One of the new products will be software designed to work with Windows 95, Microsoft's long and eagerly awaited successor to Windows 3.1.

In February 1995, Hummingbird brought to market a new version of eXceed 4 for Windows NT. The release made Hummingbird the first to offer a Windows NT-based PC X server supporting dial-up capability and providing a scripting language. In April, Hummingbird acquired Beame & Whiteside Software Inc., a provider of PC-to-UNIX networking solutions, for $11.5-million (U.S.). By combining Hummingbird's product line with Beame & Whiteside's TCP/IP and NFS (Network File System) technologies, Hummingbird has broadened its portfolio of PC-to-UNIX connectivity products and can provide solutions to a wider spectrum of customers. Later in the month, eXceed 4 for Windows was selected by BellSouth Telecommunications Inc. of Georgia to provide company-wide integration of its personal computers and enterprise computing network. In May, U.S. broker Charles Schwab & Co. Inc. chose the eXceed 4 software to let brokers access real-time market data from Windows NT workstations.

Relative strength to TSE300 / Price / Volume (in 1000's of board lots)

Rank (Profit/Revenue/Assets)
277   620   631

Fred Sorkin
Chairman President & C.E.O.

Inder P.S. Duggal
C.F.O. & Chief Controller

Address
1 Sparks Avenue
North York
ON
M2H 2W1
(416) 469-2200

Fax: (416) 496-2207
01003414/G/15.2

I.S.G. TECHNOLOGIES INC.

Exchanges	Price (Jun29'95)	5 .00	Trailing P/E	nm	Stock Symbol
TQ	Trailing Yield (%)	0 .00	Trailing EPS	(0.18)	**ISO**

Period Ending	Jun94	Jun93	Jun92	Jun91	Jun90	Business:
Yearly Statistics						I.S.G. TECHNOLOGIES is a medical company
Price-Close	8 .50	14 .75	10 .75	12 .56	1 .98	which designs, manufactures and markets full
Price-High	17 .50	19 .38	18 .50	na	na	solution medical imaging workstations. Its
Price-Low	8 .50	6 .00	10 .13	na	na	flagship product is a compact interactive
P/E-Close	nm	nm	nm	4 ,187 .50	nm	workstation for two and three dimensional
Dividends per Share	0 .00	0 .00	0 .00	0 .00	0 .00	analysis of data from computer-based imaging
Dividend Yield (%)	0 .00	0 .00	0 .00	0 .00	0 .00	techniques such as CAT or CT scanners and
Sales per Share	1 .34	1 .14	1 .57	1 .90	1 .10	magnetic resonance imagers.
EPS before extra. item	(0.17)	(0.14)	(0.11)	0 .00	(0.43)	
Cash Flow per Share	(0.08)	(0.09)	(0.06)	0 .05	(0.40)	
Book Value per Share	3 .34	3 .49	3 .64	0 .40	0 .24	
O/S Common Shares	12 ,580	12 ,101	11 ,834	6 ,255	5 ,736	
Total Revenue	19 ,963	18 ,364	15 ,805	12 ,957	7 ,304	
Income before extra.	(2 ,085)	(1 ,673)	(917)	16	(2 ,498)	

Date	EPS	DPS	Tot Rev	Inc Bex
Mar 95	(0.14)	0 .00	4 ,522	(1 ,743)
Dec 94	(0.05)	0 .00	5 ,591	(653)
Sep 94	0 .00	0 .00	5 ,571	32
Jun 94	0 .01	0 .00	6 ,564	156
Mar 94	(0.02)	0 .00	5 ,394	(253)
Dec 93	(0.06)	0 .00	4 ,603	(689)
Sep 93	(0.11)	0 .00	3 ,558	(1 ,298)
Jun 93	(0.05)	0 .00	5 ,038	(644)

	Jun94	Jun93	Jun92	
Cash Flow	(962)	(1 ,057)	(517)	
Debt/Equity	nd	nd	0 .04	
Return on Capital (%)	(4 .92)	(3 .80)	(3 .22)	
Ret. on Com. Equity (%)	(4 .95)	(3 .92)	(4 .02)	
% Change Profit	(24 .6)	(82 .5)	(5 ,875 .6)	
% Change Revenue	8 .7	16 .2	22 .0	
% Change Assets	(1 .6)	(6 .0)	474 .9	

Synopsis:

ISG Technologies Inc. reported that revenues for the third quarter ended March 31, 1995, were $4.4-million, down from revenues of $5.3-million in last year's third quarter. The loss for the quarter was 14 cents a share, compared with a loss of 2 cents a share last year. Delays in the release of several new products had a negative impact on sales, earnings, and margins in the third quarter. These delays, of six to nine months duration, reflected both internal product development and market introduction plans of some of ISG's original equipment manufacturers corporate partners. Sales of products introduced last year, such as the Viewing Wand and the Imaging Applications Platform (IAP), are on track. In April 1994, ISG received approval from the U.S. Food and Drug Administration to market its surgical guiding device, the Viewing Wand, which is now being used at over 80 sites. In February 1995, ISG and partner Mitsui & Co. Ltd received approval for the commercial release of the Wand in Japan. The company's IAP is fast becoming the industry standard. In the first half of fiscal 1995, to complement the deals signed with General Electric Co. and Philips Electronics, ISG entered into new contracts to supply IAP to four of the world's largest medical imaging equipment manufacturers: Analogic Corp.; E.I. Dupont de Nemours; Siemens Medical Systems; and Hitachi Medical Corp. Together, these companies represent roughly 60% of the global software market for medical imaging scanners.

On April 24, 1995, ISG said it would work with AESCULAP AG of Germany to develop an advanced image-guided surgical system based on core technology built by ISG. The AESCULAP system, called SPOCS (Surgical Planning and Orientation Computer System) will be marketed around the world. It is commercially available now in Europe and is being used for neurological, craniofacial, and ear, nose, and throat surgery at several university hospitals. Clinical trials in the U.S. are scheduled to begin later this year in preparation for the regulatory clearance process required by the Federal Drug Administration.

Preferred Div. Coverage	np	np	np
Total Div. Coverage	na	na	na
Interest Coverage	0 .0	0 .0	0 .0
Current Ratio	16 .9	13 .3	9 .2
Operating Margin	(20 .4)	(29 .3)	(11 .0)
Asset Turnover	0 .4	0 .3	0 .3
5 YEAR RATIOS (%)			
Return on Capital	(17 .8)	(43 .8)	(93 .1)
Return on Com. Equity	(21 .5)	(86 .3)	na
Profit Growth	na	na	na
Revenue Growth	52 .4	75 .6	123 .9
Asset Growth	55 .9	93 .9	93 .8
BALANCE SHEET (000)			
Cash	21 ,842	25 ,583	28 ,666
Current Assets	38 ,088	37 ,600	43 ,197
Net Fixed Assets	3 ,189	3 ,134	672
Invest's & Advances	2 ,715	3 ,958	3 ,935
Total Assets	44 ,293	44 ,992	47 ,854
Short Term Debt	0	0	1 ,779
Current Liabilities	2 ,248	2 ,818	4 ,717
Long Term Debt	0	0	26
Total Liabilities	2 ,248	2 ,818	4 ,743
Total Equity	42 ,045	42 ,174	43 ,111
Total Liab. & Equity	44 ,293	44 ,992	47 ,854
CAPITAL (000)			
Total Debt	0	0	1 ,805
Preferred Equity	0	0	0
Common Equity	42 ,045	42 ,174	43 ,111

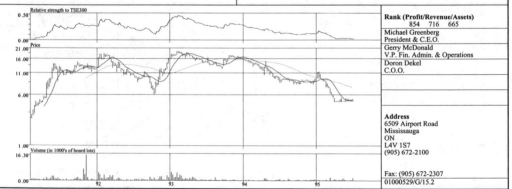

Rank (Profit/Revenue/Assets)
854 716 665

Michael Greenberg
President & C.E.O.

Gerry McDonald
V.P. Fin. Admin. & Operations

Doron Dekel
C.O.O.

Address
6509 Airport Road
Mississauga
ON
L4V 1S7
(905) 672-2100

Fax: (905) 672-2307
01000529/G/15.2

For further company information, call Globe Information Services 1-800-268-9128 or (416) 585-5345

OCS TECHNOLOGIES CORP.

Exchanges	Price (Jun29'95)	0.38	Trailing P/E	3.45	Stock Symbol
TV	Trailing Yield (%)	0.00	Trailing EPS	0.11	OCS

Period Ending	Apr94	Apr93	Apr92	Apr91	Apr90	Business:
Yearly Statistics						OCS TECHNOLOGIES CORP. is a provider of
Price-Close	3.35	4.20	4.15	1.95	na	software and related services to the public
Price-High	4.75	4.75	4.60	na	na	safety and justice markets. OCS products are
Price-Low	3.20	3.00	2.40	na	na	designed for law enforcement, fire and
P/E-Close	23.93	nm	nm	12.19	nt	emergency medical services agencies and
Dividends per Share	0.00	0.00	0.00	0.00	0.00	include computer-aided dispatch products,
Dividend Yield (%)	0.00	0.00	0.00	0.00	0.00	record management systems and jail/court
Sales per Share	2.49	1.57	0.49	0.35	1.03	management systems.
EPS before extra. item	0.14	(2.98)	(0.63)	0.16	0.11	
Cash Flow per Share	0.32	(0.74)	(0.02)	0.16	0.14	
Book Value per Share	1.21	1.13	1.59	0.73	0.29	
O/S Common Shares	14,367	10,121	5,184	3,414	2,110	
Total Revenue	30,891	12,465	2,115	1,172	1,556	
Income before extra.	1,798	(23,403)	(2,723)	541	166	

Date	EPS	DPS	Tot Rev	Inc Bex
Jan 95	0.04	0.00	9,766	298
Oct 94	0.04	0.00	11,643	795
Apr 94	(0.01)	0.00	9,726	(117)
Jan 94	0.04	0.00	6,537	596
Oct 93	0.05	0.00	6,982	670
Jul 93	na	0.00	7,281	648
Apr 93	(1.67)	0.00	3,564	(13,819)
Jan 93	(1.06)	0.00	3,920	(7,919)

	Apr94	Apr93	Apr92
Cash Flow	3,925	(5,814)	(67)	526	208
Debt/Equity	1.10	0.40	0.10	nd	0.17
Return on Capital (%)	9.29	(185.88)	(46.63)	38.34	41.07
Ret. on Com. Equity (%)	12.45	(237.80)	(50.84)	34.90	36.41
% Change Profit	107.7	0.0	(603.1)	226.5	174.5
% Change Revenue	147.8	489.3	80.5	(24.7)	44.7
% Change Assets	94.8	130.8	161.5	248.8	116.2
Preferred Div. Coverage	np	np	np
Total Div. Coverage	na	na	na
Interest Coverage	4.8	0.0	0.0
Current Ratio	2.3	1.6	2.8
Operating Margin	7.5	(142.6)	(5.0)
Asset Turnover	0.6	0.5	0.2
5 YEAR RATIOS (%)			
Return on Capital	(28.8)	na	na
Return on Com. Equity	(41.0)	na	na
Profit Growth	97.1	na	na
Revenue Growth	95.7	na	na
Asset Growth	145.1	na	na
BALANCE SHEET (000)			
Cash	4,463	184	0
Current Assets	27,878	18,285	6,724
Net Fixed Assets	4,634	2,527	863
Invest's & Advances	1,998	43	2,296
Total Assets	48,122	24,705	10,705
Short Term Debt	891	3,034	776
Current Liabilities	12,376	11,646	2,427
Long Term Debt	18,329	1,594	60
Total Liabilities	30,704	13,240	2,486
Total Equity	17,418	11,465	8,218
Total Liab. & Equity	48,122	24,705	10,705
CAPITAL (000)			
Total Debt	19,220	4,628	836
Preferred Equity	0	0	0
Common Equity	17,418	11,465	8,218

Synopsis:

OCS Technologies Corp. stated that due to a continuing cash flow shortfall, the company won't be able to make the June 30, 1995, interest payment on its 8.25% convertible debentures. The amount due is about $722,000, but because the company doesn't have the funds available, OCS has received a note of default, giving it 15 days to correct the default and make payments to debenture holders. The company said it continues to pursue permanent financing, but hasn't received any firm proposals. On June 30, 1995, OCS announced that it had arranged for short term financing of $650,000 (U.S.) from a group made up of two Canadian based financial firms. These funds will be used to pay normal operating expenses and not the interest payment due to the convertible debenture holders. The group providing this short term financing will be granted security by the Company's wholly owned U.S. subsidiary. This security will rank second behind the existing bank line of credit of $2,275,000 (U.S.). OCS has made significant efforts to reduce its operating costs, however, it continues to suffer cashflow shortfalls and requires additional financing to complete its reorganization plans.

After having spent millions of dollars buying the 911 dispatch and justice software divisions of Bell Atlantic, U.S. West, and GTE, OCS found that it had inherited costly problems with some of the U.S. contracts. Accounts receivables sky-rocketed to $25-million, profit fell below market expectations, and the stock plummeted. Bell Atlantic later agreed to pay $1.4-million to cover some of the costs on former Bell accounts, plus $500,000 to revise software documentation.

In May 1995, OCS engaged Marathon Securities Ltd. to identify an investor or strategic partner to provide $5-million of additional financing to alleviate the company's pressing cash shortfall. OCS also agreed with the guarantor to consider a restructuring proposal whereby the convertible debt of $17.5-million plus accrued interest would be converted to common shares at a price of 25 cents per share. Both the restructuring proposal and the additional financing are subject to regulatory approval.

Relative strength to TSE300

Price

Volume (in 1000's of board lots)

Rank (Profit/Revenue/Assets)
586   647   644

Robert D. Standerwick
Chairman & C.E.O.

Address
Suite 106
7011 Elmbridge Way
Richmond
BC
V7C 4V5
(604) 273-8045

Fax: (604) 273-0301

01003101/G/15.2

SHL SYSTEMHOUSE INC.

Exchanges	Price (Jun29'95)	9.37	Trailing P/E	46.85	Stock Symbol
TMQ	Trailing Yield (%)	0.00	Trailing EPS	0.20	SHK

Period Ending	Aug94	Aug93	Aug92	Aug91	Aug90
Yearly Statistics					
Price-Close	6.88	13.38	9.63	5.38	7.13
Price-High	14.50	15.75	17.13	na	12.00
Price-Low	6.63	7.25	4.60	na	4.70
P/E-Close	23.71	nm	nm	nm	nm
Dividends per Share	0.00	0.00	0.00	0.00	0.00
Dividend Yield (%)	0.00	0.00	0.00	0.00	0.00
Sales per Share	18.98	19.44	19.01	18.34	18.70
EPS before extra. item	0.29	(3.09)	(0.25)	(0.53)	(1.10)
Cash Flow per Share	1.14	(0.01)	0.32	0.55	0.28
Book Value per Share	5.55	4.29	6.42	5.99	6.66
O/S Common Shares	69,064	51,628	43,291	37,846	37,222
Total Revenue	1,163,213	915,466	743,970	694,063	698,430
Income before extra.	17,519	(145,121)	(9,521)	(19,892)	(40,585)
Cash Flow	69,506	(249)	12,450	20,585	10,311
Debt/Equity	0.59	1.06	0.69	0.63	0.37
Return on Capital (%)	7.57	(26.44)	1.38	(1.07)	(5.77)
Ret. on Com. Equity (%)	5.79	(58.09)	(3.77)	(8.38)	(15.18)
% Change Profit	112.1	(1,424.2)	52.1	51.0	(429.8)
% Change Revenue	27.1	23.1	7.2	(0.6)	9.0
% Change Assets	16.0	13.3	22.0	14.2	(11.2)

Preferred Div. Coverage	np	np	na
Total Div. Coverage	na	na	na
Interest Coverage	1.8	0.0	0.4
Current Ratio	1.3	1.0	1.4
Operating Margin	3.3	1.0	0.9
Asset Turnover	1.4	1.3	1.2
5 YEAR RATIOS (%)			
Return on Capital	(4.9)	(4.1)	2.2
Return on Com. Equity	(15.9)	(16.0)	(3.7)
Profit Growth	7.3	na	na
Revenue Growth	12.6	30.6	33.3
Asset Growth	10.1	9.9	23.5
BALANCE SHEET (000)			
Cash	83,054	63,128	65,791
Current Assets	452,713	394,802	366,950
Net Fixed Assets	155,451	115,153	80,211
Invest's & Advances	42,319	38,497	32,152
Total Assets	837,312	722,132	637,542
Short Term Debt	120,609	123,506	107,317
Current Liabilities	345,429	384,334	263,720
Long Term Debt	105,412	111,998	86,549
Total Liabilities	453,717	500,541	354,676
Total Equity	383,595	221,591	282,866
Total Liab. & Equity	837,312	722,132	637,542
CAPITAL (000)			
Total Debt	226,021	235,504	193,866
Preferred Equity	0	0	4,813
Common Equity	383,595	221,591	278,053

Business:

SHL SYSTEMHOUSE is in the business of transformational outsourcing which enables its customers to re-engineer their business processes and sustain competitive advantage through information technology. The company provides a full range of seamless systems management services anywhere in the world, working with customers during planning, building and ongoing management.

Date	EPS	DPS	Tot Rev	Inc Bex
Feb 95	0.04	0.00	332,839	2,586
Nov 94	0.05	0.00	307,625	3,300
Aug 94	0.02	0.00	297,054	1,520
May 94	0.09	0.00	305,650	5,896
Feb 94	0.10	0.00	292,756	5,445
Nov 93	0.09	0.00	267,753	4,658
Aug 93	(3.18)	0.00	225,743	(148,995)
May 93	0.05	0.00	246,348	2,304

Synopsis:

SHL Systemhouse's second 1995 quarter gross revenues grew 14% to $332.3-million from $292-million in the second quarter of 1994. Net income fell to $2.6-million from $5.4-million a year ago. Severance costs due to staff reductions, and the reorganization of the U.K. and international operations had a significant impact on the bottom line. In the first quarter, Systemhouse sold two business units in Mexico and Britain, to reduce operating losses and to focus on its core business. SHL expects to save more than $20-million annually in non-operating costs from trimming 400 positions. The company streamlined its business into three operating units: technology deployment and educational services; systems integration and transformational services; and outsourcing services.

1995 is proving to be a busy year for Systemhouse. In February, the company was awarded a three-year multimillion dollar contract by Student Loans Co., of the U.K., for computer outsourcing. Systemhouse also signed a five-year multimillion dollar contract with American Savings Bank to provide strategic technology services and networked systems management. As well, in February, the Nova Scotia government lured Systemhouse's data processing centre to Sydney from Ottawa with a $1.75-million grant and a $550,000 loan. The move created 90 jobs, and an additional 100 jobs will be created over the next four years.

In March, Systemhouse announced a joint venture in Japan with Mitsui Engineering & Shipbuilding Co. and Mitsui & Co. The venture will license use of SHL's multimedia education and systems development software technology to the Japanese companies. In May, Systemhouse signed a seven-year contract worth over $100-million with FMC Corp. of Chicago. Systemhouse will provide computer outsourcing services to FMC. The recent major licensing and reseller agreements with Mitsui, FMC, Bell Atlantic and AT&T Global Information Solutions have positioned the company for strong earnings growth in 1995.

Relative strength to TSE300

Price

Volume (in 1000's of board lots)

Rank (Profit/Revenue/Assets)
227   110   170

John R. Oltman
Chairman & C.E.O.

William W. Linton
Exec. V.P. & C.F.O.

Address
50 O'Connor Street
5th Floor
Ottawa
ON
K1P 6L2
(613) 236-1428

Fax: (613) 238-4029
S0006061/G/15.2

For further company information, call Globe Information Services 1-800-268-9128 or (416) 585-5345

SOFTKEY SOFTWARE PRODUCTS INC.

Exchanges	Price (Jun29'95)	43 .50	Trailing P/E	67 .97	Stock Symbol
T	Trailing Yield (%)	0 .00	Trailing EPS	0 .64	**SSK**

Period Ending	Dec93	Jan93	Jan92	Jan91	Nov90
Yearly Statistics	11M				14M
Price-Close	5 .50	10 .25	7 .75	3 .05	2 .65
Price-High	11 .50	11 .00	8 .00	5 .25	5 .25
Price-Low	4 .10	6 .00	2 .95	2 .00	2 .00
P/E-Close	nm	22 .28	20 .95	10 .17	8 .55
Dividends per Share	0 .00	0 .00	0 .00	0 .00	0 .00
Dividend Yield (%)	0 .00	0 .00	0 .00	0 .00	0 .00
Sales per Share	1 .89	2 .71	2 .49	1 .38	1 .29
EPS before extra. item	(1 .52)	0 .46	0 .37	0 .35	0 .31
Cash Flow per Share	(0 .61)	0 .58	0 .56	0 .34	0 .34
Book Value per Share	1 .94	3 .43	2 .16	0 .74	0 .69
O/S Common Shares	24 ,824	24 ,651	18 ,994	10 ,645	10 ,583
Total Revenue	42 ,851	62 ,612	36 ,891	16 ,092	13 ,097
Income before extra.	(37 ,780)	10 ,446	6 ,105	3 ,510	3 ,069
Cash Flow	(13 ,725)	13 ,119	8 ,250	3 ,960	3 ,467
Debt/Equity	0 .29	0 .17	0 .33	0 .15	0 .22
Return on Capital (%)	(47 .65)	14 .84	27 .85	41 .25	58 .75
Ret. on Com. Equity (%)	(62 .19)	16 .56	24 .48	39 .49	60 .09
% Change Profit	(494 .5)	71 .1	102 .9	(2 .0)	137 .3
% Change Revenue	(25 .3)	69 .7	167 .5	5 .3	26 .0
% Change Assets	(21 .2)	77 .4	465 .6	5 .2	96 .1

Preferred Div. Coverage	np	np	56 .0
Total Div. Coverage	na	200 .9	56 .0
Interest Coverage	0 .0	na	14 .9
Current Ratio	1 .4	4 .0	2 .6
Operating Margin	(81 .9)	16 .7	25 .4
Asset Turnover	0 .5	0 .5	0 .6
5 YEAR RATIOS (%)			
Return on Capital	19 .0	42 .8	(35 .8)
Return on Com. Equity	15 .7	45 .8	(33 .1)
Profit Growth	na	84 .1	na
Revenue Growth	35 .0	127 .0	126 .6
Asset Growth	74 .8	151 .0	117 .1
BALANCE SHEET (000)			
Cash	19 ,036	24 ,639	1 ,580
Current Assets	37 ,814	55 ,316	19 ,598
Net Fixed Assets	6 ,492	7 ,266	4 ,753
Invest's & Advances	0	0	1 ,527
Total Assets	89 ,844	113 ,944	64 ,246
Short Term Debt	345	433	193
Current Liabilities	26 ,550	13 ,788	7 ,669
Long Term Debt	13 ,361	14 ,006	13 ,378
Total Liabilities	41 ,738	29 ,505	22 ,452
Total Equity	48 ,106	84 ,439	41 ,794
Total Liab. & Equity	89 ,844	113 ,944	64 ,246
CAPITAL (000)			
Total Debt	13 ,706	14 ,439	13 ,571
Preferred Equity	0	0	723
Common Equity	48 ,106	84 ,439	41 ,071

Business:

SOFTKEY SOFTWARE PRODUCTS INC. is in the business of developing and marketing consumer software for home computers. The Company has over 220 titles and offices in the United States, Canada, United Kingdom, Ireland, Germany and Japan.

Date		EPS	DPS	Tot Rev	Inc Bex
Mar 95	US	0 .45	0 .00	41 ,004	10 ,019
Sep 94	US	(0 .09)	0 .00	28 ,029	(1 ,712)
Jun 94	US	(0 .05)	0 .00	27 ,796	(821)
Mar 94	US	0 .33	0 .00	35 ,304	6 ,291
Dec 93	US	(4 .62)	0 .00	2 ,270	(38 ,302)
Oct 93	US	0 .00	0 .00	9 ,742	29
Jul 93	US	0 .09	0 .00	8 ,381	832
Apr 93	US	(0 .06)	0 .00	13 ,801	(455)

Synopsis:

Softkey Software Products earned net income of $4-million on revenues of $41-million in the first quarter of 1995 as compared to net income of $3.8-million on revenues of $31.6-million in the first quarter of 1994. These results were aided by strong CD-ROM sales, which accounted for nearly 81% of publishing revenues. The growth in CD-ROM sales came from Softkey's over 200 existing consumer titles, a successful series of product upgrades, and the release of several new multimedia CD offerings. At March 31, 1995, total assets were $242.4-million and total liabilities were only $43.3-million. Softkey's working capital rose from $15.5-million at year end to $32.8-million at March 31, 1995, and its cash position grew to $18.6-million. This increase is largely due to cash generated from operations and cash from the exercise of employee stock options.

In January 1994, Softkey merged with U.S. software houses, Wordstar International and Spinaker Software Corp. The merged company is called Softkey International Inc., based in Cambridge, Massachusetts, and controls 100% of the common shares of Softkey Software Products in Canada. The merger established Softkey as one of the largest software companies in North America. In June 1995, after the IBM-Lotus takeover, rumours began about other acquisition targets for IBM, with Softkey a very likely candidate. A week earlier, Softkey filed for registration for a public offering of 2.4-million common shares.

In March 1995, Softkey signed a deal with K-Mart Corp. to put its "One Stop CD Shop" retail CD-ROM racks in all 2,208 of K-Mart's U.S. stores. In June, Warner Publisher Services agreed to distribute Softkey's Platinum Line of CD-ROM software products in the United States. The Platinum Line should hit the market July 1, 1995, and will include a collection of twelve pre-packed titles of Softkey's best-sellers. Softkey currently markets over 250 software titles in over 48 countries including the Sports Illustrated Swimsuit Calendar, MPC Wizard, and the Time Almanac.

Rank (Profit/Revenue/Assets)		
985	563	507

Michael Perik
Chairman & C.E.O.

Kevin O'Leary
President

Scott Murray
V.P. Finance & C.F.O.

Address
201 Broadway
Cambridge
MA
02139
(617) 494-1200

Fax: (617) 494-1219
01002103/G/15.2

SYSTEMS XCELLENCE INC.

Exchanges	Price (Jun29'95)	5.37	Trailing P/E	nm	Stock Symbol
T	Trailing Yield (%)	0.00	Trailing EPS	(0.20)	**SXC**

Period Ending	Feb95	Apr94	Feb94	Apr93	Apr92
Yearly Statistics			50W		
Price-Close	3.25	0.60	0.42	0.35	0.50
Price-High	3.75	0.85	0.85	0.55	na
Price-Low	0.42	0.30	0.25	0.22	na
P/E-Close	9.85	nm	5.06	nm	nm
Dividends per Share	0.00	0.00	0.00	0.00	0.00
Dividend Yield (%)	0.00	0.00	0.00	0.00	0.00
Sales per Share	1.82	0.15	0.88	0.20	0.47
EPS before extra. item	0.33	(0.20)	0.08	(0.06)	(0.37)
Cash Flow per Share	0.33	(0.11)	0.12	(0.03)	(0.21)
Book Value per Share	0.80	1.52	741.27	1.71	1.78
O/S Common Shares	6,946,347	2,485,647	400	2,485,647	2,472,314
Total Revenue	8,552,330	531,971	3,593,474	753,692	1,494,287
Income before extra.	1,492,690	(491,856)	296,503	(159,618)	(904,619)
Cash Flow	1,516,818	(268,746)	435,442	(73,787)	(524,427)
Debt/Equity	0.04	nd	0.09	0.03	0.34
Return on Capital (%)	54.58	(23.39)	17.90	(1.98)	(13.03)
Ret. on Com. Equity (%)	32.09	(24.21)	13.54	(3.68)	(18.60)
% Change Profit	403.5	(259.5)	293.2	82.4	(363.4)
% Change Revenue	1,507.7	(85.8)	395.9	(49.6)	(45.8)
% Change Assets	95.4	170.9	(67.9)	(26.1)	(13.6)
Preferred Div. Coverage	np	np	np		
Total Div. Coverage	na	na	na		
Interest Coverage	na	0.0	na		
Current Ratio	2.6	29.5	1.1		
Operating Margin	27.9	(168.5)	1.7		
Asset Turnover	1.1	0.1	2.4		
5 YEAR RATIOS (%)					
Return on Capital	6.8	(2.1)	3.4		
Return on Com. Equity	(0.2)	(5.3)	(0.0)		
Profit Growth	34.2	na	(4.8)		
Revenue Growth	25.5	(29.0)	4.9		
Asset Growth	1.7	(11.0)	(24.3)		
BALANCE SHEET					
Cash	2,810,744	2,199,317	101,367		
Current Assets	4,992,494	2,354,552	1,180,185		
Net Fixed Assets	2,210,762	1,445,953	239,920		
Invest's & Advances	7,381	46,168	0		
Total Assets	7,518,028	3,846,673	1,420,105		
Short Term Debt	111,994	0	27,994		
Current Liabilities	1,891,764	79,892	1,123,598		
Long Term Debt	89,000	0	0		
Total Liabilities	1,980,764	79,892	1,123,598		
Total Equity	5,537,264	3,766,781	296,507		
Total Liab. & Equity	7,518,028	3,846,673	1,420,105		
CAPITAL					
Total Debt	200,994	0	27,994		
Preferred Equity	0	0	0		
Common Equity	5,537,264	3,766,781	296,507		

Business:

SYSTEMS XCELLENCE INC. designs, sells and installs microcomputer based applications and solutions, including communications hardware and software. The company's products include executive information systems, treasury management systems, office automation systems, and communications gateways. The company has customers in Canada, the United States and worldwide.

Date	EPS	DPS	Tot Rev	Inc Bex
Oct 94	(0.06)	0.00	89	(139)
Jul 94	(0.03)	0.00	138	(64)
Apr 94	(0.08)	0.00	180	(209)
Jan 94	(0.04)	0.00	139	(89)
Oct 93	(0.04)	0.00	118	(77)
Jul 93	(0.04)	0.00	95	(116)
Apr 93	(0.04)	0.00	143	(103)
Jan 93	(0.04)	0.00	144	(89)

Synopsis:

The merger of Systems Xcellence Ltd. and BMB Compuscience Canada Ltd. resulted in the formation of Systems Xcellence Inc. in January 1995. Under the agreement, Systems Xcellence shareholders received one BMB Compuscience share for each Systems Xcellence share held. The company supplies expertise and software products for electronic payment systems and health care claims processing. In the year ended February 28, 1995, it posted a profit of $1.5-million, or 33 cents per share, on revenue of $8.3-million.

In April 1995, the company settled all litigation with TXN Solution Integrators with the dismissal of all claims and counter-claims between the companies.

Rank (Profit/Revenue/Assets)
692   872   966

Malcolm P. Rigby
Chairman, President & C.E.O.

Donald J. Page
C.F.O., Assist. Sec. & Treas.

Address
555 Industrial Drive
Milton
ON
L9T 5C2
(905) 876-4741

Fax: (905) 876-4741
B0020506/G/15.2

546   **For further company information, call Globe Information Services 1-800-268-9128 or (416) 585-5345**

TELEGLOBE INC.

Exchanges	Price (Jun29'95)	19.75	Trailing P/E	14.42	Stock Symbol
TMV	Trailing Yield (%)	1.72	Trailing EPS	1.37	**TGO**

Period Ending	Dec94	Dec93	Dec92	Dec91	Dec90
Yearly Statistics					
Price-Close	19.00	20.00	13.75	10.88	7.88
Price-High	23.88	20.50	13.94	11.00	10.75
Price-Low	16.50	13.63	11.00	7.38	7.50
P/E-Close	13.97	16.13	nm	20.14	39.38
Dividends per Share	0.35	0.31	0.28	0.28	0.28
Dividend Yield (%)	1.84	1.55	2.04	2.58	3.56
Sales per Share	8.64	7.77	8.03	7.15	9.93
EPS before extra. item	1.36	1.24	(1.19)	0.54	0.20
Cash Flow per Share	3.74	3.33	2.35	3.18	2.13
Book Value per Share	11.69	10.72	9.23	10.26	9.16
O/S Common Shares	56,819	56,764	52,099	39,578	40,694
Total Revenue	664,300	565,200	471,400	459,400	408,700
Income before extra.	90,900	75,500	(50,600)	25,700	8,000
Cash Flow	217,500	185,300	100,400	129,700	86,600
Debt/Equity	0.68	0.93	0.92	1.00	1.01
Return on Capital (%)	11.52	12.45	1.53	9.74	5.17
Ret. on Com. Equity (%)	12.49	12.76	(12.77)	5.68	1.91
% Change Profit	20.4	249.2	(296.9)	221.3	(60.2)
% Change Revenue	17.5	19.9	2.6	12.4	9.9
% Change Assets	9.4	17.7	8.2	20.5	7.7

Business:

TELEGLOBE INC. designs, makes and markets data communcations products and services worldwide for customers in the banking, insurance, health care and transportation industries. The company also provides computer systems integration services. The company's subsidiary, Teleglobe Canada of Montreal, is Canada's sole overseas telecommunications carrier.

Date	EPS	DPS	Tot Rev	Inc Bex
Mar 95	0.23	0.10	379,800	16,700
Dec 94	0.41	0.09	173,725	27,184
Sep 94	0.37	0.09	167,634	24,867
Jun 94	0.36	0.09	155,854	24,504
Mar 94	0.22	0.08	145,742	14,371
Dec 93	0.45	0.08	103,077	27,612
Sep 93	0.33	0.08	134,105	20,549
Jun 93	0.25	0.08	134,157	15,123

Preferred Div. Coverage	8.0	12.6	0.0
Total Div. Coverage	2.9	3.2	0.0
Interest Coverage	2.7	2.4	0.4
Current Ratio	0.9	0.7	0.7
Operating Margin	23.6	23.6	17.5
Asset Turnover	0.3	0.2	0.2
5 YEAR RATIOS (%)			
Return on Capital	8.1	7.2	7.5
Return on Com. Equity	4.0	2.6	2.3
Profit Growth	35.2	17.6	na
Revenue Growth	12.2	8.2	6.0
Asset Growth	12.5	14.2	11.7
BALANCE SHEET (000)			
Cash	14,500	15,000	6,000
Current Assets	357,300	289,000	257,300
Net Fixed Assets	1,331,700	1,237,700	1,030,200
Invest'& Advances	13,900	17,000	1,600
Total Assets	1,934,400	1,768,200	1,502,400
Short Term Debt	35,000	49,500	21,000
Current Liabilities	414,800	392,100	355,900
Long Term Debt	561,400	599,000	506,500
Total Liabilities	1,052,200	1,066,800	928,800
Total Equity	882,200	701,400	573,600
Total Liab. & Equity	1,934,400	1,768,200	1,502,400
CAPITAL (000)			
Total Debt	596,400	648,500	527,500
Preferred Equity	218,000	93,000	93,000
Common Equity	664,200	608,400	480,600

Synopsis:

Teleglobe is committed to becoming a world leader in the intercontinental telecommunications industry. In the continuing free-trade discussions between Canada and the U.S., Teleglobe has asked the Canadian government to obtain asymmetrical access to the U.S. market for the intercontinental telecommunications sector on a temporary basis. During this period, Teleglobe would get the necessary time to attain an acceptable amount of activity, and thus establish a genuine climate of competition in the sector. At the end of 1994, Teleglobe filed a proposal with the CRTC calling for the replacement of its current regime, which controls profitability by means of an authorized rate of return on shareholder investment, with a scheme that would set a maximum on the Company's prices. This would help Teleglobe remain price-competitive with other North American carriers. Teleglobe has also reached important milestones in network development, particularly with transatlantic cable. Its cables will provide the only true information superhighway between North America and Europe.

In addition, the company has established market presence in world wide mobile services, through projects such as ORBCOMM and ODYSSEY. On April 3, 1995, Teleglobe and Orbital Sciences launched the ORBCOMM system's first two low-earth orbit satellites. For personal communications, Teleglobe formed a joint venture with TRW Inc. to construct, launch and operate the ODYSSEY personal communications satellite system. ODYSSEY's medium earth orbit configuration represents the most cost effective method of providing superior quality, satellite-based mobile communications.

The Caisse de depot et placement du Quebec has decided not to proceed with a $107.5-million deal announced August 31, 1994, to pool more than half its stake in Teleglobe Inc. with the shares held by Telesystems Telecom. The deal would have required a complex reorganization of Telesystems, which is a holding company incorporated to hold shares of Teleglobe Inc. The Caisse currently owns 16.3% of Teleglobe's shares.

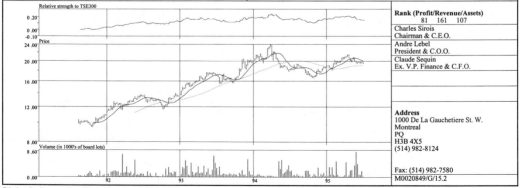

Rank (Profit/Revenue/Assets)
81   161   107
Charles Sirois
Chairman & C.E.O.
Andre Lebel
President & C.O.O.
Claude Sequin
Ex. V.P. Finance & C.F.O.

Address
1000 De La Gauchetiere St. W.
Montreal
PQ
H3B 4X5
(514) 982-8124

Fax: (514) 982-7580
M0020849/G/15.2

| | | | EARNINGS PER SHARE | | |
| | | Fiscal | Last | Estimate | Estimate |
Page	Company		year end	Year	this year	next year
551	Brenda Mines		Dec-94	(0.59)	1.15	1.15
552	DMR Group		May-94	(0.24)	0.36	0.45
553	FCA International		Jun-94	0.12	na	na
554	Intera Information Technologies	$US	Sep-94	(1.38)	na	na
555	Phoenix International Life Sciences		Aug-94	0.56	0.35	0.48
556	Versacold		Dec-94	0.55	0.70	0.85

Estimates from First Call Corporation, 22 Pittsburgh Street, Boston, MA 02210   (800) 366-9992   Fax (617) 261-5679

BRENDA MINES LTD.

Exchanges	Price (Jun29'95)			15.00	Trailing P/E		nm	Stock Symbol
TV	Trailing Yield (%)			0.00	Trailing EPS		(0.44)	BND

Period Ending	Dec94	Dec93	Dec92	Dec91	Dec90
Yearly Statistics					
Price-Close	15.50	15.75	13.00	14.25	12.25
Price-High	16.50	16.50	14.00	15.68	20.25
Price-Low	14.25	12.50	12.50	11.00	11.50
P/E-Close	nm	11.50	22.41	nm	nm
Dividends per Share	0.00	0.00	0.00	0.00	0.00
Dividend Yield (%)	0.00	0.00	0.00	0.00	0.00
Sales per Share	2.74	2.05	0.46	1.26	6.63
EPS before extra. item	(0.59)	1.37	0.58	(0.38)	(0.30)
Cash Flow per Share	1.41	1.75	1.01	1.49	2.19
Book Value per Share	21.28	21.87	20.51	19.92	20.31
O/S Common Shares	4,887	4,887	4,887	4,887	4,887
Total Revenue	20,134	17,963	8,830	14,227	50,621
Income before extra.	(2,895)	6,677	2,852	(1,871)	(1,476)
Cash Flow	6,910	8,565	4,914	7,292	10,697
Debt/Equity	nd	nd	nd	nd	nd
Return on Capital (%)	(7.57)	9.38	2.81	(2.70)	(0.88)
Ret. on Com. Equity (%)	(2.75)	6.45	2.89	(1.90)	(1.48)
% Change Profit	(143.4)	134.1	252.4	(26.8)	84.3
% Change Revenue	12.1	103.4	(37.9)	(71.9)	(30.0)
% Change Assets	8.2	0.3	3.0	4.7	(6.2)

Preferred Div. Coverage	np	np	np
Total Div. Coverage	na	na	na
Interest Coverage	nd	nd	nd
Current Ratio	82.4	120.7	40.9
Operating Margin	(110.0)	7.7	(243.3)
Asset Turnover	0.1	0.1	0.0
5 YEAR RATIOS (%)			
Return on Capital	0.2	(0.5)	2.2
Return on Com. Equity	0.6	(0.6)	0.9
Profit Growth	na	(14.5)	(13.4)
Revenue Growth	(22.6)	(29.0)	(37.3)
Asset Growth	1.8	(2.4)	(0.8)
BALANCE SHEET (000)			
Cash	113,186	108,879	102,098
Current Assets	122,976	119,249	114,411
Net Fixed Assets	474	206	1,903
Invest's & Advances	0	0	0
Total Assets	130,950	121,014	120,673
Short Term Debt	0	0	0
Current Liabilities	1,493	988	2,798
Long Term Debt	0	0	0
Total Liabilities	26,949	14,118	20,454
Total Equity	104,001	106,896	100,219
Total Liab. & Equity	130,950	121,014	120,673
CAPITAL (000)			
Total Debt	0	0	0
Preferred Equity	0	0	0
Common Equity	104,001	106,896	100,219

Business:

BRENDA MINES LTD. is a natural resources company. Its mining and milling operation in British Columbia is currently in the reclamation stage. The company's Process Technology Division provides mechanical maintenance, equipment sales, and environment and process control services to mining companies worldwide. Noranda Inc. owns 76% of the company.

Date	EPS	DPS	Tot Rev	Inc Bex
Mar 95	0.33	0.00	5,547	1,590
Dec 94	(1.39)	0.00	5,461	(6,825)
Sep 94	0.32	0.00	6,023	1,563
Jun 94	0.30	0.00	5,182	1,470
Mar 94	0.18	0.00	3,468	897
Dec 93	0.39	0.00	2,210	1,888
Sep 93	0.26	0.00	5,070	1,276
Jun 93	0.45	0.00	6,118	2,199

Synopsis:

In 1994, Brenda Mines Ltd. incurred a net loss of $2.9-million or $0.59 per share, compared to earnings of $6.7-million or $1.37 per share in 1993. The 1994 results reflect an additional pre-tax provision of $14.7-million for mine closure and rehabilitation costs. As well, there were no earnings from Australian oil interests in the year as the company sold these in late 1993. Earnings from the Process Technology division and increased interest and dividend income partially offset these factors.

Operations at Brenda's copper and molybdenum mine, located near Peachland, B.C., were discontinued in 1990 when its ore reserves were exhausted. Expenditures-to-date for mine closure and site rehabilitation total $26-million. The company estimates an additional amount of $25.2-million is sufficient to complete the reclamation of the site and to install and operate facilities which to collect and treat effluent water.

Brenda's Process Technology division achieved revenues in excess of $13-million in 1994 from an expanded customer base in Canada, the United States, and five overseas countries. Approximately $9-million of the revenue was from sales to foreign countries. The company generated these earnings principally from the sale and installation of process development and control and instrumentation systems as well as from equipment installation and mechanical maintenance contracts.

Brenda, with current business activity in Guyana, China, Chile, the Dominican Republic, Panama, Nicaragua, and Indonesia, intends to continue efforts to build and sustain an expanded national and international customer base.

At year end 1994, Brenda Mines had $113.2-million in cash and investments and no debt.

Rank (Profit/Revenue/Assets)
877   714   422

Bernard O. Brynelsen
Chairman

David L. Bumstead
President

Address
1 Adelaide St. E.
Suite 2700
Toronto
ON
M5C 2Z6
(416) 982-7111

Fax: (416) 982-3525
B0003445/G/15.3

DMR GROUP INC.

Exchanges	Price (Jun29'95)	4.05	Trailing P/E	12.39	Stock Symbol
TM	Trailing Yield (%)	0.00	Trailing EPS	0.33	**DR.A**

Period Ending	May94	May93	May92	May91	May90
Yearly Statistics					
Price-Close	5.25	5.75	5.63	4.65	2.95
Price-High	6.63	6.00	6.00	4.75	4.50
Price-Low	4.75	4.05	4.45	2.60	2.55
P/E-Close	nm	17.42	16.07	10.81	nm
Dividends per Share	0.00	0.00	0.00	0.00	0.00
Dividend Yield (%)	0.00	0.00	0.00	0.00	0.00
Sales per Share	17.44	16.98	16.04	15.50	13.31
EPS before extra. item	(0.24)	0.33	0.35	0.43	(0.03)
Cash Flow per Share	0.17	0.74	0.64	0.73	0.26
Book Value per Share	3.45	3.48	3.14	2.75	2.35
O/S Common Shares	14,138	13,856	13,401	12,898	12,879
Total Revenue	240,911	230,083	211,800	202,291	171,072
Income before extra.	(3,358)	4,474	4,632	5,557	(442)
Cash Flow	2,332	10,012	8,487	9,438	3,304
Debt/Equity	0.41	0.33	0.42	0.31	0.35
Return on Capital (%)	(2.04)	17.32	19.11	28.91	9.77
Ret. on Com. Equity (%)	(6.93)	9.92	11.95	16.92	(1.45)
% Change Profit	(175.1)	(3.4)	(16.6)	1,357.2	(117.0)
% Change Revenue	4.7	8.6	4.7	18.2	34.1
% Change Assets	12.5	11.1	27.4	20.2	20.9

Date	EPS	DPS	Tot Rev	Inc Bex
Feb 95	0.05	0.00	65,665	690
Nov 94	0.10	0.00	73,660	1,488
Aug 94	0.08	0.00	66,021	1,069
May 94	0.10	0.00	68,108	1,360
Feb 94	(0.46)	0.00	56,460	(6,389)
Nov 93	0.06	0.00	62,278	834
Aug 93	0.06	0.00	56,854	837
May 93	0.14	0.00	61,782	1,905

Preferred Div. Coverage	np	np	np
Total Div. Coverage	na	na	na
Interest Coverage	0.0	6.4	6.8
Current Ratio	1.4	1.5	1.6
Operating Margin	3.1	5.4	5.8
Asset Turnover	1.9	2.1	2.1
5 YEAR RATIOS (%)			
Return on Capital	14.6	18.6	16.8
Return on Com. Equity	6.1	9.2	8.3
Profit Growth	na	26.7	2.9
Revenue Growth	13.5	17.7	21.4
Asset Growth	18.2	21.3	21.9
BALANCE SHEET (000)			
Cash	4,595	0	1,892
Current Assets	80,229	69,349	62,782
Net Fixed Assets	13,710	13,448	10,797
Invest's & Advances	3,242	5,894	3,494
Total Assets	125,194	111,259	100,149
Short Term Debt	1,844	1,428	867
Current Liabilities	56,197	46,459	39,615
Long Term Debt	17,880	14,669	16,880
Total Liabilities	76,452	63,103	58,073
Total Equity	48,742	48,156	42,076
Total Liab. & Equity	125,194	111,259	100,149
CAPITAL (000)			
Total Debt	19,724	16,097	17,747
Preferred Equity	0	0	0
Common Equity	48,742	48,156	42,076

Business:

DMR GROUP INC. provides information technology services to business and public enterprises in Canada, the United States, Asia-Pacific and Europe. The Company's services include information technology planning, enterprise architecture, knowledge transfer, outsourcing and systems development.

Synopsis:

Unexpected events in fiscal 1994 produced a net loss of $3.4-million for DMR Group Inc. The net loss was caused by write-offs totalling $17.9-million, before tax. DMR underwent a turnaround in the first three quarters of 1995. The company was back in the black with net income at $3.2-million or $0.23 per share for the nine-month period, compared to a net loss of $4.7-million or $0.34 a year earlier. Canadian operations led the turnaround with steady revenue gains during the period. In the Asia-Pacific region, revenues increased but profit was still lagging. Sales at the United States division were down and DMR's European operations showed modest improvements.

In 1995, DMR established two business units to leverage its expertise in specific industry sectors. One unit will focus exclusively on selling its services to departments of motor vehicles (DMVs) in North America, based on its successful implementation work in vehicle licensing and registration in Quebec, Oregon, and Washington. A second unit will market its applications development and maintenance outsourcing services. In early 1995, DMR also signed a seven-year contract to provide applications management services to Air Canada worth more than $80-million.

In 1994, DMR's net revenue by industry sector were: Utilities, telecommunications and public enterprises, 25%; government sector, 22%; manufacturing, distribution and retail, 21%; financial services, 14%; transportation, 13%; and resource sector and other, 5%. By service provided, revenues were: Systems development and systems integration, 53%; outsourcing, 16%; IT strategy, enterprise architecture and benefits management, 18%; and Knowledge transfer, 13%. Gross revenues by region in 1994 were: Canada, 53%; Asia Pacific, 20%; United States, 19%; and Europe, 8%.

Relative strength to TSE300 / Price / Volume (in 1000's of board lots) charts 92–95

Rank (Profit/Revenue/Assets)
886 291 435

Pierre Y. Ducros
Chairman President & C.E.O.

Steve Perrone
V.P. Finance & Treasurer

Address
1200 McGill College Ave.
Suite 2300
Montreal
PQ
H3B 4G7
(514) 877-3301

Fax: (514) 866-0423
D0000026/G/15.3

FCA INTERNATIONAL LTD.

Exchanges	Price (Jun29'95)		3 .10	Trailing P/E		14 .76	Stock Symbol
TM	Trailing Yield (%)		0 .00	Trailing EPS		0 .21	FC

Period Ending	Jun94	Jun93	Jun92	Jun91	Jun90
Yearly Statistics					
Price-Close	3 .75	3 .15	7 .13	6 .25	10 .38
Price-High	4 .25	7 .38	8 .50	11 .00	11 .75
Price-Low	2 .90	2 .50	3 .85	6 .00	8 .88
P/E-Close	31 .25	nm	nm	nm	nm
Dividends per Share	0 .00	0 .00	0 .05	0 .04	0 .08
Dividend Yield (%)	0 .00	0 .00	0 .70	0 .64	0 .77
Sales per Share	7 .49	6 .84	7 .23	6 .34	6 .77
EPS before extra. item	0 .12	(0 .33)	(0 .18)	(1 .10)	(0 .29)
Cash Flow per Share	0 .48	0 .21	0 .29	(0 .58)	0 .21
Book Value per Share	2 .91	2 .79	3 .75	3 .85	5 .11
O/S Common Shares	9 ,782	10 ,370	10 ,497	10 ,371	10 ,363
Total Revenue	76 ,395	71 ,710	75 ,557	66 ,659	72 ,008
Income before extra.	1 ,137	(3 ,414)	(1 ,853)	(11 ,416)	(3 ,056)
Cash Flow	4 ,870	2 ,134	2 ,984	(6 ,010)	2 ,157
Debt/Equity	nd	nd	nd	nd	nd
Return on Capital (%)	6 .04	(8 .51)	(4 .94)	(22 .92)	(10 .13)
Ret. on Com. Equity (%)	3 .96	(10 .00)	(4 .68)	(24 .60)	(5 .55)
% Change Profit	133 .3	(84 .2)	83 .8	(273 .5)	(9 .0)
% Change Revenue	6 .5	(5 .1)	13 .3	(7 .4)	(0 .6)
% Change Assets	13 .3	(20 .7)	2 .9	(19 .0)	(7 .0)
Preferred Div. Coverage	np	np	np		
Total Div. Coverage	na	na	0 .0		
Interest Coverage	nd	nd	nd		
Current Ratio	3 .1	3 .8	3 .7		
Operating Margin	1 .3	(3 .2)	(2 .5)		
Asset Turnover	1 .6	1 .7	1 .4		
5 YEAR RATIOS (%)					
Return on Capital	(8 .1)	(11 .1)	(8 .9)		
Return on Com. Equity	(8 .2)	(9 .9)	(7 .4)		
Profit Growth	na	na	na		
Revenue Growth	1 .1	(2 .1)	(2 .6)		
Asset Growth	(7 .0)	(11 .0)	(7 .1)		
BALANCE SHEET (000)					
Cash	11 ,403	11 ,783	12 ,475		
Current Assets	24 ,021	21 ,074	22 ,306		
Net Fixed Assets	6 ,957	9 ,614	19 ,867		
Invest's & Advances	0	0	0		
Total Assets	47 ,704	42 ,116	53 ,142		
Short Term Debt	0	0	0		
Current Liabilities	7 ,747	5 ,600	6 ,083		
Long Term Debt	0	0	0		
Total Liabilities	19 ,209	13 ,230	13 ,759		
Total Equity	28 ,495	28 ,885	39 ,383		
Total Liab. & Equity	47 ,704	42 ,116	53 ,142		
CAPITAL (000)					
Total Debt	0	0	0		
Preferred Equity	0	0	0		
Common Equity	28 ,495	28 ,885	39 ,383		

Business:

FCA INTERNATIONAL LTD. through its subsidiaries, acts as a full service collection agency. It provides services for commercial, retail, institutional, medical and government clients. The company has operations across Canada and the United States and in the United Kingdom.

Date	EPS	DPS	Tot Rev	Inc Bex
Mar 95	0 .08	0 .00	21 ,682	824
Dec 94	0 .03	0 .00	20 ,125	288
Sep 94	0 .04	0 .00	19 ,944	352
Jun 94	0 .06	0 .00	20 ,365	562
Mar 94	0 .05	0 .00	19 ,726	553
Dec 93	0 .00	0 .00	18 ,147	(58)
Sep 93	0 .01	0 .00	18 ,156	132
Jun 93	(0 .08)	0 .00	17 ,870	(786)

Synopsis:

In 1994, FCA International Limited reported revenue gains in each of its operating divisions, for a 6%, $4.6-million increase over 1993. The company also posted a 10% improvement in revenue for the nine-month period ending March 31, 1995. Earnings before other expenses for the period amounted to $4.1-million, up 30% from the previous year. The gain was the result of improved performance in the U.S., where earnings before other expenses rose by approximately $1.4-million. Earnings before other expenses in the United Kingdom operations were down $500,000. The company's figures for Canadian operations were approximately the same as a year earlier. During the nine-month period, accounts accepted for collection increased to $1.9-billion compared with $1.7-billion for the same period a year earlier.

In 1994, FCA pursued opportunities in non-traditional collection operations: purchase of accounts receivable portfolios, outsourcing, and accounts receivable management. In the U.S., the company negotiated a $10-million (U.S.) revolving line of credit with a major U.S. bank which will be used exclusively for the purchase of settled personal injury claims paid by the New Jersey Joint Underwriting Association.

In April 1995, FCA renewed a three-year contract with its largest client, which accounted for 11% of its revenue in 1994. Due to rate ceilings in the new contract, FCA says revenues will fall marginally in the last quarter of 1995, and will drop approximately $1-million in fiscal 1996.

FCA expects to feel pressure on profit margins in 1995 and 1996 stemming from industry competition. Some large issuers of credit are more closely managing their own receivables and/or sharing their placement of collection accounts among more than one agency. In response, the company is continues with plans to reduce overheads while investing in technology and marketing.

Relative strength to TSE300

Price

Volume (in 1000's of board lots)

Rank (Profit/Revenue/Assets)		
643	463	648

W. Edwin Jarmain
Chairman

Mark S. Lubotta
Mng. Director FCA Internationa

John Moynan
President

Robert Disante
Exec V.P. Fin. & Corp. Serv.

Address
376 Victoria Ave.
Westmount
PQ
H3Z 1C3
(514) 485-4525

Fax: (514) 485-5178
F0000304/G/15.3

INTERA INFORMATION TECHNOLOGIES CORPORATION

Period Ending	Sep94	Sep93	Sep92	Sep91	Sep90	Business:
Yearly Statistics	US	US	US	US	US	**INTERA INFORMATION TECHNOLOGIES**
Price-Close	5.50	10.00	7.25	12.00	13.88	CORPORATION develops and sells advanced
Price-High	10.00	12.50	13.60	19.75	24.00	scientific and engineering services, computer
Price-Low	5.00	6.00	4.50	10.25	10.25	software and digital mapping products to major
P/E-Close	nm	19.13	nm	nm	12.72	oil companies and governments. The company's
Dividends per Share	0.00	0.00	0.00	0.00	0.00	operating segments are Petroleum and Resource
Dividend Yield (%)	0.00	0.00	0.00	0.00	0.00	Management and Mapping and
Sales per Share	12.20	13.28	12.91	13.60	12.53	Reconnaisance.
EPS before extra. item	(1.38)	0.32	(0.65)	(0.21)	0.80	
Cash Flow per Share	1.20	1.44	0.68	1.13	1.98	
Book Value per Share	4.30	5.67	5.95	7.08	7.35	
O/S Common Shares	5,549	5,538	5,453	5,453	5,372	
Total Revenue	67,660	73,262	71,154	73,794	52,283	
Income before extra.	(7,679)	1,777	(3,573)	(1,145)	3,493	

Date		EPS	DPS	Tot Rev	Inc Bex
Cash Flow *(6,675)* ...					

Cash Flow	6,675	7,926	3,755	6,142	8,281	
Debt/Equity	0.51	0.44	0.40	0.44	0.36	
Return on Capital (%)	(12.35)	8.98	(3.05)	3.24	12.52	
Ret. on Com. Equity (%)	(27.78)	5.57	(10.06)	(2.93)	15.01	
% Change Profit	(532.1)	149.7	(212.1)	(132.8)	44.9	
% Change Revenue	(7.6)	3.0	(3.6)	41.1	22.6	
% Change Assets	(20.1)	(0.5)	(16.9)	3.7	45.5	

Date		EPS	DPS	Tot Rev	Inc Bex
Mar 95	US	0.00	0.00	15,455	29
Dec 94	US	0.08	0.00	16,366	426
Sep 94	US	(1.11)	0.00	14,836	(8,940)
Jun 94	US	0.05	0.00	15,946	277
Mar 94	US	0.09	0.00	17,222	497
Dec 94	US	0.09	0.00	19,302	487
Sep 93	US	0.01	0.00	17,946	46
Jun 93	US	0.05	0.00	17,775	262

	Sep94	Sep93	Sep92	
Preferred Div. Coverage	np	np	np	
Total Div. Coverage	na	na	na	
Interest Coverage	0.0	3.1	0.0	
Current Ratio	1.5	1.2	1.2	
Operating Margin	(4.9)	5.5	0.7	
Asset Turnover	1.4	1.2	1.2	
5 YEAR RATIOS (%)				
Return on Capital	1.9	6.2	na	
Return on Com. Equity	(4.0)	8.6	na	
Profit Growth	na	(1.1)	na	
Revenue Growth	9.6	13.4	na	
Asset Growth	(0.1)	6.7	na	
BALANCE SHEET (000)				
Cash	2,587	316	583	
Current Assets	25,858	28,456	25,386	
Net Fixed Assets	16,068	25,144	28,517	
Invest's & Advances	0	0	0	
Total Assets	46,885	58,676	58,953	
Short Term Debt	6,995	9,422	8,008	
Current Liabilities	17,836	23,034	21,046	
Long Term Debt	5,169	4,242	5,050	
Total Liabilities	23,005	27,276	26,508	
Total Equity	23,880	31,400	32,445	
Total Liab. & Equity	46,885	58,676	58,953	
CAPITAL (000)				
Total Debt	12,164	13,664	13,058	
Preferred Equity	0	0	0	
Common Equity	23,880	31,400	32,445	

Synopsis:

Intera Information Technologies Corporation saw declines in revenue and earnings for the first two quarters of 1995 and fiscal 1994. The slide reflects weak results in the mapping and reconnaissance segment, and, to a lesser degree, the petroleum and resource management arm. Total bank debt as of March 1995, net of cash, was reduced to $4.8-million from $9.6-million in March 1994, largely attributable to reduction in investment in working capital.

Intera's STAR-1 airborne radar image mapping system was used in 1994 for the mapping of ten African national parks. However, in the fourth quarter, the system was out of service for refurbishing. For the first half of 1995, the company secured few large mapping projects for the STAR-1 system. Also, Intera's six-year reconnaissance contract with the federal government, which employed its STAR-2 radar reconnaissance system, expired in March 1995.

Earnings in petroleum and resource management dropped as a result of a planned increase in research and development expenditures related to the three new software products it is introducing in 1995.

In 1994, revenues by country were: United States, 18%; Canada, 38%; United Kingdom, 44%. Business segment revenues were: petroleum and resource management, 72%; mapping and reconnaissance, 28%.

Levels of government spending, world oil and gas prices, changing technology and competition can effect Intera's results. As the availability of affordable and powerful computers grows, Intera feels its complex software and services will be of use to an increasingly broad market. Intera aims to build revenue by use of its services and technologies in the emerging economies in Asia, Eastern Europe, and Central and South America. Intera feels its planned diversification into such areas as forestry and environmental and regional planning will mitigate its exposure to general economic and energy fluctuations.

Relative strength to TSE300 / Price / Volume (in 1000's of board lots)

Rank (Profit/Revenue/Assets)
946   436   585
H.A. Hampson
Chairman
B.L. Bullock
President & C.E.O.
S. Secreti
V.P. C.F.O. & Sec.-Treasurer

Address
Suite 1000
645 - 7th Avenue S.W.
Calgary
AB
T2P 4G8
(403) 266-0900

Fax: (403) 265-0499
01002942/G/15.3

PHOENIX INTERNATIONAL LIFE SCIENCES INC.

Exchanges	Price (Jun29'95)		8 .75	Trailing P/E		na	Stock Symbol
TM	Trailing Yield (%)		na	Trailing EPS		na	PHX

Period Ending	Aug94	Aug93	Aug92	
Yearly Statistics				
Price-Close	n t	n t	n t	
Price-High	n t	n t	n t	
Price-Low	n t	n t	n t	
P/E-Close	n t	n t	n t	
Dividends per Share	0 .00	0 .02	0 .00	
Dividend Yield (%)	0 .00	na	0 .00	
Sales per Share	2 .71	1 .74	0 .36	
EPS before extra. item	0 .56	0 .31	0 .17	
Cash Flow per Share	0 .73	0 .48	0 .08	
Book Value per Share	0 .27	0 .12	0 .06	
O/S Common Shares	45 ,000	45 ,000	45 ,000	
Total Revenue	38 ,119	22 ,990	16 ,349	
Income before extra.	7 ,030	3 ,860	2 ,136	
Cash Flow	9 ,137	5 ,976	3 ,664	
Debt/Equity	1 .32	1 .74	3 .05	
Return on Capital (%)	51 .67	46 .46	na	
Ret. on Com. Equity (%)	80 .69	97 .30	na	
% Change Profit	82 .1	80 .7	na	
% Change Revenue	65 .8	40 .6	na	
% Change Assets	69 .9	47 .9	na	

Preferred Div. Coverage	np	np	np	
Total Div. Coverage	na	3 .9	na	
Interest Coverage	10 .0	7 .6	5 .2	
Current Ratio	1 .5	1 .5	1 .7	
Operating Margin	20 .0	20 .9	22 .1	
Asset Turnover	1 .0	1 .1	1 .2	
5 YEAR RATIOS (%)				
Return on Capital	na	na	na	
Return on Com. Equity	na	na	na	
Profit Growth	na	na	na	
Revenue Growth	na	na	na	
Asset Growth	na	na	na	
BALANCE SHEET (000)				
Cash	0	0	1 ,000	
Current Assets	19 ,063	10 ,390	9 ,072	
Net Fixed Assets	13 ,633	8 ,884	3 ,324	
Invest's & Advances	1 ,022	761	164	
Total Assets	34 ,648	20 ,390	13 ,790	
Short Term Debt	5 ,943	1 ,331	1 ,873	
Current Liabilities	12 ,563	6 ,778	5 ,378	
Long Term Debt	9 ,899	8 ,056	5 ,875	
Total Liabilities	22 ,621	14 ,993	11 ,253	
Total Equity	12 ,027	5 ,397	2 ,537	
Total Liab. & Equity	34 ,648	20 ,390	13 ,790	
CAPITAL (000)				
Total Debt	15 ,842	9 ,387	7 ,748	
Preferred Equity	0	0	0	
Common Equity	12 ,027	5 ,397	2 ,537	

Business:

PHONEIX INTERNATIONAL LIFE SCIENCES INC. is a multi-service contract research organization which provides bioanalytical research, clinical studies, animal metabolism studies as well as regulatory affairs services to pharmaceutical and biotechnology companies in the United States and Canada.

Date	EPS	DPS	Tot Rev	Inc Bex
Nov 94	0 .10	0 .08	10 ,331	1 ,354
Nov 93	0 .10	0 .00	6 ,488	1 ,299

Synopsis:

Phoenix International Life Sciences, founded in 1989, is a contract research organization that carries out research for drug and biotechnology companies. About 90% of its business is with U.S. companies. The company went public in November 1994 with an issue of 8.5 million shares at $5 each, raising $42.5-million, with a net of $25.9-million to Phoenix.

The pharmaceutical industry is quickly changing. Profit margins on brand-name drugs are being squeezed by health management organizations (HMO's), generic drugs are gaining market share, and the regulatory burden continues to increase. The industry's response has been to contract out some of the development work on new drugs.

There are currently about 400 contract research firms in the United States. Companies such as Phoenix are retained by drug developers to design studies and collect and analyse data in order to evaluate the efficacy and safety of new drugs. Phoenix is focussing on the more difficult clinical work, since it tends to generate higher margins. The company is also developing scientific software, specifically for Laboratory Information Management Systems (LIMS), and is developing an automated high-speed extraction system for biological fluids.

Phoenix's historical five year revenue growth rate is about 50%, with contract revenues of $6.8-million in 1990 (year-ended August 31) and $33.9-million in 1994. On the basis of $21.7-million of revenues in the six months ended February 28, 1995, fiscal 1995 revenues could reach $50-million. The company's revenue in the second quarter was up 57% from the $13.8-million in the same period in 1994.

In March 1995, Phoenix opened a 220 bed Clinical Research Center in Cincinnati, Ohio. With this and continuing strong demand, further growth is anticipated in the volume of clinical studies. Demand for the company's bioanalytical services is accelerating, and more equipment is being purchased to process an increased volume of booked business by August 1995.

Relative strength to TSE300 / Price / Volume (in 1000's of board lots)

Rank (Profit/Revenue/Assets)
366   604   730

John Hooper
Chairman & President

Address
4625 Dobrin Street
Saint-Laurent
PQ
H4R 2P7
(514) 333-0033

01003761/G/15.3

VERSACOLD CORPORATION

Exchanges	Price (Jun29'95)	11.00	Trailing P/E	20.00	Stock Symbol
T	Trailing Yield (%)	0.00	Trailing EPS	0.55	ICE

Period Ending	Dec94	Dec93	Dec92	Dec91
Yearly Statistics				
Price-Close	10.25	11.00	n t	n t
Price-High	12.63	11.00	n t	n t
Price-Low	9.25	9.00	n t	n t
P/E-Close	18.64	12.94	n t	n t
Dividends per Share	0.00	na	na	na
Dividend Yield (%)	0.00	na	na	na
Sales per Share	9.08	8.47	10.31	5.36
EPS before extra. item	0.55	0.85	0.31	0.17
Cash Flow per Share	1.28	0.90	1.04	0.78
Book Value per Share	5.38	3.43	(0.62)	(0.87)
O/S Common Shares	9,753	7,782	4,800	4,800
Total Revenue	78,822	54,698	49,490	25,763
Income before extra.	4,768	4,225	1,483	822
Cash Flow	10,987	5,647	5,009	3,750
Debt/Equity	2.39	1.90	na	na
Return on Capital (%)	12.26	19.21	17.80	na
Ret. on Com. Equity (%)	12.05	35.69	na	na
% Change Profit	12.9	184.9	80.4	na
% Change Revenue	44.1	10.5	92.1	na
% Change Assets	110.3	51.6	1.8	na

Preferred Div. Coverage	np	np	np
Total Div. Coverage	na	3.4	2.9
Interest Coverage	2.0	2.2	1.5
Current Ratio	1.1	3.1	1.4
Operating Margin	19.1	19.6	18.2
Asset Turnover	0.4	0.5	0.8
5 YEAR RATIOS (%)			
Return on Capital	na	na	na
Return on Com. Equity	na	na	na
Profit Growth	na	na	na
Revenue Growth	na	na	na
Asset Growth	na	na	na
BALANCE SHEET (000)			
Cash	13,472	27,018	4,285
Current Assets	28,320	32,907	10,046
Net Fixed Assets	170,671	61,781	50,693
Invest's & Advances	725	0	0
Total Assets	207,617	98,745	65,131
Short Term Debt	11,262	1,939	1,905
Current Liabilities	25,736	10,637	7,336
Long Term Debt	113,874	48,627	47,315
Total Liabilities	155,144	72,073	68,125
Total Equity	52,473	26,672	(2,994)
Total Liab. & Equity	207,617	98,745	65,131
CAPITAL (000)			
Total Debt	125,136	50,566	49,220
Preferred Equity	0	0	0
Common Equity	52,473	26,672	(2,994)

Business:

VERSACOLD CORPORATION is a supplier of public refrigerated warehousing and distribution services. The company provides food processing, cold storage, transportation and logistics services to customers in Canada and the United States.

Date	EPS	DPS	Tot Rev	Inc Bex
Mar 95	0.10	0.00	24,750	968
Dec 94	0.20	0.00	26,581	1,936
Sep 94	0.19	0.00	24,919	1,746
Jun 94	0.06	0.00	13,961	460
Mar 94	0.08	0.00	13,148	626
Dec 93	0.12	0.00	13,781	688
Sep 93	0.57	0.00	16,707	2,743
Jun 93	0.12	0.00	12,559	596

Synopsis:

Versacold Corporation doubled its public refrigerated warehousing and distribution capacity in 1994 with the acquisition of Trans Canada Freezers (TCF). With the $96-million purchase, Versacold became the largest supplier of refrigerated and frozen logistics service in Canada. Versacold sales increased 46.6% in 1994, reflecting the immediate results of five months of TCF operations. In 1994, Versacold also built two new facilities: one in Brampton, Ontario, which is already slated for expansion in 1995, and another in Vancouver.

In 1994, revenues derived from product category were: packaged goods, 58.3%; fruit and vegetable, 15.2%; fish, 12.2%; meat and poultry, 12.2%; and other, 2.1%. After a downturn in 1994 in the West Coast salmon fishery and an average berry crop in 1994, Versacold is continuing to focus on its non-cyclical sectors of the food industry, such as packaged foods and meats for more consistent sales levels.

Versacold is well positioned for the expanding industry-wide Efficient Consumer Response (ECR) initiative. With ECR, the food industry is gradually adopting practices and technology to create a streamlined distribution of products from manufacturer all the way through the distribution chain to store shelves. As a result of ECR initiatives, Versacold has set up a logistics division to meet the changing needs of food manufacturers, distributors and retailers. Third-party logistics, or outsourcing, is gaining widespread use within the food industry. By using the logistics services of Versacold to warehouse, track, and distribute products, food service companies can maintain lower overhead expenses and achieve greater efficiency in operations. In 1994, 18% of Versacold's sales were from third-party logistics, and the company expects significant expansion in this area of operations in the next few years.

Relative strength to TSE300

Price

Volume (in 1000's of board lots)

Rank (Profit/Revenue/Assets)
430   458   349

Samuel H. Gudewill
Chairman

John F. Morgan
President & C.E.O.

Verne D. Pecho
Exec. V.P. C.F.O. & Secretary

Robert J. Thompson
V.P. Sales & Marketing

Address
2115 Commissioner Street
Vancouver
BC
V5L 1A6
(604) 255-4656

Fax: (604) 255-4330
01003515/G/15.3

				EARNINGS PER SHARE		
Page	Company		Fiscal year end	Last Year	Estimate this year	Estimate next year
561	Agra Industries		Jul-94	(0.36)	0.60	0.90
562	Alliance Communications		Mar-94	0.96	1.36	1.51
563	Arbor Memorial Services		Oct-94	0.90	0.98	1.13
564	Astral Communications		Aug-94	0.80	0.82	1.10
565	Atlantis Communications		Dec-94	0.87	0.91	1.09
566	Banister Foundation		Dec-94	0.61	0.65	1.47
567	Bovar Inc.		Dec-94	0.09	0.13	0.16
568	Bracknell Corp.		Oct-94	(0.62)	0.23	0.35
569	CGC Inc.		Dec-94	0.46	na	na
570	Chai-Na-Ta Corp.		Nov-94	0.30	na	na
571	Cineplex-Odeon	$US	Dec-94	(0.10)	(0.04)	0.10
572	Cinram Ltd.		Dec-94	0.81	0.89	1.12
573	Derlan Industries		Dec-94	(0.53)	0.10	0.45
574	Dorel Industires		Dec-94	0.68	0.88	0.95
575	Extendicare		Dec-94	0.73	0.82	0.97
576	Four Seasons Hotels		Dec-94	0.54	0.88	0.90
577	Imax Corp.		Dec-94	(0.81)	0.15	0.90
578	Inter-City Products		Dec-94	(0.09)	0.08	0.32
579	Journey's End		Jul-94	(0.89)	na	na
580	Kaufel Group		Aug-94	0.23	0.41	0.58
581	Lafarge Canada		Dec-94	3.31	na	na
582	Livent Inc.		Dec-94	0.48	0.68	0.83
583	Loewen Group	$US	Dec-94	0.97	1.23	1.54
584	MDS Health Group		Oct-94	1.11	1.30	1.44
585	Moore Corporation	$US	Dec-94	1.22	1.41	1.65
586	Philip Environmental		Dec-94	0.60	0.71	0.84
587	Premdor Inc.		Dec-94	0.78	0.90	1.09
588	Prudential Steel		Dec-94	2.11	1.69	1.78
589	Scott Paper		Dec-94	0.70	0.80	1.80
590	Shaw Industries		Dec-94	1.45	1.30	1.45
591	SNC-Lavalin Group		Dec-94	1.75	2.13	2.42
592	St. Lawrence Cement		Dec-94	0.30	0.80	0.88
593	Unican Security Systems		Jun-94	1.62	1.67	2.03

Estimates from First Call Corporation, 22 Pittsburgh Street, Boston, MA 02210   (800) 366-9992   Fax (617) 261-5679

AGRA INDUSTRIES LIMITED

Exchanges	Price (Jun29'95)	7.00	Trailing P/E	nm	Stock Symbol
TM	Trailing Yield (%)	2.29	Trailing EPS	(0.12)	**AGR.B**

Period Ending	Ju l94	Ju l93	Ju l92	Ju l91	Ju l90
Yearly Statistics					
Price-Close	6.50	7.25	7.13	8.00	8.00
Price-High	10.25	8.70	9.00	9.30	9.75
Price-Low	5.75	5.60	7.13	5.70	7.00
P/E-Close	nm	60.42	nm	nm	114.29
Dividends per Share	0.15	0.16	0.16	0.15	0.12
Dividend Yield (%)	2.31	2.21	2.25	1.88	1.50
Sales per Share	36.93	33.11	24.16	21.18	16.79
EPS before extra. item	(0.36)	0.12	(0.49)	(0.07)	0.07
Cash Flow per Share	0.07	0.73	1.10	1.66	1.03
Book Value per Share	9.33	9.62	9.16	9.64	9.88
O/S Common Shares	20,546	17,873	17,854	17,742	17,721
Total Revenue	721,008	594,863	430,266	375,596	274,181
Income before extra.	(7,044)	2,185	(8,689)	(1,240)	1,188
Cash Flow	1,322	13,120	19,574	29,501	16,888
Debt/Equity	1.03	0.90	1.02	0.55	0.37
Return on Capital (%)	(1.45)	2.20	1.40	5.54	6.61
Ret. on Com. Equity (%)	(3.87)	1.30	(5.19)	(0.72)	0.71
% Change Profit	(422.4)	125.1	(600.6)	(204.4)	118.8
% Change Revenue	21.2	38.3	14.6	37.0	11.0
% Change Assets	22.5	1.4	32.2	2.5	6.9

Preferred Div. Coverage	np	np	np
Total Div. Coverage	0.0	0.8	0.0
Interest Coverage	0.0	0.7	0.4
Current Ratio	1.4	1.4	1.4
Operating Margin	(0.2)	2.2	3.9
Asset Turnover	1.3	1.3	1.0
5 YEAR RATIOS (%)			
Return on Capital	2.9	3.5	5.2
Return on Com. Equity	(1.6)	(1.7)	(0.8)
Profit Growth	na	(18.7)	na
Revenue Growth	23.8	20.7	15.6
Asset Growth	12.4	17.2	22.3
BALANCE SHEET (000)			
Cash	35,316	42,201	38,063
Current Assets	265,829	220,278	200,702
Net Fixed Assets	166,550	161,010	151,218
Invest's & Advances	58,445	21,521	44,731
Total Assets	545,086	444,885	438,762
Short Term Debt	53,164	46,368	47,967
Current Liabilities	195,935	156,537	139,113
Long Term Debt	144,662	107,770	118,642
Total Liabilities	353,300	272,901	275,203
Total Equity	191,786	171,984	163,559
Total Liab. & Equity	545,086	444,885	438,762
CAPITAL (000)			
Total Debt	197,826	154,138	166,609
Preferred Equity	0	0	0
Common Equity	191,786	171,984	163,559

Business:

AGRA INDUSTRIES LTD. is an international corporation based in Canada which provides services in engineering, the environment, construction, technology and resource recovery to industrial, commercial and government clients in North America, Asia, Africa, Europe, the Caribbean and the Middle East.

Date	EPS	DPS	Tot Rev	Inc Bex
Apr 95	0.07	0.04	165,539	1,452
Jan 95	0.08	0.04	170,568	1,975
Oct 94	0.22	0.04	210,196	4,230
Jul 94	(0.49)	0.04	195,616	(9,521)
Apr 94	(0.05)	0.04	177,135	(781)
Jan 94	(0.07)	0.04	157,987	(1,280)
Oct 93	0.25	0.04	188,105	4,538
Jul 93	0.06	0.04	172,403	1,103

Synopsis:

Agra's net earnings for the first nine months ended April 30, 1995, increased 209% to $7,657,000 compared to $2,477,000 for the same period last year. Agra attributed the increase to better performance in both the Engineering, Construction & Technology and the Resource Recovery & Recycling Sectors. Resource Recovery & Recycling revenues rose by 26% over the same period last year. Asset Development revenues rose by 9% over the same period last year.

In April 1995, Monenco Agra Inc. was contracted by Compania Boliviana de Energia Electrica S.A. to carry out engineering, procurement, construction supervision, and project management for the expansion of hydroelectric facilities in the Zongo Valley near La Paz, Bolivia. The total capital cost of the expansion program is estimated at $105-million (U.S.). The expansion should be completed by mid 1998.

In March 1995, Monenco Agra Inc. was awarded multiple contracts totalling more than $2-million. Monenco Agra will provide systems integration services and support for the Ontario Ministry of Northern Development and Mines for its earth resources and land information system.

In March 1995, the World Bank awarded Agra's environmental and geotechnical engineering subsidiary, Agra Earth & Environmental Limited, a $1-million contract to study the clean up one of the world's largest oil spills. The spill is in the Komi Republic of the Commonwealth of Independent States. The contract is being financed by the Canadian government.

In January 1995, Agra Earth & Environmental Inc. was awarded two contracts worth $12.5-million by the U.S. Army. Agra will provide services for hazardous and toxic waste, and clean up an underground storage tank at a former military site on the Columbia River, in Oregon. The contract is worth $500,000. Meanwhile, in Alaska, Agra will work on a $12-million, three-year general services contract awarded by the Alaska Corps of Engineers.

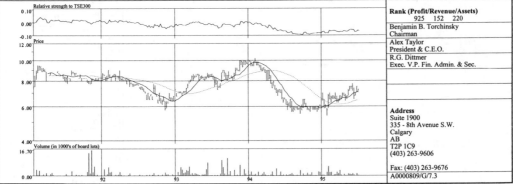

Rank (Profit/Revenue/Assets)
925   152   220
Benjamin B. Torchinsky Chairman
Alex Taylor President & C.E.O.
R.G. Dittmer Exec. V.P. Fin. Admin. & Sec.

Address
Suite 1900
335 - 8th Avenue S.W.
Calgary
AB
T2P 1C9
(403) 263-9606

Fax: (403) 263-9676
A0000809/G/7.3

ALLIANCE COMMUNICATIONS CORPORATION

Exchanges	Price (Jun29'95)	10.75	Trailing P/E	7.90	Stock Symbol
TM	Trailing Yield (%)	0.00	Trailing EPS	1.36	**AAC**

Period Ending	Mar94	Mar93	Mar92
Yearly Statistics			9M
Price-Close	13.50	n t	n t
Price-High	16.00	n t	n t
Price-Low	12.00	n t	n t
P/E-Close	13.37	n t	n t
Dividends per Share	0.00	0.05	0.00
Dividend Yield (%)	0.00	n t	0.00
Sales per Share	15.69	25.05	21.99
EPS before extra. item	1.01	0.96	0.69
Cash Flow per Share	1.52	1.40	1.04
Book Value per Share	8.59	2.28	1.98
O/S Common Shares	8,180	5,708	3,688
Total Revenue	108,985	132,161	83,874
Income before extra.	7,345	5,065	3,509
Cash Flow	10,582	7,391	3,984
Debt/Equity	0.00	1.24	1.60
Return on Capital (%)	20.26	29.82	na
Ret. on Com. Equity (%)	17.64	na	na
% Change Profit	45.0	8.3	na
% Change Revenue	(17.5)	18.2	na
% Change Assets	92.0	52.2	na
Preferred Div. Coverage	np	np	na
Total Div. Coverage	na	15.3	na
Interest Coverage	27.4	9.3	5.5
Current Ratio	1.6	1.0	0.9
Operating Margin	9.3	5.7	5.6
Asset Turnover	0.6	1.4	1.8
5 YEAR RATIOS (%)			
Return on Capital	na	na	na
Return on Com. Equity	na	na	na
Profit Growth	na	na	na
Revenue Growth	na	na	na
Asset Growth	na	na	na
BALANCE SHEET (000)			
Cash	31,936	2,051	0
Current Assets	101,729	54,550	35,119
Net Fixed Assets	2,930	1,925	789
Invest's & Advances	75,962	38,934	26,465
Total Assets	185,513	96,604	63,478
Short Term Debt	0	7,429	5,439
Current Liabilities	62,558	56,365	37,938
Long Term Debt	285	8,720	7,779
Total Liabilities	115,269	83,584	55,193
Total Equity	70,244	13,020	8,285
Total Liab. & Equity	185,513	96,604	63,478
CAPITAL (000)			
Total Debt	285	16,149	13,218
Preferred Equity	0	0	1,000
Common Equity	70,244	13,020	7,285

Business:

ALLIANCE COMMUNICATIONS CORPORATION is a fully-integrated producer and distributor of television programmes and feature films, providing development, production and international distribution services, production financing, broadcasting (Showcase Network), and music publishing.

Date	EPS	DPS	Tot Rev	Inc Bex
Mar 95	0.40	0.00	89,560	3,846
Dec 94	0.39	0.00	73,085	3,842
Sep 94	0.24	0.00	38,490	2,353
Jun 94	0.33	0.00	32,676	2,934
Mar 94	0.31	0.00	28,709	2,218
Dec 93	0.16	0.00	33,298	1,830

Synopsis:

Alliance Communications reported record revenues from all its core divisions for the fiscal year ending March 31, 1995. Total revenue rose 115%, net earnings were up 77%, and profit-per-share climbed 35%. Alliance operates four divisions: Productions; Releasing; International; and Equicap, a brokerage house arranging structured financing for independent third-party producers. Recent Alliance Productions credits include: ReBoot, a computer-animated children's series; Harlequin Romance TV movies; Due South on CBS and CTV; CBC's North of 60; and feature films Exotica and Johnny Mnemonic. As of March 1995, Alliance had earmarked $90-million for further productions in 1995.

Alliance Releasing's market share grew in fiscal 1995 due to its distribution of box office hits such as Dumb and Dumber, Pulp Fiction, and The Mask. Alliance International formed a joint venture with MDP Worldwide of Los Angeles in order to jointly acquire and licence international rights to feature films. In 1994, it also formed Le Monde Entertainment, a division that distributes films for the home video market.

In fiscal 1995, revenues by business segment were: productions, 50%; international distribution, 14%; domestic distribution, 25%; production financing fees, 10%; and broadcasting and music publishing, 1%.

Alliance won approval in April 1995 to reclassify its shares, allowing it to raise equity in the United States. The new non-voting shares should be listed on NASDAQ by the end of 1995. Alliance also arranged for a $75-million bank credit line, to be used for working capital, production financing and currency hedging.

In June 1995, Alliance and its strategic partner Liberty Media Inc. were considering purchase of the broadcasting assets of John Labatt Ltd. The assets include the Discovery Channel, Labatt's 25% stake in Viewer's Choice pay-per-view, and Dome Productions, a TV production house.

Rank (Profit/Revenue/Assets)
358   410   368

Robert Lantos
Chairman & C.E.O.
Richard Miller
C.F.O.
Gordon Haines
C.O.O

Address
Suite 400
920 Yonge Street
Toronto
ON
M4W 3C7
(416) 967-1174

Fax: (416) 960-0971
01003413/G/16.1

For further company information, call Globe Information Services 1-800-268-9128 or (416) 585-5345

ARBOR MEMORIAL SERVICES INC.

Exchanges	**Price (Jun29'95)**		19 .50	**Trailing P/E**		21 .91	**Stock Symbol**
T	**Trailing Yield (%)**		0 .21	**Trailing EPS**		0 .89	**ABO.B**

Period Ending	Oc t94	Oc t93	Oc t92	Oc t91	Oc t90	Business:
Yearly Statistics						ARBOR MEMORIAL SERVICES INC.
Price-Close	17 .00	15 .50	13 .00	9 .00	7 .00	through its related companies owns and
Price-High	19 .25	16 .00	13 .00	10 .13	9 .00	operates cemetaries, cremetoria and funeral
Price-Low	12 .13	12 .00	9 .00	6 .50	6 .50	service establishments in Canada.
P/E-Close	18 .89	20 .67	16 .05	15 .52	9 .09	
Dividends per Share	0 .08	0 .05	0 .00	0 .00	0 .00	
Dividend Yield (%)	0 .47	0 .32	0 .00	0 .00	0 .00	
Sales per Share	11 .85	11 .81	10 .89	9 .27	10 .28	
EPS before extra. item	0 .90	0 .75	0 .81	0 .58	0 .77	
Cash Flow per Share	1 .49	0 .54	2 .60	1 .60	1 .90	
Book Value per Share	11 .41	10 .38	9 .68	8 .87	8 .28	
O/S Common Shares	8 ,788	7 ,788	7 ,773	7 ,773	7 ,773	
Total Revenue	107 ,817	100 ,591	94 ,289	83 ,803	93 ,098	

Income before extra.	7 ,372	5 ,847	6 ,326	4 ,545	5 ,980	Date	EPS	DPS	Tot Rev	Inc Bex
Cash Flow	12 ,188	4 ,205	20 ,208	12 ,403	14 ,749	Apr 95	0 .28	0 .00	29 ,032	2 ,432
Debt/Equity	0 .27	0 .34	0 .37	0 .47	0 .62	Jan 95	0 .21	0 .00	24 ,885	1 ,847
Return on Capital (%)	13 .05	14 .29	14 .97	11 .42	15 .72	Oct 94	0 .21	0 .04	28 ,253	1 ,797
Ret. on Com. Equity (%)	8 .14	7 .49	8 .78	6 .82	9 .74	Jul 94	0 .19	0 .00	26 ,549	1 ,510
% Change Profit	26 .1	(7 .6)	39 .2	(24 .0)	(47 .8)	Apr 94	0 .32	0 .00	28 ,971	2 ,489
% Change Revenue	7 .2	6 .7	12 .5	(10 .0)	(7 .8)	Jan 94	0 .20	0 .00	24 ,044	1 ,576
% Change Assets	12 .6	3 .5	5 .0	3 .1	0 .3	Oct 93	0 .16	0 .05	28 ,074	1 ,291
						Jul 93	0 .14	0 .00	25 ,167	1 ,063

				Synopsis:
Preferred Div. Coverage	np	np	np	
Total Div. Coverage	12 .0	15 .0	na	In 1994, Arbor Memorial Services set down a mission statement to establish an
Interest Coverage	5 .7	5 .6	5 .3	integrated group of funeral homes, cemeteries, and crematoria in each community
Current Ratio	2 .2	2 .6	3 .1	it serves. To that end, through openings of new funeral homes, in 1995 it brought
Operating Margin	12 .3	15 .3	17 .1	to 10 the number of funeral homes located on the company's cemetery properties.
Asset Turnover	0 .3	0 .3	0 .3	In 1994-1995, it also acquired eight funeral homes in Ontario for a total cost of
5 YEAR RATIOS (%)				$15.3-million and two parcels of land adjacent to its current cemeteries for future
Return on Capital	13 .9	16 .2	15 .6	development. Arbor invested a further $7.8-million in upgrading its funeral homes
Return on Com. Equity	8 .2	10 .9	10 .2	and cemeteries.
Profit Growth	(8 .5)	26 .3	15 .7	Although cash flow improved in 1994, operating margins declined due to
Revenue Growth	1 .2	3 .6	4 .3	acquisitions and newly opened funeral homes, increased depreciation, and
Asset Growth	4 .7	2 .4	3 .8	increased corporate expenses. Cemetery sales, both pre-need and at-need
BALANCE SHEET (000)				exceeded the company's sales targets, while funeral sales declined slightly.
Cash	5 ,939	3 ,373	10 ,583	However, for the period ended January 31, 1995, funeral revenues and profit
Current Assets	44 ,457	42 ,664	53 ,036	margins increased, with a net contribution from the funeral sector 38% higher
Net Fixed Assets	105 ,314	84 ,902	70 ,890	than for the same period a year earlier. Arbor disposed of its remaining cemetery
Invest's & Advances	19 ,975	18 ,569	22 ,802	in the United States in 1994, as part of its plan to temporarily withdraw from the
Total Assets	335 ,639	298 ,187	288 ,189	U.S. market.
Short Term Debt	2 ,028	2 ,047	1 ,982	The company continues to build its pre-arranged services segment and to expand
Current Liabilities	20 ,563	16 ,545	16 ,862	in Canada by building funeral homes within its cemeteries where possible.
Long Term Debt	24 ,532	25 ,109	26 ,183	Excluding acquisitions, Arbor's 1995 capital expenditure budget is $20-million,
Total Liabilities	235 ,407	217 ,384	212 ,955	including $8.5-million for crypts and niches and cemetery development.
Total Equity	100 ,232	80 ,803	75 ,234	In 1994, 60% of revenues were derived from cemetery operations and 39%
Total Liab. & Equity	335 ,639	298 ,187	288 ,189	funeral operations. About 1% of revenues were derived from corporate and U.S.
CAPITAL (000)				operations.
Total Debt	26 ,560	27 ,156	28 ,165	
Preferred Equity	0	0	0	
Common Equity	100 ,232	80 ,803	75 ,234	

Rank (Profit/Revenue/Assets)
357   412   274

Daniel J. Scanlan
Chairman
John F. Gillies
President & C.E.O.

Address
2 Jane Street
Toronto
ON
M6S 4W8
(416) 763-4531

Fax: (416) 763-0381
A0002718/G/16.3

ASTRAL COMMUNICATIONS INC.

Exchanges	Price (Jun29'95)	11.62	Trailing P/E	14.18	Stock Symbol
TM	Trailing Yield (%)	2.58	Trailing EPS	0.82	ACM.A

Period Ending	Aug94	Aug93	Feb92	Feb91	Feb90
Yearly Statistics		18M			
Price-Close	15.75	17.00	11.00	9.38	11.00
Price-High	20.25	19.00	12.50	11.88	14.75
Price-Low	13.50	11.00	9.75	8.25	9.75
P/E-Close	19.21	27.16	16.67	11.57	11.58
Dividends per Share	0.30	0.45	0.25	0.25	0.23
Dividend Yield (%)	1.91	2.65	2.27	2.67	2.05
Sales per Share	28.59	31.30	33.94	33.33	36.36
EPS before extra. item	0.82	0.94	0.66	0.81	0.95
Cash Flow per Share	1.98	1.93	1.41	1.48	2.31
Book Value per Share	12.51	11.16	10.70	10.29	9.74
O/S Common Shares	13,060	11,510	8,503	8,499	8,455
Total Revenue	354,974	478,549	289,214	283,380	287,642
Income before extra.	10,187	9,591	5,599	6,902	7,467
Cash Flow	24,488	29,475	11,951	12,543	18,225
Debt/Equity	0.01	0.07	0.58	0.74	0.40
Return on Capital (%)	13.41	11.31	7.95	10.95	13.26
Ret. on Com. Equity (%)	6.98	5.83	6.28	8.13	10.82
% Change Profit	59.3	14.2	(18.9)	(7.6)	76.1
% Change Revenue	11.3	10.3	2.1	(1.5)	8.4
% Change Assets	14.2	4.1	(5.5)	12.3	13.5

Preferred Div. Coverage	np	np	np
Total Div. Coverage	2.8	2.0	2.6
Interest Coverage	66.3	7.6	1.9
Current Ratio	1.3	1.2	1.1
Operating Margin	5.9	5.3	4.0
Asset Turnover	1.4	1.4	1.3

5 YEAR RATIOS (%)

Return on Capital	11.4	11.9	11.1
Return on Com. Equity	7.6	7.8	7.7
Profit Growth	19.2	18.8	22.1
Revenue Growth	5.9	10.2	9.9
Asset Growth	7.4	12.2	13.7

BALANCE SHEET (000)

Cash	14,819	9,626	5,412
Current Assets	113,843	101,768	78,868
Net Fixed Assets	47,880	24,486	24,216
Invest's & Advances	4,799	7,048	7,468
Total Assets	261,086	228,527	219,532
Short Term Debt	364	689	1,479
Current Liabilities	87,271	83,894	69,779
Long Term Debt	1,355	8,398	51,385
Total Liabilities	97,756	100,044	128,581
Total Equity	163,330	128,483	90,951
Total Liab. & Equity	261,086	228,527	219,532

CAPITAL (000)

Total Debt	1,719	9,087	52,864
Preferred Equity	0	0	0
Common Equity	163,330	128,483	90,951

Business:

ASTRAL COMMUNICATIONS offers pay and basic television broadcasting, video wholesaling, distribution of features films and other filmed or videotaped programs for theatre, television, home video and related markets. It also offers video duplication, and sound mixing and duplication services. It is also retails photofinishing services and photographic equipment and supplies.

Date	EPS	DPS	Tot Rev	Inc Bex
Feb 95	0.14	0.15	100,848	1,793
Nov 94	0.14	0.00	106,465	1,830
Aug 94	0.33	0.15	88,243	4,255
May 94	0.21	0.00	88,630	2,746
Feb 94	0.14	0.15	84,343	1,684
Nov 94	0.13	0.00	93,758	1,502
Aug 93	0.28	0.15	91,643	3,049
May 93	0.19	0.00	82,416	2,214

Synopsis:

Astral Communications Inc. began 1995 with the launch of two new specialty cable channels, Moviepix and the French-language Canal D. Astral now holds seven licences. The broadcasting group realized revenue increases of 7.4% during the three months ended February 28, 1995, mainly due to the new channels. The entertainment group contributed to the overall increase in revenues through its increased sales in video wholesaling and duplication and its new Boca Raton CD replication facility, acquired in 1994.

In fiscal 1994, Astral benefited from increased revenues and earnings in both its broadcasting and entertainment groups. In the photographic retail segment, however, revenues dropped 5% and earnings 75% compared to the same 12-month period in 1993. For fiscal 1994, revenues by segment were: broadcasting, 27%; entertainment, 59%; and retail 14%. In addition, Astral's long-term debt-to-equity ratio improved to 0.01:1 during the year.

In December 1994, Astral predicted a 15% increase in fiscal 1995's revenue, profit and cash flow, and stated that its profit would grow 50% to 70% over the next three years. In order to achieve growth, the company is actively seeking acquisitions, particularly in the broadcast and entertainment sectors. Astral is currently assessing its retail business to determine whether it will remain part of its core business.

Astral is part of a consortium of communications companies that is launching a direct-to-home satellite service. The venture will deliver pay-per-view, pay and other programming to mostly rural, uncabled homes.

In 1994, Astral's capital expenditures rose to $30.7-million. Of that amount, $18.3-million was used to equip the Boca Raton CD facility. Another $6.2-million went to AstraTech Inc.'s video duplication centre and its sound post-production, lab and dubbing facilities. As well, $1.4-million went to a point-of-sale system for the retail segment.

Relative strength to TSE300 / Price / Volume (in 1000's of board lots) chart, 1992–1995

Rank (Profit/Revenue/Assets)		
296	232	310

Harold Greenberg
Chairman & C.E.O.

Ian Greenberg
President & C.O.O.

Claude Gagnon
Vice President Finance

Address
Maison Astral
2100 Rue Ste-Catherine Ouest
Bureau 900
Montreal
PQ
H3H 2T3
(514) 939-5000
Fax: (514) 939-1515
A0003324/G/16.1

564

ATLANTIS COMMUNICATIONS INC.

Exchanges	Price (Jun29'95)	6 .62	Trailing P/E	7 .20	Stock Symbol
T	Trailing Yield (%)	0 .00	Trailing EPS	0 .92	ATV

Period Ending	Dec94	Dec93	Dec92	Dec91
Yearly Statistics				
Price-Close	9 .75	14 .63	n t	n t
Price-High	16 .50	14 .66	n t	n t
Price-Low	8 .25	13 .75	n t	n t
P/E-Close	10 .71	14 .77	n t	n t
Dividends per Share	0 .00	0 .00	0 .00	0 .00
Dividend Yield (%)	0 .00	0 .00	0 .00	0 .00
Sales per Share	13 .27	12 .90	9 .15	8 .20
EPS before extra. item	0 .91	0 .99	0 .73	0 .34
Cash Flow per Share	12 .42	11 .98	8 .31	7 .30
Book Value per Share	7 .55	5 .54	1 .38	0 .67
O/S Common Shares	9 ,602	7 ,997	5 ,900	5 ,900
Total Revenue	115 ,217	76 ,090	53 ,089	48 ,378
Income before extra.	7 ,864	5 ,874	4 ,210	1 ,958
Cash Flow	107 ,828	70 ,669	48 ,210	43 ,077
Debt/Equity	1 .69	1 .58	5 .35	3 .97
Return on Capital (%)	7 .55	12 .91	22 .26	na
Ret. on Com. Equity (%)	13 .47	22 .39	69 .67	na
% Change Profit	33 .9	39 .5	115 .0	na
% Change Revenue	51 .4	43 .3	9 .7	na
% Change Assets	79 .1	76 .5	24 .0	na

Date	EPS	DPS	Tot Rev	Inc Bex
Mar 95	0.18	0.00	27 ,452	1 ,717
Dec 94	0.54	0.00	55 ,926	4 ,745
Sep 94	0.09	0.00	13 ,317	733
Jun 94	0.11	0.00	22 ,900	872
Mar 94	na	na	na	na
Dec 93	0.52	0.00	40 ,074	3 ,121
Sep 93	0.17	0.00	13 ,277	970

Preferred Div. Coverage	np	np	np
Total Div. Coverage	na	na	na
Interest Coverage	8 .1	14 .8	13 .2
Current Ratio	2 .2	2 .6	1 .1
Operating Margin	9 .4	14 .1	15 .0
Asset Turnover	0 .4	0 .5	0 .6
5 YEAR RATIOS (%)			
Return on Capital	na	na	na
Return on Com. Equity	na	na	na
Profit Growth	na	na	na
Revenue Growth	na	na	na
Asset Growth	na	na	na
BALANCE SHEET (000)			
Cash	3 ,400	24 ,721	1 ,847
Current Assets	70 ,591	48 ,550	25 ,403
Net Fixed Assets	7 ,730	3 ,769	3 ,280
Invest's & Advances	119 ,588	58 ,585	28 ,962
Total Assets	280 ,307	156 ,503	88 ,662
Short Term Debt	8 ,402	4 ,904	8 ,562
Current Liabilities	31 ,794	18 ,840	22 ,434
Long Term Debt	114 ,164	65 ,069	35 ,041
Total Liabilities	207 ,865	112 ,182	80 ,514
Total Equity	72 ,442	44 ,322	8 ,148
Total Liab. & Equity	280 ,307	156 ,503	88 ,662
CAPITAL (000)			
Total Debt	122 ,566	69 ,974	43 ,603
Preferred Equity	0	0	0
Common Equity	72 ,442	44 ,322	8 ,148

Business:

ATLANTIS COMMUNICATIONS INC. directly, and through its subsidiaries, is a producer of television programs. The company coordinates and manages all of its television programs from their conception, writing, direction, production, financing, and finally, distribution.

Synopsis:

Atlantis Communications is an internationally focused company that concentrates on the production and distribution of series and movies, mostly for television. The company has grown rapidly over the past 17 years. Both revenues and net earnings have increased by a compounded average of 50% per year.

Atlantis sees specialty broadcasting as a key component in its strategy to diversify earnings beyond its core business of television distribution and production. As part of this strategy, in 1994, Atlantis bought a controlling interest in Life Network, a cable lifestyle channel. It also plans to apply to the Canadian Radio-Television and Telecommunications Commission (CRTC) in 1995 for a licence to operate a science fiction specialty channel.

With globalization, Atlantis sees strong growth potential in international markets. While the United States is already a strong market for Atlantis, television in South America, China, New Zealand and Australia is just beginning to expand.

In 1994, Atlantis acquired a 28% interest in YTV Canada, a children's network. It also bought Soundmix Limited, a company specializing in post-production sound mixing, dubbing of dialogue, musical tracks, and special effects. Soundmix should provide cost savings for Atlantis productions and generate revenue through a roster of outside clients.

Atlantis' 1994 revenue of $115-million included $69.2-million derived from non-Canadian sources. Recent Atlantis productions include Following Her Heart, Avalanche, Trust in Me, TekWar, The Outer Limits, Squawk Box, Neon Rider, Trial at Fortitude Bay and Destiny Ridge.

Rank (Profit/Revenue/Assets)
341   398   295

Michael MacMillan
Chairman & C.E.O.

Kevin Shea
President & C.O.O.

Mona L. Stirling
C.F.O. & Treasurer

Address
65 Heward Avenue
Toronto
ON
M4M 2T5
(416) 462-0246

Fax: (416) 462-0254
01003524/G/16.1

BANISTER FOUNDATION INC.

Exchanges	Price (Jun29'95)	11.75	Trailing P/E	18.36	Stock Symbol
TMZA	Trailing Yield (%)	0.00	Trailing EPS	0.64	**BAC**

Period Ending	Dec94	Dec93	Dec92	Dec91	Dec90
Yearly Statistics					
Price-Close	14.50	17.00	8.88	7.00	8.63
Price-High	20.75	17.25	9.25	9.50	12.50
Price-Low	13.25	8.50	7.00	5.68	7.75
P/E-Close	23.77	10.43	7.34	6.25	nm
Dividends per Share	0.00	0.00	0.00	0.00	0.00
Dividend Yield (%)	0.00	0.00	0.00	0.00	0.00
Sales per Share	67.56	74.67	58.19	70.28	117.49
EPS before extra. item	0.61	1.63	1.21	1.12	(1.43)
Cash Flow per Share	1.74	2.13	2.59	2.32	(0.52)
Book Value per Share	13.92	13.38	11.66	10.45	9.31
O/S Common Shares	7,751	7,653	5,953	5,953	5,953
Total Revenue	527,453	469,332	348,014	421,725	700,697
Income before extra.	4,691	10,140	7,174	6,648	(8,517)
Cash Flow	13,469	13,306	15,395	13,786	(3,082)
Debt/Equity	0.42	0.58	0.32	0.38	0.68
Return on Capital (%)	7.34	15.25	14.19	11.09	(4.21)
Ret. on Com. Equity (%)	4.46	11.80	10.90	11.30	(14.28)
% Change Profit	(53.7)	41.3	7.9	178.1	(61.7)
% Change Revenue	12.4	34.9	(17.5)	(39.8)	8.2
% Change Assets	25.2	58.3	(2.7)	(32.5)	(5.5)

Preferred Div. Coverage	np	np	np
Total Div. Coverage	na	na	na
Interest Coverage	3.1	7.4	6.6
Current Ratio	1.2	1.3	1.3
Operating Margin	1.3	3.4	3.2
Asset Turnover	1.6	1.8	2.2
5 YEAR RATIOS (%)			
Return on Capital	8.7	6.4	4.3
Return on Com. Equity	4.8	2.4	0.1
Profit Growth	(5.6)	93.4	44.5
Revenue Growth	(4.1)	5.1	11.2
Asset Growth	4.2	7.2	0.9
BALANCE SHEET (000)			
Cash	45,374	17,195	12,822
Current Assets	227,752	156,604	86,800
Net Fixed Assets	70,300	75,246	59,181
Invest's & Advances	0	0	3,294
Total Assets	318,536	254,436	160,770
Short Term Debt	28,534	34,796	2,624
Current Liabilities	192,818	121,642	64,876
Long Term Debt	16,576	24,239	19,438
Total Liabilities	210,686	152,037	91,365
Total Equity	107,850	102,399	69,405
Total Liab. & Equity	318,536	254,436	160,770
CAPITAL (000)			
Total Debt	45,110	59,035	22,062
Preferred Equity	0	0	0
Common Equity	107,850	102,399	69,405

Date	EPS	DPS	Tot Rev	Inc Bex
Mar 95	(0.17)	0.00	151,361	(1,299)
Dec 94	0.24	0.00	146,893	1,819
Sep 94	0.28	0.00	164,998	2,190
Jun 94	0.29	0.00	132,264	2,234
Mar 94	(0.20)	0.00	82,897	(1,552)
Dec 93	0.90	0.00	127,717	5,730
Sep 93	0.42	0.00	178,490	3,074
Jun 93	0.14	0.00	90,882	825

Business:

BANISTER FOUNDATION INC. is a construction company specializing in civil, pipeline, utility, nuclear, industrial, and building construction. The company's four major divisions are active across Canada, in the United States, and internationally including India, Romania, South Korea and the Caribbean.

Synopsis:

In May 1995, Banister Foundation's Nicholls-Radtke Ltd. received contracts valued at about $80-million from TransCanada PipeLines Ltd. of Calgary. Nicholas-Radtke will build power generation plants in Kapuskasing and North Bay, Ontario. Construction should be completed by December 1996. Also in May, Jackson-Lewis Co. signed a $12-million construction contract by St. Hilda's Anglican Church and the St. Hilda's Towers Community of Toronto.

In April, Banister's Foundation Building West Inc. was awarded a $38-million contract by B.C. Building Corp. for the construction of its Forensic Psychiatric Institute in Port Coquitlam, B.C. Construction will be completed by December 1996.

Also in April, Cliffside Utility Contractors was awarded several contracts for utility work in Southern Ontario. The contracts, which total more than $26.5-million, will be completed within 24 months. The company said it received a pipeline contract for 40 kilometres of 12-inch pipe for Chatham-based Union Gas Ltd. It also said its contracts with Union Gas for new and replacement mains in the Hamilton and Waterloo regions were renewed for an additional 12 months. Cliffside also received four contracts with Bell Canada for work in Toronto, York Region and the Niagara Peninsula.

In December 1994, Foundation Building West signed two B.C. contracts totalling more than $35-million. Banister said one contract involves the construction of the Ford Theatre for the Performing Arts in Vancouver for Georgia Strait Live Entertainment Inc. The other contract is for the construction of the Walter C. Koerner Central Library at the University of British Columbia.

In November 1994, Jackson-Lewis Co. was awarded several contracts for work in the Toronto area. These contracts are worth more than $20-million. All projects are currently under way. Also in November, Banister Majestic Inc. signed a $65-million contract by Nova Gas Transmission Ltd. The contract calls for the construction of about 270 kilometres miles of steel pipe.

Rank (Profit/Revenue/Assets)
433 192 279

J.R. McCaig
Chairman

E.R. Austin
President & C.E.O.

Meier Miller
V.P. Finance, C.F.O.

Address
3660 Midland Avenue
Scarborough
ON
M1V 4V3
(416) 754-8735

Fax: (416) 754-8736
B0000364/G/7.3

For further company information, call Globe Information Services 1-800-268-9128 or (416) 585-5345

BOVAR INC.

Period Ending	Dec94	Dec93	Dec92	Dec91	Dec90
Yearly Statistics					
Price-Close	1.05	1.25	0.90	1.10	0.60
Price-High	1.55	1.40	1.55	1.70	0.65
Price-Low	0.90	0.85	0.80	0.50	0.20
P/E-Close	11.67	nm	90.00	13.75	nm
Dividends per Share	0.00	0.00	0.00	0.00	0.00
Dividend Yield (%)	0.00	0.00	0.00	0.00	0.00
Sales per Share	1.03	0.74	0.92	1.51	1.39
EPS before extra. item	0.09	0.00	0.01	0.08	(0.20)
Cash Flow per Share	0.23	0.11	0.12	0.20	0.18
Book Value per Share	0.35	0.05	0.05	(0.99)	(1.12)
O/S Common Shares	81,963	67,500	67,289	34,950	34,915
Total Revenue	80,929	50,396	48,786	55,576	48,917
Income before extra.	7,051	(64)	773	4,367	(4,951)
Cash Flow	18,113	7,204	6,417	6,950	6,141
Debt/Equity	2.99	31.88	18.02	na	na
Return on Capital (%)	11.10	3.99	9.12	21.56	4.42
Ret. on Com. Equity (%)	44.57	(2.04)	na	na	na
% Change Profit	nm	(108.3)	(82.3)	188.2	(4,706.8)
% Change Revenue	60.6	3.3	(12.2)	13.6	37.0
% Change Assets	6.5	50.5	18.1	0.1	(7.0)

Date	EPS	DPS	Tot Rev	Inc Bex
Mar 95	0.02	0.00	20,256	1,473
Dec 94	0.03	0.00	25,657	2,538
Sep 94	0.03	0.00	20,827	2,492
Jun 94	0.02	0.00	19,730	1,592
Mar 94	0.01	0.00	14,930	429
Dec 93	0.00	0.00	14,109	(85)
Sep 93	0.00	0.00	12,663	(428)
Jun 93	0.00	0.00	11,437	126

	Dec94	Dec93	Dec92
Preferred Div. Coverage	np	np	np
Total Div. Coverage	na	na	na
Interest Coverage	2.4	0.6	0.9
Current Ratio	1.0	0.8	0.7
Operating Margin	14.5	7.6	10.3
Asset Turnover	0.6	0.4	0.6
5 YEAR RATIOS (%)			
Return on Capital	10.0	10.6	(1.2)
Return on Com. Equity	na	na	na
Profit Growth	na	na	na
Revenue Growth	17.7	(20.8)	(23.6)
Asset Growth	11.9	1.9	(22.0)
BALANCE SHEET (000)			
Cash	2,585	2,006	668
Current Assets	29,009	23,701	23,968
Net Fixed Assets	96,956	93,432	52,527
Invest's & Advances	0	0	0
Total Assets	129,537	121,656	80,844
Short Term Debt	11,941	13,558	13,043
Current Liabilities	27,966	31,099	34,711
Long Term Debt	73,095	87,390	43,022
Total Liabilities	101,061	118,489	77,733
Total Equity	28,476	3,167	3,111
Total Liab. & Equity	129,537	121,656	80,844
CAPITAL (000)			
Total Debt	85,036	100,948	56,065
Preferred Equity	0	0	0
Common Equity	28,476	3,167	3,111

Business:

BOVAR INC. is an environmental and waste management company providing consulting and technical services. BOVAR is an owner/operator of waste management facilities and manufactures multi-gas monitoring instrumentation and control equipement. BOVAR offers cost effective engineering solutions for challenging environmental problems.

Synopsis:

In April 1995, Bovar Inc. and its Malaysian partner, Progressive Impact Corp. Sdn Bhd, signed a 20-year multi-million dollar contract to build and operate an air and water quality monitoring and data management system in Malaysia. Bovar will supply at least 50 air quality monitoring stations within five years. It will also provide technical assistance and training. Bovar will hold a 25% interest in the new operating company, Alam Sekitar Malaysia Sdn Bhd.

In February 1995, Bovar received approval from the Alberta government to import special waste from other provinces for treatment at the its Alberta Special Waste Treatment Centre in Swan Hills. As well, Bovar Biomedical Services Inc. gained approval to import biomedical waste from other provinces for processing at the Biomedical Waste Treatment Facility in Beiseker, Alberta. This facility can treat 6,500 tones of biomedical waste a year, more than enough to meet the demand in Canada's four western provinces.

Significant achievements during 1994 were recorded in each of Bovar's three operating divisions. As a result, Bovar reported major increases in both revenues and profitability. Revenues in 1994 rose by 60% compared to the previous year. Net income was $7.1-million compared with a loss of $0.1-million in 1993.

Early in 1994, Bovar completed the merger of Bovar Environmental Services with Concord Corporation of Toronto, forming Bovar-Concord Environmental Services. Bovar-Concord is one of Canada's largest consulting firms specializing in environmental management, assessment and research.

Net capital spending dropped to $15.5-million during 1994 from $48.2-million the previous year. This was largely to the completion of the capital construction phases for both the Swan Hills and Beiseker facilities.

Rank (Profit/Revenue/Assets)		
364	452	429

Jeffrey J. McCaig
Chairman

Paul Fee
President & C.E.O.

Daryl W. Ferko
V.P. Finance & C.F.O.

Monty Davis
Chief Operating Officer

Address
4 Manning Close N.E.
P.O. Box 6620, Station D
Calgary
AB
T2E 7N5
(403) 235-8300

Fax: (403) 248-3306
B0005970/G/8.1

BRACKNELL CORPORATION

Exchanges	Price (Jun29'95)	2.80	Trailing P/E	nm	Stock Symbol
T	Trailing Yield (%)	0.00	Trailing EPS	(0.17)	**BRK**

Period Ending	Oc t94	Oc t93	Oc t92	Oc t91	Oc t90
Yearly Statistics					
Price-Close	2.75	4.20	5.00	3.20	1.37
Price-High	5.88	9.00	6.00	3.30	2.00
Price-Low	2.20	3.90	2.95	1.10	1.25
P/E-Close	nm	14.48	10.42	5.16	2.64
Dividends per Share	0.00	0.00	0.00	0.60	0.00
Dividend Yield (%)	0.00	0.00	0.00	18.75	0.00
Sales per Share	8.28	7.67	10.50	11.90	11.44
EPS before extra. item	(0.62)	0.29	0.48	0.62	0.52
Cash Flow per Share	(0.81)	0.33	0.77	0.81	0.59
Book Value per Share	2.16	2.78	1.95	1.05	1.05
O/S Common Shares	26,281	26,281	23,281	17,160	15,219
Total Revenue	217,851	192,697	225,413	203,958	174,665
Income before extra.	(16,262)	7,130	10,138	10,535	7,930
Cash Flow	(21,321)	8,133	16,386	13,735	8,924
Debt/Equity	nd	nd	nd	0.31	0.37
Return on Capital (%)	(44.51)	18.93	54.52	57.30	44.07
Ret. on Com. Equity (%)	(25.05)	12.03	31.98	62.06	65.79
% Change Profit	(328.1)	(29.7)	(3.8)	32.9	58.0
% Change Revenue	13.1	(14.5)	10.5	16.8	13.7
% Change Assets	6.5	16.8	40.0	4.6	31.6

Preferred Div. Coverage	np	np	np
Total Div. Coverage	na	na	na
Interest Coverage	nd	nd	nd
Current Ratio	1.4	2.4	1.9
Operating Margin	(13.4)	4.9	7.7
Asset Turnover	1.6	1.5	2.1
5 YEAR RATIOS (%)			
Return on Capital	26.1	47.8	46.2
Return on Com. Equity	29.4	55.2	54.9
Profit Growth	na	114.5	181.5
Revenue Growth	7.2	283.6	148.3
Asset Growth	19.0	127.6	118.6
BALANCE SHEET (000)			
Cash	26,645	38,295	29,733
Current Assets	106,289	107,411	98,297
Net Fixed Assets	2,950	3,537	2,947
Invest's & Advances	12,504	12,678	3,862
Total Assets	134,186	126,016	107,861
Short Term Debt	0	0	0
Current Liabilities	75,768	44,334	53,083
Long Term Debt	0	0	0
Total Liabilities	77,393	52,961	62,383
Total Equity	56,793	73,055	45,478
Total Liab. & Equity	134,186	126,016	107,861
CAPITAL (000)			
Total Debt	0	0	0
Preferred Equity	0	0	0
Common Equity	56,793	73,055	45,478

Business:

BRACKNELL CORPORATION is an industrial specialty services company. Bracknell's main business is condusted through the State Group which provides construction technical services (or multi-trade contracting services) and management services to commercial, industrial and institutional clients. Bracknell recently acquired Village Communication and its wholly owned affiliate Cablecom International.

Date	EPS	DPS	Tot Rev	Inc Bex
Apr 95	0.04	0.00	71,006	1,021
Jan 95	0.04	0.00	62,848	1,007
Oct 94	(0.22)	0.00	54,796	(5,757)
Jul 94	(0.03)	0.00	59,739	(783)
Apr 94	(0.28)	0.00	54,588	(7,482)
Jan 94	(0.09)	0.00	51,246	(2,240)
Oct 93	0.13	0.00	52,492	3,324
Jul 93	0.03	0.00	46,071	822

Synopsis:

Bracknell's Construction Technical Services reported revenues of $169.5-million in 1994, compared to $133-million in 1993. Both institutional and industrial revenues improved, while commercial revenues fell by $13.2-million (30.9%). This was mainly due to high vacancy rates in Canada's commercial properties. Institutional revenue soared by $17.5-million or 95.1%, despite cutbacks in all government sectors. However, this increase contributed to a decline in institutional backlog, down $23.7-million to $22.1-million in 1994. Higher institutional revenues resulted from major projects such as the Princess Margaret Hospital in Toronto and the DCC Laboratory in Winnipeg. Industrial revenue jumped $32.2-million, or 44.8%, as a result of major automotive projects undertaken for the Ford Motor Company of Canada in Oakville and Windsor. These projects, combined with work of Chrysler Canada in Windsor, drove industrial backlog up by $9.2-million to $33.9-million during 1994. Commercial backlog increased $24.2-million to $36.3-million.

Bracknell Construction Management Services' revenues fell 30.8% from $50.5-million in 1993 to $34.9-million in 1994. The decline was due to the completion of the Cardinal project and the start of the Jager oriented strandboard plant project late in the year. The backlog for construction management services at year end of 1994 was $52.6-million, down from $67.3-million at October 31, 1993. The current backlog consists primarily of the Hibernia and the Jager strandboard plant projects. Revenues from infrastructure and Facility Management Services doubled to $13.1-million, from $7.4-million in 1993. This was the result of the CMB program, a joint venture with SNC Lavalin for the installation and maintenance of Canada Post's community mailboxes. At October 31, 1994, the backlog was $56.9-million. This was up from $52.6-million the previous year. Major projects the support services backlog include the Canada Post Community Mailbox Program, Canada Post facilities management, and the Air Canada Cargo Centre.

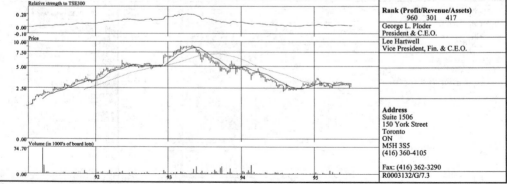

Rank (Profit/Revenue/Assets)
960   301   417

George L. Ploder
President & C.E.O.

Lee Hartwell
Vice President, Fin. & C.E.O.

Address
Suite 1506
150 York Street
Toronto
ON
M5H 3S5
(416) 360-4105

Fax: (416) 362-3290
R0003132/G/7.3

CGC INC.

Exchanges	Price (Jun29'95)	8.00	Trailing P/E	14.29	Stock Symbol
TM	Trailing Yield (%)	2.50	Trailing EPS	0.56	**GYP**

Period Ending	Dec94	Dec93	Dec92	Dec91	Dec90
Yearly Statistics					
Price-Close	8.75	10.75	7.60	7.75	8.50
Price-High	12.00	10.75	10.50	11.13	14.13
Price-Low	7.50	7.13	6.25	7.38	7.13
P/E-Close	19.02	44.79	69.09	17.22	11.81
Dividends per Share	0.20	0.20	0.44	0.74	0.84
Dividend Yield (%)	2.29	1.86	5.79	9.55	9.88
Sales per Share	7.47	6.16	5.97	6.64	8.00
EPS before extra. item	0.46	0.24	0.11	0.45	0.72
Cash Flow per Share	0.62	0.40	0.29	0.63	0.89
Book Value per Share	2.03	1.77	1.80	2.14	2.43
O/S Common Shares	25,345	25,342	25,342	25,342	25,342
Total Revenue	189,232	156,231	151,803	168,338	203,336
Income before extra.	11,682	5,980	2,727	11,343	18,283
Cash Flow	15,622	10,251	7,410	15,938	22,679
Debt/Equity	0.30	0.59	0.49	0.39	0.16
Return on Capital (%)	30.55	16.32	6.16	26.64	43.93
Ret. on Com. Equity (%)	24.25	13.20	5.46	19.61	28.35
% Change Profit	95.4	119.3	(76.0)	(38.0)	(52.3)
% Change Revenue	21.1	2.9	(9.8)	(17.2)	(19.4)
% Change Assets	2.1	6.9	(8.4)	(2.4)	(34.8)

Preferred Div. Coverage	np	np	np
Total Div. Coverage	2.3	0.9	0.2
Interest Coverage	14.5	9.2	na
Current Ratio	1.0	0.9	0.9
Operating Margin	11.2	7.3	2.5
Asset Turnover	1.8	1.5	1.6
5 YEAR RATIOS (%)			
Return on Capital	24.7	33.7	49.5
Return on Com. Equity	18.2	22.5	30.9
Profit Growth	(21.1)	(33.9)	(45.1)
Revenue Growth	(5.6)	(10.6)	(11.9)
Asset Growth	(8.7)	(7.3)	(6.0)
BALANCE SHEET (000)			
Cash	0	0	0
Current Assets	33,944	33,827	27,598
Net Fixed Assets	45,430	45,212	45,740
Invest's & Advances	0	0	0
Total Assets	105,345	103,182	96,497
Short Term Debt	12,799	23,310	19,262
Current Liabilities	33,891	39,102	31,612
Long Term Debt	2,875	2,911	2,942
Total Liabilities	53,846	58,322	50,775
Total Equity	51,499	44,860	45,722
Total Liab. & Equity	105,345	103,182	96,497
CAPITAL (000)			
Total Debt	15,674	26,221	22,204
Preferred Equity	0	0	0
Common Equity	51,499	44,860	45,722

Business:

CGC INC. is a building materials company and operates two divisions. CGC Gypsum makes and markets gypsum wallboard and related products. CGC Interiors makes suspended ceilings, acoustic tile, linear ceilings and other components.

Date	EPS	DPS	Tot Rev	Inc Bex
Mar 95	0.18	0.05	46,396	4,503
Dec 94	0.15	0.05	48,960	3,878
Sep 94	0.15	0.05	52,085	3,875
Jun 94	0.08	0.05	45,226	2,069
Mar 94	0.07	0.05	42,961	1,860
Dec 93	0.05	0.05	40,508	1,248
Sep 93	0.09	0.11	40,518	2,167
Jun 93	0.03	0.11	35,313	811

Synopsis:

CGC Inc. reorganized its three business units into two divisions at the beginning of 1995. The creation of the two divisions, Canadian Gypsum Company and CGC Interiors, allows CGC to focus on gypsum and ceiling products, its two core businesses. The Canadian Gypsum Company division integrates the major business units of the CGC Industries division, other than ISG Safety Gratings which was sold in early 1995.

CGC Inc. reported revenue of $46.4-million for the three months ended March 31, 1995, compared with $43-million a year earlier. Net profit for the first quarter of 1995 was $4.5-million compared to $1.9-million for the first quarter of 1994. Included in the 1995 first quarter results is a net gain on sale of the ISG Safety Grating Products division of approximately $2.1-million. Export opportunities and continued growth in repair and renovations should offset the continuing low level of new residential construction activity.

CGC's Montreal facility began using synthetic gypsum on a continuous basis in 1994. Kronos Canda Inc. supplies about 25% of the plant's synthetic gypsum. A new source of synthetic gypsum was secured when CGC entered into a multi-year agreement with the New Brunswick Power Corporation. In 1994, construction of a plant in Belledune, N.B., began and gypsum processing should begin by the end of 1995. With the new operation CGC expects improved operating costs at the plant.

CGC's revenue jumped to $189.2-million in 1994 compared to only $156.2-million in 1993. The key contributors to the improved sales and profitability during 1994 were increased volumes, particularly exports, and prices for gypsum wallboard. Growth in the United States and Canadian economies should continue in 1995, which could stir growth in the construction industry. It is also anticipated that export opportunities will remain favourable in 1995. Further increases in paper prices are expected in 1995. These prices increase CGC's manufacturing costs.

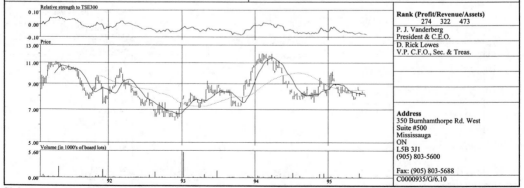

Rank (Profit/Revenue/Assets)
274   322   473

P. J. Vanderberg
President & C.E.O.
D. Rick Lowes
V.P. C.F.O., Sec. & Treas.

Address
350 Burnhamthorpe Rd. West
Suite #500
Mississauga
ON
L5B 3J1
(905) 803-5600

Fax: (905) 803-5688
C0000935/G/6.10

Industrial,nec - 569

CHAI-NA-TA CORP.

Exchanges	Price (Jun29'95)	2.35	Trailing P/E	10.68	Stock Symbol
TQ	Trailing Yield (%)	0.00	Trailing EPS	0.22	CC

Period Ending	Nov94	Nov93	May93	May92	May91
Yearly Statistics		6M			
Price-Close	4.00	6.00	6.50	5.25	1.90
Price-High	7.00	7.75	8.88	6.13	2.47
Price-Low	3.00	6.00	4.90	2.20	1.33
P/E-Close	13.33	nm	27.08	30.88	21.11
Dividends per Share	0.00	0.00	0.00	0.00	0.00
Dividend Yield (%)	0.00	0.00	0.00	0.00	0.00
Sales per Share	1.34	0.31	0.80	0.68	0.31
EPS before extra. item	0.30	(0.11)	0.24	0.17	0.09
Cash Flow per Share	0.85	0.30	0.56	0.53	0.25
Book Value per Share	1.66	1.29	1.34	1.10	0.76
O/S Common Shares	14,401	13,736	13,287	12,427	10,937
Total Revenue	19,717	2,099	10,485	7,971	3,484
Income before extra.	4,275	(1,495)	3,085	2,006	1,040
Cash Flow	12,007	2,076	7,422	6,145	2,800
Debt/Equity	0.92	1.01	0.37	0.19	0.36
Return on Capital (%)	16.00	(14.55)	20.87	29.31	19.47
Ret. on Com. Equity (%)	20.57	(16.83)	19.63	18.33	13.60
% Change Profit	242.9	(196.9)	53.8	93.0	(10.4)
% Change Revenue	369.8	(60.0)	31.5	128.8	(7.7)
% Change Assets	42.3	34.9	48.3	51.8	42.8

Business:

CHAI-NA-TA CORP. is an agricultural company involved in the cultivation and harvesting of ginseng root and is currently the largest grower of ginseng in North America. The company also has a processing and grading operation in mainland China, operated through a joint venture with the China National Foreign Trade Corporation and a marketing company in Hong Kong.

Date	EPS	DPS	Tot Rev	Inc Bex
Feb 95	0.05	0.00	3,480	687
Nov 94	0.20	0.00	10,520	2,935
Aug 94	(0.02)	0.00	1,366	(342)
May 94	(0.01)	0.00	2,344	(120)
Feb 94	0.13	0.00	5,489	1,802
Nov 93	(0.08)	0.00	1,246	(1,102)
Aug 93	(0.03)	0.00	872	(393)
May 93	0.14	0.00	4,427	1,857

Preferred Div. Coverage	np	np	np		
Total Div. Coverage	na	na	na		
Interest Coverage	11.2	0.0	26.0		
Current Ratio	1.3	2.2	1.9		
Operating Margin	31.5	(81.6)	40.4		
Asset Turnover	0.3	0.1	0.3		
5 YEAR RATIOS (%)					
Return on Capital	14.2	16.6	22.3		
Return on Com. Equity	11.1	10.4	15.3		
Profit Growth	29.8	na	51.2		
Revenue Growth	39.2	21.6	50.2		
Asset Growth	43.8	41.6	50.5		
BALANCE SHEET (000)					
Cash	458	8,013	762		
Current Assets	26,256	20,091	10,790		
Net Fixed Assets	28,530	20,124	18,830		
Invest's & Advances	326	56	0		
Total Assets	58,252	40,926	30,337		
Short Term Debt	12,782	7,383	4,314		
Current Liabilities	19,834	9,051	5,569		
Long Term Debt	9,051	10,435	2,341		
Total Liabilities	34,417	23,199	12,513		
Total Equity	23,835	17,727	17,824		
Total Liab. & Equity	58,252	40,926	30,337		
CAPITAL (000)					
Total Debt	21,832	17,817	6,655		
Preferred Equity	0	0	0		
Common Equity	23,835	17,727	17,824		

Synopsis:

Chai-Na-Ta Corp. has established four primary objectives for 1995. The company plans to increase distribution of its products throughout China, complete the Dalian facility and begin production of pharmaceutical products, expand the distribution of the Unique Formulations' line of products made with Chai-Na-Ta North American ginseng, and begin to investigate other markets in Southeast Asia.

In 1994, Chai-Na-Ta signed a business agreement with another Canadian company, the China Hua Yuan Group, to open a new processing facility in the city of Dalian. Dalian is a special economic zone in China. The agreement enables Chai-Na-Ta to fast track the development of its vertical integration program in China. For example, the Dalian venture obtained a business license in six weeks, while most companies operating in China can wait nine to twelve months. The Dalian venture was the first 100% foreign-owned company to receive a pharmaceutical license in China. This license permits the company to manufacture ginseng based pharmaceutical products under the Pegasus brand name. Renovations are underway at the Dalian facility to bring it up to internationally recognized standards for pharmaceutical manufacturing. Production is expected to begin during 1995.

In November 1994, Chai-Na-Ta opened a new wholesale showroom outlet in Shanghai, China. The Shanghai showroom will be the marketing centre for the Chinese national distribution program. It will serve future satellite offices throughout China. The marketing centre will offer Chai-Na-Ta products from Canada, the United States, and China.

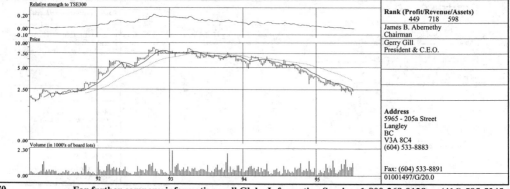

Rank (Profit/Revenue/Assets)
449 718 598

James B. Abernethy
Chairman

Gerry Gill
President & C.E.O.

Address
5965 - 205a Street
Langley
BC
V3A 8C4
(604) 533-8883

Fax: (604) 533-8891
01001497/G/20.0

CINEPLEX ODEON CORPORATION

Exchanges	Price (Jun29'95)	3.20	Trailing P/E	nm	Stock Symbol
T	Trailing Yield (%)	0.00	Trailing EPS	(0.26)	**CPX**

Period Ending	Dec94	Dec93	Dec92	Dec91	Dec90
Yearly Statistics	US	US	US	US	US
Price-Close	3.85	3.75	2.42	3.60	2.60
Price-High	5.63	4.95	4.20	7.13	8.50
Price-Low	3.20	1.40	1.97	2.03	2.15
P/E-Close	nm	nm	nm	nm	nm
Dividends per Share	0.00	0.00	0.00	0.00	0.00
Dividend Yield (%)	0.00	0.00	0.00	0.00	0.00
Sales per Share	4.70	4.94	5.81	9.59	12.89
EPS before extra. item	(0.13)	(0.07)	(0.48)	(1.38)	(2.85)
Cash Flow per Share	0.25	0.36	0.03	(0.21)	(0.96)
Book Value per Share	1.71	1.83	1.96	2.56	3.53
O/S Common Shares	114,746	109,258	101,380	83,362	47,691
Total Revenue	539,859	549,270	519,497	535,398	582,160
Income before extra.	(14,173)	(7,372)	(41,349)	(77,212)	(135,934)
Cash Flow	27,011	38,158	2,618	(11,595)	(45,782)
Debt/Equity	2.01	1.97	2.27	2.26	3.37
Return on Capital (%)	3.65	3.59	(0.84)	(3.56)	(8.86)
Ret. on Com. Equity (%)	(7.15)	(3.69)	(20.04)	(40.43)	(57.98)
% Change Profit	(92.3)	82.2	46.4	43.2	(72.9)
% Change Revenue	(1.7)	5.7	(3.0)	(8.0)	(7.8)
% Change Assets	(1.6)	(6.0)	(7.9)	(6.1)	(22.5)
Preferred Div. Coverage	np	np	np		
Total Div. Coverage	na	na	na		
Interest Coverage	0.6	0.8	0.0		
Current Ratio	0.2	0.2	0.3		
Operating Margin	4.6	5.4	(0.9)		
Asset Turnover	0.8	0.8	0.7		
5 YEAR RATIOS (%)					
Return on Capital	(1.2)	(2.3)	(1.2)		
Return on Com. Equity	(25.9)	(29.1)	(26.1)		
Profit Growth	(39.7)	na	na		
Revenue Growth	(3.1)	(2.9)	0.8		
Asset Growth	(9.1)	(11.2)	(4.4)		
BALANCE SHEET (000)					
Cash	1,191	1,268	1,350		
Current Assets	20,876	29,176	30,653		
Net Fixed Assets	606,850	619,309	658,598		
Invest's & Advances	10,782	3,775	5,613		
Total Assets	685,753	697,105	741,652		
Short Term Debt	7,277	51,089	30,991		
Current Liabilities	91,274	139,669	120,106		
Long Term Debt	386,664	343,482	420,303		
Total Liabilities	489,578	496,718	542,686		
Total Equity	196,175	200,387	198,966		
Total Liab. & Equity	685,753	697,105	741,652		
CAPITAL (000)					
Total Debt	393,941	394,571	451,294		
Preferred Equity	0	0	0		
Common Equity	196,175	200,387	198,966		

Business:

CINEPLEX ODEON CORP. is engaged in exhibiting and distributing motion pictures. The company operates theatre complexes across North America. MCA Inc. of Universal City, California, and investors related to the Claridge Group of companies are the company's major shareholders.

Date		EPS	DPS	Tot Rev	Inc Bex
Mar 95	US	(0.13)	0.00	109,964	(15,109)
Dec 94	US	(0.07)	0.00	128,937	(7,171)
Sep 94	US	0.05	0.00	163,781	5,878
Jun 94	US	(0.11)	0.00	116,374	(12,492)
Mar 94	US	0.00	0.00	130,767	(388)
Dec 93	US	0.00	0.00	130,771	59
Sep 93	US	0.03	0.00	166,956	2,732
Jun 93	US	0.01	0.00	133,313	678

Synopsis:

Cineplex Odeon saw declines in revenue and earnings for the quarter ending March 31, 1995, due to weaker admission and concession operations. Cash flow from operations amounted to a net outflow of $12.8-million (U.S.) compared to a net inflow of $2-million (U.S.), a year earlier. Reduced cash flows resulted from reduced theatre attendance, with few high-grossing films, and an increase in interest on long-term debt. As a result, the corporation failed to meet certain financial covenants under its bank credit facilities in March 1995. Cineplex Odeon's bankers granted waivers of the covenant violations and agreed to further amendments of covenants further into 1995.

During the first quarter, attendance dropped in the United States by 15.8%. Admissions revenue fell 15.2%, and concession revenue fell 19.5% from the previous year. In Canada, attendance declined 13.6% and revenue-per-patron fell 1.4%. The company attributed the attendance decline to poor film product in both the U.S. and Canada.

Cineplex Odeon's results for fiscal 1994 also showed declines. Since the company derives 30% of its revenues from Canada but reports in U.S. dollars, the drop in the Canadian dollar negatively affects revenues. Concession sales (representing 35% of revenues) fell in 1994, largely due to negative publicity on the fat content of popcorn made with coconut oil. Cineplex switched to corn oil in May 1994.

Despite recent revenue declines, Cineplex sees potential growth in both the teenage and babyboomer segments. Cineplex plans to cater to these fast-growing markets with new megaplexes. The bigger movie theatres will have fancier food, more comfortable seats, and video games in the lobby. Cineplex Odeon will open a megaplex in Universal City, Florida, in 1998. In 1995 and 1996, the company hopes to open to 30 new theatre locations and refurbish 25 theatres for approximately $55-million.

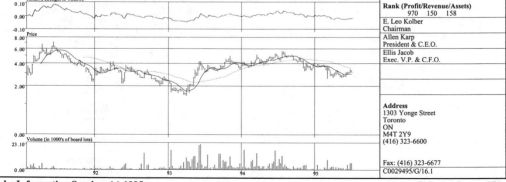

Rank (Profit/Revenue/Assets)		
970	150	158

E. Leo Kolber
Chairman

Allen Karp
President & C.E.O.

Ellis Jacob
Exec. V.P. & C.F.O.

Address
1303 Yonge Street
Toronto
ON
M4T 2Y9
(416) 323-6600

Fax: (416) 323-6677
C0029495/G/16.1

CINRAM LTD.

Exchanges	Price (Jun29'95)	17.50	Trailing P/E	20.83	Stock Symbol
TM	Trailing Yield (%)	0.69	Trailing EPS	0.84	**CRW**

Period Ending	Dec94	Dec93	Dec92	Dec91	Dec90
Yearly Statistics					
Price-Close	11.50	11.88	9.06	7.19	3.50
Price-High	12.00	15.50	9.25	7.84	3.56
Price-Low	7.75	9.00	7.13	3.38	2.69
P/E-Close	14.20	19.47	20.14	16.15	10.00
Dividends per Share	0.12	0.12	0.12	0.10	0.06
Dividend Yield (%)	1.04	0.97	1.27	1.39	1.71
Sales per Share	6.48	5.11	3.96	3.54	2.39
EPS before extra. item	0.81	0.61	0.45	0.45	0.35
Cash Flow per Share	1.25	1.14	0.91	0.69	0.57
Book Value per Share	4.34	3.69	3.12	3.20	1.95
O/S Common Shares	22,335	22,335	22,152	19,144	19,144
Total Revenue	147,080	115,307	88,754	69,198	47,978
Income before extra.	17,997	13,520	9,784	8,535	6,743
Cash Flow	28,019	25,340	19,717	13,268	11,004
Debt/Equity	nd	nd	nd	0.01	0.02
Return on Capital (%)	25.88	24.37	23.54	21.24	27.64
Ret. on Com. Equity (%)	20.09	17.84	15.01	17.32	19.48
% Change Profit	33.1	38.2	14.6	26.6	157.3
% Change Revenue	27.6	29.9	28.3	44.2	11.2
% Change Assets	21.7	17.3	22.7	49.8	19.9

Preferred Div. Coverage	np	np	np		
Total Div. Coverage	6.7	5.1	4.4		
Interest Coverage	nd	nd	nd		
Current Ratio	2.3	2.6	2.5		
Operating Margin	14.4	14.7	14.8		
Asset Turnover	1.1	1.0	0.9		
5 YEAR RATIOS (%)					
Return on Capital	24.5	22.7	22.3		
Return on Com. Equity	17.9	15.9	15.4		
Profit Growth	46.9	31.7	23.6		
Revenue Growth	27.7	23.4	24.3		
Asset Growth	25.7	23.9	23.6		
BALANCE SHEET (000)					
Cash	50,121	41,969	36,752		
Current Assets	83,900	63,943	55,651		
Net Fixed Assets	51,134	44,322	40,579		
Invest's & Advances	0	0	0		
Total Assets	137,306	112,857	96,230		
Short Term Debt	0	0	0		
Current Liabilities	36,142	25,022	21,968		
Long Term Debt	0	0	0		
Total Liabilities	40,461	30,511	27,040		
Total Equity	96,845	82,346	69,190		
Total Liab. & Equity	137,306	112,857	96,230		
CAPITAL (000)					
Total Debt	0	0	0		
Preferred Equity	0	0	0		
Common Equity	96,845	82,346	69,190		

Business:

CINRAM LTD. is the largest custom-manufacturer of compact discs and pre-recorded audio and video casette tapes in Canada and is a principal supplier of these products to most of the major record companies in the country.

Date	EPS	DPS	Tot Rev	Inc Bex
Mar 95	0.15	0.03	37,467	3,343
Dec 94	0.35	0.03	48,357	7,797
Sep 94	0.21	0.03	39,574	4,696
Jun 94	0.13	0.03	30,933	2,881
Mar 94	0.12	0.03	28,216	2,624
Dec 93	0.28	0.03	40,131	6,295
Sep 93	0.15	0.03	28,761	3,269
Jun 93	0.09	0.03	23,631	1,966

Synopsis:

In early 1995 Cinram Ltd. acquired two leading video cassette duplication companies in France, Duplication France S.A. and Video Pouce, S.A. Cinram expects the impact of these acquisitions will be reflected in the 1995 second quarter. Cinram acquired Duplication France, S.A. for approximately $4.5-million, and estimates working capital requirements to be approximately $4-million. Cinram's plans for this company call for a cost reduction program, a strong new management team, and an aggressive marketing and sales effort. Video Pouce was acquired for $1.5-million and Cinram expects the company will be self-supporting and will not need any additional working capital.

Production began in early March 1995, at the Cinram's joint venture in Mexico City. The joint venture was renamed Cinram LatinoAmericana, S.A. de C.V. to better reflect strategic plans for a broader market. Imported compact discs currently dominate the Latin America. Cinram feels as a domestic manufacturer the joint venture can penetrate this market by providing more efficient service and more competitive pricing than imports can deliver. The company had planned an original production capacity of 20 million units annually but has reduced this to 15 million units, reflecting the impact of the devaluation of the peso on the Mexican economy. Increased capacity will be phased in as demand grows.

Compact disc unit sales of in 1994 grew 41% overall when compared to 1993, in part due to the increasing popularity of CD-ROM which accounted for one-third of the increase. Audio CDs increased 27% compared to an estimated 34% increase in the overall industry. Cinram forecasts higher demand for CDs in 1995, especially CD-ROMs, and a continued drop in selling prices. Much of the growth should be generated in the U.S. About 56% of Cinram's increase in CD unit sales in 1994 could be attributed to its U.S. facility. Cinram will double the capacity at its Richmond, Indiana, plant in 1995.

Relative strength to TSE300

Price

Volume (in 1000's of board lots)

Rank (Profit/Revenue/Assets)
225   363   416
Isidore Philosophe
Chairman Of The Board
Lewis Ritchie
Secretary V.P. Fin. & C.F.O.

Address
2255 Markham Road
Scarborough
ON
M1B 2W3
(416) 298-8190

Fax: (416) 298-0612
01000468/G/6.10

For further company information, call Globe Information Services 1-800-268-9128 or (416) 585-5345

DERLAN INDUSTRIES LIMITED

Exchanges	Price (Jun29'95)	2.95	Trailing P/E	nm	Stock Symbol
T	Trailing Yield (%)	4.75	Trailing EPS	(0.15)	DRL

Period Ending	Dec94	Dec93	Dec92	Dec91	Dec90	Business:
Yearly Statistics						DERLAN INDUSTRIES LTD. is a North
Price-Close	3.30	5.38	4.65	5.75	6.13	American industrial corporation that enhances
Price-High	5.75	5.50	7.00	8.25	9.50	technology-based manufacturing companies.
Price-Low	3.10	3.10	4.60	5.25	6.00	The company assumes majority equity positions
P/E-Close	nm	nm	nm	nm	8.06	in each of its subsidiaries, while leaving
Dividends per Share	0.14	0.25	0.28	0.28	0.28	operating management responsible for
Dividend Yield (%)	4.24	4.56	6.02	4.87	4.57	day-to-day operations. The company has
Sales per Share	16.49	17.84	18.50	17.85	16.33	interests in the aerospace and specialty
EPS before extra. item	(0.29)	(2.67)	(0.63)	(0.39)	0.76	manufacturing industries in the United States,
Cash Flow per Share	1.06	1.52	0.86	0.60	1.90	Canada, and Mexico.
Book Value per Share	3.33	4.05	7.02	7.55	8.21	

	Dec94	Dec93	Dec92	Dec91	Dec90
O/S Common Shares	18,213	17,484	15,127	15,396	15,771
Total Revenue	313,029	317,725	283,329	276,640	275,476
Income before extra.	(704)	(43,288)	(5,701)	(3,925)	12,247
Cash Flow	19,503	26,392	13,226	9,301	30,750

Date	EPS	DPS	Tot Rev	Inc Bex
Mar 95	0.14	0.04	80,286	(1,361)
Dec 94	(0.21)	0.04	76,878	(2,589)
Sep 94	(0.27)	0.04	74,110	(3,974)
Jun 94	0.19	0.04	85,193	4,706
Mar 94	0.00	0.04	77,947	1,153
Dec 93	(2.53)	0.04	87,060	(44,264)
Sep 93	0.01	0.07	76,481	1,274
Jun 93	0.01	0.07	81,139	1,140

	Dec94	Dec93	Dec92	Dec91	Dec90
Debt/Equity	1.64	1.60	1.08	0.99	1.07
Return on Capital (%)	4.95	(9.78)	1.34	1.97	10.57
Ret. on Com. Equity (%)	(5.93)	(52.48)	(8.09)	(4.96)	9.61
% Change Profit	98.4	(659.3)	(45.2)	(132.0)	90.2
% Change Revenue	(1.5)	12.1	2.4	0.4	(33.8)
% Change Assets	(7.1)	0.7	(8.0)	11.1	(2.0)

				Synopsis:
Preferred Div. Coverage	0.0	0.0	0.0	Derlan determined its outlook for 1995 after assessing the impact of the three
Total Div. Coverage	0.0	0.0	0.0	main risk areas affecting the accomplishment of its objectives for 1995. Timing is
Interest Coverage	1.3	0.0	0.4	the most significant risk, especially relating to Derlan Aerospace Canada shipping
Current Ratio	1.4	1.5	1.4	its large backlog. The recent rise in interest rates has been taken into account by
Operating Margin	1.8	4.5	3.9	the company, recognizing that 70% of its debt is subject to floating rates. Foreign
Asset Turnover	1.0	0.9	0.9	exchange rates relating to variations in the value of the Canadian dollar and
5 YEAR RATIOS (%)				Mexican peso can affect the company's borrowing capacity. Derlan has set its
Return on Capital	1.8	2.6	7.5	targets for 1995 after assessing these risks.
Return on Com. Equity	(12.4)	(10.2)	2.8	
Profit Growth	na	na	na	In 1994, substantial initiatives were taken by the company. Going into 1995
Revenue Growth	(5.6)	(2.0)	0.6	Derlan's backlog was approximately $250-million, an increase of almost
Asset Growth	(1.3)	2.8	4.6	$120-million from a year ago. Derlan, supported by a strong economy, expects to
BALANCE SHEET (000)				profit in the coming year. Higher sales and earnings, adjusted to exclude Hallmark
Cash	4,342	4,170	3,200	Tools sold in 1993, were reported by The Specialty Manufacturing Sector.
Current Assets	139,827	154,920	124,866	However due to lower Aerospace sales, consolidated sales of $304-million in
Net Fixed Assets	107,703	124,182	118,383	1994 were marginally lower than the $310-million reported in the previous year.
Invest's & Advances	8,949	14,071	8,472	The restructuring of the United States Aerospace Group included the
Total Assets	310,600	334,454	332,062	consolidation of four of Derlan's smaller California subsidiaries into Energy
Short Term Debt	60,886	67,286	55,862	Container Corporation, a manufacturer of fuel tanks and cryogenic valves
Current Liabilities	96,974	105,224	86,616	acquired in early 1994.
Long Term Debt	96,585	102,769	97,576	
Total Liabilities	214,396	228,169	190,292	General Electric Co.'s GE Aircraft Engines awarded a $24-million contract to
Total Equity	96,204	106,285	141,770	Derlan Aerospace Canada in December 1994. Derlan will supply accessory gear
Total Liab. & Equity	310,600	334,454	332,062	boxes and power takeoff assemblies plus additional gears and spares for GE's
CAPITAL (000)				CF34 turbine engines. The total contract is for 350 of these products to be
Total Debt	157,471	170,055	153,438	supplied beginning in July. This brings the backlog of Derlan Aerospace Canada
Preferred Equity	35,553	35,553	35,553	to about $140-million. Derlan Industries decided not to pay its regular 3.5 cent
Common Equity	60,651	70,732	106,217	quarterly dividend on its common shares. The dividend was last paid in December 1994.

Relative strength to TSE300

Price

Volume (in 1000's of board lots)

Rank (Profit/Revenue/Assets)
807   251   282
Dermot G. Coughlan
Chairman & C.E.O.
Michael P. Forsayeth
V.P. & C.F.O.

Address
Suite 500
145 King Street East
Toronto
ON
M5C 2Y7
(416) 364-5852

Fax: (416) 362-5334
D0000375/G/6.10

DOREL INDUSTRIES INC.

Exchanges	Price (Jun29'95)	8.75	Trailing P/E	12.32	Stock Symbol
TM	Trailing Yield (%)	0.00	Trailing EPS	0.71	**DII.A**

Period Ending	Dec94	Dec93	Dec92	Dec91	Dec90
Yearly Statistics					
Price-Close	7.75	11.38	11.00	6.13	n t
Price-High	13.00	14.00	11.00	6.13	n t
Price-Low	7.00	10.38	6.00	2.80	n t
P/E-Close	11.40	18.06	25.00	10.04	n t
Dividends per Share	0.00	0.00	0.00	0.00	0.00
Dividend Yield (%)	0.00	0.00	0.00	0.00	0.00
Sales per Share	28.22	21.99	17.93	18.69	17.28
EPS before extra. item	0.68	0.63	0.44	0.61	0.15
Cash Flow per Share	1.56	1.22	0.94	1.11	0.60
Book Value per Share	6.33	5.37	4.59	3.93	2.89
O/S Common Shares	11,832	11,827	11,817	11,756	9,083
Total Revenue	333,803	259,966	211,556	172,917	156,887
Income before extra.	8,068	7,496	5,135	5,607	1,376
Cash Flow	18,457	14,377	11,068	10,250	5,477
Debt/Equity	1.68	1.28	1.34	1.20	2.47
Return on Capital (%)	12.15	12.33	11.39	16.30	12.52
Ret. on Com. Equity (%)	11.66	12.73	10.23	15.47	5.37
% Change Profit	7.6	46.0	(8.4)	307.5	(68.9)
% Change Revenue	28.4	22.9	22.3	10.2	16.1
% Change Assets	43.9	14.0	22.9	8.3	37.8

Preferred Div. Coverage	np	np	np
Total Div. Coverage	na	na	na
Interest Coverage	2.6	3.1	2.3
Current Ratio	2.1	2.4	3.1
Operating Margin	6.3	6.4	6.1
Asset Turnover	1.4	1.5	1.4
5 YEAR RATIOS (%)			
Return on Capital	12.9	14.4	12.8
Return on Com. Equity	11.1	12.8	10.6
Profit Growth	12.7	79.0	17.0
Revenue Growth	19.8	39.4	42.0
Asset Growth	24.6	18.4	44.3
BALANCE SHEET (000)			
Cash	63,082	0	0
Current Assets	145,314	103,940	94,488
Net Fixed Assets	77,248	60,991	50,009
Invest's & Advances	0	0	0
Total Assets	241,558	167,829	147,227
Short Term Debt	30,759	22,411	12,998
Current Liabilities	68,474	43,132	30,694
Long Term Debt	94,876	58,850	59,707
Total Liabilities	166,692	104,296	93,035
Total Equity	74,866	63,534	54,192
Total Liab. & Equity	241,558	167,829	147,227
CAPITAL (000)			
Total Debt	125,635	81,261	72,705
Preferred Equity	0	0	0
Common Equity	74,866	63,534	54,192

Business:

DOREL INDUSTRIES INC. is a full line manufacturer and distributor of children's furniture and accessories. The company is also a leading manufacturer of ready-to-assemble furniture.

Date	EPS	DPS	Tot Rev	Inc Bex
Mar 95	0.19	0.00	101,600	2,300
Dec 94	0.23	0.00	91,240	2,740
Sep 94	0.21	0.00	87,395	2,491
Jun 94	0.08	0.00	80,046	1,004
Mar 94	0.16	0.00	75,119	1,836
Dec 93	0.11	0.00	65,754	1,357
Sep 93	0.10	0.00	62,876	1,208
Jun 93	0.19	0.00	62,941	2,265

Synopsis:

Dorel's ready-to-assemble division was a major contributor to the company's financial results in 1994. A $7-million plant and equipment expansion program at Charleswood Corporation added 60% to the operating unit's productive capacity. In addition, the realignment of the company's Montreal plant to focus on the production of bunk beds for the juvenile market resulted in an increase in this business and future market growth. To offset increases in the cost of raw material, operating units in this segment streamlined operations and implemented product price increases.

Renewed growth in the company's juvenile products segment has been attributed to demographics -- first births, as a percentage of total births have increased since the baby boom years -- and the spending patterns associated with first births and dual-income families. In the near future, Dorel expects to replace the older products currently being offered for sale with new higher margin goods.

Ready-to-assemble furnitures sales were strong in the company's first quarter 1995. However, the company expects sales to slow somewhat during the traditional weaker second quarter as inventory reduction programs imposed by most major customers make an impact. Dorel anticipates that this situation will ease as new product lines introduced to market will raise strong orders during the second half of 1995.

In August 1994, Dorel completed the purchase of Maxi-Miliaan B.V., an infant car seat manufacturer based in the Netherlands. Dorel will use the synergy that has developed between this acquisition and Cosco Inc., a juvenile products unit, to move existing Cosco products into Europe. In addition, Dorel (U.K.), which has been negatively affected by trading conditions, declining consumer spending, and price cutting at supplier levels, will be rationalized and combined with Maxi's U.K. business.

Relative strength to TSE300

Price

Volume (in 1000's of board lots)

Rank (Profit/Revenue/Assets)
332 243 326

Martin Schwartz
President & C.E.O.
Jeffrey Schwartz
V.P. Finance & Secretary
Alan Schwartz
V.P. Operations

Address
4750 Boul Des Grandes Prairies
St-Leonard
PQ
H1R 1A3
(514) 323-5701

Fax: (514) 323-9444
01001323/G/5.8

For further company information, call Globe Information Services 1-800-268-9128 or (416) 585-5345

EXTENDICARE INC.

Exchanges	Price (Jun29'95)		12 .50	Trailing P/E		14 .88	Stock Symbol
TM	Trailing Yield (%)		0 .00	Trailing EPS		0 .84	EXE.A

Period Ending	Dec94	Dec93	Dec92	Dec91	Dec90
Yearly Statistics					
Price-Close	9 .88	6 .50	2 .90	0 .76	2 .80
Price-High	10 .13	7 .13	3 .15	3 .85	6 .88
Price-Low	8 .50	2 .40	0 .63	0 .50	1 .65
P/E-Close	13 .53	nm	nm	25 .33	5 .83
Dividends per Share	0 .00	0 .00	0 .00	0 .23	0 .30
Dividend Yield (%)	0 .00	0 .00	0 .00	29 .61	10 .71
Sales per Share	22 .96	30 .94	89 .69	66 .92	25 .23
EPS before extra. item	0 .73	(0 .30)	(0 .88)	0 .03	0 .48
Cash Flow per Share	1 .73	2 .11	(1 .15)	3 .26	2 .55
Book Value per Share	2 .69	1 .66	1 .94	4 .74	8 .32
O/S Common Shares	55 ,265	52 ,033	40 ,856	40 ,840	40 ,811
Total Revenue	1 ,249 ,058	1 ,086 ,810	2 ,577 ,044	2 ,907 ,217	758 ,945
Income before extra.	54 ,470	(4 ,712)	(19 ,598)	19 ,152	43 ,362
Cash Flow	92 ,708	72 ,771	(32 ,934)	132 ,997	73 ,023
Debt/Equity	1 .76	1 .99	1 .65	0 .90	0 .72
Return on Capital (%)	15 .57	5 .77	1 .59	6 .92	4 .57
Ret. on Com. Equity (%)	39 .59	(23 .58)	(37 .25)	1 .48	6 .75
% Change Profit	1 ,256 .0	76 .0	(202 .3)	(55 .8)	(17 .5)
% Change Revenue	14 .9	(57 .8)	(11 .4)	283 .1	1 .6
% Change Assets	16 .3	1 .3	686 .6	(6 .6)	

Preferred Div. Coverage	6 .9	0 .0	0 .0
Total Div. Coverage	6 .9	0 .0	0 .0
Interest Coverage	2 .9	1 .2	0 .4
Current Ratio	1 .1	1 .1	1 .5
Operating Margin	7 .7	6 .8	5 .4
Asset Turnover	1 .2	1 .2	0 .3
5 YEAR RATIOS (%)			
Return on Capital	6 .9	5 .6	5 .2
Return on Com. Equity	(2 .6)	(8 .6)	(4 .1)
Profit Growth	0 .7	na	na
Revenue Growth	10 .8	9 .8	28 .8
Asset Growth	(3 .7)	(6 .6)	37 .5
BALANCE SHEET (000)			
Cash	37 ,853	54 ,579	209 ,147
Current Assets	227 ,592	204 ,019	354 ,079
Net Fixed Assets	574 ,104	491 ,452	447 ,239
Invest's & Advances	122 ,938	119 ,476	7 ,806 ,239
Total Assets	1 ,021 ,601	878 ,556	9 ,138 ,911
Short Term Debt	43 ,309	23 ,596	102 ,471
Current Liabilities	212 ,889	179 ,229	239 ,002
Long Term Debt	436 ,630	403 ,573	354 ,097
Total Liabilities	748 ,580	663 ,385	8 ,861 ,737
Total Equity	273 ,021	215 ,171	277 ,174
Total Liab. & Equity	1 ,021 ,601	878 ,556	9 ,138 ,911
CAPITAL (000)			
Total Debt	479 ,939	427 ,169	456 ,568
Preferred Equity	124 ,420	128 ,609	197 ,774
Common Equity	148 ,601	86 ,562	79 ,400

Business:

EXTENDICARE INC. is a provider in North America of long-term care to the elderly through its nursing and retirement centres. It also offers other health care services including home care, the provision of institutional pharmacy and medical supplies, and hospital management and development. The company also owns 32.2% of Crown Life Insurance Company.

Date	EPS	DPS	Tot Rev	Inc Bex
Mar 95	0 .25	0 .00	336 ,607	17 ,990
Dec 94	0 .23	0 .00	323 ,808	16 ,380
Sep 94	0 .19	0 .00	322 ,101	14 ,177
Jun 94	0 .17	0 .00	308 ,651	12 ,912
Mar 94	0 .14	0 .00	292 ,577	11 ,001
Dec 93	(0 .06)	0 .00	286 ,931	(33 ,700)
Sep 93	0 .15	0 .00	277 ,568	11 ,093
Jun 93	0 .11	0 .00	661 ,443	9 ,013

Synopsis:

Extendicare Inc.'s revenue for the quarter ended March 31, 1995, was $336.6-million. This represented an increase of 15% over revenue of $292.6-million during the corresponding period in 1994. Earnings from operations were $17.8-million, representing an increase of 32% from a year earlier. The increase in earnings was derived primarily from U.S. operations as a result of 1994 acquisitions, continued expansion of the company's sub-acute care and rehabilitative therapy services, and growth in pharmacy operations. Extendicare's share of earnings of its 32% ownership of Crown Life Insurance Company was $1.7-million for the quarter compared to $1-million a year earlier.

Extendicare achieved growth in fiscal 1994 through acquisition, construction, and the internal expansion of services. Revenues (earnings before interest and income tax) by geographical segment for the fiscal year were: United States, 73.5% (72%); Canada, 25.5% (25%); United Kingdom, 1% (3%).

In 1995, Extendicare expects to generate between 8% and 10% more revenue than in 1994, and forecasts a 20% increase in earnings from its health care operations. The company intends to invest all of its cash flow in new projects rather than paying dividends. In early 1995, Extendicare acquired a British nursing centre, was awarded a contract to manage an Ontario retirement centre, and agreed to buy a nursing and rehabilitation centre in Pennsylvania for $1.8-million (U.S.). The company expects to invest a total of $50-million in 1995 to build nursing centres, nursing centre additions and therapy units.

Extendicare feels that as governments deal with their financing and deficit difficulties, opportunities for the company to manage public sector health care will expand. Additionally, the aging population and the U.S. trend to move patients quickly out of hospital and into nursing care or rehabilitative centres, will add to the company's growth.

Relative strength to TSE300
Price
Volume (in 1000's of board lots)

Rank (Profit/Revenue/Assets)
108   103   152

David J. Hennigar
Chairman

Frederick B. Ladly
President & C.E.O.

Barry L. Stephens
V.P. Finance, C.F.O. & Sec.

J. Wesley Carter
Executive V.P. & C.O.O.

Address
3000 Steeles Avenue East
Suite 700
Markham
ON
L3R 9W2
(905) 470-4000

Fax: (905) 470-4002
C0038384/G/16.2

FOUR SEASONS HOTELS INC.

Exchanges	Price (Jun29'95)	16.75	Trailing P/E	50.76	Stock Symbol
TM	Trailing Yield (%)	0.66	Trailing EPS	0.33	**FSH**

Period Ending	Dec94	Dec93	Dec92	Dec91	Dec90
Yearly Statistics					
Price-Close	16.25	13.00	19.38	17.50	16.00
Price-High	17.25	19.38	21.88	20.50	21.00
Price-Low	10.25	12.63	16.13	14.50	13.00
P/E-Close	56.03	nm	60.55	134.62	18.61
Dividends per Share	0.11	0.11	0.11	0.11	0.11
Dividend Yield (%)	0.68	0.85	0.57	0.63	0.69
Sales per Share	1.53	1.37	3.73	6.29	7.81
EPS before extra. item	0.29	(4.30)	0.32	0.13	0.86
Cash Flow per Share	1.41	0.57	0.10	0.51	1.30
Book Value per Share	4.91	4.52	8.89	6.23	5.50
O/S Common Shares	28,423	27,775	27,739	22,198	20,088
Total Revenue	132,473	112,042	158,168	180,771	200,768
Income before extra.	8,022	(119,233)	7,721	2,837	17,322
Cash Flow	39,506	15,752	2,598	11,167	26,175
Debt/Equity	2.20	2.82	1.24	1.07	0.61
Return on Capital (%)	8.62	(18.35)	1.74	2.85	15.32
Ret. on Com. Equity (%)	6.05	(64.09)	4.01	2.28	16.95
% Change Profit	106.7	(1,644.3)	172.2	(83.6)	15.2
% Change Revenue	18.2	(29.2)	(12.5)	(10.0)	(8.3)
% Change Assets	(4.9)	(13.4)	78.8	39.6	4.9

Business:
FOUR SEASONS HOTELS INC. operates a network of five-star luxury hotels and resorts, 38 medium-sized urban hotels and resorts within major business centres and key leisure destinations in 16 countries, and seven other properties under construction or development in six countries. It also holds a number of minority equity investments in properties under its management.

Date	EPS	DPS	Tot Rev	Inc Bex
Mar 95	0.09	0.00	31,216	2,596
Dec 94	0.02	0.06	38,870	658
Sep 94	0.12	0.00	32,951	3,166
Jun 94	0.10	0.06	32,659	2,897
Mar 94	0.05	0.00	25,869	1,301
Dec 93	(4.49)	0.06	29,445	(124,405)
Sep 93	0.02	0.06	26,851	398
Jun 93	0.09	0.06	26,905	2,524

Preferred Div. Coverage	na	na	na		
Total Div. Coverage	2.6	0.0	2.8		
Interest Coverage	1.4	0.0	0.6		
Current Ratio	1.1	1.0	0.8		
Operating Margin	34.2	(102.9)	(11.3)		
Asset Turnover	0.1	0.1	0.2		
5 YEAR RATIOS (%)					
Return on Capital	2.0	3.9	12.2		
Return on Com. Equity	(7.0)	(4.8)	12.0		
Profit Growth	(11.8)	na	(7.4)		
Revenue Growth	(9.6)	(14.2)	(7.2)		
Asset Growth	16.6	21.6	26.1		
BALANCE SHEET (000)					
Cash	9,436	11,926	15,704		
Current Assets	50,872	40,446	47,620		
Net Fixed Assets	68,052	72,606	72,176		
Invest's & Advances	188,497	218,819	286,165		
Total Assets	497,536	522,900	603,652		
Short Term Debt	876	4,646	13,897		
Current Liabilities	45,780	40,899	59,578		
Long Term Debt	307,721	352,898	291,995		
Total Liabilities	357,031	396,113	355,892		
Total Equity	140,505	126,787	247,760		
Total Liab. & Equity	497,536	522,900	603,652		
CAPITAL (000)					
Total Debt	308,597	357,544	305,892		
Preferred Equity	919	1,226	1,241		
Common Equity	139,586	125,561	246,519		

Synopsis:

Four Seasons Hotels Inc. showed strong signs of recovery in fiscal 1994 after enduring a sluggish lodging industry, profit erosion, and climbing debt in recent years. The company underwent a program of reducing its equity position in hotel properties, concentrating instead on hotel management. This focus led to its 1992 purchase of Regent International Hotels Ltd. The investment gave the company immediate revenues from 10 hotels and a geographical diversification in Asia. Return on the Regent investment in 1994 after related interest expense was more than 29%.

In 1994, the company sold its real estate interests in several properties, raising $65-million, used in its entirety to pay down debt. In 1995, it expects to raise $49- to $59-million from its disposition program, also ear-marked for debt reduction. In September 1994, Four Seasons sold a 25% interest to Prince Alwaleed of Saudi Arabia for $165-million.

With very little new construction in the luxury hotel market, Four Seasons/Regent is currently in a positive supply and demand position. In the first quarter of 1995, the company had a yield increase of 13% over the previous year. (Yield is occupancy multiplied by achieved room rate.) The company continues a strategy of rate increases and improved yield techniques. It is currently exploring development opportunities in the Middle East, Europe, China, Asia, Central, and South America. At the same time, it is looking for existing hotels to manage which would create immediate revenues.

In 1995, the company opened The Regent Chiang Mai in Thailand and the Regent Jakarta. Four Seasons Hotels in Istanbul, Berlin, Hualalai, Hawaii, and Indonesia are scheduled to open in 1996. By the end of 1997, the company expects to add up to eight new operations to the company's current stable of hotels and resorts. Segmented revenues in 1994 were: United States, 45%; Canada, 6%; United Kingdom and Europe, 23%; Asia, 22%; South Pacific, 4%. Hotel management accounted for 62% of revenue and hotel ownership, 38% of revenue.

Rank (Profit/Revenue/Assets)
334   378   225
Isadore Sharp
Chairman & President
Douglas L. Ludwig
C.F.O. & Treasurer

Address
1165 Leslie Street
Toronto
ON
M3C 2K8
(416) 449-1750

Fax: (416) 441-4374
F0000479/G/12.7

For further company information, call Globe Information Services 1-800-268-9128 or (416) 585-5345

IMAX CORPORATION

Exchanges	Price (Jun29'95)		15 .75	Trailing P/E		nm	Stock Symbol
TQ	Trailing Yield (%)		0 .00	Trailing EPS		(0 .80)	**IMX**

Period Ending	Dec94	Dec93	Dec92
Yearly Statistics	10M		
Price-Close	12 .38	n t	n t
Price-High	14 .88	n t	n t
Price-Low	11 .88	n t	n t
P/E-Close	nm	n t	n t
Dividends per Share	0 .00	0 .00	0 .00
Dividend Yield (%)	0 .00	0 .00	0 .00
Sales per Share	11 .53	16 .38	11 .32
EPS before extra. item	(1 .38)	1 .45	0 .57
Cash Flow per Share	1 .63	3 .91	3 .92
Book Value per Share	5 .27	(0 .26)	(1 .31)
O/S Common Shares	14 ,087	5 ,755	5 ,694
Total Revenue	99 ,647	94 ,109	66 ,713
Income before extra.	(13 ,315)	8 ,301	3 ,333
Cash Flow	13 ,773	22 ,410	22 ,851
Debt/Equity	1 .31	na	na
Return on Capital (%)	(12 .43)	116 .63	na
Ret. on Com. Equity (%)	(43 .95)	na	na
% Change Profit	(292 .5)	149 .1	na
% Change Revenue	27 .1	41 .1	na
% Change Assets	200 .6	(14 .6)	na

Preferred Div. Coverage	na	np	np
Total Div. Coverage	na	na	na
Interest Coverage	0 .0	8 .1	3 .2
Current Ratio	2 .0	0 .5	0 .8
Operating Margin	(11 .8)	17 .9	10 .0
Asset Turnover	0 .5	1 .1	0 .7
5 YEAR RATIOS (%)			
Return on Capital	na	na	na
Return on Com. Equity	na	na	na
Profit Growth	na	na	na
Revenue Growth	na	na	na
Asset Growth	na	na	na
BALANCE SHEET (000)			
Cash	79 ,831	5 ,308	12 ,843
Current Assets	111 ,780	27 ,315	39 ,687
Net Fixed Assets	36 ,370	36 ,366	37 ,208
Invest's & Advances	16 ,547	10 ,205	11 ,755
Total Assets	258 ,963	86 ,144	100 ,850
Short Term Debt	2 ,488	3 ,890	3 ,429
Current Liabilities	56 ,211	49 ,722	50 ,728
Long Term Debt	96 ,050	15 ,377	15 ,662
Total Liabilities	183 ,515	87 ,623	108 ,326
Total Equity	75 ,448	(1 ,479)	(7 ,476)
Total Liab. & Equity	258 ,963	86 ,144	100 ,850
CAPITAL (000)			
Total Debt	98 ,538	19 ,267	19 ,091
Preferred Equity	1 ,256	0	0
Common Equity	74 ,192	(1 ,479)	(7 ,476)

Business:

IMAX CORPORATION is a designer and supplier of projection and sound systems and a producer and distributor of films for large-screen theatres.

Date		EPS	DPS	Tot Rev	Inc Bex
Mar 95	US	0 .01	0 .00	17 ,957	278
Dec 94		(0 .08)	0 .00	32 ,343	(987)
Sep 94		(0 .38)	0 .00	18 ,734	(5 ,407)
Jun 94		(0 .35)	0 .00	36 ,012	(4 ,988)
Mar 94	US	(0 .30)	0 .00	15 ,724	(4 ,362)
Dec 93		na	0 .00	16 ,448	(1 ,447)
Sep 93		0 .05	0 .00	41 ,971	794
Jun 93		0 .16	0 .00	23 ,850	2 ,351

Synopsis:

In March 1994, Imax Corp. changed ownership. To finance the acquisition and provide additional working capital, the company completed a $70-million (U.S.) offering 10% senior notes. It raised approximately $18-million (U.S.) through the sale of preferred shares which were later converted to common shares. In June, Imax completed its initial public stock offering generating net proceeds of $40.8-million (U.S.).

Throughout 1994 and into early 1995, the company announced a number of strategic alliances. It entered a joint venture with Capital Cities/ABC, Inc., to develop IMAX films. Imax made two strategic alliances in Europe to develop commercial IMAX theatres and IMAX RIDEFILM theatres. Imax also entered into an agreement with SEGA Enterprises Ltd. to launch IMAX RIDEFILM theatres in two venues in Japan.

In 1994, Imax completed the integration of its motion simulation ride subsidiary Ridefilm Corporation into Imax and began marketing and film production for IMAX RIDEFILM motion simulation rides.

Imax considered the opening of SONY IMAX Theatre in New York City in November 1994 a significant commercial success for the company. As a result of this success there has been a marked increase in number of customer inquires for commercial IMAX theatres. In addition, Imax's institutional theatre business continues to prosper as museums and institutions seeking new revenue sources and new ways to educate and entertain their visitors turn to Imax products.

In 1994, the company increased its sales backlog by 35% to $113.2- million, a new all-time high. Imax opened 13 permanent theatre systems in the year increasing the permanent theatre network to 119 at December 31, 1994. Ten new IMAX format films were produced in 1994 bringing the total to 107 films.

Relative strength to TSE300 / Price / Volume (in 1000's of board lots) chart

Rank (Profit/Revenue/Assets)
958 391 311
Bradley J. Wechsler
Chairman
Robert J. Corrigan
C.E.O. & President
John M. Davison
C.F.O.

Address
45 Charles Street East
Toronto
ON
M4Y 1N1
(416) 960-8509

Fax: (416) 960-8596
01003767/G/16.1

INTER-CITY PRODUCTS CORPORATION

Exchanges	Price (Jun29'95)	3 .40	Trailing P/E	nm	Stock Symbol
TA	Trailing Yield (%)	0 .00	Trailing EPS	(0 .18)	**IPR**

Period Ending	Dec94	Dec93	Dec92	Dec91	Dec90
Yearly Statistics	US	US			
Price-Close	3 .30	4 .40	7 .13	5 .88	3 .20
Price-High	5 .25	8 .38	10 .13	6 .38	8 .75
Price-Low	2 .95	3 .00	5 .50	2 .70	2 .45
P/E-Close	nm	nm	nm	nm	0 .11
Dividends per Share	0 .00	0 .00	0 .00	0 .00	0 .00
Dividend Yield (%)	0 .00	0 .00	0 .00	0 .00	0 .00
Sales per Share	26 .70	26 .79	36 .19	53 .88	98 .02
EPS before extra. item	(0 .29)	(1 .00)	(0 .40)	(1 .13)	28 .90
Cash Flow per Share	0 .49	(0 .16)	0 .79	1 .38	5 .43
Book Value per Share	2 .85	2 .94	5 .00	4 .20	6 .81
O/S Common Shares	38 ,650	24 ,931	24 ,619	17 ,227	7 ,227
Total Revenue	690 ,500	663 ,900	818 ,800	670 ,100	674 ,300
Income before extra.	(7 ,500)	(21 ,000)	(4 ,200)	(9 ,100)	203 ,000
Cash Flow	12 ,800	(4 ,000)	17 ,900	17 ,100	37 ,200
Debt/Equity	2 .32	1 .94	1 .00	2 .03	1 .89
Return on Capital (%)	3 .54	(3 .26)	2 .43	2 .08	40 .17
Ret. on Com. Equity (%)	(8 .16)	(29 .01)	(9 .31)	(23 .05)	92 .33
% Change Profit	64 .3	(546 .8)	53 .8	(104 .5)	299 .6
% Change Revenue	4 .0	4 .9	22 .2	(0 .6)	(10 .1)
% Change Assets	(0 .4)	22 .2	(5 .0)	27 .1	(57 .3)

Date		EPS	DPS	Tot Rev	Inc Bex
Mar 95	US	(0 .14)	0 .00	138 ,300	(5 ,500)
Dec 94	US	(0 .21)	0 .00	160 ,600	(7 ,000)
Sep 94		0 .05	0 .00	204 ,100	2 ,000
Jun 94		0 .12	0 .00	208 ,700	3 ,800
Mar 94	US	(0 .29)	0 .00	95 ,729	(6 ,407)
Dec 93	US	0 .82	0 .00	186 ,252	(21 ,444)
Sep 93		0 .06	0 .00	185 ,900	2 ,600
Jun 93		0 .05	0 .00	184 ,200	2 ,200

	Dec94	Dec93	Dec92
Preferred Div. Coverage	np	0 .0	0 .0
Total Div. Coverage	na	0 .0	0 .0
Interest Coverage	0 .6	0 .0	0 .7
Current Ratio	1 .8	2 .0	1 .7
Operating Margin	2 .6	1 .2	2 .6
Asset Turnover	1 .5	1 .4	1 .6
5 YEAR RATIOS (%)			
Return on Capital	9 .0	10 .4	12 .3
Return on Com. Equity	4 .6	8 .4	15 .8
Profit Growth	na	na	na
Revenue Growth	3 .5	3 .6	(13 .5)
Asset Growth	(8 .9)	(11 .0)	(23 .6)
BALANCE SHEET (000)			
Cash	13 ,700	12 ,100	12 ,000
Current Assets	322 ,000	307 ,900	294 ,700
Net Fixed Assets	130 ,000	137 ,300	184 ,500
Invest's & Advances	0	0	0
Total Assets	476 ,200	478 ,300	518 ,300
Short Term Debt	85 ,400	47 ,300	50 ,700
Current Liabilities	177 ,300	150 ,400	168 ,700
Long Term Debt	170 ,000	184 ,700	134 ,100
Total Liabilities	365 ,900	358 ,800	334 ,200
Total Equity	110 ,300	119 ,500	184 ,100
Total Liab. & Equity	476 ,200	478 ,300	518 ,300
CAPITAL (000)			
Total Debt	255 ,400	232 ,000	184 ,800
Preferred Equity	0	46 ,100	61 ,000
Common Equity	110 ,300	73 ,400	123 ,100

Business:

INTER-CITY PRODUCTS CORPORATION manufactures heating and cooling equipment through its Heil, KeepRite, Tempstar, Arcoaire Comfortmaker and ZonaAire brands. It also makes spiral welded steel pipe for water transmission projects under the name Thomspson Pipe & Steel and refrigeration products under the KeepRite name.

Synopsis:

Inter-City Products had first-quarter 1995 furnace sales of 63,000 units. This was down 3% due to the unseasonably warm winter weather in the company's North American markets. Air conditioner sales increased from 106,000 units sold in the first quarter 1994 to 149,000 during the same period in 1995. Cooling products that were previously shipped and recorded as pre-season sales during the fourth quarter were reflected as sales closer to the selling season. In addition, the company's reduction in credit terms on sales to distributors effective April 1995 encouraged distributors to purchase products prior to the change. This change in terms is part of the company's ongoing strategy to reduce financing costs and improve asset management.

In January 1995, U.S. subsidiary, Inter-City Products Corporation (USA), completed a refinacing of its existing revolving credit facility. The refinacing involved a revolving trade receivables securitization transaction in the amount of $100-million (U.S.) for a term of five years and a revolving inventory credit facility of $40-million (U.S.) for a three-year term. Funds from the refinacing were used to repay the subsidiary's existing revolving credit facility. According to the company, its financing cost savings on an annual basis should be $2-million (U.S.).

Production of a new furnace product aimed at the builder market is scheduled to start in the second quarter of 1995. Inter-City feels that this product will further expand it furnace product lines to encompass all price points.

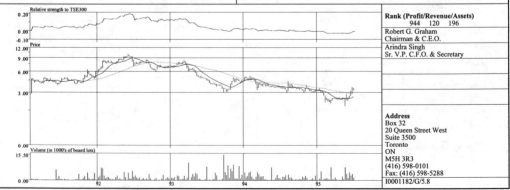

Rank (Profit/Revenue/Assets)
944 120 196

Robert G. Graham
Chairman & C.E.O.

Arindra Singh
Sr. V.P. C.F.O. & Secretary

Address
Box 32
20 Queen Street West
Suite 3500
Toronto
ON
M5H 3R3
(416) 598-0101
Fax: (416) 598-5288
I0001182/G/5.8

For further company information, call Globe Information Services 1-800-268-9128 or (416) 585-5345

JOURNEY'S END CORPORATION

Exchanges	Price (Jun29'95)	2.00	Trailing P/E	nm	Stock Symbol
TM	Trailing Yield (%)	0.00	Trailing EPS	(0.33)	**JEM**

Period Ending	Ju l94	Ju l93	Ju l92	Ju l91	Ju l90
Yearly Statistics					
Price-Close	1.83	3.65	2.55	6.50	8.75
Price-High	4.00	6.13	7.13	9.00	21.75
Price-Low	1.60	2.45	2.45	4.80	8.63
P/E-Close	nm	nm	nm	nm	13.26
Dividends per Share	0.00	0.00	0.65	0.20	0.20
Dividend Yield (%)	0.00	0.00	25.49	3.08	2.29
Sales per Share	3.44	2.78	2.54	6.85	7.17
EPS before extra. item	(0.89)	(0.57)	(1.77)	(0.80)	0.66
Cash Flow per Share	(0.27)	0.19	0.52	0.60	0.80
Book Value per Share	0.68	1.50	2.00	4.37	5.34
O/S Common Shares	10,313	10,280	10,130	10,128	10,117
Total Revenue	31,760	28,887	26,103	70,536	88,945
Income before extra.	(9,155)	(5,902)	(17,938)	(8,127)	6,638
Cash Flow	(2,462)	1,974	5,258	6,065	8,129
Debt/Equity	16.67	6.49	4.89	2.55	1.77
Return on Capital (%)	(7.59)	(6.84)	(12.59)	(5.04)	8.68
Ret. on Com. Equity (%)	(81.56)	(33.06)	(55.60)	(16.54)	12.74
% Change Profit	(55.1)	67.1	(120.7)	(222.4)	(38.5)
% Change Revenue	9.9	10.7	(63.0)	(20.7)	(13.0)
% Change Assets	8.5	(3.7)	(21.9)	(4.7)	24.8

Preferred Div. Coverage	np	np	np
Total Div. Coverage	na	na	0.0
Interest Coverage	0.0	0.0	0.0
Current Ratio	1.0	1.1	1.4
Operating Margin	(12.5)	(6.4)	(67.5)
Asset Turnover	0.2	0.2	0.2
5 YEAR RATIOS (%)			
Return on Capital	(4.7)	0.1	4.9
Return on Com. Equity	(34.8)	(13.8)	(3.1)
Profit Growth	na	na	na
Revenue Growth	(20.9)	(17.3)	(12.9)
Asset Growth	(0.6)	(1.0)	11.5
BALANCE SHEET (000)			
Cash	1,119	1,142	1,888
Current Assets	33,580	30,032	35,771
Net Fixed Assets	69,582	62,137	63,353
Invest's & Advances	9,976	11,854	11,629
Total Assets	137,671	126,906	131,748
Short Term Debt	20,719	15,677	12,939
Current Liabilities	34,346	27,106	25,185
Long Term Debt	96,303	84,373	86,280
Total Liabilities	130,649	111,479	111,465
Total Equity	7,022	15,427	20,283
Total Liab. & Equity	137,671	126,906	131,748
CAPITAL (000)			
Total Debt	117,022	100,050	99,219
Preferred Equity	0	0	0
Common Equity	7,022	15,427	20,283

Business:

JOURNEY'S END CORPORATION is involved in the management of its chain of limited-service motel, hotel and all-suite properties. The Company also derives income from property ownership interests, development services and franchise operations. The Company participates in the hotel franchise business through its 50 per cent ownership of Choice Hotels Canada Inc.

Date	EPS	DPS	Tot Rev	Inc Bex
Apr 95	(0.22)	0.00	10,200	(2,966)
Jan 95	(0.28)	0.00	na	(2,811)
Oct 94	0.13	0.00	12,143	1,292
Jul 94	(0.42)	0.00	na	(4,351)
Apr 94	(0.26)	0.00	6,300	(2,662)
Jan 94	(0.25)	0.00	na	(2,598)
Oct 93	0.04	0.00	9,357	456
Jul 93	(0.44)	0.00	na	(4,555)

Synopsis:

Journey's End reported a net loss of $4.5-million for the period ended April 30, 1995, compared to a loss of $4.8-million for the same period a year earlier. In its property ownership division, revenues were $18.4-million compared to $12.4-million in 1994. In its management operations, revenue was $4.3-million compared to $4.1-million in 1994. Under its 50% ownership of Choice Hotels Inc., the company posted franchise revenues of $5.5-million for the period compared to $5-million in 1994, an increase of 8.8%.

Journey's End has undergone restructuring and cost-cutting since reporting substantial losses since fiscal 1991, related to the industry's slow recovery from the recession. The hotel industry experienced little growth in 1993-94. However, the reservation volume in its Canadian-managed properties increased by 29% in fiscal 1994. The company attributes its decreased loss for the 1995 nine month period to: consolidation of operations of nine motels acquired at the beginning of the 1995 fiscal year; improvements in operations from its property in Windsor; and chain-wide cash flow improvements through direct property ownership, general partner, and limited partner interests.

In early 1995, a favourable advanced ruling from Revenue Canada allowed Journey's End to convert $47-million of debt into Distress Preferred Shares. In June 1995, the corporation's principal bank also converted $13.5-million of debt into 1.7 million common shares. Journey's End is continuing to restructure debt and dispose of non core and under-performing assets. The company is exploring joint venture opportunities that do not require capital or financial risk in selected Latin American and Pacific rim countries.

Consolidated revenues for fiscal 1994 by geographical segment were: Canada, $33.4-million (80%); United States $8.4-million (20%).

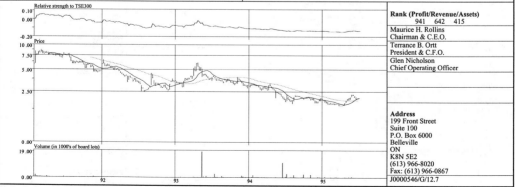

Rank (Profit/Revenue/Assets)
941   642   415

Maurice H. Rollins
Chairman & C.E.O.

Terrance B. Ortt
President & C.F.O.

Glen Nicholson
Chief Operating Officer

Address
199 Front Street
Suite 100
P.O. Box 6000
Belleville
ON
K8N 5E2
(613) 966-8020
Fax: (613) 966-0867
J0000546/G/12.7

KAUFEL GROUP LTD.

Exchanges	Price (Jun29'95)	4.40	Trailing P/E	20.00	Stock Symbol
TM	Trailing Yield (%)	0.00	Trailing EPS	0.22	KGL.A

Period Ending	Aug94	Aug93	Aug92	Aug91	Aug90	Business:
Yearly Statistics						KAUFEL GROUP LTD. is a Quebec-based
Price-Close	5.00	8.00	6.00	6.00	7.25	company specializing in the design,
Price-High	9.50	8.75	9.00	8.25	12.63	manufacturing and distribution of lighting
Price-Low	5.50	7.63	4.90	5.63	7.00	products and systems for a wide range of
P/E-Close	21.74	38.10	16.67	19.36	14.22	industrial, residential, institutional, recreational,
Dividends per Share	0.00	0.00	0.00	0.00	0.00	mass transit and municipal applications. It is the
Dividend Yield (%)	0.00	0.00	0.00	0.00	0.00	largest manufacturer and supplier of emergency
Sales per Share	8.94	10.49	8.35	7.82	8.16	lighting systems and backup power equipment
EPS before extra. item	0.23	0.21	0.36	0.31	0.51	in North America.
Cash Flow per Share	0.51	0.68	0.65	0.56	0.65	
Book Value per Share	7.00	6.37	6.11	5.70	5.57	
O/S Common Shares	19,231	14,738	14,698	14,698	14,698	
Total Revenue	171,987	154,279	122,690	114,924	120,129	
Income before extra.	4,312	3,036	5,226	4,492	7,430	
Cash Flow	9,860	10,036	9,623	8,290	9,493	

Date	EPS	DPS	Tot Rev	Inc Bex
Feb 95	0.11	0.00	46,208	2,103
Nov 94	0.10	0.00	47,180	1,845
Aug 94	0.09	0.00	47,045	1,647
May 94	(0.08)	0.00	44,055	(1,446)
Feb 94	0.11	0.00	38,825	2,110
Nov 93	0.11	0.00	42,062	2,001
Aug 93	(0.09)	0.00	43,058	(1,305)
May 93	0.08	0.00	46,531	1,166

	Aug94	Aug93	Aug92	Aug91	Aug90
Debt/Equity	0.50	0.93	0.84	0.71	0.75
Return on Capital (%)	5.17	5.86	7.15	6.59	9.67
Ret. on Com. Equity (%)	3.78	3.30	6.02	5.42	9.50
% Change Profit	42.0	(41.9)	16.3	(39.5)	(39.3)
% Change Revenue	11.5	25.7	6.8	(4.3)	9.8
% Change Assets	8.0	13.7	19.1	(1.0)	11.5

				Synopsis:
Preferred Div. Coverage	np	np	np	
Total Div. Coverage	na	na	na	
Interest Coverage	2.0	1.4	2.1	
Current Ratio	2.1	1.4	1.9	
Operating Margin	6.6	6.6	9.0	
Asset Turnover	0.7	0.7	0.7	
5 YEAR RATIOS (%)				
Return on Capital	6.9	9.5	13.1	
Return on Com. Equity	5.6	9.1	14.6	
Profit Growth	(18.8)	(22.3)	(5.5)	
Revenue Growth	9.4	11.7	16.8	
Asset Growth	10.0	14.6	25.1	
BALANCE SHEET (000)				
Cash	25,448	21,207	23,240	
Current Assets	134,600	119,829	105,318	
Net Fixed Assets	41,105	40,847	39,831	
Invest's & Advances	0	0	0	
Total Assets	230,083	213,054	187,403	
Short Term Debt	36,299	51,678	32,959	
Current Liabilities	64,843	83,405	54,434	
Long Term Debt	30,720	35,721	42,265	
Total Liabilities	95,563	119,126	97,581	
Total Equity	134,520	93,928	89,822	
Total Liab. & Equity	230,083	213,054	187,403	
CAPITAL (000)				
Total Debt	67,019	87,399	75,224	
Preferred Equity	0	0	0	
Common Equity	134,520	93,928	89,822	

Synopsis:

Kaufel Group Ltd., now that the profitability of operations is under stricter control, strongly feels that it must concentrate its efforts on improving the cash flow. A systematic reduction in its inventories will result in additional positive cash flow for the coming year. The company does not expect the reduction of all the increased inventory levels in the current year. The high level of inventories came from the closing of the Puerto Rican plant and the transfer of its operations to Montreal. Prior to the move, the Montreal facility had to increase its inventory to provide an uninterrupted supply for orders placed in Puerto Rico. Although these inventories were available at the Puerto Rico factory, management felt that transferring them ran the risk of intensified labour problems and potential disappearance.

Kaufel's consolidated sales rose by 12% to $172-million compared to $154-million in 1993. Sales of emergency lighting products were up by $11-million. Sales of general lighting products increased by about $7-million, reflecting results of the recently acquired Powerlite division. The company reported disappointing operating results in its French companies, due to a continuing weak French economy and lengthy delays in completing the consolidation of the division's manufacturing facilities. These delays stemmed from the untimely death of the French General Manager in the middle of the process. The consolidation is now complete. The company is confident that once the new management is in place, Kaufel's French company's profits will improve.

In the fiscal year ended August 1994, 79% of Kaufel's sales were concentrated in its emergency lighting division, 14% in its general lighting divisions, and 7% in its plastics and metal processing and fabrication divisions. About 39% of the total revenues were generated in the United States, 38% in Canada and 22% in Europe. Facilities in Hong Kong and Barbados accounted for approximately 1% of the company's operations. The company incurred restructuring costs of $1.4 million in the 1994 fiscal year.

Relative strength to TSE300 / Price / Volume (in 1000's of board lots)

Rank (Profit/Revenue/Assets)
446 336 331

Bruce J. Kaufman
President & C.E.O.

Aslam Khatri
V.P. Finance

Muguette Gagnier
Sr. V.P. & Secretary

Address
1811 Hymus Blvd.
Dorval
PQ
H9P 1J5
(514) 685-2270

Fax: (514) 685-0378
K0000322/G/6.10

580   **For further company information, call Globe Information Services 1-800-268-9128 or (416) 585-5345**

LAFARGE CANADA INC.

Exchanges	Price (Jun29'95)		26 .50	Trailing P/E		nc	Stock Symbol
TM	Trailing Yield (%)		nc	Trailing EPS		3 .82	**LCI.PR.E**

Period Ending	Dec94	Dec93	Dec92	Dec91	Dec90
Yearly Statistics					
Price-Close	26 .00	30 .00	18 .50	16 .13	15 .88
Price-High	35 .25	30 .00	21 .63	19 .25	23 .00
Price-Low	22 .75	18 .75	14 .13	14 .25	13 .25
P/E-Close	nc	nc	nc	nc	nc
Dividends per Share	nc	nc	nc	nc	nc
Dividend Yield (%)	nc	nc	nc	nc	nc
Sales per Share	81 .59	73 .57	70 .78	74 .35	91 .08
EPS before extra. item	3 .31	1 .71	1 .83	0 .76	7 .07
Cash Flow per Share	7 .23	8 .14	5 .44	5 .83	11 .29
Book Value per Share	60 .11	56 .81	55 .10	54 .10	53 .34
O/S Common Shares	12 ,008	12 ,008	12 ,008	12 ,000	12 ,000
Total Revenue	993 ,005	891 ,255	863 ,631	896 ,124	1 ,103 ,592
Income before extra.	44 ,975	25 ,476	26 ,518	14 ,202	84 ,816
Cash Flow	86 ,822	97 ,713	65 ,312	70 ,015	135 ,511
Debt/Equity	0 .03	0 .01	0 .03	0 .05	0 .06
Return on Capital (%)	9 .72	6 .67	5 .55	4 .43	19 .95
Ret. on Com. Equity (%)	5 .66	3 .06	3 .35	1 .41	13 .14
% Change Profit	76 .5	(3 .9)	86 .7	(83 .3)	(32 .6)
% Change Revenue	11 .4	3 .2	(3 .6)	(18 .8)	(4 .3)
% Change Assets	5 .3	4 .4	0 .7	(0 .6)	5 .1

Preferred Div. Coverage	8 .5	5 .1	5 .8
Total Div. Coverage	8 .5	5 .1	5 .8
Interest Coverage	73 .9	15 .7	11 .5
Current Ratio	3 .0	3 .0	3 .3
Operating Margin	6 .6	6 .9	3 .2
Asset Turnover	0 .9	0 .8	0 .8
5 YEAR RATIOS (%)			
Return on Capital	9 .3	13 .9	19 .7
Return on Com. Equity	5 .3	9 .0	13 .9
Profit Growth	(18 .6)	(25 .8)	(21 .2)
Revenue Growth	(3 .0)	(3 .0)	(2 .7)
Asset Growth	2 .9	4 .9	5 .9
BALANCE SHEET (000)			
Cash	182 ,994	135 ,574	105 ,100
Current Assets	557 ,039	477 ,039	440 ,922
Net Fixed Assets	479 ,536	505 ,488	515 ,545
Invest's & Advances	49 ,121	51 ,071	46 ,014
Total Assets	1 ,124 ,676	1 ,067 ,711	1 ,022 ,555
Short Term Debt	20 ,049	2 ,086	6 ,460
Current Liabilities	183 ,527	158 ,071	131 ,989
Long Term Debt	1 ,557	1 ,979	19 ,096
Total Liabilities	298 ,829	282 ,266	259 ,127
Total Equity	825 ,847	785 ,445	763 ,428
Total Liab. & Equity	1 ,124 ,676	1 ,067 ,711	1 ,022 ,555
CAPITAL (000)			
Total Debt	21 ,606	4 ,065	25 ,556
Preferred Equity	104 ,046	103 ,347	101 ,853
Common Equity	721 ,801	682 ,098	661 ,575

Business:

LAFARGE CANADA INC. produces cement and concrete-related products. The company operates seven cement plants in Canada and serves principal markets from coast to coast. The company also makes ready- mix concrete, aggregates and construction materials such as concrete pipe, block and paving stone. Lafarge Corp. of Reston, Va., owns all of the company's common shares.

Date	EPS	DPS	Tot Rev	Inc Bex
Mar 95	(1 .77)	nc	127 ,281	(20 ,137)
Dec 94	1 .56	nc	281 ,338	20 ,559
Sep 94	3 .17	nc	351 ,358	38 ,024
Jun 94	0 .86	nc	247 ,103	10 ,367
Mar 94	(1 .99)	nc	112 ,859	(23 ,975)
Dec 93	0 .23	nc	248 ,297	5 ,531
Sep 93	2 .76	nc	319 ,084	33 ,190
Jun 93	0 .97	nc	222 ,143	12 ,382

Synopsis:

Lafarge Canada Inc. reported sales of $979.7-million in 1994 compared to $883.3-million in 1993. Cement shipments increased 7% to 2.7 million metric tonnes, reflecting an increase in domestic shipments and higher export shipments to the Great Lakes area of the U.S. Selling price increases in eastern Canada helped offset a deterioration of prices in the western provinces, resulting in an average net sales price improvement of 1%. The Construction Materials group had a net sales increase of 7%.

In 1994, Lafarge closed a waste-derived fuels transfer station in Quebec, and suspended efforts to permit another facility in Nova Scotia. The dwindling waste volumes and higher permit costs have altered the economic viability of the waste fuels business.

Lafarge's Western region saw an increase in profits from the previous year. Performance varied across the area. Concrete volumes for the region slipped 2% while aggregate volumes declined 1%. The ready-mix operations in the Vancouver-area and Northern Alberta had lower contributions to the regions' bottom line but all other areas turned in a better performance than the previous year.

The company sees 1995 shaping up to be a better year in Central and Eastern Canada. It expects volume to grow in Ontario, but demand should remain flat in the Atlantic provinces except for the bridge being built between New Brunswick and Prince Edward Island. That project will consume more than 370,000 cubic meters of concrete, plus 170,000 metric tons of Lafarge cement over a three year period. The Canadian Portland Cement Association is forecasting growth of 7% in cement consumption for Ontario and Quebec in 1995. For 1995, the Construction Materials Group should show improvement because of volume growth in Ontario and concrete and aggregate shipments to the fixed link bridge project.

Relative strength to TSE300

Price

Volume (in 1000's of board lots)

Rank (Profit/Revenue/Assets)
120   119   146
John D. Redfern
Chairman Of The Board
Michel Rose
President & C.E.O.
Jean-Pierre Cloiseau
Exec. V.P. & C.F.O.

Address
Suite 800
606 Cathcart Street
Montreal
PQ
H3B 1L7
(514) 861-1411

Fax: (514) 861-1123
C0001384/G/6.6

LIVENT INC.

Period Ending	Dec94	Dec93	Dec92	Dec91	Business:
Yearly Statistics					LIVENT INC. is engaged in the business of
Price-Close	10.75	15 .50	n t	n t	acquiring domestic and international rights to
Price-High	16 .88	18 .25	n t	n t	musical works and producing, licensing and
Price-Low	10 .25	8 .50	n t	n t	marketing such properties for live theatre and
P/E-Close	21 .50	18 .68	n t	n t	other forms of entertai nment. The Company
Dividends per Share	0 .00	0 .00	0 .00	0 .00	owns and operates the Pantages Theatre in
Dividend Yield (%)	0 .00	0 .00	0 .00	0 .00	Toronto, the Ford Centre for the Performing
Sales per Share	14 .96	14 .53	nm	nm	Arts in North York, and the Ford Centre
EPS before extra. item	0 .50	0 .83	na	na	opening in Vancouver in December 1995.
Cash Flow per Share	2 .05	2 .34	nm	nm	
Book Value per Share	4 .19	3 .40	nm	nm	

O/S Common Shares	11 ,960	11 ,504	0	0
Total Revenue	175 ,198	129 ,478	103 ,705	81 ,175
Income before extra.	5 ,835	7 ,370	3 ,669	(1 ,194)
Cash Flow	24 ,024	20 ,873	13 ,853	8 ,263

Date	EPS	DPS	Tot Rev	Inc Bex
Mar 95	0 .11	0 .00	49 ,618	1 ,282
Dec 94	(0 .18)	0 .00	69 ,129	(2 ,077)
Sep 94	0 .36	0 .00	44 ,005	4 ,157
Jun 94	0 .22	0 .00	33 ,529	2 ,583
Mar 94	0 .10	0 .00	28 ,536	1 ,176
Dec 93	0 .14	0 .00	39 ,871	1 ,811
Sep 93	0 .30	0 .00	31 ,176	2 ,978
Jun 93	0 .27	0 .00	30 ,718	2 ,171

Debt/Equity	0 .35	0 .66	na	na
Return on Capital (%)	14 .75	26 .97	18 .68	na
Ret. on Com. Equity (%)	13 .08	50 .73	na	na
% Change Profit	(20 .8)	100 .9	407 .3	na
% Change Revenue	35 .3	24 .9	27 .8	na
% Change Assets	13 .8	18 .6	27 .4	na

					Synopsis:
Preferred Div. Coverage	np	np	np		Recent theatrical productions from Live Entertainment of Canada Inc. (Livent)
Total Div. Coverage	na	na	na		include "The Phantom of the Opera", "Joseph and the Amazing Technicolor
Interest Coverage	5 .2	4 .0	1 .9		Dreamcoat", "Kiss of the Spider Woman", "Show Boat", and "Sunset Boulevard",
Current Ratio	0 .4	0 .4	0 .2		scheduled to open October 1995. Livent has also acquired the rights to "Ragtime"
Operating Margin	5 .6	12 .2	7 .3		and "The Sweet Smell of Success". Livent owns and operates the Pantages
Asset Turnover	1 .2	1 .0	1 .0		Theatre and manages the Ford Centre for the Performing Arts, both in Toronto.
5 YEAR RATIOS (%)					Livent will manage and have an ownership interest in a new Vancouver theatre,
Return on Capital	na	na	na		the Ford Centre for the Performing Arts, due to open in December 1995.
Return on Com. Equity	na	na	na		
Profit Growth	na	na	na		Productions of Phantom, Joseph and Show Boat have had record breaking sales in
Revenue Growth	na	na	na		North America. However returns from Kiss have been weak. The company's 1994
Asset Growth	na	na	na		income before taxes was down 33% from 1993. This reflected Livent's
BALANCE SHEET (000)					$11.9-million non-cash writedowns of pre-production costs in 1994, of which
Cash	0	0	0		$8.9-million related to pre-production costs of Kiss.
Current Assets	20 ,159	12 ,395	16 ,237		
Net Fixed Assets	77 ,987	75 ,961	72 ,188		Livent continues to build on its success with touring productions, the faster
Invest's & Advances	12 ,310	10 ,259	10 ,165		growing segment of the theatre industry. Costs associated with traveling and
Total Assets	143 ,322	125 ,909	106 ,132		new-city marketing are significantly less than building the original show and
Short Term Debt	0	0	16 ,510		generating first-time awareness among the ticket-buying public.
Current Liabilities	46 ,689	30 ,586	70 ,307		In early 1995, two limited partnerships managed by Thomas H. Lee Company of
Long Term Debt	17 ,716	25 ,856	45 ,853		Boston made a total investment of $31-million in Livent. The net proceeds from
Total Liabilities	93 ,189	86 ,828	116 ,160		the sale were used in part to retire bank indebtedness and put toward the working
Total Equity	50 ,133	39 ,081	(10 ,028)		capital of the company.
Total Liab. & Equity	143 ,322	125 ,909	106 ,132		Livent's 1994 revenues were derived from the following segments: ticket sales,
CAPITAL (000)					78%; merchandise and concession, 8%; other (corporate sponsorship, royalty and
Total Debt	17 ,716	25 ,856	62 ,363		fees for theatre management), 10%; and joint venture projects, 4%. Revenue from
Preferred Equity	0	0	0		its directly managed productions accounted for about 20% of the North American
Common Equity	50 ,133	39 ,081	(10 ,028)		theatre industry's box office in 1994.

Rank (Profit/Revenue/Assets)
398   331   404
Garth H. Drabinsky
Chairman & C.E.O.
Myron I. Gottlieb
President & C.O.O.
Gordon Eckstein
V.P. Finance & Administration

Address
Suite 600
165 Avenue Road
Toronto
ON
M5R 3S4
(416) 324-5800

Fax: (416) 324-5495
01003369/G/16.1

For further company information, call Globe Information Services 1-800-268-9128 or (416) 585-5345

LOEWEN GROUP INC. (THE)

Exchanges	Price (Jun29'95)	48.25	Trailing P/E	34.19	Stock Symbol
TMQ	Trailing Yield (%)	0.31	Trailing EPS	1.04	**LWN**

Period Ending	Dec94	Dec93	Dec92	Dec91	Dec90	Business:
Yearly Statistics	US	US				LOEWEN GROUP INC. owns and operates
Price-Close	36.75	33.25	19.63	15.63	12.50	funeral home locations, cemeteries and
Price-High	37.50	36.25	20.00	17.63	13.88	crematoria across North America.
Price-Low	30.38	19.00	14.63	10.50	8.38	
P/E-Close	27.67	33.38	25.49	25.62	24.51	
Dividends per Share	0.07	0.05	0.04	0.02	0.00	
Dividend Yield (%)	0.19	0.14	0.20	0.13	0.00	
Sales per Share	10.52	8.28	8.35	6.85	5.26	
EPS before extra. item	0.97	0.77	0.77	0.61	0.51	
Cash Flow per Share	1.72	1.46	1.40	1.10	0.83	
Book Value per Share	10.02	8.43	8.79	6.96	5.49	
O/S Common Shares	41,015	38,647	35,534	32,754	28,391	
Total Revenue	418,013	303,011	290,542	219,497	136,500	
Income before extra.	38,494	28,182	26,125	19,066	12,864	

					Date		EPS	DPS	Tot Rev	Inc Bex
Cash Flow	68,113	53,275	48,606	35,129	21,636	Mar 95	US	0.34	0.04	129,774	14,057
Debt/Equity	1.27	1.06	1.06	1.14	1.38	Dec 94	US	0.29	0.02	120,048	11,668
Return on Capital (%)	11.53	11.09	11.83	12.03	13.10	Sep 94	US	0.19	0.00	105,758	7,751
Ret. on Com. Equity (%)	10.45	9.80	9.67	9.94	11.09	Jun 94	US	0.22	0.05	95,918	8,613
% Change Profit	36.6	39.6	37.0	48.2	78.6	Mar 94	US	0.27	0.03	96,910	10,530
% Change Revenue	38.0	34.9	32.4	60.8	80.3	Dec 93	US	0.23	0.01	87,205	8,739
% Change Assets	51.1	39.8	35.6	30.2	109.3	Sep 93	US	0.15	0.00	73,552	5,497
						Jun 93	US	0.18	0.00	70,914	6,391

	Dec94	Dec93	Dec92	Synopsis:
Preferred Div. Coverage	np	np	np	Consolidated revenue for the Loewen Group increased 37.8% to $417.5-million in 1994 from $303-million in 1993. Funeral revenue grew 28.6%, and cemetery revenue increased 127.8%. Consolidated gross profit increased 38.1% to $159-million in 1994 from $115.1-million in 1993. Funeral gross profit grew 32.4% and cemetery gross profit increased 129.2%. All amounts are in U.S. dollars.
Total Div. Coverage	13.4	16.6	19.1	
Interest Coverage	2.7	3.0	2.7	
Current Ratio	1.1	1.9	1.9	
Operating Margin	22.7	22.1	22.7	
Asset Turnover	0.4	0.4	0.4	
5 YEAR RATIOS (%)				The company attributes its strong performance to acquisitions in 1993-1994. Loewen bought 105 funeral homes and 46 cemeteries in the United States in 1994. It also paid $26.3-million for a 26% interest in Arbor Memorial Services Inc., a large public Canadian cemetery and funeral home operator. Through its acquisitions, Loewen added $331.2-million in assets. It currently owns and operates 702 funeral homes and 153 cemeteries across North America.
Return on Capital	11.9	12.7	14.2	
Return on Com. Equity	10.2	10.9	13.0	
Profit Growth	47.2	51.8	68.9	
Revenue Growth	48.1	51.1	59.7	
Asset Growth	50.8	52.8	49.4	
BALANCE SHEET (000)				As of December 1994, 52% of Loewen's outstanding common shares are held by shareholders of record resident in the United States. Therefore, it began reporting its earnings in U.S. dollars. U.S.-based operations contributed 88.4% of 1994 consolidated revenue compared with 84.9% in 1993. On a yearly basis, more than 90% of the company's revenue is generated in the United States, a trend Loewen expects to continue.
Cash	15,349	18,167	16,093	
Current Assets	109,868	90,744	86,815	
Net Fixed Assets	540,899	394,402	408,126	
Invest's & Advances	114,607	33,808	16,915	
Total Assets	1,115,736	738,445	699,182	
Short Term Debt	49,229	11,007	14,685	In 1994, Loewen issued 2 million common shares for gross proceeds of $43.3-million. It also issued $75-million Cumulative Monthly Income Preferred Securities (MIPS) in the United States.
Current Liabilities	97,665	48,959	45,298	
Long Term Debt	471,125	335,405	316,100	
Total Liabilities	704,597	412,555	386,842	
Total Equity	411,139	325,890	312,340	Loewen is continuing to develop its focus on advanced planning services, whereby people arrange for funeral services in advance of need. Currently the largest funeral services company in Canada and the second largest in the United States, Loewen plans to continue to expand through acquisitions in 1995 and 1996.
Total Liab. & Equity	1,115,736	738,445	699,182	
CAPITAL (000)				
Total Debt	520,354	346,412	330,785	
Preferred Equity	0	0	0	
Common Equity	411,139	325,890	312,340	

Rank (Profit/Revenue/Assets)
111   178   126

Raymond L. Loewen
Chairman & C.E.O.

Tim Hogenkamp
President & C.O.O.

Paul Wagler
Sr. V.P. Finance & C.F.O.

Address
4126 Norland Avenue
Burnaby
BC
V5G 3S8
(604) 299-9321

Fax: (604) 473-7330
L0001127/G/16.3

MDS HEALTH GROUP LIMITED

Exchanges	Price (Jun29'95)		17.50	Trailing P/E		12.68	Stock Symbol
T	Trailing Yield (%)		0.87	Trailing EPS		1.38	**MHG.B**

Period Ending	Oct 94	Oct 93	Oct 92	Oct 91	Oct 90
Yearly Statistics					
Price-Close	14.38	14.00	14.63	17.25	13.00
Price-High	15.00	16.75	21.00	22.50	14.75
Price-Low	12.00	10.63	14.00	13.00	11.75
P/E-Close	11.23	280.00	10.91	20.29	18.57
Dividends per Share	0.16	0.15	0.15	0.14	0.13
Dividend Yield (%)	1.11	1.04	0.99	0.78	0.96
Sales per Share	24.13	24.68	17.44	14.15	16.20
EPS before extra. item	1.28	0.05	1.34	0.85	0.70
Cash Flow per Share	2.69	2.36	2.07	1.66	1.43
Book Value per Share	12.41	11.15	11.28	9.89	8.00
O/S Common Shares	26,237	26,022	25,822	25,676	21,508
Total Revenue	637,959	644,613	477,335	343,496	304,569
Income before extra.	33,458	1,352	34,615	19,951	13,100
Cash Flow	70,271	61,113	52,668	38,962	26,027
Debt/Equity	0.68	0.81	0.73	0.45	0.68
Return on Capital (%)	10.20	4.71	17.87	13.12	16.07
Ret. on Com. Equity (%)	10.87	0.47	12.70	9.36	9.52
% Change Profit	2,374.7	(96.1)	73.5	52.3	20.3
% Change Revenue	(1.0)	35.0	39.0	12.8	31.8
% Change Assets	(0.1)	13.2	53.0	25.3	30.9

Preferred Div. Coverage	np	np	np
Total Div. Coverage	8.4	0.4	9.8
Interest Coverage	3.1	1.4	4.8
Current Ratio	1.5	1.6	2.0
Operating Margin	9.6	9.5	12.2
Asset Turnover	0.9	0.9	0.7
5 YEAR RATIOS (%)			
Return on Capital	12.4	13.3	16.8
Return on Com. Equity	8.6	na	na
Profit Growth	25.7	(36.7)	27.8
Revenue Growth	22.4	25.0	22.5
Asset Growth	23.2	32.4	33.4
BALANCE SHEET (000)			
Cash	104,481	92,942	88,977
Current Assets	333,492	329,573	247,258
Net Fixed Assets	161,510	164,823	165,268
Invest's & Advances	73,823	70,216	83,122
Total Assets	720,083	720,472	636,426
Short Term Debt	95,259	72,165	32,907
Current Liabilities	229,011	211,314	124,237
Long Term Debt	125,435	161,650	178,303
Total Liabilities	394,536	430,416	345,233
Total Equity	325,547	290,056	291,193
Total Liab. & Equity	720,083	720,472	636,426
CAPITAL (000)			
Total Debt	220,694	233,815	211,210
Preferred Equity	0	0	0
Common Equity	325,547	290,056	291,193

Business:

MDS HEALTH GROUP LIMITED is a technology-based health care company providing professionally directed testing and measurement services and systems to physicians, hospitals, nursing homes, industry and government. It operates a network of clinical laboratories in Canada, produces and supplies radioisotope products, and makes and distributes mass spectrometry instruments and medical supplies.

Date	EPS	DPS	Tot Rev	Inc Bex
Apr 95	0.40	0.08	161,861	10,363
Jan 95	0.30	0.00	154,322	7,746
Oct 94	0.40	0.08	161,331	10,544
Jul 94	0.28	0.00	158,364	7,190
Apr 94	0.35	0.07	163,078	9,154
Jan 94	0.25	0.00	155,186	6,570
Oct 93	(0.66)	0.07	162,973	(16,896)
Jul 93	0.20	0.00	158,499	5,071

Synopsis:

In fiscal 1994 and the first two quarters of 1995, MDS Health Group Limited took a number of actions consistent with its objective of sustained domestic and international growth. MDS is focused on automation of laboratory services and expanding its balance of products, services, and investments. In 1994, international sales provided more than 30% of MDS revenues.

In the first sixth months of fiscal 1995, the company's net income increased 15% to $18.1-million, while net revenues of $316.2-million were virtually unchanged from the same period in 1994. MDS's Nordion International division operates in Europe producing, supplying and distributing isotope products. The company benefited from a 1994 agreement with DuPont Pharma Radiopharmaceuticals, whereby DuPont Pharma assumed responsibility for the sales and distribution of certain Nordion products. As a result of the agreement, Nordion reduced its expenses and increased its manufacturing capacity.

In May 1995, the company's analytical equipment division, Sciex, moved into a new manufacturing facility in Toronto. This greatly increased its production capacity. Sciex also launched two new spectrometers for the pharmaceutical and biotechnology fields.

MDS is currently placing emphasis on expanding its base of emerging environmental services. To this end, in 1994 the company acquired TSL Laboratories and Environmental Protection Laboratories. Environmental revenues now total $12-million annually.

During the year ending October 31, 1994, MDS Health paid cash dividends of $0.135 per Class A Common Share and $0.16 per Class B Non-Voting Share. This reflected a $0.015 increase in the semi-annual dividend, effective September 1994.

Relative strength to TSE300

Price

Volume (in 1000's of board lots)

Rank (Profit/Revenue/Assets)
143 169 187

Wilfred G. Lewitt
Chairman & C.E.O.

John A. Rogers
President & C.O.O.

Douglas M. Phillips
Sr. V.P. Finance & C.F.O.

Address
100 International Blvd.
Etobicoke
ON
M9W 6J6
(416) 675-7661

Fax: (416) 213-4220
M0003011/G/16.2

For further company information, call Globe Information Services 1-800-268-9128 or (416) 585-5345

MOORE CORPORATION LIMITED

Exchanges	Price (Jun29'95)	30.37	Trailing P/E	8.29	Stock Symbol
TMN	Trailing Yield (%)	4.29	Trailing EPS	2.70	MCL

Period Ending	Dec94	Dec93	Dec92	Dec91	Dec90
Yearly Statistics	US	US	US	US	US
Price-Close	26.75	25.50	21.88	23.25	25.75
Price-High	28.50	28.13	26.13	32.63	35.63
Price-Low	22.50	19.13	17.63	21.75	25.00
P/E-Close	11.69	nm	nm	19.48	14.88
Dividends per Share	0.94	0.94	0.94	0.94	0.94
Dividend Yield (%)	4.81	4.77	5.22	4.63	4.26
Sales per Share	24.13	23.41	24.56	25.69	29.08
EPS before extra. item	1.22	(0.78)	(0.02)	0.91	1.27
Cash Flow per Share	1.98	2.58	1.76	2.10	2.78
Book Value per Share	13.71	13.19	14.83	16.21	16.05
O/S Common Shares	99,570	99,524	99,469	97,744	95,814
Total Revenue	2,447,060	2,352,429	2,454,764	2,544,275	2,854,072
Income before extra.	121,400	(77,606)	(2,327)	88,074	120,629
Cash Flow	197,325	256,474	174,099	203,642	265,062
Debt/Equity	0.08	0.07	0.07	0.06	0.06
Return on Capital (%)	12.40	(5.32)	2.27	9.02	13.45
Ret. on Com. Equity (%)	9.07	(5.57)	(0.15)	5.64	8.10
% Change Profit	256.4	(3,235.0)	(102.6)	(27.0)	(40.2)
% Change Revenue	4.0	(4.2)	(3.5)	(10.9)	2.9
% Change Assets	2.9	(2.3)	(4.5)	(2.2)	7.8

Preferred Div. Coverage	np	np	np
Total Div. Coverage	1.3	0.0	0.0
Interest Coverage	13.6	0.0	2.7
Current Ratio	2.3	2.2	3.0
Operating Margin	5.9	5.7	4.2
Asset Turnover	1.2	1.2	1.2
5 YEAR RATIOS (%)			
Return on Capital	6.4	8.1	13.2
Return on Com. Equity	3.4	4.6	8.7
Profit Growth	(9.7)	na	na
Revenue Growth	(2.5)	(1.9)	1.1
Asset Growth	0.2	1.3	0.8
BALANCE SHEET (000)			
Cash	266,865	261,737	311,993
Current Assets	1,009,714	1,010,441	1,063,144
Net Fixed Assets	607,096	617,341	655,665
Invest's & Advances	348,035	274,905	230,388
Total Assets	2,031,336	1,974,032	2,020,715
Short Term Debt	32,328	20,840	42,883
Current Liabilities	446,608	451,011	352,491
Long Term Debt	77,495	67,608	59,718
Total Liabilities	666,162	661,136	545,207
Total Equity	1,365,174	1,312,896	1,475,508
Total Liab. & Equity	2,031,336	1,974,032	2,020,715
CAPITAL (000)			
Total Debt	109,823	88,448	102,601
Preferred Equity	0	0	0
Common Equity	1,365,174	1,312,896	1,475,508

Business:

MOORE CORP. LTD. makes and distributes business forms and related services. The company operates in 58 countries with major markets in the United States, Canada, Europe, Australasia and South America. Its products include business forms, labels, equipment and electronic forms solutions. The company also provides information management services in direct and database management and business communication.

Date		EPS	DPS	Tot Rev	Inc Bex
Mar 95	US	1.77	0.24	904,771	181,464
Dec 94	US	0.39	0.24	652,623	39,193
Sep 94	US	0.31	0.24	591,493	30,510
Jun 94	US	0.23	0.24	584,527	25,440
Mar 94	US	0.26	0.24	619,647	26,257
Dec 93	US	(1.39)	0.24	604,492	(138,235)
Sep 93	US	0.17	0.24	573,277	16,500
Jun 93	US	0.21	0.24	577,438	20,968

Synopsis:

Moore Corporation Limited reported an increase in net earnings for the first quarter of 1995, compared to the first three months of 1994. Net earnings of $181.5-million represented an improvement of $155.2-million from the first quarter of 1994. Net earnings for the first quarter of 1995 includes a gain of $146.4-million after tax realized on the reduction of Moore's interest in Toppan Moore from 45% to 10%. Customer Communication Services revenues increased 9%, from $123-million for first quarter 1994 compared to $134-million for first quarter 1995 and was lead by the international sector.

Moore sold a 35% interest in Toppan Moore Co., Ltd., its Japanese joint venture, to its partner Toppan Printing Co., Ltd. of Japan for $355-million. The proceeds provide the company with an additional source of funds to invest in growth segments world-wide. Moore agreed to start a joint venture with Shanghai Jielong Industry Corporation Limited to make and market business forms and information handling systems for the Shanghai area. Moore will hold a 60% equity interest. Moore acquired a 20% equity interest in JetForm Corporation, the leader in open systems electronic forms software, for $18.7-million.

Moore announced with Electronic Data Systems Corp. of Dallas, two separate 10-year contracts worth up to $1-billion for Moore, to provide services to EDS, and up to $700-million for EDS, to provide services to Moore. Moore and Indigo NV of the Netherlands will work together to develop the markets for high-performance digital offset colour products.

Contributions to sales (segment operating profit) for 1994 by industry segment were: Forms, Systems and Services, 79% (74%); Customer Communication Services, 21% (26%). Contribution to sales (segment operating profit) for 1994 by geographic segment were: Canada, 8% (6%); United States, 61% (74%); Europe, 14% (10%); Latin America, 9% (7%); and Asia Pacific, 8% (3%).

Relative strength to TSE300 / Price / Volume (in 1000's of board lots)

Rank (Profit/Revenue/Assets)
41 46 74

Reto Braun
Chairman President & C.E.O.

Stephen A. Holinski
Sr. V.P. & C.F.O.

Address
1 First Canadian Place
P.O. Box 78
72nd Floor
Toronto
ON
M5X 1G5
(416) 364-2600
Fax: (416) 364-1667
M0005091/G/6.9.2

PHILIP ENVIRONMENTAL INC.

Exchanges	Price (Jun29'95)	9.62	Trailing P/E	12.50	Stock Symbol
TMQ	Trailing Yield (%)	0.00	Trailing EPS	0.77	**PEN**

Period Ending	Dec94	Dec93	Dec92	Dec91	Dec90
Yearly Statistics					
Price-Close	7.50	7.25	10.00	8.88	n t
Price-High	8.75	12.50	10.50	12.13	n t
Price-Low	6.50	6.25	7.75	7.75	n t
P/E-Close	10.00	12.08	16.67	17.40	n t
Dividends per Share	0.00	0.00	0.00	0.05	0.00
Dividend Yield (%)	0.00	0.00	0.00	0.56	0.00
Sales per Share	15.75	7.72	5.18	3.93	2.08
EPS before extra. item	0.75	0.60	0.60	0.51	0.55
Cash Flow per Share	1.94	1.11	1.10	0.80	0.55
Book Value per Share	6.95	6.43	5.38	4.44	1.86
O/S Common Shares	37,272	34,732	31,812	28,927	19,315
Total Revenue	572,560	255,297	157,665	102,439	36,816
Income before extra.	27,038	19,742	18,273	12,987	9,540
Cash Flow	70,165	36,541	33,314	20,481	9,540
Debt/Equity	1.62	1.53	0.66	0.59	0.84
Return on Capital (%)	10.26	8.80	14.36	18.86	39.97
Ret. on Com. Equity (%)	11.21	10.01	12.21	15.82	36.40
% Change Profit	37.0	8.0	40.7	36.1	4.4
% Change Revenue	124.3	61.9	53.9	178.2	16.5
% Change Assets	19.9	106.2	33.7	231.5	166.5

Preferred Div. Coverage	np	np	np	
Total Div. Coverage	na	na	na	
Interest Coverage	2.5	2.8	4.8	
Current Ratio	1.8	1.2	1.3	
Operating Margin	12.1	15.5	23.6	
Asset Turnover	0.7	0.4	0.5	

5 YEAR RATIOS (%)			
Return on Capital	18.4	na	na
Return on Com. Equity	17.1	na	na
Profit Growth	24.2	na	na
Revenue Growth	78.5	na	na
Asset Growth	96.3	na	na

BALANCE SHEET (000)			
Cash	15,804	11,279	230
Current Assets	204,958	127,603	45,397
Net Fixed Assets	336,517	294,941	186,212
Invest's & Advances	837	0	0
Total Assets	860,583	717,925	348,101
Short Term Debt	16,594	29,551	5,574
Current Liabilities	116,689	107,037	35,428
Long Term Debt	402,488	311,947	107,421
Total Liabilities	601,531	494,510	177,093
Total Equity	259,052	223,415	171,008
Total Liab. & Equity	860,583	717,925	348,101
CAPITAL (000)			
Total Debt	419,082	341,498	112,995
Preferred Equity	0	0	0
Common Equity	259,052	223,415	171,008

Business:

PHILIP ENVIRONMENTAL INC. is a fully integrated waste management company specializing in recycling and is one of Canada'a largest recyclers. The company has operations throughout Canada and the United States.

Date	EPS	DPS	Tot Rev	Inc Bex
Mar 95	0.12	0.00	173,965	4,520
Dec 94	0.20	0.00	169,582	7,370
Sep 94	0.26	0.00	145,223	9,248
Jun 94	0.19	0.00	141,576	6,792
Mar 94	0.10	0.00	116,179	3,628
Dec 93	0.23	0.00	112,878	7,900
Sep 93	0.22	0.00	55,859	7,086
Jun 93	0.15	0.00	49,968	4,752

Synopsis:

In May 1995, Philip Environmental said it will dump Intersan, the largest garbage-removal company in Quebec. Philip will use the expected $70-million from the sale to pay down debt and put money on the balance sheet. This will place the company in a strong position to pounce when strategic acquisitions appear.

Philip stated in May 1995 that it is in the process of repositioning itself. For example, it is considering more profitable recycling technologies. Beginning next year, Philip Environmental will recycle electric arc furnace (EAF) residues for the steel industry. It will convert these to base metal products including zinc, lead, and iron for resale. More than 750,000 tonnes of EAF residues are generated each year in North America and larger quantities are stockpiled. The company spent three years developing the process in conjunction with a Westinghouse Electric Corp. subsidiary and will begin construction of the first conversion unit in May. Because of demand for the metals, Philip expects the output to be pre-sold before the plant is operational next year.

In December 1994, Philip Environmental agreed to acquire the hazardous waste management assets of Northwest EnviroService Inc. of Seattle. The company expects that the acquired business will generate revenue in excess of $18-million (U.S.) a year.

In November 1994, Philip Environmental bought Delsan Environmental Group Inc. Philip would not disclose the total purchase price, but revealed it included the issuance of 919,842 common shares. The acquisition will accelerate the company's move into Delsan's market for a comprehensive demolition service that includes site clean-up and industrial recycling of materials. Delsan is expected to have sales next year of more than $35-million, making a positive impact on Philip Environmental's share profit. The acquisition of Delsan will increase Philip's staff by 200, to a total of 3,200 people.

Relative strength to TSE300

Price

Volume (in 1000's of board lots)

Rank (Profit/Revenue/Assets)
175   179   169

Howard Beck
Chairman

Allen Fracassi
President & C.E.O.

Marvin Boughton
Exec. V.P. & C.F.O.

Philip Fracassi
Exec. V.P. And C.O.O.

Address
651 Burlington Street East
P.O. Box 423
Depot 1
Hamilton
ON
L8L 7W2
(905) 544-6687
Fax: (905) 548-8444
P0003131/G/8.1

PREMDOR INC.

Exchanges	Price (Jun29'95)		10.25	Trailing P/E		12.97	Stock Symbol
TMN	Trailing Yield (%)		0.00	Trailing EPS		0.79	PDI

Period Ending	Dec94	Dec93	Dec92	Dec91	Dec90
Yearly Statistics					
Price-Close	10.38	15.13	8.88	5.75	1.70
Price-High	19.00	15.63	9.25	5.75	4.30
Price-Low	9.50	8.25	5.00	1.50	1.50
P/E-Close	13.30	26.54	31.70	nm	nm
Dividends per Share	0.00	0.00	0.00	0.00	0.04
Dividend Yield (%)	0.00	0.00	0.00	0.00	2.35
Sales per Share	20.63	16.56	13.53	14.36	17.58
EPS before extra. item	0.78	0.57	0.28	(0.09)	(0.14)
Cash Flow per Share	1.04	0.85	0.44	0.04	0.02
Book Value per Share	6.20	5.34	3.75	2.65	2.11
O/S Common Shares	36,318	35,874	32,346	26,182	13,622
Total Revenue	744,256	538,916	417,212	285,322	239,437
Income before extra.	28,177	18,447	8,516	(1,734)	(1,889)
Cash Flow	37,385	27,736	13,535	874	303
Debt/Equity	0.69	0.26	0.34	1.12	2.48
Return on Capital (%)	16.84	17.08	11.83	2.92	7.75
Ret. on Com. Equity (%)	13.52	11.80	8.93	(3.53)	(6.45)
% Change Profit	52.7	116.6	591.1	8.2	48.9
% Change Revenue	38.1	29.2	46.2	19.2	29.8
% Change Assets	54.1	45.0	14.9	53.9	(17.3)

Preferred Div. Coverage	np	np	np		
Total Div. Coverage	na	na	na		
Interest Coverage	8.0	7.0	4.2		
Current Ratio	3.5	2.7	2.4		
Operating Margin	7.0	6.4	4.4		
Asset Turnover	1.6	1.8	2.1		
5 YEAR RATIOS (%)					
Return on Capital	11.3	8.2	8.2		
Return on Com. Equity	4.9	(0.3)	(0.4)		
Profit Growth	105.7	40.6	8.0		
Revenue Growth	32.1	31.6	24.5		
Asset Growth	26.7	35.9	28.4		
BALANCE SHEET (000)					
Cash	16,475	6,949	0		
Current Assets	284,457	193,600	123,612		
Net Fixed Assets	134,748	85,763	66,301		
Invest's & Advances	1,894	2,276	2,357		
Total Assets	454,407	294,938	203,444		
Short Term Debt	10,821	20,850	11,626		
Current Liabilities	80,897	71,247	51,948		
Long Term Debt	143,630	28,570	29,677		
Total Liabilities	229,098	103,488	82,119		
Total Equity	225,309	191,450	121,325		
Total Liab. & Equity	454,407	294,938	203,444		
CAPITAL (000)					
Total Debt	154,451	49,420	41,303		
Preferred Equity	0	0	0		
Common Equity	225,309	191,450	121,325		

Business:

PREMDOR INC. manufactures and distributes wood and steel doors for residential construction, home repair, renovation, remodelling and commercial use. The company also distributes a complete line of wood mouldings in Canada.

Date	EPS	DPS	Tot Rev	Inc Bex
Mar 95	0.16	0.00	203,700	5,800
Dec 94	0.21	0.00	204,944	7,625
Sep 94	0.22	0.00	188,034	8,151
Jun 94	0.20	0.00	186,968	7,163
Mar 94	0.15	0.00	164,310	5,238
Dec 93	0.16	0.00	143,379	5,158
Sep 93	0.17	0.00	139,995	5,533
Jun 93	0.14	0.00	129,537	4,584

Synopsis:

Despite an overall slow down in North American economic activity and a large drop in housing starts, Premdor reported a 24% sales increase in the first quarter 1995 over the same period in 1994. Premdor said the increase was the result of its recent acquisitions and internal growth of 11.5%. Premdor expects home improvement expenditures to continue to rise and housing starts to show improvement as interest rates decline.

Premdor's strategy continues to focus on the manufacture and distribution of doors and expansion in international markets for these products. Consistent with this strategy, Premdor Inc. completed the purchase of Magri S.A. Of Thigonville, France, for approximately $4.5-million, in January 1995. A specialty manufacturer of plastic laminate interior doors, with annual sales of approximately $15-million, Magri S.A. is Premdor's third door manufacturing facility in France. Premdor feels the purchase of Magri complements existing product lines in France, and that European sales could exceed $75-million in 1995.

In March 1995, Premdor signed a letter of intent to form a 50-50 Joint Venture in Monterey, Mexico, with Grupo IMSA SA de CV. Premdor expects the joint venture to establish a mass production manufacturing facility in Monterey to produce both exterior steel and interior wood doors primarily for the Mexican residential and commercial markets. According to Premdor, Grupo IMSA is a leader in Mexico in the manufacture of steel and aluminum products, steel wall and roof panels, steel doors, and power storage and construction systems. Grupo IMSA's exterior steel door manufacturing operation, currently carried on by its Multypanel S.A. De. C.V. subsidiary, will be expanded and will form part of the joint venture along with a new interior wood door manufacturing operation. Total investment in the joint venture will reach about $10-million (U.S.).

Relative strength to TSE300

Price

Volume (in 1000's of board lots)

Rank (Profit/Revenue/Assets)
168   149   237

Saul M. Spears
Chairman

Philip S. Orsino
President & C.E.O.

Robert V. Tubbesing
V.P. & C.F.O.

Address
4120 Yonge Street
Suite 402
Willowdale
ON
M2P 2B8
(416) 250-8933

Fax: (416) 250-9269
P0000487/G/5.8

PRUDENTIAL STEEL LTD.

Exchanges	Price (Jun29'95)		11.37	Trailing P/E		5.60	Stock Symbol
T	Trailing Yield (%)		3.51	Trailing EPS		2.03	PTS

Period Ending	Dec94	Dec93	Dec92
Yearly Statistics			
Price-Close	12.88	n t	n t
Price-High	15.00	n t	n t
Price-Low	9.00	n t	n t
P/E-Close	6.10	n t	n t
Dividends per Share	4.90	3.00	2.00
Dividend Yield (%)	38.06	n t	n t
Sales per Share	21.47	16.20	7.96
EPS before extra. item	2.11	1.27	na
Cash Flow per Share	2.46	1.52	(0.05)
Book Value per Share	6.02	4.71	6.44
O/S Common Shares	10,000	10,000	10,000
Total Revenue	214,739	162,939	80,893
Income before extra.	21,096	12,653	(3,080)
Cash Flow	24,598	15,198	(504)
Debt/Equity	nd	0.15	0.09
Return on Capital (%)	57.81	31.69	na
Ret. on Com. Equity (%)	39.34	22.69	na
% Change Profit	66.7	510.8	na
% Change Revenue	31.8	101.4	na
% Change Assets	19.0	(4.2)	na

	Preferred Div. Coverage	Total Div. Coverage	Interest Coverage	Current Ratio	Operating Margin	Asset Turnover

Preferred Div. Coverage	np	np	np
Total Div. Coverage	0.4	0.4	0.0
Interest Coverage	1,002.8	na	na
Current Ratio	2.2	2.1	4.4
Operating Margin	15.4	11.6	(7.1)
Asset Turnover	2.3	2.1	1.0
5 YEAR RATIOS (%)			
Return on Capital	na	na	na
Return on Com. Equity	na	na	na
Profit Growth	na	na	na
Revenue Growth	na	na	na
Asset Growth	na	na	na
BALANCE SHEET (000)			
Cash	1,667	0	10,410
Current Assets	64,496	55,787	57,284
Net Fixed Assets	25,683	19,739	21,578
Invest's & Advances	0	0	0
Total Assets	91,911	77,207	80,596
Short Term Debt	0	7,225	5,864
Current Liabilities	29,180	27,026	13,009
Long Term Debt	0	0	0
Total Liabilities	31,734	30,126	16,168
Total Equity	60,177	47,081	64,428
Total Liab. & Equity	91,911	77,207	80,596
CAPITAL (000)			
Total Debt	0	7,225	5,864
Preferred Equity	0	0	0
Common Equity	60,177	47,081	64,428

Business:

PRUDENTIAL STEEL LTD. is a producer of carbon steel tubular products used in the oil and gas industry and is a producer of certain industrial products used in construction, mining, fabrication and agricultural industries.

Date	EPS	DPS	Tot Rev	Inc Bex
Mar 95	0.48	0.10	53,884	4,750
Dec 94	0.56	0.10	66,861	5,561
Sep 94	0.54	0.10	56,088	5,414
Jun 94	0.45	0.10	43,642	4,453
Mar 94	0.57	0.50	48,428	5,669
Dec 93	0.45	2.00	54,425	4,451
Sep 93	0.34	0.00	39,187	3,435
Jun 93	0.18	1.00	29,535	1,835

Synopsis:

With its No. 3 mill operating at close to designed capacity, Prudential Steel expects to derive cost benefits from the mill for the balance of the year. Prudential expects its costs for steel to increase through the second and third quarters of the year, even with recent steel price reductions in the U.S. With the relatively strong demand for energy related products, Prudential should be able to pass on most of its increased costs to customers.

Hollow structural sections (HSS) are round, square, or rectangular shaped steel tubes used in non-residential construction, as well as agriculture, mining, and metal fabricating. Until 1994, Prudential bought HSS of various shapes and sizes from outside producers. With the No. 3 mill in operation, Prudential is able to produce these products and increase its overall gross margin for the product. Prudential can use space from the planned 1995 closure of mill No. 1 as a storage facility for HSS products. This will allow it to consistently offer customers a rust-free product.

Sales revenues for the first quarter ended March 31, 1995, were up 11% from the same period last year to $53.88-million. Tonnage shipments of energy related products were virtually unchanged from the same period in 1994. Drilling continued strong in the first quarter 1995. Prudential, due to low levels of finished goods inventories that were insufficient to support the strong demand as a result of late delivery from some suppliers, showed a 26% drop in shipments of Energy Related Products over the previous quarter. The company's use of cash from operating activities in the first quarter of 1995 was $6.9-million, up from $2.3-million a year ago. Prudential intends to use this increased cash to build up inventory in early 1995. This would enable it to react promptly to customer requirements and improve customer service.

Prudential forecasts that demand for Energy Related Products will decline through the second quarter due to season drilling fluctuations. The company expects to operate at relatively high levels of activity despite the decline in drilling.

Rank (Profit/Revenue/Assets)
206   305   503

Joseph S. Badyk
Chairman

J. Donald Wilson
President & C.E.O.

R. Douglas McIntosh
Sr. V.P. & C.F.O.

Address
P.O. Box 1510
Calgary
AB
T2P 2L6
(403) 267-0345

Fax: (403) 265-3426
01003641/G/6.10

SCOTT PAPER LIMITED

Exchanges	Price (Jun29'95)			19 .37	Trailing P/E		176 .14	Stock Symbol
TMV	Trailing Yield (%)			0 .52	Trailing EPS		0 .11	**SPL**

Period Ending	Dec94	Dec93	Dec92	Dec91	Dec90
Yearly Statistics					
Price-Close	13 .00	10 .50	9 .50	19 .00	16 .75
Price-High	14 .50	14 .00	20 .00	23 .13	19 .50
Price-Low	10 .13	8 .88	8 .88	16 .63	15 .75
P/E-Close	130 .00	47 .73	nm	23 .46	18 .41
Dividends per Share	0 .10	0 .10	0 .40	0 .38	0 .34
Dividend Yield (%)	0 .77	0 .95	4 .21	2 .00	2 .03
Sales per Share	27 .98	26 .47	26 .15	28 .45	31 .28
EPS before extra. item	0 .10	0 .22	(0 .38)	0 .81	0 .91
Cash Flow per Share	1 .40	1 .94	1 .25	2 .59	2 .82
Book Value per Share	8 .47	8 .48	8 .36	9 .14	8 .71
O/S Common Shares	15 ,281	15 ,281	15 ,281	15 ,281	15 ,281
Total Revenue	427 ,618	404 ,488	399 ,590	434 ,791	477 ,993
Income before extra.	1 ,462	3 ,314	(5 ,792)	12 ,321	13 ,847
Cash Flow	21 ,428	29 ,688	19 ,175	39 ,535	43 ,135
Debt/Equity	1 .05	1 .14	1 .36	1 .14	1 .32
Return on Capital (%)	5 .23	6 .56	2 .18	12 .32	13 .64
Ret. on Com. Equity (%)	1 .13	2 .58	(4 .33)	9 .04	10 .75
% Change Profit	(55 .9)	157 .2	(147 .0)	(11 .0)	(22 .9)
% Change Revenue	5 .7	1 .2	(8 .1)	(9 .0)	7 .3
% Change Assets	1 .8	(4 .6)	(0 .3)	(2 .1)	3 .0

Date	EPS	DPS	Tot Rev	Inc Bex
Apr 95	0 .17	0 .03	105 ,939	2 ,608
Dec 94	0 .19	0 .03	107 ,783	2 ,850
Oct 94	(0 .43)	0 .03	108 ,604	(6 ,538)
Jul 94	0 .18	0 .03	106 ,129	2 ,737
Apr 94	0 .16	0 .03	105 ,122	2 ,413
Dec 93	0 .17	0 .03	97 ,542	2 ,577
Oct 93	0 .14	0 .03	104 ,183	2 ,100
Jul 93	0 .04	0 .03	101 ,517	651

Preferred Div. Coverage	np	np	np
Total Div. Coverage	1 .0	2 .2	0 .0
Interest Coverage	1 .2	1 .3	0 .4
Current Ratio	1 .0	1 .4	1 .2
Operating Margin	3 .3	4 .7	1 .6
Asset Turnover	1 .1	1 .0	1 .0
5 YEAR RATIOS (%)			
Return on Capital	8 .0	10 .9	14 .1
Return on Com. Equity	3 .8	6 .7	9 .2
Profit Growth	(39 .5)	(27 .2)	na
Revenue Growth	(0 .9)	5 .2	6 .7
Asset Growth	(0 .5)	11 .5	15 .2
BALANCE SHEET (000)			
Cash	44	48	48
Current Assets	110 ,621	99 ,310	107 ,678
Net Fixed Assets	286 ,294	292 ,055	303 ,802
Invest's & Advances	0	0	0
Total Assets	402 ,142	395 ,201	414 ,198
Short Term Debt	23 ,445	13 ,692	34 ,118
Current Liabilities	105 ,749	72 ,809	89 ,216
Long Term Debt	112 ,591	133 ,724	139 ,850
Total Liabilities	272 ,686	265 ,686	286 ,469
Total Equity	129 ,449	129 ,515	127 ,729
Total Liab. & Equity	402 ,142	395 ,201	414 ,198
CAPITAL (000)			
Total Debt	136 ,036	147 ,416	173 ,968
Preferred Equity	0	0	0
Common Equity	129 ,449	129 ,515	127 ,729

Business:

SCOTT PAPER LTD. makes and markets household and commercial paper products including bathroom tissue, paper towels and facial tissue. Plant facilities are located in New Westminster, British Columbia, and in Lennoxville, Crabtree, and Hull, Quebec. The company has sales offices across Canada.

Synopsis:

Scott Paper reported a slight improvement in income after taxes for the first three months of 1995, compared to the first quarter of 1994. After-tax earnings were $2,608,000 for the first three months of 1995 compared to $2,413,000 in the first quarter of 1994. The rising cost for fibre were offset by the cost savings from the 1994 restructuring program. Sales volumes were lower than the same period last year due mostly to production difficulties associated with the implementation of some parts of its plan. As a result of a thorough review of its business, Scott identified further cost reduction and business growth opportunities which it intends to pursue during 1995. Scott will incur a new restructuring charge of between $8-million and $10-million in the second quarter of 1995 but should achieve annual cost savings of between $12-million and $15-million as a result of these initiatives.

Scott's industry is plagued with over-capacity but operating rates in the Canadian tissue industry increased slightly in 1994 as a result of market growth and a decline in the Canadian dollar. Average operating rates were in the range of 84% to 86% of full capacity during 1994. This made it difficult to increase prices, as industry participants continued to seek opportunities to fill-out machine capacity. Selling prices remained relatively unchanged in 1994 over 1993, while volume of domestic sales of finished product grew by 7.2%.

Major productivity programs started in 1994 should reduce ongoing annual costs by $22-million. The restructuring plan involved the consolidation of manufacturing converting operations in eastern Canada from three sites to two sites. Operations at the two sites will be rebalanced along product lines and business segments. About 80% of the expected annual savings should be realized in 1995.

Relative strength to TSE300

Price

Volume (in 1000's of board lots)

Rank (Profit/Revenue/Assets)
614   208   250

Richard Nicolosi
Chairman

Lee Griffith
President & C.E.O.

David Erskine
Corp. V.P. & C.F.O.

Address
P.O. Box 3600
Suite 2300
1066 West Hastings Street
Vancouver
BC
V6B 3Y7
(604) 688-8131
Fax: (604) 643-5543
S0000990/G/6.9.1

SHAW INDUSTRIES LTD.

Exchanges	Price (Jun29'95)	10.37	Trailing P/E	7.35	Stock Symbol
T	Trailing Yield (%)	1.31	Trailing EPS	1.41	**SHL.A**

Period Ending	Dec94	Dec93	Dec92	Dec91	Dec90
Yearly Statistics					
Price-Close	12.87	12.50	10.00	14.83	9.00
Price-High	14.13	15.00	16.75	15.00	9.17
Price-Low	10.87	9.50	8.50	8.33	5.54
P/E-Close	8.58	18.38	20.83	9.43	10.31
Dividends per Share	0.14	0.12	0.12	0.11	0.09
Dividend Yield (%)	1.10	0.97	1.21	0.74	1.00
Sales per Share	14.88	11.07	9.93	14.09	10.27
EPS before extra. item	1.50	0.68	0.48	1.57	0.87
Cash Flow per Share	1.92	1.23	1.10	2.17	1.31
Book Value per Share	7.91	6.55	5.93	5.45	4.04
O/S Common Shares	20,062	20,600	20,538	20,452	20,088
Total Revenue	302,159	227,738	203,588	285,540	204,788
Income before extra.	30,452	14,056	9,862	31,883	17,411
Cash Flow	38,901	25,287	22,620	44,053	26,136
Debt/Equity	0.09	0.06	0.08	0.11	0.29
Return on Capital (%)	31.77	19.51	15.28	46.96	33.58
Ret. on Com. Equity (%)	20.75	10.95	8.45	33.11	23.85
% Change Profit	116.6	42.5	(69.1)	83.1	40.9
% Change Revenue	32.7	11.9	(28.7)	39.4	20.5
% Change Assets	28.2	10.7	(4.4)	20.1	14.9

Preferred Div. Coverage	np	np	np
Total Div. Coverage	11.0	5.8	4.1
Interest Coverage	81.3	77.5	45.1
Current Ratio	2.2	2.7	2.4
Operating Margin	16.6	11.8	9.6
Asset Turnover	1.3	1.3	1.3
5 YEAR RATIOS (%)			
Return on Capital	29.4	29.6	29.2
Return on Com. Equity	19.4	19.4	19.5
Profit Growth	19.8	17.9	28.1
Revenue Growth	12.1	13.6	18.2
Asset Growth	13.3	14.9	11.8
BALANCE SHEET (000)			
Cash	32,533	36,697	18,654
Current Assets	156,844	114,289	90,099
Net Fixed Assets	67,589	63,843	70,523
Invest's & Advances	4,404	0	0
Total Assets	229,379	178,895	161,644
Short Term Debt	14,589	7,573	8,827
Current Liabilities	70,194	42,806	36,966
Long Term Debt	274	742	1,073
Total Liabilities	70,685	44,061	39,830
Total Equity	158,694	134,834	121,814
Total Liab. & Equity	229,379	178,895	161,644
CAPITAL (000)			
Total Debt	14,863	8,315	9,900
Preferred Equity	0	0	0
Common Equity	158,694	134,834	121,814

Business:

SHAW INDUSTRIES LTD. supplies goods and services to the energy industry. The company has operations in North America, Saudi Arabia, the United Kingdom, and Australia. Products include drill string components, geophones, wire, cable, tubing, and heat-shrinkable polymeric products. Services include pipeline corrosion protection, thermal insulation systems, and pipeline inspection and repair.

Date	EPS	DPS	Tot Rev	Inc Bex
Mar 95	0.20	0.00	88,112	4,108
Dec 94	0.44	0.07	85,053	8,973
Sep 94	0.44	0.00	80,699	8,825
Jun 94	0.33	0.07	74,150	6,752
Mar 94	0.29	0.00	62,257	5,902
Dec 93	0.18	0.06	58,105	3,770
Sep 93	0.06	0.00	50,440	1,325
Jun 93	0.18	0.06	59,249	3,654

Synopsis:

Shaw Industries had an excellent year in 1994. Consolidated revenue reached a new record of $302.2-million compared to $227.7-million during 1993. The record performance, a level last achieved in 1991, resulted from a surge of activity in the Canadian energy sector in combination with improved performance at Shaw's foreign operations. The strategy of diversifying the core businesses in the energy industry along with an effort to expand internationally has proven successful. The capabilities and competitiveness of Shaw Industries will improve with these changes together with the restructuring of the company's operating divisions, implemented early in 1994. Shaw hopes to take advantage of the energy industry's growing demand for new equipment and technologies needed to maintain the increased levels of consumption anticipated during this decade.

With the acquisition of an equity interest in Arabian Pipecoating Company Ltd. in Saudi Arabia, the pipe coating division moved into international markets. Shaw established a joint venture with this pipe coating company to undertake a major offshore project in Thailand, providing the division with a major foothold in the rapidly growing Far Eastern pipeline market. The international presence of other divisions also expanded last year. Canusa secured major pipeline projects in the Middle East, North Africa, and Latin America. Guardian's facility in Scotland added capacity, while Shawflex increased its distribution and marketing capabilities in the U.S.

Shaw merged its three existing business units into two, in 1994. Shaw Pipe Protection, OMSCO Industries, and Guardian Oilfield Services were combined under Pipeline and Tubular Products. Mark Products, Canusa, Canusa-EMI, and Shawflex were combined under Energy Products.

Relative strength to TSE300

Price

Volume (in 1000's of board lots)

Rank (Profit/Revenue/Assets)
157   257   332

Leslie E. Shaw
Chairman

Geoffrey F. Hyland
President & C.E.O.

B.J. Conroy
V.P. Finance

Address
25 Bethridge Road
Rexdale
ON
M9W 1M7
(416) 743-7111

Fax: (416) 743-8194

S0001899/G/6.10

SNC-LAVALIN GROUP INC.

Exchanges	Price (Jun29'95)	26.00	Trailing P/E	14.52	Stock Symbol
TM	Trailing Yield (%)	0.92	Trailing EPS	1.79	SNC.A

Period Ending	Dec94	Dec93	Dec92	Dec91	Dec90
Yearly Statistics					
Price-Close	22.75	18.75	10.50	16.25	13.63
Price-High	23.00	19.75	19.00	20.00	14.63
Price-Low	14.50	9.88	7.88	11.63	9.38
P/E-Close	13.00	17.36	16.41	47.79	6.52
Dividends per Share	0.32	0.23	0.18	0.36	0.34
Dividend Yield (%)	1.41	1.23	1.71	2.22	2.50
Sales per Share	54.10	53.03	51.08	46.39	41.40
EPS before extra. item	1.75	1.08	0.64	0.34	2.09
Cash Flow per Share	3.34	3.03	2.35	2.13	3.91
Book Value per Share	14.09	12.55	11.66	11.22	9.33
O/S Common Shares	15,677	15,573	14,670	14,514	11,087
Total Revenue	857,278	803,646	758,418	581,411	447,628
Income before extra.	27,331	16,241	9,309	4,197	22,893
Cash Flow	52,215	45,598	34,421	26,723	42,256
Debt/Equity	0.05	0.23	0.67	1.00	0.99
Return on Capital (%)	21.15	13.76	9.87	7.62	24.42
Ret. on Com. Equity (%)	13.13	8.87	5.58	3.15	24.64
% Change Profit	68.3	74.5	121.8	(81.7)	(12.6)
% Change Revenue	6.7	6.0	30.4	29.9	22.7
% Change Assets	23.2	6.8	(4.0)	90.0	14.7
Preferred Div. Coverage	np	np	np		
Total Div. Coverage	7.6	4.6	3.5		
Interest Coverage	14.0	4.6	2.3		
Current Ratio	1.2	1.2	1.1		
Operating Margin	5.3	5.0	3.6		
Asset Turnover	1.1	1.2	1.2		
5 YEAR RATIOS (%)					
Return on Capital	15.4	15.6	9.8		
Return on Com. Equity	11.1	15.9	4.9		
Profit Growth	0.9	11.7	na		
Revenue Growth	18.5	20.1	13.0		
Asset Growth	22.4	17.6	12.7		
BALANCE SHEET (000)					
Cash	187,102	117,450	32,160		
Current Assets	622,342	445,845	378,844		
Net Fixed Assets	98,431	129,094	140,336		
Invest's & Advances	26,064	13,821	13,585		
Total Assets	793,357	643,753	602,506		
Short Term Debt	2,029	3,214	34,809		
Current Liabilities	525,013	384,235	338,625		
Long Term Debt	9,140	41,288	79,604		
Total Liabilities	572,549	448,359	431,478		
Total Equity	220,808	195,394	171,028		
Total Liab. & Equity	793,357	643,753	602,506		
CAPITAL (000)					
Total Debt	11,169	44,502	114,413		
Preferred Equity	0	0	0		
Common Equity	220,808	195,394	171,028		

Business:

SNC-LAVALIN GROUP INC. provides engineering, procurement, construction and project management services in Canada and abroad. SNC Industrial Technologies Inc. makes products for the military, para-military, and industrial markets worldwide. Securiplex Technologies produces electronic fire and control systems for naval and industrial markets worldwide.

Date	EPS	DPS	Tot Rev	Inc Bex
Mar 95	0.41	0.10	217,506	6,449
Dec 94	0.35	0.09	286,301	5,473
Sep 94	0.46	0.07	175,225	7,187
Jun 94	0.57	0.07	217,820	8,868
Mar 94	0.37	0.05	180,038	5,803
Dec 93	0.25	0.05	216,065	3,879
Sep 93	0.23	0.05	225,498	3,553
Jun 93	0.43	0.05	183,752	6,366

Synopsis:

In May 1995, SNC-Lavalin signed an agreement with the government of Kazakhstan to build a $476-million (U.S.) oil processing plant in the northwestern region of the country. The plant will separate sulphur and gas from sour crude produced at the Zhanazhol oil fields. Output from Zhanazhol is set to rise to five million tonnes a year from two million within three years of the project's completion.

In May, SNC-Lavalin's board authorized a normal course issuer bid to purchase up to 1,441,479 class A subordinate voting shares, representing about 10% of the public float. Although it ranks third among the top 10 world engineering companies in its return on average shareholders' equity, its price-earnings ratio of 12 to 13 times is well below its publicly traded competitors. Some competitors have ratios of more than 21 times earnings. The company said that part of the problem is that its shares are illiquid and trade only on the Toronto and Montreal stock exchanges. For that reason, it may list in the United States.

In January, Libya's Implementation Authority of the Great Man-Made River awarded SNC-Lavalin a contract valued at $230-million (U.S.) to build water wells. Work began in March, 95 and is scheduled to be completed within 26 months. In December 1994, SNC-Lavalin won a turnkey contract to build an international airport in the northwest Kenyan town of Eldoret, 400 kilometres from Nairobi. The Kenyan government contract has an estimated value of $115-million.

In November 1994, SNC-Lavalin International Inc. signed a memorandum of agreement with China Newtech Development & Trade Corp. to provide technology, engineering, procurement of equipment, and certain other services to the Dandong pulp mill in the province of Liaoning, China. The capital value of the project is estimated at more than $150-million. The company's fees will range between 10% and 15% of the capital cost of the project.

Relative strength to TSE300 / Price / Volume (in 1000's of board lots)

Rank (Profit/Revenue/Assets)
174   127   177

William I.M. Turner
Chairman

Guy Saint-Pierre
President & C.E.O.

Pierre Robitaille
Exec. V.P. & C.F.O.

Taro Alepian
Exec. V.P.

Address
2 Place Felix-Martin
Montreal
PQ
H2Z 1Z3
(514) 393-1000

Fax: (514) 875-4877
S0019889/G/7.3

ST. LAWRENCE CEMENT INC.

Exchanges	Price (Jun29'95)	9.00	Trailing P/E	29.03	Stock Symbol
TM	Trailing Yield (%)	0.00	Trailing EPS	0.31	**ST.A**

Period Ending	Dec94	Dec93	Dec92	Dec91	Dec90
Yearly Statistics					
Price-Close	9.88	10.75	6.63	12.25	12.75
Price-High	12.88	11.75	13.00	17.00	19.63
Price-Low	9.00	5.00	6.50	11.88	11.00
P/E-Close	32.92	nm	nm	nm	21.25
Dividends per Share	0.00	0.00	0.38	0.76	0.76
Dividend Yield (%)	0.00	0.00	5.73	6.20	5.96
Sales per Share	13.08	11.61	10.89	12.33	15.47
EPS before extra. item	0.30	(0.20)	(0.94)	(0.14)	0.60
Cash Flow per Share	1.13	0.62	(0.20)	0.71	1.51
Book Value per Share	7.32	7.00	7.19	8.42	9.14
O/S Common Shares	44,137	43,880	43,551	42,252	40,810
Total Revenue	575,660	507,333	467,085	504,479	629,970
Income before extra.	13,679	(7,836)	(39,869)	(5,728)	24,194
Cash Flow	49,668	27,259	(8,415)	29,106	61,470
Debt/Equity	0.53	0.76	0.82	0.62	0.47
Return on Capital (%)	7.33	1.42	(6.94)	2.02	11.55
Ret. on Com. Equity (%)	4.12	(2.75)	na	(1.57)	6.45
% Change Profit	274.6	80.3	(596.0)	(123.7)	(66.4)
% Change Revenue	13.5	8.6	(7.4)	(19.9)	(13.4)
% Change Assets	(3.5)	(4.6)	2.4	2.4	0.5

Preferred Div. Coverage	19.5	0.0	na
Total Div. Coverage	19.5	0.0	0.0
Interest Coverage	2.7	0.5	0.0
Current Ratio	2.2	2.8	2.9
Operating Margin	6.8	1.6	(5.8)
Asset Turnover	0.9	0.7	0.6
5 YEAR RATIOS (%)			
Return on Capital	3.1	7.0	14.0
Return on Com. Equity	na	na	na
Profit Growth	(28.3)	na	na
Revenue Growth	(4.6)	(7.1)	(7.7)
Asset Growth	(0.6)	1.3	5.0
BALANCE SHEET (000)			
Cash	0	0	0
Current Assets	218,106	219,065	231,975
Net Fixed Assets	384,826	391,081	412,916
Invest's & Advances	36,512	56,585	62,437
Total Assets	672,333	696,542	729,955
Short Term Debt	1,440	2,702	3,510
Current Liabilities	100,020	77,564	81,273
Long Term Debt	174,624	237,614	260,177
Total Liabilities	339,145	379,290	406,825
Total Equity	333,188	317,252	323,130
Total Liab. & Equity	672,333	696,542	729,955
CAPITAL (000)			
Total Debt	176,064	240,316	263,687
Preferred Equity	10,003	10,003	10,003
Common Equity	323,185	307,249	313,127

Business:

ST. LAWRENCE CEMENT INC. manufactures and distributes cement, concrete and aggregates to markets in Quebec, Ontario, the Maritimes and the eastern United States. Operations include cement and ready-mix concrete plants, distribution terminals and quarries and sand pits. Holderbank Financiere Glaris Ltd. of Switzerland, through a subsidiary, controls 60% of the company's shares.

Date	EPS	DPS	Tot Rev	Inc Bex
Mar 95	(0.30)	0.00	73,892	(12,968)
Dec 94	0.13	0.00	174,801	5,673
Sep 94	0.29	0.00	197,481	12,964
Jun 94	0.19	0.00	149,000	8,600
Mar 94	(0.31)	0.00	54,400	(13,500)
Dec 93	0.04	0.00	144,333	2,064
Sep 93	0.08	0.00	174,000	3,900
Jun 93	0.01	0.00	131,200	500

Synopsis:

Despite two work stoppages during labour negotiations at its Mississauga cement plant, St. Lawrence Cement significantly improved its first quarter revenue results from $54.5-million in 1994 to $73.9-million in 1995. This increase was due to the inclusion of joint venture revenues from infrastructure work in Ontario as well as higher cement sales volumes and prices in all markets, particularly those in the U.S. The company expects continued improvement in shipment volumes and cement prices together with expanding participation in joint ventures for large scale infrastructure work in the Toronto region. This should lead to further improvement in 1995 revenue figures.

During the fall of 1994 St. Lawrence Cement introduced a "Better Cost Management" program to encourage employees to analyze and improve costs on a continuous basis. This program will be implemented in all units during 1995 and will become permanent.

The company is in the process of introducing an integrated information system for the entire organization. This system conversion should take two years and will facilitate the daily management of company operations. In 1994, St. Lawrence Cement invested $35.8-million in its operations. These expenditures included a $2-million upgrade of the company ready-mix truck fleet, and another $1.4-million spent to automate the Milton Quarry in Ontario. The company looked towards long term development through the $3-million purchase of new stone reserves in both Canada and the United States.

Despite a slow economic recovery St. Lawrence Cement ended 1994 with good earnings. These results are due to better market conditions and the benefits of initiatives undertaken in 1993 and developed throughout 1994. While the Canadian markets showed only marginal signs of improvement, the U.S. markets posted a significant rise in sales. This kept the company's two U.S. cement plants in a sold out position for most of the year.

Rank (Profit/Revenue/Assets)
257   176   195

Peter Byland
Chairman

Frank J. Dewitt
President & C.E.O.

Guy Turgeon
Sr. V.P. & C.F.O.

Address
1945 Graham Boulevard
Mont-Royal
PQ
H3R 1H1
(514) 340-1881

Fax: (514) 342-8154
S0000263/G/6.6

UNICAN SECURITY SYSTEMS LTD.

Exchanges	Price (Jun29'95)		25.87	Trailing P/E		15.13	Stock Symbol
TM	Trailing Yield (%)		0.65	Trailing EPS		1.71	UCS.B

Period Ending	Jun94	Jun93	Jun92	Jun91	Jun90
Yearly Statistics					
Price-Close	20.00	17.50	9.25	8.50	9.00
Price-High	23.63	17.50	9.25	9.13	11.25
Price-Low	17.00	9.00	7.75	6.25	9.00
P/E-Close	12.35	16.36	14.92	56.67	50.00
Dividends per Share	0.14	0.11	0.10	0.10	0.10
Dividend Yield (%)	0.70	0.63	1.08	1.18	1.11
Sales per Share	20.13	19.03	16.94	15.94	16.82
EPS before extra. item	1.62	1.07	0.62	0.15	0.18
Cash Flow per Share	2.34	1.97	1.67	1.01	1.08
Book Value per Share	9.17	7.67	5.81	5.25	5.24
O/S Common Shares	8,460	8,434	7,434	7,434	7,388
Total Revenue	173,123	145,402	126,780	118,146	124,498
Income before extra.	13,696	8,108	4,612	1,076	1,332
Cash Flow	19,750	14,912	12,443	7,481	7,983
Debt/Equity	0.34	0.41	0.87	1.13	1.22
Return on Capital (%)	22.72	17.91	13.01	8.84	10.25
Ret. on Com. Equity (%)	19.25	15.03	11.22	2.77	3.43
% Change Profit	68.9	75.8	328.6	(19.2)	(70.9)
% Change Revenue	19.1	14.7	7.3	(5.1)	(1.1)
% Change Assets	14.9	11.8	(2.9)	(2.6)	(4.0)

Preferred Div. Coverage	np	np	np	
Total Div. Coverage	12.1	9.8	6.2	
Interest Coverage	14.3	5.5	2.9	
Current Ratio	2.8	3.2	2.2	
Operating Margin	11.5	10.0	8.4	
Asset Turnover	1.3	1.3	1.2	
5 YEAR RATIOS (%)				
Return on Capital	14.5	13.1	12.5	
Return on Com. Equity	10.3	9.0	8.6	
Profit Growth	24.5	12.4	(3.6)	
Revenue Growth	6.5	5.2	4.4	
Asset Growth	3.1	3.5	5.3	
BALANCE SHEET (000)				
Cash	4,669	8,527	0	
Current Assets	84,145	71,866	59,109	
Net Fixed Assets	39,436	35,410	36,913	
Invest's & Advances	3,101	3,153	2,675	
Total Assets	131,185	114,143	102,090	
Short Term Debt	6,716	5,568	11,561	
Current Liabilities	29,559	22,328	26,476	
Long Term Debt	19,346	20,718	25,960	
Total Liabilities	53,586	49,431	58,876	
Total Equity	77,599	64,712	43,214	
Total Liab. & Equity	131,185	114,143	102,090	
CAPITAL (000)				
Total Debt	26,062	26,286	37,521	
Preferred Equity	0	0	0	
Common Equity	77,599	64,712	43,214	

Business:

UNICAN SECURITY SYSTEMS LTD. is the parent of a group of international companies engaged in the manufacture of security products and zinc die cast hardware.

Date	EPS	DPS	Tot Rev	Inc Bex
Mar 95	0.39	0.00	51,903	3,294
Dec 94	0.44	0.00	48,819	3,698
Sep 94	0.37	0.17	45,714	3,153
Jun 94	0.51	0.00	47,089	4,390
Mar 94	0.32	0.00	42,657	2,703
Dec 93	0.40	0.14	46,264	3,386
Sep 93	0.38	0.00	35,923	3,217
Jun 93	0.14	0.00	107,629	674

Synopsis:

Unican Security Systems Ltd. continued to show increases in the third quarter ended March 31, 1995. Its sales were $145.9-million, an increase of 19% over the same period in 1994. All sectors of the company recorded significant sales increases. All business units are currently operating close to capacity, and building expansion plans are currently being considered for two facilities to accommodate continued growth.

During fiscal 1994, Unican's sales of electronic key and card-based security systems was $19.5-million, nearly four times the previous year's sales. This trend has continued in 1995 as sales of electronic hotel locks accelerated. The company has undertaken major efforts to increase production to meet the sales volume, and are now producing a significant amount of the printed circuit boards in-house.

Unican is one of the few companies which can make a completed device or component from molten metal to its finished state in one facility. The company's mill located in Rocky Mount, North Carolina, is the only company in the world that produces in-house metal for key blanks and then reuses all the on-site waste. Unican believes that this in-house capability also stimulated the development of ILCO SILVER, which combines copper, zinc, and nickel. Its excellent appearance and mechanical properties are contributing to its acceptance by leading lockmakers in Europe, Japan, and the United States. The company is increasing its penetration into the original equipment manufacturer markets with a number of its products, mostly key blanks and contract die castings.

Rank (Profit/Revenue/Assets)
256   334   421

Aaron M. Fish
Chairman & C.E.O.

Peter M. Blaikie
President & C.O.O.

Carl Emond
V.P. Finance

Address
7301 Decarie Boulevard
Montreal
PQ
H4P 2G7
(514) 735-5411

Fax: (514) 735-0428
U0000354/G/6.10

Report on Business 1000

20/20 FINANCIAL CORPORATION

(Public)   INVESTMENT COMPANIES AND FUNDS
Exchanges: T M   Stock Symbol: TTF
Suite 500, 2010 Winston Park Drive, Oakville, ON,
L6H 5R7   (905) 829-2020
20/20 FINANCIAL CORPORATION is a holding company which conducts its business through 20/20 Group Financial Inc., a mutual fund management company. 20/20 Group Financial Inc. is in the business of sponsoring, managing and distributing mutual funds in Canada.
Larry R. Lunn, Chairman

TOTAL ASSETS ($000)	72,025
TOTAL REVENUE ($000)	62,374
NET INCOME ($000)	(2,116)
EMPLOYEES	4
RANK (Profit/Revenue/Assets)	858/500/557

3M CANADA INC.

(Private)   MISC. CONSUMER PRODUCTS
1840 Oxford Street East, P.O. Box 5757, London, ON,
N6A 4T1   (519) 451-2500
3M CANADA INC. is a diversified manufacturing company.
R.L. Harms, President & General Manager

TOTAL ASSETS ($000)	401,700
TOTAL REVENUE ($000)	709,597
NET INCOME ($000)	30,411
EMPLOYEES	2,071

A & A FOODS LTD.

(Public)   WHOLESALE DISTRIBUTORS
Exchanges: V   Stock Symbol: AA
1560 Broadway Street, Port Coquitlam, BC, V3C 6E6 (604) 942-6613
A & A FOODS LTD. is involved in the importing, manufacturing, and distribution of specialty cheese and food products. The company through its subsidiaries is also involved in real estate development.
Giovanni Canporese, Chairman President & C.E.O.

TOTAL ASSETS ($000)	19,055
TOTAL REVENUE ($000)	11,826
NET INCOME ($000)	(2,209)
EMPLOYEES	60
RANK (Profit/Revenue/Assets)	861/782/879

A & W FOOD SERVICES OF CANADA LTD.

(Private)   FOOD SERVICES
171 West Esplanade, Suite 300, North Vancouver, BC,
V7M 3K9   (604) 988-2141
A & W FOOD SERVICES OF CANADA LTD. is a franchisor and operator of fast food hamburger restaurants and a franchisor and marketer of soft drinks. The company is wholly owned by U L Canada Inc.
J.J. Mooney, President

TOTAL ASSETS ($000)	na
TOTAL REVENUE ($000)	317,000
NET INCOME ($000)	na
EMPLOYEES	3,259

A.G.F. MANAGEMENT LIMITED

(Public)   INVESTMENT COMPANIES AND FUNDS
Exchanges: T   Stock Symbol: AGF.PR.B
31st Floor, TD Bank Tower, Toronto-Dominion Centre, Toronto, ON,
M5K 1E9   (416) 367-1900

A.G.F. MANAGEMENT LIMITED is engaged in the field of investment management. The company has a diversified group of funds designed to meet a variety of investment objectives, including aggressive growth, stable growth, and high income. The funds provide professional management of investments in Canada, the U.S., Europe, Japan, and other countries in Southeast Asia.
C. Warren Goldring, Chairman & C.E.O.

TOTAL ASSETS ($000)	218,020
TOTAL REVENUE ($000)	80,338
NET INCOME ($000)	15,898
EMPLOYEES	286
RANK (Profit/Revenue/Assets)	238/454/340

A.L. VAN HOUTTE LTEE

(Public)   FOOD PROCESSING
Exchanges: M   Stock Symbol: VH
8300 - 19th Avenue, Montreal, PQ, H1Z 4J8   (514) 593-7711
A.L. VAN HOUTTE LTEE operates a roasting and distribution of coffee business. The company also operates, either directly or via franchises, 84 cafe-bars and cafe-bistros.
Pierre Van Houtte, Chairman of the Board

TOTAL ASSETS ($000)	52,917
TOTAL REVENUE ($000)	44,791
NET INCOME ($000)	4,011
EMPLOYEES	75
RANK (Profit/Revenue/Assets)	465/571/619

A.R.C. RESINS INTERNATIONAL CORP.

(Public)   PRECIOUS METALS
Exchanges: V   Stock Symbol: ASR
Suite 850, 885 Dunsmuir St., Vancouver, BC,
V6C 1N5   (604) 681-9100
A.R.C. RESINS INTERNATIONAL CORP. is involved in the acquisition, exploration, and development of precious metal properties.
T.H. Reissner, Chairman

TOTAL ASSETS ($000)	16,012
TOTAL REVENUE ($000)	10,818
NET INCOME ($000)	(1,086)
EMPLOYEES	50
RANK (Profit/Revenue/Assets)	825/791/934

ABBEY WOODS DEVELOPMENTS LTD.

(Public)   DEVELOPERS
Exchanges: T V   Stock Symbol: AWD
Suite 700, 1177 West Hastings Street, Vancouver, BC,
V6E 2K3   (604) 685-2868
ABBEY WOODS DEVELOPMENTS LTD. is a Canadian company that operates as a property investor and developer. The company develops commercial and residential properties through subsidiaries as well as through joint ventures and partnerships.
Kuok Khoon Ho, Chairman

TOTAL ASSETS ($000)	27,133
TOTAL REVENUE ($000)	10,363
NET INCOME ($000)	211
EMPLOYEES	10
RANK (Profit/Revenue/Assets)	734/798/799

ABER RESOURCES LTD.

See page 27 for a full company profile.

ABITIBI-PRICE INC.
See page 151 for a full company profile.

ABL CANADA INC.
(Public)   ELECTRICAL & ELECTRONIC
Exchanges: T M   Stock Symbol: ABL
8550 Cote de Liesse, St-Laurent, PQ, H4T 1H2   (514) 344-5432
ABL CANADA INC. designs, manufactures and markets a diversified range of products for the telecommunications industry that enables the delivery of multimedia services. Among it products are network access systems, including digital audio and video codecs, fibre optic multiplexers as well as broadband switches and network management systems.
Walter Steel, Chairman

TOTAL ASSETS ($000)	27,822
TOTAL REVENUE ($000)	11,561
NET INCOME ($000)	(23,432)
EMPLOYEES	148
RANK (Profit/Revenue/Assets)	974/784/791

ACC TELENTERPRISES LTD.
(Public)   TELECOMMUNICATIONS
Exchanges: T M   Stock Symbol: ACL
Suite 401, 5343 Dundas Street West, Etobicoke, ON,
M9B 6K5   (416) 236-3636
ACC TELENTERPRISES LTD. is a telecommunications holding company providing, through wholly owned subsidiaries, switched long distance and leased line voice and data services to business and residential customers in Ontario, Quebec, British Columbia, Alberta and Manitoba.
Richard T. Sayers, Chairman

TOTAL ASSETS ($000)	41,951
TOTAL REVENUE ($000)	95,531
NET INCOME ($000)	(11,002)
EMPLOYEES	181
RANK (Profit/Revenue/Assets)	948/429/682

ACCORD FINANCIAL CORP.
(Public)   FINANCE AND LEASING
Exchanges: T V   Stock Symbol: ACD
18th Floor, 77 Bloor Street West, Toronto, ON,
M5S 1M2   (416) 961-0007
ACCORD FINANCIAL CORP. through its subsidiaries in Canada and the United States, provides factoring services to companies primarily in textiles, apparel, temporary staff placement, transportation, footwear, floor coverings, toys and sporting goods. These services include credit investigation and guarantees, receivables collection, record-keeping, and financing.
Ken Hitzig, President

TOTAL ASSETS ($000)	32,140
TOTAL REVENUE ($000)	18,610
NET INCOME ($000)	2,631
EMPLOYEES	90
RANK (Profit/Revenue/Assets)	533/725/754

ACCUGRAPH CORPORATION
(Public)   COMPUTER SOFTWARE & PROCESSING
Exchanges: T   Stock Symbol: ACU.A
5822 Cromo Drive, El Paso, TX, 79912   (915) 581-1171
ACCUGRAPH CORP. is engaged in design and development of computer-based software products, specifically addressing the computer-aided design, computer-aided manufacturing, and computer-aided

engineering markets. The company sells its software in combination with computer hardware purchased from third party manufacturers.
Hector Holguin, Chairman & C.E.O.

TOTAL ASSETS ($000)	14,740 (US)
TOTAL REVENUE ($000)	24,880 (US)
NET INCOME ($000)	5,090 (US)
EMPLOYEES	100
RANK (Profit/Revenue/Assets)	372/625/864

ACIER LEROUX INC.
(Public)   WHOLESALE DISTRIBUTORS
Exchanges: M   Stock Symbol: LER
1331 Graham Bell Street, Boucherville, PQ, J4B 6A1 (514) 641-4360
ACIER LEROUX INC. operates one of the principal steel service centres in Quebec. In this capacity the company acts as a distributor of steel products and also processes certain products in order to meet the needs of its clientele.
Raymond Leroux, President & C.E.O.

TOTAL ASSETS ($000)	127,872
TOTAL REVENUE ($000)	162,150
NET INCOME ($000)	6,122
EMPLOYEES	450
RANK (Profit/Revenue/Assets)	389/346/432

ACKLANDS LIMITED
See page 401 for a full company profile.

ADRIAN RESOURCES LTD.
(Public)   PRECIOUS METALS
Exchanges: T V   Stock Symbol: ADL
11th Floor, 808 West Hastings Street, Box 10, Vancouver, BC,
V6C 2X4   (604) 688-3008
ADRIAN RESOURCES LTD. is engaged in the exploration and development of mineral prospects in British Columbia and the Yukon.
Murray Pezim, Chairman

TOTAL ASSETS ($000)	24,229
TOTAL REVENUE ($000)	144
NET INCOME ($000)	(2,731)
EMPLOYEES	12
RANK (Profit/Revenue/Assets)	873/984/824

ADS ASSOCIES LTEE
(Public)   MANAGEMENT AND DIVERSIFIED
Exchanges: M   Stock Symbol: AAL
1220 Boul. Lebourgneuf, Bureau 200, Quebec, PQ,
G2K 2G4   (418) 626-1688
ADS ASSOCIES LTEE is a multidisciplinary group operating mainly in the engineering and construction, technology, and manufacturing sectors.
Paul Drouin, Chairman & C.E.O.

TOTAL ASSETS ($000)	27,235
TOTAL REVENUE ($000)	39,630
NET INCOME ($000)	1,457
EMPLOYEES	350
RANK (Profit/Revenue/Assets)	615/593/798

ADVANCED GRAVIS COMPUTER TECHNOLOGY LTD.
(Public)   ELECTRICAL & ELECTRONIC
Exchanges: T V Q   Stock Symbol: AED
3750 North Fraser Way, Suite 101, Burnaby, BC,
V5J 5E9   (604) 431-5020
ADVANCED GRAVIS COMPUTER TECHNOLOGY LTD. designs, develops, manufactures and markets high quality computer input devices and accessories for entertainment applications. The company distributes its products in the United States, Canada, Europe and Asia.
Grant Russell, C.E.O.

TOTAL ASSETS ($000)	16,237
TOTAL REVENUE ($000)	23,645
NET INCOME ($000)	(776)
EMPLOYEES	230
RANK (Profit/Revenue/Assets)	811/693/930

ADVANCED MATERIAL RESOURCES LIMITED
(Public)   NON-BASE METAL MINING
Exchanges: T Z   Stock Symbol: QSA
Suite 810, 121 King Street West, Toronto, ON,
M5H 3T9   (416) 367-8588
ADVANCED MATERIAL RESOURCES LIMITED has secured control of and operates modern high quality rare earth processing facilities in China.
Peter V. Gundy, Chairman President & C.E.O.

TOTAL ASSETS ($000)	24,927 (US)
TOTAL REVENUE ($000)	5,121 (US)
NET INCOME ($000)	(1,153) (US)
EMPLOYEES	600
RANK (Profit/Revenue/Assets)	838/833/729

ADVENTURE ELECTRONICS INC.
(Public)   SPECIALTY STORES
Exchanges: T M   Stock Symbol: AVN
8155 Larrey Street, Ville d'Anjou, PQ, H1J 2L5   (514) 352-5000
ADVENTURE ELECTRONICS INC. is a specialty retailer of brand-name consumer electronics products in the provinces of Quebec and Ontario.
Robert Fragman, Chairman President & C.E.O.

TOTAL ASSETS ($000)	93,008
TOTAL REVENUE ($000)	236,982
NET INCOME ($000)	8,002
EMPLOYEES	1,400
RANK (Profit/Revenue/Assets)	337/293/499

AETNA LIFE INSURANCE COMPANY OF CANADA
(Private)   INSURANCE - LIFE
P.O. Box 120, 79 Wellington St. W., Aetna Tower TD Center,
Toronto, ON, M5H 1N9   (416) 864-8000
AETNA LIFE INSURANCE COMPANY OF CANADA is a major Canadian life insurance company offering a comprehensive range of life, annuity and health products to individuals and groups across Canada.
Fraser M. Fell, Chairman

TOTAL ASSETS ($000)	2,138,600
TOTAL REVENUE ($000)	536,900
NET INCOME ($000)	8,200
EMPLOYEES	na

AGNICO-EAGLE MINES LIMITED
See page 28 for a full company profile.

AGRA INDUSTRIES LIMITED
See page 561 for a full company profile.

AGRINOVE, COOPERATIVE AGRO-ALIMENTAIRE
(Non-fin Co-op)   AGRICULTURE
180 Boul. Begin, C.P. 4600, Ste-Claire, PQ, G0R 2V0 (418) 883-3301
AGRINOVE, COOPERATIVE AGRO-ALIMENTAIRE is a dairy co-operative suppling capital management services, transportation and sales support to its members. Agrinove has an interest in Groupe Lactel.
Herman Bolduc, Chairman

TOTAL ASSETS ($000)	32,939
TOTAL REVENUE ($000)	155,325
NET INCOME ($000)	(817)
EMPLOYEES	45

AGRITEK BIO INGREDIENTS CORPORATION
(Public)   BIOTECHNOLOGY & PHARMACEUTICALS
Exchanges: M   Stock Symbol: AGK
Suite 630, 1980 Sherbrooke St. West, Montreal, PQ,
H3H 1G1   (514) 935-2581
AGRITEK BIO INGREDIENTS CORPORATION is a developer and global distributor of natural biotechnology based feed additives and waste management products for the poultry, livestock and environmental industries.
James D. Raymond, Chairman

TOTAL ASSETS ($000)	14,874
TOTAL REVENUE ($000)	4,801
NET INCOME ($000)	(141)
EMPLOYEES	60
RANK (Profit/Revenue/Assets)	770/868/945

AGRIUM INC.
See page 283 for a full company profile.

AGROMEX INC.
(Public)   AGRICULTURE
Exchanges: M   Stock Symbol: AOX
2950 rue Ontario Est, Montreal, PQ, H2K 1X3   (514) 527-9661
AGROMEX INC. is engaged exclusively in the business of reproducing, fattening and slaughtering hogs.
Robert Desilets, Chairman & President

TOTAL ASSETS ($000)	27,955
TOTAL REVENUE ($000)	60,820
NET INCOME ($000)	348
EMPLOYEES	170
RANK (Profit/Revenue/Assets)	721/506/788

AGROPUR, COOPERATIVE AGRO-ALIMENTAIRE
(Non-fin Co-op)   AGRICULTURE
510 Principale Street, P.O. Box 6000, Granby, PQ,
J2G 7G2   (514) 375-1991
AGROPUR, COOPERATIVE AGRO-ALIMENTAIRE is a Quebec-dairy based cooperative. It operates in two divisions: industrial; and fine cheese. The cooperative serves 4,900 members. A subsidiary, Natrel Inc., produces and distributes consumer milk products.
Jacques Cartier, Chairman

TOTAL ASSETS ($000)	279,508
TOTAL REVENUE ($000)	1,016,206

NET INCOME ($000)   3,877
EMPLOYEES   2,500

AINSWORTH LUMBER CO. LTD.
See page 152 for a full company profile.

AIR CANADA
See page 321 for a full company profile.

AIT ADVANCED INFORMATION TECHNOLOGIES CORPORATION

(Public)   ELECTRICAL & ELECTRONIC
Exchanges: T   Stock Symbol: AIV
9 Auriga Drive, Nepean, ON, K2E 7T9   (613) 226-7800
AIT ADVANCED INFORMATION TECHNOLOGIES CORPORA-TION is involved in the design and manufacture of advanced software-based electronic systems for the personal identification and security systems market. The company's other areas of operation are the provision of simulation and training systems for air traffic control and of engineering and project management services provided to the Canadian Space Agency.
Stephen H. Sandler, Chairman & C.E.O.

TOTAL ASSETS ($000)	32,617
TOTAL REVENUE ($000)	34,000
NET INCOME ($000)	4,022
EMPLOYEES	225
RANK (Profit/Revenue/Assets)	464/626/752

AJ PERRON GOLD CORP.
(Public)   PRECIOUS METALS
Exchanges: T   Stock Symbol: AJP
Kerr Mine/Mill Site, P.O. Box 390, Virginia Town, ON,
P0K 1X0   (705) 634-2121
AJ PERRON GOLD CORP. is involved in the mining, milling, refining, exploration and development of precious metals.
Alexander H. Perron, President & C.E.O.

TOTAL ASSETS ($000)	19,593
TOTAL REVENUE ($000)	8,542
NET INCOME ($000)	(6,922)
EMPLOYEES	150
RANK (Profit/Revenue/Assets)	924/818/877

AKITA DRILLING LTD.
(Public)   OIL AND GAS FIELD SERVICES
Exchanges: T   Stock Symbol: AKT.A
Suite 1110, 505 - 3rd Street S.W., Calgary, AB,
T2P 3E6   (403) 292-7979
AKITA DRILLING LTD. offers contract drilling services to the oil and gas industry.
Ronald D. Southern, Chairman

TOTAL ASSETS ($000)	41,999
TOTAL REVENUE ($000)	62,623
NET INCOME ($000)	7,024
EMPLOYEES	600
RANK (Profit/Revenue/Assets)	367/498/680

ALBERTA ENERGY COMPANY LTD.
See page 71 for a full company profile.

ALBERTA NATURAL GAS COMPANY LTD
See page 507 for a full company profile.

ALBERTA OIL AND GAS LIMITED
(Public)   OIL AND GAS PRODUCERS
Exchanges: Z   Stock Symbol: AOG
Suite 1200, 700 - 4th Avenue S.W., Calgary, AB,
T2P 3J4   (403) 269-3779
ALBERTA OIL AND GAS LIMITED is involved in the acquisiton and development of oil and gas properties.
Paul Stauffer, Chairman

TOTAL ASSETS ($000)	29,969
TOTAL REVENUE ($000)	8,612
NET INCOME ($000)	(290)
EMPLOYEES	0
RANK (Profit/Revenue/Assets)	779/816/774

ALBERTA POWER LIMITED
(Private)   ELECTRICAL UTILITIES
10035 - 105 Street, Edmonton, AB, T5J 2V6   (403) 420-7310
ALBERTA POWER LIMITED is engaged in the generation, transmission and distribution of electrical energy in Alberta and the Yukon Territory. Alberta Power is 100% owned by Canadian Utilities Limited of Alberta.
J.D. Wood, Chairman & C.E.O.

TOTAL ASSETS ($000)	1,930,355
TOTAL REVENUE ($000)	599,007
NET INCOME ($000)	106,104
EMPLOYEES	1,554

ALBERTA WHEAT POOL
(Non-fin Co-op)   AGRICULTURE
Box 2700, 505 - 2nd Street S.W., Calgary, AB,
T2P 2P5   (403) 290-4910
ALBERTA WHEAT POOL is a farmer-owned cooperative that provides fully integreted grain handling, grain marketing and farm supply services to its members through facilities in Alberta and northeastern British Columbia. It also owns and operates an export grain terminal in Vancouver, British Columbia.
G.E.M. Cummings, Chief Executive Officer

TOTAL ASSETS ($000)	522,177
TOTAL REVENUE ($000)	1,174,472
NET INCOME ($000)	4,269
EMPLOYEES	1,421

ALCAN ALUMINIUM LIMITED
See page 3 for a full company profile.

ALERT CARE CORPORATION
(Public)   MEDICAL SERVICES
Exchanges: Z   Stock Symbol: ACH
145 Murray Drive, Aurora, ON, L4G 2C7   (905) 841-2745
ALERT CARE CORPORATION is involved in the construction, development, sale and management of retirement homes.
W. Wayne Barton, President

TOTAL ASSETS ($000)	18,242
TOTAL REVENUE ($000)	4,537
NET INCOME ($000)	10

EMPLOYEES na
RANK (Profit/Revenue/Assets) 754/872/893

ALGO GROUP INC.
See page 203 for a full company profile.

ALGOMA CENTRAL CORPORATION
See page 322 for a full company profile.

ALGOMA STEEL INC.
See page 237 for a full company profile.

ALGONQUIN MERCANTILE CORPORATION
(Public) MANAGEMENT AND DIVERSIFIED
Exchanges: T Stock Symbol: AM
Unit 11, 668 Millway Avenue, Concord, ON, L4K 3V2 (905) 660-7688
ALGONQUIN MERCANTILE CORP. is a diversified company engaged directly or through subsidiaries in the retailing of drugs and related products and wholesaling, packaging and distribution of fresh produce.
Michael Blair, Chief Executive Officer
TOTAL ASSETS ($000) 26,654
TOTAL REVENUE ($000) 119,231
NET INCOME ($000) 2,465
EMPLOYEES 15
RANK (Profit/Revenue/Assets) 539/393/803

ALIMENTATION COUCHE-TARD INC.
(Public) FOOD STORES
Exchanges: M Stock Symbol: ATD.A
1600 St. Martin Blvd. East, Tower B, Suite 280, Laval, PQ,
H7G 4S7 (514) 662-3272
Alimentation Couche-Tard Inc. operates a network of 300 convenience stores through its wholly owned subsidiary, Magasins Couchetard Inc. and Depan Escompte Couchetard Inc.
Alain Bouchard, Chairman
TOTAL ASSETS ($000) 41,038
TOTAL REVENUE ($000) 150,804
NET INCOME ($000) 637
EMPLOYEES 1,450
RANK (Profit/Revenue/Assets) 683/359/687

ALLELIX BIOPHARMACEUTICALS INC.
(Public) BIOTECHNOLOGY & PHARMACEUTICALS
Exchanges: T M Stock Symbol: AXB
6850 Goreway Drive, Mississauga, ON, L4V 1V7 (905) 677-0831
ALLELIX is engaged in the discovery, development and subsequent commercialization of pharmaceutical products. These products are developed by applying chemical approaches to disease targets identified and defined through advanced biological techniques. Allelix's research programs focus on the development of anti-virals, anti-inflammatories and central nervous system therapies.
John R. Evans, Chairman
TOTAL ASSETS ($000) 31,609
TOTAL REVENUE ($000) 5,819
NET INCOME ($000) (10,818)
EMPLOYEES 125
RANK (Profit/Revenue/Assets) 947/849/759

ALLIANCE COMMUNICATIONS CORPORATION
See page 562 for a full company profile.

ALLIANCE FOREST PRODUCTS INC.
See page 153 for a full company profile.

ALLIANCE RO-NA HOME INC.
(Private) WHOLESALE DISTRIBUTORS
34 Henry Street, St. Jacobs, ON, N0B 2N0 (519) 677-0831
ALLIANCE RO-NA HOME INC. is a buyer of merchandise for its two 50% shareholders, Le Groupe Ro-Na Dismat Inc. and Home Hardware Stores Limited. Volume purchase rebates earned are allocated to the shareholders.
TOTAL ASSETS ($000) 116,167
TOTAL REVENUE ($000) 1,253,458
NET INCOME ($000) 7
EMPLOYEES na

ALLIEDSIGNAL CANADA INC.
(Private) TRANSPORTATION EQUIP & COMPNTS
240 Attwell Drive, Etobicoke, ON, M9W 6L7 (416) 798-6729
ALLIEDSIGNAL CANADA INC. is engaged in three industries: areospace, automotive and chemicals. AlliedSignal Canada is wholly owned by Allied Signal Inc.
Basile Papaevangelou, Chairman & President
TOTAL ASSETS ($000) 132,088
TOTAL REVENUE ($000) 179,494
NET INCOME ($000) 17,488
EMPLOYEES 2,200

ALLSTATE INSURANCE COMPANY OF CANADA
(Private) INSURANCE - PROPERTY & CASUALTY
10 Allstate Parkway, Markham, ON, L3R 5P8 (905) 477-6900
ALLSTATE INSURANCE COMPANY OF CANADA is an insurance carrier. The company is a wholly owned subsidiary of Allstate Life Insurance Company of Northbrook, Illinois.
J. Terrence Kelaher, Chairman & C.E.O.
TOTAL ASSETS ($000) 915,797
TOTAL REVENUE ($000) 445,912
NET INCOME ($000) (2,495)
EMPLOYEES 1,471

ALPHANET TELECOM INC.
(Public) OTHER SERVICES
Exchanges: T Stock Symbol: FAX
Suite 260, 55 St. Clair Ave. W., Toronto, ON,
M4V 2Y7 (416) 923-2222
ALPHANET TELECOM INC. is engaged in the design, development, installation, operation and worldwide marketing of fax messaging and information services to the hotel industry, the business traveller and users of personal computers and personal digital assistants.
Alastair T. Gordon, Chairman & Chief Tech. Officer
TOTAL ASSETS ($000) 17,487 (US)
TOTAL REVENUE ($000) 5,675 (US)
NET INCOME ($000) (528) (US)
EMPLOYEES na
RANK (Profit/Revenue/Assets) 808/826/826

ALPINE OIL SERVICES CORPORATION

(Public)   OIL AND GAS FIELD SERVICES
Exchanges: T Z   Stock Symbol: ASL
Suite 1100, 202 - 6th Avenue S.W., Calgary, AB,
T2P 2R9   (403) 266-2010
ALPINE OIL SERVICES CORPORATION and its subsidiaries operate in the oil and gas service industry, primarily in Western Canada but also in other petroleum producing countries. The main domestic market segments in which the Company competes are drillstem testing and wireline services and production testing.
Rodney J. Hauser, President & C.E.O.

TOTAL ASSETS ($000)	21,562
TOTAL REVENUE ($000)	14,514
NET INCOME ($000)	2,738
EMPLOYEES	157
RANK (Profit/Revenue/Assets)	523/763/858

ALTA GENETICS INC.

(Public)   BIOTECHNOLOGY & PHARMACEUTICALS
Exchanges: T   Stock Symbol: AGI
R.R. 2, Balzac, AB, T0M 0E0   (403) 226-0666
ALTA GENETICS INC. is engaged in the production and marketing of products and services based on cattle genetics designed to increase the efficiency of milk and meat production. The Company specializes in bull semen, cow embryos, live cattle and reproductive technologies.
Eric Baker, Chairman

TOTAL ASSETS ($000)	25,212
TOTAL REVENUE ($000)	23,253
NET INCOME ($000)	2,055
EMPLOYEES	230
RANK (Profit/Revenue/Assets)	562/694/813

AMERADA HESS CANADA LTD.

(Private)   OIL AND GAS PRODUCERS
700 - 9th Avenue S.W., Suite 1900, Calgary, AB,
T2P 4B3   (403) 267-6910
AMERADA HESS CANADA LTD. is involved in oil and gas exploration and production.
L. Hess, Chairman

TOTAL ASSETS ($000)	682,284
TOTAL REVENUE ($000)	236,645
NET INCOME ($000)	23,661
EMPLOYEES	314

AMERICAN ECO CORPORATION

(Public)   CONSULTING
Exchanges: T A   Stock Symbol: ECX
1325 South Creek Drive, Houston, TX, 77084   (713) 647-0080
AMERICAN ECO and its subsidiaries engage in industrial services and consulting for environmental remediation, and waste management, principally in the southwestern U.S. Its subsidiary, C.A. Turner Construction Company provides construction and maintenance in the petroleum, refining and chemical production industries.
Mark White, Chairman

TOTAL ASSETS ($000)	15,007 (US)
TOTAL REVENUE ($000)	7,565 (US)
NET INCOME ($000)	322 (US)
EMPLOYEES	900
RANK (Profit/Revenue/Assets)	708/806/868

AMERICAN SENSORS INC.

(Public)   MISC. CONSUMER PRODUCTS
Exchanges: T Q   Stock Symbol: ASZ
100 Tempo Avenue, Toronto, ON, M2H 2N8   (416) 496-5900
AMERICAN SENSORS INC. develops, manufactures and markets carbon monoxide detectors, smoke detectors and other hazardous gas detectors, which monitor indoor air quality.
Bill Koyle, Chairman & Director

TOTAL ASSETS ($000)	26,043
TOTAL REVENUE ($000)	17,033
NET INCOME ($000)	1,592
EMPLOYEES	400
RANK (Profit/Revenue/Assets)	601/740/807

AMISCO INDUSTRIES LTD.

(Public)   HOME FURNISHINGS
Exchanges: M   Stock Symbol: IAC
33 5e Rue, Ville de L'Islet, PQ, G0R 2C0   (418) 247-5025
AMISCO INDUSTRIES LTD. is a manufacturer of home furnishings which are sold under the trademark Amisco. The easy to assemble furniture is made of steel tubing. Amisco's products are sold in 10 Canadian provinces and all American states.
Martin Poitras, Chairman & C.E.O.

TOTAL ASSETS ($000)	12,660
TOTAL REVENUE ($000)	19,842
NET INCOME ($000)	339
EMPLOYEES	180
RANK (Profit/Revenue/Assets)	722/717/1000

AMOCO CANADA PETROLEUM COMPANY LTD.

(Private)   OIL AND GAS PRODUCERS
240 - 4th Avenue S.W., P.O. Box 200, Calgary, AB,
T2P 4H4   (403) 233-1313
AMOCO CANADA PETROLEUM COMPANY LTD. is engaged in the exploration for and production of crude oil and natural gas, the production and purchase of natural gas liquids, the marketing of liquified petroleum gases, the production and sale of sulphur and the development of mineral properties.
Don Stacey, Chairman & President

TOTAL ASSETS ($000)	5,875,000
TOTAL REVENUE ($000)	4,407,000
NET INCOME ($000)	309,000
EMPLOYEES	na

ANCHOR LAMINA INC.

(Public)   MISC. INDUSTRIAL PRODUCTS
Exchanges: T   Stock Symbol: AKC
2590 Ouellette Avenue, Windsor, ON, N8X 1L7   (519) 966-4431
ANCHOR LAMINA INC. is engaged in the production and sale of die sets and related products and services to the metal working and plastic mould industries throughout the world.
Clare Winterbottom, Chairman; President & C.E.O.

TOTAL ASSETS ($000)	74,103
TOTAL REVENUE ($000)	75,462
NET INCOME ($000)	8,433
EMPLOYEES	700
RANK (Profit/Revenue/Assets)	325/466/552

ANDERSON EXPLORATION LTD.

See page 72 for a full company profile.

ANDRES WINES LTD.
See page 183 for a full company profile.

ANGLO-CANADIAN TELEPHONE COMPANY
See page 341 for a full company profile.

APEX LAND CORPORATION
(Public)	DEVELOPERS
Exchanges: T	Stock Symbol: AXD.A

Suite 1100, 500 - 4th Avenue S.W., Calgary, AB,
T2P 0L6   (403) 264-3232
APEX LAND CORPORATION is involved in residential land development.
Frank Boyd, C.E.O.

TOTAL ASSETS ($000)	37,008
TOTAL REVENUE ($000)	19,316
NET INCOME ($000)	1,519
EMPLOYEES	8
RANK (Profit/Revenue/Assets)	607/720/718

ARAKIS ENERGY CORPORATION
(Public)	OIL AND GAS PRODUCERS
Exchanges: V Q	Stock Symbol: AKS

Suite 1800, 1500 West Georgia Street, Vancouver, BC,
V6C 2Z6   (604) 685-7933
ARAKIS ENERGY CORP. is engaged in the acquisition, exploration and development of oil and gas properties. The company operates primarily in the Appalachian Basin of the U.S. It also explores and develops major petroleum concessions in the Republic of Sudan, the Sultanate of Oman, and Papua New Guinea.
J. Terry Alexander, Chairman President & C.E.O.

TOTAL ASSETS ($000)	50,691 (US)
TOTAL REVENUE ($000)	2,227 (US)
NET INCOME ($000)	(3,601) (US)
EMPLOYEES	25
RANK (Profit/Revenue/Assets)	907/901/561

ARBOR MEMORIAL SERVICES INC.
See page 563 for a full company profile.

ARCHER RESOURCES LTD.
See page 73 for a full company profile.

ARGUS CORPORATION LIMITED
(Public)	MANAGEMENT AND DIVERSIFIED
Exchanges: T	Stock Symbol: AR.PR.A

10 Toronto Street, Toronto, ON, M5C 2B7   (416) 363-8721
ARGUS CORPORATION LIMITED is involved in a single business activity which is the investment of funds in companies, dividend and interest earning deposits.
Conrad M. Black, Chairman & C.E.O.

TOTAL ASSETS ($000)	335,170
TOTAL REVENUE ($000)	13,608
NET INCOME ($000)	10,458
EMPLOYEES	na
RANK (Profit/Revenue/Assets)	292/768/275

ARIEL RESOURCES LTD.
(Public)	PRECIOUS METALS
Exchanges: T V	Stock Symbol: AU

Suite 1135, 1188 West Georgia Street, Vancouver, BC,
V6E 4A2   (604) 682-2201
ARIEL RESOURCES LTD. operates the Matapalo Mill located 95 kilometres northwest of San Jose, Costa Rica. The mill processes ore from Ariel's two mines, the Tres Hermanos and the San Martin.
William C. Bennett, President

TOTAL ASSETS ($000)	9,443 (US)
TOTAL REVENUE ($000)	4,397 (US)
NET INCOME ($000)	180 (US)
EMPLOYEES	170
RANK (Profit/Revenue/Assets)	729/845/999

ARIMETCO INTERNATIONAL INC.
See page 4 for a full company profile.

ARMBRO ENTERPRISES INC.
(Public)	CONTRACTORS
Exchanges: T	Stock Symbol: ARE

25 Van Kirk Drive, Unit 8, Brampton, ON, L7A 1A6   (905) 454-3737
ARMBRO ENTERPRISES INC. operates in a variety of areas including: road building; heavy civil construction and aggregates.
John M. Beck, Chairman & C.E.O.

TOTAL ASSETS ($000)	41,549
TOTAL REVENUE ($000)	52,083
NET INCOME ($000)	(19,163)
EMPLOYEES	400
RANK (Profit/Revenue/Assets)	967/540/684

ARMSTRONG WORLD INDUSTRIES CANADA LTD.
(Private)	MISC. CONSUMER PRODUCTS

6911 Decarie Boul., Montreal, PQ, H3W 3E5   (514) 733-9981
ARMSTRONG WORLD INDUSTRIES CANADA LTD. is a wholly owned subsidiary of Armstrong World Industries, Inc. The principal activities include the manufacture and sale of floor covering materials and accoustical and decorative ceiling products. The corporation is also engaged in production of crude pyrophillite ore.
Gordon Levering, President

TOTAL ASSETS ($000)	51,108
TOTAL REVENUE ($000)	148,936
NET INCOME ($000)	5,056
EMPLOYEES	na

ARTISAN DRILLING LTD.
(Public)	OIL AND GAS FIELD SERVICES
Exchanges: T	Stock Symbol: ADR

1426 Meridian Road N., Calgary, AB, T2A 2N9   (403) 235-4000
ARTISAN DRILLING LTD. is engaged in contract drilling of oil and gas wells, wireline services, production testing, engineering and well optimization, and custom manufacturing of oilfield production equipment in western Canada.
Donald R. Seaman, Chairman

TOTAL ASSETS ($000)	30,226
TOTAL REVENUE ($000)	56,206
NET INCOME ($000)	5,751
EMPLOYEES	500
RANK (Profit/Revenue/Assets)	402/524/773

Canada Company Handbook

ASBESTOS CORPORATION LIMITED

(Public) OTHER MINES
Exchanges: T M Stock Symbol: AB
840 Ouellet Blve. West, Thetford-Mines, PQ,
G6G 7A5 (418) 338-5195
ASBESTOS CORPORATION LIMITED is engaged in the mining and milling of asbestos fibre through a Limited Partnership with Bell Asbestos Mines, Ltd., Lac d'Amiante du Canada, Ltee and Camchib Mines Inc.
M. De Rouin, President and C.E.O.

TOTAL ASSETS ($000)	37,156
TOTAL REVENUE ($000)	5,211
NET INCOME ($000)	1,980
EMPLOYEES	7
RANK (Profit/Revenue/Assets)	573/862/715

ASCENTEX ENERGY INC.

(Public) OIL AND GAS PRODUCERS
Exchanges: T Stock Symbol: AEN
500 Canada Place, 407 - 2nd Street S.W., Calgary, AB,
T2P 2Y3 (403) 265-3320
ASCENTEX ENERGY INC. is involved in the acquisition, exploration and development of oil and gas properties, primarily in Western Canada.
Ed A. Beaman, President & C.E.O.

TOTAL ASSETS ($000)	16,986
TOTAL REVENUE ($000)	3,485
NET INCOME ($000)	(61)
EMPLOYEES	10
RANK (Profit/Revenue/Assets)	761/890/914

ASEA BROWN BOVERI INC.

(Private) ELECTRICAL & ELECTRONIC
3000 Halpern, St-Laurent, PQ, H4S 1R2 (514) 856-6222
ASEA BROWN BOVERI INC. is an electrical engineering company which develops, provides, sells and services a wide range of systems and products generally related to the production, distribution and application of electricity. ABB is a wholly owned subsidiary of ABB Asea Brown Boveri Ltd. of Switzerland.
Peter S. Janson, President & C.E.O.

TOTAL ASSETS ($000)	336,000
TOTAL REVENUE ($000)	557,000
NET INCOME ($000)	na
EMPLOYEES	2,800

ASHTON MINING OF CANADA INC.

(Public) OTHER MINES
Exchanges: T M Stock Symbol: ACA
Unit 123, 930 W. 1st Street, North Vancouver, BC,
V7P 3N2 (604) 987-7107
ASHTON MINING OF CANADA INC. is a diamond exploration company which has interests in a number of exploration properties in Canada and in the United States.
David A. Robertson, Chairman

TOTAL ASSETS ($000)	28,148
TOTAL REVENUE ($000)	1,123
NET INCOME ($000)	(1,195)
EMPLOYEES	30
RANK (Profit/Revenue/Assets)	826/942/786

ASSINIBOINE CREDIT UNION LIMITED

(Fin. Co-op) CREDIT UNIONS
200 Main Street, 6th Floor, P.O. Box 2, Winnipeg, MB,
R3C 2G1 (204) 958-8550
ASSINIBOINE CREDIT UNION LIMITED offers deposit, loan, and retail financial services to its members.
Richard Feist, General Manager

TOTAL ASSETS ($000)	311,877
TOTAL REVENUE ($000)	27,599
NET INCOME ($000)	2,012
EMPLOYEES	180

ASTRAL COMMUNICATIONS INC.
See page 564 for a full company profile.

AT PLASTICS INC.
See page 284 for a full company profile.

AT&T GLOBAL INFORMATION SOLUTIONS

(Private) ELECTRICAL & ELECTRONIC
320 Front Street West, Toronto, ON, M5V 3C4 (416) 599-4627
AT&T GLOBAL INFORMATION SOLUTIONS provides a wide variety of Customer Focused Solutions to help businesses better understand and serve their customers by more effectively getting, moving and using customer information. These solutions are targeted to six key industries: financial services; retail; communications; consumer goods manufacturing; transportation and the public sector.
Ron S. Smith, President & C.E.O.

TOTAL ASSETS ($000)	269,025
TOTAL REVENUE ($000)	322,393
NET INCOME ($000)	(10,990)
EMPLOYEES	1,800

ATCO LTD.
See page 508 for a full company profile.

ATCOR RESOURCES LTD.
See page 74 for a full company profile.

ATI TECHNOLOGIES INC.
See page 535 for a full company profile.

ATLANTA GOLD CORPORATION

(Public) PRECIOUS METALS
Exchanges: T Stock Symbol: AAG
Suite 1440, 625 Howe Street, Vancouver, BC,
V6C 2T6 (604) 669-0016
ATLANTA GOLD CORPORATION is involved in the acquisition, exploration and development of precious metal properties. The company's principal project is in Idaho.
Karl Rollke, President

TOTAL ASSETS ($000)	13,546
TOTAL REVENUE ($000)	75
NET INCOME ($000)	(399)
EMPLOYEES	na
RANK (Profit/Revenue/Assets)	783/987/982

ATLANTIC SHOPPING CENTRES LIMITED
(Public) PROPERTY MGMNT & INVESTMENT
Exchanges: T Stock Symbol: ATS.PR.A
115 King St., Stellarton, NS, B0K 1S0 (902) 755-4440
ATLANTIC SHOPPING CENTRES LIMITED, directly and through subsidiaries, is engaged primarily in the acquisition, development and management of commercial real estate comprised mainly of shopping centres and office buildings located in the Atlantic Provinces.
P.D. Sobey, Chairman President & C.E.O.

TOTAL ASSETS ($000)	610,850
TOTAL REVENUE ($000)	77,285
NET INCOME ($000)	3,857
EMPLOYEES	na
RANK (Profit/Revenue/Assets)	471/462/208

ATLANTIS COMMUNICATIONS INC.
See page 565 for a full company profile.

ATOMIC ENERGY OF CANADA LIMITED
(Crown) MACHINERY
344 Slater Street, Ottawa, ON, K1A 0S4 (613) 237-3270
ATOMIC ENERGY OF CANADA's commercial operations consist of nuclear power engineering and design, project management, operating plant support services, and manufacturing of radiostopes. Research and development operations consist of basic and applied nuclear research and development and contract research and development services.
Robert Nixon, Chairman

TOTAL ASSETS ($000)	848,428
TOTAL REVENUE ($000)	465,446
NET INCOME ($000)	(138,720)
EMPLOYEES	3,922

ATS AUTOMATION TOOLING SYSTEMS INC.
(Public) MISC. INDUSTRIAL PRODUCTS
Exchanges: T Stock Symbol: ATA
250 Royal Oak Road, Box 32100 Preston Centre, C, Cambridge, ON, N3H 5M2 (519) 653-6500
ATS AUTOMATION TOOLING SYSTEMS INC. is involved in the custom engineering and production of industrial automated manufacturing systems. In addition, the company manufactures related precision components and subassemblies.
Lawrence G. Tapp, Chairman

TOTAL ASSETS ($000)	83,855
TOTAL REVENUE ($000)	93,396
NET INCOME ($000)	3,918
EMPLOYEES	930
RANK (Profit/Revenue/Assets)	469/432/525

AUBERGES DES GOUVERNEURS INC.
(Public) LODGING
Exchanges: M Stock Symbol: AUB
777 University, Suite 800, Montreal, PQ, H3C 3Z7 (514) 875-8822
AUBERGES DES GOUVERNEURS INC. and its franchisees operate hotels in the province of Quebec under the trademarks Hotel Des Gouverneurs and Radisson Gouverneurs.
Jacques Goupil, Chairman and C.E.O.

TOTAL ASSETS ($000)	65,010
TOTAL REVENUE ($000)	38,443
NET INCOME ($000)	(5,654)
EMPLOYEES	1000
RANK (Profit/Revenue/Assets)	913/600/574

AUDREY RESOURCES INC.
(Public) METAL MINES
Exchanges: T M Q Stock Symbol: AUY
800 Rene-Levesque Blvd. W., Suite 850, Montreal, PQ, H3B 1X9 (514) 878-3166
AUDREY RESOURCES INC. is a producer of zinc, copper, gold and silver. The company is also involved in the acquisition, exploration and development of mineral properties.
Guy Hebert, President & C.E.O.

TOTAL ASSETS ($000)	79,584
TOTAL REVENUE ($000)	40
NET INCOME ($000)	(2,086)
EMPLOYEES	16
RANK (Profit/Revenue/Assets)	855/990/531

AULT FOODS INC.
See page 184 for a full company profile.

AUR RESOURCES INC.
See page 29 for a full company profile.

AURIZON MINES LTD.
(Public) PRECIOUS METALS
Exchanges: T M V Stock Symbol: ARZ
Suite 1000, 1177 West Hastings Street, Vancouver, BC, V6E 2K3 (604) 687-6600
AURIZON MINES LTD. is a precious metal mining company. It owns a 50% interest in The Sleeping Giant Mine, an interest in the Beaufor property, both in Quebec and a 100% interest in the La Reyna Project in Mexico. The Company has investments in Aurex Resources Corp., Granduc Mining Corporation and La Esperanza Gold Explorations Ltd. which provide opportunities in Chile, Manitoba and Mexico.
Frank A. Lang, Chairman

TOTAL ASSETS ($000)	24,072
TOTAL REVENUE ($000)	14,831
NET INCOME ($000)	6,090
EMPLOYEES	10
RANK (Profit/Revenue/Assets)	391/759/827

AUTO WORKERS' COMMUNITY CREDIT UNION LIMITED
(Fin. Co-op) CREDIT UNIONS
322 King St. W., P.O. Box 158, Oshawa, ON, L1H 7L1 (905) 728-5187
AUTO WORKERS' COMMUNITY CREDIT UNION LIMITED offers full financial services including savings, loans, mortgages and RRSPs/RRIFs to its members.
Steve Nimigom, President

TOTAL ASSETS ($000)	197,382
TOTAL REVENUE ($000)	15,062
NET INCOME ($000)	(7,385)
EMPLOYEES	na

AUTOSTOCK INC.

(Public)   SPECIALTY STORES
Exchanges: T M   Stock Symbol: OTO
8288 Boul. Pie IX, Montreal, PQ, H1Z 3T6   (514) 593-8300
AUTOSTOCK INC. comprises eight divisions and subsidiaries engaged in the sale and installation of auto parts: Autopoint Inc., Autostock Distribution, Du-Ro Vitres d'autos, Glenayre Communications, Lebeau Vitres d'autos, Lebeau Technicentre, Mister Muffler Tires and Brakes and Octo Freins et Silencieux.
Gerard Lebeau, Chairman of the Board

TOTAL ASSETS ($000)	93,669
TOTAL REVENUE ($000)	178,607
NET INCOME ($000)	8,605
EMPLOYEES	1,227
RANK (Profit/Revenue/Assets)	319/327/498

AVCO FINANCIAL SERVICES CANADA LIMITED

(Private)   FINANCE AND LEASING
201 Queens Avenue, London, ON, N6A 1J1   (519) 672-4220
AVCO FINANCIAL SERVICES CANADA LIMITED is engaged in the provision of financial and insurance services. Financial services include consumer loans, sales financing and mortgages. Insurance operations are carried out through a subsidiary, London and Midland General Insurance Company. Avco Financial Services is a wholly owned subsidiary of Avco Financial Services Inc. (U.S.).
Murray Wallace, President

TOTAL ASSETS ($000)	1,346,171
TOTAL REVENUE ($000)	260,758
NET INCOME ($000)	28,731
EMPLOYEES	1,197

AVCORP INDUSTRIES INC.

(Public)   TRANSPORTATION EQUIP & COMPNTS
Exchanges: M   Stock Symbol: AVP
Suite 200, 1001 Autoroute 440 West, Chomedey, PQ,
H7L 3W3   (514) 629-5506
AVCORP INDUSTRIES INC. is engaged in the design, manufacture and sale of an extensive range of aerospace products comprised of four product groups: composite and plastic components, metal structures, aircraft engine overhaul and remanufacture and aerospace design engineering.
Robert A. Utting, Chairman

TOTAL ASSETS ($000)	14,693
TOTAL REVENUE ($000)	31,143
NET INCOME ($000)	8,479
EMPLOYEES	300
RANK (Profit/Revenue/Assets)	322/645/953

AVENOR INC.

See page 154 for a full company profile.

AVESTEL CREDIT UNION LIMITED

(Fin. Co-op)   CREDIT UNIONS
688 Queensdale Avenue East, Hamilton, ON,
L8V 1M1   (905) 387-0770
AVESTEL CREDIT UNION LIMITED provides financial products, services and programs.
Jan Koops, President & Chair

TOTAL ASSETS ($000)	320,379
TOTAL REVENUE ($000)	26,182

NET INCOME ($000)	1,349
EMPLOYEES	153

AVON CANADA INC.

(Private)   MISC. CONSUMER PRODUCTS
5500 Trans Canada Highway, Pointe Claire, PQ,
H9R 1B6   (514) 695-3371
AVON CANADA INC. is a manufacturer and distributor of cosmetics, fragrances, fashion jewellery, and audio and video cassettes, and lingerie. Avon Canada is a wholly owned subsidiary of Avon International of New York, NY.
Y. Quinion, President & C.E.O.

TOTAL ASSETS ($000)	72,389
TOTAL REVENUE ($000)	174,624
NET INCOME ($000)	6,608
EMPLOYEES	984

AZTEC RESOURCES LTD.

(Public)   OIL AND GAS PRODUCERS
Exchanges: T   Stock Symbol: AZL
Suite 1000, 400 - 5th Avenue S.W., Calgary, AB,
T2P 0M2   (403) 234-8882
AZTEC RESOURCES LTD. is involved in the acquisition, exploration and development of oil and gas properties in western Canada.
Gregory S. Fletcher, C.E.O.

TOTAL ASSETS ($000)	32,836
TOTAL REVENUE ($000)	4,669
NET INCOME ($000)	858
EMPLOYEES	12
RANK (Profit/Revenue/Assets)	593/810/749

B. C. TREE FRUITS LIMITED

(Non-fin Co-op)   FOOD PROCESSING
1473 Water Street, Kelowna, BC, V1Y 1J6   (604) 762-2604
B.C. TREE FRUITS is involved in the marketing and sale of fresh fruit received from British Columbia Fruit Growers' Association member growers through packaging houses with which the company has contracts.
Allan Earl, C.E.O.

TOTAL ASSETS ($000)	7,438
TOTAL REVENUE ($000)	6,323
NET INCOME ($000)	113
EMPLOYEES	56

B.C. BANCORP

See page 441 for a full company profile.

B.C. CENTRAL CREDIT UNION

(Fin. Co-op)   CREDIT UNIONS
1441 Creekside Drive, Vancouver, BC, V6J 4S7   (604) 734-2511
B.C. CENTRAL CREDIT UNION is a financial services and trade association for credit unions operating in British Columbia.
Mike Tarr, Chairperson

TOTAL ASSETS ($000)	2,370,326
TOTAL REVENUE ($000)	148,691
NET INCOME ($000)	7,407
EMPLOYEES	226

B.C. PACIFIC CAPITAL CORPORATION

(Public)   MANAGEMENT AND DIVERSIFIED
Exchanges: V   Stock Symbol: BPQ.A
Suite 1632, 1055 West Georgia Street, P.O. Box 11179 Royal
Centre, Vancouver, BC, V6E 3R5   (604) 669-3141
B.C. PACIFIC CAPITAL CORP. is a British Columbia based financial
and investment corporation providing management services to corporations encountering financial difficulties, considering merger or acquisition initiatives or requiring operational evaluations. The company also
owns a 62.75% interest in BRL Enterprises Inc., an oil and gas exploration and investment company.
Brian G. Kenning, Managing Partner & Chairman

TOTAL ASSETS ($000)	216,011
TOTAL REVENUE ($000)	22,493
NET INCOME ($000)	15,219
EMPLOYEES	na
RANK (Profit/Revenue/Assets)	241/701/343

BALLARD POWER SYSTEMS INC.

(Public)   MISC. INDUSTRIAL PRODUCTS
Exchanges: T   Stock Symbol: BLD
Suite 107, 980 West 1st Street, North Vancouver, BC,
V7P 3N4   (604) 986-9367
BALLARD POWER SYSTEMS INC. is engaged in the research and
development of alternate energy sources including high energy lithium
batteries and fuel cells. The company currently manufactures and sells
advanced lithium batteries for specialty applications and is involved in
the development of fuel cells which convert hydrogen fuel directly into
electricity with pure water and heat as the only bi-products.
Geoffrey Ballard, Chairman

TOTAL ASSETS ($000)	40,928
TOTAL REVENUE ($000)	19,981
NET INCOME ($000)	(5,211)
EMPLOYEES	120
RANK (Profit/Revenue/Assets)	910/715/689

BALLISTIC ENERGY CORPORATION

(Public)   OIL AND GAS PRODUCERS
Exchanges: T   Stock Symbol: BAL
Suite 600 Bow Valley Square II, 205 - 5th Avenue S.W., Calgary, AB,
T2P 2V7   (403) 290-0777
BALLISTIC ENERGY CORPORATION is active in the exploration,
development and production of oil and gas.
Martin G. Abbott, Chairman & Corp. Secretary

TOTAL ASSETS ($000)	75,887
TOTAL REVENUE ($000)	22,032
NET INCOME ($000)	4,782
EMPLOYEES	36
RANK (Profit/Revenue/Assets)	429/704/544

BANISTER FOUNDATION INC.
See page 566 for a full company profile.

BANK OF MONTREAL
See page 442 for a full company profile.

BANK OF NOVA SCOTIA (THE)
See page 443 for a full company profile.

BANQUE NATIONALE DE PARIS (CANADA)

(Private)   BANKS
BNP Tower, 1981 McGill College Avenue, Montreal, PQ,
H3A 2W8   (514) 285-6000
BANQUE NATIONALE DE PARIS (CANADA) provides a range of
corporate financial services including private banking, leasing, securities
and trade financing.
Jacques H. Wahl, Chairman

TOTAL ASSETS ($000)	2,157,463
TOTAL REVENUE ($000)	130,449
NET INCOME ($000)	(29,973)
EMPLOYEES	307

BARRICK GOLD CORPORATION
See page 30 for a full company profile.

BARRINGTON PETROLEUM LTD.
See page 75 for a full company profile.

BATON BROADCASTING INCORPORATED
See page 369 for a full company profile.

BAXTER FOODS LTD.

(Private)   FOOD PROCESSING
91 Millidge Ave, Saint John, NB, E2K 2M3   (506) 632-6600
BAXTER FOODS LIMITED processes a full line of fluid milk, cream
and ice creams. It also manufactures margarine and other edible oil
products, and misty mountain natural spring water.
Malcolm R. Baxter, Chairman President & C.E.O.

TOTAL ASSETS ($000)	39,113
TOTAL REVENUE ($000)	165,055
NET INCOME ($000)	na
EMPLOYEES	660

BAY MILLS LIMITED

(Private)   MISC. INDUSTRIAL PRODUCTS
305 Church Street, Suite 200, Oakville, ON, L6J 1N9 (905) 842-8808
BAY MILLS LIMITED is a Canadian based North American manufacturer of engineered fiber/polymer composite materials serving the transportation, marine, aerospace, electronics, sporting goods and
construction markets.
Bradford C. Mattson, President & C.E.O.

TOTAL ASSETS ($000)	99,249
TOTAL REVENUE ($000)	123,845
NET INCOME ($000)	8,811
EMPLOYEES	0

BC GAS INC.
See page 342 for a full company profile.

BC GAS UTILITY LTD.
See page 343 for a full company profile.

BC SUGAR REFINERY, LIMITED
See page 185 for a full company profile.

BC TEL
See page 344 for a full company profile.

BC TELECOM INC.
See page 345 for a full company profile.

BCE INC.
See page 346 for a full company profile.

BCE MOBILE COMMUNICATIONS INC.
See page 370 for a full company profile.

BEAMSCOPE CANADA INC.
See page 402 for a full company profile.

BEARCAT EXPLORATIONS LTD.
(Public)   OIL AND GAS PRODUCERS
Exchanges: Z   Stock Symbol: BEA
Suite 1200, 520 - 5th Avenue S.W., Calgary, AB,
T2P 3R7   (403) 265-6161
BEARCAT EXPLORATIONS LTD. operates in the oil and gas industry in Canada and the United Kingdom. It also operates in the mining industry in Canada and the United States.
John W. McLeod, President

TOTAL ASSETS ($000)	26,669
TOTAL REVENUE ($000)	3,011
NET INCOME ($000)	(3,473)
EMPLOYEES	na
RANK (Profit/Revenue/Assets)	890/902/802

BEATRICE FOODS INC.
(Private)   FOOD PROCESSING
295 The West Mall, Suite 600, Etobicoke, ON,
M9C 4Z4   (416) 626-5500
BEATRICE FOODS INC. is a dairy and food processing company with operations in Ontario, Quebec, Manitoba, Alberta, Saskatchewan and in the United States. The company is 98% owned by Merrill Lynch Capital Partners of New York. The remaining 2% is owned by management.
Don McCarthy, Chairman President & C.E.O.

TOTAL ASSETS ($000)	683,200
TOTAL REVENUE ($000)	854,700
NET INCOME ($000)	na
EMPLOYEES	3,000

BEAU CANADA EXPLORATION LTD.
See page 76 for a full company profile.

BECKER MILK COMPANY LIMITED (THE)
See page 413 for a full company profile.

BELL CANADA
(Public)   TELEPHONE UTILITIES
Exchanges: T M   Stock Symbol: BC.PR.A
19th Floor, 1050 Beaver Hall Hill, Montreal, PQ,
H2Z 1S4   (514) 870-1511
BELL CANADA is engaged in the business of providing telecommunications services in Canada.
J.V. Raymond Cyr, Chairman

TOTAL ASSETS ($000)	18,902,900
TOTAL REVENUE ($000)	8,066,200
NET INCOME ($000)	793,400
EMPLOYEES	51,503
RANK (Profit/Revenue/Assets)	6/15/17

BEMA GOLD CORPORATION
See page 31 for a full company profile.

BENEFICIAL CANADA HOLDINGS INC.
(Private)   FINANCE AND LEASING
8500 Leslie St., Suite 600, Thornhill, ON, L3T 7P1   (905) 882-5050
BENEFICIAL CANADA HOLDINGS INC. is the parent of Beneficial Canada Inc., a consumer loan business, and Beneficial Realty Ltd., a mortgage business.
David J. Farris, Chairman

TOTAL ASSETS ($000)	686,948
TOTAL REVENUE ($000)	125,615
NET INCOME ($000)	14,448
EMPLOYEES	na

BENSON PETROLEUM LTD.
(Public)   OIL AND GAS PRODUCERS
Exchanges: T   Stock Symbol: BEN
Suite 950, 633 - 6th Avenue S.W., Calgary, AB,
T2P 2Y5   (403) 269-5158
BENSON PETROLEUM LTD. is involved in oil and gas exploration and development. The company owns interests in producing oil and gas properties in Alberta and British Columbia.
Stephen V. Benediktson, Chairman

TOTAL ASSETS ($000)	21,841
TOTAL REVENUE ($000)	7,460
NET INCOME ($000)	526
EMPLOYEES	14
RANK (Profit/Revenue/Assets)	691/828/853

BENVEST CAPITAL INC.
(Public)   INVESTMENT COMPANIES AND FUNDS
Exchanges: M   Stock Symbol: BCI
1 Place Ville Marie, Suite 3230, Montreal, PQ,
H3B 3Y2   (514) 877-4299
BENVEST CAPITAL INC. is a merchant bank.
W. John Bennett, Chairman & C.E.O.

TOTAL ASSETS ($000)	31,999
TOTAL REVENUE ($000)	3,089
NET INCOME ($000)	538
EMPLOYEES	7
RANK (Profit/Revenue/Assets)	690/900/755

BERKLEY PETROLEUM CORP.
(Public)   OIL AND GAS PRODUCERS
Exchanges: Z   Stock Symbol: BKP
Suite 1250, 202 - 6th Avenue S.W., Calgary, AB,
T2P 2R9   (403) 269-6488
BERKLEY PETROLEUM CORP. is involved in the acquisition, exploration and development of oil and gas properties.
John N. Woods, Chairman & C.E.O.

TOTAL ASSETS ($000)	19,600
TOTAL REVENUE ($000)	5,542
NET INCOME ($000)	1,206
EMPLOYEES	8
RANK (Profit/Revenue/Assets)	637/856/875

BESTAR INC.

(Public)   HOME FURNISHINGS
Exchanges: M   Stock Symbol: BES
4220 rue Villeneuve, Lac-Megantic, PQ, G6B 2C3   (819) 583-1017
BESTAR manufactures ready-to-assemble furniture. It designs, manufactures and sells over 120 models of ready-to-assemble furniture used mainly as shelving for consumer electronics equipment. The company also designs, manufactures and sells juvenile furniture and home-office furniture.
Paulin Tardif, Chairman President & C.E.O.

TOTAL ASSETS ($000)	21,418
TOTAL REVENUE ($000)	38,472
NET INCOME ($000)	2,226
EMPLOYEES	290
RANK (Profit/Revenue/Assets)	554/599/859

BGR PRECIOUS METALS INC.
See page 461 for a full company profile.

BICC PHILLIPS INC.
See page 238 for a full company profile.

BIG V PHARMACIES CO. LIMITED

(Private)   SPECIALTY STORES
1005 Wilton Grove Road, London, ON, N6A 5G1   (519) 686-5081
BIG V PHARMACIES CO. LIMITED is an employee-owned retail pharmacy.
Norman Puhl, Chairman President & C.E.O.

TOTAL ASSETS ($000)	160,439
TOTAL REVENUE ($000)	514,346
NET INCOME ($000)	12,765
EMPLOYEES	4,092

BIOCHEM PHARMA INC.
See page 227 for a full company profile.

BIOMIRA INC.
See page 228 for a full company profile.

BIONAIRE INC.

(Public)   MISC. CONSUMER PRODUCTS
Exchanges: T M   Stock Symbol: ION
2000 - 32nd Avenue, Lachine, PQ, H8T 3H7   (514) 636-0790
BIONAIRE INC. is involved in the design, manufacture and marketing of air and water treatment and purification products. Its products have been sold principally for home and office use, but it has also developed and is distributing products which have computer and industrial applications. Products are sold through the company's subsidiaries and independent distributors on a worldwide basis.
F. Ross Johnson, Chairman

TOTAL ASSETS ($000)	40,352
TOTAL REVENUE ($000)	73,196
NET INCOME ($000)	3,369
EMPLOYEES	na
RANK (Profit/Revenue/Assets)	498/470/693

BIOVAIL CORPORATION INTERNATIONAL

(Public)   BIOTECHNOLOGY & PHARMACEUTICALS
Exchanges: T   Stock Symbol: BVF
460 Comstock Road, Scarborough, ON, M1L 4S4   (416) 285-6000
BIOVAIL CORPORATION is engaged in pharmaceutical product development services and communications. Its operations include: developing novel drug delivery systems, including controlled research release products; pharmaceutical contract research operations including, labratory testing, clinical research and regulatory services; pharmaceutical manufacturing services; and electronic info systems.
Eugene N. Melnyk, Chairman

TOTAL ASSETS ($000)	35,925
TOTAL REVENUE ($000)	35,543
NET INCOME ($000)	13,262
EMPLOYEES	50
RANK (Profit/Revenue/Assets)	260/617/725

BIRD CONSTRUCTION COMPANY LIMITED

(Public)   CONTRACTORS
Exchanges: W   Stock Symbol: BIRD
Suite 206, 5405 Eglinton Avenue West, Etobicoke, ON,
M9C 5K6   (416) 620-7122
BIRD CONSTRUCTION COMPANY LIMITED is engaged in construction on a contract basis in British Columbia, Alberta, Saskatchewan, Manitoba and Ontario, and is also involved in the selling of building supplies in Manitoba.
R.A. Bird, Chairman

TOTAL ASSETS ($000)	42,132
TOTAL REVENUE ($000)	140,960
NET INCOME ($000)	1,319
EMPLOYEES	200
RANK (Profit/Revenue/Assets)	627/371/679

BLACK & DECKER CANADA INC.

(Private)   APPLIANCES
125 Mural Street, Richmond Hill, ON, L4B 1M4   (905) 886-9511
BLACK AND DECKER CANADA INC. is engaged in the manufacture of household appliances and power tools. The company is a subsidiary of Black & Decker Corporation.
Donald McGuire, V.P. Finance & Administration

TOTAL ASSETS ($000)	133,741
TOTAL REVENUE ($000)	273,815
NET INCOME ($000)	3,564
EMPLOYEES	600

BLACK HAWK MINING INC.

(Public)   METAL MINES
Exchanges: T   Stock Symbol: BHK
Suite 2001, 44 Victoria Street, Toronto, ON, M5C 1Y2 (416) 363-2911
BLACK HAWK MINING INC. is a natural resource company which owns several mines. The Keystone Gold Project in Manitoba is currently in production and is 50% owned by Black Hawk Mining Inc. The Redstone Mine located in Ontario is currently the subject of a feasibility study. Black Hawk is also engaged in the exploration and development of several other mineral properties.
Gordon F. Bub, Chairman & C.E.O.

TOTAL ASSETS ($000)	19,752
TOTAL REVENUE ($000)	5,154
NET INCOME ($000)	96

EMPLOYEES 7
RANK (Profit/Revenue/Assets) 744/863/873

BLACKWOOD HODGE (CANADA) LIMITED
(Private) MACHINERY
P.O. Box 1004, Station A, Weston, ON, M9N 3N5 (416) 244-2531
BLACKWOOD HODGE (CANADA) LIMITED is engaged in the sale, rental, manufacture and service of heavy equipment in Canada. The equipment is primarily used in the construction industry.
John Letwin, President & C.E.O.
TOTAL ASSETS ($000) 88,227
TOTAL REVENUE ($000) 139,163
NET INCOME ($000) (30,556)
EMPLOYEES na

BLUE RANGE RESOURCE CORPORATION
(Public) OIL AND GAS PRODUCERS
Exchanges: T Z Stock Symbol: BBR.A
SUITE 1100, 801 - 6TH AVENUE S.W., Calgary, AB,
T2P 3W2 (403) 264-7422
BLUE RANGE RESOURCE CORPORATION is involved in the exploration, development, production, processing and marketing of natural gas and petroleum reserves in Canada.
Gary Unrau, Chairman
TOTAL ASSETS ($000) 98,030
TOTAL REVENUE ($000) 25,849
NET INCOME ($000) 4,487
EMPLOYEES 37
RANK (Profit/Revenue/Assets) 442/672/490

BMTC GROUP INC.
(Public) WHOLESALE DISTRIBUTORS
Exchanges: M Stock Symbol: GBT.A
8500 Place Marien, Montreal-Est, PQ, H1B 5W8 (514) 335-0260
BMTC GROUP INC. is a holding company. Through its subsidiaries, Brault et Martineau Inc., Ameublements Tanguay Inc. and Colonial Furniture Company (Ottawa) Ltd., the company manages and operates a retail sales network of furniture and household and electronic appliances.
Yves Des Groseillers, Chairman President & C.E.O.
TOTAL ASSETS ($000) 142,909
TOTAL REVENUE ($000) 359,408
NET INCOME ($000) 9,209
EMPLOYEES na
RANK (Profit/Revenue/Assets) 311/231/405

BOC CANADA LIMITED
(Private) CHEMICALS
89 Queensway West, 4th & 5th Floors, Mississauga, ON,
L5B 2V2 (905) 273-7700
BOC CANADA LIMITED manufactures and distributes industrial and medical gases, welding equipment and filler metals, medical equipment, high vacuum equipment and anaesthetic drugs. It is a wholly owned subsidiary of BOC Group plc of Surrey, England.
Robert W. Stevens, Chairman of the Board
TOTAL ASSETS ($000) 177,934
TOTAL REVENUE ($000) 154,908
NET INCOME ($000) 8,148
EMPLOYEES 623

BOLIVAR GOLDFIELDS LTD.
(Public) PRECIOUS METALS
Exchanges: T V Stock Symbol: BVG
Suite 725, 888 Dunsmuir Street, Vancouver, BC,
V6C 3K4 (604) 688-8525
BOLIVAR GOLDFIELDS LTD. is involved in the acquisition, exploration and development of precious base metal properties in Venezuela, Columbia and Cuba.
Ian MacFarlane Gray, President & Director
TOTAL ASSETS ($000) 46,134 (US)
TOTAL REVENUE ($000) 1,528 (US)
NET INCOME ($000) (1,774) (US)
EMPLOYEES 7
RANK (Profit/Revenue/Assets) 866/919/577

BOMBARDIER INC.
See page 255 for a full company profile.

BONAR INC.
See page 293 for a full company profile.

BOREAL INSURANCE INC.
(Private) INSURANCE - PROPERTY & CASUALTY
1100 RENE-LEVESQUE BLVD. W., MONTREAL, PQ,
H3B 4P4 (514) 392-6000
BOREAL INSURANCE INC. provides property and casualty insurance coverage for individuals and organizations.
Jean-Denis Talon, Chairman of the Board
TOTAL ASSETS ($000) 704,009
TOTAL REVENUE ($000) 448,419
NET INCOME ($000) 14,672
EMPLOYEES 779

BOUTIQUES SAN FRANCISCO INCORPOREES (LES)
(Public) CLOTHING STORES
Exchanges: M Stock Symbol: SF.A
50 De Lauzon, Boucherville, PQ, J4B 1E6 (514) 449-1313
LES BOUTIQUES SAN FRANCISCO INCORPOREES is primarily involved in the retail sale of men's, women's and children's clothing. Its target customers are fashion-conscious men, women, and children who wish to purchase reasonably priced good quality clothes.
Paul Delage Roberge, Chairman & C.E.O.
TOTAL ASSETS ($000) 58,275
TOTAL REVENUE ($000) 93,853
NET INCOME ($000) 204
EMPLOYEES 1,500
RANK (Profit/Revenue/Assets) 735/431/597

BOVAR INC.
See page 567 for a full company profile.

BOWATER CANADIAN LIMITED
(Private) EAST COAST FORESTRY
P.O. Box 1150, Liverpool, NS, B0T 1K0 (902) 354-3411

Don McNeil, President & Gen. Manager
TOTAL ASSETS ($000) 275,018
TOTAL REVENUE ($000) 152,261

NET INCOME ($000)   (10,841)
EMPLOYEES   na

BRACKNELL CORPORATION
See page 568 for a full company profile.

BRAMPTON BRICK LIMITED
(Public)   MISC. INDUSTRIAL PRODUCTS
Exchanges: T M   Stock Symbol: BBL.A
225 Wanless Drive, Brampton, ON, L7A 1E9   (905) 840-1011
BRAMPTON BRICK manufactures clay bricks and concrete blocks.
The main operations are in Brampton. The bricks are marketed mainly
in Ontario and Quebec. Concrete blocks are marketed in southern
Ontario. The company's products are used in residential, institutional,
commercial and industrial projects. The company owns a 38.2% equity
interest in the largest producer of concrete bricks in Ontario.
Jeffrey G. Kerbel, President & C.E.O.
TOTAL ASSETS ($000)   69,848
TOTAL REVENUE ($000)   23,769
NET INCOME ($000)   (667)
EMPLOYEES   140
RANK (Profit/Revenue/Assets)   803/691/566

BRANDSELITE INTERNATIONAL CORPORATION
(Public)   WHOLESALE DISTRIBUTORS
Exchanges: T   Stock Symbol: BNT
100 Granton Drive, Richmond Hill, ON, L4B 1H7   (905) 886-8300
BRANDSELITE INTERNATIONAL CORP. operates as the exclusive
agent and distributor of certain leading brands of fragrances, cosmetics,
liquor and luxury gifts, free of all duties and sales and excise taxes, to
airport duty free shops, land border duty free shops, airlines, cruise lines
and the diplomatic corps in Canada and the United States. The company
also markets its own proprietary liquor products.
Sam Ghazouli, C.E.O. & President
TOTAL ASSETS ($000)   13,607
TOTAL REVENUE ($000)   23,863
NET INCOME ($000)   739
EMPLOYEES   44
RANK (Profit/Revenue/Assets)   675/690/977

BRASCADE RESOURCES INC.
See page 509 for a full company profile.

BRASCAN LIMITED
See page 510 for a full company profile.

BREAKWATER RESOURCES LTD.
See page 32 for a full company profile.

BRENDA MINES LTD.
See page 551 for a full company profile.

BRITISH COLUMBIA FERRY CORPORATION
(Crown)   TRANSPORTATION
1112 Fort Street, Victoria, BC, V8V 4V2   (604) 381-1401
BRITISH COLUMBIA FERRY CORPORATION is a government of
British Columbia crown corporation which operates coastal ferry serv-
ices.

Frank A. Rhodes, President & C.E.O.
TOTAL ASSETS ($000)   603,972
TOTAL REVENUE ($000)   334,300
NET INCOME ($000)   (21,780)
EMPLOYEES   4,232

BRITISH COLUMBIA HYDRO AND POWER AUTHORITY
(Crown)   ELECTRICAL UTILITIES
18th Floor 333 Dunsmuir Street, Vancouver, BC,
V6B 5R3   (604) 623-4465
BRITISH COLUMBIA HYDRO AND POWER AUTHORITY is a
provincial crown corporation which generates, transmits and distributes
electricity to a service area which contains more than 92% of B.C.'s
population.
John N. Laxton, Chairman
TOTAL ASSETS ($000)   10,453,000
TOTAL REVENUE ($000)   2,395,000
NET INCOME ($000)   190,000
EMPLOYEES   5,430

BRITISH COLUMBIA PETROLEUM CORPORATION
(Crown)   OIL AND GAS PRODUCERS
Suite 1650, Commerce Place, 400 Burrard Street, Vancouver, BC,
V6C 3A6   (604) 681-5395
BRITISH COLUMBIA PETROLEUM CORPORATION is responsi-
ble for monitoring the operations of the deregulated natural gas market-
place to ensure that the public interest is protected and that all participants
in the market place are treated fairly. Administrative functions include:
the issuing of acquisition orders, the issuing of findings of producer
support, collection of data and collection of the levy.
William R. Strachan, Chairman
TOTAL ASSETS ($000)   3,356
TOTAL REVENUE ($000)   25,327
NET INCOME ($000)   1,949
EMPLOYEES   na

BRITISH COLUMBIA RAILWAY COMPANY
(Crown)   TRANSPORTATION
P.O. Box 8770, Vancouver, BC, V6B 4X6   (604) 986-2012
BRITISH COLUMBIA RAILWAY COMPANY is a provincial crown
corporation which provides a fully-integrated rail freight service within
B.C. One subsidiary, BCR Properties Ltd., owns and manages the
group's non-operating real estate assets. The operating railway subsidi-
ary, B.C. Rail Ltd., derives its revenue mainly from the transport of forest
products, coal, ore, petrochemicals and general freight.
David A. Jiles, Chairman
TOTAL ASSETS ($000)   1,457,312
TOTAL REVENUE ($000)   334,776
NET INCOME ($000)   3,401
EMPLOYEES   2,380

BRITISH COLUMBIA SYSTEMS CORPORATION
(Crown)   COMPUTER SOFTWARE & PROCESSING
4000 Seymour Place, Victoria, BC, V8X 4S8   (604) 389-3101
BRITISH COLUMBIA SYSTEMS CORPORATION is a provincial
crown corporation providing information technology services for the
public sector. Created in 1977 with the enactment of the System Act, BC
Systems offers data processing, professional staff services, data and voice
communications and information access services.

V. Collins, Chairman

TOTAL ASSETS ($000)	99,010
TOTAL REVENUE ($000)	197,088
NET INCOME ($000)	9,276
EMPLOYEES	1,226

BRITISH COLUMBIA TRANSIT

(Crown)   TRANSPORTATION

13401 - 108th Avenue, Vancouver, BC, V6P 6M2   (604) 540-3000

BRITISH COLUMBIA TRANSIT is a crown corporation that serves more than 2.8 million people throughout British Columbia. The corporation's 29 conventional transit systems, in greater Vancouver, greater Victoria and 27 communities across the province, carry 129 million passengers annually. The largest contributor to this total is the Vancouver Regional Transit System with 104.5 million passengers.

Derek Corrigan, Chair

TOTAL ASSETS ($000)	1,859,189
TOTAL REVENUE ($000)	544,800
NET INCOME ($000)	1,961
EMPLOYEES	4,590

BRITISH GROUP HOLDINGS INC.

(Public)   DEVELOPERS

Exchanges: V   Stock Symbol: BHS.A

36A-3033 King George Hwy., Surrey, BC, V4P 1B8   (604) 541-2701

BRITISH GROUP HOLDINGS INC. is involved in land and real estate development.

Henry John Block, Chairman of the Board

TOTAL ASSETS ($000)	16,119
TOTAL REVENUE ($000)	7,346
NET INCOME ($000)	354
EMPLOYEES	6
RANK (Profit/Revenue/Assets)	719/831/933

BRITISH STEEL CANADA INC.

(Private)   STEEL

2255 Cavendish Blvd, Montreal, PQ, H4B 2L8   (514) 481-8145

BRITISH STEEL CANADA INC. is engaged in the selling and distributing of metal products. The company is a wholly owned subsidiary of British Steel Canada Holdings Inc.

Irving Gubitz, President

TOTAL ASSETS ($000)	80,457
TOTAL REVENUE ($000)	126,791
NET INCOME ($000)	1,577
EMPLOYEES	na

BRL ENTERPRISES INC.
See page 511 for a full company profile.

BRUNCOR INC.
See page 347 for a full company profile.

BRUNSWICK MINING AND SMELTING CORPORATION LIMITED
See page 5 for a full company profile.

BT CANADA SECURITIES INC.

(Public)   INVESTMENT COMPANIES AND FUNDS

Exchanges: T   Stock Symbol: BTA.R

Suite 1700, North Tower, Royal Bank Plaza, Toronto, ON, M5J 2J2

BT CANADA SECURITIES INC. is affiliated with BT Bank of Canada.

TOTAL ASSETS ($000)	16,277
TOTAL REVENUE ($000)	8,050
NET INCOME ($000)	4,187
EMPLOYEES	0
RANK (Profit/Revenue/Assets)	455/821/928

BUDD CANADA INC.
See page 215 for a full company profile.

BURNS FOODS (1985) LIMITED

(Private)   FOOD PROCESSING

Box 2520, Station M, Calgary, AB, T2P 3X4   (403) 265-8140

BURNS FOODS (1985) LIMITED is engaged in food processing and distributing.

A.J.E. Child, Chairman

TOTAL ASSETS ($000)	na
TOTAL REVENUE ($000)	793,561
NET INCOME ($000)	na
EMPLOYEES	3,600

BURNS FRY HOLDINGS CORPORATION

(Private)   INVESTMENT HOUSES

Suite 5000, P.O. Box 150, 1 First Canadian Place, Toronto, ON, M5X 1H3   (416) 359-4000

BURNS FRY HOLDINGS CORPORATION owns 100% of Burns Fry Limited, a full service investment banking and securities dealing firm.

Richard J. Lawrence, Chairman

TOTAL ASSETS ($000)	4,617,120
TOTAL REVENUE ($000)	416,877
NET INCOME ($000)	25,650
EMPLOYEES	na

C CORP. INC.

(Private)   FOOD STORES

3100 Cote-Vertu, St-Laurent, PQ, H4R 2J8   (514) 333-5110

C CORP. INC. is a franchisor of five convenience store chains in Quebec, Ontario and Alberta, under the names Provi-Soir, Pinto, Red Rooster, Winks and Winks Express. The company is also involved in the wholesale and retail sale of petroleum products.

Jean Bernier, President

TOTAL ASSETS ($000)	134,677
TOTAL REVENUE ($000)	342,659
NET INCOME ($000)	(43)
EMPLOYEES	na

C.I. FUND MANAGEMENT INC.

(Public)   INVESTMENT COMPANIES AND FUNDS

Exchanges: T   Stock Symbol: CIX

151 Yonge Street, Eighth Floor, Toronto, ON, M5C 2Y1   (416) 364-1145

C.I. FUND MANAGEMENT INC., through its wholly owned subsidiary, Canadian International Fund Management Inc., promotes and manages mutual funds.

A. Warren Moysey, Chairman & C.E.O.

TOTAL ASSETS ($000)	29,182
TOTAL REVENUE ($000)	54,188
NET INCOME ($000)	3,962
EMPLOYEES	200
RANK (Profit/Revenue/Assets)	468/533/777

C-MAC INDUSTRIES INC.
See page 256 for a full company profile.

CABANO TRANSPORTATION GROUP INC.
(Public)   TRANSPORTATION
Exchanges: M   Stock Symbol: KBN
6600 Chemin St-Francois, St-Laurent, PQ, H4S 1B7 (514) 332-4341
CABANO TRANSPORTATION GROUP INC., through its subsidiaries, carries on its operations in the areas of general transport and specialized transport of both short and long distances in Ontario, Quebec, the Maritimes, and the United States.
J. Norman Morrisson, Chairman & C.E.O.

TOTAL ASSETS ($000)	95,217
TOTAL REVENUE ($000)	146,206
NET INCOME ($000)	(1,426)
EMPLOYEES	1,658
RANK (Profit/Revenue/Assets)	832/365/495

CABLETEL COMMUNICATIONS CORP.
(Public)   WHOLESALE DISTRIBUTORS
Exchanges: T   Stock Symbol: TTV
120 Gibson Drive, Markham, ON, L3R 2Z3   (905) 475-1020
CABLETEL COMMUNICATIONS CORP. is a full-service distributor of broadband communications equipment used in the cable television and telecommunications industries. The company's core business focuses on the distribution and sale of over 5,000 products required to construct, build, maintain and upgrade cable television and telecommunications systems.
Arnold S. Tenney, Chairman

TOTAL ASSETS ($000)	17,047
TOTAL REVENUE ($000)	48,301
NET INCOME ($000)	1,484
EMPLOYEES	81
RANK (Profit/Revenue/Assets)	612/557/912

CABRE EXPLORATION LTD.
See page 77 for a full company profile.

CADBURY BEVERAGES CANADA INC.
(Private)   FOOD PROCESSING
2700 Matheson Blvd.East, East Tower, Suite 400, Mississauga, ON, L4W 4X1   (905) 629-1899
CADBURY BEVERAGES CANADA INC. makes and distributes fruit-based and carbonated beverages.
Ron Segal & David Irwin, Presidents

TOTAL ASSETS ($000)	na
TOTAL REVENUE ($000)	212,155
NET INCOME ($000)	na
EMPLOYEES	na

CAE INC.
See page 257 for a full company profile.

CAISSE CENTRALE DESJARDINS DU QUEBEC (LA)
(Fin. Co-op)   CREDIT UNIONS
1 Complexe Desjardins, Suite 2822, Montreal, PQ, H5B 1B3   (514) 281-7070
The CAISSE CENTRALE has a threefold mandate. Its primary mandate is to act as financial agent within the Desjardins Group. Increasing and diversifying sources of funds and income needed to fulfill its role in the Desjardins Group and to insure its own group is the second mandate of the Caisse. Its third mandate is to participate in the development of services offered by the Group to large companies.
Claude Beland, Chairman of the Board

TOTAL ASSETS ($000)	5,428,000
TOTAL REVENUE ($000)	387,000
NET INCOME ($000)	17,000
EMPLOYEES	206

CAISSE DE DEPOT ET PLACEMENT DU QUEBEC
(Crown)   INVESTMENT COMPANIES AND FUNDS
1981 avenue McGill College, Montreal, PQ, H3A 3C7 (514) 842-3261
The CAISSE is a public pension and insurance fund manager. Its dual mandate consists in achieving an optimal financial return and in contributing through its actions to the dynamism of the Quebec economy, while ensuring the security of capital under its management.
Jean-Claude Delorme, Chairman of the Board

TOTAL ASSETS ($000)	45,940,000
TOTAL REVENUE ($000)	2,769,000
NET INCOME ($000)	2,717,000
EMPLOYEES	na

CALDWELL PARTNERS INTERNATIONAL INC. (THE)
(Public)   CONSULTING
Exchanges: T   Stock Symbol: CWL.A
64 Prince Arthur Avenue, Toronto, ON, M5R 1B4   (416) 920-7702
CALDWELL PARTNERS INTERNATIONAL INC. is an executive search consulting firm specializing in the recruitment of executives on behalf of its clients. The firm's clients include a broad range of business enterprises, public and private institutions, governments and government agencies.
C. Douglas Caldwell, Chairman & Managing Director

TOTAL ASSETS ($000)	13,870
TOTAL REVENUE ($000)	14,670
NET INCOME ($000)	2,850
EMPLOYEES	50
RANK (Profit/Revenue/Assets)	517/762/966

CALEDONIA MINING CORPORATION
See page 33 for a full company profile.

CALGARY CO-OPERATIVE ASSOCIATION LIMITED
(Non-fin Co-op)   DEPARTMENT STORES
8818 Macleod Trail S.E., Calgary, AB, T2H 0M5   (403) 299-4000
CALGARY CO-OPERATIVE ASSOCIATION LIMITED is a consumer cooperative. It operates 14 one-stop shopping centres, which retail food, drugs, petroleum, hardware, dry goods and services. In addition, the co-op has five home improvement centres, and travel services with seven offices.
Bruno A. Friesen, Chairman of the Board

TOTAL ASSETS ($000)	138,714
TOTAL REVENUE ($000)	517,786

NET INCOME ($000)	13,961
EMPLOYEES	3,475

CALIAN TECHNOLOGY LTD.
(Public)   ELECTRICAL & ELECTRONIC
Exchanges: T   Stock Symbol: CTY
300 Legget Drive, Kanata, ON, K2K 1Y5   (613) 599-7200
CALIAN TECHNOLOGY LTD. is involved in the design, manufacture and integration of electronic systems with applications in the mobile satellite communications, space and defense markets.
Larry O'Brien, Chairman & C.E.O.

TOTAL ASSETS ($000)	33,536
TOTAL REVENUE ($000)	45,452
NET INCOME ($000)	2,645
EMPLOYEES	999
RANK (Profit/Revenue/Assets)	530/570/742

CALL-NET ENTERPRISES INC.
See page 371 for a full company profile.

CAM-NET COMMUNICATIONS NETWORK INC.
(Public)   TELECOMMUNICATIONS
Exchanges: V Q   Stock Symbol: CWK
Suite 795, 885 Dunsmuir Street, Vancouver, BC,
V6C 1N5   (604) 684-9016
CAM-NET COMMUNICATIONS NETWORK INC., through its subsidiaries, provides alternative long distance voice and data telecommunication services to business and residential customers in the provinces of B.C., Ontario, Quebec and Alberta.
Daryl Buerge, Chairman & C.E.O.

TOTAL ASSETS ($000)	55,521
TOTAL REVENUE ($000)	48,028
NET INCOME ($000)	(18,913)
EMPLOYEES	137
RANK (Profit/Revenue/Assets)	964/558/607

CAMBERLY ENERGY LTD.
(Public)   OIL AND GAS PRODUCERS
Exchanges: T   Stock Symbol: CEL
Suite 2400, 125 - 9th Avenue S.E., Calgary, AB,
T2G 0P6   (403) 265-5997
CAMBERLY ENERGY LTD. is involved in the acquisition, exploration and development of oil and gas properties principally in Alberta and Saskatchewan.
Michael K. Duggan, President & C.E.O.

TOTAL ASSETS ($000)	23,431
TOTAL REVENUE ($000)	12,000
NET INCOME ($000)	374
EMPLOYEES	15
RANK (Profit/Revenue/Assets)	718/781/833

CAMBIEX EXPLORATION INC.
(Public)   PRECIOUS METALS
Exchanges: T M   Stock Symbol: CBX
Suite 850, 800 Rene-Levesque Blvd., Montreal, PQ,
H3B 1X9   (514) 878-3166
CAMBIEX EXPLORATION INC. is involved in the acquisition, exploration and development of mining properties located in Quebec and belonging to Cambior Inc.

Come Carbonneau, Chairman

TOTAL ASSETS ($000)	18,120
TOTAL REVENUE ($000)	150
NET INCOME ($000)	(1,395)
EMPLOYEES	na
RANK (Profit/Revenue/Assets)	830/982/897

CAMBIOR INC.
See page 34 for a full company profile.

CAMBRIDGE SHOPPING CENTRES LIMITED
See page 303 for a full company profile.

CAMCO INC.
See page 204 for a full company profile.

CAMDEV CORPORATION
See page 304 for a full company profile.

CAMECO CORPORATION
See page 6 for a full company profile.

CAMPBELL RESOURCES INC.
See page 35 for a full company profile.

CAMPBELL SOUP COMPANY LTD
(Private)   FOOD PROCESSING
60 Birmingham Street, Toronto, ON, M8V 2B8   (416) 251-1131
CAMPBELL SOUP CO. LTD. is engaged in the manufacture of convenience foods such as soups, frozen meals and desserts, juices, sauces and gravies. Its brand names include 's, Le Menu, Swanson, Pepperidge Farm, Prego, A1, Franco American, V-8, Habitant and Pace. The company is wholly owned by Soup Co. of the United States.
R.F. Bernstock, Chairman

TOTAL ASSETS ($000)	335,179
TOTAL REVENUE ($000)	441,239
NET INCOME ($000)	na
EMPLOYEES	1,300

CAMVEC CORPORATION
(Public)   OTHER SERVICES
Exchanges: T   Stock Symbol: CV
1190 Meyerside Drive, Mississauga, ON, M5T 1R7   (416) 795-3457
CAMVEC CORPORATION, through its operating subsidiaries, is involved in the household moving business as well as commercial office relocation.
Arthur W. Walker, Chairman & C.E.O.

TOTAL ASSETS ($000)	18,879
TOTAL REVENUE ($000)	21,414
NET INCOME ($000)	1,074
EMPLOYEES	1,200
RANK (Profit/Revenue/Assets)	651/709/882

CANABRAVA DIAMOND CORPORATION
(Public)   OTHER MINES
Exchanges: V   Stock Symbol: CNB
Suite 1280, 1055 West Hastings Street, Vancouver, BC,
V6E 2E9   (604) 683-4504

CANABRAVA DIAMOND CORPORATION is involved in mineral exploration and holds a 60% interest in a gold and silver property in the Iskut River area of British Columbia.
George Vooro, President & C.E.O.

TOTAL ASSETS ($000)	12,732
TOTAL REVENUE ($000)	273
NET INCOME ($000)	18
EMPLOYEES	4
RANK (Profit/Revenue/Assets)	752/976/998

CANADA LIFE ASSURANCE COMPANY (THE)
(Private) INSURANCE - LIFE
330 University Avenue, Toronto, ON, M5G 1R8 (416) 597-1456
THE CANADA LIFE ASSURANCE COMPANY offers products and services to meet its clients' needs for financial protection in the event of certain risks including life, medical, dental, disability and general insurance, accumulation of assets in the form of annuity, pension and investment products and financial and investment management.
E.H. Crawford, Chairman

TOTAL ASSETS ($000)	24,898,024
TOTAL REVENUE ($000)	4,609,276
NET INCOME ($000)	111,638
EMPLOYEES	3,412

CANADA MALTING CO. LIMITED
See page 186 for a full company profile.

CANADA MORTGAGE AND HOUSING CORPORATION
(Crown) FINANCE AND LEASING
National Office, 700 Montreal Road, Ottawa, ON,
K1A 0P7 (613) 748-2000
CANADA MORTGAGE AND HOUSING is a Crown Corporation with the authority to act for the Government of Canada in all matters prescribed by housing legislation, principally the National Housing Act. CMHC's purpose, as embodied in the National Housing Act, is to promote the construction of new houses, the repair and modernization of existing housing, and the improvement of housing and living conditions.
Claude F. Bennett, Chairman of the Board

TOTAL ASSETS ($000)	13,857,947
TOTAL REVENUE ($000)	1,309,482
NET INCOME ($000)	(93,497)
EMPLOYEES	2,975

CANADA PORTS CORPORATION
(Crown) TRANSPORTATION
99 Metcalfe Street, 8th Floor, Ottawa, ON, K1A 0N6 (613) 957-6787
CANADA PORTS CORPORATION describes a federal system of ports administered pursuant to the Canada Ports Corporation Act. It handles nearly half of the overall Canadian port traffic and more than 95% of container traffic.
Arnold E. Masters, Chairman of the Board

TOTAL ASSETS ($000)	249,562
TOTAL REVENUE ($000)	64,297
NET INCOME ($000)	5,289
EMPLOYEES	na

CANADA POST CORPORATION
(Crown) OTHER SERVICES
Canada Post Place, 2701 Riverside Drive, Ottawa, ON,
K1A 0B1 (613) 734-8440

CANADA POST CORPORATION is a Canadian company meeting the advertising, communications and physical distribution needs of Canadian and international customers. CANADA POST handles 10 billion messages and parcels annually.
Donald H. Lander, Chairman

TOTAL ASSETS ($000)	2,612,837
TOTAL REVENUE ($000)	4,117,948
NET INCOME ($000)	(270,390)
EMPLOYEES	62,878

CANADA SAFEWAY LIMITED
(Private) FOOD STORES
1020 - 64th Avenue N.E., Calgary, AB, T2E 7V8 (403) 730-3500
CANADA SAFEWAY LIMITED operates in the grocery industry. The company's retail stores are located in Western Canada and Ontario.
Grant Hansen, President & C.O.O.

TOTAL ASSETS ($000)	1,153,900
TOTAL REVENUE ($000)	4,628,300
NET INCOME ($000)	na
EMPLOYEES	30,000

CANADA SOUTHERN PETROLEUM LTD.
See page 78 for a full company profile.

CANADA STARCH COMPANY (1990) INC.
(Private) FOOD PROCESSING
401 The West Mall, Etobicoke, ON, M9C 5H9 (416) 620-2300
CANADA STARCH COMPANY (1990) INC. manufactures more than 60 brand name foods and household products, and more than 200 corn wet milling products. It services more than 60 basic industries in Canada.
M.R. Pyatt, Chairman of the Board

TOTAL ASSETS ($000)	363,948
TOTAL REVENUE ($000)	457,121
NET INCOME ($000)	(5,801)
EMPLOYEES	1,128

CANADA TRUST INCOME INVESTMENTS
See page 462 for a full company profile.

CANADA TRUSTCO MORTGAGE COMPANY
See page 444 for a full company profile.

CANADA TUNGSTEN INC.
See page 7 for a full company profile.

CANADA 3000 AIRLINES LIMITED
(Private) TRANSPORTATION
27 Fasken Drive, Toronto, ON, M9W 1K7 (416) 620-2300
CANADA 3000 AIRLINES LIMITED operates a domestic and international charter airline service.

TOTAL ASSETS ($000)	72,576
TOTAL REVENUE ($000)	229,661
NET INCOME ($000)	3,912
EMPLOYEES	na

CANADEX RESOURCES LIMITED
(Public) TRANSPORTATION
Exchanges: T Stock Symbol: CDX
10 Sun Pac Boulevard, Brampton, ON, L6S 4R5 (800) 265-6942

Canada Company Handbook

CANADEX RESOURCES is involved in busing, vehicle leasing, warehousing, and freight. It has interests in oil and gas properties and various other investments.

J.A. Riddell, President

TOTAL ASSETS ($000)	12,767
TOTAL REVENUE ($000)	10,424
NET INCOME ($000)	853
EMPLOYEES	260
RANK (Profit/Revenue/Assets)	666/796/996

CANADIAN AIRLINES CORPORATION
See page 323 for a full company profile.

CANADIAN AIRLINES INTERNATIONAL LTD.
(Private)　　　　　　　　　TRANSPORTATION
Suite 2800, 700 - 2nd Street S.W., Calgary, AB,
T2P 2W2　　　　　　　　　(403) 294-2000
CANADIAN AIRLINES INTERNATIONAL LTD. is involved in the airline transportation industry. It is a wholly owned subsidiary of Canadian Airlines Corporation .

Rhys T. Eyton, Chairman

TOTAL ASSETS ($000)	2,352,300
TOTAL REVENUE ($000)	2,770,000
NET INCOME ($000)	(22,300)
EMPLOYEES	14,914

CANADIAN BANK NOTE COMPANY, LIMITED
(Public)　　　　　　PUBLISHING & PRINTING
Exchanges: T　　　　Stock Symbol: CBK
145 Richmond Road, Ottawa, ON, K1Z 1A1　　(613) 722-3421
CANADIAN BANK NOTE COMPANY, LIMITED is a producer of bank notes. In addition, it is a major producer of passports, postage stamps, securities certificates, lottery products and other high security documents. The company markets its products to government agencies and authorities as well as institutional and other customers in more than forty countries.

Douglas R. Arends, Chairman & C.E.O.

TOTAL ASSETS ($000)	83,274
TOTAL REVENUE ($000)	67,578
NET INCOME ($000)	3,402
EMPLOYEES	521
RANK (Profit/Revenue/Assets)	495/489/526

CANADIAN BROADCASTING CORPORATION
(Crown)　　　　　　　　　　BROADCASTING
P.O. Box 8478, 1500 Bronson Avenue, Ottawa, ON,
K1G 3J5　　　　　　　　　(613) 724-1200
The CBC's objective is to develop and provide a national broadcasting service for all Canadians in both official languages, in television and radio, and to provide an international service. Both services should be primarily Canadian in content and character.

William Neville, Interim Chairman

TOTAL ASSETS ($000)	1,582,041
TOTAL REVENUE ($000)	374,410
NET INCOME ($000)	(152,376)
EMPLOYEES	na

CANADIAN CO-OPERATIVE WOOL GROWERS LIMITED
(Non-fin Co-op)　　　WHOLESALE DISTRIBUTORS
Box 130, Carleton Place, ON, K7C 3P3　　(613) 257-2714
CANADIAN CO-OPERATIVE WOOL GROWERS is involved in wool marketing, retail clothing, and animal health products and equipment.

Donna Zeman, Executive Director

TOTAL ASSETS ($000)	2,043
TOTAL REVENUE ($000)	3,037
NET INCOME ($000)	48
EMPLOYEES	30

CANADIAN COMMERCIAL CORPORATION
(Crown)　　　　　　　　　OTHER SERVICES
Metropolitan Centre, 11th Floor, 50 O'Connor Street, Ottawa, ON,
K1A 0S6　　　　　　　　　(613) 996-0034
CANADIAN COMMERCIAL provides a government-to-government export contracting service to the private and public sectors in Canada. It also provides a contract management service to foreign governmental clients in order to ensure their satisfaction as to the quality, cost and delivery of Canadian goods and services.

Ranald Quail, President

TOTAL ASSETS ($000)	390,631
TOTAL REVENUE ($000)	880,565
NET INCOME ($000)	1,195
EMPLOYEES	na

CANADIAN CONQUEST EXPLORATION INC.
(Public)　　　　　　OIL AND GAS PRODUCERS
Exchanges: T Z　　　　Stock Symbol: CCN
Suite 1100, 736 - 8th Avenue S.W., Calgary, AB,
T2P 1H4　　　　　　　　　(403) 260-6300
CANADIAN CONQUEST EXPLORATION INC. is an oil and gas company headquartered in Calgary, Alberta. It focuses its operations on the exploration and development of petroleum and natural gas reserves in Alberta and Saskatchewan.

Daniel A. Mercier, President & C.E.O.

TOTAL ASSETS ($000)	43,729
TOTAL REVENUE ($000)	15,408
NET INCOME ($000)	2,383
EMPLOYEES	42
RANK (Profit/Revenue/Assets)	547/752/669

CANADIAN CRUDE SEPARATORS INC.
(Public)　　　　OIL AND GAS FIELD SERVICES
Exchanges: Z　　　　Stock Symbol: CCR
Suite 1750, 521 - 3 Avenue S.W., Calgary, AB,
T2P 3T3　　　　　　　　　(403) 233-7565
CANADIAN CRUDE SEPARATORS INC. provides environmental services to the oil and gas industry in Western Canada.

David P. Werklund, President & C.E.O.

TOTAL ASSETS ($000)	18,435
TOTAL REVENUE ($000)	12,673
NET INCOME ($000)	1,659
EMPLOYEES	120
RANK (Profit/Revenue/Assets)	597/775/888

CANADIAN DAIRY COMMISSION (THE)

(Crown)   AGRICULTURE
1525 Carling Avenue, Suite 300, Ottawa, ON,
K1A 0Z2   (613) 998-9490
THE CANADIAN DAIRY COMMISSION has the authority to purchase, store, process, or dispose of dairy products; make payments to milk and cream producers for the purpose of stabilizing the price of industrial milk and cream; investigate matters relating to the production, processing or marketing of any dairy product; help promote the use of dairy products; and receive funds for the disposal of dairy products.
Gilles Pregent, Chairman & C.E.O.

TOTAL ASSETS ($000)	176,429
TOTAL REVENUE ($000)	330,148
NET INCOME ($000)	13,544
EMPLOYEES	58

CANADIAN FILM DEVELOPMENT CORPORATION

(Crown)   FINANCE AND LEASING
Tour de la Banque Nationale, 600 rue de la Gauchetiere O., 14e etage, Montreal, PQ, H3B 4L8   (514) 283-6363
CANADIAN FILM DEVELOPMENT CORP. is a Crown corporation with a mandate to develop and promote Canada's film, television and video industry. Through Telefilm Canada, the Government of Canada provides support, as a partner, to the private sector for the production of film and broadcast material, either in the form of investment funds or through a variety of resources at Telefilm's disposal.
Robert Dinan, Chairman

TOTAL ASSETS ($000)	39,236
TOTAL REVENUE ($000)	940
NET INCOME ($000)	(118,254)
EMPLOYEES	178

CANADIAN FRACMASTER LTD.

See page 79 for a full company profile.

CANADIAN GENERAL INVESTMENTS LIMITED

See page 463 for a full company profile.

CANADIAN HUNTER EXPLORATION LTD.

(Private)   OIL AND GAS PRODUCERS
Suite 2000, 605 - 5th Avenue S.W., Calgary, AB,
T2P 3H5   (403) 260-1000
CANADIAN HUNTER EXPLORATION LTD. is involved in the exploration, development and production of oil and gas, primarily in Western Canada, and acts as agent and operator of the Canadian Hunter Exploration Ltd. joint venture. The company is a wholly owned subsidiary of Noranda Inc.
J.K. Gray, Chairman

TOTAL ASSETS ($000)	826,775
TOTAL REVENUE ($000)	287,615
NET INCOME ($000)	25,129
EMPLOYEES	273

CANADIAN HYDRO DEVELOPERS, INC.

(Public)   ELECTRICAL UTILITIES
Exchanges: T Q Z   Stock Symbol: KHD
Suite 200, 622 - 5th Avenue S.W., Calgary, AB,
T2P 0M6   (403) 269-9379

CANADIAN HYDRO DEVELOPERS, INC. is a developer, owner and operator of independent hydroelectric power projects.
Jack D. McCleary, President

TOTAL ASSETS ($000)	21,656
TOTAL REVENUE ($000)	1,548
NET INCOME ($000)	(495)
EMPLOYEES	7
RANK (Profit/Revenue/Assets)	793/935/856

CANADIAN IMPERIAL BANK OF COMMERCE

See page 445 for a full company profile.

CANADIAN JOREX LIMITED

(Public)   OIL AND GAS PRODUCERS
Exchanges: T   Stock Symbol: CJX
2870 Bow Valley Square IV, 250 - 6th Avenue S.W., Calgary, AB,
T2P 3H7   (403) 266-0930
CANADIAN JOREX LIMITED is involved in oil and gas exploration and production. The Company's areas of major interest are Thorsby and Brant/Farrow, Alberta.
Louis J. Schneider, President & C.E.O.

TOTAL ASSETS ($000)	35,538
TOTAL REVENUE ($000)	10,479
NET INCOME ($000)	953
EMPLOYEES	20
RANK (Profit/Revenue/Assets)	662/795/728

CANADIAN LIQUID AIR LTD.

(Private)   MISC. INDUSTRIAL PRODUCTS
1155 Sherbrooke St. W., Montreal, PQ, H3A 2N3   (514) 842-5431
CANADIAN LIQUID AIR LTD. is a producer and marketer of industrial, medical and specialty gases and welding equipment. It is a member of the Air Liquide group of companies which operates in 58 countries on five continents and is headed by L'Air Liquide S.A. of France.
Norman M. Seagram, Chairman & C.E.O.

TOTAL ASSETS ($000)	434,916
TOTAL REVENUE ($000)	316,224
NET INCOME ($000)	17,371
EMPLOYEES	na

CANADIAN MANOIR INDUSTRIES LIMITED

See page 205 for a full company profile.

CANADIAN MAPLE LEAF FINANCIAL CORPORATION INC.

(Public)   INVESTMENT COMPANIES AND FUNDS
Exchanges: T   Stock Symbol: CNF.A
Suite 850, 999 West Hastings Street, Vancouver, BC,
V6C 2W2   (604) 684-7411
CANADIAN MAPLE LEAF FINANCIAL CORPORATION is a specialty corporate finance company. Its operational focus is high growth mid-market investment and investment management. The company has extensive experience in Western Canada and the Pacific Rim.
Steven Funk, Chairman & C.E.O.

TOTAL ASSETS ($000)	31,159
TOTAL REVENUE ($000)	9,057
NET INCOME ($000)	1,735
EMPLOYEES	14
RANK (Profit/Revenue/Assets)	620/832/763

CANADIAN MARCONI COMPANY
See page 258 for a full company profile.

CANADIAN NATIONAL RAILWAY SYSTEM
(Crown)   TRANSPORTATION
935 Rue de la Gauchetiere O., Montreal, PQ,
H3B 2M9   (514) 399-5430
CANADIAN NATIONAL RAILWAY is a federal crown corporation
engaged primarily in railway transportation and distribution. The major
activity of the company, rail transportation, is conducted across Canada
and the United States. Other operating divisions encompass real estate
and international consulting.
Brian R.D. Smith, Chairman

TOTAL ASSETS ($000)	7,809,000
TOTAL REVENUE ($000)	4,696,000
NET INCOME ($000)	245,000
EMPLOYEES	32,400

CANADIAN NATURAL RESOURCES LIMITED
See page 80 for a full company profile.

CANADIAN NORTHSTAR CORPORATION
(Public)   OIL AND GAS PRODUCERS
Exchanges: T Z   Stock Symbol: CNX
Suite 750, 1111 Melville Street, Vancouver, BC,
V6E 3V6   (604) 669-7624
CANADIAN NORTHSTAR CORP. is a diversified investment com-
pany. The company is active in merchant banking and investment
activities in Canada.
Ian Cockwell, Chairman & President

TOTAL ASSETS ($000)	77,225
TOTAL REVENUE ($000)	6,232
NET INCOME ($000)	4,909
EMPLOYEES	100
RANK (Profit/Revenue/Assets)	426/840/538

CANADIAN OCCIDENTAL PETROLEUM LTD.
See page 81 for a full company profile.

CANADIAN OVERSEAS PACKAGING INDUSTRIES LIMITED
(Private)   PACKAGING AND CONTAINERS
44 Prince William St, Suite 900, Saint John, NB,
E2L 4S6   (506) 669-7624

TOTAL ASSETS ($000)	295,154
TOTAL REVENUE ($000)	144,247
NET INCOME ($000)	28,402
EMPLOYEES	na

CANADIAN PACIFIC ENTERPRISES LIMITED
(Private)   MANAGEMENT AND DIVERSIFIED
Ste 800, Place du Canada, Montreal, PQ, H3C 3A4   (514) 395-6913
CANADIAN PACIFIC ENTERPRISES LIMITED is a diversified Canadian company which operates internationally through its subsidiaries.
These subsidiaries operate in the following segments: oil and gas, mines
and minerals, forest products, iron and steel, real estate, food processing
and financial. Most operations are carried out in North America and serve
the world market.

TOTAL ASSETS ($000)	10,246,300
TOTAL REVENUE ($000)	2,416,800
NET INCOME ($000)	159,100
EMPLOYEES	na

CANADIAN PACIFIC EXPRESS & TRANSPORT LTD.
(Private)   TRANSPORTATION
2255 Sheppard Avenue East, Willowdale, ON,
M2J 4Y1   (416) 497-7900
CANADIAN PACIFIC EXPRESS & TRANSPORT LTD. carries out
the trucking services of Canadian Pacific Limited, operating as CP
Trucks. It provides truckload and less-than-truckload freight service,
primarily in Canada. CP Trucks operates in 143 locations in Canada, and
its fleet consists of about 1,200 trucks, 3,300 highway trailers and 1,000
tractors. About 43% of 1992 revenues were generated in Ontario.
Ralph Teoli, President & C.E.O.

TOTAL ASSETS ($000)	138,302
TOTAL REVENUE ($000)	284,363
NET INCOME ($000)	na
EMPLOYEES	na

CANADIAN PACIFIC HOTELS & RESORTS INC.
(Private)   LODGING
One University Avenue, Suite 1400, Toronto, ON,
M5J 2P1   (416) 367-7111
CANADIAN PACIFIC HOTELS operates over 25 hotels, which it
owns, leases or manages. Hotels are located in city centre and resort
locations across Canada.
Robert S. DeMone, Chairman President & C.E.O.

TOTAL ASSETS ($000)	1,070,316
TOTAL REVENUE ($000)	475,409
NET INCOME ($000)	33,059
EMPLOYEES	7,100

CANADIAN PACIFIC LIMITED
See page 512 for a full company profile.

CANADIAN PIONEER ENERGY INC.
(Public)   OIL AND GAS PRODUCERS
Exchanges: T   Stock Symbol: CEQ
Suite 1700, 333 - 5th Avenue S.W., Calgary, AB,
T2P 3B6   (403) 265-9471
CANADIAN PIONEER ENERGY INC. is involved in the acquisition,
exploration, development and production of hydrocardon reserves in
Canada.
James W. Beckerleg, Chairman

TOTAL ASSETS ($000)	111,619
TOTAL REVENUE ($000)	18,881
NET INCOME ($000)	(51,729)
EMPLOYEES	35
RANK (Profit/Revenue/Assets)	988/722/459

CANADIAN REAL ESTATE INVESTMENT TRUST
(Public)   PROPERTY MGMNT & INVESTMENT
Exchanges: T   Stock Symbol: REF.UN
Suite 2012, 200 King Street West, P.O. Box 26, Toronto, ON,
M5H 3T4   (416) 971-7771
CANADIAN REAL ESTATE INVESTMENT TRUST is an equity real
estate trust, which acquires and owns a portfolio of income-producing
properties. The company specializes in the acquisition and ownership of

community shopping centres and warehouse properties across Canada. Its principal objective is to consistently provide increasing quarterly distributions of rental income along with capital appreciation to unitholders.

Gary M. Samuel, President

TOTAL ASSETS ($000)	37,482
TOTAL REVENUE ($000)	6,424
NET INCOME ($000)	1,488
EMPLOYEES	6
RANK (Profit/Revenue/Assets)	610/837/710

CANADIAN REYNOLDS METALS COMPANY LIMITED
(Private) METAL FABRICATORS
Room 802, 1420 Sherbrooke St. W., Montreal, PQ,
H3G 1K9 (514) 842-6487
CANADIAN REYNOLDS METALS COMPANY is a producer of primary aluminum and fabricated finished and semi-finished aluminium products. The company is a wholly owned subsidiary of Reynolds Metals Company of Richmond, Virginia.

William O. Bourke, Chairman & C.E.O.

TOTAL ASSETS ($000)	1,437,849
TOTAL REVENUE ($000)	862,833
NET INCOME ($000)	(32,468)

CANADIAN SATELLITE COMMUNICATIONS INC.
See page 372 for a full company profile.

CANADIAN TIRE CORPORATION, LIMITED
See page 414 for a full company profile.

CANADIAN ULTRAMAR LIMITED
(Private) INTEGRATED OILS
1356 Pleasant Street, Eastern Passage, NS,
B2Y 3Y9 (902) 465-6340
CANADIAN ULTRAMAR LTD. through its wholly owned subsidiary is engaged in petroleum refining and marketing.

Garry Garcin, Senior Vice President

TOTAL ASSETS ($000)	1,233,179
TOTAL REVENUE ($000)	1,746,753
NET INCOME ($000)	59,601
EMPLOYEES	1,400

CANADIAN UTILITIES LIMITED
See page 348 for a full company profile.

CANADIAN WESTERN BANK
See page 446 for a full company profile.

CANADIAN WESTERN NATURAL GAS COMPANY LIMITED
See page 349 for a full company profile.

CANADIAN 88 ENERGY CORP.
(Public) OIL AND GAS PRODUCERS
Exchanges: T Z Stock Symbol: EEE
Canterra Tower, Suite 700, 400 - 3rd Avenue S.W., Calgary, AB,
T2P 4H2 (403) 974-8800
CANADIAN 88 ENERGY CORP. is involved in the pursuit of diversified developments and business opportunities in the areas of oil and gas

exploration, gas plants, refining and petrochemical development throughout Western Canada through its wholly owned subsidiaries.

James D. Raymond, Chairman

TOTAL ASSETS ($000)	107,947
TOTAL REVENUE ($000)	29,168
NET INCOME ($000)	4,099
EMPLOYEES	45
RANK (Profit/Revenue/Assets)	460/653/468

CANAM MANAC GROUP INC. (THE)
See page 239 for a full company profile.

CANARC RESOURCE CORP.
(Public) PRECIOUS METALS
Exchanges: T V Q Stock Symbol: CCM
Suite 800, 850 West Hastings Street, Vancouver, BC,
V6C 1E1 (604) 685-9700
CANARC RESOURCE CORP. is involved in the acquisition, exploration and development of precious metal properties. The company has exploration projects in Canada, Costa Rica, Venezuela, Guyana and Surinam.

Bradford James Cooke, President & C.E.O.

TOTAL ASSETS ($000)	21,448 (US)
TOTAL REVENUE ($000)	258 (US)
NET INCOME ($000)	(2,472) (US)
EMPLOYEES	18
RANK (Profit/Revenue/Assets)	884/966/775

CANBRA FOODS LTD.
(Public) FOOD PROCESSING
Exchanges: T Stock Symbol: CBF
2415 - 2nd Avenue A. North, Lethbridge, AB,
T1H 0G7 (403) 329-5500
CANBRA FOODS LTD. is a fully-integrated oilseed crushing, refining, processing and packaging company. The company's major products include cooking and salad oil, margarine, shortening and a full line of proteins. Products are sold in packaged form to retailers, to distributors in the foodservice industry and in bulk form as a key ingredient for food applications.

Robert A. Wisener, Chairman

TOTAL ASSETS ($000)	64,441
TOTAL REVENUE ($000)	155,259
NET INCOME ($000)	3,526
EMPLOYEES	250
RANK (Profit/Revenue/Assets)	488/353/579

CANFOR CORPORATION
See page 155 for a full company profile.

CANGENE CORPORATION
(Public) BIOTECHNOLOGY & PHARMACEUTICALS
Exchanges: T Stock Symbol: CNJ
6280 Northwest Drive, Mississauga, ON, L4V 1J7 (905) 673-0200
CANGENE CORPORATION is a biotechnology company involved in the commercialization of innovative technology, discovered and developed at Cangene, in the field of diagnostics and therapeutics.

Donald S. Layne, Chairman

TOTAL ASSETS ($000)	14,408
TOTAL REVENUE ($000)	2,166

NET INCOME ($000) (7,176)
EMPLOYEES 95
RANK (Profit/Revenue/Assets) 927/916/955

CANGOLD RESOURCES INC.
(Public) PRECIOUS METALS
Exchanges: T M V Stock Symbol: CGR
1389 Dundas St. W., Toronto, ON, M6J 1Y4 (416) 361-3505
CANGOLD RESOURCES INC. is involved in mineral exploration and development.
David J. Birkenshaw, C.E.O.
TOTAL ASSETS ($000) 12,736
TOTAL REVENUE ($000) 3,590
NET INCOME ($000) 1,509
EMPLOYEES na
RANK (Profit/Revenue/Assets) 609/886/997

CANLAN INVESTMENT CORPORATION
(Public) DEVELOPERS
Exchanges: T Stock Symbol: CAI
Suite 1180, 1333 West Broadway, Vancouver, BC,
V6H 4C1 (604) 736-9152
CANLAN INVESTMENT CORPORATION is an investment company. It generates revenue primarily from developing land and oper ating revenue properties.
John B. Ross, President & C.E.O.
TOTAL ASSETS ($000) 101,561
TOTAL REVENUE ($000) 47,798
NET INCOME ($000) 4,103
EMPLOYEES 266
RANK (Profit/Revenue/Assets) 459/559/480

CANON CANADA INC.
(Private) WHOLESALE DISTRIBUTORS
6390 Dixie Road, Mississauga, ON, L5T 1P7 (905) 795-1111
CANON CANADA INC. is wholly owned by Canon U.S.A. Inc. The company sells consumer electronic and business products sales.
H. Murase, Chairman
TOTAL ASSETS ($000) 263,460
TOTAL REVENUE ($000) 516,023
NET INCOME ($000) na
EMPLOYEES 1,400

CANSTAR SPORTS INC.
(Private) LEISURE GOODS AND SERVICES
5705 Ferrier Street, Suite 200, Mont-Royal, PQ,
H4P 1N3 (514) 738-3011
CANSTAR SPORTS INC., through its subsidiaries, makes and markets ice skates under the Bauer, Micron, Daoust, Mega and Lange brands. The company also makes and distributes hockey equipment under the Cooper, Bauer and Flak brands, skate blades, Bauer in-line roller skates and multi-purpose helmets. Canstar has manufacturing facilities in Canada and Europe. Its main markets are the United States, Europe and Canada.
Icaro Olivieri, Chairman
TOTAL ASSETS ($000) 159,247
TOTAL REVENUE ($000) 203,594
NET INCOME ($000) 15,329
EMPLOYEES na

CANUTILITIES HOLDINGS LTD.
(Public) ELECTRICAL UTILITIES
Exchanges: T M Z Stock Symbol: CH.PR.A
1600 Canadian Western Centre, 909 - 11th Avenue S.W., Calgary, AB, T2R 1N6 (403) 292-7550
CANUTILITIES HOLDINGS LTD. is a single purpose holding company which owns controlling shares in Canadian Utilities Limited.
Ronald D. Southern, Chairman President & C.E.O.
TOTAL ASSETS ($000) 3,714,900
TOTAL REVENUE ($000) 1,822,800
NET INCOME ($000) 62,900
EMPLOYEES 0
RANK (Profit/Revenue/Assets) 99/74/59

CANWEST GAS SUPPLY INC.
(Private) WHOLESALE DISTRIBUTORS
1285 West Pender Street, Seventh Floor, Vancouver, BC,
V6E 4B1 (604) 661-3321
CANWEST GAS SUPPLY INC., is a marketing company that purchases natural gas primarily in British Columbia, and markets gas throughout B.C., Central Canada and the U.S. CanWest is owned by a group of natural gas producers who hold long term natural gas sales contracts with the company and who have subscribed for shares in the company.
Edward W. Best, Chairman
TOTAL ASSETS ($000) 58,542
TOTAL REVENUE ($000) 625,927
NET INCOME ($000) na
EMPLOYEES 50

CANWEST GLOBAL COMMUNICATIONS CORP.
See page 373 for a full company profile.

CAPE BRETON DEVELOPMENT CORPORATION
(Crown) NON-BASE METAL MINING
P.O. Box 2500, Sydney, NS, B1P 6K9 (902) 564-2848
CAPE BRETON DEVELOPMENT CORPORATION is a federal crown corporation. It operates two coal mines, Prince Colliery and Phalen Colliery and is the largest coal producer in eastern Canada.
G.S. Khattar, Q.C., Chairman of the Board
TOTAL ASSETS ($000) 379,926
TOTAL REVENUE ($000) 231,800
NET INCOME ($000) (18,766)
EMPLOYEES 2,200

CAPILANO INTERNATIONAL INC.
(Public) OIL AND GAS FIELD SERVICES
Exchanges: T Stock Symbol: KPA
6204 6A Street S.E., Calgary, AB, T2H 2B7 (403) 258-0066
CAPILANO INTERNATIONAL INC. is a geophysical service company.
M.V. Little, President & C.E.O.
TOTAL ASSETS ($000) 59,406
TOTAL REVENUE ($000) 41,766
NET INCOME ($000) 3,110
EMPLOYEES 400
RANK (Profit/Revenue/Assets) 507/581/595

CAPITAL CITY SAVINGS & CREDIT UNION LTD.
(Fin. Co-op)   CREDIT UNIONS
8723 - 82nd Avenue, Suite 300, Edmonton, AB,
T6C 0Y9   (403) 496-2000
CAPITAL CITY SAVINGS & CREDIT UNION LTD. is a full service
credit union.
Ernie Jacobson, Chairman

TOTAL ASSETS ($000)	763,075
TOTAL REVENUE ($000)	63,634
NET INCOME ($000)	3,801
EMPLOYEES	401

CARA OPERATIONS LIMITED
See page 415 for a full company profile.

CARENA DEVELOPMENTS
See page 305 for a full company profile.

CARGILL LIMITED
(Private)   WHOLESALE DISTRIBUTORS
300 - 240 Graham Avenue, P.O. Box 5900, Winnipeg, MB,
R3C 4C5   (204) 947-0141
CARGILL LIMITED, is an agricultural based company which owns
country grain elevators, feed, seed, fertilizer, beef processing and grain
terminal facilities in seven provinces. Cargill is a wholly owned subsidiary of Cargill Incorporated of Minneapolis, Minnesota.
K.L. Hawkins, President

TOTAL ASSETS ($000)	na
TOTAL REVENUE ($000)	2,600,000
NET INCOME ($000)	na
EMPLOYEES	3,000

CARIBGOLD RESOURCES INC.
(Public)   PRECIOUS METALS
Exchanges: T   Stock Symbol: CG
Suite 1000, 36 Toronto Street, Toronto, ON, M5C 2C5(416) 350-2338
CARIBGOLD RESOURCES INC. is engaged in the business of explor-
ing for precious and base metals in the Republic of Cuba.
Paul N. Zyla, Chairman

TOTAL ASSETS ($000)	12,311 (US)
TOTAL REVENUE ($000)	385 (US)
NET INCOME ($000)	84 (US)
EMPLOYEES	12
RANK (Profit/Revenue/Assets)	742/955/905

CARLSON MARKETING GROUP LTD.
(Private)   OTHER SERVICES
3300 Bloor Street West, Centre Tower, Suite 1400, Toronto, ON,
M8X 2Y2   (416) 236-2338
CARLSON MARKETING GROUP LTD. is a leading full service
incentive marketing and promotions company. It develops marketing
incentive campaigns, group travel, event marketing, direct marketing
such as credit card protection, consumer promotions, retail vacation and
corporate travel through P. Lawson Travel.
Curtis L. Carlson, Chairman

TOTAL ASSETS ($000)	33,217
TOTAL REVENUE ($000)	507,508
NET INCOME ($000)	1,774
EMPLOYEES	220

CARLSON WAGONLIT TRAVEL
(Private)   OTHER SERVICES
3300 Bloor Street West, Centre Tower, Suite 1200, Toronto, ON,
M8X 2Y2   (416) 236-1921
CARLSON WAGONLIT TRAVEL is a travel agency serving both
corporate and vacation clients.
Alan Bromfield, Managing Director

TOTAL ASSETS ($000)	17,198
TOTAL REVENUE ($000)	514,304
NET INCOME ($000)	na
EMPLOYEES	850

CARMANAH RESOURCES LTD.
(Public)   OIL AND GAS PRODUCERS
Exchanges: T Z   Stock Symbol: CKM
Suite 1905, 421 - 7th Avenue S.W., Calgary, AB,
T2P 4K9   (403) 266-4975
CARMANAH RESOURCES LTD. is invovled in the acquisition, ex-
ploration and development of oil and gas properties in Alberta, Saskatch-
ewan and Indonesia.
Richard A. Gusella, Chairman & C.E.O.

TOTAL ASSETS ($000)	16,405
TOTAL REVENUE ($000)	0
NET INCOME ($000)	0
EMPLOYEES	11
RANK (Profit/Revenue/Assets)	735/907/927

CASCADES INC.
See page 156 for a full company profile.

CASCADES PAPERBOARD INTERNATIONAL INC.
See page 294 for a full company profile.

CASCADIA BRANDS INC.
(Public)   DISTILLERIES
Exchanges: T V   Stock Symbol: CBH
Suite 214, 1285 West Broadway, Vancouver, BC,
V6H 3X8   (604) 738-9463
CASCADIA BRANDS INC. (formerly International Potter Distilling
Corp) manufactures and supplies beer, wine and spirits to Canadian
markets.
Ian C. Tostenson, President

TOTAL ASSETS ($000)	33,596
TOTAL REVENUE ($000)	32,223
NET INCOME ($000)	1,005
EMPLOYEES	200
RANK (Profit/Revenue/Assets)	656/637/738

CASSIDY'S LTD.
(Public)   WHOLESALE DISTRIBUTORS
Exchanges: T M   Stock Symbol: CYL
95 Eastside Drive, Toronto, ON, M8Z 5N7   (416) 231-1222
CASSIDY'S LTD. is engaged in the distribution of hospital, hotel and
restaurant equipment, giftware and floor coverings. Operations of the
company are conducted in Canada with a small percentage of distribution
in the United States. The company is represented in every province except
Saskatchewan, Manitoba and Prince Edward Island.

A.W. Brodeur, Chairman

TOTAL ASSETS ($000)	51,463
TOTAL REVENUE ($000)	102,296
NET INCOME ($000)	1,041
EMPLOYEES	440
RANK (Profit/Revenue/Assets)	652/419/624

CATHEDRAL GOLD CORPORATION

(Public)   PRECIOUS METALS

Exchanges: T   Stock Symbol: CAT

Suite 420, 355 Burrard Street, Vancouver, BC,
V6C 2G8   (604) 684-4659

CATHEDRAL GOLD CORP. is engaged in the acquisition, exploration and development and operation of precious metal properties. The company owns 90% of the Sterling Gold Mine located in Nevada. The company acquired 90% of the Kaburi-Eldorado Gold Project in Guyana, South America. In addition, the company has interests in gold exploration properties in British Columbia.

N. Murray Edwards, Chairman of the Board

TOTAL ASSETS ($000)	15,729
TOTAL REVENUE ($000)	4,038
NET INCOME ($000)	257
EMPLOYEES	2
RANK (Profit/Revenue/Assets)	728/879/935

CCL INDUSTRIES INC.
See page 295 for a full company profile.

CELANESE CANADA INC.
See page 285 for a full company profile.

CENTRA GAS INC.

(Private)   GAS UTILITIES

1333 West Georgia Street, Vancouver, BC, V6E 3K9 (604) 691-5500

CENTRA GAS INC. is a natural gas distributor, supplying gas to markets in Ontario, Manitoba, Alberta and British Columbia. It also operates an electrical power distribution system in Yellowknife, Northwest Territories, and a secondary oil pipeline in Manitoba. It is a wholly owned subsidiary of Westcoast Energy Inc.

Michael Phelps, President & C.E.O.

TOTAL ASSETS ($000)	1,768,414
TOTAL REVENUE ($000)	1,154,706
NET INCOME ($000)	61,646
EMPLOYEES	na

CENTRA GAS MANITOBA INC.

(Private)   GAS UTILITIES

444 St. Mary Avenue, 5th Floor, Winnipeg, MB,
R3C 3T7   (204) 944-9920

CENTRA GAS MANITOBA INC. is a natural gas distribution company.

M.E.J. Phelps, Chairman

TOTAL ASSETS ($000)	323,133
TOTAL REVENUE ($000)	282,553
NET INCOME ($000)	13,417
EMPLOYEES	663

CENTRA GAS ONTARIO INC.
See page 350 for a full company profile.

CENTRAL CAPITAL CORPORATION
See page 464 for a full company profile.

CENTRAL FUND OF CANADA LIMITED
See page 465 for a full company profile.

CENTREFUND REALTY CORPORATION
See page 306 for a full company profile.

CFCF INC.
See page 374 for a full company profile.

CFM INTERNATIONAL INC.

(Public)   MISC. CONSUMER PRODUCTS

Exchanges: T   Stock Symbol: CFM

475 Admiral Boulevard, Mississauga, ON, L5T 2N1 (905) 670-7777

CFM INTERNATIONAL INC. is an integrated manufacturer of a full range of gas, both natural and propane, fireplaces and related components.

Heinz R. Rieger, Chairman

TOTAL ASSETS ($000)	55,428
TOTAL REVENUE ($000)	40,422
NET INCOME ($000)	7,727
EMPLOYEES	350
RANK (Profit/Revenue/Assets)	345/586/608

CFS GROUP INC.

(Public)   MISC. INDUSTRIAL PRODUCTS

Exchanges: T M   Stock Symbol: CFZ

550 Marshall Avenue, Dorval, PQ, H9P 1C9   (514) 631-7731

CFS GROUP INC. is principally involved in manufacturing and selling coatings, adhesives and refractories. Its main markets are steel mills, iron foundries, aluminum and other nonferrous smelters, furniture manufacturers, the construction and woodworking industries, the packaging industry and the home improvement and sporting goods industries.

Michael Kawaja, President

TOTAL ASSETS ($000)	34,375
TOTAL REVENUE ($000)	54,860
NET INCOME ($000)	(431)
EMPLOYEES	30
RANK (Profit/Revenue/Assets)	786/531/731

CGC INC.
See page 569 for a full company profile.

CGI GROUP INC. (THE)

(Public)   CONSULTING

Exchanges: T M   Stock Symbol: GIB.A

1130 Sherbrooke Street West, Suite 700, Montreal, PQ,
H3A 2M8   (514) 841-3200

CGI GROUP provides consulting services in information systems, telecommunications and management, and a range of services in systems management and outsourcing.

Serge Godin, Chairman President & C.E.O.

TOTAL ASSETS ($000)	41,961
TOTAL REVENUE ($000)	91,294
NET INCOME ($000)	1,250
EMPLOYEES	1,200
RANK (Profit/Revenue/Assets)	634/437/681

CHAI-NA-TA CORP.
See page 570 for a full company profile.

CHAMPION ROAD MACHINERY LIMITED
(Public)   MISC. INDUSTRIAL PRODUCTS
Exchanges: T M   Stock Symbol: CHN
Box 10- Maitland Road, Goderich, ON, N7A 3Y6   (519) 524-2601
CHAMPION ROAD MACHINERY LIMITED is a road construction
equipment company. On January 1, 1994, this company was formed by
the amalgamation of CRML Acquisition Ltd. and Champion Road
Machinery Ltd.
Arthur Church, President & C.E.O.

TOTAL ASSETS ($000)	74,184
TOTAL REVENUE ($000)	176,335
NET INCOME ($000)	9,293
EMPLOYEES	662
RANK (Profit/Revenue/Assets)	309/329/551

CHANCELLOR ENERGY RESOURCES INC.
(Public)   OIL AND GAS PRODUCERS
Exchanges: T Z   Stock Symbol: CHC
Suite 950, 333 - 5th Avenue S.W., Calgary, AB,
T2P 3B6   (403) 233-8426
CHANCELLOR ENERGY RESOURCES INC. is a Calgary based
resource company primarily engaged in the acquisition, exploration and
development of oil and gas leases in North America. Exploration efforts
are concentrated in Western Canada.
Robert G. Peters, Chairman

TOTAL ASSETS ($000)	71,352
TOTAL REVENUE ($000)	24,388
NET INCOME ($000)	2,977
EMPLOYEES	20
RANK (Profit/Revenue/Assets)	512/683/559

CHARLWOOD GROUP (THE)
(Private)   MANAGEMENT AND DIVERSIFIED
135 - 10551 Shelbridge Way, Richmond, BC,
V6X 2W9   (604) 273-2721
THE CHARLWOOD GROUP is a management company.
Gary Charlwood, C.E.O.

TOTAL ASSETS ($000)	na
TOTAL REVENUE ($000)	2,200,000
NET INCOME ($000)	na
EMPLOYEES	na

CHARTERWAYS TRANSPORTATION LTD.
(Private)   TRANSPORTATION
248 Pall Mall Street, Suite 500, Station Park, London, ON,
N6A 5P6   (519) 679-9150
CHARTERWAYS TRANSPORTATION LTD. is a school bus operator. Charterways' Canadian fleet comprises approximately 2,500 vehicles operating out of 41 facilities in Ontario. It also operates a freight
services business and a storage and distribution business.
Geoff Davies, President & C.E.O.

TOTAL ASSETS ($000)	230,037
TOTAL REVENUE ($000)	213,019
NET INCOME ($000)	na
EMPLOYEES	na

CHASE MANHATTAN BANK OF CANADA (THE)
(Private)   BANKS
150 King St. W., 16th Floor, P.O. Box 68, Toronto, ON,
M5H 1J9   (416) 585-3300
CHASE MANHATTAN BANK OF CANADA is a wholly owned
subsidiary of Chase Manhattan Overseas Banking Corp., with the ultimate parent The Chase Manhattan Corporation. The company is licensed
to operate as a Schedule II bank. The bank specializes in corporate finance
and advisory services.
Thomas C. Gardner, President & C.E.O.

TOTAL ASSETS ($000)	352,139
TOTAL REVENUE ($000)	33,661
NET INCOME ($000)	13,636
EMPLOYEES	33

CHASE RESOURCE CORPORATION
(Public)   METAL MINES
Exchanges: T   Stock Symbol: CQS
Suite 1910, 400 Burrard Street, Vancouver, BC,
V6C 3A6   (604) 685-6851
CHASE RESOURCE CORPORATION is involved in the acquisition,
exploration and development of mineral resource properties.
Ian T. Rozier, President & C.E.O.

TOTAL ASSETS ($000)	17,692
TOTAL REVENUE ($000)	570
NET INCOME ($000)	(451)
EMPLOYEES	60
RANK (Profit/Revenue/Assets)	790/954/901

CHATEAU STORES OF CANADA LTD.
See page 416 for a full company profile.

CHAUVCO RESOURCES LTD.
See page 82 for a full company profile.

CHC HELICOPTER CORPORATION
See page 324 for a full company profile.

CHEVRON CANADA LIMITED
(Private)   INTEGRATED OILS
1500 - 1050 West Pender Street, Vancouver, BC,
V6E 3T4   (604) 668-5300
CHEVRON CANADA LIMITED, is a refiner and marketer of petro-
leum products and is wholly owned by Chevron Corporation of San
Francisco, California.
Patricia Woertz, President & C.E.O.

TOTAL ASSETS ($000)	na
TOTAL REVENUE ($000)	994,809
NET INCOME ($000)	na
EMPLOYEES	435

CHEVRON CANADA RESOURCES LIMITED
(Private)   OIL AND GAS PRODUCERS
500 - 5th Avenue S.W., Calgary, AB, T2P 0L7   (403) 234-5000
CHEVRON CANADA RESOURCES LTD. is engaged in oil and gas
exploration and production. Chevron Canada Resources is a wholly
owned subsidiary of Chevron Corporation of San Francisco, California.

Donald L. Paul, President

TOTAL ASSETS ($000)	2,124,000
TOTAL REVENUE ($000)	1,154,000
NET INCOME ($000)	na
EMPLOYEES	1,056

CHIEFTAIN INTERNATIONAL, INC.
See page 83 for a full company profile.

CHRYSLER CANADA LTD.
(Private)   AUTOMOTIVE
P.O. Box 1621, Chrysler Centre, Windsor, ON,
N9A 4H6   (519) 973-2000
CHRYSLER CANADA LTD. manufactures, distributes and sells automobiles and related parts. The company is 100% owned by Chrysler Corporation of Highland Park, Michigan.
G. Yves Landry, President & C.E.O.

TOTAL ASSETS ($000)	4,317,800
TOTAL REVENUE ($000)	15,762,300
NET INCOME ($000)	201,700
EMPLOYEES	14,200

CHUBB INSURANCE COMPANY OF CANADA
(Private)   INSURANCE - PROPERTY & CASUALTY
One Financial Place, 1 Adelaide Stree East, Toronto, ON,
M5C 2V9   (416) 863-0550
CHUBB INSURANCE COMPANY OF CANADA is a property and casualty insurer operating in all provinces and territories. The company is a wholly owned subsidiary of The Chubb Corporation.
Percy Chubb III, Chairman

TOTAL ASSETS ($000)	456,112
TOTAL REVENUE ($000)	215,947
NET INCOME ($000)	32,093
EMPLOYEES	335

CHUM LIMITED
See page 375 for a full company profile.

CHURCHILL CORPORATION (THE)
(Public)   CONTRACTORS
Exchanges: Z   Stock Symbol: CUQ
Suite 2280, Manulife Place, 10180 - 101 Street, Edmonton, AB,
T5J 3S4   (403) 424-8230
THE CHURCHILL CORPORATION is a diversified investment and holding company whose principal business activities are corporate investment, commercial construction, real estate development and financial and advisory services.
Stanton K. Hooper, Chairman

TOTAL ASSETS ($000)	60,386
TOTAL REVENUE ($000)	146,694
NET INCOME ($000)	227
EMPLOYEES	na
RANK (Profit/Revenue/Assets)	731/364/593

CIBA-GEIGY CANADA LTD.
(Private)   CHEMICALS
6860 Century Avenue, Mississauga, ON, L5N 2W5   (905) 821-4420
CIBA-GEIGY CANADA LTD. is a chemical company engaged in the pharmaceuticals, agricultural chemicals, plastics, and additives industries. The company is wholly owned by CIBA-GEIGY Limited of Switzerland.
Leon Jacobs, President & C.E.O.

TOTAL ASSETS ($000)	274,585
TOTAL REVENUE ($000)	425,439
NET INCOME ($000)	5,312
EMPLOYEES	1,500

CIC CANOLA INDUSTRIES CANADA INC.
(Public)   FOOD PROCESSING
Exchanges: T   Stock Symbol: CCJ
Suite 401, 1101 - 5th Street, P.O. Box 147, Nisku, AB,
T0C 2G0   (403) 955-8822
CIC CANOLA INDUSTRIES CANADA INC. is an integrated canola processing company with crushing, refining and packaging capabilities.
John W. Channon, Chairman

TOTAL ASSETS ($000)	30,402
TOTAL REVENUE ($000)	16,724
NET INCOME ($000)	52
EMPLOYEES	130
RANK (Profit/Revenue/Assets)	748/742/770

CIMARRON PETROLEUM LTD.
See page 84 for a full company profile.

CINAR FILMS INC.
(Public)   ENTERTAINMENT SERVICES
Exchanges: T M   Stock Symbol: CIF.A
1207 St. Andre Street, Montreal, PQ, H2L 3S8   (514) 843-7070
CINAR FILMS INC. is fully-integrated and involved in development, production, post-production and international distribution of animated and international distribution of animated and live-action children's television programming.
Micheline Charest, Chairman & C.E.O.

TOTAL ASSETS ($000)	37,106
TOTAL REVENUE ($000)	25,572
NET INCOME ($000)	3,434
EMPLOYEES	150
RANK (Profit/Revenue/Assets)	492/675/716

CINEPLEX ODEON CORPORATION
See page 571 for a full company profile.

CINRAM LTD.
See page 572 for a full company profile.

CIRCO CRAFT CO. INC.
See page 259 for a full company profile.

CITIBANK CANADA
(Private)   BANKS
Citibank Place, Suite 1900, 123 Front Street West, Toronto, ON,
M5J 2M3   (416) 947-5500
CITIBANK CANADA, a wholly owned subsidiary of Citibank, N.A., is licensed to operate in Canada as a Schedule II bank with full banking powers. The company and its subsidiaries offer leasing and investment dealing services through offices across Canada.

Richard E. Lint, Chairman & C.E.O.

TOTAL ASSETS ($000)	4,210,761
TOTAL REVENUE ($000)	463,477
NET INCOME ($000)	(40,847)
EMPLOYEES	900

CIVIL SERVICE CO-OPERATIVE CREDIT SOCIETY, LIMITED

(Fin. Co-op)	CREDIT UNIONS
400 Albert Street, Ottawa, ON, K1R 5B2	(613) 560-6600

CIVIL SERVICE CO-OPERATIVE CREDIT SOCIETY LIMITED provides full financial services for members, who are employees of the federal government. Through ATM and branch locations, it offers savings, RRSP, loan services, mortgages and a variety of other financial services.

Ronald G.E. Fitzgerald, General Manager & C.E.O.

TOTAL ASSETS ($000)	828,783
TOTAL REVENUE ($000)	63,716
NET INCOME ($000)	3,410
EMPLOYEES	281

CLAIRVEST GROUP INC.

(Public)	FINANCE AND LEASING
Exchanges: T	Stock Symbol: CVG
22 St. Clair Avenue East, Suite 1700, Toronto, ON,	
M4T 2S3	(416) 925-9270

CLAIRVEST GROUP INC. is organized to provide merchant banking services to emerging businesses. These merchant banking services include advisory services and the facilitation of financings. The company makes direct investments for its own account in these businesses.

Joseph L. Rotman, Chairman & C.E.O. & Pres.

TOTAL ASSETS ($000)	85,874
TOTAL REVENUE ($000)	59,641
NET INCOME ($000)	2,612
EMPLOYEES	7
RANK (Profit/Revenue/Assets)	535/515/516

CLEARLY CANADIAN BEVERAGE CORP.

(Public)	FOOD PROCESSING
Exchanges: V Q	Stock Symbol: CLV
Suite 1900, 999 West Hastings Street, Vancouver, BC,	
V6C 2W2	(604) 683-0312

CLEARLY CANADIAN BEVERAGE CORPORATION is involved in manufacturing and distributing bottled mineral water and a line of natural fruit-flavored sparkling waters.

Douglas L. Mason, President & C.E.O.

TOTAL ASSETS ($000)	62,686
TOTAL REVENUE ($000)	120,949
NET INCOME ($000)	387
EMPLOYEES	0
RANK (Profit/Revenue/Assets)	716/388/586

CLEARNET COMMUNICATIONS INC.

(Public)	TELECOMMUNICATIONS
Exchanges: T M Q	Stock Symbol: NET.A
625 Granite Court, Pickering, ON, L1W 3K1	(905) 831-6222

CLEARNET COMMUNICATIONS INC. is an operator of specialized mobile radio wireless communications networks in Canada.

Robert C. Simmonds, Chairman

TOTAL ASSETS ($000)	25,816
TOTAL REVENUE ($000)	0
NET INCOME ($000)	0
EMPLOYEES	220
RANK (Profit/Revenue/Assets)	740/729/808

CLUBLINK CORPORATION

(Public)	ENTERTAINMENT SERVICES
Exchanges: T	Stock Symbol: LNK
15765 Dufferin Street, King City, ON, L7B 1K5	(905) 841-3730

CLUBLINK CORPORATION is involved in the acquisition, management and development of golf-related recreational facilities and real estate.

Robert M. Franklin, Chairman

TOTAL ASSETS ($000)	87,432
TOTAL REVENUE ($000)	14,162
NET INCOME ($000)	2,777
EMPLOYEES	375
RANK (Profit/Revenue/Assets)	520/765/510

CML INDUSTRIES LTD.

(Public)	PAPER PRODUCTS
Exchanges: T	Stock Symbol: CNO
550 Cochrane Drive, Unionville, ON, L3R 8E2	(905) 513-8511

CML INDUSTRIES's principal business consists of investing in and managing secondary manufacturing businesses. The company, through its wholly owned subsidiaries, is involved in the manufacturing of envelopes and specialty papers.

Claude Theberge, Chairman & C.E.O.

TOTAL ASSETS ($000)	13,407
TOTAL REVENUE ($000)	24,911
NET INCOME ($000)	413
EMPLOYEES	200
RANK (Profit/Revenue/Assets)	710/678/984

CO-OP ATLANTIC

(Non-fin Co-op)	DEPARTMENT STORES
P.O. Box 750, Moncton, NB, E1C 8N5	(506) 858-6000

CO-OP ATLANTIC is a wholesale central co-operative involved in meat, grocery, produce, hardware, family fashions, petroleum, and agricultural products in Atlantic Canada.

Francis Porelle, Chairman & President

TOTAL ASSETS ($000)	104,359
TOTAL REVENUE ($000)	483,453
NET INCOME ($000)	4,128
EMPLOYEES	1,000

CO-OPERATIVE CREDIT SOCIETY OF MANITOBA

(Fin. Co-op)	CREDIT UNIONS
P.O. Box 9900, 215 Garry St., Winnipeg, MB,	
R3C 3E2	(204) 985-4700

CO-OPERATIVE CREDIT SOCIETY OF MANITOBA serves the needs of its member credit unions primarily in the areas of: depository for liquidity reserves, centralized services such as cheque clearing, training, dataprocessing, and advertising, and representation with related organization and all levels of government.

Herb Boyce, President of the Board

TOTAL ASSETS ($000)	624,810
TOTAL REVENUE ($000)	44,777

NET INCOME ($000)   3,642
EMPLOYEES   na

CO-OPERATIVE HAIL INSURANCE COMPANY LIMITED

(Fin. Co-op)   INSURANCE - PROPERTY & CASUALTY
P.O. Box 777, 2709 - 13th Avenue, Regina, SK,
S4P 3A8   (306) 522-8891
CO-OPERATIVE HAIL INSURANCE's principal business is the sale of hail insurance to farmers in Manitoba and Saskatchewan.
W. Bruce Lutz, Chairman & President
TOTAL ASSETS ($000)   40,220
TOTAL REVENUE ($000)   60,878
NET INCOME ($000)   (896)
EMPLOYEES   20

CO-OPERATIVE TRUST COMPANY OF CANADA

(Fin. Co-op)   TRUST, SAVINGS AND LOAN
333 - 3rd Avenue North, Saskatoon, SK, S7K 2M2   (306) 956-1800
CO-OPERATIVE TRUST COMPANY OF CANADA is a national financial institution owned by the Canadian Credit Union system. The company delivers deposit, retirement, mortgage and trust services through the credit union system. Co-operative Trust has 10 branch offices across Canada.
R.W. McVeigh, Chairman
TOTAL ASSETS ($000)   1,078,929
TOTAL REVENUE ($000)   96,021
NET INCOME ($000)   2,738
EMPLOYEES   198

CO-OPERATORS DATA SERVICES LIMITED

(Non-fin Co-op)   COMPUTER SOFTWARE & PROCESSING
1900 Albert Street, Regina, SK, S4P 4K8   (306) 761-4000
CO-OPERATORS DATA SERVICES LIMITED provides information system operation, and management, development and support of software products, and professional services related to use of information systems and management of telecommunication facilities. It specializes in delivering solutions to Canadian and international financial services and health care markets.
Jack Morneau, Chairman of the Board
TOTAL ASSETS ($000)   33,367
TOTAL REVENUE ($000)   77,567
NET INCOME ($000)   2,100
EMPLOYEES   515

CO-OPERATORS GENERAL INSURANCE COMPANY

(Fin. Co-op)   INSURANCE - PROPERTY & CASUALTY
Priory Square, Guelph, ON, N1H 6P8   (519) 824-4400
CO-OPERATORS GENERAL INSURANCE COMPANY is licenced to transact general insurance in all provinces and territories except Quebec.
Gordon Sinclair, Chairman
TOTAL ASSETS ($000)   1,964,798
TOTAL REVENUE ($000)   898,339
NET INCOME ($000)   42,027
EMPLOYEES   na

CO-OPERATORS GROUP LIMITED (THE)

(Fin. Co-op)   INSURANCE - PROPERTY & CASUALTY
Priory Square, Guelph, ON, N1H 6P8   (519) 824-4400

THE CO-OPERATORS GROUP LIMITED provides a wide range of services including life, property & casualty insurance, annuities & structured settlements, and investment counselling. The company is also engaged in real estate development and property management, data services and communications.
Wayne McLeod, Chairman
TOTAL ASSETS ($000)   3,094,607
TOTAL REVENUE ($000)   1,270,999
NET INCOME ($000)   43,903
EMPLOYEES   na

CO-OPERATORS LIFE INSURANCE COMPANY

(Fin. Co-op)   INSURANCE - LIFE
1920 College Avenue, Regina, SK, S4P 1C4   (306) 347-6200
CO-OPERATORS LIFE INSURANCE COMPANY provides life insurance protection. It is part of The Co-operators Group Limited.
James MacConnell, Chairman of the Board
TOTAL ASSETS ($000)   1,084,417
TOTAL REVENUE ($000)   313,315
NET INCOME ($000)   2,028
EMPLOYEES   334

CO-STEEL INC.

See page 240 for a full company profile.

COBI FOODS INC.

(Public)   FOOD PROCESSING
Exchanges: T   Stock Symbol: CFJ
P.O. Box 393, Hantsport, NS, B0P 1P0   (902) 684-1430
COBI FOODS INC. is a food processor engaged in the freezing and distribution of vegatables and beverages.
George E. Bishop, Chairman of the Board
TOTAL ASSETS ($000)   24,315
TOTAL REVENUE ($000)   39,106
NET INCOME ($000)   (11,177)
EMPLOYEES   100
RANK (Profit/Revenue/Assets)   949/595/821

COCA-COLA BEVERAGES LTD.

See page 187 for a full company profile.

COGECO CABLE INC.

See page 376 for a full company profile.

COGECO INC.

See page 377 for a full company profile.

COGNOS INCORPORATED

See page 536 for a full company profile.

COHO ENERGY INC.

See page 85 for a full company profile.

COLES BOOK STORES LIMITED

(Private)   SPECIALTY STORES
90 Ronson Drive, Rexdale, ON, M9W 1C1   (416) 243-3132
COLES BOOK STORES LIMITED is a retail bookstore chain. It is a subsidiary of Chapters Inc.

TOTAL ASSETS ($000)	110,611
TOTAL REVENUE ($000)	226,188
NET INCOME ($000)	2,395
EMPLOYEES	2,450

COLORTECH CORPORATION

(Public) MISC. INDUSTRIAL PRODUCTS
Exchanges: T M Stock Symbol: CLR.A
8027 Dixie Road, Brampton, ON, L6T 3V1 (905) 792-0333
COLORTECH CORPORATION is involved in the manufacture of colour and additive concentrates for the plastic industry.
Howard W. Taylor, Chairman

TOTAL ASSETS ($000)	14,360
TOTAL REVENUE ($000)	32,808
NET INCOME ($000)	560
EMPLOYEES	50
RANK (Profit/Revenue/Assets)	689/634/956

COMINCO LTD.

See page 8 for a full company profile.

COMINCO RESOURCES INTERNATIONAL LIMITED

(Private) PRECIOUS METALS
Suite 400, 200 Burrard Street, Vancouver, BC, V6C 3L7 (604) 682-0611
COMINCO RESOURCES INTERNATIONAL LIMITED operates in the mining industry producing ferro-nickel, copper, gold and silver and conducting exploration for base metals, precious metals and industrial minerals. The company is actively exploring mineral properties in the U.S., Chile, Mexico, Peru, Bolivia, Guatemala and Turkey. Cominco Ltd.holds a 55.7% interest in the company.
George D. Tikkanen, President

TOTAL ASSETS ($000)	118,882
TOTAL REVENUE ($000)	15,467
NET INCOME ($000)	(6,067)
EMPLOYEES	400

COMMCORP FINANCIAL SERVICES INC.

(Private) FINANCE AND LEASING
P.O. Box 5060, 5050 South Service Road, Burlington, ON, L7R 4C8 (905) 335-7555
COMMCORP FINANCIAL SERVICES is in the business of asset-based finance and management services.
T. Iain Ronald, Chairman

TOTAL ASSETS ($000)	677,911
TOTAL REVENUE ($000)	147,766
NET INCOME ($000)	14,639
EMPLOYEES	340

COMMERCIAL UNION LIFE ASSURANCE COMPANY OF CANADA

(Private) INSURANCE - LIFE
P.O. Box 370, Station A, Scarborough, ON, M1K 5C3 (416) 296-0700
COMMERCIAL UNION LIFE ASSURANCE COMPANY OF CANADA offers life, accident and sickness insurance.
Gerry S. Stafford, Chairman & C.E.O.

TOTAL ASSETS ($000)	704,874
TOTAL REVENUE ($000)	223,896
NET INCOME ($000)	10,004
EMPLOYEES	146

COMMONWEALTH PLYWOOD CO. LTD.

(Private) MISC. INDUSTRIAL PRODUCTS
PO Box 90, Ste-Therese, PQ, J7E 4H9 (514) 435-6541
COMMONWEALTH PLYWOOD CO. LTD., is a wholesale plywood distributor and manufacturer of plywood, veneer and lumber. Commonwealth is wholly owned by Soaring Phoenix Inc.
William P. Caine, President

TOTAL ASSETS ($000)	112,210
TOTAL REVENUE ($000)	228,529
NET INCOME ($000)	na
EMPLOYEES	2,000

COMPAQ CANADA INC.

(Private) WHOLESALE DISTRIBUTORS
111 Granton Drive, Suite 101, Richmond Hill, ON, L4B 1L5 (416) 733-7876
COMPAQ CANADA INC., a wholly owned subsidiary of Compaq Computer Corp. of Houston, Texas, markets and services industry-leading portable, desktop and server computer technologies and services. The company has offices in Vancouver, Calgary, Ottawa, and Montreal. Its products are sold and supported through a network of more than 2,300 marketing partners across Canada.
Donald Woodley, President

TOTAL ASSETS ($000)	na
TOTAL REVENUE ($000)	527,000
NET INCOME ($000)	na
EMPLOYEES	160

COMPAS ELECTRONICS INC.

(Public) ELECTRICAL & ELECTRONIC
Exchanges: T Stock Symbol: CMN
1245 California Avenue, Brockville, ON, K6V 5Y6 (613) 342-5041
COMPAS ELECTRONICS INC. is a Canadian manufacturer of hybrid micro circuits for the computer, communication, test instrumentation, medical electronics, and various other industries.
Donald B. Green, Chairman & C.E.O.

TOTAL ASSETS ($000)	28,742
TOTAL REVENUE ($000)	45,630
NET INCOME ($000)	(2,521)
EMPLOYEES	200
RANK (Profit/Revenue/Assets)	867/568/781

COMPUTALOG LTD.

See page 86 for a full company profile.

COMPUTING DEVICES CANADA LTD.

(Private) ELECTRICAL & ELECTRONIC
2700 Matheson Blvd. E., Suite 600- West Tower, Mississauga, ON, L4W 4V9 (905) 629-5100
COMPUTING DEVICES CANADA LTD. is a global systems integrator with 36 years of experience operating in multi-vendor computer environments. It applies leading edge computer technology to help customers find simple solutions to complex problems.
Jan Kaminski, President

TOTAL ASSETS ($000)	120,590
TOTAL REVENUE ($000)	238,305
NET INCOME ($000)	8,268
EMPLOYEES	200

COMSTATE RESOURCES LTD.

(Public) OIL AND GAS PRODUCERS
Exchanges: T Stock Symbol: CSR
Suite 901, 1015 - Fourth Street S.W., Calgary, AB,
T2R 1J4 (403) 237-8868
COMSTATE RESOURCES LTD. is involved in oil and gas production.
G.F. Fink, President

TOTAL ASSETS ($000)	22,977
TOTAL REVENUE ($000)	9,859
NET INCOME ($000)	3,033
EMPLOYEES	5
RANK (Profit/Revenue/Assets)	509/805/840

CONNAUGHT LABORATORIES LIMITED

(Private) BIOTECHNOLOGY & PHARMACEUTICALS
1755 Steeles Ave. W., North York, ON, M2R 3T4 (416) 667-2701
CONNAUGHT LABORATORIES LIMITED is engaged in the development, manufacturing and commercialization of vaccines and therapeutics for human health care.
Georges Hibon, Chairman & C.E.O.

TOTAL ASSETS ($000)	494,000
TOTAL REVENUE ($000)	408,000
NET INCOME ($000)	na
EMPLOYEES	750

CONSOLIDATED CANADIAN EXPRESS LIMITED

See page 466 for a full company profile.

CONSOLIDATED CARMA CORPORATION

See page 307 for a full company profile.

CONSOLIDATED ENFIELD CORP. LTD.

See page 513 for a full company profile.

CONSOLIDATED EUROCAN VENTURES LTD.

(Public) OIL AND GAS PRODUCERS
Exchanges: T V Stock Symbol: KEU
Suite 1320, 885 West Georgia Street, Vancouver, BC,
V6C 3E8 (604) 689-7842
CONSOLIDATED EUROCAN VENTURES LTD. is engaged in the exploration for, and development of oil and gas in Latin America with exploration properties in Columbia, Chile, Argentina and Peru. The company also has oil and gas production from its 30% interest in the Las Monas area in Columbia, where it is operator-elect.
Lukas H. Lundin, Chairman & President

TOTAL ASSETS ($000)	16,937 (US)
TOTAL REVENUE ($000)	5,563 (US)
NET INCOME ($000)	(3,852) (US)
EMPLOYEES	na
RANK (Profit/Revenue/Assets)	911/827/843

CONSOLIDATED FIVE STAR RESOURCES LTD.

(Public) OIL AND GAS PRODUCERS
Exchanges: V Stock Symbol: CFR
Unit 2, 215 Shields Court, Markham, ON, L3R 8V2 (905) 305-0222
CONSOLIDATED FIVE STAR RESOURCES LTD. is engaged in the exploration of mineral claims in the Northwest Territories, Prince Rupert and Slave Lake areas. It also has oil and gas interests in Queensland, Australia.

Edward H.K. Tan, Chairman & President

TOTAL ASSETS ($000)	33,585
TOTAL REVENUE ($000)	2,414
NET INCOME ($000)	(435)
EMPLOYEES	10
RANK (Profit/Revenue/Assets)	787/910/740

CONSOLIDATED HCI HOLDINGS CORPORATION

See page 308 for a full company profile.

CONSOLIDATED MERCANTILE CORPORATION

(Public) PACKAGING AND CONTAINERS
Exchanges: T Q Stock Symbol: CMC
106 Avenue Road, Toronto, ON, M5R 2H3 (416) 920-0500
CONSOLIDATED MERCANTILE CORPORATION operates in two industry segments. It manufactures specialty covers and packaging materials. It also manufactures furniture. The company has operations and markets in Canada and the United States.
Fred A. Litwin, President

TOTAL ASSETS ($000)	22,497
TOTAL REVENUE ($000)	43,153
NET INCOME ($000)	393
EMPLOYEES	na
RANK (Profit/Revenue/Assets)	714/579/846

CONSOLIDATED NEVADA GOLDFIELDS CORPORATION

(Public) PRECIOUS METALS
Exchanges: T Q Stock Symbol: KNV
Suite 1620, 1801 Broadway, Denver, CO, 80202 (303) 296-3200
CONSOLIDATED NEVADA GOLDFIELDS CORPORATION is involved in the operation, exploration and development of precious metal properties. Its major area of activity is Nevada, South Carolina and Alaska.
Wendell W. Robinson, Chairman

TOTAL ASSETS ($000)	27,177 (US)
TOTAL REVENUE ($000)	14,587 (US)
NET INCOME ($000)	(11,638) (US)
EMPLOYEES	63
RANK (Profit/Revenue/Assets)	957/719/708

CONSOLIDATED RAMBLER MINES LIMITED

(Public) EAST COAST FORESTRY
Exchanges: T Stock Symbol: CRR
P.O. Box 937, 300 Union Street, Saint John, NB,
E2L 4E3 (506) 632-7171
CONSOLIDATED RAMBLER MINES LIMITED is engaged in the development and harvesting of timberland in Maine, and the exploration of minerals primarily in Newfoundland.
W.D. Jamieson, President

TOTAL ASSETS ($000)	37,422
TOTAL REVENUE ($000)	3,189
NET INCOME ($000)	568
EMPLOYEES	na
RANK (Profit/Revenue/Assets)	688/898/711

CONSOLIDATED RAMROD GOLD CORPORATION

See page 87 for a full company profile.

CONSOLTEX GROUP INC.
See page 206 for a full company profile.

CONSUMERS CO-OPERATIVE REFINERIES LIMITED
(Private)　　　　　　　　　　　OIL AND GAS PRODUCERS
P.O. Box 1050, Saskatoon, SK, S7K 3M9　　　　(306) 244-3311
CONSUMERS' CO-OPERATIVE REFINERIES LIMITED manages the Co-op Refinery/ Upgrader Complex in Regina, Saskatchewan. It and the Government of Saskatchewan jointly own the upgrader through NewGrade Energy Inc. Consumers' Co-operative Refineries Limited is a wholly owned subsidiary of Federated Co-operatives Limited.
Vern Leland, President

TOTAL ASSETS ($000)	80,341
TOTAL REVENUE ($000)	336,020
NET INCOME ($000)	(357)
EMPLOYEES	na

CONSUMERS PACKAGING INC.
See page 296 for a full company profile.

CONSUMERS' GAS COMPANY LTD. (THE)
See page 351 for a full company profile.

CONTINENTAL CANADA GROUP (THE)
(Private)　　　　INSURANCE - PROPERTY & CASUALTY
1 Adelaide Street East, Toronto, ON, M5C 2V9　　(416) 350-4400
THE CONTINENTAL CANADA GROUP provides a full range of property and casualty insurance coverages and services for both commercial and personal lines. The group is wholly owned by Fairfax Financial Holdings Ltd.
Byron Messier, Chairman President & C.E.O

TOTAL ASSETS ($000)	1,038,425
TOTAL REVENUE ($000)	457,688
NET INCOME ($000)	36,139
EMPLOYEES	725

CONTINENTAL GRAIN COMPANY (CANADA) LIMITED
(Private)　　　　　　　　WHOLESALE DISTRIBUTORS
2500-200 Granville Street, Vancouver, BC, V6C 1S4　(604) 684-7292
CONTINENTAL GRAIN COMPANY (CANADA) LIMITED, is in the business of buying, trading, selling and transporting of export grain, grain byproducts and pulses in Canada. It owns and operates elevator facilities. Its parent is Continetal Grain Company.
Gerald L. McClintock, President & C.E.O.

TOTAL ASSETS ($000)	21,992
TOTAL REVENUE ($000)	160,391
NET INCOME ($000)	702
EMPLOYEES	56

CONTINENTAL PHARMA CRYOSAN INC.
(Public)　　　　BIOTECHNOLOGY & PHARMACEUTICALS
Exchanges: T M　　　　　　Stock Symbol: CPM.A
5485 Pare Street, Mont-Royal, PQ, H4P 1P7　　(514) 344-4004
CONTINENTAL PHARMA CRYOSAN is a biotechnology business, through its subsidiary Ibex Technologies Inc. Through another subsidiary, Conpharma Home Healthcare Inc., the company operates a home health care business in the United States.

Thomas O. Hecht, Chairman, President & C.E.O.

TOTAL ASSETS ($000)	61,381
TOTAL REVENUE ($000)	49,950
NET INCOME ($000)	2,011
EMPLOYEES	435
RANK (Profit/Revenue/Assets)	570/549/589

CONTRANS CORP.
(Public)　　　　　　　　　　　　TRANSPORTATION
Exchanges: T　　　　　　　　Stock Symbol: CSS.A
1179 Ridgeway Road, P.O. Box 1210, Woodstock, ON,
N4S 8P6　　　　　　　　　　　　(519) 421-4600
CONTRANS CORP. is engaged in the truckload movement of a wide range of general freight as well as specialized commodities in bulk or by flatbed throughout Ontario and Quebec, Eastern Canada and the United States.
Stan G. Dunford, Chairman & President

TOTAL ASSETS ($000)	27,395
TOTAL REVENUE ($000)	64,126
NET INCOME ($000)	2,006
EMPLOYEES	207
RANK (Profit/Revenue/Assets)	572/495/796

CONWEST EXPLORATION COMPANY LIMITED
See page 88 for a full company profile.

COOPERATIVE FEDEREE DE QUEBEC
(Public)　　　　　　　　　　　　　AGRICULTURE
Exchanges: M　　　　　　　Stock Symbol: CFU.PR.A
9001 boul. de l'Acadie, bureau 200, Montreal, PQ,
H4N 3H7　　　　　　　　　　　　(514) 384-6450
COOPERATIVE FEDEREE DE QUEBEC is an agricultural cooperative with operations in meat packing, poultry products, dairy products, fruits and vegetables, petroleum products, feeds and fertilizers, agricultural supplies and farm implements.
Jean-Marc Bergeron, Chief Executive Officer

TOTAL ASSETS ($000)	430,990
TOTAL REVENUE ($000)	1,491,189
NET INCOME ($000)	2,852
EMPLOYEES	5,361
RANK (Profit/Revenue/Assets)	516/83/243

CORBY DISTILLERIES LIMITED
See page 188 for a full company profile.

COREL CORPORATION
See page 537 for a full company profile.

CORNUCOPIA RESOURCES LTD.
See page 36 for a full company profile.

CORONET CARPETS INC.
(Private)　　　　　　　　　　　HOME FURNISHINGS
7605 Bath Road, Mississauga, ON, L4T 3T1　　(905) 678-9595
CORONET CARPETS INC. is a manufacturer of tufted broadloom carpet in Canada. Its manufacturing operation is vertically integrated from yarn processing through carpet finishing in one facility in Farnham, Quebec.

Jan Lembregts, President

TOTAL ASSETS ($000)	139,270
TOTAL REVENUE ($000)	373,566
NET INCOME ($000)	309
EMPLOYEES	460

CORPORATE FOODS LIMITED
See page 189 for a full company profile.

COSCAN DEVELOPMENT CORPORATION
See page 309 for a full company profile.

COSCIENT GROUP INC.
(Public) ENTERTAINMENT SERVICES
Exchanges: M V Stock Symbol: CST.A
300 Rue Leo-Pariseau, Bureau 2400, C.P. 1145, Montreal, PQ,
H2W 2P4 (514) 284-2525
COSCIENT GROUP INC. is an independent producer in Quebec of television series, documentaries of all sorts intended for the television market as well as commercial and promotional audiovisual materials for corporate clients and institutions.
Yves Moquin, Chairman

TOTAL ASSETS ($000)	64,129
TOTAL REVENUE ($000)	27,379
NET INCOME ($000)	(111)
EMPLOYEES	75
RANK (Profit/Revenue/Assets)	765/661/580

COSMAIR CANADA INC.
(Private) MISC. CONSUMER PRODUCTS
2115 Crescent Street, Montreal, PQ, H3G 2C1 (514) 335-8000
COSMAIR CANADA INC. is a manufacturer and supplier of cosmetics, toilet preparations and fragrances. Cosmair Canada is 75.3% owned by L'Oreal of France.
G. Peyrelongue, Chairman

TOTAL ASSETS ($000)	82,086
TOTAL REVENUE ($000)	197,232
NET INCOME ($000)	9,752
EMPLOYEES	800

COTT CORPORATION
See page 190 for a full company profile.

COUNSEL CORPORATION
See page 514 for a full company profile.

COUNSEL REAL ESTATE INVESTMENT TRUST
(Public) INVESTMENT COMPANIES AND FUNDS
Exchanges: T Stock Symbol: REI.UN
Exchange Tower, Suite 1310 P.O Box 436, 2 First Canadian Place, Toronto, ON, M5X 1E3 (416) 866-3000
COUNSEL REAL ESTATE INVESTMENT TRUST is involved in the ownership of income producing real properities across Canada with the intention of maximizing tax-sheltered income and yield for its unitholders.
Edward Sonshine, Chairman President & C.E.O.

TOTAL ASSETS ($000)	130,773
TOTAL REVENUE ($000)	15,852

NET INCOME ($000)	(1,702)
EMPLOYEES	8
RANK (Profit/Revenue/Assets)	845/745/424

CREDIT SUISSE OF CANADA
(Private) BANKS
Credit Suisse Centre, Suite 1300, 525 University Avenue, Toronto, ON, M5G 2K6 (416) 351-3500
CREDIT SUISSE OF CANADA is a wholly owned subsidiary of Credit Suisse of Zurich, Switzerland. It is licenced to operate in Canada under the Bank Act.
Sudolf W. Hug, Chairman of the Board

TOTAL ASSETS ($000)	3,698,553
TOTAL REVENUE ($000)	171,574
NET INCOME ($000)	2,005
EMPLOYEES	124

CREDIT UNION CENTRAL ALBERTA LIMITED
(Fin. Co-op) CREDIT UNIONS
350N; 8500 Macleod Trail S.E., Calgary, AB,
T2H 2N1 (403) 258-5900
CREDIT UNION CENTRAL ALBERTA LIMITED provides leadership and services to member credit unions in Alberta.
Marcel Chorel, Chairman

TOTAL ASSETS ($000)	638,502
TOTAL REVENUE ($000)	56,147
NET INCOME ($000)	4,501
EMPLOYEES	240

CREDIT UNION CENTRAL OF CANADA
(Fin. Co-op) CREDIT UNIONS
300 The East Mall, 5th Floor, Toronto, ON, M9B 6B7 (416) 232-1262
CREDIT UNION CENTRAL OF CANADA is the national financial facility for the credit union system in Canada. It was established to provide liquidity for the credit union system in Canada. It coordinates, on a national scale, programs related to marketing, communications, government relations and the payments system and electronic network services.
Tod Manrell, Chairman

TOTAL ASSETS ($000)	952,621
TOTAL REVENUE ($000)	50,515
NET INCOME ($000)	3,221
EMPLOYEES	na

CREDIT UNION CENTRAL OF NOVA SCOTIA
(Fin. Co-op) CREDIT UNIONS
P.O. Box 9200, Station A, 6074 Lady Hammond Road, Halifax, NS, B3K 5N3 (902) 453-0680
CREDIT UNION CENTRAL OF NOVA SCOTIA provides corporate financial services to Credit Unions, development support, education and training services, marketing, printing and data processing services.
Donald H. Barry, Chairman

TOTAL ASSETS ($000)	426,657
TOTAL REVENUE ($000)	43,275
NET INCOME ($000)	538
EMPLOYEES	na

CREDIT UNION CENTRAL OF ONTARIO LIMITED
(Fin. Co-op) CREDIT UNIONS
2810 Matheson Blvd. East, Mississauga, ON,
L4W 4X7 (905) 238-9400
CREDIT UNION CENTRAL OF ONTARIO LIMITED is a financial service and trade association for about 400 credit unions in Ontario.
Joe Worona, Chairman

TOTAL ASSETS ($000)	1,247,951
TOTAL REVENUE ($000)	92,139
NET INCOME ($000)	3,476
EMPLOYEES	260

CREDIT UNION CENTRAL OF PRINCE EDWARD ISLAND
(Fin. Co-op) CREDIT UNIONS
P.O. Box 968, 281 University Avenue, Charlottetown, PE,
C1A 7M4 (902) 566-3350
CREDIT UNION CENTRAL OF PRINCE EDWARD ISLAND is a financial cooperative responsible for providing financial and other services, as well as leadership, to its members in a manner responsive to the social needs of people.
Gerard T. Dougan, C.E.O. & Managing Director

TOTAL ASSETS ($000)	31,334
TOTAL REVENUE ($000)	3,676
NET INCOME ($000)	772
EMPLOYEES	9

CREDIT UNION CENTRAL OF SASKATCHEWAN
(Fin. Co-op) CREDIT UNIONS
P.O. Box 3030, Regina, SK, S4P 3G8 (306) 566-1200
CREDIT UNION CENTRAL OF SASKATCHEWAN is the trade and financial services association for credit unions in Saskatchewan.
Sid Bildfell, Chief Executive Officer

TOTAL ASSETS ($000)	1,485,035
TOTAL REVENUE ($000)	103,732
NET INCOME ($000)	5,528
EMPLOYEES	318

CRESTAR ENERGY INC.
See page 89 for a full company profile.

CRESTBROOK FOREST INDUSTRIES LTD.
See page 157 for a full company profile.

CROWN LIFE INSURANCE COMPANY
See page 493 for a full company profile.

CS RESOURCES LIMITED
See page 90 for a full company profile.

CSA MANAGEMENT INC.
(Public) MANAGEMENT AND DIVERSIFIED
Exchanges: T V Stock Symbol: CSA.A
Suite 2700, 145 King Street West, Toronto, ON,
M5H 1J8 (416) 865-0326
CSA MANAGEMENT INC.'s principal focus is the investment in precious natural resources and the management of related financial products. The company's principal assets are its 18% holding of Goldcorp Inc. and its 40% holding of Lexam Explorations Inc. The company provides investment management and administrative services to two mutual funds, Goldfund Ltd. and Goldtrust.
Robert R. McEwen, Chairman President & C.E.O.

TOTAL ASSETS ($000)	33,776
TOTAL REVENUE ($000)	5,831
NET INCOME ($000)	4,756
EMPLOYEES	4
RANK (Profit/Revenue/Assets)	431/848/736

CT FINANCIAL SERVICES INC.
See page 447 for a full company profile.

CTV TELEVISION NETWORK LTD.
(Private) BROADCASTING
45 Charles St. East, Toronto, ON, M4Y 1T5 (416) 928-6000

John Cassady, President & C.E.O.

TOTAL ASSETS ($000)	54,355
TOTAL REVENUE ($000)	153,901
NET INCOME ($000)	2,619
EMPLOYEES	na

CUBE ENERGY CORP.
(Public) OIL AND GAS PRODUCERS
Exchanges: T Stock Symbol: CUK
Suite 800, 926 - 5th Avenue S.W., Calgary, AB,
T2P 0N7 (403) 264-4405
CUBE ENERGY CORP. is a Calgary based Canadian controlled company whose business is the exploration for, and the development and production of petroleum and natural gas. The company operates primarily in Western Canada.
Steven P. Dobrowolski, President & C.E.O.

TOTAL ASSETS ($000)	21,996
TOTAL REVENUE ($000)	10,915
NET INCOME ($000)	2,020
EMPLOYEES	10
RANK (Profit/Revenue/Assets)	568/789/852

CULINAR INC.
(Private) FOOD PROCESSING
2 Complexe Desjardins, Suite 2700, P.O. Box 32, Montreal, PQ,
H5B 1B2 (514) 288-3101
CULINAR INC. manufactures and markets a broad range of food products. Its main sectors of activity include bakery, confectionery, cookies, crackers, and dry bread products. It has manufacturing and distribution networks across Canada and in the northeastern United States.
Bruno Riverin, Chairman of the Board

TOTAL ASSETS ($000)	235,635
TOTAL REVENUE ($000)	497,255
NET INCOME ($000)	(27,647)
EMPLOYEES	4,500

CUMIS GROUP LIMITED (THE)
(Private) INSURANCE - LIFE
P.O. Box 5065, Burlington, ON, L7R 4C2 (905) 632-1221
CUMIS GROUP LIMITED is a holding company with interests in: Cumis Life Insurance Company; Cumis General Insurance Company; and Canadian Northern Shield Insurance Company.

William Halfpenny, Chairman of the Board

TOTAL ASSETS ($000)	418,976
TOTAL REVENUE ($000)	141,957
NET INCOME ($000)	5,948
EMPLOYEES	560

CZAR RESOURCES LTD.
See page 91 for a full company profile.

DAKOTA MINING CORPORATION
See page 37 for a full company profile.

DALMYS (CANADA) LIMITED
See page 417 for a full company profile.

DATAMARK INC.
(Public)   BUSINESS FORMS
Exchanges: M   Stock Symbol: DMK
909 Upton, LaSalle, PQ, H8R 2V1   (514) 366-0652
DATAMARK INC. is engaged in the design, manufacture and distribution of high quality business forms and pressure sensitive labels. Datamark also provides complementary services including warehousing, forms distribution and form management computerized control systems. Other activities include commercial printing, direct marketing promotional printing and senstrip products.
Frank Heller, C.E.O. & Chairman

TOTAL ASSETS ($000)	51,196
TOTAL REVENUE ($000)	79,849
NET INCOME ($000)	1,001
EMPLOYEES	0
RANK (Profit/Revenue/Assets)	657/455/626

DAVALDOU HOLDINGS INC.
(Private)   MANAGEMENT AND DIVERSIFIED
5 Place Ville Marie, Suite 1700, Montreal, PQ,
H3B 2G2   (514) 366-0652
Davaldou Holdings Inc. is a management company with operations in Canada.

TOTAL ASSETS ($000)	104,558
TOTAL REVENUE ($000)	197,592
NET INCOME ($000)	7,085
EMPLOYEES	na

DAVIS DISTRIBUTING LIMITED
(Public)   WHOLESALE DISTRIBUTORS
Exchanges: T   Stock Symbol: DAD.B
7171 Jane Street, Concord, ON, L4K 1A7   (905) 738-6226
DAVIS DISTRIBUTING LIMITED is a wholesale distributor of tobacco products, groceries, confectionery, health and beauty aids, and sundries to some 3,000 retailers, most of which are located in Southern Ontario.
Bernard J. Davis, President

TOTAL ASSETS ($000)	30,601
TOTAL REVENUE ($000)	211,113
NET INCOME ($000)	(120)
EMPLOYEES	na
RANK (Profit/Revenue/Assets)	767/307/768

DAYTON MINING CORPORATION
(Public)   PRECIOUS METALS
Exchanges: T   Stock Symbol: DD
Suite 1610, 200 Burrard Street, Vancouver, BC,
V6C 3L6   (604) 662-8383
DAYTON MINING CORPORATION is constructing a large open pit gold mine in Chile projected to produce 140,000 ounces of gold in 1996.
Wayne D. McClay, Chairman, President & C.E.O.

TOTAL ASSETS ($000)	109,750
TOTAL REVENUE ($000)	1,032
NET INCOME ($000)	(1,687)
EMPLOYEES	100
RANK (Profit/Revenue/Assets)	843/945/465

DECOMA INTERNATIONAL INC.
(Private)   AUTOMOTIVE
355 Wildcat Rd., Toronto, ON, M3J 2S3   (416) 738-5264
DECOMA INTERNATIONAL INC. manufactures plastic components, trim items, and cast aluminum wheels. It is a subsidiary of Magna International Inc.

TOTAL ASSETS ($000)	274,615
TOTAL REVENUE ($000)	493,190
NET INCOME ($000)	18,458
EMPLOYEES	na

DELRINA CORPORATION
See page 538 for a full company profile.

DELTA HOTELS & RESORTS
(Private)   LODGING
350 Bloor Street East, Suite 300, Toronto, ON,
M4W 1H4   (416) 926-7800
DELTA HOTELS & RESORTS is a Canadian hospitality company with hotels and resorts in Canada, Cuba, the United States, and Asia.
Jonas J. Prince, Chairman & C.E.O.

TOTAL ASSETS ($000)	na
TOTAL REVENUE ($000)	308,360
NET INCOME ($000)	na
EMPLOYEES	5,200

DENBRIDGE CAPITAL CORPORATION
(Public)   INVESTMENT COMPANIES AND FUNDS
Exchanges: T   Stock Symbol: DNB
Suite 2320, 130 Adelaide Street West, Toronto, ON,
M5H 3P5   (416) 862-7444
DENBRIDGE CAPITAL CORPORATION is a growth-oriented management company with active investments in digital electronics, digital entertainment and natural gas production.
James S. Anthony, Chairman & C.E.O.

TOTAL ASSETS ($000)	38,695
TOTAL REVENUE ($000)	18,015
NET INCOME ($000)	(20,603)
EMPLOYEES	140
RANK (Profit/Revenue/Assets)	972/727/703

DENISON MINES LIMITED
See page 9 for a full company profile.

DENNINGHOUSE INC.
(Public)   SPECIALTY STORES
Exchanges: T   Stock Symbol: DEH
Suite 201, 350 Creditstone Road, Concord, ON,
L4K 3Z2   (905) 738-3180
DENNINGHOUSE INC. is principally an operator of more than 115 dollar stores in Canada. The company operates company-owned stores as well as franchises stretched across 7 provinces.
Dennis Klein, Chairman President & C.E.O.

TOTAL ASSETS ($000)	15,370
TOTAL REVENUE ($000)	10,396
NET INCOME ($000)	1,898
EMPLOYEES	94
RANK (Profit/Revenue/Assets)	579/797/939

DERLAN INDUSTRIES LIMITED
See page 573 for a full company profile.

DESJARDINS LAURENTIAN FINANCIAL CORPORATION
See page 467 for a full company profile.

DESJARDINS LIFE ASSURANCE COMPANY INC.
(Fin. Co-op)   INSURANCE - LIFE
200 ave. des Commandeurs, Levis, PQ, G6V 6R2   (418) 838-7870
DESJARDINS LIFE ASSURANCE CO. INC. offers the full range of life and health insurance services, on an individual and group basis, through various intermediaries, life underwriters, brokers, specialized consultants or direct distribution network. In addition, the company offers coverage services designed for members, employees and directors of Desjardins Caisses. It does business mainly in Quebec.
Yves Malo, Chairman

TOTAL ASSETS ($000)	3,913,382
TOTAL REVENUE ($000)	937,544
NET INCOME ($000)	43,668
EMPLOYEES	1,530

DESJARDINS TRUSTCO INC.
(Private)   TRUST, SAVINGS AND LOAN
1 Complexe Desjardins, C.P. 34 Succursale Desjardins, Montreal,
PQ, H5B 1E4   (514) 286-3434
DESJARDINS TRUSTCO INC. is the result of arrangements by Mouvement Desjardins to make Desjardins Trustco Inc. the parent corporation of Desjardins Trust (Fiducie Desjardins) and of Desjardins Commercial and Industrial Credit Inc. (Credit Industriel Desjardins Inc.).
Alain Contant, Chairman of the Board

TOTAL ASSETS ($000)	2,820,347
TOTAL REVENUE ($000)	291,877
NET INCOME ($000)	(33,296)
EMPLOYEES	na

DESJARDINS-LAURENTIAN LIFE GROUP
(Private)   INSURANCE - LIFE
200, ave. des Commandeurs, Levis, PQ, G6V 6R2   (418) 838-7870
DESJARDINS-LAURENTIAN LIFE GROUP is a life insurance holding company. Its subsidiaries include Aeterna-Life, Desjardins-Laurentian Life, Imperial Life Assurance, and Laurier Life.

Michel Therien, President & C.E.O.

TOTAL ASSETS ($000)	8,857,637
TOTAL REVENUE ($000)	na
NET INCOME ($000)	na
EMPLOYEES	na

DEVELCON ELECTRONICS LTD.
See page 260 for a full company profile.

DEVRAN PETROLEUM LTD.
(Public)   OIL AND GAS PRODUCERS
Exchanges: T V   Stock Symbol: DVP
#460, 200 Queen's Avenue, London, ON, N6B 1J3   (519) 672-5520
DEVRAN PETROLEUM LTD. is involved in both conventional oil and gas exploration in Ontario and in horizontal drilling projects in Alberta. The company's projects include: a joint venture in Essex and Kent Counties in Ontario; a horizontal drilling development in Alberta; a 45% interest in 130 wells in Saskatchewan and a 40% interest in a natural gas exploration program in Alberta.
John F. Cowan, C.E.O

TOTAL ASSETS ($000)	33,594
TOTAL REVENUE ($000)	9,116
NET INCOME ($000)	1,631
EMPLOYEES	11
RANK (Profit/Revenue/Assets)	598/812/739

DEVTEK CORPORATION
(Public)   ELECTRICAL & ELECTRONIC
Exchanges: T M   Stock Symbol: DEK.A
100 Allstate Parkway, Suite 500, Markham, ON,
L3R 6H3   (905) 477-6861
DEVTEK CORPORATION is an international developer and manufacturer of systems and components for the automotive, aircraft and industrial and defence markets.
Helmut Hofmann, Chairman & C.E.O.

TOTAL ASSETS ($000)	145,661
TOTAL REVENUE ($000)	226,005
NET INCOME ($000)	3,328
EMPLOYEES	1,700
RANK (Profit/Revenue/Assets)	499/297/401

DEXLEIGH CORPORATION
See page 515 for a full company profile.

DIA MET MINERALS LTD
See page 10 for a full company profile.

DIAMOND FIELDS RESOURCES INC.
(Public)   OTHER MINES
Exchanges: T   Stock Symbol: DFR
Suite 1900, 355 Burrard Street, Vancouver, BC,
V6C 2G8   (604) 682-2113
DIAMOND FIELDS RESOURCES INC. is involved in the acquisition, exploration and development of natural resources properties with a focus on diamond properties. The Company has operations in Namibia, South Africa, Sierra Leone, the United States and Canada.
Jean R. Boulle, Chairman, C.E.O. & President

TOTAL ASSETS ($000)	32,625
TOTAL REVENUE ($000)	664

NET INCOME ($000) (3,179)
EMPLOYEES na
RANK (Profit/Revenue/Assets) 882/952/751

DIGITAL EQUIPMENT OF CANADA LIMITED
(Private) ELECTRICAL & ELECTRONIC
4110 Yonge Street, Willowdale, ON, M2P 2C7 (416) 730-7000
DIGITAL EQUIPMENT OF CANADA LIMITED and its partners provide industry leading open client/server solutions to businesses and governments across Canada. Digital's Alpha platforms, personal computers, storage, networking, software and services, together with industry focused solutions from business partners help organizations compete.
Ronald H. Larkin, Chairman of the Board
TOTAL ASSETS ($000) 451,288
TOTAL REVENUE ($000) 1,212,688
NET INCOME ($000) (27,192)
EMPLOYEES 3,000

DISCOVERY WEST CORP.
See page 92 for a full company profile.

DISYS CORPORATION
(Public) MISC. CONSUMER PRODUCTS
Exchanges: T Stock Symbol: DCY
Number 10, Airport Square, 2600 Skymark Avenue, Mississauga, ON, L4W 5B2 (905) 625-7393
DISYS CORPORATION designs, and markets radio frequency based wireless solutions to assist business in transmitting data throughout their organizations.
William R.C. Blundell, Chairman
TOTAL ASSETS ($000) 16,861
TOTAL REVENUE ($000) 24,125
NET INCOME ($000) (3,335)
EMPLOYEES 15
RANK (Profit/Revenue/Assets) 885/687/918

DMR GROUP INC.
See page 552 for a full company profile.

DOFASCO INC.
See page 241 for a full company profile.

DOMAN INDUSTRIES LIMITED
See page 158 for a full company profile.

DOMCO INDUSTRIES LTD.
(Public) HOME FURNISHINGS
Exchanges: T M Stock Symbol: DOC
1001 Yamaska Street East, Farnham, PQ, J2N 1J7 (514) 293-3173
DOMCO INDUSTRIES LIMITED is a manufacturer of resilient floor coverings and vinyl tiles in North America. The company produces vinyl floorings which are sold to retail specialty stores, mass merchandisers and home improvement centres as well as builders and the re-modelling trades.
Georgio Cefis, Chairman
TOTAL ASSETS ($000) 285,431
TOTAL REVENUE ($000) 281,828
NET INCOME ($000) 18,500

EMPLOYEES 1,300
RANK (Profit/Revenue/Assets) 224/265/293

DOMINION EXPLORERS INC.
(Public) OIL AND GAS PRODUCERS
Exchanges: T V Stock Symbol: DMN
Suite 1250, 255 - 5th Avenue S.W., Bow Valley Square III, Calgary, AB, T2P 3G6 (403) 571-1100
DOMINION EXPLORERS INC. holds producing oil and gas interests in west-central Alberta and interests in mineral exploration properties across Canada.
C. Alan Smith,
TOTAL ASSETS ($000) 17,093
TOTAL REVENUE ($000) 3,257
NET INCOME ($000) 435
EMPLOYEES 11
RANK (Profit/Revenue/Assets) 704/896/910

DOMINION TEXTILE INC.
See page 207 for a full company profile.

DOMTAR INC.
See page 159 for a full company profile.

DONOHUE INC.
See page 160 for a full company profile.

DOREL INDUSTRIES INC.
See page 574 for a full company profile.

DORSET EXPLORATION LTD.
See page 93 for a full company profile.

DOVER INDUSTRIES LIMITED
See page 191 for a full company profile.

DRAMEX CORPORATION
(Public) METAL FABRICATORS
Exchanges: M Stock Symbol: DRX.A
3555 Pitfield Boulevard, St-Laurent, PQ, H4S 1H3 (514) 745-7360
DRAMEX CORPORATION is a consortium of diversified manufacturing companies. Expanded Metal Corporation manufactures expanded metal products in Canada. Dramex International Inc. manufactures expanded metal products in the United States. Braidwood Gear Limited manufactures industrial gears and distributes power transmission products.
Alan B. Pearson, Chairman & President
TOTAL ASSETS ($000) 18,897
TOTAL REVENUE ($000) 22,096
NET INCOME ($000) 1,269
EMPLOYEES 81
RANK (Profit/Revenue/Assets) 631/703/881

DRAXIS HEALTH INC.
See page 229 for a full company profile.

DRECO ENERGY SERVICES LTD.
See page 94 for a full company profile.

DRUG ROYALTY CORPORATION INC.

(Public)   BIOTECHNOLOGY & PHARMACEUTICALS
Exchanges: T   Stock Symbol: DRI
Suite 202, 8 King Street East, Toronto, ON, M5C 1B5 (416) 863-1865
DRUG ROYALTY CORPORATION INC. provides expertise and
financial assistance to help develop existing and emerging pharmaceuti-
cals around the world in return for royalty positions.
William C. Garriock, Chairman

TOTAL ASSETS ($000)	27,852
TOTAL REVENUE ($000)	1,859
NET INCOME ($000)	(111)
EMPLOYEES	6
RANK (Profit/Revenue/Assets)	766/930/790

DRUG TRADING COMPANY LIMITED

(Private)   WHOLESALE DISTRIBUTORS
1960 Eglinton Avenue East, Scarborough, ON,
M1L 2M5   (416) 288-1100
DRUG TRADING COMPANY LIMITED is a wholesaler of pharma-
ceuticals and drug store sundry products.
M.A. Sparrow, Chairman

TOTAL ASSETS ($000)	170,501
TOTAL REVENUE ($000)	730,182
NET INCOME ($000)	(2,617)
EMPLOYEES	885

DUKE SEABRIDGE LIMITED

(Private)   MANAGEMENT AND DIVERSIFIED
#505, Kapilano 100, 100 Park Royal,
West Vancouver, BC, V7T 1A2   (604) 926-0167
DUKE SEABRIDGE LIMITED is a wholesaler of construction materi-
als and industrial equipment and a real estate developer. The company is
wholly owned by the Guinness Family.
Antoine Laoun, President

TOTAL ASSETS ($000)	106,105
TOTAL REVENUE ($000)	278,476
NET INCOME ($000)	3,599
EMPLOYEES	500

DUNDEE BANCORP INC.

See page 468 for a full company profile.

DUPONT CANADA INC.

See page 286 for a full company profile.

DY 4 SYSTEMS INC.

See page 261 for a full company profile.

DYLEX LIMITED

See page 418 for a full company profile.

DYNACARE INC.

(Public)   MEDICAL SERVICES
Exchanges: T   Stock Symbol: DNA.B
Suite 1600, 20 Eglinton Avenue West, Toronto, ON,
M4R 2H1   (416) 487-1100
DYNACARE INC. provides a variety of health care related services,
including medical diagnostic laboratory services, retirement residence

services and home care services. The company operates in Canada and
the United States.
Albert Latner, Chairman & C.E.O.

TOTAL ASSETS ($000)	384,229
TOTAL REVENUE ($000)	166,554
NET INCOME ($000)	(36,846)
EMPLOYEES	2,900
RANK (Profit/Revenue/Assets)	982/342/256

E.D.S. OF CANADA LTD.

(Private)   COMPUTER SOFTWARE & PROCESSING
33 Yonge Street, Suite 810, Toronto, ON, M5E 1G4   (416) 814-4500
EDS CANADA provides its customers with a wide range of business
information technology services including systems management, systems integration, systems development and consulting. EDS Canada is
100% owned by Electronic Data Systems Corporation of the United
States.
Sheelagh Whittaker, President & C.E.O.

TOTAL ASSETS ($000)	210,349
TOTAL REVENUE ($000)	356,050
NET INCOME ($000)	na
EMPLOYEES	2,000

E-L FINANCIAL CORPORATION LIMITED

See page 494 for a full company profile.

EAGLE PRECISION TECHNOLOGIES INC.

(Public)   AUTOMOTIVE
Exchanges: T M   Stock Symbol: EGL
565 West Street, P.O. Box 786, Brantford, ON,
N3T 5R7   (519) 756-5223
EAGLE PRECISION TECHNOLOGIES designs and manufactures
metal tube end forming machines, computer numerically controlled
metal tube bending machines and machines used in the manufacture of
automotive exhaust systems, catalytic converters, shock absorbers and
suspension struts. Its customers include the automotive, aircraft, and
furniture industries.
A. Alex Kepecs, Chairman & President

TOTAL ASSETS ($000)	40,803
TOTAL REVENUE ($000)	32,751
NET INCOME ($000)	2,988
EMPLOYEES	300
RANK (Profit/Revenue/Assets)	511/635/690

EATON CREDIT CORPORATION

(Private)   FINANCE AND LEASING
1 Dundas Street West, Toronto, ON, M5B 1C8   (416) 756-5223

TOTAL ASSETS ($000)	858,054
TOTAL REVENUE ($000)	163,362
NET INCOME ($000)	17,865
EMPLOYEES	na

ECHO BAY MINES LTD.

See page 38 for a full company profile.

ECLIPSE CAPITAL CORPORATION

(Public)   MANAGEMENT AND DIVERSIFIED
Exchanges: T   Stock Symbol: ECP
148-A James Street, Bracebridge, ON, P1L 1R7   (905) 841-7418

ECLIPSE CAPITAL's principal business is its investment in Alert Care Corporation, a 56% owned subsidiary which manages retirement homes.
W. Wayne Barton, President

TOTAL ASSETS ($000)	17,460
TOTAL REVENUE ($000)	4,551
NET INCOME ($000)	(10)
EMPLOYEES	na
RANK (Profit/Revenue/Assets)	758/870/903

ECONOMIC INVESTMENT TRUST LIMITED

(Public)   INVESTMENT COMPANIES AND FUNDS
Exchanges: T   Stock Symbol: EVT
10th Floor, 165 University Avenue, Toronto, ON,
M5H 3B8   (416) 947-2578
ECONOMIC INVESTMENT TRUST LIMITED is an investment corporation whose portfolio includes investments in banks and trust companies and the financial, insurance & funds, food, manufacturing, metals & mining, oil, gas & pipelines, communications and transportation industries.
J. Christopher Barron, Chairman of the Board

TOTAL ASSETS ($000)	160,335
TOTAL REVENUE ($000)	4,177
NET INCOME ($000)	3,735
EMPLOYEES	6
RANK (Profit/Revenue/Assets)	476/876/385

ECONOMICAL MUTUAL INSURANCE COMPANY

(Private)   INSURANCE - PROPERTY & CASUALTY
111 Westmount Road South, P.O. Box 2000, Waterloo, ON,
N2J 4S4   (519) 570-8200
ECONOMICAL MUTUAL INSURANCE COMPANY is a property and casualty insurance company.
P.H. Sims, Chairman of the Board

TOTAL ASSETS ($000)	1,301,968
TOTAL REVENUE ($000)	694,782
NET INCOME ($000)	29,577
EMPLOYEES	1,092

EDEN ROC MINERAL CORP.

(Public)   PRECIOUS METALS
Exchanges: T   Stock Symbol: EDN
P.O. Box 955, 4776 Bridge Street, Niagara Falls, ON,
L2E 6V8   (905) 356-9112
EDEN ROC MINERAL CORP. is involved in the acquisition, exploration and development of precious mineral properties located in Cote d'Ivoire, West Africa.
Peter Crossgrove, Chairman

TOTAL ASSETS ($000)	32,827
TOTAL REVENUE ($000)	10,266
NET INCOME ($000)	(3,530)
EMPLOYEES	na
RANK (Profit/Revenue/Assets)	892/800/750

EDMONTON POWER

(Crown)   ELECTRICAL UTILITIES
10065 Jasper Avenue, Suite 1700, Edmonton, AB,
T5J 3B1   (403) 448-3401
EDMONTON POWER is a fully integrated electric utility, from generation to transmission.

Jack Cresseyerack, Chairman

TOTAL ASSETS ($000)	1,860,956
TOTAL REVENUE ($000)	471,495
NET INCOME ($000)	30,102

EDMONTON TELEPHONES CORPORATION

(Crown)   TELEPHONE UTILITIES
Suite 1270, 44 Capital Boulevard, 10044 - 108 Street, Edmonton,
AB, T5J 3S7   (403) 441-2000
EDMONTON TELEPHONES CORPORATION is the largest municipally owned and independent telephone system in Canada. It is a fully integrated operation, providing a complete range of telecommunications products and services to residential and business clients within the Edmonton corporate boundaries. It sells consulting services and terminal products around the world.
J.L. Schlosser, Chairman

TOTAL ASSETS ($000)	446,589
TOTAL REVENUE ($000)	311,766
NET INCOME ($000)	25,628

EDPER GROUP LIMITED (THE)
See page 469 for a full company profile.

EICON TECHNOLOGY CORPORATION
See page 539 for a full company profile.

EL CONDOR RESOURCES LTD.

(Public)   PRECIOUS METALS
Exchanges: V Q   Stock Symbol: ECN
Suite 1020, 800 West Pender Street, Vancouver, BC,
V6C 2V6   (604) 684-6365
EL CONDOR RESOURCES LTD. is focused on the development of a large scale copper-gold project in Western Canada. Engineering and permitting programs are now underway.
Robert G. Hunter, Chairman & C.E.O.

TOTAL ASSETS ($000)	17,220
TOTAL REVENUE ($000)	145
NET INCOME ($000)	(965)
EMPLOYEES	12
RANK (Profit/Revenue/Assets)	818/983/907

ELAN ENERGY INC.
See page 95 for a full company profile.

ELECTROHOME LIMITED
See page 262 for a full company profile.

ELI LILLY CANADA INC.

(Private)   CHEMICALS
3650 Danforth Avenue, Scarborough, ON, M1N 2E8 (416) 694-3221
ELI LILLY CANADA INC. develops, manufactures and markets life science products of which 77% are pharmaceuticals. The company is wholly owned by Eli Lilly and Co. of the United States.
Roy A. Cage, Chairman

TOTAL ASSETS ($000)	110,380
TOTAL REVENUE ($000)	272,602
NET INCOME ($000)	15,542

ELLIS-DON CONSTRUCTION LTD.
(Private)   CONTRACTORS
2045 Oxford Street East, London, ON, N5V 2Z7   (519) 455-6770
ELLIS-DON CONSTRUCTION LTD. operates as a general in the construction business. The company is 100% employee owned.
Donald J. Smith, Chairman & C.E.O.

TOTAL ASSETS ($000)	230,000
TOTAL REVENUE ($000)	753,000
NET INCOME ($000)	na
EMPLOYEES	1,500

EMCO LIMITED
See page 242 for a full company profile.

EMERSON ELECTRIC CANADA LIMITED
(Private)   ELECTRICAL & ELECTRONIC
9999 Highway 48, Markham, ON, L3P 3J6   (905) 294-9340
EMERSON ELECTRIC CANADA LIMITED is engaged in two industry segments: commercial and industrial components; and consumer products. The company is a wholly owned subsidiary of Emerson Electric Co. of the United States.
Lawrence C. Barrett, President

TOTAL ASSETS ($000)	235,777
TOTAL REVENUE ($000)	299,672
NET INCOME ($000)	22,329
EMPLOYEES	2,000

EMJ DATA SYSTEMS LTD.
See page 403 for a full company profile.

EMPIRE COMPANY LIMITED
See page 419 for a full company profile.

EMPIRE LIFE INSURANCE COMPANY (THE)
(Private)   INSURANCE - LIFE
259 King Street East, Kingston, ON, K7L 3A8   (613) 548-1881
THE EMPIRE LIFE INSURANCE COMPANY markets a full range of financial products and services designed to meet the needs of individuals and businesses in Canada.
James W. McCutcheon, Chairman of the Board

TOTAL ASSETS ($000)	2,108,127
TOTAL REVENUE ($000)	321,052
NET INCOME ($000)	19,695
EMPLOYEES	535

ENCAL ENERGY LTD.
See page 96 for a full company profile.

ENERFLEX SYSTEMS LTD.
(Public)   MACHINERY
Exchanges: T   Stock Symbol: EFX
7720 - 48th Street S.E., Calgary, AB, T2C 2V6   (403) 236-6800
ENERFLEX SYSTEMS LTD. manufactures, services and leases compressor packages necessary for the production and processing of natural gas.
P. John Aldred, President & C.E.O.

TOTAL ASSETS ($000)	102,505
TOTAL REVENUE ($000)	218,214

NET INCOME ($000)	17,779
EMPLOYEES	500
RANK (Profit/Revenue/Assets)	226/300/478

ENERPLUS RESOURCES FUND
(Public)   INVESTMENT COMPANIES AND FUNDS
Exchanges: T M   Stock Symbol: ERF.G
Suite 3200 West Tower, 150 - 6th Avenue S.W., Calgary, AB,
T2P 3Y7   (403) 269-7070
ENERPLUS RESOURCES FUND has been established to purchase and hold, as its sole efforts petroleum royalty units, series B of Enerplus resources corporation on behalf of the holders of the trust units, series B.

TOTAL ASSETS ($000)	94,829
TOTAL REVENUE ($000)	40,206
NET INCOME ($000)	1,813
EMPLOYEES	0
RANK (Profit/Revenue/Assets)	585/589/497

ENERTEC RESOURCE SERVICES INC.
(Public)   OIL AND GAS FIELD SERVICES
Exchanges: T   Stock Symbol: ERS
3024 - 49th Avenue S.E., Calgary, AB, T2B 2X4   (403) 569-9222
ENERTEC RESOURCE SERVICES INC. is engaged in the business of seismic data acquisition and seismic data processing principally in Canada and the United States.
J. Haig de B. Farris, Chairman

TOTAL ASSETS ($000)	31,344
TOTAL REVENUE ($000)	22,965
NET INCOME ($000)	1,829
EMPLOYEES	319
RANK (Profit/Revenue/Assets)	583/697/761

ENSCOR INC.
See page 216 for a full company profile.

ENSERV CORPORATION
See page 97 for a full company profile.

ENSIGN RESOURCE SERVICE GROUP INC.
See page 98 for a full company profile.

ENVIRONMENTAL TECHNOLOGIES INTERNATIONAL INC.
(Public)   ENVIRONMENTAL SERVICES
Exchanges: T   Stock Symbol: ETK
Suite 202, 190 Attwell Drive, Etobicoke, ON,
M9W 6H8   (416) 674-0573
ENVIRONMENTAL TECHNOLOGIES INTERNATIONAL INC. owns and operates a number of manufacturing and process-oriented divisions in the water and wastewater environmental industry. ETI provides financial, marketing, operational, planning, technical, and general management resources to these divisions.
Ron Williams, Chairman & C.E.O.

TOTAL ASSETS ($000)	14,755
TOTAL REVENUE ($000)	25,860
NET INCOME ($000)	(3,735)
EMPLOYEES	6
RANK (Profit/Revenue/Assets)	897/671/951

EPIC DATA INTERNATIONAL INC.
(Public)   ELECTRICAL & ELECTRONIC
Exchanges: T   Stock Symbol: EKD
7280 River Road, Richmond, BC, V6X 1X5   (604) 273-9146
EPIC DATA INC. designs, manufactures, markets and services electronic data collection systems and products, primarily for the factory data collection market.
Helmut M. Eppich, Chairman

TOTAL ASSETS ($000)	21,660
TOTAL REVENUE ($000)	22,831
NET INCOME ($000)	(1,687)
EMPLOYEES	151
RANK (Profit/Revenue/Assets)	843/698/855

EQUITABLE LIFE INSURANCE COMPANY OF CANADA
(Private)   INSURANCE - LIFE
One Westmount Rd. N., Waterloo, ON, N2J 4C7   (519) 886-5110
EQUITABLE LIFE INSURANCE COMPANY OF CANADA is an independent mutual life insurance company offering a full range of life insurance, annuities and group plans for individuals and businesses.
Robert J. Collins-Wright, Chairman of the Board

TOTAL ASSETS ($000)	783,967
TOTAL REVENUE ($000)	184,102
NET INCOME ($000)	5,483
EMPLOYEES	250

EQUITY SILVER MINES LIMITED
See page 39 for a full company profile.

ERICSSON COMMUNICATIONS INC.
(Private)   WHOLESALE DISTRIBUTORS
8400 Decarie Blvd., Montreal, PQ, H4P 2R4   (514) 738-8300
L. Hurtubise, President & C.E.O.

TOTAL ASSETS ($000)	118,392
TOTAL REVENUE ($000)	202,696
NET INCOME ($000)	14,626
EMPLOYEES	na

ESPALAU MINING CORPORATION
(Public)   CONSULTING
Exchanges: M   Stock Symbol: EPU
3200 Industrial Blvd., P.O. Box 220, Val d'Or, PQ,
J9P 4P3   (819) 825-1111
ESPALAU INC. specializes in services and products for the mining and construction industries. The company operates through subsidiaries. Espalau Gold Mines Inc. is involved in gold production. Ross Finlay Ltd. specializes in the execution of mining works. Quebco Homes Inc. manufactures modular units for the residential, commercial, and industrial sectors.
Normand Cliche, President, C.E.O. & Secretary

TOTAL ASSETS ($000)	41,397
TOTAL REVENUE ($000)	46,311
NET INCOME ($000)	(5,799)
EMPLOYEES	475
RANK (Profit/Revenue/Assets)	915/565/685

ESSTRA INDUSTRIES CORP.
(Public)   MISC. CONSUMER PRODUCTS
Exchanges: V   Stock Symbol: ESS
Suite 218, 10458 Mayfield Road, Edmonton, AB,
T5P 4P4   (403) 484-3794
ESSTRA INDUSTRIES CORP. is involved in a 122 unit luxury rental townhouse project in Minneapolis, construction of townhomes in Vancouver for sale, and merchant banking, bridge loans, and equity placements.
Peter G. Dickson, President & C.E.O.

TOTAL ASSETS ($000)	13,876
TOTAL REVENUE ($000)	2,308
NET INCOME ($000)	(547)
EMPLOYEES	na
RANK (Profit/Revenue/Assets)	795/912/965

ESTEE LAUDER COSMETICS LTD.
(Private)   MISC. CONSUMER PRODUCTS
161 Commander Blvd., Agincourt, ON, M1S 3K9   (416) 961-1919
ESTEE LAUDER COSMETICS LTD. is a distributor of cosmetic products. It is a wholly owned subsidiary of Estee Lauder International Inc..
Anton McBurnie, Exec. V.P. & Managing Director

TOTAL ASSETS ($000)	437,437
TOTAL REVENUE ($000)	804,056
NET INCOME ($000)	18,153
EMPLOYEES	na

EURO-NEVADA MINING CORPORATION LIMITED
See page 40 for a full company profile.

EXCEL ENERGY INC.
See page 99 for a full company profile.

EXCO TECHNOLOGIES LIMITED
(Public)   MISC. INDUSTRIAL PRODUCTS
Exchanges: T   Stock Symbol: XTC
60 Spy Court, Markham, ON, L3R 5H6   (905) 477-3065
EXCO TECHNOLOGIES LIMITED is a producer of large and precision-engineered tooling for the automotive and construction industries. The company's operations are comprised of three divisions: automotive; aluminum extrusion; and plastic mould components.
Arthur A. Kennedy, Chairman of the Board

TOTAL ASSETS ($000)	62,169
TOTAL REVENUE ($000)	57,660
NET INCOME ($000)	7,747
EMPLOYEES	300
RANK (Profit/Revenue/Assets)	344/521/588

EXPORT DEVELOPMENT CORPORATION
(Crown)   FINANCE AND LEASING
151 O'Connor Street, Ottawa, ON, K1A 1K3   (613) 598-2500
EXPORT DEVELOPMENT CORPORATION is a Canadian crown corporation whose purpose or goal is to facilitate and develop Canada's export trade within the framework of the Export Development Act. The company pursues its purpose by providing insurance guarantee and financing facilities, allowing Canadian firms to compete effectively abroad.

Alexander K. Stuart, Chairman

TOTAL ASSETS ($000)	9,375,000
TOTAL REVENUE ($000)	844,000
NET INCOME ($000)	171,000
EMPLOYEES	590

EXPORT PACKERS COMPANY LIMITED
(Private) WHOLESALE DISTRIBUTORS
107 Walker Drive, Brampton, ON, L6T 5K5 (905) 792-9700
EXPORT PACKERS COMPANY LIMITED is engaged in food wholesaling. The company is wholly owned by the Rubenstein family of Toronto, Ontario.
Max Rubenstein, Chairman

TOTAL ASSETS ($000)	88,500
TOTAL REVENUE ($000)	389,000
NET INCOME ($000)	na
EMPLOYEES	130

EXTENDICARE HEALTH SERVICES INC.
(Private) BIOTECHNOLOGY & PHARMACEUTICALS
3000 Steeles Avenue East, Suite 700, Markham, ON, L3R 9W2 (905) 470-1400
EXTENDICARE HEALTH SERVICES INC. is a provider in North America of long-term care to the elderly through its nursing and retirement centres. It also offers other health care services including home care, the provision of institutional pharmacy and medical supplies, and hospital management and development.
Fredende Ladly, President & C.E.O.

TOTAL ASSETS ($000)	195,780
TOTAL REVENUE ($000)	298,873
NET INCOME ($000)	20,288
EMPLOYEES	na

EXTENDICARE INC.
See page 575 for a full company profile.

FAHNESTOCK VINER HOLDINGS INC.
See page 470 for a full company profile.

FAIRFAX FINANCIAL HOLDINGS LIMITED
See page 495 for a full company profile.

FALCONBRIDGE LIMITED
See page 11 for a full company profile.

FAMOUS PLAYERS INC.
(Private) ENTERTAINMENT SERVICES
146 Bloor Street West, Toronto, ON, M5S 1P3 (416) 969-7800
FAMOUS PLAYERS INC. is engaged in the exhibition of motion pictures. The company is a subsidiary of Paramount Pictures (Canada) Inc.
J. Bailey, Executive V.P.

TOTAL ASSETS ($000)	148,172
TOTAL REVENUE ($000)	197,169
NET INCOME ($000)	1,967
EMPLOYEES	300

FARM CREDIT CORPORATION
(Crown) TRUST, SAVINGS AND LOAN
P.O. Box 4320, 1800 Hamilton Street, Regina, SK, S4P 4L3 (306) 780-8100
FARM CREDIT's role is to provide mortgage, credit and complimentary financial services on a breakeven basis to enable Canadian farmers to establish, develop and maintain viable farm enterprises.
C. Gerald Penney, President & C.E.O.

TOTAL ASSETS ($000)	3,773,613
TOTAL REVENUE ($000)	373,125
NET INCOME ($000)	28,311
EMPLOYEES	764

FARMERS CO-OPERATIVE DAIRY LTD.
(Non-fin Co-op) FOOD PROCESSING
P.O. Box 8118, Halifax, NS, B3K 5Y6 (902) 835-3373
FARMERS CO-OPERATIVE DAIRY LTD. processes and distributes a full range of dairy products including milk, cream, yogurt, cheese and margarine.
Ralph T. Ballam, Chairman

TOTAL ASSETS ($000)	41,332
TOTAL REVENUE ($000)	133,955
NET INCOME ($000)	0
EMPLOYEES	550

FCA INTERNATIONAL LTD.
See page 553 for a full company profile.

FCMI FINANCIAL CORPORATION
(Public) INVESTMENT COMPANIES AND FUNDS
Exchanges: T Stock Symbol: FCM.A
181 Bay Street, Suite 250, Toronto, ON, M5J 2T3 (416) 364-1171
FCMI FINANCIAL CORPORATION is engaged in providing management and/or advisory services to specialized funds, from which it derives fee income.
Albert D. Friedberg, Chairman & President

TOTAL ASSETS ($000)	18,130
TOTAL REVENUE ($000)	5,534
NET INCOME ($000)	966
EMPLOYEES	58
RANK (Profit/Revenue/Assets)	661/857/896

FEDERAL BUSINESS DEVELOPMENT BANK
(Crown) TRUST, SAVINGS AND LOAN
800 Victoria Square, Tour de la Place Victoria, P.O. Box 335, Montreal, PQ, H4Z 1L4 (800) 361-2126
FEDERAL BUSINESS DEVELOPMENT BANK is a crown corporation that helps create and develop Canadian small and medium-sized businesses. FBDB provides specialized financing for commercially viable business projects including term loans, Venture Loans and venture capital, as well as a wide range of business counselling, training and mentoring services. FBDB has 78 branches available across Canada.
P.J. Lavelle, Chairman

TOTAL ASSETS ($000)	3,021,273
TOTAL REVENUE ($000)	310,333
NET INCOME ($000)	4,131
EMPLOYEES	1,000

FEDERATED CO-OPERATIVES LIMITED
(Non-fin Co-op)   WHOLESALE DISTRIBUTORS
Box 1050, 401 - 22nd Street East, Saskatoon, SK,
S7K 3M9   (306) 244-3311
FEDERATED CO-OPERATIVES LIMITED operates from its base in
Saskatchewan to coordinate the procurement, processing, manufacturing
and distribution of goods, and the provision of services to its member-
owners. The cooperative operates in several business segments including
food, petroleum, hardware building materials, crop supplies, feed sup-
plies and family fashions.
V.J. Leland, President of the Board
TOTAL ASSETS ($000)   749,102
TOTAL REVENUE ($000)   1,933,588
NET INCOME ($000)   112,036
EMPLOYEES   2,514

FEDERATION DES CAISSES POPULAIRES DESJARDINS DE MONTREAL ET DE L'OUEST-DU-QUEBEC
(Private)   FINANCE AND LEASING
1 Complexe Desjardins, Case Postale 35, Succursale Desjardins,
Montreal, PQ, H5B 1E7   (514) 281-8666
FEDERATION DES CAISSES POPULAIRES DESJARDINS DE
MONTREAL ET DE L'OUEST-DU-QUEBEC is involved in a com-
prehensive range of savings and credit services. It coordinates the
operation of 323 caisses populaires with a global asset of more than 16
billion dollars and over two million members.
Jocelyn Proteau, President & C.E.O.
TOTAL ASSETS ($000)   4,325,078
TOTAL REVENUE ($000)   338,717
NET INCOME ($000)   18,986
EMPLOYEES   10,949

FEDNAV LIMITED
(Private)   TRANSPORTATION
1000 Rue de la Gauchetiere O., Bureau 3500, Montreal, PQ,
H3B 4W5   (514) 878-6500
FEDNAV LIMITED is engaged in ocean transportation of commercial
cargo on a world wide basis.
Laurence G. Pathy, President & C.E.O.
TOTAL ASSETS ($000)   336,178 (US)
TOTAL REVENUE ($000)   436,000 (US)
NET INCOME ($000)   12,718 (US)
EMPLOYEES   230

FIBERGLAS CANADA INC.
(Private)   MISC. INDUSTRIAL PRODUCTS
4100 Yonge Street, Willowdale, ON, M2P 2B6   (416) 733-1600
FIBERGLAS CANADA INC.'s operations consist of two segments. The
insulation group manufactures thermal insulation for residential, com-
mercial and industrial buildings, as well as roof insulation, accoustic
products and other insulation products. The textiles, reinforcements and
chemicals group provides a variety of materials primarily to the glass
fibre reinforced plastics industry.
R. Jones, President & C.E.O.
TOTAL ASSETS ($000)   312,960
TOTAL REVENUE ($000)   351,916
NET INCOME ($000)   11,412
EMPLOYEES   na

FIDUCIE DESJARDINS INC.
(Public)   TRUST, SAVINGS AND LOAN
Exchanges: M   Stock Symbol: FID.PR.A
1 Complexe Desjardins, P.O. Box 34, Desjardins Station, Montreal,
PQ, H5B 1E4   (514) 286-9441
DESJARDINS TRUST INC. provides specialty trust and financial serv-
ices to consumers, corporations and other institutions.
Alain Contant, Chairman of the Board
TOTAL ASSETS ($000)   1,911,532
TOTAL REVENUE ($000)   204,369
NET INCOME ($000)   (37,956)
EMPLOYEES   620
RANK (Profit/Revenue/Assets)   984/311/109

FINNING LTD.
See page 404 for a full company profile.

FIRAN CORPORATION
(Public)   AUTOMOTIVE
Exchanges: T   Stock Symbol: FNG
353 Iroquois Shore Road, Oakville, ON, L6H 1M3   (905) 844-2870
FIRAN CORPORATION is engaged in: the manufacture of a full line
of recreational vehicles, marketed through an independent franchised
dealer network throughout North America; the design and manufacture
of communications & navigation systems for the international air traffic
control market; and the manufacture of printed circuit boards for the
North American electronics industry.
D. Morgan Firestone, Chairman & C.E.O.
TOTAL ASSETS ($000)   96,394
TOTAL REVENUE ($000)   193,813
NET INCOME ($000)   3,627
EMPLOYEES   1,100
RANK (Profit/Revenue/Assets)   482/320/493

FIRST B SHARES INC.
(Public)   INVESTMENT COMPANIES AND FUNDS
Exchanges: T M V   Stock Symbol: XFB.E
2 First Canadian Place, Suite 3100, P.O. Box 21, Toronto, ON,
M5X 1J9   (416) 869-3707
FIRST B SHARES INC. is a mutual fund company.
Stuart W. Henry, President
TOTAL ASSETS ($000)   196,758
TOTAL REVENUE ($000)   17,086
NET INCOME ($000)   8,521
EMPLOYEES   na
RANK (Profit/Revenue/Assets)   321/738/360

FIRST CALGARY SAVINGS & CREDIT UNION LTD.
(Fin. Co-op)   FINANCE AND LEASING
Suite 200, 510 - 16th Avenue N.W., Calgary, AB,
T2E 1K4   (403) 230-2783
FIRST CALGARY SAVINGS & CREDIT UNION is a full service open
bond credit union.
Ron Gilmore, Chairman
TOTAL ASSETS ($000)   607,851
TOTAL REVENUE ($000)   48,487
NET INCOME ($000)   1,254
EMPLOYEES   330

FIRST MARATHON INC.
See page 471 for a full company profile.

FIRST MARITIME MINING CORPORATION LIMITED
(Public)   METAL MINES
Exchanges: T   Stock Symbol: FMM
P.O. Box 937, 300 Union Street, Saint John, NB,
E2L 4E3   (506) 632-7171
FIRST MARITIME MINING CORPORATION LIMITED is a holding company with investments in Brunswick Mining and Smelting Corporation Limited, Alantic Coast Copper Corporation Limited and Consolidated Rambler Mines Limited.
W.D. Jamieson, President

TOTAL ASSETS ($000)	16,606
TOTAL REVENUE ($000)	515
NET INCOME ($000)	381
EMPLOYEES	2
RANK (Profit/Revenue/Assets)	717/956/925

FIRST MERCANTILE CURRENCY FUND, INC. (THE)
(Public)   INVESTMENT COMPANIES AND FUNDS
Exchanges: T   Stock Symbol: FMF.UN
347 Bay Street, Suite 404, Toronto, ON, M5H 2R7   (416) 364-2724
FIRST MERCANTILE CURRENCY FUND is a closed-end trust devoted to investment in foreign currencies. These investments are made primarily through the interbank market in the form of forward contracts. A key objective of the fund is to correctly anticipate relative movements, both upward and downward, in the exchange rates of various currencies, earning profits on the changing spreads between them.
Herbert Alpert, Chairman of the Board

TOTAL ASSETS ($000)	17,091
TOTAL REVENUE ($000)	3,305
NET INCOME ($000)	2,632
EMPLOYEES	0
RANK (Profit/Revenue/Assets)	532/893/911

FIRSTSERVICE CORPORATION
(Public)   OTHER SERVICES
Exchanges: T   Stock Symbol: FSV
Suite 4000, 1140 Bay Street, Toronto, ON, M5S 2B4   (416) 960-2724
FIRSTSERVICE CORPORATION is a provider of brand name residential and commercial services. The company's brands include College Pro Painters, Certa ProPainters, ChemLawn, Green Lawn Care, Cleanol Services, Superior Pool and Itercon Security.
Jay S. Hennick, President & C.E.O.

TOTAL ASSETS ($000)	64,823
TOTAL REVENUE ($000)	88,375
NET INCOME ($000)	2,353
EMPLOYEES	5,400
RANK (Profit/Revenue/Assets)	549/440/576

FLEET AEROSPACE CORPORATION
See page 263 for a full company profile.

FLETCHER CHALLENGE CANADA LIMITED
See page 161 for a full company profile.

FLETCHER CHALLENGE INVESTMENTS II INC.
(Public)   INVESTMENT COMPANIES AND FUNDS
Exchanges: T   Stock Symbol: FII.B
Pacific Centre 9th Floor, 700 West Georgia Street, P.O. Box 10058,
Vancouver, BC, V7Y 1J7   (604) 654-4372
FLETCHER CHALLENGE INVESTMENTS II INC.'s principal assets consist of long term investments in companies within the Fletcher Challenge group. The majority of the company's revenues are received by way of dividends or interest on these long-term investments in related companies.
Bruce D. Cooper, President & C.E.O.

TOTAL ASSETS ($000)	98,216
TOTAL REVENUE ($000)	13,315
NET INCOME ($000)	10,645
EMPLOYEES	3
RANK (Profit/Revenue/Assets)	289/770/489

FLETCHER'S FINE FOODS LTD.
(Private)   FOOD PROCESSING
8385 Fraser Street, Suite 3000, Vancouver, BC,
V5X 3X8   (604) 321-4372
FLETCHER'S FINE FOODS LTD. is a pork producer with operations in Red Deer, Edmonton, Vancouver and the United States. It is wholly owned by Alberta Pork Producers Development Corporation.
Brian Perkins, Chairman

TOTAL ASSETS ($000)	38,000
TOTAL REVENUE ($000)	250,000
NET INCOME ($000)	na
EMPLOYEES	1,000

FLUOR CONSTRUCTORS CANADA LTD.
(Private)   CONTRACTORS
10101 Southport Road S.W., Box 8799 S-F, Calgary, AB,
T2J 4B4   (403) 321-4372

TOTAL ASSETS ($000)	16,529
TOTAL REVENUE ($000)	180,726
NET INCOME ($000)	2,643
EMPLOYEES	na

FLUOR DANIEL CANADA INC.
(Private)   CONTRACTORS
Box 8799, Station F, Calgary, AB, T2J 4B4   (403) 259-1110
FLUOR DANIEL CANADA INC. is engaged in engineering, procurement, construction management and maintenance. Fluor Daniel Canada's ultimate parent is Fluor Corporation of the United States.
John Gallagher, General Manager Operations

TOTAL ASSETS ($000)	85,905
TOTAL REVENUE ($000)	180,226
NET INCOME ($000)	na
EMPLOYEES	na

FONOROLA INC.
(Public)   TELECOMMUNICATIONS
Exchanges: T M   Stock Symbol: FON
Suite 305, 500 Rene-Levesque Blvd. West, Montreal, PQ,
H2Z 1W7   (514) 954-3666
FONOROLA INC. is a reseller of long distance voice and data telecommunications services to and from Quebec, Ontario, British Columbia, Alberta and the United States.

Michael Boyd, Chairman

TOTAL ASSETS ($000)	71,051
TOTAL REVENUE ($000)	107,986
NET INCOME ($000)	(7,888)
EMPLOYEES	350
RANK (Profit/Revenue/Assets)	935/411/562

FOOTHILLS PIPE LINES LTD.

(Private) GAS PIPELINES

3100 - 707 8th Ave SW, Postal Station M, Calgary, AB,
T2P 3W8 (403) 294-4111

FOOTHILLS PIPE LINES LTD. was established to construct the Canadian portion of the Alaska Natural Gas Transportation System. It transports Canadian natural gas for export to U.S. markets. It is owned in equal shares by Nova Corporation of Alberta and Westcoast Energy Inc.

R.L. Pierce, C.E.O. & Chairman

TOTAL ASSETS ($000)	1,054,562
TOTAL REVENUE ($000)	142,322
NET INCOME ($000)	21,999
EMPLOYEES	80

FORD CREDIT CANADA LIMITED

(Private) FINANCE AND LEASING

The Canadian Road, Oakville, ON, L6J 5C7 (905) 845-2511

FORD CREDIT CANADA LIMITED provides wholesale and retail financing support to Ford automotive dealers and their customers. It is an affiliate of Ford Motor Company of Canada, Limited.

William E. Odom, Chairman of the Board

TOTAL ASSETS ($000)	4,529,501
TOTAL REVENUE ($000)	677,695
NET INCOME ($000)	38,377
EMPLOYEES	546

FORD ELECTRONICS MANUFACTURING CORPORATION

(Private) ELECTRICAL & ELECTRONIC

7455 Birchmount Road, Markham, ON, L3R 5C2 (905) 474-4203

FORD ELECTRONICS MANUFACTURING CORPORATION is the manufacturer of electronic automotive products for Ford Motor Company worldwide. The company is a wholly owned subsidiary of Ford Motor Company of Michigan.

C. Szuluk, President

TOTAL ASSETS ($000)	222,996
TOTAL REVENUE ($000)	427,154
NET INCOME ($000)	na
EMPLOYEES	1,725

FORD MOTOR COMPANY OF CANADA, LIMITED

See page 217 for a full company profile.

FORDING COAL LIMITED

(Private) NON-BASE METAL MINING

10th Floor, 205 - 9th Avenue S.E., Calgary, AB,
T2G 0R4 (403) 264-1063

FORDING COAL LIMITED mines and processes metallurgical and thermal coal for markets including blast furnace steel producers, utilities and other coal consumers worldwide. Mine sites are located in Alberta and southeastern British Columbia. The company is a wholly owned subsidiary of Canadian Pacific Limited of Montreal, Quebec.

J.G. Gardiner, President & C.E.O.

TOTAL ASSETS ($000)	1,192,147
TOTAL REVENUE ($000)	624,516
NET INCOME ($000)	61,647
EMPLOYEES	1,600

FOREMOST INDUSTRIES INC.

(Public) TRANSPORTATION EQUIP & COMPNTS

Exchanges: T Stock Symbol: FMO

1225 - 64 Avenue N.E., Calgary, AB, T2E 8P9 (403) 272-3322

FOREMOST INDUSTRIES INC. specializes in the design, manufacture and sales of high-mobility all-terrain vehicles, mineral exploration drilling equipment and associated parts and service, and most recently the energy services business. It serves a broad range of global market segments, including oil and gas, utilities, mineral exploration, defense, environmental protection and frontier development.

J.H. Nodwell, Chairman & C.E.O.

TOTAL ASSETS ($000)	36,978
TOTAL REVENUE ($000)	64,475
NET INCOME ($000)	8,461
EMPLOYEES	175
RANK (Profit/Revenue/Assets)	323/494/719

FORESBEC INC.

(Public) EAST COAST FORESTRY

Exchanges: M Stock Symbol: FBC.A

1750 Rue Haggerty, Drummondville, PQ, J2C 5P8 (819) 477-8787

FORESBEC INC. is a major producer of hardwoods for export markets.

Guy Boisse, Chairman, President & C.E.O.

TOTAL ASSETS ($000)	27,528
TOTAL REVENUE ($000)	39,798
NET INCOME ($000)	1,513
EMPLOYEES	100
RANK (Profit/Revenue/Assets)	608/591/795

FORTIS INC.

See page 352 for a full company profile.

FORTUNE ENERGY INC.

(Public) OIL AND GAS PRODUCERS

Exchanges: T Stock Symbol: FEY

Suite 1000, 833 - 4th Avenue S.W., Calgary, AB,
T2P 3T5 (403) 297-0230

FORTUNE ENERGY INC. is engaged in the exploration and production of oil and natural gas.

Gordon F. Dixon, Chairman & Secretary

TOTAL ASSETS ($000)	33,608
TOTAL REVENUE ($000)	7,636
NET INCOME ($000)	111
EMPLOYEES	13
RANK (Profit/Revenue/Assets)	743/825/737

FORZANI GROUP LTD. (THE)

(Public) SPECIALTY STORES

Exchanges: T M Stock Symbol: FGL

824 - 41st Avenue N.E., Calgary, AB, T2E 3R3 (403) 230-8200

THE FORZANI GROUP LTD. is a national Canadian specialty retailer of general sporting goods, including athletic, leisure and recreational footwear and apparel.

John M. Forzani, Chairman President & C.E.O.
TOTAL ASSETS ($000)	133,893
TOTAL REVENUE ($000)	296,721
NET INCOME ($000)	7,669
EMPLOYEES	3,000
RANK (Profit/Revenue/Assets)	346/260/418

FOSSIL OIL & GAS LIMITED
(Public)   OIL AND GAS PRODUCERS
Exchanges: T   Stock Symbol: FOL
Suite 530, 635 - 8th Avenue S.W., Calgary, AB,
T2P 3M3   (403) 290-0288
FOSSIL OIL & GAS LIMITED participates in the acquisition, exploration and development of oil and gas properties.
Kenneth R. King, President & C.E.O.
TOTAL ASSETS ($000)	25,209
TOTAL REVENUE ($000)	5,580
NET INCOME ($000)	972
EMPLOYEES	7
RANK (Profit/Revenue/Assets)	659/854/814

FOUR SEASONS HOTELS INC.
See page 576 for a full company profile.

FPI LIMITED
See page 192 for a full company profile.

FRANCO-NEVADA MINING CORPORATION LIMITED
See page 41 for a full company profile.

FREEWEST RESOURCES CANADA INC.
(Public)   PRECIOUS METALS
Exchanges: T M   Stock Symbol: FWR
Suite 1525, 800 Rene-Levesque Blvd. W., Montreal, PQ,
H3B 1X9   (514) 878-3551
FREEWEST RESOURCES CANADA is a mining exploration company, exploring for precious and base metals in Ontario, Quebec, and New Brunswick.
Mackenzie I. Watson, President
TOTAL ASSETS ($000)	24,222
TOTAL REVENUE ($000)	309
NET INCOME ($000)	(465)
EMPLOYEES	5
RANK (Profit/Revenue/Assets)	791/969/825

FT CAPITAL LTD.
See page 496 for a full company profile.

FUNDY CABLE LTD.
See page 378 for a full company profile.

FUTURE SHOP LTD.
See page 420 for a full company profile.

G.T.C. TRANSCONTINENTAL GROUP LTD.
See page 379 for a full company profile.

GAINERS INC.
(Private)   FOOD PROCESSING
12525 - 66 Street, Edmonton, AB, T5J 2H8   (403) 471-0611
GAINERS INC. is engaged in meat packing.
Ian Strang, Chairman & C.E.O.
TOTAL ASSETS ($000)	na
TOTAL REVENUE ($000)	420,963
NET INCOME ($000)	na

GALTACO INC.
(Public)   AUTOMOTIVE
Exchanges: T   Stock Symbol: GMI
Suite 300, 174 Stanley St., Brantford, ON, N3S 7S3   (519) 751-1691
GALTACO INC., through its controlled subsidiary Redlaw Industries, is involved in metal stampings and assemblies for the automotive industry, thermoplastics injection molded parts and thermoset plastic parts for the shoe industry and recreational vehicle industry, and also the manufacture of industrial apparel textiles through its investment in Johnston Industries Inc.
David L. Chandler, Chairman President & C.E.O.
TOTAL ASSETS ($000)	37,044
TOTAL REVENUE ($000)	3,700
NET INCOME ($000)	650
EMPLOYEES	3
RANK (Profit/Revenue/Assets)	682/883/717

GAN COMPANY OF CANADA LIMITED (THE)
(Private)   INSURANCE - PROPERTY & CASUALTY
649 North Service Road West, P.O. Box 5012, Burlington, ON,
L7R 4L5   (905) 681-4903
THE GAN COMPANY OF CANADA LIMITED is a financial services holding company providing home and automobile insurance to individuals in Canada, and property, automobile, professional liability and casualty insurance to business and commercial accounts. GAN also manages a significant surety portfolio.
Roy J. Lever, Chairman President & C.E.O.
TOTAL ASSETS ($000)	528,536
TOTAL REVENUE ($000)	254,759
NET INCOME ($000)	(27,653)
EMPLOYEES	520

GANDALF TECHNOLOGIES INC.
See page 264 for a full company profile.

GARBELL HOLDINGS LIMITED
(Public)   INVESTMENT COMPANIES AND FUNDS
Exchanges: T   Stock Symbol: GBH.PR.A
Suite 2402 Royal Trust Tower, P.O. Box 53, Toronto-Dominion Centre, Toronto, ON, M5K 1E7   (416) 947-1100
GARBELL HOLDINGS LIMITED is an investment holding company.
George R. Gardiner, Chairman
TOTAL ASSETS ($000)	40,959
TOTAL REVENUE ($000)	1,807
NET INCOME ($000)	1,526
EMPLOYEES	7
RANK (Profit/Revenue/Assets)	606/932/688

GARDINER OIL AND GAS LIMITED

(Public)   OIL AND GAS PRODUCERS
Exchanges: T   Stock Symbol: GO
#1600, 333 - 7th Avenue S.W., Calgary, AB, T2P 2Z1 (403) 781-2222
GARDINDER OIL AND GAS LIMITED is involved in the acquisition, exploration and development of natural gas and petroleum properties principally in Alberta.
George R. Gardiner, Chairman

TOTAL ASSETS ($000)	112,466
TOTAL REVENUE ($000)	32,007
NET INCOME ($000)	4,144
EMPLOYEES	34
RANK (Profit/Revenue/Assets)	458/640/457

GAZ METROPOLITAIN AND COMPANY, LIMITED PARTNERSHIP

See page 333 for a full company profile.

GAZ METROPOLITAIN, INC.

(Private)   GAS UTILITIES
1717 Du Havre Street, Montreal, PQ, H2K 2X3   (514) 598-3324
GAZ METROPOLITAIN, INC. is involved in the operation of an integrated system for the distribution, storage and transportation of natural gas through underground pipelines. The territory it operates in, which was attributed exclusively by law, includes substantially all the current and potential natural gas users in the Province of Quebec.
Yves Rheault, Chairman

TOTAL ASSETS ($000)	824,777
TOTAL REVENUE ($000)	126,303
NET INCOME ($000)	21,822
EMPLOYEES	1,603

GE PLASTICS (CANADA) LIMITED

(Private)   MISC. INDUSTRIAL PRODUCTS
Box 10 Norman Rd., Cobourg, ON, K9A 4K2   (905) 372-6801

Randy Morris, Plant Manager

TOTAL ASSETS ($000)	1,294,070
TOTAL REVENUE ($000)	1,632,444
NET INCOME ($000)	15,054
EMPLOYEES	na

GEAC COMPUTER CORPORATION LIMITED

See page 540 for a full company profile.

GEDDES RESOURCES LIMITED

(Public)   METAL MINES
Exchanges: T   Stock Symbol: GDD
Suite 1400, Pender Place, 700 West Pender Street, Vancouver, BC, V6C 1G8   (604) 682-2392
GEDDES RESOURCES LIMITED is engaged in mining exploration and development.
Howard E. Cadinha, Chairman

TOTAL ASSETS ($000)	45,970
TOTAL REVENUE ($000)	(101)
NET INCOME ($000)	(683)
EMPLOYEES	0
RANK (Profit/Revenue/Assets)	805/1000/653

GENDIS INC.

See page 421 for a full company profile.

GENECAN FINANCIAL CORPORATION

See page 448 for a full company profile.

GENERAL ACCIDENT ASSURANCE COMPANY OF CANADA

(Private)   INSURANCE - PROPERTY & CASUALTY
2 First Canadian Place, Suite 2600, P.O. Box 410, Toronto, ON, M5X 1J1   (416) 368-4733
GENERAL ACCIDENT ASSURANCE COMPANY OF CANADA is a property and casualty insurer. The company is 100% owned by General Accident Holdings (Canada) Limited.
D.W.Pretty, Chairperson of the Board

TOTAL ASSETS ($000)	1,815,405
TOTAL REVENUE ($000)	1,064,480
NET INCOME ($000)	75,862
EMPLOYEES	1,544

GENERAL CHEMICAL CANADA LTD.

(Private)   CHEMICALS
201 City Centre Dr, Mississauga, ON, L5B 3A3   (905) 896-9595
Brian Herner, President

TOTAL ASSETS ($000)	110,955
TOTAL REVENUE ($000)	152,217
NET INCOME ($000)	na
EMPLOYEES	475

GENERAL ELECTRIC CANADA INC.

(Private)   ELECTRICAL & ELECTRONIC
2300 Meadowvale Boulevard, Mississauga, ON, L5N 5P9   (905) 858-5100
GENERAL ELECTRIC CANADA INC. is engaged in the manufacture and distribution of appliances, motors, lighting products and other electrical products. The company is a wholly owned subsidiary of General Electric Company of the United States.
Robert T.E. Gillespie, Chairman & C.E.O.

TOTAL ASSETS ($000)	1,264,558
TOTAL REVENUE ($000)	1,652,635
NET INCOME ($000)	31,322
EMPLOYEES	6,200

GENERAL ELECTRIC CAPITAL CANADA INC.

(Private)   FINANCE AND LEASING
2300 Meadowvale Boulevard, Mail Drop T-50, Mississauga, ON, L5N 5P9   (905) 858-5281
GENERAL ELECTRIC CAPITAL CANADA INC. and its subsidiaries provide time sales, loans, equipment lease financing and real estate financing. It is a wholly owned subsidiary of General Electric Capital Corp. of the United States.
Robert T.E. Gillespie, President

TOTAL ASSETS ($000)	4,165,417
TOTAL REVENUE ($000)	912,921
NET INCOME ($000)	50,231
EMPLOYEES	0

GENERAL LEASEHOLDS LIMITED
(Public)   DEVELOPERS
Exchanges: T   Stock Symbol: GLL
Suite 600, 2 St. Clair Avenue West, Toronto, ON,
M4V 1L5   (416) 929-1003
GENERAL LEASEHOLDS LIMITED is a public real estate development company with holdings in Northern and Southern Ontario including major shopping centres and office buildings.
Morey I. Speigel, Chairman & C.F.O.

TOTAL ASSETS ($000)	68,271
TOTAL REVENUE ($000)	12,126
NET INCOME ($000)	(12,227)
EMPLOYEES	23
RANK (Profit/Revenue/Assets)	951/779/570

GENERAL MILLS CANADA, INC.
(Private)   FOOD PROCESSING
1330 Martin Grove Road, P.O. Box 505, Rexdale, ON,
M9W 4X4   (416) 743-8110
GENERAL MILLS CANADA, INC. conducts operations through six divisions. They are: Lancia-Bravo Foods division; Blue Water Seafoods division; Grocery Products division; Parker Brothers division; Eddie Bauer; and Izod division.
Stephen Demeritt, President & C.E.O.

TOTAL ASSETS ($000)	231,439
TOTAL REVENUE ($000)	449,015
NET INCOME ($000)	(40,901)
EMPLOYEES	na

GENERAL MOTORS ACCEPTANCE CORPORATION OF CANADA LIMITED
(Private)   FINANCE AND LEASING
3300 Bloor Street West, Suite 2800, Toronto, ON,
M8X 2X5   (416) 234-6600
GENERAL MOTORS ACCEPTANCE CORPORATION OF CANADA LIMITED is engaged in automotive financial services to and through General Motors Dealers in Canada and their customers. GMAC of Canada is wholly owned by GMAC of Detroit, Michigan.
W. James Watson, President

TOTAL ASSETS ($000)	6,587,081
TOTAL REVENUE ($000)	1,045,998
NET INCOME ($000)	41,102
EMPLOYEES	705

GENERAL MOTORS OF CANADA LIMITED
(Private)   AUTOMOTIVE
1908 Colonel Sam Drive, Oshawa, ON, L1H 8P7   (905) 644-5000
GENERAL MOTORS OF CANADA LIMITED designs, manufactures, assembles and sells cars and trucks. It is a wholly owned subsidiary of General Motors Corp.
V. Maureen Kempston Darkes, President & General Manager

TOTAL ASSETS ($000)	8,050,837
TOTAL REVENUE ($000)	24,964,020
NET INCOME ($000)	1,026,380
EMPLOYEES	37,519

GENNUM CORPORATION
See page 265 for a full company profile.

GENTRA INC.
See page 449 for a full company profile.

GEORGE WESTON LIMITED
See page 422 for a full company profile.

GEORGE WIMPEY CANADA LIMITED
(Private)   CONTRACTORS
80 North Queen Street, Weston, ON, M8Z 5Z6   (416) 233-5811
GEORGE WIMPEY CANADA LIMITED is engaged in construction and real estate development. The company is wholly owned by George Wimpey plc of London, England.
Randy Roe, Secretary

TOTAL ASSETS ($000)	220,418
TOTAL REVENUE ($000)	252,585
NET INCOME ($000)	na
EMPLOYEES	655

GESCO INDUSTRIES INC.
(Public)   WHOLESALE DISTRIBUTORS
Exchanges: T   Stock Symbol: GSD
1965 Lawrence Ave. West, Weston, ON, M9N 1H5   (416) 243-0040
GESCO INDUSTRIES INC. has substantially all of its operations in the floor-covering industry. The company is a distributor of a product line that includes carpeting, resilient flooring, cushioned flooring, undercushion and supplies.
Norman Shnier, Chairman

TOTAL ASSETS ($000)	33,571
TOTAL REVENUE ($000)	115,158
NET INCOME ($000)	851
EMPLOYEES	250
RANK (Profit/Revenue/Assets)	667/399/741

GIBRALTAR MINES LIMITED
See page 12 for a full company profile.

GLAMIS GOLD LTD.
See page 42 for a full company profile.

GLAXO CANADA INC.
(Private)   CHEMICALS
7333 Mississauga Road North, Mississauga, ON,
L5N 6L4   (905) 819-3000
GLAXO CANADA INC. is a manufacturer of pharmaceuticals. It is a wholly owned subsidiary of Glaxo Holdings, plc.
P.N. Lucas, President & C.E.O.

TOTAL ASSETS ($000)	na
TOTAL REVENUE ($000)	335,300
NET INCOME ($000)	na
EMPLOYEES	1,020

GLENEX INDUSTRIES INC.
(Public)   MANAGEMENT AND DIVERSIFIED
Exchanges: V Q   Stock Symbol: GXI
185 Davenport Road, Toronto, ON, M5R 1J1   (416) 962-9292
GLENEX INDUSTRIES operates in two industry segments: entertainment; and oil and gas exploration and development in Canada and the U.S. Entertainment options include video production and graphics facilities to the television, advertising and communication industries.

Norman Glick, President & C.E.O.

TOTAL ASSETS ($000)	17,114
TOTAL REVENUE ($000)	5,629
NET INCOME ($000)	5
EMPLOYEES	30
RANK (Profit/Revenue/Assets)	756/852/909

GLENTEL INC.
See page 266 for a full company profile.

GLOBAL STONE CORPORATION
See page 13 for a full company profile.

GLOBELLE CORPORATION
(Public)   WHOLESALE DISTRIBUTORS
Exchanges: T   Stock Symbol: GLP
57 Adesso Drive, Concord, ON, L4K 3C7   (905) 660-1616
GLOBELLE CORPORATION is a distributor of micro-computers and related hardware products.
Geoffrey Matus, Chairman

TOTAL ASSETS ($000)	131,585
TOTAL REVENUE ($000)	483,895
NET INCOME ($000)	3,783
EMPLOYEES	300
RANK (Profit/Revenue/Assets)	473/197/420

GOLDCORP INC.
See page 43 for a full company profile.

GOLDEN KNIGHT RESOURCES INC.
See page 44 for a full company profile.

GOLDEN RULE RESOURCES LTD.
(Public)   PRECIOUS METALS
Exchanges: T   Stock Symbol: GNU
Suite 1450, 125 - 9th Avenue S.E., Calgary, AB,
T2G 0P6   (403) 233-7898
GOLDEN RULE RESOURCES LTD. is engaged in the acquisition and exploration of precious metals, base metals, and diamond properties in Canada and Latin America, mainly through subsidiary companies. The company holds interests in deposits in Saskatchewan, the NWT, B.C., Quebec, Mexico, and Venezuela.
Glen Harper, President

TOTAL ASSETS ($000)	27,815
TOTAL REVENUE ($000)	847
NET INCOME ($000)	15
EMPLOYEES	4
RANK (Profit/Revenue/Assets)	752/951/792

GOLDEN STAR RESOURCES LTD.
See page 45 for a full company profile.

GOLDFARB CORPORATION (THE)
(Public)   CONSULTING
Exchanges: T   Stock Symbol: GDF.A
Suite 1700, 4950 Yonge Street, North York, ON,
M2N 6K1   (416) 221-9200

THE GOLDFARB CORPORATION is a diversified company that owns and operates an international network of behavioral and marketing research offices. The company is also involved in equity investments.
Martin Goldfarb, Chairman President & C.E.O.

TOTAL ASSETS ($000)	76,594
TOTAL REVENUE ($000)	52,579
NET INCOME ($000)	9,536
EMPLOYEES	350
RANK (Profit/Revenue/Assets)	304/537/539

GOODFELLOW INC.
(Public)   MISC. INDUSTRIAL PRODUCTS
Exchanges: M   Stock Symbol: GDL
225 Rue Goodfellow, Delson, PQ, J0L 1G0   (514) 635-6511
GOODFELLOW INC. is a diversified distributor and re-manufacturer of timber, dressed and rough lumber, prefinished and unfinished flooring and composite and veneer based wood panel products. It also re-manufactures wood products provided by kiln drying, wood preservation and milling. The company serves customers throughout Canada, the United States and abroad.
Stephen A. Jarislowsky, Chairman

TOTAL ASSETS ($000)	82,129
TOTAL REVENUE ($000)	216,378
NET INCOME ($000)	2,677
EMPLOYEES	370
RANK (Profit/Revenue/Assets)	527/303/528

GOODYEAR CANADA INC.
(Private)   AUTOMOTIVE
10 Four Seasons Place, Etobicoke, ON, M9B 6G2   (416) 626-4611
GOODYEAR CANADA INC. is a tire and rubber company. Products include new tires and tubes, retreads, automotive belts and hoses, automotive molded parts, auto repair services, industrial rubber, and plastic products and films. The company has operations in Ontario, Quebec and Alberta and store locations across Canada. Goodyear Tire and Rubber Co. of Ohio is the company's major shareholder.
Eugene R. Culler, President & C.E.O.

TOTAL ASSETS ($000)	521,800
TOTAL REVENUE ($000)	817,900
NET INCOME ($000)	na
EMPLOYEES	4,800

GORAN CAPITAL INC.
See page 497 for a full company profile.

GRAD & WALKER ENERGY CORPORATION
See page 100 for a full company profile.

GRANDUC MINING CORPORATION
(Public)   METAL MINES
Exchanges: T   Stock Symbol: GDC
Suite 2000, 95 Wellington Street West, Toronto, ON,
M5J 2N7   (416) 363-7370
GRANDUC MINING LIMITED is engaged in the exploration for and development of minerals, primarily copper, gold and silver.
J.C. Lamacraft,

TOTAL ASSETS ($000)	21,158
TOTAL REVENUE ($000)	4,841
NET INCOME ($000)	(2,105)

EMPLOYEES 0
RANK (Profit/Revenue/Assets) 856/867/862

GRANGES INC.
See page 46 for a full company profile.

GRAYMONT LIMITED
(Private) MANAGEMENT AND DIVERSIFIED
999 West Hastings Street, Suite 1160, Vancouver, BC,
V6C 2W2 (604) 687-0131
GRAYMONT LIMITED is an investment holding company with diverse interests in Canada and the United States.
Stuart F. Wolfe, President & C.E.O.
TOTAL ASSETS ($000) 345,900
TOTAL REVENUE ($000) 204,478
NET INCOME ($000) 12,310
EMPLOYEES na

GREAT ATLANTIC AND PACIFIC TEA COMPANY, LIMITED (THE)
(Private) FOOD STORES
5559 Dundas Street West, Etobicoke, ON, M9B 1B9 (416) 239-7171
THE GREAT ATLANTIC AND PACIFIC TEA COMPANY, LIMITED operates a chain of retail food stores and is a wholly owned subsidiary of Great Atlantic & Pacific Tea Company, Inc. of Montvale, New Jersey.
J.D. Moffatt, Chairman & C.E.O.
TOTAL ASSETS ($000) 788,433
TOTAL REVENUE ($000) 2,487,860
NET INCOME ($000) (41,287)
EMPLOYEES na

GREAT EASTERN CORPORATION LIMITED (THE)
(Public) INVESTMENT COMPANIES AND FUNDS
Exchanges: V Stock Symbol: GTN.PR.A
Suite 2104, Box 60, 1969 Upper Water Street, Halifax, NS,
B3J 3R7 (902) 423-8414
THE GREAT EASTERN CORP. LTD. is an investment company.
Fred S. Fountain, President
TOTAL ASSETS ($000) 86,823
TOTAL REVENUE ($000) 17,613
NET INCOME ($000) 13,197
EMPLOYEES na
RANK (Profit/Revenue/Assets) 261/733/513

GREAT LAKES POWER INC.
See page 516 for a full company profile.

GREAT LAKES REINSURANCE COMPANY (THE)
(Private) INSURANCE - LIFE
390 Bay Street, 21st Floor, Toronto, ON, M5H 2Y2 (416) 364-2851
GREAT LAKES REINSURANCE HOLDINGS LTD. is an investment and holding company. Its principal investments are in companies engaged in the property and casualty reinsurance business. The company's main consolidated investments are The Great Lakes Reinsurance Company and Great Lakes Reinsurance (U.K.) PLC.
J.C.C. Wansbrough, Chairman
TOTAL ASSETS ($000) 330,887
TOTAL REVENUE ($000) 194,271

NET INCOME ($000) (8,104)
EMPLOYEES 8

GREAT PACIFIC ENTERPRISES INC.
See page 297 for a full company profile.

GREAT-WEST LIFE ASSURANCE COMPANY (THE)
See page 498 for a full company profile.

GREAT-WEST LIFECO INC.
See page 499 for a full company profile.

GREEN FOREST LUMBER CORPORATION
(Public) WHOLESALE DISTRIBUTORS
Exchanges: Stock Symbol:
194 Merton Street, Toronto, ON, M4S 3B5 (416) 489-3336
GREEN FOREST LUMBER CORPORATION is a leading independent North American wholesale distributor of lumber and waferboard. The company also operates two sawmills in Chapleau, Ontario.
R.D. Tuckey, President
TOTAL ASSETS ($000) 111,183
TOTAL REVENUE ($000) 377,375
NET INCOME ($000) 11,704
EMPLOYEES 550

GREENSTONE RESOURCES LTD.
(Public) PRECIOUS METALS
Exchanges: T Q Stock Symbol: GRE
Ste. 910, 26 Wellington St. E., Toronto, ON, M5E 1S2 (416) 862-7300
GREENSTONE RESOURCES LTD. is involved in the acquisition, exploration and development of precious metal properties. The company has properties in Columbia, Panama, Costa Rica, and Canada.
Hugh R. Snyder, Chairman
TOTAL ASSETS ($000) 48,450
TOTAL REVENUE ($000) 2,897
NET INCOME ($000) (3,114)
EMPLOYEES 8
RANK (Profit/Revenue/Assets) 906/874/638

GREYHOUND LINES OF CANADA LTD.
See page 325 for a full company profile.

GREYVEST CAPITAL INC.
See page 472 for a full company profile.

GRILLI PROPERTY GROUP INC.
(Public) DEVELOPERS
Exchanges: M Stock Symbol: GG.A
3535 Boul. Saint Charles, Bureau 200, Kirkland, PQ,
H9H 5B9 (514) 694-0463
GRILLI PROPERTY GROUP is involved in the building and marketing of residential, commercial and industrial properties as well as promoting and selling land for development. It also has operations in the manufacturing industry through its kitchen cabinet and concrete divisions.
Mario Grilli, Chairman & C.E.O.
TOTAL ASSETS ($000) 210,110
TOTAL REVENUE ($000) 51,882
NET INCOME ($000) 20

EMPLOYEES 135
RANK (Profit/Revenue/Assets) 751/542/347

GROUPE BOCENOR INC.
(Public) MISC. CONSUMER PRODUCTS
Exchanges: M Stock Symbol: GBO
274 Rue Duchesnay, P.O. Box 1000, Ste-Marie de Beauce, PQ,
G6E 3C2 (418) 387-7723
GROUPE BOCENOR is a manufacturer and distributor of a complete
line of windows and doors. The company is also engaged in the distri-
bution of construction materials and renovation in Sainte-Isidore de
Beauce . The company sells its products in Quebec, the Maritimes,
Ontario, and Western Canada, under the Bonneville brand.
Jean-Louis Bonneville, Chairman & C.E.O.
TOTAL ASSETS ($000) 20,032
TOTAL REVENUE ($000) 46,423
NET INCOME ($000) 459
EMPLOYEES 450
RANK (Profit/Revenue/Assets) 700/564/869

GROUPE FOREX INC. (LE)
(Public) EAST COAST FORESTRY
Exchanges: M Stock Symbol: FOX
689 - 3e Avenue, C.P. 296, Val d'Or, PQ, J9P 4P3 (819) 825-4841
GROUPE FOREX is a lumber and OSB manufacturer which operates
one sawmill and two OSB plants in Quebec. The company has sales in
Canada and the United States as well as overseas.
Jean-Jacques Cossette, Chairman President & C.E.O.
TOTAL ASSETS ($000) 219,731
TOTAL REVENUE ($000) 210,485
NET INCOME ($000) 33,043
EMPLOYEES 450
RANK (Profit/Revenue/Assets) 145/308/338

GROUPE LAPERRIERE & VERREAULT INC.
(Public) MISC. INDUSTRIAL PRODUCTS
Exchanges: M Stock Symbol: LV.B
3100 Rue Westinghouse, Parc Industriel No 2, Trois-Rivieres, PQ,
G9A 5E1 (819) 371-8265
GROUPE LAPERRIERE & VERREAULT INC. is involved in the
design, manufacture and installation of equipment for the pulp and paper
industry, mines, and aluminum plants. The company is also involved in
processing waste water and other environmental projects.
Laurent Verreault, Chairman, President & C.E.O.
TOTAL ASSETS ($000) 77,926
TOTAL REVENUE ($000) 99,456
NET INCOME ($000) 1,608
EMPLOYEES 535
RANK (Profit/Revenue/Assets) 599/421/537

GROUPE POMERLEAU
(Private) CONTRACTORS
521 Sixieme Avenue, C.P. 8, St-Georges de Beauce, PQ,
G5Y 5C4 (418) 228-6688
GROUP POMERLEAU is a general contractor.
Herve Pomerleau, President & Director General
TOTAL ASSETS ($000) 320,000
TOTAL REVENUE ($000) 205,000
NET INCOME ($000) na
EMPLOYEES 1,000

GROUPE PROMUTUEL
(Fin. Co-op) INSURANCE - PROPERTY & CASUALTY
1091 Chemin Saint-Louis, Bureau 300, Sillery, PQ,
G1S 1E2 (418) 683-1212
GROUPE PROMUTUEL FEDERATION DE SOCIETES MU-
TUELLES D'ASSURANCE GENERALE as a federation of insurance
companies, is a provider of property and casualty insurance in the
province of Quebec. It has offered information processing services and
life insurance. Since 1992, it has offered property and casualty reinsur-
ance services.
Normand Fontaine, President
TOTAL ASSETS ($000) 10,362
TOTAL REVENUE ($000) 9,696
NET INCOME ($000) (84)
EMPLOYEES 998

GROUPE RO-NA DISMAT INC. (LE)
(Public) SPECIALTY STORES
Exchanges: M Stock Symbol: RON.PR.A
1250 Rue Nobel, Boucherville, PQ, J4B 5K1 (514) 599-5100
LE GROUPE RO-NA DISMAT INC. operates several stores under the
names Le Quincaillier Ro-Na, Le Renovateur Ro-Na, Botanix, Le Quin-
cailleur, Dismat and Ro-Na L'Entrepot. It also operates Ro-na Home
Center and Ro-Na Hardware in Ontario.
Henri Drouin, Chairman
TOTAL ASSETS ($000) 87,058
TOTAL REVENUE ($000) 567,018
NET INCOME ($000) 7,069
EMPLOYEES 354
RANK (Profit/Revenue/Assets) 363/181/512

GROUPE SANI MOBILE INC.
(Public) ENVIRONMENTAL SERVICES
Exchanges: M Stock Symbol: SNB.A
Bureau 350, 6500 boul. de la Rive-Sud, Levis, PQ,
G6V 7M5 (418) 835-3750
GROUPE SANI MOBILE INC. engages in activities related to the
environmental protection, pumping and industrial cleaning sectors.
Louis Lariviere, Chairman & President
TOTAL ASSETS ($000) 44,524
TOTAL REVENUE ($000) 59,802
NET INCOME ($000) 1,347
EMPLOYEES 650
RANK (Profit/Revenue/Assets) 624/514/662

GROUPE VAL ROYAL INC.
(Public) SPECIALTY STORES
Exchanges: M Stock Symbol: VR
159 Jean-Talon Ouest, Montreal, PQ, H2R 2X2 (514) 270-8111
GROUPE VAL ROYAL is a Montreal-area retailer of products related
to construction, renovation and decoration. The company operates Val
Royal stores, Brico Centre stores and six Reno-Depot warehouse stores.
The stores sell a broad range of brand name and private label goods.
Pierre Michaud, Chairman & C.E.O.
TOTAL ASSETS ($000) 96,933
TOTAL REVENUE ($000) 338,750
NET INCOME ($000) 185
EMPLOYEES 2,500
RANK (Profit/Revenue/Assets) 738/240/492

GROUPE VIDEOTRON LTEE (LE)
See page 380 for a full company profile.

GST TELECOMMUNICATIONS INC.
(Public)   TELECOMMUNICATIONS
Exchanges: V   Stock Symbol: GTE.U
Suite 900, 999 West Hastings St., Vancouver, BC,
V6C 2W2   (604) 689-1428
GST TELECOMMUNICATIONS INC. is involved in the development
of fibre optic telecommunication networks in the United States and
Canada, as well as the manufacture of telecommunication switching and
network management equipment.
Ian Watson, Chairman, President & C.E.O.

TOTAL ASSETS ($000)	26,769 (US)
TOTAL REVENUE ($000)	5,179 (US)
NET INCOME ($000)	(3,491) (US)
EMPLOYEES	100
RANK (Profit/Revenue/Assets)	901/836/726

GSW INC.
(Public)   APPLIANCES
Exchanges: T M   Stock Symbol: GSW.B
20 Eglinton Avenue West, Suite 1903, P.O. Box 2047, Toronto, ON,
M4R 1K8   (416) 489-0640
GSW operates in two industries. Water products includes pumps and
water heaters. Building products includes metal and vinyl eavestroughs,
factory built chimneys, fireplaces, stovepipes, and barbecue accessories.
R.M. Barford, Chairman

TOTAL ASSETS ($000)	114,167
TOTAL REVENUE ($000)	244,859
NET INCOME ($000)	8,110
EMPLOYEES	1,000
RANK (Profit/Revenue/Assets)	330/289/452

GUARANTEE COMPANY OF NORTH AMERICA (THE)
(Private)   INSURANCE - PROPERTY & CASUALTY
Ste. 1560, Place du Canada, Montreal, PQ, H3B 2R4 (514) 866-6351
GUARANTEE COMPANY OF NORTH AMERICA is engaged in
general insurance with emphasis on providing property, casualty and
automobile insurance and fidelity and surety bonds.
Bruno Desjardins, Q.C., Chairman

TOTAL ASSETS ($000)	442,273
TOTAL REVENUE ($000)	162,412
NET INCOME ($000)	7,572
EMPLOYEES	270

GUARDIAN CAPITAL GROUP LIMITED
(Public)   INVESTMENT COMPANIES AND FUNDS
Exchanges: T   Stock Symbol: GCG.A
18th Floor, 110 Yonge Street, Toronto, ON, M5C 1T4 (416) 364-8341
GUARDIAN CAPITAL GROUP LIMITED is a financial services and
investment company. Through Canadian and international affiliates,
subsidiaries and advisors, the company manages portfolios for pension
funds, private clients and publicly registered investment funds, and
provides administrative and other financial services.
Anthony G.S. Griffin, Chairman

TOTAL ASSETS ($000)	54,059
TOTAL REVENUE ($000)	24,681
NET INCOME ($000)	5,859

EMPLOYEES	140
RANK (Profit/Revenue/Assets)	397/681/615

GUARDIAN INSURANCE COMPANY OF CANADA
(Private)   INSURANCE - PROPERTY & CASUALTY
Ste. 700, 181 University Ave., Toronto, ON, M5H 3M7(416) 941-5050
GUARDIAN INSURANCE COMPANY OF CANADA is a property
and casualty insurance company.
V.M. Yerril, Chairman

TOTAL ASSETS ($000)	758,801
TOTAL REVENUE ($000)	459,312
NET INCOME ($000)	17,758
EMPLOYEES	960

GUILLEVIN INTERNATIONAL INC.
(Private)   WHOLESALE DISTRIBUTORS
400 Boul. Montpelier, St-Laurent, PQ, H4N 2G7   (514) 747-9851
GUILLEVIN INTERNATIONAL is a wholesale distributor of electrical
material, health and safety products and equipment, industrial supplies
and equipment, and automation products.
Jeannine Guillevin Wood, Chairman & C.E.O.

TOTAL ASSETS ($000)	138,898
TOTAL REVENUE ($000)	421,786
NET INCOME ($000)	1,029
EMPLOYEES	1,089

GULF CANADA RESOURCES LIMITED
See page 101 for a full company profile.

GULFSTREAM RESOURCES CANADA LIMITED
(Public)   OIL AND GAS PRODUCERS
Exchanges: T   Stock Symbol: GUR
Suite 3465, 855 - 2nd St. SW, Calgary, AB, T2P 4J8   (403) 264-8288
GULFSTREAM RESOURCES CANADA LIMITED is inolved in the
acquisition, exploration and development of international oil and gas
projects.
J. Angus McKee, Chairman, President & C.E.O.

TOTAL ASSETS ($000)	13,017
TOTAL REVENUE ($000)	2,441
NET INCOME ($000)	1,745
EMPLOYEES	9
RANK (Profit/Revenue/Assets)	589/909/991

GWIL INDUSTRIES INC.
(Public)   METAL FABRICATORS
Exchanges: T M V   Stock Symbol: GWS
Suite 650 - West Tower, 555 West 12th Avenue, Vancouver, BC,
V5Z 3X7   (604) 874-4945
GWIL INDUSTRIES INC. is involved in crane services and rentals; the
manufacture of polyester resins and related raw materials; wholesale
industrial products; analysis of coal samples for the mining industry and
management services to the structural steel fabricating industry.
Hugh A. Magee, Chairman & C.E.O.

TOTAL ASSETS ($000)	49,791
TOTAL REVENUE ($000)	52,020
NET INCOME ($000)	4,867
EMPLOYEES	123
RANK (Profit/Revenue/Assets)	428/541/632

H. PAULIN & CO. LIMITED

(Public) MISC. INDUSTRIAL PRODUCTS
Exchanges: T Stock Symbol: PAP.A
55 Milne Avenue, Scarborough, ON, M1L 4N3 (416) 694-3351
H. PAULIN & CO., LIMITED manufactures and distributes industrial fasteners and automotive parts, bolts, nuts, screws and fluid system components to customers in the automotive industry, both original equipment and the aftermarket, agricultural, electrical and appliance industries.
Arthur Paulin, Chairman

TOTAL ASSETS ($000)	38,914
TOTAL REVENUE ($000)	64,484
NET INCOME ($000)	1,165
EMPLOYEES	na
RANK (Profit/Revenue/Assets)	640/493/700

HALEY INDUSTRIES LIMITED

See page 267 for a full company profile.

HALIFAX PORT CORPORATION

(Crown) TRANSPORTATION
P.O. Box 336, Halifax, NS, B3J 2P6 (902) 426-2711
HALIFAX PORT CORPORATION provides port facilities and services in Halifax, Nova Scotia.
Merv Russell, Chairman

TOTAL ASSETS ($000)	67,507
TOTAL REVENUE ($000)	11,694
NET INCOME ($000)	495
EMPLOYEES	88

HALLMARK TECHNOLOGIES INC.

(Public) AUTOMOTIVE
Exchanges: T Stock Symbol: HTI
2187 Huron Church Rd., PO Box 7040, Windsor, ON,
N9C 3Y6 (519) 966-4050
HALLMARK TECHNOLOGIES INC. engineers, designs and manufactures customized steel molds used in the injection molding of precision plastic components. Currently more than 95 per cent of these molds are produced for use in the automotive industry.
R. Douglas Balint, Chairman, C.E.O. & President

TOTAL ASSETS ($000)	24,463
TOTAL REVENUE ($000)	24,354
NET INCOME ($000)	2,754
EMPLOYEES	150
RANK (Profit/Revenue/Assets)	522/685/818

HALOZONE TECHNOLOGIES INC.

(Public) ENVIRONMENTAL SERVICES
Exchanges: T Stock Symbol: HLZ
400 Nashua Drive, Mississauga, ON, L4V 1P8 (905) 405-8200
HALOZONE TECHNOLOGIES INC. has an exclusive license to a patented technology which captures, recovers and reclaims halogenated hydrocarbons, such as chlorofluorocarbons, for recycling.
Henry Lubaszka, Chairman

TOTAL ASSETS ($000)	13,649
TOTAL REVENUE ($000)	2,005
NET INCOME ($000)	(3,548)
EMPLOYEES	6
RANK (Profit/Revenue/Assets)	893/921/973

HAMMOND MANUFACTURING COMPANY LIMITED

(Public) ELECTRICAL & ELECTRONIC
Exchanges: T Stock Symbol: HMM.A
394 Edinburgh Road North, Guelph, ON, N1H 1E5 (519) 822-2960
HAMMOND MANUFACTURING COMPANY LIMITED manufactures transformers and cabinetry for manufacturers of electrical and electronic equipment, utilities and electrical contractors.
Robert F. Hammond, President & C.E.O.

TOTAL ASSETS ($000)	65,293
TOTAL REVENUE ($000)	136,731
NET INCOME ($000)	260
EMPLOYEES	1,200
RANK (Profit/Revenue/Assets)	727/375/573

HARBOUR PETROLEUM COMPANY LIMITED

(Public) OIL AND GAS PRODUCERS
Exchanges: T Stock Symbol: HRP
Ste. 2200, 605 - 5th Ave. SW, Calgary, AB, T2P 3H5 (403) 265-5522
HARBOUR PETROLEUM COMPANY LIMITED is an oil and gas exploration and development company which has all of its properties located in Alberta.
Ronald A. Howard, Chairman

TOTAL ASSETS ($000)	76,132
TOTAL REVENUE ($000)	15,343
NET INCOME ($000)	(846)
EMPLOYEES	31
RANK (Profit/Revenue/Assets)	813/753/541

HARRIS STEEL GROUP INC.

See page 243 for a full company profile.

HARROWSTON INC.

See page 517 for a full company profile.

HARTCO ENTERPRISES INC.

(Public) SPECIALTY STORES
Exchanges: T M Stock Symbol: HTC
9001 Louis H. Lafontaine Blvd, Anjou, PQ, H1J 2C5 (514) 354-3810
HARTCO ENTERPRISES INC. is a franchisor of 160 computer stores in Canada, operating under the names of Microage, Compucentre, Microvar, Compuco, Northwest Digital, and Compusmart. These locations serve the business, government, corporate, professional and home markets. The company also owns and operates 31 junior department stores, and 21 telephone boutiques in Quebec and Ontario.
Harry Hart, President & C.E.O.

TOTAL ASSETS ($000)	86,284
TOTAL REVENUE ($000)	324,936
NET INCOME ($000)	6,009
EMPLOYEES	1,017
RANK (Profit/Revenue/Assets)	394/246/514

HAWKER SIDDELEY CANADA INC.

See page 244 for a full company profile.

HAYES-DANA INC.

(Private) AUTOMOTIVE
One St. Paul, PO Box 3029, St. Catharines, ON,
L2R 7K9 (905) 687-4200

HAYES-DANA INC. is a manufacturer and distributor of both new and replacement components for trucks, automobiles, off-highway vehicles and industrial equipment. The company markets its products to heavy truck and car makers, warehouse distributors, mass merchandisers and industrial distributors and equipment suppliers. The company has facilities in Ontario, Quebec, Manitoba, Alberta and B.C.
S.J. Morcott, Chairman

TOTAL ASSETS ($000)	253,982
TOTAL REVENUE ($000)	654,707
NET INCOME ($000)	22,978
EMPLOYEES	2,504

HCO ENERGY LTD.
(Public)   OIL AND GAS PRODUCERS
Exchanges: T Z   Stock Symbol: HCE
Ste. 3201, 400 - 3rd Ave. SW, Calgary, AB, T2P 4H2 (403) 269-8980
HCO ENERGY LTD. has moved away from gas exploration and is currently focusing on oil property acquisition and development.
Daryl H. Connolly, President & C.E.O.

TOTAL ASSETS ($000)	70,189
TOTAL REVENUE ($000)	26,590
NET INCOME ($000)	4,886
EMPLOYEES	30
RANK (Profit/Revenue/Assets)	427/667/564

HEALTH CARE AND BIOTECHNOLOGY VENTURE FUND (THE)
(Public)   BIOTECHNOLOGY & PHARMACEUTICALS
Exchanges: T   Stock Symbol: HCB.UN
c/o MDS HEALTH VENTURES INC., 100 International Boulevard, Etobicoke, ON, M9W 6J6   (416) 675-6777
THE HEALTH CARE AND BIOTECHNOLOGY VENTURE FUND is a closed-end investment trust which makes investments in private and public emerging companies in the health care and biotechnology industries.

TOTAL ASSETS ($000)	24,778
TOTAL REVENUE ($000)	0
NET INCOME ($000)	0
EMPLOYEES	na
RANK (Profit/Revenue/Assets)	641/931/817

HEES INTERNATIONAL BANCORP INC.
See page 473 for a full company profile.

HELIX CIRCUITS INC.
See page 268 for a full company profile.

HEMLO GOLD MINES INC.
See page 47 for a full company profile.

HEMOSOL INC.
(Public)   BIOTECHNOLOGY & PHARMACEUTICALS
Exchanges: T   Stock Symbol: HML
115 Skyway Avenue, Etobicoke, ON, M9W 4Z4   (416) 798-0700
HEMOSOL INC. is involved in the development of human blood substitutes derived from human hemoglobin.
Edward K. Rygiel, Chairman

TOTAL ASSETS ($000)	28,831
TOTAL REVENUE ($000)	1,357

NET INCOME ($000)	(10,419)
EMPLOYEES	59
RANK (Profit/Revenue/Assets)	945/939/780

HEPCOE CREDIT UNION LIMITED
(Fin. Co-op)   CREDIT UNIONS
700 University Ave., Hydro Place, Toronto, ON,
M5G 1X6   (416) 597-1050
HEPCOE CREDIT UNION LIMITED is one of Canada's largest credit unions. It is a member-owned self-sustained financial cooperative whose purpose is to provide a full range of financial services to its members.
G.E. Patterson, Chairman of the Board

TOTAL ASSETS ($000)	621,854
TOTAL REVENUE ($000)	49,392
NET INCOME ($000)	2,076
EMPLOYEES	225

HEROUX INC.
(Public)   TRANSPORTATION EQUIP & COMPNTS
Exchanges: M   Stock Symbol: HRX
755 Thurber Street, Longueuil, PQ, J4H 3N2   (514) 679-5450
HEROUX INC. specializes in the design, development, manufacture, and repair of products for the industrial and aerospace sectors. Additional facilities are located in Florida and Ohio. More than 85% of company sales are to the United States.
Gilles Labbe, President, C.E.O. & Chairman

TOTAL ASSETS ($000)	103,676
TOTAL REVENUE ($000)	77,946
NET INCOME ($000)	(7,874)
EMPLOYEES	644
RANK (Profit/Revenue/Assets)	934/460/477

HEWITT EQUIPMENT LIMITED
(Private)   WHOLESALE DISTRIBUTORS
5001 Trans Canada, Pointe-Claire, PQ, H9R 1B8   (514) 630-3100
HEWITT EQUIPMENT LIMITED is a heavy equipment and material handling dealer.
James Hewitt, Chairman

TOTAL ASSETS ($000)	161,365
TOTAL REVENUE ($000)	269,058
NET INCOME ($000)	9,029
EMPLOYEES	900

HEWLETT-PACKARD (CANADA) LTD.
(Private)   ELECTRICAL & ELECTRONIC
5150 Spectrum Way, Mississauga, ON, L4W 5G1   (905) 206-4725
HEWLETT-PACKARD (CANADA) is engaged in the design and manufacture of precision electronic equipment for measurement, analysis and computation. The company is a wholly owned subsidiary of Hewlett-Packard Company of the United States.
George B. Cobbe, Chairman of the Board

TOTAL ASSETS ($000)	421,981
TOTAL REVENUE ($000)	1,004,844
NET INCOME ($000)	13,496
EMPLOYEES	1,400

HIGH RIVER GOLD MINES LTD.
(Public)   PRECIOUS METALS
Exchanges: T   Stock Symbol: HRG
Ste. 1700, 155 University Ave., Toronto, ON,
M5H 3B7   (416) 947-1440
HIGH RIVER GOLD MINES LTD. is involved in the acquisition, exploration and development of precious metal properties. The company has projects in Manitoba and Burkina Faso.
Donald A. Whalen, Chairman & C.F.O.

TOTAL ASSETS ($000)	16,790
TOTAL REVENUE ($000)	21
NET INCOME ($000)	(336)
EMPLOYEES	2
RANK (Profit/Revenue/Assets)	781/992/921

HIGHLAND VALLEY COPPER
(Private)   METAL MINES
P.O. Box 1500, Logan Lake, BC, V0K 1W0   (604) 575-2443
HIGHLAND VALLEY COPPER is a partnership between Cominco Ltd. (50%), Rio Algom Limited (33.6%) and Teck Corporation (13.9%) (including 2.5% from Highmont) and 2.5% for Highmont Mining Company (excluding Teck's 2.5%).
W.J. Robertson, Chairman

TOTAL ASSETS ($000)	na
TOTAL REVENUE ($000)	464,500
NET INCOME ($000)	na
EMPLOYEES	1,101

HIGHRIDGE EXPLORATION LTD.
(Public)   OIL AND GAS PRODUCERS
Exchanges: T   Stock Symbol: HRE.A
Ste. 1710, 530 - 8th Ave. SW, Calgary, AB, T2P 3S8   (403) 269-2229
HIGHRIDGE EXPLORATION LTD. is involved in oil and gas exploration and production in Canada and the United States.
Robert T.M. Vanderham, Chairman

TOTAL ASSETS ($000)	28,977
TOTAL REVENUE ($000)	9,402
NET INCOME ($000)	1,695
EMPLOYEES	5
RANK (Profit/Revenue/Assets)	594/809/779

HIGHWOOD RESOURCES LTD.
(Public)   OTHER MINES
Exchanges: T Q   Stock Symbol: HWD
12th Floor, 20 Toronto Street, Toronto, ON, M5C 2B8 (416) 869-0772
HIGHWOOD RESOURCES is engaged in the acquisition, exploration and development of mineral properties in Canada and in Greenland.
G. Farquharson, President

TOTAL ASSETS ($000)	13,572
TOTAL REVENUE ($000)	2,464
NET INCOME ($000)	449
EMPLOYEES	0
RANK (Profit/Revenue/Assets)	702/908/980

HIL CORPORATION LTD.
See page 518 for a full company profile.

HILLCREST RESOURCES LTD.
(Private)   OIL AND GAS PRODUCERS
Ste. 1800, 407 - 2nd St. SW, Calgary, AB, T2P 2Y3   (403) 299-2222
HILLCREST RESOURCES is engaged in oil and gas exploration and production. The company has oil and gas properties in Alberta and British Columbia and mining properties in the Northwest Territories.
James Palmer, Chairman

TOTAL ASSETS ($000)	78,954
TOTAL REVENUE ($000)	31,238
NET INCOME ($000)	7,383
EMPLOYEES	na

HILLSBOROUGH RESOURCES LIMITED
(Public)   NON-BASE METAL MINING
Exchanges: T   Stock Symbol: HLB
120 Railroad Street, Brampton, ON, L6X 1G8   (905) 456-0734
HILLSBOROUGH RESOURCES LIMITED conducts its activities through a mine operation division and a mine contracting division. The company's contracting division provides contracting and engineering services to the mining industry. Its mine operation division operates the Quinsam Mine, a thermal coal mine near River, B.C.
C. Alan Smith, Chairman

TOTAL ASSETS ($000)	45,169
TOTAL REVENUE ($000)	25,400
NET INCOME ($000)	(3,724)
EMPLOYEES	250
RANK (Profit/Revenue/Assets)	896/676/658

HOECHST CANADA INC.
(Private)   CHEMICALS
800 Boul. Rene-Levesque Ouest, 23rd Floor, Montreal, PQ,
H3R 1Z1   (514) 871-5511
HOECHST CANADA INC., is a manufacturer and wholesaler of chemicals and pharmaceuticals. Its major products are specialty chemicals, pharmaceuticals, fibres, films, pigment, dyestuff and plastic resins. Hoechst Canada is a wholly owned subsidiary of Hoechst AG of Frankfurt, Germany.
A.W. Schuele, President

TOTAL ASSETS ($000)	108,128
TOTAL REVENUE ($000)	164,044
NET INCOME ($000)	4,414
EMPLOYEES	282

HOLLINGER INC.
See page 381 for a full company profile.

HOME CAPITAL GROUP INC.
See page 474 for a full company profile.

HOME OIL COMPANY LIMITED
See page 102 for a full company profile.

HOME PRODUCTS INC.
(Public)   SPECIALTY STORES
Exchanges: T   Stock Symbol: HPI
Ste. 850, 1450 Creekside Dr., Vancouver, BC,
V6J 5B3   (604) 739-8484
HOME PRODUCTS INC. is a manufacturer, distributor and retailer of consumer products, primarily for in-home use.

Wanda Dorosz, Chairman

TOTAL ASSETS ($000)	32,389
TOTAL REVENUE ($000)	37,866
NET INCOME ($000)	(13,175)
EMPLOYEES	411
RANK (Profit/Revenue/Assets)	954/605/753

HONDA CANADA INC.

(Private)   AUTOMOTIVE
715 Milner Avenue, Scarborough, ON, M1B 2K8   (416) 284-8110
HONDA CANADA INC. is involved in the assembly and distribution of vehicles and the distribution of motorcycles, all-terrain vehicles, small engines and parts to dealers throughout Canada.
K. Amemiya, Chairman & C.E.O.

TOTAL ASSETS ($000)	na
TOTAL REVENUE ($000)	2,636,251
NET INCOME ($000)	na
EMPLOYEES	2,100

HONEYWELL LIMITED

(Private)   ELECTRICAL & ELECTRONIC
The Honeywell Centre, 155 Gordon Baker Road, North York, ON, M2H 3N7   (416) 502-5200
HONEYWELL LTD. is Canada's leading controls company, offering home and building automation systems, energy management systems for commercial buildings and offices, process control solutions for industrial plants and navigation controls used in aviation and space.
Dave Larkin, Chairman

TOTAL ASSETS ($000)	392,667
TOTAL REVENUE ($000)	463,461
NET INCOME ($000)	na
EMPLOYEES	3,000

HONGKONG BANK OF CANADA

(Private)   BANKS
Suite 300, 885 West Georgia Street, Hongkong Bank of Canada Bldg., Vancouver, BC, V6C 3E9   (604) 685-1000
HONGKONG BANK OF CANADA is an indirectly held, wholly owned subsidiary of HSBC Holdings PLC of London, England.
John R.H. Bond, Chairman

TOTAL ASSETS ($000)	16,021,222
TOTAL REVENUE ($000)	1,050,010
NET INCOME ($000)	85,868
EMPLOYEES	3,167

HORSHAM CORPORATION (THE)
See page 103 for a full company profile.

HUBBARD HOLDING INC.

(Public)   CLOTHING AND TEXTILES
Exchanges: M   Stock Symbol: HUB
425 avenue Marien, Montreal-est, PQ, H1B 4V7   (514) 645-8833
HUBBARD HOLDING INC. is engaged in the business of applying dyes and finishes to woven and knitted fabrics.
Robert Lemire, Chairman

TOTAL ASSETS ($000)	14,830
TOTAL REVENUE ($000)	10,148
NET INCOME ($000)	(96)
EMPLOYEES	155
RANK (Profit/Revenue/Assets)	764/802/947

HUDSON BAY DIECASTING LIMITED

(Public)   MISC. INDUSTRIAL PRODUCTS
Exchanges: T   Stock Symbol: HBT
230 Orenda Road, Brampton, ON, L6T 1E9   (905) 453-5010
HUDSON BAY DIECASTING LIMITED is a diecasting supplier. Its main source of revenue is door entry systems and exterior trim for autos. It also produces diecast electronic chassis for the radio and computer industry and diecast plumbing hardware for specialty distributors.
Patrick Petracca, President

TOTAL ASSETS ($000)	26,860
TOTAL REVENUE ($000)	40,341
NET INCOME ($000)	(3,621)
EMPLOYEES	600
RANK (Profit/Revenue/Assets)	894/588/801

HUDSON BAY MINING AND SMELTING CO., LIMITED

(Private)   INTEGRATED MINES
Toronto Dominion Centre, 1906 - 201 Portage Avenue, Winnipeg, MB, R3B 3K6   (204) 949-4261
HUDSON BAY MINING AND SMELTING CO. LTD. is a natural resources company. The company mines and processes copper, zinc, gold, silver and nickel at sites in northern Manitoba. It also operates a zinc oxide plant in Ontario. Minorce beneficially owns all of the company's common shares
John J. Ellis, Chairman

TOTAL ASSETS ($000)	426,643
TOTAL REVENUE ($000)	399,984
NET INCOME ($000)	13,208
EMPLOYEES	na

HUDSON'S BAY COMPANY
See page 423 for a full company profile.

HUDSON'S BAY COMPANY ACCEPTANCE LIMITED

(Private)   FINANCE AND LEASING
501 - 10310 Japer Avenue, Edmonton, AB, T5J 3P7 (403) 423-1311
HUDSON'S BAY COMPANY ACCEPTANCE LIMITED is engaged in the business of purchasing accounts receivable arising out of retail credit sales of Hudson's Bay Company and an affiliate, Zeller's Inc. It is a wholly owned subsidiary within the Hudson's Bay Company group.
Gary J. Lukassen, Chairman

TOTAL ASSETS ($000)	950,637
TOTAL REVENUE ($000)	223,572
NET INCOME ($000)	27
EMPLOYEES	1

HUGHES AIRCRAFT OF CANADA LIMITED

(Private)   TRANSPORTATION EQUIP & COMPNTS
3715 - 8th Street N.E., Calgary, AB, T2E 7H7   (403) 295-6604
HUGES AIRCRAFT OF CANADA LIMITED is an aerospace and electronics company. It is a subsidiary of Hughes Aircraft Company.
G.C.C. Chang, Chairman

TOTAL ASSETS ($000)	214,500
TOTAL REVENUE ($000)	236,500
NET INCOME ($000)	na
EMPLOYEES	1,040

HUMBOLDT CAPITAL CORPORATION
(Public)   OIL AND GAS PRODUCERS
Exchanges: V   Stock Symbol: HMB
Ste. 2100, 144 - 4th Ave. SW, Calgary, AB, T2P 3N4 (403) 750-4440
HUMBOLDT CAPITAL is an investment holding company investing
in the resource industry in Canada. Its largest asset is its 15% shareholding
of Orbit Oil & Gas Ltd.
R.W. Lamond, Chairman of the Board

TOTAL ASSETS ($000)	17,284
TOTAL REVENUE ($000)	2,737
NET INCOME ($000)	2,681
EMPLOYEES	0
RANK (Profit/Revenue/Assets)	526/904/904

HUMBOLDT FLOUR MILLS INC.
(Public)   AGRICULTURE
Exchanges: Z   Stock Symbol: HFM
P.O. Box 400, Humboldt, SK, S0K 2A0   (306) 682-2577
HUMBOLDT FLOUR MILLS INC. is involved in the processing and
marketing of a variety of mustard seed and peas and lentils, together with
the sale and distribution of farm chemical and fertilizer.
Wilfred Chamney, President

TOTAL ASSETS ($000)	13,937
TOTAL REVENUE ($000)	33,708
NET INCOME ($000)	481
EMPLOYEES	40
RANK (Profit/Revenue/Assets)	697/628/964

HUMMINGBIRD COMMUNICATIONS LTD.
See page 541 for a full company profile.

See page 541 for a full company profile.

HUSKY INJECTION MOLDING SYSTEMS LTD.
(Private)   MISC. INDUSTRIAL PRODUCTS
500 Queen St. South, Bolton, ON, L7E 5S5   (905) 951-5000
HUSKY INJECTION MOLDING SYSTEMS LTD. is engaged in
supplying high technology plastic injection molding systems (including
machines, molds, robots and product handling equipment), hot runners
and related services. Husky Injection is 79% owned by an employee
group and 21% by Komatsu Ltd.
Robert Schad, President & C.E.O.

TOTAL ASSETS ($000)	381,705
TOTAL REVENUE ($000)	519,879
NET INCOME ($000)	na
EMPLOYEES	1,500

HUSKY OIL LTD.
(Private)   INTEGRATED OILS
707 - 8th Avenue S.W., P.O. Box 6525, Postal Station D, Calgary,
AB, T2P 3G7   (403) 298-6111
HUSKY OIL LTD., is a Canadian-based oil and gas company engaged
in the exploration, development, production, purchase, transportation,
processing, upgrading and marketing of crude oil, natural gas, natural gas
liquids, and sulphur. Husky also refines crude oil and markets and
transports refined petroleum products.
V.T.K. Li, Co-Chairman

TOTAL ASSETS ($000)	3,689,049
TOTAL REVENUE ($000)	890,714
NET INCOME ($000)	(238,267)
EMPLOYEES	1,400

HY & ZEL'S INC.
(Public)   SPECIALTY STORES
Exchanges: T   Stock Symbol: HZI
7171 Yonge St., Thornhill, ON, L3T 2A9   (905) 886-7171
HY & ZEL'S, through its subsidiary, The Warehouse Drug Store Ltd.,
operates 14 retail stores in the Southern Ontario region under the name
Hy & Zel's The Supermarket Drug Store.
Zelick Goldstein, C.E.O.

TOTAL ASSETS ($000)	26,540
TOTAL REVENUE ($000)	147,464
NET INCOME ($000)	2,664
EMPLOYEES	800
RANK (Profit/Revenue/Assets)	529/362/804

HYAL PHARMACEUTICAL CORPORATION
(Public)   BIOTECHNOLOGY & PHARMACEUTICALS
Exchanges: T Q   Stock Symbol: HPC
2425 Skymark Ave., Unit 1, Mississauga, ON,
L4W 4Y6   (905) 678-6800
HYAL PHARMACEUTICAL CORPORATION is engaged in the development of Hyaluronic acid formulations, which enhance, improve and
control the delivery and ultization of active drug compounds in the human
body, while reducing the toxicity of the drug. Hyal is concentrating on
the treatment of pain, both topically and intravenously, and the treatment
of skin cancer.
Donald C. Webster, Chairman

TOTAL ASSETS ($000)	22,199
TOTAL REVENUE ($000)	1,774
NET INCOME ($000)	(4,645)
EMPLOYEES	24
RANK (Profit/Revenue/Assets)	905/933/849

HYDRO-QUEBEC
(Crown)   ELECTRICAL UTILITIES
75 Boul. Rene-Levesque O., Montreal, PQ, H2Z 1A4 (800) 363-7443
HYDRO-QUEBEC is a Quebec government owned electrical utility that
ensures the generation, transmission and distribution of almost all the
electricity sold in Quebec. The company has power stations which serve
the needs of the province and allow the company to export power to the
United States.
Richard Drouin, Chairman & C.E.O.

TOTAL ASSETS ($000)	51,608,000
TOTAL REVENUE ($000)	7,374,000
NET INCOME ($000)	667,000
EMPLOYEES	26,781

HYDROMET ENVIRONMENTAL RECOVERY LTD.
(Public)   ENVIRONMENTAL SERVICES
Exchanges: T   Stock Symbol: HME.A
Ste. 2850, 205 - 5th Ave. SW, Calgary, AB, T2P 2V7 (403) 266-1313
HYDROMET ENVIRONMENTAL RECOVERY LTD. is involved in
the residue management/resource recovery sector in North America and
of selling products produced by such processes on a worldwide basis.
Dallas E. Hawkins, Chairman & C.F.O.

TOTAL ASSETS ($000)	14,173
TOTAL REVENUE ($000)	161
NET INCOME ($000)	399
EMPLOYEES	na
RANK (Profit/Revenue/Assets)	713/980/957

I.M.P. GROUP INTERNATIONAL INC.

(Private) TRANSPORTATION EQUIP & COMPNTS
Ste 400, 2651 Dutch Village Rd, Halifax, NS, B3L 4T1 (902) 453-2400
I.M.P. GROUP INTERNATIONAL INC. is the parent of a diversified group of companies in aerospace, aviation, aircraft engineering, manufacturing, repair and overhaul, hotels, and industrial, marine and medical supplies.
K.C. Rowe, Chairman President & C.E.O.

TOTAL ASSETS ($000)	na
TOTAL REVENUE ($000)	300,000
NET INCOME ($000)	na
EMPLOYEES	2,400

I.S.G. TECHNOLOGIES INC.
See page 542 for a full company profile.

IBM CANADA LTD - IBM CANADA LIMITEE

(Private) ELECTRICAL & ELECTRONIC
3600 Steeles Avenue East, Markham, ON, L3R 9Z7 (905) 316-9000
IBM CANADA LTD. is a leader in the information technology industry. IBM Canada is wholly owned by IBM World Trade Corp. of the United States.
Bill Etherington, Chairman

TOTAL ASSETS ($000)	na
TOTAL REVENUE ($000)	8,440,000
NET INCOME ($000)	155,000
EMPLOYEES	9,985

ICI CANADA INC.

(Private) CHEMICALS
C-I-L House, 90 Sheppard Avenue East, P.O. Box 200 Station A, North York, ON, M2N 6H2 (416) 229-7000
ICI CANADA INC. is engaged in the manufacturing of explosives, paints, agrochemicals, fertilizers and chloralkali products. The company is a wholly owned subsidiary of Imperial Chemical Industries PLC of the United Kingdom.
C.H. Hantho, Chairman & C.E.O.

TOTAL ASSETS ($000)	582,000
TOTAL REVENUE ($000)	738,000
NET INCOME ($000)	na
EMPLOYEES	na

IDEAL METAL INC.

(Public) WHOLESALE DISTRIBUTORS
Exchanges: M Stock Symbol: IDM
3399 Francis-Hughes Avenue, Laval, PQ, H7L 5A5 (514) 385-0111
IDEAL METAL INC. is a major non-ferrous metal distribution and processing service centre supplying the metal requirements of manufacturing and other key industries in Canada.
Jacques E. Daccord, Chairman

TOTAL ASSETS ($000)	49,255
TOTAL REVENUE ($000)	111,049
NET INCOME ($000)	1,738
EMPLOYEES	286
RANK (Profit/Revenue/Assets)	590/406/633

IMASCO LIMITED
See page 519 for a full company profile.

IMAX CORPORATION
See page 577 for a full company profile.

IMPERIAL LIFE ASSURANCE COMPANY OF CANADA (THE)
See page 500 for a full company profile.

IMPERIAL METALS CORPORATION

(Public) PRECIOUS METALS
Exchanges: T Stock Symbol: IPM
Suite 420, 355 Burrard St., Vancouver, BC, V6C 2G8 (604) 669-8959
IMPERIAL METALS CORPORATION is a mineral exploration and development company with operations in Canada and the United States. The company owns, or has significant influence over, three public mineral exploration and development companies. It also holds non-operated, producing oil and gas properties and provides technical services to its affiliates.
K. Peter Geib, Chairman

TOTAL ASSETS ($000)	37,238
TOTAL REVENUE ($000)	14,807
NET INCOME ($000)	1,144
EMPLOYEES	13
RANK (Profit/Revenue/Assets)	642/760/713

IMPERIAL OIL LIMITED
See page 104 for a full company profile.

IMPERIAL OIL RESOURCES LIMITED

(Private) OIL AND GAS PRODUCERS
237- 4th Avenue S.W., Calgary, AB, T2P 0H6 (403) 237-3737
IMPERIAL OIL RESOURCES LIMITED is the oil and gas production division of Imperial Oil Limited.

TOTAL ASSETS ($000)	5,924,000
TOTAL REVENUE ($000)	2,297,000
NET INCOME ($000)	167,000
EMPLOYEES	na

IMPERIAL PARKING LIMITED

(Public) OTHER SERVICES
Exchanges: T Stock Symbol: IPK
Ste. 300, 601 Cordova St., Vancouver, BC, V6B 1G1 (604) 681-7311
IMPERIAL PARKING LIMITED operates over 1,000 parking locations across Canada, as well as in Minneapolis/St. Paul, Minnesota, and Milwaukee, Wisconsin. The company, through wholly owned subsidiaries, is involved in the manufacture and marketing of parking lot equipment in both Canada and the United States.
Paul T.C. Clough, Chairman, President & C.E.O.

TOTAL ASSETS ($000)	38,710
TOTAL REVENUE ($000)	111,881
NET INCOME ($000)	34
EMPLOYEES	1,300
RANK (Profit/Revenue/Assets)	749/402/702

IMPERIAL TOBACCO LIMITED

(Private) TOBACCO
3810 St Antoine St. West, Montreal, PQ, H4C 1B5 (514) 932-6161
IMPERIAL TOBACCO LIMITED manufactures tobacco products.

Canada Company Handbook

Don Brown, Chairman, President & C.E.O.

TOTAL ASSETS ($000)	na
TOTAL REVENUE ($000)	2,586,000
NET INCOME ($000)	592,000
EMPLOYEES	2,600

INCO LIMITED
See page 14 for a full company profile.

INDUSTRA SERVICE CORPORATION
(Public)   OTHER SERVICES
Exchanges: T   Stock Symbol: IND
401 Salter Street, New Westminster, BC, V3M 5Y1   (604) 521-3322
INDUSTRA SERVICE CORPORATION operates in Canada and the United States in two industry segments. It repairs, maintains, and modifys of boilers, pressure vessels, and tubing used in industrial facilities. It also provides engineering services and refractory products.
Wayne E. Shaw, Chairman, President & C.E.O.

TOTAL ASSETS ($000)	25,316
TOTAL REVENUE ($000)	65,116
NET INCOME ($000)	(2,949)
EMPLOYEES	250
RANK (Profit/Revenue/Assets)	878/491/812

INDUSTRIAL-ALLIANCE LIFE INSURANCE COMPANY
(Private)   INSURANCE - LIFE
C.P. 1907, Succersale Terminus, Quebec City, PQ,
G1K 7M3   (418) 684-5000
INDUSTRIAL-ALLIANCE LIFE INSURANCE COMPANY is a major Canadian mutual life insurance company and through its wholly owned subsidiaries, owns or has majority interest in the following companies: National Life Assurance Company of Canada; North West Life Assurance Company of Canada; North West Life Assurance Company of America; Unindal Inc.; and IST Group Inc.
Robert Begin, Chairman

TOTAL ASSETS ($000)	6,694,102
TOTAL REVENUE ($000)	1,702,397
NET INCOME ($000)	51,050
EMPLOYEES	1,046

INDUSTRIAL-ALLIANCE LIFE MANAGEMENT CORPORATION
(Private)   INSURANCE - LIFE
1080 St-Louis Road, Sillery, PQ, G1K 7M3   (418) 684-5000
INDUSTRIAL-ALLIANCE LIFE MANAGEMENT CORPORATION is a group of three companies that provide life insurance. The three companies are The National Life Assurance Company of Canada, The North West Life Assurance Company of Canada and North West Life Assurance Company of America. These three companies operate in Ontario and Western Canada as well as in the northwestern United States.
Robert Begin, Chairman

TOTAL ASSETS ($000)	2,401,227
TOTAL REVENUE ($000)	516,760
NET INCOME ($000)	8,074
EMPLOYEES	380

INGERSOLL-RAND CANADA INC.
(Private)   MACHINERY
3501 St. Charles Blvd., Suite 202, Kirkland, PQ,
H9H 4S3   (514) 695-9040

INGERSOLL-RAND CANADA INC. is engaged in the manufacture, distribution and marketing of machinery and equipment. The company is wholly owned by Ingersoll-Rand Company of Woodcliff Lake, New Jersey.
S.J. Zalzal, President & C.E.O.

TOTAL ASSETS ($000)	427,872
TOTAL REVENUE ($000)	240,178
NET INCOME ($000)	39,544
EMPLOYEES	812

INMET MINING CORPORATION
See page 15 for a full company profile.

INSURANCE CORPORATION OF BRITISH COLUMBIA
(Crown)   INSURANCE - PROPERTY & CASUALTY
151 West Esplanade, North Vancouver, BC,
V7M 3H9   (604) 661-2800
INSURANCE CORPORATION OF BRITISH COLUMBIA is a crown corporation which has the power and capacity to act as an insurer and reinsurer in all classes of insurance.
Leonard J. DeVito, Chairman of the Board

TOTAL ASSETS ($000)	4,353,385
TOTAL REVENUE ($000)	2,428,434
NET INCOME ($000)	140,890
EMPLOYEES	3,800

INTELCOM GROUP INC.
(Public)   TELECOMMUNICATIONS
Exchanges: V   Stock Symbol: INL
Suite 200, 4245 - 97 Street, Edmonton, AB, T6E 5Y7 (403) 465-5959
INTELCOM GROUP, INC. principal business activities are in the communications and oil and gas industries.
Bill Becker, Chairman

TOTAL ASSETS ($000)	201,991 (US)
TOTAL REVENUE ($000)	58,556 (US)
NET INCOME ($000)	(23,867) (US)
EMPLOYEES	910
RANK (Profit/Revenue/Assets)	980/456/303

INTENSITY RESOURCES LTD.
See page 105 for a full company profile.

INTER-CITY PRODUCTS CORPORATION
See page 578 for a full company profile.

INTERA INFORMATION TECHNOLOGIES CORPORATION
See page 554 for a full company profile.

INTERMETCO LIMITED
(Public)   MANAGEMENT AND DIVERSIFIED
Exchanges: T   Stock Symbol: INT
519 Parkdale Avenue North, Hamilton, ON, L8H 5Y6 (905) 548-9700
INTERMETCO LIMITED is the largest recycler of metal products in Canada. The company manufactures spiral-weld pipe in Georgia and Pennsylvania and distributes tubular piping, prime pipe piling, beams and hollow structual tubing, and warehouses and packages galvannealed steel.

Marvin E. Goldblatt, Chairman

TOTAL ASSETS ($000)	75,195
TOTAL REVENUE ($000)	170,029
NET INCOME ($000)	1,357
EMPLOYEES	250
RANK (Profit/Revenue/Assets)	621/338/546

INTERNATIONAL COLIN ENERGY CORPORATION
See page 106 for a full company profile.

INTERNATIONAL FOREST PRODUCTS LIMITED
See page 162 for a full company profile.

INTERNATIONAL GOLD RESOURCES CORPORATION
(Public)   PRECIOUS METALS
Exchanges: T   Stock Symbol: IGC
3rd Floor, 172 King St. E., Toronto, ON, M5A 1J3   (416) 947-9208
INTERNATIONAL GOLD RESOURCES CORPORATION is involved in the acquisition, exploration and development of precious metal properties principally in the western United States and Ghana, West Africa.

TOTAL ASSETS ($000)	22,579 (US)
TOTAL REVENUE ($000)	1,384 (US)
NET INCOME ($000)	(1,085) (US)
EMPLOYEES	na
RANK (Profit/Revenue/Assets)	835/927/757

INTERNATIONAL MAHOGANY CORP.
(Public)   PRECIOUS METALS
Exchanges: T   Stock Symbol: IMY.B
1305 - 1090 W. Georgia St., Vancouver, BC,
V6E 3V7   (604) 685-9316
INTERNATIONAL MAHOGANY CORP. and its subsidiaries are engaged in the exploration and development of mineral resource properties in Canada, United States and Chile.
Anton Hendriksz, Chairman

TOTAL ASSETS ($000)	14,748
TOTAL REVENUE ($000)	854
NET INCOME ($000)	(6,127)
EMPLOYEES	0
RANK (Profit/Revenue/Assets)	919/950/952

INTERNATIONAL MINERALS & CHEMICAL CORP. (CANADA) LTD.
(Private)   OTHER MINES
General Delivery, Esterhazy, SK, S0A 0X0   (306) 745-4200
INTERNATIONAL MINERALS & CHEMICAL CORP. (CANADA) LTD.'s business consists primarily of potash mining in Canada. It is a wholly owned subsidiary of IMC GLOBAL OPERATIONS INC.
W.F. Bueche, Chairman

TOTAL ASSETS ($000)	331,600
TOTAL REVENUE ($000)	182,758
NET INCOME ($000)	1,960
EMPLOYEES	848

INTERNATIONAL MUREX TECHNOLOGIES CORPORATION
See page 230 for a full company profile.

INTERNATIONAL MUSTO EXPLORATIONS LTD.
(Private)   METAL MINES
Suite 1320, 885 West Georgia Street, Vancouver, BC,
V6C 3E8   (604) 689-7842
INTERNATIONAL MUSTO EXPLORATIONS LTD. is engaged in the acquisition, exploration and development of natural resource properties.
Lukas Lundin, C.E.O. & President

TOTAL ASSETS ($000)	50,482 (US)
TOTAL REVENUE ($000)	1,863 (US)
NET INCOME ($000)	302 (US)
EMPLOYEES	67

INTERNATIONAL OILTEX LTD.
(Public)   OIL AND GAS PRODUCERS
Exchanges: T   Stock Symbol: ILO
Ste. 910, 400 - 5th Ave. SW, Calgary, AB, T2P 0L6   (403) 266-1094
INTERNATIONAL OILTEX LTD. is involved in the exploration for and the development and production of oil and gas in Western Canada.
Christopher K.G. Rowe, Chairman

TOTAL ASSETS ($000)	17,157
TOTAL REVENUE ($000)	6,108
NET INCOME ($000)	2,090
EMPLOYEES	na
RANK (Profit/Revenue/Assets)	560/841/908

INTERNATIONAL PANORAMA RESOURCE CORP.
(Public)   OIL AND GAS PRODUCERS
Exchanges: V   Stock Symbol: ILP
Suite 600, 555 West Georgia Street, Vancouver, BC,
V6B 1Z5   (604) 687-7294
INTERNATIONAL PANORAMA RESOURCE CORP. is a mining exploration company. It has projects in southern Colorado, Grass Valley, California and Voisey Bay, Labrador.
Adrian Hartmann, President

TOTAL ASSETS ($000)	11,687 (US)
TOTAL REVENUE ($000)	1 (US)
NET INCOME ($000)	(94) (US)
EMPLOYEES	3
RANK (Profit/Revenue/Assets)	768/994/931

INTERNATIONAL PEDCO ENERGY CORPORATION
(Public)   OIL AND GAS PRODUCERS
Exchanges: T   Stock Symbol: IPP
Ste. 1600, 520 - 5th Ave. SW, Calgary, AB, T2P 3R7   (403) 262-2720
INTERNATIONAL PEDCO ENERGY CORPORATION is involved in the acquisition, exploration and development of oil and gas properties.
Thomas J. Jacobsen, Chairman & C.E.O.

TOTAL ASSETS ($000)	20,677
TOTAL REVENUE ($000)	4,975
NET INCOME ($000)	1,024
EMPLOYEES	na
RANK (Profit/Revenue/Assets)	654/864/863

INTERNATIONAL PETROLEUM CORPORATION
See page 107 for a full company profile.

INTERNATIONAL UNP HOLDINGS LTD.
(Public) INVESTMENT COMPANIES AND FUNDS
Exchanges: T Stock Symbol: IUN
Ste. 409, 120 Adelaide St. W., Toronto, ON, M5H 1T1 (416) 364-4184
INTERNATIONAL UNP HOLDINGS LTD. is in the business of investing in existing profitable companies in Poland.
L. George Bonar, Chairman, President & C.E.O.

TOTAL ASSETS ($000)	48,707
TOTAL REVENUE ($000)	32,810
NET INCOME ($000)	68
EMPLOYEES	3
RANK (Profit/Revenue/Assets)	746/633/637

INTERNATIONAL VERIFACT INC.
See page 269 for a full company profile.

INTERNATIONAL WALLCOVERINGS LTD.
(Public) MISC. CONSUMER PRODUCTS
Exchanges: T M Stock Symbol: IWL
151 East Drive, Brampton Drive, ON, L6T 1B5 (905) 791-1547
INTERNATIONAL WALLCOVERINGS LTD. designs, manufactures and distributes residential wallcoverings.
Francis P. Baker, Chairman & C.E.O.

TOTAL ASSETS ($000)	33,787
TOTAL REVENUE ($000)	49,379
NET INCOME ($000)	5,071
EMPLOYEES	250
RANK (Profit/Revenue/Assets)	422/552/735

INTERTAPE POLYMER GROUP INC.
See page 298 for a full company profile.

INTRAWEST CORPORATION
See page 310 for a full company profile.

INVERNESS PETROLEUM LTD.
See page 108 for a full company profile.

INVERPOWER CONTROLS LTD.
(Public) MISC. INDUSTRIAL PRODUCTS
Exchanges: T Stock Symbol: IPW
835 Harrington Court, Burlington, ON, L7N 3P3 (905) 639-4692
INVERPOWER CONTROLS LTD. designs, builds and services electrical power conditioning systems, and electromagnetic stirring systems, servicing the steel industry, telecommunication supplies, high energy physics, and medical areas and other industrial markets.
Shashi B. Dewan, President & C.E.O.

TOTAL ASSETS ($000)	14,858
TOTAL REVENUE ($000)	15,751
NET INCOME ($000)	2,051
EMPLOYEES	150
RANK (Profit/Revenue/Assets)	563/748/946

INVESTORS GROUP INC.
See page 475 for a full company profile.

IPL ENERGY INC.
See page 334 for a full company profile.

IPL INC.
(Public) PACKAGING AND CONTAINERS
Exchanges: M Stock Symbol: IPI
140 rue Commerciale, St-Damien, PQ, G0R 2Y0 (418) 789-2880
IPL is a major manufacturer of injection and extrusion moulded plastic products. The company manufactures and commercializes a wide range of rigid packaging containers and pails, as well as beverage cases and handling boxes designed for various uses within the food, fishing, chemical, forestry, petrochemical, construction and recycling industries. The company also supplies the automotive industry.
Remi Metivier, Chairman of the Board

TOTAL ASSETS ($000)	60,623
TOTAL REVENUE ($000)	75,617
NET INCOME ($000)	2,623
EMPLOYEES	500
RANK (Profit/Revenue/Assets)	534/465/592

IPSCO INC.
See page 245 for a full company profile.

IRWIN TOY LIMITED
See page 208 for a full company profile.

ISLAND TELEPHONE COMPANY LIMITED (THE)
See page 353 for a full company profile.

ISM INFORMATION SYSTEMS MANAGEMENT CORPORATION
(Private) COMPUTER SOFTWARE & PROCESSING
One Research Drive, University of Regina Campus, Regina, SK, S4S 7H1 (306) 781-5151
ISM INFORMATION SYSTEMS MANAGEMENT CORPORATION is Canada's largest full service information technology company providing total solutions to meet the changing information systems management needs of private and public sector organizations.
J. Gordon Garrett, Chairman & C.E.O.

TOTAL ASSETS ($000)	233,103
TOTAL REVENUE ($000)	524,436
NET INCOME ($000)	11,941
EMPLOYEES	3,400

ISRAEL DISCOUNT BANK OF CANADA
(Private) BANKS
Ste. M100, 150 Bloor St. W., Toronto, ON, M5S 2Y5 (416) 926-7200
ISRAEL DISCOUNT BANK OF CANADA is a schedule II bank.
Aron Kahana, Chairman

TOTAL ASSETS ($000)	92,205
TOTAL REVENUE ($000)	6,556
NET INCOME ($000)	224
EMPLOYEES	21

ITOCHU CANADA LTD.
(Private) WHOLESALE DISTRIBUTORS
770 - 999 Canada Place, Vancouver, BC, V6C 3E1 (604) 683-5764
ITOCHU CANADA LTD. is involved in the import and export business and real estate business. It is a wholly owned subsidiary of Itochu International Inc.

Yushin Okazaki, President & C.E.O.

TOTAL ASSETS ($000)	37,550
TOTAL REVENUE ($000)	978,299
NET INCOME ($000)	2,035
EMPLOYEES	35

ITT CANADA LIMITED
(Private) AUTOMOTIVE
P.O. Box 138, TD, Toronto, ON, M5K 1H1 (416) 863-9666
ITT CANADA is a diversified manufacturing, distribution and service company engaged principally in the manufacture and distribution of automotive parts, pumps, valves, controls and electronic components and in the provision of financial and hotel services.
Gerald B. Fedchun, Chairman President & General Counsel

TOTAL ASSETS ($000)	740,034
TOTAL REVENUE ($000)	554,558
NET INCOME ($000)	9,984
EMPLOYEES	7,300

ITW CANADA INC.
(Private) METAL FABRICATORS
115 Ridgetop Road, Scarborough, ON, M1P 2K3 (416) 293-2411
ITW CANADA INC. is a wholly owned subsidiary of Illinois Tool Works Inc. of Chicago, Illinois.
R.F. Palach, President

TOTAL ASSETS ($000)	74,128
TOTAL REVENUE ($000)	140,699
NET INCOME ($000)	4,302
EMPLOYEES	623

IVACO INC.
See page 246 for a full company profile.

JAMES RICHARDSON & SONS, LIMITED
(Private) WHOLESALE DISTRIBUTORS
Richardson Building, One Lombard Place, Winnipeg, MB, R3B 0Y1 (204) 934-5811
JAMES RICHARDSON & SONS, LIMITED is a grain, financial and management holding company. The company's subsidiaries engage in grain operations, the investment securities industry, real estate, construction, oil and gas and shipping. The company is wholly owned by the Richardson family.
George T. Richardson, Chairman & Managing Dir.

TOTAL ASSETS ($000)	4,934,408
TOTAL REVENUE ($000)	2,354,417
NET INCOME ($000)	47,669
EMPLOYEES	3,000

JANNOCK LIMITED
See page 520 for a full company profile.

JASCAN RESOURCES INC.
(Public) METAL MINES
Exchanges: T Stock Symbol: JSC
Ste. 2000, 95 Wellington St. W., Toronto, ON, M5J 2N7 (416) 362-6721
JASCAN RESOURCES INC. is engaged in the acquisition, exploration and development of mineral properties with the primary focus being gold, silver and copper.

John C. Lamacraft, President

TOTAL ASSETS ($000)	16,632
TOTAL REVENUE ($000)	2,339
NET INCOME ($000)	1,585
EMPLOYEES	na
RANK (Profit/Revenue/Assets)	602/911/924

JEAN COUTU GROUP (PJC) INC. (THE)
See page 424 for a full company profile.

JIM PATTISON GROUP (THE)
(Private) MANAGEMENT AND DIVERSIFIED
1055 W. Hastings St., Ste. 1600, Vancouver, BC, V6E 2H2 (604) 688-6764
THE JIM PATTISON GROUP is a diversified organization with consumer oriented lines of businesses that include food, broadcasting, packaging, transportation and financial services.
Jim Pattison, C.E.O. & Managing Director

TOTAL ASSETS ($000)	1,500,000
TOTAL REVENUE ($000)	3,300,000
NET INCOME ($000)	na
EMPLOYEES	16,000

JOHN DEERE LIMITED
(Private) WHOLESALE DISTRIBUTORS
South Service Road, Grimsby, ON, L3M 4H5 (905) 945-9281
JOHN DEERE LIMITED is a manufacturer and wholesaler of agricultural equipment, and a wholesaler of industrial equipment and consumer products.
G.J. Clark, President & C.E.O.

TOTAL ASSETS ($000)	1,197,255
TOTAL REVENUE ($000)	1,076,627
NET INCOME ($000)	58,403
EMPLOYEES	985

JOHN FORSYTH COMPANY INC. (THE)
(Public) CLOTHING AND TEXTILES
Exchanges: T Stock Symbol: JFC
36 Horner Avenue, Toronto, ON, M8Z 5Y1 (416) 252-6231
THE JOHN FORSYTH COMPANY INC. is a supplier of dress shirts, knitwear, outerwear and neckwear to Canadian and U.S. markets. The company manufactures garments at its Cambridge, Ontario, facility and imports finished products from off-shore suppliers. The company markets its products under exclusive licensing labels, proprietary brand labels and private labels.
Oskar Rajsky, President & C.E.O.

TOTAL ASSETS ($000)	71,757
TOTAL REVENUE ($000)	125,937
NET INCOME ($000)	(1,742)
EMPLOYEES	1,050
RANK (Profit/Revenue/Assets)	846/384/558

JOHN LABATT LIMITED
See page 521 for a full company profile.

JOHNSON & JOHNSON INC.
(Private) CHEMICALS
2155 Pie IX Boulevard, Montreal, PQ, H1V 2E4 (514) 251-5151

JOHNSON & JOHNSON INC. is a consumer health care products company.
G. Ostrou, Chairman & C.E.O.

TOTAL ASSETS ($000)	215,394
TOTAL REVENUE ($000)	376,740
NET INCOME ($000)	19,200
EMPLOYEES	900

JORDAN PETROLEUM LTD.
See page 109 for a full company profile.

JORDEX RESOURCES INC.
(Public)   METAL MINES
Exchanges: T   Stock Symbol: JDX
Suite 2660, 1221 Brickell Ave., Miami, FL, 33131   (305) 530-1875
JORDEX RESOURCES INC. is involved in the acquisition, exploration and development of mineral properties.
Brian Hinchcliffe, President & C.E.O.

TOTAL ASSETS ($000)	13,633
TOTAL REVENUE ($000)	1,458
NET INCOME ($000)	(3,142)
EMPLOYEES	10
RANK (Profit/Revenue/Assets)	881/936/974

JOURNEY'S END CORPORATION
See page 579 for a full company profile.

K MART CANADA LIMITED
(Private)   DEPARTMENT STORES
8925 Torbram Road, Brampton, ON, L6T 4G1   (905) 792-4400
K MART CANADA LIMITED is a general merchandise retailer. K Mart Canada is a wholly owned subsidiary of K Mart Corporation of Troy, Michigan.
D. Perkins, Chairman

TOTAL ASSETS ($000)	642,137
TOTAL REVENUE ($000)	1,262,552
NET INCOME ($000)	8,765
EMPLOYEES	12,000

KACEE EXPLORATION INC.
(Public)   OIL AND GAS PRODUCERS
Exchanges: Z   Stock Symbol: KCX
Ste. 1600, 311 - 6th Ave. SW, Calgary, AB, T2P 3H2   (403) 234-7703
KACEE EXPLORATION INC. is involved in the acquisition, exploration and development of oil and gas properties in western Canada.
Brian A. Skinner, Chairman & President

TOTAL ASSETS ($000)	13,620
TOTAL REVENUE ($000)	2,959
NET INCOME ($000)	(75)
EMPLOYEES	7
RANK (Profit/Revenue/Assets)	762/903/975

KALIUM CANADA, LTD.
(Private)   CHEMICALS
Suite 1200, 1801 Hamilton St., Regina, SK, S4P 4B5 (306) 347-9100
KALIUM CANADA is involved in potash mining and distribution.
J.P. Sullivan, Chairman & C.E.O.

TOTAL ASSETS ($000)	258,618
TOTAL REVENUE ($000)	133,183

NET INCOME ($000)	12,780
EMPLOYEES	175

KANEMATSU (CANADA) INC.
(Private)   WHOLESALE DISTRIBUTORS
6430 Vipond Dr, Mississauga, ON, L5T 1W8   (905) 670-1977
D.M. Sugiura, President

TOTAL ASSETS ($000)	18,548
TOTAL REVENUE ($000)	144,340
NET INCOME ($000)	(292)
EMPLOYEES	27

KAP RESOURCES LTD.
(Public)   METAL MINES
Exchanges: V   Stock Symbol: KAR
Ste. 407, 325 Howe St., Vancouver, BC, V6C 1Z7   (604) 669-7995
KAP RESOURCES Ltd. is a mineral exploration company.

TOTAL ASSETS ($000)	18,726
TOTAL REVENUE ($000)	0
NET INCOME ($000)	(689)
EMPLOYEES	na
RANK (Profit/Revenue/Assets)	806/996/885

KAUFEL GROUP LTD.
See page 580 for a full company profile.

KERR ADDISON MINES LIMITED
See page 16 for a full company profile.

KIMPEX INTERNATIONAL INC.
(Public)   WHOLESALE DISTRIBUTORS
Exchanges: T M   Stock Symbol: KPX
5355 St-Roch Street, Drummondville, PQ, J2B 6V4   (819) 472-3326
KIMPEX INTERNATIONAL INC. is a North American product developer and distributor of proprietary replacement parts and accessories for winter and summer recreational vehicles.
P.T. Joseph, Chairman

TOTAL ASSETS ($000)	43,482
TOTAL REVENUE ($000)	55,216
NET INCOME ($000)	1,784
EMPLOYEES	193
RANK (Profit/Revenue/Assets)	587/529/670

KINROSS GOLD CORPORATION
See page 48 for a full company profile.

KOMDRESCO CANADA INC.
(Private)   WHOLESALE DISTRIBUTORS
160 Boul de l'industrie, Quebec, PQ, J5R 1J3   (514) 659-1961
KOMDRESCO CANADA INC. is a wholesaler of equipment and machinery. Komdresco Canada is a wholly owned subsidiary of Komatsu Dresser Company.
Mr. J. Webster, General Manager

TOTAL ASSETS ($000)	74,199
TOTAL REVENUE ($000)	140,100
NET INCOME ($000)	na
EMPLOYEES	185

KRAFT GENERAL FOODS CANADA INC.
(Private)   FOOD PROCESSING
95 Moatfield Drive, Don Mills, ON, M3B 3L6   (416) 441-5000
KRAFT GENERAL FOODS CANADA INC. is a packaged food products manufacturer. The company is part of the North American group of companies of Kraft General Foods Inc. of the United States. The company's ultimate parent is Philip Morris Companies of New York.
Douglas Smith, President

TOTAL ASSETS ($000)	1,191,846
TOTAL REVENUE ($000)	1,788,165
NET INCOME ($000)	136,912
EMPLOYEES	4,593

KRG MANAGEMENT INC.
See page 501 for a full company profile.

KRONOS CANADA, INC.
(Private)   CHEMICALS
4 Place Ville-Marie, Ste. 500, Montreal, PQ,
H3B 4M5   (514) 397-3501
KRONOS CANADA INC. manufacturers and wholesales pigments and chemicals.
R.P. Beaulne, Chairman

TOTAL ASSETS ($000)	332,257
TOTAL REVENUE ($000)	172,455
NET INCOME ($000)	16,242
EMPLOYEES	500

KRUGER INC.
(Private)   EAST COAST FORESTRY
3285 Rue Bedford, Montreal, PQ, H3S 1G5   (514) 737-1131
KRUGER INC. is a producer of newsprint, coated paper, groundwood specialties, 100% recycled linerboard, corrugated containers, tissue products and lumber.
Joseph Kruger II, Chairman & C.E.O.

TOTAL ASSETS ($000)	1,743,524
TOTAL REVENUE ($000)	953,398
NET INCOME ($000)	26,536
EMPLOYEES	4,500

KUEHNE & NAGEL INTERNATIONAL LTD.
(Private)   TRANSPORTATION
6303 Airport Rd, Mississauga, ON, L4V 1S9   (905) 673-3981
KUEHNE & NAGEL INTERNATIONAL LTD. provides warehousing and transportation services. It is a wholly owned subsidiary of Kuehne & Nagel Holding of Quebec.
Gerd Stoppenbrink, President

TOTAL ASSETS ($000)	77,558
TOTAL REVENUE ($000)	644,409
NET INCOME ($000)	5,303
EMPLOYEES	na

KWG RESOURCES INC.
(Public)   PRECIOUS METALS
Exchanges: M Q   Stock Symbol: KWG
Suite 3200, 630 Rene-Levesque Blvd. West, Montreal, PQ,
H3B 1S6   (514) 866-6001
KWG RESOURCES INC. is involved in the acquisition, exploration and development of precious metal and diamond properties.

Pierre R. Gauthier, Chairman

TOTAL ASSETS ($000)	31,658
TOTAL REVENUE ($000)	9,016
NET INCOME ($000)	4,286
EMPLOYEES	0
RANK (Profit/Revenue/Assets)	447/813/758

LA TEKO RESOURCES LTD
(Public)   PRECIOUS METALS
Exchanges: V Q   Stock Symbol: LAO
180 East 2100 South, Suite 204, Salt Lake City, UT,
84115   (801) 466-1437
LA TEKO RESOURCES LTD. is involved in the acquisition, exploration and development of precious metal properties.
Jack Layne, President

TOTAL ASSETS ($000)	13,124 (US)
TOTAL REVENUE ($000)	10 (US)
NET INCOME ($000)	(1,326) (US)
EMPLOYEES	na
RANK (Profit/Revenue/Assets)	848/999/890

LAFARGE CANADA INC.
See page 581 for a full company profile.

LAIDLAW INC.
See page 522 for a full company profile.

LAMINCO RESOURCES INC.
(Public)   PRECIOUS METALS
Exchanges: T   Stock Symbol: LMR
SUITE 2380, 1055 West Hastings Street, Vancouver, BC,
V6E 2E9   (604) 684-6508
LAMINCO RESOURCES INC. is involved in the acquisition, exploration and development of mineral properties.
Kelsey L. Boltz, President & C.E.O.

TOTAL ASSETS ($000)	16,957
TOTAL REVENUE ($000)	139
NET INCOME ($000)	(820)
EMPLOYEES	25
RANK (Profit/Revenue/Assets)	812/985/915

LANTIC SUGAR LIMITED
(Private)   FOOD PROCESSING
1 Westmount Square, Westmount, PQ, H3Z 2P9   (514) 939-3939
LANTIC SUGAR LIMITED is engaged in refining and sales of sugar.
W.C. Brown, Chairman and C.E.O.

TOTAL ASSETS ($000)	252,923
TOTAL REVENUE ($000)	303,145
NET INCOME ($000)	36,911
EMPLOYEES	540

LASSONDE INDUSTRIES INC.
(Public)   FOOD PROCESSING
Exchanges: M   Stock Symbol: LAS.A
170 5e Avenue, Rougemont, PQ, J0L 1M0   (514) 878-1057
LASSONDE INDUSTRIES INC., through its subsidiaries, is engaged in the business of transforming, conditioning, packaging and marketing food products, consisting mainly of fruit juices and fruit beverages. It is

the largest apple juice manufacturer and distributor in Quebec and the Atlantic provinces.

Pierre-Paul Lassonde, Chairman

TOTAL ASSETS ($000)	82,477
TOTAL REVENUE ($000)	136,856
NET INCOME ($000)	6,972
EMPLOYEES	500
RANK (Profit/Revenue/Assets)	371/374/527

LATERAL VECTOR RESOURCES INC.
(Public)   OIL AND GAS PRODUCERS
Exchanges: T   Stock Symbol: LVR
Suite 120, 1230 Blackfoot Dr., Regina, SK, S4S 7G4 (306) 569-1700
LATERAL VECTOR RESOURCES INC. specializes in the redevelopment of oil properties, primarily through the process of horizontal re-entry development drilling.

Robert B. Knight, Chairman & C.E.O.

TOTAL ASSETS ($000)	16,889
TOTAL REVENUE ($000)	5,743
NET INCOME ($000)	1
EMPLOYEES	10
RANK (Profit/Revenue/Assets)	757/851/916

LAURENTIAN BANK OF CANADA
See page 450 for a full company profile.

LEBLANC & ROYLE ENTERPRISES INC.
(Private)   METAL FABRICATORS
514 Chartwell Road, Box 880, Oakville, ON, L6J 5C5 (905) 844-1242
LEBLANC & ROYLE ENTERPRISES INC. is a telecommunications equipment company.

TOTAL ASSETS ($000)	224,656
TOTAL REVENUE ($000)	235,354
NET INCOME ($000)	na
EMPLOYEES	na

LEDCOR INDUSTRIES LIMITED
(Private)   CONTRACTORS
1066 West Hastings Street, Suite 1000, Vancouver, BC, V6C 3X1   (604) 681-7500
LEDCOR INDUSTRIES LIMITED is a construction company.

David Lede, Chairman & C.E.O.

TOTAL ASSETS ($000)	na
TOTAL REVENUE ($000)	275,870
NET INCOME ($000)	na
EMPLOYEES	1,500

LEHNDORFF CANADIAN PROPERTIES
(Public)   PROPERTY MGMNT & INVESTMENT
Exchanges: T   Stock Symbol: LCP.UN
390 Bay Street, Suite 1900, Toronto, ON, M5H 2V6   (416) 869-7800
LEHNDORFF CANADIAN PROPERTIES is a real estate limited partnership established in 1979. It allows individual and institutional investors to participate on a limited liability basis in the ownership of a large and diversified portfolio of income-producing properties in Canada.

John Coleman, Chairman

TOTAL ASSETS ($000)	30,698
TOTAL REVENUE ($000)	3,273
NET INCOME ($000)	(642)

EMPLOYEES	0
RANK (Profit/Revenue/Assets)	802/894/767

LEITCH TECHNOLOGY CORPORATION
(Public)   ELECTRICAL & ELECTRONIC
Exchanges: T   Stock Symbol: LTV
220 Duncan Mill Road, Suite 301, North York, ON, M3B 3J5   (416) 445-9640
LEITCH TECHNOLOGY CORPORATION designs, manufactures and markets electronic equipment used to distribute, process and switch high quality video and audio signals required by television broadcast facilities and independent production or post-production studios.

Robert A. Lehtonen, President & C.E.O.

TOTAL ASSETS ($000)	30,770
TOTAL REVENUE ($000)	39,771
NET INCOME ($000)	6,368
EMPLOYEES	385
RANK (Profit/Revenue/Assets)	380/592/766

LEON'S FURNITURE LIMITED
See page 425 for a full company profile.

LEP INTERNATIONAL INC.
(Private)   TRANSPORTATION
401 The West Mall, 6th Flr., Etobicoke, ON, M9C 5J5 (416) 620-6570
LEP INTERNATIONAL INC. is an international freight forwarder and customs broker.

Peter Brown, C.E.O. & President

TOTAL ASSETS ($000)	26,178
TOTAL REVENUE ($000)	235,597
NET INCOME ($000)	2,673
EMPLOYEES	190

LESSARD, BEAUCAGE, LEMIEUX INC.
(Public)   CONTRACTORS
Exchanges: M   Stock Symbol: LBL
225 Montee de Liesse, St-Laurent, PQ, H4T 1P5   (514) 737-4533
LESSARD, BEAUCAGE, LEMIEUX INC. is a building contractor specializing in the manufacture and installation of windows, greenhouses, atria, curtain-walls and entrances for commercial and industrial buildings. It designs, assembles, manufactures and installs the glass covered portions of buildings.

Camille Lessard, President & C.E.O.

TOTAL ASSETS ($000)	13,419
TOTAL REVENUE ($000)	21,472
NET INCOME ($000)	(1,054)
EMPLOYEES	200
RANK (Profit/Revenue/Assets)	823/708/983

LGS GROUP INC.
(Public)   COMPUTER SOFTWARE & PROCESSING
Exchanges: M   Stock Symbol: LGS.A
1253 McGill College Avenue, Suite 1070, Montreal, PQ, H3B 2Y5   (514) 392-9193
LGS GROUP INC. provides information management consulting services. Its fields of activity include systems integration, data processing, office automation and related products.

Raymond Lafontaine, President

TOTAL ASSETS ($000)	23,255
TOTAL REVENUE ($000)	59,899

NET INCOME ($000)   (1,428)
EMPLOYEES   1,000
RANK (Profit/Revenue/Assets)   833/512/837

LIGNUM LIMITED
(Private)   WHOLESALE DISTRIBUTORS
1090 West Georgia St., Suite 1200, Vancouver, BC,
V6E 3V7   (604) 687-2425
LIGNUM LIMITED, is engaged in lumber manufacturing and wholesale lumber brokerage. Lignum is owned 100% by Leslie J. Kerr. Ltd.
John Kerr, Chairman & C.E.O.

TOTAL ASSETS ($000)	56,000
TOTAL REVENUE ($000)	140,000
NET INCOME ($000)	na
EMPLOYEES	286

LILYDALE CO-OPERATIVE LIMITED
(Non-fin Co-op)   AGRICULTURE
7727 - 127 Avenue, Edmonton, AB, T5C 1R9   (403) 476-6261
LILYDALE CO-OPERATIVE is an Alberta based cooperative designed to build and maintain a financially viable system of processing and marketing poultry products for Alberta and BC farmers. The company operates a processing division, a hatchery division, a farm division, a further-processing division and a table egg division.
T. Donkersgoed, Chairman

TOTAL ASSETS ($000)	82,351
TOTAL REVENUE ($000)	297,257
NET INCOME ($000)	3,245
EMPLOYEES	1,600

LINAMAR CORPORATION
See page 270 for a full company profile.

LIQUID CARBONIC INC.
(Private)   CHEMICALS
255 Brimley Rd, Scarborough, ON, M1M 3J2   (416) 266-3161
LIQUID CARBONIC INC. is a manufacturer of industrial & medical gases and electrodes. Liquid Carbonic is a wholly owned subsidiary of CBI Industries Inc. of the United States.
W.L. Wallace, Chairman

TOTAL ASSETS ($000)	306,840
TOTAL REVENUE ($000)	141,659
NET INCOME ($000)	1,878
EMPLOYEES	600

LIQUIDATION WORLD INC.
(Public)   SPECIALTY STORES
Exchanges: T   Stock Symbol: LQW
3900 - 29th Street N.E., Calgary, AB, T1Y 6B6   (403) 250-1222
LIQUIDATION WORLD INC. is a company specializing in marketing merchandise from distress situations, such as bankruptcies, receiverships, closeouts, inventory overruns and insurance claims. The retail outlets are located in Alberta, B.C., Ontario and Washington State.
Dale Gillespie, Chairman, President & C.E.O.

TOTAL ASSETS ($000)	13,223
TOTAL REVENUE ($000)	35,930
NET INCOME ($000)	1,113
EMPLOYEES	430
RANK (Profit/Revenue/Assets)	647/614/989

LITTON SYSTEMS CANADA LIMITED
(Private)   ELECTRICAL & ELECTRONIC
25 Cityview Drive, Rexdale, ON, M9W 5A7   (416) 249-1231
LITTON SYSTEMS CANADA LIMITED is a defence contractor providing electronic products and repair services as well as other goods and services.
Thomas J. McGuigan, President

TOTAL ASSETS ($000)	126,498
TOTAL REVENUE ($000)	136,145
NET INCOME ($000)	na
EMPLOYEES	na

LIVENT INC.
See page 582 for a full company profile.

LIVINGSTON GROUP INC.
(Private)   MANAGEMENT AND DIVERSIFIED
405 The West Mall, Etobicoke, ON, M9C 5K7   (416) 626-2828
LIVINGSTON GROUP INC. provides warehousing, distribution and customs brokerage services. Livingston Group is 91.1% owned by Ivest Corporation of London, Ontario.
R.M. Ivey, Chairman

TOTAL ASSETS ($000)	359,627
TOTAL REVENUE ($000)	170,197
NET INCOME ($000)	na
EMPLOYEES	2,500

LLOYD'S NON-MARINE UNDERWRITERS
(Private)   INSURANCE - PROPERTY & CASUALTY
1155 University, Suite 1400, Montreal, PQ, H3B 1S3   (514) 861-8361
LLOYD'S NON-MARINE UNDERWRITERS is a property and casualty insurer.
John David Rowland, Chairman of Lloyd's

TOTAL ASSETS ($000)	897,387
TOTAL REVENUE ($000)	533,142
NET INCOME ($000)	113,671
EMPLOYEES	90

LOBLAW COMPANIES LIMITED
See page 426 for a full company profile.

LOEB INC.
(Private)   FOOD STORES
400 Industrial Avenue, Ottawa, ON, K1G 3K8   (613) 737-1485
LOEB INC. operates a franchise network of 116 LOEB IGA, LOEB and IGA stores which are supplied through eight distribution centres. It also operates 22 cash and carry outlets that cater to corner stores and institutional customers. LOEB operates in Ontario and western and northwestern Quebec. The company is a wholly owned subsidiary of Provigo Inc.
W. Kipp, President

TOTAL ASSETS ($000)	627,700
TOTAL REVENUE ($000)	1,648,400
NET INCOME ($000)	(62,100)
EMPLOYEES	1,850

LOEWEN GROUP INC. (THE)
See page 583 for a full company profile.

LOF GLASS OF CANADA LTD.

(Private)   AUTOMOTIVE
Libby-Owens-Ford Company, P.O. Box 799, Toledo, OH,
43695   (419) 247-3731
Ronald W. Skeddle, President & C.E.O.

TOTAL ASSETS ($000)	137,997
TOTAL REVENUE ($000)	124,069
NET INCOME ($000)	2,390
EMPLOYEES	na

LOGISTEC CORPORATION

(Public)   TRANSPORTATION
Exchanges: T M   Stock Symbol: LGT.A
360 rue St-Jacques, bureau 1500, Montreal, PQ,
H2Y 1P5   (514) 844-9381
LOGISTEC CORPORATION and its subsidiaries provides specialized services to the marine community and industrial companies. Its services include: cargo-handling at various port terminals in Eastern Canada, the Great Lakes and the U.S. East Coast; agency services to foreign shipowners and operators calling Canadian ports; marine transportation services; and, on-site decontamination services.
Jacques Paquin, Chairman

TOTAL ASSETS ($000)	45,257
TOTAL REVENUE ($000)	74,187
NET INCOME ($000)	2,535
EMPLOYEES	na
RANK (Profit/Revenue/Assets)	537/468/657

LOKI GOLD CORP.

(Public)   PRECIOUS METALS
Exchanges: T   Stock Symbol: LKI
Suite 800, 900 West Hastings Street, Vancouver, BC,
V6C 1E5   (604) 684-8123
LOKI GOLD CORPORATION is involved in the acquisition, exploration and development of precious metal properties.
Ronald K. Netolitzky, President & C.E.O.

TOTAL ASSETS ($000)	13,680
TOTAL REVENUE ($000)	191
NET INCOME ($000)	(243)
EMPLOYEES	10
RANK (Profit/Revenue/Assets)	777/979/971

LONDON INSURANCE GROUP INC.

See page 502 for a full company profile.

LONDON LIFE INSURANCE COMPANY

(Private)   INSURANCE - LIFE
255 Dufferin Avenue, London, ON, N6A 4K1   (519) 432-5281
LONDON LIFE INSURANCE COMPANY offers life and annuity products to individuals. It also offers life, health and pension products to groups in Canada, and reinsurance.
Melvin M. Hawkrigg, Chairman

TOTAL ASSETS ($000)	13,972,000
TOTAL REVENUE ($000)	3,844,000
NET INCOME ($000)	96,000
EMPLOYEES	5,719

LOUIS DREYFUS CANADA LTD.

(Private)   WHOLESALE DISTRIBUTORS
810-360 Main St, The Commedity Exchange Tower, Winnipeg, MB,
R3C 3Z3   (204) 968-8610
LOUIS DREYFUS CANADA LTD. is a grain distribution company. It is a wholly owned subsidiary of Louis Dreyfus Corporation.

TOTAL ASSETS ($000)	59,751
TOTAL REVENUE ($000)	178,638
NET INCOME ($000)	3,484
EMPLOYEES	na

LSI LOGIC CORPORATION OF CANADA, INC.

(Public)   ELECTRICAL & ELECTRONIC
Exchanges: T M   Stock Symbol: LSC
Ste. 3410, 150 - 6th Ave. SW, Calgary, AB, T2P 3Y7   (403) 262-9292
LSI LOGIC CORPORATION OF CANADA markets application-specific circuits, customer-specific integrated circuits and application-specific standard products. LSI Logic's CoreWare methodology and leading-edge ASIC technology enables customers to build complete systems on a chip. LSI Logic applies these advanced technologies to fast-growing vertical markets such as digital video and networking.
Pierre Nadeau, President & C.E.O.

TOTAL ASSETS ($000)	55,968
TOTAL REVENUE ($000)	54,881
NET INCOME ($000)	10,792
EMPLOYEES	75
RANK (Profit/Revenue/Assets)	286/530/605

LYNX ENERGY SERVICES CORP.

(Public)   OIL AND GAS FIELD SERVICES
Exchanges: T M Z   Stock Symbol: LYX.A
Ste. 500, 622 - 5th Ave. SW, Calgary, AB, T2P 0M6   (403) 233-0888
LYNX ENERGY SERVICES CORP. is involved in the business of providing oilfield services.
J. Verne Lyons, Chairman & C.E.O.

TOTAL ASSETS ($000)	72,396
TOTAL REVENUE ($000)	78,896
NET INCOME ($000)	7,286
EMPLOYEES	5
RANK (Profit/Revenue/Assets)	359/457/556

LYTTON MINERALS LIMITED

See page 17 for a full company profile.

M-CORP INC.

(Public)   FOOD SERVICES
Exchanges: T M   Stock Symbol: MKI
Ste. 310, 8250 Decarie Blvd., Montreal, PQ, H4P 2P5 (514) 341-5544
M-CORP INC. is a full support franchise management company operating a network af 134 Mikes Restaurants, which feature Italian food with full table service in a family setting.
William M. Reim, President & C.E.O.

TOTAL ASSETS ($000)	34,100
TOTAL REVENUE ($000)	17,529
NET INCOME ($000)	2,388
EMPLOYEES	34
RANK (Profit/Revenue/Assets)	545/735/733

MAAX INC.
(Public)   MISC. CONSUMER PRODUCTS
Exchanges: T M   Stock Symbol: MXA
600 Route Cameron, Ste-Marie, PQ, G6E 1B2   (418) 387-3646
MAAX INC. designs, manufactures and markets fiberglass bathtubs,
showers, acrylic whirlpools, bathtubs, and showers and shower doors.
Placide Poulin, Chairman, President & C.E.O.

TOTAL ASSETS ($000)	35,870
TOTAL REVENUE ($000)	33,125
NET INCOME ($000)	3,759
EMPLOYEES	500
RANK (Profit/Revenue/Assets)	475/631/727

MABAIE INC.
(Public)   DEVELOPERS
Exchanges: M   Stock Symbol: MAB
Bureau 100, 1870 Boul. des Sources, Pointe-Claire, PQ,
H9R 5N4   (514) 694-0140
MABAIE INC. is a Montreal based real estate developer operating in
residential, commercial and industrial real estate.
Bernard Gervais, Chairman President & C.E.O.

TOTAL ASSETS ($000)	42,531
TOTAL REVENUE ($000)	10,062
NET INCOME ($000)	(219)
EMPLOYEES	999
RANK (Profit/Revenue/Assets)	774/803/678

MACDONALD, DETTWILER AND ASSOCIATES LTD.
(Public)   CONSULTING
Exchanges: T V   Stock Symbol: MDA
13800 Commerce Parkway, Richmond, BC, V6V 2J3(411) 278-0140
MACDONALD, DETTWILER AND ASSOCIATES LTD. is a sys-
tems engineering company engaged in the business of designing, developing and integrating sophisticated computer-based systems for the earth
observation, resource management, aviation communications, space and
defence markets.
John S. MacDonald, Chairman

TOTAL ASSETS ($000)	63,132
TOTAL REVENUE ($000)	0
NET INCOME ($000)	0
EMPLOYEES	na
RANK (Profit/Revenue/Assets)	503/420/583

MACKENZIE FINANCIAL CORPORATION
See page 476 for a full company profile.

MACLEAN HUNTER LIMITED
(Private)   PUBLISHING & PRINTING
Maclean Hunter Bldg., 777 Bay Street, Toronto, ON,
M5W 1A7   (416) 596-5000
MACLEAN HUNTER LTD. is a diversified communications company
with operations in Canada, the United States and Europe. The company
is involved in the publishing of periodicals and newspapers, business
forms and commercial printing, radio broadcasting, cable television and
communications services. The company owns a 62% interest in Toronto
Sun Publishing Corp.
Donald G. , Chairman

TOTAL ASSETS ($000)	1,805,200
TOTAL REVENUE ($000)	1,759,400

NET INCOME ($000)	56,600
EMPLOYEES	12,381

MACMILLAN BLOEDEL LIMITED
See page 163 for a full company profile.

MACYRO GROUP INC. (THE)
(Public)   CONTRACTORS
Exchanges: M   Stock Symbol: MYO
6140 Boul. Ste-Anne, L'Ange-Gardien, PQ, G0A 2K0 (418) 822-0283
THE MACYRO GROUP INC. specializes in the construction of industrial and commercial type buildings through its subsidiary Rocois Construction Inc. Through other subsidiaries, it manufactures and installs
windows and curtain walls used in industrial and commercial construction, and doors and windows for the residential sector.
Roland LeFrancois, Chairman

TOTAL ASSETS ($000)	48,284
TOTAL REVENUE ($000)	29,646
NET INCOME ($000)	(755)
EMPLOYEES	na
RANK (Profit/Revenue/Assets)	810/651/641

MAGNA INTERNATIONAL INC.
See page 218 for a full company profile.

MAJESTIC INC.
(Private)   CONTRACTORS
P.O. Box 4947, Edmonton, AB, T6E 5G8   (403) 955-7167
MAJESTIC INC. is a cross-country pipeline contractor. The company
has been involved in major pipeline systems in Canada and the United
States, and has expertise in arctic construction. The company has also
completed projects in India, the Middle East and Malaysia. In May 1992,
the company sold its 45% interest in Monenco Group Ltd. of Montreal,
a consulting engineering company.
A.J. Cressey, Chairman of the Board

TOTAL ASSETS ($000)	77,455
TOTAL REVENUE ($000)	182,203
NET INCOME ($000)	12,766
EMPLOYEES	na

MAJOR DRILLING GROUP INTERNATIONAL INC.
(Public)   CONSULTING
Exchanges: T   Stock Symbol: MDI
1776 Elmwood Drive, R.R. #4 D-291, Moncton, NB,
E1C 8J8   (506) 857-8636
MAJOR DRILLING GROUP INTERNATIONAL INC. is involved in
mineral exploration drilling for mining and mineral exploration compa-
nies, environmental drilling for government agencies and private sector
customers, and construction drilling.
Ronald J. Goguen, President & C.E.O.

TOTAL ASSETS ($000)	22,866
TOTAL REVENUE ($000)	0
NET INCOME ($000)	0
EMPLOYEES	na
RANK (Profit/Revenue/Assets)	552/611/842

MALETTE INC.
See page 164 for a full company profile.

MALETTE QUEBEC INC.
See page 165 for a full company profile.

MALOFILM COMMUNICATIONS INC.
(Public)   ENTERTAINMENT SERVICES
Exchanges: T M   Stock Symbol: MFM
Suite 650, 3575 St. Laurent Blvd., Montreal, PQ,
H2X 2T7   (514) 844-4555
MALOFILM COMMUNICATIONS INC. is a distributor and producer of filmed entertainment.
Rene Malo, Chairman, President & C.E.O.

TOTAL ASSETS ($000)	18,360
TOTAL REVENUE ($000)	31,057
NET INCOME ($000)	1,907
EMPLOYEES	52
RANK (Profit/Revenue/Assets)	578/646/892

MANITOBA HYDRO-ELECTRIC BOARD (THE)
(Crown)   ELECTRICAL UTILITIES
PO Box 815, 820 Taylor Ave., Winnipeg, MB,
R3C 2P4   (204) 474-3311
THE MANITOBA HYDRO-ELECTRIC BOARD is a Manitoba crown corporation responsible for the generation, transmission and distribution of electricity to consumers throughout the province, except for the central portion of the City of Winnipeg.
J.S. (John) McCallum, Chairman

TOTAL ASSETS ($000)	5,928,500
TOTAL REVENUE ($000)	985,400
NET INCOME ($000)	69,500
EMPLOYEES	4,044

MANITOBA POOL ELEVATORS
(Non-fin Co-op)   AGRICULTURE
Royal Bank Building, 220 Portage Avenue, P.O. Box 9800,
Winnipeg, MB, R3C 3K7   (204) 947-1171
MANITOBA POOL ELEVATORS is a producer-owned cooperative. Departments include country operations, terminals, agri-sales and service. The Pool has 120 active locals and seven associations operating on behalf of 18,000 members.
C.H. Swanson, Chairman & President

TOTAL ASSETS ($000)	270,378
TOTAL REVENUE ($000)	163,431
NET INCOME ($000)	9,165
EMPLOYEES	781

MANITOBA PUBLIC INSURANCE CORPORATION (THE)
(Crown)   INSURANCE - PROPERTY & CASUALTY
Box 6300- 9th Floor, 330 Graham Avenue, Winnipeg, MB,
R3C 4A4   (204) 985-7000
MANITOBA PUBLIC INSURANCE CORPORATION conducts a comprehensive automobile program.
Ruth M. Konzelman, Chairperson

TOTAL ASSETS ($000)	846,499
TOTAL REVENUE ($000)	464,594
NET INCOME ($000)	8,266
EMPLOYEES	1,225

MANITOBA TELEPHONE SYSTEM (THE)
(Crown)   TELEPHONE UTILITIES
489 Empress Street, P.O. Box 6666, Winnipeg, MB,
R3C 3V6   (204) 941-7314
THE MANITOBA TELEPHONE SYSTEM is a provincially owned crown corporation that provides telecommunications services to residences and businesses in Manitoba.
Tom Stefanson, Chairman

TOTAL ASSETS ($000)	1,497,597
TOTAL REVENUE ($000)	551,264
NET INCOME ($000)	14,365
EMPLOYEES	4,257

MANNVILLE OIL & GAS LTD.
See page 110 for a full company profile.

MANUFACTURERS LIFE INSURANCE COMPANY (THE)
(Private)   INSURANCE - LIFE
200 Bloor Street East, Toronto, ON, M4W 1E5   (416) 926-0100
MANULIFE FINANCIAL is one of Canada's largest life insurance companies with total assets of $40.2-billion. The company offers a variety of insurance and investment products to individuals, families and businesses. Products include life and health insurance, immediate and deferred annuities, pension and retirement products, savings and investment instruments, personal loans, and residential mortgages.
William Blundell, Chairman

TOTAL ASSETS ($000)	40,227,183
TOTAL REVENUE ($000)	8,142,710
NET INCOME ($000)	280,854
EMPLOYEES	7,045

MAPLE LEAF FOODS INC.
See page 193 for a full company profile.

MAPLE LEAF GARDENS, LIMITED
(Public)   ENTERTAINMENT SERVICES
Exchanges: T   Stock Symbol: ML
60 Carlton Street, Toronto, ON, M5B 1L1   (416) 977-1641
MAPLE LEAF GARDENS, LIMITED operates in the entertainment industry. Besides being the home of the Toronto Maple Leafs Hockey Club, the Gardens hosts many other entertainment events.
Steve Stavro, Chairman & C.E.O.

TOTAL ASSETS ($000)	30,323
TOTAL REVENUE ($000)	66,656
NET INCOME ($000)	6,211
EMPLOYEES	650
RANK (Profit/Revenue/Assets)	404/503/771

MAPLE LODGE FARMS LTD.
(Private)   FOOD PROCESSING
R.R. 2, Norval, ON, L0P 1K0   (905) 455-8340
MAPLE LODGE FARMS is a poultry processor and manufacturer of wiener and deli products.
Robert May, C.E.O.

TOTAL ASSETS ($000)	na
TOTAL REVENUE ($000)	242,958
NET INCOME ($000)	na
EMPLOYEES	1,400

MARATHON REALTY HOLDINGS INC.
(Private)   DEVELOPERS
Suite 400, 200 Wellington Street West, Toronto, ON,
M5V 3C7   (416) 348-1500
MARATHON REALTY COMPANY LIMITED is a Canadian company which develops, owns and manages income-producing properties across Canada and the United States. Marathon's portfolio includes shopping centres and office buildings; industrial parks; and commercial and agricultural lands. Marathon is a wholly owned subsidiary of Canadian Pacific Ltd.
R.K. Garney, Chairman

TOTAL ASSETS ($000)	3,190,597
TOTAL REVENUE ($000)	521,902
NET INCOME ($000)	29,281
EMPLOYEES	900

MARINE ATLANTIC INC.
(Crown)   TRANSPORTATION
100 Cameron Street, Moncton, NB, E1C 5Y6   (506) 851-3600
MARINE ATLANTIC INC. is a federal crown corporation. Its primary business is the operation of the principle ferry services to the Atlantic provinces, under contract to Transport Canada.
A.K. Scales, Chairman of the Board

TOTAL ASSETS ($000)	403,129
TOTAL REVENUE ($000)	234,388
NET INCOME ($000)	(305)
EMPLOYEES	2,700

MARITIME LIFE ASSURANCE COMPANY
(Public)   INSURANCE - LIFE
Exchanges: T   Stock Symbol: MMF.PR.A
2701 Dutch Village Road, P.O. Box 1030, Halifax, NS,
B3J 2X5   (902) 453-4300
MARITIME LIFE ASSURANCE COMPANY is involved in the life insurance industry, providing a wide range of life insurance and annuities on an individual basis, as well as life insurance, health and annuity products on a group basis across Canada.
John Lindsay, Chairman

TOTAL ASSETS ($000)	2,676,302
TOTAL REVENUE ($000)	669,945
NET INCOME ($000)	20,878
EMPLOYEES	680
RANK (Profit/Revenue/Assets)	209/158/83

MARITIME TEL & TEL LIMITED
(Private)   TELEPHONE UTILITIES
1505 Barrington Street, P.O. Box 880 Stn Central RPO, Halifax, NS,
B3J 2W3   (902) 487-4311
MARITIME TEL & TEL LIMITED is the operating subsidiary of Maritime Telegraph and Telephone Company, Limited.

TOTAL ASSETS ($000)	1,309,935
TOTAL REVENUE ($000)	na
NET INCOME ($000)	na
EMPLOYEES	3,600

MARITIME TELEGRAPH AND TELEPHONE COMPANY, LIMITED
See page 354 for a full company profile.

MARK RESOURCES INC.
See page 111 for a full company profile.

MARK'S WORK WEARHOUSE LTD.
(Public)   CLOTHING STORES
Exchanges: T   Stock Symbol: MWW
Ste. 30, 1035 - 64th Ave. SE, Calgary, AB, T2H 2J7   (403) 255-9220
MARK'S WORK WEARHOUSE LTD. operates a chain of retail stores in Canada which cater to the workwear sector and to the casual wear sector of the market. The company's sales are comprised of three broad commodity groupings; work wear, jeans and casual wear.
Marcus W. Blumes, Chairman & C.E.O.

TOTAL ASSETS ($000)	56,395
TOTAL REVENUE ($000)	161,637
NET INCOME ($000)	1,266
EMPLOYEES	1,419
RANK (Profit/Revenue/Assets)	632/347/604

MARKBOROUGH PROPERTIES INC.
See page 311 for a full company profile.

MARLEAU, LEMIRE INC.
See page 477 for a full company profile.

MARSHALL MINERALS CORP
(Public)   PRECIOUS METALS
Exchanges: T Z   Stock Symbol: MAH
4776 Bridge St., Box 356, Niagara Falls, ON,
L2E 6T8   (905) 356-9112
MARSHALL MINERALS CORP. is involved in the exploration and development of resource properties.
Harry G. Quint, Chairman, C.E.O. & Secretary

TOTAL ASSETS ($000)	54,208
TOTAL REVENUE ($000)	11,328
NET INCOME ($000)	(2,211)
EMPLOYEES	na
RANK (Profit/Revenue/Assets)	862/786/613

MARSHALL STEEL LIMITED
See page 405 for a full company profile.

MARUBENI CANADA LTD.
(Private)   WHOLESALE DISTRIBUTORS
Canada Trust Tower BCE Place, Suite 2300, 161 Bay Street,
Toronto, ON, M5J 2S1   (416) 368-1171
MARUBENI CANADA is a trading and wholesaling company.
Masaru Mizuno, Chairman

TOTAL ASSETS ($000)	44,232
TOTAL REVENUE ($000)	1,113,439
NET INCOME ($000)	(915)
EMPLOYEES	55

MATCO RAVARY INC.
(Public)   SPECIALTY STORES
Exchanges: M   Stock Symbol: MCO
355 Sir Wilfrid Laurier Blvd., St-Basile-le-Grand, PQ,
J3N 1M9   (514) 653-7861
MATCO RAVARY INC. sells home construction and renovation supplies through its seven distribution outlets on Montreal's south shore. It

carries some 30,000 products aimed at three customer groups: building contractors; handymen; and institutions. The company is part of Le Groupe RO-NA Inc., a purchasing and services group formed by independant retailers.

Carmel Chaput, Chairman & C.E.O.

TOTAL ASSETS ($000)	32,997
TOTAL REVENUE ($000)	56,003
NET INCOME ($000)	(610)
EMPLOYEES	520
RANK (Profit/Revenue/Assets)	798/526/747

MATSUSHITA ELECTRIC OF CANADA LIMITED
(Private)   WHOLESALE DISTRIBUTORS
5770 Ambler Drive, Mississauga, ON, L4W 2T2   (905) 624-5010
MATSUSHITA ELECTRIC OF CANADA LIMITED is a distributor of electrical goods.

Syunzo Ushimaru, President

TOTAL ASSETS ($000)	139,002
TOTAL REVENUE ($000)	504,276
NET INCOME ($000)	7,301
EMPLOYEES	na

MAXWELL ENERGY CORPORATION
(Public)   OIL AND GAS PRODUCERS
Exchanges: V   Stock Symbol: MXN
Suite 3100, First Canadian Centre, 350 - 7th Avenue S.W., Calgary, AB, T2P 3N9   (403) 232-2232
MAXWELL ENERGY CORPORATION is involved in the acquisition, exploration and development of oil and natural gas properties in Western Canada.

Ted Konji, Chairman of the Board

TOTAL ASSETS ($000)	19,595
TOTAL REVENUE ($000)	6,000
NET INCOME ($000)	(473)
EMPLOYEES	25
RANK (Profit/Revenue/Assets)	792/844/876

MAXX PETROLEUM LTD.
(Public)   OIL AND GAS PRODUCERS
Exchanges: T   Stock Symbol: MXP
Ste. 1000, 112 - 4th Ave. SW, Calgary, AB, T2P 0H3 (403) 261-6666
MAXX PETROLEUM LTD. is engaged in oil and gas exploration and development in southern Alberta and southern Saskatchewan.

Burl N. Aycock, President & C.E.O.

TOTAL ASSETS ($000)	71,213
TOTAL REVENUE ($000)	26,269
NET INCOME ($000)	4,260
EMPLOYEES	36
RANK (Profit/Revenue/Assets)	450/668/560

MAYNE NICKLESS CANADA INC.
(Private)   TRANSPORTATION
1290 Hornby St., Ste. 300, Vancouver, BC, V6Z 2G4 (604) 665-4700
MAYNE NICKLESS CANADA INC. supplies armoured car/ABM services, courier small parcel air & road transport services, messenger services, and guard and patrol services. The company's parent is Mayne Nickless Limited, Melbourne, Australia.

W.T. Bytheway, Chairman

TOTAL ASSETS ($000)	79,096
TOTAL REVENUE ($000)	332,621

NET INCOME ($000)	2,256
EMPLOYEES	7,300

MAZARIN MINING CORPORATION INC.
(Public)   METAL MINES
Exchanges: M   Stock Symbol: MAZ
116 St. Pierre Street, Quebec, PQ, G1K 4A7   (418) 694-1123
MAZARIN MINING CORPORATION INC. is involved in the acquisition, exploration and development of mineral properties.

Michel Cyr, Chairman

TOTAL ASSETS ($000)	54,804
TOTAL REVENUE ($000)	14,687
NET INCOME ($000)	8,601
EMPLOYEES	10
RANK (Profit/Revenue/Assets)	320/761/611

MCCAIN FOODS LIMITED
(Private)   FOOD PROCESSING
Main Street, Florenceville, NB, E0J 1K0   (506) 392-5541
MCCAIN FOODS LIMITED is a privately owned Canadian multinational food processor.

H.Harrision McCain, Chairman

TOTAL ASSETS ($000)	1,769,157
TOTAL REVENUE ($000)	3,001,750
NET INCOME ($000)	na
EMPLOYEES	12,000

MCDONALD'S RESTAURANTS OF CANADA LTD
(Private)   FOOD SERVICES
McDonald's Place, Toronto, ON, M3C 3L4   (416) 443-1000
MCDONALD'S RESTAURANTS OF CANADA LIMITED and its affiliates operate or license and service a system of quick service restaurants. McDonald's restaurants are located in all provinces of Canada and in the Yukon and Northwest Territories of Canada.

George A. Cohon, Senior Chairman

TOTAL ASSETS ($000)	858,793
TOTAL REVENUE ($000)	1,621,927
NET INCOME ($000)	na
EMPLOYEES	60,000

MCDONNELL DOUGLAS CANADA LTD.
(Private)   TRANSPORTATION EQUIP & COMPNTS
P.O. Box 6013, Toronto A.M.F., Toronto, ON, L5P 1B7   (905) 677-4341
MCDONNELL DOUGLAS CANADA LTD. manufacturers major components for both commercial and military jet aircraft. The company is wholly owned by McDonnell Douglas Corporation.

Leslie Gordon, President

TOTAL ASSETS ($000)	197,000
TOTAL REVENUE ($000)	223,000
NET INCOME ($000)	5,000
EMPLOYEES	1,700

MCGRAW-HILL RYERSON LIMITED
(Public)   PUBLISHING & PRINTING
Exchanges: T M   Stock Symbol: MHR
300 Water Street, Whitby, ON, L1N 9B6   (905) 428-2222
MCGRAW-HILL RYERSON LIMITED operates exclusively as a publisher and distributor of general books, educational, professional, and technical reference materials and multi-media products.

E. Jacques Courtois, Chairman of the Board

TOTAL ASSETS ($000)	50,842
TOTAL REVENUE ($000)	38,281
NET INCOME ($000)	(7,318)
EMPLOYEES	173
RANK (Profit/Revenue/Assets)	928/602/628

MDC CORPORATION

(Public) CONSULTING
Exchanges: T Stock Symbol: MDZ.A
45 Hazelton Avenue, Toronto, ON, M5R 2E3 (416) 960-9000
MDC CORPORATION, through its subsidiaries, conducts business in the three divisions: Marketing and Communications Services; Security and Specialty Printing; and Catalogue and Direct Marketing.
Miles S. Nadal, Chairman, C.E.O. & President

TOTAL ASSETS ($000)	123,373
TOTAL REVENUE ($000)	69,770
NET INCOME ($000)	4,317
EMPLOYEES	1,150
RANK (Profit/Revenue/Assets)	445/481/440

MDS HEALTH GROUP LIMITED
See page 584 for a full company profile.

MEDIS HEALTH AND PHARMACEUTICAL SERVICES INC.

(Private) WHOLESALE DISTRIBUTORS
3501 St. Charles Boulevard, Suite 101, Kirkland, PQ, H9H 4S3 (514) 694-2100
MEDIS HEALTH AND PHARMACEUTICAL SERVICES INC. is engaged in the distribution of pharmaceutical products, health and beauty aids, sundries and other types of drugstore merchandise to over 4,800 pharmacy customers across Canada. Medis serves all Canadian provinces from 15 distribution centres.
Claudio F. Bussandri, President & C.E.O.

TOTAL ASSETS ($000)	353,434
TOTAL REVENUE ($000)	1,852,486
NET INCOME ($000)	na
EMPLOYEES	1,220

MELCOR DEVELOPMENTS LTD.
See page 312 for a full company profile.

MEMOTEC COMMUNICATIONS INC.

(Public) ELECTRICAL & ELECTRONIC
Exchanges: T M Stock Symbol: MCM
600 McCaffrey Street, Ville St-Laurent, PQ, H4T 1N1 (514) 738-4781
MEMOTEC COMMUNICATIONS INC. develops, manufactures and markets a wide range of products in the communication networking industry to telephone companies, network end-users and value-added systems integrators.
Dennis Wood, Chairman of the Board

TOTAL ASSETS ($000)	50,797
TOTAL REVENUE ($000)	61,748
NET INCOME ($000)	745
EMPLOYEES	340
RANK (Profit/Revenue/Assets)	673/501/629

MENTOR EXPLORATION AND DEVELOPMENT CO., LIMITED

(Public) PRECIOUS METALS
Exchanges: T Stock Symbol: MV
401 Bay Street, Suite 2302, P.O. Box 102, Toronto, ON, M5H 2Y4 (416) 947-1212
MENTOR EXPLORATION AND DEVELOPMENT CO., LIMITED conducts precious metal exploration and holds investments in precious metals companies.
Paul Penna, President

TOTAL ASSETS ($000)	29,475
TOTAL REVENUE ($000)	962
NET INCOME ($000)	(1,040)
EMPLOYEES	3
RANK (Profit/Revenue/Assets)	821/947/776

MERCEDES-BENZ CANADA INC.

(Private) WHOLESALE DISTRIBUTORS
849 Eglinton Avenue East, Toronto, ON, M4G 2L5 (416) 425-3550
MERCEDES-BENZ CANADA is a wholesaler of Mercedes-Benz automobiles. The company is wholly owned by Daimler-Benz North America Holding Corp.
S. Paul Halata, President

TOTAL ASSETS ($000)	112,053
TOTAL REVENUE ($000)	339,069
NET INCOME ($000)	na
EMPLOYEES	337

MERCHANT PRIVATE LIMITED
See page 478 for a full company profile.

MERFIN HYGIENIC PRODUCTS LTD.

(Public) MISC. INDUSTRIAL PRODUCTS
Exchanges: T Stock Symbol: MIP
7979 Vantage Way, Delta, BC, V4G 1A6 (604) 946-0677
MERFIN HYGIENIC PRODUCTS is one of the leading manufacturers in North America of air-laid paper products both in converted form and parent rolls. These products are used on a global basis for industrial wipes, premoistened wipes such as hot towels, baby wipes and household wiping products, absorbent cores in adult incontinence and feminine hygiene products.
Ivan B. Pivko, President & C.E.O.

TOTAL ASSETS ($000)	70,677
TOTAL REVENUE ($000)	46,902
NET INCOME ($000)	4,648
EMPLOYEES	153
RANK (Profit/Revenue/Assets)	434/562/563

MERIDIAN TECHNOLOGIES INC.
See page 219 for a full company profile.

METHANEX CORPORATION
See page 287 for a full company profile.

METRO-RICHELIEU INC.
See page 427 for a full company profile.

MFP TECHNOLOGY SERVICES LTD.
See page 479 for a full company profile.

MICC INVESTMENTS LIMITED
See page 503 for a full company profile.

MIDLAND WALWYN INC.
See page 480 for a full company profile.

MILES CANADA INC.
(Private)   CHEMICALS
77 Belfield Rd, Rexdale, ON, M9W 1G6   (416) 248-0771
MILES CANADA INC. is a manufacturer and distributor of health care products. It is a wholly owned subsidiary of Miles Inc. of the United States.
W.C. Garriock, President

TOTAL ASSETS ($000)	245,116
TOTAL REVENUE ($000)	630,023
NET INCOME ($000)	18,205
EMPLOYEES	na

MILLTRONICS LTD.
(Public)   MISC. INDUSTRIAL PRODUCTS
Exchanges: T   Stock Symbol: MLS
730 The Kingsway, P.O. Box 4225, Peterborough, ON,
K9J 7B1   (705) 745-2431
MILLTRONICS LTD. specializes in the design, manufacture, sale and support of sophisticated and reliable measuring equipment for a wide range of primary and secondary industrial uses.
Alan E. Gillis, Chairman, President & C.E.O.

TOTAL ASSETS ($000)	56,589
TOTAL REVENUE ($000)	77,477
NET INCOME ($000)	8,203
EMPLOYEES	na
RANK (Profit/Revenue/Assets)	329/461/602

MINERA RAYROCK INC.
See page 18 for a full company profile.

MINORCO CANADA LIMITED
(Public)   INTEGRATED MINES
Exchanges: T M   Stock Symbol: MRC.PR.B
Suite 720, 70 York Street, Toronto, ON, M5J 1S9   (416) 601-9550
MINORCO CANADA LIMITED, also known as Mincan, jointly owns Mingold Resources Inc. with Inspiration Resources Corporation.
G.E. Munera, Chairman & President

TOTAL ASSETS ($000)	30,239
TOTAL REVENUE ($000)	2,121
NET INCOME ($000)	2,022
EMPLOYEES	na
RANK (Profit/Revenue/Assets)	567/917/772

MIRAMAR MINING CORPORATION
See page 49 for a full company profile.

MITEL CORPORATION
See page 382 for a full company profile.

MITSUBISHI CANADA LIMITED
(Private)   WHOLESALE DISTRIBUTORS
P.O. Box 17, Commerce Court Postal Station, Suite 5101
Commerce Court West, Toronto, ON, M5L 1A5   (416) 362-6731
MITSUBISHI CANADA LIMITED is a wholly owned subsidiary of Mitsubishi Corp. of Japan. Mitsubishi Canada Ltd. engages in import and export trading business, including steel, machinery, metals, food, textiles, chemicals, lumber and general merchandise.
T. Miyoshi, President & C.E.O.

TOTAL ASSETS ($000)	132,261
TOTAL REVENUE ($000)	1,430,698
NET INCOME ($000)	3,872
EMPLOYEES	113

MITSUBISHI ELECTRIC SALES CANADA INC.
(Private)   ELECTRICAL & ELECTRONIC
4299 - 14th Avenue, Markham, ON, L3R 0J2   (905) 475-7728
MITSUBISHI ELECTRIC SALES CANADA INC. is a distributor of electronic components, equipment and consumer electronics and a manufacturer of colour television sets. The company is a wholly owned subsidiary of Mitsubishi Electric Corporation of Japan.
E. Nishibori, President & C.E.O.

TOTAL ASSETS ($000)	na
TOTAL REVENUE ($000)	194,948
NET INCOME ($000)	na
EMPLOYEES	220

MITSUI & CO. (CANADA) LTD.
(Private)   WHOLESALE DISTRIBUTORS
20 Adelaide St. E., Ste. 1500, Toronto, ON, M5C 2T6 (416) 947-3899
MITSUI & CO. (CANADA) LTD. is an importer and exporter of steel, non-ferous metals, machinery, chemical, foodstuff, wood products and sundry items. The company is wholly owned by Mitsui & Co., Ltd. of Japan.
Shinji Teshima, President & C.E.O.

TOTAL ASSETS ($000)	285,194
TOTAL REVENUE ($000)	2,801,959
NET INCOME ($000)	4,328
EMPLOYEES	120

MNT LTD.
(Public)   INVESTMENT COMPANIES AND FUNDS
Exchanges: T   Stock Symbol: XMN
1 First Canadian Place, Suite 5000, Toronto, ON,
M5X 1H3   (416) 813-4600
MNT LTD. invests its funds in The Bank of Montreal common shares. The net proceeds from the issue of the Capital Shares and the Equity Dividend Shares offered hereby will be used by the company to satisfy obligations relating to the purchase of BMO common shares, such that there will be one Capital Share and one Equity Dividend Share for each BMO common share purchased.
Michael M. Armstrong, President & C.E.O.

TOTAL ASSETS ($000)	85,648
TOTAL REVENUE ($000)	6,022
NET INCOME ($000)	5,952
EMPLOYEES	na
RANK (Profit/Revenue/Assets)	396/843/519

MOBIL OIL CANADA, LTD.
(Private)   OIL AND GAS PRODUCERS
P.O. Box 800, Calgary, AB, T2P 2J7   (403) 260-7910
MOBIL OIL CANADA, LTD. is engaged in exploration for and production of oil and gas. The company is wholly owned by Mobil Investments Canada Inc.
Ron Billings, President
TOTAL ASSETS ($000)   2,608,109
TOTAL REVENUE ($000)   2,124,197
NET INCOME ($000)   37,976
EMPLOYEES   na

MOFFAT COMMUNICATIONS LIMITED
See page 383 for a full company profile.

MOHAWK OIL CANADA LIMITED
(Private)   OIL AND GAS PRODUCERS
Ste. 325, 6400 Roberts St., Burnaby, BC, V5G 4G2   (604) 293-4114
MOHAWK OIL CANADA LIMITED is involved in retailing alternative automotive fuels in Canada. The company offers environmentally responsible products, including ethanol-blended gasolines which are higher octane, cleaner burning fuels than conventional gasolines.
D. Skagan, Chairman
TOTAL ASSETS ($000)   104,150
TOTAL REVENUE ($000)   308,525
NET INCOME ($000)   6,335
EMPLOYEES   240

MOLSON COMPANIES LIMITED (THE)
See page 194 for a full company profile.

MONARCH DEVELOPMENT CORPORATION
See page 313 for a full company profile.

MONSANTO CANADA INC.
(Private)   CHEMICALS
P.O Box 787, Streetsville P.O., 2330 Argentia Road, Mississauga, ON, L5M 2G4   (905) 826-9222
MONSANTO CANADA INC. is a manufacturer of industrial and agricultural chemicals, pharmaceuticals and process control equipment. Monsanto is wholly owned by Monsanto Company of St. Louis, Missouri.
W.A. Dimma, Chairman
TOTAL ASSETS ($000)   148,412
TOTAL REVENUE ($000)   384,660
NET INCOME ($000)   11,061
EMPLOYEES   750

MONT SAINT-SAUVEUR INTERNATIONAL INC.
(Public)   ENTERTAINMENT SERVICES
Exchanges: M   Stock Symbol: MSX.A
350 St-Denis Street, St-Sauveur-des-Monts, PQ, J0R 1R3   (514) 227-4671
MONT SAINT-SAUVEUR INTERNAIONAL INC. operates six ski centres, five in Quebec and one in Vermont, a summer water recreation complex, and is involved in construction, sale and rental of housing units in the form of condominiums, townhouses and single family units.

Jacques G. Hebert, Chairman President & C.E.O.
TOTAL ASSETS ($000)   48,761
TOTAL REVENUE ($000)   29,448
NET INCOME ($000)   195
EMPLOYEES   1,600
RANK (Profit/Revenue/Assets)   737/652/636

MONTREAL PORT CORPORATION
(Crown)   TRANSPORTATION
Port of Montreal Building, Wing No. 1, Cite du Havre, Montreal, PQ, H3C 3R5   (514) 283-7050
MONTREAL PORT CORPORATION is involved in the administration of the Port of Montreal.
Andre Gingras, Chairman of the Board
TOTAL ASSETS ($000)   235,363
TOTAL REVENUE ($000)   61,536
NET INCOME ($000)   8,677
EMPLOYEES   378

MONTREAL TRUSTCO INC.
See page 451 for a full company profile.

MOORE CORPORATION LIMITED
See page 585 for a full company profile.

MORDEN & HELWIG GROUP INC.
(Public)   OTHER SERVICES
Exchanges: T   Stock Symbol: MGH
155 University Ave., Ste. 600, Toronto, ON, M5H 3N5 (416) 362-6762
MORDEN & HELWIG GROUP INC. is an independent insurance holding company. Through its subsidiaries it provides claim adjusting, appraisal, and loss management services to insurance companies and self-insured organizations across Canada, the United States, and the United Kingdom.
V. Prem Watsa, Chairman of the Board
TOTAL ASSETS ($000)   95,907
TOTAL REVENUE ($000)   156,092
NET INCOME ($000)   1,037
EMPLOYEES   1,800
RANK (Profit/Revenue/Assets)   653/351/494

MORGAN FINANCIAL CORPORATION
(Public)   INSURANCE - LIFE
Exchanges: T   Stock Symbol: MFT
Ste. 301, 404 - 6th Ave. S., Calgary, AB, T2P 0R9   (403) 265-5937
MORGAN FINANCIAL is a life insurance holding company. It owns 100% of Westbury Canadian Life Insurance Company of Hamilton, Ontario.
J. Rob Collins, Chairman & C.E.O.
TOTAL ASSETS ($000)   303,252
TOTAL REVENUE ($000)   99,315
NET INCOME ($000)   5,475
EMPLOYEES   2
RANK (Profit/Revenue/Assets)   410/422/284

MORGAN HYDROCARBONS INC.
See page 112 for a full company profile.

MORRISON MIDDLEFIELD RESOURCES LIMITED

(Public)   OIL AND GAS PRODUCERS
Exchanges: T   Stock Symbol: MM
1 First Canadian Place, 58th Floor, P.O. Box 192, Toronto, ON,
M5X 1A6   (416) 362-0714
MORRISON MIDDLEFIELD RESOURCES LIMITED is involved in
the acquisition, exploration and development of oil and gas properties.
A. Gordon Stollery, Chairman & C.E.O.

TOTAL ASSETS ($000)	40,326
TOTAL REVENUE ($000)	7,923
NET INCOME ($000)	430
EMPLOYEES	10
RANK (Profit/Revenue/Assets)	705/822/694

MORRISON PETROLEUMS LTD.

See page 113 for a full company profile.

MOSAID TECHNOLOGIES INCORPORATED

(Public)   ELECTRICAL & ELECTRONIC
Exchanges: T   Stock Symbol: MSD
2171 McGee Side Road, Carp, ON, K0A 1L0   (613) 836-3134
MOSAID TECHNOLOGIES INCORPORATED designs advanced
memory chips and designs, manufactures and distributes engineering test
systems for memory chips.
Richard C. Foss, Chairman

TOTAL ASSETS ($000)	25,645
TOTAL REVENUE ($000)	14,939
NET INCOME ($000)	2,925
EMPLOYEES	na
RANK (Profit/Revenue/Assets)	515/757/810

MOTOROLA CANADA LIMITED

(Private)   ELECTRICAL & ELECTRONIC
4000 Victoria Park Ave., North York, ON, M2H 3P4   (416) 499-1441
MOTOROLA CANADA LIMITED is engaged in manufacturing and
distributing electronic equipment, systems and components.
Eric Taylor, Chairman

TOTAL ASSETS ($000)	210,823
TOTAL REVENUE ($000)	606,868
NET INCOME ($000)	(46,277)
EMPLOYEES	na

MPG INVESTMENT CORPORATION LIMITED

(Public)   INVESTMENT COMPANIES AND FUNDS
Exchanges: T M   Stock Symbol: MPG
215 Sydney Street, Cornwall, ON, K6H 3H3   (613) 932-0183
MPG INVESTMENT CORPORATION LIMITED, as a closed-end
investment corporation, invests mainly in common shares of Canadian
companies listed on recognized stock exchanges. It also has minor
investments in foreign companies, bonds and certificates of deposit and
cash.
H.P.G. Channon, Chairman

TOTAL ASSETS ($000)	55,927
TOTAL REVENUE ($000)	1,945
NET INCOME ($000)	1,261
EMPLOYEES	na
RANK (Profit/Revenue/Assets)	633/924/606

MRRM INC.

(Public)   FOOD PROCESSING
Exchanges: M   Stock Symbol: MRR
1600 Trans Canada Hwy, Suite 100, Dorval, PQ,
H9P 1H7   (514) 683-5583
MRRM INC. is involved in the food processing industry and the ship
agency business. The company's main operating subsidiaries are Les
Aliments Dainty Foods, an importer and processor of rice products in
Canada; and Robert Reford, which represents ship owners and operators
from various offices in Montreal and Toronto. The company also owns
two food brokers, one in Ontario and one in Quebec.
L.A.M. Reford, President

TOTAL ASSETS ($000)	24,276
TOTAL REVENUE ($000)	35,693
NET INCOME ($000)	1,734
EMPLOYEES	150
RANK (Profit/Revenue/Assets)	592/616/822

MSR EXPLORATION LTD.

(Public)   OIL AND GAS PRODUCERS
Exchanges: A   Stock Symbol:
CBM Building, P.O. Box 250, Cut Bank, MT, 59427   (406) 873-2235
MSR EXPLORATION LTD. is an oil and gas exploration and produc-
tion company. The company has operations in Montana, North Dakota,
Utah, Arizona, Texas and Western Canada.
Joseph V. Montalban, Chairman President & C.E.O.

TOTAL ASSETS ($000)	27,222 (US)
TOTAL REVENUE ($000)	2,969 (US)
NET INCOME ($000)	(738) (US)
EMPLOYEES	na
RANK (Profit/Revenue/Assets)	819/877/706

MSV RESOURCES INC.

(Public)   PRECIOUS METALS
Exchanges: T M   Stock Symbol: MSV
630 Rene-Levesque Blvd. West, Suite 3240, Montreal, PQ,
H3B 1S6   (514) 875-9033
MSV RESOURCES INC. is involved in the production of gold and other
base metals and of the exploration and development of mining properties.
Mario Caron, President

TOTAL ASSETS ($000)	55,244
TOTAL REVENUE ($000)	51,643
NET INCOME ($000)	3,916
EMPLOYEES	425
RANK (Profit/Revenue/Assets)	470/544/609

MTC ELECTRONIC TECHNOLOGIES CO. LTD.

(Public)   WHOLESALE DISTRIBUTORS
Exchanges: Q   Stock Symbol: MTCEF
2580 Viscount Way, Richmond, BC, V6V 2G8   (604) 278-8788
MTC ELECTRONIC TECHNOLOGIES CO. LTD. is an importer and
exporter of electronics to the People's Republic of China. MTC also holds
interests in joint ventures in China which manufacture telecommunications products and provides paging and cellular telephone services in the
People's Republic of China.
Christopher Ho, Chairman C.E.O. & Director

TOTAL ASSETS ($000)	74,597
TOTAL REVENUE ($000)	57,241
NET INCOME ($000)	2,029

EMPLOYEES	30
RANK (Profit/Revenue/Assets)	566/523/548

MTC MORTGAGE INVESTMENT CORPORATION
(Public) INVESTMENT COMPANIES AND FUNDS
Exchanges: T Stock Symbol: MTO
Suite 400, 70 University Ave., Toronto, ON, M5J 2M4 (416) 598-2665
MTC MORTGAGE INVESTMENT CORPORATION's objective is to generate a secure stream of income by investing in a portfolio of residential, industrial and commercial mortgages and other qualified investments.
Ian Sutherland, Chairman

TOTAL ASSETS ($000)	103,713
TOTAL REVENUE ($000)	6,363
NET INCOME ($000)	2,386
EMPLOYEES	0
RANK (Profit/Revenue/Assets)	546/838/476

MULLEN TRUCKING LTD.
(Public) TRANSPORTATION
Exchanges: T Stock Symbol: MTL
P.O. Box 87, #1 Maple Leaf Road, Aldersyde, AB,
T0L 0A0 (403) 652-8888
MULLEN TRUCKING LTD. is a licensed common carrier engaged in the transportation of a wide variety of common commodities throughout Canada and the continental United States.
Roland O. Mullen, Chairman

TOTAL ASSETS ($000)	73,394
TOTAL REVENUE ($000)	113,219
NET INCOME ($000)	9,780
EMPLOYEES	601
RANK (Profit/Revenue/Assets)	302/401/555

MULTI-MARQUES INC.
(Private) FOOD PROCESSING
1600 Henri-Bourassa Ouest, Bureau 510, Montreal, PQ,
H3M 3E2 (514) 333-7246
MULTI-MARQUES INC. is a manufacturer and distributor of fresh bakery products in Quebec under the trade marks: Gailuron, Durivage, Diana, Bon Matin, and Petite Douceur. It markets under the Aunt May's brand in Ontario.
Hubert Barbeau, Chairman & C.E.O.

TOTAL ASSETS ($000)	185,000
TOTAL REVENUE ($000)	284,000
NET INCOME ($000)	na
EMPLOYEES	3,450

MULTIBANC FINANCIAL CORP.
(Public) INVESTMENT COMPANIES AND FUNDS
Exchanges: T M Stock Symbol: MBK.PR.A
Ste. 400, 70 University Ave., Toronto, ON, M5J 2M4 (416) 971-7246
MULTIBANC FINANCIAL CORP. was established as a closed end investment fund to acquire a portfolio consisting of common shares of five major Canadian chartered banks. Dividends received are paid to preferred shareholders of an affiliated company, Multibanc Financial Corp. On disposition of the portfolio, capital gains, after redemption of the preferreds, accrue to the holders of Multibanc NT's capital shares.
John B. Newman, Chairman & C.E.O.

TOTAL ASSETS ($000)	20,653
TOTAL REVENUE ($000)	1,988

NET INCOME ($000)	1,888
EMPLOYEES	4
RANK (Profit/Revenue/Assets)	580/923/865

MULTIBANC NT FINANCIAL CORP.
(Public) INVESTMENT COMPANIES AND FUNDS
Exchanges: T M Stock Symbol: MIB
Suite 400, 70 University Ave., Toronto, ON, M5J 2M4 (416) 971-5402
MULTIBANC NT FINANCIAL CORP. invested the proceeds of the public issue of its capital shares and the private sale of Class A shares to Multibank Financial Corp. in a portfolio consisting of common shares of Bank of Montreal, Canadian Imperial Bank of Commerce, Bank of Nova Scotia, Royal Bank of Canada and Toronto-Dominion Bank.
John B. Newman, Chairman & C.E.O.

TOTAL ASSETS ($000)	53,657
TOTAL REVENUE ($000)	2,652
NET INCOME ($000)	2,344
EMPLOYEES	0
RANK (Profit/Revenue/Assets)	550/906/617

MUNICIPAL FINANCIAL CORPORATION
See page 481 for a full company profile.

MUNICIPAL SAVINGS AND LOAN CORPORATION
(Public) TRUST, SAVINGS AND LOAN
Exchanges: T Stock Symbol: MSL.PR.A
The Municipal Tower, P.O. Box 147, 70 Collier Street, Barrie, ON,
L4M 4S9 (705) 734-7500
MUNICIPAL SAVINGS AND LOAN CORPORATION is a financial intermediary involved in investing funds from depositors and shareholders in income-producing assets such as securities, mortgages and other loans.
Maxwell L. Rotstein, Chairman & C.E.O.

TOTAL ASSETS ($000)	1,153,638
TOTAL REVENUE ($000)	115,314
NET INCOME ($000)	(4,434)
EMPLOYEES	278
RANK (Profit/Revenue/Assets)	902/397/145

MURPHY OIL COMPANY LTD.
(Private) OIL AND GAS PRODUCERS
Ste. 2100, 555 - 4th Ave. SW, Calgary, AB, T2P 3E7 (403) 294-8000
MURPHY OIL COMPANY LTD. is engaged in the exploration, development and production of convential and heavy crude oil and natural gas with major concentration in the western Canada sedimentary basin. In association with these activities, Murphy Oil is also involved in the transportation and marketing of crude oil through pipeline and trucking facilities.
Len E. Pasychny, President & C.E.O.

TOTAL ASSETS ($000)	627,567
TOTAL REVENUE ($000)	205,116
NET INCOME ($000)	19,891
EMPLOYEES	na

MUSCOCHO EXPLORATIONS LTD.
See page 50 for a full company profile.

MUTUAL LIFE ASSURANCE COMPANY OF CANADA (THE)

(Private)   INSURANCE - LIFE
227 King Street South, Waterloo, ON, N2J 4C5   (519) 888-2290
THE MUTUAL LIFE ASSURANCE COMPANY OF CANADA is a mutual life insurance company which provides life insurance and health insurance products, annuities and a financial planning service for policy holders.
Jack V. Masterman, Chairman

TOTAL ASSETS ($000)	18,907,000
TOTAL REVENUE ($000)	3,804,000
NET INCOME ($000)	155,000
EMPLOYEES	3,113

N. M. PATERSON & SONS LIMITED

(Private)   WHOLESALE DISTRIBUTORS
167 Lombard Ave., Ste. 609, Winnipeg, MB,
R3B 0V5   (204) 956-2090
N.M. PATERSON & SONS LIMITED is engaged in grain handling and Great Lakes shipping. The company is 50% owned by the D.S. Paterson family of Winnipeg, and 50% owned by the J. Paterson family of Thunder Bay.
D.S. Paterson, Chairman

TOTAL ASSETS ($000)	70,255
TOTAL REVENUE ($000)	144,935
NET INCOME ($000)	na
EMPLOYEES	280

NABISCO LTD.

(Private)   FOOD PROCESSING
10 Parklawn Road, Etobicoke, ON, M8Y 3H8   (416) 253-3200
NABISCO LTD is one of Canada's foremost consumer food manufacturers with two main lines of business being biscuits and grocery products. Biscuits include brands such as Oreos, Peek Freans, Dad's Cookies, Triscuits, Ritz and Premium Plus crackers. Grocery products include Aylmer and Del Monte canned vegetables and fruits, as well as Milk Bone pet snacks.
Raymond J. Verdon, Chairman of the Board

TOTAL ASSETS ($000)	536,189
TOTAL REVENUE ($000)	797,315
NET INCOME ($000)	48,340
EMPLOYEES	3,500

NATIONAL BANK OF CANADA
See page 452 for a full company profile.

NATIONAL FIBRETECH INC.

(Private)   HOME FURNISHINGS
5195 Maingate Drive, Mississauga, ON, L4W 1G4   (905) 624-2604
NATIONAL FIBRETECH INC. manufactures, sells and distributes synthetic floor covering products and materials, including polypropylene fibre and yarns, polypropylene carpet, and vinyl and rubber backed mats.
Sheldon Gross, Chairman

TOTAL ASSETS ($000)	44,920
TOTAL REVENUE ($000)	58,326
NET INCOME ($000)	4,030
EMPLOYEES	na

NATIONAL LIFE ASSURANCE COMPANY OF CANADA (THE)

(Private)   INSURANCE - LIFE
522 University Avenue, Toronto, ON, M5G 1Y7   (416) 598-2122
NATIONAL LIFE ASSURANCE COMPANY OF CANADA is a 99.8% owned subsidiary of Industrial-Alliance Life Management Corporation of Quebec City. National is engaged in life and health insurance plus the administration of various segregated funds.
Raymond Garneau, Chairman & C.E.O.

TOTAL ASSETS ($000)	1,756,110
TOTAL REVENUE ($000)	421,563
NET INCOME ($000)	8,093
EMPLOYEES	380

NATIONAL SEA PRODUCTS LIMITED
See page 195 for a full company profile.

NATIONAL TRUSTCO INC.
See page 453 for a full company profile.

NAVISTAR INTERNATIONAL CORPORATION CANADA

(Private)   MACHINERY
120 King St. W., 9th Floor, Hamilton, ON, L8N 3S5   (905) 528-7700
NAVISTAR INTERNATIONAL CORPORATION CANADA is engaged in the manufacture, sale, and servicing of medium and heavy trucks.
Howard Hawkins, President

TOTAL ASSETS ($000)	243,689
TOTAL REVENUE ($000)	1,333,947
NET INCOME ($000)	na
EMPLOYEES	na

NBS TECHNOLOGIES INC.
See page 271 for a full company profile.

NEEDLER GROUP LIMITED

(Public)   CEMENT AND CONCRETE
Exchanges: T   Stock Symbol: NGL
380 Hardy Road, P.O. Box 1390, Brantford, ON,
N3T 5T6   (519) 753-3408
NEEDLER GROUP LIMITED is involved in the production of aggregates, asphalt, concrete block and paving stone and provides construction services, operating principally in the Ontario and New York state.
G.H. Christopher Needler, Chairman & C.E.O.

TOTAL ASSETS ($000)	66,883
TOTAL REVENUE ($000)	46,916
NET INCOME ($000)	(2,707)
EMPLOYEES	300
RANK (Profit/Revenue/Assets)	872/561/571

NELVANA LIMITED

(Public)   ENTERTAINMENT SERVICES
Exchanges: T M   Stock Symbol: NTV
32 Atlantic Avenue, Toronto, ON, M6K 1X8   (416) 588-5571
NELVANA LIMITED develops, produces, and distributes internationally animated television programs and feature films for the family market. The company also produces live action programs and animated television commercials.

Michael Hirsh, Chairman

TOTAL ASSETS ($000)	51,605
TOTAL REVENUE ($000)	58,323
NET INCOME ($000)	6,223
EMPLOYEES	na
RANK (Profit/Revenue/Assets)	388/517/623

NESBITT THOMSON GROUP (THE)
(Private) INVESTMENT HOUSES
Sun Life Tower, 150 King Street West, 20th Floor, Toronto, ON,
M5H 3W2 (416) 586-3600
THE NESBITT THOMSON GROUP is the holding company for investment dealer, Nesbitt Burns. Nesbitt Thomson is 75% owned by the Bank of Montreal.
Brian J. Steck, Chairman & C.E.O.

TOTAL ASSETS ($000)	18,078,179
TOTAL REVENUE ($000)	335,176
NET INCOME ($000)	50,016
EMPLOYEES	1,693

NESTLE CANADA INC.
(Private) FOOD PROCESSING
25 Sheppard Ave. West, North York, ON, M2N 6S8 (416) 218-3030
NESTLE CANADA INC., is engaged in the manufacturing and distribution of food products. Nestle is a wholly owned subsidiary of Nestle S.A. of Vevey, Switzerland.
F. Cella, Chairman, C.E.O. & Market Head

TOTAL ASSETS ($000)	488,026
TOTAL REVENUE ($000)	1,057,073
NET INCOME ($000)	na
EMPLOYEES	3,959

NEW BRUNSWICK POWER COMMISSION
(Crown) ELECTRICAL UTILITIES
P.O. Box 2000, Fredericton, NB, E3B 4X1 (506) 458-4444
THE NEW BRUNSWICK ELECTRIC POWER COMMISSION is a provincial crown corporation which provides electric power directly to customers and indirectly through sales to municipal utilities. NB Power is electrically interconnected with neighbouring utilities in Quebec, Nova Scotia, Prince Edward Island, and New England.
Raymond J. Frenette, Chairman

TOTAL ASSETS ($000)	4,358,681
TOTAL REVENUE ($000)	957,325
NET INCOME ($000)	23,730
EMPLOYEES	2,736

NEW BRUNSWICK RESEARCH AND PRODUCTIVITY COUNCIL (RPC)
(Crown) CONSULTING
921 College Hill Road, Fredericton, NB, E3B 6Z9 (506) 452-8994
RPC is an independent contract research and development organization that assists clients on a fee-for-service basis. Typical projects involve the design or formulation of innovative products, productivity improvements in resource and manufacturing operations, and prototype development. RPC also offers a wide range of analytical and testing capabilities.
Dr. Knut Grotterod, Chairman

TOTAL ASSETS ($000)	5,472
TOTAL REVENUE ($000)	8,641
NET INCOME ($000)	303
EMPLOYEES	120

NEW BRUNSWICK TELEPHONE COMPANY, LIMITED (THE)
(Private) TELEPHONE UTILITIES
P.O. Box 1430, One Brunswick Square, Saint John, NB,
E2L 4K2 (506) 694-2340
THE NEW BRUNSWICK TELEPHONE CO, LIMITED (NBTel) provides a borad range of modern telecommunications services to its residential and business customers in New Brunswick. Bruncor Inc. of Saint John owns all of the common shares of the company.
Lino Celeste, Chairman

TOTAL ASSETS ($000)	737,854
TOTAL REVENUE ($000)	359,314
NET INCOME ($000)	34,210

NEW CACHE PETROLEUMS LTD.
(Public) OIL AND GAS PRODUCERS
Exchanges: T Stock Symbol: NWA
Suite 200, 1301 - 8th Street S.W., Calgary, AB,
T2R 1B7 (403) 245-4333
NEW CACHE PETROLEUMS LTD. is a Canadian owned exploration and development company.
Robert W. Macdonald, Chairman

TOTAL ASSETS ($000)	43,114
TOTAL REVENUE ($000)	9,192
NET INCOME ($000)	523
EMPLOYEES	na
RANK (Profit/Revenue/Assets)	692/811/673

NEW INDIGO RESOURCES INC.
(Public) PRECIOUS METALS
Exchanges: Z Stock Symbol: NDR
Suite 501, 700 West Pender Street, Vancouver, BC,
V6C 1G8 (604) 682-0536
NEW INDIGO RESOURCES INC. is involved in the acquisition, exploration and development of diamond properties in the Northwest Territories. New Indigo holds a 50% interest in mineral properties covering nine million acres.
D.H.W. Dobson, Chairman & President

TOTAL ASSETS ($000)	15,310
TOTAL REVENUE ($000)	272
NET INCOME ($000)	79
EMPLOYEES	0
RANK (Profit/Revenue/Assets)	745/972/940

NEWALTA CORPORATION
(Public) ENVIRONMENTAL SERVICES
Exchanges: T Stock Symbol: NAL
Ste. 400, 333 - 11th St. SW, Calgary, AB, T2R 1L9 (403) 266-6556
NEWALTA CORPORATION provides a wide range of resource management and environmental services to the oil and gas industry through a network of eleven facilities located in Alberta and British Columbia. The company provides clean oil terminalling and emulsion treatment. It handles drilling muds, tank bottoms, workover fluids, produced sands and spills, and provides site remediation services.
Felix Pardo, Chairman of the Board

TOTAL ASSETS ($000)	55,141
TOTAL REVENUE ($000)	24,790
NET INCOME ($000)	3,664
EMPLOYEES	115
RANK (Profit/Revenue/Assets)	479/680/610

NEWBRIDGE NETWORKS CORPORATION
See page 272 for a full company profile.

NEWCOURT CREDIT GROUP INC.
See page 482 for a full company profile.

NEWFOUNDLAND AND LABRADOR CREDIT UNION
(Fin. Co-op)   CREDIT UNIONS
341 Freshwater Road, Head Office, St. John's, NF,
A1B 1C4   (709) 754-2630
NEWFOUNDLAND AND LABRADOR CREDIT UNION provides
financial services for individuals and businesses in Newfoundland and
Labrador.
Michael W. Boland, Chairman & President
TOTAL ASSETS ($000)   131,346
TOTAL REVENUE ($000)   12,052
NET INCOME ($000)   280
EMPLOYEES   96

NEWFOUNDLAND AND LABRADOR HYDRO
(Crown)   ELECTRICAL UTILITIES
P.O. Box 12400, St. John's, NF, A1B 4K7   (709) 737-1400
NEWFOUNDLAND AND LABRADOR HYDRO is incorporated un-
der a special act of the province of Newfoundland as a crown corporation.
Its principal activity is the development, generation and sale of electric
power.
James R. Chalker, Chairman
TOTAL ASSETS ($000)   2,255,800
TOTAL REVENUE ($000)   408,300
NET INCOME ($000)   24,900
EMPLOYEES   1,413

NEWFOUNDLAND CAPITAL CORPORATION LIMITED
See page 326 for a full company profile.

NEWFOUNDLAND LIGHT & POWER CO. LIMITED
See page 355 for a full company profile.

NEWFOUNDLAND TELEPHONE COMPANY LIMITED
(Private)   TELEPHONE UTILITIES
Fort William Building, P.O. Box 2110, St. John's, NF,
A1C 5H6   (709) 739-2000
NEWFOUNDLAND TELEPHONE CO. LTD. provides telecommuni-
cations and information handling services throughout Newfoundland and
Labrador. The company is a wholly owned subsidiary of NewTel
Enterprises Ltd. of St. John's.
Vincent G. Withers, Chairman, President & C.E.O.
TOTAL ASSETS ($000)   685,445
TOTAL REVENUE ($000)   263,727
NET INCOME ($000)   32,068
EMPLOYEES   1,653

NEWGROWTH CORP.
See page 483 for a full company profile.

NEWHAWK GOLD MINES LTD.
(Public)   PRECIOUS METALS
Exchanges: T   Stock Symbol: NHG
Suite 860, 625 Howe St., Vancouver, BC, V6C 2T6   (604) 687-7545
NEWHAWK GOLD MINES LTD. is involved in the acquisition,
exploration and development of precious metals mineral properties. It
holds a 60% working interest in the Bruceside Sulphurets property and
a 100% interest in the Snowfields Sulphurets property in northwestern
British Columbia.
Donald A. McLeod, President & C.E.O.
TOTAL ASSETS ($000)   18,187
TOTAL REVENUE ($000)   0
NET INCOME ($000)   (32)
EMPLOYEES   na
RANK (Profit/Revenue/Assets)   759/996/894

NEWPORT PETROLEUM CORPORATION
(Public)   OIL AND GAS PRODUCERS
Exchanges: T   Stock Symbol: NPP
Suite 1600, Bow Valley Square II, 205 - 5th Avenue S.W., Calgary,
AB, T2P 2V7   (403) 531-1530
NEWPORT PETROLEUM CORPORATION is an oil and natural gas
development and production company. It is active in the Western Cana-
dian Sedimentary Basin.
Uldis Upitis, President & C.E.O.
TOTAL ASSETS ($000)   56,552
TOTAL REVENUE ($000)   17,036
NET INCOME ($000)   2,542
EMPLOYEES   na
RANK (Profit/Revenue/Assets)   536/739/603

NEWSCOPE RESOURCES LTD.
(Public)   OIL AND GAS PRODUCERS
Exchanges: T   Stock Symbol: NEX
Ste. 2999, 300 - 5th Ave. SW, Calgary, AB, T2P 3C4 (403) 266-1101
CANADIAN NEWSCOPE RESOURCES LTD. is a junior publicly
traded natural resource company with interests primarily in Alberta,
southeastern Saskatchewan, Texas, Louisiana and Mississippi.
Wieland F. Wettstein, Chairman
TOTAL ASSETS ($000)   69,931
TOTAL REVENUE ($000)   23,224
NET INCOME ($000)   1,815
EMPLOYEES   na
RANK (Profit/Revenue/Assets)   584/695/565

NEWTEL ENTERPRISES LIMITED
See page 356 for a full company profile.

NIAGARA CREDIT UNION LIMITED
(Fin. Co-op)   CREDIT UNIONS
344 Lake St., PO Box 2157B, St. Catharines, ON,
L2N 4H4   (905) 935-1000
NIAGARA CREDIT UNION LIMITED is a member-owned and locally
controlled financial institution. The credit union operates in the Niagara
Region of Ontario.
William Goertz, Cheif Executive Officer
TOTAL ASSETS ($000)   713,984
TOTAL REVENUE ($000)   54,686
NET INCOME ($000)   1,181
EMPLOYEES   330

NII NORSAT INTERNATIONAL INC.

(Public)   ELECTRICAL & ELECTRONIC
Exchanges: T Q   Stock Symbol: NII
Suite 302, 12886 - 78th Ave., Surrey, BC, V3W 8E7   (604) 597-6200
NII NORSAT INTERNATIONAL INC. designs, manufactures, distributes, and markets electronic products used to receive broadcast communications from satellite terrestrial broadcasting systems.
John Anderson, President & C.E.O.

TOTAL ASSETS ($000)	17,956
TOTAL REVENUE ($000)	37,565
NET INCOME ($000)	818
EMPLOYEES	102
RANK (Profit/Revenue/Assets)	668/606/898

NISSAN CANADA INC.

(Private)   WHOLESALE DISTRIBUTORS
5290 Orbitor Dr., Mississauga, ON, L4W 4Z5   (905) 629-2888
NISSAN CANADA INC. is a wholesale distributor of vehicles, forklifts, outboard motors and associated parts. The company is a wholly owned subsidiary of Nissan Motor Co. of Tokyo.
Yutaka Kume, Chairman

TOTAL ASSETS ($000)	507,511
TOTAL REVENUE ($000)	854,623
NET INCOME ($000)	(1,299)
EMPLOYEES	na

NISSHO IWAI CANADA LTD

(Private)   MANAGEMENT AND DIVERSIFIED
150 King St. West, Suite 1506, P.O. Box 106, Toronto, ON,
M5H 1J9   (416) 977-8182
NISSHO IWAI CANADA LTD. is involved in the purchase and sale of merchandise. The company acts as an agent in some transactions and as principal in others. It is a wholly owned subsidiary of Nissho Iwai Corporation of Japan.
Mr. Masatake Kusamichi, President & C.E.O.

TOTAL ASSETS ($000)	49,185
TOTAL REVENUE ($000)	643,687
NET INCOME ($000)	1,117
EMPLOYEES	na

NOBLE CHINA INC.

See page 196 for a full company profile.

NOBLE PEAK RESOURCES LTD

(Public)   PRECIOUS METALS
Exchanges: Z   Stock Symbol: NPK
50 Burnhamthorpe Road West, Suite 906, Mississauga, ON,
L5B 3C2   (905) 897-9406
NOBLE PEAK RESOURCES LTD. is engaged in investigation, acquisition, exploration and development of gold, base metal and diamond projects in North America.
Maureen Jensen, President & C.E.O.

TOTAL ASSETS ($000)	16,150
TOTAL REVENUE ($000)	2
NET INCOME ($000)	(172)
EMPLOYEES	5
RANK (Profit/Revenue/Assets)	772/995/932

NOMA INDUSTRIES LIMITED

See page 273 for a full company profile.

NORANDA FOREST INC.

See page 166 for a full company profile.

NORANDA INC.

See page 523 for a full company profile.

NORANDA METALLURGY INC.

(Private)   METAL MINES
PO Box 755, 181 Bay Street, Toronto, ON, M5J 2T3   (416) 982-7111
NORANDA METALLURGY INC. manages Noranda Inc.'s wholly owned copper and zinc metallurgical facilities, and markets metal products worldwide.
David Goldman, President

TOTAL ASSETS ($000)	1,008,000
TOTAL REVENUE ($000)	na
NET INCOME ($000)	na
EMPLOYEES	na

NORANDA MINING AND EXPLORATION INC.

(Private)   METAL MINES
181 Bay Street, PO Box 755, Toronto, ON, M5J 2T3   (416) 982-7111
NORANDA MINING AND EXPLORATION INC. is a producer of zinc, copper, silver, lead and sulphuric acid. The company is wholly owned by Noranda Inc.
Michael J. Knuckey, President

TOTAL ASSETS ($000)	909,000
TOTAL REVENUE ($000)	na
NET INCOME ($000)	na
EMPLOYEES	na

NORBORD INDUSTRIES INC.

(Private)   WHOLESALE DISTRIBUTORS
1 Toronto Street, Suite 500, Toronto, ON, M5C 2W4   (416) 365-0710
NORBORD INDUSTRIES INC. manufactures, markets and distributes wood and wood/fibre composite products for construction and industrial purposes. The company operates mills in Canada, the U.S., and the U.K. and has sales offices in Canada, the U.S., the U.K., Holland, Germany and Japan.
Dominic Gammiero, President

TOTAL ASSETS ($000)	na
TOTAL REVENUE ($000)	449,100
NET INCOME ($000)	na
EMPLOYEES	2,100

NORCEN ENERGY RESOURCES LIMITED

See page 114 for a full company profile.

NORTERRA INC.

(Private)   MANAGEMENT AND DIVERSIFIED
Suite 2000, Commerce Place, 10155 - 102 Street, Edmonton, AB,
T5J 4G8   (403) 425-6900
NORTERRA INC. is a management company with holdings in the transportation and manufacturing sectors.
Pat Lyall, Chairman

TOTAL ASSETS ($000)	90,426
TOTAL REVENUE ($000)	132,130

NET INCOME ($000)   na
EMPLOYEES   1,200

NORTH AMERICAN LIFE ASSURANCE COMPANY
(Private)   INSURANCE - LIFE
5650 Yonge Street, North York, ON, M2M 4G4   (416) 229-4515
NORTH AMERICAN LIFE ASSURANCE COMPANY is a mutual
life insurance company with $145-billion of assets under management
and life insurance in force of $74-billion. The company operates through-
out Canada and the U.S., offering a range of financial products and
services, including trust, real estate asset management, investment coun-
selling, annuities and mutual funds.
G.P. Osler, Chairman
TOTAL ASSETS ($000)   9,280,387
TOTAL REVENUE ($000)   1,969,859
NET INCOME ($000)   (17,364)
EMPLOYEES   na

NORTH AMERICAN PALLADIUM LTD.
(Public)   METAL MINES
Exchanges: T Q   Stock Symbol: PDL
111 Richmond Street West, Suite 916, Toronto, ON,
M5H 2G4   (416) 867-3072
NORTH AMERICAN PALLADIUM LTD. is involved in mining ex-
ploration and development.
Dale McDoulette, President
TOTAL ASSETS ($000)   63,996
TOTAL REVENUE ($000)   16,896
NET INCOME ($000)   (3,016)
EMPLOYEES   112
RANK (Profit/Revenue/Assets)   880/741/582

NORTH CANADIAN OILS LIMITED
(Private)   OIL AND GAS PRODUCERS
715 - 5th Avenue S.W., Calgary, AB, T2P 2X7   (403) 261-3100
NORTH CANADIAN OILS LIMITED is a senior Canadian oil and gas
company. Exploration and production activities are concentrated in the
Western Sedimentary Basin in Canada, while gas marketing activities
are based throughout North America. The company is now managed by
its parent company, Northern Energy Resources Limited.
Barry D. Cochrane, Chairman
TOTAL ASSETS ($000)   1,058,036
TOTAL REVENUE ($000)   453,080
NET INCOME ($000)   (42,341)
EMPLOYEES   21

NORTH WEST COMPANY INC. (THE)
See page 428 for a full company profile.

NORTHERN REEF EXPLORATION LTD.
(Public)   OIL AND GAS PRODUCERS
Exchanges: T Z   Stock Symbol: NRF
Ste. 2600, 140 - 4th Ave. SW, Calgary, AB, T2P 3N3 (403) 269-6086
NORTHERN REEF EXPLORATION LTD. is involved in the acquisi-
tion, exploration and development of oil and gas properties.
Thomas E. Phillips, President & C.E.O.
TOTAL ASSETS ($000)   111,116
TOTAL REVENUE ($000)   36,099
NET INCOME ($000)   (62,450)

EMPLOYEES   na
RANK (Profit/Revenue/Assets)   993/613/462

NORTHERN TELECOM LIMITED
See page 384 for a full company profile.

NORTHGATE EXPLORATION LIMITED
See page 51 for a full company profile.

NORTHRIDGE EXPLORATION LTD.
(Public)   OIL AND GAS PRODUCERS
Exchanges: T   Stock Symbol: NRG
Ste. 1200, 421 - 7th Ave. SW, Calgary, AB, T2P 4K9 (403) 298-8800
NORTHRIDGE EXPLORATION LTD. is involved in the exploration,
development and production of oil and gas predominantly in west central
Alberta.
D.W. Minion, Chairman
TOTAL ASSETS ($000)   52,719
TOTAL REVENUE ($000)   13,561
NET INCOME ($000)   2,084
EMPLOYEES   29
RANK (Profit/Revenue/Assets)   561/769/621

NORTHROCK RESOURCES LTD.
See page 115 for a full company profile.

NORTHSTAR ENERGY CORPORATION
See page 116 for a full company profile.

NORTHWEST DRUG COMPANY LIMITED
(Private)   WHOLESALE DISTRIBUTORS
10931 - 177 St., PO Box 2318, Edmonton, AB,
T5J 2P9   (403) 484-0404
NORTHWEST DRUG COMPANY LIMITED is a full-line, front-store
and pharmaceutical wholesaler in Western Canada, with warehouses in
Edmonton, Vancouver, Winnipeg, and Saskatchewan.
Joe Spence, Chairman of the Board
TOTAL ASSETS ($000)   35,269
TOTAL REVENUE ($000)   125,448
NET INCOME ($000)   873
EMPLOYEES   165

NORTHWEST SPORTS ENTERPRISES LTD.
(Public)   ENTERTAINMENT SERVICES
Exchanges: M V   Stock Symbol: NSE
3rd Floor, 780 Beatty St., Vancouver, BC, V6B 2M1 (604) 681-2226
NORTHWEST SPORTS ENTREPRISES LTD., through its subsidiar-
ies, owns the Vancouver Canucks hockey team. Other operations include
a restaurant at the Pacific Coliseum and 14 gallery suites.
Arthur Robert Griffiths, Chairman & President
TOTAL ASSETS ($000)   83,990
TOTAL REVENUE ($000)   50,378
NET INCOME ($000)   921
EMPLOYEES   na
RANK (Profit/Revenue/Assets)   664/548/524

NORTHWEST TERRITORIES POWER COMMISSION
(Crown)   ELECTRICAL UTILITIES
Bag 6000, #3 Capital Rd., Hay River, NT, X0E 0R0   (403) 874-5200

NORTHWEST TERRITORIES POWER CORPORATION is a Crown corporation, which operates under the authority of the Northwest Territories Power Corporation Act. It operates diesel and hydro-electric plants to provide utility services on a self-substaining basis in the Northwest Territories.

J. H. Robertson, Chairman

TOTAL ASSETS ($000)	193,302
TOTAL REVENUE ($000)	99,541
NET INCOME ($000)	9,360
EMPLOYEES	275

NORTHWESTERN UTILITIES LIMITED
See page 357 for a full company profile.

NORWALL GROUP INC.
(Public)   MISC. CONSUMER PRODUCTS
Exchanges: M T   Stock Symbol: NGI
1055 Clark Boulevard, Brampton, ON, L6T 3W4   (905) 791-2700
NORWALL GROUP INC., through three wholly owned subsidiaries, is a fully-integrated manufacturer of residential wall coverings.
R. Derek A. Ashton, Chairman, President & C.E.O.

TOTAL ASSETS ($000)	85,777
TOTAL REVENUE ($000)	72,763
NET INCOME ($000)	(2,817)
EMPLOYEES	300
RANK (Profit/Revenue/Assets)	874/473/518

NOVA CORPORATION
See page 335 for a full company profile.

NOVA SCOTIA POWER INC.
See page 358 for a full company profile.

NOVA SCOTIA RESEARCH FOUNDATION CORPORATION
(Crown)   CONSULTING
P.O. Box 790, Dartmouth, NS, B2Y 3Z7   (902) 424-8670
NOVA SCOTIA RESEARCH FOUNDATION CORPORATION is a provincial crown corporation. Its mission is to apply science and technology to improve the economy and the quality of life in Nova Scotia by: providing scientific/technical support for industry; facilitating product commercialization; working cooperatively with others in science, technology and innovation; and ensuring superior quality in all its services.
Dr. R.F. McCurdy, President & C.O.O.

TOTAL ASSETS ($000)	8,093
TOTAL REVENUE ($000)	8,002
NET INCOME ($000)	(1,207)
EMPLOYEES	100

NOVA SCOTIA RESOURCES LIMITED
(Crown)   OIL AND GAS PRODUCERS
P.O. Box 2111, Station M, Halifax, NS, B3J 3B7   (902) 420-8800
NOVA SCOTIA RESOURCES LIMITED is a Crown corporation. It was established in 1981 to acquire and manage, in partnership with the private sector, participating interests in projects to develop petroleum, energy and mineral resources, and investments in related industrial activities.

Robert A. MacKay, Chairman

TOTAL ASSETS ($000)	58,518
TOTAL REVENUE ($000)	94,651
NET INCOME ($000)	(225,725)
EMPLOYEES	5

NOVICOURT INC.
See page 19 for a full company profile.

NOWSCO WELL SERVICE LTD.
See page 117 for a full company profile.

NQL DRILLING TOOLS INC.
(Public)   MISC. INDUSTRIAL PRODUCTS
Exchanges: T   Stock Symbol: NQL.A
1802 - 4th Street, Nisku, AB, T0C 2G0   (403) 955-8828
NQL DRILLING TOOLS INC. has two operating divisions: the Black Max Division and the Quick Lube Division. The Black Max Division manufactures and leases down hole drilling motors to the international and domestic oil and gas and utility drilling markets. The Quick Lube Division operates 10 franchised Mr. Lube oil change centres in Canada.
Walter Stelmaschuk, Chairman & President

TOTAL ASSETS ($000)	28,268
TOTAL REVENUE ($000)	34,823
NET INCOME ($000)	1,978
EMPLOYEES	162
RANK (Profit/Revenue/Assets)	574/619/784

NU-GRO CORPORATION
(Public)   MISC. CONSUMER PRODUCTS
Exchanges: T   Stock Symbol: NU
P.O. Box 1148, Woodstock, ON, N4S 8P6   (519) 456-2021
NU-GRO CORPORATION is engaged in blending, packaging, and distributing in Canada and the United States bulk packaged goods such as cat litter, lawn and garden fertilizers, potting soils, and pesticides. Nu-Gro's products are sold under the Hillview, Circle H Farms, and C-I-L brands, as well as many private labels.
Austin Beutel, Chairman

TOTAL ASSETS ($000)	17,031
TOTAL REVENUE ($000)	31,594
NET INCOME ($000)	447
EMPLOYEES	200
RANK (Profit/Revenue/Assets)	703/643/913

NUGAS LIMITED
(Public)   OIL AND GAS PRODUCERS
Exchanges: T   Stock Symbol: NGS
Ste. 2100, 421 - 7th Ave. SW, Calgary, AB, T2P 4K9   (403) 262-7034
NUGAS LIMITED is involved in the exploration, development and production of natural gas in southeastern Alberta and western Saskatchewan.
Gus A. Van Wielingen, Chairman, C.E.O. & C.F.O.

TOTAL ASSETS ($000)	45,045
TOTAL REVENUE ($000)	12,967
NET INCOME ($000)	3,427
EMPLOYEES	14
RANK (Profit/Revenue/Assets)	493/773/659

NUMAC ENERGY INC.
See page 118 for a full company profile.

OCELOT ENERGY INC.
See page 119 for a full company profile.

OCS TECHNOLOGIES CORP.
See page 543 for a full company profile.

OGY PETROLEUMS LTD.
(Public)   OIL AND GAS PRODUCERS
Exchanges: T Z   Stock Symbol: OGY
Ste. 2270, 140 - 4th Ave. SW, Calgary, AB, T2P 3N3 (403) 233-0066
OGY PETROLEUMS LTD. is involved in the acquisition, exploration
and development of oil and gas properties and mineral exploration.
Gordon Stollery, Chairman

TOTAL ASSETS ($000)	15,694
TOTAL REVENUE ($000)	5,268
NET INCOME ($000)	(6,139)
EMPLOYEES	11
RANK (Profit/Revenue/Assets)	920/861/936

OILTEC RESOURCES LTD.
(Public)   OIL AND GAS PRODUCERS
Exchanges: T   Stock Symbol: OLT
Suite 1825, 510 - 5th St. SW, Calgary, AB, T2P 3S2 (403) 266-2988
OILTEC RESOURCES LTD. is involved in the acquisition, exploration
and development of oil and gas properties in Western Canada, primarily
Alberta and Saskatchewan.
Richard A. Schuster, Chairman & C.E.O.

TOTAL ASSETS ($000)	14,797
TOTAL REVENUE ($000)	4,541
NET INCOME ($000)	581
EMPLOYEES	6
RANK (Profit/Revenue/Assets)	687/871/949

OKANAGAN SKEENA GROUP LIMITED
(Public)   CABLE
Exchanges: T V   Stock Symbol: OKS.A
4625 Lazelle Avenue, Terrace, BC, V8G 1S4   (604) 635-6316
OKANAGAN SKEENA GROUP LIMITED's businesses include cable
television, television and radio broadcasting, and real estate investment.
John , Chairman & C.E.O.

TOTAL ASSETS ($000)	34,196
TOTAL REVENUE ($000)	18,130
NET INCOME ($000)	773
EMPLOYEES	89
RANK (Profit/Revenue/Assets)	672/726/732

OLCO PETROLEUM GROUP INC.
(Public)   WHOLESALE DISTRIBUTORS
Exchanges: M   Stock Symbol: OLC.A
2561 Avenue Georges V, Montreal-Est, PQ, H1L 6J7 (514) 645-6526
OLCO is involved, directly and through its subsidiaries, in the down-
stream activity of the petroleum industry, namely the supply, trading,
marketing, storage and distribution of petroleum products.
Wilfred Kaneb, Chairman & C.E.O.

TOTAL ASSETS ($000)	114,439
TOTAL REVENUE ($000)	402,857
NET INCOME ($000)	(1,674)
EMPLOYEES	141
RANK (Profit/Revenue/Assets)	842/218/451

OLYMEL SOCIETE EN COMMANDITE
(Private)   FOOD PROCESSING
2200 Leon-Pratte, Suite 400, St-Hyacinthe, PQ,
J2S 4B6   (514) 771-0400
OLYMEL, SOCIETE EN COMMANDITE is engaged in slaughtering,
cutting and further processing pork and beef.
Jean Bienvenue, Chairman, President & C.E.O.

TOTAL ASSETS ($000)	126,142
TOTAL REVENUE ($000)	607,646
NET INCOME ($000)	na
EMPLOYEES	2,300

OLYMPIA ENERGY INC.
(Public)   OIL AND GAS PRODUCERS
Exchanges: T   Stock Symbol: OLY.A
Ste. 2020, 500 - 4th Ave. SW, Calgary, AB, T2P 2V6 (403) 265-2723
OLYMPIA ENERGY INC. is involved in the acquisition, exploration,
and development of oil and gas properties in western Canada.
John J. Brown, Chairman

TOTAL ASSETS ($000)	15,012
TOTAL REVENUE ($000)	3,786
NET INCOME ($000)	1,018
EMPLOYEES	12
RANK (Profit/Revenue/Assets)	655/881/942

OMEGA HYDROCARBONS LTD.
See page 120 for a full company profile.

ONDAATJE CORPORATION (THE)
See page 484 for a full company profile.

ONEX CORPORATION
See page 524 for a full company profile.

ONTARIO DEVELOPMENT CORPORATIONS
(Crown)   TRUST, SAVINGS AND LOAN
56 Wellesley Street West, 6th Floor, Toronto, ON,
M7A 2E7   (416) 326-1070
THE DEVELOPMENT CORPORATIONS OF ONTARIO provide
loans, investments, guarantees and advisory services, as well as a network
of industrial and technology parks. Their focus is on supporting entre-
preneurs, emerging technology companies and innovative growth firms.
As the lead development agent of the province, the Corporations manage
over $1.1-billion in loans and investments.
Matthew Gaasenbeek, Chairman, Ontario Development Corp.

TOTAL ASSETS ($000)	305,183
TOTAL REVENUE ($000)	35,944
NET INCOME ($000)	(29,968)
EMPLOYEES	170

ONTARIO HYDRO
(Crown)   ELECTRICAL UTILITIES
700 University Avenue, Toronto, ON, M5G 1X6   (416) 592-5111
ONTARIO HYDRO is a provincial crown corporation without share
capital. Its mission is to help Ontario become a world leader in developing

an energy efficient and competitive economy and a leading example of sustainable development. It supplies electric power, provides energy management services, and develops future energy technologies.
Maurice F. Strong, Chairman & C.E.O.

TOTAL ASSETS ($000)	49,495,000
TOTAL REVENUE ($000)	8,730,000
NET INCOME ($000)	855,000
EMPLOYEES	22,590

ONTARIO NORTHLAND TRANSPORTATION COMMISSION

(Crown)   TRANSPORTATION
555 Oak Street East, North Bay, ON, P1B 8L3   (705) 472-4500
ONTARIO NORTHLAND TRANSPORTATION COMMISSION is an Ontario crown corporation. Its major services include rail, marine, bus, and air transportation. It is also involved in telecommunications and real estate development.
M.D. Sinclair, Chairman

TOTAL ASSETS ($000)	280,644
TOTAL REVENUE ($000)	150,303
NET INCOME ($000)	1,032
EMPLOYEES	1,250

OPTIMA PETROLEUM CORPORATION

(Public)   OIL AND GAS PRODUCERS
Exchanges: T V Q   Stock Symbol: OPP
Suite 600, 595 Howe St., Vancouver, BC, V6C 2T5   (604) 684-6886
OPTIMA PETROLEUM CORPORATION is involved in the acquisition, exploration and development of oil and gas properties.
William C. Leuschner, Chairman

TOTAL ASSETS ($000)	24,794
TOTAL REVENUE ($000)	3,264
NET INCOME ($000)	(4,305)
EMPLOYEES	8
RANK (Profit/Revenue/Assets)	900/895/816

ORBIT OIL & GAS LTD.

(Public)   OIL AND GAS PRODUCERS
Exchanges: T   Stock Symbol: ORB
Ste. 2100, 144 - 4th Ave. SW, Calgary, AB, T2P 3N4   (403) 750-4440
ORBIT OIL & GAS LTD. is involved in the exploration, development, and production of petroleum and natural gas in Western Canada and the United States. Substantially all of the company's activities are conducted jointly with others.
Robert W. Lamond, Chairman, President & C.E.O.

TOTAL ASSETS ($000)	74,065
TOTAL REVENUE ($000)	23,875
NET INCOME ($000)	5,622
EMPLOYEES	104
RANK (Profit/Revenue/Assets)	406/689/553

ORENDA FOREST PRODUCTS LTD.

(Public)   WEST COAST FORESTRY
Exchanges: T V   Stock Symbol: OFP
Suite 409, 545 Clyde Avenue, West Vancouver, BC, V7T 1C5   (604) 926-4445
ORENDA FOREST PRODUCTS LIMITED is a British Columbia logging and forest management company. Its primary products are pulplogs and sawlogs.

Hugh W. Cooper, Chairman & President

TOTAL ASSETS ($000)	18,380
TOTAL REVENUE ($000)	26,883
NET INCOME ($000)	3,264
EMPLOYEES	18
RANK (Profit/Revenue/Assets)	502/665/891

ORVANA MINERALS CORP.

(Public)   PRECIOUS METALS
Exchanges: T   Stock Symbol: ORV
Suite 710, 1177 West Hastings Street, Vancouver, BC, V6E 2K3   (604) 682-4929
ORVANA MINERALS CORP. is involved in the acquisition, exploration and development of natural resource properties worldwide.
D. Neil Hillhouse, Chairman & C.E.O.

TOTAL ASSETS ($000)	25,499
TOTAL REVENUE ($000)	1,090
NET INCOME ($000)	(1,649)
EMPLOYEES	9
RANK (Profit/Revenue/Assets)	841/944/811

OSF INC.

(Public)   MISC. INDUSTRIAL PRODUCTS
Exchanges: Stock Symbol:
5145 Steeles Avenue West, Weston, ON, M9L 1R5   (416) 749-7700
OSF INC. manufactures and supplies a broad range of store fixtures and merchandising display products and provides display services to the retail industry.
Milton Shier, Chairman & C.E.O.

TOTAL ASSETS ($000)	64,439
TOTAL REVENUE ($000)	122,773
NET INCOME ($000)	7,754
EMPLOYEES	1,100

OSHAWA GROUP LIMITED (THE)
See page 429 for a full company profile.

OTIS CANADA INC.

(Private)   MACHINERY
710 Dorval Drive, Oakville, ON, L6J 5B7   (905) 842-6847
OTIS CANADA INC. is involved in the installation and service of elevators and escalators. It is a wholly owned subsidiary of Otis Elevator Company of the United States.
E.A. Minich, President & C.E.O.

TOTAL ASSETS ($000)	53,000
TOTAL REVENUE ($000)	136,000
NET INCOME ($000)	na
EMPLOYEES	800

OXFORD PROPERTIES CANADA LIMITED

(Public)   PROPERTY MGMNT & INVESTMENT
Exchanges: T   Stock Symbol: OXF
Suite 1700, 120 Adelaide Street West, Richmond-Adelaide Centre, Toronto, ON, M5H 1T1   (416) 865-8300
OXFORD PROPERTIES CANADA LIMITED is the owner of interests in a portfolio of commercial real estate in Toronto, Edmonton and Calgary.
G. Donald Love, Chairman

TOTAL ASSETS ($000)	416,375
TOTAL REVENUE ($000)	138,437

Canada Company Handbook

NET INCOME ($000)	(2,308)
EMPLOYEES	700
RANK (Profit/Revenue/Assets)	863/372/247

PACALTA RESOURCES LTD.
(Public)   OIL AND GAS PRODUCERS
Exchanges: T Z   Stock Symbol: PAZ
Ste. 1850, 633 - 6th Ave. SW, Calgary, AB, T2P 2Y5 (403) 266-0085
PACALTA RESOURCES LTD. is involved in the acquisition, exploration and development of oil and natural gas in Western Canada.
Michael Chernoff, President

TOTAL ASSETS ($000)	14,893
TOTAL REVENUE ($000)	7,435
NET INCOME ($000)	1,486
EMPLOYEES	6
RANK (Profit/Revenue/Assets)	611/829/944

PACCAR OF CANADA LTD.
(Private)   AUTOMOTIVE
6711 Mississauga Road North, Third Floor, Mississauga, ON, L5N 4J8 (905) 858-7000
PACCAR OF CANADA LTD. is engaged in heavy duty truck manufacturing, distribution, parts sales and truck leasing. Paccar Canada is wholly owned by Paccar Inc. of the United States.
C.M. Pigott, Chairman & President

TOTAL ASSETS ($000)	196,970
TOTAL REVENUE ($000)	748,798
NET INCOME ($000)	16,768
EMPLOYEES	1,023

PACIFIC COAST SAVINGS CREDIT UNION
(Fin. Co-op)   CREDIT UNIONS
722 Cormorant Street, Victoria, BC, V8W 1P8 (604) 380-3100
PACIFIC COAST SAVINGS CREDIT UNION is a credit union in British Columbia.
Gordon Munn, Chairman of the Board

TOTAL ASSETS ($000)	1,129,256
TOTAL REVENUE ($000)	106,299
NET INCOME ($000)	11,798
EMPLOYEES	500

PACIFIC FOREST PRODUCTS LIMITED
See page 167 for a full company profile.

PACIFIC NORTHERN GAS LTD.
See page 359 for a full company profile.

PACIFIC SENTINEL GOLD CORP.
(Public)   PRECIOUS METALS
Exchanges: V Q   Stock Symbol: PSG
800 West Pender Street, Suite 1020, Vancouver, BC, V6C 2V6 (604) 684-6365
PACIFIC SENTINEL GOLD CORP. is focused on the development of a giant open-pit copper-gold-molybdenum-silver project in Yukon Territory. Ongoing development is expected to lead to substantial metal production.
Robert G. Hunter, Chairman

TOTAL ASSETS ($000)	26,497
TOTAL REVENUE ($000)	1,174

NET INCOME ($000)	119
EMPLOYEES	30
RANK (Profit/Revenue/Assets)	741/940/805

PALLISER FURNITURE LTD.
(Private)   HOME FURNISHINGS
55-1155 Gateway Road, Winnipeg, MB, R2G 1B9 (204) 988-5600
PALLISER FURNITURE LTD. manufactures furniture. The company is wholly owned by the DeFehr family of Manitoba.
Abram A. DeFehr, Chairman

TOTAL ASSETS ($000)	149,077
TOTAL REVENUE ($000)	237,320
NET INCOME ($000)	9,199
EMPLOYEES	2,200

PALOMA PETROLEUM LTD.
(Public)   OIL AND GAS PRODUCERS
Exchanges: T   Stock Symbol: PAL
1150 Guinness House, 727 - 7th Avenue S.W., Calgary, AB, T2P 0Z7 (403) 265-9265
PALOMA PETROLEUM LTD. is involved in the exploration, development and production of petroleum and natural gas in Canada.
Terry D. Brooker, President & C.E.O.

TOTAL ASSETS ($000)	74,755
TOTAL REVENUE ($000)	24,094
NET INCOME ($000)	1,738
EMPLOYEES	22
RANK (Profit/Revenue/Assets)	590/688/547

PAN AMERICAN SILVER CORP.
(Public)   PRECIOUS METALS
Exchanges: T   Stock Symbol: PAA
Suite 1500, 625 Howe St., Vancouver, BC, V6C 2T6 (604) 684-1175
PAN AMERICAN SILVER CORP. is involved in the acquisition, exploration and development of silver mines. The company has acquired or has the right to acquire silver in four properties in the U.S.A. and Mexico.
Ross J. Beaty, Chairman

TOTAL ASSETS ($000)	13,867
TOTAL REVENUE ($000)	49
NET INCOME ($000)	(95)
EMPLOYEES	na
RANK (Profit/Revenue/Assets)	796/970/967

PAN EAST PETROLEUM CORP.
(Public)   OIL AND GAS PRODUCERS
Exchanges: T   Stock Symbol: PEC
Ste. 500, 67 Richmond St. W., Toronto, ON, M5H 1Z5 (416) 361-0737
PAN EAST PETROLEUM CORP. is involved in the acquisition, exploration and development of oil and gas properties, principally in Alberta.
Richard A. Walls, President

TOTAL ASSETS ($000)	42,779
TOTAL REVENUE ($000)	1,597
NET INCOME ($000)	240
EMPLOYEES	na
RANK (Profit/Revenue/Assets)	726/934/675

PANCANADIAN PETROLEUM LIMITED
See page 121 for a full company profile.

PANGEA GOLDFIELDS INC.

(Public)   PRECIOUS METALS
Exchanges: T   Stock Symbol: PGD
PO Box 22, Suite 709, 1 Toronto St., Toronto, ON,
M5C 2V6   (416) 350-3781
PANGEA GOLDFIELDS INC. is involved in the aquisition, exploration and development of mineral properties.
Oliver Lennox-King, Chairman

TOTAL ASSETS ($000)	20,026
TOTAL REVENUE ($000)	0
NET INCOME ($000)	0
EMPLOYEES	30
RANK (Profit/Revenue/Assets)	834/977/870

PANTORAMA INDUSTRIES INC.

(Public)   CLOTHING STORES
Exchanges: T M   Stock Symbol: PTA
2 Lake Road, Dollard-des-Ormeaux, PQ, H9B 3H9   (514) 421-1850
PANTORAMA INDUSTRIES INC. is engaged in the retail sale of casual clothing at medium prices for men and women.
Robert Wexler, Chairman of the Board

TOTAL ASSETS ($000)	38,893
TOTAL REVENUE ($000)	130,182
NET INCOME ($000)	3,553
EMPLOYEES	2,500
RANK (Profit/Revenue/Assets)	487/380/701

PARAGON ENTERTAINMENT CORPORATION

(Public)   ENTERTAINMENT SERVICES
Exchanges: T   Stock Symbol: P
Suite 900, 119 Spadina Ave. Toronto, ON, M5V 2L1   (416) 977-2929
PARAGON ENTERTAINMENT CORP. is involved in the production and distribution of television programs and development of theatrical motion pictures, marketing them to television networks in Canada, the United States and Europe.
Jonathan Slan, Chairman & C.E.O.

TOTAL ASSETS ($000)	27,897
TOTAL REVENUE ($000)	5,868
NET INCOME ($000)	233
EMPLOYEES	na
RANK (Profit/Revenue/Assets)	698/783/789

PARAGON PETROLEUM CORPORATION

(Public)   OIL AND GAS PRODUCERS
Exchanges: T   Stock Symbol: PGN
Suite 700, 407 - 8th Ave. SW, Calgary, AB, T2P 1E5   (403) 266-5075
PARAGON PETROLEUM CORPORATION is a resource company engaged in the exploration for and development and production of petroleum and natural gas in Alberta and Ontario.
Brian A. McLachlan, President & C.E.O.

TOTAL ASSETS ($000)	58,248
TOTAL REVENUE ($000)	18,815
NET INCOME ($000)	1,757
EMPLOYEES	31
RANK (Profit/Revenue/Assets)	588/723/599

PARAMOUNT RESOURCES LTD.

See page 122 for a full company profile.

PARK MEDITECH INC.

(Public)   COMPUTER SOFTWARE & PROCESSING
Exchanges: M   Stock Symbol: PKM
2 First Canadian Place, Suite 2810, P.O. Box 47, Toronto, ON,
M5X 1A9   (416) 941-8900
PARK MEDITECH INC. is involved in the development, manufacturing, and marketing of medical technologies relating to diagnostic imaging, therapy treatment planning, and medically-oriented computer systems.
Sheldon Inwentash, Chairman & C.E.O.

TOTAL ASSETS ($000)	41,881
TOTAL REVENUE ($000)	2,733
NET INCOME ($000)	(6,289)
EMPLOYEES	90
RANK (Profit/Revenue/Assets)	922/905/683

PARKLAND INDUSTRIES LTD.

(Public)   INTEGRATED OILS
Exchanges: T Z   Stock Symbol: PKI
Suite 236, Riverside Office Plaza, 4919 - 59 Street, Red Deer, AB,
T4N 6C9   (403) 343-1515
PARKLAND is an integrated Western Canadian energy company with activities in refining, retailing and transportation as well as investments in oil field services, exploration and production.
Jack C. Donald, President & C.E.O.

TOTAL ASSETS ($000)	92,848
TOTAL REVENUE ($000)	126,543
NET INCOME ($000)	3,181
EMPLOYEES	135
RANK (Profit/Revenue/Assets)	506/383/500

PARRISH & HEIMBECKER LIMITED

(Private)   WHOLESALE DISTRIBUTORS
360 Main Street, Suite 700, Winnipeg, MB, R3C 3Z3   (204) 956-2030
PARRISH & HEIMBECKER LIMITED is a wholesaler of grain and poultry. It also operates flour mills, feed mills, poultry processing plants and lake ships.
H. Heimbecker, Chairman

TOTAL ASSETS ($000)	185,737
TOTAL REVENUE ($000)	666,536
NET INCOME ($000)	na
EMPLOYEES	1,300

PATHEON INC.

(Public)   BIOTECHNOLOGY & PHARMACEUTICALS
Exchanges: T   Stock Symbol: PTI
Canterra Tower, Suite 4615, 400 - 3rd Avenue S.W., Calgary, AB,
T2P 4H2   (403) 269-6795
PATHEON INC. provides contract manufacturing and packaging services to the North American pharmaceutical industry. PANTHEON also provides clinical trial manufacturing services in connection with the research, development and approval of new pharmaceutical products.
Richard A.N. Bonnycastle, Chairman, President & C.E.O.

TOTAL ASSETS ($000)	17,729
TOTAL REVENUE ($000)	24,629
NET INCOME ($000)	1,235
EMPLOYEES	286
RANK (Profit/Revenue/Assets)	635/682/900

PC DOCS GROUP INTERNATIONAL INC.
(Public)   COMPUTER SOFTWARE & PROCESSING
Exchanges: T   Stock Symbol: DXX
85 Scarsdale Rd., Suite 200, Toronto, ON, M3B 2R2 (416) 445-4823
PC DOCS GROUP INTERNATIONAL sells computer systems and
software for business. The systems combine off-the-shelf hardware with
custom and package software developed by the company. The company
also provides ongoing support services to its customers.
Rubin I. Osten, President & C.E.O.

TOTAL ASSETS ($000)	18,633
TOTAL REVENUE ($000)	25,668
NET INCOME ($000)	(8,945)
EMPLOYEES	30
RANK (Profit/Revenue/Assets)	940/673/886

PCL CONSTRUCTION GROUP INC.
(Private)   CONTRACTORS
5410 - 99 Street, Edmonton, AB, T6E 3P4   (403) 435-9711
PCL CONSTRUCTION GROUP INC. is a general contractor. PCL
Construction Group is a wholly owned subsidiary of PCL Construction
Holdings Ltd. of Edmonton, Alberta.
R. Stollery, Chairman

TOTAL ASSETS ($000)	386,751
TOTAL REVENUE ($000)	1,310,816
NET INCOME ($000)	na
EMPLOYEES	4,000

PE BEN OILFIELD SERVICES LTD.
See page 123 for a full company profile.

PEERLESS CARPET CORPORATION
See page 209 for a full company profile.

PEGASUS GOLD INC.
See page 52 for a full company profile.

PEMBRIDGE INC.
(Public)   INSURANCE - PROPERTY & CASUALTY
Exchanges: Z   Stock Symbol: PEM
Ste. 300, 1243 Islington Ave., Etobicoke, ON,
M8X 2Y3   (416) 231-2333
PEMBRIDGE INC. is a financial services intermediary involved primar-
ily in the underwriting of niche and specialty general insurance products
and the management of investment funds derived from its insurance
opertions.
John Thompson, Chairman & Secretary

TOTAL ASSETS ($000)	111,740
TOTAL REVENUE ($000)	0
NET INCOME ($000)	0
EMPLOYEES	225
RANK (Profit/Revenue/Assets)	542/596/458

PENGROWTH GAS INCOME FUND
(Public)   INVESTMENT COMPANIES AND FUNDS
Exchanges: T M   Stock Symbol: PGF.UN
Suite 1050, 202 - 6th Avenue S.W., Calgary, AB,
T2P 2R9   (403) 233-0224
PENGROWTH GAS INCOME FUND is a closed-end energy invest-
ment trust established to earn oil and gas royalty income through pur-
chasing Penngrowth Gas Corporation royalty units. All income received
by the Fund is distributed to unitholders on a monthly basis. The
corporation and the Gas Fund is managed by Pengrowth Management
LTD.
James S. Kinnear, President

TOTAL ASSETS ($000)	88,000
TOTAL REVENUE ($000)	15,252
NET INCOME ($000)	4,177
EMPLOYEES	4
RANK (Profit/Revenue/Assets)	456/755/509

PENN WEST PETROLEUM LTD.
See page 124 for a full company profile.

PERKINS PAPERS LTD.
(Public)   PAPER PRODUCTS
Exchanges: M   Stock Symbol: PKN
2345 Autoroute des Laurentides, Laval, PQ, H7S 1Z7 (514) 688-1152
PERKINS PAPERS LTD. is engaged in the manufacture and sale of
sanitary tissue products to the Canadian consumer and industrial markets.
Paper towels, bathroom tissue, serviettes, placemats, tablecovers and
food wrap are sold in the consumer market under the Budget, Decor,
Plush and Rite brand names. A similiar range of products is offered to
food chains and merchandisers under private label or generic packaging.
R. Bramwell, President & C.E.O.

TOTAL ASSETS ($000)	127,369
TOTAL REVENUE ($000)	111,158
NET INCOME ($000)	(5,109)
EMPLOYEES	492
RANK (Profit/Revenue/Assets)	909/405/433

PERLE SYSTEMS LIMITED
(Public)   ELECTRICAL & ELECTRONIC
Exchanges: T   Stock Symbol: PL
60 Renfrew Drive, Markham, ON, L3R 0E1   (905) 475-8885
PERLE SYSTEMS LIMITED is a developer and seller of data communications connectivity products. These products facilitate communications between personal computers, networks and host computer/LAN
servers.
Joseph E. Perle, C.E.O. & President

TOTAL ASSETS ($000)	23,761
TOTAL REVENUE ($000)	0
NET INCOME ($000)	0
EMPLOYEES	70
RANK (Profit/Revenue/Assets)	575/636/830

PET VALU INC.
(Public)   SPECIALTY STORES
Exchanges: T   Stock Symbol: PVI
7300 Warden Ave., Ste. 400, Markham, ON,
L3R 9Z6   (905) 946-1200
PET VALU INC. is a specialty retailer of pet food and pet supplies.
J.W. Nevil Thomas, Chairman

TOTAL ASSETS ($000)	39,767
TOTAL REVENUE ($000)	72,786
NET INCOME ($000)	3,019
EMPLOYEES	189
RANK (Profit/Revenue/Assets)	510/472/696

PETERSBURG LONG DISTANCE INC.
See page 385 for a full company profile.

PETRO-CANADA
See page 125 for a full company profile.

PETROMET RESOURCES LIMITED
See page 126 for a full company profile.

PETROMONT & CO. LTD. PARTNERSHIP
(Private)   CHEMICALS
2931 Marie-Victorin Boulevard, Varennes, PQ,
J3X 1S7   (514) 652-2971
PETROMONT & CO. LTD. PARTNERSHIP operates three petro-
chemical plants. Petromont is 50% owned by Ethylec Inc. and 50% by
Union Carbide Chemicals and Plastics Canada Inc.
Louis M. Riopel, Chairman of the Board

TOTAL ASSETS ($000)	290,575
TOTAL REVENUE ($000)	264,293
NET INCOME ($000)	na
EMPLOYEES	588

PETROREP RESOURCES LTD.
(Public)   OIL AND GAS PRODUCERS
Exchanges: T   Stock Symbol: PRR
Ste. 1000, 630 - 6th Ave. SW, Calgary, AB, T2P 0S8 (403) 264-5100
PETROREP RESOURCES is involved in the exploration for, and the
development and production of crude oil, natural gas, and related liquids
in Canada. The company is administered and controlled by Petrorep
(Canada) Ltd. Petrorep (Canada) has a 66.4% interest in Petrorep Re-
sources.
Alastair H. Ross, Chairman

TOTAL ASSETS ($000)	78,720
TOTAL REVENUE ($000)	29,846
NET INCOME ($000)	463
EMPLOYEES	52
RANK (Profit/Revenue/Assets)	699/650/533

PETROSTAR PETROLEUMS INC.
(Public)   OIL AND GAS PRODUCERS
Exchanges: T   Stock Symbol: PPE
Ste. 3750, 700 - 2nd St. SW, Calgary, AB, T2P 2W2 (403) 265-1142
PETROSTAR PETROLEUMS INC. is an Alberta based resource de-
velopment company engaged in the exploration and development of
crude oil and natural gas reserves.
Richard G. Anderson, President & C.E.O.

TOTAL ASSETS ($000)	48,385
TOTAL REVENUE ($000)	10,709
NET INCOME ($000)	1,119
EMPLOYEES	23
RANK (Profit/Revenue/Assets)	645/792/640

PHARMA PLUS DRUGMARTS LTD.
(Private)   SPECIALTY STORES
5935 Airport Rd., Ste. 500, Mississauga, ON,
L4V 1W5   (905) 672-0600
PHARMA PLUS DRUGMARTS LTD. is involved in pharmacy sales
and sales of general merchandise. It operates 106 units in Ontario. It is a
wholly owned subsidiary of The Oshawa Group Limited.

Rochelle Stenzler, President & Gen. Manager

TOTAL ASSETS ($000)	109,500
TOTAL REVENUE ($000)	417,700
NET INCOME ($000)	na
EMPLOYEES	na

PHILIP ENVIRONMENTAL INC.
See page 586 for a full company profile.

PHILIPS ELECTRONICS LTD.
(Private)   ELECTRICAL & ELECTRONIC
601 Milner Avenue, Scarborough, ON, M1B 1M8   (416) 292-0600
PHILIPS ELECTRONICS LTD is a manufacturer & wholesaler of a
wide range of consumer and professional electric and electronic products.
Philips Electronics is a wholly owned subsidiary of Philips Canada,
which is in turn a wholly owned subsidiary of Philips Electronics N.V.
Eric Versteeg, President

TOTAL ASSETS ($000)	136,900
TOTAL REVENUE ($000)	275,300
NET INCOME ($000)	5,300
EMPLOYEES	894

PHOENIX INTERNATIONAL LIFE SCIENCES INC.
See page 555 for a full company profile.

PINNACLE RESOURCES LTD.
See page 127 for a full company profile.

PIONEER METALS CORPORATION
See page 53 for a full company profile.

PITNEY BOWES OF CANADA LTD.
(Private)   OTHER SERVICES
2200 Yonge Street, Suite 100, Toronto, ON, M4S 3E1(416) 424-2211
PITNEY BOWES is comprised of the business systems group and a
leasing division. The business systems group is Canada's leading supplier
of postage meters and mailing systems. It also supplies shipping and
inserting systems, copiers, facsimile machines and related supplies.
Pitney Bowes Leasing offers leasing programs for the full line of business
systems products and its subsidiaries.
William Ted Madden, President & C.O.O.

TOTAL ASSETS ($000)	547,629
TOTAL REVENUE ($000)	260,105
NET INCOME ($000)	19,051
EMPLOYEES	1,350

PLACE RESOURCES CORPORATION
(Public)   OIL AND GAS PRODUCERS
Exchanges: T   Stock Symbol: PLG.A
Ste. 1350, 140 - 4th Ave. SW, Calgary, AB, T2P 3N3 (403) 262-7114
PLACE RESOURCES CORPORATION is engaged in the exploration,
development and production of oil and gas. It has interests in Western
Canada.
Keith W. Hern, President & C.E.O.

TOTAL ASSETS ($000)	24,330
TOTAL REVENUE ($000)	10,211
NET INCOME ($000)	1,593
EMPLOYEES	9
RANK (Profit/Revenue/Assets)	600/801/820

PLACER DOME INC.
See page 54 for a full company profile.

PLAINTREE SYSTEMS INC.
(Public)   TELECOMMUNICATIONS
Exchanges: T   Stock Symbol: LAN
59 Iber Road, Stittsville, ON, K2S 1E7   (613) 831-8300
PLAINTREE SYSTEMS INC. develops, manufactures and markets computer networking products, which improve the performance and simplify the management of local area networks.
David M. Delaney, Chairman

TOTAL ASSETS ($000)	13,600
TOTAL REVENUE ($000)	3,538
NET INCOME ($000)	(5,994)
EMPLOYEES	105
RANK (Profit/Revenue/Assets)	917/888/978

PLANVEST CAPITAL CORP.
(Public)   MANAGEMENT AND DIVERSIFIED
Exchanges: T V   Stock Symbol: PLV
Ste. 1201, 750 W. Pender St., Vancouver, BC,
V6C 2T8   (604) 685-6299
PLANVEST CAPITAL CORP. is an investment holding company. It subsidiaries operate in the financial services industry.
C. Michael O'Brian, President & C.E.O.

TOTAL ASSETS ($000)	37,290
TOTAL REVENUE ($000)	33,350
NET INCOME ($000)	2,405
EMPLOYEES	24
RANK (Profit/Revenue/Assets)	543/630/712

PLASTI-FAB LTD.
(Public)   MISC. INDUSTRIAL PRODUCTS
Exchanges: T   Stock Symbol: PFB
Ste. 270, 3015 - 5th Ave. NE, Calgary, AB, T2A 6T8   (403) 248-9306
PLASTI-FAB LTD. is a national plastics manufacturer whose principle products are insulation and custom moulding produced from beaded foam plastics. The company services markets throughout Canada with production facilities in British Columbia, Alberta, Saskatchewan, Manitoba, and Ontario.
C. Alan Smith, Chairman & C.E.O.

TOTAL ASSETS ($000)	23,258
TOTAL REVENUE ($000)	27,233
NET INCOME ($000)	1,394
EMPLOYEES	185
RANK (Profit/Revenue/Assets)	619/663/836

PMG FINANCIAL INC.
(Public)   PACKAGING AND CONTAINERS
Exchanges: T   Stock Symbol: PMP
20 Adelaide St. E., Ste. 1300, Toronto, ON, M5C 2T6 (416) 366-1515
PMG FINANCIAL INC. is an investment company with operating subsidiaries in the commercial printing industry focusing on consumer label manufacturing, packaging and specialty niche products.
Lou Elmaleh, Chairman, President & C.E.O.

TOTAL ASSETS ($000)	47,022
TOTAL REVENUE ($000)	19,115
NET INCOME ($000)	1,933
EMPLOYEES	na
RANK (Profit/Revenue/Assets)	435/567/651

POCO PETROLEUMS LTD.
See page 128 for a full company profile.

PORT OF QUEBEC CORPORATION
(Crown)   TRANSPORTATION
150 Dalhousie, Quebec, PQ, G1K 7P7   (418) 648-3640
Port of Quebec is involved in the administration of ports in Quebec.
Rene Paquet, Chairman

TOTAL ASSETS ($000)	61,848
TOTAL REVENUE ($000)	11,666
NET INCOME ($000)	(1,987)
EMPLOYEES	82

POTASH CORPORATION OF SASKATCHEWAN INC.
See page 288 for a full company profile.

POWER CORPORATION OF CANADA
See page 485 for a full company profile.

POWER FINANCIAL CORPORATION
See page 486 for a full company profile.

PPG CANADA INC.
(Private)   CHEMICALS
30 St. Clair Avenue West, Toronto, ON, M4V 3A1   (416) 923-5441
PPG CANADA INC. is a manufacturer of flat glass, automotive glass, coatings and resins, and chemicals. The company is a wholly owned subsidiary of PPG Industries, Inc. of the United States.
Jim W. Craig, President & C.O.O.

TOTAL ASSETS ($000)	391,686
TOTAL REVENUE ($000)	627,350
NET INCOME ($000)	24,070
EMPLOYEES	2,000

PRATT & WHITNEY CANADA INC.
(Private)   TRANSPORTATION EQUIP & COMPNTS
1000 Boul. Marie-Victorin, Longueuil, PQ, J4G 1A1   (514) 677-9411
PRATT & WHITNEY CANADA INC. is engaged in the manufacture of gas turbine engines for air, sea and land applications. The company is wholly owned by United Technologies Corporation of the United States.
L. David Caplan, Chairman & C.E.O.

TOTAL ASSETS ($000)	1,277,952
TOTAL REVENUE ($000)	1,581,260
NET INCOME ($000)	na
EMPLOYEES	7,400

PRAXAIR CANADA INC.
(Private)   CHEMICALS
1 City Centre Drive, Mississauga, ON, M4P 1J3   (905) 803-1600
PRAXAIR CANADA INC. manufactures chemicals, plastics, and industrial, medical and specialty gases. The company has operations across Canada. Union Carbide Corp. of Danbury, Connecticut, holds a 75% interest in the company.
Gilbert E. Playford, President & C.E.O.

TOTAL ASSETS ($000)	818,937
TOTAL REVENUE ($000)	390,945
NET INCOME ($000)	61,178
EMPLOYEES	na

PRECISION DRILLING CORP.
See page 129 for a full company profile.

PREMDOR INC.
See page 587 for a full company profile.

PREMETALCO INC.
(Private)   WHOLESALE DISTRIBUTORS
110 Belfield Road, Rexdale, ON, M9W 1G1   (416) 245-7386
PREMETALCO INC. is engaged in industrial distribution.
V.H. Sher, Chairman

TOTAL ASSETS ($000)	108,065
TOTAL REVENUE ($000)	214,329
NET INCOME ($000)	6,626
EMPLOYEES	625

PREMIER CDN ENTERPRISES LTD.
(Public)   OTHER MINES
Exchanges: M   Stock Symbol: PRB.A
1785- 55th Avenue, Dorval, PQ, H9P 2W3   (514) 631-6700
PREMIER CDN ENTERPRISES LTD. produces and markets sphagnum peat moss. It also makes and markets peat moss based culture mediums, organic soils, and organic fertilizers.
Bernard Belanger, President & C.E.O.

TOTAL ASSETS ($000)	78,237
TOTAL REVENUE ($000)	67,617
NET INCOME ($000)	4,254
EMPLOYEES	635
RANK (Profit/Revenue/Assets)	452/488/536

PREMIER CHOIX: TVEC INC.
(Public)   BROADCASTING
Exchanges: M   Stock Symbol: PCT.A
2100 Rue Ste-Catherine Ouest, 8th Floor, Montreal, PQ,
H3H 2T3   (514) 939-3150
PREMIER CHOIX: TVEC INC. operates a French language pay TV service, Super Ecran, which shows feature films 24 hours a day. The company also provides two French language specialty channels: Canal Familie which offers programming for children and young teens in the three-to-14 age group; and Canal D, which shows documentaries.
Harold Greenberg, Chairman

TOTAL ASSETS ($000)	31,465
TOTAL REVENUE ($000)	34,447
NET INCOME ($000)	3,640
EMPLOYEES	52
RANK (Profit/Revenue/Assets)	480/621/760

PREMIER UNITED KINGDOM NT (CDN) LTD.
(Public)   INVESTMENT COMPANIES AND FUNDS
Exchanges: T   Stock Symbol: PRH
Suite 5000, P.O. Box 150, First Canadian Place, Toronto, ON,
M5X 1H3   (416) 813-4600
PREMIER UNITED KINGDOM NT (CDN) LTD. has invested its funds in Series I Preference Shares of DT Holdings Ltd. The purpose of the company is to provide a vehicle through which different investment objectives with respect to participation in the Series I Preference Shares of DT Holdings Ltd. may be satisfied.

Thomas Pippy, President & C.E.O.

TOTAL ASSETS ($000)	60,625
TOTAL REVENUE ($000)	5,557
NET INCOME ($000)	5,407
EMPLOYEES	na
RANK (Profit/Revenue/Assets)	412/855/591

PRICE COSTCO CANADA INC.
(Private)   DEPARTMENT STORES
3000 Jacques-Bureau, Laval, PQ, H7P 5P7   (514) 686-4444
PRICE CLUB CANADA INC. is a large scale bulk retailing-wholesaling store offering a diverse line of products to consumers through membership.

TOTAL ASSETS ($000)	na
TOTAL REVENUE ($000)	2,025,000
NET INCOME ($000)	na
EMPLOYEES	5,500

PRIME RESOURCES GROUP INC.
See page 55 for a full company profile.

PRIMEX FOREST PRODUCTS LTD.
(Public)   WEST COAST FORESTRY
Exchanges: T V   Stock Symbol: PXF
9924 River Road, Delta, BC, V4G 1B5   (604) 583-3665
PRIMEX FOREST PRODUCTS LTD. manufactures and markets lumber products through three operations: Acorn Forest Products Division; Specialty Products Division; and Field Sawmills Limited Partnership. All operation are located in British Columbia.
George L. Malpass, President & C.E.O.

TOTAL ASSETS ($000)	101,465
TOTAL REVENUE ($000)	191,960
NET INCOME ($000)	14,498
EMPLOYEES	536
RANK (Profit/Revenue/Assets)	248/321/481

PRINCE RUPERT PORT CORPORATION
(Crown)   TRANSPORTATION
110 Third Avenue West, Prince Rupert, BC, V8J 1K8 (604) 627-7545
PRINCE RUPERT PORT CORPORATION was established pursuant to the Canada Ports Corporation Act in 1984. The company controls the area and harbour around Prince Rupert through the regulation of cargo and ship traffic through the harbour.
Peter J. Lester, Chairman

TOTAL ASSETS ($000)	111,646
TOTAL REVENUE ($000)	13,190
NET INCOME ($000)	872
EMPLOYEES	16

PRINCETON MINING CORPORATION
See page 20 for a full company profile.

PRISM SULPHUR CORPORATION
(Private)   WHOLESALE DISTRIBUTORS
Ste. 3200, 700 - 2nd St. SW, Calgary, AB, T2P 2W2   (403) 262-8766
PRISM SULPHUR CORPORATION is an international marketer of Canadian elemental sulphur. The company is owned by 21 western Canadian oil and gas producers.

B.C. MacDonald, Chairman of the Board

TOTAL ASSETS ($000)	67,623
TOTAL REVENUE ($000)	190,916
NET INCOME ($000)	na
EMPLOYEES	10

PROCOR LIMITED
(Private)   FINANCE AND LEASING
2001 Speers Road, Oakville, ON, L6J 5E1   (905) 827-4111
PROCOR LIMITED manufactures, leases and services railway cars. Procor is wholly owned by Union Tank Car Company.
Frank D. Lester, President

TOTAL ASSETS ($000)	546,451
TOTAL REVENUE ($000)	167,405
NET INCOME ($000)	14,929
EMPLOYEES	700

PROCTER & GAMBLE INC.
(Private)   MISC. CONSUMER PRODUCTS
4711 Yonge Street, North York, ON, M2N 6K8   (416) 730-4711
PROCTER & GAMBLE INC. is a manufacturer and distributor of laundry products, household cleaning products, food and beverage products, health, beauty aids and drug products, industrial chemical products and lumber, pulp and paper products. The company is a wholly owned subsidiary of Procter & Gamble Company of Cincinnati, Ohio.
Yong H. Quek, President

TOTAL ASSETS ($000)	na
TOTAL REVENUE ($000)	1,614,704
NET INCOME ($000)	na
EMPLOYEES	na

PROFCO RESOURCES LTD.
(Public)   OIL AND GAS PRODUCERS
Exchanges: T   Stock Symbol: PSO
Ste. 1400, 340 -12th Ave. SW, Calgary, AB, T2R 1L5 (403) 266-1721
PROFCO RESOURCES LTD. is involved in the acquisition, exploration, and development of oil and gas properties.
John J. Fleming, Chairman

TOTAL ASSETS ($000)	28,493
TOTAL REVENUE ($000)	1,918
NET INCOME ($000)	406
EMPLOYEES	2
RANK (Profit/Revenue/Assets)	712/926/782

PROGAS LIMITED
(Private)   GAS UTILITIES
Ste. 4100, 400 - 3rd Ave. SW, Calgary, AB, T2P 4H2 (403) 266-0300
PROGAS LIMITED is a natural gas marketer. Progas is owned by 12 corporations each holding 8.33%.
Vern Horte, Chairman

TOTAL ASSETS ($000)	93,682
TOTAL REVENUE ($000)	697,178
NET INCOME ($000)	1,313

PROMIS SYSTEMS CORPORATION LTD.
(Public)   COMPUTER SOFTWARE & PROCESSING
Exchanges: T   Stock Symbol: PSW
Suite 500, 175 Bloor St. E., Toronto, ON, M4W 3R8   (416) 960-0960
PROMIS SYSTEMS CORPORATION LTD. develops and markets software for use by large scale manufacturers in the management of plant

floor operations designed to enhance manufacturing competitiveness through higher product quality, faster output and lower production costs.
Elliot Wassarman, President & C.E.O.

TOTAL ASSETS ($000)	26,036 (US)
TOTAL REVENUE ($000)	19,924 (US)
NET INCOME ($000)	542 (US)
EMPLOYEES	150
RANK (Profit/Revenue/Assets)	674/662/722

PROVIGO INC.
See page 430 for a full company profile.

PRUDENTIAL STEEL LTD.
See page 588 for a full company profile.

PUBLIC STORAGE CANADIAN PROPERTIES
(Public)   OTHER SERVICES
Exchanges: T   Stock Symbol: PST
Suite 310, 5399 Eglinton Avenue West, Etobicoke, ON, M9C 5K6   (416) 620-1577
PUBLIC STORAGE CANADIAN PROPERTIES is involved in the operation of storage facilities.
B. Wayne Hughes, Chairman

TOTAL ASSETS ($000)	20,026
TOTAL REVENUE ($000)	7,729
NET INCOME ($000)	3,243
EMPLOYEES	0
RANK (Profit/Revenue/Assets)	504/824/871

PUROLATOR COURIER LTD.
(Private)   OTHER SERVICES
5310 Explorer Dr., Mississauga, ON, L4W 4H6   (905) 624-5454
PUROLATOR COURIER LTD. is a courier company that delivers goods and documents.
Matthew O. Diggs Jr., Chairman

TOTAL ASSETS ($000)	314,399
TOTAL REVENUE ($000)	571,647
NET INCOME ($000)	na
EMPLOYEES	9,000

QSOUND LABS, INC.
See page 274 for a full company profile.

QSR LIMITED
See page 56 for a full company profile.

QUADRA LOGIC TECHNOLOGIES INC.
See page 231 for a full company profile.

QUADRON RESOURCES LTD.
(Public)   OIL AND GAS PRODUCERS
Exchanges: T   Stock Symbol: QRL
Ste. 1100, 250 - 6th Ave. SW, Calgary, AB, T2P 3H7 (403) 531-3100
QUADRON RESOURCES LTD. is involved in the acquisition, exploration, and development of crude oil, natural gas, and natural gas liquids primarily in southeastern and central Alberta.
Richard S.S. Wilington, Chairman of the Board

TOTAL ASSETS ($000)	38,622
TOTAL REVENUE ($000)	11,393

NET INCOME ($000)	1,279
EMPLOYEES	13
RANK (Profit/Revenue/Assets)	630/785/704

QUAKER OATS COMPANY OF CANADA LIMITED (THE)

(Private) FOOD PROCESSING
Quaker Park, Peterborough, ON, K9J 7B2 (705) 743-6330
THE QUAKER OATS COMPANY OF CANADA LIMITED manufactures a wide range of quality food products. Business divisions include foods, food services, and Gatorade sports beverage. The company is a wholly owned subsidiary of Quaker Oats Company of Chicago, Illinois.
David L. Morton, President & C.E.O.

TOTAL ASSETS ($000)	147,546
TOTAL REVENUE ($000)	277,986
NET INCOME ($000)	(2,514)
EMPLOYEES	900

QUEBEC-TELEPHONE
See page 360 for a full company profile.

QUEBECOR INC.
See page 386 for a full company profile.

QUEBECOR PRINTING INC.
See page 387 for a full company profile.

QUEENSTAKE RESOURCES LTD.

(Public) PRECIOUS METALS
Exchanges: T Stock Symbol: QTR
10th Floor, 900 West Hastings Street, Vancouver, BC,
V6C 1E5 (604) 684-1218
QUEENSTAKE RESOURCES LTD. is involved in precious metal mining. The company, along with subsidiaries, operates in Canada, the United States and Uruguay.
Gordon C. Gutrath, President & C.E.O.

TOTAL ASSETS ($000)	13,574
TOTAL REVENUE ($000)	637
NET INCOME ($000)	(1,818)
EMPLOYEES	20
RANK (Profit/Revenue/Assets)	849/953/979

QUEST CAPITAL CORPORATION

(Public) MANAGEMENT AND DIVERSIFIED
Exchanges: T M V Stock Symbol: QCC
Suite 900, 999 West Hastings Street, Vancouver, BC,
V6C 2W2 (604) 689-1428
QUEST CAPITAL CORPORATION is a mining finance house whose principal business consists of financing natural resource companies and their respective properties through direct investments to such companies.
R.A. Bruce McDonald, Chairman

TOTAL ASSETS ($000)	21,579
TOTAL REVENUE ($000)	4,784
NET INCOME ($000)	2,266
EMPLOYEES	14
RANK (Profit/Revenue/Assets)	553/869/857

QUESTAR RESOURCES CORP.

(Public) OIL AND GAS PRODUCERS
Exchanges: T Stock Symbol: QRC
14th Floor, 630 - 6th Avenue S.W., Calgary, AB,
T2P 0S8 (403) 265-0540
QUESTAR RESOURCES CORP. is involved in the acquisition, exploration and development of oil and natural gas properties in Alberta and Saskatchewan.
Barry R. Giovanetto, President & C.E.O.

TOTAL ASSETS ($000)	12,782
TOTAL REVENUE ($000)	3,567
NET INCOME ($000)	626
EMPLOYEES	11
RANK (Profit/Revenue/Assets)	685/887/994

QUNO CORPORATION
See page 168 for a full company profile.

QUORUM GROWTH INC.

(Public) INVESTMENT COMPANIES AND FUNDS
Exchanges: T Stock Symbol: QI
Sun Life Tower, 150 King Street West, P.O. Box 5, Toronto, ON,
M5H 1J9 (416) 971-6998
QUORUM GROWTH INC. is a strategic, active investor in select emerging Canadian businesses selling internationally. The company focuses on companies with a strong position, proven technology, proprietary products, or services with the potential to become dominant in domestic and international markets.
E. Peter Lougheed, Chairman

TOTAL ASSETS ($000)	74,272
TOTAL REVENUE ($000)	3,369
NET INCOME ($000)	631
EMPLOYEES	0
RANK (Profit/Revenue/Assets)	684/892/550

R.P.M. TECH INC.

(Public) MACHINERY
Exchanges: M Stock Symbol: RP
184 Route 138, Cap-Sante, PQ, G0A 1L0 (418) 285-1811
R.P.M. TECH INC. is involved in the manufacturing, distribution and maintenance of heavy machinery. The company's activities are concentrated in North America, but it also operates in Europe and China.
Marcel Papillon, President & General Manager

TOTAL ASSETS ($000)	16,516
TOTAL REVENUE ($000)	25,646
NET INCOME ($000)	517
EMPLOYEES	100
RANK (Profit/Revenue/Assets)	693/674/926

RADIOMUTUEL INC.

(Public) BROADCASTING
Exchanges: M Stock Symbol: RDA.A
1717 Rene-Levesque Blvd. East, Montreal, PQ,
H2L 4E8 (514) 529-3210
RADIOMUTUEL INC. operates French language radio stations in Quebec. It also operates Musique Plus, a French language music video channel on basic cable, and Omni Outdoor Limited Partnership, an outdoor advertising company.

Normand Beauchamp, Chairman President & C.E.O.

TOTAL ASSETS ($000)	60,939
TOTAL REVENUE ($000)	53,996
NET INCOME ($000)	(3,364)
EMPLOYEES	650
RANK (Profit/Revenue/Assets)	887/534/590

RAINY RIVER FOREST PRODUCTS INC.
See page 169 for a full company profile.

RALSTON PURINA CANADA INC.
(Private)   FOOD PROCESSING
2500 Royal Windsor Dr., Mississauga, ON, L5J 1K8   (905) 822-1611
RALSTON PURINA CANADA INC. is engaged in the production of pet food, animal and poultry feeds and battery products. The company has three divisions: Grocery Products, AGRI and Eveready. Ralston Purina Canada is a 90% owned subsidiary of Ralston Purnia International Holding Company Inc. of Delaware. Ralston Purina Overseas Battery Corp. owns the remaining 10%.
W.L. Lewis, President

TOTAL ASSETS ($000)	110,274
TOTAL REVENUE ($000)	298,414
NET INCOME ($000)	5,340
EMPLOYEES	919

RANCHMEN'S RESOURCES LTD.
See page 130 for a full company profile.

RAND A TECHNOLOGY CORPORATION
(Public)   CONSULTING
Exchanges: T   Stock Symbol: RND
5285 Solar Drive, Mississauga, ON, L4W 5B8   (905) 625-2000
RAND A TECHNOLOGY CORPORATION is a value-added reseller of mechanical computer aided design, computer aided manufacturing, and computer aided engineering solutions which encompasses systems integration, software, hardware, and support and consulting services.
Dennis Semkiw, Chairman & Treasurer

TOTAL ASSETS ($000)	47,753
TOTAL REVENUE ($000)	81,795
NET INCOME ($000)	3,395
EMPLOYEES	263
RANK (Profit/Revenue/Assets)	496/450/647

RANGER OIL LIMITED
See page 131 for a full company profile.

RAYROCK YELLOWKNIFE RESOURCES INC.
See page 57 for a full company profile.

RBC DOMINION SECURITIES LIMITED
(Private)   INVESTMENT HOUSES
P.O. Box 21, Commerce Court South, Toronto, ON,
M5L 1A7   (416) 864-4000
RBC DOMINION SECURITIES LIMITED is an investment holding company which, through subsidiaries, carries on business as a fully integrated Canadian-based investment dealer.
Anthony S. Fell, Chairman & C.E.O.

TOTAL ASSETS ($000)	18,375,233
TOTAL REVENUE ($000)	1,029,180

NET INCOME ($000)	133,300
EMPLOYEES	na

REA GOLD CORPORATION
See page 58 for a full company profile.

READER'S DIGEST ASSOCIATION (CANADA) LTD. (THE)
(Private)   PUBLISHING & PRINTING
2115 Redfern, West Mount, PQ, H3Z 2V9   (514) 934-0751
THE READER'S DIGEST ASSOCIATION (CANADA) LTD. is a magazine and book publisher.
Ralph Hancox, President & C.E.O.

TOTAL ASSETS ($000)	61,166
TOTAL REVENUE ($000)	150,729
NET INCOME ($000)	11,403
EMPLOYEES	na

REALFUND
(Public)   PROPERTY MGMNT & INVESTMENT
Exchanges: T   Stock Symbol: RFN.UN
Suite 300, 151 Yonge St., Toronto, ON, M5C 2W7   (416) 947-5105
REALFUND invests in a diversified portfolio of income producing real property investments in Canada. Investments are principally in community oriented shopping centres, commercial office buildings and industrial properties primarily through direct ownership and co-ownership.
Christopher Dingle, President

TOTAL ASSETS ($000)	276,341
TOTAL REVENUE ($000)	25,424
NET INCOME ($000)	7,547
EMPLOYEES	0
RANK (Profit/Revenue/Assets)	351/679/299

RECEPTAGEN LTD.
(Public)   BIOTECHNOLOGY & PHARMACEUTICALS
Exchanges: T   Stock Symbol: PGD
3030 Beta Ave., Burnaby, BC, V5G 4K4   (604) 291-8846
RECEPTAGEN LTD. is a development stage biotechnology company focusing on developing therapies which do not reduce the immunity of patients with life threatening diseases.
A. Charles Morgan, President & C.E.O.

TOTAL ASSETS ($000)	17,221
TOTAL REVENUE ($000)	34,091
NET INCOME ($000)	(3,392)
EMPLOYEES	58
RANK (Profit/Revenue/Assets)	889/624/906

RECOCHEM INC.
(Private)   CHEMICALS
850 Montee de Liesse, Montreal, PQ, H4T 1P4   (514) 341-3550
RECOCHEM INC. is engaged in the manufacture and sales of chemical specialty products.
Joseph Kuchar, Chairman, President & C.E.O.

TOTAL ASSETS ($000)	58,627
TOTAL REVENUE ($000)	131,179
NET INCOME ($000)	1,869
EMPLOYEES	420

REDAURUM LIMITED

(Public) OTHER MINES
Exchanges: T Stock Symbol: RRK
Suite 600, 15 Toronto Street, Toronto, ON, M5C 2R1 (416) 368-3553
REDAURUM LIMITED is involved in the acquisition, exploration and development of diamond properties. The company, through its 50% interest in Auridiam Zimbabwe (Private) Limited, has commenced commercial production of the Rover Ranch diamond property in Zimbabwe.
R. Baxter-Brown, Chairman

TOTAL ASSETS ($000)	14,003
TOTAL REVENUE ($000)	4,046
NET INCOME ($000)	(135)
EMPLOYEES	na
RANK (Profit/Revenue/Assets)	769/878/962

REDEKOP PROPERTIES INC.

(Public) DEVELOPERS
Exchanges: T V Stock Symbol: RPI
827 West Pender Street, Vancouver, BC, V6C 3G8 (604) 662-8144
REDEKOP PROPERTIES INC. is involved in the development of low-rise residential condominium properties in Greater Vancouver and other areas in the Lower Mainland region of British Columbia.
Peter Redekop, Chairman, C.E.O. & Secretary

TOTAL ASSETS ($000)	39,672
TOTAL REVENUE ($000)	0
NET INCOME ($000)	0
EMPLOYEES	na
RANK (Profit/Revenue/Assets)	555/608/697

REDFERN RESOURCES LTD

(Public) PRECIOUS METALS
Exchanges: T V Stock Symbol: RFR
Suite 205, 10711 Cambie Road, Richmond, BC, V6X 3G5 (604) 278-3028
REDFERN RESOURCES LTD is engaged in the exploration and development of mineral properties primarily located in British Columbia.
John A. Greig, Chairman & President

TOTAL ASSETS ($000)	22,529
TOTAL REVENUE ($000)	410
NET INCOME ($000)	(90)
EMPLOYEES	9
RANK (Profit/Revenue/Assets)	763/961/844

REDLAW INDUSTRIES INC.

(Public) AUTOMOTIVE
Exchanges: A Stock Symbol: RDL
174 Stanley St., Suite 300, Brantford, ON, N3S 7S3 (519) 751-1691
REDLAW INDUSTRIES INC., through subsidiaries and affiliates, is involved in the manufacture of industrial and apparel textiles through its investment in Johnston Industries Inc.
David Chandler, Chairman President & C.E.O.

TOTAL ASSETS ($000)	37,201
TOTAL REVENUE ($000)	3,700
NET INCOME ($000)	(616)
EMPLOYEES	3
RANK (Profit/Revenue/Assets)	799/883/714

REDPATH INDUSTRIES LIMITED

(Private) FOOD PROCESSING
95 Queens Quay East, Toronto, ON, M5E 1A3 (416) 366-3561

REDPATH INDUSTRIES LIMITED is engaged in the refining of sugar, and the production of molasses, animal feeds, corn products, and high intensity sweeteners. Redpath is wholly owned by Tate & Lyle PLC.
M.D. McEwen, Chairman

TOTAL ASSETS ($000)	404,181
TOTAL REVENUE ($000)	268,366
NET INCOME ($000)	na
EMPLOYEES	345

REDSTONE RESOURCES INC.

(Public) METAL MINES
Exchanges: T Stock Symbol: RR
Suite 1900, Box 2005, 20 Eglinton Avenue West, Toronto, ON, M4R 1K8 (416) 480-6497
REDSTONE RESOURCES INC. is involved in the acquisition of non-gold mineral royalties.
Pierre Lassonde, Chairman

TOTAL ASSETS ($000)	47,847
TOTAL REVENUE ($000)	4,528
NET INCOME ($000)	2,106
EMPLOYEES	999
RANK (Profit/Revenue/Assets)	559/873/646

REGIONAL CABLESYSTEMS INC.

(Public) CABLE
Exchanges: O Stock Symbol: REG
Suite 300, 710 Dorval Drive, Oakville, ON, L6K 3V7 (905) 338-3133
REGIONAL CABLESYSTEMS INC. carries on cable television operations in Canada and the United States.
Gary D. Kain, Chairman

TOTAL ASSETS ($000)	130,282
TOTAL REVENUE ($000)	39,403
NET INCOME ($000)	(28,529)
EMPLOYEES	210
RANK (Profit/Revenue/Assets)	978/594/427

REGIONAL RESOURCES LTD.

(Public) PRECIOUS METALS
Exchanges: T Stock Symbol: RGL
12th Floor, 20 Toronto Street, Toronto, ON, M5C 2B8 (416) 869-0772
REGIONAL RESOURCES LTD. is involved in the exploration and development of mineral properties in northern British Columbia and the Yukon. Its assets include a 82% interest in the Midway silver-lead-zinc property in northern British Columbia and a 36% interest in Fairfield Minerals Ltd., which is active in exploration in British Columbia.
G. Farquharson, President

TOTAL ASSETS ($000)	14,811
TOTAL REVENUE ($000)	1,939
NET INCOME ($000)	1,330
EMPLOYEES	4
RANK (Profit/Revenue/Assets)	626/925/948

REITMANS (CANADA) LIMITED

See page 431 for a full company profile.

REKO INTERNATIONAL GROUP INC.

(Public) MISC. INDUSTRIAL PRODUCTS
Exchanges: T Stock Symbol: REK
5310 Walker Road, Oldcastle, ON, N0R 1L0 (519) 737-6974

REKO INTERNATIONAL GROUP INC. designs and manufactures injection moulds and other industrial tools, such as dies, fixtures, vacuum form moulds, models, and special machines for first tier suppliers. The infection moulds are used principally for the production of interior and exterior automotive parts and for other consumer and commercial products.

Steve Reko, President & C.E.O.

TOTAL ASSETS ($000)	52,904
TOTAL REVENUE ($000)	25,294
NET INCOME ($000)	3,613
EMPLOYEES	410
RANK (Profit/Revenue/Assets)	484/677/620

REMINGTON ENERGY LTD.
(Public)   OIL AND GAS PRODUCERS
Exchanges: T   Stock Symbol: REL
Ste. 750, 550 - 6th Ave. SW, Calgary, AB, T2P 0S2   (403) 269-9309
REMINGTON ENERGY LTD. is involved in the acquisition, exploration and development of oil and gas in Alberta and British Columbia.

Royston S. Baay, Chairman

TOTAL ASSETS ($000)	36,567
TOTAL REVENUE ($000)	10,586
NET INCOME ($000)	797
EMPLOYEES	24
RANK (Profit/Revenue/Assets)	670/794/721

RENAISSANCE ENERGY LTD.
See page 132 for a full company profile.

REPADRE CAPITAL CORPORATION
(Public)   METAL MINES
Exchanges: T V   Stock Symbol: RPD
40 King Street West, Suite 5600 Scotia Plaza, Toronto, ON,
M5H 4A9   (416) 363-2410
REPADRE CAPITAL CORP. intends to concentrate its business on the creation of royalty interest primarily in natural resource industries.

Jonathan Goodman, Chairman

TOTAL ASSETS ($000)	27,578
TOTAL REVENUE ($000)	3,167
NET INCOME ($000)	808
EMPLOYEES	4
RANK (Profit/Revenue/Assets)	669/899/794

REPAP ENTERPRISES INC.
See page 170 for a full company profile.

REPUBLIC GOLDFIELDS INC.
(Public)   PRECIOUS METALS
Exchanges: V A   Stock Symbol: RGF
1 Dundas Street West, Suite 2402, Box 13, Toronto, ON,
M5G 1Z3   (416) 977-4653
REPUBLIC GOLDFIELDS INC. is involved in the acquisition, exploration and development of gold properties in Canada, the United States and Cuba.

Jack S. Belton,

TOTAL ASSETS ($000)	13,740
TOTAL REVENUE ($000)	251
NET INCOME ($000)	(49)
EMPLOYEES	6
RANK (Profit/Revenue/Assets)	760/974/970

REPUBLIC NATIONAL BANK OF NEW YORK (CANADA)
(Private)   BANKS
1981 McGill College Avenue, Montreal, PQ, H3A 3A9(514) 288-5551
REPUBLIC NATIONAL BANK OF NEW YORK (CANADA) is a full service bank.

Ezekiel Schouela, Chairman

TOTAL ASSETS ($000)	888,066
TOTAL REVENUE ($000)	23,812
NET INCOME ($000)	7,333
EMPLOYEES	150

REVENUE PROPERTIES COMPANY LIMITED
See page 314 for a full company profile.

REXFOR
(Crown)   EAST COAST FORESTRY
1195 Rue de Lavigerie, Ste-Foy, PQ, G1V 4N3   (418) 659-4530
REXFOR's stock is held by the Quebec government. Its objectives are: to salvage and exploit the forested areas of the public domain and to carry out and direct the research required for these purposes; to promote the value of, preserve and protect forest and land intended for forest use; to encourage the establishment and development of the forest products industry.

Maurice Bolduc, Chairman of the Board

TOTAL ASSETS ($000)	220,735
TOTAL REVENUE ($000)	117,078
NET INCOME ($000)	26,666
EMPLOYEES	1,600

RFC RESOURCE FINANCE CORPORATION
(Public)   METAL MINES
Exchanges: T   Stock Symbol: RFC
Aetna Tower Suite 3400, Toronto-Dominion Centre, P.O. Box 19,
Toronto, ON, M5K 1A1   (416) 361-6400
RFC RESOURCE FINANCE CORPORATION owns the Pend Oreille lead-zinc mine in Washington state. It is continuing to evaluate the economic potential of the area.

John H. Purkis, President

TOTAL ASSETS ($000)	18,429
TOTAL REVENUE ($000)	17
NET INCOME ($000)	(669)
EMPLOYEES	4
RANK (Profit/Revenue/Assets)	804/993/889

RHONDA MINING CORPORATION
(Public)   PRECIOUS METALS
Exchanges: Z   Stock Symbol: RDM
Ste. 810, 540 - 5th Ave. SW, Calgary, AB, T2P 0M2   (403) 269-5369
RHONDA MINING CORPORATION is involved in the acquisition, exploration and development of mineral resource properties in Canada and the United States. Major properties include diamond prospects in Saskatchewan, copper prospects in the Northwest Territories and a copper-gold-silver-zinc-cobalt property in Oregon.

John M. Alston, Chairman & C.E.O.

TOTAL ASSETS ($000)	14,050
TOTAL REVENUE ($000)	447
NET INCOME ($000)	(5,463)
EMPLOYEES	0
RANK (Profit/Revenue/Assets)	912/959/959

RHONE-POULENC CANADA INC.

(Private)   CHEMICALS
2000 Argentia Road, Plaza #3, Suite 400, Mississauga, ON,
L5N 1V9   (905) 821-4450
RHONE-POULENC CANADA INC. is a formulator and distributor of chemicals including specialty chemicals, food ingredients, animal nutrition and crop protection products. Rhone-Poulenc Canada is a wholly owned subsidiary of Rhone-Poulenc S.A. of Paris, France.
Bernard West, C.E.O. & Chairman

TOTAL ASSETS ($000)	na
TOTAL REVENUE ($000)	257,139
NET INCOME ($000)	na
EMPLOYEES	192

RICHELIEU HARDWARE LTD.

(Public)   WHOLESALE DISTRIBUTORS
Exchanges: T M   Stock Symbol: RCH
1910 Hymus Boulevard, Dorval, PQ, H9P 1J7   (514) 683-4144
RICHELIEU HARDWARE LTD. is an importer and distributor in Canada of cabinet hardware and related products for the kitchen cabinet and furniture markets. The company's main product categories include functional and decorative hardware items for kitchen cabinets and furniture, high-pressure laminates, veneer sheets and edgebanding products, kitchen cabinet accessories and locksets.
Jean E. Douville, Chairman

TOTAL ASSETS ($000)	51,441
TOTAL REVENUE ($000)	71,853
NET INCOME ($000)	6,069
EMPLOYEES	280
RANK (Profit/Revenue/Assets)	392/476/625

RICHEY COMMUNICATIONS LTD.

(Public)   CABLE
Exchanges: V   Stock Symbol: RHC
Suite 7, 1605 Grand Ave., San Marcos, CA, 92069 (619) 471-6225
RICHEY COMMUNICATIONS LTD., through its wholly owned subsidiary, Richey Pacific Cable Vision, owns and operates private cable television systems.
Steve K. Richey, President & C.E.O.

TOTAL ASSETS ($000)	12,700 (US)
TOTAL REVENUE ($000)	3,820 (US)
NET INCOME ($000)	(1,808) (US)
EMPLOYEES	33
RANK (Profit/Revenue/Assets)	864/865/920

RICHLAND PETROLEUM CORPORATION

(Public)   OIL AND GAS PRODUCERS
Exchanges: T Z   Stock Symbol: RLP.A
Cadillac Fairview Tower 2, Suite 1800, 321 - 6th Avenue S.W.,
CALGARY, AB, T2P 3H3   (403) 261-4080
RICHLAND PETROLEUM CORPORATION is involved in the acquisition, exploration and development of oil and gas properties. The company's principal properties are located in Alberta and Saskatchewan.
Richard A.M. Todd, President & C.E.O.

TOTAL ASSETS ($000)	42,855
TOTAL REVENUE ($000)	15,788
NET INCOME ($000)	1,834
EMPLOYEES	15
RANK (Profit/Revenue/Assets)	582/747/674

RICHMOND SAVINGS CREDIT UNION

(Fin. Co-op)   CREDIT UNIONS
Professional Centre, 5611 Cooney Road, Richmond, BC,
V6X 3J5   (604) 273-8138
RICHMOND SAVINGS CREDIT UNION offers a complete range of financial services to individuals and businesses in British Columbia. The company is active in the insurance business through a wholly owned subsidiary, Richmond Savings Insurance Services.
Peter Cihelka, Chairman

TOTAL ASSETS ($000)	1,271,265
TOTAL REVENUE ($000)	99,822
NET INCOME ($000)	7,337
EMPLOYEES	388

RICHMONT MINES INC.

(Public)   PRECIOUS METALS
Exchanges: T M   Stock Symbol: RIC
110 ave. Principale, Rouyn-Noranda, PQ, J9X 4P2   (819) 797-2465
RICHMONT MINES INC. is a vertically integrated gold mining producer. The company wholly owns the Francoeur Mine and holds an interest in 2,000 acres of land divided in four mining concessions located on the Larder Lake-Cadillac fault covering an area of 749 hectares. Richmont also wholly owns the Camflo Mill and a 36% interest in Louven Mines Inc, which is a 50% owner of the Beaufor mine.
Jean-Guy Rivard, President & C.E.O.

TOTAL ASSETS ($000)	36,369
TOTAL REVENUE ($000)	20,343
NET INCOME ($000)	4,401
EMPLOYEES	127
RANK (Profit/Revenue/Assets)	444/712/723

RIDER TRAVEL CORP.

(Private)   TRANSPORTATION
370 King St. W., Box 32, Suite 700, Toronto, ON,
M5V 1J9   (416) 351-3360
RIDER TRAVAL CORP. provides corporate travel and technology solutions for travel and high transaction service industries.
Mark Rider, Chairman

TOTAL ASSETS ($000)	16,000
TOTAL REVENUE ($000)	450,000
NET INCOME ($000)	na
EMPLOYEES	600

RIGEL ENERGY CORPORATION
See page 133 for a full company profile.

RIMOIL CORPORATION (THE)

(Public)   OIL AND GAS PRODUCERS
Exchanges: T   Stock Symbol: RO.A
Ste. 200, 665 - 8th St. SW, Calgary, AB, T2P 3K7   (403) 266-4584
THE RIMOIL CORPORATION is engaged in the exploration and development of oil and gas properties.
Frank G. Vetsch, Chairman

TOTAL ASSETS ($000)	13,988
TOTAL REVENUE ($000)	7,396
NET INCOME ($000)	998
EMPLOYEES	7
RANK (Profit/Revenue/Assets)	658/830/963

RIO ALGOM LIMITED
See page 21 for a full company profile.

RIO ALTO EXPLORATION LTD.
See page 134 for a full company profile.

RIVER GOLD MINES LTD.
(Public)   OIL AND GAS PRODUCERS
Exchanges: T   Stock Symbol: RIV
137 Church Street, Toronto, ON, M5B 1Y5   (416) 982-3519
RIVER GOLD MINES LTD. is involved in the acquisition, exploration and development of mineral resource properties. The company's most signifcant property is a 100% interest in the Eagle River property in the Mishibishu Lake area of northwestern Ontario.
Conrad Hacke, President & C.E.O.

TOTAL ASSETS ($000)	31,854
TOTAL REVENUE ($000)	336
NET INCOME ($000)	(1,714)
EMPLOYEES	5
RANK (Profit/Revenue/Assets)	839/968/756

RIVERSIDE FOREST PRODUCTS LIMITED
See page 171 for a full company profile.

RJR-MACDONALD INC.
(Private)   TOBACCO
First Canadian Place, 60th Floor, P.O. Box 111, Toronto, ON, M5X 1E8   (416) 601-7000
RJR-MACDONALD INC. is engaged in manufacturing tobacco products.
Edward J. Lang, Chairman

TOTAL ASSETS ($000)	553,170
TOTAL REVENUE ($000)	415,420
NET INCOME ($000)	66,263
EMPLOYEES	850

ROBERT MITCHELL INC.
(Public)   METAL FABRICATORS
Exchanges: M   Stock Symbol: MIT.B
350 Decarie Boulevard, St-Laurent, PQ, H4L 3K5   (514) 747-2471
ROBERT MITCHELL INC. is involved in the manufacture of fabricated metal products and the wholesale distribution of pipe, valves and fittings and equipment for environmental air control.
George H. Holland, Chairman, President & C.E.O.

TOTAL ASSETS ($000)	51,046
TOTAL REVENUE ($000)	75,870
NET INCOME ($000)	(1,853)
EMPLOYEES	563
RANK (Profit/Revenue/Assets)	850/464/627

ROCKWELL INTERNATIONAL OF CANADA LTD.
(Private)   TRANSPORTATION EQUIP & COMPNTS
Corporate Office, 135 Dundas Street, P.O. Box 843, Cambridge, ON, N1R 5X9   (519) 740-8656
ROCKWELL's businesses manufacture various automotive components for heavy duty trucks, special-purpose vehicles, light trucks and passenger cars. Its electronics businesses manufacture and market radio communication, naval combat, avionics and industrial automation sys-

tems and equipment. It is also involved in the marketing of graphic equipment.
William E. Hetherington, Chairman

TOTAL ASSETS ($000)	632,890
TOTAL REVENUE ($000)	452,170
NET INCOME ($000)	48,622
EMPLOYEES	1,650

ROGERS CANTEL MOBILE COMMUNICATIONS INC.
See page 388 for a full company profile.

ROGERS CANTEL MOBILE INC.
(Private)   TELECOMMUNICATIONS
10 York Mills Rd., North York, ON, M2P 2C9   (416) 229-1400
ROGERS CANTEL MOBILE COMMUNICATIONS INC. operates a cellular telephone network in Canada. It is a wholly owned subsidiary of Rogers Communications Inc..
Edward S. Rogers, Chairman

TOTAL ASSETS ($000)	1,738,198
TOTAL REVENUE ($000)	605,614
NET INCOME ($000)	na
EMPLOYEES	na

ROGERS COMMUNICATIONS INC.
See page 389 for a full company profile.

ROHM AND HAAS CANADA INC.
(Private)   CHEMICALS
2 Manse Rd, West Hill, ON, M1E 3T9   (416) 284-4711
ROHM AND HAAS CANADA INC. is a chemicals company. Rohm and Haas Canada is a wholly owned subsidiary of Rohm and Haas Co. of the United States.
J.D. Greulich, General Manager

TOTAL ASSETS ($000)	72,119
TOTAL REVENUE ($000)	178,226
NET INCOME ($000)	na
EMPLOYEES	219

ROINS HOLDING LIMITED
(Private)   INSURANCE - PROPERTY & CASUALTY
10 Wellington Street East, Toronto, ON, M5E 1L5   (416) 366-7511
ROINS HOLDINGS LIMITED is the holding company of Royal Insurance Canada. The company's ultimate owner is Royal Insurance Holdings PLC.
Jock K. Finlayson, Chairman

TOTAL ASSETS ($000)	2,093,341
TOTAL REVENUE ($000)	900,858
NET INCOME ($000)	46,076
EMPLOYEES	1,964

ROLLAND INC.
See page 172 for a full company profile.

ROLLS-ROYCE INDUSTRIES CANADA INC.
(Private)   TRANSPORTATION EQUIP & COMPNTS
9500 Cote de Liesse, Lachine, PQ, H8T 1A2   (514) 631-3541
ROLLS-ROYCE INDUSTRIES CANADA INC. and its subsidiary Rolls-Royce Industries Canada Inc. sell and overhaul engines and design,

manufacture and sell electrical and electronic equipment. It is a subsidiary of Rolls-Royce PLC.
Barry Eccleston, C.E.O. & President

TOTAL ASSETS ($000)	334,000
TOTAL REVENUE ($000)	497,000
NET INCOME ($000)	na
EMPLOYEES	3,500

ROMAN CORPORATION LIMITED
See page 525 for a full company profile.

ROTHMANS INC.
See page 197 for a full company profile.

ROYAL AVIATION INC.
See page 327 for a full company profile.

ROYAL BANK OF CANADA
See page 454 for a full company profile.

ROYAL CANADIAN MINT
(Crown) METAL FABRICATORS
320 Sussex Drive, Ottawa, ON, K1A 0G8 (613) 993-3500
ROYAL CANADIAN MINT is Canada's national mint and has the primary responsibility for striking Canadian general circulation and numismatic coinage. It also produces bullion investment coins, in addition to coins for foreign countries. The Mint is a major refiner of gold.
James C. Corkery, Chairman of the Board

TOTAL ASSETS ($000)	82,450
TOTAL REVENUE ($000)	310,395
NET INCOME ($000)	(3,475)
EMPLOYEES	563

ROYAL INSURANCE COMPANY OF CANADA
(Private) INSURANCE - PROPERTY & CASUALTY
10 Wellington Street East, Toronto, ON, M5E 1L5 (416) 366-7511
ROYAL INSURANCE COMPANY OF CANADA is a property and casualty insurer. The company is ultimately owned by Royal Insurance Holdings plc.
Jock K. Finlayson, Chairman

TOTAL ASSETS ($000)	1,899,300
TOTAL REVENUE ($000)	894,300
NET INCOME ($000)	49,800
EMPLOYEES	1,964

ROYAL LEPAGE LIMITED
See page 315 for a full company profile.

ROYAL OAK MINES INC.
See page 59 for a full company profile.

ROYAL PLASTICS GROUP LIMITED
(Public) MISC. INDUSTRIAL PRODUCTS
Exchanges: T Stock Symbol: RYG
4945 Steeles Avenue West, Weston, ON, M9L 1R4 (416) 749-5131
ROYAL PLASTICS GROUP LIMITED is engaged in the business of manufacturing extruded PVC building products, serving the custom profile window, door, vertical blind, siding and pipe markets.

Vittorio De Zen, Chairman, President & C.E.O.

TOTAL ASSETS ($000)	440,196
TOTAL REVENUE ($000)	460,360
NET INCOME ($000)	45,583
EMPLOYEES	2,185
RANK (Profit/Revenue/Assets)	119/203/240

RUSSEL METALS INC.
See page 526 for a full company profile.

SAINT JOHN PORT CORPORATION
(Crown) TRANSPORTATION
133 Prince William Street, P.O. Box 6429, Station A, Saint John, NB, E2L 4R8 (506) 636-4869
SAINT JOHN PORT CORPORATION manages the port of Saint John, New Brunswick.
Harry P. Gaunce, Chairman

TOTAL ASSETS ($000)	64,083
TOTAL REVENUE ($000)	12,492
NET INCOME ($000)	(20,384)
EMPLOYEES	36

SAMOTH CAPITAL CORPORATION
(Public) PROPERTY MGMNT & INVESTMENT
Exchanges: T Stock Symbol: SCF
Suite 2910, 700 West Georgia Street, Box 10064 TD Tower, Vancouver, BC, V7Y 1B6 (604) 688-0810
SAMOTH CAPITAL CORPORATION is a Canadian-based merchant banking organization that specializes in lending to hotels, multi-family residential projects and master planned community developments in selected growth markets in North America.
Peter H. Thomas, Chairman & C.E.O.

TOTAL ASSETS ($000)	40,007
TOTAL REVENUE ($000)	7,831
NET INCOME ($000)	4,000
EMPLOYEES	20
RANK (Profit/Revenue/Assets)	466/823/695

SAMUEL MANU-TECH INC.
See page 247 for a full company profile.

SANDOZ CANADA INC.
(Private) CHEMICALS
385 boul. Bouchard, Dorval, PQ, H9S 1A9 (514) 631-6775
SANDOZ CANADA INC. is a manufacturer of pharmaceutics and chemicals. Sandoz Canada is wholly owned by Sandoz Ltd. of Switzerland.
H. Mader, Managing Director

TOTAL ASSETS ($000)	130,774
TOTAL REVENUE ($000)	194,038
NET INCOME ($000)	4,411
EMPLOYEES	567

SANI-GESTION INC.
(Public) ENVIRONMENTAL SERVICES
Exchanges: M Stock Symbol: SNG
3383 Boulevard de la Chaudiere, Ste-Foy, PQ, G1X 4B8 (418) 872-8061

SANI-GESTION INC., through its subsidiaries, operates a domestic, commercial and industrial garbage collection and transportation business. It also sells garbage containers and compactors and operates three dump sites for solid and dry material garbage.
Carol Coulombe, President & G.M.

TOTAL ASSETS ($000)	22,358
TOTAL REVENUE ($000)	16,372
NET INCOME ($000)	1,118
EMPLOYEES	160
RANK (Profit/Revenue/Assets)	645/743/847

SANYO CANADA INC.
(Private)   APPLIANCES
50 Beth Nealson Drive, Toronto, ON, M5H 1M6   (416) 421-8344
SANYO CANADA INC. is involved in electronic products, including computers. It is a wholly owned subsidiary of Sanyo of Japan.
Mr. S. Maekawa, President

TOTAL ASSETS ($000)	111,155
TOTAL REVENUE ($000)	219,253
NET INCOME ($000)	1,402
EMPLOYEES	na

SASKATCHEWAN AUTO FUND
(Crown)   INSURANCE - PROPERTY & CASUALTY
2260 11th Avenue, Regina, SK, S4P 0J9   (306) 751-1200
SASKATCHEWAN AUTO FUND offers compulsory automobile insurance under the Automobile Accident Insurance Act. The fund is administered by Saskatchewan Government Insurance and also operates a salvage division.
Hon. Keith Goulet, Chairman

TOTAL ASSETS ($000)	564,773
TOTAL REVENUE ($000)	360,030
NET INCOME ($000)	(93,773)
EMPLOYEES	0

SASKATCHEWAN GOVERNMENT INSURANCE
(Crown)   INSURANCE - PROPERTY & CASUALTY
2260 - 11th Avenue, Regina, SK, S4P 0J9   (306) 751-1200
SASKATCHEWAN GOVERNMENT INSURANCE offers property and casualty insurance to Saskatchewan residents. It administers for the Government of Saskatchewan a program of compulsory automobile insurance regulated by the Automobile Accident Insurance Act. It also operates as SGI Canada.
Hon. Keith Goulet, Chairman of the Board

TOTAL ASSETS ($000)	276,525
TOTAL REVENUE ($000)	145,885
NET INCOME ($000)	18,121
EMPLOYEES	1,231

SASKATCHEWAN POWER CORPORATION
(Crown)   ELECTRICAL UTILITIES
2025 Victoria Avenue, Regina, SK, S4P 0S1   (306) 566-2121
SASKATCHEWAN POWER CORPORATION was established as a provincial crown corporation to provide electrical services throughout the province. The corporation's main functions are the generation, transmission, distribution, sale and supply of electrical energy and energy management services.
Hon. Eldon F. Lautermilch, Chairman of Board

TOTAL ASSETS ($000)	3,270,000
TOTAL REVENUE ($000)	850,000

NET INCOME ($000)	85,000
EMPLOYEES	2,576

SASKATCHEWAN TELECOMMUNICATIONS
(Crown)   TELEPHONE UTILITIES
2121 Saskatchewan Drive, Regina, SK, S4P 3Y2   (306) 777-2008
SASKTEL is a Provincial crown corporation that provides local and long distance voice, data, image and text services throughout Saskatchewan. As a member of Stentor, an alliance of Canada's major telecommunications companies, SaskTel provides a full range of national and worldwide long distance communications services.
Fred Van Parys, President & C.E.O.

TOTAL ASSETS ($000)	1,154,608
TOTAL REVENUE ($000)	629,070
NET INCOME ($000)	88,514
EMPLOYEES	3,750

SASKATCHEWAN WATER CORPORATION
(Crown)   OTHER SERVICES
111 Fairford Street East, Moose Jaw, SK, S6H 7X9   (306) 694-3900
SASKATCHEWAN WATER CORPORATION is responsible for all water management functions for the Province of Saskatchewan and also operates as a water supply utility.
Andy Renaud, Chairman

TOTAL ASSETS ($000)	63,092
TOTAL REVENUE ($000)	27,797
NET INCOME ($000)	1,424
EMPLOYEES	300

SASKATCHEWAN WHEAT POOL
(Non-fin Co-op)   AGRICULTURE
2625 Victoria Avenue, Regina, SK, S4T 7T9   (306) 569-4411
SASKATCHEWAN WHEAT POOL is Canada's largest agricultural cooperative, and one of the country's major businesses. It provides services to about 70,000 farmer-owners annually and is actively engaged in promotion and development of agricultural policy on their behalf.
Donald K. Loewen, C.E.O.

TOTAL ASSETS ($000)	994,874
TOTAL REVENUE ($000)	2,109,567
NET INCOME ($000)	40,435
EMPLOYEES	3,000

SASKATOON CREDIT UNION, LIMITED
(Fin. Co-op)   CREDIT UNIONS
Second Floor, 309 - 22nd Street East, Saskatoon, SK,
S7K 0G7   (306) 934-4000
SASKATOON CREDIT UNION, LIMITED is a credit union providing members with loan, deposit, insurance and other financial services.
Paul Duncan, C.E.O.

TOTAL ASSETS ($000)	432,986
TOTAL REVENUE ($000)	34,640
NET INCOME ($000)	1,644
EMPLOYEES	189

SAVANNA RESOURCES LTD.
(Public)   OIL AND GAS PRODUCERS
Exchanges: Z   Stock Symbol: SV
540 - 5th Ave. SW, Ste. 810, Calgary, AB, T2P 0M2   (403) 269-5369
SAVANNA RESOURCES LTD. is involved in the acquisition, exploration and development of mining claims and rights.

John M. Alston, President

TOTAL ASSETS ($000)	14,026
TOTAL REVENUE ($000)	(4)
NET INCOME ($000)	(365)
EMPLOYEES	6
RANK (Profit/Revenue/Assets)	782/998/960

SCEPTRE INVESTMENT COUNSEL LIMITED

(Public) INVESTMENT COMPANIES AND FUNDS
Exchanges: T Stock Symbol: SZ.A
12th Floor, 26 Wellington Street East, Toronto, ON,
M5E 1W4 (416) 367-9898
SCEPTRE INVESTMENT COUNSEL LIMITED is involved in the business of providing investment management services to institutional and private clients.
J. Douglas Grant, Chairman

TOTAL ASSETS ($000)	13,548
TOTAL REVENUE ($000)	27,382
NET INCOME ($000)	7,811
EMPLOYEES	59
RANK (Profit/Revenue/Assets)	343/660/981

SCEPTRE RESOURCES LIMITED
See page 135 for a full company profile.

SCHNEIDER CORPORATION
See page 198 for a full company profile.

SCINTREX LIMITED

(Public) ELECTRICAL & ELECTRONIC
Exchanges: T Stock Symbol: SCT
222 Snidercroft Road, Concord, ON, L4K 1B5 (905) 669-2280
SCINTREX LIMITED is a high-tech company engaged in the research, design and manufacture of geophysical and geochemical instrumentation, nuclear reactor and military monitoring devices, security instrumentation for explosive detection, analytical instruments for medical and environmental applications and the provision of ground and airborne exploration and consulting services worldwide.
Harold O. Seigel, Chairman

TOTAL ASSETS ($000)	14,956
TOTAL REVENUE ($000)	14,910
NET INCOME ($000)	718
EMPLOYEES	125
RANK (Profit/Revenue/Assets)	678/758/943

SCOTSBURN CO-OPERATIVE SERVICES LIMITED

(Non-fin Co-op) FOOD PROCESSING
P.O. Box 340, Scotsburn, NS, B0K 1R0 (902) 485-8023
SCOTSBURN CO-OPERATIVE SERVICES LTD. operates in two business segments: processing and distribution of dairy products; and the distribution of frozen foods.
Donald Gunn, Chairman

TOTAL ASSETS ($000)	40,029
TOTAL REVENUE ($000)	152,621
NET INCOME ($000)	476
EMPLOYEES	470

SCOTT PAPER LIMITED
See page 589 for a full company profile.

SCOTT'S HOSPITALITY INC.
See page 527 for a full company profile.

SEABOARD LIFE INSURANCE COMPANY

(Private) INSURANCE - LIFE
2165 West Broadway, P.O. Box 5900, Vancouver, BC,
V6K 4N5 (604) 734-1667
SEABOARD LIFE INSURANCE COMPANY is a member of the Worldwide Eureko Insurance Group which has assets in excess of $80 billion. The company markets its products Canada-wide and is licensed to do business in 42 states in the U.S.
Michael C.D. Hobbs, Chairman of the Board

TOTAL ASSETS ($000)	1,219,897
TOTAL REVENUE ($000)	296,704
NET INCOME ($000)	7,121
EMPLOYEES	330

SEAGRAM COMPANY LTD. (THE)
See page 528 for a full company profile.

SEARS ACCEPTANCE COMPANY INC.

(Private) FINANCE AND LEASING
222 Jarvis Street, Toronto, ON, M5B 2B8 (416) 362-1711
SEARS ACCEPTANCE COMPANY INC. purchases and handles all customer credit accounts generated by merchandise and service sales from Sears. Sears Acceptance is owned 100% by Sears Canada Inc. of Toronto, Ontario.
R.S. Davis, Chairman of the Board

TOTAL ASSETS ($000)	1,440,839
TOTAL REVENUE ($000)	335,314
NET INCOME ($000)	63,366
EMPLOYEES	0

SEARS CANADA INC.
See page 432 for a full company profile.

SECOND CUP LTD. (THE)

(Public) SPECIALTY STORES
Exchanges: T Stock Symbol: SKL
Suite 801, 175 Bloor Street East, South Tower, Toronto, ON,
M4W 3R8 (416) 975-5541
THE SECOND CUP LTD. is a retailer of specialty coffees in Canada and the United States.
Michael D. Bregman, Chairman & C.E.O.

TOTAL ASSETS ($000)	19,575
TOTAL REVENUE ($000)	15,279
NET INCOME ($000)	2,112
EMPLOYEES	40
RANK (Profit/Revenue/Assets)	557/754/878

SECURITY HOME MORTGAGE CORPORATION

(Public) TRUST, SAVINGS AND LOAN
Exchanges: T Stock Symbol: SHM.PR.A
Suite 530, Sun Life Plaza II, 140 - 4th Avenue S.W., Calgary, AB,
T2P 3N3 (403) 237-7840
SECURITY HOME MORTGAGE CORPORATION'S business is to generate income by investing in a portfolio of high quality residential and other mortgages. These investments are funded through a combination

of debt and equity issued by the company. The company is active in mortgage banking, including issuance of mortgage-backed securities.

David M. Cockfield, Deputy Chairman

TOTAL ASSETS ($000)	89,569
TOTAL REVENUE ($000)	7,107
NET INCOME ($000)	(4,837)
EMPLOYEES	40
RANK (Profit/Revenue/Assets)	916/819/508

SEMI-TECH CORPORATION
See page 210 for a full company profile.

SENVEST CAPITAL INC.
(Public)   PUBLISHING & PRINTING
Exchanges: T M   Stock Symbol: SEC
1140 Boul. de Maisonneuve O., Suite 1180, Montreal, PQ, H3A 1M8   (514) 281-8082
SENVEST CAPITAL INC. operates businesses in the electronic security and printing industries. The Sencorp Security System division is a premier integrator and installer of electronic security systems. The Trenmore Printing Inc. subsidiary provides annual reports, marketing brochures and other printing products to clients in many industries.

Victor Mashaal, Chairman & President

TOTAL ASSETS ($000)	40,510
TOTAL REVENUE ($000)	13,722
NET INCOME ($000)	4,919
EMPLOYEES	35
RANK (Profit/Revenue/Assets)	425/767/691

SERENPET INC.
See page 136 for a full company profile.

SERVICE CORPORATION INTERNATIONAL (CANADA) LIMITED
(Public)   OTHER SERVICES
Exchanges: T   Stock Symbol: SVK
3789 Royal Oak Avenue, Burnaby, BC, V5G 3M1   (604) 294-9338
SERVICE CORPORATION INTERNATIONAL (CANADA) LIMITED owns 57 funeral homes, two cemeteries and six crematoria. Approximately 70% of the company's shares are beneficially owned by SCI Canada's parent company, Service Corporation International of Houston, Texas.

W. Blair Waltrip, Chairman, President & C.E.O.

TOTAL ASSETS ($000)	152,227
TOTAL REVENUE ($000)	57,726
NET INCOME ($000)	10,099
EMPLOYEES	na
RANK (Profit/Revenue/Assets)	298/520/391

SHARP ELECTRONICS OF CANADA LTD.
(Private)   WHOLESALE DISTRIBUTORS
335 Brittannia Rd, Mississauga, ON, L4Z 1W9   (905) 890-2100
SHARP ELECTRONICS OF CANADA is a distributor of information systems and consumer electronics products.

S. Hirooka, Chairman

TOTAL ASSETS ($000)	83,996
TOTAL REVENUE ($000)	141,937
NET INCOME ($000)	631
EMPLOYEES	na

SHAW COMMUNICATIONS INC.
See page 390 for a full company profile.

SHAW INDUSTRIES LTD.
See page 590 for a full company profile.

SHELL CANADA LIMITED
See page 137 for a full company profile.

SHERMAG INC.
(Public)   HOME FURNISHINGS
Exchanges: M   Stock Symbol: SMG
2171 Rue King Ouest, Sherbrooke, PQ, J1J 2G1   (819) 566-1515
SHERMAG INC. is one of the largest furniture manufacturers in Canada. Its products include solid oak, solid maple and veneer furniture. It has seven factories in Quebec and New Brunswick.

Serge Racine, Chairman, President & C.E.O.

TOTAL ASSETS ($000)	48,772
TOTAL REVENUE ($000)	42,597
NET INCOME ($000)	1,412
EMPLOYEES	700
RANK (Profit/Revenue/Assets)	617/580/635

SHERRITT INC.
See page 529 for a full company profile.

SHERWOOD CREDIT UNION
(Fin. Co-op)   CREDIT UNIONS
1960 Albert Street, Regina, SK, S4P 2T4   (306) 780-1700
SHERWOOD CREDIT UNION LIMITED is a credit union operating in Saskatchewan providing a wide range of financial services.

Dale Hillmer, Chief Executive Offficer

TOTAL ASSETS ($000)	625,202
TOTAL REVENUE ($000)	49,591
NET INCOME ($000)	2,926
EMPLOYEES	298

SHIRMAX FASHIONS LTD.
(Public)   CLOTHING STORES
Exchanges: M   Stock Symbol: SHX
3901 Jarry Street East, Montreal, PQ, H1Z 2G1   (514) 729-3333
SHIRMAX owns and operates Shirley K. Maternity, Addition-Elle, Addition-Elle Sport, Thyme en Compagnie and Gigi. Shirley K Maternity and Thyme en Compagnie are engaged in the retail sale of maternity apparel and Addition-Elle in the retail sale of women's large-size apparel.

Max Konigsberg, Chairman, President & C.E.O.

TOTAL ASSETS ($000)	33,299
TOTAL REVENUE ($000)	109,471
NET INCOME ($000)	(6,283)
EMPLOYEES	1,313
RANK (Profit/Revenue/Assets)	921/409/744

SHL SYSTEMHOUSE INC.
See page 544 for a full company profile.

SICO INC.
See page 289 for a full company profile.

SIDUS SYSTEMS INC.

(Public)   ELECTRICAL & ELECTRONIC
Exchanges: T   Stock Symbol: SSM
66 Leek Crescent, Richmond Hill, ON, L4B 1J7   (905) 882-1600
SIDUS SYSTEMS INC. is a systems integrator, designer and custom manufacturer of high-end personal computers and workstations as well as network peripheral equipment and multi-media products.
Alojz A. Muzar, Chairman & C.E.O.

TOTAL ASSETS ($000)	84,172
TOTAL REVENUE ($000)	155,289
NET INCOME ($000)	2,803
EMPLOYEES	200
RANK (Profit/Revenue/Assets)	519/352/523

SIEMENS GROUP

(Private)   ELECTRICAL & ELECTRONIC
2185 Derry Road West, Mississauga, ON, L5N 7A6   (905) 819-8000
SIEMENS GROUP designs, manufactures, markets and services electrical and electronic products and systems and information technology for residential and commercial buildings, utilities, science, goverment, industry, automotive OEM and healthcare.
Hon. D.S. Macdonald, Chairman

TOTAL ASSETS ($000)	577,278
TOTAL REVENUE ($000)	919,771
NET INCOME ($000)	na
EMPLOYEES	4,253

SIGNAL ENERGY LTD.

(Public)   OIL AND GAS PRODUCERS
Exchanges: T Z   Stock Symbol: SNN
Ste. 400, 333 - 5th Ave. SW, Calgary, AB, T2P 3B6   (403) 262-5177
SIGNAL ENERGY LTD. is involved in the acquisition, exploration and development of oil and gas properties.
Tibor Fekete, Chairman

TOTAL ASSETS ($000)	14,106
TOTAL REVENUE ($000)	2,027
NET INCOME ($000)	(147)
EMPLOYEES	4
RANK (Profit/Revenue/Assets)	771/920/958

SIGNATURE BRANDS LIMITED

(Public)   FOOD PROCESSING
Exchanges: T   Stock Symbol: SBX
934 The East Mall, Etobicoke, ON, M9B 6J9   (416) 674-8554
SIGNATURE BRANDS LIMITED is a diversified food processor which manufactures and sells a variety of corn based snack foods and specialty food products in the private label, foodservices and retail brands markets.
Tomas J. Asensio, Chairman, President & C.E.O.

TOTAL ASSETS ($000)	22,003
TOTAL REVENUE ($000)	15,791
NET INCOME ($000)	708
EMPLOYEES	na
RANK (Profit/Revenue/Assets)	679/746/851

SILCORP LIMITED

See page 433 for a full company profile.

SIMARD-BEAUDRY INC.

(Public)   MISC. INDUSTRIAL PRODUCTS
Exchanges: M   Stock Symbol: SDB
4230 Saint-Elzear Blvd East, Laval, PQ, H7E 4P2   (514) 329-4747
SIMARD-BEAUDRY INC.'s operations are divided into three main segments. The Production segment manufactures basic building materials, namely crushed stone, concrete blocks, and asphalt. The Construction segment covers the building contractor activities. The Wholesale segment covers the company's wholesale construction materials operations.
Mario Beaulieu, Chairman

TOTAL ASSETS ($000)	62,621
TOTAL REVENUE ($000)	107,628
NET INCOME ($000)	4,174
EMPLOYEES	300
RANK (Profit/Revenue/Assets)	457/413/587

SIMMONDS COMMUNICATIONS LTD.

(Public)   WHOLESALE DISTRIBUTORS
Exchanges: T   Stock Symbol: SMM
Ste. 1050, 5255 Yonge St., Willowdale, ON,
M2N 6P4   (416) 221-1900
SIMMONDS COMMUNICATIONS LTD. operates within the communications and electronics industries. The communications segment includes distribution of two-way radio equipment in Canada, the U.S., and Europe. The electronics segment involves the distribution of electronic components in Canada.
John G. Simmonds, Chairman, President & C.E.O.

TOTAL ASSETS ($000)	53,796
TOTAL REVENUE ($000)	26,749
NET INCOME ($000)	1,305
EMPLOYEES	40
RANK (Profit/Revenue/Assets)	628/666/616

SINO PAC INTERNATIONAL INVESTMENTS INC.

(Public)   MANAGEMENT AND DIVERSIFIED
Exchanges: V   Stock Symbol: SNK
Ste. 515, 800 W. Pender St., Vancouver, BC,
V6C 2V6   (604) 682-3290
SINO PAC INTERNATIONAL INVESTMENTS INC. has investments in mineral exploration, property development and development projects.
R.W.C. Ng, President & C.E.O.

TOTAL ASSETS ($000)	12,801
TOTAL REVENUE ($000)	43
NET INCOME ($000)	(1,744)
EMPLOYEES	5
RANK (Profit/Revenue/Assets)	847/989/993

SINTRA LTD.

(Public)   CONTRACTORS
Exchanges: M   Stock Symbol: STL
4984 Place de la Savane, Montreal, PQ, H4P 2M9   (514) 341-5331
SINTRA LTD. is a construction firm whose revenues are derived from the construction of roads and related works, sewer and water lines and civil works, quarries and crushing operations, pipeline and mechanical works, ready-mix concrete operations, and the production of bituminous concrete.
Michel Roullet, Chairman

TOTAL ASSETS ($000)	68,954
TOTAL REVENUE ($000)	154,647

NET INCOME ($000)	5,725
EMPLOYEES	650
RANK (Profit/Revenue/Assets)	405/354/567

SKYJACK INC.

(Public) MISC. INDUSTRIAL PRODUCTS
Exchanges: T Stock Symbol: SJK
55 Road, Guelph, ON, N1H 1B9 (519) 837-0888
SKYJACK INC. manufactures, markets and distributes self-propelled scissor-type elevating work platforms, self-propelled boom-type work platforms, truck mounted beam-type work platforms and personnel lifts.
Wolfgang Haessler, President & C.E.O.

TOTAL ASSETS ($000)	13,320
TOTAL REVENUE ($000)	43,335
NET INCOME ($000)	3,279
EMPLOYEES	460
RANK (Profit/Revenue/Assets)	501/577/988

SLATER INDUSTRIES INC.
See page 248 for a full company profile.

SLOCAN FOREST PRODUCTS LTD.
See page 173 for a full company profile.

SNC-LAVALIN GROUP INC.
See page 591 for a full company profile.

SNC-LAVALIN INC.

(Private) CONTRACTORS
1100 Rene-Levesque Blvd. West, Montreal, PQ,
H3B 4P3 (514) 393-1000
SNC-LAVALIN INC. is engaged in engineering, procurement, construction, and related services in the power, industrial, general engineering, environment and transport sectors.

TOTAL ASSETS ($000)	428,402
TOTAL REVENUE ($000)	597,432
NET INCOME ($000)	na
EMPLOYEES	5,376

SNT LTD.

(Public) INVESTMENT COMPANIES AND FUNDS
Exchanges: T Stock Symbol: XSN
Suite 5000, P.O. Box 150, 1 First Canadian Place, Toronto, ON,
M5X 1H3 (416) 359-4630
SNT LTD. invests its funds in The Bank of Nova Scotia common shares. The purpose of the company is to provide a vehicle through which different investment objectives with respect to participation in BNS common shares may be satisfied.
Frederick J. Troop, President & C.E.O.

TOTAL ASSETS ($000)	68,744
TOTAL REVENUE ($000)	8,301
NET INCOME ($000)	8,239
EMPLOYEES	0
RANK (Profit/Revenue/Assets)	328/820/568

SOCANAV INC.

(Public) TRANSPORTATION
Exchanges: T M Stock Symbol: SVX.A
1801 Avenue McGill College, Suite 1470, Montreal, PQ,
H3A 2N4 (514) 284-9535
SOCANAV is involved in the marine transportation of bulk liquids and the sale of public transportation vehicles.
Michel Gaucher, Chairman & President

TOTAL ASSETS ($000)	43,174
TOTAL REVENUE ($000)	43,895
NET INCOME ($000)	720
EMPLOYEES	200
RANK (Profit/Revenue/Assets)	677/576/672

SOCIETE DE PORTEFEUILLE DU GROUPE DESJARDINS ASSURANCES

(Fin. Co-op) INSURANCE - PROPERTY & CASUALTY
6300, boul. de la Rive-Sud, Levis, PQ, G6V 6P9 (418) 835-4850
SOCIETE DE PORTEFEUILLE DU GROUPE DESJARDINS ASSURANCES GENERALES sells general insurance.
Michel Roy, President du Conseil

TOTAL ASSETS ($000)	454,715
TOTAL REVENUE ($000)	340,012
NET INCOME ($000)	27,380
EMPLOYEES	1,471

SOCIETE GENERALE DE FINANCEMENT DU QUEBEC

(Crown) MANAGEMENT AND DIVERSIFIED
600 Rue de la Gauchetiere O., Bureau 1700, Montreal, PQ,
H3B 4L8 (514) 876-9290
SOCIETE GENERALE DE FINANCEMENT DU QUEBEC is a management company wholly owned by the Quebec government. The group's assets are concentrated in forest products, petrochemicals, and aluminum production. SGF has direct and indirect investments in some 15 subsidiaries and affiliated companies.
Marc G. Fortier, Chairman, President & C.E.O.

TOTAL ASSETS ($000)	1,194,478
TOTAL REVENUE ($000)	517,697
NET INCOME ($000)	(35,421)
EMPLOYEES	16,000

SOCIETE QUEBECOISE D'EXPLORATION MINIERE-SOQUEM

(Crown) METAL MINES
Tour Belle Cour, Bureau 2500, 2600 Boulevard Laurier, Ste-Foy,
PQ, G1V 4M6 (418) 658-5400
SOCIETE QUEBECOISE D'EXPLORATION MINIERE-SOQUEM is involved in the acquisition, exploration and development of mineral properties.
Albert Jessop, Chairman of the Board

TOTAL ASSETS ($000)	70,492
TOTAL REVENUE ($000)	15,603
NET INCOME ($000)	8,187
EMPLOYEES	63

SOCIETE QUEBECOISE D'INITIATIVES AGRO-ALIMENTAIRES

(Crown)   AGRICULTURE
Parc Samuel Holland, 1275 Chemin Ste-Foy, Bureau 284, Quebec,
PQ, G1S 4S5   (418) 643-2238
SOCIETE QUEBECOISE D'INITIATIVES AGRO-ALIMEN-
TAIRES was founded in 1975 with a mission of contributing to the
development of the commercial fisheries and agro-food business.
Raymond Lemay, President du Conseil

TOTAL ASSETS ($000)	133,518
TOTAL REVENUE ($000)	90,738
NET INCOME ($000)	6,221
EMPLOYEES	19

SOCIETE QUEBECOISE D'INITIATIVES PETROLIERES

(Crown)   OIL AND GAS PRODUCERS
1175 Rue de Lavigerie, Suite 180, Ste-Foy, PQ,
G1V 4P1   (418) 651-9543
SOCIETE QUEBECOISE D'INITIATIVES PETROLIERES's objec-
tive is to explore for, develop, produce, store, transport, purchase, import
and sell hydrocarbons in liquid or gaseous form, directly or in partnership
with other firms.
Jacques V. Goyer, Chairman of the Board

TOTAL ASSETS ($000)	226,030
TOTAL REVENUE ($000)	43,148
NET INCOME ($000)	28,851
EMPLOYEES	26

SODARCAN, INC.

(Public)   FINANCE AND LEASING
Exchanges: M   Stock Symbol: SDO.A
1140 de Maisonneuve Blvd. West, Suite 701, Montreal, PQ,
H3A 1M8   (514) 288-0100
SODARCAN, INC. operates in three main sectors: insurance brokerage;
reinsurance brokerage; and actuarial consulting.
Robert Parizeau, Chairman, President & C.E.O.

TOTAL ASSETS ($000)	187,379
TOTAL REVENUE ($000)	94,704
NET INCOME ($000)	1,167
EMPLOYEES	1,003
RANK (Profit/Revenue/Assets)	639/430/364

SODISCO-HOWDEN GROUP INC.

See page 434 for a full company profile.

SOFTKEY SOFTWARE PRODUCTS INC.

See page 545 for a full company profile.

SOLID STATE GEOPHYSICAL INC.

(Public)   OIL AND GAS FIELD SERVICES
Exchanges: T   Stock Symbol: SSS
7309 Flint Road South East, Calgary, AB, T2H 1G3   (403) 255-9388
SOLID STATE GEOPHYSICAL INC. provides seismic data acquisition, interpretation and geodetic engineering services to the oil and gas
industry. With the purchase of Nortech Surveys (Canada) Inc., the
company expanded its business to include services based upon global
satellite positioning technology. These new products and services have
applications in several industries.

Mitchell L. Peters, President & C.E.O.

TOTAL ASSETS ($000)	45,679
TOTAL REVENUE ($000)	34,328
NET INCOME ($000)	3,692
EMPLOYEES	700
RANK (Profit/Revenue/Assets)	477/622/656

SONOR INVESTMENTS LIMITED

(Public)   INVESTMENT COMPANIES AND FUNDS
Exchanges: T   Stock Symbol: SNI.PR.A
Suite 1500, Box 810, 181 Bay Street, Toronto, ON,
M5J 2T3   (416) 369-9565
SONOR INVESTMENTS LIMITED is an investment holding com-
pany.
R. Alan Broadbent, Chairman

TOTAL ASSETS ($000)	44,302
TOTAL REVENUE ($000)	400
NET INCOME ($000)	350
EMPLOYEES	0
RANK (Profit/Revenue/Assets)	720/963/664

SONORA GOLD CORP.

See page 60 for a full company profile.

SONY OF CANADA LTD.

(Private)   WHOLESALE DISTRIBUTORS
1370 Sony Place, PO Box 9400, Winnipeg, MB,
R3C 3C3   (204) 474-5200
SONY OF CANADA LTD. is engaged in the distribution of Sony
products in Canada.
Albert D. Cohen, Chairman & C.E.O.

TOTAL ASSETS ($000)	194,814
TOTAL REVENUE ($000)	554,146
NET INCOME ($000)	13,610
EMPLOYEES	1,300

SOUTH CHINA INDUSTRIES (CANADA) INC.

See page 220 for a full company profile.

SOUTHAM INC.

See page 391 for a full company profile.

SOUTHERNERA RESOURCES LIMITED

(Public)   OTHER MINES
Exchanges: T   Stock Symbol: SUF
Suite 1014, 33 Yonge Street, Toronto, ON, M5E 1S9 (416) 359-9282
SOUTHERNERA RESOURCES LIMITED explores for diamonds.
The company operates in the Northwest Territories, Manitoba, Ontario
and in South America, Zambia, Zimbabwe, Botswana, South Africa, and
Ukraine.
Christoper M.H. Jennings, President

TOTAL ASSETS ($000)	23,309
TOTAL REVENUE ($000)	500
NET INCOME ($000)	(1,214)
EMPLOYEES	5
RANK (Profit/Revenue/Assets)	828/957/834

SOUTHLAND CANADA, INC.

(Private)   FOOD STORES
3185 Willingdon Green, Burnaby, BC, V5G 4P3   (604) 299-0711
SOUTHLAND CANADA, INC. operates convenience stores. South-
land Canada is a wholly owned subsidiary of Southland Corporation of
Dallas, Texas.
Frank Farr, President & General Mgr.

TOTAL ASSETS ($000)	141,458
TOTAL REVENUE ($000)	688,408
NET INCOME ($000)	na
EMPLOYEES	5,600

SOUTHWESTERN GOLD CORPORATION

(Public)   PRECIOUS METALS
Exchanges: T V   Stock Symbol: SWG
P.O. Box 10102, Suite 1650, 701 West Georgia Street, Vancouver,
BC, V7Y 1C6   (604) 669-2525
SOUTHWESTERN GOLD CORPORATION is involved in the acquisi-
tion, exploration and development of mining properties, especially with
respect to gold and diamonds.
George Howard Plewes, Chairman & C.F.O.

TOTAL ASSETS ($000)	24,350
TOTAL REVENUE ($000)	1,290
NET INCOME ($000)	(1,026)
EMPLOYEES	27
RANK (Profit/Revenue/Assets)	816/943/819

SPAR AEROSPACE LIMITED

See page 275 for a full company profile.

SPECTRA GROUP OF GREAT RESTAURANTS INC. (THE)

(Public)   FOOD SERVICES
Exchanges: T V   Stock Symbol: SPA
837 E Cordova St, Vancouver, BC, V6A 3R2   (604) 669-5333
SPECTRA GROUP OF GREAT RESTAURANTS INC. is a regional,
multi-concept restaurant company operating in British Columbia, Alberta, and the state of Washington.
Wayne F. Holm, V.P. & Co-C.E.O.

TOTAL ASSETS ($000)	28,985
TOTAL REVENUE ($000)	46,153
NET INCOME ($000)	1,911
EMPLOYEES	2,000
RANK (Profit/Revenue/Assets)	577/566/778

SPECTRAL DIAGNOSTICS INC.

See page 232 for a full company profile.

SPECTRUM SIGNAL PROCESSING INC.

(Public)   ELECTRICAL & ELECTRONIC
Exchanges: T Q   Stock Symbol: SSY
8525 Baxter Place, 100 Production Court, Burnaby, BC,
V5A 4V7   (604) 421-5422
SPECTRUM SIGNAL PROCESSING INC. designs and manufactures
Digital Signal Processing (DSP) computer hardware and software for a
variety of computers based on the IBM PC/XT/AT, VMEBus, SBus and
FutureBus+ platforms. Applications of Spectrum's products include
multimedia, digital cellular, digital audio, medical diagnostics, radar,

sonar, defence communications and surveillance and many other industrial uses.
Michael Mertens, Chairman

TOTAL ASSETS ($000)	15,486
TOTAL REVENUE ($000)	13,109
NET INCOME ($000)	483
EMPLOYEES	115
RANK (Profit/Revenue/Assets)	696/771/938

SPEEDWARE CORPORATION INC.

(Public)   COMPUTER SOFTWARE & PROCESSING
Exchanges: T M   Stock Symbol: SPW
150 John Street, 10th Floor, Toronto, ON, M5V 3E3   (416) 408-2880
SPEEDWARE CORPORATION INC. is a software company that
develops, markets and supports a complete product line of advanced
application development software tools, integrated accounting and executive information systems for various mid-range and personal computer platforms.
Ian Farquharson, Chairman & C.E.O.

TOTAL ASSETS ($000)	25,667
TOTAL REVENUE ($000)	28,483
NET INCOME ($000)	(1,562)
EMPLOYEES	280
RANK (Profit/Revenue/Assets)	837/657/809

SPEEDY MUFFLER KING INC.

See page 435 for a full company profile.

SPORTS EXPERTS INC.

(Private)   WHOLESALE DISTRIBUTORS
4141 Autoroute Laval Ouest, Laval, PQ, H7P 4W6   (514) 687-5200
SPORTS EXPERTS INC. is a national distributor of leisure wear and
sporting goods in Canada.
Jean-Claude Merizzi, President du conseil

TOTAL ASSETS ($000)	90,703
TOTAL REVENUE ($000)	194,843
NET INCOME ($000)	(2,374)
EMPLOYEES	1,848

SPORTSCENE RESTAURANTS INC.

(Public)   FOOD SERVICES
Exchanges: M   Stock Symbol: SPS.A
426 Rue Ste-Helene, Bureau 300, Montreal, PQ,
H2Y 2K7   (514) 849-9376
SPORTSCENE RESTAURANTS INC. owns and operates 31 La Cage
aux Sports chicken and rib restaurants, including 20 franchises. It also
owns and operates Biddle's Jazz & Ribs.
Donald W. Seal, Chairman & C.O.O.

TOTAL ASSETS ($000)	18,170
TOTAL REVENUE ($000)	27,489
NET INCOME ($000)	(1,053)
EMPLOYEES	1,800
RANK (Profit/Revenue/Assets)	822/659/895

SR TELECOM INC.

See page 276 for a full company profile.

SSQ VIE
(Private) INSURANCE - LIFE
2525 Boulevard Laurier, C.P. 10500, Ste-Foy, PQ,
G1V 4H6 (418) 651-7000
SSQ VIE provides life, accident and disability insurance and pension plans.
Yves Demers, Chairman
TOTAL ASSETS ($000) 1,116,995
TOTAL REVENUE ($000) 406,211
NET INCOME ($000) 10,446
EMPLOYEES 539

ST ANDREW GOLDFIELDS LTD.
(Public) PRECIOUS METALS
Exchanges: T Stock Symbol: SAS
166 Pearl Street, Toronto, ON, M5H 1L3 (416) 597-0969
ST ANDREW GOLDFIELDS LTD. is involved in the acquisition, exploration and development of precious metal properties. The company operates the Stock Mine and Hislop Mine both situated on the Porcupine-Destor Fault in Northern Ontario.
Herbert S. Gasser, President & C.E.O.
TOTAL ASSETS ($000) 23,597
TOTAL REVENUE ($000) 12,107
NET INCOME ($000) (2,841)
EMPLOYEES 6
RANK (Profit/Revenue/Assets) 876/780/832

ST. CLAIR PAINT & WALLPAPER CORPORATION
(Public) MISC. CONSUMER PRODUCTS
Exchanges: T Stock Symbol: SCW.A
2600 Steeles Avenue West, Concord, ON, L4K 3C8 (905) 738-0080
ST. CLAIR PAINT & WALLPAPER CORPORATION, through its subsidiaries, is a retailer of paints, wallpaper, decorative supplies and related products through its 84 company-owned and 62 franchised locations. The company is also a manufacturer of wall and window coverings.
Louis Litwin, Chairman & C.E.O.
TOTAL ASSETS ($000) 23,303
TOTAL REVENUE ($000) 71,637
NET INCOME ($000) 1,349
EMPLOYEES 699
RANK (Profit/Revenue/Assets) 623/477/835

ST. GENEVIEVE RESOURCES LTD.
(Public) OTHER MINES
Exchanges: T M Stock Symbol: SGV
630 Boul. Rene-Levesque Ouest, Bureau 3200, Montreal, PQ, H3B 1S6 (514) 866-6001
ST. GENEVIEVE RESOURCES LTD., through its subsidiaries, is involved in the recycling of tailings and contract milling and in graphite mining operations. In addition, the corporatin holds investments in various companies involved in the natural resources sector, principally in the exploration and exploitation of minerals.
Pierre R. Gauthier, Chairman & President
TOTAL ASSETS ($000) 65,597
TOTAL REVENUE ($000) 20,461
NET INCOME ($000) 516
EMPLOYEES 20
RANK (Profit/Revenue/Assets) 694/711/572

ST. JOHN'S PORT CORPORATION
(Crown) TRANSPORTATION
P.O. Box 6178, St. John's, NF, A1C 5X8 (709) 772-4664
ST. JOHN'S PORT CORPORATION manages the port of St. John's, Newfoundland.
Melvin Woodward, Chairman
TOTAL ASSETS ($000) 16,542
TOTAL REVENUE ($000) 3,325
NET INCOME ($000) 371
EMPLOYEES 13

ST. LAWRENCE CEMENT INC.
See page 592 for a full company profile.

ST. LAWRENCE SEAWAY AUTHORITY (THE)
(Crown) TRANSPORTATION
360 Albert Street, Ottawa, ON, K1R 7X7 (613) 598-4600
The mission of The St. Lawrence Seaway Authority is to construct, operate and maintain a safe and reliable deep draft waterway between the Port of Montreal and Lake Erie.
Glendon R. Stewart, President
TOTAL ASSETS ($000) 577,770
TOTAL REVENUE ($000) 76,403
NET INCOME ($000) (4,005)
EMPLOYEES 750

STACKPOLE LIMITED
(Public) AUTOMOTIVE
Exchanges: T Stock Symbol: SKD
2381 Bristol Circle, B-203, Oakville, ON, L6H 5S9 (905) 829-2050
STACKPOLE LIMITED is involved in the transformation of metal alloys in powder form into shapes and parts by manufacturing processes. The parts are primarily produced for automobile manufacturers for use in engines and transmissions at costs lower or competitive to manufactured steel or cast iron parts.
J. Samuel Parkhill, Chairman & C.E.O.
TOTAL ASSETS ($000) 112,876
TOTAL REVENUE ($000) 107,525
NET INCOME ($000) 6,101
EMPLOYEES 800
RANK (Profit/Revenue/Assets) 390/414/456

STAMPEDER EXPLORATION LTD.
See page 138 for a full company profile.

STANDARD BROADCASTING CORPORATION LIMITED
(Private) BROADCASTING
2 St. Clair Avenue West, Toronto, ON, M4V 1L6 (416) 960-9911
STANDARD BROADCASTING CORPORATION LIMITED operates seven radio stations and one television station. It also produces television programs, and is involved in cable television. Operations are carried out in Canada and the United States.
Allan Slaight, President & C.E.O.
TOTAL ASSETS ($000) 129,654
TOTAL REVENUE ($000) 239,560
NET INCOME ($000) 2,867
EMPLOYEES 1,200

STANDARD LIFE ASSURANCE COMPANY (THE)
(Private)   INSURANCE - LIFE
1245 Sherbrooke Street West, Montreal, PQ,
H3G 1G3   (514) 284-6711
THE STANDARD LIFE ASSURANCE COMPANY is a mutual insurance company with branch offices in 28 Canadian cities. The company
serves the life insurance and pension needs of the Canadian public, and
offers a complete range of financial services to its many clients and policy
holders. The company is a branch of Standard Life Assurance Co. of
Scotland.
N. Lessels, Chairman

TOTAL ASSETS ($000)	9,735,395
TOTAL REVENUE ($000)	2,220,874
NET INCOME ($000)	(19,650)
EMPLOYEES	1,500

STANLEY TECHNOLOGY GROUP INC.
(Public)   CONSULTING
Exchanges: T   Stock Symbol: STG
10160 - 112 Street, Edmonton, AB, T2K 2L6   (403) 423-4777
STANLEY TECHNOLOGY GROUP INC. provides a range of engineering and professional consulting services to private and public sector
clients in Canada, the United States and internationally. The principal
services include environmental consulting, infrastructure design and
development, industrial engineering, building and land development
services and project management.
Ronald P. Triffo, President & C.E.O.

TOTAL ASSETS ($000)	45,967
TOTAL REVENUE ($000)	88,343
NET INCOME ($000)	3,630
EMPLOYEES	900
RANK (Profit/Revenue/Assets)	481/441/654

STARTECH ENERGY INC.
(Public)   OIL AND GAS PRODUCERS
Exchanges: T   Stock Symbol: SEH
Ste. 2350, 444 - 5th Ave. SW, Calgary, AB, T2P 2T8   (403) 233-7377
STARTECH ENERGY is a natural resource enterprise, primarily active
in the acquisition, exploration, and development of oil and gas reserves
in the Western Canadian sedimentary basin.
Denis J. Cote, Chairman

TOTAL ASSETS ($000)	48,994
TOTAL REVENUE ($000)	9,877
NET INCOME ($000)	488
EMPLOYEES	17
RANK (Profit/Revenue/Assets)	695/804/634

STATE FARM GROUP
(Private)   INSURANCE - PROPERTY & CASUALTY
100 Consilium Place, Scarborough, ON, M1H 3E3   (416) 290-4100
STATE FARM GROUP is a property and casualty insurance company.

TOTAL ASSETS ($000)	1,356,613
TOTAL REVENUE ($000)	724,409
NET INCOME ($000)	64,763
EMPLOYEES	1,145

STELCO INC.
See page 249 for a full company profile.

STELLA-JONES INC.
(Public)   MISC. INDUSTRIAL PRODUCTS
Exchanges: T M   Stock Symbol: SJ
395 de Maisonneuve Blvd. West, 3rd Floor, Montreal, PQ,
H3A 1L6   (514) 848-5181
STELLA-JONES INC. is engaged in the production of pressure treated
wood products. The company specializes in the supply of treated wood
poles to utility and telecommunications companies on a national and
international basis.
Tom A. Bruce Jones, Chairman

TOTAL ASSETS ($000)	48,271
TOTAL REVENUE ($000)	51,709
NET INCOME ($000)	3,606
EMPLOYEES	230
RANK (Profit/Revenue/Assets)	485/543/642

STN INCORPORATED
(Public)   TELECOMMUNICATIONS
Exchanges: T Q   Stock Symbol: STH
Suite 200, 675 Cochrane Drive, Markham, ON,
L3R 0T2   (905) 415-9595
STN INCORPORATED is in the business of providing discounted long
distance telecommunications services, to residential and commercial
customers in Ontario, Quebec, Alberta and British Columbia.
Andreino Sartor, Chairman

TOTAL ASSETS ($000)	37,916
TOTAL REVENUE ($000)	50,548
NET INCOME ($000)	(24,587)
EMPLOYEES	420
RANK (Profit/Revenue/Assets)	976/547/707

STONE-CONSOLIDATED CORPORATION
See page 174 for a full company profile.

STRIKE ENERGY INC.
(Public)   OIL AND GAS PRODUCERS
Exchanges: T   Stock Symbol: SEN
Suite 1400, 300 - 5th Avenue S.W., Calgary, AB,
T2P 3C4   (403) 233-6400
STRIKE ENERGY INC. is involved in the acquisition, exploration and
development of oil and gas properties. The company operates in Alberta
and Saskatchewan.
Edward S. Sampson, Chairman

TOTAL ASSETS ($000)	74,352
TOTAL REVENUE ($000)	24,036
NET INCOME ($000)	3,396
EMPLOYEES	70
RANK (Profit/Revenue/Assets)	461/655/549

STUART OLSON CONSTRUCTION
(Private)   CONTRACTORS
12836 - 146 Street, Edmonton, AB, T5L 2H7   (403) 452-4260
STUART OLSON CONSTRUCTION is a western Canadian based
general contractor with offices in Edmonton, Saskatoon, Calgary and
Vancouver. It is The Churchill Corporation's largest subsidiary.
Hank Reid, Chairman & C.E.O.

TOTAL ASSETS ($000)	47,857
TOTAL REVENUE ($000)	140,382
NET INCOME ($000)	na
EMPLOYEES	600

SUMITOMO CANADA LIMITED
(Private)   WHOLESALE DISTRIBUTORS
Suite 7010, 1 First Canadian Place, Toronto, ON,
M5X 1C8   (416) 860-3800
SUMITOMO CANADA LIMITED is an international trading company.
It is a wholly owned subsidiary of Sumitomo Corporation of Japan.
T. Hirano, President & C.E.O.

TOTAL ASSETS ($000)	82,139
TOTAL REVENUE ($000)	970,645
NET INCOME ($000)	885
EMPLOYEES	57

SUMMIT RESOURCES LIMITED
See page 139 for a full company profile.

SUN ICE LIMITED
(Public)   CLOTHING AND TEXTILES
Exchanges: T Z   Stock Symbol: SIH
1001 - 1st Street S.E., Calgary, AB, T2G 5G3   (403) 261-4780
SUN ICE LIMITED designs, manufactures, markets and distributes an
extensive line of skiwear, golf outerwear and active sports and leisure
wear. These products are distributed to retail stores throughout Canada,
the United States and Europe.
Sylvia Rempel, Chairperson

TOTAL ASSETS ($000)	19,618
TOTAL REVENUE ($000)	15,508
NET INCOME ($000)	310
EMPLOYEES	150
RANK (Profit/Revenue/Assets)	724/749/874

SUN LIFE ASSURANCE COMPANY OF CANADA
(Private)   INSURANCE - LIFE
Sun Life Centre, 150 King Street West, Toronto, ON,
M5H 1J9   (416) 979-9966
SUN LIFE ASSURANCE COMPANY OF CANADA is a mutual life
insurance company offering a range of financial services and products
for groups and individuals including life, health and disability insurance,
annuities and pensions, mutual funds and savings plans, investment
management services, reinsurance, and banking and trust services. Sun
Life operates in Canada, the U.S., the U.K., and Asia.
John D. McNeil, Chairman & C.E.O.

TOTAL ASSETS ($000)	60,521,824
TOTAL REVENUE ($000)	10,148,502
NET INCOME ($000)	304,477
EMPLOYEES	8,253

SUN MICROSYSTEMS OF CANADA INC.
(Private)   ELECTRICAL & ELECTRONIC
100 Renfrew Drive, Markham, ON, L3R 9R6   (905) 979-9966
SUN MICROSYSTEMS OF CANADA INC. supplies network-based
distributed computing systems for both commercial and techinical applications.

TOTAL ASSETS ($000)	44,638
TOTAL REVENUE ($000)	125,720
NET INCOME ($000)	4,190
EMPLOYEES	160

SUN-RYPE PRODUCTS LTD.
(Non-fin Co-op)   FOOD PROCESSING
1165 Ethel, Kelowna, BC, V1Y 2W4   (604) 860-7973
SUN-RYPE PRODUCTS LTD. is a fruit-based food and beverage
manufacturer
Merv Geen, Chairman

TOTAL ASSETS ($000)	41,747
TOTAL REVENUE ($000)	72,122
NET INCOME ($000)	665
EMPLOYEES	280

SUNCOR INC.
See page 140 for a full company profile.

SUNPORT MEDICAL CORPORATION
(Public)   MEDICAL SERVICES
Exchanges: V Q   Stock Symbol: SMQ
Suite 716, 850 West Hastings St., Vancouver, BC,
V6C 1E1   (604) 682-4488
SUNPORT MEDICAL CORPORATION provides outpatient services
to physicians, hospitals and other health care providers. Its services
include radiology, physical therapy, and radiation.
W. Thomas Geralds, Chief Executive Officer

TOTAL ASSETS ($000)	10,196 (US)
TOTAL REVENUE ($000)	7,814 (US)
NET INCOME ($000)	(2,091) (US)
EMPLOYEES	76
RANK (Profit/Revenue/Assets)	875/793/972

SURREY METRO SAVINGS CREDIT UNION
See page 455 for a full company profile.

SURVIVANCE, COMPAGNIE MUTUELLE D'ASSURANCE-VIE (LA)
(Fin. Co-op)   INSURANCE - LIFE
C.P. 10000, 1555 Rue Girouard Ouest, St-Hyacinthe, PQ,
J2S 7C8   (514) 773-6051
LA SURVIVANCE, COMPAGNIE MUTUELLE D'ASSURANCE-
VIE has offices in Quebec and New Brunswick.
Lucien Brosseau, Pres. & Chef de la direction

TOTAL ASSETS ($000)	117,362
TOTAL REVENUE ($000)	42,828
NET INCOME ($000)	(1,516)
EMPLOYEES	240

SUTTON RESOURCES LTD
(Public)   METAL MINES
Exchanges: V Q   Stock Symbol: STT
Suite 205, 10711 Cambie Road, Richmond, BC,
V6X 3G5   (604) 276-2576
SUTTON RESOURCES LTD is engaged in the acquisition, exploration
and development of mineral resource properties. The company has
interests in Tanzania, Guyana, Canada and the United States of America.
James Sinclair, Chairman

TOTAL ASSETS ($000)	16,719
TOTAL REVENUE ($000)	115
NET INCOME ($000)	(632)
EMPLOYEES	8
RANK (Profit/Revenue/Assets)	801/986/923

SUZUKI CANADA INC.
(Private)   WHOLESALE DISTRIBUTORS
100 East Beaver Creek Road, Richmond Hill, ON,
L4B 1J6   (905) 889-2600
SUZUKI CANADA INC. is a wholesale distributor of automobiles, motorcycles and outboard motors. Suzuki Canada is a wholly owned subsidiary of Suzuki Motor Corporation of Japan.
M. Watanabe, President & C.E.O.

TOTAL ASSETS ($000)	71,189
TOTAL REVENUE ($000)	163,738
NET INCOME ($000)	333
EMPLOYEES	114

SUZY SHIER LIMITED
(Public)   CLOTHING STORES
Exchanges: T M   Stock Symbol: SZS
1604 St-Regis Blvd., Dorval, PQ, H9P 1H6   (514) 684-3651
SUZY SHIER LIMITED is a speciality retailer of moderately priced apparel for women, sold in its Suzy Shier and L.A. Express stores and lingerie and sleepwear sold in its La Senza stores.
Irving Teitelbaum, Chairman & C.E.O.

TOTAL ASSETS ($000)	144,109
TOTAL REVENUE ($000)	267,485
NET INCOME ($000)	11,518
EMPLOYEES	3,600
RANK (Profit/Revenue/Assets)	275/273/403

SYNERGISTICS INDUSTRIES LIMITED
(Public)   MISC. INDUSTRIAL PRODUCTS
Exchanges: T M   Stock Symbol: SGX.A
5915 Airport Road, Suite 425, Mississauga, ON,
L4V 1T1   (905) 673-1213
SYNERGISTICS INDUSTRIES LIMITED is engaged in the manufacture in Canada and the United States of high quality plastic compounds, including polyvinyl chloride compounds. These are sold directly to industrial customers who apply them in the manufacture of numerous products.
R.A. Noble, Chairman & C.E.O.

TOTAL ASSETS ($000)	97,535
TOTAL REVENUE ($000)	261,786
NET INCOME ($000)	2,666
EMPLOYEES	500
RANK (Profit/Revenue/Assets)	528/277/491

SYSTEMS XCELLENCE INC.
See page 546 for a full company profile.

TAIGA FOREST PRODUCTS LTD.
(Public)   WHOLESALE DISTRIBUTORS
Exchanges: T   Stock Symbol: TFP
Suite 1001, 4330 Kingsway, Burnaby, BC, V5H 4G7   (604) 438-1471
TAIGA FOREST PRODUCTS LTD. is a distributer of building products including lumber, panelboards, insulation, wood mouldings, and doors.
Patrick E. Hamill, President C.E.O. & C.F.O.

TOTAL ASSETS ($000)	76,314
TOTAL REVENUE ($000)	370,866
NET INCOME ($000)	4,692
EMPLOYEES	201
RANK (Profit/Revenue/Assets)	432/227/540

TALISMAN ENERGY INC.
See page 141 for a full company profile.

TARO INDUSTRIES LIMITED
(Public)   OIL AND GAS FIELD SERVICES
Exchanges: T   Stock Symbol: TIN
104; 155 Glenpeer Circle S.E., Calgary, AB, T2H 2S8 (403) 253-8511
TARO INDUSTRIES LIMITED is involved in the manufacture of oilwell pumping products; distribution of flow control products; manufacture and repair of drilling and well servicing equipment; manufacture of electronic recorders to monitor temperatures and pressures in oil and gas wells; and packaging of natural gas compression systems.
M. Kanovsky, Chairman

TOTAL ASSETS ($000)	54,147
TOTAL REVENUE ($000)	59,863
NET INCOME ($000)	3,792
EMPLOYEES	209
RANK (Profit/Revenue/Assets)	472/513/614

TARRAGON OIL AND GAS LIMITED
See page 142 for a full company profile.

TARXIEN CORPORATION (THE)
(Public)   AUTOMOTIVE
Exchanges: T   Stock Symbol: TXE
505 Finley Avenue, Ajax, ON, L1S 2E2   (905) 683-4013
TARXIEN CORPORATION is involved in the manufacture of automotive parts and consumer products.
Ralph J. Zarboni, Chairman & President

TOTAL ASSETS ($000)	36,569
TOTAL REVENUE ($000)	68,735
NET INCOME ($000)	2,848
EMPLOYEES	525
RANK (Profit/Revenue/Assets)	518/484/720

TASEKO MINES LIMITED
(Public)   PRECIOUS METALS
Exchanges: V Q   Stock Symbol: TKO
Suite 1020, 800 West Pender Street, Vancouver, BC,
V6C 2V6   (604) 684-6365
TASEKO MINES LIMITED is focused on the development of Canada's largest copper-gold project, the Fish Lake deposit.
Robert G. Hunter, Chairman

TOTAL ASSETS ($000)	44,071
TOTAL REVENUE ($000)	162
NET INCOME ($000)	(439)
EMPLOYEES	35
RANK (Profit/Revenue/Assets)	788/980/667

TCG INTERNATIONAL INC.
See page 221 for a full company profile.

TECK CORPORATION
See page 61 for a full company profile.

TECSYN INTERNATIONAL INC.
(Public)   MISC. INDUSTRIAL PRODUCTS
Exchanges: T   Stock Symbol: TSN
113 - 115 Cushman Road, Unit 62, Box 845, St. Catharines, ON,
L2R 6Z4   (905) 687-8811
TECSYN INTERNATIONAL INC. is a North American manufacturing
company which produces polypropylene twine and automotive netting
products and advanced powdered metal production technologies.
Brian A. Robbins, Chairman
TOTAL ASSETS ($000)   53,160
TOTAL REVENUE ($000)   57,896
NET INCOME ($000)   7,529
EMPLOYEES   400
RANK (Profit/Revenue/Assets)   352/518/618

TEE-COMM ELECTRONICS INC.
See page 277 for a full company profile.

TEL NT LTD.
(Public)   INVESTMENT COMPANIES AND FUNDS
Exchanges: T   Stock Symbol: TLD
P.O. Box 21, Commerce Court South, Toronto, ON,
M5L 1A7   (416) 687-8811
TEL NT LTD. will invest its funds in TELUS common shares. The
purpose of the company is to provide a vehicle through which different
investment objectives with respect to participation in TELUS common
shares may be satisfied.
Douglas G. Hall, President & C.E.O.
TOTAL ASSETS ($000)   78,300
TOTAL REVENUE ($000)   5,919
NET INCOME ($000)   5,819
EMPLOYEES   0
RANK (Profit/Revenue/Assets)   399/846/535

TELE-METROPOLE INC.
See page 392 for a full company profile.

TELEBEC LTEE
(Private)   TELEPHONE UTILITIES
7151 Jean-Talon East, Anjou, PQ, H1M 3N8   (418) 684-3006
TELEBEC LTEE operates a provincially regulated telephone utility in
Quebec.
Louis A. Tanguay, Chairman & C.E.O.
TOTAL ASSETS ($000)   447,864
TOTAL REVENUE ($000)   183,226
NET INCOME ($000)   21,463
EMPLOYEES   1,145

TELEGLOBE CANADA INC.
(Private)   TELECOMMUNICATIONS
1000 De La Gauchetiere, Montreal, PQ, H3B 4X5   (514) 868-7272
TELEGLOBE CANADA, a wholly owned subsidiary of Teleglobe Inc.,
is Canada's international telecommunications carrier. It uses advanced
technology to link Canada to over 200 countries via satellite, fibre optics
and conventional cable. Customers range from large corporations to
domestic carriers and resellers.
Charles Sirois, Chairman of the Board
TOTAL ASSETS ($000)   1,211,700
TOTAL REVENUE ($000)   401,300

NET INCOME ($000)   65,200
EMPLOYEES   950

TELEGLOBE INC.
See page 547 for a full company profile.

TELEMEDIA INC.
See page 393 for a full company profile.

TELESAT CANADA
(Private)   TELECOMMUNICATIONS
1601 Telesat Court, Gloucester, ON, K1B 5P4   (613) 748-0123
TELESAT CANADA is a national communications common carrier
providing telecommunications and broadcast distribution services. Tele-
sat is 96% owned by an alliance of Canadian telephone companies and
Spar Aerospace Limited.
Raymond Cyr, Chairman & C.E.O.
TOTAL ASSETS ($000)   961,648
TOTAL REVENUE ($000)   217,866
NET INCOME ($000)   8,959
EMPLOYEES   512

TELESYSTEM TELECOM LTD.
(Public)   TELECOMMUNICATIONS
Exchanges: T M   Stock Symbol: TT.PR.A
1000 de La Gauchetiere St. W., 25th Floor, Montreal, PQ,
H3B 4W5   (514) 397-9797
TELESYSTEM TELECOM LTD. was incorporated for the sole purpose
of reorganizing and combining the investments of National Telesystem
in Teleglobe. As at May 31, 1993, the assets of the company consisted
mainly of common shares of Teleglobe. National Telesystem is a holding
and management company specialized in the telecommunications busi-
ness. The company is one of National Telesystem's subsidiaries.
Charles Sirois, Chairman & President
TOTAL ASSETS ($000)   146,640
TOTAL REVENUE ($000)   12,130
NET INCOME ($000)   10,993
EMPLOYEES   0
RANK (Profit/Revenue/Assets)   281/778/398

TELULAR CANADA INC.
(Public)   ELECTRICAL & ELECTRONIC
Exchanges: T   Stock Symbol: TC
89 Skyway Avenue, Suite 208, Etobicoke, ON,
M9W 6R4   (416) 675-0660
TELULAR CANADA INC. provides integrated communications and
computing solutions with value-added services. Using a consultative
approach, the company creates custom design solutions for the accessing,
capturing and sharing data and voice information. The company is
focused on creating single-source solutions for field force automation,
stationary wireless communications and other emerging technologies.
C. Ian Ross, Chairman
TOTAL ASSETS ($000)   22,524
TOTAL REVENUE ($000)   8,635
NET INCOME ($000)   1,845
EMPLOYEES   40
RANK (Profit/Revenue/Assets)   581/815/845

TELUS CORPORATION
See page 361 for a full company profile.

TEMBEC INC.
See page 175 for a full company profile.

TESCO CORPORATION
(Public)   OIL AND GAS FIELD SERVICES
Exchanges: T   Stock Symbol: TEO
Suite 3600, 350 - 7th Avenue S.W., Calgary, AB,
T2P 3N9   (403) 233-0757
TESCO CORPRATION is an oilfield services company with two main
operating divisions: Tesco Drilling Technology and Gris Gun Manufac-
turing. Tesco designs and manufactures a portable top drive drilling
system, while Gris Gun supplies high performance perforating guns and
charges used routinely in oil and gas well completions and workovers.
John A. Tessari, Chairman

TOTAL ASSETS ($000)	22,022
TOTAL REVENUE ($000)	20,138
NET INCOME ($000)	(183)
EMPLOYEES	122
RANK (Profit/Revenue/Assets)	773/705/850

TESMA INTERNATIONAL INC.
(Private)   AUTOMOTIVE
300 Edgeley Boulevard, Concord, ON, L4K 3Y3   (905) 669-5444
TESMA INTERNATIONAL INC. is one of four principal subsidiaries
of Magna International Inc. The company manufactures engine and
transmission components, automotive systems and other products.

TOTAL ASSETS ($000)	108,694
TOTAL REVENUE ($000)	259,195
NET INCOME ($000)	30
EMPLOYEES	1,262

TEXACO CANADA PETROLEUM INC.
(Private)   OIL AND GAS PRODUCERS
Suite 3100, 150 - 6th Avenue S.W., Calgary, AB,
T2P 4M5   (403) 234-2900
TEXACO CANADA PETROLEUM INC. is a Calgary based company
active in the exploration, development, production and marketing of
crude oil and natural gas, primarily in Western Canada. The company
was incorporated in Canada in September 1988, and began operating in
January 1989.
Alan C. Cocks, President & C.E.O.

TOTAL ASSETS ($000)	114,009
TOTAL REVENUE ($000)	38,383
NET INCOME ($000)	1,175
EMPLOYEES	73

TEXAS STAR RESOURCES CORPORATION
(Public)   OTHER MINES
Exchanges: T V Q   Stock Symbol: TXS
Suite 510, 2000 S. Dairy Ashford, Houston, TX,
77077   (713) 870-9882
TEXAS STAR RESOURCES CORPORATION is principally engaged
in exploring for and acquiring and developing diamond regions in North
America and Russia.

J. David Edwards, President

TOTAL ASSETS ($000)	14,018
TOTAL REVENUE ($000)	311
NET INCOME ($000)	(2,114)
EMPLOYEES	2
RANK (Profit/Revenue/Assets)	857/967/961

TEXTRON CANADA LIMITED
(Private)   ELECTRICAL & ELECTRONIC
40 Westminster Street, Providence, RI, 02903   (401) 421-2800
TEXTRON CANADA LIMITED is comprised of various manufactured
product businesses, which include the Canadian operations of Bell
Helicopter Textron, Homelite, Townsend, Davidson Instrument Panel
and Colonial Tool. Textron Canada is owned 65% by Ex-Cello Corporation and 35% by Textron Inc.
B.F. Dolan, Chairman

TOTAL ASSETS ($000)	394,800
TOTAL REVENUE ($000)	949,300
NET INCOME ($000)	39,000
EMPLOYEES	2,500

TFH INTERNATIONAL INC.
(Public)   INSURANCE - PROPERTY & CASUALTY
Exchanges: T   Stock Symbol: TFH
130 Adelaide St W, Ste 900, Toronto, ON, M5H 3P5   (416) 364-0919
TFH INTERNATINAL INC. through its wholly owned subsidiary
underwrites insurance exclusively for the trucking industry.
Barrett A. Macdonald, Chairman

TOTAL ASSETS ($000)	90,083
TOTAL REVENUE ($000)	38,159
NET INCOME ($000)	2,036
EMPLOYEES	na
RANK (Profit/Revenue/Assets)	565/603/505

THERATECHNOLOGIES INC.
(Public)   BIOTECHNOLOGY & PHARMACEUTICALS
Exchanges: T M   Stock Symbol: TH.B
7701 - 17th Avenue, Montreal, PQ, H2A 2S5   (514) 729-7904
THERATECHNOLOGIES INC. is a healthcare-oriented biotechnology
company which holds exclusive worldwide manufacturing and marketing rights to R&D projects comprised of diagnostic test kits, therapeutic
products, medical instrumentation and software packages. Theratechnologies is a publicly traded company listed on the Montreal Exchange.
Terrance A. Mailloux, Chairman & C.E.O.

TOTAL ASSETS ($000)	24,271
TOTAL REVENUE ($000)	17,742
NET INCOME ($000)	(4,560)
EMPLOYEES	15
RANK (Profit/Revenue/Assets)	903/730/823

THIRD CANADIAN GENERAL INVESTMENT TRUST LIMITED
(Public)   INVESTMENT COMPANIES AND FUNDS
Exchanges: T   Stock Symbol: THD
Suite 1601, 110 Yonge Street, Toronto, ON, M5C 1T4 (416) 366-2931
THIRD CANADIAN GENERAL INVESTMENT TRUST LIMITED
is a closed-end investment company. The company operates primarily
as a holding company. Its investment portfolio is comprised mainly of
the shares of two related closed-end funds – Canadian General Invest-

ments Limited and Canadian World Fund Limited. The company also
has a diversified portfolio of Canadian and foreign securities.
E. Louise Morgan, Chairman

TOTAL ASSETS ($000)	84,200
TOTAL REVENUE ($000)	2,262
NET INCOME ($000)	1,397
EMPLOYEES	0
RANK (Profit/Revenue/Assets)	618/914/522

THOMSON CONSUMER ELECTRONICS CANADA, INC.
(Private) APPLIANCES
5925 Airport Road, 10th Floor, Mississauga, ON,
L4V 1W1 (905) 405-3010
THOMSON CONSUMER ELECTRONICS CANADA, INC. is a
manufacturer and distriutor of RCA and GE brand consumer electronic
products and GE brand audio and communication products.
C. David Geise, President

TOTAL ASSETS ($000)	96,683
TOTAL REVENUE ($000)	291,546
NET INCOME ($000)	(8,545)
EMPLOYEES	75

THOMSON CORPORATION (THE)
See page 394 for a full company profile.

THUNDERWOOD RESOURCES INC.
(Public) PRECIOUS METALS
Exchanges: T Stock Symbol: THS
Suite 2501, 1 Adelaide Street East, Toronto, ON,
M5C 2V9 (416) 362-8730
THUNDERWOOD RESOURCES INC. is a Canadian mineral explora-
tion company specializing in the exploration and development of gold
and base metal deposits.
James W. Gill, Chairman

TOTAL ASSETS ($000)	14,785
TOTAL REVENUE ($000)	217
NET INCOME ($000)	(1,403)
EMPLOYEES	2
RANK (Profit/Revenue/Assets)	831/978/950

TIDAL RESOURCES INC.
(Public) OIL AND GAS PRODUCERS
Exchanges: T Stock Symbol: TID
Ste 2500, 520 - 5th Ave SW, Calgary, AB, T2P 3R7 (403) 231-1400
TIDAL RESOURCES INC. is involved in the acqusition, exploration
and development of oil and gas properties principally in western Canada,
Montana and North Dakota.
R. Paul Wanklyn, President

TOTAL ASSETS ($000)	23,601
TOTAL REVENUE ($000)	5,278
NET INCOME ($000)	212
EMPLOYEES	15
RANK (Profit/Revenue/Assets)	733/860/831

TIMBERWEST FOREST LIMITED
See page 176 for a full company profile.

TIMMINCO LIMITED
(Public) MISC. INDUSTRIAL PRODUCTS
Exchanges: T M Stock Symbol: TIM
10 Bay Street, 9th Floor, Toronto, ON, M5J 2R8 (416) 364-5171
TIMMINCO LIMITED is involved in the production of specialty non-
ferrous metals and alloys of magnesium, calcium and strontium. The
company serves a broad spectrum of industries worldwide, from primary
and secondary producers of aluminum, steel and lead to manufacturers
of automotive castings and batteries, as well as industries producing
pharmaceuticals and aerospace components.
J. Thomas Timmins, President & C.E.O.

TOTAL ASSETS ($000)	45,802
TOTAL REVENUE ($000)	49,553
NET INCOME ($000)	1,687
EMPLOYEES	224
RANK (Profit/Revenue/Assets)	596/550/655

TIOMIN RESOURCES INC.
(Public) OTHER MINES
Exchanges: M Stock Symbol: TIO
One Toronto Street, Suite 709, Box 22, Toronto, ON,
M5C 2V6 (416) 350-3779
TIOMIN RESOURCES INC. is a heavy mineral sand development
company.
Jean-Charles Potvin, C.E.O.

TOTAL ASSETS ($000)	13,812
TOTAL REVENUE ($000)	249
NET INCOME ($000)	(707)
EMPLOYEES	30
RANK (Profit/Revenue/Assets)	809/975/968

TNT FINANCIAL LTD.
(Public) INVESTMENT COMPANIES AND FUNDS
Exchanges: T Stock Symbol: XTN
Suite 5000, P.O. Box 150, 1 First Canadian Place, Toronto, ON,
M5X 1H3 (416) 359-4630
TNT FINANCIAL LTD. invests its fund in TransAlta common shares.
Michael M. Armstrong, President & C.E.O.

TOTAL ASSETS ($000)	85,823
TOTAL REVENUE ($000)	5,849
NET INCOME ($000)	5,807
EMPLOYEES	1
RANK (Profit/Revenue/Assets)	400/847/517

TOLGECO GROUP INC.
(Public) METAL FABRICATORS
Exchanges: M Stock Symbol: TL
200 Boul. Industriel, Boucherville, PQ, J4B 2X4 (514) 526-2544
GROUPE TOLGECO is a holding company operating through subsidiaries primarily in the manufacturing of steel cladding, industrial profiles,
joists and studs which are primarily used in industrial, commercial,
agricultural and residential construction. The company is also engaged
in the manufacturing and distribution of materials and specialized products for the construction industry.
J. Serge Vezina, Chairman & V.P. Development

TOTAL ASSETS ($000)	33,483
TOTAL REVENUE ($000)	61,103
NET INCOME ($000)	420
EMPLOYEES	250
RANK (Profit/Revenue/Assets)	707/505/743

Canada Company Handbook

TOMBILL MINES LIMITED

(Public)   OIL AND GAS PRODUCERS
Exchanges: T   Stock Symbol: TBL.B
P.O. Box 160, Inglewood, ON, L0N 1K0   (519) 927-9271
TOMBILL MINES LIMITED is involved in the exploration and production of oil and gas. The company also holds mineral properties and investments.
S.R. Horne, President

TOTAL ASSETS ($000)	20,585
TOTAL REVENUE ($000)	3,197
NET INCOME ($000)	1,582
EMPLOYEES	1
RANK (Profit/Revenue/Assets)	603/897/866

TOMBSTONE EXPLORATIONS CO. LTD.

(Public)   PRECIOUS METALS
Exchanges: T V   Stock Symbol: TSO
Suite 1112, 409 Granville Street, Vancouver, BC,
V6C 1T2   (604) 682-1545
TOMBSTONE EXPLORATIONS CO. LTD. is involved in the acquisition, exploration and development of precious metal properties.
Richard Clark, President & C.E.O.

TOTAL ASSETS ($000)	25,206
TOTAL REVENUE ($000)	290
NET INCOME ($000)	(278)
EMPLOYEES	6
RANK (Profit/Revenue/Assets)	778/971/815

TOMEN CANADA INC.

(Private)   WHOLESALE DISTRIBUTORS
Suite 1770, 1500 West Georgia Street, Vancouver, BC,
V6G 2Z6   (604) 682-7436
TOMEN CANADA INC. is an import and export company.
S. Oe, President

TOTAL ASSETS ($000)	25,356
TOTAL REVENUE ($000)	208,029
NET INCOME ($000)	577
EMPLOYEES	27

TOROMONT INDUSTRIES LTD.

See page 250 for a full company profile.

TORONTO AREA TRANSIT OPERATING AUTHORITY

(Crown)   TRANSPORTATION
20 Bay Street; Suite 600, Toronto, ON, M5J 2W3   (416) 869-3600
TORONTO AREA TRANSIT OPERATING AUTHORITY (GO Transit) is a Crown Agency established to design and operate interregional transit, and to encourage convenient and efficient meshing of the transit systems operating in the Greater Toronto Area with the GO Transit network.
D.G. Hobbs, Chairman

TOTAL ASSETS ($000)	1,084,984
TOTAL REVENUE ($000)	99,590
NET INCOME ($000)	(5,000)
EMPLOYEES	na

TORONTO HYDRO-ELECTRIC SYSTEM

(Crown)   ELECTRICAL UTILITIES
Toronto Hydro, 14 Carlton Street, Toronto, ON,
M5B 1K5   (416) 599-0400
TORONTO ELECTRIC COMMISSIONERS is Canada's largest municipal electric utility, distributing electricity to 210,000 customers in the city of Toronto. It is a public body consisting of five commissioners. It is a local board of the City of Toronto.
Catherine Cherrard, Chair

TOTAL ASSETS ($000)	684,700
TOTAL REVENUE ($000)	764,290
NET INCOME ($000)	26,802
EMPLOYEES	1,593

TORONTO SUN PUBLISHING CORPORATION

See page 395 for a full company profile.

TORONTO-DOMINION BANK (THE)

See page 456 for a full company profile.

TORRINGTON RESOURCES LTD.

(Public)   OIL AND GAS PRODUCERS
Exchanges: T   Stock Symbol: TRN
Suite 2600, 801 - 6 Avenue S.W., Calgary, AB,
T2P 3W2   (403) 263-9767
TORRINGTON RESOURCES LTD. is involved in the acquisition, exploration and development of oil and gas properties in western Canada.
Glenn D. Hockley, Chairman

TOTAL ASSETS ($000)	23,967
TOTAL REVENUE ($000)	6,527
NET INCOME ($000)	2,270
EMPLOYEES	5
RANK (Profit/Revenue/Assets)	551/835/828

TORSTAR CORPORATION

See page 396 for a full company profile.

TOTAL PETROLEUM (NORTH AMERICA) LTD.

See page 143 for a full company profile.

TOYOTA CANADA INC.

(Private)   WHOLESALE DISTRIBUTORS
One Toyota Place, Scarborough, ON, M1H 1H9   (416) 438-6320
TOYOTA CANADA INC. is the Canadian distributor of Toyota and Lexus vehicles, parts and forklift trucks.
T. Kunii, President

TOTAL ASSETS ($000)	284,282
TOTAL REVENUE ($000)	1,616,671
NET INCOME ($000)	na
EMPLOYEES	476

TRACER PETROLEUM CORPORATION

(Public)   OIL AND GAS PRODUCERS
Exchanges: V Q   Stock Symbol: TCP
Suite 1570, 609 Granville, P.O. Box 10345, Vancouver, BC,
V7Y 1G5   (604) 682-7507
TRACER PETROLEUM CORPORATION is involved in the acquisition, exploration and development of international oil and gas properties with an emphasis on Indonesia. The company's management has had

extensive experience in Indonesia and is currently drilling on the island of Borneo.
Roland C. Siouffi, Chairman

TOTAL ASSETS ($000)	21,396
TOTAL REVENUE ($000)	2,301
NET INCOME ($000)	(1,545)
EMPLOYEES	10
RANK (Profit/Revenue/Assets)	836/913/860

TRANSALTA CORPORATION
See page 362 for a full company profile.

TRANSALTA UTILITIES CORPORATION
See page 363 for a full company profile.

TRANSAT A.T. INC.
(Public)   TRANSPORTATION
Exchanges: T M   Stock Symbol: TRZ
300 Leo Pariseau, Bureau 400, Montreal, PQ,
H2W 2P6   (514) 987-1616
TRANSAT A.T. INC. is a service organization operating, through its subsidiaries and affiliates, in the tourism and holiday travel industry. The company's markets are throughout Canada and Europe.
Jean-Marc Eustache, President & C.E.O.

TOTAL ASSETS ($000)	176,500
TOTAL REVENUE ($000)	524,565
NET INCOME ($000)	5,567
EMPLOYEES	1,526
RANK (Profit/Revenue/Assets)	407/193/373

TRANSCANADA PIPELINES LIMITED
See page 336 for a full company profile.

TRANSWEST ENERGY INC.
See page 144 for a full company profile.

TREASURY BRANCHES DEPOSITS FUND
(Crown)   BANKS
9925 - 109 Street, 1200 ATB Plaza, Edmonton, AB,
T5K 2J8   (403) 493-7300
ALBERTA TREASURY BRANCHES is an Alberta crown agency providing banking services to over 225 locations in the province. It operates under the authority of the Treasury Branches Act, revised statutes of Alberta 1980.
A.O. Bray, Superintendent & C.O.O.

TOTAL ASSETS ($000)	8,195,728
TOTAL REVENUE ($000)	665,936
NET INCOME ($000)	24,461
EMPLOYEES	3,210

TRENTON INDUSTRIES INC.
(Public)   MACHINERY
Exchanges: T   Stock Symbol: TII
P.O. Box 698, Douglas Drive, Trenton, ON,
K8V 5W6   (613) 394-4861
TRENTON INDUSTRIES INC. is engaged in the precision machining of component parts for a broad range of industries, including manufacturers of office equipment, power generation, forestry, pipeline and areospace products.

Bruce M. Westwood, Chairman of the Board

TOTAL ASSETS ($000)	15,171
TOTAL REVENUE ($000)	26,122
NET INCOME ($000)	(5,028)
EMPLOYEES	200
RANK (Profit/Revenue/Assets)	908/670/941

TRI LINK RESOURCES LTD.
See page 145 for a full company profile.

TRIAM AUTOMOTIVE INC.
(Public)   AUTOMOTIVE
Exchanges: T   Stock Symbol: TRU
Suite 2206, 130 Adelaide Street West, Toronto, ON,
M5H 3P5   (416) 777-2728
TRIAM AUTOMOTIVE INC. is an auto parts supplier. The company designs, engineers and manufactures stamped metal parts and assembles injection mould plastic parts and metal/plastic assemblies for sale to automotive manufacturers.
James Nicol, Chairman & C.E.O.

TOTAL ASSETS ($000)	47,979
TOTAL REVENUE ($000)	22,780
NET INCOME ($000)	(142)
EMPLOYEES	0
RANK (Profit/Revenue/Assets)	784/485/645

TRIDEL ENTERPRISES INC.
(Public)   DEVELOPERS
Exchanges: T M   Stock Symbol: TDZ
4800 Dufferin Street, Downsview, ON, M3H 5S9   (416) 661-9290
TRIDEL ENTERPRISES is a diversified residential builder and construction technology distribution company engaged in two businesses. The residential real estate division develops high-rise condominium lifestyle projects primarily in the greater Metropolitan Toronto area. The construction technology division is a supplier of products to the concrete construction industry.
Angelo Delzotto, Chairman & C.E.O.

TOTAL ASSETS ($000)	586,927
TOTAL REVENUE ($000)	251,602
NET INCOME ($000)	(51,229)
EMPLOYEES	750
RANK (Profit/Revenue/Assets)	987/284/213

TRILLION RESOURCES LTD.
(Public)   PRECIOUS METALS
Exchanges: T   Stock Symbol: TLQ
Suite 800, 900 West Hastings Street, Vancouver, BC,
V6C 1E5   (604) 684-2822
TRILLION RESOURCES LTD. is involved in the exploration and development of mineral properties in Africa. The company, through a subsidiary, owns a 50% interest in Jena Mines (Private) Limited, a joint venture which operates a gold mine in Zimbabwe.
Jens E. Hansen, President

TOTAL ASSETS ($000)	12,951
TOTAL REVENUE ($000)	486
NET INCOME ($000)	(445)
EMPLOYEES	0
RANK (Profit/Revenue/Assets)	789/958/992

TRILON FINANCIAL CORPORATION
See page 487 for a full company profile.

TRIMAC LIMITED
See page 328 for a full company profile.

TRIMARK FINANCIAL CORPORATION
See page 488 for a full company profile.

TRIMIN ENTERPRISES INC.
(Public)   METAL FABRICATORS
Exchanges: T   Stock Symbol: TRM
Suite 638, 375 Water Street, Vancouver, BC,
V6B 5C6   (604) 688-4693
TRIMIN ENTERPRISES INC. is a management company with investments in two companies, Tritech Precision Inc. and Uniplast Industries Inc. Trimin's strategy is to acquire large equity interests in operating businesses, and build value for its shareholders through a combination of the established financial skills of its corporate management and its strong operating management teams.
James D. Meekison, Chairman

TOTAL ASSETS ($000)	130,950
TOTAL REVENUE ($000)	167,576
NET INCOME ($000)	6,504
EMPLOYEES	6
RANK (Profit/Revenue/Assets)	378/340/422

TRIONICS INDUSTRIES LTD.
(Public)   MANAGEMENT AND DIVERSIFIED
Exchanges: V   Stock Symbol: TIL
8527 Eastlake Drive, Lake City Business Park, Burnaby, BC,
V5A 4T7   (604) 421-7202
TRIONICS INDUSTRIES LTD. is involved in developing, manufacturing and marketing electronic revenue control systems. A key feature of these systems is their ability to process credit card transactions instantly. Through a subsidiary, the company is involved in injection molding.
Douglas Smith, Chairman & C.E.O.

TOTAL ASSETS ($000)	21,263
TOTAL REVENUE ($000)	6,776
NET INCOME ($000)	(2,036)
EMPLOYEES	30
RANK (Profit/Revenue/Assets)	851/839/861

TRITECH PRECISION INC.
(Public)   MISC. INDUSTRIAL PRODUCTS
Exchanges: T M   Stock Symbol: TCH
Suite 3400, 2 Bloor Street West, P.O. Box 79, Toronto, ON,
M4W 3E2   (416) 963-8880
TRITECH is a precision casting company engaged in the design, manufacture and distribution of metal castings to automotive, commercial and mining industries. TRITECH also holds 44% of Haley Industries Ltd., a manufacturer of magnesium and aluminum castings for the aerospace industry.
James D. Meekison, Chairman

TOTAL ASSETS ($000)	75,896
TOTAL REVENUE ($000)	99,090
NET INCOME ($000)	5,735
EMPLOYEES	705
RANK (Profit/Revenue/Assets)	403/423/543

TRITON MINING CORPORATION
(Public)   PRECIOUS METALS
Exchanges: T   Stock Symbol: TTM
Suite 1620, 1140 West Pender Street, Vancouver, BC,
V6E 4G1   (604) 689-9554
TRITON MINING CORPORATION is engaged in the acquisition, exploration and development of mineral properties in Central and South America.
Arnaldo Ismay, President & C.E.O.

TOTAL ASSETS ($000)	27,396
TOTAL REVENUE ($000)	3,505
NET INCOME ($000)	(1,734)
EMPLOYEES	320
RANK (Profit/Revenue/Assets)	871/937/872

TRIUMPH ENERGY CORPORATION
(Public)   OIL AND GAS PRODUCERS
Exchanges: T Z   Stock Symbol: TPH
Suite 410, 635 - 8 Avenue S.W., Calgary, AB,
T2P 3M3   (403) 266-1227
TRIUMPH ENERGY CORPORATION is involved in the acquisition, exploration and development of oil and gas properties in Alberta and British Columbia.
William A. Friley, President & C.E.O.

TOTAL ASSETS ($000)	20,244
TOTAL REVENUE ($000)	3,605
NET INCOME ($000)	414
EMPLOYEES	8
RANK (Profit/Revenue/Assets)	708/885/867

TRIZEC CORPORATION LTD.
See page 316 for a full company profile.

TROJAN TECHNOLOGIES INC.
(Public)   ENVIRONMENTAL SERVICES
Exchanges: T   Stock Symbol: TUV
3020 Gore Road, London, ON, N5V 4T7   (519) 457-3400
TROJAN TECHNOLOGIES INC. provides technological solutions to the environmental problem of microbial and toxic pollution in water. The company specializes in ultraviolet light applications for disinfecting water and waste water.
Henry J. Vander Laan, President & C.E.O.

TOTAL ASSETS ($000)	27,964
TOTAL REVENUE ($000)	22,713
NET INCOME ($000)	2,044
EMPLOYEES	94
RANK (Profit/Revenue/Assets)	564/699/787

TRUAX RESOURCES CORPORATION
(Public)   OIL AND GAS PRODUCERS
Exchanges: T Z   Stock Symbol: TUX
Suite 1500, 700 - 4th Avenue S.W., Calgary, AB,
T2P 3J4   (403) 233-7122
TRUAX RESOURCES CORPORATION is involved in the acquisition, exploration and development of oil and gas properties mainly in Western Canada.
Leo G. Schnitzler, President & C.E.O.

TOTAL ASSETS ($000)	13,338
TOTAL REVENUE ($000)	2,110

NET INCOME ($000)	393
EMPLOYEES	6
RANK (Profit/Revenue/Assets)	715/918/987

TRUSCAN REALTY LIMITED
(Private) PROPERTY MGMNT & INVESTMENT
Suite 1200, 380 Wellington Street, London, ON,
N6A 4S4 (519) 667-6947
TRUSCAN REALTY LIMITED is a wholly owned subsidiary of
Canada Trustco Mortgage Company and a member of the Canada Trust
group of companies. Its principal business is the management of real
estate, both for investment puposes and for occupancy by CT Financial
Services Inc. and its subsidiaries.
H. Purdy Crawford, Chairman

TOTAL ASSETS ($000)	923,683
TOTAL REVENUE ($000)	145,281
NET INCOME ($000)	9,126
EMPLOYEES	9

TSB INTERNATIONAL INC.
(Public) Computer Software and Processing
Exchanges: T Stock Symbol: TSB
Ste 115, 5399 Eglinton Ave. W., Etobicoke, ON,
M9C 5K6 (416) 622-7010
TSB International Inc. is a telecommunications management company.
Its products and services manage network planning, performance, and
cost-allocation.
Jeremy Purbrick, Chairman President & C.E.O.

TOTAL ASSETS ($000)	34,035
TOTAL REVENUE ($000)	33,989
NET INCOME ($000)	1,133
EMPLOYEES	200
RANK (Profit/Revenue/Assets)	644/627/734

TSC SHANNOCK CORP.
(Public) WHOLESALE DISTRIBUTORS
Exchanges: T Stock Symbol: TSH
4222 Manor Street, Burnaby, BC, V5G 1B2 (604) 433-3331
TSC SHANNOCK's principal business is as a wholesale distributor of
video movies, accessories, cassettes, compact discs and laser videos.
William G. McCartney, President & C.E.O.

TOTAL ASSETS ($000)	17,936
TOTAL REVENUE ($000)	72,454
NET INCOME ($000)	592
EMPLOYEES	170
RANK (Profit/Revenue/Assets)	686/475/899

TVX GOLD INC.
See page 62 for a full company profile.

TWINPAK INC.
(Private) PACKAGING AND CONTAINERS
1840 Route Trans-Canada, Dorval, PQ, H9P 1H7 (514) 684-7070
TWINPAK INC. is a Canadian leader in plastic, paper and composite
material packaging with substantial sales in the U.S. The company is a
wholly owned subsidiary of Amcor Limited of Australia.
Chris D.V. Nixon, Chairman

TOTAL ASSETS ($000)	na
TOTAL REVENUE ($000)	214,000

NET INCOME ($000)	na
EMPLOYEES	1,200

UAP INC.
See page 406 for a full company profile.

ULSTER PETROLEUMS LTD.
See page 146 for a full company profile.

UNI-SELECT INC.
(Public) WHOLESALE DISTRIBUTORS
Exchanges: T M Stock Symbol: UNS
170 Boulevard Industriel, Boucherville, PQ, J4B 2X3 (514) 641-2440
UNI-SELECT INC. is involved in the wholesale distribution and mar-
keting of spare parts for motor vehicles, equipment, tools and accessories.
It carries on business in the provinces of Quebec, Ontario, Nova Scotia,
New Brunswick, P.E.I., Manitoba, Saskatchewan, and British Columbia.
Distribution is carried out mainly through its members, all of whom are
shareholders of Uni-Select.
Jean-Louis Dulac, Chairman

TOTAL ASSETS ($000)	110,689
TOTAL REVENUE ($000)	296,592
NET INCOME ($000)	11,161
EMPLOYEES	418
RANK (Profit/Revenue/Assets)	280/261/463

UNIBOARD CANADA INC.
(Private) MISC. INDUSTRIAL PRODUCTS
Suite 370, 1195 De La Vigerie, Ste-Foy, PQ,
G1V 4N3 (418) 659-5240
UNIBOARD CANADA INC. is a manufacturer of particleboard, MDF
panel, and decorative panel.
Jacques J. Giasson, Chairman

TOTAL ASSETS ($000)	249,932
TOTAL REVENUE ($000)	228,640
NET INCOME ($000)	na
EMPLOYEES	620

UNICAN SECURITY SYSTEMS LTD.
See page 593 for a full company profile.

UNICAP COMMERCIAL CORP.
(Public) MANAGEMENT AND DIVERSIFIED
Exchanges: Z Stock Symbol: UCP.A
106 Avenue Road, Toronto, ON, M5R 2H3 (416) 920-0500
UNICAP COMMERCIAL CORP. is a management holding company
operating in three industry segments. It manufactures specialty covers.
It manufactures packaging materials. It manufactures furniture.
Mark I. Litwin, President

TOTAL ASSETS ($000)	30,815
TOTAL REVENUE ($000)	56,141
NET INCOME ($000)	(385)
EMPLOYEES	0
RANK (Profit/Revenue/Assets)	755/578/838

UNICORP ENERGY CORPORATION
See page 364 for a full company profile.

UNILEVER CANADA LTD.
(Private)   MANAGEMENT AND DIVERSIFIED
160 Bloor St. East, Suite 1500, Toronto, ON,
M4W 3R2   (416) 964-1857
UNILEVER CANADA LTD. is engaged in the manufacture and distribution of food products, detergents, personal products and specialty chemicals. Unilever Canada also operates a national chain of restaurants.
R.A. Goldstein, Chairman & C.E.O.

TOTAL ASSETS ($000)	816,778
TOTAL REVENUE ($000)	1,258,708
NET INCOME ($000)	na
EMPLOYEES	6,822

UNION BANK OF SWITZERLAND (CANADA)
(Private)   BANKS
154 University Avenue, Toronto, ON, M5H 3Z4   (416) 343-1800
UNION BANK OF SWITZERLAND (CANADA) is a schedule II bank. The bank is a wholly owned subsidiary of Union Bank of Switzerland.
Mathis Cabiallavetta, Chairman

TOTAL ASSETS ($000)	2,040,800
TOTAL REVENUE ($000)	211,465
NET INCOME ($000)	3,520
EMPLOYEES	na

UNION GAS LIMITED
(Public)   GAS UTILITIES
Exchanges: T M   Stock Symbol: UNG.PR.B
50 Keil Drive North, P.O. Box 2001, Chatham, ON,
N7M 5M1   (519) 352-3100
UNION GAS LIMITED owns and operates a fully integrated system of natural gas transmission, distribution and storage. It serves over 650,000 residential, commercial and industrial customers throughout southwestern Ontario. The storage and transmission facilities are an important component in the delivery of Western Canada gas to Eastern Canada. The company is regulated by the Ontario Energy Board.
Michael J. Phelps, Chairman

TOTAL ASSETS ($000)	2,432,300
TOTAL REVENUE ($000)	1,432,300
NET INCOME ($000)	98,300
EMPLOYEES	2,585
RANK (Profit/Revenue/Assets)	76/88/90

UNITED CANADIAN SHARES LIMITED
(Public)   CLOTHING AND TEXTILES
Exchanges: T   Stock Symbol: UCD
1601 Church Avenue, Winnipeg, MB, R2X 1G9   (204) 633-7042
UNITED CANADIAN SHARES LIMITED is engaged in leather tanning with approximately 60% of its sales from exports.
Robert H. Jones, Chairman of the Board

TOTAL ASSETS ($000)	42,569
TOTAL REVENUE ($000)	82,792
NET INCOME ($000)	2,394
EMPLOYEES	450
RANK (Profit/Revenue/Assets)	544/449/677

UNITED CO-OPERATIVES OF ONTARIO
(Non-fin Co-op)   WHOLESALE DISTRIBUTORS
P.O. Box 527, Station A, 5600 Cancross Court, Mississauga, ON,
L5A 3A4   (905) 890-8500

UNITED CO-OPERATIVES OF ONTARIO is the largest farm supply and marketing cooperative in the province. The role of the cooperative is as a wholesaler, manufacturer, distributor, and retailer in farm products, supplies, and services.
Gordon Cummings, C.E.O.

TOTAL ASSETS ($000)	80,000
TOTAL REVENUE ($000)	400,000
NET INCOME ($000)	0
EMPLOYEES	300

UNITED CORPORATIONS LIMITED
See page 489 for a full company profile.

UNITED DOMINION INDUSTRIES LIMITED
See page 530 for a full company profile.

UNITED FARMERS OF ALBERTA CO-OPERATIVE LTD.
(Non-fin Co-op)   WHOLESALE DISTRIBUTORS
1016 - 68th Avenue S.W., Calgary, AB, T2V 4J2   (403) 258-4500
UNITED FARMERS OF ALBERTA CO-OPERATIVE LTD. is a member owned farm cooperative. An extensive and diversified range of farm production inputs are distributed by the cooperative which is recognized as the largest farm supply cooperative in Alberta. Farm supplies are available from the 33 farm supply centres, and petroleum products are marketed through 126 petroleum outlets and member associations.
T. Semeniuk, Chief Executive Officer

TOTAL ASSETS ($000)	146,291
TOTAL REVENUE ($000)	435,717
NET INCOME ($000)	21,830
EMPLOYEES	600

UNITED GRAIN GROWERS LIMITED
(Public)   AGRICULTURE
Exchanges: T W   Stock Symbol: UGG
P.O. Box 6600, 2800 - 201 Portage Avenue, Winnipeg, MB,
R3C 3A7   (204) 944-5411
UNITED GRAIN GROWERS LIMITED (UGG) has four separate but related business operations: grain handling and marketing, with 224 country elevator locations and four port terminals; crop production services, which provides fertilizers, agricultural chemicals, seed and crop management services; livestock services; and communications and information services, including farm publications and grain market information.
T.M. Allen, Chairman of the Board

TOTAL ASSETS ($000)	579,338
TOTAL REVENUE ($000)	1,224,221
NET INCOME ($000)	7,049
EMPLOYEES	1,531
RANK (Profit/Revenue/Assets)	365/107/216

UNITED KENO HILL MINES LIMITED
See page 63 for a full company profile.

UNITED RAYORE GAS LTD.
(Public)   OIL AND GAS PRODUCERS
Exchanges: T V   Stock Symbol: URG
Ste 1120, 520 - 5th Ave SW, Calgary, AB, T2P 3R7   (403) 262-7677

UNITED RAYORE GAS LTD. is involved in the exploration for and development of oil, gas and minerals.

Robert L. Bell, President & C.E.O.

TOTAL ASSETS ($000)	26,296
TOTAL REVENUE ($000)	15,067
NET INCOME ($000)	(623)
EMPLOYEES	11
RANK (Profit/Revenue/Assets)	800/756/806

UNITED TIRE & RUBBER CO. LIMITED

(Public)   AUTOMOTIVE

Exchanges: T   Stock Symbol: UDT

275 Belfield Road, Rexdale, ON, M9W 5C6   (416) 675-3077

UNITED TIRE & RUBBER CO. LIMITED designs, manufactures, retreads, and distributes tires. The company is a supplier of tires and other rubber products to the mining, construction and forestry industries with branches across Canada and the United States.

Robert Scolnick, Chairman

TOTAL ASSETS ($000)	14,459
TOTAL REVENUE ($000)	36,778
NET INCOME ($000)	4,280
EMPLOYEES	90
RANK (Profit/Revenue/Assets)	448/610/954

UNITEL COMMUNICATIONS HOLDINGS INC.

(Private)   TELECOMMUNICATIONS

200 Wellington Street West, Suite 1601, Toronto, ON, M5V 3C7   (416) 345-2256

UNITEL COMMUNICATIONS HOLDINGS INC. is a telecommunications company. Unitel offers businesses and residential callers a variety of products and services for long-distance voice communications, as well as data and message services. Unitel has a fully digital, cross-Canada network which uses both fibre-optic and microwave technologies.

TOTAL ASSETS ($000)	1,126,002
TOTAL REVENUE ($000)	427,166
NET INCOME ($000)	na
EMPLOYEES	3,546

UNIVERS INFO INC.

(Public)   WHOLESALE DISTRIBUTORS

Exchanges: M   Stock Symbol: UNV

9601 rue Clement, Ville LaSalle, PQ, H8R 4B4   (514) 368-0414

UNIVERS INFO INC. is involved in the distribution of microcomputer products directly and through its subsidiaries.

Jean-Luc Lussier, Chairman

TOTAL ASSETS ($000)	16,832
TOTAL REVENUE ($000)	26,149
NET INCOME ($000)	934
EMPLOYEES	116
RANK (Profit/Revenue/Assets)	663/669/919

UPTON RESOURCES INC.

(Public)   OIL AND GAS PRODUCERS

Exchanges: T   Stock Symbol: URC

322 - 4th Street, Estevan, SK, S4A 0T8   (306) 634-6484

UPTON RESOURCES INC. produces crude oil and associated natural gas, and also acts as contract operator and administrator for other oil companies in southeast Saskatchewan.

William R. Dutton, Chairman

TOTAL ASSETS ($000)	27,294
TOTAL REVENUE ($000)	12,579
NET INCOME ($000)	1,288
EMPLOYEES	20
RANK (Profit/Revenue/Assets)	629/776/797

URBCO INC.

(Public)   DEVELOPERS

Exchanges: Z   Stock Symbol: UBC

Ste 110, 6131 - 6th St SE, Calgary, AB, T2H 1L9   (403) 531-0720

URBCO INC. is a real estate development and management company. Holdings include properties in Yellowknife, Northwest Territories, and Calgary, Alberta. Development properties include subdivisions in Okotoks and Calgary, Alberta.

Roy G. Wilson, Chairman

TOTAL ASSETS ($000)	18,759
TOTAL REVENUE ($000)	5,605
NET INCOME ($000)	420
EMPLOYEES	9
RANK (Profit/Revenue/Assets)	706/853/883

UTILITY CORP.

(Public)   ELECTRICAL UTILITIES

Exchanges: T   Stock Symbol: UTC.A

Box 433, Commercial Union Tower, Toronto-Dominion Centre, Toronto, ON, M5K 1M2   (416) 863-7411

UTILITY CORP. was formed as a financial intermediary corporation to invest its funds in a fixed portfolio of common shares and debt securities of selected Canadian utility companies.

Donald W. Paterson, Chairman

TOTAL ASSETS ($000)	205,948
TOTAL REVENUE ($000)	13,028
NET INCOME ($000)	12,296
EMPLOYEES	0
RANK (Profit/Revenue/Assets)	271/772/353

VAN WATERS & ROGERS LTD.

(Private)   WHOLESALE DISTRIBUTORS

9800 Van Horne Way, Richmond, BC, V6X 1W5   (604) 273-1441

VAN WATERS & ROGERS LTD. is a wholesale chemical distributor. The company is wholly owned by Univar Corp. (U.S.).

A.C. McHeight, Chairman

TOTAL ASSETS ($000)	140,826
TOTAL REVENUE ($000)	339,625
NET INCOME ($000)	na
EMPLOYEES	450

VANCOUVER CITY SAVINGS CREDIT UNION

(Fin. Co-op)   CREDIT UNIONS

515 West 10th Avenue, Vancouver, BC, V5Z 4A8   (604) 877-7000

VANCOUVER CITY SAVINGS CREDIT UNION is Canada's largest credit union offering a full range of financial services to members.

Shirley Y. Chan, Chairman

TOTAL ASSETS ($000)	4,083,662
TOTAL REVENUE ($000)	345,424
NET INCOME ($000)	21,207
EMPLOYEES	963

VANCOUVER PORT CORPORATION

(Crown) TRANSPORTATION
1900 Granville Square, 200 Granville Street, Vancouver, BC,
V6C 2P9 (604) 666-3226
VANCOUVER PORT CORPORATION is a crown corporation responsible for administering the lands and waterways of the Port of Vancouver. The VPC also owns five cargo and cruise terminals, and actively markets port services worldwide. The VPC maintains harbour safety and security through the offices of the Harbour Master and Ports Canada police.
Patrick Reid, Chairman

TOTAL ASSETS ($000)	382,919
TOTAL REVENUE ($000)	66,284
NET INCOME ($000)	15,807
EMPLOYEES	na

VARITECH INVESTORS CORPORATION

(Public) INVESTMENT COMPANIES AND FUNDS
Exchanges: T Stock Symbol: VRI.PR.A
BCE Place Suite 4500, 181 Bay Street, P.O. Box 770, Toronto, ON,
M5J 2T3 (416) 865-0430
VARITECH INVESTORS CORPORATION invests in premium high yielding securities of Canadian corporations according to investment guidelines established by the board of directors. Such securities primarily include preferred shares and convertible preferred shares.
Marlene J. Davidge, Chairman

TOTAL ASSETS ($000)	196,517
TOTAL REVENUE ($000)	11,022
NET INCOME ($000)	10,972
EMPLOYEES	20
RANK (Profit/Revenue/Assets)	282/787/361

VARITY CORPORATION

See page 251 for a full company profile.

VELAN INC.

(Private) METAL FABRICATORS
2125 Ward Avenue, Montreal, PQ, H4M 1T6 (514) 748-7743
VELAN INC. is a manufacturer of industrial valves.
A.K. Velan, President & C.E.O.

TOTAL ASSETS ($000)	142,029
TOTAL REVENUE ($000)	174,759
NET INCOME ($000)	17,194
EMPLOYEES	1,167

VENCAP EQUITIES ALBERTA LTD.

(Public) INVESTMENT COMPANIES AND FUNDS
Exchanges: Z Stock Symbol: VCE
Ste 1980, 10180 - 101 St, Edmonton, AB, T5J 3S4 (403) 420-1171
VENCAP EQUITIES ALBERTA LTD. is a private placement equity specialist serving western Canada and the northwestern United States.
Donald A. Carlson, Chairman

TOTAL ASSETS ($000)	294,030
TOTAL REVENUE ($000)	28,147
NET INCOME ($000)	791
EMPLOYEES	20
RANK (Profit/Revenue/Assets)	671/658/289

VENGOLD INC.

See page 64 for a full company profile.

VENTRA GROUP INC.

(Public) AUTOMOTIVE
Exchanges: T Stock Symbol: VTA
1 Mitten Court, P.O. Box 126, Cambridge, ON,
N1R 5S9 (519) 658-6777
VENTRA GROUP INC. provides design and manufacturing expertise for parts and components used in the passenger car, light truck and heavy truck industry sectors. The company operates from three groups: Metal Components; Plastic Components; and Heavy Truck Components.
Kenneth R. Nichols, Chairman & C.E.O.

TOTAL ASSETS ($000)	98,670
TOTAL REVENUE ($000)	129,685
NET INCOME ($000)	9,327
EMPLOYEES	1,053
RANK (Profit/Revenue/Assets)	308/381/488

VERITAS ENERGY SERVICES INC.

(Public) CONSULTING
Exchanges: T Stock Symbol: VES
Ste 300, 615 - 3rd Ave SW, Calgary, AB, T2P 0G6 (403) 266-9350
VERITAS ENERGY SERVICES INC. is involved in land-based seismic acquittion, seismic data processing and petroleum exploration and development information services in Canada, the United States and South America.
David B. Robson, Chairman President & C.E.O.

TOTAL ASSETS ($000)	64,011
TOTAL REVENUE ($000)	122,632
NET INCOME ($000)	6,294
EMPLOYEES	743
RANK (Profit/Revenue/Assets)	386/387/581

VERSA SERVICES LTD.

(Private) FOOD SERVICES
P.O. Box 950, Station U, Etobicoke, ON, M8Z 5Y7 (416) 255-1331
VERSA SERVICES LTD. is a diversified management company providing dietary, food service, vending, office coffee systems, laundry, housekeeping, and maintenance and material management to clients in health care, business, education, and public markets. Its businesses operate across Canada. Its subsidiaries include Major Foods Limited, Modern Building Cleaning Inc., and Versabec Inc.
Dixon S. Chant, Chairman

TOTAL ASSETS ($000)	111,503
TOTAL REVENUE ($000)	395,750
NET INCOME ($000)	5,494
EMPLOYEES	15,000

VERSACOLD CORPORATION

See page 556 for a full company profile.

VICEROY HOMES LIMITED

(Public) MISC. CONSUMER PRODUCTS
Exchanges: T Stock Symbol: VHL.A
30 Melford Drive, Scarborough, ON, M1B 1Z4 (416) 298-2200
VICEROY HOMES LIMITED is engaged in the design, manufacture and distribution of precut packaged and factory built custom homes as well as the manufacture and distribution of PVC windows. These products are manufactured in Canada and sold in both Canada and the United States.

Gaylord G. Lindal, President

TOTAL ASSETS ($000)	30,821
TOTAL REVENUE ($000)	24,386
NET INCOME ($000)	(2,138)
EMPLOYEES	213
RANK (Profit/Revenue/Assets)	859/684/765

VICEROY RESOURCE CORPORATION
See page 65 for a full company profile.

VITRAN CORPORATION INC.
(Public)   TRANSPORTATION
Exchanges: T   Stock Symbol: VTN.A
24 Mobile Drive, Toronto, ON, M4A 1H9   (416) 752-1411
VITRAN CORPORATION INC. operates a North American freight distribution system that provides logistical solutions through a network of companies located in Canada and the United States. The company provides many services, including less-than-truckload (LTL), truckload (TL), container cartage, inter-modal, dedicated contract cartage, warehousing and inventory management.
Anthony F. Griffiths, Chairman of the Board

TOTAL ASSETS ($000)	64,502
TOTAL REVENUE ($000)	164,689
NET INCOME ($000)	3,666
EMPLOYEES	1,500
RANK (Profit/Revenue/Assets)	497/357/578

VOLKSWAGEN CANADA INC.
(Private)   WHOLESALE DISTRIBUTORS
1940 Eglinton Avenue East, Scarborough, ON,
M1L 2M2   (416) 288-3000
VOLKSWAGEN CANADA INC. is engaged in importing and distributing automobiles and their related parts and manufacturing automotive components. Volkswagen Canada is 100% owned by Volkswagen AG of Germany.
John E. Kerr, Chairman

TOTAL ASSETS ($000)	399,480
TOTAL REVENUE ($000)	720,396
NET INCOME ($000)	(11,036)
EMPLOYEES	922

VOLVO CANADA LTD.
(Private)   AUTOMOTIVE
175 Gordon Baker Road, North York, ON, M2H 2N7 (416) 493-3700
VOLVO CANADA LTD. is a manufacturer of automobiles. The company is a wholly owned subsidiary of Volvo Canadian Holdings Ltd.
Mats Ola Palm, Chairman

TOTAL ASSETS ($000)	96,488
TOTAL REVENUE ($000)	365,498
NET INCOME ($000)	8,613
EMPLOYEES	200

W. G. THOMPSON & SONS LTD.
(Private)   WHOLESALE DISTRIBUTORS
122 George Street, Blenheim, ON, N0P 1A0   (519) 676-5411
W.G. THOMPSON & SONS LTD. operates country grain elevators and is involved in grains, seeds, fertilizers, pulses and agricultural chemicals.
W.D. Thompson, Chairman & President

TOTAL ASSETS ($000)	na
TOTAL REVENUE ($000)	290,000

NET INCOME ($000)	na
EMPLOYEES	290

WAJAX LIMITED
See page 407 for a full company profile.

WAL-MART CANADA INC.
(Private)   DEPARTMENT STORES
33 Adelaide Street West, Toronto, ON, M5H 1P5   (416) 361-2111
WAL-MART CANADA INC. is engaged in merchandise retailing. Its parent company is Wal-Mart Stores Inc.
William K. Lavin, Chairman

TOTAL ASSETS ($000)	1,034,968
TOTAL REVENUE ($000)	2,143,355
NET INCOME ($000)	3,109
EMPLOYEES	na

WALL FINANCIAL CORPORATION
See page 317 for a full company profile.

WASCANA ENERGY INC.
See page 147 for a full company profile.

WAWANESA MUTUAL INSURANCE COMPANY (THE)
(Private)   INSURANCE - PROPERTY & CASUALTY
191 Broadway Ave, Winnipeg, MB, R3C 3P1   (204) 985-3811
THE WAWANESA MUTUAL INSURANCE COMPANY offers property and casualty insurance.
V.M. Binkley, Chairman

TOTAL ASSETS ($000)	1,548,355
TOTAL REVENUE ($000)	733,701
NET INCOME ($000)	77,280
EMPLOYEES	1,264

WELDWOOD OF CANADA LIMITED
See page 177 for a full company profile.

WEST FRASER TIMBER CO. LTD.
See page 178 for a full company profile.

WEST KOOTENAY POWER LTD.
(Public)   ELECTRICAL UTILITIES
Exchanges: T   Stock Symbol: WKP.PR.A
1290 Esplanade, Box 130, Trail, BC, V1R 4L4   (604) 368-3321
WEST KOOTENAY POWER LTD. is a public utility engaged in the business of generating, transmitting, distributing, and selling electricity in the southern interior of British Columbia. The company supplies 90% of the electricity purchased by industrial, commercial and residential customers in its service area and is regulated by the British Columbia Utilities Commission.
J.A. Drennan, Chairman, President & C.E.O.

TOTAL ASSETS ($000)	258,306
TOTAL REVENUE ($000)	110,924
NET INCOME ($000)	8,809
EMPLOYEES	390
RANK (Profit/Revenue/Assets)	316/407/312

WESTAR GROUP LTD.
See page 329 for a full company profile.

WESTBURNE INC.
See page 408 for a full company profile.

WESTCOAST ENERGY INC.
See page 337 for a full company profile.

WESTERN CO-OPERATIVE FERTILIZERS LIMITED
(Non-fin Co-op)   WHOLESALE DISTRIBUTORS
P.O. Box 2500, Calgary, AB, T2P 2N1   (403) 279-1100
WESTERN CO-OPERATIVE FERTILIZERS LIMITED is involved in
the distribution of fertilizer.
K. Komitsch, President & C.E.O.

TOTAL ASSETS ($000)	44,053
TOTAL REVENUE ($000)	191,523
NET INCOME ($000)	20,641
EMPLOYEES	64

WESTERN QUEBEC MINES INC.
(Public)   PRECIOUS METALS
Exchanges: T M   Stock Symbol: WQM
137 Church Street, Toronto, ON, M5B 1Y5   Fax: (416) 368-0141
WESTERN QUEBEC MINES INC. is involved in the acquisition,
exploration and development of mineral properties.
Murray H. Pollitt, Chairman

TOTAL ASSETS ($000)	13,614
TOTAL REVENUE ($000)	5,322
NET INCOME ($000)	29
EMPLOYEES	na
RANK (Profit/Revenue/Assets)	750/859/976

WESTERN STAR TRUCK HOLDINGS LTD.
See page 222 for a full company profile.

WESTFAIR FOODS LTD.
See page 436 for a full company profile.

WESTFIELD MINERALS LIMITED
(Public)   METAL MINES
Exchanges: T   Stock Symbol: WFD
1632 - 1055 West Georgia St., P.O. Box 11179, Royal Centre,
Vancouver, BC, V6E 3R5   (604) 669-3141
WESTFIELD MINERALS LIMITED is an investment company and
holds a substantial portfolio of resource investments.
Terry A. Lyons, President & C.E.O.

TOTAL ASSETS ($000)	28,410
TOTAL REVENUE ($000)	1,142
NET INCOME ($000)	(514)
EMPLOYEES	0
RANK (Profit/Revenue/Assets)	794/941/783

WESTINGHOUSE CANADA INC.
(Private)   ELECTRICAL & ELECTRONIC
P.O. Box 2510, Hamilton, ON, L8N 3K2   (905) 528-8811
WESTINGHOUSE CANADA INC. competes globally in the manufac-
ture and sale of gas & steam turbines, furniture systems, electronic and
mechanical products and services. The company is a wholly owned
subsidiary of Westinghouse Electric Corp.
Mr. Gary Graham, President

TOTAL ASSETS ($000)	487,747
TOTAL REVENUE ($000)	483,692
NET INCOME ($000)	(21,021)
EMPLOYEES	2,395

WESTMIN RESOURCES LIMITED
See page 22 for a full company profile.

WESTMINSTER CREDIT UNION
(Fin. Co-op)   CREDIT UNIONS
422 Sixth Street, New Westminster, BC, V3L 3B2   (604) 525-7384
WESTMINSTER SAVINGS CREDIT UNION is a full service credit
union operating in the suburban Vancouver area.
Barry W. Forbes, President & C.E.O.

TOTAL ASSETS ($000)	475,262
TOTAL REVENUE ($000)	41,001
NET INCOME ($000)	4,399
EMPLOYEES	220

WESTROCK ENERGY INCOME FUND I
(Public)   INVESTMENT COMPANIES AND FUNDS
Exchanges: T M   Stock Symbol: WRE.UN
Suite 3300, Scotia Centre, 700 - 2nd Street S.W., Calgary, AB,
T2P 2W2   (403) 269-0500
WESTROCK ENERGY INCOME FUND I is a closed-end investment
trust established to receive royalties from Canadian oil and gas properties
acquired on behalf of Fund unitholders.
James B. Walker, Chairman of the Board

TOTAL ASSETS ($000)	27,051
TOTAL REVENUE ($000)	9,412
NET INCOME ($000)	2,760
EMPLOYEES	0
RANK (Profit/Revenue/Assets)	521/808/800

WESTROCK ENERGY INCOME FUND II
(Public)   INVESTMENT COMPANIES AND FUNDS
Exchanges: T M   Stock Symbol: WRF.UN
Suite 3300 Scotia Centre, 700 - 2nd Street S.W., Calgary, AB,
T2P 2W2   (403) 269-0503
WESTROCK ENERGY INCOME FUND II is a closed-end investment
trust created to receive royalties from Canadian oil and gas properties
acquired on behalf of Fund unitholders.
James B. Walker, Chairman

TOTAL ASSETS ($000)	47,502
TOTAL REVENUE ($000)	13,937
NET INCOME ($000)	2,470
EMPLOYEES	0
RANK (Profit/Revenue/Assets)	538/766/650

WESTWARD ENERGY LTD.
(Public)   OIL AND GAS PRODUCERS
Exchanges: T   Stock Symbol: WEL.A
Suite 2100, Canterra Tower, 400 - 3rd Avenue S.W, Calgary, AB,
T2P 4H2   (403) 262-5260
WESTWARD ENERGY LTD. is involved in the acquisition, explora-
tion and development of oil and gas properties.

Roger W. Hume, Chairman President & C.E.O.

TOTAL ASSETS ($000)	13,128
TOTAL REVENUE ($000)	4,208
NET INCOME ($000)	657
EMPLOYEES	18
RANK (Profit/Revenue/Assets)	681/875/990

WFI INDUSTRIES LTD.
(Public)   MISC. CONSUMER PRODUCTS
Exchanges: T V   Stock Symbol: WFI
9000 Conservation Way, Fort Wayne, IN, 46809   (219) 478-5667
WFI INDUSTRIES LTD. is a manufacturer and distributor of residential geothermal heating and cooling systems.
James Shields, Chairman

TOTAL ASSETS ($000)	32,861
TOTAL REVENUE ($000)	40,035
NET INCOME ($000)	916
EMPLOYEES	200
RANK (Profit/Revenue/Assets)	665/590/748

WHARF RESOURCES LTD.
See page 66 for a full company profile.

WHEATON RIVER MINERALS LTD.
(Public)   PRECIOUS METALS
Exchanges: T   Stock Symbol: WRM
Suite 515, 330 Bay Street, Toronto, ON, M5H 2S8   (416) 860-0919
WHEATON RIVER MINERALS LTD. is involved in the acquisition, exploration and development of mineral resource properties in Canada and the United States.
Ian J. McDonald, Chairman

TOTAL ASSETS ($000)	22,227
TOTAL REVENUE ($000)	17,198
NET INCOME ($000)	(3,236)
EMPLOYEES	114
RANK (Profit/Revenue/Assets)	883/737/848

WHITE ROSE CRAFTS AND NURSERY SALES LIMITED
See page 437 for a full company profile.

WIC WESTERN INTERNATIONAL COMMUNICATIONS LTD.
See page 397 for a full company profile.

WILLISTON WILDCATTERS OIL CORPORATION
(Public)   OIL AND GAS PRODUCERS
Exchanges: T   Stock Symbol: WIL
619 Souris Avenue, Box 270, Arcola, SK, S0C 0G0   (306) 455-2777
WILLISTON WILDCATTERS OIL CORPORATION is involved in the acquistion, exploration and horizontal drilling of oil and gas properties in Saskatchewan. Williston also owns and operates drilling rigs, a fleet of semi-trailers, and other oil field equipment.
Mary A. Tidlund, President & C.E.O.

TOTAL ASSETS ($000)	39,028
TOTAL REVENUE ($000)	15,901
NET INCOME ($000)	(605)
EMPLOYEES	60
RANK (Profit/Revenue/Assets)	797/744/699

WINPAK LTD.
See page 299 for a full company profile.

WINZEN INTERNATIONAL INC.
(Public)   DEVELOPERS
Exchanges: V   Stock Symbol: WZI
301 King Street West, Toronto, ON, M5V 1J5   (416) 598-0959
WINZEN INTERNATIONAL INC. is involved in real estate brokerage and property management and development.
Victor Zenkovich, President

TOTAL ASSETS ($000)	21,782
TOTAL REVENUE ($000)	8,577
NET INCOME ($000)	(1,059)
EMPLOYEES	20
RANK (Profit/Revenue/Assets)	824/817/854

XCAN GRAIN POOL LTD.
(Non-fin Co-op)   WHOLESALE DISTRIBUTORS
201 Portage Avenue, Suite 1200, Winnipeg, MB, R3B 3K6   (204) 949-1388
XCAN GRAIN POOL LTD. is a marketer of grains and foodstuffs. Xcan is jointly owned by Alberta Wheat Pool, Manitoba Pool Elevators and Saskatchewan Wheat Pool.
C.H. Swanson, Chairman & President

TOTAL ASSETS ($000)	118,202
TOTAL REVENUE ($000)	823,110
NET INCOME ($000)	4,536
EMPLOYEES	122

XEROX CANADA INC.
See page 278 for a full company profile.

XL FOODS LTD.
(Public)   AGRICULTURE
Exchanges: T Z   Stock Symbol: XLF
Suite 250, 1209 - 59th Avenue S.E., Calgary, AB, T2H 2P6   (403) 258-3233
XL FOODS operates primarily in agribusiness beef production, which consists of raising, feeding, slaughtering and processing cattle, as well as feed and grain production.
John K. Church, Chairman

TOTAL ASSETS ($000)	43,213
TOTAL REVENUE ($000)	328,679
NET INCOME ($000)	2,013
EMPLOYEES	400
RANK (Profit/Revenue/Assets)	569/245/671

YAMAHA MOTOR CANADA LTD.
(Private)   WHOLESALE DISTRIBUTORS
480 Gordon Baker Rd, Willowdale, ON, M2H 3B4   (416) 498-1911
Yamaha Motor Canada Ltd. imports and distributes Yahama products.
Mr. I. Saguchi, President

TOTAL ASSETS ($000)	46,400
TOTAL REVENUE ($000)	180,663
NET INCOME ($000)	4,578
EMPLOYEES	159

ZARGON OIL & GAS LTD.

(Public)   OIL AND GAS PRODUCERS
Exchanges: T Z   Stock Symbol: ZAR
Ste 2820, 250 - 6th Ave SW, Calgary, AB, T2P 3H7 (403) 264-9992
ZARGON OIL & GAS LTD. is involved in the acquisition, exploration
and development of oil and gas properties.
John O. McCutcheon, Chairman

TOTAL ASSETS ($000)	12,777
TOTAL REVENUE ($000)	5,747
NET INCOME ($000)	723
EMPLOYEES	5
RANK (Profit/Revenue/Assets)	676/850/995

ZELLERS INC.

(Private)   DEPARTMENT STORES
5100 de Maisonneuve Blvd. West, Montreal, PQ,
H4A 1Y6   (514) 483-7600
ZELLERS INC. is a national chain of discount department stores. It
targets the budget minded customer. It operates 292 stores across Canada,
mainly in shopping malls. The company is a wholly owned subsidiary
of Hudson's Bay Company of Toronto.
Paul S. Walters, President

TOTAL ASSETS ($000)	1,593,700
TOTAL REVENUE ($000)	3,374,800
NET INCOME ($000)	na
EMPLOYEES	33,949

ZENON ENVIRONMENTAL INC.

(Public)   ENVIRONMENTAL SERVICES
Exchanges: T   Stock Symbol: ZEN
845 Harrington Court, Burlington, ON, L7N 3P3   (905) 639-6320
ZENON ENVIRONMENTAL INC. develops, manufactures and markets environmental control technologies and operates an environmental
testing laboratory. The company specializes in water and waste water
treatment processes.
Andrew Benedek, Chairman & C.E.O.

TOTAL ASSETS ($000)	40,394
TOTAL REVENUE ($000)	59,964
NET INCOME ($000)	456
EMPLOYEES	342
RANK (Profit/Revenue/Assets)	701/510/692

ZURICH CANADA

(Private)   INSURANCE - PROPERTY & CASUALTY
400 University Avenue, Toronto, ON, M5G 1S7   (416) 586-2736
ZURICH CANADA is a property and casualty insurer. The company is
a wholly owned subsidiary of Zurich Group of Switzerland.
H.J. Saunders, Chairman

TOTAL ASSETS ($000)	1,893,699
TOTAL REVENUE ($000)	1,043,081
NET INCOME ($000)	(21,125)
EMPLOYEES	2,275

ZURICH LIFE INSURANCE COMPANY OF CANADA

(Private)   INSURANCE - LIFE
2225 Sheppard Avenue East, Willowdale, ON,
M2J 5C4   (416) 502-3600
ZURICH LIFE INSURANCE COMPANY OF CANADA is a life and
health insurance company.

Harry J. Saunders, Chairman of the Board

TOTAL ASSETS ($000)	659,061
TOTAL REVENUE ($000)	194,828
NET INCOME ($000)	6,637
EMPLOYEES	400

Definitions of Financial Terms

Stock Market Information

Price: Closing price of the stock on the date indicated.

Trailing P/E: Price divided by the sum of earnings per share before extraordinary items from the last four quarters listed.

Trailing Yield: The sum of dividends per common share from the last four quarters listed divided by Price, multiplied by 100.

Trailing EPS: The sum of earnings per share before extraordinary items from the last four quarters listed divided by Price.

Yearly Statistics (5 years)

All Companies

Price-Close: Market price as of balance sheet date.

Price-High and Price-Low: High and low market prices during the indicated fiscal year.

P/E Close: Closing market price as of balance sheet date divided by earnings per share before extraordinary items during the indicated fiscal year.

Dividends per Share (Dividends per common share): Presented for annual results for the indicated fiscal year.

Dividend Yield: Dividends per common share divided by closing market price as of balance sheet date, multiplied by 100.

Sales per Share: Main source(s) of revenue, net of excise taxes, trade discounts, returns, and allowances, divided by common shares outstanding at end of indicated fiscal year.

EPS before extra. item (Earnings per share): Earnings before extraordinary items, less preferred-share dividends, divided by average common shares outstanding during indicated fiscal year.

Cash Flow per Share: Cash flow from operations divided by common shares outstanding at end of indicated fiscal year.

Book Value per Share: Common shareholders' equity divided by common shares outstanding at end of indicated fiscal year.

O/S Common Shares (Common shares outstanding at year-end): Total number of common shares outstanding. Includes shares held by subsidiaries and other inter-company holdings. Net of treasury stock.

Total Revenue: Total revenue from operations, less sales and excise taxes, plus income from investments and any other pre-tax income during indicated fiscal year.

Income before extra. (Earnings before extraordinary items): Earnings excluding extraordinary gains and losses during indicated fiscal year.

Cash Flow (Cash flow from operations): Income before extraordinary items plus non-cash items, such as equity income and depreciation, for continuing operations.

Debt/Equity (Debt/equity ratio): Short and long term interest-bearing debt (including capital lease obligations) divided by shareholders' equity. Indicates the extent to which a company is financing its assets with debt, a more risky source of capital than equity.

Return on Capital (Return on average capital): Earnings before extraordinary items, interest expense and income taxes, divided by average capital. Shows how effectively a company is employing its capital to generate profit.

Ret. on Com. Equity (Return on average common equity): Earnings before extraordinary items, less preferred-share dividends, divided by average common shareholders' equity. Shows the rate of return on the investment for the company's common shareholders, the only providers of capital who do not have a fixed return.

% Change Profit: Percentage change in earnings before extraordinary items during the indicated fiscal period.

% Change Revenue: Percentage change in total revenue during the indicated fiscal period.

% Change Assets: Percentage change in total assets during the indicated fiscal period.

Yearly Ratios (3 years)

All Companies

Preferred Div. Coverage (Preferred dividend coverage): Earnings before extraordinary items, divided by preferred-share dividends. Shows how many times over a company can cover its preferred-share dividend obligations from earnings.

Total Div. Coverage (Total dividend coverage): Earnings before extraordinary items, divided by total dividends. Shows how many times over a company can pay its dividends from earnings.

General Companies

Interest Coverage: Earnings before extraordinary items plus income taxes and interest expense, divided by total interest expense. Shows how many times over a company can cover its interest obligations from earnings.

Current Ratio: Ratio of current assets divided by current liabilities. It is a measure of short term liquidity.

Operating Margin: Operating revenues less operating expenses, divided by operating revenues and multiplied by 100. Shows the percentage of operating revenues a company retains after operating expenses.

Asset Turnover: Total sales divided by total assets. Shows a company's ability to employ its assets productively.

Banks

Capital Ratio: Year-end assets divided by year-end total equity (capital plus reserves). Shows the proportion of a bank's assets that are financed by shareholders' equity and reserves, as opposed to debt or deposits. A higher proportion can make the bank vulnerable to downturns in the business cycle.

Operat. Costs/$100 of Assets (Operating costs per $100 of assets): Operating costs (salaries and benefits, amortization and depreciation, and other expenses) divided by year-end assets. The higher the ratio, the more the bank has spent on operations in relation to its size.

Real Estate Companies

Income prop. (% tot. prop.) and Develop. prop. (% tot. prop.) (Income producing and development properties as a percentage of total property): Shows the proportion of company's total property in income producing and development properties.

5 Year Ratios (3 years)

All Companies

Return on Capital (Five year return on average capital): Simple average of return on capital for the past five years. Shows how well a company has employed its capital over the long term.

Return on Com. Equity (Five year return on average common equity): Simple average of the return on common equity for the past five years. Shows the rate of return on the shareholders' investment over the long term.

Profit Growth (Five year profit growth): Compounded growth rate of earnings before extraordinary items over last five years.

Revenue Growth (Five year revenue growth): Compounded growth rate of total revenue over last five years.

Asset Growth (Five year asset growth): Compounded growth rate of total assets over last five years.

Balance Sheet (3 years)

General Companies

Cash (Cash and short term investments): Includes cash, short term investments, and marketable securities. Does not include cash held in trust.

Current Assets (Total current assets): As presented by the company.

Net Fixed Assets: Gross fixed assets less accumulated depreciation / depletion / amortization plus assets under capital lease, deferred exploration and resource development costs, and mining and oil and gas interests.

Invest's & Advances (Investments and advances): Includes long-term marketable securities, investments at cost, receivables under equipment leases, and all long-term interest-bearing receivables and advances. Includes cash surrender value of life insurance. Also includes non-current investments in unconsolidated subsidiaries, investments at equity, joint venture investments, and advances to and receivables from related entities. Includes dues from employees or other related entities under a share purchase plan. Includes cost investments where the company considers the investment to be in "affiliate."

Total Assets: As presented by the company.

Short Term Debt: Includes bank indebtedness, notes payable, loans and advances payable, cheques issued and outstanding, and other short term interest bearing debt. Includes current portion of long term debt as defined in non-current liabilities. Includes current portion of obligations under capital leases. Includes loans and advances from related entities not in the nature of trade. "Related entities" includes employees, directors, shareholders, and related companies.

Current Liabilities (Total current liabilities): As presented by the company.

Long Term Debt: Includes long term debt, advances, obligations under capital lease, secured debt, mortgages payable, and other interest-bearing long term debt.

Total Liabilities: Total of all liability accounts, excluding preferred shares not presented as equity (rarely used).

Total Equity: As presented by the company.

Total Liab. & Equity (Total liabilities and shareholders' equity): As presented by the company.

Banks

Cash (Cash and deposits): Includes cash and term deposits. May include short term investments.

Total Loans: Includes bank loans and mortgage loans as presented by the bank, and includes all loans and receivables, other than accounts receivable. Includes receivables under equipment leases and secured loans receivable. Does not include accrued interest receivable.

Net Fixed Assets: Gross fixed assets less accumulated depreciation / depletion / amortization.

Total Assets: As presented by the bank.

Total Deposits: Includes demand deposits, short-term deposits, RSP deposits, guaranteed investment certificates and guaranteed accounts.

Subordinated Debt: As presented by the bank.

Total Liabilities: Includes total deposits, liabilities of subsidiaries other than deposits, unspecified deferred credits and subordinated debt.

Total Equity: As presented by the company.

Total Liab. & Equity (Total liabilities and shareholders' equity): As presented by the company.

Finance Companies

Cash (Cash and deposits): Includes cash and term deposits and short term deposits.

Total Loans (Total mortgages and loans): Includes mortgage loans as presented by the company and all other loans and receivables, other than accounts receivable. Includes receivables under equipment leases and secured loans receivable. Does not include accrued loans receivable.

Net Fixed Assets: Includes gross fixed assets less accumulated depreciation / depletion / amortization.

Invest's & Advances: (Investments and advances) Includes bonds, stocks, and other marketable securities, and securities

purchased under agreements to resell. Also includes investments in companies accounted for at cost, gold bullion, share exchange memberships, and other investments.

Total Assets: As presented by the company.

Total deposits: Includes demand deposits, short-term deposits, RSP deposits, guaranteed investment certificates and guaranteed accounts.

Insurance Liability: Includes "present value of liabilities under insurance contracts" and "amounts required to provide for unmatured obligations" as presented on the balance sheet of insurance companies. Also includes benefits in course of payment, provision for unreported claims, policyholders' amounts left on deposit, provision for future policy dividends, and experience rating refunds. May include segregated investment fund liabilities.

Long Term Debt: Includes long term debt, advances, obligations under capital lease, secured debt, mortgages payable, and other interest-bearing long term debt.

Total Liabilities: Total of all liability accounts, excluding preferred shares not presented as equity (rarely used).

Total Equity: As presented by the company.

Total Liab. & Equity (Total liabilities and shareholders' equity): As presented by the company.

Real Estate Companies

Cash (Cash and short term investments): Includes cash, short term investments, and marketable securities. Does not include cash held in trust.

Total Real Estate Assets: Includes net income from producing properties after depreciation, properties under development as presented by the company, land and properties held for development as presented by the company, and land and properties held for resale as presented by the company.

Invest's & Advances (Investments and advances): Includes long term marketable securities, investments at cost, receivables under equipment leases, and all long term interest-bearing receivables and advances. Includes cash surrender value of life insurance. Also includes non-current investments in unconsolidated subsidiaries, investments at equity, joint venture investments, and advances to and receivables from related entities. Includes dues from employees or other related entities under a share purchase plan. Includes cost investments where the company considers the investment to be in "affiliate."

Total Assets: As presented by the company.

Bank Indebtedness: Includes bank indebtedness, notes payable, loans and advances payable, cheques issued and outstanding, and other short term interest bearing debt. Includes all items specified as bank debt by the company.

Long Term Debt: Includes long term debt, advances, obligations under capital lease, secured debt, mortgages payable, and other interest-bearing long term debt.

Total Liabilities: Total of all liability accounts, excluding preferred shares not presented as equity (rarely used).

Total Equity: As presented by the company.

Total Liab. & Equity (Total liabilities and shareholders' equity): As presented by the company.

Capital (3 years)

All Companies

Preferred Equity: As presented by the company.

Common Equity: Total equity less preferred equity, as presented by the company.

General Companies

Total Debt: Includes bank indebtedness, notes payable, loans and advances payable, cheques issued and outstanding, and other short term interest bearing debt. Also includes current portion of long term debt, current advances from related entities, and long term debt, advances, obligations under capital lease, secured debt, mortgages payable, and other interest bearing long term debt.

Banks

Total External Debt: Includes subordinated debt as presented by the bank, and liabilities of subsidiaries other than deposits.

Finance Companies

Total Debt: Includes bank indebtedness, notes payable, loans and advances payable, cheques issued and outstanding, and other short term interest bearing debt. Also includes current portion of long term debt, current advances from related entities, and long term debt, advances, obligations under capital lease, secured debt, mortgages payable, and other interest-bearing long-term debt. For investment houses, includes call and other loans due to clients / brokers and dealers.

Real Estate Companies

Total Debt: Includes bank indebtedness, notes payable, loans and advances payable, cheques issued and outstanding, and other short term interest bearing debt. Also includes current portion of long term debt, current advances from related entities, and long-term debt, advances, obligations under capital lease, secured debt, mortgages payable, and other interest-bearing long term debt.

Quarterly Information (8 quarters)

All Companies

EPS (Earnings per share): Earnings (or income) before extraordinary items, less preferred-share dividends, divided by average common shares outstanding.

DPS (Dividends per common share): Presented for fiscal period indicated.

Tot Rev (Total revenue): Total revenue from operations, less sales taxes and excise taxes, plus income from investments and any other pretax income.

Inc Bex (Income before extraordinary items): Earnings excluding extraordinary gains and losses.

Earnings Estimates Information

From I/B/E/S, the Institutional Brokers Estimate System.

Latest year end: Year-end date (year/month) of the actual earnings per share presented.

Earnings per Share Actual: Most recent earnings per share as reported by I/B/E/S. It is the net income of the company divided by the number of shares outstanding.

Earnings per Share Est. this year: Mean or consensus earnings estimates for the next fiscal year end. It is the arithmetic average of all the earnings forecasts for that period. It most closely represents "what Wall Street is saying."

Earnings per Share Est. next year: Mean or consensus earnings estimates for the fiscal year end two years forward. It is the arithmetic average of all the earnings forecasts for that period. It most closely represents "what Wall Street is saying."

Synopsis Information

Banks and Trusts

Capital ratio on risk-adjusted basis: Comprises of Tier 1 and Tier 2 capital as a percentage of risk-adjusted assets. Under the Bank for International Settlements Guidelines, banks are required to maintain a minimum level of capital based on their risk-adjusted assets. A solid capital base protects depositors and creditors allowing the bank to withstand losses incurred in the normal course of business. This contributes to favorable credit ratings and permits expansion and new initiatives.

Interest rate spread: Net interest income (adjusted to a taxable equivalent basis) divided by average total assets. Net interest income is the difference between interest earned on loans and securities and the interest paid on deposits and/or debentures. There is an inverse relationship between interest rates and the interest rate spread.

Non-performing loans: Those loans and loan substitution securities which have been placed on a non-accrual basis, generally due to non-payment of interest or principal for 90 days or where the collectibility of principal or interest is in significant doubt by management. These loans also include loans which have been re negotiated at a reduced rate.

Mines and Precious Metals

Probable reserves: Probable ore is ore in place for which the tonnage and grade have been computed partly from specific measurements, samples or production data, and partly from projection for a reasonable distance on geological evidence.

Proven or proved reserves: Proven ore is ore in place for which the tonnage and grade have been computed from dimensions revealed in outcrops or trenches or underground workings or drill holes and for which the grade is computed from the results of adequate sampling.

Reserve grade: Estimated metal content of an ore body, based on reserve calculations.

Reserves life index: Reserves remaining at the end of a given year divided by production in that year. Gives the remaining life in years of current reserves at the current production level.

Management and Diversified

Equity investments: Represents between 20% and 50% of the ownership interest in an investee. The choice of equity method reflects the investor's ability to influence the operations of the investee.

Instant Fax Back Order Form

To order the ☞ Report on Business Canada Company Handbook simply complete this handy order form, detach and fax to:

(416) 585-5249

☐ I would like to order another copy of the **Report on Business Canada Company Handbook, 1995** edition at the renewal rate of $49.95 (reg. $59.95). Plus $5.00 postage and handling, plus GST and PST (Ontario only) per copy. *(For a 2nd copy of the book or for a friend...)* **Total $**_____

☐ I would like to order the **Report on Business Canada Company Handbook, 1996** edition at the renewal rate of $49.95 (reg. $59.95) (Price valid until June 30, 1996).

☐ Please have a Sales Representative call me about other Globe Information Services Investor Products.

NAME: _____

TITLE: _____

COMPANY: _____

ADDRESS: _____

_____

_____ CITY: _____

PROVINCE: _____ POSTAL CODE: _____

BUS TELEPHONE: (_____) _____

FAX: (_____) _____

◯ VISA   ◯ MASTER CARD   ◯ AMEX

CHARGE CARD NO: _____

EXP. DATE: _____

SIGNATURE: _____
               REQUIRED TO VALIDATE ORDER

OR MAIL TO: _____

GLOBE INFORMATION SERVICES
444 FRONT STREET WEST, TORONTO, ONTARIO
CANADA M5V 2S9 OR CALL TOLL-FREE: 1-800-268-9128

GLOBE INFORMATION SERVICES
Where Information Becomes Intelligence.®